DETROIT PUBLIC LIBRARY
W9-BSJ-761

DETROIT
PUBLIC
LIBRARY

# ROGET
# A to Z

Edited by
Robert L. Chapman

 For information address HarperCollins Publishers, Inc., 10 East 53rd Street, New York, New York 10022.

HarperCollins books may be purchased for educational, business, or sales promotional use. For information, please write to: Special Markets Department, HarperCollins Publishers, Inc., 10 East 53rd Street, New York, N.Y. 10022

FIRST EDITION

*Designed by C. Linda Dingler*

Library of Congress Cataloging-in-Publication Data

Roget A to Z / edited by Robert L. Chapman. — 1st ed.

p. cm.

Roget's international thesaurus in alphabetical format.

ISBN 0-06-270058-8

1. English language—Synonyms and antonyms. 2. English language—Dictionaries. 3. Roget's international thesaurus. I. Chapman, Robert L. II. Roget's international thesaurus.

PE1591.R712 1994

423'.1—dc20 94-9501

94 95 96 97 98 ❖/RM 10 9 8 7 6 5 4 3 2 1

# Publisher's Preface

For many years, HarperCollins, publisher of the definitive Roget's International Thesaurus ®, has been extensively researching how words are actually used in order to be able to provide the most current reflection for the users of its thesaurus books.

After the successful publication of the latest edition of Roget's International Thesaurus ®, many readers asked us to provide this wealth of material from our database in an alphabetical form and Roget A to Z is the result of that effort.

Here are the useful features:

Headwords in boldface

Complete, in-depth entries requiring no cross references

Words identified by part of speech with closely associated words grouped together

Most frequently used words printed in boldface for quick reference

Quotations from literature conveying the essence of many entry words, with their attributions

Common foreign words with clear language identification

Slang words identified as <nonformal> with groupings in shaded boxes

As always, a book such as this would not be possible without the contributions of many. The publisher wishes to particularly thank Eugene Ehrlich who did the lion's share of the editorial work and George Alexander for his valuable computer technology work. Special thanks also to John Day, Manager, Electronic Publishing for Reference, for supervising this complex project; to C. Linda Dingler, Senior Art Director of Interior Design, for design and composition of these pages; to Elaine Verriest, Supervisor, Reference Production; to Dennis Sawicki for running computer programs against the files; and to Joe Ford and Jim Hornfischer for proofreading.

CAROL COHEN
*Vice President and Publisher*
*HarperReference*

# A

**abandon** NOUNS 1 unrestraint, unconstraint, noncoercion, nonintimidation; **unreserve,** irrepressibleness, irrepressibility, uninhibitedness, exuberance VERBS 2 **desert, forsake; quit, leave,** leave behind, take leave of, depart from, absent oneself from, turn one's back upon, say goodbye to, bid a long farewell to, walk away, **walk** *or* **run out on** <nonformal>, **leave flat** *and* leave high and dry *or* holding the bag *or* in the lurch <all nonformal>, leave one to one's fate, throw to the wolves <nonformal>

**abandoned** ADJS 1 **neglected,** unattended to, untended, unwatched, unchaperoned, uncared-for; **ignored, slighted;** half-done, undone, left undone; deserted 2 **unrestrained, unconstrained, unforced,** uncompelled, uncoerced; unmeasured, **uninhibited, unsuppressed, unrepressed, unreserved,** go-go <nonformal>, exuberant; **uncurbed, unchecked, unbridled,** unmuzzled; **unreined,** reinless

**abashed** ADJS perturbed, disquieted, discomforted, discomposed, agitated; **chagrined, embarrassed,** discomfited, **disconcerted, upset, confused,** mortified, **put-out,** out of countenance, cast down, chapfallen

**aabbé** NOUNS **clergyman,** man of the cloth, **divine, ecclesiastic, churchman, cleric,** clerical; parson, pastor, *curé* <Fr>, **rector,** curate, man of God, servant of God, shepherd

**abbess** NOUNS prioress; **mother superior,** lady superior, superioress, the reverend mother, holy mother; canoness, regular *or* secular canoness

**abbey** NOUNS **cloister, monastery, house,** friary; priory, priorate; lamasery; **convent, nunnery**

**abbreviate** VERBS **shorten, cut; reduce**; **abridge, condense,** compress, contract, **boil down,** abstract, sum up, synopsize, epitomize, encapsulate, capsulize; **curtail,** truncate, retrench; bowdlerize; elide, **cut short,** cut down

**abdicate** VERBS renounce the throne, give up the crown; **give up, relinquish, surrender, yield,** waive, **forgo, resign, renounce,** throw up, **abjure, forswear, give up on, have done with,** wash one's hands of, **write off,** drop, drop all idea of, drop like a hot potato

**abdomen** NOUNS **stomach, belly** <nonformal>, **midriff,** diaphragm; swollen *or* distended *or* protruding *or* prominent belly, *embonpoint* <Fr>, **paunch,** ventripotence

**abdominal** ADJS **digestive;** stomachal, stomachic; ventral, celiac, **gastric,** ventricular; big-bellied

**abduct** VERBS **kidnap,** snatch <nonformal>, carry off; shanghai

**aberration** NOUNS **deviation,** deviance *or* deviancy, deviousness, **departure, digression,** diversion, **divergence,** divarication, branching off, divagation, declination, aberration, aberrancy, **variation,** indirection, exorbitation; **straying,** errantry, pererration

**abet** VERBS **advance, further,** expedite, **encourage, hearten, embolden,** pat *or* clap on the back, stroke <nonformal>; **foster, nurture,** nourish, feed, **aid, help, assist,** comfort, **succor,** relieve, **ease,** doctor, remedy; be of some help, put one's oar in <nonformal>; do good, do a world of good, **benefit, avail;** aid and abet, encourage, hearten, embolden, comfort <old>

**abhor** VERBS **dislike,** disrelish, have no taste for, not stomach, not have the stomach for, not be one's cup of tea; be hostile to, have it in for <nonformal>; **hate, detest, loathe,** execrate, **abominate,** take an aversion to, be death on, not stand the sight of, not stomach, scorn, **despise**

**abhorrent** ADJS **offensive, objectionable, odious, repulsive,** repellent, rebarbative, **repugnant, revolting,** forbidding; **disgusting, sickening, loathsome,** gross *and* yucky *and* grungy *and* scuzzy <all nonformal>, beastly <nonformal>, **vile, foul, nasty, nauseating**; fulsome, mephitic, miasmal, miasmic, malodorous, stinking, fetid, noisome, noxious

**abide** VERBS **await,** wait, wait for, wait on *or* upon; have *or* keep an eye out for, lie in wait for; watch, watch and wait; **bide one's time,** bide, **mark time;** cool one's heels <nonformal>; be on tenterhooks, be on pins and needles, hold one's breath, bite one's nails, sweat *or* sweat out *or* sweat it *or* sweat it out <all nonformal>; **endure, bear, stand,** support, sustain, **suffer, tolerate,** live with; **bear up under, bear the brunt, bear with, put up with, stand for,** carry *or* bear one's cross, take what comes, take the bitter with the sweet

**ability** NOUNS **skill,** skillfulness, **expertness, expertise, proficiency,** craft, **cleverness; dexterity,** dexterousness *or* dextrousness; **adroitness, adeptness, deftness,** handiness; **competence,** capability, capacity, ability; **facility, prowess**

**abject** ADJS **penitent, repentant; penitential,** penitentiary; **contrite,** abject, humble, humbled, **sheepish, apologetic,** touched, softened, melted

**able** ADJS **competent, capable, efficient, qualified, fit, fitted, suited, worthy;** fit *or* fitted for; effective, effectual, efficient, efficacious; productive; **proficient, equal to, up to;** up to snuff <nonformal>, up to the mark <nonformal>, *au fait* <Fr>

**ably** ADVS **skillfully, expertly, proficiently,** excellently, well; **dexterously, adroitly, deftly, adeptly,** aptly, handily; agilely, nimbly, featly, spryly; **competently, capably,** efficiently; **masterfully**

**abnormal** ADJS unnatural, irregular, divergent, deviative, deviant, different, exceptional; unconventional; **irregular,** deviative, divergent, **different**; **aberrant,** stray, straying, wandering; heteroclite, heteromorphic

**abnormality** NOUNS 1 anomaly, unnaturalness, irregularity, deviation, deviancy, differentness, divergence, aberration; **nonconformity,** unconventionality
2 **oddity, curiosity, wonder,** funny *or* peculiar *or* strange thing; **anomaly**

**aboard** ADVS **on board,** on shipboard, on board ship, all aboard, afloat; **on deck,** topside; aloft; in sail; before the mast

**abode** NOUNS **habitation, place, dwelling,** dwelling place, abiding place, place to live, where one lives *or* resides, where one is at home, roof, roof over one's head, **residence,** place of residence, **domicile,** *domus* <L>; **lodging,** lodgment, lodging place

**abolish** VERBS **repeal, revoke, rescind, reverse, strike down, abrogate;** renege, renig *and* go back on *and* welsh <all nonformal>; suspend; do away with; **invalidate,** vacate, void, make void, declare null and void

**abominable** ADJS **wicked, evil, vicious, bad, naughty, wrong, sinful, iniquitous,** peccant, reprobate; dark, black; **base, low, vile,** foul, rank, flagrant, arrant, nefarious, **heinous,** villainous, criminal, up to no good, knavish, flagitious

**aborigine** NOUNS **primitive, aboriginal,** bushman, autochthon; **cave man,** cave dweller, troglodyte; bog man, bog body, Lindow man; Stone Age man, Bronze Age man, Iron Age man

**abort** VERBS **miscarry,** be stillborn, die aborning; **go amiss,** go astray, **go wrong,** go on a wrong tack, take a wrong turn, derail, go off the rails

**abortion** NOUNS 1 **miscarriage,** miscarrying, abortive attempt, vain attempt; glitch <nonformal>; **dud** <nonformal>
2 **monstrosity, monster,** miscreation, teratism, abnormal *or* defective birth, abnormal *or* defective fetus

**abortive** ADJS **fruitless,** gainless, profitless, bootless, otiose, **unrewarding,** rewardless; barren, sterile, unproductive; failed, *manqué* <Fr>; fruitless, bootless, no-win <nonformal>, futile, useless; lame, **ineffectual,** ineffective, inefficacious

**abound** VERBS **teem with,** overflow with, **abound with,** burst with, bristle with, pullulate with, **swarm with,** throng with, creep with, **crawl with, be alive with,** be lousy with <nonformal>, bristle with; **have coming out of one's ears** *and* **have up the gazoo** *and* **kazoo** <both nonformal>

**about** ADVS 1 **approximately,** nearly, some, circa; more or less, *plus ou moins* <Fr>, by and large, upwards of
2 **near, nigh, close;** hard, at close quarters; **nearby, close by,** hard by, fast by, not far *or* far off, in the vicinity *or* **neighborhood of,** at hand, at close range, **near** *or* **close at hand;** thereabout *or* thereabouts, hereabout *or* hereabouts

**above** ADJS 1 **superior, greater,** better, finer; **higher,** ascendant, in the ascendant, in ascendancy, coming <nonformal>; **previous, prior, early, earlier,** *ci-devant* or *ci-dessus* <Fr>, **former,** fore, prime, first, **preceding,** foregoing, anterior, **anticipatory,** antecedent; **preexistent**

ADVS 2 **on high,** high up, high; **aloft,** aloof; **up,** upward, upwards, straight up, to the zenith; on the shoulders of; supra, *ubi supra* <L>, hereinabove, hereinbefore, *supra* <L>, *ante* <L>
3 **beyond, plus; extra,** on the side <nonformal>, for lagniappe; **more, moreover,** *au reste* <Fr>, *en plus* <Fr>, thereto, farther, further, **furthermore,** at the same time, then, again, yet; similarly, likewise, by the same token, by the same sign; item; therewith, withal <old>; all included, altogether; among other things, *inter alia* <L>

**aboveboard** ADJS 1 **straight, square,** foursquare, straight-arrow <nonformal>, honest and aboveboard, right as rain; **fair and square; square-dealing,** square-shooting, straight-shooting, up-and-up, **on the up-and-up** *and* **on the level,** *and* on the square <all nonformal>
ADVS 2 **openly, overtly,** before one, **before one's eyes** *or* very eyes, under one's nose <nonformal>; **publicly,** in public; **in the open,** out in the open, **in plain sight,** in broad daylight, for all to see, in public view, in plain view

**abrasion** NOUNS 1 **trauma, wound, injury,** hurt, lesion; **laceration,** mutilation; scuff, scrape, chafe, gall; frazzle, fray; run, **rip,** rent, slash, **tear; bruise, contusion,** ecchymosis, **black-and-blue mark; black eye,** shiner *and* mouse <both nonformal>
2 **attrition, erosion, wearing away, wear,** detrition, ablation; rubbing away *or* off *or* out; **grinding, filing,** rasping, limation; fretting; galling; **chafing, chafe**

**abrasive** ADJS **unpleasant, disagreeable; unlikable,** dislikable; unattractive, unappealing, unengaging, uninviting, unalluring

**abreast** ADJS 1 **informed, enlightened, instructed,** versed, well-versed, educated, schooled, **taught;** posted, briefed, primed, trained; **up on,** up-to-date, abreast of, *au courant* <Fr>
ADVS 2 **in parallel;** side-by-side, alongside; equidistantly, nonconvergently, nondivergently

**abridge** VERBS **shorten, condense, cut, clip; summarize,** synopsize, wrap up <nonformal>; **sketch,** sketch out, hit the high spots; capsule, capsulize, encapsulate; **put in a nutshell**

**abridgment** NOUNS **condensation,** compression, conspectus, epitome, epitomization, summary, summation, précis, abstract, recapitulation, recap <nonformal>, wrapup, synopsis, encapsulation; **curtailment,** truncation, retrenchment; elision, ellipsis, syncope, apocope; foreshortening; **deletion,** erasure, cancellation, omission; editing, blue-penciling, striking *or* striking out; expurgation, bowdlerization, censoring *or* censorship; abbreviation

**abroad** ADJS 1 **nonresident,** not in residence, from home, **away from home,** on leave *or* vacation *or* holiday, on tour, on the road; overseas
ADVS 2 **far and wide,** far and near, distantly and broadly, widely

**abrogate** VERBS **abolish,** void, annihilate, annul, tear up, repeal, revoke, negate, invalidate, **undo, cancel,** cancel out, bring to naught, put *or* lay to rest; **repeal, revoke, rescind, reverse, strike down,** suspend

**abrupt** ADJS **sudden,** precipitant, **precipitate; hasty,** headlong, impulsive, impetuous; **unexpected**, unanticipated, unpredicted, unforeseen, unlooked-for; **gruff, brusque, curt,** short, sharp, snippy <nonformal>, **blunt,** bluff, brash, cavalier

**abruptly** ADVS **precipitately,** precipitantly, slap-bang; **suddenly,** abruptly; **impetuously, impulsively, rashly; headlong,** headfirst, head over heels, *à corps perdu* <Fr>; **gruffly, brusquely, curtly,** shortly, sharply, snippily <nonformal>, bluntly, bluffly, brashly, cavalierly

**abscess** NOUNS **sore, lesion;** pustule, papule, papula, fester, **pimple,** hickey *and* zit <both nonformal>; pock; ulcer, ulceration; fistula; suppuration

**abscond** VERBS **flee, fly, take flight,** take wing, fugitate, **run, cut and run** <nonformal>, make a precipitate departure, **run off** *or* **away,** run away from, bug out <nonformal>, **decamp,** pull up stakes, **take to one's heels,** make off, **depart**, do the disappearing act, make a quick exit, **beat a retreat** *or* **a hasty retreat, turn tail**

**absence** NOUNS 1 **nonattendance, absenting, leaving,** taking leave, **departure**; **truancy, hooky** <nonformal>, French leave, **cut** <nonformal>;

absence without leave *or* AWOL; **absenteeism,** truantism

*to leave is to die a little*
FRENCH SAYING

*Say, is not absence death to those who love?*
POPE

2 **want, lack, need, deficiency, deficit, shortage, shortfall,** wantage, **incompleteness,** defectiveness, shortcoming, imperfection

**absent** ADJS not present, nonattendant, **away, gone,** departed, disappeared, vanished, absconded, out of sight; **missing,** among the missing, wanting, **lacking,** not found, nowhere to be found, omitted, taken away, subtracted, deleted

**absentminded** ADJS **forgetful, forgetting,** inclined to forget, **memoryless, unremembering, unmindful, oblivious,** insensible to the past, with a mind *or* memory like a sieve; amnesic, amnestic; **abstracted, bemused,** museful <old>, **musing, preoccupied, absorbed, engrossed,** taken up; **absent,** faraway, elsewhere, somewhere else, not there; pensive, meditative; **lost in thought,** wrapped in thought

**absolute** ADJS 1 **downright, outright, out-and-out; utter, perfect, consummate,** superlative, surpassing, the veriest, positive, definitive, classical, pronounced, decided, regular <nonformal>, proper <Brit nonformal>, precious, profound, stark; **unmitigated,** unqualified, unrelieved, unspoiled, undeniable, unquestionable, unequivocal
2 **unrestricted, unconfined, uncircumscribed,** unbounded, unmeasured; **unlimited,** limitless, illimitable

**absolutely** ADVS 1 **certainly, surely, assuredly, positively, definitely,** decidedly; without batting an eye <nonformal>; decisively, distinctly, clearly, unequivocally, unmistakably
2 **exactly, precisely,** to a T, expressly; **just, dead,** right, straight, even, square, **plumb,** directly, squarely, point-blank; unerringly, undeviatingly; in every respect, in all respects, for all the world, neither more nor less

**absolve** VERBS 1 **acquit, clear, exculpate, exonerate,** give absolution, bring in *or* return a verdict of not guilty; **pardon, excuse, forgive;** remit, grant remission, remit the penalty of; wipe the slate clean; **whitewash,** decontaminate; destigmatize
2 **confess,** make confession, receive absolution; **shrive,** hear confession; administer absolution; administer extreme unction

**absorb** VERBS 1 **assimilate,** engross, digest, **drink,** imbibe, take up *or* in, drink up *or* in, slurp up, swill up; blot, **blot up, soak up,** sponge; osmose; infiltrate, filter in; **soak in, seep in,** percolate in
2 **understand, comprehend, apprehend,** have, **know, conceive, realize,** appreciate, have no problem with, ken <Scots>, savvy <nonformal>, sense, make sense out of, make something of; **fathom, follow; grasp, seize**

**absorbed** ADJS **engrossed,** single-minded, **occupied, preoccupied, engaged,** devoted, devoted to, intent, intent on, monopolized, obsessed, monomaniacal, swept up, taken up with, **involved, caught up in,** wrapped in, **wrapped up in,** engrossed in, **absorbed in** *or* with *or* by, **lost in, immersed in,** submerged in, buried in

**absorbing** ADJS **deep, profound;** pervasive, pervading; **engrossing,** consuming, **gripping,** riveting, holding, **arresting,** engaging, attractive, **fascinating, enthralling, spellbinding,** enchanting, magnetic, hypnotic, mesmerizing, mesmeric; obsessive, obsessing

**abstain** VERBS refrain, **refrain from, forbear, forgo,** spare, withhold, hold back, **avoid, shun,** eschew, **pass up** <nonformal>, **keep from,** keep *or* stand *or* hold aloof from, have nothing to do with, take no part in, have no hand in, **let alone,** let well enough alone, let go by, **deny oneself,** do without, go without, make do without, not *or* never touch, keep hands off

**abstinence** NOUNS **asceticism, austerity, self-denial,** self-abnegation, **rigor; puritanism,** eremitism, anchoritism, anchorite *or* anchoritic monasticism, monasticism, monachism; **continence** *or* continency; abstemiousness, abstaining; celibacy; **virginity,** intactness, maidenhood, maidenhead

**abstract** NOUNS 1 **abridgment,** compendium, *abrégé* <Fr>, **condensation,** condensed version, abbreviation, abbre-

viature, brief, digest, epitome, **précis, capsule,** capsulization, encapsulation, thumbnail sketch, **synopsis,** conspectus, syllabus, *aperçu* <Fr>, **survey, review,** pandect; **outline,** skeleton
VERBS 2 **abbreviate, cut; reduce; abridge, condense,** compress, contract, **boil down,** abstract, sum up, summarize, recapitulate, recap <nonformal>, synopsize, epitomize, encapsulate, capsulize; **curtail,** truncate, retrench; bowdlerize
ADJS 3 **recondite, abstruse,** transcendental; **profound, deep; hidden;** arcane, **esoteric,** occult; **secret; general, generalized, nonspecific,** generic, **indefinite,** indeterminate, vague, nebulous, unspecified, undifferentiated, featureless, uncharacterized, bland, neutral

**abstracted** ADJS absorbed *or* engrossed in thought, **absorbed, engrossed,** introspective, rapt, **wrapped in thought, lost in thought,** immersed in thought, buried in thought, engaged in thought, occupied, **preoccupied**

**abstraction** NOUNS 1 **abstract idea,** general idea, generality, abstract; **generalization,** general idea, generalized proposition
2 **thoughtfulness,** contemplativeness, speculativeness, reflectiveness; **pensiveness,** wistfulness, reverie, musing, melancholy; **preoccupation, absorption, engrossment,** brown study, intense *or* deep *or* profound thought

**absurd** ADJS 1 **humorous, funny, amusing; witty; droll, whimsical,** quizzical; **laughable,** risible, good for a laugh; **ludicrous, ridiculous, hilarious, absurd,** quaint, eccentric, incongruous, bizarre; **nonsensical,** insensate, ridiculous, laughable, ludicrous
2 **impossible, not possible,** beyond the bounds of possibility *or* reason, contrary to reason, at variance with the facts; **inconceivable, unimaginable, unthinkable, not to be thought of, out of the question**

**abundance** NOUNS **plenty,** plenitude, plentifulness, plenteousness; myriad, myriads, numerousness; **amplitude,** ampleness; substantiality, substantialness; **copiousness; wealth, opulence** *or* opulency, richness, affluence; **prevalence,** profuseness, **profusion,** riot; **superabundance**

**abundant** ADJS **much, many,** beaucoup <nonformal>, ample, copious, generous, overflowing, superabundant, multitudinous, plentiful, **numerous,** countless; **plentiful,** plenty, **plenteous,** plenitudinous; **bountiful,** bounteous, **lavish, generous, liberal, extravagant, prodigal; luxuriant,** fertile, productive, **rich,** fat, **wealthy, opulent, affluent**

**abuse** NOUNS 1 misuse, misusage, abuse; misapplication; **mishandling,** mismanagement, poor stewardship; malversation, breach of public trust, maladministration; diversion, defalcation, misappropriation, conversion, **embezzlement,** peculation, pilfering
2 **mistreatment, ill-treatment, maltreatment, ill-use,** ill-usage; **molesting, molestation,** child abuse *or* molestation; **berating,** rating, tongue-lashing; **revilement, vilification,** blackening, **execration, vituperation,** invective, contumely, hard *or* cutting *or* bitter words; **tirade, diatribe,** jeremiad, screed, philippic
VERBS 3 **exploit, take advantage of, use,** make use of, **use for one's own ends; manipulate,** work on, work upon, stroke, play on *or* upon; play both ends against the middle; **impose upon,** presume upon
4 **misuse, misemploy, misapply; mishandle,** mismanage, maladminister; divert, misappropriate, convert, defalcate <old>, embezzle, pilfer, peculate, feather one's nest <nonformal>; pervert, prostitute; profane, violate, pollute, foul, foul one's own nest, befoul, desecrate, defile, debase
5 **vilify, revile,** vituperate, blackguard, call names, epithet, epithetize; **swear at,** damn, cuss out <nonformal>

**abusive** ADJS **condemnatory, censorious,** censorial, damnatory, **denunciatory, reproachful,** blameful, reprobative, objurgatory, priggish; reviling; **disparaging, derogatory,** derogative, depreciative, deprecatory, slighting, belittling, minimizing, detractory, pejorative, backbiting, catty *and* bitchy <both nonformal>, contumelious, contemptuous, derisive, derisory, ridiculing

**abut** VERBS adjoin, **join, conjoin,** connect, **butt, abut on *or* upon, be contiguous, be in contact;** neighbor, **border,** border on *or* upon, **verge on *or* upon**

**abyss** NOUNS 1 **pit, deep, depth, hole,** hollow, **cavity,** shaft, well, **gulf, chasm,** abysm
2 **ocean depths, the deep sea, the deep,** trench, deep-sea trench, hadal zone, **the deeps, the depths,** bottomless depths, inner space; bottom waters

**academic** NOUNS 1 **professor,** member of academy; don <Brit>, fellow; guide, docent; rabbi, *melamed* <Heb>, pandit, pundit, guru, *mullah* <Persian>, *starets* <Russ>
ADJS 2 **studious, scholarly,** scholastic, professorial, tweedy, donnish <Brit>; owlish; rabbinic, mandarin; pedantic, dry as dust; bookish; diligent

**accelerate** VERBS **speed up, step up** <nonformal>, **hurry up, quicken; hasten**; **rush,** quicken, hustle <nonformal>, bustle, bundle, precipitate, forward; **dispatch, expedite; intensify, heighten, deepen,** enhance, **strengthen,** aggravate, exacerbate; **reinforce,** double, redouble; **complicate,** ramify, make complex; give a boost to, **step up** <nonformal>

**accent** NOUNS 1 brogue, twang, burr, drawl, broad accent; **foreign accent;** accentuation, stress accent; **emphasis, stress, word stress;** ictus, beat, rhythmical stress; rhythm, rhythmic pattern, **cadence**
VERBS 2 emphasize, stress, lay emphasis or stress upon, feature, highlight, place emphasis on, give emphasis to, **accentuate, punctuate, point up,** bring to the fore, put in the foreground

**accept** VERBS 1 **condone, countenance;** overlook, not make an issue of, let go by, let pass; **reconcile oneself to,** resign oneself to, yield *or* submit to, obey; accustom *or* accommodate *or* adjust oneself to, sit through; accept one's fate, lay in the lap of the gods, take things as they come, roll with the punches <nonformal>

2 <nonformal> **take it,** take it on the chin, take it like a man, not let it get one down, stand the gaff; bite the bullet; hold still *or* stand still for, swallow, stick, **hang in, hang in there, hang tough,** tough *or* stick it out; lump it

3 **assent,** give *or* yield assent, **acquiesce, consent**, **comply, accede, agree,** agree to *or* with, have no problem with; find it in one's heart; take kindly to *and* hold with <both nonformal>; buy <nonformal>, take one up on <nonformal>; **subscribe to,** acquiesce in, abide by; **say 'yes' to; ratify, endorse,** sign off on, second, support, **certify, confirm, validate, authenticate,** give the nod *or* the green light *or* the go-ahead *or* the OK <all nonformal>, give one's imprimatur, permit, give permission, **approve**; sanction, **authorize,** warrant, accredit

**acceptable** ADJS **tolerable, goodish, fair, fairish,** moderate, tidy <nonformal>, **decent,** respectable, presentable, good enough, **pretty good, not bad,** not amiss, not half bad, not so bad, **adequate, satisfactory, all right,** OK *or* okay <nonformal>; better than nothing; admissible, **passable,** unobjectionable, unexceptionable

**accepted** ADJS 1 **approved,** received; acknowledged, admitted, allowed, granted, conceded, recognized, professed, confessed, avowed, warranted; self-confessed; **ratified, endorsed, certified,** confirmed, validated, authenticated
2 **customary, wonted,** consuetudinary; traditional, time-honored; familiar, everyday, ordinary, **usual; established,** received, accepted; set, prescribed, prescriptive; **conventional**; conformist, conformable

**accepting** ADJS 1 **patient,** armed with patience, with a soul possessed in patience, patient as Job, Job-like, Griselda-like

*like patience on a monument*
*smiling at grief*
SHAKESPEARE

2 **submissive, compliant,** compliable <old>, complaisant, complying, **acquiescent,** consenting; **assenting,** agreeable; subservient, abject, **obedient**

**access** NOUNS 1 entree, entrée, in <nonformal>, entry, **entrance**, opening, **open door,** open arms; a foot in the door, an opening wedge, the camel's nose under the wall of the tent; **opening**
2 accessibility, approachability, openness, reachableness, come-at-ableness *and* get-at-ableness <both nonformal>; **penetrability,** perviousness; **availability, donability, procurability,** procur-

ableness, securableness, getableness, acquirability
VERBS 3 **enter, go in** *or* **into,** cross the threshold, **come in,** find one's way into, put in *or* into; be admitted, gain admission *or* admittance, have an entree, have an in <nonformal>; **set foot in,** step in, walk in

**accessible** ADJS 1 **handy, convenient; available, ready, at hand,** to hand, **on hand,** on tap, on deck <nonformal>, on call, at one's call *or* beck and call, at one's elbow, at one's fingertips, just around the corner, at one's disposal
2 **communicative, talkative**, gossipy, newsy; **sociable; unreserved, unreticent,** unshrinking, **unrestrained, unconstrained,** unhampered, unrestricted; demonstrative, expansive, effusive

**accessory** NOUNS 1 **belongings, appurtenances,** trappings, paraphernalia, appointments, accessories, perquisites, appendages, appanages, choses local
2 **attendant,** concomitant, corollary, appendage; **adjunct; accomplice,** cohort, confederate, fellow conspirator, coconspirator, partner *or* accomplice in crime; *particeps criminis, socius criminis* <both L>; accessory before the fact, accessory after the fact
ADJS 3 **additional, supplementary, supplemental; extra,** plus, further, farther, fresh, **more,** new, **other,** another, ulterior; **auxiliary,** ancillary, supernumerary, contributory, collateral; **surplus,** spare
4 **accompanying, attending, attendant, concomitant,** collateral

**accident** NOUNS **misfortune, mishap,** ill hap, **misadventure, mischance,** *contretemps* <Fr>, grief; **disaster, calamity, catastrophe,** meltdown, cataclysm, **tragedy; happening,** hap, happenstance; **fortuity,** casualty, adventure, hazard

**accidental** ADJS 1 **incidental, occasional, casual;** parenthetical, by-the-way; **unessential,** inessential *or* nonessential, unnecessary, nonvital, superfluous; **accessory, extra,** collateral, auxiliary, supernumerary; adventitious, appurtenant, adscititious
2 **circumstantial,** conditional, provisional; **incidental,** occasional, contingent, adventitious, **accidental, chance,** fortuitous, casual, aleatory, unessential *or* inessential *or* nonessential

**acclaim** NOUNS 1 **applause,** plaudit, éclat, **acclamation; popularity;** ovation, standing ovation; **repute, reputation; fame,** famousness, **renown; kudos,** report, **glory; celebrity,** recognition, a place in the sun; popular acceptance *or* favor, vogue

*the bubble reputation*
**SHAKESPEARE**

*that last infirmity of noble mind*
**MILTON**

VERBS 2 **applaud, hail; clap,** clap one's hands, give a hand *or* big hand, have *or* hear a hand *or* big hand for, hear it for <nonformal>; root for <nonformal>, cheer on

**acclaimed** ADJS **distinguished,** distingué; **famous,** famed, honored, **renowned, celebrated, popular,** much acclaimed, sought-after, hot *and* world-class <both nonformal>, **notorious, well-known,** best-known, on everyone's tongue *or* lips

**accommodate** VERBS 1 **be kind,** show kindness; treat well, do right by; favor, oblige; **conform, comply, correspond,** accord, harmonize; **adapt,** adjust, bend, meet, suit, fit, shape; **adapt to,** adjust to, gear to, assimilate to, **accommodate to** *or* **with; reconcile,** settle, compose
2 **provide, supply,** find, dish up *and* rustle up <both nonformal>, **furnish;** invest, endow, fund, subsidize

**accommodating** ADJS **considerate, thoughtful,** mindful, heedful, regardful, solicitous, attentive, delicate, tactful, mindful of others; complaisant, accommodative, at one's service, **helpful,** agreeable, **obliging,** indulgent, tolerant, lenient; **courteous, polite, civil, urbane, gracious,** graceful, agreeable, affable, fair

**accommodation** NOUNS 1 **compromise,** adjustment, settlement, mutual concession, give-and-take; bargain, deal <nonformal>, arrangement, understanding; **concession,** giving way, yielding
2 accommodations, facilities; **lodgings; room and board,** bed and board; **subsistence,** keep, fostering

**accompaniment** NOUNS **supplement,** complement, continuation, extrapolation, extension; offshoot, side issue, corollary, sidebar <nonformal>, side effect, spin-off <nonformal>, **concomi-**

tant, **additive,** adjuvant; **adjunct, addition,** increase, **increment**

**accompany** VERBS 1 **agree,** match, go along with, go hand in hand, keep pace with, keep in step; **coincide,** concur; **coexist;** coextend; **synchronize,** isochronize
2 **result, ensue, issue, follow,** attend; **turn out, come out,** fall out, redound, **work out,** pan out <nonformal>, fare

**accomplice** NOUNS **participator, participant, partaker, player, sharer;** party, **a party to,** accessory; cohort, confederate, coconspirator, partner in crime; *particeps criminis, socius criminis* <both L>; **abettor**

**accomplish** VERBS 1 **achieve, effect, effectuate,** compass, consummate, **do, execute, produce, deliver, make,** enact, **perform, discharge, fulfill, realize, attain,** run with *and* hack *and* swing <all nonformal>; **work,** work out
2 **complete,** bring to completion *or* fruition, mature; **fill in, fill out,** piece out, top off, eke *or* eke out, round out

**accomplished** ADJS 1 **achieved, effected,** effectuated, implemented, **consummated, executed, discharged, fulfilled, realized,** compassed, **attained**
2 **skilled; practiced;** trained, coached, prepared, primed, finished; at one's best, at concert pitch

**accomplishment** NOUNS **act, action, deed, doing,** thing, thing done; **turn; feat, stunt** *and* **trick** <both nonformal>; **master stroke,** *tour de force* <Fr>, **exploit,** adventure, gest, **enterprise, initiative,** track record <nonformal>; accomplished fact, *fait accompli* <Fr>, done deal <nonformal>; **achievement, fulfillment, performance, execution, effectuation,** implementation, carrying out *or* through, **discharge, dispatch, consummation, realization, attainment,** production, fruition

**accord** NOUNS 1 **unanimity,** unanimousness, universal *or* univocal *or* unambiguous assent; **like-mindedness, meeting of minds,** one *or* same mind; **concurrence, consent,** general consent, common assent *or* consent, consentaneity, accordance, **concord,** concordance, **agreement,** general agreement; **consensus;** *consensus omnium* <L>, universal agreement *or* accord, *consensus gentium* <L>, agreement of all, shared sense, sense of the meeting
2 **compact, pact, contract,** legal contract, valid contract, **covenant,** convention, transaction, paction <Scots>, formal agreement, legal agreement, undertaking, stipulation; adjustment, accommodation; **understanding, arrangement, bargain,** dicker *and* **deal** <both nonformal>
VERBS 3 **permit, allow, admit, let,** leave <nonformal>, give permission, give leave, make possible; **allow** *or* **permit of;** give *or* leave room for, open the door to; consent; **grant,** vouchsafe
4 **agree, harmonize, concur**, have no problem with, go along with <nonformal>, **cooperate, correspond, conform,** coincide, parallel, intersect, overlap, **match,** tally, hit, register, lock, interlock, check <nonformal>, square, dovetail, jibe <nonformal>; **assent**, come to an agreement, be of one *or* the same *or* like mind, see eye to eye, sing in chorus, have a meeting of the minds, climb on the bandwagon

**accordingly** ADVS **in that case, in that event, at that rate,** that being the case, such being the case, that being so, **under the circumstances,** the condition being such, as it is, as matters stand, as the matter stands, **therefore, consequently; hence, wherefore,** wherefrom, whence, then, thence, *ergo* <L>, for which reason; **consequently**

**account** NOUNS 1 **record, recording,** documentation, written word; **chronicle, annals,** history, story; letters, correspondence; **vestige, trace,** memorial, token, relic, remains; **story, tale, yarn, narrative,** narration, chronicle; **anecdote,** anecdotage; **epic,** epos, **saga**
2 **reckoning, tally, score;** account current; account rendered, *compte rendu* <Fr>; **reckoning, check,** *l'addition* <Fr>, score *or* tab <both nonformal>

**accountable** ADJS **responsible, answerable; liable,** amenable, unexempt from, chargeable, on one's head, at one's doorstep, on the hook <nonformal>; **attributable, assignable, ascribable, imputable,** traceable, referable, explicable

**accountant** NOUNS cost accountant, cost keeper; certified public accountant *or* CPA; chartered accountant *or* CA <Brit>; **auditor,** bank examiner

**accrue** VERBS 1 **grow, increase, advance,** appreciate; **spread, widen,**

broaden; **intensify, develop,** gain strength, strengthen; accumulate; **multiply, proliferate,** breed, teem; run *or* shoot up, **boom, explode**
2 **result from,** be the effect of, be due to, originate in *or* from, **come from,** come out of, grow from, **grow out of,** follow from *or* on, proceed from, descend from, emerge from, issue from, ensue from, emanate from, flow from, **derive from,** accrue from, rise *or* arise from, take its rise from, **spring from, stem from,** sprout from; **depend on,** hinge *or* pivot *or* turn on, hang on, be contingent on

**accumulate** VERBS cumulate, **amass,** mass, bulk, batch; agglomerate, conglomerate, aggregate; **combine, network, join, bring together,** get together, **gather together,** draw *or* lump *or* batch *or* bunch together, pack, pack in, cram, cram in; **bunch,** bunch up; **cluster,** clump

**accuracy** NOUNS **correctness,** care for truth, attention to fact, right, subservience to the facts *or* the data, **rightness, rigor, rigorousness, exactness, exactitude**

**accurate** ADJS **meticulous, exacting, scrupulous, conscientious,** religious, punctilious, punctual, **particular, fussy, critical, attentive,** scrutinizing; **thorough,** thoroughgoing, thoroughpaced; **finical,** finicking, finicky; **exact, precise,** precisionistic, precisianistic, prissy, **correct**

**accurately** ADVS **meticulously, exactingly, scrupulously, conscientiously,** religiously, punctiliously, punctually, fussily; strictly, rigorously

**accusation** NOUNS finger-pointing <nonformal>, accusal, **charge, complaint,** plaint, count, **blame, imputation,** delation, reproach, taxing; **accusing, bringing of charges,** laying of charges, bringing to book; **denunciation,** denouncement; **impeachment, arraignment, indictment,** bill of indictment, true bill

**accuse** VERBS 1 **charge, press charges, prefer** *or* **bring charges,** lay charges; complain, **lodge a complaint,** lodge a plaint; **impeach, arraign, indict,** bring in *or* hand up an indictment, return a true bill, article, **cite,** cite on several counts; book; **denounce,** denunciate; **finger** *and* point the finger at *and* put *or* lay the finger on <all nonformal>, **inform on** *or* **against**
2 **censure,** reprehend; **blame,** lay *or* cast blame upon; **bash** *and* trash *and* rubbish <all nonformal>; **reproach,** impugn; **condemn,** damn, take out after; damn with faint praise; fulminate against, anathematize, anathemize

**accuser** NOUNS accusant, accusatrix; incriminator, delator, allegator, impugner; informer; impeacher, indictor; **plaintiff, complainant,** claimant, appellant, petitioner, libelant, suitor; **prosecutor,** the prosecution

**accustomed** ADJS **wont, wonted, used to; conditioned,** trained, seasoned; experienced, **familiarized,** naturalized <old>, broken-in, run-in <nonformal>; **usual, regular; customary,** habitual, **normative,** prescriptive, standard, regulation, conventional

**ache** NOUNS 1 aching, throbbing, throbbing ache *or* pain; **pain, distress, grief,** stress, stress of life, suffering, passion, dolor; pang, wrench, throes, cramp, spasm; wound, injury, hurt; **sore,** sore spot, tender spot, lesion; cut, stroke; shock, blow, hard *or* nasty blow
VERBS 2 **suffer, feel pain,** feel the pangs, anguish; **hurt,** have a misery <nonformal>, ail; **smart,** tingle; throb, pound; shoot; twinge, thrill, twitch; **wince,** blanch, shrink, make a wry face, grimace; **agonize,** writhe; **suffer anguish; agonize;** go hard with, have a bad time of it, go through hell; quaff the bitter cup, drain the cup of misery to the dregs, be nailed to the cross
3 **wish for, hope for, yearn for,** yen for *and* have a yen for <both nonformal>, **itch for,** lust for, pant for, **long for, pine for,** hone for <nonformal>, ache for, be hurting for <nonformal>, weary for, languish for, **be dying for,** thirst for, sigh for, gape for <old>; cry for, clamor for; spoil for <nonformal>

**achieve** VERBS 1 **succeed with,** crown with success; **make a go of it; accomplish,** compass, **achieve**; **bring off, carry off, pull off** <nonformal>, turn *or* do the trick <nonformal>, **put through,** bring through; **put over** *or* **across** <nonformal>; get away with it *and* get by <both nonformal>
2 **arrive,** arrive at, arrive in, come, **come** *or* **get to,** approach, access, **reach, hit** <nonformal>; find, **gain,** attain, attain to, accomplish, make, **make it** <nonformal>, fetch, fetch up

at, get there, reach one's destination, come to one's journey's end, end up
3 **perform, do,** work, act, execute, **accomplish, deliver,** come through with, realize, engineer, effectuate, **bring about,** bring to fruition *or* into being, cause; mass-produce, volume-produce, industrialize; overproduce; underproduce; **be productive**

**achievement** NOUNS **exploit, feat, deed, enterprise, adventure,** gest, **bold stroke,** heroic act *or* deed; aristeia; **performance, execution, doing, accomplishment,** productive effort *or* effect, realization, bringing to fruition, fructification, effectuation, operation

**Achilles' heel** NOUNS weak point, vulnerable place, chink in one's armor, weak link; **fault,** *faute* <Fr>, **defect, deficiency, inadequacy,** imperfection, kink, defection <old>; **flaw,** hole, bug <nonformal>; something missing; catch <nonformal>, fly in the ointment, problem, little problem, curate's egg <Brit>, snag, drawback; **crack,** rift; **weakness,** frailty, infirmity, failure, **failing, foible, shortcoming; blemish,** taint

**acid** NOUNS 1 **bitterness, bitter resentment,** bitterness of spirit, heartburning; **rancor,** virulence, **acrimony,** acerbity, asperity; causticity; **choler,** gall, bile, spleen, acidity, acidulousness

2 <nonformal terms for LSD> big D, blotter, blue acid, blue cheer, blue heaven, California sunshine, cap, cubes, D, deeda, dots, electric Kool-Aid, haze, L, mellow yellows, orange cubes, pearly gates, pink owsley, strawberry fields, sugar, sunshine, tabs, yellow

ADJS 3 acidulous, acidulent, acidulated; acetic, acetous, acetose
4 **pungent, piquant, poignant; sharp, keen,** piercing, penetrating, nose-tickling, stinging, **biting, acrid,** astringent, irritating, harsh, rough, severe, asperous, cutting, trenchant; **caustic,** vitriolic, mordant, escharotic; **bitter**; acerbic, **sour**

**acknowledge** VERBS 1 **admit, own, confess, allow,** avow, **grant,** warrant, **concede,** yield <old>; **accept, recognize**
2 **thank, extend gratitude** *or* **thanks,** bless; give one's thanks, **express one's appreciation; offer** *or* **give thanks,** tender *or* render thanks, return thanks

**acknowledged** ADJS **accepted, approved,** received; admitted, allowed, granted, conceded, recognized, professed, confessed, avowed, warranted; self-confessed; **ratified, endorsed, certified,** confirmed, validated, authenticated; certificatory, confirmatory, validating, warranting; **signed,** sealed, signed and sealed, countersigned, underwritten; stamped; sworn to, notarized, affirmed, sworn and affirmed

**acme** NOUNS **summit,** top; **tip-top, peak,** pinnacle; **crest, brow;** ridge, edge; **crown,** cap, **tip,** point, spire, pitch; highest pitch, no place higher, **apex,** vertex, *ne plus ultra* <Fr>, **zenith, climax,** apogee; **culmination**

**acoustic** ADJS acoustical, phonic; **auditory,** audio, audile, **hearing, aural,** auricular, otic; **sonic;** subsonic, supersonic, ultrasonic, hypersonic; transonic *or* transsonic

**acquaint** VERBS **inform, tell, speak on** *or* **for,** apprise, **advise, advertise,** advertise of, **give word,** mention to, **enlighten,** familiarize, brief, verse, give the facts, give an account of, give by way of information

**acquaintance** NOUNS 1 casual acquaintance; pickup <nonformal>; close acquaintance; confidant, confidante, repository; **intimate,** familiar, **close friend,** intimate *or* familiar friend; **bosom friend,** friend of one's bosom, inseparable friend, **best friend**
2 **knowledge,** knowing, knowingness, ken; **command,** reach; **familiarity,** intimacy; private knowledge, privity

**acquiesce** VERBS **be willing, be game** <nonformal>, be ready; be of favorable disposition, take the trouble, find it in one's heart, find one's heart <old>, have a willing heart; **incline, lean;** look kindly upon; **bite the bullet; knuckle down** *or* **under,** take it, swallow it; grin and bear it, make the best of it, take the bitter with the sweet, shrug, shrug off, **live with it;** obey

**acquiescent** ADJS **assenting, agreeing,** acquiescing, **compliant,** consenting, consentient, consensual, submissive, unmurmuring, conceding, concessive, assentatious, **agreed, content**

**acquire** VERBS **get, gain, obtain, secure, procure; win,** score; **earn,** make; **reap, harvest; receive,** have, come by, be in receipt of, be on the receiving end; **obtain**

**acquisition** NOUNS **taking,** possession, taking possession, taking away; **claiming,** staking one's claim; **reception**

**acquit** VERBS **clear, exculpate, exonerate, absolve,** bring in *or* return a verdict of not guilty; **vindicate,** justify; grant *or* extend amnesty; **discharge, release, dismiss, free, set free,** let off <nonformal>, let go; withdraw the charge; shrive, purge; wipe the slate clean

**acquittal** NOUNS acquittance; **exculpation,** disculpation, verdict of not guilty; **exoneration, absolution, vindication, remission,** compurgation, purgation, purging; **discharge, release,** dismissal, setting free; quashing of the charge *or* indictment

**acrimonious** ADJS **harsh,** fierce, **rigorous,** severe, rough, stringent, astringent, strident, **sharp, keen,** sharpish, incisive, trenchant, **cutting,** biting, stinging, **scathing,** stabbing, **piercing, poignant,** penetrating, edged, double-edged

**across** ADJS 1 **transverse,** crosswise *or* crossways, thwart, athwart; **diagonal,** bendwise; catercorner *or* **catercornered** *or* cattycorner *or* cattycornered *or* kittycorner *or* kittycornered
ADVS 2 **crosswise** *or* crossways *or* crossway, decussatively; **cross, crisscross,** thwart, thwartly, thwartways, **athwart,** athwartwise, overthwart; **transverse,** transversely, transversally; obliquely; **sideways** *or* sidewise; across the grain, against the grain

**act** NOUNS 1 **process, procedure,** proceeding, course; step, measure, initiative, *démarche* <Fr>, move, maneuver, motion
2 **law,** *lex, jus* <both L>, **statute,** rubric, **canon,** institution; **ordinance;** measure, legislation; **rule, ruling; prescript,** prescription; **regulation,** *règlement* <Fr>; **dictate,** dictation; bylaw; **edict, decree**; **bill**
VERBS 3 **perform, do,** work, execute, **bring about,** bring to fruition *or* into being, cause; **be productive; behave,** go on; **behave oneself, conduct oneself,** manage oneself, **handle oneself,** guide oneself, **comport oneself, deport oneself**
4 **take action, take steps** *or* **measures; proceed,** proceed with, go ahead with, go with, go through with; do something, go *or* swing into action, **do something about,** take it on, run with it <nonformal>, get off the dime *or* one's ass *or* one's dead ass <nonformal>
5 **play,** playact, tread the boards, strut one's stuff <nonformal>; appear, **appear on the stage;** emote <nonformal>; pantomime, mime

**acting** NOUNS 1 **action, activity**, act, willed action *or* activity; **sham, fakery,** faking, falsity, feigning, pretending; feint, pretext, **pretense,** hollow pretense, **pretension, false pretense** *or* **pretension**
ADJS 2 performing, practicing, serving, functioning, functional, operating, operative, operational, working; **deputy,** deputative

**action** NOUNS **activity**, act, willed action *or* activity; **acting, doing,** activism, direct action, not words but action; **undertaking, enterprise, operation,** work, **venture, project,** proposition *and* deal <both nonformal>; **program, plan**; **affair, business, matter, task**, concern, interest; **initiative,** effort, attempt

**active** ADJS 1 **operating, operational, working, functioning,** operant, functional, running, **going,** going on, ongoing; **in operation,** in action, **in practice, in force,** in play, in exercise, at work, on foot
2 **lively, animated, spirited,** bubbly, ebullient, effervescent, **vivacious, sprightly,** chipper *and* perky <both nonformal>, pert; **spry, breezy, brisk, energetic,** eager, keen, can-do <nonformal>; full of life, **peppy** *and* snappy *and* zingy <all nonformal>; frisky, bouncing, bouncy

**activist** NOUNS 1 **man** *or* **woman of action, doer; hustler** *and* self-starter <both nonformal>, bustler; go-getter *and* ball of fire *and* live wire *and* powerhouse *and* human dynamo *and* spitfire <all nonformal>; **eager beaver** <nonformal>; take-charge guy <nonformal>
ADJS 2 **enterprising, aggressive, dynamic,** proactive, driving, forceful, **pushing,** pushful, **pushy, up-and-coming, go-ahead** *and* **hustling** <both nonformal>

**activity** NOUNS 1 **action,** activeness; **movement,** motion, **stir; proceedings, doings, goings-on**
2 **occupation, work,** business, **function,** enterprise, undertaking, **work,**

**affairs,** labor; thing *and* bag <both nonformal>

**actor** NOUNS **actress, player,** stage player *or* performer, playactor, histrion, histrio, thespian, theatrical <nonformal>, trouper; mummer, pantomime, pantomimist; monologist, diseur, diseuse, reciter; mime, mimer, mimic; character actor *or* actress; **villain,** antagonist, **bad guy** *or* **heavy** *or* black hat <all nonformal>; juvenile, ingenue; soubrette; straight man; matinee idol <nonformal>; romantic lead

**actual** ADJS **real,** factual, veritable, for real <nonformal>, de facto, simple, sober, **hard; self-evident,** axiomatic; accepted, conceded, stipulated, given; admitted, well-known, **established, inescapable, indisputable, undeniable; demonstrable,** provable; empirical, **objective,** historical

**actuality** NOUNS **fact, reality**, the real world; the true, ultimate truth; eternal verities; truthfulness, veracity; **the present,** presentness, present time, the here and now; **now,** the present juncture *or* occasion, the present hour *or* moment, this instant *or* second *or* moment

**actually** ADVS **truly, really, in truth,** in good *or* very truth, historically, objectively, impersonally, rigorously, strictly, strictly speaking, unquestionably, without question, **in reality, in fact,** factually, technically, in point of fact, as a matter of fact

**acute** ADJS 1 **painful;** hurtful, **hurting,** distressing, afflictive; **sharp,** piercing, stabbing, shooting, stinging, biting, gnawing; **poignant,** pungent, **severe,** cruel, harsh, grave, hard; **agonizing, excruciating,** martyrizing, **harrowing, cutting,** knifelike; sharp as a razor *or* needle *or* tack

*sharp as a two-edged sword*
BIBLE

2 **sagacious, astute,** longheaded, argute; **understanding, discerning,** penetrating, incisive, trenchant, cogent, piercing; **perspicacious,** perspicuous; **perceptive, percipient,** apperceptive, appercipient
3 **urgent, imperative,** imperious, **compelling, pressing,** high-priority, high-pressure, crying, clamorous, insistent, exigent; crucial, critical, pivotal

**adamant** ADJS **unyielding, unbending, inflexible, hard, hard-line,** inelastic, impliable, ungiving, **firm, stiff, rigid,** rigorous, stuffy; rock-ribbed, rock-hard, rock-like; adamantine; unmoved, unaffected; iron, cast-iron, flinty, steely

**adapt** VERBS **accustom, habituate,** wont; **condition,** season, **train;** familiarize, naturalize <old>, break in <nonformal>, orient, orientate; acclimatize, acclimate; inure, harden, case harden; adjust, accommodate

**adaptable** ADJS **versatile, ambidextrous,** two-handed, **all around** <nonformal>, broad-gauge, **well-rounded, many-sided,** generally capable; **pliant, pliable, flexible,** flexile, flexuous, **plastic, elastic**, **ductile,** sequacious *or* facile <both old>, tractile, **tractable, yielding,** giving, bending; **malleable,** moldable

**add** VERBS 1 **combine, unite, unify,** couple, link, yoke, yoke together; **incorporate, amalgamate, consolidate,** assimilate, **integrate,** solidify, coalesce, compound, put *or* lump together, roll into one, come together, make one, unitize
2 **calculate, compute, estimate, reckon, figure,** reckon at, put at, cipher, cast, tally, score

**addict** NOUNS 1 **drug addict, narcotics addict, user, drug user,** drug abuser, junkie *and* head *and* druggy *and* doper *and* toker *and* fiend *and* freak *and* space cadet <all nonformal>; cocaine user, cokie *and* coke head *and* crackhead *and* sniffer *and* snow drifter *and* flaky <all nonformal>
2 **enthusiast, zealot,** infatuate, energumen, rhapsodist; faddist; **fanatic; devotee,** votary, aficionada, aficionado, **fancier**

**addiction** NOUNS **substance abuse, drug abuse,** narcotics abuse, drug use, glue-sniffing, solvent abuse; **addictedness, drug addiction,** narcotic addiction, drug habit, drug habituation, drug dependence, physical addiction *or* dependence, psychological addiction *or* dependence, jones *and* monkey on one's back *and* Mighty Joe Young <all nonformal>

**addition** NOUNS accession, annexation, affixation, suffixation, prefixation, agglutination, attachment, junction, **joining**, adjunction, uniting; **increase**; **augmentation, supplementation, complementation,** reinforcement

**additional** ADJS **supplementary, supplemental; extra,** plus, further, farther, fresh, **more,** new, **other**; **auxiliary,** ancillary, supernumerary, contributory, **accessory,** collateral

**addled** ADJS **muddled,** in a muddle; fuddled <nonformal>, **befuddled;** muddleheaded, fuddlebrained <nonformal>; adrift, at sea, foggy, fogged, in a fog, hazy, muzzy <nonformal>, misted, misty, cloudy, beclouded

**address** NOUNS 1 **remark, statement,** earful *and* crack *and* one's two cents' worth <all nonformal>, **word,** say, **saying, utterance, observation, reflection, expression; assertion,** averment, allegation, affirmation, pronouncement, position, dictum
2 **speech,** speeching, speechification <nonformal>, **talk, oration,** declamation, harangue; public speech *or* address, formal speech, set speech, prepared speech *or* text; **tirade,** screed, **diatribe,** jeremiad, philippic, invective
VERBS 3 **speak to, talk to,** bespeak, beg the ear of; **appeal to,** invoke; apostrophize; **approach; buttonhole,** take by the button *or* lapel; take aside, talk to in private, closet oneself with; **greet, hail, accost; salute,** make one's salutations
4 **make a speech, give a talk, deliver an address,** speechify <nonformal>, **speak, talk, discourse;** stump <nonformal>, go on *or* take the stump; platform, soapbox; take the floor

**add up** VERBS 1 **sum up,** sum, summate, say it all <nonformal>; **figure up,** cipher up, reckon up, **count up,** foot up, cast up, score up, **tally up**
2 **be right, be correct,** be just right, get it straight; **hit the nail on the head,** hit it on the nose *or* on the money *and* say a mouthful <all nonformal>, hit the bull's-eye, score a bull's-eye

**adept** NOUNS 1 **expert; artist, craftsman,** artisan, skilled workman, journeyman; technician; seasoned *or* experienced hand; shark *or* sharp *or* sharpy *and* no slouch *and* tough act to follow <all nonformal>
ADJS 2 **skillful, good,** goodish, excellent, **expert, proficient; dexterous,** callid <old>, **adroit, deft, coordinated,** well-coordinated, **apt,** no mean, **handy;** quick, ready; **clever,** cute *and* slick *and* slick as a whistle <all nonformal>, neat, clean

**adequate** ADJS 1 **satisfactory, satisfying; sufficient**, sufficing, **enough,** commensurate, proportionate, ample, equal to
2 **tolerable, goodish, fair, fairish,** moderate, tidy <nonformal>, **decent,** respectable, presentable, good enough, **pretty good, not bad,** not amiss, not half bad, not so bad, **satisfactory, all right,** OK *or* okay <nonformal>; **acceptable,** admissible, **passable,** workmanlike

**adhere** VERBS 1 **join, connect, unite, meet,** meet up, link up, merge, converge, **come together;** knit, grow together; cohere, hang *or* hold together
2 **stick, cling,** cleave, hold; **persist,** stay, stay put <nonformal>; cling to, freeze to <nonformal>; hang on, hold on; take hold of, clasp, grasp, hug, embrace, clinch; **stick together**

**adhesive** NOUNS 1 **fastening, binding,** bonding, gluing, sticking, tying, lashing, splicing, knotting, linking, trussing, girding, hooking, clasping, zipping, buckling, buttoning
ADJS 2 **viscous, viscid,** viscose, slabby; **sticky, tacky,** tenacious, clingy, clinging, tough; gluey, gluelike, **gummy, syrupy;** treacly <Brit>; mucilaginous, clammy, slimy, slithery; gooey *and* gunky *and* gloppy *and* goopy *and* gooky <all nonformal>

**adjacent** ADJS **next,** immediate, contiguous, **adjoining, abutting; neighboring,** neighbor; **juxtaposed,** juxtapositional; **bordering,** conterminous *or* coterminous, connecting

**adjoin** VERBS 1 **connect,** butt, **abut,** abut on *or* upon, be contiguous, be in contact; **neighbor,** border, **border on** *or* **upon,** verge on *or* upon; lie by, stand by
2 **border, edge, bound, rim, skirt, hem, hem in, ringe,** befringe, lap, list, margin, marge, marginate, march, verge, line, side

**adjoining** ADJS **adjacent,** contiguous, **abutting; neighboring; juxtaposed,** juxtapositional; **bordering,** connecting

**adjourn** VERBS **postpone, delay, defer, put off,** give one a rain check <nonformal>, shift off, hold off *or* up <nonformal>, prorogue, put on hold *or* ice *or* the back burner <all nonformal>, reserve, waive, **suspend,** hang up, stay, hang fire

**adjunct** NOUNS 1 **addition,** increase, **increment,** augmentation, supplemen-

tation, complementation, *additum* <L>, additament, additory, addendum, addenda <pl>, accession, fixture; **appendage,** appendant, pendant, appanage, coda
2 **component, constituent, ingredient,** integrant, makings *and* fixings <both nonformal>, **element, factor, part,** player, module, part and parcel; appurtenance
ADJS 3 **added,** affixed, add-on, **attached,** annexed, appended, appendant; adjoined, conjoined, subjoined

**adjust** VERBS 1 **reconcile, bring to terms, bring together,** reunite, heal the breach; bring about a détente; **harmonize,** restore harmony, put in tune; **iron** *or* **sort out,** settle, compose, accommodate, arrange matters, settle differences, resolve, compromise; **patch things up**
2 **modify;** adapt; modulate, accommodate, fine-tune, fit, **qualify; vary, diversify; convert, renew, recast, revamp** <nonformal>, change over, exchange, **revive;** remake, reshape, re-create, redesign, **rebuild,** reconstruct, restructure

**adjustable** ADJS 1 **conformable, adaptable,** adaptive; **compliant,** pliant, complaisant, malleable, flexible, plastic, acquiescent, unmurmuring, other-directed, submissive, tractable, obedient
2 **changeable, alterable,** alterative, modifiable; mutable, permutable, impermanent, transient, **transitory; variable,** checkered, ever-changing, many-sided, kaleidoscopic

**adjusted** ADJS **used to; conditioned,** trained, seasoned; experienced, **familiarized,** broken-in, run-in <nonformal>, oriented, orientated; acclimated, acclimatized; **fitted, adapted, suited; qualified, fit, competent, able, capable,** proficient; checked out <nonformal>; well-qualified, well-fitted, well-suited

**adjustment** NOUNS accommodation, resolution, composition of differences, compromise, arrangement, settlement; **alteration, modification; realignment, adaptation,** accommodation, fitting

**ad lib** NOUNS 1 **improvisation, extemporization,** improvision, improvising, extempore <old>, **impromptu, ad-lib,** ad-libbing *and* playing by ear <both nonformal>; temporary measure *or* arrangement, **stopgap, makeshift**
ADVS 2 **extemporaneously, extemporarily,** extempore, *à l'improviste* <Fr>, **impromptu, offhand,** by ear, off the top of one's head *and* off the cuff <both nonformal>

**ad-lib** VERBS 1 **improvise, extemporize,** improvisate, improv *and* tapdance *and* talk off the top of one's head <all nonformal>, speak off the cuff, think on one's feet, make it up as one goes along, play it by ear <nonformal>, throw away *or* depart from the prepared text, throw away the speech, scrap the plan, **do offhand,** wing it <nonformal>, vamp, fake <nonformal>, play by ear <nonformal>
ADJS 2 **extemporaneous, extemporary,** extempore, **impromptu,** unrehearsed, **improvised,** improvisatory, improvisatorial, improviso, *improvisé* <Fr>; *ad libitum* <L>; **ad-hoc,** stopgap, makeshift, jury-rigged; **offhand,** off the top of one's head *and* off-the-cuff <both nonformal>, **spur-of-the-moment**

**administer** VERBS 1 **govern, regulate; wield authority; command, head, lead,** be master, be at the head of, **preside over,** chair; **direct, manage, supervise**
2 **bestow, confer, award, allot, render,** bestow on; **grant,** accord, **allow,** vouchsafe, yield, afford, make available; **tender,** proffer, offer, extend, come up with <nonformal>; **issue, dispense;** serve, help to; **distribute;** deal, dole, mete; **give out, deal out, dole out, mete out, hand** *or* dish out <nonformal>, fork *or* shell out <nonformal>

**administration** NOUNS **governance, authority, jurisdiction, control, command, power, rule, reign,** regnancy, **dominion, sovereignty,** empire, empery, raj <India>, imperium, **swa;** direction, management, dispensation, disposition, oversight, **supervision**

**administrator** NOUNS **director,** *directeur* <Fr>, director general, **governor,** rector, **manager,** intendant, **conductor**

**admirable** ADJS **endearing, lovable, likable, adorable, lovely,** lovesome, sweet, winning, winsome; **charming; praiseworthy,** worthy, **commendable,** estimable, **laudable,** meritorious, creditable; exemplary, model, unexceptionable

**admire** VERBS 1 **respect,** entertain respect for, accord respect to, **regard, esteem,** hold in esteem *or* consideration, favor, think much of, think highly of, have *or* hold a high opinion of; think well of, take kindly to; **sanction, accept;** endorse, bless, sign off on <nonformal>, OK

**admirer** NOUNS 1 **enthusiast, zealot,** infatuate, energumen, rhapsodist; **fanatic; devotee,** votary, aficionada, aficionado, **fancier, follower; disciple,** worshiper, idolizer, idolater
2 infatuate, **suitor, wooer,** pursuer, follower; **flirt,** coquette

**admission** NOUNS 1 admittance, acceptance; **installation,** installment, inauguration, initiation; baptism, investiture, ordination; enrollment, induction
2 **acknowledgment, admission,** avowal, self-admission, self-concession, self-avowal, owning, owning up *and* coming clean <both nonformal>, unbosoming, unburdening oneself, getting a load off one's mind <nonformal>, fessing up <nonformal>, making a clean breast, baring one's breast

**admit** VERBS 1 **take in; let in,** intromit, give entrance *or* admittance to; **welcome,** bid welcome, give a royal welcome, roll out the red carpet
2 **acknowledge,** tell all, avow, concede, grant, **own, own up** <nonformal>, let on, implicate *or* incriminate oneself, come clean <nonformal>; spill *and* spill it *and* spill one's guts <all nonformal>; **tell the truth,** tell all, admit everything, let it all hang out <nonformal>
3 **permit, allow, let,** give permission, give leave, make possible; **allow** *or* **permit of;** give *or* leave room for, open the door to; consent; say *or* give the word <nonformal>

**admonish** VERBS **warn, caution, advise; give warning,** give fair warning, utter a caveat, address a warning to, put a flea in one's ear <nonformal>, have a word with one, say a word to the wise; tip *and* tip off <both nonformal>

**ado** NOUNS **hubbub, Babel, tumult,** turmoil, **uproar, racket,** riot, **disturbance, rumpus** <nonformal>, ruckus *and* ruction <both nonformal>, commotion, **fracas, hassle,** shindy <nonformal>, rampage; to-do <nonformal>, trouble, bother, pother, dustup <Brit nonformal>, stir <nonformal>, **fuss,** brouhaha, foofaraw <nonformal>

**adolescent** NOUNS 1 **youth, juvenile,** youngling, young'un <nonformal>; **stripling,** slip, sprig, sapling; fledgling; hopeful, young hopeful; **teenager,** teener, teenybopper <nonformal>
ADJS 2 **immature, unripe,** underripe, unripened, impubic, **raw, green,** callow, wet behind the ears, unseasoned, unmellowed; half-grown, juvenile, puerile; half-baked <nonformal>; half-cocked *and* at half cock <both nonformal>

**adopt** VERBS **appropriate, assume, usurp,** arrogate, accroach; **take possession of,** possess oneself of, take for oneself, arrogate to oneself, take up, **take over, help oneself to,** make use of, make one's own, make free with, dip one's hands into

**adorable** ADJS **desirable,** sought-after, much sought-after, to be desired, **much to be desired; enviable,** worth having; **likable, pleasing,** after one's own heart; **attractive,** taking, winning, sexy <nonformal>, dishy <Brit nonformal>, **seductive, provocative,** tantalizing, exciting; appetizing, tempting, toothsome, mouth-watering; **lovable**

**adore** VERBS **cherish, hold dear,** hold in one's heart *or* affections, think much *or* the world of, prize, treasure; **admire, regard,** esteem, revere; **appreciate, value,** prize; **revere, reverence,** hold in reverence, **venerate, honor, look up to, defer to, bow to,** exalt, put on a pedestal, worship the ground one walks on

**adorn** VERBS **decorate, dress, trim, garnish,** array, **deck,** bedeck, dizen <old>, bedizen; prettify, **beautify; embellish, furbish,** embroider, enrich, grace, set off *or* out, paint, color, blazon, emblazon, paint in glowing colors; **spruce up** *and* gussy up *and* doll up *and* fix up <all nonformal>, **primp up,** prink up, prank up, trick up *or* out, deck out

**adrift** ADJS 1 **unanchored,** afloat, floating, free, free-floating; **unfastened, unbound,** uncaught, unfixed, **undone, loose, free,** loosened, unloosened, clear
2 **bewildered, dismayed,** distracted, distraught, abashed, **disconcerted, embarrassed,** discomposed, **put-out, disturbed, upset,** perturbed, **bothered,** all hot and bothered <nonformal>
ADVS 3 **separately,** severally, piecemeal, one by one; **apart,** asunder, **in two,** in twain; apart from, away from, aside from; abstractly, in the abstract, objectively, impersonally

**adult** NOUNS 1 **grownup,** mature man *or* woman, grown man *or* woman, big boy *and* big girl <both nonformal>; *legalis homo* <L>
ADJS 2 **mature, of age,** grown, **grown-up;** old enough to know better; **marriageable,** of marriageable age, nubile

**adulterate** VERBS **corrupt,** contaminate, **debase,** denaturalize, pollute, denature, bastardize, **tamper with,** doctor *and* doctor up <both nonformal>

**adulterer** NOUNS **cheater, fornicator; adulteress,** fornicatress, fornicatrix

**adulterous** ADJS freeloving; illicit, extramarital, premarital; incestuous

**adultery** NOUNS **love affair, affair,** affair of the heart, **amour, romance,** something between, thing <nonformal>, liaison, entanglement, intrigue; **dalliance,** amorous play, hanky-panky, lollygagging <nonformal>; adulterous affair, **unfaithfulness, infidelity, cuckoldry**

**advance** NOUNS 1 advancement; upward mobility; **promotion, furtherance,** preferment; **rise,** ascent, **lift, uplift,** uptick <nonformal>, upswing, uptrend, upbeat; **enhancement, enrichment; restoration,** revival, recovery
2 **offer,** offering, proffer, presentation, **bid,** submission; **overture,** approach, invitation; hesitant *or* tentative *or* preliminary approach, feeling-out, **feeler** <nonformal>
VERBS 3 **progress, proceed, go,** go *or* move forward, step forward, go on, **go ahead,** go along, push ahead, pass on *or* along; move, travel; go fast; **make progress,** come on, **get along,** come along <nonformal>, **get ahead;** further oneself
4 **improve, better,** change for the better, make an improvement; transform, transfigure; improve upon, refine upon, **mend, amend,** emend; meliorate, **ameliorate; promote,** foster, favor, nurture, forward, bring forward
5 **propose, submit,** prefer; **suggest,** recommend, commend to attention, **propound, pose, put forward,** bring forward, put *or* set forth, put it to, put *or* set *or* lay *or* bring before, dish up *and* come out *or* up with <both nonformal>; put a bee in one's bonnet, put ideas into one's head
6 **lend, loan,** accommodate with

**advanced** ADJS **contemporary, present-day,** present-time, latter-day, space-age, neoteric, now <nonformal>, **newfashioned,** fashionable, modish, mod, *à la mode* <Fr>, **up-to-date, up-to-the-minute, in,** abreast of the times; **avant-garde**

**advancement** NOUNS **progress,** going, going forward; **furtherance,** furthering; **promotion, advance,** step-up *and* upping <both nonformal>, rise, elevation, upgrading, jump, step up, step up the ladder

**advantage** NOUNS 1 vantage, odds, leg up *and* inside track *and* pole position <all nonformal>; **upper hand,** whip hand; start, head *or* flying *or* running start; **edge,** bulge *and* jump *and* drop <all nonformal>
2 **benefit, use, service, avail, profit,** point, percentage *and* mileage <all nonformal>, what's in it for one <nonformal>, convenience

**advantageous** ADJS **helpful,** of help; **to one's advantage** *or* **profit, profitable,** remuneratory, beneficial; **gainful,** productive, **profitable, remunerative, lucrative,** fat, **paying,** worthwhile

**advent** NOUNS **coming,** forthcoming; flowing toward, afflux, affluxion; imminence

**adventure** NOUNS **exploit, feat, deed, enterprise, achievement,** gest, **bold stroke,** heroic act *or* deed; aristeia; **happening,** hap, happenstance; **fortuity, accident,** casualty, hazard; contingent, contingency

**adventurer** NOUNS **daredevil, madcap,** harumscarum *and* fire-eater <both nonformal>; adventuress, adventurist; brazen-face

**adversary** NOUNS 1 **enemy, foe,** foeman, **antagonist;** bitter enemy; sworn enemy; open enemy; public enemy; archenemy, devil; **bane,** bête noire
ADJS 2 **oppositional, opponent, opposing, opposed;** contra, confrontational, confrontive; at odds, at loggerheads; **adverse,** adversarial, adversative, oppugnant, antithetic, antithetical, repugnant, **set** *or* **dead set against**

**adverse** ADJS **untoward, detrimental, unfavorable;** sinister; hostile, antagonistic, inimical; contrary, counter, counteractive, conflicting, opposing, opposed, opposite, in opposition

**adversity** NOUNS adverse circumstances, difficulties, hard knocks *and* rough going <both nonformal>, **hardship,**

**trouble,** troubles, **rigor,** vicissitude, care, stress, pressure, stress of life; hard case *or* plight, **hard life,** dog's life, vale of tears; wretched *or* miserable *or* hard *or* unhappy lot, tough *or* hard row to hoe <nonformal>

*sea of troubles*
**Shakespeare**

**advertise** VERBS **promote,** build up, cry up, sell, puff <nonformal>, **boost** <nonformal>, **plug** <nonformal>, **ballyhoo** <nonformal>; **publicize,** give publicity; go public with <nonformal>; bring *or* drag into the limelight, throw the spotlight on <nonformal>

**advice** NOUNS **counsel, recommendation, suggestion; direction, instruction,** guidance, briefing; **exhortation,** hortation <old>, enjoinder, expostulation, remonstrance; **tip** *and* tip-off *and* **pointer** <all nonformal>, clue, cue; steer <nonformal>; whisper, passing word, **word to the wise,** word in the ear, bug in the ear <nonformal>, bee in the bonnet <nonformal>

**advisable** ADJS **expedient, desirable,** to be desired, much to be desired, **politic,** recommendable; **appropriate, meet, fit, fitting,** befitting, **right, proper,** good, **becoming,** seemly, likely, congruous, **suitable,** sortable, feasible, doable, swingable <nonformal>, **convenient,** happy, heaven-sent, felicitous

**advise** VERBS **counsel, recommend, suggest, advocate,** propose, submit; **instruct,** coach, guide, direct, brief; prescribe; weigh in with advice <nonformal>, give a piece of advice, give a hint *or* broad hint, hint at, intimate, insinuate, put a flea in one's ear <nonformal>, have a word with one, speak words of wisdom

**adviser** NOUNS **counsel, counselor, consultant,** professional consultant, expert, maven <nonformal>, boffin <Brit nonformal>; instructor, guide, **mentor,** nestor, orienter; confidant, personal adviser; Polonius <Shakespeare>, preceptist

**advisory** ADJS **consultative,** consultatory; directive, instructive; **admonitory,** monitory, monitorial, cautionary, **warning**

**advocate** NOUNS 1 **lawyer, attorney, attorney-at-law,** barrister, barrister-at-law, **counselor,** counselor-at-law, **counsel,** legal counsel *or* counselor, legal adviser, legal expert, **solicitor;** member of the bar, legal practitioner, officer of the court; smart lawyer, pettifogger, Philadelphia lawyer; **defender,** pleader; successful advocate *or* defender, proponent, **champion**

VERBS 2 **urge, press, push,** work on <nonformal>, twist one's arm <nonformal>; **sell,** flog <Brit>; **insist,** push for, not take no for an answer, **importune, nag, pressure, high-pressure,** bring pressure to bear upon, throw one's weight around, jawbone *and* build a fire under <both nonformal>, talk round *or* around; **encourage,** hearten, embolden, comfort <old>; hold a brief for <nonformal>, countenance, keep in countenance, **endorse**

**aerate** VERBS **air,** air out, **ventilate,** cross-ventilate, wind, refresh, freshen

**aerosol** NOUNS **solution;** decoction, infusion, mixture; chemical solution; lixivium, leach, leachate; **suspension,** colloidal suspension; atomizer, spray

**aesthete** NOUNS person of taste, lover of beauty

**aesthetic** ADJS **tasteful, in good taste,** in the best taste; excellent, of quality, of the best, of the first water; artistic, pleasing, well-chosen, choice, of choice; pure, chaste; classic *or* classical, Attic, restrained, understated, unobtrusive, quiet, subdued, simple, unaffected

**aesthetics** NOUNS **aesthetic** *or* **artistic taste,** virtuosity, virtu, **expertise,** expertism, connoisseurship; aesthetic *or* artistic criticism, aesthetic *or* artistic evaluation, aesthetic *or* artistic analysis, aesthetic *or* artistic interpretation

**afar** ADVS **far, far off,** far away, afar off, a long way off, a good ways off <nonformal>, a long cry to, as far as the eye can see, out of sight

*over the hills and far away*
**John Gay**

**affable** ADJS 1 **good-natured,** well-natured, **good-humored, good-tempered,** bonhomous, **sweet, sweet-tempered; courteous, polite, civil, urbane, gracious,** graceful, agreeable, fair; complaisant; obliging, accommodating; **thoughtful, considerate,** tactful, solicitous

2 **sociable, social,** social-minded, fit for

society, fond of society, **gregarious; companionable,** companionate, compatible, *gemütlich* <Ger>, **congenial**

**affair** NOUNS 1 **concern, matter,** thing, concernment, interest, **business,** job <nonformal>, **transaction,** proceeding; cause célèbre, matter of moment
2 **social gathering, social,** sociable, social affair, social hour, hospitality hour, affair, gathering, get-together <nonformal>; **reception,** at home, salon, levee, soiree; matinee; reunion, family reunion; wake
3 **love affair, romance,** romantic tie *or* bond, liaison, entanglement, intrigue; **dalliance,** amorous play, the love game, hanky-panky; illicit *or* unlawful love, adulterous affair, adultery, unfaithfulness, infidelity, cuckoldry

**affect** NOUNS 1 **feeling, emotion, sentiment,** affection, affections; affective faculty, affectivity; emotional charge, cathexis
VERBS 2 **touch, move, stir; melt, soften,** melt the heart, choke one up, give one a lump in the throat; **penetrate,** pierce, go through one, go deep; touch a chord, **touch a sympathetic chord, touch one's heart,** tug at the heart *or* heartstrings
3 **impress, strike, hit,** smite, rock; **make an impression, get to one** <nonformal>; make a dent in, make an impact upon, sink in <nonformal>, strike home; **influence,** make oneself felt, weigh with, **sway,** bias, bend, incline, dispose, predispose, **move,** prompt, lead
4 **assume, put on,** assume *or* put on airs, wear, **pretend, simulate, counterfeit, sham, fake** <nonformal>, **feign,** make out like <nonformal>, make a show of, play, playact <nonformal>, act *or* play a part, put up a front <nonformal>, dramatize

**affectation** NOUNS **affectedness; pretension, pretense, airs,** putting on airs, put-on <nonformal>; **show, false show,** mere show; front, false front <nonformal>, **facade,** mere facade, **image,** public image; **pretentiousness, mannerism,** posiness <Brit>, manneredness, artifice, artfulness, **artificiality,** unnaturalness

**affection** NOUNS **friendship, friendliness; amicability,** amicableness, amity, peaceableness, unhostility; **amiability,** amiableness, **congeniality; attachment, devotion, fondness,** sentiment, warm feeling, soft spot in one's heart, weakness <nonformal>, like, **liking,** fancy, shine <nonformal>; **partiality, predilection; passion,** tender feeling *or* passion, **ardor,** ardency, fervor, heart, flame

**affectionate** ADJS **kind, kindly, benign,** benignant; good as gold, **good, nice, decent; gracious; kindhearted, warm, warmhearted,** softhearted, tenderhearted, tender, loving

**affiliate** NOUNS 1 **branch, organ, division,** wing, arm, offshoot; **chapter,** lodge, post; chapel; **local;** branch office
2 **member,** insider, initiate, one of us, cardholder, card-carrier, card-carrying member
VERBS 3 **join,** join up <nonformal>, **enter, go into,** come into, get into, make oneself part of, swell the ranks of; **enlist, enroll, sign up** *or* **on** <nonformal>, take up membership, take out membership
4 band, league, ally, **combine, unite,** fuse, merge, coalesce, amalgamate, federate, confederate, consolidate; hook up *and* tie up *and* tie in <all nonformal>; **join together,** club together, league together, band together

**affiliation** NOUNS **alliance, allying, alignment, association,** consociation, combination, **union,** unification, **coalition,** fusion, merger, coalescence, coadunation, amalgamation, **league, federation, confederation,** confederacy, consolidation, incorporation, inclusion, integration; hookup *and* tie-up *and* tie-in <all nonformal>

**affinity** NOUNS 1 **inclination, penchant, partiality, fancy, favor, predilection, preference,** propensity, proclivity, **leaning, bent,** turn, tilt, bias; special affinity, mutual affinity
2 **kinship,** family resemblance *or* likeness, generic *or* genetic resemblance

**affirm** VERBS 1 **assert,** asseverate, **aver,** protest, avow, **declare,** say loud and clear, sound off <nonformal>, have one's say, speak one's piece *or* one's mind, speak up *or* out, **state,** put in one's two-cents worth <nonformal>; **allege,** profess
2 **ratify, endorse,** sign off on, second, support, **certify, confirm, validate, authenticate, accept,** give the nod *or*

the green light *or* the go-ahead *or* the OK <all nonformal>, give a nod of assent, give one's imprimatur, permit, give permission, **approve**

**affirmative** NOUNS 1 **yes,** yea, aye, amen; nod, nod of assent; thumbs-up; **affirmativeness,** affirmative attitude, yea-saying
ADJS 2 affirming, affirmatory, certifying, certificatory; **assertive, declarative,** declaratory; **consenting, assenting,** amenable, persuaded, approving, agreeing, favorable, accordant; sanctioning, endorsing, ratifying; **acquiescent, compliant,** submissive

**afflict** VERBS **sicken, indispose; weaken, enfeeble,** enervate, reduce, debilitate, devitalize; **invalid,** incapacitate, **disable;** lay up; **distress, afflict, trouble,** burden, give one a tough row to hoe, **perturb, disquiet, discomfort, agitate, upset; pain,** give *or* inflict pain, **hurt, wound; irritate, inflame,** harshen, exacerbate, intensify

**affliction** NOUNS 1 **disease, illness, sickness, malady, ailment, indisposition, disorder,** complaint, morbidity, affection, **infirmity; disability,** defect, handicap
2 **adversity,** adverse circumstances, difficulties, hard knocks *and* rough going <both nonformal>, **hardship, trouble,** troubles, **rigor,** vicissitude, care, stress, pressure, stress of life

**affluent** ADJS **wealthy, rich, moneyed** *or* **monied,** in funds, **well-to-do, well-off, well-situated, prosperous,** comfortable, provided for, well provided for, fat, **flush,** flush with *or* of money, abounding in riches, worth a great deal, rich as Croesus

**afford** VERBS 1 **provide, supply,** find, dish up *and* rustle up <both nonformal>, **furnish;** invest, endow, fund, subsidize; donate, give, contribute, kick in <nonformal>, yield, present; make available
2 **have money,** command money, **be loaded** *and* have deep pockets <both nonformal>, have the wherewithal, have means, have independent means

**affordable** ADJS **cheap, inexpensive,** unexpensive, **low, low-priced,** frugal, reasonable, sensible, manageable, modest, moderate, to fit the pocketbook, budget, easy, economy, economic, economical; within means, within reach *or* easy reach

**affront** NOUNS **provocation, offense;** *casus belli* <L>, raw nerve, the quick, where one lives; **indignity, injury,** humiliation; scurrility, contempt, contumely, despite, flout, flouting, mockery, jeering, jeer, mock, scoff, gibe, taunt, brickbat <nonformal>; **insult, aspersion,** slap *or* kick in the face, left-handed *or* backhanded compliment, damning with faint praise; cut

*head and front of one's offending*
SHAKESPEARE

**afire** ADJS **fervent, fervid, passionate, impassioned,** intense, **ardent; hearty, cordial,** enthusiastic, exuberant, unrestrained, vigorous; keen, breathless, **excited; lively**

**afraid** ADJS fearful; **cowardly;** timid, timorous, overtimorous, overtimid, rabbity *and* mousy <both nonformal>; **fainthearted,** weakhearted, chicken-hearted, henhearted, pigeonhearted; white-livered *and* lily-livered *and* chicken-livered *and* milk-livered <all nonformal>; **yellow** *and* yellow-bellied *and* with a yellow streak <all nonformal>

**afresh** ADVS **newly,** freshly, **anew,** once more, from the ground up, from scratch <nonformal>, *ab ovo* <L>, *de novo* <L>, **again**

**African American** NOUNS **black man** *or* **woman, black,** colored person, person of color, Negro

**aft** ADJS 1 **rear,** rearward, **back,** backward, retrograde, **posterior,** postern, tail; after; **hind; hindmost,** rearmost
ADVS 2 **after;** abaft, baft, astern; aback

**after** ADJS 1 **subsequent, later,** after-the-fact, *post factum* and *ex post facto* <both L>, posterior, **following, succeeding,** successive, sequent, consecutive, attendant
ADVS 2 **subsequently, afterwards, later, next,** since; **thereafter,** thereon, thereupon, therewith, **then;** at a subsequent *or* later time, in the aftermath; *ex post facto* <L>; hard on the heels *or* on the heels

**afterlife** NOUNS **the hereafter,** the afterworld, the afterlife, life after death

**aftermath** NOUNS **sequel, follow-up,** sequelae; **consequence, effect,** result, resultant, **consequence,** consequent, sequent, sequence, sequel, sequela, sequelae; **upshot, outcome,** logical outcome, possible outcome

**afternoon** NOUNS 1 *post meridiem* <L> *or* **PM;** this afternoon, this PM <nonformal>
ADJS 2 postmeridian

**afterthoughts** NOUNS **change of mind;** second thoughts, better thoughts, mature judgment

**afterwards** ADVS **in the future, afterward** *or* afterwards, **later,** at a later time, after a time *or* while, anon; **by and by,** in the sweet by-and-by <nonformal>; **in the near** *or* **immediate future,** just around the corner, **imminently, soon, before long**

**afterworld** NOUNS **the hereafter,** the great hereafter, Paradise, Heaven, Elysian Fields, Happy Isles, the Land of Youth *or* Tir na n'Og, Valhalla; Hades, the Underworld, Hell, Gehenna; **the next world,** the world to come, life *or* world beyond the grave, the great beyond, the great unknown, **the grave,** home *or* abode *or* world of the dead

*the good hereafter*
**WHITTIER**

**again** ADVS 1 another time, **once more,** once again, over again, yet again, *encore, bis* <both Fr>; **anew,** afresh, freshly, newly
2 **additionally, in addition, also,** and then some, even more, more so, and also, and all <nonformal>, and so, **as well, too,** else, beside, **besides, to boot, not to mention, let alone, into the bargain**

**against** ADJS **disapproving,** unapproving, turned-off, **displeased, dissatisfied,** less than pleased, discontented, disgruntled

**agape** ADJS **astonished, amazed, surprised, astounded,** flabbergasted <nonformal>, **bewildered,** puzzled, confounded, **dumbfounded,** dumbstruck, staggered, overwhelmed, unable to believe one's senses *or* eyes; **in awe,** in awe of; spellbound, fascinated, captivated, beguiled, enthralled, enraptured, enchanted, entranced, bewitched, hypnotized, mesmerized, stupefied, lost in wonder *or* amazement

**age** NOUNS 1 years; time of life; **lifetime, life,** life's duration, life expectancy, lifespan, expectation of life, all the days of one's life; all one's born days *or* natural life <nonformal>

*the days of our years*
**BIBLE**

*the measure of my days*
**BIBLE**

2 **era, epoch**
VERBS 3 **grow old, get on** *or* **along in years,** be over the hill <nonformal>, turn gray *or* white; **decline,** wane, fade, fail, sink, waste away; **live to a ripe old age,** cheat the undertaker <nonformal>; be in one's dotage *or* second childhood

**ageless** ADJS **perpetual, everlasting,** everliving, permanent, perdurable, indestructible; **eternal,** sempiternal, **infinite;** dateless, timeless, immemorial; **endless,** unending, never-ending, without end, **interminable**

**agency** NOUNS 1 **instrumentality;** machinery, **mechanism,** modality; gadgetry <nonformal>; mediation, going between, intermediation, service; **expedient,** recourse, resort, device
2 **deputation; assignment,** consignment; **errand, task, office; responsibility,** purview, jurisdiction; **mission,** legation, embassy

**agenda** NOUNS **schedule** *or* program of operation, **order of the day,** things to be done; protocol; laundry list *and* wish list <both nonformal>

**agent** NOUNS 1 **intermediary,** link, **connecting link,** tie, connection, **go-between,** liaison; **instrument, tool, implement, appliance,** device; contrivance, lever, mechanism; **vehicle, organ;** medium, mediator, intermedium, intermediary, intermediate, interagent, liaison, go-between
2 **actor's agent,** playbroker, ten-percenter <nonformal>; **booking agent;** publicity man *or* agent

**aggrandize** VERBS **increase, enlarge, amplify, augment, extend,** maximize, **add to; expand, inflate; raise,** exalt, boost <nonformal>, hike *and* hike up *and* jack up *and* jump up <all nonformal>; **build, build up**

**aggravate** VERBS 1 **worsen,** make worse; **exacerbate,** embitter, sour; deteriorate; **intensify, heighten,** step up, sharpen, make acute *or* more acute, bring to a head, deepen,

**increase,** enhance, amplify, enlarge, magnify, build up; augment; rub salt in the wound, twist the knife, add insult to injury, pour oil on the fire, add fuel to the fire *or* flame

2 **vex, irk, annoy,** exasperate, provoke; **trouble, worry,** give one gray hair, plague, harass, bother, hassle

**aggravating** ADJS aggravative; **exasperating,** exasperative; **annoying, irritating**; provocative; contentious

**aggravation** NOUNS 1 **worsening; exacerbation,** embittering, embitterment, souring; deterioration; **intensification, heightening,** magnification, augmentation

2 **annoyance, vexation,** exasperation, *tracasserie* <Fr>; **nuisance, pest, bother,** botheration <nonformal>, public nuisance, **trouble, problem,** pain <nonformal>, difficulty, hot potato <nonformal>

**aggregate** NOUNS 1 **sum,** summation, **number, count;** account, cast, **score, reckoning, tally,** tale, the bottom line <nonformal>, **amount,** quantity; **whole, total**; box score <nonformal>

ADJS 2 **whole, total, entire,** gross, all; **inclusive,** all-inclusive, **exhaustive,** comprehensive, omnibus, all-embracing

**aggression** NOUNS **aggressiveness,** killer instinct, force, forcefulness, **pushiness, push, drive, hustle, go,** getup, get-up-and-get *or* **get-up-and-go** <both nonformal>, go-ahead, go-getting, go-to-itiveness <nonformal>

**aggressive** ADJS 1 **enterprising, dynamic,** activist, proactive, driving, forceful, **pushing,** pushful, **pushy, up-and-coming, go-ahead** *and* **hustling** <both nonformal>

2 **harsh,** rough, severe; **combative, contentious; belligerent, pugnacious, truculent, bellicose,** scrappy <nonformal>, full of fight; offensive; **antagonistic,** inimical; unfriendly; **quarrelsome**

**aggressor** NOUNS invader, raider; **assailant,** assailer, **attacker;** mugger <nonformal>

**aghast** ADJS **appalled, astounded; terrified,** terror-stricken; awestricken, awestruck; **horrified,** horror-stricken, horror-struck; frightened out of one's wits *or* mind, **scared to death, scared stiff** *or* **shitless** *or* spitless <nonformal>; unnerved, unstrung, unmanned, undone, **cowed,** awed, **intimidated; stunned, petrified, stupefied,** white as a sheet, ashen, pallid

**agile** ADJS **nimble, spry,** sprightly, fleet, pert, graceful, nimble-footed, light-footed, sure-footed

**aging** NOUNS 1 senescence, **maturation, development,** growth, ripening, blooming, blossoming, flourishing; **mellowing,** seasoning, tempering

ADJS 2 growing old, senescent, **getting on** *or* **along,** getting on *or* along *or* up in years, not as young as one used to be, long in the tooth; **declining,** wasting

**agitated** ADJS **perturbed, disturbed, troubled, disquieted, upset,** antsy <nonformal>, unsettled, **discomposed, flustered,** ruffled, **shaken**; **jittery** <nonformal>, **jumpy,** twittery, skittish, skittery, **agitated;** shaking, trembling, shook up *and* all shook up <both nonformal>

**agitation** NOUNS **perturbation,** ferment, **turbulence, turmoil,** tumult, uproar, **commotion,** disturbance, ado, *brouhaha* <Fr>

**agitator** NOUNS **fomenter, instigator, inciter,** exciter; **provoker,** *provocateur* <Fr>, *agent provocateur* <Fr>, catalyst; agitprop; **rabble-rouser,** firebrand, incendiary

**agnostic** NOUNS 1 **skeptic, doubter, doubting Thomas,** scoffer

ADJS 2 **skeptical, doubtful, dubious, incredulous,** from Missouri <nonformal>; **distrustful, mistrustful, untrustful,** mistrusting, untrusting

**ago** ADJS 1 **past, gone,** by, **gone-by, bygone,** departed, passed, passed away, elapsed, lapsed, vanished, faded, no more, irrecoverable, never to return, not coming back

ADVS 2 **since,** gone by; back, back when; backward, to *or* into the past; **retrospectively,** reminiscently, retroactively

**agog** ADJS **eager, anxious,** all agog; **avid, keen,** forward, prompt, quick, ready, ready and willing, alacritous, bursting to, dying to, raring to; impatient

**agonize** VERBS excruciate, **torture, torment,** desolate

**agony** NOUNS **anguish, torment, torture,** exquisite torment *or* torture, the rack, excruciation, crucifixion, martyrdom, martyrization, excruciating *or* agonizing *or* atrocious pain

**agree** VERBS **concur, accord,** coincide, **agree with,** agree in opinion; **see eye to**

**eye, be at one with,** be of one mind with, go with, **go along with,** fall *or* chime *or* strike in with, conform to, side with, join *or* identify oneself with

**agreeable** ADJS 1 **pleasant, pleasing, pleasureful, pleasurable;** fair, fair and pleasant, **enjoyable,** pleasure-giving; **likable, desirable,** to one's liking, to one's taste, to *or* after one's fancy, after one's own heart; genial, congenial, cordial, *gemütlich* <Ger>
2 **acceptable,** admissible, unobjectionable, unexceptionable, tenable, viable; **OK** *and* okay *and* all right <all nonformal>; **passable,** good enough
3 **willing, willinghearted, ready, game** <nonformal>; **disposed, inclined, minded, willed,** fain *and* prone <both old>; **well-disposed,** well-inclined, favorably inclined *or* disposed; predisposed; amenable, tractable, docile, pliant

**agreement** NOUNS 1 **accord**, accordance; **concord,** concordance; **harmony, cooperation**, peace, *rapport* <Fr>, concert, consort, **consonance,** unisonance, **unison,** union, chorus, oneness
2 **similarity, likeness,** alikeness, **sameness,** similitude; **resemblance,** semblance; **analogy, correspondence,** conformity, accordance, comparability, comparison, **parallelism, parity,** community, alliance

**agree to** VERBS 1 **assent,** give *or* yield assent, **acquiesce, consent**, **comply, accede, agree,** agree to *or* with, have no problem with; find it in one's heart; take kindly to *and* hold with <both nonformal>
2 **strike a bargain,** make a bargain, **make a deal,** put through a deal, shake hands, shake on it <nonformal>; **come to terms**

**agree with** VERBS 1 **concur, accord,** coincide, **agree,** agree in opinion; **see eye to eye, be at one with,** be of one mind with, go with, **go along with,** join *or* identify oneself with; cast in one's lot, fall in *or* into line, lend oneself to, play *or* go along, take kindly to; get on the bandwagon <nonformal>
2 **make for health,** conduce to health, **be good for**

**agricultural** ADJS **rustic, rural, country, provincial, farm, pastoral, bucolic,** Arcadian, **agrarian,** agrestic

**agriculture** NOUNS **farming,** husbandry; cultivation, culture, tillage, tilth

**ahead** ADJS 1 **front, frontal, anterior; full-face, full-frontal; fore, forward,** forehand; foremost, headmost; first, earliest, **pioneering, trail-blazing, advanced; leading,** up-front <nonformal>, **in front,** one-up, one jump *or* move ahead
2 **superior, greater,** better, finer; **higher,** upper, over, super, above; ascendant, in the ascendant, in ascendancy, coming <nonformal>
ADVS 3 **before,** out *or* up ahead, **in front,** in the front, in the lead, in the van, in advance, **in the forefront,** in the foreground; **to the fore,** to the front

**aid** NOUNS 1 **help, assistance, support, succor, relief, comfort,** ease, remedy; mutual help *or* assistance; **service, benefit**
VERBS 2 **help, assist,** comfort, abet <old>, **succor,** relieve, **ease,** doctor, remedy; be of some help, put one's oar in <nonformal>; do good, do a world of good, **benefit, avail**; **favor, befriend; give help,** render assistance, offer *or* proffer aid, come to the aid of, rush *or* fly to the assistance of, lend aid, **give** *or* **lend** *or* **bear a hand** *or* **helping hand,** stretch forth *or* hold out a helping hand

**aide** NOUNS **assistant, helper,** auxiliary, paraprofessional; **help, helpmate, helpmeet;** deputy, **agent**; **attendant, second,** acolyte

**ail** VERBS **feel ill,** feel under the weather, feel awful <nonformal>, feel something terrible, not feel like anything <nonformal>, look green about the gills <nonformal>

**ailment** NOUNS **disease, illness, sickness, malady, indisposition, disorder,** complaint, morbidity, *morbus* <L>, **affliction,** affection, **infirmity**

**aim** NOUNS 1 **direction,** directionality; **line,** direction line, line of direction, point, quarter, **way,** track, range, **bearing,** azimuth, compass reading, **heading, course**
2 **motive, reason, cause,** source, spring, mainspring; matter, score, consideration; end, end in view, telos, final cause
VERBS 3 **direct, point, turn, bend, train,** fix, set, determine; point to *or* at, hold on, fix on, sight on; take aim, aim at
4 **intend, purpose, plan,** purport, **mean,** think, **propose; resolve,** determine; project, **design,** destine; aim at,

take aim at, draw a bead on, set one's sights on, have designs on, go for, drive at, aspire to *or* after

**aimless** ADJS 1 **useless,** of no use, no go <nonformal>; meaningless, **purposeless,** of no purpose, **pointless,** feckless
2 **causeless,** designless, driftless, undirected, objectless, unmotivated, mindless; **haphazard, random,** stray, inexplicable, unaccountable, promiscuous, indiscriminate

**air** NOUNS 1 ether; ozone <nonformal>; thin air; **milieu, ambience, atmosphere, climate,** aura, spirit, feeling, feel, quality, color, sense
2 manner, manners, demeanor, mien, *maintien* <Fr>, **carriage, bearing,** port, poise, posture, guise, address, presence; tone, style, lifestyle
3 aria, **tune, melody,** line, melodic line, refrain, note, **song,** solo, lay, descant, lilt, **strain,** measure
VERBS 4 air out, **ventilate,** cross-ventilate, refresh, freshen; **aerate,** airify; oxygenate, oxygenize
5 **divulge, reveal, make known, tell,** breathe, utter, vent, ventilate, give vent to, **give out,** let get around, come out with; let in on *or* to, **confide,** confide to, let one's hair down <nonformal>, unbosom oneself, let into the secret
6 **discuss, debate, reason, deliberate,** deliberate upon, exchange views *or* opinions, talk, **talk over, hash over** <nonformal>, talk of *or* about, rap <nonformal>, comment upon, **consider, treat,** dissertate on, handle, deal with, take up, **go into, examine,** investigate, talk out, **analyze,** sift, **study,** canvass, review, ventilate, consider pro and con; **kick** *or* **knock around** <nonformal>

**airing** NOUNS 1 **walk,** ramble, amble, **hike, tramp,** traipse <nonformal>; **stroll,** saunter; **promenade;** *passeggiata* <Ital>; jaunt; **constitutional** <nonformal>, stretch; turn
2 **debate, deliberation,** exchange of views, canvassing, ventilation, review, **treatment, consideration,** investigation, **examination, study, analysis, forum,** open forum, town meeting

**airless** ADJS **stuffy,** breathless, breezeless, windless; **close, oppressive, stifling, suffocating;** ill-ventilated, unventilated, unvented

**airlift** VERBS ferry, **fly,** be airborne, wing, take wing, wing one's way, take *or* make a flight, take to the air, volitate

**air out** VERBS **ventilate,** cross-ventilate, refresh, air, freshen; **aerate**

**airplane** NOUNS aeroplane <Brit>, **aircraft, plane, ship,** fixed-wing aircraft, flying machine <old>, *avion* <Fr>; aerodyne, heavier-than-air craft

**air pollution** NOUNS atmospheric pollution, smog, **miasma, mephitis,** malaria <old>; effluvium, exhaust, exhaust gas

**airport** NOUNS **airdrome,** aerodrome <Brit>, drome, port, air harbor <Can>, aviation field, **landing field,** airship station; **air terminal, jetport; air base,** air station, naval air station; airpark; **heliport,** helidrome

**airs** NOUNS lofty airs, airs and graces, highfalutin *or* highfaluting ways <nonformal>, side; **pretensions,** vain pretensions; **show, false show,** mere show; front, false front <nonformal>, **facade,** mere facade, **image,** public image; artificiality, unnaturalness, insincerity

**airship** NOUNS **aerostat,** lighter-than-air craft; ship, dirigible balloon, **blimp** <nonformal>; rigid airship, semirigid airship; **dirigible,** zeppelin, Graf Zeppelin; gasbag, ballonet; **balloon,** *ballon* <Fr>

**airsick** NOUNS **nauseated, queasy,** squeamish, qualmish, qualmy; **sick to one's stomach**

**airtight** ADJS **close, tight, compact,** fast, shut fast, **snug,** staunch, firm; **sealed;** hermetically sealed; dustproof

**airy** ADJS 1 **lighthearted,** light, lightsome; **buoyant, jaunty,** perky, **debonair, carefree,** free and easy; **breezy**
2 **light,** unheavy, imponderous; **weightless; ethereal; volatile;** frothy, foamy, spumy, spumous, spumescent, bubbly, yeasty
3 **immaterial,** nonmaterial; **unsubstantial**, insubstantial, **intangible,** impalpable, imponderable; **incorporeal,** incorporate, incorporeous; **bodiless,** unembodied, **disembodied**

**aisle** NOUNS **alley, lane; channel, conduit;** opening, aperture; access

**ajar** ADJS half-open, cracked; **gaping, yawning,** agape, oscitant, slack-jawed, openmouthed

**akimbo** ADJS **angular;** cornered, **crooked, hooked, bent,** flexed, flexural; knee-shaped, geniculate, geniculated; crotched, furcate, furcal, forked; sharp-cornered, **sharp, pointed**

**akin** ADJS **related, kindred;** consanguineous *or* consanguinean *or* consanguineal, consanguine, by *or* of the blood; allied, affiliated, congeneric; intimately *or* closely related, remotely *or* distantly related

**alarm** NOUNS 1 **fear, fright,** affright; **scare, consternation, dismay; dread,** unholy dread, **awe; terror, horror,** horrification, mortal *or* abject fear
2 **warning, caution,** caveat, **admonition,** monition, admonishment; alarum, alarm signal *or* bell, **alert;** hue and cry
VERBS 3 **frighten,** fright, affright, funk <nonformal>, frighten *or* scare out of one's wits; **scare,** spook <nonformal>, scare one stiff *or* shitless *or* spitless <nonformal>, scare the life out of, scare the pants off of *and* scare the hell out of *and* scare the shit out of <all nonformal>

**alarming** ADJS 1 **frightening, frightful; fearful,** fearsome, fear-inspiring, nightmarish, hellish; **scary,** scaring, chilling; **startling,** disquieting, dismaying, disconcerting; **unnerving, daunting**
2 **dangerous,** dangersome <nonformal>, **perilous,** periculous, parlous, jeopardous, bad, ugly, serious, critical, explosive, attended *or* beset *or* fraught with danger

**albino** NOUNS **whiteness, white, whitishness;** albescence; **lightness, fairness;** paleness; silveriness; snowiness, frostiness; chalkiness; pearliness

**album** NOUNS photograph album; scrapbook; **compilation,** omnibus; symposium; collection, collectanea, miscellany; **miscellanea,** analects; chrestomathy, delectus

**alchemy** NOUNS **sorcery, necromancy, magic,** sortilege, **wizardry,** theurgy, gramarye <old>, rune

**alcohol** NOUNS **spirits, liquor,** intoxicating liquor, adult beverage, **hard liquor, whiskey,** whisky, firewater, spiritus frumenti, usquebaugh <Scots>, schnapps, ardent spirits, strong waters, **intoxicant,** toxicant, inebriant, **potable,** potation, **beverage, drink, strong drink,** strong liquor, alcoholic drink *or* beverage, aqua vitae, water of life, brew, **grog,** social lubricant, nectar of the gods

*the luscious liquor*
MILTON

**alcoholic** NOUNS 1 **drinker,** imbiber, **social drinker,** tippler, bibber; winebibber, oenophilist; **drunkard, drunk, inebriate, sot,** toper, guzzler, swiller, soaker, lovepot, tosspot, barfly, thirsty soul, **serious drinker,** devotee of Bacchus; **dipsomaniac, problem drinker,** chronic alcoholic
ADJS 2 **spirituous, ardent, strong, hard,** with a kick <nonformal>

**alcoholism** NOUNS **dipsomania,** oenomania, alcoholic psychosis *or* addiction, pathological drunkenness, problem drinking, heavy drinking, habitual drunkenness, ebriosity

**alcove** NOUNS **recess,** recession, **niche, nook,** inglenook, corner; cove; bay

**alert** NOUNS 1 **warning sign, premonitory sign, danger sign;** preliminary sign *or* signal *or* token; **symptom,** early symptom, premonitory symptom, prodrome, prodroma, prodromata <pl>; **precursor**; **omen**
VERBS 2 **tip** *and* tip off *and* **give one a tip** <all nonformal>; confide to, entrust with information, give confidential information, mention privately *or* confidentially, whisper, buzz, breathe, whisper in the ear, **put a bug in one's ear** <nonformal>
ADJS 3 **attentive, heedful, mindful, regardful,** advertent; observant; watchful, aware, conscious; open-eared, open-eyed, **all eyes, all ears,** all eyes and ears

**alfresco** ADVS **outdoors, out of doors, outside,** abroad; in the open, **in the open air,** *en plein air* <Fr>

**alias** NOUNS **pseudonym,** anonym, **assumed name,** false *or* fictitious name, *nom de guerre* <Fr>; **pen name, nom de plume;** stage name, *nom de théâtre* <Fr>

**alibi** NOUNS 1 **pretext, pretense, pretension,** lying pretension, **show,** ostensible *or* announced *or* public *or* professed motive; **sham**; **excuse,** apology, protestation, poor excuse, lame excuse; cover story
VERBS 2 **excuse,** offer excuse for, give as an excuse, cover with excuses, **explain,** offer an explanation; alibi out of <nonformal>, crawl *or* worm *or* squirm out of, lie out of, have an out *or* alibi *or* story <all nonformal>

**alien** NOUNS 1 **stranger, foreigner, outsider,** non-member, not one of us, not our sort, not the right sort, the other,

outlander, *Uitlander* <Afrikaans>, tramontane, ultramontane, barbarian, foreign devil <China>, *gringo* <Sp Amer>
ADJS 2 **unrelated, unconnected,** unallied, unlinked, **unassociated,** unaffiliated *or* disaffiliated; **isolated,** insular; **foreign,** strange, exotic, outlandish
3 **extraterrestrial,** exterrestrial, extraterrene, extramundane, space

**alienate** VERBS 1 **antagonize,** set against, set at odds, set at each other's throat, sick on each other <nonformal>; estrange; be alienated *or* estranged, draw *or* grow apart
2 **separate, divide, disjoin, disunite,** draw apart, dissociate, disassociate, grow apart, **disjoint,** disengage, disarticulate, **disconnect;** uncouple, unyoke

**alienation** NOUNS 1 **falling-out, breach of friendship,** parting of the ways, bust-up <nonformal>; **estrangement, disaffection,** disfavor; **breach, break, rupture, schism, split, rift,** cleft, **disunity, disunion, disruption,** separation, cleavage, divergence, division, dividedness
2 **aloneness,** loneness, **loneliness, lonesomeness,** singleness; separateness, aloofness, detachment, seclusion, sequestration, **withdrawal,** standing *or* moving *or* keeping apart, **isolation**

**align** VERBS **level, flatten, even, equalize,** smooth *or* smoothen, level out, smooth out, flush

**alike** ADJS 1 **identical,** identic; **same, selfsame,** one, **one and the same,** all the same, all one, of the same kidney; **indistinguishable,** without distinction, without difference, undifferent, undifferentiated
ADVS 2 **identically,** synonymously; coincidentally, correspondingly, congruently; **likewise,** the same way, just the same, as is, ditto, same here <nonformal>; *ibid* and *ibidem* <both L>

**alive** ADJS 1 **living,** having life, live, very much alive, alive and well, alive and kicking <nonformal>, conscious, breathing, quick <old>, **animate,** animated, **vital,** zoetic, instinct with life, imbued *or* endowed with life, vivified, enlivened, inspirited; capable of life *or* survival, viable
2 **alert, on the alert,** on the *qui vive* <Fr>, **on one's toes, on top** *and* **on the job** *and* on the ball <all nonformal>, **attentive;** quick on the trigger *or* draw *or* uptake <all nonformal>; **smart, bright, keen, sharp**
3 **remembered, recollected, recalled; retained,** kept in remembrance, enduring, lasting, **unforgotten;** lodged in one's mind, stamped on the memory; vivid, eidetic, fresh, green

**all** NOUNS 1 **the whole, the entirety, everything,** all the above *or* all of the above <both nonformal>, the aggregate, the assemblage, one and all, all and sundry, each and every <nonformal>; A to Z, A to izzard, everything from soup to nuts *and* everything but the kitchen sink <both nonformal>

*alpha and omega*
BIBLE

2 <nonformal> **whole bunch, whole mess, whole caboodle, the kit and caboodle, whole kit and caboodle,** whole kit and boodle, whole bit *or* shtick, whole megillah, **whole shooting match,** whole hog, whole animal [old], **whole deal,** whole schmear, **whole shebang,** whole works, the works, whole ball of wax, whole show, whole nine yards

3 **limit, end, extremity,** extreme, **acme,** apogee, climax, **maximum,** max <nonformal>, ceiling, **peak,** summit, **pinnacle,** crown, top; **utmost,** uttermost, utmost extent, highest degree, nth degree *or* power, *ne plus ultra* <L>; **the whole**
4 **everyone, everybody, each and everyone, one and all,** all comers *and* all hands *and* every man Jack *and* every mother's son <all nonformal>, every living soul, **all the world,** *tout le monde* <Fr>, totality; you name it *and* what have you *and* all the above <all nonformal>
ADJS 5 **whole, total, entire,** aggregate, gross; integral, integrated; **exhaustive,** comprehensive, omnibus, all-embracing
6 **every,** any, whichever, whichsoever; **each,** each one; every one, each and every, each and all, **one and all, all and sundry**
ADVS 7 **wholly, entirely**; **totally,** *in toto* <L>, from start to finish, from soup to nuts <nonformal>, from A to Z, from A to izzard, across the board; **altogether,**

**all put together,** in its entirety, *tout ensemble* <Fr>; lock, stock, and barrel; hook, line, and sinker

**allay** VERBS **relieve,** give relief; **ease,** ease matters; **relax,** slacken; **alleviate, mitigate, palliate,** soften, pad, cushion, assuage, subdue, soothe; salve, pour balm into, pour oil on; temper the wind to the shorn lamb; **pacify, conciliate, placate, propitiate, appease, mollify,** dulcify; **calm, settle, soothe,** tranquilize; smooth one's feathers; pour oil on troubled waters, pour balm on, take the edge off of, take the sting out of; cool <nonformal>, defuse; clear the air

**allege** VERBS 1 **state, declare, assert,** aver, affirm, asserverate; **say,** make a statement, send a message; proclaim
2 **accuse,** bring accusation; **charge, press charges, prefer** *or* **bring charges,** lay charges; complain, **lodge a complaint, impeach, arraign, indict,** bring in *or* hand up an indictment, return a true bill, article, **cite; finger** *and* point the finger at *and* put *or* lay the finger on <all nonformal>

**alleged** ADJS 1 **affirmed, asserted,** asseverated, avouched, avowed, averred, **declared;** professed; predicated
2 **supposed,** suppositive, **assumed, presumed, conjectured, inferred,** understood, deemed, **reputed,** putative, accounted as; **presumptive;** given, granted, taken as *or* for granted, agreed, stipulated

**allegiance** NOUNS 1 **deference**, servility; eagerness *or* readiness *or* willingness to serve, **dutifulness,** duteousness; fealty, **loyalty,** faithfulness, faith
2 **fidelity, constancy, steadfastness,** staunchness, firmness; good faith, *bona fides* <L>, *bonne foi* <Fr>

**allegorical** ADJS 1 **symbolic,** symbolical, allegoric, figural, figurative, **metaphoric,** metaphorical, anagogic, anagogical
2 **fictional,** fictionalized; mythical, mythological, **legendary, fabulous; romantic,** romanticized; historicized

**allergic** ADJS anaphylactic; **sensitive,** responsive, sympathetic, compassionate; empathic, empathetic; **oversensitive, thin-skinned;** oversensible, hyperesthetic, hyperpathic, hypersensitive, supersensitive, overtender, overrefined; **irritable, touchy,** quick on the draw *or* trigger *or* uptake, itchy, ticklish, prickly

**allergy** NOUNS allergic disorder; allergic rhinitis, **hay fever,** rose cold, pollinosis; **asthma,** bronchial asthma; **hives,** urticaria; eczema

**alleviate** VERBS **mitigate, palliate,** soften, pad, cushion, assuage, allay, defuse, lay, appease, mollify, subdue, soothe; salve, pour balm into, pour oil on; **dull, deaden,** dull *or* deaden the pain, numb, benumb, anesthetize; sedate, narcotize, dope *or* dope up <nonformal>

**alley** NOUNS **passageway, pass, passage, defile; avenue, artery; corridor, aisle, lane; channel, conduit**; access, inlet; exit, outlet; connection, communication; covered way, gallery, arcade, portico, colonnade, cloister, ambulatory

**alliance** NOUNS 1 **coalition, league, union;** council; **bloc, partnership; federation, confederation,** confederacy; grouping, assemblage; **combination,** combine
2 **treaty,** international agreement, *entente, entente cordiale* <both Fr>, concord, concordat, cartel, convention, paction, capitulation; **league**

**allied** ADJS 1 **joined, united, connected,** copulate, **coupled,** linked, knit, bridged, tight-knit, knitted, bracketed, associated, conjoined, incorporated, integrated, **merged,** gathered, assembled, accumulated, **collected**
2 **affiliated,** affiliate, associate, corporate; federated, confederated, federate, confederate; **in league,** in cahoots <nonformal>, in with, coupled, linked, linked up

**allocate** VERBS **allot,** lot, **assign, appoint, set,** detail; make assignments *or* allocations; **set apart** *or* **aside, earmark,** tag, mark out for

**allocation** NOUNS **allotment, assignment, appointment,** setting aside, **earmarking,** tagging

**allot** VERBS **bestow, confer, award, render,** bestow on; **grant,** accord, **allow,** vouchsafe, yield, afford, make available; **tender,** proffer, offer, extend; deal, dole, mete; **give out, deal out, dole out, mete out, hand** *or* dish out <nonformal>, fork *or* shell out <nonformal>

**allotment** NOUNS **portion, share, interest, part,** stake, stock, **piece,** bit, segment; **bite** *and* **cut** *and* **slice** *and* **chunk** *and* slice of the pie *or* melon *and* piece of the action <all nonformal>, **lot, pro-**

**portion, percentage,** measure, quantum, **quota,** deal *or* dole <both old>, meed, moiety, mess, helping

**all-out** ADVS **actively, busily; lively,** sprightly, **briskly, breezily, energetically, animatedly, vivaciously, spiritedly,** with life and spirit, with gusto; full tilt, in full swing; like a house afire

**allow** VERBS 1 **grant,** accord, yield, afford, make available; make a present of, give as a gift; **give generously,** give the shirt off one's back; be generous *or* liberal with, give freely; heap, lavish
2 **acknowledge, admit, own, confess,** avow, **grant,** warrant, **concede; accept, recognize;** agree in principle, express general agreement, go along with, agree provisionally *or* for the sake of argument; assent grudgingly *or* under protest
3 **make allowance for,** make room for, provide for, open the door to, take account of, **take into account** *or* **consideration, consider,** consider the circumstances; admit exceptions, **waive, set aside,** ease, lift temporarily

**allowable** ADJS **permissible, admissible;** justifiable, warrantable, sanctionable; licit, **lawful, legitimate, legal,** legitimized, legalized

**allowance** NOUNS 1 **fee, stipend,** emolument, tribute; retainer, retaining fee
2 **discount, cut, deduction,** slash, abatement, price reduction, price-cut, rollback <nonformal>; **rebate**

**allowed** ADJS **permitted,** admitted; tolerated, on sufferance; unregulated, unchecked

**alloy** NOUNS **compound, mixture, admixture,** intermixture, immixture, commixture, **composite, blend,** meld, amalgam

**all-powerful** ADJS **omnipotent, almighty;** plenipotentiary, absolute, unlimited, **sovereign**

**all right 1 tolerable, fair,** moderate, tidy <nonformal>, **decent,** respectable, presentable, good enough, **pretty good, not bad,** not amiss, not half bad, not so bad, **adequate, satisfactory,** OK *or* okay <nonformal>; better than nothing; **acceptable,** admissible, **passable**
2 **well,** doing nicely, up and about, sitting up and taking nourishment, alive and well

**all things considered** PHRS **on the whole, taking one thing with another,** on balance, taking everything into consideration *or* account; everything being equal, other things being equal, *ceteris paribus* <L>, taking into account

**allude to** VERBS **call attention to,** direct attention to, **bring under** *or* **to one's notice,** hold up to notice, bring to attention, **mention,** mention in passing, touch on; mention in passing, touch on, cite

**alluring** ADJS **fascinating, captivating, riveting, charming, glamorous,** exotic, **enchanting,** spellbinding, **entrancing,** ravishing, **intriguing, enthralling, bewitching; attractive, interesting, appealing,** dishy <Brit nonformal>, sexy <nonformal>, engaging, taking, eye-catching, catching, fetching, winning, winsome, prepossessing

**allusion** NOUNS **implication, connotation, import,** latent *or* underlying *or* implied meaning, ironic suggestion *or* implication, what is read between the lines; **suggestion;** coloration, tinge, undertone, overtone, undercurrent, more than meets the eye *or* ear, something between the lines, intimation, touch, nuance, innuendo; undermeaning, **subtext;** cryptic *or* hidden *or* esoteric *or* arcane meaning

**ally** NOUNS 1 military ally, cobelligerent, treaty partner; satellite; **associate, confederate, colleague,** bedfellow, cohort, comrade in arms, **comrade**
VERBS 2 **affiliate, associate,** consociate; **federate, confederate,** federalize, centralize; **join forces,** join *or* unite with, join *or* come together, join up with <nonformal>, hook up with <nonformal>, tie up *or* in with <nonformal>, **throw in with** <nonformal>, stand up with, be in cahoots <nonformal>, **pool one's interests, join fortunes with,** stand together, close ranks, make common cause with

**alma mater** NOUNS **college, university,** institution of higher education *or* learning; academe, academia, the groves of Academe, **the campus,** the halls of learning *or* ivy, ivied halls

**almighty** ADJS 1 **omnipotent, all-powerful;** absolute, unlimited, **sovereign; supreme**
ADVS 2 **exceedingly,** awfully *and* terribly *and* terrifically <all nonformal>, **quite,** just, so, **really,** real *and* right <both nonformal>, mightily, **mighty**

*and* almighty *and* powerfully *and* powerful <all nonformal>

**almost** ADVS **nearly, near,** pretty near <nonformal>, close, **closely;** all but, not quite, as good as; **well-nigh, just about;** nigh

**alms** NOUNS pittance, **charity, dole, handout** <nonformal>, widow's mite; Peter's pence; **offering,** offertory, votive offering; tithe

**almsgiver** NOUNS **giver, donor,** bestower, grantor, vouchsafer; fairy godmother, Lady Bountiful, Santa Claus, sugar daddy <nonformal>

**aloft** ADVS **on high,** high up, high; **above, over,** o'er, **overhead;** supra

**aloha** NOUNS Godspeed; **adieu,** one's adieus, **farewell, good-bye;** parting *or* Parthian shot; swan song; viaticum; stirrup cup, one for the road, *doch-an-dorrach* or *doch-an-dorris* <Gaelic>

**alone** ADJS 1 **solitary,** solo, *solus* <L>; **isolated,** insular, apart, separate, separated, alienated, withdrawn, aloof, standoffish, detached, removed; **private,** reserved, reticent, reclusive, shy, nonpublic, ungregarious
ADVS 2 **independently, by oneself,** all by one's lonesome <nonformal>, under one's own power *or* steam, **on one's own** *and* **on one's own hook** <both nonformal>, on one's own initiative; **on one's own account** *or* **responsibility,** on one's own say-so <nonformal>; of one's own accord, of one's own volition, at one's own discretion
3 **singly, individually,** particularly, severally, one by one, one at a time; **singularly,** in the singular; **by oneself,** by one's lonesome <nonformal>, under one's own steam, **single-handedly, solo, unaided;** separately

**along** ADVS **forward, forwards, onward, onwards, forth, on, ahead;** on the way to, on the road *or* high road to, en route to *or* for

**alongside** ADJS 1 **side, lateral;** flanking, skirting; **beside,** to the side, off to one side; **parallel**
ADVS 2 **aside,** on one side, **to one side,** to the side, sidelong, on the side, on the one hand, on the other hand; in parallel, side-by-side

**aloof** ADJS 1 **standoffish, distant, remote,** withdrawn, removed, detached, Olympian; **cool,** cold, cold-fish, frigid, chilly, icy, frosty
ADVS 2 **at a distance, away, off,** at arm's length; distantly, remotely

**aloud** ADVS **loudly,** loud, lustily; **boomingly, thunderously, thunderingly; noisily,** uproariously; at the top of one's voice, in full cry

**alp** NOUNS **mountain,** mount, hump, tor, height, dizzying height, nunatak, dome; **peak, pinnacle, summit**, mountaintop, point, topmost point *or* pinnacle, **crest,** *pic* <Fr>, *pico* <Sp>; crag, spur, the roof of the world

*the beginning and the end*
*of all natural scenery*
RUSKIN

**alphabet** NOUNS **writing system, script, letters;** letters of the alphabet, **ABC's; phonetic alphabet,** International Phonetic Alphabet *or* IPA; Initial Teaching Alphabet *or* ITA

**alphabetize** VERBS **catalog,** list, file, tabulate, rationalize, **index,** digest, codify; **categorize,** put down as, **pigeonhole,** place, **group, arrange**, range; **order,** put in order, rank, rate, **grade; sort,** assort

**alpine** ADJS **mountainous,** mountained, alpen, alpestrine, alpigene; subalpine

**already** ADVS **until now, hitherto,** till now, thitherto, **hereunto,** heretofore, until this time, by this time, **up to now,** up to the present, up to this time, to this day, to the present moment, to this very instant, **so far,** thus far, **as yet, to date**

**also** ADVS **additionally, in addition,** and then some, even more, more so, and also, and all <nonformal>, and so, **as well, too,** else, beside, **besides, to boot, not to mention, let alone, into the bargain**

**altar** NOUNS **Lord's table,** holy table, **Communion table,** chancel table, table of the Lord, God's board; rood altar

**alter** VERBS 1 **change, mutate; modify;** adapt; modulate, accommodate, adjust, fine-tune, fit, **qualify; vary, diversify; convert, renew, recast, revamp** <nonformal>, change over, exchange, **revive; about-face,** do an about-face, do a 180 <nonformal>, reverse oneself, turn one's coat, sing *or* dance to a different tune, flip-flop <nonformal>
2 **castrate,** geld, emasculate, eunuchize, neuter, spay, fix <nonformal>, unsex, deball <nonformal>

**alteration** NOUNS **modification, change; variation,** variety, difference, diversity, diversification; **deviation,** diversion, aberrance *or* aberrancy, **divergence; switch, switchover, changeover, turn,** turnabout, about-face, **reversal,** flip-flop <nonformal>; realignment, **adaptation, adjustment,** accommodation, fitting; **reform,** reformation, **improvement,** amelioration, melioration, mitigation, constructive change, **betterment,** change for the better

**alternate** NOUNS 1 **substitute,** sub <nonformal>, **substitution, replacement,** backup, second *or* third string <nonformal>, secondary, utility player, succedaneum; fill-in, **stand-in, understudy, pinch hitter** *or* runner <nonformal>
VERBS 2 reciprocate, swing, **go to and fro,** to-and-fro, **come and go,** ebb and flow, wax and wane, ride and tie, hitch and hike, back and fill
ADJS 3 **reciprocal,** reciprocative; **back-and-forth, to-and-fro,** up-and-down

**alternative** NOUNS 1 **option, discretion, pleasure,** possible choice, alternate choice
ADJS 2 **elective;** volitional, voluntary; **optional,** discretional

**although** ADVS, CONJ **notwithstanding,** all the same <nonformal>, still, yet, even; **however, nevertheless,** nonetheless; when, though; **at all events,** in any event, **in any case,** at any rate; **be that as it may,** for all that, even so, **on the other hand,** rather, again, at the same time, all the same, just the same, **however, that may be;** after all, after all is said and done

**altitude** NOUNS **height,** vertical *or* perpendicular distance; **highness, tallness, elevation,** ceiling; **loftiness,** sublimity, exaltation; hauteur, toploftiness

**altogether** ADVS 1 **in addition,** and then some, even more, more so, and also, and all <nonformal>, and so, **as well, too,** else, beside, **besides, to boot, not to mention, let alone, into the bargain; beyond, plus; moreover,** thereto, farther, further, **furthermore,** at the same time, then, again, yet; similarly, likewise, by the same token, by the same sign
2 **wholly, entirely,** all; **totally,** *in toto* <L>, from start to finish, from soup to nuts <nonformal>, from A to Z, from A to izzard, across the board; *tout ensemble* <Fr>; **in all,** on all counts, in all respects, at large; **as a whole, in the aggregate,** in bulk, in the mass, *en masse* <Fr>, *en bloc* <Fr>; lock, stock, and barrel; hook, line, and sinker
3 **generally, in general; generally speaking,** speaking generally, **broadly,** broadly speaking, **roughly,** roughly speaking, as an approximation; **usually, as a rule, ordinarily, commonly, normally,** routinely, as a matter of course; **by and large,** at large, overall, over the long haul <nonformal>, **all things considered,** taking one thing with another, taking all things together, **all in all,** taking all in all, **on the whole,** as a whole, **in the long run,** for the most part, for better or for worse

**altruistic** ADJS 1 **benevolent, charitable, beneficent, philanthropic,** humanitarian; **bighearted,** greathearted; **generous**; eleemosynary
2 **unselfish, selfless;** self-unconscious, self-forgetful, self-abasing, self-effacing; **humble; unpretentious, modest**; **self-denying,** self-renouncing, self-abnegating; **self-sacrificing,** devoted, dedicated, committed, consecrated, unsparing of self, disinterested

**alumna** *and* **alumnus** NOUNS **graduate,** grad <nonformal>; alumni, alumnae; old boy <Brit>; **graduate student,** grad student <nonformal>, **postgraduate,** postgrad <nonformal>; college graduate, college man *or* woman

**always** ADVS 1 **all along, all the time,** all the while, at all times, *semper et ubique* <L, always and everywhere>; **invariably,** without exception, *semper eadem* <L, ever the same; Elizabeth I>
2 **constantly, continually**, **steadily,** sustainedly, **regularly,** as regular as clockwork, every time one turns around, right along <nonformal>, unvaryingly, uninterruptedly, **incessantly,** unceasingly, **ceaselessly,** without cease *or* ceasing, perennially, all the time, at all times, ever, ever and anon, without letup *or* break *or* intermission, without stopping

**amalgamation** NOUNS **affiliation, alliance, allying, alignment, association,** consociation, combination, **union,** unification, **coalition,** fusion, merger, coalescence, **league, federation, confederation,** confederacy, consolidation, incorporation, inclusion, integration

**amass** VERBS **store up, stock up, lay up,** put up, **save up,** hoard up, treasure up, garner up, **heap up,** pile up, build up a stock *or* an inventory; **accumulate,** cumulate, **collect, stockpile**

**amateur** NOUNS 1 **nonprofessional, layman,** member of the laity, laic
2 **dilettante, half scholar,** sciolist, **dabbler,** dabster, trifler, smatterer
ADJS 3 **avocational,** hobby, nonprofessional

**amateurish** ADJS **unskilled, unaccomplished, untrained,** untaught, unschooled, untutored, uncoached, unimproved, uninitiated, **unprepared,** unprimed, unfinished, unpolished; **untalented, ungifted, unendowed;** unprofessional, unbusinesslike, semiskilled

**amaze** VERBS **astonish, astound, surprise,** startle, stagger, **bewilder, perplex**, flabbergast <nonformal>, confound, overwhelm, **boggle, boggle the mind; dumbfound,** strike dumb, strike dead; knock one's socks off *and* bowl down *or* over <both nonformal>, dazzle, bedazzle, daze, bedaze

**amazement** NOUNS **wonder,** wonderment, sense of wonder, marveling, **astonishment;** stupefaction; **surprise; awe,** sense of mystery, admiration; beguilement, fascination; bewilderment

**ambassador** NOUNS **diplomat,** diplomatist, diplomatic agent; **emissary, envoy, legate, minister,** foreign service officer; ambassador-at-large; envoy extraordinary, plentipotentiary, **minister plenipotentiary;** nuncio, internuncio, apostolic delegate

**ambidextrous** ADJS ambidextral, ambidexter; dextrosinistral, sinistrodextral

**ambience** NOUNS 1 **environment, surroundings, environs,** surround, circumambiencies, **circumstances,** environing circumstances, *alentours* <Fr>; **precincts,** ambit, purlieus; **neighborhood, vicinity,** vicinage
2 **milieu, atmosphere, climate, air,** aura, spirit, feeling, feel, quality, color, local color, sense, sense of place, note, tone, overtone, undertone

**ambiguity** NOUNS ambiguousness; **equivocalness,** equivocacy; **double meaning,** amphibology, multivocality, polysemy, polysemousness; double entendre; inexplicitness, uncertainty

**ambiguous** ADJS **equivocal,** multivocal, polysemous, polysemantic; two-edged, two-sided, either-or, betwixt and between; obscure, enigmatic; self-contradictory, **paradoxical,** antinomic, oxymoronic, ambivalent, **ironic**

**ambition** NOUNS 1 ambitiousness, vaulting ambition; climbing, status-seeking, social climbing, careerism; opportunism; power-hunger

*the mind's immodesty*
D'AVENANT

*the way in which a vulgar man aspires*
HENRY WARD BEECHER

2 **aim, goal**, end, end in view, telos, final cause; aspiration, inspiration, guiding light *or* star, lodestar

**ambitious** ADJS 1 **aspiring,** upward-looking, high-reaching; high-flying, social-climbing, careerist, careeristic, on the make <nonformal>; power-hungry
2 **ostentatious, pretentious;** vaunting, **lofty, highfalutin** *and* highfaluting <both nonformal>, **high-flown; high-toned,** tony <both nonformal>

**ambivalence** NOUNS **irresolution, indecision,** unsettledness, irresoluteness, **indecisiveness,** undecidedness, infirmity of purpose; mugwumpery, mugwumpism, fence-sitting, fence-straddling; capriciousness, mercuriality, fickleness; change of mind, second thoughts, tergiversation

**amble** NOUNS 1 ramble, **hike, tramp,** traipse <nonformal>; **stroll,** saunter; **promenade;** *passeggiata* <Ital>; **constitutional** <nonformal>
VERBS 2 **go slow** *or* **slowly,** go at a snail's pace, take it slow, get no place fast <nonformal>; **drag,** drag out; **creep, crawl;** laze, idle; get nowhere fast; inch, inch along; shuffle *or* stagger *or* totter *or* toddle along; traipse *and* **mosey** <both nonformal>; **saunter, stroll,** waddle, toddle <nonformal>

**ambush** NOUNS 1 **ambuscade,** *guet-apens* <Fr>; blind, stalking-horse; booby trap, trap
VERBS 2 ambuscade, **waylay; lie in ambush,** lay wait for, **lie in wait for,** lay for <nonformal>; stalk; set a trap for

**ameliorate** VERBS **improve, better,** change for the better, make an improvement; transform, transfigure; improve upon, refine upon, **mend, amend,**

emend; meliorate; **civilize,** acculturate, socialize; enlighten, edify; **educate**

**amenable** ADJS 1 **consenting, assenting,** affirmative, persuaded, approving, agreeing, favorable, accordant, consentient, consentual; **acquiescent, compliant, willing, agreeable,** content
2 **persuadable,** persuasible, open-minded, pervious, accessible, receptive, responsive; **plastic, pliant,** pliable, malleable; **suggestible, susceptible, impressionable,** weak

**amend** VERBS **revise,** redact, **revamp, rewrite,** redraft, **rework,** work over; **emend,** emendate; **edit,** blue-pencil; **redress,** make good *or* right, **put right,** set right, put *or* set to rights, put *or* set straight, make all square; requite, restitute

**amendment** NOUNS **revision,** revise, **emendation, correction, corrigenda, rectification;** editing, redaction, recension, revampment; touching up, putting on the finishing touches, putting the gloss on, finishing, perfecting, tuning, fine-tuning

**amenities** NOUNS 1 **creature comforts, comforts, conveniences,** good things of life, cakes and ale, egg in one's beer <nonformal>, all the comforts of home; all the heart can desire, luxuries, the best
2 **etiquette,** social code, rules *or* code of conduct; **formalities,** social procedures, social conduct, what is done, what one does; **manners,** good manners, exquisite manners, quiet good manners, **politeness,** *politesse* <Fr>, natural politeness, comity, civility; civilities, **social graces, mores, proprieties;** decorum, good form

**amiable** ADJS affable, genial, cordial; gentle, mild, mild-mannered; easy, easy-natured, easy to get along with, able to take a joke, **agreeable, good-natured,** well-natured, **good-humored, good-tempered,** bonhomous, **sweet, sweet-tempered**

**amicable** ADJS **in accord, harmonious, in harmony,** congruous, congruent, in tune, attuned, agreeing, in concert, **in rapport,** *en rapport* <Fr>; friendly, frictionless; **sympathetic,** simpatico <nonformal>, empathic, empathetic, **understanding**

**amiss** ADJS 1 **disorderly, in disorder,** disordered, **disorganized, disarranged, discomposed,** dislocated, deranged, convulsed; **upset, disturbed,** perturbed, unsettled, discomfited, disconcerted
2 **erroneous, untrue,** not true, **not right;** unfactual, **wrong,** all wrong; peccant, perverse, corrupt; straying, astray, adrift
ADVS 3 **astray, beside the mark,** beside the point, far from it, to no purpose, in vain, vainly, fruitlessly, bootlessly; **erroneously, falsely,** by mistake, fallaciously; **mistakenly;** on the wrong track

**amity** NOUNS **concord,** concordance, **harmony,** symphony; **rapport;** good vibrations <nonformal>, good vibes <nonformal>, good karma; **fellowship,** kinship, togetherness, **affinity; congeniality, compatibility**

**ammunition** NOUNS **ammo** <nonformal>, **powder and shot**

**amnesia** NOUNS **loss of memory, memory loss,** memory failure; **memory gap,** blackout <nonformal>; fugue

**amnesty** NOUNS 1 **pardon,** excuse, sparing, indemnity, exemption, immunity, reprieve, grace; **absolution,** shrift, remission, remission of sin
VERBS 2 **forgive, pardon, excuse,** give *or* grant forgiveness, spare; grant amnesty to, grant immunity *or* exemption; **absolve,** remit, give absolution, shrive, grant remission

**amok** ADJS **rabid, maniac** *or* **maniacal,** raving mad, stark-raving mad, **frenzied, frantic,** frenetic; **berserk,** running wild

**amoral** ADJS **unconscientious,** unconscienced, conscienceless, unconscionable, shameless, without shame *or* remorse, **unscrupulous, unprincipled,** unethical, immoral

**amorous** ADJS amatory, amative, erotic; **sexual; passionate, ardent,** impassioned; desirous; lascivious

**amortization** NOUNS **payment, paying,** paying off, paying up <nonformal>, payoff; **defrayment,** defrayal; **discharge, settlement, clearance, liquidation,** amortizement, retirement, satisfaction

**amount** NOUNS 1 quantity, **sum, number,** count, group, total, reckoning, **measure,** parcel, passel <nonformal>, **part, portion,** clutch, ration, share, issue, allotment, lot, deal
2 **price, cost, expense,** expenditure, **charge,** damage *and* score *and* tab <all nonformal>

**amphibian** NOUNS batrachian, croaker, paddock <nonformal>; **frog,** tree toad *or* frog, bullfrog; **toad,** hoptoad *or* hoppytoad; newt, salamander; **tadpole, polliwog**
**ample** ADJS **spacious, roomy, commodious, capacious; extensive,** expansive, extended; **abundant,** copious, plenteous, **plentiful**, **sufficient,** sufficing; **enough,** substantial, **plenty, satisfactory, adequate,** decent, due
**amplify** VERBS **expatiate, dilate, expand,** enlarge, **enlarge on,** expand on, **elaborate;** relate *or* rehearse in extenso; detail, particularize
**amputate** VERBS **sever, dissever,** cut off *or* away *or* loose, shear off, hack through, hack off, ax; **cleave, split**
**amulet** NOUNS **talisman, charm, fetish,** periapt, phylactery; **voodoo, hoodoo,** juju, obeah, mumbo jumbo; **good-luck charm,** good-luck piece, **lucky piece,** rabbit's-foot, lucky bean, four-leaf clover, whammy <nonformal>
**amusement** NOUNS **entertainment, diversion,** solace, divertisement, *divertissement* <Fr>, **recreation, relaxation,** regalement; **pastime,** *passe-temps* <Fr>; **mirth**; **pleasure, enjoyment**
**amusing** ADJS **entertaining, diverting,** beguiling; **fun,** funsome *and* more fun than a barrel of monkeys <both nonformal>; recreative, recreational; **delightful,** titillative, titillating; humorous
**anachronism** NOUNS chronological *or* historical error, **mistiming, misdating,** misdate, postdating, antedating; parachronism, metachronism, prochronism; prolepsis
**anagram** NOUNS logogram, logogriph, metagram; acrostic, double acrostic; amphiboly, amphibologism
**analogy** NOUNS **likening,** comparing; **comparison,** compare, examining side by side, matching, matchup, holding up together, proportion <old>, comparative judgment *or* estimate; parallelism; correlation
**analysis** NOUNS 1 analyzation, **breakdown,** breaking down, breakup, breaking up; anatomy, anatomizing, dissection; separation, **division, subdivision,** segmentation, reduction to elements *or* parts; **examination, study,** logical analysis; logical discussion, dialectic
2 a priori reasoning, a fortiori reasoning, a posteriori reasoning; discursive reasoning; **deduction, deductive reasoning,** syllogism, syllogistic reasoning; hypothetico-deductive method; **induction, inductive reasoning,** epagoge
3 **psychoanalysis,** the couch <nonformal>; psychoanalytic therapy, psychoanalytic method
**analyst** NOUNS 1 **analyzer, examiner**; taxonomist; **critic,** interpreter, exegete, explicator, theoretician, aesthetician; reviewer
2 **psychoanalyst; shrink** *and* headshrinker *and* shrinker <all nonformal>; **counselor,** psychological counselor; **psychologist; psychotherapist, therapist,** psychotherapeutist; **psychiatrist,** alienist, somatist; neuropsychiatrist; psychopathist, psychopathologist
**analytic** ADJS 1 **analytical;** segmental; classificatory, enumerative; schematic; **inquiring, questioning, querying,** quizzing; **rational,** ratiocinative *or* ratiocinatory
2 dialectic, dialectical, maieutic; syllogistic, syllogistical, enthymematic, enthymematical, soritical, epagogic, inductive, deductive, inferential, synthetic, synthetical, discursive
**analyze** VERBS 1 **break down,** break up, anatomize, dissect, atomize, unitize; **divide, subdivide,** segment; assay; separate, make discrete, isolate, reduce, reduce to elements, resolve; **reason; deduce, infer, generalize; synthesize; theorize,** hypothesize; philosophize; syllogize
2 **discuss, debate, reason, deliberate,** deliberate upon, exchange views *or* opinions, talk, **talk over, hash over** <nonformal>, talk of *or* about, **consider, treat,** dissertate on, **go into, examine,** investigate, talk out, sift, **study,** review, ventilate, thresh out, consider pro and con; **kick** *or* **knock around** <nonformal>
**anarchist** NOUNS anarch; antinomian; **nihilist,** syndicalist *and* anarcho-syndicalist <both old>
**anarchy** NOUNS anarchism; **disorderliness, unruliness,** misrule, **disorder,** disruption, disorganization, confusion, **turmoil, chaos,** primal chaos, tohubohu; antinomianism; **nihilism;** syndicalism *and* anarcho-syndicalism *and* criminal syndicalism <all old>, lynch law, mob rule *or* law, mobocracy, ochlocracy; **law of the jungle**

**anatomy** NOUNS 1 **body,** frame, bodily *or* corporal *or* corporeal entity, physical self, physical *or* bodily structure, physique, soma; organism, organic complex
2 form; **morphology,** science of structure; **structure, construction,** architecture, tectonics, architectonics, **frame,** make, **build,** fabric, tissue, warp and woof *or* weft, web, weave, texture, contexture, mold, **shape, pattern, plan,** fashion, arrangement, **organization**; organism, organic structure, **constitution, composition**

**ancestor** NOUNS procreator, begetter; natural *or* birth *or* biological parent; grandparent; ancestress, progenitress, progenitrix; **predecessor,** forebear, precedent, antecedent

**ancestry** NOUNS progenitorship; parentage, parenthood; patrocliny, matrocliny; patrilineage, matrilineage; patriliny, matriliny; **blood relationship,** blood, ties of blood, consanguinity, common descent *or* ancestry, biological *or* genetic relationship, **kinship,** kindred, **relation, relationship,** sibship

**anchor** NOUNS 1 mooring, hook *and* mudhook <both nonformal>; **anchorage,** moorings; **berth,** slip; mooring buoy
2 newscaster, sportscaster; commentator, news commentator, news reader <Brit>; news anchor, anchor man *or* woman
VERBS 3 come to anchor, lay anchor, **cast anchor,** let go the anchor, drop the hook; carry out the anchor; kedge, kedge off; **dock, tie up; moor,** pick up the mooring

**ancient** NOUNS 1 man *or* woman *or* person of old, **prehistoric mankind;** preadamite, antediluvian; **primitive, aboriginal,** aborigine, bushman, autochthon; **caveman,** cave dweller, troglodyte
ADJS 2 **aged, elderly, old,** grown old in years, along *or* up *or* advanced *or* on in years, years old, advanced, advanced in life, **at an advanced age,** geriatric, gerontic; **venerable,** old as Methuselah *or* as God *or* as the hills

**anemic** ADJS 1 **feeble,** debilitated; **strengthless,** sapless, marrowless, pithless, sinewless, listless, out of gas <nonformal>, nerveless, lustless; **impotent, powerless**
2 dull, flat, mat, dead, dingy, muddy, leaden, lusterless, lackluster; **faded, washed-out,** dimmed, discolored, etiolated; **pale, dim,** weak, **faint; pallid, wan, sallow**

**anesthetic** NOUNS 1 general anesthetic, local anesthetic, analgesic, anodyne, balm, ointment, **pain killer,** painreliever, antiodontalgic
ADJS 2 **deadening,** numbing, dulling; analgesic, narcotic; stupefying, stunning, numbing, mind-boggling *or* -numbing; anesthetizing, narcotizing

**anesthetize** VERBS **deaden, numb,** benumb, blunt, dull, obtund, **desensitize; put to sleep,** slip one a Mickey *or* Mickey Finn <nonformal>, chloroform, etherize; narcotize, drug, dope <nonformal>

**angel** NOUNS 1 celestial, celestial *or* heavenly being; messenger of God; **seraph,** seraphim <pl>, angel of love; **cherub, cherubim** <pl>, angel of light
2 **innocent,** baby, babe, babe in arms, newborn babe, infant, babe in the woods, lamb, dove
3 **backer, sponsor, patron, supporter,** Maecenas; cash cow *and* staker *and* grubstaker <all nonformal>, meal ticket <nonformal>

**angelic** ADJS 1 **seraphic, cherubic; heavenly, celestial**
2 **endearing, lovable, likable, adorable,** admirable, **lovely,** lovesome, sweet, winning, winsome

**anger** NOUNS 1 **wrath, ire,** *saeva indignatio* <L>; angriness, irateness, wrathfulness, soreness <nonformal>; infuriation, enragement

*a transient madness*
HORACE

VERBS 2 **lose one's temper,** become irate, forget oneself, let one's angry passions rise; get one's blood up, **bridle,** bridle up, **bristle,** bristle up, raise one's hackles, get one's back up; reach boiling point, boil over, climb the wall, go through the roof

3 <nonformal> **get mad** *or* **sore,** get one's Irish *or* dander *or* hackles up, get one's monkey up <Brit>; **see red, get hot under the collar,** flip out, work oneself into a lather *or* sweat *or* stew, get oneself in a tizzy, do a slow burn; **work oneself up,** work oneself into a sweat, lather, have a short fuse, get hot

under the collar, run a temperature, race one's motor, get into a dither *or* tizzy *or* swivet *or* pucker *or* stew; blow up, **blow one's top** *or* stack *or* cool, **flip,** flip out, flip one's lid *or* wig, pop one's cork, wig out, blow a gasket, fly off the handle, **hit the ceiling,** go ape, go hog wild, go bananas, lose one's cool, go off the deep end

4 **make angry, make mad,** raise one's gorge *or* choler; make one's blood boil

5<nonformal> **piss** *or* tee off, tick off, piss, **get one's goat, get one's Irish** *or* back *or* dander *or* hackles up, **make sore,** get one's mad up, make one hot under the collar, put one's nose out of joint, burn one up, burn one's ass *or* butt, steam

**angle** NOUNS 1 **viewpoint, standpoint, point of view,** vantage, vantage point, point *or* coign of vantage, where one stands
2 **slant,** spin <nonformal>; bias, leaning, inclination, tendentiousness; unequal *or* preferential treatment, discrimination, inequality

**angry** ADJS 1 angered, **incensed, indignant, irate,** ireful; **livid,** livid with rage, beside oneself, **wroth, wrathful,** wrathy, **cross,** wrought-up, worked up, riled up <nonformal>; **out of humor,** out of temper, out of sorts

2 <nonformal> **mad, sore,** mad as a hornet *or* as a wet hen *or* as hell, sore as a boil, pissed; **pissed-off** *or* PO'd; teed off *or* TO'd; ticked off, browned-off, waxy *and* stroppy <both Brit>, **hot,** het up, **hot under the collar,** burned up, hot and bothered, boiling, boiling *or* hopping *or* fighting *or* roaring mad, fit to be tied, good and mad, steamed, hacked, bent out of shape, in a lather *or* lava *or* pucker, red-assed

**anguish** NOUNS 1 **wretchedness, despair,** bitterness, infelicity, **misery, agony, woe,** woefulness, woesomeness <old>, bale, balefulness
VERBS 2 **suffer, hurt, ache, bleed; suffer anguish; agonize,** writhe; have a bad time of it, go through hell; aggrieve, oppress, **grieve, sorrow,** plunge one into sorrow, embitter; **break one's heart, make one's heart bleed;** desolate

**animal** NOUNS 1 **creature,** critter <nonformal>, living being *or* thing; **brute, beast,** varmint <nonformal>, dumb animal *or* creature, dumb friend
ADJS 2 **ruthless**; **brutal,** brutish, brute, bestial, beastly, animalistic; **mindless, soulless,** insensate, senseless, subhuman, dehumanized, brutalized

**animal kingdom** NOUNS **animal life, brute creation, fauna, Animalia** <zoology>, **animality; wild animals** *or* **beasts, beasts of field, wildlife, denizens of the forest** *or* **jungle** *or* **wild, furry creatures**

**animate** VERBS 1 **energize,** dynamize; **invigorate, enliven, liven, liven up,** vitalize, quicken, goose *or* jazz up <nonformal>; **exhilarate, stimulate,** hearten, galvanize, electrify, charge up, psych *or* pump up <nonformal>, **pep** *or* snap *or* jazz *or* zip *or* perk up <nonformal>
ADJS 2 **living, alive,** having life, live, very much alive, alive and well, alive and kicking <nonformal>, conscious, breathing, quick <old>, animated, **vital,** zoetic; viable

**animated** ADJS **active, lively, spirited,** bubbly, ebullient, effervescent, **vivacious, sprightly,** chipper *and* perky <both nonformal>, pert; **spry, breezy, brisk, energetic,** eager, keen, can-do <nonformal>; **peppy** *and* snappy *and* zingy <all nonformal>; frisky, bouncing, bouncy

**animism** NOUNS **animistic religion** *or* cult; voodooism, voodoo, hoodoo, wanga, juju, jujuism, obeah, obeahism; shamanism; fetishism, totemism; nature worship, naturism; primitive religion

**animosity** NOUNS animus; **ill will,** ill feeling, bitter feeling, **hard feelings,** no love lost; **bitterness,** sourness, soreness, **rancor,** acrimony, virulence, venom, vitriol

**annals** NOUNS **chronicle, chronology, register,** registry, record; journal, diary

**annex** NOUNS 1 **adjunct, addition,** increase, **increment,** augmentation, *additum* <L>, addendum, addenda <pl>, accession; annexation; **appendage,** appendant, pendant, appanage, tailpiece, coda
2 <building> wing, **addition,** extension, ell *or* L

VERBS 3 **take possession, appropriate, take up,** take over, make one's own, move in *or* move in on <nonformal>

**annihilate** VERBS **exterminate**, eradicate, extirpate, **eliminate,** liquidate, **wipe out, stamp out,** waste *and* take out *and* nuke *and* zap <all nonformal>, put an end to

**annihilation** NOUNS **extinction, extermination, elimination, eradication,** extirpation; rooting out, deracination, uprooting, tearing up root and branch; **snuffing out; liquidation, purge; suppression**

**anniversary** NOUNS **commemoration;** immovable feast, annual holiday; jubilee, silver jubilee, golden jubilee, diamond jubilee; centennial, centenary

**annotation** NOUNS **comment, word of explanation;** notation, **note,** note of explanation, footnote, gloss, scholium; exegesis; *apparatus criticus* <L>; commentary

**announce** VERBS 1 **herald, harbinger, forerun,** run before; give notice, notify, talk about; **state, declare, assert,** aver, affirm, asseverate, allege; make a statement, send a message; tell the world; nuncupate

**announcement** NOUNS **pronouncement, proclamation,** annunciation, enunciation; predication, predicate; utterance, dictum, *ipse dixit* <L>; **affirmation,** affirmance, **assertion, asseveration,** averment, **declaration,** vouch <old>, allegation; manifesto, position paper; statement of principles, **creed**

**annoy** VERBS **irk, vex, nettle, provoke, pique,** miff *and* peeve <both nonformal>, distemper, **ruffle, disturb,** discompose, **roil,** rile, **aggravate,** make a nuisance of oneself, **exasperate,** exercise, try one's patience, try the patience of a saint; **put one's back up,** make one bristle; **bug** <nonformal>, be on the back of *and* be at *and* ride <all nonformal>, **pester, tease, needle,** devil, get after *or* get on <nonformal>, **bedevil, pick on** <nonformal>, **plague,** beset, beleaguer

**annoyance** NOUNS **vexation,** exasperation, *tracasserie* <Fr>, **aggravation; nuisance, pest, bother,** botheration <nonformal>, public nuisance, **trouble, problem,** pain <nonformal>, difficulty, hot potato <nonformal>; **pain in the neck** *or* **in the ass** <nonformal>; **harassment,** molestation, harrying; bedevilment; vexatiousness

**annoying** ADJS **irritating,** galling, **provoking, aggravating** <nonformal>, **exasperating; vexatious,** vexing, irking, **irksome,** tiresome, wearisome; **troublesome, bothersome, worrisome,** bothering, troubling, **pesky** *and* pesty *and* pestiferous <all nonformal>; tormenting, harassing, worrying

**annual** NOUNS 1 **periodical, serial, journal,** gazette; ephemeris; yearbook
ADJS 2 **yearly;** biennial, triennial, decennial, etc

**annuity** NOUNS **subsidy,** subvention, subsidization, support; **allowance, stipend,** allotment; pension, old-age insurance, retirement benefits, social security, remittance; **insurance,** variable annuity

**annul** VERBS **abolish, nullify,** void, abrogate, annihilate, tear up, repeal, revoke, negate, invalidate, **undo, cancel,** cancel out, bring to naught, put *or* lay to rest; countermand, **abolish,** do away with; vacate, declare null and void; **overrule,** override

**annulment** NOUNS 1 **divorce,** civil divorce, **separation,** legal *or* judicial separation, separate maintenance; interlocutory decree; dissolution of marriage
2 **neutralization, nullification,** cancellation, voiding, invalidation, vitiation, frustration, thwarting, undoing

**annunciation** NOUNS **announcement,** enunciation; **proclamation,** pronouncement, pronunciamento; public declaration *or* statement, **notice, notification,** public notice; encyclical, encyclical letter; manifesto, position paper; broadside; ukase, edict

**anoint** VERBS 1 **install,** instate, induct, **inaugurate,** invest, put in, place, **place in office;** crown, throne, enthrone
2 **perform a rite,** perform service *or* divine service; administer a sacrament
3 **oil,** grease; salve, unguent, embrocate, dress, pour oil *or* balm upon; smear, daub

**anonymity** NOUNS **privacy,** retirement, isolation, sequestration, seclusion; **confidentialness,** confidentiality; **anonymousness, namelessness; incognito**

**anonymous** ADJS **private, privy, closed-door; intimate, inmost,** innermost, interior, inward, **personal; privileged,** protected; **secluded, sequestered,** isolated, withdrawn, retired; incognito

**another** NOUNS 1 **a different thing,** a different story <nonformal>, **something else,** something else again <nonformal>, *tertium quid* <L, a third something>, *autre chose* <Fr>, another kettle of fish <nonformal>, another tune, different breed of cat <nonformal>, horse of a different color
ADJS 2 **other,** whole nother <nonformal>, else, otherwise, other than *or* from; not the same, not the type <nonformal>, not that sort, of another sort, of a sort *and* of sorts <both nonformal>

**answer** NOUNS 1 **reaction, response,** respondence, feedback; reply, **rise** <nonformal>; **reflex,** reflection, **reflex action;** reverberation, resonance, sympathetic vibration; riposte, **uptake** <nonformal>, **retort, rejoinder,** reaction, return, **comeback** *and* **take** <both nonformal>, back talk
2 **solution,** resolution, **reason, explanation**; **finding,** conclusion, determination, ascertainment, verdict, judgment; **outcome, upshot,** denouement, **result,** issue, end, end result
VERBS 3 respond *or* reply to, get back to; **communicate with, get in touch** *or* **contact with, contact** <nonformal>, **make contact with,** raise, reach, get to, get through to, get hold of, make *or* establish connection, get in connection with; **refute, confute, confound, rebut,** parry, **answer conclusively,** dismiss, dispose of
4 **avail,** be of use, be of service, serve, **suffice, do, answer** *or* **serve one's purpose,** serve one's need, fill the bill *and* do the trick <both nonformal>

**answerable** ADJS **responsible; liable, accountable,** amenable, unexempt from, chargeable, on one's head, at one's doorstep, on the hook <nonformal>; responsible for, at the bottom of; to blame

**ant** NOUNS emmet <nonformal>, pismire, pissant *and* antymire <both nonformal>; red ant, black ant, fire ant, house ant, agricultural ant, carpenter ant, army ant; slave ant, slave-making ant; **termite,** white ant; queen, worker, soldier

**antagonism** NOUNS **hostility,** oppugnancy, oppugnance *and* oppugnation <both old>, **antipathy,** enmity, bad blood, inimicalness; **contrariness, contrariety,** orneriness <nonformal>, repugnance *or* repugnancy, perverseness, **obstinacy**; fractiousness, refractoriness, recalcitrance; **disagreement, discord,** discordance *or* discordancy; **disharmony,** unharmoniousness; dissonance, dissidence; **dissent**, negation, contradiction

**antagonist** NOUNS **opponent, adversary, assailant, foe, enemy,** archenemy; opposite *or* opposing side, **the opposition,** the loyal opposition; **combatant**

**antagonize** VERBS set against, set at odds, set at each other's throat, sick on each other <nonformal>; **provoke,** envenom, **embitter,** infuriate, madden; **alienate,** estrange; be alienated *or* estranged, draw *or* grow apart

**ante** NOUNS 1 **bet, wager, stake,** hazard, lay; long shot; parlay, double or nothing; **poker bet**
VERBS 2 **bet, wager, gamble, hazard, stake,** punt, lay, lay down, put up, **make a bet, lay a wager,** give *or* take *or* lay odds, make book, get a piece of the action <nonformal>; plunge <nonformal>

**antebellum** ADJS prewar, before the war; prerevolutionary

**antecedent** NOUNS 1 **precursor, forerunner,** *voorlooper* <Dutch>, vaunt-courier, avant-courier; trailblazer *or* trailbreaker, guide; **predecessor,** forebear, precedent, **ancestor;** innovator, groundbreaker
ADJS 2 **prior,** antecedent, anterior, **leading**; **preliminary,** precursory, prevenient, prefatory, exordial, prelusive, preludial, proemial, preparatory, initiatory, propaedeutic, inaugural; **preceding**, foregoing, above, anterior, **anticipatory,** antecedent; **preexistent**

**antedate** VERBS **predate,** backdate; **be prior,** be before *or* early *or* earlier, come on the scene *or* appear earlier, **precede, antecede, forerun,** come *or* go before, set a precedent; **herald,** usher in, proclaim, announce

**anthem** NOUNS 1 **paean,** laud; hosanna, hallelujah, alleluia; **hymn,** hymn of praise, **doxology, psalm,** motet, canticle, chorale; **chant,** versicle; antiphon, antiphony; offertory, offertory sentence *or* hymn

**anthology** NOUNS **compilation,** omnibus; symposium; collection, collectanea, miscellany; **miscellanea,** analects; ana; chrestomathy; garland, florilegium; *Festschrift* <Ger>

**anthropoid** NOUNS 1 preadamite, antediluvian; humanoid, primate, fossil man, protohuman, prehuman, missing link, apeman, hominid; **primitive, aboriginal,** aborigine, bushman, autochthon; **caveman,** cave dweller, troglodyte
ADJS 2 **manlike,** humanoid, hominid; anthropomorphic

**antibiotic** NOUNS 1 ampicillin, bacitracin, penicillin, etc; **miracle drug, wonder drug,** magic bullets; bacteriostat; **sulfa drug,** sulfa, sulfanilamide, sulfonamide
ADJS 2 **antidotal,** alexipharmic; **antitoxic;** bacteriostatic, antimicrobial

**antic** NOUNS **prank, trick, practical joke,** waggish trick, *espièglerie* <Fr>, caper, frolic; **monkeyshines** *and* **shenanigans** <both nonformal>

**anticipate** VERBS **foresee,** previse, see the handwriting on the wall, pave the way for; forerun, go before, get a head start, steal a march on, beat someone to the punch *or* the draw <nonformal>; **jump the gun,** go off half-cocked <nonformal>; take the words out of one's mouth

**anticipation** NOUNS 1 **carefulness, care, heed, concern, regard; attention**; **heedfulness,** regardfulness, mindfulness, **thoughtfulness;** circumspection; forethought
2 **prevision,** divination, forecast; **prediction**; **foreglimpse, prospect;** sagacity, providence, discretion, preparation, provision, prudence

**antidepressant** ADJS **psychochemical,** psychoactive; ataractic; mood drug

**antidote** NOUNS counterpoison, alexipharmic, theriaca *or* theriac; **counteractant,** counteractive, **counteragent;** counterirritant; **neutralizer,** nullifier, offset

**antipathy** NOUNS **hostility,** antagonism, **enmity**; **hatred, hate**; **aversion, repugnance,** repulsion, allergy <nonformal>, grudge, abomination, **abhorrence, horror,** mortal horror

**antipodes** NOUNS 1 **opposites,** polar opposites, contraries; **poles,** opposite poles, antipoles, counterpoles, North Pole, South Pole
2 jumping-off place *and* godforsaken place *and* God knows where *and* the middle of nowhere <all nonformal>, remotest corner of the world; outpost, outskirts; the sticks *and* the boondocks *and* the boonies <all nonformal>

**antiquarian** NOUNS antiquary, *laudator temporis acti* <L>; dryasdust, the Rev Dr Dryasdust, Jonathan Oldbuck <both Sir Walter Scott>, Herr Teufelsdröckh <Carlyle>; antique dealer, antique collector, antique-car collector; archaist

**antiquated** ADJS 1 **past, gone,** by, **gone-by, bygone,** gone glimmering, bypast, ago, **over,** departed, passed, passed away, elapsed, lapsed, vanished, faded, no more, irrecoverable, never to return, not coming back; dead as a dodo, expired, extinct, dead and buried, defunct, deceased; **passé, obsolete,** has-been, dated, antique
2 grown old, **superannuated, old,** age-encrusted; antediluvian; **fossil,** fossilized, petrified

**antique** NOUNS **antiquity,** archaism; **relic,** relic of the past; **remains,** survival, vestige, ruin *or* ruins; old thing, oldie *and* golden oldie <nonformal>
ADJS 2 **ancient,** venerable, hoary; of old, of yore; dateless, timeless, ageless; **immemorial,** old as Methuselah *or* Adam, old as God, old as the hills

**antiquity** NOUNS 1 **ancient times,** time immemorial, ancient history, remote age *or* time, remote *or* far *or* dim *or* **distant past,** distance of time
2 **oldness, age,** eld <old>, hoary eld; **ancientness,** dust of ages, rust *or* cobwebs of antiquity; venerableness, eldership, primogeniture, great *or* hoary age

**anti-Semitism** NOUNS **discrimination,** social discrimination, minority prejudice; xenophobia, know-nothingism; **chauvinism,** ultranationalism, superpatriotism; fascism

**antiseptic** NOUNS 1 microbicide, germicide, antiseptic, disinfectant
ADJS 2 **sanitary, hygienic, prophylactic; sterile,** aseptic, **uninfected;** disinfected, decontaminated, sterilized; pasteurized

**antisocial** ADJS **misanthropic,** people-hating, Timonist, Timonistic, cynical; unsociable; **man-hating,** misandrist; **woman-hating,** misogynic, misogynistic, misogynous; solitary, reclusive

**anus** NOUNS rectum; **asshole** *and* bumhole *and* bunghole <all nonformal>; bung

**anxiety** NOUNS **anxiousness; apprehension, apprehensiveness,** antsyness <nonformal>, misgiving, foreboding, forebodingness, suspense, strain, tension, stress, nervous strain *or* tension; **dread, fear**; **concern,** concernment, anxious concern, **solicitude**; perturbation, disturbance, upset, **agitation, disquiet,** disquietude, inquietude, unquietness; **nervousness**; malaise, angst

**anxious** ADJS **concerned, apprehensive,** foreboding, misgiving, suspenseful, strained, tense, tensed up <nonformal>, nail-biting, white-knuckle <nonformal>; **fearful**; uneasy, perturbed, disturbed, disquieted, agitated; **on pins and needles,** on tenterhooks, on shpilkes <nonformal>, on the anxious seat *or* bench

**any** NOUNS 1 **anything,** any one, aught, either; **anybody, anyone**
ADJS 2 **every, all,** whichever, whichsoever; **each,** each one; every one, each and every, each and all, **one and all, all and sundry,** all and some

**anybody** NOUNS any one, aught, either; **anyone**

**anyhow** ADVS **anyway,** anywise, in any way, **by any means, by any manner of means;** in any event, at any rate, leastways <nonformal>, in any case; **nevertheless, nonetheless, however, regardless**

**anyone** NOUNS **whoever,** whoso, **whosoever, whomever,** whomso, **whomsoever,** no matter who

**anything** NOUNS **any,** any one, aught, either

**anytime** ADVS **whenever,** whene'er, whensoever, whensoe'er, **at whatever time,** at any time, no matter when; if ever, once; **imminently,** impendingly; any time now, any moment, any second, any minute, any hour, any day; **to be expected,** as may be expected, as may be

**anywhere** ADVS anyplace <nonformal>; **wherever,** where'er, **wheresoever,** wheresoe'er, whithersoever, wherever it may be

**apart** ADJS 1 **secluded, seclusive, retired, withdrawn; isolated,** shut off, insular, **separate,** separated, detached, removed
ADVS 2 **away, aside,** wide apart; **separately,** severally, piecemeal, one by one; apart from, away from, aside from

**apartheid** NOUNS **discrimination,** social discrimination, minority prejudice; **color line,** color bar; **segregation**

**apartment** NOUNS **flat,** tenement, chambers <Brit>, rooms; studio apartment *or* flat; bed-sitter <Brit>, granny flat, flatlet; garden apartment; duplex apartment; railroad flat

**apathy** NOUNS **indifference, unconcern,** lack of caring, disinterest; withdrawnness, **aloofness, detachment,** ataraxy *or* ataraxia; **passiveness,** passivity, supineness, insouciance, nonchalance; **listlessness, spiritlessness,** burnout, blah *or* blahs <nonformal>; **lethargy,** hebetude, **dullness,** sluggishness, languor, languidness

**ape** NOUNS 1 **primate, simian; monkey**
2 **imitator,** simulator, me-tooer <nonformal>, **impersonator, impostor, mimic,** mimicker, mimer, mime, **mocker; parrot,** polly, poll-parrot *or* polly-parrot, aper
VERBS 3 **mimic, impersonate,** mime, **parrot,** copycat <nonformal>; take off, hit off, hit off on, take off on

**aperture** NOUNS **opening, hole,** hollow, **cavity, orifice; slot,** split, crack, check, leak

**apex** NOUNS **summit,** top; **tip-top, peak,** pinnacle; **crest, brow;** ridge, edge; **crown,** cap, **tip,** point, spire, pitch; **acme,** *ne plus ultra* <Fr>, **zenith, climax,** apogee, pole

**aphorism** NOUNS **maxim, apothegm, epigram, dictum, adage, proverb,** gnome, words of wisdom, **saw, saying,** witticism, sentence, expression, phrase, catchword, catchphrase, word, byword, mot, motto, moral

**aphrodisiac** NOUNS 1 **love potion, philter,** love philter; cantharis, blister beetle, Spanish fly
ADJS 2 aphroditous, **arousing,** stimulating, eroticizing, venereal

**aplomb** NOUNS **equanimity,** equilibrium, equability, balance; **levelheadedness,** level head, well-balanced *or* well-regulated mind; **poise, self-possession, self-control,** self-command, self-restraint, restraint, possession, **presence of mind**

**apocalypse** NOUNS **revelation, divine revelation; inspiration,** afflatus, divine inspiration; theophany, theophania, epiphany; **prophecy,** prophetic revelation

**apocryphal** ADJS **unauthoritative, unauthentic, unofficial,** nonofficial; **uncertified, unverified,** unchecked, unconfirmed, uncorroborated, unauthenticated, unvalidated, unattested, unwarranted; **undemonstrated, unproved**

**apologetic** ADJS **penitent, repentant; penitential,** penitentiary; **contrite,** abject, humble, humbled, **sheepish,** touched, softened, melted

**apologize** VERBS **beg pardon, ask forgiveness,** beg indulgence, express regret; take back; get *or* fall down on one's knees

**apology** NOUNS **excuse,** regrets; acknowledgment, penitence, contrition, breast-beating, *mea culpa* <L>, confession; abject apology, apologia, apologetic

**apoplexy** NOUNS **paralysis,** palsy, impairment of motor function; **stroke;** motor paralysis, sensory paralysis; hemiplegia, paraplegia, diplegia, quadriplegia

**apostate** NOUNS 1 **turncoat,** turnabout, **recreant, renegade,** renegado, renegate *or* runagate <old>, **defector,** tergiversator, tergiversant
ADJS 2 **recreant,** renegade, tergiversating, tergiversant; **treasonous, treasonable, traitorous,** forsworn; collaborating; faithless, **disloyal**

**apostle** NOUNS 1 **disciple, follower;** convert, proselyte; **evangelist, disciple,** saint

**appall** VERBS **horrify,** shock; make the flesh creep *or* crawl, make one shudder; **repel,** put off, turn off <nonformal>, **revolt, disgust,** nauseate, sicken, make one sick, make one sick to *or* in the stomach, make one vomit *or* puke *or* retch, turn the stomach, gross out <nonformal>

**appalling** ADJS **terrible,** terrific, tremendous; **horrid, horrible, horrifying,** horrific, horrendous; **dreadful, dread,** dreaded; **hideous, ghastly,** morbid, grim, grisly, gruesome, ghoulish, macabre

**apparatus** NOUNS **device,** contrivance, contraption <nonformal>, gadget, gizmo, gimcrack, gimmick <nonformal>, means

**apparel** NOUNS 1 **clothing, clothes, wear, wearing apparel, daywear, dress,** dressing, **raiment,** garmenture, **garb, attire, array,** habit, habiliment, fashion, style, guise, **costume,** costumery, gear; **vestment,** vesture, investment, investiture; **garments,** robes, robing, rags <nonformal>, drapery, finery, feathers; toggery *or* togs *or* **duds** *or* threads <all nonformal>

**apparent** ADJS **manifest, evident, self-evident,** axiomatic, indisputable, **obvious, plain, clear,** perspicuous, distinct, palpable, patent, tangible; **visible, perceptible, perceivable, discernible,** seeable, observable, **noticeable, much in evidence**

**apparently** ADVS 1 **seemingly, ostensibly,** to *or* by all appearances, to *or* by all accounts, to the eye; on the face of it, *prima facie* <L>; on the surface, outwardly, superficially; at first sight *or* view, at first blush
2 **manifestly, evidently, obviously, patently, plainly, clearly,** distinctly, **unmistakably,** expressly, explicitly, palpably, tangibly; **visibly, perceptibly,** perceivably, discernibly, observably, **noticeably**

**appeal** NOUNS 1 **delightfulness,** exquisiteness, loveliness; **charm,** winsomeness, grace, **attractiveness;** sexiness <nonformal>; **glamour;** captivation, enchantment, entrancement, bewitchment, witchery, enravishment, **fascination**
2 **entreaty, plea, bid,** suit, call, cry, clamor, *cri du c<oe>ur* <Fr>, beseeching, impetration, obtestation; **supplication, prayer,** rogation, **beseechment,** imploring, imploration, obsecration, obtestation, adjuration, imprecation
VERBS 3 **attract, interest, engage,** impress, charismatize, fetch <nonformal>, catch *or* get one's eye, command one's attention, rivet one, attract one's interest, be attractive, take *or* tickle one's fancy
4 **entreat, implore, beseech, beg,** crave, **plead, pray, supplicate,** impetrate, obtest; adjure, conjure; invoke, imprecate <old>, **call on** *or* **upon,** cry on *or* upon, **appeal to,** cry to, run to; go cap *or* hat in hand to

**appealing** ADJS 1 **delightful, exquisite, lovely; thrilling,** titillative; **charming, attractive, endearing, engaging,** prepossessing, heartwarming, sexy <nonformal>, **enchanting,** bewitching, witching, entrancing, enthralling, intriguing, fascinating
2 **imploring, entreating, beseeching, begging, pleading,** precatory, precative, adjuratory

**appear** VERBS 1 become visible; **arrive, make one's appearance,** make *or* put in an appearance, appear on the scene, **show up** <nonformal>, **turn up,** come, **materialize,** present oneself, present

oneself to view, **come to light,** see the light, see the light of day; **emerge,** issue, issue forth, stream forth, come forth, come to the fore, come out, come forward, come one's way, come to hand
2 be published, **come out,** break, hit the streets <nonformal>, **issue,** go *or* come forth, find vent, **see the light,** see the light of day, become public; **circulate, spread,** spread about, have currency, **get around** *or* about, **go the rounds,** pass from mouth to mouth, be on everyone's lips

**appearance** NOUNS 1 **appearing,** showing-up, coming forth, coming on the scene, making the scene <nonformal>, putting in an appearance; **emergence,** issuing, issuance; **disclosure, exposure,** opening, unfolding, showing
2 exterior, externals, **mere externals, facade,** outside, **show, outward show, image,** display, front <nonformal>, outward *or* external appearance, surface appearance, surface show, vain show, apparent character, public image, window dressing, cosmetics
3 <thing appearing> **apparition,** phenomenon; **vision, image, shape, form,** figure, presence; false image, mirage, specter, **phantom**

**appease** VERBS **pacify, conciliate, placate, propitiate, mollify,** dulcify; **calm, settle, soothe,** tranquilize; smooth over *or* out, smooth down, smooth one's feathers; pour oil on troubled waters, pour balm on, take the sting out of

**append** VERBS affix, attach, annex, adjoin, conjoin, subjoin, prefix, suffix, infix, postfix, tag, tag on, **tack on** <nonformal>, slap on <nonformal>, hitch on <nonformal>

**appendage** NOUNS 1 **external organ; head, arm, leg,** etc
2 **adjunct, addition,** increase, **increment,** augmentation, supplementation, complementation, *additum* <L>, addendum, addenda <pl>, accession, fixture; **annex,** annexation; appurtenance, appurtenant; **accessory,** attachment; **supplement,** complement, continuation, extrapolation, extension

**appendix** NOUNS vermiform appendix *or* process; **sequel,** sequela *or* sequelae, sequelant, sequent, sequitur, **consequence**; **continuation,** continuance, **follow-up** *or* **follow-through** <nonformal>; **supplement,** addendum, back matter

**appetite** NOUNS 1 **craving, coveting, lust; hunger, thirst, appetency** *or* appetence; aching void; **itch, itching,** prurience *or* pruriency; **sexual desire; mania**

*appetite, an universal wolf*
**Shakespeare**

2 **eagerness, enthusiasm, avidity,** avidness, keenness <chiefly Brit>, forwardness, prothymia, **readiness,** promptness, quickness, **alacrity,** cheerful readiness, *empressement* <Fr>; **zest,** zestfulness, gusto

**appetizer** NOUNS *apéritif* <Fr>; foretaste, *antipasto* <Ital>, *Vorspeise* <Ger>; **hors d'oeuvre;** *crostato* <Ital>; smorgasbord; canapé; **dip**

**appetizing** ADJS mouth-watering, piquant; **alluring, fascinating, captivating, riveting, charming, glamorous,** exotic, **enchanting,** spellful, spellbinding, **entrancing,** ravishing, **enravishing, intriguing, enthralling,** witching, **bewitching; tempting**

**applaud** VERBS 1 **cheer,** give a cheer, give three cheers, **cry, shout, yell,** cry for joy, yell oneself hoarse; shout hosanna *or* hallelujah
2 **congratulate, felicitate,** bless, **compliment,** tender *or* offer one's congratulations *or* felicitations *or* compliments; shake one's hand, pat one on the back

**applause** NOUNS plaudit, éclat, **acclaim, acclamation; clapping,** handclapping, clapping of hands; **cheer**; burst of applause; **round of applause, hand, big hand; ovation,** standing ovation

**appliance** NOUNS **implement,** device; contrivance, lever, mechanism; fixture; labor-saving device

**applicable** ADJS 1 **usable, utilizable;** appliable; practical, operable
2 **relevant, pertinent,** appertaining, **germane, apposite,** cogent, material, admissible, applying, pertaining, belonging, involving, appropriate, **apropos,** *à propos* <Fr>, to the purpose, **to the point**

**applicant** NOUNS **petitioner, supplicant,** suppliant, suitor; solicitant, claimant; **aspirant, candidate,** postulant

**application** NOUNS 1 **industry,** industriousness, assiduousness, **assiduity, diligence,** concentration, laboriousness, sedulity, **sedulousness,** unsparingness,

relentlessness, zealousness, ardor, fervor, vehemence
2 **use, employment,** utilization, employ <old>, **usage; exercise, exertion,** active use; good use; expenditure, expending, using up, exhausting, dissipation, dissipating, **consumption**
3 **request,** asking; desire, wish, expressed desire; **petition,** petitioning, impetration, address

**apply** VERBS 1 **put to use** *or* **good use,** carry out, put into execution, **put into practice** *or* **operation,** put in force, enforce; bring to bear upon
2 **petition,** present *or* prefer a petition, sign a petition, circulate a petition; **pray,** sue
3 **relate, associate, connect,** interconnect, ally, link, link up, wed, marry, marry up, weld, bind, tie, couple, bracket, equate, identify

**appoint** VERBS 1 **elect, vote in,** place in office
2 **equip, furnish, outfit,** gear, **prepare, fit,** fit up *or* out, fix up <nonformal>, **rig,** rig up *or* out, **turn out,** accouter, clothe, dress; man, staff

**appointment** NOUNS 1 **engagement, date** <nonformal>, double date *and* blind date <both nonformal>
2 **position, job,** employment, gainful employment, situation, **office, post, place,** station, berth, billet, engagement, gig <nonformal>

**apportion** VERBS **portion, parcel, partition, part, divide,** share; share with, cut *or* deal one in <nonformal>, share and share alike, divide with; divide into shares, divide up, divvy *or* divvy up *or* out <nonformal>, **split,** split up, carve, cut, slice, carve up, slice up, cut up, cut *or* slice the pie *or* melon <nonformal>

**appraisal** NOUNS **stocktaking, assay,** assaying; **assessment,** determination, rating, valuation, evaluation

**appreciable** ADJS **substantial,** substantive; **solid, concrete; tangible,** sensible, palpable, ponderable; **material**; **real**

**appreciate** VERBS 1 **enjoy,** be pleased with, receive *or* derive pleasure from, take delight *or* pleasure in, get a kick *or* boot *or* bang *or* charge *or* lift *or* rush out of <nonformal>; feast on, gloat over *or* on; **relish,** savor, smack the lips
2 **be grateful, be obliged,** feel *or* be *or* lie under an obligation, be obligated *or* indebted, be in the debt of, give credit *or* due credit; **be thankful,** thank one's lucky stars, thank *or* bless one's stars; be appreciative of
3 **grow, increase, advance; gain,** get ahead; wax, swell, balloon, bloat, mount, **rise,** go up, crescendo, snowball

**appreciative** ADJS **grateful, thankful; obliged, much obliged,** beholden, indebted to, crediting, under obligation, acknowledging, cognizant of; **approbatory, approbative, commendatory, complimentary, laudatory,** acclamatory, eulogistic, panegyric, panegyrical, encomiastic

**apprehend** VERBS 1 **arrest,** make an arrest, put under arrest, pick up; catch flat-footed; catch with one's pants down *or* hand in the till <nonformal>, catch one in the act *or* red-handed *or* in flagrante delicto, catch *or* have one dead to rights
2 **know, perceive,** prehend, cognize, recognize, discern, see, make out; conceive, conceptualize; **realize, appreciate, understand, comprehend,** fathom; dig <nonformal>

**apprehension** NOUNS 1 apprehensiveness, **misgiving, qualm,** qualmishness, funny feeling; foreboding; **misgiving,** chill *or* quiver along the spine
2 **arrest,** pinch *and* bust *and* collar <all nonformal>; **capture, seizure**

**apprehensive** ADJS **concerned,** foreboding, misgiving, suspenseful, strained, tense, tensed up <nonformal>, nail-biting, white-knuckle <nonformal>; **fearful**; **on pins and needles,** on tenterhooks

**apprentice** NOUNS 1 **novice,** novitiate *or* noviciate, **tyro,** abecedarian, alphabetarian, **beginner**, entrant, **neophyte, tenderfoot** *and* **greenhorn** <both nonformal>, freshman, **fledgling;** catechumen, initiate, debutant
VERBS 2 **train; drill, exercise; prepare,** ready, **condition, groom,** fit, put in tune, form, **lick into shape** <nonformal>; indenture, article, bind, bind over
ADJS 3 **indentured,** articled, bound over; **apprenticed**

**apprise** VERBS **inform, advise, advertise,** mention to, **acquaint, enlighten,** familiarize, brief, verse, give the facts, give an account of, give by way of information; **give** *or* **lead one to believe** *or* **understand;** notify, give notice *or* notification, serve notice; **communicate**; bring *or* send *or* leave word; **disclose**

**approach** NOUNS 1 **approaching, coming** *or* going toward, coming *or* going near, **access,** accession, nearing; **advent, coming,** forthcoming; imminence; approximation
2 **entrance,** entry, gate, door, portal, **entranceway,** entryway; **inlet,** ingress, intake, adit, **access,** means of access, in <nonformal>, way in; a foot in the door, an opening wedge, the camel's nose under the wall of the tent
3 **manner, way, means, mode,** modality, **fashion, style,** tone, guise <old>; **method,** methodology, **system;** algorithm <math>
4 **offer,** proffer, presentation, **bid; advance, overture,** approach, invitation; **feeler** <nonformal>; asking price
VERBS 5 **near, draw near** *or* nigh, go *or* come near, go *or* come toward, come closer *or* nearer; **accost,** encounter, confront
6 **communicate with, get in touch** *or* **contact with, contact** <nonformal>, **make contact with,** raise, reach, get to, get through to, get hold of, make *or* establish connection, get in connection with
7 **bribe,** throw a sop to; grease *and* **grease the palm** *or* **hand** *and* oil the palm *and* tickle the palm <all nonformal>; buy *and* **buy off** *and* pay off <all nonformal>; suborn, **corrupt,** tamper with; reach *and* get at *and* get to <all nonformal>

**appropriate** VERBS 1 **steal, thieve, purloin, take,** snatch, palm, **make off with,** walk off with, run off *or* away with, abstract; have one's hand in the till; **pilfer, filch**
ADJS 2 **apposite, suitable;** applicable, relevant, likely, sortable, seasonable, opportune; **fitting,** befitting, **suiting,** becoming; **fit,** fitted, qualified, **suited,** adapted, geared, tailored, dovetailing, meshing

**approval** NOUNS 1 **respect, regard,** consideration, appreciation, favor; **esteem,** estimation, prestige
2 **approbation; sanction,** acceptance, countenance, **favor; admiration, esteem, respect**; endorsement

*Our polite recognition of another's resemblance to ourselves*
AMBROSE BIERCE

**approve** VERBS **adopt;** ratify, pass, carry, endorse, sign off on <nonformal>; accept, **embrace,** espouse; **approve of,** think well of, take kindly to; **sanction, accept; admire, esteem, respect; favor,** view with favor

**approximate** VERBS 1 approach, near, come near, come close; **compare with,** stack up with <nonformal>; **correspond, match, parallel**
ADJS 2 **approaching,** nearing, approximating, proximate, proximal

**approximately** ADVS nearly, some, about, circa; more or less, *plus ou moins* <Fr>, by and large

**approximation** NOUNS **estimation,** estimate, rough measure, ballpark figure <nonformal>; **appraisal,** appraisement, **assay,** assaying; rough idea, sketch; coordinate, reciprocal, obverse, equivalent; correlate, correlative; **likeness,** like, the like of *or* **the likes of** <nonformal>; suchlike, such; simulacrum; **close match, match-up**

**apropos** ADJS 1 **germane, apposite,** cogent, material, admissible, applicable, applying, pertaining, belonging, involving, **appropriate,** *à propos* <Fr>, to the purpose, **to the point,** in point, *ad rem* <L>
ADVS 2 **incidentally, by the way, by the by;** speaking of, *à propos* <Fr>; **in passing,** *en passant* <Fr>; parenthetically, by way of parenthesis

**apt** ADJS 1 **apposite, appropriate, suitable;** applicable, relevant, likely, sortable, seasonable, opportune; **fitting,** befitting, **suiting,** becoming; to the point, to the purpose, on the button *and* on the money <both nonformal>
2 **teachable, instructable, educable,** schoolable, trainable; quick, **ready,** ripe for instruction; **receptive, willing,** motivated; docile, **malleable, moldable,** pliable, facile, plastic, **impressionable,** susceptible, formable

**aptitude** NOUNS 1 flair; **bent, turn,** propensity, **leaning,** inclination, tendency; turn for, capacity for, gift for, genius for; an eye for, an ear for, a hand for, a way with; ready wit, quick wit, sprightly wit, *esprit* <Fr>
2 **fitness** *or* fittedness, **suitability, appropriateness,** propriety, admissibility; **aptness,** qualification

**aquatic** ADJS **water-dwelling,** water-living, water-growing, water-loving; **swim-**

**ming,** balneal, natant, natatory, natatorial; **watery,** waterish, **aqueous**

**aqueous** ADJS watery, aquatic; **liquid;** splashy, **plashy, sloppy; hydraulic**

**arbiter** NOUNS **connoisseur,** *connaisseur* <Fr>, *cognoscente* <Ital>; **judge,** good judge, **critic, expert,** authority, maven <nonformal>, arbiter, arbiter of taste, *arbiter elegantiarum* <L>, tastemaker, trend-setter; **epicure,** epicurean; **gourmet, gourmand,** *bon vivant* <Fr>

**arbitrary** ADJS **capricious, whimsical,** freakish; **fanciful, notional,** fantastic *or* fantastical, maggoty, **crotchety,** kinky, harebrained, cranky, flaky <nonformal>, quirky; petulant; unrestrained

**arbitrator** NOUNS arbiter, impartial arbitrator, third party, unbiased observer; **moderator; umpire, referee, judge; go-between, middleman, intermediary, medium,** intermediate, **internuncio,** broker; **negotiator;** mediator

**arc** NOUNS 1 **curve,** sinus; **bow; crook, hook;** parabola, hyperbola; ellipse; catenary, festoon, swag
VERBS 2 **curve, turn,** sweep; **crook, hook,** loop; incurve, incurvate; recurve, decurve, bend back, retroflex; sag, swag <nonformal>; **bend,** flex; deflect, inflect; reflect, reflex; **bow,** embow; **arch,** vault; dome; **hump**

**arcade** NOUNS **corridor, hall,** hallway; passage, **passageway; gallery,** loggia; colonnade, pergola, cloister, peristyle; areaway; breezeway

**arcane** ADJS esoteric, occult, cabalistic, hermetic; enigmatic, mysterious; **secret,** close, closed, closet; cryptic, dark; unuttered, unrevealed, undivulged, undisclosed, unspoken, untold

**arch** NOUNS 1 **span, vault,** vaulting, concameration, camber; ogive; apse; **dome,** cupola; arched roof, ceilinged roof
2 **pillar,** stele *or* stela, shaft, column, memorial column, rostral column, manubial column; war memorial; memorial arch, triumphal arch
VERBS 3 vault; dome; **hump,** hunch; wind, curl; round; **curve, turn,** arc, sweep; **crook, hook,** loop; incurve, incurvate; recurve, decurve, bend back, retroflex; sag, swag <nonformal>; **bend,** flex; deflect, inflect; reflect, reflex; **bow**
ADJS 4 **chief, main, principal,** paramount, **foremost,** headmost, **leading, dominant,** crowning, capital, **cardinal;** master, magisterial; central, focal, prime, **primary,** primal, first; **preeminent**
5 **cunning, crafty, artful, wily,** guileful, **sly,** insidious, **shifty, smooth, slick** *and* slick as a whistle <both nonformal>, **slippery,** snaky, serpentine, **foxy,** vulpine, feline; **canny, shrewd,** knowing, sharp, razor-sharp, cute, acute, astute, **clever**

**archdiocese** NOUNS **diocese, see,** bishopric, archbishopric; province

**architecture** NOUNS 1 architectural design, building design, the art and technique of building; **architectural science,** architectural engineering, architectural technology

*frozen music*
GOETHE

*the art of significant forms in space*
CLAUDE BRAGDON

2 **structure, construction,** tectonics, architectonics, **frame,** make, **build,** fabric, tissue, texture, contexture, mold, **shape, pattern, plan,** fashion, arrangement, **organization**; organism, organic structure

**archives** NOUNS public records, government archives, government papers, presidential papers, historical documents, historical records, memorabilia

**arctic** ADJS 1 **northern,** north, northernmost, northerly, northbound, boreal, hyperborean; **southern,** south, southernmost, southerly, southbound, meridional, **antarctic,** austral
2 **cold, freezing,** freezing cold, **crisp, brisk,** nipping, **nippy, snappy** <nonformal>, **raw, bleak, keen, sharp,** bitter, biting, pinching, cutting, **piercing,** penetrating; **frigid,** bitter *or* bitterly cold, gelid, algid; numbing; Siberian, boreal, hyperborean

**ardent** ADJS 1 **industrious, assiduous, diligent, sedulous,** laborious, **hardworking;** hard, unremitting, unsparing, relentless, zealous, fervent, vehement; tireless, unwearied, unflagging, indefatigable
2 **amorous,** amatory; **passionate,** impassioned

**arduous** ADJS **laborious, toilsome, strenuous,** operose, onerous, oppressive, burdensome; wearisome; tough <non-

formal>, uphill, **backbreaking,** grueling, punishing, crushing, killing, Herculean

**area** NOUNS 1 **region, zone,** belt, **territory,** terrain; **district, quarter, section,** department, division; precincts, environs, milieu
2 **vocation**; **forte, métier, strong point,** long suit; specialism, specialization; cup of tea *and* bag *and* thing *and* weakness <all nonformal>

**arena** NOUNS **scene of action, site,** scene, setting, background, **field, ground,** terrain, sphere, place, locale, milieu, precinct, purlieu; athletic field, field, playing field; stamping ground, turf, bailiwick

**argue** VERBS **dispute,** polemicize, **bandy words, plead,** pettifog <nonformal>, join issue, give and take, cut and thrust, try conclusions, cross swords, lock horns, **contend, contest,** spar, **bicker, wrangle,** hassle <nonformal>, have it out

**argument** NOUNS 1 **quarrel, dispute,** polemic, **controversy,** altercation, **fight, squabble, contention,** strife, **tussle,** bicker, wrangle, snarl, **tiff, spat,** fuss
2 *argumentum* <L>; **case, plea,** pleading, *plaidoyer* <Fr>, brief

**aria** NOUNS **air, tune, melody,** line, melodic line, refrain, note, **song, strain**

**arise** VERBS 1 **emerge, come out, issue,** issue forth, come into view, extrude, **come forth; surface,** rise to the surface; **originate,** be born, come into the world, **become,** come to be, get to be <nonformal>, see the light of day
2 **rise,** ascend, mount, uprise, **rise up, get up,** get to one's feet; **revolt, rebel,** kick over the traces, reluct, reluctate; rise up, rise up in arms, mount the barricades

**aristocracy** NOUNS **nobility,** titled aristocracy, hereditary nobility, noblesse; **elite, upper classes** *or* circles, **upper crust** <nonformal>

**aristocrat** NOUNS **patrician,** Brahmin, blue-blood, socialite, swell *and* uppercruster <both nonformal>, grandee, grand dame, dowager, magnifico, lord of creation

**aristocratic** ADJS **upper-class, patrician, upscale; highborn,** highbred; born to the purple, born with a silver spoon in one's mouth; **noble,** of rank, high, exalted

*to the manner born*
SHAKESPEARE

**arm** VERBS **equip, furnish, outfit,** gear, **prepare, fit,** fit up *or* out, fix up <nonformal>, **rig,** rig up *or* out

**armada** NOUNS **fleet,** flotilla, argosy, squadron, escadrille, division, task force, task group

**armed** ADJS armed and ready, in arms, up in arms; in battle array, mobilized; **provided, equipped; readied,** available

**arms** NOUNS **weapons,** instruments of destruction, offensive weapons, **military hardware,** matériel, **weaponry, armament, munitions, ordnance,** munitions of war, *apparatus belli* <L>

**army** NOUNS forces, troops, host, array, legions; ranks, rank and file; **standing army, regular army,** professional *or* career soldiers

**aroma** NOUNS **fragrance, perfume,** scent, redolence, **incense, bouquet, odor;** muskiness; fruitiness

**aromatic** ADJS **fragrant,** odoriferous, redolent, **perfumed, scented,** sweet-smelling, sweet-scented, savory, balmy, ambrosial; **odorous**; fruity; musky

**around** ADVS round, **about,** in the neighborhood *or* vicinity *or* vicinage

**arouse** VERBS **excite, impassion, rouse, stir, stir up,** set astir, stir the feelings, stir the blood, cause a stir *or* commotion, play on the feelings; **foment, incite**; turn on <nonformal>

**arrange** VERBS 1 **prepare, make** *or* **get ready,** prep <nonformal>, **ready, fix** <nonformal>; fix *or* ready up <both nonformal>, put in *or* into shape, get one's ducks in a row <nonformal>; **put** *or* **set to rights, get it together** <nonformal>, **pull it together,** put in *or* into shape, whip into shape <nonformal>
2 **settle; adjust,** fine-tune, accommodate, reshuffle, rejigger <nonformal>, **compose,** fix, make up, straighten out, put *or* set straight

**arrangement** NOUNS **ordering,** structuring, shaping, forming, configurating, configuration, constitution; **disposition, disposal, deployment,** placement, **formation,** formulation, **configuration,** form, array; **order; organization**; **disposition,** disposal, deployment, marshaling

**arrears** NOUNS arrearage, back debts, back payments; **deficit,** default, deferred payments; cash *or* credit crunch <nonformal>

**arrest** VERBS 1 **slow, slow down** *or* **up,**

**let down** *or* **up, ease off** *or* **up, slack off** *or* **up, slacken,** relax, moderate, taper off, lose speed *or* momentum; **put on the brakes**
2 make an arrest, put under arrest, pick up; take prisoner, apprehend, capture, seize, net <nonformal>, **take into custody**

3<nonformal> **bust, pinch,** make a pinch, nab, pull in, **run in,** collar

4 **impede, inhibit, check,** countercheck, scotch, **curb,** snub; **resist, oppose**

**arrive** VERBS arrive at, arrive in, come, **come** *or* **get to,** approach, access, **reach, hit** <nonformal>; find, **gain,** attain, attain to, accomplish, achieve, make, **make it** <nonformal>, reach one's destination

**arrogant** ADJS **overbearing, superior,** domineering, **proud, haughty;** high-flown, high-falutin *and* high-faluting <both nonformal>; **condescending, patronizing,** *de haut en bas* <Fr>

**arsonist** NOUNS **incendiary,** torcher <nonformal>; pyromaniac, firebug <nonformal>

**art** NOUNS 1 **representation, delineation,** presentment, drawing, **portrayal, portraiture, depiction,** depictment, rendering, rendition, limning, imaging; **realization;** imagery
2 **visual arts; artwork,** the arts; **fine arts,** *beaux arts* <Fr>; **design,** art form; abstract art, representational art
3 **artistry, talent,** artistic skill, artistic flair, artistic invention
4 craftiness, **artfulness, artifice, wiliness,** wiles, guile, **slyness,** insidiousness, **foxiness,** slipperiness, shiftiness, trickiness

**artery** NOUNS **passageway, pass,** passage, defile; **avenue;** corridor, aisle, alley, lane; **channel,** conduit

**artful** ADJS **wily,** guileful, **sly,** insidious, **shifty,** pawky <Brit>, arch, **smooth, slick** *and* slick as a whistle <both nonformal>, **slippery,** snaky, serpentine, **foxy,** vulpine, feline; **canny, shrewd,** knowing, sharp, manipulative, manipulatory; **deceitful**

**article** NOUNS 1 **news item,** piece of news; **story,** piece; copy
2 **object, thing,** material thing, affair, something; artifact

**artifact** NOUNS **relic, fossil; product,** end product, production, manufacture; **work,** *œhuvre* <Fr>, **handiwork; object, thing,** material thing

**artificial** ADJS **affected, pretentious, mannered,** *maniéré* <Fr>; **unnatural,** insincere

**artillery** NOUNS **cannon,** cannonry, ordnance, engines of war, howitzer; field artillery; heavy artillery, mountain artillery, coast artillery, anti-aircraft artillery

**artisan** NOUNS **skilled worker, journeyman,** mechanic; **craftsman, handicraftsman;** artificer; *fabbro* <Ital>

**artist** NOUNS **entertainer,** public entertainer, performer; artiste; **musician,** performer, interpreter, concert artist, **virtuoso; vaudevillian,** dancer, **stripteaser,** singer

**artistic** ADJS **aesthetic,** pleasing, choice; pure, chaste; classic *or* classical, Attic, restrained, understated, unobtrusive, quiet, subdued, simple, unaffected; painterly

**artistry** NOUNS **competence,** capability, capacity, ability; **facility, prowess;** grace, style, finesse; **art, talent,** artistic skill, flair, artistic flair, artistic invention

**artwork** NOUNS **work of art,** objet d'art, art object, piece, **work, study, design, composition;** creation, brainchild; virtu, article *or* piece of virtu; **masterpiece,** *chef d'œhuvre* <Fr>, masterwork, old master, classic

**ascend** VERBS **rise, mount,** arise, up, uprise, levitate, upgo, **go up,** rise up, come up; stand up, **rear,** rear up, **tower,** loom

**ascending** ADJS in the ascendant, **mounting, rising,** uprising, upgoing, upcoming; climbing, scandent, scansorial; **uphill, upgrade;** acclivous, acclivitous, acclinate

**ascertain** VERBS **learn, gain knowledge,** pick up information, gather *or* collect *or* glean knowledge *or* learning; **find out, discover,** find, determine; **become informed,** gain knowledge *or* understanding of, acquire information *or* intelligence about, **learn about, find out about**

**ascetic** NOUNS 1 **recluse, loner,** solitary; cloistered monk *or* nun; **hermit,** eremite, anchorite; stylite
2 **abstainer,** abstinent; **teetotaler,** teetotalist

ADJS 3 austere, self-denying, self-abnegating, **rigorous, puritanical,** eremitic, anchoritic

**aseptic** ADJS **sanitary, hygienic, prophylactic; sterile,** antiseptic, **uninfected;** disinfected, decontaminated, sterilized

**asexual** ADJS **sexless, neuter,** neutral; castrated, emasculated, eunuchized; **cold, frigid**

**ashamed** ADJS **humiliated,** humbled, mortified <old>, **embarrassed, chagrined, abashed, crushed, red-faced,** shamed, ashamed of oneself, shamefaced

**ashen** ADJS **colorless, hueless,** toneless, uncolored, achromic, achromatic, achromatous; **faded, washed-out,** dimmed, discolored, etiolated; **pale, dim,** weak, **faint; pallid, wan, sallow;** white as a sheet; ashy, ashen-hued, cinereous, cineritious, gray, griseous

**ashore** ADVS **on land,** on dry land, on terra firma

**asinine** ADJS **foolish, fatuous,** fatuitous, inept, **inane;** futile; **senseless, witless, thoughtless,** insensate, brainless

**ask** VERBS 1 **request,** make a request, **ask for,** order, put in an order for, bespeak, call for, trouble one for; demand

2 **invite, call, summon,** extend *or* issue an invitation, request the presence of, request the pleasure of one's company

**askance** ADVS 1 **warily, charily,** cagily <nonformal>; distrustfully

2 **disapprovingly, unfavorably;** critically, reproachfully, rebukingly; captiously

**askew** ADVS 1 **awry,** askance, askant, asquint, squinting, **cockeyed** <nonformal>; **crooked**

2 **disorderly, in disorder,** disordered, **disorganized, disarranged, discomposed,** dislocated, deranged, convulsed; **out of kilter** *or* **kelter** <nonformal>, **out of whack** <nonformal>, out of gear, out of joint, out of tune, on the fritz <nonformal>

**asleep** ADJS 1 **sleeping, slumbering,** in the arms *or* lap of Morpheus, in the land of Nod; **sound asleep, fast asleep,** dead to the world

2 **unalert, unwary, unwatchful, unvigilant,** uncautious, incautious; nodding, napping, **asleep at the switch** *and* asleep on the job *and* **not on the job** *and* goofing off; daydreaming, woolgathering

**aspect** NOUNS look, view; effect, impression, **form, shape,** figure, configuration, gestalt; **respect, regard,** reference, light

**aspersion** NOUNS slur, **remark, reflection,** imputation, **insinuation,** suggestion, innuendo, disparaging *or* uncomplimentary remark, slap *or* kick in the face

**asphalt** NOUNS **pavement,** paving; macadam, blacktop, bitumen, tarmacadam, tarmac, tarvia, bituminous macadam

**asphyxiation** NOUNS **suffocation,** smothering, asphyxia; **choking**

**aspirant** NOUNS **applicant,** solicitant, claimant; seeker; postulant; **candidate,** hopeful *and* political hopeful <both nonformal>, office seeker *or* hunter, baby kisser <nonformal>

**aspire** VERBS **be ambitious;** aspire to, try to reach; aim high, keep one's eyes on the stars, raise one's sights, set one's sights, reach for the sky

*hitch one's wagon to a star*
EMERSON

**aspiring** ADJS **ambitious,** on the make <nonformal>; **hopeful, hoping, in hopes,** full of hope

**ass** NOUNS 1 **donkey, burro,** Rocky Mountain canary <W US>; **jackass,** jenny; **mule,** sumpter mule, sumpter; hinny, jennet

2 **fool, damn fool,** tomfool, perfect fool, born fool; *schmuck* <Yiddish>; jackass, stupid ass

3 **sex object;** piece *and* meat *and* piece of meat *and* piece of ass *and* hot number <all nonformal>

4 <nonformal> arse *and* bum <both chiefly Brit>, behind, backside, **butt, can,** cheeks, hind end, nether cheeks, stern, tail, rusty-dusty, **fanny,** prat, keister, popo, rear, rear end, tuchis *or* tushy *or* tush

**assail** VERBS 1 **attack, assault,** harry, assume *or* take the offensive; commit an assault upon

2 criticize, reprove, **castigate, flay,** skin alive <nonformal>, lash, slash, **excoriate,** fustigate, **roast** <nonformal>, blister

**assailant** NOUNS assailer, **attacker;** assaulter, mugger <nonformal>; **aggressor**

**assassin** NOUNS **killer, slayer, slaughterer, butcher, murderer, cutthroat,** gorilla <nonformal>, hired killer, hit man *or* button man *or* gun *or* trigger man *or* torpedo *or* gunsel <all nonformal>; **hatchet man**

**assassination** NOUNS murder, bloody murder <nonformal>; serial killing; hit *and* bump-off *and* bumping-off <all nonformal>, gangland-style execution; kiss of death; foul play

**assault** NOUNS 1 **attack; offense, offensive; strike;** surgical strike, first strike
2 **berating,** rating, tongue-lashing; **revilement, vilification,** blackening, **execration, abuse, vituperation,** invective, contumely, hard *or* cutting *or* bitter words; **tirade, diatribe,** screed, philippic
VERBS 3 **attack, assail,** harry, assume *or* take the offensive; commit an assault upon; **strike, hit, pound; launch out against, fall on** *or* **upon, set on** *or* **upon, descend on** *or* upon, come down on, swoop down on; pounce upon; blitz

**assay** NOUNS 1 **analysis,** chemical analysis, assaying, resolution, titration, qualitative analysis, quantitative analysis, volumetric analysis, gravimetric analysis
2 **test, trial, try;** essay; acid test, litmus *or* litmus-paper test; ordeal, crucible
VERBS 3 **measure, guage, quantify,** quantitate, quantize, take the measure of, mensurate,triangulate, apply the yardstick to; **estimate,** make an approximation; **assess, rate, appraise, valuate, value,** evaluate, appreciate, prize

**ass-backwards** ADJS 1 **backward,** reversed, reflex, **turned around,** back; wrong-way, wrong-way around, counter, bassackwards <nonformal>; misinterpreted
ADVS 2 **backwards,** backward, **hindwards,** hindward, **rearwards,** rearward, arear, astern

**assemble** VERBS gather; drum up, muster, rally, **mobilize; accumulate,** cumulate, **amass,** mass, bulk, batch; agglomerate, conglomerate, aggregate; **combine, gather together,** draw *or* lump *or* batch *or* bunch together, pack, pack in, cram, cram in; **bunch,** bunch up; **cluster,** clump

**assembly** NOUNS 1 **council,** conclave, *concilium* <L>, deliberative *or* advisory body; deliberative assembly, consultative assembly
2 **collection, gathering,** ingathering, **congregation;** concourse, concurrence, conflux, confluence, convergence; assemblage

**assent** NOUNS 1 acquiescence, concurrence, concurring, concurrency, **compliance, agreement,** acceptance, accession
VERBS 2 **acquiesce, consent, comply, accede, agree,** agree to *or* with, have no problem with; find it in one's heart; take kindly to *and* hold with <both nonformal>; **accept,** receive, buy <nonformal>, take one up on <nonformal>; **subscribe to,** acquiesce in

**assert** VERBS assever <old>, asseverate, **aver,** protest, lay down, avouch, avow, **declare,** say loud and clear, sound off <nonformal>, have one's say, speak one's piece *or* one's mind, speak up *or* out, **state,** set down, put in one's two-cents worth <nonformal>; **maintain, contend,** argue, **insist, hold,** submit, maintain with one's last breath

**assertive** ADJS **affirmative,** affirming, affirmatory; **positive,** absolute, emphatic, decided, table-thumping <nonformal>, unambiguously, unmistakably

**assess** VERBS **price,** place a value on, **value, evaluate,** valuate, **appraise, rate,** prize, apprize; **classify,** class, **categorize**

**assets** NOUNS **means, resources, worth,** net worth, what one is worth; circumstances, funds; wealth

**asshole** NOUNS

<nonformal> **jerk, horse's ass,** creep, **shit,** shithead, shitface, fart, **louse, meanie, heel, shitheel, rat, stinker,** dirtbag, dork, geek, dweeb, twerp, sleaze

**assiduous** ADJS **diligent, sedulous,** industrious; dogged, plodding, slogging, plugging; **pertinacious, tenacious, stick-to-itive** <nonformal>; **unswerving,** unremitting, unabating, unintermitting, uninterrupted; **unfaltering, unwavering,** relentless, **indefatigable,** undaunted, indomitable

**assign** VERBS 1 **allot,** lot, **appoint, set,** detail; **allocate,** tag, mark out for; set off, mark off, portion off; assign to, appropriate to *or* for; give *or* make an assignment, set a task

2 **transfer, convey, deliver,** hand, pass, negotiate; **hand over, turn over, pass over; consign,** confer, settle, settle on; cede, bequeath; **make over, sign over,** sign away; **deed,** deed over, give title to

**assignment** NOUNS 1 **allotment, appointment,** setting aside, **earmarking,** tagging; **allocation; task, work, stint, job,** labor, piece of work, **chore,** chare, odd job; homework
2 **transfer,** transference; **conveyance,** conveyancing; **consignment,** settling, settlement; entailment

**assist** NOUNS 1 **helping hand, hand, lift; boost** *and* leg up <both nonformal>; help in time of need
VERBS 2 minister to, act for, act in the interests of, **promote, advance, forward,** facilitate; **aid, help,** comfort, **succor,** relieve, **ease,** doctor, remedy; give help, render assistance, come to the aid of, rush *or* fly to the assistance of, **give** *or* **lend** *or* **bear a hand** *or* **helping hand,** hold out a helping hand

**assistance** NOUNS 1 **aid, help, support, succor, relief, comfort,** ease, remedy; mutual help *or* assistance; **service, benefit**
2 **subsidy,** subvention, subsidization, support, **allowance, stipend,** allotment; financial assistance; **help,** pecuniary aid

**assistant** NOUNS **helper,** auxiliary, aide, paraprofessional; **help, helpmate, helpmeet;** deputy, **agent**; **attendant, second,** acolyte

**associate** NOUNS 1 **confederate,** consociate, **colleague,** fellow member, **companion, fellow,** bedfellow, **crony,** consort, cohort, compatriot, **ally,** adjunct, coadjutor
ADJS 2 **related, connected; associated, affiliated,** filiated, **allied,** affiliate; interlocked, **interrelated,** interlinked, involved, implicated, overlapping, interpenetrating, **correlated**

**association** NOUNS 1 **association of ideas,** chain of ideas, concatenation, mental linking
2 **society,** body; **alliance, coalition, league, union;** council; **bloc,** axis; **partnership; federation, confederation,** confederacy; grouping, assemblage

**assorted** ADJS 1 **diversified, varied,** heterogeneous; **various,** divers <old>, diverse, sundry, **several, many;** of all sorts *or* conditions *or* kinds *or* shapes *or* descriptions *or* types
2 **classified, cataloged,** indexed, sorted, **graded, grouped,** ranked, rated, stratified, hierarchic

**assortment** NOUNS 1 **miscellany,** miscellanea, collectanea; **medley, variety, mixture**; hodgepodge, conglomerate, **conglomeration, odds and ends**
2 **grouping, classification**, categorization, taxonomy; **sorting,** sorting out, sifting, screening, triage, culling

**assume** VERBS 1 **undertake,** accept, **take on, take upon oneself,** take upon one's shoulders
2 **appropriate, adopt, usurp,** arrogate, accroach; **take possession of,** possess oneself of, take for oneself, arrogate to oneself
3 **suppose, presume, surmise,** expect, **suspect, infer, understand, gather, conclude, deduce, consider,** reckon, divine, imagine, **fancy,** dream, conceive, **believe, deem,** repute, feel, **think,** be inclined to think, opine, daresay

**assumed name** NOUNS **alias, pseudonym,** anonym, false *or* fictitious name, *nom de guerre* <Fr>; **pen name, nom de plume;** stage name, *nom de thé[aca]tre* <Fr>, professional name

**assumption** NOUNS 1 **appropriation, taking over, takeover** <nonformal>, **adoption, usurpation,** arrogation
2 **presumption, imposition; license,** licentiousness, **undue liberty,** liberties

**assurance** NOUNS 1 **confidence,** confidentness, conviction, belief, fixed *or* settled belief, **sureness, assuredness,** surety, security, certitude
2 **insurance; annuity, social security**

**assure** VERBS 1 **secure, guarantee, guaranty, warrant, insure,** ensure, bond, **certify; endorse**
2 **satisfy;** put one's mind at rest on; sell *and* sell one on <both nonformal>; make *or* carry one's point, bring *or* drive home to; inspire belief *or* confidence

**assuring** ADJS 1 **comforting, consoling,** consolatory, of good comfort; **reassuring,** supportive; **encouraging, heartening; cheering**
2 **persuasive,** impressive, satisfying, satisfactory, confidence-building; decisive, absolute, conclusive, determinative

**astonish** VERBS **amaze, astound, surprise,** startle, stagger, **bewilder, perplex**, flabbergast <nonformal>, confound, overwhelm, **boggle the mind; awe,** strike with wonder *or* awe; **dumb-**

**found,** strike dumb; knock one's socks off *and* bowl down *or* over <all nonformal>, dazzle, bedazzle; **stun, stupefy**

**astonishing** ADJS **amazing, surprising,** startling, **astounding,** confounding, staggering, stunning <nonformal>, eye-opening, breathtaking, overwhelming, mind-boggling *or* -numbing; **remarkable, outstanding,** extraordinary, **superior, marked,** of mark, signal, conspicuous, **striking; marvelous,** wonderful, formidable, exceptional, uncommon, appalling, humongous <nonformal>, fabulous, fantastic, incredible, egregious

**astound** VERBS **dismay, disconcert, appall,** confound, abash, discomfit, put out, take aback; **stun, stupefy**

**astounding** ADJS **terrible,** terrific, tremendous; **dreadful, dread,** dreaded; **awful;** awesome, awe-inspiring; **shocking, appalling; dire,** direful, fell; formidable, redoubtable

**astray** ADJS 1 **lost,** abroad, adrift, **at sea,** off the track, out of one's bearings, disoriented
ADVS 2 **amiss, beside the mark,** beside the point, to no purpose, vainly, fruitlessly, bootlessly; on the wrong track

**astrology** NOUNS astromancy, **horoscopy;** astrodiagnosis; natural astrology; judicial *or* mundane astrology

**astronaut** NOUNS astronavigator, cosmonaut, **spaceman, spacewoman,** space crew member, space traveler, rocketeer, rocket pilot

**astronomical** ADJS **vast, enormous,** astronomic, humongous *and* jumbo <both nonformal>, tremendous, prodigious, stupendous; **innumerable, numberless,** unnumbered, **countless,** uncounted, uncountable, unreckonable, untold, incalculable, immeasurable, unmeasured, measureless, inexhaustible, endless, infinite, without end *or* limit, more than you can shake a stick at <nonformal>

**astronomy** NOUNS **stargazing,** uranology, astrognosy, astrography, uranography, uranometry

**astute** ADJS **sagacious,** longheaded, argute; **understanding, discerning,** penetrating, incisive, acute, trenchant, cogent, piercing; **perspicacious,** perspicuous; **perceptive, percipient,** apperceptive, appercipient

**asunder** ADJS 1 **distant, remote, removed, far, far-off,** away, **faraway,** way-off, at a distance, separated, apart
ADVS 2 **separately,** severally, piecemeal, one by one; **apart,** adrift, **in two,** in twain

**asylum** NOUNS 1 **insane asylum,** lunatic asylum, **madhouse,** mental institution, mental home, bedlam; **bughouse** *and* nuthouse *and* laughing academy *and* **loonybin** *and* **booby hatch** *and* funny farm <all nonformal>
2 **refuge, sanctuary,** safehold, **haven, port,** harborage, **harbor;** port in a storm, snug harbor, safe haven; stronghold

**asymmetry** NOUNS 1 unsymmetry, disproportion, lopsidedness, imbalance, irregularity, **deviation**
2 **inconsistency, incongruity,** inconsonance, incoherence; **incompatibility,** irreconcilability, incommensurability

**atavistic** ADJS **reversionary, regressive, retrogressive, retrograde;** recidivist *or* recidivistic, recidivous, lapsarian

**atelier** NOUNS **study,** studio, *atelier* <Fr>, workroom; **office,** workplace

**atheist** NOUNS 1 **unbeliever, disbeliever,** nonbeliever; **infidel, pagan, heathen;** nullifidian
ADJS 2 **unbelieving, disbelieving, faithless; infidel,** infidelic; **pagan, heathen; atheistic;** nullifidian

**athlete** NOUNS jock <nonformal>, **player,** competitor, sportsman; letter man

**athletics** NOUNS **sport, sports,** athletic competition, game, sports activity

**atmosphere** NOUNS 1 aerosphere, gaseous envelope *or* environment *or* medium *or* blanket, welkin, lift <nonformal>; atmospheric layer *or* stratum *or* belt
2 **milieu, ambience, climate, air,** aura, spirit, feeling, feel, quality, local color, sense, note, tone, overtone, undertone

**atoll** NOUNS **island, isle; islet,** holm; oceanic island; **reef,** coral reef, coral head; coral island

**atomic energy** NOUNS **nuclear energy** *or* **power,** thermonuclear power

**atomize** VERBS 1 **disintegrate, decompose, decay,** dissolve, come apart, disorganize, **break up**, go to rack and ruin, crack up, disjoin, unknit, split, fission, **come** *or* **fall to pieces**
2 **vaporize, evaporate,** volatilize, **gasify;** sublimate, sublime; distill, fractionate; etherify; **etherize**

**atom smasher** NOUNS **accelerator, parti-**

**cle accelerator,** atomic accelerator, atomic cannon

**atone** VERBS **atone for, propitiate, expiate,** compensate, restitute, recompense, redress, redeem, repair, satisfy, give satisfaction, **make amends, make reparation** *or* **compensation** *or* **expiation** *or* **restitution,** make good *or* right, set right

**atonement** NOUNS **reparation, amends,** making amends, **restitution, propitiation, expiation, redress, recompense,** compensation, setting right, making right *or* good, making up, squaring, redemption, reclamation, satisfaction, quittance; expiatory offering *or* sacrifice, piaculum, peace offering

**atop** ADVS **on top,** at *or* on the top, topside <nonformal>; on top of the roost *or* heap; on the crest *or* crest of the wave; at the peak *or* pinnacle *or* summit

**atrocious** ADJS **horrible,** horrific, **horrifying,** horrendous, unspeakable, beyond words; **dreadful, terrible, rotten,** awful *and* beastly <both nonformal>

**atrocity** NOUNS 1 **act of cruelty,** cruelty, brutality, bestiality, barbarity, inhumanity
2 **iniquity, evil,** bad, wrong, error, obliquity, villainy, knavery, reprobacy, peccancy, **abomination, infamy,** shame

**atrophy** VERBS **waste, waste away, wither away,** consume, emaciate

**attach** VERBS 1 **annex; confiscate,** sequester, sequestrate, impound; expropriate, exercise the right of eminent domain
2 **fasten, fix, affix,** annex, put to, set to; graft, engraft; **secure,** anchor, moor; cement, knit, set, grapple, belay, **make fast**

**attaché** NOUNS commercial attaché, military attaché, **consul,** consular agent; chargé, chargé d'affaires ad interim

**attachment** NOUNS 1 **affection, devotion, fondness,** sentiment, warm feeling, soft spot in one's heart, weakness <nonformal>, like, **liking,** fancy, shine <nonformal>; **partiality, predilection; passion,** tender feeling *or* passion, **ardor,** ardency, fervor; charity, *caritas* <L>, brotherly love, Christian love, agape, loving concern, **caring**
2 **addition,** accession, annexation, affixation, suffixation, prefixation, agglutination, junction, **joining,** adjunction, uniting; **binding,** bonding, gluing, sticking, tying, lashing, splicing, knotting, linking, trussing

**attack** NOUNS 1 **seizure,** access, visitation; arrest; blockage, stoppage, occlusion, thrombosis, thromboembolism; **stroke,** ictus, apoplexy; **spasm, throes, fit, paroxysm, convulsion,** eclampsia, frenzy
2 **assault, offense, offensive; aggression; onset, onslaught; strike;** descent on *or* upon; **charge,** rush, dead set at, run at *or* against; **drive, push** <nonformal>; **sally, sortie;** *coup de main* <Fr>; frontal attack *or* assault, head-on attack, flank attack; mass attack, kamikaze attack; banzai attack *or* charge, suicide attack *or* charge; hit-and-run attack
3 **berating,** rating, tongue-lashing; **revilement, vilification,** blackening, **execration, abuse, vituperation,** invective, contumely, hard *or* cutting *or* bitter words; **tirade, diatribe,** jeremiad, screed, philippic
VERBS 4 **tackle;** engage *or* contract *or* obligate *or* commit oneself; **put** *or* **set** *or* **turn one's hand to, engage in, devote oneself to, apply oneself to,** address oneself to, give oneself up to; busy oneself with; **go** *or* **swing into action, set to, turn to, buckle to, fall to; pitch into** <nonformal>, plunge into, fall into, **launch into** *or* **upon**
5 **assault,** assume *or* take the offensive; commit an assault upon; **strike, hit, pound; go at, come at,** have at, **launch out against,** make a set *or* dead set at; gang up on, attack in force; surprise, **ambush; blitz**
6 **assail; castigate, flay,** skin alive <nonformal>, lash, slash, **excoriate,** fustigate, scathe, **roast** <nonformal>, scorch, blister

7 <nonformal> **pitch into, light into, lambaste,** pile into, sail into, wade into, lay into, plow into, tie into, rip into; **let one have it,** let one have it with both barrels; **land on,** land on like a ton of bricks, climb all over, crack down on, lower the boom on, tee off on; **mug,** jump, bushwhack, sandbag, scrag; swipe at, lay at, **go for, go at;** blindside, blind-pop, sucker-punch; **take a swing** *or* **crack** *or* **swipe** *or* **poke** *or* punch *or* **shot at**

**attacker** NOUNS **assailant,** rapist, mugger <nonformal>; **aggressor;** invader, raider

**attain** VERBS **achieve, effect, effectuate, compass, consummate, do, execute, produce, deliver, make,** enact, **perform, discharge, fulfill, realize,** run with *and* hack *and* swing <all nonformal>

**attainable** ADJS **practicable, practical, feasible; workable,** realizable, operable, negotiable, doable; **viable; achievable;** surmountable, superable

**attempt** NOUNS 1 **trial, effort, essay,** *coup d'essai* <Fr>; **endeavor, undertaking;** approach, move; coup, stroke, step

2 <nonformal> **try, whack, fling, shot, crack,** bash, belt, go, stab, lick, rip, ripple, cut, hack, smack

3 VERBS **try, essay,** try one's hand *or* wings, **undertake**, come to grips with, engage, take the bull by the horns; venture, chance; **make an attempt** *or* **effort,** lift a finger *or* hand

4 <nonformal> **tackle, take on, make a try, give a try,** have a go <chiefly Brit>, take a shot *or* stab *or* crack *or* try *or* whack at; try on for size, **go for it,** go for the brass ring, **have a fling** *or* **go at,** give a fling *or* a go *or* a whirl, **make a stab at,** have a shot *or* stab *or* crack *or* try *or* whack at

**attend** VERBS 1 **be at,** be present at, find oneself at, **go** *or* **come to; appear**, turn up, set foot in, show up <nonformal>, show one's face, make *or* put in an appearance, give the pleasure of one's company, make a personal appearance, **visit, take in** *and* do *and* catch <all nonformal>

2 **serve, work for,** be in service with; minister *or* administer to, pander to, do service to; **help**; **care for,** do for <nonformal>, **look after,** wait on hand and foot, take care of

3 **heed,** be heedful, tend, **mind, watch, observe, regard,** look, see, view, mark, remark, **note, notice,** take note *or* notice, get a load of <nonformal>

**attendant** NOUNS **assistant, helper,** auxiliary, aide; **help, helpmate, helpmeet;** deputy, **agent; second,** acolyte; adjutant, aide-de-camp; lieutenant, executive officer

**attention** NOUNS **attentiveness,** mindfulness, regardfulness, heedfulness; **heed,** ear; consideration, thought, mind; **observation,** observance, advertence, advertency, **note, notice,** remark, **regard,** respect; **intentness,** intentiveness, concentration

**attentive** NOUNS **heedful, mindful, regardful,** advertent; intent, on top of <nonformal>, diligent, assiduous, intense, earnest, concentrated; watchful, aware, conscious, alert; **meticulous**, nice, finical, finicky, finicking, niggling

**attest** VERBS **depose,** depone; **testify,** take the stand, witness; **warrant,** certify, **guarantee, assure; vouch, vouch for, swear, swear to,** swear the truth, **assert under oath;** make *or* take one's oath, **vow;** swear by bell, book, and candle

**attic** NOUNS attic room, **garret, loft,** sky parlor; cockloft, hayloft

**Attic** ADJS **elegant, tasteful, graceful, polished,** finished, round, terse; **restrained; clear,** lucid, limpid, pellucid, perspicuous; **simple, unaffected, natural,** unlabored, fluent, flowing, **easy; pure,** chaste

**Attila** NOUNS **brute,** monster, monster of cruelty, **devil,** devil incarnate; **sadist,** torturer, tormenter

**attitude** NOUNS mental attitude; psychology; **position, posture,** stance; **way of thinking; feeling, sentiment,** the way one feels; opinion

**attorney** NOUNS **lawyer, attorney-at-law,** barrister, **counselor,** counselor-at-law, **counsel,** legal counsel *or* counselor, legal adviser, legal expert, **solicitor, advocate, pleader;** member of the bar, legal practitioner, officer of the court

**attract** VERBS 1 **interest, appeal, engage,** impress, charismatize, fetch <nonformal>, catch *or* get one's eye, command one's attention, rivet one, attract one's interest, be attractive, take *or* tickle one's fancy; **invite,** summon, beckon

2 **pull, draw,** drag, tug, pull *or* draw towards, have an attraction; **lure;** adduct

**attraction** NOUNS 1 **allurement, allure, enticement, inveiglement,** invitation, come-hither <nonformal>, blandishment, cajolery; **temptation,** tantalization; **seduction,** seducement; **beguilement,** beguiling; **fascination, captivation,** enthrallment, entrapment, snaring

2 mutual attraction *or* magnetism; magnetism; gravity, gravitation; centripetal force; capillarity, capillary attraction

**attractive** ADJS 1 **delightful, exquisite, lovely; thrilling,** titillative; **charming, endearing, engaging, appealing,** prepossessing, heartwarming, sexy <nonformal>, **enchanting,** bewitching, witching, entrancing, enthralling, intriguing, fascinating; **beautiful, beauteous,** endowed with beauty; **pretty, handsome,** pulchritudinous, **lovely, graceful,** gracile
2 drawing, pulling, dragging, tugging; **magnetic;** charismatic; **alluring;** adductive, adducent

**attribute** NOUNS 1 **characteristic, peculiarity, singularity,** particularity, specialty, individualism, **character,** nature, **trait,** quirk, point of character, bad point, good point, saving grace, redeeming feature, mannerism, keynote, trick, **feature,** distinctive feature, lineament
VERBS 2 **assign, ascribe, impute,** give, place, put, apply, attach, refer

**attrition** NOUNS 1 **weakening, enfeeblement, debilitation,** exhaustion, inanition; **devitalization,** enervation; attenuation, extenuation
2 **reduction, diminution,** decrease, build-down, phasedown, drawdown, decrement, impairment, **cut** *or* **cutting,** curtailment, shortening, truncation
3 **abrasion, erosion, wearing away, wear,** detrition, ablation; ruboff; erasure, erasing, rubbing away *or* off *or* out; **grinding, filing,** rasping, limation; fretting; galling

**attune** VERBS **harmonize,** coordinate, bring into line, accord, make uniform, equalize, assimilate, homologize; **adjust, set,** regulate, **accommodate, reconcile,** synchronize, sync <nonformal>

**attuned** ADJS **harmonious,** harmonic, symphonious; harmonizing, **concordant,** consonant, accordant, according, **in accord,** in concord, in concert; synchronous, synchronized

**atypical** ADJS **unusual,** unordinary, **uncustomary,** unwonted, **uncommon, unfamiliar,** atypic, unheard-of, *recherché* <Fr>; **out of the ordinary,** out of this world, out-of-the-way, **off the beaten track,** offbeat

**auction** NOUNS 1 auction sale, vendue, outcry, sale at *or* by auction, sale to the highest bidder
VERBS 2 **auction off, auctioneer,** sell at auction, sell by auction, put up for auction, **put on the block,** bring under the hammer; knock down, sell to the highest bidder

**audible** ADJS hearable; **distinct, clear,** plain, definite, articulate

**audience** NOUNS 1 **audition,** hearing, tryout, call <all nonformal>, **interview,** conference; attention, favorable attention, ear
2 **house, congregation;** studio audience, live audience

**audit** NOUNS 1 **auditing; accounting, accountancy**
VERBS 2 **be taught, receive instruction,** be tutored, undergo schooling, pursue one's education, attend classes, go to *or* attend school, take lessons, matriculate; monitor
3 **verify, confirm,** test, prove, validate, **check,** check up *or* on *or* out <nonformal>, check over *or* through, **double-check,** triple-check, cross-check, recheck, check and doublecheck

**audition** NOUNS 1 **hearing;** sense of hearing, auditory *or* aural sense, ear; listening, heeding, attention
2 **tryout,** workout, **rehearsal,** practice; **dry run,** road test; **trial run,** practical test

**auditorium** NOUNS **theater, playhouse, house,** odeum; **opera house,** opera; **hall,** music hall, concert hall

**auditory** ADJS **aural,** auricular, otic; audio-visual; audible; acoustic, acoustical, phonic

**augment** VERBS **increase, enlarge,** aggrandize, **amplify, extend,** maximize, supplement, **add to; expand,** lengthen, broaden, fatten, fill out, thicken; build up; **reinforce,** strengthen, fortify, beef up <nonformal>; swell the ranks of

**augur** NOUNS 1 prophesier, soothsayer, *vates* <L>; **diviner,** divinator; prophetess, seeress, divineress, pythoness; Druid; **fortuneteller,** haruspex *or* aruspex, astrologer; Cassandra
VERBS 2 hint, divine <old>; **foretoken, preindicate,** presignal, **prefigure,** betoken, token, typify, **signify, mean,** spell, **indicate,** point to, **be a sign of,** show signs of

**augury** NOUNS 1 **omen, portent;** auspice, soothsay, prognostic, prognostication; foreshadowing, adumbration
2 **divination,** divining; haruspication, haruspicy, pythonism; **fortunetelling,** crystal gazing, palm-reading, palmistry; crystal ball; sorcery; clairvoyance

**august** ADJS worthy, **venerable; dignified, stately, imposing, grand, courtly,** magisterial, aristocratic

**aura** NOUNS 1 **ambience, atmosphere, climate, air,** spirit, feeling, feel, quality, color, sense, tone, overtone, undertone
2 **luster,** brilliance, radiance, splendor, resplendence *or* resplendency, refulgence *or* refulgency, **glory,** blaze of glory, nimbus, halo, envelope; charisma, mystique, glamour, numinousness

**aurora** NOUNS 1 **dawn, daybreak, sunrise, sunup** <nonformal>, cockcrowing *or* cocklight <Brit nonformal>, light, first light, daylight; **break of day,** peep of day, **crack of dawn,** first blush *or* flush of the morning, brightening *or* first brightening
2 polar lights; **northern lights, aurora borealis;** southern lights, **aurora australis;** aurora polaris

**auspices** NOUNS **patronage, fosterage, tutelage, sponsorship, backing,** aegis, coattails <nonformal>, care, guidance, **championing, championship,** seconding; **backing**

**auspicious** ADJS of good omen, of happy portent; **propitious, favorable,** favoring, fair, good; **promising,** of promise, full of promise

**austere** ADJS 1 self-denying, self-abnegating, **rigorous, rigoristic; puritanical,** eremitic, anchoritic
2 **simple, plain,** bare, bare-bones *and* no-frills <both nonformal>, mere; **single,** uniform, homogeneous, of a piece; **pure,** simon-pure, pure and simple

**austerity** NOUNS **severity, harshness, stringency,** astringency, **hard line; discipline,** strict *or* tight *or* rigid discipline, regimentation, spit and polish; Spartanism; demandingness, exactingness

**authentic** ADJS **genuine,** veridic, veridical, **real, natural, realistic, naturalistic,** true to reality, **true to nature, lifelike,** true to life, verisimilar, veristic

**authenticate** VERBS **confirm,** affirm, **substantiate, authenticate, validate, certify,** ratify, **verify; document;** probate, prove

**authenticity** NOUNS **genuineness,** bona fides, bona fideness, **legitimacy; honesty, sincerity**

**author** NOUNS **writer,** scribe <nonformal>, composer, inditer; authoress, penwoman; **creative writer,** *littérateur* <Fr>, literary artist, literary craftsman *or* artisan *or* journeyman, belletrist, man of letters, literary man

**authoritarian** ADJS **strict, exacting,** exigent, demanding, not to be trifled with, **stringent,** astringent; **severe, harsh,** dour, unsparing; despotic, **dictatorial; totalitarian**

**authoritative** ADJS 1 clothed *or* vested *or* invested with authority, **commanding, imperative; governing, controlling, ruling; preeminent, supreme,** leading, **superior; influential, prestigious, weighty,** momentous, consequential, eminent, substantial, considerable
2 **authentic,** magisterial, **official;** ex cathedra; standard, approved, accepted, received, pontific; from *or* straight from the horse's mouth

**authority** NOUNS 1 **prerogative, right, power,** faculty, competence *or* competency; **mandate,** popular authority *or* mandate, people's mandate, electoral mandate
2 **expert,** savant, scholar, connoisseur, maven <nonformal>; pundit
3 **influence,** influentiality; **power,** force, clout <nonformal>, potency, pressure, effect, indirect *or* incidental power, **say,** the final say, the last word, say-so *and* a lot to do with *or* to say about <all nonformal>, veto power

**authorize** VERBS **sanction, warrant;** give official sanction *or* warrant, legitimize, validate, legalize; empower, give power, enable, entitle; **license**

**autocratic** ADJS **arbitrary, peremptory,** imperative; absolute, absolutist, absolutistic; **dictatorial, authoritarian; bossy** <nonformal>, **domineering, high-handed, overbearing,** overruling; **despotic, tyrannical;** tyrannous

**autograph** NOUNS **signature,** hand, **John Hancock** <nonformal>

**automatic** ADJS **unpremeditated,** unmeditated, **uncalculated,** undeliberated, **spontaneous, undesigned, unstudied;** unintentional, unintended, inadvertent, unwilled, undeliberate; **unconsidered,** unadvised, snap, casual, offhand, throwaway <nonformal>; **involuntary, instinctive, mechanical,** reflex, reflexive, knee-jerk <nonformal>, conditioned

**automation** NOUNS automatic control;

robotization, cybernation; **self-action,** self-activity; self-movement, self-motion, **self-propulsion;** self-direction

**automobile** NOUNS **car, auto,** motorcar, motocar, autocar, **machine,** motor, motor vehicle, *voiture* <Fr>

**automotive** ADJS **vehicular,** transportational

**autonomous** ADJS **independent,** self-dependent; free-spirited, freewheeling, free-floating, free-standing; **self-determined,** self-directing, one's own man; self-governed, **self-governing,** sovereign

**autonomy** NOUNS **independence, self-determination, self-government,** self-direction, home rule; autarky, autarchy, self-containment, self-sufficiency; **self-reliance,** self-dependence

**autopsy** NOUNS **postmortem, inquest,** postmortem examination, ex post facto examination, necropsy, necroscopy

**autumn** NOUNS **fall,** fall of the year, harvest time

*Season of mists and mellow fruitfulness!*
KEATS

ADJS 2 autumnal; **seasonal,** in season and out of season

**auxiliary** NOUNS 1 **helper,** aide, paraprofessional; **help, helpmate, helpmeet; attendant, second,** acolyte
ADJS 2 **helping,** assisting, serving; **assistant,** adjuvant, subservient, subsidiary, ancillary, accessory; fostering, nurtural

**availability** NOUNS **accessibility,** access, **approachability, openness,** reachableness; **penetrability,** perviousness

**available** ADJS 1 **idle,** fallow, otiose; **unemployed, unoccupied,** disengaged, **jobless, out of work,** out of a job, out of harness; free, at liberty, at leisure; at loose ends
2 **accessible, approachable, reachable,** within reach; **open, penetrable,** pervious; **obtainable, attainable,** procurable, securable

**avalanche** NOUNS 1 **snowslide,** snowslip <Brit>; **slide; slip,** slippage; **landslide,** mudslide, landslip, subsidence
VERBS 2 **slide, slip,** slip *or* slide down

**avant-garde** NOUNS 1 vanguard, avant-gardist, innovator, groundbreaker; **precursor, forerunner,** foregoer, *voorlooper* <Dutch>; pathfinder, explorer, point, point man, trailblazer *or* trailbreaker, guide
ADJS 2 **advanced,** progressive, forward-looking, modernizing, ultramodern, ahead of its time, far out, way out

**avenge** VERBS **take** *or* **exact revenge,** have one's revenge, wreak one's vengeance; **retaliate, even the score, get even with**

**avenger** NOUNS **vindicator;** revanchist

**avenue** NOUNS **artery; corridor, aisle, alley, lane; channel, conduit;** opening, aperture; access

**average** NOUNS 1 **mean, median, middle**; **golden mean,** *juste milieu* <Fr>; **medium,** happy medium; middle of the road, middle course, *via media* <L>; middle state *or* ground *or* position *or* echelon *or* level *or* point, midpoint; **run of the mill;** any Tom, Dick, or Harry <nonformal>; Everyman
VERBS 2 average out, **split the difference,** take the average, strike a balance, pair off; strike *or* hit a happy medium
ADJS 3 **ordinary,** normal, **common, commonplace,** garden *and* garden-variety <both nonformal>, run-of-the-mill; **unexceptional, unremarkable, unnoteworthy,** unspectacular, nothing *or* nobody special *and* no great shakes <all nonformal>, no prize, no prize package, no brain surgeon, no rocket scientist

**aversion** NOUNS 1 **repugnance,** repulsion, **antipathy,** abomination, **abhorrence, horror,** mortal horror; **disgust, loathing;** nausea; distaste
2 **anathema, abomination,** detestation, abhorrence, antipathy, execration, hate; peeve, pet peeve; phobia

**avert** VERBS **prevent, prohibit, forbid; bar;** save, help, **keep from; deter, discourage,** dishearten; **parry, keep off, ward off, stave off, fend off,** fend, repel, deflect, turn aside; **forestall,** foreclose, **preclude,** exclude, debar, **obviate**

**avoid** VERBS **evade, dodge,** duck <nonformal>, shun, turn aside *or* to the side, draw aside, **turn away,** jib, shy, shy off; **avert; steer clear of,** make way for, get out of the way of

**avoidable** ADJS **escapable,** eludible; evadable; preventable

**await** VERBS have *or* keep an eye out for, lie in wait for; wait around *or* about, watch, watch and wait; **wait up for,** stay up for, sit up for; **loom,** threaten; lie ahead

**awake** VERBS 1 **awaken, wake, wake up, get up,** rouse, come alive <nonformal>; open one's eyes, stir <nonformal>
2 **come to life,** come into existence *or* being, come into the world, see the light; **revive, come to,** come alive, show signs of life
ADJS 3 conscious, **up;** alert, **on the alert,** on the *qui vive* <Fr>, **on one's toes, on top** *and* **on the job** *and* on the ball <all nonformal>, **attentive;** wakeful, **wide-awake,** sleepless, unsleeping, unblinking, alive, ready, prompt, quick, agile, nimble, quick on the trigger *or* draw *or* uptake <all nonformal>

**awaken** VERBS 1 **waken, rouse, arouse,** awake, wake, **wake up,** shake up, roust out <nonformal>
2 **excite, impassion, arouse, rouse, stir, stir up,** set astir, stir the feelings, stir the blood, cause a stir *or* commotion, play on the feelings; **foment, incite**; turn on <nonformal>
3 **disillusion, disenchant,** unspell, uncharm, break the spell *or* charm; **disabuse, undeceive;** correct, **set right** *or* **straight,** put straight, tell the truth, enlighten, let in on, put one wise <nonformal>; open one's eyes

**awakening** NOUNS 1 **wakening,** rousing, **arousal;** rude awakening, rousting out <nonformal>
2 **disillusionment,** disillusion, **disenchantment,** return to reality, loss of innocence, cold light of reality, enlightenment, bursting of the bubble; debunking <nonformal>

**award** NOUNS 1 **giving, donation,** bestowal, bestowment; **endowment, presentation,** presentment; awarding; grant, granting
2 **reward, prize;** first prize, second prize, etc; blue ribbon; consolation prize; booby prize; Nobel Prize, Pulitzer Prize; Oscar, Academy Award
VERBS 3 **give, present, donate,** slip <nonformal>, let have; **bestow, confer, allot, render,** bestow on; **grant,** accord, **allow,** vouchsafe, yield, afford, make available; **tender,** proffer, offer, extend, come up with <nonformal>; **give out, deal out, dole out, mete out, hand** *or* dish out <nonformal>, fork *or* shell out <nonformal>

**aware** ADJS **perceptive; conscious,** cognizant, sensitive to, alive to, **attentive, heedful, mindful, regardful,** advertent; on top of <nonformal>, diligent, assiduous, intense, earnest, concentrated; watchful, conscious, alert

**away** ADJS 1 **gone,** gone away, past and gone, extinct, missing, lost to sight *or* view, long-lost, **out of sight; unaccounted for**
ADVS 2 **elsewhere,** somewhere else, not here

**awe** NOUNS 1 **wonder,** wonderment, sense of wonder, marveling, marvel, **astonishment, amazement;** dumbfoundment, stupefaction
2 dread, unholy dread; **terror, horror,** horrification, mortal *or* abject fear
VERBS 3 **astonish, amaze, astound, surprise,** startle, stagger, **bewilder, perplex**, flabbergast <nonformal>, confound, overwhelm, **boggle, boggle the mind;** strike with wonder *or* awe; **dumbfound; stun, stupefy**

**awe-inspiring** ADJS 1 **awesome,** awful, awing; **mysterious,** numinous; weird, eerie, uncanny, bizarre
2 **imposing, impressive,** larger-than-life, awful, awesome; **sumptuous, elegant, elaborate, luxurious,** extravagant, deluxe

**awesome** ADJS 1 **magnificent, splendid, glorious,** superb, fine, superfine, fancy, superfancy, swell <nonformal>; **imposing, impressive,** larger-than-life, awful, awe-inspiring
2 **sacred, holy,** numinous, **sacrosanct, religious, spiritual,** heavenly, divine; **venerable,** awful; **ineffable,** unutterable, unspeakable, inexpressible

**awful** ADJS **terrible, dreadful,** dire, horrible, horrid; atrocious, outrageous, heinous, villainous, nefarious; monstrous; **deplorable,** lamentable, regrettable, pitiful, pitiable, woeful, grievous; flagrant, **scandalous,** shameful, **shocking,** infamous, **notorious,** arrant, **egregious**

**awkward** ADJS **bungling, blundering,** blunderheaded, bumbling, fumbling, mistake-prone, accident-prone; **clumsy, uncoordinated,** maladroit, unhandy, **all thumbs; ungainly,** uncouth, **ungraceful,** graceless, inelegant, *gauche* <Fr>; **inconvenient, incommodious**

**awning** NOUNS **shade,** shader, **screen, light shield, curtain,** drape, drapery, blind

**ax** VERBS **sever, dissever,** cut off *or* away

*or* loose, shear off, hack through, hack off, amputate; **cleave, split,** fissure; sunder, cut in two, dichotomize, halve, bisect; **chop, hew,** hack, **slash;** gash, whittle, butcher

**axiomatic** ADJS **evident, self-evident,** indisputable, **obvious, plain, clear,** perspicuous, distinct, palpable, patent, tangible; **aphoristic, proverbial,** epigrammatic, epigrammatical, **axiomatical; sententious, pithy,** gnomic, pungent, succinct, terse, crisp, pointed

**axis** NOUNS 1 **center,** centrum; **middle, heart, core, nucleus; core of one's being, where one lives; kernel; pith,** marrow, medulla; **nub, hub,** nave, pivot 2 **alliance, coalition, league, union;** council; **bloc; federation, confederation,** confederacy; **combination,** combine

# B

**babble** NOUNS 1 **chatter, jabber,** gibber, babblement, prate, **prating, prattle, palaver,** chat, natter <Brit>, **gabble,** blab, **blabber, blather,** cackle
VERBS 2 **chatter, chat, prate, prattle, patter,** palaver, **gab** <nonformal>, natter <Brit>, **gabble, jabber, blab, blabber, blather,** spout *or* **spout off** <nonformal>, pour forth, **gush,** have a big mouth <nonformal>, love the sound of one's own voice

**baby** NOUNS 1 **newborn; infant, babe,** babe in arms, little darling *or* angel *or* doll *or* cherub, bouncing baby, puling infant, mewling infant, babykins <nonformal>, baby bunting; **toddler**
ADJS 2 **infant, infantile, babyish; newborn,** neonatal; tied to mother's apron strings

**bachelor** NOUNS bach <nonformal>, confirmed bachelor, **single man**

**back** NOUNS 1 dorsum, ridge; dorsal region, lumbar region; hindquarter; loin
VERBS 2 **secure, guarantee, guaranty, warrant, assure, insure,** ensure, bond, **certify; back up, sponsor, endorse;** sign, cosign, **underwrite; stand behind, stand back of** *or* in back of, get behind; **stand by,** stick by *and* **stick up for** <both nonformal>, **champion; finance, fund, sponsor, patronize, support,** provide capital *or* money for, pay for, bankroll <nonformal>
3 **bet, wager, gamble, hazard, stake,** punt, lay, lay down, put up, **make a bet, lay a wager,** get a piece of the action <nonformal>; plunge <nonformal>
ADJS 4 **backward, reversed,** reflex, **turned around**
5 **rear,** rearward, backward, retrograde, **posterior**

**backbone** NOUNS 1 **pluck, spunk** <nonformal>, **mettle, grit,** true grit, spirit, **stamina, guts** *and* moxie <both nonformal>, bottom, **toughness** <nonformal>
2 **support; mainstay,** spine

**backbreaking** ADJS **strenuous,** painful, effortful, operose, troublesome, onerous, oppressive, burdensome

**backdrop** NOUNS **setting, background,** ground, surround, field, scene, arena, theater, locale; back, rear, hinterland, distance

**backer** NOUNS **supporter, upholder,** maintainer, sustainer; support, **mainstay, standby** <nonformal>, stalwart, reliance, dependence

**background** NOUNS 1 **setting,** backdrop, scene, arena, theater, locale; stage setting, stage set, *mise-en-scène* <Fr>
2 **experience, practice,** practical knowledge *or* skill, hands-on experience <nonformal>
3 **source, origin,** genesis, original, origination, **derivation, rise, beginning,** conception, inception, provenance, provenience

**backhanded** ADJS **circuitous, roundabout, out-of-the-way, devious, oblique, indirect,** meandering; equivocatory; evasive; vacillating

**backlash** NOUNS **counteraction, counterworking; opposition, antipathy, conflict, friction;** reaction, repercussion, recoil

**backlog** NOUNS 1 **reserve, reserves,** reservoir, resource; **stockpile, cache,** backup, reserve supply, something in reserve *or* in hand, something to fall back on, reserve fund, **nest egg, savings,** sinking fund
VERBS 2 **store up, stock up, lay up,** put up, **save up,** hoard up, treasure up, garner up, **heap up,** pile up, build up a stock *or* an inventory

**backslapper** NOUNS **flatterer; cajoler, wheedler;** back scratcher; ass-kisser <nonformal>, brown-noser, **sycophant**

**backslide** VERBS **relapse, lapse, slip back,** sink back, **fall back,** have a relapse, **revert to,** yield again to, fall again into, recidivate

**back talk** NOUNS **retort, rejoinder,** reaction, return, **comeback** *and* **take** <both nonformal>, clever *or* ready *or* witty reply *or* retort, snappy comeback <nonformal>; sass *and* lip <both nonformal>

**backtrack** VERBS backpedal, back off *or* away; reverse one's field; have second thoughts, think better of it, cut one's losses

**backup** NOUNS 1 **support, backing, aid; upholding, upkeep,** carrying, carriage, maintenance, **sustaining,** sustainment, sustenance; **reinforcement;** subsidy, subvention
ADJS 2 **substitute, alternate, alterna-**

**tive,** equivalent, token, dummy, pinch, utility, secondary

**backward** ADJS 1 **reversed,** reflex, **turned around,** back, **backward;** wrong-way, wrong-way around, counter, ass-backwards *and* bassackwards <both nonformal>
2 **undeveloped, unfinished,** unlicked, unformed; unfashioned, unwrought, unlabored, unworked, unprocessed, untreated; **underdeveloped;** arrested, stunted
ADVS 3 **inversely, conversely,** contrarily, contrariwise, **vice versa,** the other way around, **backwards,** turned around
4 **rearward,** rearwards, to the rear, **hindward,** hindwards, backwards

**backwater** NOUNS back stream, gurge, **swirl,** twirl, whirl; countercurrent, counterflow, counterflux, backflow, reflux, refluence, regurgitation, backwash, snye <Can>

**backwoods** NOUNS 1 **hinterland, back country,** outback <Australia>, up-country, boonies *and* boondocks <both nonformal>, outback <Australia>, wilderness

**bacterial** ADJS **microbic,** microbial, **microorganic;** animalcular; microzoic

**bad** NOUNS 1 **evil, wrong, ill; harm, hurt, injury, damage, detriment; destruction**; abomination, grievance, vexation, blight; ills the flesh is heir to

*something rotten in the state of Denmark*
SHAKESPEARE

ADJS 2 **evil, ill,** untoward, black, sinister; **wicked, wrong,** peccant, iniquitous, **vicious; sinful**

**bad person** NOUNS 1 disreputable person, **undesirable, good-for-nothing, no-good, rascal**

2 <nonformal> **asshole, prick, bastard, son of a bitch** *or* SOB, **jerk, horse's ass,** creep, motherfucker, mother, dork, **shit,** turd, birdturd, shithead, shitface, cuntface, dickhead, fart, **louse, meanie, heel, shitheel, rat, stinker,** stinkard, pill, bugger, dirtbag, dork, geek, dweeb, twerp, sleaze, sleazoid, sleazebag, bad lot <Brit>; **hood, hooligan**

**bad-mouth** VERBS <nonformal> put down, trash, rubbish, dump on, dig at, dis, roast, slam, hurl a brickbat

**bad taste** NOUNS **tastelessness, impropriety,** indecorousness, unseemliness; **coarseness, unrefinement,** roughness, grossness, rudeness, crudeness, uncouthness

**baffled** ADJS **at an impasse, at one's wit's end, at a loss, perplexed, bewildered,** mystified, stuck *and* stumped <both nonformal>, stymied

**bag** NOUNS **sack,** sac, poke <nonformal>; **pocket,** fob; **purse, wallet, pocketbook, handbag,** porte-monnaie; **take, catch,** seizure, **haul;** booty

**bagatelle** NOUNS **trifle, triviality, oddment,** fribble, **gimcrack, gewgaw,** frippery, **trinket,** bibelot, curio, **bauble,** gaud, toy, **knickknack,** knickknackery, kickshaw, folderol

**baggage** NOUNS 1 **impedimenta, luggage, dunnage,** bag and baggage, traps, tackle, apparatus, truck, gear, kit, outfit, duffel
2 **strumpet, trollop, wench, hussy, slut, jade,** *cocotte* <Fr>, grisette

**baggy** ADJS **drooping, droopy,** limp, loose, nodding, floppy <nonformal>; **sagging,** saggy; **bagging,** ballooning; **shapeless,** nondescript, lumpy, lumpish

**bail** NOUNS 1 bond, vadimonium; surety; **pledge, gage,** *pignus, vadium* <both L>
VERBS 2 **ladle, dip, scoop;** bucket; **dish, shovel, pour**

**bail out** VERBS 1 **parachute, jump,** make a parachute jump, hit the silk, sky-dive
2 **get out, get out of,** get well out of; **break loose,** cut loose, break away, break one's bonds *or* chains, shake off the yoke; **jump** *and* **skip** <both nonformal>; fly the coop <nonformal>
3 **give an assist, give a leg up** *or* lift *or* boost <nonformal>; **save,** redeem, **rescue**; see one through

**bait** NOUNS 1 **lure,** charm, **come-on** <nonformal>, attention-getter *or* -grabber, **attraction, draw** *or* drawer *or* crowd-drawer, crowd-pleaser; drawing card; **decoy**
VERBS 2 **heckle,** pick *or* prod at, badger, hector, bullyrag, worry, worry at, nip at the heels of, chivy, hardly give one time to breathe, make one's life miserable, keep on at, **pester, tease, needle,** devil, get after *or* get on <nonformal>, **bedevil**

**baker** NOUNS *boulanger* <Fr>, pastry cook, pastry chef, *patissier* <Fr>

**balance** NOUNS 1 **moderation,** moderateness; **restraint,** constraint, control;

**judiciousness,** prudence; steadiness, evenness, equilibrium, **stability**; **temperateness**
2 **stability, firmness, soundness, substantiality, solidity; security,** reliability; **steadiness,** steadfastness; constancy, invariability, undeflectability; **imperturbability,** unflappability <nonformal>
3 **remainder, leftover, extra, spare,** something extra *or* to spare
VERBS 4 regularize, balance off, compensate; harmonize; **proportion,** equalize; **offset**, set off, **counteract,** countervail, **counterbalance,** counterweigh, counterpoise, play off against
5 balance accounts, balance the books, strike a balance; close the books, close out

**balcony** NOUNS gallery, terrace; **peanut gallery**

**bald** ADJS 1 **hairless,** depilous; acomous; bald as a coot, bald as an egg; **baldheaded,** bald-pated
2 **plain,** common; **simple,** unadorned, unvarnished, pure, neat; bare, stark, Spartan

**ball** NOUNS 1 **sphere;** orb, orbit, **globe,** rondure; geoid; spheroid, globoid, ellipsoid, oblate spheroid, prolate spheroid
2 **dance,** *bal* <Fr>; masked ball, masque, mask, *bal masqué* <Fr>, *bal costumé* <Fr>, fancy-dress ball, cotillion; promenade, **prom** <nonformal>, formal <nonformal>
3 **fun,** action, big time *and* **high time** *and* high old time, picnic *and* laughs *and* lots of laughs, time of one's life <all nonformal>

**ballad** NOUNS popular song *or* air *or* tune, hit, song hit, hit tune; lay, *Lied* <Ger>, *chanson* <Fr>, carol, **ditty,** canticle, ballade, *ballata* <Ital>; *canzone* <Ital>; canzonet, *canzonetta* <Ital>

**ballerina** NOUNS **ballet dancer;** danseuse, coryphée; *première danseuse* <Fr>; figurante

**balloon** NOUN 1 **aerostat,** lighter-than-air craft; **airship,** ship, dirigible balloon, **blimp** <nonformal>; **dirigible,** zeppelin, *ballon* <Fr>
VERBS 2 **grow, increase, advance,** appreciate; **spread, widen,** broaden; wax, swell, bloat, mount, **rise,** go up, crescendo, snowball; **multiply, proliferate,** breed, teem

**ballooning** NOUNS lighter-than-air aviation

**ballot** NOUNS 1 **vote,** voting, **suffrage,** franchise, enfranchisement, right to vote; **voice, say;** representation; **poll,** polling, canvass, canvassing, counting heads *or* noses, exit poll; **plebiscite, referendum;** voice vote, *viva voce* vote; rising vote; show of hands
2 **slate, ticket,** proxy <nonformal>
VERBS 3 **vote, cast one's vote,** cast a ballot; exercise one's suffrage *or* franchise, stand up and be counted

**ballroom** NOUNS **dance hall,** dancery; dance palace; casino

**balls** NOUNS 1 **genitals,** genitalia, sex organs, reproductive organs, pudenda, private parts, privy parts, privates, meat <nonformal>; gonads; **testes, testicles,** balls *and* nuts *and* rocks *and* ballocks *and* family jewels <all nonformal>

2 <nonformal> **guts,** intestinal fortitude, spunk, brass balls, cojones, moxie, **backbone,** chutzpah

**balm** NOUNS 1 **lotion, salve, ointment, unguent,** *unguentum* <L>, cerate, unction, balsam, oil, emollient, demulcent
2 **condolence, condolences,** condolement, **consolation,** comfort, soothing words, **commiseration, sympathy**

**balmy** ADJS **bright, sunny,** fair, mild; halcyon

**baloney** NOUNS

<nonformal> **bunk**, **bunkum;** hooey, hoke, **hokum**, **bosh**, bull, **bullshit**, crap, flimflam, smoke and mirrors, claptrap, moonshine, eyewash, hogwash

**bamboozle** VERBS **dupe, gull,** pigeon, play one for a fool *or* sucker, snow *and* **hornswoggle** *and* diddle *and* scam <all nonformal>, **humbug, take in, put something over** *or* **across,** slip one over on <nonformal>, pull a fast one on

**ban** NOUNS 1 **prohibition, forbidding,** forbiddance; **ruling out, disallowance,** denial, rejection; refusal; injunction, **proscription,** inhibition, **interdict,** *interdictum* <L>, interdiction
VERBS 2 **prohibit, forbid; disallow, rule out** *or* **against;** deny, **reject**; say no to, **refuse**; **bar,** debar, preclude, exclude, exclude from, shut out, shut *or* close the door on, **prevent**; put under the ban, **outlaw, inhibit, interdict**
3 **ostracize,** exclude, send down, **black-**

**ball,** spurn, turn thumbs down on, snub, cut, give the cold shoulder, send to Coventry, give the silent treatment; **excommunicate;** rusticate

**banal** ADJS **trite;** corny *and* square <both nonformal>, platitudinous, **stereotyped,** stock, set, **commonplace, common,** twice-told, **familiar,** bromidic <nonformal>, old hat <nonformal>, back-number, bewhiskered, warmed-over, **cut-and-dried; hackneyed, stale,** moth-eaten

**bandage** NOUNS 1 bandaging, **tourniquet;** tape, **adhesive tape**
VERBS 2 **gird,** girt, belt, girdle, cinch; **tie up,** bind up, do up; **bandage,** bandage up, swathe, swaddle

**band-aid** NOUNS 1 **front,** mask, cloak, veil; **cosmetics,** mere cosmetics, gloss, varnish, color, coat of paint, whitewash <nonformal>; **cover,** cover-up, cover story, alibi; expedient
ADJS 2 **makeshift, stopgap,** improvised, improvisational, **jury-rigged; last-ditch; ad hoc;** quick and dirty <nonformal>

**bandit** NOUNS **brigand,** dacoit; **thug, hoodlum**

**bane** NOUNS 1 **curse, affliction, plague, pestilence,** pest, calamity, scourge, **torment,** open wound, running sore, grievance, woe, burden, crushing burden; thorn in the flesh *or* side, pea in the shoe; bugbear, **bête noire,** nemesis
2 **destroyer, ruiner, wrecker,** demolisher; **vandal,** hun; exterminator

**bang** NOUNS 1 **detonation, blast, explosion,** fulmination, **discharge, burst, pop, crack;** volley, salvo, fusillade
VERBS 2 **crack, clap, crash,** wham, slam, clash; **knock, rap, tap,** smack, whack, thwack, whop, whap, whomp, splat
ADVS 3 **suddenly,** sudden, **all of a sudden, all at once: abruptly,** sharp; precipitately, precipitantly, impulsively, impetuously, hastily; dash; on short notice, without notice *or* warning, like a bolt from the blue

**banish** VERBS **expel, cast out, ostracize,** exclude, send down, **blackball,** spurn, turn thumbs down on, snub, cut, give send to Coventry, **excommunicate; expatriate, deport**

**bank** NOUNS 1 **slope, declivity,** steep, versant, incline, rise, talus
2 **shoal, shallow,** shallows, **bar,** sandbank, sandbar, tombolo
3 **lending institution,** savings and loan association *or* thrift *or* thrift institution *or* savings institution
VERBS 4 **store, stow,** lay in store; **lay in, deposit, cache,** stash <nonformal>, bury away

**banker** NOUNS **money dealer,** moneymonger; money broker; moneylender

**bankroll** VERBS **finance, back, fund, sponsor, patronize, support,** provide for, capitalize, provide capital *or* money for, **stake** *or* **grubstake** <both nonformal>; subsidize

**bankrupt** NOUNS 1 **insolvent,** failure; **loser**
VERBS 2 **ruin, break,** bust *and* wipe out <both nonformal>; put out of business, drive to the wall, impoverish
ADJS **insolvent,** in receivership, in the hands of receivers, belly-up <nonformal>, broken, **broke** *and* busted <both nonformal>, **ruined,** failed, on the rocks

**bankruptcy** NOUNS **insolvency,** receivership, Chapter 11, **failure; crash,** collapse, bust <nonformal>

**banner** NOUNS 1 **flag,** oriflamme, **standard, pennant,** pennon, pennoncel, banneret, banderole, swallowtail, burgee, **streamer; bunting**
ADJS 2 **leading, dominant,** crowning, capital, **cardinal; preeminent, predominant,** preponderant, prevailing

**banquet** NOUNS **feast,** festal board; lavish *or* Lucullan feast; blow *or* blowout <nonformal>, groaning board

**banter** NOUNS 1 **badinage, persiflage, pleasantry, raillery,** rallying, **sport,** good-natured banter, harmless teasing; **byplay**
2 <nonformal> **kidding,** joshing, jollying, jiving, fooling around; **ribbing,** ragging, razzing, **roasting**
VERBS 3 **twit, chaff,** rally, **joke, jest,** jape, **tease,** haze

**baptize** VERBS 1 **christen;** dip, immerse; sprinkle, asperge
2 **name, denominate,** nominate, **designate, call, term, style, dub,** specify; christen

**bar** NOUNS 1 **stripe, striping, streak, streaking;** striation, striature, stria
2 barroom, *bistro* <Fr>, **tavern, pub,** gin mill <nonformal>, **saloon,** watering hole <nonformal>
3 **obstruction, clog, block,** blockade,

sealing off, **blockage,** strangulation, choking, choking off, **stoppage,** stop, **barrier, obstacle,** impediment

4 legal profession, members of the bar; representation, counsel

VERBS 5 **exclude,** debar, lock out, **shut out, keep out,** close the door on, close out, cut off, preclude; **reject, repudiate,** blackball *and* turn thumbs down on <both nonformal>; **ban,** prohibit, proscribe

6 **obstruct, get** *or* **stand in the way; block,** put up a roadblock, blockade, occlude; **debar,** shut out

**barbarian** NOUNS 1 brute; troglodyte; **alien, stranger, foreigner, outsider,** ultramontane, foreign devil <China>, *gringo* <Sp Amer>

ADJS 2 **unrefined, unpolished, uncouth,** unkempt, uncombed, unlicked; **uncultivated, uncultured; uncivilized, barbarous,** barbaric, troglodytic

**barbaric** ADJS sadistic; **ruthless**; **brutal,** brutish, brute, bestial, beastly, animal, subhuman; **barbarous,** uncivilized, unchristian; **savage, ferocious,** feral

**barber** NOUNS hairdresser, *coiffeur, coiffeuse* <both Fr>

**barbiturates** NOUNS

<nonformal> barbs, black beauties, candy, dolls, downers, downs, goofballs, nimbies, pink ladies, purple hearts

**bare** ADJS 1 **naked, nude; in the raw** <nonformal>, *in puris naturalibus* <L>, in a state of nature, in one's birthday suit, **in the buff** *and* stripped to the buff *and* **in the altogether** <all nonformal>, **stark-naked,** bare-ass <nonformal>, naked as a jaybird <nonformal>

**bare-bones** ADJS **plain,** bare, no-frills <nonformal>, mere; of a piece; **pure,** simon-pure, pure and simple; **austere,** chaste, unadorned, uncluttered, spare, stark, severe

**barefoot** ADJS barefooted, unshod; discalced, discalceate

**barely** ADVS **scarcely, hardly,** not hardly <nonformal>, only just, **narrowly,** closely, nearly, **by the skin of one's teeth,** by a hair, **slightly,** exiguously, scantily, inconsequentially, **insignificantly, negligibly,** minimally, inappreciably, **little**

**bargain** NOUNS 1 **compromise,** accommodation, settlement, mutual concession, give-and-take

2 advantageous purchase, **buy** <nonformal>, **good buy, steal** <nonformal>; money's worth

VERBS 3 **treat with, negotiate,** make terms, sit down with, sit down at the bargaining table; **drive a bargain, haggle,** chaffer, **deal, dicker,** hack out *or* work out *or* hammer out a deal

**barker** NOUNS **pitchman, pitchwoman,** spieler, ballyhooer

**bar mitzvah** NOUNS **confirmation;** bas mitzvah

**barn** NOUNS **stable,** stall; **cowbarn,** cowshed, byre

**barnacle** NOUNS **parasite,** leech, limpet, remora; **sponger,** sponge <nonformal>, freeloader <nonformal>

**barometer** NOUNS **feeler, probe,** sound, sounder; **trial balloon,** *ballon d'essai* <Fr>, pilot balloon; weather vane

**barracks** NOUNS **camp, encampment,** *Lager* <Ger>; bivouac; barrack *or* **barracks,** casern, *caserne* <Fr>

**barrage** NOUNS 1 **volley, salvo,** burst, spray, **fusillade, cannonade,** cannonry, **broadside,** enfilade

VERBS 2 **bombard, blast, strafe, shell,** cannonade, mortar, blitz; pepper, fusillade, fire a volley; rake, enfilade; pour a broadside into

**barren** NOUNS 1 **wasteland, waste,** desolation, **barrens,** barren land

ADJS 2 **fruitless,** profitless, bootless, otiose, **unprofitable,** unremunerative, sterile, unproductive

**barricade** VERBS **fortify,** garrison, man the garrison *or* trenches *or* barricades; bulwark, wall, palisade, fence; castellate, crenellate

**barrier** NOUNS 1 **boundary, bound, limit,** limitation, extremity; block, claustrum; delimitation, hedge, break *or* breakoff point, cutoff, cutoff point, terminus; **limiting factor,** determinant, limit *or* boundary condition

2 **obstruction, clog, block,** blockade, sealing off, **blockage,** strangulation, choking, choking off, **stoppage,** stop, **bar, obstacle,** impediment; **bottleneck,** chokepoint

**bartender** NOUNS mixologist, barkeeper, barkeep, barman <Brit>, tapster

**barter** NOUNS 1 **trading, swapping** <nonformal>; trade, swap <nonformal>, even trade, even-steven trade

VERBS 2 **trade, deal, traffic, truck, do business; exchange,** give in exchange, take in exchange, **swap** <nonformal>; horse-trade <nonformal>

**base** NOUNS 1 **bottom**, lowest point, nadir
2 **pedestal; stand,** standard
3 **headquarters** *or* **HQ,** central office, main office, central administration, seat, **base of operations,** center of authority
VERBS 4 **establish, fix, plant, site,** pitch, seat, **set; found,** ground, lay the foundation
ADJS 5 **low, mean, ignoble,** vile, scurvy, sorry, scrubby, beggarly; low-minded, base-minded; below par, subpar, not up to scratch *or* snuff *or* the mark, **worthless**

**baseless** ADJS **groundless,** ungrounded, **without foundation,** unfounded, built on sand; ill-founded, unbased, **untenable, unsupportable,** unsustainable

**basement** NOUNS **cellar,** cellarage; subbasement; wine cellar, potato cellar, storm cellar, cyclone cellar

**bash** NOUNS

1 <nonformal> **brawl,** blast, clambake, wingding, blowout, shindig

VERBS 2 **injure, hurt;** rough up <nonformal>, make mincemeat of, maul, batter, savage; maul, pound, beat, beat black and blue

3 <nonformal> **sock,** bang, bat, belt, bust, clip, clout, duke, swat, larrup, paste, lick, biff, wallop, whop, slam, slug

4 **censure,** reprehend; trash *and* rubbish <both nonformal>; **reproach,** impugn

**bashful** ADJS **shy, timid,** timorous, **coy, demure,** self-conscious

**basic** ADJS 1 basal, **underlying, essential,** of the essence, **fundamental; substantive,** substantial, material; **vital, all-important,** crucial, of vital importance, life-and-death *or* life-or-death; **central,** focal
2 **original, primary,** primal, primitive, pristine, primeval, aboriginal, **rudimentary,** germinal, seminal

**basics** NOUNS **essentials, rudiments, elements, nuts and bolts** <nonformal>; **principles,** principia, first principles, first steps, **outlines, primer, ABC's,** abecedarium

**basis** NOUNS **motive, reason, cause,** source, spring, mainspring; **foundation,** *fond* <Fr>, firm foundation, **base, footing,** grounds, **principle, premise**

**bask** VERBS insolate; **sun,** bask in the sun, sun oneself, sunbathe

**basket** NOUNS **container, receptacle;** receiver, holder, vessel, utensil; box, case

**bass** ADJS **deep,** deep-toned, deep-pitched, deep-sounding, deepmouthed, deep-echoing; low, low-pitched, low-toned, grave, heavy

**bastard** NOUNS 1 illegitimate *or* bastard child, whoreson, by-blow, child born out of wedlock *or* without benefit of clergy *or* on the wrong side of the blanket, natural *or* love child, *nullius filius* <L>
ADJS 2 **illegitimate, spurious,** false; misbegot, **misbegotten,** miscreated, baseborn, born out of wedlock

**bastion** NOUNS **stronghold,** strong point, **fastness,** keep, ward, donjon, **citadel, castle,** tower, tower of strength, strong point

**batch** NOUNS 1 **amount,** quantity, **sum, number,** count, group, total, reckoning, **measure,** parcel, passel <nonformal>, bunch, heap <nonformal>, gob *and* chunk *and* hunk <all nonformal>
VERBS 2 **assemble, gather; accumulate,** cumulate, **amass,** mass, bulk; agglomerate, conglomerate, aggregate; pack, pack in, cram, cram in; **bunch,** bunch up; **cluster,** clump

**bathe** VERBS 1 **wash,** bath <Brit>, lave; **steep**
2 **swim,** go in swimming *or* bathing; skinny-dip

**bathing suit** NOUNS **swimwear;** swim suit, swimming suit, tank suit, tank top, *maillot* <Fr>; **trunks;** bikini, string bikini *or* string

**bathroom** NOUNS **latrine,** convenience, **toilet,** water closet *or* WC <nonformal>; **john** *and* johnny *and* **can** *and* crapper <all nonformal>; loo <Brit nonformal>; **lavatory,** washroom, **rest room,** powder room <nonformal>; men's *or* boys' *or* little boys' room <nonformal>; head; privy, outhouse

**baths** NOUNS **health resort, spa, watering place;** mineral spring, warm *or* hot spring

**baton** NOUNS **staff,** stave; **cane, stick, walking stick,** handstaff, shillelagh

**batten** VERBS **secure,** make sure *or* secure, tie up, chain, tether; **make fast, fasten,** fasten down; batten down

4 **thrive, flourish,** boom; blossom, bloom, flower

**battered** ADJS **dilapidated, ramshackle, tumbledown, broken-down, rundown,** in ruins, derelict; beaten up, **beat-up** <nonformal>, bruised, wounded

**battery** NOUNS 1 **artillery, cannon,** cannonry, ordnance, engines of war, Big Bertha, howitzer

2 **corporal punishment, whipping, beating, thrashing, flogging,** flagellation, flailing, trouncing, basting, drubbing, buffeting

**battle** NOUNS 1 **fight, fray,** affray, combat, action, conflict, embroilment; **clash; brush, skirmish,** scrimmage; tussle, **scuffle, struggle,** scramble

VERBS 2 **contend against,** combat, clash with, rival, compete with *or* against, vie with *or* against; **resist, offer resistance**

**battle-ax** NOUNS **shrew, vixen,** virago, termagant, fury, witch, beldam, cat, tigress, she-wolf, she-devil, spitfire; **scold,** common scold

**battle cry** NOUNS **call to arms, call-up,** call to the colors, **rally;** war cry, war whoop, rebel yell; banzai, gung ho, Geronimo, go for broke; remember the Maine *or* the Alamo *or* Pearl Harbor

**battlefield** NOUNS **battleground,** battle site, **field,** combat zone, **field of battle;** field of slaughter, field of blood *or* bloodshed, aceldama, killing ground *or* field, shambles

**battleship** NOUNS battlewagon <nonformal>, capital ship; **cruiser,** battlecruiser; **destroyer,** can *or* tin can <nonformal>

**bauble** NOUNS **trinket,** gewgaw, **knickknack** *or* nicknack, **gimcrack**

**bawdy** ADJS **obscene, lewd, adult,** ithyphallic, **ribald, pornographic, salacious,** lurid, **dirty, smutty,** raunchy <nonformal>, blue, unclean, **foul, filthy, nasty,** vile, fulsome, offensive, unprintable, **foulmouthed**

**bay** NOUNS **inlet, cove,** arm of the sea, loch <Scots>, **fjord,** bight; cove; **estuary,** firth *or* frith, bayou, mouth

VERBS 2 cry, call; **howl,** yowl, yawp, yawl <nonformal>, ululate; bay at the moon

**bayonet** VERBS **stab, stick** <nonformal>, **run through, impale,** spit, **transfix,** transpierce

**bazaar** NOUNS rummage sale, white elephant sale, garage sale, flea market, flea fair, street market, **mart, market, open market**

**beach** NOUNS 1 **shore, coast,** *côte* <Fr>; **strand,** *playa* <Sp>, beachfront, plage, lido, riviera

VERBS 2 **shipwreck,** wreck, **go** *or* **run aground,** strand, run on the rocks

**beachcomber** NOUNS **vagabond, vagrant,** loafer, idler; beach bum, surf bum

**beacon** NOUNS **signal, sign;** signal fire, beacon fire, parachute flare; rocket, signal rocket, Roman candle

**beaded** ADJS **beady,** bead-shaped, beadlike; **ornamented, adorned, decorated, embellished, bedecked,** decked out, tricked out, garnished, spangled, jeweled, bejeweled; studded

**beaked** ADJS **hooked, crooked, aquiline,** aduncous; **hook-shaped,** hooklike, uncinate, unciform

**beam** NOUNS 1 **smile,** smiling; bright smile, gleaming *or* glowing smile; **grin,** ear-to-ear grin

2 **timber,** pole, spar

3 **ray,** radiation, **gleam, pencil, patch,** ray of light, beam of light

VERBS 4 exude cheerfulness, radiate cheer, not have a care in the world, glow; **smile**

5 **broadcast,** radiate, **transmit,** send

**beanery** NOUNS eating place, eating house; eatery *and* hashery *and* hash house *and* greasy spoon <all nonformal>; **fast-food restaurant,** hamburger joint <nonformal>

**beanpole** NOUNS <thin person> **slim, lanky; skeleton,** walking skeleton, beanstalk, broomstick

**bear** NOUNS 1 bar <nonformal>; grizzly, polar bear

2 short, short seller

VERBS 3 **give birth,** bear *or* have young, **have; have a baby,** bear a child; lie in, be confined, labor

4 **endure, stand,** support, sustain, **suffer, tolerate, abide,** bide, persevere; **bear up under, bear the brunt, bear with, put up with, stand for,** tolerate

5 **transport, convey,** freight, conduct, **take; carry,** pack, tote *and* lug <both nonformal>

6 **yield, produce,** furnish; **bring forth;** fruit, **bear fruit,** fructify
7 **support,** carry, **hold, sustain, maintain, bolster, reinforce,** back, back up, shoulder, give *or* furnish *or* afford *or* supply *or* lend support

**bearable** ADJS **tolerable, endurable, supportable, sufferable**

**bear arms** VERBS **serve,** do duty; fulfill one's military obligation, wear the uniform; **soldier,** see *or* do active duty

**beard** NOUNS 1 **whiskers;** beaver <nonformal>; chin whiskers, side whiskers; **sideburns,** burnsides, **muttonchops; goatee, Vandyke**
VERBS 2 **brave, face, confront,** affront, front, look one in the eye, say to one's face, **face up to, meet head-on** *or* boldly, stand up to *or* against, go eyeball-to-eyeball *or* one-on-one with <nonformal>

**bearing** NOUNS 1 **look, air, mien,** demeanor, carriage, port, posture, stance, poise, presence
2 **direction,** directionality; **orientation,** lay, lie

**bearings** NOUNS **position, orientation,** lay, lie, set, **attitude,** aspect, position line *or* line of position; **fix**

**bear market** NOUNS **declining market,** sagging market, retreating market, **slump,** sag; break in the market

**bear witness** VERBS 1 **be pious, be religious; have faith,** trust in God, love God, fear God
2 **testify, attest, give evidence, give** *or* **bear witness; depose,** depone, **warrant, swear,** allege, asseverate

**beastly** ADJS 1 **offensive, objectionable, odious, repulsive,** repellent, rebarbative, **repugnant, revolting**
2 **gruff, brusque, curt,** short, sharp, snippy <nonformal>, abrupt, **blunt,** bluff, brash, bearish, churlish
3 **brutish, brutal,** brute; **bestial,** beastlike; swinish

**beast of burden** NOUNS **pack** *or* **draft animal,** pack horse *or* mule, sumpter, sumpter horse *or* mule

**beat** NOUNS 1 **pulsation, pulse, throb;** beating, throbbing; systole, diastole
VERBS 2 **best, beat out, defeat, whip,** give a whipping *or* beating *or* thrashing, **thrash, flog,** whale; **smite,** thump, trounce, baste, **pummel,** lay on
3 <nonformal> beat all hollow, trounce, clobber, take to the cleaners, smoke, skin, skin alive, worst, whip, lick, have it all over, cut down to size
4 **pulsate, pulse, throb, palpitate,** go pit-a-pat

ADJS 5 <nonformal> **pooped, bushed,** frazzled, tuckered, tuckered out, done in, all in, dead, dead beat, dead on one's feet, gone; **pooped out,** knocked out, wiped out, run ragged, played out

6 <nonformal> **clobbered, licked, whipped,** trimmed, sandbagged, banjaxed, done in, lathered, creamed, shellacked, trounced, lambasted, settled, fixed; skinned alive; thrown for a loss

**beaten** ADJS **defeated, worsted, bested, outdone; discomfited,** put to rout, **routed,** scattered, stampeded, panicked; **undone, done for** <nonformal>, **ruined,** kaput *and* on the skids <both nonformal>, *hors de combat* <Fr>

**beater** NOUNS **agitator,** shaker, jiggler, vibrator; paddle, whisk, eggbeater; churn; blender

**beatify** VERBS **sanctify, hallow; purify,** cleanse, wash one's sins away; **bless; glorify,** exalt, ensky; saint, canonize; deify, apotheosize

**beating** NOUNS 1 **defeat;** drubbing, thrashing; clobbering *and* hiding *and* lathering *and* whipping *and* lambasting *and* trimming *and* licking <all nonformal>, trouncing; Waterloo; failure
2 **corporal punishment, whipping, thrashing, spanking, flogging,** flagellation, scourging, flailing, trouncing, basting, drubbing, buffeting, belaboring
ADJS 3 **drumming, thrumming, pounding, thumping; throbbing;** sputtering, spattering, spluttering

**beat it** VERBS

<nonformal> **split,** scram, buzz off, buzz along, bug out, fuck off *or* f off, get rolling, hightail it, pull up stakes, check out, clear out, cut out, haul ass, hit the road *or* trail, get lost, get going, shove off, push along, push off, get the hell out, make oneself scarce, vamoose

**beatitude** NOUNS **sanctification, hallowing; purification;** blessing; **glorification,** exaltation, enskying; **consecration,** dedication, canonization, enshrinement

**beatnik** NOUNS **nonconformist, original,** eccentric, gonzo <nonformal>, deviant, maverick <nonformal>, Bohemian, hippie, hipster, freak <nonformal>, flower child, street people, yippie

**beat up** VERBS

<nonformal> rough up, clobber, marmelize <Brit>, work over, lick, larrup, wallop, whop, swinge, beat one's brains out, whale, whale the tar out of, beat *or* kick the shit out of, beat to a jelly, **beat black and blue, knock one's lights out, nail,** welt, trim, flax, lather, leather, **hide,** tan, **tan one's hide,** dress down, **kick ass,** give a dressing-down, knock head, knock heads together; **paddle; lambaste, clobber,** dust one's jacket, give a dose of birch oil *or* strap oil *or* hickory oil *or* hazel oil, take it out of one's hide *or* skin

**beau** NOUNS **inamorato, swain,** man, gallant, cavalier, squire, *caballero* <Sp>; *amoroso, cavaliere servente* <both Ital>; gigolo; **boyfriend** *and* **fellow** *and* young man *and* flame <all nonformal>; old man <nonformal>; Prince Charming, Lothario, Romeo; Casanova, Don Juan; Beau Brummel

**beautified** ADJS **improved, bettered;** changed for the better, adorned, decorated

**beautiful** ADJS **artistic,** painterly; **aesthetic; decorative, ornamental**; **beauteous,** endowed with beauty; **pretty, handsome, attractive**, pulchritudinous, **lovely, graceful,** gracile; elegant; aesthetically appealing

**beautiful people** NOUNS **society,** *société* <Fr>, fashionable society, **polite society, high society,** *beau monde, haut monde* <both Fr>; best people, right people; **smart set** <nonformal>; the Four Hundred, **upper crust** <nonformal>; café society, jet set, beautiful people, in-crowd, the glitterati <nonformal>

**beauty** NOUNS 1 **beautifulness,** beauteousness, **prettiness, handsomeness, attractiveness, loveliness, pulchritude, charm,** grace, elegance, exquisiteness
2 **charmer, glamour girl,** cover girl, sex goddess; **belle,** reigning beauty, great beauty, enchantress

3 <nonformal> **doll, dish, cutie,** angel, angelface, babyface, beaut, honey, dream, looker, good-looker, stunner, dazzler, dreamboat, fetcher, bird *and* crumpet <both Brit>, peach, knockout, raving beauty, centerfold, pinup girl, pinup, bunny, cutie *or* cutesy pie, cute *or* slick chick, pussycat, sex kitten, ten

4 <famous beauties> Venus, Venus de Milo; Aphrodite, Hebe; Adonis, Appollo, Apollo Belvedere, Hyperion, Antinoüs, Narcissus; Astarte; Balder, Freya; Helen of Troy, Cleopatra; the Graces, houri, peri

*truth's smile when she beholds her own face in a perfect mirror*
TAGORE

*God's handwriting*
EMERSON

**beckon** VERBS attract one's interest, be attractive, take *or* tickle one's fancy; **invite,** summon; **tempt, tantalize, titillate,** whet the appetite, make one's mouth water, dangle before one

**become** VERBS 1 **originate,** come into the world, get to be <nonformal>, see the light of day, rise, **arise,** take rise, **come forth, issue,** issue forth
2 be converted into, **turn into** *or* **to, change into, grow into,** ripen into, **develop** *or* **evolve into,** merge *or* blend *or* melt into

**becoming** ADJS **decorous,** proper, **seemly,** fitting, appropriate, suitable, meet, happy, felicitous; **decent, modest,** delicate, elegant, proper

**bedazzle** VERBS **confuse,** throw into confusion *or* chaos, entangle, **mix up, fluster;** flummox <nonformal>, **flutter,** put into a flutter, **flurry, rattle, ruffle**

**bedding** NOUNS **bedclothes, blanket, coverlet,** cover, covers, **spread,** robe, **afghan, bedspread; bedcover; linen,** bed linen

**bedlam** NOUNS 1 **racket, din, clamor; cacophony,** din, noise, static, racket; outcry, **uproar,** hue and cry, noise and shouting
2 **insane asylum,** lunatic asylum, **madhouse,** mental institution, mental home; **bughouse** *and* nuthouse *and* laughing academy *and* **loonybin** *and* **booby hatch** *and* funny farm <all nonformal>; mental hospital

**bedraggled** ADJS **untidy, unsightly,** unneat, slobby *and* scuzzy <both non-

formal>, **unkempt; sloppy** <nonformal>, scraggly, poky, seedy <nonformal>, **shabby,** grubby <nonformal>, **frowzy, blowzy,** tacky <nonformal>

**bedridden** ADJS **bedfast, sick abed; down,** prostrate, flat on one's back; **laid up, invalided,** hospitalized

**bedrock** NOUNS 1 **rock bottom,** bed, hardpan; **grass roots;** substratum, underlayer, lowest level *or* layer *or* stratum, the pits <nonformal>
ADJS 2 **bottom,** bottommost, **undermost,** nethermost, lowermost, deepest, deepmost, profoundest, **lowest**

**bedroom** NOUNS **boudoir,** chamber, sleeping chamber, **bedchamber,** cubicle, cubiculum

**bedtime** NOUNS **sleep, slumber; repose,** silken repose, *somnus* <L>, the arms of Morpheus; bye-bye *or* beddy-bye <both nonformal>; **land of Nod,** slumberland, sleepland, dreamland; sack time <nonformal>

**beef** NOUNS 1 *bœuf* <Fr>; roast beef, *rosbif* <Fr>; Kobe beef
2 **power, potency, might;** oomph *and* punch *and* bang *and* clout *and* steam <all nonformal>; **strength; energy;** muscle power, sinew, might and main
3 **objection, protest;** protestation; **remonstrance, remonstration,** expostulation; **reservation, scruple,** compunction, qualm, twinge *or* qualm of conscience; **complaint, grievance; exception**
VERBS 4 **object, protest, kick** <nonformal>, put up a struggle *or* fight; **bitch** *and* **squawk** *and* howl *and* holler *and* put up a squawk <all nonformal>; make *or* create *or* raise a stink about <all nonformal>; yell bloody murder <nonformal>; **remonstrate,** expostulate

**beef up** VERBS **intensify, heighten, deepen,** enhance, **strengthen; exaggerate,** blow up *and* puff up <both nonformal>, **magnify;** augment, supplement; swell the ranks of

**beep** NOUNS 1 **blare,** shriek, peal; **toot,** tootle, **honk,** blat, trumpet
VERBS 2 **blare;** shriek; **toot,** tootle, sound, peal, wind, blow, blat; **honk,** honk *or* sound *or* blow the horn

**beeper** NOUNS **alarm, alert;** buzzer; automobile alarm; fire alarm

**beer** NOUNS lager, light beer; brew *and* brewskie *and* suds <all nonformal>, bitter <Brit>

**befitting** ADJS **expedient, desirable,** to be desired, much to be desired, **advisable, politic,** recommendable; **appropriate, meet, fit, fitting, right, proper, becoming,** seemly, likely, congruous, **suitable,** sortable, feasible, doable, swingable <nonformal>, **convenient,** happy, heaven-sent, felicitous; worthwhile, worth one's while

**beforehand** ADVS **early, beforetime,** early on, betimes, **ahead of time,** foresightedly, in advance, in anticipation, **with time to spare**

**befriend** VERBS 1 **make friends with,** gain the friendship of, **strike up a friendship,** take up with <nonformal>, **get acquainted,** make acquaintance with

2 <nonformal> **be buddy-buddy** *or* **palsy-walsy with,** click, have good *or* great chemistry, team up; **get next to, get palsy** *or* **palsy-walsy with,** get cozy with, cozy *or* snuggle up to, get close to, get chummy with, buddy *or* pal up with, play footsie with

**beg** VERBS 1 **entreat, implore, beseech,** crave, **plead, appeal, pray, supplicate,** impetrate, obtest; clamor for, cry for, cry out for
2 **scrounge, cadge; mooch** *and* **bum** *and* **panhandle** <all nonformal>; **hit** *and* hit up *and* **touch** *and* put the touch on *and* make a touch <all nonformal>

**beget** VERBS 1 **procreate, generate, breed,** get, **engender; propagate, multiply;** proliferate; sire; reproduce in kind
2 **cause,** be the cause of, lie at the root of; **bring about, bring to pass,** effectuate, **effect,** bring to effect, realize; establish, inaugurate, institute

**beggar** NOUNS 1 **mendicant,** scrounger, **cadger; bum** *and* bummer *and* **moocher** *and* **panhandler** <all nonformal>; *schnorrer* <Yiddish>
2 **wretch, poor devil,** *pauvre diable* <Fr>, poor creature, *mauvais sujet* <Fr>; **sad case,** sad sack *and* sad sack of shit <both nonformal>

**begin** VERBS **commence, start; start in, start off, start out, set out,** set to *or* about, go *or* swing into action, get to *or* down to, **turn to,** fall to, pitch in <nonformal>, dive in <nonformal>, plunge into, head into <nonformal>, **go**

**ahead,** fire *or* blast away <nonformal>, get the show on the road <nonformal>, get *or* set *or* start the ball rolling <nonformal>

**beginner** NOUNS **neophyte, tyro;** newcomer, new arrival, Johnny-come-lately <nonformal>; **novice,** novitiate, probationer, catechumen; **recruit,** raw recruit, rookie <nonformal>

**beginning** NOUNS 1 **commencement, start,** running *or* flying start, starting point, square one <nonformal>, **outset,** outbreak, **onset,** oncoming; **origin,** genesis
ADJS 2 **initial,** initiatory *or* initiative; **incipient,** inceptive, **introductory,** inchoative, inchoate; inaugural *or* inauguratory

**begrudge** VERBS 1 **envy,** be envious *or* covetous of, **covet,** cast envious eyes, desire for oneself; resent; **grudge**
2 **stint, scrimp, skimp, scamp,** scant, **pinch, pinch pennies,** rub the print off a dollar bill

**beguile** VERBS **fascinate, captivate, charm,** becharm, spell, spellbind, cast a spell, put under a spell, **intrigue, enthrall,** infatuate, **enrapture, transport, enravish, entrance, enchant,** witch, **bewitch**, astound

**beguiling** ADJS **alluring, fascinating, captivating, riveting, charming, glamorous,** exotic, **enchanting,** spellbinding, **entrancing,** ravishing, **enravishing, intriguing, enthralling, bewitching**

**behave** VERBS **behave oneself, conduct oneself,** manage oneself, **handle oneself,** guide oneself, **comport oneself, deport oneself,** demean oneself, **bear oneself, carry oneself**

**behavior** NOUNS **conduct, deportment, comportment, manner, manners, demeanor, mien, carriage, bearing,** poise, posture, guise, **air,** address, presence

**behead** VERBS decapitate, decollate, guillotine, bring to the block

**behest** NOUNS **command, commandment, order,** direct order, command decision, **bidding,** imperative, **dictate,** dictation, **will, pleasure,** say-so <nonformal>, **authority**

**behind** NOUNS 1 **rear, rear end, hind end,** hind part, hinder part, afterpart, rearward, **posterior,** breech, stern, tail, tail end

2 <nonformal> **ass,** backside, **butt, can,** cheeks, hind end, tail, **fanny,** prat, keister

ADJS 3 **retarded,** slowed-down, eased, slackened; set back, backward
ADVS 4 **after,** in the rear, in the train *or* wake of; in back of; behind one's back
5 **late, behindhand, belatedly,** backward, slow, in arrears *or* arrear, **behind time;** none too soon, in the nick of time, under the wire

**beholden** ADJS **grateful, thankful; appreciative,** appreciatory, sensible; **obliged, much obliged,** indebted to, under obligation

**being** NOUNS 1 **person, human, human being, man, woman, child,** member of the human race *or* family, Adamite, daughter of Eve
2 **existence;** subsistence, entity, essence, *Ding-an-sich* <Ger, thing-in-itself>, noumenon; **occurrence,** presence

**belabor** VERBS overemphasize, overstress, overaccentuate, harp on, dwell on; make a big deal *or* Federal case of <nonformal>

**belch** NOUNS 1 **burp** <nonformal>, belching, wind, gas, eructation
VERBS 2 **erupt, burst forth** *or* **out, break out, blow out** *or* **open,** eruct, **burp** <nonformal>, eructate

**belfry** NOUNS **tower; turret,** *tour* <Fr>; campanile, bell tower, **spire,** church spire

**belief** NOUNS 1 religious belief *or* faith, teaching, doctrine, creed, credo, theology, orthodoxy; system of beliefs
2 credence, credit, trust; **confidence,** assuredness, convincedness, persuadedness, **assurance; credulity**

**believable** ADJS **credible; tenable,** conceivable, **plausible,** colorable; reliable; unimpeachable, unexceptionable, **unquestionable**

**believe** VERBS 1 **have faith,** bear witness, affirm; keep the faith, fight the good fight, be observant, follow righteousness
2 credit, trust, accept, receive, buy <nonformal>; give credit *or* credence to, put faith in, take stock in *or* set store by <nonformal>, take to heart, attach weight to; **buy** *and* **buy into** <both nonformal>, **swallow**; **be certain**

**believer** NOUNS pietist, religionist, saint, theist; **devotee,** devotionalist, votary;

**zealot,** zealotist, fundamentalist, militant; **disciple,** follower, servant, faithful servant; **fanatic**

**belittle** VERBS **disparage, depreciate,** slight, minimize, make little of, degrade, debase, **run** *or* **knock down** <nonformal>, **put down** <nonformal>; **discredit,** bring into discredit

**belle** NOUNS **beauty, charmer,** *charmeuse* <Fr>; reigning beauty, great beauty, lady fair; toast of the town; enchantress

**belles lettres** NOUNS **literature, letters,** humane letters, *litterae humaniores* <L>, republic of letters

**belligerent** NOUNS 1 **combatant, fighter, battler,** scrapper <nonformal>; **contestant, contender, competitor, rival;** disputant, wrangler, squabbler
ADJS 2 **contentious, quarrelsome**; **disputatious,** controversial, litigious, polemic, polemical; **argumentative,** scrappy <nonformal>; **quarrelsome**

**bellow** NOUNS 1 **cry, call, shout, yell,** hoot
VERBS 2 **bawl,** roar; cry *or* yell *or* scream bloody murder *or* blue murder

**belly** NOUNS 1 **abdomen; stomach, midriff,** diaphragm, **paunch**

2 <nonformal> goozle, guzzle; tum, tummy, tum-tum, breadbasket, **gut,** bulge, fallen chest <nonformal>, corporation, spare tire, bay window, **pot,** potbelly, potgut, beerbelly, German *or* Milwaukee goiter, pusgut, swagbelly; **guts,** tripes, stuffings

VERBS 3 **bulge,** balloon, **pouch, swell, swell up, dilate, distend,** billow; swell out, **belly out**

**belong** VERBS hold membership, be a member, be on the rolls, be inscribed, subscribe, hold *or* carry a card, be in <nonformal>

**belongings** NOUNS **personal effects,** chattels personal, movables, choses transitory

**beloved** NOUNS 1 **sweetheart, loved one,** dearly beloved, well-beloved, object of one's affections, light of one's eye *or* life
ADJS 2 **loved, dear, darling, precious;** pet, favorite; **adored, admired, cherished,** prized, treasured, held dear

**below** ADVS **down, downward, downwards,** from the top down, *de haut en bas* <Fr>; down below

**bemused** ADJS **abstracted,** museful <old>, **musing, preoccupied, absorbed, engrossed,** taken up; **absentminded, absent,** faraway, elsewhere, somewhere else, not there; lost, **lost in thought,** wrapped in thought; **daydreaming,** daydreamy

**bench** NOUNS 1 **seat of justice, judgment seat,** mercy seat, siege of justice <old>
2 reserves, second team, second string, third string
3 workbench; **counter,** bar, buffet; **desk,** writing table; **lectern,** reading stand, ambo, reading desk

**bend** VERBS 1 **comply with,** agree with, tally with, chime *or* fall in with, go by, be guided *or* regulated by, observe, follow, yield, take the shape of; straighten, rectify, correct, **discipline**
2 **crouch, duck,** cringe, **cower; stoop, stoop down, squat,** squat down, get down, hunker *and* hunker down *and* get down on one's hunkers <all nonformal>

**Benedict Arnold** NOUNS **traitor,** treasonist, **betrayer, quisling, rat** <nonformal>, **snake in the grass, double-crosser** <nonformal>, double-dealer; Judas, Judas Iscariot, Quisling, Brutus

**benediction** NOUNS **thanks, thanksgiving,** praise, laud, hymn, paean; **blessing,** benison, invocation, benedicite

**benefactor** NOUNS benefactress, **benefiter,** succorer, befriender; ministrant, ministering angel; Samaritan, **good Samaritan; helper,** aider, assister, help, aid, helping hand

**beneficial** ADJS 1 **healthful, healthy, salubrious, salutary, wholesome,** health-enhancing, life-promoting, benign, bracing, refreshing, invigorating, tonic
2 **helpful, useful,** utile; **profitable, salutary,** good for; remedial, therapeutic; **serviceable, useful**; **constructive, positive**

**benefit** NOUNS 1 benefaction, benevolence, **blessing, favor, boon,** grace; **good, welfare,** well-being
2 benefit performance, **performance, show, presentation,** presentment, **production,** entertainment
VERBS 3 **avail,** be of use, be of service, serve, **suffice, do,** answer, **answer** *or* **serve one's purpose,** serve one's need, fill the bill *and* do the trick <both nonformal>

**benevolent** ADJS **beneficent, philanthropic, altruistic,** humanitarian; **big-**

**hearted,** greathearted; **generous**; eleemosynary; **magnanimous**
**benign** ADJS 1 **kind, kindly;** benignant; kindhearted, warm, warmhearted, softhearted, tenderhearted, tender, loving, affectionate
2 **harmless,** unhurtful; well-meaning, well-meant; **innocuous,** nonmalignant
**bent** NOUNS 1 **disposition, character, nature, temper, temperament,** mettle, constitution, stamp, type, stripe, kidney, make, mold; **turn, bias,** slant, cast, warp, twist
ADJS 2 **distorted, contorted, warped, twisted, crooked;** tortuous, labyrinthine, buckled, sprung, bowed; unsymmetric, unsymmetrical, asymmetric, asymmetrical, nonsymmetric, nonsymmetrical; irregular, deviative
**bequeath** VERBS **will, leave, devise, will to,** hand down, hand on, pass on, transmit; make a bequest
**bequest** NOUNS bequeathal, **legacy,** devise; inheritance; patrimony, birthright; heirloom
**berserk** ADJS **amok,** running wild; **rabid, maniac** *or* **maniacal,** raving mad, stark-raving mad, **frenzied, frantic,** frenetic; **raving, raging,** ranting; frothing *or* foaming at the mouth
**berth** NOUNS **anchor,** mooring, **anchorage,** moorings; slip; mooring buoy
**beseech** VERBS **entreat, implore, beg,** crave, **plead, appeal, pray, supplicate,** impetrate, obtest; **plead for,** clamor for, cry for, cry out for
**besiege** VERBS **lay siege to,** encompass, surround, **encircle,** set upon on all sides, get in a pincers, close the jaws of the pincers *or* trap
**besmirch** VERBS **vilify, revile, defile, sully, soil, smear,** smirch, bespatter, tarnish, **blacken,** denigrate, blacken one's good name, give a black eye <nonformal>; stigmatize; **muckrake, throw mud at,** heap dirt upon, drag through the mud
**bespoke** ADJS tailored, custom-made
**best** NOUNS 1 **the best,** the very best, the best ever, the top of the heap *or* the line <nonformal>, the tops <nonformal>; cream of the crop, *crème de la crème* <Fr>, salt of the earth; *pièce de résistance* <Fr>; paragon, nonpareil
VERBS 2 **defeat**; beat all hollow <nonformal>, trounce, clobber *and* take to the cleaners *and* smoke *and* skin *and* skin alive <all nonformal>, worst, whip *and* lick *and* have it all over *and* cut down to size <all nonformal>; **triumph over**
ADJS 3 very best, greatest *and* top-of-the-line <both nonformal>, **prime,** optimum, optimal; **choice, select, elect,** elite, **picked,** handpicked; **prize, champion; unsurpassed,** surpassing, unparalleled, unmatched, unmatchable, matchless, **peerless**
**bestial** ADJS **brutal,** brutish, brute, beastly, animal; insensate, senseless, subhuman, dehumanized, brutalized; **barbarous,** barbaric, uncivilized, **inhuman,** inhumane, unhuman; fiendish, fiendlike
**bestow** VERBS **give, present, donate,** slip <nonformal>, let have; **confer, award, allot, render,** bestow on; impart, let one know, communicate; **grant,** accord, **allow,** vouchsafe, yield, afford, make available
**bet** NOUNS 1 **wager, stake,** hazard, **ante;** parlay, double or nothing
VERBS 2 **wager, gamble, hazard, stake,** punt, lay, lay down, put up, **make a bet, lay a wager,** give *or* take *or* lay odds, make book, get a piece of the action <nonformal>; plunge <nonformal>
**bête noire** NOUNS **bane, curse,** infliction, visitation, **plague, pestilence,** pest, calamity, scourge, **torment,** crushing burden; bugbear, bogy, bogeymen, nemesis, arch-nemesis
**betray** VERBS inform, **inform on**, talk *and* peach <both nonformal>; rat *and* stool *and* sing *and* squeal <all nonformal>, turn state's evidence; leak <nonformal>, spill <nonformal>, **spill the beans** <nonformal>; **let the cat out of the bag** <nonformal>, speak before one thinks, be unguarded *or* indiscreet, kiss and tell, **give away** *and* give the show away *and* give the game away <all nonformal>, betray a confidence, tell secrets, reveal a secret; have a big mouth *or* bazoo <nonformal>, **blab** *or* blabber <nonformal>; babble, **tattle,** tell *or* tattle on, tell tales, **tell tales out of school;** talk out of turn, let slip, let fall *or* drop; **blurt, blurt out**
**betrayer** NOUNS **informer, betrayer,** double-crosser <nonformal>, delator <old>; **snitch** *and* snitcher <both nonformal>; whistle-blower <nonformal>; **tattler,**

**tattletale, telltale, talebearer; blab** *or* blabber *or* blabberer *or* blabbermouth <all nonformal>; **squealer** *and* preacher *and* **stool pigeon** *and* stoolie *and* **fink** *and* rat <all nonformal>, nark <Brit nonformal>; **spy**

**betrothed** NOUNS 1 **fiancé, fiancée,** bride-to-be, affianced, future, intended <nonformal>
ADJS 2 **engaged, plighted, affianced,** intended; **promised, pledged, bound, committed,** compromised, **obligated; sworn**

**better** VERBS 1 **improve,** change for the better, make an improvement; transform, transfigure; improve upon, refine upon, **mend, amend,** emend; meliorate, **ameliorate**
ADJS 2 **superior, greater,** finer; **higher,** upper, over, above; ascendant, in the ascendant, in ascendancy, coming <nonformal>; **ahead,** a cut *or* stroke above, more than a match for

**bettor** NOUNS **gambler, player,** gamester, wagerer, punter; high-stakes gambler, money player, high roller, plunger; petty gambler, low roller, piker *and* tinhorn *and* tinhorn gambler <all nonformal>

**beverage** NOUNS drink, thirst quencher, potation, potable, **liquor,** liquid

**bevy** NOUNS **company, group,** grouping, groupment, network, **party, band, knot, gang, crew,** complement, cast, outfit, pack, cohort, troop, troupe, tribe, **body,** corps, stable, bunch *and* mob *and* crowd <all nonformal>

**bewildered** ADJS **dismayed,** distracted, distraught, abashed, **disconcerted, embarrassed,** discomposed, **put-out, disturbed, upset,** perturbed, **bothered,** all hot and bothered <nonformal>; clueless, without a clue, guessing, like a chicken with its head cut off <nonformal>; **nonplussed, baffled, perplexed,** mystified

**bewildering** ADJS **confusing, distracting, disconcerting,** discomposing, **dismaying, embarrassing,** disturbing, **upsetting, perplexing, baffling, mystifying, mysterious, puzzling,** confounding; **enigmatic**

**bewitching** ADJS **alluring, fascinating, captivating, riveting, charming, glamorous,** exotic, **enchanting,** spellful, spellbinding, **entrancing,** ravishing, **enravishing, intriguing, enthralling,** witching; **tantalizing,** teasing, titillating, titillative, tickling; **provocative,** *provoquant* <Fr>

**bias** NOUNS 1 **bend,** bent, **crook, warp, twist, turn, skew,** slue, **veer,** sheer, **swerve,** lurch
2 **partiality, onesidedness;** leaning, inclination, tendentiousness; partisanship, **slant,** angle, spin <nonformal>
VERBS 3 **prejudice,** prejudice against, **jaundice, influence, sway,** bias one's judgment; warp, twist, bend, distort
ADJS 4 **slant, biased, biaswise** *or* biasways; **transverse,** crosswise *or* crossways, thwart, athwart, across; **diagonal**
ADVS 5 **diagonally, on the bias,** biaswise; catercornerways *or* **catercorner** *or* cattycorner *or* kittycorner

**bicker** VERBS **quibble, cavil,** boggle, chop logic, **split hairs,** nitpick, pick nits; **shuffle, dodge,** shy, **evade,** sidestep, hedge, skate around <nonformal>, pussyfoot <nonformal>, evade the issue

**bid** NOUNS 1 **offer,** offering, proffer, presentation, submission; **invitation**
VERBS 2 **command, order, dictate, direct, instruct,** mandate, **enjoin, charge,** commission, call on *or* upon; give an order *or* a direct order, issue a command
3 make a bid, offer, offer to buy, make an offer; give the asking price; bid up; bid in

**bier** NOUNS litter, catafalque

**big** ADJS 1 **large, sizable, great, grand, substantial,** bumper; as big as all outdoors; numerous; largish, biggish
2 **adult, mature, of age,** out of one's teens, grown, **grown-up;** old enough to know better
3 **magnanimous,** great-souled *or* -spirited; **generous,** generous to a fault, openhanded, **liberal; bighearted**

**bigamous** ADJS digamous; **polygamous,** polygynous, polyandrous; morganatic

**bighearted** ADJS openhearted, greathearted, **magnanimous; liberal, free,** free with one's money, free-spending; **generous, munificent,** large, princely, handsome; **openhanded,** freehanded, open; **giving**

**bigmouthed** ADJS **talkative, loquacious, talky,** overtalkative, garrulous, chatty; gabby *and* windy *and* gassy <all nonformal>, all jaw <nonformal>; **long-winded, prolix, verbose**

**bigot** NOUNS **racist,** racial supremacist, white *or* black supremacist; **chauvinist,** ultranationalist, jingo, superpatriot

**big shot** NOUNS 1 **superior, chief, head, boss,** honcho <nonformal>, commander, **ruler, leader,** dean, *primus inter pares* <L, first among equals>

2 <nonformal> wheel, **big wheel,** big cheese, big noise, big-timer, big-time operator, **bigwig,** big man, big gun, **high-muck-a-muck** *or* high-mucketymuck, **VIP,** brass hat, high man on the totem pole

**bile** NOUNS 1 digestive secretion, gastric juice, pancreatic juice, intestinal juice
2 **bitterness, bitter resentment,** bitterness of spirit, heartburning; **rancor,** virulence, **acrimony,** acerbity, asperity; causticity

**bilge** NOUNS 1 garbage, swill, slop, slops
2 **sink;** sump, **cesspool,** cesspit, septic tank; catchbasin; **sewer,** drain, *cloaca* and *cloaca maxima* <both L>

**bilk** VERBS **cheat, victimize, gull, swindle, defraud,** euchre, **con,** finagle, **fleece,** mulct, **cheat out of, do out of,** obtain under false pretenses

**bill** NOUNS 1 **snout, proboscis,** antlia, **trunk;** rostrum; **bill** *and* pecker <both nonformal>
2 **statute,** rubric, **canon,** institution; **ordinance; act, enactment, measure,** legislation
3 **paper money;** dollar bill, etc; **note,** negotiable note, legal-tender note; **bank note,** Federal Reserve note
4 statement, account, ledger, books
VERBS 5 send a statement; **invoice;** call, call in, demand payment, **dun**

**billboard** NOUNS **poster, bill, placard, sign,** show card, banner, *affiche* <Fr>; highway sign

**billow** VERBS **surge, swell,** heave, lift, rise, toss, **roll,** wave, **undulate;** comb, break, dash, crash, smash; rise and fall, ebb and flow; balloon, distend

**bin** NOUNS storage, **depository, repository,** conservatory <old>, reservoir, repertory; bunker, bay, crib; rack, rick; crate, box; chest, **locker,** hutch

**bind** NOUNS 1 **predicament, plight,** spot of trouble, **strait,** straits, parlous straits, tightrope, knife-edge, thin edge; **embarrassment,** embarrassing position *or* situation; **complication,** imbroglio; the devil to pay
VERBS 2 **edge, bound, rim, skirt, hem, hem in,** fringe, lap, line, side
3 **restrain, tie,** tie up, put the clamps on, **strap,** lash, leash, pinion, fasten, secure, make fast
4 **obligate, oblige, require,** make incumbent *or* imperative, tie, pledge, commit, saddle with, put under an obligation
5 **stick together, cement, colligate, paste, glue,** agglutinate, conglutinate, gum

**binding** NOUNS 1 **edging, bordering, trimming,** skirting; fringe, fimbriation, fimbria; **hem,** selvage, frill, frilling
ADJS 2 **obligatory, imperative,** peremptory, mandatory, must, *de rigueur* <Fr>; **necessary,** required

**binge** NOUNS

<nonformal> **drunk,** bust, tear, **bender, toot, bat,** jag, brannigan, guzzle, rip

**binoculars** NOUNS **spy glass,** terrestrial telescope, glass, **field glass;** zoom binoculars, opera glasses

**biodegradable** ADJS degradable, decomposable, putrefiable, putrescible, disintegrable

**biography** NOUNS memoir, **life,** story, **life story,** adventures, fortunes, experiences; **autobiography, profile, biographical sketch**

**biologist** NOUNS **naturalist,** life scientist; **botanist,** plant scientist, plant biologist, phytobiologist, phytologist; **zoologist,** animal biologist, animal scientist

**biology** NOUNS biological science, life science, the science of life, the study of living things; **botany,** plant biology, phytobiology, phytology, plant science; **zoology,** animal biology, animal science

**bionics** NOUNS autonetics, automatic *or* automation technology, automatic electronics, automatic engineering, automatic control engineering, servo engineering, **servomechanics,** system engineering

**biorhythm** NOUNS **life force, soul,** spirit, indwelling spirit, force of life, living force, *vis vitae* or *vis vitalis* <both L>, **vital force** *or* energy, animating force *or* power *or* principle, biological clock, life cycle

**biotic** ADJS **organic,** organismic; organized; **animate, living,** vital, zoetic

**birdbrained** ADJS **superficial, shallow, unprofound;** shallow-witted, shallow-minded, shallow-brained, shallow-headed, shallow-pated; **frivolous,** dizzy *and* ditzy <both nonformal>, flighty, light, volatile, frothy, fluffy, **feather-brained, birdwitted**

**birth** NOUNS 1 **nativity,** nascency, **childbirth, childbearing, having a baby, giving birth, birthing,** parturition, the stork <nonformal>; **confinement,** lying-in, being brought to bed, **childbed,** *accouchement* <Fr>; **labor,** travail, birth throes *or* pangs; **delivery,** blessed event <nonformal>; the Nativity; multiparity; **hatching;** littering, whelping, farrowing
2 **generation, genesis; development;** procreation; **heredity, heritage, inheritance;** patrocliny, matrocliny; endowment, inborn capacity *or* tendency *or* susceptibility *or* predisposition; diathesis; inheritability, heritability, heredity
ADJS 3 **kindred, akin;** consanguineous *or* consanguinean *or* consanguineal, consanguine, by *or* of the blood; **biological,** genetic; **natural,** by birth; cognate, uterine, agnate, enate; intimately *or* closely related, remotely *or* distantly related

**birth control device** NOUNS **contraceptive,** prophylactic; condom; **rubber** *and* skin *and* bag <all nonformal>; oral contraceptive, **birth control pill, the pill** <nonformal>, morning-after pill, abortion pill; diaphragm, pessary; spermicide, spermicidal jelly, contraceptive foam; intrauterine device *or* IUD, Dalkon shield <trademark>, Lippes loop

**birth defect** NOUNS congenital defect; abnormality, condition, pathological condition; complication, secondary disease *or* condition

**birthmark** NOUNS strawberry mark, port-wine stain, vascular nevus, nevus, hemangioma; beauty mark *or* spot

**birthplace** NOUNS **fatherland,** *Vaterland* <Ger>, *patria* <L>, *la patrie* <Fr>, **motherland,** mother country, **native land,** native soil, one's native heath *or* ground *or* soil *or* place, the old country, country of origin, **birthplace,** cradle; **home, homeland,** homeground, God's country

*home is where one starts*
T S Eliot

**biscuit** NOUNS sinker <nonformal>; hardtack, sea biscuit, ship biscuit, pilot biscuit *or* bread; **cracker,** soda cracker *or* saltine, graham cracker, *biscotto* <Ital>, cream cracker, nacho, potato chip, potato crisp <Brit>, sultana, water biscuit, butter cracker, oyster cracker, pilot biscuit; wafer; rusk, zwieback, melba toast, Brussels biscuit; pretzel

**bisexuality** NOUNS bisexualism, ambisexuality, ambisextrousness, amphierotism, swinging both ways <nonformal>; **sexual preference; sexual orientation**

**bishop** NOUNS <Mormon> deacon, teacher, priest, elder, Seventy, high priest, patriarch, apostle; Aaronic priesthood, Melchizedek priesthood

**bisque** NOUNS **ceramic ware, ceramics; pottery, crockery; china, porcelain;** enamelware; refractory, cement; biscuit

**bistro** NOUNS **bar,** barroom, *bistro* <Fr>, cocktail lounge; taproom; **tavern, pub,** pothouse, alehouse, rumshop, grogshop, dramshop, groggery, gin mill <nonformal>, **saloon,** drinking saloon, saloon bar <Brit>; café

**bit** NOUNS 1 **distance;** stone's throw, spitting distance <nonformal>, bowshot, gunshot, pistol shot; earshot, earreach, a whoop *and* a whoop and a holler *and* two whoops and a holler <all nonformal>, ace
2 **little,** little *or* wee *or* tiny bit <nonformal>, bite, **particle,** fragment, spot, **speck,** flyspeck, fleck, point, dot, jot, tittle, **iota,** ounce, **dab** <nonformal>, mote, **mite** <nonformal>; whit, ace, **hair,** scruple, groat, farthing, pittance, dole, trifling amount, **smidgen** *and* skosh *and* smitch <all nonformal>, pinch, gobbet, dribble, driblet, dram, drop, drop in a bucket *or* in the ocean, nutshell
3 **piece, particle, scrap**, bite, **fragment, morsel, crumb,** shard, potsherd, snatch, snack; **cut,** cutting, clip, clipping, paring, shaving, rasher, snip, snippet, chip; **tatter, shred,** stitch; **splinter,** sliver; **shiver, smithereen** <nonformal>
4 **short time, little while,** little, **instant, moment**, mo <nonformal>, small space, span, spurt, **short spell;** no time, less than no time; bit *or* **little bit,** a breath, the wink of an eye, pair of winks <nonformal>; **two shakes** *and* two shakes of a lamb's tail <both nonformal>

5 **binary digit,** infobit, kilobit, megabit, gigabit, terbit; **byte,** kilobyte, megabyte

**bitch** NOUNS 1 **shrew, vixen,** virago, termagant, brimstone, fury, witch, beldam, cat, tigress, she-wolf, she-devil, spitfire; fishwife; **scold,** common scold; battle-ax <nonformal>
2 **dog, canine, pooch** *and* bow-wow <both nonformal>; **pup, puppy,** puppy-dog *and* perp <both nonformal>, **whelp;** gyp <S US>, slut
3 **tough proposition** *and* tough one *and* toughie <all nonformal>, large *or* tall order <nonformal>; **hard job, tough job** *and* heavy lift <both nonformal>, backbreaker, ballbuster <nonformal>, **chore,** man-sized job; brutal task, Herculean task, Augean task; **uphill work** *or* **going,** rough go <nonformal>, **heavy sledding,** hard pull <nonformal>, dead lift <old>; tough lineup to buck <nonformal>, hard road to travel; hard *or* tough nut to crack *and* hard *or* tough row to hoe *and* hard row of stumps <all nonformal>
VERBS 4 **object, protest, kick** *and* **beef** <both nonformal>, put up a struggle *or* fight; **bitch** *and* **beef** *and* **squawk** *and* howl *and* holler *and* put up a squawk *and* raise a howl <all nonformal>; exclaim *or* cry out against, make *or* create *or* raise a stink about <all nonformal>; yell bloody murder <nonformal>; **remonstrate,** expostulate; raise *or* press objections, raise one's voice against, enter a protest; **complain,** exclaim at, state a grievance, air one's grievances; **dispute, challenge,** call in question

**bitchy** ADJS 1 **spiteful,** despiteful; **catty,** cattish; **snide**

2 <nonformal> **crabby, grouchy,** cantankerous, crusty, grumpy *or* grumpish, cussed, huffy *or* huffish, mean, mean as a junkyard dog, ornery, cussed, feisty, ugly, miffy, salty, scrappy, shirty <Brit>, soreheaded

**bite** NOUNS 1 **morsel, taste,** swallow; mouthful, gob <nonformal>; a nibble, a bite, munchies; cud, quid; bolus; **chew,** chaw <nonformal>; nip, nibble; munch; gnash; champ, chomp <nonformal>; snap
2 **light meal, refreshments,** light repast, light lunch, spot of lunch <nonformal>, collation, **snack** *and* nosh <both nonformal>, *casse-croûte* <Fr>
3 **zest,** zestfulness, zestiness, **briskness,** liveliness, raciness; **nippiness, tanginess,** snappiness; **spiciness,** pepperiness, hotness, fieriness; **tang, spice,** relish; **nip;** punch, snap, zip, ginger; **kick,** guts <nonformal>
4 **bit, scrap, fragment, morsel, crumb,** shard, potsherd, snatch; cutting, clip, clipping, paring, shaving, rasher, snip, snippet, chip
VERBS 5 **pain,** sting; nip, tweak, pinch; pierce, prick, stab, cut, lacerate; **irritate, inflame,** harshen, exacerbate, intensify

**biting** ADJS 1 **painful;** hurtful, **hurting,** distressing, afflictive; **acute, sharp,** piercing, stabbing, shooting, stinging, gnawing; **poignant,** pungent, **severe,** cruel, harsh, grave, hard; griping, cramping, spasmic, spasmatic, spasmodic, paroxysmal; **agonizing, excruciating,** exquisite, atrocious, torturous, tormenting, martyrizing, racking, **harrowing**
2 **pungent, piquant, poignant; sharp, keen,** piercing, penetrating, nose-tickling, stinging, **acrid,** astringent, irritating, harsh, rough, severe, asperous, cutting, trenchant; **caustic,** vitriolic, mordant, escharotic; **bitter**; acerbic, acid, **sour**

**bitter** ADJS 1 **sharp, keen,** piercing, penetrating, nose-tickling, stinging, **biting, acrid,** astringent, irritating, harsh, rough, severe, asperous, cutting, trenchant; **caustic,** vitriolic, mordant, escharotic
2 **resentful,** resenting; embittered, rancorous, virulent, **acrimonious,** acerb, acerbic, acerbate; caustic; **choleric,** splenetic, acid, acidic, acidulous, acidulent; **sore** <nonformal>, rankled, burning *and* stewing <both nonformal>

**bitterly** ADVS **caustically,** mordantly, mordaciously, corrosively, corrodingly; **acrimoniously,** acridly, acidly, acerbly, acerbically, tartly; **sharply,** keenly, incisively, trenchantly, **cuttingly,** penetratingly, piercingly, bitingly, **stingingly,** stabbingly, **scathingly,** scorchingly, witheringly, thersitically, scurrilously, abusively

**bivouac** NOUNS 1 campground *or* campsite, camp, encampment, tented field
VERBS 2 **camp, encamp,** tent; pitch,

**pitch camp,** pitch one's tent, drive stakes <nonformal>; camp out, sleep out, rough it

**bizarre** ADJS 1 **humorous, funny, amusing; witty; droll, whimsical,** quizzical; **laughable,** risible, good for a laugh; **ludicrous, ridiculous, hilarious,** quaint, eccentric, incongruous
2 **absurd, nonsensical,** insensate, ridiculous, laughable, ludicrous; **foolish, crazy;** preposterous, cockamamie <nonformal>, fantastic, fantastical, grotesque, monstrous, wild, weird, **outrageous,** incredible, beyond belief, *outré* <Fr>, extravagant

**blabbermouth** NOUNS **informer, betrayer,** double-crosser <nonformal>, delator <old>; **snitch** *and* snitcher <both nonformal>; whistle-blower <nonformal>; **tattler, tattletale, telltale, talebearer; blab** *or* blabber *or* blabberer *or* blabbermouth <all nonformal>; **squealer** *and* preacher *and* **stool pigeon** *and* stoolie *and* **fink** *and* rat <all nonformal>, nark <Brit nonformal>

**black** NOUNS 1 **blackness,** nigritude, nigrescence; inkiness; **sable, ebony;** melanism; darkness
ADJS 2 **ebony;** deep black, of the deepest dye; **pitch-black, pitch-dark,** pitchy, black *or* dark as pitch, tar-black, tarry; night-black, night-dark, black *or* dark as night; midnight, black as midnight; **inky,** inky-black, atramentous, ink-black, black as ink; **jet-black,** jetty; **coal-black,** coaly, black as coal, coal-black; sloe, sloe-black, sloe-colored; raven, **raven-black,** black as a crow; **dark**

*cyprus black as e'er was crow*
SHAKESPEARE

3 <comparisons> ebony *or* ebon <old>, jet, ink, sloe, pitch, tar, coal, charcoal, smoke, soot, smut, raven, crow, night, hell, sin, one's hat <Brit>
4 **dark-skinned,** black-skinned, **dark-complexioned; colored;** melanian, melanic, melanotic, melanistic, melanous
5 **bad, evil, ill,** untoward, sinister; **wicked, wrong,** peccant, iniquitous, **vicious**

**blackball** VERBS **ostracize,** turn thumbs down, disfellowship; **reject, repudiate,** blackball *and* turn thumbs down on <both nonformal>, read *or* drum out, ease *or* freeze out *and* leave *or* keep out in the cold <all nonformal>, **exile, banish**; **proscribe, ban, outlaw**, put under the ban; **boycott,** blacklist

**blacken** VERBS 1 black, nigrify, melanize, denigrate; **darken,** bedarken; shade, shadow; blackwash, ink, charcoal, cork; **smudge,** smutch, **smirch,** besmirch, murk, blotch, blot, dinge; smut, soot; smoke, oversmoke; ebonize
2 **vilify, revile, defile, sully, soil, smear,** smirch, besmirch, bespatter, tarnish, denigrate, blacken one's good name, give a black eye <nonformal>; **call names,** give a bad name, give a dog a bad name, stigmatize; **muckrake, throw mud at,** mudsling, heap dirt upon, drag through the mud; engage in personalities
3 **darken,** bedarken; **obscure,** obfuscate, adumbrate; **eclipse,** occult, occultate, block the light; **black out,** brown out

**black eye** NOUNS **stigma,** stigmatism, onus; **brand,** badge of infamy; **slur,** reproach, censure, reprimand, imputation, aspersion, reflection, stigmatization; pillorying; black mark; **disparagement**; **stain, taint,** attaint, **tarnish,** blur, **smirch,** smutch *or* smooch, smudge, **smear,** spot, blot, blot on *or* in one's escutcheon *or* scutcheon; shiner *and* mouse <both nonformal>

**black humor** NOUNS **humor,** sick humor, gallows humor

**blacklist** VERBS **ostracize,** turn thumbs down, disfellowship; **reject, exile, banish**; **proscribe, ban, outlaw**, put under the ban; **boycott, blackball**

**black magic** NOUNS **Satanism,** diabolism, devil-worship, **demonism, devilry, diablerie, demonry;** demonomy, demonianism; the black art; Black Mass; sorcery; demonolatry, demon *or* devil *or* chthonian worship; demonomancy; demonology, diabolology *or* diabology, demonography, devil lore

**blackmail** NOUNS 1 **extortion, shakedown** <nonformal>, bloodsucking, vampirism; protection racket; badger game
VERBS 2 **extort, exact,** squeeze, screw, **shake down** <nonformal>, levy blackmail, badger *and* play the badger game <both nonformal>

**black-market** ADJS **illegal, unlawful, illegitimate, illicit,** nonlicit, nonlegal, lawless, wrongful, fraudulent, creative <nonformal>, **against the law; outlaw, outlawed; contraband,** bootleg; under-the-table, under-the-counter

**blackout** NOUNS 1 **unconsciousness, loss of memory, memory loss, amnesia,** failure; **memory gap;** fugue; agnosia, unrecognition, body-image agnosia, ideational agnosia, astereognosis *or* astereocognosy; paramnesia, retrospective falsification, false memory, misremembrance; amnesiac
2 **power failure,** power cut, power loss; **brownout,** dimout, voltage drop, voltage loss

**blade** NOUNS 1 **leaf, frond;** lamina, spear, spire, pile, flag; **needle,** pine needle
2 **sword,** good *or* trusty sword; steel, **cold steel;** Excalibur; **knife; dagger; axe**
3 **dandy, fop,** coxcomb, macaroni, gallant, dude *and* swell *and* sport <all nonformal>, ponce *and* toff <both Brit nonformal>, exquisite, blood, fine gentleman, puppy, jackanapes, jack-a-dandy, fribble, clotheshorse, fashion plate; beau, Beau Brummel, spark, ladies' man, lady-killer <nonformal>, masher, cocksman <nonformal>; man-about-town, boulevardier

**blahs** NOUNS **listlessness, spiritlessness,** burnout, blah *or* blahs <nonformal>, heartlessness, plucklessness, spunklessness; **blues** *and* blue devils *and* mulligrubs <all nonformal>, mumps, **dumps** <nonformal>, **doldrums,** dismals, dolefuls <nonformal>, blahs *and* mopes *and* megrims *and* sulks <all nonformal>

**blame** NOUNS 1 **censure, reprehension,** stricture, reprobation, **denunciation,** denouncement, decrying, decrial, bashing *and* trashing <both nonformal>, impeachment, arraignment, indictment, **condemnation,** damnation, fulmination, anathema; castigation, flaying, skinning alive <nonformal>, fustigation, excoriation; pillorying
VERBS 2 **censure,** reprehend; lay *or* cast blame upon; **bash** *and* trash *and* rubbish <all nonformal>; **reproach,** impugn; **condemn,** damn, take out after; damn with faint praise; fulminate against, anathematize, anathemize, put on the Index; **denounce,** denunciate, **accuse, decry,** cry down, impeach, arraign, indict, call to account, exclaim *or* declaim *or* inveigh against, peg away at, cry out against, cry out on *or* upon, cry shame upon, raise one's voice against, raise a hue and cry against, shake up <old>; reprobate, hold up to reprobation; animadvert on *or* upon, reflect upon, cast reflection upon, cast a reproach *or* slur upon, complain against; throw a stone at, cast *or* throw the first stone

**blameless** ADJS **innocent;** unfallen, unlapsed, prelapsarian; **unguilty,** not guilty, **guiltless, faultless,** reproachless, **sinless,** offenseless, with clean hands; clear, in the clear; without reproach, *sans reproche* <Fr>; innocent as a lamb, lamblike, dovelike, angelic, childlike; unacquainted with *or* untouched by evil, uncorrupted, incorrupt, pristine, undefiled

**bland** ADJS 1 **insipid, tasteless, flavorless,** spiceless, **savorless,** sapless, unsavory, unflavored; pulpy, pappy, gruelly; **weak, thin,** mild, **wishy-washy,** milk-toast, washy, watery, watered, watered-down, diluted, dilute, milk-and-water; **flat, stale,** dead, *fade* <Fr>; vapid, inane, jejune; indifferent, neither one thing nor the other, featureless, unrelieved, characterless, insipid

> *weary, flat, stale, and unprofitable*
> SHAKESPEARE

2 **mild,** soft, **gentle,** tame; mild as milk *or* mother's milk, mild as milk and water, gentle as a lamb

**blank** ADJS **inexpressive,** unexpressive, impassive, po-faced <Brit>; uncommunicative; **expressionless; vacant, empty;** glassy, glazed, glazed-over, fishy, wooden; deadpan, poker-faced <nonformal>

**blanket** NOUNS 1 **coverlet,** coverlid <nonformal>, space blanket, cover, covers, **spread,** robe, buffalo robe, **afghan,** rug <Brit>; lap robe; **bedspread; bedcover;** counterpane, counterpin <nonformal>; comfort, **comforter, down comforter, duvet, continental quilt** <Brit>, **quilt,** feather bed, eiderdown; patchwork quilt; **bedding, bedclothes,** clothes; **linen,** bed linen; **sheet,** sheeting, bedsheet, fitted sheet, contour sheet; **pillowcase,** pillow slip, case, slip; duvet cover
VERBS 2 **conceal, hide,** ensconce; **cover, cover up,** blind, **screen, cloak,**

veil, screen off, curtain, shroud, enshroud, envelop; **disguise, camouflage, mask,** dissemble; plain-wrap, wrap in plain brown paper; whitewash <nonformal>; **paper over,** gloss over, varnish, slur over; distract attention from; **obscure,** obfuscate, cloud, becloud, befog, throw out a smoke screen, shade, throw into the shade
ADJS 3 **comprehensive, sweeping, complete**; whole; **all-comprehensive,** all-inclusive; without omission *or* exception, **overall,** universal, global, wall-to-wall <nonformal>, around-the-world, **total,** omnibus, across-the-board; encyclopedic, compendious; synoptic; bird's-eye, panoramic

**blare** NOUNS 1 **blast,** shriek, peal; **toot,** tootle, **honk,** beep, blat, trumpet; bay, bray; **whistle,** tweedle, squeal; trumpet call, trumpet blast *or* blare, sound *or* flourish of trumpets, Gabriel's trumpet *or* horn, **fanfare,** tarantara, tantara, tantarara; tattoo; taps
VERBS 2 blast; shriek; **toot,** tootle, sound, peal, wind, blow, blat; pipe, trumpet, bugle, clarion; bay, bell, bray; **whistle,** tweedle, squeal; **honk,** honk *or* sound *or* blow the horn, beep; sound taps, sound a tattoo

**blaring** ADJS **noisy,** noiseful, rackety, clattery, clangorous, clanging, **clamorous,** clamoursome <Brit nonformal>, clamant, blatant, brassy, brazen, blatting; uproarious, **tumultuous,** turbulent, blustering, brawling, **boisterous,** rip-roaring, rowdy, mafficking <Brit>, strepitous, strepitant, obstreperous; vociferous

**blasé** ADJS 1 **nonchalant, indifferent,** insouciant, unconcerned; **casual, offhand, relaxed, laid-back** *and* throwaway <both nonformal>; **easygoing,** easy, free and easy, devil-may-care, lackadaisical, *dégagé* <Fr>; splenetic <old>, melancholy, melancholic, life-weary, world-weary, tired of living; **listless, dispirited**
2 **disillusioned, disenchanted,** unspelled, uncharmed, **disabused,** undeceived, stripped *or* robbed of illusion, enlightened, set right, put straight

**blasphemy** NOUNS **sacrilege,** blaspheming, impiety; **profanity,** profaneness; sacrilegiousness, blasphemousness; **desecration, profanation;** tainting, pollution, contamination

**blast** NOUNS 1 **noise,** loud noise, tintamarre, **racket, din, clamor;** outcry, **uproar,** hue and cry, noise and shouting; howl; clangor, clatter, clap, jangle, rattle; roar, thunder, thunderclap; **crash, boom,** sonic boom; **bang,** percussion; brouhaha, **tumult, hubbub,** bobbery <India>; fracas, **brawl,** commotion, drunken brawl; **pandemonium,** bedlam, hell *or* bedlam let loose; charivari, shivaree <nonformal>; discord
2 **detonation, explosion,** fulmination, **discharge, burst, bang, pop, crack,** bark; **shot,** gunshot; volley, salvo, fusillade
3 **gust,** wind gust, blow, flaw, **flurry,** scud <Scots>
VERBS 4 **blare;** shriek; **toot,** tootle, sound, peal, wind, blow, blat; pipe, trumpet, bugle, clarion; bay, bell, bray; **whistle,** tweedle, squeal; **honk,** honk *or* sound *or* blow the horn, beep; sound taps, sound a tattoo
5 **detonate, explode, discharge, burst,** go off, **bang, pop, crack,** bark, fulminate; burst on the ear
6 **blow; blow up a storm;** bluster, squall; **storm,** rage, blow great guns, blow a hurricane

*blow, winds, and crack your cheeks, rage, blow*
SHAKESPEARE

**blastoff** NOUNS **rocket launching** *or* **firing,** ignition, launch, shot, shoot; countdown; **lift-off;** guided *or* automatic control, programming; flight, trajectory; **burn; burnout,** end of burning

**blaze** NOUNS 1 **fire; flame,** ingle, devouring element; **combustion, ignition,** ignition temperature *or* point, flash *or* flashing point; **conflagration;** flicker, wavering *or* flickering flame; smoldering fire, sleeping fire; marshfire, fen fire, ignis fatuus, will-o'-the-wisp; fox fire; witch fire, St Elmo's fire, corposant; **cheerful fire,** cozy fire, crackling fire; **roaring fire,** blazing fire; **raging fire,** sheet of fire, sea of flames

*whirlwinds of tempestuous fire*
MILTON

2 **flash, flare, gleam, glint, glance;** blaze *or* flash *or* gleam of light; green flash; solar flare, solar prominence, facula; Bailey's beads

VERBS 3 **mark,** make a mark, put a mark on; blaze a trail
4 **burn,** torrefy, **scorch, parch, sear; singe,** swinge; **blister,** vesicate; **cauterize,** brand, burn in; **char,** coal, carbonize
5 **flame,** fulgurate; **radiate,** shoot, shoot out rays, send out rays; spread *or* diffuse light; be bright, shine brightly, beacon

**bleach** NOUNS 1 bleacher, bleaching agent *or* substance; decolorant, decolorizer, achromatizer
VERBS 2 decolor, decolorize, discolor, achromatize, etiolate; **fade, wash out; dim, dull, tarnish,** tone down; **pale, whiten,** blanch, drain, drain of color; **lose color, fade**

**bleak** ADJS 1 **gloomy, dismal, murky, grim, somber,** sombrous, **solemn, grave;** sad, *triste* <Fr>, **funereal,** funebrial, crepehanging <nonformal>, saturnine; **dark,** black, gray; **dreary,** drear, drearisome; weary, weariful, wearisome
2 **hopeless,** unhopeful, without hope, affording no hope, worst-case, grim, dismal, cheerless, comfortless; **desperate, despairing, in despair;** despondent; disconsolate
3 **windblown,** blown; **windswept,** raw, exposed

**bleat** VERBS cry, call; **howl,** yowl, yawp, yawl <nonformal>, ululate; wail, whine, pule; **squeal,** squall, scream, screech, screak, squeak; blate, blat

**bleed** VERBS 1 **hemorrhage,** lose blood, **shed blood,** spill blood; bloody; ecchymose
2 **suffer, hurt, ache;** anguish, **suffer anguish; agonize,** writhe; go hard with, have a bad time of it, go through hell; quaff the bitter cup, drain the cup of misery to the dregs, be nailed to the cross
3 **draw off, draft off,** draft, draw, draw from; **suck,** suck out *or* up, **siphon off;** pipette; pump, pump out; tap, broach; let, let out; let blood, venesect, phlebotomize; milk; **drain,** decant; exhaust, empty
4 **take advantage of, use,** make use of, **use for one's own ends;** make a paw *or* cat's-paw of, sucker *and* play for a sucker <both nonformal>; **manipulate,** work on, work upon, stroke, play on *or* upon; play both ends against the middle; **impose upon,** presume upon; use ill, ill-use, abuse, misuse; batten on; milk, bleed white <nonformal>; drain, suck the blood of *or* from, suck dry; exploit one's position, feather one's nest <nonformal>, **profiteer, strip,** strip bare *or* clean, **fleece** <nonformal>, skin *and* pluck <both nonformal>, flay, **despoil, divest,** pick clean, pick the bones of

**blemish** NOUNS **disfigurement,** disfiguration, **defacement;** scar, keloid, cicatrix; needle scar, track *or* crater <both nonformal>; scratch; scab; blister, vesicle, bulla, bleb; weal, wale, welt, wen, sebaceous cyst; port-wine stain *or* mark, hemangioma, strawberry mark; pock, pustule; pockmark, pit; nevus, birthmark, mole; freckle, lentigo; milium, whitehead, blackhead, comedo, pimple, hickey, sty; wart, verruca; **crack,** craze, check, rift, split; **deformity,** deformation, warp, twist, kink, **distortion; flaw, defect, fault, stigma; eyesore,** blot, blot on the landscape

**blend** NOUNS 1 **compound, mixture, admixture,** intermixture, immixture, commixture, **composite,** meld, composition, confection, concoction, **combination,** combo <nonformal>, ensemble, marriage; amalgam, alloy
VERBS 2 **mix,** admix, commix, immix, **intermix, mingle,** bemingle, commingle, immingle, **intermingle,** interlace, interweave, intertwine, interlard; syncretize; interblend, stir in; **amalgamate, integrate,** alloy, coalesce, **fuse, merge,** meld, compound, compose, conflate, concoct; **combine**; mix up, hash, stir up, **scramble,** conglomerate, shuffle, **jumble,** jumble up, mingle-mangle, throw *or* toss together; knead, work; homogenize, emulsify

**bless** VERBS **sanctify, hallow; purify,** cleanse, wash one's sins away; beatify; **glorify,** exalt, ensky; **consecrate,** dedicate, devote, set apart; **beatify, saint, canonize;** enshrine

**blessed** ADJS 1 **sanctified, hallowed;** consecrated, devoted, dedicated, set apart; **glorified, exalted,** enskied; **saintly,** sainted, beatified, canonized
2 **fortunate, lucky, providential; in luck;** blessed with luck, favored; born under a lucky star, born with a silver spoon in one's mouth, born on the sunny side of the hedge; out of the woods, over the hump; **auspicious**

**blessing** NOUNS 1 **approval, approba-**

**tion; sanction,** acceptance, countenance, **favor;** endorsement, vote, favorable vote, yea vote, yea, voice, adherence, seal of approval, nod, stamp of approval, **OK**
2 **benediction,** benison, invocation, benedicite; sign of the cross; laying on of hands
3 **good fortune** *or* **luck,** happy fortune, **fortune, luck,** the breaks <nonformal>; **fortunateness, luckiness,** felicity <old>; smiles of fortune, fortune's favor

**blighted** ADJS **ruined, destroyed, wrecked, blasted, undone,** down-and-out, broken, bankrupt; spoiled; irremediable; fallen, overthrown; **devastated, desolated, ravaged,** wasted; ruinous, in ruins; gone to wrack and ruin

**blind** NOUNS 1 **stratagem, artifice,** art <old>, **craft, wile,** strategy, **device,** wily device, **contrivance, expedient, design, scheme, trick,** cute trick, fetch, fakement <nonformal>, gimmick <nonformal>, **ruse, red herring, shift,** tactic, **maneuver, stroke,** stroke of policy, master stroke, **move,** coup, gambit, **ploy, dodge,** artful dodge; **game,** little game, racket *and* grift <both nonformal>; **plot,** conspiracy, **intrigue;** sleight, feint, jugglery; method in one's madness; **subterfuge,** dust in the eyes; chicanery, knavery, deceit, trickery
2 **shade,** shader, **screen, light shield, curtain,** drape, drapery, veil; cover
VERBS 3 **hoodwink,** blindfold, blind one's eyes, blear the eyes of <old>, throw dust in one's eyes, **pull the wool over one's eyes**
ADJS 4 **sightless, unsighted,** ablepticaI, eyeless, visionless, **unseeing,** undiscerning, unobserving, unperceiving; in darkness, rayless, bereft of light, dark <nonformal>; **stone-blind,** stark blind, **blind as a bat,** blind as a mole *or* an owl; amaurotic; dim-sighted; hemeralopic; nyctalopic; color-blind; mind-blind, soul-blind, mentally *or* psychically *or* spiritually blind, benighted, unenlightened

*dark, dark, dark, amid the blaze of noon*
MILTON

5 **unpersuadable,** deaf; closed-minded; positive; dogmatic
6 **undiscerning, unperceptive,** imperceptive, impercipient, insensible, unapprehending, uncomprehending, nonunderstanding; **shortsighted,** myopic, nearsighted, dim-sighted; purblind, mind-blind, blind as a bat; blinded, blindfold, blindfolded

**blinding** ADJS obscuring; **dazzling,** bedazzling; **bright, brilliant, vivid, splendid,** splendorous, splendent, **resplendent,** bright and shining; fulgid <old>, fulgent, effulgent, refulgent; **flamboyant,** flaming; **glaring,** glary, garish

**blind spot** NOUNS **narrow-mindedness, small-mindedness, shortsightedness,** nearsightedness, purblindness; blind side, tunnel vision, blinders; closed mind, mean mind, petty mind, shut mind; narrow views *or* sympathies, cramped ideas; *parti pris* <Fr>, an ax to grind

**blink** VERBS 1 **wink,** nictitate, bat the eyes <nonformal>
2 **flinch, shrink, shy,** shy away from, draw back, recoil, funk <nonformal>, **quail, cringe, wince, blench,** say *or* cry uncle; put one's tail between one's legs

**blip** NOUNS radar signal; trace, reading, return, **echo, bounce, pip;** spot, CRT spot

**blissful** ADJS 1 **cheerful, gay**; blessed; thrice happy; happy as a lark, happy as a king, happy as the day is long, happy as a baby boy, happy as a clam at high water, happy as a pig in shit <nonformal>, happy as a sand boy <Brit>

*thrice and four times blessed*
VERGIL

2 beatific, saintly, divine; sublime; **heavenly,** paradisal, paradisiac, paradisiacal, paradisic, paradisical, empyreal *or* empyrean, Elysian; out of sight *or* of this world <nonformal>

**blister** NOUNS 1 **bubble,** bleb, **globule;** vesicle, bulla, blood blister, fever blister; balloon, bladder
VERBS 2 **sear; singe,** swinge; vesicate; **cauterize,** brand, burn in; **char,** coal, carbonize; scorify; calcine; pyrolyze

**blithe** ADJS **cheerful, cheery,** of good cheer, in good spirits, vogie <Scots>; in high spirits, exalted, elated, exhilarated, high <nonformal>; irrepressible; blithesome; **glad, gladsome; happy,** happy as a clam *or* a sand boy *or* a lark, on top of the world

**blithering** ADJS babbling, driveling, slobbering, drooling, dithering, maundering, burbling

**blitz** NOUNS 1 blitzkrieg, lightning attack, lightning war, panzer warfare, sudden *or* devastating *or* crippling attack, deep strike, shock tactics; **pass rush** <football>
VERBS 2 **attack, assault, strike, hit, pound;** attack in force; surprise; attack *or* hit like lightning; **blow up,** blast, spring, explode, blow to pieces *or* bits *or* smithereens *or* kingdom come, bomb, bombard

**blizzard** NOUNS **snowstorm,** snow blast, snow squall, snow flurry, flurry

**bloated** ADJS 1 **distended, dilated, inflated,** sufflated, **blown up, puffed up, swollen,** swelled, turgid, tumid, plethoric, incrassate; **puffy,** pursy; flatulent, gassy, windy, ventose; tumefacient; dropsical, edematous; enchymatous; fat; puffed out, bouffant, bouffed up *and* bouffy <both nonformal>; **bulging, swelling,** distended, potbellied, bellying, pouching; bagging, baggy
2 **pompous, stuffy** <nonformal>, **self-important,** impressed with oneself, pontific, pontifical; **inflated, swollen,** tumid, turgid, flatulent, gassy <nonformal>, stilted; grandiloquent, **bombastic**; solemn, formal

**blob** NOUNS **ball;** globule, globelet, orblet; glomerulus; **pellet;** boll; knob, knot; **gob,** glob <nonformal>, gobbet; **lump,** clump, bunch

**bloc** NOUNS **alliance, coalition, league;** axis; **partnership; federation, confederation,** confederacy; grouping, assemblage; **combination,** combine; *Bund, Verein* <both Ger>

**block** NOUNS 1 **obstacle, obstruction,** obstructer; **hang-up** <nonformal>; blockade, cordon, curtain; **difficulty,** hurdle, hazard; **deterrent,** determent; **drawback,** objection; **stumbling block,** stumbling stone, stone in one's path; fly in the ointment, one small difficulty, **hitch, catch,** joker <nonformal>, a "but,"a "however"
VERBS 2 **delay, retard, detain,** make late, slacken, lag, drag, drag one's feet *and* stonewall <both nonformal>, slow down, **hold up** <nonformal>, hold *or* keep back, check, **stay, stop,** arrest, impede, hinder, obstruct, throw a monkey wrench in the works <nonformal>, confine; tie up with red tape
3 **obstruct, get** *or* **stand in the way; dog,** block the way, put up a roadblock, blockade, block up, occlude; **jam,** crowd, pack; **bar,** barricade, bolt, lock; **debar,** shut out; shut off, **close,** close off *or* up, close tight, shut tight; constrict, squeeze, squeeze shut, **strangle,** strangulate, **stifle,** suffocate, **choke,** choke off, chock; stop up

**blockade** NOUNS 1 **siege, besiegement, beleaguerment;** encompassment, investment, encirclement, envelopment; blockading; cutting of supply lines; vertical envelopment; pincer movement
2 block, block the way, put up a roadblock, block up, occlude; shut off, **close,** close off *or* up, close tight, shut tight; constrict, squeeze, squeeze shut, **strangle,** strangulate, **stifle,** suffocate, **choke,** choke off

**blockage** NOUNS 1 stoppage, occlusion, thrombosis, thromboembolism; embolism, embolus; infarct, infarction; **stroke,** ictus, apoplexy; constipation, obstipation, costiveness
2 **obstruction,** blocking, blockage, clogging, occlusion; **bottleneck,** traffic jam, gridlock; constriction, squeeze, stricture, cramp, stranglehold; **closure,** closing up *or* off; obstructionism, bloody-mindedness <Brit>, negativism, foot-dragging <nonformal>; nuisance value

**blockbuster** NOUNS **surprise,** surprisal; surpriser, startler, shocker, **blow,** staggerer <nonformal>, **eye-opener,** revelation; **bolt out of** *or* **from the blue,** thunderbolt, thunderclap; **bombshell,** bomb; earthshaker; sudden turn *or* development, *peripeteia* <Gk>, switch; surprise ending, kicker *or* joker *or* catch <all nonformal>; surprise package; surprise party

**bloodbath** NOUNS **carnage, massacre, decimation,** saturnalia of blood; **mass murder, mass destruction,** mass extermination, wholesale murder, pogrom, race-murder, genocide, race extermination, **the Holocaust,** the final solution, ethnic cleansing

**bloodcurdling** ADJS **terrifying,** terrorful, terror-striking, terror-inspiring, terror-bringing, terror-giving, terror-breeding, terror-breathing, terror-bearing, terror-fraught; **hair-raising** <nonformal>; petrifying, paralyzing, stunning, stupefying; **terrorizing, terror, terroristic;** *schrecklich* <Ger>

**bloodsucker** NOUNS 1 parasite; **leech;**

**tick,** wood tick, deer tick; **mosquito,** skeeter <nonformal>, culex; bedbug, housebug <Brit>
2 **extortionist,** extortioner, **blackmailer,** racketeer, shakedown artist <nonformal>, leech, **vampire; predator,** raptor, bird of prey, beast of prey; **vulture,** shark; profiteer

**bloodthirsty** ADJS **murderous,** slaughterous; cutthroat; redhanded; **homicidal,** man-killing, death-dealing; biocidal, genocidal; suicidal, self-destructive; soul-destroying; cruel; bloody-minded; **bloody, gory,** sanguineous, sanguinary; Draconian, Tartarean

**blood vessel** NOUNS **artery,** aorta, pulmonary artery, carotid; **vein,** jugular vein, vena cava, pulmonary vein; portal vein, varicose vein; venation; **capillary;** arteriole, veinlet, veinule, venule

**bloody** ADJS 1 **sanguine,** sanguineous, **blood-red,** blood-colored, bloody-red, gory, red as blood; **bloodstained,** blood-spattered, sanguinary, ensanguined; **bleeding,** hemorrhaging; ecchymosed
2 **savage, fierce, ferocious, vicious, murderous, cruel, atrocious, mindless, brutal,** brutish, **bestial,** mindless, insensate, monstrous, mutant, inhuman, pitiless, ruthless, merciless, sanguinary, kill-crazy <nonformal>

**bloom** NOUNS 1 **flower, posy, blossom,** blow <old>; floweret, floret, floscule; **wildflower**
2 **glow,** incandescence, fieriness; **flush, blush,** redness, rubicundity, rosiness
VERBS 3 **enjoy good health,** have a clean bill of health, be in the pink; be in the best of health; **feel good,** feel fine, feel fit, feel like a million dollars *or* like a million <nonformal>, never feel better; feel one's oats, be full of pep; burst with health, glow, flourish
4 **flower,** be in flower, **blossom,** be in bloom, blow, effloresce, floreate, burst into bloom

**blooper** NOUNS

<nonformal> **goof, boo-boo,** muff, flub, foozle, bloomer, bloop, boot, bobble, boner, bonehead play *or* trick, dumb trick, boob stunt, fool mistake; howler, clanger <Brit>, screamer; fuck-up, screw-up, foul-up, snafu, muck-up, balls-up <Brit>, louse-up; pratfall, whoops

**blossom** NOUNS 1 **flowering,** florescence, efflorescence, flowerage, **blossoming, blooming;** inflorescence; **bloom,** blowing, blow; unfolding, unfoldment; anthesis, full bloom
VERBS 2 **grow, develop,** wax, **increase**; gather, brew; **grow up,** mature, maturate, spring up, ripen, come of age, **shoot up,** sprout up, upshoot, upspring, upsprout, upspear, overtop, tower; grow like a weed <nonformal>; burgeon, **sprout**, reproduce, procreate, grow out of, germinate, pullulate; vegetate; **flourish, thrive;** mushroom, balloon

**blot** NOUNS 1 **stain, taint, tarnish;** mark, brand, **stigma;** maculation, macule, macula; **spot,** blur, **blotch,** patch, speck, speckle, fleck, flick, flyspeck; daub, dab; **smirch, smudge,** smutch *or* smouch, smut, **smear;** splotch, splash, splatter, spatter; bloodstain; eyesore
VERBS 2 **absorb,** adsorb, chemisorb *or* chemosorb, **assimilate,** engross, digest, **drink,** imbibe, take up *or* in, drink up *or* in, slurp up, swill up; **blot up, soak up,** sponge; osmose; infiltrate, filter in; **soak in, seep in,** percolate in

**blotchy** ADJS **spotted, spotty,** maculate, maculated, macular, blotched, splotched, splotchy; **speckled,** speckly, bespeckled; freckled, freckly, freckle-faced; spattered, splattered, splashed

**blow** NOUNS 1 **slap,** smack, whack, whomp, **cuff, box,** buffet, belt, sock; **rap on the knuckles,** box on the ear, slap in the face; slap on the wrist, token punishment
2 **misfortune, mishap,** ill hap, **misadventure, mischance,** *contretemps* <Fr>, grief; **disaster, calamity, catastrophe,** meltdown, cataclysm, **tragedy; shock,** hard *or* nasty *or* staggering blow
VERBS 3 **blare,** blast; shriek; **toot,** tootle, sound, peal, wind, blat; pipe, trumpet, bugle, clarion
4 **squander, lavish,** slather, play ducks and drakes with; **dissipate,** scatter <old>, sow broadcast, scatter to the winds; **run through,** go through; **throw away,** throw one's money away, throw money around, **spend money like water,** hang the expense, let slip *or* flow through one's fingers, spend as if money grew on trees, spend money as if it were going out of style, throw money around, spend like a drunken sailor; gamble away; burn the candle at both ends;

seize the day, live for the day, let tomorrow take care of itself

**blow one's mind** VERBS

1 <nonformal> **go crazy, go bats,** go cuckoo, go bughouse, go nuts, go nutso, go out of one's gourd *or* skull *or* tree, go off one's nut *or* rocker, go off the track *or* trolley, go off the deep end, blow one's top *or* stack, pop one's cork, flip one's lid *or* wig, wig out, go ape *or* apeshit, schiz out, go bananas, go crackers *and* go bonkers <both Brit>, go bonzo, freak out, flip out, go hog wild, go round the bend <Brit>, lose one's marbles

2 **go on a trip**, freak out <both nonformal>; **hallucinate;** expand one's consciousness

**blowout** NOUNS 1 **explosion, discharge,** blowup, detonation, fulmination, **blast, burst, report**; flat tire
2 **eruption,** eructation, extravasation, **outburst;** outpour, jet, spout, spurt

**blow the whistle** VERBS 1 **have no patience with,** be out of all patience; **lose patience,** run out of patience, call a halt, have had it <nonformal>

2 <nonformal> tell on, blab, snitch, squeal, peach <old>, sell out, sing, rat, stool, fink, nark, finger, put the finger on, shop <Brit>, dime, drop a dime, spill one's guts, spill the beans, squawk, weasel

**blowup** NOUNS 1 **outburst,** outburst of anger, burst, **explosion,** eruption, blowup *and* **flare-up** <both nonformal>, access, blaze of temper; **storm, scene,** high words
2 **explosion, discharge, blowout,** detonation, fulmination, **blast, burst, report;** backfire
3 **enlargement; print,** photoprint, positive

**blowzy** ADJS **slovenly, slipshod, careless, loose, slack,** nonformal, negligent; **untidy, unsightly,** unneat, slobby *and* scuzzy <both nonformal>, **unkempt; messy** <nonformal>, mussy <nonformal>, **sloppy** <nonformal>, scraggly, poky, seedy <nonformal>, **shabby,** shoddy, schlocky <nonformal>, lumpen, chintzy, grubby <nonformal>, **frowzy,** tacky <nonformal>; **slatternly, sluttish, frumpish,** frumpy, draggletailed, drabbletailed, draggled, bedraggled

**blue** ADJS 1 **melancholy,** melancholic, splenetic <old>, funky <nonformal>; atrabilious, atrabiliar; **pensive, wistful,** tristful; **nostalgic,** homesick
2 **obscene, lewd, adult, bawdy,** ithyphallic, **ribald, pornographic, salacious,** sultry <nonformal>, lurid, **dirty, smutty,** raunchy <nonformal>, smoking-room, impure, unchaste, unclean, **foul, filthy, nasty,** vile, fulsome, offensive, unprintable, unrepeatable, not fit for mixed company; scurrilous, scurrile, Fescennine; **foulmouthed,** foul-tongued, foul-spoken; Rabelaisian

**blue blood** NOUNS **aristocrat, patrician,** Brahmin, thoroughbred, member of the upper class, socialite, swell *and* upper-cruster <both nonformal>, grandee, grand dame, dowager, magnifico, lord of creation; **gentleman, lady,** person of breeding

**blue-collar worker** NOUNS **worker, toiler,** moiler; member of the working class, proletarian, prole <Brit nonformal>, blue-collar *or* lunch-bucket worker, laboring man, stiff *and* working stiff <both nonformal>; **workman, workingman; workwoman, workingwoman,** workfolk, workpeople; working girl, workgirl; **factory worker,** industrial worker; autoworker, steelworker; construction worker; **laborer,** common laborer, **unskilled laborer,** navvy <Brit>, day laborer, roust-about; casual, casual laborer; **labor force, work force,** shop floor <Brit>; labor market

**blueprint** NOUNS **plan, scheme, design,** method, **program,** device, contrivance, game, envisagement, conception, enterprise, **idea, notion;** organization, rationalization, systematization, schematization; charting, mapping, graphing; **planning,** calculation, figuring; **master plan,** the picture *and* the big picture <both nonformal>; approach, attack, plan of attack; way, procedure; **arrangement,** prearrangement, system, disposition, layout, setup, lineup; **schedule,** timetable, time-scheme, time frame; deadline; plan of work; **schema,** schematism, scheme of arrangement; **guideline, guidelines,** program of action; methodology; working plan, ground plan, tactical plan, strategic plan; tactics, **strategy,** game plan <nonformal>; contingency plan

**blue ribbon** NOUNS 1 **award, reward, prize;** first prize, second prize, etc; sweepstakes; jackpot; Oscar, Academy Award; **decoration,** decoration of honor, order, ornament; ribbon

**blues** NOUNS

1 <nonformal> blue devils, mulligrubs, mumps, **dumps, doldrums,** dismals, dolefuls, blahs, mopes, sullens, megrims, sulks

2 music; the blues, talking blues, country blues, city blues

**bluff** NOUNS 1 **precipice, cliff, sheer** *or* yawning cliff *or* precipice *or* drop, steep, wall, face, scar; crag, craig <Scots>; scarp, **escarpment; palisade,** palisades
2 **sham, fakery,** faking, falsity, feigning, pretending; feint, pretext, **pretense,** hollow pretense, **pretension, false pretense** *or* **pretension;** humbug, humbuggery; bluffing, four-flushing <nonformal>; speciousness, meretriciousness; cheating, fraud; imposture; deception, delusion; acting, playacting; representation, **simulation,** simulacrum; dissembling, **dissemblance, dissimulation;** seeming, semblance, appearance, face, ostentation, **show, false show,** outward show, false air; window dressing, front, **false front, facade,** gloss, varnish; color, coloring, false color; masquerade, disguise; posture, pose, posing, attitudinizing
3 **bluster,** blustering, hectoring, bullying, **swagger,** swashbucklery, side; **bravado,** rant, rodomontade, fanfaronade; sputter, splutter; fuss, bustle, fluster, flurry; bluster and bluff; intimidation; **boastfulness**
VERBS 4 swear falsely; **bluster,** hector; **swagger,** swashbuckle; bully; bounce, vapor, roister, rollick, gasconade, kick up a dust <nonformal>; sputter, splutter; rant, rage, rave, rave on, storm; slang <Brit>; bluster and bluff, put up a bluff <nonformal>

*out-herod Herod*
SHAKESPEARE

**blunder** NOUNS 1 **bungle, botch,** flub, boner *and* bonehead play <both nonformal>, boggle, bobble *and* boo-boo *and* screw-up *and* fuck-up <all nonformal>, foozle <nonformal>, bevue; **fumble, muff,** fluff, miscue <nonformal>; **faux pas,** gaffe, solecism; stupidity, indiscretion; **slip,** trip, stumble; *gaucherie, étourderie, balourdise* <all Fr>; **hash** *and* **mess** <both nonformal>; bad job, sad work, clumsy performance; off day; **error, mistake**
VERBS 2 **make a blunder, make a faux pas,** blot one's copy book, make a colossal blunder, make a false *or* wrong step, make a misstep; **misspeak,** misspeak oneself, trip over one's tongue; embarrass oneself, have egg on one's face <nonformal>; blunder into; **botch, bungle**

**blundering** ADJS **bungling,** blunderheaded, bumbling, fumbling, mistake-prone, accident-prone; **clumsy, awkward, uncoordinated,** maladroit, unhandy, left-hand, left-handed, heavy-handed, ham-handed <nonformal>, ham-fisted *and* cack-handed <both Brit nonformal>, clumsy-fisted, butterfingered <nonformal>, **all thumbs,** fingers all thumbs, with a handful of thumbs; stiff; **ungainly,** uncouth, **ungraceful,** graceless, inelegant, *gauche* <Fr>; **gawky,** gawkish; **lubberly, loutish, oafish,** boorish, clownish, lumpish, slobbish <nonformal>; **sloppy, careless**; **ponderous, cumbersome,** lumbering, hulking, hulky; **unwieldy**

**blunt** ADJS 1 **dull,** obtuse, obtundent; bluntish, dullish; **unsharp,** unsharpened; **unedged,** edgeless; rounded, faired, smoothed, streamlined; **unpointed,** pointless; blunted, dulled; blunt-edged, dull-edged; blunt-pointed, dull-pointed, blunt-ended; bluff, abrupt
2 straight <both nonformal>, **forthright,** downright, straight-out <nonformal>; plain, broad, round; **unreserved,** unrestrained, unconstrained, unchecked; unguarded, uncalculating; free; **outspoken, plain-spoken,** free-spoken, free-speaking, free-tongued; explicit, unequivocal; bluff, brusque; heart-to-heart

**blur** NOUNS 1 **indistinctness, unclearness,** unplainness, **faintness,** paleness, feebleness, weakness, **dimness,** bedimming, bleariness, darkness, shadowiness, **vagueness,** vague appearance, indefiniteness, obscurity, uncertainty, indistinguishability; **blurriness,** soft

focus, defocus, **fuzziness, haziness,** mistiness, filminess, fogginess
VERBS 2 **dim, pale,** soften, film, mist, fog; defocus, lose resolution *or* sharpness *or* distinctness, go soft at the edges; **confound, confuse,** mix, mix up, muddle, tumble, jumble, jumble together, blur distinctions, overlook distinctions

**blurred** ADJS **formless, shapeless,** featureless, characterless, nondescript, inchoate, lumpy, lumpish, blobby *and* baggy <both nonformal>, inform; amorphous, **chaotic, orderless,** disorderly, unordered, unorganized, confused, anarchic; kaleidoscopic; **indeterminate, indefinite,** undefined, indecisive, vague, misty, hazy, fuzzy, blurred *or* blurry, unclear, obscure; obfuscatory

**blush** VERBS **flush,** mantle, **color,** change color, color up, redden, crimson, turn red, have a red face, get red in the face, blush up to the eyes; stammer; squirm with self-consciousness *or* embarrassment

**bluster** NOUNS 1 blustering, hectoring, bullying, **swagger,** swashbucklery, side; **bravado,** rant, rodomontade, fanfaronade; sputter, splutter; fuss, bustle, fluster, flurry; bluff, bluster and bluff; intimidation; **boastfulness**
VERBS 2 swagger, **show** *or* **put up a bold front,** throw out one's chest, strut, crow, look big, stand with arms akimbo; **boast, brag,** make a boast of, vaunt, flourish, gasconade, vapor, toot one's own horn, sing one's own praises, exaggerate one's own merits

**board** NOUNS 1 food and drink, sustenance, kitchen stuff, victualage, **comestibles, edibles,** eatables, viands; **fare,** cheer, creature comfort; provision, provender; table, spread <nonformal>
VERBS 2 **feed, dine,** wine and dine, mess; sustain; provision; mess with, break bread with; furnish accommodations; house, lodge
3 **go aboard,** go on board; go on shipboard, take ship

**boarder** NOUNS board-and-roomer, **transient,** transient guest *or* boarder; **lodger, roomer,** paying guest

**boardinghouse** NOUNS **lodging house,** rooming house; *pension* <Fr>, *pensione* <Ital>

**boardwalk** NOUNS walkway, catwalk, skybridge *or* skywalk *or* flying bridge *or* walkway; **sidewalk, walk,** fastwalk, *trottoir* <Fr>, foot pavement <Brit>

**boastful** ADJS **boasting, braggart, bragging,** thrasonical, thrasonic, bigmouthed <nonformal>, vaunting, vaporing, gasconading, Gascon, fanfaronading, fanfaron; vain, conceited; **vainglorious**

**boat** NOUNS ark, canoe, gondola, kayak, lifeboat, motorboat, shell, skiff, whaleboat, workboat; vessel, craft, bottom, bark, argosy, hull, hulk, keel, watercraft; tub *and* bucket *and* rustbucket *and* hooker <all nonformal>, packet

**boating** NOUNS water travel, travel by water, marine *or* ocean *or* sea travel, **navigation,** navigating, passage-making, voyaging, **cruising,** coasting, gunkholing <nonformal>; **yachting,** motorboating, canoeing, rowing, sculling

**bob** VERBS **shorten, cut; cut short,** cut off short; **dock,** shear, shave, trim, clip, snub, nip; mow, reap, **crop; prune,** poll, pollard; stunt, check the growth of; telescope; foreshorten

**bode** VERBS **forebode,** portend, croak; **threaten, menace, lower,** look black, spell trouble; **warn, forewarn,** raise a warning flag, give pause; have a premonition *or* presentiment, apprehend, preapprehend, fear for

**body** NOUNS 1 **person, human, human being, man, woman, child,** member of the human race *or* family, Adamite, daughter of Eve; ethnic; **mortal,** life, **soul,** living soul; **being,** creature, clay, ordinary clay; **individual;** somebody, one, someone
2 **corpse,** dead body, dead man *or* woman, dead person, **cadaver, carcass;** *corpus delicti* <L>; **stiff** <nonformal>; **the dead,** the defunct, **the deceased,** the departed, the loved one; **decedent,** late lamented; **remains,** mortal *or* organic remains, bones, skeleton, dry bones, relics, reliquiae; dust, ashes, earth, clay, tenement of clay
3 **substantiality,** substantialness; materiality; **substance,** mass; **solidity,** density, concreteness, **tangibility,** palpability, ponderability; **sturdiness, stability,** soundness, firmness, steadiness, stoutness, toughness, **strength,** durability

**bodybuilding** NOUNS **exercise,** motion, movement, maneuver; **program,** routine, drill, work-out; **exercise systems;**

**warm-up, stretching,** warm-down; **calisthenics,** free exercise, setting-up exercise *or* set-ups, physical jerks <Brit>, daily dozen <nonformal>, constitutional; weightlifting, weight training, pumping iron <nonformal>, bench press, arm raise, curl, wrist curl

**bodyguard** NOUNS safeguard; **convoy, escort;** guards, praetorian guard; guardsman; yeoman *or* yeoman of the guard *or* beefeater, gentleman-at-arms, Life Guardsman <all England>; Secret Service agent

**body language** NOUNS **gesture, gesticulation; motion,** movement; carriage, bearing, posture, poise, pose, stance, way of holding oneself

**bog** NOUNS **marsh,** marshland, **swamp,** swampland, fen, fenland, **morass,** mere *or* marish <both old>, *marais* <Fr>, *maremma* <Ital>, **bog, mire, quagmire,** sump <nonformal>, wash, baygall; glade, everglade; slough, swale, wallow, hog wallow, buffalo wallow, sough <Brit>; bottom, **bottoms,** bottomland, slob land, holm <Brit>, water meadow, meadow; **moor,** moorland, moss <Scots>, peat bog; salt marsh; quicksand; taiga; mud flat

**bogeyman** NOUNS **frightener, scarer, hair-raiser;** scarebabe, **bogey, bugaboo,** bugbear; hobgoblin; **scarecrow; horror, terror,** holy terror; **ogre,** ogress, **monster,** vampire, werewolf, ghoul, bête noire, fee-faw-fum; incubus, succubus, nightmare; witch, goblins; **ghost,** specter, phantom, revenant; Frankenstein, Dracula, Wolf-man; mythical monsters

**boggle the mind** VERBS 1 **astonish, amaze, astound, surprise,** startle, stagger, **bewilder, perplex**, flabbergast <nonformal>, confound, overwhelm, **boggle; awe,** strike with wonder *or* awe; **dumbfound** *or* dumbfounder, strike dumb, strike dead; strike all of a heap *and* throw on one's beam ends *and* knock one's socks off *and* bowl down *or* over <all nonformal>, dazzle, bedazzle, daze, bedaze; **stun, stupefy,** petrify, paralyze

2 **be unbelievable,** be incredible, be hard to swallow, defy belief, pass belief, be hard to believe, strain one's credulity, **stagger belief;** shake one's faith, undermine one's faith; stagger, fill with doubt

**bogus** ADJS **false, untrue, truthless, not true,** void *or* devoid of truth, contrary to fact, in error, **fallacious, erroneous**; unfounded; disinformative; **vicarious,** ersatz, mock, phony *and* fake *and* bogus <all nonformal>, counterfeit, imitation

**Bohemian** NOUNS 1 **nonconformist,** unconformist, **original,** eccentric, gonzo <nonformal>, deviant, deviationist, maverick <nonformal>, dropout, beatnik, hippie, hipster, freak <nonformal>, flower child, street people, yippie; **misfit,** square peg in a round hole, ugly duckling, fish out of water

ADJS 2 **unconventional, unorthodox, eccentric,** gonzo <nonformal>, heterodox, heretical; offbeat <nonformal>, way out *and* far out *and* kinky *and* out in left field <all nonformal>, fringy, breakaway, **out-of-the-way; original,** maverick, beat, hippie, counterculture; **nonformal,** free and easy <nonformal>

*at ease and lighthearted*
WHITMAN

**boil** NOUNS 1 furuncle, furunculus; carbuncle; canker; canker sore; cold sore, fever blister; sty; abscess, gathering, aposteme <old>; gumboil, parulis; whitlow, felon, paronychia; bubo; chancre; soft chancre, chancroid

2 **agitation, perturbation,** fidgets *and* jitters *and* ants in the pants <all nonformal>, antsiness *and* jitteriness <both nonformal>, jumpiness, nervousness, yips <nonformal>, nerviness <Brit>, nervosity, twitter, upset; **disquiet,** disquietude, inquietude, discomposure; **stir, churn, ferment,** fermentation, foment; seethe, seething, ebullition, boiling; embroilment, roil, turbidity, fume, **disturbance, commotion,** moil, **turmoil, turbulence**, **swirl, tumult,** tumultuation, hubbub, shemozzle <Brit nonformal>, rout, fuss, row, to-do, bluster, fluster, flurry, flutteration, hoo-ha *and* flap <both nonformal>, bustle, brouhaha, bobbery, hurly-burly; maelstrom; **disorder**

3 VERBS **seethe, fume,** foam, simmer, stew, ferment, stir, churn

**boisterous** ADJS 1 **noisy,** noiseful, rackety, clattery, clangorous, clanging, **clamorous,** clamoursome <Brit nonformal>, clamant, blatant, blaring, brassy, brazen, blatting; uproarious, **tumultuous,** turbu-

lent, blustering, brawling, rip-roaring, mafficking <Brit>, strepitous, strepitant, obstreperous; vociferous
2 **rampageous, rambunctious** <nonformal>, rumbustious, roisterous, wild, rollicking, **rowdy,** rough, hoody <nonformal>, harum-scarum <nonformal>; knockabout, rough-and-tumble, knock-down-and-drag-out <nonformal>

**bold** ADJS 1 **courageous, plucky, brave, valiant, valorous, gallant, intrepid,** doughty, **hardy,** stalwart, stout, stouthearted, ironhearted, lionhearted, greathearted, bold-spirited, bold as a lion; **heroic, manly,** manful, virile, macho; **audacious;** forward, bold, **presumptuous; daring,** daredevil, fire-eating, death-defying; adventurous
2 **immodest,** unmodest; exhibitionistic; **shameless,** dead *or* lost to shame, unashamed, unembarrassed, unabashed, unblushing, **brazen,** brazenfaced, brassy, bold as brass <nonformal>; **forward,** bold, pert, procacious <old>, bumptious; **flagrant,** notorious, scandalous

**bolt** NOUNS 1 **lock,** bar, padlock, catch, safety catch; barrier
2 **lightning, flash** *or* **stroke of lightning,** fulguration, fulmination, lightning strike, **bolt of lightning,** bolt from the blue, **thunderbolt,** thunderstroke, thunderball, fireball, firebolt, levin bolt *or* brand
VERBS 3 **gobble, gulp,** wolf, gobble *or* gulp *or* bolt *or* wolf down
4 **flee, fly, take flight,** take to flight, take wing, fugitate, **run, cut and run** <nonformal>, make a precipitate departure, **run off** *or* **away,** run away from, bug out <nonformal>, **decamp,** pull up stakes, **take to one's heels,** make off, **depart**, do the disappearing act, make a quick exit, **beat a retreat** *or* **a hasty retreat, turn tail,** show the heels, show a clean *or* light pair of heels; **run for it, run for one's life;** make a run for it; **take French leave,** go AWOL, slip the cable; **desert; abscond,** levant <Brit>, **elope,** run away with; skip *or* jump bail

*show it a fair pair of heels and run for it*
SHAKESPEARE

6 **hook,** hitch; lock, latch; **pin,** skewer, peg, nail, nail up, tack, staple, toggle, screw, rivet; batten, batten down; cleat

**bomb** NOUNS 1 bombshell; antipersonnel bomb, atomic bomb *or* atom bomb *or* A-bomb, atomic warhead, blockbuster, depth charge *or* depth bomb *or* ash can <nonformal>, fire bomb *or* incendiary bomb *or* incendiary, grenade, hand grenade, hydrogen bomb *or* H-bomb, letter bomb, Molotov cocktail, napalm bomb, neutron bomb, nuclear warhead, pipe bomb, plastic *or* plastique bomb, plutonium bomb, smart bomb, stench *or* stink bomb, time bomb; clean bomb, dirty bomb; **mine**
VERBS 2 drop a bomb, lay an egg <nonformal>; dive-bomb, glide-bomb, skip-bomb, pattern-bomb, etc; atom-bomb, hydrogen-bomb; **blow up,** blast, spring, explode, blow to pieces *or* bits *or* smithereens *or* kingdom come, bombard, blitz; mine; self-destruct

3 <nonformal> **lose out,** get left, **not make it,** not hack it, not get to first base, drop the ball, go for a Burton *and* come a cropper <both Brit>, **flop,** flummox, fall flat on one's ass, lay an egg, go over like a lead balloon, draw a blank, drop a bomb; fold, fold up; take it on the chin, take the count; crap out; take the collar, strike out, fan, whiff

**bombastic** ADJS 1 **stiff, stilted, formal,** Latinate, *guindé* <Fr>, **labored,** ponderous, elephantine, lumbering, cumbrous, leaden, heavy, unwieldy, sesquipedalian, inkhorn, pompous; **forced,** awkward, cramped, halting; crabbed
2 fustian, mouthy, **inflated, swollen,** swelling, turgid, turgescent, tumid, tumescent, flatulent, windy *and* gassy <both nonformal>; overadorned, fulsome

**bomber** NOUNS **destroyer, ruiner, wrecker, bane,** wiper-out, demolisher; **vandal,** hun; exterminator, annihilator; **iconoclast,** idoloclast, idol breaker; biblioclast; nihilist; terrorist, syndicalist; **bomber,** bombardier, dynamiter, dynamitard; burner, arsonist

**bombshell** NOUNS **eye-opener,** revelation; **bolt out of** *or* **from the blue,** thunderbolt, thunderclap; bomb; blockbuster, earthshaker; sudden turn *or* development, *peripeteia* <Gk>, switch; surprise ending, kicker *or* joker *or* catch <all nonformal>; surprise package; surprise party

**bona fide** ADJS **genuine, authentic,**

veridic, veridical, **real, natural, realistic, naturalistic,** true to reality, **true to nature, lifelike,** true to life, verisimilar, veristic; **literal,** following the letter, letter-perfect, *au pied de la lettre* <Fr>, true to the letter; verbatim, verbal, word-perfect, **word-for-word;** true to the spirit; **legitimate,** rightful, lawful; card-carrying <nonformal>, **good,** sure-enough <nonformal>, **sincere, honest; unadulterated**; **pure,** simon-pure; **sterling,** twenty-four carat, all wool and a yard wide <nonformal>

**bond** NOUNS 1 **security, surety,** indemnity, **guaranty, guarantee, warranty, insurance,** warrant, assurance; **obligation**, full faith and credit; **bond,** tie; stocks and bonds
2 **relation, relationship, connection;** relatedness, connectedness, **association**, **affiliation,** filiation, union, alliance, **tie,** tie-in <nonformal>, link, linkage, linking, linkup, liaison
VERBS 3 **put together, join,** conjoin, **unite,** unify, **connect,** associate, league, band, merge, **assemble,** accumulate; **join up,** become a part of, associate oneself, enter into, come aboard <nonformal>; **couple,** pair, accouple, copulate, conjugate, marry, wed, tie the knot <nonformal>, **link,** link up, build bridges, yoke, knot, splice, tie, chain, bracket; glue, tape, cement, solder, weld

**bone** ADJS **skeleton, skeletal;** osteal; **bony,** osseous, ossiferous; ossicular; ossified; **spinal,** myelic; cartilage, cartilaginous

**bonehead** NOUNS

<nonformal> **blockhead, airhead,** bubblehead, fluffhead, featherhead, woodenhead, dolthead, dumbhead, dummy, dum-dum, dumbo, dumb cluck, dodo head, doodoohead, dumbbell, dumb bunny, stupidhead, dullhead, bufflehead, jughead, thickhead, thickskull, numskull, putz, lunkhead, chucklehead, knucklehead, chowderhead, headbanger *and* jolterhead <both Brit>, muttonhead, beefhead, meathead, noodlehead, thimblewit, pinhead, pinbrain, peabrain, cabbagehead, pumpkin head, fathead, blubberhead, muddlehead, puzzlehead, addlebrain, addlehead, addlepate, tottyhead <old>, puddinghead, stupe, mushhead, blunderhead, dunderhead, dunderpate, clodpate, clodhead, clodpoll, jobbernowl *and* gaby *and* gowk <all Brit>

**bonfire** NOUNS **cheerful fire,** crackling fire; **roaring fire,** blazing fire

*bright-flaming, heatfull fire*
DU BARTAS

**bonnet** NOUNS **hat,** bonnet, cap, hood, coif

**bonus** NOUNS 1 **extra,** something extra, extra dash, extra added attraction, something into the bargain, something for good measure, baker's dozen; **padding,** stuffing, filling; trimming, **frill,** flourish, filigree, decoration, ornament; bells
2 **premium, fringe benefit** *or* **benefits,** bounty, perquisite, perquisites, perks <nonformal>, gravy <nonformal>, lagniappe, solatium; **tip**; overtime pay

**bon voyage!** PHRS **farewell!, pleasant journey!, have a nice trip!,** *tsetchem leshalom!* <Heb>, *glückliche Reise!* <Ger>, happy landing!; Godspeed!, peace be with you!, *pax vobiscum!* <L>; all good go with you!, God bless you!

**boo** VERBS **hiss, hoot,** catcall, give the raspberry *or* Bronx cheer <nonformal>, give the bird <nonformal>, whistle at

**boob** NOUNS

<nonformal> **chump,** booby, sap, prize sap, klutz, basket case, dingbat, dingdong, ding-a-ling, **ninny,** ninnyhammer, **nincompoop,** looby, noddy, saphead, mutt, jerk, jerk-off, asshole, goof, schlemiel, sawney <Brit>, galoot, gonzo, dumbo, dweeb, dropshop, dipshit, nerd, twerp, yo-yo

**boo-boo** NOUNS **bungle, blunder, botch,** flub, **error, mistake**

**booby trap** NOUNS **ambush,** ambushment, **ambuscade,** *guet-apens* <Fr>; surveillance, shadowing; lurking hole *or* place; blind, stalking-horse; **trap, gin; pitfall,** trapfall, deadfall; flytrap, mousetrap, mole trap, rattrap, bear trap; deathtrap, firetrap; Venus's flytrap, Dionaea; spring gun, set gun; baited trap; **mine; decoy;** springe, snare, tripwire

**book** NOUNS 1 **volume, tome;** publication, writing, **work, opus, production; title;** opusculum, opuscule; **trade book; textbook,** schoolbook; **reference book,**

playbook; songbook; notebook; storybook, **novel; best seller;** coffee-table book; nonbook; **children's book,** juvenile book, juvenile; picture book; coloring book, sketchbook; prayer book, psalter, psalmbook; **classic,** the book, the bible, magnum opus, great work, standard work, definitive work
VERBS 2 **charge, press charges, prefer** *or* **bring charges,** lay charges; complain, **lodge a complaint,** lodge a plaint; **impeach, arraign, indict,** bring in *or* hand up an indictment
3 **schedule, line up** <nonformal>, **slate,** book in, bill, program, calendar, docket, budget, put on the agenda; arrange for, reserve, prearrange

**bookie** NOUNS **bookmaker,** turf accountant; **tout,** turf consultant

**booking** NOUNS **engagement,** playing engagement, booking; **run; stand,** one-night stand *or* one-nighter; **circuit,** vaudeville circuit, borscht circuit; **tour, bus-and-truck, production tour;** date

**bookish** ADJS 1 **studious,** devoted to studies, **scholarly,** scholastic, academic, professorial, tweedy, donnish <Brit>; owlish; rabbinic, mandarin; pedantic, dryasdust; diligent
2 **book-learned,** book-read, **literary,** book-taught, book-fed, book-wise, book-smart, booky, book-minded; book-loving, bibliophilic, bibliophagic; **pedantic,** inkhorn; **bluestocking**

**bookkeeper** NOUNS **accountant; clerk,** actuary <old>, registrar, recorder, journalizer; calculator, reckoner; cost accountant, cost keeper; **auditor,** bank examiner; bank accountant; accountant general; comptroller *or* controller

**booklet** NOUNS **pamphlet, brochure, chapbook, leaflet, folder, tract;** circular; comic book

**booklover** NOUNS philobiblist, bibliophile, bibliolater, book collector, bibliomane, bibliomaniac, bibliotaph; **bookworm,** bibliophage; book-stealer, biblioklept

**books** NOUNS **account book, ledger, journal,** daybook; **register,** registry, **record book;** inventory, catalog; **log,** logbook; **cashbook; bankbook,** passbook; balance sheet; cost sheet, cost card

**bookshelf** NOUNS **bookholder, bookrest,** book support, **book end; bookcase,** revolving bookcase *or* bookstand, bookrack, bookstand; stack, bookstack; book table, book tray, book truck

**bookstore** NOUNS **bookshop,** *librairie* <Fr>, bookseller's; **bookstall,** bookstand; **book club**

**bookworm** NOUNS 1 **booklover,** philobiblist, bibliophile, bibliolater, book collector, bibliomane, bibliomaniac, bibliotaph
2 **nerd** *and* grind *or* greasy grind <all nonformal>, swotter *or* mugger <both Brit nonformal>

**boomerang** NOUNS 1 **missile, projectile,** bolt; brickbat, stone, rock, alley apple *and* Irish confetti <both nonformal>; bola; throwing-stick, throw stick, waddy <Austral>
VERBS 2 **recoil, rebound,** resile; **bounce, bound, spring; spring** *or* **fly back,** bounce *or* bound back, snap back; repercuss, have repercussions; **kick,** kick back, kick like a mule <nonformal>, recalcitrate <old>; **backfire;** backlash, lash back; ricochet, carom, cannon *and* cannon off <both Brit>

**booming** ADJS 1 **thundering, thunderous,** thundery, fulminating, tonitruous, tonitruant, thunderlike; pealing, rumbling, rolling, roaring; cannonading, volleying
2 **thriving, flourishing, prospering;** vigorous, exuberant; in full swing, going strong <nonformal>; halcyon, palmy, balmy, rosy, piping, clear, fair; blooming, blossoming, flowering, fruiting; fat, sleek, in good case; fat, dumb, and happy <nonformal>

**boon** NOUNS **godsend, blessing;** manna, manna from heaven, loaves and fishes, gift from on high; **benefit,** benefaction, benevolence, **favor,** grace

**boondocks** NOUNS **hinterland, back country,** outback <Australia>, up-country, boonies *and* boondocks <both nonformal>; **the bush,** bush country, bushveld, **woods,** woodlands, **backwoods,** forests, timbers, the big sticks <nonformal>, brush; wilderness, wilds, uninhabited region, virgin land *or* territory; **wasteland**

**boorish** ADJS 1 **churlish,** carlish, **loutish,** redneck <nonformal>, lubberly, lumpish, cloddish, clownish, loobyish, yokelish; rowdy, **rowdyish, ruffianly,** roughneck <nonformal>, hooliganish, raffish, raised in a barn
2 **ill-bred, ungenteel,** ungentle, cad-

dish; **ungentlemanly,** ungentlemanlike; **unladylike,** unfeminine; **vulgar, unrefined, inconsiderate, unsolicitous, tactless, insensitive; gross,** offensive, crass, **coarse, crude,** loutish, nasty

**boost** NOUNS 1 **promotion, preferment, advancement, advance,** step-up *and* upping <both nonformal>, rise, elevation, upgrading, jump, step up, step up the ladder; **raise;** kicking *or* bumping upstairs <nonformal>; exaltation, aggrandizement; pay raise
2 **commendation,** good word, acknowledgment, recognition, appreciation; boost *and* buildup <both nonformal>
VERBS 3 **cheer, gladden, brighten,** put in good humor; **encourage, hearten,** pick up <nonformal>; **inspire,** inspirit, warm the spirits, **raise the spirits,** elevate one's mood, buoy up, give a lift <nonformal>, put one on top of the world *and* on cloud nine <both nonformal>; **exhilarate,** animate, invigorate, liven, enliven, vitalize; **rejoice,** rejoice the heart, do the heart good
4 **publicize, advertise, promote,** build up, cry up, sell, puff <nonformal>, **plug** <nonformal>, **ballyhoo** <nonformal>
5 **elevate, raise, rear,** escalate, up, boost *and* hike <both nonformal>; **erect, heighten, lift,** levitate, boost <nonformal>, **hoist,** heist <nonformal>, heft, heave; raise up, rear up, lift up, hold up, set up; stick up, cock up, perk up; buoy up, upbuoy; **upraise, uplift**

**booster** NOUNS 1 injection; broken dose; booster dose, recall dose, booster shot
2 **promoter,** plugger <nonformal>; **ballyhooer** *or* **ballyhoo man** <nonformal>; **barker,** spieler <nonformal>, skywriter; billposter; sign-painter; sandwich boy *or* man

**booth** NOUNS **stall, stand;** newsstand, kiosk, news kiosk

**bootlegger** NOUNS **black marketeer,** gray marketeer; bootlegger, moonshiner <nonformal>; pusher *and* dealer <both nonformal>

**bootlicker** NOUNS

<nonformal> **apple-polisher, ass-kisser, brown-nose,** brown-noser, brownie, ass-licker, ass-wiper, suck-ass; **backslapper,** backscratcher, clawback, back-patter; bootlick; **handshaker; yes-man, stooge**

**booty** NOUNS spoil, **spoils, loot, swag** <nonformal>, ill-gotten gains, **plunder,** prize, haul, take, pickings, stealings, stolen goods, hot goods *or* items <nonformal>; **boodle** *and* squeeze *and* **graft** <all nonformal>

**booze** NOUNS 1 **spirits, liquor,** intoxicating liquor, adult beverage, **hard liquor, whiskey,** firewater, spiritus frumenti, usquebaugh <Scots>, schnapps, ardent spirits, strong waters, **intoxicant,** toxicant, inebriant, **potable,** potation, **beverage, drink, strong drink,** strong liquor, alcoholic drink *or* beverage, **alcohol,** aqua vitae, water of life, brew, **grog,** social lubricant, nectar of the gods; **rum,** the Demon Rum, John Barleycorn; the bottle, the cup, the cup that cheers, little brown jug; punch bowl, the flowing bowl

*the ruddy cup*
SIR WALTER SCOTT

VERBS 2 <nonformal> swig, swill, moisten *or* wet one's whistle; **liquor, liquor up,** lush, souse, tank up, **hit the booze** *or* **bottle** *or* **sauce,** exercise *or* bend *or* crook *or* raise the elbow, dip the beak, splice the main brace; chug-a-lug, chug

**border** NOUNS 1 **frontier, borderland,** border ground, marchland, march, marches; outskirts, outpost; frontier post; iron curtain, bamboo curtain, Berlin wall; Pillars of Hercules; three-mile *or* twelve-mile limit
2 bed, **flower bed,** ornamental border
VERBS 2 **edge, bound, rim, skirt, hem, hem in, ringe,** befringe, lap, list, margin, marge, marginate, march, verge, line, side; **adjoin; frame,** enframe, set off; trim, bind; purl; purfle

**bore** NOUNS 1 crashing bore <nonformal>, frightful bore; **pest, nuisance;** dryasdust; proser, twaddler; buttonholer

2 <nonformal> **wet blanket; drag, drip, pill,** flat tire, deadass, deadfanny, dull tool; **headache,** pain in the neck *or* ass

VERBS 3 leave one cold, set *or* send to sleep; **bore stiff** *or* to tears *or* to death *or* to extinction <nonformal>, bore to distraction, bore out of one's life, bore out of all patience; buttonhole

4 **excavate, dig,** dig out, **scoop,** scoop out, **gouge,** gouge out, grub, shovel, spade, dike, delve, scrape, scratch, scrabble; dredge; **trench,** trough, furrow, groove; **tunnel, burrow;** drive <min>, sink, lower; **mine,** sap; quarry; drill

**boring** ADJS **wearying,** wearing, **tiring; wearisome,** weariful, fatiguing, **tiresome, irksome; boresome,** stupefyingly boring, stuporific, yawny <nonformal>; **monotonous, humdrum,** unrelieved, repetitive, drab, gray, ho-hum <nonformal>, samey <Brit nonformal>, usual, as usual; tedious

**born** ADJS given birth; **hatched;** cast, dropped, whelped, foaled, calved, etc; née; newborn; stillborn

*cast naked upon the naked earth*
PLINY THE ELDER

**born-again** ADJS **redeemed, saved,** converted, regenerated, regenerate, justified, reborn, renewed; circumcised, spiritually purified *or* cleansed, sanctified

**borrow** VERBS borrow the loan of, get on credit *or* trust, get on tick *and* get on the cuff <both nonformal>; get a loan, float *or* negotiate a loan, go into the money market, **raise money; touch** *and* **hit up** *and* hit one for *and* put the arm *or* bite *or* touch on <all nonformal>; run into debt; pawn

**bosom** NOUNS 1 **heart, soul, spirit,** *esprit* <Fr>, **breast,** inmost heart *or* soul, heart of hearts, secret *or* inner recesses of the heart, secret places, heart's core, heartstrings, cockles of the heart, bottom of the heart, being, innermost being, core of one's being

2 **breast, bust, chest,** crop, brisket; **breasts,** dugs, teats; **nipple,** papilla, pap, mammilla, *mamelon* and *téton* <both Fr>; mammillation, mamelonation; mammary gland, udder, bag

**boss** NOUNS 1 **superior, chief, head, superintendent; supervisor, foreman,** monitor, **head,** headman, overman, chief, gaffer *and* ganger <both Brit nonformal>, taskmaster; sirdar <India>, **overseer,** overlooker; **straw boss** <nonformal>; slave driver; **master, lord, lord and master,** overlord, seigneur, paramount, lord paramount, liege, liege lord, *padrone* <Ital>, *patron* and *chef* <both Fr>, patroon; sahib <India>, *bwana* <Swah>; employer

2 <nonformal> **honcho,** big enchilada, biggest frog in the pond, top *or* high man on the totem pole, top dog, Mr Big, head cheese, his nibs, himself, man upstairs

VERBS 3 **direct, manage, supervise, superintend, oversee,** overlook, ride herd on <nonformal>, stand over, keep an eye on *or* upon, keep in order; cut work out for; straw-boss <nonformal>; take care of; **regulate, conduct, carry on, handle, run** <nonformal>; **control, command, head, govern**, head up *and* pull the strings *and* **mastermind** *and* quarterback *and* call the signals <all nonformal>; lay down the law, make the rules, call the shots *or* tune <nonformal>

**bossy** ADJS arrogant; **arbitrary, peremptory,** imperative; **dictatorial, authoritarian; domineering, high-handed, overbearing,** overruling; autocratic, monocratic; **tyrannical**, tyrannous, grinding, oppressive; repressive, suppressive; strict, severe

**botany** NOUNS plant biology, phytobiology, phytology, plant science; **plant kingdom,** vegetable kingdom; **plants**, flora, plant life, vegetation; vegetable life; herbage, flowerage, verdure, greenery, greens

**botch** VERBS 1 **do carelessly,** do by halves, do in a half-assed way <nonformal>, do in a slip-shod fashion, do anyhow, do in any old way <nonformal>; **bungle**; **do offhand,** dash off, knock off *and* throw off <both nonformal>, **toss off** *or* **out** <nonformal>; **roughhew,** roughcast, rough out; **knock out** <nonformal>, hammer *or* pound out, bat out <nonformal>; toss *or* **throw together,** knock together, throw *or* slap together, cobble up, patch together, patch, patch up, fudge up, fake up, whomp up <nonformal>, lash up <Brit nonformal>, slap up <nonformal>

2 **blunder, make a blunder, make a faux pas,** blot one's copy book, make a colossal blunder, make a false *or* wrong step, make a misstep; embarrass oneself, have egg on one's face <nonformal>; **bungle**

**bother** NOUNS 1 **nuisance, pest,** botheration <nonformal>, public nuisance, **trouble, problem,** pain <nonformal>, difficulty, hot potato <nonformal>;

**inconvenience; headache** <nonformal>; **pain in the neck** *or* **in the ass** <nonformal>
VERBS 2 **annoy, irk, vex, nettle, provoke, pique,** miff *and* peeve <both nonformal>, distemper, **ruffle, disturb,** discompose, **roil,** rile, **aggravate,** make a nuisance of oneself, **exasperate,** exercise, try one's patience, try the patience of a saint; give one a pain <nonformal>; get, get one down, **get one's goat,** get under one's skin, get in one's hair, tread on one's toes; burn up *and* brown off <both nonformal>; **torment, molest,** pother; **harass,** harry, drive up the wall <nonformal>, **hound,** dog, nag, nobble <Brit nonformal>, nudzh <nonformal>; **heckle,** pick *or* prod at, rub it in *and* rub one's nose in it <both nonformal>, badger, hector, bait, bullyrag, worry, worry at, nip at the heels of, chivy, hardly give one time to breathe, make one's life miserable, keep on at, fash <Scots>; **bug** <nonformal>, be on the back of *and* be at *and* ride <all nonformal>, **pester, tease, needle,** devil, get after *or* get on <nonformal>, **bedevil, pick on** <nonformal>, tweak the nose, pluck the beard, give a bad time to <nonformal>

**bottle** NOUNS **container, receptacle;** basin, pot, pan, cup, glass, ladle; cask

**bottleneck** NOUNS **hindrance,** hindering, **hampering; check, arrest,** arrestment, arrestation; fixation; **impediment,** holdback; **resistance, opposition**; suppression, **repression, restriction, restraint**; **obstruction,** blocking, blockage, clogging, occlusion; traffic jam, gridlock; **interruption,** interference; **retardation,** retardment, **detention,** detainment, **delay,** holdup, setback; **inhibition;** constriction, squeeze, stricture, cramp, stranglehold; **closure,** closing up *or* off; obstructionism, bloody-mindedness <Brit>, negativism, foot-dragging <nonformal>

**bottomless** ADJS 1 **piggish, hoggish,** swinish, a hog for, greedy as a hog; **gluttonous**; omnivorous, all-devouring; insatiable, insatiate, unsatisfied, unsated, unappeased, unappeasable, limitless, unquenchable, quenchless, unslaked, unslakeable, slakeless
2 **abysmal,** abyssal, yawning, cavernous, gaping, plunging; without bottom, soundless, unsounded, plumbless, **fathomless,** unfathomed, unfathomable; deep as a well, deep as the sea *or* ocean, deep as hell
3 **plentiful, full,** replete, well-filled, running over, overflowing; inexhaustible, exhaustless; **profuse,** profusive, effuse, diffuse

**the bottom line** NOUNS **salient point,** cardinal point, high point, great point; important thing, chief thing, **the point, main point,** main thing, essential matter, **essence,** the name of the game *and* what it's all about *and* where it's at <all nonformal>, substance, gravamen, *sine qua non* <L>, issue, real issue, front-burner issue <nonformal>, prime issue; **essential,** fundamental, substantive point, material point; **gist, nub** <nonformal>, **heart,** meat, pith, kernel, **core; crux,** crucial *or* pivotal *or* critical point, pivot; turning point, **climax, cusp, crisis;** summation, **score, reckoning, tally,** tale, the story *and* whole story *and* all she wrote <all nonformal>

**boudoir** NOUNS **bedroom,** chamber, sleeping chamber, **bedchamber,** sleeping room

**bough** NOUNS **branch,** fork, **limb; twig, sprig,** switch; spray; **shoot,** offshoot, spear, frond; scion; **sprout,** sprit, slip, burgeon, thallus; sucker

**bounce** NOUNS 1 **buoyancy,** buoyance, resilience, resiliency, springiness; springy step; **jauntiness,** perkiness, debonairness, carefreeness; **breeziness,** airiness, pertness, chirpiness, light heart
VERBS 2 **bound, spring; spring** *or* **fly**

**bouncer** NOUNS **ejector,** expeller; **ouster,** evictor; chucker <nonformal>, chucker-out <Brit nonformal>

**bound** VERBS 1 circumscribe, surround, limit, enclose, divide, separate; **border, edge, rim, skirt, hem, hem in, ring,**
2 **leap, jump, vault, spring, skip, hop,** bounce; upleap, upspring, updive; leap over, jump over, etc; overleap, overjump, overskip, leapfrog; **hurdle,** clear, negotiate
ADJS 3 **limited, restricted, bounded, finite; confined**
4 **promised, pledged, committed,** compromised, **obligated; sworn,** warranted, **guaranteed,** assured, underwritten; contracted; **engaged, plighted, affianced, betrothed,** intended
5 **joined, united, connected, coupled,** linked, knit, bridged, tight-knit, knitted, bracketed, associated, conjoined, incorporated, integrated, **merged,** gathered,

assembled, accumulated, **collected; associated,** joined up, on board; **allied,** leagued, banded together; hand-in-hand, hand-in-glove, intimate; unseparated, undivided; **wedded,** matched, married, paired, yoked, mated; **tied,** knotted, spliced, lashed

**boundary** NOUNS **limitation, limiting, restriction,** restricting, confinement, prescription, proscription, restraint, discipline, moderation, continence; bounds, limit; time-limit, time constraint; small space; **fence, wall, barrier;** stone wall; paling, palisade; rail, railing

**boundless** ADJS **infinite, endless, limitless,** termless, shoreless; unbounded, uncircumscribed, **unlimited,** illimited, infinitely continuous *or* extended, stretching *or* extending everywhere, without bound, without limit *or* end, no end of *or* to; illimitable, **interminable,** interminate; **immeasurable,** incalculable, unreckonable, innumerable, incomprehensible, unfathomable; measureless, countless, sumless; **unmeasured,** unmeasurable, immense, unplumbed, untold, unnumbered, without measure *or* number *or* term; exhaustless, inexhaustible; **all-inclusive,** all-comprehensive, **universal**; **perpetual, eternal**

*as boundless as the sea*
SHAKESPEARE

**bounty** NOUNS bountifulness, bounteousness; **openhandedness,** freehandedness, open *or* free hand, easy purse strings; **givingness;** open-heartedness, bigheartedness, largeheartedness, greatheartedness, freeheartedness; open heart, big *or* large *or* great heart, heart of gold; **magnanimity**

**bouquet** NOUNS 1 **fragrance,** fragrancy <old>, **perfume, aroma,** scent, redolence, balminess, **incense,** nosegay <old>, sweet smell, sweet savor; **odor**; spice, spiciness; muskiness; fruitiness
2 **nosegay, posy,** boughpot, flower arrangement; **boutonniere,** buttonhole <Brit>; **corsage; spray; wreath;** festoon; **garland,** chaplet, lei

**bourgeois** NOUNS 1 member of the middle class, white-collar worker, salaried worker; pillar of society, solid citizen
2 **conformist,** conformer, sheep, trimmer, parrot, yes-man, organization man; **conventionalist,** Mrs Grundy, Babbitt, Philistine, middle-class type, button-down *or* white-bread type <nonformal>, Middle American, *parvenu, arriviste, nouveau riche* <all Fr>; plastic person *and* clone *and* square <all nonformal>, three-piecer *and* yuppie <both nonformal>, Barbie Doll <trademark> <nonformal>
ADJS 3 **capitalist, capitalistic,** individualistic, nonsocialistic, free-enterprise, private-enterprise
4 **conformist, conventional**, plastic *and* square *and* straight *and* white-bread *and* white-bready *and* button-down *and* buttoned-down <all nonformal>

**bout** NOUNS **fight, match,** battle, duel, slugfest

**bow** NOUNS 1 **obeisance,** reverence, homage; **nod, bob,** bend, inclination, inclination of the head, **curtsy, salaam, kowtow,** scrape, bowing and scraping, making a leg; **genuflection,** kneeling, bending the knee; prostration; salute, salutation, namaste; presenting arms, dipping the colors *or* ensign, standing at attention
2 **prow, stem,** rostrum, figurehead, nose, beak; bowsprit, jib boom
VERBS 3 **make obeisance, salaam, kowtow,** make one's bow, bow down, **nod,** incline *or* bend *or* bow the head, bend the neck, **bob,** bob down, **curtsy,** bob a curtsy, bend, make a leg, scrape, **bow and scrape; genuflect, kneel,** bend the knee, get down on one's knees, throw oneself on one's knees, fall on one's knees, fall down before, fall at the feet of, prostrate oneself, kiss the hem of one's garment

**bowel movement** NOUNS **defecation,** dejection, **evacuation,** voidance; movement, BM, number two <nonformal>, **stool, feces,** feculence, **ordure,** night soil, jakes <Brit nonformal>, shit *and* crap <both nonformal>, turd <nonformal>; dingleberry <nonformal>; **diarrhea,** loose bowels, flux; trots *and* runs *and* shits *and* GI's *and* GI shits <all nonformal>; tourista *and* Montezuma's revenge <both nonformal>; lientery; **dysentery,** bloody flux; catharsis, purgation, purge

**bowels** NOUNS 1 small intestine, odenum, jejunum, ileum; blind gut, cecum; foregut, hindgut; midgut, mesogaster;

large intestine, colon, sigmoid flexure, rectum; anus

2 **depths,** deeps, bowels of the earth; bottomless pit; infernal pit, hell, nether world, underworld; dark *or* unknown *or* yawning *or* gaping depths, unfathomed deeps

**bowl** NOUNS 1 **cavity,** concavity, concave; **hollow,** hollow shell, shell; **hole, pit, depression, basin,** trough; **crater;** antrum

2 **arena, theater, amphitheater,** circus, **hippodrome, coliseum,** colosseum, **stadium**; Cotton Bowl, Gator Bowl, Orange Bowl, Rose Bowl, Sugar Bowl, Super Bowl

**bowlegged** ADJS bandy-legged, bandy; rickety, rachitic

**box** NOUNS 1 **container, receptacle;** receiver, holder, vessel, utensil; case

VERBS 2 **package, pack, parcel;** box up, case, encase, crate, carton; enwrap, bundle; shrink-wrap

3 **cuff,** buffet; strike; box the ears; **fight,** punch, spar, mix it up <nonformal>, shadowbox

**boxer** NOUNS **fighter,** pugilist, prizefighter, pug *and* palooka <both nonformal>, slugger, mauler

**boxing** NOUNS **prizefighting,** fighting, pugilism, noble *or* manly art of self-defense, the noble *or* sweet science, fisticuffs, the fistic sport, the fights *and* the fight game <both nonformal>, the ring

**box office** NOUNS **attendance,** frequenting, frequence; number present; turnout *and* box office *and* draw <all nonformal>

**boy** NOUNS **lad, youth,** manchild, manling, young man, *garçon* <Fr>, *muchacho* <Sp>, schoolboy, schoolkid <nonformal>, fledgling, hobbledehoy

**boycott** NOUNS 1 **proscription, ban;** boycottage; **blackball,** blackballing, blacklist; **rejection, exclusion, barring,** debarring, debarment, preclusion

VERBS 2 **ostracize,** turn thumbs down; **proscribe, ban, outlaw**, put under the ban; **blackball,** blacklist

**boyfriend** NOUNS **fellow** *and* young man *and* flame <all nonformal>

**boyish** ADJS **childish,** childlike, kiddish <nonformal>, **puerile;** boylike, beardless; puppyish, puppylike, puplike, calflike, coltish, coltlike; ungrown, half-grown, juvenile, puerile

**bra** NOUNS **brassiere,** bandeau, under-bodice, *soutien-gorge* <Fr>, uplift brassiere

**brace** NOUNS 1 **two,** twain <old>; **couple, pair, matching pair, twosome,** set of two, duo, duet, team, span, yoke, double harness

VERBS 2 **strengthen, invigorate, fortify,** beef up <nonformal>, buttress, prop, shore up, support, undergird, brace up; refresh, revive, recruit one's strength

**bracelet** NOUNS armlet, wristlet, wristband, anklet

**bracket** VERBS parenthesize, precede and follow, bookend; interconnect, ally, link, marry, marry up, weld, bind, tie, couple

**brag** VERBS 1 **boast,** make a boast of, vaunt, flourish, gasconade, vapor, puff, draw the longbow, advertise oneself, **blow one's own trumpet, toot one's own horn,** sing one's own praises, exaggerate one's own merits; bluster, swagger

2 <nonformal> **blow,** blow off, mouth off, **blow hard, talk big,** sound off, blow off *and* toot *or* blow one's own horn, **bullshit,** shoot the shit, spread oneself, lay it on thick, brag oneself up; jaw, talk trash

**Brahman** NOUNS **nobleman, noble, gentleman; peer; aristocrat, patrician, blue blood,** thoroughbred, silk-stocking, lace-curtain, swell *and* upper-cruster <both nonformal>

**Brahmin** NOUNS **elitist; highbrow** *and* egghead <both nonformal>, mandarin; **intellectual, intellect,** intellectualist, literate, member of the intelligentsia, white-collar intellectual; wise man

*someone whose mind watches itself*
CAMUS

**braid** NOUNS 1 plait, twist; **pigtail,** rat's-tail *or* rat-tail, tail; **wreath,** wreathwork

VERBS 2 plait, pleach, **wreathe,** raddle, **knit,** twist, mat, wattle

**brain** NOUNS 1 seat *or* organ of thought; sensory, sensorium; encephalon; gray matter, noodle *or* noggin *or* bean *or* upper story <all nonformal>

2 **intellectual, intellect,** intellectualist, member of the intelligentsia; rocket scientist <all nonformal>

VERBS 3 blow *or* knock *or* dash one's brains out, poleax

**brainstorm** NOUNS **good idea, great idea,** not a bad idea; **bright thought,** bright *or* brilliant idea, **insight; inspiration**

**brainwash** VERBS **condition, program, indoctrinate,** reindoctrinate, counterindoctrinate

**braise** VERBS **cook, brown,** embrown, infuscate; sauté, scorch

**bramble** NOUNS **thorn, brier, nettle,** burr, prickle, sticker <nonformal>; scrub, brier bush

**branch** NOUNS 1 **ramification,** stem, offshoot; fork, **limb, bough**
2 **stream, waterway, watercourse, channel**; meandering stream, flowing stream, lazy stream, racing stream, braided stream
3 arm, offshoot, **affiliate; chapter,** lodge, post; branch office, local office
VERBS 4 **fork,** furcate, bifurcate, trifurcate, divaricate; ramify, branch off *or* out

**brand** NOUNS 1 **stamp,** feather, color, stripe, line, grain, kidney; **make,** mark, label, shape, cast, form, mold
VERBS 2 **stigmatize; disparage, defame**; censure, reprimand, **give a black eye** <nonformal>, give a black mark, put in one's bad *or* black books; **skewer,** impale, crucify

**brass** NOUNS 1 **rashness, brashness, imprudence, indiscretion,** injudiciousness, improvidence; overconfidence, oversureness, overweeningness; **impudence,** insolence; **gall** *and* brass *and* cheek *and* chutzpah <all nonformal>; hubris
2 top brass; top people, the great; ruling circle, lords of creation

**brassy** ADJS **brazen,** brazenfaced, boldfaced, barefaced, **bold,** bold as brass <nonformal>, unblushing, unabashed, **shameless;** swaggering

**brat** NOUNS **urchin; minx, imp,** puck, elf, gamin, little monkey, **whippersnapper,** young whippersnapper, *enfant terrible* <Fr>, little terror, holy terror

**bravado** NOUNS **audacity,** boldness, bold front, brash bearing, brashness, brassiness <nonformal>, brazenness, bravado, insolence; rant, rodomontade, fanfaronade

**brave** ADJS **courageous, plucky, bold, valiant, valorous, gallant, intrepid,** doughty, **hardy,** stalwart, stout, stouthearted, ironhearted, lionhearted, greathearted, bold-spirited, bold as a lion

**bravery** NOUNS **courage,** courageousness, **nerve,** pluck, braveness, ballsiness *and* gutsiness *or* guttiness <all nonformal>, **boldness, valor**

**brawl** NOUNS 1 free-for-all, knock-down-and-drag-out <nonformal>**, broil, melee, scrimmage,** fracas, **riot**
VERBS 2 be quarrelsome *or* contentious, be thin-skinned, be touchy *or* sensitive, get up on the wrong side of the bed; broil; riot; **fight, battle, put up a fight** <nonformal>**; wage war**

**brawny** ADJS well-built, well-set, well-set-up <nonformal>, well-knit, of good *or* powerful physique, broad-shouldered; **muscular,** well-muscled, heavily muscled, thickset, burly

**brazen** VERBS 1 **brave, face, confront,** affront, look one in the eye, say to one's face, **meet head-on** *or* boldly, square up to, stand up to *or* against, go eyeball-to-eyeball *or* one-on-one with <nonformal>; brazen out *or* through
ADJS 2 loud <nonformal>, **blatant, flagrant,** shameless, brazenfaced, lurid, extravagant, sensational, **spectacular,** glaring, flaring, flaunting, screaming <nonformal>, obtrusive, vulgar, crude

**breach** NOUNS 1 **violation, infraction,** breaking; **infringement, transgression, trespass,** contravention; breach of promise, breach of contract, breach of trust *or* faith, breach of the peace
2 **break,** breakage, burst, **rupture, fracture; crack,** cleft, **fissure, cut, split,** slit; slash, slice; **gap, rift,** rent, rip, tear; chip, splinter, scale
VERBS 3 **violate, break; infringe, transgress, trespass,** contravene, trample on *or* upon, trample
4 rupture; **break open,** force *or* pry *or* prize open, crack *or* split open, rip *or* tear open; break in, burst in, bust in <nonformal>

**breadth** NOUNS **width,** broadness, wideness, fullness, amplitude, latitude, distance across *or* crosswise *or* crossways, extent, **span, expanse, spread;** beam; broad gauge, latitude

**breadwinner** NOUNS **worker, workman, workingman; workwoman, workingwoman; jobholder,** wageworker, **wage earner,** salaried worker

**break** NOUNS 1 breakage, **breach,** burst,

**rupture, fracture; crack,** cleft, **fissure, cut, split,** slit
2 **interruption, suspension,** gap, hiatus, lacuna, caesura; **interval, pause,** interim, lull, cessation, letup <nonformal>, **intermission**
3 **stroke of luck,** piece of good luck; **fluke** *and* lucky strike *and* **break** <all nonformal>, **good** *or* **lucky break** <nonformal>
VERBS 4 **break up,** fracture, **come apart,** come unstuck, **come** *or* **fall to pieces, fall apart; shatter,** fragment, fragmentize, fragmentate, fall to pieces, shard, **disintegrate**
5 **take a rest, take a break, take time out** *and* grab some R and R <both nonformal>, pause, lay off, **knock off** <nonformal>, recess, **take a recess,** take ten *and* take five <both nonformal>
6 **domesticate, tame,** bust *and* gentle <both nonformal>, break in, break to harness

**breakable** ADJS **fragile,** frangible, destructible, shattery, crumbly, brittle, fragmentable, fracturable; **unsubstantial, flimsy;** delicate, flimsy, frangible

**breakdown** NOUNS **collapse, crackup** <nonformal>, **prostration,** exhaustion; nervous prostration *or* breakdown *or* exhaustion, neurasthenia

**breakfast** NOUNS *petit déjeuner* <Fr>, continental breakfast, English breakfast

**breakthrough** NOUNS progress, headway; quantum jump *or* leap; **advance,** advancement; **innovation,** leap

**break wind** VERBS **fart** <nonformal>, let *or* lay *or* cut a fart <nonformal>, let wind

**breast** NOUNS 1 **bosom, bust, chest,** crop, brisket; thorax; pigeon breast; **breasts,** dugs, teats

2 <nonformal> **tits,** titties, **boobs,** boobies, bubbies, jugs, headlights, **knockers,** knobs, *nénés* <Fr>, bazooms, bags, bazongas, coconuts, hooters

**breath** NOUNS 1 **murmur,** murmuring, murmuration; sigh, exhalation, aspiration
2 **puff,** puff of air *or* wind, breath of air, flatus, waft, capful of wind, whiff, whiffet, stir of air

**breathtaking** ADJS **exciting, thrilling,** thrilly <nonformal>, **stirring, moving,** eye-popping <nonformal>; suspensive, **suspenseful,** cliff-hanging <nonformal>; mind-boggling

**breed** NOUNS 1 **kind, sort, ilk, type,** breed of cat <nonformal>, lot <nonformal>, **variety, species, genus,** *genre* <Fr>, phylum; tribe, clan, race, strain, blood, kin, breed
VERBS 2 **raise,** rear, grow, hatch, feed, nurture, fatten

**breeze** NOUNS light *or* gentle wind *or* breeze, softblowing wind, **zephyr,** gale <old>, air, light air, moderate breeze; fresh *or* stiff breeze; cool *or* cooling breeze; sea breeze, onshore breeze, ocean breeze

**breezy** ADJS 1 **lighthearted,** light; **jaunty,** perky, **debonair, carefree,** free and easy
2 **windy, blowy; drafty,** airy, airish; brisk, fresh

**brevity** NOUNS **conciseness,** concision, briefness, brachylogy; **pithiness,** succinctness

*the soul of wit*
SHAKESPEARE

**brew** NOUNS 1 **beer,** brew *and* brewskie *and* suds <all nonformal>, swipes <Brit nonformal>; small beer
2 **concoction,** decoction, *decoctum* <L>, **confection; mixture,** combination
VERBS 3 **distill;** bootleg, moonshine <nonformal>; **plot, scheme, intrigue,** be up to something; **conspire, connive,** collude; gather

**bribable** ADJS corruptible, purchasable, buyable; approachable; fixable; on the take *and* on the pad <both nonformal>; **venal, corrupt,** bought and paid for, in one's pocket

**bribe** NOUNS 1 bribe money, sop, sop to Cerberus, gratuity, gratification <old>, payoff <nonformal>, boodle <nonformal>; payola <nonformal>

2 VERBS <nonformal>grease, **grease the palm,** oil the palm, tickle the palm; **purchase, take care of buy, buy off,** pay off; **fix**

**bribery** NOUNS bribing, subornation, **corruption, graft**

**bridal** ADJS **matrimonial, marital, conjugal, connubial, nuptial,** wedded, married, hymeneal; epithalamic

**bride** NOUNS **newlywed;** plighted bride, blushing bride

**bridegroom** NOUNS **newlywed; groom**

**bridesmaid** NOUNS wedding attendant;

bridemaiden, maid *or* matron of honor

**bridge** NOUNS 1 **span, viaduct;** cantilever bridge, clapper bridge, drawbridge, footbridge, pontoon bridge, rope bridge, skybridge *or* skywalk *or* flying bridge *or* walkway *or* skywalk, suspension bridge, toll bridge; overpass
2 auction bridge, contract bridge, rubber bridge, duplicate *or* tournament bridge
VERBS 3 **extend over,** span, bestride, bestraddle, arch over, overarch, hang over, overhang

**bridle** VERBS 1 **anger, get one's gorge up,** get one's blood up, bridle up, **bristle,** bristle up, raise one's hackles, get one's back up
2 **restrain, curb, check, arrest,** get under control, rein, snub, snub in

**brief** NOUNS 1 **argument,** *argumentum* <L>; **case, plea,** pleading, *plaidoyer* <Fr>; special pleading
VERBS 2 give a briefing; debrief; **acquaint, enlighten,** familiarize, verse, give the facts, give an account of, give by way of information
ADJS 3 **short, abbreviated,** abbreviatory; **concise**; **succinct, summary,** synoptic, synoptical, compendious, compact

*short and sweet*
THOMAS LODGE

**briefing** NOUNS **instructions, directions, orders;** final instructions

**briefly** ADVS **shortly,** summarily, *tout court* <Fr>, in brief compass, economically, sparely, curtly, succinctly, in a nutshell, in two *or* a few words

**brier** NOUNS **thorn, bramble, nettle,** burr, prickle, sticker <nonformal>; shrub, bush; scrub, bramble, brier bush

**brig** NOUNS **military prison, guardhouse, stockade; prison camp,** internment camp, detention camp

**bright** ADJS 1 **sunny,** fair, mild, balmy; halcyon, Saturnian; **brilliant, vivid, splendid,** splendorous, splendent, **resplendent,** bright and shining
2 **smart, brainy** <nonformal>, **brilliant,** scintillating; **clever,** apt, **gifted,** talented; **sharp,** keen; smart as a whip, sharp as a tack <nonformal>; nobody's fool *and* no dumbbell *and* not born yesterday <all nonformal>

**brilliant** ADJS 1 **bright, vivid,** intense, **rich,** exotic, burning, **gorgeous**
2 **illustrious,** lustrous, glorious, radiant, splendid, splendorous, splendrous, splendent, resplendent, bright, shining; charismatic, glamorous; scintillating; **gifted,** talented; **dazzling,** bedazzling

**brim** NOUNS **border, edge, verge, brink,** brow, **rim, margin,** marge, **skirt, fringe, lip,** flange

**brindle** ADJS **striped,** stripy; **streaked,** streaky; brindled, brinded; marbled, marbleized

**brine** NOUNS **saltiness, salinity,** brininess; brackishness; **salt; preservative,** preservative medium

**bring** VERBS **fetch, go get,** go and get, go to get, **go after,** go fetch, **go for,** call for, pick up; **get,** obtain, procure, secure; **bring back, retrieve;** chase after, run after, shag, fetch and carry; **be sold, sell,** bring, realize, sell for

**brink** NOUNS **verge, brim, rim, margin,** marge, **skirt, fringe,** side

**brinkmanship** NOUNS **foreign policy,** playing with fire, flirting with death, courting disaster, stretching one's luck, going for broke <nonformal>, tightrope walking

**brisk** ADJS **refreshing,** refreshful, **fresh,** crisp, crispy, zesty, zestful, **bracing, tonic, exhilarating, stimulating, invigorating,** energizing

**bristle** NOUNS **spike,** spikelet, spicule, spiculum; **spine;** quill; **needle**
VERBS **anger, get one's blood up, bridle,** bridle up, bristle up, get one's back up; **ruffle,** rub the wrong way, go against the grain, set on edge

**Britain** NOUNS **Great Britain, United Kingdom, the UK,** Britannia, Albion, Blighty <Brit nonformal>, Tight Little Island, Land of the Rose

*This royal throne of kings, this scepter'd isle, This earth of majesty, this seat of Mars, This other Eden, demi-paradise*
SHAKESPEARE

**britches** NOUNS **pants, trousers,** pair of trousers *or* pants, trews <Scots>, **breeches,** breeks <Scots>

**brittle** ADJS 1 **fragile,** frangible, **breakable,** destructible, shattery, crumbly, fragmentable, fracturable
2 <comparisons> eggshell, matchwood, old paper, piecrust, glass, glass jaw, china, parchment, ice, bubble, glass house, house of cards, hothouse plant

**broad** NOUNS

1 <nonformal> **gal, dame,** hen, biddy, skirt, jane, doll, babe, chick, wench, bird <Brit>, tomato, bitch, minx, momma, mouse, sister, squaw, toots

ADJS 2 **wide,** deep; wide-ranging, exhaustive, comprehensive, in-depth, extensive; spread-out, **expansive;** widespread; **loose, lax, inexact,** inaccurate, imprecise; nonspecific, unspecified; **general,** sweeping; inchoate, disordered, orderless, chaotic, incoherent

*broad as the world*
JAMES RUSSELL LOWELL

**broadcast** NOUNS 1 **publication, promulgation,** evulgation, **propagation, dissemination, diffusion, broadcasting, spread, spreading,** spreading abroad, **circulation,** ventilation, airing; **dispersion** *or* **dispersal, scattering; radiobroadcast,** radiocast, **radio program**
VERBS 2 **communicate, impart, tell,** lay on one <nonformal>, **convey, transmit,** transfer, send, send word, deliver *or* send a signal *or* message, **disseminate,** pass, **pass on** *or* **along, publish, promulgate, propagate, circulate,** circularize, **diffuse, disseminate,** distribute, **spread,** spread around *or* about, spread far and wide, publish abroad, **pass the word around,** put about, **bandy about, noise about,** cry about *or* abroad, noise *or* sound abroad

**broadly** ADVS **generally, in general; generally speaking,** speaking generally, broadly speaking, **roughly,** roughly speaking, as an approximation; **vaguely, indefinitely,** indeterminably, indefinably, **indistinctly,** indecisively

**broad-minded** ADJS wide-minded, large-minded, **broad, wide,** wide-ranging, broad-gauged, catholic, spacious of mind; cosmopolitan, ecumenistic, ecumenical

**brochure** NOUNS circular; **booklet, pamphlet, chapbook, leaflet, folder, tract**

**brogue** NOUNS **accent,** regional accent, twang, burr, drawl, broad accent

**broke** ADJS 1 **insolvent, bankrupt,** in receivership, in the hands of receivers, belly-up <nonformal>, broken, **ruined,** failed, out of business, unable to pay one's creditors, unable to meet one's obligations, on the rocks; destitute

2 <nonformal> **dead broke,** busted, **flat, flat broke,** flat on one's ass, flat-ass, down for the count, stone *or* stony broke, stony, **strapped,** skint <Brit>, beat; down to one's last penny *or* cent, cleaned out, tapped out, Tap City, oofless, wasted, wiped out, without a pot to piss in

**broken** ADJS 1 **subdued, quelled,** crushed, reduced, mastered, overmastered, humbled, humiliated, brought to one's knees, brought low, made to grovel; **tamed, domesticated,** broken to harness, gentled
2 **in disrepair,** out of working order, out of condition, out of repair, inoperative

**brokenhearted** ADJS **overcome,** crushed, borne-down, overwhelmed, inundated, **stricken, cut up** <nonformal>, **desolated,** prostrate *or* prostrated, undone; **heart-stricken,** heart-struck; heartbroken

**broken-in** ADJS **accustomed, wont, wonted, used to; conditioned,** trained, seasoned; experienced, **familiarized,** naturalized <old>, run-in <nonformal>, oriented

**broker** NOUNS **go-between, middleman, intermediary, medium,** intermediate; connection <nonformal>, **contact;** arbitrator, mediator; **stockbroker,** sharebroker <Brit>, stockjobber, dealer, stock dealer; Wall Streeter; stock-exchange broker, *agent de bourse* <Fr>

**brokerage** NOUNS **stockbrokerage,** brokerage house, brokerage office; wire house; bucket shop *and* boiler room <both nonformal>

**brooch** NOUNS **gem,** pin, stickpin, breastpin, scatter pin, chatelaine

**brood** NOUNS 1 **family,** progeny, issue, offspring, fruit, seed, breed; heirs, inheritors, sons, **children, kids** <nonformal>
VERBS 2 introspect, be abstracted; fall into a brown study, retreat into one's mind *or* thoughts; **grieve, sorrow; mope, fret**

**brook** NOUNS 1 **stream,** branch; kill, bourn, run <Brit nonformal>, **creek,** crick <nonformal>; **rivulet,** rill, **streamlet,** brooklet, runlet, runnel

**brothel** NOUNS **house of prostitution,** house of assignation, house of joy *or* ill repute *or* ill fame, **whorehouse,** bawdyhouse, massage parlor, sporting house, disorderly house, **cathouse, bordello,** bagnio, stew, dive, den of vice, den *or* sink of iniquity, crib, joint

**brotherhood** NOUNS fellow feeling, **sympathy,** fraternal feeling, feeling of kinship; compassion; humaneness, humanity; charitableness; **fellowship, fraternity,** fraternalism, sodality, confraternity

**brotherly love** NOUNS charity, *caritas* <L>, Christian love, agape, loving concern, **caring**

**brow** NOUNS **countenance,** face, visage, feature, favor, physiognomy; **forehead,** lofty brow

**brownie** NOUNS **elf, pixie, gremlin,** ouphe, hob, cluricaune, puca *or* pooka *or* pwca, kobold, nisse, peri

**brown-nose** NOUNS 1 **yes-man,** toady, creature, ass-licker *and* ass-kisser *and* brown-nose *and* brown-noser *and* bootlicker <all nonformal>
VERBS 2 **fawn, truckle; flatter; toady; bootlick** <nonformal>, lick one's shoes, lick the feet of; **grovel,** crawl, creep, cower, cringe, crouch, stoop, kneel, bend the knee, fall on one's knees, prostrate oneself, throw oneself at the feet of, fall at one's feet, kiss *or* lick *or* suck one's ass *and* brown-nose <all nonformal>; **kowtow, bow and scrape**

**browse** VERBS 1 **dip into,** thumb over *or* through, run over *or* through, glance *or* run the eye over *or* through, turn over the leaves, have a look at, hit the high spots
2 **shop, market, go shopping,** go marketing; **shop around;** window-shop, comparison-shop

**bruise** NOUNS 1 contusion, ecchymosis, **black-and-blue mark; black eye,** shiner *and* mouse <both nonformal>; **discoloration,** discolorment, discolor <old>
VERBS 2 **hurt, wound, hurt one's feelings; injure, traumatize;** contuse, bung *and* bung up <both nonformal>; **buffet,** batter, bash <nonformal>, maul, pound, beat, beat black and blue; give a black eye

**bruiser** NOUNS

<nonformal> **roughneck, tough,** mug, mugger, bozo, ugly customer, **hoodlum, hood, hooligan,** gorilla, ape, plug-ugly, strong-arm man, muscle man, **goon**

**brunt** NOUNS **shock; impact, collision, clash; concussion,** percussion

**brush** NOUNS 1 **touch;** graze, grazing; stroke, gentle *or* tentative contact, caress, nudge
2 skirmish, scrimmage; tussle, **scuffle, struggle,** shoving match; **quarrel**
3 barren land, treeless plain; bush, outback <Australia>
VERBS 4 graze, brush by, glance, scrape, skim, sideswipe, skirt, shave
5 **sweep,** sweep up *or* out, brush off, whisk, broom

**brush up** VERBS **refresh the memory, review,** restudy, **rub up,** polish up *and* bone up <both nonformal>, get up on

**brutal** ADJS **savage, fierce, ferocious, vicious, murderous, cruel, atrocious, mindless,** brutish, **bestial,** mindless, insensate, monstrous, mutant, inhuman, pitiless, ruthless, merciless, bloody, sanguinary

**brutality** NOUNS mindless *or* senseless brutality, brutalness, **brutishness, bestiality, animality,** beastliness; **savagery, viciousness, violence,** fiendishness

**brutalize** VERBS **terrorize,** sow terror, vandalize, barbarize; **rape,** violate; **attack, assault,** batter, savage, mug, maul, hammer

**brute** NOUNS 1 **beast, animal, monster,** monster of cruelty, **devil,** devil incarnate; **sadist,** torturer, tormenter; Attila, Torquemada, the Marquis de Sade; **savage, barbarian, beast, animal, devil, demon, fiend; rapist, mugger, killer**
ADJS 2 **brutish, brutal,** brutelike; **bestial, beastly,** beastlike

**bubble** NOUNS 1 **globule;** vesicle, bulla, **blister,** blood blister, fever blister; balloon, bladder; air bubble, soap bubble
VERBS 2 bubble up, burble; **effervesce, fizz, fizzle;** bubble over

**bubbly** ADJS frothy, foamy, spumy, spumous, spumescent, bubbly, yeasty; burbly, **bubbling,** burbling; **effervescent,** spumescent, **fizzy, sparkling,** *mousseux* <Fr>, *spumante* <Ital>

**buck** VERBS **contend against,** strive against, struggle against, labor against, **take on** <nonformal>, grapple with, join battle with, close with, come to close quarters with, go the the mat with <nonformal>, antagonize <old>, **fight, counter**

**buckle** VERBS 1 **distort, twist,** turn,

screw, wring, wrench, wrest; writhe; **warp**
2 **hook,** hitch; **clasp,** hasp, clip, snap; **button,** zipper; lock, latch

**Buddha** NOUNS the Blessed One, the Teacher, **the Lord Buddha,** bodhisattva, Gautama Buddha

**budding** NOUNS 1 germination, pullulation; burgeoning, sprouting
ADJS 2 unseasoned, unfledged, callow, unripe, ripening, raw, green, virginal, naive, ingenuous, undeveloped

**buddy** NOUNS **coworker, workfellow, workmate, fellow worker,** butty <Brit nonformal>; **teammate,** shopmate

**budge** VERBS **move, stir; progress,** advance; shift, change, shift *or* change place

**budget** NOUNS 1 **funds, finances, moneys,** exchequer, purse, pocket
VERBS 2 **ration;** allowance, put on an allowance; schedule, cost, cost out
ADJS 3 **cheap, inexpensive,** unexpensive, **low, low-priced,** frugal, reasonable, sensible, manageable, modest, moderate, affordable, to fit the pocketbook, budget, easy, economy, economic, economical

**buff** NOUNS 1 devotee, **zealot, enthusiast,** fancier, follower

2 <nonformal> **fan, freak,** hound, fiend, demon, nut, bug, head, junkie, groupie, rooter, booster

VERBS 3 **burnish, polish,** rub up, smooth, dress, shine, furbish

**buffer** NOUNS 1 **guard; bulwark**; backstop; **fender,** mudguard, **bumper, cushion,** pad, padding
VERBS 2 **neutralize, nullify, annul, cancel,** cancel out, negate, negative, invalidate, vitiate, void, frustrate, thwart, come *or* bring to nothing, undo; **offset, counterbalance**

**buffer zone** NOUNS demilitarized zone, neutral territory

**bug** NOUNS 1 **germ,** pathogen, contagium, bug <nonformal>, disease-causing agent, disease-producing microorganism
2 **insect, beetle, mite, tick**
3 **fault,** *faute* <Fr>, **defect, deficiency, inadequacy,** imperfection, kink, defection <old>; **flaw,** hole; fly in the ointment, problem, little problem, snag, drawback; **malfunction,** glitch <nonformal>
VERBS 4 **listen in; eavesdrop,** wiretap, tap, intercept, bug <nonformal>
5 **harass,** badger, hector, be on the back of *and* be at *and* ride <all nonformal>, **pester, tease, needle,** devil, get after *or* get on <nonformal>; hassle <nonformal>

**build** NOUNS 1 **muscularity,** brawn, sinew, sinews, thew, thews; physique, body-build; body
VERBS 2 put up, set up; expand, extend, widen, broaden, build up; **construct**

**building** NOUNS **structure, edifice, construction,** construct, erection, establishment, fabric

**buildup** NOUNS development, widening, spread, broadening, elevation, **extension,** aggrandizement, access, accession, **increment,** accretion; **addition**; **expansion**; proliferation, productiveness; appreciation, waxing, snowballing, **rise** *or* raise, fattening *and* boost *and* hike <all nonformal>; **promotion, buildup** *and* promo <both nonformal>

**bulging** ADJS swelling, distended, bloated, potbellied, bellying, pouching; bagging, baggy; rounded, hillocky, hummocky, moutonnée; billowing, billowy, bosomy, ballooning, pneumatic; **swollen**, bursting, bursting at the seams, ready to burst, full to bursting, fit to bust <nonformal>

**bulk** NOUNS 1 mass, substance, matter, magnitude, amplitude, **extent; bulkiness,** hulkingness *or* hulkiness, **massiveness,** lumpishness, clumpishness; **substance,** gist, meat, essence, thrust, gravamen
VERBS 2 develop, bulk up; inflate, sufflate, **blow up,** puff up, pump up

**bulkhead** NOUNS **partition, wall, barrier;** brattice <mining>; diaphragm, septum; **buffer; bulwark,** rampart; **embankment,** bank, retaining wall, bulkheading, piling

**bulky** ADJS **hulky,** hulking, lumpish, lumpy, lumping <nonformal>, clumpish, lumbering, lubberly; **massive,** massy; **ponderous,** cumbrous, cumbersome; **clumsy,** awkward, **unwieldy;** clunky <nonformal>

**bull** NOUNS

1 <nonformal> **humbug, bunk, bunkum;** hooey, hoke, **hokum, bullshit**, crap, baloney

2 **decree,** decreement <old>, decretum, decretal, rescript, fiat, **edict,** *edictum* <L>; **proclamation,** pronouncement, pronunciamento, **declaration,** ukase; diktat
VERBS 3 **talk nonsense, gas** *and* bull *and* **bullshit** *and* throw the bull *and* shoot off one's mouth *and* shoot the bull <all nonformal>

**bulldoze** VERBS **intimidate,** bully, **cow,** walk all over, **browbeat,** bludgeon, dragoon; **demoralize;** steamroller, flatten, smash, prostrate, raze to the ground

**bulletin** NOUNS **report,** news report, flash; **brief, statement, account,** accounting

**bullfighter** NOUNS toreador, *torero* <Sp>; banderillero, picador, matador

**bullion** NOUNS ingot, bar

**bull session** NOUNS **chinfest** *and* **chinwag** *and* **talkfest** *and* **bull session** <all nonformal>; **dialogue,** duologue, trialogue

**bullshit** NOUNS 1 **absurdity,** absurdness, **ridiculousness;** ludicrousness; **nonsense,** nonsensicality, stuff and nonsense, codswallop <Brit nonformal>, horseshit <nonformal>
VERBS 2 **talk nonsense, twaddle, piffle,** waffle <Brit>, **blather, blabber, babble, gabble,** gibble-gabble, **jabber, gibber,** prate, **prattle,** rattle; gas *and* bull *and* throw the bull *and* shoot off one's mouth *and* shoot the bull <all nonformal>

**bully** NOUNS 1 **tormentor,** torturer; harasser, harrier, badgerer, **heckler,** plaguer, persecutor; molester
VERBS 2 **intimidate, cow, browbeat, hector, harass,** huff; **terrorize,** threaten; **demoralize**

**bulwark** NOUNS 1 **fortification,** work, defense work, **rampart, fence, barrier; enclosure; safeguard,** palladium, **guard; shield, screen;** umbrella, protective umbrella

**bum** NOUNS 1 **vagabond, vagrant,** vag <nonformal>; **bum** *or* bummer <nonformal>, loafer, wastrel, losel <old>, *lazzarone* <Ital>; **tramp,** turnpiker, piker, knight of the road, easy rider, **hobo** *or* bo <nonformal>, rounder <nonformal>, stiff *or* bindlestiff <nonformal>; ski bum, beach bum, surf bum, tennis bum
VERBS 2 **tramp,** hobo, go on the bum <nonformal>, vagabond, vagabondize, take to the road, beg, **scrounge, cadge; mooch** *and* **panhandle** <both nonformal>; **hit** *and* hit up *and* **touch** *and* put the touch on *and* make a touch <all nonformal>

*travel the open road*
WHITMAN

**bumbler** NOUNS **bungler, blunderer,** blunderhead, boggler, slubberer, **fumbler, botcher**

**bump** NOUNS 1 **knock, rap, tap,** smack, whack, thwack, whop, whap, swap <nonformal>, whomp, splat, crump <Brit nonformal>, slap, slat <Brit nonformal>, flap, flop
2 **rising, lump,** clump, bunch, blob; thank-you-ma'am *and* whoopdedoo <both nonformal>, cahot <Can>; speed bump, sleeping policeman <Brit>
VERBS 3 **knock, rap, tap,** smack, whack, thwack, whop, whap, swap <nonformal>, whomp, splat, crump <Brit nonformal>, slat <Brit nonformal>, slap, flap; **collide,** come into collision, be on a collision course, **clash,** meet, encounter, confront each other, impinge; **hit, strike, knock, bang; run into, bump into,** bang into, slam into, smack into, **crash into, impact,** smash into; rear-end

**bumper** NOUNS 1 **buffer, cushion,** pad, padding
ADJS 2 **large, sizable, considerable, goodly,** healthy, tidy <nonformal>, **substantial**

**bumpy** ADJS **rough, unsmooth; uneven,** ununiform, unlevel, inequal, **broken,** irregular, textured; jolty, rutty, rutted, pitted, pocky, potholed; **jolting,** jolty, **joggling,** joggly, jogglety, jouncy, **bouncy,** choppy, rough; **jarring,** bone-bruising

**bunch** NOUNS 1 **batch,** heap <nonformal>, pack, mess <nonformal>, gob *and* chunk *and* hunk <all nonformal>; agglomeration, cluster, mass, clot
2 **clique, coterie,** group; **crew** *and* mob *and* **crowd** *and* **bunch** *and* outfit <all nonformal>; ingroup, we-group
VERBS 3 **cluster,** mass, **cohere, adhere, stick, cling,** cleave, hold; **stick together, hang** *or* **hold together;** solidify, set, conglomerate, agglomerate, conglobate; **congeal,** coagulate, clabber <nonformal>, **clot**

**bundle** NOUNS 1 bindle <nonformal>, **pack, package,** packet, deck, budget,

**parcel,** fardel <nonformal>, sack, bag, poke <nonformal>, rag-bag <nonformal>, bale, truss, **roll,** rouleau, bolt; fagot, fascine, fasces
2 hoard, store; wealth; **big bucks,** megabucks, gigabucks, big money, serious money, gobs, heaps, heavy lettuce, heavy jack, heavy money, important money, pot, potful, power, mint, barrel, raft, load, **loads,** pile, wad, wads, nice hunk of change, packet <Brit> <all nonformal>
VERBS 3 bundle up, **package,** parcel, parcel up, **pack,** bag, sack, truss, truss up; bale; wrap, **wrap up,** do *or* tie *or* bind up; roll up
4 **snuggle, nestle, cuddle,** cuddle up, curl up; nest; snuggle up to, snug up *or* together <old>

**bungalow** NOUNS **cottage,** cot *or* cote, box; **cabin,** log cabin; **second home, vacation home;** chalet, lodge, snuggery

**bungle** NOUNS 1 **blunder, botch,** flub, boner *and* bonehead play <both nonformal>, boggle, bobble *and* boo-boo *and* screw-up *and* fuck-up <all nonformal>, foozle <nonformal>, bevue; **fumble, muff,** fluff, miscue <nonformal>; **slip,** trip, stumble; *gaucherie, étourderie, balourdise* <all Fr>; **hash** *and* **mess** <both nonformal>; bad job, sad work, clumsy performance
VERBS 2 **blunder,** bumble, boggle, **muff,** muff one's cue *or* lines, **fumble,** be all thumbs, have a handful of thumbs; **flounder,** muddle, lumber; stumble, **slip,** trip, trip over one's own feet, get in one's own way, miss one's footing, miscue; commit a *faux pas,* commit a gaffe; **botch,** mar, **spoil, butcher, murder,** make sad work of; play havoc with, play mischief with

3 <nonformal> **goof, pull a boner,** bobble, lay an egg, put *or* stick one's foot in it, stub one's toe, step on one's schvantz *or* pecker, drop the ball, drop a brick, bonehead into it; **blow,** blow it, bitch, bitch up, hash up, **mess up,** flub, flub the dub, **make a mess** *or* **hash of,** foul up, fuck up, goof up, bollix up, **screw up, louse up, gum up,** gum up the works, bugger, bugger up, play the deuce *or* devil *or* hell *or* merry hell with; go at it ass-backwards; put one's foot in one's mouth

**bunk** NOUNS

1 <nonformal>**humbug,** humbuggery; **bunkum;** hooey, hoke, **hokum, bosh,** bull, **bullshit,** crap, baloney, flimflam, flam, smoke and mirrors, claptrap, moonshine, eyewash, hogwash, gammon <Brit nonformal>, *blague* <Fr>, jiggery-pokery <Brit>

VERBS 2 **room,** crash <nonformal>, berth, doss down <Brit>; perch *and* roost *and* squat <all informal>

**bunker** NOUNS **bastion,** donjon; pillbox, blockhouse, garrison *or* trenches *or* barricades; garrison house; air-raid shelter, bomb shelter

**bunny** NOUNS **rabbit, bunny** *and* bunny rabbit <both nonformal>, lapin; cottontail

**bunting** NOUNS **flag, banner,** oriflamme, **standard,** gonfalon *or* gonfanon, guidon, *vexillum* <L>, *labarum* <L>; **pennant,** pennon, pennoncel, banneret, banderole, swallowtail, burgee, **streamer**

**buoy** NOUNS **marker,** aid to navigation, bell, gong, lighted buoy, nun, can, spar buoy, wreck buoy, junction buoy

**burden** NOUNS 1 **affliction,** infliction; **curse, woe,** distress, grievance, **sorrow,** *tsures* <Yiddish>; **trouble,** peck *or* pack of troubles; **care,** burden of care, cankerworm of care; **oppression, cross, cross to bear** *or* **be borne, load,** fardel <old>, encumbrance, weight, albatross around one's neck, millstone around one's neck

*all the ills that men endure*
ABRAHAM COWLEY

2 **duty, obligation,** charge, **onus,** mission, devoir, must, ought, imperative, bounden duty, proper *or* assigned task, what ought to be done, what one is responsible for, where the buck stops <nonformal>, workload

*stern daughter of the voice of God*
WORDSWORTH

VERBS 3 **distress, afflict, trouble,** give one a tough row to hoe, load with care, **bother, disturb, perturb, disquiet, discomfort, agitate, upset,** put to it; **worry,** give one gray hair

4 **load, lade,** freight; **encumber,** cumber, lumber, **saddle with,** weigh *or* weight down, press down

**burdened** ADJS **weighted, weighed** *or* **weighted down; oppressed, laden,** cumbered, **encumbered,** charged, loaded, fraught, freighted, taxed, saddled, hampered; **overburdened,** overloaded, overladen, overcharged, overfreighted, overfraught, overweighted, overtaxed; borne-down, sinking, foundering

**burdensome** ADJS **onerous, oppressive,** incumbent *or* superincumbent, **cumbersome,** cumbrous; massive; lumpish, **unwieldy**

**bureau** NOUNS **office, department;** secretariat, ministry, commissariat; municipality, bailiwick

**bureaucracy** NOUNS **officialism; red-tapeism** *and* red-tapery *and* **red tape** <all nonformal>

**bureaucratic** ADJS **executive, administrative,** ministerial; official; **supervisory, directing, managing**

**burglar** NOUNS yegg *and* cracksman <both nonformal>; housebreaker, cat burglar, cat man, second-story thief *or* worker; **safecracker,** safebreaker, safeblower; pete blower *or* pete man *or* peterman <all nonformal>

**burglary** NOUNS burglarizing, housebreaking, **breaking and entering,** break and entry, break-in, unlawful entry; second-story work <nonformal>; safebreaking, **safecracking, safeblowing**

**burial** NOUNS **interment,** burying, inhumation, sepulture, **entombment;** encoffinment, inurning, inurnment, urn burial; disposal of the dead; burial *or* funeral *or* funerary customs

**buried** ADJS **concealed, hidden, hid,** occult, recondite <old>, blind; **covered; covert, under cover,** under wraps <nonformal>; code-named; **obscured,** obfuscated, clouded, beclouded, befogged; secluded, secluse, sequestered; **obscure,** abstruse, mysterious; **secret;** unknown, latent

**burlesque** NOUNS **exaggeration,** travesty, caricature; **lampoon,** squib, **parody, satire, farce,** mockery, imitation, wicked imitation *or* pastiche, takeoff <nonformal>, **caricature**
VERBS 2 **lampoon,** satirize, parody, caricature, travesty, hit *or* take off on; send up <nonformal>; dip the pen in gall
ADJS 3 **farcical, broad,** slapstick; parodic, caricatural, macaronic, doggerel

**burly** ADJS muscular, well-muscled, heavily muscled, thickset, **brawny;** muscle-bound, all muscle

**burn** VERBS **catch fire,** catch on fire, catch, take fire, **flame,** combust, blaze, **blaze up, burst into flame; shine,** shine forth, **give light,** incandesce; scald, scorch, singe, sear

**burnish** NOUNS 1 **polish, gloss, glaze, shine, luster,** finish; **patina**
VERBS 2 **polish, shine, furbish,** sleek, slick, slick down, gloss, glaze, glance, luster; **rub,** scour, **buff;** wax, varnish; finish

**burnout** NOUNS **fatigue, weariness;** end of one's tether, overtiredness, overstrain; jadedness; lassitude, languor; combat fatigue; mental fatigue, brain fag <nonformal>; **listlessness, spiritlessness,** blah *or* blahs <nonformal>

**burn out** VERBS **get tired, grow weary, tire, weary,** fatigue, jade; **flag, droop,** faint, sink, feel dragged out, wilt; **play out,** run out, run down; **go out, die,** die out *or* down *or* away; fizzle *and* **fizzle out** <both nonformal>

**burp** NOUNS 1 **belch,** belching, wind, gas, eructation; **hiccup**
VERBS 2 **belch,** eruct, eructate; **hiccup**

**burrow** NOUNS 1 **lair, den,** cave, **hole,** covert, mew, form; tunnel, earth, run, couch, lodge
VERBS 2 **excavate, scoop,** scoop out, **gouge,** gouge out, grub, shovel, spade, dike, delve, scrape, scratch, scrabble; dredge; **trench,** trough, furrow; **tunnel,** dig

**burst** NOUNS 1 **report, crash, crack, clap, bang,** wham, slam, clash; **detonation, blast, explosion,** fulmination, **discharge, bang, pop, crack,** bark; **shot,** gunshot; volley, salvo, fusillade
VERBS 2 **break, break up,** fracture, **come apart,** come unstuck, **come** *or* **fall to pieces, fall apart, explode, blow up,** go off, go up, blow out, blast, bust <nonformal>; **detonate,** fulminate
ADJS 3 **broken,** busted <nonformal>, **ruptured,** dissilient; sprung; **shattered,** broken up, broken to pieces *or* bits, fragmentized, fragmented, in shards, in smithereens <nonformal>

**bursting** ADJS **teeming, swarming,**

**crowding,** thronging, overflowing, overcrowded, overwhelming, **crawling, alive with,** lousy with <nonformal>, populous, prolific, proliferating, crowded, packed, jammed, bumper-to-bumper <nonformal>, jam-packed, like sardines in a can <nonformal>, thronged, studded, bristling, rife, lavish, prodigal, superabundant, **profuse,** in profusion, thick

**bury** VERBS **inter,** inhume, sepulture, inearth <old>, **lay to rest, consign to the grave,** lay in the grave *or* earth, lay under the sod, put six feet under <nonformal>; tomb, **entomb,** ensepulcher, hearse; enshrine; inurn; encoffin, coffin; hold *or* conduct a funeral
2 **secrete, hide away,** keep hidden, put away, store away, stow away, file and forget, bottle up, lock up, seal up, put out of sight; **keep secret**; **cache,** stash <nonformal>, deposit, plant <nonformal>

**bus** NOUNS omnibus, chartered bus, autobus, motorbus, motor coach, articulated bus, jitney <nonformal>; express bus, local bus; schoolbus

**bush** NOUNS 1 **the bush,** bush country, bushveld, **woods,** woodlands, **backwoods,** forests, timbers, the big sticks <nonformal>, brush
2 **shrub;** scrub, bramble, brier, brier bush; topiary

**business** NOUNS 1 **undertaking, enterprise, operation,** work, **venture, project,** proposition *and* deal <both nonformal>; **affair, matter, task**, concern, interest; **vocation, occupation, work, line, line of work,** line of business *or* endeavor, number <nonformal>, walk, **walk of life, calling**
2 **company, firm, business firm, concern, house,** *compagnie* <Fr>, *compañía* <Sp>, *Aktiengesellschaft* <Ger>, *aktiebolag* <Swed>; **industry,** business establishment, commercial enterprise
3 business dealings *or* affairs *or* relations, commercial affairs *or* relations; the business world, the world of trade *or* commerce, the marketplace
ADJS 4 **commercial,** mercantile; entrepreneurial; **mercantile,** merchant

**businessman** NOUNS businesswoman, businessperson, businesspeople; enterpriser, entrepreneur; big businessman, magnate, tycoon <nonformal>, baron, king, top executive, business leader

**bust** NOUNS 1 **breast, bosom, chest,** crop, brisket; pigeon breast; **breasts,** dugs, teats
VERBS 2 **domesticate, tame, break,** bust *and* gentle <both nonformal>, break in, break to harness; housebreak
3 **go bankrupt, fail,** break, bust <nonformal>, crash, collapse, **fold, fold up,** belly up *and* go up *and* go belly up *and* **go under** <all nonformal>, shut down, shut one's doors, go out of business

**bustle** NOUNS 1 **haste, hurry, scurry, rush, race,** dash, drive, scuttle, scamper, **scramble,** hustle <nonformal>, flutter, **flurry,** hurry-scurry, helter-skelter; no time to be lost
VERBS 2 **hurry up,** hustle up <nonformal>, **rush,** quicken, hustle <nonformal>, bundle, precipitate, forward; rush along, speed along, **speed on its way; push through,** railroad through <nonformal>, steamroll

**busy** ADJS **occupied,** working; workaday, workday, prosaic

**busybody** NOUNS **meddler,** intermeddler; **pry,** Paul Pry, prier, Nosey Parker *or* nosey Parker *or* Nosy Parker <all nonformal>, snoop *or* snooper, *yenta* <Yiddish>, **kibitzer** *and* backseat driver <both nonformal>

**butch** NOUNS 1 <mannish female> **amazon,** virago, androgyne; lesbian, butch *and* dyke <both nonformal>; **tomboy,** hoyden, romp
ADJS 2 lesbian, sapphic, tribadistic; mannish, butch *and* dykey <both nonformal>

**butcher** NOUNS 1 **killer, slayer, slaughterer,** bloodshedder; massacrer; **murderer, cutthroat,** gorilla <nonformal>; professional killer, hired killer, hit man *or* button man *or* gun *or* trigger man *or* torpedo *or* gunsel <all nonformal>; **hatchet man;** exterminator, eradicator
VERBS 2 **slaughter, massacre, decimate,** commit carnage, depopulate, murder *or* kill *or* slay en masse; commit mass murder *or* destruction, murder wholesale, commit genocide
3 **botch,** mar, **spoil, murder,** make sad work of; play havoc with

**butchered** ADJS **botched, bungled,** fumbled, muffed, spoiled, murdered; **ill-managed,** ill-done, **mutilated,** garbled, hashed, **mangled**

**butler** NOUNS **major-domo, steward,** house steward, chamberlain, *maître d'hôtel* <Fr>, seneschal

**butt** NOUNS 1 **cigarette;** cig *and* **fag** *and* coffin nail *and* cancer stick <all nonformal>; cigarette butt, stub; snipe <nonformal>
2 **laughingstock, figure of fun,** joke, target, stock, **goat** <nonformal>, **fair game,** victim, dupe, fool, everybody's fool, monkey, mug <Brit nonformal>
VERBS 3 **adjoin,** join, conjoin, **connect, abut,** abut on *or* upon, be contiguous, be in contact; **border on** *or* **upon,** verge on *or* upon; lie by, stand by
4 **push, shove,** thrust; bunt; shunt; pole, row; pedal, treadle

**butterfingers** NOUNS

<nonformal> **goof,** goofer, goofball, goofus, foul-up, bonehead, dub, foozler, clumsy, fumble-fist, klutz, stumblebum, stumblebunny, duffer, lummox, **slob,** lump, dub

**butterflies** NOUNS

<nonformal> **jitters,** willies, **heebie-jeebies,** jimjams, **jumps, shakes,** quivers, trembles, dithers, collywobbles, butterflies, shivers, cold shivers, creeps, sweat, cold sweat; antsyness, ants in one's pants, yips

**butt in** VERBS **talk out of turn,** speak inopportunely, interrupt, **put one's foot in one's mouth** <nonformal>, intrude, butt in *and* stick one's nose in <both nonformal>, **go off half-cocked** <nonformal>, open one's big mouth *or* big fat mouth <nonformal>

**buttocks** NOUNS 1 **rump,** bottom, posterior, derrière; croup, crupper; podex; haunches; gluteal region; nates

2 <nonformal> **ass,** arse *and* bum <both chiefly Brit>, behind, backside, **butt, can,** cheeks, hind end, nether cheeks, stern, tail, rusty-dusty, **fanny,** prat, keister, popo, rear, rear end, tuchis *or* tushy *or* tush

**button** VERBS **fasten,** secure; button up; put *or* slap the lid on, **cover**

**butt out** VERBS

<nonformal> **get off one's back** *or* **one's case** *or* **one's tail,** get out of one's face *or* hair, **back off,** leave be, call off the dogs, keep one's nose out, get lost, take a walk

**buxom** ADJS **shapely,** well-built, built, well-shaped, well-proportioned, well-made, well-formed, stacked *or* well-stacked <both nonformal>, curvaceous, curvy <nonformal>, pneumatic, amply endowed, built for comfort *or* built like a brick shithouse <both nonformal>

**buy** NOUNS 1 **bargain,** advantageous purchase, **buy** <nonformal>, **good buy, steal** <nonformal>; money's worth
VERBS 2 **purchase,** procure, make *or* complete a purchase, make a buy, make a deal for, blow oneself to <nonformal>; buy out; buy in, buy into, buy a piece of; buy back; buy on credit, buy on the installment plan
3 **believe, credit, trust, accept,** give credit *or* credence to, put faith in, take stock in *or* set store by <nonformal>, take to heart, attach weight to; believe without reservation, take for granted, take as gospel truth <nonformal>, take on faith, take on trust *or* credit, pin one's faith on; take at face value; **take one's word for,** trust one's word, take at one's word; **buy** *and* **buy into** <both nonformal>, **swallow**

**buyer** NOUNS purchaser, emptor, **consumer,** vendee; **shopper,** marketer; window-shopper, browser; purchasing agent, customer agent

**buzz** NOUNS 1 **rasp, scratch, scrape,** grind; crunch, craunch, scranch <old>, scrunch, crump; burr, chirr
2 **report, rumor,** flying rumor, unverified *or* unconfirmed report, **hearsay,** *on-dit* <Fr>, **scuttlebutt** *and* latrine rumor <both nonformal>; **talk, whisper, rumble**
VERBS 3 whisper, buzz, breathe, whisper in the ear, **put a bug in one's ear** <nonformal>

**bypass** NOUNS 1 **detour,** roundabout way; back way, back road, back street
VERBS 2 **go roundabout,** meander, deviate, go around Robin Hood's barn, take *or* go the long way around, twist and turn; **detour,** make a detour, **go around,** go round about, go out of one's way

**by-product** NOUNS **effect, result,** resultant, **consequence,** consequent, sequent, sequence, sequel, sequela, sequelae; development, corollary; derivative, derivation; secondary *or* incidental product, spin-off, outgrowth, offshoot; **residue,** leavings, waste, waste product, industrial waste, solid waste, lees, dregs, ash

**bystander** NOUNS **witness, eyewitness,** spectator, earwitness; passerby

**byte** NOUNS **bit, binary digit,** infobit, kilobit, megabit, gigabit, terbit; kilobyte, megabyte

**byword** NOUNS **catchword,** catch phrase, shibboleth, slogan, cry; **pet expression,** cliché; **buzzword,** vogue word, fad word, in-word

**Byzantine** ADJS **scheming, calculating, designing, contriving, plotting, intriguing;** manipulatory, **manipulative;** opportunist, **opportunistic;** Machiavellian; insinuating, insidious, devious, calculating

# C

**cab** NOUNS taxicab, taxi, hack <nonformal>, gypsy cab <nonformal>; rental car; hired car, limousine, limo *and* stretch limo <both nonformal>

**cabal** NOUNS **intrigue,** web of intrigue, **plot, scheme,** deep-laid plot *or* scheme; **conspiracy,** confederacy, covin, complot <old>; junta

**cabaret** NOUNS **tavern, roadhouse; nightclub,** night spot *or* nitery *and* hot spot <all nonformal>, *boîte, boîte de nuit* <both Fr>; juke joint <nonformal>, discothèque *or* disco <nonformal>

**cabdriver** NOUNS **driver,** Jehu; cabman, cabby <nonformal>, hackman, hack *or* hacky <nonformal>

**cabin** NOUNS **cottage,** cot *or* cote, **bungalow,** box; log cabin; **second home, vacation home;** chalet, lodge, snuggery

**cabinet** NOUNS 1 **container, receptacle;** receiver, holder; box, case; cupboard

2 **council,** conclave, *concilium* <L>, deliberative *or* advisory body; divan, council of ministers, council of state, US Cabinet, British Cabinet; kitchen cabinet, camarilla; staff

**cable** NOUNS 1 **cord, line, rope, wire,** braided rope, twisted rope, flattened-strand rope, wire rope, locked-wire rope, wire cable

2 **telegram, telegraph, wire** <nonformal>, telex; **cablegram; radiogram,** radiotelegram; **day letter, night letter;** fast telegram

VERBS 3 **telegraph,** telegram, flash, **wire** *and* send a wire <both nonformal>, telex; Teletype

**cache** NOUNS 1 **hiding place,** stash <nonformal>; cubbyhole, cubby, pigeonhole

2 **stockpile,** backup, reserve supply, something in reserve *or* in hand, something to fall back on, reserve fund

VERBS 3 **secrete, hide away,** keep hidden, put away, bury away, store away, stow away, stash <nonformal>, deposit, plant <nonformal>

**cad** NOUNS bounder *and* rotter <nonformal>; **boor,** churl, clown, **lout,** looby

**cadaver** NOUNS **corpse,** dead body, dead man *or* woman, dead person, **body;** *corpus delicti* <L>; **stiff** <nonformal>; **the dead, remains,** mortal *or* organic remains, bones, skeleton, dry bones, relics, reliquiae

**cadaverous** ADJS **deathly, deathlike,** deadly; pale, deathly pale, wan, lurid, blue, livid, haggard; corpselike

**café** NOUNS **restaurant,** *trattoria* <Ital>; *caffè* <Ital>; *bistro* <Fr>; **coffeehouse,** coffeeroom, **coffee shop,** coffee bar, coffee-pot <nonformal>; pub, tavern; **bar,** barroom, *bistro* <Fr>; waterhole *or* watering hole <nonformal>; **nightclub**

**cafeteria** NOUNS **restaurant,** eating place, eating house; eatery *and* beanery *and* hashery *and* hash house *and* greasy spoon <all nonformal>; **fast-food restaurant,** hamburger joint <nonformal>; **lunchroom; tearoom,** *bistro* <Fr>; **coffee shop; tea shop,** tea-room, tea-garden, teahouse; **lunch counter,** quick-lunch counter; **snack bar,** *buvette* <Fr>, *cantina* <Sp>; milk bar; automat

**cage** NOUNS 1 **place of confinement,** close quarters, not enough room to swing a cat; pound, pinfold *or* penfold; **enclosure,** pen, coop

VERBS 2 **confine, shut in,** shut away, coop in, hem in, fence in *or* up, wall in *or* up, rail in; **shut up, coop up, pen up,** box up, mew up, bottle up, cork up, seal up, **impound;** pen, coop, pound <old>, crib, mew, cloister, immure, cage in, encage; **hold, keep in,** hold *or* keep in custody, keep in detention, constrain, ground, **restrain,** hold in restraint; check, inhibit; restrict

**cagey** ADJS **wary, chary, cagey** <nonformal>, **leery** <nonformal>, **suspicious,** suspecting, **distrustful,** mistrustful, shy

**cajole** VERBS **wheedle, blandish,** palaver; slaver *or* slobber over, beslobber, beslubber

**calamity** NOUNS **disaster, catastrophe,** meltdown, cataclysm, **tragedy; shock, blow,** hard *or* nasty *or* staggering blow

**calculate** VERBS **compute, estimate, reckon, figure,** reckon at, put at, cipher, cast, tally, score; **figure out,** work out, dope out <nonformal>; take account of, figure in *and* figure on <both nonformal>

**calculating** ADJS **scheming, designing, contriving, plotting, intriguing;** manipulatory, **manipulative;** opportunist, **opportunistic;** Machiavellian, Byzantine; **conniving,** connivent <old>, conspiring, collusive

**calf** NOUNS dogie, leppy <both W US>, weaner; heifer, yearling, fatling, stirk <Brit>

**call** NOUNS 1 **cry, shout, yell,** hoot; bawl, bellow, roar; **scream, shriek,** screech, squeal, squall, caterwaul; summons; whistle; moose call, bird call, duck call, hog call, goose call, crow call, hawk call, dog whistle; **bugle call,** trumpet call

2 **visit, social call;** formal visit, duty visit, required visit; look-in

VERBS 3 **cry, shout, yell, holler** <nonformal>, hoot; **bawl, bellow,** roar, roar *or* bellow like a bull; cry *or* yell *or* scream bloody murder *or* blue murder; caterwaul

4 **invite, ask, summon, call in, bid come,** extend *or* issue an invitation

**calligraphy** NOUNS **handwriting, hand, script,** fist <nonformal>, chirography, autography; fine writing, elegant penmanship, **good hand,** fine hand, good fist <nonformal>

**calling** NOUNS **vocation, occupation, business, work, line, line of work,** line of business *or* endeavor, number <nonformal>, walk, **walk of life,** mission, **profession, practice, pursuit, specialty,** specialization, *métier* <Fr>, **trade,** racket *and* game <both nonformal>; **career,** lifework, life's work

**callous** ADJS **calloused, insensitive,** Philistine; **thick-skinned,** pachydermatous; **hard, hard-hearted, hardened,** case-hardened, coarsened, brutalized, indurated, stony, stony-hearted, flint-hearted, flinty, steely, impervious, inured, armored *or* steeled against; **uncontrite,** unabject; untouched, unsoftened, unmelted

**calm** NOUNS 1 **lull,** lull *or* calm before the storm

VERBS 2 calm down, **stabilize, tranquilize, pacify,** mollify, appease, dulcify; **quiet,** hush, still, rest, compose, **lull, soothe,** gentle, rock, cradle, rock to sleep; cool, **subdue,** quell; keep the peace, be the dove of peace, pour oil on troubled waters

ADJS 3 **placid,** quiet, **tranquil, serene,** peaceful; **cool, coolheaded,** cool as a cucumber <nonformal>; philosophical

**camaraderie** NOUNS **fellowship, companionship, comradeship,** colleagueship; comradery, male bonding; community of interest, *esprit de corps* <Fr>

**camouflage** NOUNS 1 **cover, disguise,** protective coloration; **false colors, false front**; smoke screen; masking, dissimilation

VERBS 2 **cover, disguise,** dissimilate, **mask,** dissemble; plain-wrap, wrap in plain brown paper; whitewash <nonformal>; **paper over,** gloss over, varnish, slur over; distract attention from; **obscure,** obfuscate, cloud, throw out a smoke screen; do a cosmetic job on

**camp** NOUNS 1 **encampment,** *Lager* <Ger>; bivouac; barrack *or* **barracks,** casern, *caserne* <Fr>, cantonment, lines <Brit>; hobo jungle *or* camp; detention camp, concentration camp, *Konzentrationslager* <Ger>; campground *or* campsite

2 **vulgarity,** campiness, high *or* low camp; kitsch

3 **party, interest, side; faction,** division, **sect,** wing, splinter, splinter group, breakaway group, offshoot; **political party**

VERBS 4 **encamp,** tent; pitch, **pitch camp,** pitch one's tent, drive stakes <nonformal>; bivouac; go camping, camp out, sleep out, rough it

ADJS 5 **comic, light;** tragicomical, **farcical, slapstick;** camp *or* campy <nonformal>

**campaign** NOUNS 1 war, **drive, expedition,** hostile expedition; **crusade,** holy war, jihad

2 all-out campaign, hard-hitting campaign, hoopla *or* hurrah campaign <nonformal>; **canvass, solicitation;** front-porch campaign; grass-roots campaign; **whistle-stop campaign** <nonformal>; TV *or* media campaign

VERBS 3 **electioneer; stump** *and* take the stump *and* take to the stump *and* stump the country *and* take to the hustings *and* hit the campaign trail *and* **whistle-stop** <all nonformal>

**camp follower** NOUNS **follower,** hanger-on, satellite, creature, lackey, flunky, stooge <nonformal>, jackal, minion, myrmidon; yes-man <nonformal>, sycophant

**canal** NOUNS **trench, trough, channel, ditch,** dike <old>, fosse, cut, gutter, kennel <Brit>

**cancel** VERBS **nullify,** void, abrogate, annul, tear up, repeal, revoke, negate, invalidate, **undo,** cancel out, bring to naught, put *or* lay to rest; strike out, cross out, scratch, scratch out, rule out;

blue-pencil; **delete** *or* dele, kill; write off; expunge, censor, censor out, blank out

**cancer** NOUNS **growth,** neoplasm; **tumor,** intumescence; malignant tumor, malignant growth, metastatic tumor, sarcoma, carcinoma; **blight,** blast; canker

**cancerous** ADJS tumorous; malignant; **carcinogenic,** tumorigenic

**candid** ADJS **frank, sincere,** genuine, ingenuous, frankhearted; **open,** openhearted, transparent, open-faced; artless; **straightforward, direct,** up-front *and* straight <both nonformal>, **forthright,** downright, straight-out <nonformal>; plain, broad, round; **unreserved,** unrestrained, unconstrained, unchecked; unguarded, uncalculating; free; **outspoken, plain-spoken,** free-spoken, free-speaking, free-tongued; explicit, unequivocal; **blunt,** bluff, brusque; heart-to-heart

**candidate** NOUNS **aspirant,** hopeful *and* political hopeful *and* wannabee <all nonformal>, office seeker *or* hunter, baby kisser <nonformal>; running mate; leading candidate, head of the ticket *or* slate; **dark horse;** stalking-horse; favorite son; presidential timber

**candor** NOUNS **candidness, frankness,** plain dealing; sincerity, genuineness, authenticity; ingenuousness; artlessness; **openness,** openheartedness; freedom, freeness; **unreserve,** unrestraint, unconstraint; **forthrightness, directness, straightforwardness; outspokenness,** plain speaking; **bluntness,** bluffness, brusqueness

**candy** NOUNS **sweets,** sweet stuff, **confectionery; sweet; confection**

**cane** NOUNS 1 **staff,** stave; **stick, walking stick,** handstaff, shillelagh; Malacca cane
2 rush, reed, bamboo

**cannibal** NOUNS **man-eater,** anthropophagite

**cannon** NOUNS **artillery,** cannonry, ordnance, engines of war, Big Bertha, howitzer

**canny** ADJS **cunning, crafty, artful, wily,** callid <old>, guileful, **sly,** insidious, supple <Scots>, **shifty,** pawky <Brit>, arch, **smooth, slick** *and* slick as a whistle <both nonformal>, **foxy, shrewd,** knowing, sharp, razor-sharp

**canon** NOUNS 1 **rule, law, maxim,** dictum, moral, moralism; **norm, standard;** formula, form; rule of action *or* conduct, moral precept; commandment, *mitzvah* <Heb>; **guideline,** ground rule, rubric, protocol, working rule, working principle, standard procedure; guiding principle
2 **literary works, complete works, oeuvre, literary canon, author's canon, body of knowledge,** corpus, body of learning, store of knowledge, system of knowledge; literature of a field, publications; bibliography

**cant** NOUNS 1 **hypocrisy,** hypocriticalness; Tartuffery, Tartuffism, Pecksniffery, pharisaism, **sanctimony**, sanctimoniousness, religiosity, false piety; mummery, snuffling <old>, **mouthing;** sweet talk *and* soft soap <both nonformal>
2 **jargon, slang, argot, patois, patter, vernacular;** vocabulary, phraseology

**cantankerous** ADJS **perverse, contrary, wrongheaded, wayward, froward, difficult,** cross-grained, feisty, ornery <nonformal>; sullen, sulky, stuffy; irascible; bloody-minded <Brit>, contrary, crosswise

**canter** NOUNS 1 lope; **trot,** extended trot, dogtrot, jog trot
VERBS 2 amble, pace, tittup, lope

**cantilever** NOUNS **overhang, overhanging,** impendence *or* impendency, **projection,** beetling, jutting

**canvass** NOUNS 1 **survey, inquiry, questionnaire,** questionary; exit poll; **poll, public-opinion poll,** opinion poll *or* survey, statistical survey, opinion sampling
VERBS 2 go to the voters *or* electorate, solicit votes, ring doorbells; shake hands and kiss babies

**canyon** NOUNS **ravine, gorge,** box canyon, *arroyo* <Sp>, barranca, bolson, coulee, gully, gulch, combe <Brit>, dingle, rift, rift valley, kloof, donga, graben, gully, draw, wadi, basin, cirque, corrie, hanging valley

**cap** NOUNS 1 **headdress,** headgear, headwear, headclothes, headtire; **millinery;** headpiece, **chapeau, hat;** lid <nonformal>
2 top; **crown, tip,** point, spire, pitch; upper extremity, highest point, very top
3 **cover, lid, top, screw-top;** operculum; stopper
VERBS 4 **top,** put the lid on, cork, stopper, plug; roof, roof in *or* over

5 crown, climax, culminate; **give the finishing touches** *or* **strokes,** put the finishing touches *or* strokes on, finalize, put the icing on the cake

**capable** ADJS **competent, able, efficient, qualified, fit, fitted, suited, worthy; equal to, up to;** up to snuff <nonformal>, up to the mark <nonformal>, *au fait* <Fr>; well-qualified, well-fitted, well-suited

**capacity** NOUNS 1 **ability, capability,** faculty, facility, fitness, qualification, talent; mental capacity, **mentality,** caliber, reach *or* compass *or* scope of mind
2 **volume, content,** holding capacity, cubic footage *or* yardage etc, accommodation, room, space, measure, limit; gallonage, tankage; poundage, tonnage, cordage; stowage

**caper** NOUNS **prank, trick, practical joke,** waggish trick, *espièglerie* <Fr>, antic, frolic; **monkeyshines** *and* **shenanigans** <both nonformal>; frisk, gambol, dido <nonformal>

**capital** NOUNS 1 **architectural topping,** head, crown, cap; bracket capital; cornice
2 capital city, **seat,** seat of government; **county seat** *or* county site, county town *or* shiretown <Brit>
3 **fund;** moneyed capital; principal, corpus; circulating capital, floating capital; fixed capital, working capital, equity capital, **risk** *or* **venture capital**

**capitalism** NOUNS capitalistic system, **free enterprise,** private enterprise, free-enterprise economy, free-enterprise system, free economy; finance capitalism; *laissez-faire* <Fr>, laissez-faireism

**capitalize** VERBS **finance, back, fund, sponsor, patronize, support,** provide for, provide capital *or* money for, pay for, bankroll <nonformal>, angel <nonformal>, put up the money; subsidize; set up, set up in business

**capital punishment** NOUNS **execution;** legal *or* judicial murder; **hanging,** the gallows, the rope *or* noose; summary execution; **electrocution,** the chair <nonformal>, the hot seat <nonformal>; gassing, the gas chamber; lethal injection; **decapitation,** decollation, beheading, the guillotine, the ax, the block; **shooting,** fusillade, firing squad; **burning,** burning at the stake; stoning, lapidation; defenestration

**capitol** NOUNS **statehouse;** city hall

**capricious** ADJS **whimsical,** freakish, humorsome, vagarious; **fanciful, notional,** fantasied <old>, fantastic *or* fantastical, maggoty, **crotchety,** kinky, harebrained, cranky, flaky <nonformal>, quirky; wanton, wayward, vagrant; **arbitrary, unreasonable,** motiveless; **moody, temperamental;** petulant

**capsize** VERBS **upset,** overset, **overturn,** turn over, turn turtle, upset the boat, keel, keel over *or* up; **sink, founder,** be lost, go down, go to the bottom, go to Davy Jones's locker; scuttle

**capsule** NOUNS 1 **pill,** bolus, **tablet,** lozenge, troche
2 **condensation,** condensed version, digest, **abstract,** epitome, **précis,** nutshell *or* capsule version, capsulization, encapsulation
VERBS 3 **abridge, shorten, condense, cut, clip; summarize,** synopsize, wrap up <nonformal>; capsulize, encapsulate; **put in a nutshell**
ADJS 4 abridged, compressed, condensed, epitomized, digested, abstracted, capsulized, encapsulated

**captivate** VERBS **fascinate, charm,** becharm, spell, spellbind, cast a spell, put under a spell, **beguile, intrigue, enthrall,** infatuate, **enrapture, transport, enravish, entrance, enchant,** witch, **bewitch;** carry away, sweep off one's feet, turn one's head, knock one's socks off <nonformal>

**captivating** ADJS **alluring, fascinating, riveting, charming, glamorous,** exotic, **enchanting,** spellful, spellbinding, **entrancing,** ravishing, **enravishing, intriguing, enthralling,** witching, **bewitching; attractive, interesting, appealing,** dishy <Brit nonformal>, sexy <nonformal>, engaging, taking, eye-catching, catching, fetching, winning, winsome, prepossessing; **seductive,** seducing, **beguiling, enticing, inviting,** come-hither <nonformal>

**captive** NOUNS 1 **prisoner,** *détenu* <Fr>, cageling; arrestee; **convict,** con <nonformal>; **jailbird** <nonformal>, gaolbird <Brit nonformal>, stir bird <nonformal>; **detainee; internee; prisoner of war** *or* POW
ADJS 2 **in subjection, in bondage, in captivity,** in slavery, in bonds, in chains; under the lash, under the heel; **in one's power,** in one's control, in one's hands *or* clutches, in one's pocket, **under one's**

**thumb,** at one's mercy, at one's beck and call

**capture** VERBS 1 **apprehend, collar** <nonformal>, run down, run to earth, **nab** <nonformal>, grab <nonformal>, lay by the heels, take prisoner; **arrest,** place *or* put under arrest, take into custody; pick up *or* take in *or* run in <all nonformal>

**car** NOUNS 1 **automobile, auto,** motorcar, motocar, autocar, **machine,** motor, motor vehicle, motorized vehicle, *voiture* <Fr>

2 <nonformal> **jalopy,** banger, bus, buggy, wheels, tub, tuna wagon, heap, boat, short, crate, wreck, clunker, junker, junkheap, junkpile

**caravan** NOUNS **procession, train, column, line, string, cortege;** cavalcade, motorcade

**carbohydrate** NOUNS carbo *or* carbs <nonformal>, simple carbohydrate, complex carbohydrate; **sugar; starch**

**carbonated** ADJS **bubbly,** burbly, **bubbling,** burbling; **effervescent,** spumescent, **fizzy, sparkling,** *mousseux* <Fr>, *spumante* <Ital>

**carbuncle** NOUNS pock, furuncle, boil, wen

**carcinogenic** ADJS tumorous; cancerous, malignant; tumorigenic

**cardholder** NOUNS **member,** affiliate, belonger, insider, initiate, card-carrier, card-carrying member

**cardinal** ADJS **principal,** paramount, **foremost,** headmost, **leading, dominant,** crowning, capital; central, focal, prime, **primary,** primal, first; **preeminent,** supereminent

**cardsharp** NOUNS **cheat, cheater; skillful gambler, sharp, shark,** sharper, dean *and* professor *and* river gambler *and* dice gospeller *and* sharpie <all nonformal>; cardshark, cardsharper; **card counter**

**care** NOUNS 1 **custody,** custodianship, keep <old>, **keeping, change, ward,** guarding, hold, protective *or* preventive custody; protection, safekeeping; **support, maintenance, nurture, fostering,** nurturance, nourishment, mothering, parenting, rearing, fosterage, fostercare, **caring,** care-giving, tender loving care *or* TLC <nonformal>

2 **caution, cautiousness;** slowness to act *or* commit oneself *or* make one's move; **heed, solicitude; carefulness, heedfulness,** mindfulness, regardfulness, thoroughness; paying mind *or* attention

VERBS 3 **mind, heed,** reck, think, consider, regard, pay heed to, take heed *or* thought of; **take an interest,** be concerned; **pay attention**

**careen** VERBS **list, heel,** tilt, tip, cant, heave *or* lay down, stagger, totter, trip, flounder; set on its beam ends, set on its ears

**career** NOUNS lifework, life's work

**carefree** ADJS **lighthearted,** light, lightsome; **buoyant,** corky <nonformal>, resilient; **jaunty,** perky, **debonair,** free and easy; **breezy,** airy, without care, *sans souci* <Fr>

**careful** ADJS 1 **heedful, regardful, mindful, thoughtful, considerate, caring,** solicitous, loving, tender, curious <old>; circumspect; **attentive**; **cautious**

2 **economical, thrifty, frugal,** economic, unwasteful, conserving, **saving,** economizing, spare, **sparing; prudent,** prudential, provident, forehanded

**caregiver** NOUNS **nurse,** sister *or* nursing sister <both Brit>; hospice caregiver; practical nurse; registered nurse *or* RN; steward, **keeper, caretaker,** warder <Brit>, attendant

**careless** ADJS **heedless, unheeding, unheedful, disregardful,** disregardant, regardless, **unsolicitous, uncaring;** tactless, respectless, **thoughtless, unthinking, inconsiderate,** untactful, undiplomatic, mindless of, **unmindful,** forgetful, oblivious; **reckless**; **indifferent**; perfunctory, cursory, casual, offhand; **lax, slack, loose,** relaxed; imprecise, sloppy <nonformal>, slipshod; remiss, negligent; indifferent

**caress** NOUNS 1 gentle *or* tentative contact, brush, nudge, kiss, rub, graze

VERBS 2 **pet,** pat; feel *or* feel up <nonformal>, **fondle,** dandle, coddle, cocker, cosset; pat on the head *or* cheek, chuck under the chin

**caretaker** NOUNS **guardian, warden,** governor; **custodian,** steward, **keeper,** warder <Brit>, attendant; **curator,** conservator; janitor; castellan

**cargo** NOUNS payload; lading, load; freight, charge, burden; payload

**caricature** NOUNS 1 **burlesque, lampoon,** squib, **parody, satire, farce,**

mockery, imitation, wicked imitation *or* pastiche, takeoff <nonformal>, **travesty; cartoon**
VERBS 2 **misrepresent,** overstate, exaggerate, overdraw, blow up, blow out of all proportion; travesty, parody, burlesque

**caring** NOUNS 1 **sympathy, fellow feeling, sympathetic response,** responsiveness, relating, warmth, concern; **empathy,** identification; involvement, sharing; pathos; charity, *caritas* <L>, brotherly love, Christian love, agape, loving concern
2 **nurture, fostering,** nurturance, nourishment, nutriture <old>, mothering, parenting, rearing, fosterage, fostercare, **care,** care-giving
ADJS 3 regardful, mindful, thoughtful, considerate, solicitous, loving, tender; circumspect; **attentive**

**carnage** NOUNS **massacre, bloodbath, decimation,** saturnalia of blood; **mass murder, mass destruction**

**carnal** ADJS 1 carnal-minded, fleshly, bodily, physical; Adamic, fallen, lapsed, postlapsarian; animal, animalistic; brutish, brutal, brute; bestial, beastly, beastlike; Circean; coarse, gross; swinish; orgiastic; earthy, unspiritual, nonspiritual, material, materialistic
2 **lascivious, lecherous, sexy, salacious, sexual, lustful,** ithyphallic, **hot,** horny *and* sexed-up *and* hot to trot <all nonformal>; prurient, itching, itchy <nonformal>; concupiscent, libidinous, randy, horny <nonformal>, lubricious

**carnival** NOUNS **festival, fair;** kermis; *Oktoberfest* <Ger>; Mardi Gras; Saturnalia; **amusement park,** Tivoli, fun fair; fairground

**carnivorous** ADJS **flesh-eating, meat-eating,** omophagous, predacious

**carom** VERBS **rebound,** resile; ricochet, cannon *and* cannon off <both Brit>

**carouse** VERBS **go on a spree; go on a binge** *or* **drunk** *or* **toot** *or* **bat** *or* **bender** <nonformal>, **spree, revel,** roister, wassail, debauch, paint the town red <nonformal>

*eat, drink, and be merry*
BIBLE

**carousel** NOUNS merry-go-round, roundabout, ride, whirligig, whip, flying horses

**carp** VERBS **pick** *or* **pull** *or* **tear to pieces; tear down, cavil,** quibble, **nitpick,** pick nits, pettifog

**carpet** NOUNS **rug,** floor cover *or* covering; carpeting, wall-to-wall carpet *or* carpeting

**carpetbagger** NOUNS **defrauder,** shyster *and* pettifogger <both nonformal>; land shark, land pirate, land grabber

**carping** NOUNS **faultfinding,** taking exception, caviling, pettifogging, quibbling, captiousness, niggling, nitpicking, pestering, nagging; hypercriticism, hairsplitting

**carriage** NOUNS 1 **look, air, mien,** demeanor, bearing, port, posture, stance, poise, presence
2 **vehicle, conveyance,** carrier, means of carrying *or* transporting, means of transport, medium of transportation

**carrier** NOUNS 1 vector, biological vector, mechanical vector; Typhoid Mary
2 conveyer; transporter, hauler, carter, wagoner, drayman, shipper, trucker, common carrier, truck driver; letter carrier; cupbearer, Ganymede, Hebe; **dispatch-bearer,** nuncio <old>, **courier,** diplomatic courier, **runner,** express <Brit>, dispatch-rider, pony-express rider, *estafette* <Fr>; bicycle *or* motorcycle messenger

**carry** VERBS bear, pack, tote *and* lug <both nonformal>, manhandle

**carry on** VERBS 1 **misbehave,** get into mischief; **act up**

2 <nonformal> **kick up a row,** kick up a shindy *or* a fuss *or* a storm, piss up a storm, **raise the devil,** raise the deuce *or* dickens, raise a rumpus *or* a storm, raise a ruckus, raise Cain, **raise hell,** raise sand, raise the roof, whoop it up, hell around, horse around *or* about; go on, maffick <Brit>; **cut up,** cut up rough, **roughhouse**

3 **continue,** keep *or* stay with it, keep *or* stay at it; **go on,** go along, **keep on,** keep on keeping on, keep going, see it through, stay on, hold on, hold one's way *or* course *or* path, hold steady, slog on, plug away <nonformal>

**cart** NOUNS oxcart, horsecart, ponycart, dogcart; dumpcart; **handcart;** jinrikisha, ricksha

**carte blanche** NOUNS blank check <nonformal>, **full authority,** full power, free hand, open mandate; no holds barred; rope, long rope *or* tether, rope enough to hang oneself

**cartel** NOUNS **combination,** combine, **amalgamation, consolidation, alliance,** affiliation, **association,** hookup <nonformal>; **synthesis,** syncretism, syneresis; **conspiracy,** cabal

**cartographer** NOUNS mapmaker, mapper; chorographer, topographer, oceanographer

**carve** VERBS **shape,** whittle, cut, chisel, hew, hew out; **slice,** carve up, slice up, **cut up,** cut *or* slice the pie *or* melon <nonformal>

**Casanova** NOUNS **libertine, swinger** <nonformal>, **profligate, rake,** rakehell, rip <nonformal>, **roué,** wanton, womanizer, cocksman <nonformal>, walking phallus, debauchee, rounder <old>, **wolf** <nonformal>, woman chaser, skirt chaser <nonformal>, gay dog, gay deceiver, gallant, philanderer, lover-boy <nonformal>, lady-killer, Lothario, Don Juan

**cascade** NOUNS 1 **waterfall, cataract,** fall, **falls, Niagara,** force <Brit>, linn <Scots>, sault; nappe; watershoot
VERBS 2 **overflow,** inundate, engulf, swamp, sweep, whelm, overwhelm, **flood,** deluge, submerge

**case** NOUNS 1 **lawsuit, court case,** cause, cause in court, legal case
2 casing, encasement; **sheath,** sheathing; **box,** crate, **package,** container
3 **instance,** relevant instance, typical example *or* case, case in point, object lesson

**cash** NOUNS 1 **money, currency, legal tender, medium of exchange,** circulating medium, sterling <Brit>, hard cash, cold cash
VERBS 2 cash in <nonformal>, liquidate, convert into cash

**cashier** NOUNS 1 financial officer, bursar, purser, purse bearer, cashkeeper
VERBS 2 **dismiss, discharge, expel,** drum out, disemploy, outplace, separate forcibly *or* involuntarily, **lay off,** suspend, surplus, furlough, turn off, make redundant, riff <nonformal>, turn out, release, let go, let out, remove, displace, replace, strike off the rolls, give the pink slip

**casino** NOUNS 1 **ballroom, dance hall,** dancery; dance palace
2 **gambling house, house,** store *and* shop <both nonformal>, gaming house, betting house, betting parlor, gambling den, gambling hall; luxurious casino

**casket** NOUNS **coffin,** burial case, box, kist <Scots>; wooden kimono *or* overcoat <nonformal>; **sarcophagus;** mummy case

**Cassandra** NOUNS **pessimist, cynic,** malist, nihilist; killjoy, gloomy Gus *and* calamity howler *and* worrywart <all nonformal>, seek-sorrow, Job's comforter, prophet of doom, Eeyore

*one who is always building dungeons in the air*
JOHN GALSWORTHY

**cassette** NOUNS **recording,** tape recording; tape, tape cassette; tape cartridge, cartridge; video-cassette recorder *or* VCR

**cast** NOUNS 1 cast of characters, characters, persons of the drama, *dramatis personae* <L>; supporting cast
2 **disposition, bent, turn, bias,** slant, warp, twist
VERBS 3 **throw, fling, sling, pitch, toss, hurl, heave, chuck,** chunk *and* peg <both nonformal>, lob, shy, fire, burn, pepper <nonformal>, launch, dash, let fly, let go, let rip, let loose

**caste** NOUNS **rank, standing, level,** footing, **status,** station; **social class,** social group *or* grouping, status group, accorded status, social category, order, grade, estate, rank

**castle** NOUNS **mansion,** palatial residence, stately home <Brit>; **villa, château,** *hôtel* <Fr>, tower; **stronghold,** hold, safehold, fasthold, strong point, **fastness,** keep, ward, **bastion,** donjon, **citadel**

**castoff** NOUNS **reject,** throwaway, castaway, rejectamenta <pl>

**castrate** VERBS geld, emasculate, eunuchize, unman, neuter, spay, fix *or* alter <both nonformal>, unsex, deball <nonformal>

**casual** ADJS **nonchalant, blasé, indifferent,** unconcerned; **offhand, relaxed, laid-back** *and* throwaway <both nonformal>; **easygoing,** easy, free and easy, devil-may-care, lackadaisical, *dégagé* <Fr>; perfunctory, cursory, offhand; **occasional, incidental**

**cat** NOUNS **feline,** pussy *and* **puss** *and* **pussycat** <all nonformal>, tabby, grimalkin; house cat; **kitten, kitty** *and* kitty-cat <both nonformal>; **tomcat,** tom; mouser; ratter; Cheshire cat, Chessycat <nonformal>; Maltese cat; tiger cat, tabby cat; tortoise-shell cat, calico cat; alley cat

**cataclysm** NOUNS **debacle, disaster, catastrophe; breakup,** breaking up; **upheaval, convulsion; tragedy**

**catacombs** NOUNS **tomb, sepulcher; crypt, vault,** burial chamber; ossuary *or* ossuarium

**catalog** NOUNS 1 **description,** specification, particularization, details, itemization, cataloging; **narration**
VERBS 2 **classify,** class, **categorize,** sort, sort out, sift, group, factor, winnow, thrash out; **list, enumerate, itemize, tabulate,** tally

**catalyst** NOUNS **alterant,** alterer, alterative, **agent,** catalytic agent; **instigator, inciter,** exciter, urger; **provoker,** *provocateur* <Fr>, *agent provocateur* <Fr>

**catapult** NOUNS 1 arbalest, ballista, trebuchet
VERBS 2 **throw, fling, sling,** launch, let fly, let go, let rip, let loose

**catastrophe** NOUNS **debacle, disaster, cataclysm; disaster, calamity,** meltdown, **tragedy; shock, blow,** hard *or* nasty *or* staggering blow

**catch** NOUNS 1 **trick, artifice,** gimmick, joker; curve ball; **Catch-22,** kicker, zinger, snag <all nonformal>; fly in the ointment
2 **good thing,** find <nonformal>, *trouvaille* <Fr>; godsend, windfall; conquest
VERBS 3 **trap,** entrap, gin, catch out, catch in a trap; **ensnare, snare,** hook, **hook in,** sniggle, noose; inveigle

**catchword** NOUNS catch phrase, shibboleth, slogan, cry; **pet expression,** byword, cliché; **buzzword,** vogue word, fad word, in-word; euphemism, **code word**

**catchy** ADJS **melodious,** melodic; fine-toned, **pleasant-sounding,** agreeable-sounding, pleasant, appealing, agreeable, singable; **euphonious** *or* euphonic, **lyric, lyrical,** melic

**catechism** NOUNS creedal *or* doctrinal statement, formulated *or* stated belief; gospel

**categorical** ADJS **classificational, taxonomic** *or* **taxonomical,** typologic *or* typological; **unrestricted,** uncircumscribed, unmitigated, straight, **unreserved,** without reserve

**categorize** VERBS **classify,** class, catalog, sort, sort out, sift, group, factor, winnow, thrash out; weigh, weigh up, **evaluate, judge,** gauge, assess, appraise

**category** NOUNS **class, head, order, division,** branch, set, **group,** grouping, bracket, pigeonhole; **subdivision,** subgroup

**cater to** VERBS **wait on** *or* **upon,** wait on hand and foot, dance attendance, do service, fetch and carry, do the dirty work of, do *or* jump at the bidding of; favor, please, gratify, satisfy; **pamper,** cosset, **coddle,** mollycoddle

**catharsis** NOUNS purgation, abreaction, motor abreaction, psychocatharsis, **emotional release,** relief of tension, outlet; release therapy, acting-out, psychodrama; imaging

**cathartic** NOUNS 1 **laxative, physic, purge, purgative,** aperient, carminative, diuretic
ADJS 2 laxative, purgative, aperient; carminative; diuretic
3 **relieving, easing, alleviative,** alleviating, alleviatory, **mitigative,** mitigating

**catholic** ADJS **universal, all-inclusive,** all-including, **all-embracing,** all-encompassing, all-comprehensive, all-comprehending, all-pervading; **broad-minded,** wide-minded, large-minded, **broad, wide,** wide-ranging, broad-gauged

**catty** ADJS **spiteful,** despiteful; cattish, bitchy <nonformal>; **snide; disparaging, derogatory,** slighting, belittling, minimizing, pejorative, back-biting, catty *and* bitchy <both nonformal>

**caught** ADJS **stuck, fast,** stuck fast, **fixed, transfixed,** fastened, tied, chained, tethered, anchored, moored, held, inextricable; **fascinated,** enthralled, rapt, spellbound, charmed, enchanted, mesmerized, **hypnotized,** fixed, riveted, **arrested,** switched on <nonformal>

**caulk** VERBS **stop, stop up; obstruct, clog,** clog up; **dam,** dam up; stanch, stench <Scots>; chink

**cause** NOUNS 1 **occasion,** antecedents, **grounds,** ground, background, stimulus, base, **basis,** element, principle, factor; **determinant,** determinative; causation, causality, cause and effect; etiology
2 **principle,** interest, issue, burning issue, commitment, faith, great cause, lifework; reason for being, *raison d'être* <Fr>; **movement,** mass movement,

activity; **drive, campaign, crusade;** zeal, passion, fanaticism
VERBS 3 **compel, force, make;** have, cause to; **constrain, bind,** tie, tie one's hands; **restrain**; enforce, **drive,** impel; dragoon, use force upon, force one's hand, hold a pistol *or* gun to one's head

**caustic** ADJS mordant, mordacious, corrosive, corroding; **acrimonious,** acrid, acid, acidic, acidulous, acidulent, acerb, acerbate, acerbic, **bitter,** tart; **sharp,** sharpish, keen, incisive, trenchant, **cutting,** penetrating, piercing, biting, **stinging,** stabbing, **scathing, scorching,** withering, scurrilous, abusive, thersitical, foulmouthed, harsh-tongued

**cauterize** VERBS **burn,** torrefy, **sear; singe,** swinge; brand, burn in; **char,** scorify

**caution** NOUNS 1 **warning,** caveat, **admonition,** monition, admonishment; **notice,** notification; **word to the wise,** *verbum sapienti* <L>, verb sap, enough said
2 **cautiousness;** slowness to act *or* commit oneself *or* make one's move; **care, heed, solicitude; carefulness, heedfulness,** mindfulness, regardfulness, thoroughness; paying mind *or* attention; **guardedness; prudence,** prudentialness, **circumspection, discretion,** canniness <Scots>
VERBS 3 **warn, advise, admonish; give warning,** give fair warning, utter a caveat, address a warning to, put a flea in one's ear <nonformal>, have a word with one, say a word to the wise; tip *and* tip off <both nonformal>; **alert,** warn against, put on one's guard, warn away *or* off; **give the high sign** <nonformal>; **put on alert,** cry havoc, sound the alarm

**cautious** ADJS **careful, heedful, regardful, mindful, thoughtful, considerate, caring,** solicitous, loving, tender, curious <old>; circumspect; **attentive**

**cave** NOUNS 1 **cavern,** cove <Scots>, **hole, grotto,** grot, antre, subterrane; lair; **tunnel, burrow,** warren; subway; bunker, foxhole, dugout, *abri* <Fr>; sewer
VERBS 2 **collapse, cave in,** fall in; fold, fold up; implode; **deflate**

**cavity** NOUNS concavity, concave; **hollow,** hollow shell, shell; **hole, pit, depression, dip,** sink, fold <Brit>; scoop, pocket; **basin,** trough, **bowl, crater**

**cavort** VERBS **frolic, rollick, gambol, frisk, romp, caper,** cut capers <nonformal>, lark about <Brit nonformal>, antic, curvet, caracole, flounce, trip, skip, dance; **cut up** <nonformal>, cut a dido <nonformal>, horse around <nonformal>, fool around, carry on <nonformal>

**cease** NOUNS 1 **cessation, discontinuance,** discontinuation, phaseout, phasedown, scratching *and* scrubbing *and* breakoff <all nonformal>; **desistance,** desinence, surcease, **ceasing,** ending, halting, stopping, termination
VERBS 2 **discontinue, end, stop, halt,** end-stop, terminate, close the books on, close the books, put paid to <Brit>, abort, cancel, scratch *and* scrub <both nonformal>, hold, **quit,** stay, belay <nonformal>; **desist, refrain,** leave off, lay off <nonformal>, give over, **have done with**

**ceaseless** ADJS **endless,** unending, never-ending, without end, **interminable,** nonterminous, nonterminating; **continual,** continuous, steady, **constant, ceaseless,** nonstop, unceasing, neverceasing, **incessant,** unremitting, unintermitting, uninterrupted

**cede** VERBS **surrender,** renounce, abandon, relinquish, give over, hand over

**ceiling** NOUNS **limit, end, extremity,** extreme, **acme,** apogee, climax, **maximum,** max <nonformal>, roof, **peak,** summit, **pinnacle,** crown, top; *plafond* <Fr>, overhead

**celebrate** VERBS **observe, keep, mark,** solemnly mark, **honor; commemorate,** memorialize; **solemnize,** signalize, hallow, mark with a red letter; **make merry;** kill the fatted calf; sound a fanfare, blow the trumpet, beat the drum, fire a salute; sound *or* resound the praises of, ring one's praises, sing the praises of, trumpet; praise to the skies, *porter aux nues* <Fr>

**celebrated** ADJS **notable, noteworthy, remarkable, marked, standout** <nonformal>, of mark, signal; **memorable,** unforgettable, never to be forgotten; striking, telling, salient; **eminent, prominent,** conspicuous, noble, **outstanding, distinguished;** prestigious, esteemed, estimable, reputable; **extraordinary,** *extraordinaire* <Fr>, out of the ordinary, **exceptional, special,** rare

**celebration** NOUNS celebrating; **observance,** formal *or* solemn *or* ritual observance, **solemnization;** marking *or* honoring the occasion; **commemoration,** memorialization, remembrance, memory; jubilee; red-letter day, **holiday**; anniversaries; **festivity; revel**; rejoicing; **ceremony,** rite; religious rites; ovation, triumph; **tribute;** testimonial, testimonial banquet *or* dinner; toast; roast; **salute;** salvo; flourish of trumpets, fanfare, fanfaronade

**celebrity** NOUNS 1 **publicity,** publicness, **notoriety, fame,** famousness, notoriousness, notice, public notice, *réclame, éclat* <both Fr>
2 man *or* woman of mark *or* note, person of note *or* consequence, **notable, notability, luminary, great man** *or* **woman,** master spirit, worthy, name, **big name,** figure, public figure, **somebody; important person, VIP** *and* **standout** <both nonformal>, personage, one in a hundred *or* thousand *or* million etc; **star, superstar,** megastar, hot stuff <nonformal>

**celestial** ADJS **heavenly,** heavenish; **paradisal, paradisaic, paradisaical,** paradisiac, paradisiacal, paradisic, paradisical; supernal, ethereal; Elysian, Olympian

**celibate** ADJS **monastic,** monachal, **monkish;** misogamic, misogynous; sexually abstinent *or* continent, abstinent, abstaining

**cellar** NOUNS cellarage, **basement;** subbasement; wine cellar, potato cellar, storm cellar, cyclone cellar; coal bin *or* hole, hold, hole, bunker

**cemetery** NOUNS **graveyard, burial ground** *or* **place,** burying place *or* ground, *campo santo* <Ital>, boneyard *and* bone orchard <both nonformal>, burial yard, necropolis, polyandrium, **memorial park,** city *or* village of the dead; **churchyard,** God's acre; **potter's field;** Golgotha, Calvary

**censor** NOUNS 1 **critic**, captious critic, criticizer, **nitpicker** <nonformal>, smellfungus, belittler, censurer, carper, caviler, quibbler, petti-fogger
VERBS 2 bowdlerize, expurgate; bleep *or* bleep out <nonformal>, silence; sit on *and* sit down on *and* slap *or* smack down <all nonformal>

**censorship** NOUNS expurgation, bowdlerization, censoring; blackout <nonformal>; bleeping *or* bleeping out <nonformal>

**censure** VERBS **condemn, damn, doom; denounce,** denunciate; reprimand, **give a black eye** <nonformal>, give a black mark, put in one's bad *or* black books; pick holes in, pick to pieces

**census** NOUNS head count; population statistics, demography, demographics; **numeration, enumeration, numbering, counting,** tallying

**centennial** NOUNS **anniversary,** centenary; centennium

**center** NOUNS 1 **middle ground,** neutral ground *or* territory, center; meeting ground, interface; **middle of the road**
2 **moderate,** moderatist, moderationist, **centrist,** middle-of-the-roader <nonformal>; independent
3 nucleus, focus, kernel, **core, pith,** meat; **heart,** soul, heart and soul, spirit, sap, marrow
VERBS 4 **converge, come together,** approach, run together, **meet,** unite, connect, merge; centralize, **come to a center;** center on *or* around, concentralize, concenter, **concentrate**

**central** ADJS centric, **middle**; centermost, middlemost, **midmost; equidistant;** centralized, concentrated; axial, **essential,** fundamental, indispensable, basic, substantive, bedrock, material; **central,** focal, **pivotal,** key; core, nuclear; equidistant, halfway, midway, equatorial

**centrifuge** VERBS **separate, whirl, spin,** spin like a top *or* teetotum, whirl like a dervish; centrifugate

**centrist** NOUNS **moderate,** moderatist, moderationist, middle-of-the-roader, neutral, compromiser

**ceramics** NOUNS **pottery;** potting; **ceramic ware**

**cereal** NOUNS 1 breakfast food, dry cereal, hot cereal
2 cereal plant, farinaceous plant, **grain,** corn <Brit>

**cerebral** ADJS **mental, intellectual, rational, reasoning, thinking,** noetic, conceptive, conceptual, phrenic

**ceremonious** ADJS **ceremonial; red-carpet; ritualistic, ritual;** hieratic, hieratical, sacerdotal, liturgic; **grave, solemn**; **pompous**; **stately**; well-mannered; **conventional,** decorous

**ceremony** NOUNS 1 **formality, form, formalness;** ceremonial, **ceremoniousness; the red carpet; ritual,** rituality;

**dignity,** gravity, *gravitas* <L>, weighty dignity, staidness, reverend seriousness, **solemnity**; **pomp**
2 **rite, ritual,** rituality, **liturgy,** holy rite; order of worship; observance, ritual observance; **sacrament,** sacramental

**certain** ADJS **sure,** sure-enough <nonformal>; bound; **positive, absolute, definite,** perfectly sure, apodictic; decisive, conclusive; clear, clear as day, clear and distinct, unequivocal, unmistakable, unambiguous, nonambiguous, univocal; **necessary,** determinate, ineluctable, predetermined, predestined, **inevitable**; **true**

**certainty** NOUNS 1 **certitude,** certainness, **sureness,** surety, **assurance, assuredness,** certain knowledge; **positiveness, absoluteness, definiteness,** dead *or* moral *or* absolute certainty; unequivocalness, unmistakableness, unambiguity, nonambiguity, univocity, univocality; **infallibility,** infallibilism, inerrability, inerrancy; **necessity,** determinacy, determinateness, noncontingency, Hobson's choice, ineluctability, predetermination, predestination, **inevitability**; **truth**; **proved fact,** probatum

2 <nonformal> **sure thing,** dead certainty, dead-sure thing, sure bet, sure card, aces wired, cinch, lead-pipe cinch, dead cinch, lock, mortal lock, shoo-in, open-and-shut case

**certificate** NOUNS certification, **ticket; authority,** authorization; **credential, voucher, warrant,** warranty, testimonial; note; **affidavit,** sworn statement, notarized statement, deposition, witness, attestation, *procès-verbal* <Fr>; **visa,** *visé* <Fr>; **bill of health,** clean bill of health; navicert <Brit>; **diploma,** sheepskin <nonformal>; certificate of proficiency, testamur <Brit>; birth certificate, death certificate

**certify** VERBS substantiate, **verify, ratify, endorse,** sign off on, second, support, **confirm, validate, authenticate, accept,** give the nod *or* the green light *or* the go-ahead *or* the OK <all nonformal>, give a nod of assent, give one's imprimatur, permit, give permission, **approve**; sanction, **authorize,** warrant, vouch for, accredit; **sign,** undersign, sign on the dotted line, put one's John Hancock on <nonformal>, initial, put one's mark *or* X *or* cross on; **set one's hand and seal**

**cesspool** NOUNS sump, cesspit, septic tank; bilge *or* bilges; **sewer,** drain, *cloaca* and *cloaca maxima* <both L>

**chafe** VERBS 1 **pain,** gall, fret, rasp, rub, grate; gnaw, grind; fester, rankle <old>
2 **be impatient,** hardly wait; itch to, burn to; **champ at the bit, pull at the leash,** not be able to sit down *or* stand still; **fret, fuss,** squirm; **stew,** sweat, sweat and stew, get into a dither, get into a stew <nonformal>, work oneself into a lather *or* sweat <nonformal>, get excited

**chagrin** NOUNS **distress; embarrassment, abashment, discomfiture,** egg on one's face <nonformal>, disconcertion, disconcertment, discountenance, discomposure, disturbance, confusion; **humiliation, shame,** shamefacedness, mortification, red face

**chain** NOUNS 1 **series, succession, connection, concatenation,** catenation, catena, chaining, linkup, articulation, reticulation, nexus
2 **curb, check,** countercheck, arrest, **stay, stop,** damper, holdback; **brake,** clog, drag, drogue, remora; shackle, fetter, trammel
VERBS 3 **bind, restrain,** put the clamps on, **strap,** lash, pinion, fasten, secure, make fast; **hamper, trammel,** entrammel; rope; enchain; **shackle, fetter, manacle,** gyve, **put in irons**

**chair** NOUNS 1 **chairman,** chairwoman, convener <Brit>, speaker, presiding officer
VERBS 2 **officiate; preside,** preside over, preside at the board; occupy the chair

**challenge** NOUNS 1 **dare,** double dare; fighting words; **defy** *or* defi; gage, gage of battle, gauntlet, glove, chip on one's shoulder, slap of the glove, invitation *or* bid to combat
VERBS 2 dare, defy, fly in the teeth of, throw down the gauntlet, ask for trouble, start something, do something about it
3 **dispute,** call in question; **demur, scruple,** boggle, dig in one's heels; contest; cast doubt on, greet with skepticism, keep one's eye on, treat with reserve, bring *or* call into question, raise a question, throw doubt upon, awake a doubt *or* suspicion

4 **contend, vie, compete with** *or* **against, vie with,** enter into competition with, give a run for one's money

**challenging** ADJS **provocative, provoking,** piquant, **exciting,** prompting, **rousing, stirring, stimulating, defiant,** defying

**chamber** NOUNS 1 **compartment,** space, enclosed space; **cavity,** hollow, hole, concavity; **cell, crypt, vault**
2 **bedroom, boudoir,** sleeping chamber, **bedchamber,** cubicle, cubiculum
3 **council,** conclave, *concilium* <L>, deliberative *or* advisory body, **assembly;** deliberative assembly, consultative assembly; house

**champion** NOUNS 1 champ <nonformal>, title-holder, world champion; **record holder,** world-record holder; laureate; medal winner, Olympic medal winner, medalist, award winner, prizeman, prizetaker, **prizewinner;** hall of famer
2 **defender, advocate; upholder; guardian angel, supporter**; vindicator, apologist; **protector**; paladin; **justifier,** proponent
VERBS 3 **safeguard, protect**; stand by the side of; **advocate,** go to bat for <nonformal>, espouse, join *or* associate oneself with, stand *or* stick up for, speak up for, contend for, speak for, argue for, urge reasons for, put in a good word for

**chance** NOUNS 1 happenstance, hap; **luck;** good luck *or* fortune, serendipity, happy chance, dumb luck <nonformal>, rotten *and* tough luck <both nonformal>; **fortune,** fate, **destiny,** whatever comes, *moira* <Gk>, lot; **fortuity, randomness,** fortuitousness, adventitiousness, flip of a coin, the breaks <nonformal>, run of luck, the luck of the draw, the way the cards fall, the way the cookie crumbles *or* the ball bounces <both nonformal>

*heedless hap*
SPENSER

VERBS 2 **take chances, take a chance, risk, gamble,** hazard, press *or* push one's luck, **run the chance** *or* **risk** *or* **hazard;** risk one's neck, run a risk, go out on a limb, stick one's neck out<nonformal>, **expose oneself,** bare one's breast, lower one's guard, **lay oneself open to,** leave oneself wide open, open the door to, let oneself in for; **tempt Providence** *or* **fate,** forget the odds, **defy danger,** skate on thin ice, dance on the razor's edge, put one's head in the lion's mouth, throw caution to the wind
ADJS 3 chancy <nonformal>, dicey <Brit nonformal>, **risky** <nonformal>; **fortuitous, accidental,** aleatory

**change** NOUNS 1 **alteration, modification; variation,** variety, difference, diversity, diversification; **deviation,** diversion, aberrance *or* aberrancy, **divergence; switch, switchover, changeover, turn,** turnabout, about-face, **reversal,** flip-flop <nonformal>
VERBS 2 **fluctuate, vary; shift; alternate, vacillate,** oscillate, pendulate, waffle <Brit nonformal>, blow hot and cold <nonformal>; ebb and flow, wax and wane; go through phases, waver, shuffle, swing, sway, wobble, wobble about, flounder, stagger, teeter, totter, **seesaw,** back and fill, turn, blow hot and cold
3 **change over,** switch *and* switch over <both nonformal>, **shift; transform,** transmute; **change into, turn into, become,** resolve into, assimilate to, change one's tune, sing a different tune, dance to another tune

**changeable** ADJS **alterable,** alterative, modifiable; mutable, permutable, impermanent, transient, **transitory; variable,** checkered, ever-changing, many-sided, kaleidoscopic; **movable,** mobile, motile; plastic, malleable, rubbery, fluid; **inconstant, shifting,** uncertain, inconsistent; whimsical, **capricious, fickle**, off-again-on-again; **erratic, eccentric,** freakish; volatile, giddy, dizzy, ditzy <nonformal>, scatterbrained, mercurial, moody, flighty, impulsive, impetuous

**change of life** NOUNS **menopause,** climacteric, grand climacteric

**channel** NOUNS 1 **conduit, duct,** canal, course; **way, passage, passageway;** trough, troughway, troughing; tunnel; ditch, trench; adit; ingress, entrance; egress, exit; **stream**
2 **informant, informer, source,** news source, teller, interviewee, enlightener; the grapevine
VERBS 3 **conduct, convey,** put through; pipe, funnel, siphon; trench; direct; **guide, steer, drive, run** <nonformal>; herd, shepherd

**chant** NOUNS 1 **refrain,** burden, undersong, chorus, bob; versicle
VERBS 2 intone, intonate; **croon**

**chaos** NOUNS **formlessness,** confusion, messiness, mess, muddle, orderlessness, untidiness; **anarchy,** anarchism; **disorderliness, unruliness,** misrule, **disorder,** disruption, disorganization, confusion, **turmoil,** primal chaos, tohubohu; **turbulence, turmoil,** upset

**chaotic** ADJS **anarchic, anarchical,** anarchial, anarchistic; **unruly, disorderly,** disorganized; **turbulent, tumultuous, raging,** hellish, **storming,** stormy, **tempestuous,** troublous; **confused, muddled, jumbled,** in a mess

**chaperon** NOUNS 1 duenna; **governess;** escort
VERBS 2 **escort, conduct,** have in tow <nonformal>, marshal, **usher,** shepherd, **guide, lead; convoy,** guard; **squire,** esquire, **attend**

**chaplain** NOUNS **clergyman,** clergywoman, man *or* woman of the cloth, **divine, ecclesiastic, churchman, cleric,** minister, pastor, parson

**chapter** NOUNS **branch, organ, division,** wing, arm, offshoot, **affiliate;** lodge, post; chapel; **local**

**character** NOUNS 1 **letter, written character, sign, symbol,** graph, digraph, grapheme, allograph, alphabetic character *or* symbol, phonetic character *or* symbol
2 **disposition, nature, temper, temperament,** mettle, constitution, complexion *and* humor <both old>, makeup, stamp, type, stripe

**characteristic** NOUNS 1 **peculiarity, singularity,** particularity, specialty, individualism, **character,** nature, **trait,** quirk, point of character, bad point, good point, saving grace, redeeming feature, mannerism, keynote, trick, **feature,** distinctive feature, lineament
ADJS 2 **peculiar, singular,** single, quintessential, intrinsic, unique, qualitative, **distinctive,** marked, distinguished, notable, nameable; appropriate, proper; idiosyncratic, idiocratic, **in character, true to form**

**charade** NOUNS dumb show, **pantomime; riddle, conundrum**

**charge** NOUNS 1 **power, potency** *or* potence, prepotency, **force, might,** mightiness, **vigor,** vitality, vim, push, drive, puissance <old>
2 <nonformal> **kick,** boot, bang, belt, blast, flash, hit, jolt, large charge, rush, upper, lift; jollies
3 **injunction,** commission, **mandate**
4 **dependent, ward,** client, protégé, encumbrance; public charge, ward of the state; foster child
5 **attack, assault,** assailing, assailment; **offense, offensive; aggression;** rush, drive, push <nonformal>
6 **accusation,** accusal, finger-pointing <nonformal>, **complaint,** plaint, count, **blame, imputation,** delation, reproach, **bringing of charges,** laying of charges, bringing to book
7 **fee, dues, toll, charges, demand, exaction,** exactment, scot, shot, scot and lot; duty, tax, task; **burden,** weight, freight, cargo, load, onus
8 **electric** *or* **electrical charge,** positive charge, negative charge; live wire
VERBS 9 **exhilarate, stimulate,** hearten, galvanize, electrify, fire, build a fire under, inflame, warm, kindle, charge up, psych *or* pump up <nonformal>, rouse, arouse, act like a tonic, be a shot in the arm <nonformal>, **pep** *or* snap *or* jazz *or* zip *or* perk up <nonformal>, put pep *or* zip into it <nonformal>
10 **burden,** burthen <old>, **load,** load down *or* up, lade, cumber, **encumber, freight,** tax, handicap, hamper, saddle
11 **command, order, dictate, direct, instruct,** mandate, **bid, enjoin,** commission, call on *or* upon; issue a writ *or* an injunction
12 rush, **rush at, fly at,** run at, dash at, make a dash *or* rush at; tilt at, go full tilt at, make *or* run a tilt at, ride full tilt against; **jump off,** go over the top <nonformal>
13 **accuse,** bring accusation; **press charges, prefer** *or* **bring charges,** lay charges
14 charge to one's account, keep an account with, go on tick <nonformal>, buy on credit, buy on the cuff <nonformal>, buy on the installment plan, buy on time, put on the lay-away plan

**charisma** NOUNS **allure, attraction, interest, charm, glamour, appeal,** magnetism; star quality; personality, leadership, enchantment

**charismatic** ADJS **alluring, persuasive,**

suasive, personable, **winning,** magnetic, charming, enchanting, **attractive, magnetic**

**charitable** ADJS 1 philanthropic, eleemosynary; giving, generous to a fault, liberal, **generous**
2 **tolerant**, tolerating; **indulgent, lenient**, **condoning;** compassionate, sympathetic, sensitive

**charity** NOUNS **benevolence,** benevolentness, benevolent disposition, well-disposedness, **beneficence,** charitableness, **philanthropy; altruism,** philanthropy, philanthropism, almsgiving; **goodwill,** grace, brotherly love, Christian charity *or* love, *caritas* <L>, love of mankind, good will to *or* toward man, love, *agape* <Gk>; **generosity**; giving

**charm** NOUNS 1 **loveableness, likeableness,** lovability, likability, loveliness; attractiveness, desirability, agreeability; **appeal,** allurement; winsomeness, winning ways
2 **spell,** magic spell, glamour, weird *or* cantrip <both Scots>, wanga
3 **amulet, talisman, fetish,** periapt, phylactery; **voodoo, hoodoo,** juju, obeah, mumbo jumbo; **good-luck charm,** good-luck piece, **lucky piece,** rabbit's-foot, four-leaf clover, whammy <nonformal>; love charm, philter; scarab, scarabaeus, scarabee
VERBS 4 **fascinate, captivate,** becharm, spell, spellbind, cast a spell, put under a spell, **beguile, intrigue, enthrall,** infatuate, **enrapture, transport, enravish, entrance, enchant,** witch, **bewitch**

**charmer** NOUNS entrancer, **enchanter,** befuddler, hypnotizer, mesmerizer; **tempter, seducer, enticer,** inveigler, fascinator, tantalizer, teaser; coquette, **temptress,** enchantress, seductress, **siren;** Siren, Circe, Lorelei, Parthenope

**charming** ADJS **delightful, exquisite, lovely; attractive, endearing, engaging, appealing,** prepossessing, heartwarming, sexy <nonformal>, **enchanting,** bewitching, witching, entrancing, enthralling, intriguing, fascinating; **winning,** winsome, taking, fetching

**chart** NOUNS 1 **diagram, plot, blueprint,** graph, bar graph, pie *or* circle graph *or* chart, area graph; flow diagram, flow chart; **map**
VERBS 2 **plot; map, blueprint; diagram,** graph; map out, plot out, **lay out,** set out, mark out; lay off, mark off

**chase** NOUNS 1 **pursuit,** pursuing, pursuance, prosecution <old>; **quest,** seeking, hunting, searching; **following,** follow, follow-up; tracking, trailing, tracking down, dogging, shadowing, stalking; hot pursuit; hue and cry
VERBS 2 **pursue, follow,** go after *or* behind, come after *or* behind, move behind; **shadow** *and* **tail** <both nonformal>, **trail,** trail after, follow in the trail of, camp on the trail of, breathe down the neck of, follow in the wake of

**chasm** NOUNS **gap,** gape, **abyss,** abysm, **gulf,** void; **breach, break,** fracture, rupture

**chassis** NOUNS **frame,** underframe, infrastructure, **skeleton; mounting,** mount

**chaste** ADJS **immaculate, spotless, pure; clean,** squeaky-clean <nonformal>; guiltless, **innocent; abstinent,** abstentious, sexually abstinent, celibate

**chastened** ADJS **subdued, tame,** tamed, broken, housebroken, domesticated; **restrained,** constrained, limited, controlled, tempered, **softened,** hushed, quelled

**chastise** VERBS **correct,** rap on the knuckles, spank, turn over one's knees; **take to task,** give one a tongue-lashing, tonguelash

**chastity** NOUNS **virtue,** virtuousness, honor; **purity,** cleanness, cleanliness; **immaculacy,** immaculateness, spotlessness, stainlessness; sexual innocence, innocence

**chat** NOUNS 1 **talk,** gab *and* jaw-jaw <both nonformal>, blab, **blabber, blather,** blether, blethers <Scots>, clatter, talkee-talkee
VERBS 2 **talk,** gossip, **gab, blab, blabber, blather,** blether, clatter, twaddle, twattle, rattle, clack, natter *and* haver <both Brit>, dither

**château** NOUNS **villa,** *hôtel* <Fr>, **castle**

**chattel** NOUNS 1 **subject, vassal,** liege, liege man, liege subject, homager; **slave,** servant, chattel slave, **bondsman,** bondman, **bondslave,** theow, thrall
2 **property, properties, possessions, holdings,** havings, goods, chattels, goods and chattels, **effects,** household possessions *or* effects, lares and penates

**chatter** NOUNS 1 clack, clacket <nonformal>; racket; conversation; **palaver, prattle, gab** *and* jaw-jaw <both nonfor-

mal>; rapping *and* yakking *and* yakkety-yak <all nonformal>
VERBS 2 **chat, prate, prattle, patter,** palaver, **babble, gab** <nonformal>, natter <Brit>, **gabble, gibble-gabble,** tittle-tattle, **jabber,** gibber, **blab, blabber, blather,** blether, clatter, twaddle, twattle, rattle, clack
3 quake, shake, tremble, shudder, didder <Brit nonformal>; have a chill, have the cold shivers

**chauvinist** NOUNS 1 **patriot;** nationalist; ultranationalist; chauvin, **jingo,** jingoist; patrioteer <nonformal>, flag waver, superpatriot; **bigot, racist, sexist,** male chauvinist, male chauvinist pig *or* MCP <nonformal>, female chauvinist, womanist, **dogmatist,** fanatic
ADJS 2 **chauvinistic,** chauvinist, **jingoistic,** jingoist, jingoish, jingo

**cheap** ADJS 1 shoddy, trashy
2 **stingy, illiberal, ungenerous, chintzy, miserly,** save-all, **tight** *and* narrow <both nonformal>, **closefisted,** closehanded <old>, tightfisted, **penny-pinching**
3 **inexpensive,** unexpensive, **low, low-priced,** frugal, reasonable, sensible, manageable, modest, moderate, affordable, to fit the pocketbook, budget, easy, economy, economical; within means, within reach *or* easy reach; nominal, token; worth the money, well worth the money; cheap *or* good at the price, cheap at half the price
ADVS 4 **cheaply,** on the cheap <Brit nonformal>; **inexpensively,** reasonably, moderately, nominally; **at a bargain,** *à bon marché* <Fr>, for a song *or* mere song <nonformal>, for pennies *or* nickels and dimes *or* peanuts <all nonformal>

**cheapen** VERBS depreciate, devaluate, lower, reduce, **mark down, cut prices, cut,** slash, shave, trim, pare, underprice, knock the bottom out of <nonformal>; devalue, coarsen, vulgarize, drag in the mud; adulterate, water, water down

**cheat** NOUNS 1 **cheater;** two-timer <nonformal>; **swindler, defrauder,** cozener, juggler; **sharper, sharp, confidence man, confidence trickster; cardsharp,** cardsharper
2 chicanery, chicane, **skulduggery** <nonformal>, **trickery,** dodgery, pettifogging, pettifoggery, *supercherie* <Fr>, **artifice,** sleight, machination; **sharp practice, underhand dealing, foul play;** connivery, connivance, collusion, conspiracy, covin <law>

3 <nonformal> **gyp,** diddle, diddling, scam, flimflam flam, ramp <Brit>, scam, snow job, song and dance, number, bill of goods, burn, the business, dipsy-doodle, double cross, fiddle, hosing, the old army game, reaming, suckering, sting

VERBS 4 **victimize, gull,** pigeon, fudge, **swindle, defraud,** practice fraud upon, euchre, **con,** finagle, **fleece,** mulct, fob <old>, **bilk,** cozen, cog <old>, chouse, **cheat out of, do out of,** chouse out of, beguile of *or* out of; deceive; falsify

5 <nonformal> **gyp, clip, scam,** rope in, hose, shave, beat, rook, flam, flimflam, diddle, dipsy-doodle, do a number on, hustle, fuck, screw, have, pull something, pull a trick *or* stunt, give the business, ramp <Brit>, stick, sting, burn, gouge, chisel, hocus, hocus-pocus, play *or* take for a sucker, make a patsy of, do, run a game on, slicker, take for a ride

6 **be promiscuous,** sleep around *and* swing <both nonformal>; **debauch, wanton,** rake, chase women, womanize, whore, sow one's wild oats; **philander; commit adultery,** get a little on the side <nonformal>

**check** NOUNS 1 **restraint, constraint; control, curb,** rein, arrest, arrestation; **retardation,** deceleration, slowing down; clampdown *and* crackdown <both nonformal>, proscription, **prohibition**
2 **negotiable instrument** *or* **paper,** cheque <Brit>; blank check; bank check, teller's check; treasury check; cashier's check, certified check; traveler's check *or* banker's check
VERBS 3 look after; **check out,** scope, scope on *or* out <all nonformal>, check into, check on, check out, nose into, see into; poke about, root around *or* about, scratch around *or* about, cast about *or* around; keep under observation, spy on, have an eye out, keep an eye out, keep an eye on, keep a weather eye on, follow, tail *and* shadow <both nonformal>, stake out
4 **curb, arrest, bridle,** get under con-

trol, rein, snub, snub in; **retard,** slow down, decelerate; **cool** *and* **cool off** *and* **cool down** <all nonformal>; retrench, curtail; **hold** *or* **keep in check, hold at bay,** hold in leash, tie one down, tie one's hands
5 **verify, confirm,** test, prove, audit, **collate,** validate, check up *or* on *or* out <nonformal>, check over *or* through, **double-check,** triple-check, cross-check, recheck, check and doublecheck, check up and down

*make assurance double sure*
SHAKESPEARE

**cheek** NOUNS **brashness, impudence,** insolence; **gall** *and* brass *and* cheek *and* chutzpah <all nonformal>; **temerity,** temerariousness

**cheer** NOUNS 1 **cry, call, shout, yell,** hoot; **whoop, holler** <nonformal>; **hurrah;** burst of applause, peal *or* thunder of applause; **round of applause, hand, big hand; ovation,** standing ovation
2 **cheerfulness,** cheeriness, **good cheer,** cheery vein *or* mood; **happiness**; sanguinity, sanguine humor, euphoric *or* eupeptic mein
VERBS 3 **cry, call, shout, yell, holler** <nonformal>, hoot; **whoop, applaud, acclaim, hail;** clap one's hands, give a hand *or* big hand, have *or* hear a hand *or* big hand for, hear it for <nonformal>; root for <nonformal>, cheer on
4 **gladden, brighten,** put in good humor; **encourage, hearten,** pick up <nonformal>; **inspire,** inspirit, warm the spirits, **raise the spirits,** elevate one's mood, buoy up, boost, give a lift <nonformal>, put one on top of the world *and* on cloud nine <both nonformal>; do the heart good

**cheerful** ADJS **happy, glad, joyful, joyous,** flushed with joy, radiant, beaming, glowing, starry-eyed, sparkling, laughing, smiling, smirking, smirky, chirping, purring, singing, dancing, leaping, capering, **cheerful, gay**

**cheerless** ADJS **pathetic,** affecting, touching, moving, saddening, poignant; comfortless, discomforting, uncomfortable; **desolate,** dreary, joyless, dismal, bleak

**cheesecake** NOUNS **photograph,** pinup <nonformal>, beefcake <nonformal>

**chef** NOUNS **cook,** *cuisinier* or *cuisinière* <Fr>, kitchener, culinarian, culinary artist; **chief cook, head chef,** *chef de cuisine* <Fr>

**cherish** VERBS 1 **hold dear,** hold in one's heart *or* affections, think much *or* the world of, prize, treasure; **admire, regard,** esteem, revere; **adore, idolize,** worship, dearly love, think worlds *or* the world of, love to distraction
2 **foster, nurture,** nourish, mother, care for, lavish care on, feed, parent, rear, sustain, cultivate; take to the bosom

**chestnut** NOUNS **platitude, cliché, saw, old saw, commonplace, banality,** bromide, corn <nonformal>, tired phrase, trite saying, hackneyed *or* stereotyped saying; old joke

**chew** VERBS chew up, chaw <nonformal>, bite into; **masticate,** manducate; ruminate, chew the cud; **bite,** grind, champ, chomp <nonformal>; **munch;** gnash; nibble, **gnaw;** mouth, mumble; gum

**chic** NOUNS 1 **smartness,** elegance
ADJS 2 **well-dressed,** well-groomed, *soignée* or *soigné* <both Fr>, stylish, modish, well-turned, well turned-out, **smart,** elegant; style-conscious, clothes-conscious

**chicanery** NOUNS **trick, artifice, device,** ploy, gambit, stratagem, **scheme,** design, *ficelle* <Fr>, **subterfuge,** blind, **ruse, wile,** chouse <nonformal>, shift, **dodge,** artful dodge, sleight, pass, feint, fetch

**chicken** NOUNS 1 chick, chicky *and* chickabiddy <both nonformal>; **cock, rooster,** chanticleer; **hen,** biddy <nonformal>, partlet; cockerel, pullet; setting hen, brooder, broody hen; capon, poulard
2 **coward,** jellyfish, invertebrate, **weakling,** weak sister <nonformal>, milksop, milquetoast, mouse, **sissy, wimp** <nonformal>, baby, **big baby**
VERBS 3 **lose one's nerve,** lose courage, **get cold feet** <nonformal>, **show the white feather;** falter, boggle, funk <nonformal>; put one's tail between one's legs, back out, funk out <nonformal>, **wimp** *or* **chicken out** <both nonformal>
ADJS 4 **afraid, fearful;** timid, timorous, overtimorous, overtimid, rabbity *and* mousy <both nonformal>; **faint-hearted,** weakhearted, chicken-hearted, henhearted, pigeonhearted; **weak-kneed,** afraid of one's shadow; weak, soft; **wimpy** *or* wimpish <nonformal>

**chide** VERBS **reprove, rebuke, reprimand,** reprehend, put a flea in one's ear, **scold,** rate, **admonish, upbraid,** objurgate, have words with, take a hard line with

**chief** NOUNS 1 **superior, boss,** honcho <nonformal>, commander, **ruler, leader,** dean, *primus inter pares* <L, first among equals>, **master**; higher-up <nonformal>, senior, principal, big shot <nonformal>; chieftain, high chief
ADJS 2 **main, principal,** paramount, **foremost,** headmost, **leading, dominant,** crowning, capital, **cardinal, first, foremost,** front, up-front <nonformal>, **head, principal,** premier, **leading, main,** flagship

**chiefly** ADVS **mainly, in the main,** in chief; dominantly, **predominantly; mostly, for the most part; principally, especially, particularly,** peculiarly; **primarily, in the first place,** first of all, **above all; indeed,** even, more than ever, all the more, *a fortiori* <L>; substantially, essentially, effectually, **for the most part,** almost entirely, for all practical purposes, **virtually;** approximately, nearly, all but; **broadly,** broadly speaking, **roughly,** roughly speaking, as an approximation; **usually, as a rule, ordinarily, commonly, normally,** routinely, as a matter of course, in the usual course; **by and large,** at large, altogether, overall, over the long haul <nonformal>, **all things considered,** taking one thing with another

**child** NOUNS **simple soul,** unsophisticate, naïf, **ingenue, innocent, babe,** baby, newborn babe, babe in the woods, babe in arms, mere child, lamb, dove, angel

**childhood** NOUNS babyhood, **boyhood; girlhood**

**childlike** ADJS **artless, ingenuous, unsophisticated, naive;** born yesterday; **innocent,** innocent as a lamb

**children** NOUNS **young people, youth,** young, **younger generation,** rising *or* new generation, young blood, young fry <nonformal>, *ragazze* <Ital>; tots, childkind; small fry *and* **kids** *and* **little kids** *and* little guys <all nonformal>

**chill** NOUNS 1 **aloofness, remoteness,** coolness, coldness, frigidity, chilliness, iciness, frostiness; cold shoulder
VERBS 2 **discourage; pour** *or* **dash** *or* **throw cold water on,** throw *or* lay a wet blanket on, damp, dampen, demotivate, **cool,** quench, blunt; **refrigerate**

**chilly** ADJS **aloof, standoffish,** offish, standoff, **distant, remote,** withdrawn, removed, detached, Olympian; **cool,** cold, cold-fish, frigid, icy, frosty; shivering, shivery, shaky, dithery; chilled to the bone

**chime** NOUNS 1 **ringing,** tintinnabulation, **pealing, chiming, tinkling,** tingling, **jingling,** dinging, donging; **ring, peal**
VERBS 2 tintinnabulate, **peal,** sound; **toll,** knell, sound a knell; **tinkle,** tingle, **jingle,** ding, dingdong, dong

**china** NOUNS **ceramic ware, ceramics; pottery, crockery; porcelain**

**chink** NOUNS **crack,** cranny, check, craze, chap, **crevice,** fissure, scissure, incision, notch, score, cut, gash, slit, split, **rift,** rent; vulnerable point, **weak link, weak point, soft spot,** heel of Achilles, chink in one's armor

**chintzy** ADJS **stingy, illiberal, ungenerous, miserly,** save-all, **cheap** *and* **tight** *and* narrow <all nonformal>, **near, close, closefisted,** closehanded <old>, tightfisted; messy <nonformal>, mussy <nonformal>, **sloppy** <nonformal>, scraggly, poky, seedy <nonformal>, **shabby,** shoddy, schlocky <nonformal>, lumpen, grubby <nonformal>

**chip** NOUNS 1 **cut,** cutting, clip, clipping, paring, shaving, rasher, snip, snippet, slice, collop, dollop, scoop
VERBS 2 split, check, craze, fissure; scale, exfoliate

**chirp** VERBS **stridulate;** crick, creak, chirk, cheep, peep, pip, chirrup

**chivalry** NOUNS chivalrousness, knightliness; military *or* martial spirit, soldierly quality *or* virtues; **gallantry,** gallantness; courtliness, courtly behavior *or* politeness; *noblesse oblige* <Fr>; errantry, knight-errantry

**choice** NOUNS 1 **selection, election,** preference, decision, **pick, choosing,** free choice; alternativity; co-option, co-optation; **will,** volition, free will; preoption, first choice; the pick; **discrimination**
2 **pick, select, elect, elite,** *corps d'élite* <Fr>, chosen; **cream, flower,** fat; cream of the crop, *crème de la crème* <Fr>, salt of the earth
ADJS 3 **best,** greatest *and* top-of-the-line <both nonformal>, **prime,** optimum, optimal; **select, elect,** elite, **picked,** handpicked; **prize, champion; supreme,** paramount, **unsurpassed,**

unmatched, matchless, **peerless;** quintessential

**choke** VERBS 1 strangle, strangulate, choke off; garrote, **throttle,** burke; **suffocate, stifle, smother, asphyxiate**
2 **overload, overfill,** stuff, crowd, cram, jam, pack, jam-pack, **congest,** constrict, squeeze, squeeze shut; stop up

**choked** ADJS contracted, constricted, choked off, choked up, squeezed shut, strangulated, **obstructed,** infarcted, **blocked; plugged,** plugged up; **clogged,** clogged up; choked up, strangulated, strangled; packed, jammed, bumper-to-bumper <nonformal>, jam-packed, like sardines; **congested,** stuffed up

**choose** VERBS **select, elect,** pick, go with <nonformal>, opt, opt for, co-opt, make *or* take one's choice, make choice of, have one's druthers <nonformal>, use *or* take up *or* exercise one's option; **shop around** <nonformal>, pick and choose

**choosy** ADJS **fastidious, particular, scrupulous, meticulous, conscientious,** exacting, precise, punctilious, spit-and-polish; **sensitive, discriminating**, discriminative; **selective,** picky <nonformal>, choicy <nonformal>; critical

*nothing if not critical*
SHAKESPEARE

**chop** NOUNS 1 **whack, smack, thwack,** smash, dash, swipe, swing, **punch, poke, jab,** dig, drub, thump, pelt, cut, slog
VERBS 2 **sever, dissever,** cut off *or* away *or* loose, shear off, hack through, hack off, ax, amputate; hew, hack, **slash**

**choppy** ADJS **rough, unsmooth; uneven, nonuniform,** irregular, ragged, erose, jerky, jagged, rough, disorderly, unsystematic; **sporadic,** patchy, spotty, scrappy, snatchy, catchy, **broken, disconnected, discontinuous**

**choral** ADJS **vocal,** singing; choric

**chorale** NOUNS **hymn,** hymn of praise, **doxology, psalm, anthem,** motet, canticle; choral fantasy, anthem

**chore** NOUNS 1 **task, work, stint, job,** labor, piece of work, chare, odd job; **assignment, charge,** project, errand, **mission,** commission, **duty,** service, exercise
2 **hard job, tough job** *and* heavy lift <both nonformal>, backbreaker, ballbuster <nonformal>

**chorus** NOUNS 1 general voice, vox pop, *vox populi* <L>, ensemble; agreement, accord, *rapport* <Fr>, concert, consort, **consonance,** unisonance, **unison,** union, oneness, harmony, one *or* single voice
2 **verse, stanza;** burden, bourdon; **refrain,** response

**chosen** NOUNS 1 **choice, pick, select, elect, elite,** *corps d'élite* <Fr>; cream of the crop, *crème de la crème* <Fr>, salt of the earth
ADJS 2 **selected, picked;** select, elect; handpicked, singled-out; **elected,** unanimously elected, elected by acclamation

**chow** NOUNS

<nonformal> **grub,** grubbery, **eats,** chuck, groceries, the nosebag, scarf *or* scoff, tuck, victuals *or* vittles

**chronic** ADJS **confirmed, inveterate, established,** long-established, **fixed, settled, rooted,** thorough; incorrigible, irreversible; **deep-rooted, deep-seated, infixed, ingrained,** fast

**chronicle** NOUNS 1 **chronology, register,** registry, record; **annals,** journal, diary; story, tale, yarn, narrative
VERBS 2 write history, historify; historicize; biograph, biography, biographize; immortalize; **record**

**chronology** NOUNS 1 **history, annals, chronicles,** memorabilia, record; **chronicle, register,** registry, record; journal, diary

**chubby** ADJS **chunky** <nonformal>, **fat,** tubby <nonformal>, dumpy; **squat,** squatty, squattish; **pudgy,** podgy

**chuckle** NOUNS 1 **laugh;** chortle; cackle; **snicker,** snigger, snort
VERBS 2 **laugh,** chortle; cackle; **snicker,** snigger, snort

**chum** NOUNS

<nonformal> **pal, buddy,** bud, buddy-boy, bosom buddy, ace, mate *and* butty <both Brit>

**chummy** ADJS

<nonformal> pally, palsy, palsy-walsy, buddy-buddy

**chump** NOUNS

<nonformal> **sucker, patsy,** pigeon, chicken, fall guy, pushover, mark, easy pickings, boob, schlemiel, sap, saphead, prize sap, easy touch, soft touch

**chunk** NOUNS **lump,** clump, wodge <Brit nonformal>; **bite**

**chunky** ADJS **stubby, thickset, stocky,** blocky, **chubby,** tubby <nonformal>, dumpy; **squat, pudgy,** podgy

**churn** NOUNS 1 **mixer, blender,** beater, agitator, food processor
VERBS 2 **seethe, boil, fume,** foam, simmer, stew, ferment, stir
3 whip, whisk, beat, paddle; work up, shake up, churn up, whip up, beat up; roil, rile <nonformal>

**chutzpah** NOUNS **impudence,** insolence; **gall** *and* brass *and* cheek <all nonformal>; hubris; **temerity,** temerariousness

**cigar** NOUNS seegar <nonformal>; rope *and* stinker <both nonformal>; **cheroot, stogie,** corona, belvedere, Havana, panatella, colorado, trichinopoly; cigarillo

**cigarette** NOUNS

<nonformal>butt, cig, **fag**, coffin nail, cancer stick

**cinch** NOUNS 1 sure success, foregone conclusion, sure-fire proposition <nonformal>; **winner** *and* **natural** <both nonformal>; shoo-in *and* **sure thing** *and* sure bet *and* lead-pipe cinch <all nonformal>; **snap,** pushover, breeze, waltz, duck soup, velvet, picnic, pie, cherry pie, apple pie, cakewalk, piece of cake <all nonformal>
2 VERBS **set at rest;** clinch *and* cinch *and* nail down <all nonformal>; **prove one's point,** make one's case, bring home to, make good, have *or* make out a case

**cinema** NOUNS **motion-picture theater, movie theater,** movie palace, dream palace <nonformal>, **motion picture, movie, film**

**cipher** NOUNS 1 **code; secret writing,** coded message, cryptogram, cryptograph
2 **a nobody, insignificancy,** hollow man, jackstraw <old>, **nonentity,** empty suit *and* nebbish <both nonformal>, a nothing; lightweight, mediocrity

**circa** ADVS **approximately,** nearly, some, about; more or less, *plus ou moins* <Fr>, by and large

**circle** NOUNS 1 **sphere,** hemisphere, orb, **orbit,** ambit; **clique, coterie, set,** ring, group
VERBS 2 **encircle,** ensphere, belt, belt in, zone, cincture, encincture; **girdle,** ring, band

**circuit** NOUNS **route, path, way, itinerary, course,** track, run, line, road; tour; walk, beat, round, **round,** revolution, **circle,** full circle, go-round, **cycle,** orbit, ambit; round trip; **network,** circuit network

**circular** NOUNS 1 **booklet, pamphlet, brochure, chapbook, leaflet, folder, tract**
ADJS 2 **round,** rounded, circinate, annular, annulate ring-shaped, ringlike; **circuitous, roundabout**

**circulate** VERBS **publish, promulgate, propagate,** circularize, **diffuse, disseminate,** distribute, **broadcast,** televise, telecast, videocast, air, **spread,** spread around *or* about, spread far and wide, publish abroad, **spread a report,** launch a rumor, whisper, **rumor about,** whisper *or* buzz about

**circumference** NOUNS **periphery, fringe,** outline, lineaments, border; periphery; **compass,** circumscription

**circumscribe** VERBS **bound,** surround, limit, enclose, divide, separate; **mark off** *or* mark out, stake out, lay off, rope off; **demarcate,** delimit, delimitate, draw *or* mark *or* set *or* lay out boundaries, circle in, hedge in, set the limit, mark the periphery; **restrict, limit, narrow, confine,** tighten

**circumstance** NOUNS **pomp,** pride, **state,** solemnity, formality; **pomp and circumstance,** condition, occurrence, occasion, event, **incident**

**circumstantial** ADJS conditional, provisional; **incidental,** occasional, contingent, adventitious, **accidental, chance,** fortuitous, casual, aleatory, unessential *or* inessential *or* nonessential

**circumvent** VERBS **avoid, shun, fight shy of, shy away from,** keep from, **keep away from,** keep clear of, avoid like the plague, **steer clear of** <nonformal>, skate around <Brit informal>, **give a wide berth,** keep remote from, stay detached from; get round *or* around, **evade,** stonewall <nonformal>,

**elude, frustrate, foil,** give the slip *or* runaround <nonformal>

**circus** NOUNS **amphitheater, hippodrome, coliseum,** colosseum, **stadium, bowl; carnival**

**cite** VERBS 1 **impeach, arraign, indict,** bring in *or* hand up an indictment, return a true bill, article, cite on several counts; book
2 **itemize, specify,** circumstantiate, particularize, **spell out, detail,** go *or* enter into detail, descend to particulars, give full particulars; instance, adduce, document, give *or* quote chapter and verse; **mention,** specify, mention in passing, touch on, **refer to,** allude to

**citizen** NOUNS **national,** subject; **naturalized citizen,** nonnative citizen, citizen by adoption; hyphenated American, citizen of the world

**city** NOUNS 1 metropolis, metro, metropolitan area, greater city, megalopolis, supercity, conurbation, urban complex, spread city, urban sprawl, urban corridor, strip city, **municipality,** *urbs* <L>, *polis* <Gk>
ADJS 2 **urban, metropolitan, municipal,** metro, burghal, **civic,** oppidan; citywide; downtown, uptown, midtown; **inner-city,** core, core-city, ghetto; small-town; boom-town

**civic** ADJS **public-spirited; patriotic; nationalistic; political,** politic; governmental

**civil** ADJS **courteous, polite, urbane, gracious,** graceful, agreeable, affable, fair; complaisant; obliging, accommodating; **thoughtful, considerate,** tactful, solicitous; respectful, deferential, attentive

**civilization** NOUNS **culture, society; folkways, mores,** system of values, **ethos, culture pattern**

**civilized** ADJS **cultivated,** cultured, **refined,** polished; **learned, erudite, educated, cultured,** cultivated, lettered, literate

**civil servant** NOUNS **official, officer,** officiary, functionary, *fonctionnaire* <Fr>, apparatchik; **public official,** public servant; government *or* public employee; **bureaucrat,** mandarin

**claim** NOUNS 1 **demand, call; requisition,** requirement, stated requirement, order; legal claim, lien
VERBS 2 **demand, ask, ask for,** make a demand; **call for,** call on *or* upon one for, appeal to one for; call out for, cry *or* cry out for, clamor for; challenge, **require; requisition,** make *or* put in requisition; **demand,** ask, exact

**clairvoyance** NOUNS **extrasensory perception** *or* ESP; lucidity, second sight, insight, precognition, sixth sense; intuition; foresight; premonition; clairsentience, clairaudience

**clammy** ADJS **sweaty,** perspiry <nonformal>; sweating, perspiring; wet with sweat, beaded with sweat, **sticky** <nonformal>; bathed in sweat, drenched with sweat; sudatory, sudoric, sudorific, diaphoretic

**clamor** NOUNS **outcry, vociferation;** hullabaloo, hubbub, brouhaha, **uproar; hue and cry**

**clan** NOUNS **people, folk, family, house, tribe, nation; caste,** race, strain, blood, kin, sept; **subdivision,** subgroup, suborder

**clank** NOUNS 1 **ringing,** clang, clangor, twang, twanging
VERBS 2 clank, clang, clangor, twang

**clannish** ADJS **exclusive,** selective, **select,** elect, elite; **cliquish, snobbish,** snobby

**clap** NOUNS 1 **report, crash, crack, bang,** wham, slam, clash, burst; handclap, **clapping,** handclapping, clapping of hands
VERBS 2 **crack, crash,** wham, slam, **bang,** clash; clap one's hands, give a hand *or* big hand; **poke, punch, jab,** thwack, **smack,** crack, swipe, **whack**

**claque** NOUNS **booster** <nonformal>, puffer, promoter; **applauder,** *claqueur* <Fr>; rooter *and* fan *and* buff <all nonformal>, adherent

**clarity** NOUNS **clearness; plainness, distinctness,** explicitness, definition; **lucidity,** limpidity, pellucidity, crystal *or* crystaline clarity, crystallinity, perspicuity, transpicuity, transparency; **simplicity,** straightforwardness, directness, unequivocalness, unambiguousness

**clash** NOUNS 1 **jangle, jar; noise,** mere noise, confusion *or* conflict *or* jarring *or* jostling of sounds; jangle, clashing; **fight, battle, fray,** affray, combat, action, conflict, **brush, skirmish,** scrimmage; tussle, **scuffle, struggle,** scramble, shoving match; exchange of blows, *passage d'armes* <Fr>, passage at *or* of arms, clash of arms; **quarrel**
VERBS 2 **jangle, clash, jar;** conflict, collide, fight, jostle; **disagree, differ,** vary, not see eye-to-eye, be at cross-pur-

poses, tangle assholes <nonformal>, **disaccord**, jostle, collide

**clasp** NOUNS 1 **grasp, grip, hug, embrace,** bear hug; tight grip, iron grip, grip of iron *or* steel
VERBS 2 hug, embrace; cling, cling to, cleave to, stick to, adhere to, freeze to; **hold on to,** hold fast *or* tight, hang on to, keep a firm hold upon; **enfold,** bosom, embosom, put *or* throw one's arms around, take to *or* in one's arms, press to the bosom

**class** NOUNS 1 **social class, economic class,** social group *or* grouping, status group, accorded status, social category, order, grade, caste, estate, rank; **status, social status, economic status,** socioeconomic status *or* background, standing, footing, prestige, rank, ranking, place, station, position, level, degree, stratum; **category, group,** grouping, bracket, pigeonhole
2 **goodness, excellence, quality,** class <nonformal>; **virtue,** grace; **merit,** desert; **value, worth**
VERBS 3 **classify,** assign, designate; **categorize,** type, put down as, **pigeonhole,** place, **group, arrange**, range; **order**, rank, rate

**classic** ADJS 1 **model, exemplary,** precedential, typical, paradigmatic, representative, standard, normative; ideal
2 classic *or* classical, Attic, restrained, understated, unobtrusive, quiet, subdued, simple, unaffected; masterly, masterful, expert, proficient; **consummate,** quintessential, archetypical, exemplary, model

**classification** NOUNS **categorization,** classing, placement, ranging, **pigeonholing, sorting, grouping; grading,** stratification, ranking, rating, classing; division, subdivision; **cataloging,** codification, tabulation, rationalization, indexing, filing; **taxonomy,** typology; analysis, **arrangement**

**classify** VERBS class, **categorize,** catalog, sort, sort out, sift, group, factor, winnow, thrash out; weigh, weigh up, **evaluate, judge,** gauge, assess, appraise

**classy** ADJS **high-toned,** tony <both nonformal>, **fancy, dapper,** dashing, jaunty, braw <Scots>; sharp *and* spiffy *and* nifty *and* snazzy <all nonformal>

**clean** VERBS 1 **cleanse, purge,** deterge, depurate; **purify,** lustrate; sweeten, **freshen;** whiten, bleach; clean up *or* out, clear out, sweep out, clean up after; houseclean, clean house, spring-clean; spruce, **tidy**; scavenge; **wipe,** wipe up *or* out, wipe off; dust, dust off; steam-clean, **dry-clean, wash,** launder
ADJS 2 **pure; immaculate, spotless,** stainless, white, fair, dirt-free, soil-free; **unsoiled, unsullied,** unmuddied, unsmirched, unbesmirched, unblotted, unsmudged, unstained, untarnished, **unspotted,** unblemished; **unpolluted,** nonpolluted, untainted, unadulterated; **sqeaky-clean** *and* clean as a whistle *or* a new penny *or* a hound's tooth <all nonformal>

**clean up** VERBS 1 **make money;** rake it in *and* coin money *and* make a bundle *or* pile *or* killing *or* mint *and* clean up <all nonformal>
2 tidy, **tidy up,** neaten, trim, **put in trim,** trim up, trig up <chiefly Brit>, **straighten up,** fix up <nonformal>, police *and* police up <both nonformal>

**clear** VERBS 1 **extricate, free, release,** get out; **disengage,** disentangle, untangle, unsnarl, unravel, disentwine, disinvolve, unknot, disembarrass, disembroil; dislodge
2 **profit, make** *or* **draw** *or* **realize** *or* **reap profit, come out ahead, make money;** realize; make a fast *or* quick buck <nonformal>
3 **acquit, exculpate, exonerate, absolve,** give absolution, bring in *or* return a verdict of not guilty; **vindicate,** justify; **pardon, excuse, forgive;** remit, grant remission, remit the penalty of
ADJS 4 **distinct, plain, obvious, evident, patent,** unmistakable, not to be mistaken, much in evidence, plain to be seen, for all to see, showing for all to see, plain as a pikestaff, plain as the nose on one's face, plain as day, clear as day, plain as plain can be, big as life and twice as ugly; **crystal-clear,** clear as crystal, clear as day
5 **transparent,** transpicuous, light-pervious; show-through, see-through, peekaboo, revealing; **lucid,** pellucid, limpid

**clearance** NOUNS 1 **latitude, scope, room,** range, way, field, maneuvering space *or* room, room to swing a cat <nonformal>; **margin, space,** open space *or* field, elbowroom, breathing space, **leeway** <nonformal>
2 **authorization, authority, sanction, licensing,** countenance, **warrant,** war-

ranty, fiat; empowerment, security clearance

**clear-cut** ADJS **definite,** defined, well-defined, clean-cut, crisp; **direct, literal;** simple, **straightforward; explicit, express; unmistakable, unequivocal,** univocal, unambiguous, unconfused

**clearing** NOUNS opening up, unstopping, uncorking, throwing open, laying open, broaching, cutting through; **gap,** gape, yawn, hiatus, lacuna, gat, space, interval; **clearance,** clearage

**clearly** ADVS 1 **distinctly,** with clarity *or* crystal clarity, **plainly,** obviously, patently, definitely, unmistakably; conspicuously, undisguisedly, unconcealedly, prominently, pronouncedly, glaringly, starkly, staringly; **positively, decidedly,** manifestly, unambiguously, decisively, distinctly, patently, **obviously,** visibly, audibly, unquestionably, observably, **noticeably,** demonstrably, sensibly, quite

**clear up** VERBS **clarify, elucidate,** clear the air, **cover** *and* cover the waterfront *or* the territory <all nonformal>, **make clear,** make plain; **illuminate,** enlighten, **shed** *or* **throw light upon**

**cleft** NOUNS **crack,** cranny, chink, check, craze, chap, **crevice,** fissure, scissure, incision, notch, score, cut, gash, slit, split, **rift,** rent
2 **breach, break, rupture, schism, split, rift, disunity, disunion, disruption,** separation, cleavage, divergence, division

**clemency** NOUNS **leniency** *or* lenience, lenientness, lenity; clementness, **mercifulness,** mercy, **humaneness,** humanity, pity, **compassion**

**clench** VERBS **hold, grip, grasp, clutch,** clip, **clinch; clasp, hug, embrace; cling, cling to,** cleave to, stick to, adhere to, freeze to; **hold on to,** hold fast *or* tight, keep a firm hold upon

**clergy** NOUNS **ministry,** the cloth; clerical order, clericals; **priesthood;** priestery; presbytery; prelacy; Sacred College; rabbinate

**clerical** ADJS **ecclesiastic, ecclesiastical, churchly; ministerial,** sacerdotal, **pastoral; priestly,** priestish; episcopal, episcopalian; canonical; rabbinic, rabbinical

**clever** ADJS 1 **skillful, cute** *and* slick *and* slick as a whistle <all nonformal>, neat; **canny, shrewd,** knowing, sharp, razor-sharp, cute *or* cutesy *or* cutesy-poo <nonformal>, acute, astute
2 smart, brilliant, scintillating, sparkling, sprightly; keen, sharp, rapier-like, pungent, pointed, biting, mordant

**cliché** NOUNS 1 **platitude, saw, old saw, commonplace, banality,** bromide, **chestnut** <nonformal>, corn <nonformal>, triticism <old>, tired phrase, trite saying, hackneyed *or* stereotyped saying, *lieu commun* <Fr>, *locus communis* <L>, **familiar tune** *or* **story, old song** *or* **story,** twice-told tale
ADJS 2 banal, tired, trite, tritical <old>, **platitudinous**

**client** NOUNS **advisee,** counselee; **customer, patron**

**cliff** NOUNS **precipice, sheer** *or* yawning cliff *or* precipice *or* drop, steep, bluff, wall, face, scar; crag, craig <Scots>; scarp, **escarpment; palisade,** palisades

**climate** NOUNS **weather,** clime; **the elements,** forces of nature; microclimate, macroclimate; mental *or* intellectual climate, spiritual climate, moral climate, mores, norms, climate of opinion

**climax** NOUNS 1 **crucial moment,** critical moment, loaded *or* charged moment, decisive moment, kairotic moment, kairos, pregnant moment, defining moment, turning point, climax, **moment of truth,** crunch *and* when push comes to shove <both nonformal>, when the balloon goes up <Brit nonformal>; **orgasm,** sexual climax
VERBS 2 **come,** achieve satisfaction, achieve *or* reach orgasm; **ejaculate,** get off <nonformal>; **culminate,** consummate

**climb** NOUNS 1 **ascent,** climbing, upclimb, anabasis, clamber, escalade
VERBS 2 climb up, upclimb, **mount,** clamber, **clamber up,** scramble *or* scrabble up, claw one's way up, struggle up, inch up, shin, shinny *or* shin up <nonformal>, work *or* inch one's way up, climb the ladder; **scale,** escalade, scale the heights

**clinch** VERBS 1 **hold, grip, grasp, clutch,** clip, **clench; clasp, hug, embrace; cling, cling to,** cleave to, stick to, adhere to, freeze to; **hold on to,** hold fast *or* tight, hang on to, keep a firm hold upon
2 **make sure, make certain,** make sure of, make no doubt; lock in *and* nail down *and* clinch *and* cinch <all nonformal>

**cling** VERBS **hold, cling to,** cleave to, stick to, adhere to, freeze to; **hold on to,** hold fast *or* tight, hang on to, keep a firm hold upon; **hold on, hang on** <nonformal>, hold on like a bulldog, stick like a leech; **cohere, adhere, stick,** cleave, hold; hug, embrace, clinch

**clip** NOUNS 1 **extract,** film clip, outtake, sound bite <nonformal>
VERBS 2 **cut off** *or* **away,** shear *or* take *or* strike *or* knock *or* lop off, truncate; **amputate,** mutilate, abscind; **prune,** pare, peel, crop, bob, dock, lop, nip, shear
3 **overcharge; hold up** *and* **soak** *and* **stick** *and* **sting** *and* **clip** <all nonformal>, **make pay through the nose, gouge**

**clique** NOUNS **coterie, set, circle,** ring, junto, junta, cabal, camarilla, **clan,** group; cadre, inner circle; closed *or* charmed circle; ingroup, we-group; elite, elite group; leadership group; **old-boy network**

**clobber** VERBS **best, beat, beat out, defeat**; beat all hollow <nonformal>, trounce, take to the cleaners *and* smoke *and* skin *and* skin alive <all nonformal>, worst, whip *and* lick *and* have it all over *and* cut down to size <all nonformal>

**clock** NOUNS 1 horologe, horologium; Big Ben, ticker <nonformal>, **watch,** turnip; **timepiece,** timekeeper, **timer, chronometer**
VERBS 2 **time, fix** *or* **set the time,** mark the time; **keep time,** mark time, measure time, beat time

**clod** NOUNS 1 **lump,** clump, **hunk** *and* **chunk** <both nonformal>, wodge <Brit nonformal>; **mass,** piece, **gob** *and* glob <both nonformal>, gobbet
2 **bungler,** clodhopper, clodknocker, yokel; clot <Brit>, **dolt,** blockhead; awkward squad; **oaf, lout,** boor, lubber, oik <Brit>, **gawk,** gawky, **lummox,** yokel, rube, hick, hayseed, bumpkin

**clog** NOUNS 1 **obstruction, block,** blockade, sealing off, **blockage,** strangulation, choking, choking off, **stoppage,** stop, **bar, barrier, obstacle,** impediment; **bottleneck,** chokepoint; **congestion,** jam, traffic jam, gridlock
VERBS 2 **obstruct, bar,** stay; **block,** block up; clog up, foul; **choke,** choke up *or* off; **congest,** stuff up; **plug,** plug up; constipate, obstipate, bind

**cloister** NOUNS 1 **monastery, house, abbey,** friary; priory, priorate; lamasery; **convent, nunnery**
VERBS 2 **confine, immure;** pen, coop, pound <old>, crib, mew, cage, cage in, encage

**clone** NOUNS 1 **duplicate, duplication; double,** cookie-cutter copy
VERBS 2 **reproduce,** copy, reduplicate, **duplicate,** ditto <nonformal>; replicate

**close** NOUNS 1 **completion,** completing, **finish,** finishing, **conclusion, end,** ending, **termination,** terminus, cessation, **windup** <nonformal>, topping off, wrapping up, wrap-up, finalization
VERBS 2 **shut,** occlude; close up, shut up, contract, constrict, strangle, strangulate, choke, choke off, squeeze, squeeze shut; put *or* slap the lid on, **cover; shut the door; end, terminate,** determine, close out, close the books on, phase out *or* down, **finish, conclude,** finish with, resolve, finish *or* wind up <nonformal>; **put an end to,** put a period to, put paid to <Brit>, put *or* lay to rest, **make an end of,** bring to an end
ADJS 3 **stuffy, airless,** breathless, breezeless, windless; **oppressive, stifling, suffocating;** stirless, unstirring, not a breath of air, not a leaf stirring
4 **tight, confined,** constricted; **cramped;** intimate, cheek-by-jowl, side-by-side, hand-in-hand, arm-in-arm, *bras-dessus-bras-dessous* <Fr>
5 **imminent, near,** immediate, instant, soon to be, **at hand,** near at hand, close at hand; **in the offing,** on the horizon, **in prospect, in the wind,** in the cards <nonformal>
ADVS 6 **near, nigh;** hard, at close quarters; **nearby, close by,** hard by, fast by, not far *or* far off, in the vicinity *or* **neighborhood of,** at hand, at close range, **near** *or* **close at hand; within reach** *or* **range,** a stone's throw away

**closed-minded** ADJS **unpersuadable,** positive; dogmatic; **narrow-minded,** narrow, narrow-gauged, closed, cramped, constricted; provincial, insular, parochial

**closemouthed** ADJS **secretive,** close-lipped, secret, close, dark; discreet; evasive, shifty; **uncommunicative**

**close shave** NOUNS **narrow escape,** hairbreadth escape, **close call** <nonformal>, **near miss,** near go *or* thing <Brit nonformal>, near *or* narrow squeak <Brit

nonformal>, close *or* tight squeeze <nonformal>, squeaker <nonformal>

**closet** NOUNS 1 clothes closet, wardrobe, cloakroom; checkroom; linen closet
VERBS 2 **confine, immure;** cramp, straiten, encase; cloister, cabin, crib
ADJS 3 **secret,** close, closed; unuttered, unrevealed, undivulged, undisclosed, unspoken, untold; undisclosable, unbreatheable, unutterable

**closure** NOUNS **completion, fulfillment, consummation,** culmination, perfection, realization, actualization, **accomplishment**

**clot** VERBS **thicken,** thick <old>; inspissate, incrassate; **congeal, coagulate,** set, concrete; **curdle,** curd, clabber, lopper <nonformal>; cake, lump, clump, cluster, knot

**cloth** NOUNS **material, fabric, textile,** textile fabric, texture, tissue, stuff, weave, weft, woof, web, **material, goods,** *étoffe, tissu* <both Fr>

**clothe** VERBS enclothe, **dress, garb, attire,** tire, array, **apparel,** raiment, garment, habilitate, **tog** *and* tog out <both nonformal>, dud <nonformal>, robe, enrobe, invest, endue, **deck,** bedeck, dight, rag out *or* up <nonformal>

**clothes** NOUNS **clothing, apparel, wear, wearing apparel, daywear, dress,** dressing, **raiment,** garmenture, **garb, attire, array,** habit, habiliment, fashion, style, guise, **costume,** costumery, gear, fig *or* full fig <both Brit>, toilette, trim, bedizenment; **garments,** robes, robing, rags <nonformal>, drapery, finery, feathers; toggery *or* togs *or* **duds** *or* threads <all nonformal>

**cloud** NOUNS high fog; fleecy cloud, cottony cloud, billowy cloud; haze, fog, mist

*islands on a dark-blue sea*
SHELLEY

**cloudless** ADJS **clear,** serene; unclouded, unobscured

**cloud nine** NOUNS **bliss,** blissfulness; paradise, heaven, seventh heaven

**cloudy** ADJS nebulous, nubilous, nimbose, nebulosus; **clouded,** overclouded, **overcast;** dirty, heavy, lowering *or* louring; dark; **gloomy**; cloud-flecked; cirrous, cirrose; cumulous, cumuliform, stratous, stratiform

**clout** NOUNS **influence,** influentiality; **power**, force, potency, pressure, effect, indirect *or* incidental power, **say,** the final say, the last word, say-so *and* a lot to do with *or* to say about <all nonformal>, veto power; **weight,** moment, consequence, importance, eminence

**clown** NOUNS 1 **bungler, blunderer,** blunderhead, boggler, slubberer, bumbler, **fumbler, botcher;** oaf, gawk, boor, **clod,** clot <Brit>, **dolt,** blockhead; **fool, damn fool,** tomfool, perfect fool, born fool
2 **buffoon,** *buffo* <Ital>, **fool, jester, zany, merry-andrew,** jack-pudding, pickle-herring, **motley fool,** motley, wearer of the cap and bells; harlequin
VERBS 3 **be foolish;** be stupid; **act** *or* **play the fool; fool** *or* **horse around** <nonformal>, dick around <nonformal>, clown around; **make a fool of oneself,** make a monkey of oneself <nonformal>, play the buffoon

**club** NOUNS 1 **haunt,** purlieu, **hangout** <nonformal>, **stamping ground** <nonformal>; gathering place, rallying point, meeting place, clubhouse; casino, gambling house; country club
2 **rod, stick, switch; paddle,** ruler, ferule, pandybat
3 **fellowship, brotherhood, fraternity,** confraternity, confrerie, fraternal order *or* society; **sisterhood, sorority**
VERBS 4 cudgel, blackjack, sandbag, cosh <Brit>

**clue** NOUNS **cue, key,** tip-off <nonformal>, telltale, smoking gun <nonformal>, straw in the wind; **trace, vestige, spoor,** scent, whiff; **lead** *and* hot lead <both nonformal>; **hint,** gentle hint, **intimation, indication, suggestion, mere** *or* **faint suggestion, suspicion, inkling,** whisper

**clump** NOUNS 1 **bunch, cluster,** knot; tuft, wisp; tussock, hassock; shock
VERBS 2 **congeal, coagulate, clot,** set, concrete; **curdle,** curd, clabber, lopper <nonformal>; cake, lump, cluster, knot

**clumsy** ADJS **awkward, uncoordinated,** maladroit, unhandy, left-hand, left-handed, heavy-handed, ham-handed <nonformal>, ham-fisted *and* cack-handed <both Brit nonformal>, clumsy-fisted, butterfingered <nonformal>, **all thumbs**

**clunk** NOUNS 1 **thud,** dull thud; **thump,** flump, crump, clop, clump, plunk, tunk, plump, bump

VERBS 2 **thud, thump,** clop, clump, plunk, flump, crump

**cluster** NOUNS 1 **bunch, group,** grouping, groupment, crop, **clump,** knot; **batch, lot,** slew <nonformal>, **mess** <nonformal>; agglomeration, bunch, mass, clot
VERBS 2 **come together, assemble, congregate, collect,** come from far and wide; muster, **meet, gather, forgather,** gang up <nonformal>, mass; bunch, bunch up, clot, clump; gather around, gang around <nonformal>

**clutch** NOUNS 1 **hold, purchase, grasp, grip, clamp, clinch, clench;** seizure; **clasp, hug, embrace,** bear hug; firm hold, tight grip, iron grip, grip of iron *or* steel, death grip
2 **predicament, pinch, bind,** pass, situation, emergency; pretty pass, nice *or* pretty predicament, pretty *or* fine state of affairs, **sorry plight; complication,** imbroglio
VERBS 3 **hold, grip, grasp,** clip, **clinch, clench; clasp, hug, embrace; cling, cling to,** cleave to, stick to, adhere to, freeze to; **hold on to,** hold fast *or* tight, hang on to, keep a firm hold upon

**clutter** NOUNS 1 **jumble, litter, hodgepodge**, rat's nest, mare's nest, hurrah's nest <nautical>
VERBS 2 **litter,** scatter, crowd, jam, pack, overwhelm, overflow

**coach** NOUNS 1 trainer, instructor, mentor, teacher; **tutor,** tutorer; coacher; athletic coach
VERBS 2 **instruct,** guide, direct, **tutor; prime, cram** <nonformal>

**coagulate** VERBS **congeal, clot; cluster,** mass, bunch; **thicken,** inspissate, incrassate, curdle, clot, clabber *and* lopper <both nonformal>

**coalition** NOUNS **front, movement,** political front; popular front, people's front, grass-roots movement, ground swell; **alliance, league, union;** council; **bloc,** axis

**coarse** ADJS **gross, rude, crude, crass,** offensive, crass, loutish, nasty, raw, rough, **earthy;** ribald; raunchy <nonformal>, **obscene**; meretricious, **loud** <nonformal>, **gaudy**

**coast** NOUNS 1 **shore,** *côte* <Fr>; **strand,** *playa* <Sp>, **beach,** beachfront, plage, lido, riviera, sands, berm; **waterfront;** shoreline, coastline; **seashore, seacoast, seaside, seaboard,** seabeach, seacliff, seabank, sea margin, oceanfront, oceanside, seafront, seaside, shorefront, coastland, littoral
VERBS 2 **glide, skim,** sweep, flow; **slide,** slip, skid, skitter, sideslip, slither, glissade
3 **not lift a finger** *or* **hand, sit back, sit on one's hands** *or* ass *or* dead ass *or* butt *or* duff <nonformal>, sit on the sidelines, drift, lay down on the job <nonformal>, idle; **take it easy,** take things as they come, go with the flow, eat the bread of idleness, lie *or* rest on one's oars

**coat** NOUNS 1 **overcoat,** greatcoat, **topcoat,** surcoat; raincoat, slicker
VERBS 2 **cover,** spread on, **spread with;** smear, **smear on,** besmear, slap on, dab, daub, bedaub, plaster, beplaster; flow on, pour on; lay on, lay it on thick, slather; undercoat, prime

**coax** VERBS **urge,** wheedle, cajole, blandish, plead with, sweet-talk and soft-soap <both nonformal>, exhort, call on or upon, advocate, recommend, put in a good word, buck for and hype <both nonformal>

**cobweb** NOUNS **filament; web,** gossamer, spider *or* spider's web

**cocaine** NOUNS

<nonformal> basuco, bernice, big C, blow, C, charlie, coke, crack, crack cocaine, jumps, dust, flake, girl, gold dust, her, jay, joy powder, lady, lady snow, nose candy, snow, star dust, toot, white, white girl, white lady

**cockeyed** ADJS **cross-eyed,** swivel-eyed <nonformal>, goggle-eyed, bug-eyed *and* popeyed <both nonformal>, **walleyed;** askance, askant, asquint, squinting; in disorder, skewgee *and* slaunchways *and* skygodlin <all nonformal>; **silly,** knocked silly; **groggy** <nonformal>, **dopey** <nonformal>, woozy <nonformal>

**cocksure** ADJS **confident, convinced,** persuaded, positive; **unhesitating,** unfaltering, unwavering; **undoubting**; **self-confident, self-assured, self-reliant,** sure of oneself; poised; unafraid

**cocktail** NOUNS **drink,** mixed drink; *apéritif* <Fr>

**cocky** ADJS **conceited,** big-headed *and* too big for one's shoes *or* britches *and* biggety <all nonformal>, jumped-up <chiefly Brit nonformal>; **impudent,** bumptious, cheeky *and* **fresh** *and* facy *and* crusty *and* nervy <all nonformal>; **saucy,** sassy <nonformal>; smart *or* smart-alecky <nonformal>, smart-ass *or* wise-ass <nonformal>

**coddle** VERBS **pamper,** cosset, mollycoddle, pet, make a lap dog of, **spoil;** spare the rod

**code** NOUNS 1 **canon, maxim,** dictum, moral, moralism; **norm, standard;** formula, form; rule of action *or* conduct, moral precept; ethical *or* moral code, **ethic,** code of morals *or* ethics, ethical system, value system, axiology
VERBS 2 encode, encipher, cipher

**codify** VERBS **classify,** rationalize, **index; normalize, standardize, regularize;** formalize

**coerce** VERBS use violence, ride roughshod, intimidate, bully, bludgeon, blackjack; bully, cow, bulldoze <nonformal>, walk over, walk all over; keep down, hold *or* keep a tight hand upon, rule with a rod of iron, rule with an iron hand *or* fist; compel

**cogent** ADJS striking, telling, effective, impactful, valid, operative, in force; **relevant, pertinent,** appertaining, **germane, apposite,** material, admissible, applicable, applying, pertaining, belonging, involving, appropriate, **apropos,** *à propos* <Fr>, to the purpose, **to the point,** in point, *ad rem* <L>; weighty, authoritative

**cognizant** ADJS **knowing,** knowledgeable, informed; **conscious, aware, mindful, sensible; perceptive,** insightful, apperceptive, percipient, perspicacious, appercipient

**coherent** ADJS **clear, crystal-clear,** clear as crystal, clear as day, clear as the nose on one's face; **plain, distinct,** microscopically distinct, plain as pikestaffs; defined, well-defined, **clear-cut,** clean-cut; connected, consistent

**cohesive** ADJS cohering, coherent; adhering, **sticking, clinging,** inseparable, cleaving, holding together; **indivisible,** nondivisible, undividable, **inseparable,** indissoluble; unified

**cohort** NOUNS **henchman,** hanger-on, buddy *and* sidekick <both nonformal>; **accomplice,** confederate, fellow conspirator, coconspirator, partner *or* accomplice in crime

**coiffure** NOUNS **hairdo, hairstyle, haircut,** coif, headdress; wave; marcel, marcel wave; **permanent,** permanent wave

**coil** NOUNS **whorl,** roll, **curl,** curlicue, ringlet, pigtail, **spiral,** helix, volute, volution, involute, evolute, gyre, scroll; **kink, twist, twirl;** screw, corkscrew; tendril, cirrus; whirl, swirl, vortex

**coin** NOUNS 1 **specie,** hard money; piece, piece of money, piece of silver *or* gold
VERBS 2 **mint; counterfeit, forge**
3 innovate, invent, **make from scratch *or* from the ground up, new-mint, mint, inaugurate; neologize, neoterize**

**coincide** VERBS 1 **correspond,** agree, chime with, match, tally, go hand in glove with, twin
2 co-occur, concur; **coexist;** coextend; **synchronize,** isochronize, put *or* be in phase, be in time, keep time, time; contemporize; **accompany**, **agree,** match, go along with, go hand in hand, keep pace with, keep in step

**coitus** NOUNS **copulation, sex act,** having sex, having intercourse, *le sport* <Fr>, coupling, mating, coition, pareunia, venery, copula <law>, **sex, intercourse, sexual intercourse,** cohabitation, commerce, sexual commerce, congress, sexual congress, sexual union, sexual relations, relations, marital relations, marriage act, act of love, sleeping together *or* with; screwing *and* balling *and* nookie *and* diddling *and* making it with <all nonformal>

*making the beast with two backs*
SHAKESPEARE

**colander** NOUNS **filter; strainer, sifter, sieve, screen,** riddle, cribble, bolter, grate, grating

**cold** ADJS 1 **cool, chill,** nippy, crisp, brisk, sharp
2 **freezing;** frigid, icy, **shivering,** shivery, shaky, dithery; algid, aguish, aguey; **frozen**, half-frozen, frozen to death, chilled to the bone, blue with cold

3 <nonformal> **cold as hell,** cold as a welldigger's ass, cold as a witch's tit *or* kiss, cold enough to freeze the tail *or* balls off a brass monkey, cold as a bastard *or* a bitch, colder than hell *or* the deuce *or* the devil

4 **unfeeling, unemotional,** nonemotional, emotionless, affectless, emotionally dead *or* numb *or* paralyzed, anesthetized, drugged, narcotized; **unpassionate, frigid, unresponsive,** unresponding, **unsympathetic**
5 **aloof, standoffish, distant, remote,** withdrawn, removed, detached, Olympian; inaccessible, unapproachable; **unfriendly, inimical, uncordial,** unsociable

**cold feet** NOUNS weak knees, **faintheart,** chicken heart, **yellow streak** <nonformal>, white feather

**coldhearted** ADJS **unfeeling, unemotional,** nonemotional, emotionless, affectless, emotionally dead *or* numb *or* paralyzed, anesthetized, drugged, narcotized; passionless, **spiritless, heartless,** soulless; lukewarm, Laodicean; **cold, cool, frigid,** frozen, chill, chilly, arctic, frosty, frosted, icy, **cold-blooded,** cold as charity

**cold shoulder** NOUNS **aloofness, standoffishness,** offishness, withdrawnness, **remoteness,** distance, detachment; **repulse, rebuff; dismissal,** snub, spurning, brush-off, cut; kiss-off <nonformal>; turn-off <nonformal>; **ostracism,** ostracization, thumbs-down, thumbing-down, *pollice verso* <L>, blackballing, silent treatment, sending to Coventry

**cold turkey** NOUNS **withdrawal, withdrawal sickness,** withdrawal syndrome, withdrawal symptoms, bogue *and* coming down *and* crash <both nonformal>, abrupt withdrawal *and* cold turkey <both nonformal>; **detoxification** *or* detox <nonformal>, drying out, taking the cure

**colicky** ADJS **aching,** achy, **throbbing;** stomachachy, griping

**collaborate** VERBS 1 **cooperate,** do business *and* **play ball** <both nonformal>, coact, concur; concert, harmonize, concord; be in league, **go into partnership with,** go partners <nonformal>, go *or* be in cahoots with; **work together,** get together *and* team up *and* buddy up <all nonformal>, work as a team, act together, act in concert, **pull together; hold together, hang together,** keep together, **stand together,** stand shoulder to shoulder
2 **act the traitor,** turn against, go over to the enemy, turn one's coat, sell oneself, sell out <nonformal>; fraternize

**collaborator** NOUNS 1 **subversive; saboteur, fifth columnist, collaborationist,** fraternizer; fifth column, underground; Trojan horse
2 cooperator; coauthor; **collaborationist**

**collapse** NOUNS **breakdown, crackup** <nonformal>, **prostration,** exhaustion, cave-in; nervous prostration *or* breakdown *or* exhaustion, neurasthenia; circulatory collapse
2 **defeat; fall, downfall,** smash, crash, **undoing, ruin,** debacle, derailing, derailment; **destruction**; deathblow, quietus; Waterloo; failure; **insolvency, bankruptcy,** receivership, **failure;** bust <nonformal>
VERBS 3 **weaken,** crumble, go to pieces, disintegrate; go downhill, hit the skids <nonformal>, give way, break, cave in <nonformal>, **break down, founder;** crash <nonformal>, cave *or* fall in, come crashing *or* tumbling down, topple, totter, sway
4 **go bankrupt, go broke** <nonformal>, go into receivership, become insolvent *or* bankrupt, **fail,** break, bust <nonformal>, crash, **fold, fold up,** belly up *and* go up *and* go belly up *and* **go under** <all nonformal>, shut down, shut one's doors, go out of business, **be ruined,** go to ruin, go on the rocks, go to the wall

**collapsible** ADJS **contractive, compressible,** condensable, reducible; foldable; deflationary

**collar** NOUNS 1 **arrest,** arrestment, arrestation, pinch *and* bust <nonformal>; **capture, apprehension, seizure,** netting <nonformal>
VERBS 2 **capture, apprehend, collar** <nonformal>, run down, run to earth, **nab** <nonformal>, grab <nonformal>, lay by the heels, take prisoner; **arrest,** place *or* put under arrest, take into custody; pick up *or* take in *or* run in <all nonformal>

**colleague** NOUNS **associate, confederate,** consociate, fellow member, **companion, fellow,** bedfellow, **crony,** consort, cohort, compeer, compatriot, confrere, brother, brother-in-arms, **ally,** adjunct, coadjutor; comrade in arms, **comrade, partner**

**collect** VERBS **gather, glean, pick, pluck,** cull, **take up,** pick up, get *or* gather in, gather to oneself, bring *or* get together, scrape together; heap up, amass, assemble, accumulate

**collection** NOUNS 1 **gathering,** gleaning, bringing together, assembling, putting *or* piecing together, **accumulation,** cumulation, **amassment,** heaping up, grubbing
2 **donation,** donative; **contribution, subscription; alms,** pittance, **charity, dole, handout** <nonformal>, alms fee, widow's mite; Peter's pence; **offering,** offertory, votive offering
3 **compilation,** omnibus; collectanea, miscellany; collected works, *œuvres* <Fr>, canon; **miscellanea,** analects; chrestomathy, delectus; **anthology,** *Festschrift* <Ger>
4 collector's items, collectibles; **holdings,** fund, treasure; collectanea

**collective bargaining** NOUNS **negotiation, bargaining, haggling,** higgling, **dickering, chaffering,** chaffer, haggle; hacking out *or* working out *or* hammering out a deal, coming to terms; package bargaining, pattern bargaining

**collector** NOUNS gatherer, accumulator, connoisseur, fancier, enthusiast, pack rat *and* magpie <both nonformal>

**college** NOUNS **university,** institution of higher education *or* learning, degree-granting institution; academe, academia, the groves of Academe, **the campus,** the halls of learning *or* ivy, ivied halls; alma mater

**collegiate** ADJS **scholastic, academic,** institutional, **school,** classroom; **university;** intercollegiate, extramural; intramural

**collide** VERBS come into collision, be on a collision course, **clash,** meet, encounter, confront each other, impinge; percuss, concuss; **bump, hit, strike, run into, bump into,** bang into, slam into, smack into, **crash into, impact,** smash into, dash into, carom into; rear-end; **sideswipe** <nonformal>; **crash,** smash, crump, whomp; smash up *or* crack up *or* crunch <all nonformal>

**collision** NOUNS **crash, crack-up,** prang <Brit nonformal>; **impact, clash,** appulse, **encounter,** meeting, impingement, **bump, crash,** crump, whomp; **carom,** carambole, cannon; sideswipe <nonformal>; smash *and* crunch <both nonformal>

**colloquial** ADJS **vernacular, conversational, unliterary, nonformal,** demotic, spoken, vulgar, vulgate

**collusion** NOUNS **chicanery,** connivery, connivance, conspiracy, covin <law>; **intrigue,** web of intrigue, **plot, scheme,** deep-laid plot *or* scheme, underplot, game *or* little game <both nonformal>, trick, stratagem, finesse; counterplot; **conspiracy,** confederacy, covin, complot <old>, cabal; **complicity,** finagling <nonformal>, machination, manipulation

**cologne** NOUNS **toilet water,** Florida water; rose water, *eau de rose* <Fr>; lavender water, *eau de lavande* <Fr>; *eau de jasmin* <Fr>; cologne water, eau de Cologne; bay rum

**color** NOUNS 1 **hue; tint,** tinct, tincture, **tinge, shade, tone,** cast; key; **coloring, coloration; colorfulness,** bright color, pure color; coloring, colorant, tinction, tincture, **pigment, stain**
VERBS 2 **redden,** turn *or* grow red, color up, **mantle, blush, flush, crimson;** flame, glow

**colored** ADJS 1 hued, in color, in Technicolor <trademark>; **tinged, tinted,** tinctured, tinct, toned; **painted, enameled; stained, dyed;** tie-dyed; imbued
2 **dark-skinned, dark-complexioned;** melanian, melanic, melanotic, melanistic, melanous

**colorful** ADJS **bright, vivid,** intense, **rich,** exotic, **brilliant,** burning, **gorgeous, gay,** bright-hued, bright-colored, rich-colored, gay-colored, high-colored, deep-colored

**colorless** ADJS 1 **hueless,** toneless, uncolored, achromic, achromatic, achromatous; neutral; dull, flat, mat, dead, dingy, muddy, leaden, lusterless, lackluster; **faded, washed-out,** dimmed, discolored, etiolated; **pale, dim,** weak, **faint; pallid, wan, sallow,** fallow; pale *or* blue *or* green around the gills
2 **dull, dry,** dusty, dry as dust; **stuffy, stodgy,** wooden, stiff; characterless, pointless

**colossal** ADJS **huge,** great big, larger than life, Homeric, mighty, titanic, monumental, heroic, heroical, epic, epical, towering, mountainous

**colt** NOUNS **horse;** foal, filly

**column** NOUNS **pillar,** post, pier, pilaster; colonnette, columella; caryatid; atlas, atlantes <pl>; telamon, telamones

**coma** NOUNS **stupor,** sopor, **swoon,** lethargy <old>, soporifousness, comatoseness, torpidness, torpor, torpidity, stupefaction, **trance;** narcosis, narcohypnosis, narcoma, narcotization, narcotic stupor *or* trance; catalepsy, catatony *or* catatonia

**comatose** ADJS **unconscious, senseless, oblivious,** asleep, **dead to the world,** cold, out, **out cold;** catatonic, cataleptic; **lethargic, phlegmatic,** hebetudinous, **dull,** desensitized, sluggish, torpid, languid, slack, soporific, **stupefied,** in a stupor, **numb,** numbed, benumbed

**combat** NOUNS 1 **contention, contest,** contestation, **fighting, conflict, strife, war, struggle,** blood on the floor, cut and thrust; fighting at close quarters, infighting; **warfare**; **hostility,** enmity; **fighting,** scrapping *and* hassling <both nonformal>; **quarreling, bickering, wrangling, squabbling;** oppugnancy, contentiousness
VERBS 2 **contend, contest,** jostle; **fight, battle, war, declare** *or* **go to war,** take *or* take up arms, put up a fight <nonformal>; wage war; make the fur *or* feathers fly, **tussle, scuffle;** clash, collide; **come to blows,** close, **mix it up** *and* go toe-to-toe <both nonformal>, exchange blows

**combatant** NOUNS **fighter, battler,** scrapper <nonformal>; **contestant, contender, competitor, rival;** disputant, wrangler, squabbler, bickerer, quarreler; struggler, tussler, scuffler; **belligerent,** militant

**combative** ADJS **offensive,** on the offensive *or* attack; **aggressive, contentious, quarrelsome,** testy, feisty <nonformal>, ill-humored

**combination** NOUNS combine, combo <nonformal>, composition; **union, unification,** linking, linkage, yoking; **amalgamation, consolidation,** assimilation, **integration,** solidification, **encompassment,** inclusion, ecumenism; **alliance,** affiliation, reaffiliation, **association**, **merger,** league, hookup <nonformal>, tie-up <nonformal>

**combine** VERBS **unite, unify,** marry, wed, couple, link, yoke, yoke together; **incorporate, amalgamate, consolidate,** assimilate, **integrate,** solidify, coalesce, compound, put *or* lump together, roll into one, come together, make one, unitize; **connect, join**; **mix; add**; **merge,** meld, **blend,** stir in, merge *or* blend *or* meld *or* shade into, **fuse,** flux, melt into one, conflate

**combustible** ADJS **flammable, inflammable,** burnable

**come** VERBS 1 **appear,** become visible; **arrive, make one's appearance,** make *or* put in an appearance, appear on the scene, make the scene *and* weigh in <both nonformal>, appear to one's eyes, meet *or* catch *or* strike the eye, **come in sight** *or* **view, show,** show oneself, show one's face, nip in <nonformal>, **show up** <nonformal>, **turn up,** come, **materialize,** present oneself, present oneself to view, **manifest oneself,** become manifest, **reveal oneself,** discover oneself, uncover oneself, declare oneself, expose *or* betray oneself
2 **climax,** achieve satisfaction, achieve *or* reach orgasm; **ejaculate,** get off <nonformal>

**comeback** NOUNS 1 **recovery, rally,** return; **recuperation, convalescence; retaliation, reciprocation,** exchange, interchange, give-and-take; **retort, reply,** return, comeback <nonformal>
2 **gibe, cut,** cutting remark, verbal thrust; gibing retort, rude reproach, short answer, back answer, parting shot, Parthian shot

**comedian** NOUNS comedienne, **comic, funnyman;** farcist, farcer, *farceur, farceuse* <both Fr>; stand-up comic *or* comedian <nonformal>, light comedian, genteel comedian, low comedian, slapstick comedian

**comedown** NOUNS **disappointment,** setback, **letdown** <nonformal>; failure, fizzle <nonformal>, fiasco; **disillusionment;** descent, deflation, wounded or humbled pride; self-abasement, shamefacedness

**comedy** NOUNS **humor,** black humor, sick humor, gallows humor; comic relief, comedy relief; comic muse, Thalia; sock, coxcomb, cap and bells, motley, bladder, slapstick

**comeuppance** NOUNS **desserts,** just desserts, deservings, merits, dues, due reward *or* punishment, all that is coming to one; retaliation, vengeance

**comfort** NOUNS 1 **ease, well-being;** contentment; clover, velvet <nonformal>, bed of roses; life of ease; solid comfort
2 **consolation, solace,** solacement, easement, heart's ease, **encouragement,** aid and comfort, **assurance, reassur-**

**ance,** support, crumb *or* shred of comfort, condolence, sympathy; **relief**

*kind words and comfortable*
WILLIAM COWPER

VERBS 3 **console, solace,** give *or* bring comfort, bear up; condole with, sympathize with, extend sympathy; ease, **put** *or* **set at ease;** bolster, support; relieve; **assure, reassure; encourage, hearten,** pat on the back; **cheer**; wipe away the tears

**comfortable** ADJS comfy <nonformal>; contented; **easy,** easeful; **restful,** reposeful, peaceful, **relaxing;** soft, cushioned, cushy <nonformal>, cushiony; comfortable as an old shoe; **cozy, snug,** snug as a bug in a rug; **homelike,** homey *and* down-home <both nonformal>, homely, lived-in; **commodious,** roomy, convenient; luxurious; comfortably situated, **easy;** on Easy Street *and* in Fat City *and* in hog heaven <all nonformal>, **in clover** *and* **on velvet** <both nonformal>, on a bed of roses, in luxury, high on the hog <nonformal>

**comic** NOUNS 1 **comedian,** comedienne, **funnyman;** stand-up comic *or* comedian <nonformal>, light comedian, low comedian, slapstick comedian
ADJS 2 **comical; farcical,** slapstick, broad; **burlesque**; tragicomic, seriocomic, mock-heroic; **light;** tragicomical

**comics** NOUNS **comic strip;** comic section, funny paper *and* funnies <both nonformal>; comic book

**command** NOUNS 1 **commandment, order,** direct order, command decision, **bidding,** behest, hest <old>, imperative, **dictate,** dictation, **will, pleasure,** say-so <nonformal>, word, word of command, *mot d'ordre* <Fr>; special order; **authority**
2 **control, mastery, mastership, power, jurisdiction, dominion, domination; hold, grasp,** grip, gripe; hand, hands, iron hand, clutches; talons, claws; helm, reins of government
3 **understanding, comprehension, apprehension,** intellection, prehension; **grasp,** mental grasp, grip, mastery
VERBS 4 **order, dictate, direct, instruct,** mandate, **bid, enjoin, charge,** commission, call on *or* upon; issue a writ *or* an injunction; **decree, rule, ordain,** promulgate; give an order *or* a direct order, issue a command, say the word, give the word *or* word of command; call the shots *or* tune *or* signals *or* play <nonformal>; order about *or* around

**commanding** ADJS imperious, imperative, jussive, peremptory, abrupt; **directive, instructive; mandating,** dictating, compelling, obligating, **prescriptive,** preceptive; decretory, decretive, decretal; **authoritative; governing, controlling, regulating,** regulative, regulatory; **ruling, reigning, sovereign,** regnant

**commemorative** ADJS **celebrative,** celebratory, celebrating; commemorating; memorial; solemn

**commencement** NOUNS 1 **beginning, start,** running *or* flying start, starting point, square one <nonformal>, **outset,** outbreak, **onset,** oncoming; dawn; **launching,** launch; **opening,** jump-off *and* send-off *and* start-off *and* take-off *and* blast-off *and* git-go *and* square one <all nonformal>
2 commencement exercises, graduation, graduation exercises, baccalaureate service

**commend** VERBS **speak well** *or* **highly of,** speak in high terms of, speak warmly of, have *or* say a good word for; boost *and* give a boost to <both nonformal>, puff, promote, cry up; plug *and* tout *and* hype; pour *or* spread *or* lay it on thick <all nonformal>

**commendable** ADJS **praiseworthy,** worthy, estimable, **laudable,** admirable, meritorious, creditable; exemplary, model, unexceptionable; deserving, well-deserving; beyond all praise, *sans peur et sans reproche* <Fr>

**commensurate** ADJS **comparative, relative, comparable,** commensurable, parallel, matchable, **analogous;** analogical; **correlative**

**comment** NOUNS **1 word of explanation; annotation,** notation, **note,** note of explanation, footnote, gloss, scholium; exegesis; *apparatus criticus* <L>; commentary, commentation <old>
VERBS 2 **remark, observe, note; mention,** speak <old>, let drop *or* fall, say by the way, make mention of; refer to, allude to, touch on, make reference to, call attention to; interject; blurt, blurt out, exclaim

**commentary** NOUNS commentation <old>; **comment, remark; criticism,**

critique, *compte-rendu critique* <Fr>, analysis; **review,** critical review, **report,** notice, **write-up** <nonformal>; **editorial,** leading article *or* leader <both Brit>; gloss, running commentary

**commerce** NOUNS **trade, traffic,** truck, intercourse, **dealing, dealings; business,** business dealings *or* affairs *or* relations, commercial affairs *or* relations; the business world, the world of trade *or* commerce, the marketplace; merchantry

**commercial** NOUNS 1 **advertisement, ad** <nonformal>, advert <Brit nonformal>, notice; **commercial,** message, important message, message *or* words from the sponsor; spot commercial *or* spot, network commercial; commercial announcement, commercial message, plug <nonformal>
ADJS 2 **business, trade,** trading, **mercantile,** merchant; commercialistic, mercantilistic; **salable, marketable,** merchandisable

**commiserate** VERBS **condole with, sympathize with,** feel with, empathize with, express sympathy for, send one's condolences; pity; **console,** wipe away one's tears, comfort

**commission** VERBS **authorize,** empower, accredit; **delegate,** devolute, devolve, devolve upon, vest, invest; depute, **deputize; assign,** consign, **commit, charge, entrust,** give in charge; license, charter, warrant

**commit** VERBS 1 consign, commit to prison, send to jail, send up *and* send up the river <both nonformal>; commit to an institution, institutionalize; recommit, remit, remand
2 **engage,** undertake, obligate, bind, **agree to,** answer for, be answerable for, take on oneself, be responsible for, be security for, go bail for, accept obligation *or* responsibility, bind oneself to, put oneself down for; have an understanding; enter into a gentlemen's agreement; shake hands on; contract; **obligate, oblige,** make incumbent *or* imperative, tie, **bind,** pledge, saddle with, put under an obligation; call to account, hold responsible *or* accountable *or* answerable

**commitment** NOUNS 1 **devotion,** devoutness, devotedness, dedication, committedness; **earnestness, seriousness,** sincerity; loyalty, faithfulness, faith, fidelity
2 **obligation, agreement, engagement,** undertaking, recognizance; **understanding,** gentlemen's agreement; verbal agreement, nonformal agreement, pactum <law>; tacit *or* unspoken agreement; **contract;**

**commit suicide** VERBS **take one's own life, kill oneself,** die by one's own hand, do away with oneself, put an end to oneself; blow one's brains out, take an overdose <of a drug>, overdose *or* OD <nonformal>; commit hara-kiri *or* seppuku; sign one's own death warrant, doom oneself

**committed** ADJS **devoted,** dedicated, **fast,** steadfast, constant, faithful, staunch; tried, true, **tried and true,** true-blue, tested; bound, duty-bound, in duty bound, tied, pledged, saddled, beholden, bounden; **obliged to,** beholden to, bound *or* bounden to, **indebted to**

**commodity** NOUNS **ware,** vendible, **product, article, item,** article of commerce *or* merchandise; staple, staple item, standard article

**common** ADJS 1 **commonplace, ordinary;** plebeian; homely, homespun; **general, public, popular,** pop <nonformal>; prosaic, prosy, **matter-of-fact,** everyday, workaday, household, garden, common- *or* garden-variety; **unexceptional, unremarkable, unnoteworthy,** unspectacular, nothing *or* nobody special *and* no great shakes <all nonformal>; **prevalent, prevailing, current,** running
2 **mutual,** commutual, **joint, communal,** shared, sharing, conjoint; respective, two-way

**common man** NOUNS **commoner,** little man, **little fellow, average man,** ordinary man, typical man, **man in the street,** one of the people, man of the people, Everyman; **plebeian,** pleb <slang>; **proletarian,** prole <Brit nonformal>, *roturier* <Fr>; ordinary *or* average Joe *and* Joe Doakes *and* Joe Sixpack <all nonformal>, John Doe, Jane Doe, John Smith, Mr *or* Mrs Brown *or* Smith; a nobody

**commonplace** ADJS 1 **trite;** corny *and* square *and* square-John *and* Clyde <all nonformal>, fade, **banal,** unoriginal, platitudinous, **stereotyped,** stock, set, **common,** truistic, twice-told, **familiar,** bromidic <nonformal>, old hat <nonformal>, back-number, bewhiskered,

warmed-over, **cut-and-dried; hackneyed,** hackney; **stale,** musty, fusty; **worn,** timeworn, well-worn, moth-eaten, threadbare, **worn thin**
2 **common, ordinary;** plebeian; homely, homespun; pedestrian, **unimaginative**; insipid, vapid, flat; **general, public, popular,** pop <nonformal>; Babbittish, Philistine, bourgeois; **simple, plain, ordinary, nondescript, prosaic,** prosy, **matter-of-fact, homely, homespun,** everyday, humdrum, tiresome

**common sense** NOUNS **reasonableness,** reasonability, **logicalness,** logicality, **rationality, sensibleness, soundness,** justness, justifiability, admissibility, cogency; **sense,** sound sense, sweet reason, **logic, reason;** plausibility

**commonwealth** NOUNS community, society, **nation,** constituency, body politic, electorate; **republic,** people's republic, commonweal

**commotion** NOUNS **hubbub, Babel, tumult,** turmoil, **uproar, racket,** riot, **disturbance, rumpus** <nonformal>, ruckus *and* ruction <both nonformal>, **fracas, hassle,** shemozzle <Brit nonformal>, shindy <nonformal>, rampage; **row** *and* hassle <both nonformal>

**commune** NOUNS **community, family,** extended family, nuclear family, binuclear family; colony, settlement; communal ownership; ashram

**communicate** VERBS 1 **be in touch** *or* **contact,** be in connection *or* intercourse, have intercourse, hold communication; **intercommunicate,** interchange, commune with; grok <nonformal>; commerce with, **deal with, traffic with, have dealings with, have truck with** <nonformal>; **speak, talk,** be in a speech situation, **converse**, pass the time of day
2 **impart, tell,** lay on one <nonformal>, **convey, transmit,** transfer, send, send word, deliver *or* send a signal *or* message, **disseminate,** broadcast, pass, **pass on** *or* **along, hand on; report, render, make known,** get across *or* over; give *or* send *or* leave word; **signal;** share, share with; **leak,** let slip out, **give**; tell

**communication** NOUNS communion, congress, **commerce, intercourse; speaking, speech**, utterance, speech act, talking, linguistic intercourse, speech situation, speech circuit, converse, **conversation**; **contact, touch, connection; interpersonal communication, intercommunication,** intercommunion, grokking <nonformal>, **interplay,** interaction; **exchange,** interchange; answer, response, reply; one-way communication, two-way communication; **dealings,** dealing, **traffic, truck** <nonformal>; information; message; correspondence; social intercourse

**communicative** ADJS **talkative**, gossipy, newsy; **sociable; unreserved, unreticent,** unshrinking, **unrestrained, unconstrained,** unhampered, unrestricted; demonstrative, expansive, effusive; **candid, frank**; **open,** free, outspoken, free-speaking, free-spoken, free-tongued; **accessible, approachable,** easy to speak to

**communiqué** NOUNS **message, dispatch, word, communication,** advice, press release, release

**communism** NOUNS **Bolshevism, Marxism,** Marxism-Leninism, Leninism, Trotskyism, Stalinism, Maoism, Titoism, Castroism

**Communist** NOUNS 1 Bolshevist; Bolshevik, **Red** *and* commie *and* bolshie <all nonformal>; Marxist, Leninist, Marxist-Leninist, Trotskyite *or* Trotskyist, Stalinist, Maoist, Titoist, Castroite; card-carrying Communist, avowed Communist; fellow traveler, Communist sympathizer, comsymp <nonformal>
ADJS 2 **communistic,** Bolshevik, Bolshevist, commie *and* bolshie *and* Red <all nonformal>; **Marxist,** Leninist, Marxist-Leninist, Trotskyite *or* Trotskyist, Stalinist, Maoist, Titoist, Castroite

**community** NOUNS **society, commonwealth;** body; **kinship group, clan,** sept <Scots>, moiety, totemic *or* totemistic group, phyle, phratry *or* phratria, gens, caste, subcaste, endogamous group; **family,** extended family, nuclear family, binuclear family; order, **class, social class**, economic class; colony, settlement; **commune,** ashram

**commuter** NOUNS **traveler, passenger,** straphanger <nonformal>

**compact** VERBS 1 compress, **consolidate, concentrate,** squeeze, press, crowd, cram, jam, ram down
ADJS 2 **compressed,** cramped, compacted, concentrated, condensed, consolidated, solidified

**companion** NOUNS 1 **fellow,** fellow com-

panion, **comrade,** *camarade* <Fr>, amigo <nonformal>, mate <Brit>, comate, company, **associate**, consociate, compeer, confrere, consort, **colleague, partner,** copartner, side partner, **crony;** girlfriend <nonformal>; boyfriend <nonformal>
2 **escort, chaperon,** duenna; travel companion

**company** NOUNS 1 **fellowship, companionship, society;** fraternity, **fraternization**
2 **firm, business firm, concern, house,** *compagnie* <Fr>, *compañía* <Sp>, *Aktiengesellschaft* <Ger>, *aktiebolag* <Swed>; **business, industry, enterprise,** business establishment, commercial enterprise; cast, acting company, troupe, repertory company, stock company

**comparable** ADJS commensurable; correlative; **like,** homologous, **similar; analogous**

**compare** VERBS **liken,** assimilate, similize, liken to, compare with; **make** *or* **draw a comparison,** run a comparison, do a comparative study, bring into comparison; **analogize,** bring into analogy; **relate**; metaphorize; **draw a parallel,** parallel; **be comparable, compare to** *or* **with,** not compare with, admit of comparison, be commensurable, be of the same order *or* class, be worthy of comparison, be fit to be compared; **measure up to, come up to,** stack up with <nonformal>, hold a candle to <nonformal>

**comparison** NOUNS compare, examining side by side, matching, matchup, holding up together, proportion <old>, comparative judgment *or* estimate; **likening,** comparing, **analogy;** correlation; simile, similitude, metaphor, allegory, figure *or* trope of comparison

**compassion** NOUNS **sensitivity, sensitiveness;** perceptivity, perceptiveness; responsiveness; **sympathy;** empathy, identification; **concern,** solicitousness, solicitude; **pity**, **mercy; humaneness,** humanity; charitableness

**compatible** ADJS **in accord,** accordant <old>, **harmonious, in harmony,** congruous, congruent, in tune, attuned, agreeing, in concert, **in rapport,** *en rapport* <Fr>; frictionless; **sympathetic,** simpatico <nonformal>, empathic, empathetic, **understanding; like-minded,** akin, of the same mind, of one mind, at one, united, together; concordant, corresponding; agreeable, congenial

**compel** VERBS 1 **force, make;** have, cause, cause to; **constrain, bind,** tie, tie one's hands; **restrain**; enforce, **drive,** impel; dragoon, use force upon, force one's hand, hold a pistol *or* gun to one's head; **necessitate, oblige,** dictate, **constrain;** insist upon

2 <nonformal> **twist one's arm, armtwist, twist arms, knock** *or* bang heads, knock *or* bang heads together, strong-arm, steamroller, bulldoze, **pressure,** high-pressure, lean on, squeeze; put the screws on *or* to, get one over a barrel *or* under one's thumb, hold one's feet to the fire, put the heat on; pull rank; ram *or* cram down one's throat

**compensate** VERBS make compensation, make good, set right, restitute, make up for, counterpoise; countervail, counterbalance, cancel, rectify, **make up for; make amends,** expiate, do penance, atone; **recompense,** pay back, repay, indemnify, cover; **trade off,** give and take; **retaliate; pay,** render, tender; **recompense, remunerate,** satisfy

**compete** VERBS **contend, vie,** try conclusions *or* the issue, jockey <nonformal>; **compete with** *or* **against, vie with, challenge,** cope <old>, enter into competition with, give a run for one's money, **meet;** try *or* test one another; **rival,** emulate, outvie; keep up with the Joneses

**competent** ADJS **capable, able, efficient, qualified, fit, fitted, suited, worthy;** journeyman; fit *or* fitted for; **equal to, up to;** up to snuff <nonformal>, up to the mark <nonformal>, *au fait* <Fr>; well-qualified, well-fitted, well-suited

**competitive** ADJS competing, **vying,** rivaling, **rival,** rivalrous, emulous, in competition, in rivalry; **cutthroat**

**competitor** NOUNS **contestant, contender,** corrival, vier, player, entrant; **rival,** arch-rival; emulator

**compilation** NOUNS omnibus; symposium; collection, collectanea, miscellany; **miscellanea,** analects; ana; chrestomathy, delectus; **anthology,** garland, florilegium

**compile** VERBS **put together,** make up,

compile, colligate; **codify,** digest; publish

**complacent** ADJS **smug, self-complacent, self-satisfied,** self-content, **self-contented**; self-sufficient

**complain** VERBS 1 **groan; grumble, murmur, mutter,** growl, clamor, croak, grunt, yelp; **fret,** fuss, make a fuss about, fret and fume; air a grievance, lodge *or* register a complaint; fault, find fault; **object, protest,** remonstrate, **dispute,** challenge, complain loudly, exclaim at

2 <nonformal> **beef, bitch, kick, kvetch,** bellyache, crab, gripe, grouch, grouse, grump, have an attitude, kick, holler, howl, moan, piss, make a stink, squawk, yap; raise a howl, put up a squawk *or* howl, take on, cry *or* yell *or* scream bloody murder, give one a hard time, piss *or* kick up a storm *or* row *or* fuss, raise a stink

**complainer** NOUNS 1 **malcontent,** *frondeur* <Fr>; complainant, **faultfinder, grumbler,** growler, smellfungus, griper, croaker, peevish *or* petulant *or* querulous person, whiner

2 <nonformal> **grouch, kvetch,** kicker, griper, moaner, moaning Minnie <Brit>, crank, crab, grouser, beefer, bellyacher, bitcher, sorehead, picklepuss, sourpuss

**complaint** NOUNS 1 **grievance, peeve,** pet peeve, **groan; dissent,** objection, **protest**; hard luck story <nonformal>, tale of woe; **complaining,** scolding, groaning, **faultfinding**, sniping, destructive criticism, **grumbling, murmuring;** whining, petulance, peevishness, querulousness

2 <nonformal> **beef, kick, gripe,** kvetch, grouse, bellyache, howl, holler, **squawk,** bitch; **beefing, grousing, kicking, griping,** kvetching, **bellyaching,** squawking, **bitching,** yapping

**complementary** ADJS **reciprocal,** reciprocative, tit-for-tat, seesaw, seesawing; **completing, fulfilling,** filling; completive *or* completory, consummative *or* consummatory, culminative, perfective; complemental

**complete** VERBS 1 **perfect, finish, finish off, conclude, terminate, end,** bring to a close, carry to completion, prosecute to a conclusion; **get through, get done; round off** *or* **out, wind up** <nonformal>, **top off;** top out, crown, cap; climax, culminate; **give the finishing touches** *or* **strokes,** put the finishing touches *or* strokes on, lick *or* whip into shape, finalize, put the icing on the cake

ADJS 2 **undivided,** uncut, unsevered, unclipped, uncropped, unshorn; **undiminished,** unreduced; **whole, total,** global, **entire,** intact, solid; **full, full-fledged,** full-dress, **full-scale;** full-grown, mature, matured, ripe, developed; unabbreviated, undiminished, unexpurgated; **terminated,** concluded, finished, perfected, settled, decided, set at rest; **over, all over,** all up <nonformal>; **finished**

**completely** ADVS **fully, in full, in detail,** minutely, specifically, particularly, in particular, wholly, *in toto* <L>, **at length,** *in extenso* <L>, *ad nauseam* <L>

**completion** NOUNS completing, **finish,** finishing, **conclusion, end,** ending, **termination,** terminus, **close, windup** <nonformal>, rounding off *or* out, topping off, wrapping up, wrap-up, finalization; **perfection,** culmination; **fulfillment,** consummation, culmination, perfection, realization, actualization, **accomplishment**, closure

**complex** ADJS **complicated,** many-faceted, multifarious, ramified, perplexed, **confused,** confounded, **involved,** implicated, crabbed, **intricate,** elaborate, involuted, convoluted, multilayered, multilevel; **tangled,** entangled, tangly, embrangled, **snarled,** knotted, matted, twisted, raveled; **labyrinthine,** labyrinthian, meandering; **devious,** roundabout, deep-laid, Byzantine, subtle

**complicate** VERBS **involve, perplex,** ramify; **confound, confuse,** muddle, **mix up,** mess up *and* ball up *and* bollix up *and* screw up *and* foul up *and* fuck up *and* snafu *and* muck up *and* louse up <all nonformal>, implicate; **tangle,** entangle, embrangle, **snarl, snarl up,** ravel, knot, tie in knots

**complication** NOUNS **abstruseness,** reconditeness; crabbedness, crampedness, knottiness; **complexity,** intricacy; **profundity,** profoundness, deepness; esotericism, esotery; **complexity,**

**involvement,** complexness, involution, convolution, tortuousness, Byzantinism, *chinoiserie* <Fr>, tanglement, **entanglement,** perplexity, **intricacy,** intricateness, ramification, crabbedness, technicality, subtlety; **predicament, embarrassment,** embarrassing position *or* situation; imbroglio

**complicity** NOUNS **collusion,** connivance; artifice; **contrivance,** contriving; **guilt, guiltiness;** guilty *or* wrongful *or* criminal involvement; censurability, censurableness, reproachability, reproachableness, reprovability, reprovableness, inculpation, implication, involvement, impeachability, impeachableness, indictability

**compliment** NOUNS 1 polite commendation, complimentary *or* flattering remark, stroke <nonformal>; **bouquet** *and* posy <both nonformal>
VERBS 2 **pay a compliment,** make one a compliment, give a bouquet *or* posy <nonformal>, say something nice about; hand it to *and* have to hand it to <both nonformal>, pat on the back, take off one's hat to, doff one's cap to, congratulate

**complimentary** ADJS **approbatory, approbative, commendatory, laudatory,** acclamatory, eulogistic, panegyric, panegyrical, encomiastic, **appreciative, appreciatory; admiring, regardful, respectful**; flattering
2 **gratuitous, gratis, free, free of charge,** for free, **for nothing,** free for nothing, free for the asking, free gratis *and* free gratis for nothing <both nonformal>, for love, free as air; on the house

**comply** VERBS **acquiesce, comply with,** fall in with, take one up on <nonformal>, be persuaded, come round *or* around, come over, come to <nonformal>, see one's way clear to; **conform, correspond,** accord, harmonize; **comply with,** agree with, tally with, chime *or* fall in with, go by, be guided *or* regulated by, observe, follow, bend, yield, take the shape of

**component** NOUNS **constituent, ingredient,** integrant, makings *and* fixings <both nonformal>, **element, factor, part**, player, module, part and parcel; appurtenance, adjunct; **feature,** aspect, specialty, circumstance, detail, item

**composed** ADJS 1 **collected,** recollected, **levelheaded; poised,** together <nonformal>, in equipoise, equanimous, equilibrious, **balanced,** well-balanced; **self-possessed,** self-controlled, self-restrained; confident, assured, **self-confident, self-assured**
2 **arranged, ordered, disposed,** configured, constituted, fixed, placed, aligned, ranged, arrayed, marshaled

**composite** NOUNS 1 **compound, mixture, admixture,** intermixture, immixture, commixture, **blend,** meld, composition, confection, concoction; amalgam, alloy
ADJS 2 blended, compounded, amalgamated; **combined**; compound; **conglomerate,** pluralistic, heterogeneous, varied, **miscellaneous,** medley, motley, dappled, patchy; **scrambled, jumbled,** thrown together; syncretic, eclectic

**composition** NOUNS 1 **constitution, construction, formation,** fabrication, fashioning, shaping, organization; **embodiment,** incorporation, incarnation; **make, makeup,** getup *or* setup <both informal>; **assembly,** assemblage, putting *or* piecing together; synthesis, syneresis; **mixture**
2 **creation; invention,** origination, coinage, mintage *or* new mintage, brainchild; **concoction,** opus

**compost** NOUNS **fertilizer,** dressing, top dressing, enricher, richener; organic fertilizer, manure, muck, night soil, dung, guano, leaf litter, leaf mold, humus, peat moss, castor-bean meal, bone meal

**composure** NOUNS countenance; **calm, calmness,** calm disposition, **placidity, serenity,** tranquility, soothingness, peacefulness; mental composure, peace *or* calm of mind; calm *or* quiet mind, easy mind; **quiet,** quietness of mind *or* soul, quietude; **coolness,** coolheadedness, cool <nonformal>, sangfroid; possession, aplomb

**compound** NOUNS 1 **mixture, admixture,** intermixture, immixture, commixture, **composite, blend,** meld, composition, confection, concoction, **combination**
VERBS 2 **combine, consolidate,** assimilate, **integrate,** solidify, coalesce, put *or* lump together, roll into one, come together, make one, unitize; **synthesize,** syncretize

**comprehensive** ADJS **sweeping, complete**; whole; **all-comprehensive,** all-inclusive; without omission *or* exception, **overall,** universal, global, wall-to-wall <nonformal>, around-the-world, **total,** blanket, omnibus, across-the-board; encyclopedic, compendious; thorough

**compress** VERBS 1 **squeeze,** clamp, cramp, cramp up, tighten; **press,** pressurize, crush
2 **abridge, condense, boil down,** abstract, sum up, summarize, recapitulate, recap <nonformal>, synopsize, epitomize, encapsulate, capsulize

**compressed** ADJS **contracted,** cramped, compact *or* compacted, concentrated, condensed, consolidated, solidified; **squeezed; abridged,** condensed, epitomized, digested, abstracted, capsule, capsulized, encapsulated, **concise, brief, short**

**compromise** NOUNS 1 adjustment, accommodation, settlement, mutual concession, give-and-take; abatement of differences; bargain, deal <nonformal>, arrangement, understanding; **concession,** giving way, yielding; adaptation, mutual adjustment, coaptation, arbitration, arbitrament
VERBS 2 make *or* reach a compromise, compound, compose, accommodate, adjust, settle, make an adjustment *or* arrangement, **make a deal** <nonformal>, do a deal <Brit nonformal>, come to an understanding, strike a bargain, do something mutually beneficial; plea-bargain; strike a balance, take the mean, **meet halfway,** split the difference, go fifty-fifty <nonformal>
3 **endanger, jeopardize,** put in danger, **put in jeopardy,** put on the spot *and* lay on the line <both nonformal>; **expose,** lay open; incur danger, run into *or* encounter danger

**compulsion** NOUNS **obligation,** obligement; **command**; **necessity**; **inevitability**; **irresistibility, compulsiveness; forcing,** enforcement; command performance; **constraint,** coaction; **restraint; impulse,** impulsion, impelling force, impellent; **drive,** driving force *or* power, urge

**compulsive** ADJS **compelling; overfastidious,** queasy, **overparticular, overscrupulous, overconscientious,** overmeticulous, **overnice,** overprecise; **compulsive,** anal, anal-compulsive, **obsessive,** obsessional

**compulsory** ADJS **mandatory,** mandated, **imperative,** prescript, prescriptive, **obligatory,** must <nonformal>; compulsive, compulsatory, **compelling;** constraining, coactive; restraining; irresistible

**compute** VERBS **calculate, estimate, reckon, figure,** reckon at, put at, cipher, cast, tally, score; **figure out,** work out, dope out <nonformal>; **add, subtract, multiply, divide,** multiply out, algebraize, extract roots

**computer** NOUNS electronic data processor, information processor, electronic brain, digital computer, general purpose computer, analog computer, hybrid computer, machine, **hardware,** computer hardware, microelectronics device

**comrade** NOUNS **companion, fellow,** fellow companion, *camarade* <Fr>, amigo <nonformal>, mate <Brit>, comate, company, **associate**, consociate, compeer, confrere, consort, **colleague, partner,** copartner, side partner, **crony**

**con** NOUNS 1 **cheating,** cheating scheme, cheating method, angle, grift *and* move *and* racket *and* scam *and* sting <all nonformal>; deception
VERBS 2 **cheat, victimize, gull,** pigeon, fudge, **swindle, defraud,** practice fraud upon, euchre, finagle, **fleece,** mulct, fob <old>, **bilk,** cozen, cog <old>, chouse, **cheat out of, do out of,** chouse out of, beguile of *or* out of

**concave** ADJS concaved, **incurved,** incurving, incurvate; **sunk,** sunken; retreating, recessed, retiring; **hollow,** hollowed, empty; palm-shaped; dish-shaped, dished, dishing, dishlike, bowl-shaped; bowllike, crater-shaped, craterlike, saucer-shaped

**conceal** VERBS **hide,** ensconce; **cover, cover up,** blind, **screen, cloak, veil,** screen off, curtain, blanket, shroud, enshroud, envelop; **disguise, camouflage, mask,** dissemble; **paper over,** gloss over, varnish, slur over; **obscure,** obfuscate, cloud, becloud, befog, throw out a smoke screen, shade, throw into the shade; **eclipse,** occult

**concede** VERBS **acknowledge, admit, own, confess, allow,** avow, **grant,** warrant, yield <old>; go along with, not oppose *or* deny, agree provisionally *or* for the sake of argument; bring oneself to agree, assent grudgingly *or* under protest

**conceited** ADJS **vain,** vogie <Scots>; haughty, **arrogant**; **boastful, boasting, braggart, bragging,** thrasonical, thrasonic, big-mouthed <nonformal>, vaunting, vaporing, gasconading, Gascon, fanfaronading, fanfaron

**conceivable** ADJS **knowable,** recognizable, **understandable, comprehensible,** apprehendable, apprehensible, graspable, seizable, discernible, appreciable, perceptible, ascertainable, discoverable; credible, reasonable; **plausible,** colorable, apparent <old>; **imaginable, thinkable, supposable**

**conceive** VERBS 1 **understand, realize,** appreciate, have no problem with, ken <Scots>, savvy <nonformal>, sense, make sense out of, make something of; grasp, seize, get hold of, grasp *or* seize the meaning, be seized of, take, **take in,** catch, **catch on,** get the meaning of, get the hang of
2 **imagine, fancy,** conceptualize, ideate, figure to oneself; **invent, create, originate, make,** think up, dream up, shape, mold, coin, hatch, concoct, fabricate, produce

**concentrate** NOUNS 1 **extract,** extraction; **essence, quintessence, spirit, elixir;** decoction; **distillate,** distillation; concentration; infusion; refinement, purification
VERBS 2 concentrate the mind *or* thoughts, concentrate on *or* upon, attend closely to, brood on, **focus on** *or* **upon,** give *or* devote the mind to, glue the mind to, cleave to the thought of, fix the mind *or* thoughts upon, bend the mind upon, bring the mind to bear upon; get to the point; gather *or* collect one's thoughts, pull one's wits together, focus *or* fix one's thoughts, marshal *or* arrange one's thoughts *or* ideas
3 **intensify, heighten, condense, compress,** compact, **consolidate,** come to a head; **congest; squeeze, press, crowd,** cram, jam, ram down; steeve; pack *or* jam in; **solidify**

**concept** NOUNS **idea; thought,** mental *or* intellectual object, **notion,** conception, conceit, fancy; **opinion**; supposition, **theory**

**conception** NOUNS 1 **source, origin,** genesis, original, origination, **derivation, rise, beginning,** inception, commencement
2 invention, originating, engenderment, engendering, genesis, beginning; **devising,** hatching, fabrication, **concoction,** coinage, mintage, **contriving,** contrivance
3 **creative thought; visualization, envisioning,** envisaging, picturing, objectification, imaging, calling to *or* before the mind's eye, figuring *or* portraying *or* representing in the mind; depicting *or* delineating in the imagination; conceptualization; **picture, vision, image,** mental image, mental picture, visual image, vivid *or* lifelike image, eidetic image, concept, mental representation *or* presentation, *Vorstellung* <Ger>

**concern** NOUNS 1 **sympathy, fellow feeling, sympathetic response,** responsiveness, relating, warmth, **caring**; concernment, anxious concern, **solicitude,** zeal
2 **affair, matter,** thing, concernment, interest, **business,** job <nonformal>, **transaction,** proceeding, doing; cause célèbre, matter of moment; subject, subject of thought, **matter, subject matter,** what it is about, focus of interest *or* attention, discrete matter, topic of the day
VERBS 3 give concern, **trouble, bother, distress, disturb, upset,** frazzle, **disquiet, agitate;** rob one of ease *or* sleep *or* rest, keep one on edge *or* on tenterhooks *or* on pins and needles *or* on shpilkes <nonformal>
4 **interest,** involve in *or* with, affect the interest, give pause; pique one's interest, excite interest, excite *or* whet one's interest, arouse one's passion *or* enthusiasm, turn one on <nonformal>

**concert** NOUNS 1 **performance,** musical performance, **program,** musical program, program of music; symphony concert, chamber concert; philharmonic concert, philharmonic; popular concert, pops *and* pop concert <both nonformal>; promenade concert; band concert; **recital**
2 **harmony, cooperation**, peace, *rapport* <Fr>, **consonance,** unisonance, **unison,** union, chorus, oneness

**concession** NOUNS giving way, yielding; surrender, desertion of principle, evasion of responsibility, cop-out <nonformal>

**concise** ADJS **brief, short, condensed, compressed,** tight, close, compact; compendious; **curt,** brusque, **crisp,**

**terse,** summary; taciturn; reserved; **pithy, succinct; laconic,** Spartan; **abridged, abbreviated,** vest-pocket, synopsized, shortened, clipped, cut, pruned, contracted, truncated, docked; elliptic; sententious, epigrammatic, epigrammatical, gnomic, aphoristic<al>, **pointed,** to the point

*short and sweet*
THOMAS LODGE

**conclude** VERBS draw a conclusion, be forced to conclude, **come to** *or* **arrive at a conclusion, come up with a conclusion** *and* **end up** <both nonformal>; find, hold; deduce, derive, take as proved *or* demonstrated, extract, **gather,** collect, glean, fetch; **infer,** draw an inference; put two and two together

**conclusion** NOUNS 1 **end,** end point, ending, perfection, be-all and end-all, **termination, terminus, terminal,** terminating, term, period, **expiration,** expiry, phaseout, phasedown, discontinuation, closeout, **cessation**, ceasing, consummation, culmination, **finish, finis, finale,** the end, finishing, finalizing *or* finalization, a wrap <nonformal>, quietus, stoppage, windup *and* payoff <both nonformal>, curtain, curtains <nonformal>, all she wrote <nonformal>, fall of the curtain, end of the road *or* line <nonformal>
2 **deduction, inference,** consequence, consequent, corollary; derivation, illation; induction

**conclusive** ADJS 1 **completing,** completive, completory, **finishing,** consummative, culminating, terminative, **concluding,** fulfilling, finalizing, crowning; ultimate, **last, final,** terminal
2 **convincing,** convictional, well-founded, **persuasive,** assuring, impressive, satisfying, satisfactory, confidence-building; decisive, absolute, determinative; authoritative

**concoct** VERBS 1 **plot, hatch, hatch up,** cook up <nonformal>, brew, hatch *or* lay a plot
2 **invent, create, originate, make,** think up, dream up, shape, mold, coin, hatch, fabricate, produce; **suppose**; **fantasize;** fictionalize

**concrete** ADJS **substantial,** substantive; **solid; tangible,** sensible, appreciable, palpable, ponderable; **material, dense, compact;** compacted, consolidated, concentrated

**concur** VERBS **collaborate,** coact, **cowork,** synergize; **cooperate**; conspire, collude, connive, be in cahoots <nonformal>; **combine**, **unite, associate**, coadunate, join, conjoin; harmonize; **coincide,** synchronize, happen together; **accord**, correspond, **agree**

**condemn** VERBS **damn, doom; denounce,** denunciate; **censure**; **convict,** find guilty, bring home to; proscribe, excommunicate, anathematize; blacklist, put on the Index; pronounce judgment; **sentence,** pronounce sentence, pass sentence on; penalize; attaint; sign one's death warrant

**condense** VERBS 1 **abridge, shorten**, **cut, clip; summarize,** synopsize, wrap up <nonformal>; **outline, sketch,** sketch out, hit the high spots; capsule, capsulize, encapsulate; **put in a nutshell**
2 **densify,** inspissate, densen; **compress,** compact, **consolidate, concentrate,** come to a head; **congest; squeeze, press, crowd,** cram, jam, ram down; steeve; pack *or* jam in; **solidify**

**condiment** NOUNS **flavoring, flavor,** flavorer; **seasoning,** seasoner, **relish, spice,** condiments

**condition** NOUNS 1 **stipulation, provision,** proviso; **terms;** exception, reservation; **qualification**
VERBS 2 **accustom, habituate,** wont; season, **train;** familiarize, naturalize <old>, break in <nonformal>, orient, orientate
3 **train; prepare,** ready, **groom,** fit, put in tune, form, **lick into shape** <nonformal>
4 **make conditional,** make contingent; make it a condition, attach a condition *or* proviso, **stipulate;** insist upon, make a point of

**conditional** ADJS **undecided, undetermined, unsettled,** unfixed, unestablished; pendent, dependent, **pending,** depending, contingent, conditioned

**conditioning** NOUNS **habituation, accustoming;** seasoning, training; **familiarization,** naturalization <old>, breaking-in <nonformal>, orientation; **domestication, taming,** breaking, housebreaking; **inculcation, indoctrination,** catechization, inoculation, **implantation,** infixation, infixion, **impression, instillment,** instillation, impregnation, brainwashing; reindoctrination

**condolence** NOUNS **condolences,** condolement, **consolation,** comfort, balm, soothing words, **commiseration, sympathy,** sharing of grief *or* sorrow

**condom** NOUNS **contraceptive,** birth control device, prophylactic; **rubber** *and* skin *and* bag <all nonformal>

**condone** VERBS **overlook, disregard, ignore,** accept, take *and* swallow *and* let go <all nonformal>, pass over, give one another chance, let one off this time *and* let one off easy <both nonformal>, close *or* shut one's eyes to, **blink** *or* **wink at,** connive at; allow for, make allowances for; bear with, endure, regard with indulgence; pocket the affront, leave unavenged, turn the other cheek, bury *or* hide one's head in the sand

**conducive** ADJS **instrumental, implemental;** agential, agentive, agentival; **useful,** utile, handy, **helpful; contributory,** contributing, **constructive, positive,** promotional

**conduct** NOUNS 1 **behavior, deportment, comportment, manner, manners, demeanor, mien,** *maintien* <Fr>, **carriage, bearing,** port, poise, posture, guise, **air,** address, presence; tone, style, lifestyle; modus vivendi; **actions,** acts, goings-on, doings, what one is up to, movements, moves, tactics
VERBS 2 **channel,** channelize, canalize, **convey,** put through; **direct, manage, regulate, carry on, handle, run** <nonformal>; **control, command, head, govern, boss** *and* head up *and* pull the strings *and* **mastermind** *and* quarterback *and* call the signals <all nonformal>; **escort,** have in tow <nonformal>, marshal, **usher,** shepherd, **guide, lead; convoy,** guard

**conduit** NOUNS **channel, duct,** canal, course; **way, passage, passageway;** trough, troughway, troughing; tunnel; ditch, trench; adit; ingress, entrance; egress, exit

**confederacy** NOUNS **affiliation, alliance,** consociation, combination, union, unification, **coalition,** fusion, merger, coalescence, coadunation, **federation, confederation,** consolidation, incorporation, inclusion, integration

**confederate** NOUNS **associate,** consociate, **colleague,** fellow member, **companion, fellow,** bedfellow, **crony,** consort, cohort, compeer, compatriot, confrere, brother, brother-in-arms, **ally,** adjunct, coadjutor; comrade in arms, **comrade; accomplice,** cohort, fellow conspirator, coconspirator, partner *or* accomplice in crime; *particeps criminis, socius criminis* <both L>

**confer** VERBS 1 hold a conference, parley, palaver, powwow, sit down together, meet around the conference table, **go into a huddle** <nonformal>, deliberate, take counsel, counsel, **lay** *or* **put heads together;** collogue; **confer with,** sit down with, **consult with, advise with, discuss with, take up with,** reason with; **discuss,** talk over; **consult,** refer to, call in; **compare notes,** exchange observations *or* views; have conversations; negotiate, bargain
2 **transfer, convey, deliver,** hand, pass, negotiate; **hand over, turn over, pass over; assign, consign,** settle, settle on; bequeath; entail; **make over, sign over,** sign away; transmit, **hand down, hand on, pass on,** devolve upon; **deed,** deed over, give title to

**conference** NOUNS 1 **congress, convention, parley, palaver, confab** <nonformal>, confabulation, **conclave, powwow, huddle** <nonformal>, **consultation,** *pourparler* <Fr>, **meeting; council,** council of war; **discussion; interview, audience; news conference,** press conference; high-level talk, conference at the summit, summit, summit conference; summitry
2 **discussion, deliberation,** panel discussion, open discussion, joint discussion, symposium, colloquium, seminar; forum, open forum, **assembly,** *assemblée* <Fr>, **gathering, forgathering, congregation,** congress, convocation, concourse, **meeting,** meet, **get-together** *and* turnout <both nonformal>

**confess** VERBS break down and confess, **admit, acknowledge,** tell all, avow, concede, grant, **own, own up** <nonformal>, let on, implicate *or* incriminate oneself, come clean <nonformal>; spill *and* spill it *and* spill one's guts <all nonformal>; **tell the truth,** tell all, admit everything, let it all hang out <nonformal>, throw off all disguise; **unbosom oneself, make a clean breast, get it off one's chest** <nonformal>, **get it out of one's system** <nonformal>, disburden *or* unburden one's mind *or* conscience *or* heart, **get a load off one's mind** <nonformal>, fess up <nonformal>; out with it *and* spit it out *and* open up <all nonformal>

**confession** NOUNS confessing, shrift, **acknowledgment, admission,** concession, avowal, self-admission, self-concession, self-avowal, owning, owning up *and* coming clean <both nonformal>, unbosoming, unburdening oneself, getting a load off one's mind <nonformal>, fessing up <nonformal>, making a clean breast, baring one's breast; rite of confession

**confidant** NOUNS **counselor, mentor,** nestor, orienter; personal adviser; admonisher, monitor, Dutch uncle; **friend, acquaintance,** close acquaintance; confidante, repository; **intimate,** familiar, **close friend,** intimate *or* familiar friend; **bosom friend,** friend of one's bosom, inseparable friend, **best friend**

**confide** VERBS **divulge, reveal,** let in on, confide to, let one's hair down <nonformal>, unbosom oneself, let into the secret; entrust with information, give confidential information, mention privately *or* confidentially, whisper, buzz, breathe, whisper in the ear, **put a bug in one's ear** <nonformal>

**confidence** NOUNS 1 **poise,** aplomb, **self-possession, self-control,** self-command, self-restraint, restraint, possession, **presence of mind;** assurance, **self-confidence, self-assurance**
2 **secret,** private *or* personal matter, privity <old>; confidential *or* **privileged information** *or* **communication;** dark secret; solemn secret; guarded secret, hush-hush matter, classified information, eyes-only *or* top-secret information, restricted information; inside information

**confident** ADJS **sure,** secure, **assured,** reassured, decided, determined; **convinced,** persuaded, positive, **cocksure; unhesitating,** unfaltering, unwavering; **undoubting**; **self-confident, self-assured, self-reliant,** sure of oneself; poised; unafraid; **overconfident, oversure,** overweening, hubristic

**confidential** ADJS auricular, **inside** <nonformal>, esoteric; *in petto* <Ital>, close to one's chest *or* vest <nonformal>, under one's hat <nonformal>; **off the record,** not for the record, within these four walls, for no other ears, eyes-only, between us; not to be quoted, not for publication *or* release

**configuration** NOUNS **arrangement, ordering,** structuring, shaping, forming, configurating, constitution; **formation,** formulation, form, array; **constellation**

**confine** VERBS **shut in,** shut away, coop in, hem in, fence in *or* up, wall in *or* up, rail in; **shut up, coop up, pen up,** box up, mew up, bottle up, cork up, seal up, **impound;** pen, coop, pound <old>, crib, mew, cloister, immure, cage, cage in, encage; **enclose**; **hold, keep in,** hold *or* keep in custody, **detain,** keep in detention, constrain, ground, **restrain,** hold in restraint; check, inhibit; restrict; shackle

**confinement** NOUNS 1 **birth, childbirth, childbearing, having a baby, giving birth, birthing,** parturition, the stork <nonformal>; lying-in, being brought to bed, **childbed,** *accouchement* <Fr>; **labor,** travail, birth throes *or* pangs; **delivery,** blessed event <nonformal>
2 locking-up, lockup, caging, penning, putting behind bars, impoundment, **restraint,** restriction; check, **restraint, constraint**

**confirm** VERBS affirm, **attest,** warrant, uphold <Brit nonformal>, **substantiate, authenticate, validate, certify,** ratify, **verify;** circumstantiate, **corroborate, bear out,** support, buttress, **sustain,** fortify, bolster, back, back up, reinforce, undergird, strengthen; **document;** probate, prove

**confirmation** NOUNS **substantiation,** proof, proving, proving out, bearing out, affirmation, attestation, **authentication, validation, certification,** ratification, **verification; corroboration, support,** supporting evidence, corroboratory evidence, fortification, buttressing, bolstering, backing, backing up, reinforcement, undergirding, strengthening, circumstantiation, fact sheet; **documentation**

**confirmed** ADJS **inveterate, chronic, established,** long-established, **fixed, settled, rooted,** thorough; incorrigible, irreversible; **deep-rooted,** deep-set, deep-settled, **deep-seated,** deep-fixed, deep-dyed; **infixed, ingrained,** fast, dyed-in-the-wool; implanted, inculcated, instilled; set, **set in one's ways,** settled in habit

**confiscate** VERBS **attach, annex;** sequester, sequestrate, impound; **commandeer,** press, **impress;** expropriate, nationalize, socialize, communalize, communize, collectivize; exercise the right of eminent domain, exercise the right of angary; replevy, replevin; garnishee, garnish

**conflict** NOUNS 1 **disaccord, discord,** open conflict *or* war, **friction,** rub; jar, **jarring,** jangle, clash, clashing; touchiness, strained relations, **tension;** bad blood; **unpleasantness;** mischief; **contention**; **enmity**; psychological stress VERBS 2 **disagree, differ**, vary, not see eye-to-eye, be at cross-purposes, tangle assholes <nonformal>, **disaccord,** clash, **jar,** jangle, jostle, collide, square off, cross swords, break, break off

**conform** VERBS observe the proprieties, play the game, follow the rules, fall in *or* into line; comply, correspond, accord, harmonize; **adapt,** adjust, **accommodate,** bend, meet, suit, fit, shape; **comply with,** agree with, tally with, chime *or* fall in with, go by, be guided *or* regulated by, observe, follow, bend, yield, take the shape of; **adapt to,** adjust to, gear to, assimilate to, **accommodate to** *or* **with; reconcile,** settle, compose; rub off corners; **make conform,** shape, lick into shape, mold, force into a mold; straighten, rectify, correct, **discipline**

**conformist** NOUNS conformer, sheep, trimmer, parrot, yes-man, organization man; **conventionalist,** Mrs Grundy, Babbitt, Philistine, middle-class type, button-down *or* white-bread type <nonformal>, **bourgeois,** Middle American, plastic person *and* clone *and* square <all nonformal>, three-piecer *and* yuppie <both nonformal>, Barbie Doll <trademark> <nonformal>

**confound** VERBS **confuse,** mix, mix up, muddle, tumble, jumble, jumble together, **blur,** blur distinctions, overlook distinctions; **thwart, frustrate, foil, cross, balk; discomfit,** upset, **disrupt,** flummox <nonformal>, **disconcert, baffle,** nonplus, perplex, stump <nonformal>

**confront** VERBS **meet, meet with,** meet up with <nonformal>, come face to face with, meet head-on *or* eyeball to eyeball, be on a collision course; **accost,** encounter; front, fly in the teeth *or* face of, **face up to,** face down, face out; affront, say right to one's face, square up to, go eyeball-to-eyeball *or* one-on-one with <nonformal>;

**confused** ADJS **chaotic,** anarchic, **muddled, jumbled,** scattered, helter-skelter <nonformal>, higgledy-piggledy, hugger-mugger, skimble-skamble, in a mess; **topsy-turvy,** arsy-varsy, upside-down, ass-backwards <nonformal>; **mixed up, balled** *or* **bollixed up** <nonformal>, **screwed up** <nonformal>, mucked up <nonformal>, **fouled up** *and* fucked up *and* snafu <all nonformal>; **bewildered, dismayed,** distracted, distraught, abashed, **disconcerted, embarrassed,** discomposed, **put-out, disturbed, upset,** perturbed, **bothered,** all hot and bothered <nonformal>

**confusion** NOUNS **fluster,** flummox <nonformal>, **flutter,** flurry, ruffle; disorientation, **muddle, muddlement,** fuddle *and* fuddlement <both nonformal>, befuddlement, muddleheadedness, daze, maze <nonformal>; unsettlement, disorganization, **disorder,** chaos, **mess** *and* mix-up *and* snafu <all nonformal>, balls-up *and* shemozzle <both Brit nonformal>, shuffle, jumble, **discomfiture, discomposure, disconcertion,** discombobulation <nonformal>, **bewilderment, embarrassment, disturbance,** perturbation, **upset,** frenzy, pother, bother, botheration *and* stew <both nonformal>, pucker <old>; tizzy *and* swivet *and* sweat <all nonformal>; haze, fog, mist, cloud; maze; **perplexity**

**con game** NOUNS **confidence game, skin game** <nonformal>, **bunco game; shell game,** thimblerig, thimblerigging; bucket shop, boiler room <nonformal>; bait-and- switch, the wire

**congeal** VERBS **cohere,** coagulate, clabber <nonformal>, **clot; freeze; thicken,** thick <old>; inspissate, incrassate; set, concrete; gelatinize, gelatinate, jelly, jellify, **jell,** gel

**congenial** ADJS **friendly,** friendlike; **amicable, peaceable,** unhostile; **harmonious**; **amiable,** *simpático* <Sp>, *simpatico* <Ital>, *sympathique* <Fr>, compatible, pleasant, agreeable, favorable, well-intentioned, well-meaning, well-meant; sociable; symbiotic

**congenital** ADJS **innate, inborn; born, consummate,** unmitigated, unalloyed, perfect, veritable, egregious, deep-dyed, dyed-in-the-wool; **native, natural,** natural to, connatural, native to, indigenous; hereditary, inherited, bred in the bone, in the blood, running in the blood *or* race *or* strain, radical, rooted; connate, connatal, coeval

**congested** ADJS **glutted,** gorged, overfed, bloated, replete, swollen, **satiated, stuffed,** overstuffed, **crowded, overcrowded, crammed,** jammed, packed, jam-packed, like sardines in a can *or* tin, bumper-to-bumper <nonformal>; choked, stuffed up; overblown, distended, **swollen, bloated**

**conglomeration** NOUNS 1 **hodgepodge,** hotchpotch, hotchpot; **medley, miscellany,** mélange, pastiche, *pasticcio* <Ital>, **assortment,** assemblage, mixed bag, ragbag, grab bag, olio, *olla podrida* <Sp>, **scramble, jumble,** mingle-mangle, **mix,** mishmash, **mess,** can of worms <nonformal>, dog's breakfast <Can nonformal>, mare's nest, rat's nest, hurrah's nest <nautical nonformal>, hash, patchwork, salad, gallimaufry, salmagundi, **potpourri,** stew, sauce, slurry, omnium-gatherum

2 **combination, incorporation,** aggregation, agglomeration, congeries; **amalgamation, consolidation,** assimilation, **integration,** solidification, **encompassment,** inclusion, ecumenism

**congratulate** VERBS **felicitate,** bless, **compliment,** tender *or* offer one's congratulations *or* felicitations *or* compliments; shake one's hand, pat one on the back; **rejoice with one,** wish one joy; **applaud**, **praise**, flatter

**congratulations** NOUNS 1 **felicitation,** blessing, **compliment,** pat on the back; good wishes, best wishes; **applause**, **praise**, flattery

2 <nonformal> **congrats!, all right!, aw right!, right on!,** way to go!, attaboy!, attagirl!, good deal!, looking good!, nice going!, that's my boy!, that's my girl!

**congregate** VERBS **come together, assemble, collect,** come from far and wide, come *or* arrive in a body; league, ally; **unite**; muster, **meet, gather, forgather,** gang up <nonformal>, mass; **merge,** converge, flow together, fuse; flock together; herd together; **throng, crowd,** swarm, teem, hive, surge, seethe, mill, stream, horde

**congregation** NOUNS **lay persons,** flock, fold, sheep; parishioners, churchgoers, assembly; *minyan* <Heb>; **parish,** society; **assembly,** *assemblée* <Fr>, **gathering, forgathering,** congress

**congress** NOUNS **legislature,** legislative body; **parliament, assembly,** general assembly, house of assembly, legislative assembly, **national assembly, chamber of deputies,** federal assembly, diet; **upper chamber** *or* **house**

**conjecture** NOUNS 1 **guess,** unverified supposition, perhaps, speculation, guesswork, surmise, educated guess; guesstimate *and* hunch *and* shot *and* stab <all nonformal>; rough guess, wild guess, blind guess, bold conjecture, shot in the dark <nonformal>

VERBS 2 **guess,** guesstimate <nonformal>, give a guess, talk off the top of one's head <nonformal>, hazard a conjecture, venture a guess, risk assuming *or* stating, tentatively suggest, go out on a limb <nonformal>

**conjugal** ADJS **matrimonial, marital, connubial, nuptial,** wedded, married, hymeneal; epithalamic; **spousal;** husbandly, uxorious; bridal, wifely, uxorial

**conjure** VERBS **conjure up,** evoke, invoke, raise, summon, call up; **call up spirits,** conjure *or* conjure up spirits, summon spirits, raise ghosts, evoke from the dead

*call spirits from the vasty deep*
SHAKESPEARE

**conjurer** NOUNS **trickster,** tricker; **juggler,** sleight-of-hand performer, magician, illusionist, **prestidigitator,** *escamoteur* <Fr>; **sorcerer, necromancer, wizard,** warlock, theurgist; diviner

**con man** NOUNS

<nonformal> **gyp,** gypper, gyp artist, flimflammer, flimflam man, blackleg, bilker, fleecer, diddler, crook, sharpie, shark, jackleg, slicker, con artist, bunco, bunco artist, bunco steerer, scammer, hustler

**connect** VERBS **adjoin,** join, conjoin, butt, **abut,** abut on *or* upon, be contiguous, be in contact; border, **border on** *or* **upon,** verge on *or* upon; lie by, stand by; unite, meet, meet up, link up, merge, converge, **come together;** communicate, intercommunicate

**connection** NOUNS 1 **intermediary,** intermedium, mediary, medium; link, **connecting link,** tie, **go-between,** liaison; **mediator; contact, touch; passageway, conduit**; access, communication; alliance, **family connection** *or* tie; **marriage relationship,** affinity, marital affinity; marriage connection, matrimonial connection; **relation, relationship, association**
2 **relevance, pertinence,** pertinency, cogency, relatedness, materiality, **apposíteness,** germaneness; reference, **bearing,** concern; **continuum,** plenum; concatenation, catenation

**connive** VERBS **conspire,** collude, be in cahoots <nonformal>, complot <old>, cabal; **hatch, hatch up,** cook up <nonformal>, brew, concoct, hatch *or* lay a plot; **maneuver,** machinate, finesse, operate <nonformal>, engineer, rig, wangle <nonformal>, angle, finagle <nonformal>

**connoisseur** NOUNS *connaisseur* <Fr>, *cognoscente* <Ital>; **judge,** good judge, **critic, expert,** authority, maven <nonformal>, arbiter, arbiter of taste, *arbiter elegantiarum* <L>, tastemaker, trend-setter; **epicure,** epicurean; **gourmet, gourmand,** *bon vivant* <Fr>, good *or* refined palate

**connotation** NOUNS **implication, import,** latent *or* underlying *or* implied meaning, ironic suggestion *or* implication, more than meets the eye, what is read between the lines; meaning; **suggestion,** allusion; coloration, tinge, undertone, overtone, undercurrent, more than meets the eye *or* ear, something between the lines, intimation, touch, nuance, innuendo; **inference, supposition,** presupposition, assumption, presumption; secondary *or* transferred *or* metaphorical sense; undermeaning, undermention, subsidiary sense, subsense, **subtext**

**connubial** ADJS **matrimonial, marital, conjugal, nuptial,** wedded, married, hymeneal; epithalamic; **spousal;** husbandly, uxorious; bridal, wifely, uxorial

**conquer** VERBS **vanquish,** quell, **suppress, put down, subdue, subjugate,** put under the yoke, master; **reduce,** prostrate, fell, **flatten, break, smash, crush, humble,** bend, **bring to terms, humble,** humiliate, take down a notch *or* peg, bend, **bend to one's will**

**conqueror** NOUNS **victor, winner,** victress, victrix, triumpher; defeater, **vanquisher,** subduer, subjugator, *conquistador* <Sp>; master of the situation; conquering hero

**conscience** NOUNS grace, **sense of right and wrong;** inward monitor, inner arbiter, moral censor, censor, ethical self, superego; **voice of conscience,** still small voice within, guardian *or* good angel; tender conscience; clear *or* clean conscience; social conscience; conscientiousness; twinge of conscience

**conscientious** ADJS **meticulous, exacting, scrupulous,** religious, punctilious, punctual, **particular, fussy, critical, attentive,** scrutinizing; **thorough,** thoroughgoing; **finical,** finicking, finicky; **strict,** rigid, **rigorous,** exigent, demanding

**conscious** ADJS 1 **living, alive,** having life, live, very much alive, alive and well, alive and kicking <nonformal>, breathing, quick <old>, **animate,** animated, **vital,** zoetic, instinct with life, imbued *or* endowed with life, viable
2 **intentional,** considered, studied, advised, calculated, contemplated, envisaged, envisioned, premeditated, knowing, witting; watchful, aware, alert

**conscript** VERBS **call to arms, call up,** call to the colors; recruit; draft, induct, press, impress, commandeer; **mobilize,** call to active duty; **muster,** levy, raise, muster in

**consecrate** VERBS **dedicate, commit, devote,** set apart; **ordain,** frock, **canonize**

**consecutive** ADJS **successive,** successional, back-to-back <nonformal>; progressive; **serial,** ordinal, seriate, catenary; sequent, **sequential;** linear, lineal, in-line

**consensus** NOUNS general agreement, *consensus omnium* <L, consent of all> *and consensus gentium* <L, consent of the people>, sense, **unanimity**; **like-mindedness,** meeting *or* intersection *or* confluence of minds, sense of the meeting

**consent** NOUNS 1 **assent, agreement,** accord <old>, acceptance, approval, blessing, approbation, sanction, **endorsement,** ratification, backing; affirmation, affirmative, affirmative voice *or* vote, yea, aye, **nod** *and* **okay** *and* **OK** <all nonformal>; **leave, per-**

**mission,** readiness, promptness, promptitude, eagerness, tacit *or* unspoken *or* silent *or* implicit consent
VERBS 2 **assent,** give *or* yield assent, **acquiesce, comply, accede, agree,** agree to *or* with, have no problem with; find it in one's heart; take kindly to *and* hold with <both nonformal>; **subscribe to,** acquiesce in, abide by; yes, **say 'yes'**

**consequence** NOUNS **effect, result,** resultant, consequent, sequent, sequence, sequel, sequela, sequelae; event, eventuality, eventuation, **upshot, outcome,** logical outcome, possible outcome, scenario; **outgrowth,** spin-off, offshoot, offspring, issue, aftermath, legacy; **weight,** moment, importance, eminence

**conservation** NOUNS **preservation,** preserval, **saving, salvation,** salvage, **keeping, safekeeping,** maintenance, upkeep, support; environmental conservation; nature conservation *or* conservancy, soil conservation, forest conservation, etc

**conservationist** NOUNS **environmentalist,** preservationist, nature-lover, environmental activist, doomwatcher <Brit>, duck-squeezer *and* ecofreak *and* tree-hugger *and* eagle freak <all nonformal>

**conservative** NOUNS **rightist, rightwinger;** dry <Brit nonformal>, standpat *and* standpatter <both nonformal>; hard hat; social Darwinist; ultraconservative, arch-conservative, extreme right-winger, **reactionary,** reactionarist, reactionist, diehard; **royalist, monarchist,** Bourbon, Tory, imperialist; **right, right wing; radical right**

*the leftover progressive of an earlier generation*
EDMUND FULLER

2 **moderate,** moderatist, moderationist, middle-of-the-roader, **centrist,** neutral, compromiser
ADJS 3 **right-wing,** right of center, dry <Brit nonformal>; old-line, die-hard, unreconstructed, standpat <nonformal>, unprogressive, nonprogressive; ultraconservative, **reactionary,** reactionist

**consider** VERBS 1 **care, mind, heed,** reck, think, regard, pay heed to, take heed *or* thought of; **take an interest,** be concerned; **pay attention**
2 **discuss, debate, reason, deliberate,** deliberate upon, exchange views *or* opinions, talk, **talk over, hash over** <nonformal>, talk of *or* about, rap <nonformal>, comment upon, reason about, discourse about, **treat,** dissertate on, handle, deal with, take up, **go into, examine,** investigate, talk out, **analyze,** sift, **study,** canvass, review
3 **allow for, make allowance for,** make room for, provide for, open the door to, take account of, **take into account** *or* **consideration,** consider the circumstances

**considerable** NOUNS 1 **lot, lots,** deal, no end of, **good** *or* **great deal,** sight, **heap, pile, stack,** loads, **raft, slew,** whole slew, spate, wad, **batch,** mess, mint, peck, pack, pot, **tidy sum,** quite a little
ADJS 2 **sizable, big, great, grand,** tall <nonformal>, **goodly,** healthy, tidy <nonformal>, **substantial,** bumper; **numerous, many, manifold,** not a few, no few; **very many,** full many, **ever so many,** quite some <nonformal>

**considerably** ADVS **greatly, largely,** to a large *or* great extent, in great measure, on a large scale; **much,** muchly <nonformal>, pretty much, very much, so, so very much, ever so much, ever so, never so; considerable <nonformal>; abundantly, plenty <nonformal>, no end of, no end, not a little, galore <nonformal>, **a lot,** a deal <nonformal>, **a great deal,** *beaucoup* <Fr>

**considerate** ADJS **thoughtful,** mindful, heedful, regardful, solicitous, attentive, delicate, tactful, mindful of others; complaisant, **accommodating,** accommodative, at one's service, **helpful,** agreeable, **obliging,** indulgent, tolerant, lenient

**consign** VERBS **assign,** confer, settle, settle on; **make over, sign over,** sign away; transmit, **hand down, hand on, pass on,** devolve upon

**consistent** ADJS **connected;** continuous, **serial,** uninterrupted, contiguous, sequential, sequent, **consecutive**; orderly, tight; **joined; sound, well-grounded, well-founded,** conforming to the facts *or* the data *or* the evidence *or* reality, hard, solid, substantial; self-consistent, logical

**consolation** NOUNS **solace,** solacement, easement, heart's ease, **encouragement,** aid and comfort, **assurance, reassur-**

**ance,** support, **comfort,** crumb *or* shred of comfort, condolence, sympathy; **relief**

*kind words and comfortable*
WILLIAM COWPER

**console** VERBS **comfort, solace,** give *or* bring comfort, bear up; condole with, sympathize with, extend sympathy; ease, **put** *or* **set at ease;** bolster, support; relieve; **assure, reassure; encourage, hearten,** pat on the back; **cheer**; wipe away the tears

*rejoice with them that do rejoice, and weep with them that weep*
BIBLE

**consolidate** VERBS **incorporate, amalgamate,** assimilate, **integrate,** solidify, coalesce, compound, put *or* lump together, roll into one, come together, make one, unitize

**conspicuous** ADJS **noticeable, notable,** ostensible, **prominent, bold, pronounced, salient,** in relief, in bold *or* high *or* strong relief, **striking, outstanding,** in the foreground, sticking *or* hanging out

**conspiracy** NOUNS **intrigue,** web of intrigue, **plot, scheme,** deep-laid plot *or* scheme, underplot, game *or* little game <both nonformal>, trick, stratagem, finesse; counterplot; confederacy, covin, complot <old>, cabal; **scheming,** schemery, plotting; finagling <nonformal>, **machination,** manipulation, **maneuvering,** engineering, rigging; frame-up <nonformal>; wire-pulling <nonformal>

**conspirator** NOUNS **schemer, plotter,** counterplotter, finagler <nonformal>, Machiavellian; **intriguer,** *intrigant, intrigante* <both Fr>, cabalist; **conspirer,** coconspirator, **conniver;** maneuverer, machinator, operator <nonformal>, opportunist, exploiter; wire-puller <nonformal>

**conspire** VERBS **plot, scheme, intrigue,** be up to something; **connive,** collude, complot <old>, cabal; **hatch, hatch up,** cook up <nonformal>, brew, concoct, hatch *or* lay a plot; **maneuver,** machinate, finesse, operate <nonformal>, engineer, rig, wangle <nonformal>, angle, finagle <nonformal>

**constant** ADJS 1 **faithful, loyal,** devoted, allegiant; **true, true-blue,** true to one's colors; **steadfast,** unswerving, steady, consistent, stable, unfailing, staunch, firm, solid
2 **continual**, **perennial; steady,** sustained, **regular; incessant, ceaseless, unceasing,** unintermitting, unintermittent *or* unintermitted, unremitting, relentless, unrelenting, unchanging, unvarying, uninterrupted, unstopped, unbroken

**constellation** NOUNS **configuration,** asterism; zodiacal constellation; **star cluster,** galactic cluster, open cluster, globular cluster, stellar association, supercluster; Magellanic clouds

**consternation** NOUNS **fear, fright,** affright; **scare, alarm, dismay; dread,** unholy dread, **awe; terror, horror,** horrification, mortal *or* abject fear; **phobia** <see list>, funk *or* blue funk <both nonformal>; **panic,** panic fear *or* terror; stampede; **cowardice**

**constituency** NOUNS **electorate,** electors; constituents; bailiwick, vantage, stamping ground, footing, **territory,** turf, home turf, **power base**

**constituent** NOUNS **component, ingredient,** integrant, makings *and* fixings <both nonformal>, **element, factor, part**, player, module, part and parcel; appurtenance, adjunct; **feature,** aspect, specialty, circumstance, detail, item; elector

**constitute** VERBS **compose,** construct, fabricate; **incorporate,** embody, incarnate; **form, organize,** structure, shape, shape up; **consist of,** be a feature of, form a part of, combine *or* unite in, merge in; **consist,** be made up of, be constituted of, contain

**constraint** NOUNS **restraint; inhibition;** legal restraint, injunction, enjoining, enjoinder, interdict; **control, curb, check,** rein, arrest, arrestation; **retardation,** deceleration, slowing down; cooling *and* cooling off *and* cooling down <all nonformal>; retrenchment, curtailment; self-control; **hindrance**

**constrict** VERBS **narrow,** constrict, diminish, draw in, go in; restrict, limit, straiten, confine; shut off, **close,** close off *or* up, close tight, shut tight; constrict, squeeze, **stifle,** stop up

**construct** VERBS **build; structure; organize; form**, fabricate

**construction** NOUNS 1 **structure, formation,** conformation, **format; arrangement**, configuration; **composition**; making, building, creation, production, forging, fashioning, molding, fabrication, manufacture
2 **interpretation, reading,** way of seeing *or* understanding *or* putting; **explanation, definition,** sense-distinction; **phrase, expression, locution, utterance,** usage, term, verbalism

**constructive** ADJS **helpful, useful,** utile, aidful <old>; **profitable, salutary,** good for, **beneficial**; remedial, therapeutic; **serviceable, useful**; **contributory,** contributing, conducive, **positive,** promotional

**construe** VERBS **interpret,** put a construction on, **take;** understand, **understand by, take to mean,** take it that; **read; read into,** read between the lines; see in a special light, read in view of, take an approach to, **define, describe**; **translate, render**

**consular** ADJS **diplomatic,** ambassadorial, ministerial, plenipotentiary

**consulate** NOUNS **office, embassy,** legation, chancery, chancellery

**consult** VERBS **confer,** sit down together, **go into a huddle** <nonformal>, deliberate, take counsel, counsel, **lay** *or* **put heads together;** collogue; **consult with, advise with, discuss with, take up with,** reason with; **discuss,** talk over; refer to, call in

**consultant** NOUNS **adviser, counsel, counselor,** professional consultant, expert, maven <nonformal>, boffin <Brit nonformal>; instructor, guide, **mentor,** nestor, orienter; confidant, personal adviser

**consultation** NOUNS **conference, congress, convention, parley, palaver, confab** <nonformal>, confabulation, **conclave, powwow, huddle** <nonformal>, *pourparler* <Fr>, **meeting;** interview, audience

**consume** VERBS **spend, expend, use up;** absorb, assimilate, digest, ingest, eat, **eat up,** swallow, swallow up, gobble, gobble up; burn up; **finish,** finish off; **exhaust, deplete,** impoverish, drain, drain of resources; suck dry, bleed white <nonformal>, suck one's blood; wear away, erode, erode away, ablate; waste away; **throw away, squander**

**consumer** NOUNS **user,** employer; **buyer,** purchaser, emptor, vendee; **shopper,** marketer

**consumption** NOUNS 1 **consuming, using** *or* **eating up;** burning up; absorption, assimilation, digestion, ingestion, **expenditure,** expending, spending; squandering, wastefulness; finishing; **depletion,** drain, exhausting, **exhaustion,** impoverishment; **waste,** wastage, wasting away, erosion, ablation, wearing down, wearing away, attrition; throwing away
2 **tuberculosis** *or* **TB,** white plague, phthisis

**contact** NOUNS 1 **touch,** touching, *attouchement* <Fr>, taction, tangency, contingence; gentle *or* tentative contact, caress, brush, glance, nudge, kiss, rub, graze; impingement, impingence; osculation; **communication,** communion, congress, **commerce, intercourse**
2 **go-between, middleman, intermediary, medium,** intermedium, intermediate, interagent, **internuncio,** broker; connection <nonformal>; **negotiator,** negotiant; interpleader; arbitrator, mediator
VERBS 3 **come in contact, touch, feel, impinge,** bump up against, hit; osculate; **graze,** caress, kiss, nudge, rub, brush, glance, scrape, sideswipe, skim, skirt, shave; grope *and* feel up *and* cop a feel <all nonformal>; have a near miss, brush *or* graze *or* squeak by
4 **communicate with, get in touch** *or* **contact with, make contact with,** raise, reach, get to, get through to, get hold of, make *or* establish connection, get in connection with; **make advances,** make overtures, **approach,** make up to <nonformal>; relate to; keep in touch *or* contact with, maintain connection; **answer,** respond *or* reply to, get back to; **question,** interrogate; **correspond,** drop a line

**contagious** ADJS **infectious,** infective, **catching,** taking, spreading, **communicable,** zymotic, inoculable; pestiferous, pestilential, **epidemic,** epidemial, pandemic; epizootic, epiphytotic; endemic; sporadic

**contain** VERBS **enclose,** close in, bound, include; compass, encompass; **surround,** encircle; **shut** *or* **pen in,** coop in; **fence in,** wall in, wall up, rail in, rail off, screen off, curtain off; **hem** *or* **hedge in,** box in, pocket; shut *or* coop *or* mew up; pen, coop, corral, cage, impound, mew; **imprison,** incarcerate, jail, lock up, lock down; **besiege,** beset, beleaguer, leaguer, cordon, cordon off, quarantine, blockade

**container** NOUNS **receptacle;** receiver, holder, vessel, utensil; basin, pot, pan, cup, glass, ladle, bottle; cask; box, case; basket

**contaminate** VERBS **defile, foul, befoul; sully;** foul one's own nest, shit where one eats <nonformal>, nasty *or* benasty <both nonformal>, mess *and* mess up <both nonformal>; **pollute, corrupt, infect; taint,** tarnish; **adulterate, debase,** denaturalize, pollute, denature, bastardize, **tamper with, doctor** *and* doctor up <both nonformal>; **irradiate**

**contemplate** VERBS **consider, speculate, reflect, study, ponder,** perpend, **weigh, deliberate, debate, meditate, muse, brood, ruminate,** chew the cud <nonformal>, digest; introspect, be abstracted; wrinkle one's brow; fall into a brown study, retreat into one's mind *or* thoughts; **toy with, play with,** play around with, flirt *or* coquet with the idea

**contemporary** ADJS **modern, present-day,** present-time, twentieth-century, latter-day, space-age, neoteric, now <nonformal>, **newfashioned,** fashionable, modish, mod, *à la mode* <Fr>, **up-to-date,** up-to-datish, **up-to-the-minute, in,** abreast of the times; **advanced,** progressive, forward-looking, modernizing, **avant-garde;** ultramodern, ultra-ultra, ahead of its time, far out, way out, modernistic

**contempt** NOUNS **disdain, scorn,** contemptuousness, disdainfulness, superciliousness, snootiness, snottiness, sniffiness, toploftiness, scornfulness, despite, contumely, sovereign contempt; snobbishness; clannishness, cliquishness, exclusiveness, exclusivity; hauteur, airs, arrogance; **ridicule**; **insult**; **disparagement**

**contemptible** ADJS **offensive, objectionable, odious, repulsive,** repellent, rebarbative, **repugnant, revolting,** forbidding; **obnoxious, abhorrent, hateful, abominable,** heinous, **despicable,** detestable, execrable, beneath *or* below contempt, **base,** ignoble

**contemptuous** ADJS **disdainful,** dismissive, **supercilious,** contumelious, cavalier, you-be-damned <nonformal>; **arrogant**, uppish *and* uppity <both nonformal>; abusive, offensive, humiliating, degrading, calumnious; **disparaging, derogatory,** derogative, **depreciatory,** depreciative, deprecatory, slighting, belittling, minimizing, detractory, pejorative, backbiting

**content** NOUNS 1 **contents,** what is contained *or* included *or* comprised; **insides**, innards <nonformal>, guts; **components, constituents, ingredients,** elements, **items, parts, divisions,** subdivisions
2 **capacity, volume,** holding capacity, cubic footage *or* yardage etc, accommodation, room, space, measure, limit, burden; gallonage, tankage; poundage, tonnage, cordage; stowage; **quantity**
3 **contentment,** contentedness, satisfiedness; **satisfaction,** entire satisfaction, fulfillment; ease, peace of mind, composure; comfort; well-being, euphoria; **happiness**; **acceptance,** resignation, reconcilement, reconciliation
ADJS 4 **contented, satisfied; pleased**; happy; **easy, at ease,** at one's ease, easygoing; composed; **comfortable**, of good comfort; euphoric, eupeptic; carefree, without care, *sans souci* <Fr>; accepting, resigned, reconciled; uncomplaining, unrepining; **willing, agreeable**

**contest** NOUNS 1 **game,** play, engagement, **match,** trial, test; **fight,** bout
VERBS 2 **deny, not admit, not accept,** refuse to admit *or* accept; **disclaim, disown, disaffirm, disavow, disallow, dispute,** gainsay, **oppose, counter,** go counter to, take issue with, join issue upon, run counter to

**context** NOUNS **circumstances,** total situation, existing conditions *or* situation, set of conditions, terms of reference, **environment**, environing circumstances, frame, setting, surrounding conditions, parameters; **the picture,** the whole picture, full particulars

**contingent** ADJS **dependent, depending;** contingent on, **dependent on, depending on,** predicated on, based on, hanging *or* hinging on, turning on, revolving on; depending on circumstances; circumscribed by, hedged *or* hedged about by; boxed in <nonformal>; **subject to,** incidental to, incident to; adventitious, incidental, iffy <nonformal>

**continual** ADJS continued, continuing;

**cyclical,** repetitive, **recurrent,** periodic; **constant, perennial**

**continuation** NOUNS **sequel,** continuance, **follow-up** *or* **follow-through** <nonformal>; **protraction, prolongation,** extension, lengthening, **postponement, deferment** *or* **deferral,** prorogation, putting-off, tabling, protraction, extension of time; **adjournment** *or* adjournal, adjournment sine die; **persistence, perseverance**; **endurance, stamina,** staying power; **continuity**; **repetition**

**continue** VERBS 1 **lengthen, prolong,** prolongate, **elongate, extend,** produce, **protract;** lengthen out, let out, **draw** *or* drag *or* stretch *or* string *or* spin out; last, **endure,** go *or* run *or* flow on
2 **postpone, delay, defer, put off,** give one a rain check <nonformal>, shift off, hold off *or* up <nonformal>, prorogue, put on hold *or* ice *or* the back burner <all nonformal>, reserve, waive, **suspend,** hang up, stay, hang fire; protract, drag *or* stretch out <nonformal>; **hold over,** lay over, stand over, let the matter stand, **put aside,** lay *or* set *or* push aside, lay *or* set by, **table,** lay on the table, pigeonhole, **shelve,** put on the shelf, put on ice <nonformal>

**continuing** ADJS **durable,** perdurable, **lasting, enduring,** perduring, **abiding,** remaining, staying, **stable**, persisting, **persistent,** perennial; inveterate, agelong; **steadfast, constant,** intransient, immutable, unfading, evergreen, sempervirent, **permanent**, perennial, **long-lasting,** long-standing, of long duration *or* standing; long-term; **long-lived**

**continuity** NOUNS logical order, serial order; **degree**; **hierarchy, gradation,** subordination, superordination, rank, place; **sequence**

**continuous** ADJS continued, **continual,** continuing; **uninterrupted, unintermittent,** unintermitted, featureless, unrelieved, monotonous; **connected, joined**, linked, chained, concatenated, catenated, articulated; **unbroken,** serried, **uniform**, **incessant, constant,** steady, stable, **ceaseless,** unceasing, **endless,** unending, never-ending, **interminable,** perennial; **perpetual, everlasting,** everliving, ever-being, ever-abiding, ever-during, ever-durable, permanent, perdurable, indestructible; **infinite, abiding**

**contortion** NOUNS **distortion,** torsion, twist, twistedness, **crookedness,** tortuosity; unsymmetry, disproportion, lopsidedness, imbalance, irregularity, **deviation; twist,** quirk, turn, screw, wring, wrench, wrest; **warp,** buckle; knot, gnarl

**contraband** NOUNS smuggled goods; narcotics, drugs, dope <nonformal>, jewels, cigarettes; bootleg liquor; stolen goods *or* property, hot goods *or* items <nonformal>

**contraceptive** NOUNS birth control device, prophylactic; condom; **rubber** *and* skin *and* bag <all nonformal>; oral contraceptive, **birth control pill, the pill** <nonformal>, morning-after pill, abortion pill; diaphragm, pessary; spermicide, spermicidal jelly, contraceptive foam; intrauterine device *or* IUD

**contract** NOUNS 1 **compact, pact,** legal contract, valid contract, **covenant,** convention, transaction, paction <Scots>, accord, **agreement,** mutual agreement, agreement between *or* among parties, signed *or* written agreement, formal agreement, legal agreement, undertaking, stipulation; bond, binding agreement, ironclad agreement, covenant of salt
VERBS 2 **catch, get,** take, sicken for <Brit>, **come down with** <nonformal>, be stricken *or* seized by, fall a victim to; catch cold; take one's death <nonformal>
3 **compress,** cramp, compact, condense, concentrate, consolidate, solidify; **reduce, decrease**; abbreviate, curtail, **shorten**; **constrict, narrow,** draw, draw in *or* together; choke, choke off

**contraction** NOUNS 1 contracture; systole; **compression,** compressure, pressurizing, pressurization; **compacting,** compaction, compactedness; **condensation, concentration,** consolidation, solidification; **circumscription, narrowing;** reduction, diminuendo, **decrease**; abbreviation, curtailment, shortening; **constriction,** stricture *or* striction, astriction, strangulation, **choking,** choking off; bottleneck, chokepoint, hourglass, hourglass figure
2 **abbreviation,** shortening, clipping, cutting, pruning, truncation

**contradict** VERBS **deny, not admit, not accept,** refuse to admit *or* accept; **disclaim, disown, disaffirm, disavow,**

**disallow,** abjure, forswear, **renounce, retract,** take back, recant; revoke, nullify, **repudiate;** fly in the face of, cross, assert the contrary, contravene, controvert, impugn, **dispute,** gainsay, **oppose, counter,** go counter to, contest, take issue with, join issue upon, run counter to; belie, give the lie to, give one the lie direct *or* in his throat

**contradiction** NOUNS **denial, disavowal, disaffirmation, disownment,** disallowance; disclamation, disclaimer; **renunciation, retraction,** retractation, **repudiation,** recantation; revocation, nullification, annulment, abrogation; abjuration, abjurement, forswearing; flat *or* absolute contradiction, contravention, contrary assertion, controversion, countering, crossing, gainsaying, impugnment; **refutation, disproof**

**contraption** NOUNS **tool, instrument, implement, utensil; apparatus, device,** mechanical device, contrivance, contraption <nonformal>, gadget, gizmo, gimcrack, gimmick <nonformal>, means, mechanical means; gadgetry

**contrary** ADJS 1 perverse, **opposite,** antithetic, antithetical, **contradictory,** counter, contrapositive, contrasted; **converse, reverse,** obverse, inverse; **adverse,** adversative *or* adversive, adversarial, **opposing, opposed,** oppositive, oppositional; **antagonistic,** repugnant, oppugnant, perverse, contrarious, ornery <nonformal>, nay-saying, negative, hostile, combative, bellicose, belligerent, inimical, antipathetic, antipathetical, discordant
ADVS 2 **opposite, poles apart,** at opposite extremes; contrariwise, counter; just opposite, **face-to-face,** vis-à-vis, *front à front* <Fr>, nose to nose, one on one, eyeball-to-eyeball, back to back

**contrast** VERBS **make** *or* **draw a comparison,** run a comparison, do a comparative study, bring into comparison; weigh *or* measure against; confront, bring into confrontation, **oppose,** set in opposition, set off against, set in contrast, **put** *or* **set over against,** set *or* place against, counterpose

**contribute** VERBS 1 **participate, take part, partake,** chip in, involve *or* engage oneself, get involved; **have** *or* **take a hand in,** get in on, have a finger in, have a finger in the pie, have to do with, have a part in, be an accessory to, be implicated in, be a party to, be a player in; **join, join in,** figure in, make oneself part of, join oneself to, associate oneself with, play *or* perform a part in, play a role in, get in the act <nonformal>
2 **subscribe, chip in** *and* kick in *and* pony up *and* pay up <all nonformal>, give one's share *or* fair share; put oneself down for, pledge; contribute to, give to, **donate to,** gift *and* gift with <both nonformal>; put something in the pot, sweeten the kitty

**contribution** NOUNS 1 **participation, partaking, sharing,** having a part *or* share *or* voice, association; **involvement,** engagement; complicity
2 **donation,** donative; **subscription; alms,** pittance, **charity, dole, handout** <nonformal>, alms fee, widow's mite; Peter's pence; **offering,** offertory, votive offering, collection; tithe

**contrite** ADJS **penitent, repentant; penitential,** penitentiary; abject, humble, humbled, **sheepish, apologetic,** touched, softened, melted

**contrive** VERBS **plan, devise, design,** frame, shape, cast, concert, lay plans; **arrange,** prearrange, make arrangements, set up, work up, work out; **maneuver, manipulate,** pull strings *or* wires; **machinate,** angle <nonformal>, **jockey, engineer;** play games <nonformal>

**control** NOUNS 1 **mastery, mastership, command, power, jurisdiction, dominion, domination; hold, grasp,** grip, gripe; hand, hands, iron hand, clutches; talons, claws; helm, reins of government
VERBS 2 **restrain, constrain, govern,** guard, contain, keep under control, put *or* lay under restraint; **inhibit,** straiten <old>; enjoin, clamp *or* crack down on <nonformal>, proscribe, prohibit; **curb, check, arrest, bridle,** get under control, rein, snub, snub in; **retard,** slow down, decelerate; **cool** *and* **cool off** *and* **cool down** <all nonformal>; hold, **hold in,** keep, withhold, hold up <nonformal>; **direct, manage, regulate, conduct, carry on, handle, run** <nonformal>; **command, head, govern, boss** *and* head up *and* pull the strings *and* **mastermind** *and* quarterback *and* call the signals <all nonformal>

**controlling** ADJS **restraining, constraining; inhibiting,** inhibitive; **suppressive, repressive,** stultifying; controlling, on top of <nonformal>; **managing, managerial; commanding, governing**; leading, guiding

**controversial** ADJS 1 **contentious, quarrelsome**; **disputatious,** litigious, polemic, polemical; **argumentative,** argumental; on the warpath, looking for trouble; scrappy <nonformal>; cat-and-doggish, cat-and-dog; **bellicose, belligerent**
2 **debatable,** moot, arguable, disputable, contestable, controvertible, refutable, confutable, deniable; suspect; open to question *or* doubt

**controversy** NOUNS **quarrel,** open quarrel, dustup, **dispute, argument,** polemic, argy-bargy *and* slanging match <both Brit>, fliting <old>, altercation, **fight, squabble, contention,** strife, **tussle,** bicker, wrangle, snarl, **tiff, spat,** fuss

**convalescence** NOUNS **recovery, rally, comeback** <nonformal>, return; **recuperation**

**convene** VERBS **meet,** hold a meeting *or* session, sit; **convoke,** summon, call together

**convenience** NOUNS 1 **facility, accommodation, appliance,** amenity, appurtenance; advantage
2 **handiness, wieldiness, manageability,** manageableness, maneuverability; practicality; **flexibility,** pliancy, **pliability;** adaptability, feasibility

**convenient** ADJS **handy; available,** accessible, **ready, at hand,** to hand, **on hand,** on tap, on deck <nonformal>, on call, at one's call *or* beck and call, at one's elbow, at one's fingertips, just around the corner, at one's disposal; **timely, well-timed, seasonable, opportune; expedient,** meet, fit, fitting, befitting, suitable, sortable, appropriate

**convent** NOUNS **cloister, house, abbey;** priory, priorate; lamasery; **nunnery**

**convention** NOUNS 1 **custom,** use, **usage,** standard usage, standard behavior, **wont,** wonting, **way,** established way, time-honored practice, **tradition,** standing custom, **folkway,** manner, **practice,** praxis, prescription, **observance,** ritual, consuetude, what is done, **social convention; rule, law, canon, maxim,** dictum, moral, moralism; **norm, standard;** formula, form; rule of action *or* conduct, moral precept; commandment, *mitzvah* <Heb>; **principle,** principium, settled principle, general principle *or* truth, tenet
2 **conference, congress, parley, palaver, confab** <nonformal>, confabulation, **conclave, powwow, huddle** <nonformal>, **consultation,** *pourparler* <Fr>, **meeting**

**conventional** ADJS **decorous,** orthodox, **correct,** right, **right-thinking, proper,** decent, seemly, meet; **accepted, recognized,** acknowledged, received, admitted, approved, being done; *comme il faut, de rigueur* <both Fr>; **traditional, customary;** formal; **conformist,** bourgeois, plastic *and* square *and* straight *and* white-bread *and* white-bready *and* button-down *and* buttoned-down <all nonformal>

**converge** VERBS **come together,** approach, run together, **meet,** unite, connect, merge; **cross, intersect**; fall in with, link up with; be on a collision course; go toward, narrow the gap, close with, close, close up, close in; funnel; taper, pinch, nip; centralize, center, **come to a center;** center on *or* around, concentralize, concenter, **concentrate,** come *or* tend to a point; **come to a focus**

**conversation** NOUNS conversing; interlocution, colloquy; **exchange;** verbal intercourse, conversational interchange, interchange of speech, give-and-take, cross-talk, rapping <nonformal>, **repartee,** backchat; **discourse,** colloquial discourse; **communion, intercourse, communication**

**convert** NOUNS 1 **proselyte,** neophyte, catechumen, disciple
VERBS 2 **redeem,** regenerate, reform, save, give salvation
3 **convince; win over,** lead one to believe, bring over, bring round, talk over, talk around, bring to reason, bring to one's senses, **persuade, lead to believe, give to understand**

**convertible** ADJS changeable, resolvable, transmutable, **transformable, transitional, modifiable;** reformable, reclaimable, renewable; liquid, negotiable

**convex** ADJS **rotund, round,** rounded, rounded out, round as a ball; bellied, bellylike; bulging

**convey** VERBS 1 **transport,** freight, conduct, **take; carry, bear,** pack, tote *and* lug <both nonformal>; **channel,** channelize, canalize, **conduct,** put through; pipe, funnel, siphon
2 **communicate, impart, tell,** lay on one <nonformal>, **transmit,** transfer, send, send word, deliver *or* send a signal *or* message, **disseminate,** broadcast, pass, **pass on** *or* **along, hand on; report, render, make known,** get across *or* over

**convict** NOUNS 1 **prisoner, captive,** *détenu* <Fr>, cageling; con <nonformal>; **jailbird** <nonformal>, gaolbird <Brit nonformal>, stir bird <nonformal>; political prisoner, prisoner of conscience; lifer <nonformal>; trusty
VERBS 2 **bring in a verdict, pass** *or* **pronounce sentence**; penalize

**conviction** NOUNS 1 **trust, confidence, faith,** assured faith, belief, fixed *or* settled belief, **reliance,** dependence; assurance
2 **condemnation, damnation, doom,** guilty verdict, verdict of guilty; judgment

**convince** VERBS **persuade,** wean, bring over, sweep off one's feet <nonformal>, **win over;** seem true, ring true, sound true, **carry conviction,** hold *or* have the ring of truth

**convocation** NOUNS **summons,** convoking; calling forth, **ecclesiastical council, conclave, consistory, convention; assembly**

**convoy** NOUNS **escort, guard;** outrider

**convulsion** NOUNS **spasm, paroxysm,** throes; **seizure,** grip, attack, **fit,** access, ictus

**cool** NOUNS 1 **composure,** countenance; **calm, calmness,** calm disposition, **placidity, serenity,** tranquility, soothingness, peacefulness; mental composure, peace *or* calm of mind; calm *or* quiet mind, easy mind; **coolness,** coolheadedness, sangfroid; icy calm
VERBS 2 **calm, settle, soothe,** tranquilize; smooth, smooth over *or* out, smooth down, smooth one's feathers; allay, lay, lay the dust; pour oil on troubled waters, pour balm on, take the edge off of, take the sting out of; defuse; clear the air
3 **refrigerate; chill;** refresh, freshen; water-cool, air-cool; **air-condition;** ventilate
ADJS 4 **indifferent, halfhearted,** perfunctory, fervorless; **cold**; tepid, **lukewarm,** Laodicean; neither hot nor cold, neither one thing nor the other, **neuter, neutral; calm, placid,** quiet, **tranquil, serene,** peaceful; **coolheaded,** cool as a cucumber <nonformal>; philosophical
5 **aloof, standoffish,** standoff, offish <nonformal>, chilly, distant, remote, above all that; Olympian
6 coolish, temperate; chill, **chilly,** parky <Brit nonformal>; **fresh,** brisk, crisp, bracing, sharpish, **invigorating,** stimulating

**cooperation** NOUNS **collaboration, coaction,** concurrence, synergy, synergism; **consensus, commonality; community,** harmony, concordance, concord, fellowship, fellow feeling, solidarity, concert, **teamwork;** pulling *or* working together, communal *or* community activity, joining of forces, pooling, pooling of resources, joining of hands; joint effort, common effort, combined *or* joint operation, common enterprise *or* endeavor, collective *or* united action, mass action; **cooperativeness,** team spirit, morale, esprit, *esprit de corps* <Fr>

**cooperative** ADJS **cooperating,** cooperant, **hand in glove; collaborative,** coactive, coacting, coefficient, synergistic

**coordinate** VERBS 1 **harmonize,** bring into line, accord, make uniform, equalize, similarize, assimilate, homologize; **adjust, set,** regulate, **accommodate, reconcile,** synchronize, sync <nonformal>, integrate, proportion
2 **organize,** methodize, **systematize,** rationalize, regularize, get *or* put one's house in order; **regulate,** fix, settle; **plan,** chart, codify

**cop** NOUNS

<nonformal> copper, John Law, bluecoat, bull, flatfoot, gumshoe, gendarme, shamus, dick, pig, flattie, bizzy *and* bobby *and* peeler <all Brit>; the cops, the law, the fuzz; New York's finest

**cope** VERBS **support oneself,** make one's way; **make ends meet, keep body and soul together, keep the wolf from the door,** keep *or* hold one's head above water, keep afloat; **survive, subsist, eke out,** make out, scrape along, manage, get by; **deal with,** come to grips with, take on, tackle <nonformal>, contend with, do with

**copious** ADJS **abundant,** ample, plenteous, **plentiful**, thick on the ground <Brit>; **prolific,** proliferous, uberous, **teeming,** swarming, bursting, bursting out, plenteous, **plentiful,** generous, bountiful, **abundant**, **luxuriant, exuberant, lush,** superabundant

**copulate** VERBS couple, **mate,** unite in sexual intercourse, **have sexual relations, have sex,** make out <nonformal>, perform the act of love *or* marriage act, come together, cohabit, shack up <nonformal>, be intimate; sleep with, lie with, go to bed with; fuck *and* screw *and* lay *and* ball *and* frig *and* diddle *and* **make it with** <all nonformal>, go all the way, go to bed with, lie together; cover, mount, serve *or* service <of animals>; **make love**

**copy** NOUNS 1 **reproduction, duplication, imitation**, dummy, mock-up, **replica,** facsimile, representation, paraphrase, approximation, model, version, knockoff <nonformal>; **counterfeit**, forgery, fake *and* phony <both nonformal>
2 **the same, selfsame,** carbon copy, very same, one and the same, identical same, a distinction without a difference, the same difference <nonformal>; **duplicate,** double, clone *and* cookie-cutter dead ringer <nonformal>, the image of, the picture of, spitting image *and* spit and image <both nonformal>, facsimile
VERBS 3 **imitate, repeat,** ditto <nonformal>; do like <nonformal>, do <nonformal>, act *or* go *or* make like <nonformal>; **mirror, reflect; echo,** reecho, chorus; **borrow,** steal one's stuff <nonformal>, take a leaf out of one's book; assume, **affect;** counterfeit, fake <nonformal>, hoke *and* hoke up <both nonformal>, forge, plagiarize, crib, lift <nonformal>; **parody,** pastiche; **paraphrase,** approximate
4 **reproduce,** replicate, **duplicate,** dupe <nonformal>; clone; reduplicate; **transcribe;** trace; double; triplicate, quadruplicate, etc; stat <nonformal>, facsimile, fax <nonformal>, Xerox <trademark>; microcopy, microfilm

**copycat** NOUNS **imitator,** simulator, me-tooer <nonformal>, **impersonator, impostor**, **mimic,** mimicker, mimer, mime, **mocker;** mockingbird, cuckoo; **parrot,** polly, poll-parrot *or* polly-parrot, **ape,** aper, monkey; **copier,** copyist, counterfeiter, forger, plagiarist

**cord** NOUNS **line, rope, wire,** braided rope, twisted rope, flattened-strand rope, wire rope, locked-wire rope, **cable,** wire cable; **yarn,** spun yarn, skein, hank; **string, twine;** electric wire, electric cord, power cord, power cable

**cordial** NOUNS 1 **liqueur,** brandy, flavored brandy
ADJS 2 amiable, affable, genial; gentle, mild, mild-mannered; easy, easy-natured, easy to get along with, able to take a joke, **agreeable; genial,** hearty, ardent, warm, warmhearted, affable; hospitable

**core** NOUNS **center,** centrum; **middle, heart, nucleus; core of one's being, where one lives; kernel; pith,** marrow; **nub, hub,** nave, axis, pivot; **essence, substance,** stuff, very stuff, inner essence, essential nature, quiddity; crux, crucial *or* pivotal *or* critical point, pivot

**corner** NOUNS 1 **nook, cranny, niche, recess,** cove, bay, oriel, alcove
2 **angle,** point, bight; vertex, apex; quoin, coin, nook; **crook, hook,** crotchet
VERBS 3 run *and* drive into a corner <both nonformal>, **tree** <nonformal>, chase up a tree *or* stump <nonformal>, drive *or* force to the wall, push one to the wall, put one's back to the wall, have one on the ropes <nonformal>; get a corner on, **corner the market;** monopolize, engross; buy up, absorb

**cornerstone** NOUNS **foundation stone,** footstone; **keystone,** headstone, first stone, quoin; **salient point,** cardinal point, high point, great point; important thing, chief thing, **the point, main point,** main thing, essential matter, **essence,** the name of the game *and* the bottom line *and* what it's all about *and* where it's at <all nonformal>, substance, gravamen

**cornucopia** NOUNS horn of plenty, horn of Amalthea, endless supply, bottomless well

**corny** ADJS **trite;** corny *and* square *and* square-John *and* Clyde <all nonformal>, fade, **banal,** unoriginal, platitudinous, **stereotyped,** stock, set, **commonplace, common,** truistic, twice-told, **familiar,** bromidic <nonformal>, old hat <nonfor-

mal>, back-number, bewhiskered, warmed-over, **cut-and-dried; hackneyed,** hackney; **stale,** musty, fusty

**coronation** NOUNS **installation,** installment, **instatement,** induction, placement, **inauguration,** investiture, taking office; **accession,** accedence; enthronement

**corpse** NOUNS dead body, dead man *or* woman, dead person, **cadaver, carcass, body;** *corpus delicti* <L>; **stiff** <nonformal>; **the dead,** the defunct, **the deceased,** the departed, the loved one; **decedent,** late lamented; **remains,** mortal *or* organic remains, **mummy**

**corpulent** ADJS **stout, fat, overweight,** fattish, **obese,** adipose, gross, fleshy, beefy, meaty, hefty, porky, porcine; paunchy, paunched, bloated, puffy, blowzy, distended, swollen, pursy; abdominous, big-bellied, full-bellied, potbellied, gorbellied <old or dial>, swag-bellied, pot-gutted *and* pussle-gutted <both nonformal>

**corral** VERBS **enclose,** pen, coop, cage, impound, mew; round up, drive together; **drive, herd,** drove <Brit>, herd up, punch cattle, ride herd on; spur, goad, prick, lash, whip; wrangle

**correct** VERBS 1 **revise,** redact, recense, **revamp, rewrite,** redraft, **rework,** work over; **emend, amend,** emendate, **rectify, edit,** blue-pencil

2 rap on the knuckles, **chastise,** spank, turn over one's knees; **take to task,** call to account, bring to book, call on the carpet, read the riot act, give one a tongue-lashing, tonguelash; straighten out

ADJS 3 **meticulous, thorough,** thoroughgoing, thoroughpaced; prissy, **accurate; strict,** rigid, **rigorous,** spit-and-polish; **mannerly, well-mannered,** good-mannered, **well-behaved,** well- *or* fair-spoken; correct in one's manners *or* behavior

4 **orthodox,** orthodoxical; received, approved; right, proper; **accurate, right,** proper, just; dead right, on target *and* on the money *and* on the nose <all nonformal>, bang on <Brit nonformal>, straight, straight-up-and-down

**correction** NOUNS 1 **revision, emendation, amendment, corrigenda, rectification;** editing, redaction, recension, revampment; **polishing,** touching up, putting on the finishing touches, putting the gloss on, finishing, perfecting, tuning, fine-tuning; retrofitting

2 **reproof,** reproval; **punishment,** punition, **chastisement, chastening, correction, discipline,** disciplinary measure *or* action, **castigation,** infliction, scourge, ferule, what-for <nonformal>

**correlation** NOUNS **reciprocation,** reciprocity, reciprocality, two-edged sword, relativity; **mutuality,** communion, community, commutuality; **correspondence, equivalence,** equipollence, coequality

**correspondence** NOUNS letter writing, written communication, exchange of letters, epistolary intercourse *or* communication; personal correspondence, business correspondence

**correspondent** NOUNS 1 **letter writer,** writer, communicator; pen pal <nonformal>; addressee; **foreign correspondent,** war correspondent, special correspondent, stringer

ADJS 2 **reciprocal, corresponding,** answering, analogous, homologous, equipollent, tantamount, equivalent, coequal; **complementary,** complemental

**corridor** NOUNS 1 **airway, air lane, air line,** air route, skyway, flight path, lane, path

2 **hall,** hallway; passage, **passageway; gallery,** loggia; arcade, colonnade, pergola, cloister, peristyle; areaway; breezeway

**corrosion** NOUNS **disintegration, decomposition, erosion,** crumbling, dilapidation, wear, wear and tear, waste, wasting, wasting away, ablation, ravagement, ravages of time

**corrosive** ADJS **caustic,** mordant, mordacious, corroding; **acrimonious,** acrid, acid, acidic, acidulous, acidulent, acerb, acerbate, acerbic, **bitter,** tart; corroding; erosive, eroding, **damaging, injurious**; pollutive; corruptive, corrupting, corroding

**corrugated** ADJS **rugged,** ragged, harsh; rugose, rugous, wrinkled, crinkled, crumpled; **furrowed, grooved,** scratched, scored, incised, cut, gashed, gouged, slit, striated

**corrupt** VERBS 1 **debase, degrade,** degenerate, **deprave, debauch, defile,** violate, desecrate, deflower, ravish, ravage, despoil; **contaminate,** confound, **pollute, vitiate, poison, infect, taint;**

**pervert,** warp, twist, distort; prostitute, misuse; denature; **cheapen,** devalue; coarsen, vulgarize, drag in the mud; adulterate, alloy, water, water down; **sully, soil, defile;** demoralize
ADJS 2 corrupted, vice-corrupted, polluted, morally polluted, rotten, tainted, contaminated, vitiated; warped, perverted; **decadent,** debased, degraded, reprobate, **depraved, debauched, dissolute, degenerate,** profligate, abandoned, gone to the dogs, sunk *or* steeped in iniquity, rotten at *or* to the core, in the sewer *or* gutter

**corruption** NOUNS 1 **perversion,** misdirection, misrepresentation, misinterpretation, misconstruction; **falsification**; **twisting,** false coloring, bending the truth, **spin,** spin control, slanting, straining, torturing; misuse
2 **bribery,** bribing, subornation, **graft,** bribery and corruption; corruptedness, corruptness, rottenness, moral pollution, lack *or* absence of moral fiber

**corset** NOUNS foundation garment, corselet; **girdle,** undergirdle, panty girdle

**cosmetic** ADJS 1 **shallow, surface,** on *or* near the surface, merely surface; **superficial, cursory,** slight, light, merely cosmetic, thin, jejune, trivial
2 **beautifying;** decorative; cosmetized, cosmeticized, beautified, made-up, mascaraed, titivated

**cosmetics** NOUNS **makeup, beauty products, beauty-care products;** war paint *and* drugstore complexion <both nonformal>

**cosmic** ADJS **universal,** cosmic *or* cosmical, heaven-wide, galactic, planetary, world-wide, transnational, planet-wide, **global; total, all-inclusive,** all-including, **all-embracing,** all-encompassing, all-comprehensive, all-comprehending, all-filling, all-pervading, all-covering

**cosmopolitan** NOUNS 1 **sophisticate,** man of experience, **man of the world;** slicker *and* city slicker <both nonformal>; man-about-town; cosmopolite, citizen of the world
ADJS 2 **traveled,** well-traveled, **worldly, worldly-wise,** world-wise, wise in the ways of the world, knowing, **sophisticated,** cosmopolite, blasé

**cosmos** NOUNS **universe, world;** creation, created universe, created nature, all, **all creation,** all tarnation <nonformal>, all *or* everything that is, all being, totality, totality of being, sum of things; omneity, allness

**cost** NOUNS 1 **expense,** burden of expenditure; **price,** expenditure, **charge,** damage *and* score *and* tab <all nonformal>; rate, figure, amount
VERBS 2 **sell for, fetch, bring,** bring in, stand one *and* set *or* move one back <all nonformal>, knock one back <Brit nonformal>; **come to,** run to *or* into, **amount to,** mount up to, come up to, total up to

**costly** ADJS **expensive, dear,** of great cost, dear-bought, **high, high-priced,** premium, at a premium, top; big ticket <nonformal>, **fancy** *and* stiff *and* steep <all nonformal>, pricey; beyond one's means, not affordable, more than one can afford; upmarket, upscale <nonformal>, rich, sumptuous, executive *and* posh <both nonformal>, **luxurious,** gold-plated

**costume** NOUNS 1 **clothing, wearing apparel, raiment, garb, attire, array,** habit, habiliment, fashion, style, guise, costumery, gear, fig *or* full fig <both Brit>, toilette, trim, bedizenment; **vestment,** vesture, investment, investiture; habit, bib and tucker <nonformal>
VERBS 2 **outfit;** equip, **accouter,** uniform, caparison, rig, rig out *or* up, fit, **fit out,** turn out, habit, suit; **tailor,** tailor-make, make to order; order, bespeak

**couch** NOUNS sofa, **bed;** the sack *and* the hay *and* kip *and* doss <all nonformal>; bedstead; **litter, stretcher,** gurney

**counsel** NOUNS 1 **advice, recommendation, suggestion;** proposal; advising, advocacy; **direction, instruction,** guidance, briefing; **exhortation,** hortation <old>, enjoinder, expostulation, remonstrance; **admonition,** monition, monitory *or* monitory letter, caution, caveat, **warning; idea,** thought, opinion; **counseling;** guidance counseling, educational counseling, vocational guidance
2 **adviser, counselor, consultant,** professional consultant, expert, maven <nonformal>, boffin <Brit nonformal>; instructor, guide, **mentor,** nestor
3 **lawyer, attorney, attorney-at-law,** barrister, barrister-at-law, **counselor,** counselor-at-law, legal counsel *or* counselor, legal adviser, legal expert, **solicitor, advocate, pleader;** member of the bar, legal practitioner, officer of the court

VERBS 4 **advise, recommend, suggest, advocate,** propose, submit; **instruct,** coach, guide, direct, brief; prescribe; weigh in with advice <nonformal>, give a piece of advice

**count** NOUNS 1 **sum,** summation, difference, product, **number;** account, cast, **score, reckoning, tally,** tale, the story *and* whole story *and* all she wrote <all nonformal>, the bottom line <nonformal>
VERBS 2 **matter,** import <old>, signify, **tell, weigh, carry weight,** cut ice *and* cut some ice <both nonformal>, be prominent, stand out, mean much; be something, be somebody, amount to something; have a key to the executive washroom; be featured, star, get top billing
3 **enumerate, tell, tally,** give a figure to, put a figure on, call off, name, call over, run over; **count noses** *or* **heads** <nonformal>, call the roll

**counter** NOUNS 1 **token,** slug; **coupon; check, ticket,** tag
2 workspace, working space; **bench,** workbench, worktable; worktop; bar, buffet
VERBS 3 **retaliate, retort, strike back,** hit back at <nonformal>, give in return; **reciprocate,** give in exchange, give and take; **get** *or* **come back at** <nonformal>, turn the tables upon
4 **go contrary to, run counter to, contradict,** contravene, controvert, fly in the face of, be *or* play at cross-purposes, go against; **oppose,** be opposed to, go *or* run in opposition to, side against
ADJS 5 contrary, counteractive, conflicting, opposing, opposed, opposite, in opposition

**counteract** VERBS **offset**, set off, countervail, **counterbalance,** counterweigh, counterwork, counterpoise, **balance,** play off against, set against, set over against, equiponderate; **square,** square up

**counterfeit** NOUNS 1 counterfeit money, funny *or* phony *or* bogus money <nonformal>, false *or* bad money, queer <nonformal>, base coin, green goods <nonformal>; **forgery,** bad check, rubber check *and* bounced check *and* kite <all nonformal>
2 **copy, imitation**, forgery, fake *and* phony <both nonformal>
VERBS 3 **imitate,** copy, **simulate,** fake; forge; phony up <nonformal>, fabricate
ADJS 4 **imitation, mock, sham,** copied, fake *and* phony <both nonformal>, forged, plagiarized, unoriginal, ungenuine; **pseudo,** synthetic, synthetical, ersatz, hokey *and* hoked-up <both nonformal>, quasi; **vicarious,** ersatz, mock

**counterpart** NOUNS **analogue, parallel;** cognate, congener; **complement, correspondent,** pendant, similitude, tally

**counterproductive** ADJS counteractive *or* counteractant, **counteracting, counterworking,** countervailing; **opposing,** oppositional; **inexpedient, undesirable, inadvisable,** impolitic, impolitical, unpolitic, not to be recommended, contraindicated; **impractical, impracticable,** dysfunctional, unworkable; **ill-advised, ill-considered, unwise;** distressing, **injurious, damaging, detrimental,** deleterious, **pernicious,** mischievous

**countless** ADJS 1 **much, many,** beaucoup <nonformal>, ample, **abundant,** copious, generous, overflowing, superabundant, multitudinous, plentiful, **numerous**
2 **innumerable, numberless,** unnumbered, uncounted, uncountable, unreckonable, untold, incalculable, immeasurable, unmeasured, measureless, inexhaustible, endless, infinite, without end *or* limit, more than one can tell, more than you can shake a stick at <nonformal>, no end of *or* to; countless as the stars *or* sands

**country** NOUNS 1 land; **nation,** nationality, **state,** nation-state, sovereign nation *or* state, polity, **body politic; power,** superpower, world power; microstate; **republic,** people's republic, **commonwealth,** commonweal; **kingdom,** sultanate; **empire,** empery; **realm,** dominion, domain; **principality,** principate; duchy, dukedom
ADJS 2 **rustic, rural, provincial, farm, pastoral, bucolic,** Arcadian, **agrarian,** agrestic; **agricultural**

**countryman** NOUNS **fellow citizen,** fellow countryman, **compatriot,** congener, countrywoman, *landsman* <Yiddish>, *paesano* <Ital>, *paisano* <Sp>; fellow townsman, home boy *and* home girl *and* hometowner <all nonformal>

**countryside** NOUNS **the country,** agricultural region, farm country, farmland, arable land, grazing region *or* country, rural district, rustic region, province *or* **provinces,** woodland, grassland, woods and fields, meadows and pastures, the soil, grass roots; **the sticks** *and* the tall corn *and* yokeldom *and* hickdom <all nonformal>

**coup** NOUNS **attempt, trial, effort, essay,** assay <old>, first attempt, *coup d'essai* <Fr>; **endeavor, undertaking;** stroke, step; gambit; **stratagem, artifice,** art <old>, **craft, wile,** strategy, **device,** wily device, **contrivance, expedient, design, scheme, move,** gambit, **ploy, dodge,** artful dodge; **plot,** conspiracy, **intrigue**
2 **seizure,** power grab <nonformal>, coup d'état, seizure of power

**couple** NOUNS 1 **two,** twain <old>; **pair, matching pair, twosome,** set of two, duo, duet, brace, team, span, yoke, double harness; match, matchup, mates
VERBS 2 **copulate, mate,** unite in sexual intercourse, **have sexual relations, have sex,** make out <nonformal>, perform the act of love *or* marriage act, come together, cohabit, shack up <nonformal>, be intimate; commit adultery, fornicate
3 **put together, join,** conjoin, **unite,** unify, bond, **connect,** associate, league, band, merge, **assemble,** accumulate; **join up,** become a part of, associate oneself, enter into, come aboard <nonformal>; pair, accouple, **link,** link up, build bridges, yoke, knot, splice, tie, chain, bracket

**coupon** NOUNS **scrip, check, ticket,** tag; hat check, baggage check

**courage** NOUNS courageousness, **nerve,** pluck, **bravery,** braveness, ballsiness *and* gutsiness *or* guttiness <all nonformal>, **boldness, valor,** valorousness, valiance, valiancy, **gallantry,** conspicuous gallantry, gallantry under fire *or* beyond the call of duty, gallantness, **intrepidity,** intrepidness, **prowess,** virtue; doughtiness, stalwartness, stoutness, **manliness,** manfulness, **manhood,** virility, machismo

*fear holding on a minute longer*
GEORGE PATTON

*doing without witnesses that which we would be capable of doing before everyone*
LA ROCHEFOUCAULD

**courageous** ADJS **plucky, brave, bold, valiant, valorous, gallant, intrepid,** doughty, **hardy,** stalwart, stout, stout-hearted, ironhearted, lionhearted, great-hearted, bold-spirited, bold as a lion; **heroic,** herolike

**course** NOUNS 1 **serving,** service; **portion, helping,** help; second helping; dish, plate
2 heading, vector; compass heading *or* course, compass direction, magnetic heading, true heading *or* course
3 onward course, **surge, gush, rush,** onrush, spate, run, race; **route, path, way, itinerary,** track, run, line, road
4 **policy,** polity, principles, guiding principles; **procedure,** line, plan of action
5 **study,** branch of learning; course of study, **curriculum; subject; major, minor;** requirement *or* required course, elective course, refresher course; gut course <nonformal>

**court** VERBS 1 **curry favor, pay court to,** make court to, run after <nonformal>, dance attendance on; **shine up to,** make up to <nonformal>; **suck up to** *and* **play up to** *and* act up to <all nonformal>; be a yes-man <nonformal>, agree to anything; fawn upon, fall over *or* all over <nonformal>; **handshake** *and* back-scratch *and* **polish the apple** <all nonformal>
2 **solicit, canvass; seek, bid for,** look for; **fish for,** angle for
3 **woo,** sue, press one's suit, **pay court** *or* **suit to,** make suit to, cozy up to <nonformal>, eye up *and* chat up <Brit nonformal>, pay one's court to, address, pay one's addresses to, pay attention to, lay siege to, fling oneself at, throw oneself at the head of; **pursue,** follow; chase <nonformal>; set one's cap at *or* for <nonformal>; serenade; spark <nonformal>

**courteous** ADJS polite, civil, urbane, gracious, graceful, agreeable, affable, fair; complaisant; obliging, accommodating; **thoughtful, considerate,** tactful, solicitous; respectful, deferential, attentive

**courtesy** NOUNS courteousness, common courtesy, **politeness, civility,** *politesse* <Fr>, amenity, agreeableness, urbanity, comity, affability; **graciousness,** gracefulness; complaisance; **thoughtfulness, considerateness, tactfulness,** tact, consideration, **solicitousness, solicitude; respect,** respectfulness, deference

**courtly** ADJS **dignified, stately, imposing, grand,** magisterial, aristocratic; **noble,** lordly, princely; **majestic,** regal; worthy, **august, venerable;** statuesque; **sedate, solemn**, sober, grave

**courtship** NOUNS **courting, wooing;** court, suit, suing, amorous pursuit, addresses

**cove** NOUNS **inlet,** creek <Brit>, arm of the sea, arm, armlet, canal, reach, loch <Scots>, **bay, fjord,** bight; **gulf; estuary,** firth *or* frith, bayou, mouth, *boca* <Sp>; **harbor,** natural harbor; road *or* roads, roadstead; **strait** *or* straits, kyle <Scots>, **narrow** *or* **narrows,** euripus, belt, gut, narrow seas; **sound**

**cover** NOUNS 1 **covering,** coverage, covert, coverture, housing, hood, cowl, cowling, **shelter; screen,** shroud, shield, veil, pall, mantle, curtain, hanging, drape, drapery; **coat,** cloak, mask, guise; vestment

2 **lid, top, cap, screw-top;** operculum; stopper

3 **blanket, coverlet,** coverlid <nonformal>, space blanket, covers, **spread,** robe, buffalo robe, **afghan,** rug <Brit>; lap robe; **bedspread; bedcover;** counterpane, counterpin <nonformal>; comfort, **comforter, down comforter, duvet, continental quilt** <Brit>, **quilt,** feather bed, eiderdown; patchwork quilt

4 **concealment, hiding, secretion;** burial, burying, interment, putting away; **covering,** covering up, masking, screening; mystification, obscuration; darkening, obscurement, clouding; **subterfuge, deception, disguise, camouflage,** protective coloration

VERBS 5 **extend, reach, stretch,** sweep, spread, run, **go** *or* **go out,** carry, **range,** lie; **reach** *or* stretch *or* thrust out; span, straddle, take in, hold, encompass, surround, environ

6 **traverse, cross, travel over** *or* through, pass through, **go** *or* **pass over,** measure, transit, track, range, range over *or* through, course, do, perambulate, peregrinate, overpass, go over the ground

7 cover up; apply to, **put on,** lay on; **superimpose,** superpose; **lay over,** overlay; **spread over,** overspread; **clothe, cloak,** mantle, muffle, blanket, canopy, cope, cowl, hood, **veil,** curtain, **screen, shield,** screen off, mask, cloud, obscure, fog, befog, fuzz; block, eclipse, occult

8 **include, comprise, contain, comprehend,** hold, **take in;** cover a lot of ground <nonformal>, occupy, take up, fill; fill in *or* out, build into, **complete**

**cover-up** NOUNS **veil of secrecy, veil,** curtain, pall, wraps; iron curtain, bamboo curtain; wall *or* barrier of secrecy; **suppression,** repression, stifling, smothering; **censorship,** blackout <nonformal>, **hush-up**

**covet** VERBS **crave, hunger after,** thirst after, crave after, **lust after,** have a lech for <nonformal>, pant after, run mad after, **hanker for** *or* **after** <nonformal>; crawl after; aspire after, be consumed with desire; have an itchy *or* itching palm *and* have sticky fingers <all nonformal>; **envy,** be envious *or* covetous of, cast envious eyes, desire for oneself

**coward** NOUNS jellyfish, invertebrate, **weakling,** weak sister <nonformal>, milksop, milquetoast, mouse, **sissy, wimp** <nonformal>, baby, **big baby, chicken** <nonformal>; **yellow-belly,** *and* white-liver *and* lily-liver *and* chicken-liver <all nonformal>, white feather; fraid-cat *and* **fraidy-cat** *and* scaredy-cat <all nonformal>; funk *and* funker <both nonformal>

*one who in a perilous emergency thinks with his legs*
AMBROSE BIERCE

**cowardly** ADJS **fearful,** fearing, fearsome, **in fear, afraid; timorous, timid, shy,** rabbity *and* mousy <both nonformal>, afraid of one's own shadow; **skittish,** skittery <nonformal>, gun-shy, jumpy, goosy <nonformal>; **tremulous,** trembling, trepidant, shaky, shivery; **yellow** *and* yellow-bellied *and* with a yellow streak <all nonformal>; **weak-kneed, chicken** <nonformal>, afraid of one's shadow; weak, soft;

**cowboy** NOUNS cowgirl, puncher *or* cowpuncher *or* cowpoke <all nonformal>, *vaquero, gaucho* <both Sp>; broncobuster <nonformal>, buckaroo

**cower** VERBS **quail, cringe, crouch, skulk, sneak, slink, crouch, duck,** cringe; hunch, hunch down, hunch over, scrooch *or* scrouch down <nonformal>

**coy** ADJS **shy, timid,** timorous, **bashful,** shamefaced, shamefast, pudibund *and* verecund *and* verecundious <all old>; **demure,** skittish, mousy; self-conscious,

conscious, confused; stammering, inarticulate; **coquettish,** come-hither

**cozy** ADJS snug, snug as a bug in a rug; friendly, warm; **homelike,** homey *and* down-home <both nonformal>, homely, lived-in; **commodious,** roomy, convenient; **intimate, familiar,** chatty, *tête-à-tête* <Fr>

**crack** NOUNS 1 **cleft,** cranny, chink, check, craze, chap, **crevice,** fissure, scissure, incision, notch, score, cut, gash, slit, split, **rift,** rent; **opening,** excavation, cavity, concavity, hole; **breach, break,** fracture, rupture; fault, flaw, craze, check, rift, split
2 **witticism, crack** *and* smart crack *and* **wisecrack** <all nonformal>; **quip, mot, bon mot,** smart saying, stroke of wit, one-liner *and* zinger <both nonformal>; **gibe, dirty** *or* **nasty crack** <nonformal>; persiflage
VERBS 3 **cleave,** check, incise, craze, **cut, cut apart,** gash, slit, **split,** rive, rent, rip open; **open; gap,** breach, break, fracture, rupture; slot, groove, furrow, ditch, trench
ADJS 4 **skillful,** excellent, **expert,** crackerjack <nonformal>

**cracked** ADJS **impaired, damaged,** chipped, crazed, checked

**crackle** NOUNS 1 **snap, crack;** snapping, cracking, crackling, crepitation, decrepitation, sizzling, spitting; rale
VERBS 2 **snap, crack;** crepitate, decrepitate; spit

**crackpot** NOUNS

<nonformal> freak, character, nut, screwball, weirdie, weirdo, kook, queer potato, oddball, flake, strange duck, odd fellow, crank, bird, goofus, wack, wacko

**craft** NOUNS 1 **skill,** skillfulness, **expertness, expertise, proficiency,** dexterity, dexterousness *or* dextrousness; **craftsmanship,** workmanship, artisanship; skill; technique, art, handicraft
2 **cunning,** cunningness, **craftiness,** callidity <old>, **artfulness, art, artifice, wiliness,** wiles, guile, **slyness,** insidiousness, **foxiness**

**crafty** ADJS **cunning, artful, wily,** callid <old>, guileful, **sly,** insidious, supple <Scots>, **shifty,** pawky <Brit>, arch, **smooth, slick** *and* slick as a whistle <both nonformal>, **slippery,** snaky, serpentine, **foxy,** vulpine, feline; **canny, shrewd,** knowing, sharp, razor-sharp, cute *or* cutesy *or* cutesy-poo <nonformal>, acute, astute, **clever;** resourceful, ingenious, inventive, **scheming, designing; manipulative,** manipulatory; **deceitful**

**cram** VERBS 1 **stuff, gorge,** pig out <nonformal>, engorge, glut, guttle, eat one's fill, stuff *or* gorge oneself, gluttonize
2 **study up, get up,** study up on, read up on, get up on; **review, brush up,** polish up <nonformal>, rub up, **cram** *or* cram up <nonformal>, **bone up** <nonformal>
3 **fill, charge, load,** lade, freight, weight; **stuff, wad,** pad, **pack,** crowd, am, jam-pack, ram in, chock; **fill up,** fill to the brim, brim, top up *or* top off, fill to overflowing

**cramp** NOUNS **pain, distress, grief,** stress, stress of life, suffering, passion, dolor; ache, aching; pang, wrench, throes, spasm

**cramped** ADJS **limited, restricted,** bound, **bounded, finite; confined,** prescribed, proscribed, strait, straitened, narrow; close-fitting; **restricted,** limited, circumscribed, **confined,** constricted; incapacious, incommodious, crowded; **forced,** awkward; crabbed

**cranky** ADJS 1 **crotchety,** quirky, dotty, maggoty <Brit>, crank, crankish, whimsical, twisted

2 <nonformal> **grouchy, kvetchy,** beefing, crabby, crabbing, grousing, griping, bellyaching, bitching

**cranny** NOUNS **nook, corner, niche, recess,** cove, bay, oriel, alcove; cubicle, roomlet, carrel, hole-in-the-wall <nonformal>, cubby, **cubbyhole,** snuggery, hidey-hole <nonformal>

**crap** NOUNS 1 **feces,** feculence; defecation, movement, bowel movement *or* **BM; stool, shit** <nonformal>, **ordure,** night soil, jakes <Brit nonformal>, crap *and* ca-ca *and* doo-doo <all nonformal>; turd <nonformal>; dingleberry <nonformal>; **manure, dung, droppings;** cow pats, cow flops <nonformal>; cow chips, buffalo chips; guano; coprolite, coprolith

2 <nonformal> **bullshit,** shit, horseshit, horsefeathers, bull, poppycock, bosh, tosh <Brit>, applesauce, bunkum, bunk,

garbage, guff, jive, bilge, piffle, moonshine, flapdoodle, a crock *or* a crock of shit, claptrap, tommyrot, rot, hogwash, malarkey, double Dutch, hokum, hooey, bushwa, blah, balls <Brit>, baloney, blarney, tripe, hot air, gas, wind, waffle <Brit>

VERBS 3 **defecate, shit** <nonformal>, **evacuate,** void, **stool,** dung, have a bowel movement *or* BM, take a shit *or* crap <nonformal>, ca-ca *or* number two <both nonformal>

**crash** NOUNS 1 **noise,** loud noise, roar, thunder, thunderclap; **boom,** sonic boom

2 **crack-up,** prang <Brit nonformal>; crash landing; collision, mid-air collision

3 **collapse,** smash, comedown, breakdown, derailment, **fall,** pratfall <nonformal>, stumble, tumble, **downfall,** cropper <chiefly Brit nonformal>; nose dive *and* tailspin <both nonformal>; bursting of the bubble, **bear market,** bearishness; break in the market; selloff

VERBS 4 <nonformal> **hit the hay, hit the sack,** turn in, crawl in, flop, sack out, sack up, kip down *or* doss down <both Brit>

5 **crack up,** prang <Brit nonformal>, spin in, fail to pull out

6 **collapse;** cave *or* fall in, come crashing *or* tumbling down, topple, topple down *or* over; **go bankrupt, go broke** <nonformal>, go into receivership, become insolvent *or* bankrupt, **fail,** break, bust <nonformal>, **fold, fold up,** belly up *and* go up *and* go belly up *and* **go under** <all nonformal>, shut one's doors, go out of business, **be ruined,** go to ruin, go on the rocks, go to the wall; take a bath *and* be taken to the cleaners *and* be cleaned out *and* lose one's shirt *and* tap out <all nonformal>

**crave** VERBS **covet, hunger after,** thirst after, crave after, **lust after,** have a lech for <nonformal>, pant after, run mad after, **hanker for** *or* **after** <nonformal>; crawl after; aspire after, be consumed with desire; have an itchy *or* itching palm *and* have sticky fingers <all nonformal>

**crawl** NOUNS 1 **slow motion, leisurely gait,** snail's *or* tortoise's pace; **creep**

VERBS 2 **feel creepy,** feel funny, **have the creeps** *or* **cold creeps** *or* the heebie-jeebies <nonformal>; have gooseflesh *or* goose bumps; give one the creeps *or* the willies <nonformal>

3 **go slow** *or* **slowly,** go at a snail's pace, take it slow, get no place fast <nonformal>; **drag,** drag out; **creep;** inch, inch along; worm, worm along; poke, **poke along;** shuffle *or* stagger *or* totter *or* toddle along; **linger on,** linger, tarry, go on, **go on and on, wear on,** drag, **drag on,** drag along

**craze** NOUNS 1 **infatuation, enthusiasm,** passion, fascination, crazy fancy, bug <nonformal>, rage, furor

VERBS 2 **madden,** dement, make mad, send mad, **unbalance,** unhinge, undermine one's reason, **derange,** distract, frenzy, shatter, **drive insane** *or* mad *or* **crazy,** put *or* send out of one's mind, overthrow one's mind *or* reason, drive up the wall <nonformal>

**crazy** ADJS 1 **mentally deficient,** mentally defective, mentally handicapped, retarded, **mentally retarded,** backward, arrested, subnormal, not right in the head, **not all there** <nonformal>; **simpleminded,** simplewitted, simple, simpletonian; **half-witted,** half-baked <nonformal>; **idiotic, moronic, imbecile,** imbecilic, cretinous, cretinistic; crackbrained, cracked; babbling, driveling, slobbering, drooling, blithering, dithering, maundering, burbling

2 <nonformal> **nutty,** daffy, dotty, dippy, crazy as a bedbug *or* coot *or* loon, loony, loony-tune, goofy, wacky, balmy *or* barmy, flaky, kooky, potty, batty, ape, apeshit, wiggy, lunchy, out to lunch, bonzo, bats, nuts, nutso, nutty as a fruitcake, fruity, fruitcakey, screwy, screwball, screwballs, crackers, bananas, bonkers <Brit>, loopy, beany, buggy, bughouse, bugs, cuckoo, slaphappy, flipped, freaked-out, off-the-wall, gaga, haywire, off in the upper story, off one's nut *or* rocker, off the track *or* trolley, off the hinges, round the bend <Brit>, minus some buttons, nobody home, with bats in the belfry, just plain nuts, loco, mental <Brit>, psycho, cracked, not right in the head, tetched, off one's head, out of one's head, out of one's gourd *or* skull, out of one's tree, not all there, *meshuggah*

<Yiddish>, not tightly wrapped, three bricks shy of a load, rowing with one oar in the water, up the wall, off the wall, schizzy, schizoid, schizo

**cream** NOUNS 1 lotion, cold cream, cleansing cream; **ointment, balm, salve, unguent,** unguentum, inunction, inunctum, unction, chrism
2 **the best,** flower, fat; cream of the crop, *crème de la crème* <Fr>, salt of the earth; *pièce de résistance* <Fr>; nonesuch, paragon, nonpareil; gem of the first water

**create** VERBS **originate, invent; innovate; occasion, make, engender,** generate, give origin to, give occasion to, **give rise to,** spark, spark off, set off, trigger, trigger off

**creation** NOUNS **work of art, object of art,** objet d'art, art object, art work, artistic production, piece, **work, study, design, composition;** brainchild

**creative** ADJS **originative,** causative, **productive, constructive,** formative, fabricative, demiurgic; inventive; generative; **imaginative,** conceptual, conceptive, ideational, ideative, notional; originative, ingenious; productive, fertile, fecund, prolific, seminal, germinal, teeming, pregnant; **inspired,** visioned

**creativity** NOUNS **originality, novelty,** newness, innovation, freshness, uniqueness; inventiveness, creativeness, originality, **ingenuity;** productivity, **fertility,** fecundity

**credential** NOUNS **recommendation, reference,** letter of reference, voucher, **testimonial; identification; voucher, warrant,** warranty; **diploma,** sheepskin <nonformal>

**credible** ADJS **believable; tenable,** conceivable, **plausible,** colorable; worthy of faith, trustworthy, trusty; reliable; unimpeachable, unexceptionable, **unquestionable**

**credit** NOUNS 1 **trust,** tick <nonformal>; borrowing power *or* capacity; commercial credit, cash credit, bank credit, book credit, tax credit, investment credit; credit line, line of credit; installment plan, installment credit, consumer credit, store credit, hire purchase plan <Brit>, never-never <Brit nonformal>
2 **due,** one's due, what one merits *or* is entitled to, what one has earned, what is owing, what one has coming, what is coming to one, acknowledgment, cognizance, recognition, crediting
VERBS 3 acknowledge, make acknowledgments of, recognize, give *or* render credit *or* recognition; credit with; credit to one's account, place to one's credit *or* account
4 **believe, trust, accept,** receive, buy <nonformal>; give credit *or* credence to, give faith to, put faith in, take stock in *or* set store by <nonformal>, take to heart, attach weight to

**creditable** ADJS **praiseworthy,** worthy, **commendable,** estimable, **laudable,** admirable, meritorious, **reputable,** noble, sterling, manly, yeomanly; **respectable,** highly respectable

**creed** NOUNS **system of belief; religion, faith**, belief-system; **school, cult, ism, ideology,** *Weltanschauung* <Ger>, world view; political faith *or* belief *or* philosophy; **credo,** credenda; articles of religion, articles of faith, formulated *or* stated belief

**creek** NOUNS **waterway,** crick <nonformal>; rivulet, rill, streamlet, brooklet, runlet, runnel, rundle <nonformal>, rindle <Brit nonformal>, beck <Brit>, gill <Brit>, burn <Scots>, sike <Brit nonformal>

**creep** VERBS **crawl,** scramble, scrabble, grovel, **go on hands and knees,** go on all fours; worm, worm along, worm one's way, snake; inch, inch along; **sneak, steal,** steal along; pussyfoot *and* gumshoe <both nonformal>, slink, sidle, pad, prowl, nightwalk; **tiptoe,** tippytoe, go on tiptoe

**creepy** ADJS **spooky, eerie, weird, uncanny,** unco *or* uncolike <both Scots>

**cremation** NOUNS **incineration, burning,** reduction to ashes; suttee, self-cremation, self-immolation; the stake, burning at the stake, *auto da fé* <Pg>

**crescendo** NOUNS **loudness,** intensity, volume, amplitude, fullness; sonorousness, sonority; surge of sound, surge, swell, swelling

**crescent** NOUNS 1 **semicircle,** scythe, sickle, meniscus; crescent moon, halfmoon; lunula, lunule; horseshoe
ADJS 2 **increasing, rising,** on the upswing, on the increase, on the rise; growing, fast-growing, flourishing, burgeoning, blossoming, waxing, swelling; **crescent-shaped,** crescentlike, crescen-

tic, crescentiform; **semicircular,** semilunar; horn-shaped, hornlike, horned, corniform

**crest** NOUNS **summit,** top; **tip-top, peak,** pinnacle; **brow;** ridge, edge; **crown,** cap, **tip,** point, spire, pitch; **apex,** vertex

**crevice** NOUNS **crack, cleft,** cranny, chink, check, craze, chap, fissure, scissure, incision, notch, score, cut, gash, slit, split, **rift,** rent

**crew** NOUNS **aircrew,** flight crew; **staff, personnel, employees,** help, hired help, the help, **gang,** men, force, servantry, retinue; rowing crew; **cast,** company; complement, outfit, pack, cohort, troupe, tribe, stable, bunch *and* mob *and* crowd <all nonformal>

**crib** NOUNS 1 booth, stall, manger
2 **translation, pony** *and* trot <both nonformal>; interlinear, interlinear translation
3 **storeroom,** bin, bunker, bay; corncrib
VERBS 4 **borrow,** steal one's stuff <nonformal>, take a leaf out of one's book; counterfeit, fake <nonformal>, hoke *and* hoke up <both nonformal>, forge, plagiarize, lift <nonformal>, cheat

**crime** NOUNS **wrongdoing, evildoing, wickedness,** misdoing <old>, wrong conduct, **misbehavior, misconduct,** misdemeaning, misfeasance, malfeasance, malversation, **malpractice,** evil courses, machinations of the devil; **sin, criminality,** lawbreaking, feloniousness; misdemeanor, felony

*the transgression of the law*
BIBLE

**criminal** NOUNS 1 **felon, perpetrator, crook** *and* perp <both nonformal>, public enemy, **lawbreaker,** scofflaw; **gangster** *and* mobster *and* wiseguy <all nonformal>, **racketeer; swindler**; thief; thug; **desperado,** desperate criminal; **outlaw,** fugitive, **convict,** jailbird, gaolbird <Brit>; gallows bird <nonformal>
ADJS 2 **illegal, unlawful, illegitimate, illicit,** nonlicit, nonlegal, lawless, wrongful, fraudulent, creative <nonformal>, **against the law; felonious; outlaw, outlawed**

**cringe** VERBS **flinch, shrink, shy,** shy away from, draw back, recoil, funk <nonformal>, **quail, wince, blench, blink,** say *or* cry uncle; **cower**

**crinkle** NOUNS 1 **wrinkle, corrugation,** ridge, **furrow, crease, crimp,** ruck, **pucker,** cockle; crankle, rimple, ripple, wimple; crumple, rumple; crow's-feet
VERBS 2 **wrinkle, corrugate,** shirr, ridge, **furrow, crease,** crimp, crimple, cockle, cocker, **pucker, purse; knit;** ruck, ruckle; **crumple,** rumple; rimple, ripple, wimple

**cripple** NOUNS 1 **handicapped person,** incapable; amputee; paraplegic, quadriplegic, paralytic; deformity; the crippled, the handicapped
VERBS 2 **lame,** maim; **hamstring,** hobble; wing; emasculate, castrate; incapacitate, **disable; handicap,** put at a disadvantage; hamstring

**crisis** NOUNS **critical point,** crunch, crucial period, climax, climacteric; **turning point,** hinge, turn, turn of the tide, cusp; **emergency, exigency,** juncture *or* conjuncture *or* convergence of events, critical juncture, crossroads; **pinch,** clutch <nonformal>, rub, push, pass, strait, extremity, spot <nonformal>; **emergency,** state of emergency, red alert, race against time

**crisp** ADJS 1 **refreshing,** refreshful, **fresh,** brisk, zesty, zestful, **bracing, tonic,** cordial; analeptic; **exhilarating, stimulating, stimulative, stimulatory, invigorating,** rousing, energizing; **cool,** coolish, temperate; chill, **chilly,** parky <Brit nonformal>
2 **brittle,** crispy; **fragile, frail,** delicate, flimsy, **breakable,** frangible, crushable, crackable, crunchable, fracturable; crumbly; fissile, scissile; brittle as glass

**criterion** NOUNS 1 **measure,** measuring instrument, **meter, instrument, gauge,** barometer, **rule, yardstick,** measuring rod *or* stick, **standard,** norm, canon, test, touchstone, check
2 **model, pattern, standard,** classic example, rule, mirror, paradigm

**critic** NOUNS 1 interpreter, exegete, analyst, explicator, theoretician, aesthetician; reviewer
2 criticizer; connoisseur, *cognoscente* <Ital>; literary critic, man of letters; textual critic; editor; social critic, muckraker; captious critic, smellfungus, caviler, carper, faultfinder; criticaster, criticule, critickin

**critical** ADJS 1 **faultfinding,** carping, picky *and* nitpicky <both nonformal>, caviling, quibbling, pettifogging, cap-

tious, cynical; nagging, niggling; hypercritical, ultracritical, overcritical, hairsplitting, trichoschistic
2 evaluative, interpretive, exegetical, analytical, explicative
3 **crucial,** pivotal, climactic, climacteric *or* climacterical, decisive; pregnant, kairotic, loaded, charged; exigent, emergent

**criticism** NOUNS 1 adverse *or* harsh *or* hostile criticism, flak <nonformal>, bad notices, bad press, animadversion, imputation, reflection, **aspersion,** stricture, obloquy; **knock** *and* **swipe** *and* **slam** *and* **rap** *and* hit <all nonformal>, home thrust; minor *or* petty criticism, niggle, cavil, quibble, exception, nit <nonformal>; **faultfinding,** taking exception, carping, caviling, pettifogging, quibbling, captiousness, niggling, nitpicking, pestering, nagging; hypercriticism, hypercriticalness, hairsplitting, trichoschistism
2 **censure**; **approval**; **critique,** review, notice, critical notice, report, comment

**criticize** VERBS **pan** *and* **knock** *and* **slam** *and* hit *and* rap *and* take a rap *or* swipe at <all nonformal>, snipe at, strike out at, tie into *and* tee off on *and* rip into *and* open up on *and* plow into <all nonformal>; critique, evaluate, interpret, explicate, analyze, judge; theorize; pick holes in, pick to pieces; **approve**; **review;** comment upon, annotate; moralize upon; pontificate

**crony** NOUNS **companion, fellow,** fellow companion, **comrade,** *camarade* <Fr>, amigo <nonformal>, mate <Brit>, comate, company, **associate**, consociate, compeer, confrere, consort, **colleague**

**crook** NOUNS 1 **staff,** pastoral staff, **crosier, cross,** cross-staff, paterissa
2 **criminal, crook** *and* perp <both nonformal>, public enemy, **lawbreaker,** scofflaw; **gangster** *and* mobster *and* wiseguy <all nonformal>, **racketeer; swindler**; thief; thug

**crop** NOUNS 1 **harvest,** harvesting, **reaping, gleaning,** gathering, cutting; yield; cash crop, root crop
VERBS 2 **cut off** *or* **away,** shear *or* take *or* strike *or* knock *or* lop off, truncate; **amputate,** mutilate, abscind; **prune,** pare, peel, clip, bob, dock, lop, nip, shear, shave, strip, strip off *or* away

**cross** NOUNS 1 crux, cruciform; **crucifix,** rood, tree *or* rood tree <old>; X *or* ex, exing, T, Y; **swastika,** gammadion, fylfot, *Hakenkreuz* <Ger>; crossbones
VERBS 2 **oppose, counter,** go *or* act in opposition to, **go against,** run against, **run counter to,** fly in the face of, fly in the teeth of
3 **hybridize, crossbreed, interbreed,** miscegenate, mongrelize
ADJS 4 **angry,** angered, **incensed, indignant, irate,** ireful; **livid,** livid with rage, beside oneself, **wroth, wrathful,** wrathy, wrought-up, worked up, riled up <nonformal>

**cross-eyed** ADJS **cockeyed,** swivel-eyed <nonformal>, goggle-eyed, bug-eyed *and* popeyed <both nonformal>, **walleyed,** saucer-eyed, glare-eyed; moon-eyed

**crossroads** NOUNS 1 **village, hamlet;** ham *and* thorp *and* wick <all old>; country town, wide place in the road

*a little one-eyed, blinking sort o' place*
THOMAS HARDY

2 **crisis, critical point,** crunch, crucial period, climax, climacteric; **turning point,** hinge, turn, turn of the tide, cusp; **emergency, exigency,** juncture *or* conjuncture *or* convergence of events, critical juncture

**cross section** NOUNS sample, random sample, sampling

**crotch** NOUNS 1 **genitals,** crutch <Brit>, groin, pubic region, perineum, pelvis
2 **fork, prong,** trident; **branch, ramification,** stem, offshoot; crutch

**crotchety** ADJS **capricious,** kinky, harebrained, cranky, flaky <nonformal>, quirky; dotty, maggoty <Brit>, crank, crankish, whimsical, twisted; antisocial

**crouch** VERBS duck, cringe, **cower; stoop, bend, stoop down, squat,** squat down, get down, hunker *and* hunker down *and* get down on one's hunkers <all nonformal>; hunch, hunch down, hunch over, scrooch *or* scrouch down <nonformal>

**crow** VERBS **exult,** triumph, glory, delight, joy, jubilate; **crow** *or* crow over, crow like a rooster *or* cock; **gloat,** gloat over

**crowd** NOUNS 1 **clique, coterie, set, circle,** ring, junto, junta, cabal, camarilla, **clan,** group; **crew** *and* mob *and* **bunch** *and* outfit <all nonformal>; inner circle;

closed *or* charmed circle; ingroup, we-group; **old-boy network**
2 **throng,** press, crush, flood, spate, deluge, mass; mob, rabble, rout, ruck, jam, *cohue* <Fr>, everybody and his uncle *or* his brother <nonformal>
VERBS 3 **throng,** swarm, teem, hive, surge, seethe, mill, stream, horde; **be crowded,** be mobbed, burst at the seams, be full to overflowing

**crown** NOUNS 1 **summit,** top; cap, **tip,** point, spire, pitch; highest pitch, no place higher, **apex,** vertex, **acme,** *ne plus ultra* <Fr>, **zenith, climax,** apogee, pole; **culmination**
2 **championship,** laurels, palms, first prize, blue ribbon, new high, record
3 royal crown, coronet, tiara, diadem
VERBS 4 **top,** top off, **cap,** crest, **head,** tip, peak, surmount; overtop *or* outtop, have the top place *or* spot, over-arch; **culminate,** consummate, climax
5 **install,** instate, induct, **inaugurate,** invest, put in, place, **place in office;** throne, enthrone, anoint

**crowning** ADJS **topping,** heading, surmounting, overtopping *or* outtopping, overarching; **culminating,** consummating, perfecting, climaxing

**crucial** ADJS **critical,** pivotal, climactic, decisive

**crucify** VERBS **torture, torment, agonize, harrow,** savage, **rack,** scarify, impale, excruciate, prolong the agony, kill by inches, martyr, martyrize

**crude** ADJS **unfinished,** rude, coarse, unpolished, unrefined; uncultivated, uncultured

**cruel** ADJS cruel-hearted, sadistic; **ruthless**; **brutal,** brutish, brute, bestial, beastly, animal, animalistic; **mindless, soulless,** insensate, senseless, subhuman, dehumanized, brutalized

**cruelty** NOUNS cruelness, sadistic *or* insensate cruelty, sadism, wanton cruelty; **brutality,** mindless *or* senseless brutality, brutalness, **brutishness, bestiality, animality,** beastliness

**cruise** NOUNS 1 **voyage,** ocean *or* sea trip, sail; course, **run, passage; crossing;** shakedown cruise
VERBS 2 **navigate, sail,** steam, run, **seafare, voyage,** ply, go on shipboard, go by ship, go on *or* take a voyage

**crumb** NOUNS **scrap,** tatter, snip, **snippet,** snick, chip, nip; **morsel,** *morceau* <Fr>

**crumble** VERBS **weaken,** go to pieces, disintegrate; go downhill, hit the skids <nonformal>, give way, break, collapse, cave in <nonformal>, surrender, cry uncle <nonformal>

**crumbly** ADJS **pulverable, pulverizable,** pulverulent, triturable; **friable**

**crummy** ADJS **base, low,** low rent *and* low ride *and* low-down *and* cotton-picking <all nonformal>, **mean**

**crunch** NOUNS 1 **embarrassed** *or* **reduced** *or* **straitened circumstances,** tight squeeze, hard pinch, crunch <nonformal>, cash *or* credit crunch <nonformal>
2 **crucial moment,** critical moment, **moment of truth,** when push comes to shove <nonformal>; **pickle,** pretty pickle, fine kettle of fish <all nonformal>

**crusade** NOUNS 1 **campaign,** war, **drive, expedition,** hostile expedition; holy war, jihad
VERBS 2 **campaign for, crusade for,** put on a drive for, devote *or* dedicate oneself to, spend *or* give *or* sacrifice oneself for

**crush** NOUNS 1 **infatuation;** case <nonformal>; **puppy love** *and* calf love <both nonformal>; love at first sight
2 **crowd,** press, flood, spate, deluge, mass
VERBS 3 **deject, depress,** press down, hit one like a ton of bricks <nonformal>, **cast down,** lower, lower the spirits, get one down <nonformal>, take the wind out of one's sails, rain on one's parade, burst one's bubble, **discourage, dishearten,** take the heart out of, **dispirit,** overcome, prostrate
4 **subdue, master,** overmaster, **quell, reduce,** beat down, **break,** break down, overwhelm; tread underfoot, trample on *or* down, trample underfoot, roll in the dust, trample in the dust

**crusty** ADJS **surly,** bearish, beastly, churlish; **crusted,** incrusted

**crutch** NOUNS **supporter, support;** staff, stave, cane, stick, walking stick, alpenstock, crook

**crux** NOUNS **salient point,** cardinal point, high point, great point; **gist, nub** <nonformal>, **heart,** meat, pith, kernel, **core;** knotty point, knot, node, nodus

**cry** NOUNS 1 **call, shout, yell, whoop, holler** <nonformal>; **cheer, hurrah; howl,** yowl, yawl <Brit nonformal>;

**scream, shriek,** screech, squeal, squall, caterwaul
2 **appeal, plea,** call, clamor, *cri du cœur* <Fr>, beseeching, impetration, obtestation
VERBS 3 **weep, sob, bawl;** whimper, snivel; **shed tears,** burst into tears, burst out crying, dissolve in tears, cry one's eyes out
4 **call, shout, yell, holler** <nonformal>, hoot; hail, halloo, hollo; **whoop; cheer**; **howl,** yowl, yammer, yawl <Brit nonformal>; squawk, yawp; **bawl, bellow,** roar, roar *or* bellow like a bull; cry *or* yell *or* scream bloody murder *or* blue murder

**crypt** NOUNS **tomb, vault,** burial chamber; ossuary *or* ossuarium; charnel house, bone house; **mausoleum**

**cryptic** ADJS **secret,** close, closed, closet; dark; unuttered, unrevealed, undivulged, undisclosed, unspoken, untold; arcane, esoteric, occult, enigmatic, mysterious

**cryptography** NOUNS cryptoanalysis, cryptoanalytics; **code, cipher;** secret language; code book, code word, code name; **secret writing,** coded message, cryptogram, cryptograph

**crystallize** VERBS 1 **form, take form,** take order, **take shape, shape up;** arrange *or* range itself, **fall** *or* **drop into place,** come together
2 **solidify, set,** thicken; granulate; petrify, lithify, harden

**cubbyhole** NOUNS **nook,** cubicle, roomlet, carrel, hole-in-the-wall <nonformal>, cubby, snuggery, hidey-hole <nonformal>

**cuddle** VERBS **snuggle, nestle,** nuzzle; lap; bundle

**cuddly** ADJS **endearing, lovable, likable, adorable,** admirable, **lovely,** lovesome, sweet, winning, winsome; **charming;** caressable, kissable; cuddlesome

**cue** NOUNS **reminder,** remembrancer; **prompt,** prompter, tickler; prompting, hint; jogger <nonformal>, flapper

**cuff** NOUNS 1 **slap, smack,** flap; **box,** buffet; **spank**
VERBS 2 **slap,** smack, whack, whomp, **box,** buffet; strike; box the ears, give a rap on the knuckles

**cuisine** NOUNS **cooking, cookery, culinary art;** food preparation; culinary science; catering; nutrition

**culinary** ADJS **cooking,** kitchen

**cull** VERBS **collect, pick, pluck, take up,** pick up, get *or* gather in, gather to oneself, bring *or* get together, scrape together; isolate, set on the side

**culmination** NOUNS **completion, fulfillment, consummation,** perfection, height, top, acme, ultimate, summit, pinnacle, realization, actualization, **accomplishment**, topping-off, closure

**culpable** ADJS **blameworthy,** blamable, to blame, at fault, much at fault; chargeable, impeachable, accusable, indictable, arraignable, imputable

**culprit** NOUNS **wrongdoer, malefactor, sinner,** transgressor, delinquent; offender; evildoer

**cult** NOUNS **ism;** cultism; cultus; **mystique**

**cultivate** VERBS 1 cultivate the friendship of, **court,** pay court to, pay addresses to, seek the company of, **run after** <nonformal>, **shine up to,** make up to <nonformal>, play up to *and* suck up to <both nonformal>, hold out *or* extend the right of friendship *or* fellowship
2 **grow,** culture, **dress, work, till,** till the soil, dig, delve, spade

**cultivated** ADJS cultured, **refined,** polished, civilized; **educated, learned, erudite, scholarly,** scholastic, studious

**cultural** ADJS **educational,** educative, educating, teaching, **instructive,** instructional, **tuitional,** tuitionary; **edifying, enlightening,** illuminating

**culture** NOUNS **society, civilization; ethos, culture pattern;** cultural change; cultural lag; culture conflict; **cultivation, refinement, polish,** civility; cultivation of the mind; **refinement,** finesse, refined *or* cultivated *or* civilized taste

**cultured** ADJS **improved, bettered;** changed for the better, advanced, ameliorated, enhanced, enriched; developed, perfected; beautified, embellished; upgraded; gentrified; **reformed; transformed,** transfigured, converted; **cultivated, refined,** polished, civilized; **educated**

**culvert** NOUNS **watercourse, waterway, aqueduct,** water channel, water gate, water carrier, irrigation ditch

**cumbersome** ADJS **onerous, oppressive, burdensome,** incumbent *or* superincumbent, cumbrous; massive; lumpish, **unwieldy**

**cumulative** ADJS **additive,** additional,

additory; accumulative; summative *or* summational

**cunning** ADJS **crafty, artful, wily,** callid <old>, guileful, **sly,** insidious, supple <Scots>, **shifty,** pawky <Brit>, arch, **smooth, slick** *and* slick as a whistle <both nonformal>, **slippery,** snaky, serpentine, **foxy,** vulpine, feline

**cup** NOUNS 1 **container, receptacle;** receiver, holder, vessel, utensil; basin, pot, pan, glass
2 **trophy,** loving cup, pot <nonformal>

**Cupid** NOUNS Love, Amor, Eros, Kama; Venus, Aphrodite, Astarte, Freya

**curable** ADJS **remediable;** medicable, treatable; emendable, amendable, **correctable,** rectifiable, corrigible; **reparable,** repairable, **mendable, fixable**

**curb** NOUNS 1 **pavement,** curbstone, kerbstone <Brit>, edgestone; kerb <Brit>, curbing; gutter, kennel <Brit>
VERBS 2 **control, check,** rein, arrest; **retard,** slow down; **hinder, impede, inhibit,** countercheck, scotch, snub

**cure** NOUNS 1 **remedy, corrective,** alterative, remedial measure, sovereign remedy; **relief, help, aid, assistance,** succor; balm, balsam; healing agent; restorative, analeptic; healing quality *or* virtue; specific, specific remedy; **prescription,** recipe, receipt
VERBS 2 remedy; prescribe; treat
3 **preserve,** salt, brine, marinate *or* marinade, pickle, corn, **dry, dry-cure,** jerk, dry-salt; dehydrate, anhydrate, evaporate, desiccate; vacuum-pack; **smoke,** fume, **smoke-cure,** smoke-dry, kipper

**cure-all** NOUNS **panacea,** universal remedy, theriac, catholicon; broad-spectrum drug *or* antibiotic; elixir, elixir of life, *elixir vitae* <L>

**curio** NOUNS conversation piece; museum piece; **oddity, curiosity, wonder,** funny *or* peculiar *or* strange thing; **abnormality, anomaly**

**curiosity** NOUNS 1 intellectual curiosity, thirst for knowledge, lust for learning; eagerness; interest, **concern,** concernment; **enthusiasm,** passion, ardor, zeal; cathexis; matter of interest, special interest
2 **oddity, abnormality, anomaly; rarity,** improbability, exception, one in a thousand *or* million; **prodigy,** prodigiosity

**curious** ADJS 1 **odd, queer, peculiar, absurd, singular, oddball** <nonformal>, weird *and* kooky *and* freaky *and* freaked-out <all nonformal>, quaint, **eccentric,** gonzo <nonformal>, funny, rum <Brit nonformal>; **strange, outlandish,** off-the-wall <informal>, surreal, not for real <nonformal>, passing strange, **weird,** unearthly; off, out

*wondrous strange*
SHAKESPEARE

2 **inquisitive,** inquiring, interested, quizzical; **alert,** tuned in <nonformal>, **attentive**; burning with curiosity, eaten up *or* consumed with curiosity, curious as a cat; gossipy; overcurious, supercurious; morbidly curious, **morbid, ghoulish**

**curl** NOUNS 1 **lock, tress;** flowing locks, flowing tresses; **ringlet,** earlock, *payess* <Yiddish>; lovelock
VERBS 2 wind, **curve, turn,** arc, sweep; **crook, hook,** loop; incurve, incurvate; recurve, decurve, bend back, retroflex; **hump,** hunch; coil; kink, crimp

**curly** ADJS **curled; kinky,** kinked; **frizzly,** frizzy, frizzled, frizzed

**currency** NOUNS **money, legal tender, medium of exchange,** circulating medium, sterling <Brit>, **cash,** hard cash, cold cash; specie, coinage, mintage, coin of the realm, gold; **silver; the wherewithal,** the wherewith; lucre, **filthy lucre** <nonformal>, the almighty dollar, pelf, root of all evil, mammon

**current** NOUNS 1 **electric current,** current flow, amperage, electric stream *or* flow, juice <nonformal>
ADJS 2 **fashionable, in fashion, smart, in style, in vogue; all the rage,** all the thing; **popular,** prevalent, current; **up-to-date,** up-to-datish, up-to-the-minute, switched-on *and* hip *and* with-it <all nonformal>, trendy <nonformal>, newfashioned, modern; **in the swim;** sought-after, much sought-after

**curry** VERBS **tend; groom,** rub down, brush, currycomb; gentle, handle, manage; tame, train, break

**curse** NOUNS 1 **affliction,** infliction; **woe,** distress, grievance, **sorrow,** *tsures* <Yiddish>; **trouble,** peck *or* pack of troubles, **burden, oppression, cross, cross to bear** *or* **be borne, load,** fardel <old>, encumbrance, weight, albatross around one's neck, millstone around one's neck;

thorn, thorn in the side, crown of thorns
2 **malediction,** malison, damnation, denunciation, commination, imprecation, execration; blasphemy; anathema, fulmination, thundering, excommunication; ban, proscription; hex, evil eye, *malocchio* <Ital>, whammy <nonformal>; **hex, jinx**
3 **oath,** profane oath; cuss *or* cuss word *and* dirty word *and* four-letter word *and* **swearword** <all nonformal>, naughty word, no-no <nonformal>, foul invective, **expletive, epithet,** dirty name <nonformal>, dysphemism, obscenity
VERBS 4 accurse, **damn,** darn, **confound,** blast, anathematize, fulminate *or* thunder against, execrate, imprecate; excommunicate; call down evil upon, call down curses on the head of; put a curse on; curse up hill and down dale; curse with bell, book, and candle; blaspheme; hex, give the evil eye, throw a whammy <nonformal>
5 **swear, cuss** <nonformal>, curse and swear, execrate, rap out *or* rip out an oath, take the Lord's name in vain; swear like a trooper, cuss like a sailor, make the air blue, swear till one is blue in the face; **talk dirty** <nonformal>, scatologize, coprologize, dysphemize, use strong language

**curt** ADJS **gruff, brusque,** short, sharp, snippy <nonformal>, abrupt, **blunt,** bluff, brash, cavalier; **harsh,** rough, severe; truculent, aggressive; **surly,** crusty, bearish, beastly, churlish

**curtain** NOUNS **veil,** curtain, **cover, screen**; fig leaf; **wraps** <nonformal>; **disguise, veil of secrecy,** pall, wraps; iron curtain, bamboo curtain; wall *or* barrier of secrecy; **suppression,** repression, stifling, smothering; **censorship,** blackout <nonformal>, **hush-up, cover-up**

**curtsy** NOUNS 1 **bow, nod, bob,** bend, inclination, inclination of the head, **salaam, kowtow,** scrape, bowing and scraping, making a leg; **genuflection,** kneeling, bending the knee; salute, salutation, namaste
VERBS 2 **bow, make obeisance, salaam, kowtow,** make one's bow, bow down, **nod,** incline *or* bend *or* bow the head, bend the neck, **bob,** bob down, bob a curtsy, bend, make a leg, scrape, **bow and scrape**

**curve** NOUNS 1 **bend,** curve, swerve, veer, inflection, deflection; ell, L; cant
VERBS 2 **turn,** arc, sweep; **crook, hook,** loop; incurve, incurvate; recurve, decurve, bend back, retroflex; sag, swag <nonformal>; **bend,** flex; deflect, inflect; reflect, reflex; **bow,** embow; **arch,** vault; dome; **hump,** hunch; wind, curl; round
ADJS 3 **curved,** curvate, curvated, **curving,** curvy, curvaceous <nonformal>, curvesome, curviform; curvilinear, curvilineal; wavy, undulant, billowy, billowing; sinuous, tortuous, serpentine, mazy, labyrinthine, meandering

**cushion** NOUNS 1 **pillow,** bolster; **safeguard, fender,** mudguard, **bumper, buffer,** pad, padding
VERBS 2 absorb the shock, **soften the blow,** break the fall, deaden, damp *or* dampen, soften, suppress, neutralize, offset; show pity *or* mercy *or* consideration *or* sensitivity, temper the wind to the shorn lamb; **soften,** soften up; **ease**

**custodian** NOUNS 1 **cleaner,** cleaner-up, cleaner-off, cleaner-out; **janitor,** janitress; cleaning woman *or* lady *or* man, daily *or* daily woman *and* charwoman *or* char <all Brit>
2 **guardian, warden,** governor; steward, **keeper, caretaker,** warder <Brit>, attendant; caregiver; next friend, prochein ami, guardian *ad litem;* **curator,** conservator; janitor; castellan

**custody** NOUNS **preservation,** preserval, **conservation, saving, salvation,** salvage, **keeping, safekeeping,** maintenance, upkeep, support; custodianship, keep <old>, **keeping, care, change, ward,** guarding, hold, protective *or* preventive custody; protection, safekeeping

**custom** NOUNS **convention,** use, **usage,** standard usage, standard behavior, **wont,** wonting, **way,** established way, time-honored practice, **tradition,** standing custom, **folkway,** manner, **practice,** praxis, prescription, **observance,** ritual, consuetude, **mores;** proper thing, what is done, **social convention**; bon ton, **fashion**; manners, etiquette; way of life, lifestyle; conformity; **generalization,** labeling, stereotyping

**customary** ADJS **wonted;** traditional, time-honored; familiar, everyday, ordinary, **usual; established,** received, accepted; set, prescribed, prescriptive; **normative, normal; standard,** regular, stock, regulation; prevalent, prevailing, widespread, obtaining, generally accepted, popular, **current**; **conventional**; conformist, conformable

**cut** NOUNS 1 incision, scratch, gash; puncture, stab, stab wound; flesh wound; **laceration,** mutilation; abrasion, scuff, scrape, chafe, gall; frazzle, fray; run, **rip,** rent, slash, **tear**
2 **indignity, affront, offense, injury,** humiliation; scurrility, contempt, contumely, despite, flout, flouting, mockery, jeering, jeer, mock, scoff, gibe, taunt, brickbat <nonformal>; **insult, aspersion,** uncomplimentary remark, slap *or* kick in the face, left-handed *or* backhanded compliment, damning with faint praise

*most unkindest cut of all*
SHAKESPEARE

3 **portion, share, bite** *and* **cut** *and* **slice** *and* **chunk** *and* slice of the pie *or* melon *and* piece of the action <all nonformal>, **lot, allotment; commission,** rake-off <nonformal>
4 **discount, deduction,** slash, abatement, reduction, price reduction, price-cutting, price-cut, rollback <nonformal>; underselling
VERBS 5 **pain,** give *or* inflict pain, **hurt, wound, afflict, distress; burn;** sting; nip, bite, tweak, pinch; pierce, prick, stab, lacerate; **offend, give offense, give umbrage,** affront, outrage; grieve, aggrieve; wound, hurt, cut to the quick, hit one where one lives <nonformal>, **sting,** hurt one's feelings; step *or* tread on one's toes
6 **delete,** erase, expunge, **cancel,** omit; **edit,** edit out, blue-pencil; strike, strike out *or* off, rub *or* blot out, cross out *or* off, kill; void, rescind; **censor,** bowdlerize, expurgate; abridge, abbreviate
7 **notch, nick, incise, gash,** slash, chop, crimp, scotch, **score,** blaze, jag, scarify; **indent**; **scallop,** crenellate, crenulate, machicolate; serrate, pink, mill, knurl, tooth, picot
8 **cheapen, depreciate, devaluate,** lower, reduce, **mark down, cut prices,** slash, shave, trim, pare, underprice, knock the bottom out of <nonformal>
9 **adulterate, corrupt,** contaminate, **debase,** denaturalize, pollute, denature, bastardize, **tamper with, doctor** *and* doctor up <both nonformal>; **fortify,** spike <nonformal>, lace; **dilute,** water, water down <nonformal>
10 **turn off, shut off,** shut, shut down, close; **phase out,** phase down, taper off, wind up *or* down; **kill,** cut off short, switch off
ADJS 11 **diluted, reduced, thinned,** rarefied, attenuated; adulterated; watered, watered-down
12 **pained, grieved,** aggrieved; **wounded, hurt,** injured, **bruised,** mauled; cut to the quick; **stung;** anguished, aching, bleeding
13 **cleft,** cloven, **cracked,** sundered, rift, rent, chinky, chapped, crazed; **slit, split;** gaping, gappy; hiatal, caesural, lacunar; fissured, fissural
14 **abridged, abbreviated,** vest-pocket, synopsized, shortened, clipped, pruned, contracted, truncated, docked

**cut back** VERBS **retrench, cut down,** cut *or* pare down expenses, **curtail expenses; cut corners, tighten one's belt,** roll back, take a reef, slow down; downsize

**cute** ADJS pretty as a picture, **pretty, attractive, lovely, graceful,** gracile

**cutoff** NOUNS **stop,** stoppage, **halt, stay, arrest,** check; stand, **standstill;** full stop, dead stop, screaming *or* grinding *or* shuddering *or* squealing halt

**cut-rate** ADJS **reduced,** cut, cut-price, slashed, **marked down;** giveaway <nonformal>, sacrificial

**cutthroat** NOUNS 1 **killer,** thug, desperado, bravo, gorilla <nonformal>, apache, gunman; professional killer, hired killer, hit man *or* button man *or* gun *or* trigger man *or* torpedo *or* gunsel <all nonformal>
ADJS 2 **competitive,** extortionate, **gouging, usurious,** exacting

**cutting** ADJS **acrimonious, harsh,** fierce, **rigorous,** severe, rough, stringent, astringent, strident, **sharp, keen,** sharpish, incisive, trenchant, biting, stinging, **scathing,** stabbing, **piercing, poignant,** penetrating, edged, double-edged

**cycle** NOUNS **succession, round,** rotation, routine, the daily grind <nonformal>, recurrence, periodicity, revolution, **circle,** full circle, go-round, orbit, ambit

**cyclical** ADJS **continuous,** continued, **continual,** repetitive, **recurrent,** periodic; **recurrent,** recurring, **returning,**

reappearing, revenant, ubiquitous, ever-recurring, periodic, serial, isochronal, metronomic

**cyclone** NOUNS **whirlwind,** whirlblast, tourbillon, wind eddy; **tornado, twister,** rotary storm, typhoon, *baguio* <Sp>; **storm, tempest,** squall, line squall, **tornado, hurricane,** tropical cyclone, typhoon, storm-center, tropical storm

**cynic** NOUNS **pessimist,** malist, nihilist; killjoy, gloomy Gus *and* calamity howler *and* worrywart <all nonformal>, seek-sorrow, Job's comforter, prophet of doom, Cassandra, Eeyore; doubter, doubting Thomas

*a man who feels bad when he feels good for fear he'll feel worse when he feels better*
GEORGE BURNS

**cynical** ADJS **pessimistic,** pessimist, downbeat <nonformal>, nihilistic; **critical, faultfinding,** carping, picky *and* nitpicky <both nonformal>, caviling, quibbling, pettifogging, captious; **gloomy,** dismal, crapehanging, funereal, lugubrious; negative, negativistic; defeatist; Cassandran *or* Cassandrian, Cassandra-like

# D

**daily** NOUNS 1 **newspaper,** news, **paper,** sheet *or* rag <both nonformal>, **gazette,** daily newspaper
ADJS 2 **recurrent,** recurring, **returning,** reappearing, revenant, ubiquitous, ever-recurring, circadian, thick-coming, frequent, incessant

**dainty** ADJS **delicate, gossamer, diaphanous; subtle,** subtile, tenuous, thin, rarefied; **fine, exquisite,** flower-like

**dairy** NOUNS **larder, pantry,** buttery <nonformal>; dairy house *or* room, creamery

**dais** NOUNS **platform; stage,** estrade, floor; **rostrum, podium, pulpit,** speaker's platform *or* stand, **soapbox** <nonformal>; hustings, **stump**

**dam** NOUNS 1 **barrier,** weir, barrage, milldam, beaver dam, cofferdam, wicket dam, shutter dam
VERBS 2 **stop, stop up; obstruct, bar,** stay; **block,** block up; **clog,** clog up, foul; **choke,** choke up *or* off; dam up

**damage** NOUNS 1 **impairment, injury, harm,** mischief, scathe, **hurt, detriment,** loss, weakening, sickening; disablement, incapacitation; **malfunction,** glitch <nonformal>; mayhem, mutilation, crippling, hobbling, hamstringing
VERBS 2 **impair, injure, harm, hurt,** irritate; **worsen,** make worse, disimprove, deteriorate, put *or* set back, aggravate, exacerbate, embitter; **weaken; dilapidate;** add insult to injury, rub salt in the wound

**dame** NOUNS **noblewoman, peeress, gentlewoman**

**damn** VERBS 1 doom, send *or* consign to hell, cast into hell, doom to perdition, condemn to hell *or* eternal punishment
ADJS 2 **cursed,** accursed, bloody <Brit nonformal>, **damned, damnable,** goddamned, goddamn, **execrable**

**damned** ADJS **cursed,** accursed, bloody <Brit nonformal>, **damn, damnable,** goddamned, goddamn, **execrable; execrable, damnable;** accursed, cursed; infernal, hellish, devilish, fiendish

**damp** NOUNS 1 **moisture,** wet; **dampness, moistness,** moistiness, **wetness,** wettedness, wettishness, **wateriness,** humor *or* humectation <both old>; soddenness, soppiness, soppingness, sogginess
ADJS 2 **moist,** moisty; dampish; **wet,** wettish; **humid, dank, muggy, sticky**

**dance** NOUNS 1 **dancing,** terpsichore; the light fantastic; **choreography; ball,** *bal* <Fr>; masked ball, masque, mask, masquerade ball, masquerade, *bal masqué* <Fr>, *bal costumé* <Fr>, fancy-dress ball, cotillion
VERBS 2 **trip the light fantastic,** trip, skip, hop, foot, prance <nonformal>, **hoof** <nonformal>, clog

*trip it as we go, on the light fantastic toe*
Milton

**dancer** NOUNS danseur, terpsichorean, **hoofer** <nonformal>, step dancer, tap dancer, clog dancer, **ballet dancer; ballerina,** danseuse, coryphée; **chorus girl, chorine,** chorus boy *or* man; nautch

**dandruff** NOUNS **flake,** flock, floccule, flocculus; **scale, scurf**

**dandy** NOUNS 1 **fop,** coxcomb, macaroni, gallant, dude *and* swell *and* sport <all nonformal>, ponce *and* toff <both Brit nonformal>, exquisite, blood, clotheshorse, fashion plate; beau, Beau Brummel, spark, blade, ladies' man, man-about-town, boulevardier

ADJS 2 <nonformal> **great,** swell, jim dandy, neat, cool, super, super-duper, groovy, out of sight, something else, hot, nifty, sexy, spiffy, spiffing, ripping

**danger** NOUNS **peril, endangerment, imperilment, jeopardy, hazard, risk,** cause for alarm, **menace, threat**; **crisis, emergency,** hot spot, nasty *or* tricky spot, pass, pinch, strait, plight, predicament; powder keg, time bomb

**dangerous** ADJS dangersome <nonformal>, **perilous,** periculous, parlous, jeopardous, ugly, serious, critical, explosive, attended *or* beset *or* fraught with danger

**dangle** VERBS **hang,** hang down, fall; **depend,** pend; swing, flap, flop <nonformal>; flow, drape, cascade; **droop**

**dangling** ADJS **pendent,** pendulous, pendulant, pendular, penduline, pensile; swinging, falling loosely; shaky, rickety; hanging, drooping

**dank** ADJS **humid, muggy, sticky;** dewy, bedewed

**dapper** ADJS 1 dashing, jaunty, braw <Scots>

2 <nonformal> sharp, spiffy, classy, nifty, snazzy; swank, swanky, swell

**dapple** ADJS **mottled, motley; pied, piebald,** skewbald, pinto; **dappled**

**dare** NOUNS 1 **challenge,** double dare; fighting words; gage, gauntlet, glove, chip on one's shoulder, slap of the glove
VERBS 2 **venture, make bold to,** make so bold as to, take risks, walk the tightrope, **have the nerve, have the guts** *or* the balls <nonformal>, have the courage of one's convictions

**daring** NOUNS 1 derring-do, deeds of derring-do; **bravado,** bravura; daredeviltry, daredevilry, fire-eating; playing with fire, flirting with death, courting disaster, stretching one's luck, going for broke <nonformal>, **audacity,** audaciousness, overboldness; **venturousness,** venturesomeness, risk-taking, tightrope walking, funambulism
ADJS 2 **audacious,** overbold; **adventurous, venturous, venturesome,** adventuresome, enterprising; foolhardy, daredevil, fire-eating, death-defying; adventurous

**dark** NOUNS 1 **dark, lightlessness; obscurity,** tenebrosity, tenebrousness; **night**, dead of night, deep night; **pitch-darkness,** pitch-blackness, Cimmerian *or* Stygian *or* Egyptian darkness, Erebus

*darkness visible*
**Milton**

ADJS 2 dark-colored, **darkish,** darksome, blackish; nigrescent; darksome, darkling; **lightless,** beamless, rayless, unlighted, **unilluminated,** unlit; **swarthy,** swart; **dusky,** dusk; **somber,** sombrous, **sober, grave,** sad, funereal; hostile, sullen, angry

**dark horse** NOUNS **small chance,** little chance, **poor prospect** *or* prognosis, poor lookout <nonformal>, little opportunity, poor possibility, **unlikelihood, improbability**, hardly a chance, not half a chance; **off chance, outside chance** <nonformal>, **remote possibility,** bare possibility, a ghost of a chance, slim chance, long shot <nonformal>, hundred-to-one shot <nonformal>

**dark-skinned** ADJS black-skinned, **dark-complexioned;** melanian, melanic, melanotic, melanistic, melanous

**darling** ADJS **beloved, loved, dear, precious;** pet, favorite; **adored, admired,** esteemed, revered; **cherished,** prized, treasured, held dear

**darn** VERBS **repair, mend, fix,** put in repair, set to rights, put in order *or* condition; patch, **patch up;** sew up

**dash** NOUNS 1 **vim, verve,** fire, adrenalin, **drive; aggressiveness, enterprise,** initiative, proactiveness, thrust, spunk
2 **rush,** plunge, headlong rush *or* plunge, **race, scurry, scamper,** scud, scuttle, **spurt,** burst, **burst of speed**
3 **showiness, flashiness,** flamboyance, panache, jazziness <nonformal>, jauntiness, sportiness <nonformal>, gaiety, glitter, glare, dazzle
VERBS 4 **sadden,** damp *or* dampen the spirits; knock down, beat down; plunge one into despair; **unnerve, unman, undo, unstring,** unbrace, reduce to jelly, **demoralize, shake, upset,** psych out <nonformal>, knock down *or* flat, **crush,** overcome, prostrate; throw a wrench in the machinery, upset one's applecart; take the wind out of one's sails, cut the ground out from under one
5 **rush, tear,** dart, shoot, hurtle, bolt, fling, **scamper, scurry,** scour, scud, scuttle, scramble, **race,** careen

**dashing** ADJS **showy, flaunting, flashy,** snazzy, jaunty, rakish

**dastardly** ADJS dastard; hit-and-run; **pusillanimous,** base, craven, recreant, caitiff

**data** NOUNS **information,** database, data capture, database management, file, record, data bank

**date** NOUNS 1 **appointment, engagement,** double date *and* blind date <both nonformal>; point of time, time, day
VERBS 2 be dated, date at *or* from, date back, bear a date of, bear the date of; fix *or* set the date, make a date; **predate,** backdate, antedate; **postdate; update**
3 **age,** grow old, grow *or* have whiskers; **antiquate,** fossilize, **superannuate,** outdate; obsolesce, go out of use *or* style, lose currency *or* novelty; become obsolete *or* extinct

**dated** ADJS **old-fashioned,** old-fangled, old-timey <nonformal>, **out-of-date, outdated, outmoded,** out of style *or* fashion, out of use, disused, out of season, **unfashionable, behind the times,**

old hat *and* back-number *and* has-been <all nonformal>

**daunt** VERBS **deter,** shake, stop, stop in one's tracks, set back; **discourage, dishearten;** faze <nonformal>, terrorize; **awe, overawe**

**dawdle** VERBS **linger, loiter, tarry, delay, dally, dillydally,** shilly-shally, lollygag, waste time, **take one's time,** take one's own sweet time

**dawn** NOUNS the dawn of day, dawning, **daybreak,** dayspring, day-peep, **sunrise, sunup** <nonformal>, cockcrowing *or* cocklight <Brit nonformal>, light, first light, daylight, aurora; **break of day, crack of dawn,** first blush *or* flush of the morning

**day** NOUNS **period, point, juncture,** stage; **time,** while, **moment,** minute, instant, hour, **season;** psychological moment; **age, generation,** time, date, cycle; **daylight,** dayshine, day glow, light of day

**daydream** NOUNS 1 fantasy, pipe dream <nonformal>; reverie
VERBS 2 **muse, moon** <nonformal>, **dream,** pipe-dream <nonformal>, fantasy; abstract oneself, be lost in thought, let one's attention wander, let one's mind run on other things, dream of *or* muse on other things; **woolgather,** be somewhere else, be out of it *and* be not with it <both nonformal>

**daze** NOUNS **trance,** stupor; dream state, reverie, daydreaming; hypnotic trance; fugue, fugue state; disorientation, **muddle, muddlement,** fuddle *and* fuddlement <both nonformal>, befuddlement, muddleheadedness, maze <nonformal>

**dazed** ADJS **stupefied, stunned,** bedazed; **dazzled,** fuddled

**dazzle** NOUNS 1 **showiness, flashiness,** flamboyance, panache, dash, jazziness <nonformal>, jauntiness, sportiness <nonformal>, gaiety, glitter, glare
VERBS 2 **astonish, amaze, astound, surprise,** startle, stagger, **bewilder, perplex**, flabbergast <nonformal>, confound, overwhelm, **boggle, boggle the mind;** knock one's socks off *and* bowl down *or* over <all nonformal>, bedazzle

**dazzling** ADJS **gorgeous, ravishing; brilliant,** bright, radiant, shining, beaming, glowing, blooming, abloom, sparkling

**deactivate** VERBS **demilitarize, demobilize, disband,** reconvert, decommission

**dead** ADJS 1 **inanimate,** inanimated, unanimated, exanimate, azoic, nonliving, **lifeless,** soulless; inert; insentient, unconscious, nonconscious, **insensible,** insensate, senseless, unfeeling; **defunct,** extinct; **ended, at an end, terminated, concluded, finished, complete**, perfected, settled, decided, set at rest; **over, all over,** all up <nonformal>; **extinct,** gone out, gone-by, past
2 **lackluster, lusterless; dull,** deadened, **lifeless,** somber, **drab,** wan, **flat,** mat

**deadbeat** NOUNS **parasite,** barnacle, leech; **sponger,** sponge <nonformal>, freeloader <nonformal>, smell-feast

**deaden** VERBS 1 **numb,** benumb, blunt, dull, obtund, **desensitize;** paralyze, palsy; **anesthetize, put to sleep,** slip one a Mickey *or* Mickey Finn <nonformal>, chloroform, etherize
2 **muffle, mute, dull, soften,** quietize, cushion, baffle, damp, **dampen, soft-pedal,** put on the soft pedal

**dead end** NOUNS impasse, corner *and* box *and* hole <all nonformal>, **cleft stick;** cul-de-sac, blind alley, **dead-end street;** extremity, end of one's rope *or* tether, **wit's end, nowhere to turn;** stalemate, **deadlock; stand, standoff, standstill, halt, stop**

**deadline** NOUNS **bound, limit,** limitation, extremity; cutoff, cutoff point, terminus; time limit, time frame, term, deadline, target date, terminal date, time allotment

**deadly** ADJS **deathly,** deathful, **killing, destructive,** death-dealing, death-bringing, feral <old>; internecine; **fatal, mortal, lethal, malignant,** malign, **virulent, pernicious,** baneful; **life-threatening, terminal**

**deaf** ADJS **hard-of-hearing,** dull *or* thick of hearing, deaf-eared, dull-eared; surd <old>; deafened, stunned; **stone-deaf,** deaf as a stone, deaf as a door *or* a doorknob *or* doornail, **deaf as a post,** deaf as an adder; **unhearing;** earless; word-deaf; tone-deaf

**deafening** ADJS **loud,** loud-sounding, forte, fortissimo; loudish; **resounding,** ringing, plangent, pealing; full, sonorous; ear-deafening, **ear-splitting,** head-splitting, ear-rending, ear-piercing, piercing; **thunderous, crashing, booming**; window-rattling, earthshaking, enough to wake the dead *or* the seven sleepers

**deal** NOUNS 1 **undertaking, enterprise, operation,** work, **venture, project,** proposition <nonformal>; **understanding, arrangement, bargain; settlement,** negotiated settlement; binding agreement, ironclad agreement, covenant of salt; gentleman's *or* gentlemen's agreement
VERBS 2 **trade, traffic, truck, buy and sell, do business; barter; exchange,** change, interchange, give in exchange, take in exchange, **swap** <nonformal>, switch; swap horses *and* horse-trade <both nonformal>; **bargain, drive a bargain, negotiate, haggle,** higgle, chaffer, huckster, **dicker,** make a deal, hack out *or* work out *or* hammer out a deal

**dealer** NOUNS 1 **merchant,** merchandiser, marketer, **trader,** trafficker, monger, chandler; **tradesman,** tradeswoman; **storekeeper, shopkeeper**
2 pusher <nonformal>, narcotics *or* dope *or* drug pusher <nonformal>; **drug lord**

**dear** NOUNS 1 **sweetheart, loved one, love, beloved, darling, dear one,** dearly beloved, well-beloved, truelove, beloved object, **object of one's affections,** light of one's eye *or* life, light of love
ADJS 2 **beloved, loved, darling, precious;** pet, favorite; **adored, admired,** esteemed, revered; **cherished,** prized, treasured, held dear
3 **expensive, costly,** of great cost, dear-bought, **high, high-priced,** premium, at a premium, top; **fancy** *and* stiff *and* steep <all nonformal>, pricey; upmarket, upscale <nonformal>
ADVS 4 **dearly;** at a high price, at great cost, at a premium, at a great rate, at heavy cost, at great expense

**death** NOUNS 1 somatic death, clinical death, biological death, abiosis, **decease, demise;** brain death; **passing away,** passing, passing over, leaving life, ending, **end**, end of life, cessation of life, end of the road *or* line <nonformal>; **sleep, rest,** eternal rest *or* sleep, last sleep, last rest; reward, last debt; last muster, last roundup, curtains <nonformal>

*the undiscovered country from whose bourn no traveler returns*
SHAKESPEARE

*a debt we all must pay*
EURIPIDES

*that good night*
DYLAN THOMAS

**deathless** ADJS **immortal,** everlasting, undying, never-dying, **imperishable,** incorruptible, amaranthine; **indestructible, imperishable;** immortal, undying

**debacle** NOUNS **disaster, cataclysm, catastrophe; breakup,** breaking up; **breakdown, collapse; fall, downfall,** collapse, smash, crash, **undoing, ruin, destruction**

**debase** VERBS **abase, crush,** abash, **degrade, reduce,** diminish, **demean,** lower, **bring low,** bring down, trip up, take down, set down, put in one's place, put down, dump *and* dump on <both nonformal>; take down a peg *or* notch or two <nonformal>, make a fool *or* an ass *or* a monkey of one <nonformal>

**debatable** ADJS **doubtful,** iffy <nonformal>; **in doubt,** *in dubio* <L>; dubitable, doubtable, **dubious, questionable, problematic, problematical, speculative,** conjectural, suppositional; moot, arguable, disputable, contestable, controvertible, **controversial,** refutable, confutable, deniable

**debate** NOUNS 1 **discussion,** debating, **deliberation, nonformalogue,** exchange of views, canvassing, ventilation, airing, review, **examination, study, analysis,** logical analysis; logical discussion, dialectic; **argumentation, argument, controversy, dispute, disputation, polemic, contention, wrangling, bickering,** hubbub, bicker, verbal engagement *or* contest
VERBS 2 **discuss, reason, deliberate,** deliberate upon, exchange views *or* opinions, **talk over, consider, treat,** dissertate on, take up, **go into, examine,** investigate, talk out, **analyze,** sift, **study,** pass under review, controvert

**debauch** VERBS **corrupt, debase, degrade,** degenerate, **deprave, defile,** violate, desecrate, deflower, ravish, ravage, despoil; **be promiscuous,** sleep around *and* swing <both nonformal>; **wanton,** rake, womanize, whore, sow one's wild oats; **philander; dissipate**; fornicate, **cheat, commit adultery**

**debilitated** ADJS **decrepit, infirm,** weak,

feeble, the worse for wear, run to seed; **doddering,** doddery, doddered, tottering, tottery, rickety, shaky, palsied; on one's last legs, with one foot in the grave

**debit** NOUNS **loss, privation, expense, cost, debit;** detriment, injury, damage; **ruin,** perdition, total loss, dead loss; **expenditure, spending,** expense, disbursal, **disbursement**

**debris** NOUNS detritus, ruins, **remainder, residue,** residuum; refuse, trash, odds and ends, scraps, rags, **rubbish, waste,** orts, candle ends; scourings

**debt** NOUNS **indebtedness, obligation, liability,** financial commitment, due, **dues,** score, pledge, unfulfilled pledge, amount due, outstanding debt

**debug** VERBS **straighten out, iron out,** sort out, puzzle out; unscramble, undo, untangle, disentangle, untwist, unspin, unweave, **unravel,** ravel, ravel out

**debunk** VERBS **disabuse, undeceive;** correct, **set right** *or* **straight,** put straight, tell the truth, enlighten, let in on, put one wise <nonformal>; knock the props out from under, take the ground from under; expose, show up

**debut** NOUNS 1 **coming out** <nonformal>, presentation; premiere, premier performance; **launching,** unveiling; first appearance; maiden speech, inaugural address

VERBS 2 make one's debut *or* bow, come out; **enter on** *or* **upon** *or* **into, embark in** *or* **on** *or* **upon,** take up, go into, have a go at <chiefly Brit>, take a crack *or* whack *or* shot at <nonformal>

**decay** NOUNS 1 **decomposition, disintegration, dissolution,** resolution, degradation, biodegradation, breakup, disorganization, **corruption, spoilage, dilapidation; rot, rottenness, foulness, putridness,** putridity, rancidness, rancidity, rankness, **putrefaction,** putrescence, spoilage

VERBS 2 **decompose, disintegrate;** go *or* fall into decay, go *or* fall to pieces, break up, crumble, crumble into dust; **spoil,** corrupt, canker, **go bad; rot, putrefy,** putresce; molder, molder away, rot away, rust away, mildew

**deceased** NOUNS 1 dead person, **cadaver, carcass, body; the dead,** the defunct, **the deceased,** the departed, the loved one; **decedent,** late lamented; **remains,** mortal *or* organic remains, bones, skeleton, dry bones, relics, reliquiae

ADJS 2 **dead,** without life, inanimate, exanimate, without vital functions; **demised, defunct,** croaked <nonformal>, departed, departed this life, destitute of life, **gone, passed on,** gone the way of all flesh, dead and gone, done for <nonformal>, dead and done for <nonformal>, **at rest,** out of one's misery; **called home,** gone to a better world *or* place *or* land, gone to glory, joined the choir invisible, with the saints, sainted, numbered with the dead

*gathered to his fathers*
BIBLE

**deceitful** ADJS **false; fraudulent, sharp, guileful, insidious,** slippery, slippery as an eel, **shifty, tricky,** trickish, cute, finagling, chiseling <nonformal>; underhand, **underhanded, furtive, surreptitious,** indirect; **falsehearted, two-faced**

**deceive** VERBS **beguile, trick, hoax, dupe,** gammon, **gull,** pigeon, play one for a fool *or* sucker, **bamboozle** *and* snow *and* **hornswoggle** *and* diddle *and* scam <all nonformal>, take in, put on <nonformal>, string along, **put something over** *or* **across,** slip one over on <nonformal>, pull a fast one on

**decent** ADJS **kind, kindly, benign,** benignant; good as gold, **good, nice; kindhearted, warm, warmhearted,** humane, human; **honest, upright,** uprighteous, **upstanding,** erect, right, **righteous, virtuous, good,** clean, squeaky-clean <nonformal>; **modest, decorous,** delicate, elegant, proper, becoming, seemly

**deception** NOUNS 1 calculated deception, **deceptiveness, subterfuge,** gimmickry *or* gimmickery, **trickiness; fooling,** befooling, tricking, **kidding** *and* putting on <both nonformal>; bluffing; ensnarement, entrapment, enmeshment, entanglement

2 **hoax,** spoof <nonformal>, **humbug,** flam, **fake** *and* fakement, **rip-off** <nonformal>, **sham;** mare's nest

**deceptive** ADJS **deceiving, misleading,** beguiling, **false, fallacious,** delusive, delusory; hallucinatory, illusive, **illusory;** tricky, **fishy** <nonformal>, questionable, dubious

**decide** VERBS **determine; find,** hold, ascertain; **resolve, settle,** fix; make a decision, come to a decision, **make up one's mind,** settle one's mind, come down <nonformal>

**decision** NOUNS **resolution,** resolve, resolvedness, **determination,** fixed *or* firm resolve, **will,** purpose; **resoluteness, determinedness,** determinateness, decisiveness, decidedness, **purposefulness;** definiteness; **judgment, verdict**

**decisive** ADJS **resolute, resolved, determined,** bound *and* bound and determined <both nonformal>, **decided, purposeful;** single-minded, relentless, persistent, tenacious, persevering; **critical, crucial,** pivotal, climactic, climacteric *or* climacterical

**deck** NOUNS 1 **platform; terrace,** step terrace
VERBS 2 **fell, drop, bring down,** fetch down, down <nonformal>, take down, take down a peg, lay low; **raze,** rase, raze to the ground; **level,** lay level; **knock down,** dash down, send headlong, **floor,** lay out <nonformal>, **bowl down** *or* **over** <nonformal>

**declaration** NOUNS **statement,** allegation, allegation *or* statement of facts, procès-verbal; **deposition,** affidavit

**declare** VERBS **state, assert,** swear, swear to God <nonformal>, **affirm,** vow, avow, avouch, warrant, asseverate, confess, profess, express the belief, swear to a belief; depose, make an affidavit *or* a sworn statement

**decline** NOUNS 1 **deterioration, decadence** *or* decadency, **degradation, debasement,** derogation, deformation; **degeneration,** degeneracy, degenerateness, effeteness; declination, declension, comedown, **descent,** downtick <nonformal>, downtrend, downward trend, downturn, depreciation, **decrease, drop, fall, plunge,** free-fall, falling-off, lessening, slippage, slump, lapse, fading, dying, failing, failure, wane, ebb
VERBS 2 sink, fail, fall, slip, fade, die, wane, ebb, subside, lapse, **run down,** go down, **go downhill, fall away, fall off,** go off <nonformal>, slide, slump, hit a slump, take a nose dive <nonformal>, go into a tailspin, take a turn for the worse; hit the skids <nonformal>; reach the depths, hit *or* touch bottom, hit rock bottom, have no lower to go
3 **refuse,** refuse consent, **reject, turn down** <nonformal>, decline to accept, **not have,** not buy <nonformal>; not hold with, not think *or* hear of; **say no,** say nay, vote nay, vote negatively *or* in the negative, side against, disagree, beg to disagree, dissent; **turn thumbs down on;** be unwilling

**decode** VERBS **solve, resolve,** find the solution *or* answer, **clear up,** get, get right, do, work, **work out, find out, figure out,** dope *and* dope out <both nonformal>; **straighten out, iron out,** sort out, puzzle out; **unriddle,** riddle, unscramble, undo, untangle, disentangle, untwist, unspin, unweave, **unravel,** ravel, ravel out; **decipher,** decrypt, crack

**decompose** VERBS **disintegrate, decay,** dissolve, come apart, disorganize, **break up,** go to rack and ruin, crack up, disjoin, unknit, split, fission, atomize, **come** *or* **fall to pieces;** wear *or* waste away, molder, crumble, crumble into dust

**decor** NOUNS **decoration, adornment, embellishment,** embroidery, elaboration; **interior decoration** *or* decorating, room decoration, interior design

**decorate** VERBS 1 **ornament, adorn, embellish, embroider,** enrich; paint in glowing colors, tell in glowing terms; elaborate, convolute, involve
2 **honor, do honor,** pay regard to, give *or* pay *or* render honor to, **recognize;** pin a medal on; crown, crown with laurel; hand it to *or* take off one's hat to one <nonformal>, pay tribute, praise

**decoration** NOUNS 1 **adornment, embellishment,** embroidery, elaboration; **interior decoration** *or* decorating, room decoration, interior design
2 **insignia, regalia,** ensign, **emblem, badge,** marking, attribute; badge of office, mark of office, chain, chain of office, collar; medal

**decorative** ADJS **ornamental,** adorning, embellishing

**decorum** NOUNS **decorousness,** decency, properness, propriety, rightness, right thinking, **seemliness,** becomingness, fittingness, fitness, appropriateness, suitability, meetness, civility, urbanity; **social convention, convention,** conventional usage, what is done, what one does, **social usage, form, formality; custom**; **conformism, conformity**; **propriety**

**decoy** NOUNS **lure,** charm, **come-on**

<nonformal>, attention-getter *or* -grabber, **attraction, draw** *or* drawer *or* crowd-drawer, crowd-pleaser, headliner; hook *and* gimmick <both nonformal>; **bait, snare,** trap

**decrease** NOUNS 1 **diminishment,** diminution, **reduction, lessening, lowering,** waning, shrinking *or* shrinkage, withering, withering away, scaling down, scaledown, downsizing, build-down; **letup** <nonformal>, abatement, easing, easing off
VERBS 2 **diminish, lessen; let up,** bate, abate; **decline, subside,** shrink, wane, wither, ebb, ebb away, dwindle, languish, sink, sag, die down *or* away, wind down, taper off *and* trail off *or* away *and* tail off *or* away <all nonformal>; **reduce,** shorten, curtail, retrench, lessen, **decrease,** phase down, impair, bate, abate; **depreciate,** disparage, detract, derogate; **erode,** abrade, eat *or* wear *or* rub *or* shave *or* file away; **extract,** leach, drain, wash away; thin, thin out, weed; **refine,** purify

**decree** NOUNS 1 decretum, decretal, rescript, fiat, **edict,** *edictum* <L>; **law; rule, ruling,** dictum, ipse dixit; **proclamation,** pronouncement, pronunciamento, **declaration,** ukase; bull; **verdict,** holding
VERBS 2 **rule, ordain,** promulgate; give an order *or* a direct order, issue a command, say the word, give the word *or* word of command; proclaim, declare, pronounce; **pass judgment, pronounce judgment,** utter a judgment, deliver judgment; pronounce on, act on, **pronounce,** report; **sentence,** pass sentence, hand down a sentence, doom, condemn

**decrepit** ADJS **dilapidated, ramshackle,** tottery, **tumbledown, broken-down, run-down,** in ruins, ruinous, ruined, derelict, gone to wrack and ruin, the worse for wear; **senile,** doddering, doddery

**decriminalize** VERBS **legalize, legitimize,** legitimatize, legitimate, make legal, declare lawful; **authorize, sanction**

**dedicate** VERBS **commit, devote, consecrate,** set apart; **consecrate**

**dedicated** ADJS **devoted,** committed, **fast,** steadfast, constant, faithful, staunch; **tried and true,** true-blue, tested; **blessed,** consecrated, devoted, set apart

**dedication** NOUNS resolve, **determination,** fixed *or* firm resolve, **will,** purpose; **earnestness, seriousness,** sincerity, devotion, commitment, total commitment; single-mindedness, relentlessness, persistence, tenacity, perseverance; **self-sacrifice,** sacrifice, self-immolation, self-devotion, consecration

**deduce** VERBS **conclude,** draw a conclusion, **come to** *or* **arrive at a conclusion; derive, infer,** draw an inference; put two and two together

**deduct** VERBS **subtract,** subduct, take away, take from, **remove,** withdraw, abstract; **reduce,** shorten, curtail, retrench, lessen, **diminish, decrease,** phase down; **discount, cut, take off,** write off, charge off; **depreciate,** reduce

**deduction** NOUNS 1 **conclusion, inference,** consequence, consequent, corollary
2 **subtraction,** subduction, **removal,** taking away; **discount, cut,** slash, abatement, reduction, price reduction, price-cutting, price-cut, rollback <nonformal>; **depreciation**

**deed** NOUNS 1 **exploit, feat, enterprise, achievement, adventure,** gest, **bold stroke,** heroic act *or* deed; aristeia
VERBS 2 **transfer, convey,** deed over, give title to; exchange, barter, trade, trade away

**deemphasize** VERBS **minimize,** minify, **belittle,** detract from; dwarf, bedwarf; play down, underplay, downplay; deprecate, depreciate; **trivialize**

**deep** ADJS 1 deep-toned, deep-pitched, deep-sounding, deepmouthed, deep-echoing; **hollow, sepulchral; low,** low-pitched, low-toned, grave, heavy
2 **profound,** deep-down; deepish, deepsome; **deep-going,** deep-lying, deep-reaching; **deep-set,** deep-laid; **deep-seated, deep-rooted; recondite, abstruse,** abstract, transcendental
3 **wise, sage,** sapient, seasoned, **knowing; learned**; wise as Solomon; **learned, erudite, educated, cultured,** cultivated, lettered, literate, civilized, **scholarly,** studious

**deepen** VERBS **intensify, heighten,** enhance, **strengthen,** beef up <nonformal>, aggravate, exacerbate; **broaden, widen; lower, depress, sink**

**deep-seated** ADJS **confirmed, inveterate, chronic, established,** long-established, **fixed, settled, rooted,** thorough; incorrigible, irreversible; **deep-rooted,** deep-set, **infixed, ingrained,** fast, dyed-in-the-wool; **entrenched,** vested, **confirmed, inveterate**

**deface** VERBS **blemish, disfigure, flaw, mar;** scab; scar, cicatrize, scarify; **crack,** craze, check, split; blot, spoil; dysphemize

**de facto** ADJS 1 **real, actual,** factual, veritable, for real <nonformal>, **established, inescapable, indisputable, undeniable; empirical, objective**
ADVS 2 **really, actually; factually; genuinely,** veritably, **truly; in reality,** in actuality, in effect, in fact, in point of fact, as a matter of fact

**default** NOUNS 1 **nonpayment, delinquency,** nondischarge of debts, nonremittal, failure to pay; defection
VERBS 2 **not pay;** dishonor, repudiate, disallow, protest, stop payment, refuse to pay; **welsh** <nonformal>, levant

**defeat** NOUNS 1 **beating,** drubbing, thrashing; clobbering *and* hiding *and* lathering *and* whipping *and* lambasting *and* trimming *and* licking <all nonformal>, trouncing; **vanquishment, conquest, conquering,** mastery, subjugation, subduing, subdual; **frustration, thwarting, balking, foiling; discomfiture, disconcertion,** bafflement, confounding; upset
VERBS 2 **triumph over, prevail over,** best, **get the better** *or* **best of; surmount, overcome,** outmatch, rise above; **thwart, frustrate, baffle,** foil, cross

3 <nonformal> **clobber, trim, skin alive, beat,** skunk, drub, massacre, marmelize <Brit nonformal>, lick, whip, thrash, knock off, trim, hide, cut to pieces, run rings *or* circles around, throw for a loss, lather, trounce, **lambaste,** skin alive; fix, settle, settle one's hash, make one say 'uncle,' do in, lick to a frazzle, beat all hollow, beat one's brains out, cook one's goose, make hamburger *or* mincemeat out of, mop up the floor with, sandbag, banjax, bulldoze, steamroller, **smear,** paste, cream, **shellac,** whup, whop, whomp, shut out

**defect** NOUNS 1 **fault, deficiency, inadequacy,** imperfection, kink; **flaw,** hole, bug <nonformal>; **failing, foible, shortcoming;** weak point, Achilles' heel, chink in one's armor, weak link; **blemish,** taint; **blemish, disfigurement; malfunction,** glitch <nonformal>
VERBS 2 secede, bolt, break away; pull out <nonformal>, withdraw one's support; sell out *and* sell down the river <both nonformal>, **betray**; turn one's back on; apostatize

**defective** ADJS **imperfect, faulty, inadequate, deficient,** short, flawed, not all it's cracked up to be <nonformal>, lacking, wanting, found wanting

**defend** VERBS offer *or* say in defense, allege in support *or* vindication, **support, uphold, sustain, maintain,** assert; **plead for,** make a plea, offer as a plea, plead one's case *or* cause, put up a front *or* a brave front; **advocate,** champion, go to bat for <nonformal>, espouse, speak up for, put in a good word for; **protect, guard, safeguard, secure, keep,** bless, make safe, keep from harm

**defendant** NOUNS **accused,** respondent, codefendant, corespondent, libelee, suspect, prisoner

**defender** NOUNS **champion, advocate; upholder; guardian angel, supporter**; vindicator, apologist; **protector**; **guard**; paladin

**defense** NOUNS 1 **protection**; self-defense, self-protection, self-preservation; deterrent capacity; defense in depth; the defensive; covering one's ass *or* rear-end <nonformal>; psychological defenses, defense mechanism, avoidance reaction
2 **bulwark, rampart,** buffer, bulkhead, parapet, breastwork, work, earthwork, mound

**defensive** ADJS defending, **guarding,** shielding, screening; **protective**; self-defensive, self-protective, self-preservative

**defer** VERBS **postpone, delay, put off,** give one a rain check <nonformal>, hold off *or* up <nonformal>, prorogue, put on hold *or* ice *or* the back burner <all nonformal>, reserve, waive, **suspend,** hang up, stay, hang fire

**deference** NOUNS **respect, regard,** consideration, appreciation, favor; approbation, approval; **esteem,** estimation, prestige; **reverence, veneration,** awe; deferential *or* reverential regard; self-abnegation, submission, submissiveness; servility

**defiance** NOUNS **refractoriness, recalcitrance** *or* recalcitrancy, recalcitration, defiance of authority, defying, contumacy, **contumaciousness, obstreperousness, unruliness,** restiveness, fractiousness, orneriness *and* feistiness <both nonformal>; wildness; **obstinacy, stubbornness**

**deficiency** NOUNS **inadequacy, mediocrity**, imperfection, insufficiency; **incompetence,** *or* incompetency, maladroitness, unskillfulness; underdevelopment, hypoplasia; want, **lack, need, deficit,** defect, **shortage,** shortfall, underage; **shortcoming**

**deficient** ADJS **inadequate, mediocre,** imperfect, **insufficient; incompetent,** unskillful, maladroit; half-assed <nonformal>, botched; **incomplete, uncompleted,** defective, unfinished, imperfect, unperfected, **inadequate; wanting, lacking,** needing, missing, **partial,** part, failing

**deficit** NOUNS default, deferred payments; cash *or* credit crunch <nonformal>; unfavorable trade balance *or* balance of payments; **shortfall; shortage,** short measure, underage

**define** VERBS **characterize, distinguish, differentiate, describe; mark, earmark,** mark off, mark out, demarcate, **set apart,** make special *or* unique; keynote <nonformal>, sound the keynote, set the tone *or* mood, set the pace; be characteristic, **be a feature** *or* **trait of**

**definite** ADJS **fixed, defined,** distinct, different as night and day, determinate, certain, absolute; detailed; **particular, special, especial, specific, express,** precise, **concrete; singular, individual,** individualist *or* individualistic; **positive, absolute, flat,** definitive, determinate, decided, decisive, conclusive

**definition** NOUNS **circumscription, limiting,** circumscribing, **bounding, demarcation,** delimitation, determination, specification; **interpretation, construction, reading,** way of seeing *or* understanding *or* putting; description; **meaning**; **explanation,** sense-distinction, **interpretation**

**deflate** VERBS **humiliate, humble;** mortify <old>, **embarrass**; put out, put out of face *or* countenance; prick one's balloon; **reduce, decrease, diminish, lessen,** take from; depreciate, let the air out of, take the wind out of; puncture, **shoot** *or* **poke full of holes, cut to pieces, cut the ground from under;** cut the ground from under one's feet, not leave a leg to stand on

**deformity** NOUNS deformation, **malformation,** malconformation, monstrosity, teratology, freakishness, misproportion, **misshapenness,** misshape; **disfigurement, defacement;** mutilation, truncation; warp, twist, kink, **distortion; flaw, defect, fault**

**defray** VERBS **finance, fund**; defray expenses; pay the bill, **foot the bill** *and* pick up the check *or* tab *and* spring *or* pop for <all nonformal>; pay one's way; pay one's share, chip in <nonformal>

**defrock** VERBS **unfrock,** unchurch; strike off the roll, read out of; **unseat,** unsaddle; **dethrone,** disenthrone, unthrone, uncrown, discrown; **humiliate**; **degrade, debase**, deplume, displume, bring low

**deft** ADJS **skillful, expert, proficient; dexterous, adroit, adept, coordinated,** well-coordinated, **apt,** no mean, **handy; masterly, masterful; ingenious,** resourceful, daedal, Daedalian

**defuse** VERBS **alleviate, mitigate, palliate,** soften, pad, cushion, assuage, allay, lay, appease, mollify, subdue, soothe; take the edge off of, take the sting out of; cool <nonformal>; **moderate, restrain,** constrain, control, **keep within bounds; modulate,** abate, **diminish, reduce,** de-escalate, slacken, lessen, slow down

**defy** VERBS **confront, challenge,** dare, fly in the teeth of, throw down the gauntlet, ask for trouble, start something, do something about it; **disobey,** not mind, not heed, not keep *or* observe, not listen *or* hearken, pay no attention to, **ignore, disregard,** set at defiance, fly in the face of, snap one's fingers at, scoff at, flout

**degenerate** NOUNS 1 **reprobate,** recreant, **miscreant,** bad egg *and* wrongo *and* wrong number <all nonformal>, pervert

VERBS 2 **deteriorate, sicken, worsen, get** *or* **grow worse,** get no better fast <nonformal>, disimprove; **fall on evil days, go** *or* **come down in the world,** go downhill, be on the skids <nonformal>; run *or* go to seed, sink, decline; **go to pot** <nonformal>, go to the dogs

ADJS 3 **decadent,** debased, degraded, reprobate, **depraved, debauched, dissolute,** profligate, abandoned, gone to the bad *or* dogs, rotten at *or* to the core

**degrade** VERBS **abase, debase, crush,** abash, **demean,** lower, **bring low,** bring down, trip up, take down, set down, put in one's place, put down, dump *and* dump on <both nonformal>; **corrupt, debase,** degenerate, **deprave, debauch, defile,** violate, desecrate, deflower, ravish, ravage, despoil

**degree** NOUNS **extent, measure,** amount, proportion, stint, standard, height, pitch, reach, remove, compass, range, scale, scope, caliber; **shade,** shadow, nuance

**deify** VERBS **exalt,** elevate, ensky, raise, uplift, set up, **ennoble,** aggrandize, magnify, exalt to the skies; apotheosize, apotheose; **lionize**

**deity** NOUNS **divinity,** divineness; **godliness,** godlikeness; **god,** *deus* <L>; immortal, heathen god, pagan deity *or* divinity; **idol,** false god, devil-god

**dejected** ADJS **depressed, downhearted, down, downcast, cast down,** bowed down, subdued; **discouraged, disheartened, dispirited,** dashed; **low, feeling low,** low-spirited, **in low spirits; down in the mouth** <nonformal>, **in the doldrums, down in the dumps** *and* **in the dumps** <both nonformal>, in the depths; **despondent,** desponding; **despairing**, weary of life, suicidal, world-weary; pessimistic; spiritless, heartless, **woebegone**

**delay** NOUNS 1 stoppage, jam *and* logjam <both nonformal>, obstruction, tie-up *and* bind <both nonformal>, **block,** blockage, **hang-up** <nonformal>; **wait, halt, stay, stop,** down-time, break, pause, interim, respite; reprieve, moratorium; **retardation,** retardment, **detention,** detainment, holdup, setback
VERBS 2 **retard, detain,** make late, slacken, lag, drag, drag one's feet *and* stonewall <both nonformal>, slow down, **hold up** <nonformal>, hold *or* keep back, check, **stay, stop,** arrest, impede, **block,** hinder, obstruct, throw a monkey wrench in the works <nonformal>, **postpone, defer, put off,** prorogue, put on hold *or* ice *or* the back burner <all nonformal>, reserve, waive, **suspend,** hang up, stay, hang fire

**delegation** NOUNS **deputation, commission, mission**

**delete** VERBS **erase, expunge, cancel,** omit; **edit,** edit out, blue-pencil; strike, strike out *or* off, rub *or* blot out, cross out *or* off, kill, cut; void, rescind; **censor,** bowdlerize, expurgate; abridge, abbreviate

**deliberate** VERBS 1 **consider, contemplate, speculate, reflect, study, ponder,** perpend, **weigh, debate, meditate,** chew the cud <nonformal>, digest; introspect, be abstracted; wrinkle one's brow
ADJS 2 **intentional, intended,** proposed, purposed, telic, **projected, designed,** of design, aimed, aimed at, **meant, purposeful,** purposive, **willful, voluntary; leisurely, unhurried,** laid-back <nonformal>, unhasty, hasteless, easy, relaxed

**delicacy** NOUNS 1 **dainty, goody** <nonformal>, treat, kickshaw, **tidbit,** titbit; **morsel,** choice morsel
2 **sensibility, sensitivity, sensitiveness,** fineness of feeling, tenderness, affectivity, susceptibility, impressionability; attentiveness, **solicitousness,** solicitude, thought, regard, concern, **sensitivity,** tact, tactfulness
3 **sickliness,** peakedness <nonformal>, **feebleness,** fragility, **frailty**; **infirmity, unsoundness,** chronic ill health, invalidity, **invalidism**

**delicious** ADJS **tasty,** good, fit to eat *and* finger-lickin' good <both nonformal>, good-tasting, **savory,** savorous, **palatable, toothsome,** sapid, **good,** good to eat, nice, agreeable, likable, pleasing, to one's taste, delightful, delectable, exquisite; succulent, **luscious,** lush; ambrosial, nectarous, nectareous; scrumptious *and* yummy <both nonformal>

**delight** NOUNS 1 **happiness, felicity, gladness,** delectation; **cheer,** cheerfulness, exhilaration, **exuberance, high spirits, glee,** sunshine; **enchantment,** unalloyed happiness; elation, exaltation
VERBS 2 **tickle, titillate, thrill, enrapture, enthrall, enchant,** entrance, fascinate, captivate, bewitch, **charm,** becharm; enravish, ravish, imparadise; ecstasiate, transport, carry away; tickle, titillate, tickle the fancy; **rejoice,** jubilate, **exult**

3 <nonformal> **give one a bang** *or* kick *or* charge *or* rush, knock out, knock off one's feet *or* dead *or* for a loop, knock

one's socks off, thrill to death *or* to pieces, tickle to death, tickle pink, **wow,** slay, send, freak out; **stroke,** massage one's ego

**delinquent** NOUNS 1 **defaulter,** nonpayer; **welsher** <nonformal>, levanter; tax evader, tax dodger *or* cheat <nonformal>; **wrongdoer, malefactor, sinner,** transgressor; malfeasor, misfeasor, nonfeasor; misdemeanant, misdemeanist ADJS 2 **defaulting,** nonpaying, in arrear *or* arrears; criminal, illegal, unlawful; fraudulent

**delirious** ADJS out of one's head <nonformal>, off one's head <nonformal>, off; **giddy,** dizzy, lightheaded; **wandering, rambling, raving, ranting,** babbling, incoherent

**deliver** VERBS 1 **transfer, convey,** hand, pass, negotiate; **hand over, turn over, pass over; assign, consign,** confer, settle, settle on; transmit, **hand down, hand on, pass on,** devolve upon 2 **perform, do,** work, act, execute, **accomplish, achieve**, come through with, realize, engineer, effectuate, **bring about,** bring to fruition *or* into being; formulate, put into words, couch, phrase; **present**

**deliverer** NOUNS **savior, redeemer, liberator,** rescuer, freer, **emancipator,** manumitter

**delusion** NOUNS **deception,** self-deception, fond illusion, wishful thinking, willful misconception; vision, hallucination, phantasm, mirage, will-o'-the-wisp, delusiveness, illusion

**deluxe** ADJS **sumptuous, elegant, elaborate, luxurious,** extravagant; plush *and* posh *and* ritzy *and* swank *and* swanky <all nonformal>, Corinthian

**demagogue** NOUNS **instigator, inciter,** exciter, urger; **agitator, fomenter,** inflamer; **rabble-rouser,** rouser

**demand** NOUNS 1 **claim, call; ultimatum,** nonnegotiable demand; notice, warning; **question, query, inquiry, interrogation,** interrogatory; interrogative VERBS 2 ask, ask for, make a demand; **call for,** call on *or* upon one for, appeal to one for; call out for, cry *or* cry out for, clamor for; **oblige, necessitate, require,** exact, **dictate,** impose, call for; leave no option *or* escape, admit of no option; **levy, exact**

**demanding** ADJS **exacting,** exigent; draining, taxing, exorbitant, extortionate, grasping; **insistent,** instant, **importunate,** urgent, pertinacious, pressing, loud, clamant, crying, clamorous; persistent; **strict, exacting,** exigent, not to be trifled with, **stringent,** astringent; **difficult,** difficile; no picnic; rigorous, brutal, severe

**demeaning** ADJS **disgraceful, shameful,** pitiful, deplorable, opprobrious, sad, sorry, too bad; degrading, debasing, beneath one, beneath one's dignity, *infra indignitatem* <L>, infra dig <nonformal>, unbecoming, unworthy of one

**demented** ADJS **insane,** unsane, **mad,** stark-mad, mad as a hatter, mad as a march hare, **stark-staring mad,** maddened, **sick,** crazed, **lunatic,** moonstruck, **daft, non compos mentis,** non compos, *baca* <Japanese>, **unsound,** of unsound mind, **deranged,** deluded, disoriented, unhinged, **unbalanced,** unsettled, distraught, wandering, mazed, crackbrained, brainsick, sick *or* soft in the head, not right, not in one's right mind, **touched,** touched in the head, **out of one's mind,** out of one's senses *or* wits, bereft of reason, reasonless, irrational, deprived of reason, senseless, witless

**demobilize** VERBS **demilitarize,** deactivate, **disband,** decommission, demob <nonformal>, muster out

**democracy** NOUNS representative government, representative democracy, direct *or* pure democracy, town-meeting democracy

*government of the people, by the people, for the people*
LINCOLN

*the recurrent suspicion that more than half of the people are right more than half of the time*
E B WHITE

**demolish** VERBS **wreck,** total *and* rack up <both nonformal>, undo, unbuild, unmake, **dismantle, disassemble; take apart, tear apart, tear asunder, rend, take** *or* **pull** *or* **pick** *or* **tear to pieces,** pull in pieces, tear to shreds *or* rags *or* tatters; sunder, cleave, **split; disintegrate, fragment,** break to pieces, make mincemeat of, reduce to rubble, atomize, pulverize, **smash,** shatter

**demon** NOUNS **fiend,** fiend from hell, **devil,** Satan, daeva, rakshasa, dybbuk, shedu, gyre <Scots>, bad *or* evil *or* unclean spirit; **ghoul,** lamia, Lilith, yogini, Baba Yaga, **vampire,** the undead

**demonstrate** VERBS 1 **protest, kick** *and* **beef** <both nonformal>, put up a struggle *or* fight; demonstrate against, rally, march, sit-in, teach-in, boycott, strike, picket; **rebel**
2 **manifest, show, exhibit, display,** breathe, unfold, develop; **present,** represent <old>, **evince, evidence; indicate,** give sign *or* token, token, betoken, mean; illustrate, exhibit, manifest, display, express, set forth; **prove,** afford proof of, prove to be, prove true

**demonstration** NOUNS **objection, protest; kick** *and* **beef** *and* **bitch** *and* squawk *and* howl <all nonformal>, protestation; **remonstrance, remonstration,** expostulation; protest demonstration, counterdemonstration, **rally,** march, boycott, strike, picketing; **explanation,** explication, unfolding, **elucidation,** illumination, enlightenment, light, **clarification,** *éclaircissement* <Fr>; **illustration,** exemplification

**demoralize** VERBS **unnerve, unman, undo, unstring,** unbrace, reduce to jelly, **shake, upset,** psych out <nonformal>, dash, knock down *or* flat, **crush,** overcome, prostrate; vitiate, drive to the dogs

**demote** VERBS **degrade,** disgrade, downgrade, debase, abase, humble, humiliate, **lower, reduce,** bump *and* bust <both nonformal>; strip of rank, cut off one's spurs, deplume, displume

**demure** ADJS **shy, timid,** timorous, **bashful,** shamefaced, **coy,** skittish, **overmodest, straitlaced, puritanical**

**den** NOUNS 1 **lair,** cave, **hole,** covert, mew, form; **burrow,** tunnel, earth, run, couch, lodge
2 **retreat,** recess, hiding place, **hideaway,** hideout, hidey-hole <nonformal>; **sanctum, inner sanctum, sanctum sanctorum,** holy ground, holy of holies, adytum; private place, **ivory tower;** study, library

**denial** NOUNS **disavowal, disaffirmation, disownment,** disallowance; disclamation, disclaimer; **renunciation, retraction,** retractation, **repudiation,** recantation; revocation, nullification, annulment, abrogation; palinode, palinody

**denomination** NOUNS **sect,** sectarism, religious order, **persuasion,** faction, **church,** communion, community, group, fellowship, affiliation, order, school, party, society, body, organization; branch, variety, version, segment

**denote** VERBS **mean, signify,** spell, have the sense of, be construed as, have the force of; mean something, mean a lot, indicate, signify, signalize, symptomatize, mark, **betoken, point to,** give indication of

**denounce** VERBS **condemn, damn, doom;** denunciate; **censure**; blacklist, put on the Index; pronounce judgment

**dense** ADJS **compact, close;** close-textured, close-knit, close-woven, tight-knit; **condensed, compressed,** compacted, concrete, consolidated, concentrated; **crowded, jammed,** packed, jam-packed, packed *or* jammed in, packed *or* jammed in like sardines; **solid,** firm, substantial, massive; impenetrable, impermeable

**dent** NOUNS 1 **indentation,** indent, indention, indenture, dint; gouge, **furrow**; sunken part *or* place, **dimple; pit,** pock, pockmark; impression, impress
VERBS 2 **indent,** dint, **depress,** press in, stamp, tamp, punch, punch in, impress, imprint; **pit;** pock, pockmark; dimple

**deny** VERBS 1 **recant, retract, repudiate, withdraw, take back,** unswear, renege, welsh <nonformal>, **abjure, disavow, disown;** disclaim, unsay, unspeak; **back down** *or* **out,** climb down, crawfish out <nonformal>, backwater, weasel; **withhold,** hold back; grudge, begrudge; close the hand *or* purse; deprive one of

**depart** VERBS 1 **deviate, depart from, vary, diverge,** divaricate, branch off, angle, angle off; **digress,** divagate, turn aside, go out of the way, detour, take a side road
2 make off, begone, be off, take oneself off *or* away, take one's departure, take leave *or* take one's leave, **leave, go, go away, go off, get off** *or* **away,** get under way, **pull out;** decamp, pull up stakes, **take to one's heels,** make off, **depart**, do the disappearing act, make a quick exit, **beat a retreat** *or* **a hasty retreat, turn tail,** show the heels

3 <nonformal> **beat it, split,** scram, up and go, trot, toddle, stagger along,

mosey *or* sashay along, buzz off, buzz along, bug out, bugger off <Brit>, fuck off *or* f off, get rolling, hightail it, pull up stakes, check out, clear out, cut out, haul ass, hit the road *or* trail, piss off <chiefly Brit>, get lost, flake off, get going, shove off, push along, push off, get out, get *or* git, clear out, get the hell out, make oneself scarce, vamoose, take off, skip, skip out, lam, take it on the lam, powder, take a powder, take a runout powder, skedaddle, absquatulate <old>

**departure** NOUNS 1 **leaving, going,** passing, **parting; exit,** walkout <nonformal>; egress; **withdrawal,** removal, retreat, retirement; evacuation, abandonment, desertion; decampment; escape, flight, getaway <nonformal>; exodus, hegira; defection, voting with one's feet
2 **digression,** deviation, **discursion,** excursion, excursus, sidetrack

**depend** VERBS hang, rest, hinge; **depend on** *or* **upon, hang on** *or* **upon, rest on** *or* **upon,** rest with, repose upon, lie on, lie with, stand on *or* upon, be based on, be contingent *or* conditional on, hang in the balance, be touch and go

**dependable** ADJS **reliable, sure,** surefire <nonformal>, **trustworthy, trusty,** faithworthy, **to be depended** *or* **relied upon,** to be counted *or* reckoned on; predictable, calculable; **secure, solid, sound, firm,** fast, **stable, substantial,** staunch, steady, **steadfast, faithful, unfailing;** true to one's word

**dependent** NOUNS 1 **charge, ward,** client, protégé, encumbrance; pensioner, pensionary; **retainer,** follower; myrmidon, yeoman
ADJS 2 **subject,** tributary, client; **subservient, subordinate, inferior;** servile; relying, depending, reliant; **contingent, depending;** contingent on, **dependent on, depending on,** predicated on, based on, hanging *or* hinging on, turning on, revolving on

**deplete** VERBS **exhaust,** impoverish, drain, drain of resources; suck dry, bleed white <nonformal>, suck one's blood; **throw away, squander**

**deplore** VERBS **regret, repine; rue,** rue the day; **bemoan, bewail; lament, mourn, moan, grieve,** give sorrow words

**deploy** VERBS **locate, situate, site, place, position;** emplace, spot <nonformal>, **install,** put in place; **allocate,** collocate, **dispose,** assign; spread, **spread out,** outspread, splay, fan out; mobilize, marshal, marshal *or* deploy one's forces *or* resources

**deport** VERBS **banish, expel, cast out,** thrust out, exile, expatriate, transport, send away, **extradite**

**deposit** NOUNS 1 down payment, earnest, earnest money, binder
2 mineral deposit, pay dirt; **vein, lode,** seam, dike, ore bed
VERBS 3 **store, stow,** lay down, salt down *or* away *and* sock away *and* squirrel away <all nonformal>; reposit, lodge; **cache,** stash <nonformal>, bury away

**deposition** NOUNS 1 **placement, positioning, emplacement, situation, location, siting,** localization, **locating, placing,** putting; reposition, **deposit,** disposal, dumping
2 **sworn statement, affidavit,** statement under oath, notarized statement, sworn testimony, affirmation; **vouching, swearing; attestation;** certification; **testimony, declaration, statement,** allegation, allegation *or* statement of facts, procès-verbal

**depot** NOUNS **storehouse, storeroom,** stock room, lumber room, store, storage, **depository, repository,** conservatory <old>, reservoir, repertory, supply depot, supply base, magazine, *magasin* <Fr>, warehouse, godown; bonded warehouse, entrepôt

**depravity** NOUNS **turpitude, moral turpitude; decadence** *or* decadency, debasement, **degradation,** demoralization, abjection; **degeneracy,** degenerateness, degeneration, reprobacy, **dissoluteness, profligacy;** abandonment, abandon

**depreciate** VERBS 1 **subtract, deduct,** subduct, take away, take from, **remove,** withdraw, abstract; **reduce,** shorten, curtail, retrench, lessen, **diminish, decrease,** phase down, impair, bate, abate
2 **cheapen, devaluate,** lower, reduce, **mark down, cut prices, cut,** slash, shave, trim, pare, underprice, knock the bottom out of <nonformal>

**depress** VERBS 1 **sadden,** darken, cast a pall *or* gloom upon, weigh *or* weigh heavy upon; **deject, oppress, crush,**

press down, hit one like a ton of bricks <nonformal>, **cast down,** lower, lower the spirits, get one down <nonformal>, take the wind out of one's sails, rains on one's parade, burst one's bubble, **discourage, dishearten,** take the heart out of, **dispirit**
2 **lower,** let *or* take down, debase, **sink,** bring low, reduce, couch; pull *or* haul down, take down a peg <nonformal>; thrust *or* press *or* push down, detrude

**depression** NOUNS 1 **dejection, oppression,** dejectedness, **downheartedness,** downcastness; **discouragement, disheartenment,** dispiritedness; *Schmerz* and *Weltschmerz* <both Ger>; lowness *or* depression *or* oppression of spirit, downer *and* down trip <both nonformal>; **low spirits,** drooping spirits, sinking heart; despondence *or* **despondency,** spiritlessness
2 **hard times,** bad times, sad times; **recession,** slow-down, cooling off, slump *and* bust <both nonformal>, downturn, downtick <nonformal>
3 **lowering; sinking;** ducking, submergence, pushing *or* thrusting under, down-thrust, down-thrusting, detrusion, pushing *or* pulling *or* hauling down

**deprivation** NOUNS **loss, losing, privation,** getting away, losing hold of; **bereavement,** taking away, stripping, dispossession, despoilment, despoliation, spoliation, robbery; divestment, denudation; **destitution, privation, deprivation; neediness, want,** need, lack, pinch, impoverishment

**deprive** VERBS **take from,** take away from, **deprive of,** do out of <nonformal>, relieve of, disburden of, lighten of, ease of; **bereave, divest;** tap, milk, mine, drain, bleed, curtail

**depth** NOUNS **deepness;** deep-downness, deep-seatedness, deep-rootedness; bottomlessness; **profundity,** profoundness, **wisdom,** wiseness, sageness, sapience

**deputy** NOUNS 1 **proxy, representative, substitute,** vice, vicegerent, **alternate,** backup *and* stand-in <both nonformal>, alter ego, **surrogate,** procurator, secondary, understudy, pinch hitter <nonformal>, utility man *or* woman, the bench <nonformal>; second in command, executive officer
2 peace officer, law enforcement agent, arm of the law; deputy sheriff

**derelict** NOUNS 1 **bum,** stiff <nonformal>, skid-row bum, Bowery bum, *lazzarone* <Ital>; drifter, vagrant, hobo, tramp; beggar; castoff; jetsam, flotsam, lagan, **flotsam and jetsam;** waifs and strays
ADJS 2 **negligent, neglectful,** neglecting, culpably negligent; inadvertent, uncircumspect; **inattentive**; unwary, unwatchful, asleep at the switch, off-guard, unguarded; **remiss,** lax
3 **abandoned, forsaken, deserted,** left; disused; castaway, jettisoned; marooned; junk, junked, discarded

**deride** VERBS **ridicule,** ride <nonformal>, make a laughingstock *or* a mockery of; roast <nonformal>, **insult**; **make fun** *or* **game of, poke fun at,** make merry with, put one on *and* pull one's leg <both nonformal>; **laugh at,** laugh in one's face, hold in derision, hoot down; point the finger of scorn; pillory

**derivation** NOUNS 1 **etymology, origin,** word origin, word history, semantic history
2 **source, origin,** genesis, original, origination, **rise, beginning,** conception, inception, commencement, provenance, provenience

**derive** VERBS **elicit,** educe, deduce, induce, obtain, procure, secure; **get from,** get out of; **draw out** *or* **forth,** bring out *or* forth, pry *or* prize out; extract, **gather,** collect, glean

**derogatory** ADJS **disparaging,** derogative, **depreciatory,** depreciative, deprecatory, slighting, belittling, minimizing, detractory, pejorative, back-biting, catty *and* bitchy <both nonformal>, contumelious, contemptuous, derisive, derisory, ridiculing

**derrick** NOUNS **lifter, erector;** crane, gantry crane, crab; **hoist,** lift, hydraulic lift

**descend** VERBS **go** *or* **come down,** down, dip down, lose altitude, dump altitude <nonformal>; gravitate; **fall, drop,** precipitate, rain, rain *or* pour down, fall *or* drop down; **collapse,** crash; **swoop,** stoop, pounce; **pitch, plunge, plummet;** cascade, cataract; parachute; come down a peg <nonformal>; **fall off,** drop off; go downhill

**descendant** NOUNS **offspring, child, scion; son,** son and heir, a chip of *or* off the old block, sonny; **daughter,** heiress; grandchild, grandson, granddaughter; stepchild, stepson, stepdaughter; foster child

**descent** NOUNS 1 **descending, dropping, falling,** plummeting, **drop, fall, free-fall,** *chute* <Fr>, **downfall,** debacle, **collapse,** crash; **decline,** declination, declension, comedown, downtrend, downward trend, downturn, depreciation, **decrease, drop, fall, plunge,** free-fall, falling-off, lessening, slippage, slump, lapse, fading, dying, failing, failure, wane, ebb
2 **lineage, line, bloodline,** descendancy, line of descent, ancestral line, succession, **extraction,** derivation, birth, **blood,** breed, **family,** house, **strain,** sept, **stock,** race, stirps, seed

**describe** VERBS **portray, picture,** render, **depict, represent, delineate,** limn, **paint,** draw; evoke, bring to life, make one see; outline, sketch; **characterize,** character; **express,** set forth, give words to; **write**

**descriptive** ADJS **depictive,** expositive, **representative, delineative; expressive, vivid, graphic,** well-drawn; realistic, naturalistic, true to life, lifelike, faithful

**desecrate** VERBS **profane,** dishonor, unhallow, commit sacrilege; **corrupt, debase, degrade,** degenerate, **deprave, debauch, defile,** violate, deflower, ravish, ravage, despoil

**desensitize** VERBS **deaden, numb,** benumb, blunt, dull, obtund, hebetate; freeze, **stupefy, stun,** bedaze, besot

**desert** NOUNS wilderness, back country, boonies *and* boondocks <both nonformal>, outback <Austral>; Sahara, karroo <Africa>, badlands, dust bowl, salt flat, Death Valley, Arabia Deserta, lunar waste *or* landscape

*a barren waste, a wild of sand*
ADDISON

**desert** VERBS **abandon, forsake; quit, leave,** leave behind, take leave of, depart from, absent oneself from, turn one's back upon, turn one's tail upon, say goodbye to, bid a long farewell to, walk away, **walk** *or* **run out on** <nonformal>, **leave flat** *and* leave high and dry *or* holding the bag *or* in the lurch <all nonformal>, leave one to one's fate, throw to the wolves <nonformal>; **withdraw, back out, drop out** <nonformal>, pull out, stand down <nonformal>; **go back on, go back on one's word; vacate,** evacuate; quit cold <nonformal>, toss aside; jilt, throw over <nonformal>; **defect,** renege, wimp *or* chicken *or* cop out <nonformal>, turn one's coat, apostatize, change one's colors, turn against, turn traitor; leave *or* desert a sinking ship

**deserter** NOUNS **apostate, turncoat,** turnabout, **recreant, renegade,** renegado, renegate *or* runagate <old>, **defector,** tergiversator, tergiversant; **bolter, seceder,** secessionist, **separatist,** schismatic

**deserts** NOUNS **reprisal, requital, retribution; recompense, compensation, reward,** comeuppance <nonformal>, **just deserts,** what is merited, what is due *or* condign, what's coming to one *and* a dose of one's own medicine <both nonformal>; quittance, return of evil for evil; **punishment**

**deserve** VERBS **merit,** earn, rate *and* be in line for <both nonformal>, **be worthy of,** be deserving, richly deserve

**deserving** ADJS **due, entitled to,** with a right to; **deserving,** well-deserving, **meriting, meritorious, worthy of**

**design** NOUNS **treatment; composition,** arrangement; styling, patterning, planning, shaping

*the conscious effort to impose meaningful order*
VICTOR PAPANEK

VERBS 2 **plan, devise, contrive,** frame, shape, cast, concert, lay plans; organize, rationalize, systematize, schematize, methodize, configure, pull together, sort out; make up, get up, prepare, compose, write, indite, devise, concoct, compound, churn out *and* crank out *and* pound out *and* hammer out *and* grind out *and* rustle up *and* gin up <all nonformal>; think up, think out, dream up, set one's wits to work

**designate** VERBS **specify;** denominate, name, denote; **symbolize, stand for,** typify, be taken as, symbol, emblematize, figure <old>; **point to,** refer to, advert to, allude to, make an allusion to; pick out, select; **point out,** point at, put *or* lay one's finger on, finger <nonformal>; **classify,** class, assign

**desirable** ADJS sought-after, much sought-after, to be desired, **much to be desired; enviable,** worth having; **lik-**

**able, pleasing,** after one's own heart; **agreeable,** acceptable, unobjectionable; palatable; **attractive,** taking, winning, sexy <nonformal>, **seductive, provocative,** tantalizing, exciting; appetizing, tempting, toothsome, mouth-watering; **lovable,** adorable

**desire** NOUNS 1 **wish,** wanting, **want, need,** desideration; **hope; fancy; will, mind, pleasure,** will and pleasure; heart's desire; **urge,** drive, libido; concupiscence; passion, ardor, sexual desire; something to be desired
VERBS 2 be desirous of, **wish,** lust after, bay after, kill for *and* give one's right arm for <both nonformal>, die for <nonformal>, **want,** have a mind to, choose <nonformal>; would fain do *or* have <old>, would be glad of; **like,** have *or* acquire a taste for, fancy, take to, **take a fancy** *or* a shine to, have a fancy for; have an eye to, have one's eye on

**desirous** ADJS desiring, **wanting, wishing,** needing, hoping; dying to <nonformal>; tempted; appetitive, desiderative, optative, libidinous, libidinal; **eager;** lascivious, **lustful, passionate, ardent,** impassioned

**desk** NOUNS **table,** board, **stand;** writing table, **secretary,** *secrétaire* <Fr>, escritoire; **lectern,** reading stand, ambo, reading desk

**desolation** NOUNS 1 **wretchedness, despair,** bitterness, infelicity, **misery, anguish, agony, woe,** woefulness, bale, balefulness; **melancholy,** melancholia, **depression, sadness, grief**; suicidal despair, black night of the soul, **despondency,** despond, prostration; depth of misery; **destruction, ruin, ruination,** rack, **rack and ruin,** blue ruin <nonformal>; devastation, ravage, havoc, holocaust, firestorm, hecatomb, carnage, shambles, slaughter, bloodbath

*Slough of Despond*
**BUNYAN**

2 **wasteland, waste,** barren *or* **barrens,** barren land, **depopulation,** dispeoplement, unpeopling

**despair** NOUNS 1 **desperation,** desperateness; no way <nonformal>, no way out, no exit, despondency; disconsolateness; forlornness
VERBS 2 despair of, **despond**, falter, lose hope, **lose heart, abandon hope,** give up hope, **give up,** give up all hope *or* expectation, give way *or* over, fall *or* sink into despair, give oneself up *or* yield to despair, throw up one's hands in despair, turn one's face to the wall; curse God and die

**desperate** ADJS **hopeless,** unhopeful, without hope, affording no hope, worst-case, bleak, grim, dismal, cheerless, comfortless; **despairing, in despair;** despondent; disconsolate; forlorn; **reckless,** devil-may-care; **furious,** wild, wanton; **at the end of one's rope** *or* **tether**

**despicable** ADJS **offensive, objectionable, odious, repulsive,** repellent, rebarbative, **repugnant, revolting,** forbidding; detestable, execrable, beneath *or* below contempt, **base,** ignoble, pitiable, pathetic, **contemptible,** beneath contempt, **miserable, wretched,** beggarly, vile, **shabby**

**despise** VERBS **disdain, scorn,** hold in contempt, contemn, vilipend, disprize, misprize, rate *or* rank low, be contemptuous of, feel contempt for, **hold in contempt,** hold cheap, look down upon, think little *or* nothing of, feel superior to, be above, hold beneath one *or* beneath contempt, look with scorn upon

**despondent** ADJS **hopeless,** unhopeful, without hope, affording no hope, worst-case, bleak, grim, dismal, cheerless, comfortless; **desperate, despairing, in despair;** disconsolate; forlorn; apathetic

**destination** NOUNS **goal,** bourn <old>; port, haven, harbor, anchorage, **journey's end;** end of the line, terminus, **terminal,** terminal point; stop, stopping place, last stop; **objective, object, aim, end, goal**

**destiny** NOUNS **fate,** doom, karma, kismet, what bodes *or* looms, what is fated *or* destined *or* doomed, what is written, what is in the books

*whatever limits us*
**EMERSON**

**destroy** VERBS **devastate, desolate,** waste, **lay waste, ravage,** havoc, wreak havoc, despoil, depredate; deal *or* unleash destruction, unleash the hurricane, nuke <nonformal>; **ruin,** ruinate <nonformal>, bring to ruin, lay in ruins, play *or* raise hob with

**destroyer** NOUNS **ruiner, wrecker, bane,**

demolisher; exterminator, annihilator; **iconoclast;** terrorist

**destructive** ADJS destroying; **ruinous,** ruining; demolishing, demolitionary; **devastating, desolating,** ravaging, wasting, wasteful, spoliative, depredatory; subversive, subversionary; nihilist, nihilistic; internecine

**detach** VERBS **remove,** disengage, take *or* lift off, doff; **unfasten, undo,** unattach, unfix; **untie,** unbind, unknit, unbandage, unlace, unzip, unstrap, unchain

**detached** ADJS **separated,** disjoined, disjoint, disjointed, disjunct, **disconnected,** disengaged, **disunited, divided,** removed, divorced, **alienated,** estranged, distanced, **segregated,** sequestered, isolated, cloistered, withdrawn, aloof, standoffish

**detail** NOUNS **particular, instance, item,** point, count, case, fact, matter, article, datum, element, part, ingredient, factor, facet, aspect, thing; minutia, minutiae <pl>, trifle, petty *or* trivial matter; incidental, minor detail; **feature,** aspect, specialty, circumstance

**detain** VERBS **delay, retard,** make late, slacken, lag, drag, drag one's feet *and* stonewall <both nonformal>, slow down, **hold up** <nonformal>, hold *or* keep back, check, **stay, stop,** arrest, impede, **block,** hinder, obstruct, throw a monkey wrench in the works <nonformal>, confine; tie up with red tape

**detectable** ADJS **visible,** visual, **perceptible,** perceivable, **discernible, seeable,** viewable, witnessable, beholdable, observable, noticeable, recognizable, to be seen; **in sight,** in view, in plain sight, in full view, **evident,** in evidence, **manifest, apparent;** revealed, disclosed, unhidden, unconcealed, unclouded, undisguised

**detective** NOUNS 1 **operative, investigator, sleuth,** Sherlock Holmes <A Conan Doyle>; **plainclothesman;** private detective, private investigator *or* PI

2 <nonformal> **dick,** gumshoe, gumshoe man, hawkshaw, sleuthhound, beagle, flatfoot, tec; eye, private eye; skip tracer, spotter

**detention** NOUNS **jailing,** incarceration, **internment,** immurement, immuration; **captivity,** duress, durance, durance vile; suspension, holdup <nonformal>, detainment, **delay,** holdup, setback

**deter** VERBS **daunt,** shake, stop, stop in one's tracks, set back; **discourage, dishearten;** faze <nonformal>; **disincline, indispose,** disaffect, repel, turn from, turn away *or* aside; divert, deflect; distract, put off *and* turn off <both nonformal>; **discourage; pour** *or* **dash** *or* **throw cold water on,** take the starch out of, take the wind out of one's sails

**deteriorate** VERBS **sicken, worsen, get** *or* **grow worse,** get no better fast <nonformal>, disimprove, **degenerate;** slip back, **retrogress,** retrograde, regress, relapse, fall back

**determined** ADJS **resolute, resolved,** bound *and* bound and determined <both nonformal>, **decided,** decisive, **purposeful; earnest, serious,** sincere; devoted, dedicated, committed, wholehearted; single-minded, relentless, persistent, tenacious, persevering; fixed, **settled,** nailed down <nonformal>, ascertained; predetermined, **predestined,** predestinate, foreordained; foregone

**deterrent** NOUNS **obstacle, obstruction,** obstructer; **hang-up** <nonformal>; **difficulty,** hurdle, hazard; determent; **stumbling block,** fly in the ointment, **hitch, catch**

**detest** VERBS **hate, loathe, abhor,** execrate, **abominate,** hold in abomination, take an aversion to, shudder at, utterly detest, be death on, not stand, not stand the sight of, not stomach; scorn, **despise**

**detestable** ADJS **offensive, objectionable, odious, repulsive,** repellent, rebarbative, **repugnant, revolting,** forbidding; **obnoxious, abhorrent, hateful, abominable,** heinous, **contemptible, despicable,** execrable

**detour** NOUNS 1 **bypass, roundabout way,** roundabout, circuit, the long way around, digression, deviation, excursion
VERBS 2 **go roundabout,** meander, deviate, take *or* go the long way around; make a detour, **go around,** go round about, go out of one's way, **bypass**

**detrimental** ADJS **disadvantageous,** unadvantageous, **unfavorable;** deleterious, injurious, harmful, prejudicial, counterproductive, **pernicious,** mischievous; **adverse, untoward, unfavorable**

**devalue** VERBS **corrupt, cheapen,**

coarsen, vulgarize, drag in the mud; adulterate, alloy, water, water down

**devastate** VERBS **destroy,** desolate, waste, **lay waste, ravage,** havoc, wreak havoc, despoil, depredate; vandalize; **decimate;** gut, gut with fire, incinerate, vaporize, ravage with fire and sword; **depopulate,** dispeople, unpeople

**devastation** NOUNS **destruction, ruin, ruination,** rack, **rack and ruin,** ravage, havoc, holocaust, firestorm, hecatomb, carnage, shambles, slaughter, bloodbath, **desolation;** decimation; **depopulation,** dispeoplement, unpeopling; desolation

**develop** VERBS **intensify,** gain strength, strengthen; accrue, accumulate; **grow,** wax, **increase**; burgeon, **sprout**, blossom, **flourish, thrive,** grow like a weed; mushroom; **mature,** flourish, unfold; elaborate; open out, fill in, flesh out, evolve, unfold; work out, explicate

**development** NOUNS **refinement,** elaboration, **perfection;** beautification, embellishment; maturation, coming-of-age, ripening, evolution, seasoning; **training, preparation,** readying <nonformal>, **conditioning, grooming,** cultivation, improvement; growth, rise, incremental change, developmental change, natural growth *or* development; flowering, blossoming

**deviant** NOUNS 1 sexual pervert; **pervert,** deviate, sex *or* sexual pervert, sexual psychopath; sodomist, sodomite, pederast
ADJS 2 **perverted, deviative,** deviatory, deviating, aberrant, aberrational, aberrative, shifting, turning, swerving, veering; abnormal, aberrant, deviationist

**deviate** VERBS **depart from, vary, diverge,** divaricate, branch off, angle, angle off; **digress,** divagate, turn aside, go out of the way, detour, take a side road; **swerve, veer,** sheer, curve, **shift, turn,** trend, bend, heel, bear off; alter one's course, make a course correction, tack

**device** NOUNS 1 **trick, artifice,** ploy, gambit, stratagem, **scheme,** design, *ficelle* <Fr>, **subterfuge,** blind, **ruse, wile,** tactic, contrivance, sleight, pass, feint, fetch, chicanery
2 **mark, earmark,** hallmark, **badge,** banner, stamp, signature, sigil, seal
3 apparatus, mechanical device, contraption <nonformal>, gadget, gizmo, gimcrack, gimmick <nonformal>, means, mechanical means

**devil** NOUNS 1 **mischief-maker, rogue,** knave, **rascal,** rapscallion, scapegrace, **scamp; imp, elf, puck,** pixie, **minx,** bad boy, bugger <nonformal>, little devil, little rascal, little monkey, *enfant terrible* <Fr>
2 **demon, fiend,** fiend from hell, Satan, daeva, rakshasa

**devious** ADJS **oblique;** deviant, deviative, divergent, digressive, divagational, deflectional, excursive; **indirect,** left-handed, sinister, sinistral, shady <nonformal>, up to no good, not kosher <nonformal>, unsavory, dark, sinister, insidious, indirect, slippery, devious, tricky, shifty, evasive, unstraightforward

**devoted** ADJS dedicated, committed, **fast,** steadfast, constant, faithful, staunch; tried, true, **tried and true,** true-blue, tested; **devout,** worshipful, **reverent,** reverential, venerative, venerational, adoring, solemn

**devour** VERBS **swallow,** ingest, **consume,** take in, tuck in *or* away *and* tuck into <all nonformal>, down, take down, get down, put away <nonformal>; **eat up;** dispatch *or* dispose of *and* get away with <all nonformal>; surround *and* put oneself outside of <both nonformal>

**devout** ADJS **pious,** pietistic; **religious,** religious-minded; theistic; devoted, worshipful, prayerful, reverential, venerative, venerational; faithful, dutiful; **observant, practicing**

**diagnosis** NOUNS **examination, physical examination; interpretation, construction, reading,** way of seeing *or* understanding *or* putting; **determination, finding,** holding; prognosis

**diagonal** ADJS oblique, transverse, bias, bend <heraldry>, oblique line, slash, **slant,** virgule, scratch comma, separatrix, solidus

**diagram** NOUNS 1 **plot, chart, blueprint,** graph, bar graph, pie *or* circle graph *or* chart, area graph; flow diagram, flow chart; **outline, delineation,** skeleton, figure, profile
VERBS 2 **plot; map, chart**, **blueprint,** graph; **sketch,** sketch in *or* out, draw up a plan; map out, plot out, **lay out,** set out, mark out; lay off, mark off

**dialect** NOUNS **diction,** words, wordage, verbiage, word-usage, **usage,** *usus loquendi* <L>, use *or* choice of words, formulation, way of putting *or* couching, word garment, word dressing; parlance, locution, expression; **idiom;** class dialect; regional *or* local dialect, subdialect; patois

**dialogue** NOUNS **talk, palaver, speech, words;** confabulation, **confab** <nonformal>; **chinfest** *and* **chinwag** *and* **talkfest** *and* **bull session** <all nonformal>; duologue, trialogue; **interview,** question-and-answer session; reasoning together, dialectic

**diarrhea** NOUNS loose bowels, flux; trots *and* runs *and* shits *and* GI's *and* GI shits <all nonformal>; turistas *and* Montezuma's revenge <both nonformal>; **dysentery,** bloody flux

**diary** NOUNS **chronicle, chronology, annals,** journal

**dice** NOUNS 1 <nonformal> **bones**, rolling bones, ivories, babies, cubes, devil's bones *or* teeth, galloping dominoes, golf balls, marbles, Memphis dominoes, Mississippi marbles, Missouri marbles
VERBS 2 **square, quadrate,** form *or* make four; form fours *or* squares; **cube**

**dicker** VERBS **bargain, drive a bargain, negotiate, haggle,** higgle, chaffer, huckster, **deal,** make a deal, hack out *or* work out *or* hammer out a deal

**dictate** VERBS 1 **command, order, direct, instruct,** mandate, **bid, enjoin, charge,** commission, call on *or* upon; issue a writ *or* an injunction; **decree, rule, ordain,** promulgate; give an order *or* a direct order, issue a command, say the word, give the word *or* word of command; call the shots *or* tune *or* signals *or* play <nonformal>; order about *or* around
2 **oblige, necessitate, require,** exact, demand, impose, call for; take *or* brook no denial; leave no option *or* escape, admit of no option

**dictatorial** ADJS **authoritarian; lordly, imperious,** aristocratic, totally self-assured; hubristic; masterful, magisterial, **high-and-mighty;** elitist

**diction** NOUNS words, wordage, verbiage, word-usage, **usage,** *usus loquendi* <L>, use *or* choice of words, formulation, way of putting *or* couching, word garment, word dressing; locution, expression

**dictionary** NOUNS word list, **lexicon, glossary, wordbook, Webster's; glossary,** gloss, **vocabulary,** onomasticon, nomenclator; **thesaurus**

**die** NOUNS 1 **mold, form**, cast, template, matrix, negative; punch, stamp, intaglio, seal, mint
VERBS 2 **decease, succumb, expire, perish,** be taken by death, up and die <nonformal>, cease to be *or* live, part, depart, quit this world, make one's exit, go, go the way of all flesh, go out, pass, pass on *or* over, **pass away, meet one's death** *or* **end** *or* **fate,** end one's life *or* days, depart this life

3 <nonformal> **croak,** go west, kick the bucket, kick in, pop off, conk off, conk out, cop it, drop off, step off, go to the wall, go home feet first, knock off, pipe off, kick off, shove off, bow out, pass out, peg out, push up daisies, go for a burton <Brit>, belly up, go belly up, bite the dust, take the last count; check out, check in, cash in, hand *or* pass *or* cash in one's checks *or* chips; turn up one's toes; slip one's cable; buy the farm *or* the ranch, farm, have one's time *and* have it *and* buy it <all Brit>

4 **come to an end, draw to a close,** end up, land up; lapse, become void *or* extinct *or* defunct, run out, run its course, have its time *and* have it <both nonformal>, die away, wear off *or* away, go out, blow over, be all over, be no more

**diet** VERBS **slenderize, reduce,** reduce *or* lose *or* take off weight, watch one's weight, lose flesh, weight-watch, count calories; slim, **slim down,** thin down

**dietary** ADJS dietetic, dietic <old>; regiminal

**differ** VERBS **vary,** diverge, stand apart, be distinguished *or* distinct; **deviate from,** diverge from, divaricate from, depart from; **disagree with,** disaccord with, conflict with, contrast with, clash with, jar with; not be like, bear no resemblance to, not square with, not accord with

**difference** NOUNS **disagreement, difficulty, misunderstanding,** difference of opinion, agreement to disagree, **variance,** division, dividedness; cross-purposes; polarity of opinion, polarization; **disparity,** diversity, divergence, gap, **contrast**

**different** ADJS differing; unlike, not like, **dissimilar**; **distinct,** distinguished, differentiated, discriminated, discrete, separated, separate, disjoined, widely apart; **various,** variant, varying, varied, heterogeneous, multifarious, motley, assorted, variegated, diverse, divers, **diversified; novel, original, unique;** strange, unusual, uncommon; unfamiliar, unheard-of

**differentiate** VERBS **distinguish, make a distinction, discriminate, secern; separate,** sever, severalize, segregate, divide; **demarcate,** mark, mark out *or* off, set off, set apart, draw a line, set limits; **characterize, define**

**difficult** ADJS 1 **perverse, contrary, wrongheaded, wayward, froward,** cross-grained, cantankerous, feisty, ornery <nonformal>; irascible
2 **hard to understand, hard,** tough <nonformal>, beyond one, **over one's head,** beyond *or* out of one's depth; knotty, cramp, crabbed; intricate, **complex,** overtechnical, perplexed, **complicated**
3 troublesome, troublous, hard, trying, rigorous, stressful; wretched, miserable; **not easy;** harmful

**difficulty** NOUNS 1 **disagreement, misunderstanding, difference,** difference of opinion, agreement to disagree, **variance,** division, dividedness; cross-purposes
2 **abstruseness,** reconditeness; crabbedness, crampedness, knottiness; **complexity,** intricacy, **complication**; **hardness; profundity,** profoundness
3 **adversity,** adverse circumstances, difficulties, hard knocks *and* rough going <both nonformal>, **hardship, trouble,** troubles, **rigor,** vicissitude, care, stress, pressure

**diffuse** ADJS 1 diffusive; **formless,** unstructured; **profuse,** profusive; **redundant,** pleonastic, repetitive, reiterative, iterative, tautologous, parrotlike
2 **dispersed, scattered, distributed,** dissipated, disseminated, strown, strewn, broadcast, **spread,** dispread; **widespread,** discrete, sparse; **diluted,** thinned, thinned-out, watered, watered-down, weakened; **sporadic**

**dig** VERBS 1 **excavate,** dig out, **scoop,** scoop out, **gouge,** gouge out, grub, shovel, spade, dike, delve, scrape, scratch, scrabble; dredge; **trench,** trough, furrow, groove; **tunnel, burrow**
2 **prod, goad, poke, punch, jab,** nudge

**digest** NOUNS 1 **abridgment, condensation,** short *or* shortened version, condensed version, abbreviation, abbreviature, brief, **abstract,** epitome, **précis, capsule,** encapsulation, **synopsis,** conspectus, pandect
VERBS 2 **absorb,** adsorb, chemisorb *or* chemosorb, **assimilate,** engross, ingest
3 **consider, contemplate, speculate, reflect, study, ponder,** perpend, **weigh, deliberate, debate, meditate, muse, brood, ruminate,** chew the cud <nonformal>

**dignified** ADJS **stately, imposing, grand, courtly,** magisterial, aristocratic; worthy, **august, venerable; sedate, solemn**, sober, grave

**dignify** VERBS **honor,** confer *or* bestow honor upon; adorn, grace; **distinguish,** signalize, confer distinction on, give credit where credit is due

**dignity** NOUNS **stiffness, stiltedness,** primness, prissiness, rigidness, starchiness, buckram <old>, gravity, weight, *gravitas* <L>, weighty dignity, staidness, reverend seriousness, **solemnity**; **pomp**; pomposity

**digression** NOUNS **obliquity,** obliqueness; **deviation**, deviance, divergence, divagation, vagary, excursion, skewness, aberration, squint, declination; deflection, deflexure

**dike** NOUNS **barrier,** bank, embankment, levee

**dilapidated** ADJS **ramshackle,** decrepit, shacky, tottery, slummy <nonformal>, **tumbledown, broken-down, rundown,** in ruins, ruinous, ruined, derelict, gone to wrack and ruin, the worse for wear

**dilemma** NOUNS Scylla and Charybdis, the devil and the deep blue sea; *embarras de choix* <Fr>; choice of Hercules; Hobson's choice, **no choice,** only choice, zero option; horns of a dilemma, double bind, damned-if-you-do-and-damned-if-you-don't, no-win situation, **quandary,** nonplus

**dilettante** NOUNS **half scholar,** sciolist, **dabbler,** dabster, amateur, trifler, smatterer; grammaticaster, philologaster, criticaster, philosophaster, Latinitaster

**diligent** ADJS **industrious, assiduous, sedulous,** laborious, **hardworking;** hard, unremitting, unsparing, relentless, zealous, ardent, fervent, vehement; **energetic,** strenuous; tireless, unwearied, unflagging, indefatigable

**dilute** VERBS **cut** <nonformal>, **reduce, thin,** thin out, attenuate, rarefy; **water,** water down, adulterate, **weaken,** dilute, attenuate, extenuate; **dissipate, dispel,** dissolve

**dim** VERBS 1 **blur, pale,** soften, film, mist, fog; defocus, lose resolution *or* sharpness *or* distinctness, go soft at the edges; **darken,** bedarken; **obscure,** obfuscate, obumbrate
ADJS 2 **dim-sighted,** dull-sighted, dim-eyed, half-blind, sand-blind; bleary-eyed, blear-eyed
3 half-visible, semivisible, low-profile; **indistinct, unclear,** unplain, **indefinite,** undefined, ill-defined, ill-marked, **faint,** pale, feeble, weak, dark, **shadowy, vague, obscure,** indistinguishable, half-seen, merely glimpsed
4 **dull,** dull of mind, **dopey** <nonformal>, **obtuse,** blunt, wooden, heavy, sluggish, slow, **slow-witted,** hebetudinous, **dim-witted, dull-witted, thick-witted,** thick-headed

**dimension** NOUNS **extent,** spread, breadth; proportion; **dimensions, proportions,** caliber, scantling, proportion; **measure,** expanse, **scope,** reach, range, ballpark <nonformal>, spread, coverage, area, cirumference, ambit, girth, diameter, radius, boundary, border, periphery

**diminish** VERBS **decrease, lessen; let up,** bate, abate; **decline, subside,** shrink, wane, wither, ebb, ebb away, dwindle, languish, sink, sag, die down *or* away, wind down, taper off *and* trail off *or* away *and* tail off *or* away <all nonformal>; **reduce, lower, depress,** damp, dampen, **step down** *and* tune down *and* phase down *or* out *and* scale back *or* down *and* roll back *or* down <all nonformal>

**din** NOUNS **noise,** loud noise, **blast**, tintamarre, **racket, clamor;** outcry, **uproar,** hue and cry, noise and shouting; howl; clangor, clatter, clap, jangle, rattle; **pandemonium,** bedlam, hell *or* bedlam let loose

**dine** VERBS **feed,** wine and dine, mess; satisfy, gratify; regale

**diner** NOUNS 1 **eater,** feeder, consumer, devourer; gourmand, trencherman, **glutton**
2 **restaurant,** eating place, eatery *and* beanery *and* hashery *and* hash house *and* greasy spoon <all nonformal>; **fast-food restaurant,** hamburger joint <nonformal>; **lunch counter,** quick-lunch counter; dog wagon <nonformal>; **kitchen;** dining car

**dingy** ADJS **grimy, smoky,** sooty, fuliginous, **smudgy,** smutty, blotchy, dirty, **muddy,** murky, smirched, besmirched

**dining room** NOUNS *salle à manger* <Fr>, dinette, dining hall, refectory, mess *or* messroom *or* mess hall, commons

**diocese** NOUNS **see,** archdiocese, bishopric, archbishopric; province; synod, conference; **parish**

**dip** NOUNS 1 **bath;** acid bath, mercury bath, fixing bath; sheepdip; duck, souse
2 **declivity, descent,** drop, fall, falling-off *or* -away, **decline; downgrade, downhill**
VERBS 3 **incline, descend, decline,** drop, fall, fall off *or* away, **go downhill**
4 **submerge,** submerse, **immerse,** immerge, merge, **sink,** bury, engulf, **inundate,** deluge, drown, overwhelm, whelm; **duck, dunk** <nonformal>, douse, souse, plunge in water; baptize

**diploma** NOUNS **certificate,** sheepskin <nonformal>; certificate of proficiency, testamur <Brit>

**diplomacy** NOUNS **tact, tactfulness, diplomacy;** *savoir-faire* <Fr>; diplomatics; shirt-sleeve diplomacy; shuttle diplomacy; dollar diplomacy, gunboat diplomacy; brinkmanship

*the police in grand costume*
NAPOLEON

**diplomatic** ADJS tactful, politic, statesmanlike

**dire** ADJS grim, baleful, baneful; appalling, shocking, disgusting; direful, fell; **ill-fated,** ill-starred, evil-starred, star-crossed; **terrible, dreadful,** awful <nonformal>, horrible, horrid; fatal, doomful, **ominous, inauspicious**

**direct** VERBS 1 **govern**, **rule, control**, order, **regulate,** guide; **determine,** decide, dispose; have the say *or* say-so, have veto power over, have the last word, call the shots *and* be in the driver's seat *and* wear the pants <all nonformal>
ADJS 2 undeviating, unswerving, unbending, undeflected; single-hearted, single-minded; bluff, blunt, outspoken; **unaffected, unpretentious,** unpretending, unassuming, unfeigning, straightforward, honest, candid; unadorned,

gracile, no-frills *and* vanilla *and* plain vanilla <all nonformal>, up-front *and* straight <both nonformal>, **forthright,** downright, straight-out <nonformal>
ADVS 3 **directly, straight, straightforward, undeviatingly,** unswervingly, unveeringly; straight as an arrow

**direction** NOUNS 1 **line,** direction line, line of direction, point, quarter, **aim, way,** track, range, **bearing,** azimuth, compass reading, **heading, course**
2 **directive, instruction, rule, regulation;** prescript, prescription, **precept; management, managing,** handling, **running** <nonformal>, **conduct;** governance, **command, control, chiefdom, government**, controllership
3 **trend, drift, course, current,** *Tendenz* <Ger>, flow, stream, mainstream, main current, movement, motion, run, **tenor,** tone, **set,** set of the current, swing, bearing, line, the general tendency *or* drift, the course of events, the way the wind blows, **the way things go**

**director** NOUNS *directeur* <Fr>, director general, **governor,** rector, **manager, administrator,** intendant, **conductor;** person in charge, responsible person; impresario, producer; auteur

**dirge** NOUNS **funeral** *or* **death song,** coronach, keen, elegy, epicedium, requiem, monody, threnody, threnode, knell, death knell, passing bell, funeral march, muffled drums

**dirt** NOUNS 1 **grime;** dust; soot, smut; **mud**
2 **land, ground,** landmass, earth, glebe <old>, **sod,** clod, **soil,** dust, clay, marl
3 **scandal, malicious gossip,** juicy morsel, tidbit, choice bit of dirt <nonformal>; **scandalmongering;** character assassination

*gossip made tedious by morality*
OSCAR WILDE

**dirty** VERBS 1 dirty up, grime, **begrime;** muck, muck up <nonformal>; **muddy,** mire, bemire; **stain,** bestain, **discolor,** smirch, besmirch, **taint,** attaint, **tarnish; mark, stigmatize,** brand; smear, besmear, daub, bedaub, slubber <Brit nonformal>; blur, slur <nonformal>; **darken, blacken; soil**
ADJS 2 **dingy, grimy, smoky,** sooty, fuliginous, **smudgy,** smutty, blotchy, **muddy,** murky, smirched, besmirched
3 blasphemous, **profane, foul, foulmouthed, vile,** thersitical, **obscene,** dysphemistic, scatologic, scatological, coprological, toilet, sewer, cloacal; ribald, Rabelaisian, raw, risqué
4 **unfair,** not fair; **unsporting,** unsportsmanly, **unsportsmanlike,** not done, not kosher <nonformal>, not cricket <Brit nonformal>; foul, below the belt; **base, low, mean,** crummy

**disabled** ADJS **incapacitated; crippled,** hamstrung; disqualified, invalidated; disarmed; paralyzed; hog-tied <nonformal>; prostrate, **on one's back,** on one's beam-ends

**disadvantage** NOUNS **drawback, liability; detriment,** impairment, prejudice, loss, damage, hurt, harm, mischief, injury; **a step back** *or* **backward,** a loss of ground; **handicap**, disability; drag, millstone around one's neck

**disagree** VERBS **differ,** differ in opinion, hold opposite views, disaccord, **be at variance,** not get along, pull different ways, be at cross-purposes, have no measures with, misunderstand one another

**disagreeable** ADJS **unsavory, unpalatable, unappetizing,** untasteful, untasty, ill-flavored, foul-tasting, **distasteful,** dislikable, unlikable, uninviting, unpleasant, unpleasing, displeasing; perverse, fractious, cross-grained

**disappear** VERBS **vanish,** vanish from sight, do a vanishing act <nonformal>, depart, fly, **flee**, go, be gone, **go away,** pass, pass out *or* away, pass out of sight, exit, pull up stakes <nonformal>, leave the scene *or* stage, clear out, pass out of the picture, pass *or* retire from sight, become lost to sight, be seen no more; dematerialize, evaporate, evanesce, **vanish into thin air,** go up in smoke

**disappointed** ADJS bitterly *or* sorely disappointed; **let down,** betrayed, ill-served, ill done-by; **dashed,** blighted, blasted, crushed; **balked,** bilked, **thwarted, frustrated,** baffled, crossed, defeated, foiled

**disapprove** VERBS **disapprove of,** not approve, raise an objection, go *or* side against, go contra; **disfavor, view with disfavor, raise one's eyebrows, frown at** *or* **on,** look black upon, look askance at, make a wry face at, grimace at, **turn up one's nose at,** shrug one's shoulders at; **take a dim view of** <nonformal>, not think much of, think ill of, think little of, not take kindly to, not hold with, hold no brief for *and* not sign off on <both nonformal>

**disarm** VERBS lay down one's arms, unarm, turn in one's weapons, down *or* ground one's arms, sheathe the sword, turn swords into plowshares; **demilitarize,** deactivate, **demobilize, disband,** reconvert, decommission

**disaster** NOUNS **debacle, cataclysm, catastrophe; breakup,** breaking up; **breakdown, collapse; crash,** smash, **smashup,** crack-up <nonformal>; **wreck,** wrack, shipwreck; cave-in, cave; washout; total loss

**disastrous** ADJS **calamitous, catastrophic, cataclysmic,** cataclysmal, **tragic,** ruinous, wreckful <old>, fatal, dire, black, woeful, sore, baneful, grievous

**disbelief** NOUNS **unbelief,** nonbelief, discredit; refusal *or* inability to believe; **incredulity**; **unpersuadedness,** lack of conviction; misbelief, heresy; infidelity, atheism, **agnosticism**; minimifidianism, nullifidianism

**discard** VERBS **reject, throw away, throw out,** chuck *or* chuck away *and* shit-can *and* eighty-six <all nonformal>, cast, cast off *or* away *or* aside; **get rid of,** get quit of, get shut *or* shet of <nonformal>, rid oneself of, shrug off, **dispose of,** slough, **dump, ditch** <nonformal>, **jettison, throw** *or* **heave** *or* **toss overboard,** deep-six <nonformal>, throw out the window, throw *or* cast to the dogs, cast to the winds

**discharge** NOUNS 1 **detonation, blast, explosion,** fulmination, **burst, bang, pop, crack,** bark; **shot,** gunshot; volley, salvo, fusillade
2 **exculpation,** disculpation, verdict of acquittal *or* not guilty; **pardon, excuse, forgiveness, free pardon; release, dismissal,** setting free; quashing of the charge *or* indictment
3 **dismissal,** forced separation, *congé* <Fr>; outplacement; **firing** *and* canning <both nonformal>, **cashiering,** drumming out, dishonorable discharge; **lay-off,** removal, suspension; **the sack** *and* the chuck <both Brit nonformal>; the boot *and* the gate *and* the ax <all nonformal>; walking papers *or* ticket <nonformal>, pink slip <nonformal>
VERBS 4 **blast, detonate, explode, burst,** go off, **bang, pop, crack,** bark, fulminate
5 **emit,** give off; eject, throw *or* hurl forth
6 **perform, practice,** do, execute, carry out *or* through, do one's duty, do one's office, fulfill one's role, discharge one's function
7 release, dismiss, free, set free, let off <nonformal>, let go; quash the charge *or* indictment, withdraw the charge

**disciple** NOUNS **worshiper,** idolizer, idolater; **evangelist, apostle,** follower, servant, faithful servant

**discipline** NOUNS 1 **self-control,** control, restraint, constraint; composure, possession, aplomb; strict *or* tight *or* rigid discipline, regimentation, spit and polish; **punishment,** punition, **chastisement, chastening, correction,** disciplinary measure *or* action, **castigation,** infliction
2 **field,** field of inquiry, concern, province, domain, area, arena, sphere, branch *or* field of study, branch *or* department of knowledge, specialty, academic specialty, academic discipline
VERBS 3 **punish, chastise, chasten, correct, castigate, penalize; take to task,** bring to book, bring *or* call to account; deal with, settle with, settle *or* square accounts, teach *or* give one a lesson; pillory; **make conform,** shape, lick into shape, mold, force into a mold; straighten, rectify, correct

**disclosure** NOUNS disclosing; **revelation,** revealing, making public, publicizing, broadcasting; apocalypse; manifestation; exposure, **exposé; baring,** stripping, stripping *or* laying bare; outing <nonformal>

**discomfort** NOUNS displeasure, dissatisfaction, uncomfortableness, malaise, **painfulness; disquiet,** inquietude, **uneasiness,** unease, discomposure, vexation of spirit

**disconnected** ADJS 1 **separated,** disjoined, disjoint, disjointed, disjunct, disengaged, detached, **disunited, divided,** removed, divorced, **alienated,** estranged, distanced, **segregated,** sequestered, isolated, cloistered, shut off; **incoherent, inconsistent, uncohesive, unconsolidated,** tenuous
2 **sporadic,** patchy, spotty, scrappy, snatchy, catchy, choppy, **broken, discontinuous**

**discontent** NOUNS 1 **dissatisfaction,** unsatisfaction, unfulfillment; **resentment, envy; restlessness, restiveness, uneasiness,** unease; malaise; **disgruntlement,** sulkiness, sourness, petulance, peevishness, querulousness
VERBS 2 **dissatisfy, disgruntle, displease,** fail to satisfy, be inadequate, not fill the bill, disappoint, leave much *or* a lot to be desired, dishearten, put out <nonformal>

**discontinue** VERBS **cease, end, stop, halt,** terminate, close the books on, close the books, put paid to <Brit>, abort, cancel, scratch *and* scrub <both nonformal>, hold, **quit,** stay, belay <nonformal>

**discord** NOUNS discordance *or* discordancy, **dissonance** *or* dissonancy, diaphony, **cacophony;** stridor; **inharmoniousness,** unharmoniousness; **disaccord, conflict,** open conflict *or* war, **friction,** rub; jar, **jarring,** jangle, clash, clashing; touchiness, strained relations, **tension;** bad blood; **unpleasantness;** mischief; **contention**; **enmity**

**discount** NOUNS 1 **cut, deduction,** slash, abatement, reduction, price reduction, price-cutting, price-cut, rollback <nonformal>; underselling; **rebate,** rebatement
VERBS 2 disregard, leave out of account; consider the source, take with a grain of salt; waive, ignore, not hear of, wave aside, brush away *or* aside, refuse to consider; **cut, deduct,** bate, abate; **take off,** write off, charge off; **depreciate,** reduce; rebate, **refund,** kick back <nonformal>

**discourage** VERBS **daunt, deter,** shake, stop, stop in one's tracks, set back; **dishearten;** faze <nonformal>; **awe, overawe; pour** *or* **dash** *or* **throw cold water on,** throw *or* lay a wet blanket on, damp, dampen, demotivate, **cool, chill,** quench, blunt; take the starch out of, take the wind out of one's sails

**discover** VERBS **find,** get; strike, hit; put *or* lay one's hands on, lay one's fingers on, **locate**; **hunt down,** search out, trace down, track down, **run down, run** *or* **bring to earth;** trace; **learn, find out,** determine, become cognizant *or* conscious of, become aware of; discover *or* find oneself; invent

**discreet** ADJS **reticent, reserved,** restrained, nonassertive, low-key, low-keyed, constrained; guarded; **secretive,** close-lipped, secret, close, dark; **uncommunicative, close-mouthed**

**discrepancy** NOUNS inconsistency, inconsonance, incongruity, discongruity, unconformity *or* nonconformity, disconformity, **strangeness**, unorthodoxy, incompatibility, irreconcilability; **disparity,** inequality

**discrete** ADJS **separate, distinct; unjoined, unconnected, unattached,** unaccompanied, unattended, unassociated; discontinuous, noncontiguous, divergent; **isolated,** insular, detached, detachable, free-standing, free-floating, autonomous

**discretion** NOUNS **volition; free choice,** one's own will *or* choice *or* discretion *or* initiative, **option, pleasure, free will**; **reserve,** reservedness, restraint, low key, **constraint;** guardedness, discreetness, **uncommunicativeness**; **circumspection**

**discriminate** VERBS **distinguish,** draw *or* make distinctions, contradistinguish, secern, distinguish in thought, **separate,** separate out, divide, analyze, subdivide, **segregate,** sever, severalize, **differentiate,** demark, demarcate, set off, **set apart,** sift, sift out, sieve, sieve out, winnow, screen, screen out, sort, classify, sort out

**discriminating** ADJS **discriminate,** discriminative, selective; discriminatory; **tactful, sensitive;** appreciative, appreciatory; **critical; distinguishing;** differential; precise, accurate, exact; nice, fine, delicate, subtle, subtile, refined; fastidious; distinctive, contrastive

**discuss** VERBS **debate,** reason, deliberate, deliberate upon, exchange views *or* opinions, talk, **talk over, hash over** <nonformal>, talk of *or* about, rap <nonformal>, comment upon, reason about, discourse about, **consider, treat,** dissertate on, handle, deal with, take up, **go into, examine,** investigate, talk out, **analyze,** sift, **study,** canvass, review, pass under review, controvert, ventilate, air, thresh out, consider pro and con; **kick** *or* **knock around** <nonformal>

**discussion** NOUNS **debate,** debating, **deliberation,** exchange of views, canvassing, ventilation, airing, review, **treatment, consideration,** investigation, **examination, study, analysis,** logical analysis; logical discussion, dialectic

**disease** NOUNS **illness, sickness, malady, ailment, indisposition, disorder,** complaint, morbidity, *morbus* <L>, **affliction,** affection, **infirmity**

**disengage** VERBS **extricate, free, release, clear,** get out; disentangle, untangle, unsnarl, unravel, disentwine, disinvolve, unknot, disembarrass, disembroil; dislodge, break out *or* loose, cut loose, tear loose

**disfavor** NOUNS **falling-out, breach of friendship,** parting of the ways, bust-up <nonformal>; **alienation, estrangement, disaffection; disapproval, disapprobation,** disesteem, disrespect; rejection, thumbs-down, exclusion, ostracism, blackballing, blackball, ban

**disgrace** NOUNS 1 **scandal, humiliation; shame,** dirty shame *and* low-down dirty shame <both nonformal>, crying *or* burning shame; **reproach,** byword, byword of reproach, a disgrace to one's name
VERBS 2 **dishonor, discredit,** reflect discredit upon, bring into discredit, reproach, cast reproach upon, be a reproach to; **shame, put to shame,** impute shame to, hold up to shame; hold up to public shame *or* public scorn *or* public ridicule, pillory, bring shame upon, **humiliate**; **degrade, debase,** deplume, displume, defrock, unfrock, bring low

**disgruntled** ADJS **discontented, dissatisfied,** unaccepting, unaccommodating, **displeased,** less than pleased, let down, disappointed; resentful, dog-in-the-manger; malcontent, malcontented, **complaining,** sour, **faultfinding,** grumbling, growling, murmuring, muttering, griping, croaking, **peevish, petulant,** sulky, **querulous,** querulant, whiny

**disguise** NOUNS 1 **cover, camouflage,** protective coloration; **false colors, false front**; dissimilation, masking
VERBS 2 **conceal, hide,** ensconce; **cover, cover up,** blind, **screen, cloak, veil,** shroud, enshroud; **camouflage, mask,** dissemble; plain-wrap, wrap in plain brown paper; **obscure,** obfuscate, cloud, becloud, befog, throw out a smoke screen, shade

**disgust** NOUNS 1 **aversion, repugnance,** repulsion, **antipathy,** allergy <nonformal>, abomination, **abhorrence, horror,** mortal horror; **loathing**
VERBS 2 **repel,** turn one's stomach, nauseate; make one's gorge rise; gross one out <nonformal>; **offend,** give offense, **repel,** put off, turn off <nonformal>, **revolt,** sicken, make one sick

**disgusting** ADJS **odious, repulsive,** repellent, rebarbative, **repugnant, revolting, sickening, loathsome,** gross *and* yucky *and* grungy *and* scuzzy <all nonformal>, beastly <nonformal>, **vile, foul, nasty, nauseating**; fulsome, mephitic, miasmal, miasmic, malodorous, stinking, fetid, noisome, noxious

**dish** NOUNS 1 **serving,** service; **portion, helping,** help; second helping; **course;** plate; *plat du jour* <Fr>
VERBS 2 **ladle, dip, scoop;** dish out *or* up

**dishevel** VERBS **disorder, disarrange, disorganize,** rumple, ruffle; tousle <nonformal>, muss *and* **muss up** <both nonformal>, mess *and* **mess up** <both nonformal>; **litter, clutter,** scatter

**dishonest** ADJS **dishonorable; unconscientious,** unconscienced, conscienceless, unconscionable, shameless, without shame *or* remorse, **unscrupulous, unprincipled,** unethical, immoral, amoral; **corrupt,** corrupted, rotten; **crooked, criminal,** felonious, **fraudulent,** underhanded; shady <nonformal>, up to no good, not kosher <nonformal>, unsavory, dark, sinister, slippery, devious, tricky, shifty; fishy <nonformal>, questionable, suspicious

**dishonor** VERBS **disgrace, discredit,** reflect discredit upon, bring into discredit, reproach, cast reproach upon, be a reproach to; hold up to public shame *or* public scorn *or* public ridicule, pillory, bring shame upon, **humiliate**; **degrade, debase, desecrate, profane,** unhallow, commit sacrilege

**disillusion** NOUNS 1 **disillusionment, disenchantment,** undeception, unspelling, return to reality, loss of one's illusions, loss of innocence, cold light of reality, bursting of the bubble; awakening, rude awakening, bringing back to earth
VERBS 2 **disenchant,** unspell, uncharm, break the spell *or* charm; **disabuse, undeceive;** correct, **set right** *or* **straight,** put straight, tell the truth, enlighten, let in on, put one wise <nonformal>; open one's eyes, awaken, wake up, rob *or* strip one of one's illusions; bring one back to earth

**disinfectant** NOUNS 1 **antiseptic,** fumigant, fumigator, **germicide,** bactericide, microbicide, antibiotic
ADJS 2 **antiseptic, germicidal,** bactericidal

**disinherit** VERBS disendow; **disown,** cut out of one's will, **cut off,** cut off without a cent

**disintegrate** VERBS **decompose, decay,** dissolve, come apart, disorganize, **break up**, go to rack and ruin, crack up, disjoin, unknit, split, fission, atomize, **come** *or* **fall to pieces; erode,** corrode, ablate, consume, wear *or* waste away, molder, molder away, crumble, crumble into dust

**disinterested** ADJS **impartial, impersonal, evenhanded,** equitable, **dispassionate,** detached, objective, lofty, Olympian; **unbiased,** uninfluenced, unswayed; **neutral; unprejudiced, unbiased, unprepossessed, unjaundiced**

**disk** NOUNS **circle,** circus, rondure, **ring,** annulus; discus, saucer; halo, glory, areola, aureole; **computer disk,** diskette, floppy disk *or* floppy, hard disk, compact disk *or* CD

**disk jockey** NOUNS **broadcaster,** DJ <nonformal>; master of ceremonies, MC *or* emcee <both nonformal>

**dislike** NOUNS 1 **distaste,** disrelish, scunner; disaffection, **disfavor,** disinclination; disaffinity; **displeasure, disapproval,** disapprobation
VERBS 2 disfavor, not like, have no liking for, be no love lost between, **have no use for** <nonformal>, **not care for,** have no time for, have a disaffinity for, want nothing to do with, not think much of, entertain *or* conceive *or* take a dislike to, take a scunner to, not be able to bear *or* endure *or* abide, not give the time of day to <nonformal>, **disapprove of; disrelish,** have no taste for, not stomach, not have the stomach for, not be one's cup of tea

**dislodge** VERBS unplace; evict; **uproot,** root up *or* out, deracinate; depose, **unseat;** throw off, buck off; displace, delocalize, break out *or* loose, cut loose, tear loose

**disloyal** ADJS **unfaithful,** faithless, of bad faith, trothless; **inconstant, unsteadfast,** fickle; unloyal; false, **untrue,** not true to; disaffected, recreant, derelict, barratrous

**dismal** ADJS **gloomy, murky, bleak, grim, somber,** sombrous, **solemn, grave;** sad, *triste* <Fr>, **funereal,** funebrial, crepe-hanging <nonformal>, saturnine; **dreary,** drear, drearisome; **hopeless,** unhopeful, without hope, affording no hope, worst-case, cheerless, comfortless

**dismantle** VERBS **disassemble,** take apart *or* down, tear down; **demolish**

**dismay** NOUNS 1 **scare, alarm, consternation; dread,** unholy dread, **awe**
VERBS 2 **distress,** grieve, mourn, lament, sorrow; pain, discomfort, try one's patience, give one a hard time *or* a pain *or* a pain in the neck *or* ass *or* butt <nonformal>; **disconcert, appall, astound, confound, abash, discomfit, put out, take aback**

**dismember** VERBS **tear** *or* **rip apart,** take *or* pull apart, **pick** *or* **rip** *or* **tear to pieces,** tear to rags *or* tatters, **shred,** rip to shreds; tear limb from limb, draw and quarter; **mangle, disjoin,** unknit, unravel

**dismiss** VERBS 1 **send off** *or* **away, turn off** *or* **away,** bundle, bundle off *or* out, hustle out, pack off, **send packing,** send about one's business, send to the showers <nonformal>; **show the door,** show the gate; **give the gate** *or* the air <nonformal>; **discharge, expel, cashier,** drum out, disemploy, outplace, separate forcibly *or* involuntarily, **lay off,** suspend, surplus, furlough, turn out, release, let go, let out, remove, strike off the rolls, give the pink slip; break, bust <nonformal>; **retire,** superannuate, put out to pasture
2 dismiss *or* drive from one's thoughts; **put out of mind,** put out of one's head *or* thoughts, **think no more of, forget,** not give it another *or* a second thought, **drop the subject,** give it no more thought; turn one's back upon, abandon, leave out in the cold <nonformal>; put *or* set *or* lay aside, put on the back burner *or* on hold <nonformal>

**disobedience** NOUNS nonobedience, **noncompliance; undutifulness,** unduteousness; willful disobedience; **insubordination,** indiscipline; **unsubmissiveness, intractability,** indocility, recusancy; **nonconformity**; **disrespect**; **lawlessness,** waywardness, frowardness, **dereliction,** delinquency, nonfeasance

**disorder** NOUNS **disorderliness, disar-**

**rangement,** derangement, disarticulation, disjunction, **disorganization; disarray,** upset, disturbance, discomfiture, disconcertedness; turbulence, perturbation; **disruption**, destabilization; **confusion,** chaos, **mess** *and* mix-up *and* snafu <all nonformal>

**disoriented** ADJS **bewildered,** distracted, distraught, **disconcerted,** discomposed, in a fix *or* stew *or* pickle *or* jam *or* scrape <nonformal>; **lost,** astray, abroad, adrift, **at sea, confused, mixed-up, flustered,** fluttered, **ruffled, rattled, upset, unsettled,** off-balance, off one's stride; **disorganized, disordered,** disorientated, in a jumble

**disown** VERBS disendow; **disinherit,** disherison, cut out of one's will, **cut off,** cut off with a cent

**disparity** NOUNS **inequality, unevenness, contrariety**, **difference**; **irregularity,** nonuniformity, heterogeneity; **disproportion,** asymmetry; **unbalance,** imbalance, disequilibrium, overbalance, overcompensation, tippiness; **injustice,** inequity

**dispatch** NOUNS 1 **speed; rapidity,** celerity, **swiftness,** fastness, **quickness,** snappiness <nonformal>, **speediness;** haste, hurry, flurry, rush, precipitation; **expedition, promptness,** promptitude, instantaneousness
2 **message, word, communication, communiqué,** advice
VERBS 3 **send,** send off *or* away, send forth; transmit, remit, consign, forward; **mail, post**

**dispensable** ADJS **superfluous, redundant; excess, in excess;** unnecessary, unessential, expendable, **needless,** unneeded, gratuitous, uncalled-for

**dispense** VERBS **parcel out, dole out, hand out, mete out,** ration out, give out, hand around, pass around; **distribute,** disperse; issue, administer; disburse, pay out

**disperse** VERBS **scatter,** diffract; **distribute, broadcast, sow,** narrowcast, disseminate, propagate, pass around *or* out, publish; **diffuse, spread,** dispread, circumfuse, strew, bestrew, dot; **radiate,** diverge; scatter to the winds; **disband, scatter, separate, part,** break up, split up; part company, go separate ways

**displace** VERBS **remove, move, relocate, shift,** send, shunt; dislodge; **take away,** cart off *or* away, carry off *or* away; succeed, replace, take the place of, **step into** *or* **fill the shoes of,** don the mantle of, assume the robe of

**displaced person** NOUNS stateless person, homeless person, man without a country, exile, drifter, vagabond, deportee; expatriate

**display** NOUNS 1 **demonstration, show, showing; presentation, exhibition, exhibit, exposition, showcase,** showcasing, unveiling, exposure, manifestation
VERBS 2 **manifest, show, exhibit, demonstrate,** breathe, unfold, develop; **present, evince, evidence; make public,** go public with <nonformal>; bring *or* lay *or* drag before the public, take one's case to the public, **give** *or* **put out,** give to the world, **make known; divulge**; **ventilate,** air, get out in the open, open up

**displeasure** NOUNS **resentment,** resentfulness; disapproval, disapprobation, dissatisfaction, **discontent; vexation,** irritation, **annoyance,** aggravation <nonformal>, exasperation

**dispossess** VERBS disseise, expropriate, foreclose; **evict, oust,** dislodge, put out, turn out, **turn out of doors,** turn out of house and home, throw into the street

**disprove** VERBS **invalidate,** disconfirm, discredit, prove the contrary, belie, give the lie to; **negate,** negative; **expose, show up; explode,** blow up, blow sky-high, **puncture,** deflate, **shoot** *or* **poke full of holes, cut to pieces, cut the ground from under; knock the bottom out of** <nonformal>, knock the props *or* chocks out from under, cut the ground from under one's feet, not leave a leg to stand on, put *or* lay to rest

**disputable** ADJS doubtable, **dubious, questionable,** moot, arguable, contestable, controvertible, controversial, refutable, confutable, deniable; open to question *or* doubt; in question, in dispute, at issue

**dispute** NOUNS 1 **quarrel,** open quarrel, **argument,** polemic, **controversy,** altercation, **fight, squabble, contention,** strife, **tussle,** bicker, wrangle, snarl, **tiff, spat,** fuss; disputation; **quarreling, bickering, wrangling, squabbling;** oppugnancy
VERBS 2 **contest,** oppugn, take issue with; **fight over, quarrel over, wrangle over, squabble over,** bicker over, strive

*or* contend about; **question,** query, **challenge, contest,** cast doubt on, greet with skepticism, keep one's eye on, bring *or* call into question, raise a question, throw doubt upon

**disqualify** VERBS **invalidate,** knock the bottom out of <nonformal>, **make impossible, rule out,** disenable, close out, **bar,** prohibit, put out of reach, leave no chance

**disregard** VERBS **overlook, ignore,** accept, take *and* swallow *and* let go <all nonformal>, pass over, give one another chance, let one off this time *and* let one off easy <both nonformal>, close *or* shut one's eyes to, **blink** *or* **wink at,** connive at; **neglect, overlook,** not heed, not attend to, take for granted; lose sight of, pay no regard to; **flout, slight,** treat with contempt, fly in the teeth *or* face of, **snap one's fingers at; thumb one's nose at**

**disreputable** ADJS **discreditable, dishonorable,** unsavory, shady, **seamy, sordid; unrespectable, ignoble, ignominious, infamous,** inglorious; notorious; unpraiseworthy

**disrespect** NOUNS 1 **disrespectfulness,** lack of respect, low estimate *or* esteem, **disesteem,** dishonor, **irreverence; ridicule**; **disparagement**; **discourtesy**; **impudence,** insolence
VERBS 2 not respect, disesteem, hold a low opinion of, rate *or* rank low, hold in low esteem, not care much for, pay a lefthanded *or* backhanded compliment, damn with faint praise; **show disrespect for,** show a lack of respect for, **be disrespectful,** treat with disrespect, be overfamiliar with; trifle with, make bold *or* free with, take liberties with, play fast and loose with; **disparage**

**disruption** NOUNS **dissolution,** abruption, cataclasm; destabilization, **disintegration**, breakup, crack-up, shattering, splintering, fragmentizing, fragmentation; **bursting, scattering,** dispersal, diffusion

**dissatisfaction** NOUNS **unpleasantness**, **lack of pleasure,** joylessness, cheerlessness; discontent; displeasure, disapproval, disapprobation, **discomfort,** uncomfortableness, malaise, **painfulness; disquiet,** inquietude, **uneasiness,** unease, discomposure, unfulfillment

**dissect** VERBS **analyze, break down,** break up, anatomize, atomize, vivisect; **divide, subdivide,** segment; reduce to elements

**dissent** NOUNS 1 **dissidence,** dissentience; nonassent, nonconsent, nonconcurrence, nonagreement, agreement to disagree; **disagreement, difference, variance,** diversity, disparity; **dissatisfaction, disapproval,** disapprobation; repudiation, **rejection;** dissension, discord; bickering, infighting, factiousness
VERBS 2 dissent from, be in dissent, say nay, **disagree,** discord with, **differ,** not agree, disagree with, agree to disagree *or* differ; divide on, be at variance; **take exception,** withhold assent, **take issue, beg to differ,** raise an objection, march to *or* hear a different drummer, swim against the tide *or* against the current *or* upstream

**dissident** NOUNS 1 **dissenter,** dissentient, recusant; **objector,** demurrer; minority *or* opposition voice; **protester,** protestant; **separatist,** schismatic; sectary, sectarian, opinionist; nonconformist; apostate
ADJS 2 **dissenting,** dissentient, recusant; **disagreeing, differing; opposing**, in opposition; at variance with, at odds with; nonconforming

**dissipate** VERBS 1 **squander, lavish,** slather, blow <nonformal>; scatter to the winds; **run through,** go through; **throw away,** throw one's money away, throw money around, **spend money like water,** spend as if money grew on trees, spend money as if it were going out of style, throw money around; burn the candle at both ends; **be promiscuous,** sleep around *and* swing <both nonformal>; **debauch, wanton,** rake, chase women, womanize, whore, sow one's wild oats
2 **dispel,** dissolve, attenuate, dilute, thin, thin out, water, water down, weaken; **evaporate,** volatilize; drive away, clear away, cast forth, blow off

**dissolve** VERBS **disintegrate, decompose, decay,** come apart, disorganize, **break up**, go to rack and ruin, crack up, disjoin, unknit, split, fission, atomize, **come** *or* **fall to pieces; liquefy,** liquidize, **melt,** colliquate; deliquesce; solve

**distance** NOUNS **remoteness,** farness, faroffness, longinquity; **separation,** separatedness, divergence, clearance, margin, leeway; **extent, length,** space, **reach,** stretch, range, compass, span, stride, haul, a way, ways *and* piece <both nonformal>; **aloofness, standoffishness,** offishness, withdrawnness, **remoteness,** detachment; **coolness,** coldness, cold shoulder; inaccessibility, unapproachability

**distant** ADJS **aloof, standoffish,** offish, standoff, **remote,** withdrawn, removed, detached, Olympian; **cool,** cold, frigid, chilly, icy, frosty; inaccessible, unapproachable; tight-assed <nonformal>; remote, out-of-the-way

**distasteful** ADJS **unsavory, unpalatable, unappetizing,** untasteful, untasty, ill-flavored, foul-tasting, unlikable, uninviting, displeasing, disagreeable; **uncongenial,** unpleasant; **not to one's taste,** not one's cup of tea

**distill** VERBS **brew;** bootleg, moonshine <nonformal>, **simplify,** streamline, purify, refine; strip, strip down

**distinct** ADJS **plain, clear, obvious, evident, patent,** unmistakable, not to be mistaken, much in evidence, plain to be seen, for all to see, plain as the nose on one's face, plain as day, plain as plain can be, big as life and twice as ugly; **definite, defined, well-defined,** well-marked, well-resolved, in focus; **clear-cut,** clean-cut; crystal-clear, clear as crystal; **audible,** hearable; **express, explicit, unmistakable**

**distinction** NOUNS **notability, noteworthiness,** remarkableness, salience, memorability; **prominence, eminence, greatness;** prestige, esteem, repute, reputation, honor, glory, renown, dignity, **fame**; celebrity

**distinguish** VERBS **discriminate,** draw *or* make distinctions, secern, **separate,** separate out, divide, analyze, subdivide, **segregate,** sever, severalize, **differentiate,** demark, demarcate, **set apart,** sift, sift out, sieve, sieve out, winnow, screen, sort; separate the sheep from the goats, separate the men from the boys; **split hairs,** draw *or* make a fine *or* overfine *or* nice *or* subtle distinction

**distinguished** ADJS distingué; **noted, notable,** marked, of note, of mark; **famous,** famed, honored, **renowned, celebrated, popular,** acclaimed, much acclaimed, sought-after, hot *and* world-class <both nonformal>, on everyone's tongue *or* lips; fabled, legendary

**distort** VERBS **contort,** turn awry; **twist,** turn, screw, wring, wrench, wrest; writhe; **warp,** buckle, crumple; knot, gnarl; **crook,** bend, spring; **misinterpret, misunderstand,** misconceive, **mistake, misapprehend; get backwards,** have the wrong way round, put the cart before the horse; quote out of context; misquote, miscite, give a false coloring, give a false impression *or* idea; **garble, pervert,** twist the words *or* meaning

**distress** NOUNS 1 **chagrin; embarrassment, abashment, discomfiture,** egg on one's face <nonformal>, disconcertment, discomposure, **humiliation,** mortification
2 **pain, grief,** stress, stress of life, suffering, passion, dolor; ache, aching; pang, wrench, throes, cramp, spasm; wound, injury, hurt; **sore,** sore spot, tender spot; **curse, woe,** grievance, **sorrow**
VERBS 3 afflict, trouble, burden, give one a tough row to hoe, load with care, **bother, disturb, perturb, disquiet, discomfort, agitate, upset,** put to it; **worry,** give one gray hair; dismay, grieve, mourn, lament, sorrow; pain, discomfort, give one a hard time *or* a pain *or* a pain in the neck *or* ass *or* butt <nonformal>

**distribute** VERBS **bestow, confer, award, allot, render,** bestow on; **tender,** proffer, offer, extend, come up with <nonformal>; **issue, dispense,** administer; serve, help to; broadcast, sow, disseminate, propagate, pass around *or* out, publish

**district** NOUNS **location, area, region**; **locality, locale,** locus; quarter, section, department, division; **neighborhood,** vicinity, vicinage, neck of the woods <nonformal>, purlieus; precincts, environs, milieu

**distrust** NOUNS 1 **suspiciousness,** suspicion, doubt, misdoubt, mistrust, distrustfulness, **wariness, chariness, cageyness** *and* **leeriness** <both nonformal>; **suspicion,** suspiciousness; **distrust,** distrustfulness, mistrust, mistrustfulness
VERBS 2 **doubt, be doubtful, be dubious, be skeptical,** doubt the truth of, beg leave to doubt, **have one's doubts,** have *or* harbor *or* entertain doubts *or* suspicions, half believe, have reservations, **take with a grain of salt,** be

from Missouri <nonformal>, mistrust, misgive, cross one's fingers

**disturb** VERBS **trouble,** beset; **bother,** pother, get one down, <nonformal>, **perturb,** irk, plague, **torment,** drive one up the wall <nonformal>, give one gray hair, make one lose sleep; **harass, vex, distress**; inconvenience, **put out,** discommode

**disturbed** ADJS **neurotic, psychoneurotic,** disordered; neurasthenic, psychasthenic; stressed; **bothered, troubled, ruffled, roiled,** riled; **irked, vexed, piqued, nettled, provoked, peeved** *and* miffed <both nonformal>, **griped, aggravated, exasperated;** burned-up *and* browned-off <both nonformal>; **agitated, perturbed, disquieted, upset,** antsy <nonformal>, unsettled, **discomposed, shaken**

**ditch** NOUNS 1 **trench, trough, channel, ditch,** dike <old>, fosse, **canal,** cut, gutter, kennel <Brit>; moat
VERBS 2 **discard, get rid of,** get quit of, get shut *or* shet of <nonformal>, rid oneself of, shrug off, **dispose of,** slough, **dump, jettison, throw** *or* **heave** *or* **toss overboard,** deep-six <nonformal>, throw out the window, throw to the dogs, cast to the winds

**ditto** NOUNS **duplicate, duplication, double,** cookie-cutter copy, clone; **reproduction, replica,** facsimile, model, **counterpart;** a chip off the old block

**dive** NOUNS 1 **tumble, fall,** *culbute* <Fr>, cropper *and* **spill** <both nonformal>, **flop** <nonformal>; **header** <nonformal>; **sprawl; pratfall** <nonformal>; **stumble,** trip; **plunge**
2 **den, lair,** den of thieves; hole *and* dump *and* **joint** <all nonformal>; gyp *or* clip joint <nonformal>
VERBS 3 **plunge, pitch, plummet, drop, fall;** skydive; bungee jump; free-fall; plump, plunk, plop; nose-dive, make *or* take a nose dive; take a header <nonformal>

**diversify** VERBS **vary,** variegate, chop and change; **differentiate,** divaricate, ramify; **differ**; dissent; **disunify,** break up, break down, fragment, partition, **analyze;** change form, change shape, shift shape, ring changes, cover the spectrum

**diversity** NOUNS **difference,** otherness, separateness, discreteness, distinctness, **distinction;** unlikeness, **dissimilarity**; **variation,** variance, variegation, variety, **mixture, heterogeneity**

**divert** VERBS **amuse, entertain,** regale, beguile, solace, recreate, refresh, enliven, exhilarate, put in good humor; **delight, tickle, titillate,** tickle pink *or* to death <nonformal>, tickle the fancy; **distract,** detract, distract the attention, divert *or* detract attention, divert the mind *or* thoughts, draw off the attention, take the mind off of, relieve the mind of

**divide** VERBS 1 **partition,** set apart, separate; **wall off,** fence off, screen off, curtain off; tear open, rent, tear, rip, rip open, part, dispart, separate, divaricate; **break with, split,** separate, **diverge, part company,** come to *or* reach a parting of the ways; **alienate, estrange, disunite,** disaffect, **come between; set against,** pit against
2 **apportion, portion, parcel,** share; share with, cut *or* deal one in <nonformal>, share and share alike, divide with, go halvers *or* fifty-fifty *or* even stephen with <nonformal>

**dividend** NOUNS **return, yield,** return on investment, payout, payback

**divine** VERBS 1 **augur,** hint; **prefigure,** betoken, token, typify, **signify, mean**, spell, **indicate,** point to, look like, **be a sign of,** show signs of
ADJS 2 **blissful,** beatific, saintly; sublime; **heavenly,** paradisal, paradisiac, paradisiacal, paradisic, paradisical, empyreal *or* empyrean, Elysian; **sacred, holy,** numinous, **sacrosanct, religious, spiritual; venerable, ineffable, marvelous, wonderful,** glorious, terrific, sensational
3 **gorgeous, ravishing; glorious,** heavenly; **resplendent,** splendorous *or* splendrous, splendiferous, **splendid,** resplendently beautiful

**division** NOUNS **separation,** decentralization; **disunity, disunion, disruption,** separation, cleavage, divergence, dividedness; **apportionment, apportioning, portioning,** partitioning, parceling, budgeting, rationing; **denomination, persuasion,** faction, branch, variety, version, segment; **segregation, separationism, differentiation,** differencing, **discrimination,** distinguishing

**divorce** NOUNS 1 divorcement, grasswidowhood, civil divorce, **separation,** legal *or* judicial separation, separate maintenance; interlocutory decree

VERBS 2 **separate,** part, split up *and* split the sheets <both nonformal>, unmarry, put away, untie the knot, sue for divorce

**dizzy** ADJS **tiddly, giddy,** muddled, addled, flustered, bemused, reeling, seeing double, muzzy, foggy, vertiginous

**dock** NOUNS 1 dockage, marina, basin; dry dock; shipyard, dockyard; **wharf, pier,** quay
VERBS 2 **land,** moor, tie up, anchor, drop anchor; go ashore, **disembark,** debark, unboat

**doctor** NOUNS 1 **physician,** Doctor of Medicine *or* **MD, medical practitioner, medical man, medico** <nonformal>, leech <old>, croaker *and* sawbones <both nonformal>
VERBS 2 **treat,** minister to, care for, give care to, physic; **cure, remedy, heal; undergo treatment,** take medicine
3 **falsify, belie, misrepresent,** miscolor; distort, strain, warp, **slant, twist,** impart spin <nonformal>; put a false appearance upon, give a false coloring, **color, tamper with**

**doctrine** NOUNS **dogma**; **creed,** credo; credenda, tenet, precept, **principle, principle** *or* **article of faith,** canon, teaching

**document** NOUNS 1 official document, legal document, legal paper, legal instrument, **instrument,** writ, **paper,** parchment, scroll, roll, **writing**
VERBS 2 **itemize, specify,** circumstantiate, particularize, **spell out, detail,** go *or* enter into detail, give full particulars; **cite,** instance, adduce, give *or* quote chapter and verse; **substantiate**

**documentation** NOUNS **evidence, proof; reason to believe,** grounds for belief; **ground, grounds,** material grounds, **facts, data,** premises, basis for belief; piece *or* item of evidence, **fact,** datum, relevant fact; body of evidence; chain of evidence

**dodge** NOUNS 1 **trick, artifice, device,** ploy, gambit, stratagem, **scheme,** design, *ficelle* <Fr>, **subterfuge,** blind, **ruse, wile,** chouse <nonformal>, shift, artful dodge, sleight, pass, feint, fetch, chicanery
VERBS 2 **duck;** take evasive action, zigzag; **sidestep,** parry, fence, ward off; **hedge,** pussyfoot <nonformal>, be *or* sit on the fence, beat around *or* about the bush, hem and haw, beg the question, tapdance <nonformal>, dance around, equivocate

**dog** NOUNS 1 **canine, pooch** *and* bow-wow <both nonformal>; **pup, puppy,** puppy-dog *and* perp <both nonformal>, **whelp;** bitch, toy dog, lap dog; working dog
VERBS 2 **pursue,** prosecute <old>, **follow,** follow up, bay after, run after, **chase, give chase,** chivy; hound

**dogged** ADJS **unfaltering, unwavering,** unflinching; relentless, **unrelenting; obstinate, stubborn**; **unrelaxing,** unfailing, **untiring,** unwearying, unflagging, never-tiring, **tireless,** weariless, **indefatigable; tenacious, persevering**

**dogmatic** ADJS didactic, **positive,** peremptory, pontifical, oracular; **opinionated,** opinionative, conceited; doctrinaire

**dole** NOUNS 1 **welfare,** public welfare, public assistance, relief, relief *or* welfare payments, welfare aid, aid to dependent children; **pittance**
VERBS 2 **parcel out, portion out,** measure out, serve out, spoon *or* ladle *or* dish out, **deal out, dole out, hand out, mete out,** ration out, give out, hand around, pass around; mete, deal; disburse, pay out

**doll** NOUNS

<nonformal> cutie, angel, angelface, babyface, beaut, honey, dream, looker, good-looker, stunner, dazzler, dreamboat, knockout, raving beauty, centerfold, pinup, pussycat <all nonformal>

**domain** NOUNS **sphere, realm,** demesne, dominion, jurisdiction, bailiwick; **province,** precinct, **field,** pale, arena, turf <nonformal>, area, discipline, subdiscipline, orb, orbit, walk; **specialty**

**dome** NOUNS **mountain,** mount, alp, hump, tor, height, dizzying height, nunatak, cupola, geodesic dome; stadium, sports dome, **arena**

**domestic** NOUNS 1 **servant,** servitor, help; domestic help, domestic servant, house servant; live-in help, day help
ADJS 2 **residential,** residentiary; domiciliary, domal; **household;** stay-at-home, homebound

**domesticate** VERBS **set up housekeeping,** keep house; domesticize; tame, break, bust *and* gentle <both nonfor-

mal>, break in, break to harness; housebreak

**dominant** ADJS **chief, main, principal,** paramount, **foremost,** headmost, **leading,** crowning, capital, **cardinal;** ascendant, in the ascendant, in ascendancy, sitting on top of the world *and* sitting pretty <both nonformal>; predominant, preponderant, **paramount, supreme,** number one <nonformal>, hegemonic, hegemonistic

**dominate** VERBS **predominate,** preponderate, prevail; **have the ascendancy, have the upper** *or* **whip hand,** get under control, dictate, lay down the law; **rule the roost** *and* wear the pants *and* crack the whip *and* ride herd <all nonformal>; take the lead

**domineering** ADJS **arrogant, overbearing, superior, proud, haughty; lofty, condescending, patronizing,** *de haut en bas* <Fr>, **bossy** <nonformal>, **highhanded**

**donate** VERBS **give, present, distribute;** deal, dole, mete; **give out, dole out, hand** *or* dish out <nonformal>; make a present of, gift *or* gift with <nonformal>, give as a gift; **give generously,** give the shirt off one's back

**done** ADJS **completed, finished, concluded, terminated, ended,** finished up; signed, sealed, and delivered; **through,** done with; all over with, all said and done, all over but the shouting; **produced, made, caused, brought about;** effectuated, executed, performed; grown, raised

**Don Juan** NOUNS **tempter, seducer, enticer,** inveigler, **charmer,** enchanter, fascinator, tantalizer, teaser; **philanderer,** woman chaser, **ladies' man,** heartbreaker; lady-killer, wolf, skirt chaser; libertine, lecher, cocksman <nonformal>, Casanova

**donkey** NOUNS **ass, burro,** Rocky Mountain canary <W US>; **jackass,** jack; jenny, jenny ass, jennet; **mule,** sumpter mule, sumpter; hinny

**donor** NOUNS **giver,** donator, presenter, bestower, conferrer, grantor, awarder, imparter, vouchsafer; fairy godmother, Lady Bountiful, Santa Claus, sugar daddy <nonformal>; **contributor, subscriber,** supporter, backer, financer, funder, angel <nonformal>; subsidizer; patron, patroness

**doodle** VERBS **scribble,** scrabble, **scratch, scrawl,** make hen tracks *or* hen *or* chicken scratches <nonformal>

**doom** NOUNS 1 **end,** death, death knell, bane, deathblow, death warrant, *coup de grâce* <Fr>, final blow, quietus, cutoff; **destiny, fate,** karma, kismet, what bodes *or* looms, what is fated *or* destined *or* doomed, what is written, what is in the books
VERBS 2 **damn,** send *or* consign to hell, cast into hell, doom to perdition, condemn to hell *or* eternal punishment; **pass judgment, sentence,** pass sentence, hand down a sentence, condemn

**door** NOUNS **entrance,** entry, gate, portal, **entranceway,** entryway; **inlet,** ingress, intake, adit, approach, **access,** means of access, in <nonformal>, way in; **outlet,** egress, **exit,** outgo, outcome, out <nonformal>, way out

**doormat** NOUNS **weakling,** pushover <nonformal>, **wimp,** poor *or* weak *or* dull tool <nonformal>; **nonentity,** hollow man, empty suit *and* nebbish *and* sad sack <all nonformal>

**dope** NOUNS 1 **drug, narcotic,** dangerous drug, controlled substance, abused substance, illegal drug, addictive drug, **hard drug**
2 **stupid person, dolt, dunce,** clod, **dullard,** *niais* <Fr>, donkey, yahoo, thickwit, **nitwit,** dimwit, lackwit, halfwit, lamebrain, putz
VERBS 3 **deaden, numb,** benumb, blunt, dull, obtund, **desensitize; anesthetize, put to sleep,** slip one a Mickey *or* Mickey Finn <nonformal>; narcotize, drug, **medicate,** drug, sedate, dope *or* dope up <nonformal>

**dormant** ADJS **inert, inactive, static,** passive, sedentary; **latent,** unaroused, suspended, abeyant, in suspense *or* abeyance; sleeping, slumbering, smoldering; **inert,** immobile, vegetative, **inactive, idle**; quiescent; hibernating, sleeping

**dose** NOUNS 1 **draft, potion,** portion, **shot,** injection; broken dose; booster, booster dose, recall dose, booster shot
2 **venereal disease** *or* VD, gonorrhea *or* clap *or* the clap *or* claps <nonformal>; dose <nonformal>
VERBS 3 **medicate,** drug, dope <nonformal>; **administer,** dose with, dish out <nonformal>, mete out, prescribe

**dot** NOUNS 1 **fleck, speckle; spot,** polka dot, macula, macule; little *or* wee *or* tiny

bit <nonformal>, bite, **particle,** fragment, spot, **speck,** flyspeck, point, jot, tittle, **iota,** ounce, **dab** <nonformal>, mote, **mite** <nonformal>
VERBS 2 **mottle, dapple,** stipple, **fleck,** flake, **speck, speckle,** bespeckle, freckle, **spot,** bespot, sprinkle, spangle, bespangle, pepper, stud, maculate

**dotty** ADJS **eccentric, queer,** queer in the head, **odd, peculiar,** strange, fey, **crotchety,** quirky, whimsical, twisted; solitary, reclusive, antisocial

**double** NOUNS 1 **perfect** *or* **exact likeness, duplicate;** match, **twin;** living image, very image, very picture, living picture, dead ringer <nonformal>, spitting image *or* spit and image <nonformal>; cookie-cutter copy, clone
2 etheric double *or* self, co-walker, *Doppelgänger* <Ger>, doubleganger, fetch, wraith
VERBS 3 **turn back,** double back, retrace one's steps; **return,** go *or* come back
4 **intensify, reinforce,** redouble, add fuel to the flame *or* the fire; **fold,** fold on itself, fold up; fold over, double over, lap over, turn over *or* under

**double-cross** VERBS **betray, double-cross** *and* two-time <both nonformal>, sell out *and* sell down the river <both nonformal>, turn in; let down *and* let down one's side <both nonformal>; inform on

**double-dealing** NOUNS 1 **treachery,** treacherousness; **perfidy,** perfidiousness, falseheartedness, two-facedness, doubleness; **duplicity, dirty work** *and* dirty pool *and* dirty trick <all nonformal>
ADJS 2 **manipulated, cooked** *and* **doctored** <both nonformal>, juggled, **rigged,** engineered; packed; **shifty,** slippery, tricky; **two-faced**

**double-edged** ADJS **sharp, keen, edged, acute,** fine, **cutting,** knifelike; razor-edged, knife-edged, sharp as broken glass; two-edged

**double-talk** NOUNS 1 **gibberish,** jargon, mumbo jumbo, amphigory, gobbledegook <nonformal>; claptrap, moonshine, empty words, double-speak
VERBS 2 **equivocate,** mystify, obscure, prevaricate, tergiversate, double-speak, tap-dance <nonformal>, palter, fence, parry, shift, **shuffle, dodge,** shy, **evade,** sidestep, hedge, skate around, pussyfoot <nonformal>, evade the issue

**doubt** NOUNS 1 **doubtfulness, dubiousness,** dubiety, dubitancy; half-belief; **reservation, question,** question in one's mind; **skepticism,** Pyrrhonism; **suspicion,** suspiciousness, wariness, leeriness, **distrust, mistrust, misdoubt,** distrustfulness, mistrustfulness, disbelief
VERBS 2 **be doubtful, be dubious, be skeptical,** doubt the truth of, beg leave to doubt, **have one's doubts,** have *or* harbor *or* entertain doubts *or* suspicions, half believe, have reservations, **take with a grain of salt,** be from Missouri <nonformal>, **distrust, mistrust,** misgive, cross one's fingers; **question,** query, **challenge, contest, dispute,** cast doubt on, greet with skepticism, keep one's eye on, treat with reserve, bring *or* call into question, raise a question, throw doubt upon, awake a doubt *or* suspicion

**doubtful** ADJS iffy <nonformal>; **in doubt,** *in dubio* <L>; dubitable, doubtable, **dubious, questionable, problematic, problematical, speculative,** conjectural, suppositional; **unsure, uncertain,** unpredictable

**doubtless** ADVS unquestionably, without question, undoubtedly, beyond the shadow of a doubt, beyond a reasonable doubt, indubitably, admittedly, undeniably, unarguably, indisputably, doubtlessly, without doubt

**doughnut** NOUNS friedcake, sinker <nonformal>, cymbal <old>, olykoek <nonformal>; French doughnut, raised doughnut; glazed doughnut; fastnacht; **cruller,** twister; jelly doughnut

**dour** ADJS **sullen, sulky, surly, morose,** mumpish, dumpish, **glum,** grum, grim; **moody,** moodish; **mopish,** mopey <nonformal>, moping; **glowering,** lowering, **scowling, frowning;** dark, black; black-browed, beetle-browed; dejected, melancholy; **severe,** austere, harsh, hard, stern, unsparing, hard-shell, obdurate, **inflexible,** ironhanded, inexorable, **unyielding,** unbending, **relentless,** unrelenting, procrustean

**douse** VERBS **submerge, dip, duck, dunk** <nonformal>, souse, plunge in water; extinguish, put out, quench, out, **snuff,** snuff out, blow out, stamp out

**dove** NOUNS **pigeon,** squab; **pacifist,** pacificist, peacenik <nonformal>, **peace lover; innocent**, angel

**dovetail** VERBS **harmonize, concur**, have no problem with, go along with <nonformal>, **correspond, conform,** coincide, parallel, intersect, overlap, **match,** tally, hit, register, lock, interlock, square, jibe <nonformal>; **be consistent,** cohere, stand *or* hold *or* hang together, fall in together, fit together

**dowager** NOUNS **woman, matron, widow,** relict; **patrician,** grand dame, lady, person of breeding

**dowdy** ADJS **shabby, shoddy, seedy,** scruffy, **tacky** <nonformal>, tatty, ratty; **out at the elbows,** out at the heels, **down-at-heel**

**down** NOUNS 1 **fluff,** flue, floss, **fuzz, fur,** pile; eiderdown, eider; swansdown; thistledown
2 **plain, moor,** moorland, **downs, heath**
3 **fell, drop, bring down,** fetch down, take down a peg, lay low
ADJS 4 **fallen,** floored, **undone, done for** <nonformal>, **ruined,** kaput *and* on the skids <both nonformal>, *hors de combat* <Fr>

**down-and-out** ADJS **destitute,** in the gutter; **penniless,** moneyless, fortuneless, out of funds, **without a sou,** without one dollar to rub against another; homeless

**downbeat** ADJS **pessimistic,** pessimist, **cynical,** nihilistic; uncheerful; negative, negativistic; defeatist

**downcast** ADJS **dejected, depressed, downhearted, down, cast down,** bowed down, subdued; **discouraged, disheartened, dispirited,** dashed; **in low spirits; down in the mouth** <nonformal>, **in the doldrums, down in the dumps** *and* **in the dumps** <both nonformal>, in the depths

**downfall** NOUNS **collapse, crash,** comedown, breakdown, derailment, **fall,** pratfall <nonformal>, stumble, tumble; nose dive *and* tailspin <both nonformal>; **undoing, ruin,** debacle

**downgrade** VERBS **demote, degrade,** disgrade, debase, abase, humble, humiliate, **lower, reduce,** strip of rank, deplume, displume

**downhearted** ADJS **dejected, depressed, down,** bowed down, subdued; **discouraged, disheartened, dispirited,** dashed; down in the mouth <nonformal>, **in the doldrums, down in the dumps** *and* **in the dumps** *and* in the doleful dumps <all nonformal>, in the depths

**downhill** ADJS 1 descending, falling, dropping, dipping; **declining,** declined; declivous, declivitous, declivate
ADVS 2 **down, downward, downwards,** from the top down, *de haut en bas* <Fr>; downgrade

**downplay** VERBS **minimize,** minify, **belittle,** detract from; play down, underplay, deemphasize, tone *or* tune down; **attach little importance to,** give little weight to; make little of, make light of, think little of, throw away, **make** *or* **think nothing of,** take no account of, set little by, set no store by, set at naught

**downpour** NOUNS **rainstorm, cloudburst,** rainburst, burst of rain, torrent of rain, torrential rain *or* downpour; waterspout, spout, rainspout, downfall, pour, pouring *or* pelting *or* teeming *or* drowning rain, **deluge,** heavy rain, driving *or* gushing rain, drenching *or* soaking rain, lovely weather for ducks

*smoky rain*
CHAUCER

**downstairs** ADVS **down, downward, downwards,** from the top down, *de haut en bas* <Fr>

**downtime** NOUNS **delay,** stoppage, **wait, halt, stay, stop,** break, pause, interim, respite

**down-to-earth** ADJS **unidealistic,** unideal, **unromantic, unsentimental, practical-minded,** sober-minded, sobersided, **hardheaded,** straight-thinking, **with both feet on the ground;** sensible, sane, reasonable, rational, sound, sound-thinking

**downtrodden** ADJS **oppressed;** kept down *or* under, ground down, overborne, trampled; henpecked, browbeaten, ordered *or* kicked around <nonformal>, regimented, tyrannized; treated like dirt under one's feet

**downturn** NOUNS **decline,** declension, **subsidence,** slump <nonformal>, lapse, **drop,** downtick <nonformal>; dwindling, wane, ebb; downtrend, retreat, remission; declination, comedown, downward trend, depreciation, **decrease, drop, fall, plunge,** free-fall, falling-off, lessening, slippage, slump

**downward** ADJS 1 descending, sinking, plunging, down-trending; descendant, on the descendant; declivitous; decurrent, deciduous; **downgoing,** downcom-

ing; down-reaching; plummeting, **sinking,** foundering, setting; declining, **subsiding**
ADVS 2 **downwards,** from the top down, *de haut en bas* <Fr>

**dowry** NOUNS **settlement,** *dot* <Fr>, portion, marriage portion; **dower,** widow's dower

**doze** VERBS **slumber,** rest in the arms of Morpheus; **drowse; nap, catnap,** take a nap, catch a wink

**drab** ADJS **lackluster, lusterless; dull, dead,** deadened, **lifeless,** somber, wan, **flat,** mat

**draft** NOUNS 1 **air current,** current of air, movement of air, stream, stream of air, flow of air
2 **conscription, drafting, induction,** impressment, press; draft call, call-up, summons, call to the colors, letter from Uncle Sam <nonformal>
VERBS 3 **draw off,** draw, draw from; **suck,** suck out *or* up, **siphon off;** tap, broach
4 **sketch,** trace; block in *or* out; rough in, rough out; **write, draw up, write out,** make out; **write down, record**
5 **conscript, induct,** press, impress, commandeer; call up, call to the colors; **recruit, muster,** levy, raise, muster in

**drag** NOUNS 1 **disadvantage, detriment,** impairment; **handicap**, disability; millstone around one's neck
VERBS 2 **pull, draw, heave, haul,** hale, lug, **tug, tow,** take in tow; draggle, snake <nonformal>; troll, trawl
3 **lag, lag behind, straggle,** lag back, trail, **trail behind,** hang back *or* behind, loiter, linger, **loiter** *or* **linger behind,** dawdle, get behind, let grass grow under one's feet, **linger on,** linger, tarry, go on, **go on and on, wear on,** crawl, creep, **drag on,** drag along

**drain** NOUNS 1 **depletion,** exhausting, **exhaustion,** sapping, depreciation, dissipation, impoverishment; **waste,** wastage, wasting away; using up, consumption, expenditure
VERBS 2 **draw off,** draft, draw, draw from; **suck,** suck out *or* up, **siphon off;** decant; exhaust, empty
3 **waste, deplete, depreciate,** dissipate, wear, wear away, erode, ablate, consume, **shrink,** dribble away; squander

**dramatic** ADJS emotive, melodramatic, theatrical, histrionic, overdramatic, hammy <nonformal>, nonrational, unreasoning; overemotional, hyperthymic

**dramatize** VERBS play up <nonformal>, splash, make a production of; overact

**drape** NOUNS 1 screen, shroud, shield, veil, pall, mantle, curtain, hanging, drapery
VERBS 2 **clothe,** enclothe, **dress, garb, attire,** tire, array, **apparel,** raiment, garment, habilitate, **tog** *and* tog out <both nonformal>, robe, enrobe, invest, endue, **deck,** bedeck, wrap, enwrap, lap, envelop, sheathe, shroud, enshroud

**drastic** ADJS **extreme,** outrageous, excessive, exorbitant, unconscionable, intemperate, immoderate, extravagant

**draw** NOUNS 1 **lure,** charm, **come-on** <nonformal>, attention-getter *or* -grabber, **attraction,** crowd-pleaser, headliner; hook *and* gimmick <both nonformal>, drawing card; **decoy,** decoy duck; **bait,** ground bait, baited trap, baited hook; **snare,** trap; **endearment**; the song of the Sirens, the voice of the tempter, honeyed words; forbidden fruit
2 **tie,** dead heat, wash <nonformal>
VERBS 3 **portray, picture,** render, **depict, represent, delineate,** limn, **paint**
4 **attract, pull,** drag, tug, pull *or* draw towards, have an attraction; **lure**

**draw and quarter** VERBS **dismember,** tear limb from limb; **mangle,** lacerate, mutilate, maim

**drawback** NOUNS **disadvantage, liability; detriment,** impairment, prejudice, loss, damage, hurt, harm, mischief, injury; **a step back** *or* **backward,** a loss of ground; **handicap**, disability; drag, millstone around one's neck; objection; **stumbling block,** fly in the ointment, one small difficulty, **hitch, catch,** joker <nonformal>

**drawing** NOUNS 1 **representation, delineation,** presentment, **portrayal, portraiture, depiction,** depictment, rendering, rendition, characterization, limning, imaging
2 **lottery,** sweepstakes *or* sweepstake *or* sweep; draft lottery; **raffle;** grab bag *or* barrel *or* box
3 **pulling,** tractional, tractive, hauling, tugging, towing, towage

**drawing card** NOUNS **lure,** charm, **come-on** <nonformal>, attention-getter *or* -grabber, **attraction, draw** *or* drawer *or* crowd-drawer, crowd-pleaser, headliner;

hook *and* gimmick <both nonformal>

**drawl** NOUNS **accent,** regional accent, brogue, twang, burr, broad accent

**drawn** ADJS **tired-looking, weary-looking, tired-eyed, tired-faced, haggard, hollow-eyed, ravaged, cadaverous, worn, wan, zombiish**

**dread** NOUNS 1 **anxiety, apprehension,** foreboding, tension, stress; **fear; agitation, disquiet,** disquietude, inquietude, unquietness; **nervousness; consternation, dismay;** unholy dread, **terror, horror,** horrification, mortal *or* abject fear; **phobia**
VERBS 2 stand in dread *or* awe of, be in mortal dread *or* terror of, stand in awe of, stand aghast; be on pins and needles, break out in a cold sweat, sweat bullets <nonformal>
ADJS 3 **terrible, horrid, horrible, horrifying,** horrific, horrendous; **dreadful,** dreaded; **awful;** awesome, grim, grisly, gruesome, ghoulish, macabre

**dreadful** ADJS **horrid, horrible,** horrific, **horrifying,** horrendous, unspeakable, beyond words; **atrocious, terrible, rotten,** awful *and* beastly <both nonformal>, **hideous; tragic;** dire, grim, baneful; appalling, shocking, disgusting

**dream** NOUNS 1 **reverie, daydream, pipe dream** <nonformal>; **brown study; vision; nightmare,** incubus, bad dream
VERBS 2 **muse, moon** <nonformal>, **daydream,** pipe-dream <nonformal>, fantasy; be lost in thought, let one's attention wander, let one's mind run on other things, dream of *or* muse on other things; **wander, stray, ramble,** divagate, let one's thoughts *or* mind wander, give oneself up to reverie, **woolgather,** be absent, be somewhere else, stargaze

**dreamland** NOUNS **sleep, slumber;** the arms of Morpheus; **land of Nod,** dreamworld, dreamscape; lotus land, land of dreams, land of enchantment, land of heart's desire, wonderland, cloudland, fairyland, slumberland; light sleep, fitful sleep, **doze, drowse,** snoozle <nonformal>

**dreamy** ADJS **dreamful; dreamy-eyed,** dreamy-minded, dreamy-souled; dreamlike; day-dreamy, **dreaming, daydreaming,** pipe-dreaming <nonformal>, castle-building

**dreary** ADJS **dull, dingy,** dismal, **somber, sober, sad; desolate,** cheerless, joyless, dismal, bleak, **gloomy, murky, grim, somber,** sombrous, **solemn, grave;** drear, drearisome; weary, weariful, wearisome; blah <nonformal>, dryasdust, dusty, **dull**

**dregs** NOUNS 1 **grounds, lees,** dross, slag, draff, scoria, feces; **residue,** leavings, waste, waste product, industrial waste, solid waste, lees, ash; **sediment, settlings, deposits,** deposition
2 **riffraff, trash,** raff, chaff, **rubbish,** sordes, offscourings, off-scum, **scum, scum of the earth, dregs** *or* **scum of society**

**drench** VERBS **soak,** imbrue, **souse, sop,** sodden; **saturate,** permeate; water-soak, waterlog; **steep,** seethe, macerate, infuse, imbue, brew, impregnate, inject; infiltrate, percolate, leach, lixiviate

**dress** NOUNS 1 **clothing, clothes, apparel, wear, wearing apparel, daywear,** dressing, **raiment,** garmenture, **garb, attire, array,** habit, habiliment, fashion, style, guise, **costume,** costumery, gear, toilette, trim
VERBS 2 **clothe,** enclothe, **garb, attire,** tire, array, **apparel,** raiment, garment, habilitate, robe, enrobe, invest, endue, **deck,** bedeck, **groom, brush up, ornament, decorate, adorn, trim, garnish,** array
3 **prepare, make** *or* **get ready,** prep <nonformal>, trim <old>, **ready, fix** <nonformal>; treat, pretreat, process

**dress up** VERBS **get up, doll** *or* **spruce up** <nonformal>, **primp** *and* prink *and* prank <all nonformal>, gussy up <nonformal>, spiff *or* fancy *or* slick up <nonformal>, pretty up <nonformal>, deck out *or* up, trick out *or* up, tog out *or* up <nonformal>

**drift** VERBS **stray,** go astray, lose one's way, err; take a wrong turn *or* turning; go adrift; **wander,** wander off, ramble, rove, straggle, divagate, excurse; meander, wind, twist, snake, twist and turn; **take it easy,** take things as they come, drift with the current, go with the flow, lie *or* rest on one's oars

**drill** NOUNS 1 **exercise,** motion, movement, maneuver; **program,** practice, routine, workout
VERBS 2 **dig,** excavate, tunnel, mine; pierce to the depths; **bore,** auger; **ream,** ream out, countersink, gouge, gouge out; trepan, trephine; punch full of holes, make look like Swiss cheese *or* a sieve, **riddle, honeycomb**

3 **study,** apply oneself to, hit the books <nonformal>; **review; dig** *and* **grind** *and* **bone** *and* bone up on <all nonformal>, **practice**

**drink** NOUNS 1**beverage,** thirst quencher; **soft drink,** nonalcoholic beverage; cold drink; alcoholic beverage, liquor
2 potation, potion, libation; draft, **swig** <nonformal>, swill *and* guzzle <both nonformal>, quaff, **sip,** tot, snort *and* slug <both nonformal>, pull <nonformal>, slurp <nonformal>; nip
VERBS 3 drink in, **imbibe,** wet one's whistle <nonformal>; **quaff, sip, sup,** bib, swig *and* swill *and* guzzle *and* pull <all nonformal>; toss off *or* down, tipple, **booze, tipple, down,** toss off *or* down, knock back, throw one back, **drink hard,** drink like a fish, drink seriously, **tope**

*follow strong drink*
**Bible**

**drip** NOUNS 1 **trickle,** tricklet, **dribble,** dripping, drop, spurtle; seeping, seepage
VERBS 2 **trickle, dribble,** dripple, drop, spurtle; seep, ooze, weep; **gurgle**

**drive** NOUNS 1 **vigor, force,** power, strength, vitality, sinew, sinewiness, nervousness, nervosity, vigorousness, forcefulness, pizzazz *and* punch *and* clout <all nonformal>; driving force *or* power; **motive power**
VERBS 2 **move, actuate,** motivate, push, shove, nudge, impel, propel; **hustle** <nonformal>, drive oneself, **push, scramble,** go all out <nonformal>, **make things hum,** step lively <nonformal>, make the sparks *or* chips fly <nonformal>; enforce, give an impetus, **set going** *or* agoing, put *or* set in motion, give momentum; motivate, incite; compel

**drivel** NOUNS **nonsense, stuff and nonsense,** pack of nonsense, **folderol, balderdash,** *niaiserie* <Fr>, flummery, trumpery, **rubbish,** trash, **humbug,** hocus-pocus; claptrap, fustian, rodomontade, bombast, absurdity

**driver** NOUNS **motorist,** automobilist; **chauffeur;** speeder, road hog <nonformal>, Sunday driver, joyrider <nonformal>; hit-and-run driver

**driving** ADJS **enterprising, aggressive, dynamic,** activist, proactive, forceful, pushing, pushy, up-and-coming, go-ahead *and* hustling <both nonformal>; ambitious; motivating, motivational, motive, moving, animating, actuating, **impelling,** impulsive; **urgent, pressing;** imperative

**droll** ADJS facetious, funny, joshing <nonformal>, **whimsical,** salty, salt, Attic

**drone** NOUNS 1 **nonworker; sponger,** freeloader, lounge lizard <nonformal>, social parasite, parasite
VERBS 2 **hum,** thrum, bombilate, bombinate, **buzz,** whiz, whir, burr, purr; **mumble, mutter,** maunder; drone on; swallow one's words, jabber, gibber, gabble

**drool** NOUNS 1 **saliva, spittle, sputum, spit, expectoration;** salivation, ptyalism, sialorrhea, sialagogue, **slobber,** slabber, slaver, **drivel,** dribble
VERBS 2 **salivate,** ptyalize; **slobber,** slabber, slaver, **drivel,** dribble, dither, blither, blather, maunder, dote, burble

**droop** VERBS **languish, pine, flag, wilt; decline,** lower, **subside,** give way, lapse, cave, cave in; slouch, **sag, slump,** slump down

**drop** NOUNS 1 **descent, descending, dropping, falling,** plummeting, **fall, free-fall,** *chute* <Fr>, **downfall,** debacle, **collapse,** crash
2 **trickle,** tricklet, **dribble, drip,** dripping, seeping, seepage; droplet, **trace,** trace amount, snip, snippet
VERBS 3 **faint, swoon,** succumb, keel over <nonformal>, fall in a faint, fall senseless, **pass** *or* zonk out <nonformal>,
4 **descend, go** *or* **come down,** down, dip down, lose altitude, dump altitude <nonformal>; **fall, fall** *or* drop down; **collapse,** crash, plunge, **plummet; decline,** dip, fall off *or* away, **go downhill; decline, drop off,** fall off, fall away, fall to a low ebb, run low
5 **fell, bring down,** fetch down, down <nonformal>, take down, take down a peg, lay low; **knock down,** dash down, send headlong, **floor,** deck *and* lay out <both nonformal>, lay by the heels, ground, **bowl over** <nonformal>; strike dead, shoot

**drop in** VERBS **visit,** look in, drop by, pop in <nonformal>; **breeze in,** come breezing in; **barge in** *or* come barging in *and* wade in <all nonformal>; intrude; make *or* pay a visit, **call on** *or* **upon,** run *or* stop in, look in, drop around *or* round

**drop in the bucket** NOUNS **pittance,** dole, scrimption <nonformal>; drop in the ocean; **mite,** bit; short allowance, short commons, half rations, cheeseparings and candle ends; mere subsistence, starvation wages; widow's mite

**drop out** VERBS **withdraw, back out,** pull out, stand down <nonformal>; quit cold *and* leave flat <both nonformal>, opt out

**drought** NOUNS **dryness, aridness,** aridity, waterlessness

**drown** VERBS go to a watery grave, go to Davy Jones's locker <nonformal>; **immerse,** immerge, merge, **sink,** bury, engulf, **inundate,** deluge

**drowsy** ADJS **sleepy,** dozy, snoozy <nonformal>, **slumberous,** slumbery, dreamy; **half asleep,** asleep on one's feet; yawny, stretchy <nonformal>, oscitant, yawning, napping, **nodding,** ready for bed

**drub** VERBS **beat, smite,** thump, trounce, baste, **pummel,** pommel, **buffet, belabor,** lay on, **batter,** baste, lambaste; thrash

**drudge** NOUNS 1 **menial,** slavey <nonformal>; scullion
VERBS 2 **grind** *and* **dig** <both nonformal>, fag <Brit>, **grub, toil,** moil, toil and moil, travail, **slog,** peg away *or* along, plug away *or* along <nonformal>, hammer away, pound away, struggle along, struggle on, work away

**drug** NOUNS 1 **medicine, medicament, medication,** medicinal, theraputant, **physic,** preparation, mixture; prescription drug, nonprescription drug; **narcotic drug, controlled substance**
2 narcotic, dope <nonformal>, dangerous drug, controlled substance, abused substance, illegal drug, addictive drug, **hard drug;** soft drug, gateway drug; **opiate; sedative, depressant,** sedative hypnotic, **antipsychotic tranquilizer; hallucinogen,** psychedelic, psychedelic drug, psychoactive drug, psychoactive chemical *or* psychochemical, psychotropic drug, psychotomimetic drug, mind-altering drug, mind-expanding drug, mind-blowing drug; **stimulant; antidepressant; inhalant,** volatile inhalant
VERBS 3 **put to sleep; lull to sleep,** rock to sleep; narcotize, dope <nonformal>; anesthetize, put under; sedate; **medicate,** dope <nonformal>, dose

**drug abuse** NOUNS **substance abuse,** narcotics abuse, drug use, glue-sniffing, solvent abuse; **addiction, addictedness, habit,** drug habit, drug habituation, drug dependence

**drugstore** NOUNS **pharmacy,** chemist *and* chemist's shop <both Brit>, apothecary's shop, dispensary, dispensatory

**drum** VERBS **beat time,** keep time, tap, tap out the rhythm; count, count the beats; beat the drum, play drum *or* the drums, thrum, beat, thump, pound; tomtom; ruffle; beat *or* sound a tattoo

**drunk** NOUNS 1 **drunkard, inebriate, sot,** toper, guzzler, swiller, soaker, lovepot, tosspot, barfly, thirsty soul, **serious drinker,** devotee of Bacchus; swigger; hard drinker, heavy drinker, **alcoholic, dipsomaniac, problem drinker,** chronic alcoholic, chronic drunk, pathological drinker; wino <nonformal>

2 <nonformal> **lush,** lusher, **soak,** sponge, hooch hound, **boozer, boozehound,** booze fighter, booze freak, dipso, juicehead, loadie, ginhound, elbow bender *or* crooker, shikker, bottle sucker, swillbelly, swillpot, swillbowl; **souse, stew,** bum, rummy, rumhound, stewbum; wino

ADJS 3 **intoxicated, inebriated,** inebriate, inebrious, **drunken,** *shikker* <Yiddish>, **tipsy**

4 <nonformal> **in one's cups, under the influence,** the worse for liquor; **tiddly, giddy, dizzy,** muddled, addled, flustered, bemused, reeling, seeing double; **besotted,** sotted, sodden, drenched, fargone; drunk as a lord; staggering drunk; **fuddled,** muzzy, **boozy,** overtaken; **swacked, plastered,** shnockered, stewed, **pickled,** pissed, **soused,** soaked, boiled, fried, canned, tanked, potted, corned, bombed, ripped, smashed; bent, **crocked,** crocko, shellacked, sloshed, sozzled, zonked, tight, lushy, squiffy, afflicted, jug-bitten, oiled, lubricated, feeling no pain, polluted, raddled, organized, **high,** elevated, high as a kite, lit, **lit up,** lit to the gills, illuminated, **loaded, stinko,** tanked, tanked-up, stinking drunk, pie-eyed, pissy-eyed, shitfaced, cockeyed, cockeyed drunk, roaring or rip-roaring

drunk, skunk-drunk; half-seas over, three sheets to the wind, **blotto, stiff** blind, paralyzed, **stoned**

**dry** VERBS 1 **desiccate,** exsiccate, dry up, **dehydrate,** anhydrate; evaporate; dehumidify; torrefy, burn, fire, kiln, **bake, parch,** scorch, sear
ADJS 2 unsweet, unsweetened, sec; **thirsty,** thirsting, athirst; parched, droughty <nonformal>
3 blah <nonformal>, **dreary,** drearisome, dryasdust, dusty, **dull; satiric, satirical; sarcastic, ironic, ironical, sardonic, cynical,** Rabelaisian; caustic
4 **unproductive, barren,** dried-up, sere, exhausted, drained, leached, sucked dry, wasted, gaunt, **waste, desolate,** jejune; arid; **bone-dry,** dry as dust, dry as a bone

**drying** NOUNS 1 **desiccation,** drying up; **dehydration,** anhydration
ADJS 2 **dehydrating, desiccative,** desiccant, exsiccative, exsiccant, siccative, siccant; evaporative

**dry run** NOUNS **tryout,** workout, **rehearsal,** practice; pilot plan *or* program; dummy run; **trial run,** practical test; shakedown, shakedown cruise, bench test; flight test, test flight *or* run; audition, hearing

**dry up** VERBS **shrivel, wither,** sear, parch; **wizen,** weazen; consume, waste, waste away, attenuate, thin, emaciate, macerate; **be consumed, be used up,** waste; **run out, give out,** peter out <nonformal>; run dry

**dubious** ADJS **doubting; skeptical, distrustful, mistrustful,** mistrusting, untrusting; **suspicious,** suspecting, wary, leery
2 **improbable, unlikely,** unpromising, logic-defying, scarcely to be expected *or* anticipated; statistically improbable; **doubtful, questionable,** dubitable, **implausible,** incredible

**duck** VERBS 1 **avoid, evade, dodge,** turn aside *or* to the side, draw aside, **turn away,** jib, shy, shy off; **steer clear of,** tapdance <nonformal>, get out of the way of; **shrink,** wince, cringe, flinch
2 **dip, duck, dunk** <nonformal>, douse, souse, plunge in water; baptize

**dud** NOUNS 1 thing of naught, nullity, zero; **nonentity, nobody** *and* nonstarter *and* nebbish <all nonformal>, nonperson, unperson, cipher, man of straw, jackstraw <old>, lay figure, puppet, dummy, hollow man
2 **flop,** flopperoo, **bust, fizzle,** lemon, clinker, non-starter, **loser, washout,** turkey, bomb, flat failure, dull thud, total loss <all nonformal>

**dude** NOUNS **dandy, fop,** coxcomb, macaroni, gallant, dude *and* swell *and* sport <all nonformal>, ponce *and* toff <both Brit nonformal>, blood, fine gentleman, clotheshorse, fashion plate

**due** NOUNS 1 one's due, what one merits *or* is entitled to, what one has earned, what is owing, what one has coming, what is coming to one, acknowledgment, cognizance, recognition, credit, crediting; **right**
ADJS 2 **owed, owing, payable,** receivable, redeemable, mature, **outstanding, unpaid,** in arrear *or* arrears, back
3 fit, suitable; **proper, correct, decorous,** good, nice, decent, seemly, **appropriate,** fitting, condign, **right and proper,** as it should be, as it ought to be, *comme il faut* <Fr>; kosher *and* according to Hoyle <both nonformal>
4 **attributable, assignable, ascribable, imputable,** traceable, referable, accountable, explicable

**duel** NOUNS 1 single combat, monomachy, satisfaction, **affair of honor,** *affaire d'honneur* <Fr>; **fight, match, bout,** battle, slugfest <nonformal>
VERBS 2 fight a duel, give satisfaction; feud; skirmish; fight the good fight

**dues** NOUNS **fee, toll, charge, charges, demand, exaction,** exactment, scot, shot, scot and lot; **deserts,** just deserts, deservings, merits, due reward *or* punishment, **comeuppance** <nonformal>, all that is coming to one

**duet** NOUNS **couple, pair, matching pair, twosome,** set of two, duo, brace, team, span, yoke, double harness; match, matchup, mates

**duffer** NOUNS 1 **incompetent,** incapable; mediocrity, hacker <nonformal>, no great shakes, no prize, no prize package, no brain surgeon, no rocket scientist
2 **golfer,** player, dub *or* hacker <nonformal>

**dugout** NOUNS **shelter, cover, covert,** coverture; concealment; *abri* <Fr>, cave, earth, foxhole; **bunker**

**dull** ADJS 1 flat, mat, dead, dingy, muddy, leaden, lusterless, lackluster; **faded,**

**washed-out,** dimmed, discolored, etiolated; **pale, dim,** weak, **faint**
2 **lethargic, phlegmatic,** hebetudinous, desensitized, sluggish, torpid, languid, slack, soporific, comatose, **stupefied,** in a stupor, **numb,** numbed, benumbed; blah <nonformal>, **dreary,** drearisome, dry as dust, dusty; humdrum, tiresome
3 dull of mind, **dopey** <nonformal>, **obtuse,** blunt, dim, wooden, heavy, sluggish, slow, **slow-witted,** hebetudinous, **dim-witted, dull-witted, thick-witted,** thick-headed

**dumb** ADJS 1 **mute, mum,** voiceless, tongueless, **speechless,** wordless, breathless, at a loss for words, choked up; inarticulate; **tongue-tied,** dumbstruck, dumbstricken, stricken dumb, **dumbfounded**
2 instinctual *or* instinctive, mindless, nonrational, animal
3 **foolish,** fool <nonformal>, foolheaded <nonformal>, **stupid,** clueless <Brit nonformal>, **asinine, silly,** fatuous, fatuitous, inept, **inane;** futile

**dumbfound** VERBS **astonish, boggle the mind; dumbfound** *or* dumbfounder, strike dumb, strike dead; knock one's socks off *and* bowl over <both nonformal>, **stun, stupefy**

**dummy** NOUNS 1 **figure, figurine; mannequin** *or* manikin, model, lay figure; **fake, rip-off** <nonformal>, **sham, mock, imitation,** simulacrum
ADJS 2 **substitute, alternate, alternative,** other, tother <nonformal>, equivalent, token, pinch, utility, backup, secondary; ad hoc, provisional

**dump** NOUNS 1 **hovel,** rathole, hole, sty, pigsty, pigpen, tumbledown shack
2 **trash pile,** rubbish heap, junkheap *and* junkpile <both nonformal>, scrap heap, dustheap, midden, kitchenmidden; waste-yard, **junkyard** <nonformal>, scrapyard, dumpsite, garbage dump, landfill, sanitary landfill, toxic waste dump
VERBS 3 **discard, reject, throw away, throw out,** chuck *or* chuck away *and* shit-can *and* eighty-six <all nonformal>, cast, cast off *or* away *or* aside; **get rid of, dispose of,** slough, **ditch** <nonformal>, **jettison, throw** *or* **heave** *or* **toss overboard,** deep-six <nonformal>, throw to the dogs, cast to the winds
4 **sell,** unload, flood the market with; sacrifice, sell at a sacrifice *or* loss; undersell, undercut, **unload**

**dumpling** NOUNS ravioli, *kreplach* <Yiddish pl>, won ton; spaetzle, dim sum, gnocchi, matzo balls, *knaydlach* <Yiddish>

**dumps** NOUNS **sulks,** sullens, mumps, grumps <nonformal>, frumps <Brit nonformal>, **blues,** blue devils, mulligrubs, dorts *or* dods <both Scots>, **pouts, doldrums,** dismals, dolefuls <nonformal>, blahs *and* mopes *and* megrims <all nonformal>

**dumpy** ADJS **stubby,** stubbed, stumpy <nonformal>, undergrown, **thickset, stocky,** blocky, **chunky** <nonformal>, **fat, chubby,** tubby <nonformal>; **squat,** squatty, squattish

**dun** VERBS **importune, press,** pressure <nonformal>, prod, prod at, apply *or* exert pressure, push, **ply; beset, buttonhole,** besiege, take *or* grasp by the lapels; pester, plague, nag, nag at, make a pest *or* nuisance of oneself, try one's patience, bug <nonformal>, nudge; **bill,** send a statement; demand payment

**dunce** NOUNS **stupid person, dolt,** clod, Boeotian, **dullard,** *niais* <Fr>, donkey, yahoo, thickwit, **dope, nitwit,** dimwit, lackwit, half-wit, lamebrain, putz, lightweight, witling; **ignoramus, know-nothing;** no scholar, puddinghead, fool

**dune** NOUNS **hill, knoll,** hummock, hammock, eminence, rise, mound, swell, barrow, tumulus, kop, tel, jebel; sand dune, sandhill

**dung** NOUNS **feces,** feculence; **manure, droppings;** cow pats, cow flops <nonformal>; cow chips, buffalo chips; guano

**dunghill** NOUNS **manure pile,** midden, mixen <Brit nonformal>, colluvies

**dunk** VERBS **submerge,** submerse, **immerse,** immerge, merge, **sink,** bury, engulf, **inundate,** deluge, drown, overwhelm, whelm; **dip, duck,** douse, souse

**dupe** NOUNS 1 **gull,** gudgeon, *gobemouches* <Fr>; **victim;** gullible *or* dupable *or* credulous person, trusting *or* simple soul, innocent, *näif* <Fr>, babe, babe in the woods; **figure of fun, butt,** target, stock, **goat** <nonformal>, **fair game,** fool, everybody's fool, monkey, mug <Brit nonformal>; trusting soul; sucker *and* patsy *and* easy mark *and* pushover <all nonformal>
VERBS 2 **deceive, trick, hoax,** gammon, **gull,** pigeon, play one for a fool *or* sucker, **bamboozle** *and* snow *and*

**hornswoggle** *and* diddle *and* scam <all nonformal>, **take in,** put on *and* hocus-pocus <both nonformal>, string along, **put something over** *or* **across,** slip one over on <nonformal>, pull a fast one on

**duplicate** NOUNS 1 **copy, duplication,** dupe *and* ditto <both nonformal>; **double,** cookie-cutter copy, clone; representation, **reproduction, replica,** repro <nonformal>, facsimile, model
VERBS 2 **copy, reproduce,** replicate, dupe <nonformal>; clone
ADJS 3 **identical,** identic; **alike,** just alike, exactly alike, like two peas in a pod; reduplicated, twin

**durable** ADJS **lasting, enduring,** perduring, **abiding, continuing,** remaining, staying, **stable**, persisting, **persistent,** perennial; inveterate, agelong; **steadfast, constant,** intransient, immutable, unfading, evergreen, sempervirent, **permanent**, perennial, **long-lasting,** of long duration *or* standing, diuturnal; **tough, resistant;** shockproof, shock-resistant, impactproof, impact-resistant; **heavy-duty;** hard *or* tough as nails; **strong, hardy,** vigorous

**duration** NOUNS **time,** *durée* <Fr>, lastingness, continuity, term, while, tide, space; **period**, time frame; **chronology**, **term, tenure,** spell

**duress** NOUNS **coercion,** intimidation, scare tactics, headbanging *and* arm-twisting <both nonformal>; **the strong arm** *and* strong-arm tactics <both nonformal>, a pistol *or* gun to one's head, the sword, the mailed fist, the bludgeon, the boot in the face, the jackboot, the big stick, the club, *argumentum baculinum* <L>; **pressure, high pressure,** high-pressure methods; **compulsion**

**dusk** NOUNS dusking time *or* -tide, dusk-dark *and* dust-dark *and* dusty-dark <all nonformal>, **twilight,** evening twilight, crepuscule, crepuscular light, **semidarkness,** semidark, partial darkness, bad light, dim light, half-light, *demi-jour* <Fr>; gloam, **gloaming,** glooming; owl-light *or* owl's light

*the pale dusk of the impending night*
LONGFELLOW

**dust** NOUNS 1 **dirt, grime; powder, soot, smut; particle, particulate,** particulates, airborne particles, air pollution; fallout; cosmic dust
VERBS 2 **clean, cleanse, purge,** deterge, depurate; clean house, spruce, **tidy**; dust off

**dusty** ADJS 1 **dirty, grimy, grubby,** grungy <nonformal>, smirchy, dingy, messy <nonformal>; scruffy, slovenly, untidy; **stale, fusty, musty,** rusty
2 **powdery,** pulverulent, pulverous, lutose; **pulverized,** pulverant, powdered, disintegrated, comminute, gone to dust, reduced to powder; sandy

**duty** NOUNS 1 **obligation,** charge, **onus, burden,** mission, devoir, must, ought, imperative, bounden duty, proper *or* assigned task, what ought to be done, what one is responsible for, where the buck stops <nonformal>

*stern daughter of the voice of God*
WORDSWORTH

2 **task, work, stint, job,** labor, piece of work, **chore,** chare, odd job; **assignment, charge,** project, errand, **mission,** commission; things to do, matters in hand, irons in the fire, fish to fry; homework; busywork, makework

**dwarf** NOUNS 1 **midget,** midge, **pygmy,** manikin, homunculus, atomy, micromorph, hop-o'-my-thumb; Lilliputian, Tom Thumb; **gnome**
VERBS 2 **minimize,** minify, **belittle,** detract from; bedwarf; play down, underplay, downplay, deemphasize

**dwell** VERBS **reside, live, live in, lodge, stay,** remain, abide, hang *or* hang out <nonformal>, domicile, domiciliate

**dwelling** NOUNS **abode, habitation, place,** dwelling place, abiding place, place to live, where one lives *or* resides, where one is at home, roof, roof over one's head, **residence,** place of residence, **domicile,** *domus* <L>; **lodging,** lodgment, lodging place

**dwindle** VERBS **decrease, diminish, lessen; let up,** bate, abate; **decline, subside,** shrink, wane, wither, ebb, ebb away, languish, sink, sag, die down *or* away, wind down, taper off *and* trail off *or* away *and* tail off *or* away <all nonformal>; **drop,** drop off, fall off, fall away, fall to a low ebb, run low

**dying** ADJS **terminal,** expiring, going, slipping, slipping away, sinking, sinking fast, low, despaired of, given up, given up for dead, not long for this world, hopeless, bad, **moribund,** near death, near one's end, at the end of one's rope <nonformal>, done for <nonformal>, at the point of death, **at death's door,** at the portals of death, *in articulo mortis* <L>, *in extremis* <L>, in the jaws of death, facing *or* in the face of death; **on one's last legs** <nonformal>, with one foot in the grave

**dyke** NOUNS lesbian, butch <nonformal>; **amazon,** virago, androgyne

**dynamic** ADJS **kinetic, kinetical, kinematic, kinematical;** geodynamic, radiodynamic, electrodynamic, etc; **enterprising, aggressive,** activist, proactive, driving, forceful, **pushing, up-and-coming, go-ahead** *and* **hustling** <both nonformal>

**dynasty** NOUNS **posterity,** offspring, descendant, heir, inheritor; **successor;** replacement, line, **lineage,** family

# E

**eager** ADJS **active, lively, animated, spirited,** bubbly, ebullient, effervescent, **vivacious, sprightly,** chipper *and* perky <both nonformal>, pert; **spry, breezy, brisk, energetic,** keen, can-do <nonformal>; **enterprising,** venturesome, adventurous, plucky; psyched *or* pumped up <nonformal>, champing at the bit

**eagle eye** ADJS **sharp eye,** keen eye, piercing *or* penetrating eye, gimlet eye, X-ray eye; hawkeye, peeled eye <nonformal>, watchful eye; **weather eye; guard,** guardedness

**earlier** ADJS 1 **previous, prior, early**, *ci-devant* or *ci-dessus* <Fr>, **former,** fore, prime, first, **preceding**, foregoing, above, anterior, **anticipatory,** antecedent; **preexistent**
ADVS 2 **formerly, previously, before,** before now, erenow, erst, whilom, erewhile, **hitherto, heretofore,** thitherto, aforetime, beforetime, **in the past,** in times past

**early** ADJS 1 **former,** past, fore, **previous,** late, recent, **once, onetime,** sometime, **erstwhile,** then, quondam; **prior**; **ancient, immemorial,** primitive, primeval, prehistoric; **old,** olden
ADVS 2 **bright and early, beforehand, beforetime,** early on, betimes, precociously, **ahead of time,** foresightedly, in advance, in anticipation, ahead, before, **with time to spare**

**earmark** VERBS **allot,** lot, **assign, appoint, set,** detail; **allocate,** make assignments *or* allocations, schedule; **set apart** *or* **aside,** tag, mark out for; set off, mark off, portion off; assign to, appropriate to *or* for; reserve, restrict to, restrict; **ordain, destine, fate**

**earn** VERBS 1 **deserve, merit,** rate *and* be in line for <both nonformal>, **be worthy of,** be deserving, richly deserve
2 **be paid, draw wages,** be salaried, work for wages, be remunerated, collect for one's services, get an income, pull down *and* drag down <both nonformal>

**earnest** ADJS **sincere, serious;** loyal, faithful; intent, intent on, resolute; on top of <nonformal>, diligent, assiduous, intense, concentrated

**earnings** NOUNS **gains, profits,** winnings, return, returns, proceeds, **bottom line** <nonformal>, **income; pay,** remuneration, compensation, salary, wage, **wages,** hire

**earth** NOUNS 1 **land, ground,** landmass, **sod,** clod, **soil, dirt,** dust, clay, marl; *terra* <L>, **terra firma;** terrain
ADJS 2 **terrestrial,** earthly, telluric, tellurian

**earthly** ADJS **secular, worldly,** earthy, terrestrial, **mundane,** here-and-now, temporal; **unspiritual, profane,** carnal, materialistic; humanistic, secular-humanistic

**earthy** ADJS **vulgar, uncouth, coarse, gross,** rank, raw, broad, low, foul, gutter; frank, pulling no punches

**ease** NOUNS 1 **rest, repose, relaxation,** slippered *or* unbuttoned ease, decompression <nonformal>; **comfort**; restfulness, quiet, tranquility; inactivity; peace of mind, composure; well-being; contentment; clover, velvet <nonformal>, bed of roses; life of ease; **smoothness, facility; casualness,** offhandedness, **easiness**
VERBS 2 **extenuate, mitigate, palliate,** soften, lessen, diminish, mince; **relax,** unbend; **ease up,** ease off, **let up,** let down; abate, bate, remit, mitigate; **facilitate, grease the wheels** <nonformal>, **smooth, smooth** *or* **pave the way,** ease the way, cushion

**easy** ADJS **slow, leisurely,** slack, moderate, gentle, deliberate, unhurried, laid-back <nonformal>, relaxed, gradual, tentative, cautious, reluctant, foot-dragging <nonformal>; facile, effortless, smooth, painless

2 <nonformal> **cinch, snap,** pushover, breeze, waltz, duck soup, velvet, picnic, pie, cherry pie, apple pie, cakewalk, piece of cake <Brit>, kid stuff, turkey shoot, no-brainer, setup

**easygoing** ADJS **casual, offhand, relaxed, laid-back** *and* throwaway <both nonformal>; easy, free and easy, devil-may-care, lackadaisical, *dégagé* <Fr>

**eat** VERBS **feed,** fare, take, partake, partake of, break bread, break one's fast; refresh *or* entertain the inner man, feed one's face *and* put on the feed bag <both nonformal>, fall to, pitch in <nonformal>

**eavesdrop** VERBS **listen in;** wiretap, tap, intercept, bug <nonformal>; **keep one's ears open,** be all ears <nonformal>, listen with both ears, strain one's ears

**ebb** VERBS **diminish,** decline, sink, shrink, dwindle, **fade,** wane; go out with the tide, fade into the distance; **subside,** wither, ebb away, dwindle, languish, sink, sag, die down *or* away, wind down, taper off *and* trail off *or* away *and* tail off *or* away <all nonformal>

**eccentric** NOUNS 1 erratic, character; odd person; **nonconformist**, recluse
ADJS 2 **erratic,** idiocratic, idiocratical, idiosyncratic, idiosyncratical, **queer,** queer in the head, **odd, peculiar,** strange, fey, singular, anomalous, freakish, funny; unnatural, abnormal, irregular, divergent, deviative, deviant, different, exceptional; unconventional; solitary, reclusive, antisocial

3 <nonformal> **kooky, goofy,** birdy, funny, kinky, loopy, goofus, haywire, squirrely, screwy, screwball, nutty, wacky, flaky, oddball, wacky, wacko, lunch, out to lunch, nobody home, weird

**ecclesiastic** ADJS **ecclesiastical, churchly; ministerial, clerical,** sacerdotal, **pastoral**

**echo** NOUNS 1 **reverberation, resounding;** rebound, resound, reecho
VERBS 2 **reverberate, resound,** sound, **rumble,** roll, boom, reecho, rebound, bounce back, be reflected, be sent back, echo back, send back, return; **respond, react,** be moved, be affected *or* touched, be inspired, catch the flame *or* infection, be in tune; **mirror, reflect; reproduce, duplicate**, reduplicate, double, redouble, ditto <nonformal>, **parrot**

**eclipse** NOUNS 1 occultation; total eclipse, partial eclipse, central eclipse, annular eclipse; solar eclipse, lunar eclipse; blocking, blotting out, eclipsing
VERBS 2 **overshadow, throw into the shade,** extinguish; **cover,** cover up; obscure, block, occult, occultate, block the light

**economical** ADJS **thrifty, frugal,** unwasteful, conserving, **saving,** economizing, spare, **sparing; prudent,** prudential, provident, forehanded; careful, chary, canny; scrimping, skimping <nonformal>, cheeseparing; penny-wise; **parsimonious; cost-effective, cost-efficient; efficient,** labor-saving, time-saving, money-saving

**economics** NOUNS economic science, the dismal science; political economy; dynamic economics; theoretical economics, plutology; classical economics; Keynesian economics, Keynesianism; supply side economics

**economy** NOUNS 1 **thrift, thriftiness, frugality,** frugalness; tight purse strings; parsimony, **parsimoniousness**; care, chariness, canniness; **prudence,** providence, forehandedness; **husbandry,** management, good management *or* stewardship, prudent administration; **austerity,** austerity program, belt-tightening
2 **economic system,** capitalist *or* capitalistic economy, free-enterprise *or* private-enterprise economy, market economy, socialist *or* socialistic economy, collectivized economy

**ecstasy** NOUNS 1 **passion,** passionateness, strong feeling, powerful emotion; **ardor, ardency,** *empressement* <Fr>, warmth of feeling, **warmth, heat, fire, excitement**
2 **trance,** ecstasis, transport, mystic transport; **rapture;** yoga trance, dharana, dhyana, samadhi

**ecstatic** ADJS **overjoyed,** brimming *or* bursting with happiness, on top of the world; **rapturous,** raptured, **enraptured, enchanted,** entranced, enravished, ravished, rapt, possessed; sent *and* high *and* freaked-out <all nonformal>, **in raptures,** transported, in a transport of delight, **carried away,** rapt *or* ravished away, beside oneself, beside oneself with joy, all over oneself <nonformal>; **elated,** elate, exalted, jubilant, exultant, flushed

**edge** NOUNS **border,** limbus, bordure <heraldry>, limb, **verge, brink,** brow, **brim, rim, margin, fringe,** selvage *or* selvedge; **advantage,** vantage, odds, leg up *and* inside track *and* pole position <all nonformal>; **upper hand,** whip hand
2 **sharpness, keenness,** acuteness, acuity; **pointedness,** acumination
VERBS 3 **border, bound, rim, skirt, hem in,** befringe, marginate, verge, trim, bind
4 **go sideways, sidle,** lateral, lateralize, **veer, angle, slant, skew,** sidestep

**edgy** ADJS **nervous, uneasy, apprehensive,** qualmish, nail-biting, white-knuckle <nonformal>, nervous as a cat; **irritable, on edge,** nerves on edge, on the ragged edge <nonformal>, panicky, **fearful, frightened**

**edible** ADJS **eatable,** comestible, gustable, esculent; **palatable**

**edict** NOUNS **decree,** decretum, decretal, rescript, fiat, *edictum* <L>; **proclamation,** pronouncement, pronunciamento, **declaration,** ukase; bull, brevet <old>; diktat

**edit** VERBS **comment upon,** commentate, remark upon; **annotate,** gloss; **revise,** redact, recense, **revamp, rewrite,** redraft, **rework,** work over; blue-pencil

**edition** NOUNS issue; volume, number; **printing,** impression, print order, print run; copy; library edition; **trade edition,** subscription edition; school edition, text edition

**editorial** NOUNS **commentary,** criticism, critique, *compte-rendu critique* <Fr>, analysis; **review,** critical review, **report,** notice, **write-up** <nonformal>; leading article *or* leader <both Brit>

**educate** VERBS **teach, instruct,** give instruction, give lessons in, **school; edify, enlighten,** civilize, illumine; **direct, guide; inform**; enlarge *or* broaden the mind; **ground,** teach the rudiments *or* elements *or* basics; catechize

**educated** ADJS **informed, enlightened, instructed,** versed, well-versed, schooled, **taught; learned, erudite, cultured,** cultivated, lettered, literate, civilized, **scholarly,** scholastic, studious

**education** NOUNS **teaching, instruction, schooling, tuition; edification, enlightenment,** illumination; tutelage, **pedagogy,** pedagogics, didactics, didacticism; catechization; **learning,** acquisition of knowledge

**educational** ADJS **informative,** informing, informational; **instructive, enlightening;** educative, advisory, monitory

**eerie** ADJS **creepy, weird, uncanny,** unco *or* uncolike <both Scots>; unearthly, unworldly, otherworldly; fey; mysterious, macabre; **spooky** *and* spookish *and* hairy <all nonformal>

**effect** NOUNS 1 **result,** resultant, **consequence,** consequent, sequent, sequence, sequel, sequela, sequelae; event, eventuality, eventuation, **upshot, outcome,** logical outcome, possible outcome, scenario; **outgrowth,** spin-off, offshoot, offspring, issue, aftermath, legacy; **product, fruit,** first fruits, development, by-product
VERBS 2 effectuate, **make; bring about,** bring to pass, **bring off, produce, deliver** <nonformal>, **do the trick,** put across *or* through; swing *or* swing it *and* hack it *and* cut it *and* cut the mustard <all nonformal>; **cause,** be the cause of, lie at the root of; **bring about, bring to pass,** realize; **occasion, engender,** generate, breed, **induce,** lead, procure, get, obtain, contrive, **bring on**

**effective** ADJS **effectual,** active, efficient, efficacious, operative, telling; **practical,** practicable, pragmatic *or* pragmatical, banausic; feasible, workable, operable, realizable

**effects** NOUNS **property, possessions, holdings,** havings, goods, chattels, goods and chattels, estate and effects, what one can call one's own, what one has to one's name, all one owns *or* has, all one can lay claim to, one's all; household possessions *or* effects, lares and penates

**effeminate** ADJS **frail, slight, delicate, dainty,** puny; light, lightweight; womanish, **unmanly,** soft, prissy, **sissified,** sissy, **sissyish**

*delicately weak*
POPE

**effervescent** ADJS **bubbly,** burbly, **bubbling,** burbling; spumescent, **fizzy, sparkling,** *mousseux* <Fr>, *spumante* <Ital>; carbonated; ebullient, lively, animated, spirited, **vivacious, sprightly,** chipper *and* perky <both nonformal>, pert; alive, live, full of life, **peppy** *and* snappy *and* zingy <all nonformal>; frisky, bouncing, bouncy

**efficiency** NOUNS **capacity,** potentiality, faculty, facility, fitness, qualification, talent, flair, genius, caliber, **competence,** competency, adequacy, sufficiency, efficacy; **utility, usefulness,** avail, good, serviceability, functionality, **practicability,** practicality, practical utility, **effectiveness**

**efficient** ADJS 1 **competent, capable, able, qualified, fit, fitted, suited, worthy;** up to snuff <nonformal>, up to the mark <nonformal>, *au fait* <Fr>

2 **practical,** practicable, pragmatic *or* pragmatical, banausic; feasible, workable, operable, realizable; effective, **effectual**

**effort** NOUNS **endeavor,** striving, struggle, strain; **all-out effort,** best effort, college try *or* old college try <nonformal>; **exertion, energy,** elbow grease; **trouble, pains;** great *or* mighty effort, might and main, muscle, one's back, nerve, and sinew, hard *or* strong *or* long pull

*a long pull, a strong pull, and a pull all together*
DICKENS

**egghead** NOUNS **intellectual, intellect,** member of the intelligentsia, white-collar intellectual; **brain** *and* rocket scientist *and* brain surgeon <all nonformal>; pointy-head <nonformal>; **highbrow** <nonformal>

*someone whose mind watches itself*
CAMUS

**ego** NOUNS **egotism, egoism,** egoisticalness, egotisticalness, self-interest, individualism, **egocentricity,** egocentrism, self-centeredness, self-centerment, self-obsession; selfishness; **self, oneself,** the self, the I

*the tongue of vanity*
CHAMFORT

**egotistical** ADJS **egotistic,** egoistic, egoistical, self-interested; **egocentric,** egocentristic, self-centered, self-obsessed, narcissistic

**ego trip** NOUNS **self-satisfaction, self-content,** self-approbation, self-congratulation, self-gratulation, self-complacency, **smugness,** complacency; **narcissism, self-love,** self-devotion, self-jealousy, **self-consideration,** self-absorption, self-occupation

**eject** VERBS **expel, discharge,** extrude, obtrude, detrude, exclude, **reject,** cast, remove; **oust, bounce** *and* give the hook <both nonformal>, **put out, turn out,** thrust out; **throw out,** run out <nonformal>, cast out, chuck out, toss out, heave out; kick *or* boot out <nonformal>; give the bum's rush *or* give the old heave-ho *or* throw out on one's ear <all nonformal>; defenestrate; jettison

**eke out** VERBS **support oneself,** make one's way; **make ends meet, keep body and soul together, keep the wolf from the door,** keep *or* hold one's head above water, keep afloat; **survive, subsist, cope,** make out, scrape along, manage, get by; fill out, piece out, top off, round out

**elaborate** VERBS **develop, work out,** enlarge, enlarge on *or* upon, amplify, **expand,** expand on *or* upon, detail, go *or* enter into detail, go into, flesh out, **pursue,** spell out <nonformal>; complete

**elaborate** ADJS 1 **painstaking, diligent, assiduous,** sedulous, **thorough, thoroughgoing,** operose, industrious
2 **complex, ramified, intricate,** involuted, convoluted, multilayered, multilevel

**elapse** VERBS lapse, **pass, expire,** run its course, run out, go *or* pass by; **flow,** tick away *or* by *or* on, run, proceed, advance, roll *or* press on, flit, fly, slip, slide, glide; **continue**, last, **endure,** go *or* run *or* flow on

**elastic** ADJS resilient, springy, bouncy; **stretchable, stretchy,** stretch; extensile; **flexible**; flexile; **adaptable,** adaptive, responsive; buoyant; lively

**elate** VERBS **exalt,** elevate, lift, uplift, flush; **make proud,** do one's heart good, do one proud <nonformal>, **gratify,** turn one's head

**elbow** VERBS **bump,** jog, joggle, jolt, shake, rattle; **jostle,** shoulder

**elder** ADJS **older,** senior, major, dean

**elect** NOUNS 1 **the best,** the very best, the best ever, the top of the heap *or* the line <nonformal>, the tops <nonformal>; **choice, pick, select, elite,** chosen; **cream, flower,** cream of the crop, *crème de la crème* <Fr>, salt of the earth
VERBS 2 **choose,** pick, go with <nonformal>, opt, opt for, co-opt, make *or* take one's choice, make choice of, have one's druthers <nonformal>, use *or* take up *or* exercise one's option; vote in, place in office

**election** NOUNS **choice, selection,** preference, decision, **pick, choosing,** free choice; appointment; general election, by-election; congressional election, presidential election

**elective** ADJS volitional, voluntary, volitive; **optional,** discretional; **alternative,** disjunctive

**electric chair** NOUNS death chair, the chair <nonformal>, hot seat <nonformal>

**electrify** VERBS **stimulate,** hearten, **galvanize,** fire, build a fire under, inflame, charge up, psych *or* pump up <nonformal>, rouse, arouse, act like a tonic, be a shot in the arm <nonformal>, pep *or* snap *or* jazz *or* zip *or* perk up <nonformal>, put pep *or* zip into it <nonformal>

**elegance** NOUNS elegancy; **grace,** gracefulness, gracility; **taste,** tastefulness, good taste; **correctness,** seemliness, comeliness, **propriety,** aptness, fittingness; **refinement,** precision, exactitude, lapidary quality, finish; **smartness, chic**

**elegant** ADJS graceful, gracile, gracious; **refined, polished, cultivated,** civilized, **cultured;** nice, fine, delicate, dainty, **subtle, sophisticated, discriminating**, fastidious

**elegy** NOUNS **dirge, funeral** *or* **death song,** coronach, keen, epicedium, requiem, monody, threnody, threnode, muffled drums

**element** NOUNS **component, constituent, ingredient,** integrant, makings *and* fixings <both nonformal>, **factor, part**, module, part and parcel; appurtenance, adjunct; **feature,** aspect, specialty, circumstance, detail, item

**elementary** ADJS **original, primary,** primal, primitive, pristine, primeval, aboriginal, elemental, **basic,** basal, **rudimentary,** crucial, central, radical, **fundamental;** embryonic, germinal, seminal

**elementary school** NOUNS **grade school** *or* graded school, the grades; **primary school;** junior school <Brit>; **grammar school;** folk school, *Volksschule* <Ger>

**elevate** VERBS **raise, rear,** escalate, up, boost *and* hike <both nonformal>; **erect, heighten, lift,** levitate, boost <nonformal>, **hoist,** heft, heave; raise up, rear up, lift up, hold up, set up; stick up, cock up, perk up; buoy up, upbuoy; **upraise, uplift, exalt,** ensky; deify, apotheosize; put on a pedestal

**elicit** VERBS educe, deduce, induce, derive, obtain, procure, secure; **get from,** get out of; rouse, arouse, stimulate; **draw out** *or* **forth,** bring out *or* forth, pry *or* prize out, drag out, worm out, bring to light; **prompt, provoke, evoke,** call forth, inspire; bring about, cause

**eligible** ADJS **qualified, fit,** fitted, **suitable,** acceptable, admissible, worthy, desirable; with voice, with vote, with voice and vote, enfranchised

**eliminate** VERBS get rid of, rid oneself of, **get quit of,** get shut of <nonformal>, **dispose of, remove,** abstract, eject, expel, give the bum's rush <nonformal>, cast off *or* out, chuck <nonformal>, throw over *or* overboard <nonformal>; **weed out,** pick out; **cut out,** strike off *or* out, elide; eradicate, root up *or* out; **purge, liquidate**

**elite** NOUNS 1 **the best,** the very best, the best ever, the top of the heap *or* the line <nonformal>, the tops <nonformal>; nonesuch, paragon, nonpareil; gem of the first water
ADJS 2 **exclusive,** selective, **select,** elect; socially prominent, in society, high-society; jet-set; lace-curtain, silk-stocking; **choice, select, elect,** hand-picked

**eloquence** NOUNS **rhetoric, silver tongue,** eloquent tongue; **articulateness;** gift of gab <nonformal>, **glibness,** smoothness, slickness; **felicitousness,** felicity; **oratory**; expression, **expressiveness,** command of words *or* language, gift of gab *or* of the gab <nonformal>, gift of expression

**elude** VERBS **evade,** get away from, give the runaround *or* the slip <nonformal>; throw off the scent; lead one a merry chase, frustrate, foil, **circumvent**

**emancipated** ADJS **liberated, freed, released;** delivered, rescued, ransomed, redeemed; extricated, unbound, untied, unshackled

**emasculate** VERBS **unman, unnerve, enervate,** exhaust, incapacitate, **disable**, etiolate; cut the balls off <nonformal>, demasculinize, effeminize; castrate, geld, eunuchize, neuter, spay, fix *or* alter <both nonformal>, unsex, deball <nonformal>

**embankment** NOUNS **shore,** bank; roadway, roadbed, retaining wall, bulkhead, bulkheading, plank buttress, piling, levee, dike

**embargo** NOUNS **ban, enjoinder, injunction,** prohibitory injunction, **proscription,** inhibition, **interdict,** *interdictum* <L>, interdiction; **restriction,** prohibition

**embark** VERBS **go aboard,** board, go on board; go on shipboard, take ship; hoist the blue Peter; **entrain,** enplane *or* emplane, embus; weigh anchor, up-anchor, put to sea

**embarrass** VERBS **chagrin, abash, discomfit, disconcert,** discompose, confuse, throw into confusion *or* a tizzy, **upset,** pother, **bother,** flummox <nonformal>, confound, cast down, mortify, put out, put out of face *or* countenance, put to the blush; **mortify,** humiliate, disturb; **hamper, impede, cramp, put in a hole** <nonformal>, put in a spot <nonformal>

**embarrassed** ADJS **distressed, uncomfortable,** uneasy, ill at ease; **chagrined,** abashed, discomfited, **disconcerted, upset, confused,** mortified, **put-out,** out of countenance, cast down, chapfallen; in debt, plunged in debt, in difficulties, in embarrassed circumstances, in the hole *and* in hock <both nonformal>, in the red; **bewildered, dismayed,** distracted, distraught, discomposed, perturbed, **bothered,** all hot and bothered <nonformal>

**embassy** NOUNS **foreign office, legation;** consulate, chancery, chancellery

**embattled** ADJS battled, **engaged,** at grips, in combat; **arrayed, deployed,** ranged, in battle array, in the field; war-ravaged, war-torn

**embed** VERBS internalize, put in, keep within; enclose, surround, contain, comprise, include, enfold, take to heart, assimilate; infix, ingrain, set in, plant, implant, engraft, bed

**embellish** VERBS **develop,** elaborate; beautify, furbish, embroider, enrich, grace, set off *or* out, paint, color, blazon, emblazon, paint in glowing colors; **dress up; spruce up** *and* gussy up *and* doll up *and* fix up <all nonformal>, **ornament, decorate, adorn,** enrich; paint in glowing colors, tell in glowing terms

*to gild refined gold, to paint the lily, to throw a perfume on the violet*
SHAKESPEARE

**embellishment** NOUNS **ornamentation, decoration, adornment,** embroidery, elaboration; nonfunctional addition *or* adjunct; garnish, garnishment, garniture; **ornament,** grace, arabesque, *fioritura* <Ital>; **padding, filling;** pleonasm, tautology; verbosity, prolixity

**ember** NOUNS live coal, brand, firebrand, burning ember

**embezzle** VERBS divert, **misappropriate,** convert, defalcate <old>, peculate, feather one's nest <nonformal>; pervert, prostitute; have one's hand in the till; **pilfer, filch**

**emblem** NOUNS **symbol, icon, token, insignia, regalia,** ensign, **badge,** logo <nonformal>, marking, attribute

**embodiment** NOUNS **incarnation,** materialization, substantiation, concretization, hypostasis, reification; **essence, substance,** stuff, very stuff, inner essence, essential nature, quiddity; **quintessence, epitome,** perfect example *or* exemplar; **whole, totality, entirety,** collectivity; integration, incorporation

**embody** VERBS incarnate, **materialize,** concretize, lend substance to, reify, entify, hypostatize; **compose, constitute,** construct, fabricate; **incorporate,** embody, corporify, personify

**embossed** ADJS **in relief,** chased, bossed, hammered, toreutic; *repoussé* <Fr>; **infixed,** inwrought; impressed, indelibly impressed, imprinted; engraved, etched, graven

**embrace** NOUNS 1 **hug, squeeze,** fond embrace, embracement, clasp, enfoldment, bear hug <nonformal>
VERBS 2 **hug, clasp, press, squeeze** <nonformal>, fold, **enfold,** bosom, embosom, put *or* throw one's arms around, take to *or* in one's arms, fold to the heart, press to the bosom
3 **comprise, comprehend,** hold, **take in;** encompass, enclose, encircle, incorporate, assimilate, embody, admit, receive, envisage

**embroider** VERBS **ornament, embellish,** enrich; festoon, weight down with ornament, gild the lily, trick out, varnish; paint in glowing colors, tell in glowing terms

**embryo** NOUNS zygote, oösperm, oöspore, blastula; *Anlage* <Ger>; **fetus,** germ, rudiment; **larva,** nymph

**emerge** VERBS **come out, issue,** issue forth, come into view, extrude, **come forth; surface,** rise to the surface; sally, sally forth, come to the fore; emanate, effuse, arise, come; debouch, disembogue; jump out, leap out, hop out; bail out; **burst forth, break forth, erupt;** break cover, **come out in the open;** protrude

**emergency** NOUNS exigency, juncture *or* conjuncture *or* convergence of events, critical juncture, crossroads; **pinch,** clutch <nonformal>, rub, push, pass, strait, extremity, spot <nonformal>; state of emergency, red alert, race against time; **crisis,** hot spot, nasty *or* tricky spot, pass, pinch, strait, plight, predicament

**emergent** ADJS **emerging, issuing,** arising, surfacing, coming, forthcoming; emanating, emanent, emanative, transient; projected, plotted, planned, looked- *or* hoped-for, desired, **predicted,** prophesied, foreseen, anticipated, anticipatory, previsional, prevenient, envisioned, envisaged, probable, extrapolated

**emigrant** NOUNS **migrant,** migrator, trekker; out-migrant, *émigré* <Fr>; expatriate; **evacuee,** exile; outgoer, leaver, departer

**emigrate** VERBS **leave home,** go from home; leave the country, out-migrate, expatriate, defect; vote with one's feet; burn one's bridges

**eminent** ADJS **prominent,** outstanding, standout, high, elevated, towering, soaring, overtopping, exalted, **lofty,** sublime; august, majestic, noble, distinguished; **magnificent,** magnanimous, heroic, godlike, superb; famous, renowned, lauded, glorious; **distinguished;** prestigious, esteemed, estimable, reputable; **extraordinary,** *extraordinaire* <Fr>, out of the ordinary, **exceptional, special,** rare

**emissary** NOUNS envoy, legate, minister, foreign service officer; envoy extraordinary, plentipotentiary, nuncio, internuncio, apostolic delegate

**emit** VERBS **exude,** transude; effuse, extravasate; **issue, bring out, put out, get out,** put *or* give *or* send forth; put *or* set forth, pour forth; give vent to, give out *or* off, throw off, blow off

**emotion** NOUNS **feeling, affect, sentiment,** affection, affections; affective faculty, affectivity; emotional charge, cathexis; **feelings, sensitiveness, sensibility,** susceptibility, thin skin; the logic of the heart; feeling tone, affectivity, emotivity

**emotional** ADJS **affective,** emotive, affectional, **feeling;** soulful, of soul, of heart, of feeling, of sentiment; visceral, gut <nonformal>; demonstrative, overdemonstrative; **excitable,** highly emotional, overemotional, hyperthymic, perturbable, flappable <nonformal>, agitable

**empathy** NOUNS **affinity,** identification; involvement, sharing; pathos; identity, feeling of identity, fellow feeling, **fellowship,** kinship, togetherness

**emphasis** NOUNS **accent,** accentuation, rhythmical accent *or* accentuation, ictus, stress arsis, thesis

**emphasize** VERBS **stress,** lay emphasis *or* stress upon, feature, highlight, bright-line, place emphasis on, give emphasis to, **accent, accentuate, punctuate, point up,** bring to the fore, put in the foreground; prioritize; **highlight,** spotlight; harp on; dwell on, belabor; attach too much importance to, make a big deal *or* Federal case of <nonformal>, make a mountain out of a molehill

**emphatic** ADJS **decided, positive, forceful,** forcible; **emphasized, stressed,** accented, accentuated, punctuated, pointed; underlined, underscored, italicized; red-letter, in red letters, in letters of fire

**employ** VERBS 1 **use, utilize, make use of,** do with; practice, ply, work, manage, handle, manipulate, operate, **wield,** play; **occupy, engage, busy,** devote, spend, occupy oneself, busy oneself, go about one's business, devote oneself
2 **hire,** give a job to, take into employment, take into one's service, take on <nonformal>, recruit, headhunt <nonformal>, **engage,** sign up *or* on <nonformal>

**employee** NOUNS hired man, hired hand, man *or* girl Friday, right-hand man, assistant; **worker, laborer, toiler,** moiler; member of the working class, blue-collar *or* lunch-bucket worker, stiff *and* working stiff <both nonformal>; staff member

**empower** VERBS **enable;** invest, clothe, invest *or* clothe with power, deputize; enfranchise; endue, endow, **commission, authorize,** accredit; arm

**empty** ADJS **vacant,** hollow, inane, **bare, vacuous, void,** without content, with nothing inside, devoid, null, null and void; **blank,** clear, white, bleached; featureless, unrelieved, characterless, bland, insipid; **barren, vain, futile,** hollow, fatuous, fatuitous; **baseless, groundless,** ungrounded, **unfounded,**

ill-founded, unbased, **unsupported,** unsustained, **without foundation,** without basis *or* sound basis; **untenable, unsupportable,** unsustainable; **unwarranted,** idle, inane, vacuous

**enable** VERBS **empower,** give power, entitle; **license; make possible, permit, clear the road** *or* path for, smooth the way for, open the way for, open the door to, open up the possibility of

**enact** VERBS **perform, execute; transact; discharge, dispatch;** conduct, **manage, handle;** dispose of, take care of, **deal with,** cope with; **make, accomplish,** complete; effect, effectuate, compass, consummate, do, deliver, fulfill, realize, attain; **legislate,** make *or* enact laws, **pass,** constitute, ordain, put in force; **put through, jam** *or* **steamroller** *or* **railroad through** <nonformal>, lobby through

**enamored** ADJS **charmed,** becharmed, **fascinated, captivated,** bewitched, enraptured, enchanted; **infatuated,** infatuate; **smitten,** heartsmitten, heartstruck, lovestruck

**enchant** VERBS **delight,** delectate, **tickle, titillate, thrill, enrapture, enthrall,** entrance, fascinate, captivate, bewitch, **charm,** becharm; enravish, ravish, imparadise; ecstasiate, transport, carry away

**enchanted** ADJS **charmed,** becharmed, charmstruck, charm-bound; **spellbound,** spell-struck, spell-caught; **fascinated,** captivated; **hypnotized, mesmerized;** under a spell, in a trance

**enclose** VERBS **close in,** bound, include, **contain;** compass, encompass; **surround,** encircle; **shut** *or* **pen in,** coop in; **fence in,** wall in, wall up, rail in, rail off, screen off, curtain off; **hem** *or* **hedge in,** box in, pocket; shut *or* coop *or* mew up; **embrace,** encompass, encircle, incorporate, assimilate, embody

**enclosure** NOUNS 1 **confinement,** containing, containment, circumscription, immurement, walling- *or* hedging- *or* hemming- *or* boxing- *or* fencing- *or* walling-in; **imprisonment,** incarceration, jailing, locking-up, lockdown; inclusion; **envelopment**
2 close, **confine,** precinct, enclave, pale, paling, list, cincture; **cloister; pen, coop,** fold

**encompass** VERBS **extend,** span, straddle, take in, hold, surround, environ; **envelop,** enfold, lap, wrap, enwrap, embrace, **encircle**, girdle; **include, number, comprise, contain, comprehend; cover,** incorporate, assimilate, embody, admit, receive, envisage; **total, amount to, come to, run to** *or* **into,** mount up to, add up to, tot *or* tot up to <nonformal>, tote *or* tote up to <nonformal>, reckon up to <nonformal>, aggregate to; aggregate

**encore** NOUNS 1 repeat performance, repeat, **reprise;** replay, replaying, return match
ADVS 2 **again,** over, over again, **once more,** *encore, bis* <both Fr>, two times, twice over, ditto; **anew,** *de novo* <L>, afresh; from the beginning, *da capo* <Ital>
INTER 3 **bravo!,** bravissimo!, **well done!,** *¡ole!* <Sp>, *bene!* <Ital>, hear, hear!, bis!

**encounter** NOUNS 1 **meeting,** meeting up, joining, joining up; near-miss, collision course, near thing, narrow squeak *or* brush; **contest, engagement, match, trial, test,** *concours* and *rencontre* <both Fr>
VERBS 2 **meet, come across, run across,** meet up, fall across, cross the path of; **come upon,** run upon, fall upon, light *or* alight upon; come among, fall among; **meet with,** meet up with <nonformal>, come face to face with, **come** *or* **go up against**

**encourage** VERBS **hearten, embolden,** give encouragement, pat *or* clap on the back, stroke <nonformal>; **invite,** ask for; **abet,** aid and abet, countenance, keep in countenance; **foster, nurture,** nourish, feed; **inspire,** inspirit; buck *or* brace up <nonformal>

**encouraging** ADJS **heartening,** heartwarming; **inspiring,** inspiriting; **exhilarating,** animating, enlivening, invigorating; cheerful, cheery, glad, joyful; **auspicious, propitious**; cheering, reassuring, supportive

**encroach** VERBS **intrude,** obtrude, **interlope;** infringe, impinge, **trespass,** trespass on *or* upon, trench, entrench, overstep the bounds, go too far, know no bounds, invade, infiltrate; **break in upon,** break in, burst in, charge in, crash in, smash in, storm in; **barge in**

**encumbered** ADJS **burdened, oppressed,** laden, cumbered, charged, loaded, fraught, freighted, taxed, saddled, hampered; **overburdened,** overloaded, overladen, overfraught, overweighted, overtaxed; **in debt,** plunged in debt, in difficulties, embarrassed, in embarrassed circumstances, in the hole *and* in hock <both nonformal>, in the red, mortgaged, mortgaged to the hilt, tied up, involved

**encyclopedic** ADJS **comprehensive, sweeping, complete**; whole; **all-comprehensive,** all-inclusive; without omission *or* exception, **overall,** universal, global, wall-to-wall <nonformal>, around-the-world, **total,** blanket, omnibus, across-the-board; compendious; synoptic; pansophic, polymath *or* polymathic, polyhistoric

**end** NOUNS 1 end point, ending, perfection, be-all and end-all, **termination, terminus, terminal,** terminating, term, period, **expiration,** expiry, phaseout, phasedown, discontinuation, closeout, **cessation**, ceasing, consummation, culmination, **conclusion, finish, finis, finale,** the end, finishing, finalizing *or* finalization, a wrap <nonformal>, quietus, stoppage, windup *and* payoff <both nonformal>, curtain, curtains <nonformal>, end of the road *or* line <nonformal>

VERBS 2 **put an end to,** make an end of, **finish,** finish off <nonformal>, put paid to <Brit>, give the *coup de gr[aca]ce* <Fr> to, give the quietus to, deal a deathblow to, dispose of, get rid of, do in, do away with; **complete, perfect, finish, finish off, conclude, terminate,** bring to a close, carry to completion, prosecute to a conclusion

3 **cease, discontinue, stop, halt,** terminate, close the books, put paid to <Brit>, abort, cancel, scratch *and* scrub <both nonformal>, hold, **quit,** stay; **desist, refrain,** leave off, lay off <nonformal>, **have done with;** cut it out *and* drop it *and* knock it off <all nonformal>

**endeavor** NOUNS 1 **effort,** striving, struggle, strain; **all-out effort,** best effort, college try *or* old college try <nonformal>; **exertion**; determination, resolution; **enterprise,** undertaking

VERBS 2 **strive, struggle,** strain, sweat, sweat blood, labor, get one's teeth into, come to grips with, take it on, make an all-out effort, move heaven and earth, **exert oneself,** apply oneself, use some elbow grease <nonformal>; **try**

**endless** ADJS **infinite, boundless, limitless,** termless, shoreless; unbounded, uncircumscribed, **unlimited,** illimited, stretching *or* extending everywhere, without bound, without limit *or* end, no end of *or* to; **interminable,** interminate; **immeasurable,** incalculable, unreckonable, innumerable, incomprehensible, unfathomable; **perpetual, everlasting,** permanent, perdurable, indestructible; sempiternal, **infinite**, aeonian *or* eonian; dateless, ageless, timeless, immemorial; continuous, steady, **constant, ceaseless,** nonstop, unceasing, never-ceasing, **incessant,** unremitting

*continuous as the stars that shine*
WORDSWORTH

**endorse** VERBS **ratify,** sign off on, second, support, **certify, confirm, validate, authenticate, accept,** give the nod *or* the green light *or* the go-ahead *or* the OK <all nonformal>, give a nod of assent, give one's imprimatur, permit, give permission, **approve**; sanction, **authorize,** warrant, accredit; **sign,** undersign, sign on the dotted line, put one's John Hancock on <nonformal>, cosign, countersign; advocate, hold a brief for <nonformal>, countenance, keep in countenance, **lend oneself to,** lend one's name to, give one's support *or* countenance to, **support, back** *and* **back up** <both nonformal>, come out for

**endow** VERBS invest, vest; endow with, favor with, bless with, grace with, vest with; **settle on** *or* **upon; dower; establish, found,** constitute, institute

**endowed** ADJS **talented, gifted,** with a flair; dowered, invested

**endurance** NOUNS fortitude, intestinal fortitude <nonformal>, **toughness**, **stamina,** staying *or* sticking power, stick-to-it-iveness <nonformal>; **sufferance, stoicism,** patience of Job; **perseverance, persistence** *or* persistency, insistence *or* insistency, singleness of purpose; **pertinacity, tenacity,** tenaciousness, **doggedness**

*a minor form of despair, disguised as a virtue*
AMBROSE BIERCE

**endure** VERBS 1 **last** *or* **last out,** bide,

**abide,** dwell, perdure, **continue,** run, extend, **go on,** carry on, hold on, keep on, stay on, run on, stay the course, go the distance, go through with, grind *or* slog on, grind *or* plug away; live, **live on,** continue to be, subsist, exist, tarry; get *or* keep one's head above water; **persist;** hang in *and* hang in there *and* hang tough <all nonformal>; maintain, sustain, **remain, stay,** keep, hold, stand, prevail, last long, hold out; **survive,** defy *or* defeat time; live to fight another day; perennate; **survive,** live on, live through; wear, wear well

2 <nonformal> **take it,** take it on the chin, take it like a man, not let it get one down, stand the gaff; bite the bullet; hold still *or* stand still for, swallow, stick, **hang in, hang in there, hang tough,** tough *or* stick it out; lump it

**enemy** NOUNS **foe,** foeman, **adversary, antagonist;** bitter enemy; sworn enemy; open enemy; public enemy; archenemy, devil; the other side, the opposition; **bane**, bête noire

**energetic** ADJS **vigorous, strenuous, forceful, forcible, strong, dynamic,** kinetic, intense, acute, keen, incisive, trenchant, vivid, vibrant; **enterprising, aggressive,** proactive, activist, can-do *and* gung ho *and* take-over *and* take-charge <all nonformal>; **active, lively,** living, **animated, spirited,** go-go <nonformal>, **vivacious,** brisk, bright-eyed and bushy-tailed <nonformal>, lusty, **robust,** hearty, enthusiastic, mettlesome, zesty, zestful, impetuous, spanking, smacking; pumped *and* pumped up *and* jazzed-up *and* charged up *and* switched on <all nonformal>

**energy** NOUNS 1 **vigor, force, power, vitality,** strenuousness, **intensity, dynamism,** demonic energy; **potency**; **strength**; actual *or* kinetic energy; dynamic energy; potential energy

2 <nonformal> **pep,** bang, biff, get-up-and-go, ginger, gism, jazz, sizzle, kick, moxie, oomph, pepper, piss and vinegar, **pizzazz,** poop, punch, push, snap, spizzerinctum, starch, steam, zing, zip, zizz

**enforce** VERBS **discharge, fulfill,** render, administer; **carry out,** carry through, put through, prosecute; effect, effectuate, set in motion, implement; put in force; **abide by, honor, live up to,** adhere to, live by, **observe**

**enfranchise** VERBS **liberate, free, deliver, set free,** set at liberty, set at large; **emancipate,** manumit, disenthrall; affranchise; empower, give power, enable, entitle; charter, patent, franchise

**engage** VERBS 1 **take on** <nonformal>, go against *or* up against, close with, try conclusions with, enter the ring *or* arena with, put on the gloves with, match oneself against; **join issue** *or* **battle, do** *or* **give battle,** engage in battle *or* combat

2 **engross, absorb,** immerse, **occupy, preoccupy,** involve, monopolize, exercise, take up; **grip, hold, arrest, hold the interest, fascinate, enthrall,** spellbind, **hold spellbound,** grab <nonformal>, charm, enchant, mesmerize, hypnotize, catch; absorb the attention, claim one's thoughts, engage the attention, involve the interest, occupy the attention, monopolize one's attention, engage the mind *or* thoughts

**engaging** ADJS **engrossing, absorbing,** consuming, **gripping, arresting,** attractive, **fascinating,** enchanting, magnetic

**engrave** VERBS **grave, tool, enchase, incise, sculpture, inscribe,** character, **mark,** line, crease, score, scratch, scrape, cut, carve, chisel

**engrossed in** VERBS **absorbed,** totally absorbed, single-minded, **occupied, preoccupied, engaged,** devoted, devoted to, intent, intent on, monopolized, obsessed, monomaniacal, swept up, taken up with, **involved, caught up in,** wrapped in, **wrapped up in, absorbed in** *or* with *or* by, **lost in, immersed in,** submerged in, buried in

**enhance** VERBS **intensify, heighten, deepen, strengthen,** beef up <nonformal>, **magnify; reinforce,** change for the better, make an improvement; transform, transfigure; improve upon, refine upon, **mend, amend,** emend; meliorate, **ameliorate; enrich,** fatten

**enigma** NOUNS **mystery, puzzle,** puzzlement; **matter of ignorance,** sealed book, riddle, conundrum, **vexed question,** thorny problem, knotty point, knot, crux, node, nodus, Gordian knot, poser, teaser, perplexity

*a riddle wrapped in a mystery inside an enigma*
WINSTON CHURCHILL

**enigmatic** ADJS enigmatical, cryptic, cryptical; sphinxlike; **perplexing, puzzling;** riddling; logogriphic, anagrammatic; obscure, mysterious

**enjoy** VERBS pleasure in, be pleased with, receive *or* derive pleasure from, take delight *or* pleasure in, get a kick *or* boot *or* bang *or* charge *or* lift *or* rush out of <nonformal>; **like, love,** adore <nonformal>; **delight in, rejoice in,** indulge in, luxuriate in, revel in, riot in, bask in, wallow in, swim in; groove on *and* get high on *and* freak out on <all nonformal>; feast on, gloat over *or* on; **relish, appreciate,** roll under the tongue, do justice to, savor, smack the lips; devour, eat up

**enjoyment** NOUNS **pleasure,** quiet pleasure, euphoria, well-being, good feeling, **contentment,** content, **ease, comfort**; **gratification, satisfaction,** great satisfaction, hearty enjoyment, keen pleasure *or* satisfaction; **self-gratification,** self-indulgence; **relish, zest, gusto,** *joie de vivre* <Fr>; sweetness of life, *douceur de vivre* <Fr>; intellectual pleasure, pleasures of the mind; **strokes** *and* stroking *and* ego massage <all nonformal>

**enlarge** VERBS **increase,** aggrandize, **amplify, augment, extend,** maximize, **add to; expand, inflate; build, build up;** pyramid, parlay; develop, bulk *or* bulk up; **stretch, distend, dilate, swell, inflate,** sufflate, **blow up,** puff up, huff, puff, bloat; pump, pump up; **amplify, expatiate, dilate, expand, enlarge on,** expand on, **elaborate**

**enlightening** ADJS **educational, cultural, edifying,** illuminating; informative; didactic, preceptive; **liberalizing, liberating, broadening**

**enlist** VERBS **install,** instate, inaugurate, initiate, invest, ordain; enroll, induct, sign up, sign on; **participate, take part, partake, contribute,** chip in, involve *or* engage oneself, get involved; **join up,** sign on; **conscript, draft,** press, impress

**enmity** NOUNS **unfriendliness,** inimicality; **uncordiality,** unamiability, ungeniality, disaffinity, incompatibility, incompatibleness; personal conflict, strain, **tension;** coolness, coldness, chilliness, chill, frost, iciness, the freeze; inhospitality, unsociability

**enormity** NOUNS **outrage, atrocity, baseness, lowness, meanness, vileness,** foulness, rankness, fulsomeness, grossness, nefariousness, heinousness, **atrociousness,** monstrousness

**enormous** ADJS **large, immense, huge**; **gigantic,** mountainous, titanic, colossal, mammoth, Gargantuan, gigantesque, monstrous, outsize, sizable, larger-than-life, overgrown, king-size, monumental; **massive,** massy, weighty, bulky, voluminous; **vast,** vasty, boundless, **infinite**, immeasurable, cosmic, astronomical, galactic; **tremendous,** stupendous, awesome, prodigious; astronomical, humongous *and* jumbo <both nonformal>, prodigious, stupendous, larger than life, Homeric, mighty

**enough** NOUNS 1 **sufficiency,** sufficientness, **adequacy,** adequateness, competence *or* competency; satisfactoriness, satisfaction, satisfactory amount, enough to go around; good *or* adequate supply
ADJS 2 **sufficient,** sufficing; **ample,** substantial, **plenty, satisfactory, adequate,** decent, due;
ADVS 3 **sufficiently, amply,** substantially, **satisfactorily;** competently, **adequately**

**enraptured** ADJS **overjoyed, rapturous,** raptured, **enchanted,** entranced, enravished, ravished, rapt, possessed; **in raptures,** transported, in a transport of delight, **carried away,** rapt *or* ravished away, beside oneself, beside oneself with joy, **ecstatic,** in ecstasies, **enamored, charmed,** becharmed, **fascinated, captivated,** bewitched, enchanted

**enrich** VERBS **improve, better,** change for the better, make an improvement; **enhance,** fatten, enlighten, edify; **embellish, furbish,** embroider, grace, **ornament, decorate, adorn, gild,** trick out; paint in glowing colors, tell in glowing terms; elaborate; **fertilize,** richen, fatten, feed

**enroll** VERBS **install,** instate, inaugurate, initiate, invest, ordain; enlist, induct, sign up, sign on; **enlist, sign up** *or* **on** <nonformal>

**ensemble** NOUNS 1 **furniture,** furnishings, **suite, set of furniture,** decor
2 **cast,** cast of characters, characters,

persons of the drama, *dramatis personae* <L>; supporting cast; **company,** acting company, **troupe; orchestra, band,** combo <nonformal>, group; **chorus, chorale, choir,** choral group, choral society

**enslave** VERBS **subjugate, subject, subordinate; dominate**; enthrall, hold in thrall, make a chattel of; take captive, lead captive *or* into captivity; **hold in subjection,** hold in bondage, **hold captive,** hold in captivity; **conquer,** overrun, occupy

**ensue** VERBS **succeed, follow,** come *or* go after, **come next;** issue, emanate, attend, result; follow up, trail, track, come close on *or* tread on the heels of

**ensure** VERBS **guarantee, assure, insure,** bond, **certify;** countersecure; **sponsor,** be sponsor for, sign for, sign one's note, **back,** stand behind *or* back of, stand up for; **endorse;** sign, cosign, **underwrite,** undersign, subscribe to; confirm, attest

**entail** VERBS **imply, implicate, involve,** import, connote; involve, assume, presume, presuppose, subsume, affect, take in, contain, comprise, **call for, require,** lead to; **necessitate,** require; contribute to, lead to, conduce to

**enter** VERBS **go in** *or* **into,** access, cross the threshold, **come in,** find one's way into, put in *or* into; be admitted, gain admission *or* admittance, have an entree, have an in <nonformal>; **set foot in,** step in, walk in; **get in,** jump in, leap in, hop in; **drop in,** look in, drop by *or* in, pop in <nonformal>; **barge in** *or* come barging in *and* wade in <all nonformal>; thrust in, push *or* press in, crowd in, jam in, wedge in, pack in, squeeze in; irrupt, intrude; take in, admit; insert, **penetrate; put in, stick in,** interject; make an entry, insert, write in

**enterprise** NOUNS 1 dynamism, **initiative,** aggression, **aggressiveness,** killer instinct, force, forcefulness, pushfulness, pushingness, **pushiness, push, drive, hustle, go,** getup, **get-up-and-go** <nonformal>, go-ahead, go-getting, go-to-itiveness <nonformal>
2 **undertaking, venture, project,** proposition *and* deal <both nonformal>; **exploit, feat, deed, achievement, adventure,** gest, **bold stroke,** heroic act *or* deed; **business, industry,** business establishment, commercial enterprise

**entertain** VERBS entertain guests, guest; host, preside, do the honors <nonformal>; give a party, throw a party <nonformal>; **amuse, divert,** regale, beguile, solace, recreate, refresh, enliven, exhilarate, put in good humor

**entertainment** NOUNS **amusement, diversion,** divertisement, *divertissement* <Fr>, **recreation, relaxation,** regalement; **pastime,** *passe-temps* <Fr>; **mirth**; **pleasure, enjoyment**

**enthusiasm** NOUNS **eagerness, avidity,** avidness, forwardness, prothymia, **readiness,** promptness, quickness, **alacrity,** cheerful readiness, *empressement* <Fr>; keen desire, **appetite; zest,** zestfulness, gusto, **liveliness,** life, **vitality,** vivacity, élan, spirit, animation; **vehemence, passion,** impassionedness, **ardor,** ardency

**enthusiastic** ADJS 1 **energetic, active, lively,** living, **animated, spirited,** go-go <nonformal>, **vivacious,** brisk, bright-eyed and bushy-tailed <nonformal>, lusty, **robust,** hearty, mettlesome, zesty, zestful, impetuous; snappy *and* zingy *and* zippy *and* peppy <all nonformal>, hearty, cordial, exuberant, unrestrained, vigorous; enthused <nonformal>, glowing, full of enthusiasm; enthusiastic about, infatuated with

2 <nonformal> **gung ho, wild about, crazy about, mad about,** ape about *or* over, gone on, all in a dither over, gaga over, starry-eyed over, all hopped up about, hepped up over, hot about *or* for *or* on, steamed up about, **turned-on, switched-on;** hipped on, **cracked on,** bugs on, freaked-out, **nuts on** *or* **over** *or* **about, keen on** *or* **about,** crazy *or* mad *or* nuts about; spanking, smacking; pumped, pumped up, jazzed-up, charged up

**entice** VERBS **lure,** allure, **seduce, inveigle, lead on;** come on to *and* give the come-on *and* give a come-hither look *and* bat the eyes at *and* make goo-goo eyes at <all nonformal>, flirt with, flirt; coax, cajole, blandish; draw in, suck in *and* rope in <both nonformal>; bait, offer bait to, bait the hook

**entire** ADJS **complete, whole, total,** global, intact, solid; **full, full-fledged,** full-dress, **full-scale; uncut,** unabbreviated, undiminished, unexpurgated

**entitled** ADJS **authorized,** empowered; **warranted, sanctioned; justified,** qualified, worthy; **deserved, merited,** richly deserved, earned, well-earned

**entity** NOUNS **something, thing,** an existence; **being,** unit, individual, entelechy, monad; **person,** persona, personality, body, soul; **creature,** created being, contingent being; **organism,** life form, living thing, **individual**

**entourage** NOUNS **following, cortege, retinue,** suite, followers, followership, rout, train, body of retainers; **court**

**entrance** NOUNS **entry,** access, entree, entrée; **ingress,** ingression; **admission, reception;** infiltration, percolation, seepage, leakage; insinuation; intrusion; introduction, **insertion**

**entrance** VERBS **fascinate, captivate, charm,** becharm, spell, spellbind, cast a spell, put under a spell, **beguile, intrigue, enthrall,** infatuate, **enrapture, transport, enravish, enchant,** witch, **bewitch;** carry away, sweep off one's feet, turn one's head, knock one's socks off <nonformal>

**entrust** VERBS assign, consign, **commit, charge,** give in charge; license, charter, warrant; sell on credit, trust

**entry** NOUNS 1 **entrance,** access, entree, entrée; **ingress,** ingression; **admission, reception**; gate, door, portal, **entranceway,** entryway; **opening; vestibule, portico, entrance hall, threshold; lobby, foyer**
2 item, line item, minute, note, notation; single entry, double entry; **credit, debit**

**enumerate** VERBS **itemize,** factorize, number, detail, break out; tabulate, catalog, tally; **register,** post, enter; **count noses** *or* **heads** <nonformal>, call the roll; quantify, quantitate, quantize

**envelop** VERBS **surround, environ,** compass, **encompass,** enclose, close; go round *or* around, compass about; enfold, lap, wrap, enwrap, embrace, enclasp, embosom, embay, involve, invest; **screen, cloak, veil,** screen off, curtain, blanket, shroud, enshroud

**envious** ADJS envying, **invidious,** green with envy; **jealous**; **covetous,** desirous of; resentful; **grudging, begrudging;** mean, mean-spirited, ungenerous

**environment** NOUNS **surroundings, environs,** surround, ambience, entourage, circle, circumjacencies, circumambiencies, **circumstances,** environing circumstances, *alentours* <Fr>, total situation, existing conditions *or* situation, set of conditions, terms of reference, context, frame, setting, surround, surrounding conditions

**the environment** NOUNS the natural world, global ecosystem, the biosphere, the ecosphere, the balance of nature

**envision** VERBS **visualize,** vision, **envisage, picture, image,** objectify; picture in one's mind, picture to oneself, **view with the mind's eye,** contemplate in the imagination, form a mental picture of, represent, **see,** have a picture of; **call up,** summon up, conjure up, **call to mind,** realize

**envoy** NOUNS **diplomat,** diplomatist, diplomatic agent; **emissary, legate, minister,** foreign service officer; **ambassador,** ambassadress, ambassador-at-large; envoy extraordinary, plentipotentiary, **minister plenipotentiary;** nuncio, internuncio, apostolic delegate; chargé d'affaires; **attaché,** commercial attaché, military attaché, **consul,** consul general, vice-consul

**envy** NOUNS 1 enviousness, **covetousness;** invidia, deadly sin of envy, **invidiousness;** grudging, grudgingness; resentment, resentfulness; meanness, meanspiritedness, ungenerousness

*the tax which all distinction must pay*
EMERSON

*a kind of praise*
JOHN GAY

VERBS 2 be envious *or* covetous of, **covet,** cast envious eyes, desire for oneself; resent; **grudge, begrudge**

**epic** NOUNS 1 **account, narrative,** narration, chronicle; epos, **saga**
ADJS 2 larger than life, Homeric, mighty, **titanic, colossal, monumental,** heroic, heroical, epical, towering

**epidemic** NOUNS 1 **plague, pestilence,** pest, pandemic, pandemia, scourge
ADJS 2 **infectious,** infective, **catching,** taking, spreading, **communicable,** zymotic; pestiferous, pestilential, epidemial, pandemic; epizootic, epiphytotic; rife, rampant, pandemic, besetting

**epiphany** NOUNS **manifestation, appearance;** theophany, angelophany, Satanophany, Christophany, pneumatophany, avatar; revelation, disclosure, showing forth, moment of illumination; **insight,** inspiration, *aperçu* <French>; *satori* <Japanese>, *buddhi* <Skt>

**episode** NOUNS **event, occurrence, incident, experience, adventure,** hap, **happening,** happenstance, **phenomenon,** fact, matter of fact, reality, particular, circumstance, **occasion,** turn of events

**epitaph** NOUNS inscription, *hic jacet* <L>, tombstone marking

**epithet** NOUNS **oath,** profane oath, curse; cuss *or* cuss word *and* dirty word *and* four-letter word *and* **swearword** <all nonformal>, naughty word, no-no <nonformal>, foul invective, **expletive,** dirty name <nonformal>, dysphemism, obscenity; **nickname, sobriquet,** agnomen

**epitome** NOUNS **quintessence,** embodiment, incarnation, model, pattern, purest type, typification, perfect example *or* exemplar, paragon; archetype, prototype, exemplar, mirror

**equal** NOUNS 1 **match,** mate, twin, fellow, **like, equivalent,** opposite number, counterpart, answer <nonformal>, vis à vis, equipollent, coequal, parallel, ditto <nonformal>; **peer,** compeer, colleague, peer group
VERBS 2 match, rival, correspond, be even-steven, be tantmount to, be equal to; **keep pace with, keep step with, run abreast; amount to,** come to, come down to, run to, reach, touch; **measure up to,** come up to, stack up with <nonformal>, match up with; lie on a level with, **balance, parallel**
ADJS 3 **equalized,** like, **alike, even,** level, par, **on a par,** at par, at parity, au pair, commensurate, proportionate; on the same level, on the same plane, on the same *or* equal footing; on terms of equality, **on even** *or* **equal terms,** on even ground; on a level playing field

**equality** NOUNS **parity,** par, equation, **identity**; equivalence *or* equivalency, convertibility, **correspondence,** parallelism , equipollence, coequality; **likeness,** levelness, evenness, coextension; **balance,** poise, equipoise, **equilibrium,** equiponderance

**equalize** VERBS **equate; even,** equal out, even up, even off, square, level, level out, level off, make both ends meet; **balance,** strike a balance, poise, balance out, balance the accounts, balance the books; **compensate,** make up for, counterpoise; countervail, counterbalance, cancel

**equate** VERBS **relate, associate, connect,** interconnect, ally, link, link up, wed, marry, marry up, weld, bind, tie, couple, bracket, identify; bring into relation with, bring to bear upon, apply; **interrelate,** relativize, **correlate**

**equilibrium** NOUNS **harmony, proportion,** symmetry, **balance,** order, orderedness, measure, measuredness, concinnity, poise, equipoise, equiponderance; steadiness, evenness, **stability**; **temperateness,** temperance, sobriety; **happy medium, golden mean,** *justemilieu* <Fr>, middle way *or* path, *via media* <L>, balancing act <nonformal>

**equip** VERBS **furnish, outfit,** gear, **prepare, fit,** fit up *or* out, fix up <nonformal>, **rig,** rig up *or* out, **turn out,** appoint, accouter, clothe, dress

**equipment** NOUNS matériel, equipage, munitions; **fixtures, fittings, appointments, accouterments, appurtenances,** installations; outfit, apparatus, rig, machinery; paraphernalia, things, **gear, stuff** <nonformal>, impedimenta <pl>, **tackle**

**equivalent** NOUNS 1 **equal, match,** mate, twin, fellow, **like,** opposite number, counterpart, answer <nonformal>, vis à vis, equipollent, coequal, parallel, ditto <nonformal>; **peer,** compeer, colleague, peer group
ADJS 2 **tantamount,** equiparant, equipollent, coequal, coordinate; **identical**; corresponding *or* correspondent; convertible, much the same, as broad as long, neither more nor less, **all one,** all the same, neither here nor there

**eradicate** VERBS **annihilate, exterminate**, extirpate, **eliminate,** liquidate, **wipe out, stamp out,** waste *and* take out *and* nuke *and* zap <all nonformal>, put an end to; root up *or* out; **purge, liquidate**

**erase** VERBS **obliterate, expunge, efface, wipe out,** wipe off the map, rub out, **blot out,** sponge out, wash away; cancel, strike out, cross out, scratch, scratch out, rule out; blue-pencil; **delete** *or* dele, kill

**erect** VERBS 1 **elevate, rear, raise,** pitch, **set up,** raise *or* lift *or* cast up; raise *or* heave *or* rear aloft; uprear, upraise, uplift, upheave; upright; **upend,** stand upright *or* on end; set on its feet *or* legs *or* base *or* bottom

ADJS 2 **vertical, upright,** bolt upright, ramrod straight, upstanding, standing up, stand-up; rearing, rampant; **upended,** upraised, upreared; downright

**erode** VERBS **decrease, waste,** wear, waste *or* wear away, crumble, ablate, corrode, consume, consume away, be eaten away; melt away, deliquesce; abrade, eat *or* wear *or* rub *or* shave *or* file away; **corrode,** eat, gnaw, eat into, eat away, nibble away

**erogenous** ADJS **erotic,** erogenic, erotogenic

**erosion** NOUNS **wear, wear and tear; weathering,** ablation, ravages of time; **waste,** wastage, **exhaustion, depletion,** sapping, depreciation, dissipation, diffusion, **wearing, wearing away,** leaching away

**erotic** ADJS **sexual,** sexy, amorous; **carnal, sensual**, voluptuous, fleshly; **lascivious, lecherous, salacious,** animal, **sexual, lustful,** ithyphallic, **hot,** horny *and* sexed-up *and* hot to trot <all nonformal>; prurient, itching, itchy <nonformal>; concupiscent, lickerish, libidinous, randy, horny <nonformal>, lubricious

**erotica** NOUNS erotic literature; pornographic literature, pornography, porn *and* hard porn *and* soft porn <all nonformal>, obscene literature, scatological literature

**err** VERBS fall into error, **go wrong, go amiss,** go astray, go *or* get out of line, go awry, stray, get off-base <nonformal>, **deviate,** wander; **lapse, slip, slip up,** trip, stumble; **miscalculate**

**errand** NOUNS **task, assignment, charge,** project, **mission,** commission, **duty,** service, exercise

**errant** ADJS **deviative,** deviatory, deviating, **deviant,** departing, aberrant, aberrational, aberrative, shifting, turning, swerving, veering; **digressive,** discursive, excursive, **circuitous; devious,** indirect, out-of-the-way; erratic, zigzag, doglegged, **wandering,** rambling, roving, winding, twisting, meandering

**erratic** ADJS **capricious,** whimsical, variable, wavering, **changeable**; **indecisive, irresolute** unnatural, abnormal, irregular, divergent, deviative, deviant, different, exceptional; unconventional; **eccentric,** idiocratic, idiocratical, idiosyncratic, idiosyncratical, **queer,** queer in the head, **odd, peculiar,** strange, fey, singular, anomalous, freakish, funny

**erroneous** ADJS **untrue,** not true, **not right;** unfactual, **wrong,** all wrong; peccant, perverse, corrupt; **false, fallacious,** self-contradictory; **illogical**; **fallible; faulty,** faultful, flawed, defective, **at fault;** out, off, all off, off the track *or* rails

**error** NOUNS 1 **erroneousness; untrueness,** untruthfulness, **untruth; wrongness, wrong; falseness, falsity; fallacy, fallaciousness,** self-contradiction; fault, **faultiness,** defectiveness; misdoing, misfeasance; errancy, aberrancy, aberration, **deviancy; heresy,** unorthodoxy, heterodoxy; **mistake,** *erratum* <L>, *corrigendum* <L>; misidentification; **misjudgment, miscalculation**; misplay

2 <nonformal> **goof, boo-boo,** muff, flub, foozle, bloomer, bloop, blooper, boot, bobble, boner, bonehead play *or* trick, dumb trick, boob stunt, fool mistake; howler, clanger <Brit>, screamer; fuck-up, screw-up, foul-up, snafu, muck-up, balls-up <Brit>, louse-up; pratfall, whoops

**erupt** VERBS **burst forth,** break forth, debouch, irrupt, explode; **pop up, bob up** <nonformal>, start up, spring up, burst upon the view; flare up, flash, gleam; **find vent,** issue forth, come forth, exit, **emerge, issue,** break out, break through; **spew,** jet, spout, squirt, **spurt**

**escapade** NOUNS **revel, lark, party**; **spree, bout, fling,** wingding *and* randan <both nonformal>; **carouse, drinking bout**

**escape** NOUNS 1 **getaway** *and* break *and* breakout <all nonformal>; **deliverance; delivery,** riddance, **release,** setting-free, freeing, **liberation, extrication, rescue;** emergence, issuance, issue, outlet, vent

VERBS 2 make *or* effect one's escape, make good one's escape; **get away, make a getaway** <nonformal>; **free oneself,** deliver oneself, gain one's liberty, **get free, get clear of,** bail out, **get out, get out of,** get well out of; **break loose,** cut loose, break away, break one's bonds *or* chains, slip the collar, shake off the yoke; **jump** *and* **skip** <both nonformal>; **break jail** *or* **prison,** fly the coop <nonformal>

**escort** NOUNS 1 **conductor, usher,** shepherd; **guide,** tourist guide, cicerone; **chaperon,** duenna; **bodyguard,** guard, **convoy;** companion, sidekick <nonformal>, travel companion
VERBS 2 **conduct,** have in tow <nonformal>, marshal, **usher,** shepherd, **guide, lead; convoy,** guard; **squire, attend,** wait on *or* upon, **take out** <nonformal>; **chaperon**

**esoteric** ADJS **occult, esoterical, mysterious,** mystic, mystical, anagogic, anagogical; metaphysic, metaphysical; cabalic, cabalistic; **paranormal, supernatural**; theosophical, theosophist, anthroposophical

**ESP** NOUNS **extrasensory perception; clairvoyance,** lucidity, second sight, insight, sixth sense; intuition; foresight; premonition; clairsentience, clairaudience, crystal vision, psychometry, metapsychosis

**espionage** NOUNS **spying,** espial, **intelligence,** military intelligence, intelligence work, cloak-and-dagger work <nonformal>; counterespionage, counterintelligence; wiretap, wiretapping, bugging <nonformal>, electronic surveillance

**esprit** NOUNS **liveliness, vivacity, vitality,** life, **animation, spiritedness, spirit,** élan, **sprightliness,** high spirits, zestfulness, zest, vim, zip <nonformal>, vigor, verve, gusto, **exuberance,** heartiness; solidarity, team spirit, *esprit de corps* <Fr>

**essence** NOUNS 1 **substance,** stuff, very stuff, inner essence, essential nature, quiddity, **core,** kernel, marrow, pith, sap, spirit, quintessence, elixir, distillate, **extract,** distillation, distilled essence; sine qua non, irreducible *or* indispensable content

2 <nonformal> **meat and potatoes,** nuts and bolts, the nitty-gritty, the guts, the name of the game, the bottom line, where it's at, what it's all about, the ball game, the payoff, the score, where the rubber meets the road

**essential** NOUNS 1 **requirement, necessity,** desideratum, desideration; prerequisite, prerequirement; **must,** must item; indispensable; the necessary, the needful; necessities, necessaries, essentials, bare necessities
ADJS 2 of the essence, **fundamental; primary,** primitive, primal, elementary, elemental, simple, bare-bones *and* no-frills *and* bread-and-butter <all nonformal>, original, *ab ovo* <L>, **basic, gut** <nonformal>, basal, underlying; **substantive,** substantial, material; constitutive, constituent

**establish** VERBS **found,** constitute, institute, install, form, **set up, organize,** equip, endow, inaugurate, realize, materialize, effect, effectuate; fix, **determine, ascertain,** make out, remove all doubt; **settle,** settle the matter

**establishment** NOUNS **foundation,** constitution, institution, installation, formation, **organization,** inauguration, **inception, setting-up,** realization, materialization, effectuation; **determination, settlement, proof**

**the Establishment** NOUNS **the authorities, the powers that be,** ruling class, the lords of creation, the interests, the power elite, **the power structure;** the inner circle; the ins *and* the in-group *and* those on the inside <all nonformal>; **top brass** <nonformal>; higher-ups *and* the people upstairs *or* in the front office <all nonformal>; the corridors of power

**esteem** NOUNS 1 estimation, **honor, regard, respect,** approval, approbation, account, favor, consideration, **credit,** points *and* Brownie points <both nonformal>; prestige, repute, reputation, honor, glory, renown, dignity, **fame**
VERBS 2 **respect,** entertain respect for, accord respect to, **regard,** hold in esteem *or* consideration, favor, **admire,** think much of, think well of, think highly of, have *or* hold a high opinion of; **appreciate, value,** prize, **rate highly, think much of,** set store by

**estimate** NOUNS 1 **estimation; view, opinion**; **assessment,** assessing, **appraisal,** appraisement, appraising, appreciation, reckoning, **stocktaking,** valuation, valuing, **evaluation,** evaluating, value judgment, evaluative criticism, analyzing, weighing, weighing up, gauging, ranking, rank-ordering, **rating;** measurement; comparison
VERBS 2 form an estimate, make an estimation; **reckon,** call, guess, figure

<nonformal>; **assess, appraise,** give an appreciation, **gauge, rate, rank,** rank-order, put in rank order, class, mark, **value, evaluate,** place *or* set a value on, weigh, weigh up, prize, appreciate; size up *or* take one's measure <nonformal>, **measure**

**et cetera** NOUNS **etc, and so forth, and so on,** *und so weiter* <Ger>; **et al,** *et alii* <L>, and all <nonformal>, and others, and other things, *cum multis aliis* <L, with many others>; and everything else, **and more of the same, and the rest, and the like;** and stuff like that *and* and all that jazz <both nonformal>; **and what not** *and* and what have you *and* and I don't know what *and* and God knows what *and* and then some *and* you name it<all nonformal>; and the following, *et sequens* <L>, et seq

**eternal** ADJS **perpetual, everlasting,** everliving, ever-being, ever-abiding, ever-during, ever-durable, permanent, perdurable, indestructible; sempiternal, **infinite**, aeonian *or* eonian; dateless, ageless, timeless, immemorial; **endless,** unending, never-ending, without end, **interminable,** nonterminous, nonterminating; **continual,** continuous, steady, **constant, ceaseless,** nonstop, unceasing, never-ceasing, **incessant,** unremitting, unintermitting, uninterrupted

**eternity** NOUNS **perpetuity,** perpetualness; eternalness, sempiternity, infinite duration; everness, foreverness, **everlastingness, permanence**, perdurability, indestructibility; timelessness; **endlessness,** never-endingness, **interminability; infinity**

**ethical** ADJS **moral,** moralistic; **honest, upright,** uprighteous, **upstanding,** erect, right, **righteous, virtuous, good,** clean, squeaky-clean <nonformal>, **decent; honorable,** full of integrity, **reputable,** estimable, creditable, worthy, noble, sterling, manly, yeomanly; **respectable,** highly respectable; principled, high-principled, high-minded, right-minded; uncorrupt, uncorrupted, inviolate

**ethics** NOUNS **principles,** standards, norms, principles of conduct *or* behavior, principles of professional practice; **morals,** moral principles; code, ethical *or* moral code, **ethic,** code of morals *or* ethics, ethical system, value system, axiology; moral climate, **ethos,** *Zeitgeist* <Ger>

**ethnic** ADJS **racial, tribal, national, family,** clannish, totemic, **lineal;** phyletic, phylogenetic, genetic

**etiquette** NOUNS social code, rules *or* code of conduct; **formalities,** social procedures, social conduct, what is done, what one does; **manners,** good manners, exquisite manners, quiet good manners, **politeness,** *politesse* <Fr>, natural politeness, comity, civility; **amenities,** decencies, civilities, elegancies, **social graces, mores, proprieties;** decorum, good form

**eulogy** NOUNS **praise,** bepraisement; **laudation,** laud; *éloge* and *hommage* <both Fr>, eulogium; **encomium,** accolade, kudos, panegyric; paean; **tribute,** homage; funeral oration

**euphemism** NOUNS **overniceness,** overpreciseness, **overrefinement, elegance,** exquisiteness, preciousness, preciosity; goody-goodyism *and* goody-goodness <both nonformal>; purism

**euphoric** ADJS **in high spirits,** exalted, **elated,** exhilarated, high <nonformal>; irrepressible; **blithe,** blithesome; **happy,** happy as a clam *or* a lark, on top of the world, sitting on top of the world, sitting pretty; sanguine, sanguineous, eupeptic; **irrepressible**

**evacuate** VERBS **vacate,** abandon, desert, turn one's back on, walk away from, leave to one's fate, leave flat *or* high and dry; **withdraw,** retreat, **beat a retreat,** retire, remove; walk away, abscond, disappear, vanish; **bow out** <nonformal>, make one's exit; jump ship

**evade** VERBS **elude,** beg, **get out of,** shuffle out of, skirt, **get around** <nonformal>, circumvent; give one the runaround; ditch *and* shake *and* shake off <all nonformal>, get away from, give the runaround *or* the slip <nonformal>; lead one a chase *or* merry chase; **equivocate,** prevaricate, tergiversate, doubletalk, doublespeak, tap-dance <nonformal>, palter, **shuffle, dodge,** shy, sidestep, hedge, evade the issue; **beat about** *or* **around the bush,** not come to the point, **beg the question**

**evaluate** VERBS **estimate,** form an estimate, make an estimation; **reckon,** call, guess, figure <nonformal>; **assess, appraise,** give an appreciation, **gauge, rate, rank,** rank-order, put in rank order, class, mark, **value,** valuate, place *or* set a value on, weigh, weigh up, prize, appreciate

**evangelical** ADJS evangelic, evangelistic, gospel; **strict,** scripturalistic; hyperorthodox, puritanical, purist *or* puristic, straitlaced

**evangelist** NOUNS revivalist, evangel, evangelicalist; **missionary,** missioner; missionary apostolic, missionary rector, colporteur; television *or* TV evangelist, televangelist <nonformal>

**evaporate** VERBS **vanish,** dematerialize, evanesce, **vanish into thin air,** go up in smoke; disperse, dispel, dissipate; cease, cease to exist, **cease to be;** leave no trace, disappear, fade, fade away *or* out, fly, flee, dissolve, melt away, die out *or* away, pass, pass away, pass out of the picture <nonformal>, turn to nothing *or* naught, peter out <nonformal>, come to an end, wind down, tail off *and* trail off <both nonformal>; volatilize

**evasion** NOUNS **prevarication, equivocation,** hedging, pussyfooting <nonformal>, **sidestepping,** tergiversation, shuffle, fencing, dodging, parrying, waffling *and* tap-dancing <both nonformal>; *suppressio veri* <L>; weasel words; elusion; **evasiveness,** subterfuge; hugger-mugger, hugger-muggery

**even** ADJS 1 **smooth;** smooth-textured *or* -surfaced, **level, plane, flat,** regular, uniform, **unbroken**
2 **equal, equalized,** like, **alike,** par, **on a par,** at par, at parity, au pair, commensurate, proportionate; **drawn, tied,** neck-and-neck <nonformal>, too close to call
ADVS 3 **exactly, precisely,** to a T, expressly; **just,** right, straight, square, **plumb,** directly, squarely, point-blank; unerringly, undeviatingly; **faithfully, strictly, rigorously,** rigidly; in every respect, in all respects, for all the world, neither more nor less

**evening** NOUNS **eve,** even, evensong time *or* hour, **eventide,** vesper; **close of day,** decline *or* fall of day, when day is done; **nightfall, sunset, sundown,** setting sun

**event** NOUNS **occurrence, incident, episode, experience, adventure,** hap, **happening,** happenstance, **phenomenon,** fact, matter of fact, reality, particular, circumstance, **occasion,** turn of events

**eventuality** NOUNS **possibility,** possibleness, **the realm of possibility,** the domain of the possible, conceivableness, **conceivability,** thinkability, thinkableness, imaginability; contingency, **chance, prospect; outside chance** <nonformal>, off chance, remote possibility

**ever** ADVS **forever, forevermore, for ever and ever,** forever and aye; forever and a day <nonformal>, now and forever, *ora e sempre* <Ital>, **evermore,** ever and anon, ever and again; **constantly, continually, steadily,** sustainedly, **regularly,** as regular as clockwork, with every other breath, every time one turns around, unvaryingly, uninterruptedly, **incessantly, ceaselessly,** without letup *or* break *or* intermission, without stopping; **perpetually, always, at all,** if at all

*yesterday and today and forever*
BIBLE

**evergreen** ADJS **perennial,** indeciduous, sempervirent, ever-new, ever-young; ever-blooming, ever-bearing

**everlasting** ADJS **perpetual,** everliving, permanent, perdurable, indestructible; **immortal, deathless,** undying, neverdying, **imperishable,** incorruptible, amaranthine; **endless,** unending, neverending, without end, **interminable, constant, ceaseless,** nonstop, unceasing, never-ceasing, **incessant,** unremitting, uninterrupted

**every** ADJS **all,** any, whichever, whichsoever; **each,** each one; every one, each and every, each and all, **one and all, all and sundry**

**everybody** NOUNS **all, everyone, each and everyone, one and all,** all comers *and* all hands *and* every man Jack *and* every mother's son <all nonformal>, every living soul, **all the world,** *tout le monde* <Fr>, **whole, totality**

**everyday** ADJS **usual, regular; common, commonplace, ordinary, average,** mediocre, familiar, household, vernacular, stock; **prevailing, predominating,** current, popular

**everyone** NOUNS **the populace, the public,** the general public, people in general, everybody; **the population,** the citizenry, the whole people, the polity, the body politic; ordinary people, **persons, folk, folks,** gentry; plain people *or* folks, the rank and file, **all, each and everyone, one and all,** every living soul

**everything** NOUNS **all, the whole, the**

**entirety,** all the above *or* all of the above <both nonformal>, the aggregate, the assemblage, one and all, all and sundry, each and every <nonformal>; everything from soup to nuts *and* everything but the kitchen sink <both nonformal>

**everywhere** ADJS 1 **omnipresent, all-present,** ubiquitous; continuous, uninterrupted, infinite
ADVS 2 **here, there, and everywhere;** in every place, in all places, in every quarter, in all quarters; **all over,** all over hell *and* all over the map *and* all over the place *and* all over town <all nonformal>, all over the world, the world over, on the face of the earth, under the sun, throughout the world

**evict** VERBS **oust,** dislodge, dispossess, put out, turn out, **turn out of doors,** turn out of house and home, turn *or* put out bag and baggage, throw into the street; unhouse, unkennel

**evidence** NOUNS **proof; reason to believe,** grounds for belief; **ground, grounds,** material grounds, **facts, data,** premises, basis for belief; piece *or* item of evidence, **fact,** datum, relevant fact; **indication, manifestation, sign, symptom,** mark, token, mute witness; body of evidence, documentation

**evil** NOUNS 1 **iniquity,** bad, wrong, error, obliquity, villainy, knavery, reprobacy, peccancy, **abomination, atrocity, infamy,** shame, disgrace, scandal, unforgivable *or* cardinal *or* mortal sin, **sin**
ADJS 2 **wicked, vicious, bad, naughty, wrong, sinful, iniquitous,** peccant, reprobate; dark, black; **base, low, vile,** foul, rank, flagrant, arrant, nefarious, **heinous,** villainous, criminal, up to no good, knavish, flagitious; abominable, atrocious, monstrous, unspeakable, execrable, damnable; shameful, disgraceful, scandalous, **infamous, unpardonable,** unforgivable

**evil eye** NOUNS **spell,** *malocchio* <Ital>, whammy <nonformal>; **hex,** evil genius, **hoodoo** *and* **jinx** <both nonformal>, **Jonah; curse,** enchantment, whammy *and* double *or* triple whammy <all nonformal>

**evince** VERBS **evidence, show,** tend to show, witness to, testify to; **demonstrate, illustrate,** exhibit, manifest, display, express, set forth; **indicate, signify,** signalize, mark, **denote, betoken, point to,** give indication of, show signs of, bear on, touch on

**evocative** ADJS elicitory, arousing; **reminiscent, mindful, remindful, suggestive,** redolent

**evoke** VERBS **call up, summon up,** call *or* summon forth, call out; rouse, arouse, stimulate; **draw out** *or* **forth,** bring out *or* forth, pry *or* prize out, drag out, worm out, bring to light; **prompt, provoke,** muster up, inspire; put one in mind of <nonformal>, remind one of, bring to mind, be reminiscent of, suggest

**evolution** NOUNS **evolving,** evolvement; evolutionary change, gradual change, step-by-step change, peaceful *or* nonviolent change; **development, growth,** rise, incremental change, natural growth *or* development; flowering, blossoming; ripening, coming of age, maturation; **advance,** advancement, furtherance

**evolve** VERBS **develop, grow,** wax, change gradually *or* step-by-step; **progress, advance,** come a long way; ripen, mellow, mature, maturate; flower, bloom, blossom

**exact** ADJS **precise,** express; even, square; absolutely *or* definitely *or* positively right; **faithful;** direct; **unerring,** undeviating, constant; **infallible,** inerrant, inerrable

**exacting** VERBS **meticulous, scrupulous, conscientious,** religious, punctilious, punctual, **particular, fussy, critical, attentive,** scrutinizing; **thorough,** thoroughgoing, thoroughpaced; **exact, precise,** precisionistic, precisianistic, prissy, **accurate, correct; strict,** exigent, demanding, not to be trifled with, **stringent,** astringent; disciplined, spit-and-polish; **severe, harsh,** dour, unsparing

**exaggerate** VERBS hyperbolize; **overstate,** overspeak <old>, overreach, **overdraw,** overcharge; overstress; **overdo, carry too far, go to extremes;** push to the extreme, indulge in overkill, overestimate; overpraise, oversell, tout, puff *and* ballyhoo <both nonformal>; **stretch,** stretch the truth, stretch the point, draw the longbow; **magnify, inflate;** pile *or* lay it on *and* pour *or* spread *or* lay it on thick *and* lay it on with a trowel <all nonformal>; talk big <nonformal>, make much of; make a

Federal case out of it <nonformal>, something out of nothing, make a mountain out of a molehill; caricature, travesty, burlesque

**exaggeration** NOUNS **overstatement,** big *or* tall talk <nonformal>, **hyperbole,** hyperbolism; **magnification, enlargement,** dilation, dilatation, **inflation,** expansion, blowing up, puffing up, aggrandizement; **stretching, heightening,** enhancement; burlesque, travesty, caricature; sensationalism, puffery *and* ballyhoo <both nonformal>, touting, huckstering; grandiloquence

**exalted** ADJS **eminent, prominent,** outstanding, standout, high, elevated, towering, soaring, overtopping, **lofty,** sublime; august, majestic, noble, distinguished; **magnificent,** magnanimous, heroic, godlike, superb; famous, renowned, lauded, glorious; blessed, consecrated, devoted; **glorified,** enskied; **saintly,** sainted, beatified, canonized

**examination** NOUNS **discussion, debate,** debating, **deliberation,** exchange of views, canvassing, ventilation, airing, review, **treatment, consideration,** investigation, **study, analysis,** logical analysis; logical discussion, dialectic; survey, **discourse,** disquisition, lucubration, étude; school examination, examen, **test, quiz;** oral examination, viva voce examination, viva <nonformal>; inspection, scrutiny

**examine** VERBS **discuss, debate, reason, deliberate,** exchange views *or* opinions, **talk over, hash over** <nonformal>, talk of *or* about, comment upon, **consider, treat,** dissertate on, handle, deal with, take up, **go into,** investigate, talk out, **analyze,** sift, **study,** canvass, review, pass under review, scrutinize, inspect, controvert, ventilate, air, thresh out, **kick** *or* **knock around** <nonformal>

**example** NOUNS exemplar; **representative,** type, symbol, emblem, exponent; **exemplification,** illustration, demonstration, explanation; **instance,** relevant instance, **case,** typical example *or* case, case in point, object lesson

**exasperate** VERBS **provoke, incense,** arouse, inflame, embitter; **vex, irritate, annoy, aggravate** <nonformal>, **nettle,** fret, chafe; **pique, peeve** *and* miff <both nonformal>, huff; **ruffle, roil, rile** <nonformal>, ruffle one's feathers, **rankle;** bristle, put *or* get one's back up, stick in one's craw <nonformal>

**excavation** NOUNS **deepening, lowering, depression;** digging, mining, tunneling; drilling, probing; **pit, well, shaft,** sump; dig, diggings, workings; mine, quarry

**exceed** VERBS **surpass, pass, top, transcend, go beyond;** overpass, overstep, overrun, **overreach,** overshoot, overshoot the mark

**excel** VERBS **surpass, exceed, transcend,** get *or* have the ascendancy, get *or* have the edge, have it all over <nonformal>, overcome, overpass, best, **better,** improve on, perfect, go one better <nonformal>; **cap,** trump; top, tower above *or* over, overtop; **predominate,** prevail, preponderate; **excel in** *or* **at, shine in** *or* **at** <nonformal>, be master of; **have a gift** *or* **flair** *or* **talent** *or* **bent** *or* **faculty** *or* **turn for,** be a natural *and* be cut out *or* born to be <both nonformal>

**excellence** NOUNS **goodness, quality,** class <nonformal>; **virtue,** grace; **superiority,** first-rateness, **skillfulness**

**excellent** ADJS **surpassing, exceeding, excelling, rivaling, eclipsing,** capping, topping, **transcending,** transcendent *or* transcendental; a cut *or* stroke above, one up on <nonformal>; more than a match for

**exception** NOUNS **exemption, immunity;** special case *or* privilege; privilege; **exclusion, barring,** debarring, debarment, preclusion, omission, nonadmission, cutting-out, leaving-out; **restriction, circumscription,** narrowing, demarcation; **reservation,** waiver

**excerpt** NOUNS **extract, selection,** extraction, excerption, snippet; passage, selected passage; **clip** <nonformal>, film clip, outtake, sound bite <nonformal>
VERBS 2 **select,** make a selection; **pick,** handpick, **pick out, single out,** choose out, smile on, give the nod <nonformal>, jump at, seize on; extract, cull, glean, winnow, sift

**excess** NOUNS 1 **surplus,** surplusage, overplus, overage; superfluity, redundancy; overestimation; exaggerated lengths, **extreme,** exorbitance, inordinacy, **overkill;** grandiloquence; **excessiveness,** too much, too-muchness <nonformal>
ADJS 2 **superfluous, redundant; in excess;** unnecessary, unessential, nonessential, expendable, dispensable,

**needless,** unneeded, gratuitous, uncalled-for; verbose, prolix; *de trop* <Fr>, supererogatory, supererogative

**exchange** NOUNS 1 **retaliation, reciprocation,** interchange, give-and-take; **retort, reply,** return, comeback <nonformal>; counterblow, counterblast, recoil, boomerang, backlash; **substitution, change,** switch, switcheroo <nonformal>, commutation, subrogation; tit for tat, *quid pro quo* <L>
VERBS 2 **interchange,** change, counterchange; alternate; **transpose;** convert, commute, permute; **trade, swap** <nonformal>, **switch;** bandy, bandy about, play at battledore and shuttlecock; **reciprocate, trade off,** compromise, settle, settle for, respond, keep a balance; give tit for tat, **retaliate**

**excitement** NOUNS emotion, excitedness, **arousal, stimulation, exhilaration;** a high <nonformal>, manic state *or* condition; **excitation, arousal,** arousing, **stirring,** stirring up, working up, working into a lather <nonformal>, lathering up, whipping up, steaming up, **agitation, perturbation**

**exciting** ADJS **thrilling,** thrilly <nonformal>, **stirring, moving, breathtaking,** eye-popping <nonformal>; agitating, agitative, perturbing, disturbing, upsetting, troubling, disquieting, unsettling, distracting, jolting, jarring; heart-stirring, heart-swelling, heart-expanding, soul-stirring, spirit-stirring, deep-thrilling, mind-blowing <nonformal>; **stimulating,** stimulative, stimulatory; exhilarating, heady, intoxicating, maddening, ravishing

**exclaim** VERBS give an exclamation, burst out, blurt, blurt out, jerk out, spout out; stammer out

**exclamation** NOUNS outburst, blurt, ecphonesis; expletive, interjection

**exclude** VERBS **bar,** debar, bar out, lock out, **shut out, keep out,** count out <nonformal>, close the door on, close out, cut out, cut off, preclude; **reject, repudiate,** blackball *and* turn thumbs down on <both nonformal>, read *or* drum out, ease *or* freeze out *and* leave *or* keep out in the cold <all nonformal>, ostracize, wave off *or* aside

**exclusive** ADJS selective, **select,** elect, elite; **cliquish,** clannish; **snobbish,** snobby; excluding, exclusory; seclusive, preclusive, exceptional, inadmissible, prohibitive, preventive, prescriptive, restrictive; narrow, insular, parochial, ethnocentric, xenophobic, snobbish

**excrement** NOUNS dejection, dejecta, **discharge,** ejection; matter; **waste,** waste matter; **excreta,** egesta, ejecta, ejectamenta; exudation, exudate; transudation, transudate; extravasation, extravasate; effluent

**excruciating** ADJS **agonizing, harrowing,** racking, rending, **desolating,** consuming; **tormenting,** torturous; **heartbreaking,** heartrending, **heartsickening**

**excursion** NOUNS **journey, jaunt, junket, outing,** pleasure trip; sight-seeing trip *or* tour, rubberneck tour <nonformal>; day-trip; round trip, circuit, turn; **cruise,** package cruise, cruise to nowhere

**excuse** NOUNS 1 **cop-out** *and* **alibi** *and* **out** <all nonformal>; lame excuse, poor excuse, likely story; escape hatch, way out; **apology,** regrets
VERBS 2 **forgive, pardon,** give *or* grant forgiveness, spare; grant amnesty to, grant immunity *or* exemption; **exonerate, exculpate;** spare, except, grant immunity, make a special case of; absolve

**execute** VERBS 1 **complete,** transact, promulgate, **make;** make out, fill out; **discharge, fulfill,** render, administer; **carry out,** carry through, put through, prosecute; effect, effectuate, set in motion, implement; enforce, put in force; **abide by, honor, live up to,** adhere to, live by, **observe**
2 **put to death,** inflict capital punishment; **electrocute,** burn *and* fry <nonformal>; send to the gas chamber; **behead, decapitate,** decollate, guillotine, bring to the block; **shoot,** execute by firing squad; burn, **burn at the stake; strangle,** garrote, bowstring; stone, lapidate; defenestrate

**execution** NOUNS 1 **completion;** transaction; carrying out, discharge, fulfillment, prosecution, effectuation; enforcement; observance
2 **capital punishment; hanging,** the gallows, the rope *or* noose; summary execution; **electrocution,** the chair <nonformal>, the hot seat <nonformal>; gassing, the gas chamber; lethal injection; **decapitation,** decollation, beheading, the guillotine, the ax, the block

**executive** NOUNS 1 officer, official; **president,** prexy <nonformal>, chief executive officer; policy-maker, agenda-setter
ADJS 2 **administrative, administrating;** ministerial; **officiating, presiding;** supervisory, directing, managing

**exempt** VERBS **free, release,** discharge, **let go** *and* **let off** <both nonformal>, set at liberty, spring <nonformal>; **excuse,** spare, except, grant immunity, make a special case of; grandfather; **dispense,** dispense from, give dispensation from; dispense with, save the necessity; remit, remise; absolve

**exemption** NOUNS exception, **immunity; release,** discharge; diplomatic immunity, congressional *or* legislative immunity; special case *or* privilege; privilege; permission

**exercise** NOUNS 1 exercising; **practice, drill, workout;** yoga; constitutional <nonformal>, stretch; violent exercise; physical education
VERBS 2 **work out,** warm up, aerobicize, stretch, lift weights, pump iron <nonformal>, jog, run, bicycle, walk, fitness-walk, power-walk
3 **use, utilize, make use of,** do with; **employ,** practice, ply, work, manage, handle, manipulate, operate, **wield,** play; **have** *or* **enjoy the use of**

**exert** VERBS **exercise, ply, employ, use, put forth,** put out *and* make with <both nonformal>; practice

**exertion** NOUNS **effort, energy,** elbow grease; **endeavor**; **trouble, pains;** great *or* mighty effort, might and main, muscle, one's back, hard *or* strong *or* long pull

**exhaust** VERBS 1 **fatigue, tire, weary,** wilt, flag, jade, harass; **wear,** wear on *or* upon, **wear down; tire out, wear out, burn out; use up; do in; wind,** put out of breath; overtire, overstrain; weaken, enervate, debilitate; weary *or* tire to death; prostrate
2 **run out,** empty, find vent; **drain,** drain out; **draw off,** draft, draw, draw from; **suck,** suck out *or* up, **siphon off**

**exhaustion** NOUNS 1 exhaustedness, draining; **collapse, prostration,** breakdown, crack-up <nonformal>, nervous exhaustion *or* prostration
2 **depletion,** drain, exhausting, impoverishment; **waste,** sapping, depreciation, dissipation, diffusion, **wearing, wearing away, erosion,** ablation, leaching away

**exhaustive** ADJS **thorough, thoroughgoing,** thorough-paced, intensive, broad-based, house-to-house *and* door-to-door <both nonformal>, A-to-Z, comprehensive, all-embracing, all-encompassing, omnibus, radical, sweeping

**exhibit** NOUNS 1 presentation, presentment, **exhibition, exposition,** retrospective
VERBS 2 **evidence, evince,** furnish evidence, **show, go to show, mean,** tend to show, witness to, testify to; **demonstrate, illustrate,** manifest, display, express, set forth; **attest; indicate, signify,** signalize, symptomatize, mark, **denote, betoken, point to,** give indication of, show signs of, bear on, touch on

**exhibition** NOUNS **display, show, demonstration,** manifestation, **parade,** *étalage* <Fr>; **pageantry,** pageant, **spectacle;** vaunt, fanfaronade, blazon, flourish, flaunt, flaunting

**exhilarate** VERBS **stimulate,** invigorate, fortify, enliven, liven up, animate, vivify, quicken; brace, **brace up,** buck up *and* pick up <both nonformal>, set on one's legs *or* feet <nonformal>; renew one's strength, put *or* breathe new life into, give a breath of fresh air, give a shot in the arm <nonformal>; **animate,** enliven

**exigency** NOUNS **urgency,** imperativeness, exigence *or* exigency; **momentousness, crucialness, cruciality;** consequentiality, consequentialness; **press,** pressure, high pressure, **stress,** tension, **pinch;** clutch *and* crunch <both nonformal>

**exile** NOUNS 1 **banishment, expatriation,** exilement; outlawing *or* outlawry; **ostracism,** ostracization, thumbs-down, thumbing-down, *pollice verso* <L>, blackballing; **deportation,** transportation, **extradition**
VERBS 2 **banish, expatriate, deport,** transport, send away, **extradite; deport; outlaw,** ban, proscribe

**exist** VERBS **be,** be in existence, be extant, have being; breathe, **live**; subsist, stand, obtain, hold, prevail, be the case; **occur,** be present, be there, be found, be met with, happen to be

**existence** NOUNS **being;** subsistence, entity, essence, absolute *or* transcendental essence, *l'être* <Fr>, pure being, *Ding-an-sich* <Ger, thing-in-itself>, noumenon; **occurrence,** presence

**exit** NOUNS 1 **egress,** egression; exodus;

outgoing, outgo, going out; emersion *or* egress <astronomy>; **departure**; extraction
VERBS 2 make an exit, **make one's exit;** egress, **go out,** get out, walk out, march out, run out, pass out, bow out *and* include oneself out <both nonformal>; walk out on, leave cold <nonformal>; **depart**

**exodus** NOUNS **egress,** egression; **exit,** outgoing, outgo, going out; **departure**; extraction; hegira

**exonerate** VERBS **acquit, clear, exculpate, absolve,** bring in *or* return a verdict of not guilty; **pardon, excuse, forgive;** remit, grant remission, remit the penalty of; amnesty, grant *or* extend amnesty

**exorbitant** ADJS **overpriced,** grossly overpriced, **excessive, extravagant, inordinate, immoderate,** undue, unwarranted, unreasonable, fancy, unconscionable, outrageous, preposterous, out of bounds, out of sight <nonformal>, **prohibitive; extortionate,** cutthroat, **gouging, usurious,** exacting

**exotic** ADJS **distant,** distal, **remote, removed, far, far-off,** away, **faraway,** way-off, at a distance, separated, apart, asunder; **alluring, fascinating, captivating, riveting, charming, glamorous, enchanting,** spellful, spellbinding, **entrancing,** ravishing, **enravishing, intriguing, enthralling,** witching, **bewitching; foreign, alien,** strange, foreign-looking

**expand** VERBS **enlarge, extend, widen, broaden,** build, build up, aggrandize, **amplify,** crescendo, **magnify, increase**, augment, add to, raise, up, scale up, hike *or* hike up; **stretch, distend, dilate, swell, inflate,** sufflate, **blow up,** puff up, huff, puff, bloat; pump, pump up; rarefy

**expanse** NOUNS **immensity,** enormousness, **vastness,** vastitude, tremendousness, boundlessness, infinity; stupendousness, formidableness, prodigiousness, humongousness <nonformal>

**expansive** ADJS **extensive;** expansional, extensional; expansile, extensile, elastic; expansible, inflatable; distensive, dilatant; inflationary; spacious, **roomy;** ample, full

**expect** VERBS be expectant, **anticipate, have in prospect,** face, think, **contemplate,** have in contemplation *or* mind, envision, envisage; **hope**; presume; dread; **take for granted;** not be surprised *or* a bit surprised; foresee

**expectation** NOUNS expectance *or* **expectancy,** state of expectancy; **predictability,** predictableness; **anticipation, prospect,** thought; probability; confidence, reliance, overreliance; certainty

**expedient** ADJS **desirable,** to be desired, much to be desired, **advisable, politic,** recommendable; **appropriate, meet, fit, fitting,** befitting, **right, proper,** good, seemly, likely, congruous, **suitable,** sortable, feasible, doable, **convenient,** happy, heaven-sent, felicitous; timely, seasonable, opportune, well-timed, in the nick of time

**expedite** VERBS **advance, further, promote,** forward, hasten, contribute to, foster, aid, facilitate, abet; **send, dispatch,** transmit, remit, consign

**expedition** NOUNS **journey, trip,** *jornada* <Sp>, peregrination, sally, **trek; adventure,** emprise, **mission;** quest, pilgrimage; exploration

**expel** VERBS **banish, cast out,** thrust out, exclude, **excommunicate; exile, expatriate, deport,** transport, send away, **extradite; deport; dismiss, discharge, cashier,** drum out, throw out, **cast forth,** send out *or* forth

**expendable** ADJS **consumable,** spendable; exhaustible; replaceable; disposable, throwaway, no-deposit, no-deposit-no-return; **superfluous, redundant;** unnecessary, unessential, nonessential, dispensable, **needless,** unneeded, gratuitous, uncalled-for

**expensive** ADJS **dear, costly,** of great cost, dear-bought, **high, high-priced,** premium, at a premium, top; big ticket <nonformal>, **fancy** *and* stiff *and* steep <all nonformal>, pricey; upmarket, upscale <nonformal> rich, sumptuous, **luxurious**, gold-plated

**experience** NOUNS 1 **practice,** practical knowledge *or* skill, hands-on experience <nonformal>, field-work; background, past experience, seasoning, tempering; **worldly wisdom,** knowledge of the world, blaséness, **sophistication; occurrence, incident, episode, adventure**
VERBS 2 **have, know, feel,** taste; **encounter, undergo, go through,** pass through, be subjected to, be exposed to, **endure, suffer,** sustain

**experienced** ADJS **practiced,** mature, matured, ripe, ripened, **seasoned,** tried, well-tried, tried and true, **veteran,** an old dog at <nonformal>; **worldly, worldly-wise,** world-wise, wise in the ways of the world, knowing, **sophisticated,** cosmopolitan, cosmopolite, blasé, dry behind the ears, not born yesterday, long in the tooth

**experiment** NOUNS 1 **experimentation;** testing, trying, trying-out, **trial; trial and error,** cut and try <nonformal>; empiricism, experimentalism, pragmatism, instrumentalism
VERBS 2 **research,** make an experiment, **run an experiment,** run a sample *or* specimen; **test, try,** essay, cut and try <nonformal>, **test** *or* **try out,** have a dry run *or* dummy run *or* rehearsal *or* test run; put to the test, **put to the proof, prove, verify,** validate, substantiate, confirm

**expert** NOUNS 1 **adept,** proficient; **specialist,** specializer, **authority,** savant, scholar, connoisseur, maven <nonformal>; technical expert, technician; pundit
ADJS 2 **skillful, good,** goodish, excellent, **proficient; dexterous, adroit, deft, adept, coordinated,** well-coordinated, **apt,** no mean, **handy;** authoritative, professional; **virtuoso,** bravura, technically superb; **brilliant**

**expertise** NOUNS **profound knowledge,** deep knowledge, total command *or* mastery; specialized *or* special knowledge; proficiency; wide *or* vast *or* extensive knowledge

**expire** VERBS 1 **perish, succumb, die, cease, end,** come to an end, go, pass, **pass away, vanish, disappear,** fade away, run out, peg *or* conk out <nonformal>, come to nothing *or* naught, be no more, be done for
2 **elapse,** lapse, **pass,** run its course, run out, go *or* pass by; **endure,** go *or* run *or* flow on

**explain** VERBS **explicate, expound,** make of, exposit; **give the meaning,** tell the meaning of; **spell out,** unfold; **account for,** give reason for; **clarify, elucidate,** clear up, clear the air, **cover** *and* cover the waterfront *or* the territory <all nonformal>, **make clear,** make plain; **simplify,** popularize; **illuminate,** enlighten, **shed** *or* **throw light upon;** rationalize, euhemerize, demythologize

**explanation** NOUNS explication, unfolding, **elucidation,** illumination, enlightenment, light, **clarification,** *éclaircissement* <Fr>, simplification; **exposition,** expounding, exegesis; **justification, vindication;** rationalization

**expletive** NOUNS **oath,** profane oath, curse; cuss *or* cuss word *and* dirty word *and* four-letter word *and* **swearword** <all nonformal>, naughty word, no-no <nonformal>, foul invective, **epithet,** dysphemism, obscenity

**explicit** ADJS **crystal-clear,** clear as crystal; **express, unmistakable,** not to be mistaken, open-and-shut <nonformal>, unequivocal; self-explanatory, self-explaining; **indubitable**

**explode** VERBS **blow up, burst,** go off, go up, blow out, blast, bust <nonformal>; **detonate,** fulminate; **expose, show up;** blow sky-high, **puncture,** deflate, **shoot** *or* **poke full of holes, cut to pieces**

**exploit** NOUNS 1 **feat, deed, enterprise, achievement, adventure,** gest, **bold stroke,** heroic act *or* deed; aristeia
VERBS 2 **take advantage of,** use, make use of, **use for one's own ends;** make a paw *or* cat's-paw of, sucker *and* play for a sucker <both nonformal>; **manipulate,** work on, work upon, stroke, play on *or* upon; exploit one's position, feather one's nest <nonformal>, **profiteer**

**exploration** NOUNS **expedition; reconnaissance; reconnoitering,** reconnoiter, **scouting; search,** searching, **quest, hunt,** stalk, stalking

**exploratory** ADJS **preceding**; preliminary, pioneering, trailblazing, door-opening, kickoff, inaugural

**explore** VERBS **seek, look for,** look around *or* about for, look for high and low, look high and low, search out, **search for,** seek for, **hunt for,** cast *or* beat about for

**explosion** NOUNS **detonation, blast,** fulmination, **discharge, burst, bang; outburst,** outburst of anger, burst, eruption, blowup *and* **flare-up** <both nonformal>, access, blaze of temper

**explosive** NOUNS 1 high explosive; cellulose nitrate, cordite, dynamite, gelignite, guncotton, gunpowder, nitroglycerin, plastic explosive *or* plastique, powder, trinitrotoluene *or* trinitrotoluol *or* TNT
ADJS 2 **excitable, emotional,** highly emotional, overemotional, hyperthymic,

perturbable, flappable <nonformal>, volcanic, eruptive, inflammable; **dangerous, perilous,** ugly, serious, critical, attended *or* beset *or* fraught with danger

**export** NOUNS 1 **transferal, transfer; transmission,** transference, transmittal, transmittance; translocation, **transplantation,** translation; exportation, exporting
VERBS 2 **transfer, transpose,** translocate, hand on, send abroad

**expose** VERBS **disclose, reveal, let out, show,** impart, discover, **leak,** let slip out, let the cat out of the bag *and* spill the beans <both nonformal>; bring out of the closet; **show up; take the lid off, bring to light,** bring into the open, hold up to view; **unmask,** tear off the mask, **uncover,** unveil, take the lid off <nonformal>, ventilate, lift *or* draw the veil, raise the curtain, let daylight in

**exposé** NOUNS **disclosure,** disclosing; **revelation,** revealment, revealing, making public, publicizing, broadcasting; **uncovering,** unwrapping, uncloaking, taking the wraps off, removing the veil, **unveiling, unmasking; exposure, baring,** stripping *or* laying bare; outing <nonformal>

**exposure** NOUNS **unclothing,** divestment, stripping, denudation; baring, stripping *or* laying bare, uncovering, exposing; indecent exposure, exhibitionism, flashing <nonformal>; **disclosure,** disclosing; **revelation,** revealing, making public, publicizing, broadcasting; **unveiling, unmasking; spotlight** <nonformal>, daylight, public eye *or* consciousness, **currency,** common *or* public knowledge

**express** VERBS **phrase,** find a phrase for, give expression *or* words to, **word,** state, **frame,** conceive, style, couch, **put in** *or* **into words,** clothe *or* embody in words, couch in terms, express by *or* in words

**expression** NOUNS **phrase, locution, utterance,** usage, term, verbalism; **saying,** witticism, sentence, catchword, catchphrase, word, byword, mot, motto, moral; golden saying, proverbial saying

**expressive** ADJS **graphic, vivid,** suggestive, imaginative; well-turned; **meaningful**

**expurgate** VERBS expunge, **edit,** edit out, blue-pencil; strike out *or* off, void, rescind; **censor,** bowdlerize

**exquisite** ADJS **delightful, lovely; thrilling,** titillative; **charming, attractive, endearing, engaging, appealing,** prepossessing, heartwarming, sexy <nonformal>, **enchanting,** bewitching, witching, entrancing, enthralling, intriguing, fascinating; *recherché* <Fr>; **overnice,** overprecise, precious, *précieuse* <Fr>, **overrefined, elegant, fine,** flowerlike, **dainty, delicate**

**extant** ADJS **remaining, surviving,** vestigial, over, left, **leftover, still around, remnant,** remanent, odd; **spare,** to spare; unused, unconsumed; **outstanding,** unmet, unresolved; **present, immediate,** current, running, existent, **existing,** actual

**extemporaneous** ADJS **extemporary,** extempore, **impromptu,** unrehearsed, **improvised,** improvisatory, improvisatorial, improviso, *improvisé* <Fr>; **ad-lib,** *ad libitum* <L>; **ad-hoc,** stopgap, makeshift, jury-rigged; **offhand,** off the top of one's head *and* off-the-cuff <both nonformal>, **spur-of-the-moment, quick and dirty** <nonformal>

**extend** VERBS **reach, stretch,** sweep, spread, run, **go** *or* **go out,** cover, carry, **range,** lie; **reach** *or* stretch *or* thrust out; span, straddle, take in, hold, encompass, surround, environ; **enlarge, expand, increase,** greaten, crescendo, **develop, widen, broaden,** bulk

**extension** NOUNS **expansion, enlargement, increase,** uptick, crescendo, upping, raising, hiking, magnification, aggrandizement, amplification, ampliation <old>, broadening, widening; **spread,** spreading, creeping, fanning out, dispersion, ripple effect; **flare,** splay; deployment; augmentation, **addition**; adjunct

**extensive** ADJS **broad, wide,** liberal, diffuse, large-scale, broad-scale, broadscope, broadly-based, wide-scale, **sweeping; widespread, far-reaching,** far-ranging, **far-flung,** wide-ranging

**extenuating** ADJS **justifying,** justificatory; **vindicative,** vindicatory, rehabilitative; refuting; **excusing,** excusatory; extenuative, **palliative, mitigating,** mitigative, assuasive, lenitive, softening

**exterior** NOUNS 1 **appearance,** externals, **mere externals, facade,** outside, **show, outward show, image,** display, front <nonformal>, outward *or* external appearance, surface appearance, surface show, vain show, apparent character, public image, window dressing, cosmetics

ADJS 2 **external;** extrinsic; **outer, outside, out, outward,** outward-facing, outlying, outstanding; **outermost,** outmost

**exterminate** VERBS **eliminate, eradicate,** deracinate, **extirpate, annihilate; do away with, wipe out** <nonformal>; uproot, pull *or* pluck up by the roots, strike at the root of; **liquidate, purge;** remove, sweep away

**external** ADJS **exterior;** extrinsic; **outer, outside, out, outward,** outward-facing, outlying, outstanding; **outermost,** outmost; surface, superficial, peripheral, **fringe,** apparent, seeming; **extraneous**

**extinct** ADJS **no more, defunct, dead,** expired, passed away; vanished, gone glimmering; perished, annihilated; all over with, had it <nonformal>, down the tube *and* down the drain <both nonformal>, done for *and* dead and done for <both nonformal>; **obsolete, passé,** gone-by, past, outworn

**extinguish** VERBS **quench, snuff out,** put out, stamp *or* trample out, trample underfoot; **smother,** choke, stifle, strangle, suffocate; silence; **suppress, quash,** squash *and* squelch <both nonformal>, **quell,** put down

**extort** VERBS **exact,** squeeze, claim, demand, screw, **shake down** <nonformal>, **blackmail,** levy blackmail, badger *and* play the badger game <both nonformal>; **wrest, wring from, wrench from, rend from,** wrest *or* tear from

**extra** NOUNS 1 **bonus, premium,** something extra, extra dash, extra added attraction, lagniappe, something into the bargain, something for good measure, baker's dozen; **surplus; supernumerary,** spear carrier <nonformal>

ADJS 2 **additional, supplementary, supplemental;** plus, further, farther, fresh, **more,** new, **other,** another, ulterior; **auxiliary,** ancillary, supernumerary, contributory, **accessory,** collateral; **surplus,** spare

ADVS 3 **in addition, also,** and then some, even more, more so, and also, and all <nonformal>, and so, **as well, too,** else, beside, **besides, to boot, not to mention, let alone, into the bargain;** on top of, over, above; **beyond, plus;** on the side <nonformal>

**extract** NOUNS 1 extraction; **essence, quintessence, spirit, elixir;** decoction; **distillate,** distillation; infusion

2 **excerpt, selection,** snippet; passage, selected passage; **clip** <nonformal>, film clip, outtake, sound bite <nonformal>

VERBS 3 **take out,** get out, **withdraw, remove;** pull, draw; **pull out, draw out,** tear out, rip out, wrest out, pluck out; smelt

4 **select, pick,** handpick, **pick out, single out,** excerpt; separate the wheat from the chaff *or* tares, separate the sheep from the goats; **free,** set free, **release, extricate, liberate**

**extradite** VERBS deport, expel; repatriate; recommit, remand; transport, send away

**extramarital** ADJS freeloving; **adulterous,** illicit

**extraneous** ADJS **foreign, alien,** strange, exotic, foreign-looking; unearthly, extraterrestrial; exterior, **external;** extrinsic; ulterior, outside, outland, outlandish; **irrelevant, unessential,** nonessential, extrinsic; incidental, parenthetical

**extraordinary** ADJS **exceptional, remarkable,** noteworthy, **wonderful, marvelous,** fabulous, mythical, legendary; **stupendous,** stupefying, prodigious, portentous, phenomenal; unprecedented, unexampled, unparalleled, indescribable, unspeakable, ineffable

**extrapolate** VERBS **predict,** foresee, envision, envisage, see ahead, previse, foretell, prophesy; **anticipate, expect,** hope, hope for, look for, look forward to, **project,** plot, plan, scheme, think ahead

**extrasensory** ADJS psychosensory; **psychic, psychical, spiritual; spiritualistic,** spiritistic; mediumistic; **clairvoyant,** second-sighted, clairaudient, clairsentient, **telepathic; telekinetic, psychokinetic**

**extraterrestrial** ADJS foreign, outlandish, **alien; otherworldly,** extramundane, transmundane, transcendental, unearthly, exterrestrial, extraterrene

**extravagant** ADJS **prodigal, lavish,** profuse, **overliberal,** overgenerous, overlavish, **spendthrift, wasteful,** profligate, dissipative; pound-foolish, penny-wise and pound-foolish; easy come, easy go; elaborate, luxurious

**extreme** NOUNS 1 **limit, end, extremity, acme,** apogee, climax, **maximum,** ceiling, **peak,** summit, **pinnacle,** crown,

top; **utmost,** uttermost, utmost extent, highest degree, nth degree *or* power, *ne plus ultra* <L>; excess
ADJS 2 **radical,** out of this world, way *or* far out <nonformal>, too much <nonformal>; **greatest,** furthest, **most, utmost,** uttermost, the max <nonformal>; **ultra,** ultra-ultra; at the height *or* peak *or* limit *or* summit *or* zenith

**extremist** NOUNS 1 **radical,** ultra, ultraist; **revolutionary,** revolutionist; subversive; extreme left-winger, left-wing extremist; **anarchist,** nihilist; mild radical, parlor Bolshevik <nonformal>, pink *and* parlor pink *and* pinko <all nonformal>; lunatic fringe
ADJS 2 **radical, extreme,** revolutionary, revolutionist; subversive; ultraconservative; extreme left-wing, anarchistic, nihilistic

**extrinsic** ADJS **external,** outward, outside, outlying; **extraneous,** foreign; **objective,** nonsubjective, impersonal, extraorganismic *or* extraorganismal; **unessential,** nonessential, extraneous; incidental, parenthetical

**extroverted** ADJS extrovert, extroversive, **outgoing,** extrospective; other-directed

**exuberant** ADJS **unrestrained, unconstrained, uninhibited, unreserved,** go-go <nonformal>; **uncurbed, unchecked, unbridled,** unmuzzled; **unreined,** reinless; **uncontrolled,** unsubdued, **unruly;** irrepressible, **effusive,** gushing, gushy; extravagant

**exult** VERBS **rejoice,** jubilate, **glory, joy, delight,** bless *or* thank one's stars *or* lucky stars, congratulate oneself, hug oneself, rub one's hands, clap hands; dance *or* skip *or* jump for joy, caper, gambol, caracole, romp; triumph, glory, delight, **crow** *or* crow over, crow like a rooster *or* cock; **gloat,** gloat over

**eye** NOUNS 1 **look, sight,** the eye *and* a look-see *and* a gander <all nonformal>, regard; sidelong look; connoisseurship, savvy <nonformal>, selectiveness, fastidiousness; **view,** sight, light
VERBS 2 **scrutinize, survey,** contemplate, look over, give the eye *or* the once-over <nonformal>; **ogle,** ogle at, **leer,** leer at, give one the glad eye; examine, **inspect**; take a close *or* careful look; take a long, hard look; size up <nonformal>; take stock of

**eyeglasses** NOUNS **spectacles, specs** <nonformal>, **glasses,** pair of glasses *or* spectacles, cheaters *and* peepers <both nonformal>; reading glasses, bifocals, trifocals, pince-nez, lorgnette, *lorgnon* <Fr>; dark glasses, shades <nonformal>; goggles, blinkers; thick glasses, Coke-bottle glasses <nonformal>; **contacts,** contact lenses, hard lenses, soft lenses

# F

**fabric** NOUNS **substance, stuff, material, matter**, medium, the tangible; **elements,** constituent elements, constituents, ingredients, components, atoms, building blocks, parts

**fabulous** ADJS **marvelous,** wonderful, formidable, exceptional, uncommon, astonishing, fantastic, incredible, egregious; fabulous, mythic, mythical, mythological, **legendary; mythopoeic, mythopoetic** *or* mythopoetical

**facade** NOUNS **exterior, face,** outer face *or* side, **front; show, false show,** outward show, false air; window dressing, front, **false front,** gloss, varnish; masquerade, disguise; posture, pose, posing, attitudinizing; mannerism, affectation

**face** NOUNS 1 **countenance,** visage; cast of countenance, facial appearance *or* expression, cast, turn; **look, air, mien,** demeanor; seeming, semblance, appearance, ostentation, **show, false show,** outward show, false air; **false front, façade,** posture, mannerism, affectation
VERBS 2 **expect,** be expectant, **anticipate, have in prospect,** think, **contemplate,** have in contemplation *or* mind, envision, envisage; **brave, confront,** affront, front, look one in the eye, say to one's face, **face up to,** meet, **meet head-on** *or* boldly, square up to, stand up to *or* against, go eyeball-to-eyeball *or* one-on-one with <nonformal>

**facet** NOUNS **particular, instance, item, detail,** point, count, case, fact, matter, article, datum, element, part, ingredient, factor, aspect, thing; **respect, regard,** angle; minutia, minutiae <pl>, trifle, petty *or* trivial matter; incidental, minor detail

**facetious** ADJS **jocular, jesting, jocose, tongue-in-cheek;** joshing <nonformal>, **whimsical, droll,** humorsome; satiric, **satirical, sarcastic, ironic,** ironical; salty, salt, Attic

**facile** ADJS **glib, smooth,** smooth-spoken, smooth-tongued, **slick; felicitous;** slick as a whistle <nonformal>, pleasing, **easy, graceful, effortless,** painless

**facilitate** VERBS **ease; grease the wheels** <nonformal>; **smooth, smooth** *or* **pave the way,** ease the way, grease *or* soap the ways <both nonformal>, prepare the way, **clear the way,** make all clear for, make way for; run interference for <nonformal>, open the way, open the door to; **speed, expedite,** quicken, hasten; **help along,** help on its way

**facilitator** NOUNS animator; **agent, instrument,** implement, implementer; expediter

**facility** NOUNS 1 **accommodation, appliance, convenience,** amenity, appurtenance; advantage
2 **ease, easiness,** facileness, **effortlessness;** lack of hindrance, **smoothness,** freedom; easy going, plain sailing, smooth *or* straight sailing; **tractability,** amenability, adaptability, **suppleness,** willowiness, **litheness**

**facing** ADJS **opposite,** opposing, confronting, confrontive, eyeball-to-eyeball, one-on-one; **fronting,** looking on *or* out on, opposite, contrapositive

**facsimile** NOUNS representation, **reproduction, replica,** reduplication, model, **counterpart;** a chip off the old block

**fact** NOUNS the case, the truth of the matter, not opinion, not guesswork, what's what *and* where it's at <both nonformal>; **matter of fact, bare fact,** naked fact, bald fact, **simple fact,** sober fact, simple *or* sober truth; **cold fact,** hard fact, **brutal fact,** painful fact, the nitty-gritty *and* the bottom line <both nonformal>

*plain, plump fact*
R BROWNING

**faction** NOUNS **party, interest, camp, side;** interest group, pressure group, ethnic group; minority group, vocal minority; silent majority; division, **sect,** wing, **caucus,** splinter, splinter group, breakaway group, offshoot, schism

**factor** NOUNS **particular, instance, item, detail,** point, count, case, fact, matter, article, datum, element, part, ingredient, facet, aspect, thing; **element, part,** player, module, part and parcel; **feature,** aspect, circumstance

**facts** NOUNS **information,** data, knowledge; general information; factual information, hard information; **evidence, proof; reason to believe,** grounds for belief; **grounds,** material grounds

**factual** ADJS **real, actual,** veritable, for real <nonformal>, de facto, simple, sober, **hard; absolute, positive; self-evident,** axiomatic; accepted, conceded, stipulated, given; admitted, well-known, **established, inescapable, indisputable, undeniable; demonstrable,** provable; empirical, **objective, true**; genuine, **authentic**

**faculties** NOUNS **wits, senses,** parts, capacities, intellectual gifts *or* talents, mother wit; consciousness

**faculty** NOUNS 1 **ability, capability, capacity,** potentiality, facility, fitness, qualification, talent, flair, genius, caliber, **competence,** competency, adequacy, sufficiency, **efficiency,** efficacy; **proficiency**; the stuff *and* the goods *and* what it takes <all nonformal>
2 faculty members, professorate, professoriate, professors, professordom, teaching staff

**fad** NOUNS **craze, rage;** wrinkle <nonformal>; new take <nonformal>; novelty; faddishness, faddiness <nonformal>, faddism

**fade** VERBS **weaken, languish, wilt,** faint, **droop,** drop, **sink, decline, flag, pine, tail away** *or* off, fail, fall *or* drop by the wayside; give out, have no staying power, run out of gas <nonformal>, conk *or* peter *or* poop *or* peg *or* fizzle out <nonformal>; come apart at the seams, come unstuck *or* unglued <both informal>; wear thin *or* away; die out *or* away, dwindle, wane, **fade out** *or* **away, lose color, pale, turn pale,** grow pale, **change color,** turn white, **whiten, blanch,** wan

**fail** VERBS 1 **weaken, sink, decline,** run down, lose strength, lose one's grip, dwindle, droop, flag, wilt, wither, wither away, fade, **languish,** waste, waste away, pine, peak, be unsuccessful, fail of success, not work *and* not come off <both nonformal>, come to grief, **lose,** not make the grade, be found wanting, not come up to the mark; not pass

2 <nonformal> **lose out,** get left, **not make it,** not hack it, not get to first base, drop the ball, go for a Burton *and* come a cropper <both Brit>, **flop,** flummox, fall flat on one's ass, lay an egg, go over like a lead balloon, draw a blank, bomb, drop a bomb; fold, fold up; take it on the chin, take the count; crap out; strike out, fan, whiff; **flunk** *and* **flunk out**

**failing** NOUNS **vice, weakness,** weakness of the flesh, **flaw,** moral flaw *or* blemish, **frailty, infirmity;** failure; weak point, weak side, foible; bad habit, besetting sin; **fault, imperfection**

**failure** NOUNS 1 **unsuccessfulness,** unsuccess; no go <nonformal>; ill success; futility, uselessness; **defeat**; losing game, **no-win situation;** nonaccomplishment; **bankruptcy, insolvency,** receivership, Chapter 11

2 <nonformal> **flop,** flopperoo, megaflop, gigaflop, **bust,** frost, **fizzle,** lemon, clinkler, dud, non-starter, **loser, washout,** turkey, bomb, flat failure, dull thud, total loss

3 <nonformal> **loser, non-starter,** born loser, **flop,** washout, false alarm, **dud,** also-ran, bum, dull tool, bust, schlemiel, turkey

**faint** NOUNS 1 **unconsciousness, senselessness;** swoon, blackout, syncope, athymia, lipothymy *or* lipothymia; **coma; stupor;** semiconsciousness, grayout
VERBS 2 **swoon,** drop, succumb, keel over <nonformal>, fall in a faint, fall senseless, **pass** *or* zonk out <nonformal>, **black out,** go out like a light; gray out
ADJS 3 faintish, lightheaded, dizzy, gone
4 **indistinct, unclear,** ill-defined, ill-marked, pale, feeble, weak, **dim,** dark, **shadowy, vague, obscure,** indistinguishable, unrecognizable

**fair** NOUNS 1 **festival, festivity,** festive occasion, *fiesta* <Sp>, **fete,** gala, **gala affair, blowout** <nonformal>, **jamboree** <nonformal>; carnival; kermis; *Oktoberfest* <Ger>; Mardi Gras; Saturnalia; gala day, feria
ADJS 2 **bright, sunny,** mild, balmy, rainless, fine, bright and fair, pleasant
3 **just,** square, **fair and square; equitable,** balanced, level <nonformal>, **even,** evenhanded; deserved, merited; meet, meet and right, right and proper, fit, **proper, good,** as it should *or* ought to be; lawful, legal
4 **mediocre, middling, indifferent, fairish, fair to middling** <nonformal>, moderate, modest, medium, betwixt and between; respectable, passable, **tolera-**

**ble; so-so,** *comme ci comme ça* <Fr>
ADVS 5 **justly, fairly,** in a fair manner; **equitably, equally, evenly,** upon even terms; **impartially, disinterestedly,** without distinction, without regard *or* respect to persons, without fear or favor

**fairy** NOUNS **sprite, fay,** fairy man *or* woman; **elf, brownie, pixie, gremlin,** ouphe, hob, cluricaune, puca *or* pooka *or* pwca, kobold, nisse, peri; **imp, goblin**; **gnome; banshee; leprechaun**

**faith** NOUNS 1 **religion,** religious belief *or* faith, **belief,** teaching, doctrine, creed, credo, theology, orthodoxy; system of beliefs; tradition
2 **confidence,** confidentness, conviction, belief, fixed *or* settled belief, **sureness, assurance, assuredness,** surety, security, certitude; subjective certainty; trust

**faithful** ADJS 1 **loyal,** devoted, allegiant; **true, true-blue,** true to one's colors; **constant, steadfast,** unswerving, steady, consistent, stable, unfailing, staunch, firm, solid; dutiful; affirming, witnessing, believing; **observant, practicing**
2 **lifelike,** speaking, living, breathing, to the life, **true to life** *or* nature; **realistic, natural**

**faith healer** NOUNS **healer,** theotherapist; Christian *or* spiritual *or* divine healer; Christian Science practitioner

**fake** NOUNS 1 **hoax, deception,** spoof <nonformal>, **humbug,** flam, **rip-off** <nonformal>, **sham;** mare's nest
2 **impostor, ringer;** sham, shammer, **humbug,** *blagueur* <Fr>, **fraud** <nonformal>, **faker** *and* **phony** <both nonformal>, **fourflusher** <nonformal>, bluff, bluffer; **charlatan, quack,** quacksalver, quackster, **mountebank,** saltimbanco
3 **copy, imitation**, **counterfeit**, forgery, phony <nonformal>; ersatz
VERBS 4 **counterfeit,** hoke *and* hoke up <both nonformal>, forge, plagiarize, crib, lift <nonformal>; **tamper with, manipulate, juggle,** sophisticate, **doctor** *and* **cook** <both nonformal>, rig, cook *or* juggle the books *or* the accounts <nonformal>
ADJS 5 **imitation, mock, sham,** copied, phony <nonformal>, counterfeit, forged, plagiarized, unoriginal, ungenuine; synthetic, synthetical, ersatz, hokey *and* hoked-up <both nonformal>

**fall** NOUNS 1 **downfall,** prostration; **overthrow, overturn, upset, upheaval,** *bouleversement* <Fr>; convulsion, **subversion,** sabotage, monkey-wrenching <nonformal>; **collapse, crash,** smash, comedown, breakdown, derailment, pratfall <nonformal>, stumble, tumble, cropper <chiefly Brit nonformal>
VERBS 2 **fall down** <nonformal>, fall *or* drop by the wayside, fall flat, fall flat on one's face; fall down on the job <nonformal>; **fall short, fall through,** fall to the ground; fall between two stools; **fall dead; collapse,** fall in; **crash,** go to smash <nonformal>

**fallacy** NOUNS logical fallacy, formal fallacy, material fallacy, verbal fallacy; fallaciousness, self-contradiction; heresy, unorthodoxy, heterodoxy; mistaking, misconstruction, misapplication, misjudgment; **misinterpretation**

**fall off** VERBS **diminish, lessen; drop,** drop off, dive, take a nose dive, plummet, plunge, fall, fall away, fall to a low ebb, run low

**fall short** VERBS **come short, run short,** stop short, not make the course, not reach; not measure up, not hack it *and* not make the grade *and* not make the cut <all nonformal>, not make it, not make out; **be found wanting,** not fill the bill, not suffice

**false** ADJS **deceitful; fraudulent, sharp, guileful, insidious,** slippery, slippery as an eel, **shifty, tricky,** trickish, cute, finagling, chiseling <nonformal>; underhand, **underhanded, furtive, surreptitious,** indirect; **falsehearted, two-faced; treacherous**

**falsehood** NOUNS **lie,** falsity, **untruth,** untruism, mendacity, **prevarication, fib,** taradiddle <nonformal>, flimflam *or* flam, a crock *and* a crock of shit <both nonformal>, *blague* <Fr>; **trumped-up story,** farrago; tall tale *and* **tall story** <both nonformal>, **cock-and-bull story,** fish story <nonformal>; half-truth, stretching of the truth, slight stretching, white lie, little white lie; a pack of lies

**falsify** VERBS **pervert, twist, garble, put a false construction upon, give a spin, give a false coloring,** color, varnish, slant, strain, torture; misrepresent, misconstrue; **fabricate, invent, manufacture, trump up, make up, hatch, concoct, cook up** *and* make out of whole cloth <both nonformal>

**falter** VERBS **despair,** despair of, **despond**, lose hope, **lose heart, abandon hope,** give oneself up *or* yield to despair; **hesitate, pause, hang back,** hover; wait to see how the cat jumps *or* the wind blows, scruple, jib, stick at, stickle, strain at; **lose one's nerve,** lose courage, **get cold feet** <nonformal>, boggle, funk <nonformal>, **chicken** <nonformal>; **flounder,** flounce, **stagger,** totter, stumble, blunder

**fame** NOUNS **repute,** famousness, **renown, kudos,** report, **glory;** éclat, **celebrity, popularity,** recognition, a place in the sun; popular acceptance *or* favor, vogue; **acclaim, public acclaim,** réclame, **publicity; notoriety,** notoriousness, talk of the town; prestige, esteem, repute, reputation, honor, renown, dignity

*that last infirmity of noble mind*
MILTON

**familiar** ADJS 1 **intimate, close,** near, inseparable, on familiar *or* intimate terms; just between the two, one-on-one, man-to-man, woman-to-woman; hand-in-hand, hand and glove *or* hand in glove; **thick, thick as thieves** <nonformal>
2 familiar as household words, household, **common, current; proverbial**

**familiarize** VERBS **inform,** apprise, advise, advertise of, **give word,** mention to, **acquaint, enlighten,** brief, verse, give the facts, give an account of, give by way of information; possess *or* seize one of the facts; notify, give notice *or* notification, serve notice; **accustom, habituate,** orient

**family** NOUNS **kinfolk** *and* **kinfolks** <both nonformal>, **kinsmen, kin,** kith and kin, **relatives, relations, people,** folks <nonformal>, connections; **posterity, progeny, issue, offspring,** fruit, seed, brood, breed; extended family, nuclear family

**famished** ADJS **hungry, ravenous,** voracious, **starved,** starving, famishing, perishing *or* pinched with hunger; unfed, underfed, undernourished

**famous** ADJS **distinguished,** distingué; **noted, notable,** marked, of note, of mark; famed, honored, **renowned, celebrated, popular,** acclaimed, much acclaimed, sought-after, hot *and* world-class <both nonformal>, **well-known,** on everyone's tongue *or* lips, talked-of, talked-about

**fan** NOUNS **supporter, upholder, follower,** maintainer, sustainer; well-wisher, favorer, encourager, sympathizer; **partisan,** sider <old>, sectary, votary; buff <nonformal>, freak *and* nut <both nonformal>, aficionado, devotee, **zealot, enthusiast**

**fanatic** NOUNS 1 infatuate, **bug** <nonformal>, **nut** <nonformal>, **buff** *and* **fan** <both nonformal>, freak <nonformal>, *fanatico, aficionado* <both Sp>, devotee, **zealot, enthusiast,** energumen; **monomaniac,** crank <nonformal>; lunatic fringe
ADJS 2 **fanatical, rabid; overzealous, overenthusiastic,** bigoted, perfervid; **extreme,** extremist, extravagant, inordinate; **unreasonable, irrational; wild-eyed**

**fanciful** ADJS **capricious, whimsical,** notional, kinky, harebrained, cranky, flaky <nonformal>, quirky; **fantastic,** fantastical, antic, **unbelievable**, **impossible, incredible,** logic-defying, incomprehensible, unimaginable, inconceivable

**fancy** NOUNS 1 **inclination, penchant, partiality, favor, predilection, preference,** propensity, proclivity, **leaning, bent,** turn, tilt, bias, **affinity;** mutual affinity *or* attraction; **sympathy,** fascination; **attachment,** fondness, sentiment, warm feeling, soft spot in one's heart, weakness <nonformal>, **liking,** shine <nonformal>
VERBS 2 **desire, want,** have a mind to, **like,** have *or* acquire a taste for, take to, **take a fancy** *or* a shine to, have a weakness *or* soft spot in one's heart for; prefer, favor
3 **imagine, conceive,** conceptualize, ideate, figure to oneself
ADJS 4 **ornate, elegant,** fine, chichi, pretty-pretty; picturesque; **elaborate,** overornamented, overornate, overelegant, labored, high-wrought; **ostentatious,** flossy <nonformal>

**fanfare** NOUNS **blare,** sound *or* flourish of trumpets, fanfaronade, Gabriel's trumpet *or* horn, tarantara, tantara, tantarara; **celebration,** celebrating; rejoicing; **ceremony,** rite

**fantastic** ADJS fantastical, fanciful, antic, **unbelievable, impossible, incredible,**

logic-defying, incomprehensible, unimaginable, unexpected, unaccountable, inconceivable; preposterous, grotesque, monstrous, wild, weird, **outrageous,** beyond belief, *outré* <Fr>, extravagant, **bizarre**

**fantasy** NOUNS wildest dream; **figment of the imagination**, phantom of the mind; **apparition, appearance; vision,** waking dream; eidolon, idolum; **imagination,** imagining, **fancy,** conceit <old>; flight of fancy, fumes of fancy; make-believe

*such stuff as dreams are made on*
**Shakespeare**

**far** ADJS 1 **distant,** distal, **remote, removed, far-off,** away, **faraway,** way-off, at a distance, separated, apart, asunder
ADVS 2 **far off,** far away, **afar,** afar off, a long way off, a good ways off <nonformal>, as far as the eye can see, out of sight; clear to hell and gone <nonformal>

**farce** NOUNS **humor, slapstick,** mere farce, slapstick humor, broad humor; visual humor; mockery, imitation, wicked imitation *or* pastiche, takeoff <nonformal>

**farewell** NOUNS 1 **leave-taking, send-off,** Godspeed; **adieu,** one's adieus, aloha, **good-bye;** valedictory address, valedictory, valediction, parting words; parting *or* Parthian shot
VERBS 2 say *or* bid good-bye *or* farewell, take leave, make one's adieus; bid Godspeed, give one a send-off *or* a big send-off, see off *or* out

*speed the parting guest*
**Pope**

ADJS 3 **departing, leaving; parting,** last, final; valedictory; outward-bound

**farfetched** ADJS **remote,** distant, out-of-the-way, strained, forced, dragged in, neither here nor there, brought in from nowhere; **imaginary**; improbable

**far-flung** ADJS **extensive,** widespread, **far-reaching,** far-ranging, wide-ranging

**farm** NOUNS 1 farmplace, farmstead, farmhold <old>, farmery <Brit>, **grange,** location <Austral>, pen <Jamaica>; **plantation,** *hacienda* <Sp>; croft; **homestead,** steading; collective farm, *kibbutz* <Heb>
VERBS 2 **ranch; grow, raise,** rear; crop; dryfarm; sharecrop
ADJS 3 **rustic, rural, country, provincial, pastoral, bucolic,** Arcadian, **agrarian,** agrestic; **agricultural**

**farmer** NOUNS **agriculturist,** granger, husbandman, **yeoman,** cultivator, tiller, sodbuster, **tiller of the soil;** boutique farmer, contour farmer, crop-farmer, dirt farmer <nonformal>, gentleman-farmer; **grower,** raiser; **planter;** tenant farmer, crofter <Brit>; sharecropper, cropper, collective farm worker, *kibbutznik* <Yiddish>; **agricultural worker, farm worker,** farmhand, farm laborer, migrant *or* migratory worker *or* laborer, bracero, picker

**farsighted** ADJS longsighted, presbyopic; **farseeing,** sagacious, prepared, ready, prudent

**fart** NOUNS 1 **flatulence** *or* flatulency, flatuosity, flatus, gas, wind
VERBS 2 let *or* lay *or* cut a fart <nonformal>, let *or* break wind

**farther** ADJS **extra,** plus, further, fresh, **more,** new, **other,** another, ulterior; **auxiliary,** ancillary, supernumerary, contributory; remoter, more distant
ADVS 2 **more, moreover,** *au reste* <Fr>, *en plus* <Fr>, thereto, further, **furthermore,** at the same time, then, again, yet

**fascinate** VERBS **captivate, charm,** becharm, spell, spellbind, cast a spell, put under a spell, **beguile, intrigue, enthrall,** infatuate, **enrapture, transport, enravish, entrance, enchant,** witch, **bewitch;** sweep off one's feet, turn one's head, knock one's socks off <nonformal>

**fascinating** ADJS **charming, enchanting, entrancing, spellbinding,** glamorous, Circean; **engrossing, absorbing,** consuming, **gripping,** riveting, holding, **arresting,** engaging, attractive, **enthralling, spellbinding,** magnetic, hypnotic, mesmerizing, mesmeric

**fascination** NOUNS **captivation,** enthrallment, entrapment, snaring; **enchantment,** witchery, bewitchery, bewitchment; **attraction, interest, charm, glamour, appeal,** magnetism; charisma; **obsession,** prepossession, preoccupation, **hang-up** <nonformal>, **fixation**

**fashion** NOUNS 1 **manner, way,** wise, **means,** modality, tone; **style,** mode, vogue, trend, prevailing taste; the swim

<nonformal>, height of fashion; the new look, the season's look; high fashion, *haute couture* <Fr>
VERBS 2 **produce, create, make, manufacture, form,** formulate, evolve, mature, elaborate, **fabricate,** prefabricate, cast, shape, configure, carve out, mold, extrude, frame; **construct,** devise, design, concoct, compound, churn out *and* crank out *and* pound out *and* hammer out *and* grind out *and* rustle up *and* gin up <all nonformal>; **put together, assemble,** piece together, slap up *or* together <both nonformal>, improvise

**fast** NOUNS 1 **abstinence,** abstention, abstainment, **abstemiousness,** refraining, refrainment, avoidance, eschewal, denying *or* refusing oneself, saying no to, passing up <nonformal>
VERBS 2 not eat, go hungry, dine with Duke Humphrey; eat sparingly
ADJS 3 **swift, speedy, rapid; fastened, fixed,** secure, firm, close, tight, set; **bonded,** glued, cemented, taped; **jammed,** wedged, stuck, frozen, seized, seized up
4 **devoted,** dedicated, committed, steadfast, constant, faithful, staunch; tried, true, **tried and true,** true-blue, tested
5 **wild,** gallant, gay, rakish; rakehell, rakehellish, rakehelly
ADVS 6 **swiftly, rapidly, quickly,** snappily <nonformal>, **speedily,** apace; at a good clip <nonformal>, **by leaps and bounds,** trippingly; **posthaste, hastily,** expeditiously, promptly, double-quick; **securely, firmly,** tight; **inseparably,** indissolubly

7 <nonformal> **like a shot, as if shot out of a cannon, like a flash,** like a streak, like a blue streak, like a streak of lightning, like lightning, like greased lightning, **like a bat out of hell, like a scared rabbit,** like a house afire, like sixty, like mad *and* **crazy** *and* fury, like sin, to beat the band *or* the Dutch *or* the deuce *or* the devil; **lickety-split**; hell-bent *and* hell-bent for election *and* hell-bent for leather

**fasten** VERBS **fix, attach, affix,** annex, put to, set to; graft, engraft; **secure,** anchor, moor; cement, knit, set, grapple, belay, **make fast;** clinch, clamp, cramp; tighten, trim, trice up, screw up; cinch *or* cinch up

**fastidious** ADJS **particular, scrupulous, meticulous, conscientious,** exacting, precise, punctilious, spit-and-polish; **sensitive, discriminating**, discriminative; **selective,** picky <nonformal>, choosy; **strict**, perfectionistic; puritanic, puritanical, priggish, prudish, prissy, strait-laced

**fasting** NOUNS abstinence from food; starvation; punishment of Tantalus; hunger strike; **asceticism, austerity, self-denial,** belt-tightening

**fat** ADJS **corpulent, stout, overweight,** fattish, **obese,** adipose, gross, fleshy, beefy, meaty, hefty, porky, porcine; paunchy, bloated, puffy, blowzy, distended, swollen, pursy; abdominous, big-bellied, potbellied, **plump, buxom,** *zaftig* <Yiddish>, pleasantly plump, full, **tubby** <nonformal>, roly-poly; **pudgy,** podgy; sleek; fat, dumb, and happy <nonformal>

**fatal** ADJS **deadly,** death-bringing, mortal, lethal, malignant, malign, **virulent, pernicious,** baneful

**fatality** NOUNS fatal accident, violent death, **casualty,** disaster, calamity; DOA *or* dead-on-arrival; **deadliness, lethality,** mortality

**fate** NOUNS **destiny**, doom, karma, kismet, what bodes *or* looms, what is fated *or* destined *or* doomed, what is written, what is in the books

*whatever limits us*
EMERSON

**father** NOUNS 1 **sire,** genitor, paternal ancestor, pater <nonformal>, governor <nonformal>, *abba* <Heb>; patriarch, paterfamilias; stepfather; foster father, adoptive father; birth father

2 <nonformal> **papa,** pa, pap, pappy, **pop,** pops, **dad, daddy,** daddums, daddyo, big daddy, the old man, the governor, pater

3 **priest,** *gallach* <Heb>, father in Christ, **padre,** cassock, presbyter; curé, parish priest; confessor, father confessor, spiritual father *or* director *or* leader
VERBS 3 **engender, beget, procreate; originate,** give origin to, give occasion to, **give rise to,** spark, spark off, set off, trigger, trigger off; sire, sow the seeds of; **conceive,** have the idea, have a bright

idea <nonformal>; found, establish, inaugurate, institute

**fatigue** NOUNS 1 **tiredness, weariness,** wearifulness; **burnout,** end of one's tether, overtiredness, overstrain; lassitude, languor; combat fatigue; mental fatigue, mental strain
VERBS 2 **tire, weary, exhaust,** wilt, flag, jade, harass; **wear,** wear on *or* upon, **wear down; tire out, wear out, burn out; use up; do in;** overtire, overweary, weaken, enervate, debilitate

**fatten** VERBS **nourish, nurture,** nutrify, aliment, foster; **nurse, suckle,** lactate, breast-feed, wet-nurse, dry-nurse; fatten up, stuff, force-feed; **raise, breed,** rear, grow, hatch, feed, nurture

**fault** NOUNS 1 **defect, deficiency, inadequacy,** imperfection, kink, **flaw; weakness,** frailty, infirmity, failure, **failing, foible, shortcoming;** weak point, Achilles' heel, vulnerable place, chink in one's armor, weak link; **malfunction,** glitch <nonformal>
VERBS 2 **deprecate,** discommend, dispraise, disvalue, not be able to say much for, denigrate, faultfind, find fault with, put down <nonformal>, pick at *or* on, pick holes in, pick to pieces; **depreciate, disparage**

**faulty** ADJS **imperfect,** not perfect; **defective,** flawed, **inadequate, deficient,** short, not all it's cracked up to be <nonformal>, lacking, wanting, found wanting

**fauna** NOUNS **animal life, animal kingdom,** brute creation, Animalia <zoology>, animality; wild animals *or* beasts, beasts of field, wildlife, denizens of the forest *or* jungle *or* wild, furry creatures

**favor** NOUNS 1 **inclination, penchant, partiality, fancy, predilection, preference,** propensity, proclivity, **leaning, bent,** turn, tilt, bias, **affinity; act of kindness, kindness,** mercy, **benefit,** benefaction, benevolence, benignity, blessing, **service,** turn, break <nonformal>, **good turn, good** *or* **kind deed,** *mitzvah* <Heb>, office, good *or* kind offices, obligation, courtesy, kindly act
2 **esteem,** estimation, **honor, regard, respect,** approval, approbation, account, consideration, **credit**
3 **token, souvenir, keepsake,** token of remembrance
VERBS 4 **prefer,** have preference, **like better** *or* **best,** prefer to, set before *or* above, regard *or* honor before; rather <nonformal>, **had** *or* **have rather;** think proper, see *or* think fit, think best, please; tilt *or* incline *or* lean *or* tend toward, have a bias *or* partiality *or* penchant
5 **resemble,** be like, bear resemblance; put one in mind of <nonformal>, remind one of, bring to mind, be reminiscent of, suggest, evoke, call up, call to mind; **look like,** mirror; **take after**

**favorable** ADJS **propitious, advantageous;** kind, kindly, kindly-disposed, all for <nonformal>, **well-disposed,** well-intentioned, well-meant, **well-meaning; approving,** favoring, in favor of, well-disposed, well-inclined, supporting, backing, **advocating**

**favorite** NOUNS 1 preference; **darling,** idol, jewel, apple of one's eye, fair-haired boy, man after one's own heart; teacher's pet; tin god, little tin god
ADJS 2 **beloved, loved, dear, darling, precious;** pet; **adored, admired,** esteemed, revered; **cherished,** prized, treasured, held dear; **well-liked,** popular; dear to one's heart, after one's heart *or* own heart

**favoritism** NOUNS **partiality,** partisanship, onesidedness, undispassionateness, undetachment

**fawning** ADJS **obsequious, flattering,** sycophantic, sycophantical, toadyish, flattering, truckling, ingratiating, smarmy <nonformal>, toadying, toadeating, **bootlicking** *and* back scratching *and* backslapping *and* ass-licking *and* brown-nosing <all nonformal>; **groveling,** sniveling, cringing, cowering, crouching, crawling

**fay** NOUNS 1 **fairy, sprite,** fairy man *or* woman; **elf, brownie, pixie, gremlin,** gnome, ouphe, hob, cluricaune, puca *or* pooka *or* pwca, kobold, nisse, peri
ADJS 2 **fairy,** faery, **fairylike,** fairyish; **elfin,** elfish, elflike; gnomish, gnomelike; pixieish

**faze** VERBS **daunt, deter,** shake, stop, stop in one's tracks, set back; **discourage, dishearten; awe, overawe**

**fear** NOUNS 1 **fright,** affright; **scare, alarm, consternation, dismay; dread,** unholy dread, **awe; terror, horror,** horrification, mortal *or* abject fear; **phobia;** funk *or* blue funk <both nonformal>
VERBS 2 **be afraid; apprehend,** have qualms, misgive, eye askance; **dread,**

stand in dread *or* awe of, be in mortal dread *or* terror of, stand in awe of, stand aghast; have one's heart in one's mouth, have one's heart stand still, have one's heart skip *or* miss a beat

**fearful** ADJS fearing, fearsome, **in fear; cowardly**; **timorous, timid, shy,** rabbity *and* mousy <both nonformal>, afraid of one's own shadow; scary; **skittish,** skittery <nonformal>, jumpy, goosy <nonformal>

**feasible** ADJS **practicable, practical, workable,** realizable, operable, doable; **viable; achievable, attainable;** adaptable

**feast** NOUNS 1 **banquet,** festal board; lavish *or* Lucullan feast; blowout <nonformal>, groaning board
VERBS 2 **banquet,** regale; eat heartily, have a good appetite, eat up, lick the platter *or* plate, do oneself proud <nonformal>, do one's duty, do justice to, polish the platter, put it away <nonformal>

**feat** NOUNS **exploit, deed, enterprise, achievement, adventure,** gest, **bold stroke,** heroic act *or* deed

**feather** NOUNS **plume,** pinion; **quill;** pinfeather; contour feather, penna, down feather, plume feather, plumule; filoplume

**feature** NOUNS 1 **component,** aspect, specialty, circumstance, detail, item; **characteristic, peculiarity, singularity,** particularity, specialty, individualism, **character,** nature, **trait,** quirk, point of character, bad point, good point, saving grace, redeeming feature, mannerism, keynote, trick, distinctive feature, lineament; **highlight,** high spot, main attraction, centerpiece, pièce de résistance; outstanding feature
VERBS 2 **emphasize, stress,** lay emphasis *or* stress upon, highlight, brightline, place emphasis on, give emphasis to, **accent, accentuate, punctuate, point up,** bring to the fore, put in the foreground; headline <nonformal>; **star,** give top billing to

**feces** NOUNS feculence; defecation, movement, bowel movement *or* **BM; stool, shit** <nonformal>, **ordure,** night soil, crap *and* ca-ca *and* doo-doo <all nonformal>; turd <nonformal>; dingleberry <nonformal>; **dregs, grounds, lees,** dross, slag, draff, scoria

**federation** NOUNS **affiliation, alliance, allying, alignment, association,** consociation, combination, **union,** unification, **coalition,** fusion, merger, coalescence, coadunation, amalgamation, **league, confederation,** confederacy, consolidation, incorporation, inclusion, integration

**fee** NOUNS **stipend, allowance,** emolument, tribute; initiation fee; retainer, retaining fee; **dues,** toll, charge, charges, demand, exaction, exactment, scot, shot, scot and lot

**feeble** ADJS 1 **weak,** weakly, debilitated, imbecile; **doddering,** doddery, doddered, tottering, tottery, rickety, shaky, on one's last legs, with one foot in the grave; **strengthless,** sapless, marrowless, pithless, sinewless, listless, frail, out of gas <nonformal>, nerveless, lustless; **impotent, powerless; soft, flabby,** flaccid, unhardened; **limp,** limber, limp *or* limber as a dishrag, floppy, rubbery
2 **faint, low, soft, gentle, subdued, dim, weak,** faint-sounding, low-sounding, soft-sounding; faint-voiced, weak-voiced; half-heard, scarcely heard; barely audible, subaudible

**feebleminded** ADJS **weak-minded,** weak, feeble, infirm, soft, soft in the head, weak in the upper story <nonformal>

**feed** NOUNS 1 **fodder, provender;** forage, pasture, eatage, pasturage; grain; corn, oats, barley, wheat; ensilage, silage
VERBS 2 **dine,** wine and dine, mess; nibble, snack, graze <nonformal>; satisfy, gratify; regale; fare, take, partake, partake of, break bread; feed one's face *and* put on the feed bag <both nonformal>, fall to, pitch in <nonformal>; **foster, nurture,** nourish

**feel** VERBS **sense,** experience, **perceive,** apprehend, intuit, be sensible of, be conscious *or* aware of, apperceive; respond, respond to stimuli; be sensitive to, have a thing about <nonformal>; entertain *or* harbor *or* cherish *or* nurture a feeling; have a sensation, get *or* receive an impression

**feeler** NOUNS **offer,** offering, proffer, presentation, **bid,** submission; hesitant *or* tentative *or* preliminary approach, feeling-out; **probe,** sound, sounder; **trial balloon,** *ballon d'essai* <Fr>, pilot balloon, barometer; weather vane; straw vote

**feeling** NOUNS 1 **emotion, affect, sentiment,** affection, affections; **feelings, sensitiveness, sensibility,** susceptibil-

ity, thin skin; emotional life; the logic of the heart; **sense,** deep *or* profound sense, gut sense *or* sensation <nonformal>; **sensation**; **impression,** undercurrent
2 **hunch** <nonformal>, sense, **presentiment, premonition,** preapprehension, intimation, foreboding; suspicion, **impression,** intuition, intuitive impression, vague feeling *or* idea, funny feeling <nonformal>, feeling in one's bones
ADJS 3 **emotional, affective,** emotive, affectional; visceral, gut <nonformal>; **intuitive,** intuitional, sensing

**feisty** ADJS **plucky, spunky** *and* gutty *or* gutsy <all nonformal>, gritty, **mettlesome,** dauntless, **game,** game to the last *or* end; **perverse, contrary, wrongheaded, wayward, froward, difficult,** cantankerous, ornery <nonformal>

**feline** NOUNS 1 **cat,** pussy *and* **puss** *and* **pussycat** <all nonformal>, tabby, grimalkin; house cat; **kitten, kitty** *and* kitty-cat <both nonformal>; **tomcat,** tom; mouser; ratter; tiger cat, tabby cat; calico cat; alley cat
ADJS 2 felid, cattish, catty, catlike; kittenish; leonine, lionlike; tigerish, tigerlike

**fellow** NOUNS 1 **companion,** fellow companion, **comrade,** *camarade* <Fr>, amigo <nonformal>, mate <Brit>, comate, company, **associate**, consociate, compeer, confrere, consort, **colleague, partner,** copartner, side partner, **crony,** old crony
ADJS 2 **accompanying, twin, joint, joined**, conjoint, hand-in-hand, hand-in-glove, mutual

**fellowship** NOUNS **companionship, comradeship,** colleagueship, chumship <nonformal>, palship <nonformal>, freemasonry, consortship, boon companionship; camaraderie; scholarship

**felon** NOUNS **criminal, perpetrator, crook** *and* perp <both nonformal>, public enemy, **lawbreaker,** scofflaw

**felony** NOUNS **crime; offense, wrong,** illegality; **violation**; **wrongdoing**; much to answer for

**feminine** ADJS **female;** gynic, gynecic, gynecoid; muliebral, distaff, **womanly, womanish, womanlike,** petticoat; **ladylike,** gentlewomanlike, gentlewomanly; **matronly,** matronal, matronlike; **girlish,** little-girlish, kittenish; maidenly

**femininity** NOUNS **womankind, woman, women, womanhood,** womenfolk *or* womenfolks <nonformal>, the distaff side; **the female sex;** the second sex, **the fair sex,** the gentle sex, the softer sex, **the weaker sex,** the weaker vessel

**feminism** NOUNS **women's rights,** rights of women; **women's liberation,** women's lib <nonformal>, womanism, women's movement *or* liberation movement, sisterhood

**fence** NOUNS 1 **wall,** boundary, **barrier;** stone wall; paling, palisade; rail, railing; balustrade, balustrading; arcade
2 receiver, **receiver of stolen goods,** swagman *and* swagsman <both nonformal>, bagman, bagwoman
VERBS 3 **wall,** fence in, fence up; pale, rail, bar; hem, hem in, hedge, hedge in, hedge out; picket, palisade; bulkhead in
4 push *and* shove <both nonformal>; **sell under the counter; black-market,** black-marketeer; bootleg, moonshine <nonformal>

**fend** VERBS **fend off, ward off, stave off, hold off, fight off,** keep off, beat off, parry, counter, turn aside; **hold** *or* **keep at bay,** keep at arm's length; **hold the fort, hold the line,** stop, check, block, hinder, obstruct; **repel, repulse, rebuff, drive back,** put back, push back

**ferment** VERBS work; **bubble,** bubble up, burble; **effervesce, fizz, fizzle;** hiss, **sparkle; foam, froth,** froth up; have a head, foam over

**ferocious** ADJS **savage, fierce, vicious, murderous, cruel, atrocious, mindless, brutal,** brutish, **bestial,** mindless, insensate, monstrous, mutant, inhuman, pitiless, ruthless, merciless, bloody, sanguinary, kill-crazy <nonformal>

**fertile** ADJS **productive, fruitful,** fructiferous, fecund; **pregnant,** seminal, **rich,** flourishing, thriving, blooming; **prolific,** proliferous, uberous, **teeming,** swarming, bursting, bursting out, plenteous, **plentiful,** copious, generous, bountiful, **abundant**, **luxuriant, exuberant, lush,** superabundant; creative

**fervent** ADJS **fervid, passionate, impassioned,** intense, **ardent; hearty, cordial,** enthusiastic, exuberant, unrestrained, vigorous; keen, breathless, **excited**; **zealous,** perfervid, **spirited, vehement, abandoned**

**fervor** NOUNS **zeal, ardor,** ardency, fervency, fervidness, spirit, warmth, fire,

heat, heatedness, **passion,** passionateness, impassionedness, heartiness, intensity, **abandon,** vehemence
**festering** ADJS 1 suppurating, suppurative, rankling, mattering; pussy, purulent
2 haunting, persistent, recurrent, nagging, plaguing, rankling; obsessing, obsessive
**festival** NOUNS **festivity,** festive occasion, *fiesta* <Sp>, **fete,** gala, **gala affair, blowout** <nonformal>, **jamboree** <nonformal>; **high jinks,** do, great doings <all nonformal>
**festive** ADJS **festal; merry,** gay, jolly, jovial, joyous, joyful, gladsome, convivial, gala, hilarious; merrymaking, on the loose <nonformal>
**festivity** NOUNS **merrymaking, merriment, gaiety, jollity,** jollification <nonformal>, **joviality, conviviality,** whoopee *and* hoopla <both nonformal>; cavorting, skylarking; **revelry,** reveling, revels; **festival,** festive occasion, gala, **gala affair;** *fête champêtre* <Fr>; *Oktoberfest* <Ger>; Mardi Gras; Saturnalia
**fetal** ADJS **embryonic, germinal,** germinant, germinative, germinational; larval; in the bud; germiparous
**fetch** VERBS **bring, go get,** go and get, go to get, **go after,** go fetch, **go for,** call for, pick up; **get,** obtain, procure, secure; **bring back, retrieve;** chase after, run after, shag, fetch and carry
**fetching** ADJS **attractive,** interesting, **appealing,** engaging, taking, eye-catching, winning, winsome, prepossessing
**fete** NOUNS **party, festivity**, at home, housewarming, soiree, reception, shindig *and* brawl <both nonformal>
**fetish** NOUNS **amulet, talisman,** periapt, phylactery; totem, joss
**fetter** VERBS **shackle, manacle,** gyve, **put in irons; handcuff, tie one's hands; tie hand and foot,** hog-tie <nonformal>; straitjacket; hobble, hopple, tether; **hamper, impede, cramp, handicap,** put at a disadvantage; hamstring
**fetus** NOUNS **embryo,** zygote, oösperm, oöspore, blastula; germ, **larva,** nymph
**feud** NOUNS 1 **vendetta,** blood feud; **quarrel,** squabble, contention, strife, **tussle,** bicker, wrangle, snarl, **tiff, spat,** fuss
VERBS 2 **quarrel, dispute,** oppugn, flite <old>, altercate, **fight, squabble,** tiff, spat, **bicker, wrangle,** spar, broil, have words, set to, join issue, make the fur fly; cross swords
**feudal** ADJS 1 **imperious,** imperial, **masterful,** authoritative, aristocratic, **lordly,** magistral, **magisterial**
2 liege, **vassal,** feudatory, feodal
**fever** NOUNS 1 **feverishness,** febrility, febricity, pyrexia; hyperpyrexia, hyperthermia; **heat, fire, fever heat;** flush, hectic flush; calenture; **fever of excitement, fever pitch,** heat, fever heat, fire; sexual excitement, rut
2 **frenzy, furor,** fury, maniacal excitement, **rage; amok,** murderous insanity *or* frenzy, homicidal mania, hemothymia
**fey** ADJS **eccentric, erratic,** idiocratic, idiocratical, idiosyncratic, idiosyncratical, **queer,** queer in the head, **odd, peculiar,** strange, singular, anomalous, freakish, funny
**fiancé** NOUNS **fiancée,** bride-to-be, affianced, betrothed, intended <nonformal>
**fiasco** NOUNS **botch,** botch-up, bungle, hash, mess, muddle, foozle *and* bollix *and* bitch-up *and* screw-up *and* fuck-up <all nonformal>
**fiat** NOUNS 1 **decree,** decretum, decretal, rescript, **edict,** *edictum* <L>; **proclamation,** pronouncement, pronunciamento, **declaration,** ukase; bull, brevet <old>; diktat
2 **authorization, authority, sanction, licensing,** countenance, **warrant,** warranty
**fibrous** ADJS **stringy,** ropy, wiry; fibered, fibroid, fibrilliform
**fickle** ADJS **flighty,** skittish, **light;** coquettish, flirtatious, toying; versatile, **inconstant, changeable**; vacillating; volatile, mercurial, quicksilver
**fiction** NOUNS narrative, narrative literature, imaginative narrative, prose fiction; **storytelling,** tale-telling, yarnspinning *and* yarning <both nonformal>; fictionalization; **figment of the imagination,** creature of the imagination, creation *or* coinage of the brain, fiction of the mind; myth, romance
**fictitious** ADJS **make-believe, figmental,** fictional, fictive, fabricated, fictionalized; nonhistorical, nonfactual, nonactual, nonrealistic
**fidelity** NOUNS **faithfulness, loyalty,** faith; **constancy, steadfastness,** staunchness, firmness; trueness, troth,

true blue; good faith, *bona fides* <L>, *bonne foi* <Fr>; **allegiance, fealty, homage;** bond, tie; attachment, adherence, adhesion; devotion, devotedness

**fidget** VERBS have the fidgets; jitter, have the jitters, etc; **tense up; tremble; twitch, jerk,** vellicate; **jig, jiggle,** jigger *or* jigget <nonformal>

**field** NOUNS 1 **sphere,** profession, province, bailiwick, turf <nonformal>, department, area, discipline, subdiscipline, orb, orbit, realm, arena, domain, walk
2 **tract,** plat, **plot, patch,** piece *or* parcel of land; cultivated land; clearing

**fiend** NOUNS 1 **monster,** fiend from hell, **demon, devil,** devil incarnate, hellhound, hellkite; **vampire,** lamia, **harpy, ghoul**
2 **brute,** hellcat, **beast,** wild beast, mad dog, wolf, monster, mutant, savage; **rapist, mugger, killer**

**fierce** ADJS **savage, ferocious,** feral, **vicious, atrocious,** truculent, fell; **inhuman,** inhumane, unhuman; fiendish, fiendlike; **violent, virulent, severe, furious, intense,** sharp, acute, keen, cutting, splitting, piercing

**fiery** ADJS **heated, inflamed,** flaming, scorching, hot, red-hot, white-hot; **fanatic, zealous,** totally committed, hard-core, hard-line, ardent, passionate; **hotheaded**

**fiesta** NOUNS **festivity,** fete, festive occasion, celebration, merrymaking, revel, revelry, jubilation, joyance

**fight** NOUNS 1 **battle, fray,** affray, combat, action, conflict, embroilment; **clash; brush, skirmish,** scrimmage; tussle, **scuffle, struggle,** scramble, shoving match; exchange of blows, clash of arms; **quarrel**; pitched battle; battle royal; **fistfight,** punch-out *and* duke-out <both nonformal>, punch-up <Brit nonformal>; **struggle,** hassle <nonformal>
VERBS 2 **struggle, strive, contend, battle,** buffet, scuffle, tussle, wrestle, hassle <nonformal>; **box,** punch, spar, mix it up <nonformal>, knock out, slug, maul

**fighter** NOUNS **combatant, battler,** scrapper <nonformal>; **contestant, contender, competitor, rival;** disputant, wrangler, squabbler, bickerer, quarreler; tussler, scuffler; brawler, **boxer,** pugilist, prizefighter, pug *and* palooka <both nonformal>, slugger, mauler

**figurative** ADJS **representational, representative, depictive, delineatory, illustrative,** pictorial, graphic, ideographic, pictographic; **symbolizing,** personifying, embodying; imitative, mimetic, simulative, apish, mimish; **symbolic,** metaphorical, allegorical, figural

**figurehead** NOUNS 1 **prow, bow, stem,** rostrum, nose, beak
2 nominal head, dummy, lay figure, front man *and* front <both nonformal>, stooge *and* Charlie McCarthy <both nonformal>, puppet, creature

**figure of speech** NOUNS **figure, image,** trope, turn of expression, manner *or* way of speaking, ornament, device, flourish, flower

**fill** NOUNS 1 **full measure,** full house, bellyful *and* skinful <both nonformal>; more than enough

> *good measure, pressed down, and shaken together, and running over*
> BIBLE

VERBS 2 fill up, **pack, load; pad,** wad, **stuff;** extend throughout, leave no void, occupy; creep *or* crawl *or* swarm with, be lousy with <nonformal>, teem with; honeycomb

**filler** NOUNS **filling, packing,** padding, wadding, **stuffing**

**filling** ADJS **completing, fulfilling,** completive *or* completory, consummative *or* consummatory; **complementary,** complemental; **satiating,** sating, satisfying, surfeiting, overfilling; jading, **cloying,** cloysome

**film** NOUNS 1 covering, **coat,** coating, veneer, patina, scum, membrane, pellicle, peel, skin, rind, hide; slick, oil slick
2 **motion picture, movie, picture,** flick *and* flicker <both nonformal>, picture show; motion-picture film, panchromatic film, monochromatic film, orthochromatic film, black-and-white film, color film

**filter** VERBS **clarify,** clear, purify, rectify, depurate, decrassify; **strain;** elute, elutriate; filtrate; **percolate,** leach, lixiviate; **sift,** separate, sieve, **screen,** bolt, winnow

**filth** NOUNS **muck,** slime, mess, sordes, foul matter; ordure, **excrement**; mucus, snot <nonformal>; scurf, furfur, dandruff; putrid matter, pus, corruption, gangrene, decay, carrion, **rot**; **obscenity,**

smut <nonformal>; **dirtiness,** bawdry, raunch <nonformal>, **ribaldry, pornography,** porno *and* porn <both nonformal>, hard *or* hard-core pornography, soft *or* soft-core pornography, salacity, **smut, dirt**

**filthy** ADJS **obscene, lewd, adult, bawdy,** ithyphallic, **ribald, pornographic, salacious,** sultry <nonformal>, lurid, **dirty, smutty,** raunchy <nonformal>, blue, smoking-room, impure, unchaste, unclean, **foul, nasty,** vile, fulsome, offensive, unprintable, unrepeatable, not fit for mixed company

**finagle** VERBS **maneuver, manipulate,** pull strings *or* wires; **machinate, contrive,** angle <nonformal>, **jockey, engineer;** play games <nonformal>; **plot, scheme, intrigue; wangle;** gerrymander

**final** ADJS **terminal,** terminating *or* terminative, determinative, definitive, **conclusive; last,** last-ditch <nonformal>, last but not least, eventual, farthest, extreme, boundary, border, limbic, limiting, polar, **endmost, ultimate;** caudal, tail, tail-end

**finale** NOUNS ending, **termination, terminus,** expiry, phaseout, phasedown, discontinuation, closeout, cessation, ceasing, consummation, culmination, **conclusion, finish, finis,** the end, finishing, finalizing *or* finalization, windup *and* payoff <both nonformal>, curtains <nonformal>, end of the road *or* line <nonformal>

**finalize** VERBS **complete, round off** *or* **out, wind up** <nonformal>, **top off;** top out, crown, cap; climax, culminate; **give the finishing touches** *or* **strokes,** put the finishing touches *or* strokes on, lick *or* whip into shape, put the icing on the cake

**finally** ADVS in fine; **ultimately, eventually, as a matter of course; lastly,** last, **at last,** at the last *or* end *or* conclusion, at length, at long last; **in conclusion, in sum;** conclusively, once and for all; **after all is said and done,** the way the cookie crumbles <nonformal>

**finance** NOUNS 1 **finances, money matters;** world of finance, financial world, financial industry, **high finance,** investment banking, international banking
VERBS 2 **subsidize, back, fund, sponsor, support,** provide for, capitalize, provide capital *or* money for, pay for, bankroll <nonformal>, angel <nonformal>, put up the money; **stake** *or* **grubstake** <both nonformal>; set up, set up in business

**find** NOUNS 1 finding, **discovery;** catch, trove, *trouvaille* <Fr>; treasure trove, buried treasure; **windfall,** windfall money, windfall profit, found money, money in the bank, **bonus, gravy** <nonformal>
VERBS 2 **discover,** get; strike, hit; put *or* lay one's hands on, lay one's fingers on, **locate**; **hunt down,** search out, trace down, track down, **run down, run** *or* **bring to earth;** trace; **learn, find out,** determine, become cognizant *or* conscious of, become aware of; discover *or* find out the hard way, discover to one's cost; discover *or* find oneself; **draw a conclusion,** hold, ascertain
3 agree on a verdict, return a verdict, hand down a verdict, **bring in a verdict,** find for *or* against

**finding** NOUNS conclusion, determination, ascertainment, judgment, **verdict, decision,** resolution <old>, **determination,** holding; **learning, finding out,** determining, becoming conscious *or* cognizant of, becoming aware of; self-discovery

**fine** ADJS 1 **healthy, healthful,** enjoying health, in health, in shape, in condition, **fit,** fit and fine; **in good** *or* **fine shape, in fine fettle,** bursting with health
2 flimsy, slight, **unsubstantial** *or* **insubstantial**; **thin, tenuous,** subtile, subtle, evanescent, fastidious, overfine, refined, rarefied
3 **good, excellent,** *bueno* <Sp>, *bon* <Fr>, bonny <Brit>, **nice,** goodly, fair; **splendid, capital, grand,** elegant <nonformal>
ADVS 4 **excellently, nicely,** finely, **capitally, splendidly, famously,** royally; **well,** very well, right, aright

**finesse** NOUNS 1 **skill,** grace, style; **tact, tactfulness, diplomacy;** *savoir-faire* <Fr>; **craftsmanship,** workmanship, technical skill, **technique, touch,** technical brilliance, technical mastery, **virtuosity,** bravura, wizardry; refinement, delicacy; **tact, tactfulness,** feel, feeling, sense, **sensitivity, sensibility**
VERBS 2 **maneuver,** machinate, operate <nonformal>, engineer, rig, wangle <nonformal>, angle, finagle <nonformal>; use one's fine Italian hand

**finger** NOUNS 1 **digit;** forefinger, index

finger, index; ring finger, annulary; middle finger, medius, dactylion; little finger, pinkie <nonformal>, minimus; thumb, pollex
VERBS 2 **touch, feel,** feel of, palpate; pass *or* run the fingers over, feel with the fingertips, thumb; **point out,** point at, put *or* lay one's finger on
3 **denounce,** denunciate; point the finger at *and* put *or* lay the finger on <all nonformal>, **inform on** *or* **against; condemn to death,** sign one's death warrant, give the kiss of death to

**finicky** ADJS **finical,** finicking, finikin; **fussy,** fuss-budgety <nonformal>; **squeamish,** pernickety *and* persnickety <both nonformal>, difficult, hard to please; **meticulous**, nice, niggling

**finish** NOUNS 1 **completion,** completing, finishing, **conclusion, end,** ending, **termination,** terminus, **close, windup** <nonformal>, rounding off *or* out, topping off, wrapping up, wrap-up, finalization; **refinement,** precision, exactitude, lapidary quality; **discrimination,** choice; **restraint; polish; conclusion, finis, finale,** the end
VERBS 2 **complete, perfect, finish off, conclude, terminate, end,** bring to a close, carry to completion, prosecute to a conclusion; **get through, get done; polish, burnish;** get it over with, **finish up; give the finishing touches** *or* **strokes,** put the finishing touches *or* strokes on, lick *or* whip into shape, finalize, put the icing on the cake

**finished** ADJS 1 **used up, consumed,** concluded, terminated, ended, finished up; signed, sealed, and delivered; **skilled, accomplished;** trained, coached, prepared, primed; **elegant, polished,** round, terse; neat, trim, **refined, exact,** lapidary *or* lapidarian; wound up <nonformal>

2 <nonformal> **belly-up, dead meat,** kaput, shot, done for, SOL *or* shit out of luck, scragged, shot down, shot down in flames, down in flames, wasted, zapped, pffft *or* phut, wiped out, washed up, down and out, down the tubes, totaled; all over but the shouting

**finite** ADJS **limited, restricted,** bound, **bounded; confined**, prescribed, proscribed, cramped, strait, straitened, narrow

**fire** NOUNS 1 **zeal, ardor, ardency, fervor, fervency, fervidness, spirit, passion,** impassionedness, intensity, **abandon,** vehemence; **inspiration,** spark; afflatus, divine afflatus
2 **blaze, flame,** ingle, devouring element; **combustion, ignition,** ignition temperature *or* point, flash *or* flashing point; **conflagration**
VERBS 3 **excite, impassion, kindle,** enkindle, light up, light the fuse, **inflame,** set fire to, set on fire, fire *or* warm the blood; fan the fire *or* flame, raise to a fever heat *or* pitch; **fire one's imagination; animate, exhilarate,** enliven
4 **shoot,** fire off, let off, let fly, **discharge,** eject; detonate; **launch,** project, blast off
5 **discharge, dismiss,** expel, **lay off,** furlough, let go, make redundant, **retire;** kick upstairs

6 <nonformal> **can, sack, bump,** bounce, kick, boot, give the ax, give the gate, give one the sack *or* the ax *or* the boot *or* the gate *or* the air *or* one's walking papers, send one to the showers, show one the door *or* gate

**firearm** NOUNS **gun;** shooting iron *and* gat *and* rod *and* heater *and* piece <all nonformal>; shoulder weapon *or* gun *or* arm

**firebrand** NOUNS **hothead,** revolutionary, **terrorist,** incendiary, bomber, guerrilla; brand, **ember,** burning ember

**fireworks** NOUNS **pyrotechnics** *or* pyrotechny; **gunfire, fire, firing,** musketry, **shooting,** gunplay <nonformal>; gunfight, shootout

**firm** NOUNS 1 **company, business firm, concern, house,** *compagnie* <Fr>, *compañía* <Sp>, *Aktiengesellschaft* <Ger>, *aktiebolag* <Swed>; **business, industry, enterprise,** business establishment, commercial enterprise
ADJS 2 **sound, stout,** sturdy, tough, hard-boiled <nonformal>, solid; sound as a dollar, solid as a rock, firm as Gibraltar, made of iron; rigid, unbreakable, infrangible; **staunch,** standup <nonformal>, steady, steadfast, constant, not to be shaken, unflappable <nonformal>; undeflectable, **unswerving,** immovable, unbending, inflexible, **unyielding**; true, loyal

**first** NOUNS 1 first ever, prime, primal,

primary, **initial,** alpha; initialization, first move, opening move, gambit, **first step,** baby step, *le premier pas* <Fr>, openers, starters
ADJS 2 **foremost,** front, up-front <nonformal>, **head, chief, principal,** premier, **leading, main,** flagship; maiden
ADVS 3 firstly, **at first,** first off, first thing, for openers *or* starters <nonformal>, as a gambit, up front <nonformal>, **in the first place,** first and foremost, before everything, *primo* <L>; **originally, in the beginning,** *in limine* <L>, **at the start,** at first glance *or* first blush, at the outset; from the ground up, from the beginning, **from scratch** <nonformal>, from the first, **from the word 'go'** <nonformal>, *ab origine* <L>, *ab initio* <L>; *ab ovo* <L>

**first-class** ADJS **first-rate,** in a class by itself; of the first *or* highest degree; unmatched, matchless; champion, record-breaking; of the first water, top of the line, highest-quality, best-quality, far and away the best, the best by a long shot *or* long chalk, head and shoulders above, of the highest type

**firsthand** ADJS **unused, original;** authentic, reliable, eye-witness

**first name** NOUNS **forename, Christian name, given name,** baptismal name

**first-rate** ADJS 1 **superlative,** top, topmost, uppermost, tip-top, top-level, top-echelon, first-class, of the first water, top of the line, in a class by itself; of the first *or* highest degree

2 <nonformal> **A-1, A number one,** primo, first-chop, tip-top, top-notch, topflight, top-drawer, tops; topping *or* top-hole <both Brit>

**fiscal** ADJS **monetary, pecuniary,** nummary, **financial;** capital

**fish** VERBS go fishing, **angle;** cast one's hook *or* net; shrimp, whale, clam, grig, still-fish, fly-fish, troll, bob, dap, dib *or* dibble, gig, jig

**fisherman** NOUNS **fisher, angler,** *piscator* <L>, piscatorian, piscatorialist; Waltonian, dibber, dibbler, troller, trawler, trawlerman, dragger, jacker, jigger, bobber, guddler, tickler, drifter, drift netter, whaler, clam digger, lobsterman

*The Compleat Angler*
IZAAK WALTON

**fission** NOUNS **severance,** disseverment *or* disseverance, **sunderance,** scission, cleavage, dichotomy; **nuclear fission,** fission reaction; **atom-smashing,** atom-chipping, **splitting the atom;** atomic reaction; thermonuclear reaction; **chain reaction**

**fissure** NOUNS **crack, cleft,** cranny, chink, check, craze, chap, **crevice,** scissure, incision, notch, score, cut, gash, slit, split, **rift,** rent; **interruption, suspension, break,** breach, gap, hiatus, lacuna, caesura

**fit** NOUNS 1 **seizure, spasm, throes, paroxysm, convulsion,** eclampsia, frenzy; **epilepsy,** falling sickness; fit of anger, fit of temper, rage, **tantrum,** temper tantrum
VERBS 2 **equip, furnish, outfit,** gear, **prepare,** fit up *or* out, fix up <nonformal>, **rig,** rig up *or* out, **turn out,** appoint, accouter, clothe, dress; adapt, tailor, measure, proportion, adjust to, trim to, cut to, gear to, key to
3 **suit,** suit *or* fit to a tee, fit like a glove, **qualify, do,** serve, answer, be OK <nonformal>, do the job *and* do the trick *and* fill the bill <all nonformal>
ADJS 3 **healthy, healthful,** enjoying health, **fine,** in health, in shape, in condition, fit and fine; **in good health,** in the pink of condition, in mint condition, **in good** *or* **fine shape, in fine fettle,** bursting with health, full of life and vigor
4 **eligible, qualified,** fitted, **suitable,** acceptable, admissible, worthy, desirable; **appropriate,** fitting, proper, correct, seemly

**fitful** ADJS **discontinuous,** broken off, fragmentary, **interrupted,** suspended; disjunctive, discrete, discretive; **intermittent,** spotty, patchy, jagged; choppy, chopped-off, herky-jerky <nonformal>, jerky, spasmodic; episodic

**fitting** ADJS **decorous,** decent, proper, right, right-thinking, **seemly, becoming,** appropriate, meet, happy, felicitous; genteel; civil, urbane; **expedient,** fit, befitting, suitable

**fix** NOUNS 1 **predicament,** plight, pass, pickle *and* picklement *and* jam *and* spot *and* bind <all nonformal>; **temporary expedient, improvisation,** ad hoc measure, **quick fix** <nonformal>, **makeshift,** stopgap, shake-up, jury-rig

2 <nonformal> **put-up job,** packed *or* rigged game *or* jury, packed deal, stacked deck, cold deck, boat race, tank job; **frame-up,** frame, setup

VERBS 3 **repair, mend,** fix up <nonformal>, do up, doctor <nonformal>, put in repair, put in shape, set to rights, put in order *or* condition; **condition, recondition, service, overhaul;** patch, **patch up;** tinker, tinker up, fiddle, fiddle around; cobble
4 **fasten, attach, affix,** annex, put to, set to; **secure,** anchor, moor; belay, **make fast; determine,** decide, **establish,** settle, lock in *and* nail down *and* clinch *and* cinch <all nonformal>, clear up, sort out, set at rest

5 <nonformal> **rig,** pack, cook, cook up; **stack the cards,** cold-deck, pack the deal; put in the bag, sew up; frame, frame-up, set up; **throw,** tank, go in the tank, hold a boat race

**fixation** NOUNS **fixity,** fixedness, fixture; infixion, implantation, embedment; **obsession,** prepossession, preoccupation, **hang-up** <nonformal>, complex, fascination; **compulsion,** morbid drive, obsessive compulsion, irresistible impulse

**fixer** NOUNS **mender,** doctor <nonformal>, restorer, renovator, repairer, **repairman, repairwoman,** maintenance man *or* woman, **serviceman, servicewoman;** trouble man *and* **troubleshooter** <both nonformal>; **wirepuller** <nonformal>; **influence peddler,** power broker

**fixings** NOUNS **constituents, ingredients,** makings *and* fixings <both nonformal>, **elements**

**fizz** NOUNS 1 **bubbling,** bubbliness, **effervescence** *or* effervescency, **sparkle,** spumescence, frothiness, frothing, foaming; fizzle, carbonation; **fermentation,** ferment
VERBS 2 **bubble,** bubble up, burble; **effervesce, fizzle;** hiss, **sparkle; ferment,** work; **foam, froth,** froth up; have a head, foam over

**flabbergast** VERBS **astonish, amaze, astound, surprise,** startle, stagger, **bewilder, perplex,** confound, overwhelm, **boggle, boggle the mind; awe,** strike with wonder *or* awe; **dumbfound** *or* dumbfounder, strike dumb, strike dead; knock one's socks off *and* bowl over <both nonformal>, dazzle

**flabby** ADJS **flaccid, limp,** rubbery, flimsy, floppy; **loose,** lax, relaxed; feeble, soft, **weak,** weak as a kitten, wimpy *or* wimpish <nonformal>

**flag** NOUNS **banner,** oriflamme, **standard,** gonfalon *or* gonfanon, guidon, *vexillum* <L>, *labarum* <L>; **pennant,** pennon, pennoncel, banneret, banderole, swallowtail, burgee, **streamer; bunting**

**flagrant** ADJS **outright,** arrant, shocking, shattering, egregious, intolerable, unbearable, unconscionable, glaring, stark-staring, rank, crass, gross; **blatant,** shameless, **brazen,** brazenfaced, lurid, glaring, flaring, flaunting, screaming <nonformal>, obtrusive, vulgar, crude

**flail** VERBS **whip,** give a whipping *or* beating *or* thrashing, **beat, thrash, spank, flog,** scourge, flagellate, whale

**flair** NOUNS **talent,** strong flair, **gift, endowment,** dowry, dower, natural gift *or* endowment, **genius,** instinct, **faculty; forte,** specialty, métier, long suit, strong point; **aptitude,** inborn *or* innate aptitude, aptness, felicity, **bent**

**flak** NOUNS **criticism,** adverse criticism, harsh *or* hostile criticism, bad notices, bad press, animadversion, imputation, reflection, **aspersion,** stricture, obloquy; **knock** *and* **swipe** *and* **slam** *and* **rap** *and* hit <all nonformal>

**flaky** ADJS 1 **fanciful, notional,** fantastic *or* fantastical, maggoty, **crotchety,** kinky, harebrained, cranky, quirky; wanton, wayward, vagrant; **arbitrary, unreasonable,** motiveless; **moody, temperamental,** prima-donnaish; petulant; unrestrained
2 flocculent; **scaly,** scurfy, squamous, lentiginous, furfuraceous, lepidote

**flamboyant** ADJS **showy, flashy, ostentatious,** gaudy, glitzy <nonformal>, meretricious, flaming, bedizened, flaunting, garish

**flame** NOUNS 1 **boyfriend** *and* **girlfriend** <both nonformal>; sweetheart, passion
2 **fire; blaze,** ingle, devouring element; **combustion, ignition,** ignition temperature *or* point, flash *or* flashing point; **conflagration;** flicker, wavering *or* flickering flame

*lambent flame*
DRYDEN

VERBS 3 **catch fire,** catch on fire, catch, take fire, **burn,** combust, blaze, **blaze up, burst into flame**

**flaming** ADJS **fiery, heated, inflamed,** scorching, hot, red-hot, white-hot; **fanatic, zealous,** totally committed, hard-core, hard-line, ardent, passionate; **hotheaded**

**flap** NOUNS 1 **bustle,** brouhaha, hurly-burly, **fuss, flurry, flutter,** fluster, scramble, ferment, stew, sweat, whirl, swirl, vortex, maelstrom, **stir,** hubbub, hullabaloo, hoo-ha *and* foofaraw <both nonformal>, ado, to-do <nonformal>, bother, botheration <nonformal>, pother
VERBS 2 **hang,** hang down, fall; **dangle,** swing, flop <nonformal>; **droop,** lop; **trail, drag, draggle,** drabble, daggle

**flare** NOUNS 1 flareup, **flash,** flash fire, **blaze,** burst, outburst; deflagration; **torch,** flaming torch, flambeau, cresset; signal flare, beacon
VERBS 2 **spread,** spread out, outspread, outstretch; flare out, broaden out, splay; spraddle, sprangle, sprawl
3 **blaze,** combust, spark, **catch fire, flame,** flame up, flare up

**flareup** NOUNS **outburst,** outburst of anger, burst, **explosion,** eruption, blowup <nonformal>, access, blaze of temper; **storm, scene,** high words

**flashy** ADJS **showy, flaunting,** snazzy, flashing, glittering, **ostentatious,** gaudy, **jazzy** *and* **glitzy** *and* gimmicky *and* splashy *and* splurgy <all nonformal>; exhibitionistic, showoffy <nonformal>, bravura; **sporty** *or* dressy <both nonformal>; **frilly, flouncy,** frothy, chichi

**flat** NOUNS 1 **apartment, rooms;** studio apartment; suite, suite *or* set of rooms; walkup, cold-water flat; railroad flat
ADJS 2 dull, mat, dead, dingy, muddy, leaden, lusterless, lackluster; **insipid, tasteless, flavorless,** bland, spiceless, **savorless,** sapless, unsavory, unflavored; stale, dead, *fade* <Fr>; vapid, inane, jejune; insipid, vapid
3 **horizontal, level,** flattened; **even,** smooth, smoothened, smoothed out

**flatten** VERBS **level, even, equalize,** align, smooth *or* smoothen, level out, smooth out, flush; grade, roll, roll flat, steamroller *or* steamroll; **raze,** rase, **fell,** smash, prostrate, raze to the ground *or* dust

**flatter** VERBS 1 adulate, conceit; **cajole, wheedle, blandish,** palaver; slaver *or* slobber over, beslobber, beslubber; oil the tongue, lay the flattering unction to one's soul, make fair weather; **praise, compliment**, praise to the skies; scratch one's back, kiss ass <nonformal>, fawn upon

2 <nonformal> **soft-soap,** butter, honey, **butter up,** soften up; stroke, massage the ego; **blarney,** jolly, pull one's leg; lay it on, pour *or* spread *or* lay it on thick *or* with a trowel, overdo it, soap, oil; string along, kid along; play up to, get around

**flatterer** NOUNS 1 commender, eulogist, eulogizer; **praiser,** lauder, extoller, encomiast, panegyrist, **booster** <nonformal>, puffer, promoter

2 <nonformal> **apple-polisher, ass-kisser, brown-nose,** brown-noser, brownie, ass-licker, ass-wiper, suck-ass; **backslapper,** backscratcher, clawback, back-patter; **bootlicker,** bootlick; **handshaker; yes-man, stooge**

**flattery** NOUNS **adulation; praise**; **blandishment,** palaver, **cajolery,** cajolement, wheedling; **blarney** *and* bunkum *and* **soft soap** <all nonformal>, oil, grease, eyewash <nonformal>; strokes *and* stroking *and* ego massage <all nonformal>, sweet talk, fair *or* sweet *or* honeyed words, pretty lies, sweet nothings

**flatulence** NOUNS **distension,** puffing, puff, puffiness, **bloating,** bloat, flatulency, gassiness, **gas,** stomach gas, gassiness, flatus, windiness, farting <nonformal>, windiness; **turgidity,** turgidness, turgescence; **vaporousness,** vaporiness

**flaunt** VERBS vaunt, **parade, display, demonstrate,** manifest, make a great show of, **exhibit,** air, put forward, put forth, hold up, flash *and* sport <both nonformal>; **wave, brandish, flourish,** shake, swing, wield

**flavor** NOUNS 1 **taste,** sapor; **smack, tang; savor, relish,** sapidity; palate, tongue, tooth, stomach
2 **flavoring,** flavorer; **seasoning,** sea-

soner, **relish, condiment, spice,** condiments
VERBS 3 savor; **season,** salt, pepper, **spice,** sauce; **tinge, tincture**

**flavorsome** ADJS **flavorful,** flavorous, flavory, well-flavored; full-flavored, full-bodied; rich-flavored; **delectable, delicious,** luscious; tasty, savory; succulent

**flaw** NOUNS **fault,** *faute* <Fr>, **defect,** imperfection, kink, hole, bug <nonformal>; fly in the ointment, problem, snag, drawback; **blemish, malfunction,** glitch <nonformal>

**flawed** ADJS **illogical, irrational, invalid,** inauthentic, unauthentic, faulty, paralogical, fallacious; defective, **blemished, disfigured,** defaced, **marred,** scarred

**flawless** ADJS **perfect, ideal, faultless,** unflawed, defectless, not to be improved, **impeccable,** absolute; **just right;** spotless, stainless, taintless, unblemished, untainted, unspotted, immaculate, **pure,** uncontaminated, unadulterated; sinless; chaste; infallible; irreproachable

**fleabag** NOUNS **flophouse** *and* fleabag <both nonformal>, dosshouse <Brit nonformal>

**fledgling** NOUNS **novice,** novitiate *or* noviciate, **tyro,** abecedarian, alphabetarian, **beginner**, entrant, **neophyte, tenderfoot** *and* **greenhorn** <both nonformal>, freshman, **rookie** *and* yardbird <both nonformal>, boot

**flee** VERBS **fly, take flight,** take to flight, take wing, fugitate, **run, cut and run** <nonformal>, run away from, bug out <nonformal>, **decamp,** pull up stakes, **take to one's heels,** make off, **depart**, do the disappearing act, make a quick exit, **beat a retreat** *or* **a hasty retreat, turn tail,** show the heels, show a clean *or* light pair of heels; **bolt, run for one's life**

**fleeting** ADJS **transient, transitory,** transitive; **temporary,** temporal; **passing,** flitting, flying, fading, dying; fugitive, fugacious

**flexible** ADJS **adaptable,** adjustable, resourceful, supple; **resilient, adaptable,** adjustable, able to roll with the punches *or* bend without breaking; **compliant,** pliant, complaisant, malleable, plastic, acquiescent, submissive, tractable, obedient

**flickering** ADJS **fluctuating,** alternating, **vacillating, wavering,** wavery, wavy, mazy, flitting, guttering, fitful, shifting, shuffling

**flier** NOUNS 1 **aviator, pilot,** air pilot, licensed pilot, private pilot, airline pilot, commercial pilot, aeronaut, flyboy *and* airplane driver *and* birdman <all nonformal>
2 **advertising matter,** leaflet, leaf, folder, handbill, bill, throwaway, handout, circular, broadside, broadsheet
3 **gamble,** chance, risk, risky thing, hazard; **speculation, venture,** plunge <nonformal>; calculated risk

**flight** NOUNS 1 **trip, run; hop** *and* **jump** <both nonformal>; powered flight; solo flight, **solo;** supersonic flight; test flight, **test hop** <nonformal>
2 exit, quick exit, making oneself scarce *and* getting the hell out <both nonformal>, bolt, disappearing act <nonformal>, hasty retreat; **decampment;** skedaddle *and* skedaddling <both nonformal>; French leave, absence without leave *or* AWOL; **desertion**; hegira

**flighty** ADJS **fickle,** skittish, **light;** coquettish, flirtatious, toying; volatile, mercurial, quicksilver; faddish; **scatterbrained**, unpredictable; **impulsive;** unreliable, undependable; whimsical, **capricious,** off-again-on-again

**flimflam** VERBS

<nonformal> **gyp, clip, scam,** rope in, hose, shave, beat, rook, diddle, do a number on, hustle, fuck, screw, have, pull something, pull a trick *or* stunt, give the business, stick, sting, burn, gouge, chisel, play *or* take for a sucker, make a patsy of, take for a ride

**flimsy** ADJS **fragile,** frangible, **breakable,** destructible, shattery, crumbly, brittle, fragmentable, fracturable; **unsubstantial,** sleazy, tacky <nonformal>, wispy, cobwebby, gossamery, papery, pasteboardy; gimcrack *and* gimcracky *and* cheap-jack *and* ticky-tacky <all nonformal>; jerry-built, jerry

**flinch** VERBS **shrink, shy,** shy away from, draw back, recoil, funk <nonformal>, **quail, cringe, wince, blench, blink,** say *or* cry uncle; put one's tail between one's legs

**fling** NOUNS 1 **revel, lark, escapade,** ploy; **celebration**; **party**; **spree, bout,**

wingding *and* randan <both nonformal>; **carouse, drinking bout**
2 **throw, toss, sling, cast, hurl,** chuck, chunk <nonformal>, lob, **heave,** shy, **pitch, toss,** peg <nonformal>
VERBS 3 **throw, sling, pitch, toss, cast, hurl, heave, chuck,** chunk *and* peg <both nonformal>, lob, shy, fire, burn, pepper <nonformal>, launch, dash, let fly, let go, let rip, let loose

**flip** NOUNS 1 **reverse, reversal,** flip-flop *and* U-turn <both nonformal>, turnabout, turnaround, **about-face,** about turn <Brit>, *volte-face* <Fr>; tergiversation, tergiversating; **change of mind;** second thoughts, better thoughts, afterthoughts, mature judgment
VERBS 2 **reverse,** transpose; **throw, fling, sling, pitch, toss, cast, hurl, heave, chuck,** chunk *and* peg <both nonformal>, lob, shy, fire, burn, pepper <nonformal>, launch, dash, let fly, let go, let rip, let loose

3 <nonformal> **blow one's top** *or* stack *or* cool, flip out, flip one's lid *or* wig, pop one's cork, blow a gasket, fly off the handle, **hit the ceiling,** go ape, go hog wild, go bananas, lose one's cool, go off the deep end

ADJS 4 **impudent, impertinent, pert,** flippant, **cocky** *and* cheeky *and* **fresh** *and* facy *and* crusty *and* nervy <all nonformal>; uncalled-for, gratuitous, biggety <nonformal>; **disrespectful,** derisive, brash, bluff; **saucy,** sassy <nonformal>; **glib,** smooth

**flirt** NOUNS 1 **coquette,** gold digger *and* vamp <both nonformal>; **trifler, dallier**
VERBS 2 **coquet; philander,** gallivant, play the field <nonformal>, run *or* play around, sow one's oats; **make eyes at, ogle,** eye, cast coquettish glances, cast sheep's eyes at, make goo-goo eyes at <nonformal>, *faire les yeux doux* <Fr>, look sweet upon <nonformal>; **trifle, dally**

**flitter** NOUNS 1 **flutter,** flit, **flicker, waver,** dance; shake, quiver; **sputter, splutter; palpitation,** throb, pit-a-pat, pitter-patter
VERBS 2 **flutter,** flit, flick, **flicker,** gutter, bicker, wave, **waver,** dance; **sputter, splutter; palpitate,** pulse, throb, pitter-patter, go pit-a-pat

**float** NOUNS 1 **raft;** balsa, balsa raft; life raft; boom; pontoon; buoy, life buoy; **life preserver**; surfboard
VERBS 2 ride, drift; **sail, scud, run,** shoot; skim, foot; ride the sea, walk the waters; float on one's back, do the deadman's float
3 **issue,** put on the market; issue stock, go public <nonformal>; float a bond issue

**flock** NOUNS 1 **tuft,** fleck; forelock, widow's peak, fetlock, cowlick
2 fold, sheep; **congregation,** parishioners, churchgoers, assembly
3 **bunch, pack,** colony, host, troop, army, **herd, drove,** drive, drift, trip; flight, **swarm,** cloud

**flood** NOUNS 1 **torrent, river,** flash flood, wall of water, waterflood, **deluge;** spate, **pour,** freshet, fresh; **overflow,** spillage, spill, spillover, overflowing, overrunning, alluvion, alluvium, **inundation,** whelming, overwhelming, engulfment, submersion; washout
VERBS 2 **overflow,** inundate, engulf, swamp, sweep, whelm, overwhelm, deluge, submerge

**floor** NOUNS 1 **story,** level, flat; first floor *or* story, ground *or* street floor, *rez-de-chaussée* <Fr>; mezzanine, mezzanine floor, *entresol* <Fr>
2 **foundation,** *fond* <Fr>, firm foundation, **base, basis, footing,** basement, pavement, **ground,** grounds, **groundwork, seat,** sill, flooring, fundament
VERBS 3 **knock down,** dash down, send headlong, deck *and* lay out <both nonformal>, lay by the heels, ground, **bowl down** *or* **over** <nonformal>; **prostrate,** supinate; **throw,** pin, pin down; **stump** *or* buffalo *or* bamboozle <all nonformal>, beat the shit out of *or* lick <both nonformal>

**floozy** NOUNS **tart** *and* **chippy** *and* broad <all nonformal>, wanton, **loose woman,** easy woman <nonformal>, easy lay <nonformal>, woman of easy virtue

**flop** NOUNS 1 **tumble, fall,** *culbute* <Fr>, cropper *and* **spill** <both nonformal>; **header** <nonformal>; **pratfall** <nonformal>
2 failure; flopperoo, megaflop, gigaflop, **bust,** frost, **fizzle,** lemon, dud, nonstarter, **loser, washout,** turkey, bomb, dull thud, total loss <all nonformal>
VERBS 3 **go down, slump,** flop down <nonformal>; plump, plop *or* plop

down, plunk *or* plunk down <both nonformal>; founder

4 <nonformal> **not make it,** not hack it, not get to first base, fall flat on one's ass, lay an egg, go over like a lead balloon, draw a blank, bomb; fold, fold up; take it on the chin, take the count; crap out; strike out, fan, whiff

**floppy** ADJS **drooping, droopy,** limp, loose, nodding, loppy, lop; **sagging,** saggy, swag, sagging in folds; **bagging,** baggy, ballooning; lop-eared

**floral** ADJS **flowery; flowered,** floreate, floriate, floriated; **flowering, blossoming, blooming,** abloom, bloomy, florescent, inflorescent, efflorescent, in flower, in bloom, in blossom; horticultural, hortulan, floricultural

**flotsam** NOUNS **derelict,** castoff; jetsam, lagan, **flotsam and jetsam;** waifs and strays; abandonee, waif, throwaway, orphan, dogie <nonformal>; **castaway;** foundling

**flounce** VERBS **caper, cut capers,** cut a dido <nonformal>, curvet, cavort, capriole, **gambol,** gambado, **frisk, trip, skip,** bob, bounce, jump about; **romp,** ramp <nonformal>; **prance;** caracole

**flounder** VERBS 1 **pitch, toss, tumble,** toss and tumble, pitch and toss, **plunge,** hobbyhorse, pound, **rear, rock, roll, reel, swing, sway, lurch, yaw, heave,** scend, **welter, wallow;** make heavy weather
2 **have difficulty, struggle**

3 <nonformal> have one's back to the wall, not know where to turn, come to a dead end *or* standstill, not know whether one is coming or going, go around in circles, swim against the current; walk a tightrope, walk on eggshells *or* hot coals, dance on a hot griddle

**flourish** NOUNS 1 **display,** vaunt, fanfaronade, blazon, flaunt, flaunting; daring, brilliancy, éclat, bravura, flair; dash *and* splash *and* splurge <all nonformal>
2 turn of expression, manner *or* way of speaking, ornament, device, flower; Gongorism, floridity, euphuism
VERBS 3 **grow, develop,** wax, **increase**; grow like a weed <nonformal>; burgeon, thrive; mushroom, balloon; **enjoy good health,** burst with health, bloom, glow
4 **display,** make a great show of, brandish, wave

**flourishing** ADJS **thriving, prospering, booming** <nonformal>; vigorous, exuberant; in full swing, going strong <nonformal>; halcyon, palmy, balmy, rosy, piping, clear, fair

**flout** VERBS disregard, **slight,** slight over, treat with contempt, set at defiance, fly in the teeth *or* face of, **snap one's fingers at; thumb one's nose at,** cock a snook at, bite the thumb at; **disdain, despise, scorn**; hold in derision, scout, scoff at, **deride**

**flow** NOUNS 1 flowing, **flux,** fluency, profluence, fluid motion *or* movement; **stream, current,** set, trend, tide, water flow; drift, driftage; **course,** onward course, **surge, gush, rush,** onrush, spate, run, race
VERBS 2 **stream, issue, pour, surge, run, course, rush, gush, flush, flood;** empty into, flow into, join; tick away *or* by *or* on, run, proceed, advance, roll *or* press on, flit, fly, slip, slide, glide; **go easily, run smoothly,** work well, work like a machine, go like clockwork

**flower** NOUNS 1 **posy, blossom, bloom;** floweret, floret, floscule
VERBS 2 be in flower, **blossom, bloom,** be in bloom, blow, effloresce, floreate, burst into bloom; **thrive, flourish,** boom; batten

**flowery** ADJS **floral; flowered,** floreate, floriate, floriated; **flowering, blossoming, blooming,** abloom, bloomy, florescent, inflorescent, efflorescent, in flower, in bloom, in blossom; florid; flamboyant, fussy, frilly, frilled, flouncy, gingerbread *or* gingerbready; mannered, figured, ornamented

**flowing** ADJS **streaming, running, pouring,** fluxive, fluxional, coursing, racing, gushing, rushing, onrushing, surging, surgy, torrential, rough, whitewater; **fluent,** profluent, affluent, defluent, decurrent, confluent, diffluent

**flub** NOUNS 1 **bungle, blunder, botch,** boner *and* bonehead play <both nonformal>, boggle, bobble *and* boo-boo *and* screw-up *and* fuck-up <all nonformal>; **fumble, muff,** fluff, miscue <nonformal>; **error, mistake**

VERBS 2 <nonformal> **goof, pull a**

**boner,** bobble, lay an egg, put *or* stick one's foot in it, stub one's toe, drop the ball, drop a brick; **blow,** blow it, bitch up, hash up, **mess up,** flub the dub, **make a mess** *or* **hash of,** foul up, fuck up, goof up, bollix up, **screw up, louse up, gum up,** go at it ass-backwards; put one's foot in one's mouth

**fluctuate** VERBS **vacillate, waver, waffle** <nonformal>, pendulate, oscillate, wobble, wobble about, teeter, dither, swing from one thing to another, **shilly-shally,** back and fill, keep *or* leave hanging in midair; blow hot and cold

**fluent** ADJS **flowing,** tripping; **smooth,** pleasing, facile, **easy, graceful, elegant**

**fluff** NOUNS 1 **down,** flue, floss, **fuzz, fur,** pile; eiderdown, eider; swansdown; thistledown; lint
2 **fumble, muff,** miscue <nonformal>; **slip,** trip, stumble; *gaucherie, étourderie, balourdise* <all Fr>; **hash** *and* **mess** <both nonformal>; **error, mistake**
VERBS 3 massage, knead, plump, plump up, fluff up, shake up

**fluffy** ADJS flossy, **downy,** pubescent, feathery; fleecy, woolly, lanate; furry

**fluid** NOUNS 1 **liquid;** liquor, drink, beverage; liquid extract, fluid extract; **juice, sap,** latex; milk, whey; water; **body fluid, blood;** semiliquid
ADJS 2 **changeable,** impermanent, transient, transitory; **variable,** plastic, malleable, fluidal, fluidic, **fluent, flowing,** runny; **liquid**

**fluke** NOUNS **fortuity, accident,** casualty, adventure, hazard; freak, freak occurrence *or* accident; chance hit, lucky shot, long shot, one in a million, lucky strike *and* scratch hit *and* **break** <all nonformal>

**flunk** VERBS **flunk out** <nonformal>; **fail,** bust *and* wash out <both nonformal>

**flunky** NOUNS **lackey,** livery *or* liveried servant; **footman,** *valet de pied* <Fr>; henchman, camp follower, hanger-on, satellite, creature, stooge <nonformal>, jackal, minion, myrmidon; menial

**flurry** NOUNS 1 haste, hurry, commotion, rush, precipitation
2 **gust,** wind gust, **blast,** blow, flaw, scud <Scots>; snow flurry

**flush** NOUNS 1 **blushing, flushing,** coloring, mantling, reddening, rubicundity, rosiness; **blush,** suffusion, red face; rush, **gush; glow,** incandescence, fieriness
ADJS 2 flushed, **rosy,** rosy-cheeked, apple-cheeked, ruddy, pink, pink-cheeked
3 **prosperous,** comfortable, provided for, well provided for, fat, flush with money, worth a great deal; **full,** filled, **replete,** plenary, capacity

**fluster** VERBS **confuse,** throw into confusion *or* chaos, entangle, **mix up;** flummox <nonformal>, **flutter,** put into a flutter, **flurry,** rattle, ruffle, **disconcert,** discomfit, **discompose,** discombobulate <nonformal>, **embarrass,** put out, disturb, perturb, bother, pother, bug <nonformal>

**flutter** NOUNS 1 **dither, tizzy** <nonformal>, swivet, foofaraw, **pucker** <nonformal>, **twitter,** twitteration <nonformal>, **fluster, fret, fuss,** pother, bother; **bustle, flurry,** scramble, ferment, stew, sweat; **palpitation,** arrhythmia, pitter-patter, pit-a-pat
2 **flicker, dance, quiver;** flickering, fluttering, bickering, guttering, dancing, quivering, lambency
VERBS 3 **agitate, disturb, perturb,** shake up, perturbate, **disquiet, discompose, upset, trouble, unsettle, stir,** swirl, flurry, flutter the dovecot, fret, roughen, ruffle, rumple, ripple, ferment, convulse; flitter, flit, flick, **flicker,** gutter, bicker, wave, **waver,** dance; **palpitate,** pulse, throb, pitter-patter, go pit-a-pat

**fly** VERBS 1 be airborne, wing, take wing, wing one's way, take *or* make a flight, take to the air, take the air, volitate, be wafted; **pilot,** control, be at the controls, fly left seat; **copilot,** fly right seat; solo; **barnstorm** <nonformal>; fly blind, fly by the seat of one's pants <nonformal>
2 **flee, take flight,** take to flight, take wing, fugitate, **run, cut and run** <nonformal>, make a precipitate departure, **run off** *or* **away,** run away from, bug out <nonformal>, **decamp,** pull up stakes, **take to one's heels,** make off, **depart,** make a quick exit, **beat a retreat** *or* **a hasty retreat, turn tail**

**fly-by-night** ADJS **untrustworthy,** unfaithworthy, untrusty, trustless, **unreliable, undependable,** irresponsible, unsure, not to be trusted, not to be depended *or* relied upon; **short-lived, ephemeral,** evanescent, volatile

**foam** NOUNS 1 **froth; spume,** sea foam, scud; **spray, surf,** breakers, white water, spoondrift *or* **spindrift, suds, lather,** soap-suds; beer-suds, head; head, collar

*stinging, ringing spindrift*
KIPLING

VERBS 2 **froth,** spume, cream; **lather,** suds, sud; scum, mantle; **aerate,** whip, beat, whisk; **seethe, fume,** stew, ferment, stir, churn

**focus** NOUNS 1 focal point, prime focus, point of convergence; **center of interest** *or* attention, focus of attention; center of consciousness; **center of attraction, centerpiece,** clou, mecca, cynosure, cynosure of all eyes; polestar, lodestar; magnet; **gist,** gravamen, **nub** <nonformal>, nucleus, center, kernel, **core, pith**
VERBS 2 focalize, come to a point *or* focus, bring to *or* into focus; bring *or* come to a head, get to the heart of the matter home in on; zero in on; draw a bead on *and* get a handle on <nonformal>; **concentrate,** concenter, get it together <nonformal>; **channel,** direct, canalize, channelize; converge

**focus on** VERBS **concentrate,** concentrate the mind *or* thoughts, concentrate on *or* upon, attend closely to, brood on, give *or* devote the mind to, glue the mind to, cleave to the thought of, fix the mind *or* thoughts upon, bend the mind upon, bring the mind to bear upon; get to the point; gather *or* collect one's thoughts, pull one's wits together, focus *or* fix one's thoughts, marshal *or* arrange one's thoughts *or* ideas

**foe** NOUNS **enemy,** foeman, **adversary, antagonist;** bitter enemy; sworn enemy; archenemy; the other side, the opposition; **bane,** bête noire

**fog** NOUNS 1 pea soup *and* peasouper *and* pea-soup fog <all nonformal>; London fog, London special <Brit nonformal>; **smog,** smaze <smoke-haze>; murkiness, murk, mistiness, mist, fogginess
VERBS 2 **blur, dim, pale,** soften, film, mist; defocus, lose resolution *or* sharpness *or* distinctness, go soft at the edges; befog; fog in; smog; **mist,** mist over, mist up, bemist, enmist; **obscure,** muddle, muddy, fuzz, **confuse**

**foggy** ADJS 1 soupy *or* pea-soupy <nonformal>, nubilous; fog-bound, fogged-in; smoggy; hazy, misty; so thick you can cut it with a knife; **murky,** cloudy, nebulous
2 **muddled,** in a muddle; adrift, at sea, fogged, in a fog, hazy, muzzy <nonformal>, misted, misty, cloudy, beclouded

**foible** NOUNS **vice, weakness,** weakness of the flesh, **flaw,** moral flaw *or* blemish, **frailty, infirmity; failing,** failure; weak point, weak side, Achilles' heel, vulnerable place, chink in one's armor, weak link

**foil** VERBS **thwart, frustrate, cross, balk;** spike, scotch, checkmate; **counter,** contravene, counteract, countermand, counterwork; **derail;** take the wind out of one's sails, steal one's thunder, cut the ground from under one

**foliage** NOUNS **leafage,** leafiness, umbrage, foliation; frondage, frondescence; vernation

**folk** NOUNS **family,** brood, **house, household,** hearth, hearthside, ménage, people, homefolk, folks *and* homefolks <both nonformal>; **common people, ordinary people** *or* **folk, persons, folks,** gentry; plain people *or* folks

**folklore** NOUNS **legend, lore,** mythical lore; myth, mythology, folktale, folk motif; racial memory, archetypal myth *or* image *or* pattern; **superstition,** popular belief, **old wives' tale**

**folksy** ADJS **informal, natural,** simple, plain, homely, homey, down-home *and* folksy <both nonformal>, *haymish* <Yiddish>; **unaffected, unassuming**; unconstrained

**follow** VERBS 1 **pursue, shadow** *and* **tail** <both nonformal>, **trail,** trail after, follow in the trail of, camp on the trail of, **heel,** tread close upon, breathe down the neck of, follow in the wake of, tailgate <nonformal>, go in the rear of, bring up the rear, eat the dust of, take *or* swallow one's dust; tag *and* **tag after** *and* tag along <all nonformal>; string along <nonformal>; **dog,** bedog, **hound,** chase, get after, take out *or* take off after, **pursue**
2 **emulate,** follow in the steps *or* footsteps of, walk in the shoes of, put oneself in another's shoes, follow in the wake of, follow the example of, follow suit; pattern after, pattern on, take after, take a leaf out of one's book
3 **observe, keep, heed,** keep the faith; **live up to,** act up to, practice what one preaches, **be faithful to,** keep faith with, do justice to, do the right thing by
4 **succeed, ensue,** come *or* go after,

**come next; inherit,** take the mantle of, step into the shoes *or* place of, take over

**follower** NOUNS **hanger-on, adherent,** dangler, appendage, **dependent, satellite,** cohort, retainer, servant, man, shadow, tagtail, **henchman,** heeler <nonformal>; successor; **disciple,** adherent, votary

**following** ADJS trailing, on the track *or* trail; succeeding, successive, sequent, lineal, consecutive, ensuing, attendant; back-to-back <nonformal>, consecutive; **pursuing,** pursuant; **questing, seeking, searching**; **in pursuit,** in hot pursuit, in full cry

**follow-through** NOUNS **sequel,** sequela *or* sequelae, sequelant, sequent, sequitur, **consequence**; **continuation,** continuance, **follow-up** <nonformal>

**follow up** VERBS **pursue, follow, go after,** take out *or* off after <nonformal>, bay after, run after, run in pursuit of, make after, go in pursuit of; **go to all lengths, go all out, go the limit** <nonformal>, go the whole way, **go the whole hog** <nonformal>, cover a lot of ground, make a federal case of *and* make a big deal of *and* do up brown *and* do with a vengeance <all nonformal>, **see it through** <nonformal>, follow *or* prosecute to a conclusion

**folly** NOUNS **foolishness,** foolery, foolheadedness, **stupidity, asininity,** *niaiserie* <Fr>; *bêtise* <Fr>; **inanity, fatuity,** fatuousness; act of folly, absurdity, *sottise* <Fr>, foolish *or* stupid thing, dumb thing to do <nonformal>; fool *or* fool's trick, dumb trick <nonformal>; **imprudence, indiscretion,** imprudent *or* unwise step; blunder

**foment** VERBS **incite, instigate, put up to** <nonformal>; ferment, **agitate, arouse,** excite, stir up, work up, whip up; **inflame,** incense, **fire,** heat, heat up, impassion; **provoke,** wave the bloody shirt

**fond** ADJS **loving,** lovesome, **adoring, devoted, affectionate,** demonstrative, **romantic, sentimental, tender,** soft <nonformal>, melting; infatuated, doting

**fondle** VERBS **stroke, pet, caress**; **nuzzle,** nose, rub noses; feel up <nonformal>; rub, rub against, massage, knead; **cherish,** entertain, treasure

**fond of** VERBS 1 **enamored of,** partial to, **in love with,** attached to, wedded to, devoted to, wrapped up in; **taken with,** smitten with, struck with

2 <nonformal> **crazy about,** mad *or* nuts *or* nutty *or* wild about, swacked on, sweet on, stuck on, gone on

**food** NOUNS 1 foodstuff, food and drink, sustenance, kitchen stuff, victualage, **comestibles, edibles,** eatables, viands, **cuisine,** tucker <Australia>, ingesta <pl>; **fare,** cheer, creature comfort; provision, provender

2 <nonformal> **grub,** grubbery, **eats, chow,** chuck, grits, groceries, the nosebag, scarf *or* scoff, tuck, victuals *or* vittles

**fool** NOUNS 1 **damn fool,** tomfool, perfect fool, born fool; *schmuck* <Yiddish>; **ass,** jackass, stupid ass, egregious ass; zany, **clown, buffoon,** doodle; sop, milksop; mome <old>, mooncalf, softhead; figure of fun; **lunatic**; **ignoramus**

2 <nonformal> **blockhead, airhead,** bubblehead, fluffhead, featherhead, woodenhead, dolthead, dumbhead, dummy, dum-dum, dumbo, dumb cluck, dodo head, doodoohead, dumbbell, dumb bunny, stupidhead, dullhead, bufflehead, bonehead, jughead, thickhead, thickskull, numbskull, putz, lunkhead, chucklehead, knucklehead, chowderhead, headbanger *and* jolterhead <both Brit>, muttonhead, beefhead, meathead, noodlehead, thimblewit, pinhead, pinbrain, peabrain, cabbagehead, pumpkin head, fathead, blubberhead, muddlehead, puzzlehead, addlebrain, addlehead, addlepate, tottyhead <old>, puddinghead, stupe, mushhead, blunderhead, dunderhead, dunderpate, clodpate, clodhead, clodpoll, jobbernowl *and* gaby *and* gowk <all Brit>

VERBS 3 befool, make a fool of, practice on one's credulity, **pull one's leg,** make an ass of; **trick; spoof** *and* **kid** *and* put one on <all nonformal>; **play a trick on,** play a practical joke upon, send on a fool's errand; fake one out <nonformal>; sell one a bill of goods, give one a snow job; toy with, fiddle with, fool with, play with

**fool around** VERBS

<nonformal> **monkey, monkey around,** fiddle, fiddle around, fiddle-faddle, frivol, horse around, fool around, play around, mess around, kid around, **screw around,** muck around, muck about <Brit>, fart around, piss around, bugger around, diddle around, frig around, mess around; jerk off

**foolhardy** ADJS **harebrained,** madcap, **wild,** wild-ass <nonformal>, madbrain, madbrained; **audacious;** forward, bold, **presumptuous; daring,** daredevil, fire-eating, death-defying; adventurous

**foolish** ADJS fool <nonformal>, fool-headed <nonformal>, **stupid, dumb** <nonformal>, clueless <Brit nonformal>, **asinine; silly,** apish, dizzy <nonformal>; **fatuous,** fatuitous, inept, **inane; senseless, witless, thoughtless,** insensate, brainless; **idiotic, insane**

**foolproof** ADJS **convenient,** goofproof <nonformal>, practical, untroublesome, user-friendly; adaptable, feasible

**foothold** NOUNS **footing, toehold,** hold, perch, **purchase**; **standing,** stand, stance, standing place, *point d'appui* <Fr>, *locus standi* <L>

**footloose** ADJS **free; at liberty, at large,** on the loose, **loose,** unengaged, disengaged, detached, unattached, uncommitted, uninvolved, clear, in the clear, go-as-you-please, easygoing, footloose and fancy-free, free and easy

**fop** NOUNS **dandy,** coxcomb, macaroni, gallant, dude *and* swell *and* sport <all nonformal>, ponce *and* toff <both Brit nonformal>, exquisite, blood, fine gentleman, puppy, jackanapes, jack-a-dandy, fribble, clotheshorse, fashion plate

**forage** VERBS **plunder, pillage,** spoliate, despoil, depredate, prey on *or* upon, **raid,** reive <Scots>, ravage, ravish, raven, maraud, foray

**foray** NOUNS **raid,** razzia; **invasion, incursion,** inroad, irruption; **pillage, plunder,** sack; **marauding,** foraging; **venture**

**forbearance** NOUNS **patience, tolerance,** toleration, **acceptance; indulgence,** longaninimity, lenience, leniency; sweet reasonableness; forbearing, refraining, forbearingness; **sufferance, endurance; temperance,** nothing in excess, sobriety, soberness, frugality, abnegation

**forbid** VERBS **prohibit; disallow, rule out** *or* **against;** deny, **reject**; say no to, **refuse**; **bar,** debar, preclude, exclude, exclude from, shut out, shut *or* close the door on, **prevent**; **ban,** put under the ban, **outlaw; repress, suppress**; **enjoin,** put under an injunction, issue an injunction against, issue a prohibitory injunction; **proscribe,** inhibit, embargo, **lay** *or* **put an embargo on; taboo**

**forbidding** ADJS **offensive, objectionable, odious, repulsive,** repellent, rebarbative, **repugnant, revolting; prohibitive,** prohibitory, prohibiting; inhibitive, inhibitory, **repressive, suppressive**; proscriptive, interdictive, interdictory; preclusive, exclusive, **preventive**

**force** NOUNS 1 **strength, might,** mightiness, powerfulness, stamina; **potency, power**; **energy**; **vigor, vitality,** vigorousness, heartiness, lustiness
2 **meaning, significance, signification,** *significatum* <L>, *signifié* <Fr>, point, **sense,** idea, **purport, import,** where one is coming from <nonformal>; effect, impact, consequence, practical consequence, response; **validity, soundness,** solidity, substantiality, **justness;** authority, **authoritativeness; cogency,** weight, persuasiveness
VERBS 3 **compel, make;** cause, cause to; enforce, **drive,** impel; dragoon, use force upon, force one's hand, hold a pistol *or* gun to one's head; **force upon,** impose by force *or* main force, strong-arm <nonformal>, force down one's throat, enforce upon

**forceful** ADJS **powerful, potent,** prepotent, powerpacked, **mighty,** irresistible, avalanchine, forcible, dynamic; **cogent,** striking, telling, effective, impactful, valid, incisive, trenchant

**forcible** ADJS **strong, forceful, mighty, powerful,** puissant <nonformal>, **potent**; **stout, sturdy, stalwart, rugged,** hale; **energetic, vigorous, strenuous, strong, dynamic,** kinetic, intense, acute, keen, incisive, trenchant, vivid, vibrant; **enterprising, aggressive,** proactive, activist, can-do *and* gung ho *and* take-over *and* take-charge <all nonformal>; **coercive,** steamroller *and* bulldozer *and* sledgehammer *and* strong-arm <all nonformal>; violent

**foreboding** ADJS **anxious, concerned, apprehensive,** misgiving, suspenseful, strained, tense, tensed up <nonformal>, nail-biting, white-knuckle <nonformal>; **ominous,** premonitory, **portentous,** portending; boding, **bodeful; inauspicious, ill-omened,** ill-boding, of ill *or* fatal omen, of evil portent, loaded *or* laden *or* freighted *or* fraught with doom, looming, looming over; **unpropitious, unpromising, unfavorable, threatening, menacing, lowering;** dire, baleful, baneful, **ill-fated,** ill-starred, evil-starred, star-crossed

**forecast** NOUNS 1 **prediction, foretelling,** foreshowing, forecasting, **prognosis,** prognostication, presage <old>, presaging; **prophecy,** prophesying, vaticination
VERBS 2 **predict,** make a prediction, **foretell, soothsay,** prefigure, **prophesy, prognosticate,** call <nonformal>, make a prophecy *or* prognosis, vaticinate, forebode, presage, see ahead, see *or* tell the future, read the future, see in the crystal ball; **foresee**

**forefathers** NOUNS **ancestors, antecedents, predecessors,** ascendants, **fathers, forebears,** progenitors, primogenitors

**forefront** NOUNS front, point, **leading edge, cutting edge, vanguard,** van; cutting edge, front line, **fore,** forepart, forequarter, foreside, forehand; **priority,** anteriority

**foregoing** ADJS **former;** aforesaid, aforementioned, beforementioned, abovementioned, aforenamed, forenamed, forementioned, said, named, same; aforegoing, **preceding**; last, latter

**foreign** ADJS **alien,** strange, exotic, foreign-looking; exterior, **external;** extrinsic; ulterior, outside, outland, outlandish; barbarian, barbarous, barbaric; foreign-born; intrusive

**foreigner** NOUNS **alien, stranger, outsider,** nonmember, not one of us, not our sort, not the right sort, the other, outlander, *Uitlander* <Afrikaans>, tramontane, ultramontane, barbarian, foreign devil <China>, *gringo* <Sp Amer>

**foremost** ADJS 1 **first,** headmost; **preceding,** antecedent; **prior**; **chief**, **leading,** up-front <nonformal>, head, prime, primary; principal, paramount, **foremost, leading, dominant,** crowning, capital, **cardinal; predominant,** preponderant, prevailing, hegemonic *or* hegemonical
ADVS 2 **before**, in front, out in front, outfront, headmost, in the the van, in the forefront, in advance

**forerunner** NOUNS **harbinger, precursor,** messenger <old>, **herald,** announcer, *buccinator novi temporis* <L>; presager, premonitor, foreshadower; **trailblazer, pathfinder;** *voorlooper* <Dutch>, vaunt-courier, avant-courier, frontrunner; ancestor

**foresee** VERBS see beforehand *or* ahead, foreglimpse, foretaste, **anticipate,** contemplate, envision, envisage, **look forward to,** look ahead, look beyond, look *or* pry *or* peep into the future; **predict**; think ahead *or* beforehand; dope *and* dope out <both nonformal>; call the turn *and* call one's shot <both nonformal>

**foreseeable** ADJS **predictable, divinable, foretellable, calculable,** anticipatable; **foreknowable,** precognizable; **probable**

**foresight** NOUNS foreseeing, looking ahead, **prevision,** divination, forecast; **prediction**; **foreglimpse,** foreglance, foregleam; **prospect,** prospection; **anticipation,** contemplation, envisionment, envisagement; **foresightedness;** sagacity, provision, forehandedness, readiness, prudence

**forest** NOUNS 1 **woodland, wood, woods, timberland; timber,** stand of timber, forest land, forest cover, forest preserve, state *or* national forest
ADJS 2 **sylvan, woodland,** forestal; dendrologic, dendrological, silvicultural, afforestational, reforestational; **wooded,** timbered, forested, arboreous; **woody,** woodsy, bosky, bushy, shrubby, scrubby; copsy, braky

**forestall** VERBS cajole, **circumvent,** get around; **monopolize,** hog *and* grab all of *and* gobble up <all nonformal>, take it all, have all to oneself, have exclusive possession of *or* exclusive rights to; engross, tie up, foreclose, **preclude,** exclude, debar, **obviate,** anticipate; rule out

**foretell** VERBS **predict,** make a prediction, **soothsay,** prefigure, **forecast, prophesy, prognosticate,** call <nonformal>, vaticinate, forebode, presage, see ahead, see *or* tell the future, read the future, see in the crystal ball; dope *and* dope out <both nonformal>; call the turn *and* call one's shot <both nonformal>

**forethought** NOUNS **foresight,** foresightedness, forehandedness, forethoughtfulness; **providence,** provision, forearming; precautions, steps, measures, steps and measures; **premeditation,** predeliberation, preconsideration; caution

**forever** NOUNS 1 **an eternity,** endless time, **time without end**

*a short parenthesis in a long period*
DONNE

ADVS 2 **forevermore, for ever and ever,** forever and aye; forever and a day <nonformal>, now and forever, **eternally, evermore,** ever and anon, ever and again; **for good,** for keeps <nonformal>, for all time; **to the end of time,** till time stops *or* runs out, till hell freezes over <nonformal>, till the cows come home <nonformal>

**forewarned** ADJS **expectant,** forearmed, forestalling, ready, prepared; **looking forward to,** looking for, watching for, on the watch *or* lookout for

**foreword** NOUNS **prelude, preamble, preface,** prologue, introduction, *avant-propos* <Fr>, protasis, proem, proemium, prolegomenon *or* prolegomena, exordium

**forfeit** VERBS **lose,** incur loss, **suffer loss,** undergo privation *or* deprivation, be bereaved *or* bereft of, have no more, let slip, let slip through one's fingers; default; **sacrifice;** go broke *and* lose one's shirt *and* take a bath *or* to the cleaners *and* tap out <all nonformal>

**forgery** NOUNS fakery, plagiarism, plagiarizing, plagiary; **fake, counterfeit,** counterfeit money, funny *or* phony *or* bogus money <nonformal>, false *or* bad money, queer <nonformal>, green goods <nonformal>; bad check, rubber check *and* bounced check *and* kite <all nonformal>

**forget** VERBS **forgive and forget,** dismiss from one's thoughts, think no more of, not give it another *or* a second thought, let it go <nonformal>, let it pass, **let bygones be bygones;** write off, charge off, charge to experience; bury the hatchet; **drop the subject,** give it no more thought; turn one's back upon, turn away from, turn one's attention from, walk away; disremember *and* disrecollect <both nonformal>, fail to remember, forget to remember, **have no remembrance** *or* **recollection of,** be unable to recollect *or* recall, draw a blank <nonformal>

**forgetful** ADJS **forgetting,** inclined to forget, **memoryless, unremembering, unmindful,** absentminded, **oblivious,** insensible to the past, with a mind *or* memory like a sieve; suffering from *or* stricken with amnesia, amnesic, amnestic; blocked, repressed, suppressed, sublimated, converted; heedless; Lethean

**forgive** VERBS **pardon, excuse,** give *or* grant forgiveness, spare; amnesty, grant amnesty to, grant immunity *or* exemption; hear confession, **absolve,** remit, give absolution, shrive, grant remission; **exonerate, exculpate**; blot out one's sins, wipe the slate clean, **write off,** absolve, **cancel,** nullify; wipe out, obliterate

**forgone** ADJS **relinquished,** released, disposed of; waived, dispensed with; forsworn, renounced, abjured, **abandoned**; recanted, retracted; **surrendered,** ceded, yielded; sacrificed

**forgotten** ADJS clean forgotten <nonformal>, **unremembered,** disremembered *and* disrecollected <both nonformal>, **unrecollected, unretained, unrecalled,** past recollection *or* recall, out of the mind, lost, erased, effaced, obliterated, gone out of one's head *or* recollection, consigned to oblivion, buried *or* sunk in oblivion; out of sight out of mind; misremembered, misrecollected

**fork** NOUNS 1 **prong,** trident; **branch, ramification,** stem, tributary, offshoot; **crotch,** crutch; **delta; groin,** inguen; furcula, furculum, **wishbone**

VERBS 2 furcate, bifurcate, trifurcate, divaricate; **branch,** stem, ramify, branch off *or* out

**forlorn** ADJS lorn; **abandoned, forsaken, deserted, desolate,** godforsaken <nonformal>, friendless, unfriended, kithless, fatherless, motherless, homeless; helpless, defenseless; outcast

**form** NOUNS 1 **shape, figure;** figuration, **configuration;** formation, **conformation; structure**; **build,** make, frame; **arrangement**; makeup, format, layout; **composition**; cut, set, stamp, type, turn, cast, mold, impression, pattern, matrix, model, mode, modality

VERBS 2 formalize, **shape, fashion,** tailor, frame, figure, **lick into shape** <nonformal>; work, knead; set, fix; **forge, mold,** model, take form, shape, **shape up, take shape;** materialize; **organize,** structure, shape up; take form, take order, crystallize, **fall** *or* **drop into place,** fall into line *or* order *or* series, fall into rank, take rank; come together, draw up, gather around

**formal** NOUNS 1 **dance, ball,** *bal* <Fr>; masked ball, masque, mask, masquerade ball, masquerade, *bal masqué* <Fr>, *bal costumé* <Fr>, fancy-dress ball, cotillion; promenade, **prom** <nonformal> ADJS 2 **orderly,** ordered, **regular, well-regulated,** uniform, **systematic, harmonious;** businesslike, routine, steady, normal, habitual, usual, en règle, in hand; **nominal,** cognominal; **titular, in name only,** nominative; **stiff, stilted,** Latinate, *guindé* <Fr>, **labored,** ponderous, elephantine, lumbering, cumbrous, leaden, heavy, unwieldy, sesquipedalian, inkhorn, turgid, bombastic, pompous

**formality** NOUNS **form, formalness; ceremony,** ceremonial, **ceremoniousness; dignity,** gravity, weight, *gravitas* <L>, weighty dignity, staidness, reverend seriousness, **solemnity**; **pomp**; pomposity

**formalize** VERBS ritualize, solemnize, **celebrate,** dignify; **observe;** conventionalize, stylize; **normalize,** standardize, regularize; **codify**

**format** NOUNS **form, shape, figure;** figuration, **configuration;** formation, **conformation; structure**; **arrangement**; makeup, layout; **composition**

**formation** NOUNS **composition, constitution, construction,** fabrication, fashioning, shaping, organization; structure, configuration, array, makeup, lineup, setup, layout; formulation, **configuration,** form, array

**former** ADJS foregoing; aforesaid, aforementioned, beforementioned, abovementioned, aforenamed, forenamed, forementioned, said, named, same; past, fore, **previous,** late, recent, **once, onetime,** sometime, **erstwhile,** then, quondam; **prior**

**formidable** ADJS **difficult,** difficile; **not easy,** no picnic; **hard, tough** *and* **rough** *and* **rugged** <all nonformal>, rigorous, brutal, severe; wicked *and* mean *and* **hairy** <all nonformal>; **arduous, strenuous, toilsome, laborious,** operose, Herculean; easier said than done, like pulling teeth; exacting, demanding

**formula** NOUNS **rule,** form; rule of action *or* conduct, moral precept; ordinance, imperative, **regulation,** *règlement* <Fr>; **principle,** principium, settled principle, general principle *or* truth, tenet, convention; **guideline,** ground rule, rubric, protocol, working rule, working principle, standard procedure; guiding principle, golden rule; **code; recipe,** receipt; **prescription;** formulary

**formulate** VERBS **say, express,** give expression, verbalize, put in words, find words to express; **word,** put into words, couch, phrase; find a phrase for, give expression *or* words to, state, **frame,** conceive, style, couch, clothe *or* embody in words, express by *or* in words; put, present, set out; formularize; **write, indite,** produce, prepare

**fornicate** VERBS **be promiscuous,** sleep around *and* swing <both nonformal>; **debauch, wanton,** rake, chase women, womanize, whore, sow one's wild oats; **philander; dissipate**; **cheat, commit adultery,** get a little on the side <nonformal>

**forsake** VERBS **abandon, desert; quit, leave,** leave behind, take leave of, depart from, absent oneself from, turn one's back upon, turn one's tail upon, say goodbye to, bid a long farewell to, walk away, **walk** *or* **run out on** <nonformal>, **leave flat** *and* leave high and dry *or* holding the bag *or* in the lurch <all nonformal>, leave one to one's fate, throw to the wolves <nonformal>

**forsaken** ADJS **abandoned, deserted,** left; disused; **derelict,** castaway, jettisoned; marooned; junk, junked, discarded; **desolate,** godforsaken <nonformal>, friendless, unfriended, fatherless, motherless, homeless

**fort** NOUNS **fortress,** post; **stronghold,** hold, safehold, fasthold, strong point, **fastness,** keep, ward, **bastion,** donjon, **citadel, castle,** tower, tower of strength, strong point

**forte** NOUNS **métier, strong point,** long suit; **specialty, line, pursuit, pet subject, field,** area, main interest; **vocation**

**forth** ADVS **forward, forwards, onward, onwards, on,** along, **ahead; out,** outward, outwards, outwardly

**forthcoming** ADJS **approaching, nearing,** advancing; attracted to, drawn to; **com-**

**ing, oncoming,** upcoming, to come; proximate, near; **issuing,** arising, surfacing

**forthright** ADJS **candid, frank, sincere,** genuine, ingenuous, frankhearted; **open,** openhearted, transparent, open-faced; artless; **straightforward, direct,** up-front *and* straight <both nonformal>, downright, straight-out <nonformal>; **outspoken, plain-spoken,** free-spoken, free-speaking, free-tongued; explicit, unequivocal; **blunt,** bluff, brusque

**fortify** VERBS **strengthen, invigorate,** beef up <nonformal>, brace, buttress, prop, shore up, support, undergird, brace up; steel, harden, caseharden, anneal, stiffen, **toughen,** temper, nerve; confirm, sustain; **doctor** *and* **doctor up** <both nonformal>; spike <nonformal>, lace

**fortitude** NOUNS **hardihood,** hardiness; **pluckiness; spunkiness** *and* grittiness *and* nerviness <all nonformal>, mettlesomeness; **gameness,** grit, **stamina,** toughness, **mettle,** bottom; **heart,** spirit, stout heart, heart of oak; **resolution**, resoluteness, tenaciousness, tenacity, pertinaciousness, pertinacity, bulldog courage

**fortress** NOUNS **stronghold,** hold, safehold, fasthold, strong point, **fastness,** keep, ward, **bastion,** donjon, **citadel, castle,** tower; **fort**

**fortuitous** ADJS **incidental,** adventitious, **accidental, chance,** casual, aleatory, unessential *or* inessential *or* nonessential; **circumstantial,** conditional, provisional

**fortunate** ADJS **lucky, providential; in luck; blessed,** blessed with luck, favored; born under a lucky star, born with a silver spoon in one's mouth, born on the sunny side of the hedge; out of the woods, over the hump; **auspicious**

**fortune** NOUNS **wealth, treasure,** handsome fortune; full *or* heavy *or* well-lined *or* bottomless *or* fat *or* bulging purse, deep pockets <nonformal>; **chance,** happenstance, fate, **destiny,** whatever comes, *moira* <Gk>, lot; **good fortune** *or* **luck,** happy fortune, **luck,** the breaks <nonformal>, fortune's favor

**forum** NOUNS **conference,** discussion group, buzz session <nonformal>, **round table, panel;** open forum, colloquium, symposium; town meeting; **powwow** <nonformal>; agora, marketplace, open forum, public square; **tribunal, board,** curia, Areopagus

**forward** VERBS 1 **advance, promote,** forward, hasten, contribute to, foster, aid, facilitate, expedite, abet; **dispatch,** transmit, remit, consign
ADJS 2 **insolent,** insulting; pushy <nonformal>, obtrusive, familiar; **self-assertive,** self-asserting, importunate; bold, pert, bumptious; **precocious, advanced,** far ahead, born before one's time
ADVS 3 **forwards, onward, onwards, forth, on,** along, **ahead;** on the way to, on the road *or* high road to, en route to *or* for; **frontward,** frontwards, vanward, **headward,** headwards

**foster** VERBS **nurture,** nourish, mother, care for, lavish care on, feed, parent, rear, sustain, cultivate, **cherish;** pamper, coddle, cosset, spoon-feed; provide for, support; take charge of, **take under one's wing,** look *or* watch out for <nonformal>, have *or* keep an eye on *or* upon, keep a sharp eye on *or* upon, **watch over,** keep watch over, **watch, mind, tend**

**foul** VERBS 1 **defile, befoul; sully;** foul one's own nest, shit where one eats <nonformal>, mess *and* mess up <both nonformal>; **pollute, corrupt, contaminate, infect; taint,** tarnish, profane, violate, desecrate, defile, debase
ADJS 2 **filthy, vile,** mucky, **nasty,** icky *and* yecchy *and* yucky *and* gross *and* grungy *and* scuzzy <all nonformal>; malodorous, mephitic, rank, **fetid**; **putrid, rotten;** pollutive; **offensive, objectionable,** repellent, rebarbative, **repugnant, revolting,** forbidding, nauseating, disgusting; **odious, repulsive, obscene,** ithyphallic, **ribald, pornographic, salacious,** lurid, **dirty, smutty,** raunchy <nonformal>, blue, smoking-room, impure, unchaste, unclean, fulsome, offensive, unprintable, unrepeatable, not fit for mixed company

**foulmouthed** ADJS **cursing, maledictory,** imprecatory, **damnatory,** denunciatory, epithetic, epithetical; **abusive,** vituperative, contumelious; calumnious, calumniatory; **scurrilous;** blasphemous, **profane, foul, vile,** thersitical, **dirty** <nonformal>, **obscene,** dysphemistic, scatologic, scatological, coprological, ribald, Rabelaisian, raw, risqué; foul-tongued, foul-spoken

**found** VERBS **inaugurate,** institute, **establish,** set up <nonformal>; constitute, install, form, **set up, organize,** equip, endow, realize, materialize, effect, effectuate

**foundation** NOUNS 1 **warrant, reason,** good reason, **cause,** call, **right, basis,** substantive *or* material basis, **ground, grounds,** substance
2 **organization,** creation, establishment

**founder** NOUNS 1 **originator,** initiator, inaugurator, introducer, institutor, motive force, instigator; **organizer,** founding father, founding *or* founder member, founding partner, cofounder
VERBS 2 **sink,** be lost, go down, go to the bottom, go to Davy Jones's locker; scuttle; **break down, collapse; slip,** go downhill, be on the skids <nonformal>

**fountain** NOUNS **fountainhead,** headwater, headstream, riverhead, springhead, headspring, **mainspring,** wellspring, wellhead, well, **spring,** fount, font; **source of supply,** source, staple, resource; **spout,** rush, gush, geyser spouter <nonformal>

**the fourth estate** NOUNS **the press,** journalism, the public press, print medium, the print media, print journalism, the print press, the public print; mass media, the communications industry, public communication

**fracas** NOUNS **commotion, hubbub, Babel, tumult,** turmoil, **uproar, racket,** riot, **disturbance, rumpus** <nonformal>, ruckus *and* ruction <both nonformal>, **hassle,** shindy <nonformal>, rampage; **brawl,** free-for-all <nonformal>, donnybrook *or* donnybrook fair, broil, embroilment, melee

**fraction** NOUNS **part, portion;** percentage; **division**; **share,** parcel, dole, quota, piece *or* piece of the action <nonformal>; cut *and* slice *and* vigorish <all nonformal>; **ratio, rate, proportion; quota,** quotum; **percentage**

**fracture** NOUNS 1 **break,** bone-fracture, comminuted fracture, compound *or* open fracture, greenstick fracture, spiral *or* torsion fracture; rupture
VERBS 2 **cleave, crack,** breach, **break, break up, come apart,** come unstuck, **come** *or* **fall to pieces,** fall apart, rupture

**fragile** ADJS 1 **flimsy,** shaky, weak, papery, paper-thin, **unsound,** infirm; **impermanent,** unenduring, undurable, nondurable, nonpermanent; frail, brittle, delicate, insubstantial, **breakable,** frangible, crushable, crackable, crunchable, fracturable
2 <comparisons> eggshell, matchwood, old paper, piecrust, glass, glass jaw, china, parchment, ice, bubble, glass house, house of cards, hothouse plant

**fragment** NOUNS **piece, particle, bit, scrap**, bite, **morsel, crumb,** shard, potsherd, snatch, snack; **tatter, shred,** stitch; **splinter,** sliver; **shiver, smithereen** <nonformal>

**fragmentary** ADJS **unsound, unsubstantial,** unsturdy, unsolid, decrepit, crumbling, fragmented, disintegrating; **shattered,** broken up, broken to pieces *or* bits, fragmentized, in shards, in smithereens <nonformal>; **discontinuous,** nonlinear, nonsequential, discontinued, broken, broken off, **interrupted,** disjunctive, discrete, discretive; **intermittent, fitful**

**fragrance** NOUNS **perfume, aroma,** scent, redolence, balminess, **incense, bouquet,** nosegay <old>, sweet smell, sweet savor; **odor**; spice, spiciness; muskiness; fruitiness

**frail** ADJS **slight, delicate, dainty,** puny; light, lightweight; **fragile,** frangible, **breakable,** destructible, shattery, crumbly, brittle, fragmentable, fracturable; **unsubstantial, flimsy,** tacky <nonformal>, wispy, cobwebby, gossamery, papery, pasteboardy; in poor health; **sickly,** peaked <nonformal>; **run-down,** reduced in health

*delicately weak*
POPE

**frame** NOUNS 1 **body,** the person, carcass, anatomy, bodily *or* corporal *or* corporeal entity, physical self, physical *or* bodily structure, physique, soma
2 put-up job *and* frame-up <both nonformal>, put-on <nonformal>; **trumped-up charge,** false witness; stacked deck *or* cold deck <both nonformal>, setup
VERBS 3 **border, edge, bound, hem in,** befringe, margin, marginate, line; enframe, set off; trim, bind; **form,** formalize, **shape, fashion,** tailor; **plan, devise, contrive, design,** shape, cast, concert, lay plans; organize, rationalize, systematize, schematize, methodize,

configure, pull together, sort out
4 **phrase, express,** find a phrase for, give expression *or* words to, **word,** state, conceive, style, couch, **put in** *or* **into words,** clothe *or* embody in words, couch in terms, express by *or* in words, find words to express; **formulate,** formularize
5 **trump up a charge, bear false witness;** frame up *and* set up *and* put up a job on <all nonformal>

**framework** NOUNS **frame,** framing; **skeleton,** fabric, cadre, chassis, shell, armature; **frame of reference,** intellectual *or* ideational frame of reference, arena, world, universe, world *or* universe of discourse, system, reference system

**franchise** NOUNS 1 **vote,** voting, **suffrage,** enfranchisement, voting right, right to vote; **voice, say;** representation; charter, liberty, diploma, patent, letters patent, brevet
2 **dealership, distributorship;** concession

**frank** ADJS **candid, sincere,** genuine, ingenuous, frankhearted; **open,** openhearted, transparent, open-faced; artless; **straightforward, direct,** up-front *and* straight <both nonformal>, **forthright,** downright, straight-out <nonformal>; **unreserved,** unrestrained, unconstrained, unchecked; **outspoken, plain-spoken,** free-spoken, free-speaking; explicit, unequivocal

**frantic** ADJS **frenzied; ecstatic,** transported, enraptured, ravished, in a transport *or* ecstasy; intoxicated, abandoned; carried away, **distracted, delirious, beside oneself,** out of one's wits; uncontrollable, running mad, amok, berserk, hog-wild <nonformal>; hectic, frenetic

**fraternity** NOUNS **affiliation,** colleagueship, collegialism, collegiality; confraternity, fraternization, fraternalism; sisterhood, sorority; **fellowship,** brotherhood, sodality; comradeship, camaraderie

**fraternize** VERBS **associate with,** assort with, sort with, consort with, hobnob with, fall in with, go around with, **mingle with, mix with, touch** *or* **rub elbows** *or* **shoulders with,** eat off the same trencher; join in fellowship; flock together, herd together, club together

**fraud** NOUNS 1 **fraudulence** *or* fraudulency, **dishonesty; imposture; imposition, cheat, cheating,** cozenage, **swindle,** dodge, fishy transaction, piece of sharp practice
2 **impostor, ringer;** sham, shammer, **humbug,** *blagueur* <Fr>, **fake** *and* **faker** *and* **phony** <all nonformal>, **four-flusher** <nonformal>, bluff, bluffer; **charlatan, quack,** quacksalver, quackster, **mountebank,** saltimbanco

**fraudulent** ADJS **illegal, unlawful, illegitimate, illicit,** nonlicit, nonlegal, lawless, wrongful, creative <nonformal>, **against the law; unauthorized,** unallowed, impermissible, unwarranted; **criminal, felonious**

**fray** NOUNS 1 **fight, battle,** affray, combat, action, conflict, embroilment; **clash; brush, skirmish,** scrimmage; tussle, **scuffle, struggle,** scramble, shoving match; **quarrel**; pitched battle; battle royal; **internal struggle**
VERBS 2 **wear, wear away, wear down, wear off;** abrade, fret, whittle away, rub off; frazzle, tatter, wear ragged

**freak** NOUNS 1 **monstrosity, monster;** miscreation, abortion, teratism, abnormal *or* defective birth, abnormal *or* defective fetus; freak of nature, *lusus naturae* <L>
2 **fanatic, bug** <nonformal>, **nut** <nonformal>, **buff** *and* **fan** <both nonformal>, *fanatico, aficionado* <both Sp>, devotee, **zealot, enthusiast,** energumen
3 **fluke** <nonformal>, freak occurrence *or* accident; chance hit, lucky shot, one in a million

**freakish** ADJS freak *or* freaky <nonformal>; **eccentric, erratic,** idiocratic, idiocratical, idiosyncratic, idiosyncratical, **queer,** queer in the head, **odd, peculiar,** strange, fey, singular, anomalous, funny; unnatural, abnormal, irregular, divergent, deviative, deviant, different, exceptional

**freak out** VERBS **crack, crack up,** go haywire, **blow one's cork** *or* mind *or* stack, **flip,** flip one's lid *or* wig, wig out, freak out, go out of one's skull; come unglued *or* unstuck, go up the wall, **go on a trip** *and* **blow one's mind** <all nonformal>; **hallucinate;** expand one's consciousness

**freckle** NOUNS **mark, marking;** lentigo; blemish, macula, **spot,** blotch, splotch, flick, patch, splash; mottle, dapple

**free** VERBS 1 **extricate, release, clear,** get out; **disengage,** disentangle, untangle, unsnarl, unravel, disentwine, disinvolve, unknot, disembarrass, disembroil; dislodge, break out *or* loose, cut loose, tear loose; grant *or* extend amnesty; **discharge, release, dismiss, set free,** let off <nonformal>, let go
ADJS 2 **at liberty, at large,** on the loose, **loose,** unengaged, disengaged, detached, unattached, uncommitted, uninvolved, clear, in the clear, go-as-you-please, easygoing, footloose, footloose and fancy-free, free and easy; free as air, free as a bird, free as the wind; scot-free; **freed, liberated, emancipated,** manumitted, released, uncaged, sprung <nonformal>; **liberal,** free with one's money, free-spending; **gratuitous, gratis,** free of charge, for free, **for nothing,** free for nothing, free for the asking, for love; **profligate, licentious,** unbridled, untrammeled, uninhibited

*afoot and lighthearted*
WHITMAN

ADVS 3 **freely, without restraint,** without stint, **unreservedly,** with abandon; **gratuitously, gratis,** free, free of charge, for nothing, for the asking, at no charge, without charge, on the house

**freebie** NOUNS **gift, present;** free gift, gimme <nonformal>; oblation; handsel; free ride <nonformal>; gimme <nonformal>; labor of love

**freedom** NOUNS **liberty; license, civil liberty,** the Four Freedoms <F D Roosevelt>: freedom of speech and expression, freedom of worship, freedom from want, freedom from fear; academic freedom

*the right to live as we wish*
EPICTETUS

**free-for-all** NOUNS **knock-down-and-drag-out** <nonformal>, **brawl,** broil, melee, scrimmage, **fracas,** riot

**free hand** NOUNS 1 **latitude, leeway** <nonformal>, free scope, full *or* ample scope, free play, free course; **carte blanche,** blank check; **full authority,** full power, open mandate
2 **liberality,** liberalness, freeness, freedom; **generosity,** generousness, largeness, **unselfishness, munificence,** largess; **openhandedness,** freehandedness, open hand, easy purse strings

**free-lance** VERBS **stand on one's own two feet, shift for oneself, fend for oneself,** stand on one's own, strike out for oneself; **go it alone, be one's own man,** pull a lone oar, play a lone hand <nonformal>, **paddle one's own canoe** <nonformal>; **be one's own boss** <nonformal>, answer only to oneself; do on one's own, do on one's own initiative, do on one's own hook *or* say-so <nonformal>, do in one's own sweet way <nonformal>; be a free agent

**freeloader** NOUNS **parasite,** barnacle, leech; **sponger,** sponge <nonformal>; cadger, bummer *and* moocher <both nonformal>, free rider, deadhead <nonformal>

**freewheeling** ADJS **independent,** self-dependent; free-spirited, free-floating, free-standing; stand-alone, self-reliant, self-sufficient, self-subsistent, self-supporting, self-contained, autarkic, autarchic

**free will** NOUNS **free choice, discretion,** option, choice, say, say-so *and* druthers <both nonformal>, free decision; absolute *or* unconditioned *or* noncontingent free will

**freeze** VERBS 1 **take fright,** be paralyzed with fear, throw up one's hands in horror; shit in one's pants *and* shit green <both nonformal>; **immobilize,** keep, retain; **transfix, stick,** stick fast; seize, seize up
2 be cold, grow cold, lose heat; **shiver, quiver,** chill, have a chill, have the cold shivers; freeze to death, freeze one's balls off <nonformal>, die *or* perish with the cold; ice, glaciate, congeal

**freezing** ADJS **cold, raw,** bitter, biting, **piercing,** penetrating; **frigid,** bitter *or* bitterly cold, gelid, algid; **frozen,** half-frozen, frozen to death, chilled to the bone, blue with cold, congealing

**freight** NOUNS **load, burden; payload; burden,** burthen <old>, pressure, **oppression, deadweight;** charge, **load,** loading, lading, cargo, bale; **encumbrance;** handicap, drag, millstone

**frenzied** ADJS feverish, perfervid, febrile, at fever *or* fevered pitch; hectic, frenetic, furious, frantic, **wild,** hysteric, hysterical, delirious; **insane**; **fanatical**

**frenzy** NOUNS **furor,** fury, maniacal excitement, fever, **rage; seizure,** attack, acute episode, episode, **fit,** paroxysm, spasm, **convulsion; snit,** *crise* <Fr>; amok, murderous insanity *or* frenzy, homicidal mania, hemothymia

**frequent** VERBS 1 **haunt,** resort to, hang *and* hang around *and* hang about *and* hang out <all nonformal>
ADJS 2 oftentime, many, many times, **recurrent, oft-repeated,** thick-coming; **common,** of common occurrence, not rare, **prevalent,** usual, routine, habitual, ordinary, everyday

**fresh** ADJS 1 **refreshing,** refreshful, brisk, crisp, crispy, zesty, zestful, **bracing, tonic,** cordial; **sweet, cleanly,** fastidious, dainty, of cleanly habits; **new,** original, pristine, fresh off the assembly line, mint, in mint condition, factory-fresh; wet behind the ears, not dry behind the ears, **untried,** fresh as a daisy, fresh as the morning dew
2 **impudent, impertinent, pert,** flip <nonformal>, flippant, **cocky** *and* cheeky *and* nervy <all nonformal>, **disrespectful,** derisive, brash, bluff; **saucy,** sassy <nonformal>; smart *or* smart-alecky <nonformal>, smart-ass *or* wise-ass <nonformal>

**freshen** VERBS **refresh,** freshen up, **air,** air out, **ventilate,** fresh up <nonformal>; **revive,** revivify, **reinvigorate,** reanimate; brace, **brace up,** buck up *and* pick up <both nonformal>, perk up *and* chirk up <both nonformal>, set up, set on one's legs *or* feet <nonformal>; renew one's strength, put *or* breathe new life into, give a breath of fresh air, give a shot in the arm <nonformal>

**fret** VERBS **sulk, mope,** mope around; grump *and* **grouch** *and* **bitch** <all nonformal>; air a grievance, lodge *or* register a complaint; fret and fume, **chafe, fuss,** squirm; **stew,** sweat, sweat and stew, get into a dither, get into a stew <nonformal>, work oneself into a lather *or* sweat <nonformal>, get excited; **nettle,** chafe; **pique, peeve** *and* miff <both nonformal>, huff; **ruffle, roil, rile** <nonformal>, ruffle one's feathers, **rankle**

**fretful** ADJS peevish, petulant, **pettish,** querulous, **resentful;** impatient, **fretting,** chafing, antsy-pantsy *and* antsy <both nonformal>, squirming, squirmy, about to pee *or* piss one's pants <nonformal>; fidgety, **restless, jumpy, unquiet, unsettled**

**friction** NOUNS 1 **discord, conflict,** open conflict *or* war, rub; contention, collision, clash, clashing
2 **rubbing,** rub, frottage; frication *and* confrication *and* perfrication <all old>; **drag,** skin friction; **resistance,** frictional resistance

**friend** NOUNS **acquaintance,** close acquaintance; confidant, confidante, repository; **intimate,** familiar, **close friend,** intimate *or* familiar friend; **bosom friend,** friend of one's bosom, inseparable friend, **best friend;** alter ego, other self

**friendly** ADJS friendlike; **amicable, peaceable,** unhostile; **harmonious**; **amiable, congenial,** *simpático* <Sp>, *simpatico* <Ital>, *sympathique* <Fr>, pleasant, agreeable, favorable, well-disposed, well-intentioned, well-meaning, well-meant

**fright** NOUNS **fear,** affright; **scare, alarm, consternation, dismay; dread,** unholy dread, **awe; terror, horror,** horrification, mortal *or* abject fear; **phobia**

**frighten** VERBS affright, frighten *or* scare out of one's wits; **scare,** spook <nonformal>, scare one stiff *or* shitless *or* spitless <nonformal>, scare the life out of, scare the pants off of *and* scare hell out of *and* scare the shit out of <all nonformal>; scare one to death, scare the daylights *or* the living daylights *or* the wits *or* the shit out of <nonformal>; give one a fright *or* scare *or* turn; **startle; unnerve, unman,** unstring; make one's flesh creep, chill one's spine, curl one's hair <nonformal>, make one's hair stand on end, make one's blood run cold

**frightening** ADJS **frightful; fearful,** fearsome, fear-inspiring, nightmarish, hellish; **scary,** scaring, chilling; **alarming, startling,** disquieting, dismaying, disconcerting; **unnerving, daunting,** deterring, disheartening, fazing, awing, overawing

**frightful** ADJS **hideous, horrid, horrible, dreadful, terrible, awful** <nonformal>; **repulsive**, repellent, repelling, rebarbative, **repugnant,** offensive, foul, forbidding, loathsome, revolting

**frigid** ADJS bitter *or* bitterly cold, gelid, algid; **unsexual,** unsexed; **unfeeling, unemotional,** nonemotional, emotionless, affectless, emotionally dead *or* numb *or* paralyzed, **unpassionate, unaffectionate,** unloving; **unrespon-**

**sive,** unresponding, **unsympathetic; aloof, standoffish,** offish, standoff, **distant, remote,** withdrawn, removed, detached

*cold as the north side of a gravestone in winter*
ANON

**frill** NOUNS trimming, flourish, filigree, decoration, ornament

**frilly** ADJS **showy, flaunting, flashy,** snazzy, flashing, glittering, **jazzy** *and* **glitzy** *and* gimmicky *and* splashy *and* splurgy <all nonformal>; exhibitionistic, showoffy <nonformal>, bravura; flouncy, frothy, chichi

**fringe** NOUNS 1 **periphery,** circumference, outline, lineaments, border; **edging, bordering,** bordure <heraldry>, **trimming,** binding, skirting; fimbriation, fimbria; **hem,** selvage, list, welt
ADJS 2 **exterior, external;** extrinsic; peripheral, roundabout

**frisk** VERBS **play, sport, disport; frolic,** rollick, **gambol, romp, caper,** cut capers <nonformal>, antic, curvet, cavort, caracole, flounce, trip, skip, dance; **cut up** <nonformal>, cut a dido <nonformal>, horse around <nonformal>, fool around, carry on <nonformal>

**frisky** ADJS **spirited,** sprightly, **lively, animated, vivacious,** vital, zestful, zippy <nonformal>, **exuberant,** hearty; antic, bouncing, bouncy, skittish, coltish, rompish, capersome; **full of beans** *and* **feeling one's oats** <both nonformal>, full of piss and vinegar <nonformal>; **sportive, playful,** playful as a kitten, kittenish, **frolicsome,** gamesome

**frivolous** ADJS **haphazard,** desultory, **erratic,** sporadic, spasmodic, fitful, promiscuous, indiscriminate, casual, capricious, random, hit-or-miss, vague, dispersed, wandering, planless, undirected, **aimless,** straggling, straggly; senseless, meaningless, gratuitous; **superficial,** light, windy, airy, frothy, dizzy *and* ditzy <both nonformal>, flighty, light, volatile, frothy, fluffy, **featherbrained, birdwitted, birdbrained**

**frizzy** ADJS **curly, curled; kinky,** kinked; **frizzly,** frizzled, frizzed

**frock** NOUNS **garment,** vestment, vesture, robe, gown, rag <nonformal>, togs *and* duds <both nonformal>, dress, rig <nonformal>, **gown**

**frolic** NOUNS 1 **play,** romp, rollick, frisk, gambol, caper, dido <nonformal>
VERBS 2 **play, sport, disport; rollick, gambol, frisk, romp, caper,** cut capers <nonformal>, antic, curvet, cavort, caracole, flounce, trip, skip, dance; **cut up** <nonformal>, cut a dido <nonformal>, horse around <nonformal>, fool around, carry on <nonformal>

**front** NOUNS 1 **fore,** forepart, forequarter, foreside, forefront, forehand; **priority,** anteriority; front office; **frontier**; **foreground;** proscenium; frontage
2 **pretext, pretense, pretension,** lying pretension, **show,** ostensible *or* announced *or* public *or* professed motive; facade, **sham; cover,** cover-up, cover story
VERBS 3 **confront, face, meet, encounter,** breast, brave, meet squarely, square up to, come to grips with, head *or* wade into, meet face to face *or* eyeball to eyeball *or* one-on-one, come face to face with, look in the face *or* eye, stare in the face, stand up to, stand fast, hold one's ground, hang tough *and* tough it out *and* gut it out <all nonformal>
ADJS 4 **frontal, anterior; full-face, full-frontal; ahead, in front,** one-up, one jump *or* move ahead

**frontier** NOUNS 1 **border, borderland,** border ground, marchland, march, marches; outskirts, outpost; frontier post; **the unknown,** frontiers of knowledge
ADJS 2 **bordering, fringing,** rimming, skirting; **bounding,** boundary, **limiting,** limit, determining *or* determinant *or* determinative; threshold, liminal, limbic; **marginal, borderline;** coastal, littoral

**front runner** NOUNS **leader,** first in line; pacesetter; **precursor,** foregoer, *voorlooper* <Dutch>, vaunt-courier, avant-courier; **vanguard,** avant-garde, avant-gardist, innovator, groundbreaker

**frosty** ADJS **unfeeling, cold, cool, frigid,** frozen, chill, chilly, arctic, frosted, icy, **coldhearted, cold-blooded,** cold as charity; **unaffectionate,** unloving; **aloof, standoffish,** offish, standoff, **distant, remote,** withdrawn, removed, detached, Olympian; cold-fish, inaccessible, unapproachable

**frothy** ADJS **light,** unheavy, imponderous; foamy, spumy, spumous, spumescent, bubbly, yeasty; **frilly, flouncy,** chichi; **superficial, shallow, unprofound;** light, volatile, fluffy

**frown** NOUNS 1 **scowl,** lower, **glower, pout,** moue, mow, grimace, wry face; sullen looks, black looks, **long face; reproving look,** dirty *or* nasty look <nonformal>
VERBS 2 **look sullen,** pull *or* make a long face; **scowl,** knit the brow, lower, **glower, pout,** make a moue *or* mow, grimace, make a wry face, make a lip, hang one's lip, thrust out one's lower lip

**frozen** ADJS frozen solid, glacial, gelid, congealed; **icy,** ice-cold, icy-cold, ice, icelike; frostbitten, frostnipped;
2 **stunned,** petrified, stupefied, paralyzed; white as a sheet, pale as death *or* a ghost, deadly pale, ashen, blanched, pallid, gray with fear; **immobile, static,** stationary, **rigid**
3 **stuck, fast,** stuck fast, **jammed,** impacted, congested, packed, wedged; seized, seized up

**frugal** ADJS **parsimonious, sparing,** cheeseparing, **stinting, scamping, scrimping,** skimping; too frugal, overfrugal, frugal to excess; **economical, thrifty,** economic, unwasteful, conserving, **saving,** economizing, spare, **sparing; prudent,** prudential, provident, forehanded

**fruit** NOUNS **yield, output,** make, production; **proceeds,** produce, product; **crop, harvest,** vintage, bearing; **posterity, progeny, issue, offspring,** seed, brood, breed, family

**fruitful** ADJS **productive,** fructiferous, fecund; **fertile, pregnant,** seminal, **rich,** flourishing, thriving, blooming; **prolific,** proliferous, uberous, **teeming,** swarming, bursting, bursting out, plenteous, **plentiful,** copious, generous, bountiful, **abundant, luxuriant, exuberant, lush,** superabundant; creative

**fruitless** ADJS gainless, profitless, bootless, otiose, **unprofitable,** unremunerative, nonremunerative; uncommercial; **unrewarding,** bootless, no-win <nonformal>, futile, useless; abortive; **barren,** sterile, unproductive

**frump** NOUNS **slob** <nonformal>, **slattern, sloven,** sloppy Joe, schlep, schlump, *Strüwelpeter* <Ger>

**frustrate** VERBS **thwart,** dash, check, deal a check to, checkmate; **circumvent,** get round *or* around, **evade,** stonewall <nonformal>, **elude, foil,** give the slip *or* runaround <nonformal>; negate, invalidate, vitiate, void, stultify, come *or* bring to nothing, undo

**frustration** NOUNS **thwarting, balking, foiling; discomfiture, disconcertion,** bafflement, confounding; **defeat,** upset; check, checkmate, balk; derailing, derailment

**fry** VERBS prepare food, cook up, fry up, deep-fry *or* deep-fat fry, griddle, pan, pan-fry; stir-fry

**fuck** VERBS **copulate,** couple, **mate,** unite in sexual intercourse, **have sexual relations, have sex,** make out <nonformal>, perform the act of love *or* marriage act, come together, cohabit, shack up <nonformal>, be intimate; sleep with, lie with, go to bed with; screw *and* lay *and* ball *and* frig *and* diddle *and* **make it with** <all nonformal>, go all the way, go to bed with, lie together

**fucked-up** ADJS **confused, chaotic, mixed up,** balled *or* bollixed up <nonformal>, screwed up <nonformal>, mucked up <nonformal>, fouled up *and* snafu <both nonformal>

**fuck up** VERBS 1 **complicate, confound, confuse,** muddle, **mix up**
2 <nonformal> **goof, pull a boner,** bobble, lay an egg, put *or* stick one's foot in it, stub one's toe, step on one's schvantz *or* pecker, drop the ball, blow it, bitch, bitch up, hash up, **mess up,** flub, flub the dub, **make a mess** *or* **hash of,** goof up, **louse up, gum up,** gum up the works, bugger, bugger up, play the deuce *or* devil *or* hell *or* merry hell with; go at it ass-backwards; put one's foot in one's mouth; mess up *and* ball up *and* bollix up *and* screw up *and* foul up *and* snafu *and* muck up *and* louse up

**fuddy-duddy** NOUNS 1 **fussbudget, fusspot** <nonformal>, fuss, fusser, granny, old woman, old maid; back number <nonformal>; pop *and* pops *and* dad <all nonformal>, dodo *and* old dodo <both nonformal>; fossil *and* antique *and* relic <all nonformal>; **fogy, old fogy,** regular old fogy, old poop *or* crock <nonformal>
ADJS 2 **old-fogyish,** fogyish, old-fogy; square *and* corny *and* cornball <all non-

formal>; **stuffy, stodgy; aged**, senile, bent *or* wracked *or* ravaged with age

**fudge** VERBS **tamper with, manipulate, fake, juggle,** sophisticate, **doctor** *and* **cook** <both nonformal>, rig, cook *or* juggle the books *or* the accounts <nonformal>; **cheat, victimize, gull,** pigeon, **swindle, defraud,** practice fraud upon, euchre, **con,** finagle, **fleece,** mulct, **bilk,** cozen, chouse, **cheat out of, do out of**

**fuel** NOUNS 1 energy source; heat source, firing, combustible *or* inflammable *or* flammable material, burnable, combustible, inflammable, flammable; fossil fuel, nonrenewable energy *or* fuel source; alternate *or* alternative energy source, renewable energy *or* fuel source; solar energy, solar radiation, insolation; wind energy; geothermal energy, geothermal heat, synthetic fuels *or* synfuels
VERBS 2 fuel up; fill up, top off; refuel; coal, oil; **stoke, feed,** add fuel to the flame

**fugitive** NOUNS **escapee,** escaper, evader; escape artist; escapologist, runaway

**führer** NOUNS **dictator,** duce, commissar, pharaoh, caesar, czar

**fulfill** VERBS **carry out,** carry through, go through, work out; **put through,** get through; **implement; put into effect,** put in or into practice, translate into action; come through <nonformal>; consummate, do, execute, produce, deliver, make, enact, **perform, discharge, realize,** fill, meet, satisfy

**fulfillment** NOUNS **accomplishment, achievement, performance,** execution, effectuation, implementation, carrying out *or* through, **discharge, dispatch, consummation, realization, attainment,** production, fruition; dutifulness, acquittal, satisfaction

**full** ADJS 1 **resonant, reverberant, vibrant, sonorous,** plangent, rolling; mellow, rich; **total,** plenary, comprehensive, exhaustive; **absolute,** perfect, unequivocal, plenary; **teeming, swarming, crawling,** bristling, populous
2 filled, **replete,** plenary, capacity, flush, round; **brimful,** brimming; **chock-full,** chock-a-block, chuck-full, **jam-packed, overcrowded;** stuffed, overstuffed, **packed, crammed,** *farci* <Fr>; **glutted; cloyed,** jaded; full of, with one's fill of, **overfull,** saturated, oversaturated, supersaturated

**full-blown** ADJS **full-grown, full-fledged,** full-formed, in full bloom, in one's prime; **mellow** *or* mellowed, seasoned, tempered, aged

**full-fledged** ADJS **full-grown, grown-up,** developed, well-developed, fully developed, **mature, adult; complete, whole, entire,** solid; **full,** full-dress, **full-scale**

**fumble** NOUNS 1 **muff,** fluff, miscue <nonformal>; **bungle, blunder, botch,** flub, boner *and* bonehead play <both nonformal>, boggle, bobble *and* booboo *and* screw-up *and* fuck-up <all nonformal>, foozle <nonformal>; *gaucherie, étourderie, balourdise* <all Fr>; bad job, sad work, clumsy performance; **error, mistake**
VERBS 2 **bungle, blunder,** bumble, boggle, **muff,** muff one's cue *or* lines, be all thumbs, have a handful of thumbs; **flounder,** muddle, lumber; commit a *faux pas,* commit a gaffe; **botch,** mar

**fume** VERBS 1 **burn, seethe, simmer,** sizzle, smoke, reek, smolder, steam; be pissed *or* pissed off *or* browned off <all nonformal>, be livid, be beside oneself, stew <nonformal>, boil, fret, chafe; breathe fire and fury; **rage, storm, rave,** rant, bluster; take on *and* go on *and* carry on <all nonformal>
2 **let out, give vent to,** give out *or* off, throw off, blow off, **emit, exhaust,** evacuate, let go; **exhale,** expire, breathe out, let one's breath out, blow, puff; steam, vapor, smoke, reek

**fumigate** VERBS **sanitize,** sanitate, hygienize; **disinfect, decontaminate,** sterilize; disinfest, delouse; **deodorize**

**fun** NOUNS funmaking, fun and games, **play, sport,** game; **good time,** lovely time, pleasant time; big time *and* **high time** *and* high old time <all nonformal>, picnic *and* laughs *and* lots of laughs *and* ball <all nonformal>, great fun, time of one's life; wild oats
ADJS 2 **amusing, entertaining, diverting,** beguiling; funsome *and* more fun than a barrel of monkeys <both nonformal>; recreative, recreational; **delightful,** titillative, titillating; humorous

**function** NOUNS 1 **use, purpose, role,** part, end use, immediate purpose, ultimate purpose, operational purpose, operation; work, duty, **office,** province, place, **role,** *rôle* <Fr>, part; obligation, charge, **onus, burden,** mission, devoir, must, ought, imperative, bounden duty,

proper *or* assigned task, what ought to be done, what one is responsible for
VERBS 2 **operate, run, work; manage, direct, conduct; carry on** *or* **out** *or* **through,** make go *or* work, carry the ball <nonformal>, perform; **handle,** manipulate, maneuver; deal with, see to, take care of; occupy oneself with; be responsible for; be effective, go into effect, have effect, take effect

**functional** ADJS **acting,** performing, practicing, serving, functioning, operating, operative, operational, working; in action; **practical,** banausic, pragmatical, **utilitarian,** of general utility *or* application

**functioning** ADJS **operating, operational, working,** operant, functional, acting, active, running, **going,** going on, ongoing; **in operation,** in action, **in practice, in force,** in play, in exercise, at work, on foot; **in process,** in the works, in the pipe *or* pipeline <nonformal>

**fund** NOUNS 1 **supply, resource, resources; means, assets,** liquid assets, balance, pluses <nonformal>, black-ink items, **capital,** capitalization, available means *or* resources *or* funds, cash flow, stock in trade; venture capital
VERBS 2 **finance, back, sponsor, patronize, support,** provide for, capitalize, provide capital *or* money for, pay for, bankroll <nonformal>, angel <nonformal>, put up the money; **stake** *or* **grubstake** <both nonformal>; subsidize; set up, set up in business; refinance

**fundamental** NOUNS 1 **essential,** principle, essential principle, premise, substantive point, material point, hypostasis, postulate, axiom; **gist,** gravamen, **nub** <nonformal>, nucleus, center, focus, kernel, **core, pith,** meat; **heart,** soul, heart and soul, spirit, sap, marrow
ADJS 2 **essential,** of the essence; **primary,** primitive, primal, elementary, elemental, foundational, simple, barebones *and* no-frills *and* bread-and-butter <all nonformal>, original, *ab ovo* <L>, **basic, gut** <nonformal>, basal, **rudimentary,** crucial, central, underlying; **substantive,** substantial, material; constitutive, constituent; radical

**funds** NOUNS **finances, moneys,** exchequer, purse, budget, pocket; treasury, treasure, substance, **assets,** resources, total assets, worth, net worth, **pecuniary resources, means,** available means *or* resources *or* funds, cash flow, wherewithal, command of money; balance; war chest; reserves, cash reserves; savings, savings account, nest egg <nonformal>

**funny** ADJS 1 **humorous, amusing; witty; droll, whimsical,** quizzical; **laughable,** risible, good for a laugh
2 **ludicrous, ridiculous, hilarious, absurd,** quaint, eccentric, incongruous, bizarre, **inexplicable, unexplainable,** uninterpretable, undefinable, indefinable, **unaccountable; suspicious,** suspect

**fur** NOUNS **pelt, hide,** fell, fleece, vair <heraldry>; imitation fur, fake fur, synthetic fur; peltry, skins

**furious** ADJS hectic, frenetic, **frenzied,** frantic, **wild,** hysteric, hysterical, delirious; **violent,** fierce, ferocious, feral; feverish; desperate, mad, wild, wanton, harum-scarum <nonformal>

**furlough** NOUNS **leave, leave of absence, liberty,** shore leave; **sabbatical,** sabbatical leave *or* year; layoff

**furnace** NOUNS **kiln, oven, stove;** fiery furnace, inferno, hell; **reactor, nuclear reactor, pile,** atomic pile, reactor pile, chain-reacting pile, chain reactor, atomic *or* nuclear furnace, neutron factory

**furnish** VERBS **supply, provide, afford,** provide for; **make available to,** put one in the way of; **accommodate with,** favor with, indulge with; **heap upon,** pour on, shower down upon, **lavish upon; bear, yield, produce; bring forth,** usher into the world; fruit, **bear fruit,** fructify

**furniture** NOUNS furnishings, movables, home furnishings, house furnishings, household effects, household goods, office furniture, school furniture, church furniture, library furniture, furnishments <old>; **fixtures,** fittings, **appointments,** accouterments, appurtenances, installations

**furor** NOUNS **fury,** furore <Brit>, fire and fury; **turbulence, turmoil,** chaos, upset, **frenzy,** maniacal excitement, fever, tempestuousness, storminess, wildness, tumultuousness, tumult, uproar, racket, cacophony, pandemonium, hubbub, **commotion, disturbance, agitation,** bluster, broil, brawl, embroilment, brouhaha, fuss, flap <nonformal>, **row, rumpus,** ruckus <nonformal>, **ferment,** fume, boil, boiling, seething, ebullition, fomentation; rabidness, **mania**

**furrow** NOUNS **groove,** scratch, crack, cranny, chase, chink, score, **cut,** gash, striation, streak, stria, **gouge,** slit, incision; sulcus, sulcation; **rut,** wheel track, well-worn groove; **wrinkle, corrugation,** ridge, **crease, crimp,** ruck, **pucker,** cockle; **crinkle,** crankle, rimple, ripple, wimple

**furry** ADJS furred; villous; villose; ciliate, cirrose; hispid, hispidulous; **woolly, fleecy,** lanate, bushy, tufty, **shaggy,** shagged, wooly; **downy,** fluffy, nappy, velvety, peachy, fuzzy, flossy

**further** VERBS **advance, promote,** forward, hasten, contribute to, foster, aid, facilitate, expedite, abet; **be useful,** stand in good stead, encourage, boost <nonformal>, favor, advantage, **facilitate,** set *or* put *or* push forward
ADJS 2 **additional, supplementary, supplemental; extra,** plus, fresh, **more,** new, **other,** another, ulterior; **auxiliary,** ancillary, supernumerary, contributory, **accessory,** collateral
ADVS 3 **additionally, in addition, also,** and then some, even more, more so, and also, and all <nonformal>, and so, **as well, too,** else, beside, **besides, to boot, not to mention, let alone, into the bargain;** on top of, over, above; **beyond, plus; extra,** on the side <nonformal>, for lagniappe; **more, moreover,** *au reste* <Fr>, *en plus* <Fr>, thereto, **furthermore,** at the same time, then, again, yet; similarly, likewise, by the same token, by the same sign; all included, altogether; among other things, *inter alia* <L>

**furtive** ADJS **stealthy,** indirect, privy, backstairs, **sly, shifty, sneaky,** sneaking, skulking, slinking, slinky, feline; **covert, clandestine,** quiet, unobtrusive, hugger-mugger, **surreptitious, undercover,** underground, under-the-counter, under-the-table, **cloak-and-dagger,** backdoor, hole-and-corner <nonformal>, underhand, **underhanded**

**fury** NOUNS **furor,** fire and fury; **ecstasy,** transport, **rapture,** ravishment; intoxication, abandon; **passion, rage,** blind *or* burning rage, raging *or* tearing passion, livid *or* towering rage *or* passion; **frenzy,** orgy, orgasm; madness, craze, **delirium,** hysteria

**fuse** NOUNS 1 **detonator,** exploder; **cap,** blasting cap, percussion cap, mercury fulminate, fulminating mercury; electric detonator *or* exploder; detonating powder; **primer,** priming; primacord; circuit breaker
VERBS 2 **come together, cluster,** bunch, bunch up, clot; **amalgamate, integrate,** alloy, coalesce, **merge,** meld, **blend,** stir in, merge *or* blend *or* meld *or* shade into, melt into one, compound, compose, conflate, concoct; **combine,** unite, unify, marry, wed, couple, link, yoke, yoke together; conflate; interfuse, interblend; **encompass,** include, comprise

**fusion** NOUNS **interfusion, conflation;** blend, blending, meld, melding; **amalgamation, integration,** coalescence; **merger,** unification, uniting, integration, combination; **admixture,** composition, commixture, immixture, intermixture, **mingling,** minglement, commingling, intermingling, interlarding; **pluralism,** melting pot, multiculturalism, ethnic *or* racial *or* cultural diversity; **melting,** liquefaction, liquefying, liquescence

**fuss** NOUNS 1 **dither, tizzy** <nonformal>, swivet, foofaraw, **pucker** <nonformal>, **twitter,** twitteration <nonformal>, **flutter, fluster,** flusteration *and* flustration <both nonformal>, **fret,** pother, bother, lather *and* stew *and* snit <all nonformal>, flap; **quarrel,** open quarrel, dustup, **dispute, argument,** polemic, **controversy,** altercation, **fight, squabble, contention,** strife, **tussle,** bicker, wrangle, snarl, **tiff, spat**
VERBS 2 **bustle,** make a fuss, stir, stir about, rush around *or* about, tear around, hurry about, buzz *or* whiz about, dart to and fro, run *or* go around like a chicken with its head cut off; **be hard to please,** want everything just so, fuss over; pick and choose; **turn up one's nose,** disdain, scorn, spurn

**fussy** ADJS **bustling,** fussing; **meticulous, exacting, scrupulous, conscientious,** religious, punctilious, punctual, **particular, critical, attentive,** scrutinizing; **thorough,** thoroughgoing; **finical,** finicking, finicky, fuss-budgety <nonformal>; difficult, hard to please, picayune, picky <nonformal>

**fusty** ADJS **malodorous,** fetid, olid, odorous, stinking, reeking, reeky, nidorous, smelling, bad-smelling, **evil-smelling,** ill-smelling, heavy-smelling, **smelly,** stenchy; **foul,** vile, putrid, **musty,** funky, frowzy, stuffy, moldy, mildewed, mildewy; **stale**

**futile** ADJS **ineffective, ineffectual, inefficacious,** feckless; **vain, inutile, useless,** unavailing, bootless, fruitless; doomed, foredoomed; hollow, empty, idle; **abortive,** miscarrying, miscarried, stillborn, died aborning; no-win <nonformal>

*weary, stale, flat, and unprofitable*
SHAKESPEARE

**futility** NOUNS vanity, emptiness, hollowness; **fruitlessness,** bootlessness, unprofitableness, otiosity, worthlessness; triviality, nugacity, nugaciousness; unproductiveness; **ineffectuality,** ineffectiveness, inefficacy; **impotence**; **pointlessness,** meaninglessness, purposelessness, aimlessness, fecklessness; the absurd, absurdity; inanity, fatuity; **much ado about nothing,** tempest in a teapot, much cry and little wool

**future** NOUNS 1 **the future,** futurity, what is to come, imminence, subsequence, eventuality, **hereafter,** aftertime, afteryears, years to come, etc; **tomorrow,** the morrow, the morning after, *mañana* <Sp>; **immediate** *or* **near future,** time just ahead, immediate prospect, offing, next period; **distant future,** remote *or* deep *or* far future; **by-and-by,** the sweet by-and-by <nonformal>; **prospect,** outlook, anticipation, expectation, project, probability, prediction, extrapolation, forward look, foresight, prevision, prevenience; what is to be *or* come

ADJS 2 **later,** hereafter; **coming, forthcoming, imminent**, approaching, nearing, **prospective; eventual**, ultimate, to-be, **to come; projected,** plotted, planned, looked- *or* hoped-for, desired, emergent, **predicted,** prophesied, foreseen, anticipated, anticipatory, previsional, prevenient, envisioned, envisaged, probable, extrapolated; **in the offing,** on the horizon, **in prospect,** already in sight, just around the corner, in view, in one's eye, in store, in reserve, **in the wind**

**fuzz** NOUNS **down, fluff,** flue, floss, **fur,** pile; **downiness,** fluffiness, velvet, velvetiness, fuzziness, peach fuzz, pubescence

# G

**gab** NOUNS 1 **chatter, jabber,** gibber, **babble,** babblement, prate, **prating, prattle, palaver,** chat, **gabble,** jaw-jaw <nonformal>, blab, **blabber, blather,** blether, clatter, clack, cackle, talkee-talkee; twaddle, twattle, **gibble-gabble, chitter-chatter, tittle-tattle,** mere talk, idle talk *or* chatter; **guff** *and* **gas** *and* **hot air** *and* blah-blah *and* yak *and* yakkety-yak <all nonformal>; **gossip**
VERBS 2 **chatter, chat, prate, prattle, patter,** palaver, **babble,** natter <Brit>, **gabble,** tittle-tattle, **jabber,** gibber, **blab, blabber, blather,** blether, clatter, twaddle, twattle, rattle, clack, dither, spout *or* **spout off** <nonformal>, pour forth, **gush,** have a big mouth <nonformal>, love the sound of one's own voice; **jaw** *and* **gas** *and* yak *and* **yakkety-yak** *and* run off at the mouth *and* beat one's gums <all nonformal>, **shoot off one's mouth** *or* **face** <nonformal>; run on, rattle on

**gad about** VERBS **wander, roam, rove,** range, nomadize, **gad,** gad around, follow the seasons, wayfare, flit, traipse <nonformal>, gallivant, knock around *or* about *and* bat around *or* about <all nonformal>, prowl, **drift, stray,** float around, straggle, **meander, ramble,** stroll, saunter, jaunt, peregrinate, divagate, go *or* run about

**gadfly** NOUNS **goad, spur, prod,** sting; **prompter, mover, prime mover,** motivator, impeller, energizer, galvanizer, inducer, **actuator, animator,** moving spirit; spark plug <nonformal>; persuader; **stimulator;** coaxer, wheedler, cajoler

**gadget** NOUNS 1 **tool, instrument, implement, utensil; apparatus, device,** mechanical device, contrivance, contraption <nonformal>, gimcrack, means, mechanical means

2 <nonformal> **thingumabob, thingumajig, doodad, dohickey,** flumadiddle, gigamaree, **gimmick, gizmo,** dingus, hickey, jigger, widget

**gaffe** NOUNS **blunder, faux pas,** solecism; stupidity, indiscretion; **botch, bungle**

**gag** NOUNS 1 **silencer, muffler,** muffle, **mute,** baffle *or* baffler, quietener, cushion; **damper,** damp; dampener; **soft pedal,** sordine, sourdine, *sordino* <Ital>; hushcloth, silence cloth; **muzzle**
2 **joke, jest,** one-liner <nonformal>, **wheeze,** jape; story, yarn, **funny story,** good story; punch line, gag line
VERBS 3 muzzle, silence, muffle, stop one's mouth, cut one short, strike dumb *or* mute, dumbfound; tonguetie; squash, squelch <nonformal>, stifle, choke, choke off, throttle, put the kibosh on <nonformal>, put the lid on *and* shut down on <both nonformal>, put the damper on <nonformal>
4 be nauseated, **sicken at,** choke on, have a bellyful of <nonformal>; **retch,** keck, heave, vomit, puke, hurl *and* upchuck *and* barf <all nonformal>

**gain** NOUNS 1 **profit,** percentage <nonformal>, **take** *or* take-in *and* piece *and* slice *and* end *and* rakeoff *and* skimmings <all nonformal>; **gains, profits,** earnings, winnings, return, returns, proceeds, bottom line <nonformal>; **income**; **receipts**; **fruits,** pickings, gleanings; **pile** *and* bundle *and* cleanup *and* killing *and* mint <all nonformal>; net *or* neat profit, clean *or* clear profit, net
VERBS 2 get ahead; wax, swell, balloon, bloat, mount, **rise,** go up, crescendo, snowball; accrue, accumulate; **improve, grow better,** look better, show improvement, meliorate, ameliorate; **advance, progress,** make progress, make headway, gain ground, go forward, get *or* go ahead, come on, come along *and* come along nicely <both nonformal>, get along; make strides *or* rapid strides, **acquire,** get, obtain, secure, procure; **receive, secure,** have, come by, be in receipt of, be on the receiving end

**gait** NOUNS **pace, walk, step, stride, tread;** saunter, stroll, strolling gait; shuffle, shamble, hobble, limp, hitch, waddle; totter, stagger, lurch; toddle, paddle; mince, mincing steps, scuttle, prance, flounce, stalk, strut, swagger; trot, gallop

**gal** NOUNS

<nonformal> **dame, chick,** tomato, **babe** *or* baby, **broad,** frail, **doll,** skirt, jill, chit, cutie, filly

**gala** NOUNS 1 **fete, gala affair, blowout** <nonformal>, **jamboree** <nonformal>; gala day, *fiesta* <Sp>
ADJS 2 **festive,** festal; merry, gay, jolly, jovial, joyous, joyful, gladsome, convivial, hilarious

**galaxy** NOUNS **island universe,** galactic nebula; spiral galaxy *or* nebula, spiral; barred spiral galaxy *or* nebula, barred spiral; elliptical *or* spheroidal galaxy; disk galaxy; irregular galaxy; radio galaxy; **the Milky Way,** the galactic circle, *Via Lactea* <L>

**gale** NOUNS **windstorm,** big *or* great *or* fresh *or* strong *or* stiff *or* high *or* howling *or* spanking wind, ill *or* dirty *or* ugly wind; **tempest,** tempestuous wind; williwaw; **blow,** violent *or* heavy blow; **squall,** thick squall, black squall, white squall; half a gale, whole gale; **hurricane,** typhoon, tropical storm

**gall** NOUNS 1 **rancor,** virulence, **acrimony,** acerbity, asperity; hard feelings, **animosity**; soreness, rankling, slow burn <nonformal>; gnashing of teeth

2 <nonformal> **cheek,** face, brass, **nerve, chutzpah,** crust

VERBS 3 **irritate, aggravate,** exacerbate, worsen, rub salt in the wound, twist the knife in the wound, step on one's corns, barb the dart; touch a soft spot *or* tender spot, touch a raw nerve, touch where it hurts; provoke, **chafe, fret,** grate, rasp; **get on one's nerves, grate on,** set on edge; **set one's teeth on edge,** go against the grain; **rub one** *or* **one's fur the wrong way**

**gallant** ADJS **chivalrous,** chivalric, knightly; **courtly; formal,** ceremonious; old-fashioned, old-world

**gallery** NOUNS **corridor, hall,** hallway; passage, **passageway;** loggia; arcade, colonnade, pergola, cloister, peristyle; areaway; breezeway; **balcony,** terrace

**gallop** NOUNS 1 **run, sprint; dash, rush,** plunge, headlong rush *or* plunge, **race, scurry, scamper,** scud, scuttle, **spurt,** burst, **burst of speed;** canter, lope; hand gallop, full gallop; **trot**
VERBS 2 **go on horseback, ride;** ride hard, clap spurs to one's horse; trot, amble, pace, canter, tittup, lope

**gallows** NOUNS **scaffold;** gallows-tree, gibbet, tree, drop; hangman's rope, noose, rope, halter, hemp, hempen collar *or* necktie *or* bridle <nonformal>; the necklace <nonformal>

**galvanize** VERBS **stimulate, whet, sharpen,** pique, provoke, quicken, enliven, liven up, animate, **exhilarate,** invigorate, give a fillip to; infuse life into, give new life to, revive, renew, resuscitate; **motivate, move,** set in motion, **actuate,** move to action, **impel,** propel; **stimulate,** energize, **animate, spark;** promote, foster

**gambit** NOUNS **trick, artifice, device,** ploy, stratagem, **scheme,** design, *ficelle* <Fr>, **subterfuge,** blind, **ruse, wile,** shift, **dodge,** artful dodge, sleight, pass, feint, fetch, chicanery; offer, **bid,** strong bid; experiment, tentative; tentation, trial and error

**gamble** NOUNS 1 **chance, risk, risky thing, hazard; gambling** *or* **gambler's chance,** betting proposition, bet, matter of chance, sporting chance, **luck of the draw,** hazard of the die, roll *or* cast *or* throw of the dice, turn *or* roll of the wheel, turn of the cards, fall of the cards, flip *or* toss of a coin, toss-up, toss; **speculation,** venture, flier *and* plunge <both nonformal>; calculated risk; uncertainty; fortune, luck
VERBS 2 **try one's luck** *or* **fortune; speculate; run** *or* **bank a game;** draw lots, draw straws, lot, cut lots, **cast lots;** cut the cards *or* deck; match coins, toss, flip a coin, call, call heads or tails; shoot craps, play at dice, roll the bones <nonformal>; play the ponies <nonformal>; punt, lay, lay down, put up, **make a bet, lay a wager,** give *or* take *or* lay odds, make book; plunge <nonformal>; **bet on** *or* **upon, back;** bet *or* play against; play *or* follow the ponies <nonformal>
3 **take chances, take a chance, chance, risk,** hazard, press *or* push one's luck, **run the chance** *or* **risk** *or* **hazard;** risk one's neck, run a risk, go out on a limb, stick one's neck out<nonformal>, **expose oneself,** bare one's breast, lower one's guard, **lay oneself open to,** leave oneself wide open, open the door to, let oneself in for; **tempt Providence** *or* **fate,** forget the odds, **defy danger,** skate on thin ice, court destruction, dance on the razor's edge, go in harm's way, hang by a hair *or* a thread, put one's head in the lion's mouth, play with fire, risk one's life, throw caution to the wind

**gambol** VERBS **caper, cut capers,** cut a dido <nonformal>, curvet, cavort, capriole, gambado, **frisk,** flounce, **trip, skip,** bob, bounce, jump about; **romp; prance;** caracole

**game** NOUNS 1 **contest, engagement, encounter, match,** matching, meet, meeting, derby, pissing match <nonformal>, **trial, test,** *concours* and *rencontre* <both Fr>; card game; board game; parlor game; **gambling game**, game of chance, friendly game
ADJS 2 **willing,** ready; **disposed, inclined, minded, well-disposed,** well-inclined, favorably inclined *or* disposed; predisposed; compliant, **consenting**; **eager;** keen, prompt, quick, ready and willing, zealous, ardent, enthusiastic, resolute, tough; in the mood *or* vein *or* humor *or* mind, in a good mood; receptive, responsive; amenable, tractable, docile, pliant; **plucky, spunky** *and* feisty *and* gutty *or* gutsy <all nonformal>, gritty, **mettlesome,** dauntless, game to the last *or* end

**gamin** NOUNS **waif,** homeless waif, dogie, stray, waifs and strays; ragamuffin, tatterdemalion; gamine, urchin, street urchin, dead-end kid <nonformal>, mudlark, guttersnipe <nonformal>

**gamut** NOUNS **range, scope, compass, reach, stretch, expanse** radius, sweep, carry, fetch; **scale,** register, diapason; **spectrum**

**gamy** ADJS **strong,** strong-flavored, strong-tasting; **high,** high-flavored, high-tasted; **rank,** high; **rancid, tainted, off,** blown, turned

**gang** NOUNS **staff, personnel, employees,** help, hired help, the help, **crew,** men, force, servantry, retinue; **unholy alliance, ring** *and* mob <both nonformal>; **company, group,** band, knot, complement, cast, outfit, pack, cohort, troop, troupe, tribe, **body,** corps, stable, bunch *and* mob *and* crowd <all nonformal>

**gangly** ADJS **lean,** lean-looking, **skinny** <nonformal>, fleshless, lean-fleshed, thin-fleshed, **spare,** meager, **scrawny,** scraggy, thin-bellied, **gaunt, lank,** rangy, **lanky,** tall as a maypole; **gangling** <nonformal>, gawky, **spindling,** spindly; all skin and bones, nothing but skin and bones; **long-legged,** long-limbed, leggy

**gangster** NOUNS **criminal, felon, perpetrator, crook** *and* perp <both nonformal>, public enemy, **lawbreaker,** scofflaw; mobster *and* wiseguy <both nonformal>, **racketeer**

**gap** NOUNS **interval, space**, intervening *or* intermediate space, **interspace,** distance *or* space between, interstice; **clearance,** margin, leeway, **room**; discontinuity, jump, leap, interruption; hiatus, caesura, lacuna; time interval, interim; **disparity,** diversity, divergence, gap, contrast, difference

**gape** NOUNS 1 **gaze, stare,** goggle, glare, glower; **gaping, yawning,** oscitation, oscitancy, dehiscence, pandiculation; **yawn**
VERBS 2 stare, stare at, stare hard, look, goggle, **gawk** *or* gawp <nonformal>, gaze open-mouthed; look straight in the eye, look full in the face, hold one's eye *or* gaze, stare down; **gaze,** drop one's jaw, look *or* stand aghast *or* agog; gap <nonformal>, **yawn,** oscitate, dehisce, hang open

**garb** NOUNS **clothing, clothes, apparel, wear, wearing apparel, daywear, dress,** dressing, **raiment,** garmenture, **attire, array,** habit, habiliment, fashion, style, guise, **costume,** costumery, gear, trim, bedizenment; **garments,** robes, robing, rags <nonformal>, drapery, finery

**garbage** NOUNS **refuse, leavings,** sweepings, **scraps,** orts; gash <nonformal>, swill, pig-swill, slop, slops, hogwash <nonformal>; rags, bones, wastepaper, shard, potsherd

**garble** VERBS **pervert, falsify, twist, put a false construction upon, give a spin, give a false coloring,** twist the words *or* meaning, color, varnish, slant, strain, torture; misrepresent, misconstrue, misinterpret, misrender, misdirect, **make unintelligible, scramble,** jumble; send *or* deliver the wrong signal *or* message

**garden** NOUNS 1 *jardin* <Fr>; bed, **flower bed,** border, ornamental border; paradise; garden spot
VERBS 2 **grow, raise;** cultivate; have a green thumb
ADJS 3 horticultural, hortulan, floricultural

**gardening** NOUNS horticulture, floriculture; landscape gardening; truck gardening, market gardening, olericulture

**garden-variety** ADJS **simple**, **plain, ordinary, nondescript, common, com-**

monplace, **prosaic,** prosy, **matter-of-fact, homely, homespun,** garden, everyday, workaday, **average**

**gargantuan** ADJS **gigantic,** mountainous, titanic, colossal, mammoth, gigantesque, monster, monstrous, outsize, sizable, larger-than-life, overgrown, king-size, monumental

**garish** ADJS **lurid,** loud, screaming, shrieking, glaring, flaring, flashy, glitzy <nonformal>, flaunting, crude, blinding, overbright, raw, gaudy

**garland** NOUNS **bouquet,** festoon; **trophy,** laurel, **laurels,** bays, palm, palms, crown, chaplet, lei, wreath, **feather in one's cap** <nonformal>

**garment** NOUNS vestment, vesture, robe, frock, gown, rag <nonformal>, togs *and* duds <both nonformal>

**garnish** NOUNS **adornment, embellishment,** embroidery, elaboration; nonfunctional addition *or* adjunct; garnishment, garniture; trimming, trim

**garret** NOUNS **attic,** attic room, **loft,** sky parlor; storeroom, junk room

**garrison** NOUNS **stronghold,** hold, safehold, fasthold, strong point, **fastness,** keep, ward, **bastion,** donjon, **citadel, castle,** tower, tower of strength, strong point; **bunker, pillbox,** blockhouse, trenches *or* barricades

**garrulous** ADJS **talkative, loquacious, talky,** big-mouthed <nonformal>, gabby *and* windy *and* gassy <all nonformal>, all jaw <nonformal>; **longwinded,** prolix, verbose; **voluble,** fluent; **effusive,** gushy; expansive

**gas** NOUNS 1 **chatter, jabber,** gibber, **babble,** babblement, prate, prating, prattle, palaver, gabble, gab *and* jaw-jaw <both nonformal>, blab, **blabber, blather; guff** *and* **hot air** *and* blah-blah *and* yak *and* yakkety-yak <all nonformal>
2 **belch, burp** <nonformal>, belching, wind, eructation; **fart** <nonformal>, **flatulence** *or* flatulency, flatuosity, flatus, wind
3 **atmosphere, air**
VERBS 4 **jaw** *and* yak *and* **yakkety-yak** *and* run off at the mouth *and* beat one's gums <all nonformal>, **shoot off one's mouth** *or* **face** <nonformal>; **talk on,** talk away, **go on** <nonformal>, run on, rattle on, ramble on; talk oneself hoarse, talk till one is blue in the face

**gasp** NOUNS 1 **breathing;** insufflation, exsufflation; **breath,** wind, breath of air; pant, puff; wheeze, asthmatic wheeze; gulp
VERBS 2 murmur, mutter, mumble, whisper, breathe, buzz, sigh; pant

**gastronomy** NOUNS gastronomics, gastrology, **epicurism,** epicureanism, gourmandise; *friandise* <Fr>

**gate** NOUNS 1 **entrance,** entry, door, portal, **entranceway,** entryway; gateway, portcullis
2 **floodgate,** flood-hatch, **head gate,** penstock, water gate, **sluice,** sluice gate; tide gate, aboiteau <Can>; weir; **lock,** lock gate, dock gate; air lock
3 **receipts,** gate receipts, box office

**gate-crasher** NOUNS **intruder,** interloper, trespasser; crasher <nonformal>, unwelcome *or* uninvited guest; moocher *and* freeloader <both nonformal>

**gather** VERBS 1 **fold,** fold on itself, fold up; **double,** ply, plicate; fold over, double over, lap over, turn over *or* under; **crease, crimp; pleat,** plait, plat <nonformal>; **tuck,** tuck up, ruck, ruck up; flounce
2 **collect, glean, pick, pluck,** cull, **take up,** pick up, get *or* gather in, gather to oneself, bring *or* get together, scrape together; heap up, amass, accumulate; **come together, congregate,** come from far and wide, come *or* arrive in a body; muster, **meet, forgather,** gang up <nonformal>, mass; flock together; herd together
3 **be imminent, impend, overhang,** hang *or* lie over, **loom,** hang over one's head, hover, **threaten, menace,** lower; brew
4 **suppose,** assume, presume, surmise, expect, suspect, infer, understand, **conclude, deduce, consider,** reckon, divine, imagine, **fancy,** dream, conceive, **believe, deem,** repute, feel, **think,** be inclined to think, opine

**gathering** NOUNS **social gathering, social,** sociable, social affair, social hour, hospitality hour, affair, get-together <nonformal>; **reception,** at home, salon, levee, soiree

**gauche** ADJS **ungainly,** uncouth, **ungraceful,** graceless, inelegant; **green,** callow, innocent, ingenuous, awkward, naive, unripe, raw

**gaudy** ADJS **tawdry;** gorgeous, colorful; **garish, loud** <nonformal>, **blatant, flagrant,** shameless, **brazen,** brazenfaced, lurid, extravagant, sensational, **spectac-**

ular, glaring, flaring, flaunting, screaming <nonformal>, obtrusive, vulgar, crude; **showy, flashy, ostentatious,** glitzy <nonformal>, meretricious, flamboyant, flaming, bedizened

**gauge** NOUNS 1 **measure,** measuring instrument, **meter, instrument,** barometer, **rule, yardstick,** measuring rod *or* stick, **standard,** norm, canon, **criterion,** test, touchstone, check
VERBS 2 **measure, quantify,** quantize, take the measure of, mensurate, apply the yardstick to; **estimate,** make an approximation; **assess,** rate, appraise, valuate, value, evaluate, appreciate, prize; size *or* size up <nonformal>

**gaunt** ADJS **lean,** lean-looking, **skinny** <nonformal>, fleshless, lean-fleshed, thin-fleshed, **spare,** meager, **scrawny,** scraggy, thin-bellied, **lank, lanky; gangling** *and* gangly <both nonformal>, gawky, **spindling,** spindly; nothing but skin and bones

**gawk** VERBS **ogle; stare,** stare at, stare hard, look, goggle, **gape,** gawp <nonformal>, gaze *or* stare open-mouthed, drop one's jaw, look *or* stand aghast *or* agog, rubber *and* rubberneck <both nonformal>

**gay** ADJS 1 **colorful, bright, vivid,** exotic, **brilliant,** burning, **gorgeous,** bright-hued, bright-colored
2 **homosexual,** homoerotic, queer *and* limp-wristed *and* faggoty <all nonformal>; lesbian, sapphic, tribadistic; effeminate
3 gay as a lark; **spirited,** sprightly, **lively, animated, vivacious,** vital, zestful, zippy <nonformal>, **exuberant,** hearty; **frisky,** antic, skittish, coltish, rompish, capersome; **full of beans** *and* **feeling one's oats** <both nonformal>, full of piss and vinegar <nonformal>; **jovial, jolly,** hearty, festive

**gaze** NOUNS 1 **stare,** gape, goggle; sharp *or* piercing *or* penetrating look; **ogle,** glad eye, come-hither look <nonformal>, bedroom eyes <nonformal>
VERBS 2 fix one's gaze, fix *or* fasten *or* rivet one's eyes upon, keep one's eyes upon, feast one's eyes on; **eye, ogle; stare,** stare at, stare hard, look, goggle, **gape, gawk** *or* gawp <nonformal>, gaze open-mouthed; strain one's eyes; look straight in the eye, look full in the face, hold one's eye *or* gaze, stare down

**gazebo** NOUNS **summerhouse,** arbor, bower, pergola, kiosk, alcove, retreat

**gear** NOUNS 1 **equipment,** paraphernalia, things, **stuff** <nonformal>, impedimenta <pl>, **tackle; kit,** duffel, effects, personal effects
2 gearing, gear train; gearwheel, cogwheel, rack; **gearshift; transmission,** gearbox; automatic transmission

**gel** NOUNS 1 **semiliquid,** semifluid; **jelly,** gelatin, jell, jam; **emulsion**
VERBS 2 **thicken, congeal,** coagulate, clot, set, concrete; gelatinize, gelatinate, jelly, jellify, **jell**

**geld** VERBS **castrate,** emasculate, eunuchize, neuter, spay, fix *or* alter <both nonformal>, unsex, deball <nonformal>

**gem** NOUNS 1 good person, fine person, good *or* fine man *or* woman *or* child, worthy, prince, nature's nobleman *or* -woman, man *or* woman after one's own heart; **treasure,** jewel, pearl, diamond
2 **precious stone, gemstone;** semiprecious stone; gem of the first water

**gender** NOUNS **sex;** maleness, masculinity, femaleness, femininity; masculine, feminine, neuter, common gender; grammatical gender, natural gender

**genealogy** NOUNS **pedigree,** stemma, *Stammbaum* <Ger>, genealogical tree, **family tree,** tree; genogram

**general** ADJS **generalized, nonspecific,** generic, **indefinite,** indeterminate, vague, abstract, nebulous, unspecified, undifferentiated, featureless, uncharacterized, bland, neutral

**generalization** NOUNS universalization, globalization, ecumenization, internationalization; **labeling,** stereotyping; general idea, **abstraction,** generalized proposition; glittering generality, sweeping statement

**generally** ADVS **in general; generally speaking,** speaking generally, **broadly,** broadly speaking, **roughly,** roughly speaking, as an approximation; **usually, as a rule, ordinarily, commonly, normally,** routinely, as a matter of course, in the usual course; **by and large,** at large, altogether, overall, over the long haul <nonformal>, **all things considered,** taking one thing with another, taking all things together, on balance, **all in all,** taking all in all, **on the whole,** as a whole, **in the long run,** for the most part, for better or for worse

**generate** VERBS **cause,** be the cause of,

lie at the root of; **bring about, bring to pass,** effectuate, **effect,** bring to effect, realize; **occasion, make, create,** engender, produce, breed, work, do; **originate,** give origin to, give occasion to, **give rise to,** spark, spark off, set off, trigger, trigger off; set afloat, **set on foot;** found, establish, inaugurate, institute

**generation** NOUNS **lifetime, life,** life's duration, life expectancy, lifespan, expectation of life, period of existence, all the days of one's life; **age**

**generous** ADJS **magnanimous,** great-souled *or* -spirited; generous to a fault, openhanded, **liberal; big, bighearted,** greathearted, largehearted, great of heart *or* soul; plenteous, **plentiful,** copious, bountiful, **abundant, luxuriant, exuberant, lush,** superabundant

**genesis** NOUNS **origin,** origination, **inception,** incipience *or* incipiency, inchoation; **divine creation,** creationism, creation science; **birth,** birthing, bearing, parturition, pregnancy, nascency *or* nascence, nativity; **source, origin,** original, origination, **derivation, rise, beginning,** conception, inception, commencement, **head;** provenance, provenience, background

**genetic** ADJS **hereditary,** patrimonial, **inherited, innate;** genic; patroclinous, matroclinous; **inbred,** bred in the bone, in the blood, running in the blood *or* race *or* strain, radical, rooted; connate, connatal, coeval

**genial** ADJS **pleasant,** congenial, cordial, *gemütlich* <Ger>, affable, amiable, amicable, gracious; good, goodly, nice, fine; cheerful, **good-natured, good-humored,** bonhomous, **sweet-tempered; agreeable; hospitable, receptive,** welcoming; **friendly,** neighborly, hearty, open, openhearted, warm, warmhearted

**genie** NOUNS **jinni,** genius, jinniyeh, afreet

**genitalia** NOUNS **genitals,** sex organs, reproductive organs, pudenda, private parts, privy parts, privates meat <nonformal>; **male organs; penis, phallus,** *lingam* <Skt>; gonads; **testes, testicles,** balls *and* nuts *and* rocks *and* ballocks *and* family jewels <all nonformal>, cullions <old>; spermary; scrotum, bag *and* basket <both nonformal>, cod <old>; **female organs; vulva,** *yoni* <Skt>, cunt <nonformal>; **vagina;** clitoris; labia, labia majora, labia minora, lips, nymphae

**genius** NOUNS **talented person, talent,** man *or* woman of parts, gifted person, prodigy, natural <nonformal>, mental genius, intellectual genius, intellectual prodigy, mental giant; rocket scientist *and* brain surgeon <both nonformal>; gifted child, **child prodigy,** wunderkind, whiz kid *and* boy wonder <both nonformal>

**genocide** NOUNS **carnage, massacre, bloodbath, decimation,** saturnalia of blood; **mass murder, mass destruction,** mass extermination, wholesale murder, pogrom, race extermination, **the Holocaust,** the final solution

**genre** NOUNS **kind, sort, ilk, type,** breed of cat <nonformal>, lot <nonformal>, **variety, species, genus,** *genre* <Fr>, phylum, denomination, designation, description, style, manner, **nature, character,** persuasion, the like *or* likes of <nonformal>

**genteel** ADJS **well-bred,** highbred, **well-brought-up; cultivated,** cultured, polished, refined, gentle; gentlemanly, gentlemanlike, ladylike

**gentile** NOUNS non-Christian; **non-Jew,** goy, goyim, non-Jewish man *or shegets* <Yiddish>, non-Jewish woman *or shiksa* <Yiddish>; non-Muslim, non-Muhammadan, *giaour* <Turk>, kaffir; non-Mormon; infidel; unbeliever

**gentle** ADJS **light, soft, delicate,** dainty, tender, **easy; lenient, mild,** mild-mannered, tender, humane, compassionate, **clement,** merciful

**gentleman** NOUNS good person, fine person, good *or* fine man, worthy, prince, nature's nobleman, man after one's own heart; **good fellow,** capital fellow, **good sort,** right sort, a decent sort of fellow; real person, real man, mensch <nonformal>; perfect gentleman, a gentleman and a scholar

**gentry** NOUNS gentlefolk, gentlefolks, gentlepeople, better sort; lesser nobility, *petite noblesse* <Fr>; *samurai* <Japanese>; landed gentry, squirearchy

**genuine** ADJS **authentic,** veridic, veridical, **real, natural, realistic, naturalistic,** true to reality, **true to nature, lifelike,** true to life, verisimilar, veristic; **bona fide,** card-carrying <nonformal>, **good,** sure-enough <nonformal>, **sin-**

**cere, honest;** unflattering, unvarnished, uncolored, unqualified; **unadulterated**

**geriatric** ADJS **aged, elderly, old,** grown old in years, along *or* up *or* advanced *or* on in years, years old, advanced, advanced in life, **at an advanced age, ancient,** gerontic; **venerable,** old as Methuselah *or* as God *or* as the hills

**germ** NOUNS pathogen, contagium, bug <nonformal>, disease-causing agent, disease-producing microorganism; **microbe,** microorganism; **virus,** filterable virus, nonfilterable virus, adenovirus, echovirus, reovirus, rhinovirus, enterovirus, picornavirus, retrovirus; rickettsia; bacterium, **bacteria,** coccus, streptococcus, staphylococcus, bacillus, spirillum, vibrio, spirochete, gram-positive bacteria, gram-negative bacteria, aerobe, aerobic bacteria, anaerobe, anaerobic bacteria

**germane** ADJS **relevant, pertinent,** appertaining, **apposite,** cogent, material, admissible, applicable, applying, pertaining, belonging, involving, appropriate, **apropos,** *à propos* <Fr>, to the purpose, **to the point,** in point, *ad rem* <L>

**germicide** NOUNS **antiseptic, disinfectant,** fumigant, fumigator, antibiotic, bactericide, microbicide

**germinate** VERBS **grow, develop,** wax, **increase**; burgeon, **sprout**, blossom, reproduce, procreate, grow out of, pullulate

**gesture** NOUNS 1 **gesticulation; motion,** movement; carriage, bearing, posture, poise, pose, stance, way of holding oneself; beck, beckon; shrug; charade, dumb show, **pantomime;** broad hint, signal, nod, wink, look, nudge, kick, prompt
VERBS 2 **gesticulate; motion,** motion to; beckon, wiggle the finger at; wave the arms, wig-wag, saw the air; shrug, shrug the shoulders; pantomime, mime, ape, take off

**get** VERBS **fetch, bring, go get,** go and get, go to get, **go after,** go fetch, **go for,** call for, pick up; obtain, procure, secure; **bring back, retrieve;** chase after, run after, shag, fetch and carry; **learn,** get hold of <nonformal>, get into one's head, get through one's thick skull <nonformal>; gain, acquire

**getaway** NOUNS **escape;** break *and* breakout <both nonformal>; **deliverance; release,** setting-free, freeing, **liberation, extrication, rescue;** jailbreak, prisonbreak, break, breakout; **flight**

**get-together** NOUNS **social gathering, social,** sociable, social affair, social hour, hospitality hour, affair, gathering

**get up** VERBS **get out of bed, arise,** rise, **rise and shine** <nonformal>, greet the day, **turn out** <nonformal>; roll out *and* pile out *and* **show a leg** *and* hit the deck <all nonformal>

**get-up-and-go** NOUNS **enterprise,** dynamism, **initiative,** aggression, **aggressiveness,** killer instinct, force, forcefulness, pushfulness, pushingness, **pushiness, push, drive, hustle, go,** getup, get-up-and-get <nonformal>, go-ahead, go-getting, go-to-itiveness <nonformal>, **up-and-comingness;** spirit, gumption *and* spunk <both nonformal>

**geyser** NOUNS **jet, spout, spurt,** spurtle, squirt, spit, spew, spray, spritz <nonformal>; rush, **gush,** flush; hot *or* warm *or* thermal spring, thermae; Old Faithful

**ghastly** ADJS **deathly, deathlike,** deadly; ghostly, ghostlike; **grisly, gruesome, macabre;** pale, deathly pale, wan, lurid, blue, livid, haggard; **cadaverous,** corpselike

**ghetto** NOUNS **slum,** the inner city, the ghetto, the slums; urban ghetto

**ghost** NOUNS **specter,** spectral ghost, **spook** <nonformal>, **phantom,** phantasm, phantasma, **wraith, shade,** shadow, fetch, **apparition,** appearance, presence, shape, form, eidolon, idolum, revenant, larva; **spirit;** sprite, shrouded spirit, disembodied spirit, departed spirit, restless *or* wandering spirit *or* soul, soul of the dead, dybbuk

**ghostly** ADJS **spectral,** specterlike; ghostish, ghosty, ghostlike; **phantomlike,** phantom, phantomic *or* phantomical, phantasmal, phantasmic, **wraithlike,** wraithy, shadowy; etheric, ectoplasmic, astral, ethereal; incorporeal

**ghoulish** ADJS **hideous, ghastly,** grim, grisly, gruesome, macabre; morbidly curious, **morbid;** infernal, hellish, devilish, fiendish, satanic, demoniac, demonic, demonical, diabolic, diabolical, unholy, ungodly

**giant** NOUNS 1 amazon, colossus, titan, *nephilim* <Heb pl>
ADJS 2 gigantic, colossal, statuesque, king-size, very large

**gibberish** NOUNS **nonsense, stuff and nonsense,** pack of nonsense, **folderol,**

**balderdash,** *niaiserie* <Fr>, flummery, trumpery, **rubbish,** trash, *narrishkeit* <Yiddish>, vaporing, fudge; jargon, mumbo jumbo, **double-talk,** amphigory, gobbledegook <nonformal>; glossolalia, speaking in tongues

**giddy** ADJS **dizzy,** vertiginous, spinning, swimming, turned around, going around in circles; lightheaded, tiddly <nonformal>, **drunk, drunken**

**gift** NOUNS 1 **present,** presentation, *cadeau* <Fr>, **offering;** tribute, **award;** free gift, freebie *and* gimme <both nonformal>; oblation; handsel; Christmas present *or* gift, birthday present *or* gift
2 peace offering; **talent, flair,** strong flair, **endowment,** dowry, dower, natural gift *or* endowment, **genius,** instinct, **faculty**

**gifted** ADJS **talented, endowed,** clever, apt, with a flair; born for, made for, cut out for <nonformal>, with an eye for, with an ear for, with a bump for <nonformal>; **smart, brainy** <nonformal>, **bright, brilliant**

**gig** NOUNS **engagement, job,** employment, gainful employment, situation, **office, post, place,** station, berth, billet, **appointment**

**gigantic** ADJS **huge,** mountainous, titanic, colossal, mammoth, Gargantuan, gigantesque, monster, monstrous, outsize, sizable, larger-than-life, overgrown, king-size, monumental; giant, giantlike, gigantean

**giggle** NOUNS 1 **laughter, titter; chuckle, chortle;** cackle, crow; **snicker,** snigger, snort; fit of laughter
VERBS 2 **laugh, titter; chuckle, chortle;** cackle, crow; **snicker,** snigger, snort

**gigolo** NOUNS fancy man; **inamorato;** lovemaker, lover-boy <nonformal>; lady-killer, ladies' man, sheik, cocksman <nonformal>; Lothario, Casanova, Don Juan

**gild** VERBS begild, engild; aurify; gild the lily, trick out, varnish; paint in glowing colors, tell in glowing terms; brighten, sweeten

**gimmick** NOUNS 1 **stratagem,** artifice, craft, wile, strategy, device, wily device, contrivance, expedient, design, **scheme, trick,** cute trick, **ruse, red herring,** tactic, **maneuver, stroke,** gambit, **ploy, dodge,** artful dodge; **device,** mechanical device, contrivance, contraption <nonformal>, gadget, gizmo, gimcrack, means, mechanical means

**gingerbread** NOUNS **ornamentation, embellishment**; frippery, froufrou, overadornment, bedizenment

**gingerly** ADVS **cautiously,** prudently, circumspectly, discreetly, judiciously; guardedly, easy <nonformal>, with caution, with care

**gird** VERBS **strengthen, invigorate,** beef up <nonformal>, brace, buttress, prop, shore up, support, undergird, brace up; gird up one's loins; steel, harden, case harden, anneal, stiffen, **toughen,** temper, nerve
2 **encircle,** begird, engird; **bind,** girt, belt, girth, girdle, band, cinch; **tie up,** bind up, do up

**girl** NOUNS 1 **maid,** maiden, **lass, lassie,** young thing, young creature, young lady, damsel in distress, **damsel,** damoiselle, demoiselle, *jeune fille* <Fr>, *mademoiselle* <Fr>, *muchacha* <Sp>, miss, missy, little missy, slip, colleen <Irish>; girlie <nonformal>; girlfriend

2 <nonformal> **gal,** dame, **chick,** tomato, **babe** *or* baby, **broad,** frail, **doll,** skirt, jill, chit, cutie, filly, heifer; teenybopper *and* weenybopper

**girlfriend** NOUNS

<nonformal> **doll, angel,** baby, babydoll, doll-baby, buttercup, ducks, ducky, pet, snookums, snooky, **girl,** best girl, dream girl; old lady

**girlish** ADJS **girl-like,** maiden, maidenly; little-girlish, kittenish; **slim,** gracile, thinnish, slenderish, slimmish; **immature,** half-grown, adolescent, juvenile, puerile

**girth** NOUNS **extent,** extension, expansion, expanse, **scope,** reach, range, spread, coverage, area, cirumference, ambit, boundary, periphery

**gist** NOUNS **substance,** pith, spirit, essence, gravamen, main point; last word, name of the game *and* meat and potatoes *and* bottom line <all nonformal>; **drift,** tenor; sum, sum and substance; **heart, soul, meat, nub**

**give** NOUNS 1 **elasticity, resilience** *or* resiliency; snap, **bounce,** bounciness; **stretch, stretchiness,** stretchability; extensibility; **spring, springiness;** rebound; **flexibility**; **adaptability,** responsiveness; **buoyancy** *or* buoyance

VERBS 2 yield; bounce, spring, spring back
3 **present, donate,** slip <nonformal>, let have; **bestow, confer, award, allot, render,** bestow on; impart, let one know, communicate; **grant,** accord, **allow,** vouchsafe, yield, afford, make available; **tender,** proffer, offer, extend, come up with <nonformal>; **give out, deal out, dole out, mete out, hand** *or* dish out <nonformal>, fork *or* shell out <nonformal>; **give generously,** give the shirt off one's back

**give birth** VERBS **bear,** bear *or* have young, **have; have a baby,** bear a child; drop, cast, throw, pup, whelp, kitten, foal, calve, fawn, lamb, yean, farrow, litter; lie in, be confined, labor, travail

**give in** VERBS **yield, cede, give way, give ground, back down, give up,** cave in <nonformal>, withdraw from *or* quit the field, break off combat, cease resistance, have no fight left

**give off** VERBS **exude,** exudate, transude, transpire, reek; **emit, discharge,** send out, give out, throw off, blow off, evacuate, let go

**give up** VERBS **relinquish, surrender, yield,** yield up, waive, **forgo, resign, renounce,** throw up, abdicate, **abjure, forswear, give up on, have done with,** give up as a bad job, cede, hand over, lay down, wash one's hands of, **write off,** drop, drop all idea of, drop like a hot potato; **cease, desist from,** leave off, give over; hold *or* stay one's hand, cry quits, acknowledge defeat, **throw in the towel** *or* **sponge**

**glacial** ADJS **icy,** icelike, **ice-cold,** ice-encrusted; **frigid,** bitter *or* bitterly cold, gelid, algid; **frozen,** frozen solid, congealed

**glad** ADJS **happy, joyful, joyous,** flushed with joy, radiant, beaming, glowing, starry-eyed, sparkling, laughing, smiling, smirking, smirky, chirping, purring, singing, dancing, leaping, capering, **cheerful, blissful,** happy as a lark, happy as a king, happy as the day is long, happy as a pig in shit <nonformal>

**glade** NOUNS **open space,** clear space; **clearing,** clearance; everglade

**glamorous** ADJS **alluring, fascinating,** captivating, riveting, charming, exotic, **enchanting,** spellbinding, **entrancing,** ravishing, **enravishing, intriguing, enthralling,** witching, **bewitching; attractive, interesting, appealing,** sexy <nonformal>, engaging, taking, eye-catching, catching, fetching, winning, winsome, prepossessing; **provocative,** *provoquant* <Fr>; irresistible, Circean

**glamour** NOUNS **allurement, allure, enticement, inveiglement,** invitation, come-hither <nonformal>, blandishment, cajolery; inducement; **temptation,** tantalization; **attraction,** interest, charm, appeal, magnetism; star quality

**glance** NOUNS 1 **glimpse,** flash, quick sight; **peek, peep;** wink, blink, flicker *or* twinkle of an eye; casual glance, **half an eye;** *coup d'œil* <Fr>; quick *or* cursory inspection, quick look, first look, once-over-lightly <nonformal>
VERBS 2 **glimpse,** glint, cast a glance, glance at *or* upon, give a *coup d'œil* <Fr>, take a glance at, take a squint at <nonformal>; sweep, **graze,** brush by, scrape, skim

**glandular** ADJS glandulous; **endocrine,** humoral, exocrine, eccrine, apocrine, holocrine, merocrine; **hormonal** *or* hormonic; adrenal, pancreatic, gonadal; ovarian; luteal; prostatic; splenetic; thymic; thyroidal

**glare** NOUNS **gaze,** sharp *or* piercing *or* penetrating look; **glower,** glaring *or* glowering look; withering look, hostile look, chilly look, the fisheye <nonformal>
VERBS 2 **glower,** look daggers, look black; give a dirty look <nonformal>, give one the evil eye, give one a whammy <nonformal>; give one the fish eye <nonformal>
3 **be bright,** shine brightly, beacon; daze, blind, dazzle, bedazzle

**glaring** ADJS 1 **conspicuous,** staring, **prominent,** pronounced, well-pronounced, in bold *or* strong *or* high relief, **flagrant,** arrant, shocking, shattering, egregious, intolerable, unbearable, unconscionable, **rank,** crass, high-profile
2 flashy, blinding, overbright

**glass** NOUNS 1 **mirror, looking glass,** reflector, speculum; cheval glass, pier glass; pane, windowpane, light, windowlight, shopwindow; vitrine
ADJS 2 **glassy,** glasslike, clear as glass, vitric, vitreous, vitriform, hyaline, hyalescent; hyalinocrystalline

**glasses** NOUNS **spectacles, eyeglasses,** cheaters <nonformal>; reading glasses, readers; bifocals, divided spectacles, trifocals, pince-nez, nippers <nonformal>; lorgnette, *lorgnon* <Fr>

**glaze** NOUNS 1 **polish, gloss,** burnish, **shine, luster,** finish; **patina**
VERBS 2 **sugarcoat,** candy; **polish, shine, burnish, furbish,** sleek, slick, slick down, gloss, luster

**glazed** ADJS 1 **polished,** burnished, furbished; buffed, rubbed, finished; varnished, lacquered, shellacked, *glacé* <Fr>; **glassy,** smooth as glass
2 **expressionless; vacant,** empty, blank; glassy, glazed-over, fishy, wooden; deadpan, poker-faced <nonformal>

**gleam** NOUNS 1 **shine,** shininess, **luster, sheen, gloss,** glint; **glow,** flush, sunset glow; lambency; **incandescence,** candescence
VERBS 2 **shine,** shine forth, **burn, give light,** incandesce; **glow, beam,** glint, luster

**glean** VERBS **collect, gather, pick, pluck,** cull, **take up,** pick up, get *or* gather in, gather to oneself, bring *or* get together, scrape together; **harvest, reap,** crop, gather in

**glee** NOUNS **merriment,** merriness; **joy,** joyfulness, joyousness; gleefulness, high glee; **jollity,** jolliness, **joviality,** jocularity, jocundity

**glen** NOUNS **valley,** vale, dale, dell, dingle; bottom, bottoms, bottom glade, intervale, wadi, grove

**glib** ADJS **eloquent, silver-tongued,** silver; **smooth,** smooth-spoken, **slick; felicitous;** facile, slick as a whistle <nonformal>, spellbinding

**glide** VERBS **coast, skim,** sweep, flow; **sail, fly,** flit; **slide,** slip, skid, slither, glissade; sailplane, sail, volplane

**glimmer** NOUNS 1 **hint,** gentle hint, intimation, indication, suggestion, **mere** *or* **faint suggestion,** suspicion, inkling, whisper, **glimmering; cue, clue,** index, **symptom, sign,** spoor, track, scent, sniff, whiff, telltale, tip-off <nonformal>
2 **glitter,** shimmer, twinkle, blink; **sparkle,** spark; **scintillation,** scintilla; coruscation; **glisten,** glister, spangle, tinsel, glittering, glimmering, shimmering, twinkling
VERBS 3 **glitter,** shimmer, twinkle, blink, spangle, tinsel, coruscate; **sparkle,** spark, **scintillate; glisten,** glister

**glimpse** NOUNS **glance,** glance *or* flick of the eye, rapid glance, cast, side-glance; flash, quick sight; **peek, peep;** wink, blink, flicker *or* twinkle of an eye; casual glance, **half an eye**

**glint** NOUNS 1 **flash,** blaze, flare, flame, gleam, glance; blaze *or* flash *or* gleam of light
VERBS 2 **shine,** shine forth, burn, give light, incandesce; **glow,** beam, gleam, luster, flash, flare, blaze, flame, fulgurate; **radiate,** shoot, shoot out rays, send out rays

**glisten** VERBS **glitter,** glimmer, shimmer, twinkle, blink, spangle, tinsel, coruscate; **sparkle,** spark, **scintillate;** glister

**glitch** NOUNS **malfunction, misfire,** flash in the pan; **dud** <nonformal>; **fault,** *faute* <Fr>, defect, deficiency, inadequacy, imperfection, kink, **flaw,** bug <nonformal>; fly in the ointment, problem, little problem, snag, drawback

**glitter** NOUNS 1 **showiness, flashiness,** flamboyance, panache, dash, jazziness <nonformal>, jauntiness, sportiness <nonformal>, gaiety, glare, dazzle, dazzlingness; **gaudiness,** gaudery, glitz *and* gimmickry *and* razzmatazz *and* razzledazzle <all nonformal>, **tawdriness,** meretriciousness
VERBS 2 **cut a dash,** make a show, put on a show, make one's mark, cut a swath, **cut** *or* **make a figure;** make a splash *or* a splurge <nonformal>; shine, glare, dazzle, gleam, glow

**glitz** NOUNS tinsel <nonformal>, gaudiness, speciousness, meretriciousness, **superficiality; garishness**

**gloat** VERBS **exult,** triumph, glory, delight, joy, jubilate; **crow** *or* crow over, crow like a rooster *or* cock; gloat over

**glob** NOUNS **lump,** clump, **hunk** *and* **chunk** <both nonformal>; **mass,** piece, **gob** <nonformal>, gobbet; batch, **wad,** block, loaf

**global** ADJS **comprehensive,** sweeping, complete; whole; **all-comprehensive,** all-inclusive; without omission *or* exception, **overall,** universal, wall-to-wall <nonformal>, around-the-world, **total,** blanket, omnibus, across-the-board; **universal,** cosmic *or* cosmical, heaven-wide, galactic, planetary, world-wide, transnational, planet-wide; **total,** allover, holistic

**globe** NOUNS **sphere; ball,** orb, orbit, rondure; oblate spheroid, prolate spheroid; globule, globelet, orblet; glomerulus; terrestrial globe, the blue planet

**gloom** NOUNS **gloominess,** darkness, murk, murkiness, dismalness, bleakness, grimness, somberness, gravity, solemnity; **dreariness,** drearisomeness; wearifulness, wearisomeness

**gloomy** ADJS **dismal,** murky, bleak, grim, somber, sombrous, **solemn, grave;** sad, *triste* <Fr>, **funereal,** funebrial, crepe-hanging <nonformal>, saturnine; **dark,** black, gray; **dreary,** drear, drearisome; weary, weariful, wearisome; **pessimistic,** pessimist, downbeat <nonformal>, **cynical,** nihilistic; uncheerful; dismal, lugubrious; negative, negativistic; defeatist

**glorified** ADJS ennobled, magnified, aggrandized; enthroned, throned; immortalized, shrined, enshrined; beatified, canonized, sainted, sanctified; **idolized, godlike, deified,** apotheosized

**glorify** VERBS glamorize; **exalt,** elevate, ensky, raise, uplift, set up, **ennoble,** aggrandize, magnify, exalt to the skies; crown; throne, enthrone; immortalize, enshrine, hand one's name down to posterity, make legendary; praise, laud, extol, magnify, bless, celebrate; beatify, canonize, saint, sanctify; **deify,** apotheosize, apotheose; **lionize**

**glorious** ADJS **grandiose,** grand, magnificent, splendid, splendiferous, superb, fine, superfine, fancy, superfancy, swell <nonformal>; **imposing, impressive,** larger-than-life, awful, awe-inspiring, awesome; **illustrious,** lustrous, brilliant, radiant, splendorous, splendrous, splendent, resplendent, bright, shining

**glory** NOUNS 1 **eminence, preeminence, majesty, loftiness, prominence,** distinction, outstandingness, consequence, notability; **magnanimity,** nobility, sublimity; **fame,** renown, **kudos,** report, celebrity; **grandeur,** grandness, grandiosity, **magnificence,** gorgeousness, splendidness, splendiferousness, resplendence, brilliance; **honor,** great honor, distinction, credit, ornament; **illustriousness, luster,** brilliance *or* brilliancy, radiance, splendor, resplendence *or* resplendency, refulgence *or* refulgency, blaze of glory
VERBS 2 **rejoice,** jubilate, **exult, joy, delight,** bless *or* thank one's stars *or* lucky stars, congratulate oneself, hug oneself

**gloss** NOUNS 1 **polish, glaze,** burnish, **shine, luster,** finish; **patina;** window dressing, front, **false front, façade, pretext,** guise, semblance; mask, cloak, veil; **cosmetics,** mere cosmetics, coat of paint, whitewash <nonformal>; **cover,** cover-up, cover story, alibi; band-aid
2 amplification, restatement, rewording; **comment,** word of explanation; **annotation,** notation, **note,** note of explanation, footnote, scholium; exegesis; *apparatus criticus* <L>; commentary
VERBS 3 **comment upon,** commentate, remark upon; **annotate**

**glossary** NOUNS **dictionary,** word list, **lexicon,** thesaurus, Roget's, vocabulary, terminology, nomenclator; promptorium, gradus

**glow** NOUNS 1 **health, well-being;** bloom, flush, rosiness
2 **shine,** shininess, **luster,** sheen, gloss, glint; **gleam,** flush, sunset glow; lambency; **incandescence,** candescence; afterglow; air glow, night glow, day glow, twilight glow
VERBS 3 **enjoy good health,** have a clean bill of health, be in the pink; be in the best of health; **feel good,** feel fine, feel fit, feel like a million dollars *or* like a million <nonformal>, never feel better; feel one's oats, be full of pep; burst with health, bloom, flourish; **look good;** look like a million *and* look fit to kill *and* knock dead *and* knock one's eyes out <all nonformal>; shine, beam
4 **thrill,** tingle, **tingle with excitement;** swell, swell with emotion, be full of emotion; thrill to; turn on to *and* get high on *and* freak out on <all nonformal>; exude cheerfulness, radiate cheer, not have a care in the world, **beam,** burst *or* brim with cheer, radiate, sparkle
5 **flush, blush,** crimson, mantle, color, redden, turn *or* get red; incandesce, bloom

**glowing** ADJS 1 **rosy,** rosy-cheeked; blooming; flushed, flush; flushed with joy, radiant, beaming; **bright, sunny,** bright and sunny, **radiant,** riant, sparkling, beaming, glowing, smiling, laughing
2 **burning,** heated, hot, volcanic, red-hot, fiery, flaming, ablaze, afire, on fire;

**alight,** aglow, lambent, suffused with light

**glue** NOUNS 1 **adhesive,** cement, mucilage, epoxy resin, paste, stickum *and* gunk <both nonformal>; **plaster,** adhesive plaster, court plaster
VERBS 2 **stick together,** cement, bind, colligate, paste, agglutinate, conglutinate, gum

**glum** ADJS **morose, sullen,** sulky, mumpish, dumpish, long-faced, crestfallen, chapfallen; **moody,** moodish, **brooding,** broody; mopish, mopey <nonformal>, **moping**

**glut** NOUNS **satiety,** satiation, satisfaction, fullness, surfeit, repletion, engorgement; **saturation,** supersaturation; saturation point; more than enough, all one can stand *or* take; too much of a good thing, much of a muchness <nonformal>

**glutton** NOUNS greedy eater, big *or* hefty *or* husky eater <nonformal>, trencherman, trencherwoman, belly-god, gobbler, greedygut *or* greedyguts <nonformal>, gorger, **gourmand,** gourmandizer, gormand, gormandizer; **hog** *and* **pig** *and* chowhound *and* khazer <all nonformal>

**gnarl** VERBS **distort, contort,** turn awry; **twist,** turn, screw, wring, wrench, wrest; writhe; knot

**gnaw** VERBS **chew,** chew up, chaw <nonformal>, bite into; **masticate,** manducate; ruminate, chew the cud; **bite,** grind, champ, chomp <nonformal>; **munch;** gnash; nibble; **pain,** give *or* inflict pain, **hurt, wound, afflict, distress**

**gnome** NOUNS **fairy,** sprite, fay, fairy man *or* woman; **elf,** brownie, pixie, gremlin, ouphe, hob, cluricaune, puca *or* pooka *or* pwca, kobold, nisse, peri; **imp, goblin**; dwarf; **sylph,** sylphid; **banshee; leprechaun**

**go** VERBS 1 **disappear, vanish,** vanish from sight, do a vanishing act <nonformal>, depart, fly, **flee**, be gone, **go away,** pass, pass out *or* away, pass out of sight, exit, pull up stakes <nonformal>, leave the scene *or* stage, clear out, pass out of the picture, pass *or* retire from sight, become lost to sight, be seen no more
2 **progress, advance, proceed,** go *or* move forward, step forward, go on, **go ahead,** go along, push ahead, pass on *or* along; move, travel

**goad** NOUNS 1 **spur, prod,** prick <old>, sting, **gadfly;** oxgoad; rowel; whip, lash, whiplash, gad <nonformal>
VERBS 2 **prod,** poke, nudge, prod at, goose <nonformal>, **spur,** prick, sting, needle; whip, lash; pick at *or* on, nibble at, nibble away at

**goal** NOUNS **objective,** object, aim, end, destination, mark, object in mind, **end in view,** telos, final cause, ultimate aim; end in itself; **score,** hit, bull's-eye; touchdown

**go away** VERBS 1 **disappear, vanish,** vanish from sight, do a vanishing act <nonformal>, depart, fly, **flee**, go, be gone, pass, pass out *or* away, pass out of sight, exit, pull up stakes <nonformal>, leave the scene *or* stage, clear out, pass out of the picture, pass *or* retire from sight, become lost to sight, be seen no more; **perish, die,** die off; die out *or* away, dwindle, wane, fade, **fade out** *or* **away,** do a fade-out <nonformal>; sink, sink away, dissolve, melt, melt away, dematerialize, evaporate, evanesce, **vanish into thin air,** go up in smoke; disperse, dispel, dissipate; cease, cease to exist, **cease to be;** leave no trace, waste, waste away, erode, be consumed, wear away; undergo *or* suffer an eclipse; **hide**
2 **depart,** make off, begone, be off, take oneself off *or* away, take one's departure, take leave *or* take one's leave, **leave, go, go off, get off** *or* **away,** get under way, come away, go one's way, go *or* get along, be getting along, go on, get on; **pull out;** decamp; exit; take *or* break *or* tear oneself away, take oneself off, take wing *or* flight

**go-between** NOUNS **middleman, intermediary, medium,** intermedium, intermediate, broker; connection <nonformal>, **contact; negotiator,** negotiant; interpleader; arbitrator, mediator

**goblin** NOUNS **elf,** brownie, pixie, gremlin, cluricaune, puca *or* pooka *or* pwca, kobold, nisse, peri; **hobgoblin,** hob, ouphe

**gobs** NOUNS **lots,** deal, no end of, **good** *or* **great deal, considerable,** sight, **heap, pile, stack,** loads, **raft, slew,** whole slew, spate, wad, **batch,** mess, mint, peck, pack, pot, **tidy sum,** quite a little; **oodles, scads**

**go crazy** VERBS

<nonformal> go bats, go cuckoo, go

bughouse, go nuts, go nutso, go out of one's gourd *or* skull *or* tree, go off one's nut *or* rocker, go off the track *or* trolley, go off the deep end, blow one's top *or* stack, pop one's cork, flip one's lid *or* wig, wig out, go ape *or* apeshit, schiz out, go bananas, go crackers *and* go bonkers <both Brit>, go bonzo, blow one's mind, freak out, flip out, go hog wild, go round the bend <Brit>, have a screw loose, have bats in one's belfry, have rocks in one's head, lose one's marbles

**god** NOUNS **hero, demigod,** phoenix; **heroine, goddess,** demigoddess; **idol** 2 *deus* <L>; **deity, divinity,** immortal, heathen god, pagan deity *or* divinity; **goddess,** *dea* <L>; deva, devi, the shining ones

**God** NOUNS Jehovah; *Yahweh, Adonai, Elohim* <all Heb>; **Allah;** the Great Spirit, Manitou

**God-fearing** ADJS faithful <old>, pious, pietistic, observant, **devout**

**God forbid!** INTER Heaven forbid!, Heaven forfend!, forbid it Heaven!; by no means!, not for the world!, not on your life!, over my dead body!, not if I know it!, nothing doing!, no way! *and* no way José! <both nonformal>, perish the thought!, I'll be hanged *or* damned if!, **shame!,** for shame!, tuttut!

**godforsaken** ADJS **out-of-the-way,** back of beyond, upcountry; out of reach, **inaccessible; abandoned,** deserted, desolate, forlorn, lorn; helpless, defenseless

**godless** ADJS **ungodly,** irreligious, unrighteous, unholy, unsaintly, unangelic, unangelical; impious; **unregenerate,** unredeemed, **unconverted,** reprobate, graceless, shriftless, **lost, damned;** lapsed, fallen, recidivist, recidivistic

**godlike** ADJS **divine, godly; magnificent,** magnanimous, heroic, superb; immortalized, shrined, enshrined; beatified, canonized, sainted, sanctified; **idolized, deified,** apotheosized

**godsend** NOUNS **boon, blessing;** manna, manna from heaven, loaves and fishes, gift from on high; windfall

**go Dutch** VERBS pay one's way; pay one's share, chip in <nonformal>, share and share alike, go halfers <nonformal>

**gofer** NOUNS **underling,** understrapper, low man on the totem pole <nonformal>, flunky, errand boy *or* girl, office boy *or* girl

**go for it** VERBS

<nonformal> **knock oneself out, break one's neck,** break *or* bust one's balls, bust a gut, bust one's ass *or* hump, rupture oneself, do it or know why not, do it or break a leg, do it or bust a gut, do *or* try one's damndest *or* darndest, go all out, go the limit, go for broke, shoot the works, give it all one's got, give it one's best shot

**go-getter** NOUNS **man** *or* **woman of action, doer,** man of deeds; **hustler** *and* self-starter <both nonformal>; ball of fire *and* live wire *and* powerhouse *and* human dynamo *and* spitfire <all nonformal>; beaver, busy bee, **eager beaver** <nonformal>; operator *and* big-time operator *and* wheeler-dealer <all nonformal>; take-charge guy <nonformal>

**goggles** NOUNS **spectacles,** specs <nonformal>, glasses, eyeglasses, pair of glasses *or* spectacles, cheaters *and* peepers <both nonformal>; blinkers; eyeshield

**gold** NOUNS **wealth, money,** lucre, pelf, mammon; **substance,** property, possessions, material wealth; yellow stuff <nonformal>; nugget, gold nugget

**goldbrick** NOUNS 1 **shirker,** shirk, **slacker,** goldbricker, goof-off <nonformal>; clock watcher; **malingerer** VERBS 2 **shirk, slack,** not pull fair, not pull one's weight; **lie down on the job** <nonformal>; duck duty, dog it <nonformal>; **malinger**

**golden** ADJS **precious, dear, valuable,** worthy, rich, worth a pretty penny <nonformal>, worth a king's ransom, worth its weight in gold, good as gold, precious as the apple of one's eye; **gold,** gilt, aureate; benign, benignant, bright, happy

**golden rule** NOUNS rule of action *or* conduct, moral precept; commandment, *mitzvah* <Heb>; **principle,** principium, settled principle, general principle *or* truth, tenet, convention; **guideline,** ground rule, rubric, protocol, working rule, working principle, standard procedure; guiding principle

**gold mine** NOUNS **source of supply,** mine, rich lode, mother lode, **bonanza,** luau <nonformal>; quarry, lode, vein; Eldorado, Golconda

**gone** ADJS 1 away, gone away, past and gone, extinct, missing, no more, lost, lost to sight *or* view, long-lost, **out of sight; absent,** not present, nonattendant, departed, disappeared, vanished, absconded, out of sight
2 **missing,** among the missing, wanting, **lacking,** not found, nowhere to be found, omitted, taken away, no longer present *or* with us *or* among us

**goner** NOUNS **lost cause, fool's errand, wild-goose chase; hopeless case;** gone goose *or* gosling *and* dead duck <all nonformal>; terminal case

**goo** NOUNS 1 **sentimentality,** mawkishness, cloyingness, maudlinness, mushiness *or* sloppiness <both nonformal>; **mush** *and* slush *and* slop *and* schmaltz <all nonformal>
2 **semiliquid,** goop *and* gook *and* gunk *and* glop <all nonformal>, sticky mess, gaum <nonformal>

**good** NOUNS 1 **welfare,** well-being, **benefit; interest,** advantage; **behalf,** behoof; blessing, benison, boon; **profit,** avail <old>, gain; world of good
ADJS 2 **healthful, healthy, salubrious, salutary, wholesome,** health-preserving, health-enhancing, life-promoting, **beneficial,** benign
3 **excellent,** *bueno* <Sp>, *bon* <Fr>, bonny <Brit>, fine, nice, goodly, fair; **splendid, capital, grand,** elegant <nonformal>, braw <Scots>, famous <nonformal>; very good, *très bon* <Fr>; commendable, laudable, **estimable**

**good-bye** NOUNS 1 **leave-taking,** leave, parting, departure, congé; **send-off,** Godspeed; **adieu,** one's adieus, **farewell,** aloha; valedictory address, valedictory, valediction, parting words; swan song; viaticum; stirrup cup, one for the road, *doch-an-dorrach* or *doch-an-dorris* <Gaelic>
INTER 2 **farewell!, adieu!, so long!, I'm outa here** <both nonformal>, cheerio! <Brit>, *au revoir!* <Fr>, *¡adios!* <Sp>, *¡hasta la vista!* <Sp>, *¡hasta luego!* <Sp>, *¡vaya con Dios!* <Sp>, *auf Wiedersehen!* <Ger>, *addio!* <Ital>, *arrivederci!, arrivederla!* <both Ital>, *ciao!* <Ital nonformal>, *do svidanye!* <Russ>, *shalom!* <Heb>, *sayonara!* <Japanese>, *vale!, vive valeque!* <both L>, aloha!

**good-for-nothing** NOUNS 1 good-for-naught, **ne'er-do-well,** wastrel; drifter, vagrant, hobo, tramp; no-good <nonformal>, *vaurien* <Fr>, worthless fellow
ADJS 2 **worthless, valueless,** good-for-naught, no-good *or* NG <nonformal>, no-account <nonformal>, dear at any price, worthless as tits on a boar <nonformal>, not worth a dime *or* a red cent *or* a hill of beans *or* shit *or* bubkes <nonformal>, not worthwhile, not worth having, not worth mentioning *or* speaking of, not worth the powder to blow it to hell, of no earthly use, fit for the junk yard <nonformal>

**good-looking** ADJS **comely,** fair, **nice-looking,** well-favored, **personable,** presentable, agreeable, becoming, pleasing, goodly, bonny, likely <nonformal>, **sightly,** braw <Scots>; pleasing to the eye, lovely to behold

**good luck** NOUNS **good fortune,** happy fortune, **fortune, luck,** the breaks <nonformal>; **fortunateness, luckiness,** felicity <old>; blessing, smiles of fortune, fortune's favor

**good-natured** ADJS **good-humored, good-tempered,** bonhomous, **sweet,** sweet-tempered; **amiable, affable,** genial, cordial; **gentle,** mild, mild-mannered; easy, easy-natured, easy to get along with, able to take a joke, **agreeable**

**goodness** NOUNS **excellence, quality,** class <nonformal>; **virtue,** grace; **merit,** desert; **value, worth; fineness,** goodliness, fairness, niceness; **superiority,** first-rateness, **skillfulness**; wholeness, **soundness,** healthiness; **virtuousness**; **kindness,** benevolence

**good person** NOUNS

<nonformal> **good guy,** crackerjack, brick, trump, good egg, stout fellow, nice guy, Mr Nice Guy, good Joe, likely lad, no slouch, doll, living doll, pussycat, **sweetheart, sweetie**

**goods** NOUNS 1 **property, properties, possessions, holdings,** havings, chattels, goods and chattels, **effects,** estate and effects, what one can call one's own, what one has to one's name, all one owns *or* has, all one can lay claim to, one's all; household possessions *or* effects, lares and penates
2 **merchandise,** commodities, wares, effects, vendibles; **consumer goods,** consumer items, retail goods, goods for sale

**good Samaritan** NOUNS **benefactor,** benefactress, **benefiter,** succorer, befriender; ministrant, ministering angel; Samaritan, **helper,** aider, assister, help, aid, helping hand, Johnny-on-the-spot <nonformal>

*a very present help in time of trouble*
BIBLE

**goodwill** NOUNS **benevolence,** grace, brotherly love, charity, Christian charity *or* love, *caritas* <L>, love of mankind, good will to *or* toward man, love, *agape* <Gk>

**goody-goody** NOUNS 1 **prude, prig,** priss, puritan, bluenose; Victorian
ADJS 2 **overnice,** overprecise, precious, *précieuse* <Fr>, exquisite, **overrefined, elegant,** mincing, simpering, namby-pamby

**gooey** ADJS 1 **sentimental,** sentimentalized, soft, **mawkish, maudlin,** cloying; sticky *and* schmaltzy *and* sappy *and* soppy <all nonformal>, oversentimental, oversentimentalized, bathetic; **mushy** *or* sloppy *or* gushing *or* teary *or* beery <all nonformal>, tearjerking <nonformal>
2 **viscous, sticky, tacky,** tenacious, adhesive, clingy, clinging, tough; gunky *and* gloppy *and* goopy *and* gooky <all nonformal>; **gelatinous,** jellylike, jellied, jelled

**goof** NOUNS 1 **mistake,** error, blunder

2 <nonformal> **boo-boo,** muff, flub, foozle, bloomer, bloop, blooper, boot, bobble, boner, bonehead play *or* trick, dumb trick, boob stunt, fool mistake; howler, screamer; fuck-up, screw-up, foul-up, snafu, muck-up, louse-up

VERBS 3 **miss, miss the mark,** miss one's aim; slip, slip up <nonformal>; blunder, foozle <nonformal>, **err**; botch, bungle; waste one's effort, run around in circles, spin one's wheels

**goof off** VERBS **idle,** do nothing, **laze,** lazy <nonformal>, take one's ease *or* leisure, take one's time, **loaf, lounge; lie around,** lounge around, loll around, sit on one's ass *or* butt *or* duff <nonformal>, stand *or* hang around, **loiter about** *or* **around,** slouch, slouch around, **bum around** *and* mooch around <both nonformal>; **shirk,** avoid work, fuck off *and* **lie down on the job** <both nonformal>

**goof-off** NOUNS **idler, loafer, lounger,** loller, couch potato <nonformal>, lotus-eater, *flâneur, flâneuse* <both Fr>, **do-nothing,** do-little, *fainéant* <Fr>, fuck-off *and* goldbrick *and* goldbricker <all nonformal>, clock watcher

**goofy** ADJS

<nonformal> **kooky,** funny, kinky, loopy, goofus, haywire, screwy, screwball, nutty, wacky, flaky, oddball, wacky, wacko, out to lunch, nobody home, weird

**goose** NOUNS 1 gander, gosling
2 **silly,** silly Billy <nonformal>, **silly ass**
VERBS 3 poke, nudge, prod at, **spur,** prick, sting, needle

**goose bumps** NOUNS **creeps** *and* **cold creeps** *and* shivers *and* **cold shivers** <all nonformal>, creeping of the flesh; horripilation, gooseflesh, goose pimples; formication

**gore** NOUNS 1 **bloodshed,** bloodletting, blood, flow of blood
VERBS 2 **perforate, pierce,** drill, auger; **ream,** ream out, countersink, gouge, gouge out; trepan, trephine

**gorge** NOUNS 1 **ravine, canyon,** box canyon, *arroyo* <Sp>, barranca, bolson, coulee, gully, gulch, combe <Brit>, dingle, rift, rift valley, kloof, donga, graben, gully, draw, wadi, basin, cirque, corrie
VERBS 2 **stuff,** pig out <nonformal>, engorge, glut, guttle, cram, eat one's fill, stuff *or* gorge oneself, gluttonize
3 **satiate,** sate, satisfy, slake, allay; **surfeit,** glut, saturate, oversaturate, supersaturate

**gorgeous** ADJS 1 **ravishing; glorious,** heavenly, divine, sublime; **resplendent,** splendorous *or* splendrous, splendiferous, **splendid,** resplendently beautiful; **brilliant,** bright, radiant, shining, beaming, glowing, blooming, abloom, sparkling, **dazzling; glamorous**

2 <nonformal> **eye-filling, easy on the eyes,** not hard to look at, long on looks, looking fit to kill, dishy <chiefly Brit>; cutesy, cutesy-poo; **raving,** devastating, **stunning,** killing

**gorilla** NOUNS

<nonformal> **roughneck, tough,** bruiser, mug, mugger, bimbo, bozo, ugly

customer, **hoodlum, hood, hooligan,** ape, plug-ugly, strong-arm man, muscle man, **goon**

**gory** ADJS **bloodstained,** blood-spattered, **bloody,** sanguinary, ensanguined

**gospel** NOUNS **the truth,** the absolute truth, the intrinsic truth, the unalloyed truth, the cast-iron truth, the hard truth, the stern truth, gospel truth, Bible truth, revealed truth

**gossamer** ADJS **frail,** dainty, delicate, diaphanous, light, airy, wispy, lacy, gauzy, papery, insubstantial, ethereal, misty, vague, flimsy, wafer-thin, **fine; threadlike,** slender as a thread; **tenuous,** subtle, rare, **rarefied;** attenuated, attenuate

**gossip** NOUNS 1 gossiping, gossipmongering, back-fence gossip <nonformal>, newsmongering; **talebearing,** taletelling; **tattle,** tittle-tattle, chitchat, **talk,** idle talk, small talk, by-talk; piece of gossip, groundless rumor, tale, story
2 **newsmonger,** rumormonger, scandalmonger, gossipmonger, gossiper, *yenta* <Yiddish>, quidnunc, **busybody,** tabby <nonformal>; **talebearer,** taleteller, telltale, **tattletale** <nonformal>, tattler, tittle-tattler
VERBS 3 talk over the back fence <nonformal>; **tattle,** tittle-tattle; clatter; retail gossip, **dish the dirt** <nonformal>, tell idle tales

**Gothic** ADJS **unrefined,** unpolished, uncouth, unkempt, uncombed, unlicked; **uncultivated, uncultured; barbarous,** barbaric, barbarian; outlandish, **fanciful, notional,** whimsical, **fantastic, fantastical,** preposterous, outlandish, wild, baroque, rococo, Alice-in-Wonderland, bizarre, grotesque

**gouge** NOUNS 1 **furrow, groove,** scratch, crack, cranny, chase, chink, score, **cut,** gash, striation, streak, stria, slit
VERBS 2 **excavate, dig,** dig out, **scoop,** scoop out, gouge out, grub, shovel, spade, dike, delve, scrape, scratch, scrabble; dredge; **trench,** trough, furrow, groove; **tunnel, burrow**
3 **overcharge, hold up** *and* **soak** *and* **stick** *and* **sting** *and* **clip** <all nonformal>, **make pay through the nose,** victimize, swindle; exploit, skin <nonformal>, **fleece,** screw *and* put the screws to <both nonformal>, bleed, bleed white

**gourmand** NOUNS **glutton,** greedy eater, big *or* hefty *or* husky eater <nonformal>, trencherman, trencherwoman, belly-god, gobbler, greedygut *or* greedyguts <nonformal>, gorger, gormand, gormandizer, guttler, cormorant; **hog** *and* **pig** *and* chow hound *and* khazer <all nonformal>

**gourmet** NOUNS 1 gastronome, epicure, connoisseur of food *or* wine, bon vivant, high liver, Lucullus, Brillat-Savarin
ADJS 2 **savory,** savorous, **palatable, toothsome,** sapid, pleasing, to one's taste, **delicious,** delightful, delectable, exquisite; for the gods, ambrosial, nectarous, nectareous; fit for a king, gourmet, fit for a gourmet, of gourmet quality

**govern** VERBS **regulate; wield authority; command,** officer, captain, **head, lead,** be master, be at the head of, **preside over,** chair; **direct, manage, supervise, administer,** administrate; discipline; **rule, control**, order, **regulate,** direct, guide

**governess** NOUNS **chaperon,** duenna; escort

**government** NOUNS governance, **discipline, regulation; direction, management, administration,** dispensation, disposition, oversight, **supervision**; **regime,** regimen; **rule, sway, sovereignty, reign,** regnancy; empire, empery; social order, civil government, political government

**governor** NOUNS **ruler; captain, master, commander,** commandant, commanding officer, intendant, castellan, chatelain, chatelaine; **director, manager, executive**

**gown** NOUNS **garment,** vestment, vesture, robe, frock, rag <nonformal>, mantle, cloak

**grab** VERBS **seize,** take *or* get hold of, **lay hold of,** catch *or* grab hold of, glom *or* latch on to <nonformal>, **get** *or* **lay hands on,** clap hands on <nonformal>, put one's hands on, get into one's grasp *or* clutches; get one's fingers *or* hands on; **grasp, grip, grapple, snatch,** snatch up, nip, nail <nonformal>, **clutch,** claw, clinch, clench

**grab bag** NOUNS **hodgepodge,** hotchpotch, hotchpot; **medley, miscellany,** mélange, pastiche, *pasticcio* <Ital>, **conglomeration, assortment,** assemblage, mixed bag, ragbag, olio, *olla podrida* <Sp>, **scramble, jumble,** mingle-mangle, **mix,** mishmash, **mess,** can of worms <nonformal>, dog's breakfast <Can nonformal>, mare's nest, rat's nest, hash, patchwork, salad, gallimaufry, salmagundi, **potpourri,** stew, sauce, slurry, omnium-gatherum, **odds and ends,** oddments, all sorts, everything but the kitchen sink <nonformal>

**grace** NOUNS 1 **charm,** winsomeness, **attractiveness, appeal, elegance,** elegancy; gracefulness, gracility; **loveliness, pulchritude,** exquisiteness
2 **benevolence, goodwill,** brotherly love, charity, Christian charity *or* love, *caritas* <L>, love of mankind, good will to *or* toward man, love, *agape* <Gk>, state of grace
3 **pardon,** excuse, sparing, **amnesty,** indemnity, exemption, immunity, reprieve; **exoneration, exculpation**
4 **prayer, invocation,** silent prayer, meditation, contemplation, communion; thanks, thanksgiving

**graceful** ADJS **agile, nimble, spry,** sprightly, fleet, featly, light, nimble-footed, light-footed, sure-footed; **elegant,** gracile, gracious

**graceless** ADJS **inelegant, clumsy, clunky** *and* **klutzy** <both nonformal>, heavy-handed, heavy-footed, ham-handed, ungraceful, ungainly, infelicitous, unfelicitous; **tasteless,** in bad taste, indecorous, unseemly, uncourtly, undignified; **unpolished, unrefined**

**gracious** ADJS **courteous, polite, civil, urbane,** graceful, agreeable, affable, fair; complaisant; obliging, accommodating; **thoughtful, considerate,** tactful, solicitous; respectful, deferential, attentive; **cordial,** amiable, **friendly,** neighborly, genial, hearty, open, openhearted, warm, warmhearted

**grade** NOUNS 1 **incline,** inclination, **slope,** gradient, pitch, **ramp,** launching ramp, bank, talus, gentle *or* easy slope, glacis; rapid *or* steep slope
2 **rank,** rating, status, estate, stratum, level, station, position
VERBS 3 **level, flatten, even, equalize,** align, smooth *or* smoothen, level out, smooth out; roll, roll flat, steamroller *or* steamroll
4 **classify,** class, assign, designate; **categorize,** type, put down as, **pigeonhole,** place, **group, arrange**, range; **order**, put in order, rank, rate, **sort,** assort

**gradual** ADJS **slow, leisurely,** slack, moderate, gentle, **easy,** deliberate, go-slow, unhurried, relaxed, gradual, circumspect, tentative, cautious, reluctant, foot-dragging <nonformal>; **gradational,** calibrated, graduated, phased, staged, tapered, scalar

**graduate** NOUNS 1 grad <nonformal>; **alumnus,** alumni, alumna, alumnae; **graduate student,** grad student <nonformal>, **postgraduate,** postgrad <nonformal>; college graduate
VERBS 2 **promote, advance,** up *and* boost <both nonformal>, elevate, upgrade; pass

**graduation** NOUNS **convocation;** commencement, commencement exercises; graduation exercises; baccalaureate service

**graffito** NOUNS **inscription,** epigraph

**graft** NOUNS 1 grafting, engrafting, transplant, transplantation; infixing, implantation, embedment, tessellation, impactment, impaction; **insert,** insertion; **inset, inlay;** scion *or* cion
2 **bribery,** bribing, subornation, **corruption,** bribery and corruption; **spoils of office;** boodle <nonformal>; slush fund <nonformal>; public tit *and* public trough <both nonformal>; spoils system
VERBS 3 engraft, **implant,** bud; inarch

**grain** NOUNS 1 **particle,** fragment, spot, **speck,** flyspeck, fleck, point, dot, jot, tittle, **iota,** ounce, **dab** <nonformal>, mote, **mite** <nonformal>; granule, pebble
2 **texture,** surface texture; **surface; finish,** feel; granular texture, fineness *or* coarseness of grain
3 **cereal,** cereal plant, farinaceous plant; **kernel,** berry

**grammar** NOUNS rules of language, linguistic structure, syntactic structure; **traditional grammar, school grammar;** descriptive grammar, **structural grammar**

*the rule and pattern of speech*
HORACE

**grammar school** NOUNS **elementary school, grade school** *or* graded school, the grades; **primary school;** junior school <Brit>; folk school, *Volksschule* <Ger>

**grammatical** ADJS **syntactical,** formal, structural; correct, well-formed; tagmemic, glossematic

**granary** NOUNS **garner,** grain bin, elevator, grain elevator, **silo;** mow, haymow, hayloft, hayrick; crib, corncrib

**grand** ADJS 1 **great, considerable,** consequential; **mighty,** powerful, strong, irresistible, intense; main, maximum, **total, full,** plenary, comprehensive, exhaustive
2 **grandiose, magnificent, splendid,** splendiferous, **glorious,** superb, fine, superfine, fancy, superfancy, swell <nonformal>; **noble, proud, stately, majestic,** princely; **sumptuous, elegant, elaborate, luxurious,** extravagant, deluxe; palatial, Babylonian

**grandeur** NOUNS grandness, grandiosity, **magnificence,** gorgeousness, **splendor,** splendidness, splendiferousness, resplendence, brilliance, glory; nobility, proudness, **state, stateliness, majesty;** impressiveness, imposingness; **sumptuousness, elegance, elaborateness, lavishness, luxuriousness;** barbaric *or* Babylonian splendor

**grandfather** NOUNS 1 grandsire, grandpa, gramps; old man; great-grandfather

2 <nonformal> **grandpa,** grampa, gramper, gramp, gramps, grandpapa, grandpap, grandpappy, **granddad,** granddaddy, granddada, granfer, gramfer, granther, pop, grandpop

**grandiose** ADJS **imposing, impressive,** larger-than-life, awful, awe-inspiring, awesome; **sumptuous, elegant, elaborate, luxurious,** extravagant, deluxe; executive *and* plush *and* posh *and* ritzy *and* swank *and* swanky <all nonformal>

**grandmother** NOUNS 1 grandam; old woman, old lady, dowager, matriarch; great-grandmother

2 <nonformal> **grandma,** granma, old woman, grandmamma, grandmammy, **granny,** grammy, gammy, grannam, gammer

**grandstand** NOUNS 1 **stands,** boxes, lower deck, upper deck, outfield stands, bleachers
VERBS 2 **show off** <nonformal>, hotdog *and* showboat <both nonformal>, play to the gallery *or* galleries <nonformal>, please the crowd; strut one's stuff <nonformal>, go through one's paces, show what one has

**grange** NOUNS **farm,** farmplace, farmstead, farmhold <old>, farmery <Brit>, location <Austral>, pen <Jamaica>

**grant** NOUNS 1 **concession;** charter, franchise, liberty, diploma, patent, letters patent, brevet; royal grant
2 **subsidy,** subvention, subsidization, support, grant-in-aid, bounty; **allowance, stipend,** allotment; scholarship, fellowship; honorarium
VERBS 3 **give,** present, bestow, confer, award, allot, render, bestow on; accord, **allow,** vouchsafe, yield, afford, make available; **tender,** proffer, offer, extend, come up with <nonformal>; **issue, dispense,** administer; serve, help to; **distribute**, give out, deal out, dole out, mete out, hand *or* dish out <nonformal>, fork *or* shell out <nonformal>; make a present of, gift *or* gift with <nonformal>, give as a gift
4 allow, **concede,** admit, admit exceptions, see the special circumstances; **waive, set aside,** ease, lift temporarily, pull one's punches <nonformal>

**granulated** ADJS **granular, grainy,** granulate, **sandy, gritty,** sabulous, arenarious, arenaceous

**grapevine** NOUNS **report, rumor,** flying rumor, unverified *or* unconfirmed report, **hearsay,** *on-dit* <Fr>, **scuttlebutt** *and* latrine rumor <both nonformal>; grapevine telegraph, bush telegraph <Australia>; **pipeline;** a little bird *or* birdie

**graph** NOUNS 1 **diagram,** plot, chart, blueprint, bar graph, pie *or* circle graph *or* chart, area graph; flow diagram, flow chart
VERBS 2 **plot; map, chart**, **blueprint; diagram,** plot out, **lay out,** set out

**graphic** ADJS **descriptive, depictive,** expositive, representative, delineative; expressive, vivid, suggestive, imaginative, well-drawn; realistic, naturalistic, true to life, lifelike, faithful

**grapple** VERBS **contend, wrestle,** rassle <nonformal>, grapple with, go to the mat with; **seize, grab, grasp, grip,** gripe <old>, **snatch,** snatch up, nip, nail <nonformal>, **clutch,** claw, clinch, clench

**grasp** NOUNS 1 **hold,** purchase, grip, clutch, clamp, clinch, clench; **clasp,** hug, embrace, firm hold, tight grip
2 **understanding, comprehension, apprehension,** intellection, prehension; mental grasp, grip, **command,** mastery; intelligence, wisdom

VERBS 3 **seize,** take *or* get hold of, **lay hold of,** catch *or* grab hold of, glom *or* latch on to <nonformal>, **grab,** grip, gripe <old>, grapple, snatch, snatch up, nip, nail <nonformal>, **clutch,** claw, clinch, clench; **clasp,** hug, embrace
4 **understand,** comprehend, apprehend, have, **know, conceive, realize,** appreciate, have no problem with, ken <Scots>, savvy <nonformal>, sense, make sense out of, make something of; **fathom, follow; seize,** get hold of, grasp *or* seize the meaning, **catch on,** get the meaning of, get the hang of; **master, learn**

**grasping** ADJS **greedy,** avaricious, avid, voracious, rapacious, cupidinous, esurient, ravening, **grabby** <nonformal>, graspy, acquisitive, mercenary, sordid, overgreedy; miserly, money-hungry, money-grubbing, money-mad, venal

**grass** NOUNS

<nonformal terms for marijuana> Acapulco gold, aunt mary, bomb, boo, bush, doobie, gage, ganja, grefa, hay, hemp, herb, Indian hay, J, jane, kif, mary, maryjane, mary warner, meserole, mighty mezz, moota, muggles, pod, pot, smoke, snop, tea, Texas tea, weed, yerba

**grassland** NOUNS grass; parkland; **meadow,** meadow land, mead <old>, swale, lea, vega; **pasture,** pastureland, pasturage, pasture land, park <Brit nonformal>; **range,** grazing, grazing land; **prairie, savanna, steppe,** steppeland, **pampas,** pampa, campo, llano, **veld,** grass veld

**grate** VERBS 1 **rasp, scratch, scrape,** grind; crunch, craunch, scranch <old>, scrunch, crump
2 **irritate,** touch a soft spot *or* tender spot, touch a raw nerve, touch where it hurts; provoke, **gall,** chafe, fret, rasp; **get on one's nerves, grate on,** set on edge; set one's teeth on edge, go against the grain; **rub one** *or* **one's fur the wrong way**

**grateful** ADJS **thankful; appreciative,** appreciatory, sensible; **obliged, much obliged,** beholden, indebted to, crediting, under obligation, acknowledging, cognizant of; gratifying, pleasing

**gratify** VERBS **satisfy,** sate, satiate; slake, appease, allay, assuage, quench; regale, feed, feast; do one's heart good, warm the cockles of the heart; **make proud,** do one's heart good, do one proud <nonformal>, **elate,** flush, turn one's head; favor, please, **cater to**

**gratifying** ADJS **pleasing,** satisfying, rewarding, heartwarming, grateful; **agreeable,** desirable, acceptable

**grating** ADJS **irritating,** irritative, irritant; **chafing, galling,** fretting, rasping, boring, grinding, stinging, scratchy; **jarring; rasping,** raspy; strident, shrill, harsh, raucous

**gratis** ADJS 1 **gratuitous,** free, free of charge, for free, **for nothing,** free for nothing, free for the asking, complimentary, **on the house,** comp
ADVS 2 **gratuitously,** free, **free of charge,** for nothing, for the asking, at no charge, without charge, with the compliments of the management, as our guest, on the house

**gratitude** NOUNS **gratefulness,** thankfulness, appreciation, appreciativeness; obligation, sense of obligation *or* indebtedness

**gratuitous** ADJS unnecessary, unessential, nonessential, expendable, dispensable, **needless,** unneeded, uncalled-for

**gratuity** NOUNS **largess, bounty,** liberality, donative, sportula; perquisite, perks <Brit nonformal>; consideration, fee <old>, **tip,** *pourboire* <Fr>, *Trinkgeld* <Ger>, sweetener, inducement; grease *and* salve *and* palm oil <all nonformal>; honorarium

**grave** NOUNS 1 **tomb, sepulcher;** gravesite, burial, pit, deep six <nonformal>; resting place, last home, long home, narrow house, house of death, low house, low green tent; **crypt, vault,** burial chamber

*the lone couch of his*
*everlasting sleep*
SHELLEY

ADJS 2 **solemn,** dignified, sober, unsmiling, weighty, somber, frowning, **grim; sedate, staid;** demure, decorous; **serious, earnest, thoughtful; sober-minded,** sober-sided; straight-faced, long-faced, grim-faced, grim-visaged, stone-faced; sober as a judge, grave as an undertaker; **formal**

**graven** ADJS **engraved,** graved, tooled, enchased, inscribed, incised, marked, lined, creased, cut, carved, glyphic, **sculptured,** insculptured, **printed,** imprinted, impressed, stamped

**graveyard** NOUNS **cemetery, burial ground** *or* **place,** burying place *or* ground, *campo santo* <Ital>, boneyard *and* bone orchard <both nonformal>, burial yard, necropolis, polyandrium, **memorial park,** city *or* village of the dead; **churchyard,** God's acre; **potter's field;** Golgotha, Calvary

**gravitate** VERBS **descend**, drop, plunge, precipitate, sink, settle, subside; tend, tend to go, **incline,** point, head, lead, lean

**gravity** NOUNS **importance, significance, consequence,** consideration, **import,** note, mark, **moment, weight;** graveness, seriousness, solemnity, weightiness; *gravitas* <L>; no joke, no laughing matter, hardball <nonformal>

**gray** ADJS dull, flat, mat, dead, dingy, muddy, leaden, lusterless, lackluster; **faded, washed-out,** dimmed, discolored, etiolated; **pale, dim,** weak, **faint; pallid, wan, sallow,** fallow; pale *or* blue *or* green around the gills; **ashen,** ashy, ashen-hued, cinereous, cineritious, griseous; **grayish,** gray-colored, gray-hued, gray-toned, grayed, **grizzly,** grizzled

**gray area** NOUNS **ambiguity,** ambiguousness; **equivocalness,** equivocacy, equivocality; **double meaning,** amphibology; twilight zone, inexplicitness, uncertainty, borderline case

**gray matter** NOUNS **intellect, mind,** *mens* <L>; mental *or* intellectual faculty, nous, **reason, rationality,** rational *or* reasoning faculty, power of reason, *Vernunft* <Ger>, *esprit* <Fr>, *raison* <Fr>, **intelligence,** mentality, mental capacity, **understanding,** reasoning, intellection, conception; **brain, brains,** brainpower, smarts <nonformal>

**graze** VERBS **touch lightly,** touch upon; kiss, **brush,** sweep, brush by, glance, scrape, skim

**grease** NOUNS 1 **flattery, adulation; blarney** *and* bunkum *and* **soft soap** *and* soap *or* butter salve <all nonformal>, oil, eyewash <nonformal>; strokes *and* stroking *and* ego massage <all nonformal>, sweet talk, fair *or* sweet *or* honeyed words, soft *or* honeyed phrases, ass-kissing <nonformal>, **fawning, sycophancy; gratuity,** sweetener, inducement; salve *and* palm oil <both nonformal>
2 **oil,** *oleum* <L>; **fat,** lipid, sebum, tallow, vegetable oil, animal oil
VERBS 3 **bribe,** throw a sop to; **grease the palm** *or* **hand** *and* oil the palm *and* tickle the palm <all nonformal>; buy *and* **buy off** *and* pay off <all nonformal>; suborn, **corrupt,** tamper with; reach *and* get at *and* get to <all nonformal>; approach, try to bribe; **fix, take care of**
4 **facilitate, ease; grease the wheels** <nonformal>; grease *or* soap the ways <both nonformal>, prepare the way, **clear the way,** make all clear for, make way for; open the way, open the door to; **lubricate,** make frictionless *or* dissipationless, remove friction, oil; **speed, expedite,** quicken, hasten; **help along,** help on its way; **aid; explain,** make clear; **simplify**

**grease paint** NOUNS theatrical makeup, **makeup,** cosmetics, beauty products, beauty-care products; war paint <nonformal>; pancake makeup

**greasy** ADJS 1 **slippery,** slippy, **slick,** slithery *and* sliddery <both nonformal>, slippery as an eel; lubricious, lubric, oily, oleaginous, buttery, soaped; lubricated, oiled, greased
2 **oily; unctuous,** unctional; unguinous; **oleaginous,** oleic; unguentary, **unguent,** unguentous

**greasy spoon** NOUNS eatery *and* beanery *and* hashery *and* hash house <all nonformal>; hamburger joint <nonformal>; **lunchroom,** luncheonette; lunch wagon, dog wagon <nonformal>

**great** ADJS 1 **grand, considerable,** consequential; **mighty,** powerful, strong, irresistible, intense; main, maximum, **total, full,** plenary, comprehensive, exhaustive; grave, **serious,** heavy, deep; arch, banner, master, magisterial; topflight, highest-ranking, ranking; **star,** superstar, stellar, world-class
2 **important,** major, consequential, momentous, significant, substantial, material, big; superior, world-shaking, earthshaking; big-time *and* big-league *and* major-league *and* heavyweight <all nonformal>; high-powered <nonformal>, double-barreled <nonformal>

3 <nonformal> swell, dandy, bitchin', jim dandy, neat, cool, super, super-duper, bully <old>, tough, mean, gnarly, heavy, bad, groovy, out of sight, fab, fantabulous, marvy, gear, something

else, ducky, dynamite, keen, killer, hot, nifty, sexy, spiffy, spiffing, ripping, nobby, peachy, peachy-keen, delicious, scrumptious, not too shabby, tits, out of this world, hunky-dory, crackerjack, boss, stunning, corking, smashing, solid, all wool and a yard wide; rum *or* wizard <both Brit>, bonzer <Austral>; bang-up, jam-up, slap-up, ace-high, fine and dandy, just dandy, but good, OK, okay, A-OK

**greed** NOUNS greediness, graspingness, **avarice,** cupidity, avidity, voracity, rapacity, lust, avariciousness, *avaritia and cupiditas* <both L>; money-grubbing; avidness, esurience, wolfishness; voraciousness, ravenousness, rapaciousness, sordidness, **covetousness,** acquisitiveness; itching palm; grasping; **piggishness,** hoggishness, swinishness; **gluttony**, *gula* <L>; inordinate desire, furor, craze, fury *or* frenzy of desire, overgreediness; insatiable desire, insatiability; incontinence, intemperateness

**greedy** ADJS **avaricious,** avid, voracious, rapacious, cupidinous, esurient, **ravening, grasping, grabby** <nonformal>, graspy, acquisitive, mercenary, sordid, overgreedy; ravenous, gobbling, devouring; miserly, money-hungry, money-grubbing, money-mad, venal; **covetous,** coveting; **piggish, hoggish,** swinish, a hog for, greedy as a hog; **gluttonous**; omnivorous, all-devouring; insatiable, insatiate, unsatisfied, unsated, unappeased, unappeasable, limitless, bottomless, unquenchable, quenchless, unslaked, unslakable, slakeless

**green** NOUNS 1 **lawn;** grassplot, greenyard; grounds; **common, park, village green;** golf course *or* links, fairway; bowling green, putting green
ADJS 2 **verdant,** verdurous; grassy, leafy, leaved, foliaged; springlike, summerlike, summery, vernal, vernant, aestival; **greenish,** viridescent, virescent; **grass-green,** green as grass; glaucous, glaucescent, glaucous-green
3 **jealous, jaundiced,** jaundice-eyed, yellow-eyed, green-eyed, yellow, green with jealousy; invidious, **envious**
4 **immature, unripe,** underripe, unripened, impubic, **raw,** callow, wet behind the ears, unfledged, fledgling, unseasoned, unmellowed; **ignorant, inexperienced**; innocent, ingenuous, gauche, awkward, naive

**greenery** NOUNS **plants, vegetation;** herbage, flowerage, verdure, greens

**greenhorn** NOUNS **newcomer, new arrival,** *novus homo* <L>; *arriviste* <Fr>, Johnny-come-lately <nonformal>, new boy <Brit>; **tenderfoot;** settler, immigrant; recruit, rookie <nonformal>

**greenhouse** NOUNS **nursery; conservatory,** glasshouse <Brit>, forcing house, summerhouse, lathhouse, **hothouse,** coolhouse

**greenroom** NOUNS **anteroom,** antechamber; **waiting room,** *salle d'attente* <Fr>; **reception room,** presence chamber *or* room, audience chamber; lounge, wardroom

**greet** VERBS **hail, accost,** address; **salute,** make one's salutations; **bid** *or* **say hello,** bid good day *or* good morning, etc; exchange greetings, **pass the time of day; give one's regards**; shake hands, shake *and* give one some skin *and* give a high *or* a low five <all nonformal>, press the flesh <nonformal>, press *or* squeeze one's hand

**greetings** NOUNS **regards, compliments, respects,** *égards, devoirs* <both Fr>; **salutations,** salaams; **best wishes,** one's best, good wishes, best regards, kind *or* kindest regards, love, best love; remembrances, kind remembrances; compliments of the season

**gregarious** ADJS **sociable, social,** social-minded, fit for society, fond of society, **affable; companionable,** companionate, compatible, genial, *gemütlich* <Ger>, **congenial; communicative**; amiable, **friendly;** civil, urbane, courteous

**gremlin** NOUNS **imp, pixie,** sprite, elf, puck, kobold, *diablotin* <Fr>, tokoloshe, poltergeist, Dingbelle, Fifinella, **bad fairy,** bad peri

**grid** NOUNS **network,** hachure *or* hatchure, hatching, cross-hatching; grate, grating; grille, grillwork; gridiron

**griddle** VERBS fry, deep-fry *or* deep-fat fry, pan, pan-fry; sauté, stir-fry; broil, grill, pan-broil

**gridlock** NOUNS **blockage,** strangulation, choking, choking off, **stoppage,** stop, **bar, barrier, obstacle,** impediment; **bottleneck,** chokepoint; **congestion,** jam, traffic jam, bottleneck; impasse

**grief** NOUNS **pain, distress,** stress, stress of life, suffering, passion, dolor; **melan-**

**choly,** melancholia, depression, sadness, heartache, aching heart, heavy heart, bleeding heart, broken heart, agony of mind *or* spirit; **distressfulness,** distress, grievousness; **painfulness,** pain; **sorrow,** sorrowing, **care, woe;** heartgrief, heartfelt grief; prostrating grief, prostration; **lamentation**

**grievance** NOUNS **complaint, peeve,** pet peeve, **groan; dissent, protest**; hard luck story <nonformal>, tale of woe; **complaining,** scolding, groaning, **faultfinding**, sniping, destructive criticism, grumbling, murmuring; **injustice,** wrong, injury, disservice; raw *or* rotten deal *and* bad rap <all nonformal>; imposition; mockery *or* miscarriage of justice; great wrong, grave *or* gross injustice

**grieve** VERBS **sorrow; weep,** mourn; be dumb with grief; **pine,** pine away; **brood over,** mope, fret, take on <nonformal>; **eat one's heart out,** break one's heart over; **agonize,** ache, bleed; **lament,** moan, keen, weep over, bewail, bemoan, deplore, repine

**grill** VERBS 1 fry, deep-fry *or* deep-fat fry, griddle, pan, pan-fry; sauté, stir-fry; sear, blacken, braise, brown; broil, pan-broil
2 **interrogate,** question, **pump,** pump for information, shoot questions at, pick the brains of, worm out of; interview; draw one out

**grille** NOUNS **network, net,** netting; **mesh,** meshes; **web,** webbing; lattice, latticework; hachure *or* hatchure, hatching, cross-hatching; grillwork; **grid,** gridiron; tracery, fretwork

**grim** ADJS **sullen,** sulky, surly, morose, dour, mumpish, dumpish, **glum, moody,** moping; **glowering,** lowering, **scowling, frowning; gloomy,** dismal, murky, bleak, somber, sombrous, **solemn,** grave; **hopeless,** unhopeful, without hope, affording no hope, worst-case, bleak, dismal, cheerless, comfortless

**grimace** NOUNS 1 **wry face,** wry mouth, rictus, snarl; moue, mow, pout
VERBS 2 **make a face,** make a wry face *or* mouth, pull a face, **screw up one's face,** mug <nonformal>, mouth, make a mouth, mop, mow <old>, mop and mow <old>; pout

**grime** NOUNS **dirt;** dust; soot, smut; **mud**

**grimy** ADJS **dirty, grubby,** grungy <nonformal>, smirchy, dingy, messy <nonformal>; scruffy, slovenly, untidy; miry, **muddy**; **dusty;** smutty, smutchy, smudgy; sooty, smoky; snuffy

**grin** NOUNS 1 **smile,** silly smile *or* grin; grinning; broad grin, ear-to-ear grin, toothful grin; stupid grin, idiotic grin; sardonic grin, **smirk, simper**
VERBS 2 **smile,** beam, smile brightly; grin like a Cheshire cat *or* chessy-cat <nonformal>; **smirk, simper**

**grind** NOUNS 1 **routine,** rut, groove, well-worn groove; **treadmill,** squirrel cage; the working day, nine-to-five, the daily grind <nonformal>; **study, studying,** application; **brainwork, headwork,** lucubration, mental labor; grinding *and* boning <both nonformal>, **cramming** *and* cram <both nonformal>
2 **drudge,** grub, hack, fag, plodder, slave, galley slave, **workhorse,** beast of burden, slogger; greasy grind <nonformal>; **bookworm**
VERBS 3 **grate,** rasp, scratch, scrape; **sharpen, edge,** acuminate, aculeate, spiculate, taper; **whet, hone,** oilstone, file; **pulverize, powder,** comminute, triturate, contriturate, levigate, bray, pestle, disintegrate, reduce to powder *or* dust, grind to powder *or* dust, grind up

**grip** NOUNS 1 **control,** mastery, mastership, command, power, jurisdiction, dominion, domination; hold, grasp, hand, hands, iron hand, clutches; talons, claws; steady hand; firm hold, tight grip, iron grip, grip of iron *or* steel, death grip; **handle, hold,** grasp, haft, helve
VERBS 2 **hold,** grasp, clutch, clip, clinch, clench; bite, nip; **clasp,** hug, embrace; **cling, cling to,** cleave to, stick to, adhere to, freeze to; **hold on to,** hold fast *or* tight, hang on to, keep a firm hold upon; **hold on, hang on** <nonformal>, hold on like a bulldog, stick like a leech, hang on for dear life; keep hold of, never let go; **seize**
3 **engross,** absorb, immerse, occupy, preoccupy, engage, involve, monopolize, exercise, take up; **obsess; hold,** arrest, hold the interest, fascinate, enthrall, spellbind, hold spellbound, grab <nonformal>, charm, enchant, mesmerize, hypnotize, catch; absorb the attention, claim one's thoughts, monopolize one's attention, engage the mind *or* thoughts

**gripe** NOUNS

<nonformal> **beef, kick, gripe,** kvetch, grouse, bellyache, howl, holler, **squawk,** bitch; **beefing,** grousing, kicking, griping, kvetching, bellyaching, squawking, **bitching,** yapping

**gripping** ADJS **engrossing,** absorbing, consuming, riveting, holding, arresting, engaging, attractive, fascinating, enthralling, **spellbinding,** enchanting, magnetic, hypnotic, mesmerizing, mesmeric; obsessive, obsessing

**grisly** ADJS **deathly, deathlike,** deadly; **weird,** eerie, uncanny, unearthly; ghostly, ghostlike; **ghastly,** gruesome, macabre; **repulsive**, repellent, repelling, rebarbative, **repugnant,** offensive, foul, forbidding, loathsome, revolting

**grit** NOUNS **pluck, spunk** <nonformal>, mettle, backbone <nonformal>, true grit, spirit, **stamina, guts** *and* moxie <both nonformal>, bottom, **toughness** <nonformal>; pluckiness, spunkiness <nonformal>, **gameness,** feistiness <nonformal>, mettlesomeness; courage

**gritty** ADJS **rough**, coarse, gross, unrefined, coarse-grained; grained, **grainy,** granular, granulated, gravelly; **plucky, spunky** *and* feisty *and* gutty *or* gutsy <all nonformal>, **mettlesome,** dauntless, **game,** game to the last *or* end; **courageous**

**grizzled** ADJS **white, hoary,** hoar, grizzly, canescent; **gray, grayish,** griseous; grizzle

**groan** NOUNS 1 **lament,** plaint, *planctus* <L>; **murmur,** mutter; **moan,** whine, wail, wail of woe; **sob,** *cri du coeur* <Fr>, **cry,** outcry, scream, **howl,** yowl, bawl, yawp, keen, ululation; **complaint,** grievance
VERBS 2 **moan, howl,** yowl, **cry,** squall, bawl, yawp, yell, scream, shriek; cry out, make an outcry; **complain,** grumble, murmur, mutter, growl, clamor, croak, grunt, yelp

**groceries** NOUNS **provisions,** provender, supplies, stores, larder, food supply; food items, edibles, victuals, baked goods, packaged goods, canned goods

**groggy** ADJS **dazed,** in a daze; **silly,** knocked silly, **dopey** <nonformal>, woozy <nonformal>; **punch-drunk** *and* punchy *and* **slap-happy** <all nonformal>

**groom** NOUNS 1 **stableman,** stableboy, hostler, equerry
VERBS 2 dress, fettle <Brit nonformal>, **brush up; preen,** plume, titivate; manicure; **prepare,** ready, **condition,** fit, put in tune, form, **lick into shape** <nonformal>; rub down, brush, curry, currycomb

**groomed** ADJS **prepared, ready,** well-prepared, prepped <nonformal>, in readiness *or* ready state, all ready, good and ready, prepared and ready; coached; **readied,** available

**groove** NOUNS **furrow,** scratch, crack, cranny, chase, chink, score, **cut,** gash, striation, streak, stria, **gouge,** slit, incision; sulcus, sulcation; **rut,** wheeltrack, well-worn groove; wrinkle; **corrugation;** flute, fluting; rifling

**groovy** ADJS

<nonformal> **hep, hip,** on the beam, go-go, **with it,** into, really into; chic, clued-up, clued in, in the know, trendy

**grope** VERBS 1 **touch, feel, impinge,** bump up against, hit; osculate; **graze,** nudge, rub, brush, glance, scrape, sideswipe, skim, skirt, shave; feel up *and* cop a feel <both nonformal>; **search, hunt, explore;** dig, delve, burrow, root, pick over, poke, pry; look round *or* around, poke around, nose around, smell around; beat the bushes
2 **be uncertain, feel unsure;** be at one's wit's end, not know which way to turn, be of two minds, be at sixes and sevens, not know where one stands, be in a dilemma *or* quandary, flounder, beat about, thrash about, not know whether one is coming or going

**gross** NOUNS 1 **receipts,** revenue, profits, earnings, returns, proceeds, **take,** takings; gate receipts, gate, box office; gross receipts
VERBS 2 **make money;** rake it in *and* coin money *and* make a bundle *or* pile *or* killing *or* mint *and* clean up <all nonformal>; **realize**
ADJS 3 **offensive,** coarse, crude, obscene; obnoxious, abhorrent, hateful, abominable, heinous, **contemptible, despicable,** detestable, execrable, beneath *or* below contempt, **base,** ignoble

**grotesque** ADJS **freakish,** freak *or* freaky <nonformal>; **monstrous, deformed,**

malformed, misshapen, **misbegotten,** teratogenic, teratoid; **bizarre,** baroque, rococo; preposterous, cockamamie <nonformal>, fantastic, fantastical, wild, weird, **outrageous,** incredible, beyond belief, *outré* <Fr>, extravagant

**grotto** NOUNS **cave,** cavern, hole, grot, antre, subterrane

**grouch** NOUNS **sorehead,** curmudgeon, grump, crank, crosspatch, wasp, **bear,** grizzly bear, pit bull, junkyard dog <nonformal>; **spoilsport,** malcontent

**grouchy** ADJS

<nonformal> **crabby,** cantankerous, crusty, grumpy *or* grumpish, huffy *or* huffish, mean, mean as a junkyard dog, ornery, bitchy, cussed, feisty, ugly, miffy, salty, scrappy, shirty <Brit>, soreheaded

**groundless** ADJS **baseless,** ungrounded, **unfounded,** ill-founded, unbased, **unsupported,** unsustained, **without foundation,** without basis *or* sound basis; **untenable, unsupportable,** unsustainable; **unwarranted,** idle, empty, vain

**grounds** NOUNS 1 **dregs, lees,** dross, slag, draff, scoria, feces; **sediment, settlings, deposits,** deposition; alluvium, alluvion, diluvium

2 **evidence, proof; reason to believe,** grounds for belief; **ground,** material grounds, **facts, data,** premises, basis for belief

**group** NOUNS 1 **bunch,** grouping, groupment, crop, **cluster, clump,** knot; **batch, lot,** slew <nonformal>, **mess** <nonformal>; **set**

VERBS 2 **classify**, categorize; **grade,** gradate, rank, subordinate; **sort,** sort out <chiefly Brit>, assort; **separate,** divide; collate

**groupie** NOUNS

<nonformal> **fan, buff, freak,** hound, fiend, demon, nut, bug, head, junkie, rooter, booster, great one for

**grouping** NOUNS **classification**, categorization, taxonomy; **gradation,** subordination, superordination, **ranking,** placement; **sorting,** sorting out, assortment, sifting, screening, triage, culling, selection, shakeout

**grove** NOUNS **woodlet;** holt <nonformal>, hurst, tope <India>, shaw <nonformal>, bosk <old>; **orchard;** wood lot; coppice, copse; *bocage* <Fr>

**grovel** VERBS **fawn,** truckle; **toady,** toad-eat; **bootlick** <nonformal>, lickspittle, lick one's shoes, lick the feet of; **crawl,** creep, cower, cringe, crouch, stoop, kneel, bend the knee, fall on one's knees, prostrate oneself, throw oneself at the feet of, fall at one's feet, kiss *or* lick *or* suck one's ass *and* brown-nose <all nonformal>, kiss one's feet, kiss the hem of one's garment, lick the dust, make a doormat of oneself; **kowtow,** bow, **bow and scrape**

**grow** VERBS **develop,** wax, **increase**; gather, brew; **grow up,** mature, maturate, spring up, ripen, come of age, **shoot up,** sprout up, upshoot, upspring, upsprout, upspear, overtop, tower; grow like a weed <nonformal>; burgeon, **sprout**, blossom, reproduce, procreate, grow out of, germinate, pullulate; **flourish, thrive;** mushroom, balloon

**growl** VERBS **snarl,** grumble, gnarl, snap; show one's teeth, spit

**grownup** NOUNS **adult,** mature man *or* woman, grown man *or* woman, big boy *and* big girl <both nonformal>; **man, woman;** no chicken *and* no spring chicken <both nonformal>

**growth** NOUNS **development;** bodily development, **maturation,** maturing, coming of age, growing up, upgrowth; burgeoning, sprouting; budding, gemmation; outgrowth, excrescence; overgrowth

**grow up** VERBS **mature,** grow, **develop, ripen,** flower, flourish, bloom, blossom; fledge, leave the nest, put up one's hair, not be in pigtails, put on long pants; **come of age,** come to maturity, attain majority, **reach one's majority,** reach the age of consent, reach manhood *or* womanhood, put on long trousers *or* pants, assume the toga virilis, come into years of discretion, be in the prime of life, cut one's wisdom teeth *or* eyeteeth <nonformal>, have sown one's wild oats, settle down; **mellow,** season, temper

**grubby** ADJS **dirty, grimy,** grungy <nonformal>, smirchy, dingy; smutty, smutchy, smudgy; **messy** <nonformal>, mussy <nonformal>, **sloppy** <nonformal>, scraggly, poky, seedy <nonformal>, **shabby,** shoddy, schlocky <nonformal>, lumpen, chintzy, grubby <nonformal>, **frowzy, blowzy,** tacky <nonformal>; **infested,** wormy, ratty

**grudge** NOUNS **aversion, repugnance,** repulsion, **antipathy,** allergy <nonformal>, abomination, **abhorrence; spite,** crow to pick *or* pluck *or* pull, bone to pick

**grudging** ADJS **envious,** envying, **invidious,** green with envy; **jealous**; **covetous,** desirous of; resentful; **begrudging;** mean, mean-spirited, ungenerous; **reluctant,** renitent, **loath;** unenthusiastic, unzealous, indifferent, apathetic, perfunctory; balky, balking, restive; **niggardly,** niggard, pinchpenny, penurious, **mean,** mingy, shabby, sordid

**grueling** ADJS **fatiguing, wearying,** wearing, **tiring,** straining, stressful, trying, **exhausting,** draining, punishing, killing; **tiresome,** fatiguesome, **wearisome,** weariful; **backbreaking,** punishing, crushing, killing, Herculean

**gruesome** ADJS **deathly,** deathlike, deadly; **ghastly,** grisly, macabre; **repulsive**, repellent, repelling, rebarbative, **repugnant,** offensive, foul, forbidding, loathsome

**gruff** ADJS **brusque, curt,** short, sharp, snippy <nonformal>, abrupt, **blunt,** bluff, brash, cavalier; **harsh,** rough, severe; truculent, aggressive; **surly,** crusty, bearish, beastly, churlish

**grumble** VERBS **complain,** groan; **murmur, mutter,** growl, clamor, croak, grunt, yelp; **fret,** fuss, make a fuss about, fret and fume; air a grievance, lodge *or* register a complaint; fault, find fault

**grumbling** ADJS malcontent, malcontented, **complaining,** sour, **faultfinding,** growling, murmuring, muttering, griping, croaking, **peevish, petulant,** sulky, **querulous,** querulant, whiny; out of humor

**grump** NOUNS 1 **sorehead,** grouch, curmudgeon, crank, crosspatch, grizzly bear, pit bull, junkyard dog <nonformal>
VERBS 2 **sulk, mope,** mope around; grizzle <chiefly Brit nonformal>, **grouch** *and* **bitch** <both nonformal>, **fret;** get oneself in a sulk

**grungy** ADJS **offensive,** repellent, rebarbative, repugnant, revolting, forbidding; **disgusting, sickening, loathsome,** gross *and* yucky *and* scuzzy <all nonformal>, beastly <nonformal>, **vile, foul, nasty, nauseating**

**guarantee** NOUNS 1 **oath,** vow, word, assurance, **warrant,** solemn oath *or* affirmation *or* word *or* declaration; **pledge**
VERBS 2 **secure,** warrant, assure, insure, ensure, bond, certify; countersecure; **sponsor,** be sponsor for, sign for, sign one's note, **back,** stand behind *or* back of, stand up for; **endorse;** sign, cosign, **underwrite**

**guaranty** NOUNS **security, surety,** indemnity, **warranty, insurance,** warrant, assurance; **obligation**, full faith and credit

**guard** NOUNS 1 **defender,** champion, advocate; upholder; guardian angel, supporter; vindicator, apologist; **protector;** paladin; **bodyguard, convoy; safeguard,** palladium, shield, screen, aegis; umbrella, protective umbrella
VERBS 2 **defend, shield,** screen, secure, guard against; defend tooth and nail *or* to the death *or* to the last breath; **safeguard, protect**; stand by the side of, flank; **advocate, champion**; **defend oneself,** cover one's ass *or* rear-end <nonformal>, CYA *or* cover your ass <nonformal>

**guarded** ADJS **vigilant, wary,** prudent, **watchful,** lidless, sleepless, observant; **on the watch, on the lookout,** *aux aguets* <Fr>; **on guard,** on one's guard; discreet; **suspicious, suspecting,** wary, leery, cautious; **protected,** safeguarded, defended; **sheltered, shielded,** screened, covered, cloaked

**guardian** NOUNS **warden,** governor; **custodian,** steward, **keeper, caretaker,** warder <Brit>, attendant; caregiver; next friend, prochein ami, guardian *ad litem;* **curator,** conservator; janitor; castellan; **shepherd,** herd, cowherd; **game warden,** gamekeeper; guardian angel

**guardian angel** NOUNS **defender,** champion, advocate; upholder; **supporter**; vindicator, apologist; **protector**; **guard**; paladin; **voice of conscience,** still small voice within; guardian spirit, good angel, ministering angel, **fairy godmother**

**guerrilla** NOUNS **irregular,** casual; partisan, franctireur; **bushfighter,** bushwhacker <nonformal>; underground, resistance, maquis; *maquisard* <Fr>, underground *or* resistance fighter

**guess** NOUNS 1 **conjecture,** unverified supposition, perhaps, speculation,

guesswork, surmise, educated guess; guesstimate *and* hunch *and* shot *and* stab <all nonformal>; rough guess, wild guess, blind guess, bold conjecture, shot in the dark <nonformal>
VERBS 2 **conjecture,** guesstimate <nonformal>, talk off the top of one's head <nonformal>, hazard a conjecture, venture a guess, risk assuming *or* stating, tentatively suggest, go out on a limb <nonformal>

**guest** NOUNS **visitor,** visitant; **caller,** company; invited guest, invitee; uninvited guest, gate-crasher <nonformal>; moocher *and* freeloader <both nonformal>

**guidance** NOUNS **advice,** counsel, recommendation, suggestion; proposal; **direction,** instruction, briefing; **counseling;** guidance counseling, educational counseling, vocational guidance

**guide** NOUNS 1 guider; **shepherd,** tour guide, tour director *or* conductor, cicerone, tourist guide, dragoman; **escort, conductor, usher**
VERBS 2 **steer, drive, run** <nonformal>; channel; **escort, conduct,** have in tow <nonformal>, marshal, **usher,** shepherd, **lead; convoy,** guard; **govern, rule, control**, order, **regulate,** direct

**guidebook** NOUNS **handbook, manual,** enchiridion, vade mecum, gradus, how-to book <nonformal>; field guide; travel book, handbook, Baedeker

**guideline** NOUNS **rule,** ground rule, rubric, protocol, working rule, working principle, standard procedure; guiding principle, golden rule; code

**guidepost** NOUNS **pointer,** index, **direction, guide; signpost,** finger post, direction post; milepost; blaze; guideboard, signboard

**guild** NOUNS **fellowship,** sodality; **society,** order; **brotherhood, fraternity,** confraternity, confrerie, fraternal order *or* society; **sisterhood, sorority**

**guilt** NOUNS **guiltiness; criminality,** peccancy; guilty *or* wrongful *or* criminal involvement; **culpability,** reprehensibility, blameworthiness; bloodguilt *or* -guiltiness, red-handedness, dirty hands, red *or* bloody hands

**guiltless** ADJS **innocent;** unfallen, unlapsed, prelapsarian; **unguilty,** not guilty, **faultless, blameless,** reproachless, **sinless,** offenseless, with clean hands, clear, in the clear; innocent as a lamb, lamblike, dovelike, angelic, childlike; uncorrupted, incorrupt, pristine, undefiled

*blameless in life and pure of crime*
HORACE

**guilty** ADJS 1 guilty as hell, peccant, **criminal, to blame, at fault, culpable,** reprehensible, censurable, reproachable, reprovable, inculpated; red-handed, bloodguilty; caught in the act *or* flat-footed *or* red-handed, caught with one's pants down *or* with one's hand in the till *or* with one's hand in the cookie jar <nonformal>

**guinea pig** NOUNS **subject, experimental subject,** experimentee, testee, patient, sample; laboratory animal, experimental *or* test animal

**guise** NOUNS **pretext,** pretense, pretension, lying pretension, show, ostensible *or* announced *or* public *or* professed motive; **front,** facade, **sham; excuse,** apology, protestation, poor excuse, lame excuse; **subterfuge,** refuge, device, stratagem, feint, dipsy-doodle <nonformal>, **trick**; dust thrown in the eye, smoke screen, **screen, cover,** stalking-horse, **blind;** semblance; mask, cloak, veil; **cover,** cover-up, cover story, alibi

**gulf** NOUNS **sea,** tributary sea, bay, arm of the sea, fjord, bight; cove; **chasm, abyss,** abysm

**gull** VERBS **deceive,** beguile, trick, hoax, **dupe,** gammon, pigeon, play one for a fool *or* sucker, **bamboozle** *and* snow *and* **hornswoggle** *and* diddle *and* scam <all nonformal>, take in, put on *and* hocus-pocus <both nonformal>, string along, **put something over** *or* **across,** slip one over on <nonformal>, pull a fast one on, **cheat,** victimize, **swindle,** defraud, practice fraud upon, euchre, **con,** finagle, **fleece,** mulct, fob <old>, **bilk,** cozen, chouse, **cheat out of, do out of,** chouse out of; **make a fool of,** make a monkey of <nonformal>

**gullible** ADJS **dupable,** cullible <old>, deceivable, exploitable, seducible, persuadable, **simple; ingenuous,** unsophisticated, green, naive

**gullible person** NOUNS **dupe, gull,** gudgeon, *gobe-mouches* <Fr>; **victim;** dupable *or* credulous person, trusting *or* simple soul, innocent, *naïf* <Fr>, babe, babe in the woods

**gully** NOUNS **ravine,** gorge, canyon, box

canyon, *arroyo* <Sp>, barranca, bolson, coulee, gulch, combe <Brit>, dingle, rift, rift valley, kloof, donga, graben, draw, wadi, basin, cirque, corrie, hanging valley

**gulp** NOUNS 1 draft, dram, drench, **swig** <nonformal>, swill *and* guzzle <both nonformal>, quaff, **sip,** sup, suck, tot, bumper, snort *and* slug <both nonformal>, pull <nonformal>, lap, slurp <nonformal>; swallow
VERBS 2 **gobble, bolt,** wolf, gobble *or* gulp *or* bolt *or* wolf down; gulp down, swill, swill down

**gum** NOUNS **resin;** gum resin; oleoresin; hard *or* varnish resin, vegetable resin; synthetic resin, plastic, resinoid; chewing gum, bubble gum; chicle, chicle gum

**gummy** ADJS **adhesive,** sticky, tacky, gluey, **viscid,** glutinous; **resinous,** gummous, gumlike; gooey *and* gunky *and* gloppy *and* goopy *and* gooky <all nonformal>

**gumption** NOUNS **adventurousness,** venturousness, venturesomeness, adventuresomeness; spirit, **spunk** <nonformal>

**gun** NOUNS **firearm;** shooting iron *and* gat *and* rod *and* heater *and* piece <all nonformal>; shoulder weapon *or* gun *or* arm; stun gun; automatic, BB gun, blunderbuss

**gunfire** NOUNS **fire, firing,** musketry, **shooting,** fireworks *or* gunplay <both nonformal>; gunfight, shoot-out; **shot,** discharge; detonation; **salvo, volley,** fusillade, tattoo, spray; bowshot, gunshot, stoneshot, potshot

**gung-ho** ADJS **enthusiastic,** enthused *and* big <both nonformal>, glowing, full of enthusiasm; enthusiastic about, infatuated with

**gunk** NOUNS **slime, slop,** scum, sludge, slush; glop <nonformal>, **muck, mire,** ooze

**gunman** NOUNS **killer,** slayer, slaughterer, butcher, bloodshedder; massacrer; **manslayer, homicide, murderer,** mankiller, bloodletter, Cain; **assassin,** assassinator; **cutthroat,** thug, desperado, bravo, gorilla <nonformal>, apache; professional killer, hired killer, hit man *or* button man *or* gun *or* trigger man *or* torpedo *or* gunsel <all nonformal>; **hatchet man**

**gunrunning** NOUNS **smuggling,** contrabandage, contraband

**gunshot** NOUNS **shot,** discharge; ejection; detonation; gunfire; gun, cannon; bullet; **salvo, volley,** fusillade, tattoo, spray; bowshot, stoneshot, potshot

**guru** NOUNS **mentor;** pandit, pundit, *mullah* <Persian>, *starets* <Russ>; holy man; great soul, mahatma; *rishi* <Skt>; Brahman, pujari, purohit, bashara, vairagi *or* bairagi, sannyasi; yogi, yogin; bhikshu, bhikhari

**gush** NOUNS 1 **flow,** flowing, **flux,** fluency, profluence, fluid motion *or* movement; **course,** onward course, **surge, rush,** onrush, spate, run, race
VERBS 2 **be enthusiastic, rave, enthuse** *and* be big for <both nonformal>; **rhapsodize, carry on over** *and* rave on <both nonformal>, make much of, **make a fuss over,** make an ado *or* much ado about, make a to-do over *and* take on over <both nonformal>, be *or* go on over *or* about <nonformal>, rave about *and* whoop it up about <both nonformal>; go nuts *or* gaga *or* ape over <nonformal>; gush over; effervesce, bubble over

**gushing** ADJS 1 **sentimental,** sentimentalized, soft, **mawkish, maudlin,** cloying; sticky *and* gooey *and* schmaltzy *and* sappy *and* soppy <all nonformal>, oversentimental, oversentimentalized, bathetic; **mushy** *or* sloppy *or* teary *or* beery <all nonformal>; fulsome, slobbery, protesting too much, smarmy <nonformal>, **unctuous**
2 **flowing, streaming, running, pouring,** coursing, racing, rushing, onrushing, surging, surgy, torrential

**gust** NOUNS wind gust, **blast,** blow, flaw, **flurry,** scud <Scots>

**gusto** NOUNS **relish,** zest, *joie de vivre* <Fr>; taste, gust <Scots>; **liveliness,** vivacity, vitality, life, animation, spiritedness, spirit, esprit, élan, **sprightliness,** high spirits, zestfulness, zest, vim, zip <nonformal>, vigor, verve, **exuberance,** heartiness

**gusty** ADJS **windy,** blowy; **breezy,** drafty, airy, airish; brisk, fresh; blasty, puffy, flawy; **squally;** blustery, blustering, blusterous

**gut** NOUNS 1 goozle, guzzle; tum, tummy, tum-tum, breadbasket, bulge, fallen chest <nonformal>, corporation, spare tire, bay window, **pot,** potbelly, potgut, beerbelly, German *or* Milwaukee goiter, swagbelly <all nonformal>

VERBS 2 **eviscerate,** disembowel; **devastate,** desolate, waste, lay waste, ravage, havoc, wreak havoc, despoil, depredate; gut with fire, incinerate, vaporize, ravage with fire and sword; dissolve, lyse

ADJS 3 **emotional, affective,** emotive, affectional, **feeling;** soulful, of soul, of heart, of feeling, of sentiment; visceral

4 **primary,** primitive, primal, elementary, elemental, simple, bare-bones *and* no-frills *and* bread-and-butter <all nonformal>, original, *ab ovo* <L>, **basic,** basal, underlying; **substantive,** substantial, material

**gutless** ADJS **uncourageous,** unvalorous, unheroic, undaring, unable to say 'boo' to a goose; **pluckless,** spunkless *and* gritless <both nonformal>, spiritless, heartless

**gut reaction** NOUNS **impulse;** natural impulse, blind impulse, **instinct,** urge, drive; vagrant *or* fleeting impulse; hunch; involuntary impulse, reflex, knee jerk, automatic response

**guts** NOUNS 1 **insides, innards** <nonformal>, inwards, internals; inner mechanism, what makes it tick *and* works <both nonformal>; **vitals, viscera,** *kishkes* <Yiddish>, giblets; entrails, bowels

2 **pluck,** spunk <nonformal>, mettle, backbone <nonformal>, **grit,** true grit, spirit, **stamina,** moxie <nonformal>; pluckiness, spunkiness <nonformal>, **gameness,** feistiness <nonformal>, mettlesomeness; courage; **balls,** intestinal fortitude, spunk, brass balls, cojones, moxie, spizzerinctum, **backbone,** chutzpah <all nonformal>

**gutsy** ADJS 1 **gritty, mettlesome,** dauntless, **game,** game to the last *or* end; **courageous**

2 <nonformal> **plucky, spunky** *and* feisty; **ballsy,** gutty, stand-up, dead game, gritty, spunky, nervy

**gutter** NOUNS 1 **trough,** eave *or* eaves trough; **flume,** chute, shoot; pentrough, penstock; guide; **drain,** sluice, scupper; kennel

ADJS 2 **vulgar, uncouth, coarse, gross,** rank, raw, broad, low, foul; **earthy,** frank, pulling no punches

**guttersnipe** NOUNS **waif,** homeless waif, ragamuffin, tatterdemalion; **gamin,** gamine, urchin, street urchin, dead-end kid <nonformal>, mudlark

**guy** NOUNS

1 <nonformal> **fellow,** feller, lad, chap, cat, bird, duck, stud, joker, jasper, bugger, bastard, customer, party, character, warm body, bean, cookie, dude, gent, Joe

2 **stay, prop,** fulcrum, **bracket, brace,** bracer, guywire *or* guyline, shroud, rigging, standing rigging

**guzzle** VERBS **tipple, drink,** nip; grog, gargle; **imbibe,** have a drink *or* nip *or* dram *or* guzzle *or* gargle, soak, bib, quaff, sip, sup, lap, lap up, take a drop, slake one's thirst, cheer *or* refresh the inner man, drown one's troubles *or* sorrows, commune with the spirits

**gymnasium** NOUNS **gym** <nonformal>, **fitness center, health club,** health spa, work-out room, weight room, exercise track *or* trail, *parcourse* or *parcours* <both Fr>

**gymnastics** NOUNS **exercise,** free exercise, setting-up exercise *or* set-ups, daily dozen <nonformal>, constitutional; **gymnastic exercise; isometrics,** isometric *or* no-movement exercise; **aerobic exercise, aerobics,** aerobic dancing *or* dance, dancercize *or* dancercizing, fitaerobics, jazz ballet *or* jazzercise *and* popmobility <all Brit>; **bodybuilding,** weightlifting, weight training, pumping iron <nonformal>; calisthenics, eurythmics

**gyp** NOUNS 1 trick, hoax, deceptive, fraud

VERBS 2 **cheat, deceive, trick, hoax,** dupe

3 <nonformal> **clip,** scam, beat, rook, flam, flimflam, diddle, do a number on, hustle, fuck, screw, have, pull something, pull a trick *or* stunt, give the business, stick, sting, burn, gouge, chisel, play *or* take for a sucker, make a patsy of, run a game on, slicker, take for a ride

**gypsy** NOUNS Bohemian, Romany, *zingaro* <Ital>, *Zigeuner* <Ger>, *tzigane* <Fr>

**gyrate** VERBS **rotate, revolve, spin, turn,** round, **go round** *or* **around,** turn round *or* around; **spiral,** gyre; circumrotate, circumvolute; pirouette, turn a pirouette; wind, twist, screw, crank; wamble

# H

**habit** NOUNS 1 **clothing,** clothes, apparel, wear, wearing apparel, daywear, dress, dressing, **raiment,** garmenture, **garb, attire, array,** habiliment, **costume**
2 **substance abuse, drug abuse,** narcotics abuse, drug use, glue-sniffing, solvent abuse; drug habit, drug habituation, drug dependence, physical addiction *or* dependence, psychological addiction *or* dependence, jones *and* monkey on one's back *and* Mighty Joe Young <all nonformal>
3 **mannerism,** *minauderie* <Fr>, **trick of behavior,** trick, **quirk,** peculiarity, peculiar trait, idiosyncrasy, trademark

**habitat** NOUNS home, **range,** stamping grounds, locality, native environment

**habitual** ADJS **regular,** frequent, constant, persistent; repetitive, recurring, recurrent; stereotyped; knee-jerk <nonformal>, goose-step, lockstep, automatic; **routine,** nine-to-five, workaday, well-trodden, well-worn, beaten

**habitué** NOUNS **frequenter,** haunter

**hack** NOUNS 1 **cabdriver,** cabman, cabby <nonformal>, hackman, hacky <nonformal>; **cab, taxicab, taxi,** gypsy cab <nonformal>
2 **hack writer,** literary hack, penny-a-liner, scribbler <nonformal>, potboiler <nonformal>; **drudge,** grub, plodder
3 **two-bit** *or* **peanut politician** <nonformal>, politicaster, political dabbler; **party hack**
ADJS 4 **incompetent,** incapable; dull tool, mediocrity, dub *and* duffer <both nonformal>, no great shakes, no prize, no prize package, no brain surgeon, no rocket scientist
VERBS 5 **sever, dissever,** cut off *or* away *or* loose, shear off, hack through, hack off, ax, amputate; **chop,** hew, slash; gash, butcher

**hack it** VERBS **achieve one's purpose, gain one's end** *or* **ends,** secure one's object, attain one's objective, do what one set out to do, reach one's goal, bring it off, pull it off *and* swing it <both nonformal>; **pass muster,** get by <nonformal>, make it *and* cut the mustard <both nonformal>, meet *or* satisfy requirements

**hackneyed** ADJS **trite;** corny *and* square *and* square-John *and* Clyde <all nonformal>, fade, **banal,** unoriginal, platitudinous, **stereotyped,** stock, set, **commonplace, common,** truistic, twice-told, **familiar,** bromidic <nonformal>, old hat <nonformal>, back-number, bewhiskered, warmed-over, **stale,** musty, fusty

**hag** NOUNS **crone,** witch, beldam, frump <nonformal>, old wife; **witch, vixen,** hellhag, hellcat, she-devil, virago, brimstone, termagant, grimalkin, Jezebel, she-wolf, tigress, wildcat, siren, fury

**haggard** ADJS tired-looking, weary-looking, tired-eyed, tired-faced, hollow-eyed, ravaged, drawn, cadaverous, worn, wan, zombiish

**haggle** VERBS **bargain,** drive a bargain, negotiate, higgle, chaffer, huckster, **deal, dicker,** make a deal, hack out *or* work out *or* hammer out a deal; drive a hard bargain

**hail** NOUNS 1 hailstone; soft hail, graupel, snow pellets, tapioca snow; **hailstorm**
VERBS 2 **applaud,** acclaim; **cheer**; root for <nonformal>, cheer on; **signal,** give a signal, make a sign; hail and speak; **accost, call to,** halloo, greet, salute, speak
3 sleet, snow

**hair** NOUNS pile, **fur**, coat, pelt, **fleece,** wool, camel's hair, horsehair; **mane;** shag, tousled *or* matted hair, **mat of hair;** pubic hair; hairlet, villus, capillament, cilium, ciliolum; seta, setula; bristle

**haircut** NOUNS **hairdo, hairstyle, coiffure,** coif, headdress

**hairdresser** NOUNS **beautician,** beautifier, cosmetologist; *coiffeur, coiffeuse* <both Fr>; barber

**hairless** ADJS depilous; **bald,** acomous; bald as a coot, bald as an egg; **bald-headed,** bald-pated, tonsured

**hairpiece** NOUNS **wig, peruke, toupee,** rug *and* divot *and* doormat <all nonformal>; **periwig**

**hairsplitting** NOUNS **quibbling, caviling,** boggling, captiousness, nit-picking, **bickering; logic-chopping,** trichoschistism; **equivocation,** tergiversation, prevarication, **evasion, hedging, pussyfooting** <nonformal>, **sidestepping,** dodging, shifting, shuffling, fencing, parrying, boggling, paltering

**hairy** ADJS 1 **hirsute,** barbigerous, crinose, crinite, pubescent; pilose, pilous, pileous; **furry,** furred; villous; villose; ciliate, cirrose; hispid, hispidulous; woolly-headed, woolly-haired, ulotrichous; bushy, tufty, **shaggy,** shagged; matted, tomentose
2 **difficult,** difficile; **not easy,** no picnic; **hard, tough** *and* **rough** *and* **rugged** <all nonformal>, rigorous, brutal, severe; wicked *and* mean <both nonformal>, **formidable; arduous,** strenuous, toilsome, laborious, operose, Herculean; delicate, ticklish, tricky, sticky <nonformal>, critical, easier said than done, like pulling teeth; exacting, demanding; intricate, complex; abstruse

**hale** ADJS **hearty,** hale and hearty, **robust,** robustious, robustuous, vital, **vigorous, strong,** strong as a horse *or* an ox, bionic <nonformal>, stalwart, stout, sturdy, **rugged,** rude, hardy, lusty, bouncing, well-knit; **fit,** in condition *or* shape

**half** NOUNS 1 moiety; hemisphere, semisphere, semicircle, **fifty percent;** half-and-half *and* fifty-fifty <both nonformal>
ADJS 2 **part, partly, partial,** halfway

**half-assed** ADJS **slipshod,** slipshoddy, **slovenly,** sloppy *and* **messy** <both nonformal>, sluttish, untidy; **clumsy, bungling**; **haphazard, promiscuous, hit-or-miss,** hit-and-miss; deficient, botched

**half-baked** ADJS **premature,** unpremeditated, unmeditated, ill-considered, **half-cocked** <nonformal>, immature, undeveloped, unjelled, uncrystallized, not firm; **precocious, forward, advanced,** far ahead, born before one's time

**halfhearted** ADJS **indifferent,** zealless, perfunctory, fervorless; **cool, cold**; tepid, **lukewarm,** Laodicean; neither hot nor cold, neither one thing nor the other

**half-truth** NOUNS exaggeration; stretching of the truth, slight stretching, white lie, little white lie

**halfway** ADJS 1 **middle, medial, intermediate,** intermediary; equidistant, midway, equatorial; partly, partial
ADVS 2 **midway, in the middle,** betwixt and between <nonformal>, halfway in the middle <nonformal>; plump *or* smack *or* slap- *or* smack-dab in the middle <nonformal>; half-and-half, neither here nor there, *mezzo-mezzo* <Ital>

**half-wit** NOUNS **stupid person, dolt,** dunce, clod, Boeotian, **dullard,** *niais* <Fr>, donkey, yahoo, thickwit, dope, **nitwit,** dimwit, lamebrain, putz, lightweight, witling

**hall** NOUNS 1 assembly hall, exhibition hall, convention hall; gallery; meetinghouse, meeting room; **auditorium; concert hall; theater,** music hall; dance hall; ballroom, grand ballroom
2 **corridor,** hallway; passage, **passageway; gallery,** loggia; arcade, colonnade, pergola, cloister, peristyle

**hallelujah** NOUNS hosanna, alleluia, paean, paean *or* chorus of cheers

**hallmark** NOUNS **sign,** telltale sign, sure sign, tip-off <nonformal>, **index,** indicant, **indicator,** signal <old>, measure; **symptom;** note, keynote, **mark,** earmark, badge, device, banner, stamp, signature, sigil, seal, trait, **characteristic,** character, peculiarity, idiosyncrasy, **property,** differentia

**hallow** VERBS **sanctify; purify,** cleanse, wash one's sins away; **bless**; **glorify,** exalt, ensky; **consecrate,** dedicate, devote, set apart; **beatify,** saint, canonize; enshrine

**hallucinate** VERBS **go on a trip** *and* **blow one's mind** <both nonformal>, freak out <nonformal>; expand one's consciousness

**hallucinogen** NOUNS **psychoactive drug, psychedelic,** psychedelic drug, psychoactive drug, psychoactive chemical *or* psychochemical, psychotropic drug, psychotomimetic drug, mind-altering drug, mind-expanding drug, mind-blowing drug

**halo** NOUNS nimbus, aura, **aureole,** circle, ring, glory; **rainbow,** solar halo, lunar halo, ring around the sun *or* moon; **illustriousness, luster,** brilliance *or* brilliancy, radiance, splendor, resplendence *or* resplendency, refulgence *or* refulgency, refulgentness, **glory,** blaze of glory

**halt** VERBS 1 **put a stop to, call a halt to,** get it over with, blow the whistle on <nonformal>, **put an end to**, put paid to <Brit nonformal>, call off the dogs <nonformal>; **stop,** stay, arrest, check, flag down, wave down; block, brake, dam, stem, stem the tide *or* current; pull up, draw rein, put on the brakes, hit the

brake pedal; **bring to a stand** *or* **standstill,** bring to a close *or* halt, bring up short, **stop dead** *or* dead in one's tracks, set one back on his heels, stop cold, stop short, cut short, check in full career
ADJS 2 **crippled,** game <nonformal>, bad, handicapped, **lame,** halting, hobbling, limping; **disabled, incapacitated**

**halve** VERBS **bisect,** divide in half *or* by two, transect, subdivide; cleave, fission, **divide** *or* split *or* **cut in two,** share and share alike, go halfers *or* go Dutch <both nonformal>, **dichotomize;** bifurcate, fork, ramify, branch

**ham** NOUNS ham actor <nonformal>; grimacer; **amateur radio operator,** ham operator <nonformal>, radio amateur

**hamlet** NOUNS **village;** country town, crossroads, wide place in the road

*a little one-eyed, blinking sort o' place*
THOMAS HARDY

**hammer** VERBS **attack, assault,** batter, savage, mug, maul; plug away *or* along <nonformal>, hammer away, pound away, struggle along, struggle on, work away; drum, beat, pound; drum into, say over and over

**hamper** VERBS **impede, cramp,** embarrass; trammel, entrammel, enmesh, entangle, ensnarl, entrap, entwine, involve, entoil, toil, net, lime, tangle, snarl; fetter, shackle; **handcuff,** tie one's hands; **encumber,** cumber, **burden,** lumber, **saddle with,** weigh *or* weight down, press down; hang like a millstone round one's neck; **handicap,** put at a disadvantage

**hamstring** VERBS **cripple, lame,** cripple, maim; hobble; wing; emasculate, castrate; incapacitate, **disable**

**hand** NOUNS **worker, laborer, toiler,** moiler; employee, servant; workhand

**handbook** NOUNS **manual,** enchiridion, vade mecum, gradus, how-to book <nonformal>; nature book, field guide; travel book, **guidebook,** gazetteer, reference book

**handcuff** VERBS **hamper, impede, cramp,** embarrass; fetter, shackle; tie one's hands

**handful** NOUNS 1 **a few,** too few, mere *or* piddling *or* piddly few, only a few, **small number,** limited *or* piddling *or* piddly number, not enough to count *or* matter, not enough to shake a stick at, **scattering,** sprinkling, trickle
2 **tough proposition** *and* tough one *and* toughie <all nonformal>, large *or* tall order <nonformal>; **uphill work** *or* **going,** rough go <nonformal>, **heavy sledding,** hard pull <nonformal>; bitch <nonformal>; all one can manage

**handicap** NOUNS 1 **impediment,** embarrassment, hamper; encumbrance, cumbrance; **trouble,** difficulty; disadvantage, inconvenience, penalty; white elephant; **burden,** imposition, onus, cross, weight, deadweight, ball and chain, millstone around one's neck; disability
VERBS 2 **penalize,** put *or* impose *or* inflict a penalty *or* sanctions on; **punish**; put at a disadvantage; **encumber,** cumber, **burden,** lumber, **saddle with,** weigh *or* weight down, press down

**handicraft** NOUNS **craft, manual art,** industrial art, artisan work, craftwork, artisanship; woodcraft, woodwork, metalcraft, stonecraft; handiwork, handwork, crafting

**handkerchief** NOUNS headcloth, **kerchief,** coverchief

**handle** NOUNS 1 **hold,** grip, grasp, haft, helve; **name, moniker** <nonformal>; **label, tag; epithet,** byword; **title, honorific**
VERBS 2 **touch, finger,** pass *or* run the fingers over, feel with the fingertips, thumb; palm, paw
3 **manipulate,** wield; **deal with,** cope with, conduct, **manage; employ,** practice, ply, work, manage, operate
4 **deal in,** trade in, traffic in, carry, be in; market, merchandise, **sell,** retail, wholesale, job

**handmade** ADJS **made,** man-made; **homemade,** homespun, handcrafted, handicrafted, self-made, DIY *or* do it yourself; **custom-made,** custom-built, made to order, bespoke

**hand-me-down** ADJS **secondhand, used,** worn, previously owned, unnew, not new, pawed-over; reach-me-down <nonformal>

**handout** NOUNS **press release,** release, bulletin, official bulletin, notice; **leaflet,** leaf, folder, handbill, bill, flier, throwaway, **circular,** broadside
2 alms, pittance, **charity,** dole, alms fee, widow's mite; Peter's pence; **offering,** offertory, votive offering

**handsome** ADJS 1 **generous, munificent,** large, princely; **unsparing, unstinting,** stintless, unstinted; **openhanded,** free-handed, open; **giving**
2 **attractive**, pulchritudinous, **lovely, graceful,** gracile; elegant; aesthetically appealing; **cute;** pretty as a picture; tall, dark and handsome

**handwriting** NOUNS **hand, script,** fist <nonformal>, chirography, **calligraphy,** autography; **manuscript; autograph,** holograph; **penmanship,** penscript, pencraft; stylography

**handy** ADJS **convenient; available,** accessible, **ready, at hand,** to hand, **on hand,** on tap, on deck <nonformal>, on call, at one's call *or* beck and call, at one's elbow, at one's fingertips, just around the corner, at one's disposal; versatile, adaptable, all-around <nonformal>, of all work; crude but effective, quick and dirty <nonformal>

**hang** NOUNS 1 **knack, art, trick,** way; **touch,** feel
VERBS 2 hang down, fall; **depend,** pend; **dangle,** swing, flap, flop <nonformal>; flow, drape, cascade; **droop,** lop; nod, weep; **sag,** swag, bag; **trail, drag, draggle,** drabble, daggle
3 hang by the neck; **string up** *and* scrag *and* stretch <all nonformal>; gibbet, noose, neck, bring to the gallows; **lynch;** hang, draw, and quarter
4 **depend,** all depend, be contingent *or* conditional on, hang on *or* upon; **hang in the balance,** be touch and go, tremble in the balance, **hang in suspense; hang by a thread,** cliffhang, hang by a hair, hang by the eyelids

**hangar** NOUNS housing, dock, airdock, shed, airship shed; mooring mast

**hanger-on** NOUNS **adherent,** dangler, appendage, **dependent, satellite, follower,** cohort, retainer, servant, man, shadow, tagtail, **henchman,** heeler <nonformal>; camp follower, groupy <nonformal>

**hang in** VERBS **persist, persevere,** keep at it, stick it out, stick to it, stick with it, never say die, see it through, hang tough *and* not know when one is licked <both nonformal>; survive, make out, manage, get along, get on, eke out an existence, keep the even tenor of one's way; go on with the show <nonformal>, press on

**hanging** NOUNS 1 **pendency,** pendulousness *or* pendulosity, pensileness *or* pensility; **suspension,** dangling *or* danglement, suspense, dependence *or* dependency
2 **screen,** shroud, shield, veil, pall, mantle, curtain, drape, drapery
3 the gallows, the rope *or* noose; summary execution; **lynching,** necktie party *or* sociable <nonformal>, vigilanteism, vigilante justice; the necklace
ADJS 4 **pendent,** pendulous, pendulant, pendular, penduline, pensile; **suspended,** hung; pending, depending, dependent; **dangling,** swinging, falling loosely

**hangman** NOUNS **executioner,** executionist, deathsman <old>; **lyncher**

**hang on** VERBS **keep alive,** keep body and soul together, endure, survive, persist, last, last out, hang in <nonformal>, cheat death; **stay with it, hold on,** hold fast, hang on like a bulldog *or* leech, **stick to one's guns;** not give up, **never say die,** not give up the ship, not strike one's colors; **stay it out, stick out, hold out;** hold up, last out, **bear up,** stand up; stay the distance *or* the course; brazen it out

**hangout** NOUNS **resort, haunt,** purlieu, **stamping ground** <nonformal>; gathering place, meeting place, clubhouse, club

**hang out** VERBS 1 **frequent, haunt,** resort to, hang *and* hang around *and* hang about <all nonformal>
2 **be manifest,** be there for all to see, make an appearance, be no secret *or* revelation, **surface,** lie on the surface, be seen with half an eye; stand out, stick out, stick out a mile, stick out like a sore thumb

**hang tough** VERBS **remain firm, stand fast** *or* **firm, hold out,** hold fast, get tough <nonformal>, **take one's stand,** set one's back against the wall, **stand** *or* **hold one's ground,** keep one's footing, hold one's own, hang in *and* hang in there <both nonformal>, dig in, dig one's heels in; **stick to one's guns,** stick, stick with it, stick fast, stick to one's colors, adhere to one's principles

**hang-up** NOUNS 1 **delay,** stoppage, jam *and* logjam <both nonformal>, obstruction, tie-up *and* bind <both nonformal>, **block,** blockage
2 **obsession,** prepossession, preoccupation, **fixation,** complex, fascination; hypercathexis

**hankering** NOUNS 1 **yearning, yen** <nonformal>; **longing,** desiderium, **pining,** aching
ADJS 2 **wistful,** wishful; **longing,** yearning, yearnful, languishing, pining

**hanky-panky** NOUNS **affair,** affair of the heart, **amour, romance,** romantic tie *or* bond, something between, thing <nonformal>, liaison, entanglement, intrigue; **dalliance,** amorous play, the love game, flirtation, lollygagging <nonformal>

**haphazard** ADJS **slipshod,** sloppy *and* **messy** *and* half-assed <all nonformal>; **promiscuous;** deficient, botched; **irregular,** desultory, **erratic,** sporadic, spasmodic, fitful, indiscriminate, casual, frivolous, capricious, random, hit-or-miss, vague, dispersed, wandering, planless, undirected, **aimless,** straggling, straggly

**hapless** ADJS **unfortunate, unlucky, unprovidential,** unblessed, **unprosperous,** sad, unhappy, luckless; **out of luck,** short of luck; **down on one's luck** <nonformal>, badly *or* ill off, down in the world, in adverse circumstances

**happen** VERBS **occur,** hap, eventuate, **take place,** come *or* go down <nonformal>, go on, **transpire,** be realized, come, **come off** <nonformal>, **come about,** come true, **come to pass,** pass, pass off, go off, fall, **befall,** betide; fall to one's lot, be one's fate

**happening** NOUNS 1 **event,** occurrence, incident, episode, experience, adventure, hap, happenstance, **phenomenon,** fact, matter of fact, reality, particular, circumstance, **occasion,** turn of events
ADJS 2 **occurring, current, actual,** passing, taking place, on, **going on,** ongoing <nonformal>, **prevalent, prevailing,** that is, that applies, in the wind, afloat, afoot, under way

**happy** ADJS **glad, joyful, joyous,** flushed with joy, radiant, beaming, glowing, starry-eyed, sparkling, laughing, smiling, smirking, smirky, chirping, purring, singing, dancing, leaping, capering, **cheerful, gay**; **blissful;** happy as a lark, happy as a king, happy as the day is long, happy as a pig in shit <nonformal>

**happy-go-lucky** ADJS **improvident, prodigal,** unproviding; **thriftless, unthrifty,** uneconomical; grasshopper; **shiftless, feckless, thoughtless, heedless**

**hara-kiri** NOUNS **disembowelment,** ritual suicide, *seppuku* <Jap>, suttee, sutteeism; **suicide,** autocide, self-murder, self-homicide, self-destruction, death by one's own hand, felo-de-se, self-immolation, self-sacrifice; car of Jagannath *or* Juggernaut

**harangue** NOUNS 1 **speech,** speeching, speechification <nonformal>, **talk, oration, address,** declamation; **tirade,** screed, **diatribe,** jeremiad, philippic, invective; peroration
VERBS 2 **declaim,** hold forth, **orate,** spout <nonformal>, spiel <nonformal>, mouth; **rant,** tub-thump, perorate, rodomontade; demagogue, rabble-rouse

**harass** VERBS harry, drive up the wall <nonformal>, **hound,** dog, nag, nudzh <nonformal>, **persecute; heckle,** pick *or* prod at, rub it in *and* rub one's nose in it <both nonformal>, badger, hector, bait, bullyrag, worry, worry at, nip at the heels of, chivy, hardly give one time to breathe, make one's life miserable, keep on at; **bug** <nonformal>, be on the back of *and* be at *and* ride <all nonformal>, **pester, tease, needle,** devil, get after *or* get on <nonformal>, **bedevil, pick on** <nonformal>, give a bad time to <nonformal>; **plague,** beset, beleaguer

**harbor** NOUNS **haven, port, seaport,** port of call, free port, treaty port, home port; hoverport; harborage, **anchorage,** anchorage ground, protected anchorage, moorage, moorings; **roadstead,** road, roads; berth, slip; **dock,** dockage, marina, basin; dry dock; shipyard, dockyard; **wharf, pier,** quay

**hard** ADJS 1 **hardened,** case-hardened, **obdurate,** inured, indurated; **callous,** calloused, **seared; hardhearted,** heartless; **shameless,** lost to shame, blind to virtue, lost to all sense of honor, conscienceless, unblushing, **brazen; difficult,** troublesome, troublous, trying, rigorous, stressful; wretched, miserable; **solid,** lacking give, **tough**; resistive, resistant, steely, steellike, iron-hard, ironlike
2 <comparisons> stone, rock, adamant, granite, flint, marble, diamond; steel, iron, nails; concrete, cement; brick; oak, heart of oak; bone

**hard-boiled** ADJS **firm, obdurate,** tough, **hard,** hard-set, hard-mouthed, hard-bitten, hard-nosed <nonformal>, hard as nails

**hard-core** ADJS **unyielding, unbending, inflexible, hard, hard-line,** inelastic, impliable, ungiving, **firm, stiff, rigid,** rigorous, stuffy; rock-ribbed, rock-hard, rock-like; **immovable,** not to be moved; **uncompromising,** intransigent, irreconcilable, hard-shell <nonformal>; **fanatic, zealous,** totally committed, hard-line, ardent, passionate

**harden** VERBS indurate, stiffen, work-harden, firm, **toughen**; **callous; temper,** anneal, oil-temper, heat-temper, **case-harden,** steel; season; **petrify,** fossilize; lithify; vitrify; calcify; ossify; cornify, hornify

**hardened** ADJS **hard,** steeled, case-hardened, **obdurate,** inured, indurated, **toughened,** tempered, annealed; seasoned; **callous,** calloused, **seared; hardhearted,** heartless; **shameless,** lost to shame, blind to virtue, lost to all sense of honor, conscienceless, unblushing, **brazen**

**hard feelings** NOUNS **animosity,** animus; **ill will,** ill feeling, bitter feeling, no love lost; **bad blood,** ill blood, feud, blood feud, vendetta; **bitterness,** sourness, soreness, **rancor,** acrimony, virulence, venom, vitriol

**hard hat** NOUNS **patriot; chauvinist,** chauvin, **jingo,** jingoist; patrioteer <nonformal>, flag waver, superpatriot, hundred-percenter, hundred-percent American; hawk; **helmet,** crash helmet

**hardheaded** ADJS **obstinate,** stubborn, pertinacious, restive; willful, self-willed, strong-willed, headstrong, strong-headed, *entêté* <Fr>; **dogged,** bull-dogged, **tenacious,** persevering; **bull-headed,** bulletheaded, **pigheaded, mulish** <nonformal>, stubborn as a mule; set, **set in one's ways,** case-hardened, stiff-necked; balky, balking; unregenerate, uncooperative; dogmatic, opinionated, **sophisticated, wise,** practical, realistic, tough-minded; nobody's fool, not born yesterday, nobody's sucker *or* patsy <nonformal>

**hardhearted** ADJS **callous, calloused, insensitive,** Philistine; **thick-skinned,** pachydermatous; **hard, hardened,** coarsened, brutalized, indurated, stony, stony-hearted, flinthearted, flinty, steely, impervious, inured, armored *or* steeled against, as hard as nails

**hard-line** ADJS **unyielding, unbending,** inflexible, inelastic, ungiving, firm, stiff, rigid, rigorous; rock-ribbed, rock-hard, rock-like; **adamant,** adamantine; **immovable,** not to be moved; **uncompromising,** intransigent, irreconcilable, hard-shell *and* hard-core <both nonformal>; authoritarian

**hard-nosed** ADJS **obdurate,** tough, **hard,** hard-set, hard-mouthed, hard-bitten, hard-boiled <nonformal>

**hard-pressed** ADJS **straitened,** reduced to dire straits, in desperate straits, **pinched,** sore *or* sorely pressed, **hard up** <nonformal>, **up against it** <nonformal>; **desperate,** at the end of one's rope *or* tether; **hurried, rushed,** pushed, pressed, crowded, **pressed for time**

**hard sell** NOUNS **persuasion,** suasion; exhortation, hortation, preaching, preachment; **selling,** sales talk, salesmanship, high pressure, huckstering; jawboning *and* arm-twisting <both nonformal>; **lobbying; coaxing,** wheedling, working on <nonformal>, cajolery, cajolement, conning, snow job *and* smoke and mirrors <both nonformal>

**hardworking** ADJS **industrious,** assiduous, diligent, sedulous, laborious; unremitting, unsparing, relentless, zealous, ardent, fervent, vehement; never idle; tireless, unwearied, unflagging, indefatigable

**hardy** ADJS **hale, robust,** robustious, robustuous, vital, **vigorous, strong,** strong as a horse *or* an ox, bionic <nonformal>, stalwart, stout, sturdy, **rugged,** rude, lusty, bouncing; **fit,** in condition *or* shape

**harebrained** ADJS **capricious, whimsical,** freakish, vagarious; **fanciful, notional,** fantastic *or* fantastical, maggoty, **crotchety,** kinky, cranky, flaky <nonformal>, quirky; **foolhardy,** madcap, **wild,** daredevil; **scatterbrained,** rattlebrained, rattleheaded, rattlepated, scramblebrained, featherbrained, featherheaded; **witless,** empty-headed

**harem** NOUNS **seraglio,** serai, gynaeceum; zenana, purdah

**harlot** NOUNS **prostitute, whore,** *fille de joie* <Fr>, call girl *and* B-girl <both nonformal>, **scarlet woman,** unfortunate woman, painted woman, fallen woman, erring sister, **streetwalker,** hustler *and* **hooker** <both nonformal>, stew, meretrix

**harm** NOUNS 1 **impairment,** damage,

injury, mischief, scathe, **hurt, detriment,** loss, weakening, sickening; **worsening,** disimprovement; disablement, incapacitation; encroachment, inroad, infringement; evil
VERBS 2 **impair, damage,** endamage, injure, hurt, irritate; disadvantage; work evil, do ill; **injure,** scathe, wound, **damage; wrong,** do wrong, do wrong by, aggrieve, do evil, do a mischief, do an ill office to; **molest,** afflict; lay a hand on; **abuse,** bash <nonformal>, batter, outrage, violate, maltreat, mistreat

**harmful** ADJS **hurtful,** scatheful, **baneful,** baleful, distressing, **injurious, damaging, detrimental,** deleterious, counterproductive, **pernicious,** mischievous; **malignant,** malign, malevolent, malefic, vicious; prejudicial, disadvantageous, disserviceable; corruptive, corrupting, corrosive, corroding; deadly, lethal; ominous

**harmless** ADJS hurtless, unhurtful; well-meaning, well-meant; **uninjurious,** undamaging, **innocuous,** innoxious, innocent; inoffensive; nonmalignant, **benign**

**harmonious** ADJS **in accord, in harmony,** congruous, congruent, in tune, attuned, agreeing, in concert, amicable; frictionless; **sympathetic,** simpatico <nonformal>, empathic, empathetic, **understanding; like-minded,** akin, of the same mind, of one mind, at one, united, together; concordant, corresponding; agreeable, congenial, **compatible; peaceful**

**harmonize** VERBS **reconcile, bring to terms, bring together,** reunite, heal the breach; bring about a détente; restore harmony, put in tune; **iron** *or* **sort out,** adjust, settle, compose, accommodate, arrange matters, settle differences, resolve, compromise; **patch things up,** fix up <nonformal>, patch up a friendship *or* quarrel; **agree,** accord, concur, have no problem with, go along with <nonformal>, **cooperate, correspond, conform,** coincide, parallel, intersect, overlap, **match,** tally, hit, register, lock, interlock, check <nonformal>, square, dovetail, jibe <nonformal>

**harmony** NOUNS **cooperation, collaboration,** concurrence, synergy, synergism; **consensus, commonality; community,** concordance, concord, fellowship, fellow feeling, solidarity, concert, **teamwork;** pulling *or* working together, communal *or* community activity, joining of forces, pooling, pooling of resources, joining of hands; **accord,** accordance, **rapport;** good vibrations <nonformal>, good vibes <nonformal>, good karma; **proportion,** symmetry, **balance,** equilibrium, order, orderedness, measure, measuredness, concinnity; **euphony,** sweetness, beauty

**harness** NOUNS 1 caparison, trappings, **tack,** tackle; panoply
VERBS 2 **yoke, hitch up,** hook up; harness up; halter, bridle; saddle; tether, fetter

**harp on** VERBS **harp upon, dwell on** *or* **upon,** harp upon one *or* the same string, play *or* sing the same old song *or* tune, play the same broken record, beat a dead horse, have on the brain, constantly recur *or* revert to, labor, belabor, hammer away at, always trot out, never hear the last of; **thrash** *or* **thresh over,** cover the same ground, go over again and again, go over and over

**harried** ADJS **tormented,** plagued, harassed, dogged, hounded, persecuted, beset; nipped at, worried, chivied, **heckled,** badgered, hectored, baited, bullyragged, ragged, **pestered,** teased, needled, deviled, bedeviled, picked on <nonformal>, **bugged** <nonformal>

**harrowing** ADJS **agonizing,** excruciating, racking, rending, desolating, consuming; **tormenting,** torturous; **heartbreaking,** heartrending, heartsickening

**harsh** ADJS 1 fierce, **rigorous,** severe, rough, stringent, astringent, strident, **sharp, keen,** sharpish, incisive, trenchant, **cutting,** biting, stinging, **scathing,** stabbing, **piercing, poignant,** penetrating, edged, double-edged; **discordant,** strident, shrill, raucous
2 **oppressive, burdensome, crushing,** trying, onerous, heavy, weighty; wearing, wearying, exhausting; overburdensome, tyrannous, grinding; **heartless,** hard, hard as nails, steely, flinty, savage, **cruel**

**harvest** NOUNS 1 **yield, output,** make, production; **proceeds,** produce, product; **crop,** fruit, vintage, bearing; second crop, aftermath; bumper crop; harvesting, **reaping, gleaning,** gathering, cutting
VERBS 2 **reap,** crop, **glean, gather,** gather in, bring in, get in the harvest,

reap and carry; **pick,** pluck; dig, grabble <S US>; mow, cut

**has-been** NOUNS back number <nonformal>; dodo *and* old dodo <both nonformal>; fossil *and* antique *and* relic <all nonformal>; **mossback** <nonformal>, antediluvian; old liner, old believer, conservative, hard-shell, traditionalist, reactionary; **fogy, old fogy,** regular old fogy, **fud** *and* **fuddy-duddy** <both nonformal>

**hash** NOUNS **medley, miscellany,** mélange, pastiche, mixed bag, ragbag, jumble, mingle-mangle, **mix,** mishmash, can of worms <nonformal>, dog's breakfast <Can nonformal>, mare's nest, rat's nest, patchwork, gallimaufry, salmagundi, **potpourri,** everything but the kitchen sink <nonformal>

**hashish** NOUNS <nonformal> black hash, black Russian, hash

**hassle** NOUNS 1 **commotion,** hubbub, Babel, tumult, turmoil, uproar, racket, riot, **disturbance, rumpus** <nonformal>, ruckus *and* ruction <both nonformal>, **fracas,** shindy <nonformal>, rampage; **ado,** to-do <nonformal>, trouble, bother, pother, stir <nonformal>; **contention,** wrangling, bickering, hubbub, bicker, set-to <nonformal>, rhubarb <nonformal>
VERBS 2 **trouble, worry,** give one gray hair, plague, harass, bother, pick on *and* pick at <all nonformal>, bug <nonformal>; **contend,** contest, spar, bicker, wrangle

**haste** NOUNS **hurry,** scurry, rush, race, dash, drive, scuttle, scamper, **scramble,** hustle <nonformal>, **bustle,** flutter, **flurry,** hurry-scurry, helter-skelter; no time to be lost; **hastiness,** hurriedness, overeagerness, overzealousness, overenthusiasm

**hasty** ADJS **hurried,** festinate, **quick,** flying, **expeditious,** prompt; quick-and-dirty <nonformal>, **immediate,** instant, on the spot; onrushing, swift, speedy; **urgent;** furious, feverish; slap-bang, slapdash, **cursory,** passing, cosmetic, snap <nonformal>, superficial; spur-of-the-moment, last-minute

**hat** NOUNS **headdress,** headgear, headwear, headpiece, **chapeau, cap;** lid <nonformal>

**hatch** VERBS **be born,** have birth, come forth, issue forth, see the laight of day, come into the world; **breed,** engenger, beget, spawn, give rise to

**hatchet man** NOUNS **killer,** slayer; **disparager,** depreciator, decrier, detractor, basher *and* trasher <both nonformal>, belittler, debunker, deflater, slighter, derogator, **knocker** <nonformal>, caustic critic; **slanderer,** libeler, defamer, backbiter; calumniator, traducer; **muckraker, mudslinger,** social critic

**hate** NOUNS 1 **hatred;** dislike; **detestation,** abhorrence, aversion, antipathy, repugnance, **loathing,** execration, **abomination,** odium; **spite,** spitefulness, despite, despitefulness, **malice, malevolence,** malignity; vials of hate *or* wrath; scorn, despising, **contempt**
VERBS 2 **detest,** loathe, abhor, execrate, abominate, hold in abomination, take an aversion to, shudder at, utterly detest, be death on, not stand, not stand the sight of, not stomach; scorn, **despise**

**hateful** ADJS **loathsome,** detestable; despiteful; unlikable; **contemptible; malicious,** maleficent, malefic; **malignant,** malign; **mean** *and* ornery *and* cussed *and* bitchy <all nonformal>, nasty, baleful, beneath contempt, invidious; **wicked,** iniquitous; **harmful,** noxious

**hatred** NOUNS **hate;** dislike; **detestation,** abhorrence, aversion, antipathy, repugnance, **loathing,** execration, **abomination,** odium; **spite,** spitefulness, malice, **malevolence,** malignity; vials of hate *or* wrath; scorn, despising, **contempt**

**haughty** ADJS **arrogant,** overbearing, superior, domineering, proud; high-flown, high-falutin *and* high-faluting <both nonformal>; **stuck-up** *and* **uppish** *and* uppity *and* **upstage** <all nonformal>; **hoity-toity,** big, big as you please, six feet above contradiction; on one's high horse; **condescending,** patronizing, *de haut en bas* <Fr>

**haul** NOUNS 1 **booty,** spoil, spoils, loot, swag <nonformal>, ill-gotten gains, **plunder,** prize, take, pickings, stealings, stolen goods, hot goods *or* items <nonformal>; **boodle** *and* squeeze *and* **graft** <all nonformal>
VERBS 2 **strain, pull,** tug, heave; strain the muscles, strain every nerve *or* every nerve and sinew; put one's back into it <nonformal>; sweat blood; take on too much, spread oneself too thin, overexert, overstrain, overtax, overextend

**haunt** NOUNS 1 **hangout** <nonformal>,

**stamping ground** <nonformal>; gathering place, rallying point, meeting place, clubhouse, club
VERBS 2 **frequent,** hang *and* hang around *and* hang about *and* hang out <all nonformal>
3 **worry,** upset, vex, fret, agitate, get to <nonformal>, **torment,** dog, hound, plague, persecute, beset

**haunted** ADJS 1 **worried,** tormented, dogged, hounded, persecuted, beset, plagued; worried sick, worried to a frazzle, worried stiff <nonformal>; unable to forget, obsessed, nagged, rankled
2 spooked *and* spooky <both nonformal>, spirit-haunted, ghost-haunted, specter-haunted; **possessed,** ghost-ridden

**haunting** ADJS **unforgettable,** never to be forgotten, never to be erased from the mind, **indelible,** indelibly impressed on the mind, fixed in the mind; persistent, recurrent, nagging, plaguing, rankling, festering; obsessing, obsessive

**haven** NOUNS **refuge, sanctuary,** safehold, asylum, **port,** harborage, **harbor;** harbor of refuge, port in a storm, snug harbor, safe haven; game sanctuary, bird sanctuary, preserve, forest preserve, game preserve; stronghold

**havoc** NOUNS **detriment;** destruction; despoliation; mischief; outrage, atrocity

**hawk** NOUNS 1 **militarist, warmonger,** war dog *or* hound, war hawk
VERBS 2 **vend,** dispense, **peddle, huckster**

**haze** NOUNS 1 gauze, film; vapor; confusion
VERBS 2 **banter,** twit, chaff, rally, joke, jest, jape, **tease**

**hazy** ADJS **indistinct, unclear,** unplain, **indefinite,** undefined, ill-defined, **blurred, blurry,** bleared, bleary, blear, **fuzzy,** misty, filmy, foggy; **murky,** cloudy, foggy, fogbound, nebulous

**head** NOUNS 1 **supervisor,** foreman, monitor, headman, overman, **boss,** chief, taskmaster
2 **brain**, gray matter, pate *and* sconce *and* noddle <all nonformal>; noodle *or* noggin *or* bean *or* upper story <all nonformal>; **intelligence, intellect,** mentality, consciousness
VERBS 3 **direct,** manage, regulate, conduct, carry on, handle, run <nonformal>; **control,** command, govern, boss *and* head up *and* pull the strings *and* mastermind *and* quarterback *and* call the signals <all nonformal>; head up, office, captain, skipper <nonformal>
ADJS 4 headmost, capital, chief, paramount, supreme, preeminent; **top-level,** highest level, top-echelon, top-flight, top-ranking, top-drawer <nonformal>; **principal,** premier, **leading, main,** flagship

**headache** NOUNS 1 cephalalgia, misery in the head <nonformal>; splitting headache, **sick headache, migraine,** megrim, hemicrania
2 **nuisance,** pest, bother, botheration <nonformal>, public nuisance, **trouble, problem,** pain <nonformal>, difficulty, hot potato <nonformal>; **pain in the neck** *or* **in the ass** <nonformal>

**head count** NOUNS **roll call,** muster, **census,** nose count <nonformal>, **poll,** questionnaire, returns, census report *or* returns

**headhunter** NOUNS executive search agency *or* firm; executive recruiter, executive recruitment consultant, executive development specialist; body snatcher *and* flesh peddler *and* talent scout <all nonformal>

**heading** NOUNS 1 **direction,** directionality; **line,** direction line, line of direction, point, quarter, **aim, way,** track, range, **bearing,** azimuth, compass reading, **course**
2 **caption,** title, head, superscription, rubric; **headline**

**headline** NOUNS 1 banner, banner head *or* line, streamer; **scarehead,** screamer; drop head, running head *or* title; **subhead, subheading**
VERBS 2 **star, feature** <nonformal>, bill, give top billing to

**headlong** ADJS 1 **reckless,** devil-may-care; careless; **impetuous,** hotheaded; **hasty,** hurried, overeager, overzealous, overenthusiastic; **furious,** desperate, mad, wild, wanton, harum-scarum <nonformal>; precipitate, **precipitous,** precipitant; **breakneck**
ADVS 2 **impulsively,** impetuously, hastily, suddenly, quickly, **precipitately,** recklessly, rashly

**headquarters** NOUNS **HQ,** central station, central office, main office, central administration, seat, base, **base of operations,** center of authority; general headquarters *or* **GHQ,** command post *or* **CP,** company headquarters

**head start** NOUNS **earliness,** early hour, time to spare; running start, ground floor, first crack, beginnings, first *or* early stage, very beginning, preliminaries; advance notice, lead time, a stitch in time, readiness, preparedness, preparation

**headstrong** ADJS **obstinate,** stubborn, pertinacious, restive; willful, self-willed, strong-willed, hardheaded, strong-headed, *entêté* <Fr>; bullheaded, bullet-headed, **pigheaded, mulish** <nonformal>, stubborn as a mule; **set in one's ways,** case-hardened, stiff-necked

**headway** NOUNS **improvement,** betterment, bettering, change for the better; melioration, amelioration; **progress,** progression; **advance,** advancement; **rise,** ascent, **lift, uplift,** uptick <nonformal>, upswing, uptrend, upbeat

**headwear** NOUNS **headdress,** headgear, headclothes, headtire; **millinery;** headpiece, chapeau, cap, **hat;** lid <nonformal>; headcloth, **kerchief,** coverchief

**heady** ADJS **exciting,** thrilling, stirring, moving, breathtaking, eye-popping <nonformal>; heart-stirring, heart-swelling, heart-expanding, soul-stirring, mind-blowing <nonformal>; **stimulating,** stimulative, stimulatory; exhilarating, intoxicating, maddening, ravishing; self-willed, willful, headstrong

**heal** VERBS 1 **cure,** work a cure, **remedy, restore to health,** heal up, knit up, bring round *or* around, pull round *or* around, give a new *or* fresh lease on life, make better, make well, fix up, pull through, set on one's feet *or* legs; snatch from the jaws of death
2 **heal over,** close up, scab over, cicatrize, granulate; heal *or* right itself; **knit, set**

**health** NOUNS **well-being; fitness,** health and fitness, physical fitness; bloom, flush, glow, rosiness; mental health, emotional health; physical condition; **wholesomeness,** propriety, regularity

**healthy** ADJS 1 enjoying health, **fine,** in health, in shape, in condition, **fit,** fit and fine; **in good health,** in the pink of condition, in mint condition, **in good** *or* **fine shape, in fine fettle,** bursting with health, full of life and vigor, feeling one's oats; eupeptic
2 <nonformal> **in the pink,** in fine whack, in fine *or* high feather, chipper, **fit as a fiddle;** alive and kicking, bright-eyed and bushy-tailed; full of beans *or* of piss and vinegar

**heap** NOUNS 1 **lot, lots,** deal, no end of, **good** *or* **great deal, considerable,** sight, **pile, stack,** loads, **raft, slew,** whole slew, spate, wad, **batch,** mess, mint, peck, pack, pot, **tidy sum,** quite a little; **oodles, gobs, scads**
VERBS 2 **pile,** pile on, stack, heap *or* pile *or* stack up; mound, hill, bank, bank up; rick; pyramid; drift

**hear** VERBS 1 catch, get <nonformal>, take in; **overhear; hear of,** hear tell of <nonformal>; get an earful <nonformal>, get wind of; have an ear for
2 **sit in judgment,** hold the scales, hold court; give a hearing to; **try**; **referee, umpire,** officiate; arbitrate

**hearing** NOUNS 1 sense of hearing, auditory *or* aural sense, ear; heeding, attention, hushed attention, rapt attention, eager attention; auscultation, aural examination, examination by ear; audibility, **earshot,** earreach, range, auditory range, reach, carrying distance, **sound of one's voice**
2 **audition,** tryout, call <all nonformal>, **audience, interview,** conference; attention, favorable attention, ear; **listening,** listening in; **eavesdropping,** wiretapping, electronic surveillance, bugging <nonformal>
3 **trial,** jury trial, trial by jury, trial at the bar, inquiry, inquisition, inquest, assize; court-martial; **examination,** cross-examination

**hearsay** NOUNS 1 **report, rumor,** flying rumor, unverified *or* unconfirmed report, *on-dit* <Fr>, **scuttlebutt** *and* latrine rumor <both nonformal>; **talk, whisper,** idea afloat, news stirring; common talk, town talk, **talk of the town,** topic of the day, *cause célèbre* <Fr>; **grapevine; canard,** roorback
ADJS 2 circumstantial, presumptive, nuncupative, cumulative, ex parte

**heart** NOUNS 1 **soul, spirit,** *esprit* <Fr>, **breast, bosom,** inmost heart *or* soul, heart of hearts, secret *or* inner recesses of the heart, secret places, heart's core, heartstrings, cockles of the heart, bottom of the heart, being, innermost being, core of one's being; viscera, pit of one's stomach, **gut** *or* guts <nonformal>; bones

2 **passion,** tender feeling *or* passion, **ardor,** ardency, fervor, flame; **regard,** admiration
3 **sum and substance,** stuff, material, matter, medium, building blocks, fabric; **gist,** soul, meat, nub; the nitty-gritty *and* the bottom line *and* the name of the game <all nonformal>, **core,** kernel, marrow, pith, sap, spirit, **essence,** quintessence

**heartache** NOUNS **wretchedness,** aching heart, heavy heart, bleeding heart, broken heart, agony of mind *or* spirit; suicidal despair, black night of the soul, **despondency,** despond

**heartbreaker** NOUNS **philanderer,** philander, woman chaser, **ladies' man;** man chaser; masher, lady-killer, wolf, skirt chaser, man *or* woman on the make *and* make-out artist <both nonformal>

**heartening** ADJS **cheering,** gladdening; **encouraging,** heartwarming; **inspiring,** inspiriting; **exhilarating,** animating, enlivening, invigorating; cheerful, cheery, glad, joyful

**heartfelt** ADJS **deep-felt,** deepgoing, from the heart; **deep, profound;** indelible; pervasive, pervading, absorbing; penetrating, penetrant, piercing; **poignant,** keen, sharp, acute

**hearth** NOUNS **home,** home sweet home; **fireside,** hearth and home, hearthstone, fireplace, *foyer* <Fr>, chimney corner, ingle, ingleside *or* inglenook; **household,** ménage; **homestead,** home place, home roof, roof, rooftree; paternal roof *or* domicile, family homestead, ancestral halls

**heartland** NOUNS the Middle West, Middle America; the Great Plains, the heartlands

**heartless** ADJS **unfeeling,** unnatural, unresponsive, insensitive, **cold,** cold of heart, coldhearted, **cold-blooded; hard,** hardened, hard of heart, hardhearted, stony-hearted, marble-hearted, flint-hearted; **callous,** calloused; obdurate, indurated; **unmerciful; shameless,** lost to shame, blind to virtue, lost to all sense of honor, conscienceless

**heartrending** ADJS **agonizing,** excruciating, harrowing, racking, rending, **desolating,** consuming; **heartsickening,** heartwounding, **pitiful,** pitiable, pathetic, piteous, touching, moving, affecting, grievous, doleful

**heartsick** ADJS **disconsolate,** inconsolable, unconsolable, comfortless, prostrate *or* prostrated, **forlorn; desolate,** *désolé* <Fr>; sick, **sick at heart,** soul-sick, heartsore

**heartstrings** NOUNS **heart, bosom,** inmost heart *or* soul, heart of hearts, secret *or* inner recesses of the heart, secret places, heart's core, cockles of the heart, bottom of the heart, being, innermost being, core of one's being

**heartthrob** NOUNS

<nonformal> **sweetie, honey,** honeybunch, honeypie, sweetie-pie, sweet patootie, tootsie, tootsy-wootsy, dearie, baby, dreamboat, poopsy, sugar, sugarbun, sweets

**heart-to-heart** NOUNS 1 **chat,** cozy chat, friendly chat *or* talk, **little talk,** coze, causerie, *tête-à-tête* <Fr>, **heart-to-heart talk;** pillow-talk, intimate discourse
ADJS 2 **candid, frank, sincere,** genuine, ingenuous, frankhearted; **open,** openhearted, transparent, open-faced; **unreserved,** unrestrained, unconstrained, unchecked; unguarded, uncalculating

**heartwarming** ADJS **cheering,** gladdening; **encouraging,** heartening; **inspiring,** inspiriting; **exhilarating,** animating, enlivening, invigorating; cheerful, cheery, glad, joyful

**hearty** ADJS **vigorous,** nervy, **lusty,** bouncing, full- *or* red-blooded; **active,** lively, living, animated, spirited, go-go <nonformal>, vivacious, brisk, bright-eyed and bushy-tailed <nonformal>, lusty, **robust,** enthusiastic, mettlesome, zesty, zestful, impetuous, spanking, smacking; **hale,** hale and hearty

**heat** NOUNS 1 **fever of excitement, fever pitch,** fever, fever heat, fire; sexual excitement, rut; **anger,** more heat than light <nonformal>; **hotness,** heatedness; **warmth,** warmness
VERBS 2 raise *or* increase the temperature, **warm,** warm up, fire, fire up, stoke up

**heated** ADJS **passionate, warm, hot,** red-hot, flaming, burning, glowing, fervent, fervid; **fiery,** inflamed, flaming, scorching, white-hot; **fanatic, zealous,** totally committed, hard-core, hard-line, ardent; **hotheaded**

**heathen** NOUNS 1 **unbeliever,** disbeliever,

nonbeliever; **atheist,** infidel, pagan; nullifidian, minimifidian; secularist
ADJS 2 **pagan, paganish,** paganistic; **heathenish; unbelieving,** disbelieving, faithless; **infidel,** infidelic; **atheistic,** atheist; nullifidian, minimifidian

**heat up** VERBS **incite, stir up,** work up, whip up; **inflame,** incense, **fire,** heat, impassion; lash into a fury *or* frenzy; feed the fire, fan the flame; **aggravate,** exacerbate, heat up, **provoke,** envenom, **embitter,** infuriate, madden

**heave** VERBS **throw,** fling, sling, pitch, toss, cast, hurl, chuck, peg <nonformal>, lob, shy, fire, burn, pepper <nonformal>, launch, dash, let fly, let go, let rip, let loose

**heaven** NOUNS 1 **utopia,** paradise, heaven on earth
2 **the heavens,** heaven, **sky, firmament;** vault, cope, vault *or* canopy of heaven, celestial sphere, starry heaven *or* heavens

*this majestical roof fretted with golden fire*
SHAKESPEARE

**Heaven** NOUNS **the hereafter,** the great hereafter, a better place, Paradise, Heaven, Elysian Fields; **the afterworld,** the otherworld, **the next world,** the world to come, life *or* world beyond the grave, **the beyond,** the great beyond, the unknown, the great unknown, eternal home; **afterlife, postexistence,** future state, **life to come,** life after death

*the good hereafter*
WHITTIER

**heavenly** ADJS 1 **blissful,** beatific, saintly, divine; sublime; paradisal, paradisiac, paradisiacal, paradisic, paradisical, empyreal *or* empyrean, Elysian; **sacred, holy,** numinous, **sacrosanct,** religious, spiritual, divine; out of sight *or* of this world <nonformal>
2 **glorious,** heavenly, divine, sublime; **resplendent,** splendorous *or* splendrous, splendiferous, **splendid,** resplendently beautiful; **brilliant,** bright, radiant, shining, beaming, glowing, blooming, abloom, sparkling, **dazzling; glamorous**

**heavy** NOUNS 1 **actor, villain,** antagonist, **bad guy** *or* black hat <both nonformal>; villainess
ADJS 2 **ponderous, massive,** massy, weighty, hefty <nonformal>, fat; **leaden,** heavy as lead; deadweight; overweight

**heavy-handed** ADJS **inelegant,** clumsy, clunky and klutzy <both nonformal>, heavy-footed, ham-handed, graceless, ungraceful, infelicitous, unfelicitous; **tasteless,** in bad taste, offensive to polite ears; indecorous, unseemly, uncourtly, undignified; **unpolished, unrefined**

**heckle** VERBS **harass,** harry, drive up the wall <nonformal>, **hound,** dog, nag, pick *or* prod at, rub it in *and* rub one's nose in it <both nonformal>, badger, hector, bait, bullyrag, worry, worry at, nip at the heels of, chivy, hardly give one time to breathe, make one's life miserable, **pester, tease, needle,** devil, get after *or* get on <nonformal>, **bedevil, pick on** <nonformal>, tweak the nose, pluck the beard, give a bad time to <nonformal>

**hectic** ADJS **overactive,** hyperactive, hyper <nonformal>; frenzied, frantic, frenetic; hyperkinetic

**hedge** NOUNS 1 **qualification, limitation, limiting, restriction,** circumscription, **modification,** hedging, hedging one's bets, cutting one's losses; setting conditions, conditionality, provisionality, circumstantiality
VERBS 2 **condition,** qualify, hedge about; pussyfoot <nonformal>, be *or* sit on the fence, beat around *or* about the bush, hem and haw, beg the question, tapdance <nonformal>, dance around, equivocate; provide a hedge, hedge one's bets, cut one's losses; keep something for a rainy day

**heed** VERBS **obey, mind, keep, observe,** listen *or* hearken to; **comply, conform,** walk in lockstep; stay in line *and* not get out of line *and* not get off base <all nonformal>, **toe the line** *or* mark, fall in, fall in line, obey the rules, follow the book, **do what one is told**

**heedless** ADJS **careless, unheeding, unheedful, disregardful,** disregardant, regardless, **unsolicitous, uncaring;** tactless, respectless, **thoughtless, unthinking, inconsiderate,** untactful, undiplomatic, mindless of, **unmindful,** forgetful, oblivious

**heft** NOUNS 1 **weight, heaviness, weight-**

**iness, ponderousness,** ponderosity, ponderability, leadenness, heftiness <nonformal>; body weight, avoirdupois <nonformal>, fatness, beef *and* beefiness <both nonformal>
VERBS 2 **weigh,** weight; **balance,** weigh in the balance, strike a balance, hold the scales, put on the scales, lay in the scales; **elevate, raise, rear,** escalate, up, boost *and* hike <both nonformal>; **erect, heighten, lift,** levitate, boost <nonformal>, **hoist,** heist <nonformal>, heave; raise up, rear up, lift up, hold up, set up

**hefty** ADJS **heavy, ponderous, massive,** massy, weighty, fat; **leaden,** heavy as lead; deadweight; heavyweight; overweight

**heifer** NOUNS **calf,** yearling, fatling, stirk <Brit>

**heights** NOUNS **elevation,** eminence, **rise,** raise, **uprise,** lift, rising ground, vantage point *or* ground; soaring *or* towering *or* Olympian heights, aerial heights, dizzy *or* dizzying heights; upmost *or* uppermost *or* utmost *or* extreme height; sky, stratosphere, ether, heaven *or* heavens; **zenith, apex, acme**

**heir** NOUNS heritor, inheritor, *heres* <L>; **heiress,** inheritress, inheritrix; coheir, joint heir, fellow heir, coparcener; **heir apparent,** apparent heir; **heir presumptive,** presumptive heir; statutory next of kin; **successor,** next in line

**heirloom** NOUNS **inheritance,** heritance <old>, heritage, patrimony, birthright, legacy, bequest, bequeathal; hereditament, corporeal *or* incorporeal hereditament; **heritable**

**heist** NOUNS

<nonformal> **stickup,** job, stickup job, bag job, boost, burn, knockover, **ripoff**

**held** ADJS **possessed, owned;** in seisin, in fee, in fee simple, **free and clear; own,** of one's own; **in one's possession, in hand,** in one's grip *or* grasp, at one's command *or* disposal; on hand, by one, in stock, in store; **believed,** credited, trusted, accepted; received, of belief; **obsessed, possessed,** prepossessed, **infatuated,** preoccupied, fixated, **hung up** <nonformal>, besotted, gripped; **fascinated, enthralled, rapt, spellbound,** charmed, enchanted, mesmerized, **hypnotized,** fixed, caught, riveted, **arrested,** switched on <nonformal>

**hell** NOUNS 1 **depths,** deeps, bowels, bowels of the earth; bottomless pit; dark *or* unknown *or* yawning *or* gaping depths, unfathomed deeps; **perdition, inferno,** the pit, **the bottomless pit,** the abyss, **nether world,** lower world, underworld, infernal regions, abode *or* world of the dead, abode of the damned, place of torment, the grave, shades below; **purgatory; limbo**

*a vast, unbottom'd, boundless pit*
ROBERT BURNS

2 **Hades** Sheol, Gehenna, Tophet, Abaddon, Naraka, jahannan, avichi, **perdition,** Pandemonium, **inferno,** the pit, **the bottomless pit,** the abyss

**hellcat** NOUNS 1 **daredevil,** devil, hellraiser, **madcap,** madbrain, wild man, hotspur, rantipole, harum-scarum *and* fire-eater <both nonformal>; **adventurer,** adventuress, adventurist; brazenface
2 **witch, hag, vixen,** hellhag, she-devil, virago, brimstone, termagant, grimalkin, Jezebel, beldam, she-wolf, tigress, wildcat, bitch-kitty <nonformal>, siren, fury

**hellish** ADJS **fearful,** fearsome, fear-inspiring, nightmarish; **scary,** scaring, chilling; demoniac *or* demoniacal, diabolic, diabolical, devilish, satanic, infernal; sulfurous, brimstone, fire-and-brimstone; chthonic, chthonian

**helm** NOUNS **control, grasp,** grip, hand, hands, iron hand, clutches; reins of government

**help** NOUNS 1 **aid,** assistance, support, succor, relief, comfort, ease, remedy; mutual help *or* assistance; **bailout** <nonformal>, **rescue; financial assistance;** pecuniary aid; scholarship, fellowship; **welfare,** public welfare, public assistance, relief, relief *or* welfare payments, welfare aid, dole, aid to dependent children
2 **staff,** personnel, employees, hired help, the help, **crew, gang,** men, force, servantry, retinue
VERBS 3 **aid, assist,** comfort, abet <old>, **succor,** relieve, **ease,** doctor, remedy; be of some help, put one's oar in <nonformal>; do good, do a world of

good, **benefit, avail**; **favor, befriend; give help,** render assistance, offer *or* proffer aid, come to the aid of, rush *or* fly to the assistance of, lend aid, **give** *or* **lend** *or* **bear a hand** *or* **helping hand,** stretch forth *or* hold out a helping hand; **give an assist, give a leg up** *or* lift *or* boost <nonformal>

**helper** NOUNS **assistant,** auxiliary, aider, aide, paraprofessional; **help,** helpmate, helpmeet; **servant, employee**

**helpful** ADJS **useful,** utile; **profitable,** salutary, good for, beneficial; remedial, therapeutic; serviceable, **useful**; **contributory,** contributing, conducive, **constructive, positive,** promotional

**helping** NOUNS 1 **serving,** service; **portion,** help; second helping; **course;** dish, plate; **portion,** share, interest, part, stake, stock, piece, bit, segment; **bite** *and* **cut** *and* **slice** *and* **chunk** *and* slice of the pie *or* melon *and* piece of the action <all nonformal>, **lot, allotment, end** <nonformal>, **proportion, percentage,** measure, quantum, **quota,** deal *or* dole <both old>, meed, moiety, mess
ADJS 2 assisting, serving; **assistant, auxiliary,** adjuvant, subservient, subsidiary, ancillary, accessory; ministerial, ministering, ministrant; fostering, nurtural; care, caring, care-giving; instrumental

**helpless** ADJS **defenseless, unprotected;** vulnerable, like a sitting duck <nonformal>, aidless, friendless, unfriended; fatherless, motherless; leaderless, guideless; **untenable,** pregnable, vulnerable

**helter-skelter** ADJS 1 **confused, chaotic,** anarchic, **muddled, jumbled,** scattered, higgledy-piggledy, hugger-mugger, skimble-skamble, in a mess; **mixed up, balled** *or* **bollixed up** <nonformal>, **screwed up** <nonformal>, mucked up <nonformal>, **fouled up** *and* fucked up *and* snafu <all nonformal>
ADVS 2 **in disorder, in disarray, in confusion,** Katy bar the door <nonformal>, in a jumble, in a tumble, in a muddle, in a mess; higgledy-piggledy, hugger-mugger, skimble-skamble, willy-nilly <nonformal>, all over, all over hell <nonformal>, **all over the place, all over the shop** <nonformal>

**hem** NOUNS **edging,** fringe, fimbriation, fimbria; selvage, list, welt; frill, frilling

**hemisphere** NOUNS **half,** moiety; semisphere, semicircle, **fifty percent;** half-and-half *and* fifty-fifty <both nonformal>

**hemmed-in** ADJS **restricted,** limited, confined; circumscribed, hedged in *or* about, boxed in; landlocked; **shut-in, enclosed,** closed-in; bound, immured, cloistered, pent-up, penned, cooped, mewed, walled- *or* hedged- *or* fenced-in, fenced, walled, paled, railed, barred

**hemorrhage** NOUNS 1 hemorrhea, **bleeding;** nosebleed; ecchymosis, petechia
VERBS 2 **bleed,** lose blood, **shed blood,** spill blood; bloody; ecchymose

**henchman** NOUNS cohort, hanger-on, buddy *and* sidekick <both nonformal>; heeler *and* **ward heeler** <both nonformal>; hanger-on, satellite, creature, lackey, flunky, stooge <nonformal>, jackal, minion, myrmidon

**henpeck** VERBS **nag,** niggle, **carp at, fuss at, fret at,** yap *or* **pick at** <nonformal>, peck at, nibble at, **pester, pick on** *and* pick at <all nonformal>, bug *and* hassle <nonformal>

**henpecked** ADJS **tied to one's apron strings,** on a string, on a leash, in leading strings; wimpish <nonformal>; milktoast *or* milquetoast, Caspar Milquetoast

**hep** ADJS

< nonformal> **hip,** on the beam, go-go, **with it,** into, really into, groovy; chic, clued-up, clued in, in the know, trendy

**herald** NOUNS 1 **harbinger,** forerunner, vaunt-courier; evangel, evangelist, bearer of glad tidings; herald angel, Gabriel, *buccinator* <L>
VERBS 2 **harbinger, forerun,** run before; speak of, announce, proclaim, preannounce; give notice, notify, talk about; usher in, **anticipate,** antedate, predate; **preexist**

**heraldry** NOUNS **pomp,** circumstance, pride, **state,** solemnity, formality; **pomp and circumstance;** armory, blazonry, sigillography, sphragistics

*trump and solemn heraldry*
COLERIDGE

**herbicide** NOUNS **poison,** defoliant, Agent Orange, paraquat, weed killer

**herculean** ADJS **arduous,** strenuous, toilsome, laborious, operose

**herd** NOUNS 1 **the masses,** *hoi polloi* <Gk>, the many, **the multitude,** the crowd, the horde, the million, the mass of the people, the great unnumbered, the great unwashed, **the vulgar** *or* **common herd**
VERBS **guide,** steer, drive, run <nonformal>; herd up, punch cattle, **shepherd,** ride herd on; wrangle, round up

**hereafter** NOUNS 1 **the future,** future, futurity, what is to come, imminence, subsequence, eventuality, aftertime, afteryears, **time to come,** years to come; **distant future,** remote *or* deep *or* far future; **by-and-by,** the sweet by-and-by <nonformal>
ADVS 2 in future, hereinafter, thereafter, **henceforth, henceforward** *or* henceforwards, thence, **thenceforth,** thenceforward *or* thenceforwards, over the long haul *or* short haul <nonformal>, from this time forward, from this day on *or* forward, from this point, from this *or* that time, from then on, **from here** *or* **now on, from now on in** <nonformal>, from here in *or* out <nonformal>, from this moment on

**the hereafter** NOUNS the afterworld, the afterlife, life after death; **destiny, fate,** doom, karma, kismet, what bodes *or* looms, what is fated *or* destined *or* doomed, what is written, what is in the books, the great hereafter, **the next world,** the world to come, life *or* world beyond the grave, **the beyond,** the great beyond, the unknown, the great unknown

**hereditary** ADJS patrimonial, **inherited, innate;** genetic, genic; bred in the bone, in the blood, running in the blood *or* race *or* strain, radical, rooted; patroclinous, matroclinous

**heredity** NOUNS **heritage, inheritance, birth;** patrocliny, matrocliny; endowment, inborn capacity *or* tendency *or* susceptibility *or* predisposition

**heresy** NOUNS false doctrine, **misbelief; fallacy, error;** heterogeneity, heterodoxy, unorthodoxy, **unconventionality**

**heritage** NOUNS **inheritance,** heritance <old>, patrimony, birthright, legacy, bequest, bequeathal

**hermaphrodite** NOUNS 1 **intersex,** sexintergrade, epicence; pseudohermaphrodite; androgyne, gynandroid; transsexual
ADJS 2 hermaphroditic, pseudohermaphrodite, pseudohermaphroditic, epicene, monoclinous; androgynous, androgynal, gynandrous, gynandrian

**hermit** NOUNS **recluse,** eremite, anchorite, anchoret; marabout; hermitess, anchoress; ascetic; stylite, pillarist, pillar saint

**hero** NOUNS **god, demigod,** phoenix; **heroine, goddess,** demigoddess; **idol,** popular idol, tin god *or* little tin god <nonformal>; popular hero, pop hero <nonformal>, folk hero, superhero; **star, superstar,** megastar, hot stuff <nonformal>; cult figure; **immortal;** brave, stalwart, man *or* woman of courage *or* mettle, **celebrity,** person of note *or* consequence, **notable, notability, luminary, great woman,** worthy, name, **big name,** figure, public figure, **somebody**

**heroic** ADJS **valorous,** gallant, intrepid, doughty, **hardy,** stalwart, stout, stouthearted, ironhearted, lionhearted, greathearted, bold-spirited, bold as a lion; herolike

**heroin** NOUNS

<nonformal> big H, boy, brown, caballo, crap, doojee, flea powder, garbage, H, hard stuff, henry, him, his, horse, hombre, jones, junk, mojo, P-funk, scag, schmeck, smack, white stuff

**heroism** NOUNS **courage,** courageousness, **nerve,** pluck, **bravery,** braveness, ballsiness *and* gutsiness *or* guttiness <all nonformal>, **boldness, valor,** valorousness, valiance, valiancy, **gallantry,** conspicuous gallantry, gallantry under fire *or* beyond the call of duty, gallantness, **intrepidity,** intrepidness, **prowess,** virtue; stoutheartedness, lionheartedness, greatheartedness; heroicalness

**hero worship** NOUNS overpraise, excessive praise, idolizing, idolatry, deification, apotheosis, adulation, lionizing

**hesitant** ADJS hesitating, pikerish; faltering; shilly-shallying; diffident, tentative, timid, cautious; scrupling, jibbing, sticking, straining, stickling; **tentative,** unprecipitate, cool; **deliberate**

**hesitate** VERBS **pause, falter, hang back,** hover; shilly-shally, hum and haw, **hem and haw;** wait to see how the cat jumps *or* the wind blows, scruple, jib, stick at, stickle, strain at; think twice about, stop to consider, ponder, wrinkle one's brow; pull back, drag one's feet; **flinch, shy**

away from, shy, back off <nonformal>; not face up to, hide one's head in the sand; **procrastinate,** be dilatory, let something slide, hang, hang back, hang fire

**heterogeneous** ADJS **various,** variant, varying, varied, multifarious, motley, assorted, variegated, diverse, divers, **diversified; conglomerate,** pluralistic, multiracial, multicultural, multiethnic, multinational, **miscellaneous**

**heterosexual** NOUNS **straight** *and* breeder <both nonformal>

**hex** NOUNS 1 **curse, malediction,** malison, damnation, denunciation, commination, imprecation, execration; blasphemy; anathema, fulmination, thundering, excommunication; ban, proscription; evil eye, *malocchio* <Ital>, whammy <nonformal>
2 **spell,** magic spell, **charm,** glamour, wanga; evil eye, *malocchio* <Ital>, whammy <nonformal>; jinx, curse
VERBS 3 bring bad luck; hoodoo *and* jinx *and* Jonah *and* put the jinx on <all nonformal>; put the evil eye on, whammy <nonformal>

**hiatus** NOUNS **interruption, suspension, break,** fissure, breach, gap, lacuna, caesura; **interval, pause,** interim, lull, cessation, letup <nonformal>, **intermission**

**hibernate** VERBS **lie idle, lie fallow;** aestivate, lie dormant; lie *or* lay off, charge *or* recharge one's batteries <nonformal>; have nothing to do

**hick** NOUNS **oaf, lout,** boor, lubber, oik <Brit>, **gawk,** gawky, **lummox,** yokel, rube, hayseed, bumpkin, clod, clodhopper

**hick town** NOUNS

<nonformal terms> **one-horse town,** jerkwater town, one-gas-station, **tank town** or station, **whistle-stop,** jumping-off place; rube town podunk; hoosier town; wide place in the road

**hickey** NOUNS **sore, lesion;** pustule, papule, papula, fester, **pimple,** zit <both nonformal>; pock; blister, bleb, bulla, blain

**hidden** ADJS **secret,** close, closed, closet; cryptic, dark; unuttered, unrevealed, undivulged, undisclosed, unspoken, untold; **hush-hush, top secret,** supersecret, eyes-only, classified, restricted, under wraps <nonformal>, under security *or* security restrictions; latent, ulterior, concealed

**hide** NOUNS 1 **fur, pelt,** fell, fleece; peltry, skins; **leather,** rawhide
VERBS 2 **conceal,** ensconce; **cover, cover up,** blind, **screen, cloak, veil,** screen off, curtain, blanket, shroud, enshroud, envelop; **disguise, camouflage, mask,** dissemble; plain-wrap, wrap in plain brown paper; whitewash <nonformal>; **obscure,** obfuscate, cloud, becloud, befog, throw out a smoke screen, shade, throw into the shade; put out of sight, sweep under the rug, keep under cover
3 **hide out, conceal oneself, take cover,** hide away, **go into hiding,** go to ground; stay in hiding, **lie hid** *or* **hidden,** lie *or* lay low <nonformal>, lie *perdue,* lie snug *or* close <nonformal>, lie doggo *and* sit tight <both nonformal>, burrow <old>, **hole up** <nonformal>, **go underground**

**hideaway** NOUNS **retreat, cell, ivory tower,** hidey-hole <nonformal>, lair, sanctum, sanctum sanctorum, inner sanctum

**hideous** ADJS **horrid, horrible,** frightful, dreadful, terrible, awful <nonformal>; **repulsive,** repellent, repelling, rebarbative, **repugnant,** offensive, foul, forbidding, loathsome, loathly <old>, revolting; **ghastly,** gruesome, grisly

**hideout** NOUNS **hiding place, hideaway,** hiding, concealment, **cover,** secret place; safe house; drop, accommodation address <Brit>; **asylum,** sanctuary, retreat, refuge

**hierarchy** NOUNS class structure, power structure, pyramid, establishment, pecking order; natural hierarchy, order *or* chain of being

**high** NOUNS 1 **intoxication, inebriation, inebriety,** insobriety, besottedness, sottedness, **drunkenness, tipsiness,** befuddlement, fuddle, fuddlement, fuddledness, tipsification *and* tiddliness <both nonformal>; **excitement,** emotion, excitedness, **arousal, stimulation, exhilaration;** manic state *or* condition
ADJS 2 **overjoyed,** overjoyful, overhappy, brimming *or* bursting with happiness, on top of the world; **rapturous,** raptured, **enraptured, enchanted,** entranced, enravished, ravished, rapt, possessed; sent *and* freaked-out <both

nonformal>, **in raptures,** transported, in a transport of delight, **carried away,** rapt *or* ravished away, beside oneself, beside oneself with joy, all over oneself <nonformal>; **ecstatic,** in ecstasies, ecstasiating; rhapsodic, rhapsodical; imparadised, **in paradise,** in heaven, in seventh heaven, on cloud nine <nonformal>; **elated,** elate, exalted, jubilant, exultant, flushed

3 **intoxicated,** under the influence, **drugged**

4 <nonformal> bent, blasted, blind, bombed out, bonged out, buzzed, coked, coked out, flying, fried, geared, geared up, geezed, gonged, gorked, hopped-up, in a zone, junked, luded out, maxed, noddy, ripped, smashed, snowed, spaced, space out, spacey, stoned, strung out, switched on, tanked, totaled, tranqued, tripping, trippy, wired, zoned, zoned out, zonked, zonked out

ADVS 5 **on high,** high up; **aloft,** aloof; **up,** upward, upwards, straight up, to the zenith; **above, over,** o'er, **overhead;** above one's head, over head and ears; skyward, airward, in the air, in the clouds; on the peak *or* summit *or* crest *or* pinnacle

**highball** NOUNS **drink,** long drink, mixed drink; **eye-opener** <nonformal>, **nightcap** <nonformal>, sundowner <Brit nonformal>

**highbrow** NOUNS **snob, prig; elitist;** egghead <nonformal>, Brahmin, mandarin; **intellectual, intellect,** intellectualist, literate, member of the intelligentsia, white-collar intellectual; namedropper, tufthunter <chiefly Brit old>

**high-class** ADJS **superior,** above par, head and shoulders above, **crack** <nonformal>; **high-grade,** high-quality, high-caliber, high-test, **world-class**

**highest** ADJS **superlative, supreme, greatest, best,** maximal, maximum, most, utmost, outstanding, stickout <nonformal>; top, topmost, **uppermost,** tip-top, top-level, top-echelon, top-notch *and* top-of-the-line <both nonformal>, **first-rate,** first-class, of the first water, top of the line, highest-quality, best-quality, far and away the best, the best by a long shot *or* long chalk, head and shoulders above

**highfalutin** ADJS **ostentatious, pretentious;** vaunting, **lofty,** highfaluting <nonformal>, **high-flown,** high-flying; **high-toned,** tony <both nonformal>, **fancy,** classy <nonformal>, flossy <nonformal>

**high-handed** ADJS **imperious,** bossy <nonformal>, domineering, overbearing, overruling; tyrannous, grinding, oppressive; repressive, suppressive; strict, severe

**highlands** NOUNS **uplands,** highland, upland, high country, elevated land, dome, **plateau, tableland,** upland area, piedmont, moor, moorland, **hills, heights,** hill *or* hilly country, downs, wold, foothills, rolling country, **mountains,** mountain *or* mountainous country, high terrain, peaks, range, *massif* <Fr>

**highlight** NOUNS 1 **feature,** high spot, main attraction, centerpiece, pièce de résistance; outstanding feature

VERBS 2 **illuminate, spotlight, feature,** bring to the fore, place in the foreground, bring out in bold *or* strong *or* high relief; **flaunt,** dangle, wave, **flourish,** brandish, parade; make a show *or* a great show of; **single out,** pick out, lift up, focus on, call *or* bring to notice, direct to the attention

**high-minded** ADJS **principled,** high-principled, right-minded; true-dealing, true-disposing, true-devoted; noble-minded, **idealistic**

**high society** NOUNS **society,** fashionable society, **polite society,** high life, *beau monde, haut monde* <both Fr>, good society; best people, people of fashion, right people; *monde* <Fr>, world of fashion, Vanity Fair; **smart set** <nonformal>; the Four Hundred, **upper crust** *and* upper cut <both nonformal>; **cream of society,** *crème de la crème* <Fr>, elite, carriage trade; café society, jet set, beautiful people, the glitterati <nonformal>

**high-spirited** ADJS **high-strung,** highly strung, mettlesome, high-mettled; **mischievous,** mischief-loving, full of mischief, full of the devil *or* old nick; **playful,** sportive

**high-strung** ADJS **excitable, emotional,** highly emotional, overemotional, hyperthymic, perturbable, flappable <nonformal>, agitable; highly strung, high-spirited, mettlesome, high-mettled; irritable, edgy, **on edge,** nerves on edge, on the ragged edge <nonformal>

**hijack** VERBS shanghai, dragoon; **coerce,** use violence, ride roughshod, intimidate, bully

**hike** NOUNS 1 **walk,** ramble, amble, **tramp,** traipse <nonformal>
VERBS 2 **march,** mush, footslog, **tramp,** backpack, trail-hike; route-march
3 **increase, raise,** exalt, boost <nonformal>, hike up *and* jack up *and* jump up <all nonformal>, mark up, put up, **up** <nonformal>

**hilarious** ADJS **merry,** mirthful; **joyful, joyous,** rejoicing; **gleeful,** gleesome; **jolly,** buxom; **jovial,** jocund, jocular; **frivolous**

**hill** NOUNS down <chiefly Brit>; brae *and* fell <both Scots>; **hillock, knob,** butte, kopje, kame, monticle, monticule, monadnock, **knoll,** hummock, hammock, eminence, rise, mound, swell, barrow, tumulus, kop, tel, jebel; **dune,** sand dune

**hillbilly** NOUNS **provincial, hick** *and* yokel *and* rube *and* hayseed *and* shitkicker <all nonformal>, **bumpkin,** country bumpkin, clod, **clodhopper** <nonformal>, **boor,** clown, lout, looby

**hill of beans** NOUNS **trifle, triviality,** pin, button, hair, straw, rush, feather, fig, bean, molehill, row of pins *or* buttons <nonformal>, pinch of snuff; a continental, a hoot *and* a damn *and* a darn *and* a shit <all nonformal>, a tinker's damn

**hilly** ADJS **rolling,** knobby, undulating; **mountainous,** montane, alpine

**hindrance** NOUNS hindering, **hampering,** let, let or hindrance; **check, arrest,** arrestment, arrestation; fixation; **impediment,** holdback; **resistance, opposition**; suppression, **repression, restriction, restraint**; **obstruction,** blocking, blockage, clogging, occlusion; **interruption,** interference; **retardation,** retardment, **detention,** detainment, **delay,** holdup, setback

**hindsight** NOUNS **remembering, remembrance, recollection,** recollecting, exercise of memory, **recall,** recalling; reflection, reconsideration; **retrospect,** retrospection, looking back

**hinge** NOUNS 1 **joint,** join, joining, **juncture, union, connection,** link, connecting link, **coupling, accouplement;** clinch, embrace; **pivot**
VERBS 2 **depend,** hang, rest; **depend on** *or* **upon, hang on** *or* **upon, rest on** *or* **upon,** rest with, repose upon, lie on, lie with, stand on *or* upon, be based on, be

**hint** NOUNS 1 gentle hint, **intimation, indication, suggestion,** mere or faint suggestion, suspicion, inkling, whisper, **glimmer, glimmering; cue, clue,** index, **symptom, sign,** spoor, track, scent, sniff, whiff, telltale, tip-off <nonformal>; **implication, insinuation, innuendo;** broad hint, gesture, signal, nod, wink, look, nudge, kick, prompt
VERBS 2 **intimate,** suggest, insinuate, imply, indicate, adumbrate, lead *or* leave one to gather, justify one in supposing, give *or* drop *or* throw out a hint, give an inkling of, **hint at; leak,** let slip out; allude to, make an allusion to

**hinterland** NOUNS **back country,** outback <Australia>, up-country, boonies *and* boondocks <both nonformal>; **the bush,** bush country, bushveld, **woods,** woodlands, **backwoods,** forests, timbers, the big sticks <nonformal>, brush; wilderness, wilds, uninhabited region, virgin land *or* territory; **wasteland**; **frontier,** borderland, outpost

**hip** ADJS **fashionable, all the rage,** all the thing; **popular,** prevalent, current; **up-to-date,** up-to-datish, up-to-the-minute, switched-on *and* with-it <both nonformal>, trendy <nonformal>, newfashioned, modern, new; **in the swim;** sought-after, much sought-after; **hep,** on the beam, **with it,** into, really into, groovy <all nonformal>

**hippie** NOUNS 1 **nonconformist,** unconformist, **original,** eccentric, gonzo <nonformal>, deviant, deviationist, maverick <nonformal>, dropout, Bohemian, beatnik, hipster, freak <nonformal>, flower child, street people, yippie
ADJS 2 **unconventional, unorthodox, eccentric,** gonzo <nonformal>, heterodox, heretical; offbeat <nonformal>, way out *and* far out *and* kinky *and* out in left field <all nonformal>, fringy, breakaway, Bohemian, beat, counterculture

**hire** VERBS **employ,** give a job to, take into employment, take into one's service, take on <nonformal>, recruit, headhunt <nonformal>, **engage,** sign up *or* on <nonformal>; retain, **rent,** lease, job, **charter; sublease,** sublet

**hiss** NOUNS 1 **hissing,** siss, sissing, white

noise; **boo,** booing, hoot, catcall; **Bronx cheer** *and* **raspberry** *and* razz <all nonformal>; the bird <nonformal>
VERBS 2 **boo, hoot,** catcall, give the raspberry *or* Bronx cheer <nonformal>, give the bird <nonformal>

**historical** ADJS **historic,** historied, historically accurate; fact-based; historicized; historiographical; cliometric; **chronicled,** empirical, **objective, real,** actual

**history** NOUNS the historical discipline, the investigation of the past, the record of the past, the story of mankind; **annals, chronicles,** memorabilia, chronology; chronicle, record; **the past,** past, foretime, former times, past times, times past, water under the bridge, **days** *or* **times gone by,** bygone times *or* days, yesterday, yesteryear; recent past, just *or* only yesterday

*a set of lies agreed upon*
NAPOLEON

**hit** NOUNS 1 **blow,** stroke, knock, rap, slam, bang, crack, whack, smack, thwack, smash, dash, swipe, swing, punch, poke, jab, dig, drub, thump, pelt, cut, chop
2 hit show, success, critical success, audience success, word-of-mouth success; song hit, hit tune
VERBS 3 **strike, knock,** knock down *or* out, smite; land a blow, draw blood; **poke, punch, jab,** thwack, **smack,** clap, crack, swipe, **whack;** deal, fetch, swipe at, take a punch at, throw one at <nonformal>, deal *or* fetch a blow, hit a clip <nonformal>, let have it

4 <nonformal> **sock,** bang, bash, bat, belt, bonk, bust, clip, clout, duke, swat, yerk , plunk larrup, paste, lick, biff, clump, clunk, clonk, wallop, whop, bonk, slam, slug

**hitch** NOUNS 1 **obstacle, obstruction,** obstructer; **hang-up** <nonformal>; **difficulty,** hurdle, hazard; **drawback,** objection; **stumbling block,** stumbling stone, stone in one's path; fly in the ointment, one small difficulty, **catch,** joker <nonformal>
2 **term,** time; **tenure,** continuous tenure, tenure in *or* of office; **enlistment,** tour; prison term, stretch <nonformal>

**hitchhike** VERBS **hitch** <nonformal>, **thumb** *or* **thumb one's way** <nonformal>, **catch a ride;** hitch *or* hook *or* bum *or* cadge *or* thumb a ride <nonformal>

**hit man** NOUNS **killer,** slayer, slaughterer, butcher, bloodshedder; **homicide, murderer,** man-killer, bloodletter, Cain; **assassin,** assassinator; professional killer, contract killer, hired killer, hired gun, button man *or* gun *or* trigger man *or* torpedo *or* gunsel <all nonformal>; **hatchet man**

**hit-or-miss** ADJS **slipshod,** haphazard, hit-and-miss; half-assed <nonformal>, indiscriminate, casual, frivolous, capricious, random, vague, dispersed, wandering, planless, undirected, trial-and-error, cut-and-try

**hit the spot** VERBS

<nonformal> be just the ticket, be just what the doctor ordered, **make a hit,** go over big, go over with a bang

**hoard** NOUNS 1 **store, treasure,** wealth, treasury; plenty, plenitude, abundance, cornucopia; heap, mass, stack, pile, dump, rick; **collection, accumulation,** cumulation, amassment, stockpile
VERBS 2 **store up,** stock up, lay up, put up, **save up,** hoard up, treasure up, garner up, **heap up,** pile up, build up a stock *or* an inventory; **accumulate,** cumulate, **collect, amass, stockpile;** treasure, save, keep, hold, squirrel, squirrel away; hide, secrete

**hoarse** ADJS **raucous,** raucid, **harsh,** harsh-sounding; coarse, rude, rough, gruff, ragged; **husky,** cracked, dry; **guttural,** thick, throaty, croaky, croaking

**hoary** ADJS hoar, **grizzled,** grizzly, griseous, canescent; **gray-haired,** gray-headed, silver-headed; **old, age-old,** old-time, **ancient, antique,** venerable; **frosty, frosted,** rimed, hoar-frosted, rime-frosted

**hoax** NOUNS **deception,** spoof <nonformal>, **humbug,** flam, **fake** *and* fakement, **rip-off** <nonformal>, **sham;** mare's nest

**hobby** NOUNS **avocation,** hobbyhorse <old>, sideline, by-line, side interest, pastime, spare-time activity; amateur pursuit, amateurism; unpaid work, volunteer work

**hobgoblin** NOUNS **frightener, bogey,**

bogeyman, **bugaboo,** bugbear; **goblin,** hob, ouphe

**hobo** NOUNS drifter, vagrant, tramp; vagabond, drifter, derelict, homeless person, bum <nonformal>

**hock** VERBS **pledge, pawn,** put in pawn, **put in hock** <nonformal>; mortgage, hypothecate, bond

**hodgepodge** NOUNS hotchpotch, hotchpot; **medley, miscellany,** mélange, pastiche, *pasticcio* <Ital>, **conglomeration, assortment,** assemblage, mixed bag, ragbag, grab bag, jumble, mingle-mangle, **mix,** mishmash, **mess,** can of worms <nonformal>, rat's nest, hash, patchwork, everything but the kitchen sink <nonformal>

**hog** NOUNS 1 **swine, pig,** porker; **shoat,** piggy, piglet, pigling; sucking *or* suckling pig; gilt; **boar, sow;** barrow; wild boar, tusker, razorback; warthog, babirusa
2 **glutton,** greedy eater, big *or* hefty *or* husky eater <nonformal>, trencherman, trencherwoman, gorger, **gourmand,** gourmandizer, gormand, gormandizer; **pig** *and* chow hound *and* khazer <all nonformal>
VERBS 3 **monopolize,** grab all of *and* gobble up <both nonformal>, take it all, have all to oneself, have exclusive possession of *or* exclusive rights to

**hogwash** NOUNS

<nonformal> **humbug,** humbuggery; **bunk, bunkum;** hooey, hoke, **hokum, bosh,** bull, **bullshit,** crap, baloney, flimflam, flam, smoke and mirrors, claptrap, eyewash

**hoist** NOUNS 1 **lift, boost** *and* **hike** <both nonformal>, heave; hydraulic lift; forklift; hydraulic tailgate; lever; windlass
VERBS 2 **elevate, lift,** levitate, boost <nonformal>, heist <nonformal>, heft, heave; raise up, rear up, lift up

**hokey** ADJS **imitation, mock, sham,** copied, fake *and* phony <both nonformal>, counterfeit, forged, plagiarized, unoriginal, ungenuine; ersatz, hoked-up <nonformal>

**hold** NOUNS 1 **purchase,** grasp, grip, clutch, clamp, clinch, clench; toehold, foothold, footing; **clasp, hug, embrace,** bear hug; firm hold, tight grip, iron grip, grip of iron *or* steel, death grip
2 **influence, authority,** control, domination; **sway,** reign, rule; **mastery,** ascendancy, supremacy, dominance, predominance, preponderance; upper hand, whip hand, trump card; leverage
VERBS 3 **keep, harbor,** bear, have, have and hold, hold on to; **cherish,** embrace, hug, cling to

**holding** NOUNS 1 **retention,** retainment, **keeping,** maintenance, preservation; **share, lot;** holdings, stockholding, stockholdings
2 **verdict,** decision, determination, finding; dictum

**holdover** NOUNS **remainder,** remains, remnant, residue, residuum, rest, balance; lame duck

**holdup** NOUNS 1 bank robbery; **armed robbery,** assault and robbery
2 **delay,** stoppage, tie-up *and* bind <both nonformal>, **block,** blockage, **hang-up** <nonformal>; **detention,** suspension, obstruction, hindrance; delaying action; **wait,** halt, stay, stop, downtime, pause

**hole** NOUNS 1 **perforation,** penetration, piercing, empiercement, **puncture,** goring, boring, puncturing, punching, pricking, lancing, broach, transforation, terebration; bore, borehole, drill hole
2 **omission,** gap, hiatus, vacuum, break, lacuna, discontinuity, interval

**holiday** NOUNS 1 **day off; red-letter day,** gala day, fete day, festival day, day of festivities; national holiday, legal holiday, bank holiday <Brit>
VERBS 2 **vacation,** get away from it all, take a holiday, weekend

**holier-than-thou** ADJS **sanctimonious,** sanctified, **pious,** pietistic, pietistical, self-righteous, pharisaic, pharisaical

**holistic** ADJS **whole, total, entire,** aggregate, gross, all; integral, integrated; **one,** one and indivisible; **inclusive,** all-inclusive, **exhaustive,** comprehensive, omnibus, all-embracing; universal

**hollow** NOUNS 1 **valley,** vale, glen, dale, dell, holler <nonformal>, flume
2 **opening,** aperture, hole, cavity, orifice
ADJS 3 **vacant, empty,** inane, **bare, vacuous, void,** without content, with nothing inside, devoid, null, null and void; hollowed, empty

**holocaust** NOUNS extermination, destruction, mass killing, genocide; mass murder

**holy** ADJS **sacred,** numinous, **sacrosanct, religious, spiritual,** heavenly, divine; inviolable, **inviolate,** untouchable; **inef-**

**fable,** unutterable, unspeakable, inexpressible, inenarrable; **godly**

**homage** NOUNS **respect,** approbation, approval; **reverence, veneration,** awe; **deference,** deferential *or* reverential regard; **honor,** duty; great respect, high regard, **admiration; service,** servitium, fealty, **allegiance, loyalty,** faithfulness, faith; **encomium,** accolade, kudos, panegyric; paean; **tribute**

**home** NOUNS 1 home sweet home; **fireside, hearth,** hearth and home, hearthstone; **household,** ménage; **homestead,** home place, roof; family homestead, ancestral halls; **habitat, range,** stamping grounds, locality, native environment

*the place where, when you go there,*
*They have to take you in*
ROBERT FROST

ADJS 2 **residential,** residentiary; domestic, domiciliary, domal; **household**

**homeland** NOUNS **fatherland,** *Vaterland* <Ger>, *patria* <L>, *la patrie* <Fr>, **motherland,** mother country, **native land,** native soil, one's native heath *or* ground *or* soil *or* place, the old country, country of origin, **birthplace,** cradle; **home,** homeground, God's country

**homeless** ADJS **destitute, down-and-out,** in the gutter; **penniless,** moneyless, fortuneless, out of funds, **without a sou,** without a penny to bless oneself with, without one dollar to rub against another; propertyless, landless; **friendless,** kithless, rootless, companionless

**the homeless** NOUNS **the underprivileged,** the disadvantaged, the poor, the wretched of the earth, outcasts, the dispossessed, the powerless, the underclass

**homely** ADJS **unattractive, unhandsome,** unpretty, unlovely, uncomely, inelegant; **plain;** not much to look at, not much for looks, short on looks <nonformal>, hard on the eyes <nonformal>; homely as a mud fence, homely enough to sour milk, homely enough to stop a clock

**homemade** ADJS homespun, **handmade,** handcrafted, handicrafted, self-made, DIY *or* do it yourself

**homemaker** NOUNS housewife, househusband, houseperson, goodwife <Scots>, lady of the house

**homeowner** NOUNS **householder,** houseowner, proprietor, freeholder; cottager, cotter, cottier, crofter; head of household

**homesick** ADJS **wistful,** wishful; **longing, yearning,** yearnful, **hankering** <nonformal>, **languishing, pining,** honing <nonformal>; **nostalgic**

**homespun** ADJS **simple**, plain, ordinary, nondescript, common, commonplace, prosaic, prosy, **matter-of-fact, homely,** everyday, workday, workaday, household, garden, common- *or* garden-variety; rustic

**homesteader** NOUNS **settler,** *habitant* <Canadian & Louisiana Fr>; **colonist,** colonizer, colonial, immigrant, planter; **squatter,** nester; **pioneer;** sooner

**homestretch** NOUNS **close,** closing, cessation; decline, lapse; **last lap** *or* **round** *or* **inning** <nonformal>, last stage; beginning of the end

**homework** NOUNS **assignment, exercise,** task, set task

**homey** ADJS **comfortable,** comfy <nonformal>; contented; **restful,** reposeful, peaceful, **relaxing;** comfortable as an old shoe; **cozy, snug,** snug as a bug in a rug; friendly, warm; **homelike,** down-home <nonformal>, homely, lived-in; simple, plain, unpretending

**homicidal** ADJS **murderous,** slaughterous; man-killing, death-dealing; biocidal, genocidal; cruel; **bloodthirsty,** bloody-minded; **bloody, gory,** sanguinary

**homicide** NOUNS **manslaughter; negligent homicide; murder,** bloody murder <nonformal>; serial killing; hit *and* bump-off *and* bumping-off <all nonformal>, gangland-style execution; kiss of death; foul play; **assassination;** removal, elimination; liquidation, purge, purging; justifiable homicide

**homily** NOUNS **lesson,** teaching, instruction, lecture, discourse, talk, **sermon,** preachment; **moral,** morality, moralization, moral lesson

**homogeneous** ADJS **identical,** identic; **same,** selfsame, one, one and the same, all the same, all one, of the same kidney; **indistinguishable,** without distinction, without difference, undifferent, undifferentiated; **alike, all alike, like**, just alike, exactly alike, like two peas in a pod; consubstantial, consonant, **alike,** all alike, all of a piece, of a piece, monolithic

**homosexual** NOUNS 1 gay person, homosexualist, homophile; catamite, *mignon* <Fr>, Ganymede; **bisexual,** bi-guy <nonformal>; **lesbian,** sapphist, tribade, fricatrice <old>
ADJS 2 homoerotic, gay, queer *and* limp-wristed *and* faggoty <all nonformal>; **bisexual,** bisexed, ambisexual, ambisextrous, amphierotic, AC-DC <nonformal>, autoerotic; lesbian, sapphic, tribadistic; mannish, butch *and* dykey <both nonformal>; effeminate; transvestite

3 <nonformal> homo, queer, faggot, fag, fruit, flit, fairy, pansy, nance, auntie, queen, drag queen, closet queen, fruitcake, poof *and* poofter *and* poove <all Brit>; <nonformal terms for female homosexuals> dyke, bull dyke, butchfemme, boondagger, diesel-dyke, lesbo, lez

**honcho** NOUNS

<nonformal> **boss,** big enchilada, biggest frog in the pond, top *or* high man on the totem pole, top dog, Mr Big, head cheese, his nibs, himself, man upstairs

**hone** VERBS **sharpen, edge,** acuminate, aculeate, spiculate, taper; **whet,** oilstone, file, grind; strop, strap; set, reset; **point;** barb, spur, file to a point

**honest** ADJS **veracious, truthful,** true, true to one's word, veridical; truth-telling, truth-speaking, truth-declaring, truth-passing, truth-bearing, truth-loving, truth-seeking

**honesty** NOUNS **veracity,** veraciousness, verity, **truthfulness,** truth, veridicality, truth-telling, truth-speaking; truth-loving; credibility, absolute credibility

**honk** NOUNS 1 **blare, blast,** shriek, peal; **toot,** tootle, beep, blat, trumpet
VERBS 2 **blare,** blast; shriek; **toot,** tootle, sound, peal, wind, blow, blat; honk *or* sound *or* blow the horn, beep

**honor** NOUNS 1 great honor, distinction, glory, credit, ornament; **esteem,** estimation, **prestige; dignity; rank, standing,** stature, high place, position, station, face, **status; chastity, virtue,** virtuousness; sexual innocence, innocence
VERBS 2 confer *or* bestow honor upon; **dignify,** adorn, grace; **distinguish,** signalize, confer distinction on, give credit where credit is due; hold in high esteem, crown with laurels

**honorable** ADJS **reputable,** highly reputed, **estimable, esteemed,** much *or* highly esteemed, honored; **meritorious,** worth one's salt, noble, worthy, creditable; respected, respectable, highly respectable; revered, reverend, venerable, venerated, worshipful; **well-thought-of,** highly regarded, held in esteem, in good odor, in favor, in high favor

**honorary** ADJS **honorific, honorable; titular,** titulary; honorific

**hood** NOUNS 1 **cover, covering,** coverage, covert, coverture, housing, cowl, cowling, **shelter;** cloak, mask, guise; vestment
2 **gangster, roughneck, tough**

3 <nonformal> bruiser, mug, mugger, bimbo, bozo, ugly customer, **hoodlum, hooligan,** gorilla, ape, plug-ugly, strong-arm man, muscle man, **goon;** gun, gunsel, trigger man, rodman, torpedo, hatchet man <all nonformal>

**hoodlum** NOUNS **rowdy,** ruffian, hood <nonformal>, hooligan; **gangster** *and* mobster <both nonformal>; racketeer; **thug**

**hoodwink** VERBS blindfold, blind, blind one's eyes, throw dust in one's eyes, **pull the wool over one's eyes**

**hoofer** NOUNS **dancer,** danseur, terpsichorean, step dancer, tap dancer, clog dancer, etc; **chorus girl, chorine,** chorus boy *or* man

**hook** NOUNS 1 **lure,** charm, **come-on** <nonformal>, attention-getter *or* -grabber, **attraction, draw** *or* drawer *or* crowd-drawer, crowd-pleaser, headliner; clou, gimmick <nonformal>, drawing card, drawcard; **decoy,** decoy duck; **bait, snare**
VERBS 2 **trap,** entrap, gin, catch, catch out, catch in a trap; **ensnare, snare,** hook in, sniggle, noose; inveigle; **set** *or* **lay a trap for,** bait the hook, spread the toils; **lure,** allure, **decoy**

**hooked** ADJS 1 **addicted,** on the needle <nonformal>; dependency-prone
2 **crooked, aquiline,** aduncous; **hook-shaped,** hooklike, uncinate, unciform; hamulate, hamate, hamiform; **hook-nosed,** beak-nosed, parrot-nosed,

aquiline-nosed, Roman-nosed, crooknosed, crookbilled

**hooker** NOUNS **prostitute, harlot, whore,** *fille de joie* <Fr>, call girl *and* B-girl <both nonformal>, **streetwalker,** hustler <nonformal>, *poule* <Fr>, stew, meretrix, Cyprian, Paphian

**hooky** NOUNS **absence,** nonattendance, **absenting, leaving,** taking leave, **departure**; **truancy,** French leave, **cut** <nonformal>; **absence without leave** *or* AWOL; **absenteeism,** truantism

**hooligan** NOUNS **mischief-maker, rowdy,** ruffian, hoodlum, hood <nonformal>

**hoopla** NOUNS **publicity,** publicness, **notoriety, fame,** famousness, notoriousness, notice, public notice, **celebrity,** *réclame, éclat* <both Fr>; **limelight** *and* **spotlight** <both nonformal>, daylight, bright light, glare, public eye *or* consciousness, **exposure, currency,** common *or* public knowledge, widest *or* maximum dissemination; **ballyhoo** <nonformal>; **festivity,** merrymaking, merriment, gaiety, jollity, jollification <nonformal>, **joviality, conviviality,** whoopee <nonformal>

**hope** NOUNS 1 **hopefulness,** hoping, **hopes,** fond *or* fervent hope, good hope, good cheer; aspiration, **desire**; prospect, **expectation**; sanguine expectation, happy *or* cheerful expectation; the light at the end of the tunnel; **possibility,** possibleness, **the realm of possibility,** the domain of the possible, conceivableness, **conceivability,** thinkability, thinkableness, imaginability; outside hope, small hope, slim odds; **good possibility, good chance,** even chance; bare possibility

*the second soul of the unhappy*
GOETHE

VERBS 2 be *or* live in hopes, have reason to hope, entertain *or* harbor the hope, cling to the hope, cherish *or* foster *or* nurture the hope; look for, prognosticate, **expect**; **trust,** confide, presume, feel confident, rest assured; pin one's hope upon, put one's trust in, hope in, rely on, count on, lean upon, bank on, set great store on; hope for, **aspire to, desire**; **hope against hope,** hope and pray, hope to God <nonformal>

**hopeful** ADJS **hoping, in hopes,** full of hope, in good heart, of good hope, of good cheer; **aspiring**; **expectant**; **sanguine,** fond; **confident,** assured; undespairing; **promising,** fair

**hopeless** ADJS unhopeful, without hope, affording no hope, worst-case, bleak, grim, dismal, cheerless, comfortless; **desperate, despairing, in despair;** despondent; disconsolate; forlorn; apathetic; **dying, terminal,** sinking, sinking fast, low, despaired of, given up, given up for dead, not long for this world, **moribund,** near death, near one's end, at the end of one's rope <nonformal>, done for <nonformal>

**horde** NOUNS **throng, multitude,** host, heap <nonformal>, army, panoply, legion; **crowd,** press, crush, flood, spate, deluge, mass; **mob,** rabble, rout, ruck, jam, *cohue* <Fr>, everybody and his uncle *or* his brother <nonformal>

**horizon** NOUNS **skyline,** rim of the horizon; sea line; the far horizon, where the earth meets the sky, vanishing point, background

**horizontal** ADJS **level, flat,** flattened; **even,** smooth, smoothened, smoothed out; table-like, tabular; **plane,** plain; flat as a pancake, flat as a board

**horn** NOUNS 1 **projection,** spur, jag, **snag,** snaggle; antler; cornicle
2 **alarm,** fog signal *or* alarm, foghorn

**horny** ADJS **lustful,** prurient, hot, steamy, sexy, concupiscent, lickerish, libidinous, salacious, **passionate,** hot-blooded, itching, hot to trot *and* sexed-up <both nonformal>, randy, goatish; sex-starved, unsatisfied; lascivious

**horrendous** ADJS **terrible,** horrid, horrible, horrifying, horrific; **dreadful,** dread, dreaded; **awful; shocking,** appalling, astounding; **hideous, ghastly,** morbid, grim, grisly, gruesome, ghoulish, macabre

**horrible** ADJS **hideous,** horrid, frightful, dreadful, terrible, awful <nonformal>; **repulsive**, repellent, repelling, rebarbative, **repugnant,** offensive, foul, forbidding, loathsome, revolting; **ghastly,** gruesome, grisly

**horrified** ADJS **terrified,** terror-stricken, terror-struck, terror-smitten, terror-ridden; horror-stricken, horror-struck; frightened out of one's wits *or* mind, **scared to death, scared stiff** *or* **shitless** *or* spitless <nonformal>; unnerved, unstrung, unmanned, undone, **cowed,** awed, **intimidated; stunned, petrified, stupefied,** paralyzed, frozen

**horrify** VERBS **terrify, awe,** strike terror into; **appall, shock,** make one's flesh creep; **frighten out of one's wits** *or* **senses;** strike dumb, **stun, stupefy, paralyze, petrify,** freeze

**horror** NOUNS 1 **aversion,** repugnance, repulsion, antipathy, allergy <nonformal>, grudge, abomination, **abhorrence,** mortal horror; **terror, mortal** *or* abject fear; **phobia**
2 **abomination,** terrible thing; **scandal,** disgrace, shame, pity, atrocity, profanation, desecration, violation, sacrilege, infamy, ignominy; **eyesore,** blot, blot on the landscape, blemish, **sight** <nonformal>, **fright**

**horseplay** NOUNS **misbehavior, misconduct,** unsanctioned *or* nonsanctioned behavior; **rowdiness,** rowdyism, riotousness, ruffianism, hooliganism, roughhouse; shenanigans *and* monkey tricks *and* monkeyshines <all nonformal>

**horse racing** NOUNS **the turf,** the sport of kings, the turf sport, the racing world *or* establishment; **flat racing; harness racing,** trotting, pacing; steeplechase, the jumps

**horticulture** NOUNS **gardening;** landscape gardening, landscape architecture, groundskeeping; truck gardening, market gardening, olericulture; flower gardening, flower-growing, floriculture; viniculture, viticulture; orcharding, fruit-growing, pomiculture

**hospice** NOUNS youth hostel, elder hostel; **asylum, home,** retreat; hospitium; rest home, nursing home, old soldiers' home, sailors' snug harbor; halfway house; life-care home, continuing-care retirement community *or* CCRC

**hospitable** ADJS **receptive,** welcoming; **cordial,** amiable, gracious, **friendly,** neighborly, genial, hearty, open, openhearted, warm, warmhearted; **generous,** liberal

**hospital** NOUNS **clinic,** *hôpital* <Fr>, treatment center; infirmary; sanitarium; sick bay *or* berth; trauma center; wellness center

**hospitality** NOUNS hospitableness, receptiveness; honors *or* freedom of the house; **cordiality,** amiability, graciousness, **friendliness,** neighborliness, geniality, heartiness, bonhomie, **generosity,** liberality, openheartedness, warmth, warmness, warmheartedness; open door

**host** NOUNS 1 mine host; hostess, receptionist, greeter; landlord
2 **throng, multitude, horde,** heap <nonformal>, army, panoply, legion; **crowd,** press, crush, flood, spate, deluge, mass; an abundance of, all kinds *or* sorts of, no end of, quite a few
VERBS 3 **entertain,** entertain guests; preside, do the honors <nonformal>; give a party, throw a party <nonformal>; spread oneself <nonformal>

**hostile** ADJS **antagonistic,** repugnant, antipathetic, set against, snide, spiteful, despiteful, malicious, malevolent, malignant, hateful, full of hate *or* hatred; virulent, **bitter,** sore, rancorous, acrid, caustic, venomous, vitriolic; conflicting, clashing, colliding; quarrelsome; **provocative,** off-putting; belligerent

**hot** ADJS 1 **heated, torrid; sweltering,** sweltry, canicular; **burning,** parching, scorching, searing, scalding, blistering, baking, roasting, toasting, broiling, grilling, simmering; **boiling,** seething, ebullient; **piping hot,** scalding hot, burning hot, roasting hot, scorching hot, sizzling hot, smoking hot; **red-hot,** white-hot; hot as hell *or* blazes, hot as the hinges of hell, so hot you can fry eggs on the sidewalk <nonformal>
2 **passionate,** fiery, glowing, fervent, fervid; **sexually excited,** in rut, lustful, ithyphallic, horny *and* sexed-up *and* hot to trot <all nonformal>; prurient, itching, itchy <nonformal>; randy, horny <nonformal>, lubricious; burning with excitement, het up <nonformal>, hot under the collar <nonformal>; seething, boiling, boiling over, steamy, steaming
3 **stolen,** pilfered, purloined; pirated, plagiarized

**hot-blooded** ADJS warm-blooded; **lustful, prurient, hot,** steamy, sexy, concupiscent, lickerish, libidinous, **salacious, passionate,** itching, **horny** *and* hot to trot *and* sexed-up <all nonformal>, randy, goatish

**hot dog** VERBS **exercise skill,** handle oneself well, demonstrate one's ability, **strut one's stuff <nonformal>,** go through one's paces, show what one has, grandstand *and* showboat *and* show off <all nonformal>, play to the gallery *or* galleries <nonformal>, please the crowd; exhibit *or* parade one's wares <nonformal>

**hotel** NOUNS **inn,** hostel, hostelry, **tavern,** *posada* <Sp>; tourist hotel, *parador* <Sp>; **roadhouse,** caravansary *or* caravanserai

**hotheaded** ADJS **hot-tempered, passionate,** hot, fiery, peppery, feisty, spunky <nonformal>, **quick-tempered, short-tempered;** hasty, quick, explosive, volcanic, combustible

*sudden and quick in quarrel*
SHAKESPEARE

**hothouse** NOUNS **nursery; conservatory, greenhouse,** glasshouse <Brit>, forcing house, summerhouse, lathhouse, coolhouse

**hound** VERBS **pursue, follow,** follow up, **go after,** take out *or* off after <nonformal>, bay after, run after, run in pursuit of, make after, go in pursuit of; **chase, give chase,** chivy; dog; **worry, upset, vex,** fret, agitate, get to <nonformal>, **harass,** harry, **torment,** plague, persecute, haunt, beset

**house** NOUNS 1 **dwelling,** dwelling house, *casa* <Sp & Ital>; house and grounds, house and lot, homesite; **building, structure, edifice,** manor house, hall; town house, *rus in urbe* <L>; country house, *dacha* <Russ>, country seat; ranch house, farmhouse, sod house, adobe house; split-level; parsonage, **rectory,** vicarage, deanery, manse; official residence, White House, 10 Downing Street
VERBS 2 domicile, domiciliate; provide with a roof, **accommodate,** furnish accommodations; have as a guest *or* lodger, shelter, harbor; **lodge, quarter, put up,** billet, room, bed, berth, bunk; stable

**housebreaker** NOUNS **burglar,** yegg *and* cracksman <both nonformal>; cat burglar, cat man, second-story thief *or* worker

**housebroken** ADJS **conditioned,** trained, seasoned; domesticated, **subdued, tame,** tamed, broken, housebroke; potty-trained

**household** NOUNS 1 **family,** brood, nuclear family, binuclear family, extended family, one-parent *or* single-parent family; **house,** hearth, hearthside, ménage, people, **folk,** homefolk, folks *and* homefolks <both nonformal>; **children,** issue, descendants, progeny, **offspring,** kids <nonformal>
ADJS 2 **well-known,** well-recognized, **widely known,** commonly known, universally recognized, generally *or* universally admitted; **familiar,** familiar as household words, **common, current; proverbial;** public, notorious; known by every schoolboy; talked-of, talked-about, in everyone's mouth, **on everyone's tongue** *or* **lips**

**housekeeping** NOUNS **domestic management,** homemaking, housewifery, ménage, househusbandry; domestic economy, home economics

**housewarming** NOUNS **gathering, get-together** *and* turnout <both nonformal>; **party, festivity**, fete, at home, reception

**housewife** NOUNS **matron,** homemaker, goodwife <Scots>, lady of the house, chatelaine

**housing** NOUNS **shelter, living quarters; lodgings,** lodging, lodgment; diggings *and* digs <both Brit nonformal>, pad *and* crib <both nonformal>, room; **rooms,** berth, roost, accommodations; shelter, *gîte* <Fr>; **cover, covering,** coverage

**hovel** NOUNS **dump** <nonformal>, rathole, hole, sty, pigsty, pigpen, tumbledown shack

**hover** VERBS **be imminent, impend, overhang,** hang *or* lie over, **loom,** hang over one's head, **threaten, menace,** lower; be on the horizon, be in the offing, be just around the corner, await, face, stare one in the face, be in store, breathe down one's neck, be about to be borning; float, levitate

**howl** NOUNS 1 **screech, whine,** wail, ululation, yammer; waul, caterwaul
VERBS 2 **screech, whine,** wail, wrawl <Brit nonformal>, yammer, ululate; waul, caterwaul

**hub** NOUNS **center,** centrum; **middle**, heart, core, nucleus; core of one's being, where one lives; **pith, nub,** nave, axis, pivot; bull's-eye; dead center

**hubris** NOUNS overconfidence, oversureness, overweeningness; **gall** *and* brass *and* cheek *and* chutzpah <all nonformal>; pride, arrogance, pomposity, self-importance

**huckster** NOUNS **vendor, peddler, hawker,** butcher <old>, higgler, cadger <Scots>, colporteur, chapman <Brit>; adman *and* pitchman <both nonformal>

**huddle** VERBS **stay near,** keep close to; **cling to,** clasp, hug; go into a huddle, close ranks

**hue** NOUNS **color; tint,** tinct, tincture, **tinge, shade, tone,** cast; **way, habit,** tenor, cast, grain, vein, streak, stripe, mold, brand, stamp; **kind,** sort, type, ilk

**huffy** ADJS **provoked,** vexed, piqued; **peeved** *and* miffed <both nonformal>, **nettled, irritated, annoyed,** aggravated <nonformal>, exasperated, put-out

**hug** NOUNS 1 **embrace, squeeze,** fond embrace, embracement, clasp, enfoldment, bear hug <nonformal>
VERBS 2 **embrace,** clasp, press, squeeze <nonformal>, fold, **enfold,** bosom, embosom, put *or* throw one's arms around, take to *or* in one's arms, fold to the heart, press to the bosom; take hold of, clinch

**huge** ADJS 1 **immense, vast, enormous,** astronomic, astronomical, humongous *and* jumbo <both nonformal>, king-size, queen-size, tremendous, prodigious, stupendous, macro, mega, giga; great big, larger than life, Homeric, mighty, **titanic, colossal, monumental,** heroic, heroical, epic, epical, towering, mountainous

2 <nonformal> **whopping, walloping, whaling, whacking,** spanking, slapping, lolloping, thumping, thundering, bumping, banging

**hulking** ADJS **bulky, hulky,** lumpish, lumpy, lumping <nonformal>, clumpish, lumbering, lubberly; **massive,** massy; **ponderous,** cumbrous, cumbersome; **clumsy,** awkward, **unwieldy;** clunky <nonformal>

**hullabaloo** NOUNS **outcry,** vociferation, clamor; hubbub, brouhaha, **uproar**; **hue and cry**

**hum** NOUNS 1 **humming,** thrumming, low rumbling, booming, bombilation, bombination, **droning, buzzing,** whizzing, whirring, purring
VERBS 2 thrum, boom, bombilate, bombinate, **drone, buzz,** whiz, whir, burr, purr

**human** NOUNS 1 **person,** human being, man, woman, child, member of the human race *or* family, Adamite, daughter of Eve; **mortal,** life, **soul,** living soul; **being,** creature, clay, ordinary clay; **individual,** personage, **personality, personhood,** individuality
ADJS 2 hominal; creaturely, creatural; Adamite *or* Adamitic; **frail, weak,** fleshly, finite, **mortal; only human;** earthborn, of the earth, earthy, tellurian, unangelic; humanistic; homocentric, anthropocentric

**humane** ADJS **kind, kindly,** kindly-disposed; **benign,** benignant; good as gold, good, nice, **decent; kindhearted,** warm, warmhearted, softhearted, tenderhearted, tender, loving, affectionate; **sympathetic,** sympathizing, **compassionate**, merciful; **lenient,** mild, gentle, mild-mannered, tender, compassionate, **clement,** merciful

**humanitarian** NOUNS 1 **philanthropist, altruist,** benevolist, person of good will, **do-gooder,** bleeding heart <nonformal>, well-doer, power for good; almsgiver, almoner; Robin Hood, Lady Bountiful
ADJS 2 **benevolent,** charitable, beneficent, philanthropic, altruistic; **bighearted,** largehearted, greathearted, freehearted; **generous**; almsgiving, eleemosynary

**humanity** NOUNS **humankind,** mankind, man, human species, **human race,** race of man, human family, the family of man, human beings, mortals, mortality, flesh, mortal flesh, clay; **human nature;** frail *or* fallen humanity, Adam, the generation of Adam, Adam's seed *or* offspring; **humanness,** mortality

**humankind** NOUNS **mankind, man,** human species, **human race,** race of man, human family, the family of man, **humanity,** human beings, mortals, mortality, flesh, mortal flesh, clay; homo, genus Homo, **Homo sapiens**

*the plumeless genus of bipeds*
PLATO

**human nature** NOUNS **humanity;** frail *or* fallen humanity, Adam, the generation of Adam, Adam's seed *or* offspring; the way you are; human frailty, weakness, **human weakness,** weakness of the flesh, the weaknesses human flesh is heir to; human equation

**humble** VERBS 1 **humiliate,** bring low, **bring to terms,** take down a notch *or* peg, bend, **bring one to his knees,** bend to one's will; mortify <old>, **embarrass**; put out, put out of face *or*

countenance; **deflate,** prick one's balloon; tread *or* trample underfoot, trample down, ride down, ride *or* run roughshod over, override; have one's way with
ADJS 2 **lowly,** low, **poor, mean,** small, inglorious, undistinguished; unimportant; innocuous; **modest, unpretentious**; **plain, simple,** homely; humble-looking, humble-visaged; humblest, lowliest, lowest, least

**humbug** NOUNS

<nonformal> **bunk bunkum;** hooey, hoke, **hokum, bosh,** bull, **bullshit,** crap, baloney, flimflam, flam, smoke and mirrors, claptrap, moonshine, eyewash, hogwash, jiggery-pokery <Brit>

**humdinger** NOUNS

<nonformal> **dandy,** jim dandy, dilly, pip, pippin, peach, beaut, **lulu,** doozy, honey, sweetheart, dream, lollapaloosa, crackerjack, hot shit *or* poo, pisser, pistol, corker, whiz, **crackerjack,** knockout, something else, something else again, barn-burner, killer, killer-diller, the nuts, the cat's pajamas *or* balls *or* meow, whiz, whizbang, wow

**humdrum** ADJS **tedious, monotonous,** singsong, jog-trot, treadmill, unvarying, invariable, uneventful, broken-record, parrotlike, harping, everlasting, too much with us <nonformal>; tiresome, blah <nonformal>, **dreary,** drearisome, dry, dryasdust, dusty, **dull**

**humidity** NOUNS humidness, **dankness,** dankishness, **mugginess,** stickiness, sweatiness; absolute humidity, relative humidity; dew point; humidification

**humiliate** VERBS 1 **humble;** mortify <old>, **embarrass**; put out, put out of face *or* countenance; **shame, disgrace,** put to shame, put to the blush, give one a red face; **deflate;** dishonor, treat with indignity; **add insult to injury**

2 <nonformal> beat *or* knock *or* **cut one down to size,** take the shine *or* starch out of, take the wind out of one's sails; put one's nose out of joint, put a tuck in one's tail, make one sing small; prick one's balloon

**humility** NOUNS **humbleness,** meekness; **lowliness,** lowlihood, poorness, meanness, smallness, ingloriousness; unimportance; innocuousness; **modesty,** unpretentiousness

**humor** NOUNS 1 **wit,** pleasantry, *esprit* <Fr>, salt, spice *or* savor of wit; Attic wit *or* salt, Atticism; ready wit, quick wit, nimble wit, agile wit, pretty wit; dry wit, subtle wit; **comedy**; black humor, sick humor, gallows humor; slapstick humor, broad humor; visual humor
2 **mood,** feeling, feelings, temper, frame of mind, state of mind, morale, tone, note, **vein**
VERBS 3 **indulge, oblige;** favor, please, gratify, satisfy, **cater to; give way to,** yield to, let one have his own way; **pamper,** cosset, **coddle,** mollycoddle

**humorist** NOUNS **wit,** satirist, ironist; burlesquer, caricaturist, parodist, lampooner

**humorless** ADJS **unhappy, uncheerful,** uncheery, **cheerless, joyless, unjoyful,** unsmiling; mirthless, unmirthful, infestive; funny as a crutch <nonformal>; **out of humor,** out of sorts, in bad humor *or* spirits

**humorous** ADJS **funny,** amusing; witty; droll, whimsical, quizzical; **laughable,** risible, good for a laugh; **ludicrous,** ridiculous, hilarious, absurd, quaint, eccentric, incongruous, bizarre

**hump** NOUNS **bulge,** bilge, bow, convex; **bump;** thank-you-ma'am *and* whoopdedoo <both nonformal>, cahot <Can>; speed bump, sleeping policeman <Brit>; hill, mountain; hunch

**hunch** NOUNS **guess, conjecture,** unverified supposition, perhaps, speculation, guesswork, surmise, educated guess; guesstimate *and* shot *and* stab <all nonformal>; blind guess, bold conjecture, shot in the dark <nonformal>

**hunchbacked** ADJS **humpbacked,** bunchbacked, crookbacked, crookedbacked, camelback, humped, gibbous, kyphotic

**hung** ADJS **pendent,** pendulous, pendulant, pendular, penduline, pensile; **suspended**

**hunger** NOUNS **appetite,** stomach, relish, taste; hungriness; the munchies <nonformal>; **yen,** lech <nonformal>, thirst; instinct *or* feeling for, sensitivity to

**hungry** ADJS hungering, peckish <Brit nonformal>; empty <nonformal>, unfilled; ravening, **ravenous,** voracious, sharp-set, **wolfish,** dog-hungry <nonfor-

mal>, hungry as a bear; **starved, famished,** starving, famishing, perishing *or* pinched with hunger; fasting; half-starved, half-famished

**hunk** NOUNS

1 <nonformal> **he-man,** *and* two-fisted man <both nonformal>, jockstrap *and* jock <both nonformal>, man with hair on his chest; caveman *and* bucko <both nonformal>

2 **batch,** bunch, heap <nonformal>, pack, mess <nonformal>, gob *and* chunk <both nonformal>

**hunt** NOUNS 1 **search,** searching, **quest,** hunting, stalk, stalking, still hunt, dragnet, posse, search party
VERBS 2 go hunting, hunt down, chase, run, shikar <India>, sport; engage in a blood sport; shoot, gun; course; ride to hounds, follow the hounds; **track,** trail; **stalk; search for,** seek for, **hunt for,** cast *or* beat about for

**hunter** NOUNS **huntsman,** sportsman, **Nimrod;** huntress, sportswoman; stalker; courser; trapper; big game hunter, shikari <India>, white hunter; jacklighter, jacker

**hurdle** NOUNS **obstacle, obstruction,** obstructer; **hang-up** <nonformal>; **block,** blockade, cordon, curtain; **difficulty,** hazard; **stumbling block,** stumbling stone, stone in one's path; fly in the ointment, one small difficulty, **hitch**

**hurl** VERBS **throw,** fling, sling, pitch, toss, cast, heave, chuck, chunk *and* peg <both nonformal>, lob, shy, fire, burn, pepper <nonformal>, launch, dash, let fly, let go, let rip, let loose

**hurrah** NOUNS 1 **cheer, huzzah,** hurray, hooray, yippee, rah; **cry, shout, yell;** hosanna, hallelujah, alleluia, paean, paean *or* chorus of cheers; **applause**

**hurricane** NOUNS **storm, tempest,** squall, line squall, **tornado, cyclone,** tropical cyclone, typhoon, storm-center, tropical storm, eye of the storm *or* hurricane, war of the elements

*Nature's elemental din*
THOMAS CAMPBELL

**hurried** ADJS **rushed,** pushed, pressed, crowded, **pressed for time,** hard-pushed *or* -pressed, hard-run; double-time, double-quick, on *or* at the double

**hurry** NOUNS 1 **haste, scurry, rush, race,** dash, drive, scuttle, scamper, **scramble,** hustle <nonformal>, **bustle,** flutter, **flurry,** hurry-scurry, helter-skelter
VERBS 2 **hasten,** haste, make haste, hie, post; march in quick *or* double-quick time; **make time,** make good time, **cover ground,** get over the ground, **make strides** *or* **rapid strides**

**hurry up** VERBS 1 **accelerate,** speed up, step up <nonformal>, **quicken; hasten**; crack on, put on, put on steam, pour on the coal, put on more speed, open the throttle; quicken one's pace; pick up speed

2 <nonformal> **step on it, snap to it,** hop to it, hotfoot, bear down on it, shake it up, **get moving** *or* **going,** get a move on, get cracking <chiefly Brit>, get *or* shake the lead out, get the lead out of one's ass, get one's ass in gear, give it the gun, hump, hump it, hump oneself, shag ass, tear ass, **get a hustle** *or* **move** *or* **wiggle on,** stir one's stumps, not spare the horses

**hurt** VERBS 1 **pain,** give *or* inflict pain, **wound, afflict, distress; chafe,** gall, fret, rasp, rub, grate; gnaw, grind; **gripe; torture, torment,** rack, put to torture, put *or* lay on the rack, **agonize, harrow,** crucify, martyr, martyrize, excruciate; **suffer, feel pain,** feel the pangs, anguish; **ache,** have a misery <nonformal>, ail
ADJS 2 **pained,** in pain, hurting, **suffering,** afflicted, wounded, distressed, in distress; **tortured,** tormented, racked, agonized, harrowed, lacerated; **impaired, damaged,** injured, harmed

**hurtle** VERBS **speed, rush, tear,** dash, dart, shoot, bolt, fling, **scamper, scurry,** scour, scud, scuttle, scramble, **race,** careen

**husband** NOUNS 1 **married man,** man, benedict, goodman <old>, old man <nonformal>
VERBS 2 **manage,** husband one's resources; live frugally, get along on a shoestring, get by on little; keep *or* stay within one's means *or* budget, balance income with outgo, live within one's income, make ends meet, cut one's coat according to one's cloth, keep *or* stay ahead of the game; **save up,** save for a rainy day

**hush** NOUNS **silence,** silentness, **soundlessness,** noiselessness, **stillness, quietness,** quietude, quiescence, **quiet, still,** peace, mum; golden silence; hush *or* dead of night

*lucid stillness*
**T S Eliot**

**hushed** ADJS **silent, still,** stilly, **quiet,** quiescent, **soundless,** noiseless; quiet as a mouse, silent as the grave *or* tomb; hushed-up

**husky** ADJS **strong,** hunky *and* hefty *and* beefy <all nonformal>, strapping, doughty <nonformal>, **hardy,** hard, hard as nails, cast-iron, iron-hard, steely; **robust,** robustious, gutty *and* gutsy <both nonformal>; **hoarse,** roupy <Scots>, cracked, dry; **guttural,** thick, throaty, croaky, croaking

**hussy** NOUNS **strumpet,** trollop, wench, slut, jade, baggage, *cocotte* <Fr>, grisette; **tart** *and* **chippy** *and* **floozy** *and* broad <all nonformal>, bitch, drab, trull, quean, harridan, Jezebel, wanton, whore <nonformal>, bad woman, **loose woman,** easy woman <nonformal>

**hustle** NOUNS 1 **enterprise,** dynamism, **initiative,** aggression, aggressiveness, pushiness, push, drive, go, **get-up-and-go** <both nonformal>, go-ahead, go-getting, go-to-itiveness <nonformal>, **up-and-comingness**
VERBS 2 drive oneself, **push, scramble,** go all out <nonformal>, **make things hum,** step lively <nonformal>, make the sparks *or* chips fly <nonformal>; go full steam ahead, **hasten,** haste, **hurry, speed; work hard; scratch** *and* **sweat** <both nonformal>, slave away, toil away

3 <nonformal> **hump,** get cutting, break one's neck, bear down on it, put one's back into it, get off the dime, get off one's ass *or* duff *or* dead ass, **hit the ball,** pour it on, lean on it, shake a leg, go to town, get the lead out, floor it

**hustler** NOUNS 1 **man** *or* **woman of action,** doer; self-starter <nonformal>, bustler; go-getter *and* ball of fire *and* live wire *and* powerhouse *and* human dynamo *and* spitfire <all nonformal>; beaver, busy bee, **eager beaver** <nonformal>
2 **streetwalker, hooker** <nonformal>; **cheater,** cheat, grifter *and* mechanic *and* mover *and* rook *and* worker <all nonformal>

**hut** NOUNS hutch, **shack, shanty,** crib, hole-in-the-wall <nonformal>, **shed; lean-to;** Quonset hut *or* Nissen hut; hutment

**hybrid** NOUNS **crossbreed,** cross, mixed-blood, mixblood, **half-breed,** half-bred, half blood, half-caste

**hygiene** NOUNS hygienics; sanitation; public health, epidemiology; health physics; **preventive medicine,** prophylaxis, preventive dentistry, prophylactodontia

**hygienic** ADJS **healthful,** healthy, salubrious, salutary, wholesome, health-preserving, health-enhancing, life-promoting, **beneficial,** benign, good, **good for; hygienical,** hygeian, sanitary

**hymn** NOUNS **thanks, thanksgiving,** praise, laud, paean, benediction; grace, prayer of thanks; hymn of praise, **doxology, psalm, anthem,** motet, canticle, chorale; offertory, offertory sentence *or* hymn; hymnody, hymnology, hymnography, psalmody

**hype** NOUNS 1 **commendation,** good word, acknowledgment, recognition, appreciation; boost *and* buildup <both nonformal>; **puff,** promotion; **blurb** *and* **plug** *and* promo <all nonformal>
VERBS 2 boost *and* give a boost to <both nonformal>, puff, promote, cry up; plug *and* tout; pour *or* spread *or* lay it on thick <all nonformal>; **recommend, advocate,** put in a word *or* good word for, support, back, lend one's name *or* support *or* backing to, make a pitch for <nonformal>

**hyperactive** ADJS **overactive,** hyper <nonformal>; hectic, frenzied, frantic, frenetic; hyperkinetic

**hypnotic** ADJS 1 **mesmeric;** odylic; narcohypnotic; soporific, somniferous, somnifacient, sleep-inducing
2 **engrossing, absorbing,** consuming, **gripping,** riveting, holding, **arresting,** engaging, attractive, **fascinating, enthralling, spellbinding,** enchanting, magnetic, mesmerizing, mesmeric; obsessive, obsessing

**hypnotist** NOUNS **mesmerist,** hypnotizer, mesmerizer; Svengali, Mesmer

**hypnotize** VERBS **mesmerize,** magnetize; **entrance,** trance, put in a trance; **cast a**

**spell,** spell, **spellbind; have influence** *or* power *or* a hold over, lead by the nose, **twist** *or* **turn** *or* **wind around one's little finger; grip,** hold, arrest, hold the interest, fascinate, enthrall, hold spellbound, grab <nonformal>, charm, enchant

**hypochondria** NOUNS hypochondriasis, valetudinarianism; morbid anxiety

**hypocrisy** NOUNS hypocriticalness; Tartuffery, Tartuffism, Pecksniffery, pharisaism, **sanctimony**, sanctimoniousness, religiosity, false piety, ostentatious devotion, pietism, Bible-thumping <nonformal>; **falseness,** insincerity, duplicity, two-facedness

**hypocrite** NOUNS **phony** <nonformal>, sanctimonious fraud, pharisee, whited sepulcher, **canter,** snuffler, mealymouth; Tartuffe <Molière>, Pecksniff *and* Uriah Heep <both Charles Dickens>; **pietist,** religionist, religious hypocrite, canting hypocrite, pious fraud, religious *or* spiritual humbug, **pharisee**

*a saint abroad and a devil at home*
BUNYAN

**hypocritical** ADJS **insincere,** mealymouthed, unctuous, oily, disingenuous, smarmy <nonformal>; dishonest; **empty, hollow; sanctimonious,** sanctified, pious, pietistic, pietistical, self-righteous, pharisaic, pharisaical, **holier-than-thou, false**

**hypodermic** NOUNS **injection,** hypodermic injection, shot *and* bing <both nonformal>, hypospray *or* jet injection; booster, booster shot <nonformal>, needle <nonformal>

**hypothesis** NOUNS **theory, explanation,** proposed *or* tentative explanation, proposal, proposition, statement covering the facts or evidence; working hypothesis

**hypothetical** ADJS **theoretical,** hypothetic; postulatory, notional; **speculative, conjectural;** merely theoretical, academic, moot; impractical, armchair

**hysteria** NOUNS **fury, furor,** furore <Brit>, fire and fury; **passion, rage,** raging *or* tearing passion, towering rage *or* passion; madness, craze, **delirium**

**hysterical** ADJS **emotionalistic,** emotive, overemotional, hysteric, sensational, sensationalistic, melodramatic, theatric, theatrical, histrionic, dramatic, overdramatic, hammy <nonformal>, nonrational, unreasoning; overemotional, hyperthymic, in hysterics

# I

**ice** NOUNS 1 frozen water; ice needle *or* crystal; **icicle**
VERBS 2 **refrigerate; cool, chill;** ice-cool; ice up, ice over, glaze, glaze over

**iced** ADJS **cooled, chilled; air-conditioned,** ice-cooled

**icing** NOUNS **topping,** frosting

**icky** ADJS

<nonformal> **nasty,** yecchy, yucky, gross, grungy, scuzzy

**icon** NOUNS **image, likeness; effigy,** idol; **symbol,** emblem, token, type; **alterpiece,** diptych, triptych

**iconoclast** NOUNS **destroyer, ruiner, wrecker, bane,** wiper-out, demolisher; idoloclast, idol breaker; **irreligionist**

**idea** NOUNS **thought,** mental *or* intellectual object, **notion, concept,** conception, conceit, fancy; **perception, sense, impression,** mental impression, image, **mental image,** picture in the mind, mental picture, representation, recept; imago; memory trace; **sentiment,** apprehension; reflection, observation; **opinion**; supposition, **theory**

**ideal** NOUNS 1 ideal type, acme, highest *or* perfect *or* best type; cynosure, apotheosis, idol; **shining example, hero, superhero; model,** the very model, role model, mirror, paragon, epitome
ADJS 2 **idealized;** utopian, Arcadian, Edenic, paradisal; pie in the sky <nonformal>; heavenly, celestial; millennial; **perfect, faultless, flawless,** unflawed, defectless, not to be improved, **impeccable,** absolute; **just right;** beyond all praise, irreproachable, unfaultable, *sans peur et sans reproche* <Fr>, **matchless, peerless**

**idealist** NOUNS **visionary;** utopian, utopianist, utopianizer

**idealize** VERBS utopianize, quixotize, rhapsodize; **romanticize,** romance; paint pretty pictures of, paint in bright colors; see through rose-colored glasses; **build castles in the air** *or* **Spain**

**identical** ADJS **same, selfsame,** one, **one and the same,** all the same, all one, of the same kidney; **indistinguishable,** without distinction, without difference, undifferent, undifferentiated; **alike, all alike, like,** just alike, exactly alike, like two peas in a pod

**identification** NOUNS identification mark; **badge,** identification badge, identification tag, dog tag <military>, personal identification number *or* PIN number *or* PIN, **identity card** *or* **ID card** *or* **ID; card,** business card, calling card, visiting card, *carte de visite* <Fr>, press card
2 likening, unification, coalescence, combination, union, fusion, merger, melding, synthesis

**identify** VERBS **signify, betoken,** stand for, differentiate, note <old>, speak of, talk, **indicate,** be indicative of, be an indication of, be significant of, connote, denominate, argue, bespeak, be symptomatic *or* diagnostic of, symptomize, **characterize, mark,** highlight, be the mark *or* sign of, give token, **denote, mean; define; place,** have; spot *and* nail *and* peg *and* cotton on <all nonformal>

**identify with** VERBS **sympathize,** empathize, respond to, understand one another, enter into one's views, enter into the ideas *or* feelings of; **accord,** correspond

**identity** NOUNS **sameness,** identicalness, selfsameness, indistinguishability, undifferentiation, nondifferentiation, two peas in a pod; **equality, parity,** par, equation; **personality,** personship, personal identity; **oneness,** unity, singleness, singularity, individuality

**ideology** NOUNS system of ideas, body of ideas, system of theories; world view, *Weltanschauung* <Ger>; philosophy; **ethos**

**idiom** NOUNS **phrase, expression, locution, utterance,** usage, term, verbalism; idiotism, phrasal idiom; turn of phrase *or* expression, peculiar expression, manner *or* way of speaking; set phrase *or* term; conventional *or* common *or* standard phrase

**idiosyncrasy** NOUNS **mannerism,** *minauderie* <Fr>, **trick of behavior,** idiocrasy, trick, **quirk,** habit, peculiarity, peculiar trait, trademark; **characteristic,** character, peculiarity, **property,** differentia, **eccentricity**

**idiot** NOUNS driveling *or* blithering *or* adenoidal *or* congenital idiot; **imbecile,**

**moron, half-wit,** natural, natural idiot, born fool, natural-born fool, mental defective, defective; cretin, basket case <nonformal>

**idiotic** ADJS **foolish, inane;** futile; **senseless, witless, thoughtless,** insensate, brainless; moronic, imbecile, imbecilic

**idle** VERBS 1 **fritter away,** fool away, fribble away, dribble away, drivel away, **trifle away,** dally away, potter away, piss away <nonformal>, muddle away, diddle away <nonformal>, squander in dribs and drabs; idle away, while away
2 **trifle, dally; flirt, coquet; toy,** fribble, **play, fool,** play at, **putter, potter,** tinker, **piddle; dabble,** smatter; toy with, fiddle with, fool with, play with
ADJS 3 **sluggish,** languid, languorous, lazy, slothful, indolent, slouchy; **inactive,** unactive; fallow, otiose; **unemployed, unoccupied,** disengaged, *désœvré* <Fr>, **jobless, out of work,** out of a job, out of harness; free, available, at liberty, at leisure; at loose ends

**idol** NOUNS 1 **hero, god, demigod,** phoenix; **heroine, goddess,** demigoddess; false god
2 fetish, totem, joss; **graven image, golden calf;** devil-god, Baal, Jaganatha *or* Juggernaut; sacred cow

*the god of my idolatry*
SHAKESPEARE

**idolize** VERBS **cherish, hold dear,** hold in one's heart *or* affections, think much *or* the world of, prize, treasure; **admire, regard,** esteem, revere; **adore,** worship, dearly love, think worlds *or* the world of, love to distraction; **revere, reverence,** hold in reverence, **venerate,** honor, look up to, defer to, bow to, exalt, put on a pedestal, hero-worship, deify, apotheosize, worship the ground one walks on, stand in awe of

**idyllic** ADJS **pacific,** peaceful, peaceable; **tranquil, serene;** pastoral, bucolic, eclogic

**iffy** ADJS **doubtful, in doubt,** *in dubio* <L>; dubitable, doubtable, **dubious,** questionable, problematic, problematical, speculative, conjectural, suppositional; **debatable,** moot, arguable, disputable, contestable, controvertible, **controversial,** refutable, confutable, deniable; **casual,** adventitious, incidental, contingent

**ignite** VERBS **set fire to, fire, set on fire, kindle,** enkindle, inflame, **light,** light up, strike a light, apply the match *or* torch to, torch <nonformal>, touch off, **burn,** conflagrate; **build a fire;** rekindle, relight, relume; feed, feed the fire, **stoke,** stoke the fire, add fuel to the flame; bank; poke *or* stir the fire, blow up the fire, fan the flame; open the draft

**ignominious** ADJS **disreputable,** discreditable, dishonorable, unsavory, shady, **seamy, sordid; unrespectable,** ignoble, infamous, inglorious; unpraiseworthy; derogatory

**ignoramus** NOUNS **know-nothing;** no scholar, puddinghead, dunce, fool; **illiterate; lowbrow** <nonformal>; unintelligentsia, illiterati

**ignorance** NOUNS **unknowingness,** unknowing, nescience; lack of information, knowledge-gap, hiatus of learning; empty-headedness, blankmindedness, vacuousness, vacuity, inanity; tabula rasa; **unacquaintance,** unfamiliarity; **greenness,** greenhornism, rawness, callowness, unripeness, green in the eye, **inexperience**; crass *or* gross *or* primal *or* pristine ignorance

**ignorant** ADJS nescient, **unknowing,** uncomprehending, **know-nothing;** simple, **dumb** <nonformal>, empty, empty-headed, blankminded, vacuous, inane, **unintelligent**; **ill-informed,** uninformed, unenlightened, unilluminated, unapprized, unposted <nonformal>, clueless *or* pig-ignorant <both Brit nonformal>

**ignore** VERBS **slight,** pooh-pooh <nonformal>, make little of, dismiss, pretend not to see, disregard, overlook, neglect, pass by, pass up *and* give the go-by <both nonformal>, leave out in the cold <nonformal>, take no note *or* notice of, look right through <nonformal>, pay no attention *or* regard to, refuse to acknowledge *or* recognize

**ignored** ADJS **neglected,** unattended to, untended, unwatched, unchaperoned, uncared-for; **disregarded,** unconsidered, unregarded, **overlooked, missed,** omitted, passed by, passed over, passed up <nonformal>, gathering dust, **slighted;** half-done, undone, left undone; deserted, abandoned

**ilk** NOUNS **kind, sort, type,** breed of cat <nonformal>, lot <nonformal>, **variety, species, genus,** *genre* <Fr>, phylum, denomination, designation, description, style, manner, **nature, character,** persuasion, the like *or* likes of <nonformal>

**ill** ADJS **ailing, sick, unwell, indisposed,** taken ill, down, bad, on the sick list; **sickish, seedy** *and* rocky <both nonformal>, **under the weather, out of sorts** <nonformal>, below par <nonformal>, off-color, off one's feed <nonformal>; not quite right, not oneself; faint, faintish, feeling faint; feeling awful *and* feeling something terrible <both nonformal>; sick as a dog *or* a pig <nonformal>, laid low; in a bad way, critically ill, in danger, on the critical list, on the guarded list, in intensive care; mortally ill, sick unto death

ADVS 2 **unkindly, unbenignly,** unbenignantly; **unamiably,** disagreeably, uncordially, ungraciously, inhospitably, ungenially, unsympathetically, uncompassionately; **badly,** bad <nonformal>, evil, evilly, wrong, wrongly, amiss

**ill-advised** ADJS **unwise,** injudicious, **imprudent,** unpolitic, impolitic, contraindicated, **counterproductive;** indiscreet; **ill-considered,** ill-gauged, ill-judged, ill-imagined, on the wrong track, unconsidered

**illegal** ADJS **unlawful, illegitimate, illicit,** nonlicit, nonlegal, lawless, wrongful, fraudulent, creative <nonformal>, **against the law; unauthorized,** unallowed, impermissible, unwarranted, unwarrantable, unofficial; **criminal, felonious**

**illegality** NOUNS **unlawfulness,** illicitness, lawlessness, wrongfulness; unauthorization, impermissibility; legal *or* technical flaw, legal irregularity; **outlawry;** collapse *or* breakdown *or* paralysis of authority, anomie

**illegible** ADJS **unreadable, unclear; undecipherable,** indecipherable

**illegitimate** ADJS **spurious,** false; **bastard,** misbegot, **misbegotten,** miscreated, gotten on the wrong side of the blanket, baseborn, born out of wedlock, without benefit of clergy

**ill-equipped** ADJS **unfitted, unfit,** ill-fitted, **unsuited, unadapted, unqualified,** disqualified, incompetent, incapable; **unequipped, unfurnished,** unarmed, ill-furnished, **unprovided,** ill-provided

**ill-fated** ADJS **ominous, portentous,** portending; **foreboding,** boding, **bodeful; inauspicious, ill-omened,** ill-boding, of ill *or* fatal omen, of evil portent, loaded *or* laden *or* freighted *or* fraught with doom, looming, looming over; fateful, doomful; apocalyptic; **unpropitious, unpromising, unfavorable, unfortunate, unlucky; sinister,** dark, black, gloomy, somber, dreary; **threatening, menacing, lowering;** bad, evil, ill, untoward; dire, baleful, baneful, ill-starred, evil-starred, star-crossed

**ill health** NOUNS **unhealthiness,** healthlessness; poor health, delicate *or* shaky *or* frail *or* fragile health; **sickliness,** peakedness <nonformal>, **feebleness,** delicacy, weakliness, fragility, **frailty; infirmity, unsoundness,** debility, debilitation, enervation; chronic ill health, invalidity, **invalidism**

**illicit** ADJS **illegal, unlawful, illegitimate,** nonlicit, nonlegal, lawless, wrongful, fraudulent, creative <nonformal>, **against the law; unauthorized,** unallowed, impermissible, unwarranted, unwarrantable, outlaw, outlawed; **adulterous,** extramarital, premarital; incestuous

**ill-informed** ADJS **uninformed,** unenlightened, unilluminated, unapprised, unposted <nonformal>, clueless <nonformal>; **unversed,** uninitiated, **unfamiliar,** strange to

**illiterate** NOUNS 1 **ignoramus, know-nothing;** no scholar, puddinghead, dunce, fool

ADJS 2 **uneducated,** unschooled, uninstructed, untutored, unbriefed, untaught, unedified, unguided; ill-educated, functionally illiterate, unlettered, grammarless

**illness** NOUNS **disease, sickness,** malady, ailment, indisposition, disorder, complaint, morbidity, *morbus* <L>, **affliction,** affection, **infirmity; sickishness,** malaise, seediness *and* rockiness <both nonformal>; complication, secondary disease *or* condition

**illogical** ADJS **unreasonable, irrational, reasonless,** contrary to reason, **senseless,** without reason, **without rhyme or reason; unscientific,** nonscientific, unphilosophical; **invalid,** inauthentic, unauthentic, faulty, flawed, paralogical, fallacious; **inconsistent,** incongruous, contradictory, **self-contradictory,** self-annulling, self-refuting, oxymoronic

**ill repute** NOUNS **disrepute,** bad repute,

bad *or* poor reputation, evil repute *or* reputation, ill fame, shady *or* unsavory reputation, **bad name,** bad odor, bad report, bad character; **disesteem, dishonor,** public dishonor, **discredit; disfavor,** ill-favor; disapprobation

**ill-suited** ADJS **inappropriate, inapt,** unapt, inapposite, misplaced, **irrelevant,** malapropos, *mal à propos* <Fr>; **unsuited, unfitted,** ill-fitted; **maladjusted,** ill-chosen; ill-matched, ill-mated, mismatched, mismated, mismarried, misallied; **unfit,** inept, unqualified; unfitting, unbefitting; **unsuitable,** improper, **unbecoming,** unseemly; **out of place,** out of line, out of keeping, out of character, out of proportion, out of joint, out of tune, out of time, out of season, out of its element

**illuminated** ADJS luminous, **lightened,** enlightened, brightened, **lighted,** lit, **lit up,** flooded *or* bathed with light, floodlit; irradiated, irradiate; **alight, glowing,** aglow, lambent, suffused with light; lamplit, lanternlit, candlelit, torchlit, gaslit, firelit; sunlit, moonlit, starlit

**illuminating** ADJS **explanatory,** explaining, exegetic, exegetical, **explicative,** explicatory; **expository,** expositive; **clarifying, elucidative, elucidatory;** illuminative, enlightening; illumining, **lighting, lightening,** brightening

**illusion** NOUNS **delusion,** deluded belief; **deception, trick;** self-deception, self-deceit, self-delusion; dereism, autism; **misconception, misbelief,** false belief, wrong impression, warped *or* distorted conception; **bubble, chimera,** vapor, *ignis fatuus* <L>, will-o'-the-wisp; **dream,** dream vision; dreamworld, dreamland, dreamscape; **daydream;** pipe dream *and* trip <nonformal>; fool's paradise

*airy nothing*
**Shakespeare**

**illusionary** ADJS **bewitching, witching;** illusory, illusive; **enchanting, entrancing, spellbinding, fascinating,** glamorous, Circean

**illusory** ADJS **deceptive, deceiving, misleading,** beguiling, **false, fallacious,** delusive, delusory; hallucinatory, illusive, illusionary; **unreal,** unrealistic, **immaterial; imaginary,** imagined, fantastic, fanciful, fancied

**illustrate** VERBS **demonstrate, show,** exemplify; exhibit, manifest, display, express, set forth

**illustration** NOUNS **representation, delineation,** presentment, drawing, portrayal, portraiture, depiction, depictment, rendering, rendition, characterization; exemplification, demonstration; **picture**

**illustrative** ADJS **explanatory,** clarifying, elucidative; illuminating, illuminative, enlightening; **demonstrative,** exemplificative; illustrational; pictorial, graphic, vivid

**ill will** NOUNS **animosity,** animus; ill feeling, bitter feeling, **hard feelings,** no love lost; **bitterness,** sourness, soreness, **rancor,** acrimony, virulence, venom, vitriol

**image** NOUNS **likeness; resemblance,** semblance, similitude, simulacrum; **effigy,** icon, idol; **copy,** fair copy; **portrait,** likeness; **perfect** *or* **exact likeness,** representation, duplicate, double; match, fellow, mate, companion, **twin;** living image, very image, very picture, living picture, dead ringer <nonformal>, spitting image *or* spit and image *or* spit 'n' image <all nonformal>; **figure of speech,** trope

**imaginable** ADJS fanciable, **conceivable, thinkable,** cogitable; **supposable**

**imaginary** ADJS notional; **imagined, fancied; unreal,** unrealistic, nonexistent, never-never; visional, supposititious, **all in the mind; illusory**

**imagination** NOUNS imagining, imaginativeness, **fancy, fantasy,** conceit <old>; mind's eye, flight of fancy, fumes of fancy

*that inward eye which is the bliss of solitude*
**Wordsworth**

**imaginative** ADJS conceptual, conceptive, ideational, ideative, notional; **inventive, original,** originative, esemplastic, shaping, **creative, ingenious; productive, fertile,** fecund, prolific, seminal, germinal, teeming, pregnant; **inspired,** visioned

**imagine** VERBS **fancy, conceive,** conceptualize, ideate, figure to oneself; **invent,** create, originate, make, think up, dream up, shape, mold, coin, hatch, concoct, fabricate, produce; **suppose; fantasize;**

give free rein to the imagination, let one's imagination run riot *or* run wild, allow one's imagination to run away with one; experience imaginatively *or* vicariously

**imaging** NOUNS **visualization, envisioning,** envisaging, picturing, objectification, calling to *or* before the mind's eye, figuring *or* portraying *or* representing in the mind; depicting *or* delineating in the imagination; conceptualization

**imbalance** NOUNS **inequality,** disparity, unevenness, contrariety, difference; **disproportion,** asymmetry; **unbalance,** disequilibrium, overbalance, inclination of the balance, overcompensation, tippiness; **injustice,** inequity

**imbecile** NOUNS 1 **idiot,** driveling *or* blithering *or* adenoidal *or* congenital idiot; **moron, half-wit,** born fool, natural-born fool, mental defective, defective; **simpleton,** simp <nonformal>
ADJS 2 **foolish,** fool <nonformal>, foolheaded <nonformal>, **stupid, dumb** <nonformal>, **asinine;** buffoonish; **senseless,** witless, thoughtless, insensate, brainless; **idiotic,** moronic, imbecilic, **insane**

**imbue** VERBS **suffuse,** inform, transfuse, perfuse, diffuse, leaven; **infuse, infect,** inject, inoculate; **inculcate,** indoctrinate, catechize, **instill,** impregnate, **implant,** infix, impress

**imitate** VERBS **copy, repeat,** do like <nonformal>, do <nonformal>, act *or* go *or* make like <nonformal>; **mirror, reflect; echo,** reecho, chorus; **borrow,** steal one's stuff <nonformal>, take a leaf out of one's book; assume, **affect; simulate;** counterfeit, fake <nonformal>, hoke *and* hoke up <both nonformal>, forge, plagiarize, crib, lift <nonformal>; **parody,** pastiche; **paraphrase,** approximate

**imitation** NOUNS 1 **copying,** counterfeiting, repetition; **me-tooism** <nonformal>, emulation, the sincerest form of flattery, following, mirroring; copycat crime <nonformal>; **simulation**, modeling; fakery, forgery, plagiarism, plagiarizing, plagiary; **imposture, impersonation, takeoff** *and* hit-off <both nonformal>, **impression,** burlesque, pastiche, *pasticcio* <Ital>; mimesis; parody, onomatopoeia
ADJS 2 **mock, sham,** copied, fake *and* phony *and* bogus <all nonformal>, counterfeit, forged, plagiarized, unoriginal, ungenuine; **pseudo,** synthetic, synthetical, ersatz, hokey *and* hoked-up <both nonformal>

**immaculate** ADJS **chaste,** spotless, virtuous, pure; **clean,** squeaky-clean <nonformal>; blotless, stainless, taintless, white, snowy, pure *or* white as driven snow, guiltless, **innocent**

**immature** ADJS unadult; **inexperienced,** unseasoned, unfledged, new-fledged, **callow, unripe,** ripening, unmellowed, **raw, green,** vernal, primaveral, dewy, juicy, sappy, budding, tender, virginal, intact, innocent, naive, ingenuous, **undeveloped,** growing, unformed, unlicked, wet *or* not dry behind the ears; **minor,** underage, **puerile, childish;** childlike; **infantile**

**immeasurable** ADJS **vast,** vasty, boundless, **infinite**, cosmic, astronomical, galactic; **spacious,** amplitudinous, extensive; **tremendous,** stupendous, awesome, prodigious; incalculable, unreckonable, innumerable, incomprehensible, unfathomable; measureless, inexhaustible, endless, infinite, without end *or* limit, more than one can tell, more than you can shake a stick at <nonformal>, no end of *or* to

**immediate** ADJS **present,** attendant; immanent, indwelling, inherent, **available, accessible, at hand,** in view, within reach *or* sight *or* call, in place; **nearest,** nighest, **closest,** nearmost, next; **prompt, punctual, instant,** instantaneous, **quick**, speedy, swift, expeditious, summary, decisive, apt, alert, **ready,** Johnny-on-the-spot <nonformal>

**immense** ADJS **huge, vast, enormous,** astronomic, astronomical, humongous *and* jumbo <both nonformal>, king-size, queen-size, tremendous, prodigious, stupendous, macro, mega, giga; great big, larger than life, Homeric, mighty, **titanic, colossal, monumental,** heroic, heroical, epic, epical, towering, mountainous; **mammoth,** mastodonic; **gigantic, giant,** giantlike, gigantesque, gigantean

**immersion** NOUNS **submergence, submersion,** immergence, engulfment, **inundation,** burial; **dipping, ducking,** dousing, sousing, dunking <nonformal>, sinking; **baptism, baptizement; christening;** total immersion; **engross-**

**ment,** absorption, intentness, single-mindedness, **concentration, application,** study, studiousness, **preoccupation,** engagement, **involvement**

**immigrant** NOUNS **settler,** *habitant* <Canadian & Louisiana Fr>; **newcomer,** new arrival, *novus homo* <L>; greenhorn

**immigration** NOUNS in-migration, incoming population, foreign influx; border-crossing

**imminent** ADJS **impending,** impendent, **overhanging,** hanging over one's head, waiting, lurking, **threatening, looming,** lowering, **menacing,** lying in ambush; **brewing,** gathering, preparing; **coming, forthcoming, upcoming, to come,** about to be, about *or* going to happen, **approaching, nearing,** looming up, looming in the distance *or* future; **near, close,** immediate, instant, soon to be, **at hand,** near at hand, close at hand; **in the offing,** on the horizon, **in prospect,** already in sight, just around the corner, in view, in one's eye, in store, in reserve, **in the wind**

**immobile** ADJS **immovable,** unmovable, immotile, unmoving, **stationary,** frozen, not to be moved, at a standstill, on dead center; **firm, unyielding,** adamant, adamantine, rigid, **inflexible**

**immodest** ADJS unmodest; exhibitionistic; **shameless,** unashamed, unembarrassed, unabashed, unblushing, **brazen,** brazenfaced, brassy; **forward,** bold, pert, bumptious; **flagrant,** notorious, scandalous

**immolation** NOUNS **extermination,** destruction, destruction of life, taking of life, death-dealing, dealing of death, bane; ritual murder *or* killing, sacrifice; *auto-da-fé* <Sp, literally, act of faith>, martyrdom, martyrization; **oblation, offering, sacrifice,** incense; self-sacrifice, self-immolation; sutteeism

**immoral** ADJS **dishonorable;** unconscionable, shameless, without shame *or* remorse, **unscrupulous, unprincipled,** unethical, amoral; **corrupt,** corrupted, rotten

**immortal** ADJS everlasting, **deathless,** undying, never-dying, **imperishable,** incorruptible, amaranthine; fadeless, **unfading,** never-fading, ever-fresh

**immortality** NOUNS eternal life, **deathlessness,** imperishability, undyingness, incorruptibility *or* incorruption, athanasy *or* athanasia; eternal youth, fountain of youth; lasting *or* undying fame, secure place in history

**immortalize** VERBS **glorify,** glamorize; **exalt,** elevate, ensky, raise, uplift, set up, **ennoble,** aggrandize, magnify, exalt to the skies; crown; throne, enthrone; enshrine, make legendary, **perpetuate, preserve,** preserve from oblivion, keep fresh *or* alive, perennialize, **eternalize,** eternize

**immovable** ADJS unmovable, **immobile,** irremovable, stationary, frozen, not to be moved, at a standstill, on dead center; **firm, unyielding,** stubborn, adamant, adamantine, rigid, **inflexible**; pat, standpat <nonformal>

**immune** ADJS **resistant,** nonprone *or* nonsusceptible to disease; **exempt;** exempted, **released, excused,** immunized, excepted, let off <nonformal>, spared; grandfathered; permitted; dispensed; **unliable,** unsubject, irresponsible, unaccountable, unanswerable

**immunity** NOUNS **resistance,** nonproneness *or* nonsusceptibility to disease; **immunization; pardon,** excuse, impunity, sparing, **amnesty,** indemnity, exemption, reprieve, grace; **absolution,** shrift, remission, remission of sin; redemption; **exoneration, exculpation**

**immunize** VERBS **inoculate, vaccinate,** shoot <nonformal>

**immutable** ADJS **unchangeable,** not to be changed, changeless, unchanged, unchanging, unvarying, unvariable, **unalterable,** unaltered, unalterative, incommutable, inconvertible, unmodifiable; insusceptible of change; **inflexible,** unmalleable, intractable, untractable, intractile, **unbending, unyielding**, ungiving, **stubborn,** unalterable; irrevocable, indefeasible, **irreversible**

**imp** NOUNS **brat, minx,** puck, elf, gamin, little monkey, **whippersnapper,** young whippersnapper, *enfant terrible* <Fr>, little terror, holy terror; **pixie,** sprite, puck, kobold, *diablotin* <Fr>, tokoloshe, poltergeist, **gremlin**

**impact** NOUNS 1 **collision, clash,** appulse, **encounter,** meeting, impingement, **bump, crash,** crump, whomp; **carom,** carambole, cannon; sideswipe <nonformal>; smash *and* crunch <both nonformal>; **shock,** brunt; **concussion,** percussion

VERBS 2 operate on, **act on** *or* **upon, work on, affect, influence,** bear on, impact on; have to do with, treat, focus *or* concentrate on; bring to bear on; **run into,** bump into, bang into, slam into, smack into, **crash into,** smash into, carom into, **hit against,** strike against, knock against

**impacted** ADJS **stuck, jammed,** congested, packed, wedged

**impaired** ADJS **damaged,** hurt, injured, harmed; **deteriorated, worsened,** cut to the quick, aggravated, exacerbated, irritated, embittered; weakened; imperfect

**impale** VERBS **pierce, run through,** spit, **transfix,** transpierce; **spear,** lance, poniard, bayonet, saber, sword, put to the sword; spike

**impart** VERBS **communicate, tell,** lay on one <nonformal>, **convey, transmit,** transfer, send, send word, deliver *or* send a signal *or* message, **disseminate,** broadcast, pass, **pass on** *or* **along, hand on; report, render, make known,** get across *or* over; **disclose, reveal, let out, show,** discover, **leak,** let slip out, let the cat out of the bag *and* spill the beans <both nonformal>

**impartial** ADJS **impersonal, evenhanded,** fair, just, equitable, **dispassionate, disinterested,** detached, objective, lofty, Olympian; **unbiased,** uninfluenced, unswayed; **neutral**; selfless, unselfish

**impasse** NOUNS **corner** *and* **box** *and* **hole** <all nonformal>, cleft stick; cul-de-sac, blind alley, **dead end,** dead-end street; **extremity, end of one's rope** *or* **tether,** wit's end, nowhere to turn; **stalemate,** deadlock; stand, standoff, standstill, halt, stop

**impassioned** ADJS **fervent,** fervid, passionate, intense; **hearty, cordial,** enthusiastic, exuberant, unrestrained, vigorous; **zealous, ardent,** perfervid, **spirited,** vehement, abandoned, **warm,** heated, hot, hot-blooded, red-hot, fiery, white-hot, flaming, burning, afire, aflame, on fire

**impassive** ADJS **stolid,** inexcitable, **imperturbable,** undisturbable, **inexpressive,** unexpressive, unflappable <nonformal>; **dispassionate,** unpassionate; **steady;** stoic, stoical; **even-tempered;** bovine, expressionless, blank, dull; **patient**

**impatient** ADJS breathless; champing at the bit, rarin' to go <nonformal>; dying, **anxious, eager;** hopped-up *and* in a lather *and* in a sweat *or* stew <all nonformal>, excited; edgy, **on edge; restless,** restive, unquiet, uneasy, on *shpilkes* <Yiddish>; **fretful,** fretting, chafing, antsy-pantsy *and* antsy <both nonformal>, squirming, squirmy, about to pee *or* piss one's pants <nonformal>

**impeach** VERBS **denounce,** denunciate, **accuse**, decry, cry down, arraign, indict, call to account, exclaim *or* declaim *or* inveigh against, peg away at, cry out against, cry out on *or* upon, cry shame upon, raise one's voice against, raise a hue and cry against, shake up <old>

**impeachable** ADJS **blameworthy,** blamable, to blame, at fault, much at fault; **reprehensible,** censurable, reproachable, reprovable, open to criticism *or* reproach; **culpable,** chargeable, indictable, arraignable, imputable

**impeachment** NOUNS **arraignment,** indictment; **complaint, charge**; presentment; information; bill of indictment, true bill

**impeccable** ADJS **perfect, ideal, faultless, flawless,** unflawed, defectless, not to be improved, absolute; **just right;** spotless, stainless, taintless, unblemished, untainted, unspotted, immaculate, **pure,** uncontaminated, unadulterated, unmixed; chaste; beyond all praise, irreproachable, unfaultable, *sans peur et sans reproche* <Fr>, **matchless, peerless**

**impede** VERBS **hamper, cramp,** embarrass; trammel, entrammel, enmesh, entangle, ensnarl, entrap, entwine, involve, entoil, toil, net, lime, tangle, snarl; **encumber,** cumber, **burden,** lumber, **saddle with,** weigh *or* weight down, press down; hang like a millstone round one's neck; **handicap,** put at a disadvantage; cripple, hobble, hamstring

**impediment** NOUNS embarrassment, hamper; encumbrance, cumbrance; **trouble,** difficulty; **handicap,** disadvantage, inconvenience, penalty; **burden,** imposition, onus, cross, weight, deadweight, ball and chain, millstone around one's neck

**impel** VERBS give an impetus, **set going** *or* agoing, put *or* set in motion, give momentum; **drive, move,** animate, actuate, forward; **thrust,** power; drive *or* whip on; goad; motivate, incite; compel

**impending** ADJS **imminent,** impendent, **overhanging,** hanging over one's head, waiting, lurking, **threatening, looming,** lowering, **menacing,** lying in ambush, **brewing,** gathering, preparing; **coming, forthcoming, upcoming, to come,** about to be, about *or* going to happen, **approaching, nearing,** looming, looming up, looming in the distance *or* future; **near, close,** immediate, instant, soon to be, **at hand,** near at hand, close at hand; **in the offing,** on the horizon, **in prospect,** already in sight, just around the corner, in view, in one's eye, in store, in reserve, **in the wind**

**impenetrable** ADJS **impregnable, invulnerable,** inviolable, inexpugnable; **unassailable,** unattackable, insuperable, unsurmountable; resistless, **irresistible; invincible,** indomitable, **unconquerable,** incontestable, unbeatable; **dense,** thick, heavy, overgrown, overrun; **unfathomable,** inscrutable, ambiguous; **incoherent,** unconnected, rambling; **past comprehension,** beyond one's comprehension, beyond understanding; Greek to one

**imperative** NOUNS 1 **urgent need,** dire necessity; **exigency** *or* exigence, **urgency,** imperativeness, immediacy, pressingness, pressure; matter of necessity, case of need *or* emergency, **matter of life and death**

ADJS 2 **mandatory,** mandated, **compulsory,** prescript, prescriptive, **obligatory,** must <nonformal>; decisive, final, peremptory, absolute, eternal, written, hard-and-fast, carved in stone, set in concrete <nonformal>, ultimate, conclusive, binding, irrevocable, without appeal; **urgent,** imperious, **compelling, pressing,** high-priority, high-pressure, crying, clamorous, insistent, instant, exigent

**imperfect** ADJS not perfect; unperfected; **defective, faulty, inadequate, deficient,** short, not all it's cracked up to be <nonformal>, lacking, wanting, found wanting, erroneous, **fallible;** inaccurate, inexact, imprecise; **unsound, incomplete,** unfinished, partial, patchy, sketchy, uneven, unthorough; **damaged,** impaired; **blemished**; half-baked <nonformal>, immature, undeveloped; impure, adulterated, mixed

**imperious** ADJS imperial, **lordly,** magisterial; arrogant; **arbitrary,** peremptory, imperative; absolute, absolutist, absolutistic; **dictatorial,** authoritarian; **bossy** <nonformal>, **domineering,** high-handed, overbearing, overruling; autocratic, monocratic, **despotic, tyrannical;** tyrannous, grinding, oppressive

**impermeable** ADJS **impervious,** impenetrable; **impassable,** unpassable; unpierceable, unperforable

**impersonal** ADJS **reticent, reserved,** restrained, nonassertive, low-key, low-keyed, constrained; guarded, discreet; backward, **retiring,** shrinking; **aloof, standoffish,** offish <nonformal>, standoff, **distant,** remote, removed, **detached,** Olympian, withdrawn; **cool,** cold, frigid, icy, frosty, chilled, chilly; **impartial, evenhanded,** equitable, **dispassionate, disinterested,** detached, objective, lofty

**impersonate** VERBS **mimic,** ape, parrot, copycat <nonformal>; do an impression; take off, hit off, hit off on, take off on

**impersonator** NOUNS **imitator,** impostor, **mimic,** mimicker, mimer, mime, **mocker; faker,** pretender; sham, shammer, **humbug,** *blagueur* <Fr>, **fraud** <nonformal>, **fake** *and* **faker** *and* **phony** <all nonformal>, **fourflusher** <nonformal>, bluff, bluffer; poser, poseur; female impersonator

**impertinent** ADJS **impudent,** flip <nonformal>, flippant, **cocky** *and* cheeky *and* **fresh** *and* facy *and* crusty *and* nervy <all nonformal>, *chutzpadik* <Yiddish>; **rude, disrespectful,** derisive, brash, bluff; **saucy,** sassy <nonformal>; smart *or* smart-alecky <nonformal>, smart-ass *or* wise-ass <nonformal>

**impervious** ADJS **impenetrable,** impermeable; **impassable,** unpassable; unpierceable, unperforable; **uninfluenceable,** unswayable, unmovable

**impetuous** ADJS **impulsive, hasty,** overhasty, quick, sudden; quick on the draw *or* trigger *or* uptake, hair-trigger; **precipitate,** headlong; **reckless, rash**; impatient; **reckless,** devil-may-care; careless; hotheaded, volatile, giddy, dizzy, ditzy <nonformal>, scatterbrained, mercurial, moody, flighty

**impetus** NOUNS **acceleration,** quickening; step-up, speedup; thrust, drive, momentum

**impiety** NOUNS **impiousness; irrever-**

**ence,** undutifulness; **sacrilege,** blasphemy, blaspheming; **profanity,** profaneness; sacrilegiousness, blasphemousness; **desecration,** profanation

**impinge** VERBS **intrude,** encroach, infringe, trespass, trespass on *or* upon, trench, entrench, invade, infiltrate; **break in upon,** break in, **collide,** come into collision, be on a collision course, **clash,** meet, encounter, confront each other

**impish** ADJS **puckish, elfish,** elvish; mischievous

**implant** VERBS transplant; infix; fit in, **inlay; inculcate, indoctrinate,** catechize, inoculate, **instill, infuse,** imbue, impregnate, infix, impress; **impress upon the mind** *or* **memory,** urge on the mind, beat into, beat *or* knock into one's head, grind in, drill into, drum into one's head *or* skull

**implement** NOUNS 1 **instrument, tool, appliance,** device; contrivance, mechanism; **agent**; medium, mediator, intermedium, intermediary, intermediate, interagent, liaison, go-between; expediter, facilitator, animator; **cat's-paw,** puppet, dummy, pawn, creature, minion VERBS 2 **carry out,** carry through, go through, fulfill, work out; **bring off,** carry off; **put through,** get through; put into effect, **put in** *or* **into practice,** carry into effect, translate into action; effect, effectuate, set in motion, put in force

**implicate** VERBS **involve,** tangle, **entangle,** embarrass, enmesh, engage, **draw in,** drag *or* hook *or* suck into, catch up in, **make a party to;** interest, concern; **absorb**

**implication** NOUNS **connotation, import,** latent *or* underlying *or* implied meaning, ironic suggestion *or* implication, what is read between the lines; **suggestion,** allusion; coloration, tinge, undertone, overtone, undercurrent, more than meets the eye *or* ear, something between the lines, intimation, touch, nuance, innuendo; **hint**; **inference, supposition,** presupposition, assumption, presumption; undermeaning, subsidiary sense, **subtext;** cryptic *or* hidden *or* esoteric *or* arcane meaning

**implicit** ADJS **tacit, implied,** understood, taken for granted, intrinsic, **inherent,** resident, immanent, indwelling; unquestioning, undoubting, unhesitating

**implied** ADJS implicated, involved; **meant,** indicated; **suggested,** intimated, insinuated, hinted; **tacit,** implicit, understood, taken for granted

**implode** VERBS **collapse,** cave, cave in, fall in; fold, fold up; **deflate,** let the air out of, take the wind out of; puncture

**implore** VERBS **entreat,** beseech, **beg,** crave, **plead,** appeal, pray, **supplicate,** impetrate, obtest; adjure, conjure; **call on** *or* **upon,** cry on *or* upon, **appeal to,** cry to, run to; go cap *or* hat in hand to; kneel to, go down on one's knees to, fall on one's knees to, go on bended knee to, throw oneself at the feet of; **plead for,** clamor for, cry for, cry out for; call for help

**imply** VERBS **implicate, involve,** import, connote, entail; mean; **suggest, connote,** lead one to believe, bring to mind; **hint,** insinuate, infer, intimate; **allude to,** point to from afar, point indirectly to; write between the lines; **suppose, presuppose,** assume, presume, take for granted; mean to say *or* imply *or* suggest

**impolite** ADJS **discourteous,** uncourteous; unpolite; **rude, uncivil,** ungracious, ungallant, uncourtly, inaffable, uncomplaisant, unaccommodating; disrespectful; **insolent**

**import** NOUNS 1 **meaning, significance,** signification, *significatum* <L>, *signifié* <Fr>, point, **sense,** idea, where one is coming from <nonformal>; **implication, connotation,** latent *or* underlying *or* implied meaning, ironic suggestion *or* implication, what is read between the lines; meaning; **suggestion,** allusion; coloration, tinge, undertone, overtone, undercurrent, more than meets the eye *or* ear, something between the lines, intimation, touch, nuance, innuendo VERBS 2 **transfer,** transmit, transpose, translocate, transplace; **transplant,** translate; **pass,** pass over, **hand over,** turn over, carry over, make over, consign, assign; **deliver**; pass on, hand forward, hand on, relay; transfuse, perfuse, transfer property *or* right

**importance** NOUNS **significance, consequence,** consideration, **import,** note, mark, moment, weight, **gravity;** materiality; concern, concernment, interest; **first order,** high order, high rank; **priority,** primacy, precedence, preeminence, paramountcy, superiority, **supremacy;** value, worth, merit

**important** ADJS **major,** consequential, momentous, **significant, considerable,** substantial, material, **great,** grand, big; superior, world-shaking, earthshaking; big-time *and* big-league *and* major-league *and* heavyweight <all nonformal>; high-powered <nonformal>

**important person** NOUNS 1 **personage,** person of importance *or* consequence, **great man** *or* **woman,** man *or* woman of mark *or* note, **somebody, notable,** notability, figure; **celebrity,** famous person, person of renown, personality; name, big name, nabob, **mogul,** panjandrum, person to be reckoned with, very important person; mover and shaker, lord of creation; **worthy,** pillar of society, **dignitary, magnate;** tycoon <nonformal>, baron; power; brass, top brass; top people, the great; ruling circle, lords of creation

2 < nonformal> **big shot,** wheel, **big wheel,** big boy, big cat, big fish, big shot, biggie, big cheese, big noise, big-timer, big-time operator, **bigwig,** big man, big gun, **high-muck-a-muck** *or* high-muckety-muck, lion, something, **VIP** brass hat, high man on the totem pole, suit; sacred cow, little tin god, tin god; big man on campus *or* BMOC; 800-pound gorilla; queen bee, heavy mama

**impose** VERBS **prescribe,** require, demand, dictate, lay down, set, fix, appoint, make obligatory *or* mandatory; **oblige, necessitate, require,** exact, demand, **dictate,** call for; **exact,** assess, levy, **tax,** assess a tax upon, slap a tax on <nonformal>, lay *or* put a duty on, make dutiable, subject to a tax *or* fee *or* duty, collect a tax *or* duty on; tithe

**impose upon** VERBS **impose on,** take advantage of; **presume upon**; use ill, ill-use, abuse, misuse; **inconvenience,** put to inconvenience, **put out,** discommode, incommode, disoblige, **burden, embarrass; trouble, bother,** put to trouble, put to the trouble of

**imposing** ADJS **dignified, stately,** grand, courtly, magisterial, aristocratic; worthy, **august, venerable;** impressive, larger-than-life, awful, awe-inspiring, awesome; **sumptuous,** elegant, elaborate, luxurious, extravagant, deluxe; executive *and* plush *and* posh *and* ritzy *and* swank *and* swanky <all nonformal>; formidable, awe-inspiring

**imposition** NOUNS **infliction,** laying on *or* upon, charging, taxing, tasking; burdening, weighting *or* weighting down, freighting, loading *or* loading down, heaping on *or* upon, imposing an onus; **exaction, demand**; unwarranted demand, obtrusiveness, presumptuousness; inconvenience, trouble, bother; inconsiderateness

**impossibility** NOUNS impossibleness, the realm *or* domain of the impossible, **inconceivability,** unthinkability, unimaginability, what cannot be, what can never be, what cannot happen, hopelessness, Chinaman's chance *and* a snowball's chance in hell <both nonformal>, **no chance**; **self-contradiction,** absurdity, paradox, oxymoron, logical impossibility; impossible, the impossible

**impossible** ADJS **not possible,** beyond the bounds of possibility *or* reason, contrary to reason, at variance with the facts; **inconceivable,** unimaginable, unthinkable, not to be thought of, out of the question; hopeless; **absurd,** ridiculous, preposterous; **self-contradictory,** paradoxical, oxymoronic, logically impossible; **ruled-out,** excluded, closed-out, **barred,** prohibited

**impostor** NOUNS **ringer; impersonator; pretender;** sham, shammer, humbug, *blagueur* <Fr>, fraud <nonformal>, **fake** *and* **faker** *and* **phony** <all nonformal>, fourflusher <nonformal>, bluff, bluffer; **wolf in sheep's clothing,** ass in lion's skin, jackdaw in peacock's feathers; poser, poseur

**impotent** ADJS **powerless,** forceless, out of gas <nonformal>; **uninfluential;** feeble, soft, flabby, **weak,** weak as a kitten, wimpy *or* wimpish <nonformal>; **unsexual,** unsexed; **sexless,** asexual, **neuter,** neutral; castrated, emasculated, eunuchized; **cold, frigid**

**impound** VERBS **confine, shut in,** shut away, coop in, hem in, fence in *or* up, wall in *or* up, rail in; **shut up, coop up, pen up,** box up, mew up, bottle up, cork up, seal up; **confiscate,** sequester, sequestrate

**impoverished** ADJS **indigent,** poverty-stricken; **needy,** poor, necessitous, **in need, in want,** disadvantaged, deprived, underprivileged; **pauperized,**

starveling; **down at heels,** down at the heel, on *or* down on one's uppers, out at the heels, out at elbows, in rags; on welfare, on relief, on the dole <Brit>

**impractical** ADJS **impracticable,** unpragmatic, unfeasible; **unachievable,** unattainable, unrealizable, uncompassable; unpractical, inconvenient, unrealistic; dysfunctional, unworkable; **ill-advised,** ill-considered, unwise

**impregnable** ADJS impenetrable, **invulnerable,** inviolable, inexpugnable; **unassailable,** unattackable, insuperable, unsurmountable; resistless, **irresistible; invincible,** indomitable, **unconquerable,** unyielding, incontestable, unbeatable, more than a match for; overpowering, overwhelming

**impregnate** VERBS 1 **inseminate,** spermatize, knock up <nonformal>, **get with child** *or* **young; pollinate** *or* pollinize, pollen; cross-fertilize, cross-pollinate *or* cross-pollinize
2 **inculcate, indoctrinate,** catechize, inoculate, instill, infuse, imbue, **implant,** infix, impress

**impresario** NOUNS **showman,** exhibitor, **producer**

**impress** VERBS 1 **affect, strike, hit,** smite, rock; **make an impression, get to one** <nonformal>; make a dent in, make an impact upon, sink in <nonformal>, strike home, come home to, hit the mark <nonformal>; tell, have a strong effect, traumatize, strike hard, impress forcibly; **inculcate, indoctrinate,** catechize, inoculate, **instill, infuse,** imbue, **implant,** infix; **impress upon the mind** *or* **memory,** urge on the mind, beat into, beat *or* knock into one's head, grind in, drill into, drum into one's head *or* skull; **condition, brainwash, program**
2 **mark,** make a mark, put a mark on; **brand,** stigmatize; stamp, seal, punch, imprint, **print, engrave**
3 **conscript,** draft, induct, press, commandeer; **recruit, muster,** levy, raise, muster in

**impressed** ADJS 1 **affected,** moved, touched; impressed with *or* by, penetrated with, seized with, imbued with, devoured by, obsessed, obsessed with *or* by; wrought up by; stricken, wracked, racked, torn, agonized, tortured; worked up, all worked up, **excited**
2 **printed,** imprinted, stamped; indelibly impressed; engraved, etched, graven, embossed; **dyed-in-the-wool**

**impression** NOUNS **sense,** deep *or* profound sense, gut sense *or* sensation <nonformal>; **sensation**; undercurrent; hunch, feeling in one's bones, presentiment; foreboding; **perception,** mental impression, image, **mental image,** picture in the mind, mental picture, representation; intuition, intuitive impression; **opinion, sentiment,** reaction, **notion, idea, thought,** mind, thinking, **way of thinking, attitude,** stance, posture, position, mindset, **view,** point of view

**impressionable** ADJS **teachable,** instructable, educable, schoolable, trainable; docile, **malleable, moldable,** pliable, facile, plastic, susceptible, formable; **suggestible, susceptible**

**impressive** ADJS **exciting, thrilling,** thrilly <nonformal>, **stirring, moving, breathtaking,** eye-popping <nonformal>; striking, telling; **imposing,** larger-than-life, awful, awe-inspiring, awesome; **convincing,** convictional, well-founded, **persuasive,** assuring, satisfying, satisfactory, confidence-building

**imprison** VERBS **incarcerate, intern,** immure; **jail,** gaol <Brit>, jug <nonformal>, throw into jail, throw under the jailhouse <nonformal>; throw *or* cast in prison, clap in jail *or* prison, send up the river <nonformal>; **lock up,** hold captive, hold prisoner, hold in captivity; hold under close *or* house arrest

**improbable** ADJS **unlikely,** unpromising, hardly possible, logic-defying, scarcely to be expected *or* anticipated; statistically improbable; **doubtful,** dubious, **questionable,** doubtable, dubitable, more than doubtful; **implausible,** incredible; unlooked-for, unexpected, unpredictable

**impromptu** ADJS 1 **extemporaneous, extemporary,** extempore, unrehearsed, **improvised,** improvisatory, improvisatorial, improviso, *improvisé* <Fr>; **ad-lib,** *ad libitum* <L>; **ad-hoc,** stopgap, makeshift, jury-rigged; **offhand,** off the top of one's head *and* off-the-cuff <both nonformal>, **spur-of-the-moment, quick and dirty** <nonformal>
ADVS 2 **extemporaneously, extemporarily,** extempore, *à l'improviste* <Fr>, **ad lib, offhand,** out of hand; off the top of one's head *and* off the cuff <both nonformal>

**improper** ADJS **wrong,** wrongful; **incorrect, indecorous,** undue, unseemly; unfit, unfitting, unsuitable; **inappropriate; indecent,** indelicate, inelegant, unseemly, unbecoming, indiscreet

**impropriety** NOUNS **unfitness,** inappropriateness, unsuitability; **inaptness,** inaptitude, **inappositeness, irrelevance** *or* irrelevancy, infelicity, uncongeniality, inapplicability, inadmissibility; **awkwardness,** unfitness, unfittingness, wrongness, unsuitability

**improve** VERBS 1 **grow better,** look better, show improvement, **mend,** meliorate, ameliorate; **look up** *or* **pick up** *or* **perk up** <all nonformal>; **develop,** shape up; **advance, progress, make progress, make headway, gain,** gain ground, go forward, get *or* go ahead, come on, come along *and* come along nicely <both nonformal>, get along; make strides *or* rapid strides, take off *and* skyrocket <both nonformal>
2 **train; prepare,** ready, **condition, groom,** fit, put in tune, form, **lick into shape** <nonformal>; **cultivate,** develop, improve; **nurture, foster,** nurse; **discipline,** take in hand; ameliorate, meliorate, mitigate

**improvement** NOUNS **betterment,** bettering, change for the better; melioration, **amelioration; mend,** mending, **amendment; progress,** progression, headway; breakthrough, quantum jump *or* leap; **advance,** advancement; upward mobility; **promotion, furtherance,** preferment; **rise,** ascent, **lift, uplift,** uptick <nonformal>, upswing, uptrend, upbeat; **increase**, upgrade, upping *and* boost *and* pickup <all nonformal>; gentrification; **enhancement, enrichment;** euthenics, eugenics; **restoration,** revival, retro, recovery

**improvident** ADJS **prodigal,** unproviding; **thriftless, unthrifty,** uneconomical; grasshopper; hand-to-mouth; **shiftless, feckless, thoughtless, heedless;** happy-go-lucky; negligent

**improvisation** NOUNS **extemporization,** improvision, improvising, extempore <old>, **impromptu, ad-lib,** ad-libbing *and* playing by ear <both nonformal>, **ad hoc measure** *or* solution, adhocracy <nonformal>, ad hockery *or* hocery *or* hocism <nonformal>; temporary measure *or* arrangement, *pro tempore* measure *or* arrangement, **stopgap, makeshift,** jury-rig <naut>; cannibalization; bricolage

**improvise** VERBS **extemporize,** improv *and* tapdance *and* talk off the top of one's head <all nonformal>, speak off the cuff, think on one's feet, make it up as one goes along, play it by ear <nonformal>, throw away *or* depart from the prepared text, throw away the speech, scrap the plan, **ad-lib** <nonformal>, **do offhand,** wing it <nonformal>, vamp, fake <nonformal>, play by ear <nonformal>; **dash off, strike off,** knock off, throw off, toss off *or* out; make up, whip up, **cook up,** run up, rustle up *or* whomp up <nonformal>, slap up *or* together *and* throw *or* slap together <all nonformal>, lash up <Brit>, cobble up; jury-rig; cannibalize

**improvised** ADJS **makeshift,** makeshifty, **stopgap,** band-aid <nonformal>, improvisational, **jury-rigged; last-ditch; ad hoc;** quick and dirty <nonformal>; temporary, provisional, tentative

**imprudent** ADJS **unwise,** injudicious, unpolitic, impolitic, contraindicated, **counterproductive;** indiscreet; inconsiderate, thoughtless, mindless, witless, unthoughtful, unthinking, unreflecting, unreflective; **unreasonable, unsound, unsensible,** senseless, insensate, reasonless, **irrational,** reckless, inadvisable; inexpedient; **ill-advised,** ill-considered, on the wrong track, unconsidered; unadvised, misadvised, misguided

**impudent** ADJS **impertinent, pert,** flip <nonformal>, flippant, **cocky** *and* cheeky *and* **fresh** *and* facy *and* crusty *and* nervy <all nonformal>, *chutzpadik* <Yiddish>; uncalled-for, gratuitous, biggety <nonformal>; **rude, disrespectful,** derisive, brash, bluff; **saucy,** sassy <nonformal>; smart *or* smart-alecky <nonformal>, smart-ass *or* wise-ass <nonformal>

**impulse** NOUNS natural impulse, blind impulse, **instinct,** urge, drive; vagrant *or* fleeting impulse; involuntary impulse, reflex, knee jerk, automatic response; gut response *or* reaction <nonformal>; **notion, fancy; sudden thought,** flash, inspiration, brainstorm, brain wave, quick hunch

**impulsive** ADJS **impetuous, hasty,** overhasty, quick, sudden; quick on the draw *or* trigger *or* uptake, hair-trigger; **pre-**

**cipitate,** headlong; **reckless, rash;** impatient

**impure** ADJS **unclean, unwashed,** unbathed, unscrubbed, unscoured, unswept, unwiped; unpure; **polluted,** contaminated, infected, corrupted; ritually unclean *or* impure *or* contaminated, *tref* <Yiddish>, *terefah* <Heb>, nonkosher; not to be handled without gloves; **uncleanly; unchaste, unvirtuous,** unvirginal; indecent; soiled, sullied, smirched, besmirched, defiled, tainted, maculate

**impurity** NOUNS **uncleanness,** immundity; unpureness; **dirtiness,** grubbiness, dinginess, griminess, messiness *and* grunginess *and* scuzziness <all nonformal>, scruffiness, slovenliness, sluttishness, untidiness; miriness, muddiness; uncleanliness; **unchastity,** unchasteness; unvirtuousness; **indecency**

**impute** VERBS **attribute,** assign, ascribe, give, place, put, apply, attach, refer

**in** NOUNS 1 **entrée,** entry, **entrance, access,** opening, **open door,** open arms; a foot in the door, opening wedge, the camel's nose under the wall of the tent
ADJS 2 **participating, participative,** participant, participatory; involved, engaged, **in on** <nonformal>; implicated, accessory; **partaking, sharing; on good terms,** on a good footing, on friendly *or* amicable terms, **on speaking terms,** on a first-name basis, on visiting terms; **in good with,** in with *and* on the in with <both nonformal>, **in favor, in one's good graces,** in one's good books, on the good *or* right side of <nonformal>
ADVS 3 inward, inwards, inwardly; thereinto; inside, within; herein, therein, wherein

**inability** NOUNS **incapability, incapacity,** incapacitation, **incompetence** *or* incompetency, inadequacy, insufficiency, ineptitude, **inferiority**, inefficiency, unfitness; disability, disablement, disqualification; legal incapacity, wardship, minority, infancy

**inaccessible** ADJS **out-of-the-way,** godforsaken, back of beyond, upcountry; **out of reach,** unapproachable, untouchable, hyperborean, antipodean; **aloof, standoffish,** offish, standoff, **distant, remote,** withdrawn, removed, detached, Olympian

**inaccurate** ADJS **incorrect, inexact,** unfactual, **unprecise,** imprecise, unspecific, loose, lax, unrigorous; negligent; **vague;** approximate, approximative; out of line, out of plumb, out of true, out of square

**inactivate** VERBS **disarm,** unarm, put out of action, put *hors de combat;* **put out of order,** put out of commission <nonformal>, throw out of gear; bugger *and* bugger up *and* queer *and* queer the works *and* gum up *or* screw up <all nonformal>, throw a wrench *or* monkey wrench in the machinery <nonformal>, sabotage, wreck; kibosh *and* put the kibosh on <both nonformal>; spike, spike one's guns, put a spoke in one's wheels

**inactive** ADJS unactive; stationary, static, at a standstill; sedentary; **quiescent,** motionless

**inadequacy** NOUNS **unskillfulness, incompetence** *or* incompetency, inability, incapability, incapacity; ineffectiveness, **ineffectuality; shortcoming,** falling short, not measuring up, coming up short, **shortfall; insufficiency,** inadequateness, **deficiency,** lack, want, shortage

**inadequate** ADJS **insufficient,** unsufficing; found wanting, defective, incomplete, imperfect, deficient, lacking, failing, wanting; **too few,** undersupplied; **too little,** not enough, precious little, a trickle *or* mere trickle; **unsatisfactory,** unsatisfying

**inadmissible** ADJS **unacceptable,** unsuitable, undesirable, **objectionable,** exceptionable, impossible, untenable, indefensible; **intolerable**

**inadvertent** ADJS **unthinking,** unreasoning, unreflecting, uncalculating, unthoughtful, **thoughtless,** heedless, careless, inconsiderate; unguarded; arbitrary, capricious

**inadvisable** ADJS **inexpedient,** undesirable, counterproductive, impolitic, impolitical, unpolitic, not to be recommended, contraindicated; **impractical, impracticable,** dysfunctional, unworkable; **ill-advised,** ill-considered, unwise; **inappropriate,** unsuitable, unmeet, inapt, inept, unseemly, **improper, wrong,** bad, out of place, out of order, incongruous, ill-suited; malapropos, *mal à propos* <Fr>, inopportune, untimely, ill-timed, badly timed, unseasonable;

infelicitous, unfortunate, unhappy; unprofitable; futile

**inalienable** ADJS **inherent,** resident, implicit, immanent, indwelling; unalienable, unquestionable, unchallengeable, irreducible, **inseparable,** impartible, **indivisible,** undividable, indissoluble, bound up in *or* with

**inalterable** ADJS **permanent, unchanged,** unchangeable, unvaried, **unaltered,** inviolate, undestroyed, intact; **constant, persistent,** sustained, fixed, firm, solid, steadfast, like the Rock of Gibraltar, faithful

**inane** ADJS **empty-headed,** empty-minded, empty-noddled, empty-pated, empty-skulled; **vacuous,** vacant, empty, hollow, vapid, jejune, blank, airheaded *and* bubbleheaded <both nonformal>; **rattlebrained,** rattleheaded; scatterbrained; **fatuous,** fatuitous, inept

**inanimate** ADJS inanimated, unanimated, exanimate, azoic, nonliving, dead, **lifeless,** soulless; inert; insentient, unconscious, nonconscious, **insensible,** insensate, senseless, unfeeling

**inappropriate** ADJS **vulgar,** inelegant, indelicate, indecorous, indecent, improper, unseemly, unbeseeming, unbecoming, unfitting, unsuitable, **ungenteel,** undignified; **untasteful,** tasteless, in bad *or* poor taste, tacky *and* chintzy *and* Mickey Mouse <all nonformal>; **offensive,** offensive to gentle ears; malapropos, *mal à propos* <Fr>, infelicitous, unfortunate, unhappy

**inarticulate** ADJS **indistinct,** blurred, muzzy; incomprehensible

**inattentive** ADJS **unmindful,** inadvertent, thoughtless, **incurious**, **indifferent**; **heedless,** unheeding, unheedful, regardless, *distrait* <Fr>, **disregardful,** disregardant; **unobserving,** inobservant, unobservant, unnoticing, unnoting, unremarking, unmarking; **distracted**; **careless,** negligent; **scatterbrained,** giddy, flighty

**inaudible** ADJS **silent, still,** stilly, quiet, quiescent, hushed, soundless, noiseless; subaudible, below the limen *or* threshold of hearing, unhearable; quiet as a mouse, mousy; silent as a post *or* stone, so quiet that one might hear a feather *or* pin drop; **unsounded, unvoiced,** unvocalized, unpronounced, unuttered, unarticulated

**inaugurate** VERBS institute, **found, establish,** set up <nonformal>; **install,** initiate, induct; **introduce,** broach, bring up, lift up, raise; **launch,** float; **usher in,** ring in <nonformal>; **set on foot,** set abroach, set agoing, turn on, kick-start *and* jump-start <both nonformal>, start up, start going, start the ball rolling <nonformal>

**inauguration** NOUNS **establishment,** foundation, constitution, institution, installation, formation, **organization,** inception, setting-up, realization, materialization, effectuation

**inborn** ADJS **innate,** born, congenital; **native, natural,** natural to, connatural, native to, indigenous; **inbred,** genetic, hereditary, inherited, bred in the bone, in the blood, running in the blood *or* race *or* strain, radical, rooted; connate, connatal, coeval; **instinctive,** instinctual, atavistic, primal

**inbred** ADJS **innate, inborn,** born, congenital; **genetic,** hereditary, inherited, bred in the bone, in the blood, running in the blood *or* race *or* strain, radical, rooted; connate, connatal, coeval; **instinctive,** instinctual, atavistic, primal

**incalculable** ADJS **infinite,** boundless, endless, limitless, termless, shoreless; illimitable, **interminable,** interminate; **immeasurable,** unreckonable, innumerable, incomprehensible, unfathomable; measureless, countless, sumless; unmeasurable, immense, unplumbed, untold, unnumbered, without measure *or* number *or* term

**incandescent** ADJS **burning, ignited,** kindled, enkindled, **blazing,** ablaze, ardent, flaring, flaming, aflame, inflamed, alight, **afire, on fire,** in flames, in a blaze; **glowing,** aglow, in a glow, candescent, candent; sparking, scintillating, scintillant, ignescent

**incantation** NOUNS **conjuration,** magic words *or* formula; hocus-pocus, abracadabra, mumbo jumbo

**incapable** ADJS **incompetent,** unable, inadequate, unequipped, unqualified, ill-qualified, out of one's depth, outmatched, **unfit, unfitted,** unadapted, not equal *or* up to, not cut out for <nonformal>; ineffective, **ineffectual;** maladjusted

**incapacitated** ADJS **disabled; crippled,** hamstrung; disqualified, invalidated; disarmed; paralyzed; hog-tied <nonformal>; prostrate, **on one's back,** on one's beam-ends

**incarcerated** ADJS **jailed,** jugged <nonformal>, **imprisoned, interned,** immured; **in prison,** in stir <nonformal>, in captivity, **behind bars,** locked up, under lock and key, in durance vile

**incendiary** ADJS **incitive,** inciting, incentive; **instigative,** instigating; **agitative,** agitational; **inflammatory,** fomenting, rabble-rousing; incendive; arsonous

**incense** NOUNS joss stick; pastille; frankincense *or* olibanum; agalloch *or* aloeswood, calambac, lignaloes *or* linaloa, sandalwood

**incense** VERBS **provoke,** arouse, inflame, embitter; **vex,** irritate, annoy, exasperate, **nettle,** fret, chafe; **pique, peeve** *and* miff <both nonformal>, huff; **ruffle,** roil, rile <nonformal>, ruffle one's feathers, **rankle;** bristle, put *or* get one's back up, set up, put one's hair *or* fur *or* bristles up; stick in one's craw <nonformal>; **stir up, work up,** stir one's bile, stir the blood; wave the bloody shirt

**incentive** NOUNS **inducement, encouragement,** persuasive, invitation, provocation, incitement; **stimulus, stimulation,** stimulative, fillip, whet; carrot; reward, payment; bait, **lure**; palm oil <nonformal>, bribe; sweetening *and* sweetener <both nonformal>, interest, percentage, what's in it for one <nonformal>

**inception** NOUNS **origin,** origination, **genesis,** incipience or incipiency, inchoation; **birth,** birthing, bearing, parturition, pregnancy, nascency *or* nascence, nativity; beginnings, cradle; **establishment,** foundation, constitution, institution, installation, formation, **organization,** inauguration, **setting-up,** realization, materialization, effectuation

**incessant** ADJS **endless,** unending, neverending, without end, **interminable,** nonterminous, nonterminating; **continual,** continuous, steady, **constant, ceaseless,** nonstop, unceasing, neverceasing, unremitting, unintermitting, uninterrupted

**incest** NOUNS incestuousness, **sex crime; sexual abuse,** carnal abuse, molestation

**incident** NOUNS **event,** occurrence, episode, experience, adventure, **happening,** happenstance, **phenomenon,** fact, matter of fact, reality, particular, circumstance, **occasion,** turn of events; **nonevent,** pseudo-event, media event *or* happening, photo opportunity; what's happening

**incidental** NOUNS 1 **contingency,** contingent, accidental, accident, happenstance, mere chance; **superfluity,** superfluousness; fifth wheel *and* tits on a boar <both nonformal>
ADJS 2 **occasional, casual,** accidental; parenthetical, by-the-way; odd, sometime, extra, side, off, off-and-on, out-of-the-way; adventitious, **unexpected, unpredictable,** unforeseeable, unlooked-for, **unforeseen**

**incinerate** VERBS **cremate, burn,** reduce to ashes; **burn up,** incendiarize, consume, **burn to a crisp,** burn to a cinder

**incinerator** NOUNS cinerator, burner; solid-waste incinerator, garbage incinerator; **crematory,** cremator, crematorium, burning ghat; calcinatory

**incise** VERBS **engrave,** grave, tool, enchase, **inscribe, mark,** line, crease, score, scratch, scrape, cut, carve, chisel; groove, furrow; **cut,** carve, **slice,** pare, prune, trim, trim away, resect, excise; slit, snip, lance

**incision** NOUNS **furrow, groove,** scratch, crack, cranny, chase, chink, score, **cut,** gash, striation, streak, stria, **gouge,** slit

**incisive** ADJS **energetic,** vigorous, strenuous, forceful, forcible, strong, dynamic, kinetic, intense, **sharp, keen,** sharpish, trenchant, **cutting,** biting, stinging, **scathing,** stabbing, **piercing, poignant,** penetrating, edged, double-edged; **sagacious, astute,** longheaded, argute; **understanding, discerning,** penetrating, acute, cogent, **perspicacious,** perspicuous; **perceptive, percipient,** apperceptive, appercipient

**incite** VERBS **instigate, put up to** <nonformal>; set on, sic on; **foment,** ferment, **agitate,** arouse, excite, **stir up,** work up, whip up; rally; **inflame,** incense, **fire,** heat, heat up, impassion; **provoke,** pique, whet, tickle; nettle; lash into a fury *or* frenzy; wave the bloody shirt; pour oil on the fire, feed the fire, add fuel to the flame, fan, fan the flame, blow the coals, stir the embers

**inclement** ADJS **raw,** bleak, keen, sharp, bitter, biting, pinching, cutting, **piercing,** penetrating; severe, rigorous

**inclination** NOUNS **leaning,** lean, angularity; **slant,** rake, **slope; tilt, tip,** pitch, **list, cant,** swag, sway; partiality, **penchant,** fancy, favor, predilection, preference, propensity, proclivity, leaning, **bent,** turn, bias, **affinity;** mutual affinity *or* attraction; **sympathy,** fascination; **disposition,** liking, appetence, appetency, **desire**; half a mind *or* notion, idle wish, velleity; **appetite,** passion

**incline** NOUNS 1 inclination, **slope, grade,** gradient, pitch, **ramp,** launching ramp, bank, talus, gentle *or* easy slope, glacis; rapid *or* steep slope
VERBS 2 **lean; slope, slant,** rake, pitch, grade, bank, shelve; **tilt,** tip, list, cant, careen, keel, sidle, swag, sway; **ascend, rise,** uprise, climb, go uphill; **descend, decline,** dip, drop, fall, fall off *or* away, **go downhill;** retreat
3 **be willing, be game** <nonformal>, be ready; be of favorable disposition, take the trouble, find it in one's heart, look kindly upon; be open to, bring oneself, **agree,** be agreeable to; **acquiesce, consent**; not hesitate to, would as lief, would as leave <nonformal>, would as lief as not, not care *or* mind if one does <nonformal>; **play** *or* **go along** <nonformal>, do one's part *or* bit

**inclined** ADJS **moved, motivated,** prompted, impelled, actuated; stimulated, animated; minded, of a mind to, with half a mind to, **disposed,** dispositioned, predisposed, prone, given, bent, bent on, apt, likely, **minded, in the mood** *or* **humor**

**include** VERBS **comprise,** contain, comprehend, hold, take in; **cover,** cover a lot of ground <nonformal>, occupy, take up, fill; fill in *or* out, build into, **complete**; **embrace,** encompass, enclose, encircle, incorporate, assimilate, embody, admit, receive, envisage; **legitimize,** legitimatize; **share power,** enable, enfranchise, cut in *and* deal in *and* give a piece of the action <all nonformal>; **number among,** take into account *or* consideration

**including** ADJS **composed of,** formed of, **made of,** made up of, made out of, consisting of; composing, comprising, constituting, inclusive of, containing, incarnating, embodying, subsuming; contained in, embodied in

**inclusive** ADJS **including,** containing, comprising, covering, embracing, encompassing, enclosing, encircling, assimilating, incorporating, envisaging; counting, numbering; broad-brush *and* ballpark <both nonformal>

**incognito** ADJS **disguised,** camouflaged, in disguise; masked, masquerading; incog <nonformal>; in plain wrapping *or* plain brown paper <nonformal>; **anonymous; nameless, unnamed,** unidentified, undesignated, unspecified, innominate, without a name, **unknown**

**incoherent** ADJS 1 uncoherent, noncoherent, **inconsistent,** uncohesive, like grains of sand, **untenacious,** unconsolidated, tenuous; disconnected, unconnected, **disordered, chaotic, anarchic,** anomic, confused; **discontinuous,** broken, detached, discrete, disarticulated
2 **delirious,** out of one's head <nonformal>, off one's head <nonformal>, off; **giddy,** dizzy, lightheaded; **wandering,** rambling, raving, ranting, babbling

**incombustible** ADJS **noncombustible,** uninflammable, noninflammable, noncombustive, nonflammable

**income** NOUNS **pay,** payment, remuneration, compensation, total compensation, financial remuneration; **salary,** wage, wages, earnings; **receipts,** revenue, profits, earnings, returns, proceeds, **take,** takings, intake; net income, gross income; earned income, unearned income; dividends, royalties, commissions; disposable income

**incomparable** ADJS **peerless,** matchless, **unmatched,** unmatchable, unrivaled, **unequaled,** unapproachable, **unsurpassed, unexcelled;** unsurpassable; **uncomparable,** not comparable, not to be compared, inimitable, beyond compare *or* comparison, **apples and oranges, unique;** without equal *or* parallel, *sans pareil* <Fr>; in a class by itself, *sui generis* <L>, easily first, *facile princeps* <L>; second to none, *nulli secundus* <L>; **unbeatable,** invincible

**incompatible** ADJS **unfriendly,** inimical, unamicable; **disagreeable,** cross, cranky, ornery <nonformal>, negative, uncongenial; **discrepant,** inconsistent, inconsonant, incongruous, incongruent, unconformable, irreconcilable; strained, tense; disaccordant, unharmonious

**incompetence** NOUNS **inability,** incapability, incapacity, incapacitation, incompetency, inadequacy, insufficiency, ineptitude, **inferiority**, inefficiency, unfitness, imbecility; disability, disablement, disqualification; maladroitness, unskillfulness; legal incapacity

**incompetent** ADJS **incapable,** unable,

inadequate, unequipped, unqualified, ill-qualified, out of one's depth, outmatched, **unfit, unfitted,** unadapted, not equal *or* up to, not cut out for <nonformal>; ineffective, **ineffectual;** unadjusted, maladjusted

**incomplete** ADJS **uncompleted, deficient,** defective, unfinished, imperfect, unperfected, **inadequate; undeveloped,** underdeveloped, undergrown, stunted, hypoplastic, **immature,** callow, infant, arrested, embryonic, **wanting, lacking,** needing, missing, **partial,** part, failing; in default, in arrear *or* arrears; **in short supply,** scanty; **short,** scant, shy <nonformal>; **sketchy,** patchy, scrappy

**incomprehensible** ADJS **unintelligible,** ungraspable, unseizable, ununderstandable, unknowable; **unfathomable, inscrutable,** impenetrable, unsearchable, numinous; **ambiguous; incoherent,** unconnected, rambling; **inarticulate; past comprehension,** beyond one's comprehension, beyond understanding; Greek to one

**inconceivable** ADJS **fantastic,** fantastical, fanciful, antic, **unbelievable**, impossible, incredible, logic-defying, incomprehensible, unimaginable, unexpected, unaccountable

**inconclusive** ADJS **unsound, unsubstantial,** insubstantial, weak, feeble, poor, flimsy, unrigorous, unproved, unsustained, poorly argued, indecisive; **moot**

**incongruous** ADJS **ludicrous,** ridiculous, hilarious, absurd, quaint, eccentric, bizarre; **inconsistent,** inconsonant, inconsequent, incoherent, **incompatible,** irreconcilable; self-contradictory, paradoxical, oxymoronic, **absurd**

**inconsequential** ADJS **insignificant**, immaterial; nonessential, unessential, inessential, **not vital,** back-burner <nonformal>, dispensable; unnoteworthy, unimpressive; **inconsiderable,** inappreciable, negligible; irrelevant

**inconsiderate** ADJS **unthoughtful,** unmindful, unheedful, disregardful, **thoughtless,** heedless, respectless, mindless, unthinking, forgetful; **tactless,** insensitive; **unhelpful,** unaccommodating, unobliging, disobliging, uncooperative

**inconsistent** ADJS **incongruous, inconsonant,** inconsequent, incoherent, **incompatible,** irreconcilable; incommensurable, incommensurate; disproportionate, out of proportion, self-contradictory, paradoxical, oxymoronic, **absurd**

**inconsolable** ADJS unconsolable, **disconsolate,** comfortless, prostrate or prostrated, forlorn; **desolate,** *désolé* <Fr>; sick, **sick at heart, heartsick,** soul-sick, heartsore

**inconspicuous** ADJS half-visible, semivisible, low-profile; **indistinct, unclear,** unplain, **indefinite,** undefined, ill-defined, ill-marked, **faint,** pale, feeble, weak, **dim,** dark, **shadowy, vague, obscure,** indistinguishable, unrecognizable; half-seen, merely glimpsed; uncertain, confused, out of focus, **blurred, blurry,** bleared, bleary, blear, **fuzzy, hazy,** misty, filmy, foggy

**inconstant** ADJS **changeable,** changeful, changing, shifting, uncertain, inconsistent; **shifty,** unreliable, undependable; **unstable, unfixed,** infirm, restless, **unsettled,** unstaid, **unsteady,** wishy-washy, spineless, shapeless, amorphous, indecisive, irresolute, waffling <nonformal>, blowing hot and cold <nonformal>, like a feather in the wind, unsteadfast, unstable as water; **capricious, fickle**, off-again-on-again; **erratic, eccentric,** freakish; volatile, giddy, dizzy, ditzy <nonformal>, scatterbrained, mercurial, moody, flighty, impulsive, impetuous; **fluctuating,** alternating, **vacillating, wavering,** wavery, wavy, mazy, flitting, flickering, guttering, fitful, shifting, shuffling

**incontrovertible** ADJS **conclusive,** determinative, **decisive,** final, irresistible, sure, certain, absolute; indubitable, unarguable, indisputable, incontestable, **irrefutable,** unrefutable, unconfutable, irrefragable, unanswerable, unimpeachable; admitting no question *or* dispute *or* doubt *or* denial

**inconvenience** NOUNS 1 **impediment,** embarrassment, **trouble,** difficulty; **handicap,** disadvantage, penalty; white elephant; headache <nonformal>, problem, besetment; the bad part, the downside <nonformal>; **unwieldiness,** unmanageability; **unhandiness,** impracticality; **awkwardness,** clumsiness
VERBS 2 put to inconvenience, **put out, discommode,** incommode, disoblige, **burden, embarrass; trouble, bother,** put to trouble, put to the trouble of, **impose upon;** harm, disadvantage

**inconvenient** ADJS **unhandy, awkward,**

clumsy, unwieldy, troublesome; **incommodious,** discommodious; impractical
**incorporate** VERBS **embrace,** encompass, enclose, encircle, assimilate, embody, admit, receive, envisage; **number among,** take into account *or* consideration; **amalgamate,** consolidate, integrate, solidify, coalesce, compound, put *or* lump together, roll into one, come together, make one, unitize
**incorrect** ADJS **inaccurate, inexact,** unfactual, **unprecise,** imprecise, unspecific, loose, lax, unrigorous; negligent; **vague;** off-base <nonformal>; **ungrammatical,** solecistic, solecistical, barbarous; faulty, erroneous; infelicitous, improper; loose, imprecise
**incorrigible** ADJS **past hope, beyond recall,** past praying for; **irretrievable, irrecoverable, irreclaimable,** irredeemable, unsalvageable, unsalvable; irreformable; **irremediable, irreparable,** inoperable, **incurable,** cureless, remediless, immedicable, beyond remedy, terminal; recidivist, recidivistic; beyond control, out of hand, irreversible; unredeemable, unregenerate
**incorruptible** ADJS **trustworthy, trusty,** faithworthy, reliable, dependable, responsible, straight <nonformal>, sure, to be trusted, **to be depended** *or* **relied upon,** to be counted *or* reckoned on, as good as one's word; tried, true, **tried and true,** tested, proven; inviolable
**increase** NOUNS 1 **gain,** augmentation, greatening, **enlargement, amplification, growth,** development, widening, spread, broadening, elevation, **extension,** aggrandizement, access, accession, **increment,** accretion; **expansion,** proliferation, productiveness; **advance,** appreciation, ascent, mounting, crescendo, waxing, snowballing, **rise** *or* raise, fattening *and* boost *and* hike <all nonformal>, **up** *and* upping <both nonformal>, buildup; **upturn,** uptick <nonformal>, uptrend, upsurge, upswing
VERBS 2 **grow, advance,** appreciate; **spread, widen,** broaden; **gain,** get ahead; wax, swell, balloon, bloat, mount, **rise,** go up, crescendo, snowball; **intensify, develop,** gain strength, strengthen; accrue, accumulate; **multiply, proliferate,** breed, teem; run *or* shoot up, **boom, explode**
**increased** ADJS **heightened,** raised, elevated, stepped-up <nonformal>; **intensified,** deepened, reinforced, strengthened, fortified, beefed-up <nonformal>, tightened, stiffened; **enlarged, extended,** augmented, aggrandized, amplified, **enhanced,** boosted, hiked <nonformal>; broadened, widened, spread; **magnified, inflated, expanded,** swollen, bloated; **multiplied,** proliferated; **accelerated,** hopped-up *and* jazzed-up <both nonformal>
**incredible** ADJS **unbelievable,** unthinkable, **implausible,** unimaginable, inconceivable, not to be believed, **hard to believe,** hard of belief, beyond belief, unworthy of belief, not meriting *or* not deserving belief, tall <nonformal>; **defying belief,** staggering belief, passing belief; **mind-boggling,** preposterous, absurd, ridiculous, unearthly, ungodly; **doubtful, dubious,** doubtable, dubitable, **questionable,** problematic, problematical, **unconvincing,** open to doubt *or* suspicion
**incredulous** ADJS uncredulous, **hard of belief,** shy of belief, disposed to doubt, indisposed *or* disinclined to believe, unwilling to accept; impervious to persuasion, unconvincible, unpersuadable, unpersuasible; **suspicious, suspecting,** wary, leery, cautious, guarded; **skeptical**
**increment** NOUNS **increase, gain,** augmentation, greatening, enlargement, amplification, growth, development, widening, spread, broadening, elevation, **extension,** aggrandizement, access, accession, accretion; **adjunct, addition,** supplementation, complementation, *additum* <L>, additament, addendum, addenda <pl>, accession
**incriminate** VERBS **inculpate, implicate,** involve; cry out against, cry out on *or* upon, cry shame upon, raise one's voice against; attack, assail, impugn
**incubate** VERBS **be pregnant,** be gravid; gestate, breed, carry, carry young; **hatch; brood,** sit, set, cover
**inculcate** VERBS **indoctrinate,** catechize, inoculate, **instill, infuse,** imbue, impregnate, **implant,** infix, impress; **impress upon the mind** *or* **memory,** urge on the mind, beat into, beat *or* knock into one's head, grind in, drill into, drum into one's head *or* skull; **condition,** brainwash, program
**incumbent** NOUNS **officeholder,** officebearer <Brit>, jack-in-office, public ser-

vant, public official; holdover, lame duck; benefice-holder, beneficiary

**incur** VERBS **contract,** invite, welcome, run, **bring on, bring down,** bring upon *or* down upon, bring upon *or* down upon oneself; fall into, fall in with; get, gain, acquire

**incurable** ADJS **past hope, beyond recall,** past praying for; irrevocable, **irreversible; irremediable,** irreparable, inoperable, cureless, remediless, immedicable, beyond remedy, terminal; unrelievable, unmitigable; **ruined,** undone, kaput <nonformal>; lost, gone, gone to hell *and* gone to hell in a handbasket <both nonformal>

**incursion** NOUNS **raid,** foray, razzia; **invasion,** inroad, irruption; **air raid, air strike,** air attack, shuttle raid, fire raid, saturation raid

**indecency** NOUNS **indelicacy,** inelegance *or* inelegancy, **indecorousness,** indecorum, **impropriety**, inappropriateness, unseemliness, indiscretion, indiscreetness; **unchastity**

**indecent** ADJS **indelicate,** inelegant, indecorous, improper, inappropriate, unseemly, unbecoming, indiscreet

**indecisive** ADJS **wishy-washy,** tasteless, bland, **insipid,** vapid, neutral, watery, milky, milk-and-water, mushy; half-hearted, infirm of will *or* purpose, irresolute, changeable; **inconclusive, moot**

**indefatigable** ADJS **persevering,** perseverant, **persistent,** persisting, insistent; relentless, **unrelenting; unrelaxing,** unfailing, **untiring,** unwearying, unflagging, never-tiring, **tireless,** weariless, unwearied; undiscouraged, undaunted, indomitable, unconquerable, invincible, game to the last *or* to the end; **patient,** patient as Job

**indefensible** ADJS **unacceptable,** inadmissible, unsuitable, undesirable, **objectionable,** exceptionable, impossible, untenable, **unjustifiable,** unwarrantable, unallowable, unreasonable

**indefinite** ADJS **vague, indecisive,** indeterminate, indeterminable, undetermined, unpredetermined, undestined; amorphous, shapeless, blobby; inchoate, disordered, orderless, chaotic, incoherent

**indelible** ADJS **unforgettable, never to be forgotten,** never to be erased from the mind, indelibly impressed on the mind, fixed in the mind; haunting, persistent, recurrent, nagging, plaguing, rankling, festering; obsessing, obsessive

**indelicacy** NOUNS **indecency,** inelegance *or* inelegancy, **indecorousness,** indecorum, **impropriety**, inappropriateness, unseemliness, indiscretion, indiscreetness

**indemnify** VERBS **compensate,** make compensation, make good, set right, restitute, pay back, rectify, **make up for; recompense,** pay back, repay, cover

**indemnity** NOUNS **compensation, recompense,** repayment, payback, indemnification, measure for measure, rectification, restitution, **reparation; amends,** expiation, atonement

**independence** NOUNS **self-determination, self government,** self-direction, **autonomy,** home rule; autarky, autarchy, self-containment, self-sufficiency; **individualism,** rugged individualism, individual freedom; **self-reliance,** self-dependence; inner-direction

**independent** NOUNS 1 **nonpartisan,** neutral, mugwump, undecided or uncommitted voter
ADJS 2 self-dependent; free-spirited, freewheeling, free-floating, free-standing; **self-determined,** self-directing, one's own man; inner-directed, **individualistic;** self-governed, **self-governing, autonomous,** sovereign; stand-alone, self-reliant, self-sufficient, self-subsistent, self-supporting, self-contained, autarkic, autarchic; nonpartisan, neutral, **nonaligned**

**indescribable** ADJS **ineffable,** inenarrable, inexpressible, unutterable, unspeakable, noncommunicable, incommunicable, indefinable, undefinable, unnameable, innominable, unwhisperable, unmentionable

**indestructible** ADJS undestroyable, **imperishable,** nonperishable, incorruptible; **deathless,** immortal, undying; **invulnerable, invincible,** inexpugnable, impregnable, indivisible; **ineradicable,** indelible, ineffaceable, inerasable; **inextinguishable,** unquenchable, quenchless, undampable

**index** NOUNS 1 **mark,** marking, **earmark,** hallmark; listing, tabulation
VERBS 2 **catalog,** list, file, tabulate, rationalize, alphabetize, digest, codify

**Indian summer** NOUNS St Martin's summer, St Luke's summer, little summer of St Luke, St Austin's *or* St Augustine's summer

*the dead Summer's soul*
MARY CLEMMER

**indicate** VERBS **signify, mean**, spell, point to, look like, **be a sign of,** show signs of; **imply,** suggest, argue, breathe, bespeak, betoken

**indication** NOUNS signification, identification, differentiation, denotation, **designation,** denomination; characterization, highlighting; **specification,** naming, pointing, pointing out *or* to, fingering <nonformal>, picking out, selection; indicativeness; **meaning**; hint, suggestion; **expression, manifestation**; show, showing, disclosure

**indicative** ADJS indicatory; connotative, indicating, signifying, signalizing; **significant,** significative, meaningful; symptomatic, symptomatologic, symptomatological, diagnostic, pathognomonic, pathognomonical; evidential, **designative,** denotative, denominative, naming; **suggestive,** implicative; **expressive,** demonstrative, exhibitive; identifying; **emblematic, symbolic,** emblematical, symbolical

**indicator** NOUNS **sign,** telltale sign, sure sign, tip-off <nonformal>, **index,** indicant, measure; tip of the iceberg

**indict** VERBS **arraign, impeach,** find an indictment against, present a true bill, prefer *or* file a claim, have *or* pull up <nonformal>, bring up for investigation; **prefer charges**

**indictment** NOUNS **censure, reprehension,** stricture, reprobation, **blame, denunciation,** denouncement, decrying, decrial, bashing *and* trashing <both nonformal>, **condemnation,** damnation, fulmination, anathema; **impeachment, arraignment,** bill of indictment, true bill; **allegation**

**indifference** NOUNS 1 indifferentness; unconcern, halfheartedness, perfunctoriness; **coolness,** coldness, chilliness, chill, iciness, frostiness; tepidness, **lukewarmness**

2 **carelessness,** heedlessness, unheedfulness, *je-m'en-fichisme* and *je-m'en-foutisme* <both Fr>; perfunctoriness; cursoriness, hastiness, offhandedness, casualness

**indifferent** ADJS **halfhearted,** zealless, perfunctory, fervorless; **cool, cold**; tepid, **lukewarm;** neither hot nor cold, neither one thing nor the other, **nonchalant,** blasé, unconcerned; **casual,** offhand, relaxed, laid-back *and* throw-away <both nonformal>; **easygoing,** easy, free and easy, devil-may-care, lackadaisical, *dégagé* <Fr>

**indigent** ADJS **poverty-stricken; needy,** necessitous, **in need, in want,** disadvantaged, deprived, underprivileged; **impoverished, pauperized,** starveling; **down at heels,** down at the heel, on *or* down on one's uppers, out at the heels, out at elbows, in rags; on welfare, on relief, on the dole <Brit>

**indigestible** ADJS **innutritious,** unassimilable

**indignant** ADJS **disapproving, disapprobatory,** unapproving, turned-off, **displeased, dissatisfied,** less than pleased, discontented, disgruntled, **unhappy**

**indignity** NOUNS **affront, offense, injury,** humiliation; scurrility, contempt, contumely, despite, flout, flouting, mockery, jeering, jeer, mock, scoff, gibe, taunt, brickbat <nonformal>; **insult, aspersion,** uncomplimentary remark, slap *or* kick in the face, left-handed *or* back-handed compliment, damning with faint praise; cut

*most unkindest cut of all*
SHAKESPEARE

**indirect** ADJS **circuitous,** roundabout, out-of-the-way, devious, oblique, ambagious <old>, meandering, backhanded; **deviative, deviating,** digressive, discursive, excursive; equivocatory; evasive

**indiscreet** ADJS **rash,** brash, incautious, overbold, imprudent, injudicious, improvident; **unwary, unchary;** overconfident, oversure, overweening, **impudent,** insolent, brazenfaced, brazen

**indiscretion** NOUNS **rashness, brashness,** brazen boldness, incautiousness, overboldness, imprudence, injudiciousness, improvidence; **impropriety,** slight *or* minor wrong, venial sin, peccadillo, misstep, trip, slip, lapse; **blunder, faux pas,** gaffe, solecism; stupidity

**indiscriminate** ADJS **undiscriminating,** indiscriminative, undiscriminative, unselective; wholesale, general, blanket;

**uncritical,** uncriticizing, undemanding, nonjudgmental; **casual, promiscuous;** unexacting, unmeticulous

**indispensable** ADJS **vital, all-important,** crucial, of vital importance, life-and-death *or* life-or-death; earth-shattering, epoch-making; **essential,** fundamental, basic, substantive, bedrock, material

**indisposed** ADJS 1 **ill,** ailing, sick, unwell, taken ill, down, bad, on the sick list; **sickish, seedy** *and* rocky <both nonformal>, **under the weather, out of sorts** <nonformal>, below par <nonformal>, off-color, off one's feed <nonformal>; not quite right, not oneself
2 **unwilling, disinclined,** not in the mood, averse; **unconsenting**

**indisputable** ADJS **real, actual,** factual, veritable, for real <nonformal>, de facto, admitted, well-known, established, inescapable, undeniable; **demonstrable,** provable

**indistinct** ADJS **obscure, vague,** indeterminate, fuzzy, shapeless, amorphous; unclear, unplain, opaque, muddy, **clear as mud** *and* clear as ditch water <both nonformal>; **indistinguishable,** undistinguishable, undistinguished, indiscernible

**indistinguishable** ADJS undistinguishable, undistinguished, indiscernible, **indistinct,** indistinctive, **without distinction,** not to be distinguished, undiscriminated, unindividual, unindividualized, undifferentiated, **alike,** six of one and half a dozen of the other <nonformal>; standard, interchangeable, stereotyped, uniform

**individual** NOUNS 1 **person,** human, human being, man, woman, child, member of the human race *or* family, Adamite, daughter of Eve; **mortal, being,** creature, clay, ordinary clay; personage, **personality, personhood,** individuality; somebody, one, someone
ADJS 2 **personal,** private, peculiar, idiosyncratic; person-to-person, one-to-one, one-on-one; **singular,** individualist *or* individualistic; **personal,** private, intimate, inner, solipsistic, esoteric; **one, single,** singular, sole, unique, a certain, **solitary, lone**

**individualist** NOUNS **egotist,** egoist, egocentric; **free agent,** independent, free lance; rugged individualist; free spirit; loner *and* lone wolf <both nonformal>

**indivisible** ADJS nondivisible, undividable, **inseparable,** impartible, infrangible, indiscerptible, indissoluble; cohesive, coherent; unified; insoluble, indissolvable, infusible

**indoctrinate** VERBS **brainwash,** reindoctrinate, counterindoctrinate; subvert, alienate, win away, corrupt

**indoctrination** NOUNS **inculcation,** catechization, inoculation, **implantation,** infixation, infixion, **impression, instillment,** instillation, impregnation, **infusion,** imbuement; conditioning, brainwashing; reindoctrination

**indolence** NOUNS **laziness, sloth,** slothfulness, bone-laziness; inexertion, inertia; **shiftlessness,** spring fever; ergophobia

**indolent** ADJS **lazy,** bone-lazy, **slothful,** workshy, ergophobic; **do-nothing,** *fainéant* <Fr>, **laggard,** slow, **dilatory,** procrastinative, remiss, slack, lax; **shiftless,** do-less <nonformal>; **unenterprising,** nonaggressive; good-for-nothing, ne'er-do-well; dronish, parasitic, cadging, sponging, scrounging

**indomitable** ADJS **invincible, unconquerable,** unsubduable, unyielding, unbeatable, more than a match for; **persevering,** undiscouraged, undaunted, game to the last *or* to the end

**indubitable** ADJS **unarguable,** indisputable, incontestable, **irrefutable,** unrefutable, unconfutable, incontrovertible, irrefragable, unanswerable, inappealable, unimpeachable, absolute; admitting no question *or* dispute *or* doubt *or* denial

**induce** VERBS **prompt,** move one to, influence, sway, incline, dispose, carry, bring, lead, **lead one to; persuade,** jawbone *and* twist one's arm *and* hold one's feet to the fire <all nonformal>, work *or* bend to one's will; lead by the nose <nonformal>, wear down, soften up

**inducement** NOUNS enlistment, engagement, solicitation, **persuasion,** suasion; exhortation, hortation, preaching, preachment; **selling,** sales talk, salesmanship, hard sell, high pressure, hawking, huckstering; jawboning *and* arm-twisting <both nonformal>; **lobbying; coaxing,** wheedling, working on <nonformal>, cajolery, cajolement, conning, snow job *and* smoke and mirrors <both nonformal>, blandishment, sweet talk *and* soft soap <both nonformal>, soft sell <nonformal>

**induct** VERBS **install,** instate, inaugurate, initiate, invest, ordain; enlist, enroll, sign up, sign on

**indulge** VERBS 1 **humor, oblige;** favor, please, gratify, satisfy, **cater to; give way to,** yield to, let one have his own way; **pamper,** cosset, **coddle,** mollycoddle, pet, make a lap dog of, **spoil;** spare the rod
2 indulge oneself, indulge one's appetites, deny oneself nothing *or* not at all; **give oneself up to,** give free course to, give free rein to; live well *or* high, live high on the hog <nonformal>, live off the fat of the land; indulge in, luxuriate in, wallow in; roll in

*indulge in easy vices*
SAMUEL JOHNSON

**indulgent** ADJS 1 **compliant,** complaisant, **obliging, accommodating, agreeable,** amiable, gracious, generous, benignant, affable, decent, kind, kindly, benign, benevolent; **hands-off** <nonformal>, permissive, overpermissive, overindulgent
2 **intemperate, self-indulgent; overindulgent,** overindulging, unthrifty, unfrugal, **immoderate,** inordinate, **excessive,** too much, prodigal, extravagant, extreme, unmeasured, unlimited; crapulous, crapulent; undisciplined, uncontrolled, unbridled, unconstrained, uninhibited, **unrestrained; incontinent**; bibulous

**industrial** ADJS **manufacturing,** manufactural, fabricational, smokestack

**industrious** ADJS **assiduous,** diligent, sedulous, laborious, hardworking; **energetic,** strenuous; never idle; tireless, unwearied, unflagging, indefatigable; **painstaking,** thorough, thoroughgoing, operose

**inedible** ADJS **uneatable,** not fit to eat, unfit for human consumption

**ineducable** ADJS **stupid, dumb,** dullard, **doltish,** blockish, klutzy *and* klutzish <both nonformal>; **dense,** thick <nonformal>, opaque; unteachable

**ineffective** ADJS **ineffectual, inefficacious,** counterproductive, feckless, not up to scratch *or* up to snuff <nonformal>, **inadequate**; **invalid, inoperative,** of no force; nugatory, nugacious; fatuous, fatuitous; **vain, futile, inutile, useless,** unavailing, bootless, fruitless

**inefficiency** NOUNS **inability,** incapacity, incompetence *or* incompetency, inadequacy, insufficiency, ineptitude, **inferiority**, inexpertness, unproficiency, uncleverness

**inefficient** ADJS **unable,** incapable, incompetent, ineffective; **unqualified,** inept, unendowed, ungifted, untalented, **unfit,** unfitted; **unskillful,** artless, inexpert, unproficient, unclever

**inept** ADJS **incompetent,** inefficient, ineffective; **unqualified,** unendowed, ungifted, untalented, **unfit,** unfitted; out of one's depth, in over one's head; **unapt,** inapt, hopeless, half-assed *and* clunky <both nonformal>

**inequality** NOUNS **disparity, unevenness,** contrariety, difference; **irregularity,** nonuniformity, heterogeneity; **disproportion,** asymmetry; **unbalance,** imbalance, disequilibrium, overbalance, inclination of the balance, overcompensation, tippiness; **inadequacy,** insufficiency, shortcoming; **odds,** handicap; **injustice,** inequity, unfair discrimination, second-class citizenship, untouchability

**inequity** NOUNS **injustice, unjustness;** iniquity, inequitableness, iniquitousness; inequality, inequality of treatment *or* dealing; **wrong, wrongness,** wrongfulness, unmeetness, improperness, **impropriety;** what should not be, what ought not *or* must not be

**inert** ADJS **inactive, static, dormant,** passive, sedentary; **latent,** unaroused, suspended, abeyant, in suspense *or* abeyance; sleeping, slumbering, smoldering; **stagnant,** standing, foul; **torpid, languorous, languid,** apathetic, phlegmatic, **sluggish,** logy, dopey <nonformal>, groggy, heavy, leaden, **dull,** flat, slack, tame, **dead,** lifeless

**inertia** NOUNS **inertness, dormancy;** passiveness, passivity; suspense, abeyance, latency; torpor, apathy, indifference, indolence, lotus-eating, languor; **stagnation,** stagnancy, **vegetation;** stasis; entropy

**inescapable** ADJS **inevitable, unavoidable,** necessary, unpreventable, undeflectable, ineluctable, irrevocable, indefeasible; uncontrollable, unstoppable; relentless, inexorable, unyielding, inflexible; irresistible, resistless; sure as death, sure as death and taxes

**inestimable** ADJS **precious, valuable,**

worthy, rich, golden, of great price <old>, worth a pretty penny <nonformal>, worth a king's ransom, worth its weight in gold, good as gold, precious as the apple of one's eye; **priceless, invaluable,** without *or* **beyond price,** not to be had for love or money, not for all the tea in China

**inevitable** ADJS **unavoidable,** necessary, **inescapable,** unpreventable, undeflectable, ineluctable, irrevocable, indefeasible; uncontrollable, unstoppable; relentless, inexorable, unyielding, inflexible; irresistible, resistless; **certain,** fateful, **sure,** sure as fate, sure as death, sure as death and taxes

**inexcitable** ADJS **imperturbable,** undisturbable, unflappable <nonformal>; **unirritable; dispassionate,** unpassionate; **steady;** stoic, stoical; **even-tempered; impassive,** stolid; bovine, dull; **patient**

**inexcusable** ADJS **unjustifiable, unwarrantable,** unallowable, unreasonable, indefensible; unconscionable, **unpardonable, unforgivable,** inexpiable, irremissible

**inexhaustible** ADJS **infinite,** boundless, endless, limitless; unbounded, uncircumscribed, **unlimited,** illimited, infinitely continuous *or* extended, without bound, without limit *or* end, no end of *or* to; **immeasurable,** incalculable, unreckonable, innumerable, measureless, countless; **unmeasured,** unmeasurable, immense, unplumbed, untold, unnumbered, without measure *or* number *or* term; exhaustless

**inexorable** ADJS **firm,** rigid, rigorous, rigorist, rigoristic, stiff, **hard,** iron, steel, steely, hard-shell, obdurate, **inflexible,** ironhanded, dour, **unyielding,** unbending, impliable, **relentless,** unrelenting, procrustean; **uncompromising;** ironbound, rockbound, musclebound, hidebound

**inexpedient** ADJS **undesirable,** inadvisable, counterproductive, impolitic, impolitical, unpolitic, not to be recommended, contraindicated; **impractical, impracticable,** dysfunctional, unworkable; **ill-advised, ill-considered, unwise; unfit, unfitting,** unbefitting, **inappropriate, unsuitable,** unmeet, inapt, inept, unseemly, **improper, wrong,** bad, out of place, out of order, incongruous, ill-suited; inopportune, ill-timed, badly timed, unseasonable; unprofitable; futile

**inexpensive** ADJS **cheap,** unexpensive, **low, low-priced,** frugal, reasonable, sensible, manageable, modest, moderate, affordable, to fit the pocketbook, budget, easy, economy, economic, economical; within means, within reach *or* easy reach; nominal, token; worth the money, well worth the money; cheap at half the price; shabby, shoddy

**inexperienced** ADJS **unexperienced,** unversed, unconversant, **unpracticed;** undeveloped, unseasoned; **raw, green,** green as grass, unripe, callow, unfledged, immature, unmatured, fresh, wet behind the ears, not dry behind the ears, **untried;** unskilled in, unpracticed in, unversed in, unconversant with, unaccustomed to, unused to, unfamiliar *or* unacquainted with, new to, uninitiated in, a stranger to, a novice *or* tyro at; ignorant

**inexplicable** ADJS **unexplainable,** uninterpretable, undefinable, indefinable, funny, **unaccountable; insolvable,** unsolvable, insoluble, inextricable; mysterious, mystic, mystical, shrouded *or* wrapped *or* enwrapped in mystery

**infallible** ADJS **inerrable,** inerrant, unerring

**infamous** ADJS **abominable,** terrible, scandalous, disgraceful, shameful, shameless, atrocious, sacrilegious, ignoble, ignominious, inglorious, flagrant, **shocking, notorious,** arrant, **egregious,** unpardonable, unforgivable

**infamy** NOUNS infamousness; **ignominy,** ignominiousness; ingloriousness, **ignobility,** odium, obloquy, opprobrium; depluming, displuming, loss of honor *or* name *or* repute *or* face; degradation, comedown <nonformal>

**infant** NOUNS 1 **baby, babe,** babe in arms, little darling *or* angel *or* doll *or* cherub, bouncing baby, puling infant, mewling infant, babykins <nonformal>, baby bunting; papoose, *bimbo* <Ital> or *bambino* <Ital>; **toddler; suckling,** nursling, fosterling, weanling; neonate 2 **innocent,** child, mere child, newborn babe, babe in the woods, lamb, dove ADJS 3 **infantile,** infantine, **babyish,** baby; **newborn,** neonatal; in the cradle *or* crib *or* nursery, in swaddling clothes, in diapers, in nappies <Brit>, in arms, at the breast, tied to mother's apron strings; **undeveloped,** underdeveloped, **immature,** callow, arrested, embryonic

**infantile** ADJS **infant,** infantine, **babyish,** baby; **puerile,** immature, **childish;** childlike; incunabular, infantine

**infatuated** ADJS **enamored, charmed,** becharmed, **fascinated, captivated,** bewitched, enraptured, enchanted; **smitten,** heartsmitten, heartstruck, lovestruck, besotted, credulous, gulled, befooled, beguiled, fond, doting, gaga; **obsessed, possessed,** prepossessed, preoccupied, fixated, **hung up** <nonformal>, infatuate, gripped, held; sentimental, maudlin; dazed, fuddled

**infatuation** NOUNS infatuatedness, passing fancy; **crush** *and* mash *and* pash *and* case <all nonformal>; **puppy love** *and* calf love <both nonformal>; love at first sight; fondness, dotage; one's blind side

**infect** VERBS 1 **contaminate,** tarnish, confound, **pollute,** vitiate, poison, taint; **corrupt,** debase, degrade, degenerate, deprave, debauch, defile, violate, desecrate

2 **inspire,** inspirit, spirit, spirit up; fire, fire one's imagination; **animate, exhilarate,** enliven; **infuse,** inject, inoculate, imbue, inform

**infected** ADJS **diseased,** morbid, pathological, **contaminated,** tainted, peccant, **poisoned,** polluted, corrupted, septic

**infection** NOUNS **contagion,** contamination, taint, virus; **contagiousness,** infectiousness, communicability; carrier, vector

**infectious** ADJS **contagious,** infective, **catching,** taking, spreading, **communicable,** zymotic, inoculable; pestiferous, pestilential, **epidemic,** epidemial, pandemic; epizootic, epiphytotic; endemic

**infelicitous** ADJS **inelegant,** clumsy, clunky *and* klutzy <both nonformal>, heavy-handed, heavy-footed, ham-handed, graceless, ungraceful, inconcinnate *and* inconcinnous <both old>, unfelicitous, inapplicable, inadmissible; **faulty,** erroneous; **improper; careless,** slovenly, slipshod; ungrammatic, **ungrammatical,** solecistic, solecistical, **incorrect,** barbarous

**infer** VERBS **deduce,** generalize; **conclude,** draw a conclusion, **come to** *or* **arrive at a conclusion,** draw an inference; put two and two together

**inference** NOUNS **conclusion, deduction,** consequence, consequent, corollary; **connotation, import,** latent *or* underlying *or* implied meaning, more than meets the eye, what is read between the lines; undermeaning

**inferior** NOUNS 1 **underling, subordinate,** subaltern, **junior;** second fiddle *and* second stringer *and* third stringer *and* benchwarmer *and* low man on the totem pole <all nonformal>, loser *and* nonstarter <both nonformal>; lightweight, follower, pawn, cog, flunky, yes-man, creature

ADJS 2 **subordinate,** subaltern, sub, small-scale, **secondary; junior, minor;** second *or* third string *and* one-horse *and* penny-ante *and* dinky <all nonformal>, second *or* third rank, low in the pecking order, low-rent *and* downscale <both nonformal>; **subservient,** subject, servile, low, **lowly,** humble, modest; **lesser,** less, lower; **beneath one's dignity** *or* station, infra dig, demeaning; **poor,** punk <nonformal>, **base, mean, common,** coarse, cheesy *and* tacky <both nonformal>, tinny; shabby, seedy; cheap, Mickey Mouse <nonformal>, paltry

**inferiority** NOUNS 1 **subordinacy,** subordination, secondariness; **juniority,** minority; **subservience, subjection,** servility, lowliness, humbleness, humility; back seat *and* second fiddle <both nonformal>, second *or* third string <nonformal>

2 inferiorness, **poorness,** lowliness, humbleness, **baseness, meanness, commonness,** coarseness, tackiness, tack; **second-rateness,** third-rateness, fourth-rateness

**inferiority complex** NOUNS **complex; self-effacement, self-depreciation,** self-deprecation, self-detraction, undervaluing of self, self-doubt, **diffidence;** hiding one's light under a bushel; low self-esteem, weak ego, lack of self-confidence *or* self-reliance, self-distrust

**infernal** ADJS **cruel, inhuman,** fiendish, fiendlike; demoniac *or* demoniacal, diabolic, diabolical, devilish, satanic; **hellish,** sulfurous, brimstone, fire-and-brimstone; chthonic, chthonian

**inferno** NOUNS **hell, Hades,** Sheol, Gehenna, Tophet, Abaddon, Naraka, jahannan, avichi, **perdition,** Pandemonium, the pit, **the bottomless pit,** the abyss, **nether world,** lower world, underworld, infernal regions, abode *or* world of the dead, abode of the damned, place of torment, the grave, shades below; **purgatory; oven, furnace,** fiery furnace

**inferred** ADJS **supposed,** suppositive, assumed, presumed, **conjectured,** understood, deemed, **reputed,** putative, alleged, accounted as; suppositional, supposititious

**infertility** NOUNS **unproductiveness,** unproductivity, ineffectualness; **unfruitfulness, barrenness,** nonfruition, dryness, aridity, dearth, famine; sterileness, **sterility,** unfertileness, infecundity; wasted *or* withered loins, dry womb; impotence, incapacity

**infest** VERBS **beset,** invade, swarm, ravage, plague; **overrun, overswarm,** overspread; **creep with, crawl with,** swarm with; seize

**infestation** NOUNS **invasion,** swarming, swarm, teeming, ravage, plague; **overrunning, overswarming,** overspreading

**infidel** NOUNS **unbeliever,** disbeliever, nonbeliever; **atheist, pagan, heathen;** nullifidian, minimifidian; **gentile**

**infidelity** NOUNS **unfaithfulness,** unfaith, faithlessness, trothlessness, illicit *or* unlawful love, forbidden *or* unsanctified love, adulterous affair, adultery, unfaithfulness, cuckoldry; **inconstancy, unsteadfastness,** fickleness; **disloyalty,** unloyalty; **falsity,** falseness, untrueness; disaffection, recreancy, dereliction; bad faith, *mala fides* <L>, Punic faith; breach of promise, breach of trust *or* faith, barratry; breach of confidence

**infighting** NOUNS **dissension, dissent,** dissidence, bickering, factiousness, partisanship, partisan spirit; **divisiveness; quarrelsomeness;** fighting at close quarters

**infiltrate** VERBS **filter in, seep in,** percolate into, leak in, soak in, perfuse; **encroach, infringe,** impinge, **trespass,** trespass on *or* upon, trench, entrench, invade

**infinite** ADJS **boundless, endless, limitless,** termless, shoreless; unbounded, uncircumscribed, **unlimited,** illimited, infinitely continuous *or* extended, stretching *or* extending everywhere, without bound, without limit *or* end, no end of *or* to; illimitable, **interminable,** interminate; **immeasurable,** incalculable, unreckonable, innumerable, incomprehensible, unfathomable; **all-inclusive,** all-comprehensive, **universal**; **perpetual, eternal**

**infinitesimal** ADJS **microscopic,** ultramicroscopic; evanescent, thin, tenuous; inappreciable; impalpable, imponderable, intangible; imperceptible, indiscernible, invisible, unseeable

**infinity** NOUNS infiniteness, infinitude, the all, the be-all and end-all; **boundlessness, limitlessness, endlessness; immeasurability,** unmeasurability, immensity, incalculability, innumerability, incomprehensibility; measurelessness, countlessness, exhaustlessness, inexhaustibility; universality

*world without end*
BIBLE

**infirmity** NOUNS **unsoundness,** incapacity, unfirmness, unsturdiness, **instability, unsubstantiality;** decrepitude; **unsteadiness, shakiness,** ricketiness, wobbliness, wonkiness <Brit nonformal>, caducity, senility, invalidism; wishy-washiness, insipidity, vapidity, wateriness; **illness,** sickness, malady, ailment, indisposition, disorder, complaint, morbidity, affliction

**inflame** VERBS **incite, instigate,** put up to <nonformal>; set on, sic on; **foment,** ferment, **agitate, arouse, excite, stir up,** work up, whip up; rally; incense, **fire,** heat, heat up, impassion; pour oil on the fire, feed the fire, add fuel to the flame, fan, fan the flame, blow the coals, stir the embers; **ignite,** set fire to, set on fire, kindle, enkindle, **light,** light up, strike a light, apply the match *or* torch to, torch <nonformal>, touch off, **burn,** conflagrate

**inflamed** ADJS **fiery, heated,** flaming, scorching, hot, red-hot, white-hot; **fanatic, zealous,** totally committed, hard-core, hard-line, ardent, passionate; **hotheaded**

**inflammable** NOUNS 1 **fuel,** energy source; heat source, firing, combustible *or* inflammable *or* flammable material, burnable, combustible, flammable
ADJS 2 **flammable, combustible,** burnable; explosive, volcanic, eruptive

**inflammation** NOUNS **soreness, irritation,** tenderness, sensitiveness; algesia; festering; sore; sore spot; inflammatory disease

**inflammatory** ADJS inflammative, **inflaming, kindling,** enkindling, lighting; **incendiary,** incendive; arsonous; **incitive, instigative,** instigating; **agitative,** agitational; fomenting, rabble-rousing

**inflate** VERBS **puff up,** swell; go to one's head, turn one's head; **stretch, distend, dilate,** sufflate, **blow up,** huff, puff, bloat; pump, pump up; **exaggerate,** hyperbolize; **overstate,** overspeak <old>, overreach, **overdraw,** overcharge; **magnify,** amplify <old>; **heat** *or* **heat up the economy;** reflate

**inflated** ADJS **magnified, expanded,** swollen; **multiplied,** proliferated; **distended, dilated,** sufflated, blown up, puffed up, swollen, swelled, **bloated,** turgid, tumid, plethoric, incrassate; **exaggerated,** hyperbolical, aggrandized; **stretched,** disproportionate, blown up out of all proportion, **extravagant**; high-flown, grandiloquent, windy *and* gassy <both nonformal>, **bombastic, pretentious**

**inflexible** ADJS unflexible, **unpliable,** unpliant, unmalleable, **intractable,** untractable, intractile, **unbending,** unlimber, **unyielding**, ungiving, **stubborn,** unalterable, immutable; **immovable**; **adamant,** adamantine; **inelastic,** nonelastic, irresilient

**inflict** VERBS **wreak, do to,** bring, bring upon, bring down upon, bring on *or* down on one's head, visit upon

**influence** NOUNS 1 **machination, manipulation,** wire-pulling <nonformal>; political influence, behind-the-scenes influence *or* pressure; **prestige,** authority, influentialness; pressure, **weight,** weightiness, moment, **consequence**
2 make oneself felt, **affect,** weigh with, **sway,** bias, bend, incline, dispose, predispose, **move,** prompt, lead; color, tinge, tone, slant, impart spin; **persuade**, jawbone *and* twist one's arm *and* hold one's feet to the fire <all nonformal>, work, work *or* bend to one's will; lead by the nose <nonformal>, wear down, soften up

**influence peddler** NOUNS **wire-puller;** wheeler-dealer <nonformal>, lobby, lobbyist, influencer, **powerbroker; power behind the throne,** gray eminence, *éminence grise* <Fr>, hidden hand, manipulator, friend at *or* in court, kingmaker; **pressure group,** special-interest group, special interests, single-issue group, PAC *or* political action committee

**influential** ADJS **powerful**, potent, strong, to be reckoned with; **effective,** effectual, efficacious, telling; **weighty,** momentous, important, consequential, substantial, **prestigious,** estimable, authoritative, reputable; **persuasive,** suasive, personable, **winning,** magnetic, charming, enchanting, charismatic

**influx** NOUNS **inflow,** inflooding, incursion, indraft, indrawing, inpour, inrun, inroad, infiltration, inrush

**inform** VERBS **tell, speak on** *or* **for,** apprise, **advise, advertise,** advertise of, **give word,** mention to, **acquaint, enlighten,** familiarize, brief, verse, give the facts, give an account of, give by way of information; **instruct;** possess *or* seize one of the facts; let know, **give** *or* **lead one to believe** *or* **understand;** tell once and for all; notify, give notice *or* notification, serve notice; **report**; **disclose**; shed new *or* fresh light upon

**inform on** VERBS

<nonformal> **sell one out** *or* **down the river,** tell on, blab, snitch, squeal, peach <old>, sell out, sing, rat, stool, fink, nark, finger, put the finger on, blow the whistle, shop <Brit>, dime, drop a dime, spill one's guts, spell the beans, squawk, weasel

**informality** NOUNS **informalness,** unceremoniousness; **casualness,** offhandedness, **ease, easiness,** easygoingness; affability, graciousness, cordiality, sociability; Bohemianism, unconventionality; **familiarity; naturalness,** simplicity, plainness, homeliness, homeyness, folksiness <nonformal>, common touch, **unaffectedness,** unpretentiousness; unconstraint, unconstrainedness

**informant** NOUNS **informer, source,** teller, interviewee, enlightener; **adviser,** monitor; **reporter,** notifier, **announcer,** annunciator; spokesperson, spokeswoman, spokesman, press secretary, press officer, information officer, mouthpiece; **authority,** witness, expert witness; **tipster** <nonformal>, **tout** <nonformal>; newsmonger, gossipmonger; public relations officer

**information** NOUNS info <nonformal>, **facts, data, knowledge**; public knowledge, open secret, common knowledge;

general information; factual information, hard information; **enlightenment,** light; incidental information, sidelight; **intelligence; the dope** *and* the goods *and* **the scoop** *and* the skinny *and* the straight skinny *and* the inside skinny <all nonformal>; **communication**; **report, word,** message, presentation, account, **statement,** mention; **data,** database, **file,** data set, record, data record, data file, text file

**informative** ADJS informing, informational; **instructive, enlightening;** educative, educational; advisory, monitory; **communicative**

**informed** ADJS **enlightened, instructed,** versed, well-versed, educated, schooled, **taught;** posted, briefed, primed, trained; **up on,** up-to-date, abreast of, *au courant* <Fr>; informed of, in the know, clued-in *or* clued-up <nonformal>; **versed in, informed in,** read *or* well-read in, up on, strong in, at home in, master of, expert *or* authoritative in, proficient in, **familiar with,** at home with, **conversant with, acquainted with,** intimate with

**informer** NOUNS **betrayer,** double-crosser <nonformal>; **snitch** *and* snitcher <both nonformal>; whistle-blower <nonformal>; **tattler,** tattletale, telltale, talebearer; **blab** *or* blabber *or* blabberer *or* blabbermouth <all nonformal>; **squealer** *and* preacher *and* **stool pigeon** *and* stoolie *and* **fink** *and* rat <all nonformal>, nark <Brit nonformal>; **spy**

**infraction** NOUNS **violation, breach,** breaking; **infringement, transgression, trespass,** contravention; offense; breach of promise, breach of contract, breach of trust *or* faith, bad faith, breach of privilege; breach of the peace; **lawbreaking, violation,** breach *or* violation of law

**infrequent** ADJS unfrequent, **rare,** scarce, scarce as hens' teeth, scarcer than hens' teeth, **uncommon,** unique, unusual, almost unheard-of, seldom met with, seldom seen, few and far between, **sparse**; one-time, one-shot, once in a lifetime; **slow**

**infringe** VERBS **overstep,** transgress, trespass, intrude, break bounds, overstep the bounds, go too far, know no bounds, **encroach,** invade, irrupt, make an inroad *or* incursion *or* intrusion, advance upon

**infringement** NOUNS **overstepping,** transgression, trespass, incursion, intrusion, **encroachment,** infraction, **usurpation,** arrogation, appropriation, assumption

**infuriate** VERBS **enrage, madden,** drive one mad, frenzy, lash into fury, work up into a passion, make one's blood boil, **provoke,** envenom, **embitter,** madden

**infuriated** ADJS in a rage *or* passion *or* fury; **furious,** fierce, wild, savage; raving mad <nonformal>, **rabid,** foaming *or* frothing at the mouth; **fuming,** in a fume; **enraged,** raging, raving, ranting, storming

**infusion** NOUNS **insertion, introduction,** insinuation, injection, perfusion, inoculation, intromission; **steeping,** soaking, brewing; **imbuement, impregnation,** suffusion, decoction, infiltration, instillment, instillation, permeation, pervasion, interpenetration, penetration

**ingenue** NOUNS **simple soul,** unsophisticate, naïf, **innocent;** juvenile, *jeune première* <Fr>; soubrette

**ingenuity** NOUNS ingeniousness, resource, resourcefulness, wit; invention, **inventiveness,** originality, **creativity,** creativeness; rich *or* teeming imagination, fertile *or* pregnant imagination, seminal *or* germinal imagination, fertile mind

**ingenuous** ADJS **artless, simple,** plain, **guideless;** simplehearted, simple-minded; *ingénu* <Fr>; **unsophisticated, naive;** childlike, born yesterday; **innocent;** trustful, trusting, unguarded, unwary, unreserved, confiding, unsuspicious; **open,** openhearted, sincere, candid, **frank**; single-hearted, single-minded; direct, bluff, blunt, outspoken

**ingest** VERBS **eat**, tuck away, put away; imbibe, **drink; swallow, devour,** ingurgitate; **engulf,** engorge; **gulp,** gulp down, swill, swill down, wolf down, gobble; **absorb,** assimilate, digest, **eat up,** swallow, swallow up, gobble up

**ingrained** ADJS **confirmed, inveterate,** chronic, established, long-established, fixed, settled, rooted, thorough; incorrigible, irreversible; **deep-rooted,** deep-set, deep-settled, **deep-seated,** deep-dyed; **infixed,** fast, dyed-in-the-wool; in the very grain; infixed, implanted, inwrought

**ingratiating** ADJS **obsequious, flattering,** sycophantic, sycophantical, toadyish, fawning, flattering, truckling, smarmy <nonformal>, toadying, toadeating, **bootlicking** *and* back scratching *and* backslapping *and* ass-licking *and* brown-nosing <all nonformal>; **groveling,** sniveling, cringing, cowering, crouching, crawling

**ingratitude** NOUNS **ungratefulness, unthankfulness,** thanklessness, unappreciation, **unappreciativeness;** nonrecognition, denial of due *or* proper credit; grudging *or* halfhearted thanks

*benefits forgot*
SHAKESPEARE

**ingredient** NOUNS **component, constituent,** integrant, makings *and* fixings <both nonformal>, **element, factor, part**, player, module, part and parcel; appurtenance, adjunct; **feature,** aspect, specialty, circumstance, detail, item

**in-group** NOUNS **clique, coterie, set, circle,** ring, junto, junta, cabal, camarilla, **clan,** group; **crew** *and* mob *and* **crowd** *and* **bunch** *and* outfit <all nonformal>; cadre, inner circle; closed *or* charmed circle; elite, elite group; leadership group; **old-boy network;** the Establishment, powers that be, lords of creation

**ingrown** ADJS **entrenched,** vested, firmly established; **well-established,** well-founded, **well-grounded,** in *or* on bedrock; old-line, long-established; **confirmed, inveterate; infixed,** implanted, engrafted, embedded, inwrought

**inhabit** VERBS **occupy,** tenant, move in *or* into, take up one's abode, make one's home; rent, lease; **reside, live, live in, dwell, lodge, stay,** remain, abide, domicile, domiciliate; **room,** bunk, crash <nonformal>, berth, doss down <Brit>; **exist in, consist in,** subsist in, lie in, rest in, repose in, reside in, abide in, dwell in, **inhere in,** be present in, be a quality of, be comprised in, be contained in, be constituted by, be coextensive with

**inhabitant** NOUNS inhabiter, habitant; **occupant,** occupier, **dweller, tenant, denizen,** inmate; **resident,** residencer, residentiary, resider

**inhale** VERBS **draw in, suck,** suckle, suck in *or* up, aspirate; **inspire,** breathe in, puff, draw, drag <nonformal>, pull; snuff, snuffle, sniff, sniffle, snuff in *or* up, slurp

**inherent** ADJS **immediate,** immanent, indwelling, **available, accessible, at hand,** in view, within reach *or* sight *or* call, in place; **intrinsic,** resident, implicit, indwelling; **ingrained,** in the very grain; **instinctive,** natural, **innate,** unlearned

**inherit** VERBS be heir to, **come into,** come in for, come by, fall *or* step into; step into the shoes of, succeed to, take the mantle of, take over

**inheritance** NOUNS **heritage,** patrimony, birthright, legacy, bequest, bequeathal; reversion; entail; heirship; **succession,** line of succession, mode of succession, law of succession; primogeniture, ultimogeniture; **heritable; heirloom**

**inherited** ADJS **inbred, genetic, hereditary,** bred in the bone, in the blood, running in the blood *or* race *or* strain, radical, rooted; connate, connatal, coeval

**inhibit** VERBS **hinder, impede,** arrest, check, countercheck, scotch, **curb,** snub; damp, dampen, pour *or* dash *or* throw cold water; **retard,** slacken, **delay,** detain, **hold back, keep back,** set back, hold up <nonformal>; **restrain**; keep *or* hold in check, bottle up, dam up

**inhibition** NOUNS **suppression, repression,** resistance, restraint, censorship; block, psychological block, blockage, blocking; reaction formation; rigid control; **suppressed desire**

**inhospitable** ADJS unhospitable; **unreceptive,** closed; **uncordial,** ungracious, **unfriendly,** unneighborly

**inhuman** ADJS **cruel,** cruel-hearted, sadistic; **ruthless**; **brutal,** brutish, brute, bestial, beastly, animal, animalistic; inhumane, **savage,** fierce, ferocious, vicious, murderous, atrocious, mindless, insensate, monstrous, pitiless, merciless, bloody, sanguinary

**inimitable** ADJS **matchless, unmatched,** unmatchable, unrivaled, unparalleled, **unequaled,** unapproached, unapproachable, **unsurpassed,** unexcelled; **incomparable,** beyond compare *or* comparison, without equal *or* parallel, *sans pareil* <Fr>

**initial** VERBS 1 **ratify, endorse, sign,** undersign, sign on the dotted line, put one's John Hancock on <nonformal>, put one's mark *or* X *or* cross on; **letter, inscribe,** character, sign, mark
ADJS 2 **beginning,** initiatory *or* initia-

tive; **introductory,** inaugural *or* inauguratory; **original, first,** first ever, first of all; aboriginal, autochthonous

**initiate** VERBS **originate, create,** invent; **precede**, take the initiative, take the first step, take the lead, pioneer; **lead,** lead off, lead the way; **break the ice,** take the plunge, break ground, cut the first turf, lay the first stone

**initiation** NOUNS **installation,** installment, inauguration, investiture, placing in office; initialization, first move, opening move, gambit, **first step,** baby step, *le premier pas* <Fr>

**initiative** NOUNS **undertaking,** enterprise, operation, work, venture, project, proposition *and* deal <both nonformal>; **effort,** attempt, **act,** step, measure, *démarche* <Fr>, move, maneuver, motion

**inject** VERBS **insert, introduce,** insinuate, infuse, perfuse, inoculate, intromit; **enter**; **penetrate; put in, stick in,** set in, throw in, pop in, tuck in, whip in; slip in, ease in; interject

**injection** NOUNS **inoculation,** hypodermic, hypodermic injection, shot *and* bing <both nonformal>, hypospray *or* jet injection; booster, booster shot <nonformal>
2 **intrusion,** obtrusion, interposition, interposal, imposition, insinuation, **interference,** intervention, interventionism, interruption, interjection

**injunction** NOUNS **court order,** legal order; **instruction,** direction, charge, commission, dictate; **order,** command; **restraint,** constraint; **inhibition;** legal restraint, enjoining, enjoinder, interdict; proscription, **prohibition, forbidding,** forbiddance; **ban,** embargo, prohibitory injunction, *interdictum* <L>, interdiction

**injure** VERBS **mistreat,** maltreat, ill-treat, ill-use, abuse, molest; buffet, batter, bruise, **savage,** manhandle, maul, knock about, rough, rough up; **impair, damage,** endamage, **harm, hurt,** irritate

**injured** ADJS **pained, grieved,** aggrieved; **wounded,** hurt, **bruised,** mauled; **cut,** cut to the quick; **impaired,** damaged, harmed

**injurious** ADJS **harmful, hurtful,** scatheful, **baneful,** baleful, distressing, **damaging, detrimental,** deleterious, counterproductive, **pernicious,** mischievous; **malignant,** malign, malevolent, malefic, vicious

**injury** NOUNS **indignity,** affront, offense, humiliation; **violation,** outrage, violence, atrocity; **impairment,** damage, harm, mischief, scathe, detriment, loss, weakening, sickening; **offense,** injustice, **wrong; detriment,** loss, mischief

**injustice** NOUNS **unjustness; inequity,** iniquity, inequitableness, iniquitousness; inequality, inequality of treatment *or* dealing; **wrong, wrongness,** wrongfulness, unmeetness, improperness, **impropriety;** undueness; what should not be, what ought not *or* must not be; unlawfulness, illegality

**inkling** NOUNS **suggestion,** bare suggestion, suspicion, hint, sense, feeling, **feeling in one's bones, intuition,** intimation, impression, notion, mere notion, hunch *and* sneaking suspicion <both nonformal>, trace of an idea, half an idea, vague idea, hazy idea

**inlay** NOUNS 1 **insert,** insertion; **inset;** gore, godet, gusset; inlayer, inside layer, inlaying; **filling,** filler
VERBS 2 **inset;** infix; fit in; **fill,** pack, load; **line,** interline, interlineate

**inlet** NOUNS **cove,** creek <Brit>, arm of the sea, arm, armlet, canal, reach, loch <Scots>, **bay, fjord,** bight; **gulf; estuary,** firth *or* frith, bayou, mouth, *boca* <Sp>; **passageway,** opening, aperture; access

**inmate** NOUNS **occupant,** occupier, dweller, tenant, **denizen; prisoner,** jailbird <nonformal>, convict

**inmost** ADJS **interior,** innermost, intimate; visceral, gut <nonformal>; **intrinsic**; deep; central; **private,** privy, closed-door

**innards** NOUNS **viscera,** vitals, internal organs, insides, inwards, internals; inner mechanism, works <nonformal>; **guts** *and* kishkes *and* giblets <all nonformal>

**innate** ADJS **inborn,** born, congenital; **native, natural,** natural to, connatural, native to, indigenous; **constitutional,** bodily, physical, temperamental, organic; **inbred, genetic, hereditary,** inherited, bred in the bone, in the blood, running in the blood *or* race *or* strain, radical, rooted; connate, connatal, coeval; **instinctive,** instinctual, atavistic, primal

**inner** ADJS **intrinsic,** internal, inward; **inherent,** resident, implicit, immanent, indwelling; **ingrained,** in the very grain; infixed, implanted, inwrought, deep-seated; **subjective,** esoteric, private, secret

**inner circle** NOUNS **clique,** coterie, set, circle, ring, junto, junta, cabal, camarilla, **clan,** group; closed *or* charmed circle; ingroup, we-group; elite, elite group; **old-boy network**

**innermost** ADJS **interior,** inmost, intimate, private; visceral, gut <nonformal>; **intrinsic**; deep; central; **private,** inward, personal; protected

**innocence** NOUNS innocentness; unfallen *or* unlapsed *or* prelapsarian state; **guiltlessness,** faultlessness, blamelessness, reproachlessness, **sinlessness; spotlessness,** stainlessness, taintlessness, unblemishedness; **purity,** cleanness, cleanliness, whiteness, immaculateness, immaculacy, impeccability; clean hands, clean slate, clear conscience, nothing to hide; **chastity, virtue;** ingenuousness

**innocent** ADJS **artless, simple,** plain, **guileless;** simplehearted, simple-minded; **unsophisticated,** green, callow, ingenuous, naive, unripe, raw; childlike, born yesterday; trustful, trusting, unguarded, unwary, unreserved, confiding, unsuspicious; **open,** openhearted, sincere, candid, **frank**

**innocuous** ADJS **harmless,** hurtless, unhurtful; well-meaning, well-meant; **uninjurious,** undamaging, innoxious, innocent, unobjectionable; inoffensive; nonmalignant, **benign;** nontoxic, nonvenomous

**innovation** NOUNS **novelty,** newfangled device *or* contraption <nonformal>, neoism, neonism, **new** *or* **latest wrinkle** <nonformal>, **the last word** *or* **the latest thing** <both nonformal>, *dernier cri* <Fr>; **introduction,** discovery, invention, launching; neologism, neoterism, coinage; **breakthrough,** leap, quantum jump *or* leap

**innovator** NOUNS **transformer,** transmogrifier, innovationist, introducer; precursor; **alterant,** alterer, alterative, **agent,** catalytic agent, catalyst; **vanguard,** avant-garde, avant-gardist, groundbreaker

**innuendo** NOUNS **aspersion,** slur, **remark, reflection,** imputation, **insinuation,** suggestion, sly suggestion, whispering campaign; disparaging *or* uncomplimentary remark, allusion; coloration, tinge, undertone, overtone, undercurrent, more than meets the eye *or* ear, something between the lines, intimation, touch, nuance

**innumerable** ADJS **numberless,** unnumbered, **countless,** uncounted, uncountable, unreckonable, untold, incalculable, immeasurable, unmeasured, measureless, inexhaustible, endless, infinite, without end *or* limit, more than one can tell, more than you can shake a stick at <nonformal>, no end of *or* to; countless as the stars *or* sands

**inoculate** VERBS **immunize, vaccinate,** shoot <nonformal>; **insert, introduce,** inform, insinuate, inject, infuse, perfuse, intromit

**inoculation** NOUNS **vaccination; injection,** hypodermic, hypodermic injection, shot *and* bing <both nonformal>, hypospray *or* jet injection; booster, booster shot <nonformal>; antitoxin, vaccine; **insertion, introduction,** insinuation, perfusion, intromission

**inoffensive** ADJS **harmless,** hurtless, unhurtful; well-meaning, well-meant; **uninjurious,** undamaging, **innocuous,** innoxious, innocent; **benign**

**inoperative** ADJS **unusable,** unemployable, inoperable, unworkable; out of order, out of whack *and* on the blink *and* on the fritz <all nonformal>, in disrepair; **malfunctioning,** out of working order, out of condition, out of repair, out of tune, out of gear; out of joint; **broken**

**inopportune** ADJS **untimely,** unseasonable, badly timed, ill-timed, mistimed, unripe, unready, ill-considered, too late *or* soon, out of phase *or* time *or* sync; **inconvenient,** unhandy; malapropos, *mal à propos* <Fr>

**inquest** NOUNS **hearing, inquiry, inquisition,** inquiring, probing, inquirendo; inquisition; inquiring mind

**inquire** VERBS **be curious, want to know, take an interest in,** take a lively interest, burn with curiosity; interrogate, quiz, question, query; seek, dig up, dig around for, nose out, nose around for

**inquirer** NOUNS **asker, prober,** querier, querist, **questioner,** questionist, interrogator; examiner, catechist; inquisitor, inquisitionist; cross-questioner, cross-interrogator, **cross-examiner;** interlocutor; **pollster,** poller, sampler, opinion sampler; **interviewer; busybody,** gossip, **pry,** Paul Pry, **snoop,** snooper, nosy Parker <nonformal>

**inquiring** ADJS **curious, inquisitive,** interested, quizzical; **alert,** tuned in <nonformal>, **attentive**; burning with curiosity, eaten up *or* consumed with curiosity, curious as a cat; overcurious, supercurious; morbidly curious

**inquiry** NOUNS inquiring, probing, **inquest**, inquirendo; inquisition; **question,** query, interrogation, interrogatory; interrogative; vexed *or* knotty question, burning question; **canvass,** survey, questionnaire, questionary

**inquisition** NOUNS **trial, jury trial,** trial by jury, trial at the bar, **hearing, inquiry,** inquest, assize; **examination,** cross-examination; **grilling,** the grill <nonformal>; police interrogation; **the third-degree** <nonformal>

**inquisitive** ADJS **curious,** inquiring, interested, quizzical; **alert,** tuned in <nonformal>, **attentive**; burning with curiosity, eaten up *or* consumed with curiosity, curious as a cat; morbidly curious

**inroad** NOUNS **intrusion,** impingement, **infringement,** invasion, incursion, influx, irruption, infiltration; encroachment; **overstepping, transgression, trespass,** usurpation, infraction

**insane** ADJS **mad,** stark-mad, mad as a hatter, mad as a March hare, **stark-staring mad,** maddened, **sick,** crazed, **lunatic,** moonstruck, **daft, non compos mentis,** non compos, **unsound,** of unsound mind, **demented, deranged,** deluded, disoriented, unhinged, **unbalanced,** unsettled, distraught, wandering, mazed, crackbrained, brainsick, sick *or* soft in the head, not right, not in one's right mind, **touched,** touched in the head, **out of one's mind,** out of one's senses *or* wits, bereft of reason, reasonless, irrational, deprived of reason, senseless, witless; queer, queer in the head, odd, strange, off

**insanity** NOUNS insaneness, **lunacy, madness,** *folie* <Fr>, **craziness, daftness,** oddness, strangeness, queerness, abnormality; loss of touch *or* contact with reality, loss of mind *or* reason; dementia, athymia, brainsickness, mindsickness, mental sickness; **mental illness,** alienation, aberration, mental disturbance, **derangement,** distraction, disorientation, mental derangement *or* disorder, unbalance, mental instability, unsoundness, **unsoundness of mind**

**insatiable** ADJS **gluttonous, greedy,** voracious, ravenous, edacious, rapacious, polyphagic, bulimic, hyperphagic, Apician; **piggish, hoggish,** swinish; insatiate, unsatisfied, unsated, unappeased, unappeasable, limitless, bottomless, unquenchable, quenchless, unslaked, unslakable, slakeless

**inscribe** VERBS 1 **write out,** make out; **write down, record,** put *or* place upon record; enscroll; **register, enroll,** matriculate, check in; impanel; **print,** imprint, **stamp, etch,** engrave, impress; instill, infix, inculcate, impress, imprint, stamp, etch, grave, engrave
2 **impress on the mind, get into one's head,** drive *or* hammer into one's head, get across, get into one's thick head *or* skull <nonformal>

**inscription** NOUNS **epitaph,** tombstone marking; epigraph, graffito; **writing,** scrivening <old>, lettering; engrossment; inscript

**inscrutable** ADJS **unfathomable,** impenetrable, unsearchable, numinous; **unintelligible, incomprehensible,** inapprehensible, ungraspable, unknowable, incognizable; **past comprehension,** beyond one's comprehension, beyond understanding

**insecure** ADJS **unconfident,** unsure, unassured, unsure of oneself; unself-confident, unself-assured, unself-reliant; **unreliable,** undependable, untrustworthy, treacherous, **unsound,** unstable, unsteady, shaky, tottery, rocky

**inseminate** VERBS **fertilize,** fructify, fecundate, fecundify; **impregnate,** spermatize, knock up <nonformal>, **get with child** *or* **young; pollinate** *or* pollinize, pollen; cross-fertilize, cross-pollinate *or* cross-pollinize

**insensitive** ADJS **callous, calloused,** Philistine; **thick-skinned,** pachydermatous; **hard, hard-hearted, hardened,** case-hardened, coarsened, brutalized, indurated, stony, stony-hearted, marble-hearted, flinthearted, flinty, steely, impervious, inured, armored *or* steeled against, proof against, as hard as nails; **inconsiderate, unthoughtful,** unmindful, unheedful, disregardful, **thoughtless,** heedless, mindless, unthinking; **tactless**

**inseparable** ADJS impartible, **indivisible,** undividable, indissoluble, inalienable, inseverable, bound up in *or* with; **thick, thick as thieves** <nonformal>

**insert** NOUNS 1 insertion; **inset, inlay;** gore, godet, gusset; **graft,** scion *or* cion; tessera
VERBS 2 **introduce,** insinuate, inject, infuse, perfuse, inoculate, intromit; **enter**; **penetrate; put in, stick in,** set in, throw in, pop in, tuck in, whip in; slip in, ease in; **enter,** make an entry, write in

**inside** ADJS 1 **internal,** inner, inward; **innermost,** inmost, **intimate,** private; visceral, gut <nonformal>; **intrinsic**; deep; central; indoor; **confidential,** auricular, esoteric; **off the record,** not for the record, not to be minuted, within these four walls, eyes-only, between us; not for attribution; sensitive, privileged, under privilege
ADVS 2 **in, within;** herein, therein, wherein

**insider** NOUNS **member,** affiliate, belonger, initiate, one of us, cardholder, card-carrier, card-carrying member

**insides** NOUNS **innards** <nonformal>, inwards, internals; inner mechanism, what makes it tick *and* works <both nonformal>; **guts** <nonformal>, **vitals, viscera,** *kishkes* <Yiddish>, giblets; entrails, bowels, guts

**insight** NOUNS **discernment,** critical discernment, penetration, **perception,** perceptiveness, perspicacity; **flair; judgment,** acumen

**insightful** ADJS **understanding,** comprehending, perceptive, discerning, apperceptive, percipient, perspicacious, appercipient, shrewd, sagacious, wise; omniscient, all-knowing

**insignia** NOUNS **regalia,** ensign, **emblem, badge, symbol,** logo <nonformal>, marking, attribute; badge of office, mark of office, chain, chain of office, collar; wand, verge, *fasces* <L>, **mace, staff, baton**

**insignificance** NOUNS **unimportance,** inconsequence, inconsequentiality, indifference, **immateriality;** inessentiality; ineffectuality; unnoteworthiness, unimpressiveness; inferiority, secondariness, low order of importance, low priority, dispensability, expendability, marginality; **smallness,** littleness, slightness, inconsiderableness, negligibility; irrelevancy, meaninglessness; **pettiness,** puniness, pokiness, picayune, picayunishness; irrelevance

**insignificant** ADJS **small, inconsiderable,** inconsequential, immaterial, negligible, no great shakes, footling, one-horse *and* pint-size *and* vest-pocket <all nonformal>; unimportant, no skin off one's nose *or* ass, **trivial,** trifling, nugacious, nugatory, petty, mean, niggling, picayune *or* picayunish, nickel-and-dime *and* penny-ante *and* Mickey-Mouse *and* chickenshit <all nonformal>; **small, little,** minute, footling, minor, inferior; irrelevant

**insincere** ADJS **affected, pretentious,** la-di-da, posy <Brit nonformal>; **artificial,** unnatural; **deceitful;** unsincere, uncandid, unfrank, disingenuous; **false, hypocritical**

**insinuate** VERBS **hint,** intimate, suggest, imply, indicate, adumbrate, lead *or* leave one to gather, justify one in supposing, give *or* drop *or* throw out a hint, give an inkling of, **hint at; allege**

**insipid** ADJS **tasteless, flavorless,** bland, spiceless, savorless, sapless, unsavory, unflavored; pulpy, pappy, gruelly; **weak, thin,** mild, **wishy-washy,** milktoast, washy, watery, watered, watered-down, diluted, dilute, milk-and-water; **flat, stale,** dead, *fade* <Fr>; vapid, inane, jejune, hollow, empty, superficial; indifferent, neither one thing nor the other

**insist** VERBS **insist on** *or* **upon,** stick to <nonformal>, set one's heart *or* mind upon; **take one's stand upon,** stand on *or* upon, put *or* lay it on the line <nonformal>, make no bones about it; stand upon one's rights, **put one's foot down** <nonformal>; brook *or* take no denial, not take no for an answer; **maintain, contend,** assert; urge, press; **persist**

**insistence** NOUNS **exigence, importunity,** importunateness, importunacy, **demandingness,** pertinaciousness, pertinacity; pressure, pressingness, **urgency,** exigency; **persistence**

**insistent** ADJS **persevering,** perseverant, **persistent,** persisting; dogged, plodding, slogging, plugging; **pertinacious,** tenacious, stick-to-itive <nonformal>; **unswerving,** unremitting, unabating, unintermitting, uninterrupted; single-minded, utterly attentive; undiscouraged, undaunted, indomitable, game to the last *or* to the end; **importunate,**

urgent, pressing, loud, clamant, crying, clamorous

**insolence** NOUNS 1 **presumption,** presumptuousness; **audacity, effrontery,** boldness, assurance, hardihood, bumptiousness; overweeningness; **contempt, contemptuousness,** contumely; **disdain**, *sprezzatura* <Ital>; **arrogance**, uppishness *and* uppityness <both nonformal>; **impudence,** disrespect, disrespectfulness

2 <nonformal> **cheek,** face, brass, **nerve, gall, chutzpah,** crust

**insolent** ADJS insulting; **presumptuous,** presuming, overpresumptuous, overweening; **audacious, bold,** assured, hardy, bumptious; **contemptuous**, contumelious; **disdainful**, **arrogant**, uppish *and* uppity <both nonformal>; forward, pushy <nonformal>, obtrusive, pushy <nonformal>, **impudent**

**insolvent** ADJS **bankrupt,** in receivership, in the hands of receivers, belly-up <nonformal>, broken, **broke** *and* busted <both nonformal>, **ruined,** failed, out of business, unable to pay one's creditors, unable to meet one's obligations, on the rocks; destitute

**insomnia** NOUNS **wakefulness,** wake; **sleeplessness,** restlessness, tossing and turning; insomnolence *or* insomnolency, white night, all-night vigil, lidless vigil, *per vigilium* <L>

**inspect** VERBS **scrutinize, survey, eye,** contemplate, look over, give the eye *or* the once-over <nonformal>; examine, vet <Brit nonformal>; **pore,** pore over, peruse; take a close *or* careful look; take a long, hard look; size up <nonformal>; take stock of

**inspection** NOUNS **examination, scrutiny; survey, review, perusal,** look-over, once over *and* look-see <both nonformal>, perlustration, **study,** look-through, scan, run-through

**inspector** NOUNS **examiner,** examinant, **tester;** scrutinizer, scrutator, scrutineer, quality-control inspector; **monitor,** reviewer

**inspiration** NOUNS **encouragement, heartening,** inspiriting, inspiritment, emboldening, assurance, reassurance, pat *or* clap on the back; afflatus, divine inspiration

**inspire** VERBS inspirit, spirit, spirit up; fire, **fire one's imagination; animate, exhilarate,** enliven; **infuse, infect,** inject, inoculate, imbue, inform

**inspired** ADJS **fired,** afire, on fire; **well-put,** well-expressed, inspired, theopneustic

**inspiring** ADJS **inspirational,** inspiriting; infusive; animating, exhilarating, enlivening

**instability** NOUNS **inconstancy,** changefulness, unstableness, **unsteadiness,** unsteadfastness, unfixedness, unsettledness, rootlessness; **uncertainty,** undependability, inconsistency, shiftiness, unreliability; **variability,** variation, variety, restlessness, deviability; unpredictability, irregularity

**install** VERBS emplace, spot <nonformal>, put in place; **invest,** vest, place in office, put in, instate, induct, inaugurate, initiate, invest, ordain, **place in office**

**installation** NOUNS installment, **instatement,** induction, placement, **inauguration,** investiture, taking office; **accession,** accedence; coronation, enthronement

**instance** NOUNS **particular, item, detail,** point, count, fact, matter, article, datum, element, part, ingredient, factor, facet, aspect, thing; **example,** exemplar; relevant instance, **case,** typical example *or* case, case in point, object lesson

**instant** NOUNS 1 **moment, second,** split second, millisecond, microsecond, nanosecond, half a second, minute, **trice,** twinkle, **twinkling, twinkling** *or* **twinkle of an eye,** twink, **wink,** bat of an eye <nonformal>, **flash,** crack, tick, stroke, coup, breath, twitch; two shakes of a lamb's tail *and* two shakes *and* shake *and* half a shake *and* **jiffy** *and* jiff *and* half a jiffy <all nonformal>

ADJS 2 **hasty, hurried,** festinate, **quick,** flying, **expeditious,** prompt; quick-and-dirty <nonformal>, **immediate,** on the spot; onrushing, **swift, speedy; instantaneous,** momentary, **immediate,** presto, quick as thought *or* lightning; lightning-like, lightning-swift

**instantaneous** ADJS instant, momentary, **immediate,** lightning-like, lightning-swift; nearly simultaneous; simultaneous

**instigate** VERBS **incite, put up to** <nonformal>; set on, sic on; **foment,** ferment, **agitate,** arouse, excite, stir up, work up, whip up; rally; **inflame,**

incense, **fire,** heat, heat up, impassion; **provoke,** pique, whet, tickle; nettle; feed the fire, add fuel to the flame, fan, fan the flame

**instigator** NOUNS **inciter,** exciter, urger; **provoker,** *provocateur* <Fr>, *agent provocateur* <Fr>, catalyst; **agitator, fomenter,** inflamer; agitprop; **rabble-rouser,** rouser, **demagogue; firebrand, incendiary; troublemaker,** mischief-maker, ringleader

**instill** VERBS **inculcate, indoctrinate,** catechize, inoculate, **infuse,** imbue, impregnate, **implant,** infix, impress; **impress upon the mind** *or* **memory,** urge on the mind, beat into, beat *or* knock into one's head, grind in, drill into, drum into one's head *or* skull; **condition, brainwash**

**instinct** NOUNS **impulse;** natural impulse, blind impulse, urge, drive; vagrant *or* fleeting impulse

**instinctive** ADJS natural, **inherent, innate,** unlearned; unconscious, subliminal; **involuntary, automatic,** spontaneous, impulsive; **instinctual**

**institute** NOUNS 1 **organization,** establishment, foundation, **institution,** school, **educational institution,** teaching institution, academic *or* scholastic institution, teaching and research institution, **academy**
VERBS 2 **inaugurate,** found, establish, set up <nonformal>; **introduce,** broach, bring up, lift up, raise; **launch,** float; **usher in,** ring in <nonformal>; **set on foot,** set agoing, turn on, kick-start *and* jump-start <both nonformal>, start up, start going, start the ball rolling <nonformal>

**institution** NOUNS **organization,** establishment, foundation, institute; **creation,** establishing, origin, origination, setting-up, setting in motion; constitution, installation, formation, inauguration, **inception,** realization, materialization, effectuation

**institutionalize** VERBS **commit,** consign, commit to prison, send to jail, send up *and* send up the river <both nonformal>; commit to an institution, recommit, remit, remand

**instruct** VERBS **advise,** coach, brief; **teach,** give instruction, give lessons in, **educate, school; edify,** enlighten, civilize, illumine; **direct, guide;** get across, **inform; show,** show how, show the ropes, demonstrate; enlarge *or* broaden the mind; sharpen the wits, open the eyes *or* mind; teach a lesson, give a lesson to; **ground,** teach the rudiments *or* elements *or* basics; catechize; teach an old dog new tricks; reeducate

**instruction** NOUNS **teaching,** education, schooling, tuition; edification, **enlightenment,** illumination; tutelage, tutorage, tutorship; tutoring, coaching, private teaching, teacher; spoon-feeding; **pedagogy,** pedagogics, didactics, didacticism; catechization; computer-aided instruction, programmed instruction; self-teaching, self-instruction; **school**; **formal education,** coursework, schoolwork

**instructive** ADJS **informative,** informing, informational; **enlightening;** educative, educational; advisory, monitory; **communicative**

**instructor** NOUNS **teacher, educator,** preceptor, **mentor; master,** maestro; **pedagogue,** pedagogist, educationist; schoolman; **schoolteacher,** schoolmaster, schoolkeeper; **professor, academic,** member of academy; don <Brit>, fellow; guide, docent; rabbi, *melamed* <Heb>, pandit, pundit, guru, *mullah* <Persian>, *starets* <Russ>

**instrument** NOUNS **tool, implement, appliance,** device; contrivance, lever, mechanism; **vehicle,** organ; **agent**; medium, mediator, intermedium, intermediary, intermediate, interagent, liaison, go-between; expediter, facilitator, animator; **cat's-paw,** puppet, dummy, pawn, creature, minion, stooge <nonformal>; stalking horse; dupe

**instrumental** ADJS 1 **helping,** assisting, serving; **assistant, auxiliary,** adjuvant, subservient, subsidiary, ancillary, accessory; ministerial, ministering, ministrant; fostering, nurtural
2 orchestral, symphonic, concert

**insubordinate** ADJS **unsubmissive,** indocile, uncompliant, uncooperative, noncooperative, noncooperating, **intractable;** mutinous, disobedient

**insubordination** NOUNS **disobedience,** nonobedience, **noncompliance; undutifulness,** unduteousness; willful disobedience; indiscipline; mutiny

**insubstantial** ADJS **unsubstantial,** nonsubstantial, unsubstanced; intangible, impalpable, imponderable; **immaterial**; **bodiless,** incorporeal, unsolid, unconcrete; weightless; **transient**, ephemeral, fleeting, fugitive

**insufferable** ADJS **intolerable,** insupportable, unendurable, unbearable, past bearing, not to be borne *or* endured, for the birds <nonformal>, **too much** *or* a bit much <nonformal>, more than flesh and blood can bear, enough to drive one mad, enough to provoke a saint, enough to make a preacher swear <nonformal>, enough to try the patience of Job

**insufficiency** NOUNS **inadequacy,** insufficientness, inadequateness; short supply, seller's market; none to spare; nonsatisfaction, nonfulfillment, coming *or* falling short *or* shy; **undercommitment;** too little too late; a band-aid <nonformal>, a drop in the bucket *or* the ocean, a lick and a promise, a cosmetic measure; **incompetence,** incompetency, unqualification, unsuitability

**insufficient** ADJS unsufficing, **inadequate;** found wanting, defective, incomplete, imperfect, deficient, lacking, failing, wanting; **too few,** undersupplied; **too little,** not enough, precious little, a trickle *or* mere trickle; **unsatisfactory,** unsatisfying; cosmetic, merely cosmetic, surface, superficial, symptomatic, merely symptomatic; **incompetent,** unequal to, unqualified, not up to

**insular** ADJS insulated, isolated; island, islandy *or* islandish, islandlike; islanded, isleted, island-dotted; **remote, out-of-the-way,** up-country, in a backwater, out-of-the-world, out-back *and* back of beyond <both Austral>; **narrow,** parochial

**insulate** VERBS **segregate,** separate, separate out *or* off, divide, cordon, cordon off; **isolate,** seclude; **set apart,** keep apart; **quarantine,** put in isolation

**insulated** ADJS **insular,** isolated; **segregated,** separated, cordoned-off, divided; **isolated,** secluded; **set apart,** sequestered; **quarantined**

**insult** NOUNS 1 **indignity,** affront, offense, injury, humiliation; scurrility, contempt, contumely, despite, flout, flouting, mockery, jeering, jeer, mock, scoff, gibe, taunt, brickbat <nonformal>; **aspersion,** uncomplimentary remark, slap *or* kick in the face, left-handed *or* backhanded compliment, damning with faint praise; cut
VERBS 2 **offend, affront,** give offense to, disoblige, outrage, step *or* tread on one's toes; dishonor, humiliate, treat with indignity; call names, kick *or* slap in the face, take *or* pluck by the beard; **add insult to injury**

**insulting** ADJS **insolent, abusive, offensive,** humiliating, degrading, contemptuous, contumelious, calumnious; scurrilous, scurrile

**insurance** NOUNS **security, surety,** indemnity, guaranty, guarantee, warranty, warrant; assurance <Brit>; **annuity,** variable annuity; **social security**

**insure** VERBS **secure,** guarantee, guaranty, warrant, assure, ensure, bond, **certify; make sure, make certain,** make sure of, make no doubt, make no mistake; remove *or* dismiss *or* expunge *or* erase all doubt; **underwrite**

**insured** ADJS **secured,** covered, **guaranteed, warranted,** certified, ensured, **assured;** certain, sure

**insurer** NOUNS **guarantor,** warrantor, guaranty, guarantee; mortgagor; underwriter; sponsor, surety

**insurgent** NOUNS 1 **rebel,** revolter; insurrectionary, insurrecto, **insurrectionist;** malcontent, *frondeur* <Fr>; **mutineer,** agitator; extremist; revolutionary, revolutionist; traitor, subversive; freedom fighter
ADJS 2 **rebellious,** rebel, breakaway; **mutinous,** mutineering; **insurrectionary,** riotous, turbulent; factious, **seditious,** seditionary; revolutionary, revolutional; traitorous, treasonable, subversive; extreme, extremistic

**insurmountable** ADJS **unachievable,** unattainable, unrealizable, uncompassable; unsurmountable, **insuperable; beyond one,** beyond one's power, beyond one's control, out of one's depth, too much for

**insurrection** NOUNS **revolt,** rebellion, revolution, mutiny, insurgence *or* insurgency, *émeute* <Fr>, **uprising,** rising, **riot,** civil disorder; peasant revolt, *jacquerie* <Fr>; putsch, coup d'état; intifada

**intact** ADJS untouched, undamaged, all in one piece <nonformal>, unimpaired, virgin, pristine, unspoiled; **sound,** whole, entire, complete, integral; unhurt, unharmed, unscathed, with a whole skin

**intangible** ADJS **unsubstantial**, insubstantial, impalpable, imponderable; **incorporeal,** incorporate, incorporeous;

**unphysical,** nonphysical; **unfleshly;** airy, ghostly, spectral, phantom, shadowy, ethereal

**integral** ADJS integrated; **one,** one and indivisible; **inclusive,** all-inclusive, **unitary, unified,** united, rolled into one, composite; **intact,** whole, entire, complete

**integrate** VERBS **form** *or* **make a whole,** constitute a whole; unite, form a unity; **amalgamate,** alloy, coalesce, **fuse, merge,** meld, compound, compose, conflate, concoct; **combine, incorporate, consolidate,** assimilate, put *or* lump together, roll into one, come together, make one, unitize

**integrated** ADJS **combined,** united, amalgamated, incorporated, consolidated, assimilated, one, unitary, unitive, unitized, **joined**, joint, conjoint; **merged,** blended, fused; **mixed; unified,** rolled into one, composite

**integration** NOUNS **affiliation,** alliance, allying, alignment, **association,** consociation, combination, **union,** unification, **coalition,** fusion, merger, coalescence, coadunation, amalgamation, **league, federation, confederation,** confederacy, consolidation, incorporation, inclusion

**integrity** NOUNS **probity,** assured probity, **honesty,** rectitude, uprightness, upstandingness, erectness, **virtue,** virtuousness, **righteousness, goodness;** cleanness, **decency; honor,** honorableness, worthiness, estimableness, reputability, nobility; unimpeachableness, unimpeachability, irreproachableness, irreproachability, blamelessness; **soundness,** intactness, wholeness, entireness, completeness

**intellect** NOUNS **mind,** *mens* <L>; mental *or* intellectual faculty, nous, **reason, rationality,** rational *or* reasoning faculty, power of reason, *Vernunft* <Ger>, *esprit* <Fr>, *raison* <Fr>, ratio, discursive reason, **intelligence,** mentality, mental capacity, **understanding,** reasoning, intellection, conception; intellectual

*discourse of reason*
SHAKESPEARE

**intellectual** NOUNS 1 **intellect,** intellectualist, literate, member of the intelligentsia, white-collar intellectual; **brain** *and* rocket scientist *and* brain surgeon <all nonformal>; **pundit, Brahmin, mandarin,** egg-head *and* pointy-head <both nonformal>; **highbrow** <nonformal>; wise man
ADJS 2 **mental,** rational, reasoning, thinking, noetic, conceptive, conceptual, phrenic; intelligent; noological; cerebral

**intelligence** NOUNS 1 **secret service,** intelligence service, intelligence bureau *or* department; military intelligence, naval intelligence; **counterintelligence**
2 **intellect,** head, brain, mentality, consciousness; wise man, wisdom

**intelligence agent** NOUNS **secret agent,** operative, cloak-and-dagger operative, **undercover man,** inside man <nonformal>; **spy,** espionage agent; counterspy, double agent; **spotter; scout,** reconnoiterer; **intelligence officer;** spymaster; spy-catcher <nonformal>, counterintelligence agent

**intelligent** ADJS ideational, conceptual, conceptive, discursive; sophic, noetic; **knowing,** understanding, reasonable, rational, sensible, bright; sane; not so dumb <nonformal>, strong-minded

**intelligentsia** NOUNS literati, illuminati; intellectual elite; clerisy

**intelligible** ADJS **comprehensible, apprehensible,** prehensible, graspable, **knowable,** cognizable, scrutable, **fathomable,** decipherable, plumbable, penetrable, interpretable; **understandable,** easily understood, easy to understand, exoteric; readable; articulate

**intemperance** NOUNS intemperateness, **indulgence,** self-indulgence; **overindulgence,** overdoing; **unrestraint,** unconstraint, indiscipline, uncontrol; **immoderation,** immoderacy, immoderateness; inordinacy, inordinateness; **excess,** excessiveness, too much, too-muchness <nonformal>; prodigality, extravagance; crapulence *or* crapulency, crapulousness; **incontinence**; **swinishness,** gluttony; **drunkenness**

**intend** VERBS **purpose, plan,** purport, **mean,** have in mind, think, **propose; resolve,** determine; project, **design,** destine; **aim,** aim at, take aim at, draw a bead on, set one's sights on, have designs on, go for, drive at, aspire to *or* after, be after, set before oneself, purpose to oneself; harbor a design; **desire**

**intended** NOUNS 1 **fiancé, fiancée,** bride-to-be, affianced, betrothed, future

ADJS 2 **intentional,** proposed, purposed, telic, **projected, designed,** of design, aimed, aimed at, **meant, purposeful,** purposive, **willful,** voluntary, deliberate; **engaged,** plighted, affianced, betrothed

**intense** ADJS **fervent,** fervid, passionate, impassioned, ardent; **zealous,** spirited, hearty, vehement, abandoned, **passionate,** impassioned, **warm,** heated, hot, hot-blooded, red-hot, fiery, white-hot, flaming, burning, afire, aflame, on fire, like a house afire <nonformal>

**intensify** VERBS **heighten, deepen,** enhance, **strengthen,** beef up <nonformal>, aggravate, exacerbate; **exaggerate,** blow up *and* puff up <both nonformal>, **magnify;** whet, sharpen; **reinforce,** double, redouble, triple; **concentrate,** condense, consolidate; **develop,** gain strength, strengthen

**intensity** NOUNS **energy,** vigor, force, power, vitality, strenuousness, **dynamism,** demonic energy; **potency; strength; zeal,** ardor, ardency, fervor, fervency, fervidness, spirit, warmth, fire, heat, heatedness, **passion,** passionateness, impassionedness, heartiness, **abandon,** vehemence

**intensive** ADJS **thorough, thoroughgoing,** thorough-paced, exhaustive, broad-based, wall-to-wall <nonformal>, house-to-house *and* door-to-door <both nonformal>, A-to-Z, comprehensive, all-embracing, all-encompassing, omnibus, radical, sweeping

**intent** NOUNS **intention,** purpose, aim, object, design, plan

**intention** NOUNS **intent,** intendment, mindset, **aim,** effect, meaning, view, study, animus, **point, purpose,** function, set *or* settled *or* fixed purpose; **design, plan, project,** idea, notion; **quest,** pursuit; **resolve,** resolution, mind, will; **motive**

**interact** VERBS interwork, **interplay;** mesh, intermesh, engage, fit, fit like a glove, dovetail, mortise; **interweave,** interlace, intertwine; **interchange;** coact, **cooperate;** codepend

**interacting** ADJS interactive, interworking, interplaying; in gear, in mesh; dovetailed, mortised; **cooperative,** cooperating

**intercede** VERBS **mediate,** intermediate, go between; **intervene,** interpose, step in, step into the breach, declare oneself a party, involve oneself, put oneself between disputants, use one's good offices, act between; butt in *and* put one's nose in <both nonformal>; **negotiate,** bargain, **treat with,** make terms, meet halfway; **arbitrate,** moderate; **umpire, referee,** judge

**intercept** VERBS **listen in; eavesdrop,** wiretap, tap, bug <nonformal>

**interchangeable** ADJS 1 **exchangeable,** changeable, standard; equivalent; **even,** equal; returnable, **convertible,** commutable, permutable; commutative; retaliatory, equalizing; reciprocal, traded-off; mutual, give-and-take; **exchanged, transposed,** switched, **swapped** <nonformal>, traded, **interchanged**

2 **indistinguishable,** undistinguishable, indiscernible, not to be distinguished, undiscriminated, undifferentiated, **alike,** six of one and half a dozen of the other <nonformal>; standard

**interconnect** VERBS **interjoin,** intertie, interassociate, interaffiliate, **interlink,** interlock, interdigitate

**intercourse** NOUNS 1 **copulation, sex act,** having sex, having intercourse, *le sport* <Fr>, coupling, mating, coition, **coitus,** pareunia, venery, copula <law>, **sex, sexual intercourse,** cohabitation, commerce, sexual commerce, congress, sexual congress, sexual union, sexual relations, relations, marital relations, marriage act, act of love, sleeping together *or* with; screwing *and* balling *and* nookie *and* diddling *and* making it with <all nonformal>; meat *and* ass <both nonformal>, intimacy, connection, carnal knowledge

*making the beast with two backs*
SHAKESPEARE

2 **communication,** communion, congress, **commerce; speaking, speech**, utterance, speech act, talking, linguistic intercourse, speech situation, speech circuit, converse, **conversation;** social intercourse

**interdict** VERBS **prohibit, proscribe,** inhibit, put *or* lay under an interdict *or* interdiction; embargo, **lay** *or* **put an embargo on; taboo**

**interest** NOUNS 1 **premium, price, rate;** interest rate, rate of interest, prime interest rate *or* **prime rate,** bank rate,

lending rate, borrowing rate, the price of money; discount rate
2 **concern,** concernment; **curiosity**; **enthusiasm,** passion, ardor, zeal; cathexis; matter of interest, special interest
VERBS 3 **concern,** involve in *or* with, affect the interest, give pause; **pique, titillate,** tantalize, tickle, tickle one's fancy, **attract,** invite, **fascinate, provoke, stimulate, arouse, excite,** pique one's interest, excite interest, excite *or* whet one's interest, arouse one's passion *or* enthusiasm, turn one on <nonformal>

**interested** ADJS concerned; **alert to, sensitive to, on the watch; curious**; tantalized, piqued, titillated, tickled, **attracted,** fascinated, excited, turned-on <nonformal>; keen on *or* about, enthusiastic, passionate; fixating, cathectic

**interesting** ADJS **stimulating, provocative,** provoking, thought-provoking, thought-challenging, thought-inspiring; **titillating,** tickling, **tantalizing, inviting, exciting; piquant,** lively, racy, juicy, succulent, spicy, rich; readable

**interfere** VERBS **intrude,** obtrude, **interlope;** come between, **interpose**, insert oneself, insinuate, impose; **encroach, infringe,** impinge, **trespass,** trespass on *or* upon

**interference** NOUNS **intrusion,** obtrusion, **interloping;** interposition, interposal, imposition, insinuation, intervention, interventionism, interruption, injection, interjection; **encroachment,** entrenchment, trespass, trespassing, unlawful entry; impingement, **infringement,** invasion, incursion, inroad, influx, irruption, infiltration

**interfering** ADJS **intrusive,** obtrusive, intervenient, invasive, interruptive

**interim** NOUNS 1 **interval, interlude,** pause, break, **time-out,** recess, coffee break, halftime *or* halftime intermission, interruption; **lull,** quiet spell, resting point, point of repose, plateau, letup, relief; **respite**; **intermission,** entr'acte; *intermezzo* <Ital>
ADJS 2 **temporary,** tentative, provisional, provisory

**interior** NOUNS 1 **inside,** inner, inward, internal, intern; inner recess, recesses, **innermost** *or* **deepest recesses,** penetralia, intimate places, secret place *or* places; bosom, secret heart, heart, heart of hearts, soul, vitals, vital center; inner self, inner life, inner landscape, inner *or* interior man, inner nature; core, center
2 **inland,** inlands, up-country; heartland; hinterland; Middle America
ADJS 3 **internal, inner, inside, inward;** intestine; **innermost,** inmost, **intimate,** private

**interject** VERBS **interpose, interpolate,** intercalate, interjaculate; **intervene; insert in,** stick in, introduce in, insinuate in, sandwich in, slip in, inject in, implant in; **remark, mention,** let drop *or* fall, say by the way, make mention of; refer to, allude to, touch on, make reference to, call attention to

**interlace** VERBS **mix,** admix, commix, immix, **intermix, mingle,** bemingle, commingle, immingle, **intermingle,** interweave, intertwine, interlard

**interlocking** NOUNS **interconnection,** interjoinder, **interlinking,** interdigitation; **interassociation,** interaffiliation

**interloper** NOUNS **intruder, trespasser;** crasher *and* gate-crasher <both nonformal>, unwelcome *or* uninvited guest; invader, encroacher, infiltrator

**interlude** NOUNS **respite, recess,** rest, pause, halt, stay, lull, **break,** surcease, suspension, **intermission,** spell <Australia>, letup <nonformal>, **time out** <nonformal>, time to catch one's breath; **breathing spell,** breathing time, breathing place, breathing space, breath, **breather**

**intermarriage** NOUNS mixed marriage, interfaith marriage, interracial marriage; miscegenation; misalliance, *mésalliance* <Fr>, ill-assorted marriage

**intermarry** VERBS interwed, miscegenate

**intermediary** NOUNS **go-between, middleman,** medium, intermedium, intermediate, interagent, **internuncio,** broker; connection <nonformal>, **contact; negotiator,** negotiant; interpleader; arbitrator, mediator

**intermediate** NOUNS 1 **mediator,** intermediator, intermediate agent, intermedium, **intermediary,** interagent, internuncio; **intercessor,** interceder; ombudsman; **go-between, middleman**; connection <nonformal>; **negotiator,** negotiant, negotiatress *or* negotiatrix
ADJS 2 **intervening,** intermediary, intermedial, medial, mean, medium, mesne, median, **middle**

**interment** NOUNS **burial,** burying, inhumation, sepulture, **entombment;** encoffinment, inurning, inurnment, urn burial; disposal of the dead; burial *or* funeral *or* funerary customs

**interminable** ADJS **perpetual, everlasting,** everliving, ever-being, ever-abiding, ever-during, ever-durable, permanent, perdurable, indestructible; **endless,** unending, never-ending, without end, nonterminous, nonterminating; **continual,** continuous, steady, **constant, ceaseless,** nonstop, unceasing, never-ceasing, **incessant,** unremitting

**intermingle** VERBS **mix,** admix, commix, immix, **intermix, mingle,** bemingle, commingle, immingle, interlace, interweave, intertwine, interlard

**intermission** NOUNS **respite, recess, rest, pause,** halt, stay, lull, **break,** surcease, suspension, interlude, letup <nonformal>, **time out** <nonformal>, time to catch one's breath; **breathing spell, breather;** coffee break, tea break, cigarette break

**intermittent** ADJS **irregular,** unregular, unsystematic, unmethodical *or* immethodical; intermitting, **desultory, fluctuating, wavering,** wandering, rambling, veering; flickering, guttering

**intern** VERBS **imprison, incarcerate,** immure; **jail,** gaol <Brit>, jug <nonformal>, throw into jail, send up the river <nonformal>; hold captive, hold prisoner, hold in captivity; hold under close *or* house arrest

**internal** ADJS **interior,** inner, inside, inward; **innermost,** inmost, **intimate,** private; **intrinsic, inherent,** resident, implicit, immanent, indwelling

**internalize** VERBS put in, **keep within;** enclose, embed, surround, contain, comprise, include, enfold, take to heart, assimilate

**international** ADJS **universal,** worldwide, transnational, planet-wide, **global,** cosmopolitan, supernational, supranational

**interplay** NOUNS **interaction,** interworking, intercourse, intercommunication, **interweaving,** interlacing, intertwining; interpersonal communication, intercommunication, intercommunion, **exchange,** interchange

**interpose** VERBS **interject, interpolate,** intercalate, interjaculate; **mediate,** go between, **intervene;** put between, sandwich; **insert in,** stick in, introduce in, insinuate in, sandwich in, slip in, inject in, implant in; **intrude**

**interpret** VERBS **diagnose; construe,** put a construction on, **take;** understand, understand by, **take to mean,** take it that; **read; read into,** read between the lines; see in a special light, read in view of, take an approach to, **define, describe; criticize,** critique, evaluate, explicate, analyze, judge

**interpretation** NOUNS **construction, reading,** way of seeing *or* understanding *or* putting; constructionism, strict constructionism, loose constructionism; **diagnosis; definition,** description; **meaning; explanation,** sense-distinction

**interrogate** VERBS **inquire,** ask, question, query; ask after, inquire after, ask about, ask questions, put queries; inquire of, require an answer, ask a question, put a question to, pose *or* set *or* propose *or* propound a question

**interrogation** NOUNS **questioning, querying,** asking, seeking, pumping, probing, inquiring; **quiz,** quizzing, **examination;** interpellation, bringing into question; catechizing, catechization; catechetical method, Socratic method *or* induction

**interrogator** NOUNS **inquirer, asker, prober,** querier, querist, **questioner,** questionist; interviewer; interrogatrix; interpellator; **quizzer,** examiner, catechist; inquisitor, inquisitionist

**interrupt** VERBS **put in, cut in, break in;** jump in, chime in *and* chip in *and* put in one's two-cents worth <all nonformal>; **talk out of turn,** speak inopportunely, intrude, butt in *and* stick one's nose in <both nonformal>, open one's big mouth *or* big fat mouth <nonformal>; **suspend,** intermit, **break, break off,** take a break <nonformal>, cut off, break *or* snap the thread

**interruption** NOUNS **intrusion,** obtrusion; **interference,** intervention, interventionism, injection, interjection; **suspension,** interval, pause, interim, lull, cessation, letup <nonformal>, **intermission;** time-out, break in the action, breathing spell, cooling-off period; **postponement**

**intersect** VERBS **cross, crisscross,** cruciate; intercross, decussate; **cut across,** crosscut; **traverse,** transverse, lie across

**intersecting** ADJS **cross,** crossing,

crossed; **crisscross,** crisscrossed; **intersected,** intersectional; **meeting,** converging, convergent, uniting, merging; concurrent, confluent, mutually approaching, approaching

**intersperse** VERBS **interfuse,** interlard, interpenetrate; intersow, intersprinkle

**intertwine** VERBS **interweave, interlace,** interknit, interthread, intertissue, intertie, intertwist; **mix,** admix, commix, immix, **intermix, mingle,** bemingle, commingle, immingle, **intermingle,** interlard

**intertwined** ADJS **webbed,** webby, weblike, woven, interwoven, interlaced, interknit, intertissued, intertied, intertwisted

**interval** NOUNS **gap, space**, intervening *or* intermediate space, **interspace,** distance *or* space between, interstice; **clearance,** margin, leeway, **room;** discontinuity, jump, leap, interruption; hiatus, caesura, lacuna; lapse of time, time frame, space, span, timespan, stretch

**intervene** VERBS **intrude,** obtrude, **interlope;** come between, **interpose**, insert oneself, **interfere,** insinuate, impose; step in, step into the breach, declare oneself a party, involve oneself, put oneself between disputants, use one's good offices, act between; butt in *and* put one's nose in <both nonformal>

**intervening** ADJS intervenient, **interjacent,** intercurrent; **intermediate,** intermediary, medial, mean, medium, mesne, median, **middle**

**intervention** NOUNS intervenience, intercurrence, slipping-in, sandwiching; **intrusion,** interposition, **interposing,** interposal, interlocation, intermediacy, interjacence; putting oneself between, stepping in, declaring oneself in, involvement, interagency; interventionism

**interview** NOUNS 1 press conference, press opportunity, photo opportunity, photo op <nonformal>; **audition,** hearing, tryout, call <all nonformal>, **audience**
VERBS 2 **question, query; make inquiry,** take up *or* institute *or* pursue *or* follow up *or* conduct *or* carry on an inquiry, ask after, inquire after, ask about, ask questions, put queries; inquire of, ask a question, put a question to, pose *or* set *or* propose *or* propound a question

**interviewer** NOUNS **inquirer,** asker, prober, querier, querist, **questioner,** questionist, interrogator; talk-show host *or* hostess

**interweave** VERBS **mix,** admix, commix, immix, **intermix, mingle,** bemingle, commingle, immingle, **intermingle,** interlace, intertwine, interlard

**interwoven** ADJS **webbed,** webby, weblike, woven, interlaced, intertwined

**intimacy** NOUNS **familiarity,** intimate acquaintance, closeness, nearness, inseparableness, inseparability; affinity, special affinity, mutual affinity; **sex, sexual intercourse,** sexual relations, relations

**intimate** NOUNS 1 **friend, acquaintance,** close acquaintance; confidant, confidante; familiar, **close friend,** intimate *or* familiar friend; **bosom friend,** friend of one's bosom, inseparable friend, **best friend**
ADJS 2 **familiar, close,** near, inseparable, personal, on familiar *or* intimate terms; just between the two, one-on-one, man-to-man, woman-to-woman; hand-in-hand, hand and glove *or* hand in glove; **thick, thick as thieves** <nonformal>

**intimate** VERBS **hint,** suggest, insinuate, imply, indicate, adumbrate, lead *or* leave one to gather, justify one in supposing, give *or* drop *or* throw out a hint, give an inkling of, **hint at**

**intimidate** VERBS **cow, browbeat, bulldoze** <nonformal>, bludgeon, dragoon; **bully, hector, harass,** huff; **coerce,** use violence, ride roughshod, intimidate, bully, blackjack; hold a pistol to one's head, twist one's arm *and* arm-twist <both nonformal>; **terrorize,** put in bodily fear, use terror *or* terrorist tactics, pursue a policy of *Schrecklichkeit,* systematically terrorize; threaten; **demoralize**

**intimidated** ADJS **terrified,** frightened out of one's wits *or* mind, **scared to death,** scared stiff *or* shitless *or* spitless <nonformal>; unnerved, unstrung, unmanned, undone, **cowed,** awed, daunted, dismayed, unmanned

**intimidating** ADJS **threatening, menacing,** threatful, minatory, minacious; fear-inspiring, bludgeoning, muscle-flexing, saber-rattling, bulldozing, browbeating, bullying, hectoring, blustering, terrorizing, terroristic

**intolerable** ADJS **insufferable,** insupportable, unendurable, unbearable, past bearing, not to be borne *or* endured, for the birds <nonformal>, **too much** *or* a bit much <nonformal>, more than flesh and blood can bear, enough to drive one mad, enough to provoke a saint, enough to make a preacher swear <nonformal>, enough to try the patience of Job

**intolerant** ADJS bigoted, overzealous, fanatic, fanatical; dogmatic, opinionated; **unindulgent,** uncondoning, unforbearing

**intonation** NOUNS **inflection, modulation;** intonation pattern *or* contour, intonation *or* inflection of voice, speech tune *or* melody

**intoxicate** VERBS 1 **inebriate, addle, befuddle,** bemuse, besot, go to one's head, make one see double, make one tiddly; **fascinate,** titillate, take one's breath away

2 <nonformal> **plaster,** pickle, swack, crock, stew, souse, stone, polluute, tipsify, booze up, boozify, fuddle, overtake

**intoxicated** ADJS **inebriated,** inebriate, inebrious, **drunk, drunken,** *shikker* <Yiddish>, **tipsy,** in liquor, **in one's cups, under the influence,** the worse for liquor; **tiddly, giddy, dizzy,** muddled, addled, flustered, bemused, reeling, seeing double; **besotted,** sotted, sodden, drenched, far-gone; drunk as a lord, drunk as a fiddler *or* piper, drunk as an owl; crapulent, crapulous

2 <nonformal> **high,** bent, blasted, blind, bombed out, bonged out, buzzed, coked, coked out, flying, fried, geared, geared up, geezed, gonged, gorked, hopped-up, in a zone, junked, luded out, maxed, noddy, ripped, smashed, snowed, spaced, space out, spacey, stoned, strung out, switched on, tanked, totaled, tranqued, tripping, trippy, wired, zoned, zoned out, zonked, zonked out

**intoxicating** ADJS intoxicative, **inebriating,** inebriative, inebriant; **exhilarating,** heady, maddening, ravishing

**intractable** ADJS **inflexible,** unflexible, **unpliable, unpliant, unmalleable,** untractable, intractile, **unbending,** unlimber, **unyielding**, ungiving, **stubborn, unalterable,** immutable; **immovable**; **adamant,** adamantine

**intransigent** ADJS **unyielding,** unbending, inflexible, hard, hard-line, inelastic, impliable, ungiving, **firm, stiff, rigid,** rigorous, stuffy; **uncompromising,** irreconcilable, hard-shell *and* hard-core <both nonformal>; implacable, inexorable, **relentless,** unrelenting

**intrepid** ADJS **courageous,** plucky, brave, bold, valiant, valorous, **gallant,** doughty, **hardy,** stalwart, stout, stouthearted, ironhearted, lionhearted, greathearted, bold-spirited, bold as a lion

**intricacy** NOUNS **complexity, complication, involvement,** complexness, involution, convolution, tortuousness, Byzantinism, *chinoiserie* <Fr>, tanglement, **entanglement,** perplexity, intricateness, ramification, crabbedness, technicality, subtlety

**intricate** ADJS **complex, complicated,** many-faceted, multifarious, ramified, perplexed, **confused,** confounded, **involved,** elaborate, involuted, convoluted, multilayered, multilevel; **tangled,** entangled, tangly, embrangled, **snarled,** knotted, matted, twisted, raveled; mazy, daedal, **labyrinthine,** labyrinthian

**intrigue** NOUNS 1 web of intrigue, **plot, scheme,** deep-laid plot *or* scheme, underplot, game *or* little game <both nonformal>, trick, stratagem, finesse; **conspiracy,** confederacy, covin, cabal; finagling <nonformal>, **machination,** manipulation, **maneuvering,** engineering, rigging; frame-up <nonformal>; wire-pulling <nonformal>
VERBS 2 **fascinate, captivate, charm,** becharm, spell, spellbind, cast a spell, put under a spell, **beguile, enthrall,** infatuate, **enrapture, transport, enravish, entrance, enchant,** witch, **bewitch**
3 **plot, scheme,** be up to something; **conspire, connive,** collude; **maneuver,** machinate, finesse, operate <nonformal>, engineer, rig, wangle <nonformal>, angle, finagle <nonformal>; frame *or* frame up <both nonformal>

**intriguing** ADJS **charming,** attractive, endearing, engaging, appealing, prepossessing, heartwarming, sexy <nonformal>, **enchanting,** bewitching, witching, entrancing, enthralling, fascinating; **captivating,** irresistible, ravishing; **scheming,** calculating, designing, contriving, plotting; manipulatory, **manip-**

ulative; **conniving,** conspiring, collusive

**intrinsic** ADJS internal, **inner,** inward; **inherent,** resident, implicit, immanent, indwelling; **ingrained,** in the very grain; infixed, implanted, inwrought, deep-seated

**introduce** VERBS **insert,** insinuate, inject, infuse, perfuse, inoculate, intromit; **bring up, broach,** open up, launch, start, kick off <nonformal>; **present,** acquaint, make acquainted, give an introduction, give a knockdown <nonformal>, do the honors <nonformal>; **herald,** count down, run up, lead in, forerun, usher in; **pioneer**

**introductory** ADJS **beginning, initial,** initiatory *or* initiative; **incipient,** inceptive, inchoative, inchoate; inaugural *or* inauguratory; **elementary,** elemental, **fundamental,** foundational; **rudimentary,** rudimental

**introspective** ADJS absorbed *or* engrossed in thought, **absorbed, engrossed,** rapt, wrapped in thought, **lost in thought,** abstracted, immersed in thought, buried in thought, engaged in thought, occupied, **preoccupied**

**introverted** ADJS **reticent, reserved,** restrained, nonassertive, low-key, low-keyed, constrained; repressed, subdued; backward, **retiring,** shrinking; **undemonstrative,** unexpansive, unaffable, uncongenial, ungenial; modest, verecund, verecundious, *pudique* <Fr>, bashful

**intrude** VERBS obtrude, **interlope;** come between, **interpose,** insert oneself, **intervene, interfere,** insinuate, impose; **encroach, infringe,** impinge, **trespass,** trespass on *or* upon, invade, infiltrate; **break in upon,** break in, **barge in**

**intruder** NOUNS **interloper, trespasser;** crasher *and* gate-crasher <both nonformal>, unwelcome *or* uninvited guest; invader, encroacher, infiltrator

**intrusion** NOUNS obtrusion, **interloping;** interposition, interposal, imposition, insinuation, **interference,** intervention, interventionism, interruption, injection, interjection; **encroachment,** trespass, trespassing, unlawful entry; impingement, **infringement,** invasion, incursion, inroad, influx, irruption, infiltration

**intrusive** ADJS obtrusive, **interfering,** intervenient, invasive, interruptive

**intuition** NOUNS **intuitiveness, sixth sense;** intuitive reason *or* knowledge, direct perception *or* apprehension, immediate apprehension *or* perception, unmediated perception *or* apprehension, subconscious perception, unconscious *or* subconscious knowledge, immediate cognition, knowledge without thought *or* reason, flash of insight; intuitive understanding

**intuitive** ADJS intuitional, sensing, feeling; second-sighted, precognitive, clairvoyant; impressionistic, general, generalized, abstract

**inundate** VERBS **overflow,** engulf, swamp, sweep, whelm, overwhelm, **flood,** deluge, submerge; **oversupply, overprovide,** overlavish, overfurnish, overequip; flood the market, oversell

**inundated** ADJS **flooded,** deluged, engulfed, swamped, swept, whelmed, drowned, overwhelmed, afloat, awash; **overrun, overspread,** buried

**inured** ADJS **callous, hardened,** case-hardened, coarsened, brutalized, indurated, stony, stony-hearted, marble-hearted, flinthearted, flinty, steely, impervious, armored *or* steeled against, proof against, as hard as nails

**invade** VERBS **intrude,** obtrude, interlope; **encroach, infringe,** impinge, **trespass,** trespass on *or* upon, infiltrate; **break in upon,** break in, burst in, charge in; make an inroad, make an irruption into; storm, take by storm; **infest, beset,** swarm, ravage, plague

**invader** NOUNS **intruder,** interloper, trespasser; crasher *and* gate-crasher <both nonformal>, unwelcome *or* uninvited guest; encroacher, infiltrator; raider

**invalid** NOUNS **sick person,** ill person, sufferer; valetudinarian, **shut-in; patient,** case; **the sick, the infirm**

**invalid** ADJS **illogical,** unreasonable, irrational, reasonless, contrary to reason, **senseless,** without reason, **without rhyme or reason; unscientific,** nonscientific, unphilosophical; **inauthentic,** unauthentic, faulty, flawed, paralogical, fallacious; **repealed, revoked, rescinded,** struck down, set aside; void, **null and void**

**invalidate** VERBS **disprove,** disconfirm, discredit, prove the contrary, belie, give the lie to; **negate,** explode, blow up, blow sky-high, **puncture,** deflate, **shoot** *or* **poke full of holes,** cut to pieces, cut the ground from under; **knock the bottom out of** <nonformal>, knock the props *or* chocks out from under, take the ground from under, cut the ground from under one's feet, not leave a leg to stand on

**invaluable** ADJS **precious, priceless,** inestimable, without *or* **beyond price,** not to be had for love or money, not for all the tea in China

**invariable** ADJS **unchangeable, constant,** undeviating, undeflectable; **irreversible,** nonreversible, reverseless

**invasion** NOUNS **raid, incursion,** inroad, irruption; **usurpation, arrogation,** seizure, unlawful seizure, **appropriation,** assumption, adoption, infringement, encroachment, trespass, trespassing; **infestation,** infestment; swarming, swarm, teeming, ravage, plague

**invasive** ADJS **intrusive,** obtrusive, **interfering,** intervenient, interruptive; **invading,** invasionary, incursive, incursionary, irruptive

**invective** NOUNS **vilification, abuse,** revilement, **vituperation,** opprobrium, obloquy, contumely, calumny, scurrility, blackguardism; **disparagement**

**invent** VERBS **innovate,** make from scratch *or* from the ground up, coin, new-mint, mint, inaugurate, neologize, neoterize; **originate,** conceive, discover, make up, devise, contrive, concoct, fabricate, frame, hatch, hatch *or* cook up, strike out; think up, think out, dream up, **design,** plan, set one's wits to work; **generate, develop**

**inventive** ADJS **creative,** originative, causative, productive, **constructive,** formative, fabricative, demiurgic; generative; **original,** esemplastic, shaping, **ingenious; productive, fertile,** fecund, prolific, seminal, germinal, teeming, pregnant; **inspired,** visioned

**inventor** NOUNS discoverer, deviser; developer

**inventory** NOUNS 1 **list, enumeration, itemization,** listing, shopping list *and* laundry list *and* want list *and* wish list *and* hit list *and* shit list *and* drop-dead list <all nonformal>, items, **schedule, register,** registry; repertory, tally; summation, **reckoning, count,** bean-counting <nonformal>, census, head count, nose count, body count

VERBS 2 **list, enumerate, itemize,** tabulate, catalog, tally; **register,** post, enter, enroll, book; score, keep score; **schedule,** program; take stock

**inverse** NOUNS 1 **reverse, converse, opposite,** other side of the coin *or* picture, the flip side *and* B side <both nonformal>

ADJS 2 contrapositive, **opposite,** opposing, **opposed,** on opposite sides; **reverse,** obverse, converse; **antipodal**

**inversion** NOUNS turning over *or* around *or* upside down, the other way round; **reversing, reversal,** turning front to back *or* side to side; **reversion,** turning back *or* backwards, retroversion, retroflexion, revulsion

**invest** VERBS place, put, sink; **risk, venture;** make an investment, lay out money, place out *or* put out at interest; reinvest, roll over, plow back into <nonformal>; **invest in, put money in,** sink money in, pour money into, tie up one's money in; buy in *or* into, buy a piece *or* share of; financier; plunge <nonformal>, speculate

**investigation** NOUNS **research,** legwork <nonformal>, inquiry into; data-gathering, gathering *or* amassing evidence; perscrutation, **probe,** searching investigation, close inquiry, exhaustive study; police inquiry *or* investigation, criminal investigation, detective work, detection, sleuthing

**investigator** NOUNS **detective,** operative, sleuth, Sherlock Holmes <A Conan Doyle>; police detective, **plainclothesman;** private detective *or* dick, private investigator *or* PI, hotel detective, house detective, house dick <nonformal>, store detective

**investiture** NOUNS **installation,** installment, **instatement,** induction, placement, **inauguration,** taking office; **accession,** accedence; coronation, enthronement; calling, election, nomination, appointment, preferment, induction, institution, endowment, enfranchisement

**investment** NOUNS **endowment,** investment, **settlement,** foundation; **venture,** risk, plunge <nonformal>, speculation

**investor** NOUNS **financier,** moneyman, **capitalist,** finance capitalist; Wall Streeter

**invidious** ADJS **envious,** envying, green with envy; **jealous; covetous,** desirous of; resentful; **grudging, begrudging;** mean, mean-spirited, ungenerous

**invigorate** VERBS **strengthen, fortify,** beef up <nonformal>, brace, buttress, prop, shore up, support, undergird, brace up; gird, gird up one's loins; steel, harden, anneal, stiffen, **toughen,** temper, nerve; confirm, sustain; **restrengthen,** reinforce; **reinvigorate,** refresh, revive, recruit one's strength; **energize,** dynamize; **animate, enliven, liven, liven up,** vitalize, quicken, goose *or* jazz up <nonformal>

**invigorating** ADJS **refreshing,** refreshful, **fresh,** brisk, crisp, crispy, zesty, zestful, **bracing, tonic,** cordial; analeptic; **exhilarating,** stimulating, stimulative, stimulatory, rousing, energizing; regaling, cheering

**invincible** ADJS **indestructible,** undestroyable, **imperishable,** nonperishable, incorruptible; **invulnerable,** inexpugnable, impregnable, indivisible; **ineradicable,** indelible, ineffaceable, inerasable; **inextinguishable**

**invisible** ADJS **imperceptible,** unperceivable, **indiscernible,** undiscernible, undetectable, **unseeable,** viewless, unbeholdable, unapparent, insensible; **out of sight,** *à perte de vue* <Fr>; **secret; unseen,** sightless, unbeheld, unviewed, unwitnessed, unobserved, unnoticed, unperceived; disguised, camouflaged, hidden, **concealed**

**invitation** NOUNS **invite** *and* **bid** <both nonformal>, engraved invitation, bidding, biddance, **call,** calling, **summons**

**invite** VERBS 1 **ask,** call, summon, call in, bid come, extend *or* issue an invitation, request the presence of, request the pleasure of one's company, send an engraved invitation
2 **bring on, bring down,** bring upon *or* down upon, bring upon *or* down upon oneself

**inviting** ADJS **interesting,** stimulating, provocative, provoking, thought-provoking, thought-challenging, thought-inspiring; **titillating,** tickling, **tantalizing,** exciting; **piquant,** lively, racy, juicy, succulent, spicy, rich; readable

**invocation** NOUNS **prayer, supplication,** imploration, impetration, entreaty, beseechment, appeal, petition, suit, aid prayer, bid *or* bidding prayer, orison, obsecration, obtestation, rogation, **devotions; benediction, blessing,** benison, benedicite

**invoice** NOUNS 1 **bill,** statement, account; **bill of lading,** manifest, waybill
VERBS 2 **bill,** send a statement; demand payment, **dun**

**invoke** VERBS **summon, call,** demand, preconize; **conjure, conjure up,** evoke, raise, summon, call up; **call up spirits,** conjure *or* conjure up spirits, summon spirits, raise ghosts, evoke from the dead; **pray, supplicate,** petition, make supplication, *daven* <Yiddish>

**involuntary** ADJS **instinctive, automatic, mechanical,** reflex, reflexive, knee-jerk <nonformal>, conditioned; **unconscious,** unthinking, blind; **unwitting,** unintentional, independent of one's will, unwilling, unwilled, against one's will; **compulsive;** forced; **impulsive**

**involve** VERBS **implicate,** tangle, **entangle,** embarrass, enmesh, engage, **draw in,** drag *or* hook *or* suck into, catch up in, **make a party to;** interest, concern; **absorb**

**involved** ADJS **implicated;** interested, concerned, a party to; **included**

**invulnerable** ADJS **impregnable,** impenetrable, inviolable, inexpugnable; **unassailable,** unattackable, insuperable, unsurmountable; **invincible,** indomitable, **unconquerable,** unsubduable, unyielding, incontestable, unbeatable, more than a match for

**inward** ADJS 1 **interior,** internal, inner, inside; **innermost,** inmost, **intimate,** private; visceral, gut <nonformal>; **intrinsic**
ADVS 2 **inwards, inwardly,** withinward, withinwards; inland, inshore

**iota** NOUNS **little, bit,** little *or* wee *or* tiny bit <nonformal>, bite, **particle,** fragment, spot, **speck,** flyspeck, fleck, point, dot, jot, tittle, **dab** <nonformal>, mote, **mite** <nonformal>; whit, ace, **hair,** scruple, groat, farthing, pittance, dole, trifling amount, **smidgen** *and* skosh *and* smitch <all nonformal>, pinch

**irate** ADJS **angry,** angered, incensed, indignant, ireful; **livid,** livid with rage, beside oneself, **wroth, wrathful,** wrathy, **cross,** wrought-up, worked up, riled up <nonformal>

**ire** NOUNS **anger,** wrath, *saeva indignatio* <L>; angriness, irateness, wrathfulness, soreness <nonformal>

*a transient madness*
**Horace**

**iridescent** ADJS **rainbowy,** rainbowlike; **opalescent,** opaline, opaloid; nacreous, nacry, *nacré* <Fr>, nacred, **pearly,** pearlish, mother-of-pearl; iridal, iridial, iridine, iridian; irised, irisated

**irk** VERBS **vex, annoy, aggravate,** exasperate, provoke; **trouble, worry,** give one gray hair, plague, harass, bother, hassle

**irksome** ADJS **troublesome,** besetting; **bothersome,** vexatious, painful, plaguey <nonformal>, annoying; **burdensome,** oppressive, onerous, heavy *and* hefty <both nonformal>, crushing, backbreaking; **trying,** grueling

**iron** VERBS 1 **press,** hot-press, **mangle,** calender; roll
ADJS 2 **firm,** rigid, rigorous, rigorist, rigoristic, stiff, **hard,** steel, steely, hardshell, obdurate, **inflexible,** ironhanded, inexorable, dour, **unyielding,** unbending, impliable, **relentless,** unrelenting, procrustean

**ironclad** ADJS **uncompromising;** stubborn, obstinate; purist, puristic; puritan, puritanic, puritanical, fundamentalist, orthodox; ironbound, rockbound, musclebound; straitlaced, hidebound

**ironic** ADJS **satiric,** satirical; **sarcastic,** ironical, sardonic, cynical, Rabelaisian, dry; caustic; self-contradictory, **paradoxical,** antinomic, oxymoronic, ambivalent

**irony** NOUNS **sarcasm,** cynicism, satire, satiric wit *or* humor, invective, innuendo; causticity; self-contradiction, **paradox,** antinomy, oxymoron, ambivalence, enantiosis, equivocation

**irrational** ADJS 1 **unreasonable,** unsound, unsensible, senseless, insensate, reasonless, reckless, inadvisable; inexpedient; **ill-advised, ill-considered,** ill-gauged, ill-judged, ill-imagined, ill-contrived, ill-devised, on the wrong track, unconsidered
2 **unsound,** of unsound mind, **demented, deranged,** deluded, disoriented, unhinged, **unbalanced,** unsettled, distraught, wandering, mazed, crackbrained, brainsick, sick *or* soft in the head, not right, not in one's right mind, **touched,** touched in the head, **out of one's mind,** out of one's senses *or* wits, bereft of reason, reasonless, deprived of reason, senseless, witless

**irreconcilable** ADJS **inconsistent,** incongruous, inconsonant, inconsequent, incoherent, **incompatible;** disproportionate, out of proportion, self-contradictory, paradoxical, oxymoronic, **absurd**

**irreducible** ADJS **requisite,** needful, required, needed, necessary, wanted, called for, indicated; **essential,** vital, indispensable, unforgoable, irreplaceable; irreductible; prerequisite

**irrefutable** ADJS **conclusive,** determinative, **decisive,** final, incontrovertible, irresistible, indisputable, sure, certain, absolute; documented, documentary; authentic, reliable, indubitable, unarguable, incontestable, unrefutable, unconfutable, irrefragable, unanswerable, inappealable, unimpeachable

**irregular** NOUNS 1 casual; **guerrilla,** partisan, franctireur; **bushfighter,** bushwhacker <nonformal>; underground, resistance, maquis; *maquisard* <Fr>, underground *or* resistance fighter
ADJS 2 unregular, unsystematic, unmethodical *or* immethodical; **inconstant, unsteady, uneven, unrhythmical,** unmetrical, rough, unequal, uncertain, unsettled; **variable,** deviative, heteroclite; **capricious, erratic,** off-again-on-again, eccentric; **sporadic,** patchy, spotty, scrappy, snatchy, catchy, choppy, broken, disconnected, discontinuous; **intermittent,** intermitting, **desultory,** fluctuating, wavering

**irregularity** NOUNS **asymmetry,** unsymmetry, disproportion, lopsidedness, imbalance, quirk; **nonuniformity,** unevenness, raggedness, crazy-quilt, choppiness, jerkiness, **disorder; inconstancy, inconsistency,** variability, changeability, changeableness, mutability, capriciousness, mercuriality, wavering, **instability, unsteadiness**

**irrelevant** ADJS **impertinent, inapposite,** ungermane, uncogent, inconsequent, inapplicable, immaterial, inappropriate, inadmissible; wide of *or* away from the point, *nihil ad rem* <L>, **beside the point,** beside the mark, wide of the mark, **beside the question,** off the subject, not to the purpose, **nothing to do with the case,** not at issue, out-of-the-way; incidental, parenthetical

**irreligious** ADJS **ungodly,** godless, **unrighteous, unholy,** unsaintly, unangelic, unangelical; impious; **wicked, sinful**

**irreplaceable** ADJS **requisite,** needful,

required, needed, necessary, wanted, called for, indicated; **essential, vital, indispensable,** unforgoable, prerequisite

**irrepressible** ADJS **unrestrained,** unconstrained, unforced, uncompelled, uncoerced; unmeasured, **uninhibited,** unsuppressed, unrepressed, unreserved, go-go <nonformal>, exuberant; **unreined,** reinless; lax

**irreproachable** ADJS **inculpable,** unblamable, unblameworthy, irreprovable, **irreprehensible,** uncensurable, unimpeachable, unindictable, unarraignable, unobjectionable, unexceptionable, above suspicion; beyond all praise, unfaultable, *sans peur et sans reproche* <Fr>

**irresistible** ADJS **overpowering,** overcoming, overwhelming, overmastering, overmatching, avalanchine; **enchanting,** bewitching, entrancing, enthralling, intriguing, fascinating

**irresolute** ADJS irresolved, **unresolved; undecided, indecisive, undetermined,** unsettled, infirm of purpose; at loose ends, at a loose end; **of two minds,** in conflict, double-minded, ambivalent, ambitendent; capricious, mercurial, fickle

**irrespective of** ADVS in spite of, spite of <nonformal>, **despite,** in despite of, with, even with; **regardless of,** regardless, irrespective of, without respect *or* regard to; cost what it may, regardless of cost, at any cost, at all costs, whatever the cost

**irresponsible** ADJS **untrustworthy,** unfaithworthy, untrusty, trustless, **unreliable, undependable,** fly-by-night, unsure, not to be trusted, not to be depended *or* relied upon; **unrestrained, undisciplined,** uncontrolled, fast and loose

**irretrievable** ADJS **irrecoverable, irreclaimable,** irredeemable, unsalvageable, unsalvable; irrevocable, **irreversible; past hope, beyond recall,** past praying for; unrestorable

**irreverent** ADJS **disrespectful,** aweless; **discourteous; insolent, impudent;** ridiculing, **derisive; disparaging; impious,** undutiful; **profane,** profanatory; sacrilegious, blasphemous

**irreversible** ADJS **confirmed,** incorrigible; deep-rooted, deep-set, deep-settled, **deep-seated,** deep-fixed, deep-dyed; **infixed, ingrained,** fast, dyed-in-the-wool; **irrevocable,** indefeasible, nonreversible, reverseless

**irrevocable** ADJS **decisive,** final, peremptory, absolute, eternal, written, hard-and-fast, carved in stone, set in concrete <nonformal>, ultimate, conclusive, binding, without appeal

**irrigate** VERBS **water; wash,** bathe, **rinse,** rinse out, flush, flush out, sluice, sluice out

**irritable** ADJS **irascible,** excitable, flappable <nonformal>; **cross, cranky, testy;** cankered, crabbed, spiteful, spleeny, splenetic, churlish, bearish, snappish, waspish; **gruff,** grumbly, grumbling, growling; **disagreeable; perverse,** fractious, cross-grained

**irritant** NOUNS **irritation,** exacerbation, salt in the wound, twisting the knife in the wound, embitterment, **provocation;** pea in the shoe

**irritate** VERBS **aggravate,** exacerbate, worsen, rub salt in the wound, twist the knife in the wound, step on one's corns, barb the dart; touch a soft spot *or* tender spot, touch a raw nerve, touch where it hurts; provoke, **gall, chafe, fret,** grate, grit *and* gravel <both nonformal>, rasp; **get on one's nerves,** grate on, set on edge; **set one's teeth on edge,** go against the grain; **rub one** *or* **one's fur the wrong way**

**irritated** ADJS **annoyed,** bugged <nonformal>; galled, chafed; **bothered,** troubled, disturbed, ruffled, roiled, riled; **irked,** vexed, piqued, nettled, provoked, peeved *and* miffed <both nonformal>, **griped,** aggravated, exasperated; burnt-up *and* browned-off <both nonformal>, resentful, angry

**irritating** ADJS irritative, irritant; **chafing, galling,** fretting, rasping, boring, grating, grinding, stinging, scratchy; **annoying,** provoking, aggravating <nonformal>, **exasperating; vexatious,** vexing, irking, **irksome,** tiresome, wearisome

**irritation** NOUNS **aggravation,** exacerbation, worsening, salt in the wound, twisting the knife in the wound, embitterment, **provocation;** fret, gall, chafe; irritant; pea in the shoe

**Islam** NOUNS **Muslimism,** Islamism, Moslemism, Muhammadanism, Mohammedanism; Sufism, Wahabiism, Sunnism, Shiism; Black Muslimism; Muslim fundamentalism, militant Muslimism

**Islamic** ADJS **Muslim,** Moslem, Islamitic, Islamistic, Muhammadan, Mohammedan; Shiite, Sunni, Sunnite

**island** NOUNS 1 **isle; islet,** holm; continental island; oceanic island; **key,** cay; sandbank, sandbar, bar; **reef,** coral reef, coral head; coral island, atoll; archipelago, island group *or* chain
ADJS 2 **insular,** insulated, isolated; islandy *or* islandish, islandlike; islanded, isleted, island-dotted; seagirt; archipelagic *or* archipelagian

**isolate** VERBS **quarantine,** insulate, segregate, separate, seclude; **set apart,** keep apart; **put beyond the pale,** ghettoize; **cordon, cordon off,** seal off, rope off; wall off, set up barriers, put behind barriers; **reduce,** reduce to elements, resolve

**isolated** ADJS cloistered, **sequestered,** sequestrated, secluded, sheltered; **insular,** insulated; shut off, **separate,** separated, **apart,** detached, removed; **remote, out-of-the-way,** up-country, in a backwater, out-of-the-world, out-back *and* back of beyond <both Austral>; **unfrequented,** unvisited, off the beaten track; untraveled

**isolation** NOUNS **privacy,** retirement, sequestration, seclusion; **quarantine,** cordoning off, segregation, separation

**issue** NOUNS 1 **posterity, progeny, offspring,** fruit, seed, brood, breed, family
2 **cause, principle,** interest, burning issue, commitment, faith, great cause, lifework; **problem, topic,** case *or* point in question, bone of contention, controversial point, question before the house, debating point, question *or* point at issue, **moot point** *or* case, question mark, *quodlibet* <L>; vexed *or* knotty question, burning question
VERBS 3 **emerge, come out,** issue forth, come into view, extrude, **come forth; surface,** rise to the surface; come to the fore; emanate, effuse, arise, come; debouch, disembogue; **burst forth,** break forth, erupt; **come out in the open;** protrude
4 **bring out,** put out, get out, **launch** get off, emit, put *or* give *or* send forth, offer to the public, pass out

**itch** NOUNS 1 **sexual desire,** sensuous *or* carnal desire, bodily appetite, **biological urge,** venereal appetite *or* desire, sexual longing, **lust,** desire, lusts *or* desires of the flesh, lech <nonformal>; **craving,** coveting
2 lust; hunger, thirst, appetite
VERBS 3 **tingle,** thrill; scratch; **prickle,** prick, sting

**item** NOUNS **commodity, ware,** vendible, **product, article,** article of commerce *or* merchandise; **entry,** line item, minute, note, notation; **feature,** aspect, specialty, circumstance, detail

**itemize** VERBS **specify,** circumstantiate, particularize, **spell out, detail,** go *or* enter into detail, descend to particulars, give full particulars, atomize, anatomize; **descend to particulars,** get precise, get down to brass tacks *or* to cases <nonformal>, get down to the nitty-gritty <nonformal>, come to the point, lay it on the line <nonformal>

**itinerary** NOUNS **route, path, way, course,** track, run, line, road; road map, roadbook

**ivories** NOUNS 1 **teeth,** dentition
2 **piano keys,** eighty-eight <nonformal>
3 **dice; bones,** rolling bones, cubes, devil's bones *or* teeth, galloping dominoes, golf balls, marbles, Memphis dominoes, Mississippi marbles, Missouri marbles <all nonformal>

# J

**jab** NOUNS 1 **thrust, pass,** lunge, swing, cut, stab; **prod,** poke, **punch,** dig, nudge
VERBS 2 **thrust, push,** shove, boost <nonformal>; **prod,** goad, poke, punch, dig, nudge, thwack, **smack,** clap, crack, swipe, **whack**

**jabber** NOUNS 1 **chatter,** gibber, **babble,** babblement, prate, prating, prattle, **palaver,** chat, natter <Brit>, **gabble, gab** *and* jaw-jaw <both nonformal>, blab, **blabber, blather,** blether, clatter, clack, cackle, talkee-talkee; twaddle, twattle, **gibble-gabble,** bibble-babble, **chitter-chatter,** prittle-prattle, **tittle-tattle,** mere talk, idle talk *or* chatter
VERBS 2 **talk nonsense,** twaddle, piffle, blather, **blabber, babble,** gabble, gibble-gabble, jabber, gibber, prate, **prattle,** rattle; gas *and* bull *and* **bullshit** *and* throw the bull *and* shoot off one's mouth *and* shoot the bull <all nonformal>; **drivel,** vapor, run off at the mouth <nonformal>

**jaded** ADJS **worn-out, exhausted,** tired, fatigued, pooped <nonformal>, **spent,** effete, etiolated, played out, *ausgespielt* <Ger>, emptied, done *and* done up <both nonformal>; **run-down,** dragged-out <nonformal>, laid low, at a low ebb, in a bad way, far-gone, on one's last legs; **cloyed, fed up** *and* fed to the gills *or* fed to the teeth *and* stuffed to the gills <all nonformal>

**jag** NOUNS **binge, drunk,** bust, tear, **bender, toot, bat,** brannigan, guzzle, randan, rip

**jagged** ADJS **nonuniform,** ununiform, **uneven, irregular,** ragged, erose, choppy, jerky, rough, disorderly, unsystematic; scrappy, snatchy, spotty, patchy

**jail** NOUNS 1 **prison,** gaol <Brit>, jailhouse, lockup, toolbooth <Scots>, bridewell <Brit>; maximum- *or* minimum-security prison

2 <nonformal> **slammer, slam,** can, coop, cooler, hoosegow, stir, clink, pokey, brig, tank

VERBS 3 **imprison, incarcerate, intern,** immure; gaol <Brit>, jug <nonformal>, throw into jail, clap in jail *or* prison, send up the river <nonformal>; **lock up,** lock in, bolt in, put *or* keep under lock and key

**jailbreak** NOUNS **escape; getaway** *and* break *and* breakout <all nonformal>; prisonbreak

**jailer** NOUNS **gaoler** <Brit>, correctional *or* correction *or* corrections officer; **keeper, warder,** prison guard, **turnkey,** bull *and* screw <both nonformal>; **warden,** custodian, guardian; **guard**

**jalopy** NOUNS

<nonformal> banger, bus, buggy, wheels, tub, tuna wagon, heap, boat, short, crate, wreck, clunker, junker, junkheap, junkpile

**jam** NOUNS 1 comfit, confiture; **jelly,** preserve, conserve
2 **delay,** stoppage, logjam <nonformal>, obstruction, tie-up *and* bind <both nonformal>, **block,** blockage, **hang-up** <nonformal>;
3 **predicament,** fix *and* pickle *and* scrape *and* stew <all nonformal>; perturbation, **disturbance**
VERBS 4 **stop, stop up; block,** block up; **clog,** clog up, foul; **choke,** choke up *or* off; **fill,** fill up; **stuff,** pack; **congest,** stuff up; **plug,** plug up; **catch,** lodge, foul; **squeeze,** press, crowd, cram, ram down; pack *or* jam in

**jamboree** NOUNS **festival, festivity,** festive occasion, *fiesta* <Sp>, **fete,** gala, **gala affair, blowout** <nonformal>; **field day**

**jammed** ADJS **stuck, fast,** stuck fast, **fixed, transfixed, caught,** fastened, tied, chained, tethered, anchored, moored, held, inextricable; **impacted,** congested, packed, wedged; seized, seized up, frozen; aground, grounded, stranded, high and dry

**jangle** NOUNS 1 **clash, jar; noise,** mere noise, confusion *or* conflict *or* jarring *or* jostling of sounds; Babel
VERBS 2 **clash,** jar; **disagree, differ,** vary, not see eye-to-eye, be at cross-purposes, tangle assholes <nonformal>, **disaccord, conflict,** jostle, collide, square off, cross swords, break, break off

**janitor** NOUNS **cleaner,** cleaner-up, cleaner-off, cleaner-out; janitress, custodian; cleaning woman *or* lady *or* man

**jar** VERBS 1 **startle,** shock, electrify, jolt, shake, stun, stagger, **give one a turn** <nonformal>, take aback, take one's breath away; frighten
2 **differ,** differ in opinion, hold opposite views, disaccord, **be at variance,** not get along, pull different ways, be at cross-purposes, have no measures with, misunderstand one another; **conflict, clash,** collide, jostle, jangle

**jargon** NOUNS **lingo** <nonformal>, **slang,** cant, argot, patois, patter, vernacular; vocabulary, phraseology; **lingua franca, pidgin,** trade language

**jarring** ADJS **clashing, jangling,** jangly, confused, conflicting, jostling, warring, ajar; **harsh,** grating; **startling, shocking,** electrifying, staggering, stunning, jolting

**jaunt** NOUNS **walk,** ramble, amble, **hike, tramp,** traipse <nonformal>; slog, trudge, schlep <nonformal>; **stroll,** saunter; **promenade;** *passeggiata* <Ital>; airing; **constitutional** <nonformal>, stretch

**jaunty** ADJS **lighthearted,** light, lightsome; **buoyant,** corky <nonformal>, resilient; perky, **debonair, dapper,** dashing, **carefree,** free and easy, **gay,** rakish, **dashing; breezy,** airy

**jaw** NOUNS 1 **muzzle,** lips, embouchure; **jaws,** mandibles, chops, chaps, jowls
VERBS 2 **berate,** rate, betongue, clapper-claw <nonformal>, **tongue-lash, rail at,** rag, thunder *or* fulminate against, rave against, yell at, bark *or* yelp at

**jawbreaker** NOUNS long word, hard word, jawtwister *and* two-dollar *or* five-dollar word <all nonformal>, polysyllable; sesquipedalian, sesquipedalia <pl>

**jaws** NOUNS **clutches, claws, talons,** pounces, unguals; **pincers,** nippers, chelae; **tentacles;** mandibles, maxillae

**jazz** NOUNS 1 hot jazz, Dixieland, Basin Street; **swing,** jive <nonformal>; bebop, bop <nonformal>; mainstream jazz; avant-garde jazz, the new music <nonformal>; boogie *or* boogie-woogie; walking bass, stride *or* stride piano
ADJS 2 **syncopated; ragtime,** ragtimey <nonformal>; jazzy *and* jazzed *and* jazzed up <all nonformal>, hot, swingy <nonformal>

**jazz up** VERBS **stimulate,** whet, sharpen, pique, provoke, quicken, enliven, liven up, pick up, animate, **exhilarate,** invigorate, galvanize, fillip, give a fillip to; infuse life into, give new life to, revive, renew, resuscitate; key up, hop up *and* soup up <both nonformal>

**jazzy** ADJS **showy, flaunting, flashy,** snazzy, flashing, glittering, **glitzy** *and* gimmicky *and* splashy *and* splurgy <all nonformal>; exhibitionistic, showoffy <nonformal>, bravura; **syncopated; ragtime,** ragtimey <nonformal>; **jazz;** jazzed *and* jazzed up <both nonformal>, hot, swingy <nonformal>

**jealous** ADJS **jaundiced,** jaundice-eyed, yellow-eyed, green-eyed, yellow, green, green with jealousy; horn-mad; invidious, **envious; suspicious,** distrustful

**jealousy** NOUNS *jalousie* <Fr>, jealousness, heartburning, heartburn, **jaundice,** jaundiced eye, green in the eye <nonformal>, Othello's flaw, horn-madness

*green-eyed monster*
SHAKESPEARE

**jeer** VERBS **scoff,** gibe, barrack <Brit>, **mock,** revile, rail at, rally, chaff, twit, taunt, jape, flout, scout, have a fling at, cast in one's teeth

**jellied** ADJS **thickened,** inspissate *or* inspissated, incrassate; **congealed, coagulated, clotted,** grumous; **curdled,** curded, clabbered; jelled, gelatinized; coagulant, coagulating

**jeopardize** VERBS **endanger, imperil,** peril; **risk, hazard, gamble, gamble with;** jeopard, jeopardy, compromise, put in danger, **put in jeopardy,** put on the spot *and* lay on the line <both nonformal>; **expose,** lay open; incur danger, run into *or* encounter danger

**jeopardy** NOUNS **danger,** peril, endangerment, imperilment, hazard, risk, cause for alarm, **menace, threat; crisis, emergency,** hot spot, nasty *or* tricky spot, pass, pinch, strait, plight, predicament; dangerous ground, yawning *or* gaping chasm, quicksand, thin ice; hornet's nest; house of cards, hardball <nonformal>, no tea party, no picnic

**Jeremiah** NOUNS **warner,** cautioner, admonisher, monitor; prophet *or* messenger of doom, Cassandra

**jerk** NOUNS 1 **yank** <nonformal>, quick *or* sudden pull; **twitch,** tweak, pluck, hitch, wrench, snatch, start, bob; **flip,**

flick, flirt, flounce; jig, **jiggle;** jog, joggle
VERBS 2 **twitch,** vellicate; itch; **jig, jiggle,** jigger *or* jigget <nonformal>; **fidget,** have the fidgets

**jerky** ADJS herky-jerky <nonformal>, twitchy *or* twitchety, jerking, **twitching, fidgety, jumpy,** jiggety <nonformal>, vellicative; **spastic, spasmodic,** eclamptic, orgasmic, convulsive; fitful, saltatory

**jerry-built** ADJS **unsubstantial, flimsy,** sleazy, tacky <nonformal>, wispy, cobwebby, gossamery, papery, pasteboardy; gimcrack *and* gimcracky *and* cheap-jack *and* ticky-tacky <all nonformal>; jerry

**jest** NOUNS 1 **gibe, scoff, jeer,** fleer, flout, mock, barracking <Brit>, **taunt, twit,** quip, jape, put-on *and* leg-pull <both nonformal>, foolery
VERBS 2 **joke, wisecrack** *and* crack wise <both nonformal>, utter a mot, **quip,** jape, josh <nonformal>, make fun, **kid** *or* **kid around** <both nonformal>; **crack a joke,** get off a joke, tell a good story; **make fun of,** gibe at, fleer at, mock; **banter, twit, chaff,** rally, jape, **tease,** haze

**jester** NOUNS **buffoon,** *buffo* <Ital>, clown, fool, zany, merry-andrew, jack-pudding, pickle-herring, motley fool, motley, wearer of the cap and bells

**jet** NOUNS 1 **jet plane, turbojet,** ramjet, pulse-jet, blowtorch <nonformal>; single-jet, twin-jet, multi-jet; supersonic jet, supersonic transport *or* SST, Concorde
2 **spout, spurt,** spurtle, squirt, spit, spew, spray, spritz <nonformal>; rush, **gush,** flush
VERBS 3 **fly,** be airborne, wing, take wing, wing one's way, take *or* make a flight, take to the air, take the air, volitate, be wafted
4 **spout, spurt,** spurtle, **squirt,** spit, spew, spray, spritz <nonformal>, play, **gush,** well, surge; vomit, vomit out *or* forth

**jetsam** NOUNS **derelict,** castoff; flotsam, lagan, **flotsam and jetsam;** waifs and strays; abandonee, waif, throwaway, orphan, dogie <nonformal>; **castaway**

**jet set** NOUNS **society,** *société* <Fr>, fashionable society, **polite society, high society,** high life, *beau monde, haut monde* <both Fr>, good society; best people, people of fashion, right people; *monde* <Fr>, world of fashion, Vanity Fair; **smart set** <nonformal>; the Four Hundred, **upper crust** *and* upper cut <both nonformal>; **cream of society,** *crème de la crème* <Fr>, elite, carriage trade; café society, beautiful people, in-crowd, the glitterati <nonformal>

**jettison** VERBS **discard, reject, throw away, throw out,** chuck *or* chuck away *and* shit-can *and* eighty-six <all nonformal>, cast, cast off *or* away *or* aside; **get rid of,** get quit of, get shut *or* shet of <nonformal>, rid oneself of, shrug off, **dispose of,** slough, **dump, ditch** <nonformal>, **throw** *or* **heave** *or* **toss overboard,** deep-six <nonformal>, throw *or* cast to the dogs, cast to the winds

**jetty** NOUNS **barrier,** seawall, groin, mole, breakwater; bulwark, rampart, defense, buffer, bulkhead, parapet, breastwork, work, earthwork, mound; bank, embankment, levee, dike

**Jew** NOUNS **Hebrew,** Judaist, Israelite; Orthodox *or* Conservative *or* Reform Jew, Reconstructionist; Hasid; Rabbinist, Talmudist; Pharisee; Sadducee

**jewel** NOUNS 1 bijou, **gem,** stone, precious stone; rhinestone
2 **good thing,** a thing to be desired, **treasure,** boast, pride, **pride and joy;** prize, trophy, plum; winner *and* no slouch *and* nothing to sneeze at <all nonformal>; catch, find <nonformal>, *trouvaille* <Fr>; godsend, windfall

**jewelry** NOUNS bijouterie, ice <nonformal>; costume jewelry, glass, paste, junk jewelry <nonformal>

**Jewish** ADJS **Hebrew,** Judaic, Judaical, Israelite, Israelitic, Israelitish; Orthodox, Conservative, Reform, Reconstructionist; Hasidic

**Jezebel** NOUNS **strumpet,** trollop, wench, hussy, slut, jade, baggage, *cocotte* <Fr>, grisette; **tart** *and* **chippy** *and* **floozy** *and* broad <all nonformal>, bitch, drab, trull, quean, harridan, wanton, whore <nonformal>, bad woman, **loose woman**

**jibe** VERBS **agree,** accord, harmonize, concur, have no problem with, go along with <nonformal>, **cooperate, correspond, conform,** coincide, parallel, intersect, overlap, **match,** tally, hit, register, lock, interlock, check <nonformal>, square, dovetail; **be consistent,** cohere, stand *or* hold *or* hang together, fall in together, fit together, chime, chime with, chime in with

**jiffy** NOUNS **instant,** moment, second,

half a second, half a mo <Brit nonformal>, minute, **trice,** twinkle, **twinkling** *or* **twinkle of an eye,** twink, **wink,** bat of an eye <nonformal>, **flash,** crack, tick, stroke, coup, breath, twitch; two shakes of a lamb's tail *and* two shakes *and* half a shake *and* jiff *and* half a jiffy <all nonformal>

**jigger** NOUNS **drink,** dram, potation, potion, libation, **nip,** draft, drop, spot, finger or two, sip, sup, suck, drench, guzzle, gargle, peg, swig, swill, pull; **snort,** jolt, **shot,** snifter, quickie

**jiggle** NOUNS 1 **shake,** quake, quiver, quaver, falter, tremor, tremble, **shiver, shudder,** twitter, didder, dither; **wobble; bob,** bobble; **jerk, twitch,** tic, grimace, rictus; jig
VERBS 2 **twitch, jerk,** vellicate; itch; **jig,** jigger *or* jigget <nonformal>

**jilt** VERBS **abandon, desert, forsake;** turn one's back upon, turn one's tail upon, say goodbye to, walk or run out on <nonformal>, **leave flat** *and* leave high and dry *or* holding the bag *or* in the lurch <all nonformal>, leave one to one's fate, throw to the wolves <nonformal>; quit cold *and* leave flat <both nonformal>, toss aside; throw over <nonformal>; **junk,** deep-six <nonformal>, **discard**

**jilted** ADJS **unloved,** unbeloved, uncherished, loveless; **lovelorn,** forsaken, **rejected,** thrown over <nonformal>, spurned, crossed in love

**Jim Crow** NOUNS **segregation,** separation, separationism, division; racial segregation, apartheid, color bar, race hatred; **discrimination,** social discrimination, **social barrier**

**jimmy** NOUNS 1 **lever; pry,** prize <nonformal>; **bar,** pinch bar, **crowbar,** crow, pinchbar
VERBS 2 **pry,** prize, **lever,** wedge; pry *or* prize out; crowbar, pinchbar

**jingle** NOUNS 1 **ringing, tinkle,** tingle, dingle, ding, dingdong, ding-a-ling, ting-a-ling; **rhythm, cadence,** movement, lilt
VERBS 2 **ring, tinkle,** tingle, ding, dingdong, dong; clink, tink, ting, chink

**jingoistic** ADJS **chauvinistic,** chauvinist, jingoist, jingoish, jingo; **hard-line, hawkish** <nonformal>; patriotic; **nationalistic;** ultranationalist, ultranationalistic; overpatriotic, superpatriotic, flag-waving

**jinx** NOUNS 1 **bad influence,** malevolent influence, evil star, **ill wind;** evil genius, **hoodoo** <nonformal>, **Jonah; curse,** enchantment, whammy *and* double *or* triple whammy <all nonformal>, spell, hex, voodoo; **evil eye,** *malocchio* <Ital>
VERBS 2 bring bad luck; hoodoo *and* hex *and* Jonah *and* put the jinx on <all nonformal>; put the evil eye on, whammy <nonformal>

**jitters** NOUNS **agitation,** perturbation, trepidation, trepidity, fidgets *and* ants in the pants <both nonformal>, antsiness *and* jitteriness <both nonformal>, jumpiness, nervousness, yips <nonformal>, nervosity, twitter, upset

**jittery** ADJS **jumpy,** twittery, skittish, skittery, trigger-happy <nonformal>, gun-shy; **shaky,** shivery, quivery, in a quiver; tremulous, tremulant, trembly; jumpy as a cat on a hot tin roof; **fidgety,** fidgeting; shaking, trembling, quivering, shivering; shook up *and* all shook up <both nonformal>

**jive** NOUNS 1 **jazz; swing,** bebop, bop <nonformal>
VERBS 2 **syncopate,** play jazz, swing, rag <nonformal>
3 **kid,** jolly, josh, fool around, rub, put on, **razz, roast,** ride, needle <all nonformal>

**job** NOUNS 1 **position,** employment, gainful employment, situation, **office, post, place,** station, berth, billet, **appointment,** engagement, gig <nonformal>
VERBS 2 **sell, wholesale,** sell wholesale, be jobber *or* wholesaler for

**Job** NOUNS **stoic,** Spartan, man of iron; Griselda

**jock** NOUNS **athlete; real man, he-man,** *and* two-fisted man <both nonformal>, hunk *and* jockstrap <both nonformal>, man with hair on his chest; caveman *and* bucko <both nonformal>; athletic supporter, G-string <nonformal>

**jockey** NOUNS 1 **rider,** equestrian, horseman, horserider, horseback rider, horsebacker
VERBS 2 **maneuver,** manipulate, contrive, angle <nonformal>

**jocularity** NOUNS **facetiousness,** pleasantry, jocoseness, jocosity; **joking,** japery, joshing <nonformal>

**jog** NOUNS 1 **bump,** joggle, jolt; **jostle,** hustle
VERBS 2 **exercise,** run; **bump,** joggle, jolt, shake, rattle; **jostle,** hustle, hurtle

**jogger** NOUNS **reminder,** remembrancer;

**prompt,** prompter, tickler; prompting, cue, hint; *aide-mémoire* <Fr>, **memorandum**; **runner**

**john** NOUNS **latrine,** convenience, **toilet,** water closet *or* WC <nonformal>; johnny *and* **can** *and* crapper <all nonformal>; loo <Brit nonformal>; **lavatory,** washroom, public convenience

**John Doe** NOUNS 1 **alias, pseudonym,** anonym, **assumed name,** false *or* fictitious name, *nom de guerre* <Fr>; **pen name, nom de plume;** Jane Doe, Richard Roe
2 **common man, commoner,** little man, **little fellow, average man,** ordinary man, typical man, **man in the street,** one of the people, man of the people, Everyman; ordinary *or* average Joe *and* Joe Doakes *and* Joe Sixpack *and* Joe Blow <all nonformal>

**John Hancock** NOUNS **signature,** autograph, hand, mark, mark of signature, cross, christcross, X

**Johnny-come-lately** NOUNS **newcomer, new arrival,** *novus homo* <L>; *arriviste* <Fr>, new boy; **latecomer,** late arrival

***joie de vivre*** <Fr> NOUNS **animation, vivacity,** liveliness, **ardor,** glow, warmth, enthusiasm, lustiness, robustness, mettle, **zest,** zestfulness, **gusto, élan,** *brio* <Ital>, spiritedness, **briskness,** perkiness, pertness, **life, spirit,** life force, vital force *or* principle, *élan vital* <Fr>

**join** VERBS 1 **adjoin,** conjoin, **connect,** butt, **abut,** abut on *or* upon, be contiguous, be in contact; **neighbor,** border, **border on** *or* **upon,** verge on *or* upon; lie by, stand by
2 band, league, **associate, affiliate,** ally, **combine, unite,** fuse, merge, coalesce, amalgamate, federate, confederate, consolidate; hook up *and* tie up *and* tie in <all nonformal>; be in league, **go into partnership with,** go partners <nonformal>, go *or* be in cahoots with; **join together,** club together, league together, band together; **work together,** get together *and* team up *and* buddy up <all nonformal>, work as a team, act together, act in concert, **pull together; hold together, hang together,** keep together, **stand together,** stand shoulder to shoulder
3 **marry,** wed, nuptial, **unite, hitch** *and* **splice** <both nonformal>, couple, match, match up, make *or* arrange a match, join together, **unite in marriage,** join *or* unite in holy wedlock, tie the knot, tie the nuptial *or* wedding knot, make one
4 **enlist,** enroll, sign up *or* on <nonformal>

**joiner** NOUNS mixer *and* **good mixer** <both nonformal>, good *or* pleasant company, excellent companion, life of the party, bon vivant; clubman, clubwoman

**joint** NOUNS 1 **dive** <nonformal>, **den, lair,** den of thieves; hole *and* dump <both nonformal>; gyp *or* clip joint <nonformal>; **whorehouse,** cathouse <nonformal>, sporting house, brothel, bordello, stews, fleshpots
2 **marijuana cigarette;** roach, joy stick, kick stick, reefer, stick, twist <all nonformal>
3 **jail; slammer, slam, jug,** can, coop, cooler, hoosegow, stir, clink, pokey, big house, big school, big cage, big joint, brig, tank <all nonformal>
ADJS 4 **combined,** joined, **conjoint,** conjunct, conjugate, corporate, compact, cooperative, cooperating; concurrent, coincident; inclusive, comprehensive

**joke** NOUNS 1 **jest, gag** *and* one-liner <both nonformal>, **wheeze,** jape; **fun, sport, play;** story, yarn, **funny story,** good story; dirty story *or* joke, blue story *or* joke, *double entendre* <Fr>; shaggy-dog story; sick joke <nonformal>; ethnic joke; laugh, belly laugh, rib tickler, sidesplitter, thigh-slapper, howler, wow, scream, riot, panic; visual joke, sight gag <nonformal>
2 **laughingstock,** jestingstock, gazingstock, derision, mockery, **figure of fun,** byword, byword of reproach, jest, **butt,** target, stock, **goat** <nonformal>, game, **fair game,** victim, dupe, fool, everybody's fool
VERBS 3 **jest, wisecrack** *and* crack wise <both nonformal>, utter a mot, **quip,** jape, josh <nonformal>, fun <nonformal>, make fun, **kid** *or* **kid around** <both nonformal>; **make a funny** <nonformal>; **crack a joke,** get off a joke, tell a good story; **make fun of,** gibe at, fleer at, mock, scoff at, poke fun at, make the butt of one's humor, be merry with; ridicule

**joker** NOUNS **mischief-maker,** mischief, **rogue, devil,** knave, **rascal,** rapscallion, scapegrace, **scamp; wag**; buffoon; funmaker, jokester, practical joker, prankster, life of the party, **cutup** <nonformal>; gimmick, catch; curve, curveball, googly *or* bosey *or* wrong'un <all Brit nonformal>; **fooler, hoaxer,** practical joker; spoofer *and* **kidder** *and* ragger *and* leg-puller <all nonformal>

**joking** ADJS **jocular,** joky <nonformal>, **jesting,** jocose, tongue-in-cheek; **facetious,** joshing <nonformal>, **whimsical, droll,** humorsome; satiric, satirical, sarcastic, **ironic,** ironical; **keen-witted,** quick-witted, nimble-witted

**jolly** VERBS 1 **kid,** josh, fool around, jive, rub, put on; **razz, roast,** ride, needle <all nonformal>
2 **make merry, revel,** roister, lark <nonformal>, skylark, **make whoopee** <nonformal>, let oneself go, **blow** *or* **let off steam**
ADJS 3 **jovial,** hearty, festive, gay; **convivial,** boon, free and easy, hail-fellow-well-met

**jolt** NOUNS 1 **prod,** poke, punch, jab, dig, nudge; **bump,** jog, joggle, **jostle,** butt
VERBS 2 **startle,** shock, electrify, jar, shake, stun, **stagger, give one a turn** <nonformal>, give the shock of one's life, make one jump out of his skin, take aback, take one's breath away, bowl down *or* over <nonformal>, strike all of a heap <nonformal>
3 **prod,** goad, poke, punch, jab, dig, nudge; **bump,** jog, joggle, shake, rattle; **jostle,** hustle, **butt**

**jostle** NOUNS 1 **prod,** poke, punch, jab, dig, nudge; **bump,** jog, joggle; hustle; **shock, jolt,** jar
VERBS 2 **contend,** contest, **tussle, scuffle;** clash, collide; **wrestle,** rassle <nonformal>, grapple, grapple with; **disagree, differ**, vary, not see eye-to-eye, be at cross-purposes, tangle assholes <nonformal>, **conflict,** clash, **jar,** jangle, collide, square off; pick pockets

**jot** NOUNS minutia, **minutiae** <pl>, minim, **drop,** droplet, **mite** <nonformal>, mote, fleck, **speck,** flyspeck, tittle, jot nor tittle, iota, **trace,** trace amount, suspicion, *soupçon* <Fr>

**jounce** VERBS **shake,** quake, vibrate, jactitate; **tremble,** quiver, quaver, falter, shudder, shiver, twitter, didder, chatter; **shock, jolt,** jar, hustle, bounce, bump

**journal** NOUNS **periodical, magazine,** gazette; ephemeris; trade journal, trade magazine; daybook, diary; **account book,** ledger; **chronicle, annals**

**journalism** NOUNS **the press,** the public press, **the fourth estate;** print medium, the print media, print journalism, the print press, the public print; newspaper writing, editorial-writing, feature-writing, rewriting

**journalist** NOUNS **newspaperman, newspaperwoman,** newsman, newswoman, inkstained wretch, newswriter, gentleman *or* representative of the press; **reporter,** newshawk *and* newshound <both nonformal>; leg man <nonformal>; investigative reporter; **cub reporter; correspondent, foreign correspondent,** war correspondent, special correspondent, stringer; paparazzo

**journey** NOUNS 1 **trip,** *jornada* <Sp>, peregrination, sally, **trek;** progress, course, run; **tour,** grand tour; **excursion,** jaunt, junket, outing, pleasure trip; sight-seeing trip *or* tour; **pilgrimage,** hajj; **voyage**
VERBS 2 **travel,** make *or* take *or* go *or* go on a journey, **take** *or* **make a trip,** trek, jaunt, peregrinate; junket, go on a junket; **tour;** hit the trail <nonformal>, take the road, go on the road; go abroad, go to foreign places *or* shores, range the world, globe-trot <nonformal>; go on *or* make a pilgrimage

**journeyman** NOUNS 1 **skilled worker,** skilled laborer, mechanic; **craftsman, handicraftsman;** craftswoman; craftsperson; craftspeople; **artisan,** artificer
ADJS 2 **competent,** capable, able, efficient, qualified, fit, fitted, suited, worthy; well-qualified, well-fitted, well-suited

**jovial** ADJS **festive, festal; merry,** gay, jolly, joyous, joyful, gladsome, convivial, gala, hilarious

**joy** NOUNS **happiness,** joyfulness, cheer, cheerfulness, exhilaration, **exuberance,** high spirits, glee, sunshine; gaiety

**joyful** ADJS **happy, glad, joyous,** flushed with joy, radiant, beaming, glowing, starry-eyed, sparkling, laughing, smiling, smirking, smirky, chirping, purring, singing, dancing, leaping, capering, **cheerful,** gay; cheering, gladdening; **exhilarating,** animating, enlivening, invigorating; cheerful, cheery

**joyless** ADJS **pleasureless,** cheerless, depressed, grim; **sad, unhappy**; unsatisfied, unfulfilled, ungratified; **bored; desolate,** dreary, cheerless, dismal, bleak

**jubilant** ADJS **overjoyed,** brimming *or* bursting with happiness, on top of the world; **rapturous,** raptured, **enraptured, enchanted,** entranced, enravished, ravished, rapt, possessed; **in raptures,** transported, in a transport of delight, **carried away,** beside oneself with joy; **elated,** elate, exalted, exultant, flushed

**jubilee** NOUNS **celebration,** celebrating; **observance, commemoration,** memorialization, remembrance, memory; red-letter day, **festivity, revel**; rejoicing; **anniversary,** silver jubilee, golden jubilee, diamond jubilee

**Judaism** NOUNS Orthodox Judaism, Conservative Judaism, Reform Judaism, Reconstructionism; Hasidism

**Judas** NOUNS **traitor,** treasonist, **betrayer, quisling,** rat <nonformal>, serpent, snake, cockatrice, snake in the grass, **double-crosser** <nonformal>, double-dealer; Judas Iscariot

**judge** NOUNS 1 **magistrate,** justice, adjudicator, moderator; umpire, referee; good judge, **critic, expert,** authority, maven <nonformal>, arbiter
VERBS 2 **administer justice,** sit in judgment; **try,** try a case, conduct a trial, **hear,** give a hearing to, sit on; **criticize,** critique, evaluate, interpret, explicate, analyze; exercise judgment *or* the judgment; make a judgment call <nonformal>; adjudge, adjudicate

**judgment** NOUNS 1 **decision,** landmark decision; **verdict, sentence**; acquittal; condemnation, penalty, rap <nonformal>; punishment that fits the crime, condign punishment, well-deserved punishment
2 **judiciousness,** good *or* sound judgment, cool judgment, soundness of judgment; **prudence,** consideration, circumspection, circumspectness, reflection, reflectiveness, **thoughtfulness; discretion,** discernment, critical discernment, penetration, perception, perceptiveness, **insight,** perspicacity; acumen

**judgmental** ADJS **judicial, judiciary,** judicative; **evaluative,** critical; **disapproving, censorious**

**Judgment Day** NOUNS **doomsday,** doom, day of doom, day of reckoning, crack of doom, trumpet *or* trump of doom; Day of Judgment, the Judgment; eschatology, last things, **last days**

**judiciary** NOUNS judicial *or* legal *or* court system, judicature, judicatory, court, the courts; criminal-justice system; **justice,** the wheels of justice, judicial process

**judicious** ADJS **prudent,** prudential, politic, careful, provident, **considerate,** circumspect, **thoughtful,** reflective, reflecting; **discreet;** astute, discriminative, discriminating; **well-advised,** well-judged, enlightened

**jug** NOUNS 1 crock, vase, urn, bowl; prison

**juggle** VERBS **falsify, belie, misrepresent,** miscolor; misstate, misquote, misreport, miscite; **slant, twist,** impart spin <nonformal>; put a false appearance upon, give a false coloring, fudge <nonformal>; **play games** <nonformal>, **swindle,** defraud; conjure; **bluff**

**juggler** NOUNS **trickster,** tricker; sleight-of-hand performer, **swindler, defrauder,** cozener

**juice** NOUNS 1 **fluid, liquid;** liquor, drink, beverage; liquid extract, fluid extract; **sap,** latex
2 **current,** electric current, current flow, amperage, electric stream *or* flow

**juicy** ADJS **interesting,** stimulating, provocative, provoking, thought-provoking, thought-challenging, thought-inspiring; **titillating,** tickling, tantalizing, inviting, exciting; **piquant,** lively, racy, succulent, spicy, rich; sappy

**jumble** NOUNS **conglomeration, assortment,** assemblage, mixed bag, ragbag, grab bag, olio, *olla podrida* <Sp>, **scramble,** mingle-mangle, mishmash, **mess,** can of worms <nonformal>, everything but the kitchen sink <nonformal>, disorganization, **disorder,** chaos, **mess** *and* mix-up <both nonformal>

**jumbled** ADJS **confused, chaotic,** anarchic, **muddled,** scattered, helter-skelter <nonformal>, higgledy-piggledy, hugger-mugger, skimble-skamble, in a mess; **topsy-turvy,** arsy-varsy, upside-down, ass-backwards <nonformal>; **mixed up, balled** *or* **bollixed up** <nonformal>, **screwed up** <nonformal>, mucked up <nonformal>, **fouled up** *and* fucked up *and* snafu <all nonformal>

**jumbo** ADJS **huge, immense, vast, enormous,** astronomic, astronomical, humongous <nonformal>, king-size, queen-size, tremendous, prodigious, stupendous

**jump** NOUNS 1 **leap,** forward leap *or* jump, quantum jump *or* leap, spring, forward spring; **discontinuity,** interruption; **advantage,** vantage, odds, leg up *and* inside track *and* pole position <all nonformal>; **edge,** bulge *and* drop <both nonformal>
VERBS 2 **leap, vault, spring, skip, hop, bound,** bounce; **start,** startle, jump out of one's skin, jump a mile; have at, **attack**

**jumper** NOUNS leaper, hopper; broad jumper, high jumper; bungee jumper; parachute jumper, sky diver, sport jumper, paratrooper, smoke jumper

**jumping-off place** NOUNS **extremity, extreme; limit**, ultimacy, definitiveness, **boundary,** farthest bound, Thule, *Ultima Thule* <L>

**jumpy** ADJS **jittery** <nonformal>, twittery, skittish, skittery, trigger-happy <nonformal>, gun-shy; **shaky,** shivery, quivery, in a quiver; tremulous, tremulant, trembly; jumpy as a cat on a hot tin roof; **fidgety,** fidgeting; fluttery, all of a flutter *or* twitter; twitchy; **agitated;** shaking, trembling, quivering, shivering; shook up *and* all shook up <both nonformal>

**junction** NOUNS **joining,** joinder, jointure, **connection, union,** unification, bond, bonding, connectedness *or* connectivity, conjunction, conjoining, conjugation, liaison, marriage, hookup <nonformal>, splice, tie, tie-up *and* tie-in <both informal>, knotting

**juncture** NOUNS **circumstance,** conjuncture, contingency, eventuality; **joint,** join, joining, **union, connection,** link, connecting link, coupling, accouplement; **period, point,** stage; **time,** while, **moment,** minute, instant, hour, day, **season**

**jungle** NOUNS **labyrinth;** webwork, mesh; **wilderness,** morass, quagmire; mare's nest, rat's nest, can of worms <nonformal>, snake pit

**junior** NOUNS 1 **subordinate,** secondary, second-in-command, lieutenant, **inferior; underling,** understrapper, low man on the totem pole <nonformal>, errand boy, flunky, gofer <nonformal>; assistant, personal assistant, helper; **upperclassman**
ADJS 2 **inferior,** subordinate, secondary; **minor;** low in the pecking order; cadet, puisne <law>, younger

**junk** NOUNS 1 **rubbish,** rubble, trash, scrap, debris, litter
VERBS 2 **scrap,** consign to the scrap heap, throw on the junk heap <nonformal>; jettison, throw overboard, discard, throw away
ADJS 3 **abandoned, forsaken, deserted,** left; disused; **derelict,** castaway, jettisoned; junked, discarded; **worthless,** valueless, good-for-nothing; **cheap,** shoddy, trashy, **shabby**

**junket** NOUNS **tour,** excursion, jaunt, outing, pleasure trip; sight-seeing trip *or* tour

**junkie** NOUNS **addict,** drug addict, narcotics addict, user, drug user, drug abuser; head *and* druggy *and* doper *and* toker *and* freak <all nonformal>

**junkyard** NOUNS wasteyard, scrapyard, **dump,** dumpsite, garbage dump, landfill, sanitary landfill, toxic waste dump

**Junoesque** ADJS **shapely,** well-built, built, well-shaped, well-proportioned, well-made, well-formed, stacked *or* well-stacked <both nonformal>, curvaceous, curvy <nonformal>, pneumatic, amply endowed, built for comfort *or* built like a brick shithouse <both nonformal>, buxom, callipygian, callipygous; statuesque, goddess-like

**junta** NOUNS **clique,** conspiracy, ring, junto, cabal, camarilla, **clan,** group

**jurisdiction** NOUNS legal authority *or* power *or* right *or* sway, the confines of the law; **control,** mastery, mastership, command, dominion, domination; hold, grasp, grip, gripe

**jurisprudence** NOUNS **law,** legal science; nomology, nomography

**jurist** NOUNS legist, jurisprudent, jurisconsult; law member of a court-martial

**juror** NOUNS **juryman, jurywoman,** venireman *or* venirewoman, talesman; foreman of the jury, foreman; grand juror, petit juror, petty juror

**jury** NOUNS **panel,** jury of one's peers, sessions <Scots>, twelve men in a box; inquest; jury panel, jury list, venire facias; hung *or* deadlocked jury

**jury-rigged** ADJS **makeshift,** makeshifty, **stopgap,** band-aid <nonformal>, improvised, improvisational; **ad hoc;** quick and dirty <nonformal>; temporary, provisional, tentative

**just** ADJS 1 **fair,** square, **fair and square;**

**equitable,** balanced, level <nonformal>, **even,** evenhanded; **right, rightful;** justifiable, justified, warranted, warrantable, defensible; **due,** deserved, merited; meet, meet and right, right and proper, fit, **proper, good,** as it should *or* ought to be; lawful, legal
ADVS 2 **very, exceedingly,** awfully *and* terribly *and* terrifically <all nonformal>, **quite,** so, **really,** real *and* right <both nonformal>, **pretty,** only too, mightily, **mighty** *and* almighty *and* powerfully *and* powerful <all nonformal>

**justice** NOUNS 1 **justness; equity,** equitableness, level playing field <nonformal>; **evenhandedness,** measure for measure, give-and-take; balance, equality; **right, rightness,** rightfulness, meetness, properness, propriety, what is right; dueness; justification, **justifiableness,** justifiability, warrantedness, warrantability, defensibility; poetic justice; retributive justice, nemesis; summary justice, drumhead justice, rude justice; scales of justice; lawfulness, legality; **judge, magistrate,** adjudicator

**justifiable** ADJS **vindicable,** defensible; **excusable, pardonable, forgivable,** expiable, remissible, exemptible, venial; **condonable,** dispensable; **warrantable,** allowable, admissible, reasonable, colorable, legitimate

**justified** ADJS **warranted, entitled,** qualified, worthy; **deserved, merited,** richly deserved, earned, well-earned; **redeemed, saved,** converted, regenerated, regenerate, reborn, born-again, renewed

**justify** VERBS **vindicate,** do justice to, make justice *or* right prevail; **warrant,** account for, show sufficient grounds for, give good reasons for; **rationalize,** explain

**jut** VERBS **protrude,** protuberate, project, extrude; **stick out,** jut out, poke out, stand out, shoot out; **stick up,** bristle up, start up, cock up, shoot up

**jutting** ADJS **protruding, protrusive,** protrudent; protrusile, protrusible; **protuberant,** protuberating; **projecting, extruding,** outstanding; prominent, eminent, salient, bold; prognathous; protrusile, emissile

**juvenile** NOUNS 1 **youngster,** young person, **youth,** youngling, young'un <nonformal>, juvenal <old>; **stripling,** slip, sprig, sapling; fledgling; hopeful, young hopeful; **minor,** infant; **adolescent,** pubescent; **ingenue**
ADJS 2 **young,** youngling, juvenal, juvenescent, **youthful;** ungrown, half-grown, adolescent, puerile, boyish, girlish

# K

**kaput** ADJS **past hope, beyond recall,** past praying for; **ruined,** undone, gone to hell *and* gone to hell in a handbasket <both nonformal>

**karma** NOUNS **destiny**, **fate,** doom, kismet, what bodes *or* looms, what is fated *or* destined *or* doomed, what is written, what is in the books

**kayo** VERBS knock unconscious, knock senseless, **knock out,** KO *and* lay out *and* coldcock *and* knock stiff <all nonformal>

**keen** VERBS 1 **lament, mourn,** moan, grieve, sorrow, weep over, bewail, bemoan, deplore, **repine, sigh,** give sorrow words; elegize, dirge
ADJS 2 **eager, anxious,** agog, all agog; **avid,** forward, prompt, quick, ready, ready and willing, alacritous, bursting to, dying to, raring to; **zestful, lively,** full of life, vital, vivacious, vivid, spirited, **animated; impatient**
3 **sharp,** sharpish, incisive, trenchant, **cutting,** penetrating, piercing, biting, **stinging,** stabbing, **scathing, scorching,** withering, scurrilous, abusive, thersitical, foulmouthed, harsh-tongued
4 **smart, brainy** <nonformal>, **bright, brilliant,** scintillating; **clever,** apt, **gifted,** talented; **sharp,** smart as a whip, sharp as a tack <nonformal>; nobody's fool *and* no dumbbell *and* not born yesterday <all nonformal>

**keen on** ADJS **desirous of** *or* **to,** set on <nonformal>, bent on; fond of, with a liking for, partial to <nonformal>; inclined toward, leaning toward; **itching for** *or* **to,** aching for *or* to, **dying for** *or* **to;** spoiling for <nonformal>; mad on *or* for, wild to *or* for <nonformal>, crazy to *or* for <nonformal>; hipped on, **cracked on,** bugs on, freaked-out, **nuts on** *or* **over** *or* **about, keen about,** crazy *or* mad *or* nuts about <all nonformal>

**keep** NOUNS 1 **accommodations,** accommodation, facilities; **lodgings;** bed, board, full board; **room and board,** bed and board; **subsistence,** fostering
2 **prison,** correctional *or* correction facility, **penitentiary,** pen <nonformal>, penal institution, bastille, state prison, federal prison; house of detention, detention center, detention home; **jail, gaol** <Brit>, jailhouse, lockup
3 **stronghold,** hold, safehold, fasthold, strong point, **fastness,** ward, **bastion,** donjon, **citadel, castle,** tower, tower of strength, strong point
VERBS 4 **obey, mind,** heed, observe, listen or hearken to; comply, conform, walk in lockstep; stay in line *and* not get out of line *and* not get off base <all nonformal>; **observe, keep, heed, follow,** keep the faith
5 provide for, make provision *or* due provision for; prepare; support, maintain; **preserve, conserve, save,** spare; keep safe, keep inviolate *or* intact
6 **raise, breed,** rear, grow, hatch, feed, nurture, fatten; run; ranch, farm; culture

**keeper** NOUNS **jailer,** gaoler <Brit>, correctional *or* correction *or* corrections officer; **warder,** prison guard, **turnkey,** bull *and* screw <both nonformal>; **guard; protector,** protectress, safekeeper

**keep out** VERBS **exclude, bar,** debar, bar out, lock out, **shut out,** count out <nonformal>, close the door on, close out, cut out, cut off, preclude; **reject, repudiate,** blackball *and* turn thumbs down on <both nonformal>, read *or* drum out, ease *or* freeze out *and* leave *or* keep out in the cold <all nonformal>, ostracize, wave off *or* aside

**keep quiet** VERBS **be still,** lie still; stand, **stand still,** be at a standstill; stand like a post; **not stir,** not stir a step, not move a muscle; not breathe, hold one's breath

**keepsake** NOUNS **memento,** remembrance, token, trophy, souvenir, relic, favor, token of remembrance; *memento mori* <L>; **memories, memorabilia,** memorials

**keep the faith** VERBS **be hopeful,** keep one's spirits up, never say die, take heart, be of good hope, be of good cheer, keep hoping, keep hope alive; **hope for the best,** keep one's fingers crossed, allow oneself to hope; fight the good fight, let one's light shine, praise and glorify God, walk humbly with one's God

**keep the peace** VERBS remain at peace, wage peace; refuse to shed blood, keep one's sword in its sheath; forswear violence, beat one's swords into plowshares; pour oil on troubled waters; defuse

**keep time** VERBS **beat time,** tap out the rhythm; count, count the beats; mark time, measure time

**kelp** NOUNS **seaweed,** sea moss, rockweed, gulfweed, sargasso *or* sargassum, sea lentil, wrack, sea wrack

**ken** NOUNS 1 **knowledge,** knowing, knowingness; **familiarity,** intimacy; private knowledge, privity
VERBS 2 **understand, comprehend,** apprehend, have, know, conceive, realize, appreciate, have no problem with, savvy <nonformal>, sense, make sense out of, make something of

**kennel** NOUNS 1 **doghouse;** pound, dog pound; cattery
2 **drain,** sough <Brit nonformal>, sluice, scupper; **sink,** sump; piscina; **gutter, sewer,** cloaca, headchute

**kept** ADJS **reserved, preserved, saved,** conserved, put by, retained, held, withheld, held back, kept *or* held in reserve; **well-preserved,** well-conserved, **well-kept,** in a good state of preservation

**kept woman** NOUNS **mistress,** woman, kept mistress, **paramour,** concubine, doxy, playmate, spiritual *or* unofficial wife; live-in lover <nonformal>

**kerchief** NOUNS **headdress,** headcloth, coverchief; **handkerchief**

**kernel** NOUNS **substance,** sum and substance, stuff, material, matter, medium, building blocks, fabric; **gist,** heart, soul, meat, nub; the nitty-gritty *and* the bottom line *and* the name of the game <all nonformal>, **core,** marrow, pith, sap, spirit, **essence,** quintessence

**key** NOUNS 1 **island, isle; islet,** holm, cay; sandbank, sandbar, bar
2 clavis; latchkey; passkey, *passe-partout* <Fr>; master key, skeleton key; open sesame; plastic key
3 **clue, cue,** tip-off <nonformal>, telltale, smoking gun <nonformal>, straw in the wind; **lead** *and* hot lead <both nonformal>
ADJS 4 **central,** centric, **middle**; centermost, middlemost, **midmost;** axial, **pivotal**

**keyed up** ADJS **excited, stirred,** stirred up, wrought up, **worked up,** worked up into a lather <nonformal>, steamed up, hopped up <nonformal>, carried away

**keynote** NOUNS 1 **characteristic, peculiarity, singularity,** particularity, specialty, individualism, **character,** nature, **trait,** quirk, point of character, bad point, good point, saving grace, redeeming feature, mannerism, trick, **feature,** distinctive feature
VERBS 2 **characterize,** distinguish, differentiate, define, describe; **mark, earmark,** mark off, mark out, demarcate, **set apart,** make special *or* unique; sound the keynote, set the tone *or* mood, set the pace; be characteristic, **be a feature** *or* **trait of**

**keystone** NOUNS **foundation stone,** footstone; **cornerstone,** headstone, first stone, quoin; **salient point,** cardinal point, high point, great point; **essence,** linchpin, the name of the game *and* the bottom line *and* what it's all about *and* where it's at <all nonformal>, substance, gravamen

**khan** NOUNS **prince,** *Prinz, Fürst* <both Ger>, knez, atheling, sheikh, sherif, mirza, emir, shahzada <India>

**kibbutz** NOUNS **community,** communal effort *or* enterprise, cooperative society; **collectivity,** collectivism, collective enterprise, collective farm

**kibitz** VERBS **advise, counsel,** recommend, suggest, advocate, propose, submit; weigh in with advice <nonformal>, give a piece of advice, give a hint *or* broad hint, meddle

**kibitzer** NOUNS **meddler,** intermeddler; **busybody, pry,** Paul Pry, prier; buttinsky *and* yenta *and* backseat driver <all nonformal>

**kick** NOUNS 1

**thrill,** sensation; **charge,** boot, bang, belt, blast, flash, hit, jolt, large charge, rush, upper, lift; jollies

2 **boot;** punt, drop kick, place kick, kicking; **recoil, rebound,** resilience, repercussion, *contrecoup* <Fr>; **bounce, bound, spring,** bounce-back; **backlash,** backlashing, kickback, a kick like a mule <nonformal>; **backfire, boomerang**
VERBS 3 **object, protest, remonstrate,** expostulate; **complain,** exclaim at, state a grievance, air one's grievances
4 <nonformal> put up a struggle *or* fight; **bitch** *and* **beef** *and* **squawk** *and* howl *and* holler *and* put up a squawk *and* raise a howl; exclaim *or* cry out against, make *or* create *or* raise a stink about; yell bloody murder

5 **break the habit, cure oneself of,** disaccustom oneself, wean oneself from, break the pattern, break one's chains *or* fetters; **give up,** leave off, **abandon,** drop, stop, discontinue, shake <nonformal>, throw off, rid oneself of; get on the wagon, swear off
6 boot, kick about *or* around; kick downstairs <old>; kick out; **recoil, rebound,** resile; **bounce, bound, spring; spring** *or* **fly back,** bounce *or* bound back, snap back; kick back, kick like a mule <nonformal>, **backfire, boomerang;** backlash, lash back

**kicker** NOUNS **condition, provision, proviso, stipulation,** whereas; **catch** *and* joker *and* string *and* a string to it <all nonformal>

**kickoff** NOUNS 1 **beginning, commencement, start,** running *or* flying start, starting point, square one <nonformal>, **outset,** outbreak, **onset,** oncoming; **creation, foundation, establishment, establishing, institution, origin,** origination, establishment, setting-up, setting in motion; **launching,** launch, jump-off *and* send-off *and* start-off *and* take-off *and* blast-off *and* git-go *and* square one <all nonformal>, the word 'go' <nonformal>
ADJS 2 preliminary, exploratory, pioneering, trailblazing, door-opening, inaugural

**kick off** VERBS **start,** start off, start up, give a start, crank up, give a push *or* shove <nonformal>, jump-start, kick-start, **put** *or* **set in motion, set on foot,** set going *or* agoing, start going; **start the ball rolling** <nonformal>; get off the ground *or* off the mark, **launch**

**kid** NOUNS 1 **child,** nipper, kiddy *and* kiddo <both nonformal>, **little one,** little fellow *or* guy, little bugger <nonformal>, shaver *and* little shaver <both nonformal>, little squirt <nonformal>, **tot, little tot,** wee tot, pee-wee, tad *or* little tad, tyke, moppet
VERBS 2 **joke, jest, wisecrack** *and* crack wise <both nonformal>, utter a mot, **quip,** jape, josh <nonformal>, fun <nonformal>, make fun, **kid around** <both nonformal>; put on, razz, roast, ride, heckle <all nonformal>

**kidding** ADJS 1 **bantering,** chaffing, twitting; **fooling, teasing,** japing

**kidnap** VERBS **snatch** <nonformal>, hold for ransom; **abduct,** abduce, spirit away, **carry off** *or* **away,** run off *or* away with; skyjack; **shanghai,** crimp, impress

**kidnapper** NOUNS **abductor; shanghaier,** snatcher *and* baby-snatcher <both nonformal>; crimp, crimper

**kidnapping** NOUNS **abduction,** snatching <nonformal>; **shanghaiing,** impressment, crimping

**kill** NOUNS 1 bourn, run <Brit nonformal>, **creek,** crick <nonformal>
2 **quarry, game, prey,** venery, beasts of venery, victim, the hunted; big game
VERBS 3 **slay, put to death,** deprive of life, bereave of life, **take life,** take the life of, take one's life away, **do away with,** make away with, **put out of the way,** put to sleep, end, **put an end to,** end the life of, **dispatch,** do for, murder, finish, finish off, kill off, take out, **dispose of, exterminate, destroy,** annihilate; **liquidate,** purge; carry off *or* away, remove from life; put down, put away, put one out of one's misery; launch into eternity, send to glory, send to kingdom come <nonformal>; euthanatize; **execute**

4 <nonformal> **waste, zap,** nuke, rub out, croak, snuff, bump off, knock off, bushwhack, lay out, polish off, blow away, blot out, erase, wipe out, blast, do in, off, hit, ice, gun down, pick off, put to bed with a shovel, scrag, take care of, take out, take for a ride, give the business *or* works, get, fix, settle

5 **quash,** squash *and* **squelch** <both nonformal>; **smother, stifle,** suffocate, asphyxiate, strangle, throttle, choke off, **muzzle, gag;** censor, bleep *or* bleep out <nonformal>, silence; jump on *and* crack down on *and* clamp down on <all nonformal>, put *or* keep the lid on <nonformal>; **veto,** put one's veto upon, decide *or* rule against, **turn thumbs down on** <nonformal>

**killer** NOUNS **slayer, slaughterer, butcher,** bloodshedder; massacrer; **manslayer, homicide, murderer,** mankiller, bloodletter, Cain; **assassin,** assassinator; **cutthroat,** thug, desperado, bravo, gorilla <nonformal>, apache, gunman; professional killer, hired killer, hit man *or* button man *or* gun *or* trigger man *or* torpedo *or* gunsel <all nonformal>; **hatchet man**

**killing** NOUNS 1 **slaying, slaughter, dispatch, extermination, destruction,**

destruction of life, taking of life, death-dealing, dealing of death, bane; kill; **bloodshed,** bloodletting, blood, gore, flow of blood; mercy killing, euthanasia, negative *or* passive euthanasia; ritual murder *or* killing, immolation, sacrifice; *auto-da-fé* <Sp, literally, act of faith>, martyrdom, martyrization; lynching; stoning, lapidation; defenestration; braining; shooting; poisoning; execution; mass killing, biocide, ecocide, genocide; Holocaust; mass murder
2 **gain, profit; pile** *and* bundle *and* cleanup *and* mint <all nonformal>
ADJS 3 **fatiguing, wearying,** wearing, **tiring,** straining, stressful, trying, **exhausting,** draining, **grueling,** punishing; **deadly, deathly,** deathful, **destructive,** death-dealing, savage, brutal; internecine; **fatal, mortal, lethal, malignant,** malign, **virulent, pernicious,** baneful

**killjoy** NOUNS **spoilsport,** grinch *and* crapehanger *and* drag <all nonformal>; damp, damper, **wet blanket,** party pooper; gloomster *and* doomster <both nonformal>, doomsdayer, apocalypticist, Moaning Minnie <Brit nonformal>; skeleton at the feast; gloomy Gus *and* calamity howler *and* worrywart <all nonformal>, seek-sorrow, Job's comforter, prophet of doom, Cassandra

*one who is always building dungeons in the air*
JOHN GALSWORTHY

**kill oneself** VERBS **commit suicide, take one's own life,** die by one's own hand, do away with oneself, put an end to oneself; blow one's brains out, take an overdose <of a drug>, overdose *or* OD <nonformal>; commit hara-kiri *or* seppuku; sign one's own death warrant, doom oneself

**kiln** NOUNS **oven;** acid kiln, brick kiln, cement kiln, enamel kiln, muffle kiln, limekiln, reverberatory, reverberatory kiln

**kin** NOUNS **kinfolk** *and* **kinfolks** <both nonformal>, **kinsmen, kinsfolk, kindred,** kith and kin, **family, relatives, relations, people,** folks <nonformal>, connections; **blood relation** *or* **relative,** flesh, blood, flesh and blood, uterine kin, consanguinean; cognate; agnate, enate; kinsman, kinswoman, sib, sibling; german; next of kin

**kind** NOUNS 1 **sort, ilk, type,** breed of cat <nonformal>, lot <nonformal>, **variety, species, genus,** *genre* <Fr>, phylum, denomination, designation, description, style, manner, **nature, character,** persuasion, the like *or* likes of <nonformal>; **stamp, brand,** feather, color, stripe, line, grain, kidney; **make,** mark, label, shape, cast, form, mold; tribe, clan, race, strain, blood, kin, breed
ADJS 2 **kindly,** kindly-disposed; **benign,** benignant; good as gold, **good, nice, decent; gracious; kindhearted, warm, warmhearted,** softhearted, tenderhearted, tender, loving, affectionate; **sympathetic,** sympathizing, **compassionate**, merciful; brotherly, fraternal; humane, human; charitable, caritative

**kindergarten** NOUNS **preschool,** infant school <Brit>, nursery, **nursery school;** day nursery, **day-care center,** crèche; playschool

**kindhearted** ADJS **kind, kindly,** kindly-disposed; **benign,** benignant; good as gold, **good, nice, decent; warm, warmhearted,** softhearted, tenderhearted, tender, loving, affectionate; **compassionate**, merciful; charitable, caritative

**kindle** VERBS **excite, impassion,** arouse, rouse, stir, stir up, set astir, stir the feelings, stir the blood, cause a stir *or* commotion, play on the feelings; **work up,** work into a lather <nonformal>, whip up, **key up,** steam up; **move**; **foment, incite**; turn on <nonformal>; **awaken,** awake, wake, waken, wake up; light the fuse, **fire, inflame,** heat, warm, set fire to, set on fire, fire *or* warm the blood; fan, fan the fire *or* flame, add fuel to the fire *or* flame; raise to a fever heat *or* pitch; **ignite**

**kindred** NOUNS 1 **blood relationship,** blood, ties of blood, consanguinity, common descent *or* ancestry, biological *or* genetic relationship, **kinship, relation, relationship,** sibship; propinquity; cognation; agnation, enation; filiation, affiliation; **kinfolk** *and* **kinfolks** <both nonformal>, **kinsmen, kinsfolk,** kinnery <nonformal>, **kin,** kith and kin, **family,** relatives, relations, people, folks <nonformal>
ADJS 2 **akin, related,** of common source *or* stock *or* descent *or* ancestry, agnate, cognate, enate, connate, connatural, congeneric *or* congenerous, con-

sanguine *or* consanguineous, genetically related, related by blood, affinal

**kindred soul** NOUNS soul mate, kindred spirit, **companion, twin,** brother, sister; *mon semblable* <Fr>, second self, alter ego

**kinetic** ADJS **dynamic,** dynamical, kinetical, kinematic, kinematical

**king** NOUNS **potentate,** sovereign, monarch, ruler, prince, dynast, crowned head, anointed king, majesty, royalty, royal, royal personage

**kingmaker** NOUNS operator *and* finagler *and* **wire-puller** <all nonformal>; behind-the-scenes operator, gray eminence, *éminence grise* <Fr>, power behind the throne, **powerbroker**

**kingpin** NOUNS

<nonformal> **top dog,** boss man, big boy, Big Daddy, big cheese, kingfish, el supremo, honcho *or* head honcho, top banana, big enchilada, himself, herself, man *or* woman upstairs, queen bee, heavy momma, Big Momma

**king-size** ADJS **oversize,** oversized; **outsize,** outsized, giant-size, **queen-size,** record-size, **overlarge,** overbig, too big; **overgrown,** overdeveloped; **overweight,** overheavy; overfleshed, overstout, overfat, overplump, overfed, obese

**kink** NOUNS 1 **pang,** crick, hitch, cramp *or* cramps
2 **quirk, twist,** crank, quip, trick, mannerism, **crotchet,** conceit, whim, maggot, maggot in the brain, bee in one's bonnet *or* head <nonformal>

**kinky** ADJS 1 **curly, curled;** kinked; **frizzly,** frizzy, frizzled, frizzed
2 **capricious, whimsical,** freakish, humorsome, vagarious; **fanciful, notional,** maggoty, **crotchety,** harebrained, cranky, flaky <nonformal>, quirky; wanton, wayward, vagrant
3 **unconventional, unorthodox, eccentric,** gonzo <nonformal>, offbeat <nonformal>, way out *and* far out *and* out in left field <all nonformal>

**kismet** NOUNS **destiny, fate,** doom, karma, what bodes *or* looms, what is fated *or* destined *or* doomed, what is written, what is in the books

**kiss** NOUNS 1 **contact, touch,** gentle *or* tentative contact, caress, brush, glance, nudge, rub, graze; impingement, impingence; buss, smack, smooch <nonformal>, **osculation;** French kiss, soul kiss
VERBS 2 **touch lightly,** touch upon; **brush,** sweep, graze, brush by, glance, scrape, skim; buss, smack, smooch <nonformal>, **osculate;** blow a kiss

**kit** NOUNS **baggage,** bag and baggage, traps, tackle, apparatus, truck, gear, outfit, duffel; **set,** suit, suite, series

**kite** NOUNS 1 box kite, Eddy kite, Hargrave *or* cellular kite, tetrahedral kite
2 bad check, rubber check *and* bounced check <both nonformal>

**kitsch** NOUNS **vulgarity,** vulgarness, vulgarism, commonness, **untastefulness,** tastelessness, unaestheticness, unaestheticism, tackiness <nonformal>; low *or* bad *or* poor taste, *mauvais goût* <Fr>; vulgar taste, bourgeois taste, Babbittry, philistinism; popular taste, pop culture *and* pop <both nonformal>; campiness, camp, high *or* low camp

**kitten** NOUNS **cat, feline,** pussy *and* **puss** *and* **pussycat** <all nonformal>, tabby, grimalkin; **kitty** *and* kitty-cat <both nonformal>

**kittenish** ADJS **frisky,** antic, skittish, coltish, rompish, capersome; **full of beans** *and* **feeling one's oats** <both nonformal>, full of piss and vinegar <nonformal>; **sportive, playful,** playful as a kitten, **frolicsome,** gamesome; kittenlike

**kitty** NOUNS **funds, means,** available means *or* resources *or* funds, wherewithal, command of money; **pot,** jackpot, pool, stakes

**kittycornered** ADJS 1 **transverse,** crosswise *or* crossways, thwart, athwart, across; **diagonal,** bendwise; catercorner *or* **catercornered** *or* cattycorner *or* cattycornered *or* kittycorner; slant, bias, biased, biaswise *or* biasways
ADVS 2 **diagonally,** diagonalwise; **on the bias,** bias, biaswise; **cornerwise,** cornerways; catercornerways *or* **catercorner** *or* cattycorner *or* kittycorner

**klutzy** ADJS **clumsy, clunky** <nonformal>, heavy-handed, heavy-footed, ham-handed, ham-fisted <chiefly Brit>, graceless, ungraceful, inconcinnate *and* inconcinnous <both old>, infelicitous, unfelicitous; **stupid, dumb,** dullard, **doltish,** blockish, klutzish <nonformal>, duncish, duncical, cloddish, lumpish, **oafish,** boobish, sottish, **asinine,** lamebrained

**knave** NOUNS **rascal,** precious rascal, rogue, **scoundrel,** villain, blackguard, **scamp, scalawag** <nonformal>, spalpeen <Ir>, rapscallion, **devil**

**knead** VERBS **mix, blend,** interblend, work; **massage,** caress, pet, stroke; plump, plump up, fluff, fluff up, shake up; **mash, smash,** squash, pulp

**knee-high** ADJS **little, small**, smallish; **slight,** exiguous; pintsized <nonformal>, half-pint; knee-high to a grasshopper; petite; short

**kneel** VERBS **bow, bend,** genuflect, bend the knee, **curtsy,** make a low bow, make a leg, make a reverence *or* an obeisance, salaam, bob, duck; **kowtow,** prostrate oneself; crawl, grovel; wallow, welter

**knell** NOUNS 1 passing bell, death bell, funeral ring, tolling, tolling of the knell; **dirge, funeral** *or* **death song**
VERBS 2 **ring,** tintinnabulate, **peal,** sound; **toll,** sound a knell; **elegize,** dirge

**knickknack** NOUNS **trinket,** gewgaw, nicknack, **gimcrack,** kickshaw, whim-wham, **bauble,** fribble, bibelot, toy, gaud; bric-a-brac

**knife** NOUNS 1 blade, cutter, whittle; steel, cold steel, naked steel; shiv *and* pig-sticker *and* toad stabber *and* toad sticker <all nonformal>; dirk, dagger, stiletto
VERBS 2 **stab, stick** <nonformal>, **pierce,** plunge in; **run through, impale,** spit, **transfix,** transpierce

**knight** NOUNS **cavalier,** chevalier, *caballero* <Sp>, *Ritter* <Ger>, **knight-errant,** knight-adventurer

*a verray parfit gentil knight*
CHAUCER

**knightly** ADJS **courageous, valiant,** valorous, gallant, intrepid, stalwart, stout-hearted, ironhearted, lionhearted, great-hearted, bold-spirited, bold as a lion; **chivalrous,** chivalric, knightlike

**knit** VERBS 1 **heal, heal over,** close up, scab over, cicatrize, granulate; heal *or* right itself; **set; braid,** plait, pleach, **wreathe,** raddle, twist, mat, wattle, grow together
ADJS 2 **joined, united, connected,** copulate, **coupled,** linked, bridged, tight-knit, knitted, bracketed, associated, conjoined, incorporated, integrated, **merged,** gathered, assembled, accumulated, **collected; tied, bound,** knotted, spliced, lashed

**knob** NOUNS **hill,** brae *and* fell <both Scots>; **hillock,** butte, kopje, kame, monticle, monticule, monadnock, **knoll,** hummock, hammock, eminence, rise, mound, swell, barrow, tumulus, kop, tel, jebel; **boss,** bulla, button, bulb

**knock** NOUNS 1 **blow,** stroke, pound, bang, crack, **whack,** smack, thwack, smash, dash, **punch, poke, jab,** dig, drub, thump; **criticism,** adverse criticism, harsh *or* hostile criticism, flak <nonformal>, bad notices, bad press, animadversion, imputation, reflection, **aspersion,** stricture, obloquy; **swipe** *and* **slam** *and* **rap** *and* hit <all nonformal>
VERBS 2 **hit, strike,** knock down *or* out, smite; **criticize; pan** *and* **slam** *and* hit *and* rap *and* take a rap *or* swipe at <all nonformal>, snipe at, strike out at

**knockoff** NOUNS **reproduction,** duplication, imitation, copy, dummy, mock-up, **replica,** facsimile, representation, paraphrase, approximation, model, version; **parody,** burlesque, pastiche, *pasticcio* <Ital>, travesty

**knock off** VERBS 1 **take a break, take time out** *and* grab some R and R <both nonformal>, pause, lay off, take ten *and* take five <both nonformal>; stop work, suspend operations, call it a day
2 **do carelessly,** do by halves, do in a half-assed way <nonformal>, do in a slipshod fashion, do in any old way <nonformal>; **do offhand,** dash off, **toss off** *or* **out** <nonformal>; toss *or* **throw together,** knock together, throw *or* slap together

**knockout** NOUNS 1 **unconsciousness, senselessness;** stupor; KO *or* kayo <both nonformal>; semiconsciousness, grayout
2 **finishing stroke, finisher,** clincher, equalizer, crusher, settler; knockout blow <nonformal>; sockdolager, KO *or* kayo *and* kayo punch <all nonformal>; final stroke, finishing *or* perfecting *or* crowning touch, last dab *or* lick <nonformal>
3 **the best,** first-rater, wonder, world-beater
4 <nonformal> **dandy,** jim dandy, dilly, humdinger, pip, pippin, **peach,** ace, beaut, **lulu,** doozy, honey, sweetheart, dream, lollapaloosa, hot shit *or* poo, pisser, pistol, corker, whiz, blinger, **crackerjack,** something else, something

else again, barn-burner, killer, killer-diller, the nuts, the cat's pajamas *or* balls *or* meow, whiz, whizbang, wow, wowser

**knock out** VERBS 1 **anesthetize, put to sleep,** slip one a Mickey *or* Mickey Finn <nonformal>, chloroform, etherize; narcotize, drug, dope <nonformal>; freeze, **stupefy, stun,** bedaze, besot; knock unconscious, knock senseless, KO *and* kayo *and* lay out *and* coldcock *and* knock stiff <all nonformal>
2 **do carelessly,** do by halves, do in a half-assed way <nonformal>, do in a slipshod fashion, do anyhow, do in any old way <nonformal>; botch, **bungle; do offhand,** dash off, **toss off** *or* **out** <nonformal>; hammer *or* pound out, bat out <nonformal>; toss *or* **throw together,** knock together, throw *or* slap together, slap up <nonformal>

**knoll** NOUNS **hillock, knob,** butte, kopje, kame, monticle, monticule, monadnock, hummock, hammock, eminence, rise, mound, swell, barrow, tumulus, kop, tel, jebel; **dune,** sand dune, sandhill

**knot** NOUNS 1 knur, knurl, gnarl, burl, gall
2 **bunch,** group, grouping, groupment, crop, cluster, **clump**
3 **vexed question,** thorny problem, knotty point, crux, node, nodus, Gordian knot, poser, teaser, perplexity, puzzle, enigma
VERBS 4 **tangle,** entangle, embrangle, **snarl,** snarl up, ravel, tie in knots; **couple,** pair, accouple, copulate, conjugate, marry, wed, tie the knot <nonformal>, **link,** link up, build bridges, yoke, splice, tie, chain, bracket; **thicken,** cake, lump, clump, cluster

**knotty** ADJS **knotted;** knobbly, nodose, nodular, studded, lumpy; gnarled, knurled, knurly, burled, gnarly; **hard to understand, difficult, hard,** tough <nonformal>; exacting, demanding; intricate, complex; abstruse

**know** VERBS **perceive, apprehend,** prehend, cognize, recognize, discern, see, make out; conceive, conceptualize; **realize, appreciate, understand, comprehend,** fathom; dig *and* savvy <both nonformal>; ken <Scots>; have, possess, **grasp,** seize, have hold of; have knowledge of, be informed, be apprised of, have a good command of, have information about, be acquainted with, be conversant with, be cognizant of, be conscious *or* aware of; know something by heart *or* by rote *or* from memory

**know-how** NOUNS **skill,** skillfulness, expertness, expertise, proficiency, cleverness; **competence,** capability, capacity, ability; **craftsmanship,** workmanship, artisanship; savvy *and* bag of tricks <both nonformal>; technical skill, **technique, touch,** technical brilliance, technical mastery, **virtuosity,** bravura, wizardry

**knowing** ADJS 1 experienced, practiced, mature, matured, ripe, ripened, **seasoned,** tried, well-tried, tried and true, **veteran,** old, an old dog at <nonformal>; sagacious; **worldly, worldly-wise,** world-wise, wise in the ways of the world, knowing, **sophisticated,** cosmopolitan, cosmopolite, blasé, dry behind the ears, not born yesterday, long in the tooth
2 **knowledgeable, informed; cognizant, conscious,** aware, mindful, sensible; intelligent; **understanding, comprehending,** apprehensive, apprehending; **perceptive,** insightful, apperceptive, percipient, perspicacious, appercipient, prehensile; shrewd, sagacious, wise; all-knowing

**know-it-all** NOUNS 1 **swellhead** <nonformal>, **braggart**, know-all, smart-ass *and* wise-ass <both nonformal>, smart aleck, no modest violet
ADJS 2 **conceited, self-conceited,** immodest, self-opinionated; swollen-headed, **swelled-headed, big-headed** *and* too big for one's shoes *or* britches *and* biggety *and* **cocky** <all nonformal>; know-all, smart-ass *and* wise-ass <both nonformal>, smarty, smart-alecky, overwise, wise in one's own conceit; aggressively self-confident, obtrusive, bumptious

**knowledge** NOUNS knowing, knowingness, ken; **command,** reach; **acquaintance, familiarity,** intimacy; private knowledge, privity; **information,** data, database, datum, items, facts, factual base, corpus; **certainty, sure** *or* **certain knowledge**; practical knowledge, **experience, know-how, expertise**

**knowledgeable** ADJS **knowing,** informed; **cognizant,** conscious, aware, mindful, sensible; **perceptive,** insightful, apperceptive, percipient, perspicacious, appercipient, prehensile; shrewd, sagacious, wise; omniscient, all-knowing

**know-nothing** NOUNS **ignoramus;** no scholar, puddinghead, dunce, fool; **illiterate; lowbrow** <nonformal>; unintelligentsia, illiterati

**kook** NOUNS

<nonformal> freak, character, crackpot, nut, screwball, weirdie, weirdo, oddball, flake, strange duck, bird, goofus, wack, wacko

**kooky** ADJS **odd,** queer, peculiar, absurd, singular, curious, **oddball** <nonformal>, weird *and* freaky *and* freaked-out <all nonformal>, quaint, **eccentric,** gonzo <nonformal>, funny; **strange, outlandish,** off-the-wall <informal>, surreal, not for real <nonformal>, passing strange; **weird,** unearthly

**kosher** ADJS 1 **clean, pure; undefiled;** *tahar* <Heb>, ritually pure *or* clean; glatt kosher
2 **legal, legitimate,** legit <nonformal>, competent, **licit, lawful,** rightful, according to law, within the law

**kowtow** VERBS **bow, make obeisance, salaam,** make one's bow, bow down, scrape, **bow and scrape; genuflect, kneel,** bend the knee, get down on one's knees, throw oneself on one's knees, fall on one's knees, fall down before, fall at the feet of, prostrate oneself, kiss the hem of one's garment; crawl, grovel; wallow, welter

**kudos** NOUNS **praise,** bepraisement; **laudation,** laud; **glorification,** glory, exaltation, magnification, **honor; eulogy,** *éloge* and *hommage* <both Fr>, eulogium; **encomium,** accolade, panegyric; paean; **tribute,** homage, meed of praise; **citation,** mention, honorable mention

**kvetch** NOUNS 1 **malcontent, complainer,** grumbler, griper, whiner
2 <nonformal> **grouch,** kicker, moaner, moaning Minnie <Brit>, crank, crab, grouser, grump, beefer, bellyacher, bitcher, sorehead, picklepuss, sourpuss <all nonformal>
3 VERBS **be discontented, complain,** be disgruntled; **beef, bitch,** bellyache, crab, gripe, grouch, grouse, grump <all nonformal>

# L

**label** NOUNS 1 **tag;** ticket, docket <Brit>, tally; **stamp, sticker; seal,** sigil, signet; cachet; **brand, brand name,** trade name, **trademark; epithet,** byword
VERBS 2 **tag,** tab, ticket; stamp, seal; **brand, earmark; name,** denominate, nominate, designate, call, term, style, dub, color <nonformal>; specify; define, identify; stereotype

**labor** NOUNS 1 **work,** employment, industry, toil, moil, travail, toil and trouble, sweat of one's brow; **drudgery, sweat,** slavery, spadework, rat race <nonformal>; treadmill; unskilled labor, hewing of wood and drawing of water; dirty work, grunt work *and* donkey work *and* shit-work *and* scut work <all nonformal>; **makework,** tedious *or* stupid *or* idiot *or* tiresome work, humdrum toil, grind <nonformal>
VERBS 2 **work;** busy oneself; turn a hand, do a hand's turn, do a lick of work, earn one's keep; chore, do the chores

**laboratory** NOUNS **lab** <nonformal>, research laboratory, research establishment *or* facility *or* institute, experimental station, field station, research and development *or* R and D establishment; **proving ground**

**labored** ADJS 1 **elaborate,** overornamented, overornate, overelegant, high-wrought; **overelegant,** overelaborate, overlabored, overworked, overwrought, busy
2 **stiff, stilted, formal,** Latinate, *guindé* <Fr>, ponderous, elephantine, lumbering, cumbrous, leaden, heavy, unwieldy, sesquipedalian, inkhorn, turgid, bombastic, pompous; **forced,** strained, awkward, cramped, halting; crabbed

**laborer** NOUNS **worker, toiler,** moiler; member of the working class, proletarian, prole <Brit nonformal>, blue-collar *or* lunch-bucket worker, laboring man, stiff *and* working stiff <both nonformal>; **workman, workingman; workwoman, workingwoman,** workfolk, workpeople; **factory worker,** industrial worker; **jobholder,** wageworker, **wage earner,** salaried worker; common laborer, **unskilled laborer,** navvy <Brit>, day laborer, roustabout

**laborious** ADJS **toilsome, arduous, strenuous,** painful, effortful, operose, troublesome, onerous, oppressive, burdensome; wearisome; **heavy,** hefty <nonformal>, tough <nonformal>, uphill, **backbreaking,** grueling, punishing, crushing, killing, Herculean

**labor-saving** ADJS **economical, efficient,** time-saving, money-saving

**labor union** NOUNS trade union, trades union <Brit>; organized labor; **craft union,** horizontal union; **industrial union,** vertical union; **local,** union local, local union; company union

**labyrinth** NOUNS **complex,** perplex <nonformal>, **tangle,** tangled skein, **mess** *and* snafu *and* fuck-up <all nonformal>, ravel, snarl, snarl-up; **maze,** meander, Chinese puzzle; mare's nest, rat's nest, can of worms <nonformal>, snake pit

**lace** NOUNS 1 lacery, lacing, lacework; lattice, latticework; hachure *or* hatchure, hatching, cross-hatching
VERBS 2 **interweave, interlace, intertwine,** interknit, interthread, intertissue, intertie, intertwist; web, net; enlace
3 **tamper with, doctor** *and* doctor up <both nonformal>; **fortify,** spike <nonformal>

**laceration** NOUNS **cutting, slitting,** slashing, **splitting,** slicing; **rending, tearing,** ripping, hacking, chopping, butchering, mutilation

**lack** NOUNS 1 **want, need,** deficiency, deficit, shortage, shortfall, wantage, **incompleteness,** defectiveness, shortcoming, imperfection; **absence**, omission
VERBS 2 **want, need, require;** miss, feel the want of, be sent away empty-handed; run short of

**lackadaisical** ADJS **casual,** offhand, relaxed, **laid-back** *and* throwaway <both nonformal>; **easygoing,** easy, free and easy, devil-may-care, *dégagé* <Fr>

**lackey** NOUNS **flunky,** livery *or* liveried servant; **footman,** *valet de pied* <Fr>; **minion,** creature, hanger-on, stooge <nonformal>; henchman, camp follower, satellite, jackal, myrmidon

**lacking** ADJS **absent, missing,** among the missing, not found, nowhere to be found, omitted, taken away, subtracted, deleted; **undeveloped,** underdeveloped, undergrown, stunted, hypoplastic, **immature,** callow, infant, arrested, embryonic, **wanting,** needing, missing, **partial,** part, failing; **in short supply,** scanty; found wanting

**lackluster** ADJS **colorless,** dull, flat, mat, dead, dingy, muddy, leaden, lusterless, insipid, tedious; **lifeless,** somber, **drab,** wan

**laconic** ADJS **taciturn, untalkative,** unloquacious, indisposed to talk; curt, brief, terse, brusque, short, concise, **sparing of words,** economical of words, of few words

**lacquered** ADJS varnished, shellacked, glazed, *glacé* <Fr>; **glassy,** smooth as glass

**lacuna** NOUNS **omission,** gap, hole, vacuum, break, discontinuity, interval; **interruption, suspension, break,** fissure, breach, gap, hiatus, caesura; **interval, pause,** interim, lull, cessation, letup <nonformal>, **intermission**

**lad** NOUNS **boy,** laddie, **youth,** manchild, manling, young man, *garçon* <Fr>, *muchacho* <Sp>, schoolboy, schoolkid <nonformal>, fledgling, hobbledehoy; fellow; sonny, sonny boy

**laden** ADJS burdened, oppressed, cumbered, **encumbered,** charged, loaded, fraught, freighted, taxed, saddled, hampered; heavy-laden; full-laden

**ladies' man** NOUNS **philanderer,** philander, woman chaser, heartbreaker; masher, lady-killer, wolf, skirt chaser, man on the make *and* make-out artist <both nonformal>; libertine, lecher, cocksman <nonformal>, seducer, Casanova, Don Juan

**ladle** NOUNS 1 **container,** basin, pot, pan, cup, glass, bottle
VERBS 2 **dip, scoop; bail,** bucket; spoon

**lady** NOUNS matron; dowager, person of breeding, perfect lady

**ladylike** ADJS **well-bred,** highbred, **well-brought-up; cultivated,** cultured, polished, refined, genteel, gentle; quite the lady; **wellborn,** blue-blooded

**ladylove** NOUNS **inamorata,** *amorosa* <Ital>, lady, mistress, ladyfriend

**Lady Luck** NOUNS Chance, Fortune, Lady *or* Dame Fortune, wheel of fortune, Fortuna, the fickle finger of fate <nonformal>; Luck

**lag** VERBS **lag behind, straggle,** lag back, drag, trail, **trail behind,** hang back *or* behind, loiter, linger, **loiter** *or* **linger behind,** dawdle, get behind, fall behind *or* behindhand, let grass grow under one's feet

**laggard** NOUNS **slowpoke** *and* slowcoach <both nonformal>, plodder, slow goer, **lingerer, loiterer, dawdler,** dawdle, procrastinator, foot-dragger, stick-in-the-mud <nonformal>, drone, slug, sluggard, lie-abed, goof-off <nonformal>, goldbrick <nonformal>; tortoise, snail

**lagoon** NOUNS **lake,** salt pond, salina, tidal pond *or* pool; *laguna* <Sp>

**laid-back** ADJS **nonchalant,** blasé, indifferent, unconcerned; **casual,** offhand, relaxed, throwaway <nonformal>; **easy-going,** free and easy, devil-may-care, lackadaisical, *dégagé* <Fr>; **leisurely, unhurried,** unhasty, hasteless, easy; deliberate

**laid up** ADJS 1 **invalided,** hospitalized, in hospital <Brit>; **sick,** ill; **bedridden, bedfast, sick abed; down,** prostrate, flat on one's back; in childbed, confined
2 **stored, accumulated,** amassed; gathered, garnered, collected; **stockpiled;** backlogged; **hoarded,** treasured

**lair** NOUNS **den,** cave, **hole,** covert, mew, form; **burrow,** tunnel, earth, run, couch, lodge; **retreat, hideaway, cell, ivory tower,** hidey-hole <nonformal>, sanctum, sanctum sanctorum, inner sanctum

**laissez-faire** NOUNS 1 **noninterference, nonintervention; isolationism; laissez-faireism,** let-alone principle *or* doctrine *or* policy, deregulation; *laissez-aller* <Fr>; liberalism, free enterprise, free competition, self-regulating market; capitalism; free trade
ADJS 2 **passive; neutral,** neuter; standpat <nonformal>, **do-nothing;** *laissez-aller* <Fr>; permissive, overly permissive; noninterfering, nonrestrictive, hands-off; noninvasive, noninterventionist

**lake** NOUNS landlocked water, loch <Scots>, lough <Ir>, nyanza <Africa>, mere, freshwater lake; oxbow lake, bayou lake, glacial lake; volcanic lake; tarn; inland sea

**lake dweller** NOUNS **lacustrian, lacustrine dweller** *or* inhabitant, **pile dweller** *or* builder; laker

**lakefront** NOUNS 1 **shore, strand,** *playa* <Sp>, **beach,** beachfront, waterside, **waterfront;** lakeshore
ADJS 2 **littoral,** lakeshore; shorefront, shoreline; beachfront, beachside

**lambaste** VERBS **pound, beat, hammer, maul,** sledgehammer, **knock, rap, bang,** thump, **drub,** buffet, **batter,** pulverize, paste <nonformal>, patter, pommel, pummel, pelt, baste

**lame** ADJS **crippled,** game <nonformal>, bad, handicapped, maimed; **halt,** halting, hobbling, limping; **disabled,** incapacitated; **ineffectual,** ineffective, inefficacious, of no effect

**lamebrain** NOUNS **stupid person,** dolt, dunce, clod, Boeotian, dullard, *niais* <Fr>, donkey, yahoo, thickwit, **dope, nitwit,** dimwit, lackwit, half-wit, putz, lightweight

**lame duck** NOUNS **officeholder,** public official, **incumbent;** holdover

**lament** NOUNS 1 **plaint,** *planctus* <L>; **murmur,** mutter; **moan, groan; whine, whimper; wail,** wail of woe; **sob,** *cri du coeur* <Fr>, **cry,** outcry, scream, **howl,** yowl, bawl, yawp, keen, ululation
VERBS 2 **mourn, moan, grieve, sorrow,** keen, weep over, **bewail, bemoan, deplore, repine, sigh,** give sorrow words; sing the blues <nonformal>, elegize, dirge, knell

**laminate** VERBS 1 **layer,** lay down, lay up, **stratify,** arrange in layers *or* levels *or* strata *or* tiers
ADJS 2 **layered,** in layers; **laminated,** laminous; lamellated, lamellate, lamellar, lamelliform; **stratified,** stratiform; foliated, foliaceous, leaflike

**lamination** NOUNS **stratification,** lamellation; foliation; flakiness, scaliness

**lamp** NOUNS **light source,** source of light, **luminary,** illuminator, luminant, illuminant, incandescent body *or* point, **light,** glim; light bulb, electric light bulb, lantern, candle, taper, torch, flame; **fluorescent light, fluorescent tube,** fluorescent lamp

**lampoon** NOUNS 1 send-up <nonformal>, pasquinade, pasquin, pasquil, squib, lampoonery, **satire,** malicious parody, **burlesque**; poison pen, hatchet job
VERBS 2 **satirize,** pasquinade; parody, send up <nonformal>; dip the pen in gall, **burlesque**

**lance** VERBS **perforate, pierce,** empierce, **penetrate, puncture, punch, hole,** prick; **tap, broach; stab, stick,** pink, run through; **transfix,** transpierce, fix, **impale,** spit, skewer; gore, spear, spike, needle; slit, snip, scissor

**land** NOUNS 1 **ground,** landmass, earth, glebe <old>, **sod,** clod, **soil, dirt,** dust, clay, marl, mold <Brit nonformal>; *terra* <L>, **terra firma;** terrain; **dry land;** arable land; marginal land; grassland, woodland; crust, earth's crust, lithosphere; **real estate,** real property, landholdings, acres, territory, freehold; region; **country**
VERBS 2 set down <nonformal>, **alight, light,** touch down; **descend,** come down, dump altitude <nonformal>, fly down; come in, come in for a landing; **crash-land;** ditch <nonformal>; come to land, make a landfall, set foot on dry land; reach *or* make land, make port; put in *or* into, put into port; **disembark,** debark, unboat; **detrain,** debus, **deplane, disemplane**

**landed** ADJS **propertied,** proprietary; property-owning, landowning, landholding

**landed gentry** NOUNS **gentry,** gentlefolk, gentlefolks, gentlepeople, better sort; lesser nobility, *petite noblesse* <Fr>; *samurai* <Japanese>; squirearchy

**landlocked** ADJS **restricted, limited, confined;** circumscribed, hemmed in, hedged in *or* about, boxed in; cramped, stinted

**landlubber** NOUNS **landsman,** landman, **lubber**

**landmark** NOUNS **marker, mark;** bench mark; **milestone,** milepost; cairn, menhir, capstone; **salient point,** cardinal point, high point, great point; important thing, chief thing, **the point, main point,** main thing, essential matter, **essence,** the name of the game *and* the bottom line *and* what it's all about *and* where it's at <all nonformal>, substance, gravamen, *sine qua non* <L>, issue, real issue, front-burner issue <nonformal>, prime issue

**landowner** NOUNS **landlord, landlady;** lord of the manor; squire, country gentleman; landholder, property owner, propertied *or* landed person, man of property, freeholder; landed interests, landed gentry; slumlord, rent gouger; absentee landlord

**landscape** NOUNS **scene, view, scape;** waterscape, riverscape, seascape, seapiece; airscape, skyscape, cloudscape; snowscape; cityscape, townscape; farmscape

**landslide** NOUNS 1 **slide; slip,** slippage; mudslide, landslip, subsidence;

snowslide, snowslip <Brit>; **avalanche** 2 **victory,** total victory, grand slam; election returns, tidal wave

**language** NOUNS speech, tongue, *lingua* <L>, spoken language, natural language; **talk, parlance, locution,** phraseology, **idiom, lingo** <nonformal>; dialect; idiolect, personal usage, individual speech habits *or* performance, parole

**languish** VERBS **pine, droop, flag, wilt; fade,** fade away; **wither, shrivel,** shrink, diminish, wither *or* die on the vine

**languishing** ADJS **drooping,** sinking, declining, flagging, pining, fading, failing, **dying, terminal,** moribund; lovelorn, lovesick

**lanky** ADJS **lean,** lean-looking, **skinny** <nonformal>, fleshless, lean-fleshed, thin-fleshed, **spare,** meager, **scrawny,** scraggy, thin-bellied, **gaunt, lank, gangling** *and* gangly <both nonformal>, gawky, **spindling,** spindly

**lantern** NOUNS **light source,** source of light, **luminary,** illuminator, luminant, illuminant, incandescent body *or* point, **light,** glim; **lamp,** candle, taper, torch, flame

**lap** NOUNS **circuit, round,** revolution, **circle,** full circle, go-round, **cycle,** orbit, ambit; pass; round trip, *aller-retour* <Fr>; **beat,** rounds, **walk,** tour, turn, loop; bell lap, victory lap

**lapse** NOUNS 1 **decline,** declension, **subsidence,** slump <nonformal>, **drop,** downtick <nonformal>; **backsliding,** relapse, recidivism, recidivation, fall *or* lapse from grace; **omission,** nonfeasance, nonperformance, failure, **default; impropriety,** slight *or* minor wrong, venial sin, **indiscretion,** peccadillo, misstep, trip, slip
VERBS 2 **relapse, backslide,** slide back, lapse back, **slip back,** sink back, **fall back,** have a relapse, devolve, **return to, revert to,** recur to, yield again to, fall again into, recidivate; revert, **regress; fall,** fall from grace
3 **elapse, pass, expire,** run its course, run out, go *or* pass by

**lapsed** ADJS 1 erring, **fallen,** Adamic, postlapsarian; **relapsing, backsliding,** recidivist, recidivistic, fallen from grace; of easy virtue
2 **past, gone,** by, **gone-by, bygone,** gone glimmering, bypast, ago, **over,** departed, passed, passed away, elapsed, vanished, faded, no more, never to return, not coming back

**larboard** NOUNS 1 **left side, left, left hand,** left-hand side, wrong side <nonformal>, portside, port
ADJS 2 **left, left-hand,** sinister, sinistral; **port**
ADVS 3 **leftward,** leftwards, leftwardly, **left, to the left,** sinistrally, sinister, sinistrad; on the left; port, aport

**larcenous** ADJS **thievish,** thieving, light-fingered, sticky-fingered; fraudulent

**larceny** NOUNS **theft;** petit *or* petty larceny, petty theft, grand larceny, grand theft, simple larceny, mixed *or* aggravated larceny

**larder** NOUNS **provisions, groceries,** provender, supplies, stores, food supply; commissariat, **commissary; pantry,** buttery <nonformal>; spence <Brit nonformal>, stillroom <Brit>

**large** ADJS **sizable, big,** great, grand, tall <nonformal>, considerable, goodly, healthy, tidy <nonformal>, **substantial,** bumper; as big as all outdoors; numerous; largish, biggish; large-scale, larger than life; man-sized <nonformal>; large-size *or* -sized, man-sized, king-size, queen-size; good-sized, life-size *or* -sized

**largess** NOUNS **gratuity, bounty,** liberality, donative, sportula; perquisite, perks <nonformal>; consideration, fee <old>, **tip,** *pourboire* <Fr>, *Trinkgeld* <Ger>, sweetener, inducement; **liberality,** liberalness, freeness, freedom; **generosity,** generousness, largeness, **unselfishness, munificence; openhandedness,** freehandedness, open *or* free hand, easy purse strings; open-heartedness, bigheartedness, largeheartedness, greatheartedness, freeheartedness; open heart, big *or* large *or* great heart, heart of gold; **magnanimity**

**lark** NOUNS **revel, escapade,** ploy; **spree,** bout, fling, wingding and randan <both nonformal>, randy <Scots>; **carouse; songbird**

**larva** NOUNS **chrysalis,** aurelia, **cocoon,** pupa; nymph, nympha; wriggler, wiggler; caterpillar, maggot, grub

**larynx** NOUNS voice box, Adam's apple

**lascivious** ADJS **lecherous, sexy, salacious, carnal,** animal, **sexual, lustful,** ithyphallic, **hot,** horny *and* sexed-up *and* hot to trot <all nonformal>; prurient, itching, itchy <nonformal>; concupiscent, lickerish, libidinous, randy, lubricious; **lewd, bawdy,** adult, X-rated, hard, pornographic, porno <nonformal>, **dirty, obscene**; erotic, **sensual,** fleshly; goatish, satyric, priapic, nymphomaniacal

**lash** NOUNS 1 **whip, scourge,** flagellum, strap, thong, rawhide, cowhide, blacksnake, kurbash, sjambok, belt, razor strap; knout; bullwhip, bullwhack; horsewhip; crop; quirt; rope's end; cat, cat-o'-nine-tails; whiplash
VERBS 2 **whip,** give a whipping *or* beating *or* thrashing, **beat, thrash, spank, flog,** scourge, flagellate, flail, whale; **smite,** thump, trounce, baste, **pummel,** pommel, **drub, buffet, belabor,** lay on; **lace,** cut, stripe; horsewhip; knout; **strap,** belt, rawhide, cowhide

**lass** NOUNS **girl,** girlie <nonformal>, maid, maiden, **lassie,** young thing, young creature, young lady, damsel in distress, **damsel,** damoiselle, demoiselle, *jeune fille* <Fr>, *mademoiselle* <Fr>, *muchacha* <Sp>, miss, missy, little missy, slip, wench <dial or nonformal>, colleen <Irish>

**lasso** NOUNS 1 noose, **lariat; snare,** springe
VERBS 2 **catch, take,** land *and* nail <both nonformal>, hook, **snag, snare,** sniggle, ensnare, enmesh, **net,** mesh; **bag,** sack; **trap,** entrap; rope, noose

**last** NOUNS 1 **end,** last gasp *or* breath, final twitch, last throe, last legs, last hurrah <nonformal>; omega, izzard; **fate, destiny,** last things, eschatology, last trumpet, Gabriel's trumpet, crack of doom, doom
VERBS 2 **endure, last out,** bide, **abide,** dwell, perdure, **continue,** run, extend, **go on,** carry on, hold on, keep on, stay on, run on, stay the course, go the distance, go through with, grind *or* slog on, grind *or* plug away; live, **live on,** continue to be, subsist, exist, tarry; **persist;** hang in *and* hang in there *and* hang tough <all nonformal>; **survive,** defy *or* defeat time; live to fight another day
ADJS 3 **final, terminal,** terminating *or* terminative, determinative, definitive, **conclusive;** last-ditch <nonformal>, last but not least, eventual, farthest, extreme, boundary, border, limbic, limiting, polar, **endmost, ultimate**
ADVS 4 **finally,** in fine; **ultimately,** eventually, as a matter of course; **at last,** at the last *or* end *or* conclusion, at length, at long last; **in conclusion, in sum;** conclusively, once and for all

**lasting** ADJS **durable,** perdurable, **enduring,** perduring, **abiding, continuing,** remaining, staying, **stable**, persisting, **persistent,** perennial; inveterate, agelong; **steadfast, constant,** intransient, immutable, unfading, evergreen, sempervirent, **permanent**, **long-lasting,** long-standing, of long duration *or* standing, diuturnal; **long-lived,** tough, hardy, vital, longevous *or* longeval

**last-minute** ADJS **hasty, hurried,** festinate, **quick,** flying, **expeditious,** prompt; quick-and-dirty <nonformal>, **immediate,** instant, on the spot; eleventh-hour, deathbed

**last name** NOUNS **surname, family name,** cognomen, byname; **maiden name;** married name; patronymic, matronymic

**last resort** NOUNS **expedient,** means to an end, last expedient, last resource, *pis aller* <Fr>, last shift, trump, **recourse, resource, resort; hope**

**last rites** NOUNS **last offices,** last honors, funeral rites, last duty *or* service, funeral service, burial service, exequies, **obsequies; extreme unction;** viaticum

**last straw** NOUNS provocation, straw that broke the camel's back, match in the powder barrel

**Last Supper** NOUNS **Eucharist, Lord's Supper,** Communion, Holy Communion, **the Sacrament,** the Holy Sacrament

**last word** NOUNS 1 **authority**, directorship, management, jurisdiction, power, say <nonformal>; **ultimatum,** final word *or* offer, firm bid *or* price, sticking point; **substance, gist,** pith, spirit, essence, gravamen, name of the game *and* meat and potatoes *and* bottom line <all nonformal>
2 **the rage,** the thing, *le dernier cri* <Fr>, **the latest thing,** the in thing *and* the latest wrinkle <both nonformal>; **acme of perfection,** pink, pink of perfection, culmination, perfection, height, top, acme, ultimate, summit, pinnacle, peak, highest pitch, climax, consummation, *ne plus ultra* <L>, a dream come true

**latch** VERBS **fasten,** secure; **lock,** lock up, lock out, key, padlock, bolt, bar

**late** ADJS 1 **belated, tardy,** slow, slow on the draw *or* uptake *or* trigger <all nonformal>, **behindhand,** never on time, backward, back, **overdue,** long-awaited, untimely; **unpunctual,** unready; latish; **delayed,** detained, **held up** <nonformal>, **retarded, arrested,** blocked, **hung up** *and* in a bind <both nonformal>; **postponed, in abeyance,** held up, put off, **on hold** *or* put on hold <nonformal>, on the back burner *or* put on the back burner <nonformal>

ADVS 2 **behind,** behindhand, belatedly, backward, slow, **behind time,** after time; far on, deep into; late in the day, at the last minute, at the eleventh hour, none too soon, in the nick of time, under the wire

**latecomer** NOUNS late arrival, Johnny-come-lately; slow starter, dawdler, dallier, dillydallier; late bloomer *or* developer; retardee

**latent** ADJS **concealed,** hidden, invisible; unrealized, submerged; ulterior; unknown

**later** ADJS 1 **subsequent, after,** after-the-fact, *post factum* and *ex post facto* <both L>, posterior, **following, succeeding,** successive, sequent, lineal, consecutive, ensuing, attendant; **future,** hereafter; **coming,** forthcoming, imminent, approaching, nearing, latter, **prospective**

ADVS 2 **subsequently, after, afterwards,** after that, after all, **next,** since; **thereafter,** thereon, thereupon, therewith, **then;** in the process *or* course of time, at a subsequent *or* later time, in the aftermath; *ex post facto* <L>; hard on the heels *or* on the heels; in the future

**latest** ADJS **state-of-the-art, newest,** the very latest, up-to-the-minute, last, most recent, newest of the new, farthest out

**lather** NOUNS 1 **dither, tizzy** <nonformal>, swivet, foofaraw, **pucker** <nonformal>, **twitter,** twitteration <nonformal>, **flutter, fluster,** flusteration *and* flustration <both nonformal>, **fret, fuss,** pother, bother, stew *and* snit <both nonformal>, flap; emotional crisis, *crise* <Fr>

2 **foam, froth; spume,** sea foam, scud; **suds,** soapsuds

VERBS 3 **foam, froth,** spume, cream; suds, sud

**latitude** NOUNS **scope, room,** range, way, field, maneuvering space *or* room, room to swing a cat <nonformal>; **margin,** clearance, **space,** open space *or* field, elbowroom, breathing space, **leeway** <nonformal>, sea room, wide berth; **tolerance; free scope,** full *or* ample scope, **free hand,** free play, free course; **carte blanche,** blank check; no holds barred; rope, long rope *or* tether, rope enough to hang oneself

**lattice** NOUNS **network,** interlacement, intertwinement, intertexture, texture, reticulum, reticulation; **net,** netting; **mesh,** meshes; **web,** webbing; weave, weft; latticework; hachure *or* hatchure, hatching, crosshatching; **grid,** gridiron

**laud** VERBS **praise,** bepraise, talk one up <nonformal>; belaud; **eulogize,** panegyrize, pay tribute, salute, hand it to one <nonformal>; **extol, glorify,** magnify, exalt, bless; cry up, blow up, puff, puff up; boast of, brag about <nonformal>, make much of; sound *or* resound the praises of, ring one's praises, sing the praises of, trumpet; overpraise, praise to excess, idolize, deify, apotheosize, adulate; put on a pedestal

**laudable** ADJS **praiseworthy,** worthy, **commendable,** estimable, admirable, meritorious, creditable; exemplary, model, unexceptionable; deserving, well-deserving;

**laudatory** ADJS **approbatory,** approbative, commendatory, **complimentary,** acclamatory, eulogistic, panegyric, panegyrical, encomiastic, **appreciative,** appreciatory; **admiring,** regardful, respectful; flattering

**laugh** NOUNS 1 **joke,** capital joke, good one, belly laugh, rib tickler, sidesplitter, thigh-slapper, howler, wow, scream, riot, panic

VERBS 2 burst out laughing, burst into laughter, burst out, laugh outright; laugh it up <nonformal>; **titter; giggle; chuckle, chortle;** cackle, crow; **snicker,** snigger, snort; **guffaw,** belly laugh, horselaugh; cachinnate, roar with laughter, shake with laughter, shake like jelly; be convulsed with laughter, go into convulsions, break up *and* crack up <both nonformal>, **split one's sides,** laugh fit to burst *or* bust <nonformal>, bust a gut *and* pee in *or* wet one's pants laughing <both nonformal>, **be in stitches** <nonformal>, hold one's sides, roll in the aisles <nonformal>; laugh oneself sick *or* silly *or* limp, die laughing; laugh in one's sleeve, laugh up one's sleeve

**laughable** ADJS **absurd, nonsensical,** insensate, ridiculous, ludicrous; **foolish, crazy;** preposterous, cockamamie <nonformal>, fantastic, fantastical, grotesque, monstrous, wild, weird, **outrageous,** incredible, beyond belief, *outré* <Fr>, extravagant, **bizarre**

**laugh at** VERBS **ridicule, deride,** ride <nonformal>, make a laughingstock *or* a mockery of; roast <nonformal>; **make fun** *or* **game of, poke fun at,** make merry with, put one on *and* pull one's leg <both nonformal>; laugh in one's face, grin at, smile at, snicker *or* snigger at; **laugh to scorn,** hold in derision, laugh out of court, hoot down

**laughter** NOUNS **laughing, hilarity**, risibility; **laugh;** boff *and* boffola *and* yuck <all nonformal>; **titter; giggle; chuckle, chortle;** cackle, crow; **snicker,** snigger, snort; guffaw, **horselaugh; hearty laugh, belly laugh** <nonformal>, Homeric laughter, cachinnation; gales of laughter; fit of laughter, convulsion

*laughter holding both his sides*
MILTON

**launch** NOUNS 1 **beginning, commencement, start,** running *or* flying start, starting point, square one <nonformal>, **outset,** outbreak, **onset,** oncoming; **foundation,** establishing, institution, origin, origination, establishment, setting-up, setting in motion; **launching,** launch *or* launching pad
VERBS 2 **inaugurate,** institute, **found, establish,** set up <nonformal>; **start,** start off, start up, give a start, crank up, give a push *or* shove <nonformal>, jump-start, kick-start, **put** *or* **set in motion, set on foot,** set going *or* agoing, start going; **kick off** *and* **start the ball rolling** <both nonformal>; get off the ground *or* off the mark

**launder** VERBS **wash,** tub; **wash up** *or* out *or* away; **rinse,** rinse out, flush, flush out, irrigate, sluice, sluice out; **scrub; clean,** cleanse

**laundress** NOUNS **washer,** launderer; laundrywoman, **washerwoman,** washwoman, washerwife <Scots>

**laundry** NOUNS **washery,** washhouse, washshed; **coin laundry, Laundromat** <trademark>, **launderette,** coin-operated laundry, laundrette <Brit>, washateria; automatic laundry; hand laundry

**laundry list** NOUNS schedule *or* program of operation, **order of the day,** things to be done, **agenda,** list of agenda; wish list <both nonformal>

**laurels** NOUNS **championship,** crown, palms, first prize, blue ribbon, trophy, chaplet, wreath, garland, **feather in one's cap** <nonformal>; civic crown *or* garland *or* wreath; **cup,** loving cup

**lavatory** NOUNS **latrine,** convenience, **toilet,** toilet room, water closet *or* WC <nonformal>; loo <Brit nonformal>; washroom, public convenience; **bathroom, rest room,** comfort station *or* room; ladies' *or* women's *or* girls' *or* little girls' *or* powder room <nonformal>; men's *or* boys' *or* little boys' room <nonformal>

**lavish** VERBS 1 **give freely,** give cheerfully, give with an open hand, give with both hands, put one's hands in one's pockets, open the purse, loosen *or* untie the purse strings; **spare no expense,** spare nothing, not count the cost, let money be no object; **heap upon,** lavish upon, shower down upon; **squander,** slather, blow <nonformal>, play ducks and drakes with; **throw away,** throw one's money away, throw money around, **spend money like water,** hang the expense, spend as if money grew on trees, spend money as if it were going out of style, throw money around, spend like a drunken sailor
ADJS 2 **liberal, free,** free with one's money, free-spending; **generous, munificent,** large, princely, handsome; **unselfish,** ungrudging; **unsparing,** unstinting, stintless, unstinted; **bountiful,** bounteous, profuse; **openhanded,** freehanded, open; **prodigal,** extravagant, overliberal, overgenerous, overlavish, **spendthrift, wasteful,** profligate, dissipative; penny-wise and pound-foolish; easy come, easy go
3 **ornate,** purple <nonformal>, colored, **fancy; embellished, embroidered,** adorned, decorated, festooned, overcharged, overloaded, befrilled; **flowery, florid,** lush, luxuriant

**law** NOUNS **rule, canon, maxim,** dictum, moral, moralism; **norm, standard;** formula, form; rule of action *or* conduct, moral precept; guiding principle, golden rule; **code; legal system,** system of laws

**the Law** NOUNS **Old Testament,** Tenach;

Hexateuch, Octateuch; Pentateuch, Chumash, Five Books of Moses, **Torah,** the Jewish *or* Mosaic Law, Law of Moses

**the law** NOUNS

<nonformal> cop, copper, John Law, bluecoat, bull, flatfoot, gumshoe, gendarme, shamus, dick; the cops, the fuzz; New York's finest

**law-abiding** ADJS **honest, upright,** uprighteous, **upstanding,** erect, right, **righteous, virtuous, good,** clean, squeaky-clean <nonformal>, **decent; respectable,** highly respectable; **principled, high-principled,** high-minded, right-minded; uncorrupt, uncorrupted, inviolate; law-loving, law-revering

**law and order** NOUNS **peacefulness,** tranquillity, serenity, calmness, quiet, peace and quiet, quietude, quietness, quiet life, restfulness; order, orderliness

**lawbreaker** NOUNS **criminal,** felon, perpetrator, crook *and* perp <both nonformal>, public enemy, scofflaw

**lawful** ADJS **legal, legitimate,** legit *and* kosher <both nonformal>, competent, **licit,** rightful, according to law, within the law

**lawless** ADJS **illegal,** unlawful, illegitimate, **illicit,** nonlicit, nonlegal, lawless, wrongful, fraudulent, creative <nonformal>, **against the law; licentious, ungoverned,** undisciplined, unrestrained; insubordinate, mutinous, disobedient; **uncontrolled,** uncurbed, unbridled, unchecked, rampant, untrammeled, unreined, reinless, anything goes; **irresponsible,** wildcat, unaccountable

**lawmaker** NOUNS **legislator,** solon, lawgiver; **congressman,** congresswoman, Member of Congress; **senator; representative;** state senator, assemblyman, assemblywoman, freeholder, councilman, councilwoman, councilperson

**lawyer** NOUNS 1 **attorney, attorney-at-law,** barrister, barrister-at-law, **counselor,** counselor-at-law, **counsel,** legal counsel *or* counselor, legal adviser, legal expert, **solicitor, advocate, pleader;** member of the bar, legal practitioner, officer of the court; smart lawyer, pettifogger, Philadelphia lawyer; sea lawyer, latrine *or* guardhouse lawyer <nonformal>

2 <nonformal> **shyster, mouthpiece, ambulance chaser,** lip, fixer, legal eagle

**lax** ADJS **slack, loose,** relaxed; imprecise, sloppy <nonformal>, careless, slipshod; remiss, negligent; indifferent; weak; impotent; untrammeled, unrestrained

**laxative** NOUNS **cathartic, physic, purge, purgative,** aperient, carminative, diuretic

**lay** NOUNS 1 **song,** *Lied* <Ger>, *chanson* <Fr>, carol, **ditty,** canticle, lilt; **ballad,** ballade, *ballata* <Ital>; *canzone* <Ital>; canzonet, *canzonetta* <Ital>
ADJS 2 laic *or* laical; **nonecclesiastical,** nonclerical, nonministerial, nonpastoral, nonordained; nonreligious; **secular,** secularist; secularistic; temporal, popular, civil

**lay down** VERBS **store, stow,** lay in store; lay in a supply *or* stock *or* store, store away, stow away, **put away, lay away,** put *or* lay by, pack away, bundle away, salt away *and* sock away *and* squirrel away <all nonformal>

**layer** NOUNS 1 thickness; **level, tier,** stage, story, floor, gallery, step, ledge, deck; **stratum,** seam, *couche* <Fr>, belt, band, **bed, course,** measures; zone; shelf; **overlayer, superstratum,** overstory, topsoil; **underlayer, substratum,** understratum, understory
VERBS 2 lay down, lay up, **stratify,** arrange in layers *or* levels *or* strata *or* tiers, **laminate;** flake, scale; delaminate, desquamate, exfoliate

**layman** NOUNS 1 laic, member of the laity, secular, churchman, **parishioner,** church member; brother, sister, lay brother, lay sister; laywoman, churchwoman; catchumen; communicant; **amateur,** nonprofessional

**layoff** NOUNS **dismissal, discharge,** forced separation, *congé* <Fr>; outplacement; **firing** *and* canning <both nonformal>, **cashiering,** drumming out, dishonorable discharge, rogue's march; disemployment, removal, surplusing, displacing, furloughing; suspension; **retirement;** the bounce, **the sack** <nonformal>; the boot *and* the gate *and* the ax <all nonformal>; walking papers *or* ticket <nonformal>, pink slip <nonformal>

**lay off** VERBS 1 **discontinue, desist, refrain,** leave off, give over, **have done with;** cut it out *and* drop it *and* knock it off <all nonformal>, relinquish, renounce, abandon

2 **dismiss, discharge, expel, cashier,** drum out, disemploy, outplace, separate involuntarily, suspend, surplus, furlough, turn off, make redundant, riff <nonformal>, turn out, release, let go, let out, remove, displace, replace, strike off the rolls, give the pink slip

**layout** NOUNS **arrangement, formation,** structure, configuration, array, makeup, lineup, setup

**layover** NOUNS **sojourn,** sojourning, sojournment, temporary stay; **stay,** stop; **stopover,** stopoff, stayover

**lazy** ADJS **indolent,** bone-lazy, **slothful,** workshy, ergophobic; **shiftless,** do-less <nonformal>; drony, dronish, parasitic, cadging, sponging, scrounging; lackadaisical; remiss, slack

**lazybones** NOUNS lazyboots, lazylegs, indolent, lie-abed, slugabed

**leach** VERBS **percolate,** lixiviate, edulcorate <old>; **trickle, dribble,** dripple, **drip,** drop, spurtle; **filter, extract,** drain, wash away

**lead** NOUNS 1 **superiority,** preeminence, greatness, transcendence *or* transcendency, ascendancy *or* ascendance, prestige, favor, prepotence *or* prepotency, preponderance; predominance *or* predominancy

2 **clue,** hot lead <nonformal>; **evidence; hint,** intimation, suggestion

3 **role,** starring *or* lead *or* leading role, fat part, leading man, leading woman *or* lady, hero, heroine; romantic lead; juvenile lead

VERBS 4 **head,** spearhead, stand at the head, stand first, be way ahead <nonformal>, head the line; take the lead, go in the lead, **lead the way,** break the trail, be the bellwether, lead the pack; be the point *or* point man; **light the way,** show the way, beacon, guide

5 **rule, command,** possess authority, have the authority, have the say *or* the last word, have the whip hand *and* hold all the aces <both nonformal>; **govern,** regulate; **wield authority**

**leaden** ADJS 1 **colorless,** dull, flat, mat, dead, dingy, muddy, lusterless, lackluster; livid, lead-gray

2 **torpid,** languorous, languid, apathetic, phlegmatic, **sluggish,** logy, dopey <nonformal>, groggy, heavy, slack, tame, **dead,** lifeless

3 **stiff, stilted, formal,** Latinate, *guindé* <Fr>, **labored,** ponderous, elephantine, lumbering, cumbrous, heavy, unwieldy, sesquipedalian, inkhorn, turgid, bombastic, pompous

**leader** NOUNS pacemaker, pacesetter; bellwether, bell mare, bell cow, Judas goat; standard-bearer, torchbearer; **leader of men,** born leader, charismatic leader *or* figure, inspired leader; **conductor,** symphonic conductor, **music director,** director, *Kapellmeister* <Ger>; **orchestra leader,** band leader, bandmaster, band major, drum major

**leadership** NOUNS **supremacy, primacy,** paramountcy, **first place,** height, acme, zenith, be-all and end-all, summit, top spot <nonformal>; **influence,** influentiality; **prestige,** favor, good feeling, credit, esteem, repute, personality, charisma, magnetism, charm, enchantment; **weight,** moment, consequence, importance, eminence

**leading** ADJS 1 **heading,** precessional, precedent, precursory, foregoing; **first, foremost,** headmost; **preceding,** antecedent; prior; up-front <nonformal>, first, chief, head, prime, primary; **ahead, in front,** one-up, one jump *or* move ahead

2 **dominant,** predominant, predominate, preponderant, preponderate, **paramount,** supreme, number one <nonformal>, hegemonic, hegemonistic; ascendant, in the ascendant, in ascendancy; at the head, in chief; in charge

**leaf** NOUNS lamina, lamella; **sheet,** *feuille* <Fr>, foil; frond; leaflet, foliole; **blade,** spear, spire, pile, flag; **needle**

**leaflet** NOUNS **folder, handbill,** bill, flier, throwaway, handout, circular, broadside, broadsheet; **booklet,** pamphlet, brochure, chapbook, **tract**

**leafy** ADJS foliated, foliate, foliose, foliaged, leaved

**league** NOUNS affiliation, **alliance,** allying, alignment, association, consociation, combination, union, unification, **coalition,** fusion, merger, coalescence, coadunation, amalgamation, **federation, confederation,** confederacy, consolidation, incorporation, inclusion, integration

**leak** NOUNS 1 **leakage,** leaking, weeping <nonformal>; **dripping,** drippings, **drip,** dribble, drop, trickle

2 **divulgence, divulging,** divulgement, divulgation, letting out; **betrayal,** unwitting disclosure, indiscretion; communi-

cation leak; **blabbing** *and* blabbering <both nonformal>, babbling; **tattling**
VERBS 3 **leak out, drip,** dribble, drop, trickle, trill, distill
4 **disclose,** reveal, let out, show, impart, discover, let slip out, let the cat out of the bag *and* spill the beans <both nonformal>; take the lid off, **bring to light,** bring into the open, hold up to view

**leakproof** ADJS **watertight, waterproof,** moistureproof, seepproof, dripproof, stormproof, stormtight, rainproof, raintight

**leaky** ADJS exudative, exuding, transudative; percolative; porous, permeable, pervious, oozy, runny, weepy

**lean** VERBS 1 **incline; slope, slant,** slaunch <nonformal>, rake, pitch, grade, bank, shelve; **tilt, tip, list, cant,** careen, keel, sidle, swag, sway; **gravitate,** tend, tend to go, point, head, lead; **be willing, be game** <nonformal>, be ready; be disposed, **trend,** have a penchant
ADJS 2 lean-looking, **skinny** <nonformal>, fleshless, lean-fleshed, thin-fleshed, **spare,** meager, **scrawny,** scraggy, thin-bellied, gaunt, lank, lanky; **bony, rawboned,** bare-boned, rattle-boned <nonformal>, skeletal, **mere skin and bones, all skin and bones, nothing but skin and bones;** twiggy; thin, slim, slender

**leaning** NOUNS 1 **inclination,** lean, angularity; **slant,** slaunch <nonformal>, rake, **slope; tilt, tip,** pitch, **list, cant,** swag, sway; leaning tower, tower of Pisa; **preference, predilection,** proclivity, bent, affinity, prepossession, predisposition, partiality, penchant, bias, tendency, taste
ADJS 2 **inclining,** inclined, inclinatory, inclinational; recumbent; **sloping,** sloped, aslope; raking, pitched; **slanting,** slanted, slant, aslant, slantways, slantwise; **tilting,** tilted, atilt, tipped, **tipping,** tipsy, listing, **canting,** careening

**lean-to** NOUNS **hut,** hutch, **shack, shanty,** crib, hole-in-the-wall <nonformal>, **shed**

**leap** NOUNS 1 forward leap *or* jump, quantum jump *or* leap, spring, forward spring; **increase, gain,** augmentation, greatening, **enlargement, amplification, growth,** development, widening, spread, broadening, elevation, **extension,** aggrandizement, access, accession, **increment,** accretion
2 **jump,** hop, spring, skip, bound, bounce; pounce; upleap, upspring, jump-off; **hurdle; vault,** pole vault; jeté, grand jeté, tour jeté, saut de basque
VERBS 3 **jump,** vault, spring, skip, hop, bound, bounce; leap over, jump over; leapfrog; **hurdle,** clear, negotiate

**learn** VERBS **come to know, be informed** *or* **apprised of,** have it reported, get the facts, **get wise to** <nonformal>, **get hep to** *and* **next to** *and* **on to** <all nonformal>; become conscious *or* aware of, become alive *or* awake to, awaken to, tumble to <nonformal>, open one's eyes to; get into one's head, get through one's thick skull <nonformal>; **gain knowledge,** pick up information, gather *or* collect *or* glean knowledge *or* learning; stock *or* store the mind, improve *or* broaden the mind; stuff *or* cram the mind; **find out, ascertain, discover,** find, determine

**learned** ADJS **erudite, educated, cultured,** cultivated, lettered, literate, civilized, **scholarly,** scholastic, studious; wise; **profound,** deep, abstruse; **encyclopedic,** pansophic, polymath *or* polymathic, polyhistoric

**learner** NOUNS **student, pupil,** scholar, studier, educatee, **trainee,** *élève* <Fr>; tutee; **beginner,** neophyte, tyro; **apprentice**

**learning** NOUNS **enlightenment, education, schooling,** instruction, edification, illumination; attainments, accomplishments, skills; sophistication; store of knowledge; liberal education; acquisition of knowledge

**lease** NOUNS 1 **occupancy,** occupation; **tenancy,** tenantry, charter, leasehold, sublease, underlease, undertenancy; **rental, rent;** let <Brit>
VERBS 2 **rent out, rent;** lease out; let *and* let off *and* let out <all Brit>; charter; **sublease, sublet,** underlet

**leash** NOUNS 1 **tether,** spancel, lead, leading string; **rein;** hobble, hopple
VERBS 2 **bind, restrain, tie,** tie up, put the clamps on, **strap,** lash, pinion, fasten, secure, make fast; hobble, hopple, fetter, put on a lead, spancel; tether, picket, moor, anchor

**least** ADJS **smallest,** littlest, slightest, **lowest,** shortest; minimum, minimal, minim

**leatherneck** NOUNS **marine,** gyrene *and* devil dog <both nonformal>; horse marine; boot <nonformal>

**leave** NOUNS 1 **vacation,** holiday; **time off;** leave of absence, furlough; liberty, shore leave; **sabbatical,** sabbatical leave *or* year
2 **leave-taking, parting, departure,** congé; **send-off,** Godspeed; **adieu,** one's adieus, **farewell,** aloha, **good-bye;** valedictory address, valedictory, valediction, parting words; parting *or* Parthian shot
3 **permission, allowance,** vouchsafement; **consent**; permission to enter, admission, ticket, ticket of admission; **license,** liberty; **okay** *and* **OK** *and* **nod** *and* **go-ahead** *and* **green light** *and* **go sign** *and* **thumbs-up** <all nonformal>
VERBS 4 **depart,** make off, begone, be off, take oneself off *or* away, take one's departure, take leave *or* take one's leave, **go, go away, go off, get off** *or* **away,** get under way, come away, go one's way, go *or* get along, be getting along, go on, get on; move off *or* away, move out, march off *or* away; **pull out;** decamp; exit; take *or* break *or* tear oneself away, take oneself off, take wing *or* flight

5 <nonformal> **split,** bugger off, fuck off, f off, make tracks, pull up stakes, push along, scarper <Brit>, push off, skedaddle *or* absquatulate <old> **haul ass,** bag ass, **beat it, blow,** boogie, bug out, cut, **cut out,** cut and run, make tracks, peel out, piss off, *and* scarper <Brit nonformal>, scram, shove off

6 **abandon,** desert, forsake; **quit,** leave behind, take leave of, depart from, absent oneself from, turn one's back upon, turn one's tail upon, say goodbye to, bid a long farewell to, walk away, **walk** *or* **run out on** <nonformal>, **leave flat** *and* leave high and dry *or* holding the bag *or* in the lurch <all nonformal>, leave one to one's fate, throw to the wolves <nonformal>
7 **bequeath, will,** will and bequeath, **devise, will to,** hand down, hand on, pass on, transmit

**leave of absence** NOUNS **vacation, time off;** day off, week off, month off, etc; paid vacation; weekend; **leave, furlough; liberty,** shore leave; **sabbatical,** sabbatical leave *or* year

**leave-taking** NOUNS **leave, parting, departure,** congé; **send-off,** Godspeed; **adieu,** one's adieus, **farewell,** aloha, **good-bye**

**leavings** NOUNS **remainder,** remains, remnant, residue, residuum, rest, balance; **leftovers, refuse,** odds and ends, scraps, rags, **rubbish, waste,** orts, candle ends; scourings, offscourings; parings, sweepings, filings, shavings, sawdust; chaff, straw, stubble, husks; **debris,** detritus, ruins; end, fag end

**lecher** NOUNS **satyr, goat,** old goat, **dirty old man;** whorer *or* whoremonger <both old>, whoremaster, whorehound <nonformal>; Priapus; gynecomaniac; erotomaniac, eroticomaniac, aphrodisiomaniac

**lechery** NOUNS **philandering,** philander, lady-killing <nonformal>; **lasciviousness, lecherousness, lewdness,** bawdiness, **dirtiness,** salacity, salaciousness, **carnality,** animality, fleshliness, **sexuality, sexiness, lust, lustfulness**

*an expense of spirit in a waste of shame*
*is lust in action*
SHAKESPEARE

**lectern** NOUNS **reading stand,** ambo, reading desk; **table,** board, **stand**

**lecture** NOUNS 1 **lesson, teaching, instruction,** lecture-demonstration, harangue, **discourse,** disquisition, exposition, **talk,** homily, **sermon,** preachment
2 **rebuke, reprimand, reproach,** reprehension, **scolding, chiding,** rating, **upbraiding,** objurgation; **admonishment, admonition**
VERBS 3 **expound,** exposit; explain; **discourse,** harangue, hold forth, give *or* read a lesson; **preach,** sermonize; **reprove, rebuke, reprimand,** reprehend, put a flea in one's ear, **scold, chide,** rate, **admonish, upbraid,** objurgate, have words with, take a hard line with

**lecturing** NOUNS **public speaking, declamation, speechmaking, speaking,** speechification <nonformal>, speeching; **oratory,** platform oratory *or* speaking

**ledge** NOUNS **shelf,** shoulder, corbel, beam-end; mantel, mantelshelf, mantelpiece; retable, superaltar, gradin, *gradino* <Ital>, predella

**ledger** NOUNS **account book, journal,**

daybook; **register,** registry, **record book,** books; **cashbook**

**leech** NOUNS 1 **parasite,** barnacle; **sponger,** sponge <nonformal>, freeloader <nonformal>, smell-feast; beat *and* deadbeat <both nonformal>; **extortionist,** extortioner, **blackmailer,** racketeer, shakedown artist <nonformal>, **bloodsucker,** vampire; profiteer
VERBS 2 bleed, let blood, phlebotomize

**leer** NOUNS 1 **look,** the eye *and* a look-see *and* a gander <all nonformal>, eye, view, regard; sidelong look; leering look; snigger, **smirk,** sardonic grin, fleer, **sneer,** snort
VERBS 2 **scrutinize, survey, eye,** contemplate, look over, give the eye *or* the once-over <nonformal>; **ogle,** ogle at, leer at, give one the glad eye; take a long, hard look; size up <nonformal>; take stock of; wink, glance, raise one's eyebrows

**leery** ADJS **wary,** chary, cagey <nonformal>, **suspicious,** suspecting, **distrustful,** mistrustful, shy, cautious, guarded; **skeptical**

**leeway** NOUNS **room, latitude,** swing, play, way; room to spare, room to swing a cat <nonformal>, **elbowroom, margin;** breathing space; sea room; headroom, clearance

**left** NOUNS 1 **left side, left hand,** left-hand side, wrong side <nonformal>, near *or* nigh side <of a horse or vehicle>, portside, port, larboard; Gospel side, cantorial side, verso <of a book>
2 left wing, left-winger, radical, liberal, progressive
ADJS 3 **left-hand,** sinister, sinistral; near, nigh; **larboard, port;** left-wing, left-wingish, left-of-center, radical, liberal, progressive, wet <Brit nonformal>
4 **remaining, surviving, extant,** vestigial, over, **leftover,** still around, remnant, remanent, odd; **spare,** to spare; unused, unconsumed; **surplus,** superfluous; **outstanding,** unmet, unresolved; **abandoned,** forsaken, deserted
ADVS 5 **leftward,** leftwards, leftwardly, **to the left,** sinistrally, sinister, sinistrad; on the left; larboard, port, aport

**left-handed** ADJS 1 **oblique; devious,** deviant, deviative, divergent, digressive, divagational, deflectional, excursive; **indirect,** side, sidelong; sinister, sinistral, sinistromanual, sinistral, lefty *and* southpaw <both nonformal>; backhand, backhanded; circuitous; insulting
2 <nonformal> **southpaw** *and* lefty *and* portsider

**leftist** NOUNS 1 **liberal,** liberalist, wet <Brit nonformal>, **progressive,** progressivist, **left-winger; left**
ADJS 2 **liberal, liberalistic,** liberalist, wet <Brit nonformal>, bleeding-heart <nonformal>; **progressive,** progressivistic; **left-wing,** on the left, left of center

**leftover** NOUNS 1 **surplus,** surplusage, leftovers, plus, **overplus,** overstock, **overage,** overset, overrun, **overmeasure, oversupply;** margin; **remainder, balance,** extra, spare, something extra *or* to spare; bonus, dividend
ADJS 2 **remaining, surviving, extant,** vestigial, over, left, still around, remnant, remanent, odd; **spare,** to spare; unused, unconsumed; **surplus,** superfluous; **outstanding,** unmet, unresolved; net

**left wing** NOUNS **liberalism, progressivism,** leftism; **left,** progressiveness

**left-wing** ADJS **liberal, liberalistic,** liberalist, wet <Brit nonformal>, bleeding-heart <nonformal>; **progressive,** progressivistic; **leftist,** on the left, left of center

**leg** NOUNS 1 **limb, shank;** hind leg, foreleg; gamb, jamb <heraldry>

2 <nonformal> gams, stems, trotters, hind legs, underpinnings, wheels, shanks, sticks, pins, stumps

**legacy** NOUNS **bequest,** bequeathal, devise; inheritance, **heritage,** patrimony, birthright; **outgrowth,** spin-off, offshoot, offspring, issue, aftermath

**legal** ADJS **legitimate,** legit *and* kosher <both nonformal>, competent, **licit, lawful,** rightful, according to law, within the law; within the scope of the law; **enforceable,** legally binding

**legality** NOUNS **legitimacy, lawfulness,** legitimateness, licitness, rightfulness, validity, scope, applicability; **jurisdiction**; legal process, legal form, **due process**

**legalize** VERBS **legitimize,** legitimatize, legitimate, make legal, declare lawful, **decriminalize;** wash or launder money; validate; **authorize, sanction;** constitute, ordain, establish, put in force; prescribe, formulate; regulate, make a regulation

**legal system** NOUNS **law,** system of laws, legal branch *or* specialty; **judiciary,** judicial *or* court system, judicature, judicatory, court, the courts; criminal-justice system; the wheels of justice, judicial process

**legatee** NOUNS **beneficiary,** allottee, donee, grantee, patentee; assignee, **assign; devisee,** legatary <old>; stipendiary; pensioner, pensionary; annuitant

**legation** NOUNS **mission,** diplomatic mission, diplomatic staff *or* corps, *corps diplomatique* <Fr>; **embassy,** consular service; consulate, chancery, chancellery

**legend** NOUNS 1 **memory, remembrance,** blessed *or* sacred memory, heroic legend *or* myth; **immortality,** lasting *or* undying fame, niche in the hall of fame, secure place in history
2 **mythology,** mythicism; **lore, folklore,** folktale, myth, mythical lore; fairy lore, fairyism
3 **caption,** title, heading, head, superscription, rubric; motto, **epigraph**

**legendary** ADJS **famous,** famed, honored, **renowned, celebrated, popular,** acclaimed, much acclaimed, sought-after, hot *and* world-class <both nonformal>, **notorious, well-known,** best-known, in everyone's mouth, on everyone's tongue *or* lips; **extraordinary, exceptional, remarkable,** noteworthy, **wonderful, marvelous,** fabulous; fabled, mythical, folkloric; **traditional;** mythological, heroic; unwritten, oral, handed down

**legible** ADJS **decipherable, readable,** fair; uncoded, unenciphered, in the clear, clear, plaintext

**legion** NOUNS **throng, multitude, horde,** host, heap <nonformal>, army, panoply; flock, cluster, galaxy

**legislate** VERBS make *or* enact laws, **enact, pass,** constitute, ordain, put in force; **put through,** jam *or* steamroller *or* railroad through <nonformal>, lobby through; **filibuster; logroll,** roll logs

**legislation** NOUNS **lawmaking,** legislature <old>; **enactment,** enaction, constitution, passage, passing; **law,** *lex, jus* <both L>, **statute,** rubric, **canon,** institution; **ordinance; measure**

**legislator** NOUNS **lawmaker,** solon, lawgiver; **congressman,** congresswoman, Member of Congress; **senator; representative;** state senator, assemblyman, assemblywoman, freeholder, councilman, councilwoman, councilperson, city father

**legislature** NOUNS legislative body; **parliament, congress, assembly,** general assembly, house of assembly, legislative assembly, **national assembly, chamber of deputies,** federal assembly, diet, soviet, court; legislative chamber, **upper chamber** *or* **house, lower chamber** *or* **house;** state legislature, state assembly; provincial legislature, provincial parliament; city council, city board, common council, commission; representative town meeting, town meeting

**legitimate** ADJS **justifiable,** vindicable, defensible; **warrantable,** allowable, admissible, reasonable, colorable; **legal,** legit *and* kosher <both nonformal>, competent, **licit, lawful,** rightful, according to law, within the law

**leisure** NOUNS 1 **ease, convenience,** freedom; retirement, semiretirement; rest, repose; **free time, spare time,** goof-off time <nonformal>, odd moments, idle hours; **vacation, holiday,** time off, day off, recess, playtime
ADJS 2 **leisured;** idle, unoccupied, free, open, spare; retired, semiretired

**lend** VERBS **loan, advance,** accommodate with; loan-shark <nonformal>; float *or* negotiate a loan; lend-lease, lease-lend

**length** NOUNS longness, lengthiness, overall length; wheelbase; **extent,** extension, **measure,** span, reach, stretch; **distance**

**lengthen** VERBS **prolong,** prolongate, **elongate, extend,** produce, **protract,** continue; make prolix; lengthen out, let out, **draw** *or* drag *or* stretch *or* string *or* spin out; **stretch,** draw, pull

**lengthy** ADJS **long;** longish, longsome; **extensive, far-reaching,** fargoing, far-flung; sesquipedalian, sesquipedal; **time-consuming,** interminable, without end, no end of *or* to, **protracted,** extended, *de longue haleine* <Fr>, **long-drawn-out,** long-spun, spun-out, endless, unrelenting

**leniency** NOUNS lenience, lenientness, lenity; **clemency,** clementness, **mercifulness,** mercy, **humaneness,** humanity, pity, **compassion**; **mildness, gentleness,** tenderness, softness, moderateness; **easiness,** easygoingness; laxness; **forbearance,** forbearing, patience; acceptance, **tolerance**

**lenient** ADJS **tolerant,** tolerative, tolerating, accepting; condoning, understanding, **indulgent, forbearing; accommodating,** accommodative, at one's service, **helpful,** agreeable, **obliging,** indulgent

**leper** NOUNS **outcast,** social outcast, outcast of society, **pariah,** untouchable; outcaste; *déclassé* <Fr>; undesirable; *persona non grata* <L>, unacceptable person

**leprechaun** NOUNS **fairy, sprite, fay,** fairy man *or* woman; **elf,** brownie, pixie, gremlin, ouphe, hob, cluricaune, puca *or* pooka *or* pwca, kobold, nisse, peri; **imp,** goblin; **gnome,** dwarf

**lesbian** NOUNS 1 **homosexual,** gay person, homosexualist, sapphist, tribade, fricatrice <old>; butch *and* dyke <both nonformal>
ADJS 2 **homosexual,** homoerotic, sapphic, tribadistic; mannish, butch *and* dykey <both nonformal>

**lesion** NOUNS **trauma,** wound, injury, hurt; **cut,** incision, scratch, gash; puncture, stab, stab wound; flesh wound; **laceration,** mutilation; **sore,** sore spot, tender spot

**less** ADJS 1 **reduced, decreased,** diminished, lowered, dropped, fallen; bated, **abated; deflated,** contracted, shrunk, shrunken; **simplified**; scaled-down, miniaturized; minimized, belittled; **lower,** lesser, smaller, shorter
ADVS 2 **decreasingly,** diminishingly, less and less, ever less; on a declining scale, at a declining rate

**lessee** NOUNS **tenant, occupant,** occupier, incumbent, **resident; renter,** hirer <Brit>, leaseholder; subtenant, sublessee, underlessee, undertenant

**lessen** VERBS **relieve,** give relief; **ease,** ease matters; **relax,** slacken; **reduce,** abate, remit; **alleviate, mitigate, palliate,** soften, pad, cushion, assuage, allay, defuse, lay, appease, mollify, subdue, soothe; **decrease, diminish; decline, subside,** shrink, wane, wither, ebb, ebb away, dwindle, languish, sink, sag, die down *or* away, wind down, taper off *and* trail off *or* away *and* tail off *or* away <all nonformal>; **extenuate**

**lesser** ADJS **inferior, subservient,** subject, servile, low, **lowly,** humble, modest; less, lower, smaller, shorter; in the shade, thrown into the shade; **common,** vulgar, ordinary; **reduced,** decreased, diminished, lowered, fallen

**lesson** NOUNS **warning,** object lesson, **example,** deterrent example, warning piece; moral, moral of the story; **correction,** castigation, chastisement, spanking, rap on the knuckles; lecture, teaching, instruction, **talk,** homily, **sermon,** preachment

**let** VERBS **permit, allow,** admit, give permission, give leave, make possible; **allow** *or* **permit of;** give *or* leave room for, open the door to; consent; **grant,** accord, vouchsafe; **rent, lease,** hire, job, **charter; sublease, sublet,** underlet

**letdown** NOUNS **disappointment, comedown,** setback; **disillusionment,** descent, deflation, wounded *or* humbled pride; **slowdown,** slowup, **letup, slackoff,** ease-off, ease-up; bursting of the bubble

**let down** VERBS **disappoint,** defeat expectation *or* hope; **dash,** dash *or* blight *or* blast *or* crush one's hope; cast down; **disillusion; betray, double-cross** *and* two-time <both nonformal>, sell out *and* sell down the river <both nonformal>, turn in; let down one's side <nonformal>

**let go** VERBS 1 let pass, **let slip, let slide** *and* let ride <both nonformal>; **neglect,** overlook, disregard, not heed, not attend to, take for granted, **ignore;** not care for, not take care of
2 **exempt, free, release,** discharge, **let off** <nonformal>, set at liberty, set free, spring <nonformal>; **excuse,** spare, except, grant immunity, make a special case of; absolve
3 **let oneself go,** let loose *and* cut loose *and* let one's hair down <all nonformal>, **give way to,** open up, let it all hang out <nonformal>; go all out, pull out all the stops; go unrestrained, run wild, have one's fling, sow one's wild oats
4 **dismiss, discharge, expel, cashier,** drum out, disemploy, outplace, separate forcibly *or* involuntarily, **lay off,** suspend, surplus, furlough, turn off, make redundant, riff <nonformal>, turn out, release, let out, remove, displace, replace, strike off the rolls, give the pink slip

**lethal** ADJS **deadly, deathly,** deathful, killing, destructive, death-dealing, death-bringing; savage, brutal; internecine; **fatal, mortal,** malignant, malign, virulent, pernicious, baneful; **life-threatening,** terminal

**lethargic** ADJS **languid, languorous, list-**

**less,** lifeless, inanimate, enervated, debilitated, **pepless** <nonformal>, lackadaisical, slow, wan, logy, hebetudinous, supine, lymphatic, apathetic, **sluggish,** dopey <nonformal>, drugged, nodding, droopy, **dull,** heavy, leaden, lumpish, **torpid,** stultified, stuporous, **inert,** stagnant, stagnating, phlegmatic

**lethargy** NOUNS **languor,** languidness, languorousness, lackadaisicalness, lotus-eating; **listlessness,** lifelessness, inanimation, enervation, **dullness, sluggishness,** heaviness, dopiness <nonformal>, hebetude, supineness, **lassitude,** loginess

**letter** NOUNS **epistle, message,** communication, dispatch, missive; personal letter, business letter; **note, line,** chit

**letter carrier** NOUNS **postman, mailman,** mail carrier; postmaster, postmistress; postal clerk

**lettered** ADJS **learned, erudite, educated, cultured,** cultivated, literate, civilized, **scholarly,** scholastic, studious; **encyclopedic,** pansophic, polymath *or* polymathic, polyhistoric

**letter of credit** NOUNS **credit instrument;** paper credit; *lettre de créance* <Fr>, circular note; credit slip, credit memorandum, **negotiable instrument** *or* **paper,** commercial paper, paper, commercial letter of credit

**letters** NOUNS **literature, belles lettres,** polite literature, humane letters, *litterae humaniores* <L>, republic of letters; **scholarship, erudition,** eruditeness, learnedness

**letter writer** NOUNS **correspondent,** writer, communicator; pen pal <nonformal>

**letting go** NOUNS **relinquishment, release,** giving up, dispensation; **renunciation,** forgoing, forswearing, swearing off, resignation, abjuration, **abandonment; surrender,** cession, handover, turning over, **yielding**

**letup** NOUNS **pause, rest, break,** caesura, **recess, intermission,** interim, intermittence, interval, interlude, *intermezzo* <Ital>; **respite; interruption, suspension,** time-out, break in the action, breathing spell, cooling-off period

**levee** NOUNS **barrier, bar;** bank, embankment, dike

**level** NOUNS 1 **tier,** stage, story, floor, gallery, step, ledge, deck
2 **status, social status, economic status,** socioeconomic status *or* background, standing, footing, prestige, rank, ranking, place, station, position, degree, stratum
VERBS 3 **flatten, even,** align, smooth *or* smoothen, level out, smooth out, flush; grade, roll, roll flat, steamroller *or* steamroll; **raze,** rase, lay level, lay level with the ground; lay low *or* flat; **equalize;** equal out, even up, even off, square, level off, make both ends meet
ADJS 4 **horizontal, flat,** flattened; **even,** smooth, smoothened, smoothed out; table-like, tabular; **flush; plane,** rolled, trodden, squashed, rolled *or* trodden *or* squashed flat; flat as a pancake, flat as a board
5 **uniform, equable,** equal, **even; unvarying,** undeviating, unchanging, steady, stable; **consistent,** consonant, correspondent, accordant, homogeneous, **alike,** all alike, all of a piece, of a piece, consubstantial, monolithic
ADVS 6 **horizontally, flat,** flatly, flatways, flatwise; **evenly,** flush; **on a level**

**levelheaded** ADJS **sensible,** reasonable, rational, logical; **practical,** pragmatic; philosophical; commonsense, commonsensical <nonformal>; balanced, coolheaded, cool, **sound, sane,** sober, **sober-minded,** well-balanced

**leverage** NOUNS **influence,** influentiality; **power**, force, clout <nonformal>, potency, pressure, effect, indirect *or* incidental power, **say,** the final say, the last word, say-so *and* a lot to do with *or* to say about <all nonformal>, veto power; purchase; fulcrumage

**leviathan** NOUNS **behemoth, monster;** mammoth, mastodon; elephant, jumbo <nonformal>; whale; hippopotamus, hippo <nonformal>; **dinosaur**

**levitate** VERBS **ascend, rise, mount,** arise, hover, float, up, uprise, upgo, **go up,** rise up, come up

**levity** NOUNS **lightheartedness,** lightsomeness, lightness; **waggishness,** waggery; **playfulness,** sportiveness, **frivolity,** flippancy, merriment; panning *and* razzing *and* roasting *and* ragging <all nonformal>, **scoffing, jeering, sneering,** snickering, sniggering, smirking, grinning, leering, fleering, snorting, smart-aleckiness *and* joshing <both nonformal>, fooling, japery

**levy** NOUNS 1 **tax, taxation, duty,** tribute, taxes, rates <Brit>, contribution, assess-

ment, revenue enhancement, toll, **impost,** imposition
VERBS 2 **impose,** exact, demand; tax, task, charge, burden with, weight *or* freight with, weight down with, yoke with, **fasten upon,** saddle with, stick with <nonformal>; subject to

**lewd** ADJS **obscene,** adult, bawdy, ithyphallic, **ribald, pornographic, salacious,** sultry <nonformal>, lurid, **dirty, smutty,** raunchy <nonformal>, blue, smoking-room, impure, unchaste, unclean, **foul, filthy, nasty,** vile, fulsome, offensive, unprintable, unrepeatable, not fit for mixed company; **foul-mouthed,** foul-tongued, foul-spoken; Rabelaisian

**lexicon** NOUNS **vocabulary,** lexis, words, word stock, wordhoard, stock of words; phraseology; **thesaurus,** Roget's; **dictionary,** wordbook, Webster's; glossary, onomasticon, nomenclator; storehouse *or* treasury of words

**liability** NOUNS **disadvantage,** drawback; **detriment,** impairment, prejudice, loss, damage, hurt, harm, mischief, injury; **a step back** *or* **backward,** a loss of ground; **handicap**, disability; drag, millstone around one's neck; **exposure, openness,** nonimmunity, susceptibility

**liable** ADJS **likely,** prone; **probable; responsible,** legally responsible, answerable; **exposed,** susceptible, at risk, overexposed, open, like a sitting duck, **vulnerable**

**liaison** NOUNS 1 **love affair, affair,** affair of the heart, **amour, romance,** romantic tie *or* bond, something between, thing <nonformal>, entanglement, intrigue
2 **intermediary,** intermedium, mediary, medium; link, **connecting link,** tie, connection, **go-between**

**liar** NOUNS **fibber,** fibster, fabricator, fabulist, pseudologist; falsifier; **prevaricator,** equivocator, waffler <nonformal>, palterer; consummate liar, dirty liar; pathological liar, mythomaniac, pseudologue, confirmed *or* habitual liar; **perjurer,** false witness

**libel** NOUNS 1 **slander, scandal,** traducement; calumny, calumniation; backbiting, cattiness *and* bitchiness <both nonformal>
VERBS 2 **slander;** calumniate, traduce; stab in the back, backbite, speak ill of behind one's back

**liberal** NOUNS 1 **leftist,** left-winger; liberalist; libertarian; freethinker, latitudinarian, ecumenist, ecumenicist; bleeding heart, bleeding-heart liberal
ADJS 2 **free,** free with one's money, free-spending; **generous, munificent,** large, princely, handsome; **unselfish,** ungrudging; **unsparing, unstinting,** stintless, unstinted; **bountiful,** bounteous, **lavish,** profuse; **openhanded,** freehanded, open; **giving;** openhearted, **bighearted,** largehearted, greathearted, freehearted; **magnanimous**
3 **liberalistic,** liberalist, wet <Brit nonformal>, bleeding-heart <nonformal>; **progressive,** progressivistic; **leftist, left-wing,** on the left, left of center

**liberate** VERBS **free, deliver, set free,** set at liberty, set at large; **emancipate,** manumit, disenthrall; enfranchise, affranchise; **rescue; release,** loose, unloose, unleash, unfetter

**liberated** ADJS **freed, emancipated, released;** delivered, rescued, ransomed, redeemed; extricated, unbound, untied, unshackled, etc; free; on parole

**liberator** NOUNS **savior, redeemer,** deliverer, rescuer, freer, **emancipator,** manumitter

**libertarian** NOUNS 1 individualist, rugged individualist; free spirit; **liberal,** latitudinarian
ADJS 2 **liberal, liberal-minded,** liberalistic; freethinking, latitudinarian

**libertine** NOUNS **swinger** <nonformal>, **profligate, rake,** rakehell, rip <nonformal>, **roué,** wanton, womanizer, cocksman <nonformal>, walking phallus, debauchee, rounder <old>, **wolf** <nonformal>, woman chaser, skirt chaser <nonformal>, gay dog, gay deceiver, gallant, philanderer, lover-boy <nonformal>, lady-killer, Lothario, Don Juan, Casanova

**liberty** NOUNS **freedom; license,** run *and* the run of <both nonformal>; **civil liberty,** constitutional freedom; academic freedom

**libido** NOUNS **sexuality,** sexual nature, sexualism, love-life; sex drive, sexual instinct *or* urge

**library** NOUNS book depository; media center, media resource center, information center; **public library,** town *or* city *or* municipal library, county library, state library; school library, college library, university library; **special**

**library, circulating library, lending library** <Brit>; rental library; **book wagon, bookmobile**

**license** NOUNS 1 **lawlessness; licentiousness,** uncontrol, anything goes, unrestraint; indiscipline, insubordination, mutiny, disobedience; **profligacy, dissoluteness,** unbridledness, wildness, fastness, rakishness, gallantry, **libertinism,** libertinage
2 **franchise,** charter, patent, dispensation, release, waiver; **permit, warrant;** nihil obstat, imprimatur
VERBS 3 **authorize, sanction, warrant;** give official sanction *or* warrant, legitimize, validate, legalize; empower, give power, enable, entitle; charter, patent, enfranchise, franchise; accredit, certificate, certify

**licentious** ADJS **dissipated,** riotous, dissolute, debauched; free-living, high-living <nonformal>

**licit** ADJS **lawful, legitimate, legal,** legitimized, legalized, legitimated, decriminalized

**lick** VERBS 1 **lap up,** sponge *or* soak up, lap, slurp <nonformal>

2 <nonformal> **clobber, trim, skin alive, beat,** skunk, drub, massacre, whip, thrash, trim, hide, cut to pieces, lather, trounce, **lambaste**

**lid** NOUNS **cover,** top, cap, screw-top; operculum; stopper

**lie** NOUNS 1 **falsehood,** falsity, **untruth,** untruism, mendacity, **prevarication, fib,** flimflam *or* flam, a crock *and* a crock of shit <both nonformal>, *blague* <Fr>; **fiction,** pious fiction, legal fiction; half-truth, stretching of the truth, slight stretching, white lie, little white lie; a pack of lies
VERBS 2 **lie down, recline, repose,** lounge, sprawl, loll, drape *or* spread oneself, splay, lie limply; **lie flat** *or* prostrate *or* prone *or* supine, lie on one's face *or* back, lie on a level, hug the ground *or* deck
3 **fabricate,** invent, manufacture, trump up, make up, hatch, concoct, cook up *and* make out of whole cloth <both nonformal>, fudge <nonformal>, fake, hoke up <nonformal>

**lie detector** NOUNS polygraph, psychogalvanometer

**lie down** VERBS **recline**; prostrate, supinate, prone <nonformal>; flatten oneself, prostrate oneself; hit the ground *or* the dirt <nonformal>

**lieutenant** NOUNS **assistant, helper,** auxiliary, aider, **aid,** aide, paraprofessional; **attendant, second,** acolyte; adjutant, aide-de-camp; executive officer

**life** NOUNS **living, vitality,** being alive, having life, animation, animate existence; breath; liveliness, animal spirits, vivacity, spriteliness; **spirit,** verve, energy, adrenalin; pep *and* moxie *and* oomph *and* pizzazz *and* piss and vinegar <all nonformal>, **vim;** long life, longevity; life expectancy, life span; viability; lifetime; existence; **biography, memoir,** memorial, story, **life story,** adventures, fortunes, experiences

*one dem'd horrid grind*
DICKENS

*a comedy to those who think, a tragedy to those who feel*
H WALPOLE

**life force** NOUNS **soul,** spirit, indwelling spirit, force of life, living force, *vis vitae* or *vis vitalis* <both L>, **vital force** *or* energy, animating force *or* power *or* principle, inspiriting force *or* power *or* principle, archeus, élan vital, impulse of life, vital principle, **vital spark** *or* **flame,** spark of life, divine spark, life principle, vital spirit, vital fluid, anima

**lifeless** ADJS 1 **dead,** breathless, without life, inanimate, exanimate, without vital functions; **deceased, demised, defunct,** croaked <nonformal>, departed, departed this life, destitute of life, **gone, passed on,** gone the way of all flesh, gone west <nonformal>, dead and gone, done for <nonformal>, dead and done for <nonformal>, no more, finished <nonformal>, taken off *or* away, released, fallen, bereft of life
2 **lackluster,** lusterless; dull, dead, deadened, somber, **drab,** wan, **flat,** mat

**lifelike** ADJS **representative,** delineative; **expressive,** realistic, natural, naturalistic, true to life, faithful, verisimilar, veristic

**lifesaver** NOUNS **rescuer,** lifeguard; coast guard, lifesaving service, air-sea rescue; savior; lifeboat; salvager, salvor

**lifestyle** NOUNS **behavior, conduct,** deportment, comportment; tone, style;

way of life, habit of life, modus vivendi; **way, way of acting, ways;** culture pattern, behavioral norm, folkway, **custom**

**life-threatening** ADJS **deadly, deathly,** deathful, **killing, destructive,** death-dealing, death-bringing, feral <old>; **fatal,** mortal, lethal, malignant, malign, virulent, pernicious, baneful; **terminal**

**lifetime** NOUNS 1 **life,** life's duration, life expectancy, lifespan, expectation of life, period of existence, all the days of one's life; all one's born days *or* natural life <nonformal>

*threescore years and ten*
BIBLE

ADJS 2 **lifelong,** livelong, for life

**lift** NOUNS 1 **assist,** helping hand, hand; boost *and* leg up <both nonformal>; help in time of need; **elevator,** *ascenseur* <Fr>
VERBS 2 **elate, exalt,** elevate, uplift; waft, whisk, wing; **improve, better,** change for the better, make an improvement; meliorate, **ameliorate; advance, promote,** foster, favor, nurture, forward, bring forward; raise

**liftoff** NOUNS **rocket launching** *or* **firing,** ignition, launch, shot, shoot; blast-off

**light** NOUNS 1 radiant *or* luminous energy, visible radiation, radiation in the visible spectrum, **illumination, radiation, radiance** *or* radiancy, irradiance *or* irradiancy, irradiation, emanation; highlight; sidelight; light source; **invisible light,** black light, infrared light, ultraviolet light
2 **light source,** source of light, **luminary,** illuminator, luminant, illuminant, incandescent body *or* point, glim
VERBS 3 **ignite, set fire to,** fire, set on fire, kindle, enkindle, inflame, light up, strike a light, apply the match *or* torch to, torch <nonformal>, touch off, **burn,** conflagrate; **grow light,** grow bright, **lighten,** brighten
ADJS 4 **frail,** delicate, airy, wispy, lacy, gauzy, papery, gossamer, diaphanous, insubstantial, ethereal, misty, vague, flimsy, wafer-thin, **fine**
5 **agile, nimble, spry,** sprightly, fleet, featly, peart <nonformal>, graceful, nimble-footed, light-footed, sure-footed
6 **superficial, frivolous,** dizzy *and* ditzy <both nonformal>, flighty, volatile, frothy, fluffy; unburdensome

**lighten** VERBS 1 **disburden,** unburden, unweight, unload, unfreight, disencumber, disembarrass, ease one's load; **set one's mind at ease** *or* **rest,** set at ease, **take a load off one's mind,** smooth the ruffled brow of care; relieve oneself, let one's hair down, pour one's heart out, talk it out, let it all hang out *and* go public <both nonformal>, get it off one's chest; make light *or* lighter, reduce weight
2 **grow light,** grow bright, brighten; dawn, break; **illuminate,** illumine, illume, luminate, **light, light up,** enlighten, brighten, brighten up, irradiate; bathe *or* flood with light

**lightheaded** ADJS **dizzy, giddy,** vertiginous, spinning, swimming, turned around, going around in circles; tiddly <nonformal>, **drunk, drunken**

**lightning** NOUNS **flash** *or* **stroke of lightning,** fulguration, fulmination, bolt, lightning strike, **bolt of lightning,** bolt from the blue, **thunderbolt,** thunderstroke, thunderball, fireball, firebolt

**lightweight** NOUNS 1 **nonentity,** hollow man, doormat *and* empty suit *and* nebbish *and* sad sack <all nonformal>; **a nobody, insignificancy,** hollow man, jackstraw <old>, an obscurity, a nothing, cipher; mediocrity; small potato, small potatoes
ADJS 2 **uninfluential, powerless,** forceless, impotent; **weak,** wimpy *or* wimpish <nonformal>; unauthoritative; **ineffective,** ineffectual, inefficacious; **of no account,** no-account, without any weight, featherweight

**likable** ADJS **endearing,** lovable, adorable, admirable, **lovely,** lovesome, sweet, winning, winsome; **charming;** angelic, seraphic; caressable, kissable; cuddlesome, cuddly

**like** NOUNS 1 **equal, match,** mate, twin, fellow, **equivalent,** opposite number, counterpart, answer <nonformal>, vis à vis, equipollent, coequal, parallel, ditto <nonformal>
VERBS 2 **savor, relish,** love, be fond of, be partial to, enjoy, delight in, have a soft spot for, appreciate; have *or* acquire a taste for, fancy, take to, **take a fancy** *or* a shine to, have a fancy for; have an eye to, have one's eye on
ADJS 3 **similar, alike,** something like, not unlike; **resembling,** resemblant, following, favoring <nonformal>, savoring

*or* smacking of, suggestive of, **on the order of;** consimilar; **on a par,** at par, at parity, au pair, on the same level, on the same plane, on the same *or* equal footing
ADVS 4 **similarly,** correspondingly, **likewise,** either; in the same manner, **in like manner,** in kind; in that way, like that, like this; **thus**; so; by the same token, by the same sign; identically

**likelihood** NOUNS **probability,** likeliness, liability, aptitude, verisimilitude; **chance, odds; expectation, outlook,** prospect; favorable prospect, well-grounded hope, some *or* reasonable hope, fair expectation; **good chance**; presumption, tendency; probable cause, reasonable ground *or* presumption

**likely** ADJS 1 **probable, liable, apt,** verisimilar, in the cards, odds-on; **promising, hopeful,** fair, in a fair way; foreseeable, **predictable; presumable,** presumptive; **statistical,** actuarial; predictable within limits
ADVS 2 **probably, in all probability** *or* **likelihood,** most likely, very likely; as likely as not, very like *and* like enough *and* like as not <all nonformal>; **doubtlessly,** doubtless, **no doubt,** indubitably; **presumably,** presumptively; by all odds, ten to one, a hundred to one, dollars to doughnuts

**likely story** NOUNS **excuse, cop-out** *and* **alibi** *and* **out** <all nonformal>; lame excuse, poor excuse; escape hatch, way out

**like-minded** ADJS **agreeing, in agreement; in accord, concurring,** positive, affirmative, in rapport, *en rapport* <Fr>, **in harmony,** in accordance, in sync <nonformal>, **at one,** on all fours, of one *or* the same *or* like mind, consentient, consentaneous, **unanimous**, unisonous *or* unisonant; **harmonious,** accordant, **concordant,** consonant

**liken** VERBS **compare,** assimilate, similize, liken to, compare with; **make** *or* **draw a comparison,** run a comparison, do a comparative study, bring into comparison; **analogize,** bring into analogy; **draw a parallel,** parallel; **match,** match up; examine side by side, view together, hold up together

**likeness** NOUNS 1 **image, resemblance,** semblance, similitude, simulacrum; **effigy,** icon, idol; **copy**, fair copy; **portrait,** perfect *or* exact likeness, duplicate, double
2 **similarity,** alikeness, **sameness,** similitude; **analogy, correspondence,** conformity, accordance, agreement, comparability, comparison, **parallelism, parity,** community, alliance, consimilarity

**likewise** ADVS **similarly,** correspondingly, **like,** either; in the same manner, **in like manner,** in kind; in that way, like that, like this; **thus**; so; by the same token, by the same sign; identically

**lilt** NOUNS **rhythm,** beat, meter, measure, number *or* numbers, movement, **swing;** prosody, metrics; rhythmic pattern *or* phrase

**limb** NOUNS **branch,** fork, **bough; arm,** leg; **wing,** pinion

**limbo** NOUNS **hell,** purgatory; **place of confinement**

**limelight** NOUNS **publicity, celebrity,** *réclame, éclat* <both Fr>; **spotlight** <both nonformal>, daylight, bright light, glare, public eye *or* consciousness, **exposure, currency,** common *or* public knowledge, widest *or* maximum dissemination; **ballyhoo** *and* hoopla <both nonformal>

**limit** NOUNS 1 **end**, **extremity,** extreme, **acme,** apogee, climax, **maximum,** max <nonformal>, ceiling, **peak,** summit, **pinnacle,** crown, top; **utmost,** uttermost, utmost extent, highest degree, nth degree *or* power, *ne plus ultra* <L>; **the last straw,** the straw that breaks the camel's back, all one can bear *or* stand
VERBS 2 **restrict,** restrain, bound, confine, ground <nonformal>; straiten, narrow, tighten; specialize; stint, scant; **condition,** qualify, hedge, hedge about; draw the line, set an end point *or* a stopping place; discipline, moderate, contain; restrain oneself, pull one's punches <nonformal>

**limited** ADJS **restricted,** bound, **bounded, finite; confined**, prescribed, proscribed, cramped, strait, straitened, narrow; conditioned, qualified, hedged; disciplined, moderated; **deprived,** in straitened circumstances, pinched, on short commons, on short rations, strapped

**limiting** ADJS **restricting,** defining, determining, determinative, confining; limitative, limitary, definitive, exclusive; enclosing, **cloistered,** cloisterlike, claustral, parietal, surrounding; **restrictive,** narrowing, cramping; **qualifying, modifying,** modificatory, altering

**limitless** ADJS **unrestricted,** unconfined, uncircumscribed, unbounded, unmeasured; **unlimited,** illimitable; unqualified, unconditioned, **unconditional,** without strings, no strings, no strings attached; **infinite,** boundless, endless

**limp** NOUNS 1 hobble, claudication; shuffle, shamble, hitch, waddle; halt
VERBS 2 hobble, claudicate; **go slow** *or* **slowly,** go at a snail's pace, take it slow, get no place fast <nonformal>; **drag,** drag out; inch, inch along; poke, **poke along;** shuffle *or* stagger *or* totter *or* toddle along; drag along, drag one's feet
ADJS 3 **flaccid, flabby,** flimsy; limber, limp *or* limber as a dishrag, floppy, rubbery; **drooping, droopy,** loose, nodding, loppy, lop

**limpid** ADJS **clear, lucid,** pellucid, crystal-clear, crystalline, perspicuous, transpicuous, **transparent,** translucent, luminous; **coherent,** connected, consistent

**line** NOUNS 1 **strip,** cord, string, bar; stripe
2 **policy,** polity, principles, guiding principles; **party line,** party principle *or* doctrine *or* philosophy, **position**
3 **route,** path, way, itinerary, course, track, run, road; **railway, railroad,** rail, track, trackage, railway *or* railroad *or* rail line; **procession,** train, column, cortege
4 **lineage,** bloodline, descent, descendancy, line of descent, ancestral line, succession, **extraction,** derivation, birth, **blood,** breed, **family,** house, **strain, stock,** stirps, seed
5 **occupation,** business, work, **line of work,** line of business *or* endeavor, calling, mission, **pursuit,** *métier* <Fr>, **trade,** racket *and* game <both nonformal>; **specialty,** speciality, **field,** area, main interest; cup of tea *and* bag *and* thing <all nonformal>
VERBS 6 **border,** edge, bound, rim, skirt, hem, hem in, lap, list, margin, marge, marginate, march, verge, side; **align, line up,** string out, rank, array, range, get *or* put in a row

**lineage** NOUNS **line,** blood, strain, stock, stem, species, stirps, **breed,** brood, kind; **descent,** dynasty, family, succession; bloodline

**linear** ADJS **straight;** lineal, in a line; **direct, undeviating, unswerving,** unbending, undeflected; **sequential**

**lineup** NOUNS **arrangement,** prearrangement, system, disposition, layout, setup; **roll,** batting order, **roster,** rota <chiefly Brit>

**line up** VERBS 1 **align, line,** string out, rank, array, range, get *or* put in a row; **get in** *or* **get on line,** queue *or* queue up <Brit>, make *or* form a line, get in formation, **fall in,** fall in *or* into line, fall into rank, take one's place
2 **schedule, slate, book,** book in, bill, program, calendar, docket, budget, put on the agenda

**linger** VERBS **dawdle,** loiter, tarry, delay, dally, dillydally, shilly-shally, lollygag, waste time, **take one's time,** take one's own sweet time; goof off *or* around <nonformal>; lag, drag, trail; flag, falter, halt

**lingerer** NOUNS **slowpoke** *and* slowcoach <both nonformal>, plodder, slow goer, **loiterer, dawdler,** dawdle, **laggard,** procrastinator, foot-dragger, stick-in-the-mud <nonformal>, drone, slug, sluggard

**lingerie** NOUNS **underclothes,** underclothing, undergarments, bodywear, **underwear, undies** <nonformal>, skivvies, body clothes, smallclothes, unmentionables <nonformal>, **linen,** underlinen

**lingering** ADJS **dawdling,** loitering, tarrying, dallying, dillydallying, shilly-shallying, lollygagging, procrastinatory *or* procrastinative, dilatory, delaying, **lagging,** dragging; **protracted, prolonged,** extended, lengthened; lasting, languishing; long-continued, long-continuing, long-pending; drawn- *or* stretched- *or* dragged- *or* spun-out, long-drawn, **long-drawn-out**

**lingo** NOUNS **jargon,** slang, cant, argot, patois, patter, vernacular; vocabulary, phraseology

**lingua franca** NOUNS jargon, **pidgin,** trade language; auxiliary language, interlanguage; creolized language, creole language, creole; koine; pidgin English, talkee-talkee

**linguist** NOUNS linguistic scientist, linguistician, linguistic scholar; philologist, philologer, philologian; philologaster; **grammarian,** grammatist; grammaticaster; **etymologist,** etymologer; **lexicologist; polyglot,** bilingual *or* diglot, trilingual, multilingual

**linguistic** ADJS lingual, glottological; **philological;** lexicological, lexicographic, lexicographical; syntactic, syntactical, **grammatical**

**liniment** NOUNS **balm,** lotion, salve, ointment, unguent, *unguentum* <L>, cerate, unction, balsam, oil, emollient, demulcent; **embrocation**

**link** NOUNS 1 **relation, relationship, connection;** relatedness, connectedness, **association, affiliation,** filiation, bond, union, alliance, **tie,** tie-in <nonformal>, linkage, linking, linkup, liaison, **addition**, adjunct, junction, **combination**, assemblage
VERBS 2 **put together, join,** conjoin, **unite,** unify, bond, **connect,** associate, league, band, merge, **assemble,** accumulate; **couple,** pair, accouple, copulate, conjugate, marry, wed, tie the knot <nonformal>, link up, build bridges, yoke, knot, splice, tie, chain, bracket

**linkage** NOUNS **union, unification,** marriage, wedding, coupling, accouplement, linking, yoking; **fusion,** blend, blending, meld, melding; coalescence, coalition; **synthesis,** syncretism, syneresis

**linked** ADJS **joined, united,** connected, copulate, coupled, knit, bridged, tight-knit, knitted, bracketed, associated, conjoined, incorporated, integrated, **merged,** gathered, assembled, accumulated, **collected; associated,** joined up, on board

**lint** NOUNS **fluff,** flue, floss, **fuzz,** pile

**lion** NOUNS 1 **big cat, jungle cat;** Leo <nonformal>, *simba* <Swah>
2 **celebrity,** man *or* woman of mark *or* note, person of note *or* consequence, **notable, big name,** figure, public figure, somebody; **important person, VIP** *and* **standout** <both nonformal>, personage; social lion

**lionhearted** ADJS **courageous,** plucky, brave, bold, valiant, valorous, gallant, **intrepid,** doughty, stalwart, stout, stouthearted, ironhearted, greathearted, bold-spirited, bold as a lion

**lionize** VERBS **praise,** overpraise, praise to excess, idolize, deify, apotheosize, adulate, hero-worship; put on a pedestal

**lip** NOUNS 1 **border,** limbus, **edge,** verge, brink, brow, brim, rim, margin, marge, skirt, fringe, hem, list, selvage *or* selvedge, side; **labium,** labrum, labellum
2 **sauce** *and* sass, **back talk,** backchat <nonformal>

**lip service** NOUNS **mouth honor,** mouthing, lip homage *or* worship *or* devotion *or* praise *or* reverence; formalism, solemn mockery

**liquefy** VERBS liquidize, liquesce, fluidify, fluidize; **melt, run,** thaw, colliquate; melt down; deliquesce; **dissolve,** solve; solubilize; unclot, decoagulate; **infuse,** decoct, steep, soak, brew

**liqueur** NOUNS **cordial;** brandy, flavored brandy

**liquid** NOUNS 1 **fluid;** liquor, drink, beverage; liquid extract, fluid extract; **juice,** sap, body fluid
ADJS 2 **fluid,** fluidal, fluidic, **fluent, flowing,** fluxional, fluxionary, runny; watery; **juicy,** sappy
3 **convertible,** negotiable

**liquid assets** NOUNS **cash, ready money** *or* **cash,** the ready <nonformal>, available funds, money in hand, cash in hand, balance in hand, immediate resources, cash supply, **cash flow**

**liquidate** VERBS 1 **murder,** commit murder; **assassinate;** remove, **purge,** eliminate, get rid of
2 **pay in full,** discharge, settle, square, clear, **amortize,** retire, take up, lift, take up and pay off, honor, acquit oneself of <old>; **cash,** cash in <nonformal>, convert into cash; **sell,** convert, sell out, terminate the account

**liquor** NOUNS 1 **spirits,** intoxicating liquor, **hard liquor, whiskey,** firewater, spiritus frumenti, usquebaugh <Scots>, schnapps, ardent spirits, strong waters, **intoxicant,** toxicant, inebriant, **potable,** potation, **drink,** strong drink, grog, social lubricant, nectar of the gods; **alcohol,** aqua vitae, water of life, brew, **grog;** the cup that cheers

*the luscious liquor*
**Milton**

2 <nonformal> **booze, likker, hooch, juice, sauce,** tiger milk, pig *or* tiger sweat, sheepdip, moonshine, white lightning; **medicine,** snake medicine, corpse reviver; **rotgut, poison,** rat poison, formaldehyde, embalming fluid, shellac, **panther piss**

**list** NOUNS 1 **leaning,** slant, tilt, tip, pitch, **cant,** swag, sway
2 **enumeration, itemization,** listing, shopping list *and* laundry list *and* want list *and* wish list *and* hit list *and* shit list *and* drop-dead list <all nonformal>,

items, **schedule, register,** registry; waiting list; blacklist; short list
VERBS 3 **careen, heel,** tip, cant, heave *or* lay down, lie along; **stumble,** stagger, totter, tilt, trip, flounder; **incline,** lean; slope
4 **inscribe,** enscroll; **register,** enroll, catalog, calendar, **tabulate,** docket; **chronicle**

**listen** VERBS hark, **hearken,** heed, hear, attend, give attention, give ear, give *or* lend an ear, bend an ear; **listen to,** attend to, give a hearing to, give audience to, sit in on; **listen in; eavesdrop,** wiretap, tap, intercept, bug <nonformal>; **keep one's ears open,** be all ears <nonformal>, listen with both ears, hang on every word; hear out

**listener** NOUNS hearer, auditor, audient, hearkener; **eavesdropper,** overhearer, little pitcher with big ears, snoop, listener-in <nonformal>; fly on the wall

**listless** ADJS **languid, languorous,** lifeless, inanimate, enervated, debilitated, **pepless** <nonformal>, lackadaisical, slow, wan, **lethargic,** logy, hebetudinous, supine, lymphatic, apathetic, **sluggish,** dopey <nonformal>, droopy, **dull,** heavy, leaden, lumpish, **torpid,** stultified, stuporous, dormant; phlegmatic

**lit** ADJS **illuminated,** luminous, **lightened,** enlightened, brightened, lighted, it up, flooded *or* bathed with light, floodlit; **alight, glowing,** aglow, lambent, suffused with light

**litany** NOUNS **prayer, supplication, invocation,** imploration, impetration, entreaty, beseechment, appeal, petition, suit, orison, obsecration, obtestation, rogation, **devotions;** silent prayer, meditation, contemplation, communion

**literacy** NOUNS **scholarship, erudition,** eruditeness, **learnedness,** reading, letters; **intellectuality,** intellectualism; computer literacy, computeracy, numeracy; **culture, literary culture, high culture,** book learning, booklore

**literal** NOUNS following the letter, letter-perfect, *au pied de la lettre* <Fr>, true to the letter; verbatim, verbal, word-perfect, **word-for-word;** literal-minded

**literary** ADJS belletristic; classical; **bookish,** booky, book-minded; book-loving, bibliophilic, bibliophagic

**literate** ADJS **learned,** erudite, educated, cultured, cultivated, lettered, civilized, **scholarly,** scholastic, studious

**literature** NOUNS **letters, belles lettres,** polite literature, humane letters, *litterae humaniores* <L>, republic of letters; **work, literary work,** text, literary text; works, complete works, oeuvre, canon, literary canon, author's canon; serious literature

**lithe** ADJS **supple,** willowy, **limber;** lithesome, lissome, loose-limbed; resilient, springy

*as lissome as a hazel wand*
TENNYSON

**litigate** VERBS **sue, prosecute,** go into litigation, **bring suit,** put in suit, sue *or* prosecute at law, **go to law,** seek in law, appeal to the law, seek justice *or* legal redress, implead, **bring action against,** prosecute a suit against, take *or* institute legal proceedings against; take to court, bring into court, hale *or* haul *or* drag into court, bring to justice, bring to trial, **put on trial,** bring to the bar, take legal action

**litigation** NOUNS **lawsuit, suit,** suit in *or* at law; countersuit; **prosecution, action,** legal action, proceedings, legal proceedings, legal process; legal remedy; **case, court case,** cause, cause in court, legal case; **judicial process**

**litter** NOUNS 1 **rubbish,** rubble, trash, junk <nonformal>, shoddy, riffraff, **scrap,** dust <Brit>, **debris,** clamjamfry <Scots>; **clutter,** rat's nest, mare's nest, hurrah's nest <nautical>
VERBS 2 **disorder, disorganize,** throw out of order, put out of gear, dislocate, upset the apple-cart, **disarray;** mess *and* **mess up** <both nonformal>; **clutter,** scatter

**little** ADJS 1 **small**, smallish; **slight,** exiguous; **puny, trifling,** poky, piffling *and* pindling *and* piddling *and* piddly <all nonformal>, **dinky** <nonformal>; cramped, limited; one-horse, two-by-four <nonformal>; pintsized <nonformal>, half-pint; knee-high, knee-high to a grasshopper; petite; short
2 **ungenerous, illiberal,** unchivalrous, mean, small, paltry, mingy, petty; **niggardly, stingy; narrow-minded,** narrow, narrow-gauged, closed, closed-minded, cramped, constricted, small-minded, mean-minded, narrow-hearted, mean-spirited
ADVS 3 **small, slightly**, fractionally; **on**

**a small scale,** in a small compass, in a small way, on a minuscule *or* infinitesimal scale; **in miniature,** in a nutshell

**liturgy** NOUNS **rite, ritual,** rituality, holy rite; order of worship; **ceremony, ceremonial; observance,** ritual observance; solemnity; **form,** formula, formulary, form of worship *or* service, mode of worship; prescribed form; service, function, duty, office, practice; **sacrament,** sacramental, mystery

**live** VERBS 1 **exist, be,** be in existence, be extant, have being; breathe; subsist, stand, obtain, hold, prevail, be the case; **occur,** be present, be there, be found, be met with, happen to be; **endure, last** *or* **last out,** bide, **abide,** dwell, perdure, **continue,** run, extend, **go on,** carry on, hold on, keep on, stay on, run on, stay the course, go the distance, go through with, grind *or* plug away; **live on,** continue to be, subsist, exist, tarry; **persist; survive,** defy *or* defeat time; live to fight another day

ADJS 2 **living, alive,** having life, very much alive, alive and well, alive and kicking <nonformal>, conscious, breathing, quick <old>, **animate,** animated, **vital,** zoetic, instinct with life, imbued *or* endowed with life, vivified, enlivened, inspirited; in the flesh, among the living, in the land of the living, on this side of the grave, aboveground; existent, viable; full of life, full of pep *or* go *and* pizzazz *or* moxie <nonformal>; **charged, electrified,** hot

**lived-in** ADJS **comfortable,** comfy <nonformal>; **cozy, snug,** snug as a bug in a rug; friendly, warm; **homelike,** homey *and* down-home <both nonformal>, homely

**live-in** ADJS **resident,** residing, living, dwelling, commorant, lodging, **staying,** remaining, abiding, cohabiting

**livelihood** NOUNS **support,** maintenance, sustainment, sustentation, sustenance, subsistence, keep, upkeep; **living,** meat, bread, daily bread

**lively** ADJS 1 **active, animated,** spirited, bubbly, ebullient, effervescent, vivacious, **sprightly,** chipper *and* perky <both nonformal>, pert; **spry,** breezy, brisk, energetic, eager, keen, can-do <nonformal>; full of life, full of pep *or* go *and* pizzazz *or* moxie <nonformal>; **peppy** *and* snappy *and* zingy <all nonformal>; frisky, bouncing, bouncy

ADVS 2 **actively, busily;** sprightly, **briskly,** breezily, energetically, animatedly, vivaciously, **spiritedly,** with life and spirit, with gusto; full tilt, in full swing, all out <nonformal>

**liven** VERBS **invigorate, animate,** enliven, liven up, vitalize, quicken, goose *or* jazz up <nonformal>; **exhilarate, stimulate,** hearten, galvanize, electrify, fire, build a fire under, inflame, warm, kindle, charge, charge up, psych *or* pump up <nonformal>, rouse, arouse, act like a tonic, be a shot in the arm <nonformal>

**live off** VERBS **sponge** *and* **sponge on** *and* **sponge off of** <all nonformal>; feed on, fatten on, batten on, use as a meal ticket

**live wire** NOUNS **man** *or* **woman of action, doer,** man of deeds; **hustler** *and* self-starter <both nonformal>, bustler; go-getter *and* ball of fire *and* powerhouse *and* human dynamo *and* spitfire <all nonformal>

**live with** VERBS **endure, bear up under,** bear the brunt, bear with, put up with, tolerate, carry *or* bear one's cross, take what comes, take the bitter with the sweet, abide with, brook, brave, brave out, hang in there, keep it up

**livid** ADJS 1 **ghastly,** lurid, **haggard,** cadaverous, sickly, deadly *or* deathly pale; pale as death *or* a ghost *or* a corpse, pale-faced, tallow-faced, wheyfaced; black and blue

2 **angry,** angered, **incensed, indignant, irate,** ireful; livid with rage, beside oneself, **wroth, wrathful,** wrathy, **cross,** wrought-up, worked up, riled up <nonformal>

**living** NOUNS 1 **support,** keep, upkeep; **livelihood, benefice,** incumbency, glebe, advowson

ADJS 2 **alive,** having life, live, very much alive, alive and well, alive and kicking <nonformal>, conscious, breathing, quick <old>, **animate,** animated, **vital,** zoetic, instinct with life, imbued *or* endowed with life, vivified, enlivened, inspirited

**load** NOUNS 1 **lading,** cargo, freight, charge, burden; **payload;** boatload, busload, carload, cartload, container-load, shipload, trailerload, trainload, truckload, vanload, wagonload

2 **full measure, capacity,** complement, the whole bit <nonformal>; bellyful *and*

snootful <both nonformal>, skinful *or* mouthful <both nonformal>

VERBS 3 **lade,** freight, burden; fill; **stow,** store, put in storage, warehouse; **pack,** pack away; pile, dump, heap, heap up, stack, mass; bag, sack, pocket

4 **burden,** load down *or* up, lade, cumber, **encumber,** charge, freight, tax, handicap, hamper, saddle; **weigh on** *or* **upon,** weigh heavy on, bear or rest hard upon, lie hard *or* heavy upon, press hard upon

**loaded** ADJS 1 **weighted, weighed** *or* **weighted down; burdened,** oppressed, laden, cumbered, encumbered, charged, fraught, freighted, taxed, saddled, hampered; **primed,** cocked, **loaded for bear** <nonformal>

2 well-heeled *and* filthy rich *and* in the money *or* dough *and* well-fixed *and* made of money *and* **rolling in money** *and* big-rich *and* rich-rich *and* lousy rich

**loaf** VERBS **idle,** do nothing, **laze,** lazy <nonformal>, take one's ease *or* leisure, **lounge; lie around,** lounge around, loll around, sit on one's ass *or* butt *or* duff <nonformal>, stand *or* hang around, **loiter about** *or* **around,** slouch, slouch around, **bum around** *and* mooch around <both nonformal>; let the grass grow under one's feet; twiddle one's thumbs

**loafer** NOUNS **idler, lounger,** loller, layabout <Brit nonformal>, couch potato <nonformal>, lotus-eater, *flâneur, flâneuse* <both Fr>, **do-nothing,** *fainéant* <Fr>, goof-off *and* fuck-off *and* goldbrick *and* goldbricker <all nonformal>, clock watcher; **sluggard,** slug, slouch, sloucher, lubber, stick-in-the-mud <nonformal>, gentleman of leisure

**loan shark** NOUNS **moneylender,** moneymonger; **usurer,** shylock <nonformal>

**loathe** VERBS **hate, detest, abhor,** execrate, **abominate,** hold in abomination, take an aversion to, shudder at, utterly detest, be death on, not stand, not stand the sight of, not stomach; scorn, **despise**

**loathsome** ADJS **offensive,** objectionable, odious, repulsive, repellent, rebarbative, **repugnant, revolting,** forbidding; **disgusting, sickening,** gross *and* yucky *and* grungy *and* scuzzy <all nonformal>, beastly <nonformal>, **vile, foul, nasty, nauseating**; fulsome, mephitic, miasmal, miasmic, malodorous, stinking, fetid, noisome, noxious

**lob** VERBS **throw,** fling, sling, pitch, toss, cast, hurl, heave, chuck

**lobby** NOUNS 1 legislative lobby, special-interest lobby; **pressure group,** special-interest group, special interests, single-issue group, PAC *or* political action committee

2 **vestibule,** entrance hall, entranceway, **foyer**

VERBS 3 **exercise** *or* **exert influence,** use one's influence, bring pressure to bear upon, lean on <nonformal>, act on, **work on,** bear upon, throw one's weight around *or* into the scale, say a few words to the right person *or* in the right quarter; get at *or* get the ear of <nonformal>; **pull strings** *or* **wires** *or* **ropes,** lobby through

**lobbyist** NOUNS **person** *or* **woman** *or* **man of influence,** a mover and shaker <nonformal>, wheeler-dealer <nonformal>, influencer, **wire-puller** <nonformal>; **powerbroker; influence peddler**

**local** ADJS **localized,** of a place, geographically limited, topical, vernacular, parochial, provincial, insular, limited, confined

**locale** NOUNS **location,** situation, place, position, spot, *lieu* <Fr>, placement, emplacement, stead; **whereabouts,** whereabout, ubicity; **area,** district, region; **locality,** locus; **setting, background,** backdrop, ground, surround, field, scene, arena, theater

**locate** VERBS 1 **situate,** site, place, position; emplace, spot <nonformal>, **install,** put in place; narrow *or* pin down; **map, chart,** put on the map *or* chart; put one's finger on, **fix,** assign *or* consign *or* relegate to a place; **pinpoint,** zero in on, home in on; **discover, find,** get; **hunt down,** search out, trace down, track down, **run down, run** *or* **bring to earth;** trace

2 **settle, settle down,** sit down, park <nonformal>, ensconce, ensconce oneself; take up one's abode *or* quarters, make one's home, **reside, inhabit**

**location** NOUNS **situation, place, position,** *lieu* <Fr>, placement, emplacement, stead; **whereabouts,** whereabout, ubicity; **site,** situs; **spot, point,** pinpoint, exact spot *or* point, very spot *or* point; *locus classicus* <L>; locale

**lock** NOUNS 1 **tress;** flowing locks, flowing tresses; **curl, ringlet,** earlock, *payess*

<Yiddish>; lovelock; frizz, frizzle; dreadlocks
2 bolt, bar, padlock, catch, safety catch; barrier
VERBS 3 **close, shut,** lock up, lock out, key, padlock, latch, bolt, bar, barricade

**lockup** NOUNS **confinement,** locking-up, caging, penning, putting behind barriers, impoundment, **restraint,** restriction; **prison,** correctional *or* correction facility, penal institution, **jail, gaol** <Brit>, jailhouse

**lock up** VERBS **secrete, hide away,** keep hidden, put away, store away, stow away, file and forget, seal up, put out of sight; **imprison, incarcerate, intern,** immure; **jail,** jug <nonformal>, throw into jail; lock in, bolt in, put *or* keep under lock and key; hold captive, hold prisoner, hold in captivity

**lode** NOUNS **deposit,** mineral deposit, pay dirt; **vein,** seam, dike, ore bed; rich lode, mother lode

**lodestar** NOUNS **ideal,** principle, **ambition,** aspiration, inspiration, guiding light *or* star; **guiding star,** cynosure <old>, **polestar,** polar star, Polaris, **North Star**

**lodestone** NOUNS **magnet,** artificial magnet, field magnet, bar magnet, horseshoe magnet, electromagnet; magnetite

**lodge** NOUNS 1 **cabin,** log cabin; chalet, snuggery; **burrow,** tunnel, earth, run, couch
VERBS 2 **deposit,** repose, reposit, rest, **lay, put down,** set down, lay down
3 **house,** domicile, domiciliate; provide with a roof, have as a guest *or* lodger, shelter, harbor; **quarter, put up,** billet, room, bed, berth, bunk; stable

**lodger** NOUNS **roomer,** paying guest; **boarder,** board-and-roomer, **transient,** transient guest *or* boarder

**lodging** NOUNS **quarters, living quarters; lodgings,** lodgment; diggings *and* digs <both Brit nonformal>, pad *and* crib <both nonformal>, room; **rooms,** berth, roost, accommodations; **housing,** shelter, *gîte* <Fr>

**loft** NOUNS **attic,** attic room, **garret,** sky parlor; cockloft, hayloft; storeroom, junk room

**lofty** ADJS 1 **elevated,** triumphal, high, high-flown, highfalutin *and* highfaluting <both nonformal>, high-toned <nonformal>; high-minded, lofty-minded; high-headed, high-nosed <nonformal>
2 **eminent, prominent,** outstanding, standout, towering, soaring, overtopping, exalted, sublime; august, majestic, noble, distinguished; **haughty,** toplofty

**log** NOUNS 1 **journal,** ship's log, **logbook;** diary; time sheet, time book, daybook; timecard, time ticket, clock card, check sheet; datebook
VERBS 2 **make an entry,** enter, post, post up, journalize, book, docket, note, minute

**logic** NOUNS **reasonableness,** reasonability, **logicalness,** logicality, **rationality,** sensibleness, soundness, justness, justifiability, admissibility, cogency; **sense,** common sense, sound sense, sweet reason, **reason;** plausibility

**logical** ADJS **reasonable,** rational, cogent, sensible, sane, sound, well-thought-out, legitimate, just, justifiable, admissible; credible; plausible; as it should be, as it ought to be; well-argued, **well-founded,** well-grounded; consistent, self-consistent

**logjam** NOUNS **delay,** stoppage, jam <nonformal>, obstruction, tie-up *and* bind <both nonformal>, **block,** blockage, **hang-up** <nonformal>; gridlock

**logo** NOUNS **trademark,** logotype, registered trademark, trade name, service mark

**logy** ADJS **torpid,** languorous, languid, apathetic, phlegmatic, **sluggish,** dopey <nonformal>, groggy, heavy, leaden, **dull,** flat, slack, tame, **dead,** lifeless

**loiter** VERBS **dawdle, linger,** tarry, delay, dally, dillydally, shilly-shally, lollygag, waste time, **take one's time,** take one's own sweet time; goof off *or* around <nonformal>; lag, drag, trail; flag, falter, halt

**loiterer** NOUNS **lingerer, dawdler,** dawdle, laggard, procrastinator, foot-dragger, stick-in-the-mud <nonformal>, drone, slug, sluggard, lie-abed, sleepyhead, goof-off <nonformal>, goldbrick <nonformal>

**loll** VERBS **lie, lie down,** recline, repose, lounge, sprawl, drape *or* spread oneself, splay, lie limply

**lolling** NOUNS 1 **idling, loafing,** lazing, *flânerie* <Fr>, goofing off <nonformal>, goldbricking <nonformal>; *dolce far niente* <Ital>; dallying, dillydallying, mopery, dawdling; lounging

ADJS 2 **lying, reclining,** reposing, flat on one's back; sprawling, lounging; sprawled, spread, splay, splayed, draped

**lone** ADJS **solitary,** alone; **in solitude,** by oneself, all alone; **lonely,** lonesome; sole, unique, a certain

**loneliness** NOUNS **aloneness,** loneness, **lonesomeness,** soleness, singleness; **privacy,** solitariness, **solitude;** separateness, aloofness, detachment, seclusion, sequestration, **withdrawal, alienation,** standing *or* moving *or* keeping apart, **isolation**

**lonely** ADJS **solitary,** alone; **in solitude,** by oneself, all alone; **lonesome, lone;** lonely-hearts

**loner** NOUNS **recluse,** solitaire, solitary, solitudinarian; cloistered monk *or* nun; **hermit,** eremite, anchorite, anchoret; marabout; hermitess, anchoress; **ascetic;** closet cynic; stylite, pillarist, pillar saint; **individualist,** lone wolf <nonformal>

**lonesomeness** NOUNS **aloneness,** loneness, **loneliness,** soleness, singleness; **privacy,** solitariness, **solitude;** separateness, aloofness, detachment, seclusion, sequestration, **withdrawal, alienation,** standing *or* moving *or* keeping apart, **isolation**

**long** ADJS 1 **lengthy;** longish, longsome; tall; **extensive, far-reaching,** fargoing, far-flung; sesquipedalian, sesquipedal; as long as one's arm, a mile long; **time-consuming,** interminable, without end, no end of *or* to, overlong, marathon, lasting, **lingering,** languishing
ADVS 2 **for a long time, for long, interminably,** unendingly, undyingly, persistently, protractedly, enduringly; for ever so long <nonformal>, for many a long day, for life *or* a lifetime, for an age *or* ages, for a coon's *or* dog's age <nonformal>, for a month of Sundays <nonformal>, **forever and a day, forever and ever,** for years on end, **for days on end, etc;** morning, noon, and night; hour after hour, day after day, month after month, year after year; day in day out, month in month out, year in year out; till hell freezes over <nonformal>, till you're blue in the face <nonformal>, till the cows come home <nonformal>, from here to eternity, till the end of time; since time began

**longevity** NOUNS **durability, endurance,** duration, durableness, **lastingness,** *longueur* <Fr>, perenniality, abidingness, long-lastingness, perdurability; long-livedness

**longing** NOUNS 1 **yearning, yen** <nonformal>; desiderium, **hankering** <nonformal>, **pining,** honing <nonformal>, aching; **nostalgia, homesickness,** *Heimweh* <Ger>, *mal du pays* and *maladie du pays* <both Fr>; nostomania
ADJS 2 **wistful,** wishful; **yearning,** yearnful, **hankering** <nonformal>, languishing, pining, honing <nonformal>; **nostalgic, homesick**

**long-lived** ADJS **durable,** perdurable, **lasting, enduring,** perduring, **abiding, continuing,** remaining, staying, **stable,** persisting, **persistent,** perennial; long-term; tough, hardy, vital, longevous *or* longeval

**long shot** NOUNS **fluke** <nonformal>, freak, freak occurrence *or* accident; chance hit, lucky shot, one in a million, long odds, poor bet, hundred-to-one shot <nonformal>

**long-term** ADJS **steadfast, constant,** intransient, immutable, unfading, evergreen, sempervirent, **permanent**, perennial, **long-lasting,** long-standing, of long duration *or* standing, diuturnal

**long-winded** ADJS **wordy, verbose; talkative**; **prolix,** windy <nonformal>, longiloquent; **protracted,** extended, *de longue haleine* <Fr>, lengthy, long, **long-drawn-out,** long-spun, spun-out, endless, unrelenting

**long word** NOUNS hard word, jawbreaker *or* jawtwister *and* two-dollar *or* five-dollar word <all nonformal>, polysyllable; sesquipedalian, sesquipedalia <pl>; lexiphanicism, grandiloquence

**look** NOUNS 1 **sight,** the eye *and* a look-see *and* a gander <all nonformal>, eye, view, regard; sidelong look; leer, leering look; aspect, view; feature, lineaments
2 **air,** mien, demeanor, carriage, bearing, port, posture, stance, poise, presence; guise, garb, complexion, color
VERBS 3 **peer,** have a look, take a gander *and* take a look <both nonformal>, direct the eyes, turn *or* bend the eyes, cast one's eye, lift up the eyes; **look at,** take a look at, eye, **eyeball** <nonformal>, have a look-see <nonformal>, look on *or* upon, gaze at *or* upon; **watch, observe, view, regard;** keep one's eyes peeled *or* skinned, be watch-

ful *or* observant *or* vigilant, keep one's eyes open; keep in sight *or* view, hold in view; look after; **check** *and* **check out** <both nonformal>, scope <nonformal>, scope out <nonformal>; keep under observation, spy on, have an eye out, keep an eye out, keep an eye on, keep a weather eye on; **reconnoiter,** scout, get the lay of the land; **peek, peep,** pry, take a peep *or* peek

**look-alikes** NOUNS **set,** group, matching pair *or* set, his and hers <nonformal>, couple, pair, twins, two of a kind, birds of a feather, peas in a pod

**lookout** NOUNS 1 **vigilance, wariness,** prudence, **watchfulness,** watching, observance, **surveillance; watch,** vigil; *qui vive* <Fr>; **sharp eye,** weather eye, peeled eye, watchful eye, eagle eye
2 **warner,** cautioner, admonisher, monitor; **lookout man; sentinel,** sentry; **signalman,** signaler, flagman; lighthouse keeper; **watchman, watch,** watcher; watchkeeper

**looks** NOUNS **features, lineaments,** traits, lines; **countenance,** face, visage, feature, favor, brow, physiognomy; cast of countenance, **cut of one's jib** <nonformal>, facial appearance *or* expression, cast, turn

**loom** VERBS 1 **weave,** tissue; **interweave, interlace, intertwine,** interknit, interthread, intertissue, intertie, intertwist; inweave, intort
2 **appear,** become visible; heave in sight, appear on the horizon; **bulk,** loom large, bulk large, stand out; **tower above,** rise above, overtop; **exceed, transcend,** outstrip; **lower,** spell *or* mean trouble, look threatening, loom up; **be imminent**; **forebode**; **warn**

**looming** ADJS **imminent, impending,** impendent, overhanging, hanging over one's head, waiting, lurking, **threatening,** lowering, **menacing,** lying in ambush, **brewing,** gathering, preparing; **coming, forthcoming,** upcoming, to come, about to be, about *or* going to happen, **approaching, nearing,** looming up, looming in the distance *or* future; **near, close,** immediate, instant, soon to be, **at hand,** near at hand, close at hand; **in the offing,** on the horizon, **in prospect,** already in sight, just around the corner, in view, in one's eye, in store, in reserve, **in the wind,** in the womb of time; on the knees *or* lap of the gods, in the cards <nonformal>; that will be, that is to be; future

*in danger imminent*
SPENSER

**loonybin** NOUNS **insane asylum,** asylum, lunatic asylum, **madhouse,** mental institution, mental home, bedlam; **bughouse** *and* nuthouse *and* laughing academy *and* **booby hatch** *and* funny farm <all nonformal>; mental hospital, psychiatric hospital *or* ward

**loop** NOUNS 1 **circuit, round,** revolution, **circle,** full circle, go-round, **cycle,** orbit, ambit; pass; round trip, *aller-retour* <Fr>; **beat,** rounds, **walk,** tour, turn, lap
VERBS 2 **encircle, circle,** ensphere, belt, belt in, zone, cincture, encincture; **girdle,** gird, begird, engird; ring, band; wreathe, wreathe *or* twine around

**loophole** NOUNS **way out,** way of escape, hole to creep out of, escape hatch, escape clause, saving clause; pretext; **alternative,** choice

**loose** VERBS 1 **loosen, slacken, relax;** slack, slack off; ease, ease off, let up; **free,** let go, unleash; **disjoin,** unknit, unravel, dismember; **sow confusion,** open Pandora's box; unstick, unglue; **scatter,** disperse, diffuse; **open up, unclog,** unblock, unjam, unbar
ADJS 2 **adrift, afloat,** unmoored, untied, unanchored; **drooping, droopy,** limp, nodding, floppy <nonformal>, loppy, lop; **sagging,** saggy, swag, sagging in folds; baggy; **lax, slack,** relaxed; imprecise, sloppy <nonformal>, careless, slipshod; remiss, negligent; untrammeled, unrestrained
3 **wanton, wayward,** Paphian; **lax,** slack, loose-moraled, of loose morals, of easy virtue, easy <nonformal>, **light,** no better than she should be, whorish, chambering, **promiscuous**
4 **inaccurate, incorrect, inexact,** unfactual, **unprecise,** imprecise, unspecific, lax, unrigorous

**loosen** VERBS **loose,** let loose, cut loose *or* free, unloose, unloosen; **unbind, untie,** unstrap, unbuckle, unlash; **unfetter, unshackle,** unchain, unhandcuff, untie one's hands; **unleash,** untether, unhobble; unharness, unyoke, unbridle; unlock, unlatch, unbolt, unbar
2 **slacken, relax;** slack, slack off; ease,

ease off, let up; **loose, free,** let go, unleash; unstick, unglue

**loot** NOUNS 1 **booty,** spoil, **spoils, swag** <nonformal>, ill-gotten gains, **plunder,** prize, haul, take, pickings, stealings, stolen goods, hot goods *or* items <nonformal>; pork barrel, spoils of office, public trough; till, public till
VERBS 2 **plunder, pillage, sack,** ransack, rifle, freeboot, spoil, spoliate, despoil, depredate, prey on *or* upon, **raid,** reive <Scots>, ravage, ravish, raven, sweep, gut

**looter** NOUNS **plunderer, pillager, marauder,** rifler, sacker, spoiler, despoiler, spoliator, depredator, **raider,** moss-trooper, reiver <Scots>, forayer, forager, ravisher, ravager

**lop** VERBS **amputate,** mutilate, abscind; **prune,** pare, peel, clip, crop, bob, dock, nip, shear, strip, strip off *or* away

**lopsided** ADJS **unbalanced, ill-balanced,** overbalanced, off-balance, tippy, listing, heeling, leaning, canted, top-heavy; slaunchways *and* cockeyed *and* skewgee *and* skygodlin <all nonformal>

**lord** NOUNS **nobleman,** noble, gentleman; **peer; aristocrat, patrician,** Brahman, **blue blood,** thoroughbred, silk-stocking, lace-curtain, swell *and* upper-cruster <both nonformal>; **grandee,** magnifico, magnate, optimate; laird <Scots>, lordling; seignior, seigneur, *hidalgo* <Sp>; **master,** lord and master

**lordly** ADJS **imperious,** aristocratic, totally self-assured; hubristic; masterful, magisterial, **high-and-mighty;** elitist

**lore** NOUNS **body of knowledge,** corpus, body of learning, store of knowledge, system of knowledge, treasury of information; **superstition,** superstitiousness; popular belief, **old wives' tale;** tradition, folklore

**lose** VERBS lose out <nonformal>, lose the day, come off second best, **get** *or* **have the worst of it, meet one's Waterloo; fall,** succumb, tumble, bow, go down, go under, **bite** *or* **lick the dust,** take the count <nonformal>; snatch defeat from the jaws of victory; throw in the towel, say 'uncle'; have enough; incur loss, **suffer loss,** undergo privation *or* deprivation, be bereaved *or* bereft of, have no more, meet with a loss; kiss good-bye <nonformal>; let slip through one's fingers; **forfeit,** default; **mislay,** misplace; **lose everything,** go broke *and* lose one's shirt *and* take a bath *or* to the cleaners *and* tap out *and* go to Tap City <all nonformal>

**lose face** VERBS **incur disgrace,** incur disesteem *or* dishonor *or* discredit, get a black eye <nonformal>, be shamed, earn a bad name *or* reproach *or* reproof, forfeit one's good opinion, fall into disrepute, seal one's infamy; lose one's good name, lose countenance, lose credit, **lose caste; disgrace oneself,** lower oneself, demean oneself, drag one's banner in the dust, degrade *or* debase oneself, act beneath oneself, dirty *or* soil one's hands, get one's hands dirty, sully *or* lower oneself, derogate, stoop, descend, ride to a fall, fall from one's high estate, foul one's own nest

**loser** NOUNS the vanquished; good loser, game loser, sport *or* **good sport** <nonformal>; poor sport, poor loser; **underdog,** also-ran; **unfortunate,** poor unfortunate, the plaything *or* toy *or* sport of fortune, fortune's fool; sure loser *and* nonstarter <both nonformal>; hard case *and* sad sack *and* hard-luck guy <all nonformal>

**loss** NOUNS **losing, privation,** getting away, losing hold of; **deprivation, bereavement,** taking away, stripping, dispossession, despoilment, despoliation, spoliation, robbery; divestment, denudation; **sacrifice, forfeit, forfeiture,** giving up *or* over, denial; **destruction, ruin,** perdition, total loss, dead loss; **disadvantage,** drawback, liability; **detriment,** impairment, damage, hurt, harm, mischief, injury; **a step back** *or* **backward,** a loss of ground

**lost** ADJS **gone;** forfeited, forfeit; by the board, out the window *and* down the drain *or* tube <all nonformal>; **nonrenewable;** long-lost; lost to; wasted, consumed, depleted, squandered, dissipated, diffused, **expended; worn away, eroded,** ablated, used, used up, shrunken; stripped, clear-cut; squandered; irretrievable; **gone to waste,** run *or* gone to seed; down the drain *or* spout *or* rathole <nonformal>; misspent; **irreclaimable,** irredeemable, unredeemable, unregenerate, **irreformable,** incorrigible, past praying for; shriftless, graceless; **astray,** abroad, adrift, **at sea,** off the track, out of one's reckoning, out of one's bearings, disoriented

**lost cause** NOUNS **fool's errand,** wild-goose chase; **hopeless case; goner** *and* gone goose *or* gosling *and* dead duck <all nonformal>

**lot** NOUNS 1 **land,** property, grounds; parcel, plot, plat, quadrat; **portion, share,** interest, part, stake, stock, piece, bit, segment; **bite** *and* **cut** *and* **slice** *and* **chunk** *and* slice of the pie *or* melon *and* piece of the action <all nonformal>, **allotment, proportion, percentage,** measure, quantum, **quota**
2 **fate,** fatality, **fortune,** cup, **portion,** appointed lot, karma, kismet, weird, *moira* <Gk>, future; **destiny,** destination, **end,** final lot; the way the cards fall, the way the cookie crumbles *or* the ball bounces <both nonformal>

**the lot** NOUNS **all, the whole,** the entirety, everything, all the above *or* all of the above <both nonformal>, the aggregate, the assemblage, one and all, all and sundry, each and every <nonformal>; the corpus, everything from soup to nuts *and* everything but the kitchen sink <both nonformal>

**lotion** NOUNS **balm, salve,** ointment, unguent, *unguentum* <L>, cerate, unction, balsam, oil, emollient, demulcent, inunction, chrism

**lots** NOUNS **lot,** deal, no end of, **good** *or* **great deal, considerable,** sight, **heap,** pile, stack, loads, raft, slew, whole slew, spate, wad, **batch,** mess, mint, peck, pack, pot, **tidy sum,** quite a little; **oodles, gobs, scads;** bumper crop, rich harvest, bonanza, enough and to spare, enough and then some; fat of the land

**lottery** NOUNS drawing, sweepstakes *or* sweepstake *or* sweep; draft lottery; **raffle; state lottery,** Lotto, Pick Six, Pick Four; tombola <Brit>; number lottery, numbers pool, **numbers game** *or* **policy,** Chinese lottery <nonformal>; interest lottery, Dutch *or* class lottery; tontine

**loud** ADJS 1 loud-sounding, forte, fortissimo; loudish; **resounding,** ringing, plangent, pealing; full, sonorous; **deafening,** ear-deafening, **ear-splitting,** head-splitting, ear-rending, ear-piercing, piercing; **thunderous,** thundering, window-rattling, earthshaking, enough to wake the dead; **insistent,** instant, **importunate,** urgent, pertinacious, pressing, clamant, crying, clamorous; persistent
2 **gaudy, tawdry;** gorgeous, colorful; **garish, blatant, flagrant,** shameless, **brazen,** brazenfaced, lurid, extravagant, sensational, **spectacular,** glaring, flaring, flaunting, screaming <nonformal>, obtrusive, vulgar, crude; meretricious
ADVS 3 **loudly, aloud,** lustily; **boomingly,** thunderously, thunderingly; **noisily,** uproariously; ringingly, resoundingly; with a loud voice, at the top of one's voice, forte, *fortemente* <Ital>, fortissimo

**loudmouthed** ADJS **loud-voiced,** full-mouthed, full-throated, big-voiced, clarion-voiced, **stentorian,** stentorious, like Stentor

**lounge** NOUNS 1 **anteroom,** antechamber; side room, byroom; **waiting room,** *salle d'attente* <Fr>; **reception room,** presence chamber *or* room, audience chamber; greenroom, wardroom
VERBS 2 **lie, lie down,** recline, repose, sprawl, loll, drape *or* spread oneself, splay, lie limply; **idle,** do nothing, **laze,** lazy <nonformal>, take one's ease *or* leisure, take one's time, **loaf; lie around,** lounge around, loll around, sit on one's ass *or* butt *or* duff <nonformal>, stand *or* hang around, **loiter about** *or* **around,** slouch, slouch around, **bum around** *and* mooch around <both nonformal>

> *I loafe and invite my soul, I lean and loafe at my ease*
> **Walt Whitman**

**lousy** ADJS

<nonformal> punk, bum, badass, shitty, crappy, cruddy, cheesy, gross, raunchy, piss-poor, rat-ass, **crummy,** grim, icky, yecchy, stinking, stinky, creepy, hairy, god-awful, gosh-awful

**lout** NOUNS **oaf,** boor, lubber, **gawk,** yokel, rube, hick, hayseed, bumpkin, clod, clodhopper

**lovable** ADJS **endearing,** likable, adorable, admirable, lovely, lovesome, sweet, winning, winsome; **charming**

**love** NOUNS 1 **affection, attachment,** devotion, fondness, sentiment, warm feeling, soft spot in one's heart, weakness <nonformal>, like, **liking,** fancy, shine <nonformal>; passion, tender feeling *or* passion, **ardor,** ardency, fervor, heart, flame; physical love, Amor, Eros, bodily love, libido, sexual love, sex;

desire, yearning; charity, *caritas* <L>, brotherly love, Christian love, agape, loving concern, **caring;** spiritual love, platonic love; married love, conjugal love; **sweetheart, loved one,** beloved, darling, dear, dear one, dearly beloved, well-beloved, truelove, beloved object, **object of one's affections,** light of one's eye *or* life, light of love

*an insatiate thirst of enjoying a greedily desired object*
MONTAIGNE

*a spiritual coupling of two souls*
BEN JOHNSON

VERBS 2 **be fond of,** be in love with, **care for, like, fancy,** have a fancy for, take an interest in, **dote on** *or* **upon,** be desperately in love, burn with love; be partial to, have a soft spot in one's heart for, have a weakness *or* fondness for

3 <nonformal> **go for,** have an eye *or* eyes for, only have eyes for, be sweet on, have a crush *or* mash *or* case on; have it bad, carry a torch *or* the torch for

**love affair** NOUNS **affair,** affair of the heart, **amour, romance,** romantic tie *or* bond, something between, thing <nonformal>, liaison, entanglement, intrigue; **dalliance,** amorous play, the love game, flirtation, hanky-panky, lollygagging <nonformal>; illicit *or* unlawful love, forbidden *or* unsanctified love, adulterous affair, adultery, unfaithfulness, infidelity, cuckoldry

**love child** NOUNS **bastard,** illegitimate, illegitimate *or* bastard child, whoreson, by-blow, child born out of wedlock *or* without benefit of clergy *or* on the wrong side of the blanket, natural child, *nullius filius* <L>

**loveless** ADJS **unloved,** unbeloved, uncherished; **lovelorn,** forsaken, **rejected,** jilted, thrown over <nonformal>, spurned, crossed in love

**love letter** NOUNS billet-doux, mash note <nonformal>; valentine

**love life** NOUNS **sexuality,** sexual nature, sexualism; **love**, sexual activity, lovemaking, marriage; **carnality, sensuality**; **libido,** sex drive, sexual instinct *or* urge

**lovelorn** ADJS **unloved,** unbeloved, uncherished, loveless; forsaken, **rejected,** jilted, thrown over <nonformal>, spurned, crossed in love; lovesick, languishing

**lovely** ADJS **delightful,** exquisite; **charming, attractive,** endearing, engaging, appealing, prepossessing, heartwarming, **captivating,** irresistible, ravishing, enravishing; **winning,** winsome, taking, fetching, heart-robbing; inviting, tempting, tantalizing; **pretty,** pulchritudinous, **graceful**

**lovemaking** NOUNS 1 dalliance, amorous dalliance, billing and cooing; **fondling, caressing,** hugging, kissing; cuddling, snuggling, nestling, nuzzling; bundling; sexual intercourse

2 <nonformal> **making out, necking, petting,** spooning, smooching, lollygagging, canoodling, playing kissy-face *or* kissy-kissy *or* kissy-poo *or* kissy-huggy *or* lickey-face *or* spacky-lips, pitching *or* flinging woo, sucking face, swapping spit

**lover** NOUNS **admirer,** adorer, amorist; infatuate, paramour, **suitor, wooer,** pursuer, follower; **flirt,** coquette; vampire, vamp; conquest, catch; devotee; date *and* steady <both nonformal>; significant other

**loving** ADJS lovesome, **fond, adoring,** devoted, affectionate, demonstrative, romantic, **sentimental, tender,** soft <nonformal>, melting; **careful,** heedful, regardful, mindful, thoughtful, considerate, caring, solicitous; **attentive**

**low** ADJS 1 **deep,** deep-toned, deep-pitched, deep-sounding, deepmouthed, deep-echoing; **hollow, sepulchral;** low-pitched, low-toned, grave, heavy
2 feeling low, low-spirited, **in low spirits; down in the mouth** <nonformal>, in the doldrums, **down in the dumps** *and* **in the dumps** *and* in the doleful dumps <all nonformal>, in the depths; **despondent,** desponding; **despairing**, weary of life, suicidal, world-weary; pessimistic; spiritless, heartless, **woebegone; humble, lowly,** poor, mean, small, inglorious, undistinguished
3 **unelevated,** flat, low-lying; short, squat, squatty, stumpy, runty; **lowered,** debased, depressed; demoted; **reduced**; prone, supine, prostrate *or* prostrated,

couchant, crouched, stooped, recumbent; laid low, knocked flat, decked <nonformal>; low-set, low-hung; **low-built,** low-sized, low-statured, low-bodied; low-level, low-leveled; neap; knee-high, knee-high to a grasshopper <nonformal>
4 **base, mean, ignoble,** vile, scurvy, sorry, scrubby, beggarly; low-minded, base-minded
ADVS 5 **faintly, softly,** gently, subduedly, hushedly, dimly, feebly, weakly; near the ground; at a low ebb

**lowbrow** NOUNS 1 **ignoramus, know-nothing;** no scholar, puddinghead, dunce, fool
ADJS 2 **unlearned, inerudite,** unerudite, **uneducated,** unschooled, uninstructed, untutored, unbriefed, untaught, unedified, unguided; ill-educated, unlettered, **unscholarly,** unread, unbookish, bookless <old>, unbooked; nonintellectual, **unintellectual;** lowbrowed *and* lowbrowish <both nonformal>

**low-class** ADJS **inferior, poor,** punk <nonformal>, **base, mean, common,** coarse

**low-cut** ADJS low-necked, décolleté, strapless, half-clothed

**lowdown** ADJS **base,** low, mean, crummy

**the lowdown** NOUNS **inside information,** private *or* confidential information; **the inside dope** *and* inside wire *and* **hot tip** <all nonformal>

**lower** VERBS 1 **reduce,** decrease, diminish, lessen, take from; **depress,** de-escalate, damp, dampen, **step down** *and* tune down *and* phase down *or* out *and* scale back *or* down *and* roll back *or* down <all nonformal>; depreciate, **deflate; curtail,** retrench; deduct; **deepen, sink;** countersink; **demote, degrade,** debase, abase, humble, humiliate, bust <nonformal>
ADJS 2 **inferior, subordinate,** secondary; junior; second *or* third string *and* one-horse *and* penny-ante *and* dinky <all nonformal>, second *or* third rank, low in the pecking order; **lesser;** in the shade, thrown into the shade; **common,** vulgar; **reduced,** decreased, diminished, dropped, fallen

**lower class** NOUNS **lower classes,** lower orders, plebs, workers, working class, working people, proletariat, proles <Brit nonformal>, laboring class *or* classes

**lowest** ADJS **humble, lowly,** low, **poor, mean,** small, inglorious, undistinguished; humblest, lowliest; **least, smallest,** littlest, slightest, shortest; rock-bottom, bottom

**low-grade** ADJS **inferior, poor,** punk <nonformal>, base, mean, common, coarse, cheesy *and* tacky <both nonformal>, tinny; shabby, seedy; cheap, Mickey Mouse <nonformal>, paltry; low-class, low-quality

**low key** NOUNS **reserve, restraint,** constraint, backwardness, retiring disposition; low visibility, low profile

**lowlife** NOUNS **wretch,** mean *or* miserable wretch; **bum** *and* bummer *and* lowlifer *and* **mucker** <all nonformal>, caitiff, pilgarlic; **good-for-nothing,** good-for-naught, no-good <nonformal>, ne'er-do-well, wastrel, *vaurien* <Fr>, worthless fellow

**loyal** ADJS **faithful,** devoted, allegiant; **true, true-blue,** true to one's colors; **constant, steadfast,** unswerving, steady, consistent, stable, unfailing, staunch, firm, solid

**loyalist** NOUNS **partisan, party member,** party man *or* woman; regular, stalwart; wheelhorse, party wheelhorse; heeler, ward heeler, **party hack;** party faithful

**loyal opposition** NOUNS **political party, party,** minor party, opposition party

**loyalty** NOUNS **fidelity,** faithfulness, faith; constancy, **steadfastness,** staunchness, firmness; trueness, troth, true blue; **allegiance, fealty,** homage; bond, tie; attachment, adherence, adhesion; devotion, devotedness

**lozenge** NOUNS **pill,** bolus, **tablet, capsule,** troche

**LSD** NOUNS

<nonformal> acid, big D, blotter, blue acid, blue cheer, blue heaven, California sunshine, cap, cubes, D, deeda, dots, electric Kool-Aid, haze, L, mellow yellows, orange cubes, pearly gates, pink owsley, strawberry fields, sugar, sunshine, tabs, yellow

**lubricant** NOUNS **lubricator,** lubricating oil, lubricating agent, antifriction; graphite, plumbago, black lead; silicone; glycerin; wax, cerate

**lubricate** VERBS **facilitate,** ease; **grease the wheels** <nonformal>; smooth, **smooth** *or* **pave the way,** ease the way, grease *or* soap the ways <both nonformal>, prepare the way, **clear the way,** run interference for <nonformal>, open the way, open the door to; make frictionless *or* dissipationless, remove friction, grease, oil; **speed, expedite,** quicken, hasten; **help along,** help on its way

**lucid** ADJS 1 **clear, crystal-clear,** clear as crystal, clear as day, clear as the nose on one's face; **plain, distinct,** pellucid, limpid, perspicuous, transpicuous, **transparent,** translucent, luminous; **coherent,** connected, consistent; lucent, luculent
2 **sane,** sane-minded, **rational,** reasonable, sensible, normal, wholesome, clearheaded, clearminded, balanced, **sound,** mentally sound, of sound mind, *compos mentis* <L>, right, right in the head, **in one's right mind,** in possession of one's faculties *or* senses, together *and* all there <both nonformal>; in touch with reality

**luck** NOUNS **good fortune** *or* **luck,** happy fortune, **fortune,** the breaks <nonformal>; **fortunateness,** luckiness, smiles of fortune, fortune's favor

**lucky** ADJS **fortunate, providential;** in luck; blessed with luck, favored; born under a lucky star, born on the sunny side of the hedge; **auspicious**

**lucrative** ADJS **gainful,** productive, **profitable,** remunerative, remuneratory, fat, paying, well-paying, high-yield, high-yielding; advantageous, worthwhile; banausic, moneymaking, breadwinning

**lucre** NOUNS **wealth, riches,** opulence *or* opulency, richness, wealthiness; **prosperity,** prosperousness, **affluence,** comfortable *or* easy circumstances, independence; **money,** pelf, gold, mammon; **the wherewithal,** filthy lucre <nonformal>, the almighty dollar, root of all evil

**ludicrous** ADJS **absurd, nonsensical,** insensate, ridiculous, laughable; **foolish, crazy;** preposterous, cockamamie <nonformal>, fantastic, fantastical, grotesque, monstrous, wild, weird, **outrageous,** incredible, beyond belief, *outré* <Fr>, extravagant, **bizarre**

**lug** VERBS **pull,** carry, draw, heave, haul, hale, tote, tug, tow, take in tow

**luggage** NOUNS **impedimenta,** dunnage, **baggage,** bag and baggage, traps, tackle, apparatus, truck, gear, kit, outfit, duffel

**lukewarm** ADJS **indifferent, halfhearted,** zealless, perfunctory, fervorless; **cool, cold**; tepid, Laodicean; neither hot nor cold, neither one thing nor the other

**lull** NOUNS 1 **respite, recess, rest, pause,** halt, stay, **break,** surcease, suspension, interlude, **intermission,** spell <Australia>, letup <nonformal>, **time out** <nonformal>, time to catch one's breath; **breathing spell,** breathing time, breathing place, breathing space, breath; **breather;** rest; **calm,** calm before the storm
VERBS 2 **quiet,** quieten, **soothe,** quiesce, **calm,** calm down, tranquilize, pacify, passivize, pour oil on troubled waters; hush, still, rest, compose, gentle, rock, cradle, rock to sleep; ease, steady, smooth, smoothen, smooth over, smooth down, even out; pour oil on troubled waters

**lullaby** NOUNS **sleep-inducer,** sleep-producer, sleep-provoker, sleep-bringer, hypnotic, soporific, somnifacient; song

**lumber** NOUNS 1 **wood, timber,** hardwood, softwood; pole, post, beam, **board,** plank
VERBS 2 **plod,** plug <nonformal>, peg, shamble, **trudge,** tramp, stump, plod along, plug along <nonformal>, schlep <nonformal>; **flounder,** muddle; stumble, **slip; encumber,** cumber, burden, saddle with, weigh *or* weight down

**lumbering** NOUNS 1 **forestry,** arboriculture, tree farming, silviculture, forest management; Christmas tree farming; forestation, afforestation, reforestation; logging
ADJS 2 **poking,** poky, slow-poky <nonformal>; tottering, staggering, toddling, trudging, ambling, waddling, shuffling; **slow-moving,** slow-creeping, snail-paced, snail-like, tortoiselike, turtlelike, slow as slow, slow as molasses *or* molasses in January, slow as death; **bulky, hulky,** hulking, lumpish, lumpy, clumpish, lubberly; **clumsy,** awkward, **unwieldy; stiff, stilted, formal,** Latinate, *guindé* <Fr>, **labored,** ponderous, elephantine, cumbrous, leaden, heavy

**luminary** NOUNS **celebrity,** man *or* woman of mark *or* note, person of note *or* consequence, **notable,** great man *or* woman, master spirit, worthy, name, **big name,** figure, public figure, **somebody; important person, VIP** *and* **standout** <both nonformal>, personage, **idol,** popular idol, tin god *or* little tin god <nonformal>; lion, social lion; **star, superstar,** megastar, hot stuff <nonfor-

mal>; leading light, hard *or* tough act to follow <nonformal>

**luminous** ADJS **incandescent,** candescent; **lustrous, radiant,** irradiative; **shining,** shiny, burning, lamping, streaming; **beaming,** beamy; **gleaming,** gleamy, glinting

**lummox** NOUNS **oaf, lout,** boor, lubber, **gawk,** gawky, yokel, rube, hick, hayseed, bumpkin, clod, clodhopper

**lump** NOUNS clump, **hunk** *and* **chunk** <both nonformal>, **mass,** piece, **gob** *and* glob <both nonformal>, gobbet; batch, **wad,** block, loaf; pat <of butter>; clod; nugget

**lumpy** ADJS **bulky, hulky,** hulking, lumpish, lumping <nonformal>, clumpish; **congealed,** coagulated, clotted, grumous; **curdled,** curded, clabbered

**lunacy** NOUNS **insanity,** insaneness, unsaneness, **madness,** *folie* <Fr>, **craziness,** daftness, oddness, strangeness, queerness, abnormality; loss of touch *or* contact with reality, loss of mind *or* reason; dementedness, dementia, athymia, brainsickness, mindsickness, mental sickness, sickness

**lunar** ADJS **crescent-shaped,** crescentlike, crescent, crescentic, crescentiform; sickle-shaped, sickle-like, falcate, falciform; moon-shaped, moonlike, lunate, lunular, luniform

**lunatic** NOUNS 1 **madman, madwoman** dement, *fou* and *aliéné* <both Fr>, non compos, *bacayaro* <Japanese>; bedlamite, Tom o' Bedlam; **maniac,** raving lunatic; homicidal maniac, psychopathic killer, berserk *or* berserker
ADJS 2 **insane,** unsane, **mad,** stark-mad, mad as a hatter, mad as a march hare, **stark-staring mad,** maddened, **sick,** crazed, moonstruck, **daft,** non compos mentis, non compos, *baca* <Japanese>, **unsound,** of unsound mind, **demented, deranged,** deluded, disoriented, unhinged, **unbalanced,** unsettled, distraught, wandering, mazed, crackbrained, brainsick, sick *or* soft in the head, not right, not in one's right mind, **touched,** touched in the head, **out of one's mind,** out of one's senses *or* wits, bereft of reason, reasonless, irrational, deprived of reason, senseless, witless

**lunchroom** NOUNS **cafeteria,** eating place, eatery *and* beanery *and* hashery *and* hash house *and* greasy spoon <all nonformal>; luncheonette; **café,** *caffè* <Ital>; **coffee shop, lunch counter,** quick-lunch counter; **snack bar,** *buvette* <Fr>, *cantina* <Sp>; automat; **diner**

**lunge** NOUNS **thrust, pass,** swing, cut, stab, jab; feint; home thrust

**lurch** NOUNS 1 totter, stagger, **swing,** swinging, **sway,** swag; **rock,** roll, reel, careen; toss, tumble, pitch, plunge
VERBS 2 **pitch,** toss, tumble, toss and tumble, pitch and toss, **plunge,** hobbyhorse, pound, **rear,** rock, roll, reel, swing, **sway,** yaw, heave, scend, flounder, welter, **wallow; topple, stumble,** stagger, totter, careen, list, tilt, trip, flounder

**lure** NOUNS 1 charm, **come-on** <nonformal>, attention-getter *or* -grabber, **attraction, draw** *or* drawer *or* crowd-drawer, crowd-pleaser, headliner; **decoy,** decoy duck; **bait,** ground bait, baited trap, baited hook; **snare,** trap; **endearment**; the song of the Sirens, the voice of the tempter, honeyed words; forbidden fruit
VERBS 2 allure, **entice, seduce, inveigle, decoy,** draw, **draw on, lead on;** come on to *and* give the come-on *and* give a come-hither look *and* bat the eyes at *and* make goo-goo eyes at <all nonformal>, flirt with, flirt; **woo;** coax, cajole, blandish; **ensnare;** draw in, suck in *and* rope in <both nonformal>; bait, offer bait to, bait the hook, angle with a silver hook

**lurid** ADJS **sensational,** yellow, **melodramatic,** Barnumesque; spine-chilling, eye-popping <nonformal>; pale, deathly pale, wan, blue, livid, haggard; **cadaverous,** corpselike; **garish, loud** <nonformal>, blatant, flagrant, shameless, brazen, brazenfaced, extravagant, sensational, **spectacular,** glaring, flaring, flaunting, screaming <nonformal>, obtrusive, vulgar, crude; meretricious, **obscene,** lewd, adult, bawdy, ithyphallic, ribald, **pornographic, salacious,** sultry <nonformal>, **dirty, smutty,** raunchy <nonformal>

**lurk** VERBS couch; **lie in wait,** lay wait; **sneak, skulk, slink, prowl,** nightwalk, **steal, creep,** pussyfoot <nonformal>, gumshoe <nonformal>, tiptoe; stalk, shadow; **lie under the surface,** lie low, lie beneath, lie dormant, smolder

**lurking** ADJS **latent,** lying low, delitescent, **hidden**, obscured, obfuscated, veiled, muffled, covert, occult, cryptic; **underlying, under the surface,** submerged; **between the lines; imminent, impending,** impendent, **overhanging,** hanging over one's head, waiting, **threatening, looming,** lowering, **menacing,** lying in ambush

**luscious** ADJS **tasty,** delectable, delicious, flavorsome, savory; juicy, succulent

**lush** NOUNS 1 **drunk; soak,** boozer, boozehound, dipso, juicehead, loadie, ginhound, elbow bender *or* crooker, shikker, bottle sucker, swillbelly, swillpot, swillbowl; **souse, stew,** bum, rummy, rumhound, stewbum; wino <all nonformal>
ADJS 2 **luxuriant,** flourishing, **rank,** riotous, exuberant; dense, impenetrable, thick, heavy, gross; overgrown, overrun; **flowery, florid; exuberant,** superabundant

**lust** NOUNS 1 **craving,** coveting; **hunger,** thirst, appetite; **itch, itching,** prurience *or* pruriency; lech <nonformal>, **sexual desire,** lasciviousness, lechery, lecherousness, lewdness, bawdiness, dirtiness, salacity, salaciousness, carnality, animality, fleshliness, **sexuality,** sexiness, lustfulness
VERBS 2 **lust after,** itch for, have a lech *and* have hot pants for <both nonformal>, **desire; be in heat** *or* **rut,** rut, come in; get physical <nonformal>; **desire,** desiderate, be desirous of, **wish,** lust after, bay after, kill for *and* give one's right arm for <both nonformal>, die for <nonformal>, **want,** have a mind to, choose <nonformal>; **hanker for** *or* **after** <nonformal>; aspire after, be consumed with desire; have an itchy *or* itching palm *and* have sticky fingers <all nonformal>

**luster** NOUNS **illustriousness,** brilliance *or* brilliancy, radiance, splendor, resplendence *or* resplendency, refulgence *or* refulgency, refulgentness, **glory,** blaze of glory, nimbus, halo, aura, envelope; charisma, mystique, glamour, numinousness, magic; **shine,** shininess, **sheen, gloss,** glint

**lustrous** ADJS **illustrious,** glorious, brilliant, radiant, splendid, splendorous, splendrous, splendent, resplendent, bright, shiny, shining; charismatic, glamorous, numinous, magic, magical

**lusty** ADJS **strong,** vigorous, hearty, nervy, bouncing, full- *or* red-blooded, **animated, spirited, robust,** hearty, enthusiastic, mettlesome, zesty, zestful, impetuous, spanking, smacking; stalwart, stout, strapping, sturdy, **rugged,** rude, hardy, well-knit

**luxuriant** ADJS flourishing, **rank, lush,** riotous, exuberant; dense, impenetrable, thick, heavy, gross; jungly, jungled; overgrown, overrun; **rich, luxurious**

**luxuriate** VERBS **superabound,** overabound, **know no bounds, swarm,** pullulate, run riot, **teem; delight in, rejoice in,** indulge in, revel in, riot in, bask in, wallow in, swim in; groove on *and* get high on *and* freak out on <all nonformal>; feast on, gloat over *or* on; **relish, appreciate,** do justice to, savor, smack the lips

**luxurious** ADJS **ornate, elegant,** ostentatious; rich, luxuriant; **sumptuous,** elaborate, extravagant, deluxe; executive *and* plush *and* posh *and* ritzy *and* swank *and* swanky <all nonformal>, Corinthian; palatial, Babylonian, gold-plated

**luxury** NOUNS **splendor,** splendidness, splendiferousness, resplendence, brilliance, glory; impressiveness, imposingness; **sumptuousness,** elegance, elaborateness, lavishness; ritziness *or* poshness *or* plushness *or* swankness *or* swankiness <all nonformal>

**lynch** VERBS **hang,** hang by the neck; **string up** *and* scrag *and* stretch <all nonformal>; gibbet, noose, neck; hang, draw, and quarter

**lynching** NOUNS **hanging,** the rope *or* noose; summary execution; necktie party *or* sociable <nonformal>, vigilantism, vigilante justice; the necklace

**lyric** ADJS **melodious,** melodic; **musical,** music-like; **tuneful,** tunable; **euphonious** *or* euphonic, **lyrical,** melic; **lilting,** songful, songlike

**lyricist** NOUNS song writer, songsmith, librettist, lyrist

# M

**macabre** ADJS **hideous, ghastly,** morbid, grim, grisly, gruesome, ghoulish; **weird, eerie,** eldritch, **uncanny,** unearthly; **spooky** *and* spookish *and* hairy <all nonformal>

**Machiavellian** ADJS **scheming, calculating,** designing, contriving, plotting, intriguing; manipulatory, **manipulative;** opportunist, **opportunistic;** Byzantine; **conniving,** conspiring, collusive

**machination** NOUNS **manipulation, wire-pulling** <nonformal>; influence, political influence, behind-the-scenes influence *or* pressure; **maneuvering,** maneuvers, tactical maneuvers

**machismo** NOUNS **virility,** virileness, potence *or* **potency,** sexual power, manly vigor; ultramasculinity; **manliness,** manfulness, **manhood**

**macho** ADJS **virile, potent,** viripotent; ultramasculine, **he-mannish** *and* hunky <both nonformal>, two-fisted <nonformal>, broad-shouldered, hairy-chested; **manly,** manful

**mad** ADJS 1 **insane,** mad as a hatter, mad as a march hare, **stark-staring mad,** maddened, crazed, **lunatic,** moonstruck, **demented, deranged,** deluded, disoriented, unhinged, **unbalanced,** unsettled, distraught, wandering, mazed, crackbrained, brainsick, sick *or* soft in the head, not right, not in one's right mind, **touched,** touched in the head, **out of one's mind,** out of one's senses *or* wits, bereft of reason, reasonless, irrational

2 <nonformal> **sore,** mad as a hornet *or* as a wet hen *or* as hell, pissed; **pissed-off** *or* PO'd; teed off *or* TO'd; ticked off, browned-off, het up, **hot under the collar,** burned up, hot and bothered, boiling *or* hopping *or* fighting *or* roaring mad, fit to be tied, good and mad, steamed, bent out of shape, in a lather

**mad about** VERBS

< nonformal>**wild about, crazy about,** gone on, gaga over, all hopped up about, hot about *or* for *or* on, steamed up about, **turned-on,** freaked-out, **nuts on** *or* **over** *or* **about,** crazy *or* nuts about

**madam** NOUNS **procurer, pimp,** pander *or* panderer, *maquereau* <Fr>, mack *or* mackman, ponce <Brit nonformal>; **bawd;** procuress; white slaver

**maddening** ADJS **inflammatory; stimulating,** stimulative, stimulatory; exhilarating, heady, intoxicating, ravishing

**made** ADJS man-made; **manufactured,** created, crafted, formed, shaped, molded, cast, forged, machined, milled, fashioned, **built, constructed,** fabricated

**made-up** ADJS **invented,** originated, **conceived,** discovered, newfound; fabricated, coined, minted, new-minted; made out of whole cloth; cosmetized, cosmeticized, beautified, titivated

**madhouse** NOUNS **insane asylum,** asylum, lunatic asylum, mental institution, mental home, bedlam; **bughouse** *and* nuthouse *and* **loonybin** *and* **booby hatch** *and* funny farm <all nonformal>; mental hospital, psychopathic hospital *or* ward

**madman** NOUNS **lunatic,** dement, *fou* and *aliéné* <both Fr>, non compos, *bacayaro* <Japanese>; bedlamite, Tom o' Bedlam; **maniac,** raving lunatic; homicidal maniac, psychopathic killer

**maelstrom** NOUNS **eddy,** back stream, gurge, **swirl,** twirl, whirl; **whirlpool,** vortex, Charybdis; **bustle, fuss, flurry, flutter,** fluster, scramble, ferment, stew, sweat, **stir,** hubbub, hullabaloo, hoo-ha *and* foofaraw *and* flap <all nonformal>

**maestro** NOUNS **teacher,** instructor, educator, preceptor, **mentor; master**

**Mafia** NOUNS **the rackets** <nonformal>, the syndicate, **organized crime,** Cosa Nostra

**magazine** NOUNS **periodical,** serial, journal, gazette; ephemeris; review; organ, **house organ; trade journal,** trade magazine

**magic** NOUNS **sorcery, necromancy,** sortilege, **wizardry,** theurgy, gramarye <old>, rune, glamour; **witchcraft,** spellcraft, spellbinding, spellcasting; **witchery,** witchwork, bewitchery, enchantment; spell, charm; illusionism, sleight of hand, prestidigitation, magic show, magic act

**magical** ADJS **illustrious,** charismatic, glamorous, numinous; sorcerous, necromantic, **magic,** magian, numinous, thaumaturgic, thaumaturgical, **miraculous, wondrous,** wonder-working, **prodigious;** enchanted, bewitched

**magician** NOUNS mage, magus, magian; Merlin; prestidigitator, illusionist, conjurer, sleight-of-hand artist; mummer, guiser <Scots>, guisard

**magisterial** ADJS **dignified,** stately, imposing, grand, courtly, aristocratic; **noble,** lordly, princely; **majestic,** regal, royal, kingly, queenly; worthy, **august, venerable;** statuesque; **sedate, solemn**, sober, grave

**magistrate** NOUNS **judge, justice,** adjudicator, bencher, man *or* woman on the bench, **justice of the peace** *or* JP; arbiter, arbitrator, moderator

**magnanimous** ADJS great-souled *or* -spirited; **generous,** generous to a fault, openhanded, **liberal; big, bighearted,** greathearted, largehearted, great of heart *or* soul; noble-minded, **high-minded,** idealistic; **benevolent**, **noble,** princely, handsome, great, high, elevated, **lofty,** exalted, sublime; charitable, compassionate, sympathetic; sensitive

**magnate** NOUNS **businessman,** businesswoman, businessperson, big businessman, tycoon <nonformal>, baron, king, top executive, business leader; **industrialist,** captain of industry

**magnetic** ADJS **engrossing, absorbing,** consuming, **gripping,** riveting, holding, **arresting,** engaging, attractive, **fascinating,** enthralling, spellbinding, enchanting, hypnotic, mesmerizing, mesmeric; obsessive, obsessing; appealing, seductive, charismatic

**magnetize** VERBS **attract, pull, draw,** drag, tug, pull *or* draw towards, have an attraction; magnet, be magnetic; **lure;** electromagnetize

**magnificence** NOUNS **grandeur,** grandness, grandiosity, gorgeousness, **splendor,** splendidness, splendiferousness, resplendence, brilliance, glory; nobility, proudness, **state, stateliness, majesty;** impressiveness, imposingness

**magnificent** ADJS **grandiose,** grand, splendid, splendiferous, splendacious <nonformal>, **glorious,** superb, fine, superfine, fancy, superfancy, swell <nonformal>; **imposing, impressive,** larger-than-life, awful, awe-inspiring, awesome; **noble, proud,** stately, majestic, princely

**magnified** ADJS **exaggerated,** hyperbolical, amplified <old>, **inflated,** aggrandized; **stretched,** disproportionate, **blown up out of all proportion;** overstated, overdrawn; overdone, overwrought; overestimated; overlarge, overgreat; high-flown, grandiloquent

**magnify** VERBS **aggravate, intensify, heighten,** step up, sharpen, make acute *or* more acute, bring to a head, deepen, **increase,** enhance, enlarge, build up; augment; **exaggerate,** blow up *and* puff up <both nonformal>, **enlarge, expand,** extend, widen, broaden, build, build up, aggrandize; **extol, glorify,** exalt

**magnitude** NOUNS **size,** largeness, bigness, greatness, vastness, vastitude, order of magnitude, amplitude; mass, bulk, **volume,** body; **dimensions, proportions,** dimension, caliber, scantling, proportion; **extent,** extension, expansion, expanse, square footage *or* yardage etc, **scope,** reach, range

**maid** NOUNS **maidservant,** servitress, **girl,** servant girl, *bonne* <Fr>, serving girl, wench, biddy <nonformal>, hired girl; au pair girl, ayah <India>, amah <China>; live-in maid, live-out maid; **handmaid,** handmaiden; **lady's maid,** waiting maid *or* woman, gentlewoman, abigail, soubrette

**maiden** NOUNS 1 **single** *or* unmarried woman, spinster, spinstress, **old maid,** maid, bachelor girl, single girl, single woman, lone woman, maiden lady, feme sole

ADJS 2 **unmarried,** unwedded, unwed, single, sole, spouseless, husbandless; **spinsterly,** spinsterish, spinsterlike; **old-maidish,** old-maidenish; maidenly

**maidenhead** NOUNS **virginity,** maiden *or* virgin state, intactness, maidenhood

**mail** VERBS **post,** dispatch, send; airmail

**maim** VERBS **cripple,** lame; **hamstring,** hobble; wing; emasculate, castrate; incapacitate, **disable**

**main** ADJS **chief, principal,** paramount, **foremost,** headmost, **leading,** dominant, crowning, capital, cardinal; central, focal, prime, **primary,** primal, first

**mainland** NOUNS **continent,** landform, continental landform, landmass

**mainline** VERBS **inject,** shoot *and* shoot up *and* jab *and* get down *and* get off <all nonformal>, pop *and* skin pop <both nonformal>

**mainspring** NOUNS **fountainhead,** headwater, headstream, riverhead, springhead, headspring, wellspring, wellhead, well, **spring, fountain,** fount, font, *fons et origo* <L>

**mainstay** NOUNS **supporter, upholder,** maintainer, sustainer; support, standby <nonformal>, stalwart, reliance, dependence; **abettor, seconder,** second; endorser, sponsor; **backer, promoter,** angel <nonformal>, rabbi <nonformal>; **patron,** Maecenas; **champion,** defender, apologist, **advocate,** exponent, **protagonist**

**maintain** VERBS **affirm, assert,** asseverate, **aver,** protest, lay down, avouch, avow, **declare,** say, say loud and clear, say out loud, sound off <nonformal>, have one's say, speak, speak one's piece *or* one's mind, speak up *or* out, **state,** set down, express, put, put it, put in one's two-cents worth <nonformal>; **allege,** profess; **contend,** argue, **insist, hold,** submit, maintain with one's last breath
2 support, keep; sustain, uphold, **keep up,** keep alive

**maintenance** NOUNS **support, sustainment,** sustentation, **sustenance, subsistence,** provision, total support, meal ticket <nonformal>; **keep, upkeep; livelihood, living,** meat, bread, daily bread; **nurture, fostering,** nurturance, nourishment, mothering, parenting, rearing, fosterage, foster-care, **care, caring,** care-giving, tender loving care *or* TLC <nonformal>; preservation, **conservation**

**majestic** ADJS **lofty, elevated,** sublime, grand, noble, stately, grave, solemn, dignified; serious, weighty; moving, inspiring

**majesty** NOUNS **loftiness,** elevation, sublimity; grandeur, **nobility,** stateliness, gravity, *gravitas* <L>, solemnity, **dignity**

**major** ADJS **important,** consequential, momentous, significant, considerable, substantial, material, **great,** grand, big; superior, world-shaking, earthshaking; big-time *and* big-league *and* major-league *and* heavyweight <all nonformal>; high-powered <nonformal>

**majority** NOUNS 1 **maturity, adulthood,** grown-upness, full growth, mature age, legal age, voting age, driving age, drinking age, *legalis homo* <L>; age of consent; **manhood,** man's estate, virility, *toga virilis* <L>, **womanhood,** womanness, femininity, femaleness, womanliness
2 plurality, more than half, the greater number, the greatest number, **most,** preponderance *or* preponderancy, **bulk, mass;** lion's share

**make** NOUNS 1 **kind, sort, ilk, type,** breed of cat <nonformal>, **stamp, brand,** feather, color, stripe, line, grain, kidney; mark, label, shape, cast, form, mold
VERBS 2 **produce, create,** manufacture, form, formulate, evolve, mature, elaborate, fashion, **fabricate,** prefabricate, cast, shape, configure, carve out, mold, extrude, frame; **construct, build,** erect, put up, set up, run up, raise, rear

**make-believe** NOUNS 1 **fantasy; fiction,** myth, romance; wildest dreams, stretch of the imagination; **chimera, bubble, illusion**
ADJS 2 **fictitious, figmental,** fictional, fictive, fabricated, fictionalized; nonfactual, nonactual, nonrealistic; **fabulous, mythic, mythical,** mythological, legendary

**make do** VERBS **make shift,** make out <nonformal>, cope, manage, manage with, get along on, get by on, do with; do as well as *or* the best one can; use a last resort, scrape the bottom of the barrel

**make ends meet** VERBS **support oneself,** make one's way; **keep body and soul together,** *or* hold one's head above water, keep afloat; **survive, subsist, cope, eke out,** make out, scrape along, manage, get by

**makeshift** ADJS makeshifty, **stopgap,** band-aid <nonformal>, improvised, improvisational, **jury-rigged; last-ditch; ad hoc;** quick and dirty <nonformal>; temporary, provisional, tentative

**make sure** VERBS **make certain,** make sure of, make no doubt, make no mistake; remove *or* dismiss *or* expunge *or* erase all doubt; **assure, ensure,** insure, **certify; ascertain, get a fix** *or* **lock on** <nonformal>; **find out,** get at, see to it, see that; **determine,** decide, **establish,** settle, fix, lock in *and* nail down *and* clinch *and* cinch <all nonformal>, clear up, sort out, set at rest

**makeup** NOUNS 1 **disposition, character,** nature, temper, temperament, mettle, constitution, complexion *and* humor <both old>, stamp, type, stripe, kidney, make, mold; **turn of mind, inclination,** mind, **tendency,** grain, vein, set, mental

set, mindset, **leaning,** animus, propensity, proclivity, predilection, preference, predisposition
2 **cosmetics, beauty products, beauty-care products;** war paint *and* drugstore complexion <both nonformal>; pancake makeup

**make up** VERBS 1 **compose, constitute,** construct, fabricate; **incorporate,** embody, incarnate; **form, organize,** structure, shape, shape up; **enter into,** go into, go to make up; **make, build,** build up, assemble, put *or* piece together; **consist of,** be a feature of, form a part of, combine *or* unite in, merge in; **consist,** be made up of, be constituted of, contain; **synthesize; combine**; join; **mix**
2 **kiss and make up** *and* make it up *and* make matters up <all nonformal>, **shake hands,** come round, come together, come to an understanding, **come to terms,** let the wound heal, let bygones be bygones, forgive and forget, put it all behind one, settle *or* compose one's differences, meet halfway
3 **beautify, prettify,** cutify <nonformal>, pretty up *or* gussy up *or* doll up <all nonformal>, grace, **adorn; glamorize;** paint *and* put on one's face <both nonformal>, titivate, cosmetize, cosmeticize

**makings** NOUNS **component, constituent,** ingredient, integrant, fixings <nonformal>, **element, factor, part,** player, module, part and parcel; appurtenance, adjunct

**maladjusted** ADJS **incompetent, incapable,** unable, inadequate, unequipped, unqualified, ill-qualified, out of one's depth, outmatched, **unfit, unfitted,** unadapted, not equal *or* up to, not cut out for <nonformal>; ineffective, **ineffectual;** unadjusted

**malady** NOUNS **disease, illness,** sickness, ailment, indisposition, disorder, complaint, morbidity, *morbus* <L>, **affliction,** affection, distemper <old>, **infirmity**

**malaise** NOUNS **anxiety,** anxiousness; **uneasiness,** perturbation, disturbance, upset, agitation, disquiet, disquietude, inquietude, unquietness; **nervousness**; angst; **sickishness,** seediness *and* rockiness <both nonformal>

**malapropism** NOUNS antiphrasis, **solecism,** ungrammaticism, **misusage,** missaying, misconstruction, infelicity; corruption

**malcontent** NOUNS 1 **complainer,** complainant, **faultfinder, grumbler,** growler, smellfungus, **murmurer,** mutterer, griper, croaker, peevish *or* petulant *or* querulous person, whiner, *frondeur* <Fr>; reactionary, reactionist; rebel
ADJS 2 **discontented,** malcontented, complaining, complaintful, sour, **faultfinding,** grumbling, growling, murmuring, muttering, griping, croaking, **peevish, petulant,** sulky, **querulous,** querulant, whiny

**male** NOUNS 1 male being, **man,** male person, *homme* <Fr>, *hombre* <Sp>; **gentleman,** gent <nonformal>
ADJS 2 **masculine,** bull, **manly,** manlike, mannish, manful, andric; uneffeminate; **gentlemanly,** gentlemanlike

**male chauvinist** NOUNS **sexist,** male chauvinist pig *or* MCP <nonformal>, manist, masculist

**male organs** NOUNS **genitals,** genitalia, sex organs, reproductive organs, pudenda, private parts, privy parts; **crotch,** pubic region, perineum, pelvis; **male organs; penis,** phallus, *lingam* <Skt>; gonads; **testes, testicles,** balls *and* nuts *and* rocks *and* ballocks *and* family jewels <all nonformal>; spermary; scrotum, cod <old>

**malevolent** ADJS **ill-disposed,** evil-disposed, **ill-natured,** ill-affected, ill-conditioned, ill-intentioned, **hostile, antagonistic,** repugnant, antipathetic, set against, snide, spiteful, despiteful, malefic, malicious, malignant, hateful, full of hate *or* hatred; virulent, **bitter,** sore, rancorous, acrid, caustic, venomous, vitriolic

**malformed** ADJS **deformed, misshapen,** misbegotten, misproportioned, ill-proportioned, ill-made, ill-shaped, **out of shape;** dwarfed, stumpy; bloated; grotesque, **monstrous**

**malfunction** NOUNS 1 **fault,** *faute* <Fr>, **defect,** deficiency, inadequacy, imperfection, kink, defection <old>; **flaw,** hole, bug <nonformal>; **blemish,** taint; glitch <nonformal>
VERBS 2 **get out of order,** get out of gear; get out of joint; go wrong

**malice** NOUNS **maliciousness,** maleficence; malignance *or* **malignancy,** malignity; **meanness** *and* orneriness *and* cussedness *and* bitchiness <all non-

formal>, hatefulness, nastiness, invidiousness; **wickedness,** iniquitousness; deviltry, devilry, devilment; malice prepense *or* aforethought, evil intent; **noxiousness**

**malicious** ADJS maleficent, malefic; **malignant,** malign; **mean** *and* **ornery** *and* cussed *and* bitchy <all nonformal>, hateful, nasty, baleful, invidious; **wicked,** iniquitous; **harmful, noxious**

**malign** VERBS **defame, bad-mouth** *and* poor-mouth <both nonformal>; asperse, cast aspersions on, cast reflections on, injure one's reputation, damage one's good name, give one a black eye <nonformal>; **slur,** cast a slur on, do a number *or* a job on <nonformal>, tear down

**malignancy** NOUNS **virulence** *or* virulency, noxiousness, destructiveness, deadliness; **lethality,** mortality, fatality; **malignity, perniciousness,** banefulness; cancer

**malignant** ADJS **virulent, noxious,** malign, malevolent, malefic, vicious, destructive, deadly; mephitic, miasmal, miasmic, miasmatic; cancerous

**malingerer** NOUNS **slacker,** shirker, dodger, goof-off *and* goldbrick <both nonformal>, idler

**malingering** NOUNS **shirking, slacking,** goldbricking <nonformal>, soldiering, goofing *and* goofing off *and* fucking off <all nonformal>; **dodging,** ducking

**mall** NOUNS **marketplace, mart,** market, open market, market overt; **shopping center, shopping plaza** *or* **mall,** plaza, shopping *or* shop *or* commercial complex; public walk, promenade, esplanade, alameda, parade, *prado* <Sp>

**malleable** ADJS **docile, tractable,** biddable, unmurmuring, **yielding,** pliant, pliable, flexible, moldable, ductile, plastic, like putty in one's hands

**malnutrition** NOUNS undernourishment, undernutrition; **dietary deficiency,** vitamin deficiency

**malodorous** ADJS **fetid,** olid, **odorous, stinking, reeking,** reeky, nidorous, smelling, bad-smelling, **evil-smelling,** ill-smelling, heavy-smelling, **smelly,** smellful <Australia>, stenchy; **foul,** vile, putrid, bad, fulsome, noisome, fecal, feculent, excremental, offensive, repulsive, noxious, sulfurous; **rank,** strong, high, gamy; **rancid, musty,** funky, fusty, frowzy, stuffy, moldy, mildewed, mildewy; mephitic, miasmic, miasmal

**malpractice** NOUNS **misuse,** misusage, abuse; abuse of office, misconduct, malfeasance, misfeasance, malversation, wrongdoing; **negligence,** neglect; **misbehavior, misconduct**

**mammoth** ADJS **gigantic,** mountainous, titanic, colossal, Gargantuan, gigantesque, monster, monstrous, outsize, sizable, larger-than-life, overgrown, king-size, monumental; **massive,** massy, weighty, bulky, voluminous; **tremendous,** stupendous, awesome, prodigious

**man** NOUNS 1 **male,** male being; male person, *homme* <Fr>, *hombre* <Sp>; **gentleman,** gent <nonformal>; **husband, married man,** benedict, goodman <old>, old man <nonformal>; manservant, serving man, butler; valet, *valet de chambre* <Fr>, gentleman's gentleman

2 <nonformal > **guy,** fellow, felle, lad, chap, guy, cat, bird, duck, stud, joker, jasper, bugger, bastard, bloke *and* cove *and* johnny *and* bod, <all Brit nonformal> customer, party, character, warm, body, bean, cookie, dude, gent, Joe

VERBS 3 staff; garrison, man the garrison *or* trenches *or* barricades

**man about town** NOUNS **sophisticate,** man of experience, **man of the world;** boulevardier, playboy, social lion, slicker *and* city slicker <both nonformal>; **cosmopolitan,** cosmopolite

**manacle** NOUNS 1 **shackle,** restraint, **restraints, fetter, hamper,** trammel, trammels, gyves, bond, **bonds,** irons, chains, Oregon boat; **handcuffs,** cuffs
VERBS 2 **shackle, fetter,** gyve, put in irons; **handcuff,** tie one's hands; **tie hand and foot,** hog-tie <nonformal>

**manacled** ADJS **bound, tied,** bound hand and foot, tied up, tied down, strapped, hampered, trammeled, shackled, handcuffed, fettered, tethered; **in bonds,** in irons *or* chains, ironbound

**manage** VERBS 1 **direct, regulate,** conduct, carry on, handle, run <nonformal>; **control,** command, head, govern, **boss** *and* head up *and* pull the strings *and* **mastermind** *and* quarterback *and* call the signals <all nonformal>;
2 **economize, save,** make *or* enforce economies; **husband,** husband one's resources; live frugally, get along on a

shoestring, get by on little; keep *or* stay within one's means *or* budget, balance income with outgo, live within one's income, make ends meet, cut one's coat according to one's cloth, keep *or* stay ahead of the game

**manageable** ADJS **governable, controllable,** manipulable, corrigible, restrainable, untroublesome; domitable, tamable, domesticable; milk-toast *or* milquetoast; **workable,** operable, performable, actable, doable, negotiable, maneuverable; **practicable, feasible,** practical, viable

**management** NOUNS **direction, managing,** handling, running <nonformal>, conduct; governance, **regulation,** ordering, husbandry; manipulation

**manager** NOUNS **director,** *directeur* <Fr>, director general, **governor,** rector, **administrator,** intendant, **conductor;** person in charge, responsible person; executive

**mandarin** NOUNS **intellectual, intellect,** intellectualist, literate, member of the intelligentsia, white-collar intellectual; **pundit,** Brahmin, egghead *and* pointy-head <both nonformal>; **highbrow** <nonformal>; wise man; **bureaucrat,** red-tapist, *rond-de-cuir* <Fr>

**mandate** NOUNS 1 **authority, prerogative,** popular authority *or* mandate, people's mandate, electoral mandate; **injunction,** charge, commission; **dependency,** colony
VERBS 2 **command, order,** dictate, direct, instruct, bid, enjoin, charge, commission, call on *or* upon; **decree,** rule, ordain, promulgate; give an order *or* a direct order, issue a command, say the word, give the word *or* word of command; call the shots *or* tune *or* signals *or* play <nonformal>

**mandatory** ADJS **obligatory, compulsory,** must <nonformal>, imperative, required, dictated, **binding; preceptive,** didactic, instructive, moralistic, **prescriptive;** prescript, prescribed, hard-and-fast; formulary, standard, regulation, official, authoritative, canonical, statutory, rubric, rubrical, protocolary, protocolic

**maneuver** NOUNS 1 **stratagem, artifice,** craft, wile, strategy, device, wily device, contrivance, expedient, design, scheme, trick, cute trick, gimmick <nonformal>, **ruse,** red herring, shift, tactic, stroke, stroke of policy, master stroke, **move,** coup, gambit, **ploy, dodge,** artful dodge; **act,** step, measure, initiative, *démarche* <Fr>
VERBS 2 **manipulate,** pull strings *or* wires; **machinate,** contrive, angle <nonformal>, jockey, engineer; play games <nonformal>; **plot,** scheme, intrigue; **finagle,** wangle

**man Friday** NOUNS **right-hand man,** right hand, strong right hand *or* arm, fidus Achates, second self, alter ego, confidant

**manger** NOUNS **compartment,** booth, stall, crib

**mangle** VERBS **tear** *or* **rip apart,** take *or* pull apart, **pick** *or* **rip** *or* **tear to pieces,** tear to rags *or* tatters, **shred,** rip to shreds; lacerate, mutilate, maim

**mangled** ADJS **injured,** lacerated, cut, split, rent, torn, slit, slashed, mutilated, chewed-up; **smashed,** in bits, in pieces, in shards, burst, busted <nonformal>, ruptured, butchered, hacked

**manhandle** VERBS **mistreat,** maltreat, ill-treat, ill-use, abuse, injure, **molest;** do wrong to, do wrong by; outrage, do violence to, do one's worst to; mishandle; buffet, batter, bruise, **savage,** maul, knock about, rough, rough up

**man-hater** NOUNS **misanthrope,** misanthropist, people-hater, cynic, Timon, Timonist; misandrist; **sexist,** female chauvinist, chauvinist

**manhood** NOUNS **masculinity,** masculineness, maleness; **manliness,** manlihood, manfulness, manlikeness; mannishness; gentlemanliness, gentlemanlikeness; **maturity, adulthood, majority,** grown-upness, man's estate, virility, machismo, *toga virilis* <L>

**mania** NOUNS **craze, infatuation, enthusiasm,** passion, fascination, crazy fancy, bug <nonformal>, rage, furor; manic psychosis

**maniac** NOUNS **lunatic, madman, madwoman,** raving lunatic; homicidal maniac, psychopathic killer, berserk *or* berserker

**manic** ADJS **psychotic, psychopathic,** psychoneurotic, mentally ill, mentally sick, certifiable; disturbed, neurotic; schizophrenic, schizoid; manic-depressive; uncontrollable, running amok, wild

**manifest** NOUNS 1 **statement, bill,** itemized bill, invoice, bill of lading
VERBS 2 **show, exhibit,** demonstrate, display, breathe, unfold, develop;

**evince,** evidence; **indicate,** give sign *or* token, token, betoken, mean; **make plain,** make clear; bring to notice, expose to view, bring to *or* into view; **reveal,** divulge, disclose; **flaunt,** dangle, wave, **flourish,** brandish, parade; affect, make a show *or* a great show of; perform, enact, dramatize; **embody,** incarnate, **materialize**
ADJS 3 **apparent, evident,** self-evident, axiomatic, indisputable, obvious, plain, clear, perspicuous, distinct, palpable, patent, tangible; **visible,** perceptible, perceivable, discernible, observable, noticeable, **much in evidence; to be seen,** easy to be seen, plain to be seen; plain as day, plain as the nose on one's face, big as life; **crystal-clear,** clear as crystal; **express,** explicit, unmistakable, not to be mistaken, open-and-shut <nonformal>; self-explanatory, self-explaining; **indubitable**

**manifestation** NOUNS **appearance; expression,** evincement; **indication, evidence,** proof; embodiment, incarnation, bodying forth, materialization; epiphany, theophany, Christophany, avatar; **revelation, disclosure**, showing forth; dissemination, **publication**

**manifesto** NOUNS **statement of belief** *or* **principles,** position paper; solemn declaration; deposition, affidavit, sworn statement

**manikin** NOUNS **figure, figurine; mannequin,** model, dummy, lay figure

**manipulate** VERBS **maneuver,** pull strings *or* wires; **machinate,** contrive, angle <nonformal>, jockey, **engineer;** play games <nonformal>; **plot,** scheme, intrigue; finagle, wangle

**manipulative** ADJS **using, exploitive,** exploitative, manipulatory, scheming

**mankind** NOUNS **humankind, man,** men and women, people, human species, **human race,** human family, the family of man, **humanity,** human beings, mortals, mortality, flesh, mortal flesh, clay; generation of man <old>, *le genre humain* <Fr>, genus Homo, **Homo sapiens,** Hominidae, hominids

**manlike** ADJS **anthropoid,** humanoid, hominid; anthropomorphic, anthropopathic, therioanthropic

**manly** ADJS **masculine, male,** bull, **manlike, mannish,** manful, andric; uneffeminate; **gentlemanly,** gentlemanlike; virile, macho

**man-made** ADJS **made, manufactured,** created, crafted, formed, shaped, molded, cast, forged, machined, milled, fashioned, **built, constructed,** fabricated

**manna** NOUNS **godsend,** boon, blessing; manna from heaven, manna in the wilderness, gift from on high

**manned** ADJS staffed, readied, in place, **prepared; garrisoned**

**mannequin** NOUNS artist's model, dressmaker's model, photographer's model; dummy, lay figure

**manner** NOUNS **way,** wise, means, mode, modality, fashion, **style,** tone, guise <old>; **method,** methodology, **system; approach,** attack, tack; **technique,** procedure, process, proceeding, course, practice; *modus operandi* <L>, mode of operation *or* MO, manner of working, mode of procedure; **routine;** manner of speaking, mode of expression

**mannered** ADJS **affected, pretentious,** la-di-da; *maniéré* <Fr>; **artificial, unnatural,** insincere; theatrical, stagy, histrionic; overdone, overacted, hammed up <nonformal>; precious, *précieux, précieuse* <both Fr>, overnice, overrefined, overelegant, overelaborate; Gongoristic, Gongoresque

**mannerism** NOUNS *minauderie* <Fr>, **trick of behavior,** trick, **quirk,** habit, peculiar trait, idiosyncrasy, trademark; **characteristic, peculiarity, singularity,** particularity, specialty, individualism, **character,** nature, **trait**

**manners** NOUNS **mannerliness, good manners,** excellent *or* exquisite manners, good *or* polite deportment, good *or* polite behavior, *bienséance* <Fr>; *savoir-faire, savoir-vivre* <both Fr>; correctness, correctitude, **etiquette**

**mannish** ADJS **mannified; unwomanly,** unfeminine, uneffeminate, viraginous; **tomboyish,** hoyden, rompish

**man of the world** NOUNS person of fashion, fashionable, man-about-town, nob, *mondain* <Fr>; fashion plate, clotheshorse, Beau Brummel; **socialite;** clubman; jet setter; swinger <nonformal>

*the glass of fashion and the mold of form*
SHAKESPEARE

**man-of-war** NOUNS **warship,** war vessel, naval vessel; warship; man-o'-war, ship of war, armored vessel

**manse** NOUNS **parsonage,** pastorage, pastorate, **church house,** clergy house; presbytery, **rectory,** vicarage, deanery

**mansion** NOUNS **estate;** palatial residence, stately home <Brit>; **villa,** château, palace, *palais* <Fr>, *palazzo* <Ital>

**mantle** NOUNS **cover, covering,** screen, shroud, shield, veil, pall, curtain, hanging, drape, drapery; **robe,** frock, gown, cloak

**manual** NOUNS **handbook,** enchiridion, vade mecum, gradus, how-to book <nonformal>; **textbook,** text, schoolbook, manual of instruction

**manual labor** NOUNS **work, labor,** employment, industry, toil, moil, travail, toil and trouble, sweat of one's brow; **drudgery, sweat,** slavery, spadework, rat race <nonformal>; handwork, handiwork

**manufacture** VERBS **produce, create, make, form,** formulate, evolve, mature, elaborate, fashion, **fabricate,** prefabricate, cast, shape, configure, carve out, mold, extrude, frame; **put together, assemble,** piece together, patch together, whomp up *and* fudge together *and* slap up *or* together <all nonformal>

**manufactured** ADJS **made,** man-made; created, crafted, formed, shaped, molded, cast, forged, machined, milled, fashioned, **built, constructed,** fabricated; **mass-produced,** volume-produced, assembly-line; **assembled,** put together; **concocted, trumped-up, doctored**

**manufacturing** NOUNS **production, manufacture,** producing, devising, fashioning, framing, forming, formation, formulation; engineering, tooling-up; processing, conversion; **fabrication,** prefabrication

**manure** NOUNS **fertilizer,** dressing, top dressing, enricher, richener; organic fertilizer, muck, night soil, dung, guano, **droppings;** cow pats, cow flops <nonformal>; cow chips, buffalo chips; coprolite, coprolith

**many** ADJS **numerous, manifold,** not a few, no few; **very many,** full many, **ever so many,** considerable *and* quite some <both nonformal>; **multitudinous,** multitudinal, multifarious, multifold, multiple, **myriad;** numerous as the stars, a dime a dozen

**map** NOUNS 1 **chart; projection,** map projection, azimuthal equidistant projection *or* azimuthal projection, conic projection, Mercator projection
VERBS 2 **plot; chart, blueprint; diagram,** graph; **sketch,** sketch in *or* out, draw up a plan; map out, plot out, **lay out,** set out, mark out; lay off, mark off

**mapmaker** NOUNS **cartographer,** mapper; chorographer, topographer, oceanographer, photogrammetrist; **surveyor,** land surveyor

**mapped** ADJS **surveyed,** plotted, admeasured, triangulated; known by measurement

**mar** VERBS **spoil,** botch, **ruin,** wreck, blight, play havoc with, play mischief with; **blemish, disfigure**

**marathon** ADJS **protracted, prolonged,** extended, lengthened; **long,** overlong, time-consuming, interminable, lasting, **lingering,** languishing; long-continued, long-continuing

**marauder** NOUNS **plunderer, pillager, looter,** rifler, sacker, spoiler, despoiler, spoliator, depredator, **raider,** moss-trooper, free-booter, rapparee, reiver <Scots>, forayer, forager, ravisher, ravager; wrecker

**marble** NOUNS 1 **plaything,** mig, agate, steelie, taw
VERBS 2 **streak,** striate, band, bar, vein; marbleize
ADJS 3 **milk-white,** milky, lactescent; marmoreal

**march** NOUNS 1 quick *or* quickstep march, quickstep, quick time; lockstep; double march, double-quick, double time; slow march, slow time; half step; goose step
VERBS 2 mush, footslog, **tramp, hike,** backpack, trail-hike; route-march; file, defile, file off; **parade,** go on parade; goose-step, do the goose step; do the lock step

**margin** NOUNS 1 **room, latitude,** swing, play, way; room to spare, room to swing a cat <nonformal>, **elbowroom, leeway;** breathing space; headroom, clearance
2 **border,** limbus, bordure <heraldry>, **edge,** limb, **verge, brink,** brow, **brim, rim,** marge, **skirt, fringe, hem,** list, selvage *or* selvedge, side

**marginal** ADJS **borderline,** frontier; secondary, of a low order of importance, low-priority, expendable

**marijuana** NOUNS

1 <nonformal> Acapulco gold, aunt mary, bomb, boo, bush, doobie, gage, ganja, grass, grefa, hay, hemp, herb, Indian hay, J, jane, kif, mary, maryjane, mary warner, meserole, mighty mezz, moota, muggles, pod, pot, smoke, snop, tea, Texas tea, weed, yerga

2 <nonformal> joint, joy stick, kick stick, reeffer, roach, stick, twist

**marina** NOUNS **harbor, dock,** dockage, basin

**marinate** VERBS **preserve, cure,** season, brine, marinade, pickle, corn

**marine** ADJS **nautical,** maritime, naval, navigational; **seafaring,** seagoing, oceangoing, seaborne, water-borne; **oceanic,** pelagic, thalassic; nautical; oceanographic, oceanographical

**mariner** NOUNS **seaman, sailor,** sailorman, **navigator, seafarer,** seafaring man, bluejacket, sea *or* water dog <nonformal>, crewman, shipman, jack, jacky, jack afloat, jack-tar, **tar, salt** <nonformal>, hearty, lobscouser <nonformal>, *matelot* <Fr>, windsailor, windjammer

**marionette** NOUNS **puppet,** *fantoche* <Fr>, *fantoccino* and *fantoccio* <both Ital>, hand puppet, glove puppet

**marital** ADJS **matrimonial, conjugal,** connubial, nuptial, wedded, married, hymeneal; epithalamic; **spousal;** husbandly, uxorious; bridal, wifely, uxorial

**maritime** ADJS **nautical,** marine, naval, navigational; **seafaring,** seagoing, oceangoing, seaborne, water-borne; seamanly, seamanlike, **salty** <nonformal>; pelagic, oceanic

**mark** NOUNS **marking;** watermark; **scratch,** scratching, engraving, graving, **score,** scotch, cut, hack, gash, blaze; bar code; nick, notch; **scar,** cicatrix, scarification, cicatrization; **brand,** earmark; **stigma; stain,** discoloration; blemish, macula, **spot,** blotch, splotch, flick, patch, splash; mottle, dapple; **dot,** point; polka dot; tittle, jot; **speck, speckle,** fleck; tick, **freckle,** lentigo, mole; **birthmark,** strawberry mark, port-wine stain, vascular nevus, nevus, hemangioma; beauty mark *or* spot; caste mark; **check,** checkmark; prick, puncture; tattoo, tattoo mark
2 **dupe, victim;** coll *and* flat *and* john *and* lamb *and* lobster *and* monkey *and* patsy *and* **sucker** <all nonformal>
VERBS 3 make a mark, put a mark on; pencil, chalk; mark out, demarcate, delimit, define; **mark off, check, check off,** tick, tick off, chalk up; punctuate, point; **dot, spot,** blotch, splotch, dash, **speck, speckle,** fleck, freckle; mottle, dapple; blemish; **brand,** stigmatize; **stain, discolor**; stamp, seal, punch, impress, imprint, **print, engrave; score, scratch,** gash, scotch, scar, scarify, cicatrize; nick, notch; **blaze,** blaze a trail; **line, seam,** trace, **stripe, streak, striate;** hatch; **underline, underscore;** prick, puncture, tattoo, riddle, pepper
4 **destine, predestine,** necessitate, **ordain,** fate, appoint; come with the territory <nonformal>; have in store for; **doom,** foredoom

**mark down** VERBS **write down,** jot down, put down, set down, take down; **cheapen,** depreciate, devaluate, lower, reduce, **cut prices, cut,** slash, shave, trim, pare, underprice, knock the bottom out of <nonformal>

**marked** ADJS 1 **designated,** flagged; signed, signposted; monogrammed, individualized, personal; own-brand, own-label
2 **distinguished,** distingué; **noted, notable,** of note, of mark; **characteristic, peculiar, singular,** single, quintessential, intrinsic, unique, qualitative, **distinctive; destined, fated,** fateful, ordained, written in the cards, in store; **doomed,** foredoomed

**marker** NOUNS **mark;** bookmark; **landmark,** seamark; bench mark; **milestone,** milepost; cairn, menhir, catstone; **buoy,** aid to navigation, bell, gong, lighted buoy, nun, can, spar buoy, wreck buoy, junction buoy, special-purpose buoy; **monument; IOU**

**market** NOUNS 1 **mart, store, shop,** salon, boutique, emporium, house, establishment, *magasin* <Fr>; **retail store;** discount store, discount house, outlet store; **shopping center, shopping plaza** *or* **mall,** plaza, mall, shopping *or* shop *or* commercial complex
VERBS 2 **sell, merchandise,** move, turn over, sell off, make *or* effect a sale

**marketable** ADJS **salable,** retailable, merchandisable, merchantable, commercial, vendible; in demand

**marketplace** NOUNS **mart, market,** open

market, market overt; **shopping center, shopping plaza** *or* **mall,** plaza, mall, shopping *or* shop *or* commercial complex; emporium, rialto; **bazaar, fair,** trade fair, show, flea market, flea fair, street market, *marché aux puces* <Fr>

**market value** NOUNS **worth, value,** account, rate; street value; **price, quotation**

**mark off** VERBS **circumscribe, bound;** mark out, stake out, rope off; **demarcate,** delimit, draw *or* mark *or* set *or* lay out boundaries, circle in *or* out, hedge in, set the limit, mark the periphery; **define,** determine, fix, specify; **measure off, lay off,** set off, rule off; **step off,** pace off *or* out

**marksman** NOUNS **shooter,** shot; **gunner,** gun, **gunman; rifleman,** musketeer, carabineer; Nimrod, hunter; trapshooter; **markswoman,** targetshooter, **sharpshooter,** sniper; good shot, dead shot, deadeye, **crack shot**

**marooned** ADJS **stranded, grounded,** aground, **on the rocks,** high and dry; **stuck,** stuck *or* set fast; castaway, wrecked, shipwrecked

**marred** ADJS **spoiled** *or* spoilt, botched, blighted, **ruined,** wrecked; **blemished, disfigured,** defaced, scarred, scarified, scabbed, scabby; **faulty, flawed, defective**

**marriage** NOUNS 1 **matrimony, wedlock,** married status, holy matrimony, holy wedlock, match, matching, match-up, splicing <nonformal>, union, matrimonial union, alliance, marriage sacrament, sacrament of matrimony, bond of matrimony, wedding knot, conjugal bond *or* tie *or* knot, nuptial bond *or* tie *or* knot; misalliance, *mésalliance* <Fr>, ill-assorted marriage

*a world-without-end bargain*
SHAKESPEARE

2 **wedding,** marriage ceremony, nuptial mass; church wedding, civil wedding, civil ceremony; **nuptials,** spousals, espousals, hymeneal rites; white wedding; forced marriage, shotgun wedding; Gretna Green wedding, elopement

**marriageable** ADJS nubile, ripe, of age, of marriageable age, marriable

**marriage broker** NOUNS **matchmaker,** matrimonial agent, *shadchen* <Yiddish>; matrimonial agency *or* bureau

**marriage vow** NOUNS **betrothal,** betrothment, espousal, **engagement,** handfasting *and* affiance <both old>, troth, marriage contract, plighted troth *or* faith *or* love; banns, banns of matrimony; prenuptial agreement *or* contract

**married** ADJS **wedded,** one, one bone and one flesh, mated, matched, coupled, partnered, paired, hitched *and* spliced <both nonformal>; **linked,** tied, coupled, knotted, twinned, wed, married up, welded, conjugate, bracketed, bound, yoked, spliced, conjoined, conjoint, conjunct, joined

**marrow** NOUNS **center,** centrum; **middle,** heart, core, nucleus; **core of one's being,** where one lives; kernel; **pith,** medulla; **nub, hub,** nave, axis, pivot

**marry** VERBS wed, nuptial, **join, unite, hitch** *and* **splice** <both nonformal>, couple, match, match up, make *or* arrange a match, join together, **unite in marriage,** join *or* unite in holy wedlock, tie the knot, tie the nuptial *or* wedding knot, make one; give away, give in marriage; marry off, find a mate for, find a husband *or* wife for

**marsh** NOUNS marshland, **swamp,** swampland, fen, fenland, **morass,** *marais* <Fr>, *maremma* <Ital>, **bog, mire, quagmire,** sump <nonformal>, wash, baygall; glade, everglade; slough, swale, wallow, hog wallow, buffalo wallow, sough <Brit>

**marshal** VERBS **order, arrange**, get it together <nonformal>, **organize, regulate;** dispose, deploy; **form,** form up, configure, structure, array, pull it together, get *or* put one's ducks in a row <nonformal>, straighten it out, get *or* put one's house in order, line up, set up, lay out; rally

**martial** ADJS **warlike, militant,** fighting, warring, battling; **military,** soldierly, soldierlike; **combative, contentious,** gladiatorial

**martyr** NOUNS 1 **sufferer,** victim, prey; **wretch,** poor devil <nonformal>, object of compassion; redeemed *or* saved soul, soul in glory

VERBS 2 **torture, torment,** rack, put to torture, put *or* lay on the rack, **agonize, harrow,** crucify, martyrize, excruciate, wring, twist, contorse, convulse; prolong the agony, kill by inches

**marvel** NOUNS 1 **wonder, prodigy, miracle, phenomenon,** phenom <nonfor-

mal>; astonishment, amazement, marvelment, wonderment, wonderful thing, nine days' wonder, amazing *or* astonishing thing, quite a thing, really something, **sensation,** rocker *and* stunner <both nonformal>; one for the book *and* something to brag about *and* something to shout about *and* something to write home about *and* something else <all nonformal>
VERBS 2 **wonder,** be astonished *or* amazed *or* astounded, be seized with wonder; **gaze, gape,** drop one's jaw, look *or* stand aghast *or* agog, gawk, **stare,** stare openmouthed, open one's eyes, rub one's eyes, hold one's breath; not be able to account for, not know what to make of, not believe one's eyes *or* ears *or* senses

**marvelous** ADJS **wonderful, wondrous, miraculous,** fantastic, fabulous, phenomenal, **prodigious, stupendous,** unheard-of, unprecedented, extraordinary, exceptional, rare, unique, singular, **remarkable,** striking, **sensational; beguiling, fascinating**

**masculine** ADJS **male,** bull; **manly, manlike, mannish,** manful, andric; uneffeminate; **gentlemanly,** gentlemanlike

**masculinity** NOUNS masculineness, maleness; **manliness,** manlihood, **manhood,** manfulness, manlikeness; mannishness; gentlemanliness, gentlemanlikeness

**mash** NOUNS 1 **pulp, paste, mush,** smash, squash, crush
VERBS 2 **beat, pound, smash, crush,** crunch, flail, squash, scrunch <nonformal>

**mask** NOUNS 1 **cover, disguise, camouflage,** protective coloration; **masquerade,** masque, mummery; visor, vizard, false face, domino, domino mask
VERBS 2 **cover,** cloak, mantle, muffle, blanket, canopy, cope, cowl, hood, **veil,** curtain, **screen, shield,** screen off, cloud, obscure, fog, befog, fuzz
3 **disguise,** camouflage

**masque** NOUNS **ball,** *bal* <Fr>; masked ball, mask, masquerade ball, masquerade, *bal masqué* <Fr>, *bal costumé* <Fr>, fancy-dress ball, cotillion

**masquerade** VERBS **disguise oneself,** take an assumed name, assume a cover, change one's identity, go under an alias, remain anonymous, be incognito, go *or* sail under false colors, wear a mask

**mass** NOUNS 1 **bulk,** substance, matter, magnitude, amplitude, **extent, sum; volume,** mountain, load
2 **lump,** clump, **hunk** *and* **chunk** <both nonformal>, piece, **gob** *and* glob <both nonformal>, gobbet; batch, **wad,** block, loaf
3 **sacred music,** requiem mass, requiem, missa brevis, missa solemnis
4 **throng, multitude, horde,** host, heap <nonformal>, army, panoply, legion; **crowd,** press, crush, flood, spate, deluge
VERBS 5 **come together, assemble, congregate, collect,** come from far and wide, come *or* arrive in a body; **unite**; muster, **meet, gather, forgather,** gang up <nonformal>; **merge,** converge, flow together, fuse; **throng, crowd,** swarm, teem, hive, surge, seethe, mill, stream, horde
ADJS 6 **popular,** public, grass-roots, **common,** common as dirt, commonplace, **plain, ordinary, lowly,** low, mean, base

**massacre** NOUNS 1 **carnage, bloodbath, decimation,** saturnalia of blood; **mass murder, mass destruction,** mass extermination, wholesale murder, pogrom, race-murder, genocide, race extermination, **the Holocaust,** the final solution
VERBS 2 **slaughter, butcher, decimate,** commit carnage, depopulate, murder *or* kill *or* slay en masse; commit mass murder *or* destruction, murder wholesale, commit genocide

**massage** NOUNS massaging, stroking, kneading; **rubdown;** massotherapy; vibrator; facial massage, facial

**the masses** NOUNS **the hoi polloi,** *hoi polloi* <Gk>, the many, **the multitude,** the crowd, **the mob,** the horde, the million, the mass of the people, the herd, the great unnumbered, the great unwashed, **the vulgar** *or* **common herd;** *profanum vulgus, ignobile vulgus, mobile vulgus* <all L>

*the booboisie*
**H L Mencken**

**massive** ADJS 1 **large, immense, enormous, huge**; **gigantic,** mountainous, titanic, colossal, mammoth, Gargantuan, gigantesque, monster, monstrous, outsize, sizable, larger-than-life, overgrown, king-size, monumental; massy, weighty, bulky, voluminous; **vast,** vasty, boundless, **infinite**, immeasurable, cos-

mic, astronomical, galactic; **spacious,** amplitudinous, extensive; **tremendous,** stupendous, awesome, prodigious
2 **heavy, ponderous,** hefty <nonformal>, fat; **solid,** firm, substantial

**mass-produced** ADJS **manufactured,** volume-produced, assembly-line

**mast** NOUNS **spar,** timber; pole, stick *and* tree <both nonformal>; bare pole; radio *or* television mast, antenna tower; sprit, yard, yardarm

**master** NOUNS 1 lord, lord and master, overlord, seigneur, paramount, lord paramount, liege, liege lord, *padrone* <Ital>, *patron* and *chef* <both Fr>, patroon; **chief, boss,** sahib <India>, *bwana* <Swah>; employer; husband, man of the house, master of the house, goodman <old or nonformal>, paterfamilias; teacher, rabbi, guru, starets; master craftsman, master workman, master carpenter, etc
2 **wise man, wise woman, sage,** sapient, man *or* woman of wisdom; **mistress,** authority, mastermind, master spirit of the age, oracle
VERBS 3 **subdue,** overmaster, **quell, crush, reduce,** beat down, **break,** break down, overwhelm; **conquer**; bring low, **bring to terms, humble,** humiliate, take down a notch *or* peg, bend, bring one to his knees, bend to one's will
4 attain mastery of, make oneself master of, **gain command of, become adept in,** become familiar *or* conversant with, become versed *or* well-versed in, **get up in** *or* **on,** gain a good *or* thorough knowledge of, **learn all about, get down pat** <nonformal>, get down cold <nonformal>, get to the bottom *or* heart of; **get the hang** *or* **knack of; learn the ropes,** learn the ins and outs; know well
ADJS 5 highest, uppermost, topmost, toprank, ranking, of the first rank, world-class, **dominant,** predominant, controlling, **overruling,** overriding, all-absorbing

**masterful** ADJS **perfected, finished,** polished, refined; done to a T *or* to a turn; **classic, classical,** masterly, expert, proficient; **consummate,** quintessential, archetypical, exemplary, model

**mastermind** NOUNS 1 **master, past master;** master hand, world-class performer, **good hand,** skilled *or* practiced hand; **prodigy; virtuoso; genius,** man *or* woman of genius
VERBS 2 **control, command,** head, govern, boss *and* head up *and* pull the strings *and* quarterback *and* call the signals <all nonformal>; **order, prescribe;** lay down the law, make the rules, call the shots *or* tune <nonformal>; manipulate, maneuver, engineer; take command; be responsible for

**master of ceremonies** NOUNS **MC** *or* **emcee** <both nonformal>, compère <Brit>, marshal; **toastmaster;** host, master of the revels, revel master; social director

**masterpiece** NOUNS **masterwork,** *chef d'œuvre* <Fr>; **master stroke,** *coup de maître* <Fr>; **feat,** *tour de force* <Fr>, **epitome;** perfect specimen, highest type; **classic,** showpiece; **paragon**

**masturbation** NOUNS autoeroticism, self-abuse, onanism, manipulation, playing with oneself, jacking off *and* pulling off *and* hand job <all nonformal>; sexual fantasy; wet dream

**mat** NOUNS pad, rug; litter, bedstraw

**matador** NOUNS **bullfighter,** toreador, *torero* <Sp>; banderillero, picador

**match** NOUNS 1 **contest,** engagement, encounter, matching, meet, meeting, derby, pissing match <nonformal>, **trial, test,** *concours* and *rencontre* <both Fr>; **close contest, hard contest,** closely fought contest, close *or* tight one, horse race *and* crapshoot <all nonformal>; **fight, bout,** battle, duel, slugfest <nonformal>
2 **equal,** mate, twin, fellow, **like, equivalent,** opposite number, counterpart, answer <nonformal>, vis à vis, equipollent, coequal, parallel, ditto <nonformal>
3 matchstick, lucifer; friction match, locofoco *and* vesuvian *and* vesta *and* fusee *and* Congreve *or* Congreve match <all old>; safety match
VERBS 4 **equal,** rival, correspond, be even-steven, be tantmount to, be equal to; **keep pace with,** keep step with, run abreast; **measure up to,** come up to, stack up with <nonformal>, match up with; **accompany**, **agree,** go along with, go hand in hand, keep pace with, keep in step

**matching** ADJS **analogous,** comparable; **corresponding,** correspondent, equivalent; **parallel,** paralleling; cast in the same mold, of a kind, of a size, of a piece; duplicate, twin, of the same hue *or* stripe

**matchless** ADJS **peerless,** champion; **unmatched,** unmatchable, unrivaled, unparagoned, unparalleled, immortal, **unequaled,** never-to-be-equaled, unpeered, unexampled, unapproached, unapproachable, **unsurpassed, unexcelled;** unsurpassable; inimitable, **incomparable,** beyond compare *or* comparison, **unique;** without equal *or* parallel, *sans pareil* <Fr>; in a class by itself, *sui generis* <L>, easily first, *facile princeps* <L>; second to none, *nulli secundus* <L>; **unbeatable,** invincible

**matchmaker** NOUNS **marriage broker,** matrimonial agent, *shadchen* <Yiddish>; matrimonial agency *or* bureau

**mate** NOUNS 1 **spouse,** yokemate, partner, consort, **better half** <nonformal>

*bone of my bones, and flesh of my flesh*
BIBLE

2 **equal, match,** twin, fellow, **like, equivalent,** opposite number, counterpart, answer <nonformal>, **peer,** compeer, colleague

VERBS 3 **copulate,** couple, unite in sexual intercourse, **have sexual relations,** come together, cohabit, shack up <nonformal>, be intimate; cover, mount, serve *or* service <of animals>

**material** NOUNS 1 **fabric, cloth, textile,** textile fabric, texture, tissue, stuff, weave, weft, woof, web, **goods,** drapery, *étoffe, tissu* <both Fr>; **substance,** matter, medium, the tangible; **elements,** constituent elements, constituents, ingredients, components, atoms, building blocks, parts

ADJS 2 **relevant, pertinent,** appertaining, **germane, apposite,** cogent, admissible, applicable, applying, pertaining, belonging, involving, appropriate, **apropos,** *à propos* <Fr>, to the purpose, **to the point,** in point, *ad rem* <L>; telling, convincing, weighty

**materialistic** ADJS **earthy,** unspiritual, nonspiritual, material, **secularist,** secularistic, worldly, earthly, terrestrial, **mundane,** temporal; practical, realistic; banausic, moneymaking, breadwinning, utilitarian

**materialize** VERBS 1 **turn up, show up,** be found; discover itself, expose *or* betray itself; hang out <nonformal>; materialize, **come to light,** come out; come along, come to hand

2 **embody,** incarnate, concretize, body forth, lend substance to, reify, entify, hypostatize

**matériel** NOUNS **equipment,** equipage, munitions; armament, munition; **arms, weapons,** deadly weapons, instruments of destruction, offensive weapons, **military hardware,** weaponry, ordnance, munitions of war, *apparatus belli* <L>

**maternal** ADJS **native,** natal, **indigenous,** endemic, autochthonous; mother, original, aboriginal, primitive; **motherly,** motherlike

**mathematical** ADJS numeric *or* numerical, numerary, arithmetic *or* arithmetical, algebraic *or* algebraical, geometric *or* geometrical, trigonometric *or* trigonometrical, analytic *or* analytical

**mathematics** NOUNS math <US nonformal>, maths <Brit nonformal>, mathematic, **numbers, figures;** pure mathematics, abstract mathematics, applied mathematics, higher mathematics, elementary mathematics

**matriarch** NOUNS genetrix, dam, maternal ancestor, materfamilias; **matron,** lady of the house, chatelaine; great lady, first lady; dowager

**matriculate** VERBS **register, enroll,** check in

**matrimonial** ADJS **marital, conjugal,** connubial, nuptial, wedded, married, hymeneal; epithalamic; **spousal;** husbandly, uxorious; bridal, wifely, uxorial

**matrimony** NOUNS **marriage,** wedlock, married status, holy matrimony, holy wedlock, match, matching, match-up, splicing <nonformal>, union, matrimonial union, alliance, marriage sacrament, sacrament of matrimony, bond of matrimony, conjugal bond *or* tie *or* knot, nuptial bond *or* tie *or* knot; married state *or* status, wedded state *or* status, wedded bliss, weddedness; intermarriage, mixed marriage, interfaith marriage, interracial marriage; misalliance, *mésalliance* <Fr>, ill-assorted marriage

*a world-without-end bargain*
SHAKESPEARE

**matrix** NOUNS **mold, form,** cast, template, negative; **die,** punch, stamp, intaglio, seal, mint; last, shoe last

**matronly** ADJS **womanly,** matronal, matronlike; **middle-aged,** mid-life, *entre deux âges* <Fr>, fortyish

**matter** NOUNS 1 **substance, sum and substance,** stuff, material, medium, building blocks, fabric; **gist, heart,** soul, meat, nub; the nitty-gritty *and* the bottom line *and* the name of the game <all nonformal>, **core,** kernel, marrow, pith, sap, spirit, **essence,** quintessence, elixir, distillate, distillation, distilled essence; **affair, business, task**, concern, interest; printed matter, reading matter
VERBS 2 signify, **count, tell,** weigh, carry weight, cut ice *and* cut some ice <both nonformal>, be prominent, stand out, mean much; be something, be somebody, amount to something

**matter-of-fact** ADJS **prosaic,** prose, prosy, prosing, plain; unimaginative, unimpassioned, everyday, workday, workaday, household, garden, common- *or* garden-variety; unpoetical, dull, dry, unromantic, unidealistic, unimpassioned; pedestrian

**mature** VERBS 1 **grow up,** grow, **develop, ripen,** flower, flourish, bloom, blossom; fledge, leave the nest, put up one's hair, not be in pigtails, put on long pants; **come of age,** come to maturity, attain majority, **reach one's majority,** reach twenty-one, reach voting age, reach the age of consent, reach manhood *or* womanhood, put on long trousers *or* pants, come into years of discretion, cut one's wisdom teeth *or* eyeteeth <nonformal>, settle down
ADJS 2 **adult, of age,** out of one's teens, big, grown, **grown-up;** old enough to know better; **ripe,** matured, maturated, seasoned; blooming, abloom; **mellow,** full-grown, fully developed

**maturity** NOUNS **adulthood, majority,** grown-upness, full growth, mature age, legal age, voting age, driving age, drinking age, *legalis homo* <L>; age of consent; ripe age, riper years, full age *or* growth *or* bloom, flower of age, **prime, prime of life,** age of responsibility, age *or* years of discretion, age of matured powers; **manhood,** man's estate, virility, *toga virilis* <L>; **womanhood,** womanness

**maul** VERBS **pound, beat,** hammer, sledgehammer, knock, rap, bang, thump, **drub,** buffet, **batter,** pulverize, paste <nonformal>, patter, pommel, pummel, pelt, baste, lambaste; thresh, thrash; flail; spank, flap

**mausoleum** NOUNS **tomb, sepulcher;** resting place, last home, long home, narrow house, house of death, low house, low green tent; **crypt, vault,** burial chamber

*the lone couch of his everlasting sleep*
SHELLEY

**maven** NOUNS **specialist,** specializer, **expert, authority,** savant, scholar, connoisseur; technical expert; pundit, critic; amateur, dilettante; fan, buff, freak *and* nut <both nonformal>, aficionado

**maverick** NOUNS 1 **nonconformist,** unconformist, **original,** eccentric, gonzo <nonformal>, deviant, deviationist; **misfit,** square peg in a round hole, **dissenter**
ADJS 2 **unconventional,** unorthodox, eccentric, gonzo <nonformal>, original, Bohemian

**mawkish** ADJS **oversweet,** saccharine, rich, **cloying,** sickly-sweet; **sentimental,** sentimentalized, soft, **maudlin,** oversentimental, oversentimentalized, bathetic; **mushy** *or* sloppy *or* gushing *or* teary *or* beery <all nonformal>

**maxim** NOUNS **aphorism,** apothegm, epigram, dictum, adage, proverb, gnome, words of wisdom, saw, saying, witticism, sentence, expression, phrase, catchword, catchphrase, word, byword, mot, motto, moral

**maximize** VERBS **increase, enlarge,** aggrandize, **amplify,** augment, extend, **add to; expand**, inflate; **build,** build up; pyramid, parlay

**maximum** NOUNS 1 **limit, end**, extremity, extreme, **acme,** apogee, climax, max <nonformal>, ceiling, **peak,** summit, **pinnacle,** crown, top; **utmost,** uttermost, utmost extent, highest degree, nth degree *or* power, *ne plus ultra* <L>
ADJS 2 **superlative,** supreme, greatest, best, highest, veriest, maximal, most, utmost, outstanding

**mayhem** NOUNS **mutilation,** crippling, hobbling, hamstringing, laming, maiming; destruction

**maze** NOUNS **complex,** meander, Chinese puzzle, **labyrinth; perplexity**

**meadow** NOUNS **grassland,** meadow land, mead <old>, swale, lea, haugh *or* haughland <Scots>, vega; bottomland, water meadow; **pasture,** pastureland, pasturage, pasture land

**meager** ADJS **slight,** scrimpy, skimp,

skimpy, exiguous; scant, **scanty,** spare; miserly, niggardly, stingy, narrow <nonformal>, parsimonious, mean; austere, Lenten, Spartan, abstemious, ascetic; stinted, frugal, sparing; poor, impoverished; small, puny, paltry

**meal** NOUNS **repast,** feed *and* sit-down <both nonformal>, mess, spread <nonformal>, table, board, meat, *repas* <Fr>; **refreshment,** refection

**mealymouthed** ADJS **flattering,** adulatory; smooth-spoken, smooth-tongued, honey-mouthed, honey-tongued, honeyed, oily-tongued; fulsome, slimy, slobbery, gushing, protesting too much, smarmy <nonformal>, insinuating, oily, buttery <nonformal>, soapy <nonformal>, **unctuous,** smooth, bland; canting, sniveling

**mean** NOUNS 1 **median, middle**; **golden mean,** *juste milieu* <Fr>; **medium,** happy medium; middle of the road, middle course, *via media* <L>; middle state *or* ground *or* position *or* echelon *or* level *or* point, midpoint; **average,** balance, par, normal, norm, rule, run, generality

VERBS 2 **signify,** denote, connote, import, spell, have the sense of, be construed as, have the force of; **stand for,** symbolize; imply, suggest, argue, breathe, bespeak, betoken, **indicate; mean something,** mean a lot, have impact, come home, hit one where one lives *and* hit one close to home <both nonformal>

ADJS 3 **intermediate,** intermediary, medial, medium, mesne, median, **middle**

4 **low, base, ignoble,** vile, scurvy, sorry, scrubby, beggarly; low-minded, base-minded; **ungenerous, illiberal,** unchivalrous, small, little, paltry, mingy, petty; **niggardly, stingy**

**meander** VERBS **go roundabout,** deviate, go around Robin Hood's barn, take *or* go the long way around, twist and turn; digress; **talk in circles,** say in a roundabout way; equivocate, shilly-shally; dodge

**meandering** ADJS **circuitous,** roundabout, out-of-the-way, devious, oblique, indirect, ambagious <old>, backhanded; **deviating,** digressive, discursive, excursive

**meaning** NOUNS **significance, signification,** *significatum* <L>, *signifié* <Fr>, point, **sense,** idea, purport, import, where one is coming from <nonformal>; **denotation;** dictionary meaning, lexical meaning; emotive *or* affective meaning, undertone, overtone, coloring; relevance, bearing, **relation,** pertinence *or* pertinency; literal meaning, true *or* real meaning, unadorned meaning; **secondary meaning,** connotation; more than meets the eye, what is read between the lines; syntactic *or* structural meaning, grammatical meaning; symbolic meaning

**meaningful** ADJS **significant,** significative; **denotative, connotative,** denotational, connotational, intensional, extensional, associational; **referential; symbolic, metaphorical,** figurative, allegorical; **suggestive,** indicative, **expressive; pregnant,** full of meaning, loaded *or* laden *or* fraught *or* freighted *or* heavy with significance; **pithy, meaty,** sententious, substantial, full of substance; pointed

**meaningless** ADJS **senseless,** purportless, importless, **insignificant,** unsignificant; empty, inane, null; **purposeless,** aimless, designless, without rhyme or reason

**means** NOUNS 1 ways, **ways and means,** means to an end; **wherewithal,** wherewith; funds; **resources,** disposable resources, capital; bankroll <nonformal>; assets, liquid assets, balance, **capital,** available means *or* resources *or* funds, holdings, property

2 **expedient,** means to an end, provision, measure, step, action, effort; **stroke,** stroke of policy, coup, **move,** countermove, **maneuver,** demarche, course of action

**meant** ADJS **intentional, intended,** proposed, purposed, telic, projected, designed, of design, aimed, aimed at, **purposeful,** purposive, willful, voluntary, deliberate; deliberated; considered, studied, advised, **calculated,** contemplated, envisaged, envisioned, meditated, **conscious,** knowing, witting; planned; teleological

**meanwhile** ADVS **meantime, in the meanwhile** *or* **meantime,** in the interim, *ad interim* <L>; between acts *or* halves *or* periods, betweentimes, between now and then; till *or* until then; *en attendant* <Fr>, in the intervening time, at the same time, for the nonce, for a time *or* season

**measly** ADJS **base, low,** low rent *and* low ride *and* low-down *and* cotton-picking <all nonformal>, **mean,** crummy, shabby, mangy <nonformal>, cheesy <nonformal>

**measure** NOUNS 1 **amount,** quantity, large amount, small amount, **sum, number,** count, group, total, reckoning, parcel, passel <nonformal>, **part, portion,** clutch, ration, share, issue, ållotment, lot, deal
2 measuring instrument, **meter, instrument, gauge,** barometer, **rule, yardstick,** measuring rod *or* stick, **standard,** norm, canon, **criterion,** test, touchstone, check
3 **act, enactment,** legislation; **rule, ruling; prescript,** prescription; **regulation,** *règlement* <Fr>; edict, decree; **bill**
VERBS 4 **gauge, quantify,** quantitate, quantize, mete <old>, take the measure of, mensurate, triangulate, apply the yardstick to; **estimate,** make an approximation; **assess,** rate, appraise, valuate, value, evaluate, appreciate, prize; **assay**

**measurement** NOUNS **measure;** mensuration, measuring, **gauging; estimation,** estimate, rough measure, approximation, ballpark figure <nonformal>; **quantification,** quantitation, quantization; **appraisal,** appraisement, **stocktaking, assay,** assaying

**meat** NOUNS 1 flesh, red meat, *viande* <Fr>; butcher's meat, *viande de boucherie* <Fr>
2 **gist,** heart, soul, nub; the nitty-gritty *and* the bottom line *and* the name of the game <all nonformal>, **core,** kernel

**meat-eating** ADJS **flesh-eating, carnivorous,** omophagous, predacious

**meaty** ADJS **meaningful, pithy,** sententious, substantial, full of substance; pointed

**mechanic** NOUNS **skilled worker,** skilled laborer, **journeyman, artisan,** artificer

**mechanical** ADJS **involuntary,** instinctive, automatic, reflex, reflexive, knee-jerk <nonformal>, conditioned; **unconscious,** unthinking, blind; **unwitting,** unintentional, machinelike

**mechanism** NOUNS machinery, **movement,** movements, **action, motion, works,** workings, inner workings, what makes it work, innards, what makes it tick

**medal** NOUNS **military honor,** medallion; military medal, service medal, war medal, soldier's medal

**meddle** VERBS **pry, snoop,** peep, peek, spy, nose, nose into, have a long *or* big nose, poke *or* stick one's nose in; intervene, interfere, intermeddle

**meddler** NOUNS **busybody, pry,** Paul Pry, prier, Nosey Parker *or* nosey Parker *or* Nosy Parker <all nonformal>, snoop *or* snooper, **kibitzer** *and* backseat driver <both nonformal>

**meddlesome** ADJS meddling; **officious,** overofficious, self-appointed, impertinent, presumptuous; **busybody,** busy; pushing, pushy, forward; **prying,** nosy *or* nosey *and* snoopy <both nonformal>; inquisitive

**media** NOUNS **communications,** electronic communications, communications industry, communications medium *or* media, communications network

**median** NOUNS 1 **middle,** midmost, **midst; mean**
ADJS 2 **intermediate,** intermediary, medial, mean, medium, mesne, **middle; average,** normal, standard, par for the course

**mediate** VERBS intermediate, **intercede,** go between; **intervene,** interpose, step in, step into the breach, declare oneself a party, involve oneself, put oneself between disputants, use one's good offices, act between; **negotiate,** bargain, **treat with,** make terms, meet halfway; **arbitrate,** moderate; **umpire, referee,** judge

**mediator** NOUNS intermediator, intermediate agent, intermediate, intermedium, **intermediary,** interagent, internuncio; **intercessor,** interceder; ombudsman; **intervener,** intervenor; **go-between, middleman**; negotiator

**medicate** VERBS **give medicine,** drug, dope <nonformal>, dose; salve, oil, anoint, embrocate

**medication** NOUNS **medicine, medicament,** medicinal, theraputant, **drug,** physic, preparation; **therapy, therapeutics,** therapeusis, treatment, medical care *or* treatment

**medicine man** NOUNS **shaman,** shamanist; **voodoo,** voodooist, wangateur, **witch doctor,** obeah doctor, mundunugu, isangoma

**mediocre** ADJS **middling,** indifferent, fair, fairish, fair to middling <nonformal>, moderate, modest, medium, betwixt and between; respectable, passable, **tolerable; so-so,** *comme ci comme ça* <Fr>

**meditate** VERBS **consider, contemplate,** speculate, reflect, study, ponder, perpend, weigh, deliberate, debate, muse, brood, ruminate, chew the cud <nonformal>, digest; introspect, be abstracted; wrinkle one's brow

**medium** NOUNS 1 **psychic; spiritualist,** spiritist, ecstatic, spirit rapper, automatist, psychographist; necromancer
2 **substance,** stuff, fabric, material, matter, the tangible; **elements,** constituent elements, constituents, ingredients, components, atoms, building blocks, parts
ADJS 3 mean, **intermediate,** intermediary, median, medial, mid-level, middle-echelon; **average,** normal, standard, par for the course; middle-of-the-road, moderate; **middling, ordinary,** usual, routine, common, mediocre, merely adequate, passing, banal, so-so

**medley** NOUNS **miscellany,** miscellanea, collectanea; **assortment,** variety, mixture; hodgepodge, conglomerate, **conglomeration,** omnium-gatherum <nonformal>

**meek** ADJS **gentle, mild,** mild-mannered, peaceable, pacific, quiet; **subdued, chastened, tame,** tamed, broken, housebroken, domesticated; lamblike, gentle as a lamb, dovelike; humble

**meet** NOUNS 1 **contest, engagement, encounter, match,** matching, meeting, derby, pissing match <nonformal>, **trial, test,** *concours* and *rencontre* <both Fr>; tournament, tourney; rally; **game**; **games,** Olympic games, Olympics, gymkhana
2 **assembly,** *assemblée* <Fr>, **gathering, forgathering, congregation,** congress, conference, convocation, concourse, **meeting, get-together** *and* turnout <both nonformal>
VERBS 3 **encounter; come across, run across,** meet up, fall across, cross the path of; **come upon,** run upon, fall upon, light *or* alight upon; come among, fall among; **meet with,** meet up with <nonformal>, experience, come face to face with, **confront,** meet head-on *or* eyeball to eyeball; **run into, bump into** *and* run smack into <both nonformal>, join up with, come *or* run up against <nonformal>, run *and* fall foul of; be on a collision course
4 **come together, assemble, congregate, collect,** come from far and wide, come *or* arrive in a body; league, ally; **unite**; muster, **gather, forgather,** gang up <nonformal>, mass; **merge,** converge, flow together, fuse

**meeting** NOUNS 1 meeting up, joining, joining up, **encounter;** confrontation; rencontre; near-miss, collision course, near thing, narrow squeak *or* brush; **conference,** congress, convention, parley, palaver, confab <nonformal>, confabulation, **conclave, powwow, huddle** <nonformal>, **consultation,** *pourparler* <Fr>; **rendezvous,** tryst, assignation
ADJS 2 **in contact,** contacting, **touching,** contingent; impinging, impingent; tangent, tangential; osculatory; grazing, kissing, glancing, brushing, rubbing, nudging; **assembled,** collected, gathered; **joining, connecting**

**melancholy** NOUNS 1 **melancholia,** melancholiness; gentle melancholy, romantic melancholy; **pensiveness, wistfulness,** tristfulness; **nostalgia,** homesickness, *mal du pays* <Fr>
ADJS 2 melancholic, **blue** <nonformal>, life-weary, world-weary, tired of living; atrabilious, atrabiliar; **pensive, wistful,** tristful; **nostalgic,** homesick

**melee** NOUNS **commotion, hubbub,** Babel, tumult, turmoil, uproar, racket, riot, **disturbance, rumpus** <nonformal>, ruckus *and* ruction <both nonformal>, **fracas, hassle; row** *and* hassle <both nonformal>, **brawl,** free-for-all <nonformal>, donnybrook *or* donnybrook fair, broil, embroilment, scramble; **roughhouse, rough-and-tumble**

**meliorate** VERBS **improve, grow better,** look better, show improvement, **mend,** ameliorate; **look up** *or* **pick up** *or* **perk up** <all nonformal>; **advance, progress,** make progress, make headway, gain, gain ground, go forward, get *or* go ahead, come on, come along *and* come along nicely <both nonformal>, get along; make strides *or* rapid strides, take off *and* skyrocket <both nonformal>

**mellow** VERBS 1 **mature, grow up,** grow, **develop, ripen,** flower, flourish, bloom, blossom; season, temper
ADJS 2 **resonant, reverberant, vibrant, sonorous,** plangent, rolling;

rich, full; **merry,** jolly, happy, gay; **agreeable,** complaisant, harmonious, *en rapport* <Fr>, compatible; **mature, ripe,** ripened, of full *or* ripe age, **developed,** fully developed, well-developed, **full-grown,** full-fledged, fully fledged, full-blown, in full bloom, in one's prime; mellowed, seasoned, tempered, aged

**melodrama** NOUNS **theatrics,** theatricality, histrionics, dramatics, hamminess *and* chewing up the scenery <both nonformal>; **sensationalism,** emotionalism, melodramatics, blood and thunder

**melodramatic** ADJS **emotionalistic,** emotive, overemotional, hysteric, hysterical, sensational, sensationalistic, theatric, theatrical, histrionic, dramatic, overdramatic, hammy <nonformal>, nonrational, unreasoning; hyperthymic

**melody** NOUNS **tune, tone,** musical sound, musical quality, tonality; sweetness, dulcetness, mellifluence, mellifluousness

**melt** VERBS **liquefy,** liquidize, liquesce, fluidify, fluidize; **run,** thaw, colliquate; **affect, touch, move, soften,** melt the heart, choke one up, give one a lump in the throat; touch a chord, **touch a sympathetic chord,** touch one's heart, tug at the heart *or* heartstrings

**member** NOUNS 1 **appendage,** external organ; **arm; leg,** limb, wing
2 affiliate, belonger, insider, initiate, one of us, cardholder, card-carrier, card-carrying member; **enrollee,** enlistee; **associate,** socius, **fellow;** brother, sister; comrade; honorary member; life member; member in good standing, dues-paying member; charter member

**membership** NOUNS participation, partaking, sharing, cooperation; members, associates, affiliates, body of affiliates, constituency

**memento** NOUNS **remembrance,** token, trophy, souvenir, keepsake, relic, favor, token of remembrance; *memento mori* <L>; **memories, memorabilia,** memorials

**memoir** NOUNS **history, biography,** memorial, life, story, life story, adventures, fortunes, experiences; **autobiography, memoirs,** memorials

**memorabilia** NOUNS **archives,** public records, government archives, government papers, presidential papers, historical documents, historical records; biographical records, life records, biographical material, papers, ana; **annals, chronicles,** chronology; notabilia, great doings

**memorable** ADJS **notable,** noteworthy, celebrated, remarkable, marked, **standout** <nonformal>, of mark, signal; rememberable, unforgettable, never to be forgotten; striking, telling, salient

**memorandum** VERBS **memo** <nonformal>, memoir, *aide-mémoire* <Fr>, memorial; **reminder**; **note, notation,** annotation, jotting, docket, marginal note, marginalia, scholium, scholia, adversaria

**memorial** NOUNS 1 **monument,** monumental *or* memorial record; necrology, obituary, **memento,** remembrance, testimonial; **marker;** inscription; **tablet,** stone, hoarstone <Brit>, boundary stone, memorial stone; **pillar,** stele *or* stela, shaft, column, memorial column, rostral column, manubial column; war memorial; arch, memorial arch, triumphal arch; memorial statue, bust; monolith, obelisk, **pyramid; gravestone, tombstone;** memorial tablet, brass; cenotaph; cairn, mound, barrow, cromlech, dolmen, megalith, menhir, cyclolith; **shrine,** reliquary, tope, stupa
ADJS 2 **celebrative,** celebratory, celebrating; **commemorative,** commemorating

**memorialize** VERBS **celebrate,** observe, keep, mark, solemnly mark, honor; **commemorate; solemnize,** signalize, hallow, mark with a red letter

**memorize** VERBS **commit to memory,** con; **learn by heart,** get by heart, learn *or* get by rote, get word-perfect *or* letter-perfect, learn word for word, learn verbatim; know by heart *or* from memory, have by heart *or* rote, have at one's fingertips

**memory** NOUNS 1 **engram,** memory trace, traumatic trace *or* memory; unconscious memory; **remembrance,** recollection, reminiscence, fond remembrance, retrospection, musing on the past, looking back

*the remembrance of things past*
SHAKESPEARE

*la recherche du temps perdu*
PROUST

2 **computer memory, storage,** memory bank, memory chip, firmware; **main memory,** main storage *or* store, random access memory *or* RAM, core, core storage *or* store, disk pack, magnetic disk, primary storage, backing store, read/write memory, optical disk memory, bubble memory; read-only memory *or* ROM, programmable read-only memory *or* PROM

**men** NOUNS **work force,** hands, staff, personnel, employees, help, hired help, the help, **crew, gang,** force; **fighting force,** troops, units, firepower; human resources; **forces; mankind,** menfolk *or* menfolks <nonformal>, the sword side

**menace** NOUNS 1 **threat,** threateningness, threatfulness, promise of harm, knife poised at one's throat, arrow aimed at one's heart, sword of Damocles; **foreboding; warning**; saber-rattling, muscle-flexing, woofing <nonformal>, bulldozing, scare tactics, **intimidation**, arm-twisting <nonformal>
VERBS 2 **threaten,** bludgeon, bulldoze, put the heat *or* screws *or* squeeze on <nonformal>, lean on <nonformal>; hold a pistol to one's head, terrorize, **intimidate,** twist one's arm *and* arm-twist <both nonformal>; utter threats against, shake *or* double *or* clench one's fist at; hold over one's head; **lower,** spell *or* mean trouble, look threatening, loom, loom up; **be imminent**

**menacing** ADJS **threatening,** threatful, minatory, minacious; **lowering; imminent**; **ominous,** foreboding; denunciatory, comminatory, abusive; fear-inspiring, **intimidating,** bludgeoning, muscle-flexing, saber-rattling, bulldozing, browbeating, bullying, hectoring, blustering, terrorizing, terroristic

**ménage** NOUNS **family,** household, hearth, hearthside, people, **folk,** homefolk, folks *and* homefolks <both nonformal>

**menagerie** NOUNS **zoo,** *Tiergarten* <Ger>, zoological garden *or* park

**mend** VERBS 1 **get well,** recover, be oneself again, feel like a new person, get back on one's feet, get over it; recuperate; **improve, better,** change for the better
2 **repair,** fix, fix up <nonformal>, do up, doctor <nonformal>, put in repair, put in shape, set to rights, put in order *or* condition; **condition,** recondition, commission, put in commission, ready; **service, overhaul;** patch, **patch up**

**menial** NOUNS 1 **servant,** servitor, help; **domestic,** domestic help, domestic servant, house servant; live-in help, day help; drudge, slavey <nonformal>; scullion, turnspit
ADJS 2 **servile,** slavish, subservient, **base,** mean

**menopause** NOUNS **change of life,** climacteric, grand climacteric

**mental** ADJS **intellectual,** rational, reasoning, thinking, noetic, conceptive, conceptual, phrenic; intelligent; noological; **cognitive,** prehensive, thought, conceptualized, ideative, ideational

**mental block** NOUNS **block,** blocking, memory obstruction; repression, suppression, defense mechanism

**mental deficiency** NOUNS **insanity,** alienation, aberration, mental disturbance, **derangement,** distraction, disorientation, mental derangement *or* disorder, unbalance, mental instability, unsoundness, **unsoundness of mind;** unbalanced mind, diseased *or* unsound mind

**mental hospital** NOUNS psychopathic hospital *or* ward, **psychiatric hospital** *or* ward, **insane asylum,** asylum, lunatic asylum, **madhouse,** mental institution, mental home, bedlam; **bughouse** *and* nuthouse *and* laughing academy *and* **loonybin** *and* **booby hatch** *and* funny farm <all nonformal>

**mental illness** NOUNS **mental disorder,** emotional disorder, psychonosema, psychopathyfunctional nervous disorder; emotional instability; **maladjustment,** social maladjustment; nervous breakdown, crack-up <nonformal>; **insanity; psychosis;** schizophrenia; paranoia; **manic-depressive psychosis, depression,** melancholia; **neurosis, psychoneurosis,** neurotic *or* psychoneurotic disorder

**mentality** NOUNS **intellect,** mind, *mens* <L>; mental *or* intellectual faculty, nous, **reason, rationality,** rational *or* reasoning faculty, power of reason, *Vernunft* <Ger>, *esprit* <Fr>, *raison* <Fr>, ratio, discursive reason, **intelligence,** mental capacity, **understanding,** reasoning, intellection, conception

*discourse of reason*
SHAKESPEARE

**mental telepathy** NOUNS **telepathy,** mind reading, thought transference, telepathic transmission; telepathic dream, telepathic hallucination

**mention** NOUNS 1 **remark,** statement, earful *and* crack *and* one's two cents' worth <all nonformal>, **word,** say, **saying,** utterance, observation, reflection, expression; note, thought; assertion, averment, allegation, affirmation, pronouncement, position, dictum; **declaration; citation,** eulogy, honorable mention, kudos, accolade, tribute, praise
VERBS 2 **remark,** comment, observe, note; let drop *or* fall, say by the way, make mention of; refer to, allude to, touch on, make reference to, call attention to; opine <nonformal>; interject; blurt, blurt out, exclaim; direct attention to, **bring under** *or* **to one's notice,** hold up to notice, bring to attention, mention in passing

**mentor** NOUNS **adviser,** counsel, counselor, consultant, expert, maven <nonformal>; instructor, guide, nestor, orienter; confidant, personal adviser

**menu** NOUNS **bill of fare,** *carte du jour* <Fr>

**mercantile** ADJS **commercial,** business, trade, trading, merchant; commercialistic, mercantilistic

**mercenary** NOUNS 1 **hireling,** *condottiere* <Ital>, free lance, free companion, **soldier of fortune,** adventurer, myrmidon
ADJS 2 **greedy, avaricious,** avid, voracious, rapacious, cupidinous, esurient, **ravening,** grasping, grabby <nonformal>, graspy, acquisitive, sordid, overgreedy; ravenous, gobbling, devouring; miserly, money-hungry, money-grubbing, money-mad, venal; **piggish,** hoggish, swinish, a hog for, greedy as a hog; **gluttonous; employed,** hired, hireling, paid

**merchandise** NOUNS 1 **commodities,** wares, goods, effects, vendibles; **items,** oddments; **consumer goods,** consumer items, retail goods, goods for sale; **stock, stock-in-trade;** staples; **inventory; line,** line of goods; mail-order goods, catalog goods; **luxury goods,** high-ticket *or* big-ticket *or* upscale items
VERBS 2 **sell, market,** move, turn over, sell off, make *or* effect a sale

**merchandising** NOUNS **selling,** marketing; direct selling; mail-order selling, direct-mail selling, catalog selling; television *or* video selling; **vending,** peddling, hawking, huckstering

**merchant** NOUNS merchandiser, marketer, **trader,** trafficker, **dealer,** monger, chandler; **tradesman,** tradeswoman; **storekeeper,** shopkeeper

**merciful** ADJS **pitying, sympathetic,** sympathizing, commiserative, condolent, understanding; **compassionate,** ruthful, rueful, **clement,** gentle, soft, melting, bleeding, tender, **tender-hearted,** softhearted, warmhearted; **humane,** human; lenient, forbearant; charitable

**merciless** ADJS **pitiless,** unpitying, unpitiful; blind *or* deaf to pity; **unsympathetic,** unsympathizing; **uncompassionate,** uncompassioned; **unmerciful,** without mercy, unruing, **ruthless,** dog-eat-dog; unfeeling, bowelless, inclement, relentless, inexorable, unyielding, unforgiving; **heartless,** hard, hard as nails, steely, flinty, harsh, savage, **cruel**, brutal, brutish, **bestial,** mindless, insensate, monstrous, mutant, inhuman, bloody, sanguinary, kill-crazy <nonformal>; malign, malignant

**mercy** NOUNS **clemency,** clementness, mercifulness, **humaneness,** humanity, pity, **compassion**; **mildness, gentleness,** tenderness, softness, moderateness; **easiness,** easygoingness; laxness; acceptance, **tolerance**

**mercy killing** NOUNS euthanasia, negative *or* passive euthanasia

**merge** VERBS **converge,** come together, approach, run together, **meet,** unite, connect; **join,** band, league, **associate, affiliate,** ally, **combine, unite,** fuse, coalesce, amalgamate, federate, confederate, consolidate; hook up *and* tie up *and* tie in <all nonformal>; be in league, **go into partnership with,** go partners <nonformal>, go *or* be in cahoots with; **join together,** club together, league together, band together; **blend,** interblend, stir in

**merger** NOUNS **combination,** combine, combo <nonformal>, composition; **amalgamation,** consolidation, assimilation, **integration,** solidification, encompassment, inclusion, ecumenism; **alliance,** affiliation, reaffiliation, association, league, hookup <nonformal>, tie-up <nonformal>; buyout, takeover, leveraged buyout

**merit** NOUNS 1 **importance,** value, worth, excellence; **goodness,** quality, class <nonformal>; **virtue,** grace; desert; **fineness,** goodliness, fairness, niceness; **superiority,** first-rateness, **skillfulness**
VERBS 2 **deserve,** earn, rate *and* be in line for <both nonformal>, **be worthy of,** be deserving, richly deserve

**meritorious** ADJS **praiseworthy,** worthy, **commendable,** estimable, **laudable,** admirable, creditable; exemplary, model, unexceptionable; well-deserving; beyond all praise, *sans peur et sans reproche* <Fr>; **deserving,** meriting, worthy of, worth one's salt, **well-thought-of,** highly regarded, held in esteem, in good odor, in favor, in high favor; in one's good books

**mermaid** NOUNS **swimmer, bather,** natator, merman; bathing girl; bathing beauty; undine, nix, nixie, kelpie; **naiad,** limniad, fresh-water nymph; sea nymph, ocean nymph, sea-maid, sea-maiden, siren

**merry** ADJS **mirthful,** hilarious; joyful, joyous, rejoicing; **gleeful,** gleesome; **jolly,** buxom; **jovial,** jocund, jocular; **frivolous;** laughter-loving, mirth-loving, risible

*as merry as the day is long*
SHAKESPEARE

**merry-go-round** NOUNS **round of pleasure,** mad round, **whirl,** the rounds, the dizzy rounds; carousel, roundabout, ride, whirligig, whip, flying horses

**merrymaking** NOUNS **conviviality,** joviality, jollity, gaiety, heartiness, cheer, good cheer, festivity, partying, merriment, revelry

**mesa** NOUNS **plateau,** tableland, high plateau, table, table mountain, butte, moor, fell <Brit>, hammada

**mescaline** NOUNS

<nonformal> beans, big chief, buttons, cactus, mesc

**mesh** NOUNS 1 **interaction,** interworking, intercourse, intercommunication, **interplay;** meshing, intermeshing, engagement; **network, computer network,** communications network, local area network *or* LAN, workgroup computing
VERBS 2 **interact,** interwork, **interplay;** intermesh, engage, fit, fit like a glove, dovetail, mortise; **interweave,** interlace, intertwine; **interchange;** coact, **cooperate;** codepend

**mesmerize** VERBS **grip,** hold, arrest, hold the interest, fascinate, enthrall, spellbind, **hold spellbound,** grab <nonformal>, charm, enchant, hypnotize, catch; absorb the attention, claim one's thoughts, engross the mind *or* thoughts, engage the attention, involve the interest, occupy the attention, monopolize one's attention, engage the mind *or* thoughts

**mess** NOUNS 1 **meal,** repast, feed *and* sitdown <both nonformal>, spread <nonformal>, table, board, meat, *repas* <Fr>; **rations,** board, meals, commons <chiefly Brit>, allowance, allotment, food allotment, tucker <Australia>
2 **dining room,** *salle à manger* <Fr>, dining hall, refectory, messroom *or* mess hall, commons
3 **jumble,** scramble, tumble, snarl-up, bloody *or* holy *or* unholy *or* god-awful mess <nonformal> **turmoil,** welter, mishmash, hash, helter-skelter, farrago, crazy-quilt, higgledy-piggledy; **clutter,** litter, **disorder,** chaos, mix-up *and* snafu <both nonformal>;
4 **eyesore,** blot, blot on the landscape, blemish, **sight** <nonformal>, **fright, horror,** no beauty, no beauty queen, ugly duckling
5 **disarrange,** derange, misarrange; **disorder,** disorganize, throw out of order, put out of gear, dislocate, upset the applecart, **disarray; dishevel,** rumple, ruffle; tousle <nonformal>, muss *and* **muss up** <both nonformal>, **mess up** <nonformal>; **litter, clutter,** scatter

**message** NOUNS **dispatch,** word, communication, communiqué, advice, press release, release; **letter,** epistle; personal letter, business letter; **commercial,** commercial announcement, commercial message, **spot announcement,** spot *and* plug <both nonformal>

**messed up** ADJS 1 **disheveled,** mussed up <nonformal>, **rumpled,** tumbled, ruffled, snarled, snaggy; **tousled,** tously; uncombed, shaggy, matted

2 <nonformal> **goofed-up, bobbled,** bitched, bitched-up, hashed-up, **fouled-**

up, fucked-up, screwed-up, bollixed-up, loused-up, gummed-up, buggered, buggered-up, snafued; clunky, half-assed; ass-backwards

3 <nonformal> **queered, screwed up, fouled up,** loused up, snafued, buggered, buggered up, gummed up, snarled up, balled up, bollixed up, hashed up, mucked up, botched up; beat up, clapped-out <Brit>; totaled, kaput, finished, packed-up <Brit>, done for, cooked, sunk, shot

**messenger** NOUNS message-bearer, **dispatch-bearer,** commissionaire <Brit>, nuncio <old>, **courier,** diplomatic courier, carrier, **runner,** express <Brit>, dispatch-rider, pony-express rider, postboy, postrider, *estafette* <Fr>; bicycle *or* motorcycle messenger; **go-between,** emissary; Mercury, Hermes, Iris, Pheidippides, Paul Revere

**mess hall** NOUNS **dining room,** *salle à manger* <Fr>, dinette, dining hall, refectory, mess *or* messroom, commons; **cafeteria**

**messiah** NOUNS **leader of men,** born leader, charismatic leader *or* figure, inspired leader; Mahdi

**messy** ADJS **dirty,** grimy, grubby, grungy <nonformal>, smirchy, dingy; scruffy, slovenly, untidy; **slipshod,** slipshoddy, **slovenly,** sloppy *and* half-assed <both nonformal>, sluttish

**metabolize** VERBS **digest,** assimilate, absorb; predigest

**metallic** ADJS **metal,** metallike, metalline, metalloid *or* metalloidal, metalliform

**metamorphosis** NOUNS **transformation,** transmogrification; **translation;** metamorphism; **transfiguration** *or* transfigurement; **transubstantiation,** consubstantiation

**metaphor** NOUNS **comparison,** likening, comparing, **analogy;** simile, similitude, allegory, figure *or* trope of comparison

**metaphorical** ADJS **symbolic,** symbolical, allegoric, allegorical, figural, figurative, tropological, metaphorical, anagogic, anagogical, trolatitious; allusive, referential

**mete** VERBS **administer,** give, bestow; apply, put on *or* upon, lay on *or* upon, dose, dose with, dish out <nonformal>, mete out, prescribe; **force, force upon,** impose by force *or* main force, strongarm <nonformal>, force down one's throat, enforce upon

**meteoric** ADJS **brief,** short, short-time, quick, brisk, swift, fleet, speedy, cometary, flashing, flickering; short-term, short-termed

**meteorology** NOUNS weather science, aerology, aerography, air-mass analysis, weatherology, climatology, climatography, microclimatology, forecasting, long-range forecasting; barometry; anemology; nephology

**meter** NOUNS **measure,** numbers; **rhythm,** cadence, movement, lilt, jingle, swing; **accent,** accentuation, metrical accent, stress, emphasis, ictus, **beat**

**method** NOUNS 1 **plan,** scheme, design, **program,** device, contrivance, game, envisagement, conception, enterprise, **idea,** notion; organization, rationalization, systematization, schematization; tactics, **strategy,** game plan <nonformal>; methodology, **system;** algorithm <math>; **approach,** attack, tack
2 **approach,** attack, tack; **technique, procedure, process,** proceeding, course, practice; *modus operandi* <L>, mode of operation *or* MO, manner of working, mode of procedure

**methodical** ADJS **orderly,** ordered, regular, well-regulated, well-ordered, formal, regular as clockwork, uniform, **systematic,** symmetrical, **harmonious;** businesslike, routine, steady, normal, habitual, usual, *en règle,* in hand; **arranged**

**meticulous** ADJS **exacting,** scrupulous, conscientious, religious, punctilious, punctual, **particular,** fussy, critical, attentive, scrutinizing; **thorough,** thoroughgoing, thoroughpaced; **finical,** finicking, finicky; **exact,** precise, precisionistic, precisianistic, prissy, accurate, correct; **strict,** rigid, **rigorous,** spit-and-polish, exigent, demanding; nice, delicate, subtle, fine, refined, minute, detailed, exquisite; **fastidious**

**metropolis** NOUNS **capital;** metropolitan area, greater city, megalopolis, supercity, conurbation, urban complex; urban center, art center, cultural center, medical center, shopping center, shipping center, railroad center, garment center, manufacturing center, tourist center, trade center, etc

**mettle** NOUNS **pluck, spunk** <nonformal>, backbone <nonformal>, **grit,** true grit, spirit, **stamina,** guts *and* moxie <both nonformal>, pith <old>

**mettlesome** NOUNS **plucky,** spunky *and* feisty *and* gutty *or* gutsy <all nonformal>, gritty, dauntless, **game,** game to the last *or* end; **courageous**

**mews** NOUNS **barn,** stable, stall; **cowbarn,** cowhouse, cowshed, cowbyre, byre; street

**Mickey Finn** NOUNS **anesthetic,** sleeping pill *or* tablet, Mickey *and* knockout drops <both nonformal>, chloral hydrate; drug, dope <nonformal>, narcotic, opiate

**Mickey Mouse** ADJS **vulgar,** tasteless, in bad *or* poor taste, tacky *and* chintzy <both nonformal>; cheap, paltry

**microbe** NOUNS **germ,** pathogen, contagium, bug <nonformal>, disease-causing agent, disease-producing microorganism; microorganism

**microcosm** NOUNS **miniature,** mini; scaled-down *or* miniaturized version; microcosmos

**microorganism** NOUNS **germ,** pathogen, contagium, disease-causing agent, disease-producing microorganism, bug <nonformal> **microbe, virus,** filterable virus, nonfilterable virus, adenovirus, echovirus, reovirus, rhinovirus, enterovirus, picornavirus, retrovirus; rickettsia; bacterium, **bacteria,** streptococcus, staphylococcus, bacillus, spirillum, vibrio, spirochete

**microphone** NOUNS **mike** <nonformal>; radiomicrophone; concealed microphone, **bug** <nonformal>

**microscopic** ADJS **infinitesimal,** ultramicroscopic; evanescent, thin, tenuous; inappreciable; impalpable, imponderable, intangible; imperceptible, indiscernible, invisible, unseeable

**microwave** VERBS **cook,** prepare food, heat, micro-cook, nuke <nonformal>

**midday** NOUNS 1 **noon,** noonday, noontide, nooning <nonformal>, noontime, **high noon,** meridian, *meridiem* <L>, twelve o'clock, 1200 hours, eight bells; noonlight
ADJS 2 **noon,** noonday, noonish, meridian, twelve-o'clock; noonlit

**middle** NOUNS 1 median, midmost, **midst;** thick, thick of things; **center**; **heart,** core, nucleus, kernel; **mean**; interior; midriff, diaphragm; **waist,** waistline, zone, girth
ADJS 2 **medial,** median, mesial, middling, mediocre, average, **medium**, mezzo <music>, **mean,** mid; **midmost,** middlemost; **central**, core, nuclear; interior; **intermediate,** intermediary; centrist, moderate, middle-of-the-road

**middle age** NOUNS middle life, meridian of life, the middle years, the wrong side of forty, the dangerous age

**middle-class** ADJS bourgeois, *petit-bourgeois* <Fr>, petty-bourgeois, suburban

**middleman** NOUNS **go-between,** intermediary, medium, intermedium, intermediate, interagent, **internuncio,** broker; connection <nonformal>, **contact; negotiator,** negotiant; interpleader; arbitrator, mediator; wholesaler, jobber

**middle school** NOUNS **secondary school,** middle school, **junior high school,** junior high <nonformal>, intermediate school

**middling** ADJS **mediocre,** indifferent, fair, fairish, fair to middling <nonformal>, moderate, modest, medium, betwixt and between; respectable, passable, **tolerable; so-so,** *comme ci comme ça* <Fr>; of a kind, of a sort, of sorts <nonformal>; nothing to brag about, not much to boast of, nothing to write home about

**midget** NOUNS 1 **dwarf,** dwarfling, midge, **pygmy,** manikin, homunculus, atomy, micromorph, hop-o'-my-thumb
ADJS 2 **dwarf,** dwarfed, dwarfish, **pygmy,** nanoid, elfin; Lilliputian, Tom Thumb; **undersized,** undersize, squat, dumpy; **stunted,** undergrown, runty, pint-size *or* -sized *and* sawed-off <all nonformal>; **small,** tiny

**midnight** NOUNS 1 **dead of night,** hush of night, the witching hour

> *the very witching time of night*
> **Shakespeare**

ADJS 2 **nocturnal,** night, **nightly,** nighttime; nightlong, all-night; night-fallen

**midst** NOUNS **middle,** median, midmost; thick, thick of things; **center; heart, core,** nucleus, kernel; **mean**; interior

**midtown** NOUNS 1 city center, city centre <Brit>, urban center, central *or* center city, core, core city, inner city, business district *or* section, shopping center
ADJS 2 **urban,** municipal, **inner-city,** core, core-city

**midway** ADVS **halfway, in the middle,** betwixt and between <nonformal>, halfway in the middle <nonformal>; plump *or* smack *or* slap- *or* smack-dab in the middle <nonformal>; half-and-half, neither here nor there, *mezzo-mezzo* <Ital>; medially, mediumly; **in the midst of,** in the thick of

**mien** NOUNS **look, air,** demeanor, carriage, bearing, port, posture, stance, poise, presence; guise, garb, complexion, color; appearance, outward appearance, seeming, **front,** manner

**miff** VERBS **provoke, incense,** arouse, inflame, embitter; **vex, irritate, annoy, aggravate** <nonformal>, **exasperate, nettle,** fret, chafe; **pique, peeve** <nonformal>, huff; **ruffle, roil, rile** <nonformal>, ruffle one's feathers, **rankle;** put *or* get one's back up, stick in one's craw <nonformal>; **stir up, work up**

**might** NOUNS **strength,** mightiness, powerfulness, stamina; **force,** potency, power; **energy**; **vigor,** vitality, vigorousness, heartiness, lustiness, lustihood; **stoutness, sturdiness,** stalwartness, robustness, hardiness, ruggedness

**mighty** ADJS 1 **strong, forceful,** forcible, forcy <Scots>, powerful, puissant <nonformal>, potent; **stout,** sturdy, stalwart, rugged, hale; hunky *and* husky *and* hefty *and* beefy <all nonformal>, strapping, doughty <nonformal>, **hardy,** hard, hard as nails, cast-iron, iron-hard, steely; **robust,** robustious, gutty *and* gutsy <both nonformal>; strong-willed, obstinate; **vigorous, hearty,** nervy, **lusty,** bouncing, full- *or* red-blooded; bionic, sturdy as an ox, strong as a lion *or* an ox *or* a horse
ADVS 2 **very, exceedingly,** awfully *and* terribly *and* terrifically <all nonformal>, **quite,** just, so, **really,** real *and* right <both nonformal>, **pretty,** only too, mightily, almighty *and* powerfully *and* powerful <all nonformal>

**migrate** VERBS **transmigrate,** trek; flit, take wing; run <of fish>, swarm <of bees>; **emigrate,** out-migrate, expatriate; **immigrate,** in-migrate; remigrate; intermigrate

**mild** ADJS 1 **lenient, gentle,** mild-mannered, tender, humane, compassionate, **clement,** merciful; soft, moderate, **easy,** easygoing; lax; forgiving; **forbearing,** forbearant, patient; accepting, **tolerant**
2 **warm,** fair, genial; **temperate,** warmish; **tepid,** lukewarm, room-temperature

**mildew** NOUNS 1 **fetidness, mustiness,** funkiness, must, moldiness, fustiness, frowziness, stuffiness; mold, fungus, smut, rust
VERBS 2 mold, molder, molder away, rot away, rust away

**mileage** NOUNS distance; footage, yardage; infinity; perpetuity; long time; linear measures; oblongness; longitude

**milestone** NOUNS **marker,** mark; **landmark,** seamark; benchmark; milepost; cairn, menhir

**milieu** NOUNS **ambience,** atmosphere, climate, air, aura, spirit, feeling, feel, quality, color, local color, sense, sense of place, note, tone, overtone, undertone; **neighborhood,** vicinity, vicinage, neck of the woods <nonformal>, purlieus; premises, confines, precincts, environs

**militant** ADJS **warlike,** fighting, warring, battling; **martial,** military, soldierly, soldierlike; **combative,** contentious, gladiatorial; **belligerent,** pugnacious, truculent, bellicose, scrappy <nonformal>, full of fight; **aggressive,** offensive; **activist,** activistic

**military** ADJS **warlike,** militant, fighting, warring, battling; **martial,** soldierly, soldierlike

**militia** NOUNS organized militia, national militia, mobile militia, territorial militia, reserve militia; home reserve; **National Guard,** Air National Guard, state guard; minutemen

**milk** VERBS **exploit,** take advantage of, use, make use of, **use for one's own ends;** make a paw *or* cat's-paw of, sucker *and* play for a sucker <both nonformal>; **manipulate,** work on, work upon, stroke, play on *or* upon; play both ends against the middle; **impose upon,** presume upon; batten on; bleed, bleed white <nonformal>; drain, suck the blood of *or* from, suck dry; exploit one's position, feather one's nest <nonformal>, **profiteer**

**mill** NOUNS 1 **plant, factory, works,** manufacturing plant, *usine* <Fr>; sawmill, flour mill, etc
2 **pulverizer,** comminutor, triturator, levigator; crusher; grinder; granulator, pepper grinder, pepper mill
VERBS 3 **throng,** crowd, swarm, teem, hive, surge, seethe, stream, horde; gather around, gang around <nonfor-

mal>; **seethe,** mill around *or* about, stir, roil, moil, be turbulent
4 **process,** convert; machine; **pulverize, powder,** comminute, triturate, contriturate, levigate, bray, pestle, disintegrate, reduce to powder *or* dust, grind to powder *or* dust, grind up; flour

**millennium** NOUNS **thousand,** M, chiliad; **utopia** *or* Utopia <Sir Thomas More>, paradise, heaven, **heaven on earth;** kingdom come; **good times,** piping times, bright *or* palmy *or* halcyon days, days of wine and roses, rosy era; heyday; prosperity, era of prosperity; age of Aquarius

**millinery** NOUNS **headdress,** headgear, headwear, headclothes, headtire; headpiece, chapeau, cap, hat; hatmaking, hatting

**millstone** NOUNS **burden,** pressure, oppression, deadweight; handicap, drag; grinder; quern, quernstone

**Milquetoast** NOUNS **weakling,** weak *or* meek soul, weak sister <nonformal>, hothouse plant, softy <nonformal>, softling, **jellyfish,** invertebrate, gutless wonder <nonformal>, **baby,** big baby, crybaby, chicken <nonformal>, sop, **milksop,** namby-pamby, mollycoddle, mama's boy, mother's boy, mother's darling, teacher's pet; **wimp,** poor *or* weak *or* dull tool <nonformal>; **nonentity,** hollow man, doormat *and* empty suit *and* nebbish *and* sad sack <all nonformal>

**mime** NOUNS **imitator,** simulator, impersonator, impostor, **mimic,** mimicker, mimer; **impersonation,** personation; mimicry, mimicking, miming, mummer, pantomimist; pantomime, pantomiming, aping, dumb show; mimesis, **imitation**

**mimic** NOUNS 1 **imitator,** simulator, metooer <nonformal>, impersonator, impostor, mimicker, mimer, mime, **mocker;** mockingbird, cuckoo
VERBS 2 **impersonate,** mime, **ape, parrot,** copycat <nonformal>; do an impression; take off, hit off, hit off on, take off on; **imitate**, **simulate,** copy, counterfeit

**mince** VERBS 1 **strut,** swagger; sashay <nonformal>, prance, tittup, flounce, trip, skip
2 **pulverize**, grind, cut to pieces, make mincemeat of, make hamburger of <nonformal>

**mind** NOUNS 1 **will,** pleasure, will and pleasure; heart's desire; **wish, fancy,** discretion, pleasure, inclination, disposition, liking, appetence, appetency, **desire;** half a mind *or* notion; **resolve,** resolution; **turn of mind,** tendency, grain, vein, set, mental set, mindset, **leaning,** animus, propensity, proclivity, predilection, preference, predisposition
VERBS 2 **care, heed,** reck, think, consider, regard, pay heed to, take heed *or* thought of; **take an interest,** be concerned; **pay attention; care for,** take care of; **look after,** see after, attend to, minister to, look *or* see to, look *or* watch out for <nonformal>, have *or* keep an eye on *or* upon, keep a sharp eye on *or* upon, **watch over,** keep watch over, **watch**, tend

**mind-altering drug** NOUNS **hallucinogen,** psychedelic, psychedelic drug, psychoactive drug, psychoactive chemical *or* psychochemical, psychotropic drug, psychotomimetic drug, mind-expanding drug, mind-blowing drug

**mind-blowing** ADJS **hallucinatory,** hallucinative, hallucinational; hallucinogenic, psychedelic, consciousness-expanding, mind-expanding

**mind-boggling** ADJS **astonishing,** amazing, surprising, startling, **astounding,** confounding, staggering, stunning <nonformal>, eye-opening, breathtaking, overwhelming, mind-numbing; **spectacular**

**minded** ADJS **moved,** motivated, prompted, impelled, actuated; stimulated, animated; inclined, disposed, of a mind to, with half a mind to

**mindful** ADJS **attentive,** heedful, regardful, advertent; intent, intentive, on top of <nonformal>, diligent, assiduous, intense, earnest, concentrated; **careful**; **observing,** observant; watchful, aware, conscious, alert

**mindless** ADJS **purposeless, causeless,** designless, aimless, driftless, undirected, objectless, unmotivated; **haphazard,** random, dysteleological, stochastic, stray, inexplicable, unaccountable, promiscuous, indiscriminate, casual, leaving much to chance

**mind reader** NOUNS **telepathist,** mental telepathist, thought reader

**mine** NOUNS 1 mine of wealth, **gold mine,** bonanza, luau <nonformal>, lode, rich lode, mother lode, Eldorado,

Golconda, Seven Cities of Cibola
2 pit; **quarry; diggings, workings;** open cut, opencast; coal mine, colliery; strip mine; gold mine, silver mine, etc
VERBS 3 **undermine,** sap, sap the foundations of, honeycomb; plant a mine, trigger a mine
4 **take from,** tap, milk, drain, bleed, curtail; extract, pump

**mineral** NOUNS 1 inorganic substance, lifeless matter found in nature; extracted matter *or* material; mineral resources; **ore,** mineral-bearing material; unrefined *or* untreated mineral; natural *or* native mineral
ADJS 2 **inorganic,** unorganic, nonorganic; nonbiological; ore-bearing, oreforming

**mingle** VERBS **mix,** admix, commix, immix, **intermix,** bemingle, commingle, immingle, **intermingle,** interlace, interweave, intertwine, interlard; syncretize; **amalgamate,** integrate, alloy, coalesce, **fuse,** merge, meld, compound, compose, conflate, concoct

**miniature** NOUNS 1 mini; scaled-down *or* miniaturized version; microcosm, microcosmos; baby; doll, puppet, model
ADJS 2 **diminutive,** minuscule, minuscular, mini, micro, miniaturized, subminiature, minikin <old>, **small-scale,** minimal; pocket, pocket-sized, **vest-pocket**

**minimal** ADJS **least,** smallest, littlest, slightest, **lowest,** shortest; minimum, minim; **miniature,** diminutive, minuscule, minuscular, miniaturized, subminiature, **small-scale;** barely sufficient

**minimize** VERBS minify, **belittle,** detract from; play down, underplay, downplay, de-emphasize; **attach little importance to,** give little weight to; make little of, make light of, think little of, throw away, **make** *or* **think nothing of,** take no account of, set little by, set no store by; not give a shit *or* a hoot *or* two hoots for <nonformal>, not give a damn about, bad-mouth <nonformal>, deprecate, depreciate; **trivialize**

**minimum** NOUNS 1 **sufficiency,** sufficientness, **adequacy,** adequateness, **enough,** a competence *or* competency; exact measure, right amount, no more and no less; bare sufficiency, bare minimum, just enough, enough to get by on
ADJS 2 **least,** smallest, littlest, slightest, **lowest,** shortest; minimal, minim; few; sufficient for *or* to *or* unto, up to, equal to; barely sufficient

**minion** NOUNS **sycophant,** flatterer, toady, toad, toadeater, lickspit, lickspittle, **truckler, fawner,** courtier, flunky; creature, **puppet,** lap dog, **tool,** cat's-paw, dupe, instrument, hanger-on, lackey, flunky, stooge <nonformal>; peon, serf, slave, jackal, myrmidon; yes-man <nonformal>

**minister** NOUNS 1 **emissary,** envoy, legate, foreign service officer; envoy extraordinary, plentipotentiary, **minister plenipotentiary;** nuncio, internuncio, apostolic delegate
2 **clergyman,** clergywoman, man *or* woman of the cloth, divine, ecclesiastic, churchman, cleric, clerical; minister of the Gospel; chaplain
VERBS 3 **officiate,** do duty, **perform a rite,** perform service *or* divine service; administer a sacrament, administer the Eucharist, etc; anoint, chrism

**minor** NOUNS 1 **youngster,** young person, **youth, juvenile,** youngling, young'un <nonformal>; **stripling,** slip, sprig, sapling; fledgling; hopeful, young hopeful; infant; **adolescent,** pubescent; **teenager,** teener, teenybopper <nonformal>; junior, younger, youngest, baby
ADJS 2 **inferior,** subordinate, subaltern, sub, small-scale, **secondary;** junior; underage; **inconsiderable,** inappreciable, negligible

**minority** NOUNS 1 **immaturity,** undevelopment, inexperience, **callowness,** unripeness, greenness, rawness, sappiness, freshness, juiciness, dewiness; juniority, infancy, nonage; least
2 the minority, the few; racial *or* ethnic minority, minority group; persons of color

**minstrel** NOUNS **ballad singer,** balladeer, **bard,** rhapsode, rhapsodist; wandering *or* strolling minstrel, **troubadour,** trovatore, trouvère, minnesinger, scop, gleeman, fili, jongleur; street singer, wait

**mint** ADJS **new,** original, pristine, fresh, fresh off the assembly line, in mint condition, factory-fresh, **new-made,** new-built, new-wrought, new-shaped, new-minted, new-coined, uncirculated, new-begotten, untouched,

**mint condition** NOUNS **fine fettle,** fine whack <nonformal>, fine *or* high feather <nonformal>, **good shape,** good trim, fine shape, top shape <nonformal>, good condition; **newness,** freshness, maidenhood, dewiness, pristineness

**minus** ADJS **out of,** wanting, lacking; missing, less than nothing; negative, electronegative

**minuscule** ADJS **miniature,** diminutive, minuscular, mini, micro, miniaturized, subminiature, minikin <old>, **small-scale,** minimal; small-lettered, **lowercase**

**minute** NOUNS 1 **instant,** moment, second, sec <nonformal>, split second, **trice,** twinkle, twinkling, twinkling *or* twinkle of an eye, twink, **wink,** bat of an eye <nonformal>, **flash,** crack, tick, stroke, coup, breath, twitch; two shakes of a lamb's tail *and* two shakes *and* shake *and* half a shake *and* **jiffy** *and* jiff *and* half a jiffy <all nonformal>
2 ADJS **detailed,** full, particular, meticulous, fussy, finicky *or* finicking *or* finical, picayune, picky <nonformal>, nice <old>, precise, exact, specific, special

**minutes** NOUNS **report,** the record, proceedings, transactions, acta

**minutiae** NOUNS minim, **drop,** droplet, **mite** <nonformal>, **point,** vanishing point, mathematical point, point of a pin, pinpoint, pinhead, **dot;** trifle, petty *or* trivial matter; incidental, minor detail, details, minor details

**miracle** NOUNS **sign,** signs and portents, prodigy, wonder, wonderwork; thaumatology, thaumaturgy; fantasy, enchantment

**miraculous** ADJS **wondrous,** wonderworking, thaumaturgic *or* thaumaturgical, necromantic, **prodigious; magical,** enchanted, bewitched

**mirage** NOUNS **deception,** vision, hallucination, phantasm, fata morgana, looming, will-o'-the-wisp, **delusion,** delusiveness, illusion

**mire** NOUNS **swamp,** bog, quagmire, marsh; **mud,** muck, slush, slosh, sludge, slob <Ir>, squash, swill, **slime;** slop, ooze

**mirror** NOUNS 1 glass, **looking glass,** seeing glass <Brit nonformal>, reflector, speculum; hand mirror, window mirror, rear-view mirror, cheval glass, pier glass, shaving mirror; steel mirror; convex mirror, concave mirror, distorting mirror
VERBS 2 **image,** hold the mirror up to nature, reflect, figure; **embody,** body forth, incarnate, **personify,** personate, impersonate; **illustrate,** demonstrate, exemplify; **look like,** favor <nonformal>; **take after,** partake of, follow, appear *or* seem like, sound like; savor *or* smack of, be redolent of; **have all the earmarks of,** have every appearance of, have all the features of, have all the signs of, have every sign *or* indication of

**mirth** NOUNS **merriment,** merriness; **hilarity,** hilariousness; **joy,** joyfulness, joyousness; **glee,** gleefulness, high glee; **jollity,** jolliness, joviality, jocularity, jocundity; frivolity, **levity;** mirthfulness, amusement; fun; laughter

**misanthrope** NOUNS misanthropist, people-hater, cynic, Timon, Timonist; **man-hater,** misandrist; **woman-hater,** misogynist; **sexist,** male *or* female chauvinist, chauvinist

**misapprehension** NOUNS **misinterpretation,** misunderstanding, *malentente* <Fr>, misintelligence, misreading, misconstruction, mistaking, malobservation, **misconception; misrendering,** mistranslation, eisegesis; misexplanation, misexplication, misexposition; **perversion, distortion,** wrenching, twisting, contorting, torturing, squeezing, garbling

**misbegotten** ADJS **deformed,** malformed, misshapen, misproportioned, ill-proportioned, ill-made, ill-shaped, **out of shape; illegitimate,** spurious, false; **bastard,** misbegot, miscreated, gotten on the wrong side of the blanket, baseborn, born out of wedlock, without benefit of clergy

**misbehave** VERBS **misbehave oneself,** misconduct oneself, behave ill; get into mischief; **act up** *and* make waves *and* **carry on** *and* carry on something scandalous <all nonformal>, sow one's wild oats; **cut up** <nonformal>, horse around <nonformal>, roughhouse *and* cut up rough <both nonformal>; **do wrong, err,** offend; **sin,** commit sin; **transgress,** trespass

**miscalculate** VERBS **misjudge,** judge amiss, misestimate, misreckon, misappreciate, misperceive, get a wrong impression, misesteem, misthink, misconjecture; **misread,** misconstrue, put the wrong construction on things, misread the situation *or* case; **misinterpret;** err; fly in the face of facts

**miscellany** NOUNS **miscellanea,** collectanea; **assortment,** medley, variety, mixture; hodgepodge, conglomerate, mélange, pastiche, *pasticcio* <Ital>, **conglomeration,** omnium-gatherum <nonformal>; **sundries,** oddments, odds and ends

**mischief** NOUNS **mischievousness; devilment,** deviltry, devilry; **roguishness,** roguery, scampishness; **waggery,** waggishness; **impishness,** devilishness, puckishness, elfishness; **prankishness,** pranksomeness; sportiveness, playfulness, *espièglerie* <Fr>; high spirits, youthful spirits; foolishness

**mischievous** ADJS mischief-loving, full of mischief, full of the devil *or* old nick; **roguish,** scampish, scapegrace, arch, knavish; **devilish;** impish, puckish, elfish, elvish; **waggish,** prankish, pranky, pranksome, trickish, tricksy; **playful,** sportive, high-spirited, *espiègle* <Fr>

**misconception** NOUNS **misinterpretation,** misunderstanding, *malentente* <Fr>, misintelligence, misapprehension, misreading, misconstruction; misrendering, mistranslation, eisegesis; **perversion,** distortion, misuse of words, catachresis; misquotation

**misconduct** NOUNS **misbehavior,** unsanctioned *or* nonsanctioned behavior; frowned-upon behavior; **naughtiness,** badness; impropriety; venial sin; **disorderly conduct,** disorder, disorderliness, disruptiveness, disruption, **rowdiness,** rowdyism, riotousness, ruffianism, hooliganism; misfeasance, malfeasance, misdoing, delinquency, **wrongdoing**

**misconstrue** VERBS **pervert,** falsify, twist, garble, put a false construction upon, give a spin, give a false coloring, color, varnish, slant, strain, torture; put words in someone's mouth; **bias;** misrepresent, misinterpret, misrender, misdirect; misread, miss the point, **take wrong, get wrong,** get one wrong, take amiss, take the wrong way; **get backwards,** reverse, have the wrong way round, put the cart before the horse

**misdated** ADJS **anachronous** *or* anachronistical *or* **anachronistic,** parachronistic, metachronistic, prochronistic, unhistorical, unchronological; **mistimed;** antedated, foredated, postdated; ahead of time, **beforehand, early;** behind time, **behindhand, late,** unpunctual, tardy; **overdue,** past due

**misdemeanor** NOUNS **offense, wrong,** illegality; violation; wrongdoing; much to answer for; tort; delict, delictum

**misdirect** VERBS **mislead,** misguide, lead astray, lead up the garden path, **give a bum steer** <nonformal>; feed one a line <nonformal>, throw off the scent, throw off the track *or* trail, put on a false scent, drag *or* draw a red herring across the trail; throw one a curve *or* curve ball <nonformal>; **mismanage,** mishandle, misconduct, **misgovern,** misrule; be negligent

**miser** NOUNS **niggard,** tightwad *and* cheapskate <both nonformal>, hard man with a buck <nonformal>, **skinflint,** scrooge, penny pincher, pinchfist, churl, curmudgeon <old>, muckworm, save-all <nonformal>

**miserable** ADJS **wretched; woeful,** woebegone; crushed, stricken, **cut up** <nonformal>, heartsick, heart-stricken, heart-struck; deep-troubled; desolate, disconsolate, pleasureless; **paltry,** poor, common, **mean,** sorry, sad, pitiful, pitiable, pathetic, despicable, contemptible, beneath contempt, vile, **shabby,** scrubby, scruffy, shoddy, scurvy, crummy *and* cheesy <both nonformal>, **trashy,** rubbishy, garbagey <nonformal>, trumpery, gimcracky <nonformal>

**miserly** ADJS **stingy,** illiberal, ungenerous, chintzy, save-all, **cheap** *and* **tight** *and* narrow <all nonformal>, near, close, closefisted, tightfisted, pinchfisted, hardfisted; pinching, penny-pinching; avaricious

**misery** NOUNS **wretchedness,** despair, bitterness, infelicity, anguish, agony, woe, woefulness, bale, balefulness; **heartache,** aching heart, heavy heart, bleeding heart, broken heart, agony of mind *or* spirit; suicidal despair, black night of the soul, **despondency**

*Slough of Despond*
BUNYAN

**misfire** VERBS **come to nothing,** fail miserably *or* ignominiously; fizz out *and* **fizzle** *and* **fizzle out** *and* peter out *and* poop out <all nonformal>; flash in the pan, hang fire; **blow up in one's face,** explode, end *or* go up in smoke, go up like a rocket and come down like a stick

**misfit** NOUNS **nonconformist,** individualist, inner-directed person, oddball <nonformal>; a fish out of water, a square peg in a round hole <nonformal>

**misfortune** NOUNS **mishap,** ill hap, misadventure, mischance, *contretemps* <Fr>, grief; **disaster,** calamity, catastrophe, meltdown, cataclysm, **tragedy; shock, blow,** hard *or* nasty *or* staggering blow; **accident**

**misgiving** NOUNS **apprehension,** apprehensiveness, **qualm,** qualmishness, funny feeling; **anxiety**; doubt; foreboding, chill *or* quiver along the spine, creeping *or* shudder of the flesh

**misguided** ADJS **misdirected;** impolitic, ill-considered, ill-advised; negligent; **botched,** bungled, fumbled, muffed, spoiled, butchered, murdered; **ill-managed,** ill-done, ill-conducted, ill-devised, ill-contrived, ill-executed; mismanaged, misconducted

**mishandle** VERBS **mismanage,** misconduct, misdirect, misguide, **misgovern,** misrule; misadminister, maladminister; be negligent

**mishap** NOUNS **misfortune,** ill hap, **misadventure, mischance,** *contretemps* <Fr>, grief; shock, blow, hard *or* nasty *or* staggering blow; **accident,** casualty, collision, crash, smash *and* smashup *and* crack-up *and* pileup <all nonformal>

**misinform** VERBS **misteach,** misinstruct, miseducate; misadvise, **misguide,** misdirect, **mislead;** pervert, corrupt

**misinterpret** VERBS **misunderstand,** misconceive, mistake, misapprehend; misread, misconstrue, put a false construction on, miss the point, **take wrong, get wrong,** get one wrong, take amiss, take the wrong way; **get backwards,** reverse, have the wrong way round, put the cart before the horse; misapply; **misrender,** mistranslate; quote out of context; misquote, miscite, give a false coloring, give a false impression *or* idea; **garble,** pervert, distort, wrench, contort, torture, squeeze, twist the words *or* meaning, stretch *or* strain the sense *or* meaning, misdeem, **misjudge**; bark up the wrong tree

**misjudge** VERBS judge amiss, **miscalculate,** misestimate, misperceive, get a wrong impression, misevaluate, misesteem, misthink, misconjecture; **misread,** misconstrue, put the wrong construction on things, misread the situation *or* case; **misinterpret;** err; fly in the face of facts

**misleading** ADJS **deceptive,** deceiving, beguiling, **false, fallacious,** delusive, delusory; misteaching, misinstructive, miseducative, **misinforming;** misguiding, misdirecting

**mismanage** VERBS **mishandle,** misconduct, misdirect, misguide, **misgovern,** misrule; misadminister, maladminister; be negligent

**mismatched** ADJS **unsuited,** ill-suited; **unfitted,** ill-fitted; **maladjusted,** unadapted, ill-adapted; ill-sorted, ill-assorted, ill-chosen; ill-matched, ill-mated, mismated, mismarried, misallied; disproportionate, **out of proportion,** skew, skewed, asymmetric *or* asymmetrical

**misogynist** NOUNS **woman-hater; sexist,** male chauvinist, chauvinist; **misanthrope,** misanthropist, people-hater

**misogyny** NOUNS **woman-hating; sexism,** sex discrimination, sexual stereotyping, male chauvinism; **misanthropy,** misanthropism, people-hating

**misplace** VERBS **mislay,** misput; **lose,** incur loss, **suffer loss,** let slip through one's fingers

**misplaced** ADJS **mislaid,** misput; out of one's element, like a fish out of water, in the wrong place, in the wrong box *or* pew *and* in the right church but the wrong pew <all nonformal>; **inappropriate,** inapt, unapt, inapposite, **irrelevant,** malapropos, *mal à propos* <Fr>; shuffled; **out of line,** out of keeping, out of order *or* place, **out of step,** out of turn <nonformal>

**misprint** NOUNS **mistake,** error, *erratum* <L>, *corrigendum* <L>; misstatement, misquotation; misreport; **typographical error,** typo <nonformal>, printer's error, typist's error; clerical error

**misquote** VERBS **misrepresent,** misstate, misreport, put words into one's mouth, quote out of context; overstate, exaggerate

**misrepresent** VERBS **belie,** give a wrong idea, pass *or* pawn *or* foist *or* fob off as, send *or* deliver the wrong signal *or* message; put in a false light, **pervert,** distort, garble, twist, warp, wrench, slant, put a spin on, twist the meaning of;

color, miscolor, give a false coloring, put a false construction *or* appearance upon, falsify; **disguise,** camouflage; misstate, misreport, misquote, put words into one's mouth, quote out of context; overstate, exaggerate, overdraw, blow up, blow out of all proportion; understate

**miss** NOUNS 1 **girl,** girlie <nonformal>, **maid, maiden, lass,** girlchild, **lassie,** young thing, young creature, young lady, damsel in distress, **damsel,** damoiselle, demoiselle, *jeune fille* <Fr>, *mademoiselle* <Fr>, *muchacha* <Sp>, missy, little missy, slip, wench <dial or nonformal>, colleen <Irish>
2 near-miss; **slip, slipup** <nonformal>, slip 'twixt cup and lip; **error, mistake**
VERBS 3 **miss the mark,** miss one's aim; slip, slip up <nonformal>; goof <nonformal>, blunder, foozle <nonformal>, err; **botch,** bungle; **miscarry,** go amiss, go astray, miss by a mile <nonformal>; misfire; **miss out,** miss the boat *or* bus
4 **be inattentive,** pay no attention, pay no mind <nonformal>, not attend, not notice, **take no note** *or* **notice of,** take no thought *or* account of, not heed, give no heed, pay no regard to, not listen, hear nothing, not hear a word; **disregard,** overlook, ignore, pass over *or* by, have no time for, let pass *or* get by *or* get past; **want,** lack, need, require; feel the want of, be sent away empty-handed; run short of

**misshapen** ADJS **deformed, malformed,** misbegotten, misproportioned, ill-proportioned, ill-made, ill-shaped, **out of shape;** sway-backed, round-shouldered; bowlegged, bandy-legged, bandy; knock-kneed; flatfooted, splayfooted, pigeon-toed

**missile** NOUNS **projectile,** bolt; brickbat, stone, rock, alley apple *and* Irish confetti <both nonformal>; boomerang; bola; throwing-stick, throw stick, waddy <Austral>; **ballistic missile,** cruise missile, Exocet missile, surface-to-air missile *or* SAM, surface-to-surface missile, Tomahawk missile; **rocket; torpedo**

**missing** ADJS **absent,** not present, nonattendant, **away, gone,** departed, disappeared, vanished, absconded, out of sight; among the missing, wanting, **lacking,** not found, nowhere to be found, omitted, taken away, subtracted, deleted; no longer present *or* with us *or* among us; long-lost

**mission** NOUNS 1 **delegation,** deputation, commission; legation, embassy; **duty,** obligation, charge, onus, burden, devoir, must, ought, imperative, bounden duty, proper *or* assigned task, what ought to be done, what one is responsible for, where the buck stops <nonformal>; duties and responsibilities, assignment
2 **vocation,** occupation, business, work, line, line of work, line of business *or* endeavor, number <nonformal>, walk, **walk of life,** calling, **profession,** practice, pursuit, specialty, specialization, *métier* <Fr>, **trade,** racket *and* game <both nonformal>; **career,** lifework, life's work

**missionary** NOUNS **evangelist,** revivalist, evangel, evangelicalist; missioner; missionary apostolic, missionary rector, colporteur; television *or* TV evangelist, televangelist <nonformal>; **converter,** proselyter, proselytizer, apostlet

**misspeak** VERBS **blunder,** make a blunder, make a faux pas, make a colossal blunder, misspeak oneself, trip over one's tongue; embarrass oneself, have egg on one's face <nonformal>

**misspent** ADJS **wasted,** squandered, dissipated, consumed, spent, used, lost; **gone to waste,** run *or* gone to seed; down the drain *or* spout *or* rathole <nonformal>

**misstep** NOUNS **impropriety,** slight *or* minor wrong, venial sin, indiscretion, peccadillo, trip, slip, lapse; **transgression,** trespass; **sin,** cardinal *or* deadly *or* mortal sin, grave *or* heavy sin, unutterable sin, unpardonable *or* unforgivable *or* inexpiable sin; trip, **stumble,** false *or* wrong step, wrong *or* bad *or* false move

**mist** NOUNS 1 **drizzle,** mizzle; misty rain, Scotch mist; evening mist; fog drip; drizzling mist, drisk <nonformal>; mistiness, haze, fog, cloud
VERBS 2 **blur,** dim, pale, soften, film, fog; defocus, lose resolution *or* sharpness *or* distinctness, go soft at the edges; mist over, mist up, bemist, enmist; **haze**

**mistake** NOUNS **error,** *erratum* <L>, *corrigendum* <L>; **fault,** *faute* <Fr>; **misconception,** misapprehension, misunderstanding; misstatement, misquotation; misreport; **misprint,** typographical error, typo <nonformal>, printer's error, typist's error; clerical error; **misjudg-**

**ment,** miscalculation; misplay; misdeal; miscount; misuse; failure, miss, miscarriage

**mistaken** ADJS **in error, erring,** under an error, wrong, all wet <nonformal>, full of bull *or* shit *or* hot air *or* it *or* prunes *or* crap *or* beans <all nonformal>; off in one's reckoning; in the right church but the wrong pew

**mistreat** VERBS 1 **maltreat,** ill-treat, ill-use, abuse, injure, **molest;** do wrong to, do wrong by; outrage, do violence to, do one's worst to; mishandle, manhandle; buffet, batter, bruise, **savage,** maul, knock about, rough, rough up

2 <nonformal> **screw,** screw over, shaft, stiff, give the short *or* the shitty end of the stick, fuck, fuck over

**mistress** NOUNS 1 woman, **kept woman,** kept mistress, **paramour,** concubine, doxy, playmate, spiritual *or* unofficial wife; live-in lover <nonformal>
2 governess, duenna, madam; **matron, housewife,** homemaker, goodwife <Scots>, lady of the house, chatelaine; housemistress, housemother
3 instructress, educatress, preceptress; **schoolmistress; schoolma'am** *or* **schoolmarm**

**mistrust** NOUNS 1 **suspiciousness,** suspicion, doubt, misdoubt, distrust, distrustfulness; **wariness,** chariness, cageyness *and* leeriness <both nonformal>, mistrustfulness
VERBS 2 suffer pangs of jealousy, have green in the eye <nonformal>, be possessive *or* overpossessive, view with a jaundiced eye; **suspect,** distrust, doubt, **have one's doubts,** have *or* harbor *or* entertain doubts *or* suspicions, half believe, have reservations, **take with a grain of salt,** be from Missouri <nonformal>, misgive, cross one's fingers; **be uncertain; doubt one's word,** give one the lie

**misty** ADJS uncertain, confused, out of focus, **blurred, blurry,** bleared, bleary, blear, **fuzzy, hazy,** filmy, foggy; misty-moisty; **murky,** cloudy, foggy, fogbound, nebulous

**misunderstand** VERBS **misinterpret,** misconceive, mistake, misapprehend; misread, misconstrue, put a false construction on, miss the point, **take wrong, get wrong,** get one wrong, take amiss, take the wrong way; **get backwards,** reverse, have the wrong way round, put the cart before the horse; **confuse**, mix up, not distinguish

**misunderstanding** NOUNS **misinterpretation,** *malentente* <Fr>, misintelligence, **misapprehension,** misreading, misconstruction, mistaking, **misconception; misrendering,** mistranslation, eisegesis; **perversion,** distortion, wrenching, twisting, contorting, torturing, squeezing, garbling; misjudgment; **error; disagreement,** difficulty, difference, difference of opinion, agreement to disagree, **variance,** division, dividedness

**misuse** VERBS **misemploy,** abuse, misapply; mishandle, mismanage, maladminister; divert, misappropriate, convert, defalcate <old>, embezzle, pilfer, peculate, feather one's nest <nonformal>; pervert, prostitute; profane, violate, pollute, foul, foul one's own nest, befoul, desecrate, defile, debase

**mite** NOUNS 1 **little, bit,** little *or* wee *or* tiny bit <nonformal>, bite, **particle,** fragment, spot, **speck,** flyspeck, fleck, point, dot, jot, tittle, **iota,** ounce, **dab** <nonformal>, mote; whit, ace, **hair,** scruple, groat, farthing, pittance, dole, trifling amount, **smidgen** *and* skosh *and* smitch <all nonformal>, pinch, gobbet, dribble, driblet, dram, drop, drop in a bucket *or* in the ocean, tip of the iceberg; grain, granule, pebble
2 **flea,** sand flea, dog flea, cat flea, chigoe, chigger, jigger, red bug, harvest mite
3 **pittance,** drop in the bucket *or* the ocean; bit; widow's mite

**mitigate** VERBS **extenuate,** palliate, soften, lessen, diminish, **ease,** mince; **soft-pedal;** slur over, ignore, pass by in silence, give the benefit of the doubt, not hold it against one, **explain away,** gloss *or* smooth over, put a gloss upon, put a good face upon, varnish, **whitewash,** color, lend a color to, put the best color *or* face on, show in the best colors, show to best advantage; **modulate,** dampen, blunt, defuse, abate, weaken, reduce, de-escalate, slacken

**mitigating** ADJS assuaging, abating, **diminishing,** reducing, lessening, allaying, **alleviating,** relaxing, easing; tempering, **softening,** chastening, **subduing;** deadening, dulling, blunting, damping, dampening, cushioning

**mix** NOUNS 1 **medley, miscellany,** mélange, pastiche, *pasticcio* <Ital>, conglomeration, assortment, assemblage, mixed bag, ragbag, grab bag, olio, *olla podrida* <Sp>, **scramble, jumble,** mingle-mangle, mishmash, **mess,** can of worms <nonformal>, rat's nest, hash, patchwork, salad, gallimaufry, salmagundi, **potpourri,** stew, sauce, slurry, omnium-gatherum, Noah's ark, **odds and ends,** oddments
VERBS 2 admix, commix, immix, **intermix, mingle,** bemingle, commingle, immingle, **intermingle,** interlace, interweave, intertwine, interlard; syncretize; **blend,** interblend, stir in; amalgamate, integrate, alloy, coalesce, **fuse, merge,** meld, compound, compose, conflate, concoct; **combine**; mix up, hash, stir up, **scramble,** conglomerate, shuffle, **jumble,** jumble up, mingle-mangle, throw *or* toss together

**mixed** ADJS **mingled,** blended, compounded, amalgamated; combined; **composite,** compound, **complex,** many-sided, multifaceted, intricate; **conglomerate,** pluralistic, multiracial, multicultural, multiethnic, multinational, heterogeneous, varied, **miscellaneous,** medley, motley, dappled, patchy; promiscuous, indiscriminate, **scrambled, jumbled,** thrown together; syncretized, syncretistic, eclectic

**mixed bag** NOUNS **hodgepodge,** hotchpotch, hotchpot; **medley, miscellany,** mélange, pastiche, *pasticcio* <Ital>, **assortment,** assemblage, ragbag, grab bag, olio, *olla podrida* <Sp>, mishmash, **mess,** can of worms <nonformal>, dog's breakfast <Can nonformal>, hash, patchwork, salad, gallimaufry, salmagundi, **potpourri,** stew, omnium-gatherum, Noah's ark, **odds and ends,** oddments, all sorts, everything but the kitchen sink <nonformal>, what you will

**mixed marriage** NOUNS **marriage,** coverture, cohabitation; intermarriage, interfaith marriage, interracial marriage; miscegenation; misalliance, *mésalliance* <Fr>, ill-assorted marriage

**mixed-up** ADJS **confused,** crazy mixed-up <nonformal>; **flustered,** fluttered, ruffled, rattled, fussed <nonformal>; **upset, unsettled,** off-balance, off one's stride; **disorganized,** disordered, disoriented, disorientated, chaotic, jumbled, in a jumble, shuffled; **disconcerted,** discomposed, discombobulated <nonformal>, embarrassed, put-out, disturbed, perturbed, bothered, all hot and bothered <nonformal>; in a tizzy *or* swivet *or* sweat <nonformal>, in a pother; **perplexed**

**mixer** NOUNS 1 **blender,** beater, agitator, food processor; cement mixer, eggbeater, churn; homogenizer, colloid mill, emulsifier; crucible, melting pot
2 **dance, hop** <nonformal>, dancing party, **shindig** *and* shindy <both nonformal>

**mixture** NOUNS **assortment,** medley, variety; hodgepodge, conglomerate, **conglomeration,** omnium-gatherum <nonformal>; **compound,** admixture, intermixture, immixture, commixture, **composite,** blend, meld, composition, confection, concoction, **combination,** amalgam, alloy

**mix up** VERBS **confound,** confuse, muddle, mess up *and* ball up *and* bollix up *and* screw up *and* foul up *and* fuck up *and* snafu *and* muck up *and* louse up <all nonformal>, implicate; **tangle,** entangle, embrangle, **snarl, snarl up,** ravel, knot, tie in knots

**mix-up** NOUNS **confusion,** chaos, anarchy, misrule, license; **Babel,** cognitive dissonance; **muddle,** morass, foul-up *and* fuck-up *and* snafu *and* screw-up <all nonformal>, ball-up <nonformal>, hoo-ha *and* fine how-de-do <all nonformal>, pretty kettle of fish, pretty piece of business, nice piece of work

**moan** NOUNS 1 **lament,** plaint, *planctus* <L>; **murmur,** mutter; **groan; whine,** whimper; wail, wail of woe; **sob,** *cri du coeur* <Fr>, **cry,** outcry, scream, **howl,** yowl, bawl, yawp, keen, ululation
VERBS 2 **lament,** mourn, grieve, groan, sorrow, keen, weep over, **bewail,** bemoan, deplore, repine, sigh, give sorrow words; sing the blues <nonformal>, elegize, dirge, knell; **wail,** ululate

**moat** NOUNS **trench,** trough, channel, ditch, fosse, **canal,** cut, gutter, kennel <Brit>; sunk fence, ha-ha

**mob** NOUNS **throng,** multitude, horde, host, heap <nonformal>, army, panoply, legion; flock, cluster, galaxy; **crowd,** press, crush, flood, spate, deluge, mass; rabble, rout, ruck, jam, *cohue* <Fr>, everybody and his uncle *or* his brother <nonformal>

**the mob** NOUNS 1 **the masses, the hoi polloi,** *hoi polloi* <Gk>, the many, **the multitude,** the crowd, the horde, the million, **the majority,** the mass of the people, the herd, the great unnumbered, the great unwashed, **the vulgar** *or* **common herd;** *profanum vulgus, ignobile vulgus, mobile vulgus* <all L>

*the hateful, hostile mob*
PETRARCH

2 **the underworld,** gangland, gangdom, **organized crime,** organized crime family, the rackets, the syndicate, the Mafia, Cosa Nostra

**mobile** ADJS **moving,** stirring, in motion; transitional; motive, motile, movable

**mobilize** VERBS **set in motion,** move, actuate, motivate, push, shove, nudge, **drive,** impel, propel; **militarize,** activate, go on a wartime footing, gird *or* gird up one's loins, muster one's resources; reactivate, remilitarize, take out of mothballs *and* retread <both nonformal>

**mobster** NOUNS **criminal,** outlaw, felon, **crook** <nonformal>, lawbreaker, perpetrator, perp <nonformal>, gangster *and* wiseguy <both nonformal>, racketeer, thief; **bad person**; deceiver

**mock** VERBS 1 **scoff, jeer,** gibe, barrack <Brit>, revile, rail at, rally, chaff, **twit, taunt,** jape, flout, scout, have a fling at, cast in one's teeth; sneer, **sneer at,** fleer, curl one's lip
ADJS 2 **imitation, sham,** copied, fake *and* phony <both nonformal>, counterfeit, forged, plagiarized, unoriginal, ungenuine; **pseudo,** synthetic, synthetical, ersatz, hokey *and* hoked-up <both nonformal>, quasi

**mockery** NOUNS 1 **indignity,** affront, offense, injury, humiliation; scurrility, contempt, contumely, despite, flout, flouting, jeering, jeer, mock, scoff, gibe, taunt, brickbat <nonformal>; **insult, aspersion,** uncomplimentary remark, slap *or* kick in the face, left-handed *or* backhanded compliment; cut

*most unkindest cut of all*
SHAKESPEARE

2 **mimicry,** apery, parrotry, mimetism; hollow mockery; **insincerity,** uncandidness, uncandor, unfrankness, disingenuousness; **ridicule,** derision, raillery, rallying, chaffing; panning *and* razzing *and* roasting *and* ragging <all nonformal>, scoffing, sneering, snickering, sniggering, smirking, grinning, leering, fleering, snorting
3 **burlesque,** lampoon, squib, parody, satire, farce, imitation, wicked imitation *or* pastiche, takeoff <nonformal>, **travesty, caricature**

**mock-up** NOUNS **reproduction,** duplication, imitation, **copy**, dummy, **replica,** facsimile, representation, approximation, model, version, knockoff <nonformal>

**mode** NOUNS 1 **fashion,** style, vogue, trend, prevailing taste; proper thing, ton, bon ton; custom; convention; the swim <nonformal>, current *or* stream of fashion; height of fashion; the new look, the season's look; high fashion, *haute couture* <Fr>
2 **manner, way,** tenor, vein, lifestyle, way of life, preference, thing *and* bag <both nonformal>

**model** NOUNS 1 **pattern,** standard, criterion, classic example, rule, mirror, paradigm; showpiece, showplace; **original,** urtext, *locus classicus* <L>; **type,** prototype, antetype, **archetype,** genotype, biotype, type specimen, type species; **precedent**
2 **beauty,** beauty queen, beauty contest winner, Miss America, bathing beauty; **glamor girl,** cover girl; **belle,** reigning beauty, great beauty, lady fair
VERBS 3 **form,** formalize, shape, fashion, tailor, frame, figure, lick into shape <nonformal>; **mold,** sculpt *or* sculpture; carve, whittle, cut, chisel, hew, hew out; roughhew, roughcast, rough out, block out, lay out, sketch out
ADJS 4 **exemplary,** precedential, typical, paradigmatic, representative, standard, normative, classic; ideal

**moderate** NOUNS 1 moderatist, moderationist, **centrist,** middle-of-the-roader <nonformal>; independent; center, centrist, neutral; conservative
ADJS 2 centrist, middle-of-the-road <nonformal>, independent; **temperate,** sober, frugal, restrained, **sparing,** stinting, measured; nonviolent, peaceable, peaceful, pacifistic; judicious, prudent

**moderate** VERBS **restrain,** constrain, control, **keep within bounds; modulate,** mitigate, defuse, abate, weaken, diminish, reduce, de-escalate, slacken, lessen, slow down; **alleviate,** assuage, allay, lay, lighten, palliate, extenuate, **temper,** lenify; **soften,** subdue, tame, hold in check, keep a tight rein, chasten, underplay, play down, downplay, de-emphasize, tone *or* tune down

**moderator** NOUNS **mitigator,** modulator, stabilizer, temperer, assuager; **mediator,** bridge-builder, calming *or* restraining hand, wiser head; **alleviator,** alleviative, palliative, lenitive; **pacifier,** soother, comforter, peacemaker, pacificator, dove of peace, mollifier

**modern** ADJS **contemporary,** present-day, present-time, twentieth-century, latter-day, space-age, neoteric, now <nonformal>, **newfashioned,** fashionable, modish, mod, *à la mode* <Fr>, **up-to-date,** up-to-datish, up-to-the-minute, in, abreast of the times; **advanced,** progressive, forward-looking, modernizing, avant-garde

**modernize** VERBS streamline; update, **bring up to date,** keep *or* stay current, move with the times

**modest** ADJS 1 **meek;** humble; **unpretentious,** unpretending, unassuming, unpresuming, unpresumptuous, **unostentatious,** unobtrusive, unimposing, unboastful; unambitious, unaspiring; verecund, verecundious, *pudique* <Fr>, bashful; **decent, decorous,** delicate, elegant, proper, becoming, seemly
2 **cheap, inexpensive,** unexpensive, low, low-priced, frugal, reasonable, sensible, manageable, moderate, affordable, to fit the pocketbook, budget, easy, economy, economic, economical; within means, within reach *or* easy reach; **mediocre,** middling, indifferent, fair, fairish, fair to middling <nonformal>, medium, betwixt and between

**modesty** NOUNS 1 **humility,** unpretentiousness; plainness, simpleness, homeliness; **meekness;** unassumingness, unpresumptuousness, **unostentatiousness,** unambitiousness, unobtrusiveness, unboastfulness; bashfulness, pudicity, shame, pudency; expressionlessness, blankness, impassiveness, impassivity; straight *or* poker face, mask
2 **mediocrity,** mediocreness, fairishness, modestness, moderateness, middlingness, **indifference**

**modicum** NOUNS minim; **minimum; little, bit,** little *or* wee *or* tiny bit <nonformal>, bite, **particle,** fragment, moiety, spot, **speck,** flyspeck, fleck, point, dot, jot, tittle, **iota,** ounce, **dab** <nonformal>, mote, **mite** <nonformal>; whit, ace, **hair,** scruple, groat, farthing, pittance, dole, trifling amount, **smidgen** *and* skosh *and* smitch <all nonformal>, pinch, gobbet, dribble, driblet, dram, drop, drop in a bucket *or* in the ocean, grain, granule, pebble; small share

**modification** NOUNS **qualification,** limitation, limiting, restriction, circumscription, hedge, hedging; setting conditions, conditionality, provisionality, circumstantiality; specification; **allowance,** concession, cession, grant

**modify** VERBS **qualify, limit,** condition <old>, hedge, hedge about, restrict, restrain, circumscribe, set limits *or* conditions, box in <nonformal>, narrow; adjust to, regulate by; alter; **temper,** season, leaven, soften, modulate, moderate, assuage, **mitigate,** palliate, abate, reduce, diminish

**module** NOUNS **component,** constituent, ingredient, integrant, makings *and* fixings <both nonformal>, **element,** factor, part, player, part and parcel; appurtenance, adjunct; **feature,** aspect, specialty, circumstance, detail, item

**mogul** NOUNS **personage,** important person, somebody, notable, notability, figure; **celebrity,** famous person, person of renown, personality; name, big name, nabob, panjandrum, person to be reckoned with, very important person; mover and shaker, lord of creation; **dignitary,** dignity; **magnate;** tycoon <nonformal>, baron

**moisten** VERBS **dampen,** moisturize, damp, **wet,** wet down; humidify; dew, bedew; **sprinkle,** besprinkle, **spray,** spritz <nonformal>, sparge, asperge; **splash,** dash, swash, slosh, splatter, spatter, bespatter; hose, hose down; syringe, douche; sponge

**moisture** NOUNS damp, wet; **dampness,** moistness, moistiness, **wetness,** wettedness, wettishness, **wateriness;** soddenness, soppiness, soppingness, sogginess; dewiness; mistiness, raininess

**moisturizer** NOUNS wetting agent, wetting-out agent, liquidizer; humidifier

**mold** NOUNS 1 **original,** model, archetype, prototype, **pattern,** pilot model; **form**, cast, template, matrix,

negative; **die,** punch, stamp, intaglio, seal, mint; last, shoe last
2 **decay,** decomposition, disintegration, dissolution, resolution, degradation, biodegradation, breakup; mildew, fungus, smut, must, rust; rot, dry rot
VERBS 3 **form,** formalize, **shape, fashion,** tailor, frame, figure, **lick into shape** <nonformal>; work, knead; carve, whittle, cut, chisel, hew, hew out; roughhew, roughcast, rough out, block out, lay out, sketch out; **invent,** create, originate, make, think up, dream up, coin, hatch, concoct, fabricate, produce
4 **decay,** decompose, disintegrate; go *or* fall into decay, go *or* fall to pieces, break up, crumble, crumble into dust; **spoil,** corrupt, canker, **go bad; rot,** putrefy, putresce; molder, molder away, rot away, rust away, mildew

**moldy** ADJS **malodorous,** fetid, musty, funky, fusty, frowzy, stuffy, mildewed, mildewy; mephitic, miasmic, miasmal

**molehill** NOUNS **trifle,** triviality, pin, button, hair, straw, rush, feather, fig, bean, hill of beans <nonformal>, row of pins *or* buttons <nonformal>, pinch of snuff

**molest** VERBS **annoy,** torment, bother, pother; **harass,** harry, drive up the wall <nonformal>, **hound,** dog, nag, **persecute; mistreat,** maltreat, ill-treat, ill-use, abuse, injure; do wrong to, do wrong by; outrage, do violence to, do one's worst to; mishandle, manhandle

**mollify** VERBS **calm,** calm down, **stabilize, tranquilize, pacify,** appease, dulcify; **quiet,** hush, still, rest, compose, **lull, soothe,** gentle, rock, cradle, rock to sleep; ease, steady, smooth, smoothen, smooth over, smooth down, even out; keep the peace, be the dove of peace, pour oil on troubled waters, pour balm into

**mollycoddle** VERBS **indulge,** cater to; give way to, yield to, let one have his own way; **pamper,** cosset, **coddle,** pet, make a lap dog of, **spoil;** spare the rod

**molt** VERBS **shed, cast,** throw off, **slough,** slough off, exuviate

**molten** ADJS **melted,** fused, liquefied; liquated; meltable, fusible; thermoplastic

**moment** NOUNS **time,** while, minute, instant; psychological moment; pregnant *or* fateful moment, fated moment, kairos, moment of truth; **short time,** little while, mo <nonformal>, span, **short spell;** no time, less than no time; bit *or* **little bit,** a breath, the wink of an eye, pair of winks <nonformal>; **two shakes** *and* two shakes of a lamb's tail <both nonformal>

**momentary** ADJS **instantaneous,** instant, **immediate,** presto, quick as thought *or* lightning; lightning-like, lightning-swift; nearly simultaneous; simultaneous

**momentous** ADJS **important,** major, consequential, significant, considerable, substantial, material, **great,** grand, big; superior, world-shaking, earthshaking; big-time *and* big-league *and* major-league *and* heavyweight <all nonformal>; high-powered <nonformal>, double-barreled <nonformal>

**momentum** NOUNS **motion; movement,** stir, unrest, restlessness; **going,** running, stirring; **operation,** operating, **working,** ticking; **course,** passage, progress, trend, **advance,** forward motion, going *or* moving on; **motive power,** power; **force,** irresistible force; clout <nonformal>; **impetus**

**monastery** NOUNS **cloister,** house, abbey, friary; priory, priorate; lamasery

**money** NOUNS 1 **wealth,** lucre, pelf, gold, mammon; **substance,** property, possessions, material wealth; **assets;** *embarras de richesses* <Fr>, money to burn <nonformal>; **currency,** legal tender, medium of exchange, circulating medium, **cash,** hard cash, cold cash; specie, coinage, mintage, coin of the realm

2 <nonformal> **dough, bread, jack, kale,** scratch, sugar, change, mazuma, mopus, gelt, gilt, coin, spondulics, oof, ooftish, wampum, possibles, moolah, boodle, blunt, dinero, do-re-mi, **sugar,** brass, tin, rocks, simoleons, shekels, berries, chips, bucks, green, green stuff, the needful, grease, ointment, oil of palms, cabbage, whip-out, the nesessary, loot

3 <nonformal> **folding money, green stuff,** the long green, folding green, lean green, mint leaves, lettuce, greenbacks, frogskins, skins

**moneylender** NOUNS **lender,** loaner; loan officer; commercial banker; moneymonger; money broker; banker; **usurer,** Shylock *and* loan shark <both nonformal>

**mongrel** NOUNS 1 **cur,** lurcher <Brit>, **mutt** <nonformal>; pariah dog, hound, whelp
ADJS 2 **hybrid,** interbred, **crossbred,** crossed, cross; **half-breed,** half-bred, half-blooded, half-caste

**monitor** NOUNS 1 **warner,** cautioner, admonisher; prophet *or* messenger of doom, Cassandra, Jeremiah; **lookout,** lookout man; sentinel, sentry; signalman, signaler, flagman; reviewer
VERBS 2 **probe,** sound, plumb, fathom; check into, check on, check out, nose into, see into; poke about, root around *or* about, scratch around *or* about, cast about *or* around; **review,** pass under review, oversee

**monk** NOUNS **religious,** *religieux* <Fr>; monastic; brother, lay brother; cenobite, conventual; caloyer, hieromonach; **mendicant,** friar; beadsman; prior, claustral *or* conventual prior, grand prior, general prior; abbot; hermit; ascetic; celibate

**monolith** NOUNS **monument,** monumental *or* memorial record, **memorial; tablet,** stone, boundary stone, memorial stone; **pillar,** stele *or* stela, shaft, column, memorial column, rostral column, manubial column; obelisk; **gravestone,** tombstone; headstone, footstone; cenotaph; cairn, mound, barrow, cromlech, dolmen, megalith, menhir, cyclolith

**monolithic** ADJS **uniform, consistent,** consonant, correspondent, accordant, homogeneous, **alike,** all alike, all of a piece, of a piece, consubstantial; undifferentiable *or* undifferentiated, undifferenced

**monologue** NOUNS **soliloquy,** monology, self-address; aside; solo; monodrama; apostrophe; monotone, drone, dingdong, singsong

**monopolize** VERBS hog *and* grab all of *and* gobble up <all nonformal>, take it all, have all to oneself, have exclusive possession of *or* exclusive rights to; engross, forestall, tie up; **corner** *and* get a corner on *and* corner the market <all nonformal>; **take possession of,** possess oneself of, take for oneself, arrogate to oneself, take up, **take over,** help oneself to, make use of, make one's own, make free with, dip one's hands into; take all of, sit on

**monopoly** NOUNS monopolization; **corner** *and* cornering *and* a corner on <all nonformal>; exclusive possession; engrossment, forestallment; restraint of trade, corner on the market

**monotonous** ADJS **tedious, humdrum,** singsong, jog-trot, treadmill, unvarying, unrelieved, invariable, uneventful, broken-record, parrotlike, harping, everlasting, too much with us <nonformal>; **dreary,** drearisome, dry, dryasdust, dusty, **dull**; protracted, prolonged

**monotony** NOUNS **tedium,** humdrum, irksomeness, irk; **sameness,** sameliness, more of the same, the same old thing, the same damn thing <nonformal>; broken record, parrot; the daily round *or* grind, the weary round, the treadmill, the squirrel cage, the rat race <nonformal>, the beaten track *or* path; time on one's hands, time hanging heavily on one's hands

**monster** NOUNS 1 **fiend,** fiend from hell, **demon, devil,** devil incarnate, hellhound, hellkite; **vampire,** lamia, **harpy, ghoul;** werewolf, ape-man; ogre, ogress; Frankenstein's monster
ADJS 2 **huge,** immense, vast, enormous, humongous *and* jumbo <both nonformal>, tremendous, prodigious, stupendous; great big, larger than life, Homeric, mighty, **titanic,** colossal, monumental; monstrous; **mammoth,** mastodonic; **gigantic**

**monstrosity** NOUNS 1 **freakishness,** grotesqueness, grotesquerie, strangeness, weirdness, gonzo <nonformal>, monstrousness, malformation, deformity, teratism; miscreation, abortion, abnormal *or* defective birth, abnormal *or* defective fetus; **freak,** freak of nature, *lusus naturae* <L>
2 **eyesore,** blot, blot on the landscape, blemish, sight <nonformal>, fright, horror, mess, no beauty, no beauty queen, ugly duckling

**monstrous** ADJS **wicked,** abominable, atrocious, unspeakable, execrable, damnable; shameful, disgraceful, scandalous, **infamous,** unpardonable, unforgivable; **bestial,** mindless, insensate, inhuman, pitiless, ruthless, merciless; **deformed,** malformed, misshapen, **misbegotten,** teratogenic, teratoid

**monument** NOUNS **shaft,** pillar, column; sphinx, obelisk, pyramid; colossus; memorial arch, gravestone, mausoleum; cairn, menhir

**monumental** ADJS **immense,** enormous, huge; **gigantic,** mountainous, titanic, colossal, mammoth, Gargantuan, gigantesque, outsize, sizable, larger-than-life; **massive,** massy, weighty, bulky, voluminous; **spacious,** amplitudinous, extensive; **tremendous,** stupendous, awesome, prodigious, Olympian

**moocher** NOUNS **drone;** cadger, bummer *and* panhandler <nonformal>, **sponger,** freeloader, lounge lizard <nonformal>, social parasite, parasite; *schnorrer* <Yiddish>; uninvited guest, gate-crasher <nonformal>

**mood** NOUNS **humor,** feeling, feelings, temper, frame of mind, state of mind, morale, tone, note, **vein; mind,** heart, spirit *or* spirits

**moody** ADJS **glum,** grum, **morose,** sullen, sulky, mumpish, dumpish, long-faced, crestfallen, chapfallen; moodish, **brooding,** broody; mopish, mopey <nonformal>, **moping; temperamental,** primadonnaish; petulant; **volatile,** mercurial, flighty, impulsive, impetuous

**moon** NOUNS 1 **satellite;** orb of night, queen of heaven, queen of night, silvery moon; **new moon,** wet moon; **crescent moon,** crescent, increscent moon, increscent, waxing moon, waxing crescent moon; decrescent moon, decrescent, waning moon, waning crescent moon; gibbous moon; **half-moon,** demilune; **full moon,** harvest moon, hunter's moon

*that orbèd maiden*
SHELLEY

VERBS 2 **lie around,** lounge around, loll around, moon around, sit around, sit on one's ass *or* butt *or* duff <nonformal>, stand *or* hang around, **loiter about** *or* **around,** slouch, slouch around, **bum around** *and* mooch around <both nonformal>; **muse,** dream, daydream, pipe-dream <nonformal>, fantasy; abstract oneself, be lost in thought, let one's attention wander, let one's mind run on other things, dream of *or* muse on other things; **woolgather,** go woolgathering, let one's wits go bird's nesting, **be in a brown study,** be absent, be somewhere else, stargaze, be out of it *and* be not with it <both nonformal>

**moor** NOUNS 1 **plateau,** tableland, high plateau, table, mesa, table mountain, butte, moorland, moss <Scots>

VERBS 2 **anchor,** come to anchor, lay anchor, **cast dock,** tie up, drop anchor; pick up the mooring; lash, lash and tie; **secure,** make fast

**mooring** NOUNS **landing,** landfall; docking, tying up, dropping anchor; **getting off,** disembarkation, disembarkment, debarkation, coming *or* going ashore

**moot** ADJS **unproved,** not proved, unproven, **undemonstrated,** unshown, not shown; **untried,** untested; **unestablished,** unfixed, unsettled, undetermined, unascertained; **inconclusive,** sub judice; **debatable,** arguable, disputable, contestable, controvertible, **controversial,** refutable, confutable, deniable

**mop** VERBS **wash, rinse,** rinse out, flush, flush out, irrigate, sluice, sluice out; sponge, sponge down *or* off; **scrub,** scrub up *or* out, **swab,** mop up; hose out *or* down; rinse off *or* out

**mope** VERBS **sulk,** mope around; grizzle <Brit nonformal>, grump *and* grouch *and* bitch <all nonformal>, **brood over,** fret, take on <nonformal>; get oneself in a sulk, **eat one's heart out,** ache, bleed

**mopey** ADJS **glum,** grum, **morose,** sullen, sulky, mumpish, dumpish, long-faced, crestfallen, chapfallen; **moody,** moodish, brooding, broody; mopish, moping

**moral** NOUNS 1 **maxim,** aphorism, apothegm, epigram, dictum, adage, proverb, gnome, words of wisdom, **saying,** sentence, expression, phrase, catchword, catchphrase, word, byword, mot, motto

ADJS 2 **ethical,** moralistic; ethological; axiological; principled, high-principled, high-minded, right-minded; **virtuous,** good, upright, honest; **righteous,** just, straight, rightminded, right-thinking; **angelic,** seraphic; **saintly,** saintlike; **godly**

**morale** NOUNS **morality,** moral fiber *or* rectitude *or* virtue; **mood,** humor, feeling, feelings, temper, frame of mind, state of mind, tone, note, **vein**

**moralistic** ADJS **preceptive,** didactic, instructive, prescriptive; prescript, prescribed, mandatory, hard-and-fast, binding, dictated; **exhortative,** exhortatory, hortative, hortatory, preachy <nonformal>, **didactic,** sententious; **ethical,** moral; ethological; axiological

**morals** NOUNS **ethics, principles,** standards, norms, principles of conduct *or* behavior, principles of professional practice; morality, moral principles; ethical *or* moral code, **ethic,** code of morals *or* ethics, ethical system, value system, axiology; ethicality, ethicalness

**morass** NOUNS **marsh,** marshland, swamp, swampland, fen, fenland, bog, mire, quagmire, quicksand, slough; **muddle,** mix-up *and* foul-up *and* fuck-up *and* snafu *and* screw-up <all nonformal>, pretty kettle of fish; **predicament, plight,** spot of trouble, **strait,** straits, parlous straits, tightrope, knife-edge, thin edge; pretty *or* fine state of affairs, **sorry plight**

**moratorium** NOUNS **grace period;** suspension, holdup <nonformal>, **wait,** halt, stay, stop, downtime, break, pause, interim, respite; reprieve

**morbid** ADJS **unwholesome, unhealthy,** unsound, diseased, pathological, pathological, **infected, contaminated,** tainted, peccant, **poisoned,** septic; **hideous, ghastly,** grim, grisly, gruesome, ghoulish, macabre; overcurious, supercurious; morbidly curious

**more** ADVS **additionally,** in addition, also, and then some, even more, more so, and also, and all <nonformal>, and so, **as well,** too, else, beside, **besides,** to boot, not to mention, let alone, into the bargain; on top of, over, above; **beyond,** plus; extra, on the side <nonformal>, for lagniappe; **moreover,** *au reste* <Fr>, *en plus* <Fr>, thereto, farther, further, **furthermore,** at the same time, then, again, yet; similarly, likewise, by the same token, by the same sign

**mores** NOUNS **etiquette,** social code, rules *or* code of conduct; **formalities,** social procedures, social conduct, what is done, what one does; **amenities,** decencies, civilities, elegancies, social graces, proprieties; decorum, good form; **protocol,** convention, social usage

**morgue** NOUNS **mortuary,** charnel house, lichhouse <Brit nonformal>; ossuary *or* ossuarium; **funeral home** *or* **parlor,** undertaker's establishment; **crematorium,** crematory, cinerarium

**moribund** ADJS **dying, terminal,** expiring, going, slipping, slipping away, sinking, sinking fast, low, despaired of, given up, given up for dead, not long for this world, hopeless, bad, languishing, failing, near death, near one's end, at the end of one's rope <nonformal>, done for <nonformal>, at the point of death, **at death's door,** at the portals of death, *in articulo mortis* <L>, *in extremis* <L>, in the jaws of death, facing *or* in the face of death; **on one's last legs** <nonformal>, with one foot in the grave, tottering on the brink of the grave; nonviable, unviable, incapable of life

**morning** NOUNS morn, morningtide, morning time, morntime, matins, waking time, reveille, get-up time <nonformal>, **forenoon;** *ante meridiem* <L> *or* AM, this morning, this AM <nonformal>

*rosy-finger'd morn*
HOMER

**moron** NOUNS **idiot,** driveling *or* blithering *or* adenoidal *or* congenital idiot; **imbecile,** half-wit, natural, natural idiot, born fool, natural-born fool, mental defective, defective; **simpleton**

**moronic** ADJS **mentally deficient,** mentally defective, mentally handicapped, retarded, **mentally retarded,** backward, arrested, subnormal, not right in the head, **not all there** <nonformal>; **idiotic,** imbecile, imbecilic; **foolish,** fool <nonformal>, foolheaded <nonformal>, **stupid, dumb** <nonformal>, clueless <Brit nonformal>, **asinine**

**morose** ADJS **glum,** grum, **sullen,** sulky, mumpish, dumpish, long-faced, crestfallen, chapfallen; **moody,** moodish, **brooding,** broody; mopish, mopey <nonformal>, **moping**

**morphine** NOUNS

<nonformal> big M, emm, hocus, M, miss emma, miss morph, morph, moocah, white stuff

**morsel** NOUNS **bite, taste,** swallow; mouthful, gob <nonformal>; a nibble, a bite, munchies; **delicacy,** dainty, goody <nonformal>, treat, kickshaw, **tidbit,** titbit; choice morsel, *bonne bouche* <Fr>; *morceau* <Fr>, **crumb; piece,** particle, bit, scrap, **fragment,** shard, potsherd, snatch

**mortal** NOUNS 1 **person,** human, human being, man, woman, child, member of the human race *or* family, Adamite, daughter of Eve; life, **soul,** living soul; **being,** creature, clay, ordinary clay; **individual**

ADJS 2 **perishable,** subject to death, ephemeral, transient, mutable; **deadly,** deathly, deathful, killing, destructive, death-dealing, death-bringing; **fatal,** lethal, malignant, malign, virulent, pernicious, baneful; **life-threatening,** terminal
3 **human; frail,** weak, fleshly, finite, only human; earthborn, of the earth, earthy, tellurian, unangelic

**mortality** NOUNS **deadliness,** lethality, mortality, fatality; **death rate,** death toll; **humanness,** humanity; **death,** perishability, corruptibility, caducity

**mortifying** ADJS humiliating, humiliative, humbling, chastening, **embarrassing,** crushing, disconcerting, awkward, disturbing

**mosaic** ADJS **checked, checkered,** checkedy, check, **plaid,** plaided; tessellated, tessellate

**most** NOUNS 1 **maximum,** highest, *ne plus ultra* <Fr, no more beyond>, the max <nonformal>; **major part,** best part, better part; **majority,** generality, plurality; **bulk, mass,** body, main body; **lion's share; substance,** gist, meat, essence, thrust, gravamen
ADJS 2 **greatest,** furthest, **utmost,** uttermost; **ultra,** ultra-ultra; at the height *or* peak *or* limit *or* summit *or* zenith; **superlative,** supreme, greatest, best, highest, veriest, maximal, maximum, outstanding, stickout <nonformal>; **majority,** the greatest number
ADVS 3 **extremely, utterly, totally** in the extreme, *à outrance* <Fr, to the utmost>; **immeasurably,** incalculably, indefinitely, **infinitely;** beyond compare *or* comparison, **beyond measure,** beyond all bounds, all out <nonformal>, flat out <nonformal>; unconditionally, with no strings attached, unequivocally, downright, dead; with a vengeance

**mot** NOUNS **witticism,** pleasantry, *plaisanterie, boutade* <both Fr>; **play of wit,** *jeu d'esprit* <Fr>; crack *and* smart crack *and* wisecrack <all nonformal>; **quip,** conceit, bright *or* happy thought, bright *or* brilliant idea; **bon mot,** smart saying, stroke of wit, one-liner *and* zinger <both nonformal>; epigram, turn of thought, aphorism, apothegm

**mote** NOUNS fleck, **speck,** flyspeck, jot, tittle, jot nor tittle, iota, **trace,** trace amount, suspicion, *soupçon* <Fr>; **particle,** crumb, scrap, bite, snip, snippet

**motel** NOUNS motor court, motor inn, motor hotel, auto court

**mother** NOUNS 1 genetrix, dam, maternal ancestor, matriarch, materfamilias; stepmother; foster mother, adoptive mother; birth mother; surrogate mother

2 <nonformal> **mama,** mater, the old woman, mammy, mam, **ma, mom, mommy,** mummy, mumsy, mimsy, motherkin, motherkins

VERBS 3 **foster, nurture,** nourish, care for, lavish care on, feed, parent, rear, sustain, cultivate, **cherish;** pamper, coddle, cosset, fondle <old>; **nurse,** suckle, cradle
ADJS 4 **native,** natal, **indigenous,** endemic, autochthonous; maternal, original, aboriginal, primitive; native-born, home-grown, homebred, native to the soil *or* place *or* heath

**motherhood** NOUNS **maternity,** mothership; natural *or* birth *or* biological motherhood; motherliness, maternalness; adoptive motherhood; surrogate motherhood

**mothering** NOUNS **nurture, fostering,** nurturance, nourishment, parenting, rearing, fosterage, foster-care, **care, caring,** care-giving, tender loving care *or* TLC <nonformal>

**motif** NOUNS 1 ornamental motif, **figure, detail,** form, touch, repeated figure; **pattern, theme,** design, ornamental theme, ornamental *or* decorative composition; foreground detail, background detail; **background,** setting, foil, **style,** ornamental *or* decorative style, national style, **period style**
2 **passage, phrase,** musical phrase, strain, part, motive, theme, subject, figure; leitmotiv; **theme, text,** matter in hand

**motion** NOUNS 1 **movement,** moving, **momentum; stir,** unrest, restlessness; **going,** running, stirring; **operation,** operating, **working,** ticking; **activity**; kinesis, kinetics, kinematics; dynamics; kinesiatrics, kinesipathy, kinesitherapy; **actuation,** motivation; mobilization
VERBS 2 **gesture,** gesticulate; motion to; beckon, wiggle the finger at; wave the arms, wigwag, saw the air

**motionless** ADJS **unmoving,** unmoved, moveless, **immobile,** immotive; **still,** fixed, stationary, static, at a standstill; **stock-still,** dead-still; statuelike; still as a mouse

**motion picture** NOUNS **motion pictures, movies,** the movies, the pictures, moving pictures, films, the film, the cinema, the screen, the big screen, the silver screen, the flicks *and* the flickers <both nonformal>; **movie,** picture, film, flick *and* flicker <both nonformal>, picture show, motion-picture show, moving-picture show, photoplay, photodrama; cinéma vérité *or* direct cinema; vérité; magic realism; **documentary film** *or* **movie,** docudrama, docutainment; **feature,** feature film, feature-length film, main attraction; **educational film** *or* **movie,** training film, promotional film, trigger film; **underground film** *or* **movie,** experimental film *or* movie, avant-garde film *or* movie, representational film, art film *or* movie, surrealistic film *or* movie

**motivate** VERBS **move,** set in motion, **actuate,** move to action, **impel,** propel; **stimulate,** energize, galvanize, **animate, spark;** promote, foster; force, compel; ego-involve

**motivated** ADJS **moved,** prompted, impelled, actuated; stimulated, animated; minded, inclined, of a mind to, with half a mind to; inner-directed, other-directed

**motive** NOUNS **reason, cause,** source, spring, mainspring; matter, score, consideration; **ground, basis**; sake; **aim, goal**, end, end in view, telos, final cause; **ideal,** principle, **ambition,** aspiration, inspiration, guiding light *or* star, lodestar; intention; ulterior motive

**motley** ADJS **mottled; pied, piebald,** skewbald, pinto; **dappled,** dapple; calico; marbled; pepper-and-salt; **conglomerate,** pluralistic, multiracial, multicultural, multiethnic, multinational, heterogeneous, varied, **miscellaneous,** medley, patchy; promiscuous, indiscriminate, **scrambled, jumbled,** thrown together

**motor** VERBS **ride,** go for a ride *or* drive; go for a spin <nonformal>, take *or* go for a Sunday drive; **drive,** chauffeur; joyride *or* take a joyride <nonformal>

**motorcade** NOUNS **procession,** cavalcade, caravan; **parade,** pomp

**mottled** ADJS **motley; pied, piebald,** skewbald, pinto; **dappled,** dapple; calico; marbled; clouded; pepper-and-salt

**motto** NOUNS **slogan,** watchword, catchword, catchphrase, tag line; **device;** epithet; inscription, epigraph

**mound** NOUNS 1 **hillock, knob,** butte, kopje, kame, monticle, monticule, monadnock, **knoll,** hummock, hammock, eminence, rise, swell, barrow, tumulus, kop, tel, jebel; **dune,** sand dune
VERBS 2 **pile,** pile on, heap, stack, heap *or* pile *or* stack up; hill, bank, bank up; rick

**mount** NOUNS 1 **mountain,** alp, hump, tor, height, dizzying height, nunatak, dome; **peak, pinnacle, summit**, mountaintop, point, topmost point *or* pinnacle, **crest,** tor, *pic* <Fr>, *pico* <Sp>
2 **horse;** hoss <nonformal>, critter <nonformal>; **equine,** nag <nonformal>; **steed,** prancer, dobbin; charger, courser, war-horse; **pony,** Shetland pony, Shetland, shelty, Iceland pony, Galloway; cowcutting horse, stock horse, roping horse, cow pony
VERBS 3 **climb,** climb up, upclimb, clamber, **clamber up,** scramble *or* scrabble up, claw one's way up, struggle up, inch up, shin, shinny *or* shin up <nonformal>, ramp <nonformal>, work *or* inch one's way up, climb the ladder; **scale,** escalade, scale the heights
4 **get on,** climb on, back; **bestride,** bestraddle
5 **grow,** increase, advance, appreciate; **spread, widen,** broaden; **gain,** get ahead; wax, swell, balloon, bloat, **rise,** go up, crescendo, snowball; **intensify, develop,** gain strength, strengthen

**mountain** NOUNS mount, alp, hump, tor, height, dizzying height, nunatak; crag, spur, cloud-capped *or* cloud-topped *or* snow-clad peak, the roof of the world

**mourn** VERBS **lament,** moan, grieve, sorrow, keen, weep over, **bewail,** bemoan, deplore, repine, sigh, give sorrow words; sing the blues <nonformal>, elegize, dirge, knell

**mourner** NOUNS **griever,** lamenter, keener; mute, professional mourner; **pallbearer,** bearer

**mourning** NOUNS **lamentation,** lamenting, moaning, grieving, sorrowing, wailing, bewailing, bemoaning, keening, howling, ululation, **weeds,** widow's weeds, crape, black; deep mourning; sackcloth, sackcloth and ashes

*weeping and gnashing of teeth*
BIBLE

**mouth** VERBS **speak,** talk; patter *or* gab *or* wag the tongue <all nonformal>; chatter; converse; declaim

**mouthful** NOUNS 1 **bite,** morsel, taste, swallow; gob <nonformal>; a nibble, a bite, munchies; cud, quid; bolus; **chew,** chaw <nonformal>
2 **sesquipedalian word,** big *or* long word, two- dollar *or* five-dollar word <nonformal>, **jawbreaker,** jawtwister, polysyllabism, sesquipedalianism, sesquipedality

**mouthpiece** NOUNS **spokesman,** spokeswoman, spokesperson, spokespeople, official spokesman *or* -woman *or* -person, press officer, speaker, **voice**

**mouth-watering** ADJS **appetizing,** tempting, tantalizing, provocative, piquant

**mouthy** ADJS **bombastic,** fustian, inflated, swollen, swelling, turgid, turgescent, tumid, tumescent, flatulent, windy *and* gassy <both nonformal>; overadorned, fulsome

**movable** ADJS mobile, motile; **influenceable,** swayable, persuadable, persuasible, suasible, open, open-minded, pervious, accessible, receptive, responsive, amenable

**move** NOUNS 1 **operation,** proceeding, step, measure, maneuver, movement; **endeavor,** undertaking; approach, coup, stroke, step; gambit, offer, **bid,** strong bid; **expedient,** means, means to an end, **provision,** action, effort, countermove, demarche, course of action
VERBS 2 **affect,** touch, stir; melt, soften, melt the heart, choke one up, give one a lump in the throat; **penetrate,** pierce, go through one, go deep; touch a chord, **touch a sympathetic chord,** touch one's heart, tug at the heart *or* heartstrings, go to one's heart, get under one's skin; **touch to the quick,** smart, sting
3 locate, relocate, establish residence, make one's home, **take up residence,** take residence at, put up *or* live *or* stay at, quarter *or* billet at, move in, hang up one's hat <nonformal>
4 **set in motion,** actuate, motivate, push, shove, nudge, **drive,** impel, propel; mobilize

**moved** ADJS **motivated,** prompted, impelled, actuated; stimulated, animated; minded, inclined, of a mind to, with half a mind to; inner-directed, other-directed

**movement** NOUNS 1 **exercise,** motion, maneuver; moving, **momentum; stir,** unrest, restlessness; **going,** running, stirring; **operation,** operating, **working,** ticking; activity; **travel,** traveling, going, journeying, touring, moving, locomotion, transit, progress, passage, course, crossing
2 **gesture,** gesticulation; motion, beck, beckon; shrug
3 **trend,** drift, course, current, *Tendenz* <Ger>, flow, stream, mainstream, main current, glacial movement, motion, run, **tenor,** tone, **set,** set of the current, the way the wind blows, **the way things go,** trend of the times, spirit of the age *or* time, time spirit, *Zeitgeist* <Ger>

**mover** NOUNS **prompter,** prime mover, motivator, impeller, energizer, galvanizer, inducer, **actuator, animator,** moving spirit; **encourager,** abettor, **inspirer,** firer, spark, sparker, spark plug <nonformal>; persuader; stimulator, gadfly; **producer,** maker, creator, fabricator, **author**

**moving** ADJS 1 **pitiful,** pitiable, pathetic, piteous, touching, affecting, heartrending, grievous, doleful
2 **stirring,** in motion; transitional; **mobile,** motive, motile, motor, motorial, motoric; motivational, impelling, propelling, propellant, driving; traveling; **active**
3 **lofty,** elevated, sublime, grand, majestic, noble, stately, grave, solemn, dignified; serious, weighty; inspiring

**moxie** NOUNS **pluck,** spunk <nonformal>, mettle, backbone <nonformal>, **grit,** true grit, spirit, **stamina,** guts <nonformal>, pith <old>, bottom, **toughness** <nonformal>; pluckiness, spunkiness <nonformal>, **gameness,** feistiness <nonformal>, mettlesomeness; courage

**Mrs Grundy** NOUNS conventionalist, Grundy; conformist

**much** NOUNS 1 **plenty,** plenitude, plentifulness, plenteousness; great abundance, great plenty, quantities, as much as one could wish, more than one can shake a stick at, lots, a fistful <nonformal>, **scads**; an ample sufficiency, enough and to spare, enough and then some; fat of the land

ADJS 2 **many,** beaucoup <nonformal>, ample, **abundant,** copious, generous, overflowing, superabundant, multitudinous, plentiful, **numerous**, countless
ADVS 3 **greatly, largely,** to a large *or* great extent, in great measure, on a large scale; pretty much, very much, so, so very much, ever so much, ever so, never so; **considerably**

**muck** NOUNS **filth,** slime, mess, sordes, foul matter; ordure, **excrement**; **mud,** mire, slush, slosh, sludge, squash, swill

**muckraking** NOUNS **smear campaign,** mudslinging campaign, negative campaign; **whispering campaign;** mudslinging *and* dirty politics *and* dirty tricks *and* dirty pool <all nonformal>, character assassination; political canard, roorback

**muddle** NOUNS 1 **confusion, fluster,** flummox <nonformal>, flutter, flurry, ruffle; disorientation, muddlement, fuddle *and* fuddlement <both nonformal>, befuddlement, muddleheadedness, daze, maze <nonformal>; unsettlement, disorganization, **disorder,** chaos, **mess** *and* mix-up *and* snafu <all nonformal>, discomfiture, discomposure, disconcertion, discombobulation <nonformal>, **bewilderment,** embarrassment, disturbance, perturbation, **upset,** frenzy, pother, bother, botheration *and* stew <both nonformal>
VERBS 2 **confound, confuse,** mix, mix up, tumble, jumble, jumble together, **blur,** blur distinctions, overlook distinctions; **perplex, baffle,** daze, addle, fuddle, **mystify, puzzle,** nonplus, put to one's wit's end; **make uncertain,** obscure, muddy, fuzz, fog, **confuse**

**muddled** ADJS **confused,** in a muddle; fuddled <nonformal>, **befuddled;** muddleheaded, **addled,** addlepated, addlebrained; adrift, at sea, foggy, fogged, in a fog, hazy, muzzy <nonformal>, misted, misty, cloudy, beclouded

**muddle through** VERBS **manage,** make out, get on *or* along <nonformal>, **scrape along,** worry along, get by, **manage somehow;** make it <nonformal>, **make the grade,** cut the mustard *and* hack it <both nonformal>

**muddy** VERBS 1 **make uncertain,** obscure, muddle, fuzz, fog, **confuse**
ADJS 2 **dingy,** grimy, smoky, sooty, fuliginous, smudgy, smutty, blotchy, dirty, murky, smirched, besmirched
3 **obscure,** vague, indistinct, indeterminate, fuzzy, shapeless, amorphous; unclear, unplain, opaque, **clear as mud** *and* clear as ditch water <both nonformal>

**mudslinging** NOUNS **smear campaign,** mudslinging campaign, negative campaign; **whispering campaign;** muckraking, dirty politics *and* dirty tricks *and* dirty pool <all nonformal>, character assassination; political canard, roorback

**muffle** NOUNS 1 **silencer,** muffler, mute, baffle *or* baffler, quietener, cushion; **damper,** damp; dampener; **soft pedal,** sordine, sourdine, *sordino* <Ital>; hushcloth, silence cloth; **gag, muzzle**
VERBS 2 **mute,** dull, soften, deaden, quietize, cushion, baffle, damp, **dampen,** deafen; subdue, stop, tone down, **soft-pedal,** put on the soft pedal

**mufti** NOUNS civilian dress *or* clothes, **civvies** *and* cits <both nonformal>, plain clothes

**mug** NOUNS 1 **face,** facies, **visage;** physiognomy, phiz *and* dial <both nonformal>; **countenance,** features, lineaments, favor; mush *and* pan *and* kisser *and* map *and* puss <all nonformal>
VERBS 2 **make a face,** make a wry face *or* mouth, pull a face, **screw up one's face,** mouth, make a mouth, mop, mow, mop and mow; pout
3 **overact,** overdramatize, chew up the scenery <nonformal>, act all over the stage; **ham** *and* ham it up <both nonformal>; grimace; milk a scene
4 **rob;** roll, stick up <nonformal>, **attack**

**mugger** NOUNS **assailant,** assailer, attacker; assaulter; **robber,** holdup man *and* stickup man <both nonformal>; sandbagger

**muggy** ADJS **moist,** moisty; **damp,** dampish; **wet,** wettish; **humid,** dank, sticky

**mulish** ADJS **obstinate,** stubborn, pertinacious, restive; willful, self-willed, strong-willed, hardheaded, **headstrong,** strongheaded, *entêté* <Fr>; **dogged,** bulldogged, tenacious, perserving; bullheaded, bulletheaded, **pigheaded,** stubborn as a mule; set, **set in one's ways,** balky, balking

**mull over** VERBS **think over,** ponder over, brood over, muse over, reflect over, con over, **deliberate over,** run over, **meditate over,** ruminate over, chew over, digest, turn over, **revolve,** revolve *or* turn over in the mind, deliberate upon, meditate upon, muse on *or* upon, bestow thought *or* consideration upon

**multicolor** ADJS **variegated, many-colored,** many-hued, diverse-colored, **multicolored,** varicolored, polychrome, polychromic, polychromatic; parti-colored, parti-color; of all manner of colors, of all the colors of the rainbow; versicolor, versicolored

**multilateral** ADJS **many-sided,** multifaceted, polyhedral

**multilingual** NOUNS **polyglot,** linguist, **bilingual** *or* diglot, trilingual

**multiple** ADJS multiplied, multifold, **manifold**; **increased**; multinomial, polynomial <both mathematics>; **multitudinous,** multitudinal, multifarious, **myriad,** numerous as the stars, numerous as the sands, numerous as the hairs on the head

*numerous as glittering gems of morning dew*
EDWARD YOUNG

**multiplied** ADJS **increased, heightened,** raised, elevated, stepped-up <nonformal>; **intensified,** deepened, reinforced, strengthened, fortified, beefed-up <nonformal>, tightened, stiffened; **enlarged,** extended, augmented, aggrandized, amplified, **enhanced,** boosted, hiked <nonformal>; **magnified,** inflated, expanded, swollen, bloated; proliferated; **multiple,** multifold, **manifold**

**multiply** VERBS proliferate, **increase,** duplicate; **produce,** be productive, pullulate, fructify, be fruitful, spin off, engender, beget, teem; **reproduce**

**multiracial** ADJS **mixed, mingled,** blended, compounded, amalgamated; **conglomerate,** pluralistic, multicultural, multiethnic, multinational, heterogeneous, varied, **miscellaneous,** medley, motley

**multitude** NOUNS **throng, horde,** host, heap <nonformal>, army, panoply, legion; flock, cluster, galaxy; **crowd,** press, crush, flood, spate, deluge, mass; **mob,** rabble, rout, ruck, jam, *cohue* <Fr>, everybody and his uncle *or* his brother <nonformal>

**mum** ADJS **mute, dumb,** voiceless, tongueless, **speechless,** wordless, breathless, at a loss for words, choked up; inarticulate; close, **closemouthed,** close-tongued, snug <nonformal>, **tight-lipped;** close-lipped, tongue-tied, word-bound

**mumble** NOUNS 1 **murmur,** murmuring, murmuration; **mutter,** muttering; mumbling; soft voice, low voice, small *or* little voice

*still small voice*
BIBLE

VERBS 2 **murmur,** mutter, maunder; **lower one's voice,** speak under one's breath; swallow one's words

**mumbo jumbo** NOUNS 1 **incantation, conjuration,** magic words *or* formula; hocus-pocus, abracadabra; open sesame; **voodoo, hoodoo,** juju, obeah
2 **nonsense, gibberish,** jargon, double-talk, amphigory, gobbledegook <nonformal>; glossolalia, speaking in tongues

**mummy** NOUNS **corpse,** dead body, dead man *or* woman, dead person, cadaver, body; embalmed corpse

**munch** VERBS **chew,** chew up, chaw <nonformal>, bite into; **masticate,** manducate; ruminate, chew the cud; **bite,** grind, champ, chomp <nonformal>; nibble, **gnaw**

**mundane** ADJS **secularist,** secularistic, worldly, earthly, earthy, terrestrial, temporal; **plain,** common, commonplace, ordinary, unembellished; **matter-of-fact,** unromantic, unidealistic, unimpassioned; pedestrian, **unimaginative**; insipid, vapid, flat; humdrum, tiresome, **dull**

**munitions** NOUNS **arms, weapons,** deadly weapons, instruments of destruction, offensive weapons, **military hardware,** matériel, **weaponry,** armament, ordnance, munitions of war, *apparatus belli* <L>

**murder** NOUNS 1 **homicide,** manslaughter; negligent homicide; bloody murder <nonformal>; serial killing; hit *and* bump-off *and* bumping-off <all nonformal>, gangland-style execution; kiss of death; foul play; **assassination;** removal, elimination; liquidation, purge, purging; justifiable homicide
VERBS 2 commit murder; **assassinate;** remove, **purge, liquidate,** eliminate, get rid of
3 **botch,** mar, spoil, butcher, make sad work of; play havoc with, play mischief with

**murderer** NOUNS **killer,** slayer, slaughterer, butcher, bloodshedder; manslayer, homicide, man-killer, bloodletter, Cain; **assassin,** assassinator; **cutthroat,** thug, desperado, bravo, gorilla <nonformal>, apache, gunman; professional killer, hired killer, hit man *or* button man *or* gun *or* trigger man *or* torpedo *or* gunsel <all nonformal>; **hatchet man;** thrill killer, homicidal maniac; serial killer; executioner; exterminator, eradicator; death squad

**murderous** ADJS slaughterous; cutthroat; **homicidal,** man-killing, death-dealing; biocidal, genocidal; **savage,** fierce, ferocious, vicious, cruel, **atrocious,** mindless, brutal, brutish, **bestial,** insensate, monstrous, inhuman, pitiless, ruthless, merciless, bloody, sanguinary

**murky** ADJS **gloomy,** dismal, bleak, grim, somber, sombrous, solemn, grave; cloudy, **foggy,** fogbound, hazy, misty, nebulous; indefinable, undefined, ill-defined, **unclear,** unplain, **indistinct,** fuzzy, **obscure,** confused, hazy, shadowy, shadowed forth, misty, blurred, blurry, veiled; **loose, lax, inexact,** inaccurate, imprecise; nonspecific, unspecified

**murmur** NOUNS 1 murmuring, murmuration, sough; **mutter,** muttering; **mumble,** mumbling; susurration, susurrus; **whisper,** whispering, stage whisper, breathy voice
VERBS 2 **mutter,** mumble; susurrate; lower one's voice, **speak under one's breath;** whisper, whisper in the ear; **sigh,** sough

**muscle** NOUNS 1 **muscularity,** brawniness; beefiness *and* huskiness *and* heftiness *and* hunkiness <all nonformal>, thewiness, sinewiness; **brawn,** beef <nonformal>; **sinew,** sinews, thew, thews; musculature, build, physique; great *or* mighty effort, might and main, one's back, nerve and sinew, hard *or* strong *or* long pull
VERBS 2 **exert strength,** put beef *or* one's back into it <nonformal>; use force, get tough <nonformal>, manhandle *and* strong-arm <both nonformal>; bull, bulldoze, steamroller, railroad; elbow, shoulder; **butt,** bunt, buck <nonformal>, run *or* bump *or* butt against, bump up against, knock *or* run one's head against; assault

**muscular** ADJS **able-bodied, well-built,** well-set, well-set-up <nonformal>, well-knit, of good *or* powerful physique, broad-shouldered, barrel-chested, **athletic;** well-muscled, heavily muscled, thickset, burly, **brawny;** thewy, sinewy, **wiry;** muscle-bound, all muscle

**muse** NOUNS 1 **inspiration,** afflatus, divine afflatus; genius, animus, moving *or* animating spirit; the Muses; **brown study,** study, reverie, dreamy abstraction, quiet *or* muted ecstasy, trance
VERBS 2 **consider,** contemplate, speculate, reflect, study, ponder, perpend, **weigh,** deliberate, debate, meditate, brood, ruminate, chew the cud <nonformal>; **moon** <nonformal>, **dream,** daydream, pipe-dream <nonformal>, fantasy; abstract oneself, be lost in thought, let one's attention wander, let one's mind run on other things, dream of *or* muse on other things; **wander,** stray, ramble, divagate, let one's thoughts *or* mind wander, give oneself up to reverie, **woolgather,** go woolgathering, **be in a brown study,** be absent, be somewhere else, stargaze, be out of it *and* be not with it <both nonformal>

**museum** NOUNS **gallery,** art gallery, picture gallery, pinacotheca; Metropolitan Museum, National Gallery, Museum of Modern Art, Guggenheim Museum, Tate Gallery, British Museum, Louvre, Hermitage, Prado, Uffizi, Rijksmuseum; **library;** repository

**mushy** ADJS **wishy-washy,** tasteless, bland, **insipid,** vapid, neutral, watery, milky, milk-and-water; halfhearted, infirm of will *or* purpose, **indecisive,** irresolute, changeable; **sentimental,** sentimentalized, soft, **mawkish,** maudlin, cloying; oversentimental, oversentimentalized, bathetic; sloppy *or* gushing *or* teary *or* beery <all nonformal>, treacly <Brit nonformal>; tear-jerking <nonformal>

**music** NOUNS harmonious sound, **score,** musical score *or* copy, notation, musical notation, written music, copy, draft, transcript, transcription, version, edition, text, arrangement; **harmonics,** harmony; melodics; musicality

*the speech of angels*
CARLYLE

**musical** NOUNS 1 **musical theater,** music theater, lyric theater, musical stage, lyric

stage; **music drama,** lyric drama; **musical comedy;** Broadway musical
ADJS 2 **musically inclined,** musicianly, with an ear for music; **music-loving,** music-mad, musicophile, philharmonic; **melodious,** melodic; music-like; **tuneful,** lilting; fine-toned, **pleasant-sounding,** agreeable-sounding, pleasant, appealing, agreeable, catchy, singable; euphonious *or* euphonic, **lyric,** lyrical, melic; **sweet, dulcet,** sweet-sounding, achingly sweet

**musician** NOUNS **music maker,** professional musician; performer, executant, interpreter, tunester, artiste, artist, concert artist, **virtuoso,** virtuosa; maestro; recitalist; **soloist,** duettist; street musician, busker <chiefly Brit>

**must** NOUNS 1 **fetidness,** fetidity, malodourousness, **smelliness,** stinkingness, **odorousness,** noisomeness, **rankness, foulness,** putridness, offensiveness; **mustiness,** funkiness, moldiness, smut, rust, fungus, mildew, mildew, fustiness, frowziness, stuffiness
VERBS 2 **be necessary,** lie under a necessity, be one's fate; be a must <nonformal>; be obliged, **have to,** have got to <nonformal>, should, need, **need to,** have need to; not able to keep from, not able to help, **cannot help but,** cannot do otherwise; be forced *or* driven
ADJS 3 **obligatory,** binding, imperative, imperious, peremptory, mandatory, *de rigueur* <Fr>; **necessary,** required; carved in stone, set in concrete <nonformal>

**mustache** NOUNS mustachio, soup-strainer <nonformal>, toothbrush, handle bars *or* handlebar mustache, Fu Manchu mustache, Zapata mustache, walrus mustache

**muster** NOUNS 1 **enlistment,** enrollment; conscription, draft, drafting, induction, impressment, press; call, draft call, call-up, summons, call to the colors, letter from Uncle Sam <nonformal>; **recruitment,** recruiting; mustering, mustering in, levy, levying
2 **roll call,** nose *or* head count <nonformal>, **poll,** questionnaire, returns, census report *or* returns

**musty** ADJS **stale,** fusty, rusty, dusty, moldy, mildewed; **worn,** timeworn, time-scarred; **moth-eaten,** moss-grown, crumbling, moldering, gone to seed, dilapidated

**mutate** VERBS **change,** work *or* make a change, alter, modify; **adapt;** vary, **diversify; convert,** renew, recast, revamp <nonformal>, change over, exchange, remake, reshape, re-create, redesign, rebuild, reconstruct, restructure

**mute** NOUNS 1 **silencer,** muffler, muffle, baffle *or* baffler, quietener, cushion; **damper,** damp; dampener; **soft pedal,** sordine, sourdine, *sordino* <Ital>; **gag,** muzzle; soundproofing
VERBS 2 **muffle,** dull, soften, deaden, quietize, cushion, baffle, damp, **dampen,** deafen; subdue, stop, tone down, **soft-pedal,** put on the soft pedal
ADJS 3 **mum, dumb,** voiceless, tongueless, speechless, wordless, breathless, at a loss for words, choked up; inarticulate; **tongue-tied,** dumbstruck, dumbstricken, stricken dumb, **dumbfounded;** anaudic, aphasic, aphonic

**muted** ADJS **muffled,** softened, dampened, damped, **smothered,** stifled, bated, dulled, deadened, subdued; **dull,** dead, flat, *sordo* <Ital>

**mutilate** VERBS **tear** *or* **rip apart,** take *or* pull apart, pick *or* rip *or* tear to pieces, **shred,** rip to shreds; **dismember,** tear limb from limb, draw and quarter; **mangle,** lacerate, maim; **damage**

**mutinous** ADJS **rebellious,** rebel, breakaway; mutineering; **insurgent, insurrectionary,** riotous, turbulent; factious, **seditious,** seditionary; revolutionary, revolutional; traitorous, treasonable, subversive; extreme, insubordinate, disobedient

**mutiny** NOUNS 1 **revolt,** rebellion, revolution, insurrection, insurgence *or* insurgency, *émeute* <Fr>, **uprising,** rising, outbreak, general uprising, *levée en masse* <Fr>, **riot,** civil disorder; peasant revolt, *jacquerie* <Fr>; putsch, coup d'état; indiscipline, insubordination, disobedience
VERBS 2 **revolt, rebel,** kick over the traces, reluct, reluctate; **rise up,** rise, arise, rise up in arms, mount the barricades; mount *or* make a coup d'état

**mutter** VERBS **mumble,** maunder; drone, drone on; swallow one's words, speak drunkenly *or* incoherently; jabber, gibber, gabble

**mutual** ADJS commutual, **common,** joint, communal, shared, sharing, conjoint; respective, two-way; give-and-take;

**exchanged,** transposed, switched, swapped <nonformal>, traded, **interchanged**

**muzzle** NOUNS 1 **silencer, gag,** muffle, **mute,** baffle *or* baffler, quietener, cushion; **damper,** damp; dampener; **soft pedal**
2 **snout,** snoot <nonformal>, nozzle <nonformal>; **mouth;** maw, oral cavity, gob <nonformal>, gab <Scots>; jaw, lips, embouchure; bazoo *or* kisser *or* mug *or* mush *or* trap *or* yap <all nonformal>
VERBS 3 **silence,** squash, squelch <nonformal>, stifle, choke, choke off, throttle, put the kibosh on <nonformal>, put the lid on *and* shut down on <both nonformal>, put the damper on <nonformal>, **gag,** muffle, stop one's mouth, cut one short

**mysterious** ADJS **awesome,** awful, awing, awe-inspiring; **transcendent,** transcending, surpassing; numinous; weird, eerie, uncanny, bizarre; enigmatic; **inexplicable, unexplainable,** uninterpretable, undefinable, indefinable; mystic, mystical, shrouded *or* wrapped *or* enwrapped in mystery; **occult,** paranormal, supernatural; arcane, esoteric

**mystery** NOUNS **enigma,** puzzle, puzzlement; **perplexity;** mysteriousness, miraculousness, strangeness; problem, riddle, conundrum

**mystic** NOUNS 1 **occultist,** esoteric, mystagogue, cabalist, supernaturalist, transcendentalist; adept, mahatma; yogi, yogin, yogist; theosophist, anthroposophist
ADJS 2 **occult,** esoteric, esoterical, mysterious, mystical, anagogic, anagogical; metaphysic, metaphysical; cabalic, cabalistic; theosophical, theosophist, anthroposophical

**mystify** VERBS **perplex,** baffle, confound, daze, maze, addle, fuddle, muddle, **puzzle,** nonplus, put to one's wit's end; keep one guessing, keep in suspense

**mystifying** ADJS **bewildering,** confusing, distracting, disconcerting, discomposing, **dismaying,** embarrassing, disturbing, **upsetting,** perturbing, bothering; **perplexing,** baffling, mysterious, puzzling, funny, funny peculiar, confounding; **problematic** *or* problematical; intricate; **enigmatic**

**mystique** NOUNS **illustriousness,** luster, brilliance *or* brilliancy, radiance, splendor, resplendence; charisma, glamour, numinousness, magic

**myth** NOUNS **fabrication,** invention, concoction, disinformation; canard, base canard; **fiction,** figment, fable, romance, extravaganza; mythology, legend, lore, folklore, folktale, folk motif; racial memory, archetypal myth *or* image *or* pattern

**mythical** ADJS **fictional,** mythological, **legendary,** fabulous; mythopoeic, mythopoetic *or* mythopoetical; **allegorical** *or* allegoric, parabolic *or* parabolical; **romantic,** romanticized; **extraordinary,** exceptional, remarkable, noteworthy, **wonderful,** marvelous; mythified, mythicized

# N

**nadir** NOUNS **boundary,** lower limit, floor, low-water mark, the pits <nonformal>; **base, bottom**, lowest point; the lowest of the low

**nag** NOUNS 1 **nuisance, pest,** pesterer, pain *and* pain in the neck *or* ass <nonformal>, nudzh <nonformal>, *nudnik* <Yiddish>; annoyer, harasser, harrier, badgerer, **heckler,** plaguer, persecutor
2 horse; **plug,** hack, jade, crock, garron <Scots & Ir>, crowbait <nonformal>, scalawag, rosinante; balky horse, balker, jughead; stack of bones
VERBS 3 **importune,** beset, buttonhole, besiege, take *or* grasp by the lapels; work on <nonformal>, **tease,** pester, plague, nag at, make a pest *or* nuisance of oneself, try one's patience, bug <nonformal>, nudge; niggle, **carp at, fuss at,** fret at, yap *or* pick at <nonformal>, peck at, nibble at, **henpeck,** pick on *and* pick at <all nonformal>, bug *and* hassle <nonformal>

**nagging** ADJS 1 **importunate; teasing,** pesty, pesky <nonformal>, pestering, plaguing, dunning; **insistent,** demanding, urgent; **critical, faultfinding,** carping, caviling, quibbling, pettifogging, captious, cynical; niggling; hypercritical, ultracritical, overcritical, hairsplitting, trichoschistic
2 **unforgettable, never to be forgotten,** never to be erased from the mind, **indelible,** indelibly impressed on the mind, fixed in the mind; haunting, persistent, recurrent, plaguing, rankling, festering; obsessing, obsessive

**nail** VERBS 1 **catch, take,** catch flat-footed, land <nonformal>, hook, **snag, snare,** sniggle, spear, harpoon; **bag,** sack; **trap,** entrap
2 **pin,** skewer, peg, nail up, tack, staple, toggle, screw, bolt, rivet

**naive** ADJS **immature,** unadult; **inexperienced,** unseasoned, unfledged, newfledged, **callow,** unripe, **raw, green,** vernal, primaveral, dewy, juicy, sappy, budding, tender, virginal, intact, ingenuous, **undeveloped,** growing, unformed, unlicked, wet *or* not dry behind the ears; **unsophisticated,** childlike, born yesterday; **innocent;** trustful, trusting, unguarded, unwary, unreserved, confiding, unsuspicious

**naked** ADJS 1 **nude; bare,** peeled, raw <nonformal>, **in the raw** <nonformal>, *in puris naturalibus* <L>, in a state of nature, in nature's garb; in one's birthday suit, **in the buff** *and* in native buff *and* stripped to the buff *and* **in the altogether** <all nonformal>, with nothing on, without a stitch, without a stitch to one's name *or* on one's back; **stark-naked,** bare-ass <nonformal>, naked as the day one was born, naked as a jaybird <nonformal>
2 **open,** overt, open to all, open as day, out of the closet <nonformal>; **revealed,** disclosed, exposed; bare, bald

**name** NOUNS 1 **appellation,** appellative, **denomination,** designation, style, *nomen* <L>, **cognomen,** cognomination, full name; proper name *or* noun; moniker *and* handle <both nonformal>; **title,** honorific; **label,** tag; epithet, byword; middle name; eponym; namesake; secret name, cryptonym, euonym
2 **celebrity,** man *or* woman of mark *or* note, person of note *or* consequence, **notable,** notability, luminary, great man *or* woman, master spirit, worthy, **big name,** figure, public figure, **somebody**
VERBS 3 **designate, specify;** denominate, denote; stigmatize; **appoint,** assign, **nominate,** select, tab <nonformal>; **ordain**
ADJS 4 **important,** major, consequential, momentous, significant, considerable, substantial, material, **great,** grand, big; big-time *and* big-league *and* major-league *and* heavyweight <all nonformal>; high-powered <nonformal>, double-barreled <nonformal>; big-name <nonformal>, self-important

**name-dropper** NOUNS **social climber,** climber, tufthunter, status seeker, fortune hunter

**nanny** NOUNS **nurse, nursemaid,** nurserymaid, amah, ayah, mammy <nonformal>; **baby-sitter,** baby-minder <Brit>, sitter <nonformal>

**nap** NOUNS 1 **snooze** <nonformal>, **catnap,** wink, **forty winks** *and* some Zs <both nonformal>; **siesta,** blanket drill *and* sack *or* rack time <all nonformal>
2 **texture,** surface texture; **finish,** feel; **grain,** granular texture, fineness *or* coarseness of grain; pile, shag, nub, knub

VERBS 3 **sleep, slumber,** rest in the arms of Morpheus; **doze,** drowse; **catnap,** take a nap, catch a wink, sleep soundly, **sleep like a top** *or* **log,** sleep like the dead

**napping** ADJS **sleepy, slumberous,** slumbery, dreamy; **half asleep,** asleep on one's feet; yawny, stretchy <nonformal>, oscitant, yawning, **nodding,** ready for bed; asleep, **off one's guard,** caught napping, caught tripping, **asleep at the switch** *and* asleep on the job *and* **not on the job** *and* goofing off *and* looking out the window <all nonformal>; daydreaming, woolgathering

**narc** NOUNS **detective,** operative, investigator, narcotics agent; treasury agent *or* T-man <nonformal>

**narcissistic** ADJS **egotistic,** egotistical, **egocentric,** egocentristic, self-centered, self-obsessed, narcistic; selfish, self-esteeming, self-admiring; **self-centered**

**narcotic** NOUNS 1 **drug,** dope <nonformal>, dangerous drug, controlled substance, abused substance, illegal drug, addictive drug, **hard drug; opiate; sedative,** depressant, sedative hypnotic, antipsychotic tranquilizer

ADJS 2 hypnotic, **soporific,** somniferous, somnifacient; sedative, **anesthetic,** analgesic; stupefying, stunning, numbing, mind-boggling *or* -numbing; anesthetizing, narcotizing; **palliative,** alleviative, alleviatory, assuasive, lenitive, **calmative,** calmant, demulcent, anodyne

**narcotics addict** NOUNS **addict, drug addict,** user, drug user, drug abuser, junkie *and* head *and* druggy *and* doper *and* toker *and* fiend *and* freak *and* space cadet <all nonformal>; cocaine user, cokie *and* coke head *and* crackhead *and* sniffer *and* snow drifter *and* flaky <all nonformal>; opium user, opium addict, hophead *and* hopdog *and* tar distiller <all nonformal>; heroin user *or* addict, smackhead *and* smack-sack *and* schmecker <all nonformal>; methedrine user *or* methhead <nonformal>; amphetamine user, pillhead *and* pill popper *and* speed freak <all nonformal>; LSD user, acidhead *and* acid freak *and* tripper *and* cubehead <all nonformal>; marijuana smoker *and* pothead <both nonformal>

**narcotize** VERBS **numb, benumb,** paralyze, deaden, anesthetize, freeze, **stun, stupefy,** drug, sedate, dope *or* dope up <nonformal>, tranquilize, deaden, dull, blunt, obtund, take the edge off, take the sting *or* bite out

**narrate** VERBS **tell, relate,** recount, report, **recite,** rehearse, give an account of; tell a story, unfold a tale, a tale unfold, fable, fabulize

**narrative** NOUNS **story,** tale, yarn, account, narration, chronicle; **anecdote,** anecdotage; **epic,** epos, **saga**

**narrator** NOUNS **relator,** reciter, recounter, *raconteur* <Fr>; **anecdotist; storyteller,** storier, taleteller, teller of tales, spinner of yarns *and* yarn spinner <both nonformal>; word painter; **persona,** central consciousness, the I of the story

**narrow** VERBS 1 constrict, diminish, draw in, go in; restrict, limit, straiten, confine; **taper; contract**

ADJS 2 **slender;** narrowish, narrowy; **close,** near; **tight, strait,** isthmic, isthmian; close-fitting; **restricted,** limited, circumscribed, **confined,** constricted; **cramped,** cramp; incapacious, incommodious, crowded

**narrow-minded** ADJS **prudish,** priggish, prim, prissy, smug, stuffy <nonformal>, old-maidish, **overmodest,** demure, **straitlaced,** stiff-necked, hide-bound, censorious, sanctimonious, **puritanical,** Victorian, mid-Victorian; **insular,** parochial, ethnocentric, xenophobic, snobbish; narrow-gauged, closed, closed-minded, cramped, constricted, *borné* <Fr>, little-minded, small-minded, mean-spirited; **small,** little, mean, petty; uncharitable, ungenerous; bigot, **bigoted,** fanatical; **illiberal,** unliberal, uncatholic

**nasal** ADJS **stopped,** muted, checked, occlusive, nasalized, twangy, continuant, liquid, lateral, affricated; **twangy,** breathy, adenoidal, snuffling

**nasty** ADJS 1 **offensive**, fulsome, noisome, noxious, rebarbative, mawkish, cloying, brackish, **foul, vile,** bad; gross *and* icky *and* yucky <all nonformal>, **sickening, nauseating,** nauseous, nauseant, vomity *and* barfy <both nonformal>; rank, rancid, maggoty, weevily, spoiled, overripe, high, rotten, stinking, putrid, malodorous, fetid

2 **malicious,** maleficent, malefic; **malignant,** malign; **mean** *and* **ornery** *and* cussed *and* bitchy <all nonformal>, hateful, baleful, invidious; **wicked,** iniq-

uitous; **harmful,** noxious; gross, offensive, crass, **coarse, crude,** loutish

**nation** NOUNS **country,** land; nationality, **state,** nation-state, sovereign nation *or* state, polity, **body politic; power,** superpower, world power; **republic,** people's republic, **commonwealth,** commonweal; free nation, captive nation, nonaligned *or* unaligned *or* neutralist nation; developed nation, industrial *or* industrialized nation; underdeveloped nation, third-world nation

**national** ADJS **public,** general, common; communal, societal, social; state; societal; **popular,** public, mass, grass-roots; nation-wide, country-wide

**nationality** NOUNS **nativeness,** nativity, native-bornness, indigenousness *or* indigenity, aboriginality, autochthonousness; **nation,** state, nation-state, sovereign nation *or* state, polity, body politic; nationhood, peoplehood

**native** NOUNS 1 indigene, autochthon, earliest inhabitant, first comer, primitive settler; primitive; **aborigine,** aboriginal; local *and* local yokel <both nonformal>
ADJS 2 natal, **indigenous,** endemic, autochthonous; mother, maternal, original, aboriginal, primitive; native-born, home-grown, homebred, native to the soil *or* place *or* heath
3 **innate,** inborn, born, congenital; **natural,** natural to, connatural, native to, indigenous; **constitutional,** bodily, physical, temperamental, organic; **inbred,** genetic, hereditary, inherited, bred in the bone, in the blood, running in the blood *or* race *or* strain, radical, rooted; connate, connatal, coeval; **instinctive,** instinctual, atavistic, primal

**native land** NOUNS **fatherland,** *Vaterland* <Ger>, *patria* <L>, *la patrie* <Fr>, **motherland,** mother country, native soil, one's native heath *or* ground *or* soil *or* place, the old country, country of origin, **birthplace,** cradle; **home, homeland,** homeground, God's country

*home is where one starts*
**T S Eliot**

**nativity** NOUNS **birth,** genesis, nascency, **childbirth,** childbearing, having a baby, giving birth, birthing, parturition, the stork <nonformal>; **delivery,** blessed event <nonformal>; the Nativity

**natty** ADJS **tidy,** trim, neat, spruce, sleek, slick *and* slick as a whistle <nonformal>, smart, trig, snug, **well-kept,** well-kempt, well-cared-for, well-groomed; neat as a button *or* pin <nonformal>

**natural** NOUNS 1 **talented person,** talent, man *or* woman of parts, gifted person, prodigy, **genius,** mental genius, intellectual genius, intellectual prodigy, mental giant; rocket scientist *and* brain surgeon <both nonformal>; phenom <nonformal>; gifted child, **child prodigy,** wunderkind, whiz kid *and* boy wonder <both nonformal>
ADJS 2 naturelike, native; in the state of nature; primitive, primal, pristine, unspoiled, untainted, uncontaminated; **unaffected, unassuming, unpretending,** unpretentious, unfeigning, undisguising, undissembling, undesigning; **genuine,** inartificial, unadorned, unvarnished, unembellished; homespun
3 **instinctive,** inherent, innate, unlearned; unconscious, subliminal; **involuntary,** automatic, spontaneous, impulsive; **instinctual,** libidinal

**naturalize** VERBS grant *or* confer citizenship, adopt, admit, affiliate, **assimilate;** Americanize, Anglicize, etc; acculturate, acculturize; indigenize, go native <nonformal>; **domesticate,** domesticize, **tame,** break, gentle, housebreak; acclimatize, acclimate

**nature** NOUNS **character, quality,** suchness; **constitution,** composition, **characteristics,** makeup, constituents; **temperament,** temper, fiber, **disposition,** spirit, ethos, genius, dharma; **way, habit,** tenor, cast, hue, tone, grain, vein, streak, stripe, mold, brand, stamp
2 physical world, natural world

**naughty** ADJS **misbehaving,** unbehaving; bad; improper, not respectable; out-of-order *and* off-base *and* out-of-line <all nonformal>; **disorderly,** disruptive, **disobedient,** transgressive, uncomplying, wayward, froward

**nauseating** ADJS **offensive,** objectionable, odious, repulsive, repellent, rebarbative, **repugnant, revolting,** forbidding; **disgusting,** sickening, loathsome, gross *and* yucky *and* grungy *and* scuzzy <all nonformal>, beastly <nonformal>, **vile,** foul, nasty; **obnoxious,** abhorrent, hateful, abominable

**nauseous** ADJS **nasty, offensive,** fulsome, noisome, noxious, rebarbative, mawkish, cloying, brackish, **foul, vile,** bad;

gross *and* icky *and* yucky <all nonformal>, **sickening, nauseating,** nauseant; **nauseated,** queasy, squeamish, qualmish, qualmy; **sick to one's stomach;** pukish *and* puky *and* barfy <all nonformal>; seasick, carsick, airsick

**nautical** ADJS **marine,** maritime, naval, navigational; seafaring, seagoing, oceangoing, seaborne, water-borne; seamanly, seamanlike, **salty** <nonformal>; pelagic, oceanic

**naval** ADJS **nautical,** marine, maritime, navigational; seafaring, seagoing, oceangoing, seaborne, water-borne; seamanly, seamanlike

**navigate** VERBS **sail, cruise,** steam, run, seafare, voyage, ply, go on shipboard, go by ship, go on *or* take a voyage, cross, traverse, make a passage *or* run; sail round, circumnavigate; **pilot,** helm, coxswain, **steer,** guide, be at the helm *or* tiller, direct, manage, handle, run, operate, shape *or* chart a course

**navy** NOUNS naval forces, **first line of defense; fleet,** flotilla, argosy, armada, squadron, escadrille, division, task force, task group; mosquito fleet

**Neanderthal** ADJS **unrefined,** unpolished, uncouth, unkempt, uncombed, unlicked; **uncivilized,** noncivilized; **barbarous,** barbaric, barbarian; outlandish, Gothic; **savage,** brutish, bestial, animal, **mindless;** troglodytic

**near** VERBS 1 **come near,** draw near *or* nigh, **approach**, come within shouting distance; come within an ace *or* an inch; **be imminent,** impend, overhang, hang *or* lie over, **loom,** hang over one's head, hover, **threaten, menace,** lower; brew, gather; rush up on one, forthcome, be on the horizon, be in the offing, be just around the corner
ADJS 2 **close, nigh,** close-in, nearish, nighish, intimate, cheek-by-jowl, side-by-side, hand-in-hand, arm-in-arm, *bras-dessus-bras-dessous* <Fr>; **approaching,** nearing, approximate *or* approximating, proximate, proximal
ADVS 3 **nearly,** pretty near <nonformal>, close, **closely; almost,** all but, not quite, as good as, as near as makes no difference; **well-nigh,** just about; nigh, nigh hand

**nearby** ADJS 1 **handy, convenient,** neighboring, vicinal, propinquant *or* propinquous, ready at hand, easily reached *or* attained
ADVS 2 **aside,** on one side, **to one side,** to the side, sidelong, on the side, on the one hand, on one hand, on the other hand; **alongside,** in parallel, side-by-side; in juxtaposition; away

**nearest** ADJS nighest, **closest,** nearmost, next, immediate

**nearsighted** ADJS **undiscerning,** unperceptive, imperceptive, impercipient, insensible, unapprehending, uncomprehending, nonunderstanding; **shortsighted,** myopic, dim-sighted, purblind

**neat** ADJS **tidy,** trim, natty, spruce, sleek, slick *and* slick as a whistle <nonformal>, smart, trig, snug, tight, **shipshape; well-kept,** well-kempt, well-cared-for, well-groomed; neat as a button *or* pin <nonformal>

**necessary** ADJS **obligatory,** compulsory, entailed, mandatory; **exigent,** urgent, necessitous, importunate, **imperative;** choiceless, without choice, out of one's hands *or* control; **requisite,** needful, required, needed, **wanted,** called for, indicated; **essential,** vital, indispensable, unforgoable, irreplaceable

**necessity** NOUNS **obligation,** obligement; compulsoriness, **compulsion,** duress; **requirement,** requisite, requisition; **need,** want, occasion; desideratum, desideration; **prerequisite,** essential, indispensable; the necessary, the needful; necessities, necessaries, essentials, bare necessities

**need** NOUNS 1 **want,** lack, deficiency, deficit, shortage, shortfall, wantage, **incompleteness,** defectiveness, shortcoming, imperfection; **destitution,** impoverishment, beggary, deprivation
VERBS 2 **want,** lack, require; miss, feel the want of, be sent away empty-handed; run short of

**needle** NOUNS 1 **thorn,** bramble, brier, nettle, burr, prickle, sticker <nonformal>; **spike,** spikelet, spicule, spiculum; **spine;** bristle; quill; nib, neb
VERBS 2 **annoy, bug** <nonformal>, be on the back of *and* be at *and* ride <all nonformal>, **pester, tease,** devil, get after *or* get on <nonformal>, **bedevil, pick on** <nonformal>, tweak the nose, pluck the beard, give a bad time to <nonformal>; **goad, prod,** poke, nudge, prod at, goose <nonformal>, **spur,** prick, sting

**needless** ADJS **unnecessary,** unessential, nonessential, **unneeded,** gratuitous, uncalled-for, unrequired; unrecognized, neglected

**the needy** NOUNS **the poor,** the have-nots <nonformal>, the down-and-out, the disadvantaged, the underprivileged, the distressed, the underclass; the urban poor, the homeless, the ranks of the homeless; the other America; the forgotten man

*the forgotten man at the bottom of the economic pyramid*
F D ROOSEVELT

**negate** VERBS abnegate, **say 'no';** shake the head, wag *or* waggle the beard; **abolish,** nullify, void, abrogate, annihilate, annul, tear up, repeal, revoke, invalidate, **undo, cancel,** cancel out, bring to naught, put *or* lay to rest; **belie,** be contrary to, come in conflict with

**negative** ADJS **contrary;** contrarious, perverse, **opposite,** antithetic, antithetical, **contradictory,** counter, contrapositive, contrasted; **antagonistic,** repugnant, oppugnant, perverse, contrarious, ornery <nonformal>, nay-saying, hostile, combative, bellicose, belligerent, inimical, antipathetic, antipathetical, discordant; **disagreeable,** cross, cranky, ornery <nonformal>, uncongenial, incompatible

**neglect** NOUNS 1 neglectfulness, **negligence,** inadvertence *or* inadvertency, malperformance, dereliction, *culpa* <L>, culpable negligence, criminal negligence; **remissness,** laxity, laxness, slackness, looseness, laches; **disregard,** airy disregard, slighting; **inattention**; **oversight,** overlooking; **omission,** nonfeasance, nonperformance, lapse, failure, **default;** poor stewardship *or* guardianship *or* custody; procrastination
VERBS 2 **overlook, disregard,** not heed, not attend to, take for granted, **ignore;** not care for, not take care of; **pass over,** gloss over; **let slip, let slide** <nonformal>, let the chance slip by, **let go,** let ride <nonformal>, let take its course; not give a thought to, take no thought *or* account of, blind oneself to, turn a blind eye to, leave out of one's calculation; lose sight of, lose track of; **be neglectful** *or* **negligent,** fail in one's duty, **fail,** lapse, **default**

**neglected** ADJS unattended to, untended, unwatched, unchaperoned, uncared-for; **disregarded,** unconsidered, unregarded, **overlooked, missed,** omitted, passed by, passed over, passed up <nonformal>, gathering dust, **ignored, slighted;** half-done, undone, left undone; deserted, abandoned; in the cold *and* out in the cold <both nonformal>; on the shelf, shelved, pigeonholed, on hold *and* on the back burner <both nonformal>, **put** *or* **laid aside,** sidetracked *and* sidelined <both nonformal>, shunted

**negligee** NOUNS **dishabille,** *déshabillé* <Fr>, **undress,** something more comfortable; *négligé* <Fr>; **wrap,** wrapper

**negligent** ADJS **neglectful,** neglecting, derelict, culpably negligent; inadvertent, uncircumspect; **inattentive**; unwary, unwatchful, asleep at the switch, off-guard, unguarded; **remiss,** slack, lax, relaxed, laid-back <nonformal>, loose, loosey-goosey <nonformal>, unrigorous, permissive, overly permissive; slighting; slurring, scamping, skimping <nonformal>; procrastinating

**negligible** ADJS **insignificant,** small, inconsiderable, inconsequential, no great shakes, footling, one-horse *and* pint-size *and* vest-pocket <all nonformal>; unimportant, no skin off one's nose *or* ass, **trivial**

**negotiable** ADJS 1 **transferable,** conveyable, alienable; **assignable,** consignable; devisable, bequeathable; heritable, inheritable
2 **practicable,** practical, feasible; workable, actable, performable, realizable, compassable, operable, doable, swingable, bridgeable; **viable; achievable, attainable;** surmountable, superable

**negotiate** VERBS **manage,** contrive, succeed in; make out, get on *or* along <nonformal>, come on *or* along <nonformal>, go on; **scrape along,** worry along, **muddle through,** get by, manage somehow; make it <nonformal>, **make the grade,** cut the mustard *and* hack it <both nonformal>; **clear,** clear the hurdle; **engineer; swing** <nonformal>, put over <nonformal>, put through; **treat with,** bargain, make terms, sit down with, sit down at the bargaining table

**negotiation** NOUNS **bargaining,** haggling, higgling, **dickering,** chaffering, chaffer, haggle; hacking out *or* working out *or* hammering out a deal, coming to terms; collective bargaining

**negotiator** NOUNS **mediator,** intermediator, intermediate agent, intermediate, intermedium, **intermediary,** interagent, internuncio; **intercessor,** interceder; **go-between,** middleman; negotiant, negotiatress *or* negotiatrix

**neighborhood** NOUNS **vicinity,** vicinage, environs, surroundings, surround, setting, grounds, purlieus, confines, precinct; neck of the woods <nonformal>, precincts, milieu

**neighboring** ADJS **nearby,** handy, convenient, vicinal, propinquant *or* propinquous, ready at hand, easily reached *or* attained; **adjacent,** next, immediate, contiguous, **adjoining,** abutting; neighbor; **bordering,** conterminous *or* coterminous, connecting

**neighborly** ADJS **hospitable,** receptive, welcoming; **cordial,** amiable, gracious, **friendly,** genial, hearty, open, openhearted, warm, warmhearted; **generous,** liberal; neighborlike; sociable

**nemesis** NOUNS **bane,** curse, affliction, infliction, visitation, **plague,** pestilence, pest, calamity, scourge, **torment,** open wound, running sore, grievance, woe, burden, crushing burden; bugbear, **bête noire,** bogy, bogeymen, arch-nemesis

**nepotism** NOUNS **partiality,** onesidedness; **favoritism,** preference, unequal *or* preferential treatment, discrimination

**nerd** NOUNS **specialist,** specializer, **expert, authority,** savant, scholar, connoisseur, maven <nonformal>; technical expert, technician, techie <nonformal>; fan, buff, freak *and* nut <both nonformal>, aficionado

**nervous** ADJS **high-strung,** overstrung, highly strung, all nerves; **uneasy, apprehensive,** qualmish, nail-biting, white-knuckle <nonformal>; nervous as a cat; **excitable; irritable,** edgy, **on edge,** nerves on edge, on the ragged edge <nonformal>, panicky, **fearful, frightened;** jittery, jumpy, agitated, shook up, shaking, trembling

**nervous breakdown** NOUNS **collapse,** breakdown, crackup <nonformal>, **prostration,** exhaustion; nervous prostration *or* exhaustion, neurasthenia

**nervy** ADJS **impudent,** impertinent, pert, flip <nonformal>, flippant, **cocky** *and* cheeky *and* **fresh** *and* facy *and* crusty <all nonformal>, *chutzpadik* <Yiddish>; **rude,** disrespectful, derisive, brash, bluff; **saucy,** sassy <nonformal>; smart *or* smart-alecky <nonformal>, smart-ass *or* wise-ass <nonformal>

**nest egg** NOUNS **reserves,** stockpile, cache, backup, reserve supply, something in reserve *or* in hand, something to fall back on, reserve fund, **savings,** sinking fund; proved reserves; life savings

**nestle** VERBS **snuggle,** cuddle, cuddle up, curl up; nestle, nest; bundle; snuggle up to, snug up *or* together <old>

**net** NOUNS 1 **network, webwork, weaving, meshwork,** tissue, crossing over and under, interlacement, intertwinement, intertexture, texture, reticulum, reticulation; netting; **mesh; web,** webbing; trawl, dragnet, seine, purse seine, pound net, gill net; **meshes, toils**
2 **gain,** profit, take *or* take-in *and* piece *and* slice *and* end *and* rakeoff *and* skimmings <all nonformal>; net *or* neat profit, clean *or* clear profit
VERBS 3 **trap,** entrap, gin, catch, **ensnare, snare,** hook, **hook in,** sniggle, noose; mesh, enmesh, ensnarl, wind, tangle, entangle, entoil, enweb; run down, run to earth, **take captive, take prisoner,** apprehend, capture, seize, **take into custody**
4 **profit,** make *or* draw *or* realize *or* reap profit, come out ahead, make money; rake it in *and* coin money *and* make a bundle *or* pile *or* killing *or* mint *and* clean up <all nonformal>; **realize,** clear; make a fast *or* quick buck <nonformal>; **yield,** bring in, afford, pay, pay off <nonformal>, **return**
ADJS 5 **remaining,** over, left, leftover; **spare,** to spare; unused, unconsumed; **surplus**

**network** NOUNS 1 **webwork,** weaving, meshwork, tissue, crossing over and under, interlacement, intertwinement, intertexture, texture, reticulum, reticulation; **net,** netting; **mesh,** meshes; **web,** webbing; wicker, wickerwork; basketwork, basketry; lattice, latticework; hachure *or* hatchure, hatching, crosshatching; trellis, trelliswork, treillage; grate, grating; grille, grillwork; **grid,** gridiron

*Any thing reticulated or decussated, at equal distances, with interstices between the intersections*
**Samuel Johnson**

2 **source,** information medium *or* media, mass media, print media, electronic media, the press, radio, television; channel, the grapevine; information network, in-group, old-boy network; coterie, salon, clique, **set**

**neurological** ADJS **neural,** nervous, nerval; neurologic

**neurosis** NOUNS **mental disorder,** emotional disorder, emotional instability; **psychoneurosis,** neuroticism, neurotic *or* psychoneurotic disorder

**neurotic** ADJS **psychoneurotic,** disturbed, disordered; neurasthenic, psychasthenic; hysteric<al>, hypochondriac, phobic; stressed, disturbed, depressive; manic; manic-depressive

**neuter** VERBS 1 **castrate,** geld, emasculate, eunuchize, spay, fix *or* alter <both nonformal>, unsex, deball <nonformal>
ADJS 2 **unsexual,** unsexed; **sexless,** asexual, neutral; castrated, emasculated, eunuchized; **cold,** frigid; impotent

**neutral** NOUNS 1 **nonpartisan,** independent, mugwump, undecided *or* uncommitted voter; **moderate,** moderatist, moderationist, middle-of-the-roader, **centrist,** compromiser
ADJS 2 **impartial,** impersonal, evenhanded, equitable, dispassionate, **disinterested,** detached, objective, lofty, Olympian; **unbiased,** uninfluenced, unswayed; indifferent

**neutralize** VERBS **nullify,** annul, cancel, cancel out, negate, negative, negativate, invalidate, vitiate, void, frustrate, stultify, thwart, come *or* bring to nothing, undo; **offset,** counterbalance; buffer

**never** ADVS ne'er, **not ever,** at no time, on no occasion, not at all; **nevermore;** never in the world, never on earth; never in all one's born days <nonformal>, never in my life, *jamais de la vie* <Fr>

**never-ending** ADJS **perpetual, everlasting,** everliving, ever-being, ever-abiding, ever-during, ever-durable, permanent, perdurable, indestructible; **eternal,** sempiternal, infinite, **endless,** unending, without end, **interminable, continual,** continuous, steady, **constant, ceaseless,** nonstop, unceasing, neverceasing, **incessant,** unremitting, unintermitting, uninterrupted

**nevertheless** ADVS **notwithstanding,** but, all the same <nonformal>, still, yet, even; **however,** regardless, nonetheless; **although,** when, though; howbeit, albeit; **at all events,** in any event, **in any case,** at any rate; **be that as it may,** for all that, even so, **on the other hand,** rather, again, at the same time, just the same, after all, after all is said and done

**new** ADJS 1 young, **fresh,** fresh as a daisy, fresh as the morning dew; **unused,** firsthand, original; untried, untouched, unhandled, untrodden, unbeaten; virgin, virginal, intact; dewy, pristine, evernew, sempervirent, evergreen; **immature,** undeveloped, raw, callow, fledgling, unfledged, nestling

2 <nonformal> **brand-new**, fire-new, **brand-spanking new,** spanking,, **spanking new; just out; hot,** hottest, hot off the fire *or* griddle *or* spit, hot off the press; newfangled *or* newfangle

ADVS 3 **newly,** freshly, **anew,** once more, from the ground up, from scratch <nonformal>, *ab ovo* <L>, *de novo* <L>, **afresh, again;** as new

**newborn** ADJS **born,** given birth; hatched; **infant, infantile,** infantine, **babyish,** baby; neonatal, new-fledged; in the cradle *or* crib *or* nursery, in swaddling clothes, at the breast, tied to mother's apron strings

**newcomer** NOUNS **new arrival,** *novus homo* <L>; *arriviste* <Fr>, Johnny-come-lately <nonformal>, new boy <Brit>; **tenderfoot,** greenhorn; settler, emigrant, immigrant; recruit, rookie <nonformal>

**news** NOUNS **tidings, intelligence,** information, word, advice; newsiness <nonformal>; newsworthiness; a nose for news; **journalism,** reportage, coverage, news coverage; **the press,** the fourth estate, the press corps, print journalism, electronic journalism, broadcast journalism, broadcast news, radio journalism, television journalism

**newscaster** NOUNS **broadcaster,** radiobroadcaster, radiocaster; commentator, news commentator; anchor, news anchor, anchor man *or* woman; news reader <Brit>

**newsman** NOUNS **journalist,** newspaperman, newspaperwoman, newswoman, newspeople, inkstained wretch, newswriter, gentleman *or* representative of the press; **reporter,** newshawk *and* newshound <both nonformal>; leg man

<nonformal>; interviewer; investigative reporter; **cub reporter; correspondent,** foreign correspondent, war correspondent, special correspondent, own correspondent, stringer; **editor,** managing editor, city editor, news editor, sports editor, woman's editor, feature editor, **copy editor,** copyman, copy chief, slotman; **columnist**

**newspaper** NOUNS news, **paper,** sheet *or* rag <both nonformal>, **gazette,** daily newspaper, daily, weekly newspaper, weekly, neighborhood newspaper, national newspaper; newspaper of record; **tabloid,** extra, special, special edition

**next** ADJS 1 **adjacent,** immediate, contiguous, **adjoining,** abutting; neighboring, neighbor; **juxtaposed,** juxtapositional; **bordering,** conterminous *or* coterminous, connecting; **nearest,** nighest, **closest,** nearmost, immediate; **succeeding,** successive, following, ensuing, sequent, sequential, sequacious, posterior, **subsequent,** consequent; proximate
ADVS 2 **subsequently,** after, afterwards, after that, after all, **later,** since; **thereafter,** thereon, thereupon, therewith, **then;** in the process *or* course of time, as things worked out, in the sequel; at a subsequent *or* later time, in the aftermath; *ex post facto* <L>; hard on the heels *or* on the heels

**nibble** NOUNS 1 **bite,** morsel, taste, swallow; mouthful, a nibble, a bite, munchies; **chew,** chaw <nonformal>; nip, munch
VERBS 2 **pick,** peck <nonformal>, **snack** <nonformal>, munch, nosh <nonformal>; pick at, peck at <nonformal>, eat like a bird, show no appetite; gnaw

**nice** ADJS **dainty, delicate,** *délicat* <Fr>, fine, refined, exquisite, subtle; minute, detailed, exquisite; **meticulous**, finical, finicky, finicking, niggling

**nice guy** NOUNS **good guy,** crackerjack, brick, trump, good egg, stout fellow, Mr Nice Guy, good Joe, likely lad, no slouch, doll, living doll, pussycat, **sweetheart,** sweetie <all nonformal>

**nicety** NOUNS niceness, **delicacy,** delicateness, daintiness, exquisiteness, fineness, refinement, subtlety

**niche** NOUNS **nook,** corner, cranny, recess, cove, bay, oriel, alcove; cubicle, roomlet, carrel, hole-in-the-wall <nonformal>, cubby, **cubbyhole**

**nick** NOUNS 1 **notch,** nock, **cut,** cleft, **incision, gash,** hack, blaze, scotch, **score,** kerf, crena, depression, jag; **indentation**
VERBS 2 **notch,** cut, incise, gash, slash, chop, crimp, scotch, **score,** blaze, jag, scarify; **indent**; **scallop,** crenellate, crenulate, machicolate

**nickname** NOUNS **sobriquet,** byname, cognomen; epithet, agnomen; **pet name,** diminutive, hypocoristic, affectionate name

**nifty** ADJS **chic, dapper,** dashing, jaunty, braw <Scots>; sharp *and* spiffy *and* classy *and* snazzy <all nonformal>

**niggling** ADJS **insignificant,** unimportant, no skin off one's nose *or* ass, **trivial,** trifling, nugacious, nugatory, petty, mean, picayune *or* picayunish, nickel-and-dime *and* penny-ante *and* Mickey-Mouse *and* chickenshit <all nonformal>; shallow, depthless, cursory, superficial, skin-deep; **critical, faultfinding,** carping, picky *and* nitpicky <both nonformal>, caviling, quibbling, pettifogging, captious, cynical; nagging; hypercritical, ultracritical, overcritical, hairsplitting, trichoschistic

**night** NOUNS 1 **nighttime,** nighttide, lights-out, taps, bedtime, sleepy time <nonformal>, **darkness**, blackness, dark, lightlessness; tenebrosity, tenebrousness; dead of night, deep night

*sable-vested Night, eldest of things*
**MILTON**

ADJS 2 **nocturnal,** nightly, nighttime; nightlong, all-night; night-fallen; midnight

**nightclub** NOUNS **cabaret;** club, night spot; nitery *and* hot spot <both nonformal>, *boîte, boîte de nuit* <both Fr>; discothèque *or* disco <nonformal>

**nightfall** NOUNS **close of day,** decline *or* fall of day, shut of day, gray of the evening, grayness, evening's close, when day is done; **sunset, sundown,** setting sun, going down of the sun, cockshut *and* cockshut time *and* cockshut light <all nonformal>, retreat; shank of the evening <nonformal>, the cool of the evening

*the evening is spread out against the sky, Like a patient etherized upon a table*
**T S ELIOT**

**nightgown** NOUNS **nightwear,** night clothes; **nightdress,** nightie *and* shortie nightie <both nonformal>, bedgown; nightshirt; **pajamas,** pyjamas <Brit>, pj's <nonformal>; sleepers

**nightmare** NOUNS **frightener,** scarer, hair-raiser; **bogey,** bogeyman, **bugaboo,** bugbear; hobgoblin; **incubus,** succubus, bad dream

**nimble** ADJS **agile, spry,** sprightly, fleet, featly, peart <nonformal>, light, graceful, nimble-footed, light-footed, surefooted; nimble-fingered, neat-fingered, neat-handed; **quick,** adroit, dexterous; **sharp-witted,** keen-witted, needle-witted, **quick-witted,** quick-thinking, steeltrap, nimble-witted, quick on the trigger *or* uptake <nonformal>

**nincompoop** NOUNS **chump, boob,** booby, sap, prize sap, klutz, dingbat, dingdong, ding-a-ling, **ninny,** saphead, mutt, jerk, goof, schlemiel, galoot, gonzo, dumbo, dweeb, nerd, twerp, yo-yo <all nonformal>

**nip** NOUNS 1 **drink,** dram, potation, potion, libation, draft, drop, spot, finger or two, sip, sup, suck, drench, guzzle, gargle, jigger; peg, swig, swill, pull; **snort,** jolt, **shot,** snifter, quickie
2 **chilliness,** nippiness, crispness, briskness, sharpness, bite; **chill,** sharp air
VERBS 3 **bite,** cut, penetrate, bite the tongue, sting, make the eyes water, go up the nose; **chill; prune,** pare, peel, clip, crop, bob, dock, lop, shear, shave, strip, strip off *or* away; **put an end to,** nip in the bud; cut short
4 **tipple,** drink, **guzzle, imbibe,** have a drink *or* nip *or* dram *or* guzzle *or* gargle, soak, bib, quaff, sip, sup, lap, lap up, take a drop, slake one's thirst, cheer *or* refresh the inner man, drown one's troubles *or* sorrows, commune with the spirits; **down,** toss off *or* down, knock back, throw one back, drink off *or* up

**nippy** ADJS 1 **zestful,** zesty, **brisk,** lively, racy, zippy, **tangy,** with a kick; spiced, seasoned, high-seasoned; **spicy,** curried, **peppery,** hot, burning
2 **cold,** crisp, brisk, nipping, **snappy** <nonformal>, raw, bleak, keen, sharp, bitter, biting, pinching, cutting, **piercing,** penetrating

**nit** ADJS **louse,** head louse, body louse, grayback, cootie <nonformal>

**nitpick** VERBS **find fault,** take exception, fault-find, pick holes, cut up, pick *or* pull *or* tear apart, pick *or* pull *or* tear to pieces; tear down, **carp,** cavil, quibble, pick nits, pettifog, catch at straws, **split hairs**

**nitpicker** NOUNS **perfectionist,** precisian, precisianist, stickler, captious critic, **faultfinder,** smellfungus, carper, caviler, quibbler, pettifogger

**the nitty-gritty** NOUNS **sum and substance,** gist, heart, soul, meat, nub; the bottom line *and* the name of the game <both nonformal>, **core,** kernel, marrow, pith, sap, spirit, essence; sober *or* grim reality, hardball <nonformal>, not a dream, more truth than poetry; **meat and potatoes** *and* nuts and bolts *and* where the rubber meets the road <all nonformal>

**nitwit** NOUNS **stupid person,** dolt, dunce, clod, Boeotian, **dullard,** *niais* <Fr>, donkey, yahoo, thickwit, **dope,** dimwit, lackwit, half-wit, lamebrain, putz, lightweight, witling

**no** INTERJS 1 **nay,** *non* <Fr>, *nein* <Ger>, *nyet* <Russ>, certainly not, no sir, no ma'am, to the contrary, **by no means,** under no circumstances, never

2 <nonformal> nope, nix, no dice, unhunh, no sirree; no way, no way Jose, not on your life, not by a long chalk, not by a long shot *or* sight, not by a darn *or* damn sight, not a bit of it, not much, not a chance, fat chance, nothing doing, forget it, that'll be the day

**noble** NOUNS 1 **nobleman,** gentleman; peer; aristocrat, patrician, Brahman, **blue blood,** thoroughbred, silk-stocking, lace-curtain, swell *and* uppercruster <both nonformal>
2 **aristocracy,** titled aristocracy, hereditary nobility, noblesse
ADJS 3 **lofty,** elevated, sublime, grand, majestic, stately, grave, solemn, dignified; **meritorious,** worth one's salt, worthy, creditable; respected, respectable, highly respectable; **well-thought-of,** highly regarded, held in esteem, in good odor, in favor, in high favor; **eminent,** prominent, conspicuous, **outstanding,** distinguished

**nobody** NOUNS **no one,** no man, not one, not a single one *or* person, **not a soul** *or* **blessed soul** *or* **living soul,** never a one, ne'er a one, nary one <nonformal>, nobody on earth *or* under the sun, nobody present; **nonentity,** nonstarter *and* nebbish <both nonformal>, nonperson, unperson, cipher, man of straw, puppet, hollow man; **mediocrity, second-rater,** third-rater, fourth-rater, nothing *or* nobody special, no great shakes <nonformal>, no prize package, no brain surgeon, no rocket scientist, small potatoes <nonformal>

**nocturnal** ADJS night, **nightly,** nighttime; nightlong, all-night; night-fallen; midnight

**no-good** NOUNS 1 **wretch, good-for-nothing,** good-for-naught, ne'er-do-well, wastrel, *vaurien* <Fr>, worthless fellow ADJS 2 **worthless,** valueless, good-for-nothing, good-for-naught, NG <nonformal>, no-account <nonformal>, dear at any price, worthless as tits on a boar <nonformal>, not worth a dime *or* a red cent *or* a hill of beans *or* shit *or* bubkes <nonformal>, not worthwhile, not worth having, not worth a rap *or* a continental *or* a damn, not worth the powder to blow it to hell, of no earthly use

**noise** NOUNS loud noise, **blast**, tintamarre, **racket, din, clamor;** outcry, **uproar,** hue and cry, noise and shouting; howl; clangor, clatter, clap, jangle, rattle; roar, thunder, thunderclap; **crash, boom,** sonic boom; **bang,** percussion; brouhaha, **tumult,** hubbub; fracas, **brawl,** commotion, drunken brawl; **pandemonium,** bedlam, hell *or* bedlam let loose; charivari, shivaree <nonformal>; discord

**noisemaker** NOUNS snapper, cricket, clapper, clack, clacker, cracker; firecracker, cherry bomb

**noisy** ADJS noiseful, rackety, clattery, clangorous, clanging, **clamorous,** clamant, blatant, blaring, brassy, brazen, blatting; uproarious, **tumultuous,** turbulent, blustering, brawling, **boisterous,** rip-roaring, rowdy, strepitous, strepitant; vociferous

**nomad** NOUNS Bedouin; gypsy, tinker <Brit>, Bohemian, Romany, *zingaro* <Ital>, *Zigeuner* <Ger>, *tzigane* <Fr>

**nomadic** ADJS **wandering, nomad,** floating, drifting, gypsyish *or* gypsylike; **vagrant,** vagabond, vagabondish; **footloose,** footloose and fancy-free; **migratory,** migrational, transmigrant, transmigratory

**no-man's-land** NOUNS forbidden ground *or* territory, **battlefield,** battleground, battle site, **field,** combat area, **field of battle**

**nom de plume** NOUNS **pseudonym,** assumed name, **pen name**

**nomenclature** NOUNS **terminology,** orismology, glossology <old>; onomatology, onomastics; **taxonomy,** classification, binomial nomenclature, binomialism, Linnaean method, trinomialism

**nominate** VERBS **name, designate;** put up, propose, submit, name for office; **denominate,** call, term, style, dub, color <nonformal>; specify; define, identify; **title,** entitle; **label,** tag

**nominee** NOUNS **assignee,** appointee, selectee, candidate; licensee, licentiate; deputy, agent

**nonaggressive** ADJS **unbelligerent,** unhostile, unbellicose, **uncontentious,** unmilitant, unmilitary, noncombative, nonmilitant; **antiwar,** pacific, peaceable, peace-loving, dovish <nonformal>; meek, lamblike; **pacifistic,** pacifist, irenic; **nonviolent;** conciliatory

**nonalcoholic beverage** NOUNS **soft drink,** cold drink; carbonated water, soda water, sparkling water, **soda,** pop, soda pop, tonic; milk shake, frosted shake, thick shake, shake *and* frosted <both nonformal>; malted milk, malt <nonformal>

**nonaligned** ADJS **independent,** free-spirited, freewheeling, free-floating, freestanding; **self-determined,** self-directing, one's own man; self-governed, **self-governing,** autonomous, sovereign; stand-alone, self-reliant, self-sufficient, self-subsistent, self-supporting, self-contained, autarkic, autarchic; nonpartisan, neutral; third-world, third-force

**nonbeliever** NOUNS **unbeliever,** disbeliever; **atheist,** infidel, pagan, heathen; nullifidian, minimifidian; secularist; **gentile**

**nonchalant** ADJS **blasé,** indifferent, unconcerned; **casual,** offhand, relaxed, laid-back *and* throwaway <both nonformal>; **easygoing,** easy, free and easy, devil-may-care, lackadaisical, *dégagé* <Fr>

**noncombatant** NOUNS nonbelligerent, nonresistant, nonresister; **civilian,** citizen

**noncommittal** ADJS **cautious,** careful, heedful, mindful, regardful, **thorough; prudent,** circumspect, slow to act *or* commit oneself *or* make one's move, uncommitted; **discreet,** politic, judicious, Polonian; guarded, on guard, on one's guard; uncommunicative; **tentative,** hesitant, unprecipitate, cool; **deliberate**

**noncommunicable** ADJS **indescribable,** ineffable, inexpressible, unutterable, unspeakable, indefinable, undefinable, unnameable

**nonconformist** NOUNS unconformist, **original,** eccentric, gonzo <nonformal>, deviant, deviationist, maverick <nonformal>, dropout, Bohemian, beatnik, hippie, hipster, freak <nonformal>, flower child, street people, yippie; **misfit,** square peg in a round hole, ugly duckling, fish out of water; **dissenter**

**nondenominational** ADJS **nonsectarian,** undenominational; interdenominational, ecumenic *or* ecumenical

**nondescript** ADJS **simple**, plain, ordinary, common, commonplace, prosaic, prosy, **matter-of-fact,** homely, homespun, everyday, workday, workaday, household, garden, common- *or* garden-variety

**nonentity** NOUNS **a nobody, insignificancy,** hollow man, jackstraw <old>, empty suit *and* nebbish <both nonformal>, an obscurity, a nothing, cipher; lightweight; **small fry; mediocrity,** second-rater, third-rater, fourth-rater, nothing *or* nobody special, no great shakes <nonformal>, no prize, no prize package

**nonessential** NOUNS 1 inessential *or* unessential, nonvitalness, carrying coals to Newcastle, gilding the lily; **accessory, extra,** collateral; the other, not-self; **appendage,** appurtenance, auxiliary, supernumerary, **supplement,** addition, addendum, superaddition, adjunct; **subsidiary,** subordinate, secondary; **contingency,** contingent, incidental, accidental, accident, happenstance, mere chance; **superfluity,** superfluousness; fifth wheel <nonformal>
ADJS 2 **needless,** unnecessary, unessential, **unneeded,** uncalled-for, unrequired; unrecognized, neglected

**nonetheless** ADVS **nevertheless,** however, regardless; at all, nohow <nonformal>

**nonexistent** ADJS without being, nowhere to be found; **minus, missing,** lacking, wanting; **null, void,** devoid, empty, inane, vacuous; **negative,** less than nothing; **unreal,** unrealistic, unactual, never-never; supposititious, **illusory**

**nonflammable** ADJS **incombustible,** noncombustible, uninflammable, noninflammable, noncombustive

**nonliving** ADJS **inanimate,** inanimated, unanimated, exanimate, azoic, dead, **lifeless,** soulless; inert; insentient, unconscious, nonconscious, **insensible,** insensate, senseless, unfeeling

**no-no** NOUNS **prohibition,** forbidding, forbiddance; thou-shalt-not *and* don't <both nonformal>; forbidden fruit, contraband; cuss *or* cuss word *and* dirty word *and* four-letter word *and* swearword <all nonformal>, naughty word, foul invective, **expletive, epithet,** dirty name <nonformal>, dysphemism, obscenity

**nonpartisan** NOUNS 1 **independent,** neutral, mugwump, undecided *or* uncommitted voter, centrist; swing vote
ADJS 2 **independent,** neutral, mugwumpian *and* mugwumpish <both nonformal>, **on the fence**

**nonperishable** ADJS **indestructible,** undestroyable, **imperishable,** incorruptible; **ineradicable,** indelible, ineffaceable, inerasable; **inextinguishable,** unquenchable, quenchless, undampable

**nonplussed** ADJS **in a dilemma,** on the horns of a dilemma; **perplexed,** confounded, mystified, puzzled, baffled, bamboozled <nonformal>, buffaloed <nonformal>; **at a loss,** at one's wit's end, fuddled, addled, muddled, dazed, stymied

**nonpoisonous** ADJS **innocuous,** innoxious, innocent; nontoxic, nonvirulent, nonvenomous

**nonproductive** ADJS **unproductive,** nonproducing; **infertile,** sterile, unfertile *or* nonfertile, **unfruitful,** unfructuous, infecund, unprolific *or* nonprolific; **ineffectual**

**nonprofessional** NOUNS **amateur,** layman, layperson, member of the laity, laic

**nonsectarian** ADJS **undenominational,** nondenominational; interdenominational; ecumenic *or* ecumenical

**nonsense** NOUNS 1 **stuff and nonsense,** pack of nonsense, folderol, balderdash, *niaiserie* <Fr>, flummery, trumpery, **rubbish,** trash, vaporing, fudge; **humbug,** gammon, hocus-pocus; rant, claptrap, fustian, rodomontade, bombast, absurdity; stultiloquence, **twaddle**

2 <nonformal> **bullshit,** shit, crap, horseshit, horsefeathers, bull, poppycock, bosh, tosh <Brit>, applesauce, bunkum, bunk, garbage, guff, jive, bilge, piffle, moonshine, flapdoodly, moonshine, a crock *or* a crock of shit, claptrap, tommyrot, rot, hogwash, malarkey, double Dutch, hokum, hooey, bushwa, blah, balls <Brit> blah, baloney, blarney tripe, hot air, gas, wind, waffle <Brit>

**nonstop** ADJS **continuous,** ceaseless, unceasing, **endless,** unending, never-ending, **interminable,** perennial; straight, running; **round-the-clock,** twenty-four-hour, steady, **constant,** never-ceasing, **incessant,** unremitting, unintermitting, uninterrupted

**nontoxic** ADJS **harmless,** hurtless, unhurtful; **uninjurious,** undamaging, **innocuous,** innoxious, innocent; nonpoisonous, nonvirulent, nonvenomous

**nonviolent** ADJS **moderate,** temperate, sober; **mild,** soft, bland, **gentle,** tame; mild as milk *or* mother's milk, gentle as a lamb; peaceable, peaceful, pacifistic; **judicious, prudent**

**nook** NOUNS **corner,** cranny, niche, recess, cove, bay, oriel, alcove; cubicle, roomlet, carrel, hole-in-the-wall <nonformal>, cubby, **cubbyhole,** snuggery; **hiding place,** hideaway, hideout, hidey-hole <nonformal>

**noon** NOUNS **noonday,** noontide, nooning <nonformal>, noontime, **high noon, midday,** meridian, *meridiem* <L>, twelve o'clock, 1200 hours, eight bells

**noose** NOUNS lasso, lariat; **hangman's rope,** rope, halter, hemp, hempen collar *or* necktie *or* bridle <nonformal>; the necklace <nonformal>

**norm** NOUNS **rule,** procedure, **common practice,** the way things are done, form, prescribed *or* set form; common *or* ordinary run of things, matter of course, par for the course <nonformal>; standard operating procedure *or* SOP, drill <Brit>

**normal** ADJS 1 **natural; general**; typical, unexceptional; **normative,** prescribed, model, ideal, desired
2 **sane,** sane-minded, **rational,** reasonable, sensible, **lucid,** wholesome, clearheaded, clearminded, balanced, **sound,** mentally sound, of sound mind, *compos mentis* <L>, sound-minded, healthy-minded, right, right in the head, **in one's right mind,** in possession of one's faculties *or* senses, together *and* all there <both nonformal>

**normalize** VERBS **regulate,** regularize, stabilize, damp; **systematize,** methodize, standardize, routinize; **codify,** formalize

**northern lights** NOUNS polar lights, **aurora; aurora borealis,** merry dancers; aurora polaris; aurora glory; streamer *or* curtain *or* arch aurora; polar ray

**North Star** NOUNS **guiding star,** cynosure <old>, **polestar,** polar star, lodestar, Polaris

**nose** NOUNS 1 olfactory organ; **snout, snoot** <nonformal>, nozzle <nonformal>, **muzzle; proboscis,** antlia, **trunk; beak,** rostrum; **bill** *and* pecker <both nonformal>; nib, neb; smeller *and* beezer *and* bugle *and* schnozzle *and* schnoz *and* schnozzola *and* conk <all nonformal>
VERBS 2 **smell,** scent; **sniff,** snuff, snuffle, inhale, breathe, breathe in; get a noseful of, smell of, catch a smell of, get *or* take a whiff of, whiff
3 **pry,** Paul-Pry, snoop, **stick** *or* **poke one's nose in,** stick one's long nose into

**nosh** NOUNS 1 **light meal,** refreshments, light repast, light lunch, spot of lunch <nonformal>, collation, **snack** *and* **bite** <both nonformal>, *casse-croûte* <Fr>
VERBS 2 **nibble; snack** <nonformal>, pick at, peck at <nonformal>

**no-show** NOUNS **absentee,** truant

**nostalgia** NOUNS **sentimentality,** sentiment, sentimentalism, oversentimentality, oversentimentalism, bathos; nostomania; romanticism; **wistfulness,** wishfulness, yearnfulness; **homesickness,** *Heimweh* <Ger>, *mal du pays* and *maladie du pays* <both Fr>

**nostalgic** ADJS **sentimental,** sentimentalized, soft, **mawkish, maudlin,** cloying; nostomanic, **longing,** yearning, yearnful, hankering <nonformal>, languishing, pining, **homesick**

**nosy** ADJS **meddlesome,** meddling; **officious,** overofficious, self-appointed, impertinent, presumptuous; **busybody,** busy; pushing, pushy, forward; **prying,**

snooping, nosey *and* snoopy <both nonformal>; inquisitive

**notable** NOUNS 1 **celebrity,** man *or* woman of mark *or* note, person of note *or* consequence, notability, luminary, great man *or* woman, name, **big name,** figure, public figure, **somebody;** important person, VIP *and* standout <both nonformal>, personage; lion, social lion
ADJS 2 **noteworthy,** celebrated, remarkable, marked, standout <nonformal>, of mark, signal; **memorable,** rememberable, unforgettable, never to be forgotten; striking, telling, salient; **eminent,** prominent, conspicuous, noble, **outstanding,** distinguished; prestigious, esteemed, estimable, reputable; **extraordinary,** *extraordinaire* <Fr>, out of the ordinary, **exceptional,** special, rare

**notarized statement** NOUNS **deposition,** sworn statement, affidavit, statement under oath, sworn testimony, affirmation

**notary** NOUNS **notary public;** endorser, subscriber, ratifier, approver, upholder, certifier, confirmer

**notched** ADJS **nicked,** incised, gashed, scotched, scored, chopped, blazed; **indented**; serrate, serrated, serrulated, **saw-toothed,** saw-edged, sawlike; crenate, crenated, crenulate, crenellated, battlemented, embrasured; scalloped; dentate, dentated, **toothed,** toothlike, tooth-shaped; lacerate, lacerated; **jagged,** jaggy; erose

**note** NOUNS 1 **remark,** statement, thought, **mention;** letter, message, communication, missive, line, chit, billet <old>; **reply,** answer, acknowledgment
2 **distinction,** mark; importance, consequence, significance; **notability,** prominence, eminence, preeminence, greatness, conspicuousness, outstandingness; **stardom;** loftiness, high and mightiness <nonformal>
3 musical note, notes of a scale; tone; sharp, flat, natural; accidental
VERBS 4 **heed, attend,** be heedful, tend, **mind,** watch, observe, regard, look, see, view, mark, remark, **notice,** take note *or* notice, get a load of <nonformal>

**notebook** NOUNS pocket notebook, blankbook; loose-leaf notebook, spiral notebook; **memorandum book,** memo book <nonformal>, commonplace book, adversaria; address book

**noteworthy** ADJS **notable,** celebrated, remarkable, marked, standout <nonformal>, of mark, signal; striking, telling, salient; **eminent,** prominent, conspicuous, noble, **outstanding,** distinguished; prestigious, esteemed, estimable, reputable; **extraordinary,** *extraordinaire* <Fr>, out of the ordinary, **exceptional,** special, rare

**nothing** NOUNS 1 **nil,** *nihil* <L>, *nichts* <Ger>, *nada* <Sp>, **naught, aught;** zero, cipher; nothing whatever, nothing at all, nothing on earth *or* under the sun, no such thing; thing of naught, nullity
2 **nonentity, nobody** *and* nonstarter *and* nebbish <all nonformal>, nonperson, unperson, cipher, man of straw, hollow man

3 <nonformal> **ziltch, zip,** zippo, nix, goose egg, Billy be damn, diddly, shit, diddly shit, squat, diddly squat, Sweet Fanny Adams <Brit>, bubkes, beans, a hill of beans, a hoot, **a fart,** a fuck, fuck all *and* bugger all <both Brit>, jack shit, a rat's ass

**notice** NOUNS 1 **press release,** release, handout, bulletin, official bulletin; **publicity,** publicness, notoriety, fame, famousness, notoriousness, public notice, **celebrity,** *réclame, éclat* <both Fr>; **review,** critical review, report, **write-up** <nonformal>
2 **cognizance;** cognition, noesis; **recognition,** realization; **consciousness,** awareness, mindfulness, note; **observation,** observance, advertence, advertency, **note,** remark, regard, respect; **intentness,** intentiveness, concentration
VERBS 3 **see,** behold, observe, view, witness, perceive, discern, spy, espy, **sight,** have in sight, make out, pick out, descry, spot <nonformal>, discover, take notice of, have one's eye on, distinguish, recognize, **catch sight of,** get a load of <nonformal>, take in, get an eyeful of <nonformal>, **set** *or* **lay eyes on,** clap eyes on <nonformal>; **glimpse,** get *or* catch a glimpse of

**noticeable** ADJS **conspicuous,** notable, ostensible, **prominent,** bold, pronounced, salient, in relief, in bold *or* high *or* strong relief, **striking,** outstanding, in the foreground, sticking *or* hanging out

**notify** VERBS **inform,** tell, speak on *or* for,

apprise, **advise, advertise,** advertise of, give word, mention to, **acquaint,** enlighten, familiarize, brief, verse, give the facts, give an account of, give by way of information; give notice *or* notification, serve notice; **report,** disclose

**notion** NOUNS 1 **caprice,** whim, *capriccio* <Ital>, *boutade* <Fr>, humor, **whimsy,** freak, whim-wham; **fancy,** fantasy, conceit, flimflam, toy, freakish inspiration, crazy idea, fantastic notion, fool notion <nonformal>, harebrained idea, brainstorm, **vagary,** megrim; **design,** plan, project, idea
2 **suggestion,** bare suggestion, suspicion, inkling, hint, sense, feeling, feeling in one's bones, intuition, intimation, impression, mere notion, hunch *and* sneaking suspicion <both nonformal>, trace of an idea, half an idea, vague idea, hazy idea

**notoriety** NOUNS **disreputability,** disreputableness; discreditableness, dishonorableness, unsavoriness, **unrespectability;** disgracefulness, shamefulness; talk of the town

**notorious** ADJS **disreputable,** discreditable, dishonorable, unsavory, shady, **seamy,** sordid; unrespectable, ignoble, ignominious, infamous, inglorious; unpraiseworthy; derogatory; talked about

**notwithstanding** ADVS **however,** nevertheless, nonetheless; **although,** when, though; howbeit, albeit; **at all events,** in any event, in any case, at any rate; **be that as it may,** for all that, even so, on the other hand, rather, again, at the same time, all the same, just the same, **however that may be;** after all, after all is said and done

**nourish** VERBS feed, sustain, nurture; nutrify, aliment, foster; **sustain,** strengthen; **nurse,** suckle, lactate, breast-feed, wet-nurse, dry-nurse; fatten, fatten up, stuff, force-feed

**nourishment** NOUNS **nutrition,** nourishing, feeding, nurture; alimentation; **food** *or* **nutritive value,** food intake; food chain *or* cycle; **fostering,** nurturance

**nouveau riche** NOUNS **vulgarian,** low *or* vulgar *or* ill-bred fellow, *épicier* <Fr>; *parvenu, arriviste* <both Fr>, upstart; parvenu, **new-rich,** pig in clover <nonformal>; **social climber,** climber, namedropper, tufthunter, status seeker

**novel** ADJS **original,** unique, different; strange, unusual, uncommon; unfamiliar, unheard-of; **first,** first ever

**novelty** NOUNS **innovation,** newfangled device *or* contraption <nonformal>, neoism, neonism, **new** *or* **latest wrinkle** <nonformal>, the last word *or* the latest thing <both nonformal>, *dernier cri* <Fr>; what's happening *and* what's in *and* the in thing *and* where it's at <all nonformal>; new ball game; new look, latest fashion *or* fad

**novice** NOUNS novitiate *or* noviciate, **tyro,** abecedarian, alphabetarian, **beginner,** entrant, **neophyte,** tenderfoot *and* greenhorn <both nonformal>, freshman, **fledgling;** catechumen, initiate, debutant; postulant; newcomer; **recruit**

**noway** ADVS noways, **nowise,** in no wise, in no case, in no respect, **by no means,** by no manner of means, on no account, not on any account, not for anything in the world, under no circumstances, nohow <nonformal>, **not in the least,** not much, not at all, never, not by a damn sight <nonformal>, not by a long shot <nonformal>; not nearly, **nowhere near;** not a bit, not a bit of it, not a whit, not a speck, not a jot, not an iota

**nowhere** ADVS in no place, neither here nor there; nowhither

**noxious** ADJS **nasty, offensive**, fulsome, noisome, rebarbative, mawkish, cloying, brackish, **foul, vile,** bad; **sickening,** nauseating, nauseant, vomity *and* barfy <both nonformal>; poisonous, rank, rancid, maggoty, weevily, spoiled, overripe, high, rotten, stinking, putrid, malodorous, fetid

**nth degree** NOUNS **limit,** end, extremity, extreme, **acme,** apogee, climax, **maximum,** ceiling, **peak,** summit, **pinnacle,** crown, top; **utmost,** uttermost, utmost extent, highest degree, *ne plus ultra* <L>

**nuance** NOUNS **suggestion,** allusion; coloration, tinge, undertone, overtone, undercurrent, more than meets the eye *or* ear, something between the lines, intimation, touch, innuendo; **nicety, subtlety,** refinement, delicacy, nice *or* fine *or* delicate *or* **subtle distinction,** fine point; shade *or* particle of difference, hairline

**nubby** ADJS **studded,** knobbed, knobby, knoblike, nubbled, nubbly, torose; **knotty, knotted**

**nuclear power** NOUNS **atomic energy,**

**nuclear energy,** thermonuclear power; activation energy, binding energy, mass energy; energy level

**nuclear reactor** NOUNS **reactor, pile,** atomic pile, reactor pile, chain-reacting pile, chain reactor, **furnace,** atomic *or* nuclear furnace, neutron factory; fast pile, intermediate pile, slow pile

**nuclear weapons** NOUNS **atomic weapons,** thermonuclear weapons, A-weapons; weapons of mass destruction

**nucleus** NOUNS 1 **center,** centrum; **middle**, heart, core; pith, marrow, medulla; **nub, hub,** nave, axis, pivot, **gist,** gravamen, focus, kernel, meat; **heart,** soul, heart and soul, spirit, sap, marrow
2 **atomic nucleus;** cell nucleus; macronucleus, meganucleus; micronucleus; nucleolus

**nude** NOUNS 1 **work of art,** art work, artistic production, piece, **work,** study, design, composition; still life
ADJS 2 **naked,** bare, peeled, raw <nonformal>, **in the raw** <nonformal>, *in puris naturalibus* <L>, in a state of nature, in nature's garb; in one's birthday suit, **in the buff** *and* in native buff *and* stripped to the buff *and* **in the altogether** <all nonformal>, with nothing on, without a stitch; **stark-naked,** bare-ass <nonformal>, naked as the day one was born, naked as a jaybird, **undressed,** undecked, unarrayed

*in naked beauty more adorned*
MILTON

**nudge** NOUNS 1 **hint,** broad hint, gesture, signal, nod, wink, look, kick, prompt; **prod,** poke, punch, jab, dig
VERBS 2 **set in motion,** move, actuate, motivate, push, shove, **drive,** impel, propel; **goad, prod,** poke, prod at, goose <nonformal>, **spur,** prick, sting, needle; work on <nonformal>, **tease,** pester, plague, nag, nag at, make a pest *or* nuisance of oneself, try one's patience, bug <nonformal>

**nudity** NOUNS **nakedness,** bareness, undress, beauty unadorned; **the nude,** the altogether *and* the buff <both nonformal>, **the raw** <nonformal>; state of nature, **birthday suit** <nonformal>; not a stitch, not a stitch to one's name *or* back; full-frontal nudity; décolleté, décolletage, toplessness; nudism, naturism, gymnosophy

**nugget** NOUNS **lump,** clump, **hunk** *and* **chunk** <both nonformal>; **mass,** piece, gob *and* glob <both nonformal>, gobbet

**nuisance** NOUNS **annoyance,** vexation, bothersomeness, exasperation, *tracasserie* <Fr>, **aggravation; pest,** bother, botheration <nonformal>, public nuisance, **trouble,** problem, pain <nonformal>, difficulty, hot potato <nonformal>; **trial; bore,** crashing bore <nonformal>; **headache** <nonformal>; **pain in the neck** *or* **in the ass** <nonformal>

**nullify** VERBS **abolish,** void, abrogate, annihilate, annul, tear up, repeal, revoke, negate, negative, invalidate, **undo, cancel,** cancel out, put *or* lay to rest; **neutralize,** vitiate, frustrate, stultify, thwart, come *or* bring to nothing

**numb** VERBS 1 **benumb,** paralyze, **deaden,** anesthetize, freeze, **stun,** stupefy, drug, narcotize, **dull,** dull *or* deaden the pain; sedate, dope *or* dope up <nonformal>
ADJS 2 **insensible,** numbed, benumbed, dead, **deadened,** asleep, unfelt; **unfeeling,** apathetic, affectless; callous; anesthetized, narcotized; **lethargic,** phlegmatic, apathetic, hebetudinous, **dull,** desensitized, sluggish, torpid, languid, slack, soporific, comatose, **stupefied,** in a stupor

**number** NOUNS 1 **sum,** count, group, total, reckoning, **measure,** parcel, passel <nonformal>, part, **portion,** clutch, ration, share, issue, allotment, lot, deal
VERBS 2 numerate, number off, **enumerate, count,** tell, tally, give a figure to, put a figure on, call off, name, call over, run over; **count noses** *or* **heads** <nonformal>, call the roll; census, poll; page, paginate, foliate

**numerable** ADJS **calculable,** computable, **reckonable,** estimable, countable, numberable, enumerable; **measurable,** mensurable, quantifiable

**numeral** NOUNS 1 **number,** *numero* <Sp and Ital>, no *or* n, digit, binary digit *or* bit, **cipher,** character, symbol, sign, notation
ADJS 2 **numeric** *or* numerical, numerary, numerative

**numerous** ADJS **many,** manifold, not a few, no few; **very many,** full many, **ever so many,** considerable *and* quite some <both nonformal>; **multitudinous,** multitudinal, multifarious, multifold, multiple, **myriad,** numerous as the stars

**nun** NOUNS sister, *religieuse* <Fr>, clergywoman, conventual; abbess, prioress; **mother superior,** lady superior, superioress, the reverend mother, holy mother; canoness, regular *or* secular canoness; novice, postulant

**nunnery** NOUNS **convent, cloister,** house; priory, priorate

**nuptial** ADJS **matrimonial,** marital, conjugal, connubial, wedded, married, hymeneal; epithalamic; **spousal;** husbandly, uxorious; bridal, wifely, uxorial

**nuptials** NOUNS **wedding, marriage,** marriage ceremony, nuptial mass; church wedding, civil wedding, civil ceremony; spousals, espousals, hymeneal rites; white wedding; forced marriage, shotgun wedding; Gretna Green wedding, elopement

**nurse** NOUNS 1 sister *or* nursing sister <both Brit>; **probationer,** probationist; caregiver, hospice caregiver; practical nurse; registered nurse *or* RN
2 **nursemaid,** nurserymaid, nanny <chiefly Brit>, amah, ayah, mammy <nonformal>; dry nurse, wet nurse; **baby-sitter,** baby-minder <Brit>, sitter <nonformal>
VERBS 3 **foster, nurture,** nourish, mother, care for, lavish care on, feed, parent, rear, sustain, cultivate, **cherish;** suckle, cradle; dry-nurse, wet-nurse; spoon-feed; **harbor,** hold on to, bear, cling to

**nursery** NOUNS **conservatory,** greenhouse, glasshouse <Brit>, forcing house, summerhouse, lathhouse, **hothouse,** coolhouse; potting shed; force *or* forcing bed, forcing pit, **hotbed,** cold frame; **cradle,** bedroom

**nurture** NOUNS 1 **nutrition, nourishment,** nourishing, feeding; **support,** maintenance, sustainment, sustentation, **sustenance, subsistence,** provision; **fostering,** nurturance, mothering, parenting, rearing, fosterage, **care, caring,** care-giving, tender loving care *or* TLC <nonformal>; **upbringing,** bringing-up, fetching-up <nonformal>, raising, breeding
VERBS 2 **foster,** nourish, mother, care for, lavish care on, feed, parent, rear, sustain, cultivate, **cherish; nurse,** suckle, cradle; dry-nurse, wet-nurse; spoon-feed

**nut** NOUNS 1 **seed; stone,** pit; pip; fruit; **grain,** kernel, berry
2 **fanatic,** infatuate, **buff** *and* **fan** <both nonformal>, freak <nonformal>, *fanatico, aficionado* <both Sp>, devotee, **zealot, enthusiast,** energumen; **monomaniac,** crank <nonformal>; lunatic fringe

3 <nonformal> **nut,** nutso, nutter, nutball, nutbar, nutcase, loon, loony, headcase <Brit>, crazy, psycho, crackpot, screwball, weirdie, weirdo, kook, flake, crackbrain, *meshugana* <Yiddish>, fruitcake, schizo, wack, wacko, sickie, sicko

**nutrient** NOUNS nutritive, **nutriment,** food; **natural food,** health food; roughage, fiber

**nutrition** NOUNS **nourishment,** nourishing, feeding, nurture; alimentation; **food** *or* **nutritive value,** food intake; food chain *or* cycle

**nutritious** ADJS nutritive, nutrient, **nourishing;** alimentary, alimental; digestible, assimilable

**nutty** ADJS

<nonformal> **crazy,** daffy, dotty, dippy, crazy as a bedbug *or* coot *or* loon, loony, goofy, wacky, flaky, kooky, potty, batty, ape, out to lunch, bats, nuts, nutty as a fruitcake, screwy, screwball, bananas, cuckoo, flipped, freaked-out, off-the-wall, off one's nut *or* rocker, round the bend <Brit>, minus some buttons, nobody home, with bats in the belfry, cracked, not right in the head, tetched, out of one's head, out of one's gourd *or* skull, not all there, *meshuggah* <Yiddish>, three bricks shy of a load, rowing with one oar in the water

**nuzzle** VERBS **stroke,** pet, caress, fondle; **nose,** rub noses; feel up <nonformal>; rub, rub against, massage; **cuddle,** snuggle, nestle; bundle

**nymph** NOUNS nymphet, nymphlin; **dryad,** hamadryad, wood nymph; vila *or* willi; tree nymph; oread, mountain nymph; **larva**

# O

**oaf** NOUNS **lout,** boor, lubber, oik <Brit>, **gawk,** gawky, **lummox,** yokel, rube, hick, hayseed, bumpkin, clod, clodhopper

**oath** NOUNS 1 **vow,** word, assurance, guarantee, warrant, solemn oath *or* affirmation *or* word *or* declaration; **pledge**; Bible oath, ironclad oath; judicial oath, extrajudicial oath; oath of office, official oath; oath of allegiance, loyalty oath, test oath
2 **profane oath,** curse; cuss *or* cuss word *and* dirty word *and* four-letter word *and* **swearword** <all nonformal>, naughty word, no-no <nonformal>, foul invective, **expletive, epithet,** dirty name <nonformal>, dysphemism, obscenity

**obedient** ADJS **compliant,** complying, allegiant; **acquiescent,** consenting, **submissive**, deferential, self-abnegating; willing, **dutiful,** duteous; loyal, faithful, devoted; uncritical, unshakable, doglike; conforming, in conformity; law-abiding

**obese** ADJS **corpulent,** stout, fat, big, overweight, fattish, adipose, gross, dumpy, fleshy, beefy, meaty, hefty, porky, porcine; paunchy, paunched, bloated, puffy, blowzy, distended, swollen, pursy; abdominous, big-bellied, full-bellied, potbellied, swag-bellied, rotund, **tubby** <nonformal>, roly-poly; **pudgy,** podgy; **portly,** stocky, imposing; well-fed, corn-fed, grain-fed

**obey** VERBS **mind,** heed, keep, observe, listen *or* hearken to; **submit, comply,** conform, walk in lockstep; stay in line *and* not get out of line *and* not get off base <all nonformal>, **toe the line** *or* mark, fall in, fall in line, obey the rules, follow the book, **do what one is told;** do as one says, defer to, do one's bidding, lie down and roll over for <nonformal>

**obituary** NOUNS obit <nonformal>, necrology, necrologue; register of deaths, roll of the dead, death roll, mortuary roll, bill of mortality; casualty list

**object** NOUNS 1 **article, thing,** material thing, affair, something; whatsit <nonformal>, what's-its-name; something or other, *etwas* <Ger>, *eppes* <Yiddish>, *quelque chose* <Fr>; artifact
2 **intent,** intention, purpose, aim, design, plan

**object** VERBS **protest, kick** *and* **beef** <both nonformal>, put up a struggle *or* fight; bitch *and* squawk *and* howl *and* holler *and* put up a squawk *and* raise a howl <all nonformal>; exclaim *or* cry out against, make *or* create *or* raise a stink about <all nonformal>; yell bloody murder <nonformal>; **remonstrate,** expostulate; raise *or* press objections, raise one's voice against, enter a protest; **complain,** exclaim at, state a grievance, air one's grievances; **dispute,** challenge, call in question; **demur,** scruple, boggle, dig in one's heels; **demonstrate,** demonstrate against, rally, march, sit-in, teach-in, boycott, strike, picket; **rebel**

**objectionable** ADJS **offensive,** odious, repulsive, repellent, rebarbative, **repugnant, revolting,** forbidding; **disgusting,** sickening, loathsome, gross *and* yucky *and* grungy *and* scuzzy <all nonformal>, beastly <nonformal>, **vile,** foul, nasty, nauseating; fulsome, mephitic, miasmal, miasmic, malodorous, stinking, fetid, noisome, noxious; **obnoxious,** abhorrent, hateful, abominable, heinous, **contemptible, despicable,** detestable, execrable, beneath *or* below contempt, **base,** ignoble

**objective** NOUNS 1 **object,** aim, end, goal, destination, mark, object in mind, **end in view,** telos, final cause, ultimate aim; end in itself; **target,** butt, bull's-eye, quintain; quarry, prey, game; reason for being, *raison d'être* <Fr>
ADJS 2 **extrinsic,** external, outward, outside, outlying; **unprejudiced,** unbiased, unprepossessed, unjaundiced; impartial, evenhanded, **fair, just**, equitable, **dispassionate,** impersonal, detached, disinterested; indifferent, neutral; **unswayed,** uninfluenced, undazzled

**objector** NOUNS **dissenter,** dissident, dissentient, recusant; demurrer; minority *or* opposition voice; **protester,** protestant, dissident, dissentient; obstructionist, obstructive, negativist, naysayer; contra; **resister;** die-hard, bitter-ender, last-ditcher, intransigent, irreconcilable

**obligated** ADJS **obliged,** obligate, under obligation; bound, duty-bound, in duty bound, tied, pledged, committed, saddled, beholden, bounden; **obliged to,**

beholden to, bound *or* bounden to, **indebted to**

**obligation** NOUNS 1 **commitment,** agreement, engagement, undertaking, recognizance; **understanding,** gentlemen's agreement; verbal agreement, nonformal agreement, pactum <law>; tacit *or* unspoken agreement; **contract**; designation, committal, earmarking
2 **debt,** indebtedness, indebtment, **liability,** financial commitment, due, **dues,** score, pledge, unfulfilled pledge, amount due, outstanding debt; **bill, bills,** chits <nonformal>, **charges**

**obligatory** ADJS **compulsory,** imperative, mandatory, required, dictated, **binding;** involuntary; necessary; *de rigueur* <Fr>

**obliging** ADJS **considerate,** thoughtful, mindful, heedful, regardful, solicitous, attentive, delicate, tactful, mindful of others; complaisant, **accommodating,** accommodative, at one's service, **helpful,** agreeable, indulgent, tolerant, lenient

**oblique** ADJS **devious,** deviant, deviative, divergent, digressive, divagational, deflectional, excursive; **indirect,** side, sidelong; left-handed, sinister, sinistral; backhand, backhanded; circuitous

**obliterate** VERBS **expunge,** efface, erase, raze <old>, blot, sponge, **wipe out,** wipe off the map, rub out, **blot out,** sponge out, wash away; cancel, strike out, cross out, scratch, scratch out, rule out; blue-pencil; **delete** *or* dele, kill

**oblivion** NOUNS **insensibility,** insensibleness, **unconsciousness,** unawareness, obliviousness, nirvana; anesthesia, narcosis; unthinkingness, unmindfulness, forgetfulness, lack *or* loss of memory, amnesia; quietism, passivity, apathy; blank mind, fallow mind, tabula rasa; unintelligence

**oblivious** ADJS **unconscious, out,** out like a light, out cold; comatose; dormant; dead, **dead to the world;** inconsiderate, untactful, undiplomatic, mindless of, **unmindful,** forgetful; out of it *and* not with it <both nonformal>; **preoccupied**

**obnoxious** ADJS **offensive,** odious, offensive, gross, **disgusting,** repulsive, loathsome, **abominable,** detestable, despicable, contemptible, beneath contempt, hateful

**obscene** ADJS **lewd,** adult, bawdy, ithyphallic, **ribald,** pornographic, salacious, sultry <nonformal>, lurid, **dirty, smutty,** raunchy <nonformal>, blue, smoking-room, impure, unchaste, unclean, **foul, filthy,** nasty, vile, fulsome, offensive, unprintable, unrepeatable, not fit for mixed company; **foul-mouthed,** foul-tongued, foul-spoken; Rabelaisian

**obscenity** NOUNS **coarseness,** grossness, *grossièreté* <Fr>, rudeness, crudeness, crudity, **crassness,** rawness, roughness, **earthiness;** ribaldness, ribaldry; raunchiness <nonformal>; **cursing,** cussing <nonformal>, **swearing, profanity,** profane swearing, foul *or* profane *or* obscene *or* blue *or* bad *or* strong *or* unparliamentary *or* indelicate language, vulgar language, vile language, colorful language, unrepeatable expressions, dysphemism, billingsgate, evil speaking, **dirty language** *or* **talk** <nonformal>, scatology, coprology, filthy language, filth

**obscure** VERBS 1 **cover,** cover up; **clothe,** cloak, mantle, muffle, blanket, canopy, cope, cowl, hood, **veil,** curtain, **screen, shield,** screen off, mask, darken, obfuscate, cloud, fog, befog, fuzz; block, eclipse, occult; film, film over, scum; **make unintelligible, scramble,** jumble, garble; mystify, shadow; **complicate**
ADJS 2 **vague, indistinct,** indeterminate, fuzzy, shapeless, amorphous; unclear, unplain, opaque, muddy, **clear as mud** *and* clear as ditch water <both nonformal>; **dark,** dim, shadowy; **murky,** cloudy, foggy, fogbound, hazy, misty, nebulous; mysterious, enigmatic
3 **unrenowned,** renownless, nameless, inglorious, **unnotable,** unnoted, unnoticed, unremarked, undistinguished, unfamed, uncelebrated, unsung, unhonored, unglorified, unpopular; **unknown,** little known, unheard-of, *ignotus* <L>

**observant** ADJS respectful, regardful, mindful; **faithful,** devout, devoted, true, loyal, constant; dutiful, duteous; as good as one's word; **practicing,** active; compliant, conforming; punctual, punctilious, scrupulous, meticulous, conscientious

**observation** NOUNS 1 observance; **looking,** watching, viewing, seeing, witnessing, espial; **notice,** note, respect, **regard;** watch, lookout; surveillance, spying, espionage

2 **remark, statement,** earful *and* crack *and* one's two cents' worth <all nonformal>, **word,** say, saying, utterance, reflection, expression; assertion, averment, allegation, affirmation, pronouncement, position, dictum; **declaration; opinion**; supposition, **theory**

**observe** VERBS 1 **keep, heed,** follow, keep the faith; regard, defer to, **respect**, attend to, comply with, conform to; hold by, **abide by,** adhere to; **live up to,** act up to, practice what one preaches, **be faithful to,** keep faith with, do justice to, do the right thing by; **fulfill,** fill, meet, satisfy; **make good,** keep *or* make good one's word *or* promise, be as good as one's word

2 **celebrate,** keep, mark, solemnly mark, **honor; commemorate,** memorialize; **solemnize,** kill the fatted calf; sound a fanfare, blow the trumpet, beat the drum, fire a salute

3 **remark,** comment, note; mention, let drop *or* fall, say by the way, make mention of; refer to, allude to, touch on, make reference to, call attention to; muse, reflect; opine <nonformal>; interject; blurt, blurt out, exclaim

**observer** NOUNS **spectator,** looker, onlooker, looker-on, **watcher,** gazer, gazer-on, gaper, goggler, **viewer,** seer, beholder, perceiver, percipient; **witness,** eyewitness; sidewalk superintendent; kibitzer; girl-watcher, ogler, drugstore cowboy <nonformal>

**obsessed** ADJS 1 **possessed,** prepossessed, **infatuated,** preoccupied, fixated, **hung up** <nonformal>, besotted, gripped, held; monomaniac *or* monomaniacal; unable to forget, haunted, plagued, nagged, rankled

2 **engrossed, absorbed,** totally absorbed, single-minded, **occupied,** preoccupied, engaged, devoted, devoted to, intent, intent on, monopolized, swept up, taken up with, **involved,** caught up in, **wrapped up in**

**obsession** NOUNS prepossession, preoccupation, **hang-up** <nonformal>, **fixation,** tic, complex, fascination; hypercathexis; **compulsion,** morbid drive, obsessive compulsion, irresistible impulse; **monomania,** ruling passion, fixed idea, *idée fixe* <Fr>, one-track mind; **possession**, spirit control

**obsessive** ADJS obsessional; **obsessing,** possessing, preoccupying, gripping, holding; driving, impelling, **compulsive,** compelling; haunting, persistent, recurrent, nagging, plaguing, rankling, festering

**obsolete** ADJS **passé,** extinct, gone out, gone-by, dead, past, run out, **outworn**

**obstacle** NOUNS **obstruction,** obstructer; **hang-up** <nonformal>; **block,** blockade, cordon, curtain; **difficulty,** hurdle, hazard; **deterrent,** determent; **drawback,** objection; **stumbling block,** stumbling stone, stone in one's path; fly in the ointment, **hitch, catch,** joker <nonformal>

**obstinate** ADJS **stubborn,** pertinacious, restive; willful, self-willed, strong-willed, hardheaded, **headstrong,** strongheaded, *entêté* <Fr>; **dogged,** bulldogged, tenacious, perserving; bullheaded, bulletheaded, **pigheaded, mulish** <nonformal>, stubborn as a mule; **set in one's ways,** case-hardened, stiff-necked; balky, balking

**obstreperous** ADJS **defiant,** refractory, recalcitrant, contumacious, unruly, restive, impatient of control *or* discipline; fractious, ornery *and* feisty <both nonformal>; wild, untamed

**obstruct** VERBS **get** *or* **stand in the way;** dog, block, block the way, put up a roadblock, blockade, block up, occlude; **jam,** crowd, pack; **bar,** barricade, bolt, lock; **debar,** shut out; shut off, **close,** close off *or* up, close tight, shut tight; strangle, suffocate

**obstruction** NOUNS **clog, block,** blockade, sealing off, **blockage,** strangulation, choking, choking off, **stoppage,** stop, **bar, barrier, obstacle,** impediment; **bottleneck,** chokepoint; **congestion,** jam, traffic jam, gridlock, rush hour; constipation, obstipation, costiveness; infarct, infarction; embolism, embolus; **blind alley,** blank wall, **dead end,** cul-de-sac, dead-end street, impasse

**obtain** VERBS **acquire,** get, gain, secure, procure; win, score; **earn,** make; **reap,** harvest; come *or* enter into possession of, **come into, come by,** come in for, be seized of; draw, derive

**obverse** NOUNS opposite side, other side, the other side of the picture *or* coin, other face; **reverse,** inverse, converse; flip side *and* B-side <both nonformal>; **front,** head <of a coin>

**obvious** ADJS **patent,** unquestionable, unexceptionable, undeniable, self-evident, axiomatic; indubitable, unarguable, indisputable, incontestable, **irrefutable,** unrefutable, unconfutable, incontrovertible, irrefragable, unanswerable, unimpeachable, absolute; admitting no question *or* dispute *or* doubt *or* denial; **demonstrable,** provable, verifiable, testable, confirmable; well-founded, well-established, well-grounded; factual, **real,** historical, actual

**occasion** NOUNS **circumstance,** occurrence, event, **incident;** juncture, conjuncture, contingency, eventuality; **condition; opportunity,** chance, time; **necessity,** need, want

**occasionally** ADVS on occasion, **sometimes,** at times, at odd times, every so often <nonformal>, at various times, on divers occasions, **now and then,** every now and then <nonformal>, now and again, every once in a while <nonformal>, every now and again, once or twice, **from time to time;** only when the spirit moves, only now and then, at infrequent intervals, once in a blue moon <nonformal>; irregularly, sporadically, once in a while

**occult** ADJS **esoteric,** esoterical, mysterious, mystic, mystical, anagogic, anagogical; metaphysic, metaphysical; cabalic, cabalistic; **paranormal, supernatural**; theosophical, theosophist, anthroposophical

**the occult** NOUNS **supernaturalism,** supernaturalness, supernaturality, supranaturalism, supernormalness, **preternaturalism,** supersensibleness, superphysicalness, superhumanity; **the paranormal;** numinousness; **unearthliness,** unworldliness, **otherworldliness,** eeriness; the supernatural, the supersensible; **paranormality;** supernature, supranature; **mystery,** mysteriousness, miraculousness, strangeness; faerie, witchery, elfdom

**occupant** NOUNS **inhabitant,** inhabiter, habitant; occupier, **dweller,** tenant, denizen, inmate; **resident,** residencer, residentiary, resider; incumbent, *locum tenens* <L>; sojourner; addressee; squatter; homesteader

**occupation** NOUNS 1 **habitation,** inhabiting, inhabitation, habitancy, inhabitancy, **tenancy,** occupancy, residence *or* residency, residing, abiding, **living,** nesting, **dwelling,** commorancy <law>, lodging, staying, stopping, sojourning, staying over
2 **appropriation,** taking over, takeover <nonformal>, **adoption,** assumption, usurpation, arrogation; **conquest,** subjugation, enslavement, colonization
3 **vocation,** business, work, line, line of work, line of business *or* endeavor, number <nonformal>, walk, walk of life, calling, mission, **profession,** practice, pursuit, specialty, specialization, *métier* <Fr>, **trade,** racket *and* game <both nonformal>

**occupied** ADJS 1 **inhabited,** tenanted; **peopled,** empeopled, populated, colonized, settled; populous
2 **busy, engaged,** employed, working; at it; **at work,** on duty, on the job, in harness; hard at work, **hard at it;** on the move, on the go, on the run, **on the hop** *or* **jump** <nonformal>; busy as a bee *or* beaver, busier than a one-armed paper hanger <nonformal>; up to one's ears *or* elbows *or* asshole *or* neck *or* eyeballs in <nonformal>; tied up
3 absorbed *or* engrossed in thought, **absorbed,** engrossed, introspective, rapt, wrapped in thought, lost in thought, abstracted, immersed in thought, buried in thought, engaged in thought, **preoccupied**

**occupy** VERBS 1 **engage, busy,** devote, spend, **employ,** occupy oneself, busy oneself, go about one's business, devote oneself; pass *or* employ *or* spend the time; **occupy the mind** *or* **thoughts,** fasten itself on the mind, seize the mind, fill the mind; **engross, absorb,** immerse, preoccupy, involve, monopolize, exercise, take up; **obsess;** absorb the attention, claim one's thoughts, engross the mind *or* thoughts, engage the attention, monopolize one's attention, engage the mind *or* thoughts
2 **inhabit,** tenant, move in *or* into, make one's home, rent, lease, **reside, live in,** dwell, lodge, stay

**occur** VERBS **happen**, hap, eventuate, **take place,** come *or* go down <nonformal>, go on, **transpire,** be realized, come, **come off** <nonformal>, **come about,** come true, **come to pass,** pass, pass off, go off, fall, **befall,** betide; **be found,** be met with; **occur to,** come to mind, come into one's head, impinge on one's consciousness, claim one's mind *or* thoughts, pass through one's head *or* mind, dawn upon one, **enter one's mind,** cross one's mind; **strike,** strike one, strike the mind, grab one <nonformal>, **suggest itself**

**occurrence** NOUNS **event,** incident, episode, experience, adventure, hap, **happening,** happenstance, **phenomenon,** fact, matter of fact, reality, particular, circumstance, **occasion,** turn of events

**ocean** NOUNS **sea,** ocean sea, great *or* main sea, *thalassa* <Gk>, main *or* ocean main, the bounding main, tide, salt sea, salt water, blue water, deep water, open sea, the brine, the briny *and* the big pond <both nonformal>, the briny deep, **the deep,** the deep sea, the deep blue sea, drink *and* big drink <both nonformal>, **high sea, high seas**

*the great naked sea shouldering a load of salt*
**Sandberg**

*the wine-dark sea*
**Homer**

**oceanic** ADJS **marine, maritime,** pelagic, thalassic; nautical; deep-sea

**ocular** ADJS **visual,** eye, eyeball <nonformal>; **sighted,** seeing, having sight *or* vision; **optic,** optical; ophthalmic, ophthalmological; binocular, monocular

**odd** ADJS 1 **queer, peculiar,** absurd, singular, curious, oddball <nonformal>, kooky *and* freaky *and* freaked-out <all nonformal>, quaint, **eccentric,** gonzo <nonformal>, funny; **strange, outlandish,** off-the-wall <informal>, surreal, not for real <nonformal>, passing strange; **weird,** unearthly

*wondrous strange*
**Shakespeare**

2 **sole, unique,** singular, absolute, unrepeated, **alone,** lone, **only,** only-begotten, **one and only,** first and last; unpaired, azygous

**oddball** NOUNS **misfit, nonconformist,** individualist, inner-directed person; **freak,** sport, anomaly; a fish out of water, a square peg in a round hole <nonformal>

**oddity** NOUNS 1 **eccentricity,** idiosyncrasy, idiocrasy, **erraticism,** erraticness, **queerness, peculiarity,** strangeness, singularity, freakishness, freakiness, quirkiness, crotchetiness, dottiness, crankiness, crankism, crackpotism; abnormality, anomaly, unnaturalness, irregularity, deviation, deviancy, differentness, divergence, aberration
2 **curiosity,** funny *or* peculiar *or* strange thing; **abnormality,** anomaly; rarity, improbability, exception, one in a thousand *or* million; curio, conversation piece

**odds** NOUNS **gambling odds; short odds, long odds,** long shot; even chance, good chance, small chance, no chance; **probability, likelihood,** likeliness, liability, aptitude, verisimilitude; **chance**

**odious** ADJS **offensive,** objectionable, repulsive, repellent, rebarbative, **repugnant, revolting,** forbidding; **obnoxious,** abhorrent, hateful, abominable, heinous, **contemptible, despicable,** detestable, execrable, beneath *or* below contempt, **base,** ignoble

**odor** NOUNS **smell, scent,** aroma, flavor <old>, savor; **essence,** definite odor, redolence, effluvium, emanation, exhalation, fume, breath, subtle odor, whiff, trace, detectable odor; trail, spoor; **fragrance**; stink, stench

**odyssey** NOUNS **travels,** journeys, **journeyings,** wanderings, voyagings, transits, peregrinations, peripatetics, migrations, transmigrations

**off** ADJS 1 **tainted,** blown; **stale; sour,** soured, turned; **rank,** rancid, strong <nonformal>, **high,** gamy
2 **unbalanced,** unsettled, distraught, wandering, mazed, crackbrained, brainsick, sick *or* soft in the head, not right, not in one's right mind, **touched,** touched in the head, **out of one's mind,** out of one's senses *or* wits, irrational, queer, queer in the head, odd, strange
3 **below par,** below standard, below the mark <nonformal>, substandard, **not up to scratch** *or* snuff *or* the mark <nonformal>, not up to sample *or* standard *or* specification
ADVS 4 **at a distance,** away, aloof, at arm's length; distantly, remotely

**off-base** ADJS **misbehaving,** naughty, bad; improper, not respectable; out-of-order *and* out-of-line <both nonformal>; **disorderly,** disruptive, **rowdy,** rowdyish, **ruffianly**

**offbeat** ADJS **unconventional,** way out *and* far out *and* kinky *and* out in left field <all nonformal>, fringy, breakaway,

**out-of-the-way; original,** maverick, Bohemian, **nonformal,** free and easy <nonformal>

**offend** VERBS give offense, **repel,** put off, turn off <nonformal>, **revolt, disgust,** nauseate, sicken, make one sick; stick in one's throat, stick in one's crop *or* craw *or* gizzard <nonformal>; **horrify, appall,** shock; give umbrage, affront, outrage; grieve, aggrieve; wound, hurt, cut, cut to the quick, hit one where one lives <nonformal>, **sting,** hurt one's feelings; step *or* tread on one's toes; offend the eye, offend one's aesthetic sensibilities, **look bad**

**offense** NOUNS **indignity,** affront, injury, humiliation; **insult,** aspersion, uncomplimentary remark, slap *or* kick in the face, left-handed *or* backhanded compliment, damning with faint praise; **outrage,** atrocity, enormity; **misdeed, misdemeanor,** misfeasance, malfeasance, malefaction, criminal *or* guilty *or* sinful act, injustice, injury, **wrong,** iniquity, evil, peccancy, *malum* <L>; tort; **impropriety,** slight *or* minor wrong, venial sin, **indiscretion,** peccadillo, misstep, trip, slip, lapse; **transgression,** trespass

**offensive** NOUNS 1 **attack, assault,** assailing, assailment; **offense,** aggression; onset, onslaught; strike; surgical strike, first strike, preventive war; **charge,** rush, dead set at, run at *or* against; breakthrough; **counterattack,** counteroffensive; blitzkrieg, blitz, lightning attack, lightning war, panzer warfare, sudden *or* devastating *or* crippling attack

ADJS 2 **objectionable,** odious, repulsive, repellent, rebarbative, **repugnant, revolting,** forbidding; **disgusting,** sickening, loathsome, beastly <nonformal>, **vile,** foul, filthy, bawdy, nasty, nauseating; fulsome, mephitic, miasmal, miasmic, malodorous, stinking, fetid, noisome, noxious; coarse, gross, crude, obscene; **insulting,** insolent, abusive, humiliating, degrading, contemptuous, contumelious, calumnious; scurrilous

**offer** NOUNS 1 offering, proffer, presentation, **bid,** submission; **advance, overture,** approach, invitation; hesitant *or* tentative *or* preliminary approach, feeling-out, **feeler** <nonformal>; asking price; **counteroffer,** counterproposal

VERBS 2 **proffer, present,** tender, offer up, **put up, submit,** extend, prefer <old>, **hold out,** hold forth, place in one's way, lay at one's feet, put *or* place at one's disposal, put one in the way of; **bid,** make a bid, offer to buy, make an offer

**offering** NOUNS **oblation,** sacrifice, immolation, incense; burnt offering, votive *or* ex voto offering; peace offering, sacramental offering; **donation,** donative; **contribution,** subscription; alms, pittance, **charity,** dole, handout <nonformal>, alms fee, widow's mite; Peter's pence; collection; tithe

**off-guard** ADJS **unalert,** unwary, unwatchful, unvigilant, uncautious, incautious; **unprepared,** unready; **off one's guard,** napping, asleep at the switch *and* asleep on the job *and* not on the job *and* goofing off *and* looking out the window <all nonformal>; daydreaming, woolgathering

**office** NOUNS **bureau,** department; secretariat, ministry; **function,** duty, job, province, place, **role,** *rôle* <Fr>, part; **capacity,** character, **position**

**officer** NOUNS 1 **executive,** official; chief executive officer, chief executive, managing director <Brit>; functionary, *fonctionnaire* <Fr>, apparatchik; **public official,** public servant; officeholder; **commissioned officer**

2 **policeman,** constable, police officer, *flic* <Fr nonformal>, *gendarme* <Fr>, *carabiniere* <Ital>; peace officer, law enforcement agent, arm of the law; policewoman, police matron; patrolman, police constable <England>; trooper, mounted policeman; chief of police

**official** ADJS **recorded,** registered; **filed,** indexed, enrolled, **entered,** logged, booked, posted; documented; **on record,** on file, on the books; legal, of record; **authoritative, authentic,** magisterial; cathedral, ex cathedra; standard, approved, accepted, received, pontific; from *or* straight from the horse's mouth

**officiate** VERBS **function,** serve; perform as, act as, act *or* play one's part, **do duty,** discharge *or* perform *or* exercise the office *or* duties *or* functions of, serve in the office *or* capacity of; **referee, umpire,** arbitrate; **minister,** perform a rite, perform service *or* divine service; administer a sacrament, administer the Eucharist, etc; anoint, chrism

**off-limits** ADJS **prohibited,** forbidden,

forbade, *verboten* <Ger>, **barred; unpermissible,** not permitted *or* allowed, unchartered; beyond the pale, out of bounds; unauthorized, **unsanctioned,** unlicensed; banned, under the ban, **outlawed,** contraband; taboo, tabooed, untouchable; **illegal,** unlawful, illicit

**offset** VERBS set off, **counteract,** countervail, **counterbalance,** counterweigh, counterpoise, **balance,** play off against, set against, set over against, equiponderate; **square,** square up; **cushion,** absorb the shock, **soften the blow,** break the fall, deaden, damp *or* dampen, soften, suppress, neutralize

**offshoot** NOUNS **branch,** fork, limb, bough; **shoot,** spear, frond; scion; **sprout,** sprit, slip, burgeon; **branch,** organ, division, wing, arm, **affiliate; chapter,** lodge, post; branch office

**offspring** NOUNS **descendant; child,** scion; son, son and heir, a chip off the old block; **daughter,** grandchild, grandson, granddaughter

**often** ADVS **repeatedly,** frequently, recurrently, every time one turns around, with every other breath, **again and again, over and over,** over and over again, many times over, time and again, **time after time,** times without number, **ad nauseam;** year in year out, week in week out, etc, year after year, day after day, day by day; **many times,** several times, a number of times, many a time

**ogle** VERBS **scrutinize,** survey, eye, contemplate, look over, give the eye *or* the once-over <nonformal>; ogle at, **leer,** leer at, gape, give one the glad eye; take a long, hard look; size up <nonformal>; take stock of; **make eyes at,** make googoo eyes at <nonformal>, *faire les yeux doux* <Fr>, look sweet upon <nonformal>

**ogre** NOUNS **monster,** vampire, werewolf, ghoul, *bête noire;* **fiend,** fiend from hell

**oil** VERBS grease, **lubricate; anoint,** salve, unguent, embrocate, dress, pour oil *or* balm upon; smear, daub; slick, slick on <nonformal>

**oily** ADJS **greasy; unctuous,** unctional; unguinous; **oleaginous,** oleic; unguentary, **unguent,** unguentous; chrismal, chrismatory; **fat, fatty,** adipose; pinguid, pinguedinous, pinguescent; blubbery, tallowy, suety; lardy, lardaceous

**ointment** NOUNS **balm,** salve, lotion, cream, unguent, unguentum, inunction, inunctum, unction, chrism; lenitive, embrocation, demulcent, emollient

**okay** NOUNS 1 **permission,** leave, consent; **license,** liberty; **OK** *and* **nod** *and* **go-ahead** *and* **green light** *and* **go sign** *and* **thumbs-up** <all nonformal>; special permission, charter, patent, dispensation, release, waiver; zoning variance, variance

VERBS 2 **consent, assent,** give consent, say yes *or* aye *or* yea, vote affirmatively, vote aye, nod, nod assent; accept, play *or* go along <nonformal>, **agree to, sign off on** <nonformal>, go along with <nonformal>; **approve,** give one's blessing to, **OK** <nonformal>; sanction, **endorse,** ratify; **wink at,** connive at; be willing, turn a willing ear; deign, condescend; have no objection, not refuse; permit

ADJS 3 **tolerable,** goodish, fair, fairish, moderate, **decent,** respectable, presentable, good enough, **pretty good,** not bad, not amiss, not half bad, not so bad, **adequate,** satisfactory, all right, OK <nonformal>; better than nothing; **acceptable,** admissible, **passable,** unobjectionable, unexceptionable

**old** ADJS 1 **aged, elderly,** grown old in years, along *or* up *or* advanced *or* on in years, years old, advanced, advanced in life, **at an advanced age,** ancient, geriatric, gerontic; **venerable,** old as Methuselah *or* as God *or* as the hills; patriarchal; hoary, hoar, **gray,** white, gray- *or* white-haired, gray with age; wrinkled, prune-faced <nonformal>; wrinkly, with crow's feet, marked with the crow's foot

2 **antiquated,** grown old, superannuated, antique, age-encrusted, of other times

**old age** NOUNS **oldness,** elderliness, senectitude, advanced age *or* years; **ripe old age,** the golden years, senior citizenship, hoary age, gray *or* white hairs; **decline of life,** declining years; sunset *or* twilight *or* evening *or* autumn *or* winter of one's days; **dotage,** second childhood; senility, anility

*an incurable disease*
**Seneca**

**old-fashioned** ADJS old-fangled, **dated,** out-of-date, outdated, **outmoded,** out of style *or* fashion, out of use, **unfashionable,** styleless, **behind the times,** of the old school, old hat *and* back-number *and* has-been <all nonformal>

**old-line** ADJS **conservative,** diehard, standpat <nonformal>, opposed to change; backward, backward-looking, old-fashioned, **unprogressive,** nonprogressive, unreconstructed, status-quo, stuck-in-the-mud; long-established; **confirmed,** inveterate, **dyed-in-the-wool**

**omen** NOUNS **portent; augury,** auspice, soothsay, prognostic, prognostication; **warning sign,** premonitory sign, danger sign; preliminary sign *or* signal *or* token; **handwriting on the wall;** straw in the wind; presentiment, foreboding

**ominous** ADJS **portentous,** portending; **foreboding,** boding, **bodeful; inauspicious,** ill-omened, ill-boding, of ill *or* fatal omen, of evil portent, loaded *or* laden *or* freighted *or* fraught with doom, looming, looming over; fateful, doomful; **unpropitious,** unpromising, unfavorable, unfortunate, unlucky; sinister, dark, black, gloomy, somber, dreary; **threatening,** menacing, lowering; dire, baleful, baneful, **ill-fated,** ill-starred, evil-starred, star-crossed

**omit** VERBS **leave undone,** leave, **let go,** leave half-done, pretermit, **skip,** jump, **miss,** pass over, pass up <nonformal>, abandon; **ban,** prohibit, proscribe, taboo, **leave out,** ignore

**omnipotent** ADJS **almighty,** all-powerful; plenipotentiary, absolute, unlimited, **sovereign**; **supreme**; omnicompetent

**omnipresent** ADJS **all-present,** ubiquitous, everywhere; continuous, uninterrupted, infinite; **pervasive,** all-pervading, **universal**

**omniscient** ADJS **all-wise,** all-knowing, all-seeing

**omnivorous** ADJS all-devouring, pantophagous; **gluttonous**

**onerous** ADJS **oppressive,** burdensome, incumbent *or* superincumbent, **cumbersome,** cumbrous; **laborious,** toilsome, arduous, strenuous, painful, operose, troublesome, oppressive

**one-sided** ADJS **discriminatory; prejudiced,** prepossessed, biased, jaundiced, colored; **partial,** partisan; interested, nonobjective, **undetached,** undispassionate

**one-upmanship** NOUNS **cunning,** low cunning, animal cunning; gamesmanship <nonformal>; **canniness, shrewdness,** sharpness, acuteness, astuteness, **cleverness;** lifemanship, **competitive advantage**

**one-way** ADJS unidirectional, irreversible

**ongoing** ADJS **happening,** occurring, current, actual, passing, taking place, on, **going on, prevalent,** prevailing, that is, that applies, in the wind, afloat, afoot, under way, in hand, **on foot,** ado, doing; **operating,** operational, working, functioning, operant, functional, acting, active, running

**onset** NOUNS **beginning,** commencement, start, running *or* flying start, starting point, square one <nonformal>, **outset,** outbreak, oncoming

**onslaught** NOUNS **attack,** assault, assailing, assailment; **offense,** offensive; aggression; onset

**onus** NOUNS **duty,** obligation, charge, **burden,** mission, devoir, must, ought, imperative, bounden duty, proper *or* assigned task, what ought to be done, what one is responsible for, where the buck stops <nonformal>; **stigma,** stigmatism; burden of proof, *onus probandi* <L>; the proof of the pudding

**ooze** NOUNS 1 **slime, slop,** scum, sludge, slush; glop *and* gunk <both nonformal>, **muck,** mire; **seepage,** seep; perfusion; **oozing,** weeping
VERBS 2 **exude,** exudate, transude, transpire, reek; **emit,** discharge, give off; leach, lixiviate; effuse, extravasate; **seep,** bleed, weep

**opalescent** ADJS pearly, nacreous, mother-of-pearl, iridescent, opaline, opaloid

**opaque** ADJS intransparent, nontranslucent, adiaphanous, impervious to light; **dark, obscure**, cloudy, roiled, roily, turbid; **dense,** thick <nonformal>

**open** VERBS 1 **disclose,** open up, lay open, break the seal, bring into the open, get out in the open
ADJS 2 **unclosed,** uncovered; **unobstructed,** unstopped, unclogged; clear, cleared, free; wide-open, unrestricted; **disclosed**; bare, exposed, unhidden, naked, bald; candid, **frank**; self-revealing, self-revelatory; outspoken, free-speaking, free-spoken, free-tongued; **accessible, approachable,** conversable, easy to speak to; **extroverted,** outgoing
3 overt, open to all, open as day, out of the closet <nonformal>; unclassified;

**revealed,** bare, **exposed,** out in the open, naked; out on a limb <nonformal>; liable, susceptible, nonimmune

**openhearted** ADJS **open,** sincere, candid, **frank; giving,** bighearted, largehearted, greathearted; **cordial,** amiable, gracious, **friendly,** neighborly, genial, hearty, warm, warmhearted; heart-to-heart

**opening** NOUNS 1 **aperture, hole,** hollow, cavity, **orifice; slot,** split, crack, check, leak; opening up, unstopping, uncorking, clearing, throwing open, laying open, broaching, cutting through; passageway; inlet; outlet; **gap,** gape, yawn, hiatus, lacuna, gat, space, interval; **chasm,** gulf; cleft; fontanel; foramen, fenestra
2 **opportunity,** chance, time, occasion; room, scope, space, place, liberty

**open-minded** ADJS **open, receptive,** rational, admissive; **persuadable,** persuasible; **unopinionated,** unopinioned, unwedded to an opinion; **undogmatic**

**operable** ADJS **workable,** performable, actable, **doable,** manageable, compassable, negotiable, maneuverable; **practicable, feasible,** practical, viable

**operate** VERBS 1 **function,** perform, go, run, be in action *or* operation *or* commission; be effective, go into effect, have effect, take effect, militate
2 **work, move,** practice, do one's stuff *or* one's thing <all nonformal>; **plot, scheme,** intrigue, be up to something; **conspire, connive,** collude, complot <old>, cabal; **maneuver,** engineer, rig, wangle <nonformal>, angle, finagle <nonformal>

**operation** NOUNS 1 **surgery,** surgical treatment, surgical operation, surgical intervention, surgical technique *or* measure, the knife <nonformal>; unnecessary surgery, tomomania
2 **function,** use, purpose, role, part, end use, immediate purpose, ultimate purpose, operational purpose; **functioning,** action, performance, performing, **working,** work, workings, exercise, practice; **management,** direction, conduct, running, carrying-on *or* **-**out, execution, seeing to, overseeing, oversight
3 action; **mission; operations,** military operations, naval operations

**operative** NOUNS 1 **secret agent,** cloak-and-dagger operative, **undercover man,** inside man <nonformal>; **spy,** espionage agent; counterspy, double agent; **detective,** investigator, sleuth
ADJS 2 **operational,** go <nonformal>, functional, practical; effective, effectual, efficient, efficacious

**operator** NOUNS 1 **telephone operator,** switchboard operator, telephonist, **central;** long distance; PBX operator
2 **conniver;** maneuverer, machinator, opportunist, pot-hunter, exploiter; strategist, machinator, wheeler-dealer <nonformal>; finagler *and* **wire-puller** <both nonformal>; behind-the-scenes operator, gray eminence, *éminence grise* <Fr>, power behind the throne, kingmaker <nonformal>, **powerbroker**

**opiate** NOUNS **sleep-inducer,** sleep-producer, sleep-provoker, sleep-bringer, hypnotic, soporific, somnifacient; poppy, mandrake, mandragora, narcotic, opium, morphine, morphia; sedative; anesthetic

**opinion** NOUNS **sentiment,** feeling, sense, impression, reaction, **notion,** idea, thought, mind, thinking, **way of thinking,** attitude, stance, posture, position, mindset, **view,** point of view, eye, sight, lights, observation, **conception,** concept, conceit, **estimation,** estimate, consideration, **theory**, assumption, presumption, **conclusion,** judgment, personal judgment; **point of view**

**opinionated** ADJS **dogmatic,** dogmatical, dogmatizing, pronunciative, didactic, **positive,** positivistic, peremptory, pontifical, oracular; **opinioned,** opinionative, conceited; **self-opinionated,** self-opinioned; doctrinaire

**opium** NOUNS 1 **sleep-inducer,** sleep-producer, sleep-provoker, sleep-bringer, hypnotic, soporific, somnifacient; poppy, mandrake, mandragora, opiate, morphine, morphia; sedative; anesthetic

2 <nonformal> black pills, brown stuff, hop, O, tar

**opponent** NOUNS **adversary,** antagonist, assailant, foe, foeman, **enemy,** archenemy; adverse *or* opposing party, opposite camp, opposite *or* opposing side, **the opposition,** the loyal opposition

**opportune** ADJS **timely,** well-timed, in the nick of time, seasonable, convenient; **propitious,** ripe, auspicious, lucky, providential, heaven-sent, fortunate, happy, felicitous

**opportunist** NOUNS **intriguer,** *intrigant, intrigante* <both Fr>, cabalist; maneuverer, machinator, operator <nonformal>, pot-hunter, exploiter

**opportunity** NOUNS **chance,** time, occasion; opening, room, scope, space, place, liberty; equal opportunity, nondiscrimination, affirmative action; a leg up, stepping-stone, rung of the ladder; time's forelock; break <nonformal>, the breaks <nonformal>

**oppose** VERBS **counter, cross,** go *or* act in opposition to, **go against,** run against, **run counter to,** fly in the face of, fly in the teeth of; kick out against, make waves <nonformal>, **protest**; set oneself against, set one's face *or* heart against; be *or* play at cross-purposes, **obstruct,** traverse, sabotage; **take issue with,** take one's stand against, lift *or* raise a hand against, declare oneself against, stand and be counted against, side against, vote against, vote nay, veto; make a stand against; not put up with, not abide, not be content with; counteract, counterwork, countervail; **resist,** withstand

**opposed** ADJS contrapositive, **opposite,** opposing, **facing,** confronting, confrontational, confrontive, eyeball-to-eyeball, one-on-one; on opposite sides, adversarial, at loggerheads, at daggers drawn, antithetic, antithetical; **unconsenting**; dead set against

**opposing** ADJS **contradictory,** contradicting, contrary, contra, nay-saying, adversative, repugnant; **opposed,** oppositive, oppositional; anti <nonformal>, dead against

**opposite** NOUNS 1 **the opposite,** the contrary, the antithesis, the reverse, the other way round *or* around, the inverse, the converse, the obverse, the counter; **the other side,** the mirror *or* reverse image, the other side of the coin, the flip *or* B side <nonformal>; the direct *or* polar opposite, the other *or* opposite extreme; antipode, antipodes; **antonym,** opposite term, counterterm
ADJS 2 **adverse,** untoward, detrimental, unfavorable; sinister; hostile, antagonistic, inimical; contrary, counter, counteractive, conflicting, opposing, opposed, in opposition
ADVS 3 **poles apart,** at opposite extremes; contrary, contrariwise, counter; just opposite, **face-to-face,** vis-à-vis, *front à front* <Fr>, nose to nose, one on one, eyeball-to-eyeball

**opposition** NOUNS **contrariety,** oppositeness, antithesis, contrast, contraposition, counterposition, contradiction, contraindication, contradistinction; **antagonism,** repugnance, resistance, oppugnance, oppugnancy, **hostility,** perversity, nay-saying, negativeness, orneriness <nonformal>, inimicalness, **antipathy**

**oppress** VERBS 1 **burden,** weigh upon, weight down, wear one down, be heavy on one, crush one; **tire, exhaust,** weary, wear out, wear upon one; prey on the mind, prey on *or* upon; **haunt,** haunt the memory, obsess; **anguish,** afflict, torment
2 **persecute,** torment, victimize, play cat and mouse with, **harass,** get *or* keep after, get *or* keep at, harry, hound, beset

**oppressed** ADJS **weighted,** weighed *or* weighted down; burdened, laden, cumbered, **encumbered,** charged, loaded, fraught, freighted, taxed, saddled, hampered; **overburdened,** overloaded, overladen; **subjugated,** subjected, enslaved, enthralled, in thrall, captive, bond, unfree; **downtrodden,** kept down *or* under, ground down, overborne, trampled, ordered *or* kicked around <nonformal>, regimented, tyrannized; treated like dirt under one's feet

**oppression** NOUNS **persecution,** harrying, hounding, tormenting, bashing <nonformal>, harassment, victimization; **despotism,** tyranny, fascism, domineering, domination; heavy hand, high hand, iron hand, iron heel *or* boot; big stick, *argumentum baculinum* <L>

**oppressive** ADJS 1 **burdensome,** crushing, trying, onerous, heavy, weighty; **harsh,** wearing, wearying, exhausting; overburdensome, tyrannous, grinding, repressive
2 **stuffy,** airless, breathless, breezeless, windless; **close,** stifling, suffocating; stirless, unstirring, not a breath of air, not a leaf stirring

*not wind enough to twirl the one red leaf*
COLERIDGE

**oppressor** NOUNS **tyrant,** despot, hard master, driver, **slave driver,** Simon Legree <Harriet B Stowe>; **martinet,** disciplinarian, stickler

**opt** VERBS **choose,** elect, pick, go with <nonformal>, opt for, co-opt, make *or* take one's choice, make choice of, have one's druthers <nonformal>, use *or* take up *or* exercise one's option

**optimal** ADJS **best,** very best, greatest *and* top-of-the-line <both nonformal>, **prime,** optimum; **choice,** paramount, **unsurpassed,** surpassing, unparalleled, unmatched, unmatchable, matchless, makeless <old>, **peerless;** quintessential

**optimist** NOUNS hoper, Pollyanna <Eleanor Porter>, ray of sunshine <nonformal>, irrepressible optimist, Dr Pangloss <Voltaire>; utopian, perfectionist; millenarian, chiliast, millennialist, millennian

*a proponent of the doctrine that black is white*
Ambrose Bierce

**optimistic** ADJS upbeat <nonformal>, bright, sunny; **cheerful**; **rosy,** roseate, rose-colored, *couleur de rose* <Fr>; pollyannaish, Panglossian; utopian, perfectionist, millenarian, chiliastic, millennialistic

**optimum** NOUNS 1 **the best,** the very best, the best ever, the top of the heap *or* the line <nonformal>, the tops <nonformal>; **quintessence,** prime, superlative; **cream,** flower, fat; cream of the crop, *crème de la crème* <Fr>, salt of the earth; *pièce de résistance* <Fr>; nonesuch, paragon, nonpareil; gem of the first water
ADJS 2 **best,** very best, greatest *and* top-of-the-line <both nonformal>, **prime,** optimal; supreme, paramount, **unsurpassed,** surpassing, unparalleled, unmatched, unmatchable, matchless, makeless <old>, **peerless;** quintessential

**option** NOUNS 1 **discretion,** pleasure, will and pleasure; optionality; possible choice, alternative, alternate choice, say, say-so *and* druthers <both nonformal>, free decision
2 stock option, right, **put, call,** put and call, right of put and call; straddle, spread

**optional** ADJS **discretionary,** discretional, nonmandatory, elective; arbitrary; **self-determined,** self-determining, autonomous, independent, self-active, self-acting; **unforced,** uncoerced, unpressured, unrequired, uncompelled; unprompted, uninfluenced

**opulence** NOUNS **wealth,** riches, opulency, luxuriousness; richness, wealthiness; **prosperity,** prosperousness, **affluence,** comfortable *or* easy circumstances, independence; **money,** lucre, pelf, gold, mammon; **substance,** property, possessions, material wealth; **assets; fortune,** treasure, handsome fortune; *embarras de richesses* <Fr>, money to burn <nonformal>

**opulent** ADJS **luxuriant,** fertile, productive, **rich,** fat, **wealthy,** affluent

**opus** NOUNS publication, writing, **work,** production; opusculum, opuscule; **piece,** composition, production, work; **masterwork,** masterpiece, *chef d'œuvre* <Fr>, *Meisterstück* <Ger>

**oracle** NOUNS **master,** mistress, authority, mastermind, master spirit of the age; Delphic *or* Delphian oracle, Python, Pythian oracle; Delphic tripod, tripod of the Pythia; Dodona, oracle *or* oak of Dodona

**oral** NOUNS 1 **examination,** school examination, examen, **exam** <nonformal>, **test, quiz;** oral examination
ADJS 2 **speech; spoken,** uttered, said, vocalized, **voiced,** verbalized, pronounced, sounded, articulated, enunciated; vocal, voiceful; verbal, **unwritten,** *viva voce* <L>, nuncupative, parol

**orate** VERBS **declaim,** hold forth, elocute <nonformal>, spout <nonformal>, spiel <nonformal>, mouth; **harangue, rant,** tub-thump, perorate, rodomontade; demagogue, rabble-rouse

**oration** NOUNS **speech,** speeching, speechification <nonformal>, **talk, address,** declamation, harangue; public speech *or* address, formal speech; campaign speech, stump speech; **tirade,** screed, **diatribe,** jeremiad, philippic, invective; after-dinner speech; funeral oration, eulogy; allocution, exhortation, hortatory address; salutatory, salutatory address; valediction, valedictory, valedictory address; inaugural address, inaugural; peroration

**orator** NOUNS **public speaker,** platform orator *or* speaker; rhetorician, rhetor; silver-tongued orator, spellbinder; **soapbox orator,** soapboxer, stump orator

**oratory** NOUNS 1 **public speaking,** declamation, speechmaking, speaking,

speechification <nonformal>, lecturing, speeching; after-dinner speaking; platform oratory *or* speaking; campaign oratory, stump speaking, the stump, the hustings; the soap box; **elocution; rhetoric,** art of public speaking; **eloquence**; forensics, **debating; preaching,** pulpit oratory, Bible-thumping <nonformal>, the pulpit, homiletics
2 **chapel,** oratorium; chantry; sacellum, sacrarium

**orb** NOUNS **sphere,** hemisphere, **orbit,** ambit, circle; **circuit,** judicial circuit, **beat, round,** walk; **realm,** demesne, **domain,** dominion, jurisdiction, bailiwick; **province,** precinct, department; **field,** pale, arena

**orbit** NOUNS 1 **sphere of influence,** orb, ambit; bailiwick, vantage, stamping ground, footing, **territory,** turf, home turf, constituency, power base
2 **circuit,** round, revolution, **circle,** full circle, go-round, **cycle; trajectory;** circle of the sphere, great circle, small circle
VERBS 3 **circle, circuit,** describe a circle, make a circuit, move in a circle, **circulate; go round** *or* **around,** go about; **wheel,** round; make a pass; come full circle, close the circle, make a round trip, return to the starting point; circumnavigate, girdle, girdle the globe

**ordain** VERBS 1 **install,** instate, inaugurate, initiate, invest; frock, **canonize, consecrate;** saint
2 **command,** order, dictate, direct, instruct, mandate, **bid,** enjoin, charge, commission, call on *or* upon; **decree,** rule, promulgate; **proclaim,** declare, pronounce; **destine,** predestine, necessitate, fate, mark, appoint; constitute, establish, put in force

**ordained** ADJS 1 in orders, in holy orders, of the cloth
2 **destined, fated,** fateful, written, in the cards, marked, in store; **doomed,** foredoomed, devoted; inevitable

**ordeal** NOUNS **trial, tribulation,** trials and tribulations; fiery ordeal, the iron entering the soul; crucial test; acid test, litmus test; crucible

**order** NOUNS 1 **harmony,** proportion, symmetry, **balance,** equilibrium, orderedness, measure, measuredness, concinnity
2 **fellowship,** sodality; **society,** guild; **brotherhood,** fraternity, confraternity, confrerie, fraternal order *or* society; **sisterhood,** sorority; **sect,** sectarism, religious order, **denomination,** persuasion, faction, **church,** communion, community, group, affiliation, school, party, body, organization
3 **sequence,** logical sequence, **succession,** successiveness, consecution, **consecutiveness,** following, coming after; descent, lineage, line; order of succession; **priority**
VERBS 4 **command,** dictate, direct, instruct, mandate, **bid,** enjoin, charge, commission, call on *or* upon; issue a writ *or* an injunction; **decree,** rule, ordain, promulgate; give an order *or* a direct order, issue a command, say the word, give the word *or* word of command; call the shots *or* tune *or* signals *or* play <nonformal>; order about *or* around; put in *or* place an order, order up
5 **arrange,** reduce to order, **put** *or* **get** *or* **set in order,** right, prioritize, put first things first, get one's ducks in a row <nonformal>; **put** *or* **set to rights,** get it together <nonformal>, **pull it together,** put in *or* into shape, whip into shape <nonformal>, sort out <chiefly Brit>, unsnarl, make sense out of <nonformal>

**orderly** ADJS ordered, **regular,** well-regulated, well-ordered, methodical, formal, regular as clockwork, uniform, **systematic,** symmetrical, **harmonious;** businesslike, routine, steady, normal, habitual, usual, en règle, in hand; **arranged**

**ordinance** NOUNS **law;** imperative, **regulation,** *règlement* <Fr>; **decree,** decretum, decretal, rescript, fiat, **edict,** *edictum* <L>; *ordonnance* <Fr>; **proclamation,** pronouncement, pronunciamento, **declaration,** ukase; bull, diktat

**ordinary** ADJS **average,** normal, **common, commonplace,** garden *and* garden-variety <both nonformal>, run-of-the-mill; **unexceptional,** unremarkable, unnoteworthy, unspectacular, nothing *or* nobody special *and* no great shakes <all nonformal>; conventional

**ordnance** NOUNS **arms, weapons,** deadly weapons, instruments of destruction, offensive weapons, **military hardware,** matériel, **weaponry,** armament, munitions, munitions of war, *apparatus belli* <L>; **artillery, cannon,** cannonry, engines of war

**organic** ADJS **anatomic,** anatomical,

organismal; organized; **animate, living,** vital, zoetic; **biological,** biotic; physiological; **constitutional,** bodily, physical, temperamental; connate, connatal, coeval; **instinctive,** instinctual, atavistic, primal

**organism** NOUNS organization, organic being, life-form, form of life, **living being** *or* **thing,** being, creature, created being, **individual,** genetic individual, physiological individual, morphological individual; zoon, zooid; virus; aerobic organism, anaerobic organism; heterotrophic organism, autotrophic organism; microbe, microorganism

**organization** NOUNS 1 establishment, foundation, institution, institute; **composition,** constitution, construction, formation, fabrication, fashioning, shaping; **methodization,** ordering, planning, charting, codification, regulation, regularization, routinization, normalization, rationalization; **systematization,** ordination, coordination

**organize** VERBS methodize, **systematize,** rationalize, regularize, get *or* put one's house in order; **harmonize,** synchronize, **tune,** tune up; **regularize,** routinize, normalize, standardize; **regulate,** adjust, coordinate, fix, settle; **plan,** chart, codify; **establish, found,** constitute, institute, install, form, **set up,** equip, endow, inaugurate, realize, materialize, effect, effectuate; **unionize**

**organized** ADJS **arranged,** ordered, disposed, configured, composed, constituted, fixed, placed, aligned, ranged, arrayed, marshaled, grouped, ranked, **graded;** methodized, **regularized,** routinized, normalized, standardized, **systematized;** regulated, harmonized, synchronized; **classified**, categorized, **sorted,** assorted; **orderly**

**organized crime** NOUNS **the underworld,** gangland, gangdom, organized crime family, the rackets, the mob, the syndicate, the Mafia, Cosa Nostra

**organizer** NOUNS **planner, designer,** deviser, contriver, framer, projector; enterpriser, entrepreneuer; promoter, developer, expediter, facilitator, animator; **founder,** founding father, founding *or* founder member, founding partner, cofounder; union *or* labor organizer

**orgy** NOUNS **debauch,** saturnalia; **frenzy,** orgasm; madness, craze, **delirium,** hysteria

**orientation** NOUNS **habituation,** accustoming; conditioning, seasoning, training; **familiarization,** breaking-in <nonformal>; acclimation, acclimatization; adaption, adjustment, accommodation, adaptation; alignment, collimation; **bearings**

**origin** NOUNS origination, **genesis, inception,** incipience *or* incipiency, inchoation; **divine creation,** creationism, creation science; **birth,** birthing, bearing, parturition, pregnancy, nascency *or* nascence, nativity; **source,** origination, **derivation,** rise, beginning, conception, commencement

**original** ADJS **novel,** unprecedented; unique, *sui generis* <L>; new, fresh; underived, **firsthand; authentic,** genuine, veridic, veridical; imaginative, creative; **avant-garde,** revolutionary; **pioneer,** bellwether, trail-blazing

**originate** VERBS **invent, conceive,** discover, make up, devise, contrive, concoct, fabricate, coin, mint, frame, hatch, hatch *or* cook up, strike out; think up, think out, dream up, **design,** plan, set one's wits to work; **generate, develop,** mature, **evolve;** engender, beget, spawn, hatch, bring forth, give rise to, bring *or* call into being; procreate

**ornament** NOUNS 1 ornamentation, **adornment,** embellishment, elegant variation, **embroidery, frill,** colors *or* colors of rhetoric <both old>, figure, figure of speech; musical flourish, ruffles and flourishes, grace note
VERBS 2 **decorate,** adorn, dress, trim, garnish, array, **deck,** bedeck, bedizen; **redecorate,** refurbish, redo; gimmick *or* glitz *or* sex up <nonformal>; **embellish, furbish,** embroider, enrich, grace, set off *or* out, paint, color, blazon, emblazon, paint in glowing colors; **gild,** gild the lily, trick out, varnish; **dress up; spruce up** *and* gussy up *and* doll up *and* fix up <all nonformal>, **primp up,** prink up, prank up, trick up *or* out, deck out; smarten, smarten up, dandify, titivate

**ornamental** ADJS **decorative,** adorning, embellishing

**ornate** ADJS **elegant, fancy,** fine, chichi, pretty-pretty; picturesque; **elaborate,** overornate, labored; **ostentatious**; **rich,** luxurious, luxuriant; **flowery,** florid; flamboyant, fussy, frilly, frilled, befrilled, flouncy, gingerbread *or* gingerbready; **overelegant,** overelaborate, overlabored, overworked, overwrought, overornamented, busy; cluttered; **baroque,** rococo, arabesque, moresque; purple, colored, adorned, **embellished, embroidered,** lavish, festooned

**ornery** ADJS **perverse,** contrary, wrong-headed, wayward, froward, difficult, cross-grained, cantankerous, feisty; sullen, sulky, stuffy; irascible

**orphan** NOUNS abandonee, waif, dogie <nonformal>; foundling; wastrel, reject, **discard**

**orthodox** ADJS of the faith, of the true faith; **sound,** firm, faithful, true, true-blue, right-thinking; **evangelical; scriptural,** canonical; traditional, traditionalistic; literal, textual; standard, customary, conventional; **authoritative,** authentic, accepted, received, approved; correct, right, proper

**oscillate** VERBS **vibrate,** librate, nutate; pendulate; **fluctuate,** vacillate, waver, wave; resonate; **swing,** sway, swag, dangle, **reel,** rock, lurch, roll, careen, toss, pitch; **wag,** waggle; **wobble,** wamble; shake, flutter

**ostentatious** ADJS **pretentious; ambitious,** vaunting, lofty, highfalutin *and* highfaluting <both nonformal>, **high-flown,** high-flying; **high-toned,** tony <both nonformal>, **fancy,** classy <nonformal>, flossy <nonformal>, gaudy, glitzy <nonformal>, meretricious, flamboyant, flaming, bedizened, flaunting, garish

**ostracize** VERBS turn thumbs down; **reject,** exile, banish; **proscribe,** ban, outlaw, put under the ban; **boycott,** blackball, blacklist, snub, cut, give the cold shoulder, send to Coventry, give the silent treatment; **excommunicate**

**other** ADJS **another,** whole nother <nonformal>, else, otherwise, other than *or* from; not the same, not the type <nonformal>, not that sort, of another sort, of a sort *and* of sorts <both nonformal>; **fresh,** additional, further; **substitute,** alternate, alternative, tother <nonformal>, equivalent, token, dummy, pinch, utility, backup, secondary

**otherwise** ADVS in other ways, **in other respects;** elsewise, else, or else; than; other than; **on the other hand;** contrarily; alias

**otherworldly** ADJS **heavenly;** extraterrestrial, extramundane, transmundane, transcendental; Elysian, Olympian; **unearthly,** unworldly, eerie; fey; starry-eyed, dewy-eyed; in the clouds, with one's head in the clouds; airy; supernatural; **occult**

**oust** VERBS **eject,** expel, discharge, extrude, obtrude, detrude, exclude, **reject,** cast, remove; **bounce** *and* give the hook <both nonformal>, **put out, turn out,** thrust out; **throw out,** run out <nonformal>, cast out, chuck out, **evict,** dislodge, dispossess, put out, turn out, **turn out of doors,** turn out of house and home, turn *or* put out bag and baggage, throw into the street; unhouse, unkennel

**out** NOUNS 1 **excuse,** cop-out *and* alibi <both nonformal>; lame excuse, poor excuse, likely story; escape hatch, way out

ADJS 2 **asleep,** sleeping, **sound asleep,** fast asleep, in a sound sleep, flaked-out <nonformal>; **unconscious,** oblivious, out like a light, out cold; comatose; **dead to the world;** drugged, narcotized; doped *and* stoned *and* spaced out *and* strung out *and* zonked *and* zonked out *and* out of it <all nonformal>; **dead-drunk,** blind drunk, overcome, passed out <nonformal>, under the table

3 **extinguished,** quenched, snuffed; contained, under control

ADVS 4 outward, outwards, outwardly; **without,** outside

5 **at a loss, unprofitably,** to the bad <nonformal>; in the red <nonformal>; out-of-pocket

**outback** NOUNS **hinterland,** back country, up-country, boonies *and* boondocks <both nonformal>; **the bush,** bush country, bushveld, **woods,** woodlands, **backwoods,** forests, timbers, the big sticks <nonformal>, brush; wilderness, wilds, uninhabited region, virgin land *or* territory; **wasteland**; **frontier,** borderland, outpost

**outburst** NOUNS outburst of anger, burst, **explosion,** eruption, blowup *and* **flare-up** <both nonformal>, access, blaze of temper; **storm, scene,** high words

**outcast** NOUNS social outcast, outcast of society, **castaway, derelict,** Ishmael; **pariah,** untouchable, leper; outcaste; *déclassé* <Fr>; **outlaw; expellee,** evictee; displaced person *or* DP; exile, expatriate, man without a country; undesirable; *persona non grata* <L>, unacceptable person

**outcome** NOUNS **event, eventuality,** eventuation, effect, issue, result, denouement, end, end result, aftermath, **upshot,** logical outcome, possible outcome, scenario; consequence; **realization,** materialization, coming to be *or* pass, incidence

**outcry** NOUNS **vociferation,** clamor; hullabaloo, hubbub, brouhaha, uproar; **hue and cry**

**outdated** ADJS **old-fashioned,** old-fangled, old-timey <nonformal>, **dated,** out, out-of-date, **outmoded,** obsolete, out of style *or* fashion, out of use, disused, out of season, **unfashionable,** styleless, **behind the times,** of the old school, old hat *and* back-number *and* has-been <all nonformal>; superannuated, superannuate

**outdo** VERBS **outrival,** outvie, outachieve, edge out, **outclass, outshine,** overmatch, outgun <nonformal>; **outstrip,** outgo, outrange, outreach, outpoint, **outperform;** outplay, outmaneuver, outwit; outrun, outstep, outpace, outmarch, run rings *or* circles around <nonformal>; outride, outjump, outleap, outgeneral, outpoint, outsail, outfight

**outdoor** ADJS **out-of-door,** out-of-doors, **outside,** without-doors; open-air, alfresco; out and about

**outdoors** NOUNS outside, **the out-of-doors,** the great out-of-doors, the open, **the open air;** outland

**outfit** NOUNS 1 **costume,** costumery, character dress; getup *and* rig <both nonformal>; masquerade, disguise; **apparatus,** rig, machinery; paraphernalia, things, **gear, stuff** <nonformal>, impedimenta <pl>, **tackle; kit,** duffel, effects, personal effects
VERBS 2 **equip, furnish,** gear, prepare, fit, fit up *or* out, fix up <nonformal>, **rig,** rig up *or* out, **turn out,** appoint, accouter, clothe, dress

**outgoing** ADJS **unreserved,** unreticent, unshrinking, **unrestrained,** unconstrained, unhampered, unrestricted; demonstrative, expansive, effusive; **accessible, approachable,** conversable, easy to speak to; **extroverted**

**outgrowth** NOUNS **effect, result,** resultant, **consequence,** consequent, sequent, sequence, sequel, sequela, sequelae; event, eventuality, eventuation, **upshot, outcome,** logical outcome, possible outcome, scenario; **spin-off,** offshoot, offspring, issue, aftermath, legacy; derivative, derivation, by-product

**outhouse** NOUNS **latrine,** convenience, **toilet, john** *and* johnny *and* **can** *and* crapper <all nonformal>; loo <Brit nonformal>; privy, backhouse, shithouse <nonformal>

**outing** NOUNS 1 **excursion,** jaunt, junket, pleasure trip; day-trip
2 **disclosure,** disclosing; **revelation,** revealment, revealing, making public, publicizing, broadcasting

**outlandish** ADJS **strange,** off-the-wall <informal>, surreal, not for real <nonformal>, passing strange; **fantastic, fantastical,** fantasque, extravagant, preposterous, wild, baroque, rococo, florid; Alice-in-Wonderland, bizarre, grotesque

**outlast** VERBS **outstay,** last out, outwear, **outlive,** survive; **outtalk,** outspeak, **talk down,** filibuster

**outlaw** NOUNS 1 **criminal,** felon, **crook** <nonformal>, lawbreaker, perpetrator, perp <nonformal>, gangster *and* mobster <both nonformal>, racketeer, thief
VERBS 2 **prohibit, forbid; disallow,** rule out *or* against; **bar,** debar, preclude, exclude, exclude from, shut out, shut *or* close the door on, **prevent**; **ban, proscribe,** inhibit, interdict, put *or* lay under an interdict *or* interdiction

**outlay** NOUNS **spendings,** disbursements, payments, outgoings, outgo, outflow, money going out

**outlet** NOUNS egress, **exit,** outgo, outcome, out <nonformal>, way out; loophole, escape; **opening**; outfall, estuary; chute, flume, sluice, weir, floodgate; **vent,** ventage, venthole, port; **exhaust;** door

**outline** NOUNS 1 **contour,** delineation, lines, lineaments, shapes, figure, figuration, **configuration,** gestalt; **features,** main features; **profile,** silhouette
2 **plan,** scheme, schema, chart, flow chart, graph; table of contents
VERBS 3 contour; **delineate;** silhouette, profile, limn; **sketch,** sketch out, hit the high spots; capsule, capsulize, encapsulate; **put in a nutshell**

**outlook** NOUNS mental outlook; *Anschauung* <Ger>, **point of view,** viewpoint, standpoint, **perspective,** *optique* <Fr>; position, stand, place, situation; side; footing, basis; where one is *or* sits *or* stands; **view,** sight, light, eye; respect, regard; **frame of reference,** intellectual *or* ideational frame of reference, framework, arena, world, universe, world *or* universe of discourse, system, reference system

**out of order** ADJS **in disrepair, malfunctioning,** out of working order, out of condition, out of repair, inoperative; **out of kilter** *or* **kelter** <nonformal>, out of whack <nonformal>, out of gear, on the fritz <nonformal>, on the blink *and* haywire <both nonformal>

**out-of-pocket** ADJS **at a loss,** unprofitably, to the bad <nonformal>; in the red <nonformal>; out, short, **short of money** *or* **funds** *or* **cash**

**out of shape** ADJS **out of practice,** out of training *or* form, soft <nonformal>, out of condition, stiff, **rusty;** gone *or* run to seed *and* over the hill *and* not what one used to be <all nonformal>, losing one's touch, slipping, on the downgrade

**out-of-the-way** ADJS godforsaken, back of beyond, upcountry; **out of reach,** inaccessible, remote, ungetatable, unapproachable, untouchable, hyperborean, antipodean; **unfrequented,** unvisited, off the beaten track; untraveled

**outpouring** NOUNS **overflow,** flood, inundation, flow, shower, spate, stream, gush, avalanche; **prevalence,** profuseness, **profusion,** riot; **superabundance;** an ample sufficiency, enough and to spare, enough and then some

**output** NOUNS **yield,** make, production; **proceeds,** produce, product; **crop, harvest,** fruit, vintage, bearing; second crop, aftermath; bumper crop

**outrage** NOUNS 1 **injustice,** wrong, injury, grievance, disservice; raw *or* rotten deal *and* bad rap <all nonformal>; imposition; mockery *or* miscarriage of justice; great wrong, grave *or* gross injustice; atrocity, enormity
VERBS 2 **offend, affront,** give offense to, disoblige, step *or* tread on one's toes; dishonor, humiliate, treat with indignity; flout, mock, jeer at, scoff at, fleer at, gibe at, taunt; **insult,** call names, kick *or* slap in the face, take *or* pluck by the beard; **add insult to injury**

**outrageous** ADJS **disgraceful, shameful,** pitiful, deplorable, opprobrious, sad, sorry, too bad; degrading, debasing, demeaning, beneath one, beneath one's dignity, *infra indignitatem* <L>, infra dig <nonformal>, unbecoming, unworthy of one; cheap, gutter; **humiliating,** humiliative; **scandalous,** shocking, incredible, beyond belief, *outré* <Fr>

**outset** NOUNS **beginning,** commencement, start, running *or* flying start, starting point, square one <nonformal>, outbreak, **onset,** oncoming

**outside** NOUNS 1 **exterior,** external, surface
2 **outdoors,** the out-of-doors, the great out-of-doors, the open, **the open air**
ADJS 3 **exterior,** external; extrinsic; **outer,** out, outward, outward-facing, outlying, outstanding; **outermost,** outmost; surface, superficial, epidermic, cortical; cosmetic, merely cosmetic
4 **outdoor,** out-of-door, out-of-doors, without-doors; open-air, alfresco; out and about
ADVS 5 **outdoors,** out of doors, abroad; in the open, **in the open air,** alfresco, *en plein air* <Fr>

**outsider** NOUNS **alien, stranger,** foreigner, non-member, not one of us, not our sort, not the right sort, the other, outlander, *Uitlander* <Afrikaans>, tramontane, ultramontane, barbarian, foreign devil <China>, *gringo* <Sp Amer>

**outsmart** VERBS **outwit, outfox,** outguess, outfigure, **outmaneuver,** outgeneral, outflank, outplay; get the better *or* best of, go one better; pull a fast one <nonformal>, steal a march on; make a fool of, make a sucker *or* patsy of <nonformal>; be too much for, throw a curve <nonformal>

**outspoken** ADJS **communicative, open,** free, free-speaking, free-spoken, free-tongued; candid, frank; direct, bluff, blunt

**outstanding** ADJS 1 **eminent, prominent,** standout, high, elevated, towering, soaring, overtopping, exalted, **lofty,** sublime; august, majestic, noble, distinguished; **magnificent,** magnanimous, heroic, godlike, superb; famous, renowned, lauded, glorious
2 **remaining, surviving,** extant, vestigial, over, left, **leftover,** still around, remnant, remanent, odd; **spare,** to spare; unused, unconsumed; **surplus,** superfluous; unmet, unresolved

**outward** ADJS 1 **exterior,** external; **outer,** outside, out, outward-facing, outlying, outstanding; **outermost,** outmost; surface, superficial; apparent, seeming; open, public
ADVS 2 **forth; out,** outwards, outwardly

**outwit** VERBS **outfox, outsmart,** outguess, outfigure, **outmaneuver,** outgeneral, outflank, outplay; get the better *or* best of; get round *or* around, **evade,** stonewall <nonformal>, **elude, frustrate, foil,** give the slip *or* runaround <nonformal>; pull a fast one <nonformal>, steal a march on; be too much for, be too deep for; throw a curve <nonformal>

**oval** ADJS ovate, ovoid, oviform, egg-shaped, obovate

**ovation** NOUNS **applause,** plaudit, éclat, **acclaim, acclamation;** popularity; clap, handclap, **clapping,** handclapping, clapping of hands; **cheer**; burst of applause, peal *or* thunder of applause; **round of applause,** hand, big hand; standing ovation

**oven** NOUNS **kiln,** stove, furnace

**over** ADJS 1 **higher,** superior, greater; **above;** upper, upmost *or* uppermost, outtopping, overtopping
2 **past, gone,** by, gone-by, bygone, gone glimmering, bypast, ago, departed, passed, passed away, elapsed, lapsed, vanished, faded, no more, irrecoverable, never to return, not coming back; over and above; extra, spare, supernumerary
ADVS 3 **again,** over again, **once more,** *encore, bis* <both Fr>, two times, twice over, ditto; **anew,** *de novo* <L>, afresh; from the beginning, *da capo* <Ital>
4 **excessively,** inordinately, immoderately, intemperately, overweeningly, hubristically, **overly,** overmuch, too much; **too,** too-too <nonformal>; **exorbitantly,** unduly, unreasonably, unconscionably, outrageously

**overact** VERBS overdramatize, chew up the scenery <nonformal>, act all over the stage; **ham** *and* ham it up <both nonformal>; **mug** <nonformal>, grimace; spout, rant, roar, declaim; milk a scene

**overactive** ADJS hyperactive, hyper <nonformal>; hectic, frenzied, frantic, frenetic; hyperkinetic; intrusive, officious

**overall** ADVS **throughout,** all over, inside and out, through and through; **at full length,** *in extenso* <L>, *ad infinitum* <L>; every inch, every whit, every bit; **in every respect,** in all respects, you name it <nonformal>; **on all counts,** at all points, for good and all

**overbearing** ADJS **arrogant, superior,** domineering, proud, haughty; lofty, toplofty <nonformal>; high-nosed *and* stuck-up *and* uppish *and* uppity *and* upstage <all nonformal>; **hoity-toity,** big, big as you please, six feet above contradiction; **condescending,** patronizing, *de haut en bas* <Fr>

**overcast** ADJS **cloudy,** nebulous, nubilous, nimbose, nebulosus; **clouded,** overclouded; dirty, heavy, lowering *or* louring; dark; **gloomy,** glooming, dark and gloomy, Acheronian, Acherontic, **somber,** sombrous

**overcharge** NOUNS 1 surcharge, overassessment; gouging *or* price-gouging, highway robbery <nonformal>
VERBS 2 **overprice,** set the price tag too high; surcharge, overtax; **hold up** *and* **soak** *and* **stick** *and* **sting** *and* **clip** <all nonformal>, make pay through the nose, gouge; victimize, swindle; exploit, skin <nonformal>, **fleece,** screw *and* put the screws to <both nonformal>, bleed, bleed white; profiteer

**overcoat** NOUNS **outerwear; coat,** greatcoat, **topcoat,** surcoat

**overcome** VERBS 1 **unnerve,** undo, unstring, unbrace, reduce to jelly, **demoralize,** shake, upset, psych out <nonformal>, dash, knock down *or* flat, **crush,** prostrate
2 surmount; **overpower, overmaster,** overmatch; **overthrow, overturn,** overset; put the skids to <nonformal>; **upset,** trip, trip up, lay by the heels, send flying *or* sprawling; silence, floor, deck, make bite the dust; overcome oneself, master oneself; kick the habit <nonformal>
ADJS 3 crushed, borne-down, overwhelmed, inundated, **stricken,** cut up <nonformal>, **desolated,** prostrate *or* prostrated, broken-down, undone; **heart-stricken,** heart-struck; **broken-hearted,** heartbroken

**overcrowded** ADJS **teeming, swarming,** crowding, thronging, overflowing, overwhelming, bursting, **crawling, alive with,** lousy with <nonformal>, populous, prolific, proliferating, crowded, packed, jammed, bumper-to-bumper <nonformal>, jam-packed, like sardines in a can <nonformal>, thronged, studded, bristling, rife, lavish, prodigal, superabundant, **profuse,** in profusion, thick, **thick with,** thick-coming, thick as flies

**overdo** VERBS **go too far,** do it to death <nonformal>, pass all bounds, know no bounds, overact, **carry too far,** overcarry, go to an extreme, **go to extremes,** go overboard, go *or* jump off the deep end; **run** *or* **drive into the ground; overemphasize,** overstress; overplay, overplay one's hand <nonformal>; **overreact,** protest too much; overreach oneself; **overtax,** overtask, overexert, overexercise, overstrain, overdrive, overspend, exhaust, overexpend, overuse; burn the candle at both ends; **spread oneself too thin,** take on too much, have too much on one's plate, have too many irons in the fire; exaggerate; **overindulge**

**overdue** ADJS **late,** belated, tardy, slow, slow on the draw *or* uptake *or* trigger <all nonformal>, **behindhand,** never on time, backward, back, **long-awaited,** untimely; unpunctual, unready; latish; **delayed,** detained, **held up** <nonformal>, retarded, arrested, blocked, hung up *and* in a bind <both nonformal>, obstructed, stopped, jammed, congested; weather-bound

**overeat** VERBS overgorge, **overindulge,** make a pig *or* hog of oneself, pig out *or* pork out *or* scarf out <nonformal>; stuff oneself

**overflow** NOUNS 1 spillage, spill, spillover, overflowing, overrunning, alluvion, alluvium, **inundation, flood,** deluge, whelming, overwhelming, engulfment, submersion, cataclysm; **outpouring,** superabundance; enough and to spare, enough and then some
VERBS 2 flow over, wash over, **run over, well over,** brim over, lap, lap at, lap over, overbrim, overrun, pour out *or* over, **spill,** slop, slosh, spill out *or* over; **cataract,** cascade; inundate

**overgrown** ADJS 1 **gigantic,** mountainous, titanic, colossal, mammoth, Gargantuan, gigantesque, monster, monstrous, outsize, sizable, larger-than-life, king-size, monumental; hypertrophied
2 **luxuriant,** flourishing, **rank,** dense, impenetrable, thick, heavy, gross; jungly, jungled; overrun; **weedy,** unweeded, weed-choked, weed-ridden

**overhang** NOUNS 1 **overhanging,** impendence *or* impendency, **projection,** beetling, jutting; cantilever
VERBS 2 hang over, hang out, **impend,** impend over, **project,** project over, beetle, **jut,** beetle *or* jut *or* thrust over, stick out over; **overlie,** lie over
3 **be imminent,** loom, hang over one's head, hover

**overhaul** NOUNS 1 **repair,** repairing, **fixing,** mending, making *or* setting right, repair work; servicing, maintenance; overhauling
2 VERBS **repair,** mend, fix, fix up <nonformal>, do up, doctor <nonformal>, put in repair, put in shape, set to rights, put in order *or* condition; **recondition,** put in commission, ready; **service**

**overhead** NOUNS 1 **expenses, costs,** charges, disbursals, liabilities; expense, cost, burden of expenditure; operating expense *or* expenses *or* costs *or* budget, general expenses
ADVS 2 **on high,** high up, high; **aloft,** aloof; **up,** upward, upwards, straight up, to the zenith; **above, over,** o'er

**overhear** VERBS **hear,** catch, get <nonformal>, take in; **hear of,** hear tell of <nonformal>; get an earful <nonformal>, get wind of

**overjoyed** ADJS overjoyful, overhappy, brimming *or* bursting with happiness, on top of the world; **rapturous,** raptured, **enraptured,** enchanted, entranced, enravished, ravished, rapt, possessed; sent *and* high *and* freaked-out <all nonformal>, **in raptures,** transported, in a transport of delight, **carried away,** beside oneself, beside oneself with joy, in seventh heaven, on cloud nine <nonformal>; **elated,** elate, exalted, jubilant, exultant, flushed

**overkill** NOUNS **overdoing,** overcarrying, **overreaching,** supererogation; piling on <nonformal>, overimportance, overemphasis; overuse; overreaction; too much on one's plate, too many irons in the fire, too much at once

**overlap** VERBS **overlie,** lie over; lap, **lap over,** override, imbricate, jut, shingle; **extend over,** span, bridge, bestride, bestraddle, arch over, overarch, hang over, overhang

**overlook** VERBS 1 **condone,** disregard, ignore, accept, take *and* swallow *and* let go <all nonformal>, pass over, give one another chance, let one off this time *and* let one off easy <both nonformal>, close *or* shut one's eyes to, **blink** *or* **wink at,** connive at; allow for, make allowances for; bear with, endure, regard with indulgence; pocket the affront, leave unavenged, turn the other cheek, bury *or* hide one's head in the sand

2 **slight, ignore,** pooh-pooh <nonformal>, make little of, dismiss, pretend not to see, disregard, neglect, miss, pass by, pass up *and* give the go-by <both nonformal>, leave out in the cold <nonformal>, take no note *or* notice of, look right through <nonformal>, pay no attention *or* regard to, refuse to acknowledge *or* recognize

**overpowering** ADJS **irresistible,** overcoming, overwhelming, overmastering, overmatching, avalanchine

**overpriced** ADJS grossly overpriced, **exorbitant,** excessive, extravagant, inordinate, immoderate, undue, unwarranted, unreasonable, fancy, unconscionable, outrageous, preposterous, out of bounds, out of sight <nonformal>, **prohibitive; extortionate,** cutthroat, gouging, usurious

**overrated** ADJS **overestimated,** puffed up, pumped up <nonformal>, overvalued, on the high side; **exaggerated**

**overreact** VERBS make a Federal case out of it <nonformal>, make something out of nothing, make a mountain out of a molehill, protest too much

**overriding** ADJS **paramount,** highest, uppermost, topmost, toprank, ranking, of the first rank, world-class, **dominant,** predominant, master, controlling, **overruling,** all-absorbing

**overrule** VERBS **repeal,** revoke, rescind, reverse, strike down, abrogate; suspend; **waive,** set aside; countermand, counterorder; **cancel,** write off; **annul,** nullify, disannul, withdraw, **invalidate,** void, vacate, make void, declare null and void; override

**overseas** ADVS **abroad,** in foreign parts; **oversea,** beyond seas, over the water, transmarine, across the sea; on one's travels

**oversee** VERBS **supervise,** superintend, boss, ride herd on <nonformal>, stand over, keep an eye on *or* upon, keep in order; straw-boss <nonformal>; take care of

**overshadow** VERBS **eclipse,** throw into the shade, top, extinguish, take the shine out of <nonformal>; put to shame, show up <nonformal>, put one's nose out of joint, put down <nonformal>, fake out <nonformal>; **command,** dominate, overarch, command a view of; bestride, bestraddle

**oversight** NOUNS 1 **neglect,** neglectfulness, **negligence,** inadvertence *or* inadvertency, malperformance, dereliction, *culpa* <L>, culpable negligence, criminal negligence; **remissness,** laxity, laxness, slackness, looseness, laches; unrigorousness; **inattention;** overlooking; **omission,** nonfeasance, nonperformance, lapse, failure, **default;** poor stewardship *or* guardianship *or* custody
2 **supervision,** superintendence, **surveillance,** eye; **charge,** care, auspices, jurisdiction; responsibility, accountability

**overspend** VERBS spend more than one has, spend what one hasn't got; overdraw, overdraw one's account, live beyond one's means, have champagne tastes on a beer budget

**overstep** VERBS **transgress, trespass,** intrude, break bounds, overstep the bounds, go too far, know no bounds, **encroach, infringe,** invade, irrupt, make an inroad *or* incursion *or* intrusion, advance upon; usurp

**overt** ADJS **open,** open to all, open as day, out of the closet <nonformal>; **revealed,** disclosed, exposed; bare, bald, naked

**overtake** VERBS **outstrip, overhaul,** catch up, **catch up with,** come up with *or* to, gain on *or* upon, pass, lap; outpace, outrun, outsail; leave behind, leave standing *or* looking *or* flatfooted

**overthrow** VERBS **overturn; upset,** overset, upend, **subvert,** throw down *or* over; undermine, honeycomb, **sap,** sap the foundations, **weaken**

**overtone** NOUNS **meaning, signification,** emotive *or* affective meaning, coloration, coloring, tinge, undertone, undercurrent, intimation, touch, nuance, innuendo; connotation, **implication, import,** latent *or* underlying *or* implied meaning, ironic suggestion *or* implication, more than meets the eye, what is read between the lines

**overture** NOUNS 1 **prelude,** *Vorspiel* <Ger>, **introduction,** operatic overture, dramatic overture, concert overture, voluntary, descant, vamp; curtain raiser
2 **offer, advance,** approach, invitation; hesitant *or* tentative *or* preliminary approach, feeling-out, **feeler** <nonformal>

**overview** NOUNS **abstract,** epitome, **précis,** capsule, nutshell *or* capsule version, capsulization, encapsulation, sketch, thumbnail sketch, **synopsis,** conspectus, syllabus, *aperçu* <Fr>, **survey,** review, pandect, bird's-eye view

**overweight** ADJS **corpulent, stout,** fat, fattish, **obese,** adipose, gross, fleshy, beefy, meaty, hefty, porky, porcine; **heavyset,** thickset, chubby, chunky <nonformal>, dumpy; pyknic, endomorphic, overheavy; overfleshed, overstout, overfat, overplump, overfed

**overwhelmed** ADJS 1 **overcome,** crushed, borne-down, inundated, **stricken,** cut up <nonformal>, **desolated,** prostrate *or* prostrated, broken-down, undone; **heart-stricken,** heart-struck; **brokenhearted,** heartbroken; **astonished,** amazed, surprised, astounded, flabbergasted <nonformal>, **bewildered,** puzzled, confounded, **dumbfounded,** dumbstruck, staggered, unable to believe one's senses *or* eyes
2 **defeated,** worsted, bested, outdone; beaten, discomfited, put to rout, **routed,** scattered, stampeded, panicked; confounded; **overcome,** overthrown, upset, overturned, overmatched, **overpowered,** whelmed, **overmastered,** overborne, overridden; **undone,** done for <nonformal>, **ruined,** kaput *and* on the skids <both nonformal>, *hors de combat* <Fr>

**overwhelming** ADJS **exciting,** overpowering, overcoming, overmastering, more than flesh and blood can bear; **astonishing,** amazing, surprising, startling, **astounding,** confounding, staggering, stunning <nonformal>, eye-opening, breathtaking, mind-boggling *or* -numbing; incontrovertible, irresistible, indisputable, irrefutable, sure, certain, absolute

**owe** VERBS **be indebted,** be obliged *or* obligated for, be financially committed, lie under an obligation, be bound to pay

**owing** ADJS **due,** owed, payable, receivable, redeemable, mature, **outstanding, unpaid,** in arrear *or* arrears, back

**own** VERBS **have title to,** have for one's own *or* very own, have to one's name, call one's own, have the deed for, hold in fee simple

**owner** NOUNS **proprietor,** proprietary; *rentier* <Fr>; titleholder, deedholder; proprietress, proprietrix; **master,** mistress, lord, laird <Scots>

**ownership** NOUNS **title,** possessorship, *dominium* <L>, **proprietorship,** proprietary, property right *or* rights; **dominion,** sovereignty; landownership, landowning, landholding, land tenure

**oxymoron** NOUNS self-contradiction, **paradox**, antinomy, ambivalence, **irony,** enantiosis, equivocation, **ambiguity**, absurdity, logical impossibility

# P

**pacifier** NOUNS **soother,** comforter, peacemaker, pacificator, dove of peace, mollifier; **moderator,** mitigator, modulator, stabilizer, temperer, assuager; **mediator,** bridge-builder, calming *or* restraining hand, wiser head; **alleviator,** alleviative, palliative, lenitive

**pacify** VERBS **conciliate,** placate, propitiate, appease, mollify, dulcify; **calm,** settle, soothe, tranquilize; smooth, smooth over *or* out, smooth one's feathers; allay, lay, lay the dust; pour oil on troubled waters, pour balm on, take the edge off of, take the sting out of; cool <nonformal>, defuse

**pack** VERBS 1 **bundle,** bundle up, **package,** parcel, parcel up, bag, sack, truss, truss up; bale; wrap, **wrap up,** do *or* tie *or* bind up; **box, case,** encase, crate, embox; containerize; encapsulate
2 **gather together,** draw *or* lump *or* batch *or* bunch together, pack in, cram, cram in; **fill,** charge, load, lade, freight, weight; **stuff,** wad, pad, jam, jam-pack, ram in, chock; **fill up,** fill to the brim, brim, top up *or* top off, fill to overflowing, fill the measure of

**package** NOUNS **bundle,** bindle <nonformal>, pack, packet, deck, budget, **parcel,** fardel <nonformal>, sack, bag, poke <nonformal>, ragbag <nonformal>, bale, truss, **roll,** rouleau, bolt

**packed** ADJS **crowded,** crammed; bumper-to-bumper <nonformal>, jam-packed, packed *or* crammed like sardines <nonformal>; **compact,** firm, solid, dense, close, serried; **teeming,** swarming, crawling, bristling, populous, **full**

**pact** NOUNS **compact,** contract, legal contract, valid contract, **covenant,** convention, transaction, accord, **agreement,** mutual agreement, agreement between *or* among parties, signed *or* written agreement, formal agreement, legal agreement, undertaking, stipulation; **understanding,** arrangement, bargain, dicker *and* deal <both nonformal>; bond, binding agreement, ironclad agreement, covenant of salt; gentleman's *or* gentlemen's agreement

**pad** NOUNS 1 **quarters,** living quarters; lodgings, lodging, lodgment; diggings *and* digs <both Brit nonformal>, crib <nonformal>, room; **rooms,** berth, roost, accommodations; **housing,** shelter; **scratch pad**
VERBS 2 **alleviate,** mitigate, palliate, soften, cushion, assuage, allay, defuse, lay, appease, mollify, subdue, soothe
3 **protract,** extend, spin out, string out, draw out, stretch out, go on *or* be on about, **drag out,** run out, drive into the ground <nonformal>; fill out, **tautologize,** battologize

**paddy wagon** NOUNS **police van,** patrol wagon; wagon *and* Black Maria <both nonformal>

**padlock** NOUNS 1 **lock,** bolt, bar, catch, safety catch
VERBS 2 **fasten,** secure; **lock,** lock up, lock out, key, latch, bolt, bar

**paean** NOUNS laud; hosanna, hallelujah, alleluia; **hymn,** hymn of praise, **doxology,** psalm, anthem, motet, canticle, chorale; **chant,** versicle; antiphon, antiphony; offertory, offertory sentence *or* hymn

**pagan** NOUNS 1 **heathen;** allotheist; animist; idolater, idolist; **unbeliever,** disbeliever, nonbeliever; **atheist,** infidel; nullifidian, minimifidian
ADJS 2 **paganish,** paganistic; **heathen,** heathenish; pagano-Christian; allotheistic; animist, animistic; idolatrous; **unbelieving,** disbelieving, faithless; infidel, infidelic; **atheistic,** atheist; nullifidian, minimifidian

**page** NOUNS 1 **attendant,** usher, squire; errand boy *or* girl, gofer <nonformal>, office boy *or* girl, copyboy; footboy
2 **paper,** sheet, leaf
VERBS 3 **summon,** call; call for, send for *or* after, bid come

**pageant** NOUNS **display,** show, demonstration, manifestation, **exhibition,** parade, *étalage* <Fr>; **pageantry,** spectacle; vaunt, fanfaronade, blazon, flourish, flaunt, flaunting

**paid** ADJS **paid-up,** discharged, settled, liquidated, acquitted <old>, paid in full, receipted, remitted; prepaid, postpaid

**pain** NOUNS 1 **suffering,** hurt, hurting, misery <nonformal>, **distress,** *Schmerz* <Ger>, dolor <old>; **discomfort,** malaise; aches and pains
2 **grief,** stress, stress of life, passion
VERBS 3 give *or* inflict pain, **hurt,**

wound, afflict, distress; burn; sting; nip, bite, tweak, pinch; pierce, prick, stab, cut, lacerate; **irritate,** chafe, gall, fret, rasp, rub, grate; **torture,** torment, rack, put to torture, put *or* lay on the rack, **agonize,** harrow, crucify, martyr, martyrize, excruciate, wring, twist, contorse, convulse; wrench, tear, rend
4 **dismay,** grieve, mourn, lament, sorrow; discomfort, get in one's hair, try one's patience, give one a hard time *or* a pain *or* a pain in the neck *or* ass *or* butt <nonformal>

**painful** ADJS hurtful, **hurting,** distressing, afflictive; **acute,** sharp, piercing, stabbing, shooting, stinging, biting, gnawing; **poignant,** pungent, **severe,** cruel, harsh, grave, hard; griping, cramping, spasmic, spasmatic, spasmodic, paroxysmal; **agonizing,** excruciating, exquisite, atrocious, torturous, tormenting, martyrizing, racking, **harrowing**

**pain killer** NOUNS **anesthetic,** general anesthetic, local anesthetic, analgesic, anodyne, balm, ointment, pain-reliever, antiodontalgic, soothing syrup; tranquilizer, **sedative,** drug, dope <nonformal>, narcotic, opiate

**painless** ADJS **easy,** facile, effortless, smooth; plain, uncomplicated, straightforward, **simple**, Mickey Mouse <nonformal>, simple as ABC <nonformal>, easy as pie *and* easy as falling off a log <both nonformal>, downhill all the way, like shooting fish in a barrel, like taking candy from a baby; nothing to it

**painstaking** ADJS **diligent,** assiduous, sedulous, **thorough,** thoroughgoing, operose, industrious, elaborate

**paint** VERBS 1 **color,** hue, lay on color; apply paint, paint up, **coat,** cover, face; dab, **daub,** dedaub, smear, besmear, brush on paint, slap *or* slop on paint; **embellish, furbish,** embroider, enrich, grace, set off *or* out, blazon, emblazon, paint in glowing colors
2 **portray,** picture, render, **depict,** represent, delineate, limn; evoke, bring to life, make one see

**pair** NOUNS **set,** matching pair *or* set, his and hers <nonformal>, twins, lookalikes, two of a kind, birds of a feather, peas in a pod; **two,** twain <old>; **couple,** twosome, set of two, duo, duet, brace, team, span, yoke, double harness; match, matchup, mates

**pal** NOUNS

> <nonformal terms> **buddy,** bud, buddy-boy, bosom buddy, asshole buddy, main man, home boy, goombah, landsman, paesan, paesano, pally, palsy-walsy, road dog, walkboy, cobber <Austral>, pardner, pard, sidekick, tillicum, **chum,** ace, mate *and* butty <both Brit>

**palatable** ADJS **tasty,** good, fit to eat *and* finger-lickin' good <both nonformal>, good-tasting, **savory,** savorous, **toothsome,** gusty <Scots>, sapid, **good,** good to eat, nice, agreeable, likable, pleasing, to one's taste, **delicious,** delightful, delectable, exquisite; fit for a king, gourmet, fit for a gourmet, of gourmet quality; scrumptious *and* yummy <both nonformal>

**palatial** ADJS **imposing,** impressive, larger-than-life, awe-inspiring, awesome; **noble,** proud, stately, majestic, princely; **sumptuous,** elegant, elaborate, luxurious, extravagant, deluxe; executive *and* plush *and* posh *and* ritzy *and* swank *and* swanky <all nonformal>, Babylonian

**pale** VERBS 1 **lose color,** fade, fade out; **bleach,** bleach out; **turn pale,** grow pale, change color, turn white, whiten, blanch, wan
ADJS 2 **colorless,** faded, washed-out, dimmed, discolored, etiolated; **dim,** weak, faint; pallid, wan, sallow, fallow; pale *or* blue *or* green around the gills; **white,** white as a sheet; **pasty,** mealy, waxen; deathly pale, lurid, haggard; **cadaverous**

**pall** NOUNS 1 **veil of secrecy,** veil, curtain, wraps; wall *or* barrier of secrecy; **suppression,** repression, stifling, smothering
VERBS 2 **be tedious,** drag on, go on forever; have a certain sameness, be infinitely repetitive; **weary,** tire, irk, wear, wear on *or* upon, **make one tired,** fatigue, weary *or* tire to death, jade; give one a swift pain in the ass *and* give one a bellyful *and* make one fed-up <all nonformal>, **satiate,** glut

**palliative** NOUNS **alleviative,** alleviatory, lenitive, assuasive, assuager; soothing, abirritant, extenuative, saving grace; **alleviator,** pacifier, soother, comforter, peacemaker, pacificator, dove of peace, mollifier; **drug,** anodyne, dolorifuge, soothing syrup, **tranquilizer,** calmative; **sedative**; balm, salve; cushion, shock absorber

**pallor** NOUNS **paleness,** dimness, weakness, **faintness,** fadedness; pallidity, pallidness, prison pallor, **wanness, sallowness,** pastiness, ashiness; wheyface; grayness, griseousness; **haggardness,** lividness, sickly hue, sickliness, deadly *or* deathly pallor, deathly hue, cadaverousness

**palpable** ADJS **manifest,** apparent, evident, self-evident, axiomatic, indisputable, **obvious,** plain, clear, perspicuous, distinct, patent, tangible, sensible, appreciable, ponderable

**palpitation** NOUNS **trepidation,** trepidity, perturbation, fear and trembling; **uneasiness,** disquiet, disquietude, inquietude; nervousness; heartquake; flutter, **arrhythmia,** throb, pitter-patter, pit-a-pat; fibrillation, ventricular fibrillation, tachycardia, ventricular tachycardia <all medicine>

**palsy** NOUNS **paralysis,** impairment of motor function; shaking, quaking, **quivering,** quavering, shivering, trembling, tremulousness, **shuddering,** vibration; jactation, jactitation; the shakes *and* the shivers *and* the cold shivers <all nonformal>, ague, chattering

**paltry** ADJS **poor,** common, mean, sorry, sad, pitiful, pitiable, pathetic, **despicable,** contemptible, beneath contempt, **miserable, wretched,** beggarly, vile, **shabby,** scrubby, scruffy, shoddy, scurvy, scuzzy <nonformal>, scummy, crummy *and* cheesy <both nonformal>, **trashy,** rubbishy, gimcracky <nonformal>; **cheap,** worthless, valueless; tawdry, meretricious, gaudy

**pamper** VERBS **indulge,** humor, oblige; favor, please, gratify, satisfy, **cater to; give way to,** yield to, let one have his own way; cosset, **coddle,** mollycoddle, pet, make a lap dog of, **spoil;** spare the rod

**pamphlet** NOUNS **booklet,** brochure, chapbook, leaflet, folder, tract; circular

**pan** VERBS 1 **criticize; knock** *and* **slam** *and* hit *and* rap *and* take a rap *or* swipe at <all nonformal>, snipe at, strike out at, tie into *and* tee off on *and* rip into *and* open up on *and* plow into <all nonformal>
2 **mine;** pan for gold; prospect

**panacea** NOUNS **cure-all,** universal remedy, theriac, catholicon; polychrest, broad-spectrum drug *or* antibiotic; elixir, elixir of life, *elixir vitae* <L>

**pancake** NOUNS griddlecake, **hot cake,** battercake, flapcake, **flapjack,** flannel cake; buckwheat cake; chapatty <India>; blintz, cheese blintz, *crêpe, crêpe suzette* <both Fr>, *palacsinta* <Hung>, *Pfannkuchen* <Ger>, Swedish pancake

**pandemonium** NOUNS **turbulence,** turmoil, chaos, upset, **fury, furor,** *furore* <Ital>, **rage,** frenzy, passion, fanaticism, zealousness, zeal, tempestuousness, storminess, wildness, tumultuousness, **tumult,** uproar, racket, cacophony, hubbub, **commotion,** disturbance, agitation, bluster, broil, brawl, embroilment, brouhaha, fuss, flap <nonformal>, **row, rumpus,** ruckus <nonformal>, foofaraw <nonformal>, **ferment,** bedlam, hell *or* bedlam let loose; charivari, shivaree <nonformal>

**pander to** VERBS **toady to,** truckle to, cater to; **wait on** *or* **upon,** wait on hand and foot, dance attendance, do service, fetch and carry, do the dirty work of, do *or* jump at the bidding of

**Pandora's box** NOUNS **trouble,** peck of troubles; hornet's nest, can of worms <nonformal>; **evil**

**panel** NOUNS 1 **forum,** conference, discussion group, panel discussion, open discussion, buzz session <nonformal>, **round table;** open forum, colloquium, seminar, symposium; **powwow** <nonformal>
2 **jury,** jury of one's peers, sessions <Scots>, country, twelve men in a box; inquest; jury panel, jury list, venire facias

**pang** NOUNS **compunction,** qualm, qualms, qualmishness, scruples, scrupulosity, scrupulousness, pangs, **pangs of conscience,** throes, sting *or* pricking *or* twinge *or* twitch of conscience, touch of conscience, **voice of conscience,** pricking of heart, better self

**panhandle** VERBS beg, **scrounge,** cadge; mooch *and* bum <both nonformal>; **hit** *and* hit up *and* **touch** *and* put the touch on *and* make a touch <all nonformal>; pass the hat <nonformal>

**panhandler** NOUNS **beggar,** mendicant, scrounger, cadger; bum *and* bummer *and* **moocher** <all nonformal>; hobo, tramp; loafer

**panic** NOUNS 1 **fear, fright,** affright; **scare,** alarm, consternation, dismay; dread, unholy dread, **awe; terror,** horror, horrification, mortal *or* abject fear; panic fear *or* terror; stampede; **cowardice**
VERBS 2 **put in fear,** put the fear of God into, **throw a scare into** <nonformal>; stampede, send scuttling, throw blind fear into

**panicky** ADJS panic-prone, panicked, in a panic, panic-stricken, panic-struck, terror-stricken, out of one's mind with fear, prey to blind fear

**panoramic** ADJS **comprehensive,** sweeping, complete; encyclopedic, compendious; synoptic; bird's-eye

**pantomime** VERBS **impersonate,** personate; **mimic,** mime, take off, do *or* give an impression of, mock; ape, copy; **pose as, masquerade as,** affect the manner *or* guise of, pass for, pretend to be, represent oneself to be

**pantry** NOUNS **larder,** buttery <nonformal>; spence <Brit nonformal>, still-room <Brit>

**pants** NOUNS **trousers,** pair of trousers *or* pants, trews <Scots>, **breeches,** britches <nonformal>, breeks <Scots>, **pantaloons,** jeans, **slacks**

**papal** ADJS **pontific, pontifical,** apostolic, apostolical; **popish** *or* papist *or* papistic *or* papistical *or* papish <all nonformal>

**paper** NOUNS 1 **document,** official document, legal document, legal paper, legal instrument, **instrument,** writ, parchment, scroll, roll, **writing,** script, scrip; holograph, chirograph; **papers,** ship's papers; docket, **file,** personal file, **dossier;** blank, form
2 **newspaper,** news, sheet *or* rag <both nonformal>, **gazette,** daily newspaper, daily, weekly newspaper, weekly, neighborhood newspaper, national newspaper; newspaper of record; **tabloid,** extra, special, extra edition, special edition
3 **treatise,** piece, treatment, handling, tractate, tract; contribution; examination, survey, **discourse, discussion,** disquisition, descant, exposition, screed; homily; memoir; dissertation, **thesis; essay,** theme; pandect; excursus; **study,** lucubration, étude; research paper, term paper; **monograph,** research monograph

**papers** NOUNS **archives,** public records, government archives, government papers, presidential papers, historical documents, historical records, memorabilia; cartulary; biographical records, life records, biographical material, ana; parish rolls *or* register *or* records; citizenship papers

**par** NOUNS 1 **average,** balance, normal, norm, rule, run, generality; **mediocrity,** averageness, passableness, adequacy; par value
2 **equality, parity,** equation, identity; equivalence *or* equivalency, convertibility, **correspondence,** parallelism, equipollence, coequality; **balance,** poise, equipoise, **equilibrium,** equiponderance; symmetry, proportion; level playing field
ADJS 3 **equal, equalized,** like, **alike, even,** level, **on a par,** at par, at parity, au pair, commensurate, proportionate; on the same level, on the same plane, on the same *or* equal footing; on terms of equality, **on even** *or* **equal terms,** on even ground; on a level, on a level playing field, in the same boat

**parade** NOUNS 1 display, show, demonstration, manifestation, exhibition, *étalage* <Fr>; **pageantry,** pageant, pomp, spectacle; **procession,** train, column, line, string, cortege; cavalcade, caravan, motorcade; dress parade; promenade, review, march-past, funeral
VERBS 2 **flaunt,** vaunt, display, demonstrate, manifest, make a great show of, **exhibit,** air, put forward, put forth, hold up, flash *and* sport <both nonformal>; **file,** defile, file off; go on parade, promenade, march past

**paradise** NOUNS **bliss,** blissfulness; **heaven,** seventh heaven, cloud nine, **utopia, heaven on earth;** millennium, kingdom come; dreamland, lotus land, land of dreams, land of enchantment, land of heart's desire, wonderland, cloudland, fairyland, land of faerie, faerie; Eden, Garden of Eden; the Promised Land, land of promise, land of plenty, land of milk and honey, Canaan, Goshen; Shangri-la

**paradox** NOUNS **self-contradiction,** antinomy, oxymoron, ambivalence, **irony,** enantiosis, equivocation, ambiguity, equivocality, equivocalness, mixed message *or* signal, absurdity, logical impossibility

**paradoxical** ADJS **inconsistent,** incongruous, inconsonant, inconsequent, incoherent, **incompatible,** irreconcilable; disproportionate, out of proportion, self-contradictory, oxymoronic, **absurd;** abnormal, anomalous

**paragon** NOUNS **ideal,** beau ideal, nonpareil, nonesuch, person to look up to, *chevalier sans peur et sans reproche* <Fr>, **good example, role model,** shining example; exemplar, epitome; **model,** pattern, standard, norm, mirror; **standout,** one in a thousand *or* ten thousand, man of men, a man among men, woman of women, a woman among women

**parallel** VERBS 1 be parallel, coextend; run parallel, go alongside, go beside, run abreast; match, equal, **compare with,** stack up with <nonformal>; **agree,** accord, harmonize, concur, have no problem with, go along with <nonformal>, **cooperate**, correspond, conform, coincide, intersect, overlap, **match,** tally, hit, register, lock, interlock, check <nonformal>, square, dovetail, jibe <nonformal>
ADJS 2 paralleling; coextending, coextensive, nonconvergent, nondivergent, **equidistant,** equispaced, collateral, concurrent; lined up, aligned; equal, even; analogous; in the same category, of that kind *or* sort *or* ilk; **congenial,** *en rapport* <Fr>, sympathetic, compatible, affinitive

**paralyzed** ADJS **disabled,** incapacitated; crippled, hamstrung; disqualified, invalidated; hog-tied <nonformal>; prostrate, **on one's back,** on one's beam-ends; **stunned,** petrified, stupefied, frozen; **inert,** like a bump on a log <nonformal>, immobile, dormant, stagnant, stagnating, vegetative, vegetable, static, stationary, motionless, immobile, unmoving, paralytic

**parameter** NOUNS **specification,** given, *donnée* <Fr>, **limitation,** limiting condition, boundary condition; **contingency,** circumstance; **terms,** provisions; grounds; small *or* fine print *and* fine print at the bottom <all nonformal>

**paramount** ADJS **principal,** leading, foremost, main, chief, number one <nonformal>, premier, **prime, primary,** preeminent, **supreme,** cardinal; highest, uppermost, topmost, toprank, ranking, of the first rank, world-class, **dominant,** predominant, master, controlling, **overruling,** overriding, all-absorbing; **unsurpassed,** surpassing, unparalleled, unmatched, unmatchable, matchless, **peerless;** quintessential

**paranoid** NOUNS 1 **psychotic,** psycho <nonformal>, mental, mental case, certifiable case, **psychopath,** psychopathic case; psychopathic personality; paranoiac
ADJS 2 **psychotic,** psychopathic, psychoneurotic, mentally ill, mentally sick, certifiable; paranoiac

**paraphernalia** NOUNS things, **gear,** stuff <nonformal>, impedimenta <pl>, **tackle; belongings,** appurtenances, trappings, appointments, accessories, perquisites, appendages

**paraphrase** NOUNS **rephrase,** reword, restate, rehash; give a free *or* loose translation; approximate

**parasite** NOUNS 1 **nonworker,** drone; **sponger,** sponge <nonformal>, freeloader <nonformal>, social parasite, smell-feast, cadger, bummer *and* moocher <both nonformal>, beat *and* deadbeat <both nonformal>; **attendant**, satellite, hanger-on, dangler, adherent, appendage, dependent, stooge <nonformal>, flunky
2 bloodsucker; **leech; tick,** wood tick, deer tick; **mosquito,** skeeter <nonformal>, culex; bedbug, housebug <Brit>; parasitic plant, saprophyte

**parcel** NOUNS 1 **bundle,** pack, package, packet, deck, budget, fardel <nonformal>, sack, bag, poke <nonformal>, **roll,** rouleau, bolt
VERBS 2 **apportion,** divide, divide up, divvy *and* divvy up <both nonformal>, parcel up *or* out, **split,** split up, cut up, subdivide; district, zone

**parched** ADJS **dried,** dehydrated, desiccated, dried-up, exsiccated; **baked,** sunbaked, burnt, scorched, **seared,** sere, sun-dried, adust; **withered,** shriveled, wizened, weazened; **thirsty,** thirsting, athirst

**parchment** NOUNS **codex;** scroll; palimpsest, *codex rescriptus* <L>; papyrus

**pardon** NOUNS 1 excuse, sparing, **amnesty,** indemnity, exemption, immunity, reprieve, grace; **absolution,** shrift, remission, remission of sin; redemption; **exoneration, exculpation**
VERBS 2 **forgive,** excuse, give *or* grant forgiveness, spare; amnesty, grant amnesty to, grant immunity *or* exemp-

tion; hear confession, **absolve,** remit, give absolution, shrive, grant remission; **exonerate,** exculpate; blot out one's sins, wipe the slate clean

**pardonable** ADJS **excusable,** forgivable, expiable, remissible, exemptible, venial; **condonable,** dispensable; **warrantable,** allowable, admissible, reasonable, colorable, legitimate; innocuous, unobjectionable, inoffensive

**pare** VERBS 1 **peel,** skin, strip, flay, excoriate, decorticate, bark; scalp
2 **reduce,** decrease, diminish, lessen, take from; **lower,** curtail, retrench; **cut,** cut down *or* back, trim away, chip away at, whittle away *or* down, roll back <nonformal>

**parent** NOUNS 1 **progenitor, ancestor,** procreator, begetter; natural *or* birth *or* biological parent; grandparent; ancestress, progenitress, progenitrix; stepparent; adoptive parent; surrogate parent
VERBS 2 **foster, nurture,** nourish, mother, care for, lavish care on, feed, rear, sustain, cultivate, **cherish**

**parental** ADJS **ancestral,** ancestorial, patriarchal; parent; **paternal,** fatherly, fatherlike; **maternal,** motherly, motherlike; fostering

**pariah** NOUNS **outcast,** social outcast, outcast of society, castaway, derelict, Ishmael; **untouchable,** leper; outcaste; *déclassé* <Fr>; undesirable; *persona non grata* <L>, unacceptable person

**parish** NOUNS **diocese,** see, archdiocese, bishopric, archbishopric; province; synod, conference; **congregation,** parishioners, churchgoers, assembly

**parishioner** NOUNS **layman,** laic, secular, churchman, church member; brother, sister, lay brother, lay sister; laywoman, churchwoman; catchumen; communicant

**parity** NOUNS **equality,** par, equation, **identity**; equivalence *or* equivalency, convertibility, **correspondence,** parallelism , equipollence, coequality; **likeness,** levelness, evenness, coextension; **balance,** poise, equipoise, **equilibrium,** equiponderance; symmetry, proportion; level playing field; **justice**, equity

**parliamentary** ADJS **legislative,** legislatorial, lawmaking; deliberative; **congressional;** senatorial; bicameral, unicameral

**parlor** NOUNS **living room,** sitting room, morning room, drawing *or* withdrawing room, best room <nonformal>, salon

**parochial** ADJS **local, localized,** of a place, geographically limited, topical, vernacular, provincial, insular, limited, confined; narrow, insular, ethnocentric, xenophobic, snobbish

**parochial school** NOUNS **religious school,** church-related school, church school; Sunday school

**parody** NOUNS 1 **burlesque, lampoon,** squib, **satire, farce,** mockery, imitation, wicked imitation *or* pastiche, takeoff <nonformal>, travesty, caricature
VERBS 2 **burlesque, lampoon,** satirize, caricature, travesty, hit *or* take off on, send up <nonformal>; dip the pen in gall

**parole** VERBS **release,** put on parole, release from prison, spring <nonformal>; let out, let off, let go free; let out on bail

**parrot** NOUNS 1 **imitator,** simulator, metooer <nonformal>, **impersonator, impostor**, **mimic,** mimicker, mimer, mime, **mocker;** mockingbird, cuckoo; polly, poll-parrot *or* polly-parrot, **ape,** aper, monkey; **echo,** echoer, echoist
VERBS 2 **mimic,** impersonate, mime, **ape,** copycat <nonformal>; do an impression; take off, hit off, hit off on, take off on; **echo**

**parry** VERBS **fend off,** ward off, stave off, hold off, fight off, keep off, beat off, fend, counter, turn aside; **hold** *or* **keep at bay,** keep at arm's length; **hold the fort,** hold the line, stop, check, block, hinder, obstruct; **repel, repulse,** rebuff, drive back, put back, push back

**parsimonious** ADJS **sparing,** cheeseparing, **stinting,** scamping, scrimping, skimping; frugal; too frugal, overfrugal, frugal to excess; penny-wise, penny-wise and pound-foolish

**parson** NOUNS **clergyman,** clergywoman, man *or* woman of the cloth, divine, ecclesiastic, churchman, cleric, minister, pastor, rector, curate

**parsonage** NOUNS **pastorage,** pastorate, manse, **church house,** clergy house; presbytery, **rectory,** vicarage, deanery; glebe; chapter house

**part** NOUNS 1 **portion,** share, interest, stake, stock, **piece,** bit, segment; **bite** *and* **cut** *and* **slice** *and* **chunk** *and* slice of the pie *or* melon *and* piece of the action <all nonformal>, **lot, allotment,** end <nonformal>, **proportion,** percent-

age, measure, quantum, **quota,** meed, moiety, mess, helping
2 **role, lines,** side; bit, bit part, minor role; feeder, straight part; walking part, walk-on; top banana, second banana
3 **component,** constituent, ingredient, integrant, makings *and* fixings <both nonformal>, **element,** factor, player, module, part and parcel; appurtenance, adjunct
VERBS 4 **part company,** split up, dispel, disband, scatter, **disperse,** break up, break it up <nonformal>, **go separate ways,** diverge
ADJS 5 **incomplete, uncompleted, deficient,** defective, unfinished, imperfect, unperfected, **inadequate; partial,** failing; **half,** halfway; **in short supply,** scanty; **short,** scant, shy <nonformal>; **sketchy,** patchy
ADVS 6 **partly,** partially, **in part**

**partial** ADJS 1 **interested,** involved, **partisan,** unneutral, **one-sided,** all on *or* way over to one side, **biased,** tendentious, slanted
2 part; **fractional,** sectional, componential; segmentary, segmental, modular; **fragmentary;** incomplete, open-ended

**partial to** ADJS fond of, enamored of, **in love with,** attached to, wedded to, devoted to, wrapped up in; **taken with,** smitten with, struck with

**participant** NOUNS **participator,** partaker, player, sharer; party, **a party to,** accomplice, accessory; partner, copartner; shareholder

**participate** VERBS **take part,** partake, contribute, chip in, involve *or* engage oneself, get involved; **have** *or* **take a hand in,** get in on, have a finger in, have a finger in the pie, have to do with, have a part in, be an accessory to, be implicated in, be a party to, be a player in; **participate in,** partake of *or* in, **take part in,** take an active part in, **join, join in,** figure in, make oneself part of, play a part in, play a role in, get in the act <nonformal>; climb on the bandwagon; **have a voice in,** help decide, be in on the decisions

**participation** NOUNS **partaking, sharing,** having a part *or* share *or* voice, contribution, association; **involvement,** engagement; complicity

**particle** NOUNS **bit,** little *or* wee *or* tiny bit <nonformal>, fragment, spot, **speck,** flyspeck, fleck, point, dot, jot, tittle, **iota,** ounce, **dab** <nonformal>, mote, **mite** <nonformal>; crumb, scrap, bite, snip, snippet, **morsel,** shard, potsherd

**particular** NOUNS 1 **instance, item, detail,** point, count, case, fact, matter, article, datum, element, part, ingredient, factor, facet, aspect, thing; **respect, regard,** angle
ADJS 2 **special,** especial, specific, express, precise, **concrete; singular, individual,** individualist *or* individualistic; **fixed,** definite, defined, distinct, different, different as night and day, determinate, certain, absolute

**parting** ADJS **departing,** leaving; last, final, farewell; valedictory; outward-bound

**partisan** NOUNS 1 **party member,** party man *or* woman; regular, stalwart, loyalist; wheelhorse, party wheelhorse; heeler, ward heeler, **party hack;** party faithful; **fan** *and* buff <both nonformal>, aficionado, **admirer**
ADJS 2 polarizing, **divisive,** factional, factious; **quarrelsome,** bickering, disputatious, wrangling, eristic, eristical, polemical; litigious, pugnacious, combative, **aggressive,** bellicose, belligerent; feisty <nonformal>, touchy, irritable, shrewish, **irascible**
3 **party;** bipartisan, biparty, two-party; **partial,** interested, involved, unneutral, **one-sided,** all on *or* way over to one side

**partition** NOUNS 1 **dividing wall,** division, separation, *cloison* <Fr>; **wall,** barrier; bulkhead; diaphragm; septum; **border, dividing line,** property line, party wall; **buffer,** bumper, mat, fender, cushion, pad, shock pad, collision mat; buffer state
VERBS 2 set apart, separate, divide, subdivide; **wall off,** fence off, screen off, curtain off, compartmentalize, segment; **apportion,** portion, parcel, part, divide, share; divide into shares, **share out** *or* **around,** divide up, divvy *or* divvy up *or* out <nonformal>, **split,** split up, carve, cut, slice, carve up, slice up, cut up, cut *or* slice the pie *or* melon <nonformal>

**partner** NOUNS pardner *or* pard <nonformal>, copartner, side partner, buddy <nonformal>, **sidekick** *and* sidekicker <both nonformal>; **mate; business partner,** general partner, special partner, silent partner, dormant *or* sleeping partner

**partnership** NOUNS **alliance,** hookup *and* tie-up *and* tie-in <all nonformal>; copartnership, copartnery <old>, cahoots <nonformal>; colleagueship, collegialism, collegiality

**part-time** ADJS **occasional,** casual, incidental; odd, sometime, extra, side, off, off-and-on, out-of-the-way, spare, spare-time

**party** NOUNS 1 **participator,** participant, partaker, player, sharer; **a party to,** accomplice, accessory; partner, copartner; cotenant; shareholder
2 **entertainment,** party time, **festivity,** celebration, fete, at home, housewarming, soiree, reception, **dance,** ball, prom, do <chiefly Brit>; **spree, bout, fling,** randy <Scots>; **carouse,** drinking bout

3 <nonformal> **brawl, bash,** blast, clambake, wingding, hoodang, blowout, shindig, shindy, do *and* bean-feast *and* knees-up *and* rave *and* rave-up <all Brit>

4 **political party,** major party, minor party, third party, splinter party; party in power, opposition party, loyal opposition
VERBS 5 **enjoy oneself,** have a good time, have the time of one's life

6 <nonformal> **throw a party; party,** have fun, live it up, have a ball, ball, boogie, jam, kick up one's heels, make whoopee, whoop it up

7 **dissipate,** plunge into dissipation, **debauch, wanton, carouse,** run riot, live hard *or* fast, squander one's money in riotous living, burn the candle at both ends, keep up a fast *or* killing pace, sow one's wild oats, have a fling

*eat, drink, and be merry*
BIBLE

ADJS 8 **partisan,** partial, interested; **factional,** sectional, sectarian, sectary, denominational

**pass** NOUNS 1 **narrow, narrows,** strait; gap, ravine
2 **complimentary ticket,** comp <nonformal>, free pass *or* ticket, paper <nonformal>, free admission, guest pass *or* ticket, Annie Oakley <nonformal>
VERBS 3 **transfer,** pass over, **hand over,** turn over, carry over, make over, consign, assign; pass on, pass the buck <nonformal>, hand forward, hand on, relay
4 **outdistance,** distance; surpass, overpass; **get ahead,** pull ahead, shoot ahead, walk away *or* off <nonformal>; **leave behind,** leave at the post, leave in the dust, leave in the lurch; **come to the front,** have a healthy lead <nonformal>
5 **ratify,** pass on *or* upon, give thumbs up <nonformal>; amen, say amen to
6 **succeed,** graduate, qualify, win one's spurs *or* wings, get one's credentials, be blooded; pass with flying colors; **stand the test,** stand up, hold up, hold up in the wash, **pass muster,** get by <nonformal>, make it *and* hack it *and* cut the mustard <all nonformal>, meet *or* satisfy requirements
7 be past, **be a thing of the past,** elapse, lapse, slip by *or* away, be gone, fade, fade away, be dead and gone, be all over, have run its course, have run out, have had its day; **disappear, go** *or* **pass by,** get *or* shoot ahead of; bypass

**passable** ADJS **acceptable,** admissible, **agreeable,** unobjectionable, unexceptionable, tenable, viable; **OK** *and* okay *and* all right *and* alright <all nonformal>; good enough, **mediocre,** middling, indifferent, fair, fairish, fair to middling <nonformal>, moderate, modest, medium, betwixt and between; respectable, **tolerable; so-so,** *comme ci comme ça* <Fr>

**passage** NOUNS **phrase,** musical phrase, strain, part, motive, motif, theme, subject, figure; leitmotiv; **movement**

**passageway** NOUNS **entrance,** corridor, companionway, hall, hallway, way; jetway, jet bridge; gangway, gangplank; **vestibule;** aisle, alley, lane; channel, conduit; opening, aperture; covered way, gallery, arcade, portico, colonnade, cloister, ambulatory

**passé** ADJS **past, gone,** by, **gone-by, bygone,** gone glimmering, bypast, ago, **over,** departed, passed, passed away, elapsed, lapsed, vanished, faded, no more, irrecoverable, never to return, not coming back; **dead,** dead as a dodo, expired, extinct, dead and buried, defunct, deceased; run out, blown over, finished, forgotten, wound up; **obso-**

lete, has-been, dated, antique, **antiquated,** extinct, outworn

**passenger** NOUNS **traveler,** fare, **commuter,** straphanger <nonformal>; transient

**passion** NOUNS 1 passionateness, strong feeling, powerful emotion; **fervor,** fervency, fervidness, impassionedness, **ardor,** ardency, *empressement* <Fr>, tender feeling *or* passion, warmth of feeling, **warmth, heat, fire,** verve, furor, **fury,** vehemence; heartiness, gusto, relish, savor; spirit, heart, soul; **liveliness;** zeal; excitement; predilection
2 **cause, principle,** interest, issue, burning issue, commitment, faith, great cause, lifework; reason for being, *raison d'être* <Fr>; **craze,** infatuation, enthusiasm, fascination, crazy fancy, bug <nonformal>

**passionate** ADJS **fiery, vehement,** hotheaded, **impetuous,** violent, volcanic, furious, fierce, **wild;** tempestuous, stormy, tornadic; simmering, volcanic, ready to burst forth *or* explode; **impassioned,** enthusiastic, **ardent, fervent,** burning, glowing, warm; urgent, stirring, exciting, stimulating, provoking

**passive** ADJS 1 **neutral,** standpat <nonformal>, **do-nothing;** *laissez-faire, laissez-aller* <both Fr>; **inert,** like a bump on a log <nonformal>, immobile, dormant, stagnant, stagnating, vegetative, vegetable, static, stationary, motionless, immobile, unmoving, paralyzed, paralytic; procrastinating; **inactive, idle**; quiescent; quietist, quietistic, contemplative, meditative; **submissive, compliant,** complying, **acquiescent,** consenting; supine, **unresisting**
2 **uninterested,** unconcerned, disinterested, uninvolved, **indifferent, apathetic,** impassive, stolid, phlegmatic, listless

**password** NOUNS **watchword,** countersign; token; open sesame; secret grip; shibboleth

**past** NOUNS 1 **the past,** foretime, former times, past times, times past, water under the bridge, **days** *or* **times gone by,** bygone times *or* days, yesterday, yesteryear; recent past, just *or* only yesterday; **history,** past history; dead past, dead hand of the past
ADJS 2 **gone,** by, **gone-by, bygone,** gone glimmering, bypast, ago, **over,** departed, passed, passed away, elapsed, lapsed, vanished, faded, no more, irrecoverable, never to return, not coming back; **dead**, dead as a dodo, expired, extinct, dead and buried, defunct, deceased; **passé, obsolete,** has-been, dated, antique, antiquated; **former,** previous, late, recent, **once, onetime,** sometime, **erstwhile,** then, quondam

**pasta** NOUNS **spaghetti,** spaghettini, ziti, fedellini, fettuccine, radiattore, vermicelli, **macaroni,** lasagne, linguine

**paste** NOUNS 1 **fake,** imitation, simulacrum, dummy; tinsel, *clinquant* <Fr>, pinchbeck, shoddy, junk
2 **pulp,** mash, mush, smash, squash, crush; tomato paste *or* pulp; cement, glue, mucilage
VERBS 3 **stick together,** cement, bind, colligate, glue, agglutinate, conglutinate, gum

**pastime** NOUNS **amusement,** entertainment, diversion, solace, divertisement, *divertissement* <Fr>, recreation, relaxation, regalement; *passe-temps* <Fr>

**pastor** NOUNS **clergyman,** clergywoman, man *or* woman of the cloth, divine, ecclesiastic, churchman, cleric, minister, parson, rector, curate

**pastoral** ADJS **rustic,** rural, country, provincial, farm, bucolic, Arcadian, **agrarian,** agrestic; agricultural; idyllic, eclogic

**pastry** NOUNS *patisserie* <Fr>; French pastry, Danish pastry; **tart;** turnover; timbale; **pie,** *tarte* <Fr>, fruit pie, tart; *quiche* or *quiche Lorraine* <Fr>; *vol-au-vent* <Fr>; dowdy, pandowdy; cream puff, croquembouche, profiterole; cannoli, cream horn; éclair, chocolate éclair

**pat** NOUNS 1 **caress; tap,** rap, dab, chuck, touch, tip; love-tap
VERBS 2 **caress,** pet, **fondle,** dandle, coddle, cocker, cosset; pat on the head *or* cheek, chuck under the chin; **tap,** rap, dab, chuck, touch, tip

**patch** NOUNS 1 **spot,** dot, polka dot, macula, macule, blotch, splotch, splash; **mottle,** dapple; speck, speckle, fleck, flick, flyspeck
2 **plot,** plot of ground *or* land, parcel of land, plat, **tract,** field
3 **scrap,** tatter, smithereen <nonformal>, **stitch, shred,** tag

**patent** NOUNS 1 **copyright,** certificate of invention, *brevet d'invention* <Fr>; **trademark, logo** *or* logotype, registered trademark, trade name, service mark
ADJS 2 **manifest,** apparent, evident,

self-evident, indisputable, **obvious, plain,** clear, perspicuous, distinct, palpable, tangible; **unquestionable,** unexceptionable, undeniable, axiomatic; indubitable, unarguable, incontestable, **irrefutable,** incontrovertible, irrefragable

**paternal** ADJS **loving,** fond, adoring, devoted; parental, parent; fatherly, fatherlike

**paternity** NOUNS **fatherhood,** fathership; natural *or* birth *or* biological fatherhood; fatherliness, paternalness; adoptive fatherhood

**path** NOUNS **track,** trail, pathway, footpath, footway, *piste* <Fr>; walkway, catwalk, skybridge *or* skywalk *or* flying bridge *or* walkway; **sidewalk,** walk, fastwalk, *trottoir* <Fr>, foot pavement <Brit>; boardwalk; hiking trail; towpath *or* towing path; bridle path *or* road *or* trail *or* way; bicycle path; beaten track *or* path, rut, groove; garden path

**pathetic** ADJS 1 **affecting,** touching, moving, emotive, saddening, poignant; comfortless, discomforting, uncomfortable; **pitiful,** pitiable, piteous, affecting, heartrending, grievous, doleful
2 **paltry, poor,** common, mean, sorry, sad, despicable, contemptible, beneath contempt, **miserable, wretched,** beggarly, vile, **shabby,** scrubby, scruffy, shoddy, crummy *and* cheesy <both nonformal>, **trashy,** cheap, worthless, valueless; tawdry, meretricious

**pathological** ADJS **unwholesome,** unhealthy, unsound, morbid, **infected,** contaminated, tainted, peccant, **poisoned,** septic

**pathos** NOUNS **woe,** sadness, sorrowfulness, mournfulness, lamentation, woefulness, poignancy; comfortlessness, discomfort, dreariness, cheerlessness, joylessness, dismalness, **depression,** bleakness

**patience** NOUNS **tolerance,** toleration, **acceptance; indulgence,** lenience, leniency; sweet reasonableness; **forbearance,** forbearing, forbearingness; **sufferance,** endurance; long-suffering, long-sufferance, longanimity; **stoicism,** fortitude, self-control; patience of Job; waiting game, waiting it out; **perseverance**

*a minor form of despair, disguised as a virtue*
AMBROSE BIERCE

**patient** NOUNS 1 **sick person,** ill person, sufferer, victim; valetudinarian, **invalid, shut-in;** incurable, terminal case; **case;** inpatient, outpatient; **the sick,** the infirm
ADJS 2 armed with patience, with a soul possessed in patience, patient as Job, Job-like, Griselda-like; **tolerant,** tolerative, tolerating, accepting; understanding, **indulgent,** lenient; **forbearing;** philosophical; **long-suffering,** longanimous; **enduring,** endurant; disciplined, self-controlled; **persevering**

**patina** NOUNS **verdigris,** aerugo; patination; **polish,** gloss, glaze, burnish, **shine,** luster, finish; covering, **coat,** coating, veneer, film, membrane

**patois** NOUNS **jargon,** lingo <nonformal>, slang, cant, argot, patter, vernacular

**patriarch** NOUNS **old man,** elder, oldster <nonformal>; graybeard *or* greybeard, reverend *or* venerable sir; grandfather, grandsire; octogenarian, nonagenarian, centenarian; paterfamilias

**patriarchal** ADJS **ancestral,** ancestorial; **paternal,** paternalistic, patriarchic, patriarchical

**patrician** NOUNS 1 **aristocrat,** Brahmin, blue-blood, thoroughbred, member of the upper class, socialite, swell *and* upper-cruster <both nonformal>, grandee, grand dame, dowager, magnifico, lord of creation
ADJS 2 **upper-class,** aristocratic, upscale; gentle, genteel, of gentle blood; gentlemanly, gentlemanlike; ladylike, quite the lady; born to the purple, born with a silver spoon in one's mouth; **high-society,** socialite, hoity-toity <nonformal>, posh

*to the manner born*
SHAKESPEARE

**patriot** NOUNS nationalist; ultranationalist; **chauvinist,** chauvin, **jingo,** jingoist; patrioteer <nonformal>, flag waver, superpatriot, hard hat <nonformal>, hundred-percenter, hundred-percent American; hawk

**patriotic** ADJS **public-spirited,** civic; nationalistic; ultranationalist, ultranationalistic; overpatriotic, superpatriotic, flagwaving, **chauvinist,** chauvinistic, jingoist, jingoistic; hawkish

**patriotism** NOUNS love of country; **nationalism,** nationality, ultranationalism; **chauvinism,** jingoism, overpatriotism; patriotics, flag-waving; saber-rattling

**patrol** VERBS **police,** pound a beat <nonformal>, go on one's beat, reconnoiter, scout; **watch,** keep watch, keep guard, keep watch over, keep vigil, keep watch and ward; stand guard, stand sentinel; be on the lookout; mount guard; sweep, go *or* make one's rounds, scour, scour the country

**patron** NOUNS **contributor, subscriber,** supporter, backer, financer, funder, angel <nonformal>; subsidizer; patroness, Maecenas; **fan** *and* buff <both nonformal>; **customer,** client; patronizer <nonformal>, regular customer *or* buyer, regular

**patronage** NOUNS **fosterage,** tutelage, sponsorship, backing, auspices, aegis, coattails <nonformal>, care, guidance, **championing,** championship, seconding; interest, advocacy, encouragement, **backing,** abetment; **custom,** trade; **political patronage,** favors of office, pork *and* pork barrel <both nonformal>, plum, melon <nonformal>

**patronize** VERBS 1 **condescend, deign,** vouchsafe, stoop, descend, lower *or* demean oneself, trouble oneself, set one's dignity aside *or* to one side, be so good as to, so forget oneself, dirty *or* soil one's hands; deal with *or* treat *de haut en bas* <Fr, from high to low> or *en grand seigneur* <Fr, like a great lord>, talk down to, talk *de haut en bas*
2 **trade with,** deal with, traffic with, do business with, have dealings with, have truck with, transact business with; frequent as a customer, shop at, trade at, take one's business *or* trade to

**patsy** NOUNS trusting soul; **dupe;** sucker *and* easy mark *and* pushover<all nonformal>; scapegoat, fall guy <nonformal>

**patter** NOUNS 1 **rain,** rainfall, **shower,** sprinkle, flurry, pitter-patter, splatter
2 **jargon,** lingo <nonformal>, **slang,** cant, argot, patois, vernacular; vocabulary, phraseology; **sales talk,** sales pitch

**pattern** NOUNS 1 **gestalt,** figure, configuration, sensory pattern; figure-ground; **original,** archetype, prototype, **mold,** pilot model
2 **habit,** habitude, **custom,** second nature; stereotype; stereotyped behavior; force of habit; creature of habit; **knee-jerk** <nonformal>, automatism
3 **theme,** design, ornamental theme, ornamental *or* decorative composition; exemplar, epitome; **model,** standard, norm, mirror

**paucity** NOUNS **fewness,** infrequency, **sparsity,** sparseness, **scarcity,** scantiness, meagerness, miserliness, niggardliness, tightness, **dearth,** poverty; **rarity,** rareness, uncommonness

**paunch** NOUNS **abdomen; stomach,** belly <nonformal>, midriff; swollen *or* distended *or* protruding *or* prominent belly, *embonpoint* <Fr>, ventripotence

**pauper** NOUNS **poor man,** poorling, poor devil, down-and-out *or* down-and-outer, indigent, penniless man, hard case, starveling; homeless person, bag woman *or* lady, shopping-bag lady, shopping-cart woman *or* lady, homeless *or* street person; welfare client; charity case

**pause** NOUNS 1 **respite, recess, rest,** halt, stay, lull, **break,** surcease, suspension, interlude, **intermission,** spell <Australia>, letup <nonformal>, **time out** <nonformal>, time to catch one's breath; **breathing spell,** breathing time, breathing place, breathing space, breath; **breather**
2 **demur,** demurral, **scruple, qualm,** qualm of conscience, reservation, compunction; **hesitation,** hesitancy *or* hesitance, pause, boggle, **falter;** qualmishness, scrupulousness, scrupulosity; **stickling,** boggling; **faltering;** shrinking; shyness, **diffidence,** modesty, bashfulness; recoil; **protest, objection**
VERBS 3 **rest,** let up *and* take it easy <both nonformal>, **relax,** rest on one's oars; **recess,** take *or* call a recess; **take a break,** break, take ten

**paw** NOUNS 1 pad, pug, *patte* <Fr>; hand <nonformal>
VERBS 2 **touch, feel,** feel of, palpate; **handle,** palm; poke at, prod

**pawn** NOUNS 1 lightweight, follower, cog, flunky, yes-man, creature; **cat's-paw,** puppet, dummy, creature, minion, stooge <nonformal>; stalking horse; toy, plaything; dupe
VERBS 2 **pledge,** impignorate *and* handsel <both old>, **deposit,** stake, post, put in escrow, **put up,** put up as collateral, lay out *or* down; put in pawn, spout *or* put up the spout <both old>, **hock** *and* **put in hock** <both nonformal>

**pay** NOUNS 1 **payment,** remuneration,

compensation, total compensation, wages plus fringe benefits, financial package, pay and allowances, financial remuneration; rate of pay; **salary,** wage, wages, income, earnings
VERBS 2 **be profitable,** repay, pay off <nonformal>, yield a profit, show a percentage, be gainful, be worthwhile *or* worth one's while, be a good investment
3 **spend,** expend, disburse, pay out, fork out *or* over <nonformal>, shell out <nonformal>, **lay out,** outlay; **yield,** bring in, afford, **return**

4 <nonformal> **kick in, fork over,** pony up, pay up, cough up, stump up [Brit], come across, come through with, come across with, come down with, come down with the needful, plank down, plunk down, post, tickle *or* grease the palm, cross one's palm with, lay on one; pay to the tune of

**payable** ADJS **due,** owed, owing, receivable, redeemable, mature, **outstanding, unpaid,** in arrear *or* arrears, back, coming, **coming to**
**payee** NOUNS **recipient, receiver,** accepter, getter, taker, acquirer, obtainer, procurer; endorsee
**payer** NOUNS remunerator, compensator, recompenser; paymaster, purser, bursar, cashier, treasurer; defrayer; liquidator
**payment** NOUNS **paying,** paying off, paying up <nonformal>, payoff; **defrayment,** defrayal; paying out, doling out, **disbursal**; **discharge,** settlement, clearance, liquidation, amortization, amortizement, retirement, satisfaction; quittance; **debt service,** interest payment, sinking-fund payment; **remittance;** installment; **cash,** hard cash, spot cash, cash payment, cash on the nail *and* cash on the barrelhead <both nonformal>; pay-as-you-go; payment in kind
**peace** NOUNS *pax* <L>; **peacetime,** freedom from war, cessation of combat, exemption from hostilities, public tranquillity; **harmony,** accord
**peaceful** ADJS **pacific,** peaceable; tranquil, serene; idyllic, pastoral; halcyon, soft, piping, **calm, quiet,** restful, **untroubled,** orderly, **at peace;** concordant; bloodless
**peacemaker** NOUNS make-peace, reconciler, smoother-over; **pacifier,** pacificator; **conciliator,** propitiator, **appeaser**
**peace of mind** NOUNS **composure,** mental composure, calm of mind; peace of heart, peace of soul *or* spirit, peace of God

*peace which passeth all understanding*
BIBLE

**peacock** NOUNS 1 peafowl, peahen, bird of Juno
2 **strutter,** swaggerer, swash, swasher, **swashbuckler,** miles gloriosus
**peak** NOUNS 1 **summit,** top; **tip-top,** pinnacle; **summit,** mountaintop, point, topmost point *or* pinnacle, **crest,** tor, *pic* <Fr>, *pico* <Sp>; **limit,** extremity, extreme, **acme,** apogee, climax, **maximum,** ceiling, crown; **utmost,** uttermost, utmost extent, highest degree, nth degree *or* power, *ne plus ultra* <L>; **acme of perfection,** pink, pink of perfection, culmination, perfection, height
VERBS 2 **top,** top off, **crown, cap,** crest, **head,** tip, surmount; **culminate,** consummate, climax
**peaked** ADJS **haggard,** poor, puny, peaky <nonformal>, **pinched;** shriveled, withered; **wizened,** weazeny; **emaciated,** emaciate, emacerated, **wasted,** attenuated, worn to a shadow
**peal** NOUNS 1 **ring,** chime; toll, knell
VERBS 2 **ring,** tintinnabulate, sound; **toll,** knell, sound a knell; **chime**
**peanuts** NOUNS **petty cash,** pocket money, pin money, spending money, mad money, **change,** small change; nickels and dimes *and* chicken feed *and* chickenshit <all nonformal>
**pearly** ADJS **iridescent,** opalescent, nacreous, pearl-like, rainbowlike, mother-of-pearl; pearly-white, pearl-white;
**peasant** NOUNS **countryman,** countrywoman, **provincial,** son of the soil, tiller of the soil; *campesino* <Sp>, *Bauer* <Ger>, rustic; **peon,** hind, fellah, muzhik; hick *and* yokel *and* rube *and* hayseed *and* shit-kicker <all nonformal>, **bumpkin,** country bumpkin, clod, **clodhopper** <nonformal>, hillbilly *and* woodhick <both nonformal>
**peculiar** ADJS **odd, queer,** absurd, singular, curious, oddball <nonformal>, weird *and* kooky *and* freaky *and* freaked-out <all nonformal>, quaint, **eccentric,** gonzo <nonformal>; **strange,** outlandish, off-the-wall <informal>, surreal, not for real <nonformal>, passing strange

**peculiarity** NOUNS **eccentricity, idiosyncrasy,** idiocrasy, erraticism, erraticness, **queerness, oddity,** strangeness, singularity, freakishness, freakiness, quirkiness, crotchetiness, dottiness, crankiness, crankism, crackpotism; abnormality, anomaly, unnaturalness, irregularity, deviation, deviancy, differentness, divergence, aberration

**peddler** NOUNS **vendor,** huckster, hawker, butcher <old>, higgler, cadger <Scots>, colporteur, chapman <Brit>; coster *or* costermonger <both Brit>; sidewalk salesman

**pedestal** NOUNS **base; stand,** standard

**pedestrian** NOUNS 1 **walker,** walkist; foot traveler, foot passenger, hoofer <nonformal>, footbacker <nonformal>, ambulator, peripatetic
ADJS 2 **prosaic,** prosy, prosing; unpoetical, poetryless; **plain,** common, commonplace, ordinary, unembellished, mundane; **matter-of-fact,** unromantic, unidealistic, unimpassioned; **unimaginative,** insipid, vapid, flat; humdrum, tiresome, **dull**

**pedigree** NOUNS **genealogy,** stemma, *Stammbaum* <Ger>, genealogical tree, **family tree,** tree; genogram

**peek** NOUNS 1 **glance,** glance *or* flick of the eye, squiz <Australia>, slant <nonformal>, rapid glance, cast, side-glance; **glimpse,** flash, quick sight; **peep;** wink, blink, flicker *or* twinkle of an eye; casual glance, **half an eye;** *coup d'œil* <Fr>
VERBS 2 **pry, snoop,** peep, spy, nose, nose into, have a long *or* big nose, poke *or* stick one's nose in; meddle

**peel** NOUNS 1 peeling, rind; skin, epicarp; covering, **coat,** coating, veneer, film, patina, scum
VERBS 2 **pare,** skin, strip, flay, excoriate, decorticate, bark, denude

**peer** NOUNS 1 **equal, match,** mate, twin, fellow, **like, equivalent,** opposite number, counterpart, answer <nonformal>, vis à vis, equipollent, coequal, parallel, ditto <nonformal>; **compeer,** colleague, peer group; **nobleman,** noble, gentleman
VERBS 2 **look,** have a look, take a gander *and* take a look <both nonformal>, direct the eyes, turn *or* bend the eyes, cast one's eye, lift up the eyes; **look at,** take a look at, eye, **eyeball** <nonformal>, have a look-see <nonformal>, look on *or* upon, gaze at *or* upon; **watch,** observe, view, regard; keep one's eyes peeled *or* skinned, be watchful *or* observant *or* vigilant, keep one's eyes open

**peerless** ADJS **matchless, champion; unmatched,** unmatchable, unrivaled, unparagoned, unparalleled, immortal, **unequaled,** never-to-be-equaled, unpeered, unexampled, unapproached, unapproachable, **unsurpassed,** unexcelled; inimitable, **incomparable,** beyond compare *or* comparison, **unique;** in a class by itself, *sui generis* <L>, easily first, *facile princeps* <L>; second to none, *nulli secundus* <L>

**peeve** NOUNS 1 **complaint,** grievance, pet peeve, **groan; dissent,** protest; hard luck story <nonformal>, tale of woe; **grudge,** spite, crow to pick *or* pluck *or* pull, bone to pick
VERBS 2 **annoy,** irk, vex, nettle, provoke, pique, miff <nonformal>, distemper, **ruffle, disturb,** discompose, **roil,** rile, **aggravate,** make a nuisance of oneself, **exasperate,** exercise, try one's patience, try the patience of a saint

**pellet** NOUNS **sphere; ball,** orb, orbit, **globe,** rondure; **shot; bullet,** slug

**pelt** NOUNS 1 **fur, hide,** fell, fleece, vair <heraldry>
VERBS 2 **stone,** lapidate <old>, pellet; brickbat *or* egg <both nonformal>; **throw,** fling, sling, pitch, toss, cast, hurl, heave, chuck, chunk *and* peg <both nonformal>; **riddle, pepper,** pump full of lead <nonformal>; snipe, pick off

**pen** NOUNS 1 **enclosure,** close, **confine,** precinct, enclave, coop, fold; **penitentiary,** keep, penal institution
VERBS 2 **enclose,** close in, bound, include, **contain;** compass, encompass; **surround,** encircle; **shut in,** coop in, confine; coop, corral, cage, impound, mew; **imprison,** incarcerate, jail, lock up
3 **write, pencil,** drive *or* push the pen *or* pencil <nonformal>; take pen in hand; **put in writing,** put in black and white; author, **compose, indite,** formulate, produce, prepare

**penalize** VERBS put *or* impose *or* inflict a penalty *or* sanctions on; **punish; handicap,** put at a disadvantage

**penalty** NOUNS **sanctions,** penal *or* punitive measures; punishment; **reprisal,** retaliation, compensation, price; the devil to pay

**penance** NOUNS penitence, repentance;

penitential act *or* exercise, **mortification,** maceration, flagellation, lustration; **asceticism,** fasting; **purgation,** purgatory; **sackcloth and ashes;** hair shirt

**penchant** NOUNS **inclination,** partiality, fancy, favor, predilection, preference, propensity, proclivity, **leaning, bent,** turn, tilt, bias, **affinity**

**pending** ADJS **overhanging,** overhung, lowering, **impending,** impendent; pendent, dependent, depending, contingent, conditional, conditioned; **open,** in question, at issue, **in the balance,** up in the air, up for grabs <nonformal>, **in suspense,** in a state of suspense, suspenseful

**penetrate** VERBS **affect,** pierce, go through one, go deep; touch a chord, **touch a sympathetic chord,** touch one's heart, tug at the heart *or* heartstrings, go to one's heart, get under one's skin; **pervade,** permeate; **get over** *or* **across** <nonformal>, come through, register <nonformal>, sink in, soak in; **imbue,** imbrue, **infuse,** suffuse, transfuse, breathe, **instill,** infiltrate, **impregnate**

**penetrating** ADJS **piercing,** stabbing, cold, cutting, stinging, biting, keen, brisk, sharp, caustic, astringent, **striking,** incisive, trenchant, poignant, slashing, mordant, acid, corrosive; **sagacious,** discerning, acute, cogent

**penis** NOUNS **genitals,** phallus, *lingam* <Skt>; gonads

**penitent** NOUNS 1 confessor; **prodigal son,** prodigal returned; Magdalen
ADJS 2 **repentant;** penitential, penitentiary; **contrite,** abject, humble, humbled, **sheepish,** apologetic, touched, softened, melted

**penitentiary** NOUNS **prison,** prisonhouse, minimum- *or* maximum-security facility, pen <nonformal>, keep, penal institution, bastille, state prison, federal prison; maximum- *or* minimum-security prison

**pen name** NOUNS **nom de plume;** alias, pseudonym, anonym, **assumed name,** false *or* fictitious name

**pennant** NOUNS **flag, banner,** oriflamme, standard, gonfalon *or* gonfanon, guidon, *vexillum* <L>, *labarum* <L>; pennon, pennoncel, banneret, banderole, swallowtail, burgee, **streamer;** bunting

**penniless** ADJS **destitute,** broke *and* cleaned out *and* tapped out *and* wiped out <all nonformal>, down-and-out, in the gutter; moneyless, fortuneless, out of funds, **without a sou,** without a penny to bless oneself with, without one dollar to rub against another; insolvent, in the red, **bankrupt**

**penny pincher** NOUNS **niggard,** tightwad *and* cheapskate <both nonformal>, **miser,** hard man with a buck <nonformal>, **skinflint,** scrooge, pinchfist, churl, muckworm

**pension** NOUNS annuity; old-age insurance, retirement benefits, social security, remittance

**pensive** ADJS **wistful,** tristful; **thoughtful,** cogitative, **contemplative,** reflective, speculative, deliberative, meditative, ruminative, ruminant

**peon** NOUNS **peasant,** hind, fellah, muzhik

**people** NOUNS 1 **population, inhabitants,** habitancy, dwellers, **populace,** whole people, people at large, citizenry, folk, souls, living souls, body, whole body, warm bodies <nonformal>; **public,** general public; **family,** relatives, relations, folks <nonformal>
VERBS 2 empeople, **populate, inhabit,** denizen; colonize, **settle,** settle in, plant

**the people** NOUNS **the populace,** the public, the general public, people in general, everyone, everybody; **the population,** the citizenry, the whole people, the polity, the body politic; **common people,** ordinary people *or* folk, persons, folk, folks, gentry; the common sort, plain people *or* folks, the common run <nonformal>, the rank and file

**pep** NOUNS **liveliness,** life, spirit, verve, energy, adrenalin; moxie *and* oomph *and* pizzazz *and* piss and vinegar <all nonformal>, **vim**

**peppy** ADJS **spirited, lively,** gingery <nonformal>, racy, sparkling, vivacious; piquant, poignant, pungent

**perceive** VERBS **see, discern,** make out, descry; see the light, see daylight <nonformal>, wake up, wake up to, tumble to <nonformal>, come alive; **see through,** see to the bottom of, penetrate, see into, pierce, plumb; see at a glance, see with half an eye; understand, comprehend, fathom

**perception** NOUNS **sensation,** sense, feeling; sense impression, percept, sense perception; **vision,** sight, eyesight, seeing; power of sight, sense of sight, visual sense; discernment; perspicacity, perspicuity, sharp *or* acute *or* keen sight; **sagacity,** sagaciousness, **astuteness,** acumen

**perceptive** ADJS **discerning,** perspicacious, insightful; **astute,** judicious

**perch** NOUNS 1 **footing,** foothold, toehold, hold, perch, purchase; footrest
VERBS 2 **rest on,** stand on, repose on, **sit on,** ride, piggyback on; **straddle,** bestraddle, stride, bestride

**percolate** VERBS **trickle,** dribble, dripple, **drip,** drop, spurtle; **filter,** leach, lixiviate; distill, condense, sweat; seep, weep; **gurgle**

**perennial** ADJS 1 indeciduous, **evergreen,** sempervirent, ever-new, ever-young; ever-blooming, ever-bearing
2 **incessant,** constant, steady, stable, **ceaseless,** unceasing, **endless,** unending, never-ending, **interminable**

**perfect** VERBS 1 **touch up,** finish, put on the finishing touches, polish, fine down, fine-tune <nonformal>, tone up, **brush up, furbish,** furbish up, spruce, **spruce up,** freshen, vamp, vamp up, rub up, brighten up, polish, polish up, shine <nonformal>; retouch; **revive,** renovate; **repair,** fix
2 ADJS **ideal, faultless,** flawless, unflawed, not to be improved, **impeccable,** absolute; **just right;** spotless, stainless, taintless, unblemished, untainted, unspotted, immaculate, **pure,** uncontaminated, unadulterated, unmixed; sinless; chaste; indefectible, trouble-free; infallible; beyond all praise, irreproachable, unfaultable, *sans peur et sans reproche* <Fr>, **matchless,** peerless

**perfectionist** NOUNS precisian, precisianist, stickler, nitpicker <nonformal>, captious critic

**perforate** VERBS **pierce,** empierce, penetrate, puncture, punch, hole, prick; **tap,** broach; stab, stick, pink, run through; **transfix,** transpierce, fix, **impale,** spit, skewer; gore, spear, lance, spike, needle; **bore,** drill, auger; **ream,** ream out, countersink, gouge, gouge out; trepan, trephine; punch full of holes, make look like Swiss cheese *or* a sieve, **riddle,** honeycomb

**perform** VERBS **execute,** enact; transact; discharge, dispatch; conduct, **manage, handle;** dispose of, take care of, **deal with,** cope with; **make,** accomplish, complete; enact, dramatize; **act, play,** playact, tread the boards, strut one's stuff <nonformal>; appear, appear on the stage; **operate,** function, run, work

**performance** NOUNS **execution,** carrying out, enactment; **transaction; discharge,** dispatch; conduct, **handling,** management, administration; **achievement,** accomplishment, effectuation, implementation; commission, perpetration; completion; **master stroke,** *tour de force* <Fr>, exploit, adventure, gest, **enterprise,** initiative, production, track record <nonformal>; taking a role *or* part, theatrical performance, **show,** presentation, entertainment, stage presentation *or* performance

**performer** NOUNS **entertainer,** public entertainer; artist, artiste; impersonator, female impersonator; **vaudevillian,** vaudevillist; dancer, hoofer <nonformal>; song and dance man; chorus girl, show girl, chorine <nonformal>; coryphée; chorus boy *or* man; burlesque queen <nonformal>, **stripteaser,** exotic dancer, ecdysiast; **musician,** musico, **music maker,** professional musician

**perfume** NOUNS 1 **fragrance,** aroma, scent, redolence, balminess, **incense, bouquet,** sweet smell, sweet savor; odor; spice, spiciness; muskiness; fruitiness
VERBS 2 **scent,** cense, incense, thurify, aromatize, odorize, fumigate, embalm

**peril** NOUNS **danger,** endangerment, imperilment, jeopardy, hazard, risk, cause for alarm, **menace,** threat; **crisis,** emergency, hot spot, nasty *or* tricky spot, pass, pinch, strait, plight, predicament; powder keg, time bomb; gathering clouds, storm clouds

**period** NOUNS 1 **point, juncture,** stage; **interval,** lapse of time, time frame, space, span, timespan, stretch, time-lag, time-gap; **time,** while, **moment,** minute, instant, hour, day, **season;** psychological moment; pregnant *or* fateful moment, fated moment, kairos, moment of truth; **spell**
2 **menstruation,** menstrual discharge *or* flow *or* flux, catamenia, catamenial discharge, flowers <old>, **the curse** <nonformal>, the curse of Eve; **menses, monthlies,** courses, that time

**periodic** ADJS periodical, seasonal, epochal, **cyclic** *or* cyclical, serial, isochronal, metronomic; measured, steady, even, **rhythmic** *or* rhythmical; **recurrent,** recurring, reoccurring; **intermittent,** reciprocal, alternate

**periodical** NOUNS **serial, journal,** gazette; ephemeris; **magazine,** book *and* zine <both nonformal>; pictorial; review; organ, **house organ; trade journal,** trade magazine; daily, weekly, biweekly, bimonthly, fortnightly, monthly, quarterly; annual, yearbook; daybook, diary

**peripheral** ADJS **environing,** surrounding, encompassing, enclosing; **enveloping,** wrapping, enwrapping, enfolding, embracing; **encircling,** circling; bordering; circumjacent, circumferential, circumambient, ambient; circumfluent, circumfluous; circumflex; **roundabout,** suburban, neighboring

**perish** VERBS **expire,** succumb, die, cease, end, come to an end, go, pass, **pass away,** vanish, disappear, fade away, run out, peg *or* conk out <nonformal>, come to nothing *or* naught, be no more, be done for; be all over with, be all up with <nonformal>

**perishable** ADJS **impermanent,** unenduring, undurable, nondurable, nonpermanent; **passing,** fleeting, flitting, flying, fading, dying; fugitive, fugacious

**perjury** NOUNS **deceitfulness;** falseness; false swearing, oath breaking, forswearing, untruthfulness, credibility gap; **insincerity,** unsincereness, uncandidness, uncandor, unfrankness, disingenuousness; **prevarication,** equivocation

**perky** ADJS **lighthearted,** light, lightsome; **buoyant,** corky <nonformal>, resilient; **jaunty,** debonair, carefree, free and easy; **breezy,** airy

**permanent** ADJS **changeless,** unchanging, immutable, unvarying, unshifting; **unchanged,** unchangeable, unvaried, **unaltered,** inalterable, inviolate, undestroyed, intact; **constant, persistent,** sustained, fixed, firm, solid, steadfast, like the Rock of Gibraltar, faithful; unchecked, unfailing, unfading; **lasting, enduring,** abiding, remaining, staying, continuing; durable; perpetual; stable

**permeate** VERBS **pervade,** penetrate; **suffuse,** inform, transfuse, perfuse, diffuse, leaven, imbue; **fill,** extend throughout, leave no void, occupy; creep *or* crawl *or* swarm with, be lousy with <nonformal>, teem with; honeycomb

**permission** NOUNS **ratification,** endorsement, acceptance, approval, approbation, subscription, signing-off, imprimatur, **sanction,** the OK *and* the okay *and* the green light *and* the go-ahead *and* the nod <all nonformal>, **certification,** confirmation, validation, authentication, authorization, warrant; **stamp of approval**

**permissive** ADJS **indulgent,** compliant, complaisant, **obliging,** accommodating, agreeable, amiable, gracious, generous, benignant, affable, decent, kind, kindly, benign, benevolent; **hands-off** <nonformal>, overpermissive, overindulgent; **nonrestrictive,** unrestrictive

**permit** NOUNS 1 **license, warrant;** building permit, learner's permit; driver's license, marriage license, hunting license, fishing license, etc; nihil obstat, imprimatur

VERBS 2 **allow,** admit, let, give permission, give leave, make possible; **allow** *or* **permit of;** give *or* leave room for, open the door to; consent; **grant,** accord, vouchsafe; okay *and* OK *and* give the nod *or* go-ahead *or* green light *or* go sign <all nonformal>, say *or* give the word <nonformal>; **enable,** clear the road *or* path for, smooth the way for, open the way for, open the door to, open up the possibility of

**perpetrate** VERBS bring about, bring to pass, **bring off,** produce, deliver <nonformal>, **do the trick,** put across *or* through; swing *or* swing it *and* hack it *and* cut it *and* cut the mustard <all nonformal>; **achieve,** accomplish, realize; **inflict,** wreak, do to; **commit;** pull off <nonformal>; go and do, up and do *or* take and do <both nonformal>

**perpetrator** NOUNS **evildoer, wrongdoer,** worker of ill *or* evil, **malefactor,** malfeasant, malfeasor, misfeasor, malevolent, public enemy, **sinner, villain,** villainess, transgressor, delinquent; bad *or* bad guy *and* baddy *and* meany *and* wrongo *and* black hat <all nonformal>; **criminal,** outlaw, felon, **crook** <nonformal>, lawbreaker, perp <nonformal>

**perpetual** ADJS **everlasting,** everliving, ever-being, ever-abiding, ever-during, ever-durable, permanent, perdurable, indestructible; **eternal,** sempiternal, **infinite,** aeonian *or* eonian; dateless, ageless, timeless, immemorial; **endless,** unending, never-ending, without end, **interminable,** nonterminous, nonterminating; **continual,** continuous, steady, **constant, ceaseless,** nonstop, unceasing, never-ceasing, **incessant,** unremitting, unintermitting, uninterrupted

**perpetuate** VERBS **preserve,** preserve from oblivion, keep fresh *or* alive, perennialize, **eternalize,** eternize, **immortalize;** monumentalize; **sustain,** protract, prolong, extend, lengthen, spin *or* string out; **keep up,** keep going, keep alive, survive

**perplex** VERBS **baffle, confound,** daze, amaze <old>, maze, addle, fuddle, muddle, **mystify, puzzle,** nonplus, put to one's wit's end; keep one guessing, keep in suspense

**persecute** VERBS oppress, **torment,** victimize, play cat and mouse with, **harass,** get *or* keep after, get *or* keep at, harry, hound, beset; pursue, hunt

**persevere** VERBS 1 **persist, carry on,** go on, **keep on,** keep up, keep at, **keep at it,** keep going, keep driving, keep trying, try and try again, **keep the ball rolling,** keep the pot boiling, keep up the good work; not take 'no' for an answer; not accept compromise *or* defeat; **endure,** last, **continue**

2 <nonformal> **stick,** stick to it, stick with it, stick it, stick it out, hang on for dear life, hang in, hang in there, hang tough, tough it out, keep on trucking, keep in keeping on; **go the limit,** go the whole hog, go the whole nine yards, go all out, shoot the works, go for broke, go through hell and high water

**persist** VERBS **persevere,** keep at it, stick it out, stick to it, stick with it, never say die, see it through, hang in *and* hang tough *and* not know when one is licked <all nonformal>; press on; perseverate, iterate, reiterate, **harp,** go on about, chew one's ear off *and* run off at the mouth <both nonformal>, beat a dead horse

**persistent** ADJS **persevering,** perseverant, persisting, insistent; **enduring,** permanent, **constant,** lasting; continuing; resolute; **diligent,** assiduous, sedulous, industrious; dogged, plodding, slogging, plugging; **pertinacious,** tenacious, stick-to-itive <nonformal>; **unswerving,** unremitting, unabating, unintermitting, uninterrupted; **unfaltering,** unwavering, unflinching; relentless, **unrelenting; obstinate,** stubborn; **unrelaxing,** unfailing, **untiring,** unwearying, unflagging, never-tiring, **tireless,** weariless, **indefatigable,** undiscouraged, undaunted, indomitable, unconquerable, invincible, game to the last *or* to the end

**person** NOUNS **human, human being,** man, woman, child, member of the human race *or* family, Adamite, daughter of Eve; **mortal,** life, **soul,** living soul; **being,** creature, clay, ordinary clay; **individual,** personage, **personality,** personhood, individuality

**personable** ADJS **persuasive,** suasive, **winning,** magnetic, charming, enchanting, charismatic; **comely,** fair, good-looking, nice-looking, well-favored, presentable, agreeable, becoming, pleasing, goodly, bonny, likely <nonformal>, **sightly**

**personal** ADJS **individual,** private, peculiar, idiosyncratic; person-to-person, one-to-one, one-on-one; **intimate,** inmost, innermost, interior, inward

**personality** NOUNS 1 **psyche,** psychic apparatus, **self;** personage, **personhood,** individuality, personship, personal identity; **selfness,** selfhood, **egohood,** self-identity

2 **celebrity,** famous person, person of renown

**personify** VERBS **embody,** body forth, incarnate, personate, impersonate; **illustrate,** demonstrate, exemplify; metaphorize, similize; personalize; symbolize

**personnel** NOUNS **staff, employees,** human resources, help, hired help, the help, **crew, gang,** men, force, servantry, retinue

**perspective** NOUNS **vista,** view, horizon, prospect, outlook, survey; range, scan, scope; **outlook,** mental outlook; *Anschauung* <Ger>, **point of view,** viewpoint, standpoint, *optique* <Fr>; **frame of reference**

**perspiration** NOUNS **sweat,** water; exudation, exudate; diaphoresis, sudor; honest sweat, the sweat of one's brow; beads of sweat, beaded brow; cold sweat

**perspire** VERBS **sweat,** exude; break out in a sweat, **get all in a lather** <nonformal>; sweat like a trooper *or* horse, swelter, wilt

**persuade** VERBS **prevail on** *or* **upon,** prevail with, **sway,** convince, lead to believe, **bring round,** bring to reason, bring to one's senses; **win, win over,** win around, bring over, draw over, gain, gain over; **talk over, talk into,** argue into, out-talk <nonformal>; hook *and* hook in <both nonformal>, con *and* do a snow job on <both nonformal>, sell *and* sell one on <both nonformal>, **charm, captivate;** wear down, overcome one's resistance, arm-twist *and* twist one's arm <both nonformal>

**persuasive** ADJS persuading; wheedling, cajoling; hortative, hortatory; exhortative, exhortatory; **convincing,** convictional, well-founded, assuring, impressive, satisfying, satisfactory, confidence-building; decisive, absolute, conclusive, determinative

**pert** ADJS **impudent, impertinent,** saucy, flip <nonformal>, flippant, **cocky** *and* cheeky *and* **fresh** *and* facy *and* crusty *and* nervy <all nonformal>; **animated,** spirited, bubbly, ebullient, effervescent, **vivacious, sprightly,** chipper *and* perky <both nonformal>

**pertinent** ADJS **relevant,** appertaining, **germane, apposite,** cogent, material, admissible, applicable, applying, pertaining, belonging, involving, appropriate, **apropos,** *à propos* <Fr>, to the purpose, **to the point,** in point, *ad rem* <L>

**perturb** VERBS **agitate,** disturb, trouble, disquiet, discompose, discombobulate <nonformal>, unsettle, **stir, ruffle,** shake, shake up, shock, upset, make waves, jolt, jar, rock, stagger, electrify, bring *or* pull one up short, give one a turn <nonformal>; fuss <nonformal>, flutter, flurry, rattle, disconcert, **fluster**

**peruse** VERBS **study,** regard studiously, **read,** go over, have one's nose in a book <nonformal>; contemplate; **examine**; give the mind to; **pore over,** vet <nonformal>; **search into,** go into, delve into, dig into, poke into, pry into; **probe,** sound, plumb, fathom

**pervade** VERBS **permeate,** penetrate; **suffuse,** inform, transfuse, perfuse, diffuse, leaven, imbue; **fill,** extend throughout, leave no void, occupy; **overrun,** overswarm, overspread, bespread, run through, meet one at every turn, whelm, overwhelm; creep *or* crawl *or* swarm with, be lousy with <nonformal>, teem with

**pervasive** ADJS pervading, suffusive, perfusive, suffusing, all-pervading, ubiquitous, omnipresent, **universal**

**perverse** ADJS **contrary,** wrongheaded, wayward, froward, difficult, cross-grained, cantankerous, feisty, ornery <nonformal>; sullen, sulky, stuffy; irascible

**pervert** NOUNS 1 **degenerate,** sexual pervert; **deviant,** deviate, sex *or* sexual pervert, sex fiend, sex criminal, sexual psychopath; sodomist, sodomite, bugger; pederast; paraphiliac; zoophiliac; pedophiliac; sadist; masochist; sadomasochist, algolagniac; fetishist; transvestite *or* TV, cross-dresser; narcissist; exhibitionist; necrophiliac; coprophiliac; scotophiliac, voyeur; erotomaniac, nymphomaniac, satyr; rapist

VERBS 2 **falsify,** twist, garble, put a false construction upon, give a spin, give a false coloring, color, varnish, slant, strain, torture; put words in someone's mouth; **bias;** misrepresent, misconstrue, misinterpret, misrender, misdirect; misuse; send *or* deliver the wrong signal *or* message

3 **corrupt,** debase, degrade, degenerate, **deprave,** debauch, defile, violate, desecrate, deflower, ravish, ravage, despoil; warp, twist

**pesky** ADJS **annoying,** troublesome, bothersome, worrisome, bothering, troubling, disturbing, plaguing, plaguesome, plaguey <nonformal>, pestilent, pestilential, pesty *and* pestiferous <both nonformal>, pestering, plaguing, nagging, dunning

**pessimist** NOUNS **cynic,** malist, nihilist; killjoy, gloomy Gus *and* calamity howler *and* worrywart <all nonformal>, seeksorrow, Job's comforter, prophet of doom, Cassandra, Eeyore; negativist; defeatist

*one who is always building dungeons in the air*
JOHN GALSWORTHY

**pest** NOUNS **nuisance, bother,** botheration <nonformal>, public nuisance, **trouble, problem,** pain <nonformal>, bore, crashing bore <nonformal>; **drag** *and* downer <both nonformal>; **pain in the neck** *or* **in the ass** <nonformal>; **blight**

**pester** VERBS **nag,** niggle, **carp at,** fuss at, fret at, yap *or* **pick at** <nonformal>, peck at, nibble at, **henpeck, pick on** *and* pick at <all nonformal>, bug *and* hassle <nonformal>

**pesticide** NOUNS **poison,** eradicant; systemic insecticide *or* systemic, fumigant, chemosterilant

**pet** NOUNS 1 **favorite,** preference; **darling,** idol, jewel, apple of one's eye, fair-haired boy, man after one's own heart; fondling, cosset, minion; spoiled child *or* darling, *enfant gâté* <Fr>; teacher's pet
VERBS 2 **stroke, caress,** fondle; **nuzzle,** nose, rub noses; feel up <nonformal>; rub, rub against, massage, knead
3 **pamper,** cosset, **coddle,** mollycoddle, make a lap dog of, **spoil;** spare the rod
ADJS 4 **beloved,** loved, dear, darling, precious; favorite; **cherished,** prized, treasured, held dear; **well-liked,** popular; **well-beloved,** dearly beloved, dear to one's heart, after one's heart *or* own heart, dear as the apple of one's eye

**peter out** VERBS be unproductive, **come to nothing,** come to naught, hang fire, flash in the pan, fizzle out

**petite** ADJS **little, small**, smallish; **slight,** exiguous; **puny, trifling,** poky, piffling *and* pindling *and* piddling *and* piddly <all nonformal>, **dinky** <nonformal>; pintsized <nonformal>, half-pint; knee-high, knee-high to a grasshopper; short

**petition** NOUNS 1 **request,** asking; the touch <nonformal>; desire, wish, expressed desire; petitioning, impetration, address; **application; requisition,** demand
VERBS 2 present *or* prefer a petition, sign a petition, circulate a petition; **pray,** sue; **apply to,** call on *or* upon; **supplicate,** invoke, make supplication, **implore, beseech**, obtest

**pet peeve** NOUNS **complaint,** grievance, peeve, **groan;** hard luck story <nonformal>, tale of woe

**petrified** ADJS 1 **terrified,** stunned, stupefied, paralyzed, frozen
2 **hardened,** lapidified <old>, fossilized

**petty** ADJS **insignificant,** inconsequential, negligible, unimportant, **trivial,** trifling, nugacious, nugatory, mean, niggling, picayune *or* picayunish, nickel-and-dime *and* penny-ante <both nonformal>; shallow, depthless, cursory, superficial, skin-deep; **ungenerous, illiberal,** small, little, paltry, mingy, **niggardly, stingy**

**petulant** ADJS **peevish,** pettish, **querulous, fretful,** resentful; **complaining,** faultfinding

**peyote** NOUNS

<nonformal> bad seed, big chief, buttons, cactus, P, topi

**phallic** ADJS **genital;** penile, penial

**phantom** NOUNS 1 **phantasm,** phantasma, wraith, specter; shadow, shade; phantasmagoria; **fantasy,** wildest dream; **figment of the imagination**, phantom of the mind; **apparition,** appearance; vision, waking dream; shape, form, figure, presence; eidolon, idolum
ADJS 2 **spectral,** specterlike; **ghostly,** ghostish, ghosty, ghostlike; **spiritual,** psychic, psychical; **phantomlike,** phantomic *or* phantomical, phantasmal, phantasmic, **wraithlike,** wraithy, shadowy; etheric, ectoplasmic, astral, ethereal; incorporeal

**pharmacy** NOUNS **drugstore,** chemist *and* chemist's shop <both Brit>, apothecary's shop, dispensary, dispensatory

**phenomenal** ADJS **wonderful,** wondrous, marvelous, miraculous, fantastic, fabulous, **prodigious,** stupendous, unheard-of, unprecedented, extraordinary, exceptional, rare, unique, singular, **remarkable,** striking, **sensational;** incredible, inconceivable, outlandish, unimaginable, incomprehensible; **bewildering,** puzzling, enigmatic

**phenomenon** NOUNS **event,** occurrence, incident, episode, experience, adventure, hap, **happening,** happenstance, fact, matter of fact, reality, particular, circumstance, **occasion,** turn of events

**philanderer** NOUNS woman chaser, **ladies' man,** heartbreaker; masher, lady-killer, wolf, skirt chaser, man on the make *and* make-out artist <both nonformal>; libertine, lecher, cocksman <nonformal>, seducer, Casanova, Don Juan

**philanthropic** ADJS **benevolent,** charitable, beneficent, altruistic, humanitarian; **bighearted,** largehearted, greathearted, freehearted; **generous**; almsgiving, eleemosynary; giving, generous to a fault, liberal

**philanthropist** NOUNS **altruist,** benevolist, **humanitarian,** man of good will, **do-gooder,** bleeding heart <nonformal>, well-doer, power for good; Robin Hood, Lady Bountiful

**philistine** NOUNS 1 **vulgarian,** low *or* vul-

gar *or* ill-bred fellow, *épicier* <Fr>; Babbitt, bourgeois; **conventionalist**
ADJS 2 **uncultured,** uncultivated, unrefined, rude; nonintellectual, **unintellectual; lowbrow** *and* lowbrowed *and* lowbrowish <all nonformal>

**philosopher** NOUNS philosophizer, philosophe; philosophaster; **thinker,** speculator; casuist; metaphysician, cosmologist; sophist

**philosophize** VERBS reason, probe

**philosophy** NOUNS **ideology,** system of ideas, body of ideas, system of theories; world view, *Weltanschauung* <Ger>; ethos

**phlegmatic** ADJS **lethargic,** hebetudinous, **dull,** desensitized, sluggish, torpid, languid, slack, soporific, comatose, **languorous,** apathetic, logy, dopey <nonformal>, groggy, heavy, leaden, flat, slack, tame, **dead,** lifeless

**phobia** NOUNS **fear, fright,** affright; **dread,** unholy dread, **terror, horror,** horrification, mortal *or* abject fear; funk *or* blue funk <both nonformal>; **panic,** panic fear *or* terror

**phone** NOUNS 1 **telephone,** horn <nonformal>, telephone set; telephone extension, extension; wall telephone, desk telephone; dial telephone, touch-tone telephone, push-button telephone; coin telephone, pay station, pay phone; mobile telephone *or* phone <nonformal>, cellular telephone *or* phone <nonformal>
VERBS 2 **telephone, call,** call on the phone <nonformal>, put in *or* make a call, **call up, ring,** ring up, give a ring *or* buzz <nonformal>, buzz <nonformal>

**phonic** ADJS **acoustic,** acoustical, **sonic;** subsonic, supersonic, ultrasonic, hypersonic; transonic *or* transsonic, faster than sound

**phony** NOUNS **fake** *and* **fraud** <both nonformal>; affecter; mannerist; **pretender,** actor, playactor <nonformal>, performer; paper tiger, hollow man, straw man, man of straw, empty suit <nonformal>; **hypocrite,** sanctimonious fraud, pharisee
ADJS 2 **imitation,** mock, sham, copied, fake <nonformal>, counterfeit, forged, plagiarized, unoriginal, ungenuine; **pseudo,** synthetic, synthetical, ersatz, hokey *and* hoked-up <both nonformal>; **assumed,** put-on, pretended, simulated, feigned, counterfeited; spurious; hypocritical

**phosphoresce** VERBS **luminesce,** fluoresce; iridesce, opalesce

**photograph** NOUNS 1 **photo** <nonformal>, heliograph, **picture,** shot <nonformal>; **snapshot,** snap <nonformal>; black-and-white photograph; color photograph, color print, heliochrome; slide, diapositive, transparency; candid photograph; still, still photograph; photomural; montage, photomontage; **portrait;** pinup <nonformal>, cheesecake *and* beefcake <both nonformal>; police photograph, **mug** *or* mug shot <nonformal>, positive, negative, print, enlargement, contact print, photocopy
VERBS 2 **shoot** <nonformal>, take a photograph, **take a picture,** take one's picture; **snap,** snapshot, snapshoot; **film,** get *or* capture on film; **mug** <nonformal>

**phrase** NOUNS 1 **maxim,** aphorism, apothegm, epigram, dictum, adage, proverb, gnome, words of wisdom, **saw, saying,** witticism, sentence, expression, catchword, catchphrase, word, byword, mot, motto, moral; common *or* current saying, stock saying, pithy saying, wise saying *or* expression, oracle, sententious expression *or* saying
VERBS 2 express, find a phrase for, give expression *or* words to, **word,** state, **frame,** conceive, style, couch, **put in** *or* **into words,** clothe *or* embody in words, couch in terms, express by *or* in words, find words to express; put, present, set out; **formulate,** formularize

**physical** NOUNS 1 **checkup,** physical examination, physical checkup, health examination; self-examination; exploratory examination
ADJS 2 **carnal,** carnal-minded, **fleshly,** bodily; **corporeal,** corporeous, corporal, **bodily;** somatic, somatical, somatous; worldly, earthly, here-and-now, **secular,** temporal, **unspiritual,** nonspiritual

**physician** NOUNS **doctor,** doc <nonformal>, Doctor of Medicine *or* MD, medical practitioner, medical man, medico <nonformal>, leech <old>, croaker *and* sawbones <both nonformal>; **general practitioner** *or* **GP;** family doctor; country doctor; **intern; resident,** house physician, resident physician; medical attendant, attending physician; **specialist,** board-certified physician *or* specialist; health-care professional, health-care provider, therapist, therapeutist, practitioner

**physique** NOUNS **body,** the person, carcass, anatomy, frame, bodily *or* corporal *or* corporeal entity, physical self, physical *or* bodily structure, soma; **musculature,** build, body-build, somatotype, constitution, genetic makeup

**piazza** NOUNS **porch,** stoop, **veranda,** patio, lanai, gallery

**picayune** ADJS **detailed,** minute, full, particular, meticulous, fussy, finicky *or* finicking *or* finical, picky <nonformal>, nice <old>, precise, exact, specific; **petty,** puny, piddling, piffling, niggling, pettifogging, picayunish; small-beer

**pick** NOUNS 1 **choice,** selection, election, preference, decision, **choosing,** free choice

2 plectrum, plectron

3 **the best,** the very best, the best ever, the top of the heap *or* the line <nonformal>, the tops <nonformal>; **select,** elect, elite, *corps d'élite* <Fr>, chosen; **cream, flower,** fat; cream of the crop, *crème de la crème* <Fr>, salt of the earth

VERBS 4 **strum, thrum, pluck,** plunk, twang, sweep the strings

5 **choose, elect,** go with <nonformal>, opt, opt for, co-opt, make *or* take one's choice, make choice of, have one's druthers <nonformal>, use *or* take up *or* exercise one's option; pick and choose; handpick, **pick out, single out,** choose out, smile on, give the nod <nonformal>, jump at, seize on; **decide between,** cull, glean, winnow, sift; separate the wheat from the chaff, separate the sheep from the goats

6 **harvest, reap,** crop, **glean, gather,** gather in, bring in, get in the harvest, reap and carry

**picket** NOUNS 1 picketer, demonstrator, picket line; counterdemonstrator

VERBS 2 **march,** demonstrate, counterdemonstrate

**pickle** NOUNS 1 **predicament,** plight, pass, fix *and* jam *and* spot *and* bind *and* scrape *and* stew <all nonformal>; pretty pickle *and* fine kettle of fish *and* how-do-you-do *and* fine how-do-you-do <all nonformal>; **spot,** tight spot; squeeze, tight squeeze

VERBS 2 **preserve, cure,** season, salt, brine, marinate *or* marinade, corn

**pickpocket** NOUNS cutpurse, fingersmith *and* dip <both nonformal>; **purse snatcher;** light-fingered gentry

**pickup** NOUNS 1 **bracer, refresher,** reviver, tonic, hair of the dog *or* hair of the dog that bit one <nonformal>

2 **acceleration,** quickening; getaway; step-up, speedup; thrust, drive, impetus; **increase**, upgrade, upping *and* boost <both nonformal>

**picky** ADJS **selective,** choosy, choicy <nonformal>; **strict**, perfectionistic, precisianistic, puristic; **critical, faultfinding,** carping, nitpicky <nonformal>, caviling, quibbling, pettifogging, captious, cynical

**picnic** NOUNS **good time,** lovely time, pleasant time; big time *and* **high time** *and* high old time <all nonformal>, laughs *and* lots of laughs *and* ball <all nonformal>, great fun

**picture** NOUNS 1 **image, likeness,** representation, tableau; photograph; **illustration,** illumination; mental image, mental picture, visual image, vivid *or* lifelike image, eidetic image, concept, **conception,** mental representation *or* presentation, *Vorstellung* <Ger>

*a poem without words*
HORACE

VERBS 2 **describe, portray,** render, **depict,** represent, delineate, limn, **paint,** draw; evoke, bring to life, make one see; **visualize,** vision, envision, envisage, image, objectify; picture in one's mind, picture to oneself, **view with the mind's eye,** contemplate in the imagination, form a mental picture of

**picturesque** ADJS **pictorial,** pictural, graphic; picturable; **fancy,** chichi, pretty-pretty

**piddling** ADJS **petty, puny,** piffling, niggling, pettifogging, picayune, picayunish; small-beer

**piece** NOUNS 1 **particle,** bit, scrap, bite, **fragment, morsel, crumb,** shard, potsherd, snatch, snack; **cut,** cutting, clip, clipping, paring, shaving, rasher, snip, snippet, chip, slice, collop, dollop, scoop; **tatter,** shred, stitch; **splinter,** sliver; **shiver,** smithereen <nonformal>; **lump,** gob <nonformal>, gobbet, hunk, chunk

2 **sex object;** meat *and* piece of meat *and* ass *and* piece of ass *and* hot number <all nonformal>

**piecemeal** ADVS **separately,** severally, one by one; **apart,** adrift, asunder, **in two,** in twain; apart from, away from, aside from; abstractly, in the abstract, objectively, impersonally

**pie in the sky** ADJS **ideal, idealized;** utopian, Arcadian, Edenic, paradisal

**pier** NOUNS 1 **pillar, column,** post, pilaster; pier buttress, buttress pier; **shaft**, upright, post, jack, pole, staff, stanchion, pile *or* piling
2 **dock,** dockage, **wharf,** quay

**pierce** VERBS **penetrate,** interpenetrate, pass *or* go through, get through, get into, make way into, **stab, stick** <nonformal>, plunge in; **run through,** impale, spit, **transfix,** transpierce

**piercing** ADJS 1 **shrill, thin,** sharp, acute, argute, keen, keening, ear-piercing; **screechy,** screeching, shrieky, shrieking, **squeaky,** squeaking, screaky, creaky, creaking; **penetrating,** stabbing, cutting, stinging, biting, keen, brisk, sharp, caustic, astringent
2 **cold,** freezing cold, **raw,** bleak, keen, sharp, bitter, biting, pinching, cutting, penetrating

**piety** NOUNS **piousness,** pietism; **religion,** faith; religiousness, religiosity, religionism, religious-mindedness; theism; love of God, adoration; **devoutness,** devotion, devotedness, worship, worshipfulness, prayerfulness, cultism; faithfulness, dutifulness, observance, churchgoing, conformity; **reverence,** veneration

**pig** NOUNS 1 **swine, hog,** porker; **shoat,** piggy, piglet, pigling; sucking *or* suckling pig; gilt; **boar, sow;** barrow; wild boar, tusker, razorback; warthog, babirusa
2 **glutton,** greedy eater, **hog** *and* chow hound *and* khazer <all nonformal>; slob

**pig out** VERBS **overeat,** overgorge, **overindulge, make a pig** *or* **hog of oneself,** pork out *or* scarf out <nonformal>; stuff oneself

**pigsty** NOUNS **hovel,** dump <nonformal>, rathole, hole, sty, pigpen, tumbledown shack

**pile** NOUNS 1 **down, fluff,** flue, floss, fuzz, fur
VERBS 2 **pile on,** heap, stack, heap *or* pile *or* stack up; mound, hill, bank, bank up; rick; pyramid; drift

**pilfer** VERBS **steal,** thieve, purloin, appropriate, take, snatch, palm, **make off with,** walk off with, run off *or* away with, abstract, disregard the distinction between *meum* and *tuum;* have one's hand in the till; **filch;** shoplift; embezzle; defraud, swindle

**pilgrim** NOUNS **traveler,** wayfarer, journeyer, trekker; **palmer,** hajji

**pilgrimage** NOUNS **journey,** *jornada* <Sp>, peregrination, sally; **expedition,** hajj, quest

**pill** NOUNS bolus, tablet, capsule, lozenge, troche

**the pill** NOUNS **contraceptive,** birth control device, oral contraceptive, **birth control pill,** morning-after pill, abortion pill

**pillage** VERBS **plunder, loot,** sack, ransack, rifle, freeboot, spoil, spoliate, despoil, depredate, prey on *or* upon, **raid,** reive <Scots>, ravage, ravish, raven, sweep, gut; maraud, foray, forage

**pillow** NOUNS cushion, bolster

**pilot** NOUNS 1 **steersman,** helmsman, wheelman, wheelsman, boatsteerer; conner, sailing master; harbor pilot, docking pilot; river pilot, navigator, timoneer, steerman, steerer, coxswain, boatheader
2 **aviator,** airman, flier, air pilot, licensed pilot, private pilot, airline pilot, commercial pilot, aeronaut, flyboy *and* airplane driver *and* birdman <all nonformal>; captain, chief pilot; copilot, second officer; stunt flier
VERBS 3 helm, coxswain, **steer,** guide, be at the helm *or* tiller, direct, manage, handle, run, operate, **conn** *or* cond, be at *or* have the conn; **navigate,** shape *or* chart a course
4 control, be at the controls, **fly,** manipulate, drive <nonformal>, fly left seat; **copilot,** fly right seat; solo; fly blind, fly by the seat of one's pants <nonformal>; follow the beam, ride the beam, fly on instruments; fly in formation
ADJS 5 **experimental,** test, trial; testing, proving, trying; probative, probatory, verificatory; heuristic

**pimp** NOUNS 1 **procurer,** pander *or* panderer, *maquereau* <Fr>, mack *or* mackman, ponce <Brit nonformal>; **bawd;** procuress, **madam** <nonformal>; white slaver
VERBS 2 procure, pander

**pimple** NOUNS **pustule,** papule, papula, fester, hickey *and* zit <both nonformal>; **rising,** lump, bump

**pin** NOUNS 1 **brooch,** stickpin, breastpin,

scatter pin, chatelaine; tie clasp *or* clip, tie bar, tiepin *or* scarfpin, tie tack *or* tie tac; lapel pin *or* button
VERBS 2 **skewer,** peg, nail, nail up, tack, staple, toggle, screw, bolt, rivet; spread-eagle <nonformal>, pin down

**pinch** NOUNS 1 **squeezing,** compression, clamping *or* clamping down, tightening; **pressure,** press, crush; **squeeze,** tweak, nip
2 **crisis, critical point,** crucial period, climax, climacteric; **turning point,** hinge, turn, turn of the tide, cusp; **emergency, exigency,** juncture *or* conjuncture *or* convergence of events, critical juncture, crossroads; clutch *and* crunch <nonformal>, rub, push, pass, strait, extremity, spot <nonformal>, **predicament,** bind, pass, situation
VERBS 3 **pain,** give *or* inflict pain, **hurt,** wound, afflict, distress; nip, bite, tweak

**pinched** ADJS 1 **constricted,** strangled, strangulated, choked, choked off, coarcted, **squeezed,** clamped, nipped, pinched-in, wasp-waisted; puckered, pursed; knitted, wrinkled
2 **straitened,** reduced to dire straits, in desperate straits, sore *or* sorely pressed, **hard-pressed, hard up** <nonformal>, up against it <nonformal>; driven from pillar to post; **desperate,** in extremities, *in extremis* <L>, at the end of one's rope *or* tether

**pinch-hit** VERBS **substitute for,** sub for <nonformal>, subrogate; **act for,** double for *or* as, stand *or* sit in for, understudy for, fill in for, stand in the stead of, step into *or* fill the shoes of; **relieve,** spell *and* **spell off** <both nonformal>, cover for

**pine** VERBS **grieve,** sorrow; weep, mourn; be dumb with grief; pine away; **eat one's heart out,** break one's heart over; **agonize,** ache, bleed; **languish,** droop, flag, wilt; fade, fade away

**pink** NOUNS 1 **acme of perfection,** pink of perfection, culmination, perfection, height, top, acme, ultimate, summit, pinnacle, peak, highest pitch, climax, consummation, *ne plus ultra* <L>, **the last word,** a dream come true
ADJS 2 **pinkish,** pinky; pink-cheeked; fresh-faced, fresh as a daisy *or* rose, fresh as April

**pink slip** NOUNS **dismissal,** the bounce, the sack <Brit nonformal>; the boot *and* the gate *and* the ax <all nonformal>; walking papers *or* ticket <nonformal>

**pinnacle** NOUNS **limit,** extremity, extreme, **acme,** apogee, climax, **maximum,** max <nonformal>, ceiling, **peak,** summit, crown, top

**pinpoint** VERBS **locate,** put one's finger on, **fix,** assign *or* consign *or* relegate to a place; zero in on, home in on; find *or* fix *or* calculate one's position, triangulate, find a line of position, **get a fix on** *or* navigational fix, navigate; **pin on,** fix on *or* upon, attach to, accrete to, connect with, fasten upon, hang on <nonformal>, **saddle on** *or* **upon,** place upon, **father upon,** settle upon, saddle with

**pinup** NOUNS **photograph,** cheesecake *and* beefcake <both nonformal>; centerfold

**pioneer** NOUNS 1 **vanguard,** spearhead, advance guard, **cutting edge,** avant-garde, outguard; precursor; **settler,** *habitant* <Canadian & Louisiana Fr>; **colonist,** colonizer, colonial, immigrant, planter; **homesteader**
VERBS 2 **go before,** blaze *or* break the trail, break new ground, be in the van *or* vanguard; **lead,** lead *or* show the way; precede, **take the initiative,** take the first step, take the lead; **break the ice,** take the plunge, break ground, cut the first turf, lay the first stone
ADJS 3 **original,** novel, unprecedented; new, fresh; underived, **firsthand; avant-garde,** revolutionary; bellwether, trailblazing

**pious** ADJS **religious,** religious-minded; theistic; **devout,** devoted, worshipful, prayerful, cultish, cultist, cultistic; **reverent,** reverential, venerative, venerational, adoring, solemn; faithful, dutiful; affirming, witnessing, believing; **observant,** practicing

**pipe** NOUNS 1 tobacco pipe; corncob, corncob pipe, Missouri meerschaum; briar pipe, briar; clay pipe, clay, churchwarden <Brit>; meerschaum; water pipe, hookah, nargileh, kalian, hubble-bubble; peace pipe, calumet
2 **tube;** tubing, piping, tubulation; tubulure
VERBS 3 **channel,** put through channels; tube, pipeline, flume, **siphon, funnel,** tap
4 **blow a horn,** sound *or* wind the horn, sound, blow, wind, **toot,** tootle, tweedle

**pipe dream** NOUNS **airy hope,** unreal hope, dream, golden dream, bubble, chimera, fool's paradise, quixotic ideal, utopia

**pipsqueak** NOUNS **nonentity,** empty suit *and* nebbish <both nonformal>, an obscurity, a nothing, cipher; whippersnapper *and* whiffet *and* squirt *and* shrimp *and* scrub *and* runt <all nonformal>

**pique** NOUNS 1 **huff,** pet, tiff, miff *and* stew <both nonformal>, fret, **fume,** ferment
VERBS 2 **annoy,** irk, vex, nettle, provoke, miff *and* peeve <both nonformal>, distemper, **ruffle, disturb,** discompose, **roil,** rile, **exasperate,** exercise, try one's patience, try the patience of a saint
3 **stimulate,** whet, sharpen, quicken, enliven, liven up, pick up, jazz up <nonformal>, animate, **exhilarate,** invigorate, galvanize, fillip, give a fillip to

**pirate** NOUNS **corsair, buccaneer, privateer,** sea rover, rover, picaroon; air pirate, airplane hijacker, skyjacker

**pirouette** NOUNS 1 **whirl,** wheel, reel, **spin, turn,** round
VERBS 2 **spin,** turn, round, **go round** *or* **around,** turn round *or* around; turn a pirouette

**piss** NOUNS 1 **urine,** water, number one, *pish* <Yiddish>, pee *and* pee-pee *and* wee-wee *and* whizz <all nonformal>, piddle, stale
VERBS 2 **urinate,** pass *or* make water, wet, stale, piddle, pee; pee-pee *and* wee-wee *and* whizz *and* take a whizz *and* number one <all nonformal>, spend a penny, pump bilge

**pit** NOUNS 1 **well, shaft,** sump; **chasm,** gulf, abyss, abysm; **excavation,** dig, diggings, workings; mine, quarry
2 **indentation,** indent, indention, indenture, **dent,** dint; pock, pockmark
3 **stone,** nut; pip; fruit; grain, kernel
VERBS 4 **indent,** dent, dint, **depress,** press in, stamp, tamp, punch, punch in, impress, imprint; pock, pockmark; dimple

**pitch** NOUNS 1 **tone, frequency,** audio frequency *or* AF; intonation
2 **incline,** inclination, **slope, grade,** gradient, **ramp,** rapid *or* steep slope; **extent, measure,** amount, ratio, proportion, stint, standard, height, reach, remove, compass, range, scale, scope, caliber
3 **sales talk,** sales pitch, patter; spiel *or* ballyhoo <both nonformal>
VERBS 4 **toss, tumble,** toss and tumble, pitch and toss, **plunge,** hobbyhorse, pound, **rear, rock,** roll, reel, swing, sway, lurch, yaw, heave, scend, **flounder, welter, wallow;** make heavy weather
5 **incline,** lean; slope, slant, rake, grade, bank, shelve; **tilt,** tip, list, cant, careen, keel, sidle, swag, sway
6 **proposition, come on to,** hit on, put *or* make a move on, make *or* throw a pass, george, **make a play for,** play footsie with, mash <old> <all nonformal>

**pitfall** NOUNS **trap,** trapfall, deadfall; baited trap; **booby trap,** mine; decoy

**pithy** ADJS **aphoristic,** proverbial, epigrammatic, epigrammatical; **sententious,** gnomic, pungent, succinct, terse, crisp, pointed

**pittance** NOUNS dole; drop in the bucket *or* the ocean; **mite,** bit; short allowance, half rations, cheeseparings and candle ends; mere subsistence, starvation wages; widow's mite

**pitted** ADJS **rough,** jolty, **bumpy,** rutty, rutted, pocky, potholed

**pity** NOUNS 1 **sympathy,** feeling, fellow feeling in suffering, **commiseration,** condolence, condolences; **compassion, mercy,** ruth, rue, humanity; **sensitivity; clemency,** quarter, reprieve, mitigation, relief, favor, grace; **leniency,** lenity, gentleness; **kindness,** benevolence; pardon, **forgiveness**; self-pity; **pathos**
VERBS 2 **be** *or* **feel sorry for,** feel sorrow for; **commiserate,** compassionate; open one's heart; **sympathize, sympathize with,** feel for, weep for, lament for, bleed, bleed for, have one's heart bleed for *or* go out to, condole with

**pivot** VERBS **turn round** *or* **around** *or* **about,** turn, make a U-turn, turn on a dime, turn tail, **come** *or* **go about,** put about, fetch about; **swivel,** pivot about, swing, round, swing round; wheel, wheel about, whirl, spin; heel, turn upon one's heel

**pivotal** ADJS **urgent, imperative,** imperious, **compelling, pressing,** high-priority, high-pressure, crying, clamorous, insistent, instant, exigent; crucial, critical, acute

**pixie** NOUNS **imp,** sprite, elf, puck, kobold, *diablotin* <Fr>, tokoloshe, poltergeist, **gremlin,** Dingbelle, Fifinella, **bad fairy,** bad peri; little *or* young devil, devilkin, deviling; erlking

**pizazz** NOUNS **liveliness,** animation, vivacity, vivaciousness, **sprightliness,** spiritedness, bubbliness, ebullience, effervescence, **briskness,** breeziness, peppiness <nonformal>; **life,** spirit, verve, energy, adrenalin; pep *and* moxie *and* oomph *and* piss and vinegar <all nonformal>, **vim**

**placard** NOUNS **poster, bill,** sign, show card, banner, *affiche* <Fr>

**placate** VERBS **pacify,** conciliate, propitiate, appease, mollify, dulcify; **calm,** settle, soothe, tranquilize; smooth, smooth over *or* out, smooth down, smooth one's feathers; cool <nonformal>, defuse; clear the air

**place** NOUNS 1 **location, situation,** position, spot, *lieu* <Fr>, placement, emplacement, stead; **whereabouts,** whereabout, ubicity; **locality,** locale, locus; abode; **site,** situs; **point,** pinpoint, exact spot *or* point, very spot *or* point; *locus classicus* <L>
VERBS 2 **locate, situate,** site, position; emplace, spot <nonformal>, **install,** put in place; **allocate,** collocate, dispose, deploy, assign; **localize,** narrow *or* pin down; **pinpoint,** zero in on, home in on; **recognize,** know, tell, distinguish, make out; identify, have

**placement** NOUNS **positioning,** emplacement, situation, location, siting, localization, **locating, placing,** putting; allocation, collocation, **disposition,** assignment, **deployment,** posting, stationing, spotting

**placid** ADJS **calm,** quiet, **tranquil, serene,** peaceful; **cool, coolheaded,** cool as a cucumber <nonformal>; unruffled, untroubled, stolid, stoic, stoical, impassive

**plagiarize** VERBS **pirate,** borrow *and* crib <both nonformal>, steal, appropriate; **pick one's brains;** infringe, infringe a copyright

**plague** NOUNS 1 **epidemic, pestilence,** pest, pandemic, pandemia, scourge; **infestation,** infestment; **invasion,** swarming, swarm, teeming, ravage; **bane, curse,** affliction, infliction, visitation, calamity, scourge, **torment,** open wound, running sore, grievance, woe, burden, crushing burden; disease; death; evil, harm
VERBS 2 **trouble,** beset; **bother,** pother, get one down, <nonformal>, disturb, perturb, irk, **torment,** drive one up the wall <nonformal>, give one gray hair, make one lose sleep; **harass,** vex, distress; inconvenience, **put out,** put out of the way, discommode; **concern,** worry; **puzzle,** perplex; give one a hard time *and* give one a bad time *and* make it tough for <all nonformal>

**plain** NOUNS 1 **plains,** flat country, flatland, **flats,** flat, level; champaign, champaign country, open country, **wide-open spaces; prairie,** grassland, sea of grass, **steppe, pampas,** *pampa* <Sp>, savanna, tundra, vega, campo, llano, sebkha; **veld,** grass veld, bushveld, tree veld; **plateau,** upland, tableland, table, **mesa,** mesilla; peneplain; coastal plain, tidal plain, alluvial plain, delta, delta plain; mare, lunar mare
ADJS 2 **distinct,** clear, obvious, evident, patent, unmistakable, not to be mistaken, much in evidence, plain to be seen, for all to see, showing for all to see, plain as the nose on one's face, plain as day, clear as day, plain as plain can be, big as life and twice as ugly; **definite,** defined, well-defined, well-marked, well-resolved, in focus; **clear-cut,** crystal-clear, clear as crystal; **simple,** bare, bare-bones *and* no-frills <both nonformal>, mere
3 **homely,** not much to look at, not much for looks, short on looks <nonformal>, hard on the eyes <nonformal>
ADVS 4 **absolutely,** perfectly, quite, right, stark, clean, sheer, plumb <nonformal>; irretrievably, unrelievedly, irrevocably

**plaintive** ADJS **sorrowful,** sorrowing, sorrowed, **mournful,** rueful, woeful, doleful, plangent; anguished; dolorous, **grievous,** lamentable, lugubrious; **tearful**

**plan** NOUNS 1 **scheme, design,** method, **program,** device, contrivance, game, envisagement, conception, enterprise, **idea, notion;** organization, rationalization, systematization, schematization; **planning,** calculation, figuring; long-range planning, long-range plan; **master plan,** the picture *and* the big picture <both nonformal>; approach, attack, plan of attack; way, procedure; **arrangement,** prearrangement, system, disposition, layout, setup, lineup; blueprint, **guideline, guidelines,** program of action; methodology; working plan, ground plan, tactical plan, strategic

plan; tactics, **strategy,** game plan <nonformal>; contingency plan
VERBS 2 **devise,** contrive, design, frame, shape, cast, concert, lay plans; organize, rationalize, systematize, schematize, configure, pull together, sort out; **arrange,** prearrange, make arrangements, set up, work up, work out; **schedule;** lay down a plan, shape *or* mark out a course; program; **project,** cut out, make a projection, plan ahead; intend

**plant** NOUNS 1 **vegetable; weed;** angiosperm, flowering plant; monocotyledon *or* monocot *or* monocotyl; dicotyledon *or* dicot *or* dicotyl; exotic, hothouse plant; ephemeral, annual, biennial, triennial, perennial; evergreen, deciduous plant; aquatic plant, hydrophyte
2 **shill,** decoy, **come-on man** <nonformal>, capper, stool pigeon, stoolie <nonformal>; *agent provocateur* <Fr>
3 **factory, works,** manufacturing plant, *usine* <Fr>; push-button plant, automated *or* cybernated *or* automatic *or* robot factory; assembly *or* production line; defense plant, munitions plant, armory, arsenal; **power plant**
VERBS 4 **set,** put in; **sow, seed,** seed down, seminate, inseminate; **disseminate,** broadcast, sow broadcast, scatter seed; drill; bed; dibble; **transplant,** reset, pot
5 **establish,** fix, site, pitch, seat; **found, base,** ground, lay the foundation; **cache,** stash <nonformal>, deposit; **bury**

**plastic** NOUNS 1 **thermoplastic;** thermosetting plastic; resin plastic; cellulose plastic; protein plastic; cast plastic, molded plastic, extruded plastic
2 **credit card,** plastic, plastic money *or* credit, gold card, charge card, charge plate; smart card, supersmart card
ADJS 3 **compliant,** pliant, complaisant, malleable, flexible, acquiescent, unmurmuring, other-directed, submissive, tractable, obedient

**plate** VERBS chromium-plate, copperplate, gold-plate, nickel-plate, silverplate; **electroplate, galvanize,** anodize

**plateau** NOUNS 1 **tableland,** high plateau, table, mesa, table mountain, butte, moor, fell <Brit>, hammada
2 **plane,** level

**platform** NOUNS 1 **stage,** estrade, dais, floor; **rostrum,** podium, pulpit, speaker's platform *or* stand, **soapbox** <nonformal>; hustings, **stump;** tribunal; emplacement; catafalque
2 party platform, **program,** declaration of policy

**platitude** NOUNS **cliché,** saw, old saw, commonplace, banality, bromide, **chestnut** <nonformal>, corn <nonformal>, tired phrase, trite saying, hackneyed *or* stereotyped saying, commonplace expression, *locus communis* <L>, **familiar tune** *or* **story,** old song *or* story, old song and dance <nonformal>, twice-told tale

**platonic** ADJS **continent;** abstemious, abstinent

**plausible** ADJS **believable,** credible; tenable, conceivable, colorable; **possible,** within the bounds *or* realm *or* range *or* domain of possibility, humanly possible; **conceivable,** conceivably possible, **imaginable,** thinkable, cogitable

**play** VERBS 1 **perform,** execute, render, do; interpret; make music; play by ear; play at, pound out *and* saw away at <both nonformal>
2 **sport,** disport; frolic, rollick, gambol, frisk, romp, caper, cut capers <nonformal>, lark about <Brit nonformal>, antic, curvet, cavort, caracole, flounce, trip, skip, dance; **cut up** <nonformal>, cut a dido <nonformal>, horse around <nonformal>, fool around, carry on <nonformal>
3 **gamble,** game, try one's luck *or* fortune; **speculate**

**playboy** NOUNS **dissipater,** free liver, high liver <nonformal>; nighthawk *and* nightowl <both nonformal>; partyer, partygoer, man-about-town

**play down** VERBS **minimize,** underplay, downplay, de-emphasize; **soften, subdue,** tame, hold in check, keep a tight rein, chasten, tone *or* tune down

**player** NOUNS 1 **participator,** participant, partaker, sharer; party, **a party to,** accomplice, accessory; **actor, actress,** stage player *or* performer, playactor, histrion, histrio, thespian, trouper; **instrumentalist,** instrumental musician; **athlete; gambler,** gamester, sport
2 **person** *or* **woman** *or* **man** of influence, a presence, a palpable presence, a mover and shaker <nonformal>, a person to be reckoned with, a player on the scene; heavyweight, big wheel *and* biggie *and* heavy *or* long-ball hitter *and* piledriver <all nonformal>, very important person *or* VIP <nonformal>

**playful** ADJS **sportive,** sportful; **frolicsome,** gamesome, rompish, larkish, capersome; waggish

**plaza** NOUNS **square,** *place* <Fr>, *piazza* <Ital>, *campo* <Ital>, **marketplace,** market, mart, rialto, forum, agora

**plea** NOUNS **entreaty, appeal,** bid, suit, call, cry, clamor, *cri du cœur* <Fr>, beseeching, impetration, obtestation; **supplication,** prayer, rogation, **beseechment,** imploring, imploration, obsecration, obtestation, adjuration, imprecation; **invocation,** invocatory plea *or* prayer; **defense,** pleading, **case,** *plaidoyer* <Fr>, brief

**plead** VERBS **enter a plea** *or* **pleading,** argue at the bar; **plead** *or* **argue one's case,** present one's case, make a plea, tell it to the judge <nonformal>

**plead with** VERBS **coax,** wheedle, cajole, blandish, sweet-talk *and* soft-soap <both nonformal>, **exhort,** call on *or* upon, advocate, recommend, put in a good word, buck for *and* hype <both nonformal>; insist, insist upon

**pleasant** ADJS **pleasing, pleasureful,** pleasurable; fair, fair and pleasant, **enjoyable,** pleasure-giving; felicitous, felicific; **likable, desirable,** to one's liking, to one's taste, to *or* after one's fancy, after one's own heart; **agreeable,** complaisant, harmonious, *en rapport* <Fr>, compatible; **blissful;** sweet, mellifluous, honeyed, dulcet; mellow; **gratifying,** satisfying, rewarding, heartwarming, grateful; **welcome,** welcome as the roses in May; genial, congenial, cordial, *gemütlich* <Ger>, affable, amiable, amicable, gracious; cheerful

**please** VERBS 1 **pleasure, give pleasure,** afford one pleasure, be to one's liking, sit well with one, meet one's wishes, take *or* strike one's fancy, feel good *or* right, strike one right; do one's heart good, warm the cockles of one's heart; **suit,** suit one down to the ground; **indulge,** humor, oblige; favor, gratify, satisfy, **cater to**

2 <nonformal> **hit the spot,** be just the ticket, be just what the doctor ordered, **make a hit,** go over big, go over with a bang

**pleasure** NOUNS **enjoyment;** quiet pleasure, euphoria, well-being, good feeling, **contentment,** content, **ease,** comfort; **gratification, satisfaction,** great satisfaction, hearty enjoyment, keen pleasure *or* satisfaction; **self-gratification,** self-indulgence; instant gratification; kicks <nonformal>, **fun,** entertainment, amusement; intellectual pleasure, pleasures of the mind; physical pleasure, creature comforts, bodily pleasure, sense *or* sensuous pleasure

**pleat** NOUNS 1 **pleating,** plait *or* plat; accordion pleat, box pleat, knife pleat
VERBS 2 **fold,** fold on itself, fold up; **plait,** plat <nonformal>; **tuck, gather,** tuck up, ruck, ruck up

**plebeian** NOUNS 1 **common man,** commoner, **average man,** ordinary man, typical man, **man in the street,** one of the people, man of the people, Everyman; pleb <slang>; ordinary *or* average Joe *and* Joe Doakes *and* Joe Sixpack <all nonformal>, John Doe, Jane Doe, John Smith, Mr *or* Mrs Brown *or* Smith
ADJS 2 **common, commonplace,** ordinary; homely, homespun; **general,** public, popular, pop <nonformal>

**pledge** NOUNS 1 **promise,** solemn promise, troth, plight, faith, parole, **word, word of honor,** solemn declaration *or* word; **oath,** vow; **assurance,** guarantee, warranty; **gage,** *pignus, vadium* <both L>; **earnest,** earnest money, god's penny, handsel; **bail,** bond, vadimonium; **hostage,** surety
VERBS 2 **deposit, stake,** post, put in escrow, **put up,** put up as collateral, lay out *or* down; **pawn,** put in pawn, **hock** *and* **put in hock** <both nonformal>; mortgage, hypothecate, bottomry, bond; **put up** *or* **go bail,** bail out; **subscribe,** put oneself down for; **obligate,** oblige, require, make incumbent *or* imperative, tie, **bind,** commit, saddle with, put under an obligation

**plenty** NOUNS 1 plenitude, plentifulness; myriad, myriads, numerousness; **amplitude,** ampleness; **abundance,** copiousness; **bountifulness,** bounteousness, liberalness, **liberality,** generousness, **generosity; lavishness,** extravagance, prodigality; luxuriance, fertility, teemingness, productiveness; **wealth,** opulence *or* opulency, richness, affluence; more than enough; maximum; **prevalence,** profuseness, **profusion,** riot; superabundance; no end of, great abundance, great plenty, as much as one could wish, more than one can shake a

stick at, lots, a fistful <nonformal>, **scads**
ADJS 2 **sufficient,** sufficing; **enough,** ample, substantial, **satisfactory,** adequate, decent, due; plenty good enough <nonformal>; sufficient for *or* to *or* unto, up to, equal to; **plentiful,** plenteous, plenitudinous, **ample,** all-sufficing; superabundant; a dime a dozen

**pliable** ADJS **pliant, flexible,** flexile, flexuous, **plastic,** elastic, tractile, **tractable,** yielding, giving, bending; adaptable, **malleable,** moldable, shapable, fabricable, fictile; compliant, submissive; like putty *or* clay

**plight** NOUNS **predicament,** spot of trouble, **strait,** straits, parlous straits, tightrope, knife-edge, thin edge; **pinch, bind,** pass, clutch, situation, emergency; **embarrassment,** embarrassing position *or* situation; **complication,** imbroglio; the devil to pay

**plod** VERBS **plug,** plug at, plug away *or* along; pound *or* hammer away; keep one's nose to the grindstone, struggle along, struggle on, work away

**plodder** NOUNS **drudge,** grub, hack, slave, galley slave, **workhorse,** beast of burden, slogger; grind *and* greasy grind <both nonformal>

**plot** NOUNS 1 plot of ground *or* land, parcel of land, plat, **patch, tract, field;** lot
2 **intrigue,** web of intrigue, **scheme,** deep-laid plot *or* scheme, game *or* little game <both nonformal>, trick, stratagem, finesse; **conspiracy,** confederacy, covin, cabal
VERBS 3 **map,** chart, **diagram,** graph; **sketch,** sketch in *or* out, draw up a plan; map out, plot out, **lay out,** set out, mark out; lay off, mark off
4 **scheme, intrigue,** be up to something; **conspire, connive,** collude, cabal; **hatch, hatch up,** cook up <nonformal>, brew, concoct, hatch a plot; counterplot, countermine

**plow** VERBS **cultivate,** culture, **work, till,** till the soil, dig, delve, spade; plow in, plow under, plow up, list, fallow, backset <W US>; **harrow**

**ploy** NOUNS **trick,** artifice, device, gambit, stratagem, **scheme,** design, *ficelle* <Fr>, **subterfuge,** blind, **ruse,** wile, **dodge,** artful dodge, sleight, pass, feint, fetch, chicanery

**pluck** NOUNS **spunk** <nonformal>, **mettle, backbone** <nonformal>, **grit,** true grit, spirit, **stamina,** guts *and* moxie <both nonformal>, pith <old>, bottom, **toughness** <nonformal>; pluckiness, spunkiness <nonformal>, **gameness,** feistiness <nonformal>, mettlesomeness; courage

**plug** NOUNS 1 **hydrant,** fire hydrant, water plug, fireplug
2 **stopper,** stop, **stopple,** stopgap; **cork,** bung, spike, spile, spigot
3 **publicity,** ballyhoo *and* hoopla <both nonformal>; **writeup,** puff <nonformal>, **blurb** <nonformal>; promo *and* hype <both nonformal>; commendation
VERBS 4 **stop up; obstruct,** bar, stay; **block,** block up; **clog,** clog up, foul; **choke,** choke up *or* off; **fill,** fill up; **stuff,** pack, jam; **congest,** stuff up; plug up
5 **publicize,** give publicity; promote, build up, cry up, sell, puff <nonformal>, **boost** <nonformal>, **ballyhoo** <nonformal>; make a pitch for *and* beat the drum for *and* thump the tub for <all nonformal>; recommend
6 keep doggedly at, **plod,** drudge, slog *or* slog away, soldier on, put one foot in front of the other, peg away *or* at *or* on; **plug at,** plug away *or* along; pound *or* hammer away; keep one's nose to the grindstone

**plumage** NOUNS **feathers,** feather, feathering; contour feathers; breast feathers; hackle; flight feathers; remiges, primaries, secondaries, tertiaries; covert, tectrices

**plump** VERBS 1 **fatten,** fat; **gain weight,** gather flesh, take *or* put on weight, become overweight
2 knead, plump up, fluff, fluff up, shake up
ADJS 3 **overweight,** fattish, buxom, *zaftig* <Yiddish>, pleasantly plump, full, huggy <nonformal>, **tubby** <nonformal>, roly-poly; **pudgy,** podgy

**plunder** NOUNS 1 **booty,** spoil, **spoils,** loot, swag <nonformal>, ill-gotten gains, haul, take, pickings, stealings, stolen goods, hot goods *or* items <nonformal>; **boodle** *and* squeeze *and* **graft** <all nonformal>
VERBS 2 **pillage,** loot, sack, ransack, rifle, freeboot, spoil, spoliate, despoil, depredate, prey on *or* upon, **raid,** ravage, ravish, raven, sweep, gut; **fleece**

**plunge** NOUNS 1 **dive,** pitch, drop, fall; free-fall; header <nonformal>; **swoop,**

pounce; **decline,** plummet, plummeting, nose dive *and* slump *and* sag <all nonformal>, free fall
VERBS 2 **dive,** pitch, plummet; swoop, swoop down, stoop, **pounce,** pounce on *or* upon; nose-dive, make *or* take a nose dive; **fall,** decline, drop, crash, head for the bottom, sag, slump; break, give way; reach a new low

**plurality** NOUNS pluralness; a greater number, a certain number; **several,** some, a few, more; the greater number

**plus** ADJS 1 **additional,** supplementary, supplemental; extra, further, **more,** new, **other,** another, ulterior; **surplus,** spare
ADVS 2 **additionally,** in addition, also, and then some, even more, more so, and also, and all <nonformal>, and so, **as well,** too, else, beside, **besides,** to boot, not to mention, let alone, into the bargain; on top of, over, above; **beyond**

**plush** ADJS **grandiose, sumptuous,** elegant, elaborate, luxurious, extravagant, deluxe; executive *and* posh *and* ritzy *and* swank *and* swanky <all nonformal>; **velvety,** plushy, soft as silk

**pock** NOUNS **furuncle,** boil, carbuncle, pustule; **pit,** pockmark; impression, impress; **blemish**

**pocket** VERBS 1 **retain, keep, save,** save up, hip-pocket <nonformal>; **maintain,** preserve; get into one's hold *or* possession; palm; draw off, drain off; skim *and* skim off *and* take up front <all nonformal>
ADJS 2 **miniature,** diminutive, **small-scale,** pocketsized, **vest-pocket;** handy, compact

**pocketbook** NOUNS **purse,** wallet, bag, handbag, poke <nonformal>, porte-monnaie, moneybag; money belt, money clip

**pod** NOUNS **hull,** shell, capsule, case, **husk, shuck; seed vessel,** seedcase, seedbox, pericarp; **capsule,** cod <nonformal>, seed pod

**podium** NOUNS **platform; stage,** estrade, dais, floor; **rostrum,** pulpit, speaker's platform *or* stand, **soapbox** <nonformal>; hustings, **stump**

**poem** NOUNS **verse, rhyme,** verselet, versicle; **thing of beauty,** vision, picture <nonformal>, eyeful <nonformal>, **sight** *or* **treat for sore eyes** <nonformal>

*imaginary gardens with real toads in them*
MARIANNE MOORE

**poet** NOUNS **poetess,** ballad maker, balladmonger; **bard, minstrel,** scop, fili, baird, skald, **jongleur, troubadour,** *trovatore* <Ital>, trouveur, *trouvère* <Fr>, *Meistersinger* <Ger>, minnesinger; **poet laureate;** occasional poet; **lyric poet;** epic poet; pastoral poet, pastoralist, idyllist, rhapsodist, rhapsode

**poetic** ADJS **poetical,** poetlike; **lyrical, narrative,** dramatic, lyrico-dramatic; bardic; runic, skaldic; epic, heroic; pastoral, bucolic, eclogic, idyllic

**poetry** NOUNS poesy, **verse,** song, rhyme

*the rhythmic, inevitably narrative, movement from an overclothed blindness to a naked vision*
DYLAN THOMAS

**poignant** ADJS **exquisite,** acute, sharp, **keen,** vivid, intense, extreme, excruciating; **pungent,** piquant; **deep-felt,** deep-going, from the heart, heartfelt, penetrating, penetrant, piercing, acute; **pathetic,** affecting, touching, moving, saddening

**point** NOUNS 1 pinpoint, pinhead, **dot; tip,** cusp; acumination, mucro; **nib,** neb
2 **meaning, significance,** signification, *significatum* <L>, *signifié* <Fr>, **sense,** idea, purport, import, where one is coming from <nonformal>; **particular,** instance, item, detail, count, case, fact, matter, article, datum, element, part, ingredient, factor, facet, aspect, thing
VERBS 3 **direct,** aim, turn, bend, train, fix, set, determine; point to *or* at, hold on, fix on, sight on; take aim, aim at, turn *or* train upon; give a push in the right direction; tend, tend to go, **incline,** head, lead, lean

**point-blank** ADJS 1 **directly,** to the point; candidly, frankly
ADVS 2 **exactly, precisely,** to a T, expressly; **just, dead,** right, straight, even, square, **plumb,** directly, squarely

**pointless** ADJS **useless,** of no use, no go <nonformal>; **aimless,** meaningless, **purposeless,** of no purpose, feckless; **unavailing,** of no avail, failed; ineffective, **ineffectual**; impotent; **superfluous**

**point of view** NOUNS **viewpoint,** standpoint, vantage, vantage point, point *or* coign of vantage, where one stands; bird's-eye view, worm's-eye view, fly on the wall; **outlook,** angle, angle of vision, *optique* <Fr>; mental outlook; **opinion,**

sentiment, feeling, sense, impression, reaction, **notion,** idea, thought, mind, thinking, **way of thinking,** attitude, stance, posture, position, mindset, **view,** sight, lights, observation, **conception,** concept, conceit, **estimation,** estimate, consideration, **theory**, assumption, presumption, **conclusion, judgment**, personal judgment

**point out** VERBS **call attention to,** direct attention to, **bring under** *or* **to one's notice,** hold up to notice, bring to attention, **mention,** mention in passing, touch on; **single out,** pick out, lift up, focus on, call *or* bring to notice, direct to the attention, **feature,** highlight; **direct to,** address to; **point to,** point at, put *or* lay one's finger on; **excite** *or* **stimulate attention,** drum up attention

**poise** NOUNS **equanimity,** equilibrium, equability, balance; **levelheadedness,** level head, well-balanced *or* well-regulated mind; aplomb, **self-possession,** self-control, self-command, self-restraint, restraint, possession, **presence of mind;** confidence, assurance, **self-confidence,** self-assurance

**poison** NOUNS 1 **venom,** venin, virus <old>, toxic, toxin, toxicant; eradicant, **pesticide; insecticide, herbicide,** defoliant, Agent Orange, paraquat, **weed killer;** fungicide; microbicide, germicide, antiseptic, disinfectant, antibiotic
VERBS 2 envenom; **contaminate,** confound, **pollute,** vitiate, infect, taint; **pervert,** warp, twist, distort

**poisonous** ADJS **toxic,** toxicant; **venomous,** envenomed, venenate, venenous; pollutive; **virulent,** noxious, malignant, malign, destructive, deadly; pestiferous, pestilential

**poke** NOUNS 1 **hit,** blow, stroke, knock, rap, pound, slam, bang, crack, **whack, smack,** thwack, smash, dash, swipe, swing, **punch, jab,** dig, drub, thump, pelt, cut, chop, dint, slog
VERBS 2 **go slow** *or* **slowly,** go at a snail's pace, take it slow, get no place fast <nonformal>; **poke along;** drag along, drag one's feet
3 **goad, prod,** nudge, prod at, goose <nonformal>, **spur,** prick, sting, needle; **punch,** jab, thwack, **smack,** clap, crack, swipe, **whack**

**poky** ADJS **slow, leisurely,** poking, slowpoky <nonformal>; slow as molasses *or* molasses in January, slow as death

**pole** NOUNS 1 **spar,** timber; **mast,** stick *and* tree <both nonformal>
2 **extremity, extreme; limit**, ultimacy, definitiveness, **boundary,** farthest bound, jumping-off place, Thule, *Ultima Thule* <L>

**polemic** NOUNS **argumentation,** argument, controversy, dispute, disputation, debate, eristic; war of words, verbal engagement *or* contest

**police** NOUNS 1 **police force,** law enforcement agency; **constabulary;** state police, troopers *or* state troopers, highway patrol, county police, provincial police
2 policeman, constable, officer, police officer, *flic* <Fr nonformal>, *gendarme* <Fr>, *carabiniere* <Ital>; peace officer, law enforcement agent, arm of the law; military policeman *or* MP; detective; policewoman, police matron; patrolman, police constable <England>; trooper, mounted policeman; reeve, portreeve; **sheriff, marshal;** deputy sheriff, deputy, bound bailiff, catchpole, beagle <nonformal>, bombailiff <Brit nonformal>; sergeant, police sergeant; roundsman; lieutenant, police lieutenant; captain, police captain; inspector, police inspector; superintendent, chief of police; commissioner, police commissioner; government man, federal, fed *and* G-man <both nonformal>; narc <nonformal>; **bailiff,** tipstaff, tipstaves <pl>; mace-bearer, lictor, sergeant at arms; beadle; traffic officer, meter maid

3 <nonformal> cop, copper, John Law, bluecoat, bull, flatfoot, gumshoe, gendarme, shamus, dick, pig, flattie, bizzy *and* bobby *and* peeler <all Brit>, Dogberry; the cops, the law, the fuzz; New York's finest; tec, op

VERBS 4 **watch, keep watch,** keep guard, keep watch over, keep watch and ward; stand guard; be on the lookout; patrol, pound a beat <nonformal>, go on one's beat
5 tidy, **tidy up,** neaten, trim, **put in trim,** trim up, **straighten up,** fix up <nonformal>, **clean up,** police up <nonformal>, groom, spruce *and* spruce up <both nonformal>, **clear up,** clear the decks

**policy** NOUNS 1 **polity,** public policy; line, **party line,** party principle *or* doctrine *or* philosophy, **position,** bipartisan policy; **prudence,** providence; **insurance policy,** certificate of insurance

**polish** NOUNS 1 **gloss, glaze,** burnish, **shine,** luster, finish; **patina; cultivation,** culture, refinement, civility; cultivation of the mind; **refinement,** finesse, refined *or* cultivated *or* civilized taste
VERBS 2 **shine,** burnish, furbish, sleek, slick, slick down, gloss, glaze, glance, luster; **rub,** scour, **buff;** wax, varnish; finish
3 **perfect,** touch up, finish, put on the finishing touches, fine-tune <nonformal>, tone up, **brush up,** furbish, furbish up, spruce, **spruce up,** freshen, vamp, vamp up, rub up, brighten up, polish up

**polite** ADJS **courteous,** civil, urbane, gracious, graceful, agreeable, affable, fair; complaisant; obliging, accommodating; **thoughtful,** considerate, tactful, solicitous; respectful, deferential, attentive

**political** ADJS **politic,** civil, civic; **official,** bureaucratic

**politician** NOUNS politico, political leader, professional politician; party leader, party boss *and* party chieftain <both nonformal>; machine *or* clubhouse politician, **political hack,** pol <nonformal>; old campaigner, war-horse; reform politician, reformer

**politics** NOUNS 1 polity, the art of the possible; practical politics, *Realpolitik* <Ger>; empirical politics; **party** *or* **partisan politics,** partisanism; politicization; reform politics; multiparty politics; power politics, *Machtpolitik* <Ger>; machine politics, bossism <nonformal>; **interest politics,** single-issue politics, interest-group politics, pressure-group politics, PAC *or* political action committee politics; consensus politics; pork-barrel politics; ward politics
2 **political science,** poli-sci <nonformal>, **government,** civics; political philosophy, political theory

**pollute** VERBS **corrupt,** contaminate, infect; taint, tarnish; vitiate, poison, pervert, warp, twist, distort; prostitute, misuse; **cheapen,** devalue; coarsen, vulgarize, drag in the mud; adulterate, alloy, water, water down

**pollution** NOUNS **corruption,** contamination, vitiation, **defilement,** fouling, befouling; **poisoning,** perversion, prostitution, misuse; denaturing, adulteration; environmental pollution, **environmental destruction,** ecocide, ecocatastrophe

**Pollyanna** NOUNS **optimist,** hoper, ray of sunshine <nonformal>, irrepressible optimist, Dr Pangloss <Voltaire>

**poltergeist** NOUNS **imp,** pixie, sprite, elf, puck, kobold, *diablotin* <Fr>, tokoloshe, **gremlin; specter,** ghost, spectral ghost, **spook** <nonformal>, **phantom,** phantasm, phantasma, **wraith, shade,** shadow, fetch, **apparition,** appearance, presence, shape, form, eidolon, idolum, revenant

**pomade** NOUNS **ointment, balm,** salve, lotion, cream, unguent, unguentum; **brilliantine,** pomatum, hairtonic

**pommel** VERBS **pound, beat,** hammer, maul, sledgehammer, **knock,** rap, bang, thump, **drub,** buffet, **batter,** pulverize, paste <nonformal>, patter, pummel, pelt, baste, lambaste

**pomp** NOUNS circumstance, pride, **state,** solemnity, formality; **pomp and circumstance,** heraldry

**pompous** ADJS **stuffy** <nonformal>, **self-important,** impressed with oneself, pontific, pontifical; **inflated,** swollen, bloated, tumid, turgid, flatulent, gassy <nonformal>, stilted; grandiloquent, **bombastic**; solemn, formal

**pond** NOUNS **pool,** lakelet, pondlet, dew pond, linn <Scots>, *étang* <Fr>; farm pond; fishpond; millpond, millpool; salt pond, salina, tidal pond *or* pool

**ponder** VERBS **consider,** contemplate, speculate, reflect, study, perpend, **weigh,** deliberate, debate, meditate, muse, brood, ruminate, chew the cud <nonformal>, digest; introspect, be abstracted; wrinkle one's brow; fall into a brown study, retreat into one's mind *or* thoughts

**ponderous** ADJS **heavy, massive,** massy, weighty, hefty <nonformal>, fat; **leaden,** heavy as lead; deadweight; heavyweight; overweight; **solemn,** grave; cumbersome, lumbering, hulking, hulky; **unwieldy**

**pontificate** VERBS **dogmatize,** lay down the law, oracle, oraculate, proclaim

**pooch** NOUNS **dog,** canine, bow-wow <nonformal>; **pup, puppy,** puppy-dog <nonformal>, **whelp;** bitch; toy dog, lap dog; working dog; watchdog, sheep dog, shepherd *or* shepherd's dog; Seeing Eye dog, guide dog

**pooh-pooh** VERBS **slight, ignore,** make

little of, dismiss, pretend not to see, disregard, overlook, neglect, pass by, take no note *or* notice of, look right through <nonformal>, pay no attention *or* regard to; sneer at, fleer, curl one's lip

**pool** NOUNS 1 **swimming pool,** plunge, plunge bath, natatorium; swimming hole; wading pool
2 **pot,** jackpot, stakes, kitty; bank; office pool

**pool hall** NOUNS **billiard parlor, poolroom**

**pooped** ADJS **worn-out, used up** <nonformal>, worn to a frazzle, frazzled, fit for the dust hole *or* wastepaper basket; **exhausted, tired,** fatigued, **spent,** effete, etiolated, played out, *ausgespielt* <Ger>, emptied; **run-down,** dragged-out <nonformal>, laid low, at a low ebb, in a bad way, far-gone, on one's last legs

**poor** ADJS 1 **ill off,** badly *or* poorly off, hard up <nonformal>, downscale, impecunious, **unmoneyed;** reduced, in reduced circumstances; **straitened,** in straitened circumstances, feeling the pinch, strapped, **financially embarrassed** *or* distressed, **pinched,** squeezed, at the end of one's rope, on the edge *or* ragged edge <nonformal>, on Queer Street; short, **short of money** *or* **funds** *or* **cash,** out-of-pocket; unable to make ends meet, unable to keep the wolf from the door
2 **paltry,** common, **mean,** sorry, sad, pitiful, pitiable, pathetic, **despicable,** contemptible, beneath contempt, **miserable, wretched,** beggarly, vile, **shabby,** scrubby, scruffy, shoddy, scurvy, scuzzy <nonformal>, scummy, **crummy** *and* cheesy <both nonformal>, **trashy,** rubbishy, garbagey <nonformal>, trumpery, gimcracky <nonformal>

**pop** NOUNS 1 **soft drink,** soda water, sparkling water, **soda,** soda pop, tonic
VERBS 2 **bulge,** bilge, **belly,** bag, balloon; **goggle,** bug <nonformal>; **swell,** swell up, dilate, distend, billow; swell out, **belly out,** round out
ADJS 3 **common,** commonplace, ordinary; plebeian; homely, homespun; **general,** public, popular; campy, high-camp, low-camp, kitschy
ADVS 4 **all of a sudden,** all at once: abruptly, sharp; precipitately, precipitantly, impulsively, impetuously, hastily; dash; smack, bang, slap, plop, plunk, plump

**poppycock** NOUNS **foolishness, folly,** foolery, foolheadedness, **stupidity,** asininity, *niaiserie* <Fr>; **inanity,** fatuity, fatuousness; **nonsense,** tomfoolery

**populace** NOUNS **population,** inhabitants, habitancy, dwellers, **people,** whole people, people at large, citizenry, folk, souls, living souls, body, whole body, warm bodies <nonformal>; **public,** general public

**popular** ADJS **desired, wanted,** coveted; **wished-for,** hoped-for, longed-for; in demand; prevalent, prevailing, widespread, obtaining, generally accepted, current; **general,** pop <nonformal>; **famous,** famed, honored, renowned, celebrated, acclaimed, much acclaimed, sought-after, hot *and* world-class <both nonformal>, **well-known,** on everyone's tongue *or* lips, talked-of, talked-about; **prevailing,** predominating

**populate** VERBS **people,** empeople, **inhabit,** denizen; colonize, **settle,** settle in, plant

**population** NOUNS **inhabitants,** habitancy, dwellers, **populace, people,** whole people, people at large, citizenry, folk, souls, living souls, body, whole body, warm bodies <nonformal>

**porch** NOUNS stoop, **veranda,** piazza <nonformal>, patio, lanai, gallery; sleeping porch; propylaeum

**pore** NOUNS 1 **outlet,** vent, ventage, venthole
VERBS 2 pore over, peruse; take a close *or* careful look; take a long, hard look; size up <nonformal>; take stock of

**pornography** NOUNS **obscenity,** dirtiness, bawdry, raunch <nonformal>, **ribaldry,** porno *and* porn <both nonformal>, hard-core pornography, soft-core pornography, salacity, **smut,** dirt, filth; lewdness, bawdiness, salaciousness, **smuttiness,** foulness, filthiness, nastiness, vileness, offensiveness; scurrility, fescenninity; pornographic art *or* literature; blue movie *and* dirty movie *and* porno film *and* skin flick <all nonformal>, adult movie, stag film <nonformal>, X-rated movie

**porous** ADJS porose; poriferous; like a sieve, sievelike, cribose, cribriform

**port** NOUNS 1 **harbor,** haven, seaport, port of call, free port, treaty port, home port; hoverport; harborage, **anchorage,** anchorage ground, protected anchor-

age, moorage, moorings; **roadstead,** road, roads
ADJS 2 **left, left-hand,** sinister, sinistral; near, nigh; **larboard**
ADVS 3 **leftward,** leftwards, leftwardly, **left, to the left,** sinistrally, sinister, sinistrad; on the left; larboard, aport

**portable** ADJS **transferable,** conveyable; transmittable, transmissible, transmissive, consignable, deliverable; **movable,** removable; portative; transportable, transportative, transportive

**portent** NOUNS **omen; augury,** auspice, soothsay, prognostic, prognostication; **ominousness,** portentousness, bodefulness, presagefulness, suggestiveness, significance, **meaning**, meaningfulness; **forewarning,** prewarning, **premonition,** precautioning; advance warning *or* notice, **foreboding**

**porter** NOUNS **bearer,** redcap, skycap; janitor

**portfolio** NOUNS **holdings,** investment portfolio; folder

**portion** NOUNS **share,** interest, part, stake, stock, **piece,** bit, segment; **bite** *and* **cut** *and* **slice** *and* **chunk** *and* slice of the pie *or* melon *and* piece of the action <all nonformal>, **allotment,** proportion, percentage, measure, quantum, **quota,** deal *or* dole <both old>, meed, moiety, mess, helping

**portly** ADJS **corpulent,** stout, fat, overweight, fattish, **obese,** adipose, gross, fleshy, beefy, meaty, hefty, porky, porcine; paunchy; imposing

**portrait** NOUNS **likeness, description,** portrayal, portraiture, **depiction,** rendering, rendition, **delineation,** limning, representation; **word painting** *or* **picture,** picture, image, photograph; portraiture, portrayal

**portray** VERBS **represent,** delineate, depict, render, characterize, **picture,** picturize, limn, draw, paint

**pose** NOUNS 1 **posing, posturing,** attitudinizing, attitudinarianism; peacockery, peacockishness; carriage, bearing, posture, poise, stance, way of holding oneself
VERBS 2 **posture, attitudinize,** peacock, strike a pose, strike an attitude, pose for effect; sit
3 **postulate,** predicate, posit, set forth, lay down, assert; advance, **propose,** propound

**posh** ADJS **sumptuous,** elegant, elaborate, luxurious, extravagant, deluxe; plush *and* ritzy *and* swank *and* swanky <all nonformal>, Corinthian; **high-society,** socialite, hoity-toity <nonformal>

**position** NOUNS 1 **job,** employment, gainful employment, situation, **office,** post, place, station, berth, billet, **appointment,** engagement, gig <nonformal>
2 **premise,** proposition, assumed position, sumption, **assumption,** supposal, presupposition, **hypothesis,** thesis, theorem, lemma, **statement,** affirmation, categorical proposition, assertion, basis, ground, foundation; **opinion,** sentiment, feeling, sense, impression, reaction, **notion,** idea, thought, mind, thinking, **way of thinking,** attitude, stance, posture, mindset
VERBS 3 **locate,** situate, site, place; **install,** put in place; **pinpoint,** zero in on, home in on

**positive** ADJS **emphatic,** decided, forceful, forcible; **emphasized,** stressed, accented, accentuated, punctuated, pointed

**posse** NOUNS **search,** searching, **quest, hunt,** hunting, stalk, stalking, still hunt, dragnet, search party; *posse comitatus* <L>; **vigilantes,** vigilance committee

**possess** VERBS 1 **have, hold,** have and hold, possess outright *or* free and clear, **occupy, fill, enjoy,** boast; have in hand, have in one's possession
2 **demonize,** devilize, diabolize; **obsess; bewitch,** bedevil

**possessed** ADJS 1 **owned,** held; **free and clear;** in one's possession, in hand, in one's grip *or* grasp, at one's command *or* disposal; on hand, by one, in stock, in store
2 possessed with a demon *or* devil, **pixilated, bedeviled,** demonized, devil-ridden, demonic, demonical, demoniacal; ghost-ridden; obsessed

**possessive** ADJS **avaricious,** greedy, grasping, graspy *and* grabby <both nonformal>, acquisitive; **individualistic,** personalistic, privatistic

**possible** ADJS within the bounds *or* realm *or* range *or* domain of possibility, in one's power, in one's hands, humanly possible; **conceivable,** conceivably possible, **imaginable,** thinkable, cogitable; plausible; **potential**

**post** NOUNS 1 **standard,** upright; newel; signpost, milepost; stanchion; hitching post, snubbing post, Samson post; **pillar,** column, pier, pilaster

2 **position, job,** employment, gainful employment, situation, **office,** place, station, berth, billet, **appointment**
VERBS 3 **pledge,** deposit, stake, put in escrow, **put up,** put up as collateral, lay out *or* down; **put up** *or* **go bail,** bail out
4 **mail,** dispatch, send; airmail

**posterior** NOUNS 1 **rear, rear end,** hind end, hind part, hinder part, afterpart, rearward, **behind,** breech, stern, tail, tail end, **buttocks, rump,** bottom, derrière
ADJS 2 **rear,** rearward, **back,** backward, retrograde, postern, tail; after *or* aft; **hind,** hinder; hindmost, **aftermost,** aftmost, rearmost

**posterity** NOUNS **progeny,** issue, offspring, fruit, seed, brood, breed, family; **descent,** succession; lineage, blood, bloodline; **descendants,** heirs, inheritors

**postman** NOUNS **mailman,** mail carrier, letter carrier; postmaster, postmistress; postal clerk

**postmortem** NOUNS **autopsy,** inquest, postmortem examination, ex post facto examination, necropsy, necroscopy

**postpone** VERBS **delay, defer,** put off, give one a rain check <nonformal>, hold off *or* up <nonformal>, prorogue, put on hold *or* ice *or* the back burner <all nonformal>, reserve, waive, **suspend,** hang up, stay, hang fire; **hold over,** lay over, stand over, let the matter stand, **put aside,** table, pigeonhole, **shelve,** put on the shelf

**postscript** NOUNS appendix; rider, allonge, codicil; **epilogue,** envoi, postlude, conclusion, peroration

**postulate** VERBS **predicate, posit,** set forth, lay down, assert; pose, advance, **propose,** propound

**posture** NOUNS 1 **look, air, mien,** demeanor, carriage, bearing, port, stance, poise, presence; pose, posing, attitudinizing; mannerism, affectation; opinion, attitude
VERBS 2 **pose, attitudinize,** peacock, strike a pose, strike an attitude, pose for effect

**potbellied** ADJS **obese,** abdominous, bigbellied, full-bellied, swag-bellied, potgutted *and* pussle-gutted <both nonformal>

**potent** ADJS **powerful,** powerpacked, **mighty,** irresistible, **vigorous,** vital, **energetic,** puissant, ruling, in power; **cogent,** striking, telling, effective, impactful, valid, operative; **virile,** viripotent; ultramasculine, **macho, hemannish** *and* hunky <both nonformal>, two-fisted <nonformal>, broad-shouldered, hairy-chested

**potentate** NOUNS **sovereign,** monarch, ruler, prince, dynast, **crowned head,** emperor, *imperator* <L>, king-emperor, **king,** anointed king, majesty, royalty, royal, royal personage; **chief, chieftain,** high chief

**potential** NOUNS 1 **talent, flair,** power, ability, capability, capacity; the goods *and* the stuff *and* the right stuff *and* what it takes *and* the makings <all nonformal>; potentiality, virtuality
ADJS 2 **latent,** underlying, under the surface, submerged; unmanifested, virtual, possible

**potion** NOUNS **drink,** potation, libation; **nip,** draft, drop, spot, finger or two, sip, sup, suck, drench, guzzle, gargle, jigger

**potpourri** NOUNS **hodgepodge,** hotchpotch, hotchpot; **medley, miscellany,** mélange, pastiche, *pasticcio* <Ital>, **conglomeration,** assortment, assemblage, mixed bag, grab bag, olio, *olla podrida* <Sp>, **scramble,** jumble, **mix,** mishmash, **mess,** can of worms <nonformal>, rat's nest, hash, patchwork, salad, gallimaufry, salmagundi, stew, omniumgatherum, **odds and ends,** everything but the kitchen sink <nonformal>

**pottery** NOUNS **ceramic ware,** ceramics; crockery

**pounce** VERBS **plunge,** dive, pitch, plummet, drop, fall; swoop, swoop down, stoop, pounce on *or* upon

**pound** NOUNS 1 **place of confinement,** close quarters, not enough room to swing a cat; pinfold *or* penfold; **cage; enclosure,** pen, coop; dog pound
VERBS 2 **beat,** hammer, maul, sledgehammer, **knock, rap,** bang, thump, **drub,** buffet, batter, pulverize, paste <nonformal>, patter, pommel, pummel, pelt, baste, lambaste

**pour** VERBS 1 **flow,** stream, issue, surge, run, course, rush, gush, flush, flood
2 **rain, precipitate,** stream, stream down, pour with rain, **pelt,** pelt down, drum, tattoo, come down in torrents *or* sheets *or* buckets *or* curtains, **rain cats and dogs** <nonformal>

**pout** NOUNS 1 **scowl,** frown, lower, **glower,** moue, mow, grimace, wry face; sullen looks, black looks, **long face**

VERBS 2 **look sullen,** look black, look black as thunder, gloom, pull *or* make a long face; **frown, scowl,** knit the brow, lower, **glower,** make a moue *or* mow, grimace, make a wry face, make a lip, hang one's lip, thrust out one's lower lip

**poverty** NOUNS poorness, impecuniousness, impecuniosity; **straits,** difficulties, **hardship**; financial distress *or* embarrassment, **embarrassed** *or* **reduced** *or* **straitened circumstances,** tight squeeze; genteel poverty; vows of poverty, voluntary poverty; **dearth,** paucity

**powder** NOUNS 1 **dust;** efflorescence; soot, smut; **particle, particulate,** particulates, airborne particles, air pollution; cosmic dust
VERBS 2 **pulverize,** comminute, triturate, contriturate, levigate, bray, pestle, reduce to powder *or* dust, grind to powder *or* dust, grind up; come *or* fall to dust, **crumble,** crumble to *or* into dust, **disintegrate**, fall to pieces, break up; effloresce

**power** NOUNS 1 potency *or* potence, prepotency, **force, might,** mightiness, **vigor,** vitality, vim, push, drive, charge; dint, virtue; powerfulness, forcefulness; cogence *or* cogency, validity, effect, impact, **effectiveness,** effectivity, effectuality, competence *or* competency; **authority**, weight; muscle power, sinew, might and main, beef <nonformal>, strong arm
2 **nation,** nationality, **state,** nation-state, sovereign nation *or* state, polity, **body politic;** superpower, world power
3 **governance,** authority, jurisdiction, control, command, rule, reign, regnancy, **dominion,** sovereignty, sway; **influence,** force, clout <nonformal>, potency
4 **personage,** important person, person of importance *or* consequence, **great man** *or* **woman,** man *or* woman of mark *or* note, **somebody, notable,** notability, figure
VERBS 5 **impel,** give an impetus, **set going** *or* agoing, put *or* set in motion, give momentum; **drive, move,** animate, actuate, forward; **thrust; propel;** motivate, incite; compel

**power broker** NOUNS **wire-puller;** influence peddler, four-percenter, fixer <nonformal>

**the power elite** NOUNS **the authorities,** the powers that be, ruling class *or* classes, the lords of creation, **the Establishment,** the interests, **the power structure; they,** them; the inner circle

**powerful** ADJS **vigorous,** strong, **forceful,** forcible, vital, driving, sinewy, sinewed, punchy *and* full of piss and vinegar *and* zappy <all nonformal>, **striking,** telling, effective, impressive

**powerless** ADJS **impotent,** forceless, out of gas <nonformal>; feeble, soft, flabby, **weak**, weak as a kitten, wimpy *or* wimpish <nonformal>; **ineffective,** ineffectual, inefficacious; **of no account,** no-account, without any weight, featherweight, lightweight

**practical** ADJS practicable, pragmatic *or* pragmatical, banausic; feasible, workable, operable, realizable; **efficient,** effective, **effectual**

**practice** NOUNS 1 **experience,** practical knowledge *or* skill, hands-on experience <nonformal>, field-work; rehearsal, exercise, drill
2 **observance,** performance, execution, discharge, carrying out *or* through; dutifulness, acquittal, ritual observance; **rite,** ritual, rituality
VERBS 3 **put into practice,** exercise, employ, use; carry on, conduct, prosecute, wage; follow, pursue; engage in, work at, devote oneself to, **do,** turn to, apply oneself to, employ oneself in; play at; **take up,** take to, undertake, tackle, take on, address oneself to, have a go at, turn one's hand to, **go in** *or* **out for** <nonformal>, follow as an occupation, set up shop
4 **rehearse,** go through, walk *or* run through, go over; go through one's part, read one's lines

**pragmatic** ADJS **realistic,** realist, **practical;** pragmatical, scientific, scientistic, positivistic; **unidealistic,** unideal, **unromantic,** unsentimental, practical-minded, sober-minded, sobersided, **hardheaded,** straight-thinking, **down-to-earth,** with both feet on the ground

**prairie** NOUNS **grassland,** range, grazing, grazing land; **savanna,** steppe, steppeland, **pampas,** pampa, campo, llano, **veld,** grass veld

**praise** NOUNS 1 **laudation,** laud; **glorification,** glory, exaltation, magnification, **honor; eulogy,** *éloge* and *hommage* <both Fr>, eulogium; **encomium,** accolade, kudos, panegyric; paean; **tribute,** homage; congratulation

VERBS 2 **applaud,** flatter, compliment, praise to the skies; scratch one's back; hand it to *or* take off one's hat to one <nonformal>, pay tribute, **glorify,** laud, exalt, extol, magnify, bless, celebrate; sing praises, sing the praises of, sound *or* resound the praises of

**praiseworthy** ADJS worthy, **commendable,** estimable, **laudable,** admirable, meritorious, creditable; exemplary, model, unexceptionable; deserving, well-deserving

**prank** NOUNS **trick,** practical joke, waggish trick, *espièglerie* <Fr>, antic, caper, frolic; **monkeyshines** *and* **shenanigans** <both nonformal>

**prattle** NOUNS 1 **chatter,** jabber, gibber, **babble,** babblement, prate, **prating,** palaver, chat, natter <Brit>, **gabble, gab** *and* jaw-jaw <both nonformal>, blab, **blabber,** blather, clatter, clack, cackle
VERBS 2 **talk nonsense,** twaddle, piffle, **blather,** blabber, babble, gabble, gibble-gabble, **jabber,** gibber, prate, rattle; talk through one's hat; gas *and* bull *and* **bullshit** *and* throw the bull *and* shoot off one's mouth *and* shoot the bull <all nonformal>

**pray** VERBS **supplicate,** invoke, petition, make supplication, *daven* <Yiddish>; **implore,** beseech, obtest; offer a prayer, send up a prayer, commune with God; **say one's prayers;** tell one's beads, recite the rosary; **say grace**

**prayer** NOUNS **supplication, invocation,** imploration, impetration, entreaty, beseechment, appeal, petition, suit, orison, obsecration, obtestation, rogation, **devotions**

**prayer book** NOUNS **psalter, psalmbook**

**preach** VERBS **admonish,** exhort, expostulate, remonstrate; Bible-thump *and* preachify <both nonformal>, **sermonize,** read a sermon

**preacher** NOUNS sermoner, sermonizer, sermonist, homilist; pulpiter, pulpiteer; predicant, predikant; preaching friar; television *or* TV preacher, telepreacher <nonformal>

**precarious** ADJS ticklish, touchy, touch-and-go, **critical, delicate;** slippery, slippy; on thin ice, on slippery ground; hanging by a thread, trembling in the balance

**precaution** NOUNS **forethought,** foresight, foresightedness; **providence,** provision, forearming; precautions, steps, measures, steps and measures; **safeguard,** protection, preventive measure, safety net, safety valve, sheet anchor; **insurance**

**precede** VERBS antecede, **come first,** come *or* go before, **go ahead of,** go in advance, stand first, stand at the head, **head,** head up <nonformal>, front, **lead**, take precedence, have priority

**precedent** NOUNS **precursor,** forerunner, **predecessor,** forebear, antecedent, ancestor

**precept** NOUNS prescript, **prescription, teaching;** instruction, direction, charge, commission, **injunction,** dictate; **order,** command; **a belief,** tenet, dogma, **principle,** principle *or* article of faith, canon, maxim, axiom; **doctrine,** teaching

**precinct** NOUNS **sphere,** orbit, **province,** department; **field,** pale, arena, place, locale, milieu, purlieu; **election district**

**precious** ADJS 1 **dear, valuable,** worthy, rich, golden, worth a pretty penny <nonformal>, worth a king's ransom, worth its weight in gold, good as gold; **priceless, invaluable,** inestimable, without *or* beyond price, not to be had for love or money
2 **pretentious,** mannered, artificial, unnatural, studied; *précieux, précieuse* <both Fr>, overnice, overrefined, overelegant, overelaborate, hyperelegant, etc

**precipice** NOUNS **cliff, sheer** *or* yawning cliff *or* precipice *or* drop, steep, bluff, wall, face, scar; scarp, **escarpment; palisade**

**precipitate** VERBS 1 **hasten,** hurry, accelerate, speed, speed up, **hurry up,** rush, quicken, hustle <nonformal>, bustle, bundle, forward
2 deposit, sediment, sedimentate
ADJS 3 precipitant; **sudden,** abrupt; **impetuous,** impulsive, rash; headlong, breakneck; breathless, panting, hasty, **overhasty,** too soon off the mark, too quick on the draw *or* trigger *or* uptake <nonformal>

**précis** NOUNS **abridgment,** *abrégé* <Fr>, condensation, condensed version, abbreviation, abbreviature, brief, digest, **abstract,** epitome, **capsule,** nutshell *or* capsule version, capsulization, encapsulation, **synopsis,** summary, résumé, summing up

**precise** ADJS **punctilious,** scrupulous, precisian, precisionist, precious, puristic; by-the-book; exact, meticulous;

**detailed,** minute, full, particular, fussy, finicky *or* finicking *or* finical, picayune, picky <nonformal>, nice <old>, specific

**precision** NOUNS **exactness,** exactitude, accuracy, preciseness, punctuality, correctness, prissiness; **strictness, rigor,** rigorousness, spit and polish

**preclude** VERBS **prohibit,** forbid; disallow, rule out *or* against; **bar,** debar, exclude, exclude from, shut out, shut *or* close the door on; **forestall,** foreclose, **obviate,** anticipate; rule out

**precocious** ADJS **premature,** too early, too soon, oversoon; forward, advanced, far ahead, born before one's time

**precursor** NOUNS **forerunner,** foregoer, *voorlooper* <Dutch>, vaunt-courier; pioneer, *voortrekker* <Dutch>, frontiersman, bushwhacker; trailblazer *or* trailbreaker, guide; **leader**, leadoff man *or* woman, bellwether, fugleman; **herald,** announcer, *buccinator* <L>, messenger, harbinger, stormy petrel; **predecessor,** forebear, precedent, antecedent, **ancestor; vanguard,** avant-garde, avant-gardist, innovator, groundbreaker

**predecessor** NOUNS forebear, precedent, antecedent, **ancestor**

**predicament** NOUNS 1 **plight,** spot of trouble, **strait,** straits, parlous straits, tightrope, knife-edge, thin edge; **pinch, bind,** pass, clutch, situation, emergency; pretty pass, fine state of affairs, sorry plight; **embarrassment,** embarrassing position *or* situation; the devil to pay

2 <nonformal> **pickle,** crunch, hobble, pretty pickle, fine kettle of fish, how-do-you-do, fine how-do-you-do; **spot, tight spot; squeeze, tight squeeze,** ticklish *or* tricky spot, hot spot, hot seat, sticky wicket <Brit>; **scrape, jam, hot water,** tail in a gate, tit in the wringer; **mess,** holy *or* unholy mess, mix, stew; hell to pay

**predict** VERBS make a prediction, **foretell, soothsay,** prefigure, **forecast,** prophesy, prognosticate, call <nonformal>, make a prophecy *or* prognosis, vaticinate, forebode, presage, see ahead, see *or* tell the future, read the future, see in the crystal ball

**predictable** ADJS **divinable,** foretellable, calculable, anticipatable; **foreseeable,** foreknowable, precognizable; **reliable,** dependable, sure, surefire <nonformal>, trustworthy, **to be depended** *or* **relied upon,** to be counted *or* reckoned on

**predilection** NOUNS **preference,** proclivity, bent, affinity, prepossession, predisposition, partiality, inclination, leaning, tilt, penchant, bias, tendency, taste; favor, fancy; personal choice, druthers <nonformal>; chosen kind *or* sort, style, one's cup of tea <nonformal>, type, bag *and* thing <both nonformal>

**predominant** ADJS **prevalent,** prevailing, common, popular, **current,** running; regnant, reigning, **ruling,** predominating, **dominant;** rife, rampant, pandemic, epidemic, besetting; **well-connected,** favorably situated, near the seat of power

**preeminent** ADJS **paramount,** principal, leading, foremost, main, chief, number one <nonformal>, premier, **prime, primary,** supreme; highest, uppermost, topmost, toprank, ranking, of the first rank, world-class, **dominant,** predominant, master, controlling, **overruling,** overriding, all-absorbing

**preempt** VERBS **appropriate, adopt, assume, usurp,** arrogate, accroach; preoccupy, prepossess

**preen** VERBS spruce up *and* gussy up *and* doll up *and* fix up <all nonformal>, **primp up,** prink up, prank up, trick up *or* out, deck out, fig out; primp, prink, prank; smarten, smarten up, dandify, titivate

**prefer** VERBS **favor, like better** *or* **best,** prefer to, set before *or* above, regard *or* honor before; **had** *or* **have rather,** choose rather, had rather *or* sooner, had *or* would as soon; see *or* think fit, think best, please; tilt *or* incline *or* lean *or* tend toward, have a bias *or* partiality *or* penchant

**preferable** ADJS of choice *or* preference, **better,** preferred, **to be preferred,** more desirable, favored; preferential, preferring, favoring

**pregnant** ADJS 1 *enceinte* <Fr>, knocked-up <nonformal>, **with child** *or* **young, in the family way** <nonformal>, gestating, breeding, teeming, parturient; heavy with child *or* young, great *or* big with child *or* young, wearing her apron high, in a delicate condition, gravid, heavy, great, big-laden; carrying; **expecting** <nonformal>, anticipating

*and* anticipating a blessed event <both nonformal>, infanticipating <nonformal>
2 **meaningful,** meaning, **significant,** significative; full of meaning, loaded *or* laden *or* fraught *or* freighted *or* heavy with significance; **pithy, meaty,** sententious, substantial, full of substance; pointed

**prejudice** NOUNS 1 prejudgment, forejudgment, **predilection, prepossession,** preconception; **bias,** bent, leaning, inclination, twist; **jaundice,** jaundiced eye; **partiality,** partisanship, favoritism, onesidedness
VERBS 2 prejudice against, prejudice the issue, prepossess, **jaundice, influence, sway, bias,** bias one's judgment; warp, twist, bend, distort

**premature** ADJS **too early, too soon,** oversoon; previous *and* a bit previous <both nonformal>; **untimely; precipitate,** hasty, **overhasty,** too soon off the mark, too quick on the draw *or* trigger *or* uptake <nonformal>; **unprepared,** unripe, impulsive, rushed, unmatured

**premeditate** VERBS **calculate,** preresolve, predetermine, preconsider, direct oneself, forethink, work out beforehand; plan; plot, scheme

**premier** NOUNS 1 **head of state,** chief of state; prime minister, chancellor, grand vizier, dewan <India>; doge
ADJS 2 **first,** foremost, front, up-front <nonformal>, **head,** chief, principal, **leading, main,** flagship

**premiere** NOUNS premier performance, debut

**premise** NOUNS **proposition, position,** assumed position, sumption, **assumption,** supposal, presupposition, **hypothesis,** thesis, theorem, lemma, **statement,** affirmation, categorical proposition, assertion, basis, ground, foundation; major premise, minor premise

**premium** NOUNS 1 **extra, bonus,** something extra, extra dash, extra added attraction, lagniappe, something into the bargain, something for good measure, baker's dozen; **interest**
ADJS 2 **expensive,** dear, costly, of great cost, dear-bought, high, high-priced, at a premium, top; big ticket <nonformal>, **fancy** *and* stiff *and* steep <all nonformal>, pricey

**premonition** NOUNS **forewarning,** prewarning, precautioning; presentiment, hunch *and* funny feeling <both nonformal>, **foreboding; portent**

*warnings, and portents and evils imminent*
SHAKESPEARE

**preoccupy** VERBS **occupy the mind** *or* **thoughts,** engage the thoughts, monopolize the thoughts, fasten itself on the mind, seize the mind, fill the mind; **engross,** absorb, immerse, **occupy,** engage, involve, monopolize, exercise, take up

**preparation** NOUNS 1 **medicine,** medicament, medication, medicinal, therapeutant, **drug, physic,** mixture
2 **training,** readying <nonformal>, **conditioning,** grooming, cultivation, development, improvement; sagacity, providence, discretion, provision, forehandedness, readiness, prudence

**preparatory school** NOUNS **secondary school,** middle school, **academy,** *Gymnasium* <Ger>; *lycée* <Fr>, lyceum; **high school,** senior high school, senior high <nonformal>; prep school <nonformal>, public school <Brit>, seminary

**prepare** VERBS **make** *or* **get ready,** prep <nonformal>, **ready, fix** <nonformal>; **make preparations** *or* **arrangements,** clear the decks <nonformal>, clear for action, settle preliminaries, tee up <nonformal>; mobilize, marshal, deploy, marshal *or* deploy one's forces *or* resources; **prepare** *or* **provide for** *or* **against,** forearm; **guard against, make sure against,** make sure, **look before one leaps;** see how the land lies *or* the wind blows, see how the cat jumps <nonformal>

**preposterous** ADJS **absurd, nonsensical,** insensate, ridiculous, laughable, ludicrous; **foolish,** crazy; cockamamie <nonformal>, fantastic, fantastical, grotesque, monstrous, wild, weird, **outrageous,** incredible, beyond belief, *outré* <Fr>, extravagant, **bizarre;** high-flown

**prerequisite** NOUNS **condition,** provision, proviso, stipulation, whereas; **requisite,** obligation; *sine qua non* <L>, *conditio sine qua non* <L>; **must,** must item; **essential,** indispensable

**prerogative** NOUNS **right, due,** droit; power, authority, prerogative of office; natural right, presumptive right, inalienable right; divine right; vested right *or* interest

**preschool** NOUNS infant school <Brit>, nursery, **nursery school;** day nursery, **day-care center,** day care, crèche; playschool; **kindergarten**

**prescribe** VERBS **require,** demand, dictate, impose, lay down, set, fix, appoint, make obligatory *or* mandatory; decide once and for all, carve in stone, set in concrete <nonformal>; authorize

**presence** NOUNS 1 being here *or* there, hereness, thereness, physical *or* actual presence, spiritual presence; **immanence,** indwellingness, **inherence;** whereness, **immediacy;** ubiety; availability, accessibility; nearness; **occurrence**, existence
2 **person** *or* **woman** *or* **man** of influence, an influential, an affluential, a presence, a palpable presence, a mover and shaker <nonformal>, a person to be reckoned with, a player *or* player on the scene; heavyweight, big wheel *and* biggie *and* heavy *or* long-ball hitter *and* piledriver <all nonformal>, very important person *or* VIP <nonformal>; power behind the throne, gray eminence, *éminence grise* <Fr>, hidden hand, manipulator, friend at *or* in court, kingmaker

**present** NOUNS 1 **gift,** presentation, *cadeau* <Fr>, **offering;** tribute, **award;** free gift, freebie *and* gimme <both nonformal>; oblation; handsel
ADJS 2 attendant; **on hand,** on deck <nonformal>, on board; **immediate,** immanent, indwelling, inherent, **available, accessible, at hand,** in view, within reach *or* sight *or* call, in place; **extant,** prevalent, current, in force *or* effect, afoot, on foot, under the sun, on the face of the earth
3 **immediate,** latest, current, running, extant, existent, **existing,** actual, topical, being, that is, as is, that be; **present-day,** present-time, present-age, **modern**, modern-day; **contemporary,** contemporaneous; up-to-date, up-to-the-minute, fresh, **new**

**present** VERBS 1 **give, donate,** slip <nonformal>, let have; **bestow,** confer, award, allot, render, bestow on; **issue,** dispense, administer; serve, help to; **distribute;** give out, deal out, dole out, mete out, hand *or* dish out <nonformal>, fork *or* shell out <nonformal>; make a present of, gift *or* gift with <nonformal>, give as a gift; **give generously,** give the shirt off one's back; be generous *or* liberal with, give freely
2 **introduce,** acquaint, make acquainted, give an introduction, give a knockdown <nonformal>, do the honors <nonformal>

**presentable** ADJS **tolerable,** goodish, fair, fairish, moderate, tidy <nonformal>, **decent,** respectable, good enough, **pretty good, not bad,** not amiss, not half bad, not so bad, **adequate,** satisfactory, all right, OK *or* okay <nonformal>; better than nothing; **acceptable,** admissible, **passable,** unobjectionable, unexceptionable; workmanlike; sufficient

**presentiment** NOUNS **hunch** <nonformal>, sense, **premonition,** preapprehension, intimation, foreboding; suspicion, **impression,** intuition, intuitive impression, **feeling,** forefeeling, vague feeling *or* idea, funny feeling <nonformal>, feeling in one's bones

**preserve** NOUNS 1 **sweets,** sweet stuff, **confectionery; sweet,** confection; **jelly,** jam, conserve
2 **reserve,** reservation; park, paradise; forest preserve *or* reserve; wilderness preserve; Indian reservation; **refuge,** sanctuary, game preserve *or* reserve, bird sanctuary, wildlife sanctuary *or* preserve
VERBS 3 **conserve,** save, spare; **keep,** keep safe, keep inviolate *or* intact; not endanger, not destroy; not use up, not waste, not expend; **guard,** protect; **maintain,** sustain, uphold, support, **keep up,** keep alive
4 **cure,** season, salt, brine, marinate *or* marinade, pickle, corn, **dry, dry-cure,** jerk, dry-salt; dehydrate, anhydrate, evaporate, desiccate; vacuum-pack; **smoke,** smoke-cure, smoke-dry, kipper; **refrigerate,** freeze, quick-freeze, blast-freeze; freeze-dry, lyophilize; irradiate
5 **perpetuate,** preserve from oblivion, keep fresh *or* alive, perennialize, **eternalize,** eternize, **immortalize;** monumentalize; freeze, embalm

**preside** VERBS **administer,** administrate; **officiate;** preside over, preside at the board; chair, chairman, occupy the chair; **administer justice,** administer, **sit in judgment**

**president** NOUNS prexy <nonformal>, chief executive officer, chief executive, managing director <Brit>; **head of state,** chief of state; the man in the White House

**press** NOUNS 1 **extractor,** separator; wringer; cider mill
2 **pressure,** press, crush; urgency; impulse, impulsion, compulsion; **drive,** push; constraint, exigency, stress, pinch
VERBS 3 **bring pressure to bear upon,** put pressure on, bear down on, bear against, bear hard upon; **importune, urge,** pressure <nonformal>, prod, prod at, apply *or* exert pressure, push, **ply;** dun; **beset,** buttonhole, besiege, take *or* grasp by the lapels

**pressure** NOUNS 1 **coercion,** intimidation, scare tactics, headbanging *and* arm-twisting <both nonformal>, **duress; the strong arm** *and* strong-arm tactics <both nonformal>, a pistol *or* gun to one's head, the sword, the mailed fist, the bludgeon, the boot in the face, the jackboot, the big stick, the club, *argumentum baculinum* <L>; **high pressure,** high-pressure methods
2 **urgency,** imperativeness, exigence *or* exigency; **press,** high pressure, **stress,** tension, **pinch;** clutch *and* crunch <both nonformal>; **crisis, emergency;** moment of truth, turning point, climax, defining moment
VERBS 3 **urge,** press, push, work on <nonformal>, twist one's arm <nonformal>; **insist,** push for, not take no for an answer, **importune,** nag, high-pressure, bring pressure to bear upon, throw one's weight around, throw one's weight into the scale, jawbone *and* build a fire under <both nonformal>, talk round *or* around

**prestige** NOUNS **authority,** influence, influentialness; **weight,** weightiness, moment, **consequence;** eminence, **stature,** rank, seniority, preeminence, priority, precedence; **importance,** prominence; **honor;** dignity; rank, standing, stature, high place, position, station, face, **status**

**presume** VERBS 1 **assume,** venture, hazard, dare, pretend, attempt, **make bold** *or* so bold, make free, **take the liberty,** take upon oneself, go so far as to
2 **suppose,** surmise, expect, **suspect,** infer, understand, gather, conclude, deduce, consider, reckon, divine, imagine, **fancy,** dream, conceive, **believe, deem,** repute, feel, **think,** be inclined to think, opine, say, be afraid <nonformal>; **think likely,** daresay, venture to say

**presumption** NOUNS assumption, **imposition; license,** licentiousness, undue liberty, liberties, familiarity, **presumptuousness,** freedom *or* liberty abused, hubris; **conjecture,** inference, surmise, guesswork; **probability,** likelihood, likeliness, **good chance;** presumptive evidence; reasonable ground *or* presumption

**presumptuous** ADJS presuming, assuming, overweening, would-be, self-elect, self-elected, self-appointed, self-proclaimed, *soi-disant* <Fr>; **insolent,** insulting; forward, pushy <nonformal>, obtrusive, pushy <nonformal>, familiar, impertinent

**pretend** VERBS **affect,** assume, put on, assume *or* put on airs, wear, **simulate,** counterfeit, sham, fake <nonformal>, **feign,** make out like <nonformal>, make a show of, play, playact <nonformal>, act *or* play a part, play a scene, put up a front <nonformal>, dramatize, lay it on thick <nonformal>

**pretentious** ADJS **ostentatious,** vaunting, **lofty,** highfalutin *and* highfaluting <both nonformal>, **high-flown,** high-flying; **high-toned,** tony <both nonformal>, **fancy,** extravagant

**pretext** NOUNS **pretense, pretension,** lying pretension, **show,** ostensible *or* announced *or* public *or* professed motive; **front,** facade, **sham; excuse,** apology, protestation, poor excuse, lame excuse

**pretty** ADJS **beautiful,** attractive, pulchritudinous, **lovely, graceful,** gracile; **cute;** pretty as a picture

**prevail** VERBS **excel,** surpass, **predominate,** preponderate; **outweigh,** overbalance, overbear; **persist,** run true to form *or* type, continue the same

**prevail upon** VERBS **persuade,** sway, convince, lead to believe, **bring round,** bring to reason, bring to one's senses; **win, win over,** win around, bring over, **talk over,** talk into, argue into, out-talk <nonformal>

**prevalent** ADJS **prevailing, common,** popular, **current,** running; rife, rampant, pandemic, epidemic, besetting

**prevent** VERBS **prohibit,** bar, **keep from;** deter, discourage, dishearten; **avert,** parry, keep off, ward off, stave off, fend off, fend, repel, deflect, turn aside; **preclude,** exclude, debar, **obviate,** anticipate; rule out

**prevention** NOUNS **stop,** stoppage, stopping; **determent,** deterrence, discouragement; forestalling, preclusion, obviation, foreclosure

**previous** ADJS **prior,** early, **earlier,** *ci-devant* or *ci-dessus* <Fr>, **former,** fore, prime, first, **preceding**, foregoing, above, anterior, **anticipatory,** antecedent; **preexistent**

**prey** NOUNS **sufferer,** victim, **wretch,** poor devil <nonformal>, object of compassion; **quarry,** game, venery, beasts of venery, victim, the hunted

**price** NOUNS 1 **quotation;** bid-and-asked prices, bid price, asked *or* asking *or* offering price; **odds**
VERBS 2 set *or* name a price, fix the price of; place a value on, **value, evaluate,** valuate, **appraise,** assess, rate, prize, apprize; quote a price

**priceless** ADJS **precious, invaluable,** inestimable, without *or* beyond price, not to be had for love or money, not for all the tea in China

**prickly** ADJS **touchy, tetchy,** miffy <nonformal>, ticklish, quick to take offense, **thin-skinned,** sensitive, high-strung, highly strung, temperamental

**pride** NOUNS proudness, pridefulness; **self-esteem, self-respect,** self-confidence; pardonable pride; obstinate *or* stiff-necked pride, stiff-neckedness; **vanity,** conceit; haughtiness, **arrogance**

**priest** NOUNS **father,** father in Christ, **padre,** cassock, presbyter; curé, parish priest; confessor, father confessor, spiritual father *or* director *or* leader

**priesthood** NOUNS **clergy, ministry,** the cloth; clerical order, clericals; presbytery; prelacy

**prig** NOUNS **prude,** priss, puritan, bluenose, goody-goody <nonformal>

**prim** ADJS **prudish,** priggish, prissy, smug, stuffy <nonformal>, old-maidish, **overmodest,** demure, **straitlaced,** stiff-necked, hide-bound, narrow, censorious, **puritanical**

**primacy** NOUNS **supremacy,** first place, height, acme, zenith, be-all and end-all, summit, top spot <nonformal>; **sovereignty,** rule, hegemony, control

**prima donna** NOUNS **leading lady, principal, star,** headliner; **diva,** singer

**primal** ADJS **original, primary,** primitive, pristine, primeval, aboriginal, elementary, elemental, **basic,** basal, **rudimentary,** crucial, central, radical, **fundamental**

**primary** ADJS **essential,** of the essence, **fundamental;** primitive, primal, elementary, elemental, simple, bare-bones *and* no-frills *and* bread-and-butter <all nonformal>, original, *ab ovo* <L>, **basic,** gut <nonformal>, basal, underlying

**prime** NOUNS 1 **the best, quintessence,** optimum, superlative; **cream,** flower, cream of the crop, *crème de la crème* <Fr>, salt of the earth
ADJS 2 **best,** very best, greatest *and* top-of-the-line <both nonformal>, optimum, optimal; **unsurpassed,** surpassing, unparalleled, unmatched, unmatchable, matchless, **peerless;** quintessential

**primer** NOUNS **schoolbook,** alphabet book, abecedary, abecedarium; gradus, **grammar,** reader

**primitive** ADJS **primeval,** primogenial, primordial, pristine; **aboriginal,** autochthonous; **original,** primary, primal, pristine

**primp** VERBS spruce up *and* gussy up *and* doll up *and* fix up <all nonformal>, **primp up,** prink up, prank up, trick up *or* out, deck out; prink, prank, preen

**prince** NOUNS *Prinz, Fürst* <both Ger>, knez, atheling, sheikh, sherif, mirza, khan, emir, shahzada <India>; crown prince, heir apparent; heir presumptive; prince consort; prince regent

**princess** NOUNS *princesse* <Fr>, *infanta* <Sp>, rani *and* maharani *and* begum *and* shahzadi *and* kumari *or* kunwari *and* raj-kumari *and* malikzadi <all India>; crown princess

**principal** NOUNS 1 **headmaster,** headmistress; **chief; lead,** leading man *or* lady, leading actor *or* actress
2 **capital, fund;** moneyed capital; corpus; fixed capital, working capital, equity capital, **risk** *or* **venture capital**
ADJS 3 **first, foremost,** front, up-front <nonformal>, head, chief, premier, **leading, main,** flagship

**principle** NOUNS **cause,** interest, issue, burning issue, commitment, faith, great cause, lifework; reason for being, *raison d'être* <Fr>; **a belief,** tenet, dogma, precept, **principle** *or* **article of faith,** canon, maxim, axiom; **doctrine,** teaching

**print** NOUNS 1 **imprint,** stamp, impression; **impact,** force, **repercussion,** reaction
VERBS 2 **imprint,** impress, stamp, engrave; **publish,** issue, put in print, bring out, put out, get out

**prior** ADJS **previous,** early, earlier, *ci-devant* or *ci-dessus* <Fr>, **former,** fore, prime, first, **preceding**, foregoing, above, anterior, **anticipatory,** antecedent; **preexistent**

**priority** NOUNS precedence, prerogative, privilege, right-of-way; antecedence *or* antecedency, anteriority, precession; preference, urgency; top priority; primacy, preeminence

**prison** NOUNS 1 correctional *or* correction facility, minimum- *or* maximum-security facility, **penitentiary,** pen <nonformal>, keep, bastille, state prison, federal prison; **jail, gaol** <Brit>, jailhouse, lockup; **military prison,** guardhouse, stockade, brig; dungeon, oubliette, black hole; **prison camp,** internment camp, detention camp, labor camp, forced-labor camp, gulag, **concentration camp;** penal settlement *or* colony

2 <nonformal> **slammer, slam, jug,** can, coop, cooler, hoosegow, stir, clink, pokey, nick *and* quod *and* chokey <all Brit>; **joint,** big house, big school, big cage, big joint, brig, tank

**prisoner** NOUNS **captive,** *détenu* <Fr>, **convict,** con <nonformal>; **jailbird** <nonformal>, gaolbird <Brit nonformal>, **internee; prisoner of war** *or* POW

**prissy** ADJS **prudish,** priggish, prim, smug, stuffy <nonformal>, old-maidish, **overmodest,** demure, **straitlaced,** stiff-necked, hide-bound, narrow, censorious, sanctimonious, **puritanical**

**pristine** ADJS **intact,** untouched, undamaged, all in one piece <nonformal>, unimpaired, virgin, unspoiled

**privacy** NOUNS retirement, isolation, sequestration, seclusion; incognito, anonymity; **confidentialness,** confidentiality

**private** ADJS **privy,** closed-door; intimate, inmost, innermost, interior, inward, **personal; priviliged,** protected; **secluded,** sequestered, isolated, withdrawn, retired; incognito, anonymous

**privilege** NOUNS **license,** liberty, freedom, immunity; favor, indulgence, **special favor,** dispensation

**prize** NOUNS 1 **award,** reward; first prize, second prize, etc; blue ribbon; consolation prize; booby prize; Nobel Prize, Pulitzer Prize; trophy, plum

VERBS 2 **value,** esteem, treasure, appreciate, **rate highly,** think highly of, think well of, **think much of,** set store by

**probability** NOUNS **good chance,** sporting chance, good opportunity, good possibility; odds-on, odds-on chance, **likelihood, possibility**, favorable prospect, well-grounded hope

**probe** NOUNS 1 **investigation,** research, legwork <nonformal>, inquiry into; data-gathering, gathering *or* amassing evidence; perscrutation, searching investigation, close inquiry, exhaustive study; police inquiry *or* investigation, criminal investigation, detective work, detection, sleuthing

VERBS 2 **sound out,** feel out, sound, get a sounding *or* reading *or* sense, **feel the pulse,** read

**problem** NOUNS **nuisance,** pest, bother, botheration <nonformal>, public nuisance, **trouble,** pain <nonformal>, difficulty, hot potato <nonformal>; puzzling *or* baffling problem, why; enigmatic question, **perplexity; puzzler,** poser, brain twister *or* teaser <nonformal>, sticker <nonformal>; mind-boggler; **issue,** topic, case *or* point in question, bone of contention, controversial point, riddle, conundrum, mystery, enigma

**problematic** ADJS **doubtful,** iffy <nonformal>; **in doubt,** *in dubio* <L>; dubitable, doubtable, **dubious,** questionable, problematical, speculative, conjectural, suppositional

**proceed** VERBS **take action,** take steps *or* measures; proceed with, go ahead with, go with, go through with; do something, go *or* swing into action, **do something about,** act on *or* upon, take it on, get with it <nonformal>

**proceedings** NOUNS **affairs,** concerns, matters, circumstances, relations, **dealings,** doings, goings-on <nonformal>

**proceeds** NOUNS **gain, profit,** percentage <nonformal>, **take** *or* take-in *and* piece *and* slice *and* end *and* rakeoff *and* skimmings <all nonformal>; **gains,** profits, earnings, winnings, return, returns, bottom line <nonformal>

**process** NOUNS 1 **procedure,** proceeding, course; **act,** step, measure, initiative, *démarche* <Fr>, move, maneuver, motion

VERBS 2 **prepare,** make *or* get ready, prep <nonformal>, **ready, fix** <nonfor-

mal>; convert; mill, machine; **mine,** extract, pump, smelt, **refine**

**procession** NOUNS **train,** column, line, string, cortege; cavalcade, caravan, motorcade; **parade,** pomp; dress parade; progression, rotation; **continuity**

**proclaim** VERBS cry, cry out, **promulgate,** give voice to; **herald,** herald abroad; **blazon,** blare, blare forth *or* abroad, thunder, declaim, shout, trumpet, trumpet *or* thunder forth, shout from the housetops

**proclamation** NOUNS **announcement,** annunciation, enunciation; decree, pronouncement, pronunciamento; **declaration,** statement; public declaration *or* statement, **notice,** notification, public notice; circular, encyclical, encyclical letter; manifesto, position paper; broadside; rationale; white paper, white book; ukase, edict; bulletin board, notice board

**proclivity** NOUNS **inclination,** penchant, partiality, fancy, favor, predilection, preference, propensity, **leaning, bent,** turn, tilt, bias, **affinity**

**procrastinate** VERBS be dilatory, hesitate, let something slide, hang, hang back, hang fire; **temporize,** gain *or* make time, **play for time,** drag one's feet <nonformal>, hold off <nonformal>; **stall,** stall for time, tap-dance <nonformal>

**procrastinator** NOUNS **slowpoke** *and* slowcoach <both nonformal>, plodder, slow goer, **lingerer,** loiterer, dawdler, **laggard,** foot-dragger, stick-in-the-mud <nonformal>, drone, slug, sluggard, lie-abed, goof-off <nonformal>, goldbrick <nonformal>

**procure** VERBS **acquire,** get, gain, obtain, secure; pimp, pander

**prod** VERBS **goad,** poke, nudge, prod at, goose <nonformal>, **spur,** prick, sting, needle; **importune,** urge, press, pressure <nonformal>, apply *or* exert pressure, push

**prodigal** NOUNS 1 **wastrel,** waster, **squanderer; spendthrift,** spender, spendall, big-time spender <nonformal>; prodigal son
ADJS 2 **extravagant,** lavish, profuse, **overliberal,** overgenerous, overlavish, **spendthrift,** wasteful, profligate, dissipative; pound-foolish, penny-wise and pound-foolish

**prodigious** ADJS **extraordinary,** exceptional, remarkable, noteworthy, **wonderful, marvelous,** fabulous, mythical, legendary; **stupendous,** stupefying, portentous, phenomenal

**produce** NOUNS 1 **vegetables; yield,** output, make, production; **proceeds,** product; **crop, harvest,** fruit, vintage, bearing
VERBS 2 **be productive,** proliferate, pullulate, fructify, be fruitful, **multiply,** spin off, engender, beget, teem; create, make, manufacture, form, formulate, evolve, mature, elaborate, fashion, fabricate; **adduce,** advance, present, bring to bear, **offer,** proffer, invoke, **bring forward,** bring on

**product** NOUNS **commodity,** ware, vendible, **article,** item, article of commerce *or* merchandise; **effect,** result, resultant, **consequence,** consequent

**profane** ADJS **unsacred,** nonsacred, **unholy,** unhallowed, unsanctified, unblessed; **secular,** temporal, worldly, fleshly, mundane; profanatory

**profanity** NOUNS **cursing,** cussing <nonformal>, swearing, profane swearing, foul *or* profane *or* obscene *or* blue *or* bad *or* strong *or* unparliamentary *or* indelicate language, vulgar language, vile language, colorful language, unrepeatable expressions, dysphemism, billingsgate, ribaldry, evil speaking, **dirty language** *or* **talk** <nonformal>, **obscenity,** scatology, coprology, **filthy language,** filth

**profess** VERBS **state, assert,** swear, swear to God <nonformal>, declare, **affirm,** avow, avouch, asseverate, confess, be under the impression, express the belief, swear to a belief

**profession** NOUNS **vocation,** walk of life, calling, mission, **practice,** pursuit, specialty, specialization, *métier* <Fr>

**proficient** ADJS **fitted,** adapted, adjusted, suited; qualified, fit, competent, able, capable, well-qualified, well-fitted, well-suited

**profile** NOUNS 1 **outline,** contour, delineation, lines, lineaments, silhouette; **characterization,** character, character sketch
VERBS 2 **outline,** contour; **delineate;** silhouette, limn

**profit** NOUNS 1 **gain,** percentage <nonformal>, **take** *or* take-in *and* piece *and* slice *and* end *and* rakeoff *and* skimmings <all nonformal>; **gains,** earnings, winnings,

return, returns, proceeds, bottom line <nonformal>
VERBS 2 **make** *or* **draw** *or* **realize** *or* **reap profit,** come out ahead, make money; gain by, **capitalize on,** cash in on *and* make a good thing of <both nonformal>, turn to profit *or* account, **realize on,** make money by, obtain a return, turn a penny *or* an honest penny

**profitable** ADJS **gainful,** productive, **remunerative,** remuneratory, lucrative, fat, **paying,** well-paying, high-yield, high-yielding; advantageous, worthwhile; banausic, moneymaking, breadwinning

**profound** ADJS **deep-felt,** from the heart, heartfelt, **deep,** pervasive, pervading, absorbing; penetrating, penetrant, piercing; **poignant,** keen, sharp, acute; **wise,** sage, sapient, seasoned, **knowing; learned**

**profuse** ADJS **plentiful,** plenty, **plenteous,** plenitudinous, profusive, effuse, diffuse

**progeny** NOUNS **posterity,** issue, offspring, fruit, seed, brood, breed, family; **descendants,** heirs, inheritors, sons, **children,** treasures, hostages to fortune, youngsters, younglings

**prognosis** NOUNS prognostication; diagnosis; **prediction,** foretelling, foreshowing, forecasting, presaging

**program** NOUNS 1 **plan,** scheme, design, method, device, contrivance, game, envisagement, conception, enterprise, **idea,** notion; **undertaking, venture,** project, proposition *and* deal <both nonformal>; **performance,** musical performance, musical program, program of music; **software,** computer program, source program, object program
VERBS 2 **inculcate,** indoctrinate, catechize, inoculate, **instill,** infuse, imbue, impregnate, **implant,** infix, impress; **impress upon the mind** *or* **memory,** condition, brainwash
3 **schedule,** line up <nonformal>, **slate,** book, book in, put on the agenda
4 **automate,** automatize, robotize; **computerize,** digitize

**progress** NOUNS 1 **progression,** going, going forward; **course,** career, **passage,** trend, **advance,** forward motion, going *or* moving on, momentum; **improvement, betterment,** bettering, change for the better; headway
VERBS 2 **advance,** proceed, go, go *or* move forward, step forward, go on, **go ahead,** go along, push ahead, pass on *or* along; move, travel; go fast; **make progress,** come on, **get along,** come along <nonformal>, **get ahead;** further oneself

**progressive** NOUNS 1 **liberal,** progressivist, **leftist,** left-winger
ADJS 2 progressing, advancing, proceeding, **ongoing,** oncoming, onward, forward, **forward-looking,** go-ahead <nonformal>; moving

**prohibit** VERBS **forbid; disallow,** rule out *or* against; deny, reject; **bar,** debar, preclude, exclude, exclude from, shut out, shut *or* close the door on, prevent; **ban,** put under the ban, **outlaw;** repress, suppress; **enjoin,** proscribe, inhibit, **interdict,** put *or* lay under an interdict *or* interdiction; taboo

**prohibitive** ADJS prohibitory, prohibiting, **forbidding;** inhibitive, inhibitory, **repressive,** suppressive; proscriptive, interdictive, interdictory; **exorbitant,** excessive, extravagant, inordinate, immoderate, undue, unwarranted, unreasonable, fancy, unconscionable, outrageous, out of sight <nonformal>

**project** NOUNS **task,** work, stint, job, labor, piece of work, **chore,** chare, odd job; **assignment,** charge, commission

**project** VERBS **overhang,** hang over, hang out, **impend,** impend over, project over, beetle, **jut,** beetle *or* jut *or* thrust over, stick out over; **protrude,** protuberate, extrude; stick out, jut out, poke out, stand out

**proletarian** NOUNS 1 **worker,** workman, working man, working woman, working girl, laboring man, toiler, stiff *and* working stiff <both nonformal>, member of the working class
ADJS 2 **working class,** blue collar, lower-class

**proliferate** VERBS **multiply,** increase, duplicate

**prolific** ADJS **productive,** proliferous, uberous, **teeming,** swarming, bursting, bursting out, plenteous, **plentiful,** copious, bountiful; creative

**prolong** VERBS **protract,** continue, **extend,** lengthen, lengthen out, **draw out,** spin out, drag *or* stretch out; linger on, dwell on; **keep up,** keep going, keep alive

**prom** NOUNS **dance, hop** <nonformal>, cotillion; promenade, <nonformal>, formal <nonformal>

**promenade** NOUNS 1 **path,** public walk, esplanade, alameda, parade, *prado* <Sp>, mall; review, march-past
VERBS 2 **go for a walk,** perambulate, take a walk, take one's constitutional <nonformal>, take a stretch, stretch the legs; *passeggiare* <Ital>, parade

**prominent** ADJS **conspicuous,** outstanding, stickout <nonformal>, much in evidence, to the front, in the limelight <nonformal>; **important,** consequential, significant

**promiscuous** ADJS indiscriminate, **wanton,** wayward, Paphian; **loose,** lax, slack, loose-moraled, of loose morals, of easy virtue, easy <nonformal>, whorish

**promise** NOUNS 1 **pledge,** solemn promise, troth, plight, faith, parole, **word, word of honor,** solemn declaration *or* word; **oath,** vow
VERBS 2 **suggest,** hint, imply, give prospect of, make likely, give ground for expecting, raise expectation, **lead one to expect,** hold out hope, have *or* show promise, **bid fair**
3 give *or* make a promise, hold out an expectation; **pledge,** plight, troth, **vow; give one's word,** pledge *or* pass one's word, give one's parole, **give one's word of honor**

**promising** ADJS of promise, full of promise, bright with promise, pregnant of good, best-case, **favorable,** looking up; **auspicious, propitious**

**promote** VERBS **advance, further,** forward, hasten, contribute to, foster, aid, facilitate, expedite, abet; build up, cry up, sell, puff <nonformal>, **boost** <nonformal>, **plug** <nonformal>, **ballyhoo** <nonformal>

**promoter** NOUNS **booster** <nonformal>, plugger <nonformal>; organizer, developer, expediter, facilitator, animator; **backer,** angel <nonformal>, rabbi <nonformal>; **patron,** Maecenas

**prompt** VERBS 1 **provoke,** evoke, elicit, call up, summon up, muster up, call forth, **inspire;** bring about, cause; prompt the mind, give the cue
ADJS 2 **punctual,** immediate, instant, instantaneous, **quick**, speedy, swift, expeditious, summary, decisive, apt, alert, **ready,** Johnny-on-the-spot <nonformal>

**prone** ADJS 1 **recumbent,** accumbent, procumbent, decumbent; **prostrate,** flat; **supine,** resupine
2 **disposed,** dispositioned, **predisposed,** inclined, given, bent, bent on, apt, likely, **minded,** in the mood *or* humor

**pronounce** VERBS announce, annunciate, enunciate, **proclaim; maintain,** have, **contend,** argue, **insist, hold,** submit, maintain with one's last breath; **pass judgment,** pronounce judgment, utter a judgment, deliver judgment

**pronounced** ADJS **conspicuous,** noticeable, notable, ostensible, **prominent,** bold, salient, in relief, in bold *or* high *or* strong relief, **striking, outstanding,** in the foreground

**proof** NOUNS **evidence,** reason to believe, grounds for belief; **ground, grounds,** material grounds, **facts, data,** premises, basis for belief; demonstration, ironclad proof, incontrovertible proof

**prop** VERBS **support,** lend support, give *or* furnish *or* afford support; reinforce, undergird, bolster, **bolster up,** buttress, shore, shore up, prop up

**propaganda** NOUNS indoctrination; brainwashing; **disinformation**

**propagate** VERBS **procreate,** generate, breed, beget, get, **engender; multiply;** proliferate

**propel** VERBS **set in motion,** move, actuate, motivate, push, shove, nudge, **drive,** impel

**propellant** ADJS **propulsive,** propulsory, propelling; **motive; driving,** pushing, shoving

**proper** ADJS **decorous,** decent, right, right-thinking, **seemly, becoming,** fitting, appropriate, suitable, meet, happy, felicitous; genteel; civil, urbane

**property** NOUNS 1 **real estate,** realty, real property, land, land and buildings, chattels real, tenements; immoveables; *praedium* <L>, **land,** lands, grounds, acres
2 **characteristic,** quality, attribute

**prophecy** NOUNS **prediction,** foretelling, forecasting, **prognosis,** prognostication, presaging; prophesying, vaticination

**prophet** NOUNS **predictor,** foreteller, prognosticator, seer, foreseer, foreshower, **forecaster;** prophesier, soothsayer, *vates* <L>

**prophylactic** NOUNS **preventive,** preventative, protective; **contraceptive,** birth control device; condom

**proponent** NOUNS **justifier,** vindicator; defender, pleader; **advocate,** successful advocate *or* defender, **champion; apologist,** apologizer, apologetic

**proportion** NOUNS **symmetry,** symmetricalness, proportionality, **balance**, equilibrium; **percentage,** measure, quantum, **quota; harmony,** order, concinnity

**proportional** ADJS **comparable,** proportionate, proportionable; **like,** homologous

**proposal** NOUNS **proposition,** suggestion, offer, instance; **motion,** resolution; marriage proposal, offer of marriage, popping of the question

**proprietor** NOUNS **owner;** *rentier* <Fr>; titleholder, deedholder; proprietress, proprietrix; **master, mistress, lord,** laird <Scots>; **landlord, landlady**

**propriety** NOUNS **decorum, decency,** good behavior *or* conduct, correctness, correctitude, rightness, properness, decorousness, goodness, goodliness, niceness, seemliness

**propulsion** NOUNS **pushing,** propelling; shoving, butting; **drive, thrust,** motive power, driving force, means of propulsion; **push, shove**

**pro rata** ADJS and ADVS **proportionate,** proportional; prorated, *pro rata* <L> <all adjectives>; **proportionately,** in proportion, *pro rata* <L> <all adverbs>

**prosaic** ADJS **prosy;** unpoetical, poetryless; **plain,** common, commonplace, ordinary, unembellished, mundane; **matter-of-fact,** unromantic, unidealistic, unimpassioned; pedestrian, **unimaginative**; insipid, vapid, flat; humdrum, tiresome, **dull**

**proscribe** VERBS **prohibit,** inhibit, **interdict,** put *or* lay under an interdict *or* interdiction; put on the Index; embargo, **lay** *or* **put an embargo on;** taboo, ban, outlaw

**prosecute** VERBS **sue, litigate,** go into litigation, **bring suit,** put in suit, sue *or* prosecute at law, **go to law,** seek in law, appeal to the law, seek justice *or* legal redress, implead, **bring action against,** prosecute a suit against, take *or* institute legal proceedings against; **put on trial,** take before the judge

**proselytize** VERBS **convince,** persuade, wean, bring over, sweep off one's feet <nonformal>, **win over;** proselyte, evangelize; convert

**prospect** NOUNS 1 **view,** scene, sight; outlook, lookout, vista, perspective; **expectation,** expectance *or* **expectancy,** state of expectancy; **anticipation,** outlook, probability, foresight, prevision
VERBS 2 **mine;** quarry; pan, pan for gold

**prospective** ADJS **expected,** in prospect, **coming,** forthcoming, imminent, approaching, nearing

**prospectus** NOUNS **proposal,** proposition; **scenario, game plan** <nonformal>

**prosper** VERBS enjoy prosperity, **fare well,** get on well, do well, have it made *or* hacked <nonformal>, have a good thing going, have everything going one's way, get on swimmingly, go great guns <nonformal>

**prosperity** NOUNS prosperousness, thriving *or* flourishing condition; success; **well-being,** weal, happiness, felicity; a chicken in every pot, a car in every garage

**prosperous** ADJS **successful,** affluent, wealthy; **comfortable,** comfortably situated, **easy;** on Easy Street *and* in Fat City *and* in hog heaven <all nonformal>, **in clover** *and* **on velvet** <both nonformal>

**prostitute** NOUNS 1 **harlot, whore,** *fille de joie* <Fr>, call girl *and* B-girl <both nonformal>, **scarlet woman,** unfortunate woman, painted woman, fallen woman, erring sister, **streetwalker,** hustler *and* **hooker** <both nonformal>, *poule* <Fr>, meretrix
VERBS 2 **misuse,** misemploy, abuse, misapply; divert, misappropriate, pervert; profane, violate, pollute

**prostrate** ADJS **disabled,** incapacitated; **on one's back,** on one's beam-ends, flat on one's back; prostrated, **forlorn;** desolated, **brokenhearted,** heartbroken

**protect** VERBS **guard, safeguard,** secure, keep, bless, make safe, **police,** enforce the law; keep from harm; **shelter,** shield, screen

**protection** NOUNS **guard,** shielding, safekeeping; policing, law enforcement; **shelter,** cover, shade, **defense**

**protector** NOUNS **keeper,** protectress, safekeeper; patron, patroness; tower, pillar, strong arm, tower of strength, rock; champion, **defender**

**protégé** NOUNS **dependent,** charge, ward, client, protégée, encumbrance

**protest** NOUNS 1 **complaint,** grievance, peeve, pet peeve, **groan;** objection, kick *and* **beef** *and* bitch *and* squawk *and* howl <all nonformal>, protestation;

**remonstrance, remonstration,** expostulation, **dissent**
VERBS 2 **object,** kick *and* beef <both nonformal>, put up a struggle *or* fight; bitch *and* **squawk** *and* howl *and* holler *and* put up a squawk *and* raise a howl <all nonformal>; exclaim *or* cry out against; yell bloody murder <nonformal>; **remonstrate,** expostulate; raise *or* press objections, raise one's voice against, enter a protest

**protocol** NOUNS **rule, guideline,** ground rule, rubric, working rule, working principle, standard procedure; **code, etiquette,** social code, rules *or* code of conduct; **formalities,** social procedures, social conduct, what is done, what one does

**prototype** NOUNS **original, model,** archetype, **pattern, mold,** pilot model; **innovation,** new departure

**protract** VERBS **prolong,** continue, **extend, lengthen,** lengthen out, **draw out, spin out,** drag *or* stretch out; linger on, dwell on; dawdle, procrastinate, temporize, drag one's feet

**protrude** VERBS **protuberate,** project, extrude; stick out, jut out, poke out, stand out, shoot out; **stick up,** bristle up, start up, cock up, shoot up

**proud** ADJS **prideful, self-esteeming,** self-respecting; proud as Punch, proud as Lucifer, proud as a peacock

**prove** VERBS **demonstrate, show,** afford proof of, prove to be, prove true; **establish,** fix, **determine, ascertain,** make out, remove all doubt; **verify,** confirm, test, validate

**proven** ADJS **proved,** demonstrated, shown; **established,** fixed, **settled,** determined, nailed down <nonformal>, ascertained; **confirmed,** substantiated, attested, **authenticated,** certified, validated, verified

**proverb** NOUNS **maxim,** aphorism, apothegm, epigram, dictum, adage, gnome, words of wisdom, **saw, saying,** phrase, catchphrase, motto, moral

**provide** VERBS **supply,** find, dish up *and* rustle up <both nonformal>, **furnish;** support, maintain, keep

**provider** NOUNS **supplier,** furnisher; donor; patron; **purveyor,** provisioner, **caterer,** victualer, sutler

**provincial** ADJS **rustic,** rural, country, farm, pastoral, bucolic, Arcadian, **agrarian,** agrestic; insular, parochial; **hidebound,** creedbound, **straitlaced,** stuffy <nonformal>

**provision** NOUNS **condition,** proviso, stipulation, whereas; **specification,** given, *donnée* <Fr>, **limitation,** limiting condition, boundary condition; **catch** *and* joker *and* kicker *and* string *and* a string to it <all nonformal>; sagacity, providence, discretion, preparation, forehandedness, readiness, prudence

**provocative** ADJS **provoking,** piquant, **exciting,** challenging, prompting, **rousing,** stirring, stimulating, stimulant, stimulative, stimulatory, energizing, electric, galvanizing, galvanic; **encouraging,** inviting, alluring; **tempting,** teasing, titillating, titillative, tickling; *provoquant* <Fr>; thought-provoking, thought-challenging, thought-inspiring; racy, juicy, spicy

**provoke** VERBS **incense,** arouse, inflame, embitter; **vex,** irritate, annoy, aggravate <nonformal>, **exasperate,** nettle, fret, chafe; **pique,** peeve *and* miff <both nonformal>, huff; **ruffle,** roil, rile <nonformal>, ruffle one's feathers, **rankle; sow dissension,** stir up trouble, make *or* borrow trouble; **alienate, estrange,** separate, divide, disunite, disaffect, come between

**prowess** NOUNS **skill,** skillfulness, **expertness,** proficiency, craft, **cleverness; dexterity,** dexterousness *or* dextrousness; **adroitness,** address, deftness, handiness, hand, practical ability; **facility,** mastery

**prowl** VERBS **wander,** roam, rove, knock around *or* about *and* bat around *or* about <all nonformal>; **sneak,** steal, steal along; slink, sidle, pad, nightwalk

**prowler** NOUNS **thief,** robber, crook <nonformal>; larcenist, larcener; sneak thief

**proximity** NOUNS **nearness,** closeness, nighness, propinquity, intimacy, immediacy; **vicinity,** vicinage, **neighborhood,** environs, surroundings

**proxy** NOUNS **deputy,** representative, substitute, vice, vicegerent, **alternate,** backup *and* stand-in <both nonformal>, alter ego, **surrogate,** procurator, secondary, understudy, pinch hitter <nonformal>; **ballot,** proxy ballot

**prude** NOUNS **prig,** priss, puritan, bluenose, goody-goody <nonformal>

**prudent** ADJS **judicious,** judicial, judgmatic, judgmatical, prudential, politic, careful, provident, **considerate,** circumspect, **thoughtful,** reflective, reflecting; **discreet;** discriminative, discriminating

**prune** VERBS **sever, dissever,** cut off *or* away *or* loose, shear off, hack off; **cut,** incise, carve, **slice,** pare, trim, trim away, resect, excise

**pry** VERBS 1 **snoop,** peep, peek, spy, nose, nose into, have a long *or* big nose, poke *or* stick one's nose in; meddle
2 prize, **lever,** wedge

**psalm** NOUNS **hymn,** hymn of praise, **doxology,** anthem, motet, canticle, chorale; hymnody, hymnology, hymnography, psalmody

**pseudonym** NOUNS **alias,** anonym, **assumed name,** false *or* fictitious name, *nom de guerre* <Fr>; pen name, stage name, *nom de théâtre* <Fr>, professional name

**psyche** NOUNS psychic apparatus, **personality,** self, personhood; **spirit,** spiritus, **soul,** *âme* <Fr>, **heart,** mind, anima, *anima humana* <L>

**psychedelic** ADJS **psychochemical,** psychoactive; ataractic; hallucinogenic, mind-expanding, psychotomimetic, consciousness-expanding, mind-expanding, mind-blowing <nonformal>

**psyched up** ADJS **prepared,** pumped up <nonformal>, eager, keen, champing at the bit; alert, vigilant; **set** *and* **all set** <both nonformal>, on the mark *and* teed up <nonformal>; primed, loaded, cocked, **loaded for bear** <nonformal>

**psychic** NOUNS 1 **spiritualist,** spiritist, **medium,** ecstatic, spirit rapper, automatist, psychographist; necromancer
ADJS 2 **psychical,** spiritual; spiritualistic, spiritistic; mediumistic; **clairvoyant,** second-sighted, clairaudient, clairsentient, **telepathic; extrasensory,** psychosensory

**psycho** NOUNS **psychotic,** mental, mental case, certifiable case, **psychopath,** psychopathic case

**psychoactive drug** NOUNS hallucinogen, psychedelic, psychedelic drug, psychoactive drug, psychoactive chemical *or* psychochemical, psychotropic drug, psychotomimetic drug, mind-altering drug, mind-expanding drug, mind-blowing drug

**psychosis** NOUNS psychopathy, psychopathology, psychopathic condition; certifiability

**psychotic** NOUNS 1 psycho <nonformal>, mental, mental case, certifiable case, **psychopath,** psychopathic case; psychopathic personality
ADJS 2 **psychopathic,** psychoneurotic, mentally ill, mentally sick, certifiable

**psych out** VERBS **unnerve,** unman, undo, unstring, unbrace, reduce to jelly, **demoralize,** shake, upset; **unriddle,** unscramble, undo, untangle, disentangle, untwist, unspin, unweave, **unravel,** ravel, ravel out; guess, divine, guess right

**puberty** NOUNS **adolescence,** maturation, maturement, pubescence, **sexual maturity,** nubility

**public** NOUNS 1 **population,** inhabitants, dwellers, **populace, people,** whole people, people at large, citizenry, folk, souls, living souls, body, whole body, warm bodies <nonformal>; general public
ADJS 2 **general,** common; communal, societal, social; civic, civil; pop <nonformal>; mass, grass-roots; notorious; known by every schoolboy; talked-about, **on everyone's tongue** *or* **lips**

**publication** NOUNS **publishing,** promulgation, evulgation, **propagation,** announcement, dissemination, diffusion, broadcast, broadcasting, spread, spreading, spreading abroad, **circulation,** ventilation, airing, noising, bandying, bruiting, bruiting about; **printing**

**publicity** NOUNS **notoriety,** fame, famousness, notoriousness, notice, public notice, **celebrity,** *réclame, éclat* <both Fr>; **limelight** *and* **spotlight** <both nonformal>, daylight, bright light, glare, public eye *or* consciousness, **exposure, currency,** common *or* public knowledge, widest *or* maximum dissemination

**publish** VERBS **promulgate,** propagate, circulate, circularize, **diffuse, disseminate,** distribute, **broadcast,** televise, telecast, videocast, air, **spread,** spread around *or* about, spread far and wide, publish abroad, **pass the word around,** bruit, **bruit about,** advertise, repeat, retail, put about, **bandy about,** noise about; **print;** issue, put in print, bring out, put out, get out

**puerile** ADJS immature, **childish;** childlike; **infantile,** infantine; **babyish**

**pugnacious** ADJS **belligerent,** truculent, bellicose, scrappy <nonformal>, full of fight; **aggressive,** antagonistic, **quarrelsome**

**puke** VERBS **gag,** retch, keck, heave, vomit, hurl *and* upchuck *and* barf <all nonformal>

**pull** NOUNS 1 **draw,** heave, haul, tug, a long pull and a strong pull, strain, drag; **attraction,** pulling power, magnetism
VERBS 2 **draw,** heave, haul, hale, lug, **tug,** tow, take in tow; **attract,** drag, pull *or* draw towards, have an attraction; **lure**

**pull out** VERBS 1 **retreat,** sound *or* beat a retreat, beat a hasty retreat, **withdraw,** retire, pull back, exfiltrate, advance to the rear, disengage; **fall back,** move back, go back, stand back; run back; withdraw one's support
2 **extract,** draw out, tear out, rip out, wrest out, pluck out, pick out, weed out, rake out; **pry out,** prize out, **pull up,** pluck up

**pulsate** VERBS **pulse,** beat, throb, not miss a beat; **palpitate,** go pit-a-pat; drum

**pulse** NOUNS **pulsation,** beat, throb; beating, throbbing; systole, diastole; **palpitation,** flutter, arrhythmia, pitter-patter, pit-a-pat; fibrillation, ventricular fibrillation, tachycardia, ventricular tachycardia <all medicine>; **heartbeat**

**pulverize** VERBS **powder,** comminute, triturate, contriturate, levigate, bray, pestle, disintegrate, reduce to powder *or* dust, grind to powder *or* dust, grind up; **fragment,** shard, shatter; **beat,** pound, mash, smash, crush, crunch, flail, squash, scrunch <nonformal>

**pummel** VERBS **whip,** give a whipping *or* beating *or* thrashing, **beat,** thrash, spank, whale; **smite,** thump, trounce, baste, pommel, **drub,** buffet, belabor, lay on

**pump** VERBS **draw off,** suck, suck out *or* up, **siphon off;** pump out

**pumping iron** NOUNS **weightlifting,** weight training, bench press

**pun** NOUNS **play on words,** *jeu de mots* <Fr>, paronomasia, *calembour* <Fr>, punning

**punch** NOUNS 1 **power,** force, vigor, vitality, vim, push, drive, charge, oomph *and* pizazz *and* bang *and* clout *and* steam <all nonformal>
2 **hit,** blow, stroke, knock, rap, pound, slam, bang, crack, **whack,** smack, thwack, smash, dash, swipe, swing, **poke, jab**
VERBS 3 **indent, dent,** dint, depress, press in, stamp, tamp, punch in, impress, imprint
4 **fight,** box, spar, mix it up <nonformal>, knock down, knock out, slug, maul

**punctual** ADJS **prompt,** immediate, instant, instantaneous, **quick**, speedy, swift, Johnny-on-the-spot <nonformal>

**puncture** NOUNS 1 **hole,** perforation, penetration, piercing, goring, boring, puncturing, punching, pricking, lancing, broach; acupuncture, trephining, trepanning
VERBS 2 **deflate,** let the air out of, take the wind out of; **perforate, pierce,** penetrate, punch, prick; explode, blow up, blow sky-high, shoot *or* poke full of holes, cut to pieces, cut the ground from under

**pundit** NOUNS **scholar,** learned man *or* woman, giant of learning, colossus of knowledge, mastermind, **savant**

**pungent** ADJS **piquant,** poignant; sharp, keen, piercing, penetrating, nose-tickling, stinging, **biting, acrid,** astringent, irritating, harsh

**punish** VERBS **chastise,** chasten, discipline, correct, castigate, penalize; take to task, bring to book, bring *or* call to account; **give one his desserts** *or* **just desserts,** teach *or* give one a lesson, make an example of

**punishment** NOUNS **reprisal,** requital, retribution; recompense, compensation, comeuppance <nonformal>, desserts, **just desserts,** what is merited, what's coming to one *and* a dose of one's own medicine <both nonformal>

**puny** ADJS **frail,** slight, delicate, dainty; trifling, poky, piffling *and* pindling *and* piddly <all nonformal>, **dinky** <nonformal>; **petty, piddling,** piffling, niggling, pettifogging, picayune

*delicately weak*
POPE

**puppet** NOUNS **marionette,** *fantoche* <Fr>, *fantoccino* and *fantoccio* <both Ital>, hand puppet, glove puppet

**purchase** VERBS **buy,** procure, make *or* complete a purchase, make a buy, make a deal for, blow oneself to <nonformal>; buy on credit, buy on the installment plan; buy sight unseen *or* blind

**pure** ADJS **faultless,** flawless, unflawed, **impeccable,** absolute; **just right;** spotless, stainless, taintless, unblemished, untainted, unspotted, immaculate, uncontaminated, unadulterated, unmixed; sinless; chaste

**purgatory** NOUNS living death, hell, hell upon earth; limbo; **purgation**

*cold purgatorial fires*
T S Eliot

**purge** NOUNS 1 **cleansing,** cleanout, cleaning out, purging, purgation, catharsis; **purification,** purifying, lustration; expurgation, bowdlerization; **laxative,** cathartic, physic, purgative, aperient, carminative; liquidation
VERBS 2 **clean, cleanse,** deterge, depurate; expurgate, bowdlerize; overthrow; **eliminate, get rid of,** rid oneself of, **get quit of,** get shut of <nonformal>, **dispose of, remove,** abstract, eject, expel, give the bum's rush <nonformal>, throw over *or* overboard <nonformal>; clear, clear out, clear away, clear the decks; liquidate, **do away with,** exterminate, annihilate

**purify** VERBS **refine, clarify,** clear, rectify, depurate; chasten, restrain; cleanse, wash one's sins away; distill

**purist** NOUNS dogmatist, positivist, bigot, fanatic; **pedant;** formalist, precisionist, precisian, *précieux* <Fr>, **bluestocking,** *bas bleu* <Fr>, *précieuse* <Fr fem>

**purity** NOUNS immaculacy, immaculateness, spotlessness, unspottedness; **chastity;** guiltlessness, innocence; cleanness, cleanliness, impeccability; clean hands, clean slate, clear conscience, nothing to hide; **virtue,** virtuousness, honor

**purpose** NOUNS **function,** use, role, part, end use, immediate purpose, ultimate purpose, operational purpose, operation; **intent,** intention, aim, object, design, plan

**pursue** VERBS **follow,** go after *or* behind, come after *or* behind, move behind; **shadow** *and* **tail** <both nonformal>, **trail,** trail after; **practice,** put into practice, exercise, employ, use; carry on, conduct, prosecute, wage; **elaborate,** develop, work out, enlarge, enlarge on *or* upon, amplify, **expand,** expand on *or* upon, detail, go into detail

**pursuer** NOUNS pursuant, **chaser,** follower; hunter, quester, **seeker**

**pursuit** NOUNS 1 pursuing, pursuance; **quest,** seeking, hunting, searching; **following,** follow, follow-up; tracking, trailing, tracking down, dogging, shadowing, stalking; **chase,** hot pursuit; hue and cry
2 **vocation,** occupation, business, work, line, line of work, walk, **walk of life,** calling, mission, **profession,** practice, specialty, specialization, *métier* <Fr>, **trade,** racket *and* game <both nonformal>

**push** NOUNS 1 **enterprise,** dynamism, initiative, **aggressiveness,** pushiness, drive, hustle, go, getup, **get-up-and-go** <nonformal>, go-ahead, go-getting
2 **thrust,** shove, boost <nonformal>; **pressure; stress**
VERBS 3 **propel,** impel, **shove,** thrust; **drive, move,** forward, advance; sweep, sweep along

**pusher** NOUNS **drug seller** *or* dealer, contact, connection

**pushover** NOUNS **weakling,** sissy *and* pansy *and* pantywaist <all nonformal>, lightweight; **wimp,** poor *or* weak *or* dull tool <nonformal>; trusting soul; **dupe;** sucker *and* patsy *and* easy mark <all nonformal>; **cinch** *and* snap <both nonformal>

**pushy** ADJS **insolent,** forward, obtrusive, familiar; self-assertive, self-asserting, importunate

**pussyfoot** VERBS **be cautious, tiptoe, go** *or* walk on tiptoe, walk on eggs *or* eggshells *or* thin ice; **shuffle,** dodge, shy, **evade,** sidestep, hedge, skate around <nonformal>, evade the issue; **beat about** *or* **around the bush**

**put back** VERBS **turn back, restore,** replace, return, place in *status quo ante;* **reestablish,** redintegrate, reenact, **reinstate,** restitute; **reinstall,** reinvest, revest, reinstitute, reconstitute, recompose, recruit, **rehabilitate,** redevelop; give back, hand back

**put-down** NOUNS **humiliation, abasement,** debasement, setdown, afront, dig <nonformal>, insult, slap *or* kick in the face

**put down** VERBS 1 **suppress,** subdue, quell, smash, **crush; quash,** squash *and* squelch <both nonformal>; **deprecate,** discommend, denigrate, **fault,** find fault with, pick holes in, pick to pieces; **ridicule**
2 **record,** write down, mark down, jot down, set down, take down

3 **pay over,** hand over; ante, **ante up,** put up; lay down, lay one's money down, show the color of one's money

**put off** VERBS **1 offend,** give offense, **repel,** turn off <nonformal>, **revolt,** disgust, nauseate, sicken, make one sick, make one sick to *or* in the stomach

2 **not face up to,** hide one's head in the sand, not come to grips with, procrastinate, temporize, **postpone,** delay, defer, prorogue, put on hold *or* ice *or* the back burner <all nonformal>

**put-on** NOUNS 1 **gibe,** scoff, jeer, fleer, flout, mock, **taunt,** twit, quip, jest, jape, leg-pull <nonformal>, foolery

ADJS 2 **assumed, pretended,** simulated, **phony** *and* **fake** *and* **faked** <all nonformal>, feigned, counterfeited; spurious, sham; hypocritical

**put out** VERBS **inconvenience,** put to inconvenience, **discommode,** disoblige, **burden,** embarrass; trouble, bother, put to trouble, put to the trouble of, **impose upon;** harm, disadvantage

**putrid** ADJS **decayed,** decomposed; spoiled, corrupt, peccant, bad, **gone bad; rotten,** rotting, putrefied, foul

**putter** VERBS **trifle,** dabble, fribble, footle, potter, piddle, diddle, doodle; **dabble,** smatter

**put together** VERBS **join,** conjoin, **unite,** unify, bond, **connect,** associate, league, band, merge, **assemble,** accumulate; **gather,** mobilize, marshal, mass, amass, **collect,** conglobulate; fix together, lay together, piece together, clap together, tack together, stick together, lump together, roll into one

**put-upon** ADJS **distressed, afflicted,** beset, beleaguered; **troubled,** bothered, disturbed, perturbed, disquieted, discomforted, discomposed, agitated

**put up with** VERBS **endure,** bear, stand, support, sustain, **suffer,** tolerate, abide, bide, live with; persevere; **bear up under,** bear the brunt, bear with, stand for, tolerate, take the bitter with the sweet, hang in there

**puzzle** NOUNS 1 **enigma,** mystery, puzzlement; crossword puzzle, jigsaw puzzle; **problem,** puzzling *or* baffling problem, why; **perplexity;** knot, knotty point, crux, point to be solved; **puzzler,** poser, brain twister *or* teaser <nonformal>, sticker <nonformal>; mind-boggler

VERBS 2 **perplex,** baffle, confound, addle, fuddle, muddle, **mystify,** nonplus, put to one's wit's end; keep one guessing, keep in suspense

**pyramid** NOUNS **monument,** memorial; monolith, obelisk; **gravestone, tombstone;** memorial tablet, brass; headstone, footstone; mausoleum; cenotaph; cairn, mound, barrow, cromlech, dolmen, megalith, menhir, cyclolith; **shrine,** reliquary, tope, stupa

**pyromaniac** NOUNS **incendiary, arsonist,** torcher <nonformal>; firebug <nonformal>; pyrophile

# Q

**quack** NOUNS 1 **charlatan,** quacksalver, quackster, **mountebank,** saltimbanco
ADJS 2 **quackish;** charlatan, charlatanic; specious, meretricious

**quadruple** VERBS **quadruplicate,** fourfold, form *or* make four, multiply by four

**quagmire** NOUNS **marsh,** swamp, **morass,** mire, slough, quicksand

**quail** VERBS **cower,** cringe, crouch, skulk, sneak, slink; wince, blink, blench

**quaint** ADJS **odd,** queer, peculiar, absurd, **singular,** curious, oddball <nonformal>, weird *and* kooky *and* freaky *and* freaked-out <all nonformal>, **eccentric**

**quake** NOUNS 1 **earthquake,** temblor, diastrophism, epicenter, shock-wave; **shake,** quiver, quaver, falter, **tremor,** tremble, shiver, shudder
VERBS 2 **tremble,** shake, shiver, quiver, quaver; tremble *or* quake *or* shake in one's boots *or* shoes, tremble like an aspen leaf, shake all over

**qualification** NOUNS **limitation,** limiting, restriction, circumscription, **modification,** hedge, hedging; setting conditions, conditionality, provisionality, circumstantiality; specification; **mental reservation,** *arrière-pensée* <Fr>

**qualify** VERBS 1 **measure up,** meet the requirements, check out <nonformal>, have the credentials *or* qualifications *or* prerequisites; be up to *and* be just the ticket *and* fill the bill <all nonformal>
2 **limit,** hedge, hedge about, **modify,** restrict, restrain, circumscribe, set limits *or* conditions, box in <nonformal>, narrow

**quality** NOUNS **nature,** character, suchness; property, attribute; **goodness,** excellence, class <nonformal>

**qualm** NOUNS **compunction,** qualms, qualmishness, scruples, scrupulosity, scrupulousness, pang, pangs, **pangs of conscience,** throes, sting *or* pricking *or* twinge *or* twitch of conscience, **apprehension,** apprehensiveness, **misgiving,** funny feeling; qualm of conscience, reservation

**quandary** NOUNS **dilemma,** horns of a dilemma, double bind, damned-if-you-do-and-damned-if-you-don't, no-win situation, nonplus

**quantify** VERBS quantize, **count,** number off, enumerate, number, rate, fix; quantitate, **measure, gauge,** take the measure of, mensurate; compute, calculate

**quantity** NOUNS **numerousness**; quantities, much, abundance, copiousness, superabundance, superfluity, profusion, plenty, plenitude

**quantum** NOUNS **quantity,** amount, **whole**; mass, **bulk,** substance, matter, magnitude, amplitude, **extent, sum; percentage,** measure, **quota**

**quarantine** NOUNS 1 **isolation,** cordoning off, segregation, separation, sequestration, seclusion; walling in *or* up *or* off; sanitary cordon, *cordon sanitaire* <Fr>, cordon
VERBS 2 **isolate,** segregate, separate, seclude; **cordon, cordon off,** seal off, rope off; wall off, set up barriers, put behind barriers

**quarrel** NOUNS 1 open quarrel, dustup, **dispute, argument,** polemic, lovers' quarrel, **controversy,** altercation, **fight,** squabble, contention, strife, **tussle,** bicker, wrangle, snarl, **tiff, spat,** fuss; row, scrap, hassle
VERBS 2 **dispute,** oppugn, altercate, **fight, squabble,** tiff, spat, **bicker, wrangle,** spar, have words, set to, join issue, make the fur fly, make *or* kick up a row

**quarter** NOUNS 1 **district,** section, department, division; **neighborhood,** vicinity, vicinage, neck of the woods <nonformal>, purlieus
VERBS 2 **house,** domicile, domiciliate; **lodge,** put up, billet, room, bed, berth, bunk; stable
3 divide by four *or* into four; quadrisect

**quarters** NOUNS **living quarters; lodgings,** lodging, lodgment; diggings *and* digs <both Brit nonformal>, pad *and* crib <both nonformal>, **rooms,** berth, accommodations; **housing**, shelter

**quartet** NOUNS **four,** tetrad, quatern, quaternion, quaternary, quaternity, quadruplet, foursome

**quash** VERBS **cover up,** muffle up; **hush up, hush,** hush-hush, shush, hugger-mugger; **suppress,** repress, **stifle,** muffle, **smother,** squash, squelch, kill, sit on *or* upon, put the lid on <nonformal>; **censor,** black out <nonformal>

**quaver** NOUNS 1 **shake,** quake, quiver,

falter, **tremor,** tremble, shiver, shudder, twitter, didder, dither
VERBS 2 **shake,** tremble, quiver, cringe, cower, totter, teeter, dodder

**queasy** ADJS **nauseated,** nauseous, **squeamish,** qualmish, qualmy; **sick to one's stomach;** pukish *and* puky *and* barfy <all nonformal>; seasick, carsick, airsick

**queer** VERBS 1 **put out of order,** put out of commission <nonformal>, throw out of gear; bugger *and* bugger up *and* queer the works *and* gum up *or* screw up <all nonformal>, throw a wrench *or* monkey wrench in the machinery <nonformal>, sabotage, wreck
ADJS 2 **odd,** peculiar, absurd, **singular,** curious, oddball <nonformal>, weird *and* kooky *and* freaky *and* freaked-out <all nonformal>, quaint, **eccentric,** gonzo <nonformal>; queer in the head, strange, off, mentally deficient
3 **homosexual,** homoerotic, gay, limp-wristed *and* faggoty <both nonformal>; lesbian, sapphic, tribadistic

**quell** VERBS **subdue, master,** overmaster, **crush,** reduce, beat down, **break,** break down, overwhelm; cool

**quench** VERBS **gratify,** satisfy, sate, satiate; slake, appease, allay, assuage; pour *or* dash *or* throw cold water on, throw *or* lay a wet blanket on, damp, dampen, demotivate, **cool,** chill, blunt; **extinguish,** stanch, damp down, drown, kill

**query** NOUNS **question,** inquiry, interrogation, interrogatory

**quest** NOUNS **search,** searching, **hunt,** hunting, stalk, stalking, still hunt, dragnet, posse, search party

**question** NOUNS 1 **query,** inquiry, **interrogation,** interrogatory; interrogative; open question, question *or* point at issue, **moot point** *or* case; vexed *or* knotty question, burning question; leading question; feeler, trial balloon
VERBS 2 **inquire, ask,** query; make inquiry, take up *or* institute *or* pursue *or* follow up *or* conduct *or* carry on an inquiry, ask after, inquire after, ask about, ask questions, put queries; ask a question, put a question to, pose *or* set *or* propose *or* propound a question
3 **doubt,** be doubtful, be dubious, be skeptical, doubt the truth of, beg leave to doubt, **have one's doubts,** have *or* harbor *or* entertain doubts *or* suspicions, half believe, have reservations, **take with a grain of salt,** be from Missouri <nonformal>, **distrust, mistrust,** misgive, cross one's fingers; **query,** challenge, contest, dispute, cast doubt on, greet with skepticism, keep one's eye on, treat with reserve, bring *or* call into question, raise a question, throw doubt upon

**questionable** ADJS **doubtful,** iffy <nonformal>; dubitable, doubtable, **dubious,** problematic, problematical, speculative, conjectural, suppositional

**questionnaire** NOUNS **canvass,** survey, inquiry, questionary

**queue** VERBS **line up,** get in *or* get on line, queue up <Brit>, make *or* form a line, get in formation, **fall in,** fall in *or* into line

**quibble** VERBS **cavil, bicker,** boggle, chop logic, **split hairs,** nitpick, pick nits; Jesuitize; **equivocate,** mystify, obscure, prevaricate, tergiversate, doubletalk, doublespeak, tap-dance <nonformal>, palter, fence, parry, shift, **shuffle,** dodge, shy, **evade,** sidestep, hedge, pussyfoot <nonformal>, evade the issue

**quick** ADJS 1 **swift, speedy,** expeditious, snappy <nonformal>, celeritous, alacritous, **prompt,** ready, smart, sharp, quick on the draw *or* trigger *or* uptake <nonformal>; **agile,** nimble, spry
ADVS 2 **swiftly,** rapidly, quickly, snappily <nonformal>, **speedily,** with speed, **fast,** apace, at a great rate, at a good clip <nonformal>, **by leaps and bounds,** lickety-split <nonformal>

**quid pro quo** NOUNS **trade-off,** equivalent, consideration, something of value, tit for tat, give-and-take

**quiet** NOUNS 1 **silence,** silentness, **soundlessness,** noiselessness, **stillness, quietness,** quietude, quiescence, **still,** peace
VERBS 2 **silence,** put to silence, hush, hush one up, hush-hush, **shush,** quieten, **still**
ADJS 3 **silent, still,** stilly, quiescent, **hushed, soundless,** noiseless; **calm,** tranquil, peaceful, peaceable, pacific, halcyon; **placid**

**quilt** NOUNS **comforter,** down comforter, duvet, feather bed, eiderdown; patchwork quilt

**quintet** NOUNS fivesome, quintuplets, quints <nonformal>, cinquain, quincunx, pentad

**quip** NOUNS 1 **witticism, pleasantry,** conceit, bright *or* happy thought, **mot,**

bon mot, smart saying, stroke of wit, one-liner *and* zinger <both nonformal>; flash of wit, **sally,** flight of wit
VERBS 2 **joke,** jest, wisecrack *and* crack wise <both nonformal>, utter a mot, jape, josh <nonformal>, make fun, **kid** *or* **kid around** <both nonformal>

**quirky** ADJS **fanciful, notional,** fantastic *or* fantastical, maggoty, **crotchety,** kinky, harebrained, cranky, flaky <nonformal>

**quit** VERBS 1 **vacate,** evacuate, abandon, desert, turn one's back on, walk away from, leave to one's fate, leave flat *or* high and dry; leave *or* desert a sinking ship; **withdraw,** retreat, **beat a retreat,** retire, remove; walk away, abscond, disappear, vanish; **bow out** <nonformal>, make one's exit
2 **resign,** demit, leave, **vacate,** withdraw from; **retire,** superannuate, be superannuated, get the golden handshake *or* parachute <nonformal>; **tender** *or* **hand in one's resignation**

**quiver** NOUNS 1 **flutter,** flitter, flit, **flicker, waver,** dance; shake
VERBS 2 **shake,** tremble, quaver, cringe, cower, totter, teeter, dodder; **tremble,** shiver, quake, flutter, twitter, shake like an aspen leaf

**quiz** NOUNS 1 **examination,** school examination, **exam** <nonformal>, **test**
VERBS 2 **inquire,** ask, question, query; make inquiry, take up *or* institute *or* pursue *or* follow up *or* conduct *or* carry on an inquiry, ask after, inquire after, ask about, ask questions, put queries

**quota** NOUNS **part,** portion, fraction; percentage; **share,** parcel, dole, piece *or* piece of the action <nonformal>; cut *and* slice *and* vigorish <all nonformal>

**quotation** NOUNS 1 **price,** quoted price, price tag *and* ticket *and* sticker <all nonformal>
2 **citation,** reference, cross reference

**quote** VERBS **repeat,** repeat word for word *or* verbatim, quote chapter and verse

# R

**rabble** NOUNS ragtag <nonformal>, **ragtag and bobtail; riffraff, trash,** raff, chaff, **rubbish,** dregs, **scum,** scum of the earth, dregs *or* scum **of society**

*the tagrag people*
SHAKESPEARE

**rabble-rouser** NOUNS **instigator,** inciter, exciter, urger; **provoker,** *provocateur* <Fr>, *agent provocateur* <Fr>; **agitator,** fomenter, inflamer; agitprop; rouser, **demagogue**

**rabid** ADJS **maniac** *or* **maniacal,** raving mad, stark-raving mad, **frenzied, frantic,** frenetic; **mad,** madding, wild, furious, violent; **amok, berserk,** running wild

**race** NOUNS 1 contest of speed *or* fleetness; derby; **horse race;** automobile race; boat race, yacht race, regatta
2 **people,** folk, family, house, clan, tribe, nation; **lineage,** line, blood, strain, stock, stem, species, stirps, **breed,** brood, kind; **ethnicity,** tribalism, clannishness
VERBS 3 **speed, go fast,** skim, **fly,** flit, fleet; go like lightning *or* a streak of lightning; go like greased lightning; **rush, tear,** dash, dart, shoot, hurtle, bolt, fling, **scamper, scurry,** scour, scud, scuttle, scramble, careen; **run**

**racetrack** NOUNS **track,** racecourse, turf, oval, course, strip

**racial** ADJS **ethnic,** tribal, national, family, clannish, totemic, **lineal; ethnic;** phyletic, phylogenetic, genetic

**racing** NOUNS 1 **track,** track sports; **horse racing**, the turf, the sport of kings; dog racing, automobile racing
ADJS 2 **flowing,** streaming, running, pouring, fluxive, fluxional, coursing, gushing, rushing, onrushing, surging, surgy, torrential, rough, whitewater

**racism** NOUNS **discrimination,** social discrimination, minority prejudice; xenophobia, know-nothingism; racialism, race hatred, **race prejudice,** race snobbery, racial discrimination

**racist** NOUNS 1 **bigot,** intolerant, illiberal; racialist, racial supremacist, white *or* black supremacist, pig <nonformal>
ADJS 2 **prejudiced,** prepossessed, biased, jaundiced; racialist, anti-Negro, antiblack, antiwhite; anti-Semitic

**rack** NOUNS **agony,** anguish, torment, torture, exquisite torment *or* torture, the rack, the iron maiden, excruciation, crucifixion, martyrdom, martyrization, excruciating *or* agonizing *or* atrocious pain; **strain,** straining, **stress,** stressfulness, **stress and strain,** taxing, tension, stretch

**racket** NOUNS 1 **noise,** loud noise, blast, **din,** clamor; outcry, **uproar,** hue and cry, noise and shouting
2 **cheating,** cheating scheme, cheating method, angle, con *and* grift *and* move *and* scam *and* sting <all nonformal>
3 **vocation,** occupation, business, work, line, line of work, line of business *or* endeavor, number <nonformal>, walk, **trade,** game <nonformal>

**racketeer** NOUNS gangster; **black marketeer,** gray marketeer; bootlegger, moonshiner <nonformal>; pusher *and* dealer <both nonformal>, narcotics *or* dope *or* drug pusher <nonformal>

**racy** ADJS **risqué,** risky, salty, spicy, **off-color,** suggestive, scabrous; **piquant,** lively, juicy, succulent, rich; readable

**radar** NOUNS radio detection and ranging; **radar set,** radiolocator <Brit>; radarscope; radar antenna; radar reflector

**radial** ADJS **radiating,** radiate, radiated; rayed, spoked; radiative

**radiant** ADJS **happy,** glad, joyful, joyous, flushed with joy, beaming, glowing, **bright, sunny,** sparkling

**radiate** VERBS 1 radiate out, ray, ray out, beam out, diffuse, emanate, spread, disperse, scatter
2 **shine,** shine forth, **glow,** beam, gleam, glint, luster, glance; **transmit,** send

**radiation** NOUNS radiant energy; ionizing radiation; **radioactivity,** activity, radioactive radiation *or* emanation, atomic *or* nuclear radiation; natural radioactivity, artificial radioactivity; **ray,** cosmic ray bombardment, electron shower; electron emission

**radical** NOUNS 1 **extremist,** ultra, ultraist; **revolutionary,** revolutionist; extreme left-winger, left-wing extremist, **red** <nonformal>; **anarchist,** nihilist; pink *and* parlor pink *and* pinko <all nonformal>
ADJS 2 **extreme, extremist,** extremistic, ultraist, ultraistic

3 revolutionary, revolutionist; ultraconservative; extreme left-wing, **red** <nonformal>; anarchistic, nihilistic, pink <nonformal>

**radicle** NOUNS **root,** radix; radicel, rootlet; **taproot,** tap; **rhizome,** rootstock

**radio** NOUNS 1 **radio receiver;** radio telescope; **radio set, receiver,** receiving set, **wireless** *and* wireless set <both Brit>, set
VERBS 2 **broadcast,** radiobroadcast, radiocast, simulcast, **wireless** <Brit>, radiate, **transmit,** send; narrowcast; shortwave
ADJS 3 **wireless** <Brit>; radiosonic; neutrodyne; heterodyne; superheterodyne; shortwave; radio-frequency, audio-frequency

**radioactive** ADJS activated, radioactivated, irradiated, charged, **hot; contaminated,** infected, poisoned; radioluminescent, autoluminescent

**radioactive element** NOUNS **radioelement; radioisotope; tracer, tracer element, tracer atom**

**radio broadcasting** NOUNS **broadcasting,** the air waves, radiocasting; commercial radio, public radio; AM broadcasting, FM broadcasting, shortwave broadcasting; **transmission,** radio transmission

**radiology** NOUNS radiography, radioscopy, fluoroscopy, magnetic resonance imaging, MRI, mammography

**radius** NOUNS **extent,** extension, expansion, expanse, square footage *or* yardage etc, **scope,** reach, range, ballpark <nonformal>, spread, coverage, area, cirumference, ambit, girth, diameter, boundary, border, periphery

**raffle** NOUNS **lottery,** drawing, sweepstakes *or* sweepstake *or* sweep

**raft** NOUNS **float;** balsa, balsa raft, Kon Tiki; life raft, Carling float

**rag** NOUNS 1 **material,** fabric, cloth, stuff; rags; **garment,** robe, frock, gown, togs *and* duds <both nonformal>
2 **newspaper,** paper, sheet <nonformal>
VERBS 3 **berate,** rate, tongue-lash, rail at, thunder *or* fulminate against, rave against, yell at, bark *or* yelp at

**ragamuffin** NOUNS **waif,** homeless waif, tatterdemalion; **gamin,** gamine, urchin, street urchin, dead-end kid <nonformal>, guttersnipe <nonformal>

**rage** NOUNS 1 **passion; fury,** furor; livid *or* towering rage *or* passion, blind *or* burning rage, raging *or* tearing passion, furious rage
2 **fad, craze;** infatuation, enthusiasm, wrinkle <nonformal>; novelty
VERBS 3 **storm,** rant, have a fit, rave, roar; **rampage,** ramp, **tear,** tear around; go *or* carry on <nonformal>

**ragged** ADJS **shabby,** raggedy, raggedy-ass <nonformal>, **tattered,** torn; patchy; **frayed,** in rags, in tatters, in shreds

**raging** ADJS **frenzied,** raving, roaring, bellowing, ramping, storming, howling, ranting, fulminating, frothing *or* foaming at the mouth; **wild,** hog-wild <nonformal>; **enraged; stormy,** tempestuous

**rags** NOUNS **tatters,** secondhand clothes, old clothes; worn clothes, **hand-me-downs** *and* reach-me-downs <both nonformal>; **refuse,** odds and ends, scraps

**ragtime** ADJS **syncopated;** ragtimey <nonformal>

**raid** NOUNS 1 **foray,** razzia; **invasion, incursion,** inroad, irruption; **air raid,** air strike, air attack, saturation raid; escalade, scaling, boarding
VERBS 2 foray, make a raid; **invade,** inroad, make an inroad, make an irruption into; escalade, scale, scale the walls, board; storm, take by storm, overwhelm, inundate; **plunder,** pillage, loot, sack, ransack, rifle, freeboot, spoil, spoliate, despoil, depredate, prey on *or* upon, reive <Scots>, ravage, ravish, raven, sweep, gut; maraud, forage

**raider** NOUNS **plunderer,** pillager, looter, marauder, rifler, sacker, spoiler, despoiler, freebooter, rapparee, reiver <Scots>, forager, ravisher, ravager

**railroad** NOUNS **railway,** rail, line, track, trackage, railway *or* railroad *or* rail line

**railroad through** VERBS **legislate,** make *or* enact laws, **put through,** jam *or* steamroller through <nonformal>, lobby through; bring pressure to bear upon; **ram,** ram through, bull, bulldoze, muscle, steamroller

**rain** NOUNS 1 **rainfall,** fall, **precipitation,** moisture, wet, rainwater; **shower, sprinkle,** flurry, patter, pitter-patter, splatter; streams of rain, sheet of rain, splash *or* spurt of rain; **drizzle,** mizzle; **mist,** misty rain, Scotch mist
VERBS 2 **precipitate,** rain down, fall; **shower,** shower down; **sprinkle,** spit *and* spritz <both nonformal>, spatter, patter, pitter-patter; **drizzle,** mizzle; **pour,** stream, stream down, pour with

rain, **pelt,** pelt down, drum, tattoo, come down in torrents *or* sheets *or* buckets *or* curtains, **rain cats and dogs** <nonformal>

**rainbow** NOUNS **halo,** nimbus, aura, **aureole,** circle, ring, glory; solar halo, lunar halo, ring around the sun *or* moon; white rainbow *or* fogbow

**rainy** ADJS **showery;** pluvious *or* pluviose *or* pluvial; **drizzly,** drizzling, mizzly, drippy; **misty,** misty-moisty; torrential, pouring, streaming, pelting, drumming, driving, blinding, cat-and-doggish <nonformal>

**raise** NOUNS 1 **increase, gain,** augmentation; **advance,** appreciation, rise, fattening *and* boost *and* hike <all nonformal>, **up** *and* upping <both nonformal>, buildup
VERBS 2 **elevate, rear,** escalate, up, boost *and* hike <both nonformal>; **erect,** heighten, lift, levitate, boost <nonformal>, **hoist,** heist <nonformal>, heft, heave
3 **breed,** rear, grow, hatch, feed, nurture, fatten; keep, run

**raised** ADJS **lifted,** elevated; upraised, **uplifted,** upcast; **reared,** upreared; rearing, rampant; erect, upright; high

**rake** NOUNS 1 **libertine,** swinger <nonformal>, **profligate,** rakehell, rip <nonformal>, **roué,** wanton, womanizer, cocksman <nonformal>, walking phallus, debauchee, rounder <old>, **wolf** <nonformal>, gay dog, gay deceiver, philanderer, lady-killer
VERBS 2 **comb,** curry, card, hackle *or* hatchel, heckle <nonformal>; harrow, weed

**rally** NOUNS 1 **recovery,** comeback <nonformal>, return; **recuperation,** convalescence
VERBS 2 come about *or* round, **take a favorable turn,** get over <nonformal>, take a turn for the better, gain strength; come a long way <nonformal>; **recuperate,** recover
3 **scoff,** jeer, gibe, **mock,** revile, rail at, chaff, **twit, taunt,** jape, flout, scout, have a fling at
4 **come together,** assemble, congregate, collect, come from far and wide, come *or* arrive in a body; league, ally; rally around

**ram** VERBS 1 **sail into,** run down, run in *or* into; collide
2 ram down, tamp, pile drive, jam, crowd, cram

**ramble** NOUNS 1 **walk,** amble, **hike,** tramp, traipse <nonformal>; **stroll,** saunter; **promenade;** jaunt, airing
VERBS 2 **wander,** wander off, rove, straggle, divagate, excurse, pererrate; meander, wind, twist, snake, twist and turn; **digress,** wander, get off the subject, wander from the subject, get sidetracked, excurse, maunder, stray, go astray

**ramification** NOUNS **complexity,** complication, involvement, complexness, involution, convolution, tortuousness, Byzantinism, *chinoiserie* <Fr>, tanglement, **entanglement,** perplexity, **intricacy,** intricateness, crabbedness, technicality, subtlety

**ramp** NOUNS **incline,** inclination, **slope, grade,** gradient, pitch, launching ramp, bank, talus, gentle *or* easy slope, glacis

**rampage** NOUNS 1 **commotion,** hubbub, Babel, tumult, turmoil, riot, **disturbance,** rumpus <nonformal>, ruckus *and* ruction <both nonformal>, **fracas, hassle**
VERBS 2 **rage,** storm, rant, rave, roar; ramp, **tear,** tear around; go *or* carry on <nonformal>; **destroy, wreck,** wreak havoc, ruin; sow chaos *or* disorder

**rampant** ADJS **prevalent,** prevailing, common, popular, **current,** running; **rife,** pandemic, epidemic, besetting; lousy with <nonformal>, teeming; **superabundant**; a dime a dozen

**rampart** NOUNS **fortification,** work, defense work, **bulwark,** fence, barrier

**ramshackle** ADJS **dilapidated,** decrepit, shacky, tottery, **tumbledown,** broken-down, run-down, in ruins, ruinous, ruined, derelict, gone to wrack and ruin, the worse for wear

**ranch** NOUNS **farmstead;** *rancho, hacienda* <both Sp>, rancheria; **cattle ranch;** dude ranch

**rancher** NOUNS **stockman,** stock raiser, stockkeeper <Austral>; cattleman, cow keeper, cowman, **rancher,** ranchman, ranchero

**rancid** ADJS **tainted,** off, blown; **sour,** soured, turned; **rank,** strong <nonformal>, **high,** gamy

**rancor** NOUNS **virulence,** venomousness, **venom,** vitriol, gall, **acrimony,** acerbity, asperity; **bitterness,** sourness

**random** ADJS **irregular,** haphazard, desultory, **erratic,** sporadic, spasmodic, fitful, promiscuous, indiscriminate, casual, frivolous, capricious, hit-or-miss, **aimless,** straggling, straggly; dysteleological, stochastic

**range** NOUNS 1 **scope,** compass, reach, stretch, expanse, radius, sweep, carry, fetch; **gamut,** scale, register, diapason; **spectrum**
2 **habitat,** home, stamping grounds, locality, native environment; grazing, grazing land
3 **mountain range,** massif; **mountain system, chain,** mountain chain, cordillera, sierra
VERBS 4 **extend,** reach, stretch, sweep, spread, run, cover, carry, lie; **reach** *or* stretch *or* thrust out; span, straddle, take in, encompass
5 **traverse,** cross, travel over *or* through, pass through, **go** *or* **pass over, cover,** measure, transit, track, range over *or* through, course

**rank** NOUNS 1 **standing,** level, footing, **status,** station; **position,** place, sphere, orbit, echelon; **order,** estate, precedence, condition; rate, rating
VERBS 2 **size,** adjust, grade, group, range, graduate, sort, match; gauge, **measure**, proportion; hierarchize
ADJS 3 **malodorous,** fetid, olid, **odorous,** stinking, reeking, reeky, nidorous, smelling, bad-smelling, **evil-smelling,** ill-smelling, strong, high, gamy
4 **luxuriant,** flourishing, **lush,** riotous, exuberant; overgrown, overrun; **weedy,** unweeded, weed-choked, weed-ridden

**rankle** VERBS **fester,** suppurate, matter, run, weep; **ruffle,** roil, rile <nonformal>, ruffle one's feathers

**ransack** VERBS **loot,** sack, rifle, despoil, depredate, prey on *or* upon, **raid,** reive <Scots>, ravage, ravish, raven, sweep, gut

**ransom** NOUNS 1 **redemption,** salvage, trover; **retrieval,** recovery
VERBS 2 **recover,** regain, retrieve, **get back,** come by one's own; **redeem,** reclaim

**rant** VERBS **rage,** storm, rave, roar, have a fit

**rap** NOUNS 1 **sentence,** judgment, punishment
2 **tap,** pat, dab, chuck, touch, tip
3 **trifle,** a hoot *and* a damn *and* a darn *and* a shit <all nonformal>, a tinker's damn
VERBS 4 **criticize;** pan *and* knock *and* slam *and* hit *and* take a rap *or* swipe at <all nonformal>, snipe at, strike out at, tie into *and* tee off on *and* rip into *and* open up on *and* plow into <all nonformal>
5 talk, **talk over,** hash over <nonformal>, talk of *or* about, comment upon, reason about, discourse about; **kick** *or* **knock around** <nonformal>
6 **tap,** pat, dab, chuck, touch, tip

**rape** NOUNS 1 **sexual possession,** taking; sexual assault, ravishment, violation, indecent assault, date rape *or* acquaintance rape, serial rape *or* gang bang <nonformal>; statutory rape
2 **plundering,** rapine, spoliation, depredation, **raiding,** reiving <Scots>, ravage, ravaging, ravagement, ravishment
VERBS 3 **possess sexually,** take; commit rape, commit date *or* acquaintance rape, ravish, violate, assault sexually, lay violent hands on, have one's will of

**rapid** ADJS **fast,** swift, speedy; staccato

**rapport** NOUNS **good terms,** good understanding, good footing, friendly relations; **harmony,** sympathy, fellow feeling

**rapt** ADJS **gripped,** held, fascinated, enthralled, spellbound, charmed, enchanted, mesmerized, **hypnotized,** fixed, caught, riveted, **arrested,** switched on <nonformal>

**rapture** NOUNS **happiness,** ravishment, bewitchment, **enchantment,** unalloyed happiness; elation, exaltation; **ecstasy,** ecstasies, transport; **bliss,** blissfulness

**rare** ADJS 1 **underdone,** undercooked, not done, *saignant* <Fr>
2 extraordinary, exceptional, unique, singular, **remarkable,** striking, sensational; *sui generis* <L, of its own kind>; **out of the ordinary,** out of this world, out-of-the-way, out of the common, out of the pale, **off the beaten track,** offbeat, breakaway
3 rarefied; **subtle; thin,** thinned, dilute, attenuated, attenuate

**rascal** NOUNS precious rascal, rogue, knave, **scoundrel,** villain, blackguard, **scamp, scalawag** <nonformal>, spalpeen <Ir>, rapscallion, **devil**

**rash** NOUNS 1 **skin eruption,** eruption, efflorescence, breaking out
ADJS 2 **brash,** incautious, overbold, **imprudent,** indiscreet, injudicious, improvident; **unwary,** unchary; overcareless; hubristic; temerarious

**rasp** VERBS **grate,** scratch, scrape, grind; provoke, **gall,** chafe, fret, grate, irritate

**rat** NOUNS 1 **informer, squealer** *and* preacher *and* **stool pigeon** *and* stoolie *and* **fink** <all nonformal>
VERBS 2 **betray,** inform, **inform on,** talk *and* peach <both nonformal>; stool *and* sing *and* squeal <all nonformal>, turn state's evidence

**rate** NOUNS 1 **velocity,** gait, pace, tread, step, stride, clip *and* lick <both nonformal>
2 **interest,** premium, price; interest rate, rate of interest, prime interest rate *or* **prime rate,** bank rate, lending rate, borrowing rate, the price of money; discount rate
VERBS 3 **deserve,** merit, earn, be in line for <nonformal>, **be worthy of,** be deserving, richly deserve
4 **rank,** count, be regarded, be thought of, be in one's estimation

**rather** ADVS 1 to a degree, to some extent, in a way, in a measure, in some measure; somewhat, kind of <nonformal>, sort of <nonformal>, pretty, quite, fairly; a little, a bit; slightly, scarcely, to a small degree; very, extremely, to a great degree
2 **instead,** *faute de mieux* <Fr>; in its stead *or* place; in one's stead, in one's behalf, in one's place, in one's shoes; by proxy; as an alternative

**ratify** VERBS **endorse,** sign off on, second, support, **certify,** confirm, validate, authenticate, accept, give the nod *or* the green light *or* the go-ahead *or* the OK <all nonformal>, give a nod of assent, give one's imprimatur, permit, give permission, **approve**

**rating** NOUNS 1 **berating,** tongue-lashing; **revilement, vilification,** blackening, execration, abuse, vituperation, invective, contumely, hard *or* cutting *or* bitter words
2 **estimate,** estimation; **evaluation,** evaluating, value judgment, evaluative criticism, analyzing, weighing, weighing up, gauging, ranking, rank-ordering

**ration** NOUNS 1 **portion,** clutch, share, issue, allotment, lot, deal; **allowance,** budget
VERBS 2 **budget;** put on an allowance

**rational** ADJS 1 **sane,** reasonable, sensible, **lucid,** normal, wholesome, clearheaded, clearminded, balanced, **sound,** mentally sound, of sound mind, *compos mentis* <L>, sound-minded, right in the head, **in one's right mind,** in possession of one's faculties *or* senses, together *and* all there <both nonformal>
2 **logical,** reasonable, cogent, sensible, sane, sound, well-thought-out, legitimate, just, justifiable, admissible

**rationale** NOUNS **reason,** reason why, reason for *or* behind, underlying reason, rational ground, **explanation,** the why, the wherefore, **the why and wherefore**

**rationalize** VERBS 1 **organize,** methodize, systematize, get *or* put one's house in order; **regularize,** routinize, normalize, standardize
2 logicalize, logicize; provide a rationale; intellectualize; explain away

**rations** NOUNS board, meals, commons <chiefly Brit>, mess, allowance, allotment, food allotment, tucker <Australia>; emergency rations; garrison *or* field rations

**rat race** NOUNS **futility,** vanity, emptiness, hollowness; **drudgery,** sweat, slavery, spadework; treadmill

**rattle** NOUNS 1 rattling, rattletybang; **clatter,** clitter, **clitterclatter,** chatter, clack, clacket <nonformal>; racket
VERBS 2 **clatter,** clitter, **chatter,** clack; rattle around, clatter about; **blather,** blabber, babble, gabble, gibble-gabble, **jabber,** gibber, prate, **prattle**
3 **agitate,** perturb, flutter, flurry, disconcert, **fluster**

**raucous** ADJS **harsh,** harsh-sounding; coarse, rude, rough, gruff, ragged; **hoarse, husky,** roupy <Scots>, cracked, dry; **guttural,** thick, throaty, croaky, croaking

**raunchy** ADJS **obscene,** lewd, adult, bawdy, ithyphallic, **ribald,** pornographic, salacious, lurid, **dirty,** smutty, blue, smoking-room, impure, unchaste, unclean, **foul,** filthy, nasty, vile, fulsome, offensive, unprintable, unrepeatable, not fit for mixed company

**ravage** NOUNS 1 **plundering,** rapine, spoliation, depredation, **raiding,** ravaging, ravagement, rape, ravishment
VERBS 2 **plunder,** pillage, loot, sack, ransack, rifle, freeboot, spoil, spoliate, despoil, depredate, prey on *or* upon, **raid,** reive <Scots>, raven, sweep, gut; **debauch,** ravish, ruin; **violate,** abuse; **rape,** force

**rave** VERBS 1 **be enthusiastic,** enthuse *and* be big for <both nonformal>; **rhapsodize,** carry on over *and* rave on <both nonformal>, make much of, **make a fuss over,** make an ado *or* much ado about, make a to-do over *and* take on

over <both nonformal>, rave about *and* whoop it up about <both nonformal>; go nuts *or* gaga *or* ape over <nonformal>
2 **rage,** storm, rant, roar; have a fit

**ravenous** ADJS **rapacious,** ravening, vulturous, vulturine, sharkish, **wolfish,** lupine, predacious, **predatory,** raptorial; **gluttonous,** greedy, voracious, edacious, insatiable, polyphagic, bulimic, hyperphagic, Apician

**ravine** NOUNS gorge, canyon, box canyon, *arroyo* <Sp>, barranca, bolson, coulee, gully, gulch, rift, rift valley, kloof, donga, graben, draw, wadi

**ravish** VERBS 1 **delight,** enravish, imparadise; transport, carry away
2 **possess sexually,** take; **rape,** commit rape, commit date *or* acquaintance rape, violate, assault sexually, lay violent hands on, have one's will of; deflower, deflorate, devirginate
3 **plunder,** pillage, loot, sack, ransack, rifle, ravage, raven, sweep, gut

**raw** ADJS 1 **sore;** smarting, tingling, **burning; irritated,** inflamed, tender, sensitive, fiery, angry, red; algetic; chafed, galled
2 **inexperienced,** unseasoned, unfledged, new-fledged, **callow,** unripe, ripening, unmellowed, **green,** vernal, dewy, juicy, sappy, budding, tender, virginal, intact, innocent, naive, ingenuous, **undeveloped**
3 **windblown,** blown; **windswept,** bleak, exposed
4 **crude; uncooked,** unbaked, unboiled; underdone, undercooked, rare, red
5 **coarse,** gross, rude, crude, crass, rough, **earthy;** ribald; raunchy <nonformal>, **obscene**

**raw deal** NOUNS **injustice,** wrong, injury, grievance, disservice; rotten deal *and* bad rap <both nonformal>; **bad luck,** ill luck, hard luck, **tough** *or* **rotten luck** <nonformal>

**ray** NOUNS **radiation,** sunray, radius, spoke; radiance, diffusion, scattering, dispersion, emanation; halo, aureole, glory, corona

**raze** VERBS rase, **fell, level,** flatten, smash, prostrate, raze to the ground *or* dust; steamroller, bulldoze; **pull down,** tear down, take down

**razorback** NOUNS **swine;** wild boar, tusker; warthog, babirusa

**razzledazzle** NOUNS **showiness, flashiness,** flamboyance, panache, dash, jauntiness; **gaudiness,** gaudery, glitz *and* gimmickry *and* razzmatazz <all nonformal>, **tawdriness,** meretriciousness

**reach** NOUNS 1 **earshot,** earreach, **hearing,** range, auditory range, carrying distance, **sound of one's voice**
2 **range,** scope, compass, stretch, expanse radius, sweep, carry, fetch
3 **knowledge,** knowing, knowingness, ken; **command**
VERBS 4 **move, touch,** affect, **soften,** unsteel, melt, melt the heart, appeal to one's better feelings; sadden, grieve
5 **extend, stretch,** sweep, spread, run, **go** *or* **go out,** cover, carry, **range,** lie; **reach** *or* stretch *or* thrust out; span, straddle, take in, hold, encompass, surround, environ
6 **arrive at,** come at, get at, arrive upon, **come upon,** hit upon, strike upon, fall upon, light upon, pitch upon, stumble on *or* upon
7 **communicate with,** get in touch *or* contact with, **make contact with,** raise, get to, get through to, get hold of, make *or* establish connection

**reach out** VERBS **stretch out,** extend, extend out, go *or* go out, range out, carry out; outstretch, outlie, outdistance, outrange

**react** VERBS **respond,** reply, answer, riposte, snap back, come back at <nonformal>; rise to the fly, take the bait; go off half-cocked *or* at half cock

**reaction** NOUNS **impact,** force, **repercussion,** backwash, backlash, reflex, recoil, response; **answer,** riposte, uptake <nonformal>, **retort,** rejoinder, return, **comeback** *and* **take** <both nonformal>

**reactionary** NOUNS 1 ultraconservative, arch-conservative, extreme right-winger, reactionist, diehard
ADJS 2 **conservative, right-wing,** right of center, ultraconservative, reactionist

**reactive** ADJS reacting, merely reactive; **responsive,** respondent, responding, antiphonal; **quick on the draw** *or* trigger *or* uptake

**read** VERBS peruse, go over, read up *or* read up on, have one's nose in a book <nonformal>; bury oneself in, wade through, plunge into; **dig** *and* **grind** *and* **bone** *and* bone up on <all nonformal>

**ready** VERBS 1 **prepare,** make *or* get ready, prep <nonformal>, **fix** <nonformal>; **make preparations** *or* **arrange-**

**ments,** put in *or* into shape; dress; treat, pretreat, process

ADJS 2 **eager,** agog, all agog; **avid,** keen, forward, prompt, quick, ready and willing, alacritous, bursting to, dying to, raring to

3 **handy,** convenient; available, accessible, **at hand,** to hand, **on hand,** on tap, on deck <nonformal>, on call, at one's call *or* beck and call, at one's elbow, at one's fingertips, just around the corner, at one's disposal

**ready-made** ADJS ready-formed, ready-mixed, ready-furnished, ready-dressed, ready-cooked; ready-to-wear, off-the-rack; cut-and-dried *or* cut-and-dry

**real** ADJS 1 **actual,** factual, veritable, for real <nonformal>, de facto, simple, sober, **hard;** established, inescapable, indisputable, undeniable; demonstrable, provable

2 **genuine,** authentic, veridic, veridical, **natural,** realistic, naturalistic, true to reality, **true to nature,** true to life, verisimilar, veristic

**realistic** ADJS **genuine,** authentic, veridic, veridical, **real,** natural, naturalistic, true to reality, **true to nature,** lifelike, true to life, verisimilar, veristic

**reality** NOUNS **actuality,** factuality, empirical *or* demonstrable *or* objective existence, the here and now; historicity; **authenticity;** sober *or* grim reality, hardball *and* the nitty-gritty <both nonformal>

**realize** VERBS 1 **externalize,** exteriorize, bring into the open, bring out, show, display, exhibit; **objectify,** actualize, project, realize

2 clear, **profit, make** *or* **draw** *or* **realize** *or* **reap profit,** come out ahead, make money; gain by, **capitalize on,** commercialize, make capital out of, **cash in on** *and* make a good thing of <both nonformal>, turn to profit *or* account, **realize on,** make money by, obtain a return, turn a penny *or* an honest penny

3 **understand,** comprehend, apprehend, have, **know, conceive,** appreciate, have no problem with, ken <Scots>, savvy <nonformal>, sense, make sense out of, make something of

**realm** NOUNS **sphere,** demesne, **domain,** dominion, jurisdiction, bailiwick; **kingdom, empire,** dominion, domain

**ream** VERBS **bore,** drill, auger; ream out, countersink, gouge, gouge out; **call down** *or* **dress down** <both nonformal>; give the deuce *or* devil, give hell

**reap** VERBS **harvest,** crop, glean, gather, gather in, bring in, get in the harvest, reap and carry; **acquire,** gain, earn, make

**reappear** VERBS **recur,** reoccur, return, repeat, **come again,** come up again, be here again, resurface, reenter, come round again, come in its turn

**rear** NOUNS 1 **rear end,** hind end, hind part, hinder part, afterpart, rearward, **posterior, behind,** breech, stern, tail, tail end; **afterpiece,** tailpiece, heelpiece, heel; **back,** back side, reverse <of a coin or medal>, tail <of a coin>; rear guard, rear area

VERBS 2 **pitch,** toss, tumble, toss and tumble, pitch and toss, **plunge,** hobbyhorse, pound, **rock,** roll, reel, swing, sway, lurch, yaw

3 **rise,** ramp, uprear, rear up, rise on the hind legs; upheave; sit up, sit bolt upright; jump up, spring to one's feet

4 **foster, nurture,** nourish, mother, care for, lavish care on, feed, parent, sustain, cultivate, cherish; **raise, breed,** grow, hatch, feed, nurture, fatten

ADJS 5 rearward, **back,** backward, retrograde, **posterior,** postern, tail; after *or* aft; **hind,** hinder; hindmost, hindermost, hindhand, posteriormost, **aftermost,** aftmost, rearmost

**rearrange** VERBS **reorganize,** reconstitute, **reorder,** restructure, reshuffle, rejigger <nonformal>, tinker *or* tinker with, tune, tune up, fine-tune; **shake up,** shake out; redispose, redistribute, reallocate, realign

**reason** NOUNS 1 reason why, rationale, reason for *or* behind, underlying reason, rational ground, **explanation,** the why, the wherefore, **the why and wherefore,** stated cause, pretext, pretense, excuse

2 **sanity, saneness,** sanemindedness, soundness, **soundness of mind,** soundmindedness, sound mind, healthy mind, right mind <nonformal>, senses, **rationality,** reasonableness, lucidity, balance, wholesomeness; **sense,** common sense, sound sense, sweet reason, **logic**

VERBS 3 **discuss,** debate, deliberate, deliberate upon, exchange views *or* opinions, talk, **talk over,** hash over <nonformal>, talk of *or* about, reason about, discourse about, **consider, treat,** dissertate on, handle, deal with, **exam-**

**ine,** investigate, talk out, **analyze,** sift, **study,** review, pass under review, controvert, ventilate; **kick** *or* **knock around** <nonformal>

**reasonable** ADJS 1 **warrantable,** allowable, admissible, colorable, legitimate; **sensible,** logical, rational, cogent, sound, well-thought-out
2 **cheap, inexpensive,** unexpensive, low, low-priced, frugal, sensible, manageable, modest, moderate, affordable, to fit the pocketbook, budget, easy, economy, economic, economical

**reassure** VERBS **encourage,** hearten, embolden, nerve, pat *or* clap on the back, **assure,** bolster, support, cheer on, root for

**rebate** NOUNS **discount,** cut, deduction, slash, abatement, reduction, price reduction, price-cutting, price-cut, rollback <nonformal>; rebatement

**rebel** NOUNS 1 revolter; **insurgent,** insurrectionary, insurrecto, **insurrectionist;** malcontent, *frondeur* <Fr>; **mutineer,** rioter, brawler; maverick <nonformal>, troublemaker, refusenik <nonformal>; nonconformist
VERBS 2 **revolt,** kick over the traces, reluct, reluctate; **rise up,** rise, arise, rise up in arms, mount the barricades; mount *or* make a coup d'état; **mutiny**

**rebellion** NOUNS **revolt,** revolution, mutiny, insurrection, insurgence *or* insurgency, *émeute* <Fr>, **uprising,** rising, outbreak, general uprising, *levée en masse* <Fr>, **riot,** civil disorder; peasant revolt, *jacquerie* <Fr>; putsch, coup d'état; intifada

**reborn** ADJS **renascent,** redivivus, redux, resurrected, renewed, revived, resurgent, recrudescent, reappearing, phoenix-like; **redeemed, saved,** converted, regenerated, regenerate, justified, born-again

**rebound** NOUNS 1 **recoil,** resilience, repercussion, *contrecoup* <Fr>; backlash, backlashing, kickback, **kick,** a kick like a mule <nonformal>, ricochet, carom
VERBS 2 **recoil,** resile; **spring** *or* **fly back,** bounce *or* bound back, snap back; backlash, lash back; ricochet, carom

**rebuff** NOUNS 1 **repulse; dismissal,** cold shoulder, snub, spurning, brush-off, cut; kiss-off <nonformal>; turn-off <nonformal>; refusal
VERBS 2 **snub,** cut *or* cut dead <nonformal>, drop, repulse; cold-shoulder *or* turn a cold shoulder upon *or* **give the cold shoulder** <nonformal>, give *or* turn the shoulder <nonformal>, turn one's back upon

**rebuke** NOUNS 1 **reproof,** reproval, reprobation, a flea in one's ear; **reprimand,** reproach, reprehension, **scolding,** chiding, rating, **upbraiding,** objurgation
VERBS 2 **reprove,** reprimand, reprehend, put a flea in one's ear, **scold,** chide, rate, **admonish,** upbraid, objurgate, have words with, take a hard line with; **lecture,** read a lesson *or* lecture to

**rebuttal** NOUNS **counterstatement,** counterreply, counterclaim, counterblast, counteraccusation, countercharge, *tu quoque* <L, you too>, contraremonstrance; **rejoinder**

**recalcitrant** ADJS **defiant,** refractory, contumacious, obstreperous, unruly, restive, impatient of control *or* discipline; fractious, ornery *and* feisty <both nonformal>

**recall** NOUNS 1 **revocation,** retraction, recantation
2 **remembering,** remembrance, recollection, recollecting, exercise of memory, recalling
VERBS 3 **remember, recollect,** flash on *and* mind <both nonformal>; remember clearly, remember as if it were yesterday; have total recall, remember everything
4 **remind,** put in mind, refresh the memory of; **remind one of,** suggest, put one in mind of; take one back, carry back, carry back in recollection

**recant** VERBS **reject,** repudiate, abjure, forswear, **renounce**, disown, disclaim, retract; unwish

**recap** NOUNS 1 **summary,** résumé, recapitulation, rundown, run-through; **summation**
VERBS 2 **sum up,** summarize, recapitulate, rehash <nonformal>, **recount,** rehearse, recite, relate; detail, itemize, inventory

**recede** VERBS retrocede; **retreat,** retire, withdraw; **diminish,** decline, sink, shrink, dwindle, **fade, ebb,** wane

**receipt** NOUNS **reception,** taking in, receiving; **recipe; receiving,** receival, getting, taking; acquisition; **acknowledgment,** voucher

**receipts** NOUNS **income,** revenue, profits, earnings, returns, proceeds, **take,** takings, intake, take *or* take-in <nonformal>; gains; gate receipts, gate, box office; net receipts, net; gross receipts, gross

**receive** VERBS 1 **take in;** admit, let in, intromit, give entrance *or* admittance to; **welcome,** bid welcome, give a royal welcome, roll out the red carpet
2 **get,** gain, secure, have, come by, be in receipt of, be on the receiving end; **obtain,** acquire
3 **tune in,** pick up, spot, home on; pinpoint; identify, trigger; lock on

**receiver** NOUNS 1 **recipient,** accepter, getter, taker, acquirer, obtainer, procurer; payee, endorsee; addressee, consignee; holder, trustee; **hearer,** viewer, beholder, audience, auditor, listener, looker, spectator; the receiving end
2 **fence,** receiver of stolen goods, swagman *and* swagsman <both nonformal>, bagman, bagwoman
3 **radio,** radio receiver; **radio set,** receiving set, **wireless** *and* wireless set <both Brit>, set

**recent** ADJS 1 **late,** newly come, of yesterday; latter, later
2 **previous,** once, one time, former

**receptacle** NOUNS **container;** receiver, holder, vessel, utensil; basin, pot, pan, cup, glass, ladle, bottle; cask; box, case

**reception** NOUNS 1 **receiving,** receipt, getting, taking; acquisition; **assumption,** acceptance; **welcome,** welcoming
2 **social gathering, social,** at home, salon, levee, soiree

**receptionist** NOUNS **host,** mine host, hostess, greeter

**receptive** ADJS 1 recipient; welcoming, open, hospitable, cordial, inviting, invitatory; introceptive; **admissive,** admissory; receivable, receptible, admissible
2 **open-minded,** open, rational, admissive; **persuadable,** persuasible; **unopinionated,** unopinioned, unwedded to an opinion

**recess** NOUNS 1 **respite,** rest, pause, halt, stay, lull, **break,** surcease, suspension, interlude, **intermission,** spell <Australia>, letup <nonformal>, **time out** <nonformal>, time to catch one's breath
2 **nook,** corner, cranny, niche, cove, bay, oriel, alcove; cubicle, roomlet, carrel, hole-in-the-wall <nonformal>; **retreat,** hideaway; **sanctum,** inner sanctum, sanctum sanctorum
VERBS 3 **pause, rest,** let up *and* take it easy <both nonformal>, **relax,** rest on one's oars; take *or* call a recess; **take a break,** break, take ten

**recession** NOUNS 1 recedence, receding, retrocedence; **retreat,** retirement, withdrawing, withdrawal; retraction, retractation, retractility
2 **depression,** slump, economic stagnation, **bust** <nonformal>

**recharge** VERBS **reactivate,** revive, revivify, **renew,** reanimate, reinspire, **regenerate,** rejuvenate, revitalize, put *or* breathe new life into, restimulate

**recidivism** NOUNS **reversion,** reverting, retroversion, retrogradation, **retrogression,** retrocession, regress, **relapse, regression, backsliding,** lapse, slipping back, backing, recidivation

**recipient** NOUNS **receiver,** accepter, getter, taker, acquirer, obtainer, procurer; payee, endorsee; addressee, consignee

**reciprocal** ADJS **communal,** mutual, associated, **joint,** conjoint, **in common,** share and share alike; cooperative; reparative, compensatory, restitutive, recompensing, recompensive

**reciprocate** VERBS **correspond,** correspond to, respond to, answer, answer to, give in exchange, give and take, go tit-for-tat

**recital** NOUNS **narration,** narrative, relation, rehearsal, restatement, telling, retelling, recounting, recountal, review; **iteration,** reiteration, recapitulation, recap *and* wrapup <both nonformal>, rehash <nonformal>

**recite** VERBS **narrate,** tell, relate, recount, report, rehearse, give an account of; **iterate,** reiterate, recapitulate, rehash <nonformal>, **retell,** retail, **restate,** review

**reckless** ADJS devil-may-care; careless; **impetuous,** hotheaded; **hasty**, hurried, overeager, overzealous, overenthusiastic; precipitate, precipitant; headlong, breakneck; slapdash, slap-bang; accident-prone

**reckon** VERBS 1 **plan,** plan on, figure on, plan for *or* out, count on, figure out, calculate, calculate on, reckon *or* bargain on, bargain for, bank on *or* upon, make book on <nonformal>
2 **suppose,** assume, presume, surmise, expect, **suspect,** infer, understand, gather, conclude, deduce, consider, imagine, **fancy,** believe, deem, repute, feel, **think**

**reckoning** NOUNS **calculation,** computation, estimation, calculus; adding, casting, ciphering, totaling, count

**reclaim** VERBS **rehabilitate,** recondition, recover, restore, readjust

**recline** VERBS **lie, lie down,** repose, lounge, sprawl, loll, drape *or* spread oneself, splay, lie limply; **lie flat** *or* prostrate *or* prone *or* supine, lie on one's face *or* back, hug the ground *or* deck; prostrate, supinate

**recluse** NOUNS **loner,** solitaire, solitary, solitudinarian; **hermit,** eremite, anchorite, anchoret; hermitess, anchoress; **ascetic;** closet cynic; stylite, pillarist, pillar saint

**recognition** NOUNS **acknowledgment,** acceptance; appreciation; **identification,** reidentification, distinguishment; realization

**recognize** VERBS 1 **honor,** do honor, pay regard to, give *or* pay *or* render honor to; **know,** tell, distinguish, make out; identify, place, make <nonformal>
2 **know, perceive,** discern, see
3 **realize,** appreciate, understand, comprehend, be aware of, be conscious of

**recoil** NOUNS 1 **rebound,** resilience, repercussion, *contrecoup* <Fr>; **bounce,** bound, spring, bounce-back; **repulse,** rebuff; backlash, backlashing, kickback, **kick,** a kick like a mule <nonformal>, **backfire,** boomerang
VERBS 2 **rebound,** resile; **bounce,** bound, spring; spring *or* fly back, bounce *or* bound back, snap back; **kick,** kick back, kick like a mule <nonformal>, **backfire,** boomerang

**recollect** VERBS **remember,** recall, think of; **call** *or* **bring to mind,** recall to mind, call up, summon up, conjure up, evoke, recapture, call back, bring back

**recommend** VERBS 1 **advise,** counsel, suggest, advocate, propose, submit; **advance,** commend to attention, put forward, bring forward, put *or* set forth, put it to, put *or* set *or* lay *or* bring before
2 **advocate,** put in a word *or* good word for, support, back, lend one's name *or* support *or* backing to, make a pitch for <nonformal>

**recompense** NOUNS 1 **remuneration,** compensation; requital, requitement, quittance, **retribution,** reparation, redress, satisfaction, **atonement, amends,** return, restitution
VERBS 2 **compensate,** make compensation, make good, set right, restitute, pay back, rectify, **make up for; pay back,** repay, indemnify, cover; **trade off,** give and take; **retaliate**

**reconcile** VERBS bring to terms, **bring together,** reunite, heal the breach; bring about a détente; **iron** *or* **sort out,** adjust, settle, compose, accommodate, arrange matters, settle differences, resolve, compromise; **patch things up,** fix up <nonformal>

**reconciliation** NOUNS reconcilement, *rapprochement* <Fr>, **reunion,** shaking of hands, making up *and* kissing and making up <both nonformal>

**recondition** VERBS **rehabilitate,** reclaim, recover, restore, readjust; **renovate,** renew; refit, revamp, furbish, refurbish; refresh, face-lift

**reconsider** VERBS **reexamine,** review; revise one's thoughts, reappraise, revaluate, rethink; view in a new light, have second thoughts, think better of

**reconstitute** VERBS **rearrange,** reorganize, **reorder,** restructure, reshuffle, rejigger <nonformal>, tinker *or* tinker with, tune, tune up, fine-tune; redispose, redistribute, reallocate, realign

**reconstruct** VERBS **remake,** remodel, recompose, reconstitute, re-create, **rebuild,** refabricate, re-form, refashion, reassemble

**record** NOUNS 1 **phonograph record,** disc, wax, long-playing record *or* LP; transcription, electrical transcription, digital transcription, digital recording; compact disk *or* CD
2 **recording,** documentation, written word; **chronicle, annals,** history, story; roll, rolls, **register,** registry, rota, roster, scroll, catalog, inventory, table, list; **vestige,** trace
VERBS 3 put *or* place upon record; **inscribe,** enscroll; **register,** enroll, matriculate, check in; commit to *or* preserve in an archive, archive; **write,** commit *or* reduce to writing, put in writing, put in black and white, put on paper; **write down,** mark down, jot down, put down, set down, take down; note, note down, make a note, make a memorandum; put on tape, tape, tape-record; videotape; **chronicle,** write history, historify

**recording** NOUNS **record,** phonograph record, long-playing record *or* LP; transcription, electrical transcription, digital transcription, digital recording; wire recording, tape recording; tape, tape cassette, cassette; documentation, written word

**recount** NOUNS 1 election returns, **poll,** count, official count
2 **summation,** summary, summing, summing up, recounting, rehearsal, capitulation, **recapitulation,** recap *and* rehash <both nonformal>, statement, **reckoning,** count

**recount** VERBS **narrate,** tell, relate, report, **recite,** rehearse, give an account of; retell, **iterate,** reiterate, rehearse, recapitulate, rehash <nonformal>, restate

**recoup** VERBS **recover,** regain, retrieve, recuperate, **get back,** come by one's own; **repay,** pay back, restitute, **reimburse**

**recourse** NOUNS **resource,** resort; last resort *or* resource, *dernier ressort* and *pis aller* <both Fr>; **hope;** expedient

**recover** VERBS 1 **rally,** revive, get well, get over, pull through, pull round *or* around, come round *or* around <nonformal>, come back <nonformal>, make a comeback <nonformal>; get back in shape <nonformal>, be oneself again, feel like a new person
2 **regain,** retrieve, **recoup,** get back, come by one's own; **redeem,** ransom; reclaim; repossess, resume, reoccupy; **retake,** recapture, take back; replevin

**recovery** NOUNS **reclamation,** retrieval, salvage, salving; **rally,** comeback <nonformal>, return; **recuperation,** convalescence; **repossession,** resumption, reoccupation; reclaiming; upturn, uptick <nonformal>, expanding economy, **economic expansion**

**recreation** NOUNS **refreshment,** invigoration, reinvigoration, reanimation, revival, revivification, renewal; **relaxation,** regalement; **pleasure,** enjoyment

**recruit** NOUNS 1 **rookie** <nonformal>, **conscript,** draftee, inductee, selectee, enlistee, enrollee, trainee, boot <nonformal>; **raw recruit,** tenderfoot
VERBS 2 **employ, hire,** give a job to, take into employment, take into one's service, take on <nonformal>, headhunt <nonformal>, **engage,** sign up *or* on <nonformal>; **muster,** levy, raise

**rectify** VERBS **remedy,** correct, right, patch up, emend, amend, **redress,** make good *or* right, **put right,** set right, put *or* set to rights, put *or* set straight, set up, heal up, knit up, make all square

**recuperate** VERBS **get well, recover,** mend, be oneself again, feel like a new person, get back on one's feet, get over it

**recur** VERBS **repeat,** reoccur, **come again,** come round again, go round again, come up again, resurface, **return,** reappear, resume; resound, reverberate, echo; keep coming, come again and again, happen over and over; recur to the mind, return to mind, come back, reenter

**redecorate** VERBS **ornament,** decorate, adorn, dress, trim, garnish, array, **deck,** bedeck; prettify, **beautify;** refurbish, redo

**redeem** VERBS 1 **reclaim,** recover, retrieve; ransom; rescue; salvage, salve; recycle; win back, **recoup**
2 **pay in full,** meet one's obligations *or* commitments, redeem one's pledge, settle *or* square accounts; regenerate, **reform,** convert, save, give salvation

**red flag** NOUNS **warning sign,** premonitory sign, danger sign; **symptom,** early symptom, premonitory symptom, precursor; **red light**

**red-handed** ADJS 1 **guilty,** guilty as hell, peccant, criminal, to blame, at fault, faulty, on one's head; caught in the act *or* flatfooted *or* red-handed, caught with one's pants down *or* with one's hand in the till *or* with one's hand in the cookie jar <nonformal>
ADVS 2 red-hand, **in the act,** in the very act, *in flagrante delicto* <L>

**red herring** NOUNS **stratagem,** artifice, **ruse,** tactic, **maneuver, stroke,** gambit, **ploy,** dodge, artful dodge

**redneck** NOUNS 1 **vulgarian,** lout, yahoo; **ruffian,** roughneck <nonformal>, **rowdy,** hooligan
ADJS 2 rowdy, **rowdyish,** ruffianly, roughneck <nonformal>, hooliganish, raffish, raised in a barn

**redo** VERBS **remake,** make *or* do over, refashion, **reshape,** recast, rework, rejigger <nonformal>, **reconstruct,** rebuild, redesign, restructure, **revise;** redecorate, refurbish; **repeat,** do again, do a repeat

**redress** NOUNS 1 **reparation, recompense,** paying back, squaring <nonformal>; retribution, **atonement,** satisfaction, **amends,** making good, **requital**
VERBS 2 **remedy,** rectify, correct, right,

patch up, emend, amend, make good *or* right, **put right,** set right, put *or* set to rights, put *or* set straight, set up, heal up, knit up, make all square; pay reparations, requite, restitute, recompense, compensate, remunerate

**red tape** NOUNS **officialism,** bureaucracy; **red-tapism** *and* red-tapery <both nonformal>; bureaucratic delay, *paperasserie* <Fr>

**reduce** VERBS 1 **decrease,** diminish, lessen, take from; **lower,** depress, de-escalate, damp, dampen, **step down** *and* tune down *and* phase down *or* out *and* scale back *or* down *and* roll back *or* down <all nonformal>; **curtail,** retrench; **cut,** cut down *or* back, trim away, whittle away *or* down, pare
2 **conquer,** prostrate, fell, **flatten,** break, smash, crush, humble, bend, bring one to his knees; **impoverish,** pauperize, beggar

**redundant** ADJS **superfluous;** excess, in excess; unnecessary, unessential, nonessential, expendable, dispensable, **needless,** unneeded, gratuitous, uncalled-for; pleonastic, tautologous, tautological; verbose, prolix

**reek** VERBS **stink,** smell, smell bad, assail *or* offend the nostrils, smell to heaven *or* high heaven; **exude,** exudate, transude, transpire

**reel** NOUNS 1 **whirl,** wheel, **spin,** turn, round; spiral, helix, helicoid, gyre; pirouette; **swirl,** twirl, **eddy,** gurge, surge
VERBS 2 **whirl,** twirl, wheel, spin, spin like a top; **swirl,** gurge, surge, **eddy; flounder,** flounce, stagger, totter, roll, rock, lurch, careen, swing, sway

**reel off** VERBS **repeat,** rattle off, regurgitate; say again, repeat oneself, repeat word for word *or* verbatim, repeat like a broken record

**reentry** NOUNS **return,** homecoming, recursion; reentrance, remigration; Earth insertion; splashdown

**refer** VERBS **attribute,** assign, ascribe, impute, give, place, put, apply, attach; cite

**referee** NOUNS 1 **arbitrator,** arbiter, impartial arbitrator, third party, unbiased observer; **moderator; umpire,** judge
VERBS 2 **mediate,** intermediate, **intercede,** go between; **arbitrate,** moderate; **umpire,** judge

**refer to** VERBS **point to,** advert to, allude to, make an allusion to; **point out,** point at, put *or* lay one's finger on; **relate to,** apply to, bear on *or* upon, **concern,** involve, touch, affect, interest; **pertain to,** appertain, appertain to, belong to, fit

**refine** VERBS **clarify,** clear, purify, rectify, depurate, decrassify; try; **strain;** elute, elutriate; **filter,** filtrate; **process,** convert; mill, machine; extract, smelt

**reflect** VERBS 1 **image, mirror,** hold the mirror up to nature, figure; **embody,** body forth, incarnate, **personify,** personate, impersonate
2 **consider,** contemplate, speculate, study, ponder, perpend, **weigh,** deliberate, debate, meditate, muse, brood, ruminate, chew the cud <nonformal>, digest; introspect, be abstracted

**reflection** NOUNS 1 **stigma,** slur, reproach, censure, reprimand, imputation, aspersion, stigmatization; pillorying; disparagement
2 **consideration,** contemplation, speculation, meditation, musing, rumination, deliberation, lucubration, brooding, study, **pondering,** turning over in the mind
3 reflected *or* incident light; reflectance, albedo; blink, iceblink, ice sky, snowblink, waterblink, water sky

**reflex** NOUNS 1 conditioned reflex, conditioned response; simple reflex, unconditioned reflex; backwash, backlash, recoil, response; spontaneous reaction, unthinking response, knee-jerk <nonformal>
ADJS 2 **spontaneous,** unintentional, unintended, inadvertent, unwilled, **indeliberate,** undeliberate; **involuntary,** reflexive, knee-jerk <nonformal>, automatic

**reform** NOUNS 1 **reformation;** transformation; conversion; reformism, meliorism; **regeneration,** revival, reclamation, redemption, amendment, improvement, renewal, recrudescence, **rebirth,** renascence, new birth, change of heart; change of mind *or* commitment *or* allegiance *or* loyalty *or* conviction
VERBS 2 **improve, better,** change for the better, make an improvement; transform, transfigure; advance, promote, foster, favor, nurture, forward, bring forward; **lift,** elevate, **uplift,** raise, boost <nonformal>; put *or* set straight; reform oneself, turn over a new leaf, mend

one's ways, straighten out, straighten oneself out, go straight <nonformal>; get it together *and* get one's ducks in a row <both nonformal>

**reformatory** NOUNS **reform school,** correctional institution, industrial school, training school; borstal *or* borstal school *or* remand school <all Brit>

**refrain** NOUNS 1 **repeat,** repetend, bis, echo; **burden,** chant, undersong, chorus, bob
VERBS 2 **abstain,** hold, **spare,** forbear, forgo, keep from; hold *or* stay one's hand, sit by *or* idly by, sit on one's hands; **avoid,** shun, eschew, **pass up** <nonformal>, **keep from,** keep *or* stand *or* hold aloof from, have nothing to do with, take no part in, have no hand in, **let alone,** let well enough alone, **deny oneself,** do without, go without

**refresh** VERBS **freshen,** freshen up, fresh up <nonformal>; **revive,** revivify, **reinvigorate,** reanimate; **exhilarate,** stimulate, invigorate, fortify, enliven, liven up, animate, vivify, quicken; renew one's strength, put *or* breathe new life into, give a breath of fresh air, give a shot in the arm <nonformal>; renew, recreate, charge *or* recharge one's batteries <nonformal>

**refreshment** NOUNS refection, refreshing, **bracing,** exhilaration, stimulation, enlivenment, vivification, **invigoration,** reinvigoration, reanimation, revival, revivification, revivescence *or* revivescency, renewal, recreation; **tonic,** bracer, breath of fresh air, pick-me-up *and* a shot in the arm *and* an upper <all nonformal>

**refrigerant** NOUNS **coolant;** cryogen; Freon <trademark>, ether; liquid air, liquid oxygen *or* lox, liquid nitrogen, liquid helium, etc

**refrigerate** VERBS **cool,** chill; ice, ice-cool; water-cool, air-cool; **air-condition**

**refuge** NOUNS **sanctuary,** safehold, **asylum,** haven, port, harborage, **harbor;** harbor of refuge, port in a storm, snug harbor, safe haven; game sanctuary, bird sanctuary, preserve, forest preserve, game preserve

**refugee** NOUNS **emigrant,** émigré, outmigrant; defector; evacuee, boat person, *émigré* <Fr>; **displaced person** *or* DP, stateless person

**refund** NOUNS 1 **reparation,** recompense, paying back, squaring <nonformal>, repayment, reimbursement, remuneration, **compensation,** indemnification; kickback <nonformal>
VERBS 2 **recompense,** pay back, square <nonformal>, repay, reimburse, remunerate, kick back <nonformal>

**refurbish** VERBS **renovate,** renew; recondition, refit, revamp, furbish; refresh, face-lift; redecorate, redo

**refusal** NOUNS **unwillingness,** disinclination, nolition, **indisposition,** indisposedness, **reluctance,** renitency, renitence, grudgingness, grudging consent; **resistance,** dissent

**refuse** NOUNS **waste,** wastage, waste matter; leavings, sweepings, **scraps,** orts; **garbage,** slops, hogwash <nonformal>; dregs; deadwood; rags, bones, wastepaper, shard, potsherd; slag, culm, slack

**refuse** VERBS **be unwilling,** would *or* had rather not, not care to, not find it in one's heart to, not have the heart *or* stomach to; object to, draw the line at, be dead set against, **balk at;** grudge, begrudge; **disapprove,** decline, not consent, refuse consent, **reject, turn down** <nonformal>, decline to accept, not buy <nonformal>; put *or* set one's foot down, refuse point-blank *or* summarily; decline politely *or* with thanks, beg off

**refute** VERBS **confute,** confound, rebut, parry, answer, **answer conclusively,** dismiss, dispose of; argue down; silence, put *or* reduce to silence, shut up, stop the mouth of; take the wind out of one's sails; **contradict,** controvert, counter, run counter, **deny**

**regal** ADJS **stately,** imposing, grand, courtly, magisterial, aristocratic; **majestic,** royal, kingly, queenly; statuesque, fit for a king

**regale** VERBS 1 **feast, banquet,** eat heartily, lick the platter *or* plate, do oneself proud <nonformal>, put it away <nonformal>; refresh the inner man
2 **amuse,** cheer, entertain, divert, beguile, solace, recreate, refresh, enliven, exhilarate, put in good humor

**regalia** NOUNS **insignia,** ensign, **emblem,** badge, symbol, marking, attribute; badge of office, mark of office, chain, chain of office, collar; livery, uniform, mantle, dress, formal dress

**regard** NOUNS 1 **respect,** consideration, appreciation, favor; approbation, approval; **esteem,** estimation, prestige; **favor,** goodwill, good graces, mutual

regard, favorable regard, the good *or* right side of <nonformal>
2 **relevance,** pertinence, pertinency, cogency, relatedness, materiality, **appos

iteness,** germaneness; **connection,** reference, bearing, concern, concernment, interest, respect
VERBS 3 **cherish, hold dear,** hold in one's heart *or* affections, think much *or* the world of, prize, treasure; **admire,** esteem, revere; **adore, idolize,** worship, dearly love, think worlds *or* the world of, love to distraction
4 **care,** mind, heed, think, consider, pay heed to, take heed *or* thought of; **take an interest,** be concerned; pay attention
5 **contemplate,** look upon, view, see, view with the mind's eye, **envisage,** envision, visualize, imagine, image

**regardless** ADJS 1 **careless,** heedless, unheeding, unheedful, unsolicitous, uncaring; tactless, thoughtless, unthinking, inconsiderate, untactful, undiplomatic, mindless of, **unmindful,** forgetful, oblivious
ADVS 2 **anyhow,** anyway, anywise, in any way, **by any means,** by any manner of means; in any event, at any rate, in any case; **nevertheless,** nonetheless, however; at all, nohow <nonformal>

**regards** NOUNS **compliments,** respects, *égards, devoirs* <both Fr>; **best wishes,** one's best, good wishes, best regards, kind *or* kindest regards, love, best love; greetings

**regent** NOUNS ruler, governor; protector, prince regent, queen regent

**regiment** VERBS **hold** *or* **keep a tight hand upon,** keep a firm hand on, keep a tight rein on, rule with an iron hand, rule with a rod of iron, knock *or* bang heads together <nonformal>; discipline

**region** NOUNS **area,** zone, belt, **territory,** terrain; place; space; **setting,** locale, world, milieu

**regional** ADJS **territorial,** geographical, areal, sectional, zonal, topographic *or* topographical

**register** NOUNS 1 **range,** scope, compass, reach, stretch, expanse radius, sweep, carry, fetch; **gamut; spectrum**
2 **registration,** registry; **listing,** tabulation, cataloging, inventorying, indexing; **chronicle,** chronology, record
VERBS 3 be heard, **fall on the ear,** sound in the ear, catch *or* reach the ear, come to one's ear, make an impression, get across <nonformal>; **get over** *or* **across** <nonformal>, come through, **penetrate, sink in,** soak in; dawn on, be glimpsed
4 **represent,** delineate, depict, render, characterize, hit off, **portray,** picture, picturize, limn; convey an impression of
5 patent, copyright; **guard,** protect; **enroll,** matriculate, check in; impanel

**regress** VERBS go backwards, **recede,** return, revert; **retrogress,** retrograde, retroflex, retrocede; fall *or* get *or* go behind, lose ground, slip back; **backslide,** lapse, relapse, recidivate

**regret** NOUNS 1 **regrets,** regretting, regretfulness; **remorse,** remorsefulness, remorse of conscience; **shame,** shamefulness, shamefacedness, shamefastness; **sorrow,** grief; **contrition,** contriteness
VERBS 2 **deplore,** repine, be sorry for; rue, rue the day; **bemoan,** bewail; curse one's folly, **reproach oneself,** kick oneself <nonformal>, bite one's tongue, accuse *or* condemn *or* blame *or* convict *or* punish oneself, flagellate oneself, wear a hair shirt, make oneself miserable

**regrettable** ADJS much to be regretted; **deplorable,** lamentable, pitiful, pitiable, woeful, woesome <old>, grievous, sad

**regular** NOUNS 1 **customer,** client; patron, regular customer *or* buyer
ADJS 2 **habitual,** frequent, constant, persistent; **systematic** *or* systematical, methodical, ordered, orderly, regular as clockwork; **usual, customary,** accustomed, wonted, **normative,** standard, regulation, conventional

**regularity** NOUNS **constancy,** invariability, unvariation, undeviation, even tenor *or* pace, smoothness, clockwork regularity; **sameness, monotony,** undifferentiation, the same old thing <nonformal>, the daily round *or* routine, the treadmill

**regulate** VERBS **direct,** manage, conduct, carry on, handle, run <nonformal>; **control,** command, head, govern, boss *and* head up *and* pull the strings *and* mastermind *and* quarterback *and* call the signals <all nonformal>; **order,** prescribe; lay down the law, make the rules, call the shots *or* tune <nonformal>

**regulation** NOUNS 1 **direction,** directive, instruction, rule; prescript, prescription, **precept**; general order; **government,** governance, discipline

ADJS 2 **established,** received, accepted; set, prescribed, prescriptive; **standard,** regular, stock, **conventional**

**regulatory** ADJS **governing,** controlling, regulating, regulative, commanding

**rehabilitate** VERBS recondition, reclaim, recover, restore, readjust; **reeducate,** reinstruct; repatriate

**rehash** VERBS **paraphrase,** rephrase, reword, restate; **iterate,** reiterate, rehearse, recapitulate, recount, **recite,** retell, retail, review, run over

**rehearse** VERBS **practice,** go through, walk *or* run through, go over; go through one's part, read one's lines; study one's part

**reign** NOUNS 1 **governance,** authority, jurisdiction, control, command, power, rule, regnancy, **dominion, sovereignty,** empire, empery, raj <India>, imperium, **sway**

VERBS 2 **rule,** sway, wield the scepter, wear the crown, sit on the throne; rule over, govern

**reigning** ADJS **governing,** controlling, regulating, regulative, regulatory, commanding; ruling, sovereign, regnant; dominant, preponderant, **leading,** paramount, supreme, number one <nonformal>, hegemonic, hegemonistic

**reimburse** VERBS **repay,** pay back, restitute, recoup; pay in kind, pay one in his own coin, give tit for tat; **refund,** kick back <nonformal>

**reinforce** VERBS **intensify,** heighten, deepen, enhance, **strengthen,** beef up <nonformal>, aggravate, exacerbate; double, redouble, triple; bolster, back up, give *or* furnish *or* afford *or* supply *or* lend support; **corroborate,** bear out, buttress, **sustain,** fortify, undergird

**reinforcements** NOUNS **support, relief,** auxiliaries, reserves, reserve forces

**reinstate** VERBS **restore,** put back, replace, return, place in *status quo ante;* **reestablish,** redintegrate, reenact, restitute; **reinstall,** reinvest, revest, reinstitute, reconstitute, recompose, recruit, **rehabilitate,** redevelop

**reiterate** VERBS **repeat,** say again, do again; **iterate,** rehearse, recapitulate, recount, rehash <nonformal>, **recite, retell,** retail, **restate,** reword, review, run over, sum up, summarize, précis, resume, encapsulate

**reject** NOUNS 1 **discard,** throwaway, castaway, castoff, rejectamenta <pl>; **refuse**

VERBS 2 **repudiate,** abjure, forswear, **renounce,** disown, disclaim, recant; except, **exclude**, deselect, close the door on, leave out in the cold, cut out, blackball, blacklist; disregard; throw out *or* away, chuck *and* chuck out <both nonformal>, discard; categorically reject, disallow, not hear of; **turn thumbs down on** *and* thumb down <both nonformal>, ostracize, ban

**rejoice** VERBS jubilate, **exult,** glory, joy, delight, bless *or* thank one's stars *or* lucky stars, congratulate oneself, hug oneself, rub one's hands, clap hands; dance *or* skip *or* jump for joy, rollick, revel, frolic, caper, gambol, caracole, romp

**rejoice in** VERBS **delight in,** indulge in, luxuriate in, revel in, riot in, bask in, wallow in, swim in; groove on *and* get high on *and* freak out on <all nonformal>; feast on, gloat over *or* on; **relish,** appreciate, roll under the tongue, do justice to, savor, smack the lips; devour, eat up

**rejuvenate** VERBS **revive,** revivify, renew, **reanimate,** reinspire, regenerate, revitalize, put *or* breathe new life into, restimulate; **rekindle,** relight, reheat the ashes, stir the embers

**relapse** NOUNS 1 **lapse,** falling back; **reversion,** regression; reverting, retroversion, retrogradation, **retrogression,** retrocession, regress, **backsliding,** recidivism, recidivation

VERBS 2 **lapse,** backslide, slide back, lapse back, **slip back,** sink back, **fall back,** have a relapse, devolve, **return to,** revert to, yield again to, fall again into, recidivate; revert, regress; **fall,** fall from grace

**relate** VERBS **associate, connect,** interconnect, ally, link, link up, wed, marry, marry up, weld, bind, tie, couple, bracket, equate, identify; bring into relation with, bring to bear upon, apply; **parallel,** parallelize, draw a parallel; **interrelate,** relativize, **correlate**

**related** ADJS 1 **kindred, akin,** of common source *or* stock *or* descent *or* ancestry, agnate, cognate, enate, connate, connatural, congeneric *or* congenerous, consanguine *or* consanguineous, genetically related, related by blood, affinal

2 **connected; linked,** tied, coupled, knotted, twinned, wedded, wed, married *or* married up, welded, conjugate,

bracketed, bound, yoked, spliced, conjoined, conjoint, conjunct, joined

**relate to** VERBS **refer to, apply to, bear on** *or* **upon,** respect, regard, **concern, involve,** touch, affect, interest; **pertain, pertain to,** appertain, appertain to, belong to, fit; **have to do with,** have connection with, link with *or* link up with, connect, tie in with <nonformal>, deal with, treat of, touch upon

**relation** NOUNS **relationship, connection;** relatedness, connectedness, **association, affiliation,** filiation, bond, union, alliance, **tie,** tie-in <nonformal>, link, linkage, linking, linkup, liaison, **addition**, adjunct, junction, **combination**, assemblage; **positive** *or* **good relation,** affinity, rapport, mutual attraction, sympathy, accord; **closeness,** propinquity, **proximity,** approximation, contiguity, nearness, intimacy

**relative** ADJS **comparative,** relational; **relativistic,** indeterminate, uncertain, variable; **relating,** pertaining, appertaining, pertinent, referring, referable

**relax** VERBS unbend, unwind, slack, slacken, **ease; ease up, let up,** slack up, slack off, **ease off,** let down, **slow down,** take it slow, let up, take time to catch one's breath

**relay** VERBS **deliver**; pass on, pass the buck <nonformal>, hand forward, hand on

**release** NOUNS 1 **deliverance,** extrication, freeing, removal; suspension, intermission, respite, surcease, reprieve; discharge; catharsis, purging, purgation, purge, cleansing, cleansing away, emotional release
VERBS 2 **free, deliver,** reprieve, remove, free from; suspend, intermit, give respite *or* surcease; **relax,** decompress, ease, destress; act as a cathartic, **purge,** purge away, cleanse, cleanse away; give release, cut loose; **unhand,** let go, let loose, turn loose, cast loose, let out, let off, let go free; **discharge, dismiss;** let out on bail, grant bail to, go bail for <nonformal>; parole, put on parole; release from prison, spring <nonformal>; demobilize, separate from the service

**relent** VERBS **yield, give,** relax, bend, unbend, give way; submit

**relentless** ADJS **unyielding,** unbending, inflexible, hard, hard-line, inelastic, impliable, ungiving, **firm,** stiff, rigid, rigorous, stuffy; implacable, inexorable, unrelenting

**relevant** ADJS **pertinent,** appertaining, **germane, apposite,** cogent, material, admissible, applicable, applying, pertaining, belonging, involving, appropriate, **apropos,** *à propos* <Fr>, to the purpose, **to the point,** in point, *ad rem* <L>

**reliable** ADJS **dependable,** sure, surefire <nonformal>, **trustworthy,** trusty, to be depended *or* relied upon, to be counted *or* reckoned on; predictable, calculable; **secure,** solid, sound, firm, fast, **stable,** substantial, staunch, steady, **steadfast,** faithful, unfailing; true to one's word

**relic** NOUNS **memento,** remembrance, token, trophy, souvenir, keepsake, favor, token of remembrance; *memento mori* <L>

**relief** NOUNS **lightening,** easing, easement, alleviation; disburdening, disencumberment, unburdening, **unloading,** unlading, unsaddling, untaxing, unfreighting; **aid,** help, assistance, support, succor, comfort, ease, remedy

**relieve** VERBS 1 give relief; **ease,** ease matters; **relax,** slacken; **alleviate,** mitigate, palliate, soften, pad, cushion, assuage, allay, defuse, lay, appease, mollify, subdue, soothe; **dull, deaden,** dull *or* deaden the pain, numb, benumb, anesthetize; **lighten**
2 **substitute for,** subrogate; stand *or* sit in for, understudy for, fill in for, change places with, stand in the stead of, fill the shoes of; spell <nonformal>, cover for

**relieve of** VERBS **take from,** take away from, **deprive of,** do out of <nonformal>, disburden of, lighten of, ease of; **deprive,** bereave, divest

**religion** NOUNS religious belief *or* faith, **belief, faith,** teaching, doctrine, creed, credo, theology, orthodoxy; system of beliefs; tradition

**religious** ADJS 1 **pious,** pietistic; religious-minded; theistic; **devout,** devoted; **reverent,** reverential, venerative, venerational, adoring, solemn; faithful, dutiful; affirming, witnessing, believing; **observant,** practicing; **sacred, holy,** numinous, sacrosanct, spiritual
2 **conscientious,** scrupulous, punctilious, meticulous, strict

**relinquish** VERBS **give up,** surrender, yield, cede, hand *or* turn over; take one's hands off, loose one's grip on; **forgo,** do without, get along without, forswear, abjure, **renounce,** swear off; **part with,** give away, dispose of, rid oneself of, get rid of, see the last of, dump

**relish** NOUNS 1 **taste,** gusto, *goût* <Fr>; **flavor,** sapor; **smack,** tang; savor, sapidity; palate, tongue, tooth, stomach; taste in the mouth; sweetness, sourness, bitterness, bittersweetness, saltiness; aftertaste; savoriness
VERBS 2 **savor,** like, love, be fond of, be partial to, enjoy, delight in, have a soft spot for, appreciate, roll under the tongue, do justice to, smack the lips

**reluctant** ADJS **grudging,** renitent, loath; backward, laggard, dilatory, slow, slow to; unenthusiastic, unzealous, indifferent, apathetic, perfunctory; balky, balking, restive

**rely on** VERBS **trust,** confide in, depend on, repose, place trust *or* confidence in, have confidence in, **trust in**, trust utterly *or* implicitly, deem trustworthy, think reliable *or* dependable, take one's word, take at one's word

**remain** VERBS 1 **be left** *or* **left over,** survive, subsist, rest
2 **stay,** keep, hold, endure, stand, prevail, last long, hold out; defy *or* defeat time; live to fight another day; live on, live through; wear, wear well

**remainder** NOUNS **surplus,** surplusage, leftovers, plus, **overplus,** overstock, **overage,** overset, overrun, overmeasure, oversupply; **balance,** leftover, extra, spare, something extra *or* to spare

**remains** NOUNS **corpse,** dead body, mortal *or* organic remains, bones, skeleton, dry bones, relics, reliquiae

**remark** NOUNS 1 **statement,** earful *and* crack *and* one's two cents' worth <all nonformal>, **word,** say, **saying,** utterance, observation, reflection, expression; **assertion,** averment, allegation, affirmation, pronouncement, position, dictum; **declaration**
VERBS 2 **comment,** observe, note; mention, let drop *or* fall, say by the way, make mention of; refer to, allude to, touch on, make reference to, call attention to; muse, reflect

**remarkable** ADJS **outstanding,** extraordinary, **superior**, marked, of mark, signal, conspicuous, **striking; marvelous,** wonderful, formidable, exceptional, uncommon, astonishing, appalling, fabulous, fantastic, incredible, egregious

**remedial** ADJS **curative,** therapeutic, healing, corrective, alterative, restorative, analeptic

**remedy** NOUNS 1 **cure, corrective,** alterative, remedial measure, sovereign remedy; healing agent; restorative, analeptic; specific, specific remedy
VERBS 2 **rectify,** correct, right, patch up, emend, amend, **redress,** make good *or* right, **put right,** set right, put *or* set to rights, put *or* set straight, set up, heal up, knit up, make all square; **cure,** work a cure, **heal,** restore to health

**remember** VERBS **recall, recollect,** think of, call *or* bring to mind, recall to mind, call up, summon up, conjure up, evoke, recapture, call back, bring back

*call back yesterday, bid time return*
SHAKESPEARE

**remind** VERBS **put in mind,** remember, put in remembrance, bring back, bring to recollection, refresh the memory of; **jog the memory,** awaken *or* arouse the memory, flap the memory, give a hint *or* suggestion; **prompt,** give the cue, nudge

**reminder** NOUNS **remembrance,** remembrancer; **prompt,** prompter, tickler; prompting, cue, hint; jogger <nonformal>

**reminisce** VERBS rake *or* dig up the past; **remember,** look back, reflect, think of, evoke, recapture, look back upon things past

**remiss** ADJS **lax,** slack, loose, relaxed; imprecise, sloppy <nonformal>, careless, slipshod; negligent; work-shy

**remission** NOUNS 1 **pardon,** excuse, sparing, **amnesty,** indemnity, exemption, immunity, reprieve, grace; **absolution,** shrift, remission of sin; redemption; **exoneration,** exculpation; **restitution,** restoration, restoring, giving back, sending back, remitting, **return**
2 **decline,** declension, **subsidence,** dwindling, wane, ebb; downturn, downtrend, retreat; modulation, **abatement, mitigation,** diminution, **reduction,** lessening

**remit** VERBS 1 **pay,** render, tender; **recompense,** remunerate, compensate, reward, guerdon, indemnify, satisfy
2 **ease up,** ease off, abate, mitigate; **slacken,** slack, slake, slack off, slack up

**remittance** NOUNS **payment,** paying, paying off, paying up <nonformal>, payoff; paying out, **disbursal**; installment

**remnant** NOUNS **remainder,** remains,

residue, residuum, **rest, balance;** holdover

**remodel** VERBS **re-form,** reshape, refashion, recast; rehabilitate

**remorse** NOUNS **regret,** remorsefulness, remorse of conscience; **ruth,** ruefulness, guilty conscience, guilt feelings; onus, burden

**remorseless** ADJS **unregretful,** unregretting, **unremorseful,** unsorry, unsorrowful, unrueful; **merciless,** unmerciful, without mercy, unruing, **ruthless,** heartless, steely, flinty

**remote** ADJS 1 **distant,** distal, **removed,** far, far-off, away, **faraway,** way-off, at a distance, exotic, separated, apart, asunder; out-of-the-way, in a backwater; **unfrequented,** unvisited, off the beaten track
2 **aloof,** standoffish, distant, **detached,** Olympian, withdrawn; **cool,** cold, coldfish, frigid, chilly, icy, frosty; inaccessible, unapproachable
3 **farfetched,** strained, forced, dragged in, neither here nor there, brought in from nowhere; improbable

**remove** VERBS 1 **move,** relocate, shift, send, shunt; displace, delocalize, dislodge; **take away,** cart off *or* away, carry off *or* away; set *or* lay *or* put aside, put *or* set to one side, side
2 **murder,** commit murder; assassinate; **purge,** liquidate, eliminate, get rid of
3 **detach,** disengage, take *or* lift off, doff; **unfasten,** undo, unattach, unfix; **free,** release, liberate, loose, unloose, unleash, unfetter; **dismiss,** discharge, expel, cashier, drum out, separate forcibly *or* involuntarily, **lay off,** suspend, make redundant, turn out, let go, let out, give the pink slip

**removed** ADJS **aloof,** standoffish, offish, standoff, **distant, remote,** withdrawn; isolated, shut off, insular, **separate,** separated, **apart,** detached

**remunerate** VERBS **pay,** render, tender; **recompense,** compensate, reward, guerdon, indemnify, satisfy

**renaissance** NOUNS **revival,** revivification, **renewal,** resurrection, resuscitation, restimulation, reanimation, resurgence, recrudescence; renascence, **rebirth,** new birth; **rejuvenation,** rejuvenescence

**render** VERBS 1 **translate,** transcribe, transliterate, put *or* turn into, transfuse the sense of; construe
2 **describe,** portray, picture, **depict,** represent, delineate, limn, **paint,** draw; evoke, bring to life, make one see; **characterize,** character; **express,** set forth, give words to; **play,** perform, execute, do; interpret; make
3 **give, bestow,** confer, award, allot, bestow on; **deliver,** hand, pass, reach, forward, put into the hands of; transfer
4 **melt,** melt down, liquefy; refine

**rendezvous** NOUNS 1 **tryst,** assignation, meeting; trysting place, meeting place, place of assignation; assignation house; love nest <nonformal>
VERBS 2 **meet,** date; **couple,** copulate, link

**renegade** NOUNS 1 **apostate,** defector, turncoat, traitor, deserter
ADJS 2 **apostate,** recreant, tergiversating, tergiversant; **treasonous,** treasonable, traitorous, forsworn; collaborating; faithless, **disloyal**

**renege** VERBS **repeal,** revoke, rescind, reverse, strike down, abrogate; renig *and* go back on *and* welsh <all nonformal>; **be unfaithful,** not keep faith *or* troth, go back on <nonformal>, **fail,** break one's word *or* promise, go back on one's word <nonformal>, break faith

**renew** VERBS **revive,** revivify, **reanimate,** reinspire, regenerate, rejuvenate, revitalize, put *or* breathe new life into, restimulate; refresh; **renovate,** recondition, refit, revamp, furbish, refurbish; face-lift, recast, revamp <nonformal>, change over

**renounce** VERBS **swear off,** forswear, **give up,** abandon, stop, discontinue; take the pledge, get on the wagon *or* water wagon <nonformal>; **kick** *and* kick the habit <both nonformal>, dry out; relinquish

**renovate** VERBS **renew;** recondition, refit, revamp, furbish, refurbish; refresh, face-lift

**renown** NOUNS **repute,** reputation; **fame,** famousness, **kudos,** report, **glory;** éclat, **celebrity,** popularity, recognition, a place in the sun; **acclaim,** public acclaim, réclame; **notoriety,** notoriousness, talk of the town

*the bubble reputation*
SHAKESPEARE

**rent** NOUNS 1 **crack, cleft,** cranny, chink, check, craze, chap, **crevice,** fissure,

scissure, incision, notch, score, cut, gash, slit, split, **rift**
2 **rental,** lease, let <Brit>; sublease, sublet; charter
VERBS 3 **cleave, crack,** check, incise, craze, **cut, cut apart,** gash, slit, **split,** rive, rip open
4 **lease,** let <Brit>, hire, job, **charter; sublease,** sublet

**reorganize** VERBS **rearrange,** reconstitute, **reorder,** restructure, reshuffle, rejigger <nonformal>, tinker *or* tinker with, tune, tune up, fine-tune; **shake up,** shake out; redispose, redistribute, reallocate, realign

**repair** VERBS **mend, fix,** fix up <nonformal>, do up, put in repair, put in shape, set to rights, put in order *or* condition; **condition,** recondition, service, overhaul; patch, patch up

**reparation** NOUNS **recompense,** paying back, squaring <nonformal>, repayment, reimbursement, refund, remuneration, **compensation,** indemnification; retribution, **atonement,** redress, satisfaction, **amends,** making good, **requital**

**repartee** NOUNS **conversation,** verbal intercourse, conversational interchange, interchange of speech, give-and-take, cross-talk, rapping <nonformal>, backchat; clever *or* ready *or* witty reply *or* retort

**repast** NOUNS **meal,** feed *and* sit-down <both nonformal>, mess, spread <nonformal>, table, board, meat, *repas* <Fr>; **refreshment,** refection

**repay** VERBS pay back, restitute, **reimburse,** recoup; **requite,** quit, **atone,** make amends, make good, make up for, make up to, make restitution, make reparation; pay in kind, pay one in his own coin, give tit for tat

**repeal** VERBS **revoke,** rescind, reverse, strike down, abrogate; countermand, counterorder; **abolish,** do away with; **annul,** nullify, disannul, withdraw, **invalidate,** void, vacate, make void, declare null and void

**repeat** NOUNS 1 ditto <nonformal>, echo; **refrain,** burden, chant, undersong, chorus, bob; **encore,** repeat performance, **reprise;** replay, replaying
VERBS 2 **redo,** do again, do over, do a repeat, **reproduce,** duplicate, reduplicate, double, redouble, ditto <nonformal>, **echo,** parrot, reecho; come again *and* run it by again <both nonformal>, say again, repeat oneself, **quote,** repeat word for word *or* verbatim, repeat like a broken record
3 **recur,** reoccur, **come again,** come round again, go round again, come up again, resurface, reenter, **return,** reappear, resume; revert, turn *or* go back; keep coming, come again and again, happen over and over

**repeatedly** ADVS **frequently, commonly,** usually, ordinarily, routinely, habitually; **often,** oftentimes; **again and again,** time after time; **in quick** *or* **rapid succession;** often enough, not infrequently, not seldom, unseldom

**repel** VERBS 1 **disgust,** turn one's stomach, nauseate; make one's gorge rise; gross one out <nonformal>; **offend,** give offense, put off, turn off <nonformal>, **revolt,** horrify, appall, shock; make the flesh creep *or* crawl, make one shudder
2 **repulse,** rebuff, shut *or* slam the door in one's face, turn one away; **drive back,** put back, push back

**repellent** ADJS 1 **offensive,** objectionable, odious, repulsive, rebarbative, **repugnant,** revolting, forbidding; **disgusting,** sickening, loathsome, beastly <nonformal>, **vile,** foul, nasty, nauseating
2 **resistant,** resistive, resisting, renitent, up against, withstanding

**repent** VERBS **think better of,** change one's mind, have second thoughts; **plead guilty,** own oneself in the wrong, humble oneself, **apologize**, beg pardon *or* forgiveness, throw oneself on the mercy of the court; **do penance**

**repentant** ADJS **penitent,** penitential, penitentiary, repenting; **contrite,** abject, humble, humbled, **sheepish,** apologetic, touched, softened, melted

**repercussion** NOUNS **impact,** force, reaction; backwash, backlash, reflex, recoil, response; **recoil,** rebound, resilience, *contrecoup* <Fr>

**repertoire** NOUNS repertory, stock-in-trade; stock

**repetition** NOUNS **reproduction,** duplication, reduplication, doubling, redoubling; **recurrence,** reoccurrence, cyclicality, return, reincarnation, rebirth, reappearance, renewal, resumption; iteration, reiteration, echoing

**repetitive** ADJS **repetitious,** repetitional *or* repetitionary, repeating; **duplicative,** reduplicative; **imitative**, parrotlike;

echoing, reechoing, echoic; **iterative,** reiterative, reiterant; battological, tautological *or* tautologous, redundant

**replace** VERBS 1 **restore,** put back, return, place in *status quo ante;* **reestablish,** redintegrate, **reinstate,** restitute; **reinstall,** reinvest, revest, reinstitute, reconstitute, recompose, reintegrate, reconvert, reactivate; refill, replenish
2 **supplant,** supersede, succeed, **remove,** displace, supplant, oust; **dismiss,** take the place of, crowd out, cut out <nonformal>

**replacement** NOUNS **successor,** backup, backup man *or* woman, substitute, stand-in, **substitution,** succedaneum

**replay** NOUNS **encore,** repeat performance, repeat, **reprise;** replaying, return match

**replenish** VERBS **complete,** bring to completion *or* fruition, mature; **fill in, fill out,** piece out, top off, eke *or* eke out, round out; **make up,** make good, refill; fill up, restock

**replete** ADJS **full,** filled, plenary, capacity, flush, round; **ample,** well-filled, running over, overflowing; **profuse,** profusive, effuse, diffuse; **surfeited,** gorged, glutted; cloyed, jaded

**replica** NOUNS **reproduction,** duplication, imitation, **copy**, dummy, mock-up, facsimile, representation, approximation, model, version, knockoff <nonformal>

**reply** NOUNS 1 **answer, response,** responsion, replication; riposte, uptake <nonformal>, **retort,** rejoinder, reaction, return, **comeback** <nonformal>, short answer, back talk; **repartee,** snappy comeback <nonformal>
VERBS 2 **answer,** acknowledge; reply by return mail; **defend,** offer *or* say in defense, allege in support *or* vindication, **support,** uphold, sustain, maintain, assert; respond, riposte, counter

**report** NOUNS 1 **bulletin,** brief, statement, account, accounting; notice, **write-up** <nonformal>; **rumor,** unverified *or* unconfirmed report, **hearsay,** *on-dit* <Fr>, **scuttlebutt** *and* latrine rumor <both nonformal>; common talk, town talk, **talk of the town,** topic of the day, *cause célèbre* <Fr>; **grapevine**
2 **explosion,** discharge, blowout, blowup, detonation, fulmination, blast, burst
VERBS 3 give a report, give an account of, tell, relate; write up, make out *or* write up a report; gather the news, newsgather; **narrate,** tell, recount, **recite,** give an account of

**reporter** NOUNS **journalist,** newspaperman, newspaperwoman, newsman, newswoman, inkstained wretch, newswriter, gentleman *or* representative of the press; newshawk *and* newshound <both nonformal>; leg man <nonformal>; investigative reporter; cub reporter; correspondent, foreign correspondent, war correspondent, special correspondent, own correspondent, stringer

**repository** NOUNS **storehouse,** storeroom, stock room, lumber room, store, storage, **depository,** reservoir, depot, supply depot, supply base, magazine, *magasin* <Fr>, warehouse; **archives,** library, stack room

**reprehensible** ADJS **blameworthy,** blamable, to blame, at fault, much at fault; censurable, reproachable, reprovable, open to criticism *or* reproach; **culpable,** chargeable, impeachable, accusable, indictable, arraignable, imputable

**represent** VERBS 1 **describe,** portray, picture, render, **depict,** delineate
2 **act for,** act on behalf of, substitute for, appear for, answer for, speak for, be the voice of, give voice to, be the mouthpiece of <nonformal>, hold the proxy of, hold a brief for, act in the place of, stand in the stead of, serve in one's stead, pinch-hit for <nonformal>

**representation** NOUNS **description,** portrayal, portraiture, **depiction,** rendering, rendition, **delineation,** limning; **characterization,** character, character sketch, profile

**representative** NOUNS 1 **deputy,** proxy, substitute, **alternate,** backup *and* stand-in <both nonformal>, alter ego, **surrogate,** procurator, secondary, understudy, pinch hitter <nonformal>; exponent, advocate, pleader, paranymph, attorney, champion; lieutenant; **legislator,** lawmaker, solon, lawgiver; **congressman,** congresswoman, Member of Congress; **senator**
ADJS 2 **model,** exemplary, precedential, typical, paradigmatic, standard, normative, classic

**repress** VERBS **cover up,** muffle up; **hush up,** hush, hush-hush, shush, hugger-mugger; **suppress,** stifle, muffle, **smother,** squash, quash, squelch, kill, sit on *or* upon, put the lid on <nonformal>; **censor,** black out <nonformal>; **enjoin,** put under an injunction, issue an injunction against, issue a prohibitory injunction; **proscribe,** inhibit

**reprieve** NOUNS 1 **pardon,** excuse, sparing, **amnesty,** indemnity, exemption, immunity, grace; respite
VERBS 2 **release,** free, deliver, remove, free from; pardon, remit, forgive; respite, give *or* grant a reprieve

**reprimand** NOUNS 1 **reproof,** reproval, reprobation, a flea in one's ear; **rebuke,** reproach, reprehension, **scolding,** chiding, rating, **upbraiding,** objurgation; **admonition; correction,** castigation, chastisement, spanking, rap on the knuckles; lecture, lesson
VERBS 2 **reprove,** rebuke, reprehend, put a flea in one's ear, **scold,** chide, rate, **admonish,** upbraid, objurgate, have words with, take a hard line with; **lecture,** read a lesson *or* lecture to; **correct,** rap on the knuckles, **chastise,** spank, turn over one's knees

3 <nonformal> **call down** *or* **dress down, speak** *or* **talk to, tell off,** tell a thing or two, pin one's ears back, **give a piece** *or* **bit of one's mind, rake** *or* **haul over the coals,** rake up one side and down the other, give it to, let one have it, let one have it with both barrels, trim, come down on *or* down hard on, jump on *or* all over *or* down one's throat; give one a hard time *or* what for; **bawl out,** give a bawling out, chew, **chew out,** chew ass, ream, ream out, ream ass, cuss out, jack up, sit on *or* upon, lambaste, give a going-over, tell where to get off; give the deuce *or* devil, give hell, give hail Columbia

**reprisal** NOUNS **requital,** retribution; recompense, compensation, **reward,** comeuppance <nonformal>, desert, deserts, **just deserts,** what is merited, what is due *or* condign, what's coming to one *and* a dose of one's own medicine <both nonformal>

**reprise** NOUNS **encore,** repeat performance, repeat; replay, replaying

**reproach** NOUNS 1 **rebuke,** reprimand, reprehension, **scolding,** chiding, rating, **upbraiding,** objurgation
VERBS 2 **disgrace,** dishonor, discredit, reflect discredit upon, bring into discredit, cast reproach upon, be a reproach to

**reproduce** VERBS **remake,** make *or* do over, **re-create,** regenerate, resurrect, revive, re-form, refashion, **reshape,** recast, rework, rejigger <nonformal>, redo, **reconstruct,** rebuild, redesign, restructure, **revise;** reprint, reissue; repeat, restore; **copy,** replicate, **duplicate,** clone; **be productive,** proliferate, fructify, be fruitful, **multiply,** engender, beget

**reproduction** NOUNS 1 **procreation,** generation, begetting, breeding, engenderment; **propagation,** multiplication, proliferation
2 **duplication,** imitation, copy, dummy, mock-up, **replica,** facsimile, representation, paraphrase, approximation, model, version, knockoff <nonformal>

**repudiate** VERBS **recant,** retract, withdraw, take back, unswear, renege, welsh <nonformal>, **abjure,** disavow, disown; **deny,** disclaim, unsay, unspeak; **renounce,** forswear, eat one's words, eat crow, eat humble pie; **back down** *or* **out,** climb down, crawfish out <nonformal>, backwater, weasel
2 **not pay;** dishonor, disallow, protest, stop payment, refuse to pay; **default,** welsh <nonformal>, levant
3 **reject,** blackball *and* turn thumbs down on <both nonformal>, read *or* drum out, ease *or* freeze out *and* leave *or* keep out in the cold <all nonformal>, ostracize, wave off *or* aside

**repugnant** ADJS **offensive,** objectionable, odious, repulsive, repellent, rebarbative, **revolting,** forbidding; **disgusting,** sickening, loathsome, **vile,** foul, nasty, nauseating; fulsome, **contemptible,** despicable, detestable, execrable, beneath *or* below contempt, **base,** ignoble

**repulse** VERBS **rebuff,** repel, kiss one off *and* slap one in the face *and* kick one in the teeth <all nonformal>, send one away with a flea in one's ear, give one short shrift, shut *or* slam the door in one's face, turn one away; cut, **snub**

**repulsive** ADJS **offensive,** objectionable, odious, repellent, rebarbative, **repugnant,** revolting, forbidding; **disgusting,** sickening, loathsome, gross *and* yucky *and* grungy *and* scuzzy <all nonformal>, beastly <nonformal>; fulsome, mephitic, miasmal, miasmic, malodorous, stinking, fetid, noisome, noxious

**reputable** ADJS highly reputed, **estimable,** esteemed, much *or* highly esteemed, **honorable,** honored; **meritorious,** worth one's salt, noble, worthy, creditable; respected, respectable, highly respectable; **well-thought-of,** highly regarded, held in esteem, in good odor, in favor, in high favor

**reputation** NOUNS **notability,** prestige, esteem, repute, honor, glory, renown, dignity, **fame**

**repute** NOUNS 1 prestige, esteem, reputation, honor, glory, renown, dignity, fame
VERBS 2 **suppose,** assume, presume, surmise, expect, **suspect,** infer, understand, gather, conclude, deduce, consider, reckon, divine, imagine, **fancy,** dream, conceive, **believe,** deem, feel, **think,** be inclined to think, opine, say, daresay

**request** NOUNS 1 asking; desire, wish, expressed desire; **petition,** petitioning, impetration, address; application; requisition; demand
VERBS 2 **ask,** make a request, **beg leave,** make bold to ask; **desire,** wish, wish for, express a wish for, crave; **ask for,** order, put in an order for, call for, trouble one for; **requisition,** make *or* put in a requisition; make application, **apply for,** file for, **put in for;** demand

**requiem** NOUNS **dirge,** funeral *or* death song, coronach, keen, elegy, epicedium, monody, threnody, threnode, knell, death knell, passing bell, funeral *or* dead march, muffled drums; eulogy, funeral *or* graveside oration

**require** VERBS **need, want,** feel the want of, have occasion for, be in need of, be hurting for <nonformal>, stand in need of, not be able to dispense with, not be able to do without; **call for,** cry for, cry out for, clamor for

**requirement** NOUNS **requisite,** requisition; **necessity,** need, want, occasion; need for, **call for,** demand, demand for; desideratum, desideration; necessities, necessaries, essentials, bare necessities

**requisition** NOUNS 1 **demand,** requirement, request, stated requirement, order, rush order; requisite, **prerequisite,** prerequirement; **must,** must item
VERBS 2 **request, ask,** make a request, make *or* put in a requisition; make application, **apply for,** file for, **put in for;** demand

**rescind** VERBS **repeal,** revoke, reverse, strike down, abrogate; countermand, counterorder; **abolish,** annul, nullify, withdraw, **invalidate,** void, vacate, make void, declare null and void; **overrule,** override

**rescue** NOUNS 1 **deliverance,** delivery, **saving;** lifesaving; **extrication,** release, freeing, liberation; **bailout; salvation,** salvage, redemption, ransom; **recovery,** retrieval
VERBS 2 come to the rescue, **deliver, save,** be the saving of, **redeem,** ransom, **salvage; recover,** retrieve; **free,** set free, **release,** extricate, extract, **liberate**; snatch from the jaws of death; save one's neck *or* ass *and* bail one out <all nonformal>

**research** NOUNS 1 **investigation,** legwork <nonformal>, inquiry into; data-gathering, gathering *or* amassing evidence; **probe,** searching investigation, close inquiry, exhaustive study
VERBS 2 **experiment,** make an experiment, **run an experiment; test,** try, essay, cut and try <nonformal>, **test** *or* **try out,** have a dry run *or* dummy run *or* rehearsal *or* test run; put to the test, **put to the proof,** prove, verify, validate, substantiate, confirm, put to trial, bring to test, make a trial of, give a trial to

**researcher** NOUNS **experimenter,** experimentist, experimentalist, bench scientist, research worker, R and D worker; **tester,** analyst, analyzer

**resemble** VERBS be like, bear resemblance; put one in mind of <nonformal>, remind one of, bring to mind, be reminiscent of, suggest, evoke, call up, call to mind; **look like,** favor <nonformal>, mirror; **take after,** have all the earmarks of, have every appearance of, have all the features of, have all the signs of, have every sign *or* indication of; **approximate,** approach, near, come near, come close; **compare with,** stack up with <nonformal>

**resent** VERBS be resentful, feel *or* harbor *or* nurse resentment, feel hurt, smart, feel sore *and* have one's nose out of joint <both nonformal>; bear *or* hold *or* have a grudge

**reservation** NOUNS 1 **preserve,** reserve; **refuge, sanctuary**, game preserve *or* reserve, bird sanctuary, wildlife sanctuary *or* preserve
2 **stipulation,** provision, proviso, condi-

tion; exception, qualification, question, question in one's mind

**reserve** NOUNS 1 **restraint, constraint,** backwardness, retiring disposition; low key, low visibility, low profile; reservedness, **detachment,** withdrawal
2 **preserve,** reservation; park, **refuge,** sanctuary, game preserve *or* reserve, wildlife sanctuary *or* preserve
VERBS 3 keep *or* hold back, save, save up, sock *or* squirrel away, tuck away, put under the mattress, hoard; keep in hand, have up one's sleeve; restrict to, restrict

**reside** VERBS live, **live in,** dwell, lodge, stay, remain, abide, hang *or* hang out <nonformal>, domicile, domiciliate

**residence** NOUNS **abode,** habitation, place, dwelling, dwelling place, abiding place, place to live, where one lives *or* resides, where one is at home, roof, roof over one's head, place of residence, **domicile,** *domus* <L>

**resident** NOUNS 1 **inhabitant,** inhabiter, habitant; **occupant,** occupier, **dweller, tenant, denizen,** inmate; resider; writer- *or* poet- *or* artist- *or* composer-in-residence; incumbent, *locum tenens* <L>; sojourner; physician
ADJS 2 residentiary, **in residence;** residing, living, dwelling, commorant, lodging, **staying,** remaining, abiding, living in; cohabiting, live-in
3 **inherent,** implicit, immanent, indwelling

**residential** ADJS residentiary; domestic, domiciliary, domal; **home,** household

**residue** NOUNS **remainder,** remains, remnant, residuum, **rest,** balance; **leavings,** leftovers, oddments; **debris,** detritus, ruins; vestige, trace, hint, shadow, afterimage, afterglow

**resign** VERBS **quit,** leave, **vacate,** withdraw from; **retire,** superannuate, be superannuated, be pensioned *or* pensioned off, be put out to pasture, get the golden handshake *or* parachute <nonformal>; retire from office, stand down, stand *or* step aside, give up one's post; **tender** *or* **hand in one's resignation,** send in one's papers, turn in one's badge *or* uniform; **abdicate,** renounce the throne, give up the crown

**resilient** ADJS **elastic,** springy, bouncy; **stretchable,** stretchy, stretch; extensile; **flexible**; flexile; **adaptable,** adaptive, responsive; buoyant; lively

**resist** VERBS **withstand;** stand; endure; **stand up,** bear up, hold up, hold out; defy, tell one where to get off <nonformal>, throw down the gauntlet; bear up against; **repel,** repulse, rebuff

**resistance** NOUNS 1 immunity, nonproneness *or* nonsusceptibility to disease
2 withstanding, countering, renitence *or* renitency, repellence *or* repellency; **defiance; opposing,** opposition; stand; repulsion, repulse, rebuff; **objection, protest,** remonstrance, **dispute,** challenge, demur; dissent; **reluctance;** passive resistance, noncooperation
3 **irregular,** casual; **guerrilla,** partisan, franctireur; underground, maquis; underground *or* resistance fighter

**resolute** ADJS **resolved,** determined, bound *and* bound and determined <both nonformal>, **decided,** decisive, **purposeful;** devoted, dedicated, committed, single-minded, relentless, persistent, tenacious, persevering

**resolution** NOUNS 1 **adjustment,** accommodation, composition of differences, compromise, arrangement, settlement, terms
2 resoluteness, tenaciousness, tenacity, pertinaciousness, pertinacity, bulldog courage

**resolve** NOUNS 1 **intention,** intent, mindset, purpose, set *or* settled *or* fixed purpose; resolution, mind, will; determination
VERBS 2 **determine,** decide, will, purpose, make up one's mind, make *or* take a resolution, make a point of; **settle,** settle on, fix, seal; conclude, come to a determination *or* conclusion *or* decision, determine once for all; **solve,** find the solution *or* answer, **clear up,** get, get right, do, work, **work out, find out,** figure out

**resonate** VERBS **vibrate,** oscillate, librate, nutate, pulse, throb; snore

**resort** NOUNS 1 **haunt,** purlieu, hangout <nonformal>, **stamping ground** <nonformal>; gathering place, rallying point, meeting place, clubhouse, club; casino, gambling house; health resort; **spa,** baths, springs, watering place
2 **recourse,** resource; last resort *or* resource, *dernier ressort* and *pis aller* <both Fr>; **hope**

**resound** VERBS **reverberate,** sound, **rumble,** roll, boom, echo, reecho, rebound, bounce back, be reflected, be sent back, echo back, send back, return

**resource** NOUNS **reserve,** reserves, reservoir; **resort,** recourse; answer, solution

**resourceful** ADJS **ingenious,** daedal, Daedalian; **adaptable,** adjustable, flexible, ready

**respect** NOUNS 1 **regard,** consideration, appreciation, favor; approbation, approval; **esteem,** estimation, prestige; **reverence,** veneration, awe; **deference,** deferential *or* reverential regard; great respect, high regard, **admiration;** courtesy, respectfulness
VERBS 2 entertain respect for, accord respect to, **regard, esteem,** hold in esteem *or* consideration, favor, **admire,** think much of, think well of, think highly of, have *or* hold a high opinion of; **revere, reverence,** hold in reverence, **look up to,** defer to, bow to, exalt, put on a pedestal, **worship,** hero-worship, deify, apotheosize

**respectable** ADJS **reputable,** estimable, esteemed, much *or* highly esteemed, **honorable,** honored; **meritorious,** worth one's salt, noble, worthy, creditable; respected, highly respectable; **decent,** presentable, **adequate,** satisfactory, all right

**respectful** ADJS **regardful,** attentive; **deferential,** conscious of one's place, dutiful, honorific, ceremonious, cap in hand; courteous, **thoughtful,** considerate, tactful, solicitous

**respects** NOUNS **regards,** *égards* <Fr>; duties, *devoirs* <Fr>; attentions

**respite** NOUNS **recess, rest,** pause, halt, stay, lull, **break,** surcease, suspension, interlude, **intermission,** spell <Australia>, letup <nonformal>, **time out** <nonformal>, time to catch one's breath; **breathing spell,** breathing time, breathing place, breathing space, breath

**respond** VERBS 1 **react,** be moved, be affected *or* touched, be inspired, echo, catch the flame *or* infection, be in tune; **respond to,** warm up to, take *or* lay to heart, open one's heart to, be turned on to <nonformal>, feel in one's breast; enter into the spirit of, be imbued with the spirit of; empathize with, identify with, relate to emotionally, dig *and* be turned on by <both nonformal>
2 **answer,** make *or* give answer, **reply,** say in reply; **retort,** riposte, **rejoin,** return; come back *and* come back at *and* come right back at <all nonformal>, answer back *and* talk back *and* shoot back <all nonformal>

**respondent** NOUNS 1 **accused,** defendant, codefendant, corespondent, libelee, suspect, prisoner
ADJS 2 **answering,** replying, responsive, responding; rejoining, returning; echoing, echoic, reechoing

**response** NOUNS **answer,** reply; **reaction,** gut reaction <nonformal>; echo, chord, sympathetic chord, vibrations, vibes <nonformal>; **empathy,** identification

**responsibility** NOUNS incumbency; **liability, accountability,** accountableness, answerability, answerableness, amenability; product liability; **responsibleness,** dutifulness, duteousness, devotion *or* dedication to duty, sense of duty *or* obligation

**responsible** ADJS 1 **answerable; liable,** accountable, amenable, unexempt from, chargeable, on one's head, at one's doorstep, on the hook <nonformal>; responsible for
2 **trustworthy,** trusty, trustable, faithworthy, **reliable,** dependable, straight <nonformal>, sure, to be trusted, **to be depended** *or* **relied upon,** to be counted *or* reckoned on, as good as one's word

**responsive** ADJS **sensitive,** sympathetic, compassionate, amenable, receptive; empathic, empathetic; **impressionable,** impressible, susceptible; **adaptable,** adaptive

**rest** NOUNS 1 **repose,** ease, relaxation, slippered *or* unbuttoned ease, decompression <nonformal>; **comfort**; restfulness, quiet, tranquility; inactivity; sleep
2 **remainder,** remains, remnant, residue, residuum, **balance**
VERBS 3 **repose,** take rest, take one's ease, **take it easy** <nonformal>, rest from one's labors, take life easy; **pause,** relax, rest on one's oars; **take a break,** break, take ten

**restaurant** NOUNS eating place, eating house, dining room; eatery *and* beanery *and* hashery *and* hash house *and* greasy spoon <all nonformal>; fast-food restaurant

**restful** ADJS **comfortable, easy,** easeful; reposeful, peaceful, **relaxing,** relaxed; **calm,** quiet, **untroubled,** orderly, at peace; **soothing**

**restitution** NOUNS **compensation, recompense,** repayment, payback, indemnity, indemnification, measure for measure, rectification, **reparation;** reinstatement, restoration

**restless** ADJS **bustling,** fussing, fussy; **fidgety,** fretful, jumpy, unquiet, unsettled; **agitated,** turbulent

**restore** VERBS **put back,** replace, return, place in *status quo ante;* **reestablish,** redintegrate, reenact, **reinstate,** restitute; **reinstall,** reinvest, revest, reinstitute, reconstitute, recompose, recruit, **rehabilitate,** redevelop

**restrain** VERBS **constrain,** control, govern, guard, contain, keep under control, put *or* lay under restraint; **inhibit, curb,** check, arrest, bridle, get under control, rein, snub, snub in; **hold** *or* **keep in check,** hold at bay; **moderate,** keep within bounds; modulate, mitigate

**restraint** NOUNS 1 **reserve, constraint,** backwardness, retiring disposition; low key, low visibility, low profile; **reticence** *or* reticency; control, discipline; composure, possession, aplomb; restrainedness, **understatement,** unobtrusiveness, quietness, subduedness, quiet taste 2 **confinement,** locking-up, lockup, lockdown, caging, penning, putting behind barriers, impoundment, restriction; self-control, self-restraint

**restrict** VERBS **limit,** narrow, confine, tighten; ground, restrict to home; circumscribe; keep in *or* within bounds, keep from spreading, localize; **cage in,** hem, hem in, box, box in *or* up; **cramp,** stint; qualify

**restricted** ADJS **limited,** confined; circumscribed, hemmed in, hedged in *or* about, boxed in; shut-in; cramped, stinted; cloistered, enclosed

**restructure** VERBS **rearrange,** reorganize, reconstitute, **reorder,** reshuffle, rejigger <nonformal>, tinker *or* tinker with, tune, tune up, fine-tune; **shake up,** shake out; redispose, redistribute, reallocate, realign

**result** NOUNS 1 **effect,** resultant, **consequence,** consequent, sequent, sequence, sequel, sequela, sequelae; **upshot,** outcome, logical outcome; **product**, fruit, derivative
VERBS 2 **ensue,** issue, follow, attend, accompany; **turn out,** come out, fall out, redound, **work out,** pan out <nonformal>, fare; **eventuate,** terminate, end; **end up,** wind up

**resume** VERBS **recommence,** rebegin, **renew,** reestablish; **revive,** resuscitate, recrudesce; reenter, reopen, **return to,** go back to, begin again, take up again, make a new beginning, make a fresh start, have another shot *or* crack *or* go <nonformal>

**résumé** NOUNS **summary,** recapitulation, recap <nonformal>, rundown, run-through; summation; **curriculum vitae,** vita

**resurrect** VERBS **revive,** revivify, renew; **reanimate,** reinspire, regenerate, rejuvenate, revitalize, put *or* breathe new life into, restimulate; **refresh;** bring back, call back, recall to life, raise from the dead

**resuscitate** VERBS **revive,** revivify, renew, **reanimate,** reinspire, regenerate, rejuvenate, revitalize, put *or* breathe new life into, restimulate; bring to, bring round *or* around; rally, reclaim, restore

**retain** VERBS **keep, save,** save up, pocket *and* hip-pocket <both nonformal>; **maintain,** preserve; keep *or* hold in, bottle *or* cork up <both nonformal>, suppress, repress, inhibit; **keep in memory,** bear in mind, keep *or* hold in mind, hold *or* retain the memory of, **keep in view,** have in mind, hold *or* carry *or* retain in one's thoughts, store in the mind

**retainer** NOUNS 1 dependent, follower; myrmidon, yeoman; vassal, liege, liege man, feudatory, homager; inferior, **underling, subordinate,** understrapper 2 **fee,** stipend, retaining fee

**retaliate** VERBS **retort,** counter, **strike back,** hit back at <nonformal>, give in return; **reciprocate,** give in exchange, give and take; **revenge,** avenge, take *or* exact revenge, even the score, get even with

**retard** VERBS **delay, detain,** make late, slacken, lag, drag, drag one's feet *and* stonewall <both nonformal>, slow down, **hold up** <nonformal>, hold *or* keep back, check, **stay, stop,** arrest, impede, **block,** hinder, obstruct, throw a monkey wrench in the works <non-formal>

**retch** VERBS **feel disgust,** be nauseated, sicken at, choke on, have a bellyful of <nonformal>; **gag,** keck, heave, vomit, puke, hurl *and* upchuck *and* barf <all nonformal>

**reticence** NOUNS reticency; **reserve,** reservedness, restraint, low key, **constraint;** guardedness, discreetness, discretion; suppression, repression; subduedness; backwardness, retirement, low profile

**retire** VERBS 1 **go to bed;** lay me down to sleep; bed, bed down

2 <nonformal> go night-night, go bye-bye, go beddy-bye; **hit the hay, hit the sack,** crash, turn in, crawl in, flop, sack out, sack up, kip down *or* doss down <both Brit>

3 **dismiss,** discharge, expel, cashier, drum out, **lay off,** make redundant, turn out, give the pink slip; put on the retired list; pension off, superannuate, put out to pasture; read out of

**retired** ADJS in retirement, superannuated, on pension, pensioned, pensioned off, emeritus, emerita <fem>; **secluded,** seclusive, withdrawn

**retiring** ADJS **reserved,** restrained, constrained; quiet; low-keyed, keeping low visibility *or* a low profile; **backward,** shrinking

**retort** NOUNS **answer,** reply, response, responsion; riposte, uptake <nonformal>, **rejoinder,** reaction, return, **comeback** *and* **take** <both nonformal>, back talk; clever *or* ready *or* witty reply *or* retort, snappy comeback <nonformal>

**retouch** VERBS **touch up,** finish, put on the finishing touches, polish, fine down, fine-tune <nonformal>, tone up, **furbish,** furbish up, spruce, **spruce up**

**retract** VERBS **draw** *or* **pull back,** pull out, draw *or* pull in; **recant,** repudiate, withdraw, take back, unswear, renege, welsh <nonformal>, **abjure,** disavow, disown; **deny,** disclaim, unsay, unspeak; **eat one's words,** eat one's hat, swallow, eat crow, eat humble pie; **back down** *or* **out,** weasel

**retreat** NOUNS 1 **withdrawal,** strategic withdrawal, exfiltration; **fallback,** pull-out, pullback; advance to the rear; disengagement; **backing down** *or* **off** *or* **out** <all nonformal>; reneging, copping *or* weaseling out <nonformal>
2 **sanctum,** sanctum sanctorum, holy of holies; **den,** sanctuary, refuge; **hideaway,** ivory tower, lair, inner sanctum
VERBS 3 sound *or* beat a retreat, beat a hasty retreat, **withdraw, retire,** pull out *or* back, exfiltrate, advance to the rear, disengage; **fall back,** move back, go back, stand back; **draw back,** back out *or* out of *and* back off *and* back down <all nonformal>

**retrenchment** NOUNS **curtailment,** cut, cutback, drawdown, rollback, scaleback, pullback, truncation; **economizing,** reduction of expenses

**retribution** NOUNS **reprisal,** requital; recompense, comeuppance <nonformal>, desert, deserts, **just deserts,** what's coming to one *and* a dose of one's own medicine <both nonformal>; retributive justice, nemesis; reparation, redress, satisfaction, **atonement, amends,** return

**retrieval** NOUNS **reclamation,** recovery, salvage, salving; redemption, salvation

**retrieve** VERBS **recover,** regain, recuperate, **recoup,** get back, come by one's own; **redeem,** ransom; **repossess,** resume, reoccupy; **retake,** recapture, take back

**retroactive** ADJS **back,** backward, into the past; retrospective, retroactionary, *ex post facto* <L>, *a priori* <L>

**retrospect** NOUNS 1 retrospection, hindsight, looking back
VERBS 2 **think back,** go back, **look back,** carry one's thoughts back, look back upon things past, use hindsight, **see in retrospect,** hark back, retrace; review in retrospect

**return** NOUNS 1 **homecoming,** recursion, returning; reentrance, **reentry;** remigration; **recovery,** rally, comeback <nonformal>
2 **gain, profit,** earnings, winnings, returns, proceeds, bottom line <nonformal>; receipts; **fruits,** pickings, gleanings; net profit, clean *or* clear profit, net; dividend; interest; **yield,** return on investment, payout, payback
VERBS 3 **restore,** put back, replace; give back, restitute, hand back; **recur,** repeat, reappear, **come again,** come up again, be here again, resurface, reenter, **come round** *or* **around,** come round again, come in its turn; **revert,** retrovert, **regress,** retrogress, reverse, return to the fold; backslide, slip back, recidivate, lapse, lapse back, relapse
4 **reflect,** echo, bounce back

**returns** NOUNS 1 election returns, **poll,** count, official count
2 **receipts,** income, revenue, profits, earnings, proceeds, **take,** takings, intake, yield, fruits

**reunion** NOUNS **reconciliation,** reconcilement, *rapprochement* <Fr>, shaking of hands, making up *and* kissing and making up <both nonformal>; gathering, get-together <nonformal>; family reunion

**revamp** VERBS **renovate,** renew; recondition, refit, furbish, refurbish; refresh, face-lift

**reveal** VERBS **disclose,** let out, show, impart, discover, **leak,** let slip out, let the cat out of the bag *and* spill the beans <both nonformal>; manifest; bring into the open, get out in the open, bring out of the closet; **expose, show up; bare,** strip *or* lay bare, blow the lid off *and* blow wide open *and* rip open *and* crack wide open <all nonformal>; **bring to light,** bring into the open, hold up to view

**revealing** ADJS **disclosive,** revelatory, revelational; **disclosing,** showing, exposing, betraying; show-through, see-through, peekaboo; **diaphanous,** sheer, thin; **gossamer,** filmy, gauzy

**reveille** NOUNS **awakening,** wakening, rousing, arousal; rude awakening, rousting out <nonformal>; waking time, get-up time <nonformal>; **bugle call**

**revel** VERBS **make merry,** roister, jolly, lark <nonformal>, skylark, **make whoopee** <nonformal>, let oneself go, **blow** *or* **let off steam;** cut loose, let loose, let go, let one's hair down <nonformal>, whoop it up, **kick up one's heels;** celebrate; **go on a spree,** go on a bust *or* toot *or* bender *or* binge *or* rip *or* tear <all nonformal>; **carouse**

**revelation** NOUNS 1 **disclosure,** disclosing; revealment, revealing, making public, publicizing, broadcasting; exposure, exposition, **exposé**
2 **divine revelation;** inspiration, afflatus, divine inspiration; theophany, theophania, epiphany; **prophecy,** prophetic revelation, apocalypse

**revenge** NOUNS 1 **vengeance,** avengement, sweet revenge, getting even, evening of the score; revanche, revanchism; **retaliation,** reprisal; vendetta, feud, blood feud
VERBS 2 **avenge, take** *or* **exact revenge,** have one's revenge, wreak one's vengeance; **retaliate,** even the score, get even with; launch a vendetta

**revenue** NOUNS **receipts,** receipt, income, profits, earnings, returns, proceeds, **take**

**reverberate** VERBS **resound,** sound, **rumble,** roll, boom, echo, reecho, rebound, bounce back, be reflected, be sent back, echo back, send back, return

**reverence** NOUNS **respect,** regard, consideration, appreciation, favor; **veneration,** awe; **deference,** deferential *or* reverential regard; **honor, homage,** duty; adoration, breathless adoration, worship; deification, apotheosis; **obeisance,** genuflection, kneeling, bending the knee; prostration

**reverie** NOUNS **dream;** daydream, pipe dream <nonformal>; brown study, trance

**reverse** NOUNS 1 **reversal,** reversing, reversion; **backing,** backing up, backup; **about-face,** *volte-face* <Fr>, about-turn, turnaround, turnabout; tergiversation, tergiversating; **change of mind;** second thoughts, better thoughts, afterthoughts
2 opposite side, other side, the other side of the picture *or* coin, other face; **inverse,** obverse, converse
3 reversal of fortune, **setback,** check, severe check, backset *and* throwback <both nonformal>; **comedown,** descent, down
VERBS 4 go into reverse; **back, back up,** backpedal, back off *or* away; **backwater,** backtrack, reverse one's field; have second thoughts, think better of it, cut one's losses
5 **repeal,** revoke, rescind, strike down, abrogate; **annul,** nullify, disannul, withdraw, **invalidate,** void, vacate, make void, declare null and void; **overrule,** override; transpose, flip <nonformal>

**revert** VERBS **regress,** retrogress, retrograde, retrocede, **return,** return to the fold; backslide, slip back, recidivate, lapse, lapse back, relapse

**review** NOUNS 1 **criticism,** critique, *compte-rendu critique* <Fr>, analysis; critical review, **report,** notice, write-up <nonformal>; commentary
2 **study,** studying, application, conning; restudy, restudying, brushing up, boning up <nonformal>; grind *and* grinding *and* boning <all nonformal>, **cramming** *and* cram <both nonformal>
3 **reexamination,** recheck, reappraisal, revaluation, rethinking, revision, second *or* further look
VERBS 4 **brush up,** refresh the memory, restudy, **brush up,** polish up *and* bone up <both nonformal>, get up on; **cram** <nonformal>

5 **reconsider, reexamine,** revise one's thoughts, reappraise, revaluate, rethink; view in a new light, have second thoughts, think better of

6 **criticize,** critique; **censure**, pick holes in, pick to pieces; comment upon, annotate; moralize upon; pontificate

**reviewer** NOUNS **critic,** interpreter, exegete, analyst, explicator

**revise** VERBS redact, recense, **revamp,** rewrite, redraft, **rework,** work over; **emend,** amend, emendate, **rectify,** correct; **edit,** blue-pencil

**revive** VERBS revivify, **renew,** recruit; **reanimate,** reinspire, regenerate, rejuvenate, revitalize, put *or* breathe new life into, restimulate; **resuscitate,** bring to, bring round *or* around; **resurrect,** bring back, call back, recall to life, raise from the dead

**revoke** VERBS **repeal,** rescind, reverse, strike down, abrogate; renege, renig *and* go back on *and* welsh <all nonformal>; **waive,** set aside; countermand, counterorder; **annul,** nullify, withdraw, **invalidate,** void, vacate, make void, declare null and void

**revolt** NOUNS 1 **rebellion,** revolution, mutiny, insurrection, insurgence *or* insurgency, *émeute* <Fr>, **uprising,** rising, outbreak, general uprising, *levée en masse* <Fr>, **riot,** civil disorder; peasant revolt, *jacquerie* <Fr>; putsch, coup d'état; intifada

VERBS 2 **rebel,** kick over the traces, reluct, reluctate; **rise up,** rise up in arms, mount the barricades; mount *or* make a coup d'état; **mutiny; riot,** run riot; secede, break away

**revolting** ADJS **offensive,** objectionable, odious, repulsive, repellent, rebarbative, **repugnant,** forbidding; **disgusting,** sickening, loathsome

**revolution** NOUNS 1 **radical** *or* **total change,** violent change, striking alteration, sweeping change, clean sweep, clean slate, square one <nonformal>, tabula rasa; revolutionary war, war of national liberation; bloodless revolution, palace revolution; **revolt**

2 **rotation,** roll, **gyration,** spin

**revolutionary** NOUNS 1 **rebel**; anarchist, anarch, syndicalist, criminal syndicalist, terrorist; subversive

ADJS 2 **rebellious,** rebel, breakaway; **mutinous,** mutineering; **insurgent, insurrectionary,** riotous, turbulent; factious, **seditious,** seditionary; **radical,** extreme, extremist

3 **original,** novel, unprecedented; unique, *sui generis* <L>; **avant-garde,** trail-blazing

**revolve** VERBS **rotate,** spin, turn, round, **go round** *or* **around,** turn round *or* around; circumrotate, circumvolute; **swivel,** pivot, wheel

**reward** NOUNS 1 **incentive,** inducement, encouragement, carrot; payment; meed, guerdon; honorarium

VERBS 2 **pay,** render, tender; **recompense,** remunerate, compensate, guerdon, indemnify, satisfy

**rhapsodize** VERBS **be enthusiastic,** rave, enthuse *and* be big for <both nonformal>; get stars in one's eyes, **carry on over** *and* rave on <both nonformal>, make much of, **make a fuss over,** make an ado *or* much ado about; **idealize,** utopianize, quixotize

**rhythm** NOUNS **beat, meter,** measure, number *or* numbers, movement, **lilt, swing;** rhythmic pattern *or* phrase; tempo

**rich** ADJS **wealthy,** affluent, moneyed *or* monied, in funds *or* cash, **well-to-do,** well-off, well-situated, prosperous, comfortable, provided for, well provided for, fat, **flush,** flush with *or* of money, abounding in riches, worth a great deal, frightfully rich, rich as Croesus

**rickety** ADJS **unsteady, shaky,** ricketish, teetering, teetery, tottery, tottering, doddering, tumbledown, ramshackle, dilapidated, rocky <nonformal>

**rid** ADJS **quit,** clear, free, free of, clear of, quit of, rid of, shut of, shed of <nonformal>

**riddle** NOUNS **conundrum,** charade, rebus; logogriph, anagram; **matter of ignorance,** sealed book, enigma, mystery, puzzle

**ride** NOUNS 1 **drive;** spin *and* whirl <both nonformal>; joyride <nonformal>; Sunday drive; airing; lift <nonformal>, pickup <nonformal>

VERBS 2 **go for a ride** *or* **drive;** go for a spin <nonformal>, take *or* go for a Sunday drive; **drive,** chauffeur

3 **ridicule, deride,** make a laughingstock *or* a mockery of; roast <nonformal>, insult; **make fun** *or* **game of,** poke fun at, make merry with, put one on *and* pull one's leg <both nonformal>

**ride for a fall** VERBS **court danger,** mock

*or* defy danger, go in harm's way, thumb one's nose at the consequences, **tempt fate** *or* **the gods** *or* **Providence,** tweak the devil's nose, bell the cat, play a desperate game

**ridge** NOUNS ridgeline, *arête* <Fr>, chine, spine, horst, kame, esker, cuesta, serpent kame, Indian ridge, moraine, terminal moraine

**ridicule** NOUNS 1 **derision,** mockery, raillery, rallying, chaffing; panning *and* razzing *and* roasting *and* ragging <all nonformal>, **scoffing,** jeering; **banter**
VERBS 2 **deride,** ride <nonformal>, make a laughingstock *or* a mockery of; roast <nonformal>, **insult**; **make fun** *or* **game of,** poke fun at, make merry with, put one on *and* pull one's leg <both nonformal>

**ridiculous** ADJS **absurd,** nonsensical, insensate, laughable, ludicrous; **foolish,** crazy; preposterous, cockamamie <nonformal>, fantastic, **outrageous,** incredible, beyond belief, *outré* <Fr>, extravagant, **bizarre**

**rid oneself of** VERBS **give up,** leave off, **abandon,** drop, stop, discontinue, kick *and* shake <both nonformal>, throw off; **part with,** give away, dispose of, get rid of, see the last of, dump, be finished with

**rifle** NOUNS 1 **gun,** firearm; shoulder weapon *or* gun *or* arm; gun make
VERBS 2 **plunder,** pillage, loot, sack, ransack, freeboot, spoil, spoliate, despoil, depredate, prey on *or* upon, **raid,** reive <Scots>

**rift** NOUNS **falling-out,** breach of friendship, parting of the ways, bust-up <nonformal>; **breach,** break, rupture, schism, split, cleft; open rupture

**rigamarole** NOUNS **twaddle,** twiddle-twaddle, fiddle-faddle, fiddlesticks, **blather, babble,** babblement, **gabble,** gibble-gabble, **blabber,** gibber, jabber, prate, **prattle,** palaver, rigmarole, galimatias, skimble-skamble, drivel, drool

**right** NOUNS 1 rightfulness, rightness; what is right *or* proper, what should be, what ought to be, the seemly, the thing, the right *or* proper thing, the right *or* proper thing to do, what is done
2 **prerogative,** due, droit; power, authority, prerogative of office; faculty, appurtenance; **claim,** proper claim, demand, **interest, title,** pretension, pretense, prescription; birthright; natural right, presumptive right, inalienable right; divine right
VERBS 3 **remedy,** rectify, correct, patch up, emend, amend, **redress,** make good *or* right, **put right,** set right, put *or* set to rights, put *or* set straight, set up, heal up, knit up, make all square; **arrange,** order, reduce to order, **put** *or* **get** *or* **set in order,** put first things first, get one's ducks in a row <nonformal>
ADJS 4 rightful; fit, suitable; **proper,** correct, decorous, good, decent, seemly, **due, appropriate,** fitting, condign, **right and proper,** as it should be, as it ought to be, *comme il faut* <Fr>
ADVS 5 **rightward,** rightwards, rightwardly, **to the right,** dextrally, dextrad; on the right, dexter
6 **exactly, precisely,** to a T, expressly; **just,** dead, straight, even, square, **plumb,** directly, squarely, point-blank
PHRS 7 that's right, that is so, amen, that's it, *c'est ça* <Fr>; right you are, right as rain

PHRS 8 <nonformal> **right on!,** you better believe it!, you've got something there, I'll say, I'll tell the world, I'll drink to that, righto, quite, rather!, you got it!, you said it, you said a mouthful, now you're talking, you can say that again, you're not kidding, that's for sure, ain't it the truth?, you're damn tootin', don't I know it?, you're telling me?, you're not just whistling Dixie, bet your ass *or* sweet ass *or* bippy *or* boots *or* life *or* you bet the rent, fucking ay, fucking ay right

**righteous** ADJS **honest,** upright, **upstanding,** erect, right, **virtuous,** clean, squeaky-clean <nonformal>, decent; rightminded, right-thinking

**rightful** ADJS condign, appropriate, proper; fit, becoming; **fair,** just; **legal,** legitimate, legit *and* kosher <both nonformal>, **licit, lawful,** according to law, within the law

**the right stuff** NOUNS **qualifications;** talents, powers, parts; the goods *and* the stuff *and* what it takes *and* the makings <all nonformal>

**the right thing** NOUNS **right,** rightfulness, rightness; what is right *or* proper, what should be, what ought to be, the seemly, the thing, the proper thing, the right *or* proper thing to do, what is done

**rigid** ADJS **firm, rigorous,** rigorist, rigoristic, stiff, **hard,** iron, steel, steely, hard-shell, obdurate, **inflexible,** iron-handed, inexorable, dour, **unyielding,** unbending, impliable, **relentless,** unrelenting, procrustean; **uncompromising**

**rigor** NOUNS 1 **adversity,** adverse circumstances, difficulties, hard knocks *and* rough going <both nonformal>, **hardship,** trouble, troubles, vicissitude, stress, pressure
2 **rigidity,** rigidness, **firmness,** renitence *or* renitency, nonresilience *or* nonresiliency, inelasticity

**rile** VERBS **annoy,** irk, vex, nettle, provoke, pique, miff *and* peeve <both nonformal>, **ruffle,** disturb, discompose, **roil,** aggravate, make a nuisance of oneself, **exasperate,** exercise, try one's patience, try the patience of a saint

**ring** NOUNS 1 band, wedding band, engagement ring, mood ring, signet ring, school *or* class ring, circle, earring, nose ring
2 **clique,** coterie, set, circle, junto, junta, cabal, camarilla, **clan,** group
3 **halo,** nimbus, aura, **aureole,** circle, glory
VERBS 4 tintinnabulate, **peal,** sound; **toll,** knell, sound a knell; **tinkle,** tingle, **jingle,** ding, dingdong, dong; ring changes *or* peals; ring in the ear
5 **encircle, circle,** ensphere, belt, belt in, zone, cincture, encincture; **girdle,** gird, begird, engird; band

**ringleader** NOUNS **instigator,** inciter, **troublemaker,** mischief-maker

**rinse** VERBS **wash,** bathe, rinse out, flush, flush out, irrigate, sluice, sluice out

**riot** NOUNS 1 **uprising,** rising, outbreak, general uprising, *levée en masse* <Fr>, civil disorder; **free-for-all,** brawl, broil, melee, scrimmage, **fracas**
VERBS 2 **roister,** roil, carouse; **create a disturbance,** make a commotion, make trouble, cause a stir *or* commotion, create a riot, **cut loose,** run wild, run riot, run amok, go on a rampage, go berserk

**ripe** ADJS **mature,** matured, maturated, seasoned; blooming, abloom; **mellow,** full-grown, fully developed

**ripen** VERBS **mature,** maturate; bloom, blow, blossom, flourish; come to fruition, bear fruit; **mellow;** grow up, reach maturity, reach its season; bring to maturity, bring to a head

**rip off** VERBS

<nonformal> **swipe, pinch,** bag, lift, hook, crib, **cop,** nip, snitch, snare, boost, burn, clip; **knock off** *or* **over,** tip over

**rip-off** NOUNS **hoax,** deception, spoof <nonformal>, **humbug,** flam, fake *and* fakement, **sham;** mare's nest

**ripple** NOUNS 1 **splash; crinkle,** crankle, rimple, wimple
VERBS 2 **agitate,** shake, disturb, perturb, shake up, perturbate, **disquiet,** discompose, upset, trouble, unsettle, stir, swirl, flurry, flutter, fret, roughen, ruffle, rumple, convulse

**rise** NOUNS 1 **ascent,** ascension, levitation, **rising,** uprising, **uprise,** uprisal; **uplift,** elevation; **uptick** <nonformal>, increase
VERBS 2 **arise,** mount, uprise, **rise up, get up,** get to one's feet; **stand up,** stand on end; jump up, spring to one's feet; **levitate,** ascend; hover, **rise in the world,** work one's way up, step up, come *or* move up in the world, claw *or* scrabble one's way up, mount the ladder of success, pull oneself up by one's bootstraps

**risk** NOUNS 1 **investment, venture,** plunge <nonformal>, speculation
2 **gamble,** chance, risky thing, hazard; **precariousness,** danger, riskiness
VERBS 3 take a chance, run a risk, push *or* press one's luck, lay one's ass on the line *and* put one's money where one's mouth is <both nonformal>, **gamble, bet**; risk one's neck *and* shoot the works *and* go for broke <all nonformal>

**risqué** ADJS risky, **racy,** salty, spicy, **off-color,** suggestive, scabrous

**rite** NOUNS **ritual,** rituality, **liturgy,** holy rite; order of worship; **ceremony,** ceremonial; observance, ritual observance

**ritual** NOUNS 1 **ceremony,** ceremonial; **rite,** formality; solemnity, service, function, office, **observance,** performance
ADJS 2 **ceremonious,** ceremonial; ritualistic; hieratic, hieratical, sacerdotal, liturgic

**rival** NOUNS 1 **contestant,** contender, competitor
VERBS 2 **equal,** match, correspond, be even-steven, be tantamount to, be equal to; **keep pace with,** keep step with, run abreast; vie, vie with

**rivalry** NOUNS **competition,** vying, emulation; cutthroat competition; **sportsmanship,** gamesmanship, lifemanship, one-upmanship
**riveted** ADJS **fixed,** fastened, anchored; **gripped,** held, fascinated, enthralled, rapt, spellbound, charmed, enchanted, mesmerized, **hypnotized,** caught, **arrested,** switched on <nonformal>
**riveting** ADJS **engrossing,** absorbing, consuming, **gripping,** holding, **arresting,** engaging, attractive, **fascinating,** enthralling, spellbinding, enchanting, magnetic, hypnotic, mesmerizing, mesmeric; obsessing
**roam** VERBS **wander, rove,** range, nomadize, **gad,** gad around *or* about, follow the seasons, wayfare, flit, traipse <nonformal>, gallivant, knock around *or* about *and* bat around *or* about <all nonformal>, prowl, **drift, stray,** float around, straggle, **meander, ramble,** stroll, saunter, jaunt, peregrinate
**roar** NOUNS 1 **noise,** loud noise, **racket,** din, clamor; outcry, **uproar,** hue and cry, noise and shouting; howl; thunder, thunderclap
VERBS 2 **be noisy,** make a noise *or* racket, raise a clamor *or* din *or* hue and cry, noise, racket, **clamor,** clangor; **bawl,** bellow, roar *or* bellow like a bull; cachinnate, roar with laughter
**roast** VERBS **ridicule,** deride, ride <nonformal>, make a laughingstock *or* a mockery of; **insult**; make fun *or* game of, poke fun at; **castigate,** flay, skin alive <nonformal>, scorch, blister, trounce
**rob** VERBS 1 commit robbery; pick pockets, jostle; hold up; **burglarize;** burgle <nonformal>; **steal,** appropriate, **make off with,** pilfer, filch, have one's hand in the till

2 <nonformal> **swipe, pinch,** bag, **lift,** hook, crib, **cop,** nip, snitch, snare, boost, annex, borrow, burn, clip, **rip off,** nick *and* nobble <both Brit>; **heist, knock off** *or* **over,** tip over; **stick up; mug;** roll, jackroll; hijack

**robber** NOUNS **holdup man** *and* stickup man <both nonformal>; highwayman, highway robber, footpad, road agent, bushranger <Austral>
**robbery** NOUNS 1 **theft,** robbing; bank robbery; highway robbery; **armed robbery,** holdup; jostling; hijacking; purse snatching

2 <nonformal> **heist, stickup,** job, stickup job, bag job, boost, burn, knockover, **ripoff**

**robe** NOUNS frock, mantle, gown, cloak
**robot** NOUNS **automaton,** mechanical man; cyborg; bionic man, bionic woman
**robust** ADJS **hale, hearty,** hale and hearty, robustious, robustuous, vital, **vigorous, strong,** strong as a horse *or* an ox, stalwart, stout, sturdy, **rugged,** rude, hardy, lusty, bouncing, well-knit
**rock** NOUNS 1 **rock-and-roll,** rock music, rock 'n' roll, hard rock, acid rock, folk rock, country rock, full-tilt boogie
2 **stone,** igneous rock, volcanic rock, granite, basalt, sedimentary rock, metamorphic rock, schest, gneiss, crag, bedrock
VERBS 3 **agitate,** perturb, disturb, trouble, disquiet, discompose, unsettle, **stir,** ruffle, shake, shake up, shock, upset, make waves, jolt, jar, stagger, electrify, bring *or* pull one up short, give one a turn <nonformal>
4 **oscillate, vibrate,** librate, nutate; pendulate; **swing,** sway, swag, dangle, **reel,** lurch, roll, careen, toss, pitch; **wag,** waggle; **calm,** calm down, tranquilize, pacify, mollify, appease, dulcify; **quiet,** hush, still, rest, compose, **lull,** soothe, gentle, cradle, rock to sleep
5 **pitch,** toss, tumble, pitch and toss, **plunge,** pound, **rear, rock,** reel, swing, sway, lurch, yaw, heave, scend, **flounder, welter,** wallow
**rocket** NOUNS 1 **missile;** ballistic missile, guided missile; torpedo; projectile rocket, ordnance rocket, combat *or* military *or* war rocket; bird <nonformal>
VERBS 2 **shoot up,** upshoot, upstart, upspring, upleap, upspear, **skyrocket**
**rocketry** NOUNS rocket science *or* engineering *or* research *or* technology; **missilery,** missile science *or* engineering *or* research *or* technology
**rocket scientist** NOUNS **talent,** gifted person, prodigy, natural <nonformal>, **genius,** mental genius, intellectual genius, intellectual prodigy, mental giant; brain surgeon <nonformal>
**rock the boat** VERBS **not conform,** nonconform, not comply; **get out of line** *and* make waves <all nonformal>, upset

the apple cart, break step, break bounds; protest

**rocky** ADJS 1 **unsteady,** shaky, rickety, teetery, tottery, tottering, doddering, tumbledown, ramshackle, dilapidated; groggy, wobbly, staggery; **sickish,** seedy <nonformal>, **under the weather, out of sorts** <nonformal>, below par <nonformal>, off-color, off one's feed <nonformal>
2 **rugged,** ragged, harsh; **craggy,** cragged; gravelly, stony; **unreliable,** undependable, untrustworthy, treacherous, **insecure,** unsound, unstable

**rod** NOUNS 1 **scepter, staff,** wand, staff *or* rod *or* wand of office, baton, mace, truncheon, fasces; stick, switch
2 **gun, firearm;** shooting iron *and* gat *and* heater *and* convincer *and* piece <all nonformal>

**rogue** NOUNS **mischief-maker,** mischief, **devil,** knave, **rascal,** rapscallion, scapegrace, **scamp;** wag

**role** NOUNS 1 **function,** use, purpose, part, end use, immediate purpose, ultimate purpose, operational purpose, operation; work, duty, office; part, capacity, character

**role model** NOUNS **paragon,** person to look up to, *chevalier sans peur et sans reproche* <Fr>, **good example,** shining example; exemplar, epitome; **model,** pattern, standard, norm

**roll** NOUNS 1 **roster,** scroll, rota; **roll call,** muster, **census,** nose *or* head count <nonformal>
2 **swing,** swinging, **sway,** swag; **rock,** lurch, reel, careen; wag, waggle; wave, waver
VERBS 3 **reverberate, resound,** sound, **rumble,** boom, echo, reecho, rebound, bounce back, be reflected, be sent back, echo back, send back, return
4 **run smoothly,** go like clockwork *or* a sewing machine; present no difficulties, give no trouble, be painless, be effortless; flow, glide, slide, coast, sweep, sail

**roll back** VERBS **retrench,** cut down, cut *or* pare down expenses, curtail expenses; cut corners, tighten one's belt, cut back, slow down

**rolling stone** NOUNS **wanderer,** rover, roamer, gadabout <nonformal>, runabout, go-about <nonformal>; **itinerant,** peripatetic, bird of passage, visitant; **drifter** *and* **floater** <both nonformal>

**roly-poly** NOUNS 1 **fat person,** fatty *and* fatso <both nonformal>, **tub, tub of lard,** blimp <nonformal>, hippo <nonformal>
ADJS 2 **stout, obese,** adipose, gross, fleshy, beefy, abdominous, big-bellied, full-bellied, potbellied, **tubby** <nonformal>

**romance** NOUNS **love affair, affair,** affair of the heart, amour, romantic tie *or* bond, something between, thing <nonformal>, liaison, entanglement, intrigue; fiction, figment, **myth,** fable

**romantic** NOUNS 1 dreamer, daydreamer, dreamer of dreams, castle-builder, lotus-eater, **wishful thinker;** romanticist, romancer
ADJS 2 **loving,** lovesome, fond, adoring, devoted, affectionate, demonstrative, **sentimental, tender,** soft <nonformal>, melting; romanticized, romancing, romanticizing; **impractical,** unpractical, unrealistic; starry-eyed, dewy-eyed; with one's head in the clouds

**romp** NOUNS 1 **frolic,** play, rollick, frisk, gambol, caper, dido <nonformal>
VERBS 2 **play,** frolic, rollick, gambol, frisk, caper, cut capers <nonformal>, antic, cavort, caracole, flounce, trip, skip, dance; **cut up** <nonformal>, cut a dido <nonformal>, horse around <nonformal>

**roof** NOUNS roofing, roofage, top, **housetop,** rooftop

**rook** VERBS **cheat,** pluck *and* skin <both nonformal>

**rookie** NOUNS **novice,** novitiate *or* noviciate, **tyro,** abecedarian, alphabetarian, **beginner**, entrant, **neophyte,** tenderfoot *and* greenhorn <both nonformal>, freshman, **fledgling;** catechumen, initiate, debutant; **recruit,** raw recruit, inductee, yardbird<nonformal>

**room** NOUNS 1 **latitude,** swing, play, way; spare room, room to spare, room to swing a cat <nonformal>, **elbowroom,** margin, leeway
2 **chamber,** *chambre* <Fr>, *salle* <Fr>, four walls
VERBS 3 bunk, crash <nonformal>, berth; **lodge,** quarter, put up, billet, bed, bunk

**roomer** NOUNS **lodger,** paying guest; **boarder,** board-and-roomer, **transient,** transient guest *or* boarder; **renter,** tenant

**roomy** ADJS **spacious,** sizable, commodious, capacious, ample

**roost** NOUNS 1 perch, roosting place; eyrie
VERBS 2 **settle, settle down,** sit down, locate, park <nonformal>, ensconce, ensconce oneself; perch, nest, hive, burrow

**root** NOUNS 1 radix, radicle; rootlet; **tap-root,** tap; **rhizome,** rootstock; **tuber,** tubercle; **bulb,** bulbil, corm, earthnut
2 **source, origin,** genesis, original, origination, **derivation,** rise, beginning, conception, inception, commencement, etymon, primitive, radical
VERBS 3 **take root,** strike root; **stick,** stick fast
4 **cheer;** root for <nonformal>, cheer on; cheer *or* applaud to the very echo
5 look for, look around *or* about for, look for high and low, look high and low, search out, **search for,** seek for, **hunt for,** cast *or* beat about for

**rooter** NOUNS **booster** <nonformal>, applauder, *claqueur* <Fr>; claque; fan *and* buff <both nonformal>, adherent

**root out** VERBS **exterminate,** eliminate, eradicate, deracinate, **extirpate,** annihilate; wipe out <nonformal>; cut out, root up *or* out, uproot, pull *or* pluck up by the roots, cut up root and branch, strike at the root of

**rope** NOUNS 1 **cord,** line, wire, braided rope, twisted rope, **cable,** wire cable
2 **hanging,** the gallows, the rope *or* noose; **lynching,** necktie party; **hangman's rope,** noose
VERBS 3 **catch,** take, **trap,** lasso, noose; **bind,** tie, brace, truss, **lash,** leash, strap, lace, wire, chain

**rope off** VERBS **circumscribe,** bound; mark off *or* mark out, stake out, lay off; **cordon, cordon off,** seal off; set up barriers, put behind barriers

**roster** NOUNS **roll,** scroll, rota; **roll call,** muster, **census,** nose *or* head count <nonformal>; checkroll, checklist

**rosy** ADJS **optimistic,** upbeat <nonformal>, bright, sunny; cheerful; roseate, rose-colored, *couleur de rose* <Fr>

**rot** NOUNS 1 **rottenness,** foulness, putridness, putridity, rancidness, rancidity, rankness, **putrefaction,** putrescence, spoilage, decay, decomposition; dry rot, wet rot
VERBS 2 **decay,** decompose, disintegrate; go *or* fall into decay, go *or* fall to pieces, break up, crumble, crumble into dust; **spoil,** corrupt, go bad; putrefy, putresce

**rotary** ADJS **rotational,** rotatory, rotative; trochilic, vertiginous; circumrotatory, circumvolutory, circumgyratory

**rotate** VERBS **revolve,** spin, turn, round, **go round** *or* **around,** turn round *or* around; circumrotate, circumvolute; **swivel,** pivot, wheel, swing; pirouette, turn a pirouette

**rotten** ADJS **decayed,** decomposed; spoiled, corrupt, peccant, bad, **gone bad; rotting,** putrid, putrefied, foul; putrescent, **mortified,** necrosed, necrotic, sphacelated, gangrened, gangrenous; rotten at *or* to the core

**rough** ADJS 1 **unsmooth; uneven,** ununiform, unlevel, inequal, **broken,** irregular, textured; jolty, **bumpy,** rutty, rutted, pitted, pocky, potholed; **coarse,** gross, unrefined, coarse-grained; abrasive
2 **undeveloped, unfinished,** crude, unpolished, unrefined; uncultivated, uncultured

**rough-and-ready** ADJS **unarranged,** unorganized, haphazard; makeshift, **extemporaneous,** extemporized, improvised, ad-lib *and* off the top of one's head <both nonformal>; wild-and-woolly

**roughhouse** NOUNS 1 **misbehavior,** misconduct, **rowdiness,** rowdyism, riotousness, ruffianism, hooliganism; horseplay; helter-skelter, pell-mell, **rough-and-tumble**
VERBS 2 **misbehave,** cut up <nonformal>, horse around <nonformal>, cut up rough <nonformal>

**rough it** VERBS **camp,** go camping, camp out, sleep out

**roughly** ADVS approximately, nearly, some, about, circa; more or less, *plus ou moins* <Fr>, by and large, upwards of, **to the amount of,** to the tune of <nonformal>; as much as, all of <nonformal>, no less than

**roughneck** NOUNS 1 **vulgarian,** low *or* vulgar *or* ill-bred fellow, guttersnipe <nonformal>, *épicier* <Fr>; rough, **ruffian, rowdy,** hooligan; vulgarist, ribald

2 <nonformal> **tough,** bruiser, mug, mugger, bimbo, bozo, ugly customer, **hoodlum, hood, hooligan,** gorilla, ape, plug-ugly, strong-arm man, muscle man, **goon;** gun, gunsel, trigger man, rodman, torpedo, hatchet man; hellion, terror, holy terror, shtarker, ugly customer

**rough up** VERBS **mistreat,** maltreat, ill-treat, ill-use, abuse, injure, **molest;** do violence to, do one's worst to; mishandle, manhandle; buffet, batter, bruise, **savage,** manhandle, maul, knock about, rough

**round** NOUNS 1 **revolution,** rotation, cycle, circle, wheel, circuit
ADJS 2 **circular,** rounded, circinate, annular, annulate ring-shaped, ringlike; annulose; disklike, discoid

**rouse** VERBS **arouse,** raise, raise up, **waken, awaken,** wake up, turn on <nonformal>, charge *or* psych *or* pump up <nonformal>, stir, **stir up,** set astir, **pique**

**rout** NOUNS 1 **retreat,** *reculade* <Fr>, **withdrawal,** withdrawment, strategic withdrawal, exfiltration; **retirement,** fallback, pullout, pullback
VERBS 2 **overwhelm,** whelm, snow under <nonformal>, overbear, defeat utterly, deal a crushing *or* smashing defeat; **put to rout,** put to flight, scatter, stampede, panic

**route** NOUNS **path,** way, itinerary, course, track, run, line, road; trajectory, traject, *trajet* <Fr>; circuit, tour, orbit; walk, beat, round; trade route, **sea lane, air lane,** flight path

**routine** NOUNS 1 **act,** scene, number, turn, bit *and* shtick <both nonformal>
2 **order,** even tenor, standard operating procedure; **peace,** quiet, quietude, tranquillity; **round,** cycle, rotation, the daily grind <nonformal>, recurrence, periodicity, endless round; gamut, spectrum
ADJS 3 **habitual, regular,** frequent, constant, persistent; repetitive, recurring, recurrent; stereotyped; nine-to-five, workaday, well-trodden, well-worn, beaten; trite, hackneyed, **ordinary,** normal, average, usual, standard, par for the course <nonformal>

**rove** VERBS **stray,** go astray, lose one's way, err; take a wrong turn *or* turning; drift, go adrift; **wander,** wander off, ramble, straggle, divagate, excurse, perrate

**row** NOUNS 1 **train,** range, rank, **file,** line, string, thread, queue, bank, tier; windrow, swath; single file, Indian file
VERBS 2 **paddle,** ply the oar, **pull,** scull, punt

**row** NOUNS 1 **commotion,** scrap, hassle <nonformal>, **brawl,** free-for-all <nonformal>, ruckus, rhubarb <nonformal>, rumpus <nonformal>, donnybrook *or* donnybrook fair, broil, embroilment, melee, scramble; helter-skelter, pell-mell, **roughhouse,** rough-and-tumble
VERBS 2 **be noisy, make a noise** *or* **racket,** raise a clamor *or* din *or* hue and cry, noise, racket, **clamor,** roar, clangor; brawl, rumpus; **make an uproar,** kick up a dust *or* racket, kick up *or* raise a hullabaloo, raise the roof

**rowdy** NOUNS 1 **ruffian,** rough, bravo, **thug;** bully, bullyboy, bucko; hell-raiser
ADJS 2 **noisy, boisterous,** rip-roaring, strepitous, strepitant, obstreperous; **disorderly,** disruptive, rowdyish, **ruffianly**

**royal** ADJS **sovereign; regal,** majestic, purple; **kinglike,** kingly

*every inch a king*
SHAKESPEARE

**royalty** NOUNS 1 **sovereignty,** regnancy, **majesty,** kingship, kinghood; queenship, queenhood; the throne, the Crown, the purple
2 **dividend; commission,** rake-off *and* cut <both nonformal>

**rub** NOUNS 1 **bone of contention,** apple of discord, sore point, tender spot, delicate *or* ticklish issue, beef <nonformal>; **crux,** hitch, pinch, snag, catch, joker <nonformal>, where the shoe pinches
NOUNS 2 **friction,** rubbing, frottage; **resistance,** frictional resistance
VERBS 3 **stroke,** pet, caress, fondle; **nuzzle,** nose, rub noses; feel up <nonformal>; rub against, massage, knead; frictionize; polish

**rubber** NOUNS 1 **elastic;** elastomer; gum elastic; **eraser,** India rubber
2 **contraceptive,** birth control device, prophylactic; condom
ADJS 3 **rubbery,** rubberlike; rubberized

**rubberneck** NOUNS 1 **rubbernecker** <nonformal>; watcher, Peeping Tom, voyeur, scopophiliac
VERBS 2 keep one's eyes open, keep one's eye on, stare, gape, peer, gawk, rubber <nonformal>

**rubbish** NOUNS **rubble, trash,** junk <nonformal>, shoddy, riffraff, **scrap,** debris, litter, lumber; **nonsense,** stuff and nonsense, pack of nonsense, **folderol,** balderdash, *niaiserie* <Fr>, flummery, trumpery

**rub elbows with** VERBS **associate with,** assort with, sort with, consort with, hobnob with, fall in with, go around with, **mingle with,** mix with, touch elbows *or* shoulders with

**rub out** VERBS 1 **obliterate,** expunge, efface, erase, blot, sponge, **wipe out,** wipe off the map, **blot out,** sponge out, wash away
2 kill, waste *or* zap <both nonformal>

**rub the wrong way** VERBS **ruffle,** wrinkle, corrugate, crinkle, crumple, **rumple;** bristle; go against the grain, set on edge

**ruckus** NOUNS **commotion,** hubbub, Babel, tumult, turmoil, **uproar, racket,** riot, **disturbance,** rumpus <nonformal>, ruction <nonformal>, **fracas, hassle,** rampage

**ruddy** ADJS **red-complexioned,** ruddy-complexioned, warm-complexioned, red-fleshed, red-faced, ruddy-faced, apple-cheeked, rubicund, **florid,** sanguine, full-blooded

**rude** ADJS **impudent,** impertinent, pert, flip <nonformal>, flippant, cocky *and* cheeky *and* fresh *and* facy *and* crusty *and* nervy <all nonformal>; **disrespectful,** derisive, brash, bluff; **coarse,** gross, crude, crass, raw, rough, **earthy**

**rudimentary** ADJS **original,** primary, primal, primitive, pristine, primeval, aboriginal, **elementary,** elemental, **basic,** basal, crucial, central, radical, **fundamental;** embryonic

**rue** VERBS **regret,** deplore, repine, be sorry for; rue the day; **bemoan,** bewail; curse one's folly, **reproach oneself,** kick oneself <nonformal>, wear a hair shirt, make oneself miserable

**ruffian** NOUNS rough, bravo, **rowdy, thug;** bully, bullyboy, bucko; hell-raiser

**ruffle** NOUNS 1 **flurry,** bustle, stir, swirl, swirling, whirl, vortex, eddy, hurry, hurry-scurry, hurly-burly
2 **tuck,** gather; frill, ruche, ruching; flounce
VERBS 3 **agitate,** perturb, disturb, trouble, disquiet, discompose, discombobulate <nonformal>, unsettle, **stir, shake,** shake up, shock, upset, make waves, jolt, jar, rock, stagger, bring *or* pull one up short, give one a turn <nonformal>; **fluster,** rub the wrong way, go against the grain, set on edge
4 wrinkle, corrugate, crinkle, crumple, **dishevel,** rumple; tousle <nonformal>, muss *and* muss up <both nonformal>, mess *and* mess up <both nonformal>; disarrange

**rug** NOUNS 1 **carpet,** floor cover *or* covering; carpeting, wall-to-wall carpet *or* carpeting
2 **wig,** peruke, toupee, hairpiece, divot *and* doormat <both nonformal>; **periwig**

**rugged** ADJS 1 ragged, harsh; rugose, rugous, wrinkled, crinkled, crumpled, corrugated; **scratchy, abrasive,** rough as a cob <nonformal>
2 **sturdy,** stable, **solid,** sound, firm, steady, tough, stout, strong; **durable,** lasting, enduring; **well-made,** well-constructed, well-built, well-knit

**ruin** NOUNS 1 **fall, downfall,** collapse, smash, crash, **undoing,** debacle, derailing, derailment; **destruction,** perdition, total loss, dead loss
VERBS 2 **destroy,** deal *or* unleash destruction, bring to ruin, lay in ruins, play *or* raise hob with; **devastate,** desolate, waste, **lay waste,** ravage, havoc, wreak havoc, despoil, depredate
3 **bankrupt, break,** bust *and* wipe out <both nonformal>; put out of business, drive to the wall, scuttle, sink; impoverish
4 **seduce,** betray, deceive, mislead, lead astray, lead down the garden *or* the primrose path; **debauch,** ravish, ravage, despoil, deflower

**ruined** ADJS 1 **destroyed, wrecked,** blasted, undone; broke, bankrupt; spoiled

2 <nonformal> **shot, done for,** done in, finished, *ausgespielt* <Ger>, kaput; gone to pot, gone to the dogs, gone to hell in a handbasket, phut, belly up, blooey, kerflooey, dead in the water, washed up, all washed up, history, **dead meat, down the tube** *or* **tubes,** zapped, nuked, tapped out, wiped out

**ruins** NOUNS **wreck,** ruin, total loss; hulk, carcass, skeleton; mere wreck, wreck of one's former self; **remains,** vestige

**rule** NOUNS 1 **norm,** procedure, **common practice,** the way things are done, form, prescribed *or* set form; common *or* ordinary run of things, matter of course, par for the course <nonformal>
2 **law,** canon, maxim, dictum, moral, moralism; ordinance, imperative, **regulation,** *règlement* <Fr>; **principle,** principium, settled principle, general principle *or* truth, tenet, convention; **guideline,** ground rule, rubric, protocol, standard procedure

3 **government,** governance, discipline, regulation; **regime,** regimen; **sway,** sovereignty, reign, regnancy
VERBS 4 **command, lead,** possess authority, have the authority, have the say *or* the last word, have the whip hand *and* hold all the aces <both nonformal>; **take precedence,** precede; **come** *or* **rank first,** outrank, rank, rank out <nonformal>
5 **sway, reign,** bear reign, have the sway, wield the scepter, wear the crown, sit on the throne; rule over, overrule

**rulebook** NOUNS **rule, law,** principle, standard, criterion, canon, code, code of practice, maxim, prescription, guideline, the book <nonformal>

**rule out** VERBS **make impossible,** disenable, disqualify, close out, **bar,** prohibit, put out of reach, leave no chance

**ruler** NOUNS 1 **straightedge, rule;** square, T square, triangle
2 **potentate,** sovereign, monarch, prince, dynast, **crowned head,** emperor, *imperator* <L>, king; **chief,** chieftain, high chief

**ruling** NOUNS 1 **verdict,** decision, **determination,** finding, holding; **decree,** consideration, order, **pronouncement,** deliverance; dictum
ADJS 2 **prevalent,** prevailing, common, popular, **current,** running; regnant, reigning, **predominant,** predominating, **dominant**

**rumble** NOUNS 1 **reverberation,** resounding; rumbling, thunder, thundering, boom, booming, growl, growling, grumble, grumbling, reboation; **talk,** whisper, buzz, bruit, cry
2 **fight, fistfight,** punch-out *and* duke-out <both nonformal>, punch-up <Brit nonformal>; street fight
VERBS 3 **reverberate, resound,** sound, roll, boom, echo, reecho, rebound, bounce back, be reflected, be sent back, echo back, send back, return

**ruminate** VERBS **consider,** contemplate, speculate, reflect, study, ponder, perpend, **weigh,** deliberate, debate, meditate, muse, brood, chew the cud <nonformal>, digest

**rummage** VERBS **grope,** grope for, **feel for,** fumble, grabble, scrabble, feel around, poke around, pry around

**rumor** NOUNS **report,** flying rumor, unverified *or* unconfirmed report, **hearsay,** *on-dit* <Fr>, **scuttlebutt** *and* latrine rumor <both nonformal>; idea afloat, news stirring; **common talk,** town talk, **talk of the town,** topic of the day, *cause célèbre* <Fr>

**rumple** VERBS **disarrange,** derange, misarrange; **disorder,** disorganize, throw out of order, put out of gear, dislocate, upset the apple-cart, **disarray; dishevel,** ruffle

**rumpus** NOUNS **commotion, hubbub,** Babel, tumult, turmoil, **uproar,** racket, riot, **disturbance,** ruckus *and* ruction <both nonformal>, **fracas,** hassle

**run** NOUNS 1 **sprint; dash,** rush, plunge, headlong rush *or* plunge, **race,** scurry, scamper, scud, scuttle, **spurt,** burst, burst of speed
2 **journey,** trip, progress, course; **voyage,** ocean *or* sea trip, **cruise,** sail; **passage; crossing; flight,** trip, hop *and* jump <both nonformal>
3 **burrow,** tunnel, earth, couch, lodge
4 **stream,** brook, branch; kill, bourn, **creek,** crick <nonformal>; **rivulet,** rill
5 **freedom, license,** the run of <nonformal>
6 **series,** succession, **sequence,** consecution, progression, course, gradation
VERBS 7 **fester,** suppurate, matter, rankle, run, weep
8 **extend,** reach, stretch, sweep, spread, **go** *or* **go out,** cover, carry, **range,** lie; **reach** *or* stretch *or* thrust out
9 **flee,** fly, take flight, take wing, fugitate, **cut and run** <nonformal>, make a precipitate departure, **run off** *or* **away,** run away from, bug out <nonformal>, decamp, **take to one's heels,** make off, **depart**, do the disappearing act, make a quick exit
10 **flow,** stream, issue, pour, surge, course, rush, gush, flush, flood
11 **direct,** manage, regulate, conduct, carry on, handle
12 **run for office,** throw *or* toss one's hat in the ring <nonformal>, announce for, enter the lists *or* arena
13 **operate,** function, work, act, perform, go, be in action *or* operation *or* commission

**run amok** VERBS **go berserk,** go on a rampage, cut loose, run riot, run wild

**the runaround** NOUNS **avoidance,** shunning; **evasion,** elusion; side-stepping, evasive action, buck-passing *and* passing the buck <both nonformal>

**runaway** NOUNS 1 **fugitive,** fleer, person

on the run, runagate, **bolter,** skedaddler <nonformal>
ADJS 2 **fugitive,** in flight, on the lam <nonformal>, hot <nonformal>; disappearing

**run away** VERBS **run off,** run along, flee, take to flight, fly, take to one's heels, cut and run *and* hightail *and* make tracks *and* absquatulate <old> <all nonformal>

**run-down** ADJS 1 **unhealthy,** frail; weakened, with low resistance, reduced, reduced in health
2 **dilapidated,** ramshackle, decrepit, **tumbledown,** in disrepair, broken-down, in ruins, ruinous

**run into** VERBS 1 **collide,** come into collision, be on a collision course, **clash,** meet, encounter, confront each other, impinge; bump into, bang into, slam into, **crash into,** impact, smash into
2 **come across,** run across, meet with, meet up with <nonformal>, fall in with, **encounter,** bump into <nonformal>, come *or* run up against <nonformal>; **chance on** *or* **upon,** happen on *or* upon *or* across, **stumble on** *or* **upon**

**runner** NOUNS **messenger,** message-bearer, courier, diplomatic courier, carrier; **smuggler,** contrabandist; drug smuggler; gunrunner, rumrunner

**running start** NOUNS **advantage,** start, head *or* flying start; **edge,** bulge *and* jump *and* drop <all nonformal>

**runny** ADJS exudative, exuding, transudative; percolative; porous, permeable, pervious, oozy, weepy, leaky

**run-of-the-mill** ADJS **ordinary,** average, normal, **common,** commonplace, garden *and* garden-variety <both nonformal>, **unexceptional,** unremarkable, unnoteworthy, unspectacular, no great shakes <nonformal>, no prize package, no brain surgeon, no rocket scientist

**runt** NOUNS **shrimp** <nonformal>, diminutive, wisp, chit, slip, snip, snippet, **peanut** *and* **peewee** <both nonformal>

**run-through** NOUNS **summary,** résumé, recapitulation, recap <nonformal>, rundown

**runway** NOUNS **taxiway,** strip, landing strip, **airstrip,** flight strip, take-off strip; run

**rupture** NOUNS 1 **break,** breakage, **breach,** burst, **fracture; crack,** cleft, **fissure,** cut, split, slit; slash, slice; **gap, rift,** rent, rip, tear
VERBS 2 **breach,** break open, force *or* pry *or* prize open, crack *or* split open, rip *or* tear open; break into, break through; break in, burst in, bust in <nonformal>, stave *or* stove in, cave in

**rural** ADJS **pastoral,** arcadian, bucolic, rustic, country

**ruse** NOUNS **trick,** artifice, device, ploy, gambit, stratagem, **scheme,** design, *ficelle* <Fr>, **subterfuge,** blind, **wile,** dodge, artful dodge, sleight, pass, feint, fetch, chicanery, gimmick <nonformal>, **red herring,** tactic, **maneuver, stroke,** master stroke, **move,** coup

**rush** NOUNS 1 **thrill, sensation,** titillation; **tingle,** tingling; quiver, shiver, shudder, tremor, tremor of excitement, kick *and* charge <both nonformal>; flush, rush of emotion, surge of emotion
2 **torrent,** gush, spate, cascade, spurt, jet, rapids; precipitation, haste, hastiness, **overhastiness,** impulse, impulsivity, impulsiveness
VERBS 3 **make haste, hasten,** festinate, **hurry,** hurry up, run, post, **rush,** chase, tear, dash, spurt, leap, plunge, **scurry,** hurry-scurry, scamper, scramble, scuttle, hustle <nonformal>, bundle, bustle; do on the run *or* on the fly

**rust** NOUNS 1 **blight,** blast; canker, cancer; mold, fungus, mildew, smut, must
VERBS 2 **oxidize; corrode,** erode, eat, gnaw, eat into, eat away, nibble away, gnaw at the root of; canker

**rustic** ADJS **rural,** country, provincial, farm, pastoral, bucolic, Arcadian, **agrarian,** agrestic; **agricultural**

**rustle** NOUNS 1 rustling, froufrou

*a little noiseless noise among the leaves*
KEATS

VERBS 2 crinkle; **swish,** whish
3 **steal,** thieve, purloin, appropriate, take, snatch, palm, **make off with;** poach

**rustler** NOUNS cattle thief, abactor, **cattle rustler** <nonformal>

**rustle up** VERBS **cook,** prepare food, prepare, do, cook up, fry up, boil up; make up, whip up, run up, whomp up <nonformal>, slap up *or* together *and* throw *or* slap together <all nonformal>; **provide, supply,** find, dish up <nonformal>, **furnish**

**rusty** ADJS **corroded,** eroded, eaten; rust-eaten, rust-worn, rust-cankered; **out of**

**practice,** out of training *or* form, soft <nonformal>, out of shape *or* condition, stiff; **stale,** fusty, musty, dusty, moldy; gone to seed

**rut** NOUNS **furrow, groove,** ruck <nonformal>, wheeltrack, well-worn groove; **routine,** track, beaten path *or* track

**ruthless** ADJS **merciless,** unmerciful, without mercy, unruing, dog-eat-dog; **heartless,** hard, hard as nails, steely, flinty, harsh, savage, **cruel;** remorseless, unremorseful

# S

**sabotage** VERBS **disable,** disenable, unfit, **incapacitate,** put out of order, put out of commission <nonformal>, throw out of gear; bugger *and* bugger up *and* queer *and* queer the works *and* gum up *or* screw up <all nonformal>, throw a wrench *or* monkey wrench in the machinery <nonformal>, wreck

**saboteur** NOUNS **subversive;** fifth columnist, crypto

**sack** NOUNS 1 **plundering,** pillaging, looting, sacking, freebooting, ransacking, rifling, spoiling, **despoliation,** despoilment, despoiling; **pillage,** plunder
2 **bundle,** bindle <nonformal>, **pack,** package, **parcel,** fardel <nonformal>, bag, poke <nonformal>
VERBS 3 **plunder,** pillage, loot, ransack, rifle, freeboot, spoil, spoliate, despoil, depredate, prey on *or* upon, ravage, ravish, raven, sweep, gut; tackle; **fire** <nonformal>
4 **bundle,** bundle up, **package,** parcel, parcel up, **pack,** bag, truss, truss up; bale

**sack out** VERBS

<nonformal> **snooze,** get some shut-eye, get some sack time, flake out, crash, catch forty winks *or* some zs, pound the ear

**sacrament** NOUNS **rite, ritual,** rituality, **liturgy,** holy rite; order of worship; sacramental, mystery

**sacred** ADJS **holy,** numinous, **sacrosanct,** religious, spiritual, heavenly, divine; **venerable,** awesome, awful; inviolable, **inviolate,** untouchable; **ineffable,** unutterable, unspeakable, inexpressible, inenarrable

**sacred cow** NOUNS **idol; fetish,** totem, joss; **graven image,** golden calf; devil-god; little tin god, tin god

*the god of my idolatry*
SHAKESPEARE

**sacrifice** NOUNS 1 **oblation,** offering, immolation, incense; peace offering, sacramental offering, sin *or* piacular offering, whole offering; human sacrifice, self-sacrifice, self-immolation
VERBS 2 **martyr,** martyrize; immolate; make a sacrifice; **give away,** dispose of, part with; **propitiate,** make propitiation; appease; **offer sacrifice,** make sacrifice to, immolate before, offer up an oblation

**sacrilege** NOUNS **blasphemy,** blaspheming, impiety; **profanity,** profaneness; sacrilegiousness, blasphemousness; **desecration,** profanation; tainting, pollution, contamination

**sad** ADJS 1 **unhappy, uncheerful,** uncheery, **cheerless, joyless, unjoyful,** unsmiling; mirthless, unmirthful, humorless, infestive; funny as a crutch <nonformal> **grim; out of humor,** out of sorts, in bad humor *or* spirits; **sorry,** sorryish; discontented; **wretched, miserable;** pleasureless
2 saddened; sadhearted, **sad of heart;** heavyhearted, heavy; dejected, depressed, downhearted, down, in low spirits; oppressed, weighed upon, weighed *or* weighted down, bearing the woe of the world, burdened *or* laden with sorrow
3 **disgraceful,** shameful, pitiful, deplorable, opprobrious

**sadden** VERBS darken, cast a pall *or* gloom upon, weigh *or* weigh heavy upon; **deject,** depress, oppress, crush, press down, hit one like a ton of bricks <nonformal>, **cast down,** lower, lower the spirits, get one down <nonformal>, take the wind out of one's sails, **discourage,** dishearten, take the heart out of, **dispirit**

**saddle** NOUNS 1 **ridge,** hogback, hog's-back, saddleback, horseback; **helm,** driver's seat <nonformal>; seat, **chair,** bench
VERBS 2 **burden,** load, load down *or* up, lade, cumber, **encumber,** charge, freight, tax, handicap, hamper; **oppress,** weigh one down, weigh on *or* upon, weigh heavy on, bear *or* rest hard upon, lie hard *or* heavy upon

**saddle with** VERBS **obligate,** oblige, require, make incumbent *or* imperative, tie, **bind,** pledge, commit, put under an obligation; **encumber,** cumber, **burden,** weigh *or* weight down, press down; hang like a millstone round one's neck

**safe** NOUNS 1 **strongbox,** money chest, coffer, locker, chest; piggy bank; **vault,**

strong room; safe-deposit *or* safety-deposit box *or* vault
ADJS 2 **secure,** safe and sound; **protected**; on the safe side; unthreatened, unmolested; unhurt, unharmed, unscathed, intact, untouched, with a whole skin, undamaged

**safeguard** NOUNS 1 **guard; shield,** screen, aegis; umbrella, protective umbrella
VERBS 2 **protect,** guard, secure, keep, bless, make safe, **police, enforce the law;** keep from harm; **insure,** ensure, guarantee; **shelter,** shield, screen, cover, cloak

**safekeeping** NOUNS **protection,** guard, shielding; policing, law enforcement; **safeguarding,** security, **shelter,** cover, refuge; preservation

**safety** NOUNS safeness, **security,** assurance; risklessness, immunity, clear sailing; **protection,** safeguard

**safety valve** NOUNS **precaution,** precautiousness; **forethought,** foresight, foresightedness, forehandedness, forethoughtfulness; **safeguard,** protection, preventive measure, safety net

**sage** NOUNS 1 **wise man,** wise woman, sapient, man *or* woman of wisdom; great soul, mahatma, guru, rishi; **intellect,** person of intellect; mandarin, **intellectual**; savant, scholar
ADJS 2 **wise,** sapient, seasoned, **knowing;** learned; **profound,** deep; wise as an owl *or* a serpent, wise as Solomon

**sail** NOUNS 1 **canvas,** muslin, cloth, rag <nonformal>; **full** *or* **plain sail,** press *or* crowd of sail; **voyage,** ocean *or* sea trip, **cruise,** run, passage; crossing
VERBS 2 **navigate, cruise,** steam, run, **seafare,** voyage, ply, go on shipboard, go by ship, go on *or* take a voyage

*go down to the sea in ships*
BIBLE

3 **run smoothly,** work well, work like a machine, go like clockwork *or* a sewing machine; present no difficulties, give no trouble, be painless, be effortless; flow, roll, glide, slide, coast, sweep

**sailor** NOUNS **mariner,** seaman, **navigator,** seafarer, seafaring man, bluejacket, sea *or* water dog <nonformal>, crewman, shipman, jack-tar, **tar,** salt <nonformal>, windsailor, windjammer

**saint** NOUNS God-fearing man, pietist, religionist, theist; **disciple,** follower, servant, faithful servant

**sake** NOUNS **intention,** intent, mindset, **aim,** effect, meaning, view, study, animus, **point,** purpose, function, set *or* settled *or* fixed purpose

**salaam** NOUNS 1 **obeisance,** reverence, homage; **bow,** nod, bob, bend, inclination, inclination of the head, **curtsy,** kowtow, scrape, bowing and scraping, making a leg; **genuflection,** kneeling, bending the knee; prostration
VERBS 2 **bow,** bend, kneel, genuflect, bend the knee, **curtsy,** make a low bow, make a leg, make a reverence *or* an obeisance, bob, duck; **kowtow,** prostrate oneself

**salary** NOUNS **pay,** payment, remuneration, compensation, total compensation, wages plus fringe benefits, financial package, pay and allowances, financial remuneration; rate of pay; **wage,** wages, income, earnings, hire

**sale** NOUNS closing-out sale, going-out-of-business sale, inventory-clearance sale, distress sale, fire sale; bazaar; rummage sale, white elephant sale, garage sale, flea market; tax sale

**sales** NOUNS selling, market, **marketing,** merchandising, retail, retailing, wholesale, wholesaling

**salesmanship** NOUNS **promotion, advertising,** Madison Avenue, hucksterism <nonformal>; **selling,** sales talk, hard sell, high pressure, hawking, huckstering

**salesperson** NOUNS **salesman,** seller, salesclerk; **saleswoman,** saleslady, salesgirl; **clerk,** shop clerk, store clerk, shop assistant

**salient** NOUNS **conspicuous,** noticeable, notable, ostensible, **prominent,** bold, pronounced, in relief, in bold *or* high *or* strong relief, **striking,** outstanding, in the foreground, sticking *or* hanging out

**salivate** VERBS ptyalize; **slobber,** slabber, slaver, **drool,** drivel, dribble; **expectorate,** spit, spit up; spew

**sallow** ADJS **pale,** pallid, wan, fallow; **pasty,** mealy, waxen

**salt** NOUNS 1 **saltiness,** salinity, brininess; brackishness; **brine**
2 **mariner,** seaman, sailor, sailorman, navigator, seafarer, seafaring man, bluejacket, sea dog <nonformal>, jack-tar, **tar,** hearty, *matelot* <Fr>
3 **wit, humor,** pleasantry, *esprit* <Fr>; Attic wit *or* salt, Atticism

VERBS 4 **preserve,** cure, season, brine

**salt of the earth** NOUNS **the best,** the very best, the best ever, the tops <nonformal>; cream of the crop, *crème de la crème* <Fr>

**salute** NOUNS 1 **obeisance,** reverence, homage; salutation; **greeting**
VERBS 2 **do** *or* **pay homage to,** show *or* demonstrate respect for, pay respect to, pay tribute to; **eulogize,** panegyrize, pay tribute, hand it to one <nonformal>; make one's salutations

**salvage** NOUNS 1 **reclamation,** recovery, retrieval, salving; redemption, salvation
VERBS 2 **redeem,** reclaim, recover, retrieve; ransom; rescue; salve; recycle; win back, **recoup**

**salvageable** ADJS **remediable,** curable; **reparable,** repairable, mendable, fixable; restorable, recoverable, retrievable, reversible, reclaimable, recyclable, redeemable

**salvation** NOUNS **redemption,** redeemedness, conversion, regeneration, new life, reformation, adoption; spiritual purification *or* cleansing

**salve** NOUNS 1 **ointment,** balm, lotion, cream, unguent, unguentum, inunction, inunctum, unction, chrism
VERBS 2 **alleviate,** mitigate, palliate, soften, pad, cushion, assuage, allay, defuse, lay, appease, mollify, subdue, soothe; pour balm into, pour oil on

**salvo** NOUNS **volley,** burst, spray, **fusillade,** drumfire, **cannonade,** cannonry, **broadside,** enfilade

**Samaritan** NOUNS **benefactor,** benefactress, **benefiter,** succorer, befriender; ministrant, ministering angel; **good Samaritan; helper,** helping hand; good person

**same** ADJS **identical,** selfsame, one, **one and the same,** all the same, all one, of the same kidney; **indistinguishable,** without distinction, without difference, undifferent, undifferentiated; wall-to-wall, back-to-back

**sample** NOUNS 1 **specimen;** piece, taste, swatch; **cross section,** random, sampling
VERBS 2 **taste,** taste of, sample; **savor,** savor of; sip, roll on the tongue; assay
ADJS 3 **typical,** typic, typal; exemplary

**sanctify** VERBS **hallow; purify,** cleanse, wash one's sins away; **bless,** beatify; **glorify,** exalt, ensky; **consecrate,** dedicate, devote, set apart

**sanctimonious** ADJS sanctified, **pious,** pietistic, pietistical, self-righteous, pharisaic, pharisaical, **holier-than-thou; false,** insincere, hypocritical; canting, sniveling, unctuous

**sanction** VERBS **ratify, endorse,** sign off on, second, support, certify, confirm, validate, authenticate, accept, give one's imprimatur, permit, give permission, **authorize,** warrant, accredit

**sanctioned** ADJS **authorized,** empowered, entitled; **warranted,** licensed, privileged; chartered, patented; franchised, enfranchised; accredited, certificated

**sanctity** NOUNS sanctitude; **sacredness,** holiness, hallowedness, numinousness; sacrosanctness, sacrosanctity; heavenliness, transcendence, divinity, divineness; venerableness, **venerability,** blessedness

**sanctuary** NOUNS **holy of holies,** sanctum, sanctum sanctorum, adytum, sacrarium; **refuge,** safehold, **asylum,** haven, safe haven; game sanctuary, bird sanctuary, preserve, forest preserve, game preserve

**sanctum** NOUNS **sanctum sanctorum,** holy of holies, adytum; **den,** retreat, **hideaway,** cell, ivory tower, inner sanctum

**sand** NOUNS 1 grain of sand; sands of the sea; sand pile, sand dune, sand hill; sand reef, sandbar
VERBS 2 **buff,** burnish, polish, rub up, sandpaper, smooth, dress, shine, furbish, sandblast

**sandwich** NOUNS 1 *canapé* <Fr>, *smörgåsbord* <Swed>; club sandwich, dagwood; hamburger, burger; submarine *or* sub *or* hero *or* grinder *or* hoagy *or* poorboy
VERBS 2 **interpose,** interject, interpolate, intercalate, interjaculate; **intervene;** put between, **insert in,** stick in, introduce in, insinuate in, sandwich in, slip in

**sandy** ADJS **granular,** grainy, granulate, granulated; gritty, sabulous, arenarious, arenaceous

**sane** ADJS sane-minded, **rational,** reasonable, sensible, **lucid,** normal, wholesome, clearheaded, clearminded, balanced, **sound,** mentally sound, right in the head, **in one's right mind,** in possession of one's faculties *or* senses, together *and* all there <both nonformal>

**sanguine** ADJS 1 sanguineous, **blood-red,** blood-colored, bloody-red, bloody, gory, red as blood

2 **cheerful, cheery,** of good cheer, in good spirits; **hopeful,** hoping, full of hope, in good heart, of good hope, of good cheer; optimistic

**sanitary** ADJS **hygienic,** prophylactic; sterile, aseptic, antiseptic, **uninfected;** disinfected, decontaminated, sterilized

**sanity** NOUNS **saneness,** sanemindedness, soundness, **soundness of mind,** sound mind, healthy mind, right mind <nonformal>, senses, reason, **rationality,** reasonableness, lucidity, balance, wholesomeness

**sans** PREP absent, lacking; void of, empty of, free of, **without,** minus, less

**Santa Claus** NOUNS **Santa, Saint Nicholas, Saint Nick, Kriss Kringle, Father Christmas**

**sap** NOUNS

1 <nonformal> **chump, boob,** booby, prize sap, klutz, basket case, dingbat, ding-a-ling, **ninny,** nincompoop, mutt, jerk, goof, schlemiel, gonzo, dumbo, dweeb, nerd, twerp, yo-yo

VERBS 2 **weaken,** enfeeble, debilitate, unnerve, rattle, shake up <nonformal>, **devitalize, enervate,** sap the strength of, exhaust; **undermine,** mine, sap the foundations of, honeycomb

**sapling** NOUNS **sprout,** seedling, sucker, shoot, slip; **twig,** sprig, scion

**sarcasm** NOUNS **irony,** cynicism, satire, satiric wit *or* humor, invective, innuendo; causticity

**sardonic** ADJS **sarcastic,** ironic, ironical, cynical, Rabelaisian, dry; caustic

**sass** NOUNS 1 **sauce** *and* lip <nonformal>, **back talk,** backchat <nonformal>
VERBS 2 **sauce** <nonformal>, **talk back,** answer back, lip *and* give one the lip <both nonformal>, provoke

**sassy** ADJS **impudent,** impertinent, pert; **rude,** disrespectful, derisive, brash, bluff; **saucy,** smart-alecky <nonformal>, smart-ass *or* wise-ass <nonformal>

**Satan** NOUNS 1 **demon, fiend,** fiend from hell, **devil,** bad *or* evil *or* unclean spirit
2 Lucifer, Old Ned *or* Old Harry <nonformal>, the Angel of Darkness, the archenemy, the Devil, the Evil Spirit, the Tempter

**satanic** ADJS **diabolic,** diabolical, devilish, demonic, demoniac, demoniacal, Mephistophelian; **fiendish,** fiendlike

**sate** VERBS **gratify, satisfy,** satiate; slake, appease, allay, assuage, quench

**sated** ADJS **satiated,** satisfied, slaked, allayed; **surfeited, gorged,** replete, engorged, **glutted; cloyed,** jaded

**satellite** NOUNS 1 **hanger-on,** adherent, dangler, appendage, **dependent,** follower, cohort, retainer, tagtail
2 puppet regime *or* government; dependency *or* dependent state, client state, satellite state, puppet government, creature
3 **moon; artificial satellite**, unmanned satellite, sputnik; communications satellite, weather satellite, orbiting observatory, geophysical satellite, navigational satellite, geodetic satellite, research satellite

**satire** NOUNS **burlesque,** lampoon, squib, **parody,** farce, mockery, imitation, wicked imitation *or* pastiche, takeoff <nonformal>, **travesty,** caricature

**satirist** NOUNS **lampooner,** lampoonist, ironist, pasquinader

**satirize** VERBS **lampoon,** pasquinade; parody, send up <nonformal>; dip the pen in gall, **burlesque**

**satisfaction** NOUNS **gratification,** great satisfaction, hearty enjoyment, keen pleasure *or* satisfaction; **self-gratification,** self-indulgence; entire satisfaction, fulfillment; **redress,** making *or* setting right, amends, compensation, **recompense**

**satisfactory** ADJS 1 **satisfying;** pleasant, agreeable
2 **sufficient**, sufficing, **adequate,** enough, commensurate, proportionate, proportionable, ample, equal to, suitable, good enough

**satisfy** VERBS 1 **gratify,** sate, satiate; slake, appease, allay, assuage, quench; do one's heart good, warm the cockles of the heart; put *or* set at ease, set one's mind at ease *or* rest
2 **pay in full,** pay off, pay up <nonformal>, **discharge,** settle, square, **clear,** liquidate, amortize; **atone,** atone for, propitiate, expiate, compensate, restitute, recompense, redress, redeem

**satisfying** ADJS **gratifying,** rewarding, heartwarming, grateful; **welcome;** pleasant, pleasing, pleasureful, to one's liking, *en rapport* <Fr>

**saturate** VERBS **imbue,** imbrue, **infuse,** steep, decoct, brew; soak, drench, supersaturate, supercharge

**saucy** ADJS **impudent,** impertinent, pert,

sassy <nonformal>, cheeky <nonformal>

**saunter** VERBS walk, ramble, **stroll,** amble, jaunt, peregrinate

**sauté** VERBS **brown,** embrown, infuscate; fry, braise, sear, blacken, brown

**savage** NOUNS 1 **barbarian,** brute, beast, animal, tiger, shark, hyena; wild man; cannibal, man-eater, anthropophagite
ADJS 2 **fierce,** ferocious, vicious, murderous, cruel, **atrocious,** mindless, brutal, brutish, **bestial,** mindless, insensate, monstrous, inhuman, pitiless, ruthless, merciless, bloody, sanguinary; feral, **barbarous,** barbaric

**savanna** NOUNS **grassland,** prairie, steppe, steppeland, **pampas,** pampa, campo, llano, **veld,** grass veld

**savant** NOUNS scholar, connoisseur, maven <nonformal>; **intellect,** person of intellect; mandarin, intellectual; **learned man,** man of learning, giant of learning, colossus of knowledge, mastermind, pundit

**save** VERBS 1 **reserve,** conserve, keep, retain, husband, husband one's resources, keep *or* hold back, withhold; **keep in reserve,** keep in store, keep on hand, keep by one; preserve; **set** *or* **put aside,** put *or* lay *or* set by; save up, save to fall back upon, keep as a nest egg, **save for a rainy day,** provide for *or* against a rainy day
2 **rescue,** come to the rescue, **deliver,** be the saving of, **redeem,** ransom, salvage

**savings** NOUNS **reserve,** reserves, **nest egg,** sinking fund; proved reserves; life savings

**savior** NOUNS **redeemer,** deliverer, **liberator,** rescuer, freer, **emancipator,** manumitter

**savory** ADJS **delectable,** delicious, luscious; tasty, flavorsome; juicy, succulent

**savvy** NOUNS **smartness,** braininess, smarts <nonformal>, mental alertness, nous, **sharpness,** keenness, acuity, acuteness

**saw** NOUNS 1 **platitude,** cliché, old saw, commonplace, banality, bromide, **chestnut** <nonformal>, corn <nonformal>, tired phrase, trite saying, hackneyed *or* stereotyped saying, commonplace expression
VERBS 2 **sever, dissever,** cut off *or* away *or* loose, shear off, **cleave,** sunder

**say** NOUNS 1 **remark, statement,** earful *and* crack *and* one's two cents' worth <all nonformal>, **word,** saying, utterance, observation, reflection, expression
VERBS 2 **state,** declare, assert, aver, affirm, asseverate, allege; make a statement, send a message

**saying** NOUNS **maxim,** aphorism, apothegm, epigram, dictum, adage, proverb, gnome, words of wisdom, **saw,** witticism, expression, phrase

**scab** NOUNS 1 **crust,** incrustation, scale, eschar
2 **strikebreaker,** rat *and* fink *and* scissorbill <all nonformal>, **blackleg** <Brit>

**scald** VERBS **burn, scorch,** parch, **roast,** toast, cook, bake, fry, broil, boil, seethe

**scale** NOUNS 1 **extent, measure,** amount, ratio, proportion, stint, standard, height, pitch, reach, remove, compass, range, scope, caliber
2 **flake,** flock, floccule, flocculus; **scurf,** dandruff
3 **gamut,** register, compass, range, diapason; diatonic scale, chromatic scale
VERBS 4 **flake,** scale *or* flake off, desquamate, exfoliate
5 **climb,** climb up, upclimb, **mount,** clamber; escalade, scale the heights; climb over, surmount

**scalp** VERBS 1 **peel,** pare, skin, strip, flay, excoriate, decorticate, bark
2 **trade,** speculate, resell

**scam** NOUNS 1 **cheating,** cheating scheme, cheating method, angle, con *and* grift *and* move *and* racket *and* sting <all nonformal>; deception
VERBS 2 **trick,** dupe, gammon, **gull,** pigeon, play one for a fool *or* sucker, bamboozle *and* snow *and* hornswoggle *and* diddle <all nonformal>

**scamp** NOUNS **mischief-maker,** mischief, **rogue,** devil, knave, **rascal,** rapscallion, scapegrace, precious rascal

**scamper** VERBS **rush, tear,** dash, dart, shoot, hurtle, bolt, fling, **scurry,** scud, scuttle, scramble, **race,** careen

**scan** NOUNS 1 **study,** look-through, run-through
VERBS 2 **browse,** skim, dip into, thumb over *or* through, run over *or* through, glance *or* run the eye over *or* through, turn over the leaves, have a look at, hit the high spots

**scandal** NOUNS **dirt** <nonformal>, **malicious gossip;** character assassination, **slander**; whispering campaign; **disgrace,** humiliation

*gossip made tedious by morality*
Oscar Wilde

**scandalize** VERBS **incur disgrace,** make oneself notorious, put one's good name in jeopardy; compromise oneself; raise eyebrows, cause tongues to wag
**scant** ADJS **sparse,** scanty, exiguous, **infrequent,** scarce, scarce as hen's teeth <nonformal>, poor, piddling, thin, slim, **meager**
**scanty** ADJS **scarce,** sparse, in short supply, at a premium; not to be had for love or money, not to be had at any price
**scapegoat** NOUNS **goat** <nonformal>, fall guy *and* can-carrier *and* patsy *and* catch dog <all nonformal>, **whipping boy**
**scar** NOUNS 1 **mark,** cicatrix, scarification, cicatrization, keloid, cicatrix; flaw, defect, fault
VERBS 2 **mark,** score, scratch, gash, scotch, scarify, cicatrize, disfigure, deface, **flaw, mar**
**scarce** ADJS **sparse,** scanty; in short supply, at a premium; **rare,** uncommon; scarcer than hen's teeth <nonformal>; not to be had for love or money, not to be had at any price
**scarcity** NOUNS scarceness; **sparsity,** sparseness; **scantiness,** scant sufficiency; **dearth,** paucity, poverty; **rarity,** rareness, uncommonness
**scare** NOUNS 1 **fear,** fright, affright; **alarm,** consternation, dismay; dread, unholy dread; **panic,** panic fear *or* terror
VERBS 2 **frighten,** frighten *or* scare out of one's wits

3 <nonformal> spook, scare one stiff *or* shitless *or* spitless, scare the life out of, scare the pants off of, scare hell out of, scare the shit out of; scare one to death, scare the daylights *or* the living daylights *or* the wits out of

**scarecrow** NOUNS **figure,** woman *or* man of straw; gargoyle, monster, **monstrosity,** teratism
**scary** ADJS **frightening,** frightful; scaring, chilling; **alarming,** startling, disquieting, dismaying, disconcerting; **unnerving,** daunting
**scathing** ADJS **acrimonious,** acrid, acidulous, acid, **bitter,** tart, **caustic,** mordant *or* mordacious; **cutting,** biting, stinging, stabbing, **piercing,** penetrating, edged, double-edged
**scatter** VERBS **disperse,** diffract; **distribute,** broadcast, sow, disseminate, propagate; scatter to the winds; **disband,** separate, part, break up, split up; **part company,** dispel
**scatterbrain** NOUNS **rattlebrain,** rattlehead, rattlepate, **harebrain,** featherbrain, shallowbrain, **flibbertigibbet**
**scenario** NOUNS 1 **script,** screenplay, motion-picture play *or* script, treatment, original screenplay

2 <nonformal> scheme, design, program, plan, idea, strategy

**scene** NOUNS **view,** scape; landscape; waterscape, riverscape, seascape; exterior, interior; scenery
**scenery** NOUNS decor; **scene; drop,** drop scene, drop curtain, scrim, cloth; **backdrop**
**scent** NOUNS 1 **fragrance,** perfume, aroma, redolence, balminess, **incense, bouquet,** sweet smell, sweet savor; **odor**; spice, spiciness; muskiness; fruitiness
2 **track,** trail, path, course, *piste* <Fr>, line, wake; **spoor,** signs, traces
VERBS 3 catch the scent of, sniff, smell, get a whiff of <nonformal>, **get wind of;** sniff *or* scent *or* smell out, nose out; be on the right scent, have a fix on
**schedule** NOUNS 1 **program,** programma, **bill,** card, **calendar,** docket, slate; schedule *or* program of operation, **order of the day,** things to be done, **agenda,** list of agenda; laundry list *and* wish list <both nonformal>
VERBS 2 **line up** <nonformal>, **slate,** book, book in, bill, program, calendar, docket, budget, put on the agenda
**scheduled** ADJS **slated,** booked, billed, booked-in, to come
**scheme** NOUNS 1 **plan,** design, method, **program,** device, contrivance, game, envisagement, conception, enterprise, **idea,** notion; **intrigue,** web of intrigue, **plot,** deep-laid plot *or* scheme, trick, stratagem; **scheming,** schemery, plotting; finagling <nonformal>, **machination,** manipulation, **maneuvering,** engineering, rigging
VERBS 2 **plot,** intrigue, be up to something; **conspire,** connive, collude, cabal; **hatch,** cook up <nonformal>, brew,

concoct, hatch *or* lay a plot; **maneuver,** machinate, finesse, operate <nonformal>, engineer, rig, wangle <nonformal>, angle, finagle <nonformal>

**scholar** NOUNS 1 **student,** pupil, learner, studier, educatee, trainee, *élève* <Fr>
2 **learned person,** man of learning, giant of learning, colossus of knowledge, mastermind, **savant,** pundit; **mine of information,** walking encyclopedia; **academician,** schoolman; classicist, classicalist, Latinist, humanist

**scholarship** NOUNS **erudition,** eruditeness, **learnedness,** reading, letters; **intellectuality,** intellectualism; **culture,** literary culture, high culture, book learning, booklore; **bookishness,** bookiness, pedantry, pedantism, donnishness <Brit>; classicism, classical scholarship, humanism, humanistic scholarship; **fellowship**

**school** NOUNS 1 **educational institution,** teaching institution, academic *or* scholastic institution, teaching and research institution, **institute,** academy, seminary, *Schule* <Ger>, *école* <Fr>, *escuela* <Sp>; alternative school; magnet school
2 **system of belief; cult,** ism, ideology, *Weltanschauung* <Ger>, world view; political faith *or* belief *or* philosophy; **creed, credo,** credenda
VERBS 3 **teach, instruct,** give instruction, give lessons in, **educate; edify,** enlighten, civilize, illumine; **direct,** guide; **ground,** teach the rudiments *or* elements *or* basics; catechize

**schooled** ADJS **informed,** enlightened, instructed, versed, well-versed, educated, taught; **up on,** up-to-date, abreast of, *au courant* <Fr>

**science** NOUNS **art,** craft; skill; **study,** discipline; **field,** field of inquiry, concern, province, domain, area, arena, sphere, branch *or* field of study, branch *or* department of knowledge, specialty, academic specialty; natural science; applied science, pure science, experimental science; Big Science

**scientific** ADJS **exact, precise,** express; **strict,** close, severe, **rigorous,** rigid; scientifically exact; pragmatic, pragmatical, scientistic, positivistic

**scientist** NOUNS person of science; practical scientist, experimental scientist, theoretical scientist; scholar; authority, expert, researcher

**scintillating** ADJS 1 **glittering,** glimmering, shimmering, twinkling, blinking, glistening, glistering; **sparkling,** scintillant, scintillescent, coruscating, coruscant
2 **smart,** brainy <nonformal>, bright, brilliant; sharp-witted, keen-witted, needle-witted, **quick-witted,** quick-thinking, steel-trap, nimble-witted, quick on the trigger *or* uptake <nonformal>; smart as a whip, sharp as a tack <nonformal>

**scoff** VERBS **jeer,** gibe, **mock,** revile, rail at, rally, chaff, **twit,** taunt, jape, flout, scout, have a fling at, cast in one's teeth

**scold** NOUNS 1 **shrew,** vixen, virago, common scold; kvetch, **complainer**
VERBS 2 **reprove,** rebuke, reprimand, reprehend, put a flea in one's ear, **chide,** rate, **upbraid,** objurgate; **take to task,** call on the carpet, read the riot act, give one a tongue-lashing, tonguelash

**scoop** NOUNS 1 **cavity,** concavity, concave; **hollow,** hollow shell, shell; depression, dip, pocket; scoopful
2 **information,** info <nonformal>, facts, data, knowledge; **intelligence;** the dope *and* the goods *and* the scoop <all nonformal>; **news item,** article, story, piece; beat <nonformal>, exclusive; **the facts,** the information, the particulars
VERBS 3 **ladle,** dip; bail, bucket; **excavate,** dig, dig out, scoop out

**scope** NOUNS **range,** compass, reach, stretch, expanse radius, sweep, carry, fetch; **spectrum**

**scorch** VERBS **burn,** parch, scald, torrefy, sear, singe; **darken,** blacken; **cauterize,** brand, burn in

**score** NOUNS 1 **notch, nick,** cut, cleft, **gash,** hack, blaze, scotch, kerf, crena, depression; **furrow, groove,** scratch, crack, cranny, chase, chink, striation, stria, gouge
2 reckoning, **tally, aggregate, amount,** quantity; box score <nonformal>
3 musical score *or* copy, **music,** notation, musical notation, written music, transcript, transcription, arrangement
VERBS 4 **notch,** nick, cut, incise, gash, slash, chop, crimp, scotch, blaze, jag, scarify; **furrow,** groove, scratch, incise, cut, striate, streak, gouge
5 **score a success,** be successful, notch one up <nonformal>, hit it, hit the mark, ring the bell <nonformal>, turn up trumps, hit the jackpot <nonformal>

6 **calculate,** compute, estimate, reckon, figure, reckon at, put at, cipher, cast, tally

**scorn** NOUNS 1 **contempt, disdain,** contemptuousness, disdainfulness, superciliousness, snottiness, sniffiness, scornfulness, contumely
VERBS 2 **disdain, despise,** hold in contempt, contemn, vilipend, disprize, misprize, rate *or* rank low, be contemptuous of, feel contempt for, **hold in contempt,** hold cheap, look down upon, think little *or* nothing of, hold beneath one *or* beneath contempt, look with scorn upon, view with a scornful eye, give one the fish-eye *or* the beady eye <nonformal>

**scot-free** ADJS free as the wind, free as a bird, at large, **free**

**scoundrel** NOUNS **rascal,** precious rascal, rogue, knave, villain, blackguard, **scamp,** scalawag <nonformal>, spalpeen <Ir>, rapscallion

**scour** VERBS **scrub; grope,** grope for, **feel for,** fumble, grabble, scrabble, feel around, poke around, grope in the dark; sweep, scour the country

**scourge** NOUNS **epidemic,** plague, pestilence, pest, pandemic, pandemia; **bane,** curse, affliction, infliction, visitation, calamity, **torment,** burden, crushing burden

**scout** NOUNS 1 **vanguard,** point, point man; **spearhead,** advance guard, outguard; pathfinder, explorer, trailblazer *or* trailbreaker, guide
VERBS 2 **reconnoiter,** get the lay of the land

**scowl** NOUNS 1 **frown,** lower, **glower, pout,** moue, mow, grimace, wry face; sullen looks, black looks, **long face**
VERBS 2 **frown,** knit the brow, lower, **glower, pout,** make a moue *or* mow, grimace, make a wry face, make a lip

**scrabble** VERBS 1 **creep, crawl,** scramble, grovel, **go on hands and knees,** go on all fours
2 **excavate, dig,** dig out, **scoop,** scoop out, **gouge,** gouge out, grub, shovel, spade, dike, delve, scrape, scratch; **scribble,** scratch, scrawl

**scram** INTERJ 1 go away!, begone!, get you gone!, go along!, get along!, **run along!, get along with you!,** away!, away with you!, **off with you!,** off you go!, on your way!, go about your business!, be off!, **get out of here!,** get out!, clear out!, leave!, *allez!* <Fr>, *allez-vous-en!* <Fr>, *va-t'-en!* <Fr>, *raus mit dir!* <Ger>, *heraus!* <Ger>, *¡váyase!* <Sp>, *via! or va' via!* <Ital>, shoo!, scat!, git! <nonformal>

*stand not on the order of your going,*
*but go at once*
**SHAKESPEARE**

*go and hang yourself*
**PLAUTUS**

2 <nonformal> **beat it!,** buzz off!, bug off!, shoo!, skiddoo!, skedaddle!, vamoose!, cheese it!, make yourself scarce!, **get lost!,** take a walk!, take a hike!, go chase yourself!, go play in the traffic!, get the hell out!, push off!, shove off!, take a powder!, blow!

**scramble** NOUNS 1 **haste,** hurry, scurry, rush, race, dash, drive, scuttle, scamper, hustle <nonformal>, **bustle,** flutter, **flurry,** hurry-scurry, helter-skelter; no time to be lost
2 **jumble,** tumble, snarl-up, mess, bloody *or* holy *or* unholy *or* god-awful mess <nonformal>, **turmoil,** welter, mishmash, hash, helter-skelter, farrago, crazy-quilt, higgledy-piggledy
VERBS 3 **hustle** <nonformal>, **drive,** drive oneself, push, go all out <nonformal>, **make things hum,** step lively <nonformal>, make the sparks *or* chips fly <nonformal>
4 **make unintelligible,** jumble, garble; mix up, hash, stir up, conglomerate, shuffle, **jumble,** jumble up, mingle-mangle

**scrap** NOUNS 1 tatter, smithereen <nonformal>, patch, **stitch, shred,** tag; snip, **snippet,** snick, chip, nip; **morsel,** *morceau* <Fr>, crumb
2 fight; **row, rumpus,** ruckus, ruction, brannigan, set-to, run-in, **hassle,** rhubarb <all nonformal>
VERBS 3 **junk** <nonformal>, consign to the scrap heap, throw on the junk heap <nonformal>, discard, throw away, chuck, **get rid of,** dispense of, dump
4 **row, hassle,** make *or* kick up a row; mix it up, lock horns, bump heads <all nonformal>

**scrape** NOUNS 1 **rasp, scratch,** grind; burr, chirr, buzz; fix *and* jam *and* pickle *and* stew <all nonformal>; perturbation,

disturbance, upset, bother, pother
VERBS 2 **grate,** rasp, scratch, grind; **brush,** sweep, graze, brush by, glance, skim
3 **bow,** make obeisance, kowtow, **bow and scrape;** fall down before, fall at the feet of, prostrate oneself, kiss the hem of one's garment
4 **scrimp,** skimp <nonformal>, scrape and save; live frugally, get along on a shoestring, get by on little, eke out

**scrappy** ADJS **contentious,** quarrelsome; **argumentative,** argumental; on the warpath, looking for trouble

**scraps** NOUNS **leavings,** leftovers; refuse, odds and ends, rags, **rubbish,** waste

**scratch** NOUNS 1 **rasp,** scrape, grind; **furrow,** groove, crack, cranny, chase, chink, score, **cut,** gash, striation, streak, stria, **gouge,** slit, incision; sulcus, sulcation; **abrasion,** scuff
VERBS 2 **grate,** rasp, scrape, grind; **furrow,** groove, score, incise, cut, carve, chisel, gash, striate, streak, gouge, claw

**scrawl** NOUNS 1 **scribble,** scrabble, scratch, *barbouillage* <Fr>; *pattes de mouche* <Fr>, hen tracks *and* hen scratches <both nonformal>
VERBS 2 **scribble,** scrabble, scratch, make hen tracks *or* hen *or* chicken scratches <nonformal>

**scrawny** ADJS **skinny** <nonformal>, **gaunt,** lank, lanky; mere skin and bones, all skin and bones, nothing but skin and bones; twiggy

**scream** NOUNS 1 **screech,** shriek, squeal, shrill, keen, squeak, squawk, skirl; waul, caterwaul
VERBS 2 **screech,** shriek, squeal, shrill, keen; waul, caterwaul

**screen** NOUNS 1 **veil,** curtain, cover; fig leaf; **wraps** <nonformal>; disguise; **pretext,** smoke screen, stalking-horse, **blind;** guise, semblance; **shade,** light shield
VERBS 2 **cover,** cover up; **veil,** shield, screen off, mask, cloud, obscure, fog, befog, fuzz; block, eclipse, occult; **conceal,** hide, ensconce
3 **sort,** sort out, classify, select; **separate,** divide; **sift,** size, sieve, bolt, riddle

**screw up** VERBS 1 **bungle,** blunder; spoil, ruin, play havoc with

2 <nonformal> foul up, fuck up, bitch up, **blow,** louse up, queer, snafu, snarl up, balls up <Brit>, bugger, bugger up, gum up, ball up, bollix, bollix up, **mess up,** hash up, muck up; play hob with, play hell with, play merry hell with, play the devil with, rain on one's picnic *or* parade; upset the apple cart, cook, sink, shoot down in flames; **total**

**scribble** NOUNS 1 illegibility, unreadability; undecipherability, indecipherability; scrawl, **hen track** <nonformal>; scrabble, **scrawl,** scratch, *barbouillage* <Fr>; *pattes de mouche* <Fr>, hen tracks *and* hen scratches <both nonformal>
VERBS 2 scrabble, **scratch,** scrawl, make hen tracks *or* hen *or* chicken scratches <nonformal>, doodle

**scribbler** NOUNS **writer,** penman, pen, penner; pen *or* pencil driver *or* pusher <nonformal>, word-slinger, **inkslinger** *and* ink spiller *and* inkstained wretch <all nonformal>, knight of the plume *or* pen *or* quill <nonformal>; **hack writer,** hack, literary hack, potboiler <nonformal>

**scrimmage** NOUNS **free-for-all,** knock-down-and-drag-out <nonformal>, **brawl,** broil, melee, **fracas**

**scrimp** VERBS **stint,** skimp, scamp, scant, screw, **pinch,** starve, famish; **pinch pennies,** rub the print off a dollar bill, rub the picture off a nickel; live upon nothing; grudge, begrudge

**script** NOUNS 1 **handwriting,** hand, chirography, **calligraphy,** autography; **manuscript,** autograph, holograph; **penmanship,** stylography
2 **screenplay,** motion-picture play *or* script, shooting script

**scripture** NOUNS **scriptures,** sacred writings *or* texts, bible; canonical writings *or* books, sacred canon

**Scripture** NOUNS **Bible,** Holy Bible, the Scriptures, Holy Scripture, Holy Writ, the Book, the Good Book, the Book of Books, the Word, the Word of God

**scroll** NOUNS 1 **coil,** whorl, roll, **curl,** curlicue, ringlet, pigtail, **spiral,** helix, volute, volution, involute, evolute, gyre
2 **document,** official document, legal document, legal paper, legal instrument, **instrument,** writ, **paper,** parchment

**scrooge** NOUNS **niggard,** tightwad *and* cheapskate <both nonformal>, **miser,** hard man with a buck <nonformal>, **skinflint,** penny pincher, pinchfist, curmudgeon <old>

**scrounge** VERBS 1 beg, **cadge**

2 <nonformal>mooch, bum, panhandle; hit, hit up, touch, put the touch on, make a touch

**scrub** NOUNS 1 **brush,** bush, **brushwood,** shrubwood, scrubwood
VERBS 2 **wash, clean,** bathe, scrub up *or* out, **swab,** mop, mop up; **scour**
3 **discontinue,** terminate, abort, cancel, scratch <nonformal>, hold, **quit,** stay, belay <nonformal>

**scruffy** ADJS **dirty,** grimy, grubby, grungy <nonformal>, smirchy, dingy, messy <nonformal>; slovenly, untidy, **shabby,** scrubby, shoddy, scurvy, scuzzy <nonformal>, scummy, **crummy** *and* cheesy <both nonformal>

**scrumptious** ADJS **tasty,** finger-lickin' good <nonformal>, **savory,** palatable, toothsome, **luscious;** for the gods, ambrosial, nectarous, nectareous; fit for a king, yummy <nonformal>

**scruple** NOUNS 1 **compunction, qualm,** qualms, qualmishness, scruples, scrupulosity, scrupulousness, pang, pangs, **pangs of conscience,** throes, sting *or* pricking *or* twinge *or* twitch of conscience
2 **modicum,** whit, ace, hair, groat, farthing, pittance, trifling amount, **smidgen** *and* skosh *and* smitch <all nonformal>, pinch

**scrupulous** ADJS **punctilious, precise,** precisian, precisionist, precious, puristic; by-the-book; exact, meticulous; **orderly,** methodical; **conscientious,** careful

**scrutinize** VERBS **survey, eye,** contemplate, look over, give the eye *or* the once-over <nonformal>; **ogle,** ogle at, **leer,** leer at, give one the glad eye; examine, vet, inspect; **pore,** take a close *or* careful look; take a long, hard look; size up <nonformal>

**scrutiny** NOUNS overview, **survey,** contemplation; **examination,** inspection, the once-over <nonformal>, visual examination, a vetting

**scuffle** NOUNS **struggle,** fight, tussle, wrestle, hassle <nonformal>

**sculptor** NOUNS sculptress, sculpturer; figurer, *figuriste* <Fr>, **modeler,** molder, wax modeler, clay modeler

**sculpture** NOUNS 1 **figure,** bust, statue, statuette, statuary; portrait bust *or* statue; glyph; marble, bronze, terra cotta; mobile, stabile
VERBS 2 sculp *or* sculpt <nonformal>, insculpture <old>

**scum** NOUNS 1 **slime,** slop, sludge, slush; glop *and* gunk <both nonformal>, **muck,** mire, ooze; **offal,** slough, offscourings, scurf, riffraff, scum of the earth; off-scum, foam, froth; **film,** skin, scale

**scuttle** VERBS 1 **rush, tear,** dash, dart, shoot, hurtle, bolt, fling, **scamper, scurry,** scour, scud, scramble, **race,** careen
2 **sink,** send to the bottom, send to Davy Jones's locker; **founder, go down,** go to the bottom, sink like lead, go down like a stone; cook one's goose *and* cut one down to size *and* cut one off at the knees *and* pull the plug on *and* pull the rug out from under <all nonformal>

**scuttlebutt** NOUNS **report, rumor,** flying rumor, unverified *or* unconfirmed report, **hearsay,** *on-dit* <Fr>, latrine rumor <nonformal>

**sea** NOUNS **ocean,** great *or* main sea, *thalassa* <Gk>, **main** *or* ocean main, the bounding main, tide, salt sea, salt water, blue water, deep water, open sea, **the brine,** the briny *and* the big pond <both nonformal>, the briny deep

**seam** NOUNS 1 **joint,** join, joining, suture, closure; boundary, interface
2 **deposit,** mineral deposit, pay dirt; **vein,** lode

**seamless** ADJS **unvaried,** unruffled, undiversified, undifferentiated, unchanged; **unbroken,** serried, **uniform**, undifferentiated, wall-to-wall *and* back-to-back <both nonformal>, jointless, gapless, smooth

**seamstress** NOUNS **sewer,** needleworker, sempstress, needlewoman; dressmaker, modiste

**sear** VERBS **shrink,** shrivel, wither, parch, dry up; scorch, singe; **burn**

**search** NOUNS 1 searching, **quest, hunt,** hunting, stalk, stalking, still hunt, dragnet, posse, search party
VERBS 2 **seek, hunt,** look for high and low, look high and low, search out, **search for,** seek for, **hunt for,** cast *or* beat about for

**season** NOUNS 1 time of year, season of the year, **period,** annual period

*the measure of the year*
KEATS

VERBS 2 **flavor,** savor; mellow, temper, come of age, come into its own, mature, ripen, evolve
3 stiffen, work-harden, **temper,** strengthen

**seasonable** ADJS **timely,** well-timed, opportune, convenient, in the nick of time

**seasonal** ADJS in *or* out of season, off-season; early-season, mid-season, late-season; **periodic,** cyclic *or* cyclical, serial

**seasoned** ADJS **ripe,** mature, matured, maturated; **experienced,** practiced, tried, well-tried, tried and true, **veteran,** an old dog at <nonformal>; **toughened,** hardened, tempered, annealed

**seasoning** NOUNS **flavoring,** flavor, flavorer; seasoner, **relish,** condiment, spice, condiments

**seat** VERBS **place,** put, set, lay, pose, posit, site, stick <nonformal>, **station,** post; park, plump down <nonformal>

**secede** VERBS **defect, bolt,** break away; pull out <nonformal>, withdraw one's support; turn one's back on; apostatize

**secluded** ADJS **seclusive,** retired, withdrawn; isolated, shut off, insular, **separate,** separated, **apart,** detached, removed; **remote,** out-of-the-way, outback *and* back of beyond <both Austral>; **unfrequented,** unvisited, off the beaten track; untraveled

**seclusion** NOUNS reclusion, **retirement,** withdrawal, retreat, recess; **sequestration,** separation, detachment, apartness; **isolation**

> *splendid isolation*
> SIR WILLIAM GOSCHEN

**second** NOUNS 1 **instant,** moment, split second, millisecond, microsecond, nanosecond, half a second, **trice,** twinkle, twinkling *or* twinkle of an eye
VERBS 2 **ratify,** endorse, sign off on, support, **certify,** confirm, validate, authenticate, accept, give the nod *or* the green light *or* the go-ahead *or* the OK <all nonformal>, give a nod of assent, give one's imprimatur; take the part of, take up *or* adopt *or* espouse the cause of, **go to bat for** <nonformal>, side with, align oneself with

**secondary** ADJS **unessential,** subsidiary, subordinate; **incidental,** circumstantial, contingent; collateral, indirect

**secondhand** ADJS **used,** worn, previously owned, **unnew,** not new, pawed-over; hand-me-down *and* reach-me-down <both nonformal>

**second thoughts** NOUNS **irresolution,** change of mind, tergiversation, better thoughts, afterthoughts, mature judgment; **afterthought,** *arrière-pensée* <Fr>

**secrecy** NOUNS secretness, airtight secrecy, close secrecy; crypticness; **secretiveness,** closeness

**secret** NOUNS 1 **confidence;** private *or* personal matter, trade secret; confidential *or* privileged information *or* communication; deep *or* profound secret, sealed book, mystery of mysteries; skeleton in the closet *or* cupboard
ADJS 2 close, closed, closet; cryptic, dark; unuttered, unrevealed, undivulged, undisclosed, unspoken, untold; **unrevealable,** undivulgable, undisclosable, untellable, unwhisperable, unbreatheable, unutterable; arcane, esoteric, occult, cabalistic, hermetic; enigmatic, mysterious; *in petto* <L>

**secretary** NOUNS 1 amanuensis; **minister,** secretary of state, undersecretary, cabinet minister, cabinet member
2 *secrétaire* <Fr>, escritoire, **desk,** writing table

**secrete** VERBS 1 produce, give out; excrete; water; lactate; weep, tear
2 **hide away,** keep hidden, put away, store away, stow away, file and forget, bottle up, lock up, seal up, put out of sight; keep secret; **cache,** stash <nonformal>, deposit, plant <nonformal>; **bury;** squirrel away

**sect** NOUNS **faction,** division, wing, **caucus,** splinter, splinter group, breakaway group, offshoot; **school,** class, order; **denomination,** communion, confession, faith, church

**sectarian** ADJS **factional,** sectary, denominational, schismatic, schismatical

**secular** ADJS **unsacred,** nonsacred, **unholy,** unhallowed, unsanctified, unblessed; profane, **temporal, worldly,** fleshly, mundane, temporal; **unspiritual,** secularist; secularistic

**secure** VERBS 1 **guarantee,** guaranty, warrant, assure, insure, ensure, bond, **certify; sponsor,** be sponsor for, sign for, sign one's note, **back,** stand behind *or* back of, stand up for
2 make sure *or* secure, tie, tie off *or* up, chain, tether; make fast, fasten, fasten down; **anchor,** moor; batten *and* batten

down; **protect,** guard, safeguard, keep, make safe

*build one's house upon a rock*
BIBLE

ADJS 3 **fast,** fastened, fixed, firm, close, tight, set; **safe,** safe and sound; **protected;** on the safe side; unthreatened, unmolested; unhurt, unharmed, unscathed, intact, untouched, with a whole skin, undamaged

**security** NOUNS **surety,** indemnity, **guaranty,** guarantee, warranty, insurance, warrant, assurance; **stability,** firmness, soundness, substantiality, solidity; **safety,** safeness

**sedate** VERBS 1 narcotize, drug, dope <nonformal>; anesthetize, put under; tranquilize, deaden, dull, blunt, obtund, take the edge off, take the sting *or* bite out
ADJS 2 **staid,** sober, sober-minded, **serious,** grave, solemn, sobersided

**sedative** NOUNS 1 **sedative hypnotic,** depressant; sleeping pill *or* tablet *or* potion; **calmative,** tranquilizer
ADJS 2 **calmative,** calmant, depressant, **soothing,** tranquilizing, quietening; narcotic, opiatic; hypnotic, soporific, somniferous, somnifacient, sleep-inducing

**sedentary** ADJS **inert,** inactive, static, dormant, passive; **quiescent,** motionless

**sediment** NOUNS **deposit;** detritus, debris; settlings, deposits, deposition

**seduce** VERBS **betray,** deceive, mislead, lead astray, lead down the garden *or* the primrose path; **debauch,** ravish, ravage, despoil, ruin; deflower, pop one's cherry <nonformal>; **defile,** soil, sully; **violate,** abuse

**seductive** ADJS **attractive,** taking, winning, sexy <nonformal>, **provocative,** tantalizing, exciting; appetizing, tempting, toothsome, mouth-watering; seducing, **beguiling,** enticing, inviting, come-hither <nonformal>

**see** VERBS **behold,** observe, view, witness, perceive, discern, spy, espy, **sight,** have in sight, make out, pick out, descry, spot <nonformal>, discover, notice, take notice of, have one's eye on, distinguish, recognize, **catch sight of,** get a load of <nonformal>, take in, get an eyeful of <nonformal>, look on *or* upon, cast the eyes on *or* upon, **set** *or* **lay eyes on; glimpse,** get *or* catch a glimpse of; see at a glance, see with half an eye; see with one's own eyes

**seed** NOUNS 1 **sperm,** spermatozoa, semen, milt
2 **stone,** pit, nut; pip; fruit; **grain,** kernel, berry; flaxseed, linseed; bird seed
VERBS 3 **plant,** set, put in; **sow,** seed down, seminate, inseminate; **disseminate,** broadcast, sow broadcast, scatter seed; drill

**seedy** ADJS **shabby,** shoddy, scruffy, **tacky** <nonformal>, dowdy, tatty, ratty; **ragged,** tattered, torn; **frayed,** frazzled; **out at the elbows**

**seek** VERBS **quest,** quest after, seek out, look for, hunt, search, dig up, dig around for, nose out, nose around for

**seem** VERBS appear to be, seem to be, **appear, look,** feel, sound, look to be, appear to one's eyes, have *or* present the appearance of, give the feeling of, strike one as, come on as <nonformal>; have every appearance of, have all the earmarks of, have all the features of, show signs of, have every sign *or* indication of

**seemly** ADJS **appropriate,** fit, fitting, **proper,** correct, comely; **felicitous,** happy, **apt,** well-chosen; well-put, well-expressed, inspired

**seep** VERBS ooze, percolate; exude; sweat; secrete

**seesaw** VERBS **fluctuate,** vary; alternate, vacillate, oscillate, pendulate, blow hot and cold <nonformal>; go through phases, waver, shuffle, swing, sway, wobble, wobble about, flounder, stagger, teeter, totter, **teeter-totter**

**seethe** VERBS **boil, fume,** foam, simmer, stew, ferment, stir, churn; **mill,** mill around *or* about, stir, roil, moil, be turbulent

**see to** VERBS **attend to,** look to, advert to, be aware of; **pay attention to,** pay regard to, give mind to, pay mind to <nonformal>, not forget, spare a thought for, **give heed to;** occupy oneself with, concern oneself with, give oneself up to, be absorbed *or* engrossed in, be into <nonformal>; **care for,** take care of, **look after,** see after

**segment** NOUNS **portion,** share, interest, part, stake, stock, **piece,** bit

**segregate** VERBS **separate,** separate out *or* off, differentiate, demark, divide, cordon, cordon off; **isolate,** insulate, seclude; **set apart,** keep apart

**seize** VERBS take *or* get hold of, **lay hold of,** catch *or* grab hold of, glom *or* latch on to <nonformal>, **get** *or* **lay hands on,** clap hands on <nonformal>, put one's hands on, get into one's grasp *or* clutches; get one's fingers *or* hands on; **kidnap,** abduct, snatch <nonformal>

**seizure** NOUNS **attack,** access, visitation; arrest; **stroke,** ictus, apoplexy; **spasm,** throes, fit, paroxysm, convulsion, eclampsia, frenzy; **usurpation,** arrogation, assumption, taking over

**seldom** ADVS **infrequently,** unfrequently, rarely, uncommonly, scarcely, hardly, **scarcely** *or* **hardly ever,** not often, only now and then, at infrequent intervals

**select** NOUNS 1 **choice,** pick, elect, elite, *corps d'élite* <Fr>, chosen; **cream,** flower, cream of the crop, *crème de la crème* <Fr>, salt of the earth; *pièce de résistance* <Fr>; nonesuch, paragon, nonpareil
VERBS 2 make a selection; **pick,** handpick, **pick out, single out,** choose out, smile on, give the nod <nonformal>, jump at, seize on; **decide between,** choose up sides <nonformal>, cull, glean, winnow, sift
ADJS 3 **exclusive,** selective, elect, elite; **choice,** picked, handpicked; **prize,** champion

**selection** NOUNS 1 **choice,** election, preference, decision, **pick,** choosing, free choice; **specification,** naming, nomination, pointing, fingering <nonformal>, picking out
2 **excerpt, extract,** extraction, excerption, snippet; passage, selected passage

**self** NOUNS **ego; oneself,** I, me, myself, my humble self, number one <nonformal>, yours truly <nonformal>; the self

**self-confidence** NOUNS **pride,** proudness, pridefulness; **self-esteem,** self-respect, self-reliance, face, independence, self-sufficiency

**self-control** NOUNS **self-command,** self-possession, self-mastery, self-government, self-domination, **self-restraint,** self-conquest, self-discipline, **self-denial;** composure, possession, aplomb

**self-esteem** NOUNS **pride,** proudness, pridefulness; **self-respect,** self-confidence, self-reliance, face, independence, self-sufficiency; pardonable pride

**selfish** ADJS **self-seeking,** self-serving, self-advancing, self-promoting, self-advertising, ambitious for self, **self-indulgent,** self-pleasing, hedonistic, self-jealous, self-sufficient, **self-interested,** self-absorbed, wrapped up in oneself; possessive; **avaricious,** greedy, grasping, graspy *and* grabby <both nonformal>, acquisitive

**self-reliance** NOUNS **independence,** self-direction, autarky, autarchy, self-containment, self-sufficiency; self-dependence; inner-direction

**self-respect** NOUNS **self-esteem,** self-reliance, self-consequence, face, independence, self-sufficiency; pardonable pride; positive self-image

**self-righteous** ADJS **sanctimonious,** sanctified, pious, pietistic, pietistical, pharisaic, pharisaical, holier-than-thou

**self-sufficient** ADJS self-confident, self-reliant, **independent;** self-complacent, **smug,** complacent, self-contained

**sell** VERBS 1 **merchandise, market,** move, turn over, sell off, make *or* effect a sale; convert into cash, turn into money; **retail,** sell retail, sell over the counter; **wholesale,** sell wholesale, job, be jobber *or* wholesaler for; sell like hotcakes
2 **convince; win over,** lead one to believe, bring over, bring round, talk over, talk around, bring to reason, bring to one's senses, **persuade,** lead to believe, give to understand; sell one on <nonformal>

**sell out** VERBS **betray,** double-cross *and* two-time <both nonformal>, sell down the river <nonformal>, turn in; inform on

**seminar** NOUNS **discussion, panel,** panel discussion, open discussion, joint discussion, symposium, colloquium, conference; proseminar

**send** VERBS send off *or* away, send forth; **dispatch,** remit, consign, forward; **mail,** post, dispatch; **transmit,** radiate, beam

**send for** VERBS **summon, call,** demand, preconize; call for, send after, bid come; **cite,** subpoena, summon forth, call out

**send-off** NOUNS **leave-taking,** leave, parting, departure, congé; Godspeed; **adieu,** one's adieus, **farewell,** aloha, **good-bye;** valedictory address, valedictory, valediction, parting words; parting *or* Parthian shot; swan song; viaticum

**senile** ADJS decrepit, doddering, doddery; **childish,** childlike, in one's second childhood, **doting**

**senior** NOUNS 1 **superior,** higher-up

<nonformal>, principal, big shot <nonformal>; Sr, *senex* <L>, **elder,** dean, *doyen* <Fr>, *doyenne* <Fr>
ADJS 2 ranking, older, elder, dean; **oldest,** eldest

**senior citizen** NOUNS **old man,** old woman, elder, oldster <nonformal>; golden-ager, geriatric; old chap, old party, old codger <nonformal>, geezer *and* old geezer <both nonformal>, old duffer <nonformal>, old-timer <nonformal>, dotard, veteran

**seniority** NOUNS **eldership,** deanship, primogeniture; eminence, **stature,** rank, preeminence, priority, precedence

**sensation** NOUNS **sense, feeling;** sense impression, sense-datum *or* -data, percept, perception, sense perception; experience, sensory experience; **thrill,** titillation; astonishment, amazement, wonderful thing, nine days' wonder, amazing *or* astonishing thing, quite a thing, really something

**sensational** ADJS **lurid,** yellow, **melodramatic,** Barnumesque; spine-chilling, eye-popping <nonformal>; **wonderful,** wondrous, marvelous, miraculous, fantastic, fabulous, phenomenal, **prodigious,** stupendous, unheard-of, unprecedented, extraordinary, exceptional, rare, unique, singular, **remarkable,** striking

**sense** NOUNS 1 **meaning,** significance, signification, *significatum* <L>, *signifié* <Fr>, point, idea, **purport,** import, where one is coming from <nonformal>; **sensibleness,** reasonableness, reason, rationality, sanity, saneness, **soundness;** good *or* common *or* plain sense, **horse sense** <nonformal>
VERBS 2 **feel,** experience, **perceive,** apprehend, be sensible of, be conscious *or* aware of, apperceive; taste, smell, see, hear, touch; be sensitive to; **understand,** comprehend, apprehend, **know,** conceive, realize, appreciate, make sense out of, make something of; **intuit,** feel intuitively, **feel** *or* **know in one's bones** <nonformal>, **have a feeling,** have a funny feeling <nonformal>, **get** *or* **have the impression,** have a hunch <nonformal>, just know, know instinctively

**sensible** ADJS **reasonable,** rational, logical; practical, pragmatic; philosophical; commonsense, commonsensical <nonformal>; **levelheaded,** balanced, coolheaded, cool, **sound,** sane, sober, **soberminded,** well-balanced

**sensitive** ADJS 1 responsive, sympathetic, compassionate; empathic, empathetic; delicate, tactful, considerate, courteous, solicitous, refined; **oversensitive,** thin-skinned; sensible, receptive; susceptible, impressionable; **tender,** soft, tenderhearted, softhearted, warmhearted
2 irritable, edgy, touchy, prickly

**sensual** ADJS **lascivious,** lecherous, sexy, salacious, carnal, animal, **sexual,** lustful, ithyphallic, **hot,** horny *and* sexed-up *and* hot to trot <all nonformal>; prurient, itching, itchy <nonformal>; concupiscent, lickerish, libidinous, randy, horny <nonformal>, lubricious; erotic, fleshly

**sensuous** ADJS **captivating,** irresistible, ravishing, enravishing; **winning,** winsome, taking, fetching, heart-robbing; inviting, tempting, tantalizing; voluptuous, zaftig <nonformal>

**sentiment** NOUNS 1 **love,** affection, attachment, devotion, fondness, warm feeling, soft spot in one's heart, weakness <nonformal>, like, **liking,** fancy, shine <nonformal>; **passion,** tender feeling *or* passion, **ardor,** ardency, fervor, heart, flame; **regard,** admiration
2 **opinion,** feeling, sense, impression, reaction, **notion,** idea, thought, mind, attitude, stance, posture, position, mindset, **view,** point of view

**sentimental** ADJS sentimentalized, soft, **mawkish, maudlin,** cloying; sticky *and* gooey *and* schmaltzy *and* sappy *and* soppy <all nonformal>, bathetic

**sentry** NOUNS **watchman,** watch, watcher; watchkeeper; **sentinel,** picket

**separate** VERBS 1 **divide,** disjoin, disunite, draw apart, dissociate, disassociate, grow apart, **disjoint,** disengage, disarticulate, disconnect; **part,** cut the knot, **divorce,** estrange; **alienate, segregate,** separate off, factor out, sequester, isolate, curtain off, shut off, set apart *or* aside, split off, cut off *or* out *or* loose *or* adrift; **part company,** split up, disband, scatter, **disperse,** break up, break it up <nonformal>, **go separate ways,** diverge
ADJS 2 **distinct,** discrete; unjoined, unconnected, unattached, unaccompanied, unattended, unassociated; **apart,** asunder, **in two;** discontinuous, noncontiguous, divergent; **isolated,** insular,

detached, detachable, free-standing, free-floating, autonomous; **independent,** self-contained, stand-alone <nonformal>; separated, alienated, withdrawn, aloof, standoffish, detached, removed

**sequel** NOUNS sequela *or* sequelae, sequelant, sequent, sequitur, consequence; **continuation,** continuance, follow-up *or* follow-through <nonformal>; consequent, sequent, sequence, eventuality, eventuation, **upshot,** outcome

**sequence** NOUNS **series,** succession, run, consecution, progression, course, gradation; **subsequence,** posteriority, following, supervenience, supervention

**sequester** VERBS **reserve,** conserve, retain, husband, keep *or* hold back, withhold; **keep in reserve,** keep in store, keep on hand, keep by one; put in escrow; confiscate, sequestrate, impound

**seraph** NOUNS **angel,** celestial, celestial *or* heavenly being; seraphim <pl>, angel of love

**serendipity** NOUNS **discovery,** accidental *or* chance discovery, happening *or* stumbling upon, tripping over, casual discovery; good luck *or* fortune, happy chance, dumb luck <nonformal>; **fortuity,** randomness, fortuitousness

**serene** ADJS **calm,** placid, quiet, **tranquil,** peaceful, untroubled, at peace; **cool,** coolheaded, cool as a cucumber <nonformal>; philosophical

**serf** NOUNS esne; helot, villein; peon

**serial** NOUNS 1 installment, *livraison* <Fr>; **periodical,** journal, gazette; ephemeris; daytime serial, soap opera *or* soap <nonformal>
ADJS 2 **periodic** *or* periodical, seasonal, epochal, **cyclic** *or* cyclical, isochronal, metronomic; continuing

**series** NOUNS **succession,** run, **sequence,** consecution, progression, course, gradation; **continuum,** plenum

**serious** ADJS **sedate, staid,** sober, soberminded, grave, solemn, sobersided; temperate, moderate; **earnest,** thoughtful, sincere, weighty; moving, inspiring

**sermon** NOUNS **lesson,** teaching, instruction, lecture, harangue, **discourse,** disquisition, exposition, **talk,** homily, preachment; **moral,** morality, moralization, moral lesson

**serum** NOUNS serous fluid, blood serum; **antitoxin,** antitoxic serum; **antivenin;** antiserum

**servant** NOUNS 1 servitor, help; **domestic,** domestic help, domestic servant, house servant; live-in help, day help; scullion
2 **believer, disciple,** follower, faithful servant

**serve** VERBS 1 **lend** *or* **give oneself,** render service to, do service for, labor in behalf of; minister to, cater to; attend; pander to; do duty; **work for,** be in service with, serve one's every need
2 **suffice, do,** just do, **answer;** work, be equal to, **avail;** answer *or* serve the purpose, do the trick *and* fill the bill <both nonformal>, **suit**

**service** NOUNS 1 **act of kindness,** kindness, favor, mercy, **benefit,** benefaction, benevolence, benignity, blessing, turn, break <nonformal>, **good turn,** good *or* kind deed, good *or* kind offices, obligation, grace, act of grace, courtesy, kindly act, labor of love
2 **military service;** active service *or* duty; military obligation; selective service, national service <Brit>; branch of the service
3 servanthood, servitude <old>, servitorship, *servitium* <L>; **ministry,** ministration, attendance, tendance; divine service, public worship, **liturgy**, office, duty, exercises, **devotions;** church service
VERBS 4 **repair,** mend, fix, fix up <nonformal>, do up, doctor <nonformal>, put in repair, put in shape, set to rights, put in order *or* condition; **condition, recondition,** commission, put in commission, ready; **overhaul**

**serviceable** ADJS **useful,** employable, of use, of service, **functional,** utilitarian, of general utility *or* application

**servile** ADJS **slavish,** subservient, **menial,** base, mean; submissive, obsequious

**servitude** NOUNS **subjection,** compulsory *or* involuntary servitude, servility, bond service, indentureship

**session** NOUNS **meeting;** sitting, sit-down <nonformal>, séance; semester, trimester, term, academic year

**set** NOUNS 1 **clique,** coterie, circle, ring; **suit,** suite, series, outfit *and* kit <both nonformal>; group, matching pair *or* set, his and hers <nonformal>, couple, pair, twins, look-alikes, two of a kind, birds of a feather, peas in a pod
2 inclination, mind, **tendency,** grain, vein, mental set, mindset, **leaning,** propensity, proclivity, predilection, preference, predisposition

VERBS 3 **place,** put, lay, pose, posit, site, seat, stick <nonformal>, **station,** post; park, plump down <nonformal>;
4 **solidify,** conglomerate, agglomerate, conglobate; **congeal,** coagulate, clabber <nonformal>, **clot**
ADJS 5 **demarcated,** delimited, defined, definite, determined, determinate, specific, stated, fixed, **established,** stabilized, **entrenched,** vested, firmly established; **confirmed,** inveterate; settled

**setback** NOUNS **disappointment,** comedown, **letdown** <nonformal>; failure, fizzle <nonformal>, fiasco; **reverse,** reversal, devolution

**setting** NOUNS **background,** backdrop, ground, surround, field, scene, arena, theater, locale; stage, stage setting, stage set, *mise-en-scène* <Fr>; **environment**, environing circumstances, context, frame, surround, surrounding conditions; hardening, solidification

**settle** VERBS 1 **settle down,** sit down, locate, park <nonformal>, ensconce, ensconce oneself; take up one's abode *or* quarters, make one's home, **reside,** inhabit; **colonize,** populate, people
2 **sink, set**; **decline,** lower, **subside,** give way, lapse, cave, cave in; **light; land,** perch, come to rest; **arrange,** compose, patch up, adjust, straighten out, bring to terms *or* an understanding; make peace
3 **pay in full,** pay off, pay up <nonformal>, **discharge,** square, **clear,** liquidate, amortize, retire; pay the bill; settle the matter

**settlement** NOUNS 1 **peopling,** peoplement, empeoplement, **population,** inhabiting; **colonization,** plantation
2 **adjustment,** accommodation, resolution, composition of differences, compromise, arrangement, terms; **endowment,** investment, foundation; **dowry,** *dot* <Fr>, portion, marriage portion; **discharge,** clearance, liquidation, amortization, satisfaction

**settler** NOUNS **colonist,** colonizer, colonial, immigrant, planter; **homesteader;** *habitant* <Canadian & Louisiana Fr>; **squatter,** pioneer

**set up** VERBS **establish,** fix, plant, site, pitch, seat, set; found, base, ground, lay the foundation; **build,** put up; **install,** invest, vest; **inaugurate,** institute

**set upon** VERBS **attack, fall on** *or* upon, **descend on** *or* upon, come down on, swoop down on; pounce upon; lift *or* raise *or* lift a hand against

**seventh heaven** NOUNS **bliss,** blissfulness; paradise, heaven, cloud nine

**sever** VERBS **dissever,** cut off *or* away *or* loose, shear off, hack through, hack off, ax, amputate; **cleave,** split, fissure; sunder, cut in two, dichotomize, halve, bisect; **tear, rend,** rive, rend asunder

**several** ADJS divers, **sundry,** various; some five or six, etc; upwards of

**severe** ADJS 1 **harsh,** fierce, **rigorous,** rough, stringent, astringent, strident, **sharp, keen,** sharpish, cruel, dour, grave, incisive, trenchant, **cutting,** biting, stinging, **scathing,** stabbing, **piercing, poignant,** penetrating, edged, double-edged
2 **inornate,** unornate, **unelaborate,** unfancy, unfussy; austere, monkish, cloistral, stark, Spartan

**sew** VERBS **stitch,** needle; stitch up, sew up; **tailor**

**sewer** NOUNS **gutter,** pit, sink, sink of corruption; den of iniquity, den, **fleshpots,** hellhole; hole *and* joint *and* the pits <all nonformal>; Sodom, Gomorrah, Babylon; **brothel**

**sex** NOUNS 1 gender; maleness, masculinity, femaleness, femininity; **genitals,** genitalia
2 **copulation,** sex act, having sex, having intercourse, *le sport* <Fr>, coupling, mating, coition, **coitus,** pareunia, venery, **intercourse, sexual intercourse,** cohabitation, commerce, sexual commerce, congress, sexual congress, sexual union, sexual relations, relations, marital relations, marriage act, sleeping together *or* with

*making the beast with two backs*
**Shakespeare**

ADJS 3 **sexual,** sexlike, gamic, coital, libidinal; **erotic,** sexy, amorous; nuptial; venereal; **carnal, sensual**, voluptuous, fleshly

**sex appeal** NOUNS **sexual attraction** *or* attractiveness *or* magnetism, sexiness

**sexist** NOUNS 1 male chauvinist, male chauvinist pig *or* MCP <nonformal>, manist, masculist, feminist, female chauvinist, womanist
ADJS 2 **man-hating,** misandrist; **woman-hating,** misogynic, misogynis-

tic, misogynous; male- *or* female-chauvinistic

**sexless** ADJS **unsexual,** unsexed; asexual, **neuter,** neutral; castrated, emasculated, eunuchized; **cold,** frigid; impotent

**sex object** NOUNS sex queen, sex goddess; stud <nonformal>; piece *and* meat *and* piece of meat *and* ass *and* piece of ass *and* hot number <all nonformal>

**sex organs** NOUNS **genitals,** genitalia, reproductive organs, pudenda, private parts, privy parts, privates <nonformal>; **male organs; penis** phallus, *lingam* <Skt>; gonads; **testes,** testicles, balls *and* nuts *and* rocks *and* ballocks *and* family jewels <all nonformal>; scrotum, bag *and* basket <both nonformal>, cod <old>; **female organs; vulva,** *yoni* <Skt>, cunt <nonformal>; **vagina;** clitoris; labia, labia majora, labia minora, lips, nymphae; ovary; uterus, womb

**sexual** ADJS 1 gametic, gamic; **spermatic,** spermic, **seminal,** spermatozoal, spermatozoan, spermatozoic; sporal, sporous, sporoid; sporogenous
2 **lascivious,** lecherous, sexy, salacious, carnal, animal, **lustful,** ithyphallic, **hot,** horny *and* sexed-up *and* hot to trot <all nonformal>; prurient, itching, itchy <nonformal>; concupiscent, lickerish, libidinous, randy, horny <nonformal>, lubricious; **sensual,** fleshly; goatish, satyric, priapic, gynecomaniacal; **amorous,** amatory, amative, erotic

**sexual desire** NOUNS **sensuous** *or* carnal desire, bodily appetite, **biological urge,** venereal appetite *or* desire, sexual longing, **lust,** desire, lusts *or* desires of the flesh, itch, lech <nonformal>; **craving,** coveting, hunger, thirst, appetite

**sexual intercourse** NOUNS **copulation,** sex act, coupling, mating, coition, **coitus,** pareunia, venery, cohabitation, commerce, sexual commerce, congress, sexual congress, sexual union, sexual relations, relations, marital relations, marriage act, act of love, sleeping together *or* with; **lovemaking,** dalliance, amorous dalliance

**sexy** ADJS 1 **lustful,** prurient, hot, steamy, concupiscent, lickerish, libidinous, **salacious,** passionate, hot-blooded, itching, **horny** *and* hot to trot *and* sexed-up <all nonformal>, randy, goatish
2 **alluring,** fascinating, captivating, attractive, **seductive,** seducing, **beguiling,** enticing, inviting, come-hither <nonformal>; flirtatious, coquettish; **provocative,** *provoquant* <Fr>; appetizing, mouth-watering, piquant; **irresistible**

**shabby** ADJS **shoddy,** seedy, scruffy, **tacky** <nonformal>, dowdy, tatty, ratty; **niggardly,** niggard, pinchpenny, penurious, **grudging,** mean, mingy, sordid

**shack** NOUNS **hut,** hutch, **shanty,** crib, hole-in-the-wall <nonformal>, **shed;** lean-to

**shackle** NOUNS 1 restraint, **restraints,** fetter, hamper, trammel, trammels, **manacle,** gyves, bond, **bonds,** irons, chains, Oregon boat; electronic ankle bracelet *and* offender's tag *and* monitor
VERBS 2 **bind,** restrain, tie, tie up, put the clamps on, **strap,** lash, leash, pinion, fasten, secure, make fast; **fetter,** manacle, gyve, **put in irons; handcuff,** tie one's hands; tie hand and foot, hogtie <nonformal>; **hamper,** impede, cramp, embarrass; hobble, hamstring

**shade** NOUNS 1 **shadow,** shadiness; thick *or* dark shade, gloom; mere shadow; **phantom,** phantasm; nuance

*the shadow of a shade*
AESCHYLUS

VERBS 2 **screen,** veil, curtain, shutter, draw the curtains, put up *or* close the shutters; cover; **shadow**

**shading** NOUNS **gradation,** graduation, grading, staging, phasing, tapering, shadowing, overshadowing, **clouding,** overclouding, obnubilation, gathering of the clouds, overcast

**shadow** NOUNS **shade,** shadiness; umbra, umbrage, umbrageousness; thick *or* dark shade, gloom; penumbra; silhouette

**shady** ADJS 1 **disreputable,** discreditable, dishonorable, unsavory, up to no good, **seamy,** sordid; unrespectable, ignoble, ignominious, infamous, inglorious; notorious
2 **shadowy,** shadowed, shaded, darkling, umbral, umbrageous; overshadowed, overshaded, obumbrate, obumbrated; penumbral; screened, veiled, curtained

**shaft** NOUNS 1 air passage, air duct, airway, air shaft, **air hole,** air tube; **vent,** venthole, ventage, ventiduct; **ventilator,** ventilating shaft

2 **pit,** well, sump; **excavation,** dig, diggings, workings
3 **pillar,** stele *or* stela, column, memorial column, rostral column, manubial column; upright

**shaggy** ADJS **hairy,** bushy, tufty, shagged; matted, tomentose; mopheaded, burrheaded, shockheaded, unshorn; **nappy,** pily; nubby *or* nubbly; uncombed, matted

**shake** NOUNS 1 **quake,** quiver, quaver, falter, **tremor,** tremble, shiver, shudder, twitter, didder, dither; wobble
VERBS 2 tremble, quiver, quaver, cringe, cower, totter, teeter, dodder
3 **agitate,** disturb, perturb, shake up, perturbate, **disquiet,** discompose, upset, trouble, unsettle, stir, flutter the dovecote, fret, convulse; shake in one's boots *or* shoes

**shakedown** NOUNS 1 **extortion, blackmail,** bloodsucking, vampirism; protection racket; badger game
2 **tryout,** workout, **rehearsal,** practice; pilot plan *or* program; **dry run,** dummy run; *Gedankenexperiment* <Ger>; **trial run,** practical test; shakedown cruise

**shaken** ADJS **agitated,** perturbed, disturbed, troubled, disquieted, upset, unsettled, **discomposed, flustered,** ruffled

**shakeout** NOUNS **sorting,** sorting out, assortment, sifting, screening, triage, culling, selection, winnowing

**shake up** VERBS 1 **agitate,** perturb, disturb, trouble, disquiet, discompose, discombobulate <nonformal>, unsettle, **stir,** ruffle, shake, shock, upset, make waves, jolt, jar, rock, stagger, electrify, bring *or* pull one up short, give one a turn <nonformal>
2 **rearrange,** reorganize, reconstitute, **reorder,** restructure, reshuffle, tinker with; redistribute, reallocate, realign

**shaky** ADJS 1 **unsteady,** rickety, teetering, teetery, tottery, tottering, doddering, rocky <nonformal>; **tremulous,** trembling, trepidant, shivery
2 **insecure, unsound, infirm,** unsolid, **unstable,** unsubstantial, insubstantial, **unsteadfast,** desultory

**shallow** NOUNS 1 **shoal,** shallows, shallow *or* shoal water, flat, shelf
ADJS 2 **depthless,** not deep, unprofound; **surface,** on *or* near the surface, merely surface; **superficial,** cursory, slight, light, cosmetic, merely cosmetic, thin, jejune, trivial; unprofound; shallow-witted, shallow-minded, shallow-brained, shallow-headed, shallow-pated; **frivolous,** flighty, light, volatile, frothy, featherbrained, birdwitted, birdbrained

**sham** NOUNS 1 **hoax,** deception, spoof <nonformal>, **humbug,** flam, **fake** *and* fakement, **rip-off** <nonformal>; false front
VERBS 2 **pretend,** simulate, counterfeit, fake <nonformal>, **feign,** make out like <nonformal>, make a show of, play, playact <nonformal>, act *or* play a part, put up a front <nonformal>
ADJS 3 **imitation,** mock, copied, fake *and* phony <both nonformal>, counterfeit, forged, plagiarized, unoriginal, ungenuine, spurious; hypocritical

**shamble** NOUNS **leisurely gait,** snail's *or* tortoise's pace; slouch, shuffle, plod

**shame** NOUNS 1 **chagrin,** distress; embarrassment, abashment, discomfiture, egg on one's face <nonformal>, discomposure; **humiliation,** shamefacedness, mortification, disgrace, red face; dirty shame *and* low-down dirty shame <both nonformal>, crying *or* burning shame
VERBS 2 **disgrace,** put to shame, hold up to shame; hold up to public shame *or* public scorn *or* public ridicule, pillory, bring shame upon

**shameful** ADJS **disgraceful,** pitiful, deplorable, opprobrious, sad, sorry, too bad; degrading, debasing, demeaning, beneath one, beneath one's dignity, *infra dignitatem* <L>, infra dig <nonformal>, unbecoming, unworthy of one

**shameless** ADJS **brazen,** brazenfaced, boldfaced, barefaced, brassy <nonformal>, **bold,** bold as brass <nonformal>, unblushing, unabashed, aweless, dead *or* lost to shame; **blatant,** flagrant, lurid, extravagant, sensational, **spectacular,** glaring, flaring, flaunting, screaming <nonformal>, obtrusive, vulgar, crude; meretricious

**shanghai** VERBS **seize, kidnap,** abduct, snatch <nonformal>, carry off

**shanty** NOUNS **shack,** crib, hole-in-the-wall <nonformal>, **shed;** lean-to

**shape** NOUNS 1 **form,** figure; figuration, **configuration;** formation, **conformation;** structure; **build,** make, frame, **physique,** body-build
VERBS 2 **form,** formalize, **fashion,** tailor, frame, figure, **lick into shape** <nonformal>; work, knead; take form, **shape up,** take shape

3 **plan,** devise, contrive, design, frame, cast, concert, lay plans

**shapeless** ADJS **formless,** featureless, characterless, nondescript, inchoate, lumpy, lumpish, baggy <nonformal>, inform; amorphous, **chaotic,** orderless, disorderly, unordered, unorganized, confused, anarchic, inchoate

**shapely** ADJS **well-shaped,** well-proportioned, well-made, **well-formed,** well-favored; comely; trim, trig <old>, neat, spruce; well-built, built, stacked *or* well-stacked <both nonformal>, curvaceous, curvy <nonformal>, amply endowed, built for comfort *or* built like a brick shithouse <both nonformal>, callipygian, callipygous; Junoesque, statuesque

**shard** NOUNS **piece,** particle, bit, scrap, bite, **fragment,** morsel, crumb, potsherd

**share** NOUNS 1 **portion,** interest, part, stake, stock, **piece,** bit, segment; **bite** *and* **cut** *and* **slice** *and* **chunk** *and* slice of the pie *or* melon *and* piece of the action <all nonformal>, **allotment, proportion, percentage,** measure, quantum, **quota**
VERBS 2 **share in,** come in for a share, **go shares,** be partners in, have a stake in, have a percentage *or* piece of <nonformal>, **divide with,** divvy up with <nonformal>, halve, go halves; **share and share alike**

**shared** ADJS **mutual,** commutual, **common,** joint, communal, sharing, conjoint; respective, two-way

**sharing** NOUNS **apportionment,** apportioning, portioning, division, **partition,** repartition, partitionment, partitioning, parceling, budgeting, rationing, **dividing**

**shark** NOUNS **expert,** adept, proficient; sharp *or* sharpy *and* no slouch *and* tough act to follow <all nonformal>; vulture, **skillful gambler,** sharp, sharper, dean *and* professor *and* river gambler *and* dice gospeller *and* sharpie <all nonformal>; **cardsharp** *or* cardshark, cardsharper

**sharp** ADJS 1 **acrimonious, harsh,** fierce, **rigorous,** severe, rough, stringent, astringent, strident, **keen,** incisive, trenchant, **cutting,** biting, stinging, **scathing,** stabbing, **piercing,** poignant, penetrating, edged, double-edged; sharp as a razor *or* needle *or* tack
2 **steep,** precipitous, bluff, plunging, abrupt, bold, **sheer,** rapid; vertical
3 **alert,** quick, agile, nimble, quick on the trigger *or* draw *or* uptake <all nonformal>; **smart,** bright, keen; **wily,** crafty; calculating, scheming
4 **smart,** elegant; spiffy *and* classy *and* nifty *and* snazzy <all nonformal>
ADVS 5 **punctually,** precisely, exactly; **on time,** on the minute *or* instant, to the minute *or* second, **on the dot** <nonformal>

**sharpen** VERBS 1 **stimulate,** whet, pique, provoke, quicken, enliven, liven up, pick up, jazz up <nonformal>, animate, **exhilarate,** invigorate, galvanize, fillip, give a fillip to; infuse life into, give new life to, revive, renew, resuscitate
2 **edge,** acuminate, aculeate, spiculate, taper; **whet,** hone, oilstone, file, grind; strop, strap; **point;** file to a point

**shatter** VERBS **splinter,** shiver, break to *or* into pieces, fragmentize, break to *or* into smithereens <nonformal>; **smash,** crush, crunch, squash, make mincemeat of, make hamburger of <nonformal>

**sheath** NOUNS **case,** casing, encasement; sheathing

**sheathe** VERBS **clothe,** wrap, enwrap, lap, envelop, shroud, enshroud; wrap *or* bundle *or* muffle up; swathe, swaddle

**sheen** NOUNS **shine,** shininess, **luster,** gloss, glint; **glow,** gleam, flush, sunset glow

**sheep** NOUNS 1 jumbuck <Australia>; **lamb,** lambkin, yeanling; teg <Brit>; **ewe,** ewe lamb; **ram,** tup <Brit>, wether; bellwether; mutton
2 **conformist,** conformer, trimmer, parrot, yes-man, organization man

**sheepish** ADJS **contrite,** abject, humble, humbled, **apologetic,** touched, softened, melted

**sheer** ADJS 1 **steep,** precipitous, bluff, plunging, abrupt, bold, sharp, rapid; **mere,** stark, bare, bare-bones, plain, simple, unadorned, unenhanced
ADJS 2 **transparent,** transpicuous, light-pervious; show-through, see-through, peekaboo, revealing; **diaphanous,** thin; **gossamer,** gossamery, filmy, gauzy
ADVS 3 **perpendicularly,** up and down, **straight up and down;** plumb, *à plomb* <Fr>; at right angles
4 **absolutely,** perfectly, quite, right, stark, clean, plumb <nonformal>, plain

**shelf** NOUNS **ledge,** shoulder, corbel,

beam-end; mantel, mantelshelf, mantelpiece

**shell** NOUNS 1 seashell, lorication, lorica, conch; test, testa, episperm, pericarp, elytron, scute, scutum; **protective covering,** cortex, thick skin *or* hide
2 **cartridge,** cartouche, ball cartridge; blank cartridge, dry ammunition
VERBS 3 **husk,** hull, pod, shuck
4 **bombard,** blast, strafe, cannonade, mortar, barrage, blitz; rake, enfilade; pour a broadside into; cannon

**shellacking** NOUNS **utter defeat,** total defeat, overwhelming defeat, crushing defeat, smashing defeat, decisive defeat; no contest; **smearing** *and* **pasting** *and* creaming *and* **clobbering** *and* whomping <all nonformal>; whitewash *or* **whitewashing** <nonformal>, **shutout**

**shelter** NOUNS 1 **quarters,** living quarters; lodgings, lodging, lodgment; housing, **cover,** covert, coverture; concealment
VERBS 2 **protect,** guard, safeguard, secure, **shield,** screen, cover, cloak

**sheltered** ADJS **protected, guarded,** safeguarded, defended; safe; **shielded,** screened, covered, cloaked; cloistered, sequestered, sequestrated, isolated, secluded

**shelve** VERBS **put away,** lay away, **put aside,** lay *or* set *or* wave *or* cast *or* push aside, sideline <nonformal>, put *or* lay *or* set by; **pigeonhole,** put on the shelf, put in mothballs; put on ice <nonformal>

**shenanigans** NOUNS horseplay; monkey tricks *and* monkeyshines <both nonformal>

**shepherd** NOUNS 1 **herd,** herdsman, **herder,** drover, herdboy; shepherdess, **sheepherder,** sheepman
VERBS 2 **escort,** conduct, have in tow <nonformal>, marshal, **usher,** guide, lead; ride herd on <nonformal>

**shield** NOUNS 1 **cover,** covering, coverage, covert, coverture, housing, hood, cowl, cowling; **screen,** aegis, shroud, veil, pall, mantle, curtain, hanging, drape, drapery; **armor,** mail
VERBS 2 **defend,** guard, screen, secure, guard against; **safeguard,** protect; stand by the side of, flank; **shelter,** cover, cloak, shroud <old>

**shift** NOUNS 1 **moving,** removal, movement, relocation; **displacement,** delocalization, transition, **modulation,** qualification
2 work shift, **tour,** tour of duty, stint, bit, **watch, trick,** time, **turn,** relay, spell *or* turn of work; day shift, night shift, swing shift, graveyard shift <nonformal>, dogwatch, anchor watch; lobster trick; split shift
VERBS 3 **deviate,** depart from, vary, diverge, divaricate, branch off, angle, angle off; **digress,** divagate, turn aside, go out of the way, detour, take a side road; **swerve,** veer, sheer, curve, **turn,** trend, bend, heel, bear off; change horses in midstream, **change; change over,** switch over <nonformal>, switch

**shifting** ADJS **inconstant,** changeable, changeful, changing, uncertain, inconsistent; **shifty,** unreliable, undependable; **variable,** deviable, whimsical, **capricious,** fickle, off-again-on-again; **erratic,** eccentric, freakish; volatile, **fluctuating,** vacillating, wavering

**shiftless** ADJS **improvident,** thriftless, unthrifty, uneconomical; **feckless,** thoughtless, heedless; negligent, **unenterprising**

**shifty** ADJS **tricky,** trickish, cute, finagling, chiseling <nonformal>; **evasive,** slippery, slippery as an eel; **cunning,** crafty, artful, wily, devious, unstraightforward

**shill** NOUNS decoy, **come-on man** <nonformal>, plant, capper, stool pigeon, stoolie <nonformal>

**shillelagh** NOUNS **staff,** stave; **cane,** stick, walking stick, handstaff

**shimmer** NOUNS 1 **glitter,** glimmer, twinkle, blink; sparkle, spark; **scintillation,** scintilla; coruscation
VERBS 2 **glitter,** glimmer, twinkle, blink, spangle, tinsel, coruscate; **sparkle,** spark, **scintillate; glisten,** glister

**shindig** NOUNS **dance,** hop <nonformal>, dancing party, shindy <nonformal>; **party,** festivity, fete, brawl <nonformal>

**shine** NOUNS 1 shininess, **luster, sheen, gloss,** glint; **glow, gleam,** flush, sunset glow; lambency; **incandescence,** candescence
VERBS 2 shine forth, **burn, give light,** incandesce; **glow,** beam, gleam, glint, luster, glance; **buff,** burnish, polish, rub up, furbish

**shining** ADJS **illustrious,** lustrous, glorious, brilliant, splendid, splendorous, splendrous, splendent, resplendent, bright; **luminous,** incandescent, candescent; **radiant,** shiny, burning, lamping, streaming; **glossy,** glassy, *glacé* <Fr>, bright as a new penny, **polished,** burnished, shined

**shining example** NOUNS **paragon,** ideal, beau ideal, nonpareil, person to look up to, *chevalier sans peur et sans reproche* <Fr>, **good example,** role model, **hero,** superhero

**shirk** VERBS **slack,** lie *or* rest upon one's oars, not pull one's weight; **lie down on the job** <nonformal>; soldier, duck duty, **goof off** *and* dog it <both nonformal>, goldbrick <nonformal>; **malinger**

**shiver** NOUNS 1 **tingle,** tingling; quiver, shudder, tremor, tremor of excitement, rush <nonformal>; **shake,** quake, quaver, falter, **tremor, tremble,** twitter, didder, dither
VERBS 2 **tremble,** shake, quake, quiver, quaver; tremble *or* quake *or* shake in one's boots *or* shoes, tremble like an aspen leaf, shake all over

**shock** NOUNS 1 **trauma; start,** jar, jolt, turn; **concussion,** impact, crunch, smash; **blow,** hard *or* nasty *or* staggering blow
VERBS 2 **offend,** give offense, **repel,** put off, turn off <nonformal>, **revolt,** disgust, nauseate, sicken, make one sick; **horrify,** appall; **shake up,** upset, jolt, jar, rock, stagger, electrify, bring *or* pull one up short, give one a turn <nonformal>; **startle,** electrify, **give one a turn** <nonformal>, give the shock of one's life, make one jump out of his skin

**shocking** ADJS **astonishing**; eye-opening, eye-popping <nonformal>; **startling,** electrifying, staggering, stunning, jarring, jolting; **scandalous,** outrageous

**shod** ADJS shoed, booted, *chaussé* <Fr>

**shoddy** ADJS **shabby,** seedy, scruffy, **tacky** <nonformal>, dowdy, tatty, ratty; **slovenly, sloppy** <nonformal>, schlocky <nonformal>, lumpen, chintzy, grubby <nonformal>, **frowzy,** blowzy, tacky <nonformal>

**shoo-in** NOUNS sure success, foregone conclusion, sure-fire proposition <nonformal>; **winner** *and* **natural** <both nonformal>; sure thing *and* sure bet *and* cinch *and* lead-pipe cinch <all nonformal>

**shook** ADJS **startled,** shocked, electrified, jarred, jolted, shaken, staggered, **given a turn** *or* **jar** *or* **jolt,** taken aback, bowled down *or* over <nonformal>, struck all of a heap <nonformal>, able to be knocked down with a feather

**shoot** NOUNS 1 **rapids,** white water; chute, sault
2 **offshoot,** offset, **branch,** sprout, filiation; sucker, slip
VERBS 3 **fire,** fire off, let off, let fly, **discharge,** eject; **riddle,** pepper, pelt, pump full of lead <nonformal>; snipe, pick off; potshot, take a potshot

**shoot up** VERBS 1 **spring up,** jump up, **leap up,** vault up, start up, fly up, pop up, bob up; float up, surface, break water; **gush, jet,** spurt, fountain; **inject,** mainline <nonformal>
2 **inject,** mainline; jab *or* get off <nonformal>

**shop** NOUNS 1 **office;** store, boutique, specialty shop
VERBS 2 **market,** go shopping, go marketing; **shop around;** window-shop, comparison-shop, **browse**

**shore** NOUNS 1 **coast,** *côte* <Fr>; **strand,** *playa* <Sp>, beach, beachfront, beachside shingle, plage, lido, riviera; waterside, **waterfront;** shoreline, coastline; **seashore,** coast, seacoast, seaside, seaboard
ADJS 2 **coastal,** littoral, seaside, shoreside; oceanfront, oceanside; seaside, seafront, shorefront, shoreline; beachfront

**shore up** VERBS **strengthen,** invigorate, fortify, beef up <nonformal>, brace, buttress, prop, support, undergird; reinforce, undergird, bolster, **bolster up,** shore, prop up

**short** ADJS 1 **brief,** abbreviated, abbreviatory; concise; **curt,** curtate, decurtate; **succinct,** summary, synoptic, synoptical, compendious, compact; **little**

*short and sweet*
THOMAS LODGE

2 **financially embarrassed** *or* distressed, **pinched,** feeling the pinch, squeezed, on the edge *or* ragged edge <nonformal>, down to bedrock, **short of money** *or* **funds** *or* **cash,** out-of-pocket
ADVS 3 **abruptly,** suddenly, all of a sudden

**shortage** NOUNS **want,** lack, need, deficiency, deficit, shortfall, **incompleteness,** defectiveness, shortcoming, imperfection

**shortcoming** NOUNS **imperfection,** imperfectness; **unperfectedness; fault-**

**iness,** defectiveness, defectibility; **deficiency,** lack, want, shortage, **inadequacy,** inadequateness; **weakness,** frailty, infirmity, failure, **failing,** foible

**shortcut** NOUNS cut, cutoff; shortest way; **beeline**

**shorten** VERBS **abridge,** condense, reduce, compress, cut, clip; capsule, capsulize, encapsulate; **put in a nutshell**

**shortfall** NOUNS **want,** lack, need, deficiency, deficit, shortage, wantage, **incompleteness,** defectiveness, shortcoming, imperfection

**short-lived** ADJS **transient,** transitory, transitive; **temporary,** temporal; **impermanent,** unenduring, undurable, nondurable, nonpermanent; **ephemeral,** evanescent, volatile, **momentary**

**short shrift** NOUNS **repulse,** rebuff, peremptory *or* flat *or* point-blank refusal, summary negative; kiss-off *and* slap in the face *and* kick in the teeth <all nonformal>

**shortsighted** ADJS **nearsighted,** myopic; **undiscerning,** unperceptive, imperceptive, impercipient, insensible, purblind, unapprehending, uncomprehending; unforseeing, unseeing

**short temper** NOUNS **irascibility,** irritability, excitability, quick temper, short fuse <nonformal>; **crankiness,** testiness, crustiness, huffiness, huffishness, churlishness, bearishness, snappishness, waspishness; **hotheadedness,** hot blood

**short-term** ADJS **brief,** short, short-time, quick, brisk, swift, fleet, speedy

**shot** NOUNS 1 **dose,** draft, potion, portion, injection; booster, booster shot; **snort,** jolt, snifter
2 discharge; ejection; detonation; gunfire
3 **guess,** conjecture, unverified supposition, surmise, educated guess; guesstimate *and* hunch *and* stab <all nonformal>; rough guess, wild guess, bold conjecture, shot in the dark <nonformal>
ADJS 4 **unnerved,** unmanned, unstrung, undone, reduced to jelly, unglued <nonformal>, **demoralized,** shaken, upset, dashed, stricken, **crushed;** shot to pieces; **done for** *and* done in *and* finished *and ausgespielt* <Ger> *and* kaput <all nonformal>

**shoulder** VERBS **support,** bear, carry, **hold,** sustain, maintain, bolster, reinforce, back, back up, give *or* furnish *or* afford *or* supply *or* lend support

**shout** NOUNS 1 **cry,** call, yell, hoot; war cry, battle cry, war whoop, rallying cry; cheer
VERBS 2 **cry,** call, yell, holler <nonformal>, hoot; **cheer,** give a cheer, give three cheers
3 **proclaim, herald,** trumpet, shout from the housetops

**shove** NOUNS 1 **thrust,** push, boost <nonformal>; pressure
VERBS 2 **push,** propel, impel, thrust; **drive,** forward, advance; sweep, sweep along; butt

**show** NOUNS 1 **display,** demonstration, showing; presentation, showing forth, presentment, ostentation <old>, **exhibition,** exhibit, exposition, retrospective; **showcase,** showcasing, unveiling, exposure
2 **pretext,** pretense, pretension, lying pretension, ostensible *or* announced *or* public *or* professed motive; **front,** facade, sham
3 theatrical performance, **performance,** production, entertainment, stage presentation *or* performance; premiere, premier performance, debut
VERBS 4 shine out *or* through, **surface,** appear, **be visible,** be seen, be revealed, be evident, be noticeable, meet the gaze, impinge on the eye, present to the eye, meet *or* catch *or* hit *or* strike the eye
5 **prove,** demonstrate, afford proof of, prove to be, prove true; follow, follow from, follow as a matter of course

**show business** NOUNS show biz <nonformal>, the entertainment industry; **the theater,** the footlights, the stage, the boards, the bright lights, Broadway, the Great White Way

**showdown** NOUNS **confrontation,** standoff, Mexican standoff <nonformal>, clashing, collision, cross-purposes, conflict

**show off** VERBS **grandstand** *and* hotdog *and* showboat <all nonformal>, play to the gallery *or* galleries <nonformal>, please the crowd; exhibit *or* parade one's wares <nonformal>, strut one's stuff <nonformal>, go through one's paces, show what one has

**show-off** NOUNS **exhibitionist,** flaunter; **grandstander** *or* grandstand player *or* hot dog *or* **hotshot** *or* showboat <all nonformal>

**showpiece** NOUNS **model,** pattern, standard, criterion, classic example, rule, mirror, paradigm; **classic,** masterwork, masterpiece, *chef d'œuvre* <Fr>

**showstopper** NOUNS **smash, hit,** smash hit, gas, gasser, blast, boffo, barnburner, howling *or* roaring success, one for the book, wow, sensation, overnight sensation, phenom, sockeroo <all nonformal>

**show up** VERBS 1 **arrive,** make *or* put in an appearance, turn up, **surface,** pop *or* bob up *and* make the scene <all nonformal>; **overshadow,** eclipse, throw into the shade, top; put to shame, put one's nose out of joint, put down <nonformal>
2 **disprove,** invalidate, disconfirm, discredit, prove the contrary, belie, give the lie to, **expose**

**showy** ADJS **flaunting, flashy,** snazzy, flashing, glittering, **jazzy** *and* **glitzy** *and* gimmicky *and* splashy *and* splurgy <all nonformal>; exhibitionistic, showoffy <nonformal>, bravura; **frilly,** flouncy, frothy, chichi

**shred** NOUNS 1 **scrap,** tatter, smithereen <nonformal>, patch, **stitch,** tag
VERBS 2 **tear** *or* **rip apart,** take *or* pull apart, **pick** *or* **rip** *or* **tear to pieces,** tear to rags *or* tatters, rip to shreds

**shrew** NOUNS **bitch** <nonformal>, **vixen,** virago, termagant, brimstone, fury, witch, beldam, cat, tigress, she-wolf, she-devil, spitfire; fishwife; **scold,** common scold; battle-ax <nonformal>

**shrewd** ADJS **artful,** cunning, knowing, crafty, wily, guileful, canny, slick, sly, smart as a fox, foxy *and* crazy like a fox <both nonformal>; devious, Byzantine, calculating

**shriek** NOUNS 1 **screech,** scream, squeal, shrill, keen, squeak, squawk, skirl; waul, caterwaul
VERBS 2 **screech,** screak, squeak, squawk, **scream,** squeal, shrill, keen; waul, caterwaul

**shrill** ADJS **thin,** sharp, acute, argute, keen, keening, **piercing,** penetrating, ear-piercing; **screechy,** screeching, shrieky, shrieking, **squeaky,** squeaking, screaky, creaky, creaking; strident, harsh, raucous, grating

**shrine** NOUNS holy place, dagoba, naos; sacrarium, delubrum; tope, stupa; reliquary, *reliquaire* <Fr>

**shrink** NOUNS 1 **psychotherapist,** therapist, **psychiatrist, psychoanalyst,** analyst; headshrinker *and* shrinker <both nonformal>
VERBS 2 **flinch,** shy, shy away from, draw back, recoil, funk <nonformal>, **quail,** cringe, wince, blench, blink, say *or* cry uncle
3 get smaller, **diminish,** decline, sink, dwindle, **fade, ebb,** wane

**shrivel** VERBS **shrink,** wither, sear, parch, dry up; **wizen,** weazen, wrinkle; consume, waste, waste away, attenuate, emaciate

**shroud** NOUNS 1 **screen,** shield, veil, pall, mantle, curtain, hanging, drape, drapery; **coat,** cloak, mask, guise; **graveclothes,** winding sheet, cerecloth, cerements; pall
VERBS 2 **wrap,** enwrap, wrap up, wrap about *or* around; **envelop,** surround, encompass, lap, smother, enfold, embrace, invest; swathe, swaddle; **screen,** cloak, veil, screen off, curtain, blanket, enshroud, envelop; **disguise,** camouflage, mask, dissemble; hide one's light under a bushel

**shrunk** ADJS shrunken; **shriveled,** shriveled up; **withered,** sear, parched, corky, dried-up; **wasted,** wasted away, consumed, emaciated, emacerated, thin, attenuated

**shuck** VERBS **husk,** hull, pod, **shell**

**shudder** NOUNS 1 **shake,** quake, quiver, quaver, falter, **tremor,** tremble, shiver, twitter, didder, dither
VERBS 2 **shake,** quake, vibrate, jactitate; **tremble,** quiver, quaver, falter, **shiver,** twitter, didder, chatter; shake in one's boots *or* shoes

**shuffle** NOUNS 1 **slow motion,** leisurely gait, snail's *or* tortoise's pace; slouch, plod, shamble
VERBS 2 **stroll,** saunter, *flâner* <Fr>; scuff, scuffle, straggle, shamble, slouch; riffle; **dance,** shake

**shun** VERBS **avoid,** fight shy of, shy away from, keep from, keep away from, circumvent, keep clear of, avoid like the plague, **steer clear of** <nonformal>, **give a wide berth,** keep remote from, stay detached from; **abstain,** abstain from, refrain, **refrain from,** eschew, **pass up** <nonformal>, have nothing to do with, take no part in, have no hand in

**shut** VERBS 1 **close,** occlude; close up, shut up, contract, constrict, strangle, strangulate, choke, choke off, squeeze,

squeeze shut; **turn off,** shut off, shut down
ADJS 2 **closed,** unopen, unopened; unvented, unventilated; **ruled out,** barred

**shutdown** NOUNS **closure,** closing, shutting, shutting up, occlusion; shutting down; **exclusion**, shutting out, **ruling out;** blockade, embargo

**shut down** VERBS **close up** *or* **down,** shut up, shut up shop, go out of business, shutter, put up the shutters; jump on *and* crack down on *and* clamp down on <all nonformal>, put *or* keep the lid on <nonformal>; bottle up, cork, cork up; **strike,** walk out, call a strike, go *or* go out on strike

**shut-in** NOUNS **sick person,** ill person, sufferer, victim; valetudinarian, **invalid,** bedridden invalid

**shutter** VERBS **shade,** screen, veil, curtain, draw the curtains, put up *or* close the shutters; cover

**shuttle** NOUNS 1 **train,** railroad train; shuttle train; **air shuttle,** shuttle service, shuttle trip; **spacecraft,** space shuttle
VERBS 2 **alternate,** go to and fro, **come and go,** ebb and flow; shuttlecock

**shut up** VERBS 1 **confine, shut in,** shut away, coop in, hem in, fence in *or* up, wall in *or* up, rail in; **coop up, pen up,** box up, mew up, bottle up, cork up, seal up, **impound**

2 <nonformal> keep one's trap *or* yap shut, button up, button one's lip, dummy up, clam up, not let out a peep, play dumb, stonewall, say nothing

**shy** ADJS 1 **timid,** timorous, **bashful,** shamefaced, shamefast, pudibund *and* verecund *and* verecundious <all old>; **coy, demure,** skittish, mousy
2 **incomplete,** uncompleted, deficient, defective, unfinished, imperfect, unperfected, **inadequate; short,** scant

**shyster** NOUNS 1 **trickster,** shady character; horse trader, Yankee horse trader; **swindler**

2 <nonformal> **mouthpiece, ambulance chaser,** lip, fixer, legal eagle, Philadelphia lawyer

**sibling** NOUNS agnate, enate; kinsman, kinswoman, sib, brother, sister

**sick** ADJS **ill,** ailing, unwell, indisposed, taken ill, down, bad, on the sick list; **sickish,** rocky <nonformal>, **under the weather,** out of sorts <nonformal>, below par <nonformal>, off-color, off one's feed <nonformal>; **sick at heart,** heartsick, soul-sick, heartsore

**sicken** VERBS **deteriorate,** worsen, get *or* grow worse, get no better fast <nonformal>, disimprove, **degenerate**

**sickly** ADJS **unhealthy,** healthless, in poor health; **infirm,** unsound, invalid, valetudinary, valetudinarian, debilitated, cachectic, enervated, exhausted, drained; peaky *or* peaked <nonformal>; **feeble,** frail; **run-down,** reduced in health

**sickness** NOUNS **disease,** illness, malady, ailment, indisposition, **disorder,** complaint, morbidity, *morbus* <L>, **affliction,** affection, **infirmity**

**side** NOUNS 1 aspect, **facet,** angle, viewpoint, slant *and* twist *and* spin <all nonformal>
2 **party,** interest, camp; interest group, pressure group, ethnic group; minority group, vocal minority
ADJS 3 **lateral;** flanking, skirting; **beside,** to the side, off to one side; **alongside,** parallel; next-beside; extra, off, spare, sparetime, **part-time**

**sideburns** NOUNS **whiskers,** burnsides, **muttonchops**

**sidekick** NOUNS **henchman,** co hort, hanger-on, buddy <nonformal>; **partner,** side partner, sidekicker <nonformal>; companion

**sideline** NOUNS **avocation,** hobby, side interest, pastime, spare-time activity; amateur pursuit, amateurism; unpaid work, volunteer work

**sidestep** VERBS **go sideways,** sidle, lateral, lateralize, **edge,** veer, angle, slant, skew; go crabwise; **sideslip,** skid; pull away *or* clear; pull back, shrink, recoil; step aside; hedge, skate around <Brit nonformal>, pussyfoot <nonformal>, evade the issue

**sideswipe** VERBS impinge, bump up against, hit; osculate; **graze,** caress, kiss, nudge, rub, brush, glance, scrape, skim, skirt, shave; **collide,** smack into, crash into, impact, smash into, dash into; **carom**

**sideways** ADVS **laterally,** laterad; sideway, **sidewise,** sidewards, sideward, side-

long, aside, crabwise; side-to-side; **edgeways,** edgeway, edgewise
**side with** VERBS take sides with, **unite with; join,** join with, join up with *and* get together with *and* team up with <all nonformal>, strike in with <old>; **throw in with** *and* string along with *and* swing in with <all nonformal>, **go along with; line up with** <nonformal>, align with, align oneself with, range with, range oneself with, stand up with, stand in with; **close ranks with,** fall in with, make common cause with, pool one's interests with
**sidle** VERBS **go sideways,** lateral, lateralize, **edge,** veer, angle, slant, skew, sidestep; go crabwise; **sideslip,** skid
**siege** NOUNS **besiegement,** beleaguerment; encompassment, investment, encirclement, envelopment; blockading, blockade; cutting of supply lines
**sieve** NOUNS screen, strainer, colander, riddle, cribble, net; **separator,** centrifuge
**sift** VERBS **refine,** separate, sieve, **screen,** bolt, winnow; cull, glean; separate the wheat from the chaff, separate the sheep from the goats; discriminate
**sigh** NOUNS 1 **sighing,** moaning, sobbing, whining, soughing
VERBS 2 **moan,** sob, whine, sough; **whimper**
**sight** NOUNS 1 **vision,** eyesight, seeing; **sightedness; look,** the eye *and* a look-see *and* a gander <all nonformal>, eye, regard; leer, leering look
2 sighthole; finder, viewfinder; panoramic sight; bombsight; peep sight, open sight
3 **view,** scene, prospect, outlook, lookout, vista, perspective; **spectacle,** exhibit, **exhibition,** exposition, **show,** stage show, **display,** presentation, representation
4 **eyesore,** blot, blot on the landscape, blemish, **fright,** horror, mess, no beauty, no beauty queen, ugly duckling
**sightly** ADJS **comely,** fair, good-looking, nice-looking, well-favored, **personable,** presentable, agreeable, becoming, pleasing, goodly, bonny, likely <nonformal>; pleasing to the eye, lovely to behold
**sightsee** VERBS see the sights, take in the sights; **rubberneck** <nonformal>; go on a tour, join a tour
**sign** NOUNS 1 telltale sign, sure sign, tip-off <nonformal>, **index,** indicant, **indicator,** measure; **symptom; mark,** earmark, hallmark; **signal; high sign** *and* the wink *and* the nod <all nonformal>
2 symbol, significant, significant, type, token, icon; **miracle,** signs and portents, prodigy, wonder, wonderwork
VERBS 3 **shake hands** *or* shake <nonformal>, affix one's John Hancock <nonformal>, seal, formalize, make legal and binding, solemnize; **endorse;** sign, cosign, **underwrite,** undersign, subscribe to; confirm, attest
**signal** NOUNS 1 **sign;** high sign *and* the wink *and* the nod <all nonformal>; wink, flick of the eyelash, glance, leer; **implication,** insinuation, innuendo; broad hint, gesture, nod, look, nudge, kick, prompt
VERBS 2 signalize, sign, give a signal, make a sign; speak; flash; **give the high sign** *or* **the nod** *or* a high five <all nonformal>; nod; nudge, poke, kick, dig one in the ribs, touch; wink, glance, raise one's eyebrows
**signature** NOUNS **ratification,** endorsement, acceptance, approval, approbation, subscription, subscribership, signing-off, imprimatur, **sanction,** permission, the OK *and* the okay *and* the green light *and* **the go-ahead** *and* the nod <all nonformal>, **certification,** confirmation, validation, authentication, authorization, warrant; **subscription,** autograph, John Hancock <nonformal>; countersignature
**significant** ADJS **important,** major, consequential, momentous, considerable, substantial, material, **great,** grand, big
**significant other** NOUNS **lover,** admirer, adorer, amorist; infatuate, paramour; escort, companion, date *and* steady <both nonformal>; live-in lover, POSSLQ *or* person of opposite sex sharing living quarters
**signify** VERBS **betoken,** stand for, identify, differentiate, speak of, talk, **indicate,** be indicative of, be an indication of, be significant of, connote, denominate, argue, bespeak, be symptomatic *or* diagnostic of, symptomize, **characterize, mark,** highlight, be the mark *or* sign of, give token, **denote,** mean
**sign up** VERBS **join,** join up <nonformal>, **enter,** go into, come into, get into, make oneself part of, swell the ranks of; **enlist,** enroll, affiliate, sign on <nonfor-

mal>, take up membership, take out membership

**silence** NOUNS 1 **quiescence,** *or* quiescency, **stillness,** quietness, **quiet,** quietude; **taciturnity,** untalkativeness, unloquaciousness

*lucid stillness*
**T S Eliot**

VERBS 2 **put to silence,** hush, hush one up, hush-hush, **shush, quiet,** quieten, **still; soft-pedal,** put on the soft pedal; squash, squelch <nonformal>, stifle, choke, choke off, throttle, put the kibosh on <nonformal>, put the lid on *and* shut down on <both nonformal>, put the damper on <nonformal>, **gag, muzzle,** muffle; strike dumb

**silent** ADJS **still, quiet,** quiescent, hushed, soundless, noiseless; **inaudible,** quiet as a mouse, mousy; silent as a post *or* stone, silent as the grave *or* tomb, still as death; **taciturn,** untalkative, unloquacious, indisposed to talk; **speechless,** wordless, mum

**silhouette** NOUNS **outline, profile; broad lines,** vignette; shadow figure; **shadow**

**silky** ADJS **smooth;** satiny, velvety, smooth as silk *or* satin *or* velvet, smooth as a billiard ball *or* baby's ass <nonformal>; **sleek,** slick, glossy, shiny, gleaming; silken, gossamer, gossamery, flossy; silklike, sericeous, soft as silk

**silly** ADJS **nonsensical,** poppycockish <nonformal>; **foolish,** absurd; twaddling, twaddly; rubbishy, trashy; skimble-skamble; Pickwickian; **fatuous,** fatuitous, inept, **inane,** empty, vacuous; trite, vapid

**silver** NOUNS 1 **tableware,** dining utensils; **silverware,** silver plate, stainless-steel ware; **flatware,** flat silver
ADJS 2 **eloquent,** silver-tongued; well-spoken, articulate; **glib, smooth,** smooth-spoken, smooth-tongued, slick

**similar** ADJS **like, alike,** something like, not unlike; **resembling,** resemblant, following, favoring <nonformal>, savoring *or* smacking of, suggestive of, **on the order of;** something of the sort *or* to that effect

**simmer** VERBS **seethe,** sizzle, smoke, smolder, steam; **fume,** stew <nonformal>, boil, fret, chafe; **foam,** froth, froth up; **boil,** ferment, stir, churn

**Simon Legree** NOUNS **oppressor,** hard master, driver, **slave driver;** martinet, disciplinarian, stickler

**simpatico** ADJS **amiable,** congenial, *simpático* <Sp>, *sympathique* <Fr>, pleasant, agreeable, favorable, well-affected, well-disposed, well-intentioned, well-meaning, well-meant; sociable; kind

**simple** ADJS 1 **plain,** ordinary, nondescript, common, commonplace, prosaic, prosy, **matter-of-fact,** homely, homespun, everyday, workday, workaday, household, garden, common- *or* garden-variety; pure, **pure and simple,** chaste, classic *or* classical, Attic; natural, homey, down-home *and* folksy <both nonformal>; **unaffected,** unassuming
2 **ignorant,** nescient, empty, empty-headed, blankminded, vacuous, inane, unintelligent; **green,** callow, innocent, ingenuous, gauche, awkward, naive, unripe, raw; **gullible,** dupable, ingenuous, unsophisticated, green, naive

**simpleminded** ADJS **artless,** simplehearted; **ingenuous,** *ingénu* <Fr>; childlike, born yesterday; simplewitted, simple, simpletonian; **idiotic,** moronic, imbecile, imbecilic, cretinous, cretinistic

**simpleton** NOUNS **idiot,** imbecile, moron, half-wit, natural, natural idiot, born fool, natural-born fool, mental defective, defective

**simplicity** NOUNS **purity,** simpleness, **plainness,** no frills, starkness, severity; **unadulteration,** unsophistication, unspoiledness, intactness, fundamentality, elementarity, primitiveness *or* primitivity, primariness; **ingenuousness,** unsophistication; greenness, naïveness, **naïveté,** naivety; uncomplexity, uncomplicatedness

**simulate** VERBS **imitate,** counterfeit, fake <nonformal>, hoke *and* hoke up <both nonformal>; **parody,** pastiche; **affect, pretend, sham, feign,** make out like <nonformal>, make a show of, play, playact <nonformal>

**sin** NOUNS 1 **iniquity, evil,** bad, wrong, error, obliquity, villainy, knavery, reprobacy, peccancy, **abomination,** atrocity, infamy, shame, disgrace, scandal, unforgivable *or* cardinal *or* mortal sin
VERBS 2 **do wrong,** misbehave, misdemean *and* misdo <both old>, **err,** offend; commit sin; **transgress,** trespass

**sincere** ADJS **candid,** frank, genuine, honest, ingenuous, frankhearted; **open,** openhearted, transparent, open-faced; artless; **straightforward,** direct, upfront *and* straight <both nonformal>, **forthright,** downright, straight-out <nonformal>

**sinful** ADJS **wrongdoing,** evildoing, malefactory, malfeasant; **wrong,** iniquitous, wicked; **ungodly,** godless, **irreligious,** unrighteous, unholy, unsaintly, unangelic, unangelical; impious

**sing** VERBS **vocalize,** carol, descant, lilt, troll, line out *and* belt out *and* tear off <all nonformal>; **warble,** trill, tremolo

**singe** VERBS **burn,** torrefy, scorch, parch, sear; swinge; **blister,** vesicate; **cauterize,** brand, burn in

**singer** NOUNS **vocalist,** vocalizer, voice, songster, songbird, warbler, lead singer, caroler, melodist, minstrel, cantor; songstress, cantatrice, chanteuse, song stylist, canary <nonformal>; chanter, chantress

**single** ADJS 1 **unmarried,** unwedded, unwed, sole, spouseless, wifeless, husbandless; **bachelorly,** bachelorlike; **spinsterly,** spinsterish, spinsterlike; maiden, maidenly; virgin, virginal
2 **one,** singular, individual, sole, unique, a certain, **solitary, lone;** exclusive

**singular** ADJS 1 **wonderful,** wondrous, marvelous, miraculous, fantastic, fabulous, phenomenal, **prodigious,** stupendous, unheard-of, unprecedented, extraordinary, exceptional, rare, unique, **remarkable,** striking, sensational
2 **odd,** queer, peculiar, absurd, **curious,** oddball <nonformal>, weird *and* kooky *and* freaky *and* freaked-out <all nonformal>, quaint, **eccentric,** gonzo <nonformal>

**sinister** ADJS **ominous,** dark, black, gloomy, somber, dreary; **threatening,** menacing, lowering; bad, evil, ill, untoward; dire, baleful, baneful, **ill-fated,** ill-starred, evil-starred, star-crossed; shady <nonformal>, up to no good, not kosher <nonformal>, unsavory, insidious, indirect, slippery, devious, tricky, shifty, evasive

**sink** NOUNS 1 **washbasin,** washbowl, kitchen sink; sump; **sewer, hole,** pit, depression, dip; **basin,** trough, **bowl**
VERBS 2 **go down,** sink down, submerge; **set, settle,** settle down; **decline,** lower, **subside,** give way, lapse, cave, cave in; **slump,** slump down; founder; diminish, lessen; abate; shrink, wane, wither, ebb, ebb away, dwindle, languish; **deepen,** lower, depress
3 **scuttle,** send to the bottom, send to Davy Jones's locker; **founder, go down,** go to the bottom, sink like lead, go down like a stone; **slip,** go downhill, be on the skids <nonformal>

**sinner** NOUNS **wrongdoer,** malefactor, transgressor, delinquent; malfeasor, misfeasor, nonfeasor; misdemeanant, misdemeanist

**sip** NOUNS 1 **nip,** draft, drop, spot, finger or two, sup, suck, drench, guzzle, gargle, jigger
VERBS 2 **drink,** quaff, sup, bib, swig *and* swill *and* guzzle *and* pull <all nonformal>; **taste,** taste of, sample; **savor,** savor of; roll on the tongue

**sire** VERBS **engender,** beget, procreate; **give birth to,** bear, birth, bring to birth; father, mother

**siren** NOUNS 1 **tempter,** seducer, enticer, inveigler, **charmer,** enchanter, fascinator, tantalizer, teaser; coquette, flirt; **temptress,** enchantress, seductress; **vampire,** vamp <nonformal>, *femme fatale* <Fr>
2 **warning signal,** alert, red alert; klaxon, tocsin

**sissy** NOUNS 1 **milksop,** namby-pamby, mollycoddle, mama's boy, mother's boy, mother's darling, teacher's pet; pansy *and* pantywaist <both nonformal>, **wimp,** poor *or* weak *or* dull tool <nonformal>
ADJS 2 **weak-kneed, chicken** <nonformal>, afraid of one's shadow; weak, soft; **wimpy** *or* wimpish <nonformal>, unmanly, unmanful, sissified; milksoppy, milksoppish

**sister** NOUNS **nun,** *religieuse* <Fr>, clergywoman, conventual; abbess, prioress; **mother superior,** lady superior, superioress, the reverend mother, holy mother; novice, postulant

**sit** VERBS set <nonformal>, **sit down, be seated,** remain seated; perch, roost

**site** NOUNS 1 **arena,** scene of action, scene, setting, background, **field, ground,** terrain, sphere, place, locale, milieu, precinct, purlieu
VERBS 2 **situate,** place, position; emplace, spot <nonformal>, **install,** put in place; **pinpoint,** zero in on, home in on; find *or* fix *or* calculate one's posi-

tion, triangulate, find a line of position, **get a fix on**

**sitter** NOUNS **baby-sitter,** baby-minder <Brit>

**sit tight** VERBS **hold on** <nonformal>, hold one's breath; wait a minute *or* second, wait up; **wait and see,** bide the issue, see which way the cat jumps, see how the cookie crumbles *or* the ball bounces <nonformal>

**situate** VERBS **locate,** site, place, position; emplace, spot <nonformal>, **install,** put in place

**situation** NOUNS 1 **placement,** positioning, emplacement, location, siting, **locating,** placing, putting; **status,** status quo *or* status in quo, position, standing, footing, bearings, spot
2 **position,** job, employment, gainful employment, **office,** post, place, station, berth, billet, **appointment,** engagement, gig <nonformal>

**size** NOUNS **largeness,** bigness, greatness, vastness, vastitude, **magnitude,** order of magnitude, amplitude; mass, bulk, **volume,** body; **dimensions,** proportions, dimension, caliber; **measure,** measurement, gauge, **scale; extent,** scope, reach, range; depth, breadth, width

**skeleton** NOUNS 1 **frame,** framing; **framework,** fabric, cadre, chassis, shell, armature; lattice, latticework, infrastructure
2 **corpse,** dead body, dead man *or* woman, dead person, **cadaver,** carcass, body; *corpus delicti* <L>; **remains,** mortal *or* organic remains, bones, dry bones, relics, reliquiae

**skeptic** NOUNS doubter, dubitante, **doubting Thomas,** scoffer, cynic, pooh-poohер, nay-sayer, unbeliever

**sketch** NOUNS 1 **description,** portrayal, portraiture, **depiction,** rendering, rendition, **delineation,** limning, representation; vignette, cameo; **characterization,** character, character sketch, profile; **drawing;** line drawing; **draft**
VERBS 2 **describe,** portray, picture, render, **depict,** draft, represent, delineate, limn, draw; outline, sketch out, trace; **characterize,** character; **express,** set forth, give words to; **write**

**sketchy** ADJS **imperfect,** defective, faulty, inadequate, deficient, short, not all it's cracked up to be <nonformal>, lacking, wanting, found wanting; **unsound,** incomplete, unfinished, partial, patchy, uneven, unthorough; makeshift

**skew** NOUNS 1 **bias,** bend, bent, **crook,** warp, twist, turn, **veer,** sheer, **swerve,** lurch
VERBS 2 **unbalance,** disbalance, disequilibrate, overbalance, overcompensate, **throw off balance,** upset

**skewer** VERBS **pierce,** penetrate, puncture, punch, hole, prick; **tap,** broach; stab, stick, pink, run through; **transfix,** transpierce, fix, **impale,** spit; crucify; **disparage,** defame

**ski** VERBS run, schuss, traverse, turn, check

**skid** NOUNS 1 **slide; slip,** slippage; **glide,** coast, glissade; slither; sideslip
VERBS 2 **glide,** coast, skim, sweep, flow; **slide,** slip, skitter, sideslip, slither, glissade; sideslip

**skid row** NOUNS **slum** *or* **slums,** blighted area *or* neighborhood *or* section; tenderloin, red-light district, Bowery, skid road <nonformal>

**skill** NOUNS skillfulness, **expertness,** expertise, proficiency, craft, **cleverness; dexterity,** dexterousness *or* dextrousness; **adroitness,** address, **adeptness,** deftness, handiness, hand, practical ability; **competence,** capability, capacity, ability; **facility,** prowess; **craftsmanship,** workmanship, artisanship; **know-how** *and* savvy *and* bag of tricks <all nonformal>; **technique,** touch, technical brilliance, technical mastery

**skillful** ADJS **expert,** proficient; dexterous, **adroit,** deft, adept, coordinated, well-coordinated, **apt,** no mean, **handy;** masterly, masterful; authoritative, professional; **virtuoso,** bravura, technically superb; workmanlike

**skim** VERBS 1 **touch lightly,** touch upon; kiss, **brush,** sweep, graze, brush by, glance, scrape; **speed,** go fast, **fly,** flit, fleet, wing one's way, outstrip the wind; **scratch the surface,** hardly touch, skim over, hit the high spots *and* give a lick and a promise <both nonformal>, cut corners; slight
2 **cheat,** shortchange, shortweight, skim off the top; **pocket,** palm

**skimp** VERBS **stint,** scrimp, scamp, scant, screw, **pinch,** starve, famish; **pinch pennies,** live on nothing; **economize, scrape,** scrape and save; put something aside, save for a rainy day, have a nest egg

**skimpy** ADJS **meager, slight,** scrimpy, skimp, exiguous; scant, **scanty,** spare; miserly, niggardly, stingy, parsimonious, mean

**skin** NOUNS 1 dermis; **cuticle; rind; flesh;** bare skin *or* flesh, the buff; integument, tegument, tegmen, tegmentum; epicarp; bark
VERBS 2 **peel,** pare, strip, flay, excoriate, decorticate, bark; scalp

**skinny** ADJS **lean,** lean-looking, fleshless, lean-fleshed, thin-fleshed, **spare,** meager, **scrawny,** scraggy, **gaunt,** lank, lanky; twiggy; **underweight,** undersized, undernourished, spidery

**skip** NOUNS 1 **leap,** jump, hop, spring, bound, bounce
VERBS 2 **leave undone,** leave, **let go,** leave half-done, pretermit, jump, **miss,** omit, pass over, pass up <nonformal>, abandon; **slack,** shirk, malinger, goof off *and* goldbrick <both nonformal>
3 **leap,** jump, vault, spring, hop, bound, bounce; **gambol,** gambado, **frisk,** flounce, **trip,** bob, jump about

**skirmish** NOUNS **fight,** battle, fray, affray, combat, action, conflict, embroilment; **clash;** brush, scrimmage

**skirt** VERBS **border,** edge, bound, rim, hem, hem in, befringe, lap, list, margin, marge, marginate, verge; **graze,** caress, kiss, nudge, rub, brush, glance, scrape, sideswipe, skim, shave; **evade,** elude, **get out of,** shuffle out of, **get around** <nonformal>, circumvent

**skittish** ADJS **frisky,** antic, coltish, rompish, capersome; **jittery** <nonformal>, **jumpy,** twittery, skittery, trigger-happy <nonformal>, gun-shy; **coy,** demure, mousy

**skulduggery** NOUNS **chicanery,** chicane, **trickery,** dodgery, pettifogging, pettifoggery, *supercherie* <Fr>, **artifice,** sleight, machination; **sharp practice,** underhand dealing, connivery, connivance, conspiracy

**skulk** VERBS **sneak,** slink, prowl, nightwalk, **steal,** creep, pussyfoot <nonformal>, gumshoe <nonformal>, tiptoe; **cower,** quail, cringe, crouch

**sky** NOUNS **the heavens,** heaven, **firmament;** empyrean, welkin, *caelum* <L>; **the blue,** blue sky, azure, cerulean, the blue serene; **ether,** air

**skyrocket** VERBS **shoot up,** spring up, jump up, **leap up,** vault up, start up, fly up, pop up, bob up; upshoot, upstart, upspring, upleap, upspear, rocket, make rapid strides, take off <nonformal>

**slab** NOUNS plank, deal <Brit>, slat, tablet, table; puncheon

**slack** ADJS 1 **dilatory,** procrastinative, remiss, lax; **negligent,** neglectful, neglecting, derelict, culpably negligent; relaxed, laid-back <nonformal>, unrigorous, permissive, overly permissive; work-shy
2 **loose,** lax, relaxed, easy

**slacker** NOUNS **shirker,** shirk, **goldbricker,** goldbrick <nonformal>; clock watcher; **malingerer**

**slake** VERBS **satiate,** sate, satisfy, allay; **surfeit,** glut, gorge, engorge; **cloy,** jade, pall

**slam** NOUNS 1 **hit,** blow, stroke, knock, rap, pound, bang, crack, **whack,** smack, thwack, smash, dash, swipe, swing, **punch,** poke, jab, dig, drub, thump, pelt, cut, chop, dint, slog
2 **criticism;** knock *and* swipe *and* rap *and* hit <all nonformal>
VERBS 3 **crack,** clap, crash, wham, **bang,** clash
4 criticize; pan *and* knock *and* hit *and* rap *and* take a rap *or* swipe at <all nonformal>

**slammer** NOUNS

<nonformal> **slam, jug,** can, coop, cooler, hoosegow, stir, clink, pokey, **joint,** big house, brig, tank

**slander** NOUNS 1 **scandal,** libel, traducement; calumny, calumniation; backbiting, cattiness *and* bitchiness <both nonformal>; character assassination; whispering campaign
VERBS 2 **libel;** calumniate, traduce; stab in the back, backbite, speak ill of behind one's back

**slang** NOUNS **jargon,** cant, argot, patois, patter, vernacular; **colloquialism,** localism

**slant** NOUNS 1 aspect, look, view; facet, side, angle, viewpoint, twist *and* spin <both nonformal>; obliquity, bias, skew; **inclination,** leaning, **bent,** turn, tilt, cast, warp; way of looking at things, slant on things
VERBS 2 **incline,** lean; slope, rake, pitch, grade, bank; **tilt,** tip, list, cant, careen, keel, sidle, swag, sway
3 **pervert,** falsify, twist, garble, put a false construction upon, give a spin,

give a false coloring, color, varnish, put a spin on, twist the meaning of

**slap** NOUNS 1 smack, whack, whomp, **cuff, box,** buffet, belt; blow; **rap on the knuckles,** box on the ear, slap in the face; slap on the wrist, token punishment

VERBS 2 smack, whack, whomp, **cuff, box,** buffet; strike; slap the face, box the ears, give a rap on the knuckles

**slapstick** NOUNS 1 **comedy;** comic relief, comedy relief; sock, coxcomb, cap and bells, motley, bladder, buffoonery

ADJS 2 **comic** *or* **comical;** farcical, broad; burlesque

**slash** NOUNS 1 **wound,** injury, lesion; **cut,** incision, scratch, gash; **laceration,** mutilation; run, **rip,** rent, **tear**

2 **diagonal,** oblique, transverse, oblique line, **slant,** virgule, scratch comma, separatrix, solidus

VERBS 3 cut, cut *or* slant across, cut crosswise *or* transversely *or* diagonally, catercorner, diagonalize, slash across; **gash,** chop, crimp, scotch, **score,** blaze, jag, scarify; slit, scratch

4 **attack,** assail; castigate, flay, skin alive <nonformal>, **excoriate,** fustigate, scarify, scathe

5 **mark down,** cut prices, cut, shave, trim, pare, underprice, knock the bottom out of <nonformal>

**slat** NOUNS **strip,** lath, batten, spline, strake, plank

**slate** NOUNS 1 **ballot,** ticket; **schedule,** program, programma, **bill,** card, **calendar,** docket

VERBS 2 **schedule,** line up <nonformal>, **book,** book in, bill, program, calendar, docket, budget, put on the agenda

**slaughter** NOUNS 1 **butchery,** butchering, shambles, occision, slaughtering, hecatomb, holocaust

VERBS 2 **butcher,** massacre, decimate, commit carnage, depopulate, murder *or* kill *or* slay en masse; commit mass murder *or* destruction, murder wholesale, commit genocide

**slaughterhouse** NOUNS abbatoir, butchery <Brit>, shambles; stockyard; gas chamber, concentration camp, death camp, killing fields

**slave** NOUNS 1 **drudge,** grub, hack, fag, plodder, galley slave, **workhorse,** beast of burden, slogger

VERBS 2 **work hard;** scratch *and* hustle *and* sweat <all nonformal>, **sweat and slave** <nonformal>, slave away, toil away; work one's head off <nonformal>, work one's fingers to the bone, break one's back; work like a slave *or* galley slave, **work day and night,** burn the midnight oil; lucubrate, elucubrate

**slavery** NOUNS **subjection,** subjugation; **bondage,** captivity; thrall, thralldom, enthrallment; enslavement, master-slave relationship; **servitude; serfdom,** serfhood, villenage, **vassalage;** helotry, helotism; **peonage;** drudgery

**slay** VERBS 1 **kill,** put to death, deprive of life, take the life of, take one's life away, **do away with,** make away with, put out of the way, put to sleep, end, **put an end to,** end the life of, **dispatch,** do for, finish, finish off, kill off, **dispose of,** exterminate, destroy, annihilate; euthanatize; **execute**

2 **make one laugh,** strike one as funny, convulse; wow *and* knock dead *and* kill *and* break one up *and* crack one up *and* fracture one <all nonformal>; have them rolling in the aisles; keep them in stitches

**sled** NOUNS **sleigh,** *traîneau* <Fr>; snowmobile, Sno-Cat, weasel, Skimobile; toboggan

**sleep** NOUNS 1 **slumber; repose,** silken repose, *somnus* <L>, the arms of Morpheus; light sleep, fitful sleep, **doze,** drowse; beauty sleep <nonformal>; bedtime, sack time <nonformal>

VERBS 2 **slumber,** rest in the arms of Morpheus; **doze,** drowse; nap, catnap, take a nap, catch a wink, sleep soundly, **sleep like a top** *or* **log,** sleep like the dead

3 **fall asleep, go to sleep, drop off, retire,** doze off, drowse off, drift off, close one's eyes

**sleepy** ADJS **drowsy,** slumberous, slumbery, dreamy; **half asleep,** asleep on one's feet; sleepful, sleep-filled; heavy, **heavy-eyed,** heavy with sleep, sleep-swollen; **somnolent,** soporific; **lethargic,** comatose, narcose *or* narcous, stuporose *or* stuporous, in a stupor, out of it <nonformal>

**sleet** NOUNS 1 glaze, glazed frost, verglas, freezing rain

VERBS 2 **hail, frost,** ice, ice up, ice over, glaze, glaze over

**slender** ADJS **narrow,** narrowish, narrowy; **close,** near; **tight,** strait, isthmic, isthmian; **restricted,** limited, circumscribed, **confined,** constricted; **meager,** scant, scanty; **thin,** slim, gracile; **svelte,** slinky, sylphlike, willowy

**slew** NOUNS

<nonformal> **heap,** batch, pile, **stack,** loads, lots, **raft,** whole slew, spate, wad; **oodles,** gobs, scads, **mess**

**slice** NOUNS 1 **portion,** share, interest, part, stake, stock, **piece,** bit, segment; slice of the pie *or* melon *and* piece of the action <both nonformal>; **cut,** cutting, clip, clipping, paring, shaving, rasher, snip, snippet, collop
VERBS 2 **cut,** incise, carve, pare, prune, trim, trim away, resect, excise; slit, snip, lance, scissor

**slick** ADJS 1 **sleek,** glossy, shiny, gleaming; varnished, lacquered, shellacked, glazed, *glacé* <Fr>; **glassy,** smooth as glass; **slippery,** slippy, slithery *and* sliddery <both nonformal>, slippery as an eel; lubricious, lubric, oily, oleaginous, greasy, buttery, soaped; lubricated, oiled, greased
2 **cunning,** crafty, artful, wily, guileful, **sly,** insidious, **shifty,** arch, **smooth,** slick as a whistle <both nonformal>, **slippery,** snaky, serpentine; devious, Byzantine, calculating

**slide** NOUNS 1 **slip,** slippage; **glide,** coast, glissade; glissando; slither; **skid,** sideslip; **landslide,** mudslide, landslip, subsidence; **snowslide,** avalanche
VERBS 2 **slip,** slip *or* slide down; **glide,** skim, coast, glissade; **slither; skid,** sideslip; avalanche
3 **decline,** sink, fail, fall, fade, die, wane, **go downhill,** fall away, fall off, go off <nonformal>, slump, take a nosedive <nonformal>, go into a tailspin, hit the skids <nonformal>

**slight** NOUNS 1 **snub,** rebuff, repulse; humiliation, spurning, spurn, disregard, the go-by <nonformal>; cut, **the cold shoulder** <nonformal>; sneer, snort, sniff; contemptuous dismissal, kiss-off <nonformal>; **rejection**
VERBS 2 **ignore,** make little of, dismiss, pretend not to see, disregard, overlook, neglect, pass by, pass up *and* give the go-by <both nonformal>, leave out in the cold <nonformal>, take no note *or* notice of, look right through <nonformal>
3 **flout,** disregard, treat with contempt, snap one's fingers at; thumb one's nose at, cock a snook at, bite the thumb at; **disparage,** depreciate, belittle, degrade, debase, **run** *or* **knock down** <nonformal>, **put down** <nonformal>
ADJS 4 **frail,** delicate, dainty; puny; light, lightweight; **fragile,** unsubstantial, flimsy, **small**, smallish; **meager,** scrimpy, skimp, skimpy, exiguous

**slim** ADJS 1 **thin,** slender, gracile, thin-bodied, thin-set, narrow- *or* wasp-waisted; **svelte,** slinky, sylphlike, willowy; girlish, boyish; thinnish, slenderish, slimmish
ADJS 2 **meager,** scrimpy, skimp, skimpy, exiguous; scant, **scanty,** spare

**slime** NOUNS **filth,** muck, mess, sordes, foul matter; mucus, snot <nonformal>; **slop,** scum, sludge, glop *and* gunk <both nonformal>, ooze

**slimy** ADJS **filthy,** foul, vile, mucky, **nasty,** icky *and* yecchy *and* yucky *and* gross *and* grungy *and* scuzzy <all nonformal>; **odious,** repulsive; scummy <nonformal>; fulsome, slobbery, gushing, protesting too much, smarmy <nonformal>, insinuating, oily, **unctuous,** smooth, bland; **fawning,** sycophantic, obsequious

**slink** VERBS **lurk,** couch; **lie in wait,** lay wait; **sneak,** skulk, prowl, nightwalk, **steal,** creep, pussyfoot <nonformal>, gumshoe <nonformal>

**slinky** ADJS 1 **svelte,** sylphlike, willowy
2 furtive, stealthy, privy, backstairs, **sly, shifty, sneaky,** sneaking, skulking, slinking, feline

**slip** NOUNS 1 slipup *and* miscue <both nonformal>; **lapse,** *lapsus* <L>, **oversight,** omission, inadvertence *or* inadvertency, loose thread; **misstep,** trip, stumble, false *or* wrong step, wrong *or* bad *or* false move; false note; **slip of the tongue,** *lapsus linguae* <L>; **slip of the pen,** *lapsus calami* <L>
VERBS 2 **sink,** founder, go down, go under <nonformal>; go downhill, be on the skids <nonformal>; **fall,** lapse, trip; **err,** fall into error, **go wrong,** go amiss, go astray, go *or* get out of line, go awry, stray, get off-base <nonformal>, **deviate,** wander

**slippery** ADJS 1 slippy, **slick,** slithery <nonformal>, slippery as an eel; lubricious, lubric, oily, oleaginous, greasy, soaped; lubricated, oiled, greased

2 **fraudulent,** sharp, guileful, insidious, **shifty,** tricky
3 **precarious,** ticklish, touchy, touch-and-go, **critical,** delicate; on thin ice

**slipshod** ADJS **slovenly,** sloppy *and* messy *and* half-assed <all nonformal>, sluttish, untidy; **clumsy,** bungling; **haphazard,** promiscuous, hit-or-miss, hit-and-miss

**slit** NOUNS 1 **break,** breakage, **breach,** burst, **rupture,** fracture; crack, cleft, **fissure,** cut, split; **gap,** rift, rent, rip, tear
VERBS 2 **cut,** cut apart, gash, **split,** rive, rent, rip open; cut open, cleave; tear open, rent, tear, dispart, separate; slash, scratch

**slither** VERBS **slide,** slip, slip *or* slide down; **glide,** skim, coast, glissade

**sliver** NOUNS **scrap,** tatter, smithereen <nonformal>, patch, snip, **snippet,** snick; splinter, shiver; **morsel,** *morceau* <Fr>, crumb

**slob** NOUNS **slattern,** sloven, frump <nonformal>, Sloppy Joe, schlep, schlump, *Strüwelpeter* <Ger>; drab, **slut,** trollop; pig, swine; **litterbug**

**slobber** NOUNS 1 **saliva,** spittle, sputum, spit, expectoration; salivation, ptyalism, sialorrhea, sialagogue, slabber, slaver, **drivel,** dribble, drool; gush, smarm *and* smarminess <both nonformal>
VERBS 2 slabber, slaver, **drool, drivel,** dribble; dither, blither, blather, maunder, dote, burble

**slogan** NOUNS **catchword,** catch phrase, shibboleth, cry; **motto,** watchword, tag line; epithet

**slope** NOUNS 1 **declivity,** steep, versant, incline, rise, talus, brae <Scots>, mountainside, hillside, bank, gentle *or* easy slope, glacis, angle of repose, steep *or* rapid slope, fall line
VERBS 2 **incline,** lean; slant, rake, pitch, grade, bank, shelve; **tilt,** tip, list, cant, careen, keel, sidle, swag, sway

**sloppy** ADJS **slipshod,** slipshoddy, **slovenly, messy** *and* half-assed <both nonformal>, sluttish, untidy; **clumsy,** bungling; **haphazard,** promiscuous, hit-or-miss, hit-and-miss; half-assed <nonformal>

**slot** NOUNS **opening,** aperture, hole, hollow, orifice; split, crack, check; position

**sloth** NOUNS **apathy,** indifference, unconcern; **lethargy,** hebetude, sluggishness, languor, languidness; acedia, noonday demon; **indolence,** laziness, slothfulness, bone-laziness

**slouch** NOUNS 1 **bungler, blunderer,** blunderhead, boggler, slubberer, bumbler, **fumbler,** botcher; **lout,** oaf, gawk, boor, **clown**
VERBS 2 **droop,** sag, swag; **lie around,** lounge around, loll around, moon, sit on one's ass *or* butt *or* duff <nonformal>, **loiter about** *or* **around,** slouch around

**slovenly** ADJS **slipshod,** careless, loose, slack, nonformal, negligent; **untidy,** unsightly, **unkempt; messy** <nonformal>, mussy <nonformal>, **sloppy** <nonformal>, scraggly, poky, seedy <nonformal>, **shabby,** shoddy, chintzy, grubby <nonformal>, **frowzy,** blowzy, tacky <nonformal>

**slow** VERBS 1 **slow down** *or* **up,** let down *or* up, ease off *or* up, slack off *or* up, slacken, relax, moderate, taper off, lose speed *or* momentum; **decelerate,** retard, delay, **detain,** impede, obstruct, arrest, stay, **check,** curb, **hold up,** hold back
ADJS 2 **leisurely,** slack, moderate, gentle, **easy,** deliberate, go-slow, unhurried, relaxed, gradual, circumspect, tentative, cautious, reluctant, foot-dragging <nonformal>; poking, poky, slow-poky <nonformal>; **sluggish,** languid, languorous, lazy, slothful, indolent, idle, slouchy; slow as slow, slow as molasses *or* molasses in January, slow as death
ADVS 3 **slowly,** leisurely, unhurriedly, relaxedly, easily, moderately, gently; pokingly, pokily; **sluggishly,** languidly, languorously, lazily, indolently, idly, deliberately, with deliberation, circumspectly, tentatively, cautiously, reluctantly; in low gear

**slowdown** NOUNS 1 **slowing,** retardation, retardment, **slackening,** flagging, slowing down; slowup, **letup,** letdown, slack-up, slack-off, ease-off, ease-up; **delay**, detention, setback, holdup <nonformal>
2 **job action;** rulebook slowdown, sick-in *and* sickout <both nonformal>; work-to-rule, rule-book slowdown

**slug** NOUNS 1 **slowpoke** <nonformal>, plodder, slow goer, slow-foot, **lingerer,** loiterer, dawdler, dawdle, **laggard,** procrastinator, foot-dragger, stick-in-the-mud <nonformal>, drone, sluggard, lie-abed, goof-off <nonformal>, goldbrick <nonformal>
2 **shot; ball,** cannonball, rifle ball, minié ball; **bullet,** pellet

3 **token,** counter
4 **dose,** portion; shot *and* nip *and* snort *and* dram <all nonformal>
VERBS 5 **fight,** punch, spar, mix it up <nonformal>, knock down, knock out, maul

**sluggish** ADJS **languid,** languorous, listless, lifeless, inanimate, enervated, debilitated, **pepless** <nonformal>, lackadaisical, slow, wan, **lethargic,** logy, phlegmatic, hebetudinous, apathetic, dopey <nonformal>, nodding, droopy, **dull,** heavy, leaden, lumpish, torpid

**slum** NOUNS **slums,** the other side *or* the wrong side of the tracks, blighted area *or* neighborhood *or* section, run-down neighborhood, tenement district, shanty-town, hell's kitchen *or* half-acre

**slump** NOUNS 1 **sinkage,** lowering, **decline,** subsidence, submergence, lapse, decurrence; **droop,** sag; downturn, downtrend, retreat, remission; **descent,** downward trend, downturn, depreciation, **decrease,** drop, fall; **depression,** recession, economic stagnation, **bust** <nonformal>
VERBS 2 **decline,** sink, fail, fall, slip, fade, die, wane, ebb, subside, lapse, **run down,** go down, **go downhill,** fall away, fall off, go off <nonformal>, slide, take a nose dive <nonformal>, go into a tailspin, take a turn for the worse

**slur** NOUNS **aspersion,** remark, reflection, imputation, **insinuation,** suggestion, sly suggestion, innuendo, whispering campaign; disparaging *or* uncomplimentary remark

**slurp** VERBS **lap up,** sponge *or* soak up, lick, lap; snuff, snuffle, sniff, sniffle, snuff in *or* up

**slut** NOUNS **strumpet,** trollop, wench, hussy, jade, baggage, *cocotte* <Fr>, grisette; **tart** *and* **chippy** *and* **floozy** *and* broad <all nonformal>, drab, trull, quean, harridan, Jezebel, wanton, whore <nonformal>, bad woman, **loose woman,** easy woman <nonformal>, easy lay <nonformal>, woman of easy virtue, frail sister

**sly** ADJS **shrewd,** artful, cunning, knowing, crafty, wily, guileful, canny, slick, smart as a fox, crazy like a fox <both nonformal>; insinuating, insidious, devious, Byzantine, calculating

**smack** NOUNS 1 **slap,** flap; **box,** cuff, buffet; **spank**
VERBS 2 **slap,** whack, whomp, **cuff,** box, buffet; strike; slap the face, box the ears, give a rap on the knuckles
3 **kiss,** osculate, buss, smooch <nonformal>
ADVS 4 **suddenly,** precipitately, impulsively, impetuously, hastily; dash; bang, slap, plop, plunk, plump, pop; **unexpectedly**, out of a clear blue sky

**small** ADJS 1 **little,** smallish; **slight,** exiguous; **puny, trifling,** poky, piffling *and* pindling *and* piddling *and* piddly <all nonformal>, **dinky** <nonformal>; one-horse, two-by-four <nonformal>; pint-sized <nonformal>, half-pint; knee-high to a grasshopper; petite; short
2 **ungenerous,** illiberal, unchivalrous, mean, little, paltry, mingy, petty; **niggardly,** stingy; **narrow-minded,** small-minded, mean-minded, mean; uncharitable
ADVS 3 little, **slightly**, fractionally; **on a small scale,** in a small compass, in a small way, on a minuscule *or* infinitesimal scale; in a nutshell

**smart** ADJS 1 **brainy** <nonformal>, bright, brilliant, scintillating; **clever,** apt, **gifted,** talented; **sharp,** keen; **quick,** nimble, adroit, dexterous; **sharp-witted,** quick-witted, quick-thinking, nimble-witted, quick on the trigger *or* uptake <nonformal>; smart as a whip, sharp as a tack <nonformal>
2 **fashionable,** in fashion, in style, in vogue; all the rage, all the thing; **up-to-date,** up-to-the-minute, with-it <nonformal>, trendy <nonformal>

**smart aleck** NOUNS **braggart**, know-it-all *or* know-all, smart-ass *and* wise-ass <both nonformal>

**smash** NOUNS 1 **whack,** smack, thwack, swipe, swing, **punch,** poke, jab
VERBS 2 **demolish,** wreck, total *and* rack up <both nonformal>, undo, unbuild, unmake, dismantle; **disintegrate,** fragment, break to pieces, make mincemeat of, reduce to rubble, atomize, pulverize, shatter

**smattering** NOUNS **slight knowledge,** vague notion, imperfect knowledge, a little learning, glimmering, **smattering of knowledge,** smattering of ignorance, half-learning, sciolism

**smear** NOUNS 1 **defamation,** vilification, revilement, defilement, blackening, denigration; character assassination, *ad hominem* <L> *or* personal attack
VERBS 2 **vilify,** revile, defile, sully, soil,

smirch, besmirch, bespatter, tarnish, **blacken,** denigrate, blacken one's good name, give a black eye <nonformal>; **muckrake,** throw mud at, mudsling, heap dirt upon, drag through the mud

**smell** NOUNS 1 **odor,** scent, aroma, savor; **essence,** redolence, effluvium, emanation, exhalation, fume, breath, subtle odor, whiff, trace, detectable odor; trail, spoor; fragrance; stink, stench
VERBS 2 **scent,** nose; **sniff,** snuff, snuffle, inhale, breathe, breathe in; get a noseful of, smell of, catch a smell of, get *or* take a whiff of, whiff
3 **stink,** smell bad, assail *or* offend the nostrils, smell to high heaven, **reek;** smell up, stink up; stink out

**smelly** ADJS **malodorous,** fetid, olid, **odorous,** stinking, reeking, reeky, nidorous, smelling, bad-smelling, **evil-smelling,** stenchy; **foul,** vile, putrid, fulsome, noisome, fecal, feculent, excremental, offensive, repulsive, noxious, sulfurous

**smile** NOUNS 1 smiling; bright smile, gleaming *or* glowing smile, beam; silly smile *or* grin; **grin,** grinning
VERBS 2 crack a smile <nonformal>, break into a smile; **grin,** grin like a Cheshire cat *or* chessy-cat <nonformal>

**smirk** NOUNS 1 scornful laugh *or* smile, snicker, snigger, sardonic grin, leer, fleer, **sneer,** snort
VERBS 2 **smile,** crack a smile <nonformal>; simper

**smitten** ADJS **enamored,** charmed, becharmed, **fascinated, infatuated,** infatuate; heartsmitten

**smooch** VERBS **kiss, osculate,** buss, smack; blow a kiss

**smooth** VERBS 1 flatten, plane, planish, **level,** even, equalize; **dress,** dub, dab; smooth down *or* out, lay; plaster, plaster down; roll, roll smooth; harrow, drag; grade
2 **pacify,** smooth over *or* out, smooth down, smooth one's feathers; allay, pour oil on troubled waters, pour balm on; cool <nonformal>, defuse; clear the air
ADJS 3 **talkative, voluble, fluent; glib,** flip <nonformal>; gregarious, sociable
4 **even,** smoothened, smoothed out; table-like; flat, level, horizontal; velvety, smooth as silk *or* satin *or* velvet, smooth as a billiard ball *or* baby's ass <nonformal>
5 **suave,** smug, bland, **unctuous,** oily, oleaginous, fulsome, ingratiating, disarming

**smother** VERBS 1 **suppress,** repress, keep under, stifle, choke *or* hold back, fight down *or* back, inhibit; **suffocate,** stifle, asphyxiate, stop the breath
2 **extinguish,** quench, snuff out, put out, stamp *or* trample out, trample underfoot; **quash,** squash *and* squelch <both nonformal>, **quell,** put down

**smudge** NOUNS 1 **soil,** soilure, soilage, smut; **smirch,** smutch, smear, **spot,** blot, blotch, **stain**
VERBS 2 **darken,** smutch, **smirch,** besmirch, murk, blotch, blot, dinge; **smear,** blacken one's name *or* reputation, give one a black eye, tear down

**smug** ADJS **complacent,** self-complacent, self-satisfied, self-content, self-contented; **prudish,** priggish, prim, prissy, stuffy <nonformal>

**smuggler** NOUNS contrabandist, runner; drug smuggler, mule <nonformal>; gunrunner, rumrunner

**smut** NOUNS 1 **blackening,** denigration; **smudging,** smutching, smirching; smudge, smutch, smirch
2 **obscenity, ribaldry, pornography,** porno *and* porn <both nonformal>, salacity, **dirt,** filth; lewdness, bawdiness, salaciousness, **smuttiness,** foulness, filthiness, nastiness, vileness, offensiveness

**snack** NOUNS 1 **light meal,** refreshments, light repast, light lunch, nosh <nonformal>, **bite** <nonformal>
VERBS 2 nibble, pick, nosh <nonformal>; pick at, peck at <nonformal>, eat like a bird

**snag** NOUNS 1 **crux,** hitch, pinch, rub, catch, joker <nonformal>, where the shoe pinches
VERBS 2 **catch,** take, catch flatfooted, land *and* nail <both nonformal>, hook, **snare,** sniggle, spear, **bag,** trap, entrap

**snake** NOUNS 1 **serpent,** ophidian; **viper,** pit viper; sea snake; plumber's snake; snake in the grass
VERBS 2 convolve, **wind,** twine, twirl, **twist,** turn, twist and turn, meander, crinkle; serpentine, slink, worm; pluck, wrench

**snappy** ADJS **quick,** swift, speedy, expeditious, celeritous, alacritous, **prompt,** ready, smart, sharp, quick on the draw *or* trigger *or* upswing <nonformal>; **agile,** nimble, spry

**snare** NOUNS 1 springe, trap; noose, lasso, lariat; bola; **net,** trawl, dragnet, seine; cobweb; **meshes,** toils
VERBS 2 **catch, take,** catch flatfooted, land *and* nail <both nonformal>, hook, **snag,** sniggle; ensnare, enmesh, entangle, tangle, foul, tangle up with; **net,** bag, trap, entrap; lasso, rope, noose

**snarl** NOUNS 1 **grimace,** wry face, wry mouth, rictus
2 **fight,** squabble, contention, strife, **tussle,** bicker, wrangle, **tiff,** spat, fuss
3 **tangle,** tangled skein, mess *and* snafu *and* fuck-up <all nonformal>, ravel, snarl-up; can of worms <nonformal>, snake pit
VERBS 4 **growl,** gnarl, **snap,** show one's teeth, spit; **glower,** lower, scowl, **glare,** frown, give a dirty look <nonformal>, look daggers

**snatch** VERBS **seize,** snatch up, nip, nail <nonformal>, **clutch,** claw, clinch, clench; **kidnap,** hold for ransom; skyjack; **shanghai,** impress

**sneak** NOUNS 1 **dastard,** craven, poltroon, recreant, caitiff, arrant coward
VERBS 2 **creep,** steal, steal along; pussyfoot *and* gumshoe <both nonformal>, slink, sidle, pad, prowl, nightwalk; **cower,** quail, cringe, crouch, skulk

**sneaky** ADJS **underhanded;** furtive, stealthy, privy, backstairs, **sly,** shifty, sneaking, skulking, slinking, slinky; **cowering,** quailing, cringing

**sneer** NOUNS 1 scornful laugh *or* smile, snicker, snigger, **smirk,** sardonic grin, leer, fleer, snort
VERBS 2 **scoff,** jeer, **mock,** revile, **twit,** taunt, jape, flout, scout, have a fling at, cast in one's teeth; cut at; **sneer at,** fleer, curl one's lip

**snicker** NOUNS 1 scornful laugh *or* smile, snigger, **smirk,** sardonic grin, leer, fleer, **sneer,** snort
VERBS 2 chortle; cackle, crow; snigger, snort; laugh up one's sleeve, laugh in one's beard

**snide** ADJS **hostile,** antagonistic, repugnant, antipathetic, set against, spiteful, malicious, malevolent, malignant

**snip** NOUNS 1 **scrap,** tatter, smithereen <nonformal>, patch, **stitch,** shred, tag; **snippet,** snick, chip, nip
VERBS 2 **cut,** slit, lance, scissor

**snit** NOUNS **dither,** tizzy <nonformal>, swivet, foofaraw, **flutter,** fluster, **fret,** fuss, pother, bother, lather *and* stew <both nonformal>, flap

**snitch** NOUNS **informer,** betrayer, double-crosser <nonformal>, snitcher <nonformal>; whistle-blower <nonformal>; **tattler,** tattletale, telltale, talebearer; blab *or* blabber *or* blabberer *or* blabbermouth <all nonformal>; **squealer** *and* preacher *and* **stool pigeon** *and* stoolie *and* **fink** *and* rat <all nonformal>

**sniveling** ADJS **tearful,** weepy <nonformal>; lachrymal, lachrymose, lacrimatory; blubbering, whimpering; canting, unctuous, mealymouthed

**snob** NOUNS **prig;** elitist; highbrow *and* egghead <both nonformal>, Brahmin, mandarin; name-dropper

**snobbish** ADJS snobby, **priggish,** snippy <nonformal>; snooty *and* snotty *and* sniffy <all nonformal>; high-hat *and* high-hatted *and* high-hatty <all nonformal>

**snoop** NOUNS 1 **meddler,** intermeddler; **busybody,** pry, Paul Pry, prier, Nosey Parker *or* nosey Parker *or* Nosy Parker <all nonformal>, snooper, backseat driver <nonformal>
VERBS 2 **pry,** peep, peek, spy, nose, nose into, have a long *or* big nose, poke *or* stick one's nose in; meddle

**snort** NOUNS 1 **drink,** jolt, **shot,** snifter, wet; quickie
2 scornful laugh *or* smile, snicker, snigger, **smirk,** sardonic grin, leer, fleer, **sneer**
VERBS 3 snicker, snigger
4 **use,** be on; **sniff,** blow, toot, one and one <nonformal>

**snotty** ADJS **contemptuous,** disdainful, supercilious, sniffy, toplofty, toploftical, **scornful,** sneering, withering, contumelious; snobbish, snobby, priggish

**snow job** NOUNS **inducement,** coaxing, wheedling, working on <nonformal>, cajolery, cajolement, conning, smoke and mirrors <nonformal>, blandishment, sweet talk *and* soft soap <both nonformal>

**snub** NOUNS 1 **rebuff,** repulse; **slight,** humiliation, spurning, spurn, disregard, the go-by <nonformal>; cut, **the cold shoulder** <nonformal>; contemptuous dismissal, **dismissal**, kiss-off <nonformal>; **rejection**
VERBS 2 **rebuff,** cut *or* cut dead <nonformal>, drop, repulse; **high-hat** *and* upstage <both nonformal>; **look down**

one's nose at, look cool *or* coldly upon; cold-shoulder *or* turn a cold shoulder upon *or* **give the cold shoulder** <nonformal>
ADJS 3 **shortened, curtailed,** cut short, short-cut, **docked,** bobbed, sheared, shaved, trimmed, clipped, snubbed, nipped

**snug** ADJS **cozy,** snug as a bug in a rug; friendly, warm; **homelike,** homey *and* down-home <both nonformal>, homely, lived-in, intimate; **compact,** fast, shut fast

**snuggle** VERBS **nestle,** cuddle, cuddle up, curl up; nest, nuzzle; bundle; snuggle up to

**soak** VERBS 1 **overprice,** hold up *and* stick *and* sting *and* clip <all nonformal>, **make pay through the nose,** gouge
2 **drench,** imbrue, **souse,** sop, sodden; **saturate,** water-soak, waterlog; **steep,** seethe, macerate, infuse, imbue, impregnate

**soap** NOUNS **cleanser,** detergent, synthetic detergent, abstergent

**soapbox** NOUNS **platform; rostrum,** podium, pulpit, speaker's platform *or* stand; hustings, **stump**

**soar** VERBS 1 **fly,** be airborne, drift, hover; zoom, plane, kite, fly aloft
2 **tower,** rear, spire, outsoar

**sob** NOUNS 1 **cry,** *cri du coeur* <Fr>, outcry, scream, **howl,** yowl, bawl, yawp, keen, ululation
VERBS 2 **weep,** cry, **bawl,** boo-hoo; **blubber,** whimper, snivel, keen, whine, wail; shed tears, drop a tear; break down and cry, turn on the waterworks <nonformal>; cry one's eyes out

**sober** ADJS 1 **sedate,** staid, sober-minded, **serious,** grave, solemn, dignified, unsmiling, sobersided; temperate, moderate; **levelheaded,** balanced, coolheaded, cool, **sound,** sober-minded
2 in one's right mind, in possession of one's faculties; clearheaded; **unintoxicated,** uninebriated, uninebriate; cold *or* stone sober <nonformal>, **sober as a judge;** able to walk the chalk mark *or* line <nonformal>; dry, straight, temperate

**sociable** ADJS **social,** social-minded, fit for society, fond of society, **gregarious,** amiable, **friendly;** civil, urbane, courteous

**social** NOUNS 1 **social gathering,** social affair, social hour, hospitality hour, affair, gathering, get-together <nonformal>
ADJS 2 **communal,** common, general, public, collective, popular, societal; sociable

**socialism** NOUNS collective ownership, collectivization, public ownership; **collectivism;** state socialism, *Staatsozialismus* <Ger>; Fabian socialism, Fabianism; utopian socialism; Marxian socialism, Marxism

**socialite** NOUNS **aristocrat,** patrician, Brahmin, blue-blood, thoroughbred, member of the upper class, swell *and* upper-cruster <both nonformal>, grandee, grand dame, magnifico, lord of creation

**socialize** VERBS 1 **civilize,** acculturate, enlighten, edify; **educate**
2 **collectivize,** communize, communalize; nationalize, expropriate

**society** NOUNS 1 *société* <Fr>, fashionable society, **polite society, high society,** high life, *beau monde, haut monde* <both Fr>, good society; **smart set** <nonformal>; the Four Hundred, **upper crust** *and* upper cut <both nonformal>
2 **community,** commonwealth; **kinship group,** clan, totemic *or* totemistic group, phyle, phratry *or* phratria, gens, caste, subcaste, endogamous group; **class, social class**, economic class
3 **company,** association, consociation; guild, organization, fellowship, professional organization, union

**soda** NOUNS **beverage,** drink, thirst quencher; **soft drink,** nonalcoholic beverage; cold drink; carbonated water, soda water, sparkling water, pop, soda pop, tonic

**sodden** ADJS **soaked, drenched,** soused, bathed, steeped, macerated; **water-soaked,** waterlogged; soaking, sopping; wringing wet, soaking wet, sopping wet, wet to the skin, like a drowned rat; soppy, **soggy,** dripping wet

**sodomy** NOUNS **anal sex,** anal intercourse, buggery <nonformal>

**soft** ADJS 1 **faint, low,** gentle, subdued, dim, feeble, weak, faint-sounding, low-sounding, soft-sounding
2 **sentimental,** sentimentalized, **mawkish,** maudlin, cloying; sticky *and* gooey *and* schmaltzy *and* sappy *and* soppy <all nonformal>, oversentimental, oversentimentalized, bathetic
3 nonresistive, nonrigid; whisper-soft,

soft as putty *or* clay *or* dough, etc, soft as a baby's bottom

*soft as sinews of the new-born babe*
SHAKESPEARE

**soften** VERBS 1 **extenuate,** mitigate, palliate, lessen, diminish, **ease,** mince; **soft-pedal;** subdue, tame, hold in check, keep a tight rein, chasten, underplay, play down, downplay, de-emphasize, tone *or* tune down
2 **cushion,** absorb the shock, **soften the blow,** break the fall, deaden, damp *or* dampen, suppress, neutralize, offset

**softhearted** ADJS **tender,** soft, tenderhearted, warmhearted; kindhearted, warm, **sympathetic,** sympathizing, **compassionate**, merciful

**softy** ADJS **weakling,** weak *or* meek soul, weak sister <nonformal>, hothouse plant, softling, **jellyfish,** invertebrate, gutless wonder <nonformal>; **wimp,** poor *or* weak *or* dull tool <nonformal>

**soggy** ADJS **soaked,** drenched, soaking, sopping; **sodden,** soppy, soaky

**soil** NOUNS 1 soilage, smut; **smirch,** smudge, smutch, smear, **spot,** blot, blotch
2 **land, ground,** landmass, earth, **sod,** clod, **dirt,** dust, clay, marl; arable land; topsoil, subsoil
VERBS 3 **vilify,** revile, defile, sully, smear, smirch, besmirch, bespatter, tarnish, **blacken,** denigrate, blacken one's good name, give a black eye <nonformal>; **muckrake,** throw mud at, mudsling, heap dirt upon, drag through the mud; **stigmatize,** brand

**soiree** NOUNS **social gathering,** social; **reception,** at home, salon, levee

**sojourn** NOUNS temporary stay; **stay,** stop; **stopover,** stopoff, stayover, layover

**solace** NOUNS **consolation,** solacement, easement, heart's ease; support, **comfort,** crumb *or* shred of comfort; condolence, sympathy

*surcease of sorrow*
POE

**soldier** NOUNS 1 **military man** *or* **woman,** serviceman, servicewoman, navy man *or* woman; air service-man *or* -woman

2 <nonformal> **grunt, dogface,** footslogger, paddlefoot, doughfoot, blisterfoot, crunchie, line doggie, groundpounder

3 defender, champion, advocate; upholder; guardian angel, supporter; vindicator, apologist; **protector; guard;** paladin; guard dog, attack dog, junkyard dog

**sole** ADJS **unique,** singular, absolute, unrepeated, **alone,** lone, **only,** only-begotten, **one and only,** first and last; celibate

**solemn** ADJS 1 **dignified,** sober, grave, unsmiling, weighty, **somber,** frowning, **grim; sedate,** staid; **serious,** earnest, thoughtful; straight-faced, long-faced, grim-faced, stone-faced
2 **lofty,** elevated, sublime, grand, majestic, noble, stately; **reverent,** reverential, venerative, venerational, adoring

**solicit** VERBS **canvass; court,** woo, address, sue, sue for, pop the question <nonformal>; **seek,** bid for, look for; **fish for,** angle for; **make advances,** approach, **make an overture,** solicit, importune

**solicitor** NOUNS 1 **petitioner,** supplicant, suppliant, suitor; **applicant,** solicitant, claimant; **aspirant,** seeker; canvasser
2 **lawyer,** attorney, attorney-at-law, barrister, **counselor,** counselor-at-law, **counsel,** legal counsel *or* counselor, legal adviser, legal expert, **advocate,** pleader; member of the bar, legal practitioner, officer of the court

**solicitous** ADJS **considerate,** thoughtful, mindful, heedful, attentive, tactful, mindful of others; **helpful,** agreeable, **obliging,** indulgent, tolerant, lenient

**solid** NOUNS 1 solid body, body, mass; lump, clump, cluster; block, cake; node, knot
ADJS 2 **firm,** sound, stout, sturdy, hard, tough, hard-boiled <nonformal>, **staunch,** stable; sound as a dollar, solid as a rock, firm as Gibraltar, made of iron
3 **unanimous,** consentaneous, **with one voice;** agreeing, in agreement, like-minded, of one mind, of the same mind; of a piece, **at one,** at one with; **complete,** whole, total, global, **entire,** intact
4 **valid,** sound, well-grounded, well-founded, conforming to the facts *or* the data *or* the evidence *or* reality, hard, substantial

**solidarity** NOUNS **community,** harmony, concordance, concord, fellowship, fellow feeling, concert, **teamwork,** team spirit, esprit, *esprit de corps* <Fr>; solidity

**solidify** VERBS **cohere,** set, conglomerate, agglomerate, conglobate; **congeal,** coagulate, clabber <nonformal>, **clot; cluster,** mass, bunch; **integrate,** coalesce, come together, make one, unitize

**soliloquy** NOUNS monology, self-address; **monologue;** aside; monodrama; apostrophe

**solitary** ADJS **alone; in solitude,** by oneself, all alone; **lonely,** lonesome, lone; **one,** single, singular, individual, sole, unique; reclusive, antisocial

**solution** NOUNS 1 resolution, **answer,** reason, explanation; **finding,** conclusion, determination, ascertainment, verdict, judgment; **outcome,** upshot, denouement, **result,** issue, end, end result; **happy ending** *or* outcome, the answer to one's prayers, the light at the end of the tunnel; possible solution, **scenario**
2 decoction, infusion, mixture; chemical solution; lixivium, leach, leachate; **suspension,** colloidal suspension; **emulsion,** gel, aerosol

**solve** VERBS **resolve,** find the solution *or* answer, **clear up,** get, get right, do, work, **work out,** find out, figure out, dope *and* dope out <both nonformal>; **straighten out,** iron out, sort out, puzzle out; **get to the bottom** *or* **heart of,** fathom, plumb

**solvent** ADJS 1 **sound,** substantial, solid, good, sound as a dollar, creditworthy; **able to pay,** good for, unindebted, out of the hole *or* the red
2 dissolvent, resolvent, resolutive, thinning, cutting, diluent; alkahestic

**somber** ADJS **gloomy,** dismal, murky, bleak, grim, sombrous, **solemn,** grave; sad, *triste* <Fr>, **funereal,** funebrial, crepehanging <nonformal>, saturnine; sinister, dark, black, dreary; **lackluster, dull,** deadened, lifeless, **drab,** wan

**somebody** NOUNS **personage,** important person, person of importance *or* consequence, **great man** *or* **woman,** man *or* woman of mark *or* note, **notable,** notability, figure; **celebrity,** famous person, person of renown, personality

**something** NOUNS **object,** article, thing, material thing, affair; whatsit <nonformal>, what's-its-name; something or other, *etwas* <Ger>, *eppes* <Yiddish>, *quelque chose* <Fr>; artifact

**sometime** ADJS 1 **former,** past, fore, **previous,** late, recent, **once,** onetime, **erstwhile,** then, quondam; **occasional,** casual, incidental; off-and-on, spare, sparetime, **part-time**
ADVS 2 **someday,** some of these days, one of these days, some fine day *or* morning, sometime or other, somewhen, **sooner or later**

**somewhat** ADVS **to a degree,** to a certain extent, to some degree, in some measure, to such an extent, *pro tanto* <L>; **moderately,** mildly, detectably, just visibly, modestly, appreciably, visibly, **fairly,** tolerably, **partially,** partly, part, in part, incompletely

**son** NOUNS **offspring,** child, scion; son and heir, a chip of *or* off the old block, sonny; stepson, foster child

**song** NOUNS lay, *Lied* <Ger>, *chanson* <Fr>, carol, **ditty,** canticle, lilt; **ballad,** ballade, *ballata* <Ital>; *canzone* <Ital>; canzonet, *canzonetta* <Ital>

**soon** ADVS **presently,** directly, shortly, in a short time *or* while, **before long,** ere long, in no long time, in a while, **in a little while,** after a while, by and by, anon, betimes, *bientôt* <Fr>, in due time, in due course, at the first opportunity; in a moment *or* minute, *tout à l'heure* <Fr>

**soot** NOUNS **dirt,** grime; dust; smut

**soothe** VERBS **quiet,** quieten, **lull,** quiesce, **calm,** calm down, tranquilize, pacify, passivize, pour oil on troubled waters; mollify, dulcify; **settle,** smooth over *or* out, smooth down, smooth one's feathers

**soothing** ADJS **palliative,** lenitive, alleviative, assuasive, balmy, balsamic, demulcent, emollient; **sedative,** calmative, calmant, depressant, tranquilizing, **relaxing,** pacifying

**sooty** ADJS **dingy,** grimy, smoky, fuliginous, **smudgy,** smutty, blotchy, dirty, **muddy,** murky, smirched, besmirched

**sophisticated** ADJS 1 **worldly,** worldly-wise, wise in the ways of the world, knowing, cosmopolitan, cosmopolite, blasé, dry behind the ears, not born yesterday, long in the tooth
2 nice, fine, delicate, dainty, **subtle,** discriminating, fastidious

**sorcerer** NOUNS **necromancer,** wizard, wonder-worker, warlock, theurgist; warlock, male witch; thaumaturge, thaumaturgist; **conjurer**, diviner

**sorceress** NOUNS shamaness; **witch,** witchwoman <nonformal>, witchwife <Scots>, **hex, hag,** lamia

**sordid** ADJS **squalid,** wretched, shabby; **disreputable,** discreditable, dishonorable, unsavory, shady, **seamy**

**sore** NOUNS 1 pustule, papule, papula, fester; sore spot, tender spot, lesion
ADJS 2 **raw;** smarting, tingling, **burning; irritated,** inflamed, tender, sensitive, fiery, angry, red; algetic; chafed, galled; **festering; painful,** harsh, bitter, sharp

**sorrow** NOUNS sorrowing, **grief,** care, **woe;** heartgrief, heartfelt grief; **anguish,** misery, agony; **lamentation**

**sorry** ADJS 1 **regretful,** remorseful, full of remorse, **ashamed,** shamefaced, **rueful,** repining, unhappy about; **self-reproachful,** self-reproaching, self-condemning, self-convicting
2 **disgraceful,** shameful, pitiful, deplorable, opprobrious, sad; degrading, debasing, demeaning; **paltry,** poor, common, **mean,** pitiable, pathetic

**sort** NOUNS 1 **kind,** ilk, type, breed of cat <nonformal>, lot <nonformal>, **variety,** species, genus, *genre* <Fr>, phylum, denomination, designation, description, style, manner, **nature, character,** persuasion, the like *or* likes of <nonformal>
VERBS 2 **distinguish,** draw *or* make distinctions, secern, **separate,** separate out, divide, analyze, subdivide, **set apart,** sift, sift out, sieve, sieve out, winnow, screen, screen out, classify, sort out

**so-so** ADJS 1 **middling, ordinary,** usual, routine, common, mediocre, merely adequate, passing, banal
ADVS 2 **mediocrely,** middlingly, fairly, fairishly, middling well, fair to middling <nonformal>, moderately, modestly, **indifferently;** passably, **tolerably**

**soul** NOUNS 1 person, persona, body, warm body <nonformal>; **individuality,** personhood
2 **psyche,** spirit, spiritus, *âme* <Fr>, **heart, mind,** anima, *anima humana* <L>; *atman* and *purusha* and *buddhi* and *jiva* and *jivatma* <all Skt>; *ba* and *khu* <both Egyptian myth>; *ruach* and *nephesh* <both Hebrew>; spiritual being, inner man

*the Divinity that stirs within us*
ADDISON

**soul-searching** NOUNS self-analysis, examination of conscience

**sound** NOUNS 1 sonance, acoustic, acoustical *or* acoustic phenomenon; auditory phenomenon *or* stimulus, auditory effect; noise
2 **inlet, cove,** arm of the sea, arm, armlet, **bay,** fjord, bight
VERBS 3 make a sound *or* noise, give forth *or* emit a sound; **reverberate,** resound, **rumble,** roll, boom, echo
4 **take soundings,** make a sounding, heave *or* cast *or* sling the lead, **fathom, plumb,** plumb-line, plumb the depths
ADJS 5 whole, wholesome; unimpaired; sound of mind and body, sound in wind and limb, sound as a dollar <nonformal>
6 **stable,** substantial, firm, solid, stabile; solid as a rock, built on bedrock; **logical,** reasonable, rational, cogent, sensible, sane, justifiable, admissible; well-argued, well-founded, well-grounded, **valid**

**sound bite** NOUNS **excerpt,** extract, selection, extraction, excerption, snippet; selected passage; **clip** <nonformal>, film clip, outtake

**sour** VERBS 1 turn sour *or* acid, **acidify,** acidulate, acetify; acerbate, exacerbate; **embitter,** bitter, envenom
ADJS 2 soured, sourish; **tart,** tartish; crab, **crabbed;** acerb, acerbic, acerbate
3 **complaining,** faultfinding, grumbling, growling, **peevish,** petulant, sulky; **sour-tempered,** prune-faced <nonformal>

**source** NOUNS **origin,** genesis, original, origination, **derivation,** rise, beginning, conception, inception, commencement, **head;** provenance, provenience, background; **informant,** informer, teller, interviewee, enlightener

**souvenir** NOUNS **memento,** remembrance, token, trophy, keepsake, relic, favor, token of remembrance; *memento mori* <L>; **memorabilia** <pl>

**sovereign** NOUNS 1 **potentate,** monarch, ruler, prince, dynast, **crowned head,** emperor, *imperator* <L>, king-emperor, **king,** anointed king, majesty, royalty, royal, royal personage
ADJS 2 **governing,** controlling, regulating, regulative, regulatory, **commanding; ruling,** reigning, regnant; self-governing

**sow** VERBS **seed,** seed down, seminate,

inseminate; **disseminate,** broadcast, sow broadcast, scatter seed

**spa** NOUNS **health resort,** watering place, baths; mineral spring, warm *or* hot spring

**space** NOUNS 1 **extent,** extension, spatial extension, uninterrupted extension, space continuum, continuum; **expanse,** expansion; accommodation, room, measure; **margin,** clearance, open space *or* field, elbowroom, breathing space, **leeway** <nonformal>, sea room, wide berth
2 **outer space,** cosmic space, empty space, ether space, pressureless space, celestial spaces, interplanetary *or* interstellar *or* intergalactic *or* intercosmic space, metagalactic space, **the void**
VERBS 3 **interspace,** make a space, set at intervals, dot, scatter, **space out,** separate, split off, part, dispart, set *or* keep apart
ADJS 4 **spatial,** dimensional, proportional; **extraterrestrial,** extramundane, alien

**spacecraft** NOUNS **spaceship,** space rocket, rocket ship, manned rocket, interplanetary rocket; orbiter; **shuttle,** space shuttle; **capsule,** space capsule, ballistic capsule

**spacious** ADJS **sizable,** roomy, commodious, capacious, ample; spreading, **vast,** vasty, broad, **wide,** deep, high, voluminous

**span** NOUNS 1 **extent,** length, space, **reach,** stretch, range, compass, stride, haul, a way
2 **arch,** vault, vaulting, concameration, camber; ogive; apse; **bridge,** viaduct
3 **interval,** lapse of time, time frame, space, timespan, stretch, time-lag, time-gap
VERBS 4 **extend,** reach, stretch, sweep, spread, run, **reach** *or* stretch *or* thrust out; straddle, take in, hold, encompass, surround, environ

**spangled** ADJS **illuminated,** bespangled, tinseled, studded; star-spangled, star-studded

**spank** VERBS **correct,** rap on the knuckles, **chastise,** turn over one's knees; **whip,** give a whipping *or* beating *or* thrashing, **beat,** thrash, flog

**spar** VERBS **quarrel,** dispute, oppugn, altercate, **fight,** box, squabble, tiff, spat, **bicker,** wrangle, spar, broil, have words, set to, join issue, make the fur fly

**spare** VERBS 1 **forgive,** pardon, excuse, give *or* grant forgiveness; **abstain,** refrain, forgo, forbear, waive; **preserve,** conserve, save; **give away,** dispose of, part with, sacrifice
ADJS 2 **reserved,** preserved, saved, conserved, put by, kept, retained, held, withheld, held back, kept *or* held in reserve
3 **economical,** thrifty, frugal, economic, unwasteful, conserving, **saving,** economizing, **sparing; austere,** chaste, unadorned, uncluttered, stark, severe; scant, **scanty**

**spark** NOUNS 1 **inspiration,** infusion, infection; fire, firing, sparking; **immediate cause,** proximate cause, trigger; sparkle, **glitter,** glimmer, shimmer, twinkle, blink
VERBS 2 **kindle,** enkindle, **fire,** spark off, trigger, trigger off, touch off, set off, light the fuse, **enflame,** set afire *or* on fire
3 **originate,** give origin to, give occasion to, **give rise to,** spark off, set off, trigger, trigger off; **squire,** swain

**sparkle** NOUNS 1 **bubbling,** bubbliness, effervescence, spumescence, frothiness, frothing, foaming; **fizz,** fizzle, carbonation; ebullience, **spirit,** liveliness, vivacity, dash, verve, vividness
VERBS 2 **effervesce,** fizz, fizzle; scintillate, be brilliant, coruscate; **glitter,** glimmer, shimmer, twinkle, blink, spangle

**sparse** ADJS scant, **scanty,** exiguous, **infrequent,** scarce, scarce as hen's teeth <nonformal>, poor, piddling, piddly, thin, slim, meager

**Spartan** ADJS stoic, stoical, disciplined, self-controlled; austere, monkish, cloistral, severe, stark, ascetic, bare

**spasm** NOUNS **convulsion,** cramp, **paroxysm,** throes; **seizure,** grip, attack, **fit,** access, ictus

**spastic** ADJS **spasmodic,** paroxysmal, jerky, herky-jerky <nonformal>, eclamptic, orgasmic, convulsive

**spat** NOUNS **quarrel,** bicker, wrangle, snarl, **tiff,** fuss

**spatter** VERBS splatter, splash, **bespatter,** dabble, bedabble, spot, splotch; **sprinkle,** besprinkle, asperge

**spawn** VERBS **lay,** deposit, drop; breed, engender, beget, hatch; bring forth, give rise to, give being to, bring *or* call into being

**speak** VERBS **talk,** use language, communicate orally *or* verbally; use nonformal speech *or* style, colloquialize, vernacularize; jargon, jargonize, cant; patter

**speaker** NOUNS **talker,** public speaker, speechmaker, speecher, speechifier <nonformal>, spieler *and* jawsmith <both nonformal>; after-dinner speaker; **spokesman,** spokeswoman

**speak up** VERBS **speak out,** speak one's piece *or* one's mind, pipe up, open one's mouth, open one's lips, say out, say loud and clear, say out loud, sound off, lift *or* raise one's voice, break silence, find one's tongue; **have one's say,** put in one's two cents worth <nonformal>

**spear** NOUNS 1 throwing spear, javelin, assegai
VERBS 2 lance, poniard, bayonet, saber, sword, put to the sword; **catch,** take, land *and* nail <both nonformal>, hook, **snag,** snare, sniggle, harpoon

**special** ADJS **particular,** especial, specific, express, precise, **concrete; singular,** individual, individualist *or* individualistic; **distinguished,** noteworthy, **exceptional,** extraordinary

**specialty** NOUNS speciality, **line,** pursuit, pet subject, business, line of business, **field,** area, main interest; **forte,** métier, strong point, long suit

**species** NOUNS **kind,** sort, ilk, type, breed of cat <nonformal>, **variety,** genus, *genre* <Fr>, phylum, denomination, designation, description, style, manner, **nature, character,** persuasion, the like *or* likes of <nonformal>

**specific** ADJS **particular,** express, precise, **concrete; singular,** individual, individualist *or* individualistic

**specification** NOUNS **designation,** stipulation, specifying, designating, stipulating, singling-out, featuring, highlighting, focusing on, denomination; **allocation,** attribution, fixing, selection, assignment, pinning down

**specify** VERBS **designate;** denominate, name, denote; **itemize,** circumstantiate, particularize, **spell out,** detail, go *or* enter into detail, descend to particulars, give full particulars, atomize, anatomize; **call attention to,** direct attention to, **bring under** *or* **to one's notice,** hold up to notice, bring to attention, **mention,** mention in passing, touch on; **single out,** focus on, call *or* bring to notice, direct to the attention, **feature,** highlight

**specimen** NOUNS **sample,** taste, taster, little bite, little smack; **representative,** representation, **type,** typification, embodiment, **example**, exemplar; exemplification

**specious** ADJS **spurious, ostensible,** hypocritical, **fallacious,** colorable, plausible, hollow, superficially *or* apparently sound; deceptive, illusive, empty

**speck** NOUNS **dot;** mote, fleck, flyspeck, jot, tittle, iota, **trace,** trace amount, suspicion, *soupçon* <Fr>; **particle,** crumb, scrap, bite, snip, snippet; **blotch,** patch, speckle

**speckle** VERBS **spot,** bespot, **blot,** blotch, speck, bespeckle; freckle; **spatter,** splatter, splash, splotch

**spectacle** NOUNS **sight;** exhibit, **exhibition,** exposition, **show,** stage show, **display, presentation,** representation; **pageant,** pageantry; parade, pomp

**spectacular** ADJS extravagant, sensational, glaring, flaring, flaunting, screaming <nonformal>, obtrusive, vulgar, crude

**spectator** NOUNS **witness,** eyewitness; **bystander,** passerby

**specter** NOUNS **ghost,** phantom, revenant; **phantasm,** phantasma, wraith; **apparition,** appearance; shape, form, figure, presence; eidolon, idolum

**spectrum** NOUNS **range,** scope, compass, reach, stretch, expanse radius, sweep, carry, fetch; **gamut**

**speculate** VERBS **consider,** contemplate, reflect, study, ponder, perpend, **weigh,** deliberate, debate, meditate, muse, brood, ruminate, chew the cud <nonformal>, digest; **bet,** bet on, gamble

**speculator** NOUNS adventurer, operator; big operator, smart operator; **plunger,** gunslinger; **arbitrager** *or* arbitrageur; **gambler,** venturer; **theorist,** theorizer, **theoretician**

**speech** NOUNS **talk,** the power *or* faculty of speech, the verbal *or* oral faculty, talking, speaking, **discourse,** oral communication, vocal *or* voice *or* viva-voce communication, communication; rhetoric; oration, address, declamation, harangue

*a faculty given to man to conceal his thoughts*
TALLEYRAND

**speechless** ADJS **taciturn,** untalkative, **silent,** wordless, **mum; mute**, dumb, quiet; **closemouthed,** tight-lipped

**speed** NOUNS 1 **rapidity,** celerity, swiftness, fastness, **quickness,** snappiness <nonformal>, **speediness; dispatch,** expedition, promptness, promptitude, instantaneousness
2 stimulant; Adrenalin <trademark> *or* adrenaline <Brit> *or* epinephrine <US>, aloes; amphetamine sulphate, aromatic spirits of ammonia, caffeine, dextroamphetamine sulfate *or* Dexedrine <trademark>, digitalin *or* digitalis, methamphetamine hydrochloride *or* Methedrine <trademark>, smelling salts *or* salts
VERBS 3 **go fast,** skim, **fly,** flit, fleet, wing one's way, outstrip the wind; go like greased lightning; **rush, tear,** dash, dart, shoot, hurtle, bolt, fling, **scamper, scurry,** scour, scud, scuttle, scramble, **race,** careen; **hasten,** haste, **hurry,** accelerate, speed up, **hurry up,** quicken, hustle <nonformal>, bustle, bundle, precipitate, forward

4 <nonformal> **barrel,** tear along, thunder along, breeze along, tear up the road, rip, whiz, go full tilt, step on it, put the pedal to the metal, make tracks, go like blazes, get the lead out

**speedy** ADJS **quick,** swift, expeditious, snappy <nonformal>, celeritous, alacritous, dispatchful <old>, **prompt,** ready, smart, sharp, quick on the draw *or* trigger *or* upswing <nonformal>; **hasty,** hurried, festinate, **quick,** flying

**spell** NOUNS 1 magic spell, **charm,** glamour; evil eye, *malocchio* <Ital>, whammy <nonformal>; **hex,** jinx, curse
2 **interval,** lapse of time, time frame, space, span, timespan, stretch; course, series, **bout,** turn
VERBS 3 orthographize; spell *or* respell phonetically; spell out; spell backward; outspell, spell down
4 **substitute for,** relieve, cover for; ghost, **take the place of**

**spellbound** ADJS fascinated, captivated, under a charm, beguiled, enthralled, enraptured, enravished, enchanted, entranced, bewitched, hypnotized, mesmerized, stupefied, lost in wonder *or* amazement

**spend** VERBS 1 consume, expend, **pass,** employ, **put in;** devote, bestow, give to *or* give over to, devote *or* consecrate *or* dedicate to; dissipate, **exhaust,** use up
2 **expend,** disburse, pay out, fork out *or* over <nonformal>, shell out <nonformal>, **lay out,** outlay; loosen *or* untie the purse strings *and* throw money around <both nonformal>, splurge, spend money like a drunken sailor *and* spend money as if it were going out of style <both nonformal>

**spendthrift** NOUNS **prodigal,** wastrel, waster, **squanderer;** wastethrift, spender, spendall, big-time spender <nonformal>; Diamond Jim Brady; prodigal son

**spent** ADJS **devitalized,** drained, exhausted, sapped, burned-out, used up, played out, *ausgespielt* <Ger>, effete, etiolated; **wasted,** squandered, dissipated, consumed, used, lost; **gone to waste,** run *or* gone to seed; down the drain *or* spout *or* rathole <nonformal>

**spew** VERBS **erupt,** burst forth *or* out, break out, blow out *or* open, eruct, belch, **vomit,** spout, disgorge, **discharge,** eject, throw *or* hurl forth

**sphere** NOUNS 1 orb, **orbit,** ambit, circle; **realm,** demesne, **domain,** dominion, jurisdiction, bailiwick; **province,** precinct, **field,** arena
2 **ball,** globe, rondure; **pellet;** boll; **gob,** glob <nonformal>, blob, gobbet; **balloon,** bladder, bubble

**spice** NOUNS **flavoring,** flavor, flavorer; **seasoning,** seasoner, **relish,** condiment, condiments; **tang,** nip, bite; punch, snap, zip, ginger

**spicy** ADJS **zestful,** zesty, **nippy,** snappy, **tangy,** with a kick; spiced, seasoned, high-seasoned; curried, **peppery,** hot, burning, hot as pepper; musky; **risqué,** risky, **racy,** salty, **off-color,** suggestive, scabrous; piquant, lively, juicy, succulent

**spiel** NOUNS **sales talk,** sales pitch, patter; **pitch** *or* ballyhoo <both nonformal>

**spill** NOUNS 1 **overturn,** upset, overset, **overthrow,** upturn, turnover; **capsizing,** capsize, capsizal, turning turtle; **overflow,** spillage, spillover, overflowing, overrunning, alluvion, alluvium
VERBS 2 **run over,** well over, brim over, pour out *or* over, **slop, slosh,** spill out *or* over

**spin** NOUNS 1 **misrepresentation,** perversion, distortion, deformation, garbling, twisting, slanting; **coloring,** miscoloring, false coloring; falsification, spin control, disinformation; **slant,** angle

2 **whirl,** wheel, reel, **turn,** round; dizzy round, rat race
VERBS 3 **whirl,** whirligig, twirl, **wheel, reel,** spin like a top *or* teetotum, whirl like a dervish; **swirl,** eddy; **braid,** twist

**spindly** ADJS **unsteady,** shaky, rickety, spidery, teetering, teetery, tottery, tottering; gangling *and* gangly <both nonformal>, gawky, **spindling; underweight,** undersized, undernourished

**spineless** ADJS **weak-willed,** wimpy *or* wimpish <nonformal>, feeble, fainthearted, **frail,** faint, infirm; invertebrate; without a will of one's own

**spin-off** NOUNS **outgrowth,** offshoot, offspring, issue, aftermath, legacy; derivative

**spinster** NOUNS **single** *or* unmarried woman, spinstress, **old maid,** maid, maiden, bachelor girl, single girl, single woman, lone woman, maiden lady, feme sole

**spiny** ADJS **barbed,** tined, pronged; **spined,** spinous, hispid, acanthoid, acanthous

**spiral** NOUNS 1 **coil,** whorl, roll, **curl,** curlicue, ringlet, pigtail; helix, volute, volution, involute, evolute, gyre, scroll
ADJS 2 spiroid, volute, voluted; **helical,** helicoid, helicoidal; verticillate, whorled, scrolled; cochlear, cochleate

**spire** NOUNS **tower; turret,** *tour* <Fr>; campanile, bell tower, belfry; church spire

**spirit** NOUNS 1 **animation,** spiritedness, **briskness,** perkiness, pertness, **life,** life force, *élan vital* <Fr>; **zeal,** ardor, ardency, fervor, fervency, fervidness, warmth, fire, heat, heatedness, **passion;** soul, indwelling spirit, force of life, living force, *vis vitae* or *vis vitalis* <both L>, **vital force** *or* energy, vital principle, **vital spark** *or* **flame**
2 **familiar spirit,** familiar; **genius, good genius,** daemon, demon, *numen* <L>, totem; **guardian,** guardian spirit, guardian angel, angel, good angel, ministering angel, **fairy godmother**

**spirited** ADJS sprightly, **lively,** animated, vivacious, vital, zestful, zippy <nonformal>, **exuberant,** hearty; **active,** bubbly, ebullient, effervescent, chipper *and* perky <both nonformal>

**spirits** NOUNS **liquor,** intoxicating liquor, adult beverage, **hard liquor, whiskey,** firewater, spiritus frumenti, usquebaugh <Scots>, schnapps, **intoxicant,** toxicant, inebriant, strong drink, alcoholic drink *or* beverage, **booze** <nonformal>

**spiritual** ADJS 1 **godly,** godlike; God-fearing; righteous, holy
2 **ghostly,** ghostlike; **psychic,** psychical; **occult,** supernatural, astral

**spite** NOUNS spitefulness, despite, despitefulness, **malice,** malevolence, malignity, cattiness; grudge

**splash** NOUNS 1 **lap,** swash, wash, slosh, plash
VERBS 2 **spatter,** splatter, **bespatter,** dabble, bedabble, spot, splotch

**splay** VERBS **diverge,** divaricate; spread, **spread out,** outspread, fan out, deploy

**splendid** ADJS **magnificent,** splendiferous, tremendous, immense, **wonderful,** glorious, divine, heavenly, terrific, sensational; sterling, golden; **bright,** brilliant, vivid, **resplendent,** bright and shining

**splendor** NOUNS **luster,** resplendence *or* resplendency, refulgence, splendidness, **brilliance,** brightness, radiance, radiant splendor

**splice** NOUNS 1 **fastening,** attachment, affixation; bond, fastener
VERBS 2 **fasten, bind, tie,** brace, truss, **lash,** leash, rope, strap, lace

**splinter** NOUNS 1 **piece,** bit, scrap, bite, sliver; **shiver,** smithereen <nonformal>
VERBS 2 **shatter,** shiver, break to *or* into pieces, fragmentize, break to *or* into smithereens <nonformal>

**split** NOUNS 1 **breach,** break, rupture, schism, rift, cleft, splinter, **disunity,** disunion, disruption, separation, cleavage, divergence, division, dividedness
VERBS 2 **cleave,** slit, rive, rent, rip open; breach, break, fracture, rupture, sunder; **clear out,** make oneself scarce
3 **apportion,** portion, parcel, partition, part, divide, share; **split up,** carve, cut, slice, carve up, slice up, cut up, cut *or* slice the pie *or* melon <nonformal>; divide *or* split fifty-fifty

**splurge** VERBS **spend,** throw money around <nonformal>, go on a spending spree, spend money like a drunken sailor *and* spend money as if it were going out of style <both nonformal>, **squander**

**spoil** VERBS 1 **mar,** botch, **ruin,** wreck, blight, play havoc with; destroy, corrupt, canker; **butcher,** murder, make sad work of; **plunder,** pillage, loot, sack, spoliate, despoil

2 <nonformal> **screw up, foul up,** fuck up, bitch up, **blow,** louse up, queer, snafu, snarl up, balls up <Brit>, bugger, bugger up, gum up, ball up, bollix, bollix up, **mess up,** hash up, muck up; play hob with, play hell with, play merry hell with, play the devil with, rain on one's picnic *or* parade; upset the apple cart, cook, sink, shoot down in flames; **total**

3 **decay,** decompose, disintegrate; go *or* fall into decay, **go bad;** rot, putrefy, putresce; mold, molder, molder away, rot away, rust away, mildew
4 **indulge, cater to; give way to,** yield to, let one have his own way; **pamper,** cosset, **coddle,** mollycoddle, pet, make a lap dog of; spare the rod

**spoken** ADJS **vernacular,** colloquial, conversational, unliterary, nonformal, demotic, vulgar, vulgate

**spokesperson** NOUNS **spokesman,** spokeswoman, spokespeople, official spokesman *or* -woman *or* -person, press officer, speaker, **voice,** mouthpiece <nonformal>

**sponge** NOUNS 1 **parasite,** barnacle, leech; **sponger,** freeloader <nonformal>, smell-feast; beat *and* deadbeat <both nonformal>
VERBS 2 **sponge on** *and* **sponge off of** <both nonformal>; feed on, fatten on, batten on, live off of, use as a meal ticket, freeload

**sponsor** NOUNS 1 **financer,** backer, funder, **patron,** supporter, angel <nonformal>, Maecenas; cash cow *and* staker *and* grubstaker <all nonformal>, meal ticket <nonformal>
VERBS 2 **finance,** back, fund, patronize, support, provide for, capitalize, provide capital *or* money for, pay for, bankroll <nonformal>, angel <nonformal>, put up the money; **stake** *or* **grubstake** <both nonformal>

**spontaneous** ADJS **unpremeditated,** unmeditated, **uncalculated,** undeliberated, **undesigned,** unstudied; **involuntary,** automatic, impulsive; **instinctual,** libidinal

**spoof** NOUNS 1 **hoax, deception,** humbug, flam, fake *and* fakement, **rip-off** <nonformal>, sham; mare's nest
VERBS 2 **fool,** make a fool of, **pull one's leg,** make an ass of; **trick; kid** *and* put one on <both nonformal>; **play a trick on,** play a practical joke upon, send on a fool's errand

**sporadic** ADJS **irregular, haphazard,** desultory, **erratic,** fitful, promiscuous, indiscriminate, spasmodic, casual, frivolous, capricious, random, hit-or-miss

**sport** NOUNS 1 **banter,** badinage, persiflage, **raillery,** rallying, good-natured banter, harmless teasing
2 **dandy, fop,** coxcomb, macaroni, gallant, dude *and* swell <both nonformal>, jackanapes, clotheshorse, fashion plate
3 **fun,** funmaking, fun and games, **play,** game; **good time,** lovely time, pleasant time; **sports, athletics,** athletic competition, sports activity

**spot** NOUNS 1 **location,** situation, place, position, *lieu* <Fr>, placement, emplacement, stead
2 **stain, blot,** blur, **blotch,** patch, speck, speckle, fleck, flick, flyspeck
3 **tight spot;** squeeze, tight squeeze, hot spot, hot seat; **scrape,** jam, hot water, tit in the wringer; **mess,** holy *or* unholy mess; hell to pay <all nonformal>
VERBS 4 **locate,** situate, site, place, position; emplace, **install,** put in place; **dot,** blotch, splotch, dash, **speck,** speckle, fleck, freckle; **detect,** see, lay eyes on, catch sight of, **spy,** espy, descry, sense, pick up, notice, discern, **perceive,** make out, recognize, distinguish, identify

**spotless** ADJS stainless, taintless, **unblemished,** unspotted, untainted, unsoiled, unsullied, undefiled; pure, clean, **immaculate,** impeccable, squeaky-clean <nonformal>, **chaste,** virtuous

**spotlight** NOUNS 1 **celebrity,** *réclame, éclat* <both Fr>; **limelight** <nonformal>, bright light, public eye *or* consciousness
VERBS 2 **stress,** lay emphasis *or* stress upon, feature, highlight, place emphasis on, give emphasis to

**spotty** ADJS 1 **sporadic,** patchy, scrappy, snatchy, choppy, **broken,** disconnected, discontinuous; **intermittent,** desultory, fluctuating; **scattered,** sprinkled, few and far between
2 **spotted,** maculate, maculated, macular, blotched, **blotchy,** splotched, splotchy

**spouse** NOUNS **mate,** yokemate, partner, consort, **better half** <nonformal>

*bone of my bones, and flesh of my flesh*
BIBLE

**sprawl** VERBS **recline,** repose, lounge, loll, drape *or* spread oneself, splay, lie limply

**spread** NOUNS 1 **meal, repast,** feed *and* sit-down <both nonformal>, mess, table, board, *repas* <Fr>; **refreshment,** refection, treat
2 **divergence,** spreading, spreading out, splaying, fanning, fanning out, deployment; ripple effect; **enlargement,** amplification, growth, development, widening, roadening, **extension,** aggrandizement
3 **coverlet,** robe, buffalo robe, **afghan,** bedspread; bedcover; **comforter,** duvet, **quilt,** patchwork quilt
VERBS 4 spread out, outspread, outstretch; **expand,** extend, widen; open, **open up,** unfold; **flare,** flare out, broaden out, splay; spread like wildfire; overrun, overgrow

**spree** NOUNS **drinking bout,** bout, **carouse,** carousal, drunken carousal *or* revelry; bacchanal, bacchanalia, bacchanalian; debauch, orgy

**sprightly** ADJS **active,** lively, animated, spirited, bubbly, ebullient, effervescent, **vivacious,** chipper *and* perky <both nonformal>, pert; **agile,** nimble, spry, fleet; clever, brilliant, scintillating, sparkling

**spring** NOUNS 1 springtide, **springtime,** seedtime *or* budtime, Maytime, Eastertide; *primavera* <Ital>, prime of the year
2 **leap,** jump, hop, skip, bound, bounce; **elasticity,** resilience *or* resiliency, **give;** snap, bounciness

**spring up** VERBS **shoot up,** jump up, **leap up,** vault up, start up, fly up, pop up, bob up; **originate, arise,** crop up; burst forth, break out, erupt, irrupt

**sprinkle** NOUNS 1 **spray,** sparge, shower; spindrift, spume, froth, foam; **splash,** plash, swash, slosh; **splatter,** spatter
VERBS 2 **shower,** spatter, patter, pitter-patter; **drizzle,** mizzle; besprinkle, asperge, splash; **dot,** spot, speck, speckle, stud

**sprout** NOUNS 1 **seedling,** set; sucker, shoot, slip; **twig,** sprig, scion, sapling
VERBS 2 **grow, shoot up,** sprout up, upshoot, burgeon, blossom, germinate, pullulate; **flourish,** thrive, grow like a weed

**spry** ADJS **agile, nimble,** sprightly, fleet, featly, peart <nonformal>, light, graceful, nimble-footed, light-footed, sure-footed

**spunk** NOUNS **pluck,** mettle, backbone <nonformal>, **grit,** true grit, spirit, **stamina,** guts *and* moxie <both nonformal>, bottom, pluckiness, spunkiness <nonformal>, **gameness,** feistiness <nonformal>, mettlesomeness

**spur** NOUNS 1 **goad,** prod, prick <old>, sting, **gadfly;** oxgoad; rowel
2 **offshoot,** ramification, scion
VERBS 3 **goad,** prod, poke, nudge, prod at, goose <nonformal>, prick, sting, needle; whip, lash, urge

**spurious** ADJS **false,** untrue, truthless, not true, void *or* devoid of truth, contrary to fact, in error, **fallacious,** erroneous; unfounded

**spurn** VERBS **turn up one's nose at,** scorn to receive *or* accept, not want any part of; spit upon, **disdain,** scorn, **turn one's back upon,** not give one the time of day <nonformal>; **blackball,** turn thumbs down on, snub, cut, give the cold shoulder

**spur-of-the-moment** ADJS **extemporaneous,** extemporary, extempore, **impromptu,** unrehearsed, **improvised,** ad-lib, *ad libitum* <L>; **ad-hoc,** stopgap, makeshift, jury-rigged; **offhand,** off the top of one's head *and* off-the-cuff <both nonformal>, **quick and dirty** <nonformal>

**spurt** NOUNS **burst,** fit, spasm; **torrent,** rush, gush, spate, cascade; outpour, jet, spout, squirt

**spy** NOUNS 1 **secret agent,** operative, cloak-and-dagger operative, **undercover man,** inside man <nonformal>; espionage agent; counterspy, double agent; **intelligence agent** *or* **officer;** spycatcher <nonformal>, counterintelligence agent
VERBS 2 **see,** behold, observe, view, witness, perceive, discern, espy, **sight,** make out, pick out, descry, spot <nonformal>, notice, take notice of, have one's eye on, **catch sight of,** get a load of <nonformal>, get an eyeful of <nonformal>, **glimpse,** get *or* catch a glimpse of; **pry, snoop,** peep, peek, nose into

**squabble** NOUNS 1 **quarrel,** dispute, argument, **fight,** contention, strife, **tussle,** bicker, wrangle, snarl, **tiff, spat,** fuss

VERBS 2 **quarrel,** dispute, oppugn, **fight,** tiff, spat, **bicker, wrangle,** spar, have words, set to, make the fur fly

**squalid** ADJS **sordid,** wretched, shabby; slumlike, slummy

**squall** NOUNS **storm,** tempest, line squall; stormy weather, rough weather, foul weather, dirty weather; rainstorm

**squander** VERBS **lavish,** slather, blow <nonformal>, play ducks and drakes with; **dissipate,** scatter to the winds; **run through,** go through; throw one's money away, throw money around, **spend money like water,** spend like a drunken sailor

**square** NOUNS 1 **plaza,** *place* <Fr>, *piazza* <Ital>, *campo* <Ital>, **marketplace,** market, mart, rialto, forum, agora
ADJS 2 **banal,** trite, unoriginal, platitudinous, **stereotyped,** stock, set, **commonplace,** common, truistic, twice-told, **familiar,** bromidic <nonformal>, old hat <nonformal>, back-number; corny *and* square-John *and* Clyde <all nonformal>
3 **straight,** foursquare, straight-arrow <nonformal>, honest and aboveboard, right as rain; **old-fogyish,** fogyish, old-fogy; fuddy-duddy, cornball <nonformal>; **stuffy,** stodgy
4 even, quits, zero-sum, even steven <nonformal>
ADVS 5 **exactly,** precisely, to a T, expressly; **just, dead,** right, straight, even, **plumb,** directly, squarely, point-blank

**square one** NOUNS **new start,** new beginning, fresh start, clean slate, tabula rasa

**squash** VERBS **suppress, repress,** stultify; **keep down,** hold down, keep under; close *or* shut down; **subdue,** quell, put down, smash, crush; mash

**squat** VERBS 1 **crouch,** stoop, bend, stoop down, squat down, get down, hunker *and* hunker down *and* get down on one's hunkers <all nonformal>; hunch down, hunch over, scrooch *or* scrouch down <nonformal>
ADJS 2 **stubby,** stumpy <nonformal>, dumpy; squatty, squattish; flat, short, runty

**squawk** NOUNS 1 **screech,** shriek, scream, squeal; **objection,** kick *and* beef *and* bitch *and* howl <all nonformal>, protestation
VERBS 2 **screech,** shriek, scream, squeal; **object,** kick *and* beef <both nonformal>, put up a struggle *or* fight; bitch *and* howl *and* holler *and* put up a squawk *and* raise a howl <all nonformal>; exclaim *or* cry out against, make *or* create *or* raise a stink about <all nonformal>; yell bloody murder <nonformal>

**squeamish** ADJS **nauseated,** nauseous, **queasy,** qualmish, qualmy; sick to one's stomach; **demurring,** boggling, stickling, hedging, **hesitant,** hesitating, faltering

**squeeze** NOUNS 1 **embrace,** hug, fond embrace, embracement, clasp, enfoldment, bear hug <nonformal>; **tight squeeze** *and* hot spot *and* hot water <all nonformal>
VERBS 2 **embrace,** hug, clasp, press, fold, **enfold,** press to the bosom
3 compress, clamp, cramp, cramp up, tighten; roll *or* wad up, roll up into a ball, ensphere; **press,** high-pressure <nonformal>, pressurize, crush, lean on <nonformal>; **exact,** extort, blackmail

**squelch** VERBS **cover up,** muffle up; **hush up, suppress,** repress, **stifle,** muffle, **smother,** squash, quash, kill, sit on *or* upon, put the lid on <nonformal>, **muzzle,** gag; bleep *or* bleep out <nonformal>, silence

**squirm** VERBS **fidget,** have the fidgets *and* have ants in one's pants <both nonformal>; twist and turn, wriggle, wiggle, writhe; **chafe,** fret, fuss

**stab** NOUNS 1 **wound,** puncture, stab wound; flesh wound; **thrust,** pass, lunge, swing, cut; home thrust
2 **try;** whack, fling, shot, crack, bash, <all nonformal>
VERBS 3 **stick** <nonformal>, **pierce,** plunge in; **run through,** impale, spit, **transfix,** transpierce

**stabilize** VERBS **firm,** firm up <nonformal>; **steady,** balance, counterbalance, ballast; **immobilize,** freeze, keep, retain; **transfix,** stick, hold, pin *or* nail down <nonformal>

**stable** ADJS **substantial,** firm, solid, sound, stabile; solid as a rock; **steady,** unwavering, steadfast; **balanced,** in equilibrium, in a stable state; **imperturbable,** unflappable <nonformal>, unshakable, **cool** <nonformal>, impassive, stolid, stoic; **reliable**, predictable

**staccato** ADJS **drumming,** thrumming,

beating, pounding, thumping; throbbing; palpitant, fluttering; **rapid,** stuttering, chattering

**stack** NOUNS 1 **chimney, flue,** stovepipe, smokestack
VERBS 2 **load, lade,** pile, heap, heap up, mass; heap *or* pile *or* stack up; mound, hill, bank, bank up

**stadium** NOUNS **arena, amphitheater,** circus, **hippodrome,** coliseum, colosseum, **bowl**

**staff** NOUNS 1 stave; pilgrim's staff, pastoral staff, shepherd's staff, crook; pikestaff, alpenstock; quarterstaff
2 **personnel, employees,** help, hired help, the help, **crew, gang,** force, retinue

**stage** NOUNS 1 **period,** point, juncture; interval
2 **platform;** the boards; estrade, dais, floor; **rostrum,** podium, pulpit, speaker's platform *or* stand
VERBS 3 **dramatize, present,** produce, mount, put on, put on the stage; put on a show

**stagger** VERBS 1 **astonish,** amaze, astound, surprise, startle, **bewilder,** perplex, flabbergast <nonformal>, confound, overwhelm, **boggle,** boggle the mind
2 **flounder,** flounce, totter, stumble, falter, blunder, wallop; **struggle,** labor; **wallow,** welter

**staggering** ADJS 1 **astonishing,** amazing, surprising, startling, **astounding,** confounding, stunning <nonformal>, eye-opening, breathtaking, overwhelming, mind-boggling *or* -numbing
2 **wobbly,** wobbling, weaving, lurching, careening

**stagnant** ADJS **inert,** inactive, static, dormant, passive, sedentary; sleeping, slumbering, smoldering; **standing,** foul, stagnating, vegetative

**staid** ADJS **sedate,** sober, sober-minded, **serious,** grave, solemn, sobersided; temperate, moderate; **stuffy** <nonformal>; stolid

**stain** NOUNS 1 **taint, tarnish;** mark, brand, **stigma; smirch,** smudge, smutch *or* smouch, smut, **smear;** splotch, splash, splatter, spatter
VERBS 2 **soil,** besoil; black, **blacken; smirch,** besmirch, sully, **smudge,** smear; **spot**

**stainless** ADJS **spotless,** taintless, unblemished, unspotted, **untainted,** unsoiled, unsullied, undefiled; pure, clean, immaculate, impeccable, pure as driven snow, squeaky-clean <nonformal>, chaste

**stake** NOUNS 1 **portion,** share, interest, part, stock, **piece,** bit, segment; **grubstake** <nonformal>; **bet,** wager, hazard, ante
VERBS 2 **finance,** back, fund, grubstake <nonformal>; subsidize; **bet,** wager, gamble, hazard, punt, lay, lay down, put up, **make a bet,** plunge <nonformal>; ante, ante up

**stale** ADJS **fusty, musty,** rusty, dusty, moldy, mildewed; **moth-eaten,** moldering, gone to seed

**stalemate** NOUNS **tie,** deadlock, wash *and* toss-up <both nonformal>, standoff *and* Mexican standoff <both nonformal>

**stalk** VERBS **hunt,** prowl after, **search out,** hunt out, spy out, scout out, **ferret out,** fish out, root out

**stall** NOUNS 1 **booth,** stand; newsstand, kiosk, news kiosk
VERBS 2 lose power; flame out; stick, die, go dead, **conk out** <nonformal>, sputter and stop, run out of gas *or* steam, come to a dead stop
3 **temporize,** gain time, **play for time,** drag one's feet <nonformal>, hold off <nonformal>; stall off, **stall for time,** stall *or* stooge around *and* tap-dance <all nonformal>; filibuster

**stalwart** NOUNS 1 **tower of strength,** muscle man, piledriver, bulldozer, hunk <nonformal>; **hero,** heroine; brave, gallant, valiant, man *or* woman of courage *or* mettle; support, **mainstay,** standby <nonformal>
ADJS 2 **courageous,** plucky, brave, bold, valiant, valorous, gallant, intrepid, doughty, **hardy,** stout, stouthearted, lionhearted; heroic

**stamina** NOUNS **pluck,** spunk <nonformal>, **mettle,** backbone <nonformal>, **grit,** true grit, spirit, guts *and* moxie <both nonformal>, bottom, **toughness** <nonformal>; endurance, staying power

**stammer** NOUNS 1 **stammering,** stuttering, hesitation, faltering, traulism, dysphemia, *balbuties* <L>; palilalia; stutter
VERBS 2 **stutter,** stammer out; hesitate, falter, halt, stumble

**stamp** NOUNS 1 seal, sigil, signet; postage stamp
VERBS 2 **impress upon,** bring home

to, make it felt; stamp on, etch, engrave, engrave on; mint
3 seal, punch, impress, imprint, **print,** engrave
4 stomp <nonformal>, trample, tread, drub, clump, clop

**stampede** VERBS **panic,** send scuttling, throw blind fear into; **rout, put to rout,** put to flight, scatter

**stance** NOUNS **attitude,** position, posture; **way of thinking; feeling, sentiment,** the way one feels; opinion

**stanch** VERBS **suppress, extinguish,** quench, damp down, pour water on, dash *or* pour cold water on, drown, kill

**stand** NOUNS 1 **station,** status, **standing,** standpoint; **viewpoint,** *optique* <Fr>, point of reference, reference-point, angle, perspective, distance; position
2 **growth,** crop; plantation, planting; **clump,** tuft, tussock, hassock
3 **engagement,** playing engagement, booking; **run;** one-night stand *or* one-nighter; date
4 **booth,** stall; newsstand, kiosk, news kiosk
VERBS 5 **endure,** bear, support, sustain, **suffer, tolerate,** abide, bide, live with; **bear up under,** put up with, stand for, brook, brave, brave out, hang in there, keep it up
6 **stand erect,** stand up, stand upright, stand up straight, be erect, be on one's feet; stand at attention *and* stand at parade rest <both military>

**standard** NOUNS 1 **yardstick,** norm, canon, **criterion,** test, touchstone, check; **model,** pattern, mirror; **rule,** law, principle, code, maxim, prescription, guideline, rulebook
2 **flag, banner,** oriflamme, gonfalon *or* gonfanon, guidon, *vexillum* <L>, *labarum* <L>
ADJS 3 **model,** exemplary, typical, paradigmatic, representative, normative, classic; ideal
4 **usual,** regular; customary, habitual, accustomed, wonted, **normative,** prescriptive, regulation, conventional; interchangeable, stereotyped, uniform

**standardize** VERBS **make uniform,** homogenize, assimilate, stereotype; **systematize,** methodize, routinize; **normalize,** regularize; codify

**stand by** VERBS **be prepared,** be ready, stand ready, hold oneself in readiness, keep one's powder dry

*put your trust in God, my boys, and keep your powder dry*
CROMWELL

**stand for** VERBS **suffer,** countenance, have, **tolerate,** condone, brook, endure, stomach, bear, bear with, put up with, hear of *and* go along with <both nonformal>; **signify, betoken,** identify, differentiate, **indicate,** be indicative of, be an indication of, connote, denote, mean

**stand-in** NOUNS **deputy,** proxy, representative, substitute, **alternate,** backup <nonformal>, alter ego, surrogate; **understudy,** standby

**standing** NOUNS **rank,** level, footing, **status,** station; **position,** place, sphere, orbit, echelon; **prestige,** honor; dignity; stature, high place

**standoff** NOUNS **impasse,** corner *and* box *and* hole <all nonformal>, cleft stick; **stalemate,** deadlock; stand, standstill, halt, stop

**star** NOUNS 1 **winner,** star in the firmament, success, superstar *and* megastar <both nonformal>; phenom *and* comer <both nonformal>; cult figure; **lead,** leading man *or* lady, leading actor *or* actress, principal, headliner, headline *or* feature attraction
2 **quasar,** quasi-stellar radio source; **pulsar,** pulsating star, eclipsing binary, X-ray pulsar
VERBS 3 **act,** perform, play the lead, get top billing, have one's name in lights
ADJS 4 **predominant,** topflight, highest-ranking, ranking; superstar, stellar, world-class

**stare** NOUNS 1 **gaze,** gape, goggle; sharp *or* piercing *or* penetrating look; **ogle,** glad eye, come-hither look <nonformal>, bedroom eyes <nonformal>; **glare,** glower, glaring *or* glowering look
VERBS 2 **gaze,** fix one's gaze, fix *or* fasten *or* rivet one's eyes upon, **eye, ogle;** stare at, stare hard, look, goggle, **gape,** gawk *or* gawp <nonformal>, gaze openmouthed

**stark** ADJS **sheer,** bare, bare-bones, **plain,** simple, **unadorned,** unenhanced; austere, monkish, cloistral, severe, Spartan

**start** NOUNS 1 shock, jar, jolt, turn
2 starting, start-off, setoff, setout, takeoff *and* getaway <both nonformal>; the starting gun *or* pistol; break; the green light; **point of departure,** starting place

*or* point, takeoff, **base,** baseline, basis; starting line *or* post *or* gate, starting blocks; head *or* flying *or* running start; **edge,** bulge *and* jump *and* drop <all nonformal>
VERBS 3 startle, **jump,** jump out of one's skin, jump a mile, leap like a startled gazelle; **shy,** fight shy, start aside, boggle, jib; **panic,** stampede, skedaddle <nonformal>
4 **set out** *or* **off,** be off, be on one's way, **start out** *or* **off,** strike out, get off, get away, get off the dime <nonformal>; get the green light, break; set sail; **begin,** commence; start up, kick *or* click in <nonformal>; **kick off** *and* **start the ball rolling** <both nonformal>; get off the ground *or* off the mark, **launch**

**startle** VERBS **shock,** electrify, jar, jolt, shake, stun, **stagger,** give one a turn <nonformal>, give the shock of one's life, make one jump out of his skin, take aback, take one's breath away, strike all of a heap <nonformal>; frighten

**starve** VERBS **hunger,** hunger for, feel hungry; be ravenous, raven; famish; not know where one's next meal is coming from, **live from hand to mouth,** eke out *or* squeeze out a living

**stash** NOUNS 1 **hiding place, cache**; drop
VERBS 2 **secrete,** hide away, **cache,** deposit, plant <nonformal>; **bury,** bury away

**state** NOUNS 1 **country,** land; **nation,** nationality, nation-state, sovereign nation *or* state, polity, body politic
2 mode, modality; **status,** situation, status quo *or* status in quo, position, standing, footing, location, bearings, spot; condition, circumstance
VERBS 3 **declare, assert,** aver, affirm, asseverate, allege; **say,** make a statement, send a message; **announce,** tell the world; **relate,** recite; proclaim, nuncupate

**stately** ADJS **dignified,** imposing, grand, courtly, magisterial, aristocratic; **noble,** lordly, princely; **majestic,** regal, royal, kingly, queenly; worthy, **august,** venerable; statuesque; **sedate,** solemn, sober, grave

**statement** NOUNS 1 **remark,** earful *and* crack *and* one's two cents' worth <all nonformal>, **word,** say, **saying,** utterance, observation, reflection, expression; **assertion,** averment, allegation, affirmation, pronouncement, position, dictum; **declaration,** statement of facts, *procès-verbal* <Fr>
2 **bill,** itemized bill, bill of account, **account,** reckoning, invoice

**state-of-the-art** ADJS **newest, latest,** the very latest, up-to-the-minute, last, most recent, newest of the new, most advanced

**statesman** NOUNS stateswoman, solon, public man *or* woman, national leader; elder statesman

> *a successful politician who is dead*
> THOMAS B REED

**static** ADJS **inert,** inactive, dormant, passive, sedentary; **quiescent,** motionless

**station** NOUNS 1 status, **stand,** standing, standpoint; **rank,** level, footing; **position,** place, sphere, orbit, echelon; **job,** employment, gainful employment, situation, **office,** post, berth, billet
2 **terminal,** stopping point

**stationary** ADJS **immovable,** unmovable, **immobile,** immotile, unmoving, frozen, not to be moved, at a standstill, on dead center

**stationery** NOUNS **paper,** paper stock, stock; sheet, leaf, page

**statistics** NOUNS **mathematical probability,** statistical probability, predictability; **figures,** indexes *or* indices; vital statistics

**statue** NOUNS **sculpture,** bust, statuette, statuary; portrait bust *or* statue; carving, wood carving; figurehead

**statuesque** ADJS **giant**, gigantic, colossal; Junoesque, goddess-like

**stature** NOUNS **prestige,** authority, influence; **weight,** weightiness, moment, **consequence;** eminence, rank, seniority, preeminence, priority, precedence

**status** NOUNS **social status,** economic status, socioeconomic status *or* background, standing, footing, prestige, rank, ranking, place, station, position, level, degree, stratum; state, status quo *or* status in quo

**status quo** NOUNS **state,** status, situation, status in quo, position, standing, footing, location, bearings, spot; **circumstances,** total situation, existing conditions *or* situation, set of conditions, terms of reference

**statutory** ADJS **preceptive,** official, authoritative, canonical, rubric, rubrical, protocolary; **enforceable,** legally binding; statutable

**staunch** ADJS **firm,** standup <nonformal>, fixed, settled, steady, steadfast, constant, reliable, flinty, steely; unshaken, not to be shaken, unflappable <nonformal>; undeflectable, **unswerving,** not to be deflected; immovable, unbending, inflexible, **unyielding**; true, loyal

**stay** NOUNS 1 **sojourn,** sojourning, sojournment, temporary stay; stop; **stopover,** stopoff, stayover, layover; abeyance, drop, lull, lapse; truce, cease-fire, stand-down
2 **curb, check,** countercheck, arrest, **stop,** damper, holdback
VERBS 3 **stop, halt,** bring to a stop, put a stop *or* end to, bring to a shuddering *or* screeching halt <nonformal>; **block,** stall, stymie, deadlock; nip in the bud

**steadfast** ADJS **devoted,** dedicated, committed, **fast,** constant, faithful, staunch; tried, true, **tried and true,** true-blue, tested

**steady** ADJS **reliable,** dependable, sure, surefire <nonformal>, **trustworthy,** trusty; predictable, calculable; **secure,** solid, sound, firm, fast, **stable, substantial,** staunch, steady, **faithful,** unfailing; true to one's word

**steal** VERBS **thieve,** purloin, appropriate, take, snatch, palm, **make off with,** walk off with, run off *or* away with, abstract, disregard the distinction between *meum* and *tuum;* have one's hand in the till; **pilfer,** filch

**stealth** NOUNS stealthiness, **furtiveness,** clandestine behavior, **surreptitiousness,** covertness, slyness, shiftiness, sneakiness, slinkiness, underhand dealing, undercover *or* underground activity, **covert activity** *or* **operation**

**steamy** ADJS **heated,** passionate, warm, hot, red-hot, flaming, **burning,** fiery, glowing, fervent, fervid; seething, boiling, boiling over, steaming

**steep** ADJS 1 **precipitous,** bluff, plunging, abrupt, bold, **sheer,** sharp, vertical
2 **expensive,** dear, costly; fancy *and* stiff <both nonformal>, pricey; upmarket, upscale <nonformal>

**steer** VERBS **direct to,** give directions to, lead *or* conduct to, point out to, show, **show** *or* **point the way,** put on the track, put on the right track; **pilot,** helm, coxswain, guide, **navigate**

**stellar** ADJS **celestial,** heavenly, empyrean, empyreal; **astral,** starry; all-star, star quality

**stem** VERBS **put a stop to,** call a halt to; block, brake, dam, stem the tide *or* current; bring up short, cut short, check in full career; checkmate

**stench** NOUNS **stink,** funk, malodor, fetor, foul odor, offense to the nostrils

**step** NOUNS 1 **pace,** stride; footstep, footfall, tread
2 **means,** means to an end, **measure,** action, **move,** maneuver, demarche, course of action
VERBS 3 **tread,** pace, stride, pad; foot, foot it; leg, leg it; hoof it

**sterile** ADJS 1 **sanitary,** aseptic, antiseptic, **uninfected;** disinfected, decontaminated, sterilized
2 arid, barren, blank, jejune; **unproductive,** infertile, unfruitful; **impotent,** gelded; ineffectual

**stern** ADJS **strict,** exacting, grim, dour, unsparing; austere, rugged, **tough** <nonformal>

**stew** NOUNS 1 olla, olio, *olla podrida* <Sp>; meat stew, *étuvée* <Fr>; Irish stew, mulligan stew *or* mulligan <nonformal>; goulash, Hungarian goulash; ragout; *bouillabaisse* <Fr>, *paella* <Catalan>, oyster stew, chowder
2 **dither, fret, fuss,** pother, bother, lather *and* sweat *and* snit <all nonformal>, flap; **huff,** pique, pet, tiff, miff <nonformal>, ferment; **fix** *and* jam *and* pickle *and* scrape <all nonformal>
VERBS 3 **fret,** fuss, chafe, fret and fume, sweat, get into a dither; bite one's nails, walk the floor, go up the wall <nonformal>, be on tenterhooks *or* pins and needles; **seethe,** simmer, sizzle, smoke, smolder, steam

**steward** NOUNS **attendant,** flight attendant, stewardess, hostess; major-domo, house steward; **custodian,** keeper, caretaker

**stickler** NOUNS **perfectionist,** precisian, precisianist, nitpicker <nonformal>, captious critic

**the sticks** NOUNS **the country,** the tall corn *and* yokeldom *and* hickdom <all nonformal>; the boondocks *and* the boonies <both nonformal>; nowhere

**sticky** ADJS **adhesive, tenacious,** clingy; **tacky,** gluey, gummy, **viscid,** glutinous

**stiff** ADJS **stilted,** prim, prissy, rigid, starch, starchy, starched; **rigid,** firm, renitent, incompressible; nonresilient, inelastic

**stifle** VERBS **suppress, repress,** keep under, smother, choke *or* hold back, fight down *or* back, inhibit; muffle, **smother,** squash, quash, squelch, kill, sit on *or* upon, put the lid on <nonformal>; suffocate, asphyxiate, strangle, throttle, choke off, **muzzle,** gag

**stigma** NOUNS stigmatism, onus; **brand,** badge of infamy; **slur,** reproach, censure, reprimand, imputation, aspersion, reflection, stigmatization; pillorying; **black eye** <nonformal>, black mark; **stain,** taint, tarnish

**stigmatize** VERBS **brand; stain,** besmirch, smirch, tarnish, taint, **blacken,** smear, **sully,** soil, defile, vilify, **slur,** cast a slur upon, **disparage,** defame; **give a black eye** <nonformal>

**still** ADJS **silent,** quiet, quiescent, **hushed,** soundless, noiseless; **at rest,** resting, reposing; **fixed,** stationary, static, at a standstill; **stock-still,** dead-still

**stimulant** NOUNS **energizer, stimulus,** stimulator, vitalizer, arouser, needle <nonformal>, restorative; tonic; **antidepressant**

**stimulate** VERBS **whet, sharpen,** pique, provoke, quicken, enliven, liven up, pick up, jazz up <nonformal>, animate, **exhilarate,** invigorate, galvanize, energize, spark

**stimulus** NOUNS **energizer,** stimulator, vitalizer, arouser, needle <nonformal>, restorative; **cause,** occasion, grounds

**stingy** ADJS **illiberal,** ungenerous, chintzy, miserly, cheap *and* tight *and* narrow <all nonformal>, **closefisted,** tightfisted, penny-pinching

**stint** NOUNS 1 **task,** work, job, labor, piece of work, **chore,** odd job; **restriction,** limitation
VERBS 2 **scrimp,** skimp, scamp, scant, screw, **pinch,** starve, famish; grudge, begrudge

**stipulate** VERBS stipulate for, specifically provide, set conditions *or* terms, make reservations; **make conditional,** make contingent; **specify,** designate, determine, single out, feature, highlight, focus on, select

**stir** NOUNS 1 **bustle,** fuss, flurry, flutter, fluster, scramble, ferment, stew; **commotion,** hubbub, hullabaloo, hoo-ha *and* foofaraw *and* flap <all nonformal>, ado, to-do <nonformal>
VERBS 2 **awake,** open one's eyes; **excite,** impassion, arouse, rouse, **stir up,** work up, work up into a lather <nonformal>, whip up; **ruffle,** shake up, shock, upset, make waves
3 **move,** budge; **bustle,** fuss, make a fuss, stir about, rush around *or* about, tear around, run *or* go around like a chicken with its head cut off

**stock** NOUNS 1 **lineage,** line, blood, strain, species, stirps, **breed,** brood, kind; ethnicity
2 **merchandise, consumer goods,** consumer items, retail goods, goods for sale; **stock-in-trade;** staples; inventory
VERBS 3 gather *or* procure materials; **store,** stock up, lay in, restock
ADJS 4 **stereotyped,** set, **commonplace,** truistic, twice-told, **familiar,** bromidic <nonformal>, old hat <nonformal>; **standard,** regular, regulation; **conventional,** common, commonplace, ordinary, average, everyday, mediocre, household

**stockpile** NOUNS 1 **reserve, reserves,** reservoir, resource; **cache,** backup, reserve supply, something in reserve *or* in hand
VERBS 2 **store up,** lay up, put up; **accumulate,** cumulate, collect, amass; backlog

**stocky** ADJS **stubby,** thickset, blocky, **chunky** <nonformal>

**stodgy** ADJS **dull,** stuffy, wooden, stiff; **old-fogyish,** fuddy-duddy, square *and* corny *and* cornball <all nonformal>

**stoic** ADJS **imperturbable,** unflappable <nonformal>, unshakable, **cool** <nonformal>, impassive, stolid; without nerves, without a nerve in one's body, unflinching

**stoke** VERBS **ignite;** feed the fire, stoke the fire, add fuel to the flame; poke *or* stir the fire

**stolen** ADJS pilfered, purloined; pirated, plagiarized; hot <nonformal>

**stolid** ADJS **inexcitable,** imperturbable, unflappable <nonformal>; stoic, stoical; even-tempered; impassive, laid-back <nonformal>; **staid,** stuffy <nonformal>

**stomach** NOUNS 1 **abdomen, belly,** paunch

2 <nonformal> goozle, guzzle; tum, tummy, tum-tum, breadbasket, **gut,** bulge, fallen chest, corporation, spare tire, bay window, **pot,** potbelly, potgut,

beerbelly, German *or* Milwaukee goiter, pusgut, swagbelly; **guts,** tripes, stuffings

**stomp** VERBS **stamp,** trample, tread, drub, clump, clop

**stone** NOUNS 1 **jewel,** bijou, **gem,** precious stone; rhinestone
2 **monument,** marker, **tablet,** boundary stone, memorial stone; **gravestone,** tombstone; headstone, footstone

**stonewall** VERBS **delay,** retard, stall, drag one's feet <nonformal>, slow down, **hold up** <nonformal>, hold *or* keep back, check, **stay, stop,** arrest, impede, **block,** hinder, obstruct, throw a monkey wrench in the works <nonformal>

**stooge** NOUNS **hanger-on,** dangler, adherent, appendage, dependent, parasite, flunky; cat's-paw, puppet, dummy, pawn, creature, minion, figurehead

**stool pigeon** NOUNS **informer, betrayer,** double-crosser <nonformal>, snitch *and* snitcher <both nonformal>; **squealer** *and* preacher *and* stoolie *and* **fink** *and* rat <all nonformal>

**stoop** NOUNS 1 **porch,** veranda, piazza <nonformal>, front steps
2 **crouch,** bend, squat; **bow,** genuflection, kneeling, kowtow, kowtowing
VERBS 3 **condescend,** deign, vouchsafe; descend, lower *or* demean oneself, trouble oneself, set one's dignity aside *or* to one side; **grovel,** crawl, creep, cower, cringe, crouch, kneel, bend the knee, fall on one's knees, prostrate oneself, throw oneself at the feet of, **kowtow,** bow, bow and scrape

**stop** VERBS 1 **stop up; obstruct,** bar, stay; **block,** block up; **clog,** clog up, foul; **plug,** plug up; come to a stop *or* halt, **halt,** stop in one's tracks, skid to a stop, stop dead; bring to a stop, put a stop *or* end to, bring to a shuddering *or* screeching halt <nonformal>
INTERJS 2 **cease!, stop!, halt!,** *halte!* <Fr>, hold!, freeze!, stay!, desist!, quit it!; **let up!,** easy!, take it easy!, relax!, get off it!, **leave off!,** *arrâtez!* <Fr>, stop it!, forget it!, no more!, have done!, *tenez!* <Fr>, **hold everything!, hold it!,** hold to!, hold on!, whoa!, that's it!, that's enough!, that will do!, enough!, enough is enough!, all right already!, *basta!* <Ital>

3 <nonformal> **cut it out!,** cool it!, bag it!, chill out!, call it quits!, can it!, turn it off!, chuck it!, stow it!, drop it!, lay off!, all right already!, come off it!, **knock it off!,** break it off!, break it up!

**stopgap** NOUNS 1 **improvisation,** temporary measure *or* arrangement, *pro tempore* measure *or* arrangement, **makeshift,** ad hoc measure, **fix** *and* **quick fix** <both nonformal>, jury-rigged expedient
ADJS 2 **makeshift,** band-aid <nonformal>, improvised, improvisational, **jury-rigged;** ad hoc; quick and dirty <nonformal>; temporary, provisional

**stoppage** NOUNS **delay,** jam *and* logjam <both nonformal>, obstruction, tie-up *and* bind <both nonformal>, **block,** blockage, **hang-up** <nonformal>; **stop,** halt, stay, arrest, check, cutoff <nonformal>

**stopper** NOUNS 1 stop, **stopple,** stopgap; **plug, cork,** bung, spike, spill, spile, tap, faucet, spigot, valve, check valve, cock, sea cock, peg, pin
VERBS 2 **plug,** plug up; stopple, **cork,** bung, spile; put the lid on

**storage** NOUNS **stowage;** cold storage, cold store, dry storage, dead storage; storage space; **depository,** repository, depot, supply depot, warehouse; bonded warehouse, entrepôt

**store** NOUNS 1 **hoard, treasure,** treasury; plenty, plenitude, abundance, cornucopia; **market,** mart, shop, salon, boutique, wareroom, emporium
VERBS 2 **stow,** lay in store; **lay in,** lay in a supply *or* stock *or* store, store away, stow away, **put away,** lay away, put *or* lay by, pack away, bundle away, lay down, stow down, salt down *or* away *and* sock away *and* squirrel away <all nonformal>

**storm** NOUNS 1 **tempest,** squall, line squall, **tornado,** cyclone, hurricane, tropical cyclone, typhoon, tropical storm; stormy weather, rough weather, foul weather, dirty weather
VERBS 2 **rage,** rant, rave, roar; **rampage,** ramp, **tear,** tear around; go *or* carry on <nonformal>; come in like a lion; **destroy,** wreck, wreak havoc, ruin; **attack,** assault, batter, savage, mug, maul, hammer

**stormy** ADJS **turbulent,** tumultuous, raging, chaotic, hellish, anarchic, **storming,** tempestuous, **frenzied,** wild, wild-eyed, frantic, furious

**story** NOUNS **tale,** yarn, account, narrative, narration, chronicle; trumped-up story, fabrication

**stout** ADJS **corpulent,** fat, overweight, fattish, **obese,** adipose, gross, fleshy, beefy, meaty, hefty, porky, porcine; **sturdy,** stable, **solid,** sound, firm, steady, tough, strong, rugged; **durable,** lasting, enduring

**stouthearted** ADJS **courageous,** plucky, brave, bold, valiant, valorous, gallant, intrepid, doughty, **hardy,** stalwart, stout, lionhearted; heroic

**stove** NOUNS **heater,** warmer; **furnace;** cooker, cookery

**stow** VERBS **put away,** lay away, **put aside,** put *or* lay *or* set by; store

**straddle** VERBS **extend,** reach, stretch, sweep, spread, span, take in, encompass; step over, overstride

**strafe** VERBS **bombard,** blast, shell, cannonade, mortar, barrage, blitz; rake, enfilade

**straggle** VERBS **bring up the rear,** come last, **follow,** come after; trail, trail behind, lag behind, fall behind, fall back

**straight** ADJS 1 dead straight, straight as an edge *or* a ruler, ruler-straight, even, right, true, straight as an arrow; **direct,** undeviating, unswerving, unbending, undeflected
2 **square,** foursquare, straight-arrow <nonformal>, honest and aboveboard, right as rain; **square-dealing,** square-shooting, straight-shooting, **on the up-and-up** *and* **on the level,** *and* on the square <all nonformal>; **aboveboard,** open and aboveboard; undiluted, unfortified
3 **conformist, conventional**, bourgeois, plastic *and* square *and* white-bread *and* button-down *and* buttoned-down <all nonformal>
ADVS 4 unswervingly, undeviatingly, **directly;** straight to the mark; in the groove *and* on the beam *and* on the money <all nonformal>; **exactly,** precisely, to a T; **dead,** right, even, square, **plumb,** squarely, point-blank

**straightforward** ADJS **unaffected, unpretentious,** unpretending, unassuming, unfeigning, direct, honest, candid; **uncomplicated,** uninvolved, simple

**strain** NOUNS 1 **lineage, extraction,** derivation, birth, **blood,** breed, **family,** house, **stock,** race, stirps, seed
2 straining, **stress,** stressfulness, **stress and strain,** taxing, **tension,** stretch, rack; **overwork,** overexertion, overstrain
VERBS 3 **tense,** stress, stretch, tax, press, rack; take on too much, spread oneself too thin, overexert, overstrain, overextend; drive *or* whip *or* flog oneself

**strait** NOUNS narrow, **narrows; bottleneck,** chokepoint; isthmus; **pinch,** clutch <nonformal>, rub, pass, extremity, spot <nonformal>; **predicament,** plight, spot of trouble

**straitlaced** ADJS **rigorous,** inflexible, **unyielding,** unbending, impliable, **relentless,** unrelenting, procrustean; ironbound, hidebound; puritanical

**stranded** ADJS **grounded,** aground, **on the rocks,** high and dry; **stuck,** stuck *or* set fast; castaway, marooned, shipwrecked

**strange** ADJS **extraneous,** foreign, alien, exotic, foreign-looking; **outlandish,** off-the-wall <informal>, surreal, not for real <nonformal>, passing strange; **unfamiliar**

**stranger** NOUNS **outsider,** non-member, the other, they; **foreigner,** alien; not our sort, not the right sort

**strangle** VERBS garrote, **throttle,** choke, burke; **suffocate,** stifle, smother, asphyxiate, stop the breath

**stranglehold** NOUNS **hindrance,** impediment, restriction, restraint; **obstruction,** blocking, blockage, clogging, occlusion; constriction, squeeze, stricture, cramp

**strapping** ADJS **sturdy,** hunky *and* husky *and* hefty *and* beefy <all nonformal>, doughty <nonformal>, **hardy,** robust, lusty

**stratagem** NOUNS **artifice,** craft, wile, **device,** wily device, **contrivance,** expedient, design, scheme, trick, cute trick, **ruse,** red herring, tactic, **maneuver,** stroke, master stroke, gambit, **ploy,** dodge, artful dodge

**strategic** ADJS **canny,** shrewd, acute, astute, clever; **Machiavellian,** politic, tactical

**strategist** NOUNS **tactician;** maneuverer, machinator, manipulator, wire-puller <nonformal>; calculator, schemer, intriguer; wheeler-dealer <nonformal>; behind-the-scenes operator, gray eminence, *éminence grise* <Fr>, power behind the throne, kingmaker <nonformal>

**strategy** NOUNS **plan,** scheme, design, long-range planning, long-range plan; program of action; methodology; working plan, strategic plan; tactics, game plan <nonformal>

**stratum** NOUNS **social class,** economic class, **social status,** economic status, socioeconomic status *or* background, standing, footing, prestige, rank, ranking, place, station, position, level, degree; **grade,** rank, rating, status, estate

**stray** NOUNS 1 **waif,** homeless waif, dogie, waifs and strays
VERBS 2 go astray, lose one's way, err; take a wrong turn *or* turning; drift, go adrift; **wander,** wander off, ramble, rove, straggle, divagate, excurse, pererrate; **digress,** wander, **get off the subject,** get sidetracked, excurse, maunder; **go wrong,** err, deviate from the path of virtue, leave the straight and narrow

**streak** NOUNS 1 **ray,** beam, gleam, **stream,** ray of light, beam of light; string of losses *or* victories
2 **disposition, tendency,** grain, vein, set, mental set, mindset, **leaning,** animus, propensity, proclivity, predilection, preference, predisposition; **bent,** turn, bias, slant, cast, warp, twist; strain
VERBS 3 **stripe,** striate, band, bar, vein; marble, marbleize

**stream** NOUNS **current,** run, rush, onrush, ongoing; **wash,** wake, **exhaust,** jet exhaust, **vapor trail,** condensation trail, contrail; **streak,** ribbon, ribbon of light, streamer, stream of light

**streamline** VERBS **simplify,** reduce, reduce to elements *or* essentials; **modernize,** update, **bring up to date,** move with the times

**streetcar** NOUNS **trolley** *or* trolley car, **tram** *or* tramcar <both Brit>; trolley bus, trackless trolley; cable car, grip car

**street person** NOUNS homeless person; bag woman *or* lady, shopping-bag lady, shopping-cart woman *or* lady

**streetwalker** NOUNS **prostitute,** whore, hustler *and* **hooker** <both nonformal>

**strength** NOUNS strongness; **robustness,** vigorousness, ruggedness, **vitality,** lustiness, hardiness, vigor; **might,** mightiness, power, intensity; **strong-mindedness,** strength of mind, strength *or* fixity of purpose, fortitude, moral fiber

**strengthen** VERBS **invigorate, fortify,** beef up <nonformal>, brace, buttress, prop, shore up, support, undergird, brace up; **toughen,** temper, **reinforce; reinvigorate,** refresh, revive, recruit one's strength; **intensify,** heighten, deepen, enhance

**strenuous** ADJS **laborious,** toilsome, arduous, painful, effortful, operose, troublesome, onerous, oppressive, burdensome

**stress** NOUNS 1 **pain,** distress, grief, stress of life, suffering, passion, dolor; **anxiety,** apprehension, apprehensiveness, misgiving, foreboding, suspense, strain, tension, nervous strain *or* tension;
2 **accent,** accentuation, stress accent; **emphasis,** word stress
VERBS 3 **strain,** tense, stretch, tax, press, rack
4 **emphasize,** lay emphasis *or* stress upon, feature, highlight, place emphasis on, give emphasis to, **accent,** accentuate, punctuate, point up

**stretch** NOUNS 1 **range,** scope, compass, reach, expanse, radius, sweep, carry, fetch; **extent,** length, span, stride, haul
2 **interval,** lapse of time, space, span, timespan, time-lag, time-gap; **time,** while; **term,** tenure, **enlistment,** hitch <nonformal>, tour; prison term
VERBS 3 **extend,** reach, sweep, spread, run, cover; **reach** *or* stretch *or* thrust out; span, straddle, take in, hold, encompass, surround, environ
4 distend, dilate, swell, swell up, swell out, puff up, puff out, pump up, bloat, tumefy, balloon, fill out
5 **lengthen,** prolong, prolongate, **elongate,** extend, produce, **protract,** continue; draw *or* drag *or* stretch *or* string *or* spin out
6 **exaggerate,** hyperbolize; stretch the truth, stretch the point, draw the longbow

**stricken** ADJS **wretched,** miserable; crushed, heartsick; desolate, disconsolate; shaken, upset, dashed, crushed

**strict** ADJS 1 **exacting,** exigent, demanding, not to be trifled with, **stringent,** astringent; disciplined, spit-and-polish; **severe,** harsh, dour, unsparing; Spartan
2 scripturalistic, evangelical; hyperorthodox, puritanical, purist *or* puristic, straitlaced; creedbound; **dogmatic,** fundamentalist, precisianist *or* precisianistic, literalist *or* literalistic

**strident** ADJS stridulant, stridulous; strident-voiced; shrill, harsh, raucous, grating

**strife** NOUNS **contention,** contest, contestation, combat, **fighting,** conflict, war, struggle, blood on the floor, cut and thrust

**strike** NOUNS 1 **attack, assault,** assailing, assailment; **offense,** offensive; surgical strike, first strike, **preemptive strike;** blitzkrieg, blitz, lightning attack, lightning war, panzer warfare, sudden *or* devastating *or* crippling attack, deep strike
2 **walkout** *or* tie-up <both nonformal>, industrial action <Brit>, **job action;** work stoppage, sit-down strike, sitdown, wildcat strike, outlaw strike; sympathy strike; general strike
VERBS 3 **slap,** smack, whack, whomp, **cuff, box,** buffet; slap the face, box the ears, give a rap on the knuckles; **bump,** hit, knock, bang

4 <nonformal> **belt,** bat, clout, bang, slam, bash, biff, paste, wham, whop, clump, bonk, wallop, clip, cut, plunk, swat, soak, sock, slog, slug, yerk <old>, clunk, clonk

5 **go on strike,** go out, walk, walk out; hit the bricks <nonformal>, shut it down
6 **impress,** make an impression, grab <nonformal>, hit; **sink in** <nonformal>

**strikebreaker** NOUNS **scab** *and* **rat** *and* **fink** *and* scissorbill <all nonformal>, **blackleg** <Brit>

**striking** ADJS **remarkable,** outstanding, extraordinary, **superior**, marked, of mark, signal, conspicuous, **outstanding,** in the foreground

**stringent** ADJS **strict,** exacting, exigent, demanding, not to be trifled with, astringent; **severe,** harsh, dour, unsparing; **stern,** grim, austere, rugged, **tough** <nonformal>; **hard-line,** authoritarian

**strip** NOUNS 1 **runway,** taxiway, landing strip, **airstrip,** flight strip, take-off strip
2 **strap,** strop; **band,** bandage, fillet, fascia, taenia; **tape,** tapeline, tape measure
VERBS 3 **divest,** strip away, remove; uncover, uncloak, unveil, **expose,** lay open, bare, lay *or* strip bare, **denude,** denudate; fleece, shear; pluck
4 **undress,** unclothe, undrape, disarray; **disrobe;** unsheathe, discase, uncase; strip to the buff <nonformal>, do a strip-tease
5 **peel,** pare, skin, flay, excoriate, decorticate, bark; scalp

**strive** VERBS **endeavor,** struggle, strain, sweat, sweat blood, labor, get one's teeth into, come to grips with, take it on, make an all-out effort, move heaven and earth, **exert oneself,** apply oneself, use some elbow grease <nonformal>

**stroke** NOUNS 1 **seizure, attack,** access, visitation; arrest; blockage, stoppage, occlusion, thrombosis, thromboembolism; ictus, apoplexy
VERBS 2 **pet,** caress, fondle; **encourage,** hearten, embolden, give encouragement, pat *or* clap on the back; **soft-soap,** butter, honey, **butter up,** soften up; massage the ego <nonformal>

**stroll** NOUNS 1 **leisurely gait,** snail's *or* tortoise's pace; **walk,** ramble, amble, saunter
VERBS 2 **go slow** *or* **slowly,** saunter, amble, waddle, ramble, meander, *flâner* <Fr>

**stroller** NOUNS **baby carriage,** baby buggy <nonformal>, perambulator, pram <Brit>; walker

**strong** ADJS 1 **forceful,** forcible, **mighty,** powerful, potent; **robust,** vigorous, hearty, nervy, **lusty,** bouncing, full- *or* red-blooded
2 strong-smelling, strong-scented; **pungent,** penetrating, nose-piercing, sharp; reeking, reeky

**strong-arm** VERBS use force, get tough <nonformal>, muscle *and* manhandle <both nonformal>

**stronghold** NOUNS hold, safehold, fasthold, strong point, **fastness,** keep, ward, **bastion,** donjon, **citadel,** castle, tower, tower of strength, strong point; refuge, sanctuary

**structure** NOUNS 1 **building,** edifice, construction, construct, erection, establishment, fabric; **plan,** architecture, architectonics, scheme, design; **syntax,** syntactic structure, word order, word arrangement
VERBS 2 **construct,** build; organize, shape, shape up; form, configure, array, pull it together, get *or* put one's ducks in a row <nonformal>, line up, set up, lay out

**struggle** NOUNS 1 **fight,** battle, tussle, scuffle, wrestle, hassle <nonformal>
VERBS 2 **strive,** contend, fight, battle, buffet, scuffle, tussle, wrestle, hassle <nonformal>, work *or* fight one's way,

agonize, huff and puff, grunt and sweat, sweat it <nonformal>, make heavy weather of it

**strut** NOUNS 1 **swagger,** swank <nonformal>, bounce, brave show; swaggering, strutting; peacockishness, peacockery
VERBS 2 **swagger,** swank <nonformal>, prance, stalk, peacock

**stub** NOUNS **extremity,** extreme; tail, **tail end,** butt end, tag, tag end, fag end; stump, butt

**stubborn** ADJS **obstinate,** pertinacious, restive; willful, self-willed, strong-willed, hardheaded, **headstrong,** strongheaded, *entêté* <Fr>; **dogged,** bulldogged, **tenacious,** persevering; **pigheaded,** mulish <nonformal>, stubborn as a mule; **unyielding**, ungiving

**stuck** ADJS **fast,** stuck fast, **fixed,** transfixed, caught, fastened, tied, chained, tethered, anchored, moored, held, inextricable; **jammed,** impacted, congested, packed, wedged; seized, seized up, frozen; **baffled,** perplexed, bewildered, mystified, stumped <nonformal>, stymied

**stuck-up** ADJS **conceited,** self-conceited, immodest, **puffed up,** chesty <nonformal>; aggressively self-confident, obtrusive, bumptious

**studded** ADJS **knobbed,** knobby, knoblike, nubbled, nubby, nubbly, torose; **knotty,** knotted; **ornamented,** decorated, embellished; **peppered,** spotted, dotted, powdered, dusted, specked, speckled; thronged, bristling, rife

**student** NOUNS **pupil,** scholar, learner, studier, educatee, **trainee,** *élève* <Fr>; tutee; **learned man,** person of learning, giant of learning, colossus of knowledge, mastermind, **savant,** pundit

**studied** ADJS **reasoned,** advised, considered, calculated, meditated, contemplated, deliberated, weighed, thought-out; **pretentious,** mannered, artificial, unnatural

**studio** NOUNS *atelier* <Fr>; gallery; **workplace,** workroom, worksite, workshop, shop; radio station

**study** NOUNS 1 branch of learning; **discipline,** subdiscipline; **field,** specialty, academic specialty, area; **studying,** application, conning; **reading,** perusal
2 **retreat,** sanctum, **den,** lair, mew; **ivory tower;** library
VERBS 3 regard studiously, apply oneself to, crack a book *and* hit the books <both nonformal>; **read, peruse,** go over, read up *or* read up on, have one's nose in a book <nonformal>; **grind** *and* **bone** *and* bone up on <all nonformal>, lucubrate, elucubrate, **burn the midnight oil**

**stuff** NOUNS 1 **matter,** material, materiality, **substance**
VERBS 2 **gorge**, pig out <nonformal>, engorge, glut, guttle, cram, eat one's fill, stuff *or* gorge oneself, gluttonize; **fill,** pack, load; **pad,** wad, **cram,** jam, jampack, fill to the brim, overfill, make burst at the seams, surfeit

**stuffed** ADJS **full,** packed, jammed, jampacked, like sardines; stuffed to the gills <nonformal>; **congested,** stuffed up; **surfeited,** glutted, gorged, overfed, bloated, replete, swollen, **satiated**, overstuffed

**stuffy** ADJS 1 **airless,** breathless, breezeless, windless; **close,** oppressive, stifling, suffocating, sultry
2 **pompous,** self-important, impressed with oneself, pontific, pontifical; **inflated,** swollen, bloated, tumid, turgid, flatulent, gassy <nonformal>, stilted; **hidebound,** straitlaced

**stumble** VERBS **topple,** lurch, pitch, stagger, totter, careen, list, trip, flounder, **slip,** trip, trip over one's own feet, get in one's own way, miss one's footing, miscue; commit a *faux pas,* commit a gaffe; **botch,** mar, **spoil,** butcher, murder, make sad work of

**stump** NOUNS 1 **platform; rostrum,** podium, pulpit, speaker's platform *or* stand, **soapbox** <nonformal>; hustings
VERBS 2 **electioneer,** campaign; take the stump *and* take to the stump *and* stump the country *and* take to the hustings *and* hit the campaign trail *and* whistle-stop <all nonformal>
3 **thwart, disconcert, baffle,** nonplus, perplex

**stun** VERBS **deaden,** numb, benumb, blunt, dull, obtund, desensitize; **stupefy,** bedaze, besot; knock unconscious, knock senseless, **knock out,** KO *and* kayo *and* lay out *and* coldcock *and* knock stiff <all nonformal>; **startle,** shock, electrify, jar, jolt, shake

**stunning** ADJS **astonishing,** amazing, surprising, startling, **astounding,** confounding, staggering, eye-opening, breathtaking, overwhelming, mind-boggling *or* -numbing; **eye-filling** *and* long on looks *and* raving *and* devastating *and* killing <all nonformal>

**stunted** ADJS **undersized,** undergrown, runty, pint-size *or* -sized *and* sawed-off <all nonformal>; shrunk, shrunken, wizened, shriveled; meager, scrubby, scraggy

**stupefy** VERBS **stun,** bedaze, besot; knock unconscious, paralyze, **deaden,** anesthetize, drug, narcotize, anesthetize, petrify, strike dumb

**stupendous** ADJS **prodigious,** unheard-of, unprecedented, extraordinary, exceptional, rare, unique, singular, **remarkable,** striking, sensational

**stupid** ADJS 1 **dumb,** doltish, blockish, klutzy *and* klutzish <both nonformal>, cloddish, lumpish, oafish, **dense,** thick <nonformal>, opaque, bovine, thick-headed

2 <nonformal> **blockheaded,** woodenheaded, stupidheaded, dumbheaded, dunderheaded, blunderheaded, clueless *or* jolterheaded *or* joltheaded *or* jingle-brained <all Brit>, chowderheaded, chuckleheaded, beetleheaded, nitwitted, numskulled, cabbageheaded, pumpkinheaded, sapheaded, lunkheaded, muttonheaded, meatheaded, fatheaded, boneheaded, knuckleheaded, clodpated; dead from the neck up, dead above *or* between the ears, muscle-bound between the ears; featherheaded, airheaded, bubbleheaded, out to lunch, lunchy, dufus, dufus-assed, spastic, spazzy, three bricks shy of a load, without brain one, not playing with a full deck

**stupidity** NOUNS 1 stupidness, *bêtise* <Fr>, **dumbness** <nonformal>, doltishness, **density,** denseness, opacity; **obtuseness,** sluggishness, slowness, **dim-wittedness,** thick-wittedness, thick-headedness

2 **blunder,** faux pas, gaffe, solecism; indiscretion; botch, bungle

**stupor** NOUNS **coma,** swoon, **trance;** narcosis, narcohypnosis, narcoma, narcotization, narcotic stupor *or* trance; **unconsciousness,** senselessness; nothingness, oblivion, obliviousness, nirvana; torpor, torpidity, stupefaction

**sturdy** ADJS stable, **solid,** sound, firm, steady, tough, stout, **strong,** rugged; **durable,** lasting, enduring; **well-made,** well-constructed, well-built, well-knit; **well-founded,** well-established, well-grounded

**stutter** NOUNS 1 **stammering, stuttering,** hesitation, faltering, traulism, dysphemia, *balbuties* <L>; palilalia; stammer

VERBS 2 **stammer,** stammer out; hesitate, falter, halt, stumble

**style** NOUNS 1 **fashion,** mode, vogue, trend, prevailing taste; proper thing, ton, bon ton; custom; convention; height of fashion; the season's look; high fashion, *haute couture* <Fr>

2 **kind,** sort, ilk, type, manner, **nature,** character, persuasion, the like *or* likes of <nonformal>

**stylish** ADJS **modish,** voguish, vogue; dressy <nonformal>; *soigné* or *soignée* <both Fr>; *à la mode* <Fr>, in the mode

**stymie** VERBS **stop,** stay, halt, bring to a stop, put a stop *or* end to, bring to a shuddering *or* screeching halt <nonformal>; **block,** stall, deadlock; nip in the bud

**suave** ADJS **smooth,** smug, bland, **glib,** unctuous, oily, oleaginous, fulsome, ingratiating, disarming; fine-spoken, fair-spoken, smooth-tongued, oily-tongued, honey-tongued

**subconscious** NOUNS 1 **inmost mind,** inner recesses of the mind, mind's core, deepest mind, center of the mind; inner man; subconscious mind

ADJS 2 **unconscious;** subliminal, extramarginal

**subdue** VERBS **master,** overmaster, **quell,** crush, reduce, beat down, **break,** break down, overwhelm; tread underfoot, trample on *or* down, trample underfoot, trample in the dust; **suppress**; make one give in *or* say 'uncle' <nonformal>, bring low, **bring to terms,** humble, humiliate, take down a notch *or* peg, bend, **bring one to his knees,** bend to one's will

**subject** NOUNS 1 **vassal,** liege, liege man, liege subject, homager

2 **topic,** matter, subject matter, what it is about, **concern,** focus of interest *or* attention, discrete matter, category

**subjective** ADJS **introverted,** introvert, introversive, **ingoing,** inner-directed; esoteric, private, secret, internal

**subjugate** VERBS **subject,** subordinate; dominate; **enslave,** enthrall, hold in thrall, make a chattel of; **hold in sub-**

**jection,** hold in bondage, hold captive, hold in captivity; **hold down,** keep down, keep under; **keep** *or* **have under one's thumb,** vassalize, make dependent *or* tributary

**sublime** ADJS **lofty,** elevated, grand, majestic, noble, stately, grave, solemn, dignified; moving, inspiring; **gorgeous,** ravishing; glorious, heavenly, divine

**submarine** NOUNS **sub,** submersible, underwater craft; **U-boat,** *U-boot* or *Unterseeboot* <both Ger>, pigboat <nonformal>; nuclear *or* nuclear-powered submarine; Polaris submarine; Trident submarine; hunter-killer submarine

**submerge** VERBS submerse, **immerse,** immerge, merge, **sink,** bury, engulf, **inundate,** deluge, drown, overwhelm, whelm; **dip,** duck, dunk <nonformal>, douse, souse, plunge in water; baptize

**submissive** ADJS **compliant,** complaisant, complying, **acquiescent,** consenting; subservient, abject, **obedient**; servile; **resigned,** uncomplaining; unassertive; **passive,** supine, unresisting, deferential, self-abnegating

**submit** VERBS 1 **comply,** take, accept, go along with <nonformal>, suffer, bear, brook, **acquiesce,** be agreeable, accede, assent; **succumb,** resign, resign oneself, give oneself up, not resist; take one's medicine, face the music; bite the bullet; knuckle under
2 **propose,** prefer; **suggest,** recommend, **advance,** commend to attention, **propound,** pose, put forward, bring forward, put *or* set forth, put it to, put *or* set *or* lay *or* bring before, dish up *and* come out *or* up with <both nonformal>

**subordinate** NOUNS 1 **junior,** secondary, second-in-command, lieutenant, **inferior; underling,** understrapper, low man on the totem pole <nonformal>, assistant, personal assistant, helper; **servant,** employee
ADJS 2 **inferior,** subaltern, **secondary; junior,** minor; **subservient,** subject, servile, **lowly,** humble, modest; **lesser,** less, lower; subsidiary

**subscribe** VERBS 1 **contribute,** chip in *and* kick in *and* pony up *and* pay up <all nonformal>, give one's share *or* fair share; contribute to, give to, donate to
2 **belong,** hold membership, be a member, be on the rolls, be inscribed, be in <nonformal>; hold a subscription

**subsequent** ADJS **after, later,** after-the-fact, *post factum* and *ex post facto* <both L>, posterior, **following, succeeding,** successive, lineal, ensuing, attendant

**subservient** ADJS **deferential,** obeisant; obsequious, servile; crouching, prostrate, prone, on one's belly, on one's knees, on bended knee; **assistant,** auxiliary, adjuvant, subsidiary, ancillary, accessory

**subside** VERBS **cease**, wane, ebb, run *or* die down, die off, dwindle, molder; **give way,** lapse, cave, cave in; **decline,** shrink, ebb away, languish, sink, sag, die down *or* away, wind down, taper off *and* trail off *or* away *and* tail off *or* away <all nonformal>

**subsidiary** ADJS **secondary,** subordinate; **incidental,** circumstantial, contingent

**subsidize** VERBS **finance,** bankroll *and* greenback <both nonformal>, fund; angel <nonformal>; **aid,** assist, support, help, pay the bills, pick up the check *or* tab *and* spring for *and* pop for <all nonformal>

**subsidy** NOUNS subvention, subsidization, support; **grant,** grant-in-aid, bounty; **allowance,** stipend, allotment

**substance** NOUNS 1 **sum and substance,** stuff, material, matter, medium, building blocks, fabric; **essence,** quintessence, elixir, distillate, distillation, distilled essence; sine qua non, irreducible *or* indispensable content
2 **meaning, gist,** pith, spirit, essence, gravamen, last word, name of the game *and* meat and potatoes *and* bottom line <all nonformal>

**substandard** ADJS **below par,** below standard, below the mark <nonformal>, **not up to scratch** *or* snuff *or* the mark <nonformal>

**substantiate** VERBS **confirm,** affirm, **attest,** warrant, **authenticate,** validate, certify, ratify, verify; **corroborate,** bear out, support, buttress, **sustain,** fortify, bolster, reinforce, undergird, strengthen; materialize

**substitute** NOUNS 1 sub <nonformal>, **substitution,** replacement, backup, deputy; locum tenens, **relief,** fill-in, **stand-in,** understudy, pinch hitter
VERBS 2 **exchange, change,** take *or* ask *or* offer in exchange, switch, ring in <nonformal>, **put in the place of,** change for, make way for, give place to
ADJS 3 **alternate, alternative,** other,

tother <nonformal>, equivalent, token, dummy, pinch, utility, backup, secondary; **proxy;** reserve, **spare,** stopgap, temporary, provisional

**subterfuge** NOUNS **secrecy,** secretness, concealment; **secretiveness,** closeness; **evasiveness,** evasion; **deception,** calculated deception, **deceptiveness,** gimmickry *or* gimmickery, trickiness; blind, **ruse,** wile, **dodge,** artful dodge, chicanery

**subtle** ADJS **nice,** dainty, delicate, *délicat* <Fr>, fine, refined, exquisite, **sophisticated,** discriminating, fastidious

**subtract** VERBS **deduct,** subduct, take away, take from, **remove,** withdraw, abstract; **reduce,** shorten, curtail, retrench, lessen, **diminish, decrease,** phase down, impair, bate, abate

**subversive** NOUNS 1 **saboteur,** fifth columnist, crypto; security risk; **revolutionist,** revolutionary, revolutionizer
ADJS 2 revolutionary, revolutional; traitorous, treasonable; vandalish, vandalistic; subversionary

**subway** NOUNS *métro* <Fr>, tube, underground <Brit>; shuttle train, shuttle

**succeed** VERBS 1 **prevail,** be successful, be crowned with success, meet with success, do very well, do famously, deliver, come through *and* make a go of it <both nonformal>; prosper; **make a hit** <nonformal>, click *and* connect <both nonformal>, **catch on** *and* take <both nonformal>, catch fire, have legs <nonformal>; **go over** *and* go over big *or* with a bang <all nonformal>; pass, graduate, qualify, win one's spurs *or* wings, pass with flying colors
2 **come** *or* **follow** *or* **go after,** follow, follow on *or* upon, replace, take the place of, displace, overtake, supervene; **step into** *or* **fill the shoes of,** don the mantle of, assume the robe of

**succession** NOUNS 1 **accession;** rightful *or* legitimate succession; **usurpation,** arrogation, assumption, taking over, seizure; line of succession, mode of succession, law of succession; primogeniture, ultimogeniture; **lineage,** line, bloodline, descent, descendancy, line of descent, ancestral line; devolution, reversion
2 **series,** run, **sequence,** consecution, progression, course, gradation

**successive** ADJS **consecutive,** successional, back-to-back <nonformal>; **serial,** ordinal, seriate, catenary; sequent, **sequential;** linear, lineal, in-line

**successor** NOUNS **follower,** next in line; **replacement,** backup, backup man *or* woman, substitute, stand-in; **descendant,** posterity, **heir,** inheritor

**succinct** ADJS **pithy,** laconic, **sententious,** gnomic, pungent, terse, crisp, pointed

**succulent** ADJS **palatable,** delicious, dainty; **savory,** savorous, toothsome, sapid, delightful, delectable, exquisite; juicy, fleshy, **luscious,** for the gods, ambrosial, nectarous, nectareous

**succumb** VERBS 1 **perish,** expire, die, cease, end, come to an end, go, pass, **pass away, vanish, disappear,** fade away, run out, peg *or* conk out <nonformal>, come to nothing *or* naught, be no more, be done for; be all over with, be all up with <nonformal>
2 **submit,** relent, resign, resign oneself, give oneself up, not resist; take one's medicine, swallow the pill, face the music

**sudden** ADJS **abrupt,** precipitant, **precipitate; hasty,** headlong, impulsive, impetuous; speedy, swift, quick; **unexpected**, unanticipated, unpredicted, unforeseen, unlooked-for; **surprising**, startling

**suddenly** ADVS **abruptly,** all of a sudden

**sue** VERBS **litigate,** prosecute, go into litigation, **bring suit,** go to law, seek in law, appeal to the law, seek justice *or* legal redress, implead, **bring action against,** prosecute a suit against, take *or* institute legal proceedings against; take to court, bring into court, bring before a jury, bring to justice, bring to trial

**suffer** VERBS **feel pain,** feel the pangs, anguish; **hurt,** ache, have a misery <nonformal>, ail; **agonize,** writhe; **endure,** bear, stand, support, sustain, **tolerate,** bear up under, bear the brunt, bear with, put up with, brook, brave, hang in there, keep it up; **countenance,** condone, stomach; **be punished,** suffer for, **suffer the consequences** *or* **penalty,** get it *and* catch it <both nonformal>, **get one's desserts** *or* **just desserts**

**sufficient** ADJS sufficing; **enough,** ample, substantial, **plenty,** satisfactory, adequate, due

**suffocate** VERBS **stifle,** asphyxiate, stop

the breath; **smother,** choke, strangle, throttle

**suggest** VERBS 1 **promise,** hint, imply, give prospect of, make likely, give ground for expecting, raise expectation, **lead one to expect,** hold out hope, make fair promise, have a lot going for, have *or* show promise, **bid fair,** stand fair to; **advise,** counsel, recommend, advocate, propose, submit
2 **resemble,** put one in mind of <nonformal>, remind one of, bring to mind, be reminiscent of, evoke, call up, call to mind; savor *or* smack of, be redolent of; **have all the earmarks of,** have every appearance of

**suggestion** NOUNS **hint,** *soupçon* <Fr>, suspicion, intimation; **proposal,** proposition, instance; **remark,** reflection, imputation, **insinuation,** sly suggestion, innuendo, disparaging *or* uncomplimentary remark

**suit** NOUNS 1 suit of clothes, rig <nonformal>, **costume,** habit, bib and tucker <nonformal>
2 **lawsuit,** suit in *or* at law; countersuit; **litigation,** prosecution, action, legal action, proceedings, legal proceedings, legal process; legal remedy; **case,** court case, cause, legal case
VERBS 3 **outfit;** equip, **accouter,** uniform, caparison, rig, rig out *or* up, fit, **fit out,** turn out, **costume,** habit
4 fit, suit *or* fit to a tee, fit like a glove, **qualify, do,** serve, answer, be OK <nonformal>, do the job *and* do the trick *and* fill the bill *and* cut the mustard <all nonformal>

**suitable** ADJS **eligible,** qualified, fit, fitted, acceptable, admissible, worthy, desirable; **seemly,** becoming, fitting, meet, happy, felicitous; **apt,** apposite, appropriate; **expedient,** befitting; feasible, doable, swingable <nonformal>

**suitor** NOUNS **wooer,** pursuer, follower; escort, companion, date *and* steady <both nonformal>; significant other; **petitioner,** supplicant, suppliant

**sulk** VERBS **mope,** mope around; grump *and* grouch *and* bitch <all nonformal>, **fret;** get oneself in a sulk

**sullen** ADJS **morose,** mopish, mopey, uncommunicative; disobedient, recalcitrant, refractory, fractious, sulky, indocile

**sully** VERBS soil, defile; **corrupt,** seduce, deceive, **debauch, ravish,** ravage, despoil, ruin; **violate,** abuse

**sultry** ADJS **stifling,** suffocating, stuffy, close, oppressive; **humid,** sticky <nonformal>, muggy

**sum** NOUNS **total,** sum total, sum and substance, **the amount,** whole *or* gross amount, grand total; amount of money; round sum, lump sum; summation

**summarize** VERBS **restate,** reword, review, run over, sum up, précis, encapsulate; **recapitulate,** recap *and* rehash <both nonformal>, **recount,** rehearse, recite, relate; **sum up,** sum, summate, say it all <nonformal>

**summary** NOUNS **résumé,** rundown, run-through; **summation,** summing up, recounting, capitulation, **recapitulation,** recap *and* rehash <both nonformal>; sum, substance, sum and substance, wrap-up

**summer** NOUNS **summertime,** summertide, good old summertime; growing season; midsummer; **dog days,** canicular days; Indian summer

**summit** NOUNS top; **tip-top,** peak, pinnacle; **crest,** brow; **supremacy,** primacy, paramountcy, **first place,** height, acme, zenith, top spot <nonformal>; **culmination,** perfection, top, ultimate, consummation, *ne plus ultra* <L>

**summon** VERBS **call,** demand, preconize; call for, send for *or* after, bid come; **invite,** ask, call in; **convoke,** call together

**sumptuous** ADJS **grandiose,** grand, magnificent, splendid, **elegant,** elaborate, luxurious, extravagant, deluxe

**sun** NOUNS orb of day, daystar

> *the glorious lamp of Heav'n,*
> *the radiant sun*
> **DRYDEN**

**sundry** ADJS **diversified,** varied, assorted, heterogeneous; **various,** many and various, divers <old>, diverse, **several,** many; of all sorts *or* conditions *or* kinds *or* shapes *or* descriptions *or* types

**sunglasses** NOUNS colored glasses, sunspecs <nonformal>, dark glasses, shades <nonformal>

**sunk** ADJS **depressed,** lowered, debased, reduced, **fallen; sunken,** submerged; downcast, low, at a low ebb

**sunny** ADJS **bright,** fair, mild, balmy; halcyon, **radiant,** riant, sparkling, beaming, glowing, sanguine, optimistic, hopeful

**sunrise** NOUNS **dawn,** the dawn of day, dawning, daybreak, **sunup,** cockcrow, light, first light, daylight, aurora; **break of day,** peep of day, crack of dawn

**sunset** NOUNS **eventide,** vesper; **close of day,** decline *or* fall of day, shut of day, when day is done; **nightfall, sundown,** setting sun, going down of the sun, the cool of the evening

**superb** ADJS super <nonformal>, **exquisite; magnificent,** splendid, splendiferous, tremendous, immense, **marvelous,** wonderful, glorious, divine, heavenly, terrific, sensational

**superficial** ADJS **shallow,** unprofound; shallow-minded, **frivolous,** flighty, light, volatile, frothy, fluffy, **featherbrained,** birdbrained

**superfluous** ADJS **redundant;** excess, in excess; unnecessary, unessential, nonessential, expendable, dispensable, **needless,** unneeded, gratuitous, uncalled-for; pleonastic, tautologous, tautological

**superintendent** NOUNS **supervisor,** foreman, monitor, **head,** headman, taskmaster; **overseer,** inspector, proctor; **straw boss** <nonformal>

**superior** NOUNS 1 **chief,** head, boss, honcho <nonformal>, commander, **leader,** dean, *primus inter pares* <L, first among equals>, **master**; higher-up <nonformal>, senior, principal, big shot <nonformal>

ADJS 2 **greater,** better, finer; **higher,** upper, over, super, above; ascendant, in the ascendant, in ascendancy, coming <nonformal>; **surpassing,** exceeding, excellent, **excelling,** rivaling, eclipsing, capping, topping, **transcending,** transcendent *or* transcendental; **ahead,** a cut *or* stroke above, one up on <nonformal>

**superiority** NOUNS **preeminence,** greatness, **lead,** transcendence *or* transcendency, ascendancy *or* ascendance, prestige, favor, prepotence *or* prepotency, preponderance; predominance *or* predominancy, hegemony; **excellence**, virtuosity, inimitability, incomparability; **seniority,** precedence, deanship; success, accomplishment

**superlative** ADJS **supreme,** greatest, best, highest, veriest, maximal, maximum, topmost, **uppermost,** tip-top, top-level, top-echelon, top-notch *and* top-of-the-line <both nonformal>, **first-rate,** first-class, of the first water, top of the line; sublime

**supernatural** ADJS supranatural, **preternatural; supernormal,** hypernormal, preternormal, **paranormal; superhuman,** preterhuman, unhuman, nonhuman; **unearthly,** unworldly, otherworldly, eerie; fey; psychical, **spiritual,** occult; transcendental; mysterious, arcane, esoteric

**supersede** VERBS **supplant,** succeed, **replace,** displace, **take the place of,** crowd out, cut out <nonformal>

**superstar** NOUNS **first-rater,** topnotcher, world-beater; wonder, prodigy, genius, virtuoso, **star,** luminary, leading light, one in a thousand *or* a million; hard *or* tough act to follow <nonformal>

**superstitious** ADJS **credulous,** unthinking, uncritical, unskeptical

**supervise** VERBS **superintend,** boss, oversee, overlook, ride herd on <nonformal>, stand over, keep an eye on *or* upon, keep in order; **direct,** manage, administer, discipline

**supplant** VERBS **remove,** displace, outplace, replace; **supersede,** succeed, **take the place of,** crowd out, cut out <nonformal>

**supple** ADJS **adaptable,** adjustable, pliant, flexible, resourceful; limber, lithe, willowy, lithesome, lissome

**supplement** NOUNS 1 **adjunct,** addition, increase, **increment,** augmentation, supplementation, complementation, *additum* <L>, addendum, addenda <pl>, complement, continuation, extrapolation, extension

VERBS 2 **add to,** augment; **reinforce,** strengthen, fortify, beef up <nonformal>

**supply** NOUNS 1 **fund,** resource, resources; means, assets, liquid assets; **materials,** material resources *or* means; store

VERBS 2 **provide,** find, dish up *and* rustle up <both nonformal>, **furnish;** contribute, kick in <nonformal>, yield, present; make available; stock, store; provide for, make provision *or* due provision for; fill, fill up; replenish, restock

**support** NOUNS 1 **maintenance,** sustainment, sustentation, **sustenance,** subsistence, provision, total support, meal ticket <nonformal>; **keep,** upkeep; livelihood, living, meat, bread, daily

bread; **nurture,** fostering, nurturance, nourishment, **care,** caring, care-giving, tender loving care *or* TLC <nonformal>
VERBS 2 **back** *and* **back up** <both nonformal>, come out for, **endorse;** go with the party, follow the party line; **get on the bandwagon** <nonformal>; **finance,** fund, sponsor, patronize, provide for, provide capital *or* money for, bankroll <nonformal>, angel <nonformal>, put up the money; **stake** *or* **grubstake** <both nonformal>; subsidize
3 **corroborate,** bear out, buttress, **sustain,** fortify, bolster, back, back up, reinforce, undergird, strengthen; **document;** prove

**supporter** NOUNS **upholder,** maintainer, sustainer; support, **mainstay,** standby <nonformal>, stalwart, reliance, dependence; **backer,** promoter, angel <nonformal>, rabbi <nonformal>; **champion,** defender, apologist, **advocate,** exponent; **fan** *and* buff <both nonformal>, aficionado, **admirer**

**suppose** VERBS **assume,** presume, surmise, expect, **suspect,** infer, understand, gather, conclude, deduce, consider, reckon, divine, imagine, **believe,** deem, repute, feel; **think likely,** daresay, venture to say

**suppress** VERBS **repress,** keep under, choke *or* hold back, fight down *or* back, inhibit; **cover up,** hush up, stifle, muffle, **smother,** squash, quash, squelch, kill, sit on *or* upon, put the lid on <nonformal>; **conquer,** vanquish, quell, **put down,** subdue, subjugate, put under the yoke

**supremacy** NOUNS **primacy,** paramountcy, **first place,** height, acme, zenith, be-all and end-all, summit, top spot <nonformal>; **dominance,** dominion, domination; preeminence, superiority; **ascendance** *or* **ascendancy;** upper *or* whip hand, sway; **priority,** precedence

**supreme** ADJS **superlative,** greatest, best, highest, **uppermost,** first-rate, first-class, of the first water, top of the line; **governing,** preeminent, leading, **superior, peerless;** quintessential

**sure** ADJS 1 **certain,** sure-enough <nonformal>; bound; **positive,** absolute, definite, perfectly sure, apodictic; decisive, conclusive; clear, clear as day, clear and distinct, unequivocal, unmistakable, unambiguous, nonambiguous; **confident,** secure, **assured,** reassured, decided, determined; **convinced,** persuaded, positive, **cocksure; unhesitating,** unfaltering, unwavering; **self-confident,** self-assured, self-reliant, sure of oneself; poised; unafraid
ADVS 2 **surely, to be sure,** sure enough, for sure <nonformal>; sure thing *and* surest thing you know <both nonformal>

**surf** NOUNS **spray,** breakers, white water, spoondrift *or* **spindrift,** roller, curler, comber, whitecap, white horse

**surface** NOUNS 1 **exterior,** external, outside; superficies, covering, skin, outer skin *or* layer, epidermis, integument, envelope, crust, cortex, rind, shell; veneer, gloss
VERBS 2 **be revealed,** become known, come to light, appear, manifest itself, come to one's ears, transpire, **leak out,** get out, come out, out, come home to roost, come out in the wash, break forth, show its face; comes out of the closet <nonformal>, stand revealed; blow one's cover <nonformal>
ADJS 3 **apparent,** appearing, **seeming,** ostensible; outward, superficial; cosmetic, merely cosmetic; on *or* near the surface, merely surface, **nominal**

**surge** NOUNS 1 **flow,** course, onward course, **gush,** rush, onrush, spate, run, race; **upturn,** uptick <nonformal>, uptrend, upsurge, upswing; **leap,** jump; flood; **swirl,** twirl, **eddy,** gurge
VERBS 2 **flow,** stream, issue, pour, run, course, rush, flush, flood; **gush,** well, **swirl,** gurge, **eddy**

**surly** ADJS **sullen,** sulky, morose, dour, mumpish, dumpish, **glum,** grum, grim; **moody,** moodish; **mopish,** mopey <nonformal>, moping; crusty, bearish, beastly, churlish

**surmise** VERBS **suppose,** assume, presume, expect, **suspect,** infer, understand, gather, conclude, deduce, consider, reckon, divine, imagine, **fancy,** dream, conceive, **believe,** deem, repute, feel, **think,** be inclined to think, opine, daresay, be afraid <nonformal>

**surmount** VERBS **overcome,** overpower, overmaster, overmatch; overcome oneself, master oneself; kick the habit <nonformal>

**surpass** VERBS **excel,** outdo, pass, do *or* go one better; challenge comparison, make the most of

**surplus** NOUNS 1 leftovers, plus, overstock, **overage,** overset, overrun, **overmeasure,** oversupply; **remainder,** balance, leftover, extra, spare, something extra *or* to spare
ADJS 2 overplus; **remaining,** unused, **leftover;** over, over and above; extra, spare, supernumerary, as a bonus

**surprise** NOUNS 1 **astonishment;** surpriser, startler, shocker, **blow,** eye-opener, revelation; **bolt out of** *or* **from the blue,** thunderbolt, thunderclap; **bombshell,** earthshaker; sudden turn *or* development, *peripeteia* <Gk>; surprise package; surprise party; **surprise attack**
VERBS 2 **take by surprise,** do the unexpected, spring a surprise <nonformal>, **open one's eyes,** give one a revelation; **catch** *or* **take unawares,** catch *or* take short, take aback, pull up short, raise some eyebrows, **catch off-guard**, cross one up <nonformal>; throw a curve <nonformal>, **blindside** <nonformal>; **astonish**

**surreal** ADJS **strange,** outlandish, off-the-wall <informal>, not for real <nonformal>, passing strange

*wondrous strange*
SHAKESPEARE

**surrender** NOUNS 1 **capitulation;** renunciation, giving over, abandonment, relinquishment, **cession;** giving up *or* in, backing off *or* down <nonformal>, retreat, recession, recedence
VERBS 2 **give up,** capitulate, acknowledge defeat, **cry quits,** say 'uncle' <nonformal>, **throw in the towel** *or* **sponge** <nonformal>, show *or* wave the white flag; renounce, abandon, relinquish, **cede,** give over, hand over

**surreptitious** ADJS **covert,** clandestine, unobtrusive, **undercover,** underground, under-the-counter, under-the-table, **cloak-and-dagger,** backdoor, underhand, **underhanded; furtive,** stealthy, privy, backstairs, **sly,** shifty, sneaky, sneaking, skulking, slinking, slinky

**surrogate** NOUNS **deputy,** proxy, representative, substitute, vice, vicegerent, **alternate,** backup *and* stand-in <both nonformal>, alter ego, procurator, secondary, understudy, pinch hitter <nonformal>, utility man *or* woman, the bench <nonformal>; locum tenens

**surround** VERBS **environ,** compass, encircle, **encompass,** enclose, close; go round *or* around, compass about; **envelop,** enfold, lap, wrap, enwrap, embrace, enclasp, embosom, embay, involve, invest; **bound,** circumscribe, limit, girdle

**surveillance** NOUNS shadowing, following, trailing, tailing <nonformal>, 24-hour surveillance, observation, stakeout <nonformal>; **spying,** espionage, espial; wiretap, wiretapping, bugging <nonformal>, electronic surveillance

**survey** NOUNS 1 **scrutiny,** overview, contemplation; **examination,** inspection, scrutiny, the once-over <nonformal>, visual examination, a vetting <Brit nonformal>, ocular inspection, eyeball inspection <nonformal>; **discourse,** discussion, disquisition, descant, exposition, screed
2 **canvass,** inquiry, questionnaire, questionary; exit poll; **poll,** public-opinion poll, opinion poll *or* survey, statistical survey, opinion sampling, voter-preference survey; consumer-preference survey, market-research survey; consumer research, market research
VERBS 3 **scrutinize,** eye, contemplate, look over, give the eye *or* the once-over <nonformal>; examine, vet <Brit nonformal>, inspect; **watch,** put under surveillance, stake out <nonformal>

**survive** VERBS **remain,** be left *or* left over, rest; **keep alive,** keep body and soul together, endure, persist, last, last out, hang on, hang in <nonformal>, be spared; cheat death; **subsist,** cope, eke out, make out, scrape along, manage, get by; **recover,** pull through, pull round *or* around, come round *or* around <nonformal>, come back <nonformal>, make a comeback <nonformal>; weather the storm; outlive

**survivor** NOUNS heir, successor; **widow,** widower, relict, war widow, **orphan**

**susceptible** ADJS **exposed,** at risk, overexposed, open, like a sitting duck, **vulnerable**; liable, nonimmune

**suspect** VERBS 1 distrust, mistrust, doubt, misdoubt; surmise, **infer,** understand, gather, conclude, deduce, smell a rat *and* see something funny <both nonformal>; greet with skepticism, raise a question, throw doubt upon, awake a doubt *or* suspicion
ADJS 2 suspected, **under suspicion,**

under a cloud; **discredited,** exploded, rejected, **suspicious,** open to question *or* doubt; in question, in dispute, at issue

**suspend** VERBS **hang,** hang up, put up, fasten up; **interrupt,** intermit, **break,** break off, take a break <nonformal>, cut off, break *or* snap the thread; **lay off,** surplus, furlough

**suspenders** NOUNS pair of suspenders, braces <Brit>, galluses <nonformal>

**suspense** NOUNS state of suspense, cliff-hanging *and* nail-biting <both nonformal>; uncertainty, nervous expectation; **anxiety,** dread, pessimism, apprehension; abeyance, latency

**suspicion** NOUNS **suspiciousness,** doubt, misdoubt, mistrust, distrust, distrustfulness; **impression,** inkling, intuition, **feeling,** funny feeling <nonformal>, feeling in one's bones; wariness, leeriness, guardedness, skepticism

**suspicious** ADJS **incredulous,** suspecting, shy, wary, leery, cautious, guarded; suspect, funny; open to question *or* doubt

**sustain** VERBS **protract,** prolong, extend, perpetuate, lengthen, spin *or* string out; **maintain,** keep, hold, retain, preserve; **keep up,** keep going, keep alive, **survive**

**sustenance** NOUNS **nutriment,** nourishment, nurture; **support,** maintenance, sustainment, sustentation, **subsistence,** provision, total support, meal ticket <nonformal>

**svelte** ADJS **slender,** slinky, sylphlike, willowy

**swag** NOUNS **booty,** spoil, **spoils,** loot, ill-gotten gains, **plunder,** prize, haul, take, stolen goods, hot goods *or* items <nonformal>

**swagger** NOUNS 1 **strut,** side, swank <nonformal>, bounce, brave show; swaggering, strutting; peacockishness, peacockery
VERBS 2 **strut,** swank <Brit>, prance, stalk, peacock

**swallow** VERBS **ingest,** imbibe, drink; devour, ingurgitate; **gulp,** gulp down, swill, swill down, wolf down, gobble; **believe,** credit, trust, accept, buy <nonformal>

**swamp** NOUNS 1 **marsh,** marshland, swampland, fen, fenland, **morass,** bog, mire, quagmire
VERBS 2 **overflow,** inundate, engulf, sweep, whelm, overwhelm, **flood,** deluge, submerge

**swanky** ADJS **sumptuous,** elegant, elaborate, luxurious, extravagant, deluxe; plush *and* posh *and* ritzy *and* swank <all nonformal>

**swap** NOUNS 1 **trade,** horse trade <nonformal>; even trade, even-steven trade, **switch;** barter
VERBS 2 **interchange, exchange,** change, counterchange; **trade,** switch

**swarm** NOUNS 1 **invasion,** swarming, teeming, ravage, plague; **overrunning,** overswarming, overspreading
VERBS 2 **come together, throng, crowd,** teem, hive, surge, seethe, mill, stream, horde; **infest,** beset, invade, ravage, plague; **overrun,** overswarm, overspread

**swarthy** ADJS **dark,** dark-colored, **darkish,** darksome, blackish; nigrescent

**swashbuckler** NOUNS **blusterer, swaggerer,** swasher, fanfaron, bravo, **bully,** bullyboy, bucko, roisterer, cock of the walk, vaporer, blatherskite <nonformal>

**sway** NOUNS 1 **swing,** swinging, swag; **rock,** lurch, roll, reel, careen
VERBS 2 **rear,** rock, roll, reel, swing, lurch, yaw, heave, scend, **flounder,** welter, wallow
3 **induce,** prompt, move one to, influence, incline; **persuade,** prevail on *or* upon, convince, lead to believe, **bring round,** bring to reason, bring to one's senses

**swear** VERBS 1 **give one's word,** pledge *or* pass one's word, give one's parole, **give one's word of honor,** cross one's heart *and* cross one's heart and hope to die <both nonformal>; **vouch,** warrant, take one's oath, acknowledge, avow
2 **curse,** cuss <nonformal>, blaspheme, execrate, take the Lord's name in vain; swear like a trooper, cuss like a sailor; **talk dirty** <nonformal>, scatologize, coprologize, dysphemize, use strong language

**sweat** NOUNS 1 **perspiration,** water; exudation, exudate; diaphoresis, sudor; honest sweat, the sweat of one's brow; beads of sweat, beaded brow; cold sweat; **lather,** swelter, streams of sweat; sudoresis
VERBS 2 **perspire,** exude; break out in a sweat, **get all in a lather** <nonformal>; sweat like a trooper *or* horse, swelter, wilt; **fear,** break out in a cold sweat, sweat bullets <nonformal>; **stew,** get into a dither, get into a stew <non-

formal>, work oneself into a lather *or* sweat <nonformal>; wait impatiently, sweat it out <nonformal>
3 **work hard;** scratch *and* hustle <both nonformal>, **slave,** sweat and slave <nonformal>, slave away, toil away; work one's head off <nonformal>, work one's fingers to the bone, break one's back, bust one's hump *or* ass <nonformal>

**sweep** VERBS 1 sweep up *or* out, **brush,** brush off, whisk, broom; **graze,** brush by, glance, scrape, skim; go *or* make one's rounds, **scour,** scour the country
2 **glide,** coast, skim, flow; **drive,** move forward, advance; sweep along

**sweepstakes** NOUNS **lottery,** drawing, sweepstake *or* sweep; **raffle; state lottery,** Lotto, Pick Six, Pick Four; **numbers game** *or* **policy,** Chinese lottery <nonformal>; tontine

**sweet** NOUNS 1 **sweetness,** sweetishness, saccharinity; **sugariness,** syrupiness; oversweetness, mawkishness, cloyingness, sickly-sweetness
ADJS 2 sweetish, sweetened; sacchariferous; **sugary,** sugared, candied, **honeyed,** syrupy; mellifluous; honeyed, dulcet; sugarsweet, honeysweet, sweet as sugar *or* honey; sugar-coated; bittersweet
3 **endearing,** lovable, likable, adorable, admirable, **lovely,** lovesome, winning, winsome; caressable, kissable; cuddlesome, cuddly

**sweetheart** NOUNS 1 **loved one,** love, beloved, darling, dear, dear one, truelove, **object of one's affections,** light of one's eye *or* life, light of love

2 <nonformal> **sweetie, honey,** honeybunch, honey-bunny, honeypie, hon, main squeeze, sweetie-pie, sweet patootie, tootsie, tootsie-pie, tootsy-wootsy, dearie, baby, dreamboat, heartthrob, poopsy, poopsy-woopsy, sugar, sugar-bun, sweets

**swell** VERBS 1 **din;** surge, rise, crescendo, loudness
2 **billow,** surge, heave, lift, rise, send, scend, toss, popple; **bulge,** bilge, bouge <nonformal>, **belly,** bag, balloon, pouch; **swell up,** dilate, distend, swell out, **belly out,** round out

**swelter** VERBS **roast,** toast, cook, bake, fry, broil, boil, seethe, simmer, stew; **sweat,** break out in a sweat, **get all in a lather** <nonformal>; sweat like a horse, wilt

**swerve** VERBS **veer,** sheer, curve, **shift,** turn, trend, bend, heel, bear off; alter one's course, angle off *or* away, veer off, slant off, go off on a tangent

**swift** ADJS **quick,** speedy, expeditious, snappy <nonformal>, celeritous, alacritous, quick on the draw *or* trigger <nonformal>; **brief,** short, brisk, fleet; summary, decisive

**swig** NOUNS 1 **drink,** potation, potion, libation; draft, dram, drench, swill *and* guzzle <both nonformal>, quaff, **sip,** sup, suck, tot, bumper, snort *and* slug <both nonformal>, pull <nonformal>, lap, gulp, slurp <nonformal>; nip, peg
VERBS 2 **drink,** drink in, **imbibe,** wet one's whistle <nonformal>; **quaff,** sip, sup, bib, swill *and* guzzle *and* pull <all nonformal>; drink off *or* up, toss off *or* down, drain the cup; tipple, booze

**swill** NOUNS 1 **refuse,** waste, waste matter, **garbage,** pig-swill, slop, slops, hogwash <nonformal>; **mud,** muck, mire, slush, slosh, sludge, slime; slop
VERBS 2 **drink,** quaff, sip, sup, bib, swig *and* guzzle *and* pull <all nonformal>; toss off *or* down, drain the cup; tipple, **booze**

**swim** NOUNS 1 aquatics, **swimming,** bathing, natation, balneation, bathe <Brit>
VERBS 2 **bathe,** go in swimming *or* bathing; skinny-dip

**swim suit** NOUNS **swimwear; bathing suit,** tank suit, tank top, *maillot* or *maillot de bain* <Fr>, two-piece suit; bikini, string bikini *or* string

**swindle** NOUNS 1 **hoax,** cheat, fraud; **imposture; imposition,** cheating, cozenage, dodge, fishy transaction, piece of sharp practice; **graft** <nonformal>, grift <nonformal>; bunco
VERBS 2 **cheat,** victimize, gull, pigeon, fudge, **defraud,** practice fraud upon, euchre, **con,** finagle, **fleece,** mulct, **bilk,** cozen, cheat out of, do out of; bunco, play a bunco game; sell gold bricks <nonformal>

**swine** NOUNS 1 **pig,** hog, porker; **shoat,** piggy, piglet, pigling; gilt; **boar,** sow; **beast,** animal
2 bad person, animal, cur, reptile, snake

**swing** NOUNS 1 **rhythm,** beat, meter, measure, number *or* numbers, movement, **lilt;** play, range, scope, sweep

VERBS 2 **turn round** *or* **around** *or* **about,** swivel, pivot, pivot about, swing round; wheel, wheel about, whirl, spin; brandish, flourish, flaunt, shake, wield
3 **be promiscuous,** sleep around <nonformal>; **debauch, wanton,** rake, womanize, sow one's wild oats
4 **syncopate,** play jazz, jive <nonformal>

**swinger** NOUNS **libertine,** profligate, rake, **roué,** wanton, womanizer, debauchee

**swirl** NOUNS 1 **flurry,** ruffle, bustle, stir, swirling, whirl, vortex, eddy, hurry, hurry-scurry, hurly-burly
VERBS 2 **agitate,** unsettle, stir, flurry, flutter, fret, ruffle, rumple, ripple, ferment, convulse

**switch** NOUNS 1 **substitution,** exchange, change, switcheroo <nonformal>, commutation, subrogation; **replacement,** displacement; superseding, supersession
VERBS 2 **substitute,** exchange, change, take *or* ask *or* offer in exchange, ring in <nonformal>, **put in the place of,** change for, make way for, give place to

**swivel** VERBS **turn round** *or* **around** *or* **about,** pivot, pivot about, swing, round, swing round; wheel, wheel about, whirl, spin; heel, turn upon one's heel

**swollen** ADJS **distended,** dilated, inflated, sufflated, **blown up,** puffed up, swelled, **bloated,** turgid, tumid, plethoric, incrassate; **surfeited,** glutted, gorged, overfed, replete; overblown

**swoon** NOUNS 1 **unconsciousness,** senselessness; **faint,** blackout, syncope, athymia, lipothymy *or* lipothymia; semiconsciousness, grayout
VERBS 2 **faint,** drop, succumb, keel over <nonformal>, fall in a faint, fall senseless, pass *or* zonk out <nonformal>, go out like a light; gray out

**swoop** VERBS **plunge,** dive, pitch, plummet, drop, fall; plump, plunk, plop; swoop down, stoop, **pounce,** pounce on *or* upon

**sword** NOUNS **blade,** good *or* trusty sword; steel, **cold steel;** Excalibur

**sworn** ADJS **affirmed,** asserted, asseverated, avouched, avowed, averred, declared; **deposed,** warranted, **attested,** certified, vouched, **vouched for,** vowed, pledged, sworn to

**sylvan** ADJS **woodland,** forest, forestal; **wooded,** timbered, forested, arboreous; **woody,** woodsy, bosky, bushy, shrubby, scrubby; copsy, braky

**symbol** NOUNS **emblem,** icon, token, type; **representative,** exponent; **exemplification,** illustration, demonstration, explanation

**symbolic** ADJS symbolical, allegoric, allegorical, figural, figurative, tropological, **metaphoric,** metaphorical, anagogic, anagogical

**symmetrical** ADJS **symmetric,** balanced, balanced off, proportioned, eurythmic, harmonious; coequal, coordinate, equilateral; **well-balanced**

**symmetry** NOUNS **harmony,** proportion, concord, **balance,** equilibrium, order, orderedness, measure, measuredness, concinnity; **correspondence,** equivalence, equipollence, coequality

**sympathetic** ADJS **sensitive,** responsive, receptive; **comforting,** consoling, consolatory, of good comfort; condoling, condolent, condolatory; sympathizing, **compassionate**, merciful; empathic, empathetic; **congenial,** *en rapport* <Fr>, compatible, affinitive

**sympathy** NOUNS **fellow feeling,** sympathetic response, responsiveness, relating, warmth, **caring,** concern; response, echo, chord, sympathetic chord, vibrations, vibes <nonformal>; **empathy,** identification; **condolence,** condolences, **consolation,** comfort, balm, soothing words, **commiseration,** sharing of grief *or* sorrow; **compassion,** sensitivity

**symposium** NOUNS **forum,** conference, discussion group, **round table,** panel, panel discussion, seminar; open forum, colloquium

**symptom** NOUNS **warning sign,** premonitory sign, danger sign; preliminary sign *or* signal *or* token; early symptom, premonitory symptom, prodrome, prodroma, prodromata <pl>; precursor

**synagogue** NOUNS **temple,** fane; tabernacle; *shul* <Yiddish>; house of worship

**synchronized** ADJS **synchronous,** synchronic *or* synchronal, in sync <nonformal>; **in time,** in step, in tempo, in phase, with *or* on the beat

**syndicate** NOUNS commercial enterprise; **trust,** cartel, combine, pool, consortium; crime family, crime organization

**syndrome** NOUNS **signs,** symptoms, pathology, symptomatology, symptomology

**synergy** NOUNS **cooperation,** collaboration, coaction, concurrence, synergism; symbiosis, commensalism

**synopsis** NOUNS **abridgment,** condensation, short *or* shortened version, condensed version, abbreviation, **abstract,** epitome, **précis,** capsule, nutshell *or* capsule version, capsulization, encapsulation, conspectus

**synthesis** NOUNS **identification,** likening, unification, coalescence, combination, union, fusion, merger, blending, melding; syneresis, syncretism

**synthetic** NOUNS 1 **plastic;** thermoplastic, thermosetting plastic; resin plastic; cellulose plastic; protein plastic; synthetic fabric *or* textile *or* cloth
ADJS 2 **imitation,** synthetical, ersatz, hokey *and* hoked-up <both nonformal>, mock

**system** NOUNS **discipline,** method, methodology, methodicalness, systematicness; **frame of reference,** intellectual *or* ideational frame of reference, framework, arena, world, universe, world *or* universe of discourse, reference system

**systematic** ADJS **orderly,** ordered, **regular,** well-regulated, well-ordered, methodical, formal, regular as clockwork, uniform, symmetrical; businesslike, routine, steady, normal, habitual, usual

# T

**tab** NOUNS **bill,** itemized bill, bill of account, **account,** reckoning, check, *l'addition* <Fr>, score <nonformal>

**table** NOUNS 1 **plateau,** tableland, high plateau, mesa, butte, moor, hammada
2 board, **stand; bench,** workbench; **counter,** bar, buffet; **lectern,** reading stand, ambo, reading desk
VERBS 3 **postpone,** delay, defer, put off, hold off *or* up <nonformal>, prorogue, put on hold *or* ice *or* the back burner <all nonformal>; **hold over,** lay over, stand over, let the matter stand, **put aside,** lay *or* set *or* push aside, lay *or* set by, pigeonhole, **shelve,** put on the shelf, put on ice <nonformal>

**tableau** NOUNS **spectacle,** sight; **show,** display, presentation, representation; tableau vivant; **picture;** image, likeness, representation

**tabloid** NOUNS **newspaper,** paper, sheet *or* rag <both nonformal>

**taboo** NOUNS 1 **exclusion,** ban, bar, injunction; prohibition
ADJS 2 **prohibited,** forbidden, *verboten* <Ger>, barred; banned, tabooed, untouchable

**tabulate** VERBS **file,** index, **catalog,** calendar, **list,** enumerate, itemize, tally

**tacit** ADJS **wordless,** unspoken, unuttered, unexpressed, unsaid; **implicit,** implied, understood, taken for granted

**taciturn** ADJS **untalkative,** unloquacious, indisposed to talk; **silent,** speechless, wordless, **mum;** close, **closemouthed,** close-tongued, tight-lipped; close-lipped, **laconic,** curt, brief, terse, brusque, short, concise, **sparing of words,** economical of words, of few words

**tackle** NOUNS 1 **harness,** caparison, trappings, **tack; impedimenta,** luggage, dunnage, baggage, bag and baggage, traps, apparatus, truck, gear, kit, outfit, duffel
VERBS 2 **take up,** take to, **undertake,** take on, address oneself to, have a go at, turn one's hand to, **go in** *or* **out for** <nonformal>, make it one's business, follow as an occupation, set up shop; **deal with,** cope with, come to grips with, contend with; **plunge into,** dive into; light into *and* wade into *and* tear into *and* sail into <all nonformal>

**tacky** ADJS 1 **shabby,** shoddy, seedy, scruffy, dowdy, tatty, ratty; **untasteful,** tasteless, in bad *or* poor taste, chintzy *and* Mickey Mouse <both nonformal>; meretricious
2 **sticky,** tenacious, adhesive, clingy, clinging, tough; gluey, gluelike, glutinous, glutenous, glutinose

**tact** NOUNS **considerateness,** sensitivity, tactfulness; **diplomacy,** *savoir-faire* <Fr>; **thoughtfulness,** consideration, **solicitousness,** solicitude

**tactic** NOUNS **maneuver,** demarche, course of action; **device,** contrivance, artifice, stratagem, shift; gimmick *and* dodge *and* trick <all nonformal>

**tactile** ADJS tactual; touchable, **palpable,** tangible

**tag** NOUNS 1 **label,** ticket, tally; stub, counterfoil; **token,** check; **name,** brand name, trade name, trademark
2 **afterpart,** afterpiece; **wake,** trail, train, queue; **tail,** tailpiece, rear, rear end; **tail end,** butt end, tag end
VERBS 3 **label,** tab, ticket; **brand,** earmark; hallmark; bar-code; name, **designate,** call, term, style, dub; nickname

**tail** VERBS 1 **follow,** move behind; **pursue,** shadow <nonformal>, **trail,** trail after, follow on the trail of, camp on the trail of
ADJS 2 **rear,** rearward, **back,** backward, retrograde, **posterior,** postern; after *or* aft; **hind,** hinder; hindmost, hindermost, hindhand, posteriormost, **aftermost,** aftmost, rearmost
3 caudal, caudate, caudated, tailed; taillike, caudiform

**tailor** NOUNS 1 tailoress, *tailleur* <Fr>, sartor; fitter; busheler, bushelman
VERBS 2 **form,** formalize, **shape, fashion,** frame, figure; adapt, fit, measure, proportion, adjust to, trim to, cut to, gear to, key to

**taint** NOUNS 1 **stain,** tarnish; mark, brand, **stigma**
VERBS 2 **stigmatize,** brand; stain, besmirch, smirch, tarnish, blot, **blacken, smear,** bespatter, **sully,** soil, defile, vilify, **slur,** cast a slur upon

**take** NOUNS 1 **gain, profit,** percentage <nonformal>, take-in *and* piece *and* slice *and* end *and* rakeoff *and* skimmings <all nonformal>; **gains,** profits,

earnings, winnings, return, returns, proceeds, bottom line <nonformal>
2 **catch,** bag, capture, seizure, **haul;** booty
VERBS 3 **pocket,** swallow, down, stomach, eat, digest, disregard, turn a blind eye, ignore; swallow an insult, turn the other cheek, take it lying down
4 **transport, convey,** freight, conduct; **carry, bear,** pack, tote *and* lug <both nonformal>, manhandle
5 **interpret,** diagnose; construe, put a construction on, understand, **understand by,** take to mean, take it that; **read into,** read between the lines
6 possess, take possession; **get,** get into one's hold *or* possession; pocket, palm; draw off, drain off; skim *and* skim off *and* take up front <all nonformal>; **steal,** thieve, purloin, appropriate, snatch

**take back** VERBS **recant,** retract, repudiate, withdraw, unswear, renege, welsh <nonformal>, **abjure,** disavow, disown; **deny,** disclaim, unsay, unspeak; **renounce,** forswear, eat one's words, eat crow, eat humble pie; **back down** *or* **out,** climb down, crawfish out <nonformal>, backwater, weasel; **apologize,** beg pardon, ask forgiveness, beg indulgence, express regret

**take on** VERBS 1 **undertake, assume,** accept, **take upon oneself,** take in hand, take upon one's shoulders, take up, go with, **tackle,** attack; engage *or* contract *or* obligate *or* commit oneself; **contend against,** strive against, struggle against, labor against, grapple with, join battle with, go to the mat with <nonformal>, **fight,** buck <nonformal>, counter
2 **employ, hire,** give a job to, take into employment, take into one's service, recruit, **engage,** sign up *or* on <nonformal>

**take out** VERBS 1 **extract,** get out, **withdraw,** remove; **exclude,** except, cancel, cancel out, censor out, bleep out <nonformal>, rule out, bar, ban
2 **escort, conduct,** have in tow <nonformal>, marshal, **usher,** shepherd, **guide,** lead; **squire,** esquire, **attend,** date, wait on *or* upon

**take over** VERBS **take command,** take charge, take the helm, take the reins of government, take the reins into one's hand, get the power into one's hands, gain *or* get the upper hand, take the lead; **take possession,** appropriate, take up, make one's own, move in *or* move in on <nonformal>, annex; buy out; **succeed,** take the mantle of, step into the shoes *or* place of

**tale** NOUNS **story,** yarn, account, narrative, narration, chronicle; anecdote

**talent** NOUNS **flair,** strong flair, **gift,** endowment, natural gift *or* endowment, **genius,** instinct, **faculty,** bump <nonformal>; **talented person,** man *or* woman of parts, gifted person, prodigy, natural <nonformal>, **child prodigy,** wunderkind, whiz kid *and* boy wonder <both nonformal>

**talented** ADJS **gifted,** endowed, with a flair; **clever,** apt

**talisman** NOUNS **charm,** amulet, fetish, periapt, phylactery; **voodoo,** hoodoo, juju, obeah, mumbo jumbo

**talk** NOUNS 1 **palaver,** speech, words; confabulation, **confab** <nonformal>; chinfest *and* chinwag *and* talkfest *and* bull session <all nonformal>; **dialogue,** duologue, trialogue; idle talk, small talk
VERBS 2 **speak,** use language, communicate orally *or* verbally; patter *or* gab *or* wag the tongue <all nonformal>; mouth; chatter; converse; declaim; **gossip,** talk over the back fence <nonformal>

3 <nonformal> **yak,** yap, yakkety-yak, gab, spiel, chin, jaw, shoot off one's face *or* mouth, shoot *or* bat the breeze, beat *or* bat one's gums, bend one's ear, make chin music, rattle away, talk a blue streak, talk someone's ear *or* head off, flap one's jaw, natter <Brit>, spout off, sound off

**talkative** ADJS **wordy,** verbose; **prolix,** windy <nonformal>, **long-winded,** longiloquent

**talk into** VERBS **persuade,** prevail on *or* upon, **sway,** convince, lead to believe, **bring round,** bring to reason, bring to one's senses; **win, win over,** win around, bring over, draw over, gain, gain over; **talk over,** argue into, out-talk <nonformal>

**talk of the town** NOUNS **report,** rumor, **common talk,** town talk, topic of the day, *cause célèbre* <Fr>; **notoriety,** notoriousness

**tall** ADJS **long,** lengthy; longish, longsome; **rangy,** lanky, lank, tall as a maypole;

**gangling** *and* gangly <both nonformal>; **long-legged,** long-limbed, leggy

**tally** NOUNS 1 **returns,** census report *or* returns, election returns; **account,** reckoning, rendering-up, score
2 **agreement,** correspondence, coincidence, intersection, overlap, parallelism, symmetry, equivalence
VERBS 3 **coincide,** correspond, agree, chime with, match, go hand in glove with, jibe
4 **list,** enumerate, itemize, tabulate, catalog
5 **calculate,** compute, estimate, reckon, figure, reckon at, put at, cipher, cast, score

**tame** VERBS 1 **domesticate,** break, bust *and* gentle <both nonformal>, break in, break to harness; **soften,** subdue, hold in check, keep a tight rein, chasten, underplay, play down, downplay, tone *or* tune down
ADJS 2 **domesticated,** tamed, broken; **subdued,** chastened, housebroken, domesticated; lamblike, gentle as a lamb, dovelike; **mild,** soft, bland, gentle

**tamp** VERBS **depress,** press in, stamp, punch, punch in, impress, imprint

**tamper with** VERBS **adulterate,** corrupt, contaminate, **debase,** denaturalize, pollute, denature, bastardize, **doctor** *and* doctor up <both nonformal>; **fortify,** spike <nonformal>, lace; **dilute,** cut <nonformal>, water, water down <nonformal>

**tang** NOUNS **taste,** *goût* <Fr>; **flavor,** sapor; **smack,** savor, relish, sapidity; **spice,** relish

**tangent** ADJS **in contact,** contacting, **touching,** meeting, contingent; impinging, impingent; tangential

**tangible** ADJS touchable, **palpable,** tactile; **obvious,** plain, clear, perspicuous, distinct, patent, sensible, appreciable

**tangle** NOUNS 1 **complex,** tangled skein, **mess** *and* snafu *and* fuck-up <all nonformal>, ravel, snarl, snarl-up; knot, Gordian knot; **maze,** meander, Chinese puzzle, labyrinth
VERBS 2 **snag, snare,** sniggle, ensnare, enmesh, entangle, foul, tangle up with; **snarl,** snarl up, ravel, knot, tie in knots

**tank** NOUNS **well,** cistern, vat

**tantalizing** ADJS **appetizing,** mouthwatering, tempting, piquant; **provocative**, provoking, teasing; **titillating,** tickling, inviting, exciting

**tantrum** NOUNS **fit,** fit of anger, fit of temper, rage, temper tantrum; duck *or* cat fit *and* **conniption** *or* conniption fit *and* snit <all nonformal>, paroxysm, convulsion

**tape** NOUNS 1 **strip,** strap, strop; **lace,** thong; **band,** bandage, fillet, fascia, taenia; **belt,** girdle; **ribbon,** ribband; tapeline, tape measure
2 magnetic tape, videotape
VERBS 3 **put together,** concatenate, articulate, agglutinate; glue, cement
4 **record,** put on tape, tape-record

**taps** NOUNS **funeral, burial,** burying; dead march, muffled drum, last post <Brit>; dirge; decease

**tardy** ADJS **late,** belated, slow, slow on the draw *or* uptake *or* trigger <all nonformal>, **behindhand,** never on time, backward, back, **overdue,** long-awaited, untimely; unpunctual, unready

**target** NOUNS **objective,** object, aim, end, goal, destination, mark, object in mind, **end in view,** telos, final cause, ultimate aim; butt, bull's-eye, quintain; quarry, prey, game

**tarnish** VERBS **stigmatize,** brand; stain, besmirch, smirch, taint, blot, **blacken, smear,** bespatter, **sully,** soil, defile, vilify, **slur,** cast a slur upon, blow upon; dirty, **soil**

**tarry** VERBS **dawdle,** linger, loiter, delay, dally, dillydally, shilly-shally, lollygag, waste time, **take one's time,** take one's own sweet time; goof off *or* around <nonformal>; **live on,** continue to be, subsist, exist

**tart** NOUNS 1 **pastry,** turnover; timbale; **pie,** *tarte* <Fr>, fruit pie; *quiche* or *quiche Lorraine* <Fr>
2 **strumpet,** trollop, wench, hussy, slut, jade, baggage, *cocotte* <Fr>, grisette; **chippy** *and* **floozy** *and* broad <all nonformal>
ADJS 3 **sour,** soured, sourish; tartish; acerb, acerbic, acerbate; acescent; **acrimonious,** acrid, acid, acidic, acidulous, acidulent, **bitter,** sharp

**task** NOUNS **work,** stint, job, labor, piece of work, **chore,** chare, odd job; **assignment,** charge, project, **duty,** service, exercise

**taste** NOUNS 1 **sample,** taster, little bite, little smack; **relish,** gusto, gust <Scots>; **passion, weakness** <nonformal>
2 **elegance,** tastefulness, good taste; discriminating taste, aesthetic *or* artistic

judgment; palate, fine *or* refined palate
VERBS 3 taste of, sample; **savor,** savor of; sip, roll on the tongue

**tasteful** ADJS **in good taste,** in the best taste; excellent, of quality, of the best, of the first water; **aesthetic,** artistic, pleasing, well-chosen, choice, of choice; **elegant,** graceful, **polished,** finished, round

**tasteless** ADJS **insipid,** flavorless, bland, spiceless, **savorless,** sapless, unsavory, unflavored, flat; **untasteful,** in bad *or* poor taste, tacky *and* chintzy *and* Mickey Mouse <all nonformal>; **offensive,** offensive to gentle ears

**tasty** ADJS fit to eat *and* finger-lickin' good <both nonformal>, good-tasting, **savory,** savorous, **palatable,** toothsome, sapid, **delicious,** delightful, delectable, exquisite; fit for a king, gourmet; scrumptious *and* yummy <both nonformal>

**tatter** NOUNS **scrap,** smithereen <nonformal>, patch, **stitch,** shred; snip, **snippet,** sliver, shiver

**tattle** VERBS **give away** *and* give the show away *and* give the game away <all nonformal>, betray a confidence, tell secrets, reveal a secret; have a big mouth <nonformal>, **blab** *or* blabber <nonformal>; babble, tell *or* tattle on, tell tales, tell tales out of school; tittle-tattle

**tattletale** NOUNS **snitch** *and* snitcher <both nonformal>; whistle-blower <nonformal>; **tattler,** telltale, talebearer; blab *or* blabber *or* blabberer *or* blabbermouth <all nonformal>

**taught** ADJS **informed,** enlightened, instructed, versed, well-versed, educated, schooled

**taunt** NOUNS 1 **gibe,** scoff, jeer, fleer, flout, mock, barracking <Brit>, **twit,** quip, jest, jape, put-on *and* leg-pull <both nonformal>, foolery
VERBS 2 **scoff,** jeer, gibe, barrack <Brit>, **mock,** revile, rally, chaff, **twit,** jape, flout, scout, have a fling at, cast in one's teeth; hold in contempt, ridicule, deride

**taut** ADJS **tense,** tensed-up, uptight <nonformal>, **strained,** stretched tight, unrelaxed, under a strain; **tight,** unrelaxed; nonresilient, inelastic

**tawdry** ADJS **gaudy,** garish, loud <nonformal>, **flagrant,** shameless, **brazen,** brazenfaced, lurid, extravagant, sensational, obtrusive, vulgar, crude; meretricious, **trashy,** rubbishy, cheap

**tax** NOUNS 1 **charge,** duty, task; **burden,** weight, freight, cargo, load, onus
VERBS 2 **strain,** tense, stress, stretch, press, rack; **burden,** load, load down *or* up, lade, cumber, **encumber,** charge, freight, handicap, hamper, saddle; **oppress,** weigh one down, weigh on *or* upon, weigh heavy on, **overburden,** overtax, overload
3 **charge,** demand, ask, require; **exact,** assess, levy, impose; assess a tax upon, slap a tax on <nonformal>, lay *or* put a duty on, make dutiable, subject to a tax *or* fee *or* duty, collect a tax *or* duty on

**taxi** NOUNS **cab,** taxicab, hack <nonformal>, medallion cab, gypsy cab <nonformal>; hired car, limousine, limo *and* stretch limo <both nonformal>

**taxing** ADJS **demanding,** exacting, exigent; draining, exorbitant, extortionate, grasping

**taxpayer** NOUNS **good** *or* **respectable citizen,** excellent *or* exemplary citizen, good neighbor, burgher, **pillar of society,** salt of the earth

**teach** VERBS **instruct,** give instruction, give lessons in, **educate,** school; edify, enlighten, civilize, illumine; **direct,** guide; inform; **show,** show how, show the ropes, demonstrate; teach a lesson, give a lesson to; **ground,** teach the rudiments *or* elements *or* basics; catechize; teach an old dog new tricks

**teacher** NOUNS **instructor,** educator, preceptor, mentor; master, maestro; **pedagogue,** pedagogist, educationist; **schoolteacher,** schoolmaster; **professor,** academic; don <Brit>, fellow; guide, docent

**tear** NOUNS 1 **rip,** rent, slash; fissure, cut, split, slit; slash, slice; **gap,** rift, rent
2 **binge,** drunk, bust, **bender,** toot, bat, jag, guzzle <all nonformal>
VERBS 3 **cut,** chop, hew, hack, slash, rip, cut, slit; gash, **rend,** rive, rend asunder

**tear down** VERBS 1 **raze,** pull down, take down, bring down, bring down about one's ears, bring tumbling *or* crashing down; **disassemble,** take apart *or* down; **dismantle,** demolish
2 **find fault,** pick holes, pick *or* pull *or* tear apart; carp, cavil, quibble, nitpick; **slur,** cast a slur on, do a number *or* a job on <nonformal>

**tearful** ADJS teary, **weepy** <nonformal>; lachrymal, lachrymose, lacrimatory; **weeping,** sobbing, crying; **in tears,** with tears in one's eyes, bathed *or* dissolved in tears

*like Niobe, all tears*
SHAKESPEARE

**tears** NOUNS **weeping,** sobbing, crying, bawling; blubbering, whimpering, sniveling; flood of tears, fit of crying; cry *and* good cry <both nonformal>; **tearfulness,** weepiness <nonformal>, lachrymosity, melting mood

**tease** NOUNS 1 **tormentor,** torment; teaser; annoyer, harasser, harrier, badgerer, heckler
VERBS 2 pick on <nonformal>, tweak the nose, pluck the beard, give a bad time to <nonformal>; **plague,** beset, beleaguer; **twit,** chaff, **jest,** jape, haze; **needle,** devil, get after *or* get on <nonformal>, bedevil

**technical** ADJS **specialized,** specialist, specialistic; **insignificant**, inconsequential, immaterial; nonessential, unessential, inessential, not vital, negligible

**technicality** NOUNS **intricacy,** intricateness, ramification, crabbedness, subtlety; **a nothing,** nothing in particular, nothing to speak *or* worth speaking of, nothing to think twice about, nothing to write home about, thing of naught; mere technicality

**technician** NOUNS **specialist,** technical expert, techie <nonformal>, nerd <nonformal>

**technique** NOUNS **approach,** attack, tack; **procedure,** process, proceeding, course, practice; technical skill, touch, technical brilliance, technical mastery; technology

**technology** NOUNS **technique,** technic, **technics,** technical knowledge *or* skill, technical know-how <nonformal>; **mechanics,** mechanism; high technology, high-tech *or* hi-tech <nonformal>

**tedious** ADJS **monotonous,** humdrum, singsong, jog-trot, treadmill, unvarying, invariable, uneventful, broken-record, parrotlike, harping, everlasting, too much with us <nonformal>; **dreary,** drearisome, dry, dryasdust, dusty, dull, lackluster; insipid, vapid; protracted, prolonged; prolix, long-winded

**teeming** ADJS **swarming,** crowding, thronging, overflowing, overcrowded, overwhelming, bursting, **crawling, alive with,** lousy with <nonformal>, crowded, packed, jammed, jam-packed, thronged, rife, superabundant, **profuse,** in profusion, thick with; **productive,** fertile, fecund, prolific, seminal, germinal, pregnant

**teeter** VERBS **shake,** tremble, quiver, quaver, cringe, cower, totter, dodder; **vacillate,** waffle <nonformal>, fluctuate, pendulate, oscillate, wobble, wobble about, dither; **seesaw,** teeter-totter

**teetotaler** NOUNS **abstainer,** abstinent; teetotalist; Rechabite, hydropot, nondrinker

**telepathy** NOUNS **mental telepathy,** mind reading, thought transference, telepathic transmission; telepathic dream, telepathic hallucination

**telephone** NOUNS 1 **phone** *and* horn <both nonformal>, telephone set; telephony, telephonics
VERBS 2 **phone** <nonformal>, **call,** call on the phone <nonformal>, put in *or* make a call, **call up,** ring, ring up, give a ring *or* buzz <nonformal>, buzz <nonformal>

**televise** VERBS **telecast,** videocast; colorcast; simulcast

**television** NOUNS **TV, video,** telly <Brit nonformal>; the small screen *or* the tube <both nonformal>, the boob tube <nonformal>; **network television,** free television; the dream factory; subscription television, pay TV; cable television, cable TV; closed-circuit television *or* closed circuit TV; public-access television *or* public-access TV

**tell** VERBS **inform,** apprise, **advise,** advertise, advertise of, **give word,** mention to, **acquaint,** enlighten, familiarize, brief, verse, give the facts, give an account of, give by way of information; **narrate,** relate, recount, report, **recite,** rehearse, give an account of

**telling** ADJS **cogent,** effective, impactful, valid, operative, in force; impressive, striking; effectual, efficacious; material, convincing, weighty; **conclusive,** determinative, **decisive,** salient

**temper** NOUNS 1 **hot temper,** quick *or* short temper, irritable temper, warm temper, fiery temper, fierce temper, short fuse <nonformal>, pepperiness, feistiness *and* spunkiness <both nonformal>, **hotheadedness,** hot blood; dan-

der *and* Irish <both nonformal>; bad temper
2 **mood,** humor, feeling, feelings, frame of mind, state of mind, morale, vein; mind, heart, spirit *or* spirits
VERBS 3 **moderate, alleviate,** assuage, allay, lay, lighten, palliate, extenuate, lenify; **damp,** dampen, bank the fire, reduce the temperature, throw cold water on, throw a wet blanket on
4 **harden,** indurate, firm, toughen; anneal, oil-temper, heat-temper, **case-harden,** steel; season

**temperament** NOUNS **disposition,** character, nature, temper, mettle, constitution, makeup, stamp, type, stripe, kidney, make, mold; **turn of mind,** inclination, mind, grain, vein, set, mental set, mindset

**temperate** ADJS 1 **moderate,** sober, frugal, restrained, **sparing,** stinting, measured
2 **cool,** coolish; **fresh,** brisk, crisp, bracing, sharpish, **invigorating,** stimulating

**tempest** NOUNS **windstorm,** big *or* great *or* fresh *or* strong *or* stiff *or* high *or* howling *or* spanking wind, storm, stormy winds, tempestuous wind; **outburst,** outbreak, **flare-up,** explosion, eruption, irruption, upheaval, convulsion, spasm

**temple** NOUNS fane; tabernacle; synagogue, *shul* <Yiddish>; **mosque,** masjid; dewal, girja; pagoda; kiack; pantheon

**tempo** NOUNS **time, beat,** time pattern, timing; **rhythm**

**temporal** ADJS **secularist,** secularistic, worldly, earthly, earthy, terrestrial, **mundane; unspiritual,** profane, carnal, **secular;** humanistic, secular-humanistic; worldly minded, earthly minded, carnal-minded

**temporary** NOUNS 1 temporary employee, office temporary, temp <nonformal>
ADJS 2 **transient,** transitory, transitive; temporal; **impermanent,** unenduring, undurable, nondurable, nonpermanent; **short-lived,** ephemeral, fly-by-night, evanescent, volatile, momentary; **expedient**, ad-hoc, stopgap, provisional, tentative

**tempt** VERBS **attract,** interest, appeal, engage, impress, charismatize, catch *or* get one's eye, command one's attention, rivet one, attract one's interest, be attractive, take *or* tickle one's fancy; **tantalize,** titillate, tickle, **tease,** whet the appetite, make one's mouth water, dangle before one

**temptress** NOUNS **tempter,** seducer, enticer, inveigler, **charmer,** enchanter, fascinator, tantalizer, teaser; coquette, flirt; enchantress, seductress, **siren;** *femme fatale* <Fr>

**tenacious** ADJS **persevering,** perseverant, **persistent,** persisting, insistent; **diligent,** assiduous, sedulous, industrious; dogged, plodding, slogging, plugging; **pertinacious,** stick-to-itive <nonformal>; **unswerving,** unremitting, unabating, unintermitting, uninterrupted; **unfaltering,** unwavering, unflinching; relentless, unrelenting

**tenant** NOUNS 1 **occupant,** occupier, incumbent, **resident; lodger,** roomer, paying guest; **renter,** subtenant; squatter
VERBS 2 **inhabit, occupy,** move in *or* into, take up one's abode, make one's home; rent, **reside,** live, live in, dwell, lodge, stay, remain, abide

**tend** VERBS 1 have a tendency, **incline,** be disposed, **lean,** trend, have a penchant, set, verge, turn, warp, tilt, bias, bend to, work *or* gravitate *or* set toward; show a tendency *or* trend *or* set *or* direction, swing toward
2 **care for,** take care of; **look after,** see after, attend to, minister to, look *or* see to, keep an eye on *or* upon, **watch over,** keep watch over, **watch,** mind

**tendency** NOUNS **inclination,** leaning, penchant, proneness, conatus, weakness, susceptibility; liability, readiness, willingness, eagerness, aptness, aptitude, **disposition,** proclivity, propensity, predisposition, **predilection,** a thing for <nonformal>, affinity, prejudice, **liking,** delight, soft spot

**tender** VERBS 1 **offer,** proffer, present, offer up, **put up,** submit, extend, **hold out,** hold forth, place in one's way, lay at one's feet, put *or* place at one's disposal, put one in the way of
ADJS 2 **sensitive,** sensible, emotionable, delicate; responsive, sympathetic, receptive; susceptible, impressionable; **soft,** tenderhearted, softhearted, warmhearted; affectionate, demonstrative, **romantic,** sentimental

**tenement** NOUNS **apartment house,** flats; duplex, duplex house; apartment complex; high-rise apartment building *or* high rise

**tenet** NOUNS **a belief,** dogma, precept, **principle,** principle *or* article of faith, canon, maxim, axiom; **doctrine,** teaching

**tenor** 1 alto; male alto, countertenor; falsetto; lyric tenor, operatic tenor, heldentenor *or* heroic tenor *or* Wagnerian tenor
2 **trend,** tone, the general tendency *or* drift, the main course, the course of events, the way the wind blows, **the way things go,** trend of the times, spirit of the age *or* time, time spirit, *Zeitgeist* <Ger>

**tense** ADJS tensed-up, uptight <nonformal>, **strained,** stretched tight, taut, unrelaxed, under a strain; **on edge,** with bated breath, with muscles tense, quivering, keyed-up, biting one's nails

**tension** NOUNS tenseness, tautness, **strain, stress,** stress and strain, mental strain, nervous tension *or* strain, pressure; personal conflict

**tent** NOUNS canvas; top, whitetop, round top, big top; tentage

**tentacles** NOUNS **clutches,** claws, talons, pounces, unguals; **nails,** fingernails; **pincers,** nippers, chelae

**tentative** ADJS **hesitant,** hesitating, pikerish; faltering; diffident, timid, cautious; trial, experimental; unprecipitate, cool; stopgap, temporary, provisional

**tenuous** ADJS **thin,** subtile, subtle, evanescent, fine, overfine, refined, rarefied; **ethereal,** airy, windy, spirituous, vaporous, gaseous; **chimerical,** gossamer, gossamery, gauzy, shadowy, phantomlike; dreamlike, illusory, unreal

**tenure** NOUNS **term,** time, duration; spell; continuous tenure, tenure in *or* of office

**tepid** ADJS **indifferent,** halfhearted, perfunctory, fervorless; **cool,** lukewarm, Laodicean; neither hot nor cold, neither one thing nor the other

**term** NOUNS 1 **word,** phrase, utterance, lexical form *or* item, linguistic form, semantic *or* semiotic *or* semasiological unit
2 time, duration, **tenure;** spell

**terminal** NOUNS 1 **destination,** end of the line, terminus, terminal point; stop, stopping place, last stop; **airport,** air terminal
ADJS 2 **past hope,** incurable, cureless, remediless, immedicable, beyond remedy; **dying,** expiring, going, slipping, slipping away, sinking, sinking fast, low, despaired of, given up, given up for dead, not long for this world

**terminate** VERBS **end,** determine, close, close out, close the books on, phase out *or* down, **finish,** conclude, finish with, resolve, finish *or* wind up <nonformal>; **put an end to,** put a period to, put paid to <Brit>, put *or* lay to rest, **make an end of,** bring to an end, bring to a close *or* halt; **kill**, extinguish, scrag *and* waste *and* take out *and* zap <all nonformal>, **give the quietus**

**terminology** NOUNS **nomenclature,** orismology; onomatology, onomastics; vocabulary, nomenclator

**terrace** NOUNS **balcony,** gallery; step terrace, deck

**terrain** NOUNS **land,** ground, **field,** sphere, place, locale, milieu, precinct, purlieu

**terrestrial** ADJS **earth,** earthly, telluric, tellurian; earthbound; **secularist,** secularistic, worldly, earthy, **mundane,** temporal

**terrible** ADJS terrific, tremendous; **horrid,** horrible, horrifying, horrific, horrendous; **dreadful,** dread, dreaded; **awful;** awesome, awe-inspiring; **shocking,** appalling, astounding; **dire,** direful, fell

**terrific** ADJS **superb,** super <nonformal>, **superexcellent, supereminent,** superfine, **exquisite; magnificent,** splendid, splendiferous, tremendous, immense, **marvelous, wonderful,** glorious, divine, heavenly, sensational

**terrified** ADJS terror-stricken, terror-struck, terror-smitten, terror-ridden; **horrified,** horror-stricken, horror-struck; **appalled,** astounded, aghast; frightened out of one's wits *or* mind, **scared to death,** scared stiff *or* shitless *or* spitless <nonformal>; unnerved, unstrung, unmanned, undone, **cowed,** awed, **intimidated; stunned,** petrified, stupefied, paralyzed, frozen

**territory** NOUNS **region,** area, zone, belt, terrain; **sphere of influence,** orbit, ambit; bailiwick, vantage, stamping ground, footing, turf, home turf, constituency, **power base**

**terror** NOUNS **fear,** fright, affright; **scare,** alarm, consternation, dismay; dread, unholy dread, awe; horror, horrification, mortal *or* abject fear; holy terror

**terrorism** NOUNS **terrorization,** terrorizing, horrification, scaremongering, panic-mongering, scare tactics; terror *or* terroristic tactics, *Schrecklichkeit* <Ger>, rule by terror, reign of terror

**terrorist** NOUNS 1 **revolutionist,** revolutionary, revolutionizer; rebel; anarchist, anarch, syndicalist, criminal syndicalist; subversive
ADJS 2 **revolutionist,** revolutionary, anarchic *or* anarchical, syndicalist, terroristic

**terrorize** VERBS **intimidate,** put in bodily fear, use terror *or* terrorist tactics, pursue a policy of *Schrecklichkeit,* systematically terrorize; threaten; hold a pistol to one's head, sow terror, barbarize, brutalize

**terse** ADJS **laconic,** curt, brief, brusque, short, concise, **sparing of words,** economical of words, of few words; **sententious,** pithy, gnomic, pungent, succinct, crisp, pointed

**test** NOUNS 1 **trial,** try; assay; crucial test; acid test, litmus *or* litmus-paper test; ordeal, crucible; test case
VERBS 2 **try,** essay, cut and try <nonformal>, **test** *or* **try out,** have a dry run *or* dummy run *or* rehearsal *or* test run; run it up the flagpole and see who salutes <nonformal>; put to the test, put to trial, bring to test, make a trial of, give a trial to; **verify,** confirm, prove, audit, **check,** check up *or* on *or* out <nonformal>, check over *or* through, **double-check,** triple-check, cross-check, check and doublecheck
ADJS 3 **experimental,** trial; testing, proving, trying; probative, probatory, verificatory; empirical; trial-and-error, hit-or-miss, cut-and-try

**testament** NOUNS **will,** last will and testament; **bequest,** bequeathal, **legacy,** devise

**testify** VERBS **attest,** give evidence, witness, witness to, **give** *or* **bear witness;** disclose; **vouch,** state one's case, **depose,** depone, **warrant, swear,** take one's oath, acknowledge, avow, **affirm,** avouch, aver, allege, asseverate, **certify,** give one's word

**testimonial** NOUNS 1 **celebration,** tribute; testimonial banquet *or* dinner; salute
2 **recommendation,** reference, credential, letter of reference, voucher; character reference, character, certificate of character, good character

**testimony** NOUNS **attestation,** witness; **deposition,** legal evidence, sworn evidence *or* testimony; *procès-verbal* <Fr>; affidavit, sworn statement; instrument in proof, *pièce justificative* <Fr>

**test run** NOUNS **tryout,** workout, **rehearsal,** practice; pilot plan *or* program; **dry run,** dummy run; road test; **trial run,** practical test; shakedown, shakedown cruise, bench test; flight test, test flight; audition, hearing

**testy** ADJS **irascible,** irritable, excitable, flappable <nonformal>; **cross,** cranky, disagreeable; perverse, fractious, cross-grained

**tête-à-tête** NOUNS 1 **chat,** cozy chat, friendly chat *or* talk, **little talk,** coze, causerie, **visit** <nonformal>, **heart-to-heart talk** *or* heart-to-heart; pillow-talk, intimate discourse
ADJS 2 **intimate,** familiar, cozy, chatty; man-to-man, woman-to-woman

**tether** NOUNS 1 **shackle,** restraint, **restraints,** fetter, hamper, trammel, trammels, **bonds,** irons, chains; spancel, leash, lead
VERBS 2 **secure,** make sure *or* secure, tie, tie off *or* up, chain

**textile** NOUNS **material,** fabric, cloth, textile fabric, texture, tissue, stuff, weave, weft, woof, web, goods

**texture** NOUNS surface texture; **surface; finish,** feel; **grain,** granular texture, fineness *or* coarseness of grain

**thank** VERBS **extend gratitude** *or* **thanks,** bless; give one's thanks, **express one's appreciation;** offer *or* give thanks, tender *or* render thanks, return thanks; acknowledge, make acknowledgments of, credit, recognize, give *or* render credit *or* recognition

**thankful** ADJS **grateful,** appreciative, appreciatory, sensible; **obliged,** much obliged, beholden, indebted to, crediting, under obligation, acknowledging, cognizant of

**thankless** ADJS **disliked,** unappreciated, misunderstood; unsung, unwept, unlamented, unmourned, undeplored, unmissed, unregretted; **ungrateful,** unappreciative, unmindful

**thanksgiving** NOUNS **thanks,** praise, laud, hymn, paean, benediction; grace, prayer of thanks; **acknowledgment,** cognizance, **credit,** crediting, recognition; thank offering, votary offering

**thaw** NOUNS 1 **melting,** liquefaction, liquefying, liquescence, running; **thawing**
VERBS 2 **melt,** melt down, liquefy; **run,**

colliquate; thaw out, unfreeze; defrost, deice

**theater** NOUNS **the theater,** the footlights, the stage, the boards, the bright lights, Broadway, the Great White Way; **playhouse,** house, theatron, odeum; **amphitheater;** circle theater, arena theater, theater-in-the-round; vaudeville theater; burlesque theater; **little theater,** community theater; open-air theater, outdoor theater

**theatrical** ADJS **theatric,** stagy, dramatic, histrionic, thespian; **spectacular; melodramatic;** overacted, overplayed, milked <nonformal>

**theatrics** NOUNS **emotionalism,** theatricality, histrionics, dramatics, hamminess *and* chewing up the scenery <both nonformal>; **sensationalism, melodrama,** melodramatics, blood and thunder; theatricism, theatricalism, staginess

**theft** NOUNS **thievery,** stealing, thieving, **purloining;** swiping *and* lifting *and* snatching *and* snitching *and* pinching <all nonformal>; **pilfering,** pilferage, filching; sneak thievery; shoplifting, boosting <nonformal>; **robbery,** robbing

**theme** NOUNS **motif,** pattern, design, ornamental theme; **essay,** pandect; excursus; **paper,** research paper, term paper; **subject,** topic

**then** ADJS 1 **former,** past, fore, **previous,** late, recent, **once,** onetime, sometime, **erstwhile,** quondam; **ancient,** immemorial, early, primitive, primeval, prehistoric; **old,** olden
ADVS 2 thereat, thereupon, **at that time,** at that moment *or* instant, in that case *or* instance, on that occasion; **again,** at another time, at some other time, anon; **subsequently,** after, afterwards, after that, after all, **later,** next, since; **thereafter,** thereon, therewith

**theological** ADJS **religious; divine;** doctrinal, doctrinary; canonic *or* canonical

**theology** NOUNS **religion,** religious belief *or* faith, **belief,** faith, teaching, doctrine, creed, credo, orthodoxy; system of beliefs

**theoretical** ADJS **hypothetical,** hypothetic; postulatory, notional; **speculative,** conjectural; impressionistic, intuitive; general, generalized, abstract, ideal; merely theoretical, academic, moot; impractical, armchair

**theory** NOUNS theorization, *theoria* <Gk>; **hypothesis,** hypothecation, hypothesizing; **speculation,** mere theory; analysis, **explanation,** abstraction; theoretical basis *or* justification; body of theory, theoretical structure *or* construct; unified theory

**therapeutic** ADJS **remedial,** curative, healing, corrective, disease-fighting, alterative, restorative, analeptic, sanative, sanatory; all-healing, panacean; adjuvant

**therapist** NOUNS **psychotherapist,** psychotherapeutist; clinical psychologist; licensed psychologist, psychological practitioner; **psychoanalyst,** analyst; shrink *and* headshrinker *and* shrinker <all nonformal>; **counselor,** psychological counselor; therapeutist

**therapy** NOUNS **therapeutics,** therapeusis, **treatment,** medical care *or* treatment, medication; noninvasive *or* nonsurgical therapy *or* treatment; disease-fighting, healing; healing arts; psychotherapy; **cure,** curing, remedy

**thereabouts** ADVS **there,** thereat, in that place, in those parts; thereabout, in that vicinity *or* neighborhood; **thither,** thitherward, thitherwards, to that place; **near** *or* **close at hand**

**thereafter** ADVS **subsequently,** after, afterwards, after that, after all, **later,** next, since; thereon, thereupon, therewith, **then;** *ex post facto* <L>

**thereby** ADVS herewith, therewith, wherewith, wherewithal; whereby, hereby

**therefore** ADVS **accordingly,** in that case, in that event, at that rate, that being the case, such being the case, that being so, **under the circumstances,** the condition being such, as it is, as matters stand, as the matter stands, **consequently,** as a result, as a consequence, in consequence, in the event, **hence,** thence, *ergo* <L>, for which reason

**therein** ADVS **in,** inside, within; herein, wherein

**thermal** ADJS **warm,** thermic; **toasty** <nonformal>, warm as toast

**thermometer** NOUNS thermal detector; mercury, glass; thermostat

**thermonuclear reaction** NOUNS **fusion,** nuclear fusion, fusion reaction, thermonuclear fusion, laser-induced fusion, cold fusion

**thesaurus** NOUNS Roget's, storehouse *or* treasury of words; word list, lexicon, glossary

**thesis** NOUNS 1 **treatise,** treatment, handling, tractate, tract; disquisition, descant, exposition, screed; dissertation, essay, **monograph,** research monograph
2 **supposition,** supposal, supposing; **presupposition,** presupposal; **assumption,** presumption, conjecture, inference, surmise, guesswork; **postulate,** postulation, *postulatum* <L>, set of postulates; **proposition,** premise

**they** NOUNS **the authorities,** the powers that be, ruling class *or* classes, the lords of creation, **the Establishment,** the interests, the power elite, **the power structure;** them; the inner circle

**thick** ADJS 1 three-dimensional; **thickset, heavyset,** thick-bodied, broad-bodied, thick-girthed; **massive, bulky**, corpulent; coarse, heavy, gross
2 **luxuriant,** flourishing, **rank, lush,** riotous, exuberant; dense, impenetrable, overgrown, overrun; **profuse,** in profusion, thick with; **teeming,** swarming, crowding, thronging, overflowing, overcrowded, overwhelming, bursting, **crawling**
3 **familiar,** intimate, close, near, inseparable, on familiar *or* intimate terms; just between the two, hand and glove *or* hand in glove; **thick as thieves** <nonformal>
4 **stupid, dumb,** doltish, blockish, klutzy *and* klutzish <both nonformal>, cloddish, **oafish,** boobish, lamebrained, dense
ADVS 5 **densely,** compactly, **close,** closely, thickly, heavily; solidly, firmly

**thicken** VERBS grow thick, thick; incrassate, inspissate; fatten; **congeal,** condense, coagulate, clot, set, concrete; gelatinize, gelatinate, jelly, jellify, **jell,** gel; **curdle,** curd, clabber, lopper <nonformal>; cake, lump, clump, cluster, knot

**thicket** NOUNS thickset, **copse,** coppice; bosket <old>, boscage; covert

**thief** NOUNS **criminal,** outlaw, felon, **crook** <nonformal>, lawbreaker, perpetrator, perp <nonformal>

**thin** VERBS 1 thin down, thin away *or* off *or* out; **rarefy,** subtilize, **attenuate;** dilute, water, water down, weaken; **emaciate**
ADJS 2 **slender, slim,** gracile; thin-bodied, thin-set, narrow- *or* wasp-waisted; **slight,** frail, delicate, light, airy, wispy, lacy, gauzy, papery, gossamer, diaphanous, insubstantial, ethereal, misty, vague, flimsy, wafer-thin, **fine; tenuous,** subtle, rare, **rarefied;** attenuated, attenuate, **watery, weak,** diluted, watered *or* watered-down

*imperially slim*
**E A Robinson**

3 **sparse,** scant, **scanty,** exiguous, **infrequent,** scarce, scarce as hen's teeth <nonformal>, poor, piddling, piddly, **meager**

**thing** NOUNS 1 **object,** article, material thing, affair, something; whatsit <nonformal>, what's-its-name; something or other, *etwas* <Ger>, *eppes* <Yiddish>, *quelque chose* <Fr>; artifact
2 **affair,** concern, matter, concernment, interest, **business,** job <nonformal>, **transaction,** proceeding, doing; **lifestyle,** way of life, preferences; cup of tea *and* bag *and* weakness <all nonformal>

**things** NOUNS **belongings,** appurtenances, trappings, paraphernalia, appointments, accessories, perquisites, appendages, appanages, choses local; material things, mere things; **personal effects,** chattels personal, movables, choses transitory

**think** VERBS 1 **cogitate,** cerebrate, put on one's thinking *or* considering cap <nonformal>, intellectualize, ideate, conceive, conceptualize, form ideas, entertain ideas; **reason;** use one's head, use one's noodle *or* noggin <nonformal>, use *or* exercise the mind, set the brain *or* wits to work, have something on one's mind, have a lot on one's mind
2 **opine,** be of the opinion, be persuaded, be convinced; be afraid <nonformal>, **have the idea,** have an idea, **suppose,** assume, presume, judge, **guess,** surmise, suspect, have a hunch <nonformal>, have an inkling, expect <nonformal>, have an impression, conceive, **imagine,** fancy, daresay; **deem,** esteem, hold, regard, consider, maintain

**thinker** NOUNS **intellectual,** intellect; brainworker, **brain** *and* rocket scientist *and* brain surgeon <all nonformal>; **reasoner,** ratiocinator; sophist; philosopher, speculator

**thin-skinned** ADJS **touchy,** tetchy, miffy <nonformal>, ticklish, prickly, quick to take offense, **sensitive,** oversensitive, hypersensitive, high-strung, highly strung, temperamental; squeamish, susceptible

**third world** NOUNS **unaligned** *or* nonaligned nation, third force; underdeveloped nation, depressed area, chronic poverty area

**thirst** NOUNS thirstiness, dryness; polydipsia; **yen,** appetite, instinct *or* feeling for, sensitivity to

**thirsty** ADJS thirsting, athirst; **dry,** arid, parched, droughty <nonformal>; bibulous, imbibitory, soaking, blotting

**thorn** NOUNS **bramble,** brier, nettle, burr, prickle, sticker <nonformal>; **spine;** bristle; **affliction,** infliction, visitation, **torment,** grievance, woe, thorn in the flesh *or* side, pea in the shoe; bugbear, **bête noire,** bogeyman, nemesis

**thorny** ADJS **prickly,** muricate, echinate, acanaceous, aculeolate; brambly, briery, nettly, bristly; **difficult,** knotty, spiny, set with thorns; delicate, ticklish, tricky, sticky <nonformal>, critical, exacting, demanding; intricate, complex

**thorough** ADJS **thoroughgoing,** exhaustive, intensive, broad-based, A-to-Z, comprehensive, all-embracing, all-encompassing, sweeping; **unmitigated,** unqualified, unconditional, unrestricted, unreserved, **all-out,** wholesale, whole-hog <nonformal>; **utter,** absolute, total

**thought** NOUNS **thinking, cogitation,** cerebration, ideation, noesis, mentation, intellection, intellectualization, ratiocination; reasoning; **brainwork,** headwork, mental labor *or* effort, mental act *or* process, act of thought, mental *or* intellectual exercise; conceptualization; abstract thought, imageless thought; **idea;** mental *or* intellectual object, **notion,** concept, conception, conceit, fancy; consideration, mind

**thoughtful** ADJS **considerate,** mindful, heedful, regardful, solicitous, delicate, tactful, mindful of others; respectful, deferential, attentive; **prudent,** politic, careful, provident, circumspect, reflective, reflecting

**thoughtless** ADJS **inconsiderate,** unthoughtful, unmindful, heedless, respectless, mindless, unthinking, **tactless,** insensitive; **unhelpful,** unaccommodating, unobliging, uncooperative

**thought-provoking** ADJS **interesting,** stimulating, provocative, provoking, thought-challenging, thought-inspiring

**thrash** VERBS **whip,** give a whipping *or* beating *or* thrashing, **beat,** spank, flog, scourge, flagellate, flail, whale

**thread** NOUNS **filament;** fiber; **strand,** suture; filature; **string,** continuum, queue; gamut, spectrum

**threadbare** ADJS **worn,** well-worn, deep-worn, worn-down, the worse for wear, dog-eared; **worn ragged,** worn to rags, worn to threads; bare; **hackneyed,** hackney; **stale,** musty, fusty; timeworn, moth-eaten, **worn thin**

**threat** NOUNS **menace,** promise of harm, knife poised at one's throat, arrow aimed at one's heart, sword of Damocles; imminent threat, powder keg, timebomb, imminence; **intimidation**, arm-twisting <nonformal>; veiled *or* implied threat, idle *or* hollow *or* empty threat; **danger,** peril, endangerment, imperilment, jeopardy, hazard, risk, cause for alarm

**threaten** VERBS **menace,** bludgeon, bulldoze, put the heat *or* screws *or* squeeze on <nonformal>, lean on <nonformal>; hold a pistol to one's head, terrorize, **intimidate,** twist one's arm *and* arm-twist <both nonformal>; utter threats against; hold over one's head; **lower,** spell *or* mean trouble, look threatening, loom, loom up

**threshold** NOUNS **boundary line,** borderline, division line, interface, limen, limit, boundary, line of demarcation; **sill,** doorsill

**thrift** NOUNS **economy,** thriftiness, **frugality,** frugalness; tight purse strings; **prudence,** providence; **husbandry,** management, good management *or* stewardship, custodianship, prudent *or* prudential administration

**thrifty** ADJS **economical,** frugal, conserving, **saving,** economizing, spare, sparing; **prudent,** prudential, provident, careful; scrimping, skimping <nonformal>, penny-wise; parsimonious

**thrill** NOUNS 1 **sensation,** titillation; **tingle,** tingling; quiver, shiver, shudder, tremor, **tremor of excitement,** rush <nonformal>; flush, rush of emotion, surge of emotion

VERBS 2 **tickle,** thrill to death *or* to pieces, give a thrill, **give one a kick** *or* boot *or* charge *or* bang *or* lift <nonformal>; intoxicate, fascinate, titillate, take one's breath away; tingle, **tingle with excitement,** shiver, quiver, quaver, quake, flutter, twitter

**thrive** VERBS **flourish,** boom; blossom, bloom, flower; batten, fatten, grow fat; be fat, dumb, and happy <nonformal>

**throb** VERBS **pulsate,** pulse, beat, not miss a beat; **palpitate,** go pit-a-pat, pitter-patter

**throes** NOUNS **seizure,** attack, **spasm,** fit, paroxysm, convulsion, eclampsia, frenzy; **pain,** pang, wrench, cramp; **pangs of conscience,** sting *or* pricking *or* twinge *or* twitch of conscience, touch of conscience, **voice of conscience**

**throng** NOUNS 1 **multitude, horde,** host, heap <nonformal>, army, panoply, legion; flock, cluster, galaxy; **crowd,** press, crush, mass; **mob,** rabble, rout, ruck, jam, *cohue* <Fr>, everybody and his uncle *or* his brother <nonformal>
VERBS 2 **crowd,** swarm, teem, hive, surge, seethe, mill, stream, horde

**throttle** VERBS **strangle,** garrote, **choke,** burke; **suffocate,** stifle, smother, choke off, asphyxiate, stop the breath; muzzle, gag

**throw** NOUNS 1 **toss,** fling, sling, cast, hurl, chuck, chunk <nonformal>, lob, **heave,** shy, **pitch,** peg <nonformal>; **flip;** put, shot-put
VERBS 2 **fling,** sling, pitch, toss, cast, hurl, heave, chuck, chunk *and* peg <both nonformal>, lob, shy, fire, burn, pepper <nonformal>, launch, dash, let fly, let go, let rip, let loose
3 **discompose,** throw into confusion, perturb
4 **fix,** rig, go in the tank, hold a boat race <all nonformal>
5 **stump,** stick, floor, beat, beat the shit out of <all nonformal>

**throw away** VERBS **discard,** throw out, chuck *or* chuck away *and* shit-can *and* eighty-six <all nonformal>, **get rid of,** dispose of, slough, **ditch** <nonformal>, jettison, throw *or* heave *or* toss overboard, deep-six <nonformal>; **squander,** blow <nonformal>, throw one's money away

**throwback** NOUNS **reversion,** regression; **reversal,** backward deviation, devolution; **return,** recurrence, renewal, recrudescence; atavism; **setback,** check, severe check, backset

**throw out** VERBS **eject,** expel, discharge, extrude, obtrude, detrude, exclude, **reject,** cast, remove; **oust,** bounce *and* give the hook <both nonformal>, **put out,** turn out, thrust out; run out <nonformal>, cast out, chuck out, toss out, heave out, kick *or* boot out <nonformal>; give the bum's rush *or* give the old heave-ho *or* throw out on one's ear <all nonformal>; defenestrate; jettison, throw overboard, discard, junk, throw away

**thrust** NOUNS 1 **push,** shove, boost <nonformal>; **pushing,** propulsion, propelling; shoving, butting; **drive,** motive power, driving force, means of propulsion; **rocket propulsion,** reaction propulsion, jet propulsion, blast propulsion
VERBS 2 **push,** shove, boost <nonformal>; press, stress, **bear,** bear upon, bring pressure to bear upon; **drive,** force, run

**thud** NOUNS **thump,** flump, crump, clop, clump, clunk, plunk, tunk, plump, bump, dull thud

**thug** NOUNS **murderer,** man-killer, bloodletter, Cain; **assassin,** assassinator; **cutthroat,** desperado, gorilla <nonformal>, gunman; professional killer, hired killer, hit man *or* button man *or* gun *or* trigger man *or* torpedo *or* gunsel <all nonformal>; hatchet man; **bandit,** dacoit; gangster *and* mobster <both nonformal>; **hoodlum,** ruffian, rowdy; goon <nonformal>

**thump** NOUNS 1 **punch,** poke, jab, dig, drub, pelt, cut, chop, dint, slog
VERBS 2 **drum,** thrum, beat, pound, thump out, roll; palpitate, flutter; **throb,** pulsate

**thunder** NOUNS 1 thundering, clap *or* crash *or* peal of thunder, **thunderclap,** thundercrack, thunderstroke
VERBS 2 **din,** boom; **resound,** blast the ear, pierce *or* split *or* rend the ears, rend *or* split the eardrums, split one's head; rock the sky, fill the air, shake *or* rattle the windows; **peal,** rumble, grumble, growl, **roll,** roar

**thunderstruck** ADJS **dumbfounded,** dumbstruck, staggered, overwhelmed, unable to believe one's senses *or* eyes; wonder-struck, wonder-stricken, awestricken, awestruck, struck all of a heap <nonformal>

**thwart** VERBS **frustrate,** foil, cross, balk; spike, scotch, checkmate; **throw a monkey wrench into the works** <nonformal>; spike one's guns, put one's nose out of joint <nonformal>, upset one's applecart

**tiara** NOUNS crown, royal crown, coronet, diadem

**tic** NOUNS twitching, vellication; **jerk,** twitch, grimace, rictus; **fixation,** complex, fascination

**ticket** NOUNS 1 **permission,** permission to enter, admission, ticket of admission; **certificate,** certification; **summons,** parking ticket
2 **ballot,** slate; straight ticket, split ticket
3 **price,** quotation, quoted price, price tag *and* **sticker** <both nonformal>

**tickle** NOUNS 1 tickling, **titillation,** pleasant stimulation, **ticklishness,** tickliness
VERBS 2 **titillate,** delight, delectate, **thrill,** enrapture, enthrall, enchant, entrance, fascinate, captivate, bewitch, **charm,** becharm; transport, carry away; tickle pink *or* to death <nonformal>, tickle the fancy

**tickled** ADJS **pleased,** delighted; **thrilled;** tickled to death *and* tickled pink <both nonformal>, exhilarated; **gratified,** satisfied; pleased with, taken with, favorably impressed with, sold on <nonformal>; pleased as Punch

**ticklish** ADJS 1 tickling, tickly, **titillative**
2 **precarious,** touchy, touch-and-go, **critical,** delicate; on thin ice, on slippery ground; hanging by a thread, trembling in the balance; tricky, sticky <nonformal>, easier said than done, exacting, demanding

**tidal** ADJS estuarine, littoral, grallatorial; **coastal,** seaside, shore, shoreside; tideland, wetland

**tidbit** NOUNS 1 **delicacy,** dainty, goody <nonformal>, treat, kickshaw, titbit; **morsel,** choice morsel, *bonne bouche* <Fr>
2 **scandal,** dirt <nonformal>, **malicious gossip;** juicy morsel, choice bit of dirt <nonformal>

**tide** NOUNS tidal current *or* stream, tidal flow *or* flood, tide race; **riptide,** rip, tiderip, overfalls; **spring tide; high tide,** high water, full tide; **low tide,** low water; **neap tide,** neap; lunar tide, solar tide; **flood tide,** ebb tide

**tidy** VERBS 1 **tidy up,** neaten, **straighten up,** fix up <nonformal>, **clean up,** police *and* police up <both nonformal>, groom, spruce *and* spruce up <both nonformal>, clear up
ADJS 2 **trim,** natty, neat, spruce, sleek, slick *and* slick as a whistle <nonformal>, smart, **shipshape,** well-kept, well-cared-for, neat as a pin <nonformal>

**tie** NOUNS 1 **intermediary,** link, **connecting link,** connection, **go-between,** liaison; **allegiance,** bond, attachment
2 dead heat, draw, wash <nonformal>
VERBS 3 **bind,** restrain, tie up, put the clamps on, **tie one's hands; tie hand and foot,** hog-tie <nonformal>; straitjacket; **obligate,** oblige, require, make incumbent *or* imperative, pledge, commit, saddle with; **connect,** interconnect, ally, link, link up, wed, marry, marry up, weld, couple, bracket, equate
4 **equal,** match, rival, correspond, be even-steven, be tantamount to, be equal to; **keep pace with,** measure up to, come up to, stack up with <nonformal>, match up with

**tie-in** NOUNS **affiliation,** hookup *and* tie-up <both nonformal>, filiation, bond, union, alliance, **tie,** link, linkage, linking, linkup, liaison

**tier** NOUNS **layer,** thickness; **level,** stage, story, floor, step, ledge, deck; **stratum,** seam, *couche* <Fr>, belt, band

**tie up** VERBS 1 **bind,** restrain, tie, put the clamps on, **strap,** lash, leash, pinion, fasten, secure, make fast; **hamper,** trammel, entrammel; **shackle,** fetter, manacle, gyve, **put in irons; handcuff,** tie hand and foot, hog-tie <nonformal>; hobble, put on a lead <chiefly Brit>, spancel; tether
2 **monopolize,** hog *and* grab all of *and* gobble up <all nonformal>, have exclusive possession of *or* exclusive rights to; engross, forestall, corner *and* get a corner on *and* corner the market <all nonformal>
3 **wrap up,** do *or* bind up

**tiff** NOUNS **quarrel,** open quarrel, dustup, **dispute,** argument, lovers' quarrel, **spat,** fuss

**tight** ADJS 1 **narrow,** strait, isthmic, isthmian; close-fitting; **restricted,** limited, circumscribed, confined, constricted; **cramped,** cramp; incapacious, incommodious, crowded
2 **stingy,** illiberal, ungenerous, chintzy, miserly, **cheap** <nonformal>, near, close, closefisted, tightfisted, penny-pinching; miserly, niggardly
ADVS 3 **securely,** firmly, fast; **inseparably,** indissolubly

**tightwad** NOUNS **niggard, cheapskate** <nonformal>, **miser,** hard man with a buck <nonformal>, **skinflint,** scrooge, penny pincher

**till** VERBS **cultivate,** culture, **dress,** work, till the soil, dig, delve, spade; **plow,** plow under, plow up

**tilt** NOUNS 1 **leaning,** bent, turn, bias, **affinity;** mutual affinity *or* attraction; **tip,** pitch, **list, cant,** swag, sway
VERBS 2 **incline,** lean; slope, slant, pitch, grade, bank; **tip,** list, cant, careen, keel, sidle, swag, sway
3 **tend,** have a tendency, **incline,** be disposed, lean, trend, have a penchant, turn, warp, bend to; show a tendency *or* trend *or* set *or* direction

**timber** NOUNS **woodland,** timberland; stand of timber, **forest,** forest land, forest cover, forest preserve, state *or* national forest

**time** NOUNS 1 **tempo,** beat, time pattern, timing; **duration,** *durée* <Fr>, lastingness, continuity, term, while, tide, space, spell
2 **age,** generation, day, date, cycle
VERBS 3 **fix** *or* **set the time,** mark the time; **keep time,** mark time, measure time, beat time; **clock** <nonformal>

**timeless** ADJS **perpetual, everlasting,** dateless, ageless, immemorial; **endless,** unending, never-ending, without end, **interminable**

**timely** ADJS **well-timed,** seasonable, opportune, convenient; **expedient,** meet, fit, fitting, befitting, suitable, sortable, appropriate; **propitious,** ripe, auspicious, lucky, providential, heaven-sent, fortunate, happy, felicitous

**time off** NOUNS **lull,** quiet spell, resting point, point of repose, plateau, letup, relief, vacation, holiday, off-time; respite

**time-out** NOUNS **respite,** recess, rest, pause, halt, stay, lull, **break,** time to catch one's breath; **breathing spell,** breather; coffee break, tea break, cigarette break

**timepiece** NOUNS timekeeper, **timer, chronometer,** ship's watch; horologe, horologium; **clock,** Big Ben, ticker <nonformal>, **watch,** turnip

**timetable** NOUNS **plan, schedule,** time-scheme, time frame; timeline, time schedule, time chart; time scale

**timid** ADJS **fearful,** fearing, fearsome; **timorous,** shy, mousy <nonformal>, afraid of one's own shadow; **shrinking,** bashful, diffident; **hesitant,** hesitating, tentative, cautious

**timing** NOUNS **tempo,** time, beat, time pattern; synchronism, sync <nonformal>; **chronology,** timekeeping, clocking, horology

**timorous** ADJS **afraid,** fearful; timid, overtimorous, overtimid; **fainthearted,** weakhearted, chicken-hearted, lily-livered <nonformal>; **weak-kneed,** chicken <nonformal>, afraid of one's shadow; daunted, dismayed, unmanned, cowed, intimidated

**tinge** NOUNS 1 **hint,** *soupçon* <Fr>, **suspicion,** suggestion, intimation; **trace,** touch, dash, cast, **smattering,** sprinkling; tincture; coloration, undertone, overtone, undercurrent, more than meets the eye *or* ear, something between the lines, intimation, touch, nuance, innuendo
VERBS 2 **imbue,** imbrue, **infuse,** suffuse, transfuse, breathe, **instill,** infiltrate, **impregnate, permeate,** pervade, penetrate, leaven; **tincture,** entincture, temper, color, dye, flavor, tone, slant, impart spin

**tingle** NOUNS 1 tingling, thrill, buzz; **prickle,** prickles, prickling, pins and needles; **sting,** stinging, urtication
VERBS 2 thrill; **itch;** scratch; **prickle,** prick, sting; **tingle with excitement,** glow; thrill to; **throb,** palpitate, go pit-a-pat; **tremble,** shiver, quiver, quaver, quake, flutter, twitter

**tinker** VERBS **putter,** potter, **piddle; dabble,** smatter; toy with, fiddle with, fool with, play with

**tinny** ADJS **inferior,** poor, punk <nonformal>, **base,** mean, common, coarse, cheesy *and* tacky <both nonformal>; cheap, Mickey Mouse <nonformal>, paltry

**tint** NOUNS 1 **color,** hue; tinct, tincture, **tinge,** shade, tone, cast; key; **coloring,** coloration; **touch,** dash, smack, **trace,** vestige, hint, inkling
VERBS 2 **color,** hue, lay on color; **tinge,** tinct, **tincture,** tone, complexion; pigment; **stain,** dye, imbue

**tiny** ADJS teeny *and* teeny-weeny *and* eentsy-weentsy <all nonformal>, wee *and* peewee <both nonformal>, bitty *and* bitsy *and* little-bitty *and* little-bitsy *and* itsy-bitsy *and* itsy-witsy <all nonformal>; **minute,** fine

**tip** NOUNS 1 **summit,** top; **tip-top,** peak, pinnacle; **crown,** cap, cusp, point, spire,

**apex,** acme, *ne plus ultra* <Fr>, **zenith, climax,** apogee, pole
2 **tilt,** pitch, **list, cant,** swag, sway
3 piece of advice, **word of advice,** word to the wise, *verbum sapienti* <L>, verb *or* verbum sap <nonformal>, **hint,** broad hint, flea in the ear <nonformal>, a few words of wisdom, one's two cents' worth <nonformal>, intimation, insinuation
4 **gratuity,** largess, bounty, liberality, donative, sportula; consideration, *pourboire* <Fr>, *Trinkgeld* <Ger>, sweetener, inducement; grease *and* salve *and* palm oil <all nonformal>
VERBS 5 **careen,** list, heel, cant; **tilt,** dip, fall off *or* away, **go downhill**
6 tip off *and* **give one a tip** <both nonformal>, alert; **give a pointer to** <nonformal>; **let in on,** let in on the know <nonformal>; let next to *and* put next to *and* **put on to** *and* put on to something hot <all nonformal>

**tipple** VERBS **drink,** nip; **imbibe,** have a drink *or* nip *or* dram *or* guzzle *or* gargle, soak, bib, quaff, sip, sup, lap, lap up, take a drop, slake one's thirst, cheer *or* refresh the inner man, drown one's troubles *or* sorrows; **down,** toss off *or* down, knock back, throw one back, drink up, drink bottoms-up, drink deep

**tipsy** ADJS **intoxicated, inebriated,** inebriate, inebrious, **drunk,** drunken, *shikker* <Yiddish>, **in one's cups,** under the influence, the worse for liquor; **tiddly,** dizzy, muddled, addled, flustered, reeling; mellow

**tiptoe** VERBS 1 **be cautious,** make haste slowly; feel one's ground *or* way; pussyfoot, go *or* walk on tiptoe, walk on eggs *or* eggshells *or* thin ice
ADJS 2 **on tiptoe,** on tippytoe, tiptoeing, tippytoe

**tip-top** ADJS **A-1, A number one,** primo, top-notch, topflight, top-drawer, tops; topping *or* top-hole <both Brit> <all nonformal>

**tirade** NOUNS **speech,** screed, **diatribe,** jeremiad, philippic, invective

**tire** VERBS 1 **fatigue,** weary, exhaust, wilt, flag, jade, harass; **wear,** wear on *or* upon, **wear down; tire out,** wear out, burn out; wind, put out of breath; weaken, enervate, weary *or* tire to death

2 <nonformal> **beat, poop,** frazzle, fag, tucker; fag out, tucker out, knock out, do in, do up; **poop out,** peter out

**tired** ADJS 1 **weary, fatigued,** wearied, weariful, jaded, run-down, good and tired; in need of rest, ready to drop; drooping, droopy, wilting, flagging, sagging; worn to a frazzle, **exhausted, spent,** effete, etiolated, played out, *ausgespielt* <Ger>, emptied, drawn, worn, wan

2 <nonformal> **beat, pooped, bushed,** poohed, paled, frazzled, bagged, fagged, tuckered, plumb tuckered, done, done in, all in, dead, dead beat, dead on one's feet, gone; **pooped out,** knocked out, wiped out, tuckered out, played out, fagged out; run ragged; used up, done up, beat up, washed-up

3 **cliché,** banal, trite, platitudinous

**tireless** ADJS **industrious,** assiduous, diligent, sedulous, **hardworking;** unfailing, **untiring,** unwearying, unflagging, never-tiring, weariless, **indefatigable,** game to the last *or* to the end

**tiresome** ADJS **vexatious,** vexing, irking, **irksome,** wearisome; **wearying,** wearing, tiring; pedestrian, **unimaginative**; insipid, vapid, flat; humdrum, **dull**

**titanic** ADJS **gigantic,** mountainous, colossal, mammoth, Gargantuan, gigantesque, monster, monstrous, outsize, sizable, larger-than-life, overgrown; **monumental,** heroic, heroical, epic, epical, towering

**titillate** VERBS **delight,** delectate, tickle, thrill, **enrapture,** enthrall, enchant, entrance, fascinate, captivate, bewitch, **charm,** becharm; intoxicate, fascinate, take one's breath away; **tempt,** tantalize, **tease,** make one's mouth water, dangle before one; **pique,** tickle one's fancy, **provoke,** stimulate, arouse, excite, pique one's interest, turn one on <nonformal>

**title** NOUNS 1 **ownership,** *dominium* <L>, proprietorship, proprietary, **property right** *or* rights; **claim,** proper claim, demand, **interest,** pretension, pretense, prescription
2 **honorific,** honor, title of honor; **handle** *and* handle to one's name <both nonformal>; courtesy title; **caption,** heading, head, superscription, rubric
VERBS 3 **name,** denominate, nominate, **designate,** call, term, style, dub; define, identify; entitle; **label,** tag; nickname; christen; caption, subtitle

**titled** ADJS **named,** called, yclept <old>, **styled,** denominated, known as, known by the name of, designated, termed, dubbed, identified as; christened, baptized; **noble,** of rank, high, exalted; aristocratic

**TLC** NOUNS **tender loving care,** consideration, solicitude, caring, loving care, caregiving

**toady** NOUNS 1 **sycophant,** flatterer, toadeater, lickspit, lickspittle, **yes-man,** truckler, creature, ass-kisser *and* brownnose *and* bootlicker <all nonformal>
VERBS 2 **fawn,** truckle; flatter; toadeat; **bootlick** <nonformal>, lickspittle, lick one's shoes, lick the feet of; kiss one's feet, kiss the hem of one's garment, make a doormat of oneself; **kowtow,** bow, bow and scrape

**to and fro** ADVS **back and forth,** backward and forward, backwards and forwards, in and out, seesaw, from side to side, from pillar to post

**toast** VERBS 1 **drink to,** pledge, drink a toast to, drink *or* pledge the health of, give you

INTERJ 2 <toasts> *skoal!, skl!* <Norw>, *prosit!* or *prost!, à votre santé!* <Fr>, *¡salud!* <Sp>, *l'chaim!* <Heb>, *slàinte!* <Ir>, *salute!* <Ital>, *na zdorovye!* <Russ>, *nazdrowie!* <Pol>, to your health!, long life!, to life!, cheerio!, cheers!, down the hatch!, bottoms up!, here's how!, here's to you!, here's looking at you!, here's mud in your eye!, here's good luck!, here's to absent friends!, confusion to our enemies!

**today** NOUNS 1 **the present,** presentness, present time, the here and now; **now,** the present juncture *or* occasion, the present hour *or* moment, this instant *or* second *or* moment; **the present age,** this day, this day and age
ADVS 2 **now,** at present, at this point, at this juncture, at this stage *or* at this stage of the game, on the present occasion, **at this time,** at this moment *or* instant, at the present time; this day, in these days, **in this day and age,** in our time, nowadays

**to-do** NOUNS **agitation,** perturbation, ferment, **commotion,** disturbance, ado, *brouhaha* <Fr>; **bustle,** fuss, flurry, flutter, fluster, **stir,** hubbub, hullabaloo, hoo-ha *and* foofaraw *and* flap <all nonformal>; **trouble,** bother, pother

**together** ADJS 1 **composed,** collected, levelheaded; poised, equanimous, **balanced,** well-balanced; **self-possessed,** self-controlled, self-restrained; confident, assured, **self-confident,** self-assured; **like-minded,** akin, of the same mind, of one mind, at one, united
ADVS 2 **collectively, mutually,** jointly, unitedly, in conjunction, conjointly, *en masse* <Fr>, communally, corporately, **in a body,** all at once, *ensemble* <Fr>; simultaneously, coincidentally, concurrently, synchronously; **connectedly,** cumulatively

**toil** NOUNS 1 **work, labor,** industry, moil, travail, toil and trouble, sweat of one's brow; **drudgery,** sweat, slavery, spadework; dirty work, grunt work *and* donkey work *and* shit-work *and* scutwork <all nonformal>
VERBS 2 **work,** labor; **drudge,** grub, moil, toil and moil, travail, **plod,** slog, peg, plug <nonformal>, plug away *or* along <nonformal>, hammer away, pound away, struggle along, work away; keep one's nose to the grindstone

**toilet** NOUNS **latrine,** water closet; john *and* johnny *and* can *and* crapper <all nonformal>; commode, potty-chair <nonformal>; **chamber pot,** chamber, pisspot <nonformal>, potty <nonformal>; throne <nonformal>; **bathroom,** lavatory, washroom, **rest room,** comfort station; head <nautical>

**token** NOUNS 1 **symbol,** emblem, icon; **counter,** slug; **memento,** remembrance, trophy, souvenir, keepsake, relic, favor, token of remembrance
ADJS 2 **substitute,** alternate, alternative, other, tother <nonformal>, equivalent, dummy, pinch, utility, backup, secondary; ad hoc, provisional; makeshift, reserve, **spare,** stopgap, temporary, tentative

**tolerable** ADJS **goodish,** fair, fairish, moderate, **decent,** respectable, presentable, good enough, **pretty good,** not bad, not half bad, not so bad, **adequate,** satisfactory, all right, OK *or* okay <nonformal>; better than nothing; **acceptable,** admissible, **passable,** unobjectionable, unexceptionable

**tolerance** NOUNS **indulgence,** lenience *or* leniency, condonation, lenity; **forbearance,** patience, long-suffering; permissiveness; **compassion**, sympathy; sensitivity

**tolerate** VERBS **endure,** bear, stand, support, sustain, **suffer,** abide, bide, live with; **bear up under,** put up with, stand for, brook, brave, hang in there, bear with; **countenance,** condone, stomach, indulge; shut one's eyes to, **wink at,** blink at, overlook; **accept,** shut one's eyes to, look the other way

**toll** NOUNS 1 **ringing,** tintinnabulation, **pealing,** chiming, **tolling,** knelling; clangor, clanking, clanging; **ring,** peal, chime; knell

2 **fee,** charge, charges, demand, exaction, exactment; user fee; **levy,** impost, imposition

VERBS 3 **ring,** tintinnabulate, **peal,** sound; knell, sound a knell; chime

**tomb** NOUNS **sepulcher; grave,** gravesite, burial; resting place, last home, long home, narrow house, house of death; **crypt,** vault, burial chamber; ossuary *or* ossuarium; **mausoleum; catacombs;** mastaba; cist grave, box grave, passage grave, shaft grave, beehive tomb; pyramid, mummy chamber; burial mound, tumulus, barrow, cist, cromlech, dolmen

**tome** NOUNS **book,** volume; **work,** opus; **classic,** magnum opus, great work, scholarly work, standard work, definitive work

**tomorrow** NOUNS 1 **the future,** future, futurity, what is to come, imminence, subsequence, eventuality, **hereafter,** aftertime, afteryears, **time to come;** the morrow, the morning after, *mañana* <Sp>; **immediate** *or* **near future,** time just ahead, immediate prospect, offing, next period

ADVS 2 **in the future,** afterward *or* afterwards, **later,** at a later time, after a time *or* while, anon; **by and by,** in the sweet by-and-by <nonformal>; *mañana* <Sp>, the day after tomorrow; **in the near** *or* **immediate future,** just around the corner, **imminently**, soon, before long

**tone** NOUNS 1 **tint,** tinct, tincture, **tinge,** shade, cast

2 **fitness,** condition, shape, trim, fettle, aerobic fitness, anaerobic fitness, cardiovascular fitness, cardiorespiratory fitness; tonus, tonicity

3 **feeling,** emotional coloring *or* shade *or* nuance, feeling tone, note, overtone, undertone; **tone of voice; tenor,** mood, humor, feelings, temper, frame of mind, state of mind, morale, note, vein

**tone down** VERBS **muffle,** mute, dull, soften, deaden, subdue, **soft-pedal; moderate,** tame, hold in check, keep a tight rein, chasten, underplay, play down, downplay, de-emphasize

**tongue** NOUNS **language,** speech, *lingua* <L>, spoken language, natural language; **utterance,** voice

**tongue-in-cheek** ADJS **joking,** jesting, jocose; facetious, joshing <nonformal>; satiric, **satirical,** sarcastic, ironic, ironical

**tongue-tied** ADJS **speechless,** wordless, breathless, at a loss for words, choked up; inarticulate; dumbstruck, dumbstricken, stricken dumb, dumbfounded; **tight-lipped;** close-lipped, word-bound

**tonic** NOUNS 1 **bracer,** cordial, restorative, analeptic, roborant, **pick-me-up** <nonformal>; shot in the arm <nonformal>; **refresher,** reviver, hair of the dog *or* hair of the dog that bit one <nonformal>

ADJS 2 **stimulating,** bracing, invigorating, reviving, refreshing, restorative, analeptic, strengthening, roborant; remedial, **curative**

**tool** NOUNS **instrument,** implement, utensil; apparatus, device, mechanical device, contrivance, contraption <nonformal>, gadget, gizmo, gimcrack, gimmick <nonformal>, means, mechanical means

**tooled** ADJS enchased, inscribed, incised, marked, lined, creased, cut, carved, glyphic; grooved, furrowed

**too much** NOUNS 1 **superabundance,** overabundance, superflux, **plethora,** redundancy, overprofusion, too many, too much of a good thing

2 ADJS **insufferable,** intolerable, insupportable, unendurable, unbearable, excessive, past bearing, not to be borne *or* endured, for the birds <nonformal>, a bit much <nonformal>, overmuch, more than flesh and blood can bear

**toot** NOUNS 1 tootle, **honk,** beep, blat, trumpet

2 <nonformal> **binge,** drunk, bust, tear, **bender,** bat

VERBS 3 tootle, sound, peal, wind, blow, blat; pipe, trumpet; **honk,** honk *or* sound *or* blow the horn, beep

**top** NOUNS 1 top side, upper side, upside; topside *or* topsides; **peak,** summit, pinnacle, crown, perfection, height, acme, ultimate
2 **cover,** lid, cap, screw-top; stopper; **tent,** big top
3 **toy,** spinning top, teetotum
VERBS 4 top off, **crown,** cap, crest, **head,** tip, peak, surmount; have the top place *or* spot, over-arch; **culminate,** consummate, climax; ice, frost <a cake>; fill, top up; **overshadow,** eclipse, throw into the shade; **rise above,** tower above *or* over
ADJS 5 topmost, **uppermost,** upmost, overmost, **highest;** tip-top, tip-crowning, **maximum,** maximal, ultimate; **head,** headmost, capital, chief, paramount, supreme, preeminent; **top-level,** highest level, top-echelon, top-flight, top-ranking, top-drawer <nonformal>

**topic** NOUNS **subject,** matter, subject matter, what it is about, **concern,** focus of interest *or* attention, discrete matter, category; **theme,** burden, matter in hand, **question,** problem, issue; point in question, main point, gist; item on the agenda

**topical** ADJS 1 **local, localized**
2 present, immediate, **latest, current, running, extant, existent,** existing, **actual;** contemporary, **up-to-date, up-to-the-minute, fresh; thematic**

**topless** ADJS 1 **unclad,** undressed, half-clothed; low-necked, low-cut, décolleté, strapless; **seminude,** scantily clad
2 headless, crownless; **towering,** towery, soaring, monumental, colossal

**top-notch** ADJS **superlative,** top, topmost, **uppermost,** tip-top, top-level, top-echelon, top-of-the-line <nonformal>, **first-rate,** first-class, of the first water, highest-quality

**topple** VERBS **tumble,** fall, fall down; **fall over,** topple down *or* over; lurch, pitch, **stumble,** stagger, totter, careen, list, tilt, trip, flounder

**tops** ADJS

<nonformal> **A-1, A number one,** primo, first-chop, tip-top, top-notch, topflight, top-drawer; topping *or* top-hole <both Brit>

**topsy-turvy** ADJS **upside-down,** ass over elbows *and* ass over tincups *and* arsy-varsy <all nonformal>; **confused,** chaotic, **muddled,** jumbled, scattered, helter-skelter <nonformal>, in a mess; **screwed up** <nonformal>, mucked up <nonformal>

**torch** NOUNS 1 flaming torch, flambeau, cresset; **flare,** signal flare, fusee; beacon
VERBS 2 **set fire to,** fire, set on fire, kindle, enkindle, inflame, **light,** light up, strike a light, touch off, **burn,** conflagrate

**toreador** NOUNS **bullfighter,** *torero* <Sp>; banderillero, picador, matador

**torment** NOUNS 1 **torture,** excruciation, crucifixion, passion, laceration, clawing, lancination, flaying, excoriation; **worry,** worriedness; **worries,** troubles, concerns; worrying, fretting; harassment
2 **tormentor,** torturer; **nuisance,** pest, pesterer, pain *and* pain in the neck *or* ass <nonformal>, nag, public nuisance; **tease,** teaser; annoyer, harasser, harrier, badgerer, **heckler,** plaguer, persecutor
VERBS 3 **torture,** rack, put to torture, put *or* lay on the rack, **agonize, harrow,** crucify, martyr, martyrize, excruciate, wring, twist, contorse, convulse
4 **persecute,** oppress, victimize, play cat and mouse with, **harass,** get *or* keep after, get *or* keep at, harry, hound, beset; **disturb, perturb,** irk, plague, drive one up the wall <nonformal>, give one gray hair, make one lose sleep

**torn** ADJS **impaired,** lacerated, mangled, cut, split, rent, slit, slashed, mutilated, chewed-up; raggedy, raggedy-ass <nonformal>, **ragged,** tattered; **alienated,** estranged, disaffected, separated, divided, disunited

**tornado** NOUNS **storm,** tempest, squall, line squall, **cyclone,** hurricane, tropical cyclone, typhoon, tropical storm

**torrential** ADJS **pouring,** streaming, pelting, drumming, driving, blinding

**torrid** ADJS **hot,** heated, sweltering, sweltry, canicular; **burning,** parching, scorching, searing, scalding, blistering, baking, roasting, toasting, broiling, **boiling,** seething, ebullient; hot as hell *or* blazes, hot as the hinges of hell, so hot you can fry eggs on the sidewalk <nonformal>, like a furnace *or* an oven

**tortuous** ADJS **distorted,** contorted, warped, twisted, crooked; labyrinthine, buckled, sprung, bent, bowed; irregular, deviative, anamorphous; sinuous, serpentine, mazy, meandering; convoluted, overelaborate, overinvolved

**torture** NOUNS 1 **torment,** excruciation, crucifixion, passion, laceration, clawing, lancination, flaying, excoriation; **agony**
VERBS 2 **torment,** agonize, harrow, savage, **rack,** scarify, crucify, impale, excruciate, lacerate, claw, rip, bloody, lancinate, macerate, convulse, wring; prolong the agony, kill by inches, make life miserable *or* not worth living; martyr, martyrize; put on *or* to the rack; dismember, tear limb from limb; draw and quarter, break on the wheel, keelhaul

**toss** NOUNS 1 **throw,** fling, sling, cast, hurl, chuck, lob, **heave,** shy, **pitch,** peg <nonformal>; flip
2 **even chance,** even break *and* fair shake <both nonformal>, even *or* square odds, level playing field, **half a chance,** fifty-fifty; **tossup,** standoff <nonformal>
VERBS 3 **pitch,** tumble, toss and tumble, pitch and toss; **flounder,** welter, wallow; make heavy weather
4 **throw,** fling, sling, pitch, cast, hurl, heave, chuck, lob, fire, launch, dash, let fly, let go, let rip, let loose; **flip,** snap, jerk

**tossup** NOUNS **gamble,** guess, piece of guesswork, estimate, guesstimate *and* ball-park figure <nonformal>; **coin-toss** <nonformal>, **touch and go;** contingency, double contingency, possibility upon a possibility

**total** NOUNS 1 **sum,** sum total, sum and substance, **the amount,** whole *or* gross amount, grand total
VERBS 2 **compute,** add up; sum, totalize, total up, tote *and* tote up <nonformal>, tally; **amount to,** come to, run to *or* into, mount up to, add up to, tote *or* tote up to <nonformal>, aggregate to
3 **demolish,** wreck, rack up <nonformal>, **fragment,** break to pieces, make mincemeat of, reduce to rubble, atomize, pulverize, **smash,** shatter
ADJS 4 **thorough,** thoroughgoing, complete; **unmitigated,** unqualified, unrelieved, unspoiled, undeniable, unquestionable, unequivocal; **unmitigated,** unabated; unmixed, unalloyed
5 **cumulative,** accumulative, overall, without omission *or* exception; blanket, omnibus, across-the-board; **whole,** entire, aggregate, gross, all

**totaled** ADJS **wrecked,** ravaged; worthless

**totter** NOUNS 1 **flounder,** flounce, stagger, stumble, falter
VERBS 2 **flounder,** flounce, **stagger,** stumble, falter, blunder, wallop; **struggle,** labor; **wallow,** welter

**touch** NOUNS 1 **contact,** touching, *attouchement* <Fr>, taction, tangency, contingence; gentle *or* tentative contact, caress, brush, glance, nudge, kiss, rub, graze; impingement, impingence
2 **knack,** art, hang, trick, way; feel
VERBS 3 **feel,** feel of, palpate; **finger,** pass *or* run the fingers over, feel with the fingertips, thumb; **handle,** palm, paw; **manipulate,** wield, ply; poke at, prod; tap, flick; come in contact
4 **affect,** move, stir; melt, soften, melt the heart, choke one up, give one a lump in the throat; **penetrate,** pierce, go through one, go deep; touch a chord, **touch a sympathetic chord,** touch one's heart, tug at the heart *or* heartstrings, go to one's heart, get under one's skin; **touch to the quick,** smart, sting

**touch and go** NOUNS **even chance,** even break *and* fair shake <both nonformal>; **half a chance,** toss, toss-up, standoff <nonformal>

**touched** ADJS 1 **affected,** moved, impressed; impressed with *or* by, penetrated with, seized with, imbued with, devoured by, obsessed, obsessed with *or* by; **contrite,** abject, humble, humbled, **sheepish,** apologetic, softened, melted
2 **unbalanced,** unsettled, distraught, sick *or* soft in the head, not right, not in one's right mind, touched in the head, **out of one's mind,** out of one's senses *or* wits, bereft of reason, irrational, deprived of reason, senseless, witless

**touch on** VERBS **call attention to,** mention, specify, mention in passing, cite, **refer to,** allude to

**touch up** VERBS **perfect,** finish, put on the finishing touches, polish, fine-tune <nonformal>, tone up, **brush up,** furbish, furbish up, spruce, **spruce up,** freshen, brighten up, polish, polish up, shine <nonformal>

**touchy** ADJS 1 **tetchy,** ticklish, prickly, quick to take offense, **thin-skinned,** sensitive, oversensitive, hypersensitive, high-strung, highly strung, temperamental
2 **precarious,** ticklish, touch-and-go, **critical,** delicate; on thin ice, hanging by a thread, trembling in the balance

**tough** ADJS **resistant;** shockproof, shock-resistant, impact-resistant; stubborn, stiff; hard *or* tough as nails; **strong,** hardy, vigorous; cohesive, **tenacious,** viscid; **durable,** lasting; untiring

**tough break** NOUNS **bad luck,** hard luck, **rotten luck** <nonformal>, raw deal <nonformal>, bad *or* tough *or* rotten break <nonformal>, devil's own luck; **ill fortune,** evil fortune, evil star, ill wind, evil dispensation; frowns of fortune

**toupee** NOUNS **wig,** peruke, hairpiece, rug *and* divot *and* doormat <all nonformal>; **periwig**

**tour** NOUNS 1 **shift,** work shift, tour of duty, stint, bit, **watch,** trick, time, **turn,** relay, spell *or* turn of work; day shift, night shift, swing shift, graveyard shift <nonformal>; lobster trick *or* tour, sunrise watch
2 **term,** time; **tenure,** continuous tenure, tenure in *or* of office; **enlistment,** hitch <nonformal>
3 **sight-seeing,** rubbernecking <nonformal>; walking tour, bus tour, sightseeing tour *or* excursion, rubberneck tour <nonformal>
VERBS 4 **journey, travel,** make *or* take *or* go *or* go on a journey, **take** *or* **make a trip,** gad around *or* about, junket, go on a junket; campaign, go overseas, go on an expedition, go on safari; go on a sight-seeing trip, sight-see, rubberneck <nonformal>

**tourist** NOUNS **traveler,** sightseer, excursionist, rubberneck *or* rubbernecker <nonformal>

**tournament** NOUNS tourney, gymkhana, **field day;** rally; **regatta**

**tout** NOUNS 1 **booster** <nonformal>, puffer, promoter; plugger *and* touter <both nonformal>; pitchman, barker, spieler; **tipster** <nonformal>, dupester <nonformal>
VERBS 2 boost *and* give a boost to <both nonformal>, puff, promote, cry up; plug *and* hype; pour *or* spread *or* lay it on thick <all nonformal>; make a pitch for <nonformal>

**tow** VERBS **pull,** draw, heave, haul, hale, lug, **tug,** take in tow

**tower** NOUNS 1 **turret,** *tour* <Fr>; campanile, bell tower, belfry; **spire,** church spire; **lighthouse,** light tower; martello, martello tower; observation tower, fire tower; antenna tower; water tower, standpipe; Texas tower
VERBS 2 **soar,** spire; **rise,** uprise, ascend, mount, rear

**town** NOUNS 1 township; market town <Brit>; small town; twin town; boom town, ghost town
ADJS 2 **urban,** metropolitan, municipal, metro, burghal, **civic,** oppidan; small-town; boom-town

**toxic** ADJS **poisonous,** toxicant; **venomous,** envenomed, venenate, venenous; veneniferous, toxiferous; **virulent,** noisome, noxious, malignant, malign, destructive, deadly; mephitic, miasmal, miasmic, miasmatic

**toy** NOUNS 1 **plaything,** bauble, knickknack, gimcrack, gewgaw, kickshaw, whim-wham, folderol
ADJS 2 **miniature,** diminutive, minuscule, minuscular, mini, micro, miniaturized, subminiature, **small-scale,** minimal; pony, bantam

**trace** NOUNS 1 **essence,** definite odor, redolence, effluvium, emanation, exhalation, fume, breath, subtle odor, whiff, detectable odor; trail, spoor; **hint,** *soupçon* <Fr>, suspicion, suggestion, intimation, vestige; **touch,** dash, **smattering,** sprinkling; tinge, tincture
VERBS 2 **represent,** delineate, limn, draw; trace out, trace over; **sketch,** draft, outline
3 **search out,** hunt out, spy out, scout out, **ferret out,** fish out, pry out

**track** NOUNS 1 **trail,** path, course, *piste* <Fr>, line, wake; vapor trail, contrail, condensation trail; **spoor,** signs, traces, **scent**
VERBS 2 **traverse,** cross, travel over *or* through, pass through, **go** *or* **pass over,** cover, measure, transit, range, range over *or* through, course, peregrinate, overpass, go over the ground; patrol, reconnoiter, scout; sweep, go *or* make one's rounds, scour, scour the country
3 **hunt,** go hunting, hunt down, chase, run, shikar <India>, sport; trail; **stalk,** prowl after, still-hunt; hound, dog; **follow** *or* **go after, follow up,** trail, come close on *or* tread on the heels of, dog the footsteps of

**track record** NOUNS **qualification,** qualifiedness, credentials, record

**tract** NOUNS 1 **plot,** plot of ground *or* land, parcel of land, plat, **patch,** field; lot; section <square mile>, forty <sixteenth of a section>; real estate
2 **booklet,** pamphlet, brochure, chapbook, leaflet, folder; **treatise,** piece, treatment, handling, tractate

**traction** NOUNS **pulling,** drawing, draft, dragging, heaving, tugging, towing; **purchase,** hold, **foothold,** toehold, footing

**trade** NOUNS 1 **vocation,** occupation, business, work, line, line of work, line of business *or* endeavor; racket *and* game <both nonformal>
2 **trading,** doing business, trafficking; horse trading <nonformal>, **dealing,** deal-making, wheeling and dealing <nonformal>
VERBS 3 **deal,** traffic, truck, buy and sell, do business; barter; speculate, venture, operate, **play the market,** buy *or* sell *or* deal in futures; arbitrage; **swap** <nonformal>, **switch**
ADJS 4 **commercial,** business, trading, **mercantile,** merchant; commercialistic, mercantilistic

**tradition** NOUNS **custom,** immemorial usage; ancient wisdom, ways of the fathers; traditionalism *or* traditionality; lore, folklore

**traditional** ADJS **legendary,** unwritten, oral, handed down; true-blue, tried and true; **prescriptive,** customary, conventional, understood, admitted, recognized, acknowledged, received; **hallowed,** time-honored, immemorial; **venerable,** hoary, worshipful; **longstanding,** of long standing, long-established, established, fixed, inveterate, rooted; folkloric

**traffic** NOUNS **commerce,** trade, truck, intercourse, **dealing,** dealings; **business,** business dealings *or* affairs *or* relations, commercial affairs *or* relations

**tragedy** NOUNS 1 tragic drama; tragic flaw; buskin, cothurnus; tragic muse, Melpomene
2 **disaster,** calamity, catastrophe, meltdown, cataclysm**; shock,** blow, hard *or* nasty *or* staggering blow; **accident,** casualty, collision, crash, plane *or* car crash; **wreck,** shipwreck; smash *and* smashup *and* crack-up *and* pileup <all nonformal>

**tragic** ADJS **disastrous,** calamitous, catastrophic, cataclysmic, cataclysmal, **ruinous,** fatal, dire, black, woeful, sore, baneful, grievous; destructive

**trail** NOUNS 1 **path,** track, pathway, footpath, footway, *piste* <Fr>; **course,** line, wake; vapor trail, contrail, condensation trail; **spoor,** signs, traces, **scent**
VERBS 2 **follow,** go after *or* behind, come after *or* behind, move behind; **pursue,** shadow *and* tail <both nonformal>, trail after, follow on the trail of, follow *or* tread *or* step on the heels of, follow in the steps *or* footsteps *or* footprints of, tread close upon, breathe down the neck of, sit on the tail of, tailgate <nonformal>, bring up the rear, eat the dust of, take *or* swallow one's dust; tag *and* tag after *and* tag along <all nonformal>; **dog,** bedog, **hound,** chase, get after, take out *or* take off after
3 **bring up the rear,** come last, **follow,** come after; trail behind, lag behind, draggle, **straggle;** fall behind, fall back, fall astern

**train** NOUNS 1 railroad train; choo-choo *and* choo-choo train <both nonformal>; passenger train; aerotrain, bullet train, *train de haute vitesse* <Fr>; local, way train, milk train; express train, express; lightning express, flier, cannonball express <nonformal>; monorail; streamliner; rolling stock
2 **afterpart,** afterpiece; **wake,** trail, queue; body of retainers
VERBS 3 **drill,** exercise; practice, rehearse; keep in practice, keep one's hand in; **prepare,** ready, **condition,** groom, fit, put in tune, form, **lick into shape** <nonformal>; **discipline,** take in hand; put through the mill *or* grind <nonformal>; break, break in, housebreak

**trained** ADJS 1 **conditioned,** seasoned; experienced, **familiarized,** broken-in, oriented, orientated; acclimated, acclimatized; inured, hardened, case-hardened; adapted, adjusted, accommodated; housebroken, potty-trained
2 **skilled,** accomplished; practiced; coached, prepared, primed, finished; at one's best; posted, briefed, primed

**trainee** NOUNS **recruit,** rookie <nonformal>, enrollee, boot <nonformal>; **raw recruit,** tenderfoot; **apprentice,** learner

**traipse** VERBS **go slow** *or* **slowly,** poke, poke along; drag along, drag one's feet, walk, mosey <nonformal>; **saunter,** stroll, amble, waddle, toddle <nonformal>; ambulate

**trait** NOUNS **characteristic,** peculiarity, singularity, particularity, specialty, individualism, **character,** nature, quirk, point of character, bad point, good point, saving grace, redeeming feature, mannerism, keynote, trick, **feature,** distinctive feature

**traitor** NOUNS treasonist, **betrayer,** quisling, rat <nonformal>, serpent, snake, cockatrice, **snake in the grass,** double-crosser <nonformal>, double-dealer; Judas, Judas Iscariot, Benedict Arnold, Quisling, Brutus; **apostate,** turncoat, turnabout, **recreant,** renegade, **defector,** tergiversator, **deserter,** turntail, fifth columnist, collaborationist, collaborator

**tramp** NOUNS 1 **walk,** ramble, amble, **hike,** traipse <nonformal>; slog, trudge, schlep <nonformal>; **stroll,** saunter
2 **bum,** derelict; **good-for-nothing,** good-for-naught, ne'er-do-well, wastrel; drifter, vagrant, hobo, vagabond, stiff *and* bindlestiff <both nonformal>, swagman *or* sundowner <both Austral>
VERBS 3 **plod,** peg, shamble, **trudge,** stump, lumber; plod along, plug along <nonformal>, schlep <nonformal>; **hike,** backpack

**trample** VERBS **run over,** overrun; **ride over,** override, **run down,** ride down; **trample on** *or* **upon,** trample down, tread upon, step on, walk on *or* over, trample underfoot, ride roughshod over

**trance** NOUNS **daze,** stupor; catatonic stupor, catalepsy; cataplexy; dream state, reverie, daydreaming; somnambulism, sleepwalking; hypnotic trance; **ecstasy,** ecstasis, transport, mystic transport; meditation, contemplation; **rapture;** yoga trance, dharana, dhyana, samadhi; hypnosis

**tranquil** ADJS **calm,** halcyon, pacific, peaceable, placid, quiet, **serene,** peaceful; **cool,** coolheaded, cool as a cucumber <nonformal>; reposeful

**tranquilizer** NOUNS **sedative,** sleeping pill *or* tablet, knockout drop *and* Mickey Finn <both nonformal>; drug, dope <nonformal>, narcotic, opiate, calmative

**transact** VERBS **execute,** complete, promulgate, make; **discharge,** fulfill, render, administer; **carry out,** carry through, put through, prosecute; effect, effectuate, set in motion, implement

**transaction** NOUNS business *or* commercial transaction, **deal,** business deal, operation, turn; package deal; **execution,** completion

**transcend** VERBS **excel,** surpass, exceed, get *or* have the ascendancy, get *or* have the edge, have it all over <nonformal>, overcome, overpass, best, **better,** improve on, perfect, go one better <nonformal>; **predominate,** prevail, preponderate; **outweigh,** go beyond, overbalance, overbear

**transcribe** VERBS **write,** copy out, engross, make a fair copy, copy; **adapt,** make an adaptation; transpose

**transfer** NOUNS 1 transference; **conveyance,** conveyancing; **giving**; **delivery,** deliverance; **assignment,** assignation; **consignment,** consignation; **exchange,** barter, trading
VERBS 2 **transmit,** transpose, translocate, metathesize, switch; **transplant,** translate; **pass,** pass over, **hand over,** turn over, carry over, make over, consign, assign; deliver; communicate, diffuse, disseminate, spread, impart; transfuse, perfuse, transfer property *or* right

**transfix** VERBS 1 **stab,** stick, pink, run through; transpierce, fix, **impale,** spit, skewer; gore, spear, lance, spike, needle
2 **immobilize,** freeze, keep, retain; stick, hold, pin *or* nail down <nonformal>; captivate, engross, enthrall, fascinate, spellbind

**transform** VERBS **transfigure,** transmute, transmogrify; **translate;** transubstantiate, metamorphose; **do over,** redo, make over, rejigger <nonformal>; **change,** change into, turn into, become, resolve into, assimilate to, bring to, reduce to

**transgress** VERBS **violate,** break, breach; infringe, overstep, overstep the bounds, trespass, contravene, trample on *or* upon; **do wrong,** misbehave, **err,** offend; **sin,** commit sin; disobey the law, offend against the law, flout the law, make a mockery of the law, fly in the face of the law

**transient** NOUNS 1 transient guest *or* boarder, temporary lodger; **sojourner;** passer, passerby; **wanderer; vagabond,** drifter, derelict, homeless person, tramp, hobo, bum <nonformal>
ADJS 2 **transitory,** transitive; **temporary,** temporal; **impermanent,** unenduring, undurable, nondurable, nonpermanent; frail, brittle, fragile, insubstantial; changeable, **mutable,** unstable, inconstant; capricious, fickle, impulsive, impetuous; **short-lived,** ephemeral, fly-by-night, evanescent, volatile, momentary; **passing,** fleeting, flitting, flying, fading, dying; fugitive, fugacious; perishable, mortal

**transition** NOUNS **change,** switch, switchover, changeover, turn, turnabout, about-face, **reversal,** flip-flop <nonformal>; apostasy, defection, change of heart; **shift,** modulation, qualification; transit, passage

**translate** VERBS **render,** transcribe, transliterate, put *or* turn into, transfuse the sense of; construe; **transform,** transfigure, transmute, transmogrify; transubstantiate, metamorphose

**translation** NOUNS 1 transcription, transliteration; **paraphrase,** loose *or* free translation; decipherment, decoding; amplification, restatement, rewording; literal *or* verbal *or* faithful *or* word-for-word translation; **pony** *and* trot *and* crib <all nonformal>; interlinear, interlinear translation, bilingual text *or* edition
2 **apotheosis,** resurrection, gathering, **ascension,** the Ascension; **assumption,** the Assumption; removal to Abraham's bosom

**translucent** ADJS lucent, translucid, lucid, pellucid; semitranslucent, semipellucid

**transmission** NOUNS **transferal,** transfer; transference, transmittal, transmittance; translocation, **transplantation,** translation; communication, spread, spreading, dissemination, diffusion; transduction, conduction, convection; transfusion, perfusion; **radio broadcasting,** AM broadcasting, FM broadcasting, shortwave broadcasting; **gearbox,** automatic transmission, standard transmission, stick shift; synchronized shifting, synchromesh

**transmit** VERBS **transfer,** transpose, translocate, transplace, metathesize, switch; **pass,** pass over, **hand over,** turn over, carry over, make over, consign, assign; deliver; pass on, hand forward, relay; communicate, diffuse, spread, impart; **dispatch,** remit, consign, forward; expedite; **convey,** send, send word, deliver *or* send a signal *or* message, **disseminate,** broadcast, **pass on** *or* **along,** hand on; report, render, make known, get across *or* over

**transparent** ADJS transpicuous, perspicuous, translucent, light-pervious, luminous; show-through, see-through, peekaboo, revealing; **lucid,** pellucid, **clear,** limpid; **crystal-clear,** clear as crystal; **diaphanous,** sheer, thin; **gossamer,** gossamery, filmy, gauzy

**transpire** VERBS 1 **exude,** exudate, transude, reek; **emit, discharge,** give off
2 **occur,** happen, eventuate, **take place,** come *or* go down <nonformal>, go on, be realized, come, **come off** <nonformal>, **come about,** come true, **come to pass,** pass, pass off, go off, fall, **befall,** betide

**transplant** NOUNS 1 **insertion,** introduction, insinuation, injection, infusion, perfusion, inoculation, intromission; graft, grafting, engrafting, transplantation; infixing, implantation, embedment
VERBS 2 **transfer,** transmit, transpose, translocate, transplace, metathesize, switch; translate; **implant,** infix; fit in, **inlay**

**transport** NOUNS 1 **transportation,** conveyance, carrying, bearing, packing, toting *and* lugging <both nonformal>; **hauling,** haulage, portage, porterage, waft, waftage; **shipment,** shipping, transshipment
2 **trance,** ecstasy, ecstasis, mystic transport; **rapture;** yoga trance, dharana, dhyana, samadhi
VERBS 3 **convey,** freight, conduct, **take; carry, bear,** pack, tote *and* lug <both nonformal>, manhandle; lift, waft, whisk, wing, fly
4 **fascinate,** captivate, charm, becharm, spell, spellbind, cast a spell, put under a spell, **beguile,** intrigue, enthrall, infatuate, **enrapture,** enravish, entrance, enchant, witch, **bewitch;** carry away, sweep off one's feet, turn one's head, knock one's socks off <nonformal>

**transpose** VERBS **reverse,** convert; put the cart before the horse; turn into the opposite, turn about, turn the tables, turn the scale *or* balance; rotate, revolve, pronate, supinate, resupinate; **interchange,** exchange, change, counterchange

**transsexual** NOUNS **intersex,** epicene; hermaphrodite, pseudohermaphrodite; androgyne, gynandroid

**transverse** NOUNS 1 **crosspiece,** traverse, transversal, transept, transom; diagonal; **crossbar,** crossarm; oblique, bias, bend <heraldry>, oblique line, slash
ADJS 2 transversal, traverse; **across,** cross, crossway, **crosswise** *or* crossways, thwart, athwart, overthwart; oblique, **diagonal,** catercorner *or* **catercornered** *or* cattycorner *or* catty-cornered *or* kittycorner *or* kittycornered;

slant, bias, biased, biaswise *or* biasways
ADVS 3 **crosswise** *or* crossways *or* crossway, decussatively; **cross,** crisscross, across, thwart, thwartly, thwartways, **athwart,** athwartwise, overthwart; traversely; transversely, transversally; obliquely; **sideways** *or* sidewise

**trap** NOUNS 1 **ambush,** ambushment, **ambuscade,** *guet-apens* <Fr>; surveillance, shadowing; lurking hole *or* place; blind, stalking-horse; booby trap, gin; pitfall, trapfall, deadfall; **booby trap,** mine; decoy
VERBS 2 entrap, gin, catch, catch out, catch in a trap; **ensnare,** snare, hook, **hook in,** sniggle, noose; inveigle; net, mesh, enmesh, ensnarl, wind, tangle, entangle, entoil, enweb; trip, trip up; **set** *or* **lay a trap for,** bait the hook, spread the toils; **lure,** allure, **decoy**

**trappings** NOUNS **harness,** caparison, **tack,** tackle; **belongings,** appurtenances, paraphernalia, appointments, accessories, perquisites, appendages, appanages; **finery,** frippery, gaudery, trumpery, folderol, trickery, festoons, superfluity; **frills,** frills and furbelows, bells and whistles *and* gimmickry *and* Mickey Mouse *and* glitz <all nonformal>

**trash** NOUNS 1 **rubbish, junk,** refuse, waste; **nonsense,** stuff and nonsense, pack of nonsense, **folderol,** balderdash, *niaiserie* <Fr>, flummery, trumpery, vaporing, rant, claptrap, fustian, rodomontade, bombast, absurdity
VERBS 2 **censure,** reprehend; **blame,** lay *or* cast blame upon; **bash** *and* rubbish <both nonformal>; **reproach,** impugn; **denounce,** denunciate, accuse, **decry,** cry down, impeach, arraign, indict, call to account, exclaim *or* declaim *or* inveigh against, raise one's voice against, raise a hue and cry against, reprobate, hold up to reprobation

**trauma** NOUNS **wound,** injury, hurt, lesion; **laceration,** mutilation, abrasion, scuff, scrape, chafe, gall; **psychological stress,** stress; psychological *or* emotional trauma, traumatism, mental *or* emotional shock

**traumatic** ADJS **impaired,** damaged, hurt, injured, harmed; deteriorated, worsened, cut to the quick, aggravated, exacerbated, irritated, embittered; **damaging,** injurious, degenerative

**travel** NOUNS 1 traveling, going, journeying, touring, moving, **movement,** motion, locomotion, transit, progress, passage, course, crossing; world travel, globe-trotting <nonformal>; junketing; **tourism,** touristry
VERBS 2 **go,** move, pass, fare, wayfare, fare forth, fetch, flit, hie, sashay <nonformal>; progress; move on *or* along, go along; wend, **wend one's way;** betake oneself, direct one's course, bend one's steps *or* course; course, run, flow, stream; **journey,** make *or* take *or* go *or* go on a journey, **take** *or* **make a trip,** navigate, trek, jaunt, peregrinate; junket, go on a junket; tour

**travesty** NOUNS **exaggeration, burlesque,** lampoon, squib, **parody,** satire, farce, mockery, imitation, wicked imitation *or* pastiche, takeoff <nonformal>, **caricature**

**treacherous** ADJS **perfidious,** falsehearted; **shifty,** slippery, tricky; **double-dealing,** double, ambidextrous; two-faced; **unsafe,** unhealthy <nonformal>; **unreliable,** undependable, untrustworthy, **insecure,** unsound, unstable, unsteady, shaky, tottery, rocky

**treachery** NOUNS treacherousness; **perfidy,** perfidiousness, falseheartedness, two-facedness, doubleness; **duplicity,** double-dealing, foul play, dirty work *and* dirty pool *and* dirty trick *and* dirty game <all nonformal>

**tread** NOUNS 1 **gait,** pace, walk, stride; **step,** stair, footstep, rest, footrest, steppingstone
VERBS 2 **walk,** ambulate, **step,** pace, stride, pad; **stamp,** stomp <nonformal>, trample, clump, clop

**treason** NOUNS petty treason, misprision of treason, high treason; lese majesty, sedition; fifth-column activity; collaboration; apostasy, renunciation, **defection, desertion,** crossing-over, abandonment

**treasure** NOUNS 1 **wealth,** riches, opulence *or* opulency, luxuriousness; **fortune,** handsome fortune; full *or* heavy *or* well-lined *or* bottomless *or* fat *or* bulging purse, deep pockets <nonformal>; money to burn <nonformal>; substance, **assets,** resources, total assets, worth, net worth, **pecuniary resources,** means, available means *or* resources *or* funds, cash flow, wherewithal, command of money

2 **good thing,** a thing to be desired; gem, jewel, diamond, pearl; boast, pride, pride and joy
VERBS 3 **value, esteem,** prize, appreciate, **rate highly,** think highly of, think well of, **think much of,** set store by; give *or* attach *or* ascribe importance to; make much of, make a fuss *or* stir about, make an ado *or* much ado about; hold up as an example

**treasury** NOUNS **treasure house;** depository, repository; storehouse; **strongbox,** safe, money chest, coffer, locker, chest; **public treasury,** public funds, taxpayer funds *or* money, pork barrel, public crib *or* trough *or* till <nonformal>

**treat** NOUNS 1 **delicacy,** dainty, goody <nonformal>, kickshaw, **tidbit,** titbit; **morsel,** choice morsel, *bonne bouche* <Fr>; **regalement,** regale; **feast,** banquet, Lucullan feast; feast *or* banquet of the soul; **standing treat,** picking up the check *or* tab <nonformal>; paying the bills
VERBS 2 **doctor,** minister to, care for, give care to, physic; nurse; **cure,** remedy, heal; **handle,** manage, use, **deal with, cope with,** come to grips with, take on, tackle <nonformal>, contend with, do with
3 treat to, **stand treat,** go treat, pick up the check *or* tab <nonformal>, pay the bill, set up, blow to <nonformal>; stand drinks; maintain, support; subsidize

**treatise** NOUNS piece, treatment, handling, tractate, tract; examination, survey, **discourse,** discussion, disquisition, descant, exposition, screed; dissertation, **thesis;** pandect; excursus; **study,** lucubration, étude; **paper,** research paper; monograph

**treatment** NOUNS 1 medical treatment *or* attention *or* care; **cure,** curative measures; medication; **regimen,** regime, protocol; **usage,** handling, management; way *or* means of dealing; processing
2 **discussion,** consideration, investigation, **examination,** study, analysis, logical analysis; **technique,** draftsmanship, brushwork, painterliness

**treaty** NOUNS international agreement, *entente, entente cordiale* <both Fr>, concord, concordat, cartel, convention, paction, capitulation; **alliance,** league; nonaggression pact, mutual-defense treaty

**trek** NOUNS 1 **journey,** trip, *jornada* <Sp>, peregrination, sally; migration, transmigration
VERBS 2 **journey,** travel, make *or* take *or* go *or* go on a journey, **take** *or* **make a trip,** migrate, transmigrate

**tremble** NOUNS 1 **quiver,** quaver, shiver, shudder, twitter, tremble, flutter
VERBS 2 **shake,** quake, shiver, quiver, quaver; tremble *or* quake *or* shake in one's boots *or* shoes, tremble like an aspen leaf, shake all over

**tremendous** ADJS **huge,** immense, vast, enormous, astronomic, astronomical, humongous *and* jumbo <both nonformal>, prodigious, stupendous; magnificent, splendid, splendiferous, **marvelous,** wonderful, glorious, divine, heavenly, terrific, sensational

**tremor** NOUNS **shake,** quake, quiver, quaver, falter, **tremble,** shiver, shudder, twitter, didder, dither; **shock,** jolt, jar, jostle; **bounce,** bump

**trench** NOUNS **trough,** channel, ditch, entrenchment, fosse, **canal,** cut, gutter; moat; sunk fence, ha-ha; slit trench

**trend** NOUNS 1 **fashion,** style, mode, vogue, prevailing taste; current *or* stream of fashion; height of fashion; the new look, the season's look; high fashion, *haute couture* <Fr>
2 **drift,** course, current, *Tendenz* <Ger>, flow, stream, mainstream, main current, movement, glacial movement, motion, run, **tenor,** tone, **the way things go,** trend of the times, spirit of the age *or* time, time spirit, *Zeitgeist* <Ger>; the way it looks

**trendy** ADJS **fashionable,** in fashion, smart, in style, in vogue; all the rage, all the thing; **popular,** prevalent, current; **up-to-date,** up-to-datish, up-to-the-minute, switched-on *and* hip *and* with-it <all nonformal>, **in the swim;** sought-after, much sought-after; **faddish,** faddy <nonformal>

**trespass** VERBS **encroach,** infringe, impinge, trespass on *or* upon, invade, infiltrate; **transgress,** disobey the law, flout the law, **overstep,** intrude, break bounds, overstep the bounds, go too far, know no bounds

**trial** NOUNS 1 **tribulation,** trials and tribulations; **ordeal,** fiery ordeal, the iron entering the soul; cross, curse, blight, **affliction**; plight, predicament
2 **test,** *concours* and *rencontre* <both

Fr>; **experiment,** experimentation; testing, trying, trying-out
3 **jury trial,** trial by jury, trial at the bar, **hearing,** inquiry, inquisition, inquest, assize; court-martial
ADJS 4 venturesome, willing; determined, resolute; **experimental,** test; testing, proving, trying; probative, probatory, verificatory; **tentative,** provisional; empirical; trial-and-error, hit-or-miss, cut-and-try; heuristic

**tribe** NOUNS **race,** people, **folk,** family, house, clan, nation; strain, line; patriclan, matriclan, deme, sept, gens, phyle, phratry, totem

**tribunal** NOUNS **forum,** board, curia, Areopagus; judicature, judicatory, judiciary; council; inquisition, the Inquisition

**tribute** NOUNS 1 **praise,** homage, meed of praise; congratulation; adulation, lionizing, hero worship; **citation,** eulogy, kudos, **accolade**
2 **tax,** taxation, duty, taxes, rates <Brit>, contribution, **assessment,** revenue enhancement, cess <Brit>, **levy,** toll, impost, imposition

**trick** NOUNS 1 **artifice,** device, ploy, gambit, stratagem, **scheme,** design, *ficelle* <Fr>, **subterfuge,** blind, ruse, wile, **dodge,** artful dodge, sleight, pass, feint, fetch, chicanery; **knack,** art, hang, way; **prank,** practical joke, waggish trick, *espièglerie* <Fr>, antic, caper, frolic; monkeyshines *and* shenanigans <both nonformal>
2 **shift,** work shift, **tour,** tour of duty, stint, bit, **watch,** time, **turn,** relay, spell *or* turn of work; day shift, night shift, swing shift, graveyard shift <nonformal>, dogwatch, lobster trick
VERBS 3 **play a practical joke,** play tricks *or* pranks, **play a joke** *or* **trick on,** make merry with; spoof *and* kid *and* put one on <all nonformal>; **clown around,** pull a stunt *or* trick; pull one's leg <nonformal>

**trickle** NOUNS 1 tricklet, **dribble,** drip, dripping, drop, spurtle; percolation, leaching, lixiviation; seeping, seepage; **handful,** scattering, sprinkling
VERBS 2 **dribble,** dripple, **drip,** drop, spurtle; **filter,** percolate, leach, lixiviate; seep, weep

**tricky** ADJS 1 **fraudulent,** sharp, guileful, insidious, slippery, slippery as an eel, **shifty,** trickish, cute, finagling, chiseling <nonformal>; **cunning,** artful, gimmicky <nonformal>, **wily,** crafty; calculating, scheming
2 **difficult,** difficile; **not easy,** no picnic; wicked *and* mean *and* hairy <all nonformal>, **formidable;** delicate, ticklish, sticky <nonformal>, critical, easier said than done, like pulling teeth; exacting, demanding

**trifle** NOUNS **triviality,** oddment, bagatelle, fribble, **gimcrack,** gewgaw, frippery, **trinket,** bibelot, curio, **bauble,** gaud, toy, **knickknack,** knickknackery, kickshaw, folderol; hill of beans <nonformal>, molehill

**trifle with** VERBS show disrespect for, **show a lack of respect for,** be disrespectful, treat with disrespect, be overfamiliar with; make bold *or* free with, take a liberty, take liberties with, play fast and loose with

**trigger** NOUNS 1 **immediate cause,** proximate cause, spark; ultimate cause, immanent cause, causing cause, *causa causans* <L>; provocation, **last straw,** straw that broke the camel's back
VERBS 2 **cause,** be the cause of, **give rise to,** spark, spark off, set off, trigger off

**trill** VERBS **ripple,** babble, burble, bubble, **gurgle,** guggle, purl; **warble,** sing, call; chirr, roll; **twitter,** tweet, twit, chatter, chitter

**trim** NOUNS 1 **ornamentation,** decoration, **adornment,** embellishment, embroidery, elaboration; trimming
VERBS 2 **ornament,** decorate, adorn, dress, garnish, array
3 **mark down,** cut prices, cut, slash, shave, pare, underprice, knock the bottom out of <nonformal>
4 **shorten,** abbreviate, cut short, **crop,** prune, dock, shear, mow, clip
ADJS 5 **shapely,** well-shaped, well-proportioned, well-made, **well-formed,** well-favored; neat, spruce, clean, clean-cut, clean-limbed
6 **tidy,** natty, neat, spruce, sleek, slick *and* slick as a whistle <nonformal>, smart, snug, tight, **shipshape,** well-kept, well-cared-for, well-groomed; neat as a button *or* pin <nonformal>

**trinket** NOUNS gewgaw, **knickknack** *or* nicknack, knack <old>, **gimcrack,** kickshaw, whim-wham, **bauble,** fribble, bibelot, toy, gaud

**trip** NOUNS 1 **journey,** *jornada* <Sp>, peregrination, sally, trek; **tour,** grand tour; **conducted tour,** package tour *or*

holiday; **excursion,** jaunt, junket, outing, pleasure trip; sight-seeing trip *or* tour; day-trip; **cruise,** package cruise, cruise to nowhere
VERBS 2 **tumble,** fall, fall down, come *or* fall *or* get a cropper <nonformal>, take a fall *or* tumble, take a flop *or* spill <nonformal>, precipitate oneself; fall over, tumble over, trip over; **take a header** <nonformal>; fall prostrate, fall flat, fall on one's face, fall flat on one's ass <nonformal>; **stumble,** stagger, totter, careen, flounder

**trite** ADJS corny *and* square *and* square-John *and* Clyde <all nonformal>, fade, **banal,** unoriginal, platitudinous, **stereotyped,** stock, set, **commonplace,** common, truistic, twice-told, **familiar,** bromidic <nonformal>, old hat <nonformal>, back-number, bewhiskered, warmed-over, **cut-and-dried;** hackneyed, **stale,** musty, fusty; **worn,** time-worn, well-worn, moth-eaten, threadbare, **worn thin**

**triumph** NOUNS 1 **great success,** resounding triumph, brilliant success, striking success, meteoric success; **victory,** conquest, subduing, subdual; a feather in one's cap <nonformal>
VERBS 2 **prevail, be victorious,** come out ahead, come out on top <nonformal>, clean up; **win** *or* **carry** *or* **gain the day,** win the battle, come out first, finish in front, make a killing <nonformal>; **win the prize,** win the palm *or* laurels, take the cake <nonformal>
3 **exult,** glory, delight, joy, jubilate; **crow** *or* crow over, **gloat,** gloat over

**triumphant** ADJS **victorious,** triumphal, **winning,** prevailing; conquering, vanquishing, defeating, overcoming; ascendant, in the ascendant, in ascendancy, sitting on top of the world *and* sitting pretty <both nonformal>, dominant; flushed with success *or* victory

**trivial** ADJS **insignificant,** inconsiderable, inconsequential, negligible, no great shakes; unimportant, no skin off one's nose *or* ass; trifling, nugacious, nugatory, petty, mean, niggling, picayune *or* picayunish, nickel-and-dime *and* penny-ante *and* Mickey-Mouse *and* chickenshit <all nonformal>

**trolley** NOUNS **streetcar,** trolley car, **tram** *or* tramcar <both Brit>; electric car, electric <nonformal>; trolley bus, trackless trolley; horsecar

**trollop** NOUNS **strumpet,** wench, hussy, slut, jade, baggage, *cocotte* <Fr>, grisette; **tart** *and* **chippy** *and* **floozy** <all nonformal>, drab, trull, harridan, Jezebel, wanton, whore <nonformal>, **loose woman,** easy woman <nonformal>, easy lay <nonformal>, woman of easy virtue, frail sister

**trophy** NOUNS 1 laurel, **laurels,** bays, palm, palms, crown, chaplet, wreath, garland, **feather in one's cap** <nonformal>; prize, plum; **cup,** loving cup, pot <nonformal>; **belt,** championship belt, black belt, brown belt, etc; banner, flag
2 **memento,** remembrance, token, souvenir, keepsake, relic, favor, token of remembrance

**troubadour** NOUNS **minstrel,** ballad singer, balladeer, **bard,** rhapsode, rhapsodist; wandering *or* strolling minstrel, trovatore, trouveur, *trouvère* <Fr>, minnesinger, *Meistersinger* <Ger>, scop, gleeman, jongleur

**trouble** NOUNS 1 **inconvenience,** bother; encumbrance, cumbrance; difficulty; **the matter;** headache <nonformal>, problem, besetment, **inconvenience,** disadvantage; the bad part, the downside <nonformal>
VERBS 2 beset; **bother,** pother, get one down, <nonformal>, **disturb,** perturb, irk, plague, **torment,** drive one up the wall <nonformal>, give one gray hair, make one lose sleep; inconvenience, **put out,** put out of the way, discommode; **concern,** worry; **puzzle,** perplex; give one a hard time *and* give one a bad time *and* make it tough for <all nonformal>; be too much for

**troublemaker** NOUNS **instigator,** inciter, **provoker,** *provocateur* <Fr>, *agent provocateur* <Fr>, catalyst; **agitator,** fomenter, inflamer; agitprop; **rabble-rouser,** firebrand, incendiary; seditionist, seditionary; mischief-maker, ringleader

**troubleshooter** NOUNS **mender, fixer,** doctor <nonformal>, restorer, renovator, repairer, **repairman, repairwoman,** maintenance man *or* woman, **serviceman, servicewoman;** trouble man <nonformal>; Mr Fixit *and* little Miss Fixit <both nonformal>

**trough** NOUNS **trench,** channel, ditch, fosse, **canal,** cut, gutter

**trounce** VERBS **best,** beat, beat out, defeat; beat all hollow <nonformal>, clobber *and* take to the cleaners *and* smoke *and* skin *and* skin alive <all nonformal>, worst, whip *and* lick *and* have it all over *and* cut down to size <all nonformal>; **smite,** thump, baste, **pummel,** pommel, **drub,** buffet, belabor, lay on

**troupe** NOUNS **company,** acting company; repertory company, stock company; circus troupe

**trousers** NOUNS **pants,** pair of trousers *or* pants, **breeches,** britches <nonformal>, breeks <Scots>, **pantaloons,** jeans, slacks

**trousseau** NOUNS **wardrobe,** wedding clothes, bridal outfit

**trove** NOUNS **find,** finding, **discovery;** *trouvaille* <Fr>; treasure trove, buried treasure; **windfall,** windfall money, found money, money in the bank

**truce** NOUNS **armistice,** peace; pacification, suspension of hostilities, **cease-fire,** stand-down, breathing spell, cooling-off period; temporary arrangement, *modus vivendi* <L>; hollow truce, *pax in bello* <L>

**truck** NOUNS 1 lorry <Brit>, *camion* <Fr>; trailer truck, truck trailer, tractor trailer, semitrailer, rig *and* semi <both nonformal>; eighteen-wheeler <nonformal>
2 **dealings,** dealing, traffic, social intercourse; **commerce,** trade, intercourse, business, business dealings *or* affairs *or* relations, commercial affairs *or* relations

**true** ADJS **truthful;** in conformity with the facts *or* the evidence *or* reality, on the up-and-up *or* strictly on the up-and-up <nonformal>; gospel, **hard,** cast-iron; **factual,** actual, effectual, **historical,** documentary; objectively true; **certain,** undoubted, unquestionable; unrefuted, unconfuted, undenied; categorically true

**trumpet** VERBS **proclaim,** cry, cry out, **promulgate,** give voice to; blare forth *or* abroad, thunder, declaim, trumpet *or* thunder forth, shout from the housetops; celebrate, sing the praises of

**trust** NOUNS 1 investment company; investment trust, holding company; trust fund; blind trust
2 **belief,** credence, credit, faith
VERBS 3 **believe,** credit, accept, receive, buy <nonformal>; give credit *or* credence to, give faith to, put faith in, take stock in *or* set store by <nonformal>, take to heart, attach weight to; **confide in,** rely on, depend on, repose, place trust *or* confidence in, have confidence in, **trust in,** trust utterly *or* implicitly, deem trustworthy, think reliable *or* dependable, take one's word, take at one's word

**trustworthy** ADJS **trusty,** trustable, faithworthy, **reliable,** dependable, responsible, straight <nonformal>, sure, to be trusted, **to be depended** *or* **relied upon,** to be counted *or* reckoned on, as good as one's word; tried, true, **tried and true,** tested, proven

**truth** NOUNS 1 **trueness, verity,** veridicality, conformity to fact *or* reality *or* the evidence *or* the data, simple *or* unadorned truth, very truth; historical truth, **objective truth,** actuality, historicity, impersonality; **fact,** actuality, reality, the real world, the truth

2 <nonformal> **what's what,** how it is, how things are, like it is, where it's at, dinkum oil <Austral>, the straight of it, the straight goods *or* skinny *or* scoop, the honest-to-God truth, God's truth, the real thing, the very model, the genuine article, the very thing, it, the article, the goods, the McCoy, the real McCoy, chapter and verse, the gospel, the gospel truth, the lowdown, the skinny

**try** NOUNS 1 **test,** trial; essay; acid test, litmus *or* litmus-paper test; ordeal, crucible; probation
VERBS 2 **attempt,** essay; try one's hand *or* wings; **undertake,** approach, come to grips with, engage, take the bull by the horns; venture, venture on *or* upon, chance
3 try a case, conduct a trial, **hear,** give a hearing to, sit on; **judge,** sit in judgment

**trying** ADJS **oppressive,** burdensome, crushing, onerous, heavy, weighty; **harsh,** wearing, wearying, exhausting, grueling

**tryout** NOUNS workout, **rehearsal,** practice; **dry run,** dummy run; road test; **trial run,** practical test; shakedown, shakedown cruise, bench test; flight test, test flight *or* run; audition, hearing

**tryst** NOUNS **rendezvous,** assignation, meeting; trysting place, meeting place, place of assignation; assignation house; love nest <nonformal>

**tub** NOUNS **bath,** bathtub; bidet; washtub, washpot, washing pot, wash boiler

**tube** NOUNS **pipe; tubing,** piping, tubulation; tubulure
**tubular** ADJS tubate, tubiform, tubelike, pipelike; cylindrical; tubed, piped; tube-shaped
**tuft** NOUNS **flock,** fleck; forelock, widow's peak, quiff <Brit>, fetlock, cowlick; goatee; **crest,** topknot; panache; **clump,** tussock, hassock
**tug** NOUNS 1 **pull,** draw, heave, haul, a long pull and a strong pull, strain, drag
VERBS 2 **pull,** draw, heave, haul, hale, lug, **tow,** take in tow; **drag,** man-haul, draggle, snake <nonformal>; troll, trawl
**tumble** NOUNS 1 **fall,** *culbute* <Fr>, cropper *and* **spill** <both nonformal>, **flop** <nonformal>; **header** <nonformal>; sprawl; pratfall <nonformal>; **stumble,** trip; **dive,** plunge
VERBS 2 **fall,** fall down, take a fall *or* tumble, take a flop *or* spill <nonformal>, precipitate oneself; fall over, tumble over, trip over; **sprawl,** sprawl out, take a pratfall <nonformal>, spread-eagle <nonformal>, fall headlong, **take a header** <nonformal>; fall on one's face, fall flat on one's ass <nonformal>; **fall over,** topple down *or* over; **topple,** lurch, pitch, **stumble,** stagger, totter, careen, list, tilt, trip, flounder
**tumor** NOUNS **growth,** neoplasm; intumescence; benign tumor, nonmalignant tumor; malignant tumor, malignant growth, metastatic tumor, **cancer,** sarcoma, carcinoma
**tumult** NOUNS **commotion,** hubbub, Babel, turmoil, **uproar,** racket, riot, **disturbance,** rumpus <nonformal>, ruckus *and* ruction <both nonformal>
**tune** NOUNS 1 **air,** aria, **melody,** line, melodic line, refrain, note, **song,** lay, descant, lilt
VERBS 2 **tune up,** attune, atone, chord, **put in tune;** voice, string; tone up, tone down
**tunnel** NOUNS 1 **burrow,** earth, run, couch, lodge, warren; railroad tunnel, vehicular tunnel
VERBS 2 **dig,** excavate, **drill;** pierce to the depths; **trench,** burrow; drive sink, lower; **mine,** sap; drill, bore
**turbulent** ADJS **tumultuous,** tempestuous, boisterous, clamorous, uproarious; **agitated;** raging, chaotic, hellish, anarchic; **turbid,** roily
**turf** NOUNS 1 **sod,** sward, greensward
2 **field,** sphere, profession, province, bailiwick, area, discipline, orb, orbit, realm, arena, home turf, stamping ground, territory, domain, walk
**turkey** NOUNS 1 gobbler, turkey gobbler; turkey-cock, tom, tom turkey; hen turkey
2 failure, **flop** *and* bomb <both nonformal>
**turmoil** NOUNS **disorderliness,** unruliness, **disorder,** disruption, confusion, chaos; **commotion,** hubbub, Babel, tumult, disturbance
**turn** NOUNS 1 **start,** shock, jar, jolt
2 **crook,** warp, twist, skew, slue, **veer,** sheer, **swerve,** lurch
3 **aptitude,** bent, propensity, **leaning,** inclination, **turn of mind,** mind, **tendency,** grain, vein
VERBS 4 **turn round** *or* **around** *or* **about,** make a U-turn, turn on a dime, turn tail, **come** *or* **go about,** put about, fetch about; veer, veer around; **swivel,** pivot, pivot about, swing, round, swing round; wheel, wheel about, whirl, spin; heel, turn upon one's heel; **rotate,** revolve, **go round** *or* **around,** spiral, gyrate, gyre; circumrotate, circumvolute; circle
**turn down** VERBS **refuse,** decline, refuse consent, **reject,** decline to accept, **not have,** not buy <nonformal>; vote down, **turn thumbs down on;** turn one's back on, turn a deaf ear to, set oneself against, harden one's heart, resist entreaty *or* persuasion; **repudiate,** disallow, disclaim
**turning point** NOUNS **crisis,** critical point, crunch, crucial period, climax, climacteric; hinge, turn, turn of the tide, cusp; decisive moment, defining moment, **moment of truth,** when push comes to shove <nonformal>
**turn off** VERBS **offend,** give offense, **repel,** put off, **revolt,** disgust, nauseate, sicken, make one sick; distract, put off <nonformal>; **shut off,** shut, shut down, close; **phase out,** phase down, taper off, wind up *or* down; **kill, cut,** cut off short, switch off
**turn on** VERBS 1 **rouse, arouse,** raise, raise up, **waken, awaken,** wake up, charge *or* psych *or* pump up <nonformal>, stir, **stir up,** set astir, **pique**
2 **depend,** hang, rest, hinge; **depend on** *or* **upon,** hang on *or* upon, rest on *or* upon, stand on *or* upon, be based on, be contingent on

**turnout** NOUNS **attendance,** frequenting, frequence; number present; box office *and* draw <both nonformal>

**tutor** NOUNS 1 tutorer; **coach,** coacher; **private instructor,** *Privatdocent, Privatdozent* <both Ger>
VERBS 2 **coach; prime,** cram <nonformal>, cram with facts, stuff with knowledge

**TV** NOUNS **television,** video, telly <Brit nonformal>; television set, the small screen *or* the tube <both nonformal>, the boob tube <nonformal>, idiot box <nonformal>

**twang** NOUNS **accent,** regional accent, brogue, burr, drawl, broad accent

**tweak** NOUNS 1 **twitch,** pluck, hitch, wrench, snatch, start, bob
VERBS 2 **twitch,** pluck, snatch, hitch, wrench, snake <nonformal>

**twig** NOUNS sprig, scion, sapling; switch; branch, imp, bough

**twilight** NOUNS 1 **dusk,** evening twilight, crepuscule, crepuscular light, gloam, **gloaming,** glooming; **foredawn,** morning twilight, half-light, glow, first light, **the small hours;** alpenglow

*the dawn's early light*
FRANCIS SCOTT KEY

ADJS 2 **evening,** evensong, vesper, vespertine *or* vespertinal; twilighty, crepuscular; **dusk,** dusky, duskish

**twin** NOUNS 1 **the same,** selfsame, **duplicate,** double, clone *and* cookie-cutter copy <both nonformal>, *Doppelgänger* <Ger>, very image, look-alike, dead ringer <nonformal>, the image of, the picture of, spitting image *and* spit and image <both nonformal>, carbon copy; **equal,** match, mate, fellow, **equivalent,** opposite number, counterpart, coequal, parallel
ADJS 2 **identical,** identic; **same,** selfsame, one, **one and the same,** all the same; **alike,** all alike, like, just alike, exactly alike, like two peas in a pod; **duplicate,** reduplicated, of the same hue *or* stripe

**twine** NOUNS **cord,** line, rope, **string**

**twinge** NOUNS 1 **pang,** twitch, wrench, jumping pain; crick, kink, hitch, cramp *or* cramps; **nip,** thrill, pinch, tweak, bite, prick, **stab,** stitch
VERBS 2 **suffer,** feel pain, feel the pangs, **hurt,** ache, have a misery <nonformal>, ail; **smart,** tingle; thrill, twitch

**twinkle** NOUNS 1 **glitter,** glimmer, shimmer, blink; sparkle, spark; **scintillation,** scintilla; coruscation
2 **instant,** moment, second, **trice,** twinkling, twinkling *or* twinkle of an eye, **wink,** bat of an eye <nonformal>, two shakes of a lamb's tail *and* two shakes *and* shake *and* half a shake *and* **jiffy** *and* jiff *and* half a jiffy <all nonformal>
VERBS 3 **glitter,** glimmer, shimmer, blink, spangle, tinsel, coruscate; **sparkle,** spark, scintillate

**twins** NOUNS pair of twins <nonformal>, identical twins, fraternal twins, exact mates, look-alikes, dead ringers <nonformal>; Tweedledum and Tweedledee, Siamese twins

**twirl** VERBS convolve, **wind,** twine, **twist,** turn, twist and turn; **whirl,** whirligig, **wheel,** reel, spin, spin like a top *or* teetotum, whirl like a dervish

**twist** NOUNS 1 **bias,** bend, **crook,** skew, slue, **veer,** sheer, **swerve,** lurch; **quirk,** kink, crank, quip, trick, mannerism, **crotchet,** conceit, whim, bee in one's bonnet *or* head <nonformal>; **bent,** turn, slant, cast, warp; idiosyncrasy, eccentricity, individualism; strain, streak
VERBS 2 angle, **angle off,** swerve, shoot off at an angle, **veer,** sheer, sway, slue, **skew,** turn, bend, bias; wind, screw, crank
3 **pervert,** falsify, garble, put a false construction upon, give a spin, give a false coloring, color, varnish, slant, strain, torture; put words in someone's mouth; warp, bend, distort
4 **deform,** misshape, torture, disproportion

**twisted** ADJS **distorted,** contorted, warped, crooked; tortuous, labyrinthine; **falsified,** perverted, garbled, slanted, doctored, biased, strained, tortured; misrepresented, misquoted; influenced, swayed

**two-faced** ADJS **deceitful,** false; **false-hearted,** treacherous; sneaky; **cunning,** artful, gimmicky <nonformal>, **wily,** perfidious; **shifty,** slippery, tricky; double-dealing, duplicitous, hypocritical

**two-timer** NOUNS **cheat,** cheater; **traitor,** betrayer, quisling, Judas, double-dealer, **deceiver**

**two-way** ADJS **mutual,** commutual, common, joint, communal, shared, sharing, conjoint; respective

**tycoon** NOUNS **businessman,** businesswoman; big businessman, magnate, baron, king, top executive, business leader; **industrialist,** captain of industry; banker, financier; robber baron

**type** NOUNS 1 **example,** exemplar; **representative,** symbol, emblem, exponent; **exemplification,** illustration, demonstration, explanation; **kind,** sort, ilk, breed of cat <nonformal>, lot <nonformal>
VERBS 2 transcribe, copy out, engross, make a fair copy, copy
3 **classify,** class, assign, designate; **categorize,** put down as, **pigeonhole,** place, **group,** arrange

**typhoon** NOUNS **cyclone,** tornado, twister, rotary storm, *baguio* <Sp>, hurricane, tropical cyclone, tropical storm

**typical** ADJS typic, typal; exemplary, sample; **characteristic,** distinctive, distinguishing, quintessential; **natural,** normal, usual, regular, par for the course <nonformal>; **true to type,** true to form, the nature of the beast <nonformal>; paradigmatic, representative, standard, normative, classic

**typify** VERBS **designate,** specify; denominate, name, denote; **symbolize,** stand for, be taken as

**tyranny** NOUNS **despotism,** fascism, domineering, domination, oppression; heavy hand, high hand, iron hand, iron heel *or* boot

**tyrant** NOUNS **despot,** warlord; **autocrat,** autarch; absolute ruler *or* master *or* monarch, omnipotent *or* all-powerful ruler; **dictator,** duce, führer, commissar, pharaoh, caesar, czar; **oppressor,** hard master, driver, **slave driver,** Simon Legree <Harriet B Stowe>

# U

**ubiquitous** ADJS **omnipresent,** all-present, everywhere; **pervasive,** all-pervading, universal; **returning,** reappearing, revenant

**UFO** NOUNS unidentified flying object; **flying saucer**

**ugly** ADJS **unsightly,** unattractive, unhandsome, unpretty, unlovely, uncomely, inelegant; ugly as sin, ugly as hell; **uglified,** disfigured, defaced, blotted, blemished, marred, spoiled

**ulterior** ADJS 1 **thither,** yonder, yon; **farther,** further, remoter, more distant; **latent,** concealed, hidden

**ultimate** NOUNS 1 **acme of perfection,** pink, pink of perfection, culmination, perfection, height, top, acme, summit, pinnacle, peak, highest pitch, climax, consummation, *ne plus ultra* <L>, **the last word,** a dream come true
ADJS 2 **farthest, furthest,** farthest off, furthermost, extreme, remotest, most distant; **last,** final, terminal; **eventual,** coming

**ultimatum** NOUNS last *or* final word *or* offer, firm bid *or* price, sticking point

**umbrage** NOUNS **offense,** pique; glower, scowl, angry look, dirty look <nonformal>, glare, frown

**umbrella** NOUNS **shade,** shader, **screen,** light shield, curtain, drape, drapery, blind, veil; **awning,** sunblind <Brit>; **sunshade,** parasol, beach umbrella; cover; shadow; protection

**umpire** NOUNS 1 **judge,** judger, adjudicator, justice; arbiter; referee
VERBS 2 **sit in judgment,** hold the scales, hold court; **hear,** give a hearing to; try; **referee,** officiate; arbitrate

**unabashed** ADJS **brazen,** brazenfaced, boldfaced, barefaced, brassy <nonformal>, **bold,** bold as brass <nonformal>, unblushing, aweless, **shameless,** dead *or* lost to shame; **undaunted,** undismayed, uncowed, unintimidated, unawed

**unabated** ADJS **undiminished,** unreduced, unrestricted, unretarded, unmitigated; unquenched, unextinguished

**unable** ADJS **incapable, incompetent,** inefficient, ineffective; **unqualified,** inept, unendowed, ungifted, untalented, **unfit,** unfitted; **outmatched,** out of one's depth, in over one's head, outgunned; **inferior**

**unabridged** ADJS uncondensed, unexpurgated; complete

**unacceptable** ADJS inadmissible, unsuitable, undesirable, **objectionable,** exceptionable, impossible, untenable, indefensible; intolerable, not to be thought of, beyond the pale, **unwelcome,** unwanted

**unaccustomed** ADJS **new,** disaccustomed, **unused,** unwonted; **unused to,** unfamiliar with, unacquainted with, unconversant with, unpracticed, new to, a stranger to

**unadulterated** ADJS **unpolluted,** nonpolluted, untainted, **undefiled;** pure, unspoiled, untouched, intact, virgin, uncorrupted, unsophisticated, unalloyed, untinged, undiluted, unfortified

**unaffected** ADJS 1 **unmoved, untouched,** dry-eyed, unimpressed, unstruck, **unstirred,** unruffled, unanimated, uninspired; **uninfluenced,** unswayed
2 **natural,** inartificial, unartificial; **unpretentious,** unpretending, unassuming, unfeigning, direct, straightforward, honest, candid; innocent, naive

**unafraid** ADJS **unfearing,** unfearful; unapprehensive, undiffident; **confident,** fearless, dauntless, aweless, dreadless; **unfrightened,** unscared, unalarmed, unterrified; **untimid,** untimorous, unshy, unbashful

**unambiguous** ADJS **clear,** crystal-clear, clear as day, clear as the nose on one's face; explicit, express; unmistakable, unequivocal, univocal, unconfused; **loud and clear** <nonformal>

**unanimous** ADJS **solid,** consentaneous, **with one consent** *or* **voice;** unchallenged, uncontroverted, uncontested, unopposed; **of one accord;** like-minded, of one mind, of the same mind; of a piece, **at one,** at one with

**unannounced** ADJS **unexpected,** out of the blue, out of left field *and* from out in left field <both nonformal>; without warning, unheralded

**unanticipated** ADJS **unexpected,** unlooked for, unhoped for, unprepared for, undivined, unguessed, unpredicted, **unforeseen;** without warning, unheralded; **surprising**, startling, electrifying, shocking, nerve-shattering

**unappealing** ADJS **unpleasant,** unpleasing, unenjoyable; displeasing, disagreeable; unlikable, dislikable; **abrasive,** wounding, hostile, unfriendly; **undesirable,** unattractive, unengaging, uninviting, unalluring; **distasteful,** unpalatable

**unappetizing** ADJS **unsavory,** unpalatable, untasteful, untasty, ill-flavored, foul-tasting, **distasteful,** dislikable, unlikable, uninviting, unpleasant, unpleasing, displeasing, disagreeable

**unappreciated** ADJS **disliked,** unvalued, unprized, misprized, undervalued; **despised,** lowly, spat-upon, untouchable; **unpopular,** out of favor, gone begging; misunderstood; unsung, thankless; unwept, unlamented, unmourned

**unapproachable** ADJS 1 **peerless,** matchless, champion; unmatched, unmatchable, unrivaled, unparalleled, **unequaled,** never-to-be-equaled, **unsurpassed,** unexcelled; inimitable, **incomparable,** beyond compare *or* comparison, **unique;** without equal *or* parallel, *sans pareil* <Fr>; in a class by itself, *sui generis* <L>, easily first, *facile princeps* <L>; second to none, *nulli secundus* <L>; **unbeatable,** invincible
2 **out-of-the-way,** godforsaken, back of beyond, upcountry; **out of reach,** forbidding, inaccessible, untouchable, hyperborean, antipodean

**unarguable** ADJS **obvious,** patent, unquestionable, indubitable, indisputable, incontestable, **irrefutable,** unrefutable, incontrovertible, irrefragable, unanswerable, unimpeachable, absolute

**unarmed** ADJS **unprotected,** unshielded, unsheltered, **unguarded,** undefended, unattended, unwatched, unfortified; barehanded, weaponless; **defenseless,** helpless

**unashamed** ADJS **immodest,** unmodest; exhibitionistic; **shameless,** unembarrassed, unabashed, unblushing, **brazen,** brazenfaced, brassy; **forward,** bold, pert, bumptious

**unassuming** ADJS **natural,** unaffected, unpretending, unpretentious, unfeigning, undisguising, undissimulating, undissembling, undesigning; simple

**unattached** ADJS **free;** at liberty, at large, on the loose, unengaged, disengaged, detached, uncommitted, uninvolved, clear, in the clear, footloose, footloose and fancy-free; **separate,** distinct, discrete; unjoined, unconnected, unaccompanied, unattended, unassociated

**unattainable** ADJS **impracticable,** unachievable; unrealizable, insurmountable, unsurmountable, insuperable; **beyond one,** beyond one's power, beyond one's control, out of one's depth, too much for; **unobtainable,** unavailable, unprocurable, unsecurable, not to be had, **not to be had for love or money**

**unauthorized** ADJS **prohibited,** forbidden, *verboten* <Ger>, barred; beyond the pale, off limits, out of bounds; **unsanctioned,** unlicensed; banned, under the ban, **outlawed,** contraband; taboo, tabooed, untouchable; **illegal,** unlawful, illicit

**unavailable** ADJS **inaccessible,** unaccessible; **unreachable,** beyond reach, out of reach; **impenetrable,** impervious; closed to, denied to, lost to, closed forever to; **unobtainable,** unattainable, unprocurable, unsecurable, not to be had, **not to be had for love or money**

**unavoidable** ADJS **inevitable,** necessary, **inescapable,** unpreventable, ineluctable, irrevocable, indefeasible; relentless, inexorable, unyielding, inflexible; **certain,** fateful, **sure,** sure as fate, sure as death, sure as death and taxes; **destined,** fated

**unaware** ADJS **unconscious,** insensible, unknowing, incognizant; mindless, witless; **unmindful,** unwitting, unsuspecting; unperceiving, impercipient, unaware of, in ignorance of, unconscious of, unmindful of, insensible to, out of it <nonformal>, not with it <nonformal>; **blind to,** deaf to, dead to, a stranger to; **off one's guard,** caught napping, caught tripping

**unbalanced** ADJS 1 **ill-balanced,** overbalanced, off-balance, tippy, listing, heeling, leaning, canted, top-heavy; **unstable,** unsteady
2 **insane,** of unsound mind, **demented,** deranged, deluded, disoriented, unhinged, unsettled, distraught, wandering, mazed, crackbrained, brainsick, sick *or* soft in the head, not right, not in one's right mind, bereft of reason, irrational, senseless, witless

**unbearable** ADJS **insufferable,** intolerable, insupportable, unendurable, for the birds <nonformal>, **too much** *or* a bit much <nonformal>, more than flesh and blood can bear, enough to drive one mad, enough to try the patience of Job; **flagrant,** arrant, shocking, shattering, egregious, unconscionable, glaring, stark-staring, **rank,** crass, gross

**unbeatable** ADJS **irresistible; invincible,** indomitable, unconquerable, unsubduable, unyielding, incontestable, more than a match for; overpowering, overwhelming; **peerless,** matchless, champion

**unbecoming** ADJS **indecent,** indelicate, inelegant, indecorous, improper, inappropriate, **unseemly,** indiscreet

**unbefitting** ADJS **inexpedient,** undesirable, inadvisable, counterproductive, impolitic, impolitical, unpolitic, not to be recommended, contraindicated; **ill-advised,** ill-considered, unwise; **unfit,** unfitting, **inappropriate,** unsuitable, unmeet, inapt, inept, unseemly

**unbelievable** ADJS **incredible,** unthinkable, **implausible,** unimaginable, inconceivable, not to be believed, **hard to believe,** beyond belief, unworthy of belief, not meriting *or* not deserving belief, tall <nonformal>; **defying belief,** staggering belief, passing belief; **mind-boggling,** preposterous, absurd, ridiculous, unearthly, ungodly

**unbiased** ADJS **unprejudiced,** unprepossessed, unjaundiced; impartial, even-handed, **fair,** just, equitable, objective, dispassionate, impersonal, detached, disinterested; indifferent, neutral

**unburden** VERBS **lighten,** unload, unfreight, disencumber, disembarrass, ease one's load; **set one's mind at ease** *or* **rest,** set at ease, take a load off one's mind, let one's hair down, pour one's heart out, talk it out, let it all hang out *and* go public <both nonformal>, get it off one's chest

**uncalled-for** ADJS **unwelcome,** unasked, unbidden, uninvited, unasked-for; **disrespectful,** derisive, brash, bluff; **unsolicited,** needless, gratuitous

**uncanny** ADJS **creepy,** spooky, eerie, weird, unearthly, macabre

**uncaring** ADJS **apathetic,** indifferent, unconcerned, **uninterested; careless,** heedless, unheeding, unheedful, disregardful, unsolicitous; tactless, respectless, **thoughtless,** unthinking, inconsiderate, untactful, undiplomatic, mindless of, **unmindful,** forgetful, oblivious

**uncertain** ADJS **unsure; doubting,** agnostic, **skeptical,** unconvinced, unpersuaded; chancy, dicey <Brit>, touch-and-go; **equivocal,** polysemous, inexplicit, imprecise, ambiguous; unpredictable, doubtful, dubious

**unchanging** ADJS **unchangeable,** not to be changed, changeless, unchanged, unvarying, unvariable, **unalterable,** unaltered, unalterative, **immutable,** incommutable, inconvertible, unmodifiable; lasting, unremitting, permanent

**uncharitable** ADJS **unbenevolent,** unbeneficent, unphilanthropic, unaltruistic, ungenerous

**uncharted** ADJS **unknown,** uninvestigated, unexplored; unidentified, unclassified, unfathomed, unplumbed, virgin, untouched; **unfamiliar,** strange

**unchecked** ADJS **unrestrained,** unconstrained, unforced, uncompelled, uncoerced; **uncurbed,** unbridled, unmuzzled; **unreined,** uncontrolled, ungoverned, **unruly;** out of control, out of hand, out of one's power; **abandoned,** intemperate, immoderate, **incontinent,** licentious, loose, wanton, rampant, riotous, wild; irrepressible; lax

**uncivilized** ADJS **barbarous,** barbaric, unchristian; **inhuman,** inhumane, unhuman; fiendish, fiendlike; demoniac *or* demoniacal, diabolic, diabolical, devilish, satanic, hellish, infernal; **unrefined,** unpolished, uncouth, unkempt, uncombed, unlicked; noncivilized

**unclad** ADJS **undressed,** unclothed, unattired, disrobed, ungarmented, undraped, ungarbed, unrobed, unappareled, uncased; half-clothed, *en déshabillé* <Fr>, in dishabille, nudish; low-cut, décolleté, strapless, topless; scantily clad

**unclassified** ADJS **unordered,** orderless, disordered, unorganized, random, entropic, unarranged, ungraded, unsorted; unidentified, uncharted, unfathomed, unplumbed

**unclear** ADJS **indeterminate,** indefinite, undefined, indecisive, vague, misty, hazy, fuzzy, blurred *or* blurry, obscure; opaque, muddy, **clear as mud** *and* clear as ditch water <both nonformal>; **illegible,** unreadable, undecipherable, indecipherable

**unclog** VERBS **unstop,** unblock, clear, unfoul, free; **unplug,** uncork, uncap; crack; **unlock,** unlatch, undo; **purge,** clean *or* scour out, clear off *or* out *or* away, flush out, blow, blow out, sweep out; **open up,** unjam, unbar, loose

**uncomfortable** ADJS **distressed,** afflicted, put-upon, beset, beleaguered; **troubled,** bothered, disturbed, perturbed, disquieted, discomforted, discomposed, agitated; uneasy, ill at ease

**uncommitted** ADJS **neutral,** noncommitted, uninvolved; neither one thing nor the other, neither hot nor cold; **on the fence** *or* **sidelines** <nonformal>, in the middle of the road, centrist, moderate, midway; **independent,** nonpartisan; unaligned, nonaligned; **impartial**

**uncommon** ADJS **marvelous,** wonderful, formidable, exceptional, astonishing, appalling, fabulous, fantastic, incredible, egregious; strange, unusual, almost unheard-of, seldom met with, seldom seen, few and far between; **rare,** scarcer than hen's teeth <nonformal>; not to be had for love or money, not to be had at any price

**uncomplicated** ADJS **uninvolved,** incomplex, straightforward; plain, **simple**, Mickey Mouse <nonformal>, simple as ABC <nonformal>, easy as pie *and* easy as falling off a log <both nonformal>, downhill all the way, like shooting fish in a barrel, like taking candy from a baby

**uncomplimentary** ADJS **disapproving,** disapprobatory, unapproving, **unfavorable,** low, poor, **opposed**, opposing, against, agin <nonformal>, dead set against, death on, down on; unappreciative

**uncompromising** ADJS **unyielding,** unbending, inflexible, hard, hard-line, inelastic, impliable, ungiving, **firm,** stiff, rigid, rigorous, stuffy; **adamant,** adamantine; **immovable,** not to be moved; **unalterable,** unchangeable, immutable; **intransigent,** irreconcilable, hard-shell *and* hard-core <both nonformal>; implacable, inexorable, **relentless,** unrelenting; stern, grim, dour

**unconcerned** ADJS **uninterested,** turned-off, **dispassionate,** insouciant, **careless,** regardless; easygoing; incurious; mindless, **unmindful,** heedless, inattentive, disregardful; **devil-may-care,** reckless, negligent; unsolicitous, unanxious; pococurante, **nonchalant,** inexcitable; **blasé** undiscriminating, casual; **listless,** lackadaisical, sluggish; bovine; numb, **apathetic**

**unconditional** ADJS **unqualified,** unconditioned, **unrestricted,** unhampered, **unlimited,** uncircumscribed, unmitigated, **categorical,** straight, **unreserved,** without reserve; **explicit,** express, unequivocal, clear, unmistakable; **peremptory,** indisputable, **without exception,** admitting no exception; **positive,** absolute, flat, definite, definitive, determinate, decided, decisive, fixed, final, conclusive; **utter,** perfect, downright, outright, out-and-out, straight-out <nonformal>, all-out, flat-out <nonformal>

**unconfirmed** ADJS **unproved,** not proved, unproven, **undemonstrated,** not shown; **untried,** untested; **unsubstantiated,** unattested, **unauthenticated,** unvalidated, uncertified, **unverified; uncorroborated,** unsustained, **unsupported,** unsupported by evidence, **groundless,** without grounds *or* basis, unfounded; **inconclusive,** indecisive; **moot**

**unconscionable** ADJS **flagrant,** arrant, shocking, shattering, egregious, intolerable, unbearable, glaring, stark-staring, **rank,** crass, gross; **conscienceless,** shameless, without shame *or* remorse, **unscrupulous,** unprincipled, unethical, immoral, amoral; **exorbitant,** undue, outrageous, **unreasonable**

**unconscious** NOUNS 1 **subconscious,** subconscious *or* unconscious mind, submerged mind, subliminal, subliminal self; collective unconscious, racial unconscious

ADJS 2 **senseless,** oblivious, comatose, asleep, dead, **dead to the world,** cold, out, **out cold;** half-conscious, semiconscious; drugged, narcotized; **subliminal,** extramarginal; preconscious, foreconscious, coconscious; **unpremeditated,** spontaneous, undesigned, unstudied; **unaware,** insensible, unknowing, incognizant

**uncontested** ADJS **unanimous,** uncontradicted, unchallenged, uncontroverted, unopposed; **undoubted,** unquestioned, undisputed

**uncontrollable** ADJS **ungovernable,** unmanageable, indomitable, untamable, **intractable,** refractory; **recalcitrant,** contumacious; obstreperous, **unruly,** restive, wild, fractious; beyond control, out of hand; **beside oneself,** like one possessed; unstoppable; relentless, inexorable, unyielding, inflexible

**unconventional** ADJS **unorthodox, eccentric,** gonzo <nonformal>, heterodox, heretical; unfashionable, offbeat <nonformal>, way out *and* far out *and* kinky *and* out in left field <all nonformal>, fringy, breakaway, out-of-the-way; original, maverick, Bohemian, beat, hippie, counterculture

**unconvinced** ADJS **uncertain,** unsure; doubting, agnostic, **skeptical,** unpersuaded, unconverted; **hesitant,** hesitating; **indecisive,** incredulous, irresolute; **unbelieving,** disbelieving, nonbelieving

**uncooperative** ADJS **insubordinate,** unsubmissive, indocile, **uncompliant,** noncooperative, noncooperating, intractable; **unhelpful,** unaccommodating, unobliging, disobliging

**uncoordinated** ADJS **clumsy,** awkward, maladroit, unhandy, left-hand, left-handed, heavy-handed, ham-handed <nonformal>, butterfingered <nonformal>, **all thumbs,** fingers all thumbs, with a handful of thumbs

**uncouth** ADJS **unpolished,** uncultivated, uncultured, unrefined; **ungainly,** ungraceful, graceless, inelegant, *gauche* <Fr>; unrefined; **vulgar,** barbarous, barbaric, rude, **crude,** outlandish

**uncover** VERBS **unearth,** dig up, disinter, exhume, excavate; **disclose,** expose, reveal, blow the lid off, crack wide open, **bring to light;** turn up, root up, ferret out, pry out

**uncut** ADJS **complete,** whole, total, global, **entire,** intact, solid; **full,** full-fledged, full-dress, **full-scale;** unabbreviated, undiminished, unexpurgated

**undaunted** ADJS **undismayed,** uncowed, unintimidated, unappalled, unabashed, unawed; **unflinching,** unshrinking, unquailing, uncringing, unwincing, unblinking

**undecided** ADJS **irresolute,** irresolved, unresolved; **indecisive,** undetermined, unsettled, infirm of purpose; dubious, **uncertain**; at loose ends, at a loose end; **of two minds,** in conflict, double-minded, ambivalent; changeable, mutable; capricious, mercurial, fickle; **pending,** depending, contingent, conditional, conditioned; **open,** in question, at issue, **in the balance,** up in the air, up for grabs <nonformal>, **in suspense,** in a state of suspense, suspenseful

**undeclared** ADJS **unexpressed,** unpronounced, **unsaid,** unspoken, unuttered, unvoiced, wordless, silent; **unmentioned,** untalked-of, **untold,** unsung, unproclaimed, unpublished; unwritten, unrecorded

**undefeated** ADJS **unbeaten,** unvanquished, unconquered, unsubdued, unquelled, unbowed

**undemanding** ADJS **unstrict,** unexacting; unsevere, unharsh; lenient; **permissive,** overpermissive, overindulgent, **soft;** easy, easygoing, laid-back <nonformal>; **flexible,** pliant, yielding; **uncritical,** uncriticizing, nonjudgmental

**undeniable** ADJS **obvious,** patent, unquestionable, unexceptionable, self-evident, axiomatic; indubitable, unarguable, indisputable, incontestable, **irrefutable,** unrefutable, incontrovertible, irrefragable, unanswerable, unimpeachable, absolute; admitting no question *or* dispute *or* doubt *or* denial; **demonstrable,** verifiable, testable, confirmable; well-founded, well-established, well-grounded

**underbrush** ADJS **undergrowth,** underwood, copsewood, undershrubs, boscage

**undercover** ADJS 1 **covert,** clandestine, quiet, unobtrusive, hugger-mugger, **surreptitious,** underground, under-the-counter, under-the-table, **cloak-and-dagger,** backdoor, underhand, **underhanded; furtive,** stealthy, privy, backstairs, **sly,** shifty, sneaky, sneaking, skulking, slinking, slinky, feline
ADVS 2 **secretly,** in secret; in the closet; nobody the wiser; **covertly,** *à couvert* <Fr>, under the cloak of; **behind the scenes,** in the background, in a corner, in the dark; *sub rosa* <L>, under the rose; underground; *sotto voce* <Ital>, under the breath, with bated breath, in a whisper

**undercurrent** NOUNS **implication,** connotation, import, latent *or* underlying *or* implied meaning, ironic suggestion *or* implication, more than meets the eye, what is read between the lines; **suggestion,** allusion; coloration, tinge, undertone, overtone, more than meets the eye *or* ear, something between the lines, intimation, touch, nuance, innuendo; **inference,** supposition, presupposition, assumption, presumption; undermeaning, undermention, subsidiary sense, subsense, **subtext**

**undercut** VERBS **disprove, invalidate,**

disconfirm, discredit, prove the contrary, belie, give the lie to; **expose,** show up; explode, blow up, blow sky-high, **puncture,** deflate, shoot *or* poke full of holes, cut to pieces, cut the ground from under; knock the props *or* chocks out from under, cut the ground from under one's feet, not leave a leg to stand on

**undergarments** NOUNS **underclothes,** underclothing, bodywear, **underwear,** undies <nonformal>, skivvies, body clothes, smallclothes, unmentionables <nonformal>, **lingerie,** linen, underlinen

**undergo** VERBS **experience,** have, know, feel, taste; **encounter,** meet, meet with, meet up with <nonformal>, run up against <nonformal>; **go through,** pass through, be subjected to, be exposed to, stand under, labor under, **endure,** suffer, sustain

**underground** NOUNS 1 **irregular,** casual; **guerrilla,** partisan, franctireur; resistance, maquis; *maquisard* <Fr>, underground *or* resistance fighter; fifth column; underground route, underground railroad
ADJS 2 **subterranean,** subterraneous, buried, deep-buried
3 **covert,** clandestine, surreptitious, undercover, **stealthy,** sneaky, sneaking, skulking, slinking, slinky, feline; **concealed,** hidden, under cover, under wraps <nonformal>
ADVS 4 beneath the sod, six feet under <nonformal>; at rest, resting in peace
5 **secretly,** in secret, **covertly,** under the cloak of; in the dark, in darkness, behind the veil of secrecy

**underhanded** ADJS **fraudulent,** sharp, guileful, insidious, slippery, slippery as an eel, **shifty,** tricky, trickish, cute, finagling, chiseling <nonformal>; underhand, **furtive,** surreptitious, indirect; **dishonest,** dishonorable; **unscrupulous,** unprincipled, unethical, immoral, amoral; **corrupt,** corrupted, rotten; **crooked,** criminal, felonious, shady <nonformal>, up to no good, unsavory, dark, sinister, devious

**underling** NOUNS **inferior,** understrapper <Brit>, **subordinate,** subaltern, **junior;** secondary, second fiddle *and* second stringer *and* third stringer *and* benchwarmer *and* low man on the totem pole <all nonformal>, understrapper, errand boy, flunky, gofer <nonformal>

**underlying** ADJS **latent,** lurking, **hidden,** obscured, obfuscated, veiled, muffled, covert, **under the surface,** submerged; **between the lines;** hibernating, sleeping, dormant; **basic,** gut <nonformal>, basal

**undermine** VERBS **weaken,** enfeeble, debilitate, soften up <nonformal>, unbrace, unman, unnerve, rattle, shake up <nonformal>, **devitalize,** enervate, eviscerate; **sap,** sap the strength of, exhaust, gruel, take it out of <nonformal>; blunt, dull, damp *or* dampen, take the edge off; mine, sap the foundations of, honeycomb; sabotage, throw *or* toss a monkey-wrench in the works <both nonformal>; subvert, **overthrow,** overturn, overwhelm, upset, subvert, defeat, demolish

**underprivileged** ADJS **indigent,** poverty-stricken; needy, necessitous, **in need,** in want, disadvantaged, deprived, **impoverished,** depressed, pauperized, starveling

**underrated** ADJS **underestimated,** undervalued, on the low side; unvalued, unprized, misprized

**underscore** VERBS **underline,** emphasize, stress, lay emphasis *or* stress upon, feature, highlight, place emphasis on, give emphasis to, **accent,** accentuate, punctuate, point up, bring to the fore, put in the foreground; prioritize; **highlight,** spotlight; **star,** italicize; make a big deal *or* Federal case of <nonformal>

**understand** VERBS 1 **comprehend,** apprehend, have, **know,** conceive, realize, appreciate, have no problem with, make sense out of; **fathom,** follow; grasp, seize, get hold of, grasp *or* seize the meaning, **take in,** catch, **catch on,** get the meaning of, get the hang of; **suspect,** infer, gather, conclude, deduce, consider, reckon, divine

2 <nonformal> **read one loud and clear,** read, read one, dig, get the idea, be with one, be with it, get the message, get the word, get the picture, get up to speed, get into *or* through one's head *or* thick head, get, get it, catch *or* get the drift, have it taped, have it down pat, see where one is coming from, hear loud and clear, hear what one is saying, grok, have hold of, have a fix on, know like the back *or* palm of one's hand, know inside out

**understanding** NOUNS 1 entente; mutual *or* cordial understanding, consortium, *entente cordiale* <Fr>; **compact**
2 **intelligence,** comprehension, apprehension, intellection, prehension; conception, conceptualization, ideation; **grasp,** mental grasp, grip, **command,** mastery
ADJS 3 **patient,** armed with patience, with a soul possessed in patience, patient as Job; **tolerant,** tolerative, tolerating, accepting; **indulgent,** lenient; **pitying,** sympathizing, commiserative, condolent; **compassionate,** merciful, ruthful, rueful; lenient, forbearant; charitable, empathic, empathetic
4 **sagacious, astute,** discerning, penetrating, incisive, acute, trenchant, cogent, piercing; **perspicacious,** perspicuous; **perceptive,** percipient, apperceptive, appercipient, insightful

**understated** ADJS **tasteful,** in good taste, in the best taste; **restrained,** unobtrusive, quiet, subdued, simple, unaffected

**understudy** NOUNS **alternate,** backup *and* stand-in <both nonformal>, alter ego, **surrogate,** procurator, secondary, pinch hitter <nonformal>; locum tenens; **relief,** fill-in

**undertake** VERBS **assume,** accept, **take on,** take upon oneself, take upon one's shoulders, take up, go with, **tackle,** attack; engage *or* contract *or* obligate *or* commit oneself; **put** *or* **set** *or* **turn one's hand to,** engage in, devote oneself to, apply oneself to, address oneself to, give oneself up to; pitch into <nonformal>, plunge into, fall into, **launch into** *or* **upon;** go at, set at, have at <nonformal>, knuckle *or* buckle down to; put one's shoulder to the wheel

**undertaker** NOUNS **mortician,** funeral director; embalmer; gravedigger; sexton

**undertone** NOUNS **significance,** emotive *or* affective meaning, overtone, coloring; **drift,** tenor; **secondary meaning,** connotation, implied meaning, implication; **suggestion,** allusion; coloration, tinge, undercurrent, more than meets the eye *or* ear, something between the lines, intimation, touch, nuance, innuendo

**underwear** NOUNS **underclothes,** underclothing, undergarments, bodywear, **undies** <nonformal>, skivvies, body clothes, unmentionables <nonformal>, **lingerie,** linen, underlinen; woolies <nonformal>; long johns <nonformal>

**underworld** NOUNS 1 **depths,** deeps, bowels, bowels of the earth; bottomless pit; infernal pit, hell, nether world; dark *or* unknown *or* yawning *or* gaping depths, unfathomed deeps
2 **the underworld,** gangland, organized crime, gangsterism

**underwrite** VERBS **secure,** guarantee, guaranty, warrant, assure, insure, ensure, bond, **certify; sponsor,** insure, be sponsor for, sign for, sign one's note, **back,** stand behind *or* back of, stand up for; sign, cosign, subscribe to; confirm, attest

**undeserved** ADJS **unmerited,** unearned; **unwarranted,** unjustified, unprovoked; unentitled, undeserving, unmeriting, nonmeritorious, unworthy; preposterous, outrageous

**undesirable** NOUNS 1 bad person, bad man *or* woman *or* child, unworthy *or* disreputable person, unworthy, disreputable, *persona non grata* <L>, unacceptable *or* unwanted *or* objectionable person
ADJS 2 unattractive, unappealing, unengaging, uninviting, unalluring; unwelcome, thankless; **distasteful,** untasteful, **unpalatable,** unsavory; **unacceptable,** inadmissible, unsuitable, **objectionable,** exceptionable, impossible, untenable, indefensible; **intolerable**

**undetectable** ADJS **imperceptible,** unperceivable, **indiscernible,** undiscernible; behind the curtain *or* scenes; disguised, camouflaged, hidden, **concealed;** undisclosed, unrevealed, *in petto* <L>; latent, unrealized, submerged

**undeveloped** ADJS **unfinished,** unlicked, unformed; unfashioned, unwrought, unlabored, unworked, unprocessed, untreated; **underdeveloped;** backward, arrested, stunted; **crude,** rude, coarse, unpolished, unrefined; uncultivated, uncultured; rough, roughcast, roughhewn, **in the rough;** rudimentary

**undignified** ADJS **vulgar,** inelegant, indelicate, indecorous, indecent, improper, unseemly, unbeseeming, unbecoming, unfitting, inappropriate, unsuitable, ungenteel; **untasteful,** tasteless, in bad *or* poor taste, tacky *and* chintzy *and* Mickey Mouse <all nonformal>; **offensive,** offensive to gentle ears

**undiminished** ADJS unabated, unreduced, unrestricted, unretarded, unmitigated; complete, unreduced

**undisciplined** ADJS **ungoverned,** unrestrained; insubordinate, mutinous, disobedient; **uncontrolled,** uncurbed, unbridled, unchecked, rampant, untrammeled, unreined, reinless, anything goes; irresponsible, fast and loose

**undisputed** ADJS **unquestioned,** uncontested, uncontradicted, unchallenged, uncontroverted, uncontroversial; **doubtless,** beyond a shade *or* shadow of doubt, past dispute, beyond question

**undivided** ADJS uncut, unsevered, unclipped, uncropped, unshorn; **undiminished,** unreduced, complete; unseparated

**undo** VERBS 1 **take off,** remove, doff, slip *or* step out of, slip off, slough off, cast off, throw off, drop
2 **unnerve,** unman, unstring, unbrace, reduce to jelly, **demoralize,** shake, upset, psych out <nonformal>, dash, knock down *or* flat, **crush,** overcome, prostrate
3 **do for,** fix <nonformal>, settle, sink, cook *and* cook one's goose *and* cut one down to size *and* cut one off at the knees *and* pull the plug on *and* pull the rug out from under <all nonformal>, scuttle, put the kibosh on *and* put the skids under <both nonformal>, do in, poleax, torpedo, knock out, KO <nonformal>, deal a knockout blow to, zap *and* shoot down *and* shoot down in flames <all nonformal>
4 **abolish,** nullify, void, abrogate, annihilate, annul, tear up, repeal, revoke, negate, negative, invalidate, **cancel,** cancel out, bring to naught, put *or* lay to rest

**undoing** NOUNS **destruction,** ruin, ruination, **dissolution,** disintegration, breakup, disruption, disorganization, lysis; **neutralization,** nullification, annulment, cancellation, voiding, invalidation, vitiation, frustration, thwarting

**undress** NOUNS 1 **dishabille,** *déshabillé* <Fr>, something more comfortable; **negligee,** *négligé* <Fr>; **wrap,** wrapper; bareness, baldness, **nakedness,** nudity, beauty unadorned
VERBS 2 **unclothe,** undrape, **disrobe; strip,** strip to the buff <nonformal>, do a strip-tease

**undying** ADJS **immortal,** everlasting, **deathless,** never-dying, **imperishable,** incorruptible, amaranthine; **continuous**, ceaseless, unceasing, unending, endless, incessant, unremitting, steady, sustained, protracted, indefatigable

**unearthly** ADJS **deathly,** deathlike, deadly; **weird,** eerie, uncanny, unworldly; **otherworldly,** extraterrestrial, extramundane, transmundane, not of the earth, not of this world; weird, passing belief; **mind-boggling,** preposterous, absurd, ridiculous, ungodly; supernatural

**uneasy** ADJS **restless,** restive, unquiet, unsettled, unrestful, tense; **fidgety,** antsy <nonformal>, fussy, fluttery; **troubled,** bothered; perturbed, disturbed, disquieted, agitated; **apprehensive,** qualmish, nail-biting, white-knuckle <nonformal>, nervous as a cat; unpeaceful

**uneconomical** ADJS **improvident,** thriftless, unthrifty; **shiftless,** feckless, thoughtless, heedless; happy-go-lucky; negligent

**uneducated** ADJS **unlearned, inerudite,** unerudite, unschooled, uninstructed, untutored, unbriefed, untaught, unedified, unguided; **lowbrow** *and* lowbrowed *and* lowbrowish <all nonformal>

**unemotional** ADJS **unfeeling,** emotionless, affectless, emotionally dead *or* numb *or* paralyzed, anesthetized, drugged, narcotized; passionless, **spiritless,** heartless, soulless; **unresponsive,** unresponding, unsympathetic; **impassive,** impassible; immovable, untouchable; **inexcitable**

**unemployed** ADJS **idle,** fallow, otiose; **unoccupied,** disengaged, *désœuvré* <Fr>, **jobless,** out of work, out of a job, out of harness; free, available, at liberty, at leisure; at loose ends

**unending** ADJS **incessant,** constant, steady, stable, **ceaseless,** unceasing, **endless,** never-ending, **interminable,** perennial, without end

**unenlightened** ADJS **ignorant,** nescient, unknowing, uncomprehending, **know-nothing; ill-informed,** uninformed, unilluminated, unapprized, unposted <nonformal>, clueless <Brit nonformal>; **unacquainted,** unconversant, unversed, uninitiated, **unfamiliar,** strange to

**unequaled** ADJS **peerless,** matchless, champion; unmatched, unmatchable, unrivaled, unparalleled, immortal, never-to-be-equaled, unapproached, unapproachable, unsurpassed, unexcelled; unsurpassable; inimitable, **incomparable,** beyond compare *or* comparison, **unique;** without equal *or* parallel, *sans pareil* <Fr>; in a class by itself, *sui generis* <L>

**unequivocal** ADJS **certain,** sure, sure-enough <nonformal>; **positive,** absolute, definite, perfectly sure, apodictic; decisive, conclusive; clear, clear as day, clear and distinct, unmistakable, unambiguous, univocal

**unessential** ADJS inessential *or* nonessential, unnecessary, nonvital, superfluous; **accessory,** extra, collateral, auxiliary, supernumerary; adventitious, appurtenant, adscititious; **additional,** supplementary, supplemental, superadded, supervenient, make-weight; **accidental,** chance, fortuitous, casual, aleatory; extraneous, extrinsic; incidental, parenthetical

**unethical** ADJS **unconscientious,** unconscienced, conscienceless, unconscionable, shameless, without shame *or* remorse, **unscrupulous,** unprincipled, immoral, unmoral, amoral, nonmoral; **corrupt,** corrupted, rotten

**uneven** ADJS **unbalanced,** discriminatory, uneven; **inconstant,** unsteady, rough, unequal, uncertain, unsettled; **variable,** deviative, heteroclite; **capricious,** erratic, off-again-on-again, eccentric; **incomplete,** unfinished, partial, patchy, sketchy, unthorough; makeshift

**uneventful** ADJS **uninteresting,** unexciting; uninspiring; **tedious,** monotonous, humdrum, invariable; **dreary,** dry-as-dust, **dull**

**unexceptional** ADJS **ordinary,** average, normal, **common,** commonplace, garden *and* garden-variety <both nonformal>, run-of-the-mine *or* -mill; **unremarkable,** unnoteworthy, unspectacular, nothing *or* nobody special *and* no great shakes <all nonformal>, no prize package, no brain surgeon, no rocket scientist

**unexpected** ADJS **unanticipated,** unlooked for, unhoped for, unprepared for, undivined, unguessed, unpredicted, **unforeseen;** unforeseeable, unpredictable, off-the-wall <nonformal>; **improbable**; contrary to expectation, beyond *or* past expectation, more than expected, more than one bargained for; out of the blue, out of left field *and* from out in left field <both nonformal>; without warning, unheralded, unannounced; sudden

**unexplained** ADJS unascertained; uninvestigated, unexplored; undiscovered, untraced, untracked; unaccounted for, unsolved

**unexplored** ADJS **unexamined,** unstudied, unconsidered, unsearched, unscanned, unweighed, unsifted, uninvestigated, unindagated, unconned

**unfailing** ADJS **persevering,** unrelenting; **unrelaxing,** untiring, unwearying, unflagging, never-tiring, **tireless,** weariless, **indefatigable,** unwearied, unsleeping, undrooping, unnodding, unwinking, sleepless; undiscouraged, undaunted, indomitable, unconquerable, steadfast, invincible, game to the last *or* to the end; **patient,** patient as Job

**unfair** ADJS not fair; **unsporting,** unsportsmanly, unsportsmanlike, not done, not kosher <nonformal>, not cricket <Brit nonformal>; **dirty** <nonformal>, foul, below the belt

**unfaithful** ADJS faithless, of bad faith, trothless; **inconstant,** unsteadfast, fickle; **disloyal,** unloyal; false, **untrue,** not true to; disaffected, recreant, derelict, barratrous

**unfamiliar** ADJS **novel,** original, unique, different; strange, unusual; unheard-of; **first,** first ever; **uncustomary,** unwonted, **uncommon,** atypic *or* atypical, *recherché* <Fr>; **out of the ordinary,** out of this world, out-of-the-way, off the beaten track, offbeat; uninitiated, strange, strange to

**unfashionable** ADJS **old-fashioned,** old-fangled, **dated,** out, out-of-date, outdated, **outmoded,** out of style *or* fashion, out of use, disused, out of season, styleless, **behind the times,** of the old school, old hat *and* back-number *and* has-been <all nonformal>

**unfavorable** ADJS **unpropitious,** unpromising, unfortunate, unlucky; untoward, dire, baleful, baneful, **ill-fated,** ill-starred, evil-starred, star-crossed; **adverse,** detrimental

**unfeeling** ADJS **unemotional,** nonemotional, emotionless, affectless, emotionally dead *or* numb *or* paralyzed, anesthetized, drugged, narcotized; **unpassionate,** dispassionate, unimpassioned, **objective;** passionless, **spiritless,** heartless, soulless; **unaffectionate,** unloving; **unresponsive,** unresponding, unsympathetic; **impassive,** immovable, untouchable; **callous,** obdurate, indurated; **unmerciful**

**unfinished** ADJS **undeveloped,** unlicked, unformed; unfashioned, unwrought, unlabored, unworked, unprocessed, untreated; **underdeveloped;** backward, arrested, stunted; **crude,** rude, coarse, unpolished, unrefined; uncultivated, uncultured; rough, roughcast, rough-hewn, **in the rough**

**unfit** VERBS 1 **disable,** disenable, **incapacitate,** drain, de-energize; enfeeble, debilitate, weaken; cripple, maim, lame, hamstring, knee-cap, defang, pull the teeth of <nonformal>; wing, clip the wings of; **put out of order,** put out of commission <nonformal>, throw out of gear; bugger *and* bugger up *and* queer *and* queer the works *and* gum up *or* screw up <all nonformal>
ADJS 2 **incompetent,** incapable, unable, inadequate, unequipped, unqualified, ill-qualified, out of one's depth, outmatched, **unfitted,** unadapted, not equal *or* up to, not cut out for <nonformal>; ineffective, **ineffectual;** unadjusted, maladjusted

**unflappable** ADJS **inexcitable,** imperturbable, undisturbable; **unirritable,** steady; stoic, stoical; **even-tempered;** impassive, stolid; unshaken, not to be shaken, undeflectable, **well-balanced;** unshakable, **cool** <nonformal>, without nerves, without a nerve in one's body, unflinching

**unflattering** ADJS unexaggerated, undistorted; unvarnished, uncolored, unqualified

**unflinching** ADJS **unhesitating,** unhesitant, **unfaltering,** unshrinking; unquailing, uncringing, unwincing, unblinking; without nerves, without a nerve in one's body

**unfold** VERBS **unclose,** unwrap, unroll, open; **uncover,** uncase, unsheathe, unveil, undrape, uncurtain; **disclose,** expose, reveal, bare, take the lid off, **manifest,** show, exhibit, demonstrate, display, breathe, develop; **amplify,** expatiate, dilate, expand, enlarge, **enlarge on,** expand on, elaborate; **develop,** open out, fill in, flesh out, evolve, work out, explicate

**unforeseen** ADJS **unexpected,** unanticipated, unlooked for, unhoped for, unprepared for, undivined, unguessed, unpredicted; contrary to expectation, beyond *or* past expectation, more than one bargained for; out of the blue, without warning, unheralded, unannounced

**unforgettable** ADJS **never to be forgotten,** never to be erased from the mind, **indelible,** indelibly impressed on the mind, fixed in the mind; haunting, persistent, recurrent, nagging, plaguing, rankling, festering; obsessing, obsessive; **memorable,** striking, telling, salient

**unforgivable** ADJS **unjustifiable,** unwarrantable, unallowable, unreasonable, indefensible; **inexcusable,** unconscionable, **unpardonable,** inexpiable, irremissible

**unfortunate** ADJS **unlucky,** unprovidential, unblessed, **unprosperous,** sad, unhappy, hapless, fortuneless, misfortuned, luckless; **out of luck,** short of luck; **down on one's luck** <nonformal>, badly *or* ill off, down in the world, in adverse circumstances; ill-starred, evil-starred, born under an evil star, star-crossed

**unfounded** ADJS **baseless,** groundless, ungrounded, **without foundation,** not well-founded, built on sand, **unsupported,** unsustained, without basis *or* sound basis; **untenable,** unsupportable, unsustainable; **unwarranted,** idle, empty, vain

**unfriendly** ADJS **inimical,** unamicable; uncordial, unamiable, ungenial, incompatible; cool, cold, chill, chilly, frosty, icy; inhospitable; unsociable

**unfurl** VERBS unfold, unroll, unwind, unreel, uncoil, reveal, reveal *or* expose gradually

**ungainly** ADJS uncouth, **ungraceful,** graceless, inelegant, *gauche* <Fr>; **gawky,** gawkish; clumsy, clunky <nonformal>

**unglued** ADJS **unnerved,** unmanned, unstrung, undone, reduced to jelly, **demoralized,** shaken, upset, dashed, stricken, **crushed;** neurasthenic, prostrate, prostrated, overcome

**ungodly** ADJS 1 godless, **irreligious,** unrighteous, unholy, unsaintly, unangelic, unangelical; impious; **wicked,** sinful, **execrable,** damnable
2 **mind-boggling,** preposterous, absurd, ridiculous, unearthly

**ungrateful** ADJS **unthankful,** unthanking,

thankless, unappreciative, unappreciatory, unmindful, unrecognizing

**unhappy** ADJS **uncheerful,** uncheery, **cheerless,** joyless, unjoyful, unsmiling; mirthless, unmirthful, humorless; funny as a crutch <nonformal>; **grim;** out of humor, out of sorts, in bad humor *or* spirits; **sorry,** sorryish; discontented; **wretched,** miserable; unpropitious; infelicitous

**unhealthy** ADJS in poor health; **infirm,** unsound, invalid, valetudinary, valetudinarian, debilitated, cachectic, enervated, exhausted, drained; **sickly,** peaked <nonformal>; **feeble,** frail; weakened, with low resistance, **run-down,** reduced in health; **unwholesome,** unsound, morbid, diseased, pathological

**unheard-of** ADJS **unrenowned,** renownless, nameless, inglorious, **unnotable,** unnoted, unnoticed, unremarked, **undistinguished,** unfamed, uncelebrated, unsung, unhonored, unglorified, unpopular; little known, obscure, *ignotus* <L>

**uniform** NOUNS 1 **livery,** mantle, outfit, dress, monkey suit <nonformal>
ADJS 2 **equable,** equal, **even; level,** flat, smooth; **regular,** constant, steadfast, persistent, continuous; **unvarying,** undeviating, unchanging, steady, stable; cloned *or* clonish *and* cookie-cutter <all nonformal>; **consistent,** consonant, correspondent, accordant, homogeneous, **alike,** all of a piece, monolithic

**unify** VERBS reduce to unity, unitize, make one; **integrate,** unite, bond, link, yoke

**unimpeachable** ADJS **faultless,** flawless, impeccable, reliable, unexceptionable; **believable,** credible

**unimportant** ADJS **of no importance,** of little *or* small importance, of no great importance, **of no account,** of no significance, of no concern, of no matter, of little *or* no consequence, no great shakes <nonformal>; **inferior,** secondary, of a low order of importance, low-priority, expendable; marginal

**unimpressed** ADJS **unaffected,** unmoved, untouched, dry-eyed, **unstirred,** unruffled, unanimated, uninspired

**unimpressive** ADJS **insignificant**, inconsequential, immaterial; unnoteworthy; **inconsiderable,** inappreciable, negligible

**uninformed** ADJS **unsuspecting,** unaware, unwarned, unforewarned, unadvised, unadmonished; off one's guard; **ill-informed,** unenlightened, unilluminated, unapprized, unposted <nonformal>

**uninhabitable** ADJS **unhabitable,** nonhabitable, unoccupiable, untenantable, **unlivable,** unfit to live in, not fit for man or beast

**uninhibited** ADJS **unsuppressed,** unrepressed, unreserved, exuberant; **uncurbed,** unchecked, unbridled, unmuzzled; **unreined,** uncontrolled, **unruly;** out of control, out of hand; **abandoned,** intemperate, immoderate, **incontinent,** licentious, loose, wanton, rampant, riotous, wild; irrepressible

**uninspired** ADJS **unaffected,** unmoved, untouched, dry-eyed, unimpressed, unstruck, **unstirred,** unruffled, unanimated; arid, barren, infertile, infecund; **unoriginal,** undaring, unaspiring, uninventive

**uninterrupted** ADJS **continuous,** continued, **continual,** continuing; **unintermittent,** unintermitted, featureless, unrelieved, monotonous; **connected, joined**, linked, chained, concatenated, catenated, articulated; unremitting, **incessant,** constant, steady, stable, **ceaseless,** unceasing, **endless,** unending, never-ending, **interminable,** perennial

**uninvolved** ADJS **uncomplicated,** straightforward; **uninquisitive,** uninquiring; bored; inattentive; **uninterested,** unconcerned, **indifferent,** apathetic, passive, impassive, stolid, phlegmatic, listless; aloof, detached, distant, withdrawn, reclusive, sequestered, eremitic

**union** NOUNS 1 **affiliation,** alliance, allying, alignment, association, consociation, combination, unification, **coalition,** fusion, merger, coalescence, amalgamation, **league,** federation, confederation, confederacy, consolidation, incorporation, inclusion, integration; labor union; hookup *and* tie-up *and* tie-in <all nonformal>
2 **joint,** join, joining, **juncture, connection,** link, connecting link, **coupling,** interface

**unique** ADJS inimitable, **incomparable,** beyond compare *or* comparison, *sui generis* <L>; **novel,** original, different; strange, unusual, uncommon; unfamiliar, unheard-of; **first,** first ever, **sole,** singular, absolute, unrepeated, **alone,** lone, **only,** only-begotten, **one and only,** first and last

**unit** NOUNS **individual,** single, integer, entity, singleton, **item,** article, point, module

**unite** VERBS **converge,** come together, approach, run together, **meet,** connect, merge; fall in with, link up with; **join,** band, league, **associate,** affiliate, ally, **combine,** fuse, coalesce, amalgamate, federate, confederate, consolidate; hook up *and* tie up *and* tie in <all nonformal>; **close ranks,** make common cause, throw in together <nonformal>, unite efforts, join in; **integrate,** form a unity

**United States of America** NOUNS **United States,** US, USA, US of A <nonformal>, **America,** Columbia, the States, Uncle Sugar *and* Yankeeland <both nonformal>, Land of Liberty, the melting pot

**unity** NOUNS **oneness,** homogeneity, consubstantiality; **completeness,** totality; wholeness, entireness, **entirety; integrity,** integrality, undividedness, intactness, untouchedness, unbrokenness; solidity, solidarity; **indivisibility,** inseparability, impartibility, infrangibility, cohesion, coherence

**universal** ADJS cosmic *or* cosmical, heaven-wide, galactic, planetary, worldwide, transnational, planet-wide, **global;** catholic, **all-inclusive,** all-including, **all-embracing,** all-encompassing, all-comprehensive, all-comprehending

**universe** NOUNS **world,** cosmos; creation, created universe, created nature, all, **all creation,** all tarnation <nonformal>, all *or* everything that is, all being, totality, totality of being, sum of things; wide world, whole wide world; **macrocosm; frame of reference,** intellectual *or* ideational frame of reference, framework, arena, world *or* universe of discourse, system, reference system

*world without end*
**Bible**

**university** NOUNS institution of higher education *or* learning, degree-granting institution; graduate school, postgraduate school; academe, academia, the groves of Academe, **the campus,** the halls of learning *or* ivy, ivied halls; alma mater

**unjust** ADJS **inequitable,** unequitable, iniquitous, **unbalanced,** discriminatory, uneven, unequal; **wrong,** wrongful, unrightful; **undue**, unmeet, undeserved, unmerited

**unkempt** ADJS **unrefined,** unpolished, uncouth, uncombed, unlicked; **untidy,** unsightly, unneat, slobby *and* scuzzy <both nonformal>, **messy** <nonformal>

**unkind** ADJS **unkindly,** ill; **unbenign,** unbenignant; **unamiable,** disagreeable, **uncordial,** ungracious, inhospitable, **ungenial,** unaffectionate, unloving; **unsympathetic,** unsympathizing, uncompassionate, uncompassioned; malevolent

**unknown** ADJS unbeknown <nonformal>, **unheard-of,** unapprehended, unapparent, unperceived, unsuspected; uninvestigated, unexplored; unidentified, unclassified, uncharted, unfathomed, unplumbed, virgin, untouched; **undisclosed,** unrevealed, undivulged, undiscovered, unexposed, sealed; **unfamiliar,** strange

**unlawful** ADJS **illegal,** illegitimate, illicit, nonlicit, nonlegal, lawless, wrongful, fraudulent, creative <nonformal>, **against the law; unauthorized,** unallowed, impermissible, unwarranted, unwarrantable, unofficial; **criminal,** felonious; outlaw, outlawed

**unlike** ADJS **dissimilar,** unsimilar, unresembling, unresemblant; unidentical; **disparate,** diverse, divergent, **contrasting,** different; nonuniform; scarcely like, hardly like, a bit *or* mite different; **incomparable,** incommensurable, not to be compared, of different orders; apples and oranges

**unlikely** ADJS **improbable,** unpromising, hardly possible, logic-defying, scarcely to be expected *or* anticipated; statistically improbable; **doubtful,** dubious, **questionable,** dubitable, more than doubtful; **implausible,** incredible; unlooked-for, unexpected, unpredictable

**unlimited** ADJS **unrestricted,** unconfined, uncircumscribed, unbound <old>, unbounded, unmeasured; limitless, illimitable; unqualified, unconditioned, **unconditional,** without strings, no strings, no strings attached; open-ended, open, **wide-open** <nonformal>; decontrolled, deregulated; **infinite,** boundless, unbounded, undefined, omnipresent, ubiquitous

**unlivable** ADJS unhabitable, **uninhabitable,** nonhabitable, unoccupiable, untenantable, **unfit to live in,** not fit for man or beast

**unload** VERBS off-load, unlade, unpack, disburden, unburden, **discharge,** dump; **disembarrass,** disencumber, relieve, disburden, unhamper, get out from under; throw on the market, **liquidate**

**unlock** VERBS **explain,** decipher, crack, find the key to, unravel, read between the lines, read into, solve; **get to the bottom** *or* **heart of,** fathom, plumb; **unlatch,** unbolt, unbar

**unloved** ADJS unbeloved, uncherished, loveless; **lovelorn,** forsaken, **rejected,** jilted, thrown over <nonformal>, spurned, crossed in love

**unlucky** ADJS **unfortunate,** unprovidential, unblessed, **unprosperous,** sad, unhappy, hapless, fortuneless, misfortuned, luckless; **out of luck,** short of luck; **down on one's luck** <nonformal>, badly *or* ill off, down in the world, in adverse circumstances; ill-starred, evil-starred, born under a bad sign, star-crossed; **in a jam** *and* in a pickle *or* pretty pickle *and* in a tight spot *and* between a rock and a hard place <all nonformal>, between the devil and the deep blue sea; up a tree *and* up the creek *or* up shit creek without a paddle *and* up to one's ass in alligators <all nonformal>

**unmanageable** ADJS **unwieldy,** unhandy; inconvenient, impractical; **awkward,** clumsy, cumbersome, unmaneuverable; contrary, perverse, crosswise; ponderous, bulky, hulky, hulking

**unmarked** ADJS **unheeded,** unobserved, unnoticed, unnoted, unperceived, unseen, undiscerned, undescried, unremarked, unregarded, unminded, unconsidered, unthought-of, unmissed; **unmarred,** unscarred, unscratched, undefaced, unbruised; none the worse for wear

**unmarried** ADJS **unwedded,** unwed, single, sole, spouseless, wifeless, husbandless

**unmentionable** ADJS **indescribable,** ineffable, inexpressible, unutterable, unspeakable, undefinable, unnamable, unwhisperable; **atrocious,** monstrous

**unmistakable** ADJS **express,** explicit, not to be mistaken, open-and-shut <nonformal>; **unequivocal,** unambiguous, unconfused; **loud and clear** <nonformal>; **lucid,** pellucid, limpid

**unnatural** ADJS **heartless,** unfeeling, unresponsive, insensitive; **artificial,** insincere; **abnormal,** irregular, divergent, deviative, deviant, different, exceptional

**unnecessary** ADJS **unessential,** inessential *or* nonessential, nonvital, superfluous; **superfluous,** redundant; excess, in excess; expendable, dispensable, **needless,** unneeded, gratuitous, uncalled-for

**unnerving** ADJS **nerve-racking,** nerve-rending, nerve-shaking, nerve-jangling, nerve-trying, nerve-stretching; jarring, grating

**unobtainable** ADJS **inaccessible,** unattainable, unavailable, unprocurable, unsecurable; not to be had, **not to be had for love or money;** undiscoverable, unascertainable

**unoccupied** ADJS 1 **available,** open, free, unfilled, **uninhabited,** unpopulated, unpeopled, untaken, untenanted, tenantless, untended, unmanned, unstaffed; **deserted,** abandoned, forsaken, godforsaken <nonformal>
2 idle, free, open, spare; retired, semiretired

**unofficial** ADJS **unauthoritative,** unauthentic, nonofficial, apocryphal; **uncertified,** unverified, unchecked, unconfirmed, uncorroborated, unauthenticated, unvalidated, unattested, unwarranted

**unopposed** ADJS **unanimous,** solid, consentaneous, **with one voice;** uncontradicted, unchallenged, uncontroverted, uncontested, carried by acclamation

**unorganized** ADJS amorphous, **chaotic,** orderless, disorderly, unordered, confused, anarchic; **unarranged,** haphazard; makeshift, rough-and-ready, **extemporaneous,** extemporized, improvised, ad-lib *and* off the top of one's head <both nonformal>; **random,** entropic, unarranged, ungraded, unsorted, unclassified

**unorthodox** ADJS nonorthodox, **heterodox,** heretical; **unauthoritative,** unauthentic, unaccepted, unreceived, unapproved; **nonconformist,** individualistic, inner-directed, perverse; **unconventional,** eccentric, original, maverick, Bohemian

**unpardonable** ADJS **inexcusable,** unconscionable, **unforgivable,** inexpiable, irremissible; shameful, disgraceful, scandalous, **infamous,** improper, reprehensible, blamable, blameworthy, unworthy

**unplanned** ADJS **unintentional,** unintended, **unmeant,** undesigned, unpurposed, unthought-of; **unpremeditated,** unprompted, unguided, unguarded; **unwitting,** unthinking, unconscious, involuntary

**unpleasant** ADJS **unpleasing,** unenjoyable; displeasing, disagreeable; unlikable, dislikable; **abrasive,** wounding, hostile, unfriendly; unwelcome, thankless; **distasteful,** uncongenial; **not to one's taste,** against the grain, uninviting; unlovable; **abhorrent,** odious; **intolerable**

**unpopular** ADJS **disliked,** out of favor, gone begging; **unappreciated,** misunderstood; unsung, thankless; **undistinguished,** unfamed, uncelebrated, unsung, unhonored; **unknown,** little known, obscure, unheard-of, *ignotus* <L>

**unprecedented** ADJS **original,** novel; unique, *sui generis* <L>; new, fresh; underived, firsthand; **unimitated,** uncopied, **unduplicated,** unparalleled, unreproduced, unexampled; **archetypal,** archetypical, archetypic, prototypal

**unpredictable** ADJS **unexpected,** unanticipated, unlooked for, unhoped for, unprepared for, unpredicted, **unforeseen;** unforeseeable, off-the-wall <nonformal>; out of the blue, dropped from the clouds; incalculable, uncountable, unreckonable, unaccountable, undivinable; **fickle,** capricious, whimsical, **erratic,** variable

**unprejudiced** ADJS **unbiased,** unprepossessed, unjaundiced; impartial, evenhanded, **fair,** just, equitable, **objective,** dispassionate, impersonal, detached, disinterested

**unprepared** ADJS **unsuspecting,** unaware, uninformed, unwarned, unforewarned, unadvised, unadmonished; unready, off one's guard; **unskilled,** unaccomplished, untrained, untaught, unschooled, untutored, uncoached, unimproved, uninitiated, unprimed, unfinished, unpolished

**unpretentious** ADJS **modest,** meek; humble; unpretending, **unassuming,** unpresuming, unpresumptuous, **unostentatious,** unobtrusive, unimposing, unboastful; unambitious, unaspiring; **unaffected,** genuine, inartificial, unartificial, unadorned, unvarnished, unembellished

**unprincipled** ADJS **dishonest,** dishonorable; unconscionable, shameless, **unscrupulous,** unethical, immoral, amoral; **corrupt,** corrupted, rotten

**unprintable** ADJS **obscene,** foul, filthy, nasty, vile, fulsome, offensive, unrepeatable, not fit for mixed company; scurrilous, scurrile, fescennine

**unproductive** ADJS nonproductive *or* nonproducing; **infertile,** sterile, unfertile, **unfruitful,** unfructuous, infecund, unprolific; **barren,** arid, dry, dried-up, sere, exhausted, drained, leached, sucked dry, wasted, gaunt, **waste,** desolate, jejune

**unprofessional** ADJS **amateurish,** unbusinesslike, semiskilled

**unprofitable** ADJS **fruitless,** gainless, profitless, bootless, otiose, unremunerative, nonremunerative; **unrewarding,** worthless, useless; sterile, futile, unproductive

**unprovoked** ADJS **undeserved,** unmerited, unearned; **unwarranted,** unjustified; preposterous, outrageous

**unpublished** ADJS **unmentioned,** untalked-of, **untold,** unsung, unproclaimed; unwritten, unrecorded

**unqualified** ADJS 1 **incapable,** incompetent, inefficient, ineffective; inept, unendowed, ungifted, untalented, **unfit,** unfitted; disqualified
2 **unmitigated,** unrelieved, unspoiled, undeniable, unquestionable, unequivocal, unvarnished, uncolored; **flagrant,** arrant, shocking, shattering, egregious, intolerable, unbearable, unconscionable; total, utter

3 <nonformal> **no ifs, ands, or buts; no strings attached,** no holds barred, no catch *or* joker *or* kicker, no joker in the deck, no small print *or* fine print, no fine print at the bottom; downright, that's that, what you see is what you get

**unquestionable** ADJS **unmitigated,** unqualified, unrelieved, unspoiled, undeniable, unequivocal; **inalienable,** unalienable, uninfringeable, unchallengeable, unimpeachable, unexceptionable; **obvious,** patent, self-evident, axiomatic; **certain,** undoubted, categorically true

**unravel** VERBS **disentangle,** untangle, **unscramble,** unsnarl, unknot, untwist, unbraid, unweave, untwine, unwind, uncoil, unthread, ravel; **unclutter,** clarify, clear up, disambiguate, sort out, get to the core *or* nub *or* essence; **solve, resolve,** find the solution *or* answer, **clear up,** work out, find out, figure out, dope *and* dope out <both nonformal>

**unreadable** ADJS **illegible,** unclear; undecipherable, indecipherable

**unready** ADJS **unprepared,** unprimed; surprised, caught short, caught napping, caught with one's pants down <nonformal>, taken by surprise, taken aback, taken unawares, blindsided <nonformal>, caught off balance, caught off base <nonformal>, tripped up

**unreal** ADJS unrealistic, unactual, not real; merely nominal; immaterial; unsubstantial; **imaginary,** imagined, fantastic, fanciful, fancied; illusory

**unrealistic** ADJS **visionary,** idealistic, quixotic; romantic, romanticized, romancing, romanticizing; **impractical,** unpractical, starry-eyed, dewy-eyed; in the clouds, with one's head in the clouds

**unreasonable** ADJS 1 **capricious,** whimsical; **arbitrary,** motiveless; **moody,** temperamental, petulant; **unjustifiable,** unwarrantable, unallowable, indefensible; **inexcusable,** unconscionable; **unsound,** unsensible, senseless, insensate, reasonless, **irrational,** reckless, inadvisable
2 **overpriced,** grossly overpriced, **exorbitant,** excessive, extravagant, inordinate, immoderate, undue, unwarranted

**unrecognizable** ADJS **indistinct,** unclear, **indefinite,** undefined, ill-defined, ill-marked, **faint,** pale, feeble, weak, **dim,** dark, **shadowy,** vague, obscure, indistinguishable

**unrelated** ADJS **unconnected,** unallied, unlinked, **unassociated,** unaffiliated *or* disaffiliated; disrelated, disconnected, dissociated, detached, discrete, disjunct, removed, **separated,** segregated, apart, other, independent, marked off, bracketed; **foreign,** alien, strange, exotic, outlandish; extraneous

**unrelenting** ADJS **unyielding,** unbending, inflexible, hard, hard-line, inelastic, impliable, ungiving, **firm,** stiff, rigid, rigorous, stuffy; **unalterable,** unchangeable, immutable; **uncompromising,** intransigent, irreconcilable, hard-shell *and* hard-core <both nonformal>; implacable, inexorable, **relentless**

**unreliable** ADJS **undependable,** untrustworthy, unfaithworthy, treacherous, **unsure,** not to be depended *or* relied on; **insecure,** unsound, infirm, unsolid, **unstable,** unsubstantial, insubstantial, **unsteadfast,** unsteady, desultory, shaky; **precarious,** hazardous, dangerous, perilous, risky, ticklish; **unauthentic** *or* **inauthentic,** unauthoritative

**unresolved** ADJS **remaining,** outstanding, unmet; **irresolute,** irresolved, **undecided,** indecisive, undetermined, unsettled, at loose ends; changeable, mutable; capricious, mercurial, fickle

**unresponsive** ADJS **unfeeling,** emotionless, affectless, emotionally dead *or* numb *or* paralyzed, anesthetized, drugged, narcotized; **coldhearted,** cold-blooded, cold as charity; **unaffectionate,** unloving; unresponding, **unsympathetic; impassive,** dull, obtuse; **heartless,** unnatural, insensitive; **uninfluenceable,** unswayable, unmovable

**unrest** NOUNS **agitation,** perturbation, **malaise,** unease, restlessness; **disquiet,** disquietude, inquietude, discomposure; **turmoil,** turbulence, **disorder**

**unripe** ADJS **immature,** underripe, unripened, impubic, **raw, green,** callow, wet behind the ears, cub, cubbish, unfledged, fledgling, unseasoned, unmellowed

**unruly** ADJS **disorderly,** obstreperous; **unbridled;** restive, riotous, fractious, out of control, wild, rampant

**unsafe** ADJS unhealthy <nonformal>; **unreliable,** undependable, untrustworthy, treacherous, **insecure,** unsound, unstable, unsteady, shaky, tottery, rocky

**unsaid** ADJS **tacit,** wordless, unspoken, unuttered, unexpressed; **implicit**

**unsanitary** ADJS **unhealthful,** unhealthy, insalubrious, unsalutary, unwholesome, peccant, bad, **bad for;** noxious, noisome, injurious, baneful, harmful; **polluted,** contaminated, tainted, foul, septic; unhygienic, insanitary; morbific, pathogenic, pestiferous

**unsatisfactory** ADJS **unsatisfying,** ungratifying, unfulfilling; **displeasing**; disappointing, disheartening, not up to expectation, not good enough; **inadequate,** incommensurate, insufficient

**unsavory** ADJS 1 **unpalatable,** unappetizing, untasteful, untasty, ill-flavored, foul-tasting, **distasteful,** dislikable, unlikable, uninviting, unpleasant, unpleasing, displeasing, disagreeable
2 **disreputable,** discreditable, dishonorable, shady, **seamy,** sordid

**unscrupulous** ADJS 1 **unmeticulous,** unexacting, unpainstaking, unrigorous, **unconscientious,** unpunctilious, unpunctual, **unparticular,** unfussy, unfinical, uncritical
2 **dishonest,** dishonorable; conscienceless, unconscionable, shameless, without shame *or* remorse, **unprincipled,** unethical, immoral, amoral; **corrupt,** corrupted, rotten

**unseat** VERBS **dislodge,** unplace; evict; depose, unsaddle

**unseemly** ADJS **indecent,** indelicate, inelegant, indecorous, improper, inappropriate, **unbecoming,** indiscreet

**unseen** ADJS **unheeded,** unobserved, unnoticed, unnoted, undetected, unperceived, undiscerned, undescried, unmarked, unremarked, unregarded, unspied, unminded, unconsidered

**unsightly** ADJS **ugly,** unattractive, unhandsome, unpretty, unlovely, uncomely, **inelegant; disfigured,** defaced, blotted, blemished, marred, spoiled

**unskilled** ADJS **unaccomplished,** untrained, untaught, unschooled, untutored, uncoached, unimproved, uninitiated, **unprepared,** unprimed, unfinished, unpolished; **untalented,** ungifted, unendowed; amateurish, unprofessional, unbusinesslike

**unsophisticated** ADJS **artless,** simple, plain, **guideless;** simplehearted, simpleminded; **ingenuous,** *ingénu* <Fr>; **naive,** childlike, born yesterday; **innocent;** trustful, trusting, unguarded, unwary, unreserved, confiding, unsuspicious; **uncomplex,** uncomplicated, uncorrupted

**unsound** ADJS **infirm,** unfirm, **unstable,** unsubstantial, unsturdy, unsolid, decrepit, crumbling, fragmented, fragmentary, disintegrating; rotten, rotten at *or* rotten to the core; **unwholesome,** unhealthy, morbid, diseased, pathological; **insolvent,** indebted; **unreasonable,** unsensible, senseless, insensate, reasonless, **irrational,** reckless, inadvisable

**unsparing** ADJS **harsh,** severe, **stringent,** astringent, hard, stern, dour, grim, inclement; **unremitting,** relentless, zealous, ardent, fervent, vehement; **unstinting,** stintless, unstinted

**unspeakable** ADJS **indescribable,** ineffable, inenarrable, inexpressible, unutterable, noncommunicable, incommunicable, indefinable, undefinable, unnamable, unwhisperable, unmentionable; execrable, damnable; disgraceful, scandalous, **infamous,** unpardonable, unforgivable

**unspoiled** ADJS **natural,** naturelike, native; in the state of nature; primitive, primal, pristine, untainted, uncontaminated; **unaffected,** unassuming, unpretending, unpretentious, unfeigning, undisguising, undissimulating, undissembling, undesigning; **intact,** untouched, undamaged, all in one piece <nonformal>, unimpaired, virgin

**unspoken** ADJS **tacit,** wordless, unuttered, unexpressed, unsaid; **implicit**

**unsportsmanlike** ADJS **unfair,** not fair; **unsporting,** unsportsmanly, not done, not kosher <nonformal>, not cricket <Brit nonformal>; **dirty** <nonformal>, foul, below the belt

**unstable** ADJS **unsound,** infirm, **unsubstantial,** unsturdy, unsolid, decrepit, crumbling, fragmented, fragmentary, disintegrating; changeable, **mutable,** inconstant; **insecure,** unsound, insubstantial, **unsteadfast,** unsteady, desultory, shaky

**unsteady** ADJS 1 **shaky,** rickety, spindly, spidery, teetering, teetery, tottery, tottering, doddering, tumbledown, ramshackle, dilapidated, rocky <nonformal>, unstable; groggy, wobbly, staggery
2 **inconstant,** uneven, unrhythmical, unmetrical, rough, unequal, uncertain, unsettled; **variable,** deviative, heteroclite; **capricious,** erratic, off-again-on-again, eccentric

**unsuccessful** ADJS successless, failing; failed, *manqué* <Fr>; unfortunate; fruitless, bootless, no-win <nonformal>, futile, useless; lame, **ineffectual,** ineffective, inefficacious, of no effect; malfunctioning

**unsuitable** ADJS **unacceptable,** inadmissible, undesirable, unfit, **objectionable,** exceptionable, impossible, untenable, indefensible; intolerable; improper, **unbecoming,** unseemly

**unsung** ADJS **unexpressed,** unpronounced, **unsaid, unspoken, unuttered,** undeclared, unbreathed, unvoiced, wordless, silent; **unmentioned,** untalked-of, **untold,** unproclaimed, unpublished; unwritten, unrecorded; **unrenowned,** nameless, inglorious, **unnotable,** unnoticed, unremarked, **undistinguished,** uncelebrated, unhonored, unglorified, unpopular

**unsure** ADJS **uncertain,** doubting, agnostic, **skeptical,** unconvinced, unpersuaded; **unconfident,** unassured, insecure, unsure of oneself; unself-confident, unself-assured, unself-reliant

**unsurpassed** ADJS **best,** very best, greatest *and* top-of-the-line <both nonformal>, **prime,** optimum, optimal; **supreme,** paramount, surpassing, unparalleled, unmatched, unmatchable, matchless, **peerless;** quintessential

**unsuspecting** ADJS **unaware,** unconscious, insensible, unknowing, incognizant; **unmindful,** unwitting, **trusting,** trustful, **confiding,** unsuspicious, without suspicion; credulous; unwarned

**unsymmetrical** ADJS unsymmetric, **asymmetric,** asymmetrical, nonsymmetric, nonsymmetrical; **irregular,** deviative, anamorphous; ununiform *or* **nonuniform,** disproportionate, misshapen

**unsympathetic** ADJS uncompassionate; unconcerned, unsolicitous, non-caring; **unperceptive,** imperceptive, impercipient, blind; **unfeeling,** apathetic, affectless; callous; **unresponsive,** unresponding, unsympathizing, **uncompassionate,** uncompassioned

**untalented** ADJS **unqualified,** inept, unendowed, ungifted, **unfit,** unfitted; **amateurish,** unprofessional

**untangle** VERBS **extricate,** free, release, clear, get out; **disengage,** disentangle, unsnarl, unravel, disentwine, disinvolve, unknot, disembarrass, disembroil; **solve,** resolve, find the solution *or* answer, **work out,** figure out, dope *and* dope out <both nonformal>; **unriddle,** unscramble, untwist, unspin, unweave; **decipher,** decode, decrypt, crack

**untenable** ADJS **unacceptable,** inadmissible, unsuitable, undesirable, **objectionable,** exceptionable, impossible, indefensible; **unsupportable,** unsustainable

**unthinkable** ADJS **unbelievable,** incredible, **implausible,** unimaginable, inconceivable, not to be believed, **hard to believe,** hard of belief, beyond belief, unworthy of belief, not meriting *or* not deserving belief, tall <nonformal>; **defying belief,** staggering belief, passing belief

**untidy** ADJS **slovenly,** slipshod, careless, loose, slack, nonformal, negligent; **unsightly,** unneat, unkempt; **messy** <nonformal>, sloppy <nonformal>, scraggly, poky, seedy <nonformal>, **shabby,** shoddy, schlocky <nonformal>, lumpen, chintzy, grubby <nonformal>, **frowzy,** blowzy, tacky <nonformal>

**untimely** ADJS **unseasonable,** inopportune, ill-timed, ill-seasoned, mistimed, unripe, unready, ill-considered, too late *or* soon, out of phase *or* time *or* sync; **inconvenient,** unhandy; **inappropriate,** irrelevant, improper, out of line, off-base, unsuitable, **inexpedient,** unfitting, unbefitting, untoward, malapropos, *mal à propos* <Fr>, intrusive

**untoward** ADJS **adverse,** detrimental, unfavorable; sinister; hostile, antagonistic, inimical; contrary, counter, counteractive, conflicting, opposing, opposed, opposite, in opposition; **difficult,** troublesome, troublous, hard, trying, rigorous, stressful

**untried** ADJS **unproved,** not proved, unproven, **undemonstrated,** unshown, not shown; untested

**untrue** ADJS **unfaithful,** faithless, of bad faith, trothless; **inconstant,** unsteadfast, fickle; **disloyal,** unloyal; false, not true to; **erroneous,** not true, **not right**

**unusable** ADJS **unserviceable,** unemployable, inoperative, inoperable, unworkable; out of order, out of whack *and* on the blink *and* on the fritz <all nonformal>, in disrepair; inapplicable; unsuitable, unfit; functionless, nonfunctional, otiose

**unused** ADJS unutilized, **unemployed,** unapplied, unexercised; in abeyance, suspended; waived; **unspent,** unexpended, unconsumed; held back, held out, put by, put aside, saved, held in reserve, in hand, spare, to spare, extra, reserve; untapped; **new,** original, pristine, fresh, fresh off the assembly line, mint, in mint condition, factory-fresh

**unusual** ADJS unordinary, **uncustomary,** unwonted, **uncommon,** unfamiliar, atypical, *recherché* <Fr>; **rare,** out of the ordinary, out of this world, out-of-the-way, **off the beaten track,** offbeat, breakaway

**unveil** VERBS **uncover,** uncase, unsheathe, undrape, uncurtain; **disclose**, expose, reveal, bare, take the lid off, manifest, ventilate, take the wraps off, lift *or* draw the veil, raise the curtain, let daylight in, unshroud, unwrap

**unwanted** ADJS unwished, undesired; **unwelcome,** unasked, unbidden, uninvited, uncalled-for, unasked-for

**unwarranted** ADJS **baseless,** groundless, ungrounded, **unfounded,** ill-founded, unbased, **unsupported,** unsustained, **without foundation,** without basis *or* sound basis; **untenable,** unsupportable, unsustainable; idle, empty, vain

**unwavering** ADJS **confident,** sure, secure, **assured,** reassured, decided, determined; **convinced,** persuaded, positive, cocksure; **unhesitating,** unfaltering

**unwelcome** ADJS **unwanted,** unwished, undesired; **unagreeable,** undesirable, unacceptable; **uninvited,** unasked, unbidden, uncalled-for, unasked for

**unwilling** ADJS **disinclined,** indisposed, not in the mood, averse; unconsenting; dead set against, opposed; resistant; disobedient, recalcitrant, refractory, fractious, sullen, sulky, indocile, mutinous; **involuntary,** forced

**unwind** VERBS 1 **relax,** unbend, slack, slacken, **ease; ease up,** let up, slack up, slack off, **ease off,** let down, **slow down,** take it slow, take time to catch one's breath; lay back *and* kick back *and* decompress <all nonformal>
2 unfold, unroll, unfurl, unreel, uncoil, reveal, reveal *or* expose gradually

**unwise** ADJS injudicious, **imprudent,** unpolitic, impolitic, contraindicated, **counterproductive;** indiscreet; inconsiderate, thoughtless, mindless, witless, unthoughtful, unthinking, unreflecting, unreflective; **unreasonable,** unsound, unsensible, senseless, insensate, reasonless, **irrational,** reckless, inadvisable

**unwitting** ADJS **unintentional,** unintended, **unmeant,** unplanned, undesigned, unpurposed, unthought-of; **unpremeditated,** unmeditated, unprompted, unguided, unguarded; **unthinking,** unconscious, involuntary

**unworkable** ADJS **impracticable,** impractical, unpragmatic, unfeasible; unperformable, inoperable, undoable, unnegotiable, unbridgeable

**unwritten** ADJS **traditional; legendary,** oral, handed down; **customary,** conventional, understood, admitted, recognized, acknowledged, received; **hallowed,** time-honored, immemorial, long-established, established, fixed, inveterate, rooted; folk, of the folk, folkloric

**upbeat** ADJS **optimistic,** bright, sunny; cheerful; **rosy,** roseate, rose-colored, *couleur de rose* <Fr>

**update** VERBS **modernize,** streamline; **bring up to date,** keep *or* stay current, move with the times

**upgrade** VERBS **promote,** advance, boost <nonformal>, elevate, jump; kick *or* bump upstairs <nonformal>; **raise;** exalt, aggrandize

**upheaval** NOUNS **convulsion,** cataclysm, catastrophe, disaster; **revolution, break,** break with the past, sudden change, radical *or* revolutionary *or* violent *or* total change, catastrophic change, overthrow, **quantum jump** *or* **leap,** sea change; **uplift,** upcast, upthrust

**uphill** ADJS 1 **laborious,** toilsome, arduous, strenuous, painful, effortful, operose, troublesome, onerous, oppressive, burdensome; **heavy,** hefty <nonformal>, tough <nonformal>, **backbreaking,** grueling, punishing, crushing, killing, Herculean; hard-fought, hard-earned
ADVS 2 **slantingly,** slopingly, aslant, aslope, atilt, rakingly, tipsily, slantwise, on *or* at a slant; slaunchwise *and* slaunchways <both nonformal>; off plumb *or* the vertical; **upgrade**

**uphold** VERBS **buoy,** buoy up; **sustain,** hold up, bear up, upbear, uplift, upraise; **maintain,** support, **keep up,** keep alive; **defend,** offer *or* say in defense, allege in support *or* vindication, assert; **confirm,** affirm, **attest,** warrant, **substantiate,** authenticate, validate, certify, ratify, verify; **corroborate,** bear out, buttress, bolster

**upkeep** NOUNS **preservation,** conservation, saving, salvation, salvage, **keeping,** safekeeping, maintenance, support

**uplift** VERBS **elate,** exalt, elevate, lift; **buoy,** buoy up; **sustain,** hold up, bear up, uphold, upbear, upraise; raise, boost <nonformal>; **ennoble,** aggrandize, magnify, exalt to the skies

**upper class** NOUNS **upper classes,** aristocracy, patriciate, ruling class, ruling circles, elite, elect, the privileged, the classes, the better sort, upper circles, upper cut *and* upper crust *and* cream <all nonformal>, gentry, lords of creation; **high society,** high life, the Four Hundred, *haut monde* <Fr>

**upper crust** NOUNS **society,** fashionable society, **polite society,** high society, high life, *beau monde, haut monde* <both Fr>; **smart set** <nonformal>; the Four Hundred, upper cut <nonformal>; **cream of society,** *crème de la crème* <Fr>, elite, carriage trade; café society, jet set, beautiful people, in-crowd, the glitterati <nonformal>

**upper hand** NOUNS **advantage,** leg up *and* inside track *and* pole position <all nonformal>; whip hand; start, head *or* flying *or* running start; **edge,** bulge *and* jump *and* drop <all nonformal>, trump card

**uppermost** ADJS **paramount,** principal, leading, foremost, main, chief, number one <nonformal>, premier, **prime,** primary, preeminent, **supreme,** cardinal; highest, topmost, toprank, ranking, of the first rank, world-class, **dominant,** predominant, master, controlling

**uppity** ADJS **insolent,** insulting; **presumptuous,** presuming, overpresumptuous, overweening; **audacious,** bold, assured, hardy, bumptious; **contemptuous**, contumelious; **disdainful**, arrogant, uppish <nonformal>; forward, pushy <nonformal>, obtrusive, familiar

**upright** ADJS **honest,** uprighteous, **upstanding,** erect, right, **righteous,** virtuous, good, clean, squeaky-clean <nonformal>, **decent; honorable,** full of integrity, **reputable,** estimable, creditable, worthy, noble, sterling, manly, yeomanly; **respectable,** highly respectable; **ethical,** moral; principled, high-minded, right-minded; **erect**

**uprising** NOUNS **revolt,** rebellion, revolution, mutiny, insurrection, insurgence *or* insurgency, *émeute* <Fr>, rising, outbreak, general uprising, *levée en masse* <Fr>, **riot,** civil disorder

**uproar** NOUNS **commotion,** hubbub, Babel, tumult, turmoil, **racket,** riot, **disturbance,** rumpus <nonformal>, ruckus *and* ruction <both nonformal>, **fracas,** hassle, rampage

**upscale** ADJS **expensive,** dear, costly, **high-priced,** premium, at a premium, top; big ticket <nonformal>, **fancy** *and* stiff *and* steep <all nonformal>, pricey; upmarket, rich, sumptuous, executive *and* posh <both nonformal>, **luxurious,** gold-plated; **prosperous,** high-income, well-heeled <nonformal>; **affluent,** wealthy

**upset** NOUNS 1 **distress,** trouble, vexation, unease; **uneasiness,** perturbation, disturbance, **agitation,** disquiet, disquietude, inquietude, unquietness; **defeat**
2 **dislodgment;** unplacement, **unseating,** unsaddling, unhorsing; **overturn,** overthrow, **turnover,** spill <nonformal>; **capsizing,** capsize, capsizal, turning turtle
VERBS 3 **chagrin,** embarrass, abash, discomfit, disconcert, discompose, confuse, throw into confusion *or* a tizzy, confound, cast down, mortify, put out, put out of face *or* countenance; **distress,** afflict, trouble, burden, load with care, **bother,** disturb, perturb, disquiet, discomfort, agitate; **worry,** give one gray hair, vex, fret, agitate, get to <nonformal>, **harass,** harry
4 **unnerve,** unman, undo, unstring, unbrace, reduce to jelly, **demoralize,** shake, psych out <nonformal>, dash, knock down *or* flat, **crush,** overcome, prostrate
5 **overthrow,** overturn, overwhelm; upend, **subvert,** throw down *or* over; undermine, honeycomb, **sap,** sap the foundations, weaken; **disorder,** disarrange, disorganize, **confuse**, sow confusion; **discompose**, destabilize, unsettle, **disturb,** perturb
ADJS 6 **agitated,** perturbed, disturbed, troubled, disquieted, antsy <nonformal>, unsettled, **discomposed,** flustered, ruffled, shaken, **overcome,** overwhelmed, overpowered, overmastered; *bouleversé* <Fr>

**upside-down** ADJS **inverted,** topsy-turvy, ass over elbows *and* ass over tincups *and* arsy-varsy <all nonformal>; **capsized,** head-over-heels; **mixed up,** balled *or* bollixed up <nonformal>, screwed up <nonformal>, mucked up <nonformal>, **fouled up** *and* fucked up *and* snafu <all nonformal>

**upstage** VERBS **snub,** rebuff, cut *or* cut dead <nonformal>, drop, repulse; **high-hat** <nonformal>; **look down one's nose at,** look cool *or* coldly upon; steal the show, steal the spotlight

**upstart** NOUNS **parvenu,** adventurer,

sprout <nonformal>; *bourgeois gentilhomme* <Fr>, would-be gentleman; *nouveau riche* <Fr>, *arriviste* <Fr>, **newly-rich,** pig in clover <nonformal>; **social climber,** climber, name-dropper, status seeker

*an upstart crow beautified in our feathers*
ROBERT GREENE

**upsurge** NOUNS 1 **surge,** upsurgence, upleap, upshoot, uprush; **gush,** jet, spurt, spout, fountain; uptick <nonformal>, **increase,** uptrend, upswing
VERBS 2 **surge,** rise, rise up, upheave; **rear,** rear up, **tower,** loom; increase

**uptight** ADJS **tense,** tensed-up, **strained,** stretched tight, taut, unrelaxed, under a strain; pedantic, **stuffy** *and* hidebound <both nonformal>

**up-to-date** ADJS 1 **fashionable,** in fashion, smart, in style, in vogue; all the rage, all the thing; abreast of the times, up-to-the-minute, switched-on *and* hip *and* with-it <all nonformal>, trendy <nonformal>, modern, contemporary, newfashioned, new; **in the swim;** sought-after, much sought-after
2 **informed, enlightened, instructed,** versed, well-versed, educated, schooled, **taught;** posted, briefed, primed, trained; **up on,** abreast of, *au courant* <Fr>

**upturn** NOUNS **uptrend,** uptick <nonformal>, upcast, upsweep, upbend, upsurge; **increase,** gain, augmentation, **advance,** appreciation, ascent, mounting, crescendo, waxing, snowballing, **rise** *or* raise, buildup

**urban** ADJS **metropolitan,** municipal, metro, **civic,** oppidan; citywide; citified; downtown, uptown, midtown; **inner-city,** core, core-city, ghetto

**urbane** ADJS **courteous,** polite, civil, gracious, graceful, agreeable, affable, fair

**urge** NOUNS 1 urgency; impulse, impulsion, compulsion; press, **pressure,** drive, push; sudden *or* rash impulse
VERBS 2 **press,** push, work on <nonformal>, twist one's arm <nonformal>; **insist,** push for, not take no for an answer, **importune,** nag, pressure, high-pressure, bring pressure to bear upon, jawbone *and* build a fire under <both nonformal>, talk round *or* around; **lobby; coax,** wheedle, cajole, blandish, plead with, sweet-talk *and* soft-soap <both nonformal>, **exhort,** call on *or* upon, advocate, recommend, put in a good word, buck for *and* hype <both nonformal>; insist upon

**urgent** ADJS **imperative,** imperious, **compelling,** pressing, high-priority, high-pressure, crying, clamorous, insistent, instant, exigent; crucial, critical, pivotal, acute

**urinate** VERBS **pass** *or* **make water,** wet, stale, **piss** <nonformal>, piddle, pee; pee-pee *and* wee-wee *and* make *or* do *or* go number one <all nonformal>

**usable** ADJS **utilizable;** applicable, appliable; practical, operable; **reusable; exploitable;** manipulable, pliable, compliant

**usage** NOUNS 1 **custom,** convention, use, standard usage, standard behavior, **wont,** wonting, **way,** established way, time-honored practice, **tradition,** standing custom, **folkway,** manner, **practice,** praxis, prescription, **observance,** ritual, consuetude, mores
2 **treatment,** handling, management; way *or* means of dealing
3 **diction,** words, wordage, verbiage, word usage, *usus loquendi* <L>, use *or* choice of words, formulation, way of putting *or* couching, word garment, word dressing; **rhetoric,** speech, talk <nonformal>; **language,** dialect, parlance, locution, expression, grammar; **idiom**

**use** NOUNS 1 **employment,** utilization, usage; exercise, exertion, active use; good use; ill use, wrong use, misuse; hard use, hard *or* rough usage; **application,** appliance; expenditure, expending, using up, exhausting, dissipation, dissipating, **consumption**
2 **function,** purpose, role, part, end use, immediate purpose, ultimate purpose, operational purpose, operation; work, duty, office
3 **wear,** hard wear; wear and tear
VERBS 4 **utilize,** make use of, do with; **employ,** practice, ply, work, manage, handle, operate, **wield,** play; have *or* enjoy the use of; exercise, exert; **exploit,** take advantage of, **use for one's own ends;** make a paw *or* cat's-paw of, sucker *and* play for a sucker <both nonformal>; **manipulate,** work on, work upon, stroke, play on *or* upon; play both ends against the middle; use ill, ill-use, abuse, misuse

**used to** ADJS **accustomed,** wont, wonted; **familiar with,** conversant with, **at home in** *or* **with,** no stranger to, an old hand at, **habituated,** *habitué* <Fr>; **in the habit of,** never free from; in a rut

**useful** ADJS employable, of use, of service, **serviceable,** good for; **helpful,** of help; **advantageous,** to one's advantage *or* profit, profitable, beneficial, fructuous, worthwhile, worth one's while; **practical,** banausic, pragmatical, **functional,** utilitarian, of general utility *or* application; fitting, proper, appropriate, expedient; well-used, well-thumbed

**useless** ADJS of no use, no go <nonformal>; **aimless,** meaningless, **purposeless,** of no purpose, **pointless,** feckless, futile; **unavailing,** of no avail, failed; ineffective, **ineffectual,** inefficacious, of no effect; malfunctioning, worthless, unrewarding

**user** NOUNS 1 employer; **consumer,** enjoyer
2 **drug user,** drug abuser, junkie *and* head *and* druggy *and* doper *and* toker *and* fiend *and* freak *and* space cadet <all nonformal>

**user-friendly** ADJS **handy,** wieldy, **manageable,** maneuverable; **convenient,** foolproof, goofproof <nonformal>, practical, untroublesome

**usher** NOUNS 1 **attendant,** tender, usherer, usherette; ostiary
VERBS 2 **escort,** conduct, have in tow <nonformal>, marshal, shepherd, **guide,** lead; convoy, guard; **attend,** wait on *or* upon; **chaperon**

**usual** ADJS **regular; customary,** habitual, accustomed, wonted, **normative,** prescriptive, standard, regulation, conventional; **common,** commonplace, ordinary, average, everyday, mediocre, familiar, household, vernacular, stock; **prevailing,** predominating, current, popular; **universal**

**usurp** VERBS **arrogate,** seize, grab *and* latch on to <both nonformal>, **appropriate,** assume, adopt, take over, arrogate to oneself, pretend to, infringe, encroach

**usury** NOUNS **lending,** loaning; moneylending, lending at interest; loansharking *and* shylocking <both informal>; excessive *or* exorbitant interest

**utilize** VERBS **use,** make use of, do with; **employ,** practice, ply, work, manage, handle, manipulate, operate, **wield,** play; **have** *or* **enjoy the use of;** exercise, **exert**

**utmost** ADJS **superlative,** supreme, greatest, best, highest, maximal, maximum, most, outstanding, stickout <nonformal>; top, topmost, uppermost, damndest <nonformal>

**utopia** NOUNS Utopia <Sir Thomas More>, **paradise,** heaven, **heaven on earth;** land of dreams, land of enchantment, land of heart's desire, wonderland, cloudland, fairyland, Eden, Garden of Eden; the Promised Land, land of promise, land of plenty, land of milk and honey

**utopian** ADJS perfectionist, millenarian, chiliastic; **ideal,** idealized; Arcadian, Edenic, paradisal; pie in the sky <nonformal>

**utter** VERBS 1 **say,** breathe, sound, **voice,** vocalize, phonate, **articulate,** enunciate, pronounce, lip, give voice, give tongue, give utterance; **express,** give expression, verbalize, put in words, find words to express; **tell,** communicate; **convey,** impart, disclose; **issue,** deal out, retail, dispense
ADJS 2 **downright,** outright, out-and-out; **absolute,** perfect, consummate, superlative, surpassing, the veriest, positive, definitive, classical, pronounced, decided, profound, stark; **thorough,** thoroughgoing, **complete,** total

# V

**vacancy** NOUNS vacuity, voidness, **emptiness,** blankness, hollowness, inanition; **bareness,** barrenness, desolateness, bleakness, desertedness; **nonoccupancy,** nonoccupation, nonresidence; job vacancy, **opening,** open place *or* post, vacant post

**vacate** VERBS **quit,** evacuate, abandon, desert, turn one's back on, walk away from, leave to one's fate, leave flat *or* high and dry; **withdraw,** retreat, **beat a retreat,** retire, remove; walk away, abscond, disappear, vanish; **bow out** <nonformal>, make one's exit; **resign,** demit, leave, withdraw from; **abdicate,** renounce the throne, give up the crown

**vacation** NOUNS 1 holiday <Brit>; **time off;** day off, week off, month off, etc; paid vacation, paid holiday <Brit>; **leave,** leave of absence, furlough; **sabbatical,** sabbatical leave *or* year; weekend; busman's holiday; package tour *or* holiday
VERBS 2 **get away from it all,** holiday, take a holiday; **take a leave of absence,** take leave, go on leave, go on furlough, take one's sabbatical; weekend

**vacillate** VERBS **waver,** waffle <nonformal>, **fluctuate,** pendulate, oscillate, wobble, wobble about, teeter, totter <old>, dither, swing from one thing to another, **shilly-shally,** back and fill, keep off and on, keep *or* leave hanging in midair; blow hot and cold; **equivocate**, fudge; change one's mind, tergiversate; shift, change horses in midstream, **change**

**vacuum** NOUNS **void,** blank, emptiness, empty space, inanity; **nothingness;** *tabula rasa* <L>, clean slate; nothing; **omission,** gap, hiatus, hole, break, lacuna, discontinuity, interval; **vacuity,** vacuousness, vacancy, mental void, blankness, hollowness, inanity, vapidity, jejunity

**vagabond** NOUNS 1 **vagrant,** bum *or* bummer <nonformal>, loafer, wastrel, *lazzarone* <Ital>; **tramp,** turnpiker, piker, knight of the road, easy rider, **hobo** *or* bo <nonformal>, rounder <nonformal>, stiff *or* bindlestiff <nonformal>; landloper, sundowner *or* swagman *or* swagsman <all Australian nonformal>; beachcomber, idler; ski bum, beach bum, surf bum, tennis bum; **wanderer;** drifter, derelict, homeless person
ADJS 2 **wandering,** roving, roaming, ranging, **rambling,** meandering, strolling, **straying,** straggling, shifting, flitting, landloping, errant, **transient,** transitory, fugitive; **vagrant,** vagabondish; **footloose,** footloose and fancy-free

**vagrant** NOUNS 1 **bum,** stiff <nonformal>, derelict, skid-row bum, Bowery bum, *lazzarone* <Ital>; beachcomber; **good-for-nothing,** good-for-naught, **ne'er-do-well,** wastrel; drifter, hobo, tramp
ADJS 2 **inconstant,** irregular, spasmodic; **desultory,** rambling, roving, wanton, wayward, wandering, afloat, adrift; **unrestrained,** undisciplined, irresponsible, uncontrolled, fast and loose

**vague** ADJS **indefinite,** indecisive, indeterminate, indeterminable, **undetermined,** unpredetermined, undestined; **random,** stochastic, entropic, **chance,** chancy <nonformal>, dicey *and* dodgy <Brit nonformal>, aleatory *or* aleatoric, hit-or-miss; indefinable, undefined, ill-defined, **unclear,** unplain, **indistinct,** fuzzy, **obscure,** confused, hazy, shadowy, misty, foggy, fog-bound, murky, blurred, blurry, veiled; **loose,** lax, inexact, inaccurate, imprecise; nonspecific, unspecified; **broad,** general, sweeping; amorphous, shapeless, inchoate, disordered, orderless, chaotic, incoherent

**vain** ADJS 1 **vainglorious,** conceited, overproud, overweening; **self-important,** self-esteeming, self-assuming, **self-admiring,** self-delighting, self-worshiping, self-loving, self-infatuated, narcissistic; **self-satisfied,** self-content, self-contented, self-approving, self-congratulating, self-congratulatory, self-complacent, **smug,** complacent, self-sufficient
2 **futile,** hollow, empty, idle; absurd; inane, fatuous, fatuitous; **unwarranted**

*weary, stale, flat, and unprofitable*
SHAKESPEARE

**valentine** NOUNS **love letter,** billet-doux, mash note <nonformal>

**valet** NOUNS **man,** manservant, serving man, gillie <Scots>, **boy,** *garçon* <Fr>, houseboy, houseman; butler; *valet de* *chambre* <Fr>, gentleman, gentleman's gentleman

**valiant** ADJS **courageous,** plucky, brave, bold, valorous, gallant, intrepid, doughty, **hardy,** stalwart, stout, stout-hearted, ironhearted, lionhearted, great-hearted, bold-spirited, bold as a lion; **heroic,** chivalrous, chivalric, knightly, knightlike, soldierly, soldierlike; **manly,** manful, virile, macho

**valid** ADJS **sound,** well-grounded, well-founded, conforming to the facts *or* the data *or* the evidence *or* reality, hard, solid, substantial; consistent, self-consistent, logical; **good,** just, sufficient; **cogent,** weighty, authoritative; legal, lawful, legitimate, **binding**

**validate** VERBS **confirm,** affirm, **attest,** warrant, **substantiate,** authenticate, certify, ratify, **verify; corroborate,** bear out, support, buttress, **sustain,** fortify, bolster, back, back up, reinforce, undergird, strengthen; **document;** probate, prove

**valley** NOUNS vale, dale, dell, dingle; **glen,** bottom, bottoms, bottom glade, intervale, wadi, grove; trench, trough, lunar rill; gap, pass, ravine

**valor** NOUNS **courage,** nerve, pluck, **bravery,** braveness, **boldness,** valorousness, valiance, valiancy, **gallantry,** conspicuous gallantry, gallantry under fire *or* beyond the call of duty, gallantness, **intrepidity,** intrepidness, **prowess,** virtue; **heroism,** military *or* martial spirit, soldierly quality *or* virtues; **manliness,** manfulness, **manhood,** virility, machismo

**valuable** ADJS of value, all for the best, all to the good, **profitable,** yielding a return, well-spent, **worthwhile,** rewarding; gainful, remunerative; **precious,** dear, worthy, rich, golden, of great price <old>, worth a pretty penny <nonformal>, worth a king's ransom, worth its weight in gold, good as gold, precious as the apple of one's eye; **priceless,** invaluable, inestimable, without *or* beyond price, not to be had for love or money, not for all the tea in China

**value** NOUNS 1 **benefit,** use, service, avail, profit, advantage, percentage *and* mileage <all nonformal>, what's in it for one <nonformal>, convenience; worth, **preciousness,** dearness, high *or* great value, extraordinary worth, **pricelessness,** invaluableness

VERBS 2 **esteem,** treasure, prize, appreciate, **rate highly,** think highly of, think well of, **think much of,** set store by; give *or* attach *or* ascribe importance to; make much of, make a fuss *or* stir about, make much ado about; hold up as an example

**vamp** NOUNS 1 **flirt,** coquette, gold digger <nonformal>; **courtesan,** adventuress, **seductress,** femme fatale, vampire, temptress

VERBS 2 **charm,** becharm, **infatuate,** hold in thrall, command one's affection, **fascinate,** attract, allure, grow on one, strike *or* tickle one's fancy, **captivate,** bewitch, enrapture, carry away, sweep off one's feet, turn one's head, inflame with love; **seduce,** draw on, tempt, tantalize

3 **improvise,** wing it <nonformal>, fake <nonformal>, play by ear <nonformal>

**vampire** NOUNS **frightener,** scarer, hair-raiser; **ogre,** ogress, **monster,** harpy, werewolf, ghoul, bête noire; incubus, succubus, nightmare; **ghost,** specter, phantom, revenant; bloodsucker; living dead

**vandalism** NOUNS **destruction,** ruin, ruination, rack, **rack and ruin; desolation;** dissolution, disintegration, depredation, spoliation, despoliation, despoilment

**vanguard** NOUNS **forefront,** cutting edge, front line; **predecessor,** forebear, precedent, antecedent, **ancestor; avant-garde,** avant-gardist, innovator, groundbreaker; advance guard, van

**vanilla** ADJS **unadorned,** undecorated, unornamented, unembellished, ungarnished, unfurbished, unvarnished, untrimmed, plain; back-to-basics, no-frills, no-nonsense, plain-vanilla *and* white-bread *or* white-bready <all nonformal>

**vanish** VERBS **disappear,** vanish from sight, do a vanishing act <nonformal>, depart, fly, **flee,** go, be gone, **go away,** pass, pass out *or* away, pass out of sight, exit, pull up stakes <nonformal>, leave the scene, clear out, pass out of the picture, pass from sight, become lost to sight, be seen no more; **perish, die,** die off; die out *or* away, dwindle, wane, fade, **fade out** *or* **away,** do a fade-out <nonformal>; dematerialize, evaporate, evanesce, **vanish into thin air,** go up in smoke; **cease to be;** leave no trace

**vanity** NOUNS **vainness;** overproudness, overweening pride; **self-importance,** consequentiality, consequentialness, **self-esteem,** high self-esteem *or* self-valuation, **self-admiration,** self-love, *amour-propre* <Fr>, self-infatuation, narcissism, **self-satisfaction,** ego trip <nonformal>, self-approbation, self-congratulation, **smugness,** complacency, self-sufficiency; vainglory, vaingloriousness

*an itch for the praise of fools*
ROBERT BROWNING

**vapid** ADJS **insipid,** inane, superficial; **flat,** tasteless; characterless, colorless, pointless; **dead,** lifeless, spiritless, bloodless, pale, pallid, etiolated, effete; **dreary,** drearisome, dismal; **heavy,** leaden, ponderous, elephantine; inexcitable; **vacuous,** vacant, empty, hollow, inane, jejune, blank, airheaded *and* bubbleheaded <both nonformal>; **rattlebrained,** rattleheaded; scatterbrained

**vapor** NOUNS volatile; **fume,** reek, exhalation, breath, effluvium; fluid; **miasma,** mephitis, fetid air; **smoke,** smudge; **damp,** chokedamp, blackdamp, firedamp, afterdamp; **steam,** water vapor; **cloud**

**variable** ADJS **inconstant,** inconsistent, varying, **changeable,** changing, mutable, capricious, impulsive, mercurial, erratic, spasmodic, sporadic, wavery, wavering, **unstable,** unsteady; **multiform,** diversiform, versatile; **protean;** deviative, heteroclite; **capricious,** off-again-on-again, eccentric; checkered, ever-changing, many-sided, kaleidoscopic

**variation** NOUNS **inconstancy,** instability, changefulness, unstableness, **unsteadiness,** unsteadfastness, unfixedness, unsettledness, rootlessness; **variability,** variety, restlessness, deviability; unpredictability, irregularity; flightiness, impulsiveness, mercuriality, moodiness, whimsicality, **capriciousness,** fickleness; **changing,** fluctuation, vicissitude, oscillation, vacillation

**varied** ADJS **diversified,** assorted, heterogeneous; **various,** many and various, divers <old>, diverse, sundry, **several,** many; of all sorts *or* conditions *or* kinds *or* shapes *or* descriptions *or* types; **conglomerate,** pluralistic, multiracial, multicultural, multiethnic, multinational, **miscellaneous,** medley, motley, dappled, patchy

**variety** NOUNS 1 **miscellany,** miscellanea, collectanea; **assortment,** medley, mixture; hodgepodge, conglomerate, **conglomeration,** omnium-gatherum <nonformal>; **sundries,** oddments, odds and ends; **multiformity,** multifariousness, nonuniformity, **diversity,** diversification, variation, variegation, variability, versatility, proteanism, manifoldness, multiplicity, heterogeneity, pluralism
2 **kind,** sort, ilk, type, breed of cat <nonformal>, lot <nonformal>, denomination, designation, description, style, manner, **nature,** character, persuasion, the like *or* likes of <nonformal>

**various** ADJS **diversified,** varied, assorted, heterogeneous; many and various, divers <old>, diverse, sundry, **several,** many; of all sorts *or* conditions *or* kinds *or* shapes *or* descriptions *or* types; pluralistic

**vary** VERBS **differ,** diverge, stand apart, be distinguished *or* distinct; **deviate from,** diverge from, divaricate from, depart from; **disagree with,** disaccord with, conflict with, contrast with, clash with, jar with; not be like, bear no resemblance to, not square with, not accord with; **diversify,** variegate, waver, mutate; change, intermit, **fluctuate,** shift, lack regularity, go by fits and starts

**vast** ADJS **huge,** immense, enormous, astronomic, astronomical, humongous *and* jumbo <both nonformal>, tremendous, prodigious, stupendous, macro, mega, giga; great big, larger than life, Homeric, mighty, **titanic,** colossal, monumental, heroic, towering, mountainous; profound, abysmal, deep as the ocean; **mammoth,** gigantic, giant; **infinite**

**vault** NOUNS 1 **jump,** spring, saltation, leap; pole vault
2 **compartment,** chamber, space, enclosed space, **crypt,** burial chamber; arch, **span,** vaulting, concameration, camber; **dome,** cupola, geodesic dome, igloo, concha; arched roof, ceilinged roof

**veer** VERBS **swerve,** sheer, curve, **shift,** **turn,** trend, bend, heel, bear off; turn right, turn left, hang a right *or* left <nonformal>; alter one's course, make a course correction; **go sideways,** sidle, **edge,** angle, slant, skew, sidestep; go crabwise; **sideslip,** skid

**vegetable** ADJS 1 vegetal, vegetative, vegetational, vegetarian; **plantlike; herbaceous,** herbal, herbous, herbose, herby; leguminous, leguminose, leguminiform
ADJS 2 **passive;** standpat <nonformal>, do-nothing; **inert,** like a bump on a log <nonformal>, immobile, dormant, stagnant, stagnating, vegetative, static, stationary, motionless, immobile, unmoving, paralyzed, paralytic; **inactive,** idle; quiescent, torpid, comatose; phlegmatic, numb

**vegetarian** NOUNS 1 lactovegetarian, vegan, fruitarian, plant-eater, **herbivore,** phytophagan, phytophage; grass-eater, graminivore; grain-eater, granivore
ADJS 2 vegetable-eating, lactovegetarian, veganistic, fruitarian; plant-eating, **herbivorous,** phytivorous, phytophagous; grass-eating, graminivorous; grain-eating, granivorous

**vegetate** VERBS 1 **grow;** germinate, pullulate; **burgeon,** sprout, shoot; **bud,** gemmate, put forth *or* put out buds; flourish, luxuriate, riot, grow rank *or* lush
2 **stagnate,** merely exist, just be, pass the time; sleep, slumber, idle

**vegetation** NOUNS 1 **plants; flora,** plant life, vegetable life; **vegetable kingdom,** plant kingdom; herbage, flowerage, verdure, greenery, greens; **growth;** germination, pullulation; burgeoning, sprouting; budding, luxuriation
2 **mere existence,** simple existence, **vegetable existence,** mere tropism; **stagnation,** stagnancy, apathy, indolence, languor, torpor

**vehement** ADJS emphatic, **passionate,** impassioned, enthusiastic, **ardent,** fiery, **fervent,** burning, glowing, warm; urgent, stirring, exciting, stimulating, provoking

**vehicle** NOUNS **conveyance,** carrier, means of carrying *or* transporting, means of transport, medium of transportation, carriage; watercraft, aircraft; **instrument,** tool, implement, appliance, device; contrivance, lever, mechanism; organ; agent; medium, mediator, intermedium, intermediary, intermediate, interagent, liaison, go-between

**veil** NOUNS veiling; *yashmak* <Turk>, *chador* <Iranian>; mantilla; curtain, pall, **cover,** screen, wraps; fig leaf; **wraps** <nonformal>; cover, disguise; **veil of secrecy,** iron curtain, bamboo curtain; wall *or* barrier of secrecy; guise, semblance; mask, cloak, cover-up, cover story, alibi

**vein** NOUNS 1 **duct,** vessel, canal, passage; blood vessel, jugular vein, vena cava, pulmonary vein; portal vein, varicose vein; venation; veinlet, veinule, venule
2 **style; mode,** manner, strain; **way,** habit, tenor, cast, hue, tone, grain, streak, stripe, mold, brand, stamp; **mood,** humor, feeling, feelings, temper, frame of mind, state of mind, morale, note
3 **deposit,** mineral deposit, pay dirt; **lode,** seam, dike, ore bed

**velocity** NOUNS **speed; rapidity,** celerity, **swiftness,** fastness, quickness, speediness; **rate,** gait, pace, tread, step, stride, clip *and* lick <both nonformal>

**velvet** NOUNS 1 **comfort,** ease, security, well-being; clover <nonformal>, bed of roses; luxury, lap of luxury, life of ease; solid comfort
2 **smoothness**, down, **downiness,** fluff, fluffiness, velvetiness; satin, satininess; silk, silkiness; softness

**venal** ADJS **corruptible,** bribable, purchasable, on the take *and* on the pad <nonformal>, mercenary, hireling; **corrupt,** bought and paid for, in one's pocket

**vendetta** NOUNS **feud,** blood feud, **bad blood,** ill blood

**vendor** NOUNS supplier, salesman; **peddler,** huckster, hawker, butcher <old>, colporteur, chapman <Brit>; coster *or* costermonger <both Brit>; sidewalk salesman

**veneer** NOUNS **coating,** coat, gloss; **facing,** veneering, revetment; pellicle, **film,** skin, patina, scum, membrane; slick, oil slick; **lamina,** lamella; **sheet,** leaf, *feuille* <Fr>, foil

**venerable** ADJS **reverend,** estimable, honorable, worshipful, august, awe-inspiring, awesome, awful, dreadful; respected, respectable, highly respectable; revered, venerated, worshipful; time-honored, **aged,** elderly, old, hoary, grown old in years, along *or* up *or* advanced *or* on in years, **at an advanced age,** ancient, geriatric, gerontic; old as Methuselah *or* as God *or* as the hills; patriarchal

**venereal disease** NOUNS **VD, sexually-transmitted disease** *or* STD, social disease, Cupid's itch *or* Venus's curse, dose <nonformal>; chancre, chancroid; gonorrhea *or* clap *or* the clap *or* claps <nonformal>; syphilis *or* syph *or* the syph *or* the pox <nonformal>

**vengeance** NOUNS **revenge,** avengement, sweet revenge, getting even, evening of the score; **wrath;** revanche, revanchism; **retaliation,** reprisal; vendetta, feud, blood feud; the wrath of God

**venom** NOUNS **poison,** venin, toxic, toxin, toxicant; **bitterness,** sourness, **rancor,** acrimony, gall, virulence, vitriol, **animosity,** animus; **ill will,** ill feeling, bitter feeling, **hard feelings,** no love lost; **bad blood**

**vent** NOUNS 1 **outlet,** ventage, venthole, port; venting, discharge; **emission,** emitting, giving forth, giving out; emanation
VERBS 2 **reveal,** make known, tell, breathe, utter, ventilate, air, give vent to, **give out,** let out <Brit>, let get around, out with <nonformal>, come out with; **exhaust,** drain

**ventilate** VERBS 1 **air,** air out, cross-ventilate, refresh, freshen
2 **disclose,** reveal, let out, show, impart, **leak,** let slip out, let the cat out of the bag *and* spill the beans <both nonformal>; **uncover,** unveil, take the lid off <nonformal>, take the wraps off, lift *or* draw the veil, raise the curtain, let daylight in, **make public,** go public with <nonformal>; bring *or* lay *or* drag before the public, **display,** take one's case to the public, **give** *or* **put out,** give to the world, **make known;** divulge, bring into the open, get out in the open, open up, broach, give vent to

**venture** NOUNS **undertaking,** enterprise, operation, work, **project,** proposition *and* deal <both nonformal>; **program,** plan; **affair,** business, matter, task, concern, interest; **initiative,** effort, attempt; **investment,** risk, flutter, flier, plunge <nonformal>, speculation

**verbalize** VERBS **express,** give expression, put in words, find words to express; **word,** formulate, put into words, couch, phrase

**verbatim** ADJS 1 **genuine,** verisimilar, veristic; **literal,** following the letter, letter-perfect, *au pied de la lettre* <Fr>, true to the letter; word-perfect, word-for-word; **original,** unimitated, uncopied; unexaggerated, undistorted; unvarnished, uncolored, unqualified; unadulterated
ADVS 2 **exactly,** precisely, to a T, expressly; **literally,** *literatim* <L>, word for word, word by word, word for word and letter for letter, *verbatim et litteratim* <L>, in the same words, *ipsissimis verbis* <L>, to the letter, according to the letter, *au pied de la lettre* <Fr>; **faithfully,** strictly, rigorously, rigidly

**verbiage** NOUNS **diction,** words, wordage, word-usage, **usage,** *usus loquendi* <L>, use *or* choice of words, formulation, way of putting *or* couching; **rhetoric,** speech, talk <nonformal>; **language,** dialect, parlance, locution, expression, grammar; **wordiness,** verbosity, verbalism, verbality

**verdict** NOUNS **decision,** resolution <old>, **determination,** finding, holding; **pronouncement,** deliverance; **award,** action, sentence; condemnation, doom; acquittal; dictum; **judgment,** landmark decision

**verify** VERBS **confirm,** test, prove, audit, **collate,** validate, **check,** check up *or* on *or* out <nonformal>, check over *or* through, **double-check,** triple-check, cross-check, recheck, check and doublecheck, check up and down, check over and through, check in and out; **audit,** take stock, inventory

*make assurance double sure*
SHAKESPEARE

**veritable** ADJS **real,** actual, factual, for real <nonformal>, de facto, simple, sober, **hard; absolute,** positive; accepted, conceded, stipulated, given; admitted, well-known, **established,** inescapable, indisputable, undeniable; demonstrable, provable; empirical, **objective,** historical; **true,** honest-to-God <nonformal>, genuine, card-carrying <nonformal>, **authentic**

**vermin** NOUNS 1 parasite; **louse,** head louse, body louse, grayback, cootie <nonformal>; crab, crab louse; weevil
2 **riffraff,** trash, raff, chaff, **rubbish,** dregs, sordes, offscourings, off-scum, **scum,** scum of the earth, dregs *or* scum *or* off-scum *or* offscourings of society, swinish multitude

**vernacular** NOUNS **nonformal language**

*or* **speech,** nonformal standard speech, **spoken language,** colloquial language *or* speech, vernacular language *or* speech; colloquialism, colloquial usage, ordinary language *or* speech; nonformal English, conversational English, colloquial English, English as it is spoken; **jargon,** lingo <nonformal>, **slang,** cant, argot, patois, patter

**versatile** ADJS **handy,** convenient; available, accessible, **ready, at hand,** to hand, **on hand,** on tap, on deck <nonformal>, on call, at one's call *or* beck and call, at one's elbow, at one's fingertips, just around the corner, at one's disposal; adaptable; **ambidextrous,** all around <nonformal>, broad-gauge, **well-rounded,** many-sided, generally capable; adjustable, flexible, resourceful

**verse** NOUNS stanza; **poem,** rhyme; verselet, versicle

*imaginary gardens with*
*real toads in them*
MARIANNE MOORE

**version** NOUNS **rendering,** rendition; reading, lection, variant, variant reading; **edition,** critical *or* scholarly edition; variorum edition *or* variorum; conflation, composite reading *or* text; **draft,** first draft, second draft, etc, recension

**versus** ADJS vs, **opposed to,** adverse to, counter to, **in opposition to,** in conflict with, at cross-purposes with; **against,** agin <nonformal>, dead against, athwart

**vertical** ADJS **upright,** bolt upright, ramrod straight, **erect,** upstanding, standing up, stand-up; rearing, rampant; **upended,** upraised, upreared

**vertigo** NOUNS **dizziness,** vertiginousness, spinning head, swimming, swimming of the head, **giddiness,** wooziness <nonformal>, **lightheadedness;** Ménière's syndrome

**verve** NOUNS **vim,** fire, adrenalin, **dash,** drive; **liveliness,** vivacity, vitality, life, **animation,** spiritedness, spirit, esprit, élan, **sprightliness,** high spirits, zestfulness, zest, zip <nonformal>, vigor, gusto, **exuberance,** heartiness

**vessel** NOUNS 1 **duct,** canal, passage; blood vessel
2 **ship,** craft, bottom, bark, argosy, hull, hulk, keel, watercraft
3 **container,** receptacle; receiver, holder, utensil; basin, pot, pan, cup, glass, ladle, bottle

**vest** NOUNS 1 **waistcoat,** weskit <nonformal>, down vest, bulletproof vest
VERBS 2 **endow,** invest; endow with, favor with, bless with, grace with, vest with; **settle on** *or* **upon;** dower
3 **delegate,** devolute, devolve, devolve upon, invest; depute, **deputize**

**vested interest** NOUNS **pressure group,** interest group, special-interest group, political action committee *or* PAC, single-issue group; **special interest;** vested right

**vestige** NOUNS **remainder,** remains, remnant, residue, residuum, **rest,** balance; **leavings,** leftovers, oddments; survival, trace, hint, shadow, afterimage, afterglow, **spoor,** scent, whiff

**veteran** NOUNS 1 vet <nonformal>, seasoned *or* grizzled veteran, **old pro** <nonformal>; **old hand,** old-timer <nonformal> one of the old guard; old campaigner, war-horse *or* old war-horse <nonformal>; salt *and* old salt *and* old sea dog <all nonformal>, shellback <nonformal>
ADJS 2 **experienced,** practiced, mature, matured, ripe, ripened, **seasoned,** tried, well-tried, tried and true, **old,** an old dog at <nonformal>

**veto** VERBS put one's veto upon, decide *or* rule against, **turn thumbs down on** <nonformal>, negative, kill; **reject,** categorically reject, disallow, not hear of; vote down, exclude, ostracize, blackball, ban; say no to; **pocket**

**vex** VERBS **irk,** annoy, aggravate, exasperate; **trouble,** worry, give one gray hair, plague, harass, bother, hassle; **provoke,** incense, arouse, distress, inflame, embitter; **irritate,** annoy, nettle, fret, chafe; **pique,** peeve *and* miff <both nonformal>, huff; **ruffle,** roil, rile <nonformal>, ruffle one's feathers, rankle; **stir up,** work up, stir one's bile, stir the blood

**via** PREPS **through,** by, passing by *or* through, **by way of,** by the way of; over, around, round about, here and there in, all through

**viable** ADJS 1 **acceptable,** admissible, **agreeable,** unobjectionable, unexceptionable, tenable; **practicable,** feasible, practical
2 **living,** alive, having life, live, very much alive, alive and well, alive and

kicking <nonformal>, conscious, breathing, quick <old>, **animate,** animated, **vital,** zoetic, instinct with life, imbued *or* endowed with life, vivified, enlivened, inspirited; tenacious of life; capable of life *or* survival

**vibrant** ADJS **energetic,** vigorous, strenuous, forceful, forcible, strong, dynamic, kinetic, intense, acute, keen, incisive, trenchant, vivid; **resonant,** reverberant, sonorous, plangent, rolling

**vibrate** VERBS **resonate,** pulse, throb; **oscillate,** librate, nutate; **shake,** quake, jactitate; **tremble,** quiver, quaver, falter, **shudder,** shiver, twitter, didder, chatter

**vicarious** ADJS ersatz, **mock,** phony *and* fake *and* bogus <all nonformal>, counterfeit, imitation; **proxy**

**vice** NOUNS viciousness; criminality, **wrongdoing**; **immorality,** unmorality, evil; amorality; **unvirtuousness,** ungoodness; **unrighteousness,** ungodliness, unsaintliness, unangelicalness; **uncleanness,** impurity, unchastity, fallenness, fallen state, lapsedness; delinquency, moral delinquency; peccability; **weakness,** weakness of the flesh, **flaw,** moral flaw *or* blemish, **frailty,** infirmity; failing, failure; weak point, weak side, foible; bad habit, besetting sin; **fault,** imperfection

**vice versa** ADJS **inversely,** conversely, contrarily, contrariwise, the other way around, **backwards,** turned around; **reciprocally,** back and forth, backward and forward, backwards and forwards, alternately, seesaw, to and fro; counter, topsy-turvy, upside down, arsy-varsy <nonformal>, **on the other hand,** *per contra* <L>, **on** *or* **to the contrary,** *tout au contraire* <Fr>

**vicinity** NOUNS **nearness,** closeness, nighness, **proximity,** propinquity, intimacy, immediacy; approximation, approach, convergence; a rough idea <nonformal>; vicinage, **neighborhood,** environs, surroundings, surround, setting, grounds, purlieus, confines, precinct; neck of the woods <nonformal>

**vicious** ADJS **savage,** ferocious, feral, mean *and* mean as a junkyard dog <both nonformal>, fierce, **atrocious,** truculent, fell; **wicked,** evil, bad, naughty, wrong, sinful, iniquitous, peccant, reprobate; **malignant,** malign, malevolent, malefic

**victim** NOUNS 1 **sufferer,** prey; **wretch,** poor devil <nonformal>, object of compassion; martyr
2 **quarry,** game, prey, venery, beasts of venery, the hunted; **dupe,** john *and* lamb *and* mark *and* monkey *and* patsy *and* sucker <all nonformal>

**victimize** VERBS **cheat,** gull, deceive, pigeon, fudge, **swindle,** defraud, practice fraud upon, euchre, **con,** finagle, **fleece,** mulct, **bilk,** cozen, chouse, **cheat out of,** do out of, chouse out of, beguile of *or* out of; **persecute,** oppress, **torment,** harass, get *or* keep after, get *or* keep at, harry, hound, beset

**Victorian** ADJS **prudish,** priggish, prim, prissy, smug, stuffy <nonformal>, oldmaidish, **overmodest,** demure, **strait-laced,** stiff-necked, hidebound, narrow, censorious, sanctimonious, **puritanical**

**victorious** ADJS **triumphant,** triumphal, **winning,** prevailing; conquering, vanquishing, defeating, overcoming; ahead of the game, ascendant, in the ascendant, in ascendancy, sitting on top of the world *and* sitting pretty <both nonformal>, dominant; successful; flushed with success *or* victory

**victory** NOUNS **triumph,** conquest, subduing, subdual; a feather in one's cap <nonformal>; total victory, grand slam; **championship,** crown, laurels, cup, trophy, belt, blue ribbon, first prize

**video** NOUNS **television,** TV, telly <Brit nonformal>; the small screen *or* the tube <both nonformal>, the boob tube <nonformal>

**vie** VERBS **compete,** contend, **compete with** *or* **against,** vie with, challenge, enter into competition with, give a run for one's money, **meet;** try *or* test one another; **rival,** emulate, outvie; keep up with the Joneses

**view** NOUNS 1 **intention,** intent, intendment, mindset, **aim,** effect, meaning, study, animus, **point,** purpose, function, set *or* settled *or* fixed purpose; **estimate,** estimation; opinion; **assessment,** assessing, **appraisal,** appraisement, appraising, appreciation, reckoning
VERBS 2 **look,** peer, have a look, take a gander *and* take a look <both nonformal>, direct the eyes, turn *or* bend the eyes, cast one's eye, lift up the eyes; **look at,** take a look at, eye, **eyeball** <nonformal>, have a look-see <nonformal>, look on *or* upon, gaze at *or* upon; **watch,** observe, regard; **contemplate,**

look upon, regard, view with the mind's eye, **envisage,** envision, **visualize,** imagine, image

**viewpoint** NOUNS **standpoint,** point of view, vantage, vantage point, point *or* coign of vantage, where one stands; bird's-eye view, worm's-eye view, fly on the wall; **outlook,** angle, angle of vision, *optique* <Fr>; mental outlook, perspective

**vigil** NOUNS **watchfulness,** watching, observance, surveillance; watch, lookout; *qui vive* <Fr>; **sharp eye,** weather eye, peeled eye, watchful eye, eagle eye, lidless *or* sleepless *or* unblinking *or* unwinking eye; all-night vigil, lidless vigil, *per vigilium* <L>

**vigilant** ADJS **wary,** prudent, **watchful,** lidless, sleepless, observant; **on the lookout,** *aux aguets* <Fr>; **on guard,** on one's guard; with open eyes, with one's eyes open, with one's eyes peeled *or* with a weather eye open <both nonformal>; alert, sharp-eyed, Argus-eyed, eagle-eyed, hawk-eyed; all eyes, all ears, **all eyes and ears**

**vigor** NOUNS **force,** power, strength, vitality, drive, sinew, sinewiness, nervousness, nervosity, vigorousness, forcefulness, effectiveness, impressiveness, pizzazz *and* punch *and* clout <all nonformal>; incisiveness, trenchancy, cuttingness, poignancy, bitingness, bite, mordancy; strong language

*thoughts that breathe and words that burn*
THOMAS GRAY

**vile** ADJS **low,** base, mean, ignoble, scurvy, sorry, scrubby, beggarly; low-minded, base-minded; **dirty,** smutty, raunchy <nonformal>, blue, smoking-room, impure, unchaste, unclean, **foul,** filthy, nasty, fulsome, offensive, unprintable, unrepeatable, not fit for mixed company

**vilify** VERBS **revile,** defile, sully, soil, smear, smirch, besmirch, bespatter, tarnish, **blacken,** denigrate, blacken one's good name, give a black eye <nonformal>; **call names,** give a bad name, give a dog a bad name, stigmatize; **muckrake,** throw mud at, mudsling, heap dirt upon, drag through the mud; engage in personalities

**village** NOUNS **hamlet;** country town, crossroads, wide place in the road

**villain** NOUNS **malefactor,** malfeasant, malfeasor, misfeasor, malevolent, public enemy, **sinner,** villainess, transgressor, delinquent; **scoundrel,** blackguard, **scamp,** scalawag <nonformal>, spalpeen <Ir>, rapscallion, devil

**vim** NOUNS **verve,** fire, adrenalin, **dash, drive; aggressiveness,** enterprise, initiative, proactiveness, thrust, spunk; **eagerness**, zeal, heartiness, keenness, gusto; **liveliness,** vivacity, vitality, life, **animation,** spiritedness, spirit, esprit, élan, **sprightliness,** high spirits, zestfulness, zest, zip <nonformal>, vigor

**vindicate** VERBS **justify,** do justice to, make justice *or* right prevail; get off the hook <nonformal>, exculpate; **clear,** clear one's name *or* one's good name, purge, destigmatize, reinstate, restore, rehabilitate; **acquit,** exonerate, absolve, give absolution, bring in *or* return a verdict of not guilty

**vindictive** ADJS **revengeful,** vengeful, avenging; vindicatory; revanchist; **wrathful,** rancorous, grudgeful, irreconcilable, unappeasable, implacable, unwilling to forgive and forget, unwilling to let bygones be bygones; **retaliatory**

**violate** VERBS 1 **corrupt,** debase, degrade, degenerate, **deprave,** debauch, defile, desecrate, deflower, ravish, ravage, despoil; **possess sexually,** take; **rape,** abuse, commit rape, commit date *or* acquaintance rape, assault sexually, lay violent hands on, have one's will of; 2 **break** *or* **violate the law,** breach the law, infringe, contravene, infract, **transgress,** trespass, disobey the law, offend against the law, flout the law, make a mockery of the law, fly in the face of the law, circumvent the law, disregard the law, **take the law into one's own hands,** commit a crime

**violence** NOUNS **cruelty,** brutality, mindless *or* senseless brutality, brutalness, **brutishness,** bestiality, animality, beastliness; **savagery,** viciousness, fiendishness

**VIP** NOUNS **very important person, somebody;** important person, standout <nonformal>, personage, one in a hundred *or* thousand *or* million etc; cynosure, model, very model, ideal type; popular hero, folk hero; luminary, celebrity

**viper** NOUNS **serpent,** snake, ophidian; pit viper; **reptile,** vermin, varmint <non-

formal>, hyena; **swine,** pig; **skunk,** polecat; insect, worm

**virgin** NOUNS 1 virgo intacta, cherry <nonformal>; vestal, vestal virgin
ADJS 2 **natural,** native, in a state of nature, in the raw; inartificial, artless; virginal, pristine, untouched, unsullied; maidenly, vestal, intact; **undamaged,** unharmed, unhurt, uninjured, unscathed, **unspoiled,** inviolate, unimpaired

**virile** ADJS **potent,** viripotent; ultramasculine, **macho,** he-mannish *and* hunky <both nonformal>, two-fisted <nonformal>, broad-shouldered, hairy-chested; **manly,** manful

**virtual** ADJS **potential,** unmanifested, possible

**virtue** NOUNS **virtuousness,** goodness, righteousness, rectitude, right conduct *or* behavior, the straight and narrow, the straight and narrow way, the right thing; probity; **morality,** moral fiber *or* rectitude *or* virtue, morale; **saintliness,** saintlikeness; **chastity,** honor; **purity,** cleanness, cleanliness; **immaculacy,** immaculateness, spotlessness, stainlessness, taintlessness, blotlessness; uncorruptness; sexual innocence, innocence

**virtuoso** NOUNS **first-rater,** topnotcher, world-beater; wonder, prodigy, genius, **star,** superstar; luminary, leading light, one in a thousand *or* a million; hard *or* tough act to follow <nonformal>

**virtuous** ADJS **good,** moral; upright, honest; **righteous,** just, straight, right-minded, right-thinking; **angelic,** seraphic; **saintly,** saintlike; **chaste,** pure, purehearted, pure in heart; **immaculate,** spotless, blotless, stainless, taintless, white, snowy, pure *or* white as driven snow; **unsoiled,** unsullied, undefiled, untarnished, unstained, unspotted, untainted, unblemished; sexually innocent, innocent

**virulent** ADJS 1 **acrimonious,** acrid, acidulous, acid, **bitter,** tart, caustic, mordant *or* mordacious, rancorous, **violent,** vehement, vitriolic; **noxious,** malignant, malign, destructive, deadly
2 **infectious,** infective, contagious, communicable, catching, pernicious; toxic, noisome

**virus** NOUNS **infection,** contagion, contamination, taint; filterable virus, nonfilterable virus, adenovirus, echovirus, reovirus, rhinovirus, enterovirus, picornavirus, retrovirus

**visa** NOUNS entry visa, exit visa, *visé* <Fr>; **clearance,** clearance papers

**viscous** ADJS **viscid,** viscose, slabby; **thick,** heavy, stodgy, soupy, thickened, inspissated, incrassated; curdled, clotted, grumous, coagulated, clabbered *and* loppered <both nonformal>; **sticky,** tacky, tenacious, adhesive, clingy, clinging, tough; gluey, gluelike, glutinous, glutenous, glutinose; **gummy,** gummous, gumlike, syrupy; **gelatinous,** jellylike, jellied, jelled; tremelloid *or* tremellose

**vise** NOUNS contractor, constrictor, clamp, compressor, pincer, squeezer; thumbscrew

**visible** ADJS visual, **perceptible,** perceivable, **discernible,** seeable, viewable, witnessable, beholdable, observable, detectable, noticeable, recognizable, to be seen; **in sight,** in view, in plain sight, in full view, before one's eyes, under one's eyes, open, naked, outcropping, hanging out <nonformal>, exposed, showing, open *or* exposed to view; **evident,** in evidence, **manifest,** apparent; revealed, disclosed, unhidden, unconcealed, unclouded, undisguised

**vision** NOUNS 1 **sight,** eyesight, seeing; **sightedness;** eye, power of sight, sense of sight, visual sense; **perception,** discernment; perspicacity, perspicuity, sharp *or* acute *or* keen sight, visual acuity, quick sight
2 **apparition,** appearance, phenomenon; **image,** shape, form, figure, presence; false image, mirage, specter, **phantom,** phantasm, phantasma, wraith, specter; **dream;** reverie, daydream, pipe dream <nonformal>; **nightmare,** incubus, bad dream
3 **thing of beauty,** picture <nonformal>, poem, eyeful <nonformal>, sight *or* treat for sore eyes <nonformal>

**visit** NOUNS 1 **social call,** call; formal visit, duty visit, required visit; exchange visit; flying visit, look-in; visiting, visitation; round of visits; social round, social whirl, mad round
VERBS 2 make *or* pay a visit, **call on** *or* **upon,** drop in, run *or* stop in, look in, look one up, see, stop off *or* over <nonformal>, drop *or* run *or* stop by, drop around *or* round; exchange visits

**visitor** NOUNS **guest,** visitant; **caller,** company; invited guest, invitee; frequenter, habitué, haunter; uninvited guest, gate-crasher <nonformal>; moocher *and* freeloader <both nonformal>

**vista** NOUNS **view,** scene, sight; prospect, outlook, lookout, perspective; scenery, scenic view; panorama, sweep; bird's-eye view, worm's-eye view

**visual** ADJS **ocular,** eye, eyeball <nonformal>; **sighted,** seeing, having sight *or* vision; **optic,** optical; ophthalmic; revealed, disclosed, unhidden, unconcealed, unclouded, undisguised

**visualize** VERBS vision, **envision,** envisage, picture, image, objectify; picture in one's mind, picture to oneself, **view with the mind's eye,** form a mental picture of, represent, **see,** just see, have a picture of; **call up,** summon up, conjure up, **call to mind,** realize

**vital** ADJS **all-important,** crucial, of vital importance, life-and-death *or* life-or-death; earth-shattering, epoch-making; **essential,** fundamental, indispensable, basic, substantive, bedrock, material; **central,** focal; bottom-line *and* meat-and-potatoes *and* gut <all nonformal>

**vitality** NOUNS **energy,** vigor, force, power, strenuousness, **intensity,** dynamism, demonic energy; potency; strength; vim, push, drive, charge, puissance <old>; virility; **haleness,** heartiness, robustness, vigorousness, ruggedness, lustiness, hardiness; **liveliness,** life, vivacity, élan, spirit, animation

**vitriolic** ADJS **acrimonious,** acrid, acidulous, acid, **bitter,** tart, **caustic,** mordant *or* mordacious, **virulent,** violent, vehement; **rancorous; venomous,** venenate, envenomed

**vivacious** ADJS **active,** lively, living, **animated,** spirited, go-go <nonformal>, brisk, bright-eyed and bushy-tailed <nonformal>, hearty, enthusiastic, mettlesome, zesty, zestful, impetuous, spanking, smacking; pumped *and* pumped up *and* jazzed-up *and* charged up *and* switched on <all nonformal>, snappy *and* zingy *and* zippy *and* peppy <all nonformal>; vital, **exuberant,** frisky, antic, skittish, coltish, rompish, capersome; **full of beans** *and* **feeling one's oats** <both nonformal>

**vivid** ADJS **expressive,** graphic, suggestive, imaginative; well-turned; eidetic, fresh, green, alive; **bright,** brilliant, splendid, splendorous, splendent, **resplendent,** bright and shining; fulgent, effulgent, refulgent

**vocation** NOUNS **occupation,** business, work, line, line of work, line of business *or* endeavor, number <nonformal>, walk, **walk of life,** calling, mission, **profession,** practice, pursuit, specialty, specialization, *métier* <Fr>, **trade,** racket *and* game <both nonformal>; **career,** lifework, life's work; **the ministry,** call, sacred calling

**vociferous** ADJS vociferant, vociferating; **clamorous,** blatant; obstreperous, brawling; **noisy;** yelping, yapping, yappy, yammering; loud-voiced, loudmouthed, openmouthed, stentorian

**vogue** NOUNS **fashion,** style, mode, trend, prevailing taste; custom; the swim <nonformal>, current *or* stream of fashion; height of fashion; the new look, the season's look; high fashion, *haute couture* <Fr>

**voice** NOUNS *voce* <Ital>; *voce di petto* <Ital>, chest voice; *voce di testa* <Ital>, head voice; **soprano,** mezzo-soprano, dramatic soprano, soprano spinto, lyric soprano, coloratura soprano; boy soprano; male soprano, castrato; alto, contralto; tenor, lyric tenor, operatic tenor, heldentenor *or* heroic tenor *or* Wagnerian tenor; baritone, light *or* lyric baritone; **bass,** basso, basso profundo, basso cantante *or* lyric bass, basso buffo *or* comic bass; treble, falsetto

**void** NOUNS 1 **vacuum,** blank, emptiness, empty space, inanity; **nothingness;** *tabula rasa* <L>, clean slate; nothing; **gap,** gape, **abyss,** gulf, chasm

VERBS 2 **abolish,** nullify, abrogate, annihilate, annul, tear up, repeal, revoke, negate, negative, invalidate, **undo,** cancel, cancel out, bring to naught, put *or* lay to rest

3 **evacuate,** eliminate, remove; **empty,** empty out, deplete, **exhaust,** vent, drain; **clear,** purge, clean *or* scour out, clear off *or* out *or* away, clear, unfoul, unclog, flush out, blow, blow out, sweep out, make a clean sweep, clear the decks; defecate

ADJS 4 **vacant,** empty, hollow, inane, **bare,** vacuous, without content, with nothing inside, devoid, null, null and void; **repealed,** revoked, rescinded, struck down, set aside; **invalid**

**volatile** ADJS **capricious,** fickle, off-again-on-again; **erratic,** eccentric, freakish;

giddy, dizzy, scatterbrained, mercurial, moody, flighty, impulsive, impetuous; mercurial; volatilizable; **vaporable,** vaporizable, vaporescent; **evaporative,** evaporable

**volcanic** ADJS **warm,** burning, heated, hot, red-hot, fiery, flaming, glowing, ablaze, afire, on fire, boiling over, steaming, steamy; emotionally unstable; explosive, eruptive, inflammable; **impetuous,** violent, furious, fierce, **wild;** tempestuous, stormy, tornadic; simmering, ready to burst forth *or* explode; **hot-tempered,** hotheaded, passionate, peppery, feisty, combustible

**volley** NOUNS **salvo,** burst, spray, **fusillade,** drumfire, **cannonade,** cannonry, **broadside,** enfilade; **barrage,** artillery barrage

**volume** NOUNS 1 **loudness,** intensity, amplitude, fullness; sonorousness, sonority; surge of sound, surge, crescendo, swell, swelling; loudishness
2 **capacity,** content, holding capacity, cubic footage *or* yardage etc, accommodation, room, space, measure, limit, burden; gallonage, tankage; poundage, tonnage, cordage; stowage; **quantity**
3 **tome; edition,** issue; library edition; back number; **trade edition,** subscription edition, subscription book; school edition, text edition

**voluminous** ADJS **capacious,** generous, ample, copious, broad, wide, extensive, expansive, comprehensive; **spacious**

**voluntary** ADJS **volunteer;** ex gratia, gratuitous; spontaneous, free, freewill; **discretionary,** discretional, nonmandatory, **optional; unsought,** unasked, unrequested, **unsolicited,** uninvited, unbidden; unprompted, uninfluenced; **elective;** volitional, volitive

**volunteer** VERBS do voluntarily, do ex gratia, **do of one's own accord,** do of one's own volition, **do of one's own free will** *or* **choice;** do independently, **come** *or* **step forward,** offer *or* proffer *or* present oneself, not wait to be asked, not wait for an invitation, need no prodding

**voluptuous** ADJS **carnal,** sensual, sensualist, sensualistic, fleshly; zaftig <nonformal>; luxurious; sensuous; luxurious

**vomit** NOUNS 1 vomitus, **puke** *and* barf <both nonformal>, spew, egesta; the dry heaves <nonformal>; vomiturition; **vomiting,** vomition, disgorgement, **regurgitation,** egestion, emesis, the pukes *and* the heaves <both nonformal>; **retching,** heaving, gagging; nausea
VERBS 2 spew, disgorge, **regurgitate,** egest, **throw up,** bring up, be sick, cast *or* heave the gorge; **retch,** keck, heave, gag; reject; be seasick, feed the fish

3 <nonformal> **puke,** upchuck, chuck up, urp, oops, oops up, shoot *or* blow *or* toss one's cookies *or* lunch, barf, ralph, ralph up, blow grits

**voodoo** NOUNS 1 voodooism, hoodoo, wanga, juju, jujuism, obeah, obeahism; shamanism; fetishism
2 **shaman,** shamanist; voodooist, wangateur, **witch doctor,** obeah doctor, **medicine man,** mundunugu, isangoma

**voracious** ADJS **gluttonous,** greedy, ravenous, edacious, rapacious, insatiable, polyphagic, bulimic, hyperphagic, Apician; **piggish,** hoggish, swinish; **gorging,** cramming, glutting, stuffing, guzzling, wolfing, bolting, **gobbling,** gulping, gluttonizing

**vote** NOUNS 1 voting, **suffrage,** franchise, enfranchisement, voting right, right to vote; **voice,** say; **poll,** polling, canvass, canvassing, counting heads *or* noses; **ballot,** balloting, secret ballot, Australian ballot; ballot-box, voting machine; **plebiscite,** plebiscitum, referendum; endorsement
VERBS 2 **cast one's vote,** ballot, cast a ballot; have suffrage, be enfranchised, have a say *or* a voice; hold up one's hand, exercise one's suffrage *or* frachise, stand up and be counted; **poll,** canvass

**voter** NOUNS elector, **balloter;** registered voter; fraudulent voter, floater, repeater, ballot-box stuffer; proxy

**vow** NOUNS 1 **promise, pledge,** solemn promise, troth, plight, faith, parole, **word, word of honor,** solemn declaration *or* word; **oath;** avouchment; assurance, guarantee, warranty
VERBS 2 **promise,** give *or* make a promise, hold out an expectation; **pledge,** plight, troth; **give one's word,** pledge *or* pass one's word, give one's parole, **give one's word of honor,** plight one's troth *or* faith, pledge *or* plight one's honor; cross one's heart *and* cross one's heart and hope to die <both nonformal>, **swear;** vouch, avouch,

**warrant,** guarantee, assure; underwrite, countersign

**voyage** NOUNS ocean *or* sea trip, **cruise,** sail; course, **run,** passage; crossing; shakedown cruise

**voyeur** NOUNS **Peeping Tom,** watcher, scopophiliac, scoptophiliac

**vulgar** ADJS 1 **inelegant,** indelicate, indecorous, indecent, improper, unseemly, unbeseeming, unbecoming, unfitting, inappropriate, unsuitable, **ungenteel,** undignified; **untasteful,** tasteless, in bad *or* poor taste, tacky *and* chintzy *and* Mickey Mouse <all nonformal>; **offensive,** offensive to gentle ears; barbarous, barbaric, rude, **crude,** **uncouth,** Doric, outlandish; low, gross, **coarse**
2 **vernacular,** colloquial, conversational, unliterary, nonformal, demotic, spoken, vulgate; unstudied, familiar, common, everyday; **substandard,** nonformal, uneducated; dysphemistic

**vulnerable** ADJS **pregnable,** penetrable, expugnable; assailable, attackable, surmountable; conquerable, beatable <nonformal>, vincible; weak, **exposed,** susceptible, at risk, overexposed, open, like a sitting duck; **in debt, indebted,** financially burdened, heavily committed, overextended

# W-X-Y-Z

**wacky** ADJS

**kooky, goofy,** birdy, funny, kinky, loopy, goofus, haywire, screwy, screwball, nutty, flaky, oddball, wacko, out to lunch, nobody home, weird

**wad** NOUNS **accumulation,** agglomeration, conglomeration, conglomerate, agglomerate; **aggregation,** aggregate; **mass,** lump, gob <nonformal>, chunk *and* hunk <both nonformal>

**waddle** VERBS **go slow** *or* **slowly,** go at a snail's pace, take it slow, get no place fast <nonformal>; **drag,** creep, crawl; poke, **poke along;** shuffle *or* stagger *or* totter *or* toddle along; drag along, drag one's feet, toddle <nonformal>; limp, hobble, claudicate

**waffle** VERBS **vacillate,** waver, **fluctuate,** pendulate, oscillate, wobble, dither, swing from one thing to another, **shilly-shally,** back and fill, keep *or* leave hanging in midair; blow hot and cold; **equivocate,** fudge; change one's mind, tergiversate; shift, change horses in midstream; **evade,** evade the issue, duck the issue *and* **cop out** <both nonformal>

**wag** NOUNS 1 **funnyman,** comic, *bel-esprit* <Fr>, life of the party; **joker,** jokester, gagman <nonformal>, **jester,** quipster, wisecracker *and* gagster <both nonformal>; wagwit; zany, madcap, cutup <nonformal>; prankster
VERBS 2 **wiggle,** wriggle; waggle; **writhe,** squirm

**wager** NOUNS 1 **bet,** stake, hazard, lay, play *and* chunk *and* shot <all nonformal>; cinch bet *or* sure thing, mortal cinch *and* mortal lock *and* nuts <all nonformal>; long shot
VERBS 2 **bet,** gamble, hazard, stake, punt, lay, lay down, put up, **make a bet,** lay a wager, give *or* take *or* lay odds, get a piece of the action <nonformal>; plunge <nonformal>; **bet on** *or* **upon,** back; play *or* follow the ponies <nonformal>; parlay

**wagon** NOUNS 1 wain; haywagon, milkwagon; dray, van, caravan; covered wagon, prairie schooner, Conestoga wagon
2 **police car,** patrol car; prowl car, squad car, cruiser; **police van,** patrol wagon; paddy wagon *and* Black Maria <both nonformal>

**waif** NOUNS homeless waif, dogie, stray, waifs and strays; ragamuffin, tatterdemalion; **gamin,** gamine, urchin, street urchin, dead-end kid <nonformal>, mudlark, guttersnipe <nonformal>

**wail** NOUNS 1 **lament,** plaint, *planctus* <L>; **moan,** groan; whine, whimper; wail of woe; **sob,** *cri du coeur* <Fr>, **cry,** outcry, scream, **howl,** yowl, bawl, yawp, keen, ululation
VERBS 2 ululate; **moan,** groan; howl, yowl; **cry,** squall, bawl, yawp, **yell,** scream, shriek; cry out, make an outcry; bay at the moon; whine, keen, blubber, sob

**wait** NOUNS 1 **delay,** stoppage, jam *and* logjam <both nonformal>, obstruction, tie-up *and* bind <both nonformal>, **block,** blockage, **hang-up** <nonformal>; **retardation** *or* retardance, slowdown *and* slow-up <both nonformal>, slowness, lag, time lag, lagging, dragging, dragging one's feet *and* foot-dragging <both nonformal>; **halt,** stay, stop, downtime, break, pause, interim, respite; reprieve, stay of execution; moratorium
VERBS 2 **await,** wait for, wait on *or* upon, stay *or* tarry for; wait around *or* about, watch and wait; **bide one's time,** bide, abide, **mark time;** cool one's heels <nonformal>; **wait up for,** stay up for, sit up for; **be patient,** forbear, bear with composure, wait it out, play a waiting game, wait one's turn, watch for one's moment, keep one's shirt *or* pants on <nonformal>; contain oneself, possess oneself, possess one's soul in patience

**waiter** NOUNS **waitress;** carhop; counterman, soda jerk <nonformal>; busboy; headwaiter, *maître d'hôtel* <Fr>, maître d' <nonformal>

**wait on** VERBS **toady to,** truckle to, pander to, cater to; **wait upon,** wait on hand and foot, dance attendance, do service, fetch and carry, do the dirty work of, do *or* jump at the bidding of; **look after,** take care of

**waive** VERBS **give up,** relinquish, surrender, yield, yield up, **forgo,** resign, renounce, **abjure,** forswear, give up on, have done with, hand over, lay down, wash one's hands of; **not use,** do without, dispense with; prorogue, put on hold *or* ice *or* the back burner <all nonformal>, reserve, **suspend,** set aside, ease, lift temporarily, pull one's punches <nonformal>

**waiver** NOUNS special permission, charter, patent, **dispensation,** release; zoning variance, variance; suspension; waiving, setting aside

**wake** VERBS **awake,** awaken, wake up, get up, rouse, come alive <nonformal>; open one's eyes, stir <nonformal>; stir up, set astir, stir the feelings, stir the blood, cause a stir *or* commotion, play on the feelings; **work up,** work into, work up into a lather <nonformal>, lather up, whip up, **key up,** steam up; foment, incite; turn on <nonformal>

**walk** NOUNS 1 ramble, amble, **hike,** tramp, traipse <nonformal>; slog, trudge, schlep <nonformal>; **stroll,** saunter; **promenade,** *passeggiata* <Ital>; jaunt, airing; **constitutional,** turn; **march,** forced march, route march; parade
2 **path,** track, trail, pathway, footpath, footway, *piste* <Fr>; walkway, catwalk, skybridge *or* skywalk *or* flying bridge *or* walkway; **sidewalk,** *trottoir* <Fr>, foot pavement <Brit>; boardwalk; public walk, promenade, esplanade, alameda, parade, *prado* <Sp>; beaten track *or* path, rut, groove; garden path
3 **walk of life,** calling, mission, **profession,** practice, pursuit, specialty, specialization, *métier* <Fr>, **trade,** racket *and* game <both nonformal>
VERBS 4 ambulate, peripateticate, pedestrianize, traipse <nonformal>; **step,** tread, pace, stride, pad; foot, foot it; leg, leg it; hoof it, ankle, heel and toe, ride shank's mare <nonformal>, ride the shoeleather *or* hobnail express, stump it <nonformal>; peg *or* jog *or* shuffle on *or* along; perambulate; circumambulate; jaywalk; power walk, exercise walk, speed walk, race walk
5 **go free,** breathe the air of freedom; be freed, be released; be exonerated, go *or* get off scot-free
6 **strike,** go on strike, go out, walk out; hit the bricks <nonformal>, shut it down

**wall** NOUNS **fence,** boundary, **barrier;** stone wall; paling, palisade; **partition,** dividing wall, separation, *cloison* <Fr>; **dividing line,** property line, party wall

**wallop** NOUNS 1 **sock,** bang, bash, bat, belt, bust, clip, clout, duke, swat, larrup, paste, lick, biff, whop, slam, slug <all nonformal>
VERBS 2 **beat up,** rough up, clobber, work over, lick, larrup, whop, beat one's brains out, whale, whale the tar out of, beat *or* kick the shit out of, beat to a jelly, **beat black and blue,** knock one's lights out, nail, lather, **hide,** tan, **tan one's hide,** kick ass, knock heads together; **paddle;** lambaste, take it out of one's hide *or* skin <all nonformal>

**wallow** VERBS **pitch,** toss, tumble, toss and tumble, pitch and toss, **plunge,** pound, **rear,** rock, roll, reel, swing, sway, lurch, yaw, heave, scend, **flounder,** welter; make heavy weather, grovel

**Wall Street** NOUNS **stock exchange,** exchange, **stock market,** bourse, board; the Exchange, the Big Board; **financial district,** the Street

**wan** ADJS tired-looking, weary-looking, tired-eyed, tired-faced, haggard, hollow-eyed, ravaged, drawn, cadaverous, worn, zombiish <nonformal>; **pale,** dim, weak, **faint; pallid,** sallow; pale *or* blue *or* green around the gills; **pasty,** mealy, waxen; **ashen,** ashy, ashen-hued, cinereous, cineritious, gray, griseous; **lackluster,** dull, dead, deadened, **lifeless,** somber, drab

**wander** VERBS **roam,** rove, range, nomadize, **gad,** gad around *or* about, follow the seasons, wayfare, flit, traipse <nonformal>, gallivant, knock around *or* about *and* bat around *or* about <all nonformal>, prowl, **drift,** stray, float around, straggle, **meander,** ramble, stroll, saunter, jaunt, peregrinate, pererrate, divagate; **digress,** get off the subject, wander from the subject, get sidetracked, excurse, maunder, stray, go astray, woolgather, **daydream**

**wanderer** NOUNS **rover,** roamer, rambler, stroller, straggler, mover; **itinerant,** peripatetic, rolling stone, peregrine, peregrinator, bird of passage, visitant; **drifter** *and* **floater** <both nonformal>; **exile,** outcast, refugee, émigré displaced person *or* DP, *déraciné* <Fr>

**wane** VERBS **decline,** sink, fail, fall, slip, fade, die, ebb, subside, lapse, **run down,** go down, **go downhill,** fall away, fall off, slide, slump, hit a slump, take a nose dive <nonformal>, go into a tailspin

**wangle** VERBS **maneuver,** manipulate, pull strings *or* wires; **machinate,** contrive, angle <nonformal>, **jockey,** engineer; play games <nonformal>; **plot,** scheme, intrigue; finagle

**want** NOUNS 1 **lack,** need, deficiency, deficit, shortage, shortfall, wantage, **incompleteness,** defectiveness, shortcoming, imperfection; **absence**, omission; **destitution,** impoverishment, beggary, deprivation
VERBS 2 **desire,** desiderate, be desirous of, **wish,** lust after, bay after, kill for *and* give one's right arm for <both nonformal>, die for <nonformal>, **have a mind to,** choose <nonformal>; fancy, take to, **take a fancy** *or* a shine to, have a fancy for; tilt toward, have a penchant for, have a weakness *or* soft spot in one's heart for; set one's cap for, have designs on; wish very much; **lack**, want for; fall short; **require,** need, feel the want of, have occasion for, be in need of, be hurting for <nonformal>, stand in need of, not be able to dispense with, not be able to do without

**wanted** ADJS **desired,** coveted; **wished-for,** hoped-for, longed-for; in demand, popular; **welcome,** welcome as the roses in May; **called for,** indicated

**wanton** ADJS **wayward,** Paphian; **loose,** lax, slack, loose-moraled, of loose morals, of easy virtue, easy <nonformal>, **light,** no better than she should be, promiscuous; **desultory,** rambling, roving, vagrant, wandering, afloat, adrift; **unrestrained,** undisciplined, irresponsible, uncontrolled

**war** NOUNS 1 **warfare,** warring, warmaking, combat, fighting, *la guerre* <Fr>; armed conflict, armed combat, military operations, the sword, arbitrament of the sword, appeal to arms *or* the sword, resort to arms, force *or* might of arms, bloodshed; **state of war,** hostilities, belligerence *or* belligerency, open war *or* warfare *or* hostilities; **hot war,** shooting war; total war, all-out war; holy war, jihad

*a conflict which does not determine who is right—but who is left*
ANON

*politics with bloodshed*
MAO TSE-TUNG

VERBS 2 **wage war,** make war, carry on war *or* hostilities, engage in hostilities, wield the sword; battle, **fight;** spill *or* shed blood

**warden** NOUNS **jailer,** gaoler <Brit>, correctional *or* correction *or* corrections officer; **keeper,** warder, prison guard, **turnkey,** bull *and* screw <both nonformal>; custodian, guardian; **game warden,** gamekeeper

**wardrobe** NOUNS furnishings, things, accouterments, trappings; **outfit,** livery, harness, caparison; turnout *and* getup *and* rig <all nonformal>; wedding clothes, bridal outfit, trousseau; clothes closet

**warehouse** NOUNS 1 **storehouse,** storeroom, storage, **depository,** repository, depot, supply depot, supply base, magazine, *magasin* <Fr>, godown; bonded warehouse, entrepôt
VERBS 2 **store,** stow, lay in store; **lay in,** lay in a supply *or* stock *or* store, store away, stow away, **put away,** lay away, put *or* lay by, pack away, bundle away, lay down, stow down, salt down *or* away *and* sock away *and* squirrel away <all nonformal>; **deposit,** reposit, lodge; **cache,** stash <nonformal>

**wares** NOUNS **merchandise,** commodities, goods, effects, vendibles; **consumer goods,** consumer items, retail goods, goods for sale; **stock,** stock-in-trade; **line,** line of goods

**warfare** NOUNS **contention,** contest, contestation, combat, **fighting,** conflict, strife, war, struggle, blood on the floor, cut and thrust; armed conflict, armed combat, military operations, resort to arms, force *or* might of arms, bloodshed; **state of war,** hostilities, open war *or* warfare *or* hostilities

**warhead** NOUNS **payload;** nuclear *or* thermonuclear warhead, atomic warhead; multiple *or* multiple-missile warhead

**warm** VERBS 1 **heat,** raise *or* increase the temperature, warm up, fire, fire up, stoke up; take the chill off; preheat; **reheat,** warm over; mull
ADJS 2 **heated,** passionate, hot, red-hot, flaming, **burning,** fiery, glowing, fervent, fervid; feverish, febrile, hectic, flushed
3 **kind, kindly,** kindly-disposed; **benign,** benignant; good as gold, **good,** nice, decent; gracious; kindhearted,

warmhearted, softhearted, tenderhearted, tender, loving, affectionate; **cordial,** genial, hearty, ardent, warmhearted, affable; hospitable

**warmonger** NOUNS **militarist,** war dog *or* hound, war hawk, **hawk** <nonformal>; **chauvinist,** jingo, jingoist

**warn** VERBS **caution,** advise, admonish; give warning, give fair warning, utter a caveat, address a warning to, put a flea in one's ear <nonformal>, have a word with one, say a word to the wise; tip *and* tip off <both nonformal>; notify, put on notice, give notice *or* advance notice *or* advance word; tell once and for all; issue an ultimatum; **threaten; alert,** warn against, put on one's guard, warn away *or* off; **give the high sign** <nonformal>; **put on alert,** cry havoc, sound the alarm

**warning** NOUNS **caution,** caveat, **admonition,** monition, admonishment; **notice,** notification; **word to the wise,** *verbum sapienti* <L>, verbum sap, enough said; tip-off <nonformal>; **lesson,** object lesson, **example,** deterrent example, warning piece; alarm; final warning *or* notice, ultimatum; **threat**

**warp** NOUNS 1 **bias, bend,** bent, **crook,** twist, turn, skew, slue, **veer,** sheer, **swerve,** lurch; **distortion,** unsymmetry, disproportion, lopsidedness, imbalance, irregularity, deviation; idiosyncrasy, **eccentricity,** individualism; strain, streak
VERBS 2 bias, twist, distort, contort, torture, skew; put in a false light, **pervert,** garble, wrench, slant, put a spin on, twist the meaning of; **color,** miscolor, **give a false coloring,** put a false construction *or* appearance upon, falsify; **deform,** kink

**warrant** NOUNS 1 **ratification,** endorsement, acceptance, approval, approbation, subscription, signing-off, imprimatur, **sanction,** permission, the OK *and* the okay *and* the green light *and* the go-ahead *and* the nod <all nonformal>, license, nihil obstat, **certification,** confirmation, validation, authentication, authorization; **oath,** vow, **word,** assurance, guarantee, solemn oath *or* affirmation *or* word *or* declaration; pledge
2 **summons,** subpoena, writ of summons; **writ**
VERBS 3 **authorize,** sanction, give official sanction *or* warrant, legitimize, validate, legalize; empower, give power, enable, entitle; **license;** charter, patent, enfranchise, franchise
4 **state,** assert, swear, swear to God <nonformal>, declare, **affirm,** vow, avow, avouch, asseverate, confess, be under the impression, profess, express the belief, swear, swear to a belief; depose, make an affidavit *or* a sworn statement

**warranty** NOUNS **security,** surety, indemnity, **guaranty,** guarantee, insurance, assurance; **obligation**, full faith and credit; **bond,** tie; **authorization,** authority, sanction, licensing, countenance, **warrant,** fiat

**warrior** NOUNS **military man** *or* **woman,** serviceman, servicewoman, **soldier,** brave, fighting man, legionary, hoplite, **man-at-arms,** Amazon

**wary** ADJS **chary,** cagey <nonformal>, **leery** <nonformal>, **suspicious,** suspecting, distrustful, mistrustful, shy

**wash** VERBS **bathe,** bath <Brit>, shower, lave; **launder;** wash up *or* out *or* away; **rinse,** rinse out, flush, flush out, irrigate, sluice, sluice out; ritually immerse, baptize; **sponge,** sponge down *or* off; **scrub,** scrub up *or* out, **scour,** holystone; hose out *or* down

**washout** NOUNS **debacle,** disaster, **breakdown,** collapse; total loss

**waste** NOUNS 1 **refuse,** wastage, waste matter, **leavings,** sweepings, scraps, orts; **garbage,** swill, slops, lees, **dregs**; **consumption;** wasting, wasting away, atrophy, wilting, emaciation
2 **prodigality,** profligacy, **extravagance,** pound-foolishness, recklessness, reckless spending *or* expenditure; **wastefulness,** dissipation, squandering; conspicuous consumption *or* waste
VERBS 3 **waste away, wither away,** atrophy, consume, consume away, erode away, emaciate, pine away
4 **deplete, depreciate,** dissipate, wear, wear away, erode, ablate, consume, drain, **shrink,** dribble away; **spend,** expend, use up, exhaust; lose; spill, pour down the drain *or* rathole; pour water into a sieve, cast pearls before swine, kill the goose that lays the golden egg, throw out the baby with the bath water
ADJS 5 **unproductive,** nonproductive *or* nonproducing; **unfruitful,** infecund, unprolific *or* nonprolific; ineffectual; **barren,** desert, arid, dry, dried-up, sere,

exhausted, drained, leached, sucked dry, gaunt, **desolate,** jejune

**wasteful** ADJS **devastating, desolating,** ravaging, wasting, spoliative, depredatory; vandalic, vandalish, vandalistic; **prodigal,** extravagant, lavish, profuse, **overliberal,** overgenerous, overlavish, **spendthrift,** profligate, dissipative

**wasteland** NOUNS **waste,** desolation, barren *or* **barrens,** barren land; heath; **desert,** karroo <Africa>, badlands, dust bowl, salt flat, Death Valley, lunar waste *or* landscape

**watch** NOUNS 1 **vigil,** lookout; *qui vive* <Fr>; invigilation, proctoring, monitoring; **sharp eye,** weather eye, peeled eye, watchful eye, eagle eye, lidless *or* sleepless *or* unblinking *or* unwinking eye
2 **shift,** work shift, **tour,** tour of duty, stint, bit, **trick,** time, **turn,** relay, spell *or* turn of work
3 **timepiece,** timekeeper, **timer,** chronometer, ship's watch; horologe, horologium; **clock,** Big Ben, ticker <nonformal>, turnip
VERBS 4 **look, peer,** have a look, take a gander *and* take a look <both nonformal>, direct the eyes, turn *or* bend the eyes, cast one's eye, lift up the eyes; **look at,** take a look at, eye, **eyeball** <nonformal>, have a look-see <nonformal>, look on *or* upon, gaze at *or* upon; **observe,** view, regard; keep one's eyes peeled *or* skinned, be watchful *or* observant *or* vigilant, keep one's eyes open; keep in sight *or* view, hold in view; look after
5 **keep watch,** keep guard, keep watch over, keep vigil; stand guard, stand sentinel; be on the lookout; **police,** patrol, pound a beat <nonformal>, go on one's beat

**watchful** ADJS **vigilant,** wary, prudent, lidless, sleepless, observant; **on the lookout,** *aux aguets* <Fr>; **on guard,** on one's guard, guarded; alert, aware, with open eyes, with one's eyes open, with one's eyes peeled *or* with a weather eye open <both nonformal>; all eyes, all ears, **all eyes and ears;** custodial

**watchword** NOUNS **password,** countersign; catchword, catchphrase, slogan; shibboleth

**water** NOUNS 1 **fluid,** liquid; **juice,** sap; **body fluid,** semiliquid
VERBS 2 **dilute,** cut <nonformal>, water down, adulterate, irrigate *and* baptize <both nonformal>; **weaken,** attenuate, extenuate

**watery** ADJS **waterish, aqueous,** aquatic; liquid; **splashy,** plashy, sloppy; hydrous, hydrated; hydraulic

**wave** NOUNS 1 **billow,** surge, **swell,** heave, undulation, lift, rise, send, scend; trough, peak; **sea,** heavy swell, ocean swell, ground swell; **roller,** roll; **comber,** comb; **tidal wave,** tsunami; **whitecap,** white horse; standing wave
VERBS 2 **signal,** give the high sign *or* the nod <both nonformal>; wave the hand, wave a flag, **flag,** flag down
3 **undulate; brandish,** flourish, flaunt, shake, swing, wield; **flap,** flutter; wag, wigwag

**waver** VERBS **vacillate,** waffle <nonformal>, **fluctuate,** pendulate, oscillate, wobble, wobble about, teeter, dither, swing from one thing to another, **shilly-shally,** back and fill, keep off and on, keep *or* leave hanging in midair; blow hot and cold; **equivocate**, fudge; shift, change horses in midstream, **change**

**wavy** ADJS **undulant,** undulatory, undulative, undulating, undulate, undulated; **billowy,** billowing, surgy, rolling; **wavering,** wavery, flitting, flickering, guttering, fitful, shifting, shuffling

**way** NOUNS 1 **route,** path, itinerary, course, track, run, line, road; **scope, room,** range, maneuvering space *or* room, room to swing a cat <nonformal>
2 **manner,** wise, **means,** mode, modality, **fashion,** style, tone; **method,** methodology, system; **approach,** attack, tack; **technique,** procedure, process, proceeding, course, practice; *modus operandi* <L>, mode of operation *or* MO, manner of working; **habit,** tenor, cast, grain, vein, streak, stripe, mold, brand, stamp

**wayward** ADJS 1 **disobedient,** transgressive, uncomplying, violative, lawless, froward, naughty; **undisciplined,** ill-disciplined, indisciplined; **desultory,** rambling, roving, vagrant, wanton, wandering, afloat, adrift
2 **unvirtuous,** virtueless, ungood; fleshly, carnal, wanton, prodigal; erring, **fallen, lapsed,** postlapsarian

**weak** ADJS 1 weakly, **feeble,** debilitated, imbecile; **strengthless,** sapless, marrowless, pithless, sinewless, listless, out of gas <nonformal>, nerveless, lustless; **impotent,** powerless; spineless, lily-liv-

ered, whitelivered, wimpy *and* wimpish *and* chicken *and* gutless <all nonformal>, cowardly; dull, slack; **languorous,** languid, **drooping,** droopy, pooped <nonformal>; asthenic, anemic, bloodless, effete, etiolated
2 <comparisons> a kitten, a reed, thread, matchwood, a rope of sand; a house of cards, a house built on sand, a sand castle; water, milk and water, gruel, dishwater, cambric tea

*weak as water*
BIBLE

3 **faint,** low, soft, gentle, subdued, dim, feeble, faint-sounding
4 attenuated, attenuate, **watery,** diluted, watered *or* watered-down

**weaken** VERBS 1 grow weak *or* weaker, go soft <nonformal>; **languish,** wilt, faint, **droop,** drop, **sink, decline,** flag, pine, fade, tail away *or* off, fail, fall *or* drop by the wayside; crumble, go to pieces, disintegrate; give out, have no staying power, run out of gas <nonformal>, conk *or* peter *or* poop *or* peg *or* fizzle out <nonformal>; come apart, come apart at the seams, come unstuck *or* unglued <both informal>
2 **enfeeble,** debilitate, unstrengthen, unsinew, undermine, soften up <nonformal>, unbrace, unman, unnerve, rattle, shake up <nonformal>, **devitalize,** enervate, eviscerate; **sap,** sap the strength of, exhaust, gruel, take it out of <nonformal>; dilute, water, water down, attenuate, extenuate

**weakling** NOUNS **weak** *or* meek soul, weak sister <nonformal>, hothouse plant, softy <nonformal>, softling, **jellyfish,** invertebrate, gutless wonder <nonformal>, **baby,** big baby, crybaby, chicken <nonformal>, Milquetoast, sop, **milksop,** namby-pamby, mollycoddle, mama's boy, mother's boy, mother's darling, teacher's pet; sissy *and* pansy *and* pantywaist <all nonformal>, pushover <nonformal>, lightweight; **wimp,** poor *or* weak *or* dull tool <nonformal>; doormat *and* empty suit *and* nebbish *and* sad sack <all nonformal>

**wealth** NOUNS 1 **opulence** *or* opulency, richness, affluence; **prosperity,** prosperousness, thriving *or* flourishing condition

2 <nonformal> **bundle, big bucks,** megabucks, gigabucks, big money, serious money, gobs, heaps, heavy lettuce, heavy jack, heavy money, important money, pot, potful, power, mint, barrel, raft, load, **loads,** pile, wad, wads, nice hunk of change, packet <Brit>

**wealthy** ADJS 1 **rich,** affluent, moneyed *or* monied, in funds *or* cash, **well-to-do,** well-off, well-situated, prosperous, comfortable, provided for, well provided for, fat, **flush,** flush with money, abounding in riches, worth a great deal, frightfully rich, rich as Croesus; privileged, born with a silver spoon in one's mouth

2 <nonformal> **loaded, well-heeled, filthy rich,** warm <Brit>, in the money *or* dough, well-fixed, made of money, **rolling in money,** rolling *or* wallowing in it, disgustingly rich, big-rich, rich-rich, oofy, lousy rich, upscale

**wean** VERBS **disaccustom,** cure, break off, stop; **convince,** persuade, bring over, sweep off one's feet <nonformal>, win over

**wear** NOUNS 1 use, hard wear; **wear and tear;** erosion, weathering, ablation, ravages of time
VERBS 2 **have on,** be dressed in, affect, sport <nonformal>
3 **wear away,** wear down, wear off; abrade, fret, whittle away, rub off; fray, frazzle, tatter, wear ragged; **wear out;** weather, erode, ablate

**wear out** VERBS **fatigue,** tire, weary, exhaust, wilt, flag, jade, harass; **wear,** wear on *or* upon, wear down; **tire out,** burn out; use up; weaken, enervate, debilitate

**weary** ADJS **weariful; tired,** wearied, irked; good and tired, tired to death, weary unto death; **sick and tired of;** jaded, satiated, palled, fed up <nonformal>; **listless,** dispirited

**weasel** VERBS **equivocate,** waffle <nonformal>, tergiversate, evade, dodge, sidestep, say in a roundabout way, parry, duck, weasel out <nonformal>, palter; renege

**weather** NOUNS 1 **climate,** clime; **the elements,** forces of nature; microclimate, macroclimate

VERBS 2 **weather the storm,** ride, ride out, ride out a storm; erode, ablate

**weather-beaten** ADJS **weatherworn,** weathered; eroded; **faded,** washed-out

**weave** VERBS loom, tissue; **interweave,** interlace, intertwine, interknit, intertissue, intertwist; **braid,** plait, pleach, **wreathe,** raddle, **knit,** twist, mat, wattle

**web** NOUNS **cobweb,** gossamer, spider *or* spider's web

**wed** VERBS **marry,** join, unite, hitch *and* splice <both nonformal>, couple, match, match up, make *or* arrange a match, join together, **unite in marriage,** join *or* unite in holy wedlock, tie the knot, tie the nuptial *or* wedding knot, make one

**wedding** NOUNS **marriage,** marriage ceremony, nuptial mass; church wedding, civil wedding, civil ceremony; espousement, bridal; **nuptials,** spousals, hymeneal rites

**wedge** VERBS **jam,** seize; make fast, fasten, fasten down

**weed** VERBS **cultivate,** weed out, hoe, cut, prune, thin, thin out

**weep** VERBS **sob,** cry, **bawl,** blubber, whimper, snivel; shed tears, drop a tear; give way to tears, melt *or* dissolve in tears, break down, break down and cry, turn on the waterworks <nonformal>; cry one's eyes out; **drip,** seep

**weepy** ADJS **tearful,** teary; lachrymal, lachrymose, lacrimatory; in the melting mood, on the edge of tears, ready to cry; **weeping,** sobbing, crying; blubbering, whimpering, sniveling; oozy, runny, leaky

**weigh** VERBS **heft** <nonformal>, balance, weigh in the balance, strike a balance, hold the scales, put on the scales; **consider,** contemplate, speculate, reflect, study, ponder, **deliberate,** debate, meditate, muse, brood, ruminate, chew the cud <nonformal>

**weight** NOUNS 1 **heaviness,** weightiness, ponderousness, heftiness *and* heft <both nonformal>; body weight, avoirdupois <nonformal>, fatness, beef *and* beefiness <both nonformal>; poundage, tonnage; **solemnity,** gravity, moment, consequence, importance, eminence; cogency, force, persuasiveness
2 paperweight, letterweight; sinker, lead, plumb, plummet, bob; sash weight; sandbag

**weight-watching** NOUNS **reducing,** slenderizing, slimming down, dieting; calorie-counting

**weird** ADJS **eerie,** eldritch, **uncanny,** unearthly, macabre; **spooky** *and* spookish *and* hairy <all nonformal>; **absurd,** preposterous, fantastic, fantastical, grotesque, monstrous, wild, **outrageous,** incredible, beyond belief, *outré* <Fr>, extravagant, **bizarre**

**welcome** NOUNS 1 welcoming, **reception,** *accueil* <Fr>; cordial *or* warm *or* hearty welcome, pleasant *or* smiling reception, the glad hand <nonformal>, **open arms;** welcome mat
VERBS 2 make welcome, bid one welcome, make one feel welcome *or* at home *or* like one of the family, give one the freedom of the house, hold out the hand, extend the right hand of friendship; glad-hand *and* give the glad hand *and* glad eye <all nonformal>; **receive** *or* **welcome with open arms;** give a warm reception to, roll out the red carpet, give the red-carpet treatment

*kill the fatted calf*
BIBLE

ADJS 3 welcome as the roses in May, wanted, desired, wished-for; **agreeable,** desirable, acceptable

**weld** VERBS **fuse, solder,** braze; **stick together,** cement, bind, colligate

**welfare** NOUNS **well-being,** weal, happiness, felicity; quality of life; comfortable *or* easy circumstances, **comfort,** ease, security; **welfare work,** social service, social welfare, social work; commonweal, public welfare; public assistance, relief, the dole, social security <Brit>

**well** NOUNS 1 **pit,** deep, depth, hole, hollow, **cavity,** shaft, sump; oil well; wellspring, wellhead, **spring,** fountain, fount, font, *fons et origo* <L>
ADJS 2 **unailing,** unsick, unsickly, unfrail; all right, doing nicely, up and about, sitting up and taking nourishment, alive and well
ADVS 3 **ably,** capably, competently, adequately, effectively, effectually, efficiently; to the best of one's ability, as lies in one's power, so far as one can, as best one can; **successfully,** to some purpose, to good purpose; **skillfully,** expertly, proficiently, excellently

**well-being** NOUNS **health,** fitness, health and fitness, physical fitness; bloom, flush, glow, rosiness; euphoria; happiness; **comfort,** ease, contentment

**well-bred** ADJS highbred, **well-brought-up;** cultivated, cultured, polished, refined, genteel, gentle; gentlemanly, gentlemanlike, ladylike

**well-built** ADJS **sturdy,** stable, **solid,** sound, firm, steady, tough, stout, **strong,** rugged; **durable,** lasting, enduring; **well-made,** well-constructed; **shapely,** built, well-proportioned, well-formed, stacked *or* well-stacked <both nonformal>, curvaceous, curvy <nonformal>, amply endowed, built for comfort *or* built like a brick shithouse <both nonformal>, buxom

**well-known** ADJS **well-understood, well-recognized, widely known,** commonly known, universally recognized, generally *or* universally admitted; **familiar,** common, current; proverbial; public, notorious; **on everyone's tongue** *or* **lips;** commonplace, trite, hackneyed, platitudinous, truistic

**well-rounded** ADJS **versatile,** all-around <nonformal>, broad-gauge, **many-sided,** generally capable; **adaptable,** adjustable, flexible, resourceful, supple

**well-to-do** ADJS **wealthy,** well-situated, prosperous, comfortable, provided for, well-off, well provided for; independent, independently rich, independently wealthy; privileged, higher-income, upper-income

**welsh** VERBS **repudiate,** renege, dodge, duck; **not pay;** dishonor, **default,** levant <Brit>

**wet** NOUNS 1 **moisture,** damp; **dampness,** moistness, moistiness, **wetness,** soddenness; mistiness, fogginess; rainfall
VERBS 2 **moisten,** dampen, moisturize, damp, wet down; humidify, **water,** sprinkle, besprinkle, **spray,** spritz <nonformal>, sparge, asperge; **swash,** slosh, splatter, spatter, bespatter
ADJS 3 **moist,** moisty; **damp,** dampish; wettish; **humid,** dank, muggy, dewy, bedewed; rainy

**wet blanket** NOUNS **spoilsport,** killjoy, grouch, grinch *and* sourpuss <both nonformal>, malcontent, **dog in the manger** <nonformal>

**whammy** NOUNS **curse,** anathema, fulmination; hex, evil eye, jinx, *malocchio* <Ital>

**wheedle** VERBS **coax,** cajole, blandish, flatter, palaver, plead with, sweet-talk *and* soft-soap <both nonformal>

**wheel** NOUNS steering wheel; **potter's wheel,** kick wheel, pedal wheel, power wheel; **big shot** *and* big wheel *and* big-time operator *and* **bigwig** *and* big man *and* big gun *and* high-muck-a-muck *and* big man on campus *or* BMOC

**wheeler-dealer** NOUNS operator *and* finagler *and* **wire-puller** <all nonformal>; **person** *or* **woman** *or* **man** of influence, a presence, a palpable presence, a mover and shaker <nonformal>, a person to be reckoned with, a player *or* player on the scene; influencer, power-broker

**whereabouts** NOUNS 1 **location,** place, position, spot, *lieu* <Fr>, placement, emplacement, stead; whereabout, ubicity
ADVS 2 **where,** in what place, in which place

**whereas** NOUNS **condition,** provision, proviso, stipulation

**wherewithal** NOUNS **means,** ways, **ways and means,** means to an end; funds; **resources,** disposable resources, capital; **assets,** total assets, worth, net worth, **pecuniary resources,** available means *or* resources *or* funds, cash flow, command of money

**whet** VERBS **stimulate,** sharpen, pique, provoke, quicken, enliven, excite, stir, liven up, pick up, jazz up <nonformal>, animate; infuse life into, give new life to, revive, renew, resuscitate; **hone,** oilstone, file, grind; strop

**while** NOUNS **time,** duration, *durée* <Fr>, lastingness, continuity, term, tide, space; **meantime,** meanwhile, the while

**while away** VERBS **fritter away,** fool away, fribble away, dribble away, drivel away, **trifle away,** dally away, potter away, piss away <nonformal>, muddle away, diddle away <nonformal>, squander in dribs and drabs; idle away

**whim** NOUNS **caprice,** humor, **whimsy,** freak, whim-wham; **fancy,** fantasy, **conceit, notion,** flimflam, toy, freakish inspiration, crazy idea, fantastic notion, fool notion <nonformal>, harebrained idea, brainstorm, **vagary,** megrim; **quirk,** twist, kink, crank, quip, trick, mannerism, **crotchet,** maggot, maggot in the brain, bee in one's bonnet *or* head <nonformal>

**whimper** VERBS **blubber,** snivel; shed

tears, drop a tear; give way to tears, melt *or* dissolve in tears, break down, break down and cry, turn on the waterworks <nonformal>

**whimsical** ADJS **capricious,** freakish, humorsome, vagarious; **fanciful,** notional, fantastic *or* fantastical, maggoty, kinky, harebrained, cranky, flaky <nonformal>, quirky; **droll,** quizzical; **fickle,** erratic, variable, wavering, **changeable**

**whine** NOUNS 1 **lament,** plaint, *planctus* <L>; **whimper;** cry
VERBS 2 **whimper,** yammer <nonformal>, pule, grizzle <chiefly Brit nonformal>; nasalize, **speak through one's nose,** snuffle

**whip** NOUNS 1 **lash,** scourge, flagellum, strap, thong, rawhide, cowhide, blacksnake, kurbash, sjambok, belt, razor strap; knout; bullwhip, bullwhack; horsewhip; crop; quirt; cat, cat-o'-nine-tails
VERBS 2 give a whipping *or* beating *or* thrashing, **beat,** thrash, spank, flog, scourge, flagellate, flail, whale; **smite,** thump, trounce, baste, **pummel,** pommel, **drub,** buffet, belabor, lay on; **lash,** lace, cut, stripe; horsewhip; knout; **strap,** belt, rawhide, cowhide; **switch,** birch, give the stick; pistol-whip

**whippersnapper** NOUNS **brat,** urchin; minx, **imp,** puck, elf, gamin, little monkey, young whippersnapper, *enfant terrible* <Fr>, little terror, holy terror; spoiled brat; snotnose kid <nonformal>; punk *and* punk kid <both nonformal>; pipsqueak *and* squirt *and* shrimp *and* scrub *and* runt <all nonformal>

**whir** NOUNS 1 **turning,** whirling, swirling, **spinning,** wheeling, reeling
VERBS 2 **hum,** thrum, **drone,** buzz, whiz, burr, purr

**whirl** NOUNS 1 **eddy,** swirl, twirl; **bustle,** fuss, flurry, flutter, fluster, scramble, ferment, stew, sweat, vortex, maelstrom, **stir,** hubbub, hullabaloo, hoo-ha *and* foofaraw *and* flap <all nonformal>, ado, to-do <nonformal>; **round of pleasure,** mad round, merry-go-round, the dizzy rounds
VERBS 2 **eddy,** gurge, **swirl,** purl, reel, spin; **swivel,** pivot, pivot about, swing, round, swing round; wheel, wheel about, go round *or* around, circle, rotate, gyrate

**whiskey** NOUNS **spirits,** liquor, intoxicating liquor, **hard liquor,** firewater, spiritus frumenti, usquebaugh <Scots>, schnapps, ardent spirits, strong waters, **intoxicant,** toxicant, inebriant, **drink, strong drink,** strong liquor, alcoholic drink *or* beverage, **alcohol,** aqua vitae, water of life, **grog,** social lubricant, nectar of the gods; **booze** <nonformal>; **rum,** the Demon Rum, John Barleycorn; the cup that cheers

**whisper** NOUNS 1 whispering, stage whisper, breathy voice, sussuration; **hint,** gentle hint, **intimation,** indication, suggestion, **suspicion,** inkling, **glimmer,** glimmering; **implication,** insinuation, innuendo; **report,** rumor, flying rumor, unverified *or* unconfirmed report, **hearsay,** *on-dit* <Fr>, scuttlebutt *and* latrine rumor <both nonformal>; **talk,** buzz, rumble, bruit, cry; common talk, town talk, **talk of the town,** topic of the day, *cause célèbre* <Fr>
VERBS 2 **tell confidentially,** tell for one's ears only, mention privately, **breathe,** whisper in the ear; tell one a secret; confide, take aside, see one alone, talk to in private, speak in privacy; say under one's breath, **put a bug in one's ear** <nonformal>

**white** NOUNS **whiteness,** whitishness; albescence; **lightness,** fairness; paleness, chalkiness

**white elephant** NOUNS **impediment,** handicap, disadvantage, inconvenience, penalty; **burden,** imposition, cross, weight, deadweight, ball and chain, millstone around one's neck

**white flag** NOUNS **truce, surrender;** truce flag, flag of truce; offer of parley; calumet, peace pipe, **pipe of peace;** downing of arms, empty hands, hand of friendship, outstretched hand

**white lightning** NOUNS **bootleg liquor, moonshine** <nonformal>; hooch *and* shine *and* mountain dew <all nonformal>, white mule <nonformal>

**whitewash** VERBS **excuse, absolve,** vindicate, clear, exculpate, exonerate, give absolution; justify; **discharge,** release, dismiss, free, set free, let off <nonformal>, let go; quash the charge *or* indictment, withdraw the charge; clear the skirts of, shrive, purge; wipe the slate clean; **decontaminate,** destigmatize

**whittle** VERBS **shape, fashion,** carve, cut, hew, hew out; trim, pare down, gash

**whiz** NOUNS 1 **ace,** star, superstar, crackerjack, great, all-time great, topnotcher, first-rater, flash, hot stuff, pistol, no slouch, world-beater, hot rock, the one who wrote the book <all nonformal>

VERBS 2

<nonformal> **barrel,** clip, tear *or* tear along, bowl along, thunder along, breeze *or* breeze along, tear up the track *or* road, eat up the track *or* road, scorch, sizzle, rip, zip, nip, zing, highball, pour it on, shake *or* get the lead out, give it the gun, skedaddle, scoot, step on it, step on the gas, hump *or* hump it, hotfoot, hightail, make tracks, step lively, step along, carry the mail, hop along, get, git, go like a bat out of hell, run like a scared rabbit, run like mad, go at full blast, go all out, go flat out, run wide open, go at full tilt *or* steam, let her out, open her up, go hell-bent for election *or* leather, give it the gas, go like blazes *or* blue blazes, floor it, make tracks

**whole** NOUNS 1 **totality, entirety,** collectivity; complex; integration, embodiment; **unity,** integrity, wholeness; organic unity, oneness
ADJS 2 **sound,** wholesome; unimpaired; sound of mind and body, sound in wind and limb, sound as a dollar <nonformal>
3 **complete,** total, global, **entire,** intact, solid; full-grown, mature, matured, ripe, developed; **uncut,** unabbreviated, undiminished, unexpurgated

**wholehearted** ADJS **resolute,** resolved, determined, bound *and* bound and determined <both nonformal>, **decided,** decisive, purposeful; **earnest,** serious, sincere; devoted, dedicated, committed; single-minded, relentless, persistent, tenacious, persevering

**wholesome** ADJS **healthful,** healthy, salubrious, salutary, health-preserving, health-enhancing, life-promoting, **beneficial,** benign, good, **good for; hygienic,** hygienical, hygeian, sanitary; constitutional, for one's health; conditioning; bracing, refreshing, invigorating, tonic; **sound,** whole; **sane,** sane-minded, **rational,** reasonable, sensible, **lucid,** normal, clearheaded, clear-minded, balanced

**whopper** NOUNS 1 thumper *and* lunker *and* whale *and* jumbo <all nonformal>; monster, hulk
2 **monstrous lie,** consummate lie, deep-dyed falsehood, out-and-out lie, gross *or* flagrant *or* shameless falsehood, **barefaced lie,** dirty lie <nonformal>; the big lie

**whore** NOUNS 1 **prostitute,** harlot, *fille de joie* <Fr>, daughter of joy, call girl *and* B-girl <both nonformal>, **scarlet woman,** unfortunate woman, painted woman, fallen woman, erring sister, **streetwalker,** hustler *and* **hooker** <both nonformal>, strumpet, woman of the town, *poule* <Fr>, stew, meretrix, Cyprian, Paphian
VERBS 2 **be promiscuous,** sleep around *and* swing <both nonformal>; **debauch,** wanton, fornicate, **cheat,** commit adultery, get a little on the side <nonformal>

**whorehouse** NOUNS **brothel,** house of prostitution, house of assignation, house of joy *or* ill repute *or* ill fame, bawdyhouse, massage parlor, sporting house, disorderly house, **cathouse,** bordello, bagnio, stew, dive, den of vice, den *or* sink of iniquity, crib, joint

**whorl** NOUNS 1 **coil,** roll, **curl,** curlicue, ringlet, pigtail, **spiral,** helix, volute, volution, involute, evolute, gyre, scroll; screw, corkscrew; tendril, cirrus; whirl, swirl, vortex
VERBS 2 convolve, **wind, twine,** twirl, **twist, turn,** twist and turn, meander, crinkle; serpentine, snake, slink, worm; screw, corkscrew; whirl, swirl; scallop; intort; contort

**why** NOUNS 1 **enigma,** mystery, puzzle, puzzlement; **problem,** puzzling *or* baffling problem; question, question mark, vexed *or* perplexed question, enigmatic question, sixty-four dollar question <nonformal>; **perplexity; puzzler,** poser, brain twister *or* teaser <nonformal>, sticker <nonformal>; mind-boggler, **hard** *or* **tough nut to crack**
ADVS 2 whyever, how come <nonformal>, how is it that, **wherefore,** what for, for which, **on what account,** on account of what *or* which, for what *or* whatever reason, from what cause, *pourquoi* <Fr>

**wicked** ADJS 1 **evil,** vicious, bad, naughty, wrong, sinful, iniquitous, peccant, reprobate; dark, black; **base,** low, vile, foul, rank, flagrant, arrant, nefarious, **heinous,** villainous, criminal, up to no good, knavish, flagitious; abominable,

atrocious, monstrous, unspeakable, execrable, damnable; shameful, disgraceful, scandalous, **infamous,** unpardonable, unforgivable; **improper,** reprehensible, blamable, blameworthy, unworthy
2 **difficult,** difficile; **not easy,** no picnic; **hard,** tough *and* rough *and* rugged <all nonformal>, rigorous, brutal, severe; mean *and* hairy <both nonformal>, **formidable; arduous,** strenuous, toilsome, laborious, operose, Herculean; knotty, knotted; thorny, spiny, set with thorns; easier said than done, like pulling teeth; exacting, demanding; intricate, complex; abstruse

**wide** ADJS 1 **voluminous,** capacious, generous, ample, copious, broad, extensive, expansive, comprehensive; **spacious;** wide-scale, wide-ranging, exhaustive, in-depth; widespread
ADVS 2 **clear;** wide of the mark, abroad, all abroad, astray, afield, far afield

**widen** VERBS 1 **broaden,** stretch, distend, dilate, swell, inflate, sufflate, **blow up,** puff up, huff, puff, bloat; **expand,** extend, extend to the side *or* sides; **spread**, spread out *or* sidewise *or* sideways, outspread, outstretch
2 **generalize,** universalize, catholicize, ecumenicize, globalize, internationalize; make a generalization, deal in generalities *or* abstractions

**widespread** ADJS 1 **customary,** wonted, consuetudinary; traditional, time-honored; **normative,** normal; prevalent, prevailing, obtaining, generally accepted, popular, current; conventional; conformist, conformable
2 **dispersed,** scattered, distributed, disseminated, strown, strewn, broadcast, **spread,** dispread; diffuse, discrete, sparse; far-spread, **far-reaching,** far-ranging, **far-flung,** wide-flung, wide-reaching, wide-ranging

**width** NOUNS **breadth,** broadness, wideness, fullness, amplitude, latitude, distance across *or* crosswise *or* crossways, extent, **span, expanse, spread;** beam

**wield** VERBS **use,** utilize, make use of, do with; **employ,** practice, ply, work, manage, handle, manipulate, operate, play; **have** *or* **enjoy the use of;** exercise, exert; **brandish,** flourish, flaunt, shake, swing

**wieldy** ADJS **handy,** wieldable, handleable; tractable; **manageable,** maneuverable; **convenient,** foolproof, goofproof <nonformal>, practical, untroublesome, user-friendly; adaptable

**wife** NOUNS **married woman,** wedded wife, goodwife <old>, squaw, woman, lady, matron, old lady *and* old woman *and* little woman *and* ball and chain <all nonformal>, feme, feme covert, **better half** <nonformal>, **helpmate,** helpmeet, rib, wife of one's bosom; common-law wife

**wig** NOUNS **peruke,** toupee, hairpiece; rug *and* divot *and* doormat <all nonformal>; periwig

**wiggle** NOUNS 1 **wriggle;** wag, waggle; writhe, **squirm**
VERBS 2 **wriggle;** wag, waggle; **writhe, squirm,** twist and turn; have ants in one's pants <nonformal>

**wild** NOUNS 1 **wilderness,** howling wilderness, wilds
ADJS 2 **furious,** fierce, savage, untamed; raving mad <nonformal>, **rabid,** foaming *or* frothing at the mouth; **fuming,** in a fume; **enraged,** raging, raving, ranting, storming
3 **unrestrained,** unconstrained, unforced, uncompelled, uncoerced; unmeasured, **uninhibited,** unsuppressed, unrepressed, unreserved, boisterous, exuberant; **uncurbed,** unchecked, unbridled, unmuzzled; **unreined,** uncontrolled, unmastered, unsubdued, ungoverned, **unruly;** out of control, out of hand, out of one's power; **abandoned,** intemperate, immoderate, **incontinent,** licentious, loose, wanton, rampant, riotous, rowdy

**wilderness** NOUNS **wasteland,** waste, desolation, barren *or* **barrens,** barren land; howling wilderness, wild, wilds

**will** NOUNS 1 **resolution,** resolve, resolvedness, **determination,** decision, fixed *or* firm resolve, purpose; **resoluteness,** determinedness, decisiveness, **purposefulness;** single-mindedness, relentlessness, persistence, tenacity, perseverance; self-will, obstinacy; **moral fiber; iron will,** will of iron *or* steel; a will *or* mind of one's own, the courage of one's convictions, moral courage
2 **testament,** last will and testament; **bequest,** bequeathal, **legacy,** devise; inheritance
VERBS 3 **wish,** see *or* think fit, think good, think proper, **choose to,** have a mind to; have half a mind *or* notion to;

choose, determine, decide; **desire; resolve,** purpose, make up one's mind, make *or* take a resolution, make a point of
4 **bequeath,** will and bequeath, **leave,** devise, will to, hand down, hand on, pass on, transmit; make a bequest, write one's last will and testament, write into one's will

**willful** ADJS 1 **obstinate,** stubborn, pertinacious, restive; self-willed, strong-willed, hardheaded, **headstrong,** strongheaded, *entêté* <Fr>; **dogged,** bulldogged, tenacious; bullheaded, bulletheaded, **pigheaded,** mulish <nonformal>, stubborn as a mule; set, **set in one's ways,** case-hardened, stiff-necked
2 **intentional,** intended, proposed, purposed, telic, **projected,** designed, of design, aimed, aimed at, **meant,** purposeful, purposive, voluntary, deliberate

**willing** ADJS **willinghearted,** ready, game <nonformal>; **disposed,** inclined, minded, willed; **well-disposed,** well-inclined, favorably inclined *or* disposed; predisposed; **favorable,** agreeable, cooperative; compliant, **acquiescent,** consenting; in the mood *or* vein *or* humor *or* mind, receptive, responsive; amenable, tractable, docile, pliant

**will power** NOUNS **will,** volition; choice, determination, decision; **free choice,** one's own will *or* choice *or* discretion *or* initiative, **free will**; conation, conatus; **resolution**

**wilt** VERBS **languish,** pine, droop, flag; fade, fade away; **wither,** shrivel, shrink, diminish, wither *or* die on the vine, **dry up,** desiccate, wizen, wrinkle, sear

**wily** ADJS **shrewd,** artful, cunning, knowing, crafty, guileful, canny, slick, sly, smart as a fox, foxy *and* crazy like a fox <both nonformal>; insinuating, insidious, devious, Byzantine, calculating

**wimp** NOUNS **weakling,** jellyfish, milksop, milquetoast; poor *or* weak *or* dull tool <nonformal>, sissy

**wimpy** ADJS **weak,** spineless, lily-livered, whitelivered, wimpish *and* chicken *and* gutless <all nonformal>, cowardly; weak as a kitten, wimpish <nonformal>, faint-hearted

**win** NOUNS 1 **victory,** triumph, conquest, subduing, subdual; a feather in one's cap <nonformal>; **championship,** crown, laurels, cup, trophy, belt, blue ribbon, first prize
VERBS 2 **triumph,** prevail, be victorious, come out ahead, come out on top <nonformal>; **gain,** capture, carry; win out <nonformal>, **win through,** carry it, carry off *or* away; **win** *or* **carry** *or* **gain the day,** win the battle, come out first, finish in front; **win the prize,** win the palm *or* bays *or* laurels, take the cake <nonformal>, win one's spurs *or* wings
3 **acquire,** get, gain, obtain, secure, procure; score; **earn,** make; **reap,** harvest; take, catch, capture; come *or* enter into possession of, **come into,** come by, come in for, be seized of

**wince** VERBS **flinch,** shrink, shy, shy away from, draw back, recoil, funk <nonformal>, **quail,** cringe, blench, blink, say *or* cry uncle

**wind** NOUNS 1 current, **air current,** current of air, **draft,** movement of air, stream, stream of air, flow of air; updraft, uprush; downdraft, downrush, microburst; fall wind, gravity wind, katabatic wind, head wind, tail wind, following wind; jet stream, upper-atmosphere *or* upper-atmospheric wind
2 **breath,** breath of air; pant, puff; gasp, gulp; **artificial respiration,** kiss of life, mouth-to-mouth resuscitation
3 **fart** <nonformal>, flatulence *or* flatulency, flatuosity, flatus, gas; **belch,** burp <nonformal>, belching, eructation

**wind** VERBS **wander,** meander, curl, twist, snake, twist and turn; screw, crank, wind up

**windbag** NOUNS **chatterer,** chatterbox, babbler, jabberer, prater, prattler, gabbler, gibble-gabbler, **gabber** <nonformal>, **blabberer,** blatherer, patterer, word-slinger, *moulin à paroles* <Fr>; gasbag *and* windjammer *and* hot-air artist *and* motor-mouth *and* ratchet-jaw <all nonformal>; big talker <nonformal>, spendthrift of one's tongue

**windfall** NOUNS **windfall money, windfall profit, found money, money in the bank, bonus,** gravy <nonformal>; godsend

**winding** ADJS **convolutional,** twisting, twisty, **turning; meandering,** meandrous, mazy, labyrinthine; **serpentine,** snaky, anfractuous; roundabout, circuitous, ambagious, circumlocutory; labyrinthine; **tortuous,** torsional

**windup** NOUNS **completion,** completing, **finish,** finishing, conclusion, end, ending, **termination,** terminus, **close,**

rounding off *or* out, topping off, wrapping up, wrap-up, finalization

**windy** ADJS **blowy; breezy,** drafty, airy, airish; brisk, fresh; **gusty,** blasty, puffy, flawy; **squally;** blustery, blustering, blusterous; aeolian, favonian, boreal; ventose

**wine** NOUNS *vin* <Fr>, *vino* <Sp & Ital>; vintage wine, nonvintage wine; red wine, white wine, rosé wine, pink wine; dry *or* sweet wine, heavy *or* light wine, full *or* thin wine, rough *or* smooth wine, still wine, sparkling wine; jug wine, plonk <Brit>

**wing** NOUNS 1 **addition,** annex, extension, ell *or* L; **branch,** organ, division, arm, offshoot, affiliate; **offshoot,** ramification, scion, spur; pinion
2 **protectorship,** guardianship, stewardship, custodianship; **care,** charge, keeping, nurture, nurturing, nurturance, custody, fostering, fosterage; hands, safe hands

**wing it** VERBS 1 **improvise,** extemporize, improv *and* tapdance *and* talk off the top of one's head <all nonformal>, speak off the cuff, think on one's feet, make it up as one goes along, depart from the prepared text, throw away the speech, scrap the plan, **ad-lib** <nonformal>, **do offhand,** fake <nonformal>, play by ear <nonformal>
2 **do easily,** make short work of, do with one's hands tied behind one's back, do with both eyes shut, do standing on one's head, sail *or* dance *or* waltz through

**wink** NOUNS 1 casual glance, **half an eye;** flick of the eyelash, glance, leer; **hint,** broad hint, signal, nod, look; blink
2 **instant,** moment, **trice,** twinkle, twinkling, twinkling *or* twinkle of an eye, twink, bat of an eye <nonformal>
VERBS 3 **blink,** nictitate, bat the eyes <nonformal>; **signal,** give a signal, make a sign; glance, raise one's eyebrows

**winner** NOUNS 1 **victor,** victress, victrix, triumpher; **conqueror,** defeater, **vanquisher,** subduer, subjugator, *conquistador* <Sp>; top dog <nonformal>; champion, champ *and* number one <both nonformal>; easy winner, sure winner, shoo-in <nonformal>; **star,** success, superstar
2 **good thing,** a thing to be desired; no slouch *and* nothing to sneeze at <both nonformal>; catch, find <nonformal>

**winning** NOUNS 1 **acquisition,** gaining, getting, getting hold of <nonformal>, coming by, **acquirement, obtainment,** obtention, **attainment,** securement
ADJS 2 **victorious,** triumphant, triumphal, prevailing; conquering, vanquishing, defeating, overcoming; ahead of the game, ascendant, in the ascendant, in ascendancy, sitting on top of the world *and* sitting pretty <both nonformal>, dominant; successful
3 **delightful,** winsome, taking, fetching, heart-robbing; inviting, tempting, tantalizing; **attractive,** sexy <nonformal>, **seductive,** provocative, exciting; **endearing,** lovable, likable, adorable, admirable, **lovely,** magnetic, charming, enchanting, charismatic

**winnings** NOUNS **gains,** cut *and* take <both nonformal>, **profits,** earnings, return, returns, proceeds, bottom line <nonformal>, makings; **fruits,** pickings, gleanings; **booty,** spoils

**winnow** VERBS **select,** make a selection; **pick,** handpick, pick out; **decide between,** choose up sides <nonformal>, cull, glean, sift; separate the wheat from the chaff, separate the sheep from the goats

**winsome** ADJS **endearing,** lovable, likable, adorable, admirable, **lovely,** lovesome, sweet, winning; **charming;** caressable, kissable; **pleasant,** genial, irrepressible, prepossessing

**wintry** ADJS **cold,** freezing, freezing cold, **crisp,** brisk, nipping, **nippy,** snappy <nonformal>, **raw,** bleak, keen, sharp, bitter, biting, pinching, cutting, **piercing,** penetrating; **wintery,** winterlike, winterbound, hiemal, brumal, hibernal

**wipe** VERBS **wipe up** *or* out, wipe off; rub, swab, brush; towel

**wipe out** VERBS 1 **exterminate,** eliminate, eradicate, deracinate, **extirpate,** annihilate; **liquidate,** purge; remove, sweep away, wipe off the map, rub out
2 **bankrupt,** ruin, break, bust <nonformal>; put out of business, drive to the wall, scuttle, sink, impoverish; **cancel,** delete, expunge

**wire** NOUNS 1 **cable,** electric wire, electric cord, cord, power cord, power cable; **telegram,** telex; **cablegram,** day letter, night letter
VERBS 2 **electrify,** wire up; **telegraph,** telegram, send a wire <nonformal>, telex; cable

**wiretap** NOUNS 1 **surveillance,** wiretapping, bugging <nonformal>, electronic surveillance
VERBS 2 **listen in;** eavesdrop, tap, intercept, bug <nonformal>

**wiry** ADJS **well-built,** thewy, sinewy; **stringy,** ropy, fibrous

**wisdom** NOUNS ripe wisdom, seasoned understanding, mellow wisdom, wiseness, sageness, sapience, good *or* sound understanding; **profundity,** intelligence, profoundness, depth; **conventional wisdom,** received wisdom, prudential judgment, prudence

**wise** ADJS **sage,** sapient, seasoned, **knowing;** learned; **profound,** deep; wise as an owl, wise as Solomon; wise beyond one's years, in advance of one's age

**wisecrack** NOUNS 1 **witticism,** pleasantry, *plaisanterie, boutade* <both Fr>; **crack** *and* smart crack <both nonformal>; **mot,** bon mot, smart saying, stroke of wit, one-liner *and* zinger <both nonformal>; **sally,** flight of wit; **repartee,** backchat, retort, riposte, snappy comeback <nonformal>; **gibe,** dirty *or* nasty crack <nonformal>; persiflage
VERBS 2 **joke,** jest, crack wise <nonformal>, utter a mot, **quip,** jape, josh <nonformal>, fun <nonformal>, make fun, **kid** *or* **kid around** <both nonformal>; make a funny <nonformal>; **crack a joke,** get off a joke; **make fun of,** gibe at, fleer at, mock, scoff at

**wise guy** NOUNS **wiseacre,** wisehead, wiseling, **witling,** wisenheimer *or* weisenheimer <nonformal>, smart ass <nonformal>; **gangster,** hoodlum

**wise man** NOUNS **sage,** wise woman, sapient, man *or* woman of wisdom; **philosopher,** thinker, lover of wisdom; elder, wise old man, elder statesman; seer; mentor; **intellect,** man of intellect; mandarin, **intellectual**; savant; brain *and* rocket scientist *and* brain surgeon <all nonformal>; **pundit,** Brahmin, mandarin, egg-head *and* pointy-head <both nonformal>; **highbrow** <nonformal>

**wish** NOUNS 1 **desire,** wanting, **want,** need, desideration; **hope;** fancy; will, mind, pleasure, will and pleasure; heart's desire; **inclination,** disposition, liking, appetence, appetency, espressed desire
VERBS 2 **desire,** desiderate, be desirous of, ewish for, express a wish for, crave, lust after, bay after, kill for *and* give one's right arm for <both nonformal>, die for <nonformal>, **want,** have a mind to, choose <nonformal>; **like,** have *or* acquire a taste for, fancy, take to, **take a fancy** *or* a shine to, have a fancy for; lean toward, tilt toward, have a penchant for, have a weakness *or* soft spot in one's heart for

**wishful thinking** NOUNS **fantasy,** fantasizing, escape into fantasy, dreamlike thinking, autistic *or* dereistic thinking, autism, dereism; **wistfulness,** wishfulness, **nostalgia;** sheep's eyes, longing *or* wistful eye; daydream, daydreaming; **credulity,** credulousness, inclination *or* disposition to believe, ease of belief, will *or* willingness to believe, wishful belief

**wishy-washy** ADJS tasteless, bland, **insipid,** vapid, neutral, watery, milktoast, milky, milk-and-water, mushy; halfhearted, infirm of will *or* purpose, **indecisive,** irresolute, changeable; **unsteady,** spineless, shapeless, amorphous, blowing hot and cold <nonformal>, like a feather in the wind, unsteadfast

**wistful** ADJS **wishful; longing,** yearning, yearnful, **hankering** <nonformal>, **languishing,** pining, honing <nonformal>; **nostalgic,** homesick; **pensive,** tristful

**wit** NOUNS 1 **humor,** pleasantry, *esprit* <Fr>, salt, spice *or* savor of wit; Attic wit *or* salt, Atticism; ready wit, quick wit, nimble wit, agile wit, pretty wit; dry wit, subtle wit; **sense,** mother wit, natural *or* native wit, **intelligence,** intellect, understanding
2 **humorist,** funnyman, comic, *bel-esprit* <Fr>, life of the party; **joker,** jokester, gagman <nonformal>, **jester,** quipster, wisecracker *and* gagster <both nonformal>; wag, wagwit; epigrammatist; satirist, ironist; burlesquer, caricaturist, parodist, lampooner

**witch** NOUNS **hag,** vixen, hellhag, hellcat, she-devil, virago, brimstone, termagant, grimalkin, Jezebel, beldam, she-wolf, tigress, wildcat, bitch-kitty <nonformal>, siren, fury; **sorceress,** shamaness; witchwoman <nonformal>, witchwife <Scots>; witch of Endor

**witchcraft** NOUNS **sorcery,** necromancy, magic, sortilege, **wizardry,** theurgy, rune, glamour; spellcraft, spellbinding, spellcasting; **witchery,** witchwork, bewitchery, enchantment

**witch hunt** NOUNS **persecution,** oppression, harrying, hounding, tormenting, bashing <nonformal>, harassment, victimization; **witch-hunting,** redbaiting <nonformal>, McCarthyism; fishing expedition, inquisition

**withdraw** VERBS 1 **retreat,** sound *or* beat a retreat, beat a hasty retreat, **beat a retreat,** remove; **retire,** pull out *or* back, exfiltrate, advance to the rear, disengage; **fall back,** move back, draw back, back out *or* out of *and* back off *and* back down <all nonformal>
2 **retract,** draw *or* pull back, pull out, draw *or* pull in; draw in one's claws *or* horns; defer, take a back seat, play second fiddle; **shrink,** wince, cringe, flinch, shy, fight shy, duck
3 **stand alone,** stand *or* move *or* keep apart, keep oneself to oneself, alienate *or* seclude *or* sequester *or* isolate oneself, feel out of place

**withdrawal** NOUNS 1 **retreat,** *reculade* <Fr>, strategic withdrawal, exfiltration; **retirement,** removal, fallback, pullout, pullback; advance to the rear; rout; disengagement; **backing down** *or* **off** *or* **out** <all nonformal>; reneging, copping *or* weaseling out <nonformal>, **recantation,** disavowal, denial, **repudiation,** retraction
2 **aloofness,** standoffishness, distance, remoteness, **detachment,** reclusiveness, solitariness; **inaccessibility,** unapproachability; introversion; **alienation,** standing *or* moving *or* keeping apart, **isolation**
3 **resignation,** demission, **abdication,** voluntary resignation; forced resignation, deposal; relinquishment

**wither** VERBS **shrink,** shrivel, sear, parch, dry up; **wizen,** wrinkle, weazen; consume, waste, waste away, attenuate, thin, emaciate

**withhold** VERBS hold back, hold out on <nonformal>, **refrain from,** forbear, forgo, spare, **avoid,** shun, eschew, **pass up** <nonformal>, **keep from,** keep *or* stand *or* hold aloof from, have nothing to do with, take no part in, have no hand in, **let alone,** let well enough alone, let go by, **deny oneself,** do without, go without, make do without, not *or* never touch, keep hands off

**witness** NOUNS 1 **eyewitness,** spectator, earwitness; **bystander,** passerby; **deponent,** testifier, attestant, attester, attestator, voucher, swearer; **informant,** informer; character witness; cojuror, compurgator
VERBS 2 **see,** behold, observe, view, perceive, discern, spy, espy, **sight,** have in sight, make out, pick out, descry, spot <nonformal>, discover, notice, take notice of, have one's eye on, distinguish, recognize, ken <nonformal>, **catch sight of,** get a load of <nonformal>, take in, get an eyeful of <nonformal>, look on *or* upon, cast the eyes on *or* upon, **set** *or* **lay eyes on,** clap eyes on <nonformal>; **glimpse,** get *or* catch a glimpse of; see with one's own eyes
3 bear witness, affirm, **believe**; keep the faith, fight the good fight, let one's light shine, praise and glorify God, walk humbly with one's God; be observant, follow righteousness

**wits** NOUNS **senses,** faculties, parts, capacities, intellectual gifts *or* talents, mother wit; consciousness

**witticism** NOUNS **pleasantry,** *plaisanterie, boutade* <both Fr>; play of wit, *jeu d'esprit* <Fr>; **crack** *and* smart crack *and* **wisecrack** <all nonformal>; **quip, mot,** bon mot, smart saying, stroke of wit, one-liner *and* zinger <both nonformal>; epigram, turn of thought, aphorism, apothegm; flash of wit, scintillation; **sally,** flight of wit

**witty** ADJS **amusing,** humorous, comic, comical, farcical; **funny; jocular,** joking, jesting, jocose, tongue-in-cheek; facetious, joshing <nonformal>, **whimsical,** droll, humorsome; smart, clever, brilliant, scintillating, sparkling, sprightly; keen, sharp, rapier-like, pungent, pointed, biting, mordant; satiric, **satirical,** sarcastic, ironic, ironical; **keen-witted,** quick-witted, nimble-witted

**wizard** NOUNS **sorcerer,** necromancer, wonder-worker, theurgist; warlock, male witch; thaumaturge, thaumaturgist; alchemist; conjurer; diviner; dowser, water witch, water witcher; diabolist

**wobble** VERBS **fluctuate,** pendulate, oscillate, wobble about, teeter, dither, flounder, stagger, **seesaw,** teeter-totter, wamble

**woe** NOUNS **wretchedness,** despair, bitterness, infelicity, **misery,** anguish, agony, woefulness, bale, balefulness; **heartache,** aching heart, heavy heart, bleeding heart, broken heart, agony of mind *or* spirit; **despondency,** despond; **desolation,** prostration; **curse,** distress, grievance, **sorrow,** *tsuris* <Yiddish>

**wolf** NOUNS 1 timber wolf, lobo <W US>, brush wolf, prairie wolf, coyote, medicine wolf <W US>

2 masher, lady-killer, skirt chaser, man on the make *and* make-out artist <both nonformal>, gay deceiver, philanderer; libertine, lecher, cocksman <nonformal>, seducer, Casanova, Don Juan

VERBS 3 **gobble,** gulp, bolt, gobble *or* gulp *or* bolt *or* wolf down; **gorge,** engorge, glut, cram, **stuff,** batten, guttle, **devour,** raven, eat like a horse, stuff oneself *and* hog it down *and* eat one's head off *and* fork *or* shovel it in <all nonformal>, eat one out of house and home

**woman** NOUNS 1 **womankind,** women, femininity, **womanhood,** womenfolk *or* womenfolks <nonformal>, the distaff side; **the female sex;** the second sex, **the fair sex,** the gentle sex, the softer sex, **the weaker sex,** the weaker vessel

2 <nonformal> **gal, dame,** hen, biddy, skirt, jane, broad, doll, babe, chick, wench, bird <Brit>, tomato, bitch, minx, momma, mouse, sister, squaw, toots

3 **wife,** married woman, wedded wife, goodwife <old>, squaw, lady, matron, old lady *and* old woman *and* little woman *and* ball and chain <all nonformal>, feme, feme covert, **better half** <nonformal>, **helpmate,** helpmeet, rib, wife of one's bosom; wife in name only; wife in all but name, common-law wife; **mistress,** kept woman, kept mistress, paramour, concubine, doxy, playmate, spiritual *or* unofficial wife; live-in lover <nonformal>

*the female of the human species, and not a different kind of animal*
**G B Shaw**

*O fairest of creation! last and best of all God's works*
**Milton**

**womanizer** NOUNS **libertine,** swinger <nonformal>, **profligate,** rake, rakehell, **roué,** wanton, cocksman <nonformal>, debauchee, **wolf** <nonformal>, woman chaser, skirt chaser <nonformal>, gay dog, gay deceiver, gallant, philanderer, lover-boy <nonformal>, Lothario, Don Juan, Casanova

**wonder** NOUNS 1 wonderment, sense of wonder, marveling, marvel, **astonishment,** amazement; **surprise;** beguilement, fascination; bewilderment, puzzlement

2 **marvel,** prodigy, miracle, phenomenon, phenom <nonformal>; **sensation,** rocker *and* stunner <both nonformal>; one for the book *and* something to brag about *and* something to shout about *and* something to write home about *and* something else <all nonformal>; **rarity,** nonesuch, nonpareil, exception, one in a thousand, **first-rater,** topnotcher, worldbeater; hard *or* tough act to follow <nonformal>

VERBS 3 **marvel,** be astonished *or* amazed *or* astounded, be seized with wonder; **gaze,** gape, drop one's jaw, look *or* stand aghast *or* agog, gawk, **stare,** stare openmouthed, open one's eyes, rub one's eyes, hold one's breath

4 **be uncertain,** feel unsure; doubt, have one's doubts, **question,** puzzle over, agonize over; wonder whether, wrinkle one's brow; not know what to make of, not be able to make head or tail of

**wonderful** ADJS **wondrous,** marvelous, miraculous, fantastic, fabulous, phenomenal, **prodigious,** stupendous, unheard-of, unprecedented, extraordinary, exceptional, rare, unique, singular, **remarkable,** striking, sensational

**woo** VERBS **court,** sue, press one's suit, **pay court** *or* **suit to,** cozy up to <nonformal>, eye up *and* chat up <Brit nonformal>, pay one's court to, fling oneself at; **pursue,** follow; chase <nonformal>; set one's cap at *or* for <nonformal>; spark <nonformal>, squire

**wood** NOUNS **woodland,** woods, timberland; **timber,** stand of timber, **forest,** forest land, forest cover, forest preserve, state *or* national forest; **firewood,** stovewood; **kindling,** kindling wood; brush, brushwood; log, backlog, yule log *or* yule clog <old>; **lumber,** forest-product; hardwood, softwood

**wooded** ADJS **sylvan,** woodland, forest, forestal; timbered, forested, arboreous; **woody,** woodsy, bosky, bushy, shrubby, scrubby; copsy, braky

**wooden** ADJS **inexpressive,** unexpressive, impassive, uncommunicative; **expressionless; vacant,** empty, blank; glassy, glazed, glazed-over, deadpan, poker-faced <nonformal>

**woolly** ADJS **fleecy,** lanate, lanated, flocky, flocculent, floccose; bushy, tufty, **shaggy,** shagged; fuzzy

**woozy** ADJS **dazed,** mazed, **dazzled,** bedazzled, in a daze; **silly,** knocked silly, cockeyed <nonformal>; **groggy** <nonformal>, dopey <nonformal>; **punch-drunk** *and* punchy *and* slaphappy <all nonformal>

**word** NOUNS 1 **oath,** vow, assurance, guarantee, warrant, solemn oath *or* affirmation *or* word *or* declaration; pledge; **promise,** solemn promise, troth, plight, faith, parole, **word of honor**
2 **report,** message, presentation, account, **statement,** mention; **news,** tidings, intelligence, information, advice; parol, the spoken word; vocable

**wordy** ADJS **verbose;** talkative; **prolix,** windy <nonformal>, **long-winded,** longiloquent; **protracted,** extended, *de longue haleine* <Fr>, lengthy, long, **long-drawn-out,** spun-out, endless, unrelenting; padded

**work** NOUNS 1 **composition,** opus, production, literary production, literary artifact *or* artefact, lucubration, brainchild; essay, article; poem; play; novel, short story; **work of art,** object of art, objet d'art, art object, art work, artistic production, piece, **study,** design; creation, brainchild
2 **occupation,** job, employment, business, employ, **activity,** function, enterprise, undertaking, **affairs,** labor; thing *and* bag <both nonformal>; **task,** stint, job, piece of work, **chore,** odd job
VERBS 3 **labor;** busy oneself; turn a hand, do a lick of work, earn one's keep; do the chores; **operate,** function, act, perform, go, run, be in action *or* operation *or* commission; be effective, go into effect, have effect, take effect, militate; **accomplish,** achieve, **deliver,** realize, engineer, effectuate, **bring about,** bring to fruition *or* into being, cause; be productive
4 **suffice,** do, just do, serve, **answer;** be equal to, **avail;** answer *or* serve the purpose, do the trick <nonformal>, suit; **satisfy,** meet requirements; **pass muster,** make the grade *or* the cut *and* hack it *and* cut the mustard *and* **fill the bill** <all nonformal>; get by *and* scrape by <both nonformal>, do in a pinch, **pass,** pass in the dark <nonformal>
5 **cultivate,** culture, **dress,** till, till the soil, dig, delve, spade

**workable** ADJS **operable,** operatable, **performable,** actable, doable, manageable, compassable, negotiable, maneuverable; **practicable,** feasible, practical, viable

**workaday** ADJS **routine,** nine-to-five, well-trodden, well-worn, beaten; **matter-of-fact,** homely, homespun, everyday, household, garden, common- *or* garden-variety, prosaic

**workaholic** NOUNS **hustler** *and* self-starter <both nonformal>, bustler; go-getter *and* ball of fire *and* live wire *and* powerhouse *and* human dynamo *and* spitfire <all nonformal>; overachiever; beaver, busy bee, **eager beaver** <nonformal>

**worker** NOUNS **workman,** working man, working woman, working girl, proletarian, laborer, laboring man, toiler, stiff *and* working stiff <both nonformal>, artisan, mechanic, industrial worker, factory worker

**workhorse** NOUNS **drudge,** grub, hack, fag, plodder, slave, galley slave, beast of burden, slogger; grind *and* greasy grind <both nonformal>

*hewers of wood and drawers of water*
BIBLE

2 **draft horse,** dray horse, cart horse, plow horse

**working class** NOUNS **lower class,** lower classes, lower orders, plebs, workers, working people, proletariat, laboring class *or* classes, toilers, toiling class *or* classes, the other half, low-income group, wage-earners, hourly worker, blue-collar workers

**working-class** ADJS **blue-collar,** proletarian, lower-class, born on the wrong side of the tracks

**workmanlike** ADJS **skillful,** good, goodish, excellent, **expert,** proficient; dexterous, **adroit,** deft, adept, coordinated, well-coordinated, **apt,** no mean, **handy; ingenious,** resourceful, well-done; **passable,** unobjectionable, unexceptionable

**workmanship** NOUNS **skill,** skillfulness, **proficiency,** craft, **craftsmanship,** artisanship; **know-how** *and* savvy *and* bag of tricks <all nonformal>; technical skill, **technique,** touch, **mastery,** command, control, grip

**works** NOUNS 1 **benevolences,** philanthropies, charities; **good works,** public service
2 **complete works,** oeuvre, canon, literary canon, author's canon
3 **plant,** factory, manufacturing plant, *usine* <Fr>
4 **mechanism,** machinery, **movement,** movements, **action,** motion, workings, inner workings, what makes it work, innards, what makes it tick; clockworks, watchworks, servomechanism

**world** NOUNS 1 **outlook,** mental outlook; *Anschauung* <Ger>, **point of view,** viewpoint, standpoint, **perspective,** *optique* <Fr>; slant, way of looking at things, slant on things, where one is coming from <nonformal>; **frame of reference,** intellectual *or* ideational framework, arena, universe, world *or* universe of discourse, system, reference system
2 **universe,** cosmos; creation, created universe, created nature, all, **all creation,** all tarnation <nonformal>, all *or* everything that is, all being, totality, totality of being, sum of things; omneity, allness; nature, system; wide world, whole wide world; **macrocosm**

*world without end*
BIBLE

**worldly** ADJS 1 **experienced,** practiced, mature, matured, ripe, ripened, **seasoned,** tried, well-tried, tried and true, **veteran,** old, an old dog at <nonformal>; **worldly-wise,** wise in the ways of the world, knowing, **sophisticated,** cosmopolitan, cosmopolite, blasé, dry behind the ears, not born yesterday, long in the tooth
2 **unsacred,** nonsacred, **unholy,** unhallowed, unsanctified, unblessed; profane, **secular,** temporal, fleshly, mundane; unsaved, unredeemed, unregenerate, reprobate; **secularist,** secularistic, earthly, earthy, terrestrial, **materialistic,** material, Philistine

**worn** ADJS 1 **wasted, rundown,** worn-out, worn to a frazzle <nonformal>, worn to a shadow, reduced to a skeleton; tired-looking, weary-looking, haggard, hollow-eyed, ravaged, drawn, cadaverous, wan; dissipated, **eroded,** consumed, ablated; worn-down, the worse for wear, dog-eared; timeworn; **threadbare,** bare
2 **secondhand,** used, previously owned, **unnew,** not new, pawed-over; hand-me-down, reach-me-down <Brit nonformal>

**worry** NOUNS 1 worriment <nonformal>, worriedness; **worries,** worries and cares, troubles, concerns; worrying, fretting; harassment, torment
VERBS 2 **upset,** vex, fret, agitate, get to <nonformal>, **harass,** harry, **torment,** dog, hound, plague, persecute, haunt, beset; worry oneself, worry one's head about, worry oneself sick, trouble one's head *or* oneself, lose sleep; **fuss,** chafe, stew *and* take on <both nonformal>, fret and fume; bite one's nails, walk the floor, go up the wall <nonformal>, be on tenterhooks *or* pins and needles <nonformal>

**worrywart** NOUNS **worrier,** killjoy, nervous Nellie *and* gloomy Gus *and* calamity howler <all nonformal>, seeksorrow, Job's comforter, prophet of doom, Cassandra

**worse** ADJS **aggravated,** worsened, worse and worse, exacerbated, embittered, soured, deteriorated; **intensified,** heightened, stepped-up, **increased,** worse off, the worse for, all the worse for; **degenerate,** unmitigated

**worsen** VERBS get *or* grow worse, take a turn for the worse; go from push to shove, **go from bad to worse;** jump out of the frying pan and into the fire, avoid Scylla and fall into Charybdis; **deteriorate,** sicken, get no better fast <nonformal>, disimprove, **degenerate;** slip back, **retrogress,** retrograde, regress, relapse, fall back

*sow the wind and reap the whirlwind*
BIBLE

**worship** NOUNS 1 worshiping, **adoration,** devotion, homage, veneration, reverence; idolatry
VERBS 2 **adore,** reverence, venerate, revere, honor, do *or* pay homage to, pay divine honors to, do service, lift up the heart, bow down and worship, humble oneself before; idolize

**worst** ADJS flagrant, **scandalous,** shameful, **shocking,** infamous, **notorious,** arrant, **egregious; odious,** disgusting, repulsive, loathsome, **abominable,** detestable, despicable, contemptible, beneath contempt, hateful; as bad as they come, as bad as they make 'em <nonformal>, as bad as bad can be; worthless

**worth** NOUNS 1 **preciousness,** dearness, value, high *or* great value, extraordinary worth, **pricelessness,** invaluableness; **assets,** resources, total assets, net worth, **pecuniary resources,** means, available means *or* resources *or* funds, cash flow, wherewithal, command of money
2 **goodness,** excellence, quality, class <nonformal>; **virtue,** grace; **merit,** desert; **fineness,** virtuousness

**worthless** ADJS **valueless,** good-for-nothing, good-for-naught, no-good *or* NG <nonformal>, no-account <nonformal>, dear at any price, not worth a dime *or* a red cent *or* a hill of beans *or* shit <nonformal>, not worthwhile, not worth having, not worth mentioning *or* speaking of, not worth a rap *or* a continental *or* a damn, of no earthly use; unworthy, unprofitable, profitless, unrewarding, useless

**worthwhile** ADJS **valuable,** of value, all for the best, all to the good, **profitable,** fructuous, rewarding, worth one's while; gainful, remunerative, advantageous

**worthy** ADJS **warranted,** justified, entitled, qualified; **deserved,** merited, richly deserved, earned, well-earned; **reputable,** highly reputed, **estimable,** esteemed, much *or* highly esteemed, **honorable,** honored; **meritorious,** worth one's salt, noble, creditable; respected, respectable, highly respectable; **well-thought-of,** held in esteem, in good odor, in favor, in high favor

**would-be** ADJS **presumptuous,** presuming, assuming, overweening, self-elected, self-appointed, self-proclaimed; **so-called,** *soi-disant* <Fr>; **self-called,** self-styled, self-christened

**wound** NOUNS 1 **trauma,** injury, hurt, lesion; **cut,** incision, scratch, gash; puncture, stab, stab wound; flesh wound; **laceration,** mutilation; **bruise,** contusion, ecchymosis
VERBS 2 **pain,** give *or* inflict pain, **hurt,** afflict, bruise, distress; pierce, prick, stab, cut, lacerate; **grieve,** aggrieve, anguish; hurt one's feelings; wound *or* sting *or* cut to the quick; **injure,** draw blood, traumatize

**wow** NOUNS 1 belly laugh, rib tickler, sidesplitter, thigh-slapper, howler, scream, riot, panic
VERBS 2 **make one laugh,** raise a smile *or* laugh, convulse, be the death of; slay *and* knock dead *and* kill *and* break one up *and* crack one up *and* fracture one <all nonformal>; have them rolling in the aisles; keep them in stitches

**wrangle** NOUNS 1 **quarrel,** open quarrel, **dispute,** argument, polemic, lovers' quarrel, **controversy,** altercation, **fight,** squabble, contention, strife, **tussle,** bicker, snarl, **tiff,** spat, fuss; words, sharp words, war of words, logomachy
VERBS 2 **quarrel,** dispute, oppugn, altercate, **fight,** squabble, tiff, spat, **bicker,** spar, have words, set to, join issue, make the fur fly; **be quarrelsome** *or* contentious, be thin-skinned, be touchy *or* sensitive, get up on the wrong side of the bed

**wrap** NOUNS 1 **dishabille,** *déshabillé* <Fr>, undress, something more comfortable; **negligee,** *négligé* <Fr>; **wrapper,** wrapping, gift wrapping
VERBS 2 enwrap, lap, envelop, sheathe, shroud, enshroud; wrap *or* bundle *or* muffle up; swathe, swaddle; **package,** pack, parcel; box, case, encase, crate, carton; shrink-wrap; do *or* tie *or* bind up

**wrath** NOUNS **anger,** ire, *saeva indignatio* <L>; angriness, irateness, wrathfulness; vials of wrath, grapes of wrath; the wrath of God

**wreck** NOUNS 1 **nervous wreck,** a bundle of nerves; wrack, shipwreck; total loss; **accident,** casualty, collision, crash, plane *or* car crash, smash *and* smashup *and* crack-up *and* pileup <all nonformal>
VERBS 2 **spoil,** mar, botch, **ruin,** blight, play havoc with; **demolish,** total *and* rack up <both nonformal>; **take apart,** tear apart, tear asunder, rend, take *or* pull *or* pick *or* tear to pieces, tear to shreds *or* rags *or* tatters; **disintegrate,** fragment, break to pieces, make mincemeat of, reduce to rubble, atomize, pulverize, **smash,** shatter

**wrench** NOUNS 1 **pang,** throe, throes; seizure, spasm, paroxysm; **twinge,** jumping pain; **pain,** distress, grief, stress, stress of life, suffering, passion,

dolor; ache, aching; shock, blow, hard *or* nasty blow
2 **jerk,** yank <nonformal>, quick *or* sudden pull; **twitch,** tweak, pluck, hitch, snatch, start; tool
VERBS 3 **twist,** turn, screw; **wrest,** wring, **rend,** rip; **force from,** wrest from, wrench from, wring from, tear from, rip from, rend from, snatch from, pry loose from

**wrestle** VERBS **struggle,** strive, contend, fight, battle, buffet, grapple, grapple with, go to the mat with, scuffle, tussle, rassle <nonformal>, hassle <nonformal>, work *or* fight one's way, agonize, huff and puff, grunt and sweat, sweat it <nonformal>, make heavy weather of it

**wretch** NOUNS mean *or* miserable wretch, beggarly fellow, **beggar;** devil, **poor devil,** *pauvre diable* <Fr>, poor creature, *mauvais sujet* <Fr>; **sad case,** sad sack <nonformal>; **good-for-nothing,** good-for-naught, no-good <nonformal>, **ne'er-do-well,** wastrel, *vaurien* <Fr>, worthless fellow

**wretched** ADJS **miserable;** woeful, woebegone; crushed, stricken, **cut up** <nonformal>, heartsick, heart-stricken, heart-struck; deep-troubled; desolate, disconsolate; **lamentable,** deplorable, regrettable, pitiable, piteous, rueful, **sad,** sorrowful, mournful, **depressing,** depressive; **pathetic,** affecting, touching, moving, saddening, poignant; **squalid,** sordid, shabby; beggarly, vile

**wring** VERBS **agonize,** harrow, crucify, martyr, martyrize, excruciate, twist, contorse, convulse; **squeeze** *or* **press out,** express, wring out; **wrest,** wrench, **rend,** rip; **wrest from,** wrench from, rip from, rend from, snatch from, pry loose from

**wrinkle** NOUNS 1 **corrugation,** crease, crimp, ruck, pucker; **crinkle,** crankle, rimple, ripple, wimple; crumple, rumple; crow's-feet
2 **fad,** craze, rage; new take <nonformal>; novelty; fillip
VERBS 3 **corrugate,** shirr, ridge, **furrow,** crease, crimp, crimple, cockle, cocker, **pucker,** purse; knit; ruck, ruckle; **crumple,** rumple; **crinkle,** rimple, ripple, wimple
4 **age, grow old,** senesce, get on *or* along, **get on** *or* **along in years,** wither, shrivel, wizen, shrink, diminish, wither *or* die on the vine, **dry up,** desiccate, sear

**writ** NOUNS **document,** official document, legal document, legal paper, legal instrument, **instrument,** paper, parchment, scroll, roll, **writing,** script, scrip; **summons,** subpoena, writ of summons; warrant

**write** VERBS **pen,** pencil, drive *or* push the pen *or* pencil <nonformal>; spill ink <nonformal>, **scribe;** take pen in hand; **put in writing,** put in black and white; **draw up,** draft, write out, make out; **write down,** record; author, **compose,** indite, formulate, produce, prepare; dash off, knock off *or* out <nonformal>, pound *or* crank *or* grind *or* churn out; **correspond,** correspond with, **communicate with,** write to, write a letter, send a letter to, send a note, **drop a line** <nonformal>

**writer** NOUNS **author,** composer, inditer; authoress, penwoman; **creative writer,** *littérateur* <Fr>, literary artist, literary craftsman *or* artisan *or* journeyman, belletrist, man of letters, literary man; free lance, free-lance writer; ghostwriter, ghost <nonformal>; scribbler <nonformal>, penman, pen, penner; pen *or* pencil driver *or* pusher <nonformal>, wordslinger, **inkslinger** *and* ink spiller *and* inkstained wretch <all nonformal>, knight of the plume *or* pen *or* quill <nonformal>; writer's cramp, graphospasm

**writing** NOUNS 1 scrivening <old>, inscription, lettering; pen, **pen-and-ink;** inkslinging *and* ink spilling <both nonformal>, pen *or* pencil pushing <nonformal>; secret writing, cryptography
2 **composition,** the art of composition, inditing, inditement; **creative writing,** literary art, verbal art, literary composition, literary production, verse-writing, short-story writing, novel-writing, playwriting, drama-writing; essay-writing; expository writing

**wrong** NOUNS 1 **misdeed,** misdemeanor, misfeasance, malfeasance, malefaction, criminal *or* guilty *or* sinful act, **offense,** injustice, injury, **iniquity,** evil, peccancy, *malum* <L>; tort; **error,** fault, breach; **impropriety,** slight *or* minor wrong, venial sin, **indiscretion,** peccadillo, misstep, trip, slip, lapse; **transgression,** trespass; **sin,** cardinal *or* deadly *or* mortal sin
ADJS 2 **wrongful;** improper, incorrect, indecorous, undue, unseemly; unfit,

unfitting, inappropriate, unsuitable; **evil,** sinful, wicked, unrighteous; not the thing, hardly the thing, not done, **off-base** *and* **out-of-line** *and* **off-color** <all nonformal>
3 **erroneous,** untrue, not true, **not right;** unfactual, all wrong; peccant, perverse, corrupt; **false,** fallacious, self-contradictory; illogical; unproved; **faulty,** faultful, flawed, defective, **at fault;** wide of the mark, beside the mark; amiss, awry, askew, deviant, deviative, deviational; erring, errant, aberrant; mistaken, in error, erring, **all wet** <nonformal>; in the right church but the wrong pew
ADVS 4 **wrongly,** wrongfully; **improperly,** incorrectly, indecorously; **erroneously,** falsely, by mistake, fallaciously; **mistakenly;** amiss, astray, on the wrong track

**X-rated** ADJS **lascivious,** lecherous, sexy, salacious, carnal, animal, **sexual,** lustful, ithyphallic; prurient, itching, itchy <nonformal>; **lewd,** bawdy, adult, hard, pornographic, porno <nonformal>, **dirty,** obscene; erotic, **sensual,** fleshly

**yacht** NOUNS **sailboat,** sailing vessel, sailing boat, ragboat <nonformal>, sailing yacht, sailing cruiser, sailing ship, tall *or* taunt ship, sail, sailer, **windjammer** <nonformal>, windship, windboat; pleasure boat, a hole in the water into which one pours money <nonformal>

**yank** NOUNS 1 **jerk,** quick *or* sudden pull; wrench, snatch
VERBS 2 **jerk,** snatch, wrench

**Yankee** NOUNS **Northerner,** northlander; Northman; New Englander, Down-Easter Yankee

**yard** NOUNS 1 **enclosure,** close, **confine,** precinct, enclave, pale, paling, list, cincture; park, court, courtyard, curtilage, toft
2 yards, railroad yard, brickyard, shipyard, dockyard, boatyard

**yawn** NOUNS 1 **gap,** gape, hiatus, lacuna, gat, space, interval; **chasm,** gulf; **gaping, yawning,** oscitation, oscitancy, dehiscence, pandiculation; the gapes
VERBS 2 **gape,** oscitate, dehisce, hang open

**yell** NOUNS 1 **cry,** call, shout, hoot; **whoop,** holler <nonformal>; **cheer,** hurrah; howl, yowl; bawl, bellow, roar; **scream, shriek,** screech, squeal, squall, caterwaul; yelp, yap, yammer, yawp, bark; war cry, battle cry, war whoop, rallying cry
VERBS 2 **cry,** call, shout, holler <nonformal>, hoot; whoop; **cheer; howl,** yowl, yammer; squawk, yawp; **bawl,** bellow, roar, roar *or* bellow like a bull; cry *or* yell *or* scream bloody murder *or* blue murder; **scream, shriek,** screech, squeal, squall, waul, caterwaul; yelp, yap, bark; give a cheer, give three cheers, yell oneself hoarse

**yellow** ADJS 1 **sensational,** lurid, **melodramatic,** Barnumesque; spine-chilling, eye-popping <nonformal>; **jealous,** jaundiced, jaundice-eyed, yellow-eyed
2 **cowardly,** coward; **afraid,** fearful; timid, timorous, overtimorous, overtimid, rabbity *and* mousy <both nonformal>; **fainthearted,** weakhearted, chicken-hearted, yellow-bellied *and* with a yellow streak <both nonformal>; **chicken** <nonformal>, afraid of one's shadow; panicky, panic-prone, funking *and* funky <both nonformal>; daunted, dismayed, unmanned, cowed, intimidated

**yelp** NOUNS 1 **cry,** call, shout, yell, hoot; screech, squeal, squall, caterwaul; yap, yammer, yawp, bark
VERBS 2 **cry,** screech, squeal, squall, waul, caterwaul; yap, bark; **grumble,** murmur, mutter, growl, clamor, croak, grunt

**yen** NOUNS **yearning,** longing, desiderium, **hankering** <nonformal>, **pining,** aching; lech <nonformal>, hunger, thirst; instinct *or* feeling for, sensitivity to

**yeoman** NOUNS 1 **retainer,** dependent, follower; myrmidon; vassal, liege, liege man, feudatory, homager; **attendant,** tender, usher, squire; guardsman; yeoman of the guard *or* beefeater, gentleman-at-arms
2 **agriculturist,** agriculturalist; **farmer,** granger, husbandman, cultivator, tiller, sodbuster, **tiller of the soil**

**yes** INTERJS 1 yes, yea, aye, *oui* <Fr>, *sí* <Sp>, *da* <Russ>, *ja* <Ger>; yes sir, yes ma'am; why yes, *mais oui* <Fr>; **indeed,** yes indeed; **surely, certainly,** assuredly, most assuredly, **right, right you are,**

**exactly, precisely,** just so, absolutely, positively, really, truly, rather <Brit>, quite, to be sure; **all right, right, good,** well and good, good enough, **very well,** *très bien* <Fr>; naturally, *naturellement* <Fr>; **of course,** as you say, **by all means,** by all manner of means; **amen;** hear hear <Brit>

2 <nonformal> **yeah,** yep, yup, uh-huh; yes sirree, same here, likewise, indeedy, yes indeedy, sure, sure thing, sure enough, surest thing you know; right on!, righto!; OK, okay, Roger, Roger-dodger; fine; you bet!, bet your ass!, you can bet on it!, you can say that again!, you said it!, you better believe it

**yes-man** NOUNS 1 sycophant; lightweight, follower, pawn, cog, flunky, creature, lacky, hanger-on; toady, jackal, minion, myrmidon; ass-kisser *and* brown-nose *and* bootlicker <all nonformal>
2 **conformist,** conformer, sheep, trimmer, parrot, organization man

**yesterday** NOUNS 1 **the past,** past, foretime, former times, past times, times past, water under the bridge, **days** *or* **times gone by,** bygone times *or* days, yesteryear; recent past, just *or* only yesterday; **history,** past history; dead past, dead hand of the past

*a bucket of ashes*
CARL SANDBURG

ADVS 2 **formerly,** previously; **earlier,** before, before now, erenow, **hitherto,** heretofore, aforetime, beforetime, **in the past,** in times past; then; only yesterday, recently; **historically,** in historic *or* prehistoric times

**yet** ADVS 1 **additionally,** in addition, also, and then some, even more, more so, and also, and all <nonformal>, and so, **as well,** too, else, beside, **besides,** to boot, not to mention, let alone, into the bargain; on top of, over, above; **beyond,** plus; **more,** moreover, *au reste* <Fr>, *en plus* <Fr>, thereto, farther, further, **furthermore,** at the same time, then, again; similarly, likewise, by the same token, by the same sign
2 **until now,** hitherto, till now, thitherto, **hereunto,** heretofore, until this time, by this time, **up to now,** up to the present, up to this time, to this day, to the present moment, to this very instant, **so far,** thus far, **as yet,** to date, already, still, now *or* then as previously
ADVS, CONJ 3 **notwithstanding,** but, still, even; **however,** nevertheless, nonetheless; **although,** when, though; albeit; **at all events,** in any event, in any case, at any rate; **be that as it may,** for all that, even so, **on the other hand,** rather, again, at the same time, all the same, just the same; after all, after all is said and done

**yield** NOUNS 1 **output,** make, production; **proceeds,** produce, product; **crop,** harvest, fruit, vintage, bearing; bumper crop; **interest; return,** return on investment, payout, payback
VERBS 2 **give up,** relinquish, surrender, yield up, waive, **cede,** give way, give ground, back down, give up, give in, cave in <nonformal>, withdraw from *or* quit the field; **cease,** desist from, leave off, give over; cry quits, acknowledge defeat, **throw in the towel** *or* **sponge**
3 **bear,** produce, furnish; **bring forth,** usher into the world; fruit, **bear fruit,** fructify; **give,** relent, relax, bend, unbend, give way; bounce, spring, spring back

**yokel** NOUNS 1 **oaf,** lout, boor, lubber, **gawk,** gawky, **lummox,** rube, hick, hayseed, bumpkin, clod, clodhopper
ADJS 2 **hick,** hicky, hickified, from the sticks, rube, hayseed, down-home, shit-kicking, hillbilly, redneck <all nonformal>

**yonder** ADJS 1 yon; **farther,** further, remoter, more distant
ADVS 2 yon; **in the distance,** in the remote distance; **in the offing,** on the horizon, in the background

**young** NOUNS 1 **young people,** youth, **younger generation,** rising *or* new generation, young blood, young fry <nonformal>; **children,** tots, childkind; small fry *and* kids *and* little kids *and* little guys <all nonformal>
ADJS 2 youngling, youngish, **juvenile,** juvenescent, **youthful,** youthlike, in the flower *or* bloom of youth, blooming, florescent, flowering, dewy, fresh-faced; fresh as a daisy, fresh as the morning dew

**youngster** NOUNS **young person, youth,** juvenile, youngling, young'un <nonformal>; **stripling,** slip, sprig, sapling; fledgling; hopeful, young hopeful;

**minor,** infant; **adolescent,** pubescent; **teenager,** teener, teenybopper <nonformal>

**youth** NOUNS 1 **youthfulness,** juvenility, juvenescence, tenderness, tender age, early years, school age, *jeunesse* <Fr>, prime of life, flower of life, salad days, springtime *or* springtide of life, seedtime of life, flowering time

*my green age*
DYLAN THOMAS

2 **youngster,** young person, **juvenile,** youngling, young'un <nonformal>; **stripling,** slip, sprig, sapling; fledgling; hopeful, young hopeful

**yowl** NOUNS 1 **howl,** yawl <Brit nonformal>; bawl, bellow, roar; **cry,** caterwaul, outcry, scream, yawp, keen, ululation
VERBS 2 **howl,** yammer, ululate, yawl <Brit nonformal>; squawk, yawp; **bawl,** bellow, roar, roar *or* bellow like a bull; cry *or* yell *or* scream bloody murder *or* blue murder; **scream,** shriek, screech, squeal, squall, caterwaul; yelp, yap, bark

**yummy** ADJS 1 **tasty,** good, fit to eat *and* finger-lickin' good <both nonformal>, good-tasting, **savory,** savorous, **palatable,** toothsome, sapid, good to eat, nice, agreeable, likable, pleasing, to one's taste, **delicious,** delightful, delectable, exquisite; for the gods, ambrosial, nectarous, nectareous; fit for a king, gourmet, of gourmet quality; scrumptious <nonformal>
2 **fun,** kicky, chewy, dishy, drooly, sexy <all nonformal>

**yuppie** NOUNS **conventionalist,** Babbitt, Philistine, middle-class type, button-down *or* white-bread type <nonformal>, **bourgeois,** plastic person *and* clone *and* square <all nonformal>, three-piecer <nonformal>

**zap** VERBS **annihilate,** exterminate, eradicate, extirpate, **eliminate,** liquidate, **wipe out,** stamp out, waste *and* take out *and* nuke <all nonformal>, put an end to, **end, terminate,** bring to an end, bring to a close *or* halt; **dispose of,** polish off <nonformal>; put the kibosh on <nonformal>, put the skids under <nonformal>; **kill,** extinguish, **give the quietus,** put the finisher *or* settler on <nonformal>, knock on the head, knock out <nonformal>, kayo *or* KO <both nonformal>, shoot down *and* shoot down in flames <both nonformal>, wipe out <nonformal>; **cancel, delete,** expunge, censor, censor out, blank out, erase

**zeal** NOUNS **ardor,** ardency, fervor, fervency, fervidness, spirit, warmth, fire, heat, heatedness, **passion,** passionateness, impassionedness, heartiness, intensity, **abandon,** vehemence; intentness, resolution; **devotion,** devoutness, devotedness, dedication, commitment, committedness; **earnestness, seriousness,** sincerity; loyalty, faithfulness, faith, fidelity; **zealousness,** zealotry, fanaticism

**zealot** NOUNS **enthusiast,** infatuate, energumen, rhapsodist; faddist; hobbyist, collector; **fanatic;** visionary, fundamentalist, militant; **devotee,** votary, aficionada, aficionado, **fancier,** admirer, **follower; disciple,** worshiper, idolizer, idolater; devotionalist

**zenith** NOUNS **apex,** vertex, acme, *ne plus ultra* <Fr>, **climax,** apogee, pole; **culmination; extremity,** maximum, limit, upper extremity, highest point; **supremacy,** primacy, paramountcy, **first place,** height, be-all and end-all, summit, top spot <nonformal>

**zero** NOUNS **nothing,** nil, *nihil* <L>, *nichts* <Ger>, *nada* <Sp>, **naught,** aught, nullity; cipher; nothing whatever, nothing at all, nothing on earth *or* under the sun, no such thing; **nonentity,** nobody *and* nonstarter *and* nebbish <all nonformal>, nonperson, unperson, hollow man; flash in the pan, dud <nonformal>

**zero hour** NOUNS **crucial moment,** critical moment, loaded *or* charged moment, decisive moment, defining moment, turning point, climax, **moment of truth,** crunch *and* when push comes to shove <both nonformal>; H-hour, D-day, A-day, target date, deadline

**zest** NOUNS **animation,** vivacity, liveliness, **ardor,** glow, keen desire, **appetite,** savor, relish; warmth, enthusiasm, lustiness, robustness, mettle, zestfulness, **sprightliness,** high spirits, vim, zip <nonformal>, vigor, verve, **exuberance,** heartiness, **gusto,** élan, *joie de vivre* <Fr>, *brio* <Ital>, spiritedness, vitality; **briskness,** perkiness, pertness, **life,** spirit

**zigzag** NOUNS 1 zig, zag; zigzaggedness, flexuosity, **crookedness,** crankiness; switchback, hairpin, dogleg; wandering *or* twisting *or* zigzag *or* shifting course *or* path; **divergence,** divarication, branching off, divagation, declination, aberration, aberrancy
VERBS 2 zig, zag, **stagger,** wind in and out, **go to and fro,** to-and-fro, **come and go,** pass and repass, back and fill; **bend,** curve, pull, crook, dogleg, hairpin; **digress**
ADJS 3 **digressive,** discursive, excursive, **circuitous;** devious, indirect, errant, erratic, dogleg *or* doglegged, **wandering,** rambling, roving, winding, twisting, meandering, snaky, serpentine; **crooked,** zigzagged, zigzaggy <nonformal>, jagged, serrate, sawtooth *or* sawtoothed

**zilch** NOUNS

<nonformal> **zip,** zippo, nix, goose egg, diddly, diddly squat, bubkes, beans, a hill of beans, a hoot, a rat's ass

**zip** NOUNS **zest,** zestfulness, zestiness, **briskness,** liveliness, raciness; **nippiness,** tanginess, snappiness; **spiciness,** pepperiness, hotness, fieriness; **tang,** spice, relish; **nip,** bite; punch, snap, ginger; **sprightliness,** high spirits, vim, vigor, verve, gusto, **exuberance,** heartiness

**zodiac** NOUNS **band,** belt, cincture, cingulum, **girdle,** girth, girt, zone, fascia, fillet; ecliptic, equator, great circle; **orbit,** circle, trajectory; circle of the sphere, great circle, small circle; ecliptic; **signs of the zodiac**

**zombie** NOUNS **apparition,** appearance, presence, shape, form, eidolon, idolum, revenant, larva; **spirit;** unsubstantiality, immateriality, incorporeal, incorporeity, incorporeal being *or* entity; **walking dead man**

**zone** NOUNS 1 **region,** area, belt, **territory,** terrain; space; **country**, land, territoriality; territorial waters, air space; **district,** quarter, section, department, division; salient, corridor; neck of the woods <nonformal>, purlieus; confines, precincts, environs, milieu; **orbit,** circle
2 postal zone, zip code *or* zip, postal code <Canada>, postcode <Brit>

**zoo** NOUNS **menagerie,** *Tiergarten* <Ger>, zoological garden *or* park

**zoom** VERBS **speed,** skim, **fly,** flit, fleet, wing one's way, outstrip the wind; **ascend,** climb, gain altitude, mount; **soar,** plane, kite, fly aloft, chandelle